THE HISTORY OF WESTERN CIVILIZATION

VOLUME TWO

UTOPIA

Cartoon by Cesare

THE HISTORY OF WESTERN CIVILIZATION

BY HARRY ELMER BARNES PH.D.

*Lecturer on the History of Civilization
New School for Social Research, New York*

with the collaboration of

HENRY DAVID M.A.

Instructor in History, College of the City of New York

Volume Two

HARCOURT, BRACE AND COMPANY
NEW YORK

COPYRIGHT, 1935, BY
HARCOURT, BRACE AND COMPANY, INC.

All rights reserved. No part of this book may be reproduced in any form, by mimeograph or any other means, without permission in writing from the publisher.

PRINTED IN THE UNITED STATES OF AMERICA
BY QUINN & BODEN COMPANY, INC., RAHWAY, N. J.

To
JAMES THOMSON SHOTWELL
Pioneer in Social History in the United States

PREFACE

This book is a straightforward account of the development of institutions and culture in the Western world. It is not based upon any preconceived notion of social evolution, nor have I been governed by any rigid schematic conception of historical interpretation. There is no assumption of invariable or uniform "stages" in history. The book has been built upon two main convictions. The first is that the history of civilization must be founded upon a broad perspective of time and space that cannot be secured from history alone, but must be grounded in biology, archaeology, anthropology, and sociology as well. The second is that the whole story of human development should be told. Qualifying this, however, is the belief that one must not try to lay exactly the same emphasis on each department or phase of culture in every period of human development. In some epochs the mere struggle for existence has been most important. In others religion has loomed largest in the interest of peoples. In another age the struggle for wealth and power has been dominant. Among some peoples, art and things of beauty have seemed to possess most significance. When treating a particular people in any era, I have attempted to stress especially the most characteristic and illuminating traits of that age and civilization. Likewise, while all peoples who have played any prominent part in the development of Western civilization have been mentioned, considerations of common sense and space alike dictate that major attention should be given to those areas and populations through which the stream of Western culture has flowed most directly and continuously from the caves of the Old Stone Age to the metropolitan centers of the twentieth century. Peoples and regions on the periphery of this main stream of Western culture are dealt with only in so far as they have contributed their rivulets to the general current of cultural tradition in the West. While they have not been followed slavishly, two elaborate syllabuses form the basis of the organization of the book: my *Social History of the Western World* (Appleton, 1921); and *An Outline of the History of the Western European Mind,* by James Harvey Robinson, which I revised under his supervision in 1919 (Marion Press, 1919). I have also found very helpful and suggestive the *Guide to the History of European Civilization* prepared by the members of the department of history of the College of the City of New York (1932).

The history of Western civilization cannot be confined within the older historical chronology. It is now realized that man has been on the earth for at least a million years, and some learned students estimate that he has been here for a much longer period—perhaps three times as long. Hence, even in the most modest estimate, far more than 90 per cent of the period of human habitation of this planet had already passed before the arrival of what used to be known as "the Dawn of History." If we were to use the old categories of historical chronology, we would have to identify ancient history with the Eolithic and Paleolithic periods of the early Stone Age; medieval history with the Neolithic or New Stone Age; and modern history with the period since the appearance of civilization in early Egypt. From the standpoint of time and culture alike, the whole civilization of man in the West since ancient Egyptian days is "modern" in character. The term "contemporary history" might well be applied to the relatively novel culture that has arisen since 1700 as a result of the growth of science, invention, business enterprise, and world-trade. In order, however, not to clash too sharply with the conventional historical perspective and pedagogy, I have attempted to adapt the new chronological conceptions to the old terms, and one will still find in these pages references to ancient history, classical civilization, the Middle Ages, and the like. In the light of rigorous historical logic it would probably have been better to abandon all the old chronological designations, but it has been deemed inexpedient to do so.

In describing the so-called prehistoric period, special emphasis has been placed upon the rise of the arts connected with assuring material existence, the origins of human social groupings, and the beginnings of man's theories about the supernatural world.

The ancient Orient is portrayed as the geographical area and historical period that witnessed the origins of civilization, built up by a leisure class on the basis of the oppression and exploitation of a large servile group. It was also the period in which there first emerged large-scale political units founded upon territorial residence rather than real or fictitious kinship. The two civilizations of the ancient Mediterranean world diverged widely in character. The Greeks introduced skeptical thought, an appreciation of the true and the beautiful, and a secular outlook upon life. The Romans were more notable for their achievements in military conquest, administration, jurisprudence, and engineering. The Greeks were intellectual innovators; the Romans, imitators.

The medieval period was marked by a revival of supernaturalism, the dominance of agricultural society, political localism and decentralization, and the degradation of scholarship. But it was not a uniform cultural age, for growth and development characterized nearly every element of its civilization. The rise of urbanism and the middle class foretold the coming of the modern period in which political centralization, nationalism, representative government, imperialism, science, machines, secularism, and capitalism and its attendant organized exploitation and economic waste have been dominating traits. The importance of the various elements in civilization thus shifts with the different epochs of history and the historian must, accordingly, allot his space and diversify his treatment with appropriate discrimination. To give as much attention to religious items in the twentieth century as in the thirteenth would, for example, be absurd. The theory of historical causation underlying the treatment in this book is a very broad one,[1] based upon the primary obligation of being true to the facts and thoroughly aware of the shifting trends of cultural development throughout the ages.

[1] See my chapter in *Essays in Intellectual History Dedicated to James Harvey Robinson*, Harper, 1929, pp. 269-72.

PREFACE

In dealing with the last century, not only the history of Europe but also the history of the Americas has been brought into the picture, for three reasons: In the first place, any history of Western civilization in contemporary times must take account of the achievements of the Western Hemisphere. In the second place, the United States has carried certain cultural and institutional developments—particularly finance capitalism and educational experimentation—much further than any other contemporary area. In the third place, and very important from a pedagogical point of view, characteristic contemporary developments are much more teachable if they are based upon and illustrated by the American materials with which students in this country are familiar in their everyday life.

If this work is a contribution to the so-called new history, it is only because it deals with historical materials as they should always have been handled—as the complete record of man's development on our planet. This broad view of history is, fortunately, becoming less "new" as time goes on, and in another generation or two the narrowness and superficiality of much of the historical writing of the nineteenth century is likely to appear curious, if not almost incredible. At the same time, the political, legal, military, and diplomatic elements in human achievement, which occupied the whole attention of former generations of historians, are not ignored here. They are merely freed from the obscuring husk of transient personal episodes, and thereby made to stand out the more clearly in their institutional import. This is not to question the importance of personalities in history, and no outstanding personality in political or military history has been denied recognition in this book. The major weakness of the older history was not so much that it was purely political history as that it failed to make even political history intelligible or significant. Likewise, while there is little in this work about the episodes of particular wars, there is an adequate account of the evolution of the various types and stages of warfare—something all too often missing from books that elaborate the details of innumerable wars. Whether we are pacifists or militarists, there is no escaping the prevalence and importance of wars in the past, and any history of civilization must treat of the ways in which these wars were fought and of the place of warfare in the successive periods of history.

While this work has been conceived and executed without any moralistic preconceptions or any idea of a "mission" to humanity, I do believe that history has no significance except in so far as it enables the reader more intelligently to understand the present and more rationally to work for a better future. History can serve this noble purpose, first by making it clear how we have arrived at our present state of civilization, and second, by helping to lift the weight of the "dead hand" of error and superstition that has come down from the past. There are few traditional obstructions to clear thinking and sane social action that cannot be wiped away, once these obstacles are candidly examined in their historical origins.

I have tried properly to combine intellectual and social candor with due respect for the historical point of view. If this work does not regard orthodox Christianity in the twentieth century to be the pertinent force that many of its adherents deem it, yet no impartial historical work places the medieval Catholic Church more fairly in its cultural setting or more fully recognizes the genuine social service that it rendered a millennium ago. The positive contributions and ravages of capitalism are recounted with equal frankness. The attempt has been made to handle historical data both in the perspective of past ages and in their bearing on the civilization of our day.

Some readers may think they detect a note of pessimism and disillusionment in the closing section of the work, which treats of the crises in contemporary civilization. Any such interpretation does not conform to my intention. I have only sought to be realistic. A chronicler of the year 1400 who found nothing but good and vitality in feudalism, the manorial system, the guilds, the Roman Catholic Church, and the Scholastic philosophy would command little respect from a contemporary historian. We are today in a highly comparable situation. There seems to be convincing evidence that capitalism, nationalism, democracy, supernaturalism, and the like may be in their terminal stages; at least, the historian must note such evidence of this probability as lies beyond question, though it is not his province to prophesy as to the future with dogmatism. Above all, it is high time that students of history recognize that all is not well in the modern world, and accustom themselves to the idea of social change. All this does not necessarily imply any pessimism or disillusionment. Civilization went on to better things after the close of the Middle Ages, and we may also move on to a more desirable and equitable cultural and institutional life. We are the more likely to do so just in proportion as we recognize the possibility and fit ourselves for adjustment to a new age of man.

In all this preceding "frame of reference" I find myself in complete harmony with the "Conclusions and Recommendations" of the Commission on the Social Studies of the American Historical Association.

A number of factors have entered into the planning and writing of this book. It may be regarded as in part an answer to an amiable challenge. Professor Carl Becker once good-naturedly reminded me that it might be time to quit writing so much *about* the "new history" and to begin writing some *of* it. Further, it may be viewed as an incomplete and imperfect discharge of a historical debt to three of my major teachers of history, James Harvey Robinson, James Thomson Shotwell, and Franklin Henry Giddings. My debt to others, such as Dunning, Shepherd, and Beard, has in part been taken care of in other ways and places, though their influence will be evident in many parts of this book. Robinson, Shotwell, and Giddings aroused my interest in the history of thought and culture and in the problems of social evolution. It would have pleased me better if these men had seen fit to execute a project such as this one. Since they did not, my contribution may do something towards filling the lamentable gaps in the literature of historical synthesis. Finally, this mode of approach to history, calling for a broad perspective and constructive synthesis, has always appealed to me far more than the highly intensive type of historical scholarship. It has devolved upon me to participate in the latter, the type that still rates as historical scholarship par excellence, but my own capacities and tastes impel me rather to put such fragmentary contributions together in a general picture of human development. This is not to deprecate the conventional brand of historical scholarship, but merely to state my preference to leave it for others who find it more congenial than ventures on a larger scale. A miniature is as much a work of art as a panorama on a vast canvas, but they call for different qualifications and interests.

My training has also been well adapted to this kind of historical enterprise. While I took more than the required number of courses in history for my major in history in both undergraduate and graduate work, I also wandered afield and took enough work in both anthropology and sociology to qualify for the doctorate in these subjects. The exigencies of my career have compelled me to give both undergraduate and graduate courses in political science and economics, while other incidents drew me into work on the history of science. All of this was further stimulated and extended by my part in the so-called social-science movement in this country. Finally, duties as coeditor of the most extensive enterprise ever projected in a coöperative *History of Civilization* have not proved irrelevant to the preparation of these volumes.

It would be impossible in any brief space to indicate all of the sources from which the book has been drawn. It has been my good fortune to study at Columbia University and elsewhere under an unusually large number of most stimulating teachers of history, who have taken a leading part in creating the "new history" and in developing an interest in the history of civilization. A number of others, among them James Henry Breasted, J. L. Myres, M. I. Rostovstev, James Westfall Thompson, Charles Homer Haskins, George Sarton, Ferdinand Schevill, Lynn Thorndike, Preserved Smith, Carl Becker, Werner Sombart, the Webbs, the Hammonds, R. H. Tawney, Harold J. Laski, Thorstein Veblen, and J. T. Merz, I have followed closely in their writings. Their ideas and their learning have played a definite part in giving me information and in shaping my conceptions of the development of civilization.

For nearly fifteen years I offered yearly undergraduate or graduate courses in the intellectual and social history of the Western world. The preparation of material for these courses has helped much in hammering out the unifying concepts and in organizing the materials that have gone in to the making of *A History of Western Civilization*. The "Suggested Reading" and "Further References" indicate the material in the English language that I value most highly as throwing light upon the major periods of Western history.[1] I have made no attempt here to include books in foreign languages, except where there is nothing adequate in English. The majority of our American students of history are really at home only in materials written in English, and there is no point in complicating the bibliographies by the listing of numerous titles in other languages. Those who are able to handle the foreign languages are also able to locate the books written in them, as listed and described in the *Guide to Historical Literature* (Macmillan, 1931) and other more specialized

---

[1] In order to save space, full data regarding a book referred to are given only (1) the first time it is named in a footnote and (2) the first time it is listed in Suggested Reading or Further References. After that only the author's surname and the title of the book are given. Publishers are listed for foreign books only in case they maintain an American branch or agent.

bibliographies. It has been my aim to prepare, above all, discriminating and highly useful lists of supplementary readings. There is no pedantic massing of indiscriminate or obscure titles. I believe I have succeeded in compiling the most helpful and well-selected bibliography of the history of civilization for the beginner in this field that can be found anywhere. In particular, I have included references to most of the major collections of source materials in English, thus enabling the students to obtain some notion of the flavor of the original sources of history.

It may not be presumptuous or out of place here to express the opinion that the most useful supplementary reading to accompany this history, in addition to the collections of source materials, is Sir J. A. Hammerton's *Universal History of the World,* a coöperative work in eight volumes (Amalgamated Press, 1927-29) written by experts who know their materials, have some feeling for cultural history, and bring with them a perspective that enables them to handle their assignments in intelligent and illuminating fashion. It is the only history of civilization of any moderate scope in the English language that justifies the name. More old-fashioned and less useful is the *History of the World,* edited by H. F. Helmolt (Dodd, Mead, 1900, 8 vols.), but I have listed the more relevant chapters in appropriate places in the bibliography. The elaborate series, *History of Civilization,* published by Alfred A. Knopf (1924 *et seq.*), will be found very helpful in special volumes, particularly those which constituted the *Universal History of Labor* series in the original French edition. The *Encyclopædia of the Social Sciences* is almost indispensable.

This book has, with deliberate intent, been made both complete and comprehensive in the hope that it will prove adequate even if used without any additional reading. With the curtailment of individual and institutional resources for the purchasing of sufficient quantities of books for extensive supplementary reading, many prefer a basic treatment that will supply all of the necessary material. This book has been designed to meet such a demand. At the same time, there is no reason why any student of history with the preference and the library resources may not undertake elaborate reading in connection with the textual material. But these volumes, together with occasional recourse to collections of source materials, will be found adequate to any reasonable demands. Another virtue of the full treatment, especially of contemporary times, is that the book can be used both for the history of civilization and for a general introduction to the social sciences without the necessity of purchasing additional books. An elaborate system of cross-referencing in the footnotes has been introduced to give unity and coherence to the vast mass of material in the two volumes.

In the use of quotations I have been governed by my own convictions in this matter. I believe there are only three justifications for quotations: (1) an occasional inclusion of a contemporary source; (2) a definitive statement by a recognized expert on a controversial subject; and (3) an unusually brilliant or incisive handling of an important detail by a reputable scholar that presents the subject matter better than the author would be likely to do. In the third category I have not hesitated to include citations of an especially cogent character, even though the person cited did not write his doctoral dissertation on

PREFACE

the subject matter of the paragraph cited. Nor have I refused to bring in occasionally material from able but well-known manuals, if it happened to be particularly relevant and well expressed. Where I have found a particularly cogent or valuable quotation already cited by another author, I have cited it from the book where I obtained it, rather than resorting to the easy method of citing the original source as though it were an independent discovery of my own.

In conference with the publishers, it was debated at length whether to include in an appendix a long chronological summary of the ordinary facts of world-history. It was decided not to do so. It was believed that the space which would be required to produce a satisfactory piece of work in this field could be better employed in other ways. Instead, we frankly recommend the constant use of either the chronological summaries in Hammerton or, for more detail, C. J. Ploetz, *Manual of Universal History* (Houghton Mifflin, 1925). Other chronological summaries of importance are G. P. Putnam, *Handbook of Universal History* (Putnam, 1927); *Harper's Book of Facts* (Harper, 1895); Arthur Hassall, *Handbook of European History, 476-1871* (Macmillan, 1897); and G. P. Gooch, *Annals of Politics and Culture, 1492-1899* (Macmillan, 1901). For the genealogy of leading ruling houses, see H. B. George, *Genealogical Tables Illustrative of Modern History* (5th ed., Oxford Press, 1916).

There are many historians and teachers who concede the need for a general history of civilization within reasonable scope, but contend that such an aspiration is vain because the task is impossible of execution by any author. They are prone to question the "scholarship" of anyone who attempts such an enterprise. They hold that no such book can be written from the "sources," and hence cannot be truly dependable. The pages that follow are the best answer to such a philosophy of pedantic futility. Every chapter has received the approval of two or more of the leading experts in this country, both as to the adequacy and relevance of the material and as to the accuracy of the facts. The book has been based upon some examination of source material, but it is obviously founded mainly on secondary works, most of them based on original sources. If such secondary works, based upon the sources, as I have used are not reliable, then the argument for writing from source-material obviously falls down before elementary logic.

Others very well might have performed the task far better than I have done, but no candid and fair reader can deny that here is a comprehensive history of civilization which is at least intelligently planned and executed in reliable factual fashion. If it pleases any reader better to believe that the reliability of the book is to be attributed to the experts who have read the proof sheets rather than to my own contributions, such an interpretation is wholly agreeable to me.

HARRY ELMER BARNES

New School for Social Research
March 15, 1935

NOTE OF ACKNOWLEDGMENT

My indebtedness to others in the preparation of this book is as wide as the scope of the work. First and foremost must be mentioned my collaborator, Mr. Henry David of the College of the City of New York, without whose aid I could not have brought the work to completion at the present time. Beyond all his extensive labors on the book, his fine historical sense and sound judgment have saved me from many a pitfall. Yet he is not to be held responsible for any defects in the general plan, organization, or execution of the work, for which I must take full responsibility. Dr. Mildred H. Hartsough has given much time to careful editorial work on the book, especially the second volume, and her wide knowledge of economic history has been especially valuable to me. I have imposed without conscience upon the good nature and erudition of my friends and acquaintances who are specialists upon one or another period or subject. The galley proofs of both volumes were read in large part by Professor Benjamin B. Kendrick of the North Carolina College for Women and gained much from his unusual sagacity in the appraisal of historical material. Professor Ralph E. Turner of the University of Pittsburgh read the page proofs of Volume I and gave me the benefit of his very wide knowledge of historical materials and the social sciences. Professor Edward Maslin Hulme of Stanford University has cheerfully assumed a large burden of proof-reading on Volume I, and his aid has proved as notable for its efficiency as for the courtesy with which it has been rendered. Professor W. I. Brandt of the College of the City of New York read Volume One in manuscript and made many helpful suggestions.

The galley proofs of Volume I were read by the following specialists: Chapter I by Professor George Grant MacCurdy of Yale University; Chapter II by Professor Alexander Goldenweiser of the University of Oregon; Chapter III by Professor Nathaniel Schmidt of Cornell University; Chapters IV-V by Professor Sterling Tracy of Columbia University; Chapters VI-X by Professor Wallace E. Caldwell of the University of North Carolina; Chapter XI by Dr. Alexander C. Flick, State Historian of New York, Mr. John Burke O'Leary of Worcester, Massachusetts, and Professor Edward Maslin Hulme of Stanford University; Chapter XII by Professor Albert L. Guérard of Stanford University; Chapter XIII by Professor James Westfall Thompson of the University of California; Chapters XIV-XV by Professor Albert H. Lybyer of the University of Illinois and Professor Jesse E. Wrench of the University of Missouri; Chapter XVI by Professor Thompson and Professor Austin P. Evans of Columbia University (in manuscript); Chapters XVII-XVIII by Professor Thompson, Professor Hulme, and Professor Felix Flügel of the University of California; Chapter XIX by Dr. Flick, Professor Hulme, and Mr. O'Leary; Chapter XX by Professor Ernest W. Nelson of Duke University and

NOTE OF ACKNOWLEDGMENT

Professor Urban T. Holmes of the University of North Carolina; Chapters XXI-XXIII by Professor Hulme.

The galley proofs of Volume II were read by the following experts: Chapters I-III by Professor James E. Gillespie of Pennsylvania State College; Chapter IV by Professor Leo Gershoy of Long Island University; Chapter V by Professor Howard Robinson of Miami University; Chapter VI by Professor J. Salwyn Schapiro of the College of the City of New York and Professor Leland Hamilton Jenks of Wellesley College; Chapters VII-VIII by Professor Frederick C. Dietz of the University of Illinois; Chapter IX by Professor Erich W. Zimmermann of the University of North Carolina; Chapter X by Professor Harold U. Faulkner of Smith College; Chapter XI by Dr. Harry W. Laidler of the League for Industrial Democracy; Chapter XII by Professor Henry Pratt Fairchild of New York University; Chapters XIII-XIV by Professor Thomas Preston Peardon of Columbia University; Chapters XV-XVI by Professor Joseph Ward Swain of the University of Illinois and Professor Parker T. Moon of Columbia University; Chapter XVII by Professor Swain; Chapter XVIII by Professor F. Lee Benns of the University of Indiana; Chapter XIX by Professor John Herman Randall, Jr., of Columbia University; Chapter XX by Professor Zimmermann; Chapter XXI by Mr. John T. Flynn, Professor Bernhard Ostrolenk of the College of the City of New York (in manuscript), and Miss Martha Schaible of the Standard Statistics Company; Chapter XXII by Professor Peardon; Chapter XXIII by Professor Merle E. Curti of Smith College; Chapter XXIV by Dr. Laidler; Chapter XXV by Professor Jerome Davis of Yale University; and Chapter XXVI by Professors George S. Counts, Goodwin Watson, and Clyde R. Miller of Columbia University.

The page proofs of Volume I were read by the following historians: Chapters I-II by Professor Robert H. Lowie of the University of California; Chapter III by Professor Caldwell; Chapters IV-V by Professor Schmidt; Chapters VI-X by Professor A. A. Trever of Lawrence College; Chapters XI-XXIII by Professor Hulme; and Chapter XV by Professor Lybyer.

The page proofs of Volume II were read by the following scholars: Chapters I-VI by Professor Frederick L. Nussbaum of the University of Wyoming; Chapter V by Professor Randall; Chapters VII-XI by Professor Joseph M. Klamon of Washington University; Chapter XII by Mr. Louis M. Hacker; Chapters XIII-XVIII by Professor Walter Consuelo Langsam of Columbia University; Chapter XIX by Professor Max Otto of the University of Wisconsin; Chapter XX by Mr. Waldemar B. Kaempffert of the New York *Times;* Chapter XXI by Professor Klamon and Miss Schaible; Chapters XXII-XXIII by Professor Langsam; Chapter XXIV by Mr. Hacker; Chapter XXV by Professor Leslie A. White of the University of Michigan; and Chapter XXVI by Professor Otto. I have also received important aid in matters pertaining to the history of science, literary history, the history of art, and that of music, from Mr. David Dietz of the Scripps-Howard Science Service; Professor Newton Arvin of Smith College; Professor Bailey W. Diffie of the College of the City of New York; Professor Charles Julius Kullmer of Syracuse University; Dr. Homer A. Harvey, formerly of Syracuse University; Mr. Meyric R. Rogers, Director of the City Art Museum, St. Louis, Missouri; Professor Roy Dickin-

NOTE OF ACKNOWLEDGMENT

son Welch of Princeton University; and Professor Richard F. Donovan of Yale University.

Just how much these authorities added to the quality of the book will never be fully realized by anybody save themselves and the author, but it may be said here that their aid was fully proportionate to their wide knowledge and kindly patience.

The publishers of the books and magazines quoted have given their permission for the use of the material, and thanks are hereby extended to them for their courtesy. The source of illustrations is acknowledged under the pictures when permission has been necessary. For the use of photographs and other illustrations for reproduction the courtesy of the Pratt Institute Free Library, Brooklyn, New York, is gratefully acknowledged.

The author is grateful to Miss Isabel Ely Lord for the preparation of the index.

CONTENTS FOR VOLUME TWO

PART ONE: THE EXPANSION OF EUROPE

I. THE EXPANSION OF EUROPE AND THE ORIGINS OF MODERN SOCIETY   3

    I. New Perspectives on the Origins of Modern Times   3
    II. The Character and Significance of the Expansion of Europe   6
    III. The Forces behind the Expansion of Europe   8
    IV. The Interest in the Orient Created by the Crusades   10
    V. Medieval Contacts with the Far East and Their Influence on European Expansion   16
    VI. The Significant Explorations and Discoveries   21
    VII. The Rival Commercial Empires   25

II. THE COMMERCIAL REVOLUTION AND THE BEGINNINGS OF MODERN INDUSTRY AND AGRICULTURE   31

    I. The Commercial Revolution   31
    II. Causes and Effects of the Dislocation of Prices   41
    III. The New Impulses to Manufacturing Activity   43
    IV. The Rise of the Woolen Industry and the Putting-out System   46
    V. Changes in the Technique and Organization of Agriculture   48

III. CAPITALISM AND COMMERCIAL POLICIES IN THE EARLY MODERN PERIOD   57

    I. The Beginnings of Modern Capitalism   57
    II. The Rise of Modern Banking   66
    III. Insurance   69
    IV. The Origins of Produce and Stock Exchanges   70
    V. The Era of Speculation and "Bubbles"   72
    VI. Commercial Monopolies   74
    VII. Mercantilism and the Absolute State   75
    VIII. The Idea of Natural Liberty: The Physiocrats   77
    IX. The Preparation for the Industrial Revolution   79

IV. THE RISE OF THE MIDDLE CLASS AND THE EVOLUTION OF THE NATIONAL-STATE SYSTEM   82

    I. The Emergence of Nationalism   82
    II. The Rise of the Absolute Dynastic State   84

CONTENTS

   III. The Era of Absolute Monarchies   89
   IV. The Rise of the Middle Class and the Origins of Representative Government   94
   V. The Significance of the English, American, French, and Later Revolutions   98
   VI. The Revolutions of 1830, 1848, and 1905   120
   VII. The Origins of Constitutional Government and the Growing Popularity of Republics   131

V. THE LIBERATION OF THE INTELLECT IN EARLY MODERN TIMES   143

   I. The Intellectual Temper of Early Modern Times   143
   II. The Progress of Natural Science in the Sixteenth and Seventeenth Centuries   145
   III. The Leading Aspects of Scientific Development in the Eighteenth Century   150
   IV. The Emancipation of Philosophy   154
   V. The Blight of Intolerance and Censorship   163
   VI. The Growth of Toleration and Freedom of Thought   168
   VII. The Religious Revolution: Deism, Rationalism, and Materialism   172
   VIII. Secularizing Ethics   189
   IX. The Origins of the Theory of Progress   191
   X. The Romanticists and the Revolt against Reason   194
   XI. The Religious Reaction   200

VI. THE SOCIAL AND CULTURAL IMPACT OF THE NEW INSTITUTIONS AND INTELLECTUAL FORCES   212

   I. The Growth of Population and the Increasing Prominence of the Middle Class   212
   II. The Secularization of Political Philosophy   216
   III. The New Developments in Law and Legal Philosophy   222
   IV. Rationalism and Social Philosophy   226
   V. The Romanticist Reaction in Social and Political Theory   232
   VI. Utopias, Social and Revolutionary Doctrines Affecting the Lower Classes   234
   VII. The Origins of Public Relief of the Poor   237
   VIII. Major Educational Developments in Early Modern Times   240
   IX. How the New Cultural Currents Affected Literature   244
   X. Achievements in Art and Music   247
   XI. The Contributions of European Expansion and the Period of Enlightenment   255

CONTENTS

PART TWO: THE ERA OF INDUSTRIAL CAPITALISM, NATIONALISM, DEMOCRACY, AND IMPERIALISM

VII. THE NEW EMPIRE OF MACHINES AND THE RISE OF THE FACTORY SYSTEM — 263

  I. The Eve of a New Era in Human Civilization — 263
  II. The Economic Backwardness of Society in 1750 — 264
  III. The Scientific Background of Modern Industrialism — 265
  IV. The General Nature and Significance of the Industrial Revolution — 267
  V. Why the Industrial Revolution Came First to England — 270
  VI. The New Textile Machinery and Processes — 273
  VII. The Technological Revolution in the Iron and Coal Industries — 277
  VIII. The New Steel Industry — 280
  IX. Artificial Illumination in Modern Material Culture — 283
  X. The Coming of the Factory — 285
  XI. The Main Elements in the Factory System — 286
  XII. Working-Conditions in Early Factories and Mines — 289
  XIII. The Reaction of the Inventions and Factories upon Business: The Rise of Industrial Capitalism — 294

VIII. THE REVOLUTION IN POWER, TRANSPORTATION, AND COMMUNICATION — 299

  I. The New Power Resources — 299
  II. The Revolution in Transport — 303
  III. New Devices for the Transmission of Information — 317
  IV. The Liberalization of Commercial Policies — 319

IX. THE TRANSIT OF THE INDUSTRIAL REVOLUTION TO CONTINENTAL EUROPE AND THE ORIENT — 324

  I. The General Character of the Transit of the Industrial Revolution — 324
  II. The Industrial Revolution in France — 325
  III. The Industrial Revolution in Germany — 329
  IV. The Industrial Revolution in Russia — 337
  V. Economic Progress in Other European Countries — 341
  VI. The Industrial Revolution in the Orient: Japan and China — 348
  VII. Australasia and Other Areas — 351

X. THE INDUSTRIAL REVOLUTION COMES TO THE UNITED STATES — 356

  I. American Economic Life to the Civil War — 356
  II. The Growth of Large-Scale Industry since 1860 — 364
  III. The Crisis in American Agriculture — 373

CONTENTS

XI. THE DEFENSE AND CRITICISM OF EARLY INDUSTRIAL CAPITALISM — 378

I. Economic Liberalism and the Idealization of Capitalistic Individualism — 378
II. English Philosophical Radicalism and Utilitarianism — 384
III. The Rise of Opposition to Economic Liberalism — 385
IV. Early Philosophical Anarchism — 396
V. The Political Revolutions of 1848 — 397
VI. The Rise of Humanitarianism — 398

XII. SOCIAL PHASES OF THE NEW RÉGIME — 405

I. The Factory Town and the Urban Age — 405
II. Modern Industrialism and Population Trends since 1800 — 416
III. The Triumph of the Bourgeoisie — 424
IV. The Proletarian Challenge to Capitalism — 427
V. Wealth, Social Classes, and Economic Equality — 433
VI. Feminism and the Changing Status of the Sexes — 434
VII. Psychological Results of the Industrial Revolution — 438
VIII. The Dawn of a New Era of Leisure — 442
IX. The Economic Basis of Contemporary Culture — 443

XIII. THE FOUNDATIONS OF CONTEMPORARY NATIONALISM — 453

I. The Popularization of National Sentiment — 453
II. Nationalism in the Machine Age — 457
III. The Development of Contemporary Nationalism Outside Europe — 467
IV. Nationalism in the World War — 471
V. Nationalism since the World War — 473
VI. Anti-Semitism Combines Nationalistic Frenzy and Racial Vagaries — 475

XIV. THE ORIGINS OF DEMOCRACY AND THE RISE OF PARTY GOVERNMENT — 482

I. What Is Democracy? — 482
II. A Brief History of Democracy — 483
III. Obstacles to Democracy — 499
IV. The Importance of Political Parties in Modern Government — 501
V. The Nature and Function of Political Parties — 501
VI. The Historical Evolution of Political Parties — 505
VII. The Two-Party and Group Systems — 515

XV. THE COURSE OF MODERN IMPERIALISM — 521

I. The Historical Background of Modern Imperialism — 521
II. The Nature of Contemporary Imperialism — 526

CONTENTS

   III. Imperialism in Africa   528
   IV. Modern Imperialism in Western Asia   532
   V. Great Britain in India   534
   VI. Western Imperialism in the Far East   536
   VII. The United States and Latin America in Modern Imperialism   541
   VIII. Summary of Imperialistic Expansion   545
   IX. The Economics of Contemporary Imperialism   546
   X. Imperialism and the World War   549
   XI. Imperialism and World-Politics after the World War   550

XVI. THE INFLUENCE OF CONTEMPORARY IMPERIALISM ON WESTERN CIVILIZATION   559

   I. The Effects of Contemporary Expansion on Oversea Areas   559
   II. The Reaction of Contemporary Imperialism upon Europe and America   567

XVII. THE WORLD WAR, 1914-1918   575

   I. Levels and Types of Responsibility   575
   II. The Causes of Wars in General   575
   III. European Diplomacy from 1870 to 1912   578
   IV. The Diplomatic Revolution: 1912-1914   582
   V. The Eve of the World War   587
   VI. The Crisis of June-August, 1914   589
   VII. The Great Conflict: The Old and the New Warfare   593
   VIII. Propaganda in the War: The Pen Behind the Sword   599
   IX. The Tragic Balance Sheet of Hostilities   600
   X. Did the War Pay?   602

XVIII. AFTER THE WORLD WAR   606

   I. The Note of Disillusionment   606
   II. National Self-determination   607
   III. Making the World Safe for Democracy   611
   IV. The Economic Aspects of the Treaty of Versailles   613
   V. The Treaties with Austria, Hungary, Bulgaria, and Turkey   616
   VI. The Effect of Peace upon Labor   616
   VII. The French Security Pact of 1919   618
   VIII. A Warning to Future Generations   618
   IX. The Settlement of War Debts   619
   X. The Reparations Problem   622
   XI. Industrial Results of the World War   626
   XII. The Rationalization of Industry   629
   XIII. European Agriculture since 1914   632
   XIV. The Monetary Crisis and the Abandonment of the Gold Standard   636

CONTENTS

XIX. INTELLECTUAL AND CULTURAL ACHIEVEMENTS OF THE NINETEENTH CENTURY — 640

I. The Development of Natural Science — 640
II. The Rise of the Evolutionary Concept and Its Early Intellectual Effects — 653
III. The Influence of Science upon Intellectual and Religious Attitudes — 663
IV. The Rise of the Social Sciences — 665
V. Religious Movements — 672
VI. Major Trends in Philosophy — 680
VII. Educational Progress — 683
VIII. Literature — 690
IX. Trends in Art — 709
X. Achievements in Music — 712

PART THREE: THE CRISIS IN WESTERN CIVILIZATION

XX. THE SECOND INDUSTRIAL REVOLUTION — 723

I. The Meaning of the Second Industrial Revolution — 723
II. Applied Chemistry and the New Industrial Order — 726
III. New Developments in Transportation and Communication — 736
IV. The Era of Large-Scale Business Enterprise — 748
V. Mass Production and the "Speed-up" System — 752
VI. Power Production, Automatic Machines, Technological Unemployment, and the Eve of the "Third" Industrial Revolution — 756
VII. The Growth of Scientific Business Management — 762
VIII. The Chain Store and Mass Distribution — 764
IX. The Social Impact of the Machine Age — 766
X. The Spirit of Invention — 767
XI. The International Results of Increased Production — 769

XXI. FINANCE CAPITALISM — 780

I. Stages in the Evolution of Capitalism — 780
II. New Credit Institutions: Commercial and Investment Banks — 784
III. The Influence of the Corporation and the Holding Company upon Industrial Consolidation — 795
IV. Finance Capitalism and Absentee Ownership — 798
V. Speculation in Corporate Securities — 803
VI. The Concentration of Wealth and the Destruction of Mass Purchasing Power — 806
VII. The Theory of Business Enterprise and the Price System — 816
VIII. The Effect of Finance Capitalism upon Business — 822
IX. Racketeering and Organized Crime — 833
X. The Business Cycle — 836
XI. Property Rights and the Supreme Court — 842
XII. "The New Capitalism" — 847

CONTENTS

XXII. THE CRISIS IN DEMOCRACY AND PARTY GOVERNMENT — 855

  I. The Critical Test of Democratic Institutions — 855
  II. The Fundamental Assumptions of Democracy — 855
  III. Democratic Aspirations in the Light of Science and Experience — 859
  IV. The Outlook for Democracy — 870
  V. Contemporary Abuses in the Party System — 872
  VI. Efforts to Reform Party Government — 879
  VII. Graft and Waste under the Party System of Government — 884

XXIII. IN QUEST OF WORLD PEACE — 898

  I. Historic Plans for World Organization — 898
  II. The Creation of the League of Nations — 901
  III. The Structure and Operation of the League of Nations — 902
  IV. The League of Nations, Disarmament, and Militarism — 908
  V. The Vain Struggle for Disarmament — 910
  VI. The Development of the Peace Movement to 1914 — 914
  VII. The Kellogg Pact: A Challenge to the Future — 917
  VIII. The Isolation Myth in the United States — 922
  IX. Eliminating the Basic Causes of Wars — 924
  X. The "Aggressive War" Myth and Substitutes for War — 927

XXIV. CONTEMPORARY PROGRAMS OF SOCIAL AND ECONOMIC REFORM — 931

  I. The Historical Background — 931
  II. The Effect of the Idealistic Philosophy of the State — 932
  III. The Rise of Scientific Sociology — 932
  IV. The Development of Marxian or Scientific Socialism — 933
  V. The English Fabians and the Growth of "Revisionist" Socialism — 936
  VI. The Rise and Expansion of State Socialism — 938
  VII. Recent Developments in Christian Socialism — 944
  VIII. The Newer Anarchism — 946
  IX. The Development of the Coöperative Movement — 947
  X. The Expansion of Labor Unions — 948
  XI. The Development of Syndicalism and the Radical Labor Movement — 952
  XII. Guild Socialism as a Compromise Between Socialism and Syndicalism — 955
  XIII. Henry George, the Single Tax, and Land Nationalization — 955
  XIV. Bourgeois Attempts to Absorb the Radical Proletarian Movements — 957
  XV. The Great War and Policies of Reconstruction — 958
  XVI. Fascism and the Corporative State — 961
  XVII. The Pseudo-Biological Apology for Capitalism, Industrial Autocracy, and Economic Individualism — 963

CONTENTS

    xviii. Contemporary Humanitarianism: The Scientific Control of the Maladjusted ... 964
    xix. Concluding Observations ... 972

XXV. SOVIET RUSSIA ... 979

    i. The Significance of Soviet Russia in World-History ... 979
    ii. The Russian Revolution ... 980
    iii. The Political Structure of the U.S.S.R. ... 991
    iv. The Economy of Soviet Russia ... 997
    v. The Industrial Progress of Soviet Russia ... 1002
    vi. Transportation ... 1005
    vii. The Agricultural Revolution ... 1007
    viii. Soviet Trade and Commerce ... 1011
    ix. Money, Banking, and Public Finance ... 1012
    x. Summary of Economic Conditions in Soviet Russia ... 1014
    xi. The New Social Order in Russia ... 1015
    xii. A Tentative Estimate ... 1027

XXVI. INTELLECTUAL AND CULTURAL TRENDS IN THE TWENTIETH CENTURY ... 1035

    i. Outstanding Achievements in Science ... 1035
    ii. Intellectual Implications of Twentieth-Century Science ... 1049
    iii. Progress in the Social Sciences ... 1057
    iv. Outstanding Problems of Religion ... 1060
    v. Developments in Philosophy ... 1067
    vi. Some Leading Educational Advances ... 1070
    vii. Literature in Our Century ... 1079
    viii. Modernism in Art and Music ... 1094
    ix. Cultural Lag and the Human Outlook ... 1101

INDEX ... 1117

LIST OF ILLUSTRATIONS

Utopia	*frontispiece*
The First Royal Stock Exchange	72
Promoting the South Sea Bubble	72
Some Leading Thinkers: Jeremy Bentham, Adam Smith, Herbert Spencer, Robert Owen	73
Some Great Scientists: Giordano Bruno, Antoine Laurent Lavoisier, Sir Isaac Newton, Carolus Linné	152
Some Great Philosophers: Auguste Comte, John Locke, Francis Bacon, René Descartes	153
Early Spinning Machinery	300
An Early Factory	301
A Modern Factory	301
An Early Express Train	316
A Streamline Train	316
An Old-Type Reaper	317
Later Reaping Machinery	317
The Tariff Walls of Europe with Their Relative Heights	452
An Industrial Center	452
Fifth Avenue and Forty-second Street, New York City, 1850	453
Fifth Avenue, New York City, 1889	453
Leaders in Democracy: Thomas Jefferson, Andrew Jackson, Abraham Lincoln, William Jennings Bryan	484
James Ramsay MacDonald	485
Franklin Delano Roosevelt	485
Muscle Shoals	485
Some Equipment of the World War: Warship, Airplane, Big Gun, Tank	620
Some Results of the World War: Blinded and Mutilated, Ruins—The Cathedral of Arras, Losses and Gains	621

xxiv LIST OF ILLUSTRATIONS

The Big Four: Vittorio E. Orlando, David Lloyd George, Georges Clemenceau, Woodrow Wilson	636
Scientists and Philosophers: Hermann Helmholtz, Georg Wilhelm Hegel, Charles Darwin, François Marie Arouet de Voltaire	637
Modern Spinning Machinery	772
Power	772
An Old-Time Country Store	773
A Modern Chain Store	773
Andrew Mellon	804
J. Pierpont Morgan, Jr.	804
Wall Street	804
The Menace of the Gangster	804
The Way It Works	805
Benito Mussolini	964
Adolf Hitler	964
A Crowd Giving the Nazi Salute	964
The League of Nations Buildings, Geneva	965
A Three-Year-Old Fascist Soldier Salutes Mussolini	965
Josef Stalin	996
Karl Marx	996
Nikolai Lenin	996
Leon Trotsky	996
A Collective Farm, Soviet Russia	997
The Dnieprostroy Dam, Soviet Russia	997
The Empire State Building, New York City	1036
An Aerial View of Modern New York	1037
Modern Scientists and Philosophers: Sigmund Freud, Herbert George Wells, John Dewey, Albert Einstein	1052
Relativity	1053

LIST OF MAPS

Trade Routes and Routes of the Explorers	20
Origins of the Great Powers	88
Europe in 1789	112
Economic Resources of the World	348
Density and Growth of Population	420
Peoples and Languages of Modern Europe	460
The Far East	536
Europe in 1871	580
Postwar Treaty Adjustments	608
Europe in 1920	628
Danger Spots of Today	924
European Religions	1060

PART ONE

THE EXPANSION OF EUROPE

I. THE EXPANSION OF EUROPE AND THE ORIGINS OF MODERN SOCIETY

II. THE COMMERCIAL REVOLUTION AND THE BEGINNINGS OF MODERN INDUSTRY AND AGRICULTURE

III. CAPITALISM AND COMMERCIAL POLICIES IN THE EARLY MODERN PERIOD

IV. THE RISE OF THE MIDDLE CLASS AND THE EVOLUTION OF THE NATIONAL-STATE SYSTEM

V. THE LIBERATION OF THE INTELLECT IN EARLY MODERN TIMES

VI. THE SOCIAL AND CULTURAL IMPACT OF THE NEW INSTITUTIONS AND INTELLECTUAL FORCES

CHAPTER I

THE EXPANSION OF EUROPE AND THE ORIGINS OF MODERN SOCIETY

I. NEW PERSPECTIVES ON THE ORIGINS OF MODERN TIMES

Until recently, historians rather generally employed the term "modern times" to describe a very definite and well-unified historical period. They have now come to regard this division as an arbitrary one, chiefly valuable as a pedagogical necessity. Such a change in viewpoint implies a recognition of the complexity of modern civilization and of the variability in the rate of development in the different fields of human activity.

It has long since been clearly apparent to discerning historians that there was no sharp and sudden change from medieval to modern times. Many characteristic phases of medieval civilization held over in western Europe for centuries, and not a few persist to this very day.[1] Moreover, those developments in life and thought which we have come to regard as preëminently *modern* made their appearance at widely different times in various parts of Europe. For example, a degree of commercial life, middle-class strength, and representative government that had appeared in England in the last quarter of the seventeenth century arrived in Russia only at the outset of the twentieth century. In some backward parts of Europe today people live and think much as they did in the days of St. Thomas Aquinas and Philip Augustus.

While keeping in mind these necessary safeguards against exaggerating the suddenness, thoroughness, and uniformity of cultural changes in the Western world between 1450 and 1800, we are perfectly safe in declaring that striking novel features appeared in Europe during these centuries and that these constituted a more decisive break with the past than had previously taken place in the same number of years at any time in human history. The oceans were conquered for the first time. Discovery and colonization took on a world-wide character. Trade assumed a volume, variety, and geographic scope hitherto unknown in the experience of mankind. In due time, these commercial and monetary developments led to the need for machinery to produce the desired goods. This, in turn, brought into being factories and modern urban life, together with the improved methods of transportation and communication necessary to serve a world-civilization. The dominion of an aristocratic agricultural class was brought to an end. For the first time in history, with the exception of certain periods and areas in the ancient Orient, the middle class

---
[1] See above, Vol. I, pp. 871 ff.

of merchants and small business men became sufficiently strong to hold its own against the old agrarian oligarchy. In due time and in certain places, they actually overcame the latter and created a middle-class state designed to advance and protect the interests of the rising capitalistic society. The lower classes gradually cast off their servility and demanded a part in formulating a policy of the state.

In politics there were equally striking changes. The decentralization, weakness, and provincialism that had characterized the medieval feudal monarchies gave way before the rising tide of nationalism. This was effectively promoted by the religious changes of the sixteenth century and by the economic and financial developments associated with the new era of discovery and trade. The national state supplanted the feudal monarchy. It was first presided over by well-nigh absolute monarchs. The growing middle class soon found their rule burdensome and restrictive. Therefore, when the middle class became powerful enough, it challenged this absolute royal dominion and brought into existence representative government as the result of revolutions extending from 1645 in England to 1905 in Russia. Following upon this revolt of the middle class came the demand of the masses for participation in government, thus giving rise to the movement in behalf of democracy.

Quite as striking were the transformations that took place in the realm of the mind. These were in large part stimulated by the curiosity aroused as a result of the unprecedented contact of cultures brought about by discovery and colonization. Natural science underwent a development the like of which had not been known before in the mental evolution of humanity. Science gave us our first passably accurate ideas of both the heavens above and the earth under our feet. It led to the discovery of elementary truths with respect to the nature of the physical universe and the life of plants, animals, and men. Science and skepticism gradually freed the human mind to some degree from the dominion of superstition, the supernatural, and considerations based upon fears and hopes relative to a life beyond the grave. All of this opened the way for the partial triumph of human reason. Once the searchlight of reason was turned upon human ideas and institutions, the need for reform was clearly indicated and the hope of human progress kindled in the minds of men.

The enormity and complexity of such changes as these inevitably stimulated a search for their causes. A generation ago the majority of historians looked upon the capture of Constantinople by the Turks in 1453 as the key to the explanation of the genesis of modern civilization. The Greek scholars who fled before the Turks were thought to have brought the Renaissance to Italy and the Renaissance was believed to have created in turn the Protestant revolt. Moreover, the Turkish capture of Constantinople was regarded as the direct cause of the explorations designed to discover an oversea route to the Indies. We now know that those forces which produced the Italian Renaissance were already under way before Constantinople was captured. We shall make clear later the fact that the capture of Constantinople by the Turks had no primary influence in encouraging the explorations that led to the conquest of the oceans and the rise of modern colonial enterprise. Constantinople suffered a long decline before the Ottoman Turks finally captured it. Its eclipse was due to slow but sweeping changes in European economic organization, which curtailed its monopoly of markets, and to certain military movements in Asia affecting its sources of supplies.[1]

The Renaissance, the intellectual awakening of the fourteenth and fifteenth centuries, is now generally regarded as an acceleration of a cultural movement that was already well under way and had its roots far back in the Middle Ages. Its intellectual, scientific, and economic atmosphere was derived at least as much from the contemporary European situation as from the revival of the classics that has given the period its name. There is no divorcing it, as a factor in modern history, from the material facts that underlay and surrounded it. Chief among these were the economic life of the Italian cities, the invention of printing, and the great expansion of European economic contacts that began with the Crusades, merged with the explorations and colonizing projects overseas, and is still continuing in the form of the exploitation of backward regions of the earth.[2]

Historians of the Protestant revolt, that diversely timed and widespread religious movement which resulted in the breaking away of thousands of Europeans from the Roman Catholic Church, are interesting themselves more and more in such economic matters as the effect of the rapid development of trade and industry upon peasant life, politics, and the outlook of Europeans generally.[3] It is impossible to consider the revolt from the Catholic Church independent of the flood of printed books and pamphlets that would not have been possible without the inventions of the preceding century, or to peruse the pamphlets themselves without perceiving the fundamental driving force of the economic issues they discussed. The bourgeoisie—the enterprising middle class—and the national state had acquired a potential power that was bound to assert itself before very long. Whenever this took place, the overturn of the medieval system was inevitable.

From the Crusades to the present, the most impressive and constant symptom in the changes that have taken place has been the expansion of European life and cultural contacts.[4] The present-day citizen is able to familiarize himself with the more important events that have taken place throughout the world in the previous twenty-four hours. He thus finds it very difficult to comprehend that during the greater part of recorded history, the chief successive centers of the highest civilization have occupied an extremely limited geographical area and that the peoples themselves have had only the most imperfect and tardy knowledge of what was taking place contemporaneously within even this restricted area.

[1] *Cf.* J. W. Thompson, *Economic and Social History of the Middle Ages (300-1300)*, Century, 1928, pp. 414-15; and M. M. Knight, H. E. Barnes, and Felix Flügel, *Economic History of Europe*, Houghton Mifflin, 1928, Chap. III. See above, Vol. I, pp. 500 ff.

[2] *Cf.* Preserved Smith, *The Age of the Reformation*, Holt, 1920, Chap. I; and E. M. Hulme, *The Renaissance, the Protestant Revolution and the Catholic Reformation in Continental Europe*, Century, 1914, Chaps. I-IX.

[3] See, for instance, Smith, *op. cit.*, Chap. XIV; and A. F. Pollard, *Factors in Modern History*, Knopf, 1926, Chap. II.

[4] See W. R. Shepherd, "The Expansion of Europe," *Political Science Quarterly*, March-September, 1919. For an excellent survey of the expanding geographical basis of Western civilization, see J. K. Wright, *The Geographical Basis of European History*, Holt, 1928.

The oversea phase of widened social contacts began with a search for a water route to the Far East, and resulted in the discovery, exploration, and colonization of the New World as well. All this had profound results for the economic, social, and political life of western Europe. The oceanic age of Western culture came into being.[1] As a result of exploration, colonization, and mechanical invention, the subsequent history of the Western world is largely concerned with: (1) The extension of cultural interaction between peoples; (2) the breaking down of the earlier localism, isolation, provincialism, and stability of agricultural society; and (3) the effects of expanding culture and commerce upon the original European centers of civilization.

II. THE CHARACTER AND SIGNIFICANCE OF THE EXPANSION OF EUROPE

It is to the expansion of Europe, then, that we must look for a historical force sufficiently powerful and comprehensive to explain the origins of modern times. One aspect of this great movement, long a subject for historical study, is the movement of Europe outward to both the Old World and the New World. This was long regarded as the essence of the expansion movement. Attention was concentrated primarily upon discovery, colonization, and trade with oversea areas. Important as all of this may have been, however, it was less significant than the reaction of this expansion upon Europe itself. This latter phase of the expansion movement generally escaped the serious and protracted attention of historians until it was made the chief scholarly concern of a famous American historian, Professor William Robert Shepherd, of Columbia University. By developing this very important thesis he has given enterprising historians their first clear conception of what is perhaps the most dynamic and potent factor in the rise of modern civilization. This perspective is so indispensable to the understanding of the genesis of modern times that it is worth while to cite the core of Professor Shepherd's doctrines:

> Among the dominant characteristics of modern history there is none so little understood as the relationship established during the past five hundred years between Europe and the rest of the world—the interaction of European and non-European in the development of modern civilization. Not only is its significance unappreciated, but even the actual story of the stupendous movement which has brought Europeans into close and regular contact with lands and peoples all over the globe is inadequately known. Worthy of the pen of a Gibbon, the narrative of the greatest of human adventures awaits a master hand. . . .
>
> The "Renaissance," the "Reformation," the "French Revolution," the "Industrial Revolution," "Nationalism and Democracy," have been examined, described and evaluated with reference to the particular period of which they form a part. But a movement greater than these and contemporaneous with them has been comparatively ignored. Actually they seem to have been born and bred in Europe alone, and thus to have communicated their influence to the rest of the world; and yet, how far were they in reality the product of Europe's ventures beyond its own frontiers; and if not wholly the product, how far was their inception or development affected

[1] *Cf.* H. F. Helmolt, ed., *History of the World,* Dodd, Mead, 1900, 8 vols., Vol. VIII, Chap. v.

by such ventures oversea and overland in distant portions of the earth? This is a question that has remained substantially without an answer. . . .

The history of European colonization, moreover, should not be confounded with that of the expansion of Europe. Colonization has to do with the processes by which a given country has acquired, governed and utilized distant territories. . . .

The history of the expansion of Europe . . . includes colonization and vastly more. It may be regarded, in fact, as the record of the interpenetration of Europeans and non-Europeans the world over in all departments of human activity. Two fundamental concepts are inherent in its interpretation. Of these the first is that dependencies, other than mere seaports and their restricted hinterland, are the germs of new societies and possibly of new nations. Their inhabitants are communities drawn in greater or less degree from European race stocks, or else composed largely of non-Europeans. In either case they are adapting themselves to a new environment. So far as the Europeans are concerned, the environment is the natural one of the locality into which they have transplanted themselves; whereas the environment for the native peoples is that artificially established for them by the Europeans. This mutuality of environmental operation, European and non-European, works in two ways. It involves an application to native lands and peoples of ideas, institutions, usages and commodities derived from Europe, and determines the extent to which the native type of civilization or barbarism may be affected. Similarly, in a reverse sense, it connotes the adoption or adaptation by the Europeans of elements drawn from native conditions, both of country and of people, which modify what they have brought from home. Just as the Europeans influence the natives and their surroundings, so in some degree are they themselves influenced.

The second fundamental concept of the expansion of Europe is that whatever Europeans have done oversea and overland beyond their frontiers forms an essential part of the history of their particular nations and of the continent as a whole. The concept is divisible into two phases, of which one may be called the "outward," and the other the "homeward" movement. The former concerns the transmission of European ideas and institutions and the modifications they undergo in contact with their new environment. The latter betokens the results that follow for Europe itself—the influence of such activities upon European civilization proper, and in particular upon the local life and thought of the nations more directly engaged in the work of expansion. Here again a process of interaction is observable. It reveals both the impress made on the civilization of Europe by what the Europeans carry back from their distant ventures, and the manner in which these exotic contributions to European life and thought undergo a change amid new conditions of existence.

Of the two phases of the second fundamental concept, the latter is far the more significant, not only because it refers to Europe itself, but because it has been so long without recognition. Well may the European proudly tell of what he has done, or thinks he has done, for the "little brown brother" or some other beneficiary of the "white man's burden." But what has the "little brown brother" done for him? How have his land, his people, his circumstances, been of benefit or detriment to the European and his country? In what respects has the development of civilization in Europe been moulded by factors and forces born outside its geographical bounds? These indeed are paramount questions. . . .

Out of the New Worlds in the West and East the achievements of the European have brought forth a new Europe that has continued to speak the languages and cherish the traditions and customs of the former home, that has sought to be freer, richer, more tolerant, less tied to ancient prejudices, more open to progress, and that has served accordingly to influence old Europe in every phase of its existence. New things have been found, new forms of society created, new kinds of industry devised, new fields of commerce opened up, new opportunities for financial operations discovered, new ideas and new departments of knowledge made manifest and new concepts of national and international welfare evolved, all of which could not fail profoundly to affect Europe itself. Ancient civilizations aroused and energized, primitive beliefs and practices cast into modern moulds by the impact of the European, have yielded to him in return many a treasure, material and mental, by which his life and thought have become vastly enriched and diversified. From all that expansion has evoked in spirit and attainment—the zest of enterprise, eagerness for adventure, fame, wealth, new scenes and new homes, new places on the earth where a greater comfort and happiness might be assured, the introduction of the unknown and an increased use of the known—from its contact, in a word, with new lands and new peoples in America, Asia, Africa, and the isles of the sea, Europe has derived new impulses and new developments.[1]

III. THE FORCES BEHIND THE EXPANSION OF EUROPE

Of all the forces encouraging European expansion in modern times, the oldest and most enduring, if not the most important, has been the missionary impulse of Christianity. This force not only widened the area of European civilization during the period from the fall of the Roman Empire to the height of the Middle Ages, but ever since that time has maintained an amazing energy and activity. As Professors Robinson and Beard have well expressed the matter: "the way for imperialism was often explored and made smooth by preachers of the Word apparently following the command 'Go ye into all the world and preach the Gospel to every creature.' (Mark xvi, 15.)"[2]

The Crusades (1095-1291), as noted below, constitute the first notable religious movement that possesses great significance for the subsequent expansion of Europe. The intellectual and economic results of the Crusades, centering in the appropriation of Muslim culture and in the development of trading relations between East and West by Italian city-states, were much more significant for posterity than any temporary triumph of the Cross over the Crescent. Yet it is possible that without the initial religious impulse, which, among other motives, gave rise to the Crusades, there would have been a much slower development of the intellectual and economic interaction between Europe and the East. In the later period of European exploration that ushered in the Commercial Revolution, the Catholic missionaries—Franciscan and Dominican, and later Jesuit—were in the vanguard of expansion.

About the beginning of the nineteenth century the Protestant missions entered into the promotion of conversion overseas. Missionaries have carried European culture to native peoples and have done much in the way of spreading some knowledge of oversea cultures back home. Moreover, profoundly moved by a conviction of the uniqueness and the superiority of Christianity over all other forms of world-religion, these missionaries have often violated the theology and the mores of the native peoples. This has frequently been followed by the persecution or the extermination of the missionaries. Such action

---

[1] Shepherd, *loc. cit.*, pp. 43, 47, 49, 50-51, 211.
[2] J. H. Robinson and C. A. Beard, *The Development of Modern Europe*, rev. ed., 2 vols., Ginn, 1929-30, Vol. II, p. 147.

has, in turn, opened the way for the military intervention of modern governments, driven on by eager capitalists, anxiously awaiting the opportunity for exploitation or investment in these undeveloped areas. The missionary movement has always been closely linked with the expansion of European civilization and the growth of modern imperialism.

One of the most persistent and effective of all influences stimulating the process of expansion has been the desire to develop more extensive and profitable trading relations. The Italian merchants who carried the Crusaders to the Near East built up trade with the Levant and helped to produce a flourishing Mediterranean commercial activity. This was both a harbinger and a cause of the later oversea exploration. The jealousy on the part of the Western or seaboard European Powers as to the Italian monopoly of the trade with the East led to attempts, first made by the Portuguese, to discover another route to the Indies. This resulted in that great era of exploration which brought about the Commercial Revolution and the beginnings of modern world-trade. From 1550 to the present day the development of world-trade has been one of the most notable agencies promoting the expansion movement. This was especially true after it was reënforced by the increased productivity brought about by the Industrial Revolution. At the present time, in conjunction with the search for raw materials, world-trade quite overshadows all other stimuli to expansion overseas.

A powerful political motive for expansion has been found in modern nationalism, a force that has been developing with ever greater intensity since the appearance of the dynastic national states during the sixteenth and seventeenth centuries. It was nationalism that promoted the narrow and exclusive policy, known as mercantilism, that dominated European commercial and colonial methods from the close of the sixteenth century until its overthrow by the Economic Liberals after the middle of the eighteenth century. It was nationalism that combined with trade rivalry to produce the series of European wars over colonial interests in the late seventeenth century and the eighteenth century.

Another set of influences promoting European expansion was highly varied and complex. These influences may be described vaguely, but on the whole accurately, as psychological. There was, of course, plenty of psychological motivation in the desire to save the heathen, to secure markets, and to advance national power and prestige, but there were powerful psychic incentives over and beyond these. The opportunity for adventure and the possibility of achieving wealth and glory were present. Curiosity was an important factor inducing many a mariner, explorer, and settler to venture forth from his European home. Resentment over oppression—religious, political, or economic—stimulated many to seek their fortunes abroad. The general atmosphere of the age of expansion was such as to catch the imagination of the daring and roving spirits of that era, and many succumbed who were not forced by circumstances to better their lot in the new lands. Piracy was revived,[1] and some of the well-known early explorers were little more than semilegalized pirates.

[1] *Cf.* Philip Gosse, *History of Piracy,* Longmans, 1932.

All of the motives leading to oversea expansion were later strongly stimulated and given new energy by the Industrial Revolution of the eighteenth and nineteenth centuries. The term "Industrial Revolution" refers to the sweeping changes in living and business conditions that followed the introduction of steam as the basis of machine power, and the subsequent mass-production made possible by improved machinery.[1] The vast increase in the production of marketable commodities through the application of machine processes and the factory system has led to the search for wider markets. The improved methods of ocean transportation and of the communication of information have made this search for world-markets more feasible and successful. Explorations in the undeveloped areas have revealed the wealth of raw materials to be obtained from these districts, and the increase of available capital has encouraged the desire of business adventurers to develop the economic potentialities of these backward regions. This exploitation has been made easy through the fact that the industrial and scientific revolutions transformed the military as well as the economic field and created a war technique and military equipment that make it practically impossible for the less advanced peoples to resist European invasion. Modern imperialism has, then, been a historical complex of ever greater significance, which has drawn its motive power from the realms of religious zeal, commercial ambitions, national pride, and the multifarious impulses derived from modern capitalism.

The motives of European expansion may, then, be summarized admirably in Professor Shepherd's epigrammatic statement that those who left Europe for experience overseas were driven primarily by the desire to spread the Gospel, to accumulate gold, and to cover themselves and their country with glory. "Gospel, glory, and gold" were the outstanding motives, conscious or unconscious, associated with the rise of the new order.

IV. THE INTEREST IN THE ORIENT CREATED BY THE CRUSADES

The Crusades constitute the initial phase in the history of European expansion. Considered in this light, rather than as an expression of purely medieval religious fervor, the Crusades assume their proper historical significance.[2] Even though we grant the religious impulse the full measure of its importance, the Crusades should not be considered exclusively as "holy wars" or military pilgrimages to the Sepulcher of Christ. Both their nature and their underlying motivating forces were too complex and varied to support such an interpretation.[3] They were the first major steps in the European colonization of non-European lands, as well as an enormous business undertaking; in short, an anticipation of the still greater movement of expansion that Europe experienced after the close of the fifteenth century. In their own setting they constituted the climax of a general movement of European expansion in the eleventh and twelfth centuries, which took the form of an extension of Christianity.[4] In southern Italy and Sicily, for example, the

---

[1] See below, pp. 263 ff.
[2] *Cf.* W. C. Abbott, *The Expansion of Europe,* Holt, 1924, 2 vols., Vol. I, p. 34.
[3] *Cf.* Thompson, *op. cit.,* Chap. xvi.   [4] *Cf. Ibid.,* Chaps. x, xx, xxii.

Normans conquered and dispossessed the ruling Mohammedans in the course of the eleventh century. (The conflict began in 1016 and continued until 1090.) In Spain, the Christians in the North began in the last quarter of the eleventh century the struggle with the Moors that was not concluded until the days of Columbus. Much the same situation was to be observed in other regions of Europe. At the beginning of the eleventh century, the Germans were expanding eastward, and in this process Poles, Bohemians, and Hungarians were converted.

As we have observed, both the motives that led to the attempted conquest of the Holy Land and the reasons which prompted people to join the Crusades were complex and varied. Pilgrimages from western Europe to the Holy Land, regarded by the Church as a form of penance, had been made from the fourth century on. Even after the Muslim conquest of Syria in the seventh century the pilgrims in increasing numbers continued to make their way to the Holy Land. Mild, tolerant, and efficient, Muslim rule assured the pilgrims a secure and unmolested passage if they met the necessary taxes and fees and if their papers were in order.[1] In the course of the eleventh century the practice of making the journey to the Holy Land in large groups became popular. In 1065, thirty years before the first Crusade, a pilgrimage from southern Germany numbered no less than 11,000 persons.[2] Even such large bands had little complaint to make against the treatment accorded them by the Muslims.

Then came the advance of the Seljuk Turks into Syria, their capture of Jerusalem (in 1071), and their final control of almost all of Asia Minor except the region around Constantinople. These new masters of the Near East were ruder in culture than the earlier Muslims whom they displaced, and less amiable towards the native Christians in Asia Minor. To some Christians in the West it seemed that their presence threatened to place difficulties in the way of the pilgrims. The fear that the Holy Sepulcher might become inaccessible to European Christians did much to create the countless stories after 1071 of attacks and cruelties suffered by pious pilgrims at the hands of the Turks. There seems to have been little actual ground for such a fear. Professor Thompson concludes that "the Seljuk domination in Syria and Palestine entailed little change in the status of the people." Most of the tales testifying to Turkish atrocities immediately before the Crusades were entirely without foundation in fact. In modern eyes they appear to have been the product of the "anti-Islamic propaganda" current in that period. The effectiveness of such propaganda in the West was fully appreciated by Church and feudal lords, and it was freely used to arouse religious fanaticism against the Turks.[3]

Meanwhile, ringing appeals for aid to recover Asia Minor were coming to the West from the hard-pressed Byzantine Emperors in Constantinople. The answer to these entreaties came in the form of the First Crusade, preached by Pope Urban II, aided by devout agitators and fanatics like Peter the Hermit.

---

[1] *Cf.* J. W. Thompson, *The Middle Ages, 300-1500*, Knopf, 1931, 2 vols., Vol. I, pp. 565-66, and *Economic and Social History of the Middle Ages*, pp. 390 ff.

[2] *Cf.* L. J. Paetow, ed., *The Crusades, and Other Historical Essays Presented to Dana C. Munro*, Crofts, 1928, pp. 3-43.

[3] *Cf.* Thompson, *Economic and Social History of the Middle Ages*, p. 391.

Urban, however, was far more concerned with the possibilities inherent in an armed movement on the East than in the difficulties of the Byzantine Emperor, Alexius Comnenus. It offered an opportunity to Urban, who had been exiled from Rome by the Emperor Henry IV, as an episode in the investiture struggle, to regain his power as the leader and head of Christendom; it might create auspicious conditions for healing the breach between the Greek and Roman churches and thus make the Pope ruler over all Christendom; and it might enable the Church to relieve the West of the presence of large numbers of intractable feudal lords whose love of fighting among one another the Church had not succeeded in reducing to any great degree.

At the Council of Clermont (November, 1095), the Pope preached the Holy War to a considerable assemblage of churchmen and feudal nobles, most of them French. In his address, Urban astutely touched on the many motives that might induce men to join a war on the infidel for the recovery of the Holy Land. The bait, so to speak, offered in 1095 in the form of a vast religious raid on rich Eastern lands, and the type of men that responded, make it clear that the name "Crusades" sanctified interests and desires that were not always identical with those of the Church. Whatever the motives and the goals, the same means could be employed.

Granting that an element of religious piety moved some men to become Crusaders, the motives that swayed the vast number of participants were mainly nonreligious. At least one contemporary writer was acute enough to observe that "only a few could be found . . . who were actuated by a holy purpose." All those who engaged in the Crusades were assured the blessings of the Church and the remission of their sins. The feudal knights, warriors by desire and profession, were promised positive entry into Heaven for doing that which they utterly enjoyed—fighting on earth. Assurance of salvation and blessedness through fighting was a potent attraction. Picture the fortunate knight, writes Ernest Barker, who "might butcher all day, till he waded ankle-deep in blood, and then at nightfall kneel, sobbing for very joy, at the altar of the Sepulchre—for was he not red from the winepress of the Lord?"[1]

But there were other, more material attractions. If those who fell were assured of Paradise, those who survived were promised wealth and plunder. For the younger sons of feudal lords, deprived of any appreciable amount of land either by primogeniture or by excessive subdivision, there was the opportunity for carving out a feudal fief in the East. To the landless and the impoverished the Crusades promised to be an undertaking that would temporarily relieve their misery. It is of record that the years immediately preceding the Crusades (1094-95) witnessed widespread famine and pestilence. Would not the fabulous East appear to be a splendid field for emigration? So reasoned many a dejected Westerner. Many of those who joined the Crusades were actually fleeing from debts or duties that oppressed them, and many more from the punishment of their crimes. To the Italian cities, and to the trading class in general, the Crusades offered a golden opportunity for commercial expansion. In addition to the profits from marketing plunder, the payment for shipping of men and horses, and the supplying of provisions, there was the interest

---

[1] Article "Crusades," Encyclopaedia Britannica, 11th ed., p. 524.

of the Italian towns in establishing their own agencies in the cities of the Levant so as to acquire the goods of the East more directly and cheaply. To the peasants, the Crusades offered escape from the lot of serfdom. Many thousands of them, in response to appeals by "self-constituted, ignorant and passionate soap-box orators, like the notorious Peter the Hermit,"[1] broke away from the soil, and added their numbers to the armies of professional soldiers. A large number of vagrants, seizing the opportunity for adventure and spoil, joined in.

In formal theory, at least, the Crusaders were granted, through the instrumentality of the Church, decisive economic privileges: (1) They were exempted, either entirely or partially, from the payment of taxes; (2) they were permitted to alienate their lands without permission of their overlords; (3) they were relieved of debts and absolved from the payment of interest; and (4) their property and dependents were taken care of by the clergy during their absence. In addition, Crusaders could be summoned and tried only before ecclesiastical courts, which almost guaranteed them favorable treatment.

With such attractive prospects and assurances, it is no wonder that the response to the Crusades was almost instantaneous, and that thousands took the cross. The first crusading host, in fact, contained but a handful of knights. Among those who set out for the East in veritable streams between the close of the eleventh century and the last quarter of the thirteenth were representatives from every section of Western society. There were feudal nobles and knights, churchmen, whole families of peasants, merchants, hucksters, and, of course, tramps, criminals, prostitutes, bankrupts, and escaped villeins.

There were expeditions to the East for almost two centuries, but the height of the crusading period lay between 1096 and the recapture of Jerusalem by Saladin in 1187. The First Crusade lasted three years (1096-99); the Second Crusade two years (1147-49); the Third fell between 1189 and 1192; the Fourth Crusade, that commercial venture upon which we have already touched, lasted two years (1202-04); the tragic Children's Crusade occurred in 1212. There were four more expeditions in the thirteenth century, the last in 1270-72.

As military expeditions for the recovery of the Holy Land, the Crusades were never more than partially and temporarily successful, and in the end they were utter failures. Several feudal states were established in western Asia under the rule of Western princes, among which the Kingdom of Jerusalem is perhaps the best known.[2] For our purpose, the Latin kingdoms in the Holy Land are important chiefly as areas for colonization for the discontented of Europe, and for the feudal development and legal formulations that took place in them.[3] Before the thirteenth century drew to a close, the last of their possessions in the Holy Land were lost to the Christians, to be held once more by the devotees of Islam.[4]

The reasons for the failure of the Crusades [5] are not difficult to find. The

[1] Thompson, *Economic and Social History of the Middle Ages*, p. 395. The Church authorized them to appeal to the knights, not to the lower classes.
[2] *Cf.* J. L. La Monte, *Feudal Monarchy in the Latin Kingdom of Jerusalem*, Mediaeval Academy of America, 1933   [3] See above, Vol. I, pp. 579-80.
[4] The Kingdom of Cyprus, founded in 1195, however, remained an independent state until 1489.
[5] That is, with reference to the specific purpose for which they were initiated.

natural obstacles in the way of the undertaking, the lack of efficient coöperation among the Western leaders, the increasing antagonism between the Byzantine Empire and the Powers of the West (presumably allies at first), the friction and struggle between the Empire and the papacy in Europe, the conflicting interests and ambitions of the chief Crusaders, the sharp commercial rivalry among the Italian cities and towns, the precarious nature of the feudal states erected in the Holy Land, the irresponsible attitude of the Europeans, essentially interested in exploiting the East, the fact that whatever religious fervor had been present at first was soon obscured by other, more worldly motives that inevitably created bitter antipathies—these were all factors that reduced the potency of the Crusades as political, military, and religious enterprises.

It has been usual to lay primary stress upon the Crusades as military expeditions and to deal chiefly with the warfare between Muslims and Christians. But, in the last generation, historians, led by Ernest Barker, Dana C. Munro, and others, have come to see that far more important than the fighting were the peaceful contacts between Christians and Muslims for nearly two hundred years in Palestine, Syria, and Asia Minor. Commercial, cultural, and other relationships were maintained during the long interludes between active strife. The Crusaders and their Italian mercantile associates gained increasing knowledge of Muslim civilization and economic life. They also learned from the Muslims about the civilizations of the Further Orient. Even the peacetime activities of the Crusaders themselves were probably more significant than their military exploits, especially their training in systematic feudal government.[1]

One of the most spectacular results of the Crusades was the establishment of three military orders.[2] These were the Templars, founded in 1119 to protect pilgrims and to wage incessant war on the infidel; the Hospitalers of St. John of Jerusalem, organized in 1130 to succor the afflicted pilgrims and fight the unbelievers, though its existence as a charitable organization goes back half a century before the First Crusade; and the German or Teutonic order established at the close of the twelfth century with a purpose similar to that of the two older organizations. The Teutonic Knights were not very active in the Holy Land. Their main contribution lay in the conquest of the Baltic coast and East Prussia for Christianity. These societies, which were presumably charitable in purpose, soon neglected that function and became essentially military organizations. Before long they had acquired great wealth, and with their extensive holdings, armies, naval forces, and financial institutions, were like "chartered companies." They were destroyed later, mainly because their wealth aroused the avarice of kings like Philip the Fair of France.

In Europe proper, the growing French monarchy seems to have profited in prestige and renown from the Crusades, because the enterprise was so largely French. Germany was extended to the east as a result of the activities of the Teutonic order. The papacy grew in power and the Church in wealth through

---

[1] As examples of this newer emphasis, see Paetow, *op. cit.*, pp. 139-82; D. C. Munro, article "Crusades," Encyclopedia of the Social Sciences; and Ernest Barker, in Sir T. W. Arnold and Alfred Guillaume, eds., *The Legacy of Islam*, Oxford Press, 1931, pp. 40 ff.

[2] See above, Vol. I, pp. 707 ff.

the Crusades. But the papacy also experienced spiritual corruption from them.

The effect of the Crusades upon the social, economic, and cultural life of Europe is far from clear, and is still a matter of sharp difference of opinion among historians. We have already taken note of the significant and fundamental changes that took place in the structure of European civilization after the eleventh century. Some historians tend to ascribe to the Crusades the origin or at least the stimulus for these transformations.[1] Others are prone to minimize the influence of the Crusades upon European life. "The Crusades undoubtedly had a general effect upon the Christian societies," writes Seignobos; "but for all these effects there were more active and more positive causes in the peoples of the West." It is extremely difficult to distinguish between European phenomena that simply occurred contemporaneously with the Crusades, and those which were clearly influenced by them. It is true that some of the direct results usually claimed for them are not susceptible to proof. Nevertheless, the heightened contact between the Western and Eastern civilizations certainly left unmistakable, if imponderable or immeasurable, influences upon the civilization of Europe. In bringing the West into touch with civilizations unlike its own and in most ways superior to it, the Crusades performed their greatest service. From this point of view, whatever stimulus was given to Europe by the interaction of different cultures and peoples may be considered an indirect result of the Crusades. With reference to the transformations that occurred in European economic and social life, we may safely say that the Crusades served to stimulate and accelerate the already existing European movements, as well as to set in motion several new and original trends.

Among those forward-looking developments which are to be related to the Crusades, either directly or indirectly, we may note especially: (1) The discrediting of the Church, which had preached the Crusades that failed to rescue the Holy Land, and a relaxation of Church discipline through indiscriminate granting of indulgences and remission of penance in recognition of special acts of bravery and generosity; (2) further exploration and travel in the East, with the consequent increase of geographical knowledge, and what we may call the "discovery" of the Far Orient by the West before the opening of the fourteenth century; (3) the revival of trade with Syria and the increased demand for the products of the East; (4) the growth of commerce with the East, with the resulting increase in the prosperity of the Italian trading cities, the development of the great European overland trade routes, many improvements in the technique of medieval trade, and the growth of towns in northern Europe; (5) the beginnings of a money economy in Europe with all the implications that flow from so fundamental a change; (6) a body blow to the feudal system because of the lives and money lost by the nobles during the Crusades; and (7) the rise and increasing influence of the middle class in the West.

In addition, contact with the Byzantine and Muslim civilizations served to stimulate the cultural pulse of Europe. Western knowledge of mathematics

---

[1] See, for instance, Abbott, *op. cit.,* Vol. I, p. 34.

and science was broadened, new interests were aroused, new tastes in food and clothing were acquired, and some measure of skepticism and tolerance was gained.[1] Finally, the interest in exploration and discovery, so largely stimulated by the Crusades, continued unabated to reap its rewards in the period of the oversea expansion of Europe that set in at the close of the fifteenth century.

V. MEDIEVAL CONTACTS WITH THE FAR EAST AND THEIR INFLUENCE ON EUROPEAN EXPANSION

Following on the heels of the Crusades came the next important development that notably stimulated the contact of Europeans with outside areas. This was the series of medieval visits to the Far East which, spurred on mainly by religious and commercial motives, began in the middle of the thirteenth century and stirred both the curiosity and the cupidity of Westerners. Not only did the highly advanced civilizations of the Far East vastly impress the crude Europeans, but the fabulous riches of these areas suggested that much money might be made through more extended commercial contacts.

A great historical movement prompted and facilitated these travels. The so-called Tatars (Tartars) conquered the greater part of Asia and made large inroads into Muslim areas. The Christian Powers of western Europe looked to the Tatars as potential allies against the Mohammedan hosts. Miss Eileen Power has admirably summarized the significance of this Tatar conquest for subsequent medieval travel and the very significant results that flowed therefrom:

The Tartar conquests began at the beginning of the thirteenth century, when Chinghiz Khan and his hordes came down from Mongolia and attacked the Chinese Empire, taking Peking in 1214 and by degrees, in the course of the next fifty years, extending their sway until they ruled almost the whole of Eastern Asia. They first turned westward in 1218 and the flood of conquest slowly spread right across Asia, over a large part of Russia, into Poland and Hungary, and all over Persia and part of Asia Minor, until by the death of Mangu Khan in 1259 one empire stretched from the Yellow River to the banks of the Danube, and from the Persian Gulf to Siberia. Nothing like it had ever been known in history before, for the Roman Empire was a mere midget in comparison, and nothing like it was to be known again until the great land empire of Russia in the nineteenth century. . . .

After 1241 the flood of conquest rolled back, and when next it rolled West again, it was seen to overwhelm not Christian kingdoms but the caliphates of Baghdad and Syria, establishing in the '50s Tartar for Muslim rule there, sacking Baghdad and extinguishing the Caliphate in 1258. For this reason the attitude of Europe began to undergo a change, and men saw in the Tartars not a menace to Christendom but a possible ally against a common enemy. As Europeans got to know more about the Tartars, they learned that they were tolerant to all creeds, Buddhist, Muhammadan, Jewish and Christian, having no very strongly marked beliefs of their own. They began also to learn that there were large groups of Nestorian Christians still scattered throughout Asia. Europeans who visited the Tartar camp at Karakorum

---

[1] See above, Vol. I, Chapters xiv-xv; and Charles Seignobos, *History of Mediaeval and Modern Civilization,* Scribner, 1907, Chap. x.

MEDIEVAL CONTACTS WITH THE FAR EAST

brought back news of ladies of high rank, wives and mothers of khans, who professed the Christian faith. Rumours of the conversion now of the Great Khan himself in Cathay, now of one or other of the lesser khans in Persia or Russia, kept rising, and men repeated also the famous legend of Prester John.[1] All these things, together with the indisputable fact that the Tartars had laid the Muslim power low all over Asia, began to present them to Western rulers in a totally new light. Gradually there took shape the dream of converting the Tartars to Christianity and then forming a great Tartar-Christian alliance which should smite Islam hip and thigh, reconquer Palestine and Egypt, and succeed where crusades from the West alone had failed.

From the middle of the thirteenth century, therefore, it is essential to remember that Europe was no longer shrinking in terror from the Tartars, but on the contrary was looking upon them as potential converts and allies. Embassies were continually setting out to one or other of the centres of their power, Sarai on the Volga, the new Persian capital of Tabriz, or distant Cathay, from the Pope, or the King of France, or the King of England, with invitations to embrace Christianity and projects of alliance. Merchants also began to go thither to trade and Franciscan friars to preach, and by degrees a busy intercourse sprang up between East and West. . . .

The century 1245 to 1345 was indeed an heroic age in the history of travel and an epoch in the relations of East and West. But while we give our wonder and admiration to William of Rubruck, Marco Polo, John of Monte Corvino and the other travellers who first made Asia known to Europe in this brief and marvellous episode, let us not forget that it was solely and entirely due to the Tartars that they were able to do so, and let us modify in our own minds, if not indeed reverse, the unjust verdict by which history has too often ungratefully condemned them. For if the world had not caught a Tartar in the thirteenth century, it would have been the poorer for a legacy of imperishable courage and romance.[2]

The first medieval traveler to make the trip from Europe to the Far East and to return alive was John of Piano Carpini. John was an Italian friar belonging to the Franciscan order. He was sent to Tatary by Pope Innocent IV, in 1245. He was received by the Great Khan near Karakorum in Mongolia. The journal of his travels was the best of all medieval descriptions of the manners and customs of the Tatars. Having been present at the election of the Khan, he was able to include a description of the lavish and impressive ceremonies connected with it. John was absent from the West for two years, and reached the papal court on his return journey in 1247.

Nearly a decade later, William of Rubruck, a French friar from Flanders, was sent by King Louis IX of France on a mission to the Khan. He left for the Far East in 1251 and returned to France in 1255. He joined to his predecessor's capacity for accurate description a capacity to write a very entertaining narrative. But the most famous of all of these medieval travelers to the Far Orient was Marco Polo (1254-1324). Two Italian merchants, Marco's father, Nicolo, and his uncle, Maffeo, had paid a visit to the Khan and had been requested by the latter to return to the Pope and to bring back to the Far East a company of learned men who might give instruction in Western learning. They failed to enlist the desired scholars but they took back with

---

[1] A legendary Christian emperor, first believed by western Europeans to reign in India and later in Ethiopia. See Newton, *op. cit.* below, pp. 182-86, 194.
[2] In A. P. Newton, ed., *Travel and Travellers in the Middle Ages,* Knopf, 1926, pp. 126-28, 158.

them young Marco, then a lad of seventeen. Leaving Italy in November, 1271, they arrived at the court of the Khan in May, 1275. The Khan was immediately impressed with the intelligence and energy of Marco Polo and sent him on many missions to distant regions extending from Siberia to India. He was at one time governor of an important Chinese city.[1]

A keen observer, he made ample notes bearing on his striking experiences. After many years of Marco's faithful service in the employ of the Khan, the latter reluctantly consented to allow him to return in 1292, reaching Venice in the winter of 1295. He was taken prisoner after a naval encounter between Genoa and Venice in 1298. While in prison in Genoa he dictated his famous *Travels* to a fellow captive, Rusticiano of Pisa, who fortunately possessed marked literary ability. These *Travels* are among the most important journals ever written. They were not only interesting but highly comprehensive and accurate. Miss Power says of them:

> It is almost impossible to speak too highly either of the extent of his observation or of its accuracy. It is true that he repeats some of the usual travellers' tales, and that where he reports from hearsay he not infrequently makes mistakes; but where he had observed with his own eyes he was almost always accurate; he had a great opportunity, and he was great enough to take it.[2]

Though Marco Polo had been preceded by the two travelers we have already mentioned, his *Travels* added greatly to our knowledge of the Far East. The eminent authorities Professor Yule and Professor Beazley thus describe his importance in medieval geographic discovery:

> Polo was the first traveller to trace a route across the whole longitude of Asia, naming and describing kingdom after kingdom which he had seen; the first to speak of the new and brilliant court which had been established at Peking; the first to reveal China in all its wealth and vastness, and to tell of the nations on its borders; the first to tell more of Tibet than its name, to speak of Burma, of Laos, of Siam, of Cochin-China, of Japan, of Java, of Sumatra and of other islands of the archipelago, of the Nicobar and Andaman Islands, of Ceylon and its sacred peak, of India but as a country seen and partially explored; the first in medieval times to give any distinct account of the secluded Christian Empire of Abyssinia, and of the semi-Christian island of Sokotra, and to speak, however dimly, of Zanzibar, and of the vast and distant Madagascar; whilst he carries us also to the remotely opposite region of Siberia and the Arctic shores, to speak of dog-sledges, white bears, and reindeer-riding Tunguses.[3]

The profound impression that the facts contained in Marco Polo's book made upon Europeans in his day has been well summarized by Professor Gillespie:

> Those Europeans who had the opportunity in the days before printing to read Marco's book must have been considerably impressed by the contrast between the rather sordid conditions then existing in European lands and the advanced civilization and splendors of the Khan's great empire. For there were to be found great cities like Pekin, twenty-four miles square, with streets "so broad and straight that

---

[1] On Marco Polo, see E. E. Power, *Medieval People*, Houghton Mifflin, 1924, Chap. II.
[2] In Newton, *op. cit.*, p. 135.   [3] Article "Marco Polo," Encyclopaedia Britannica, 11th ed., p. 10.

from one gate another [was] visible"; or Kin-sai in the south of China, with its twelve thousand stone-bridges, its four thousand public baths, its many ships and merchants "so numerous and so rich that their wealth [could] neither be told nor believed." The vast marble palaces surrounded by beautiful parks in which the Great Khan resided amidst a magnificent court, clothed in splendid robes of gold and silk bedecked with costly jewels, the great storehouses of grain maintained as a safeguard against famine, and the Khan's messenger service, which reached to the farthest borders of his empire, were all such matters of wonder to Europeans that they were still seeking to find them centuries later when Columbus made his famous voyage of discovery. Perhaps even more to their liking was the island of Cipangu (Japan), lying to the east of the continent of Asia, where Marco reported "gold is abundant beyond all measure." Here, so it was said, was to be found a great palace completely roofed with gold and paved with great plates of gold "like slabs of stone, a good two fingers thick."[1]

Other travelers followed John, William, and Marco to the Orient. One papal legate, John of Monte Corvino (1247-1328), a Franciscan friar, attained the honor of becoming the archbishop of Peking. In 1329 the Pope sent a French Dominican, Jordanus, on a missionary enterprise to India. He was an acute observer and an excellent writer. To him and to John of Monte Corvino and Oderic of Pordenone medieval Europe owed the main additions to its knowledge of India. Far and away the most extensive traveler of all was a Muslim explorer, Ibn Battuta (1304-78), who spent some twenty-eight years in more or less continuous travel in Africa and Asia. He is estimated to have covered some 75,000 miles, and his descriptions of his travels, while at times full of imagination, are generally accurate and informing.

Widespread popular interest in these travels to the Far East was aroused by a fictitious book entitled *The Travels of Sir John Mandeville*. This first appeared in French between 1357 and 1371. It was a fanciful work, compiled indiscriminately from ancient encyclopaedists like Pliny, medieval compilers such as Vincent of Beauvais, and actual contemporary travelers to the Far East. Though a weird mixture of fact and fiction, it caught the popular imagination and did much to arouse general curiosity about the riches and wonders of the Far East. The general social and intellectual effect of these travels has been admirably summarized by Miss Power:

There is no need to labour the effect of the tremendous mass of exact knowledge which the reports of Marco Polo brought to the enterprising mercantile world of Venice and Genoa, and to the hardly less enterprising ecclesiastical world which was still cherishing its great scheme of converting the Tartars. The two friars who first penetrated to Mongolia and the three merchants who first made the great tour to Cathay by land and back to Europe by sea were only pioneers of a widespread movement. For it was by now plain that the Tartar Empire had wrought one of the most startling revolutions in the history of the world up to that date by bringing into contact for the first time the two ends of the earth, Europe and the Far East. For the next fifty years or so, roughly between 1290 and 1340, a steady stream of travellers took the Eastern road. They had need, indeed, to find new trade routes, for the collapse of the Latin power in Palestine, culminating in the loss of Acre in 1291, was seriously interrupting the old. The term "trade routes" is used advisedly,

[1] Gillespie, *History of Geographical Discovery, 1400-1800*, Holt, 1933, p. 9.

for although some of the best travel books belonging to this period were written by missionaries, the real impetus to travel was given by trade, and the most frequent journeys to Persia, India and Cathay were made by merchants.

These merchants now found themselves no longer mere clients at the closed gates of the east, loading their ships with goods brought to those termini by Muslim middlemen; they found that they could pass through the gates and themselves follow the trade routes. Direct access to the East was at last open to them, and it has been said with truth that "the unification of Asia by the Mongols was as important a fact for the commerce of the Middle Ages as the discovery of America for the men of the Renaissance. It was equivalent to the discovery of Asia." . . .

There are surely few episodes in history more remarkable and more interesting than these years, when an Italian archbishop held sway in Peking, when Genoese merchants had a *fondaco* at Zaiton and chaffered in the ports of India, when Franciscan friars set up convents in the towns of Persia and China, and mission stations in Turkestan, and when merchants and missionaries regularly took the caravan roads across Central Asia, or sailed in junks through the Indian Ocean and among the Spice Islands.[1]

In the latter part of the fourteenth century the Tatars were driven out of western Asia by the Muslims and were displaced in China by the antiforeign Ming dynasty. Thereafter, the freedom of Western Christian travelers to move to and fro from East to West came to an end. Henceforth, they could only meet with the orientals to trade at the fixed terminals of the trade routes to the Far East. But in less than a century the curiosity of Europe concerning the Orient had been enormously whetted and its knowledge of these distant areas vastly extended. While cultural contact was greatly curtailed thereafter, trading relations were maintained, and constituted the backbone of that revival of medieval commerce which we have described in the preceding volume.[2] For many years this new commerce was controlled by the city-states of the Mediterranean basin, especially those of the Italian Peninsula. In due time, however, this trade led to the rise and growth along the Atlantic seaboard in western Europe of towns that would no longer inactively tolerate the monopoly of the Mediterranean cities.

While the volume of European foreign trade during the so-called Dark Ages was greater than was once supposed,[3] it is true that the most notable revival of medieval trade in the West followed the Crusades.[4] The peoples of western Europe desired from the Malay Archipelago and the East Indies the essential spices needed to make palatable their coarse and ill-preserved food. They further wished to secure precious stones from Persia and India; drugs, perfumes, gums, dyes, and woods from the Indies, China, and Japan; and silks, draperies, cloth, rugs, and fine steel work from Syria, Persia, and Asia Minor. The demand for these commodities, awakened or at least enhanced by the contact with the East during the Crusades, was exploited first by the Italian city-states. Their traders purchased these products which had been brought from the East through the Red Sea, Asia Minor, or Turkestan, took them back to Europe, and sold them to distributing merchants.

As was noted near the beginning of this chapter, a venerable tradition in

---

[1] Power, *loc. cit.*, pp. 136, 152.
[2] See Vol. I, pp. 650 ff.
[3] See above, Vol. I, p. 657.
[4] See above, Vol. I, pp. 657 ff.

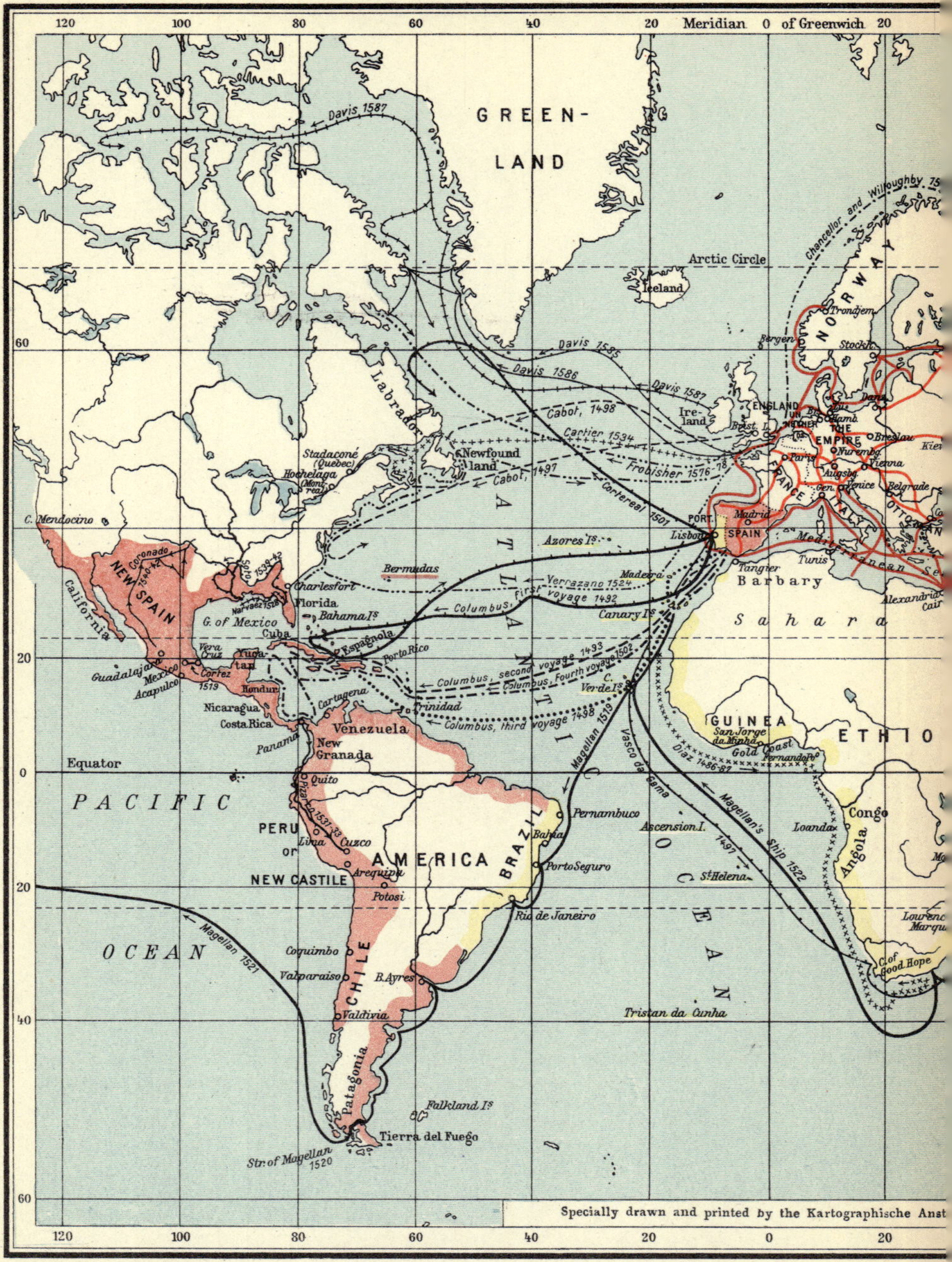

PRINTED IN GERMANY

TRADE ROUTES AND ROUTES OF THE EXPLORERS

- Spain and Spanish Discoveries in the 15th and 16th Century
- Portugal and Portuguese " " " " "
- Medieval Trade Routes

Scale of Miles along Equator

A. Brockhaus, Leipzig, Germany.

European historical writing represented the occupation of the above-mentioned Eastern trade routes by the Turks after 1453 as the chief cause of the downfall of the Italian city-states and the major reason for the subsequent attempts of western Europeans to discover new routes to the East. This conception was a phase of the catastrophic theory of the origin of modern times which made the fall of Constantinople appear the starting-point of the development of modern civilization. The Renaissance and the Reformation were once attributed to the capture of Constantinople by the Turks. It is now apparent that this event had little or nothing to do with the Renaissance, the Reformation, or oversea discoveries.

Research into the statistics of prices following 1453[1] reveals no appreciable effect of Turkish occupation on the volume or the prices of commodities coming from the Far East to Europe. This revelation makes it clear that there was no serious disruption of trade with the Far East after 1453, since the European demand for the Eastern products may be assumed to have remained constant or to have increased somewhat. Any curtailment of the supply would have forced prices up markedly. This research also calls attention to the fact that the Turks did not occupy or close the southern trade routes to the Far East until nearly a generation after oversea communication had been established with the Indies.

It seems, rather, that the chief cause of oversea exploration was the jealousy of the developing western European seaboard Powers and merchants as to the Italian monopoly of the Eastern trade. With the Portuguese and Spanish, religious motives—"crusading, conquest, and adventure"—were also very powerful.

The Portuguese under Henry the Navigator[2] and Diaz began, in the middle of the fifteenth century, the explorations that ultimately ended in the successful voyage of Vasco da Gama to India in 1498. Under Spanish auspices, Columbus discovered America in 1492, and Magellan's fleet circumnavigated the globe in 1519-22. These and subsequent explorations opened the way for further expansion and constituted the geographical foundation of the expansion of Europe, the Commercial Revolution, and the dawn of modern history.

VI. THE SIGNIFICANT EXPLORATIONS AND DISCOVERIES

1. PORTUGUESE EXPLORATION

Prince Henry the Navigator, of Portugal, while governor of Ceuta and of the southernmost Portuguese region of the Algarve, conceived the plan of exploring the West African coast beyond Cape Bojador in search of a new route to the East.[3] All available sources of information were employed, and for a continuous period of over fifty years Prince Henry sent ships to chart the African coast and the adjacent islands for the benefit of merchant vessels. By granting licenses for private enterprise, Prince Henry attracted many

[1] Especially by Professor A. H. Lybyer.
[2] See Sir C. R. Beazley, *Prince Henry the Navigator*, Putnam, 1895.
[3] Some scholars doubt if Henry ever really conceived of his project in the light of a search for a new route to the East.

profiteers, and in a few years ships were bringing slaves to Portugal. Explorations became more frequent. In 1447-48 a ship reached Cape Verde, and a decade later Diego Gomez was sent to explore the Cape Verde Islands in search of gold and a sea route to India. After Prince Henry's death these enterprises were continued intermittently, and finally in 1486 Diaz rounded the Cape of Good Hope.

Jealous of the success of the Spanish expeditions, the Portuguese under Emanuel the Fortunate outfitted a small fleet under the command of Vasco da Gama. This expedition set sail for India in 1497 by way of the Cape of Good Hope. After stopping at the Cape Verde Islands to replenish supplies, the fleet sailed southward in the Atlantic for a period of ninety-three days before landing at St. Helena's Bay, situated a hundred miles north of the Cape. Rounding the latter in November, Vasco da Gama, fighting storms, mutinies, winds, and currents, attempted to land at three different places but was driven back each time by unfriendly natives. At Melinde he made the acquaintance of an amicable sultan and secured the services of a pilot to direct him across the Indian Ocean. After sailing for twenty-three days, he finally dropped anchor at Calicut,[1] an important port on the western or Malabar coast of India, more than a year after he had left Portugal.

Following Vasco da Gama's voyage, many fleets sailed to the East. These aroused the hostility of the Muslims by taking over much of the large Muslim trade and by mistreating the Muslim natives.

Learning that the Muslims in the Levant and India were preparing to strike at Portugal, the Portuguese sent a large fleet under the command of Francisco de Almeida and vanquished them in a naval battle at Diu, February, 1509, thus gaining for Portugal the control of the Indian Ocean.

Under the leadership of the able general, Affonso de Albuquerque, successor to De Almeida as viceroy of India, the port of Goa, in north Malabar, and Malacca were successfully attacked. Forts were built, the one at Malacca controlling the Straits passage to the more remote East. Going on to the Spice Islands, Albuquerque organized trading-posts which later enabled Portuguese commerce to be carried as far as China. The next years witnessed the migration of large numbers of Portuguese to the Orient, preoccupied more with the acquisition of the riches the East offered than with the industrial and agricultural exploitation of the new colonial domains. Although a long series of trading and military posts stretched from Canton to the Straits of Gibraltar by the middle of the sixteenth century, and although the Red Sea, the Indian Ocean, and the South Atlantic were firmly controlled, the enterprise was not as profitable as it might have been. Lisbon was the center for the commercial houses of most of the European nations, and Portuguese trade secrets soon became common property. Wealth easily attained gradually tended to slacken the vigorous action that had been characteristic of these people in the earlier days of expansion overseas.

Approximately two years after Vasco da Gama's voyage, and several years after Columbus' first voyage, Portugal sent out another fleet of ships, this time numbering thirteen and manned by 1,200 sailors under the command

---

[1] Not the modern Calcutta.

of Pedro Alvarez Cabral, to take possession of the commerce in the East. Steering in an extreme southwesterly direction, Cabral sighted land, which he claimed as a Portuguese possession. This was Brazil, and Spain, which had exploited Columbus's bravery and ingenuity, was no longer the sole power in the Western Hemisphere.

2. SPANISH DISCOVERIES

Christopher Columbus, a native of Genoa, who later lived in Portugal, early became convinced that the East Indies could be reached by sailing westward—a notion already widely prevalent among geographers. Desiring to prove this, he submitted his plans to Portugal, to England, and to every other state with some maritime significance except Venice, but was rebuffed by each one in turn. Finally Queen Isabella of Castile decided to back him, and raised $100,000. With this he outfitted three ships, and on August 3, 1492, set sail westward from Palos. From the Canaries, his first stop, he proceeded westward, and thirty-three days later (October 12, 1492) sighted land, which he believed to be Asia. It was in reality one of the Bahamas, but for more than a century after Columbus Europeans failed fully to recognize the reality of a Western Hemisphere standing between them and the East Indies and China.

Magellan, a Portuguese in Spanish service, was commissioned in 1519 to lead a fleet of five ships across the Atlantic and around South America to the Spice Islands. Leaving San Lucar, he followed the eastern coast of South America southwards, spent the winter in Patagonia, crossed at the southern tip of the continent the straits that bear his name,[1] and finally emerged into the Pacific. Mutiny, desertion, starvation, scurvy, and fear of sailing over the edge of the world were some of the hardships he had to endure and combat. Two of his ships were lost. Nearing Asia, Magellan claimed the Philippines in the name of Spain, but during hostilities with the natives he and a number of his sailors were killed, and one of his three ships was burned. Of the two remaining ships one, the *Trinidad,* attempted to recross the Pacific, but was driven back to the Moluccas and its sailors were taken prisoners by the Portuguese; the other, the *Victoria,* continued the journey, sailed around the Cape of Good Hope, and at last reached Spain three years after first setting sail. The circumnavigation of the globe was a significant event in the history of the world, since it obtained added information as to its size and proved definitely that the earth was round. In addition, the vastness of the Pacific and the remoteness of America from Asia were for the first time satisfactorily demonstrated.

3. FRENCH, ENGLISH, AND DUTCH EXPLORATION

Fearful and jealous of the power and wealth being amassed by the Spanish and Portuguese, the English, French, and Dutch attempted explorations on their own accounts. Henry VII, King of England, sent John Cabot, a Venetian, to the northwest in an attempt to discover another means of reaching the Indies.[2] In 1497 he landed on the coast of North America near Labrador, and placed for England a claim to the New World. For the next hundred years

[1] *Cf.* James Bryce, *South America,* Macmillan, 1914, Chap. VIII.
[2] N. M. Crouse, *The Search for the Northwest Passage,* Columbia University Press, 1934.

England, still hopeful of finding a northern route to the Indies, continued sending ships to this region. France, inspired by England's efforts, also commissioned searches in this area, relinquishing the idea, however, much earlier than England. One of its navigators, Jacques Cartier, while exploring the eastern coast of North America sailed up the St. Lawrence River as far as the Lachine Rapids (1534-36), and thus established a French claim to Canada. These ventures, unsuccessful in their primary object, nevertheless revealed to Europe the value of the Newfoundland fisheries. Henry Hudson explored the Atlantic coast of North America for the Dutch and sailed up the Hudson River in 1609. In 1578 Francis Drake, an Englishman, while circumnavigating the globe as a plunderer of Spanish ships (1577-80), touched northern California and claimed it for England. Drake was the most intrepid and successful of English explorers. His voyage around the world in 1577-80 was rivaled only by that of Magellan among early explorations, and Drake covered much more ground than Magellan and his sailors. He touched Brazil, went through the Straits of Magellan, came up the Pacific coast of America to 48° N. lat., went westward to Java, and then rounded the Cape of Good Hope for home.

In North America during the seventeenth century the English secured colonies extending along the Atlantic coast from Canada to Florida; the Dutch had New Netherlands and were moving southward when they were halted by the English; and the French had established trading and military posts in the valleys of the St. Lawrence and the Mississippi, and in the region about the Great Lakes.

In 1553 the English sent three ships to the northeast in search of a passage to China. One, under the control of Richard Chancellor, reached Archangel, on the White Sea coast of Russia. This led to a trading agreement with the Tsar and to the establishment of the Muscovy Company. In 1584 the Dutch also established a commercial outpost at Archangel.

After England's victory over Spain and the Spanish Armada (1588), James Lancaster was sent with an expedition to make contacts in the East, and on December 31, 1600, the struggle to establish the monopoly of English commerce in the Indies was launched through the incorporation of the English East India Company. In 1602 a similar company was formed by the Dutch, and later the French, observing their success, established still a third.

In the West Indies, the Dutch had formed the Dutch West India Company in 1617-21, settled on many of the Antilles, especially Curaçao, and carried on an extensive smuggling commerce with the mainland. Not content with the progress they had made, the Dutch sent a force to conquer Brazil, Peru, and Mexico, but the attempt failed. The Spanish had negligently omitted to make proper provision for the protection of all the West Indies, and soon the English had established themselves in Barbados, St. Christopher, Jamaica, and many other islands; the Dutch in Curaçao and St. Eustatius; and the French in Martinique, Guadeloupe, part of Santo Domingo, and in other islands of less importance.

SIGNIFICANT EXPLORATIONS AND DISCOVERIES

4. RUSSIAN EXPANSION EASTWARD

Meanwhile the Russians, in an attempt to escape the unjust severity of their government and in search of sables, expanded eastward and penetrated Siberia.[1] In 1639 they reached the eastern waters and constructed a fort on the shore of the Sea of Okhotsk. In 1690, they found the Kamchatka Peninsula and heard rumors here of a strange country to the northeast. Learning of this, Peter the Great sent out expeditions to ascertain their truth. Finally, in 1740, Bering, a Danish navigator employed by Russia, sighted North America. Four years later, missionaries and exiles settled at Yakutat Bay and at Sitka in Alaska. Soon afterward ships from Spain, France, and England, as well as Russia, were cruising the waters around Alaska, drawn by the promise of acquiring the wealth to be had from seal-hunting.

In this chapter our treatment of European expansion has, for pedagogical and chronological reasons, been rather arbitrarily terminated about the year 1800. In a later chapter we shall describe the expansion movement in the nineteenth and twentieth centuries, including the European invasion of the Far East, the complete conquest of India, the occupation of Australasia, the partition of Africa, further Russian expansion over Siberia, and the like.[2]

VII. THE RIVAL COMMERCIAL EMPIRES

The epoch from 1500 to 1763 in world-politics may be most intelligently viewed as the era of the rise and struggles of those rival commercial empires whose explorations and conquests we have just briefly surveyed. This period started off with the rise of the Portuguese to commercial supremacy following the return of Vasco da Gama from India in 1499, and ended with the defeat of the French in North America and India by Great Britain in 1763.

Taking advantage of its priority in explorations in the East, Portugal occupied the Spice Islands and points along the Indian and African coasts, and built up a considerable trade. Its internal strength was not equal, however, to the strain imposed by this overextended and rapid external expansion. It lacked the naval power to defend its trading monopoly; it was unable to organize a systematic and competent distributing service for the Eastern commodities; it had few commodities to be taken East in exchange for materials purchased; and a corrupt officialdom made it impossible for it to control unscrupulous traders. Its decline invited foreign aggression, and in 1580 Portugal was annexed to Spain and held in subjection for some sixty years.

Spain vied with Portugal as an early contender for colonial and commercial supremacy, occupying the greater part of the New World, especially South America and Central America, and several groups of Pacific islands. The impressive wealth thereby secured and controlled by Spain might have made that country the greatest of modern powers had it been guided by a wise administrative and fiscal policy, but such wisdom was lacking, and the

---

[1] *Cf.* Andrei Lobanov-Rostovsky, *Russia and Asia,* Macmillan, 1933, Chaps. I-IV; and F. A. Golder, *Russian Expansion on the Pacific, 1641-1850,* A. H. Clark, 1914.
[2] See below, Chapter xv.

Spanish decline was only slightly less rapid and complete than that of Portugal.

The excessively strict regulation of the colonial trade under Spanish mercantilism [1] crippled the commerce of the colonies with the mother country and invited smuggling; a cruel and wasteful system of native labor lessened productivity in the colonies; the expulsion of Jews and Moors from Spain drove its moneyed classes beyond its borders, while repudiation of debts forced the withdrawal of German credit; religious bigotry and fiscal exaction lost Spain the rich Netherlands; the Inquisition crushed out intellectual originality and initiative; and the loss of the Armada in 1588 meant the end of Spanish naval supremacy.[2] At the beginning of the seventeenth century Spain was becoming the second-rate power that it has since remained.

Stirred to action by Spanish oppression, the Netherlands enjoyed commercial supremacy in Europe for more than a half-century following 1590, occupying most of the old Portuguese possessions in the East, as well as valuable areas in North and South America.[3] But the Dutch were apparently not equal to the task of integrating and administering a permanent empire of great extent.[4] Like the ancient Greek confederacies, the Netherlands were a loosely united group of jealous city-states rather than a compact national unit; the "Spanish Fury" helped to ruin Antwerp, and the closing of the Scheldt ended its prosperity; the Dutch devoted their energy chiefly to commercial activity, giving but little attention to permanent colonial policy; and in the contest with England under Cromwell and during the early years of the Restoration the Dutch were thoroughly worsted. Though the Dutch naval power was shattered in the middle of the seventeenth century, the Netherlands retained their predominant position in the carrying trade of the world well down into the eighteenth century—at least to 1730.

France was prevented from making an early entry into the commercial and colonial scramble by the religious divisions that led to the civil wars of the latter part of the sixteenth century. Even when it did make some systematic attempt to contend as a first-class commercial and colonizing power, its strength was sapped by the suicidal policy of Louis XIV. At the critical moment in the colonial competition Louis wasted the national energy of France in futile attempts to extend his eastern boundary and humiliate the Hapsburgs. France was immensely more rich and potentially more powerful than England in the seventeenth and eighteenth centuries, but it lost out in the final conflict because of a corrupt administration, the failure to devote its resources to the strengthening of its colonies, and the adoption of a fatally weak colonial policy—that of scattered military occupation.

Though England had, by 1763, become the leading colonial and commercial state of Europe, it was, until the time of Elizabeth, a relatively small and weak state. The rising British sea power was based upon the naval training afforded its sailors by buccaneering expeditions against the Spaniards. The extent of this power was clearly demonstrated by the destruction of the Spanish Armada

---

[1] *Cf.* W. R. Shepherd, *Latin America*, Holt, 1914, Chap. IV; and J. W. Horrocks, *Short History of Mercantilism*, Brentano's, 1925, Chap. VII.

[2] *Cf. Cambridge Modern History*, Vol. III, Chap. XV.

[3] *Cf. Ibid.*, Chap. VI; and Hendrik Van Loon, *The Fall of the Dutch Republic*, new ed., Houghton Mifflin, 1924.   [4] *Cf.* Clive Day, *History of Commerce*, Longmans, 1922, pp. 195-96.

in 1588. After the Dutch were vanquished in the middle of the seventeenth century, the hundred years' duel of England and France for colonial supremacy began. England took its colonial enterprise seriously, while France looked upon it as a "side issue" when compared to the dynastic struggle on the continent of Europe between the Bourbons and the Hapsburgs. But the chief significance of this century-long contest was that it represented a struggle between two different colonial systems—the intensive occupation and exploitation of a limited area versus the extremely meager settlement of a vast territory by a few soldiers and traders. In 1688 there were about 300,000 English colonists in the narrow piedmont region of the Atlantic Coast, while there were scarcely 20,000 Frenchmen in the vast regions of Canada and the Mississippi Valley. With the French further handicapped by futile dissipation of energy elsewhere and infinitely less efficient than the English in colonial policy, there could be only one issue to the conflict. By the Treaty of Paris of 1763 at the end of the French and Indian War, Great Britain took over the great majority of the French colonies in America.

But this very triumph of Great Britain over its traditional European enemy only involved it in a more serious struggle with its most aggressive colonial domains, the English colonies of the Atlantic Coast.[1] The occupation of the extensive territory conquered from France west of the Alleghenies forced upon England a reconstruction of its hitherto loosely organized and indifferently enforced colonial policy. This imperial organization necessitated additional expenditures, which Great Britain proposed to raise by direct taxation and through enforcement of the long-dormant navigation laws. But this fiscal policy aroused the opposition of the American colonial merchants, long accustomed to unhampered smuggling, and they united with the debtor landlords of the Southern colonies to give vitality to the aspiration for independence.[2] The revolution that ensued was in its essence a civil war within the British Empire, in which British and American liberals made common cause against conservatives and imperialists in both countries.[3] The colonial cause prevailed chiefly because of the defection of the British Whigs,[4] and through French aid begotten of the spirit of revenge for the defeat of 1756-63.

The loss of the more important British colonies in America produced a marked trend towards the granting of greater autonomy for the British colonies that remained. This changing attitude was reflected in the Quebec Acts of 1774 and 1791, the Irish Parliament Act of 1782, and the India Act of 1784, but the thoroughgoing revision of British imperial policy in a liberal direction did not take place until a half-century later, after Lord Durham's famous report following the Canadian rebellion of 1837.

In this first phase of European expansion overseas, Germany and Austria[5] failed to participate—Germany because of the distracting religious wars and

[1] See below, pp. 104 ff.
[2] Studied especially by Sydney George Fisher, A. M. Schlesinger, and Carl Becker.
[3] Cf. H. E. Barnes, *History and Social Intelligence,* Knopf, 1926, Chap. IX; and A. M. Schlesinger, *New Viewpoints in American History,* Macmillan, 1922, Chap. VII.
[4] Emphasized by G. O. Trevelyan, John Fiske, W. E. H. Lecky, and C. H. Van Tyne.
[5] The Great Elector of Brandenburg established a few posts on the west coast of Africa and the Austrian Emperor, Charles VI, financed the Ostend Company to carry on trade with the Indies.

Austria on account of isolation, inertia, or propinquity to a vast amount of unoccupied territory in Asia. The fact that these states remained outside the circle of the new commercial and colonial Powers was most important in determining the lines of their later political and economic evolution, and possessed great significance for their subsequent history and for that of the rest of the world. Though it did not participate in the oversea expansion, Russia was beginning that movement eastward through Siberia which was to make it an important participant in the second great period of colonial expansion, namely, that after 1870. Even in the eighteenth century it had, as we have seen, established outposts in Alaska.

It has been important in this preliminary chapter to call attention to the colonial activities of the European states that participated in this process of expansion. Yet, as we implied at the beginning, by far the most significant aspect of European expansion from 1500 to 1800 lay in the reaction of European experiences abroad upon European society itself. It is with the various phases of this reaction of expansion upon European conditions that we shall concern ourselves in the next several chapters.

SUGGESTED READING

Sir J. A. Hammerton, *Universal History of the World,* Amalgamated Press, 1927-29, 8 vols., Chaps. 109, 111, 132-33, 137, 146, 152

D. C. Munro, *The Kingdom of the Crusaders,* Appleton-Century (forthcoming)

R. A. Newhall, *The Crusades,* Holt, 1927

A. P. Newton, ed., *Travel and Travellers in the Middle Ages,* Knopf, 1926, Chaps. v-x

E. E. Power, *Medieval People,* Houghton Mifflin, 1924, Chap. II

J. E. Gillespie, *History of Geographical Discovery, 1400-1800,* Holt, 1933, pp. 1-63, 77-96

——*History of Europe, 1500-1815,* Knopf, 1928, Chaps. IV, XVI, XVIII

C. J. H. Hayes, *Political and Cultural History of Modern Europe,* 3d ed., Macmillan, 1934, 2 vols., Vol. I, Chaps. II, IX

William Cunningham, *Essay on Western Civilization in Its Economic Aspects,* Putnam, 1898-1900, 2 vols., Vol. II, Bk. V. Chap. III

W. C. Abbott, *The Expansion of Europe,* Holt, 1924, 2 vols., Vol. I, Chaps. III, VI, IX, XIII-XIV, XVII-XVIII, XX; Vol. II, Chaps. XXVI, XXX, XXXII

E. P. Cheyney, *The European Background of American History, 1300-1600,* Harper, 1904, Chaps. I-VI

Ramsay Muir, *The Expansion of Europe,* 3d ed. rev., Houghton Mifflin, 1928, Chaps. I-IV

W. L. Dorn, *Dynastic Ambitions and Colonial Enterprise,* Harper (forthcoming)

Clive Day, *History of Commerce,* new ed., Longmans, 1922, Pt. III, Chaps. XIX-XX, XXVI-XXVII

J. H. Robinson, *Readings in the History of Western Europe,* Ginn, 1904, 2 vols., Vol. I, Chap. XV

—— and C. A. Beard, *Readings in Modern European History,* Ginn, 1908, 2 vols., Vol. I, Chaps. VI-VII

E. P. Cheyney, ed., *Readings in English History,* new ed., Ginn, 1922, Chap. XIII

FURTHER REFERENCES

THE EXPANSION OF EUROPE AND THE ORIGINS OF MODERN SOCIETY. On the importance of the expansion of Europe for modern civilization, see W. R. Shepherd, "The Expansion of Europe," *Political Science Quarterly,* March-September, 1919. On the expansive force of Christianity, see C. H. Robinson, *History of Christian Missions* (Scribner, 1915); A. J. S. Macdonald, *Trade Politics and Christianity in Africa and the East* (Longmans, 1916).

On trade and European expansion, see Pts. II-III of J. W. Jeudwine, *Studies in Empire and Trade* (Longmans, 1923).

On the impulse of early nationalism to expansion, see Chaps. I, x, of A. F. Pollard, *Factors in Modern History* (Knopf, 1926).

On psychological factors in expansion, see Hammerton, *op. cit.,* Chap. 146.

THE CRUSADES. The best introductory treatments of the Crusades are Ernest Barker, article "Crusades," Encyclopaedia Britannica, 11th ed.; Chaps. XXI, XXV, of D. C. Munro and R. J. Sontag, *The Middle Ages, 395-1500* (Century, 1928); Chap. XX of J. W. Thompson, *The Middle Ages, 300-1500* (Knopf, 1931, 2 vols.); Newhall, *op. cit.* On the causes and motives of the Crusades, a good summary is pp. 483 ff. of A. C. Flick, *The Rise of the Mediaeval Church* (Putnam, 1909), though the judgment of the Seljuk Turks is too harsh. On the results of the Crusades, see Flick, *op. cit.,* pp. 500 ff.; Newhall, *op. cit.,* Chap. III; Hammerton, *op. cit.,* Chap. 109; pp. 265 ff. of G. B. Adams, *Civilization during the Middle Ages* (new ed., Scribner, 1922); Munro, *op. cit.*

MEDIEVAL CONTACTS WITH THE FAR EAST. On medieval travel and travelers, see Chap. IV of J. S. Keltie and O. J. R. Howard, *History of Geography* (Putnam, 1912); Newton, *op. cit.;* E. L. Guilford, *Travellers and Travelling in the Middle Ages* (Macmillan, 1924); Vols. II-III of Sir C. R. Beazley, *The Dawn of Modern Geography* (Oxford Press, 1905-06, 3 vols).

On the Turks and the expansion of Europe, see A. H. Lybyer, "The Influence of the Rise of the Ottoman Turks upon the Routes of Oriental Trade," American Historical Association, *Annual Report,* 1914, Vol. I, pp. 125-33; and "The Ottoman Turks and the Routes of Oriental Trade," *English Historical Review,* October, 1915.

EXPLORATIONS AND DISCOVERIES. For good accounts of the explorations and discoveries that brought in modern times, see Jeudwine, *op. cit.,* Pts. II-IV; Hammerton, *op. cit.,* Chap. 137; Abbott, *op. cit.,* Vol. I, Chaps. III, VI, IX; E. J. Payne, Vol. I, Chap. I, of *Cambridge Modern History* (Macmillan, 1911-32, 7 vols.); Joseph Jacobs, *The Story of Geographical Discovery* (Appleton, 1916); Gillespie, *History of Geographical Discovery;* A. P. Newton, ed., *The Great Age of Discovery* (London, 1932); J. N. L. Baker, *History of Geographical Discovery and Exploration* (Houghton Mifflin, 1932); Jeannette Mirsky, *To the North* (Viking Press, 1934); F. A. Golder, *Russian Expansion on the Pacific, 1641-1850* (A. H. Clark, 1914). The most complete and up-to-date series on the explorations and discoveries are the "Pioneer Histories," now being published by Macmillan (1933 *et seq.*). The volumes which have appeared thus far are: J. B. Brebner, *Explorers of North America, 1492-1806;* Edgar Prestage, *The Portuguese Pioneers;* Sir William Foster, *England's Quest of Eastern Trade;* A. P. Newton, *The European Nations in the West Indies, 1493-1688;* E. A. Walker, *The Great Trek;* J. C. Beaglehole, *Exploration of the Pacific;* F. A. Kirkpatrick, *Spanish Conquistadores.*

RIVAL COMMERCIAL EMPIRES. For excellent summaries on this subject, see Day, *op. cit.,* Pt. III; Cunningham, *op. cit.,* Vol. II, Bk. V, Chap. III; Muir, *op. cit.,* Chaps. III-IV; and further treatment of the struggles of rival commercial empires in Abbott, *op. cit.,* Vol. I, Chaps. III-IV, IX, XIII-XIV, XVII-XVIII, XX; Vol. II, Chaps. XXVI, XXX, XXXII; Chaps. II-III of Ramsay Muir, *Short History of the British Commonwealth* (World Book Co., 1922, 2 vols.); A. G. Keller, *Colonization* (Ginn, 1908); Vol. I, Chap. V, of H. F. Helmolt, ed., *History of the World* (Dodd, Mead, 1900, 8 vols.).

On the Spanish colonial empire, see Pt. I of W. R. Shepherd, *Latin America* (Holt, 1914); Chaps. II-III of H. E. Bolton and T. M. Marshall, *The Colonization of North America, 1492-1783* (Macmillan, 1920); E. D. Salmon, *Imperial Spain* (Holt, 1931).

For an illuminating survey of British colonial expansion, see Pollard, *op. cit.,* Chap. X; for fuller treatment, see J. A. Williamson, *Short History of British Expansion* (Macmillan, 1930); Foster, *op. cit.;* Newton, *op. cit.*

On the colonial struggle of France and England, see A. H. Buffinton, *The Second Hundred Years War* (Holt, 1929); Sir J. R. Seeley, *The Expansion of England* (Macmillan, 1895).

On the French reaction to the loss of most of the colonial empire of France, see C. L. Lokke, *France and the Colonial Question . . . 1763-1801* (Columbia University Press, 1932).

CHAPTER II

THE COMMERCIAL REVOLUTION AND THE BEGINNINGS OF MODERN INDUSTRY AND AGRICULTURE

I. THE COMMERCIAL REVOLUTION

1. IMPROVEMENTS IN NAVIGATION AND SHIPBUILDING

Perhaps the most striking immediate effect of the expansion of Europe was its influence upon European and world commerce. The results in this field constitute what is, narrowly and technically speaking, the Commercial Revolution.

The era of expansion and commercial development depended upon several important innovations in the art of navigation. In the first place, we may note the series of inventions in the field of nautical instruments, from the earlier compass and astrolabe to the development of the mariner's log in the seventeenth century and the chronometer in the eighteenth.[1] The mariner's compass, as we have seen, came to the knowledge of western Europe at the close of the twelfth century.[2] Its origin is uncertain, though many believe it was derived from China or India by way of the Muslims. The astrolabe, a graduated brass circle for estimating the altitude of heavenly bodies, was known before 800, but was first employed in Western navigation by John II of Portugal about 1485. The quadrant, which replaced the astrolabe, was an instrument with a graduated arc of 90° and was used to measure approximately the altitude of heavenly bodies. It dates from the early sixteenth century. The sextant is a much more accurate instrument for computing the altitude of heavenly bodies and for estimating their angular distances as seen in the sky. It was invented independently by Captain John Hadley of the British navy and Thomas Godfrey of Philadelphia in 1731. It supplanted the astrolabe and quadrant. The chronometer, the first instrument for telling time accurately on board ship, was invented in 1735 by an Englishman, John Harrison. This, together with earlier instruments, made it possible to estimate longitude with exactness. The provision of the mariner's compass, the quadrant and the sextant, telescopes, and other accessories enabled mariners to find their way at sea far more safely and precisely than had ever been the case in early maritime activity.

[1] *Cf.* E. P. Cheyney, *The European Background of American History, 1300-1600*, Harper, 1904, pp. 47-59; and Abbott, *The Expansion of Europe*, Vol. II, pp. 272-73.
[2] See above, Vol. I, pp. 534-35, 792-93.

Maps, charts, and tables were constantly improved, lighthouses built, harbors cleared of natural obstacles, and pilot service inaugurated. The rise of national governments marked the end of medieval strand laws, which had practically conferred upon localities the right to pillage stranded vessels.

Along with these improvements went the development of larger and more seaworthy ships. At first, the tendency was to concentrate upon building larger ships. The result was the development of the galleon, the caravel, the urca, and the carrack, vessels of from two to five decks, exceedingly well armed to beat off privateers and pirates. Ships of this sort were, however, relatively unwieldy. The Dutch and British specialized in craft somewhat smaller in size, but far swifter, more seaworthy, and more reliable than the galleon and the carrack. The Commercial Revolution rested upon these inventions and improvements connected with the art of navigation much as the later Industrial Revolution depended upon the inventions in textile machinery, steam power, and metallurgy.

2. NEW COMMODITIES FROM OVERSEAS AND THE REVOLUTION IN EUROPEAN TASTES AND CUSTOMS

The Commercial Revolution, with the accompanying growth of foreign trade and fresh cultural contacts, led to a radical change in European taste. The psychological factor of demand lies at the bottom of all economic activity, and the character of European demand for consumer's goods was transformed during this period. Even the better middle-class houses were not considered comfortable without glass windows, wooden or tiled roofs, carpets and rugs, and upholstered furniture. Wall paper was introduced from China and lacquered ware from Japan. The hammock came from the West Indies, not from one of the older civilizations. Increase in the supply of cotton fiber and the cheapening of cotton and linen cloth made possible the introduction of more comfortable and more serviceable types of clothing. Underclothing and bedclothes, commonplace conveniences of modern life, began to come into general use in Europe for the first time.

Many of the new goods contributed less to comfort in itself than to satisfaction of the desire for ostentation and adornment. Furs, such as those of the beaver, sable, musk ox, and civet cat, were used for adornment of the person—particularly the feminine person. Furs were at this time especially a symbol of wealth and social rank. The use of silks for clothing, tapestry, and so on, was considerably increased by the introduction of silk culture from the East and its rapid development in northern Italy and southern France. Ostrich feathers were brought from Africa and utilized for trimming hats and dresses. Folding fans and parasols appeared in imitation of the Orient. At the outset, the parasol was almost wholly an object of ostentation, associated as it was in the Orient with royalty. In Europe it remained an ostensible sunshade until the close of the eighteenth century, when the more practicable collapsible umbrella for protection against rain was developed. The perfumes used by both men and women, in part as a substitute for bathing, while not by any means novel in European society, were greatly increased and diversified by the new imports.

To add to the attractive appearance of dwellings, considerable attention was paid to the development of gardens, in which were planted various shrubs and flowers that had been brought from the Orient and America. Among these were the Virginia creeper, the aster, the dahlia, the nasturtium, the sunflower, and various trees and plants such as the magnolia tree, the century plant, the pepper plant, the coral tree, and the locust tree.

The range of foods habitually consumed in Europe was greatly altered and enlarged. While spices continued to be imported in very large quantities, probably the most important food product introduced into Europe was the potato. This vegetable was first brought to Europe in the sixteenth century from the Americas.[1] By the close of the seventeenth century it served as food for some people, especially the poor, as well as for live stock. It was not completely popularized as food, however, until the Napoleonic era and the decades following, when Europeans began to discover not only that the potato possesses high food value, but that it can be grown in abundance under relatively simple and cheap agricultural conditions.

Other food products new to Europe, though of somewhat less importance than the potato, were the lima bean, the yam, tapioca, and the tomato. Sugar was first extensively introduced at this time. Down to the sixteenth and seventeenth centuries the chief sweetening used for food and beverages had been honey. With the discovery of sugar cane, particularly in the West Indies and Central America, sugar came to be used in increasing quantities, especially after the opening of the nineteenth century. The demand for it was stimulated by the introduction of new beverages such as tea, coffee, and cocoa, which called for sweetening to meet the taste of most drinkers.

Important tropical fruits were now brought into Europe for the first time or in greater quantities than ever before. Among these were oranges, pineapples, bananas, and lemons. The more perishable fruits were introduced and grown in warm European areas. The coconut and the peanut were also first imported into Europe during the centuries after 1500. Indian corn (maize), while brought back to Spain by Columbus before the close of the fifteenth century, has never been as popular a crop in western Europe as in the United States. Yet it has been cultivated rather extensively as food for cattle and swine, and in parts of southern and southeastern Europe—in Rumania, for example—it is a main article of peasant diet. Several new varieties of fowl were introduced as a result of oversea contact, particularly the turkey from Mexico, the guinea fowl from Africa, and the bantam from Java. Though the turkey came from America, its outlandish appearance earned it an oriental name, since mysterious or bizarre products were usually attributed to the East, for which Turkey was a symbol.

Probably the new beverages did even more than the foods and house furnishings to alter the pattern of social contacts in Europe. To alcoholic drinks long known in Europe were added new wines from the Madeira and Canary Islands, and rum made from the sugar and molasses of the West Indies. An especially popular beverage known as punch was made of rum, sugar, lemon juice, spices, and water. Far more significant, however, were the new non-

[1] Discovered by Pizarro in South America.

alcoholic drinks. The Dutch in the East Indies learned tea-drinking from the Chinese and introduced it into Europe in the seventeenth century. Within a hundred years tea became an important commodity in world-trade. Attempts by the British East India Company to market it in the American colonies under conditions disapproved of by leading citizens will be remembered as one of the interesting episodes preliminary to our war for independence.

Europeans had discovered the virtues of coffee through contact with Arabia at the close of the Middle Ages. Mocha, the capital of the province of Yemen, on the Arabian coast of the Red Sea, was the first source of coffee for European consumption. Nearly all the coffee consumed in Europe until the close of the seventeenth century came from this area. In the following century the Dutch transplanted the industry to their East India islands, particularly Java. The Portuguese carried it to Brazil about the same time, and here it spread to other parts of tropical South America.

The third important nonalcoholic beverage was cocoa, which was made from the cacao bean imported from Mexico and Central America. Chocolate was manufactured by adding vanilla—also a new product—and sugar to cocoa.

The establishment of coffeehouses or "cafés" began a new chapter in the social life of Europe. They were great forgathering places, particularly for men. They tended to break up the home as an air-tight compartment in society. Business enterprises often originated in coffeehouses, much of the political intrigue was laid there, and authors and artists often met there.

In this connection tobacco should be mentioned also, for it had a similar if not a greater effect upon social ways. When first brought from the West Indies it was used for its alleged medicinal properties. From the first there was a great deal of opposition—supported even by royalty—to its general adoption as a form of mild indulgence. King James I of England was one of the famous and vigorous critics of the new habit. Notwithstanding, there arose an enormous demand for tobacco in Europe, which led to its cultivation on a large scale in the West Indies and the South Atlantic colonies of North America, where it early became the most important single export of many areas.

In addition to a large number of fruits, vegetables, and beverages, at first regarded as medicinal, many drugs of undoubted therapeutic value were also brought into Europe during this period. Among these should be mentioned quinine, balsam, sarsaparilla, opium, and sweet flag. Of these much the most important was quinine, which was introduced from Peru in the seventeenth century and has proved a valuable specific for malaria and various fevers. In many areas and periods prior to this time malaria attained the proportions of a plague. These new drugs affected European medicine beneficially at the time by lessening the reliance upon crude methods of bloodletting for all diseases; they stimulated the beginnings of modern medical science, and extended the materia medica.

3. INCREASE IN THE VOLUME OF TRADE

The most notable phase of the Commercial Revolution was the great increase in the volume of trade. Hitherto, the trade of Europe with the rest of the

THE COMMERCIAL REVOLUTION

world had been limited rather strictly to the products of the Orient, chiefly spices, silks, tapestries, precious stones, perfumed woods, and commodities of this sort. Most of them, with the notable exception of the spices, were articles of luxury rather than articles of common consumption. With the discovery of the new areas, particularly in the New World and the East Indies, the supply of these articles was greatly increased and a whole new range of commodities added. There was a steadily increasing European demand for such novel commodities.

For early modern times there are few trade statistics broad enough in scope or compiled with sufficient care and understanding to be worth quoting. We have to visualize the extent of economic progress chiefly in other ways. By 1600 upper-class life was profoundly affected by the influx of new goods, but the degree of innovation varied greatly from one locality to another. The new states had not yet achieved highly organized or unified economic systems, and internal lines of communication were still poor for the most part. By 1700 the middle classes, particularly in England, Holland, Spain, and Portugal, had generally changed their mode and standards of consumption, but the laboring masses were still living much as they had in the Middle Ages. It was not until the eighteenth century proper that the effects of the expansion of Europe penetrated to the very foundations of European society, stimulating a so-called Industrial Revolution that has altered the conditions of human life more profoundly than any other event in history.

In spite of their naval defeat at the hands of England a half-century before, the Netherlands remained one of the most important commercial states at the opening of the eighteenth century, and though dislodged from their primacy before 1800, persisted as a prominent state in the commerce and carrying trade of the world.

While inferior to the Dutch in commercial power and activity in the seventeenth century, England was already beginning that commercial and manufacturing development which was later to place it in a position of undisputed leadership in the industry and trade of the Old World. At the end of the seventeenth century England was importing about $27,000,000 worth of goods annually and exporting goods to the value of some $32,000,000. This trade increased about sixfold within a hundred years. In 1802, imports stood at about $157,000,000 and exports at approximately $207,000,000.

England ultimately achieved an enormous economic superiority over France and other competitors (prior to the rise of Germany after 1870) because the future lay with the two lines of activity it was beginning to cultivate: oversea trade and the manufacture of goods demanded abroad. While the commercial changes in English life were prophetic of the future, it must be borne in mind that they took place gradually. In 1700 England's oversea trade amounted to but 21 per cent of its total foreign trade, while that of France in 1716 totaled but 18 per cent. Seventy years later the proportions were 40 per cent and 33 per cent respectively. But the rapid expansion of trade and the growing predominance of exports over imports made up a definite and striking process, as is demonstrated by the following statistics:

English Trade in the Eighteenth Century [1]

Value of Imports		Value of Exports		
1720	£ 6,090,083	1705		£ 5,308,966
1730	7,780,019	1709		5,913,357
1740	6,703,778	1711		5,962,988
1750	7,772,039	1713-15	(average)	7,696,573
1760	9,832,802	1728-38	"	7,891,739
1783	11,651,281	1749-51	"	12,599,112
1789	37,784,000	1755-7	"	11,708,515
1798	42,261,000	1762-3	"	14,693,270
1802	31,400,000	1775-6	"	17,492,515
		1783-5	"	22,641,982
		1790-2	"	31,464,800
		1796-7	"	38,506,771
		1802	"	41,400,000

As Clive Day observes: "The figures show that the foreign trade of England grew between five and six fold in the course of the [eighteenth] century; that it advanced considerably in the first half, but moved with the speed of a revolution in the second." [2]

The situation at the opening of the eighteenth century is well illustrated by coffee, a commodity very rarely used in Europe a century earlier. Consumption of coffee doubled between 1710 and 1720, and again in the following decade; but in the next five years, 1730-35, it almost trebled. The breakfast coffee of the middle classes was already a fact. Coffee is only a suggestive illustration of the general situation—cloth was to prove far more important because its importation was destined to give way to its manufacture. Cloth-making was to bring iron and coal to the fore, and the new manufacturing methods involving these have revolutionized the modern world.

In the seventeenth century England carried on a large trade in salt fish with the South Atlantic colonies and the West Indies. With the Southern American colonies it had a highly developed tobacco and rice trade and had laid the foundations for a flourishing commerce in naval stores. It did a lucrative fur business with the North Atlantic colonies and the Hudson Bay region. It imported from the North Atlantic colonies furs, lumber, codfish, and oil. With the West Indies it had an immense trade in sugar, molasses, rum, dyes, spices, cotton, tropical woods, and tobacco. It divided with the Dutch a slave trade between the western coast of Africa and the American colonies. West Africa also furnished gold, gum arabic, ebony, rare woods, ostrich feathers, and ivory. From the Far East and the East Indies England imported an impressive list of commodities thus described by a contemporary annalist:

books, canes, drugs, gums, oils, indigo in large quantities; cochineal, China-ink, galls, turmeric, seed-lack, shell-lack, stick-lack, ivory, fans, cane-mats, cinnamon, cloves, mace, nutmeg, pepper, cayenne pepper, ginger, sago, sugar, tea, a little rice, coffee, preserved fruits, mother-of-pearl shell, and spoons made of it, saltpetre, arrack,

---

[1] J. B. Botsford, *English Society in the Eighteenth Century*, Macmillan, 1924, p. 33.
[2] Day, *History of Commerce*, p. 205.

cotton, cotton yarn, raw silk of Bengal and China, calicoes and muslins, cassia, ebony, sandal, satin and sapan woods . . . porcelains . . . japanned cabinets . . . ornamental furniture . . . skins of tigers and panthers . . . precious stones.[1]

Set off against these imports from overseas were the leading English exports of salt fish, wheat, woolen and cotton cloth, hardware, firearms, gunpowder, and various trinkets that were used in the trade with backward peoples.

The total foreign commerce of France appears to have been somewhat smaller than England's during the seventeenth century. For example, the total English foreign trade in 1700 amounted to about $59,000,000; in 1716 to about $65,000,000; and in 1789 to about $340,000,000. The French foreign trade totaled approximately $43,000,000 in 1716, and $230,000,000 in 1787. This becomes the more significant when we realize that the population of France was then more than double that of England. The economic life of France had just been disastrously affected by a series of religious civil wars and the destruction or emigration of a part of its most desirable industrial population, the Huguenot craftsmen. French foreign trade increased in volume at about the same rate as that of England, but somewhat less rapidly in the oversea commodities. England began dealing with the lands across the sea, tending more and more to import raw materials and export manufactured goods. France's trade remained chiefly with its European neighbors, Italy, France, England, and the Baltic states; and over two-thirds of its exports were raw materials. Its American trade in 1716 amounted to only some $5,000,000; that with Asia and Africa combined about half this figure; and all three taken together constituted only about one-fifth of its business with European countries.

In spite of its colonial and mercantile mistakes France did, however, build up a considerable foreign trade with oversea areas after 1716, amounting to some $69,000,000 in 1787, but England was outdistancing France even then. The critical period in which France lost out in oversea trade was that of the American and French revolutions and the Napoleonic period. The English well-nigh suppressed French commerce on the ocean, and France was quite unable to compete against the overwhelming British preponderance in oversea trade after 1815. English priority in the Industrial Revolution put the finishing touches on the hopelessness of French competition. As Clive Day observes: "The failure of France to manufacture goods which would hold their own in the world market must be regarded as her vital weakness." [2]

The foreign trade of the Dutch surpassed that of England in 1650, but in less than a hundred years, say about 1730, the English had moved ahead, though the total Dutch commerce did not drop much for decades thereafter. At the time when the Dutch were just holding their own the English foreign trade was moving ahead by leaps and bounds. Italian foreign commerce gradually faded out as the western seaboard towns slowly but surely tore the trade with the East from the old monopoly of Venice and other Italian trading cities. Austrian foreign trade showed no noticeable improvement during this whole period from 1500 to 1800. The Great Elector of Prussia (1640-88) had some

---

[1] Botsford, *op. cit.,* pp. 34-35.
[2] Day, *op. cit.,* p. 239. Partisans of France are prone to deny that it had any "vital weakness," and to contend France had an adequate commercial organization suitable to its peculiar conditions, which were different from those in England.

maritime, commercial, and colonial vision. Had he been able to obtain some good Baltic ports, Prussia might have become a considerable commercial power. But he failed, and Prussia remained absorbed in political and military issues until after 1871, when a period of remarkable commercial expansion set in for Germany.

4. THE WIDENING GEOGRAPHIC SCOPE OF TRADING OPERATIONS: FLUVIAL, THALASSIC, AND OCEANIC

A powerful factor promoting this marked development in the volume and variety of European trade was the revolutionary change in the geographic scope of trading operations. In the earliest period of trade it was, as we have seen,[1] carried on primarily in river basins. This stage of civilization has been called by some writers fluvial or riparian.[2] Shortly after the dawn of recorded history, some daring navigators had so far mastered the art of navigation as to venture upon the great inland seas. This trade, from the Egyptian and Aegean commerce of the fourth millennium B.C. to that around the Mediterranean in the Middle Ages, has been called thalassic or pelagic, meaning commerce along the coast of an inland sea.[3]

In the early modern period of European expansion the commerce of the Western world passed from the thalassic type, which had endured for some five thousand years, to the stage of oceanic or world-wide traffic. Only a relatively small portion of the habitable parts of the world were exploited by explorers and colonizers during this early period to 1800, but they extended enormously the range of European geographic knowledge and foreign contacts and they laid the foundations for the further colonization and discoveries of the nineteenth century. The whole period of four centuries since 1500 has been relatively brief, but during this era Europeans penetrated the majority of the land areas of the planet. Many careful thinkers, even those most hostile to modern life as compared with that of the ancient world at its best, have seized upon this world-wide system of transportation and intercommunication as one of the most distinctive and advantageous aspects of present-day civilization.[4]

5. THE GROWING SUPREMACY OF THE WESTERN SEABOARD TOWNS

As oversea exploration gathered way, chiefly under the leadership of the towns and states of the Atlantic seaboard of Europe, the centers of commercial activity were no longer Genoa, Pisa, Amalfi, and Venice, but became Lisbon, Seville, Cádiz, Bordeaux, Nantes, Dieppe, Dunkirk, St. Malo, Antwerp, Amsterdam, Bristol, Liverpool, and London. The commercial activity of Venice did not collapse as quickly as was long supposed. It maintained a prominent position in the trade with the Near Orient all through the Commercial Revolution. But in the end oceanic trade became all-important and the days of Venetian leadership were over.[5]

[1] See above, Vol. I, pp. 81 ff., 97 ff., 116 ff., 128 ff., 144 ff. [2] See above, Vol. I, pp. 81 ff.
[3] *Cf.* J. H. Rose, *The Mediterranean in the Ancient World*, Macmillan, 1933.
[4] See A. C. Flick, *Modern World History, 1776-1926*, Crofts, 1926, especially pp. 493-96.
[5] *Cf.* F. C. Lane, "Venetian Shipping during the Commercial Revolution," *American Historical Review*, January, 1933, and *Venetian Ships and Shipbuilders of the Renaissance*, Johns Hopkins Press, 1934.

The shift of commercial ascendancy from the Mediterranean to the Northwest was more than a mere economic change. It meant that new cities were to become the dominant factors in the history of mankind in the West and that the Mediterranean world, dominant for five millennia, would recede to a position of second-rate significance. Henceforth, for several centuries, the dynamic movement of Europe was to be overwhelmingly towards the West, with the main area of outstanding developments located in northwestern Europe and in the newly discovered continents. While the Near Orient was destined to remain significant for western Europe from the days of the Turkish siege of Vienna to those of the Suez Canal, the Baghdad Railroad, and the partitions of Persia, it lost its age-old position of primary commercial importance.[1]

6. THE INCREASED SUPPLY OF PRECIOUS METALS

No less revolutionary than the commercial changes were those connected with the development of new financial situations and methods. There was, of course, a very intimate and causal relationship between the rise of the new commerce and the dawn of the capitalistic age.

Down to the time of oversea expansion there had been a great scarcity of the precious metals in Europe. This had been an inevitable outcome of the situation late in the Middle Ages, when Europe had depended upon the Orient for its imports of the more expensive goods. The only practicable way to keep goods flowing westward was to find either money or goods to flow eastward in exchange. Europeans had made increasingly successful efforts to duplicate or find substitutes for the oriental imports, to mine and mint money, and to develop products of their own to exchange in the oriental trade. In spite of all, however, the extensive imports from the East were not matched in monetary value by Western exports. Hence during the later Middle Ages the Levant trade tended to drain away to the East the money and precious metals of the West, in payment for goods. At the opening of the sixteenth century, however, the money situation was already somewhat ameliorated. Europe was producing some $500,000 to $750,000 a year in precious metals, and a similar amount was being drawn from the west coast of Africa. If we accept the usual estimates of $170,000,000 to $200,000,000 as the amount of coin in circulation in Europe in 1492 or 1500, $250,000,000 is not an improbable figure for 1520. Accumulation went on constantly in spite of the drain eastward, and both European and African production of precious metals were stimulated in every possible way. This acceleration in output continued until about 1600, after which time the dearth of money was somewhat less acute and the flood of gold and silver from America had so raised prices and wages as to render many Old World mines unprofitable. In addition to the gold, silver, and copper in circulation as coinage about 1520, there was also a considerable amount of the precious metals in the form of plate and other works of art, and much was hoarded in the form of bars, coins, and so on.

Shortly after 1520 the Spaniards obtained large lump sums by the pillage of

[1] *Cf.* G. F. Renard and Georges Weulersse, *Life and Labor in Modern Europe*, Knopf, 1926, *passim*, especially pp. 276-79; and Helmolt, *History of the World*, Vol. VIII, Chap. v.

Aztec and Inca treasuries, and they also developed a steady supply of precious metals by working the mines of Peru, Bolivia, and Mexico. The annual output of the world was quadrupled between 1500 and 1550, and by the latter date the American mines were supplying more than all the others combined. A quadrupling of the yearly output of precious metals does not mean, of course, that the total European supply was quadrupled in fifty years. Gold and silver are very durable, and the stock of 1500 represented the accumulation of thousands of years. Production at such a high rate was certain, however, to tell in time. Over $1,000,000,000 worth of new money metal was mined between 1520 and 1600, and it is likely that a much larger percentage of this went into circulation as coins than was true of the stock in existence at the earlier date.

We can only speculate as to the total effect of the new monetary situation in putting the old plate and hoards into circulation, and there are no reliable figures as to the amount of gold and silver that flowed out of Europe to the Orient. The usual estimate is probably conservative enough—that the coinage of Europe increased about twelvefold during the sixteenth century. Though the general anticipation as to the volume of precious metals available in the New World was far greater than the actuality, and although many Europeans spent their lives in fruitless search for mountains of gold and silver, the actual amount brought into Europe by the close of the eighteenth century was stupendous in comparison with that existing in 1500. Spain had access to more and richer mines than the other European states, but the latter, particularly England, were able to offset this handicap to some degree by depredations upon Spanish commerce and by the seizure of scores of richly laden treasure ships. The following table gives a quantitative impression of the increase of the precious metals:

PRODUCTION OF GOLD AND SILVER IN THE WORLD FROM THE DISCOVERY OF AMERICA TO THE END OF THE EIGHTEENTH CENTURY [1]

	GOLD		SILVER	
	Total for period Value in dollars	Annual average for period Value in dollars	Total for period Coining value in dollars	Annual average Coining value in dollars
1493–1520	107,931,000	3,855,000	54,703,000	1,954,000
1521–1544	114,205,000	4,759,000	89,986,000	3,740,000
1545–1560	90,492,000	5,656,000	207,240,000	12,952,000
1561–1580	90,917,000	4,546,000	248,990,000	12,450,000
1581–1600	98,095,000	4,905,000	348,254,000	17,413,000
1601–1620	113,248,000	5,662,000	351,579,000	17,579,000
1621–1640	110,324,000	5,516,000	327,221,000	16,361,000
1641–1660	116,571,000	5,828,000	304,525,000	15,226,000
1661–1680	123,084,000	6,154,000	280,166,000	14,008,000
1681–1700	143,088,000	7,154,000	284,240,000	14,212,000
1701–1720	170,403,000	8,520,000	295,629,000	14,781,000
1721–1740	253,611,000	12,681,000	358,480,000	17,924,000
1741–1760	327,116,000	16,356,000	443,232,000	22,162,000
1761–1780	275,211,000	13,761,000	542,658,000	27,133,000
1781–1800	236,464,000	11,823,000	730,810,000	36,540,000

[1] *Statistical Abstract of the United States*, 1920.

II. CAUSES AND EFFECTS OF THE DISLOCATION OF PRICES

Gold and silver being commodities, they follow the general rule that an increase in the supply of them is accompanied by a roughly proportional decrease in their exchange value against other goods. This proportion cannot be rigidly applied, of course, even to the sixteenth century, since a standard medium of exchange, though itself a commodity, occupies a very special position in the economic order. We must not be surprised, therefore, to find that the increase in money metals is not exactly proportionate to that of prices and wages from year to year or even from decade to decade. Nearly all economic tendencies require a certain amount of time to express themselves, and they are usually counteracted, retarded, or reënforced by other factors, of which the deliberate purposes of men are often among the more important. All the western European countries had a large residuum of manorial and other non-monetary economic wealth. Hence they could absorb vast amounts of precious metals in the process of changing over to a money economy without experiencing any proportionate change in prices or wages.

The increase of precious metals in Europe after 1500 upset, therefore, the price level.[1] The mounting volume of precious metals that might be converted into specie tended to reduce the purchasing power of a given amount of gold or silver. To state the same thing in other words, prices and wages tended to rise, though not exactly at the same rate at which the new coins accumulated. Governments, for example that of Elizabeth, legislated on wages in a not altogether unsuccessful attempt to hold them arbitrarily low. Both private trading companies and states that were interested in imports from overseas made ingenious attempts to keep the prices high. Foreign trade was regulated in a way calculated to entice and retain precious metals.

The mercantilist philosophy which lay back of this agreed with the modern arguments for protective tariffs at many points.[2] Before condemning this philosophy as a whole, it is important to remember that gold, silver, and copper were almost the only money in circulation in early mercantilist days, that few nations had enough to secure the full advantages of a money economy, and that the total amount of these metals was changing rather rapidly.

While the data preserved for us are fragmentary and not to be overworked in nice points of detail, the general trend of prices from the thirteenth century to the end of the sixteenth is fairly clear. The thirteenth-century author of *Fleta* gives the average price of wheat in England at 6*d*. or about 12 cents per bushel, a figure that checks up fairly well with those of J. E. T. Rogers in his *History of Agriculture and Prices in England*.[3] Between 1261 and 1400 the average price was 5*s*. 10¾*d*. per quarter of eight bushels, or nearly 50 per cent higher than the quotation given above. Rogers's quotations for 1500-01 are mostly between 6*s*. and 8*s*., though they run as low as 4*s*. 8*d*. and as high as 10*s*. The prices increased steadily up to 1550, when they ranged between 9*s*. 6*d*.

---

[1] *Cf.* F. L. Nussbaum, *History of the Economic Institutions of Modern Europe,* Crofts, 1933, pp. 98 ff.; J. E. Gillespie, *The Influence of Oversea Expansion on England to 1700,* Columbia University Press, 1920, pp. 162-63; and E. J. Hamilton, *American Treasure and the Price Revolution in Spain, 1501-1650,* Harvard University Press, 1934. [2] See below, pp. 75 ff.

[3] Oxford Press, 1866-92, 7 vols. See especially Vol. V, pp. 787 ff.

and 16s. 1d., with many entries near the higher level. Most of Rogers's price-listings for 1600-01 are between 30s. and 40s. Comparison of this price per quarter with the 7s. or thereabouts a century earlier and the 4s. of the thirteenth century gives us some notion of the trend of prices of one of the most characteristic commodities.

The English price for eggs, another staple food product, crept up from about 4d. for 120 (slightly less than an American cent per dozen) in 1300 to $5\frac{1}{8}d$. a century later. At the opening of the sixteenth century the quotations ranged from 5d. to 10d., with an average around 7d. Here they encountered the general meteoric rise, being quoted at 3s. and 4s., and even more, by 1570.

Live stock is a commodity the units of which are much less uniform as to size and quality than grain or eggs, but the sixteenth-century price records tell the same general story. Schapiro gives an admirable brief summary of the increase of prices of such goods as foods, clothing, and spices in Germanic countries.[1] For instance, beef rose 15 per cent between 1500 and 1525, clothing 50 per cent, wheat and oats over 100 per cent, and many spices still more notably.

The extent of the price changes so early in the century is ample evidence that other powerful factors besides American gold and silver were at work. There was certainly something in the charge of contemporary writers, including Luther, that vast monopolies existed, and that society in general had not yet learned to protect itself against the newer business methods that were pushing up through the ruins of medievalism. Far more important than monopolies, however—perhaps as important as the new supply of precious metals in raising prices—was the introduction of a new system of credit and the constant depreciation of the coinage in country after country.

This marked increase in prices had many important economic and social results. In the first place, it greatly stimulated trade and speculation, culminating in the disastrous period of "bubbles," which will be described further on. It increased considerably the income of the industrial and merchant classes and of wage-earners. Salaried and wage-earning people suffered temporarily, however, because their income could not be increased as rapidly as the cost of living. This was particularly true of the wage-earners in those states where the guild system still persisted in any important way, for the rules of the guild resisted any very significant increase in the wages paid for the labor of journeymen. Some states also legislated against the increase of wages. The landed nobility who received their rent payments in kind were much less adversely affected than those who had commuted the rent to cash, since the price of farm produce increased, while the purchasing power of a given amount of money fell off. The squires who owned and worked their own farms tended to share in the prosperity because of the remarkable rise in the prices of the things they had to sell. Long-term leaseholders who paid rent in money tended to profit at the expense of their landlords because while their rents remained unchanged, the income from the land increased with the rise in prices.

In many instances governments took cognizance of these price changes and

[1] J. S. Schapiro, *Social Reform and the Reformation*, Columbia University Press, 1909, Chap. I.

wage increases and attempted legal regulation, but, as in the case of the medieval Statute of Labourers, such opposition to general economic tendencies was usually unsuccessful in the long run. Gradually, the European situation became adjusted to the larger volume of precious metals and to the corresponding changes in price levels. In general, the net result of both was a great stimulation to economic activity and achievement.

III. THE NEW IMPULSES TO MANUFACTURING ACTIVITY

One of the most important indirect results of the Commercial Revolution was its stimulation of European manufacturing, particularly in England. The new oversea markets called for increased quantities of European manufactured products, and the governments stressed the production of those to be exchanged for raw materials. No doubt the flow of goods was checked somewhat by monopoly and mercantilism, but the increased production was, nevertheless, unprecedented.

The textile industry was one of the first to be profoundly affected by the new demand for goods. The manufacture of woolens had been highly developed in Flanders in the Middle Ages and had been introduced into England after the middle of the fourteenth century. The silk industry had also grown to some proportions in Italy and France, and, to a lesser degree, in England. Not only was silk manufactured, but raw silk was successfully produced in both Italy and France. The mulberry tree and the silkworm had been introduced and cultivated satisfactorily. There was relatively little cotton manufacturing carried on in Europe until the opening of the eighteenth century, though some cotton cloth is known to have been produced in England as early as the sixteenth century.

Some of the oversea demand for European textiles came from natives, but far more of it from colonists. Among the old, established industries to profit by the new situation were English woolens and French silks. The fact that some of this textile trade was with tropical or subtropical regions led in time to a remarkable development of the cotton trade, in spite of the opposition of the vested interests in the woolen and silk industries. As early as the latter half of the sixteenth century the English began to make for export to the Indies a coarse cloth known as fustian. At the outset it was probably not cotton, certainly not all cotton, but it soon became a mixture in which cotton figured more and more as the importation of raw cotton into England increased. A considerable cotton industry also developed in the manufacturing of calico, chintz, and underclothing, but the woolen interests effectively restrained the full expansion of the new rival for a long period. Cotton came to dominate English textile industry only after the onset of the Industrial Revolution of the eighteenth century, though some pure cotton goods were being manufactured before the introduction of any of the new textile machinery that appeared after 1738.

The early development of this English production of a rough, staple cotton cloth was of great importance in facilitating the later introduction of textile machinery. The ancient traditions, craft skill, and the vested interests of the guilds in the woolen industry offered a much greater resistance to technological changes.

The revolution in dyestuffs also improved the quality as well as increasing the possible quantity of English colored fabrics. The most important of these new vegetable dyes from overseas were indigo, logwood, and cochineal.

European manufactures were also notably stimulated through the introduction, and later the imitation, of a number of new commodities from the East, particularly pottery, many types of hardware, glass, furniture (particularly upholstered furniture), tapestry, and silks. The wide use of pottery in Europe came largely from the contact of Europeans with China.[1] During the Middle Ages dishes had been made of wood, pewter, or brass. Now Europeans, while still importing some porcelain objects from China, began to manufacture imitations of these Chinese goods, and we can note the beginnings of such well-known products as Dresden ware and Delft ware. Allied with the pottery industry was the manufacture of clay pipes, which began after 1600, when tobacco was introduced from North America.

Various types of glass products and glazed ware appeared in Europe on a considerable scale from the seventeenth century onward. During the Middle Ages there had been little use of glass, except for windows in the dwellings of the rich and the notable development of stained glass for cathedral windows. The glass industry in the Orient had been important since the days of the ancient Egyptians, and European contact with the East led to the large-scale introduction of glass and glazed products. For that matter, the great glass windows of the medieval Gothic cathedrals had been constructed after the crusading expeditions to the Levant began in 1096.[2] Not only did the expansion of Europe encourage the use of glass and glazing for such purposes as windows and dishes, but many specialized products appeared, such as spectacles, burning glasses, mirrors, and other new devices brought forth as a result of the progress in the science of optics.

The leather industry increased to a marked degree, particularly notable being the enormous demand for shoes on the part of the colonists. In the year 1658 no less than 24,000 pairs of shoes were sent to Virginia alone.

There was a large market for various types of hardware in the colonies, particularly for muskets, swords, hoes, nails, various types of tools, lead, pewter, and tinware. The development of the hardware industry in turn stimulated mining, particularly the mining of iron, lead, and tin.

European taste in furniture also underwent sweeping modifications as a result of contact with outside peoples.[3] Most medieval furniture was crudely made and was rarely upholstered. A desire for sumptuous, comfortable, and richly upholstered articles now grew up as a result of voyages to the East.[4] New and admirable types of wood for such purposes came in from overseas, such as mahogany, rosewood, and cedar. Gum varnishes of similar origin were

---

[1] *Cf.* Adolf Reichwein, *China and Europe,* Knopf, 1925, pp. 23 ff.; and Botsford, *op. cit.,* pp. 102 ff.

[2] See above, Vol. I, p. 765. Stained glass had also been made in ancient Gaul and Funck-Brentano believes that Gaul rather than the Orient was the source of this medieval art. See above, Vol. I, p. 422.

[3] *Cf.* Gillespie, *op. cit.,* pp. 141 ff.; and Botsford, *op. cit.,* pp. 104 ff.

[4] *Cf.* Reichwein, *op. cit.,* pp. 23 ff.

THE NEW IMPULSES TO MANUFACTURING ACTIVITY 45

utilized to give the new furniture a high polish and an attractive finish. European contact with the Chinese and Japanese art of lacquering influenced these new developments to no inconsiderable degree. Not only was the furniture industry developed, but the new tastes were applied also to such things as wainscoting, stairways, screens, and so on, which were made of the newly imported woods and finished with the new varnishes.[1]

Floors in the medieval period were usually bare, or at best were covered by reed or straw mats. Only a few of the very rich had oriental rugs on their floors. The more general use of carpets and rugs was now introduced from the East. These, along with the new furniture and varnishes, served to bring new standards of taste and comfort into European households. The wealthy continued, as they have down to the present time, to import rugs and carpets from the Orient, but there soon developed a profitable industry in the manufacture of these products in Europe.

Silks and tapestries had been imported into western Europe from the Byzantine Empire, Syria, and Persia for a long time, and a considerable development had already taken place in the native European silk industry. These beginnings were vastly stimulated by direct contact with the East. The quantity of silk clothing and tapestries demanded was much greater, while design and workmanship both underwent sweeping changes under oriental influences.

Shipbuilding was immediately affected by the new commerce. We have already seen how the change in the construction of vessels had been one of the most important influences making possible oversea expansion.[2] Gradually but surely the ships were made more adaptable to the necessities and demands of oceanic navigation, and the progress in physics and mathematics made it possible to apply scientific rules to their construction. Improvements in the technique of shipbuilding thus tended to keep pace with the demand for more and better vessels. The expansion of English shipping is characteristic of the age. In 1560 the total tonnage of English merchant ships was 7,600. In 1691 it had increased to 500,000. This was accompanied by a remarkable growth in the tonnage of war vessels. The English naval tonnage in 1607 was 23,000, while a century later it reached over 120,000.

In addition to these major phases of industrial change resulting from the Commercial Revolution, there were others of lesser though significant proportions. One of these was the manufacture of trinkets for trade with the natives of backward countries. While this never promised to become a great and permanent national industry, it did furnish work for large numbers of individuals during the sixteenth, seventeenth, and eighteenth centuries, and was the means for defrauding the natives on a huge scale. The introduction of precious metals and stones in larger quantities, the desire for ostentatious adornment, and the increased opportunity for copying oriental work led to a marked development of the jewelry industry. The manufacture of new scientific instruments for navigation, such as the quadrant, the sextant, the chronometer, reflectors, and telescopes, was almost a new craft. Pictures were produced for market on a considerable scale for the first time. Gunpowder-making occupied a more important place than we can easily realize, the muskets being used for hunting

[1] *Cf. Ibid.* [2] See above, pp. 31 ff.

as well as for warfare—and there were many frontiers. Enormous quantities of salt had to be mined or separated from salt water, since it was the one known preservative of fish and meat at sea as well as indispensable for their preservation for any length of time on land.

IV. THE RISE OF THE WOOLEN INDUSTRY AND THE PUTTING-OUT SYSTEM

We must now describe a new type of industrial organization, which at least partly replaced the guild system in those areas where it was introduced. The new so-called domestic or putting-out system developed as early as the thirteenth century in Italy, spreading gradually into the Rhine Valley, Flanders, and England.[1] In Flanders it existed side by side with the independent guild system in the same towns, the two being applied to different industries. It will be recalled that this newer system, in which the masters often owned the tools and the journeymen were wage laborers with little hope of advancement, was first introduced in those industries which worked chiefly for exports—"export" meaning sale outside the jurisdiction of the town, not necessarily beyond "national" frontiers. The Commercial Revolution greatly increased the number of merchant capitalists who supplied manufactured goods for consumption at distant places and times, and hence furthered the encroachment of the capitalistic organization upon the craft guild already in progress. The domestic or putting-out system was introduced into England in the fifteenth century, in the new and rapidly developing woolen and worsted industries.

Instead of having the workingmen collected in the household of a guild master, the workers under this system lived in their several dwellings, either in the towns or in the adjacent countryside. The person who really controlled all phases of this manufacturing process was known as a merchant capitalist, or more technically, in the woolen industry, as a clothier. He furnished the original capital with which to establish the business and sent out the raw materials to be worked up by the laborers living in their homes and performing the work at a rate agreed upon.[2] The representatives of the merchant capitalist could then go to the homes of the contract workers, leave more raw material, and collect the finished work. This merchant capitalist was not merely superimposed upon a single craft—his type was the organizing center of the whole group of crafts in the industry. For example, the clothier bought raw wool in the market or from the raisers, sent it in turn to spinners, weavers, fullers, and dyers, and finally marketed the finished product. Blackwell Hall in London became the great English cloth market.

At first the clothiers and the buyers of their goods met in a rather informal and haphazard fashion, but about the middle of the seventeenth century a special group of so-called factors appeared. They brought buyers and sellers together, collecting a fee or commission on sales. Later the drapers, who had been both retailers and wholesalers in the Middle Ages, gave up the retail trade and became wholesalers in the modern sense. They bought finished

---

[1] See above, Vol. I, p. 674.
[2] Hence the term "putting-out" as descriptive of the system.

cloth from clothiers or factors and sold it to city retailers, provincial wholesalers, exporters, or foreign buyers. This transformation of the woolen industry and of the methods of selling cloth was completed by about 1750. England was then ready for the next step, the mechanical revolution in manufacturing technique. While the putting-out system was most completely developed in the textile industry, it was also applied in some measure to other industries, such as cutlery, leather, and iron.[1]

There were many marked differences between the guild and the putting-out systems, but the most important were those which tended to develop a capitalistic tendency on the part of the merchant, the dominant figure in the process. Incidentally, in some ways the laboring groups in the scattered homes were rendered for a while more independent than under the old guild order, where the possibility of thoroughgoing personal supervision was much greater. At the same time, particularly in the later development of the putting-out system, the workers tended to lose their independence to the merchants, who often supplied them with both materials and tools. In this phase, some of the worst evils later associated with modern industrialism put in an appearance—woman and child labor, low wages, and "sweating" of the workers.

There were also defects in the putting-out system from the standpoint of the merchant capitalists. One of the greatest of these lay in the tendency of the unsupervised workingmen to loaf, particularly following the periodic pay days, after which one or all of the members of a family sometimes got drunk and remained intoxicated until the wages were used up. This had been more difficult in the old guild days and was even less possible when the factory came in later. There was also a great waste of time and money in sending out goods for the various processes of manufacturing, and in collecting them again. Nor was it easy for the capitalist to make certain of his ability to collect his manufactured product at the time he expected delivery, and a hitch early in the series of processes, say in spinning, delayed work all along the line. It was also difficult for him to supervise closely the quality and the style of his product, which was especially a drawback when new ideas and products began to be introduced. Finally, it was fairly easy for the workers to steal a portion of the raw material or to cheapen it by putting in substitutes. Material thus saved out could either be worked up by the employee himself or sold to a class of racketeering brokers who made a regular business of buying such stolen goods.

As a result of these manifold difficulties there was a tendency to grope after some method of securing better supervision of labor than any possible improvement of the putting-out system, however sweeping, seemed to offer. This led to the appearance of some large central shops—many writers call them factories—before the modern mechanical technique had been introduced. Workingmen could be assembled in a large building with spinning-wheels, hand looms, and the primitive appliances for dyeing and fulling. Here they could be kept at work by representatives of the merchant capitalists. Viewed from the standpoint of personnel organization and discipline, this arrangement had all the advantages of the factory system, as we know it, except one—the cost

---

[1] See N. S. B. Gras, *Industrial Evolution,* Harvard University Press, 1930, Chaps. III-IV; and R. B. Westerfield, *Middlemen in English Business,* Yale University Press, 1915.

of the tools was still so slight that the craftsman in most trades still had some chance to work for himself if he thought all the employers unjust. If it had become general, there is every reason to suppose that the central shop would have exhibited most of the defects and inconveniences of the factory system, such as crowded living-conditions and the centralizing of control in the hands of a few persons. Its slow growth and its restriction to a few industries suggest that the disadvantages of centralization before machines came in must have about balanced the advantages until the Industrial Revolution threw an overwhelming weight into the scales on the side of the factory.

As we approach closer to the period of the Industrial Revolution in England, following 1738, we find that the dependence of workers upon the merchant capitalist became more complete. Fewer and fewer of the spinners and weavers were free to work for themselves and to carry on agricultural operations during part of their time. More and more, they came to be cottagers who carried on no other occupation than industrial activities under the putting-out system, and were financed by the master clothiers who gave out the materials and paid the workers for their labor when the finished products were collected. Hence the transition from the putting-out to the factory system in the textile industries of England did not call for any such complete break in the economic relations between employers and employees as was once supposed. While the numbers working in the cotton industry were not so great as those engaged in the woolen industry, the cotton workers became numerous by the eighteenth century, and were working under much the same conditions as those which existed in the woolen and worsted industries.[1]

While the domestic or putting-out system became the dominant type of organization and control in the English textile industries from the close of the sixteenth century to the rise of the factory system in the eighteenth, it was by no means so successful on the Continent. It established itself in some areas, but there was no thoroughgoing elimination of the guild system. This was not completely abandoned in France until after the Revolution, and it remained in force in parts of Germany and Austria until far into the nineteenth century.[2]

V. CHANGES IN THE TECHNIQUE AND ORGANIZATION OF AGRICULTURE

Along with the development of manufacturing as a result of the Commercial Revolution came the stimulation of other forms of industry, such as fishing and agriculture. For centuries the fisheries constituted an important element in the industrial and commercial life of Europe. They were greatly increased in scope and improved in technique by the growth of oversea trade and contacts.[3] Not only was the amount of fishing carried on in European waters notably increased, in order to supply the greater demand of the Continent itself, but new areas were opened to exploitation, particularly off Newfoundland and at other spots along the coast of North America. New markets for the products of the fisheries were discovered in the tropical and semitropical colonies, espe-

---

[1] *Cf.* G. W. Daniels, *The Early English Cotton Industry*, Longmans, 1920.
[2] See below, pp. 325 ff., 329 ff.   [3] *Cf.* Gillespie, *op. cit.*, pp. 103-05.

CHANGES IN AGRICULTURE 49

cially in the West Indies, where great quantities of salt fish were consumed. In addition to the salt fish itself, other important commodities, such as oil and whalebone, were provided through the fisheries. The greatly increased use of salt fish also stimulated, as we have seen, the development of the salt industry.

Even more revolutionary were the changes in agriculture between 1600 and 1800, most notably in England. The English developments were most significant from the standpoint of the general economic history of Europe because of their closer relationship with the Industrial Revolution.

While the connection between the new commerce and the greatly stimulated manufacturing industry on the one hand, and the expansion of Europe on the other, is clear and obvious enough, it may not appear so evident that the Agricultural Revolution, which we are about to describe, was directly related to the results of the oversea expansion. A little reflection will, however, reveal the fundamental dependence of the agricultural transformation upon the preceding developments in commerce and industry. The Crusades were the first great impulse to a money economy. Capital, which did more than anything else to break up the medieval manorial system, was accumulated chiefly as a result of the new commercial activity. It was the early modern commercial activity that produced the merchant princes who wished to secure social and political prestige through purchasing great landed estates, thus establishing themselves in the grand manner essential to social success in the England of that day. It was the money that had been acquired through commercial pursuits which enabled Thomas Coke and others like him to carry on capitalistic farming on a large scale. Finally, not a few of the new crops came from abroad. The Agricultural Revolution, then, cannot be divorced from the general complex of economic, social, and cultural changes that grew out of the expansion of Europe from the days of the Crusades onward.

The manorial system had been wiped out in England, as far as methods of landholding and class differentiation were concerned, by the fifteenth century, but the technique of agriculture, involving rudimentary tools and coöperative labor, underwent astonishingly slight changes between the twelfth century and the close of the seventeenth. In spite of the disappearance of the legal aspects of the manor and of many of its old social practices, the technique of agriculture and the distribution of arable land resembled medieval manorial practice to an astonishing extent. Our old friends the agricultural village, strip ownership of land, coöperative cultivation, common pasture, and wood-gathering rights [1] were still present in 1700 to a marked degree.

A series of remarkable changes in technique, with a sweeping reaction upon the social organization of English agriculture, took place in the eighteenth century. They may be summarized under such general headings as: (1) The introduction of new implements; (2) successful experiments with new crops; (3) improvements of stock-breeding; (4) drainage of waste land and the development of scientific notions of fertilizing the soil; and finally (5) the organization of scientific and pseudo-scientific societies for the promotion of improved agricultural technique.

As has been noted, down to the seventeenth century there had been little or

[1] See above, Vol. I, pp. 609 ff.

no improvment in the type of the medieval agricultural implements of western Europe. Above all, almost nothing new had been provided for working up the ground about the roots of crops that could be "cultivated"—not grain, of course—and for eliminating weeds. The provision of better agricultural tools and machinery is associated chiefly with the work of Jethro Tull (1674-1740).[1] Tull introduced the first successful modern drill for the sowing of grain, superseding the old and wasteful method of sowing grain broadcast by hand on top of the ground. He also stimulated (for England) the popularity of the modern practice of "cultivating," namely, working up the soil about the roots of such crops as peas, beans, beets, turnips, potatoes, and eliminating the competing weeds. We may summarize his contributions in the words of Prothero: "The chief legacies which Jethro Tull left to his successors were clean farming, economy in seedings, drilling, and the maxim that the more irons are among the roots the better for the crop."[2]

Another important advance in English farming lay in the contribution of Lord Townshend (1674-1738), who was mainly responsible for the introduction of new crops.[3] Down to this time it had been difficult to secure winter crops, or any that would not considerably reduce the fertility of the land. This deficiency had made it necessary to leave one-third or more of the ground fallow each year. An associated problem had been to secure enough fodder to carry the horses, cattle, and sheep safely through the winter season, because the "hay" was chiefly derived from unproductive natural grasses.

Townshend solved some of these problems. He introduced and rendered important services in promoting the successful cultivation of turnips and artificial grasses. Clover does not reduce fertility as do grains, and it also performs important services in gathering nitrogen, loosening the ground, and counteracting the tendency of many crops, when repeated, to render the soil unfit to reproduce them until it has been "rested," as farmers sometimes colloquially put it. The chemistry of plant growth and the results of repeated cultivation on the same spot under intensive artificial conditions are so delicate and complicated that a judicious change of crops is often as effective in preventing decline of yield as a fallow year would be. After the introduction of clover and the rotation of crops, the fallow year was gradually abandoned, and the acreage that might be cropped each year increased by some 30 per cent or more. At the same time, the appearance of clover made it possible for the first time to produce an adequate supply of fodder to carry live stock through the winter. Turnips as a new crop also helped greatly in the problem of getting enough food for cattle. They were also used as food by peasants. So great was Lord Townshend's enthusiasm for turnips that he was dubbed "Turnip Townshend."

Along with the improvements in the technique of cultivation and the care of plants and cereals came a revolutionary development of stock-breeding, very largely the result of the efforts of Robert Bakewell (1725-95).[4] The improve-

---

[1] Cf. R. W. Prothero (Lord Ernle), *English Farming, Past and Present*, 3d ed., Longmans, 1922, Chap. VII; and T. H. Marshall, "Jethro Tull and the 'New Husbandry' of the Eighteenth Century," *Economic History Review*, January, 1929. [3] Cf. *Ibid.*, Chap. VII.
[2] Prothero, *op. cit.*, p. 172.   [4] Cf. *Ibid.*, Chap. VIII.

ment in crops and cultivation made possible the feeding of a larger number of live stock than ever before. With the dawning possibility of stock-raising for profit came a new interest in producing specialized types that would bring the highest market prices as beef, mutton, and pork. This had been impossible under manorial conditions. The cultivators had used common pasture lands, so that all the stock ran together, breeding down to a common mongrel type. Something had been done in stock-breeding by monasteries and lay lords who had inclosed fields, but the shortage of hay for wintering tended to throw emphasis on hardihood rather than on quality from the consumer's point of view. Some progress had already been made in the Netherlands, where the manor had disappeared early or never existed at all, and the commerce with the Mediterranean region had bettered the breeds, particularly of cattle, horses, and sheep. In England, as in northern Europe, however, it was usual to find a single type of horse, cow, sheep, or hog, not specialized, respectively, to road or draft use, milk or beef, mutton or wool, or the best type of pork.

Bakewell thoroughly understood that no one type of animal could be adapted to all the various purposes. Therefore he started in to breed specialized horses for draft or road use, to create distinctive breeds of cattle for beef or milk, and to separate his wool sheep from his mutton sheep. While he was opposed to allowing others to imitate his methods or appropriate his secrets, it proved impossible for him to prevent it. If anything, his improvements in stock-breeding were more rapidly accepted than the innovations of Tull and Townshend in their respective fields. The Duke of Bedford (1765-1802) and Lord Somerville (1765-1819) carried on and popularized scientific stock-breeding.

Arthur Young (1741-1820) made a contribution of a different sort. He was thoroughly familiar with the work of Tull, Townshend, and Bakewell, and desired to see these promising innovations generally adopted. He understood, however, that this would not be possible so long as England was divided into many small holdings, worked according to the anachronistic coöperative methods inherited from the manorial régime, and without any adequate capital to finance capitalistic farming. His professional life was devoted mainly to the reforms that were necessary to realize these aspirations. He was the great prophet and agitator, urging on the most characteristic agrarian transformation of his time in England—the development of the inclosure or engrossing of land.[1] The consolidation of small holdings into larger farms displaced the English yeomanry and produced modern capitalistic farming between 1760 and 1830.

Further technical advances were made in such processes as draining land, mixing soils, and improvements in fertilization. The desirability of mixing soils was emphasized by Lord Townshend and carried on by Thomas Coke and other early capitalistic farmers.[2] Scientific fertilization of soils was made possible by the remarkable advances in chemistry in the seventeenth and eighteenth centuries. Perhaps the first important chemist to devote his attention to land fertilization was Sir Humphry Davy. His work was carried on, among others, by the greatest organic chemist of his age, the German scientist Justus Liebig. Chemistry enabled experts to determine just what chemicals

[1] Cf. Ibid., Chap. IX.   [2] Cf. Ibid., Chap. X.

were needed in any particular soil to insure maximum fertility and also made it possible to produce these chemicals more surely, speedily, and cheaply. Agricultural societies were organized to aid in carrying on effectively all of these progressive farming methods. Such were the famous Smithfield Club of London and the Highland Society in Scotland.

The rapidity with which the reforms were actually carried out was due to the Commercial Revolution and its results. Merchants had greatly increased in numbers and in wealth, but social prestige was still hard to achieve without membership in the landholding class. Many who had become rich in commerce were thus glad to invest their money in great landed estates as the one open door to political and social influence. It happened, not altogether by accident, that the technical improvements in agriculture mentioned above added the possibility of profits to the social and political incentives for building up the great estates that characterized English agriculture throughout the nineteenth century. Another factor in producing the concentration of estates was the higher agricultural prices that prevailed during the French Revolutionary and Napoleonic wars. These encouraged capitalistic farming in order to secure the profits promised by the price increases. These large landed holdings were created chiefly out of the purchases of land held earlier by the squires and tenant farmers, and by the occupation of leaseholds and customs holds appropriated from the peasantry.[1]

We hear much about the inclosures under the Tudor kings, but they were insignificant as compared with those which were made in the century following 1740, during some single years of which as much land was inclosed as in the entire Tudor period. To illustrate by two fairly representative decades: 469 inclosure bills were passed in 1790-99, affecting 858,270 acres; and between 1810 and 1819, 853 bills permitted the consolidation of 1,560,990 acres. After 1801, it was easy for private individuals to get such bills through a docile Parliament and to oust the peasants who had enjoyed some protection down to that time. The history of expropriation and inclosure bills from 1760 down to the General Inclosure Act of 1845 is inseparable from that of the agricultural development of the nineteenth century. The extensive inclosures interest us at this point chiefly as the culmination of the movement towards capitalistic farming in England, the first great exponent of which was Thomas Coke of Holkham (1752-1842). His notable success was a vital factor in encouraging others to adopt similar methods. In the United States George Washington and Thomas Jefferson stand out as examples of early capitalistic farming. Washington was the more successful.[2]

These agricultural changes produced revolutions in other phases of English life, most notably with respect to social classes. In seventeenth-century England the agricultural element, which made up the majority of the population, was divided into the following five classes: (1) The old noble families from feudal times, of which only about sixty remained; (2) the squires or gentry, who made up much the most numerous element in the landed aristocracy and

---

[1] *Cf.* Prothero, *op. cit.,* Chap. x.
[2] *Cf.* H. L. Ritter, *Washington as a Business Man,* Sears, 1931, Chaps. IV, VI, IX, XIII, XVI; and A. J. Nock, *Jefferson,* Harcourt, Brace, 1926, pp. 57-73, 167-71.

furnished most of the petty officers of the state and the army; (3) the yeomen or freeholders, who occupied relatively small farms; (4) the free tenants, who worked their plots on leaseholds from the squires and the landed gentry; and (5) the agricultural laborers, who worked for the great lords, the squires, and free tenants. As a result of the inclosures the agricultural classes in England were, generally speaking, reduced to three: (1) A great landed aristocracy, derived chiefly from the new mercantile class, which had invested its savings in land; (2) a middle group of renters; and (3) a great mass of agricultural laborers who were deprived of any personal landholdings.

Though these agricultural transformations as a whole increased agricultural efficiency and production, they certainly brought about a serious social loss to England in the wholesale depression of the great mass of the residents in the country. This dolorous fact has been well presented by Professor Gras:

To many students of our day, the most significant result of the agricultural revolution was not economic efficiency, not change in land tenure, and not literary culture, but the loss of well-being by the rank and file of country people. The proletarianizing of the yeomen and the customary tenants seems a great social set-back. Where they had been masters, they now became laborers, at least in many instances. And then the cottars and squatters, the traditional poor and laboring class of the village, suffered greatly when their holdings were enclosed for the new agriculture. They lost their cow, pig, and geese when the commons were enclosed, and instead of milk, pork, and fowl, they lived on bread and tea. They lost their fuel when the waste land was enclosed: and if they wanted to keep warm, they were invited to use the stables. Truly it was but slight compensation for such losses to have plenty of work offered to them and to be compelled to accept it to keep body and soul together. Industrial discipline is one of our modern acquisitions, but the price in this case and commonly is a very heavy one. The usual escape from this sad dilemma is to regard the economic gain as permanent and the human suffering as temporary. But the unescapable reflection is that the sufferers have but one life to live, and when that is gone, civilization is gone—for them. They have helped to furnish the elegant home of the gentleman farmer and they have submitted to the new discipline. They have built the poet's palace of art but they dwell not in it.[1]

The ruination of the free peasantry was a major cause of the decline of Roman society. Whether the depression of the agricultural classes will ruin England remains to be seen. The coming of the Industrial Revolution after 1738 and the employment of many of the landless in factories lessened the immediate social penalty of dispossessing the English masses of their lands.

These agricultural changes, like those in industry and commerce, were not without their relation to the Industrial Revolution. The new capitalistic farming, for the time being at least, increased the productivity of English agriculture and made it possible to maintain for a time the greatly increased urban population. Further, the great mass of peasants ousted from their lands were glad to accept any means of earning a living open to them—specifically to take up employment on the great estates or in the new factory towns at even pitifully inadequate wages and under the most exacting conditions of labor. In this way a cheap and eager industrial proletariat was provided for the new

[1] N. S. B. Gras, *History of Agriculture in Europe and America*, Crofts, 1925, p. 228.

factory towns that were created as a result of the inventive genius of Hargreaves, Crompton, and Watt, and the organizing genius of Arkwright. From the dispossessed agricultural laborers there was created a "free" labor market to facilitate the rapid expansion of a nascent industrialism.[1]

In France and Germany, as in England, the new trade stimulated by the Crusades and the impecuniousness of the feudal nobles led to a general decay of serfdom. This was checked in Germany, especially in eastern Germany, by the ravages of the Thirty Years' War (1618-48), and serfdom was actually increased for a time thereafter. It must not be forgotten that the Commercial Revolution was well under way by this time, that capitalism was developing rapidly, and hence that the growth of serfdom in eastern Germany was accompanied by the consolidation of estates considerably different from medieval manors. Junker farming had many quite modern aspects, in spite of its anachronistic labor system. Prussian cameralism, as it was called—virtually economic planning—devoted special attention to improvements in agriculture. In many respects the great Prussian estates were progressive as to methods of cultivation, with much inclosed land, well-bred stock, and an increasing amount of grain raising for market. Western Germany—especially southwestern Germany—was more like France. During French Revolutionary and Napoleonic times it became a part of the French system for a time, and never quite relapsed into the old looseness of organization or shook off the influence of the Code Napoléon.

The decay of both manorialism and serfdom was more pronounced and continuous in France than in Germany, for two main reasons, besides many lesser ones: (1) France was more involved in the expansion of Europe and the Commercial Revolution; and (2) its highly centralized national government encouraged the shift to a taxable money economy, at the same time that it sternly suppressed the feudal barons. By 1774 only about 6 per cent of the French population was in a state of even nominal serfdom, and the French finance minister, Necker, correctly characterized rural France just before the Revolution as "an immensity of small rural properties." The social structure of feudalism no longer served any logical purpose. In France the Physiocrats [2] helped to promote the same scientific interest in agriculture that Tull, Townshend, Bakewell, and Young were encouraging in England.[3]

When the Industrial Revolution began about the middle of the eighteenth century in England, the latter was not only more highly industrialized already than either France or Germany, but its agriculture had also been placed on a more thoroughly capitalistic basis. Its oversea colonies and stations gave it a great advantage in both raw materials and markets. The wars and blockades from 1792 to 1815 offered an opportunity to consolidate an enduring industrial supremacy on the basis of these advantages already won. While much of continental Europe was being laid waste by Napoleon's armies, England was safe from invasion and becoming prosperous through the sale of goods and munitions of war to the Continent. Both England and Germany had one potential superiority over France that was to become more and more apparent during the nineteenth century. Their populations were far from the

---
[1] See below, pp. 285 ff.; and Prothero, *op. cit.*, Chap. xiv.
[2] See below, pp. 77 ff.   [3] *Cf.* Gras, *op. cit.*, Chap. x.

CHANGES IN AGRICULTURE 55

maximum that the soil could support, whereas this factor had largely stabilized and crystallized French society for centuries. Swift economic change was more difficult in France for want of "elbow room."

SUGGESTED READING

Hammerton, *Universal History of the World*, Chaps. 137, 146
L. B. Packard, *The Commercial Revolution, 1400-1776*, Holt, 1927, Chap. 1
J. E. Gillespie, *The Influence of Oversea Expansion on England to 1700*, Columbia University Press, 1920, Chaps. IV-VI
—— *History of Europe, 1500-1815*, Chap. V
Hayes, *Political and Cultural History of Modern Europe*, Vol. I, pp. 466-69
F. A. Ogg and W. R. Sharp, *The Economic Development of Modern Europe*, Macmillan, 1926, Chaps. IV, VI
F. L. Nussbaum, *History of the Economic Institutions of Modern Europe*, Crofts, 1933, Pt. III, Chap. IV
Ephraim Lipson, *Economic History of England*, Macmillan, 1929-31, 2 vols., Vol. II.
J. B. Botsford, *English Society in the Eighteenth Century*, Macmillan, 1924, Chaps. I-II
P. J. Mantoux, *The Industrial Revolution in the Eighteenth Century*, Harcourt, Brace, 1928, Pt. I
H. E. Sée, *Economic and Social Conditions in France during the Eighteenth Century*, Knopf, 1927, Chaps. II, VI-IX
G. F. Renard and Georges Weulersse, *Life and Work in Modern Europe*, Knopf, 1926
Day, *History of Commerce*, Pt. II, Chaps. XV, XXI-XXIV
H. de B. Gibbins, *History of Commerce in Europe*, Macmillan, 1891, Bk. III, Chaps. I-IV
N. S. B. Gras, *History of Agriculture in Europe and America*, Crofts, 1925, Chaps. IX-X
Hutton Webster, *Historical Selections*, Heath, 1929, pp. 753-65
L. C. Marshall, *The Emergence of the Modern Order: Industrial Society*, University of Chicago Press, 1929-30, 3 vols., Vol. I, Pt. I, pp. 131-66, 175-217
A. E. Bland, P. A. Brown, and R. H. Tawney, eds., *English Economic History: Select Documents*, Macmillan, 1915, Pt. III, Sec. II

FURTHER REFERENCES

THE COMMERCIAL REVOLUTION. On the nature of the Commercial Revolution, see Packard, *op. cit.*; Helmolt and others, *History of the World*, Vol. VIII, pp. 62 ff.

On the history of ships and shipbuilding, see Abbott, *The Expansion of Europe*, Vol. I, pp. 325-26; Gillespie, *The Influence of Overseas Expansion on England*, pp. 150-53; pp. 189 ff. of *Facts and Factors in Economic History: Articles by Former Students of Edwin Francis Gay*, Harvard University Press, 1932; A. W. Kirkaldy, *British Shipping: Its History, Organization and Importance* (Dutton, 1914); Romola and R. C. Anderson, *The Sailing-Ship* (McBride, 1926); R. S. Holland, *Historic Ships* (McCrae, Smith, 1926); J. F. Meigs, *The Story of the Seaman* (Lippincott, 1924, 2 vols.); Hendrik Van Loon, *Ships and How They Sailed the Seven Seas* (Simon & Schuster, 1935).

On the new commodities and the changes in tastes and customs, see pp. 23-72 of Adolf Reichwein, *China and Europe* (Knopf, 1925); Gillespie, *op. cit.*, Chaps. II-III, XI; Botsford, *op. cit.*, Chaps. III-IV, X.

On the rise and character of modern trade, see Gillespie, *op. cit.*, Chap. IV; Botsford, *op. cit.*, Chap. II; Day, *op. cit.*, Pt. III; Helmolt and others, *op. cit.*, Vol. VIII, pp. 62 ff.; Chap. IV of J. L. LeB. and Barbara Hammond, *The Rise of Modern Industry* (Harcourt, Brace, 1926); Ogg and Sharp, *op. cit.*, Chap. III; Mantoux, *op. cit.*, Pt. I; Jeudwine, *Studies in Empire and Trade*, Pts. IV-V.

On the geographical background of commerce, see Hammond and Hammond, *op. cit.*, Chaps. I-II; Nussbaum, *op. cit.*, Pt. III, Chap. II; Helmolt, *op. cit.*, Vol. IV, Chap. I; Vol. VIII, Chap. V.

On the shifts of geographical basis of European history from a fluvial to a thalassic and then to an oceanic basis, see J. K. Wright, *The Geographical Basis of European History* (Holt, 1928).

On the precious metals in early modern times, see Nussbaum, *op. cit.*, pp. 89-105; Alexander Del Mar, *History of the Precious Metals* (Cambridge Encyclopedia Co., 1902); E. J. Hamilton, *American Treasure and the Price Revolution in Spain, 1501-1650* (Harvard University Press, 1934).

MANUFACTURING. For English industry on the eve of the Commercial Revolution, see L. F. Salzman, *England in Tudor Times* (Scribner, 1926). On the expansion of early modern manufacturing, see Gillespie, *op. cit.*, Chap. V; Nussbaum, *op. cit.*, pp. 72 ff.; Chap. XIX of H. de B. Gibbins, *Industry in England* (Scribner, 1916).

On the woolen industry, see Ephraim Lipson, *History of the Woollen and Worsted Industries* (Macmillan, 1921), and *Economic History of England*, Vols. I-II. On the silk industry, see G. B. Hertz, "The English Silk Industry in the Eighteenth Century," *English Historical Review*, October, 1909. On the cotton industry, see pp. 90 ff. of M. DeC. Crawford, *The Heritage of Cotton* (Putnam, 1931); G. W. Daniels, *The Early English Cotton Industry* (Longmans, 1920).

On the domestic or putting-out system of industry, see Nussbaum, *op. cit.*, Pt. III, Chap. IV; Chap. IV of Sir W. J. Ashley, *The Economic Organization of England* (Longmans, 1914) and Vol. II, pp. 191-243 of his *English Economic History* (Longmans, 1888-93, 2 vols.); Lipson, *op. cit.*, Vol. I, pp. 391-443 and Vol. II; George Unwin, *Industrial Organization in the 16th and 17th Centuries* (Oxford Press, 1904); R. B. Westerfield, *Middlemen in English Business* (Yale University Press, 1915).

CHANGES IN AGRICULTURE. On English agriculture on the eve of the Agricultural Revolution, see Reginald Lennard, "English Agriculture under Charles II," *Economic History Review*, October, 1932. On the agricultural changes from 1650 to 1800, see pp. 250-60 of Frederick Bradshaw, *Social History of England* (London, 1918); Chap. II of Arthur Birnie, *Economic History of Europe, 1760-1930* (Dial Press, 1930); Ogg and Sharp, *op. cit.*, pp. 31-39; pp. 102 ff. of Gilbert Slater, *The Growth of Modern England* (Houghton Mifflin, 1933); Gibbins, *op. cit.*, Chap. XVII; Chaps. VII-X of R. W. Prothero (Lord Ernle), *English Farming, Past and Present* (3d ed., Longmans, 1922); Gras, *op. cit.*, Chaps. IX-X; pp. 96 ff., 205 ff., 295 ff., of Renard and Weulersse, *op. cit.;* Bk. II, Chap. I, of Elie Halévy, *History of the English People in 1815* (Harcourt, Brace, 1924); Sée, *op. cit.*, Chap. II; L. P. Adams, *Agricultural Depression and Farm Relief in England, 1813-1852* (London, 1932).

CHAPTER III

CAPITALISM AND COMMERCIAL POLICIES IN THE EARLY MODERN PERIOD

I. THE BEGINNINGS OF MODERN CAPITALISM

One of the most striking and characteristic phases of the development of the modern order was the beginning of what is commonly called modern capitalism. We need not attempt here any technical definition of capitalism, but it may be useful and illuminating to state some of its more fundamental attributes, which are: (1) The desire for private profit rather than the service of the community or mankind; (2) the estimation of social status and success in terms of relative monetary resources; (3) the evaluation of goods and services in terms of prices set by bargaining in the market rather than by considerations of justice or intrinsic worth; (4) the accumulation of large monetary resources for investment in business ventures; (5) the existence of a free market for the sale of goods; (6) the presence of a sufficient labor market to procure the needed laborers; (7) a credit system adequate to the needs of the economic era; and (8) a reasonably thorough development of commercial and industrial life.

This capitalistic development was made possible by the creation of relatively large fortunes available for various types of economic enterprise, together with the emergence of a new spirit in economic life, which sought to exploit every possible opportunity for profit in business undertakings. The accumulation of working capital on a large scale, according to our standards, first took place in early modern times. While there were beginnings of a capitalistic régime in ancient Babylonia and Syria, and in the great cities of the Alexandrian East and the Roman Empire, nothing like the situation in even eighteenth-century Europe existed in the ancient world. In both Greece and Rome, the napkin and agrarian economy,[1] rather than the capitalistic outlook, prevailed. There was relatively little accumulation of monetary resources for the furtherance of economic enterprises. Muslim cities in Asia, Africa and

---

[1] See Vol. I, p. 211. The term "napkin" is used by some writers to describe an economic order in which savings are not usually reinvested in productive business or speculation. It is derived from Jesus' parable of the talents (Matt. 25: 14-28), in which one steward is pictured as having carefully wrapped his piece of money in a napkin rather than investing it in gainful business. According to the parable, he was sharply castigated by his lord and master. This "napkin economy" was rather general in antiquity and the Middle Ages, though in some cases, such as ancient Syria, Hellenistic Alexandria, Muslim Baghdad, and the like, there were some symptoms of incipient capitalism. The term "agrarian economy" signifies the prevalence of landed rather than business wealth and of the ideas associated with agricultural society. Western civilization existed in a primarily agrarian economy from the close of the Stone Age to the time of Columbus and Luther—and, for the most part, in a napkin economy as well.

Spain, and the Byzantine commercial centers came a little nearer to modern capitalism.

Italian financial organization in the later Middle Ages was more like modern capitalism in some respects,[1] but many of the leading Italian banking houses were family ventures, their capital was much less than that of modern concerns of equal repute, and archaic traditions and practices greatly hampered their operations. Too much of the earlier prejudice against interest-taking remained, interest rates were high and erratic, and the provision of proper security for loans had not yet been fully achieved. In several cases the private banks succumbed through the defalcation of princes too strong to be coerced. Others decayed with the families that controlled them, because the joint-stock principle[2] was not yet well enough worked out to bring in new blood and abandon outlived policies. The Peruzzi of the fourteenth century had a capital of some $800,000, the Medici of the fifteenth perhaps $5,000,000. The Fuggers of South Germany had many times as much, but the period of their greatest prosperity belongs to early modern rather than late medieval times. Their capital at the peak of their prosperity, about the middle of the sixteenth century, has been estimated at between 5,000,000 and 6,000,000 Rhenish gulden, which probably represents a purchasing power of over $50,000,000 in our money.[3]

In medieval Europe generally, and especially in northern Europe, the industrial limitations of the guild system, the lack of extensive and diversified commerce, and the prevailing theories regarding price and interest greatly limited the use of capital, and hence obstructed its accumulation. It was the era of oversea expansion, with the remarkable growth of commercial activity, and the accompanying revolutionary discoveries of precious metals, that made possible modern capitalism. Other associated factors of importance were the financial system that had been developed by the Catholic Church in raising and administering its vast funds, and the rapidly increasing financial needs of the State. These induced the controlling agencies to make use of, and hence to tolerate, the new class of capitalistic entrepreneurs. As a matter of fact, a marked increase in the income of the state accompanied the growth of private fortunes, so that private and public capitalism developed side by side. Moreover, the decay of the manorial and guild systems, which dispossessed large classes of the ownership of means of production, made labor marketable in a new sense, injecting an element of mobility and adaptability that was unique at least in degree.

There have been considerable differences of opinion as to the source of the surplus wealth that made possible the rise of modern capitalism.[4] While reliable statistical evidence for this early period is scanty, it seems most likely that the private accumulations were built up slowly, chiefly out of the new piracy, privateering, and commerce. The merchants who acquired their first surplus in trade often multiplied it by engaging in financial operations where the risks were great, but the opportunities for profit were correspondingly large. We should not, moreover, forget the part played in the rise of certain early fortunes and in the increase of public revenues by the confiscation of Church property,

---

[1] *Cf.* Richard Ehrenberg, *Capital and Finance in the Age of the Renaissance*, Harcourt, Brace, 1928, Introduction. [2] See below, pp. 62, 71. [3] *Cf.* Ehrenberg, *op. cit.*, Bk. I, Chap. 1.

[4] See particularly the works of Werner Sombart, Jakob Strieder, Max Weber, Henri Sée, and J. A. Hobson.

THE BEGINNINGS OF MODERN CAPITALISM

especially monastic property, in many Protestant countries after 1525. The confiscation of Church lands by Charles Martel helped on feudalism; the confiscation of Church property by Henry VIII eight hundred years later contributed to the growth of capitalism.

Capitalism is certainly the outstanding economic feature of the modern and contemporary era and more than any other element serves to differentiate the period since 1500 from the economy that prevailed in antiquity and the Middle Ages.[1] Certain statistics that have been gathered as to England and France well illustrate this tendency towards a marked increase of available capital. The estimated national wealth of England in 1600 was £17,000,000; in 1630, £28,000,000; in 1660, £56,000,000; and in 1688, £88,000,000. Equally illuminating is the increase of coin in England during this same period. In 1600 it is estimated that the extant coin in England was some £4,000,000; in 1625, £6,000,000; in 1660, £16,000,000; and in 1680, £18,500,000. The royal income also showed a remarkable development, particularly from the customs dues. In 1603 the customs dues of England amounted to only £36,000; by 1660, they had increased to over £4,000,000. A generation or so after this time, at the height of the prosperity of the East India Company, this great organization alone paid an annual tribute to the English treasury of some £4,000,000. It is estimated that the annual income of William III in 1700 was £4,415,360. The revenues of the British kingdom are estimated to have been £500,000 in the reign of Elizabeth; £4,000,000 in 1700; and £34,000,000 in 1801. The revenues of the kings of France increased from 10,000,000 livres in 1600 to 200,000,000 in 1700 and 500,000,000 in 1789.

Private fortunes of considerable size—some of them totaling over £1,000,000 —were built up in England and other European states during this period. They were accumulated through privateering, the slave trade and slavery in the colonies, money-lending, mining ventures, promotion and speculation, and investment in commercial and manufacturing activity.[2] In the latter part of the sixteenth century, especially, was privateering a lucrative enterprise. The voyage of Drake in 1577-80 brought in as spoils some £600,000, of which about £275,000 was handed over to the Queen as the share of the state in this form of semilegalized piracy. Besides the private fortunes accumulated through speculation in stocks, and by the promotions of new enterprisers— projectors, they were called, in early English terminology—many enriched themselves through graft in positions with the government or with trading organizations, the most notorious and successful being the "nabobs" in the East Indian service. Others amassed considerable sums as resident planters or absentee landlords of domains in the New World, particularly in the West Indies.

It should not, of course, be assumed that all of the fortunes accumulated in the seventeenth and eighteenth centuries were the product of dubious or illegitimate enterprises. Perhaps the great majority of capitalists rose from the ranks of labor mainly as the result of daring energy, application, and sagacity in constructive business and commercial ventures. The case of William Miles is representative of many members of this large new class of capitalists:

[1] *Cf.* J. A. Hobson, *Evolution of Modern Capitalism*, rev. ed., Scribner, 1926, Chap. I.
[2] *Cf.* Botsford, *English Society in the Eighteenth Century*, Chap. v.

This young man came to Bristol with three half-pence, obtained a job as a porter, and did evening work for a small shipbuilder. On the completion of his apprenticeship, by which time he had saved £15, he qualified as ship's carpenter in a Jamaica merchantman. There he bought a cask or two of sugar, which he sold in Bristol at a huge profit. With this money he stocked up with articles in greatest demand in Jamaica, and repeated his former investment. Saving his earnings, which became larger each trip, he settled down in Bristol as a sugar-merchant, in which capacity he amassed a large fortune. In 1793, his son joined him in partnership, not only in the West India trade, but in the largest sugar-refining business in Bristol. . . . Elsewhere, and in general, the capitalist manufacturer was a self-made man; and curiously enough, few who entered the trade rich were successful:

"The men who did establish themselves were raised by their own efforts, commencing in a very humble way, and pushing their advance by a series of unceasing exertions, having a very limited capital to begin with, or even none at all save that of their own labour." [1]

While the fortunes of this age were insignificant as compared to those of the late nineteenth century and the twentieth century, they far exceeded anything that had been previously known in western Europe.[2] It is, to be sure, something more than the mere size of the fortunes that characterizes modern capitalism. The extent of monetary possessions alone would scarcely distinguish the Fuggers from Croesus.

It should be remembered, moreover, that these estimates of fortunes must be interpreted in the light of the frequent and often extreme depreciation of the currency carried on by many rulers in Europe between 1500 and 1800. This tended to offset to some degree the ostensible increase of public and private fortunes during this period. Where depreciation was present the purchasing power of the increased incomes and fortunes did not keep pace with their formal and apparent growth.

Even more important was the changing conception of the nature of capital and its possible uses, particularly investment, in the expansion of business enterprises. The "theory of business enterprise" and the "price system," with their emphasis on gainful business and financial pursuits and their measurements and evaluations in terms of monetary prices, gradually triumphed over the attitudes and conceptions of the napkin and agrarian economy. This was an epoch-making transition, which has been variously and definitively analyzed by many eminent scholars.[3]

Very significant also was the depersonalization of business forces and instruments. A real distinction gradually developed between the capital and assets of a business unit and the capital and assets of the individuals involved in it. Neither the Greeks nor the Florentines had ever been able to achieve this dissociation of personality from business. It was an important incident in the transition from a need-covering economy, based on ideas of necessity and the just price, to modern economic life founded on the aspiration to make the utmost possible pecuniary profit for individuals.

---

[1] Botsford, *English Society in the Eighteenth Century*, pp. 120, 124. The last paragraph is from Gaskell, *The Manufacturing Population of England*.
[2] *Cf.* Nussbaum, *History of the Economic Institutions of Modern Europe*, pp. 114 ff.; and Ehrenberg, *op. cit.*, Bk. I, Chaps. II-III.
[3] Especially Weber, Sombart, Sée, Hobson, Webb, Tawney, Hammond, Veblen, and Commons.

Another very potent item in the developing capitalistic processes and psychology was the drive, which became ever more successful for centuries, to free economic contracts and market operations from all hampering restraints, whether of a religious, legal, or other character. It aimed, in essence, to smash every vestige of the medieval system that had sought to control economic life in the interest of the well-being of human society as a whole. The depersonalization of business helped here, since it made more difficult the application to business practices of a body of personal morality. The ideal, conscious or unconscious, was an economic society free from all restraints that might hinder a market which brought together in a mechanical fashion the forces of demand and supply.

By the close of the sixteenth century the medieval prohibition by both Church and law courts against the taking of interest had generally disappeared.[1] The increased need on the part of both State and Church for working capital was among the most important factors in producing this result. Even before the Protestant revolt the Church had ceased to inveigh against interest as such, but had retained earnest convictions about extortionate rates and various abuses of wealth that were considered to be at variance with the Christian religion. For good or ill, religious authority was weakened by the Protestant revolt at a most critical period in economic evolution. Europe went through both a religious and an economic revolution at the same time, with both religious camps needing all the social and financial support they could get. In the long run, the Christian Church as a whole—if we may speak of it thus after the Protestant revolt—probably settled down more smoothly and complacently to the new capitalistic system than would have been the case without the sixteenth-century theological upheaval to distract its attention from economic matters during the critical years of the transition.

One of the decisive factors in creating a new attitude towards interest-taking was the demand for large sums of working capital for investment in oversea trading ventures and in the larger business units in Europe that grew up with them. It was impossible, as we now see, to accumulate this essential capital without offering some appropriate material reward. Not only were the time-worn economic ideals of Aristotle and the medieval Church abandoned, but the banking class, deriving its income largely from interest, was raised to a position of unprecedented eminence and respect. Obviously there was nothing brand-new or astonishing about this—it was merely the result of the growth and spread, under exceptionally favorable circumstances, of a condition clearly visible in the Italian towns of late medieval times.

An outstanding aspect of the rise of capitalism and new business instruments was the growth and fixation of the idea of a business unit, firm or enterprise, in contrast to the older family or guild organization. Business in the ancient and medieval world had been carried on almost entirely by individuals or through family or quasi-family enterprises, though in the Roman period the fraternal partnership gave rise to various forms of business partnerships, notably the *commenda*.[2] The joint-stock principle of impersonally distributed

[1] *Cf.* Max Weber, *General Economic History*, Greenberg, 1927, Chap. XXI.
[2] See Vol. I, pp. 299 ff.

risks and profits was not entirely unknown in medieval Italy.[1] The partnership facilitated the accumulation of more capital for investment in business and, looked at from the other side, it increased the opportunities for the profitable investment of surplus wealth. But it had one grave defect, namely, the unlimited liability of the partners. In the case of the failure of a partnership any single partner who might have available resources was liable for the total indebtedness of the partnership, and would be compelled to settle the full indebtedness if his fellow partners proved insolvent. Further, a partnership was ordinarily dissolved upon the death or withdrawal of any of the partners, and thus failed to provide any real permanence of organization.

When business, and particularly commerce, began to develop on a much larger scale in the early modern period, a need was soon felt for new and more adaptable forms of business organization. Among the first to fill this need was the regulated company, best developed in England.[2] The most notable examples are the Merchant Staplers and the Merchant Adventurers, the latter belonging to the sixteenth century and the former of somewhat earlier origin. The regulated company was in reality a form of business association rather than of organization, though it exercised no little influence upon the later joint-stock companies. The Merchant Adventurers were an association of men engaged in foreign trade, particularly with the East, which secured a royal charter granting a monopoly of that particular branch of trade. There was no common pool of actual capital, but ships of the members were sent out together, and their association in a single body enabled them to secure special power and privileges. Other famous regulated companies, of a later period, were the Muscovy Company and the Levant Company.

It was out of these regulated companies, partly, that there developed the joint-stock companies, which became fairly common in the seventeenth and eighteenth centuries. The earliest joint-stock companies were, almost without exception, commercial rather than industrial enterprises. One of the first in England—the East India Company—was originally organized, in 1600, as a regulated company, but within a few years had become a true joint-stock company. This new type of organization was a great improvement over earlier forms. Its negotiable shares, split up into relatively small sums, made possible the gathering together of a far greater amount of capital than did either the partnership or the regulated company. At the same time, it provided highly centralized control, which the regulated company did not. In general, the joint-stock company possessed many of the economic advantages of the nineteenth and twentieth century corporation, but it lacked certain favorable legal characteristics of the latter. Except where expressly provided to the contrary through statutory law, the investor in a joint-stock company had the same unlimited liability that threatened the members of a partnership. Further, the joint-stock company was not a person before the law. It thus lacked many legal and economic advantages possessed by the contemporary corporation.[3]

In spite of these drawbacks, which did not become serious until later, the

---

[1] *Cf.* Thompson, *Economic and Social History of the Middle Ages*, p. 449.
[2] *Cf.* Cheyney, *The European Background of American History*, Chap. VII.
[3] See below, pp. 796 ff.

THE BEGINNINGS OF MODERN CAPITALISM

joint-stock company played no small part in the trade with the East that was so important to the early modern world, and it was very important in the settlement and exploration of the Western Hemisphere.

The foremost historian of the rise of modern capitalism, Professor Werner Sombart, has brilliantly summarized the character and leading trends in the rise of early modern capitalism. This summary will serve well to bring together the scattered threads in the analysis and description of capitalistic origins that we have presented in the preceding pages:

Two conditions must be fulfilled for a period to be regarded as dominated by "capitalism." There must be exploitation by economically active men through means of money to make a profit. And there must be steps toward a rationalizing of economic life with the idea of making as much profit as possible.

The employment of capital in the Middle Ages did not, in the main, fulfill these conditions. But a number of causes which became active about the year 1500 cooperated to hasten an alteration of European economic life. Among these may be enumerated: (1) The opening of productive gold and silver mines in Germany and Austria; (2) the discovery of America; (3) the rapid rise in the importation of precious metals; (4) a sudden increase in the exploitable population; (5) the discovery of the sea route to the Indies; (6) the expulsion of the Arabs from their position as middlemen, with the consequent possibility of a direct exploitation of the Orient; (7) the concentration of oppressed religious minorities, Jews and later the Evangelicals in the Spanish Netherlands (Antwerp); (8) the rise of modern great states; (9) the rise of modern armies; (10) advances in technique: blast furnaces, hydraulic machines, amalgam processes; and (11) the perfection of the system of double entry bookkeeping by Lucas Pacciuoli.

In consequence of these events, economic life began to be transformed in the direction of capitalism. The idea of the "firm" began to spread, and men became accustomed to regular business management. The old forms of community trade broke down, to be replaced by a new organization of the merchants in the shape of the exchange or bourse. There was a beginning of warehousing when Antwerp came to constitute the first Continental fair. Mercantile commission business arose; there was a collective organization of communication (the post office) on an international basis; and there were the first traces of large-scale industry.

More decisive were the transformations that European economic life underwent in the seventeenth century. New types of entrepreneurs arose in the shape of the steadily growing numbers of heretics and persecuted religionists. The business philosophy of capitalism was formulated by the Puritans. There was a rapid growth of civil wealth and consequent luxury demand; and a rapid increase in the standing army. This was the golden age of the mercantilist trade policy, and in technique there was notable progress: ribbon mills, calico-printing, surveying.

In consequence of these developments we may speak of the following innovations in economic organization: (1) The definite formation of capitalistic enterprise; (2) the beginning of the modern corporation in the great oversea joint-stock companies; (3) the beginning of advertisements and the commercial newspaper; (4) written and printed "price currents"; (5) purchase from sample; (6) the founding of the government post office and stagecoach; (7) the rise of banks of circulation (that is, banks with note-issuing powers); (8) the introduction of exchange instruments.

The epoch of early capitalism comes to an end with the beginning of full capitalism towards the end of the eighteenth century. And the more clearly to point the characteristics of capitalistic economy, the additional traits that had been taken on by that time may be enumerated. Economic life was completely rationalized by the struggle for profits. There was a depersonalizing of business and business management. There was a generalizing of forms of profit recognized by contract. The principle of free competition was established. There was an extension of impersonal forms of business association (the stock company), a depersonalizing of credit, the rise of drafts, of speculative trade. There was a commercializing, and "bourseanizing" of economic life. Paper money, credit banks, speculative production, and hence capital crises had made their appearance. The enterpriser had secured control of demand. Purchase at a distance took place according to sample and standard. Capitalism was extended over all fields of economic life, to agriculture, retail trade, local handwork shops. The strategic position in economic life was passing from the (organic) textile industry to the (inorganic) metal industry. A hereditary working class made its appearance. Upon one side there now stood the capitalist; upon the other a proletariat. And Europe was beginning to pass from a land of peasants to a land of industries.[1]

The rise of capitalism spelled the doom of the social-minded economic ideals of the Middle Ages. The medieval emphasis upon excellent craftsmanship, the subsistence ideal in production, the curbing of sharp dealings, and the dubiousness of financial gain without rendering any comparable service to society held over into the seventeenth century to some degree in many areas.[2] But the competitive ideal and the glorification of immediate pecuniary profits gradually but surely made headway against this higher social idealism of the Middle Ages. The central feature in this ethical revolution was the triumph of the belief that financial gain was in itself highly honorable—the complete antithesis of the medieval attitude:

> Another ethical notion of great importance for the development of capitalistic society was that of the honorableness of gain. The pious merchants, like the pious kings, began their contracts with an invocation of the Trinity and regarded their profits as the "blessing of God." . . . The primary capitalistic impulse was there, to get rich quickly; what was lacking was the rational and deliberate calculation of the fully developed capitalistic spirit.[3]

The conception of the manner in which financial gain might legitimately be made passed far from the medieval perspective. In the Middle Ages it had been regarded as improper even to sell a substantial commodity for more than it cost. Early capitalistic morality not only repudiated this and favored making money by buying and selling commodities without any addition to their value; it even stimulated and approved the accumulation of pecuniary profits through buying and selling securities which often represented no substantial value or consideration whatsoever. In short, the new economic ethics not only sanctioned sharp business practices in legitimate trading of valuable commodities; it put the stamp of its approval upon overt financial gambling. Even open lotteries were popular and publicly sanctioned. In these new attitudes we may discern the rise of that "something-for-nothing" psychology which lies at the basis of

---

[1] Translated and adapted from Sombart, *Der moderne Kapitalismus,* 4th ed., Munich, 1921-27, 4 vols., Vol. II, pp. 10-13.   [2] *Cf.* Nussbaum, *op. cit.,* pp. 150-56.   [3] *Ibid.,* pp. 151, 153.

THE BEGINNINGS OF MODERN CAPITALISM

so much of our contemporary economic and racketeering activity.[1] As Daniel Defoe complained: "It hath changed honest Commerce into Bubbling, our Traders into Projectors, our Industry into Tricking, and Applause is earned where the Pillory is deserved."[2] These words were written in January, 1732. They would be appropriate today. This shows that for two centuries the dominant ideals of capitalistic business have remained essentially unchanged. The main difference is that in 1732 there were still many men of influence in the business world who sharply criticized such practices and upheld the earlier social ideals.[3]

Religion, in the early modern period, also adjusted itself to the new economic and social developments.[4] A close relationship developed between Protestantism and capitalism, in the same way that Protestantism also came to be intimately affiliated with nationalism. The Protestants regarded business as a divine calling, and Calvin particularly stressed the divine approval of persistent industry and frugal thrift. Considerable doubt was expressed as to the divine sanction of the reckless spending of money. But there was assumed to be complete certainty as to the pleasure that the Almighty derives from witnessing the personal accumulation of pecuniary profits.[5] The rigorous code of private ethics developed by the Puritans was in large part an overcompensation for their primary absorption in the week-day processes of material gain.[6]

There was thus reëstablished that intimate association between religion and business enterprise which had characterized the civilization of ancient Mesopotamia[7] and has flowered in our own day in such assertions as those of the American coal magnate George F. Baer, to the effect that our modern plutocrats are unquestionably "those Christian men to whom God in his infinite wisdom has given the control of the property interests of the country." The line of descent is philosophically, if not genealogically, clear and direct from the priests of ancient Babylonia to John Calvin, Richard Baxter, Chancellor Day, Pastor Bigelow, and Bruce Barton.[8] In an important book R. H. Tawney has admirably summarized the transformation in the relation of religion to business between 1500 and 1660:

> When the age of the Reformation begins, economics is still a branch of ethics, and ethics of theology; all human activities are treated as falling within a single scheme, whose character is determined by the spiritual destiny of mankind; the appeal of theorists is to natural law, not to utility; the legitimacy of economic transactions is tried by reference, less to the movements of the market, than to moral standards derived from the traditional teaching of the Christian Church; the Church itself is regarded as a society wielding theoretical, and sometimes practical, authority in social affairs. The secularization of political thought, which was to be the work of the next two centuries, had profound reactions on social speculation, and by the Restoration the whole perspective, at least in England, has been revolutionized. Religion has been converted from the keystone which holds together the social edifice

---

[1] See below, pp. 833 ff.   [2] Cited by Botsford, *op. cit.*, pp. 163-64.
[3] *Cf.* Nussbaum, *op. cit.*, pp. 353-56.   [4] See above, Vol. I, pp. 861 ff.
[5] See above, Vol. I, pp. 861 ff.   [6] *Cf.* Weber, *op. cit.*, Chap. xxx; see above, Vol. I, p. 862.
[7] See above, Vol. I, pp. 128 ff., 136 ff.
[8] On Calvinism and Materialism, see G. E. Harkness, *John Calvin; the Man and His Ethics*, Holt, 1931, Chaps. VIII-IX.

into one department within it, and the idea of a rule of right is replaced by economic expediency as the arbiter of policy and the criterion of conduct. From a spiritual being, who, in order to survive, must devote a reasonable attention to economic interest, man seems sometimes to have become an economic animal, who will be prudent, nevertheless, if he takes due precautions to assure his spiritual well-being." [1]

In this way orthodox Christianity, especially Protestantism, became the strongest bulwark of materialistic philosophy in modern times.[2] Atheists and radicals have been denounced in season and out by Christian ministers for their "materialism." But, for the most part, both atheists and radicals have been singularly impecunious and idealistic persons who have repudiated any hope of earthly riches in order to serve what they believe to be a noble cause. If there is a nonmaterialistic type of person, it is the average radical agitator in any field. On the other hand, the great majority of the very wealthy bankers, industrialists, transportation magnates, utility kings, and the like have been noted for their public piety. As churches have become larger and more magnificent and church activities more costly, it has been necessary to lean more heavily upon benefactions from the very rich. Clergymen have therefore been loath to denounce "malefactors of great wealth." Rather, the latter have been showered with honors and their calling has been extolled in the sight of the Lord. The rise of capitalism and Protestantism, then, transformed Christianity from an idealistic critique of worldly riches and the profit system into a major buttress of materialism, in any sensible and practical use of that term. There have been plenty of incidental rebellions against this attitude within the Church, but they have met with no general success.

II. THE RISE OF MODERN BANKING

Intimately connected with the genesis of modern capitalism and the appearance of new forms of business organization was the development of banking.[3] The roots of the modern banking system reach back to the Jewish and Syrian money-changers of the medieval towns and fairs. They in turn were largely transplantations from the more complicated economic order of the eastern Mediterranean region, where their origins are lost in antiquity. As the hostility of Church and secular law to the taking of interest waned and the Italian merchants gradually took the leading place in European trade, money-changing and banking operations passed from the hands of the Jews into those of the Lombards and Cahorsines.[4]

Among the most important functions of the financial agents, in addition to exchanging the multifarious currencies at the fairs and markets, were the acceptance of money deposits for safe-keeping, the transferring of money from place to place, and the handling of bills of exchange. The acceptance of deposits, in England particularly, came to be one of the recognized functions

---

[1] Tawney, *Religion and the Rise of Capitalism*, Harcourt, Brace, 1926, p. 278.
[2] For a long and learned, if not very convincing, effort to refute the thesis of Weber, Tawney, Ashley, and others, see H. M. Robertson, *Aspects of the Rise of Economic Individualism*, Macmillan, 1934. [3] See above, Vol. I, pp. 675 ff.
[4] A name originally applied to the money-changers from Cahors, in southern France; later, like the term "Lombards," applied to money-changers in general.

of the goldsmiths. They of course had to provide some kind of safe-keeping for their own bullion, and from that necessity naturally came to accept deposits from others, a service for which they charged the depositor. As time went on, they were sometimes tempted by the high rates of interest to lend out these deposits, of course without the knowledge of the depositors. They were thus the ancestors of the modern deposit bankers.

Bills of exchange were in common use all during the later Middle Ages. They arose originally only out of commercial transactions, being simply promises to pay at a specified time and place. Before the end of the Middle Ages, they had become credit instruments as well, being given in return for advances of money as well as in payment for goods. One of the important reasons for this latter development was that their use concealed the collection of interest, and thus enabled the principals to avoid the accusation of usury. As both commercial and credit instruments, bills of exchange were in wide use at all the leading fairs and markets of the later Middle Ages. Dealing in these and the transferring of money were functions usually performed by merchants. They also lent money on occasion both to one another and to the princes, who were perennially in financial straits. It was also the merchants (who only gradually came to specialize in these financial operations) who served the Church's elaborate financial system. They collected money all over Europe for transfer to Rome; they lent money to Church officials, who often found themselves in need; and they sometimes accepted money from the papal curia when it had surplus funds for investment.[1] In the early modern period, they also performed a valuable service in the occasional issuance of letters of credit to pilgrims or other travelers.

As has been pointed out, it was the merchants of the Italian cities—the towns of Lombardy and Tuscany, later chiefly Venice, Genoa, and Florence—who in the later Middle Ages were the bankers of Europe, if this term may be used with reference to so early a period.[2] Florence became the great banking center of the fourteenth century, the Medici being the leading merchants and bankers. Florentine preëminence was due chiefly to the papal collections which passed through that city, and to the extended trade of Florence, particularly in cloth and the materials for making cloth. A bank was opened in Delft in 1313, one at Calais in 1320, and a third at Genoa in 1345. These institutions, as well as the earlier ones referred to, must not be thought of as banks in the modern sense; their chief functions were to accept deposits for safe-keeping and, often, to take over the public debt. They did not use the modern bank checks and they were not ordinarily allowed to issue notes or to lend out the deposits left with them. The only securities normally handled were those arising out of the public debt. The public bank of deposit of Barcelona, opened in 1401, was a closer approximation to the modern banking institution.

As the routes of trade shifted in the fifteenth and sixteenth centuries, the mercantile and financial power passed gradually to northern Europe, at first to the Fuggers, Welsers, and Baumgartners of Augsburg, and later to the

[1] *Cf.* Jakob Strieder, *Jacob Fugger the Rich Merchant and Banker of Augsburg,* Adelphi Co., 1931.
[2] See above, Vol. I, pp. 675 ff.; and Ehrenberg, *op. cit.,* Introduction and Pt. I, Chaps. II-III.

Dutch towns. Northern Europe's superior natural resources made it potentially a vastly richer country than the Mediterranean region. Throughout the Middle Ages the peopling of northern Europe and the development of variegated resources in so many places delayed the consolidation of the new or "modern" order, while at the same time its enormous unfolding possibilities prevented an effectual stabilization of the old.

The remarkable development of northwestern Europe was a cause as well as an effect of the expansion of European civilization overseas. By 1550, the Fuggers of Augsburg, well north of the Alps, were the most influential financiers in Europe. They had created their business mainly through the aid of Bohemian, Styrian, and Carinthian silver. Already in 1511, before their section of Europe had become deeply involved in oversea ventures, they had a capital of almost 200,000 gulden, a sum that had increased by 1527 to over 2,000,000 gulden (probably the equivalent in purchasing power of $20,000,000 today). At this time they were thus making about 55 per cent annually on their investments.

The critical period in the development of modern banking came, however, after the opening of the seventeenth century. By this time all of western Europe was beginning to feel the results of the new oversea trade, and was laying the foundations for the remarkable development of industry and commerce that was to characterize this century. Many important banks were established between the opening of the seventeenth century and the close of the eighteenth; some of them performed important commercial functions, others were largely government financial agencies.[1]

The development of these banks made possible the systematic accumulation of capital to be put at the disposal of enterprising merchants and manufacturers, facilitated loans and money transfers, began the process of discounting commercial paper, and in other ways rendered more effective the various financial aids to industry and commerce. To be sure, even the greatest of the seventeenth and eighteenth century banks were relatively insignificant in their control of capital as compared to the larger ones in even a second-class American city of today. Few at first lent money to manufacturers or engaged in a personal loan business. Nevertheless, these early banking houses formed the beginnings out of which have grown such establishments as our vast present-day commercial banks and such quasi-public concerns as the Bank of Amsterdam, the Bank of England, and the Federal Reserve System of the United States.

The development of banking facilitated the rise of the various types of commercial paper, the use of which has been indispensable to modern exchange, either national or international. Among these were promissory notes, drafts, checks, and bills of exchange. Important also for business operations of the newer sort was the development, originating in Italy, of modern double-entry bookkeeping, and the rise of various business auxiliaries, such as auditors, agents, and brokers.

[1] Among the more important of these early banks and the date of their establishment were: Bank of Amsterdam, 1608; Bank of Middleburg, 1616; Bank of Venice, 1619; Bank of Hamburg, 1619; Bank of Rotterdam, 1635; Bank of Sweden, 1656; Bank of Spain, 1665; Bank of England, 1694; Bank of Vienna, 1703; Bank of Berlin and Breslau, 1765.

The development of the use of checks and the perfection of double-entry bookkeeping were of vital significance in the future history of mankind. Business dealings had hitherto taken place chiefly through the transfer of cash. Then, a little later, goods were transferred on the basis of a secured pledge, such as a bill of exchange. Even the enormous increases in the supply of precious metals after 1500 did not keep pace with the expansion of trade. It became more and more evident that cash and ordinary commercial paper were not adequate to maintain the totality of the increasing volume of exchange. Therefore there slowly grew up the practice of payment in checks, based upon definite deposits of cash in a given bank. The first true checks were used in Barcelona, Venice, and Sicily early in the sixteenth century. The earliest checks in our own country were circulated in Boston in 1681. The use of checks greatly facilitated exchange because the credit resources of the banks could be expanded far beyond the actual cash on hand. In normal times only a small percentage of the reserves of a bank are actually withdrawn in cash. Today, an overwhelming majority of transactions are accomplished through checks that are balanced through the use of clearing-houses. Paper transactions have thus replaced the actual exchange of cash to a wide extent. Banknotes also came slowly into use as a substitute for metal currency.

Double-entry bookkeeping not only greatly facilitated the keeping of accounts.[1] It also helped to create a new attitude towards economic matters, stimulating a quantitative rather than a qualitative outlook and helping to make business ideals more impersonal. This innovation has been challengingly characterized by Professor Sombart:

Ideas of profit seeking and economic rationalism first became possible with the invention of double-entry bookkeeping. Through this system can be grasped but one thing—the increase in amount of values considered purely quantitatively. Whoever becomes immersed in double-entry bookkeeping must forget all qualities of goods, and services, abandon the limitations of the need-covering principle, and be filled with the single idea of profit; he may not think of boots and cargoes, meal and cotton, but only of amounts of values, increasing or diminishing.[2]

III. INSURANCE

Another branch of business, which at the present time is closely related to banking, is that of insurance. Rudimentary marine insurance, at least, was fairly well developed in Italy in the Middle Ages. The risks of sea voyages were great, as Antonio in *The Merchant of Venice* learned to his disaster. Merchants therefore came to make mutual agreements for protection. One simple way of accomplishing this was by means of a written contract among the merchants concerned to distribute or spread any losses incurred in the enterprise contemplated. All would sign their names beneath the agreement, from which practice arose the term "underwriting." Insurance was also included, without being clearly recognized as such, in early interest rates. These were high partly on account of the great risks involved in lending money.

It was only very gradually that insurance became clearly differentiated as a field of business enterprise. The maritime undertakings of the early modern

---

[1] *Cf.* Nussbaum, *op. cit.*, pp. 156 ff.   [2] Sombart, *op. cit.*, Vol. II, pp. 119-20.

period, from which the first insurance business grew, involved a vastly greater amount of risk than present ones, the science of navigation being as yet rudimentary, the ships small, and the dangers from pirates and privateers great. It was in line with the development of collective enterprise at the time to spread out the risks among a number of people, so that in case of disaster all would lose a little instead of one's losing everything. The merchants of England developed the habit of meeting in the great coffeehouses of London, especially at Lloyd's, and arranging for the insurance of ships. The next step was the organization of marine insurance companies to specialize in this type of business. The first marine insurance company was established in Paris in 1668. Such companies became relatively well systematized by the opening of the eighteenth century, and the business tended to gravitate into the hands of a few more powerful and efficient insurance companies. Two British marine insurance companies founded in 1720 are still doing business. Lloyd's in London has remained the center of the marine insurance business, but it was not incorporated until 1871, when it became legally an exchange for the regulation of marine underwriting.[1]

While maritime insurance did not develop so extensively in other European countries as in England, progress along roughly similar lines took place in all those states which shared in the oversea trade.

Other forms of insurance appeared at about the same time or a little later. There was no important development of fire-insurance companies until after the great fire of 1666 in London. This was followed by the organization of a number of such companies, the first on a joint-stock basis (1680). The Sun Fire Insurance Company, which opened its offices in 1706, was the first to carry on business on a large scale. Life-insurance companies appeared during this same period. As in the case of fire insurance, individuals had carried on a crude and sporadic life-insurance business for some time, but the first mutual company, the Friendly Society, was organized in 1684. The first great life-insurance companies were the Amicable (1706) and the Equitable (1762), both historic English concerns still in existence. The first American life-insurance company was the Insurance Company of North America, established in Philadelphia in 1796.

The insurance companies have not only been a prominent element in modern business in themselves; they have also played a great part in the evolution of modern capitalism. In our day, their investments have become nearly as important as those of the banks as a means by which cash and liquid capital are accumulated and made available for business and finance.[2]

IV. THE ORIGINS OF PRODUCE AND STOCK EXCHANGES

As a result of the same factors that brought about the development of banking came the rise, in the early modern period, of the bourse or exchange. The Middle Ages saw the beginnings of the bourse, though not on the order of the modern stock or produce exchange. The dealings in bills of exchange, already referred to, took on the character of bourse trade—that is, the mer-

---

[1] *Cf.* C. E. Fayle, *A History of Lloyd's,* Macmillan, 1928.   [2] See below, pp. 794 ff.

THE ORIGINS OF PRODUCE AND STOCK EXCHANGES

chants concerned met frequently and regularly, and the conditions of trade were fairly well standardized.[1] This trade in bills presupposed a knowledge of the currency conditions; and the reputations of the merchants had to be sufficiently well known so that the bills which they signed would be generally accepted.

In the fifteenth century, bourses more on the modern order developed, first in Lyons and in Bruges. The latter was the first to use the name "bourse." The bourse established later at Antwerp became much the most important trading-center of its time. The Bruges bourse was used mainly for dealings in bills of exchange and in money; but the Antwerp bourse of the late fifteenth century was a true merchants' bourse, open to all merchants of whatever nation trading in the city. It thus became the first international bourse.

The most important commodity dealt in on the Antwerp bourse was pepper, though many others, such as copper and alum, also figured. The trade was speculative to a higher degree than might be expected, because of the extensive risks of the spice trade. Attempts at monopoly and price-fixing were by no means unknown. In these early modern bourses the practice also developed of transacting exchanges by means of paper securities representing the commodities, instead of the more cumbersome method of trading in the commodities themselves. To make this possible it was necessary to create an elaborate system of grading and supervision of commodities offered for sale. This insured that the paper instruments corresponded to specific grades as well as amounts of goods. An inevitable accompaniment of this innovation was the appearance of the first general tendency towards speculation in the changing prices of the paper securities that represented the actual commodities. In addition to facilitating the exchange of goods, these produce exchanges thus broadened the opportunities for borrowing and investing money.

There could be no capital bourse in the modern sense, of course, until the joint-stock principle had developed sufficiently to give volume to the trade and speculation in securities. The first loans made—those to the princes—passed through the bourse only indirectly, since the princes or their representatives went to the merchants for advances. If the merchants needed to raise ready money, they did it by selling bills of exchange on the bourse. It has been said that in the middle of the sixteenth century the "Fugger bond" was considered one of the safest of investments. The Fuggers paid less for their money than any other firm, or even the city of Antwerp.[2] The "Fugger bond" was only a personal promise to pay, the value of which depended entirely upon the business reputation of the house; bonds as they are known at the present time, based on the assets of a corporation, are a development of the nineteenth century.

Though there were as yet few or no corporate stocks and bonds, there was early a considerable purchase and sale of capital on the Antwerp and later on the Amsterdam bourse, by means of the current commercial instruments. The first securities regularly dealt in there were those representing municipal indebtedness. Later, as the finances of the states were put on a sounder basis,

---

[1] *Cf.* Ehrenberg, *op. cit.*, pp. 54 ff. [2] *Cf. Ibid.*, pp. 116, 120.

their "stocks," as they were then called, were also dealt in on the bourses.[1] Until the nineteenth century public loans were the favorite form of investment. After 1800 the joint-stock banks, canals, and railroad companies began to put their securities on the market in large volume.

Quite naturally, the early capital bourse was simply one feature of the already existing produce exchange. By the end of the seventeenth century the exchange of joint-stock shares was fairly well developed, but most of the transactions took place outside of the bourses. Gradually, however, as the volume of stock transactions increased, the conveniences of a special bourse became evident, and the true stock exchange appeared. As it took on its modern form, it became more spectacular, if not more important, than the commodity exchange.

The first true stock exchange vaguely resembling the modern type was established in London in 1698. It was followed by one in Paris in 1724. The first one set up in America was opened in New York City in 1817. As in our own day, the stock exchange of the eighteenth century helped along both good and bad practices. In assisting in the collection of large quantities of capital for profitable investment, it aided in a highly valuable and constructive function; but it also invited chicanery and foolish speculation. Yet in spite of great abuses, the development of agencies for the exchange of securities did much to stimulate and carry along the development of the large trading companies of the seventeenth and eighteenth centuries.

V. THE ERA OF SPECULATION AND "BUBBLES"

In the seventeenth century the purchase and sale of securities was still a new and incalculable field of investment. The late seventeenth century and early eighteenth witnessed a veritable orgy of investment in stocks. This is not surprising, in view of the great expansion in trade and the opening up of important fresh fields to business enterprise at almost the same time that the profit-getting motive became dominant. This fever of speculation was the more dangerous because even business men, to say nothing of the general public, were as yet unfamiliar with the possible uses and abuses of the joint-stock principle. It required the great inflations and disasters of the so-called bubble period to give people some understanding of the limitations within which it is safe to buy and sell paper instruments instead of actual commodities.[2]

This age possessed all the love of pecuniary accumulation that exists today, but was without the supposedly more chastened attitudes and methods that have been produced by two centuries or so of disappointment and loss from unwise and overoptimistic investments. This speculative spirit of the period is well described by Professor Botsford in words which might have been applied to the United States in 1926-29:

The psychology of the *nouveaux riches* [newly rich] may be perceived by an understanding of their business ethics. The easiest and quickest way to make money was by speculation in the stock market. The buying and selling of stock, of course, more closely resembled gambling than the exchange of legitimate securities. There were no financial experts to enlighten popular ignorance with accurate knowledge; nor was there a vigilant board of directors to expose shams or legisla-

---

[1] *Cf.* Ehrenberg, *op. cit.*, pp. 367 ff.   [2] *Cf.* Weber, *op. cit.*, Chap. XXIV.

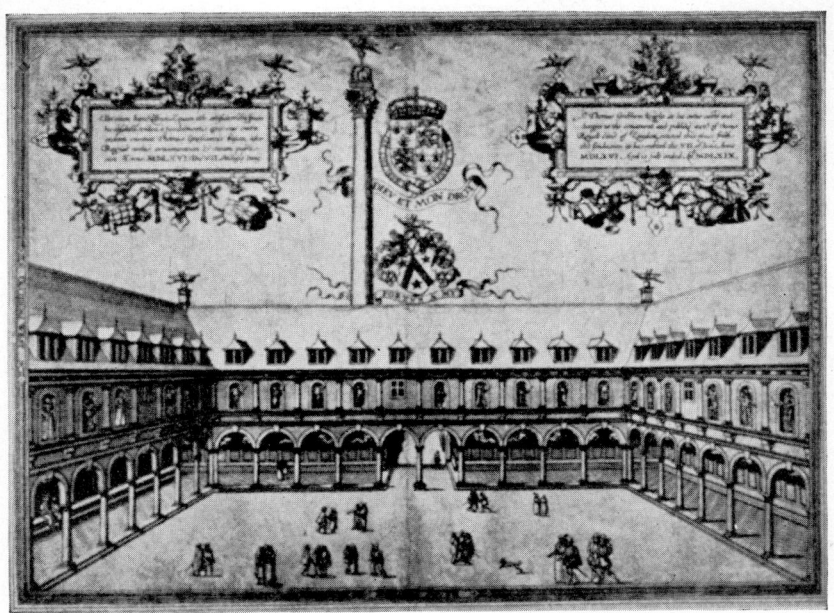

From Mottram's History of Financial Speculation, *Little, Brown & Company*
THE FIRST ROYAL STOCK EXCHANGE

From Mottram's History of Financial Speculation, *Little, Brown & Company*
PROMOTING THE SOUTH SEA BUBBLE

Keystone View Company
JEREMY BENTHAM

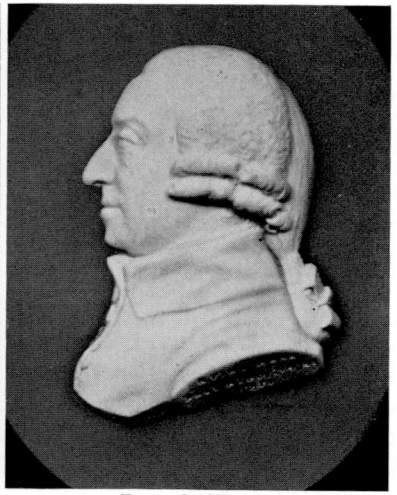

From the Wedgwood Medallion
ADAM SMITH

Ewing Galloway
HERBERT SPENCER

Wide World Photos
ROBERT OWEN

SOME LEADING THINKERS

tion to prevent the foisting of fraudulent stock on the public. On the contrary, every means was taken to fascinate the public mind by vague rumors of imaginary advantages. False reports of fabulous profits were seemingly substantiated by dividends which could never be paid from legitimate gains. Particularly in the case of the South Sea hoax, and of the thousand and one lesser bubbles, did the Government share the blame, with the stock-jobbers themselves, for the stimulation of human cupidity.[1]

The most famous of the manias of speculation of the forty years or so down to 1720 were the English South Sea Bubble and the even more sensational aftermath of John Law's financial experiment in France, sometimes called the Mississippi Bubble.

The South Sea Bubble grew out of an effort, which at first seemed legitimate, to handle the rapidly increasing government debt in England. The dominant interest in oversea trading ventures rather naturally suggested a commercial monopoly as a way out. So a company was formed by the government creditors and was known as The Governor and Company of Merchants of Great Britain Trading to the South Seas and Other Parts of America. This South Sea Company agreed to take over all the debts of the state, some £31,000,000, for which they were to receive interest at 5 per cent up to 1727 and 4 per cent thereafter. It agreed to pay the government outright £3,500,000, which was later raised to £7,500,000. In return, the company was given a monopoly on the trade with South America—a trade that was really controlled by the king of Spain. The prospect of gain for the company was grossly exaggerated at the outset. Philip V of Spain imposed severe restrictions on the British trade, and the company failed to exploit even its limited opportunities in legitimate ventures in the South American area. So the enterprise slumped. Then the government permitted, if it did not openly encourage, the promoters of the company to deceive the populace in order to boom the stock. The most absurd representations were made as to possible enterprises and profits, and the stock went up to over $5,000 a share. The greatest boom came in the spring and summer of 1720. The collapse was inevitable, and thousands were ruined. The government had to step in and liquidate the enterprise. The legitimate government creditors were settled with at about 30 cents on the dollar on their original investment before the boom.

This was only one of a number of stock enterprises floated at the time, many of which were bogus. It is estimated that about $1,500,000,000 was lost in "bubbles" and such speculation in England in the eighteenth century— a colossal sum for that period. People bought shares in enterprises for making perpetual-motion machines, for putting alchemy on a commercial basis, for exploiting "gold mines" in the Carolinas, for developing fisheries in Greenland, importing walnut trees from Virginia and even, in one case, "for an undertaking which shall in due time be revealed." The general crash that followed seriously chilled the popular interest in public companies, even those doing a legitimate business. On the other hand, it tended to concentrate capital in the hands of the more clever and more ruthless members of the community,

[1] Botsford, op. cit., pp. 162-63.

whose business methods and activities were not seriously cramped or handicapped by inability to float new companies.

Like the South Sea Bubble, the Law scheme in France had a legitimate background and an unfortunate speculative culmination. John Law was an able young Scotch financier who had developed a rational and progressive scheme for French banking and public finance. A fatal mistake was made in combining with this banking scheme a speculative company to develop trade between France and the Western world, later expanded into the Company of the Indies. An era of almost insane speculation in the shares of the company followed, rendered doubly disastrous by the fact that the paper money guaranteed by the capital of the Bank of France was inseparably involved with the affairs of the speculative trading concern. Law found it impossible to control the price of the stock or to check the issuance of notes. When the crash came, as it speedily did, the country was left flooded with a currency consisting of the company's depreciated notes, public finance was crippled for a long time, and innumerable individuals were ruined. The disaster cut short a promising beginning in modern banking and finance.[1]

VI. COMMERCIAL MONOPOLIES

A leading characteristic of the new oversea trade that was handled by large and well-knit companies was the tendency towards commercial monopolies: monopolies of the trade in certain areas, in specific commodities, or in both. There was in monopoly the obvious advantage to the company that dominated the trade in a particular commodity. Furthermore, since the source of supply of such goods was rather limited and specific, it was relatively easy to maintain a monopoly by controlling the supply at its origin. The company that first developed contacts with an area had an enormous advantage in its trade, particularly when its position was further strengthened by governmental favoritism.

In most European states, monopoly was encouraged and developed by the attitude of the governments. Trading monopolies were favored because of the greater ease and certainty of governmental control over the activities of merchants, a few great companies being far easier to supervise than a cloud of independent traders. The friendliness of governments towards trading monopolies was also due in part to the belief that this was the way to foster and encourage commerce, one of the leading aims of states under the mercantilist theory of the time. As a matter of fact, the granting of monopolies was probably a wise and necessary measure at a time when the entrepreneur had to be encouraged by the possibility of large profits in order to induce him to run the heavy risks involved in oversea trade.

---

[1] Certainly our recent experiences with speculation should prevent us from taking any superior attitude towards these eighteenth-century "bubbles." With all our subsequent experience and improved financial methods, we still lose sums through speculation that make these older "bubbles" seem child's play. The losses on the New York Stock Exchange alone from 1929 to 1933 amounted to over $75,000,000,000. The citizens of the United States hold about $18,000,000,000 worth of foreign securities today, and of these some $10,000,000,000 are in default of interest, principal, or both. Compared with such losses as these, those of the eighteenth-century "bubble" period appear trifling. See below, pp. 803 ff.

As a result of these various influences, commercial monopolies became the usual thing in the seventeenth and eighteenth centuries, and monopoly was a basic element in the organization and activities of the early trading companies. Some of the most notable of these monopolistic companies have already been mentioned. Among them were the English and Dutch East India companies, the South Sea Company, and the Hudson's Bay Company.

VII. MERCANTILISM AND THE ABSOLUTE STATE

The commercial expansion of the period 1500-1800, with its various subordinate results, had a direct and important effect upon the political tendencies of the time. This was particularly true with respect to the growth of large territorial states and the trend toward secular absolutism.[1] With the increased resources of the royal treasuries, as a result of income from privateering, customs duties, fees for chartering companies, and so on, the kings became more powerful, and were able gradually to make good their aspiration for ascendancy over feudal lords. The ability to maintain a paid, loyal army and officialdom was a basic factor in creating the early national dynastic states. This new income was also used by many states in warfare to extend their holdings in Europe and overseas. Again, the various activities of the national state in connection with commercial monopolies and maritime regulation served greatly to extend the notion of its crucial importance and the wide scope of its legitimate activities.

All of these factors help to account for the development of a definite and clear-cut national economic policy. Heretofore there had been princes who sought their own immediate benefit, and cities that looked to the furtherance of their own well-being and prosperity. But a national economic policy, looking to permanent results, was a product of the new economic and political situation. While interference with commerce by central governments had not been unknown in the medieval period, the weakness of the secular state had prevented such control from assuming any very significant proportions. With the combined and parallel growth of world-commerce and the national dynastic state, there evolved a policy of the complete governmental regulation of economic activities. This new policy, though varying in detail and extent of application, was known as mercantilism in England, as Colbertism in France, and as cameralism in Germany.

The medieval towns, in the formulation of their economic policy, had been concerned chiefly with the regulation of trade and industry in favor of their own craftsmen as against outsiders.[2] The guiding motive of the new national policy, as it developed in England, France, and Germany, was to dominate trade in the interest of the national state. Some of the old urban regulations were taken over into national policy, and it was the same fundamental selfish motive that shaped both. This has been well expressed by Schmoller, who described mercantilism as "town policy writ large in the annals of the state." Mercantilism projected into economic life the existing narrowly nationalistic conceptions and practices. Every state was assumed to be the potential com-

[1] See below, Chapter IV.   [2] See above, Vol. I, pp. 664 ff.

mercial enemy of every other. The prosperity of each was supposed to depend upon a narrow, exclusive policy of increasing its export and decreasing its import trade, monopolizing the trade of its colonies, and restricting the commerce of its neighbors as far as possible when this commerce offered any serious competition.

The fundamental assumptions of the mercantilist system were roughly as follows: 1. The precious metals are the most valid measure of the wealth of a nation. 2. Aside from mining of ore, trade is the chief means of accumulating these precious metals in the shape of specie. 3. In order that this trade may be profitable and specie accumulated, there must be a favorable balance of exports over imports. 4. To furnish markets for these exports, and thus to create a favorable balance of trade for the mother country, colonies are valuable, if not indispensable. 5. In order that the colonies may furnish markets for finished products and a source of supply of raw materials, manufacturing must be forbidden in the colonies, lest they supply their own necessities and exhaust their stock of raw materials. 6. The colonies must thus be looked upon primarily as profitable commercial enterprises of the mother country and colonial trade as a monopoly of the mother country.

We now know that this mercantilist argument was erroneous in many of its premises, particularly the notions that the supply of specie is the most important criterion of national prosperity and that a favorable balance of trade necessarily means an increase in the domestic supply of available specie. We further know that these policies and practices restricted the commercial activity and prosperity of the various European states. Inevitably, the sum of the small commercial injuries inflicted by states on each other was detrimental to the European family of nations as a whole. These facts were not understood at the time.

Mercantilism should be assessed in terms of its historical background, which helps to explain most of its assumptions. At a time when specie was being introduced into Europe in large quantities, and when Spain, which brought in much of the precious metals from the New World, occupied a leading position in the world of nations, it was natural to associate the control over large quantities of specie with the notion of national greatness. A favorable balance of trade was much more important in the seventeenth and eighteenth centuries than it is now, when a surplus of imports is usually offset or qualified by the "invisible balance" in the form of interest on foreign investments, and payments for freight, insurance, brokerage, and the like. Since colonial development had been undertaken in several instances by means of commercial companies, it is not so surprising that the colonies were looked on as commercial enterprises, and that they were expected to serve the economic interests of the mother country.

Mercantilist policy was thus a natural product of its time, but became fatally anachronistic and obstructive when states maintained it after the conditions that gave rise to it had been widely altered.

Along with the aspects and achievements of mercantilism that related directly to commercial and colonial policies and practices went very important enactments in the way of the extension of state activity in economic affairs within the home boundaries. In England such things as the Statute of Apprentices, introducing state control of labor and its conditions, the establishment of the price-fixing power of the justices of the peace, and the state control of industrial life by public proclamation are significant cases in point. In France the state enforcement of guild practices, the digging of canals, the erection of public buildings, and the reclamation of land are achievements associated with Colbert and his assistants and successors. Even more thoroughgoing was the state intervention in the field of national economic life and public finance in Prussia, which was guided by the German mercantilists or cameralists and most thoroughly executed under the aegis of Frederick the Great.

In Germany the mercantilist trend was colored by the peculiar circumstances that existed there as compared to the more commercial states like England, France, and Spain. The problem of foreign trade being far less important at that date in Germanic states, the philosophy of extensive state intervention naturally turned more towards domestic economic and political problems. This brought up the question of the technique of social improvement by means of state direction, thus giving a sociological cast to the whole movement. A number of notable German leaders of the seventeenth and eighteenth centuries helped to shape the special trend of mercantilism in that country. An American sociologist, Professor Albion W. Small, has summarized the sociological significance of the cameralists.[1] As he points out, cameralism frankly subordinated everything within the control of the state to the problem of national existence. It was an attempt to select those policies and practices which would help most to make the ruler secure at home and to strengthen him against other rulers abroad. It was soon perceived that this was not merely a matter of physical factors, but involved the training and education of the people as well. As we have already seen, cameralism greatly stimulated scientific and intensive agriculture in Germany.[2]

VIII. THE IDEA OF NATURAL LIBERTY: THE PHYSIOCRATS

Almost before mercantilism had taken definite shape as a policy, some objections began to be raised. The fundamental principle of mercantilism was regulation to achieve a desired public goal. But some of those engaged in trade soon found this regulation inimical to their interests. This was notably the case with the East India Company in England, one of the most powerful centers of commercial influence. The trade with the Orient consisted largely of the export of silver in payment for the fine merchandise brought in. The business carried on by the East India Company thus regularly resulted in an unfavorable balance of trade and in the withdrawal of specie from England. Criticisms of the company on this score were frequent, and the advocates of the company were driven, in their own interests, to question fundamentally the doctrines of mercantilism.

While the East India trade was one of the outstanding vehicles of opposi-

---

[1] Albion W. Small, article "Sociology" in Encyclopedia Americana. See also his book *The Cameralists*, University of Chicago Press, 1909, especially Chap. I.   [2] See above, p. 54.

tion to mercantilist restrictions, underneath the self-interested propaganda flowed a deep stream of new economic and social thought, some of the sources of which were far from being of a purely business nature. Though the merchant classes, including Cromwell, their arch-representative in England for a decade, started out with a firm belief in mercantilism, many changed their minds when they discerned the relationship of the system to royal absolutism and taxation. As their interests broadened out beyond what they had at first anticipated, they found their march to prosperity hampered at many points. In the same way that they had objected to arbitrary royal taxation and insisted upon the right of Parliament to decide upon these matters, so later many individuals and private groups came to chafe at any state interference whatever. As is quite common with human beings, they identified their own group advantage with alleged benefits to all human society. The pamphleteers for the most part did not base their attacks on mercantilism upon a direct and open statement of their interests, but sought for a general and social philosophy that would incidentally justify the aspirations of their class. This philosophy they found ready-made in the deductions that had grown up with modern critical thought, founded especially upon the scientific progress of their own country.

Remarkable developments in natural science from Copernicus to Newton had suggested that nature manifests itself according to certain immutable laws.[1] The thinkers who developed this new intellectual attitude came to hold that society in all its manifestations and institutions, no less than physical nature itself, is subject to the reign of natural law. Natural law was assimilated to, and regarded as identical with, divine law. It was thus assumed that the laws of nature were an expression of the divine will, and therefore benign in their operations. From this they then reasoned that man should endeavor to allow the natural order of things to govern his social, political, and economic life. This would be brought about more certainly than in any other way, they thought, by allowing free and unlimited competition to dominate all phases of economic policy and activity.

All this implied, when it did not specifically urge: (1) That the states should refrain from all activity in the economic field beyond the minimum of interference necessary to secure protection of life and property and the enforcement of contracts; (2) that all public regulation of economic activities should cease; and (3) that a régime of individualism, competition, and free trade should be instituted. The doctrine, with its implications, was first thoroughly formulated by a group of mid-eighteenth-century French writers known as the Physiocrats.

In addition to opposing all regulation of economic life that interfered with the operation of natural law,[2] the Physiocrats specifically emphasized the "productive" value of agricultural labor that brought "new" commodities into existence. They decried the "sterile" activities of commerce and industry that merely transferred already existing goods. The Physiocratic theories were taken up and elaborated by a remarkable group of English economic writers.

---

[1] See below, Chapter v, for the intellectual developments of this period.
[2] This doctrine of freedom from regulation came to be known as laissez faire, a shibboleth that is still frequently brought into economic discussions.

Adam Smith, whose *Wealth of Nations* appeared in print in 1776, was the first and most famous.

There was one notable difference in the later English interpretation. While the Physiocrats had represented mining and agriculture as the sole productive industries, the English writers adapted their doctrines to the new economic tendencies of the time and laid special stress upon labor, manufacturing, and commerce as the chief sources of income in national wealth. The economic thought of Smith, Malthus, Ricardo, and the two Mills, among others, varies so much from their French predecessors that they are usually distinguished from the Physiocrats by the term "Classical Economists." [1]

Some slight effects of these attempts to apply the idea of natural law and natural liberty to economics were visible at the outset. Turgot, the contemporary and friend of Adam Smith, attempted to reform French finances in 1774, and was willing to go to great lengths if the opportunity offered, but his initial measures proved unwelcome to the privileged classes and he was driven from office.[2] English parliamentary debates show the influence of the *Wealth of Nations* up to the French Revolution, the excesses of which gave a temporary check to the whole notion of natural liberty. It was not until the nineteenth century that serious attempts were made to achieve free trade in France, Germany, and England.

IX. THE PREPARATION FOR THE INDUSTRIAL REVOLUTION

The various commercial, financial, and industrial results of the Commercial Revolution had their most important influence upon European society in preparing the way for the great Industrial Revolution that was to transform completely the culture of the Western world in the century and a half following 1750.[3] The growing commerce created a large new supply of available capital. It hastened the growth of capitalism, credit, and credit institutions. It trained and encouraged Europeans in the way of investments, speculation, and business enterprise. It greatly stimulated European manufacturing industry, tended to weaken the old restrictive guild system, even producing a preliminary type of factory system, and developed a larger and more highly specialized industrial population. In these and various other ways the Commercial Revolution prepared the way for the Industrial Revolution.

There has been for a long time a good-natured controversy among alert economic and social historians as to whether the Commercial Revolution or the Industrial Revolution was the more important influence in modern times. This controversy is, however, essentially futile, since it implies a decision as to whether cause or effect is the more influential in history. For practical purposes, it may be said that while the Industrial Revolution has created far more sweeping changes in European society than its predecessor, these later transformations would have been impossible without the profound alterations in European society produced by the Commercial Revolution.[4]

[1] See below, pp. 378 ff.   [2] See below, p. 111.
[3] *Cf.* Renard and Weulersse, *Life and Labor in Modern Europe*, pp. 343-83; and Nussbaum, *op cit.*, Pt. III, Chaps. IV-V.
[4] For the Industrial Revolution, see below, Chapters VII-X.

CAPITALISM IN EARLY MODERN PERIOD

SUGGESTED READING

Hammerton, *Universal History of the World*, Chaps. 135, 152, 160
Packard, *The Commercial Revolution*, Chaps. II-III
F. L. Nussbaum, *Absolutism, Mercantilism and Classicism*, Harper, 1936
—— *History of the Economic Institutions of Modern Europe*, Pt. II, Chaps. I-II; Pt. III
J. W. Thompson, *Economic and Social History of Europe in the Later Middle Ages (1300-1530)*, Chaps. XVIII-XIX
Cheyney, *The European Background of American History*, Chaps. VII-VIII
Gillespie, *The Influence of Oversea Expansion on England to 1700*, Chap. VI
J. A. Hobson, *The Evolution of Modern Capitalism*, rev. ed., Scribner, 1926, Chap. I
Elgin Groseclose, *Money: A Survey of Monetary Experience*, University of Oklahoma Press, 1934, Bks. VI-VII, IX
Richard Ehrenberg, *Capital and Finance in the Age of the Renaissance*, Harcourt, Brace, 1928, Introduction and Bk. II
G. T. Warner, *Landmarks in English Industrial History*, Macmillan, 1899, Chaps. IX, XI, XIII-XIV
Sée, *Economic and Social Conditions in France in the Eighteenth Century*, Chaps. VII, X
—— *Modern Capitalism*, Adelphi Press, 1928
J. W. Horrocks, *Short History of Mercantilism*, Brentano's, 1925
Lipson, *Economic History of England*, Vol. III
Charles Gide and Charles Rist, *History of Economic Doctrines*, Heath, 1915, Bk. I
Webster, *Historical Selections*, pp. 766-75
Marshall, *The Emergence of the Modern Order: Industrial Society*, Vol. I, Pt. I, pp. 82-104, 166-75, 231-44
Bland, Brown, and Tawney, *Economic History; Select Documents*, pp. 672-83

FURTHER REFERENCES

CAPITALISM AND COMMERCIAL POLICIES IN THE EARLY MODERN PERIOD. On the rise of capitalism, see Cunningham, *Western Civilization in Its Economic Aspects*, Vol. II, Bk. V, Chap. II; *Cambridge Modern History*, Vol. I, Chap. XV; Nussbaum, *History of the Economic Institutions of Modern Europe*, Pt. II, Chap. III; Pt. III, Chaps. I, V; Renard and Weulersse, *Life and Labor in Modern Europe*, pp. 343 ff.; Chaps. XXII-XXIII, XXX of Max Weber, *General Economic History* (Greenberg, 1927); Chap. XI of Preserved Smith, *The Age of the Reformation* (Holt, 1920); Ehrenberg, *op. cit.*; Sée, *Modern Capitalism*; Hobson, *op. cit.*, Chap. I.

On early English fortunes, see Gillespie, *op. cit.*, pp. 154 ff.; Nussbaum, *op. cit.*, p. 245. On public and private fortunes outside England, see *Ibid.*, pp. 114 ff.; Ehrenberg, *op. cit.*

On the transition from a napkin economy to the theory of business enterprise, see pp. 337-43 of M. M. Knight, H. E. Barnes, and Felix Flügel, *Economic History of Europe* (Houghton Mifflin, 1928); Nussbaum, *op. cit.*, p. 46; P. T. Homan, pp. 231 ff. of H. W. Odum, ed., *American Masters of Social Science* (Holt, 1927).

On the new business units, commercial organizations, and chartered companies, see Cheyney, *op. cit.*, Chaps. VII-VIII; Thompson, *op. cit.*, Chap. XIX; David Hannay, *The Great Chartered Companies* (London, 1926).

On the origins of *The Merchant Adventurers*, see E. M. Carus-Wilson, "The Origins and Early Development of the Merchant Adventurers," *Economic History*

FURTHER REFERENCES

Review, April, 1933; George Unwin, "The Merchant Adventurers' Company in the Reign of Elizabeth," *Ibid.,* January, 1927.

MODERN BANKING. On the rise of early banking, see A. P. Usher, "The Origins of Banking: The Primitive Bank of Deposit," *Economic History Review,* April, 1934; Weber, *op. cit.,* Chap. xx; Thompson, *op. cit.,* Chap. xviii; Ehrenberg, *op. cit., passim;* Chaps. viii-ix of Sir Norman Angell, *The Story of Money* (Stokes, 1929).

INSURANCE. For the early history of insurance, see C. F. Trenerry, *The Origin and Early History of [Life] Insurance* (London, 1926); A. F. Jack, *Introduction to the History of Life Assurance* (London, 1912); C. E. Fayle, *A History of Lloyd's* (Macmillan, 1928).

PRODUCE AND STOCK EXCHANGES. On the early bourses and exchanges, see Nussbaum, *op. cit.,* pp. 200 ff.; Angell, *op. cit.,* pp. 210 ff.; Day, *History of Commerce,* Chap. xvii; Emmanuel Vidal, *History and Methods of the Paris Bourse* (United States Government Printing Office, 1910); Ehrenberg, *op. cit.,* Bk. II and pp. 357 ff.

SPECULATION AND "BUBBLES." On the early "bubbles" and speculative scandals, see Day, *op. cit.,* Chap. xvii; Pts. II-III of R. H. Mottram, *History of Financial Speculation* (Little, Brown, 1929); Angell, *op. cit.,* Chap. x; Weber, *op. cit.,* Chap. xxiv; Earl Sparling, *A Primer of Inflation* (Day, 1933). On the South Sea Bubble, see Botsford, *op. cit.,* pp. 164 ff.; Mottram, *op. cit.,* pp. 131 ff.; Lewis Melville (L. S. Benjamin), *The South Sea Bubble* (Small, Maynard, 1923). For a vivid but not too reliable biography of John Law, see Georges Oudard, *The Amazing Life of John Law* (Harcourt, Brace, 1928). On Walpole's economic policy, see N. A. Brisco, *The Economic Policy of Robert Walpole* (Macmillan, 1907).

COMMERCIAL MONOPOLIES. On early commercial monopolies, see Weber, *op. cit.,* pp. 284-85; Gibbins, *History of Commerce in Europe,* pp. 242-46; Mottram, *op. cit.,* pp. 41 ff., 77 ff.; Renard and Weulersse, *op. cit.,* index under Monopolies; Hannay, *op. cit.;* C. T. Carr, ed., *Select Charters of Trading Companies, A.D. 1530-1707* (London, 1913).

MERCANTILISM. On mercantilism, Colbertism, and cameralism, the best brief work is Horrocks, *op. cit.* See also A. J. Sargent, *The Economic Policy of Colbert* (Longmans, 1899); Lipson, *op. cit.,* Vol. III; A. W. Small, *The Cameralists* (University of Chicago Press, 1909). For an excellent summary of the acts and policies stimulated by mercantilism in England, see Bradshaw, *Social History of England,* Chaps. v-vi. On Spanish mercantilism, see *Facts and Factors in Economic History,* pp. 214 ff.

On the decline of mercantilism and the rise of economic liberalism, see Horrocks, *op. cit.,* Chap. vi; Gide and Rist, *op. cit.,* Bk. I, Chaps. i-ii; Henry Higgs, *The Physiocrats* (Macmillan, 1897); F. W. Hirst, *Adam Smith* (Macmillan, 1904); Eli Ginzberg, *The House of Adam Smith* (Columbia University Press, 1934).

CHAPTER IV

THE RISE OF THE MIDDLE CLASS AND THE EVOLUTION OF THE NATIONAL-STATE SYSTEM

I. THE EMERGENCE OF NATIONALISM

In the first volume of this work we traced the chief stages in the political evolution of mankind to the close of the Middle Ages. First, humanity was organized, for the most part, on what has been called the gentile basis, namely, tribal society.[1] Here the individual's position and the power of the rulers were founded upon blood relationship, real or assumed. One did not have rights or prestige either because he resided in a certain place or because he was protected by some overlord. He owed all his status and privileges to the fact that he was a member of a quasi-biological clan or gens. This was believed to be composed of blood brethren, irrespective of whether the relationship was traced through the male or the female line. An interloper had no rights or privileges. Those who ruled were elected by and from the blood brethren. Even the most elaborate political organizations in primitive society, such as the Iroquois tribes and confederacy, rested fundamentally on clan units that were made up of alleged kinsmen. The same was true of even the early Germanic tribes when they first appeared on the historical horizon. Real or fictitious blood relationship, then, was the foundation of primitive political organization, though family relations and local propinquity served occasionally to hold men together and secure order.

In the frequent and numerous wars that took place during the interval between primitive and historical civil society, some of these kinship groups were conquered and reconquered by others and subjected to the rule of the victors. Blood relationships were thus gradually obscured and broken down. In this age of conquest, personal loyalty to dominant personalities became ever more important. The basis for public control was the loyal support of the leader by his followers and the protection of the subordinates by the leader. In short, personal relationships, founded on superiority and subordination, on loyalty and protection, supplanted the blood-kinship basis of primitive society. The resulting political and social order was what we know as feudalism. This seems to have existed as the background of most early historical political societies, intervening between primitive tribal organization and the more highly developed political state grounded in territorial residence. Early city-states and monarchies thus appear to have arisen out of feudal origins.[2] This feudal order re-

[1] See above, Vol. I, pp. 43 ff.
[2] See above, Vol. I, pp. 87 ff., 191 ff.; Alexandre Moret and Georges Davy, *From Tribe to Empire*, Knopf, 1926, especially Pt. II; and R. H. Lowie, *The Origin of the State*, Harcourt, Brace, 1927.

THE EMERGENCE OF NATIONALISM

appeared again in Western civilization when the Greek and Roman social structure collapsed and the Northern barbarians gained control of public affairs. Medieval feudalism has been examined in detail in a preceding chapter.[1]

The earliest type of political organization which rested upon a civil and territorial basis was the city-state that appeared first in Egypt nearly five millennia before Christ. It persisted in various forms and areas down to the rise of imperial Rome, though earlier empires had sporadically blotted it out in wide sections of the ancient East. Indeed, city-state culture persisted in early modern Italy, Germany, and Holland. In the chapter on Greek society we presented an analysis of the character of the Greek city-state, perhaps the highest development attained by this form of politico-social organization.[2] Antiquity produced not only the city-state but also the patriarchal empire, created out of the conquest of many and scattered city-states. But neither the city-state nor the empire brought about a truly national psychology or political organization. The city-state was too small and provincial. The empires were too vast, embraced too many peoples and cultures, and were of too brief duration to weld their divergent cultures into a national unit. Even the Roman Empire did not attain a national, self-conscious character.

The political, social, economic, and cultural conditions of the Middle Ages were no better adapted to the creation of the national state than were those of imperial antiquity. The unit of political organization and administration was the domain of the feudal lord. This varied greatly in area, but it rarely ever approached being coextensive with any cultural or national entity. Usually a single feudal domain was but a small isolated element in the feudal hierarchy, and it made for political decentralization and local immunity rather than for national unity. The center of social life was the infinite number of isolated and minute medieval manors and the few small and scattered medieval towns. The units of agrarian and urban industry, the manors and the towns respectively, were relatively isolated, nearly self-sufficient, and narrowly selfish and provincial.[3] They were thoroughly unadapted to providing any firm economic foundations for national unity. The pivotal points in medieval culture were the royal palaces, towns, and the monasteries. The towns were too few, too poorly connected with others by means of communication, and too much governed by the spirit of localism and jealous isolation to be able to bring into being to any marked degree that general cultural homogeneity so all-essential to the existence of national unity. Nor were the monasteries any better in these respects.

With the origin of modern times, however, we have arrived at the point where we must consider the emergence of a new political entity of great import for the future of humanity, namely, the national state.

It was made clear in an earlier chapter that the feudal order was characterized, above everything else, by localism and the immunity of the feudal lord.[4] The center of power was the feudal domain, and only the most tenuous authority inhered in the average feudal monarch. Such power as he did have was

---

[1] See above, Vol. I, Chapter xv.   [2] See above, Vol. I, pp. 185 ff.
[3] The manors, of course, far more so than the towns.
[4] See above, Vol. I, pp. 564 ff.; and W. C. MacLeod, *The Origin and History of Politics*, Wiley, 1931, Chaps. VIII, XI-XIII.

primarily derived from his own position as a strong feudal lord and from the aid given to him by his subordinate feudal lords. The stronger kings of the feudal period owed their power chiefly to the creation of some sort of royal army. Each feudal lord was supreme in his own domain—that is, was immune from higher control after he had met his duties and obligations to his overlords and king. Feudalism was a testimonial to the relative unimportance of the nonlocal and impersonal aspects of life.

With the national state all this was thoroughly transformed.[1] The political power became centralized, first in monarchs and later in elective rulers. The state became absolute and all too often crushed out at will the immunities and privileges of individuals, whether lords or common men. The authority and administration radiated out from the center of the realm instead of being scattered about in outlying regions. The king hired his own army and administration instead of relying on levies of feudal troops and the administration of justice by feudal lords. Order was preserved by the monarch and his will had to be respected by all under his dominion. National sovereignty supplanted local immunity. Order gradually grew out of chaos.

It has been shown earlier, in treating the decline of feudalism, how the stronger feudal monarchs at the close of the medieval period were beginning to assert their power at the expense of the feudal lords and to lay the foundations of the national monarchy.[2] This movement was hastened by the expansion of Europe and the Commercial Revolution. These brought into play forces which served to extinguish the political aspects of feudalism and to create a system of nationalism.

With this process of building the national state we shall now concern ourselves, first tracing its appearance in the form of absolute monarchy and then indicating how absolutism was undermined by the growth of revolutionary doctrines and the rise of representative government. Republics, of course, proved no less nationalistic than the earlier monarchies. Political liberalism has not thus far consistently produced cosmopolitanism or internationalism. Progressive democracies in the twentieth century remained as nationalistic as seventeenth-century monarchies. The greatest of all the wars of the nations was fought in the second decade of our own century and democratic states entered it with as much ardor and as little provocation as the most reactionary empires.

II. THE RISE OF THE ABSOLUTE DYNASTIC STATE

During most of the Middle Ages the kings had themselves been little more than glorified feudal lords. They depended mainly upon the feudal lords for their royal revenue, for their soldiers, and, to a very large extent, for the administration of justice. Nothing could have been more natural than for the feudal barons to hesitate to make any contributions to a cause that threatened the reduction of their own power and prestige. To strengthen the monarch was no less than cutting their own institutional throat. As we made plain earlier, there was not a single outstandingly powerful feudal king who did not owe his power and success chiefly to the fact that he had managed somehow to cre-

---

[1] *Cf.* Edward Jenks, *The State and the Nation*, Dutton, 1919, Pt. III.
[2] See above, Vol. I, pp. 797 ff.

ate a fairly effective royal army that he could completely control. The feudal system was merely the best substitute that could be found for more centralized government in a primitive agricultural society without any great volume of trade or store of precious metals.

Another element that hampered the origins of nationalism during the feudal period was the power of the international ecclesiastical state—the Roman Catholic Church. This had to be disrupted before the spirit of nationalism could have full sway.

The various civil and religious wars of late medieval and early modern times killed off many of the feudal nobility and did a great deal towards reducing the power of the feudal lords. Such suicidal tendencies in feudalism were especially well illustrated by the Hundred Years' War, the later English Wars of the Roses, and the French religious wars of the sixteenth century. But this self-destruction of the power of the lords was not sufficient. What was needed in addition was a large independent source of income for the king. This was at last provided through the various benefits derived by the monarchs from oversea trade and colonization. They received, as we have seen, some income from the discovery of precious metals, some from their share in public piracy or privateering, some from fees for chartering commercial companies and the granting of monopolies, and some from customs duties on the increased foreign trade. To these new sources of revenue were added the older methods of direct taxation and other means of raising money. The old and new revenues enabled the kings to hire more officials and larger armies and thus carry forward with a new impetus the destruction of the power of the feudal lords.

At this same time, and motivated by much the same tendencies that helped the kings along towards royal absolutism, came the Protestant Revolution that broke up the unity of the Roman Catholic Church and removed the ecclesiastical barriers to nationalism and royal omnipotence.

Out of this background arose the beginnings of those relentless wars of the national monarchs against their old feudal rivals which extended from the accession of Henry VII of England in 1485 to the close of the eighteenth century. While this process involved an extensive development of royal absolutism and tyranny as an inevitable accompaniment of the growth of national centralization, the movement as a whole was one of the most important in the history of the political development of humanity.[1]

In England the feudal régime ended and a strong monarchy was established when Henry VII founded the Tudor line in 1485. In Spain the centralizing process was very well advanced by 1555 when Philip II came to the throne. Henry IV of France established the strong Bourbon dynasty in 1589, and by 1652 all serious threats of political feudalism against the absolute monarchy had practically disappeared. Russia, under Peter the Great (1689-1725), effectively imitated France. A little over a century after the establishment of the Bourbon dynasty, Peter had crushed local government in Russia and given relatively permanent centralization to the vast Slavic empire of eastern Europe. Working upon the foundations laid by the Great Elector in the last half of the previous century, Prussian rulers had created a highly centralized kingdom by

[1] See below, pp. 89 ff.

1713. In this way the national-state system emerged from the feudal order of the Middle Ages.

Nor must it be forgotten that the growth of nationalism was forwarded during the period of the Commercial Revolution by those narrow but potent nationalistic aspects of mercantilism which, as we pointed out above, persisted until the middle of the nineteenth century. These forces, it must be emphasized again, had a powerful effect in increasing national consciousness, self-interest, and jealousy and were a strong stimulant to international friction.[1]

In addition to this powerful economic impulse to nationalistic and militaristic policies, a strong intellectual influence making for national self-consciousness arose in the remarkable development of vernacular literature after the spell of the classic revival had spent its force.[2] Italy produced Machiavelli, Guicciardini, Ariosto, and Tasso; France, Rabelais, Montaigne, Corneille, Molière, and Racine; Spain, Cervantes, Lope de Vega, and Calderon; Portugal, Camoëns, Miranda, and Ferreira; England, More, Spenser, Shakespeare, Jonson, Marlowe, Bacon, and Milton; Germany, Sachs, Hutten, Opitz, and Fleming. Even Holy Scripture, once known only in the single Latin Vulgate, was no longer a unifying force in literature and religion in the troublous times of Luther's age. In the translations of Luther and the later King James version it became a powerful vehicle in aiding the development, popularization, and improvement of the vernacular languages. The vernacular Bible was thus a subtle and effective force making for nationalistic divisions. This vernacular literature not only gave expression to the growing differentiation of national cultures. It also constituted a prized national possession of first-rate cultural importance and served as a patriotic inspiration for the generations to come. When the religious divisions created by the Reformation coincided with national boundaries, as in the case of England, Spain, and Holland, they constituted a formidable psychic force making for national cohesion and self-satisfaction.

Before the end of the eighteenth century, then, political Europe had almost ceased to be either feudal or imperial in the medieval sense and had come to be preponderantly national in political organization, economic policy, and intellectual tastes and expression. What was further needed to perfect the nationalistic system was: (1) The psychological thrill furnished by the French Revolution and its results; and (2) the provision of a real "nervous system" for the new national states in the improved methods of communication and transportation that came later as a phase of the Industrial Revolution.[3]

The emergence of the national dynastic state in modern times was first manifested in the case of Tudor England, aided by the appearance in 1485 of a shrewd and vigorous monarch in the person of Henry VII. In England alone had the feudal nobility thus far been gracious and self-effacing enough to hasten their own destruction by wars of direct self-extermination—the Wars of the Roses (1455-85). Henry VII, starting off with a weakened feudal system, filled the royal coffers by taxing the feudal nobles through the use of "Morton's Fork"[4] and other ingenious devices, haled recalcitrant and rebellious feudal

---

[1] See above, pp. 75 ff.   [2] See above, Vol. I, pp. 834 ff.   [3] See below, pp. 303 ff., 317 ff., 736 ff.
[4] This refers to the ingenuity of Henry's chancellor, Cardinal Morton, who alleged that if a subject displayed wealth this was proof that he should share it with the king, while if he lived very plainly and thriftily this indicated that he must have saved much money to contribute to the crown. Some scholars now question this statement.

THE RISE OF THE ABSOLUTE DYNASTIC STATE   87

lords before the arbitrary Court of the Star Chamber, and encouraged the new commerce by trade treaties such as the "Intercursus Magnus" and by subsidizing such explorers as the Cabots. His son, Henry VIII, broke with Rome over a divorce dispute and thus added a religious cast to the growing English nationalism. Elizabeth profited by the labors of her father and grandfather. Her reign witnessed notable literary and cultural expressions of English nationalism, as well as the emergence of England as a leading naval and colonizing nation. By the close of the Tudor period (1603) England had become a highly centralized dynastic national state.[1] Feudalism in its political aspects had passed, and the middle class had so far developed its political strength that a half-century later it was able to show superiority over the Crown in the revolution of 1645.

After a brief but brilliant episode of Portuguese nationalism (1498-1580), Spain came next in the order of national development.[2] Charles V had been an imperialist rather than a nationalist and had hoped to revive the medieval empire. But Philip II (1556-98), carrying on the work of Ferdinand and Isabella, was a true Spanish nationalist and attempted to weld in one national unity not only Spain but the Spanish possessions in the Netherlands. Philip was a good example of the early paternal absolute monarch. He would brook no opposition to the royal will and he insisted upon personal supervision of most of the administrative activities in his kingdom. He linked up a spirited Spanish nationalism with almost fanatical devotion to the Catholic Church. His overardent nationalism actually brought disruption rather than centralization, and in 1568 the Dutch, led by William the Silent, broke into active revolt against Philip's oppressive measures.[3] The new Dutch national state declared its independence in 1581 and secured the European confirmation of its action at Westphalia in 1648. Philip's rivalry with England, born partially of nationalistic motives and partially of hatred of Protestantism, produced the ill-fated expedition of the Spanish Armada, its defeat by England, the destruction of Spanish primacy in sea power, and the rise of British maritime strength.[4]

About a century after England had emerged from civil war with a strong national monarch at the head of the state, Henry IV, the founder of the French Bourbon dynasty, came forth victorious over his opponents in the French religious wars and was crowned king in 1589. The religious wars had helped to decimate the French nobility and made easier the centralizing processes. Capturing not only Paris but France "by a mass," Henry began with his great minister, Sully, the building of the dynastic national state in France. Henry's career was cut short by his untimely death at the hand of the assassin Ravaillac, but his program was widened and carried on with vigor and determination by the great ecclesiastics and statesmen Richelieu and Mazarin. By the time of the suppression of the Fronde [5] in 1652, the feudal system had passed away as

[1] See H. A. L. Fisher, *Political History of England, 1485-1603*, 2 vols., Longmans, 1906; and H. D. Traill and J. S. Mann, *Social England*, 6 vols. in 12, Putnam, 1909, Vol. II, Chap. VIII; Vol. III, Chaps. IX-X.
[2] See *Cambridge Modern History*, Macmillan, 1902-12, 7 vols., Vol. III, Chap. XV.
[3] See *Ibid.*, Chap. VI.
[4] *Cf.* Sir J. S. Corbett, *Drake and the Tudor Navy*, Longmans, 1898, 2 vols.
[5] The so-called Fronde was a revolt of the feudal lords against the new centralizing policies.

a dominating political power in France. The fruits of the work of Henry, Sully, Richelieu, and Mazarin were appropriated by Louis XIV, in whose reign France not only reached the height of her dynastic centralization but also attained cultural primacy in Europe.

The Thirty Years' War (1618-48) brought with it a multitude of nationalistic movements and demonstrated the strong political element in the Protestant revolt. The stirrings of national ambitions in Bohemia (1618-20) and in Denmark (1625-29) were speedily repressed, but Sweden under Gustavus Adolphus (1594-1632) forged to the front as an important national state (1630-32) and maintained this position until it was lost through the insane ambitions of her warrior king Charles XII (1697-1718).

The Treaty of Westphalia [1] first gave general European recognition to the growing national-state system and to the existence of independent national sovereignty. It brought diversity rather than unity, however, to Germany and helped to postpone German unification until the latter part of the nineteenth century, when this belated achievement disturbed the peace of Europe.

If a unified national German state was not the product of this earlier period in the development of dynastic national states, there appeared the dynasty and the state that were ultimately to bring centralization and unity to Germany, namely, Prussia under the Hohenzollerns. After having developed from robber barons into wealthy city magnates of Nuremberg in southern Germany, the Hohenzollerns appeared upon the north-European stage through the purchase of the Mark of Brandenburg by Frederick Hohenzollern from the bankrupt Emperor Sigismund in 1415. Through fortunate marriage arrangements they secured possession of Prussia in 1618. The basis of the Prussian bureaucracy and military system was laid by Frederick William, the Great Elector (1640-88), and the process was carried to completion by King Frederick William I (1713-40). Starting with these contributions of his ancestors, Frederick the Great (1740-86) was able, by statecraft, diplomatic duplicity, and military genius, to raise Prussia to the rank of a first-rate European power. At the same time, he created that German political dualism [2] which erected an effective barrier to German national unification until Austria had been humiliated and finally ousted in 1866.

In the latter part of the seventeenth century Poland attained to a degree of power that enabled it to save Christendom from the Turks in 1683. But an unfavorable geographical situation, ethnic, religious, and social diversity, almost unrestrained feudal anarchy, and the absence of a strong middle class prevented Poland from securing permanent national unity, condemned it to a steady decline, and then led to a century and a half of dismemberment.

Even semi-Asiatic Russia did not remain immune to this general European process of national differentiation and centralization. Under its barbarous and brutal but able Tsar, Peter the Great (1682-1725), political power was centralized, a national royal army was established, European manners and customs were introduced, and Russian foreign policy was given a new westward shift.

---

[1] See *Cambridge Modern History,* Vol. IV, Chap. xiv.
[2] That is, Austro-Prussian rivalry for German leadership.

ORIGINS OF THE GREAT POWERS OF PREWAR EUROPE

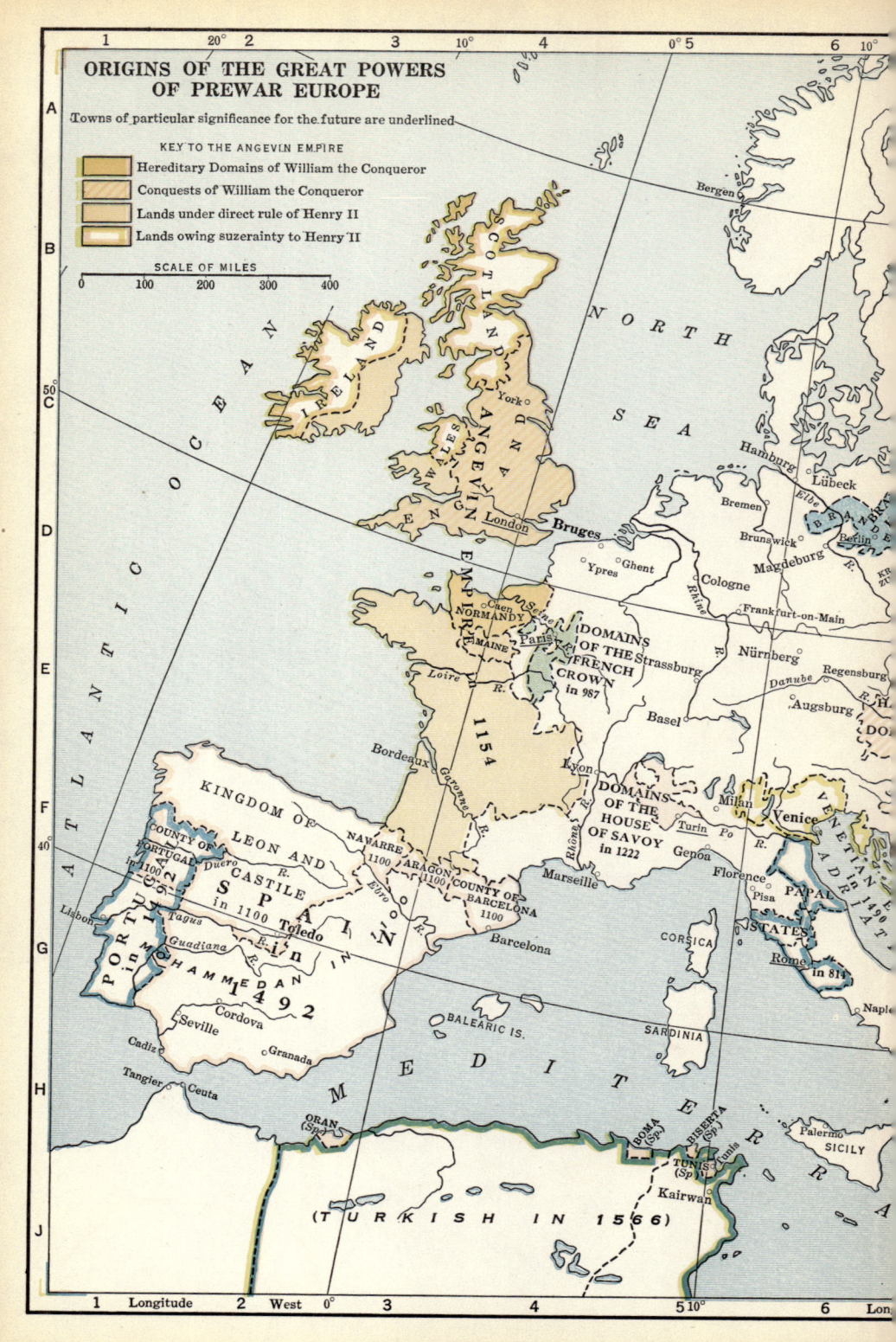

Towns of particular significance for the future are underlined

KEY TO THE ANGEVIN EMPIRE
- Hereditary Domains of William the Conqueror
- Conquests of William the Conqueror
- Lands under direct rule of Henry II
- Lands owing suzerainty to Henry II

SCALE OF MILES
0　100　200　300　400

PRINCIPALITY OF MUSCOVY in 1462

POLAND in 1569

OTTOMAN EMPIRE in 1566

BLACK SEA

AEGEAN SEA

MEDITERRANEAN SEA

PRUSSIA (To Brandenburg 1618)

Warsaw
Cracow
Kiev
Rzhew
Moscow
Nizhni Novgorod
Volga R.
Don R.
Dnepr R.
Dnestr R.
Tana
Belgrade
Danube R.
Adrianople
Constantinople
Halys R.
Angora
Trebizond
Antioch
Aleppo
Euphrates R.
Damascus
CRETE (To Venice)
CYPRUS (To Venice)
MONTENEGRO

GREAT POWERS

By 1721 the Baltic provinces had been taken from Sweden and the all-important "window to the west" secured.

While neither Prussia nor Russia was seriously affected directly by the Commercial Revolution, the growth of nationalism in these states during the seventeenth and eighteenth centuries was in some ways indirectly a result of the political reactions of this great economic movement. In both states the nationalistic policies were adopted as a direct and obvious imitation of the administrative and military methods of the Western monarchs of the new order of national states. The Great Elector could observe the centralizing policies, methods, and measures of Richelieu, Mazarin, and Louis XIV, and King Frederick I of Prussia took as his model William III of England. Peter the Great learned from England and Holland the secrets of the new industry and commerce, while from Louis XIV he obtained suggestions as to political centralization and military reorganization. Moreover, there were many Huguenots in Prussia and many Dutch and English in Russia. By the middle of the eighteenth century, then, national states had been created in most of Europe. Only in Germany, Italy, and the Balkans was this process postponed until the next century, with results rather disastrous to humanity at large.[1]

III. THE ERA OF ABSOLUTE MONARCHIES

The rise of the fairly well centralized national state in the place of the provincial and localized feudal entity was the outstanding political achievement of early modern times. Within the general framework of the national state there developed successively two widely different types of organization and control. In the first, the absolute power of the king was the conspicuous fact; in the second, this dominant authority was captured by parliaments representing the middle class. The middle class that pushed ahead in politics at this time was, of course, the wealthy or upper middle class. The petty bourgeoisie made little progress in political power or recognition until somewhat later.

While the rise of the individual ruler to power was the most striking thing about these new states as seen by contemporary observers, it was not their most permanent feature. The king was confused with the state, and often regarded himself as practically identical with it. Back of the visible clashes of kings with Popes was the more general struggle between secular and religious authority that had gone on with varying fortunes throughout the Middle Ages.[2] But the new national states were in a position ultimately to triumph completely over Church and feudal lords alike.

The "divine right" theories of the early modern kings were taken directly from the Middle Ages. Here identical claims had been made by French kings and Holy Roman Emperors and by the lawyer courtiers like Pierre Dubois and Marsiglio of Padua,[3] who supported them against papal encroachments. After the twelfth-century revival of the Roman law, which emphasized the supremacy of the State and the king,[4] the earlier advantages of the Church in the contest were pretty steadily undermined.

[1] See below, pp. 457 ff.
[2] See above, Vol. I, pp. 583 ff.
[3] See above, Vol. I, pp. 807 ff.
[4] See above, Vol. I, pp. 745, 807 ff.

Various theories of divine right were set forth. In the first half of the seventeenth century Sir Robert Filmer, in his *Patriarcha,* defended Stuart absolutism, arguing that God had bestowed absolute paternal power upon kings through His arrangements with Adam. James I himself wrote learnedly in behalf of the divine right of monarchs. An eminent French philosopher-theologian at the close of the seventeenth century, Bossuet, also supported the idea that citizens should honor their king with the same blind obedience which children theoretically accord to their parents.

The notion of divine kingship helped to capture for the national state the popular awe that had earlier attached itself to the semispiritual sway of the medieval Church and empire. Machiavelli's *Prince* laid great stress upon *Realpolitik,* or the practical methods of securing royal dominion, and also upon the supremacy of the monarch. Still later, an English philosopher, Thomas Hobbes, vigorously defended the secular absolutism of the state. Especially important in strengthening the conception of secular absolutism was the development of the idea of political sovereignty by Bodin, Hobbes, and others. In the words of Bodin, sovereignty is "the supreme power in the state, unrestrained by law." This was an awe-inspiring conception, which has been taken seriously to our own day.

In addition to its sheer might and growing wealth, the state also gained added respect and dignity through the rise of modern commerce and colonies, which greatly increased the range of problems that needed to be settled by the central civil authorities.

It should be noted at this point that the absolute state, which brooks no opposition to its authority, is not necessarily limited to absolute monarchy, or to monarchy of any kind, as is witnessed by contemporary Soviet Russia or any of the republics in the recent World War. It was the absolutism of the state itself in whatever form over any lesser organization that was established. Secular absolutism had prevailed. The absolute state and the absolute monarch appeared together in modern times, but the absolute monarch has by now faded away, while the absolute state has lingered on little impaired in either pretense or power. It has been challenged only by "Syndicalists" and "Pluralists" in recent times and here in theory only.[1]

In estimating the balance sheet of absolute monarchy in Europe we must consider both its contributions to progress and its disservice to civilization and happiness. There is no denying the fact that the rise of absolute monarchy in early modern times brought about certain definite achievements of a constructive and a progressive character.[2] Large and well-integrated political states arose on the ruins of feudal chaos. Law and order were established. The administration of states was centralized and clarified. Without such political contributions as these further political evolution would have been difficult or impossible. However costly and brutal this early centralizing process may have been, it provided the essential foundations for the future development of representative government, democracy, and internationalism. Further, in the realm

---

[1] See below, pp. 952 ff.; and C. E. Merriam and H. E. Barnes, eds., *History of Political Theories: Recent Times,* Macmillan, 1924, pp. 80 ff., 216 ff.
[2] *Cf.* Jenks, *op. cit.,* Chaps. xi-xii, xiv; Seignobos, *History of Mediaeval and Modern Civilization,* Chap. xxiii; *Persecution and Liberty: Essays in Honor of George Lincoln Burr,* Century, 1931, pp. 375-404; and Leo Gershoy, *The Enlightened Despots,* Harper (forthcoming).

of culture the work of the monarchs cannot be ignored. Though they subjected their citizens to burdensome taxation and wasted the royal income riotously in lavish display and court debauchery, while their subjects often starved, they did create luxury, and a leisure class that patronized notable works in various fields of art and letters.

As over against these more commendable contributions of the monarchs must be set the detriment that they brought to European civilization. First and foremost must be put the frequent, unnecessary, bloody, and expensive wars that the monarchs waged to enhance their personal prestige or to extend their territorial domain. For several centuries these despots kept Europe bathed in blood. Mere dynastic ambition brought death and mutilation to hundreds of thousands of otherwise peaceful peasants and townsmen and devasted thousands of square miles of rich and beautiful countryside. Next came the crushing expenses that royal life and activity (exclusive of waging wars) brought about. Among these royal expenses were the lavish sums wasted upon a riotous court life and upon favorites and mistresses. Some of the money, to be sure, found its way into beautiful and impressive public buildings, thus constituting, as we have seen, a contribution to civilization.

A particularly reprehensible aspect of the financial burdens imposed by absolutism was the inequitable system of levies by which taxes were collected mainly from those least able to pay. Powerful lords and favorites were able to evade just taxation, while the middle class and the relatively poor were crushed by arbitrary exactions. At times, the losses in royal warfare and the general financial extortion combined reduced large areas almost to a state of barbarism. This was most notably the case during the Thirty Years' War (1618-48).

The glories and the horrors of absolute monarchy are perhaps best exemplified by the reign of the "Grand Monarch," Louis XIV of France (1643-1715). The administrative and economic reforms of Colbert were among the most notable of monarchical contributions to effective centralized administration. The arts, the sciences, and letters were supported by lavish grants of money and generous bestowal of royal honor and approval. Public buildings of a number and impressiveness rivaled only by those of the later age of Napoleon were erected at Paris and Versailles. At the same time, the foolish and unnecessary dynastic wars, waged especially with the Hapsburgs, brought death and desolation to France and crushed the French populace under a terrific burden of taxation. It would be rash to contend that the great Louis left France as happy or prosperous as it had been when he assumed the government in the middle of the seventeenth century.

The finest flower of absolute monarchy appeared in the age of the so-called Enlightened Despots of the latter part of the eighteenth century—Frederick the Great of Prussia, Catherine the Great of Russia, Joseph II of Austria, and Charles III of Spain. While some of these monarchs were more despotic than they were enlightened, they all had the interests of the whole monarchy at heart and endeavored to rule in such fashion as to make their country more prosperous and powerful than before. Yet all benefits had to come at the pleasure of the monarchs; their subjects as a whole had little share in the creation and direction of policies of the state which, to an increasing degree, affected their destiny.

Frederick the Great of Prussia (1740-86) was one of the most remarkable rulers of all time. He is known chiefly as a warrior king, but between wars he devoted himself assiduously to increasing the welfare of his efficiently governed kingdom, and himself set an example of laborious and conscientious devotion to public duty. Frederick was always dominated by the obsession of strengthening the state, and humanitarianism played little part in his policies. He began a thorough reform of the Prussian legal and judicial system and took the first steps towards what ultimately became the great code of German law. He carried further the work of the Great Elector in suppressing local self-government and establishing a centralized bureaucracy, continuing the work of his predecessors in furthering the unparalleled efficiency of the Prussian civil service. Many laws were passed for the improvement of agriculture, the building of roads, the draining of swamps, and the erection of public buildings throughout Prussia. Enforcing a strict mercantilist policy (cameralism), he prohibited importation of many manufactured goods and stimulated the industrialization of Prussia by generous subsidies. Yet there was no lavish waste. These expenditures were controlled by the most rigorous considerations of efficiency and economy. State monopolies were created to increase public revenue. He believed that good subjects must be literate and he gave much attention to educational progress, even establishing elementary schools. A friend of Voltaire, he took what were for the time bold steps in establishing religious toleration. Frederick was himself a scholar and a musician and he did all in his power to encourage science, literature, and art in his realm. But, as was so often true of even the best of monarchs, these enlightened activities were offset by the bloody wars in which Frederick was involved, though he was not always the aggressor. These conflicts left their trail of blood and taxes on the body politic of Prussia.

Catherine the Great of Russia (1762-96), one of the most interesting personalities in European history,[1] ruled over a much more backward society than the colorful Prussian monarch. Nevertheless, she did actually execute a number of remarkable achievements in the way of modernizing Russia. She carried further the work of Peter the Great in centralizing and improving the system of political administration. Under the influence of Beccaria and Blackstone, she ordered the revision of the Russian criminal code to remove the more atrocious examples of barbarism and cruelty. She lightened the oppressive exploitation of the Russian masses by the Greek Catholic Church through secularizing some Church property and taking over much of the Church land. She even went so far as to discuss the possibility of providing a written constitution for Russia and abolishing serfdom. Her administrative reforms were epoch-making. Only the upper classes among the Russians could read or write, but within this group Catherine vigorously encouraged the cultivation and appreciation of art and letters, being herself a great admirer of Voltaire, Diderot, and the French Enlightenment. Catherine's failure to achieve more in the way of reform was due mainly to the reactionary character of the Russian nobility. In her earlier years as Empress she contemplated sweeping reforms, but the nobility blocked her and she turned to a foreign war in disgust.

[1] For a brilliant and not too inaccurate a characterization, see Katharine Anthony, *Catherine the Great*, Knopf, 1930.

Later, she accommodated herself to more moderate reforms, which caused great dissatisfaction to the progressive elements. Their criticism irritated Catherine and she then turned definitely to reaction and became as conservative and intolerant as the nobility who had enraged her in her youth. Russia, therefore, settled down to reaction and absolutism.

Joseph II of Austria (1765-90) was the Hapsburg representative of the enlightened despots.[1] He was probably the most enlightened and liberal of the lot, though sometimes oppressive, as in his Belgian policy. Joseph wished to carry out a most thoroughgoing administrative reform of his antique and ill-organized state. He proposed thirteen new provinces to take the place of the old illogical and irregular territorial divisions, and German was to be the language spoken throughout his realm. Centralization was to be forwarded by establishing a uniform system of government dominated by royal officials. He proposed to make inroads upon the vast vested interests of the Roman Catholic Church in Austria through nationalizing the Church, restricting the power of the Pope, limiting monasticism, and establishing religious toleration. He aimed to advance the industrial prosperity of his country by stimulating commerce, building roads, introducing equitable taxation, and abolishing serfdom. In the field of law he was profoundly impressed by the recommendations of Beccaria and ordered the revision of the Austrian criminal code in such a way as to abolish torture, and even the death penalty except for treason. He also ordered the formulation of a new and enlightened civil code. The shortness of his reign and the violent opposition of reactionaries to decency, justice, and efficiency prevented Joseph from making much headway in putting his program into operation, but it undoubtedly represented the best formulation of good royal intentions in the whole history of enlightened despotism. His failure may probably be assigned chiefly to the fact that he was too far ahead of his subjects, the oppressed as well as the privileged classes.

Charles III of Spain (1759-88) was another enlightened despot worthy of mention. He did his best to overcome the disasters that had overtaken Spain since the fatal reign of Philip II. Manufactures were fostered. Thrifty German farmers were induced to settle in Spain and teach the Spaniards improved methods of agriculture. Decent roads and navigable canals were extensively constructed. The navy was strengthened and the mercantile marine greatly extended. The horrors and cruelties of the Spanish Inquisition were severely restrained and the zealous Jesuits were expelled. Law and order were improved throughout Spain and a model police system was established for the city of Madrid. In spite of the long warfare that had been waged against any type of intellectual enlightenment in Spain, Charles made some concessions to religious toleration and patronized science. The beneficial effect of such a reign is reflected in the fact that when he died the Spanish revenues had increased threefold and the population had grown from 7,000,000 to 10,000,000. Leopold of Tuscany, Joseph I of Portugal, and Gustavus III of Sweden also carried on the same traditions of enlightened despotism.

In spite of its contributions to efficiency and well-being, enlightened despotism had its notable weaknesses. Even the best of such rulers could not wholly avert foolish and expensive wars, and moreover the enlightened despots usually

[1] *Cf.* S. K. Padover, *The Revolutionary Emperor*, Ballou, 1934.

subordinated their domestic reforms to an aggressive foreign policy. More serious than this, perhaps, was the fact that there could be no assurance that a wise and able ruler would be succeeded by a person of equally good intentions and high intelligence. Indeed, most of the enlightened despots with whom we have dealt were followed by extremely incompetent successors.

Whatever the wars, sorrow, cruelty, waste, or inefficiency of the absolute monarchs, these things were not directly the main cause of the gradual recasting of the absolute state into more flexible and responsive forms. This must be sought in the royal ineffectiveness in promoting the interests and activities of the mercantile middle class. In the latter part of the eighteenth century and throughout the nineteenth the middle class was aided by the growing discontent of the masses as the Industrial Revolution began to supplement the Commercial Revolution.[1]

IV. THE RISE OF THE MIDDLE CLASS AND THE ORIGINS OF REPRESENTATIVE GOVERNMENT

The absolute monarchs, as we have seen, had originally owed their ascendancy in no small measure to the aid of the merchant and professional classes. Remembering the depredations and persecutions that their classes had suffered at the hands of the feudal lords in the Middle Ages,[2] they joined enthusiastically with the aspiring kings to crush feudalism. In the period that followed they furnished most of the personnel of the new system of administration. In due time, however, the merchant classes found that the absolute monarchs threatened their interests and limited their independence quite as much as the feudal lords had done earlier. When the growing royal power openly challenged the interests of the merchant classes, through arbitrary taxation, trade monopolies, and the like, the merchants organized in opposition to the absolute monarchs and subjected them to constitutional limitations in many areas.

From the English revolution of 1642-49 to the Russian Revolution of 1905, the most characteristic political development in European society was the uprising of the middle class against the absolute monarchs and the resulting evolution of parliamentary institutions and constitutional government. Early historians such as Carlyle, Michelet, and Bancroft looked upon the French and American revolutions as unique epics, but we now know that these, along with the English revolutions of the seventeenth century, were but specific political manifestations of the growth of middle-class self-consciousness and power. Will Durant has admirably summarized the situation:

It was the bankers, the merchants and the manufacturers who aroused, financed and tamed the French Revolution; they who overthrew the hold of the Tory landowners upon young America in 1776; they who, in 1832, upset the ancient aristocracy of England and made themselves, inch by inch, supreme lords of the British Empire and its destiny. By Liberty they meant freedom from feudal tolls and harassing legislation; by Equality they meant that they were as good as any wig or miter in the land; by Fraternity they meant modestly to suggest their eligibility to the *salons* and *soirées* of the aristocracy.[3]

[1] See below, pp. 427 ff.   [2] See above, Vol. I, pp. 651-2.
[3] W. J. Durant, "Is Democracy Doomed?" *Saturday Evening Post,* Sept. 15, 1934, p. 78.

THE ORIGINS OF REPRESENTATIVE GOVERNMENT

In a political sense the most important item in the program of the new commercial middle class was their drive for representative government. They soon lost their faith in being able to protect their interests merely through unofficial negotiations and compromises with the monarchs. They felt that they must take an active part in government and, if possible, secure dominion over the kings. This could be done only through increasing the power of the legislative or elective branch of the government. Therefore the middle class labored mightily to establish and vindicate representative government. Only in this way could they take the place that they wished in the structure and processes of the state. This aspiration, together with active oppression by monarchs, produced a movement for political revolution that would enable the middle class to seize the government, limit the crown, and create representative government.

Representative government in Europe has had a very interesting history. It is ordinarily supposed that it grew up from the beginning as a result of a popular demand on the part of the masses. But in point of historical fact it began as a very much disliked aspect of royal oppression.[1] In the early medieval monarchies the kings would send royal representatives about the realm to investigate the degree of obedience to royal decrees and the capacity of individuals to pay taxes. These royal lieutenants would gather together representative subjects in each community to submit to this inquisition. Naturally, this was very unpopular with the persons thus summoned and with their neighbors. It meant that they must reveal local disobedience to law and expose themselves to punishment, to levies on their property, and to retaliation by resentful neighbors.

In due time, it being more convenient to the king, citizens were summoned from their localities to the temporary or permanent residence of the king to give such information. The process was still unpopular, for the king usually got everything he asked for and gave little or nothing in return. But after some experience these subjects, brought to the capital under pressure, began to ask the kings for favors and concessions by means of petitions. At first the kings scornfully ignored or rebuked such presumption on the part of their subjects. After a long and stormy period, however, the right of petition was gradually conceded.

The next step was that in which the people did not rest satisfied with merely asking the monarch to grant them favors but demanded a definite part in making the laws. They were no longer contented with arbitrary royal decrees, even when favorable. There was no guarantee that an absolute monarch would not at another time give out oppressive decrees. The people had to have control over lawmaking to protect themselves with any assurance.

It was at this stage that the battle for representative government first reached the proportions of a popular program. It is this era which we are now approaching in discussing the struggle between monarchs and merchants that began in England in the seventeenth century. Royal inquisitions, petitions by subjects, and parliamentary government are the main stages through which representative government evolved.

While the chief basis of the movement for representative government lay in

[1] See above, Vol. I, pp. 581 ff. *Cf.* A. B. White, *Self-government at the King's Commana*, University of Minnesota Press, 1933.

the desire of the middle class to escape royal exactions and oppression through taking the lawmaking into their own hands, a powerful stimulus and example came to them from the struggles over Church government during the so-called Conciliar Movement (series of Church Councils) of the fifteenth century.[1] The battle over representative government was here fought out in clerical circles a couple of centuries before it took place in the strictly political field.

In early Church theory the Pope had been regarded as a sort of absolute monarch in the Church—the vicegerent of God on earth. During the Councils the antipapal party revived the legal theory of the Roman corporation and applied it to Church government. This was a strictly representative theory. According to its tenets, the real source of ultimate authority in the Catholic Church resided in the whole body of believers. But the latter were so numerous that they could not govern directly. They had to elect representatives, namely, delegates to Church Councils. So, in practice, the active authority in the Church was the Councils. They could not sit continuously. So the Pope ruled by an implied delegated authority during the interims, but he was not authorized to undo the enactments of the Councils. This controversy, which lasted over a century or more of bitter European strife in ecclesiastical circles, furnished much material for the inspiration and guidance of the middle class in their struggle for representative institutions in politics after 1600. Even the precedent of medieval struggles of feudal lords against the kings was unhistorically but effectively involved in behalf of the merchants. Such was the revival of the Magna Charta in seventeenth-century English political propaganda.

The middle class produced a body of economic and political theory to justify their attitudes and program.[2] In the realm of economic policy they gradually came to favor complete withdrawal of the state from all types of interference with economic life. In the field of political theory they developed a related type of interpretation.[3] What they desired above all was freedom from arbitrary taxation and other forms of oppression. Hence they worked out a doctrine of the natural rights of man to "life, liberty, and property." This theory of natural rights was closely allied to the natural order that lay at the foundation of the economic philosophy of laissez faire. These natural rights of life, liberty, and property, which included, specifically, freedom from arbitrary confiscation of property, imprisonment, or taxation, were held by these middle-class writers to be inherent in the order of nature from the beginnings of human society. The state or civil authority was established not to limit or terminate these supposed inherent natural rights, but rather still more firmly to assure and protect them. No ruler had any real authority to infringe upon these natural rights.

Assaults upon absolutism were thus philosophically justified, and the middle class worked out a logical theory of the right of revolution that ran as follows: It was held that primitive men had originally lived in a state of nature. This unregulated life became confused and inconvenient because of the rise of property and the consequent development of human selfishness. Without an authoritative political superior there was no one to settle quarrels and controversies. In order to assure peace and safety, it was deemed necessary to create such a superior authority, the state, to maintain order and to preserve the natural

---

[1] See above, Vol. I, pp. 712 ff. [3] See *Cambridge Modern History*, Vol. VI, Chap. xxiii.
[2] See above, pp. 77 ff.; and below, pp. 378 ff.

THE ORIGINS OF REPRESENTATIVE GOVERNMENT

rights of every individual. This was done by a voluntary social contract on the part of all the people. A governing group, said the natural-rights philosophers, was then chosen by the people, and these newly established rulers agreed to abide by certain general terms in the governmental "compact" (or constitution) thus created. In case the rulers violated the terms of this original agreement, it was not only the right but the duty of the people to rise up and drive them from power, substituting new authorities who would agree to abide by the terms of the contract.

It was this type of theory which was developed as an apologetic for the English revolutions of the seventeenth century, and was exploited as the justification of the American and French revolutions. By far the most influential writer of the group that stressed the importance of the social and governmental contracts and the right of revolution was an English philosopher, John Locke.[1] Many of his theories were taken up and popularized in America and France by such writers as Thomas Jefferson and Jean Jacques Rousseau.

New illustrative material on the life of primitive peoples overseas appeared in the sixteenth and seventeenth centuries as a result of the reports of explorers. Though often false or misinterpreted, it seemed to many to vindicate the historical accuracy of the doctrine of an original state of nature, prior to organized society. These savages found by explorers were thought to be men who still lived in the state of nature. There is no real historical justification, however, for the seventeenth and eighteenth century contentions about natural rights or early social contracts. There is no evidence that states ever originated through contracts. Most of the assumptions about primitive liberty and equality, which are so familiar to us through the writings of Locke, Rousseau, and Jefferson, have also been swept away by modern anthropological and historical research. The vigor and success of "Rousseauism," as we might call it, had no apparent connection with the scientific truth or untruth of its doctrines. It is to be explained by the type of society that thus rationalized its interests.

The middle class threw off the bonds of royal absolutism and established representative government through a series of revolutions that lasted from 1642 in England to 1905 in Russia.[2] Some may object that these movements cover too long a time period to be lumped together. As a matter of fact, their real nature and significance can only be understood when they are considered in this fashion. Russian political development in 1905 was much closer in nature to the English political institutions of 1642 than to British politics in 1905.[3] Chronological synchronisms are usually very misleading in the study of the history of civilization, where one is concerned with general institutional growth and trends. Moreover, when one reflects that feudal developments covered the period from the fall of the Roman Empire to the sixteenth century in western Europe, it is not surprising that the rise of the middle class, the right of revolution, and the establishment of representative government required two and a half centuries for their achievement throughout Europe and America.

[1] See below, pp. 161 ff., 220 ff.
[2] For splendid introductions to the meaning of these revolutions, see G. H. Soule, *The Coming American Revolution*, Macmillan, 1934, Pt. I; E. D. Martin, *Farewell to Revolution*, Norton, 1935, Chaps. VI-XI; and E. L. Woodward, *French Revolutions*, Oxford Press, 1934.
[3] *Cf.* Erik Achorn, *European Politics and Civilization Since 1815*, Harcourt, Brace, 1934, p. 221.

V. THE SIGNIFICANCE OF THE ENGLISH, AMERICAN, FRENCH, AND LATER REVOLUTIONS

1. THE GENERAL IMPORT OF THESE REVOLUTIONS

Before examining these revolutions in any detail it will clarify the subsequent discussion to indicate briefly the manner in which they exemplified the rise of the middle class and representative government. The English Revolution of 1642-49, which was extended in its achievements by that of 1688-89, definitely ended absolute monarchy in England and established the supremacy of Parliament, the representative branch of the government. This was the essence of the middle-class political program.[1] While the powerful landlord class was far from subordinated at this time, English political and legal institutions were gradually adapted to the aspirations of the bourgeoisie. Under such ministers as Walpole and Pitt, English government and foreign policy were directed as far as possible in the interest of stimulating trade and commerce and increasing the profits of the classes that benefited thereby.[2]

The American Revolution of 1775-83, which detached the thirteen colonies of the Atlantic seaboard from the European system, was also primarily a revolt and a triumph of the commercial classes. While, as Professor Schlesinger has shown, the powerful merchant classes did not at first actually desire an open rebellion, they had hoped to intimidate England into ordering a discontinuance of the new commercial policy that it had determined upon in 1763.[3] Ultimately, the movement of protest the merchants had encouraged among the mobs of the coast towns grew into overt revolution, which they found themselves obliged to support.

After independence had been achieved, the merchant class logically gave up most of the radical notions of the revolutionary period. They framed a relatively conservative Constitution designed to restore financial stability and promote commerce, and in other ways aimed to advance the interests of the business classes. The leader of this group was Alexander Hamilton, perhaps the ablest economic statesman in the history of American capitalism. Even the Latin-American revolutions of 1812 and thereafter had a considerable economic basis, in that they were encouraged by England, whose merchants stood to profit greatly by the increased freedom of trade.

The French Revolution was also clearly an example of the increased power of the bourgeois group. In the seventeenth century the middle class had attempted to secure a reform of the policies of the state—particularly the internal economic policies—but the dynasty and the landlords were too strong. By the close of the eighteenth century the middle class had become powerful enough to defy the monarchy and successfully attack the economic and social vestiges

---

[1] *Cf.* R. H. Gretton, *The English Middle Class,* London, 1917.
[2] See *Cambridge Modern History,* Vol. VI, Chap. vi; R. H. Mottram, *History of Financial Speculation,* Little, Brown, 1929, Pt. III; and N. A. Brisco, *The Economic Policy of Robert Walpole,* Macmillan, 1907.
[3] A. M. Schlesinger, *The Colonial Merchants and the American Revolution,* Columbia University Press, 1918.

of French feudalism.[1] France was reorganized in line with the program and practices of the middle class—a tendency carried still further by Napoleon, who based his system primarily upon the notion of placating—and in some cases elevating—the bourgeoisie.

It should be kept in mind that these achievements in the way of establishing parliamentary ascendancy over absolute monarchy lacked any marked tendency towards the genuinely popular government that we call democracy. They were more a preparation for, than an actual realization of, democratic institutions. In no country could a majority of the people cast ballots for the election of representatives. Economic and political activity were still based upon the notion of privilege and position. Not until the nineteenth century, with the growth of the industrial proletariat and of the frontier element in the United States, was there any conspicuous success in the way of realizing democracy.[2]

It is also significant that during this entire period there was no systematic analysis of the meaning and implications of democracy. Nor, with the doubtful exception of Mably in France, Thomas Paine in England and America, and Jefferson in America, was there any important defense of democracy as the ideal form of government. Most of the liberals regarded a constitutional monarchy or, at the most, an aristocratic republic as the ideal form of government. Montesquieu and Rousseau, for example, both held that a democracy would be tolerable only in a very small state and could never be successful in an extensive country. Jefferson favored an aristocratic republic. In short, most of the radical political theories of the period were fragmentary contributions that could later be utilized in a systematic analysis and defense of democracy. They were not anything that could be regarded as comprehensive and thoroughgoing discussions of the nature and validity of democracy.

There will now follow a brief review of the English, American, French, and Continental revolutions with special reference to their relation to the increased power of the middle class, the assertion of the right of revolution, and the establishment of representative government. This will in no sense present a conventional chronological summary of these three revolutionary movements, a theme that is entirely aside from the purposes of this work.[3] Yet the topics and developments now to be considered probably represent the real institutional significance of these great historic revolutions of the seventeenth, eighteenth, and nineteenth centuries.

2. THE ENGLISH REVOLUTIONS OF THE SEVENTEENTH CENTURY

The effects of the expansion of Europe and the Commercial Revolution upon the rise of the middle class and the growth of parliamentary government were more quickly discernible in England than in any other major European state.

[1] See Sée, *Economic and Social Conditions in France during the Eighteenth Century*, Chap. ix; and Leo Gershoy, *The French Revolution and Napoleon*, Crofts, 1933, pp. 51 ff.

[2] See below, pp. 489 ff.

[3] These details can be followed in any of the better manuals on English, modern European and American history that have been cited. For further reading, G. B. Adams, *Constitutional History of England*, Holt, 1921; Gershoy, *op. cit.*; and C. H. Van Tyne, *The American Revolution*, Harper, 1905, and *History of the Founding of the American Republic*, Houghton Mifflin, 2 vols., 1922-29, may be especially recommended.

While Spain also entered extensively into commerce and colonization, the power of the court and of the Church was so dominant there as to stifle any significant development of the middle class or of representative government.

The underlying theme that runs through English political history from 1550 to 1750 was the conflict between royal absolutism and the drive of the middle class for representative government and the control of their own economic destiny. The kings were supported by the nobility and country gentry, as well as by the forces of the Anglican Church. The middle class was buttressed by the town artisans and by some of the peasantry. The Puritans and other Protestant Dissenters usually lined up against royalty. Towards the close of the seventeenth century the supporters of the royal party came to be known as Tories, while the middle class and their supporters were found mainly in what was called the Whig party.

While there were rumblings of discontent, there were no active clashes between the Crown and Parliament in the age of Elizabeth. The Virgin Queen encouraged the explorers and freebooters like Drake, Frobisher, and Hawkins and "split" with them the profits of their piracy. Her policies in the main were rather favorable to the rising commercial groups. When the latter openly challenged the policies of the Queen in Parliament she usually stalled for time and then graciously conceded their demands when it seemed strategic to do so.

James I (1603-25), first of the Stuart kings, was much more presumptuous than Elizabeth and much more lacking in tact and discretion. During his reign, partially because of a more lavish court, the expenses of the English Crown greatly increased while its legitimate income remained practically stationary.[1] James was a vigorous supporter of the theory of the rule of kings by divine right. Therefore the idea of asking any favors from Parliament was repugnant to him. So he turned to quasi-legal methods of increasing his income. For several hundred years it had been the privilege of the Crown to collect a considerable portion of its income from the so-called tonnage and poundage duties. These were to be levied on definite and specific types of importations and the king could not legally impose similar duties on other goods without the consent of Parliament. James proceeded, however, to levy duties on new and unspecified imports. This was a double challenge and menace to the middle class. The King ignored Parliament and thus rebuffed the idea of representative government so dear to the middle class. Further, the new taxes fell directly upon the merchants who belonged to this group, thus increasing their financial burdens and reducing their profits. In addition, James interfered with the freedom of manufacturing and trade by arbitrarily establishing industrial and commercial monopolies.[2] The stage was all set for a bitter struggle between the King and Parliament, but James died before the clash came to a head.

Charles I (1625-49) continued the faults of his father and learned nothing from the latter's experience with Parliament. He was even more extravagant and hence soon needed more money than he was legally entitled to raise. Parliament granted him an additional revenue on the basis of a probable war with Spain. Charles spent this without declaring war and then demanded further

---

[1] F. C. Dietz, *English Public Finance, 1558-1641*, Century, 1932, Chaps. VI-XII.
[2] These monopolies were not resented by the merchants who directly profited by them.

subsidies. Parliament balked and Charles tried forced loans for a time. These being inadequate, he summoned Parliament, which refused to grant him further money unless he would make definite constitutional concessions to representative government and the rights of the middle class. The latter carried on their campaign against the King in the name of the Magna Charta of 1215. This was literally unhistorical, since the Magna Charta had really been a document favoring the landed nobility, who were now lined up with the King. It had represented a feudal, not a bourgeois, triumph.[1] But it appealed to the imagination of middle-class liberals and made an excellent talking-point in favor of their program.

Charles was forced to grant the so-called Petition of Right in 1628, the first great constitutional victory in the struggle of the English middle class for political supremacy. It forbade forced loans and benevolences and bound the king not to levy further taxes without the consent of Parliament. It prohibited the billeting and quartering of soldiers in private houses without the assent of the owners. It clearly stated the supremacy of the common or civil law over martial law and ordered the king not to establish military law in time of peace. Arbitrary imprisonment was outlawed, thus removing the chief instrument whereby the king had coerced recalcitrant subjects.

Finding himself greatly hampered by parliamentary restrictions, Charles dispensed with Parliament and ruled alone for some eleven years (1629-40). He could no longer levy new direct taxes and so he resorted to other expedients. He revived old feudal laws and compelled the wealthy to apply for and pay a high fee for knighthood. He imposed fines on the basis of obsolete laws. He also disposed of extensive industrial and commercial monopolies in wines, salts, soap, and the like to favored companies in return for large sums of money. Perhaps most unpopular of all was his collection of ship money. For many centuries it had been the custom for the coast towns to provide ships or money to build ships for the royal navy. Charles now demanded this contribution and insisted upon collecting it from the inland counties of England as well as from the coast towns. This was bitterly opposed by the middle class, led by one John Hampden, who himself happened to be a wealthy landowner. The case was tried before a court packed with judges who were partisans of the King and they upheld their monarch's practices (1638). Charles was able to carry out his arbitrary measures through making wide use of the Court of the Star Chamber, an oppressive tribunal the decisions of which were determined by policy rather than law.

The economic and political struggle was complicated by religious considerations. By and large, the Anglicans supported the King, while the dissenting Protestants, especially the Puritans, lined up with the opposition. Charles particularly offended the radical Protestants by showing a definite cordiality towards the Catholics. This bias arose in part from his having a Catholic wife.

To secure imperative funds, the King found it necessary to summon Parliament in 1640. His first Parliament was quickly dissolved. Charles was compelled to call another during the same year. This met on November 3, 1640, and lasted for nearly twenty years; hence it is known in English history as the Long Parliament. It immediately proceeded to pass laws designed to curb the king and to

---

[1] See above, Vol. I, p. 799.

increase the power of Parliament. The arbitrary tribunals that the King had used, the Courts of High Commission and the Star Chamber, were abolished. Illegal financial levies like ship money were forbidden. The right of the king to dissolve Parliament was denied, and it was provided that Parliament must meet at least once every three years. A comprehensive rebuke to the King's methods and to royal pretensions was embodied in the famous Grand Remonstrance of 1641. This was a lengthy and thoroughgoing indictment of Charles and his practices. It was a ringing manifesto of the middle class in behalf of representative government. It integrated this group and incensed the supporters of royalty.

The Grand Remonstrance, together with religious disturbances, brought on in 1642 a period of civil war that lasted with brief interludes until the execution of the King in 1649. The long struggle between Charles and the middle-class parliamentarians brought about a definite alignment of the major classes in England for or against the ancient pretensions of royalty. A distinguished English constitutional historian has thus described the set-up of English classes, which ultimately produced the well-known divisions of Tories and Whigs:

The loyal adherents of Charles I. were drawn from the territorial nobles, the country gentlemen, the higher yeomanry, the Church, and the universities: the Parliament was mainly supported by the small freeholders, the inhabitants of towns, and Protestant Nonconformists. Seventy years afterwards, on the accession of George I, the same classes were distinguished by similar principles. The feudal relations of the proprietors of the soil to their tenantry and the rural population, their close connection with the Church, and their traditional loyalty, assured their adherence to the politics of their forefathers. The rustics, who looked to the squire for bounty, and to the rector for the consolations of religion and charity, were not a class to inspire sentiments favorable to the sovereignty of the people. Poor, ignorant, dependent, and submissive, they seemed born to be ruled as children, rather than share in the government of their country.

On the other hand, the commercial and manufacturing towns—the scenes of active enterprise and skilled handicraft,—comprised classes who naturally leaned to self-government, and embraced Whig principles. Merchants and manufacturers, themselves springing from the people, had no feelings or interests in common with the county-families, from whose society they were repelled with haughty exclusiveness; they were familiarized, by municipal administration, with the practice of self-government; their pursuits were congenial to political activity and progress. Even their traditions were associated with the cause of the Parliament and the people against the Crown. The stout burghers among whom they dwelt were spirited and intelligent. Congregated within the narrow bounds of a city, they canvassed, and argued, and formed a public opinion concerning affairs of state, naturally inclining to popular rights. The stern nonconformist spirit, as yet scarcely known in country villages, animated large bodies of townsmen with an hereditary distrust of authority in church and state.[1]

From 1649 to 1658 England was ruled by the so-called Commonwealth government. It was presided over by Oliver Cromwell, who had been the most successful military leader in the struggle against Charles. Most of the program of the middle-class parliamentarians was put into operation. The first written

---

[1] Sir T. E. May, *Constitutional History of England*, Longmans, 1912, 3 vols., Vol. II, p. 23.

constitution of modern times, the so-called Instrument of Government, was promulgated. This provided for constitutional government and assured the predominance of Parliament. But even this did not endure, for in 1655 Cromwell established what amounted to a military dictatorship and ruled in arbitrary fashion until his death in 1658. But in the main Cromwell governed, with or without Parliament, in a manner that was generally favorable to the mercantile middle class. He passed legislation especially advantageous to English mercantile and colonial interests, and greatly strengthened the British navy to give protection to such interests. After his death chaos prevailed, and in 1660 Charles II (1660-85), son of Charles I, was recalled from exile to revive the sway of the Stuart dynasty. Charles II followed the general policy of Elizabeth in discreetly observing "what the traffic would bear" in the royal conflict with Parliament. He gave way whenever any open clash seemed probable. Nevertheless, during his reign the divisions between the middle and upper classes became more sharply established and the Whig and Tory parties definitely came into existence.

Charles was succeeded in 1685 by his brother James II (1685-88). James was far less politic than Charles. He not only challenged the trading interests of the middle class but also distinctly sacrificed their well-being to international policies favorable to the Catholic states of Europe. He also revived Catholic practices in England. This provoked another active rebellion of the middle class, and also alienated the support of many non-Catholic Tories. As a result, James's supporters were too few and weak to carry on another civil war. The "Glorious Revolution" of 1688-89 was carried through without serious bloodshed. James's Protestant daughter Mary, and her Dutch husband William of Orange, were summoned to take over the British throne.

Parliament assumed control and proceeded to enact a number of constitutional changes that definitely and permanently established the supremacy of Parliament in English political processes. First and foremost came the famous English Bill of Rights (1689). This first condemned the policies of James II. Then it proceeded to enumerate decisively the basic rights and liberties of English citizens. It proclaimed the right of Parliament to control taxation, the army, and its own meetings and procedure. It stated that all Protestant Englishmen should have the right to bear arms. It authorized all Englishmen to petition for a redress of grievances. It condemned excessive bail and fines as well as cruel punishments. It denied the power of the king to suspend laws or to permit his subjects to disobey the laws of the realm with impunity. The financial supremacy of Parliament was insured by forbidding the king to levy taxes or to maintain an army without the consent of Parliament. The king was also forbidden to interfere with the free election of members of Parliament or with their freedom of speech in that body. The trial of Englishmen by impartial juries was guaranteed.

This Bill of Rights is probably the most important single document in the history of the triumph of the middle class and representative government. Not only was it a charter of liberty for England, but it became the inspiration for the other countries that followed in English footsteps. It was embodied in the various state constitutions adopted in America after 1776, was taken over almost bodily in the first ten Amendments to the Constitution of the United States, was frequently referred to by the French revolutionists, was incorporated in part in their Declaration of the Rights of Man, and was not ignored in the Continental revolutions of 1830 and 1848.

Further acts passed during or after the Revolution of 1688-89 were designed still more decisively to establish parliamentary domination. The Mutiny Act of 1689 insured parliamentary control of the army. Military appropriations were to last for one year only. Further, the enforcement of martial law in the army was permitted for only annual periods, and parliamentary approval was required for its renewal. This meant that the army could not be maintained and disciplined unless the king called Parliament into session every year. A definite concession was made to the middle-class Puritans in the Toleration Act of 1689, which granted religious toleration to most Protestant Dissenters but kept Roman Catholics under the ban. Finally, the Act of Settlement (1701) declared that on the death of Anne the British crown should go to the German Protestant, George I of the House of Hanover.[1] This marked the dominion of Parliament over the determination of dynastic succession in England. All these developments from 1688 to 1701 created a new conception of kingship—the tenure of the crown by sovereigns who owed their title to Parliament.

In the first half of the eighteenth century parliamentary control over the Crown was still further extended by the rise of cabinet government. Gradually the king of England became more and more of a ceremonial and sentimental figurehead, while the real executive came to be a responsible committee of Parliament, the so-called cabinet. Of course, England was still considerably removed from complete parliamentary control and middle-class dominion.[2] It required the Reform Bill of 1832 to give the middle class fair representation in Parliament, and not until the Reform Bill of 1911 did the House of Commons finally attain complete supremacy in the legislative body.

These remarkable developments establishing the right of revolution and the supremacy of the representative branch of the British government received their most notable philosophical defense in John Locke's famous *Second Treatise of Government,* the classic statement of the right of revolution and middle-class economic and political interests. Locke's doctrines were, as we have already noted, an inspiration for Thomas Jefferson and the American Revolution and for Rousseau and the French Declaration of the Rights of Man.[3]

3. THE AMERICAN REVOLUTION

The American Revolution is usually studied primarily as a movement of rebellion and secession within the British Empire. But its most important features and its greatest significance in the institutional history of the West are to be found in the rise of the mercantile middle class and its defiance of those British commercial policies which ran directly counter to American interests.

[1] The present ruling dynasty in England.
[2] *Cf.* Edward and A. G. Porritt, *The Unreformed House of Commons,* Cambridge University Press, 1903, 2 vols.
[3] *Cf.* H. J. Laski, *Political Thought in England from Locke to Bentham,* Holt, 1920; and *Cambridge Modern History,* Vol. VI, Chap. XXIII.

Before 1763 there had been considerable repressive British commercial legislation designed to restrict colonial trade and manufacture to the advantage of Britain. But most of these enactments had not been vigorously enforced. The colonists violated them freely and with impunity. Smuggling was rife all along the Atlantic coast. It is estimated that some 40,000 were engaged in this smuggling trade in the middle of the eighteenth century. Smuggling carried with it no such stigma as it does today, because even the most respectable merchants were often engaged in this illegal traffic.

This temporary paradise of the American merchant class came to a rude and sudden end at the close of the French and Indian War in 1763. This victory over France gave England a vast addition to its American territory, namely, the St. Lawrence and Mississippi valleys. It was necessary at once to reorganize the administration and defense of these vast areas. Inasmuch as the English colonists in America would profit mainly by the policing of these new territories—through being protected from the Indians and ultimately allowed to settle there—the British logically believed that the colonists should pay a part of the cost of fortifying and governing these sections in the North and West.

Therefore the British government proposed to enforce rigorously the long-dormant Navigation Acts and to collect the customs duties which these authorized. This would have brought colonial smuggling—which meant a large part of the colonial trade—to an abrupt end. The English government also proposed to add new duties and direct taxes. A stamp tax was ordered on legal and public documents. This fell mainly on the merchant and professional classes. New duties were embodied in the Sugar Act of 1764 and the Townshend Acts of 1767. The Tea Act of 1773 struck a fatal blow at the colonial smuggling trade in tea. This legislation enraged the American merchant and professional classes, and they raised the objection that Great Britain had no right to tax them without representation. When, however, the British minister Grenville proposed to Benjamin Franklin that the colonists raise the taxes themselves, Franklin was compelled to admit that there was little prospect of their doing so.

Other classes were driven by their economic interests to join with the merchants in opposing the new English financial policy. Powerful land speculators and pioneer settlers had hoped to swarm into the land west of the Alleghenies as soon as the British and the colonists had defeated the French. But the British held up this program by the royal Proclamation Line of 1763, which closed the West to immediate settlement. The British were not opposed to the ultimate settlement of this territory by colonists, but they wished to get it properly policed and fortified before colonists entered and stirred up trouble with the Indians. George Washington and Patrick Henry were the leaders of the groups that particularly opposed the closing of the West. The landlords of the South were deeply in debt to British merchants, and a British act of 1752 permitted British creditors to levy directly on the property of their American debtors. Revolution and independence offered a perfect opportunity to these Southern landlords to protect themselves against British legal action. Thomas Jefferson was the major spokesman of this group.

The poorer classes throughout the colonies, all of them living in desperate poverty and in sore oppression, welcomed any prospect of change. It seemed to them that almost anything new would be something better.[1]

These were, then, the major groups in colonial American society who opposed the new British colonial and commercial policy. Comparable to the Royalist party in England were the American Loyalists who stood with England and its new policies. They were made up chiefly of the landed gentry and the official class, which owed its position and income mainly to British appointments and support. The Loyalists pretty generally constituted the upper classes among the American colonists. As in England, religious lines were interwoven with economic and social interests. The Anglican Church lined up with Loyalism, while the Nonconformists supported independence and revolution, in part because they feared that an Anglican episcopate would be established in the colonies. There was a large class that was relatively indifferent to the controversy, chiefly the farmers of the middle colonies.

Whatever the diversity of groups encouraging independence and revolution, the merchants were the most powerful.[2] At first, they did not favor active revolution. What they wished to do was to make a show of resistance that would scare off the British and induce them to go back to the easy-going methods that prevailed before 1763. As we have seen, they carried the bluff too far. The mobs they organized to intimidate the British got out of hand. The British leaders themselves were "pig-headed" and lacking in diplomacy. Therefore war could not be averted. When the merchants realized this, they decided to go ahead with the movement for complete independence. But they had no sympathy with radical revolutionary doctrines. They planned, as soon as revolution succeeded, to regain control of policies in America and to restore law, order, and sound business procedure. This they did when they formulated and adopted our federal Constitution.

At the outset Great Britain did not intend to launch any aggressive military measures against the seceding colonists. It proposed a show of force to disguise a program of conciliation. To avert the success of this and to secure French aid, the more radical patriots put through the Declaration of Independence.[3] This was a characteristic document of middle-class revolutionary theory, based directly upon the doctrines of John Locke. The theoretical paragraphs are worth quoting because they represent a classic statement of this type of theory:

When, in the course of human events, it becomes necessary for one people to dissolve the political bands which have connected them with another, and to assume, among the powers of the earth, the separate and equal station to which the laws of nature and of nature's God entitle them, a decent respect to the opinions of mankind requires that they should declare the causes which impel them to the separation.

We hold these truths to be self-evident, that all men are created equal; that they are endowed by their Creator with certain unalienable rights; that among these are life, liberty, and the pursuit of happiness. That to secure these rights, governments

---

[1] See James Oneal, *The Workers in American History*, 4th ed., rev., Rand Book Store, 1921; J. R. Commons, ed., *Documentary History of American Industrial Society*, A. H. Clark, 1910, 10 vols., Vols. I-II; and M. W. Jernegan, *The Laboring and Dependent Classes in Colonial America, 1607-1783*, University of Chicago Press, 1931.   [2] See Schlesinger, *op. cit.*

[3] *Cf.* S. G. Fisher, *The Struggle for American Independence*, Lippincott, 1908, 2 vols.; and C. L. Becker, *The Declaration of Independence*, Harcourt, Brace, 1922.

are instituted among men, deriving their just powers from the consent of the governed; that whenever any form of government becomes destructive of these ends, it is the right of the people to alter or to abolish it, and to institute a new government, laying its foundation on such principles, and organizing its powers in such form, as to them shall seem most likely to effect their safety and happiness. Prudence, indeed, will dictate that governments long established should not be changed for light and transient causes; and accordingly all experience hath shewn, that mankind are more disposed to suffer, while evils are sufferable, than to right themselves by abolishing the forms to which they are accustomed. But when a long train of abuses and usurpations, pursuing invariably the same object, evinces a design to reduce them under absolute despotism, it is their right, it is their duty, to throw off such government, and to provide new guards for their future security. Such has been the patient sufferance of these colonies; and such is now the necessity which constrains them to alter their former systems of government.

After independence was declared the several colonies became states and enacted state constitutions. These very directly reflected the English principles that had been worked out in the previous century. They embodied specifically the English Bill of Rights and other popular limitations on executive power. They distinctly elevated the position of the legislatures, thus advancing the cause of representative government.

The social and economic changes during the Revolution were in many ways much more important than the events that took place on the battlefield.[1] Revolution wiped out at once the British regulation of colonial trade, industry, finance, and the coining of money. It eliminated the restrictions on the seizure and settlement of the land west of the Alleghenies. It abolished all quitrents to the king and proprietary families. It likewise did away with the old feudal vestiges of entail and primogeniture. In fact, it brought to a general end most of the institutions and practices connected with landed privilege. There was a wholesale confiscation of great Tory estates, valued at some $40,000,000. These were distributed among the poor American farmers. Religious freedom was forwarded through a decisive movement to disestablish the Anglican and Congregational churches and to grant religious liberty to all believers. Religious qualifications for voting persisted, however, in many states.

It has been usually assumed that the American Revolution was won on the battlefield, but this is only true in part. Many of the British, particularly in the Whig party, favored the colonial cause.[2] The capture of Cornwallis at Yorktown in 1781 was a terrific blow to the prestige of Lord North and the Tories. The Whig friends of the colonists came into power and called off the British armies and fleets. They then negotiated a treaty with the colonists which was so generous to the latter that it was vigorously opposed by our French allies.

Once independence had been won the business classes lost little time in crushing out colonial radicalism.[3] Outbreaks like Shays' Rebellion in 1787 were quickly suppressed. Leaders of the business and conservative classes, together with their legal representatives, were frightened at the prospect of dis-

[1] Cf. J. F. Jameson, *The American Revolution Considered as a Social Movement*, Princeton University Press, 1926.
[2] See Van Tyne, *The American Revolution;* and D. M. Clark, *British Opinion and the American Revolution,* Yale University Press, 1930.
[3] See C. A. and Mary Beard, *The Rise of American Civilization,* Macmillan, 1927, 2 vols., Vol. I, Chap. VII.

order and they organized a movement to revise the loose-jointed Articles of Confederation and to provide a Constitution that would promote sound business and economic conservatism. In making the new Constitution the creditor classes predominated and they were led by Washington, Franklin, Hamilton, and Madison. The most unique thing about the Constitution of the United States was the fact that it was the first important one designed to protect property against inroads from the lower classes. Hitherto, the middle class had been chiefly fearful of royalty and nobility. The radicals opposed the Constitution with vigor and with a violence of language that present-day citizens little realize.[1] The most powerful condemnation of the Constitution was contained in the so-called *Centinel Letters*. These compare fairly with the *Federalist*, written in support of the Constitution by Hamilton, Jay, and Madison. We cite here a brief but characteristic passage from these letters illustrating the flavor of opposition to the Constitution:

> The new constitution, instead of being the panacea or cure of every grievance so delusively represented by its advocates, will be found upon examination like Pandora's box, replete with every evil. The most specious clauses of this system of ambition and iniquity contain latent mischief, and premeditated villainy.

Through energetic and adroit activity of statesmen and politicians representing the propertied and creditor classes, the Constitution was adopted and prosperity and order were restored. Relative permanence was assured to the system through the very great difficulties interposed to the amendment of the Constitution. Still further protection of the new order was provided when the United States Supreme Court, following the precedent of John Marshall, assumed the right to declare congressional and state legislation unconstitutional and to prevent its execution on these grounds. Thomas Jefferson and the more progressive liberals were induced to support the Constitution on the condition that the first ten Amendments be adopted as an integral part of the document. This was a concession which the business classes were in no way loath to grant because, as we have seen, these Amendments specifically embodied the English Bill of Rights, with some elaborations. They thus put into the American Constitution the basic doctrines of the middle-class revolt from autocracy and arbitrary government.[2]

The American Revolution, then, terminated in the extinction or severe restriction of the old landed aristocracy, installed the business and legal classes in a position of predominance, and embodied the revolutionary and parliamentary ideals of the middle class in our federal government. While the executive branch was given greater power than in England, the possibility of executive tyranny was guarded against through the separation of governmental powers and the balance of departments provided for in our Constitution. Though Thomas Jefferson led a temporary rebellion against the business classes in behalf of the farmers and the principles of '76, just as soon as his party had to

---

[1] *Cf.* Barnes, *History and Social Intelligence*, pp. 332 ff.
[2] *Cf.* W. H. Black, *Our Unknown Constitution*, Real Book Company, 1933, Chaps. iv, xiv; and Leon Whipple, *Our Ancient Liberties*, H. W. Wilson, 1927, Chaps. ii-v.

take over the responsibilities of government they surrendered in large part to the strong nationalistic tendencies and economic policies of those who had framed the Constitution and launched our national government. The middle-class ideals of the opening of the nineteenth century have been elaborated and strengthened as a result of the rise of industrial and financial capitalism in our country, and though challenged from time to time have maintained themselves until our day.

4. THE FRENCH REVOLUTION AND NAPOLEON

The French Revolution was long portrayed as an epic of blood and glory. The Reign of Terror loomed as the great event of the Revolution. Guillotines, assassinations, and wars figured chiefly in the earlier presentations of this important episode in the history of European civilization. A subsequent generation of historians have tended to minimize the element of gore and confusion. They have made it clear that the French Revolution represented a very considerable collection of permanent achievements in the creation of modern society. The most important and far-reaching reforms of the Revolution were brought about before the end of the year 1791, some two years before the beginning of the Reign of Terror. The terrorism and excesses of the French Revolution were a late and incidental phase of a considerable institutional and social upheaval in France.

While more dramatic and socially more disruptive than either the English or the American Revolution, the French Revolution continued the same fundamental developments and changes in Western society. It was a movement launched and engineered primarily by the middle class in revolt against the privileges and oppression of the feudal nobility and the Catholic Church. It was a culmination of the long process of adapting French government and economics to the needs of a bourgeois society. Its basic doctrines were identical with those which had inspired and justified the English and American revolutions. Yet there were some differences in degree as between these three great upheavals. The French Revolution was far more of a social revolution than its two predecessors and it was much more of a shock to the existing social fabric than either the English or the American revolutions. Further, the peasantry of France profited far more as a result of the Revolution than did the peasantry of England as a result of the upheavals in the latter country.

We may now briefly outline the main forces and the course of events in France from the middle of the eighteenth century to the close of the reign of Napoleon. The French Revolution was the outgrowth of two major factors: (1) The abuses of the old régime;[1] and (2) the resulting increase of discontent among the French middle class. The latter had protested against exploitation by the feudal lords and the Catholic Church back in 1614, but it was far too weak to make good its resentment. The Estates-General was ignominiously dissolved in that year and not reassembled for another hundred and seventy-five years. In the interval, the political power of the French feudal nobility was

---

[1] See Sée, *op. cit.*

crushed through the centralizing policies of Henry IV, Sully, Richelieu, and Mazarin. The last important revolt of the feudal lords was suppressed in the so-called Fronde revolt of 1652. But the oppressive social and economic privileges inhering in feudal nobility were perpetuated in France down to the last quarter of the eighteenth century. In its basic essentials the French Revolution represented the final wiping-away of the social and economic aspects of feudalism, the elimination of the oppressive rights and privileges of the Catholic Church in France, the creation of an intense French nationalism, and the triumph of bourgeois ideals.

Professor A. C. Flick has given a useful summary of the nature and abuses of the old régime that provoked the revolt of France in 1789 and subsequent years:

1. The government was autocratic and inefficient, and encouraged injustice and inequality. The king's will was law, while the people, even the clergy and nobles, had little voice in national affairs. There was neither civil nor political liberty. The rights of free speech, assembly, and the press were denied. Arbitrary arrests were common, jury trial unknown, and no writ of *habeas corpus* was permitted. The laws lacked unity, uniformity, and were unwisely administered. National taxation was arbitrary, unfairly distributed, and corrupt. National funds were not spent solely for the welfare of the nation. Government officials were oppressive and open to bribery. Favoritism to the few, extravagance, and vain display characterized royal rule. Attempts were made to crush such traces of local government as remained under the powerful machinery of absolutism.

2. The church, wealthy and mighty, was closely allied with the autocratic state, and reflected its policies and practices, while its own obvious duties and opportunities were too often neglected. Freedom of worship was denied. Disbelief was rampant more especially among the scholars, higher clergy and nobles.

3. Society was based on the class distinctions and special privileges of an outgrown feudalism. The nobles and higher clergy enjoyed their feudal rights and prerogatives without giving adequate services in return. The middle class through its wealth and intelligence was emerging as the dominant power in the nation. The common people, having gained their emancipation from serfdom to a large degree, were galled and irritated by the arbitrary acts of the government and by the remnants of feudalism associated with the church, society, and the land system.

4. Economic evils accompanied a bad government and a vicious social system, and hindered industrial progress and national prosperity. Poverty and misery resulted. The peasants and town workers had to bear the brunt of the hardships of the old régime, and the parish priests suffered but little less.

5. National education was sadly neglected, and such as did exist was in the hands of the clergy. The press was closely censored, and books and pamphlets had to secure special permits for publication.

6. In short, the old régime had become but a hollow shell—a system which had come down beyond its time. Against the conditions it perpetuated, the murmur of the people increased in volume and vehemence as time passed, until, under the leadership of the middle class, it finally broke forth in the Revolution.[1]

While fully recognizing the obstacles to political freedom and social justice still existing in pre-Revolutionary France, one must be on his guard against

---

[1] Flick, *Modern World History, 1776-1926*, p. 86. For another good summary, see Sée, *op. cit.*, pp. 229 ff. For more detail on the old régime, see below, pp. 115 ff.; and Frantz Funck-Brentano, *The Old Régime in France*, Longmans, 1929.

exaggerating the backward character of France in 1788. There has been a tendency on the part of patriotic American historians to exaggerate the tyranny of George III, so as to lend additional nobility to the revolutionary resistance to him. So in France, historians of the French Revolution have blackened the old régime in order to make the great Revolution appear more glorious and sweeping. As Professor Brinton puts it:

> The men of the great French Revolution built up a myth about the Old Régime in order to justify themselves. This is a common political process, and may be compared with our own popular myths about George III., North, the Hessians. But while American historians have for some time been aware of the mythical element in their own revolution, and have been able to discount it partially, French historians have not until quite recently shown any signs of criticizing these stereotyped notions.[1]

An important force that stimulated and strengthened the movement of revolt against privilege was found in the writings of the French *philosophes,* among whom the more notable were Voltaire, Helvétius, Diderot, Montesquieu, and Rousseau. Their work was supplemented by that of the Physiocrats, whose contributions to Economic Liberalism were discussed in the preceding chapter. These writers vigorously attacked the abuses and injustices perpetrated by the vested feudal and ecclesiastical interests and ably supported the doctrines of progress and justice. Rarely or never, however, were they vigorous revolutionists. Most of them favored a limited monarchy and peaceful constitutional reforms. But their writings contributed to the general intellectual ferment that helped French thought to accept the doctrines of change and improvement and particularly stirred up resentment against the Catholic Church in France.[2]

As may repeatedly be observed in the sequence of events in revolutions, the French Revolution was provoked and brought to a head by the stupidity of the vested interests in opposing orderly and gradual reform. Louis XV (1715-74) wantonly invited revolution by his incompetent and extravagant reign and is said to have cynically forecast the consequences by proclaiming the doctrine of "After me, the deluge." His successor Louis XVI (1774-93) meant well but was incompetent and lazy, was influenced by a corrupt and recalcitrant court, and was encouraged to resist reform by a charming but irresponsible and extravagant queen, Marie Antoinette.

About the time of the American Revolution the great French publicist and statesman Turgot suggested a series of reforms that would have curbed the worst abuses of the old feudal and ecclesiastical régime, given the middle class most of the reforms they required, and, in all probability, averted the revolution that followed a little over a decade later. But Louis XVI was induced by his queen and courtiers to dismiss his able minister in 1776 and to sabotage his reform proposals. Turgot was followed by stupid or futile successors who only postponed the inevitable catastrophe. Royal expenditures increased, taxes were raised, extortion became more arbitrary and frequent, and the protests of the

[1] C. C. Brinton, review of C. D. Hazen, "The French Revolution," *American Historical Review,* July, 1933, p. 745.
[2] *Cf.* Marius Roustan, *The Pioneers of the French Revolution,* Little, Brown, 1926.

middle and lower classes gained ever increasing scope and momentum. The matter was brought to a head by the French intervention in behalf of the American revolutionists. The French had aided the colonists in part to spite England and in part to assure protection of their West Indian colonies. This aid to the American Revolution enormously increased the French expenditures and brought about a condition of near-bankruptcy in the national treasury. The last chance for peaceful reform before the Revolution came in February, 1787, when the King summoned an Assembly of Notables to pass upon reform projects suggested by his minister Calonne. As might have been expected, the reforms were curtly rejected by these representatives of the vested aristocratic interests. Calonne was dismissed and thought it best to seek safety by flight to England. This action of the "Notables" only intensified the discontent of the middle class and the masses. More revenue was indispensable, and in 1788 the King was forced to call the Estates-General for the first time since 1614.[1]

Even at this late date any serious violence might easily have been averted had the King and his advisers exhibited any degree of intelligence or straightforward statesmanship. The Estates-General, made up of 308 clergy, 285 nobles, and 621 of the third estate, met for its first session at Versailles on May 4, 1789. Louis irritated the Estates-General and his minister contented himself with lecturing them. After more than a month of futile delay, in which no significant reforms or concessions were secured, the third estate organized as a National Constituent Assembly on June 17 and on June 20 took the famous Tennis Court Oath not to disband until it had made a constitution for France and brought about significant reforms. The King finally ordered the clergy and nobility to meet with the third estate and permission was given to vote by head. This was a distinct gain for the third estate since when the estates voted as a unit the clergy and nobility outnumbered the commoners by two to one. Even when voting by head the third estate had few more votes than the combined clergy and nobility. But they counted on support from enough of the liberal clergy and nobility to get a majority vote for reform measures and thus avert a complete stalemate of the reform program. Without such a change in the voting system the reforms that followed could never have been carried. When convinced that the Assembly was determined to achieve its reform program, Louis and his councilors attempted to coerce it and to break it up by military force. This provoked retaliation and opposition from the populace, particularly the Paris mobs. The most notable uprising was on July 14, 1789, when mobs, in an attempt to secure arms, captured the Bastille, a notorious Paris prison. Early in October, 1789, the Assembly moved to Paris and was more than ever dominated by the Paris Commune and the disorderly elements at the capital.

There was, however, little serious disorder during the next two years. On August 4-5, 1789, the most important reforms of the whole French revolutionary period were launched in the Assembly. They constituted in essence the wiping-out of most of the social and economic phases of French feudalism that represented the core of the abuses and privileges of the old régime. On August 26 the Declaration of the Rights of Man was proclaimed, setting forth the the-

[1] Failure to reform the royal revenue-collecting machinery also helped on revolution. This had prevented the monarchy from getting its share of the increasing wealth of France and left it bankrupt in the midst of a wealthy society.

Specially drawn and printed by the Kartographische
Anstalt von F. A. Brockhaus, Leipzig, Germany.

PRINTED IN GERMANY

EUROPE
in 1789
at outbreak
of French Revolution

oretical justification of the principles of the middle class and the reform program. The National Assembly proceeded to draw up a new constitution for France, which was adopted in 1791. This well exemplified the middle-class insistence upon representative government. The dominating power in the new government was vested in a Legislative Assembly of one chamber. The king was retained as the formal executive, but the real executive was the Executive Council, a committee of the Assembly. That the Revolution was thus far a bourgeois and not a democratic movement is evident from the suffrage qualification in the constitution of 1791. The citizens were classified as active citizens and passive citizens. The former were those who were twenty-five years of age and paid a direct tax equal to three times the amount of a laborer's daily wage in the locality. Only the active citizens could vote.

Unfortunately, in a moment of calculated political maneuvering, the National Assembly passed what is known as the Self-denying Ordinance, namely, an act forbidding anyone who had served in the National Assembly to stand for election to the new Legislative Assembly. This meant that those who had already had two years of invaluable experience in social reform and representative government were prevented from carrying over the lessons they had learned into the new government. The latter was inevitably made up of relatively inexperienced men, thus inviting excesses and confusion.

Foreign affairs proceeded to shape up in such a fashion as deeply to influence and complicate matters within France itself. Many of the French nobles had fled to reactionary states across the Rhine and there urged the kings and emperors to intervene and put down the revolutionary movement in France. These reactionary foreign rulers were in general sympathy with such a proposal, for they saw well enough that the success of the French revolutionists imperiled the reactionary system of which they were the supreme representatives. They therefore threatened the revolutionists. In the famous Declaration of Pilnitz of August 27, 1791, the Hapsburg Emperor, Leopold, and King Frederick William of Prussia declared that the maintenance of monarchy and order in France was of profound interest to all the sovereigns of Europe. This stirred up French resentment, and in April, 1792, France declared war on Austria and Prussia.

On July 25, 1792, the stupid Duke of Brunswick, commander in chief of the Austro-Prussian forces, issued his famous "manifesto." In this he declared that the old régime must be reëstablished in France, threatened to punish French soldiers captured in battle as rebels and traitors, and declared that Paris would be destroyed if the French royal family was harmed. This suggested to the French revolutionists the existence of an alliance between the French court and foreign potentates. It provoked an uprising against the court party in Paris on August 9 and 10 and the royal family was forced to flee to the Assembly to save their lives. A radical revolutionary commune was established in Paris. At this time Danton came to dominate the revolutionary movement through his leading position in the Provisional Executive Council. On August 10 the Legislative Assembly suspended the King and called for the election of a National Convention. The mobs got out of hand, and between September 2 and 7, 1792, it is estimated that somewhere between 2,000 and 10,000 royalists were slain. A French Republic was proclaimed on September 22, 1792.

This foreign threat against the Revolution, and the declaration of war on these foreign enemies, enormously strengthened the sentiment of patriotism in France and vastly increased the element of radicalism in the Revolution. The brilliant victories of General Dumouriez against the foreign coalition electrified revolutionary France. But the dangers from abroad impressed the revolutionists with the necessity of safeguarding themselves from disloyalty and treason within the French boundaries—particularly the opposition of Royalists and Catholics. A Committee of Public Safety under the leadership of Robespierre was created to take active control of affairs, and the famous Reign of Terror resulted.[1] This was originally no wanton movement to butcher innocents. Rather, it was a serious attempt to organize France in a thorough fashion for national defense and to preserve the Revolution from its enemies both within and without. It was simply an extreme manifestation of the inevitable attempt to maintain unity and strength in a moment of extreme danger, such as we witnessed in our generation during the World War and in Russia after the Revolution of 1917. There is no doubt that the Committee of Public Safety and its associated Committee of General Security and Revolutionary Tribunal went to altogether unnecessary extremes in their tactics, but the nature and purpose of the "Terror" were logical and easily understandable.

In due time, this harsh policy subsided, partly because of the victories of the French armies, which reduced the danger from abroad, and partly because of the very excesses of the Terror, which discredited the extreme radicals. With the execution of Robespierre on July 28, 1794, the Terror collapsed.[2] A more conservative form of government was established in the so-called Directory, which succeeded the Convention in 1795. This was overthrown by Napoleon Bonaparte in 1799 when he introduced what was known as the Consulate. This lasted until 1804, when Napoleon created the First French Empire, which endured until Napoleon's banishment to Elba in 1814.

It may be helpful at this point to summarize briefly the nature of the political organization and control of France during the Revolutionary and Napoleonic periods.[3] The Estates-General lasted from May 4 to June 27, 1789. This was superseded by the National Constituent Assembly, which had control from June 27, 1789, to October 1, 1791. Then came the Legislative Assembly, which had a lifetime of approximately one year, from October 1, 1791, to September 20, 1792. The National Convention was installed on September 20, 1792, and remained in control until October 26, 1795. Then came the government of the Directory, which dominated affairs from October 27, 1795, to November 19, 1799. Napoleon ruled under the Consulate from 1799 to 1804, and under the Empire from 1804 to 1814. Down to the time of Napoleon all of these governmental experiments represented a definite victory for the middle class and the principle of representative government. Even under the personal rule of Napoleon some of the forms of representative government were preserved, and

---

[1] See, especially, Albert Mathiez, *The French Revolution*, Knopf, 1928, Bk. III, for an up-to-date interpretation.

[2] See Albert Mathiez, *The Fall of Robespierre*, Knopf, 1927, Chaps. IX-XII, and *After Robespierre, the Thermidorian Reaction*, Knopf, 1931.

[3] *Cf.* Leo Gershoy, *The French Revolution, 1789-1799*, Holt, 1932.

all the main reform measures put through by the middle class during the Revolution were perpetuated.

We may now turn to a consideration of the major reforms of the French Revolution, noticing, in particular, how they exemplified various phases of the middle-class program. It will be apparent as we go on that all the outstanding reforms were achieved before violence or terror had become characteristic of the French Revolution. The fundamental theoretical principles of the revolution were embodied in the famous Declaration of the Rights of Man enunciated on August 26, 1789.

The Declaration set forth the revolutionary version of the basic principles of human society. It declared that men are born free and equal with respect to their rights before the law. It held that all social distinctions are artificial and are only to be justified if they contribute to the well-being of the people. Government is created to preserve the natural rights of man. Liberty represents the freedom to do anything that does not injure another person. Its character and limits are determined by law, which, according to Rousseau, is a product of the general will.

The Declaration then proceeded to state the specific rights of man. It held that there should be no arbitrary imprisonment. Everybody was to be entitled to a fair legal trial. Freedom of speech and publication was guaranteed where this was not subversive of the public order. Taxes must be determined and levied by the representatives of the people. The Declaration also embodied a considerable amount of liberal rhetoric, particularly centering about the famous revolutionary slogans of Liberty, Fraternity, and Equality. Of these three principles, Fraternity received much the most emphasis during the Revolutionary period. It constituted the psychological core of the remarkable development of French nationalism in this era.

We can best appreciate the nature and significance of the French revolutionary reforms if we briefly summarize the more notable abuses of the old régime.[1] First we have the enormous extravagances of the king and the court, which formed an ever greater burden borne on the backs of the subjects. Next we have the wasteful exploitation inherent in the perpetuation of the old feudal and quasi-feudal nobility, which in 1789 numbered about 25,000 families.[2] In the medieval period, as we have seen, the nobles performed a very definite service to the state in administering justice and providing soldiers for the army. After the rise of the centralized royal administration in the seventeenth century the nobility no longer served any important purpose in French society. While compelled to abandon their pretensions to political power, the nobles still retained most of their social and economic privileges. They oppressed their peasants and serfs. They ignored the rights of the common people, often riding ruthlessly over the fields of grain when hunting, and maintaining for sporting purposes great flocks of pigeons that ravaged the fields of the neighboring farmers. They flocked to the royal court, greatly increased the expenses of the state, and thus added to the burdens that had to be met through the taxation of the middle class and the peasantry. The nobles could be largely irresponsible

[1] *Cf.* Sée, *op. cit.* [2] *Ibid.*, Chaps. IV-V.

and nonchalant in their waste and extravagance because they enjoyed wide exemption from taxation.

The Catholic Church in France was another source of vast expense and no little oppression.[1] The clergy at the time of the Revolution numbered in excess of 130,000. They owned somewhere between 6 per cent and 10 per cent of the land of France, enjoyed enormous revenues from fees, tithes, ecclesiastical dues, and the like, estimated at 100,000,000 livres annually, and were exempt from taxation. While there were many earnest and active priests, a considerable proportion of the French clergy had become worldly, lazy, and neglectful of their spiritual duties, thus losing the respect of the populace. This made the heavy burdens imposed by the Church all the more ridiculous and unpopular in the minds of many Frenchmen. The writings of Voltaire and others helped to inflame the intellectuals against the Church.

The peasants, who constituted about four-fifths of the population, had been very generally freed from serfdom.[2] There were only about a million serfs in France in 1789, and the French peasants were rather better off than the similar class elsewhere in Europe. Nevertheless, the French peasantry was subjected to an almost incredible array of diversified taxes. There were a number of direct taxes. Among these were ecclesiastical tithes and many old feudal taxes. Then there was the taille, a tax on the profits of lands held by the peasants. This was one of the most roundly hated of the direct taxes. There was also a 5 per cent income tax and the capitation or poll tax. Finally, we may note in this category the corvée or forced labor exacted of agricultural workers and farmers. There were, in addition, a large number of indirect taxes, such as the salt tax, the tobacco tax, the excise tax on wines and ciders, and custom duties levied not only at the frontier but also at the many internal customs boundaries. It has been estimated by a competent scholar that these taxes absorbed from 30 to 35 per cent of the annual income from the land, and the poorest classes paid the largest share. On top of all this was the fact that both the distribution and the collection of the taxes were grossly unequal and unjust.

The political and the legal situation of France cried equally for reform. The French administrative divisions had come down from medieval and early modern times. They were unequal in size and illogical in distribution and boundaries. There was a vast amount of overlapping and duplication in administration, thus increasing both public expenses and administrative confusion. The legal situation was extremely complicated and irrational. Roman, German, and French laws were in operation in various parts of France, thus recapitulating the whole legal experience of the country; altogether there were about four hundred different sets or bodies of law in existence. This made legal administration difficult and invited all sorts of corruption and oppression. The criminal law was still barbarous and brutal, permitting torture and cruel corporal punishments. The courts were, if anything, worse than the laws. The judges were venal and incompetent and litigation dragged out in scandalous fashion.

The National Assembly made a heroic effort to remedy the more flagrant abuses that existed in the old régime in France. Beginning with the action on

---

[1] See Sée, *op. cit.*, Chap. III.   [2] See *Ibid.*, Chaps. I-II.

the famous night of August 4-5, 1789, the more notable forms of privilege and oppression possessed by the nobility and clergy were either swept away or voluntarily surrendered. A decree was passed and signed by the King abolishing most vestiges of the feudal system in France. Its provisions constituted the most important single achievement of the whole French Revolution. Serfdom was abolished. The manorial courts were terminated. The hated hunting-rights and game laws were wiped out along with the pigeon houses and dovecotes. The flagrant exemptions of the nobility from taxation were ended, as also were the tithes and all ecclesiastical dues. The limitation of important public offices to the nobility was done away with and these offices were formally opened to all French citizens. It was once believed that the French nobles, when they surrendered their ancient privileges in August, 1789, and thereafter, were acting voluntarily and from benevolent motives. It has since been amply proved, however, that they were intimidated by threats and by rumors of peasant uprisings that were believed to endanger their property and the lives of their relatives back home.

Following on the heels of these reforms begun in early August, 1789, came a large number of other notable advances carried out under the auspices of the National Assembly. The old indirect taxes were abolished and a better system of direct taxation was installed. The old servile dues were abolished by laws of April, 1790.

Owing to the temporary difficulties in collecting direct taxes, the Church lands were seized as a source of revenue on November 2, 1789. They were further used as security for the issue of the famous French revolutionary paper money, the *assignats*.[1] In February, 1790, the monasteries and religious houses were suppressed, and on July 12, 1790, the Civil Constitution of the Clergy was proclaimed. This provided for the election of the French clergy by vote of the French citizens. The Jews and Protestants, as well as the Catholics, voted at their election—an unfair and offensive arrangement. The salaries of the clergy were to be paid by the state. These serious inroads on the ancient power of the Catholic Church in France lined up most of the clergy decisively against the Revolution. Many of them refused to take the oath of loyalty to the French government. These so-called nonjuring clergy fled from France, joined the self-exiled nobility, and coöperated in intrigue against the Revolution.

The political and legal reforms of the time were quite as striking. We have already seen how the Assembly provided France with its first constitution, that of 1791. The local administration of France was completely reorganized. The ancient and irrational administrative units were done away with and France was divided up into eighty-three new departments, approximately uniform in size and population. These were further subdivided in logical fashion. The unification, revision, and simplification of French laws was ordered, thus laying the basis for the later development of the Napoleonic code.[2] Many of the cruel criminal laws were swept away and a new system of law courts was ordered.

It will easily be seen that these measures represented most impressive gains for the French middle class and also incidentally very considerably bettered

---

[1] See *Cambridge Modern History*, Vol. VIII, Chap. XXIII; and S. E. Harris, *The Assignats*, Harvard University Press, 1930.   [2] See *Cambridge Modern History*, Vol. VIII, Chap. XXIV.

the lot of the French peasantry. These benefits were secured at the expense of the first two estates in the old French order of things—the clergy and the nobility. The victories of the French middle class were in many ways more dramatic and colorful than those won by the same class in the English or the American revolutions.

The absence of any powerful urban proletarian interests in the revolutionary policies may be seen in the passage of the law of June 14, 1791, which not only abolished guilds but also prohibited all combinations, agreements, and strikes of workingmen. But the law was passed quite as much to abolish antique labor associations as to shut off the development of the coming trade-unions.

The next important set of reforms were carried out by the National Convention between 1792 and 1795. The property of the fugitive nobility was confiscated. State control of grain prices was established. Many of the great estates of the nobles were divided up and offered for sale to poor citizens in small plots. The old ground rents were abolished. The separation of Church and State was decreed and religious toleration ordered. The work of the National Assembly in codifying and reforming the French legal code was continued with notable success. The ancient and barbarous features of the criminal code were still further pruned away. The laws of inheritance were modernized and the property rights of women recognized and protected. Slavery was abolished. A very notable program of public education, prepared by Talleyrand, Condorcet, and others, was recommended. A new and rational system of weights and measures—the metric system—was adopted.

Along with these substantial types of progress brought about by the National Convention went many unusual and amusing enactments. Revolutionary salutations, particularly "Citizen" Jones and "Citizen" Smith, were ordered. Revolutionary clothing was prescribed. A revolutionary calendar was adopted made up of twelve months of thirty days each, with five holidays at the end of the year, a division of the year very similar to the Egyptian calendar of 4241 B.C. These new months were directly related to the seasons and to the products of the various parts of the year. Even children were named after the more important dates or events of the revolutionary period, such as, for example, Fourteenth of July Smith, Tenth of August Jones, and Twentieth of June Brown. The worship of the Goddess of Reason was encouraged. But these lesser and often humorous reforms should not divert one's attention from the really notable achievements of the Convention.

Napoleon, both as First Consul and as Emperor, preserved most of the gains that the middle class had put through in the French Revolution. Himself derived from the middle class, Napoleon had little sympathy with a decadent hereditary nobility that had outgrown its usefulness. We have noted that in the case of the French Revolution the more important reforms came during the early years. The same was decisively the case in the reign of Napoleon. His most striking achievements in the field of public affairs were worked out during the Consulate.

In the purely political field he severely limited representative government and transferred most powers to the hands of the executive. But he carried on with thoroughness and success the process of reorganizing and administering the local government of France that had been begun by the Revolution. He brought to completion the centralizing processes of Richelieu and Mazarin and made France the best example of centralized government among all the major states of Europe. There was little place left for popular government or local democracy, but the system was remarkably uniform, responsible, and efficient in its operation.

Even more notable were Napoleon's legal and judicial reforms. He appointed a commission in August, 1800, to prepare a new civil code. Some five great legal codifications appeared between 1804 and 1808—the civil code, the code of criminal procedure, the commercial code, the code of civil procedure, and the penal code. These were achievements notable for both clarity of conception and simplicity of statement. They preserved most of the valuable social reforms of the Revolution, such as civil equality, religious toleration, equality of inheritance, the emancipation of the serfs, freedom of the land, legality of arrest, and trial by jury. There were some defects, such as the laws perpetuating female inferiority before the law, but in a very real sense Napoleon justified the title once conferred upon him of the "Second Justinian."

Napoleon also worked out a fairly satisfactory settlement of the Church problem, which had been hanging fire ever since the Civil Constitution of the Clergy in the early days of the Revolution. The Pope conceded the permanence of the confiscation of Church lands and the suppression of the monasteries. He also agreed to having the salaries of the clergy paid by the state. From his side, Napoleon made concessions that saved the sensibilities of the churchmen. While the bishops were to be nominated by the state, they were to be invested with the spiritual power and symbols of their office by the higher clergy. The priests were to be appointed by the bishops with the approval of the government. This settlement was made with Pope Pius VII on July 15, 1801.[1] It was known as the Concordat of 1801, and the arrangement lasted with little change until the separation of Church and State in France following 1905.

Napoleon's financial policies and legislation were so extensive and decisive that they have been known as "the new Colbertism." He carefully reorganized the system of taxation so as to lay the burden upon those best able to contribute. At first he relied chiefly on direct taxes, but the increased expenditures due to his many wars led him later to include a considerable number of indirect levies. The national debt was consolidated and stabilized. He established a very efficient administrative system in fiscal matters and severely punished corrupt officials. He created the Bank of France in 1800. He endeavored to promote industrial expansion by importing English mechanics, and offered liberal prizes for industrial inventions.[2]

Directly related to his financial policy were his distinguished achievements in the construction of public works. He built a large number of splendid commercial and military roads, including some across the Alps. He constructed many canals, canalized rivers, and built famous bridges. Marshy areas were drained and reclaimed. The leading harbors were enlarged and fortified. Espe-

[1] See H. H. Walsh, *The Concordat of 1801*, Columbia University Press, 1933.
[2] See below, pp. 326 ff.

cially notable were the public buildings he constructed in Paris as part of a general plan for making the French capital beautiful.

Napoleon also brought to completion the systematic plans for French public education that had been launched in the period of the Revolution. It was a highly centralized and supervised governmental system, about as precise and uniform as the local government of France itself. The Napoleonic educational program was improved upon somewhat by Carnot in 1848 and put into thorough operation by Jules Ferry in 1884.

Napoleon not only assured the permanence of middle-class revolutionary reforms in France but also carried these French reforms into other parts of Europe, particularly into Spain, Italy, the Rhine provinces, and Poland. Much of the stimulus to the revolutions of 1830 and 1848 in these areas can be attributed to the influence of the French Revolution operating through the so-called Napoleonic ideas. Even in areas that bitterly opposed Napoleon, the French revolutionary notions produced a powerful impact on the old régime. Most notably was this the case with Prussia, which, under Stein and Hardenberg, felt it necessary to introduce extensive political and social reforms in order to strengthen the state and effectively oppose Napoleon himself. Serfdom was ordered abolished by the edict of 1807. Even Latin America felt the reverberations of the French and Napoleonic influences, which were a powerful stimulus to the revolutionary movements throughout Latin America following 1812.

VI. THE REVOLUTIONS OF 1830, 1848, AND 1905

1. THE REVOLUTION OF 1830

We may now pass over in brief review the revolutions of 1830 and 1848 in Europe. These outbursts of middle-class feeling are sometimes treated quite independently of the English, American, and French revolutions, but in most cases they really represent the delayed Continental manifestation of the same general forces, principles, and aspirations that we have noted above in connection with these three great historic revolutionary movements. While the middle class became powerful enough to assert independence in England by the end of the eighteenth century, it was not sufficiently strong to triumph on the Continent outside of France until the middle of the nineteenth century or thereafter. In Russia the middle class did not become sufficiently potent to challenge the old order until the opening of the twentieth century.

There was a general wave of revolution over Europe in 1830.[1] The forces of reaction had been organized to oppose the principles of the French Revolution by the shrewd and alert Austrian autocrat, Prince Metternich (1773-1859), who kept the lid on for several decades after Waterloo. But the forces making for middle-class assertiveness and representative government could not be kept down indefinitely by anyone. In France, King Louis XVIII (1815-24) had been careful not to antagonize too seriously those Frenchmen who remained loyal to the achievements and institutions of the Revolutionary and Napoleonic eras, but Charles X (1824-30) was a fanatical Catholic royalist and a determined

[1] See Flick, *op. cit.*, Chap. x.

THE REVOLUTIONS OF 1830, 1848, AND 1905

supporter of the old order.[1] He desired to restore the France of the pre-Revolutionary epoch. In 1825 he appropriated nearly a billion francs to indemnify the nobility whose lands had been seized in the Revolution. He also attempted to restore the feudal system of primogeniture, which had been abolished by the Revolution. A broad law of 1826 against sacrilege raised the fear of a clerical reaction. Charles was known to be very sympathetic with the program and sentiments of the more reactionary Catholic clergy. When severe criticism arose, Charles endeavored to slap on a vigorous censorship. In 1830 he rashly issued the so-called July Ordinances, which suspended the liberty of the press, dissolved the new Chamber of Deputies, and altered the election law in such a manner as to restrict the power of the middle class and to increase that of the landed proprietors. This was too much. Active revolution broke out in Paris on July 28, 1830. The King and the royal troops were cleared out of the city in less than a week. The last Bourbon king of France was compelled to retire and a new dynasty, the House of Orléans, was given the throne in the person of Louis Philippe (1830-48). The latter was a confirmed friend of the middle class, and the Orleanist administration during the following eighteen years was a splendid example of a limited bourgeois monarchy.

Belgium had been influenced by French reforms and the spirit of nationalism. It had been annexed to Holland in 1815 but the union was never popular. In 1830 a revolution broke out. The leaders demanded independence and middle-class reforms. In 1830-31 a conference of the European Powers meeting in London finally accepted the Belgian Revolution and guaranteed the neutrality of Belgium. The Belgian constitution adopted in 1831 was widely copied in middle-class revolutions thereafter.

Among the German states Prussia and Austria remained immune to revolution, but in some of the smaller states, such as Brunswick, Saxony, Hanover, and Hesse-Cassel, revolutions broke out and constitutions and reforms were granted. Revolutions started in 1831 in northern and central Italy, but Louis Philippe was not yet sufficiently well installed in France to make it safe for him to intervene in behalf of the Italian revolutionists. This made it possible for Austria to step in and quickly crush these premature Italian uprisings.

Poland had been particularly affected by the French Revolution and Napoleon, for the latter had directly introduced into Poland many of the more notable French reforms and had distinctly stimulated Polish nationalism. The old historical Kingdom of Poland had disappeared as a result of the three partitions of 1772, 1793, and 1795. Alexander I of Russia desired to restore Poland, but Prussia and Austria refused to give up their share of the spoil. Therefore, in 1815 there were four Polands—Austrian, Prussian, and Russian Poland, and the Republic of Cracow created in 1815. In November, 1830, Russian Poland broke into active revolt.[2] The Poles had hoped for French aid but this was not forthcoming. By September, 1831, the Poles were hopelessly defeated.

In England the most important reaction of the revolutions of 1830 was to be found in the famous parliamentary Reform Bill of 1832. The supremacy of Parliament had been secured by the Revolution of 1688-89, but the representa-

[1] F. B. Artz, *France under the Bourbon Restoration*, Harvard University Press, 1931.
[2] Impelled more by nationalism than by middle-class aspirations.

tive districts for the election of the members of Parliament had not been changed since early modern times. The new industrial cities were therefore very inadequately represented, and the whole set-up of the districts notoriously favored the Tory landholding group. Hence it was much to the interest of the middle class to reconstruct the representative districts throughout England. This program was embodied in the Reform Bill of 1832, which became law on June 7 of that year. This was a crucial victory for the middle-class Whigs in British politics. They also made a lesser gain in the reform of the franchise, which was considerably extended to members of the lower middle class. Universal suffrage was not, however, secured at this time. The more prosperous city workers were given the right to vote in 1867. The better class of peasants were granted the right of suffrage in 1884. Universal manhood suffrage was not secured until late in 1918. At this time limited woman suffrage was also granted; the restrictions were removed by an act of 1928.

2. THE REVOLUTIONS OF 1848

Outside of France, Belgium, and some of the lesser German states the revolutionary movement of 1830 was abortive and unsuccessful. Between 1830 and 1848, however, the middle class grew in strength in Europe as a result of the increasing commercial and industrial activity. In some states, particularly in France, the more radical members of the middle class were aided by the new industrial workers, who had grown in numbers as a result of the beginnings of the Industrial Revolution.

At the outset, Louis Philippe of France had been inclined to establish a liberal business administration, but insurrections broke out in 1832, and in 1835 attempts were made on the life of the King himself. This led to the enactment of rather reactionary and oppressive laws in September of 1835. These weakened the Orleanist rule. The growing French working class particularly resented the increasingly reactionary policies of Louis Philippe and joined with the more radical members of the middle class in agitating for revolutionary reforms and the establishment of a republic. Dynastic elements also entered, for Louis Napoleon Bonaparte, nephew of the great Emperor, was laying plans to restore the Bonaparte dynasty. He was able to draw on the immense sentimental attachment of many Frenchmen to the glorious memories of the brilliant Napoleonic era.

To aid him in checking the growth of discontent and revolution, Louis Philippe called to his aid as Prime Minister the eminent French publicist and historian, Guizot. He remained in office from 1840 to 1848. Guizot was attached to the middle class but belonged decidedly to the conservative wing. He believed that no changes in the French system were necessary or desirable. Guizot and Louis Philippe were able to keep in control of affairs until the close of 1847, but gradually all parties joined together in the opposition—middle-class liberals, radical republicans, Socialists, and Bonapartists. Active rioting broke out late in February, 1848, and on February 24 Louis Philippe abdicated and fled to England, where he died in exile in 1850.

The Second French Republic was accordingly set up on February 24. This passed through three main stages. The first was the working-class phase, which lasted from February 24 to May 4, 1848. In this period the influence and theories of the labor leader Louis Blanc were dominant. But the more conservative republicans conspired to defeat his program and drive out the radicals. They succeeded, and a middle-class republic was set up on May 4, which lasted until December 20, 1848. Slowly but surely the sentiment for another Bonaparte grew in strength, and on December 20, 1848, Louis Napoleon was elected President of the conservative republic. He ruled under republican forms until the close of the year 1851. Then, as Napoleon III, he was able to transform the Second Republic into the Second Empire. This empire lasted until the defeat of France by Prussia in 1870-71. Though an empire, the régime of Napoleon III was really devoted to middle-class ideals and to the promotion of business prosperity. He especially favored the trading classes through liberal tariff policies. From 1848 onward it was very apparent that the old order, ruled by the king and the nobility, could never again be restored in France.

The forces making for revolution had increased so notably between 1830 and 1848 that not even Austria-Hungary was able to escape their impact in the latter year. This ancient Hapsburg monarchy was the center of European reaction. The reforms introduced by its liberal monarch Joseph II, which were described above,[1] had been cast aside, and the country still remained a medieval feudal society in most aspects of its public and economic life. Its real ruler from the Napoleonic era to the Revolution of 1848 was Prince Metternich, the most aggressive, astute, and successful opponent of the middle-class liberalism exemplified by the French Revolution and its associated developments. He was the implacable foe of both nationality and liberalism. But these principles had become so potent by 1848 that even Metternich could no longer keep them thoroughly bottled up. Revolutions broke out in the various Austrian dominions, particularly Hungary, Bohemia, and northeastern Italy. Their reverberations even reached Vienna and forced Metternich into temporary exile.

The Kingdom of Hungary had come under Austrian Hapsburg rule in 1526. Down to the middle of the nineteenth century it remained a reactionary feudal state. The first important steps taken toward reform were embodied in the program of Count István Széchenyi, a Hungarian nobleman who desired to improve the material and intellectual conditions of Hungary and to make his country one of the most powerful and prosperous states of Europe. In the field of political reform and liberalism, however, he was very timid. Consequently, leadership passed to more liberal men. Of these the most colorful was Louis Kossuth (1802-94). He was a typical liberal and patriot. He attacked the political and legal aspects of the old régime, demanding the abolition of the privileges of the nobility, equal legal rights for all citizens, trial by jury, and the reform of the criminal code. Even more advanced was the program of another Hungarian liberal leader, Ferencz Deák (1803-76). He worked for the taxation of the nobles; the control of national expenditures by the Hungarian Diet, the liberty of the press, public meetings and political associations; and Hungarian independence.

On March 3, 1848, Kossuth made a fiery speech in the Hungarian Diet condemning the old régime in Hungary and denouncing the evil influence of

[1] See above, p. 93.

Austria upon Hungary. His speech was translated into German and circulated among the Vienna mobs. The result was a riot in Vienna that frightened Metternich, and he fled to London for safety. The Hungarian Diet proceeded to pass the famous March Laws of 1848, which abolished most aspects of feudalism in Hungary; proclaimed the fundamental principles of liberalism, such as religious toleration, freedom of the press, and trial by jury; and made Hungary practically an independent nation by demanding that the only connection with Austria should be the personal dynastic union according to which the Emperor of Austria should at the same time be the King of Hungary. In all other ways Hungary was to be an independent nation. Austria, with its hands full at home, acquiesced on March 31, 1848.

The Austrian reactionaries gained in strength in the later months of 1848, and war broke out with Hungary. The Hungarians were victorious, and in the enthusiasm of their national triumph declared Hungary an independent republic with Kossuth as president. This alarmed the reactionary Russian Tsar, Nicholas I, who had no desire to have a powerful republic among his neighbors. When he was invited by the Austrian Emperor, Francis Joseph, to send an army to aid the Austrians he was only too willing to do so. The Hungarians, though greatly outnumbered, fought bravely against the Austrians and the Russians, but they were crushed in August, 1849, and their country was reduced to the status of a dependent province of Austria until 1867. The arrangements of the latter year brought into being the Austro-Hungarian Dual Monarchy, which lasted until the close of the World War, when Austria-Hungary was separated and both states were dismembered.

In Bohemia also both nationalism and middle-class liberalism were inseparably intertwined. The Czechs, a Slavic people who predominated in Bohemia, desired autonomy or independence. The middle class resented the restrictions that had hung over from the old feudal age. Encouraged by the events in Hungary, the Bohemian Diet sent a delegation to Vienna demanding political and legal liberalism, freedom of the press and religion, the power to determine their own taxation, and autonomy in local government. These demands were conceded by the Austrian Emperor on April 8, 1848.

Nationalism, however, undermined liberalism in Bohemia as it had in Hungary. In the first place, the Czechs quarreled with the Germans in Bohemia over the question of independence versus union with either Austria or Germany. Further, the Czechs called a Panslavic Congress to meet at Prague in June, 1848. This was made up of Czechs, Moravians, Ruthenians, Croats, and Serbs—the numerous Slavic peoples under the dominion of Austria. They could not understand each other when speaking in their several Slavic tongues, so, to their vast humiliation, they had to conduct their proceedings in the despised German language of their hated Austrian masters. The quarrels among these Slavs led to a riot in Prague on June 12. Taking advantage of the confusion, the Austrian general Windischgrätz stepped in and made himself dictator of Bohemia on June 17. Austria repudiated its concessions to Bohemia and the status quo was soon restored.

In Austrian Italy the revolutionary spirit of middle-class liberalism had been particularly fanned by nationalistic aspirations set forth by Giuseppe Mazzini

(1805-72) and other Italian patriots. Revolution broke out among the Austrian states in northern Italy and at first the Emperor had to acquiesce. But jealousy among the various Italian states offered Vienna its chance. The Austrian general Radetzky recovered Lombardy and Venetia after his victory at Custozza at the close of July, 1848. Revolution spread in other parts of Italy—in Tuscany, the Papal States, and Naples. Constitutional government and unity seemed imminent, but jealousy and stupidity postponed their realization until 1870.

Even in Austria itself revolution could not be averted in 1848. The liberals demanded a constitution, the protection of personal liberties, and an increase in the right of self-government. Weakened by revolution throughout the Empire, Austria was compelled to grant these demands. The Austrian Diet abolished feudalism in the Hapsburg domains on July 22, 1848. The revolutionists forced the Emperor Ferdinand I and Metternich to flee from Vienna for safety. But General Windischgrätz was recalled from Prague and suppressed the Vienna Revolution on October 31, 1848. The reactionary party, now victorious in Vienna, forced Ferdinand to resign and chose as Emperor Francis Joseph I, a nephew of Ferdinand, who was only eighteen years of age at the time. Francis Joseph had one of the longest reigns in recorded history, retaining his crown until his death in 1916 in the midst of the World War. Prince Felix Schwarzenberg succeeded the deposed Metternich as the leader of autocracy and reaction in Vienna. Therefore, though Metternich himself passed from the scene, he had the satisfaction of seeing his system restored after having withstood the shock of the mid-century revolutions.

Nevertheless, though political reaction was revived, great progress had been brought about in the social and economic realms by the revolutions of 1848. The feudal system had been outlawed throughout the Austrian possessions, though it required many years to remove all its vestiges in practice. Indeed Hungary, even in the period since the World War, is still dominated by the great landed magnates, who were able to resist the agrarian reforms proposed after the World War by Count Károlyi.

The revolutions in the Italian Peninsula were also put down through the aid of the armies of reactionary Austria. The liberal King Charles Albert of Piedmont was defeated at the battle of Novara on March 23, 1849. The Florentine Republic of Tuscany was crushed. Even supposedly liberal France came to the aid of the Pope and overthrew the Roman Republic at the end of June, 1849. In March, 1849, the King of Naples put down the revolution in Naples and Sicily and made absolutism secure for the moment in southern Italy. Only in the Kingdom of Piedmont and Sardinia did liberalism survive in Italy after the ill-fated revolutions of 1848. Here Charles Albert abandoned his throne in favor of his son, Victor Emmanuel II. The young king soon called to his assistance the shrewd and industrious statesman Count Camillo Cavour (1810-61). As a result of their joint efforts Italy attained unity in the following generation, after a struggle that culminated with the seizure of Rome from the Pope in 1870.[1] National unity and middle-class political liberalism were at last assured in the Italian Peninsula.

The revolutionary movement of 1848 also swept over the German states out-

---

[1] See below, pp. 459 ff.

side of Austrian possessions. In Prussia the people demanded the establishment of a constitutional monarchy. Frederick William IV, King of Prussia (1840-58), refused to grant this demand and dissolved the Prussian Landtag in June, 1847. A serious constitutional crisis thus existed in Prussia on the eve of the revolutions that broke out early in 1848. Barricades were erected in Berlin in the middle of March, 1848, and Frederick William was forced to agree to call the Landtag in order to draw up a constitution for Prussia. The revolutionary movement quickly spread beyond Prussia. A great parliament of liberal German delegates met at Frankfort on May 18, 1848, and remained in session for exactly thirteen months. The real purpose of the parliament was to bring about German unity and to secure a constitution for a new and united German Empire.

The Frankfort Parliament failed for a number of reasons. Few of its members had any knowledge of or experience with constitutional government. No practical program or constitution was ready to be submitted. There were many fiery patriots and liberals in the parliament who insisted upon long and frequent speeches on the general principles of liberty and patriotism, thus wasting a vast amount of precious time in eloquent but costly rhetoric. This lost time was crucial, because it was during this period that the reactionaries were regaining their hold in the Austrian domains and getting in shape to intervene elsewhere.

The Frankfort Parliament was forced to face two basic problems, namely, what should be included in the united Germany, and who should be called to head the new German Empire. If all of the Austrian possessions were included, this would produce a heterogeneous population of Germans, Slavs, and Magyars. It would be next to impossible to create a close federal union out of such a mixture of peoples spread over far-flung areas. On the other hand, to include only German Austria would break up the unity of Austria, and the latter country naturally objected to any such proposal. It was decided, nevertheless, that the new Germany should be constituted solely of Germanic states and that the non-German Austrian possessions must be excluded. This turned Austria against the proposal to unify Germany.

It was next decided to offer the title of German Emperor to King Frederick William IV of Prussia, who back in 1848 had agreed to accept it if it were ever offered to him. But now he hesitated. He disliked to take a crown as the gift of an unholy revolutionary assembly when it should have come from God or, at the very least, from a council of German princes. Further, he was fearful of the opposition of Austria and certain strong German states, such as Bavaria, Württemberg, Saxony, and Hanover. Therefore on April 28, 1849, he definitely refused the new imperial crown. The Frankfort Parliament soon had to disband in humiliation.

Frederick William then tried to form a new imperial union with Prussia at its head, roughly similar to that which came in 1871. But Prince Schwarzenberg, the reactionary leader in Austria, compelled him to abandon this plan.[1]

[1] This withdrawal of Frederick William is known as the Humiliation of Olmütz from the name of the place where Frederick William's representative had acquiesced in Schwarzenberg's demands.

Austrian supremacy within the German states was once more asserted and German unity further postponed. A young Prussian squire who was greatly distressed by this Prussian surrender to Austrian dictation, Otto von Bismarck, led the Prussians in a crushing victory over Austria in 1866 and then defeated France in 1870. The result was that Austria was driven into a subordinate position among the German states, and German unity was at last secured after a thousand years of futile efforts to attain it.[1]

In spite of the failure to secure unity and constitutional government for all the German states, Frederick William was induced to grant a constitution to Prussia in January, 1850. In 1847 he had said that he would never allow a "scrap of paper to come between him and God," but in 1850 he did so. The movements for constitutional government in other German states, especially Saxony, Baden, and the Rhenish Palatinate, were suppressed by local and Prussian troops.

In central Europe and Italy the revolutions of 1848 were brought about by the same mercantile and business classes that had many years before carried through the English, American, and French revolutions. There was as yet little of the new mechanical industry in these areas. The urban proletariat were weak and few. There was therefore little working-class radicalism or real democracy in these revolutionary movements. In France, on the other hand, we have already seen that the more progressive business liberals were aided in revolutionary activities by the urban workers.

In England in 1848, the uprising was primarily a proletarian movement.[2] This was because England was a century ahead of central Europe in its social and economic evolution. The radicalism of 1848 in England centered around what is known as the Chartist movement, which began to develop in the thirties.[3] The Chartist leaders drew up a Great Charter or proletarian Bill of Rights comprising some six points designed to advance the political rights and powers of the working classes. These six points were: (1) Universal manhood suffrage; (2) equal electoral districts; (3) the elimination of property qualifications for members of Parliament; (4) the payment of parliamentary members; (5) vote by secret ballot; and (6) annual sessions of Parliament.

The Chartists agitated for a decade. On April 10, 1848, a great Chartist demonstration was called in London. The government in alarm summoned Metternich's old friend, the aged Duke of Wellington, to lead the army against any possible rioters. A great storm made it necessary to call off the Chartist demonstration, and the movement collapsed as a result of the threat of force and the scorn of critics.[4] Nevertheless, five of these six points of the Chartists have since been secured, thus attesting to the growth of the power of the working classes and of political democracy in England. Only annual sessions of Parliament remain to be secured.

A bloody uprising took place in Paris in 1871 after the withdrawal of the

[1] See below, pp. 459 ff.
[2] See J. L. LeB. and Barbara Hammond, *The Age of the Chartists, 1832-1854*, Longmans, 1930.
[3] See F. F. Rosenblatt, *The Social and Economic Aspects of the Chartist Movement*, Columbia University Press, 1917; H. U. Faulkner, *Chartism and the Churches*, Columbia University Press, 1917; and Hammond and Hammond, *op. cit.*
[4] See P. W. Slosson, *The Decline of the Chartist Movement*, Columbia University Press, 1916.

Prussian troops. Known as the Communard Movement, it was a revolt somewhat similar to the first stages of the French Revolution of 1848, namely, an effort to introduce radical social democracy. It also aimed to give greater autonomy to the larger urban areas, especially Paris. It was brutally suppressed after a far greater loss of life and property than took place in the Reign of Terror in the first French Revolution.

3. THE RUSSIAN REVOLUTION OF 1905

Russia was even more backward in its social, economic, and political evolution than central Europe. Hence the movements for middle-class revolution and political liberalism that swept over central Europe in 1830 and 1848 did not come to Russia until the opening of the twentieth century. To be sure, serfdom had been abolished on the imperial lands in July, 1858, and on the estates of nobles by the great Edict of Emancipation of March 3, 1861. But political liberalism and representative government made little headway until the Revolution of 1905.

Beginning about 1890, Russia began slowly to introduce modern mechanical methods, the factory system, and up-to-date methods of transportation.[1] The leader in industrializing Russia was Count Sergius Witte (1849-1915), one of the ablest statesmen of modern times.

As a result of even this preliminary invasion of Russia by the new economy there developed a considerable group of middle-class capitalists and political liberals. They demanded some share in the autocratic state dominated by the Romanov tyrants and their oppressive spies and police. But, as has been usual in such instances, these demands only led to the tightening-up of the reactionary elements. Count Witte was dismissed in 1903 because of the opposition of the Russian reactionaries. The Tsar called to his aid a notorious conservative minister, V. K. Plehve, who was in sympathy with the archreactionary adviser to the Tsar, Pobiedonostsev. They organized vigorously every autocratic force in Russia in the effort to repress the liberal demands. Oppressive decrees were passed with the design of intimidating and destroying liberal opposition.

The rotten autocratic system was, however, soon discredited and undermined as a result of Russia's humiliating and rapid defeat in the Russo-Japanese War of 1904-05. Plehve was assassinated in 1904 and the Tsar was compelled to grant some minor concessions to the liberals. They were not satisfied, however, and insisted upon: (1) The granting of a constitution; (2) the establishment of the conventional liberal civil rights in Russia; (3) the guarantee of the freedom of conscience, speech, publication, and public meetings; and (4) the establishment of representative government. The Tsar refused, and as a result revolution broke out in January, 1905.

The Tsar and his associates endeavored to stem the tide of liberalism, but in October, 1905, a general strike was declared. The autocrats then gave way to some degree. In June, 1905, the Tsar had agreed to call a national assembly, and in August he provided for its creation during the coming January. He dismissed his more reactionary ministers and once more summoned Count Witte

---
[1] There had been some industrialization in Poland at an earlier date.

to act as Premier. On October 30, 1905, the Tsar issued a manifesto guaranteeing civil liberties, liberalizing the franchise for the election of the new assembly—the Duma—and conceding that henceforth no law should be executed without the consent of that body. But the Tsar and his associates were motivated by fear rather than sincerity. They did their best to insure reactionary intimidation of the Duma when it met. Witte was dismissed in April, 1906, and supplanted by conservatives, Goremykin and Stolypin.

The first Duma met on May 10, 1906. The leading group in the opposition to the Tsar were the Constitutional Democrats, or so-called Cadets. Their leader was the distinguished Russian professor of history and law, Paul Milyukov. The Duma proceeded to enact laws establishing political liberalism in Russia, and demanded that the ministry should be responsible to the Duma instead of the Tsar. The Tsar refused and dismissed the Duma on July 21, 1906. The Cadets then went to Viborg in Finland and issued the so-called Viborg Manifesto in imitation of the famous French Tennis Court Oath of 1789. They exhorted the Russian people to stand firm for constitutionalism and liberalism. But the manifesto proved ineffective and the revolution gradually collapsed. Reaction set in once more. Russia went into the World War still under autocratic rule.

The World War undermined the Romanov régime far more thoroughly than the Russo-Japanese War. The Cadet group established a constitutional monarchy in March, 1917. A more radical government, dominated by the Social Revolutionaries, the agrarian Socialist party of Russia, came into power with Kerensky in the summer of 1917. In November, 1917,[1] a group of Marxian socialists, the Bolsheviks, took over the government in the name of the city workers. They established the Soviet Russia of today.[2] The Tsar paid with his life the penalty for his reactionary policies and timidity. His associates among the Russian courtiers and nobles were either killed or driven into exile.

4. THE BOURGEOIS REVOLUTIONS PROMOTE NATIONALISM

It has been evident throughout our survey of the revolutions from 1642 to 1905 that the middle-class liberals were interested fundamentally in insuring representative government, in bringing about the guarantee of personal liberties, and in securing proper constitutional protection of property.[3] But these movements also did much to stimulate the growth of nationalism after the Treaty of Westphalia in 1648. In a later chapter we shall trace the origins of contemporary nationalism,[4] but it is in order at this place to indicate briefly the connection between these middle-class revolutions and the development of national spirit.[5]

The period of the Commonwealth under Cromwell stimulated English national spirit, particularly as a result of the brilliant naval victories over the Dutch and the suppression of revolution in Catholic Ireland. The "Glorious Revolution" of 1688-89 is the greatest event in the history of British liberalism

---

[1] October, according to the old-style Russian calendar.   [2] See below, pp. 986 ff.
[3] Cf. W. J. Durant, *Mansions of Philosophy,* Simon & Schuster, 1929, Chap. xvii; and Whipple, op. cit.   [4] See below, Chapter xiii.
[5] J. H. Rose, *Nationality in Modern History,* Macmillan, 1916, Lectures I-IV; and Julien Benda, *Discours à la nation européenne,* Paris, 1933.

and has been properly honored in perhaps the most famous of all British historical works, Macaulay's *History of England*. This revolution was followed up immediately by brilliant foreign wars, especially the War of the Spanish Succession. The merchant friends of revolution were also particularly enthusiastic in their support of colonization and of the creation of the British Empire.[1]

The American Revolution transformed thirteen jealous and quarreling colonies into the first great federal republic of human history. At the time of the Albany Congress of 1754 the colonists would not unite even for their own defense. By the time of the purchase of Louisiana in 1803 even the states-rights Jeffersonian Republicans had succumbed to centralization and the principle of nationality.

The French Revolution and the Napoleonic period in France constituted the most powerful impulse to nationalism prior to the Industrial Revolution of the nineteenth century. A psychological justification for nationalism was found in the popular slogan of Fraternity. The glorious foreign wars, replete with victories, that were fought by the revolutionists and Napoleon enormously enriched the already strong military tradition in France. The reforms of the revolutionists and Napoleon completed the process of centralizing the French administration. Napoleon's conquests carried the ideal of nationality into lands outside of France, some directly and some as a defense against French aggression. Italy and Poland were good examples of the direct transmission of nationalism from France, while Prussia, Spain, and Austria were perhaps the best illustrations of rising nationalism as a barricade against French dominion.

The element of nationality was everywhere prominent in the revolutions of 1830 and 1848. It was even more powerful than middle-class economic and political aspirations in Belgium, Poland, and Italy in 1830. In 1848 nationality so complicated the economic, political, and legal program of the middle class as to defeat most of these revolutions. In Hungary, Bohemia, and again in Italy, nationality was a more powerful force than liberalism. The inability to restrain it within discreet bounds was chiefly responsible for the collapse of the revolutions in Hungary and Bohemia, and seriously weakened those in the lesser states of Italy.

Even in Russia in 1905 nationalism played a prominent part. The patriotic resentment of the Russians over the defeat of their armies in the Far East was the main factor in preparing the groundwork of the revolution. Moreover, the Cadets linked hands enthusiastically with the most extreme Russian reactionaries in supporting the Panslavic program of the Russian nationalists.

It is thus readily apparent that middle-class revolutionary movements from the seventeenth century to the twentieth were quite as potent as the absolute monarchs of earlier times in stimulating the development and psychological power of the national-state system. It was the failure to recognize this important historical fact that did more than anything else to encourage the futile hope of many liberal pacifists before 1914 that constitutional government or democracy would constitute a safeguard against war.[2]

These developments which we have briefly summarized brought to a final

---

[1] See *Cambridge Modern History*, Vol. VI, Chap. vi.   [2] See below, pp. 612 ff., 914 ff.

conclusion one of the great stages in the evolution of human society and social institutions, namely, feudalism. The ending of feudalism is frequently obscured in accounts of contemporary battles, political maneuvers, and dynastic changes, but it is of far greater significance than all of these. The termination of feudalism was an incident in the triumph of nationalism and middle-class liberalism, the rise of the bourgeoisie, and the dominion of the new urban and business order. Looking at the matter broadly, it is true to say that the absolute monarchs put an end to feudalism in a political and legal sense, while it remained for the middle class to wipe out its economic and social vestiges.

In England feudalism had vanished in a political sense by the time of the rise of the Tudor monarchy in 1485, and its social and economic hangovers had disappeared by the close of the Revolution of 1648. But even in a social and economic sense feudalism had little sway in England after the sixteenth century. In France feudalism was wiped out politically by Richelieu and Mazarin in the first half of the seventeenth century; its social and economic vestiges were ended by the reforms of the Revolution following August 4, 1789. In Prussia political feudalism was disrupted by the centralizing policies initiated by the Great Elector (1640-88) and it was wiped out socially and economically following the Edict of Emancipation of 1807 in the period of "Regeneration." In Austria feudalism was ended in both a political and an economic sense during the Revolution of 1848, though the old landed nobility still maintain their dominion in Hungary. In Russia political feudalism was largely broken up during the eighteenth century by the centralizing activities of Peter the Great and Catherine. Serfdom was legally abolished in the middle of the nineteenth century, but the social and economic phases of feudalism actually persisted down to the Revolution of 1917. Feudalism disappeared in Italy as an aspect of the process of liberalization and unification between 1830 and 1870. In Spain political feudalism was dealt a heavy blow by Philip II (1556-98), but its social and economic aspects did not fully disappear until the Revolution of 1931.

VII. THE ORIGINS OF CONSTITUTIONAL GOVERNMENT AND THE GROWING POPULARITY OF REPUBLICS

The ideals of the middle class from the seventeenth century to the twentieth are clear enough—nationalism, freedom for business enterprise, the protection of property, and the guarantee of civil liberties. But it was necessary to do something more than to enunciate and eulogize these ideals. They had to be put where they could be applied, made permanent, and be protected. In short, it was necessary to create constitutions, which would embody these ideals and make them the basis of the law and politics of the state. Hence the growing power of the middle class and the success of revolutions was everywhere accompanied by the rise of constitutional government.

Back of the rise of all constitutions lie basic aspirations and principles. First, there is the conception of a higher or absolute law, to which any and all secular rulers are subordinate. Second, there is the notion of primordial and inalienable individual rights—such as life, liberty, and property. Finally, there is the notion of a sacred written charter, embodying the higher law and personal rights and immune to change except through a formal and indubitable expression of the public will. Constitutional government states the supreme law, enumerates individual rights, and places all on semisacred parchment.

While constitutional law and comparative government may be very difficult and technical subjects, there is no reason why one cannot make clear the general nature and significance of constitutions. A constitution may be defined in general terms as the organic instrument of government. It creates the form and functions of political institutions and machinery, and also prescribes the rights and immunities of the individual citizen. For example, a constitution determines whether or not a state will be a monarchy or a republic; it may prescribe either executive or parliamentary ascendancy in the government, or it may distribute the powers of government equally among the executive, legislative, and judicial branches as is theoretically done in the United States; it may describe in detail the nature, terms, and mode of election of the various members of each department of the government; and it may specifically enumerate the liberties and immunities of the individual citizen under the particular form of government created. In short, the constitution defines and describes the legal rights of the citizen and the structure and operation of the government that is to make him secure in the enjoyment of these rights. As Professor Hamilton puts it: "A law for the government, safeguarding individual rights, set down in writing—that is the constitution."

A constitution may be a very precise written document, worked out all at one time by a specific constitutional convention. Or it may be a collection of documents and precedents running over many centuries. Our federal Constitution is a good example of the first, and the English constitution of the second.

In the period with which we are concerned, following the middle of the seventeenth century, constitutions have been mainly the creation of the middle classes. But any dominant class can make and operate a constitution. Constitutional government may well support a landed aristocracy, as does that of Hungary today. It may just as well bring into being a proletarian régime that virtually outlaws both the landed nobility and the middle-class capitalists. Such has been the result of the constitution of Soviet Russia in our day. But thus far in modern history the movement for constitutions has been so closely linked with the program and activities of the middle class that we may almost identify the desire for, and the creation of, constitutions with the interests and strategy of that class. Down to 1789 the middle-class constitutions were designed to protect property from assault by royalty and nobility. The United States set the precedent in creating a constitution to protect property against industrial workers and peasants—that is, to protect the middle class from those below it.

The political institutions and policies of the Western world since the seventeenth century have reflected the economic, social, and political ambitions and ideals of the capitalistic middle class. These were chiefly legal protection of property, enforcement of contract, and a large degree of freedom in personal and business initiative.[1] Everywhere the bourgeoisie have been fearful of state interference with economic activities, except where this interference has been

---

[1] W. P. Larkin, *Property in the Eighteenth Century*, Dublin, 1930.

believed to foster the interests of the capitalist class. They have been opposed to social legislation designed to protect the working classes and hence likely to hamper the freedom of the employer to deal with his employees as he sees fit.

Most modern constitutions have embodied the fundamental bourgeois ideals of freedom from arbitrary governmental interference and assured the protection of personal rights and property interests. The fundamental rights and immunities for all men and the appropriate guarantees of economic liberty were embodied in the first ten Amendments to the American Constitution—really an integral part of the document, since they were all added immediately. The French Declaration of the Rights of Man, drawn up in 1789, mentions property among the "natural and imprescriptible rights of man" in Article 2, and in Article 17 also describes it as "an inviolable and sacred right."

The great advantage of a constitution to the middle-class business man is that it gives a certain fixity and permanence to the political system and renders him and his business relatively free from arbitrary change and interference on the part of the government. Neither king, peasant, noble, nor worker can arbitrarily invade business or interfere with property. Not only are life and liberty made secure within prescribed limits, but also the rights and privileges of property have been carefully defined in most constitutions since the middle of the eighteenth century. This notion of the immunity of business from governmental control has received its most notable recognition in the judicial interpretation of the "due process" clause in the Fourteenth Amendment to the Constitution of the United States. This states that no "state shall deprive any person of life, liberty or property without due process of law." In our constitutional law, business corporations have been admitted as persons in legal cases, and they are protected by the Fourteenth Amendment. "Due process of law" is so broad a conception that it opens up the widest opportunity for judges sympathetic with the propertied groups to set aside any legislation unfavorable to corporate business interests.[1]

The relative stability of constitutional governments and their specific guarantees of political and economic rights to the propertied classes have been the chief reasons why the triumph of the bourgeoisie in politics throughout the Western world has been characterized by the immediate adoption of written constitutions. The degree of fixity and rigidity in constitutional government varies greatly.[2] In Great Britain Parliament can legally amend the constitution with as little formal difficulty as it meets in passing a bill appropriating a petty sum for repairing a local bridge. In the United States the process of amendment is so extremely difficult that only eleven Amendments have been added since the original ten were embodied over a hundred and forty years ago. But even in England constitutional changes are infrequent and never undertaken in a light-hearted manner. This is due chiefly to the British reverence for precedent and their reluctance to experiment rashly. In practice, then, the English constitution is not so easy to alter in any fundamental sense. Almost without exception, constitutions have been changed slowly and infrequently, and con-

[1] See R. L. Mott, *Due Process of Law,* Bobbs-Merrill, 1926.
[2] See Charles Borgeaud, *The Adoption and Amendment of Constitutions in Europe and America.* Macmillan, 1895.

stitutional government has been characterized by relative certainty and permanence. The middle class have thus far been vindicated by historical experience in their reliance upon constitutional government as a guarantee against either royal arbitrariness or proletarian radicalism. There should be no further difficulty in understanding the vast devotion of contemporary American business men to the Constitution and its sanctity.

While the first important written constitution of modern times was the so-called Instrument of Government drawn up by Cromwell for his Commonwealth government, constitutions are by no means a product of modern history. Aristotle is said to have studied the text of some hundred and fifty-eight constitutions to serve as the basis of his book on the *Athenian Constitution*. The forerunners of modern written constitutions were the charters granted to the medieval towns, to the English colonies in America, and to chartered trading companies. The English constitution is a curious combination of various documents dating from the Magna Charta of the first quarter of the thirteenth century to the Parliamentary Reform Bill of 1911 and certain important readjustments since the World War. Among the most important of these documents are the Magna Charta (1215), the Petition of Right (1628), the Bill of Rights (1688-89) and the legislation immediately following it, the Reform Bill of 1832, the Suffrage Acts of 1867, 1884, and 1918, the Parliament Bill of 1911, and the Suffrage Acts of 1918 and 1928. In addition, there are other things that go to make up the English Constitution, such as "the privileges of Parliament," the Conventions of the Constitution, the Common Law, and the like.

The first great crop of written constitutions in modern society was of those adopted by the American states after the Declaration of Independence in 1776.[1] They were founded on the precedents of the colonial charters, the revolutionary doctrines of the British Whigs, and the Bill of Rights of 1689.[2] These early state constitutions in America almost perfectly exemplified the political ideals of the middle-class liberals. The aristocratic and monarchical elements in government were eliminated, especially the hereditary executive. Special privilege and hereditary rights were denounced. The doctrine of popular sovereignty and the assertion that all powers were originally given to the government by the people were boldly and universally proclaimed.

The French philosopher Montesquieu maintained about the middle of the eighteenth century that the chief guarantee of liberty lies in a proper separation of powers and in an elaborate system of governmental checks and balances. This doctrine was embodied very generally in these American state constitutions. The lingering fear of the king was reflected, nevertheless, in a general tendency to exalt the legislature at the expense of the executive department. Short terms for governors were the rule. John Adams said that annual elections were the only safeguard against tyranny. The laissez-faire tendencies of the Economic Liberalism of that time were accepted and the functions and powers of government were minimized and restricted. The chief purpose of government was represented as the protection of life, liberty, and property, and any extensive development beyond this was frowned upon. Yet there were

---

[1] See W. C. Morey, "The First State Constitutions," American Academy of Political Science, *Annals*, September, 1893.   [2] See Whipple, *op. cit.*, Chaps. ii-v.

THE ORIGINS OF CONSTITUTIONAL GOVERNMENT 135

some vestiges of aristocracy and privilege. Property qualification for voting and office-holding were common, and even religious qualifications for both office and the ballot were frequent. Constitution-making was carried to a wider field in the Articles of Confederation of March, 1781. But these were weak and inadequate, and a Constitution embodying strong federal principles was framed in 1787 and adopted by 1789.

In France, the French Revolution produced a number of constitutions, all profoundly influenced by British and American precedents. The most notable and influential was that of 1791, which provided for the creation of a limited monarchy under the Legislative Assembly. This was more widely followed as a model than the later and more radical constitutions because at this time limited monarchy aroused fewer objections from conservative minds than republican government. Napoleon popularized constitutional government. Even though he ruled with an iron hand, he governed under constitutional forms in France and handed out charters and constitutions to his subject territories.[1] A famous and influential constitution of the Napoleonic period was that adopted in Spain in 1812 and based on the French constitution of 1791. This constitution, proclaiming popular sovereignty and parliamentary government, was widely studied by the European liberals in their struggle for constitutions between the Congress of Vienna (1815) and the revolutions of 1848. It was also widely imitated by the Latin-American peoples. The constitution of industrial Belgium, influenced by the British constitution and adopted and approved in 1830-31, was especially admired by middle-class liberals and widely copied.

From 1815 to 1848 the battle for constitutions met many and serious rebuffs, but since 1848 every civilized state has established constitutional government, by which is meant, almost universally, representative government. The great enemy of constitutions in Europe from 1815 to 1848 was Prince Metternich. He knew that constitutions almost always entailed representative institutions, and hence he recognized their threat to the system of autocracy that maintained him in power. But after 1848 his influence waned. The Kingdom of Piedmont and Sardinia obtained a constitution in 1848, which developed into the constitution of United Italy. The King of Prussia granted a constitution in 1850, which lasted with few changes until the close of the World War. The Emperor of Austria was compelled to establish constitutional government in 1861. The minor European countries adopted constitutions at various times during the nineteenth century, particularly after 1850. The Latin-American states entered the constitution-making age in the first quarter of the nineteenth century. They usually modeled their constitutions after the Spanish constitution of 1812 and the Constitution of the United States.

Those states which adopted constitutions relatively late had a decided advantage in studying the experience of earlier constitutional systems. Most of the constitutions of Australasia embody, for example, the best features of the English and American constitutions. The some dozen new states that came into existence in Europe after the World War adopted constitutions which in many cases embodied not only previous political experience but also novel prin-

---

[1] As Guérard points out, however, all these Napoleonic constitutions spelled one word—Napoleon. *Cf.* A. L. Guérard, *Reflections on the Napoleonic Legend,* Scribner, 1924, pp. 55-60.

ciples or political science, such as proportional and vocational representation.[1] After the World War Turkey adopted a constitution that conferred remarkable powers upon the executive. In Russia and Spain, constitutional government has been recently turned against wealth and privilege and made a bulwark of proletarian radicalism.[2] The following quotation summarizes the extent and significance of this era of constitution-making:

> Between 1776 and 1850 well on towards a hundred written constitutions were created throughout the world. For the most part they represented political victories won by the people for democracy and nationality. Many of them stood as protests against the oppression of a motherland, such as the new American states against Great Britain, Spain, and Portugal. Others embodied hostility to control by other lands, as Belgium against Holland, Greece against Turkey, and Italy and Hungary against Austria. Some stood as revolts against tyrannical rulers as in France, Spain, Germany, and Austria. Others incorporated internal demands for reform as in Switzerland and Holland. Taking these documents as a whole, they measure the decline of absolutism and mark the progress of the world in liberty and equality.[3]

In the rise of Fascism and dictatorship since the World War one may note the rise of a strong tendency to abandon representative government, though there is no reason why a constitution might not readily be founded upon the most extreme Fascist principles. But the most striking aspect of the rise of Fascism is the suggested implication that the middle class has lost its confidence in representative government as a means of protecting the vested interests of property. A main reason for this lies in the increasing strength of the working class in contemporary society, and the consequent demand of this class that constitutions shall express their interests as well as those of the middle class.

Some of the characteristics of the preconstitutional age have tended to hang over into the era of constitutions. The conception of the divine right of kings has come down to us in the form of the divine status and sanctity of constitutions. The existence of constitutions has, indeed, begotten a perverted mental attitude towards them known as "constitutionalism." This has been defined by one authority as follows:

> Constitutionalism is the name given to the trust which men repose in the power of words engrossed on parchment to keep a government in order. The writing down of the fundamental law, beyond peradventure and against misunderstanding, is an important political invention. It offers exact and enduring language as a test for official conduct at the risk of imposing outworn standards upon current activities.[4]

The vested interests frequently regard a constitution that was actually created as a result of many compromises, and was looked upon by its framers as a very imperfect experiment, as a body of law divinely inspired, too sacred even to be criticized, to say nothing of being seriously altered or largely replaced.

---

[1] See H. L. McBain and Lindsay Rogers, *The New Constitutions of Europe*, Doubleday, Page, 1923, Pt. I.
[2] See MacLeod, *op. cit.*, pp. 460 ff. Less in Spain than in Russia. The Spanish Revolution has recently turned more to the right, and its ultimate results are as yet unpredictable.
[3] Flick, *op. cit.*, p. 215.
[4] W. H. Hamilton, article "Constitutionalism," Encyclopaedia of the Social Sciences, Vol. IV, p. 255.

THE ORIGINS OF CONSTITUTIONAL GOVERNMENT

The theory of the divine right of kings became archaic and out of adjustment with the social and economic interests of the seventeenth and eighteenth centuries. So, too, constitutions that were drawn up a century or a half-century ago have likewise come to be poorly adapted to the needs of a far different civilization from that which accompanied their formulation. This is a defect which is likely to become even more serious in the light of cultural alterations, which take place with far greater rapidity today than ever before. Further, constitutions, which are but a means to the end of orderly and free government, tend to be regarded as an end in themselves. It is doubtful if the excesses of divine-right panegyric under Louis XIV were greater than the absurdities of constitution eulogy in our own age. It is difficult to keep in mind or practice the basic truth, so well phrased by Thomas Jefferson, that constitutions are made to serve society and not society to serve constitutions. A characteristic product of the constitution cult is the following excerpt from an address by Henry D. Estabrook, cited in Harry F. Atwood's *Back to the Republic,* a book that has enjoyed an amazing popularity with the American plutocracy.

And so, on this great continent, which God had kept hidden in a little world—here, with a new heaven and a new earth, where former things had passed away, the people of many nations, of various needs and creeds, but united in heart and soul and mind for the single purpose, builded an altar to Liberty, the first ever built, or that ever could be built, and called it the Constitution of the United States. . . .

O marvelous Constitution! Magic parchment, transforming word, maker, monitor, guardian of mankind! Thou hast gathered to thy impartial bosom the peoples of the earth, Columbia, and called them equal. Thou hast conferred upon them imperial sovereignty, revoking all titles but that of man. Native and exotic, rich and poor, good and bad, old and young, the lazy and the industrious, those who love and those who hate, the mean and lowly, the high and mighty, the wise and the foolish, the prudent and the imprudent, the cautious and the hasty, the honest and the dishonest, those who pray and those who curse—these are "We, the people of the United States"—these are God's children—these are thy rulers, O Columbia. Into our hands thou hast committed the destinies of the human race, even to the omega of thine own destruction. And all thou requirest of us before we o'erstep boundaries blazed for guidance is what is required of us at every railroad crossing in the country: "Stop. Look. Listen." Stop and think. Look before and after and to the right and left. Listen to the voice of reason and to the small still voice of conscience.[1]

These abuses in the way of constitution worship have been most evident in the United States, in part because of the antiquity of the American Constitution and in part because of the degree to which this document is a bulwark of the vested propertied interests. This attitude appears not only in such silly brochures as the one just quoted, but also in such a pretension to sober scholarship as James M. Beck's *The Constitution of the United States.*[2] That a recognition of this state of affairs does not necessarily imply a subversive intention may be seen from the judicious criticism of the American constitutional system in William MacDonald's *A New Constitution for a New America,* the work

[1] Atwood, *op. cit.,* Laird, 1926, pp. 66-67.
[2] *Cf.* T. R. Powell, "Constitutional Metaphors," *New Republic,* Feb. 11, 1925, pp. 314-15—a review of J. M. Beck, *The Constitution of the United States.*

of an eminently conservative, respectable, and balanced writer, wholly devoid of any violently revolutionary motives.[1]

But it should be remembered that constitution worship, intellectually indefensible as it is when used as a mask for the more real motive of the advantage that it lends the vested propertied class, ought not so to antagonize its opponents that they forget that this same constitution, along with its inequitable parts, usually embodies many guarantees and safeguards of personal liberty that have been won during the age-long growth of social conscience.

The middle class have been very generally favorable to the republican form of government. Monarchy has symbolized to them, on the basis of the historical experiences of two previous centuries, arbitrary royal rule and interference with their business and prosperity. Bourgeois political supremacy has therefore generally been followed by the establishment of the republican form of government and the adoption of written constitutions. This has not been invariably true, because in certain instances the monarchical tradition has been too strong for the middle class to uproot at once. One must, of course, be on his guard lest he consider that a republic necessarily means a more liberal form of government than can exist under a constitutional monarchy. The formal monarchy of England today provides a government more democratic and more responsive to popular will than does the republic of the United States. Even Nazi Germany has seen fit as yet to retain the fiction of a republic.

Though the republican form of government has been the usual expression of middle-class political liberalism in modern times, it is well known that republics are in no sense an exclusively modern institution. The republican form of government was fairly common among the Greeks. Rome remained a republic for hundreds of years. In the Middle Ages there were city-state republics, such as Genoa. Switzerland became a republic in 1291.

But the first important republic of modern times was the Dutch Republic, which was formed in 1579 and lasted for two centuries. A far more extensive republic appeared on this side of the Atlantic when the United States of America was given permanence by the federal Constitution framed in 1787. The first French Republic came into being in 1792. The Second French Republic lasted from 1848 to 1852. The Third French Republic was declared in 1870 and assured in 1879. The revolutions in Latin America following 1810 usually brought into existence what were at least formally called republics, however dictatorial the rule of any leader. In South Africa the Dutch Boers established two republics, the Orange Free State in 1836, and the Transvaal in 1852.

Since the World War a considerable crop of new republics has sprung up in Europe. Among them are Czechoslovakia, Austria, Poland, the Baltic republics—Lithuania, Latvia, Estonia, and Finland—the Union of Socialist Soviet Republics, Portugal, and Spain. The Soviet Republics and the new Spanish Republic have well illustrated the fact that republican government need not be inseparably connected with the dominion and aspirations of the middle class. In both of these countries republican forms of government have been used to advance the interests of the radical proletariat.

[1] See also W. K. Wallace, *Our Obsolete Constitution*, Day, 1932; and W. Y. Elliott, *The Need for Constitutional Reform*, McGraw-Hill (forthcoming).

THE ORIGINS OF CONSTITUTIONAL GOVERNMENT

We have now traced the development of the major political movements associated with the origins, struggles, and triumphs of the middle class in Western society. At first, they helped the kings to crush out feudalism and to create the national state. Then they found that the absolute monarchs hampered their personal and business freedom. Thereupon they developed a theory of political revolution and proceeded to apply it. Beginning with the English achievements of the seventeenth century, they created limited monarchies and republics and brought about the supremacy of representative government. To enhance their prestige and to assure permanence for their institutions, they framed constitutions that made it more difficult to change the law and political order under which their system of business enterprise was conducted.

SUGGESTED READING

Hammerton, *Universal History of the World*, Chaps. 139-41, 143-44, 148-51, 155-57, 160, 162, 166, 169
Abbott, *The Expansion of Europe*, Chaps. IV, VIII, XXII-XXIII, XXVII
Charles Seignobos, *History of Mediaeval and Modern Civilization*, Scribner, 1907, Chaps. XXII-XXIII, XXV-XXVI
—— *History of Contemporary Civilization*, Scribner, 1909, Chaps. IV-V, X-XII
J. H. Randall, Jr., *The Making of the Modern Mind*, Houghton Mifflin, 1926, Chaps. VIII, XIV
W. E. H. Lecky, *History of the Rise and Influence of the Spirit of Rationalism in Europe*, Appleton, 1914, 2 vols., Chap. V
G. H. Soule, *The Coming American Revolution*, Macmillan, 1934, Pt. I
E. D. Martin, *Farewell to Revolution*, Norton, 1935
E. M. Hulme, *History of the British People*, Century, 1924, Chaps. X-XVIII
H. D. Traill and J. S. Mann, *Social England*, Putnam, 1909, 6 vols., Vol. III, Chaps. IX-X; Vol. IV, Chaps. XIII-XVI
G. B. Adams, *Constitutional History of England*, Holt, 1921, Chaps. X-XVI
R. H. Gretton, *The English Middle Class*, London, 1917
J. L. LeB. and B. Hammond, *The Age of the Chartists, 1832-1854*, Longmans, 1930
O. F. Christie, *The Transition from Aristocracy, 1832-1867*, Putnam, 1928
J. F. Jameson, *The American Revolution Considered as a Social Movement*, Princeton University Press, 1926
Sée, *Economic and Social Conditions in France during the Eighteenth Century*, Chaps. I-IV, X, XII-XIII
Sydney Herbert, *The Fall of Feudalism in France*, Stokes, 1921
C. E. Merriam, *Political Power: Its Composition and Incidence*, McGraw-Hill, 1934
W. C. MacLeod, *The Origin and History of Politics*, Wiley, 1931, Chaps. XXV-XXVIII
Edward Jenks, *The State and the Nation*, Dutton, 1919, Pt. III
Franz Oppenheimer, *The State*, Vanguard Press, 1926, Chaps. VI-VII
E. W. Burgess, *The Function of Socialization in Social Evolution*, University of Chicago Press, 1916, Pt. II
F. L. Schuman, *International Politics*, McGraw-Hill, 1933, Bk. I
Charles Borgeaud, *The Rise of Modern Democracy in Old and New England*, Scribner, 1894
—— *The Adoption and Amendment of Constitutions in Europe and America*, Macmillan, 1895
A. C. McLaughlin, *Constitutional History of the United States*, Appleton-Century (forthcoming)
Articles "Constitutional Conventions," "Constitutional Law," "Constitutionalism,"

"Constitutions," "Democracy," "Representation," "Republicanism," "Secularism" and "Sovereignty," Encyclopaedia of the Social Sciences
H. A. L. Fisher, *The Republican Tradition in Europe,* Putnam, 1911
Webster, *Historical Selections,* Sec. XXI
Robinson and Beard, *Readings in Modern European History,* Vol. I, Chaps. I, IV, X-XVI; Vol. II, Chaps. XVII, XIX-XX, XXV, XXVIII
Cheyney, *Readings in English History,* pp. 418-31, 451-63, 495-504, 539-50
G. B. Adams and H. M. Stephens, *Select Documents of English Constitutional History,* Macmillan, 1910
R. B. Morgan, *Readings in English Social History,* Macmillan, 1924, Bks. IV-V
William Haller, ed., *Tracts on Liberty in the Puritan Revolution,* Columbia University Press, 1934, 3 vols.
F. M. Anderson, ed., *Constitutions and Other Select Documents Illustrative of the History of France, 1789-1907,* rev. ed., H. W. Wilson, 1908
Allen Johnson, ed., *Readings in American Constitutional History, 1776-1876,* Houghton Mifflin, 1912

FURTHER REFERENCES

THE RISE OF THE MIDDLE CLASS AND THE EVOLUTION OF THE NATIONAL-STATE SYSTEM. For the major stages of political evolution, see Burgess, *op. cit.,* Pt. II; Schuman, *op. cit.,* Bk. I; Jenks, *op. cit.;* MacLeod, *op. cit.;* Oppenheimer, *op. cit.*

On the history of nationalism to 1815, see pp. 57-80 of Ramsay Muir, *Nationalism and Internationalism* (Houghton Mifflin, 1917); Chap. II of C. J. H. Hayes, *Essays on Nationalism* (Macmillan, 1926) and Chaps. II-III of *Historical Evolution of Modern Nationalism* (Long & Smith, 1931); Chaps. I-IV of J. H. Rose, *Nationality in Modern History* (Macmillan, 1916); W. S. Robertson, *History of the Latin-American Nations* (Appleton, 1925).

On the rise of royal absolutism, see good introductory surveys in Hammerton, *op. cit.,* Chap. 139; Gillespie, *History of Europe, 1500-1815,* Chaps. XIII-XV, XVII; Hayes, *Political and Cultural History of Modern Europe,* Vol. I, Chaps. I, V-VIII; Muir, *Short History of the British Commonwealth,* Vol. I, Bk. III; C. J. Friedrich, *The Emergence of the Modern State* (Harper, forthcoming).

On Henry VII, see *Cambridge Modern History,* Vol. II, Chap. XIII; Hammerton, *op. cit.,* Chap. 135. On constitutional development in Tudor England, see Adams, *op. cit.,* Chap. X; K. W. M. Pickthorn, *Early Tudor Government* (Macmillan, 1934, 2 vols.). On royal finance in England, see F. C. Dietz, *English Government Finance, 1485-1558* (University of Illinois, 1921) and *English Public Finance, 1558-1641* (Century, 1932).

On Richelieu, Mazarin, and the early Bourbons, see *Cambridge Modern History,* Vol. IV, Chaps. IV, XXI.

On the rise of Prussia, see Hammerton, *op. cit.,* Vol. II, Chap. 150; *Cambridge Modern History,* Vol. V, Chaps. XX-XXI; Chaps. I-IV of Sir J. A. R. Marriott and C. G. Robertson, *The Evolution of Prussia* (Oxford Press, 1915); Sir Richard Lodge, *Great Britain and Prussia in the Eighteenth Century* (Oxford Press, 1923).

On Russian national origins, see Hammerton, *op. cit.,* Chap. 149; Chap. XII of Sir Bernard Pares, *History of Russia* (Knopf, 1926); Frank Nowak, *Medieval Slavdom and the Rise of Russia* (Holt, 1930); Helmolt, *History of the World,* Vol. V, Chap. VII.

On the divine right of kings, see J. N. Figgis, *The Divine Right of Kings* (Macmillan, 1914); J. W. Allen, *History of Political Thought in the Sixteenth Century* (Dial Press, 1928).

On the secularization of politics in modern times, see Lecky, *op. cit.,* Chap. v.

For the cultural panorama of the age of Enlightened Despots, see Vol. II, Bk. II of Egon Friedell, *Cultural History of the Modern Age* (Knopf, 1930-32, 3 vols.).

On Louis XIV, see L. B. Packard, *The Age of Louis XIV* (Holt, 1929) and *Europe and the Bourbon Ascendancy* (Harper, 1935); Hammerton, *op. cit.,* Chap. 148; Arthur Hassall, *Louis XIV and the Zenith of the French Monarchy* (Putnam, 1895); J. E. Farmer, *Versailles and the Court under Louis XIV* (Century, 1905). For a psychological interpretation of Louis XIV, see Sisley Huddleston, *Louis XIV in Love and in War* (Harper, 1929).

On the enlightened despots, see Hayes, *op. cit.,* Vol. I, pp. 346 ff.; *Cambridge Modern History,* Vol. VI, Chaps. xii, xviii-xx; Geoffrey Bruun, *The Enlightened Despots* (Holt, 1929); Penfield Roberts, *The Cult of Stability* (Harper, forthcoming); Leo Gershoy, *The Enlightened Despots* (Harper, forthcoming); Helmolt, *op. cit.,* Vol. VII, Chap. v; A. H. Johnson, *The Age of the Enlightened Despots* (Macmillan, 1910).

On the history of revolutions, see Soule, *op. cit.,* Pt. I; Martin, *op. cit.*

On the early middle-class revolutions, for introductions see Gillespie, *op. cit.,* Chaps. xvii, xix, xxiv; Hayes, *op. cit.,* Chaps. x, xii; Chaps. vii, xiv, xvi-xviii, of C. P. Higby, *History of Europe (1492-1815)* (Houghton Mifflin, 1927); Jenks, *op. cit.,* Chap. xiii; Hammerton, *op. cit.,* Chap. 141.

On the origins of representative government, see Jenks, *op. cit.,* Chap. xiii; MacLeod, *op. cit.,* Chap. xxv; article "Representation," Encyclopaedia of the Social Sciences; A. B. White, *Self-Government at the King's Command* (University of Minnesota Press, 1933).

On natural rights and libertarianism, for the best brief analysis see Leon Whipple, *Our Ancient Liberties* (H. W. Wilson, 1927).

ENGLISH REVOLUTIONS AND CONSTITUTIONAL DEVELOPMENTS, SEVENTEENTH CENTURY. Muir, *Short History of the British Commonwealth,* Vol. I, Bk. IV, Chaps. iii-ix; Bk. V, Chaps. iv-vi; G. M. Trevelyan, *England under the Stuarts* (4th ed., Putnam, 1904); Traill and Mann, *op. cit.,* Vol. IV; *Cambridge Modern History,* Vol. IV, Chaps. viii-ix.

On Cromwell, see *Ibid.,* Vol. VI, Chap. xv; Hammerton, *op. cit.,* Chap. 144; Sir C. H. Firth, *Oliver Cromwell* (Putnam, 1900); S. R. Gardiner, *Oliver Cromwell* (Longmans, 1901) and *Cromwell's Place in History* (Macmillan, 1897).

On the constitutional developments and the triumph of representative government in England, see Adams, *op. cit.,* Chaps. xi-xvi; Borgeaud, *The Rise of Democracy in Old and New England.* On political, social, and constitutional development after 1832, see Hammond and Hammond, *op. cit.;* Christie, *op. cit.;* Julius West, *History of the Chartist Movement* (Houghton Mifflin, 1920); T. M. Hovell, *The Chartist Movement* (Longmans, 1925); Emily Allyn, *Lords versus Commons, 1830-1930* (Century, 1931).

THE AMERICAN REVOLUTION. For an especially excellent and authentic analysis of the causes of the Revolution, see Chaps. ii-iv of C. M. Andrews, *The Colonial Background of the American Revolution* (Yale University Press, 1924). On the importance of the Mississippi Valley in the controversy, see C. W. Alvord, *The Mississippi Valley in British Politics* (A. H. Clark, 1917, 2 vols.). On the nature and importance of the Revolution, see Chap. ix of H. E. Barnes, *History and Social Intelligence* (Knopf, 1926); Chap. viii of A. M. Schlesinger, *New Viewpoints in American History* (Macmillan, 1922); C. L. Becker, *The Beginnings of the American People* (Houghton Mifflin, 1915) and *The Eve of the Revolution* (Yale University Press, 1918); C. H. Van Tyne, *The History of the Founding of the American Republic* (Houghton Mifflin, 2 vols., 1922-29).

On the earliest American state constitutions, see pp. 74 ff. of C. E. Merriam, *History of American Political Theories* (Macmillan, 1903); pp. 91 ff. of W. A. Dunning, *History of Political Theories from Rousseau to Spencer* (Macmillan, 1920); W. C. Morey, "The First State Constitutions," American Academy of Political Science, *Annals,* September, 1893; W. C. Webster, "Comparative Study of the State Constitutions of the American Revolution," *Ibid.,* May, 1897.

On the economic basis of the Constitution of the United States, see J. A. Smith, *The Spirit of American Government* (Macmillan, 1907); Chaps. II-IV of C. A. Beard, *Economic Interpretation of the Constitution of the United States* (Macmillan, 1903).

THE FRENCH REVOLUTION. On the conditions preceding the Revolution, see Sée, *op. cit.,* Chaps. I-IV, X, XII-XIII; Frantz Funck-Brentano, *The Old Régime in France* (Longmans, 1929). On the Revolution and Napoleon, see Hammerton, *op. cit.,* Chaps. 156-57; Leo Gershoy, *The French Revolution and Napoleon* (Crofts, 1933); L. R. Gottschalk, *The Era of the French Revolution* (Houghton Mifflin, 1929); C. C. Brinton, *A Decade of Revolution, 1789-1799* (Harper, 1934); *Cambridge Modern History,* Vol. VIII. The latest classic treatment of the French Revolution is Albert Mathiez, *The French Revolution* (Knopf, 1928). For an ingenious attempt to reduce the French Revolution to terms of laws of social causation, see Pt. I of S. A. Reeve, *The Natural Laws of Social Convulsions* (Dutton, 1933). On the social reforms of the Revolution, see Seignobos, *History of Mediaeval and Modern Civilization,* Chap. V; Herbert, *op. cit.*

On the Napoleonic reforms, see Vol. I, Chap. VIII of August Fournier, *Napoleon the First* (Holt, 1903, 2 vols.); *Cambridge Modern History,* Vol. IX, Chaps. V-VII. On the spread of these reforms, see *Ibid.,* Vol. VIII, Chap. XXV; Vol. IX, Chaps. IV, XI, XXIV; Hammerton, *op. cit.,* Chap. 160.

For a general survey of all the French Revolutions from 1789 to 1871, see E. L. Woodward, *French Revolutions* (Oxford Press, 1934).

On Metternich and his system of reaction, see A. J. May, *The Age of Metternich* (Holt, 1933); Arthur Herman, *Metternich* (Century, 1932); Algernon Cecil, *Metternich* (Macmillan, 1933).

On the revolutions of 1830 and 1848, see Vol. I, Chaps. V-X, of C. D. Hazen, *Europe since 1815* (rev. ed., Holt, 1924, 2 vols.); Helmolt, *op. cit.,* Vol. VIII, Chap. II; F. B. Artz, *Reaction and Revolution, 1814-1832* (Harper, 1934).

On the revolutions of 1848, the best brief treatment still remains Vol. I, Chap. VIII, of C. M. Andrews, *The Historical Development of Modern Europe* (Putnam, 1896, 2 vols.). See also *Cambridge Modern History,* Vol. XI, Chaps. IV-VII; Vol. I, Chaps. V-VII, of Sir A. W. Ward, *Germany, 1815-1890* (Macmillan, 1917-20, 3 vols.).

RUSSIA. On Russia from 1860 to 1914, see *Cambridge Modern History,* Vol. XII, Chaps. XII-XIII. On the Russian Revolution of 1905, see Pares, *op. cit.,* Chap. XXIII; M. J. Olgin, *The Soul of the Russian Revolution* (Holt, 1917); Vol. II, pp. 101-261 of M. N. Pokrovsky, *Brief History of Russia* (International Publishers, 1933, 2 vols.).

CONSTITUTIONAL GOVERNMENTS. On the subject of constitutions, the best introduction is W. H. Hamilton, article "Constitutionalism," Encyclopaedia of the Social Sciences. On the history of constitutionalism, see pp. 212 ff. of A. C. Flick, *Modern World History, 1776-1926* (Knopf, 1926); Seignobos, *op. cit.,* Chap. X; MacLeod, *op. cit.,* Chap. X; Dunning, *op. cit.,* pp. 91 ff., 248 ff., Morey, *loc. cit.;* Borgeaud, *The Adoption and Amendment of Constitutions;* C. F. Strong, *Modern Political Constitutions* (Putnam, 1930); F. J. Stimson, *The Law of the Federal and State Constitutions of the United States,* Boston Book Co., 1908.

On republicanism and republics, see P. R. Rohden, article "Republicanism," Encyclopaedia of the Social Sciences; Henry Mann, *Ancient and Mediaeval Republics* (privately printed, 1879); Fisher, *op. cit.;* Robertson, *op. cit.,* Chaps. VI-XIX.

CHAPTER V

THE LIBERATION OF THE INTELLECT

IN EARLY MODERN TIMES

I. THE INTELLECTUAL TEMPER OF EARLY MODERN TIMES

We now come to the point where we may describe the most remarkable period in the intellectual development of Western civilization since the innovations that made possible the Periclean civilization of ancient Greece. Not since the era from 600 B.C. to 200 B.C. had there been any such promising intellectual ferment and cultural progress as that witnessed in western Europe from 1450 to 1800. And there were illuminating points of resemblance between these two epoch-making ages in the intellectual history of mankind. The Hellenic thinkers brought free inquiry into the world, questioned the supernaturalism of oriental antiquity, raised reason to a position of supremacy, directed philosophy towards a solution of human problems, and created a scientific habit of thought. The scientists, philosophers, and critical thinkers of the period from 1450 to 1880, carrying on the work of the more progressive late medieval thinkers, performed much the same function in freeing western Europe from the protective but smothering blanket of orthodox medievalism. They too challenged orthodox supernaturalism, elevated reason, defended free thinking, brought philosophy down to earth, and carried through the most important scientific renaissance since the days of Hellenistic Greece.[1]

It is not easy to summarize concisely the dominating psychology of early modern times, but the one deep undercurrent was the growing secularism of the age. The supernaturalism of the Catholic Church held over without any serious break, and was actually intensified by the necessity of defense against the assaults of Protestantism. In some ways the Protestants believed in a more crass and direct supernaturalism than did the Catholics.

There was, nevertheless, a steady if slow progress towards various types of secularism and Rationalism. Protestantism was very closely related to the rise of capitalism. While the Protestants were still predominantly and almost fiercely absorbed in the matter of the salvation of the soul, they did believe that one means of assuring spiritual, as well as earthly, salvation lay in industry, thrift, and the accumulation of pecuniary profits.

This was in direct opposition to the Catholic attitude during the Middle

---

[1] This liberating tendency was not, of course, *born* in the fifteenth century. It was a continuation, with gathering momentum, of the progressive intellectual tendencies of the later Middle Ages. See Vol. I, pp. 789 ff.

Ages. The Church had repudiated the desirability of worldly prosperity and had closely restrained business enterprise in the interest of social justice and human welfare, even though there were symptoms of realistic economic adjustment to the newer commercial and financial methods on the part of the later Schoolmen.

A political basis for secularism was found in the revived prestige and influence of Roman law and in the development of the social-contract conception. The first emphasized secular absolutism and the latter the mundane and human origins of political institutions. The period of discoveries created a spirit of adventure and novelty, helping along economic and social changes and serving to arouse an interest in secular matters.

In addition to these more diffused forms of assault upon the dominant supernaturalism, there existed a number of direct and immediate modes of attack. The Humanists, especially outside of Italy, were for the most part relatively pious Christians. Nevertheless, in their literary and philosophical activities they stressed the excellence of Greek and Latin literature, with its secular cast. Crotus Rubianus, in the *Letters of Obscure Men,* Ulrich von Hutten, and other later German Humanists employed the weapon of satire against the abuses in the Church. The Rationalists, while firmly believing in a sort of impersonal cosmic God, vigorously attacked orthodox Christianity and the prevailing types of supernaturalism.[1] The Rationalists and the Deists anticipated the contemporary Modernists by contrasting the teachings of Jesus with orthodox historical Christianity, both Catholic and Protestant. They repudiated historical Christianity, but found much to commend in the teachings of Jesus. They believed that they had found a great deal in common between the doctrines of Jesus and their own Rationalistic natural religion.

The rise of modern astronomy from Copernicus to Newton proved that the Sun, rather than the Earth, is the center of our system, and also gave some preliminary hint of the vast extent of the universe. Both of these innovations were a direct challenge to the orthodox theory of creation and cosmology. Francis Bacon, the great rhetorical herald of the new scientific age, called attention to the serious inadequacies of the deductive logical method of orthodox Catholic Scholastic theology as a tool for scientific research, and called for an ever greater reliance upon inductive reasoning from a mass of observed facts. Science, he believed, would be able to revolutionize the world and greatly increase human happiness. He repudiated the Scholastic dialectic as a technique for acquiring information on the ground that "nature is more subtle than any argument." The Humanists, and particularly the Rationalists, assaulted the intolerance of Catholics and Protestants alike, and some warmly defended not only toleration but complete freedom of thought.

As far as the mental climate of modern times marked a break with that of the Middle Ages, it may be said to have been characterized chiefly by a growing secularism, tolerance, and freedom, and by an increasing reliance upon the scientific method. Further, a theory of human progress replaced the Christian epic, which had been characterized by predominant interest in the Fall of Man and the Day of Judgment.

---

[1] See Sir J. A. Hammerton, *Universal History of the World,* Amalgamated Press, 1927-29, 8 vols., Chap. 154.

II. THE PROGRESS OF NATURAL SCIENCE IN THE SIXTEENTH AND SEVENTEENTH CENTURIES

The scientific achievements from Copernicus to Lavoisier were probably more remarkable and numerous than those which had taken place during the whole history of man from the Stone Age to the middle of the sixteenth century. The causes of this scientific activity are numerous and complex.

In the first place, we have to recognize more thoroughly than most historians of science have been wont to do the important work of the hitherto obscure scientists of the late medieval period. We have already referred to this briefly in the preceding volume. It was in the fourteenth century, for example, that the laws of falling bodies, the rotation and revolution of the earth, the principles of analytical geometry, and the basic ideas of the calculus were at least anticipated, and the modern approach to anatomy and physiology founded. And men like Copernicus, Galileo, Vesalius, Descartes, and others were not unfamiliar with this earlier work. Indeed, they derived much directly from it. The researches of Continental historians of science and of Professor Lynn Thorndike in this country have made it necessary to abandon the once popular doctrine that "medieval superstition" was suddenly superseded in the late fifteenth and sixteenth centuries by the rapid and unparalleled discovery of scientific truth. We are coming to see that in the field of science and criticism the Middle Ages moved gradually into modern times—a development comparable to what we have already shown to be the case with respect to the transition of medievalism into the Renaissance.[1]

Humanism produced a secular outlook more concerned with things of this world than with salvation in the next. To be sure, the Humanists were usually Christians first and lovers of pagan culture second, but their secular interests looked in a direction that could tolerate or promote scientific curiosity.[2] Although the Protestant revolt in its religious aspects was probably more intensely otherworldly than Renaissance Catholicism, it did seriously challenge Catholic authority and tradition. It certainly weakened the hold of the deductive and essentially antiscientific Scholastic philosophy. Further, Protestantism encouraged that individuality of personal expression which was closely related to the early stages of scientific progress.

The political and economic tendencies of the time also helped on the progress of science. Science cannot well flourish in times and places where physical disorder, violence, confusion, and general poverty prevail. Hence the growth of the national state and centralized administration that followed on the heels of feudalism helped to create order and justice in the social system. A degree of political stability superseded the disorder of the past. The rising capitalism

---

[1] *Cf*. Lynn Thorndike, *History of Magic and Experimental Science*, Vols. III-IV, Columbia University Press, 1934 (Vols. I-II, Macmillan).

[2] The Humanistic contributions to science should not, however, be exaggerated, as they are by certain exuberant historians of the Renaissance. The Humanists helped to check the scientific trend of the thirteenth and fourteenth centuries; they had little sympathy with the interests of the scientist, since their own outlook was poetic and esthetic; outstanding Humanists interested in science (for example, Leonardo and Pierre Ramus) were rare; and the Humanists were authoritarians, substituting one set of authorities (Plato, Cicero, Seneca, and Plutarch) for another (Aristotle and the Schoolmen).

produced a large wealthy class that had leisure for scientific pursuits or was able to subsidize scientists and their societies, academies, and journals. As the middle class accumulated more of the things of this world they came to think more extensively about its problems—which constitute the field of science.

Paradoxically enough, the very religious intolerance of the sixteenth and seventeenth centuries indirectly helped on scientific interests. The religious persecutions, the religious wars, and the witchcraft mania served to turn many of the best minds of Europe away from religion and towards a compensatory interest in the investigation of scientific problems. This was, however, but a temporary and indirect factor. In the end, the growing political stability and intellectual urbanity had a far more salutary and lasting influence on the growth of scientific activity.

There were also certain very specific aids that furthered scientific endeavor at this time. Mathematics, so essential to most scientific formulations, had been advancing since western Europe came in contact with Arabic numerals and the algebraic notation in the hands of the Muslims during the Crusades and after. The science of optics had also been carried along from the Greeks by the Muslims. Al-Hazen and other Muslim scientists had made additional contributions to this field, which were taken up and improved upon by Witelo, Roger Bacon, and others. In due time this progress in pure and applied optics made possible the telescope, the microscope, the prism, and other invaluable aids to science. Alchemy also came to lose more and more of its mystical aspects and aspirations and gradually developed into the more practical chemistry.

The new science was, as has been suggested earlier, intimately related to the expansion of Europe. The contact of cultures, which had been greatly extended by the Crusades and subsequent developments, was the most potent influence in introducing Muslim and Hellenistic science into Europe and in stimulating that curiosity which is essential to any persistent development of scientific activity. Cultural contacts and the comparative way of looking at things, which these contacts slowly engendered, also helped gradually to develop an attitude of toleration and later one of freethinking, both of great assistance to scientific progress.

Even more direct relationship between the oversea expansion and the new science is to be discerned in the extensive information brought into Europe as a result of the process of expansion. Geography was most rapidly and directly influenced. A veritable revolution was produced in the science of geography, as well as in its subordinate field of cartography. Geology was likewise stimulated through the observation of new types of earth structure and the discovery of new rocks and fossils. Before the end of the eighteenth century the revolutionary significance of this new geological knowledge was gradually coming to be apprehended.

The biological sciences ranked next to the geographical in the degree to which they were influenced by oversea discoveries. The large number of new types of animals and plants not only enriched the field of natural history and descriptive botany and biology, but also led to the necessity of devising systems of classification of biological data, of which that by Linnaeus was the most famous. Even more, the observation of unfamiliar plants and animals by Europeans remaining at home was facilitated through the establishment of botanical and zoölogical gardens. Medical science was similarly extended through the observation of new diseases and the enormous extension of the materia medica, which provided important remedies, especially quinine, for diseases hitherto treated unsuccessfully. Inoculation against smallpox was first practiced in China, India, and Muslim realms. The observation of the Turkish practice of this method by Lady Mary Wortley Montagu in Constantinople aided her in converting Dr. Keith of London to experimentation with it. This, as well as the cowpox of Gloucestershire dairymaids, helped Edward Jenner to introduce vaccination against smallpox.[1]

Astronomy was also forwarded by the new facts acquired through observing the heavenly bodies from new positions and in discovering new constellations that were visible only from the Southern Hemisphere. Modern mathematics depended almost wholly for its initial impulses upon the mathematical knowledge of the Orient that was brought in from the eleventh century onward. Physics owed not a little to the preservation of the Hellenic physical knowledge by the Muslims and its later transmission by them to the Europeans, as well as to the indispensable mathematical knowledge that had been slowly developed from earlier Hellenic and oriental beginnings. Chemistry was enriched by the discovery of new ores and chemicals, as well as by the introduction of the advanced Muslim alchemy that had embodied and extended the earlier Hellenic and oriental alchemy.

We may now turn to a brief survey of the specific contributions to scientific advance that, in their totality, constituted the most remarkable scientific renaissance in the history of mankind before the nineteenth century.

In the field of mathematics, algebra and geometry were carried far beyond the stage reached when introduced into Europe by the Muslims in the later Middle Ages. Logarithms, devised at the opening of the seventeenth century by Napier and Briggs, enormously simplified mathematical problems and astronomical computations. René Descartes (1596-1650) and Pierre de Fermat (1601-65) improved analytical geometry and laid the basis for the development of graphic methods. Together with Blaise Pascal they developed the theory of numbers. Finally, Newton and Leibnitz, in the last half of the seventeenth century, perfected the calculus, without which few of the later developments in physical science and engineering could have been achieved.

In astronomy, as we have already pointed out,[2] there were sufficient achievements to constitute a revolutionary change of man's attitude towards the whole universe. The improved astronomy meant veritably the discovery of the new heavens, in the same way that the geographical explorations had revealed a new earth. Copernicus, relying in part upon the recovery of ancient Greek astronomical knowledge and in part on astronomical discoveries of the fourteenth and fifteenth centuries, interchanged the positions of the Sun and the Earth in the medieval system of fixed, revolving, transparent spheres, thus substituting the heliocentric for the geocentric theory of the universe. Kepler showed that the planets move freely about the Sun in elliptical orbits instead

[1] *Cf.* Victor Robinson, *Pathfinders in Medicine,* Medical Life Press, 1929, Chap. XI.
[2] See above, Vol. I, pp. 793 ff.

of being restrained in the scheme of fixed transparent spheres. He also worked out the basic laws of planetary motion, which Newton combined with Galileo's law of falling bodies to constitute the famous law of universal gravitation.

It should be remembered that the progress in optics already described made possible the more complete development of the telescope, which promoted the science of astronomy in subsequent years.

In physics Galileo (1564-1642) perfected the law of falling bodies and thus founded the all-important field of dynamics. Newton took it up here. Evangelista Torricelli (1608-47) and Pascal invented the barometer in the middle of the seventeenth century to measure atmospheric pressure, and Fahrenheit devised the thermometer at the opening of the eighteenth to register temperature. Otto von Guericke (1602-86) devised the air pump and still further advanced the scientific study of atmospheric pressure. Kepler, Snell, Mariotte, Descartes, Newton, Huygens, and others further developed the science of optics. Particularly important were the origins of spectrum analysis and the scientific explanation of color by Newton and Huygens. In the middle of the seventeenth century Christiaan Huygens (1629-95) invented the first practicable pendulum clock. He thus produced a time-telling instrument that became sufficiently exact in its results to make possible the further development of dynamics.[1] Huygens himself, in 1673, made the outstanding contribution to dynamics since the days of Galileo, consisting of a new theory of the oscillations of a pendulum.

In chemistry and alchemy [2] Paracelsus, as we have seen, criticized the traditional mystical tendencies and called for a more practical attitude in this field. The foundations for subsequent progress in general chemistry were laid by the work of Robert Boyle (1627-91) and G. E. Stahl (1660-1734), who performed the indispensable service of wiping out once and for all the grossly misleading Aristotelian theory of the four basic elements—earth, air, fire, and water. In addition, Hermann Boerhaave (1668-1738) laid the foundations for later progress in the field of organic chemistry.

The achievements in biology were as revolutionary as those in astronomy. Andreas Vesalius (1514-64) put the systematic study of human anatomy on a firm basis.[3] William Harvey (1578-1657) discovered the circulation of the blood and thus established dynamic physiology. The progress in optics that made possible the microscope very notably forwarded the progress of biology.[4] Robert Hooke was thus enabled for the first time to describe clearly the cellular structure of organic matter in 1665. Marcello Malpighi (1628-94) and Nehemiah Grew (1641-1712) built upon the achievements of Hooke the first careful work in the minute anatomy of plants and animals. By the use of the micro-

---

[1] Huygens ranked next to Newton among seventeenth-century scientists. See Philipp Lenard, *Great Men of Science*, Macmillan, 1933, pp. 67 ff.
[2] For an interesting discussion of the revolution in chemistry, see J. N. Leonard, *Crusaders of Chemistry*, Doubleday, Doran, 1930, Chap. v.
[3] Leonardo da Vinci (1452-1519) had done important work here, and though it was unpublished it had some effect on the scientific work of his day and succeeding generations.
[4] On the rise of modern biology, see W. A. Locy, *The Growth of Biology*, Holt, 1925, Chaps. XI-XII.

scope Leeuwenhoek (1632-1723) isolated blood corpuscles, bacteria, and other microscopic bodies. Jan Swammerdam (1637-80) likewise carried on intensive microscopic studies of the insects, including a minute investigation of the intestinal tracts of flies and bees. Francesco Redi (1626-79) founded pathology by his studies of putrefaction, and largely discredited by experiments the theory of spontaneous generation. Giovanni Borelli (1608-79) introduced the fundamental principles of mechanics into an explanation of biological facts, including the mechanism of the human body. He gave special attention to the mechanics of breathing and of muscular motion. Scientific botany was cultivated by Leonhard Fuchs, Andrea Cesalpino, Hooke, Malpighi, and Rudolf Camerarius (1665-1721). The latter, a professor in Tübingen, discovered the fact of the sexuality of plants, rejected since Aristotle's day.

Building upon these advances in biology and chemistry, Boerhaave and others founded empirical medicine and began the long and difficult process of undermining the authority of Hippocrates and Galen. Thomas Sydenham (1624-1689) was probably the best-known physician of the age, but he paid less attention to the scientific work of the time. He neglected his contemporaries and other authorities except Hippocrates, upon whom he relied heavily. He did, however, make some use of observation and experience in his practice.

In the field of geology no little progress was made towards a recognition of the real nature of the origins of the Earth, and of the earth-building processes.[1] Nicolaus Steno (1631-86), Robert Plot, Edward Llwyd, Robert Hooke, and others began to comprehend the nature and implications of the fossil remains of extinct forms of organic life. In this way some dim inkling was gleaned of the vast antiquity of our planet, thus preparing the way for discrediting the scriptural theory of the recent creation of the Earth. Martin Lister (1638-1712) first suggested a geological map, and Hooke gave the first scientific description of earthquakes.

Epoch-making advances were made in the related field of geography.[2] The explorations and discoveries greatly extended man's knowledge of the topography and configuration of our planet. The new navigation and exploration rendered necessary better maps and charts. Accurate globes and maps were made by Ortelius (1527-98), Gerardus Mercator (1512-94), Planck, and others. The scientific methods of establishing latitude and longitude, anticipated by Hipparchus in antiquity, were now firmly established. Books like Richard Hakluyt's *Principal Navigations* (1589) and Chardin's *Travels* (1686) did much to popularize this new geographical knowledge. On the basis of the greatly extended body of information in this field, Bernhardus Varenius, in his *Geographia generalis,* founded scientific geography (1650). Between the sixteenth century and the early nineteenth Bodin, Mead, Arbuthnot, Montesquieu, and Herder made many interesting suggestions in the field of anthropogeography, emphasizing the influence of geographic factors on man and culture.[3]

[1] See H. B. Woodward, *History of Geology,* Putnam, 1911, Chap. I.
[2] See J. S. Keltie and O. J. R. Howarth, *History of Geography,* Putnam, 1912, Chaps. IV-VI.
[3] See Franklin Thomas, *The Environmental Basis of Society,* Century, 1925, pp. 48 ff., 55 ff., 58 ff., 63 ff.

These scientific advances had a profound influence upon the general thinking of the period through impressing upon the attention of man such striking considerations as the hitherto unsuspected extent of the universe, the relative insignificance of the Earth, the apparent reign of law in the development and processes of the universe, the conception of God as a lawmaking and law-abiding Being instead of an arbitrary violator of natural law, and, finally, the recognition of the antiquity of the Earth.

The advance in natural science also had significant effects upon the growth of toleration. It has often been held that it was the increasing toleration and Rationalism that made scientific activity possible. In reality, it is more true that the scientific achievements helped to create a spirit of tolerance. The seventeenth century, which saw the scientific movement in full swing, was one of the worst centuries for religious wars, persecution, and belief in witchcraft. It was chiefly the scientific advances of the seventeenth century that rendered possible the tolerance and enlightenment of the eighteenth. Some of the exponents of toleration, however, such as Montaigne, Milton, Locke, and Bayle, were little affected directly by science and were led to support toleration through their own intellectual insight or mental subtleties.

As science progressed, the technique and equipment necessary for its promotion was provided in more adequate fashion. Laboratories were constructed and equipped. Observatories were built and telescopes installed. Museums were constructed.

Organizations to encourage and advance scientific research now came into being. These were backed by scholars and by enthusiastic and learned amateurs. The first to be founded was the British Royal Society, whose meetings began about 1645. The society was incorporated in 1662. It was created on the general model of the House of Solomon, the central institution in *The New Atlantis* of Francis Bacon.[1] The Royal Society owed much at first to its versatile and industrious curator, Robert Hooke. The Dublin Philosophical Society was founded in 1684 in imitation of the Royal Society. The French Academy of Sciences was chartered in 1666, and in 1700 Leibnitz founded the Berlin Academy.

Journals devoted to scientific and philosophical discoveries and controversies soon followed.[2] The *Journal des savants* appeared in 1665, followed in the same year by the *Philosophical Transactions* of the British Royal Society. The first German publication, the *Acta eruditorum,* appeared at Leipzig in 1682.

III. THE LEADING ASPECTS OF SCIENTIFIC DEVELOPMENT IN THE EIGHTEENTH CENTURY

Natural science in the eighteenth century suffered at least momentarily because of the extensive and brilliant results achieved in the seventeenth.[3] These had been relatively so breath-taking that it almost seems as though scholarship

---

[1] See below, p. 158.
[2] Preserved Smith, *History of Modern Culture,* Holt, 1930-34, 2 vols., Vol. I, pp. 172 ff.
[3] See Sir W. C. D. Dampier-Whetham, *History of Science,* Macmillan, 1930, pp. 180 ff.; and J. H. Randall, Jr., *The Making of the Modern Mind,* Houghton Mifflin, 1926, Chap. XI.

had to pause to get its bearings. Further, the scientific progress of the seventeenth century had brought to the mind many new and strange discoveries, phenomena, and processes. This tended to provoke reflection and stimulate philosophical analysis. Scholars stopped to speculate upon the meaning of it all for human knowledge and social life.[1] Moreover, the explorations overseas brought back many new plants, animals, minerals, which required study and classification. This promoted a trend towards biological classification, natural history, and descriptive work. These factors, along with some others, strongly conditioned the developments in science during the first two-thirds of the eighteenth century.

The Deists and the Rationalists tried to discover and unravel the implications of the new science with respect to the laws of the universe, the nature of God, and the duties of man. Others, following in their train, endeavored to set forth the supposed lessons of science and theology for the social sciences and the reform of humanity. The Physiocrats and the Encyclopedists took the lead here.

The cultivation of natural history, begun by John Ray (1627-1705), was continued on a much more impressive scale by the French scientists Buffon and Cuvier. The profusion of data in botany and zoölogy made necessary some system of classification if confusion were not to reign. The Swedish naturalist Carolus Linnaeus (1707-78) rose to the occasion in his *System of Nature,* perhaps the first complete scheme of classification of natural phenomena since the days of Aristotle. The summarization, codification, and interpretation of the scientific discoveries of the previous century occupied the attention of many able scholars, in particular Diderot and his associates who compiled the *Grand Encyclopedia.*[2] As the eighteenth century wore on, however, the zeal for experimentation and rigorous scientific exploration returned, and the developments of the latter part of the century paved the way for the sweeping scientific revolution of the nineteenth century, in which we find a Helmholtz as much outdistancing Newton in the range and volume of his achievements as the latter did Copernicus.

We can here summarize only a few of the outstanding achievements. The most definitive and complete work was done in advanced phases of mathematics. The leaders were Maclaurin, Euler, the Bernoullis, D'Alembert, and Lagrange. Leonhard Euler (1707-83) was probably the most talented mathematician who ever lived, when we consider both the volume and the quality of his work. Maclaurin devoted himself to the method of fluxions, and Daniel Bernoulli (1700-82), Jean Le Rond d'Alembert (1717-83), and Joseph Lagrange (1736-1813) did their best work in analytical mechanics and certain other basic aspects of mathematical physics. The work of Lagrange was of high importance for nineteenth-century physics.

In astronomy, James Bradley (1693-1762) worked on the velocity of light and the distance of the stars and discovered the "nodding" of the Earth's pole. Lagrange and Pierre Laplace (1749-1827) cultivated celestial mechanics, and

---
[1] See Botsford, *English Society in the Eighteenth Century,* pp. 231-36.
[2] See below, pp. 184-85.

Laplace worked out his famous nebular theory of the origins of the universe. Sir William Herschel discovered the planet Uranus in 1781, and investigated the problems of double stars and nebulae.

In physics perhaps the most pregnant work was done in laying the foundations for electrophysics, which became the most striking field of progress in physics in the nineteenth and twentieth centuries. In the sixteenth and seventeenth centuries Sir Humphrey Gilbert, Gray, and Von Guericke had investigated certain rudimentary aspects of magnetism and electrophysics. Carrying on Gray's work, a Frenchman, Charles Du Fay (1698-1739), discovered the fact that there are two kinds of electricity, positive and negative. Benjamin Franklin proved that lightning is only a vast electric spark. Luigi Galvani (1737-98) discovered what was once interpreted as "animal magnetism" through experimentation with frogs' legs. Alessandro Volta (1745-1827) constructed the first important electric battery and overthrew the notion of animal magnetism. Two Dutchmen, Cunaeus and Pieter van Musschenbroek, invented the famous Leyden jar, which did much to popularize interest in the wonders of electricity as well as to aid pure science. Finally, Charles Coulomb (1736-1806) discovered that Newton's law of inverse squares (that is, universal gravitation) applies also to the attraction and repulsion of electrical charges.

The other outstanding achievements in physics were the contribution to optics made by Chester Hall's invention of the achromatic lens in 1750, Joseph Black's study of latent heat, and the foundation of acoustics by Ernst Chladni (1756-1827), who discovered that the communication of vibrations in material bodies can be reduced to mathematical laws. Hall's invention revolutionized the telescope, while Black's helped on Watt and the steam engine. Chladni started the physical explanation of sound and the conquest of communication on their way.

The most striking and important scientific discoveries of the eighteenth century in natural science were unquestionably those in the field of chemistry. Joseph Priestley (1733-1804) and Karl Wilhelm Scheele (1742-86) upset the "phlogiston theory"—the doctrine that combustible bodies are composed in part of an invisible and highly combustible substance known as phlogiston.[1] During their researches they independently discovered oxygen. Scheele also found hydrogen, but did not fully realize the nature of his disclosure. Henry Cavendish (1731-1810) completed the discovery of hydrogen and unraveled the chemical composition of water. Antoine Lavoisier (1743-94), who was a tragic sacrifice to the French Reign of Terror, founded quantitative chemistry and the theory of the conservation of mass, established the fact of the chemical cycle of life, and revolutionized chemical nomenclature. The conception of atomic and molecular weights and the elementary laws of qualitative chemistry were soon to be laid down by Proust, Berthollet, Dalton, Gay-Lussac, and Avogadro.[2] The dominion of Aristotle, alchemy, mysticism, and superstition in chemistry, challenged by Boyle and Stahl, was now at an end and the path opened for the remarkable advances of the nineteenth century.

In the field of biology much further theoretical and descriptive work was

---

[1] It was not finally obliterated until the work of Lavoisier achieved the feat.
[2] See below, pp. 644 ff.

GIORDANO BRUNO — ANTOINE LAURENT LAVOISIER

SIR ISAAC NEWTON — CAROLUS LINNÉ

SOME GREAT SCIENTISTS

From a drawing by N. I. W. De Roode, *Ewing Galloway*
Open Court Publishing Company
AUGUSTE COMTE   JOHN LOCKE

Ewing Galloway   *Ewing Galloway*
FRANCIS BACON   RENÉ DESCARTES

SOME GREAT PHILOSOPHERS

done, in large part as a result of the improvement of the microscope and the application of the new chemical discoveries to biology and physiology. John Ray (1627-1705) systematized botanical knowledge. A Dutch scientist, Ingenhousz, worked on the exchange of gases between the plants and the air, and the Swiss Horace Bénédict de Saussure (1740-99) established the basic facts of the chemistry of plant nutrition. Albrecht von Haller (1708-77) systematized physiological knowledge and did valuable original work on respiration, embryology, and muscular irritability. Embryology was still further advanced through the studies of Caspar Wolff (1733-94). François Bichat (1771-1802) contributed the important doctrine that the life of the whole body is the outcome of the activities of the constituent tissues. John Hunter (1728-93) put comparative anatomy on its feet. Giovanni Morgagni (1682-1772) carried further the work in pathology started by Redi and others. The comparative anatomy of animals was linked up with that of man through the establishment of physical anthropology by Johann Friedrich Blumenbach (1752-1840) and others.

Medicine strode ahead in the eighteenth century on the basis of the progress in biology, physiology, chemistry, and pathology.[1] The outstanding figure of the opening of the century was Hermann Boerhaave. He synthesized and criticized the medical lore of the past, endeavoring to save what was valid. To this residue he joined the scientific knowledge of his own day. He greatly extended and popularized clinical medicine and laid much stress on the value of autopsies. Auenbrugger founded physical diagnosis by discovering the significance of the percussion of the thorax. Hunter extended our knowledge of pathology in disease and greatly improved the technique of surgery, especially in the ligature of the arteries. Edward Jenner, at the close of the eighteenth century, made one of the most important discoveries in the history of preventive medicine, namely, the theory of immunization to disease through vaccination. He showed that a subject innoculated with the mild disease of cowpox was safe against the ravages of the dread smallpox.

The achievements of the geologists were not only important in their own field, but were also of great significance for the evolutionary biology which was to arise in the next century.[2] Lazzaro Moro comprehended the full significance of fossils and of the stratification of rocks in interpreting earth history. Abraham Gottlieb Werner founded the principles of stratigraphical geology. James Hutton's *Theory of the Earth,* published in 1785, systematized the geological advances up to his time, emphasized the importance of the observational method in geology, and paved the way for the classic work of Sir Charles Lyell in the following century. This pioneer work in historical geology, which for the first time threw real light on the processes of earth formation and the meaning of fossils, constituted the beginnings of decisive scientific evidence that made untenable any short-time view, however widely held previously, of the creation of the world and its inhabitants. It was a contribution not only to science but also to the reconstruction of historical perspective.

[1] See Victor Robinson, *The Story of Medicine,* Albert & Charles Boni, 1932, Chap. x, and *Pathfinders in Medicine,* Chaps. ix-xi; and F. H. Garrison, *Introduction to the History of Medicine,* 4th ed., Saunders, 1929, Chaps. viii-x.
[2] *Cf.* Woodward, *op. cit.,* Chaps. ii-iii.

Finally, scientific methods, albeit of a crude type, began to be applied within the field of social science. With the work of Montesquieu, Ferguson, Gall, the Physiocrats, Adam Smith, the Cameralists, Bentham, and others, political philosophy tended to differentiate into the several social sciences of sociology, economics, political science, jurisprudence, and ethics.[1]

Another aspect of scientific progress in this period was the gradual entry of natural science into the respectable curriculum of the universities. Scientific research came to be less a matter of individual initiative or the collaboration of enthusiastic laymen. It slowly became a part of the organized system of academic knowledge and activities, fighting its way successfully against the vested educational interests of logic, metaphysics, and the classical languages. Not until the twentieth century did the natural sciences gradually drift away from universities to commercial laboratories and highly endowed private foundations, the latter of which may be roughly compared to the academies of the seventeenth and eighteenth centuries. Even this recent movement has been limited chiefly to the United States.

IV. THE EMANCIPATION OF PHILOSOPHY

1. MICHEL EYQUEM DE MONTAIGNE

Humanism, the new astronomy, the scientific revival, and the oversea discoveries brought about notable changes in philosophic thought. Most representative, perhaps, of these innovations were the writings of Montaigne, Francis Bacon, Descartes, John Locke, and David Hume. Each of these writers presented in one or more ways a very decisive departure from the Scholastic philosophy of the Middle Ages.

Montaigne (1533-90) is regarded by many as the first important Rationalistic and critical writer.[2] Lecky calls him the first great French skeptic. Scholasticism had been characterized primarily by great technicality, much logical wrangling, and very marked dogmatism. Montaigne departed from all these. He was popular in his phraseology and expression, urbane in his attitude, and profoundly dubious of any dogmatic certainty as to the major problems of knowledge and life. He once stated that he would prefer hoeing cabbages in his garden to engaging in Scholastic disputations.

Montaigne's training and intellectual background were well suited to producing the first great representative of urbanity, skepticism, and toleration. He was brought up in a tolerant household, his father being a Catholic and his mother a Jewess converted to Protestantism. Montaigne was no closet philosopher, but a man of affairs. He was a lawyer by training and profession and at one time served as Mayor of Bordeaux. This gave him a practical contact with everyday affairs and aided in promoting a realistic trend in his thought. The two main intellectual influences that helped to shape his thinking were the ancient classics and the discoveries overseas, the latter of which were just getting thoroughly under way during his lifetime. As we have already seen,

---

[1] See Randall, *op. cit.*, Chaps. XIII-XIV; H. E. Barnes and Howard Becker, *The History of Sociological Thought*, Heath (forthcoming), Chaps. XIV-XVI; and below, pp. 665 ff.
[2] See I. C. Willis, *Montaigne*, Knopf, 1927.

the ancient pagan philosophers were highly tolerant of views that conflicted with their own and were more interested in the things of this world than in salvation in the world to come. The discoveries overseas brought sharply to Montaigne's attention the great diversity of customs and ideas among both savage and civilized peoples scattered over the world's surface. Here was a very direct challenge to the prevailing Christian idea that there could be only one right way of living and thinking.

Montaigne broke with the medieval theology and Scholastic philosophy in his whole attitude towards the fundamental problems of life and human experience. He repudiated the supernatural and otherworldly perspective of the Christians. His was a predominantly secular outlook. He held that man is a dual entity, in which the body is fully as important as the soul. He thus launched that rebellion against the typical religious view of life which is prone to contrast the "higher" things associated with the soul and those "lower" matters connected with bodily needs and expression. His attitude here was similar to that of the Greeks. He suggested a complete revolution in the whole perspective of medieval philosophy by advocating the characteristic Epicurean contention that the purpose of human learning is to teach us how to live happily and not how to die safely.

Equally original and novel was his appreciation of the element of variety and diversity in life and nature. It was here that he was primarily affected by his reflections on oversea discoveries. He was impressed by the variety in both physical nature and human conduct. Hence the theological attempt to enforce uniformity in human behavior and thought seemed stupid to him. Yet he was a practical man, and argued that it was expedient to conform outwardly to the prevailing manners and customs of any given locality. But such conformity should be purely external and not lead to any sacrifice of real intellectual and moral integrity.

The ancient Greek philosopher Xenophanes suggested that a man is wont to construct conceptions of God in terms of his own attitudes and experiences. Montaigne, at least, conceived of a God as broad-minded and tolerant as was Montaigne himself. As a famous historian of European intellectual life observed, Montaigne was the first man in western Europe to discover a God who was not minutely interested in the details of individual faith and conduct. He held that if variety and diversity were characteristic of nature and mankind, God must be responsible for this situation. Otherwise we would have to divorce God from both nature and society or imagine both to be expressing themselves in a manner repugnant to the will of God. Therefore it was hard for Montaigne to conceive of a God who would sanction any ferocious efforts to enforce uniformity in ideas or conduct.

Montaigne's contact with everyday life produced a keen interest in the conditions about him and led him to combat intolerance and oppression. Hence many of his incomparable essays are devoted to undermining the bigotry and abuses of his age. He was thus a forerunner of the great French Rationalistic reformers, such as Bayle, Voltaire, and Helvétius. But Montaigne was too detached and urbane ever to become the active crusader of the type of Voltaire. He had, nevertheless, a wide influence in promoting tolerance and humanity because of the vast popularity of his essays. These were written with such clarity and charm that they have been enthusiastically read for centuries by countless thousands. The progress of knowledge since Montaigne's time has made it possible for men to be more learned, but it is doubtful if there has ever been a better example of a truly civilized intellect than the great French essayist of the late sixteenth century. The advance that he marked over Erasmus is very striking. The latter was indeed a person of a tolerant and urbane outlook, but these qualities in his case were applied almost exclusively to issues of supernaturalism and religion. With him, philosophy still remained very completely the handmaiden of theology. With Montaigne, it was already becoming an introduction to sociology and esthetics.

2. FRANCIS BACON

Until about the middle of the second decade of our own century it was commonly held that Roger Bacon back in the thirteenth century was the first great critic of the Scholastic method in theology and the deductive method in philosophy. We have already made it clear above that Bacon was, in most of his essential attitudes and interests, a true Scholastic philosopher. The reforms and innovations he suggested were primarily related to improving rather than repressing Scholasticism. It was his fellow countryman of the same surname, Francis Bacon (1561-1626), three centuries later, who was the first distinguished and well-publicized assailant of the Scholastic interests and methods.

Like Montaigne, Bacon's interests were secular and social rather than otherworldly and religious. He was, likewise, deeply influenced, as was Montaigne, by Humanism and the oversea discoveries. But to these he added a warm emotional appreciation of the scientific attitude, which had very little part in the philosophy of Montaigne. Bacon was the outstanding literary herald of the revival of natural science in early modern times. He felt that the deductive method was inadequate to the task of discovering new knowledge. Hence he repudiated the otherworldliness and the deductive Aristotelian logic of medieval Scholasticism. He wrote more beautifully and convincingly on the significance of science and on the inductive or experimental method than most other men before or since his day. One can best appreciate the departure that Bacon made from Scholasticism by comparing his *Advancement of Learning* (1605) with the *Summa theologica* that St. Thomas Aquinas produced in the thirteenth century.

Whatever Bacon's enthusiasm for the new scientific approach, he was keenly alive to the many obstacles that would have to be overcome in order to secure its acceptance in an age which was still overwhelmingly concerned with otherworldly interests and theological disputations. Therefore he did his best to undermine respect for antiquated methods. He suggested an ingenious reformulation of our conception of the Devil. The latter might well be considered as the sum total of the traditional or archaic ideas that continually assault mankind from all sides. Even though the personal Devil of the ancient theology may be questioned, there is no doubt of the reality and ubiquity of the Devil when conceived of in the manner suggested by Bacon. Bacon also offered an ingenious argument designed to overcome our unreasoning admiration for ancient knowledge. This he summarized pungently in his observation, "We are the ancients."[1] By this he meant that the accumulated fund of knowledge becomes older and richer with each generation. Under normal circumstances each generation possesses not only the wisdom of its predecessors but such new knowledge as has been added by the generation in question. If we go back to remote antiquity we find that knowledge is both more scanty and more unreliable. As we retrace the steps of human development we uncover ignorance and superstition rather than omniscience. Bacon thus presented the most powerful of all general arguments against the exclusive worship of intellectual authority and reverence for the knowledge of antiquity.

Probably the most famous item in Bacon's analysis of the obstacles to clear scientific thinking was his conception of the four "Idols" that impede intelligent and effective thinking.[2] In the first place, we are handicapped by what Bacon called the "Idol of the Tribe." By this he meant those defects which are inherent in the thinking of the human race as a whole, namely, our limited intellectual capacity, the dominion of emotion over reason, the tendency to jump at conclusions, and the like. To these are added those difficulties which arise out of what he called the "Idol of the Cave." These represent the special handicaps which are peculiar to the thinking of any given individual, namely, the prejudices and complexes that have arisen from the circumstances of his social surroundings, education, and experience. These make it difficult for the individual to face in an unbiased fashion ideas and conceptions that radically challenge his own preconceived notions.

Next we have the "Idol of the Market-place." Here Bacon had in mind the fact that we are impeded in our thinking through the necessity of putting our thoughts into words. It is often difficult to find the right word. Further, words have different meaning and emotional implications to various persons because of their divergent life experiences. Again, there is the proclivity to be more concerned with the style of expression than with the intellectual content. This was the great defect of ancient and modern rhetoric. Throughout the history of man there has been a tendency to let words act as a substitute for clear and effective thinking. Therefore, even if a man possesses clear and defensible ideas he may find it difficult to put them in exactly the right words to express his own notions. Moreover, even if he succeeds in this, his formulations may not convey exactly the right impression to others.

Finally, we have the "Idol of the Theatre." Men are inclined to become especially enamored of a given system of thought or of particular intellectual hobbies. Their notions will revolve about these special or personal formulations, to which there is usually an emotional as well as an intellectual attachment. This last Idol produces the single-track mind and promotes emotional discipleship for particular bodies of thought or types of social reform. All of these make it very hard indeed for one to approach a problem in the unbiased and open-minded fashion insisted upon by science. Bacon was, therefore, thoroughly aware of the difficulties to be overcome in promoting the scientific point of view, but he felt that these obstacles could best be overcome if we first clearly realize their character and extent.

[1] A statement and argument which first appears in the twelfth century.
[2] Bacon, *Novum Organum*, Bk. I, Secs. 37-45. These "Idols" may have been derived in part from the four obstacles to knowledge listed by Roger Bacon. See above, Vol. I, p. 790.

Bacon's departure from medievalism is forcefully borne out by his secular interests. In the Middle Ages the leading philosophers had been chiefly absorbed with the Kingdom of God and its problems. Bacon suggested that intelligent men should shift their intellectual interests to the Kingdom of Man.[1] Instead of trying to save souls they should seek to improve human institutions and living-conditions. In the place of relying upon divine revelation they should make an effort to increase the sum total of substantial scientific knowledge. The divergence of his attitude from that of the typical Christian theologian may be clearly discerned by comparing his *The New Atlantis* with St. Augustine's *The City of God*.

At the same time, Bacon was no crusader against the prevailing religious system. He formally assigned to theology the supremacy among the sciences and conceded that ultimate causation lay beyond the field of scientific research. He thus avoided trouble in the form of persecution by religious opponents. If this attitude was a form of obscurantism, it was also a very practical example of expediency making for greater peace of mind on the part of Bacon.

Bacon's most eloquent elaboration of his idea that science might be extremely effective in bettering human conditions was contained in his unfinished Utopia, *The New Atlantis*. This pictured an imaginary ideal society on an island off the western coast of South America. Here civilization had reached a much more advanced stage than elsewhere, owing to the greater development and application of scientific activity. The center of this community was the so-called House of Solomon, which has already been mentioned.[2] This was manned and controlled by scientists who devoted their attention wholly to experimental work and scientific research. The population as a whole was alert in appropriating the discoveries made at the House of Solomon and in applying these to bettering their living-conditions.

In spite of Bacon's enthusiasm for science, the part he played was that of a zealous literary supporter of the movement rather than a real scientist in his own right. No man has ever surpassed him as an essayist in this field. At the same time, very few men formally devoted to science have ever been less capable of appreciating existing scientific activity. While writing enthusiastically in support of the scientific method, Bacon either ignored or attacked most of the actual scientific work carried on in his day. As noted before, he attempted to ridicule the Copernican system. He scoffed at the work of Gilbert, who founded the scientific study of electricity and magnetism, and he depreciated the significance of mathematics for natural science. Incredible as it may seem, he also believed in astrology and witchcraft. These facts have led to severe attacks upon Bacon's intelligence and integrity by some historians, most conspicuously Dr. John W. Draper. The flavor of Draper's criticism may be discerned from the following:

Few scientific pretenders have made more mistakes than Lord Bacon. He rejected the Copernican system, and spoke insolently of its great author; he undertook to criticise adversely Gilbert's treatise "De Magnete"; he was occupied in the condemnation of any investigation of final causes, while Harvey was deducing the circulation of the blood from Aquapendente's discovery of the valves in the veins; he was

---

[1] He here agreed with Montaigne. [2] See above, p. 150.

doubtful whether instruments were of any advantage, while Galileo was investigating the heavens with the telescope. Ignorant himself of every branch of mathematics, he presumed they were useless in science, but a few years before Newton achieved by their aid his immortal discoveries. It is time the sacred name of philosophy should be severed from its long connexion with that of one who was a pretender in science, a time-serving politician, an insidious lawyer, a corrupt judge, a treacherous friend, a bad man.[1]

While we need not carry our derogation so far, it must be admitted that Bacon himself came very close to falling a victim to his own Idols of the Market-place and the Theatre.

When all is said and done, Bacon wrote most effectively in behalf of the experimental point of view in human learning and made himself one of the major figures in that intellectual tradition which lays special emphasis upon the potency of science in human affairs. In short, he was one of those rare Humanists who praised instead of despising natural science.

3. RENÉ DESCARTES

While Bacon had either despised or ignored mathematics, the eminent French scientist and philosopher, René Descartes (1596-1650), rightly recognized that mathematics constitutes the fundamental basis of all physical science. His own work in this field put him among the dozen most distinguished figures in the history of mathematics. He did important work on the theory of equations, but he is usually remembered for his advancement of analytical geometry, thereby preparing the way for the indispensable calculus later devised by Newton and Leibnitz. The scientific discoveries of his own day also influenced Descartes's cosmology, biology, and psychology. He was most deeply affected here by Harvey's discovery of the circulation of the blood. On the basis of this and certain related findings, Descartes believed that all phenomena, from the universe as a whole to the lowest forms of life, were constructed and functioned as machines.[2] The lower animals are mere automatons—purely mechanical without any conscious reflection. In a strictly physiological sense, man is also a mere machine organized about the central pumping plant of the heart. But, because of his soul, located as Descartes believed in the pineal gland, man is a higher form of machine than the lower animals. He possesses the capacity of consciousness, and hence the power of reflective self-direction.

Descartes is important in the history of thought mainly because of his contributions to philosophical and scientific method. In his *Discourse on Method* he set forth an admirable body of principles. He held that the first step is to wipe away all earlier and accepted authority and to start out with a clear and unbiased mind. The philosopher must never accept as true anything that cannot be proved to be such. Everything must be stated at the outset in the

[1] J. W. Draper, *History of the Intellectual Development of Europe*, rev. ed., Harper, 1904, 2 vols., Vol. II, p. 60.
[2] See especially Woodbridge Riley, *From Myth to Reason*, Appleton, 1926, Bk. IV. His notions here were much less exact and scientific than the work of the Italian physiologist Borelli.

most simple and clear form, gradually and logically advancing to the more complex and involved problems. Each specific problem must be divided into as many parts as may be necessary to solve it. Thoughts and propositions must be arranged in an orderly sequence of ideas. In the end, there must be complete analysis and a sufficiently comprehensive review of the whole problem to omit nothing. This book was written in lucid French for the intelligent layman, and hence had a very wide influence on the history of philosophical thought and scientific method.

To secure support for his mathematical physics, Descartes turned from the Aristotelian position, which had an opposing physics of its own, to the Augustinian doctrine, in which God was identified with the realm of mathematics. While he went back to St. Anselm's ontological proof of God to substantiate his theism, his views of God were quite different from those of Anselm. In his correspondence, Descartes once said: "You can substitute 'the mathematical order of nature' for 'God' whenever I use the latter term"—a view not so far from that of Jeans, Eddington, and Millikan in our day. In this sense, Descartes's proofs of God were not due to "preconceived notions," as is often charged, but to the necessity of such a concept to hold his thought together—combined, of course, with the strategic desire to get the support of the most influential party of French theologians for his revolution in physics, in which aspiration he was eminently successful.

In the history of psychology Descartes is noted for his clear and uncompromising statement of the doctrine of the dualism between mind and body, that is, the dogma that they are generically separate and different. The vital characteristic of the body is essence, while that of the mind is thought. They must even be studied by different methods. There is an eternal opposition between the essential material body and the thinking self. Hence there can be no interaction between mind and body—a doctrine directly opposed to modern scientific psychology, which more accurately regards thinking as a biochemical function of the physical brain and nervous system. Descartes made his ultimate test of reality the fact of consciousness, expressed as, "I think, therefore I am."

While Descartes believed in God and was willing to admit the possibility of divine purpose in the universe, his notions on these matters would give little comfort to an orthodox theologian. To him God was not a personality but "Absolute Substance." Moreover, he held that if there was a divine purpose in the universe it must be of a truly divine order. Therefore, it would be beyond the grasp of a mere mortal like man. In his general intellectual and religious attitudes, however, Descartes was of a distinctly conservative cast of mind.

Descartes was extremely timid in publicly expressing subversive ideas. His motto was one that he lifted from the Latin writer Ovid, *Bene vixit qui bene latuit*—"He lives well who effectively hides his opinions." Nevertheless, the broad outlines of Descartes's intellectual system, as expressed in his *Discourse on Method,* were of an advanced and progressive character and had a very considerable influence upon the subsequent history of ideas.

4. JOHN LOCKE

John Locke (1632-1704), the English physician, publicist, and apologist of middle-class revolutionary sentiment, was the foremost apostle of that seventeenth-century mechanical conception of experience—known as Empiricism—of which his contemporary, Hobbes, had been the founder. According to this doctrine, all the materials of knowledge are the result of the mechanical impact of particles upon the sense organs. This empirical doctrine Locke set forth in his *Essay concerning the Human Understanding,* which has been called by an eminent historian of philosophy "The Inaugural Lecture of the Eighteenth Century."

Locke began by clearing away what he regarded as antique rubbish. He asserted that philosophy should pretend to deal only with problems and conceptions that the human mind is capable of encompassing. Admitting definite limitations to the human mind, he excluded from consideration many issues that earlier philosophers and theologians had assumed to meddle with. He vigorously assaulted the doctrine of innate ideas, contending that man is not born with any apprehension of universal truth. Indeed he questioned any such thing as the universality of knowledge.

Locke then turned to the problem of how we come by the ideas with which the mature human mind is stocked. He contended that these are the product of experience and of reflection on experience—that is, Reason. He thus expressed his historic contention in his famous *Essay concerning Human Understanding:*

> Let us then suppose the mind to be . . . white paper, void of all characters, without any ideas; how comes it to be furnished? Whence comes it by that vast store which the busy and boundless fancy of man has painted on it with an almost endless variety? Whence has it all the materials of reason and knowledge? To this I answer, in one word, from experience; in that all our knowledge is founded, and from that it ultimately derives itself. Our observation employed either about external sensible objects, or about the internal operations of our minds, perceived and reflected on by ourselves, is that which supplies our understandings with all the materials of thinking. These two are the fountains of knowledge, from whence all the ideas we have, or can naturally have, do spring.[1]

Our impressions of external objects are what might be called sensations, while consciousness of the operations of our own mind he calls reflections. These are the two sources of human knowledge. By thus basing knowledge on experience and Reason rather than innate ideas or revelation, Locke separated himself from existing philosophical tradition and theological dogma.

Yet Locke was in no sense irreligious. What he attempted to do was to bring religion into conformity with reason and experience. Luther had contended that there was a fierce conflict between reason and faith, in which the latter was always triumphant. Locke held that the only valid faith was one that could be founded upon reason. He was one of the leaders in the early struggle for religious toleration. But he was hardly able to go the whole way to Rationalism. He believed in miracles and thought they were essential

---

[1] Bk. II, Chap. 1, § 2.

to refresh religious convictions. Moreover, he did not approve of toleration for Catholics and atheists, excluding the latter, for example, on the ground that they denied the existence and the law of God, could not be bound by an oath, and thus destroyed the very foundations of morality. In his doctrines in the field of ethics Locke also exhibited symptoms of both the old and the new order. He held that human happiness rather than the salvation of the soul must be regarded as the supreme good, but he sought the origins and nature of moral law in the will and law of God. In political theory, Locke was easily the leader of the new liberalism that justified revolution against tyranny.[1]

Among the numerous and important personalities who created the Enlightenment of the eighteenth century, John Locke was rivaled only by Bayle and surpassed only by Voltaire. He was the most influential philosopher of his generation. He created a new and progressive type of psychology, led the fight against intolerance, defended Reason against Faith in a period when this was more dangerous than a century later, started the revolt in education against pedantry and classicism, and was the most important figure in the whole age in systematizing the type of political and legal theory that dominated the Enlightenment. If he did not go so far as Voltaire, the path of the latter was made easier because of Locke's earlier work. If he was timid and heavy when compared to Bayle, his thought was more profound and his influence much greater.

5. DAVID HUME

David Hume (1711-76) possessed the most devastating critical mind in the whole period of Rationalism. His philosophy represented the most extreme development of the skeptical tendency. He was particularly famous for his criticism of the accepted doctrine of causation. What Hume sought to prove was that the idea of a "necessary connection"—that is, logical necessity—is no essential part of a working theory of causation. His empirical idea of causation was merely that of a "constant conjunction" between things. The observation of this "constant conjunction" does indeed establish a workable notion of causal relation, but not any "necessary connection." It also logically creates the belief that what has been constantly conjoined will always be conjoined. While Hume thus ruled the idea of logical necessity out of the theory of causation he was not highly skeptical about the doctrine of a causal order based upon observation. Indeed, he was a thoroughgoing naturalist and determinist who used the notion of a causal order constantly in criticizing miracles and other theological conceptions. What he condemned was inference going beyond observation, on the principle that "there must be a cause" for what is observed, though the cause be unobservable. This skepticism of Hume stimulated the great German philosopher Immanuel Kant to undertake his classic *Critique of Pure Reason.*

Hume's ethical, religious, and political doctrines are examined elsewhere.[2] He rejected any absolute principles or purposes in ethics and held that conduct must be justified by its contribution to utility and human well-being. We are induced to help others through the operation of sympathy, by which we are able to project ourselves into the unhappy situation of those requiring help. True morality is that conduct which increases human happiness.

[1] See below, pp. 217 ff.   [2] See below, p. 190.

THE EMANCIPATION OF PHILOSOPHY

We have now briefly surveyed the manner in which philosophy was liberated from bondage to Aristotelianism, deductive metaphysics, and Christian dogma. It came to be concerned with problems of life here on earth, was guided by generalizations based upon human experience, and grew to have proper respect for the methods and discoveries of science.[1]

V. THE BLIGHT OF INTOLERANCE AND CENSORSHIP

The human race has been extremely intolerant of dissent and novelty. Countless thousands, since the dawn of history, have come to an untimely end or endured excruciating tortures because they have dared to think or act in a manner opposed to the ways of the majority. A heavy penalty has been placed upon nonconformity. The way of the doubter and the heretic has been far harder than that of the proverbial transgressor.[2]

Among the chief foundations of intolerance are fear and laziness. Primitive man believes that all institutions and social habits are revealed and established by the gods. Any deviation by an individual from the safe customary ways of life is highly dangerous. It will arouse the anger of the spiritual powers and bring disaster to the group. Consequently, taboos are set up, specifying what cannot be done if group customs are to be maintained unimpaired. Fierce punishment is visited upon him who dares to violate a taboo and thereby to place in jeopardy the safety and prosperity of the group. The whole primitive scheme of things depends upon a strict observance of wont and custom. While this fear of innovation and change is far greater in primitive society, much of this panicky attitude has been perpetuated in modern society. Hendrik Van Loon rightly makes much of ignorance and self-interest as causes of intolerance,[3] and they are very often the underlying causes of the fear complex.

The dominating factor in the enforcement of this attitude of conformity is the so-called instinct of the herd. Man is relatively helpless by himself. Group life and coöperative endeavor have ever been essential to human safety and progress. This has meant that group discipline must be enforced in order to make the community unified and efficient. Rules of conduct and thought must be laid down. The violator of these must suffer. This group discipline, so essential to human survival, has exacted a high price in the way of ruthlessly stamping out the innovator and the rebel. The history of civilization is, in a way, the record of the extension of the field of dissent that society will tolerate. Dr. Dietrich has well described the operation of fear-dominated herd instinct upon intolerance through the ages:

After all, intolerance is merely the manifestation of the *protective instinct of the herd*. The life of the individual is so dependent upon the life of the group, that the group, and the various individuals in the group, are afraid to let any individual say or do anything that might endanger the protective power of the group. Thus a pack of wolves is intolerant of the wolf that is different and invariably gets rid of

---

[1] See below, pp. 680 ff., 1067 ff. We have not included Spinoza, since he is more important for the history of technical philosophy than for the history of thought. He was "the philosopher's philosopher." For a reliable popular treatment, see Lewis Browne, *Blesséd Spinoza*, Macmillan, 1932. The same considerations apply to the omission of Leibnitz.

[2] *Cf.* E. P. Cheyney, *Law in History, and Other Essays*, Crofts, 1927, Chap. II.

[3] *Tolerance*, Boni & Liveright, 1925.

this offending individual. A tribe of cannibals is intolerant of the individual who threatens to provoke the wrath of the gods and bring disaster upon the whole community, and so drives him into the wilderness. The Greek commonwealth cannot afford to harbor within its sacred walls one who dares to question the very basis of its organization, and so in an outburst of intolerance condemns the offender to drink the poison. The Roman cannot hope to survive if a small group of zealots play fast and loose with laws held indispensable since the days of Romulus, and so is driven into deeds of intolerance. The Church depended in early days for her continued existence upon the absolute obedience of even the humblest of her subjects and is driven to such extremes of suppression and cruelty that many prefer the ruthlessness of the Turk to the charity of the Christian. And in a period of hysterical fear, even we Americans are assured that our government cannot withstand criticism, and so we throw into prison or deport from our shores those who dare offer it. And so it goes throughout the ages until life, which might be a glorious adventure, is turned into a horrible experience, and all this happens because human existence so far has been entirely dominated by fear.[1]

Laziness is another foundation of intolerance. The habitual and the traditional is not only the safe thing. It is also the easy thing to do. Our muscular reflexes and patterns of mental behavior are adapted to doing things in the way we have been taught to do them. It is easier to think in the old grooves to which we have become accustomed since childhood. Habit, as William James pointed out, is the great flywheel of society. We need to give but little attention to habitual modes of thought and behavior. Years of adjustment have made them natural and mainly unconscious. New ways and thoughts, on the other hand, are painful. This pain is not only psychological, but even mildly physiological, as the new science of endocrinology has made clear.[2] Any innovation upsets our whole established scheme of things, cuts across our habitual reactions, and forces a readjustment that our timid and lazy nature resents and resists.

Fear and laziness, then, beget intolerance of change and novelty. They lead us to hate the innovator. Fear doubtless produces a far more vigorous expression of intolerance than does laziness, but the latter adds its quota to the total social resentment against the person who suggests a new way of regarding an issue of morals, religion, politics, law, education, art, and the like.

We have already referred to the severe intolerance of primitive society and to the even more thoroughly organized repression of any innovation in the military-religious society of the ancient Orient.[3] In classical society a very considerable freedom of opinion and action existed for the educated and favored classes. With the rise of Christianity something approaching the intolerance of oriental antiquity once more reappeared. Christianity added a new source of fear with respect to new ideas. Before this time, there had been little concern with regard to the future life. The violator of a taboo might bring temporal disaster to his social group, but he was not so often thought of as placing immortal souls in jeopardy. With the Christians the future life came to be all-important. Earthly disaster was of slight significance compared to the

[1] J. H. Dietrich, *The Road to Tolerance*, privately published, Minneapolis, 1929.
[2] Particularly in the study of the psychology of the emotions. *Cf.* W. B. Cannon, "What Strong Emotions Do to Us," *Harper's Magazine*, July, 1922.   [3] See above, Vol. I, pp. 56 ff., 172 ff.

THE BLIGHT OF INTOLERANCE AND CENSORSHIP 165

incurring of eternal damnation. Therefore Christian opinion during the Middle Ages was resentful of innovation on double grounds. It might bring mankind immediate disaster and it might also produce the inestimable tragedy of damnation in the life to come.¹

The intolerance of the medieval Catholic Church rested on two grounds, political and religious.² The Church in an administrative sense was modeled after the Roman imperial system. It was veritably a new and greater Rome. It became the greatest international state the world had ever known, or knew down to the British Empire of the nineteenth century. Any challenge to its authority in the form of heresy was not only a doctrinal menace but politico-ecclesiastical treason. This, more than sympathy for the damned, was the foundation of the fierce treatment of medieval heretics.

On the religious side, of course, there was ample reason for the Church to be impatient with those who departed from the true unity of Christian doctrine. There was no salvation except in following precisely the literal teachings of the Church. The heretic was doomed to damnation. The more he persisted in his false teachings, the greater his punishment in Hell. Further, the longer he was permitted to teach and convert, the more souls he dragged to Hell after him. Hence there was every logical reason why the Church should stamp out heretics with expedition and no little savagery.

The attitude of the Catholic Church towards those who hold views at variance with Catholic doctrine has varied according to time and the class of persons involved. Down to the Counter-Reformation, when the repressive and protective activities of the Church were revived and extended, there was by no means any such ferocity of reaction towards somewhat daring scholars as certain Protestant and skeptical historians have asserted to be the case. Abélard's persecution was due more to his own irascible nature and to the savage personal hatred of St. Bernard than to the general policy of the Church.³ The manhandling of Roger Bacon by the Church now appears to have been somewhat exaggerated in many older historical accounts. While by no means encouraging intellectual independence, the Church was prone to overlook the heterodox views of esoteric scholars expressing their notions within the cloistered walls of the colleges and universities.

With heretics—those who attempted to start a popular doctrinal rebellion—the reaction of the Church was quite different. Here there was plenty of aggressive repression. Even repentant heretics were frequently put to death. The Crusades were in a way a manifestation of Christian intolerance on a vast scale, but the most notorious example of medieval Christian intolerance was, perhaps, the brutal extermination of the admirable Albigensian cult and Provençal culture in the thirteenth century. In Spain especially the Jews and the Moors were treated with great brutality, and many thousands put to death

---

¹ See above, Vol. I, pp. 355 ff.
² See J. H. Robinson, *Introduction to the History of Western Europe*, rev. ed., Ginn, 1924, 2 vols., Vol. I, pp. 243-47, and *Mind in the Making*, Harper, 1921, pp. 132 ff. A good summary of up-to-date opinion, correcting Lecky's views on heresy and intolerance. The most satisfactory, scholarly summary of the Catholic theory of intolerance and persecution is that by E. W. Nelson, in *Persecution and Liberty: Essays in Honor of George Lincoln Burr*, pp. 3-20.
³ See above, Vol. I, pp. 739 ff.

in the most barbarous fashion. After Protestantism was launched a new enemy rose for the Church to cope with. In many Catholic countries the Protestants were repressed with extreme alertness and cruelty. The most striking examples were the Catholic retaliations in the Thirty Years' War, the massacre of St. Bartholemew's Day in France in 1572, and the slaughter after the Revocation of the Edict of Nantes in 1685.

The chief instrument of intolerance in Catholicism was the Inquisition—an agency for the investigation and punishment of heresy and infidelity. While active in the later Middle Ages, it became especially energetic after the Counter-Reformation. The most savage and notorious of these inquisitory bodies was the Spanish Inquisition. It was founded in the latter part of the fifteenth century to curb Jews and Moors, but was later used with terrible effect against Christian heretics, real and suspect. The Church did not execute its victims. It convicted them through horrible tortures and then turned them over to the State for the infliction of the death penalty. These butcheries (*autos da fe*), literally carried on in the name of the Lord, were often made festive days for the countryside and city dwellers.

Among the early Protestants, likewise, there was little of the spirit of urbane toleration. As we have seen, Calvin burned Servetus at the stake because of a difference of opinion concerning the Trinity, and Melanchthon, the learned Protestant leader, praised this act as a model for future generations. The Protestant Tudors killed many Catholics in England, and the Stuart monarchs and Protestant Parliaments placed Catholics under severe disabilities for centuries. Tens of thousands of Irish Catholics were massacred for religious as well as political reasons by Cromwell and other Protestant leaders. Even in the English colonies in America, some of which were ostensibly established to provide religious freedom, there was persecution, often of a brutal nature.[1]

The one great weakness of the Protestants in enforcing intolerance was that there was little unity within the movement. Protestantism began in secession and it has grown up by following this practice. Those who did not like the majority policy in a particular sect could get out and found a new movement. This has gone on until today it takes several pages of the census reports to list the various Protestant sects in the United States.

The majority sect in any Protestant state could, however, turn to the state for aid and pass laws placing the minority sects under severe disadvantages, as was done in England from the seventeenth century to the nineteenth. In proceeding against Catholics and Dissenters the Protestant governments used such instruments and methods as the notorious Court of the Star Chamber in England—really the King's Council sitting in the capacity of a tribunal of summary justice. Repressive legislation was also frequent.

Down to the time of the invention of printing, intolerance was directed chiefly against the spoken word and the opinions expressed in the few books or tracts laboriously copied by hand. But printing slowly opened the way for the influence of dangerous books that might be freely circulated by the tens of thousands. At first there was little censorship, because the earliest books published were the Bible, Latin grammars, Scholastic philosophical treatises, me-

---

[1] J. M. Mecklin, *The Story of American Dissent*, Harcourt, Brace, 1934.

THE BLIGHT OF INTOLERANCE AND CENSORSHIP 167

dieval encyclopedias, and the like that had long been in existence in copied form. It soon became evident, however, that books containing novel and dangerous doctrines might be printed and sent broadcast over the land. Precautions had to be taken against such a calamity. Therefore, usually at the behest of the Church, laws were passed directing that all presses be licensed. Unlicensed printing was severely punished, in some Catholic countries by the death penalty. A printer who published a dangerous book might possibly have his license revoked, lose his means of livelihood, and be severely punished, perhaps by death. This was the reason for Osiander's protective foreword to his edition of Copernicus' epoch-making work.

The first license to operate a press was issued by the Archbishop of Mainz in 1485. In 1546 the Council of Trent put further restrictions upon unlicensed printing and in 1559 Pope Paul IV issued the first real Catholic *Index of Prohibited Books*. Other and fuller editions of the *Index* have since been issued. At first, the Catholic *Index* attempted to cover Catholic, Protestant, and infidel literature, but the present *Index* is limited chiefly to Catholic books, since the progress of printing has made the examination of all books too great a task.[1]

Protestant countries were not slow to set up a censorship of the press. The action of England is representative. The Court of the Star Chamber limited unlicensed printing by decrees of 1586 and 1637. Then, in 1643, the Long Parliament passed an act forbidding all unlicensed printing. This outrage called forth the classic defense of the freedom of publication, Milton's *Areopagitica* (1644). Yet, as evidence of human frailty in practical situations, it was not more than a decade before Milton himself was acting in a capacity dangerously close to that of a censor for the Commonwealth government. Two eminent men were brutally mutilated and imprisoned in England for their publishing activities, Alexander Leighton and William Prynne. Under the Restoration the censorship system was relaxed somewhat, but it was a half-century before any wide freedom of printing was achieved even in England. Indeed, absolute freedom of the press has not yet been won even in the United States.

Intelligent and educated persons have long since come to understand the futility of censorship. Most notions that we desire to keep from the people are not actually harmful. Even if they were, censorship usually results in far greater advertising of the ideas that we want to suppress. Moreover, all censorship is likely to be unenlightened, for ignorance and stupidity are usually implicit in the consent of persons to act as censors. Perhaps no one has put the case against censorship more concisely than did James Harvey Robinson in an interview published in the *Literary Digest* of June 23, 1923:

> I am opposed to all censorship, partly because we already have Draconian laws, and police willing to interfere on slight pretense in cases in which the public sense of propriety seems likely to be shocked; partly because, as Milton long ago pointed out, censors are pretty sure to be fools, for otherwise they would not consent to act. Then I am a strong believer in the fundamental value of sophistication. I would have boys and girls learn early about certain so-called "evils"—and rightly so-called

[1] The most recent brief and authoritative summary of the character of the Catholic *Index* is Joseph McCabe, *The History and Meaning of the Catholic Index of Forbidden Books*, Haldeman-Julius, 1931.

—so that they begin to reckon with them in time. I have no confidence in the suppression of every-day facts. We are much too skittish of honesty. When we declare that this or that will prove demoralizing, we rarely ask ourselves, demoralizing to whom and how? We have a sufficiently delicate machinery already to prevent the circulation of one of Thorstein Veblen's philosophic treatises and Mr. Cabell's highly esoteric romance. For further particulars see the late John Milton's "Areopagitica" *passim*. To judge by the conduct of some of our college heads the influence of this work is confined to a recognition of its noble phraseology, with little realization of the perennial value of the sentiments it contains.[1]

Down to this period in the history of western Europe we have treated of intolerance as something primarily related to religion, though there was plenty of political oppression as well. But the economic and social changes that we have described in preceding chapters, which are best envisaged under the general term of the rise of capitalism, led to the appearance of another ground for intolerance, namely, the economic. Private property and material wealth assumed a new importance in human thinking. The vested economic interests became as jealous of their material possessions as the medieval Church had been of its theological pretensions and responsibilities. It gradually became as audacious to challenge the institution of property and the profit motive as it had been to question the accepted theory of the Trinity. As we shall point out soon, Christianity came to the defense of capitalism, and the two combined to create the most oppressive type of modern intolerance. When it seemed as though freedom had been won from the heavy hand of the tottering supernaturalism, a new form of mental intimidation arose in the shape of capitalistic dogmas and controls. Martyrs to economic radicalism have died or been imprisoned in large numbers since 1700, a Babeuf matching a Servetus, a Tom Mooney a Roger Williams, and a Sacco a Bruno. Wholesale deportation and frequent imprisonment of economic dissenters is common even in the United States of today, while in Fascist countries their treatment recalls that of the heretics in medieval and early modern times. Even the end of capitalism would certainly not relieve us of economic intolerance, for a time at least. The Russian Communists are as intolerant of the very conception of private property in the production and distribution of goods as the capitalists have been of attacks upon it.

VI. THE GROWTH OF TOLERATION AND FREEDOM OF THOUGHT

The growth of tolerance, urbanity, and free thought constitutes the most convincing evidence of the progress of human civilization. The case for toleration may rest on one of two grounds. The first is the purely self-interested emotional protest of the minority that is being trampled on. Examples of this were the early Christians in the Roman Empire, the repressed nationalities in Europe before 1914, or the Russian Communists before 1917. In such cases, there is rarely any general intellectual comprehension of the broad merits and implications of intellectual freedom. It is merely the distressed howl of the underdog, who is all too willing to use similar methods once he gets into control.

---

[1] "Censorship or Not," *loc. cit.*, p. 29.

GROWTH OF TOLERATION AND FREEDOM OF THOUGHT

Witness, for example, the Christian proscription of paganism after Constantine, the brutal repressiveness of the present Yugoslav government in dealing with Croats and Macedonians, and the severe intolerance of economic dissent in Bolshevik Russia.

The second or intellectual justification of toleration is something quite different. It has no relationship to the possession of dominant physical or political power. In the first place, it requires a good historical sense that will enable one to recognize the absurdity of most of the propositions and policies concerning which man has been intolerant in the past. History also reveals the lack of success that has attended the majority of the efforts to put over a doctrine or policy by means of sheer physical force. In the second place, intellectual humility dictates a tolerant attitude, for such humility arises from a sense of the relative weakness of the best human intellects and the highly tentative and incomplete character of human knowledge on any topic whatsoever. We have no such absolute certainty on any point as would justify its forcible inculcation. Then, any understanding of the really adroit technique of conversion would make it clear that convincing argumentation is far better than any effort to blackjack the skeptical. Moreover, if one has real faith in the ultimate triumph of truth and right he can afford to let these win gradually and moderately, rather than to jeopardize their success by unwise ardor. Finally, the spirit of urbanity and a sense of humor are admirable safeguards against an intolerant attitude, particularly when joined to the cosmic perspective possible today.

The Catholic Church has been consistently and logically intolerant in its official policy. In actual practice, it has often been far more tolerant at certain times and in certain quarters than the Protestants. But its formal doctrine has been one of unyielding intolerance of views that diverge from what is regarded by the Church as divinely revealed truth. From St. Augustine and Cardinal Bellarmine to Father Sheen and Father Gillis in our own day, the intolerance of Catholicism has been defended as the intolerance sprung of the possession of divine truth. Granting the premises of the Church, which loyal churchmen must accept, there would seem to be no logical objection to this view. It simply happens that these premises are becoming progressively more susceptible to effective skeptical criticism.

Many of the early arguments centered about the relations of Church and State. The Catholic Church had held that the State was the servant and handmaiden of the Church. It should aid in maintaining the faith but should never assume to control religion. It had been a leading tenet of Protestantism that the State should have control over the religion of the region when it wished to assert this power. Should the State adopt and rigorously enforce the doctrines of the dominant Church? The affirmative answer was the attitude in Catholic countries and in some Protestant countries in early modern times. John Calvin, especially, asserted the power of the state to control religion in his government of Geneva. It was this state intervention that made possible effective religious intolerance. Without the civil arm to enforce its will, religion would have been powerless to maintain its decrees.

The argument against state enforcement of ecclesiastical policies was well set forth by the Socinians (later called Unitarians), the Anabaptists, the

Quakers, and the eminent philosopher John Locke.[1] The Socinians, so called because of their founders, Laelius and Faustus Socinus, favored the union of the dominant Church with the State, but held that there should be full toleration for all other sects and cults. The Anabaptists, whose chief stronghold was at Münster in Westphalia, went even further. They advocated complete separation of Church and State. This doctrine was stated in extreme fashion in the United States by Roger Williams, founder of the first truly free commonwealth—Rhode Island.[2] William Penn and the Quakers argued fervently against the right of the civil authority to coerce one in spiritual matters. Locke defended toleration on grounds of logic, his argument running as follows: There are many religions. There can be but one true religion. If we allow the state to enforce religion, this would mean that some governments would be enforcing a religion of error and consigning many souls to damnation. Far better to let religions compete freely, so that the true one may assert itself and triumph. Locke, moreover, agreed with the Quakers that the state has no legitimate power over human belief. Yet Locke was able to find sufficient reasons why there should be no toleration for Catholics or atheists.

Other writers developed ingenious arguments in support of toleration. We have already noted the earlier views of Montaigne. In his *Religion of the Protestants a Safe Way to Salvation,* published in 1637, William Chillingworth held that all that is necessary to insure salvation are a few essentials of the Christian faith. Other tenets are of indifferent character, and dissent in regard to these nonessentials should be fully and freely tolerated. The same notion was set forth a few years later by Jeremy Taylor in his *Discourse on the Liberty of Prophesying* (1647). He held that the Apostles' Creed constitutes the essential points of Christianity. Belief in this is all that is needed to secure salvation. There should be full toleration for those religions which accept this, whatever the other items in their creeds.

A more sweeping philosophical argument for toleration was set forth by Joseph Glanvill, a skeptic who nevertheless defended the belief in witchcraft. In his *Vanity of Dogmatizing,* published in 1661, he stated the case for intellectual humility and the relativity of knowledge. He emphasized the fact that human ignorance is enormous compared to the relatively weak human intellect and the slight volume of definite human knowledge. Further, what passes for final human knowledge is relative as to time and place. The dogmas of one region or period are derided in another area and epoch.[3] With the subsequent development of skepticism and indifference, the movement for toleration grew apace.

The French skeptic Pierre Bayle contributed an ironic critique of intolerance in his *Compel Them to Come In,* published in 1686.[4] Like Montaigne and Glanvill, he stressed the great diversity of opinions held with regard to any

---

[1] See A. C. McGiffert, *Protestant Thought before Kant,* Scribner, 1911, Chap. VI; and Smith, *op. cit.,* Vol. I, pp. 391 ff.; Vol. II, pp. 450 ff.

[2] See E. J. Carpenter, *Roger Williams,* Grafton Press, 1909; and M. L. Greene, *The Development of Religious Liberty in Connecticut,* Houghton Mifflin, 1905.

[3] Incidentally, Glanvill also anticipated Hume's devastating criticism of the accepted notions of causation. *Cf.* Ferris Greenslet, *Joseph Glanvill* (Macmillan, 1900).

[4] On Bayle and toleration, see Howard Robinson, *Bayle the Sceptic,* Columbia University Press, 1932, Chap. IV.

subject and pointed out that the partisans of each dogma believe it to be absolute truth. He said that while we are wont to regard our neighbors as foolish heretics, they are at the same time probably entertaining the same notions regarding us. He further pointed out that no one can be so sure of possessing absolute truth as to justify forcing its acceptance upon another person. Moreover, forcible feeding of ideas is a poor method of converting anyone to our point of view. We may club a man into admitting that he agrees with us, but in his own mind he is likely to be more than ever set against us in the end. Urbane argument is the only wise method of trying to convince another. If this fails we may as well pass on the task to someone else.[1] Bayle held that we should permit complete freedom for any type of religious or irreligious thought. If we presume to take Christianity to the Siamese we should invite the Siamese to bring their religion to us and test out the excellencies of the two cults through competition.

An English Deist, Matthew Tindal (1656-1733), defended the liberty of conscience very effectively in his *Essay on the Power of the Magistrate* (1697), and the next year in his *Liberty of the Press* he argued eloquently for freedom in religious discussion and witheringly attacked the proposal to license the press. But even he would not tolerate atheists. A satirical contribution to the cause of toleration came from the pen of Daniel Defoe. He wrote a little tract called *The Shortest Way with Dissenters* (1702). He deliberately assumed the point of view of a very intolerant English high churchman and argued for the utmost severity in repressing dissent. His work was really a reductio ad absurdum of Anglican intolerance in England. For a moment his intent was misunderstood and the book was hailed by the reactionaries as a masterpiece in defense of intolerance. Soon afterwards the hoax was discovered and Defoe was thrown into jail for a time.

A revolutionary step forward in the defense of intellectual freedom was taken by Anthony Collins (1676-1729) in his *Discourse of Free Thinking* (1713), ably supplemented by his *Inquiry concerning Human Liberty* (1715). These works took the argument beyond the case for toleration. Toleration, while a gratifying improvement over intolerance, is in reality an intellectually arrogant attitude. To tolerate anything, we more or less necessarily assume that our notions are right, but that, in our own infinite wisdom, we can afford to tolerate the errors of our brothers in darkness. Freethinking concedes the absence of any certainty or dogmatic assurance about any form of human knowledge on the part of anybody. With this approach to the issue, the question of toleration hardly emerges, for the notion of intolerance can hardly be entertained. The pursuit of knowledge is open to all comers, without restraint. Individual reason must be the supreme guide for men in the quest of knowledge and we should be willing to follow reason wherever it logically seems to lead. This is, of course, the opposite extreme from Luther's conception that reason is the Devil's most dangerous and attractive harlot. Collins's formulation of the freethinking position was adopted by most of the later Deists and received its classic popularization in Tom Paine's *The Age of Reason*.[2] How far the England of Collins's day was from the ideal that he philosophically justi-

---

[1] For Bayle as a skeptical writer, see below, pp. 179 ff.   [2] See below, pp. 178-79.

fied is seen from the fact that, following Descartes's injunction as to personal caution, he published most of his controversial works anonymously.

Not only was there notable progress in expounding the theory of toleration and free thought during the century following Francis Bacon; there was no little success as well in achieving actual toleration of heterodox thought. Here the Dutch Netherlands led the way in permitting freedom of the press, religion, and education. Holland became an asylum for the persecuted from adjacent lands. Several noteworthy steps were also taken in England. The death penalty for heresy was abolished in 1677, thus marking a break with the Theodosian legislation of the Roman Empire. The Toleration Act of 1689 permitted freedom of worship to all save Catholics and Unitarians, but kept all except Anglicans from important public offices. It was not until 1828 that the political disabilities of Dissenters were removed. A year later those of Catholics were also erased from the statute books. The censorship laws were allowed to lapse in 1694. But it was a long time before anything like real freedom of publication was attained in England. The work of Wilkes, Paine, Godwin, Huxley, and others had to intervene before this was assured.[1]

Other countries dragged along in Britain's train. France achieved little freedom of thought or religion until the time of the Third Republic after 1879. In many countries today there are vestiges of the old spirit of religious bigotry and intolerance. In Russia we have the other extreme, an intolerance of religion outside of the rôle of pure worship. In the United States our hard-won liberties are still in jeopardy. An alert organization, the American Civil Liberties Union, has to give its attention to their preservation. Even so, as Ernest Sutherland Bates has indicated, we have less liberty today than we did a generation ago, and Thomas Jefferson would be in legal and physical jeopardy today if he were now frankly proclaiming his doctrines.[2] Benjamin Gitlow, a New York Socialist, was sent to prison after the World War for expressing revolutionary sentiments that were repeatedly uttered by Jefferson. In 1933, Angelo Herndon was given an eighteen-year prison sentence in the state of Georgia for possessing literature containing doctrines not more radical than those to be found in the writings of Jefferson and Lincoln. We still need to be vigilant to safeguard the liberties that have been so slowly won for us.

VII. THE RELIGIOUS REVOLUTION: DEISM, RATIONALISM, AND MATERIALISM

1. REASON APPLIED TO RELIGION

The men of the eighteenth century took the claims of the intellect more seriously than they had ever been taken before. Buoyed up by the progress of science in the previous one hundred years, they turned with the utmost confidence to the application of the same general outlook to religion, politics, and economics. It is an impressive demonstration of just how men have assimilated scientific knowledge and have tried to adjust their general world-outlook to it.

---

[1] Even in our day books have been suppressed in England that are freely circulated in the United States. In November, 1934, England passed a Sedition Act which makes the possession of radical and pacifist literature punishable by imprisonment or a heavy fine.

[2] E. S. Bates, *This Land of Liberty*, Harper, 1930; and A. G. Hays, *Let Freedom Ring*, Liveright, 1928.

Particularly fascinating is the effect of the new way of approaching old problems of religious thinking. Both Catholicism and the new Protestantism were essentially medieval in their outlook. Neither had made any extensive effort to accommodate itself to the advancing knowledge. When independent thinkers began to busy themselves with the problem of the effect of science on religion, they were as strongly opposed by Protestants as by Catholics. And if, in the long run, the Protestants showed themselves more responsive to the new arguments, it was only because they could not, with a variety of sects, present so united and adamant a front in the cause of repression. Ultimately, the Protestants and Catholics launched a strong conservative movement known as the "Romanticist Reaction."

There is a definite progression in the history of religious thought in this period. We shall trace out the various stages under the headings of: (1) Rationalistic Supernaturalism; (2) Deism; and (3) Materialism: atheistic and devout. The one point on which most of the thinkers agreed was the necessity of promoting virtue, in the sense of honor, decency and responsibility, and not exclusively with the connotation of personal piety and chastity.

2. RATIONALISTIC SUPERNATURALISM

Rationalistic Supernaturalism was launched effectively in the writings of John Locke, especially his *The Reasonableness of Christianity*. He laid down the fundamental arguments and later writers for the most part simply clarified and elaborated them.[1] The underlying contention was that nothing in religious dogma should be accepted by an intelligent man that did not square with reason. Scrutinizing our qualities and surroundings, it appeared to Locke that there are certain general religious principles that can be deduced from the very nature of things. These are acceptable to reason, and all other religious information and principles should conform to them. These basic tenets or principles are as follows: (1) There is one God who is the Ruler of the Universe; (2) He demands that man lead a virtuous life in conformance with His will; and (3) there is a future life in which evil conduct will be punished and good conduct rewarded. The Rationalistic Supernaturalists argued that historical Christianity is fundamentally the same as the natural religion of the Deists,[2] and that whoever accepted the one should accept the other.

The question naturally arose as to what to believe about such special aspects of Christianity as revelation and miracles. If natural religion can be discovered by any unhampered intellect, why should its truths need such reënforcement, as formulated in Christianity? It was in their response to this question that the Rationalistic Supernaturalists differentiated themselves from the two other groups of religious liberals. They argued that history showed that man can lose sight of God in spite of the fact that the intellect inevitably leads one to Him. Furthermore, they contended that most men had a rather inadequate idea of their moral duty. Thirdly, they contended that worship needed simplification and purification. Lastly, they thought that some exceptional encouragement to virtue was necessary, such as future punishments or rewards. Miracles were deemed necessary on much the same grounds, for they gave unmistakable

---

[1] *Cf.* S. G. Hefelbower, *The Relation of John Locke to English Deism*, University of Chicago Press, 1918.   [2] See below, pp. 174 ff.

proof of God's encouragement of the principles the teacher was setting forth. They were "a witness of God."

Yet if it appeared that revelation and miracles were necessary to reënforce and give authority to the principles of natural religion, it was still demanded that the deductions derived from these supernatural accessories should square with the claims of reason. They could not be entirely irrational, even if they were above reason. They must appeal, in other words, to rational men in full possession of their powers. This position was taken up and elaborated in a more ecclesiastical fashion by Locke's contemporary, John Tillotson (1630-94), Archbishop of Canterbury, and by Samuel Clarke (1675-1729), who was in his time the most popular and influential philosopher in England.

It is apparent that this whole attitude is a far cry from the attitude of Luther and the early Protestants. Catholics also, from St. Peter to Gilbert Chesterton, have always tended to be suspicious of the exclusive use of reason.

The drift from Rationalistic Supernaturalism to Deism is well illustrated by the works of John Toland (1670-1722), whose most important book was *Christianity Not Mysterious* (1696). Toland was a professed disciple of Locke and, at the time he wrote this book, an opponent of Deism. He took seriously Locke's suggestion that the Bible might well be investigated to see if any of its statements failed to conform to reason. Toland found that many did thus fail. He recommended that all such statements should be rejected, since anything that the Deity did not care to reveal clearly could hardly be worth knowing. This was a complete refutation, by implication, of the hypothesis of allegory. Among such biblical matters to be rejected were many miracles, including the virgin birth of Christ. His work created a storm of protest, even impelling Locke to repudiate the more radical conclusions of his disciple. But the book had a wide influence, even on the Continent, since Voltaire was attracted by it and gave it much publicity. Anthony Collins, whom we shall consider again below, was also an avowed disciple of Locke, but his writings savor more of advanced Deism.

3. DEISM

Anyone critically examining this position of the Rationalistic Supernaturalists can see that the need of a supernatural ratification of what is claimed to be true in itself may well be questioned on both logical and historical grounds. That is precisely what happened. Those thinkers known as Deists rejected the need of supernaturalism and clung to the natural religion.[1] They rejected both revelation and miracles and claimed that the natural religion of reason was in itself sufficient to sustain human virtue.

Deism found its earliest exponent in the historian and philosopher Lord Herbert of Cherbury (1583-1648), who was an English ambassador to France and a person who could publish his views with an impunity denied to lesser men. Nevertheless, to protect himself, he published his earliest treatise on these matters in Latin. In his *Religion of the Gentiles,* completed in 1645, he formulated the basic principles of "natural religion." This religion rests upon five

---

[1] See, especially, McGiffert, *op. cit.,* Chap. x; and Smith, *op. cit.,* Vol. I, pp. 408 ff.; Vol. II, pp. 479 ff.

THE RELIGIOUS REVOLUTION

fundamental tenets:[1] (1) Belief in the existence of God; (2) encouragement of the worship of God; (3) the view that the promotion of better living is the chief end of worship; (4) the contention that better living must be preceded by the repentance of sins; and (5) the belief in a world to come, in which man will be dealt with in accordance with his daily life here on earth. This religion was justified on the ground that it was universal and reasonable, whereas Christianity had been defended upon the contention that it was unique and based on faith. Lord Herbert argued for these tenets of natural religion and then went on to deny the utility of revelation, holding that it was used to sustain all sorts of irrelevant additions to the reasonable fundamentals. He thought these irrelevancies were added chiefly to give power to scheming and self-interested priests and that the eventual result was the obscuring of the simple and easily comprehended truths of natural religion.

Another early Deist was Charles Blount (1654-93), who was the principal contributor to a collaborative volume entitled *The Oracles of Reason* (1693). Blount's work is not original, but it is probably the best summary of the essentials of Deism.[2] After setting forth the tenets of natural religion he went on to say that religion and morality are identical and that the fear and ritualistic worship of God are quite unnecessary. The main thing required of man is to shape his conduct to natural morality and to imitate the perfections of God.

A forceful statement of the whole Deistic position came in Matthew Tindal's *Christianity as Old as Creation,* published in 1730. His main contribution was to point out the evil of demanding that men conform, in the name of religion, to morally indifferent practices. If natural religion is the basic truth of the matter, then revelation cannot add anything to it. If the tenets adduced are true, their truth will appear without supernatural ratification. Therefore all the flummery that grows up, once supernaturalism is given a hand in the matter, is simply an invitation to superstition and cruelty. And certainly such a consummation would defeat the primary purpose of religion, which is the promotion of virtue (that is, honor and decency).

Having moved along to this point, the Deists next turned their critical weapons on Christianity and its claim to being a divine revelation. The burden of these attacks fell on prophecy and miracles. It had been argued by devout writers that if Christianity had validity as a divine revelation, one of the ways in which this would be proved would be by the scriptural prophecies of its coming. On the evidence in the Bible, the Deists proved that this ratification by prophecy could not be demonstrated logically or historically. This line was taken in two famous books, *A Discourse on the Grounds and Reasons of the Christian Religion* (1724), written by Anthony Collins, and a work entitled *The Moderator between an Infidel and an Apostate* (1725) by Thomas Woolston (1669-1731). It was argued that the biblical prophecies of the coming of the Messiah were valid only when interpreted in a broadly allegorical fashion. At

---
[1] These principles are remarkably similar to those of Modernist Protestantism today.
[2] Blount also wrote widely in ironic criticism of revealed religion. His *Anima mundi* contrasted religious ideas of the pagans and Christians in a manner not flattering to the latter. He was the first effective popularizer of the Deistic point of view.

the same time, it was asserted that these scriptural prophecies of Jesus were the only basis on which Christianity could pretend to be a revealed religion.

Woolston wrote a whole series of pamphlets on religious topics, attacking not only revelation but also miracles.[1] Most important were his six *Discourses* (1727-30), of which 30,000 copies are said to have been sold. He was the most prolific and effective of the early assailants of the Christian miracles. Woolston was a very witty and satirical writer, and even descended to scurrility. Yet his arguments were usually very effective, for they seemed so obviously sensible that it was difficult to get around them. An example of his style is this comment on the story of the divine blasting of the fig tree:

> What if a yeoman of Kent should go to look for pippins in his orchard at Easter (the supposed time that Jesus sought for these figs) and because of a disappointment cut down his trees? What then would his neighbors make of him? Nothing less than a laughing-stock; and if the story got into our *Publick News,* he would be the jest and ridicule of mankind.[2]

But Woolston paid the penalty for his boldness, was prosecuted for blasphemy and profaneness, fined £25, and sentenced to one year in jail. Being unable to raise the security of £4,000 demanded as a condition of his release, he eventually died in jail. His fate illustrates the fact, which must not be forgotten, that all of these men risked severe penalties for their ventures into religious criticism. They were hampered by blasphemy laws and all sorts of social and legal penalties. If the conditions in England were superior to those in many states on the Continent, they were not yet ideal for the dissenter.

Matthew Tindal (1653-1733), Thomas Chubb (1679-1746), and Henry St. John Bolingbroke (1678-1751) drew a sharp contrast between "true" and "historical" Christianity. True Christianity was made up of the teachings of Jesus. Historical Christianity was the Christian religion as it existed in the worship of the Catholics and Protestants of the seventeenth and eighteenth centuries, bearing, so these writers contended, only the most remote resemblance to the teachings of Jesus. These Deists accepted true Christianity as a valid religion because they believed it conformed to the five basic tests mentioned above, but they rejected historical Christianity without the slightest hesitation. Tindal's *Christianity as Old as the Creation* (1730) was probably the ablest philosophical defense of Deism. He attempted to justify the latter on the basis of Locke's empirical philosophy and to show the conformity of religion to the rational nature of man, dating back to the Creation. Chubb's *Discourse concerning Reason* (1731) was a forceful defense of the adequacy of a religion of reason; and his *True Gospel of Jesus Christ* (1739) endeavored to prove that the teachings of Jesus were such a religion. Chubb anticipated the "social Christianity" of today by asserting that the teachings of Jesus were designed to comfort and elevate the poor.

Conyers Middleton (1683-1750), in his *Letter from Rome* (1729), clearly pointed out for the first time the large number of pagan elements that had

---

[1] On the attack on miracles in this period, see W. E. H. Lecky, *History of the Rise and Influence of the Spirit of Rationalism in Europe,* rev. ed., Appleton, 1910, 2 vols., Vol. I, Chap. II.

[2] Cited by J. B. Bury, *History of Freedom of Thought,* Holt, 1913, p. 142.

entered into the creation of historical Christianity. The great historian Edward Gibbon (1737-94) explained the triumph of Christianity in the early centuries of our era as the result of secular historical causes rather than of divine intervention and support. In his *Introductory Discourse* and his *Free Inquiry* (1747-48), Middleton called attention to the unreliability of the Christian Fathers as historians and chroniclers of the rise of the Christian faith. He showed that theirs was a credulous age, given to forgery, allegory, and miracle-mongering, however high the moral motives of the faithful. In particular, this proved to Middleton the inadequacy of the Fathers as authorities for the post-Apostolic miracles.

Woolston, Middleton, and Hume attacked the whole conception of the miraculous and offered withering criticism of the Christian belief in miracles. Woolston held that the miracles had only allegorical reality and validity. In addition to questioning the validity of the Church Fathers as authorities for miracles, Middleton especially emphasized the fact that the miracles must be accepted in toto or not at all. Selection was illogical. Middleton also called upon the Protestant Christians to explain why the power to work miracles had ceased. Hume's arguments against miracles have probably never been surpassed, and may be regarded as the definitive Rationalistic refutation of the hypothesis of miracle-working and its services to the faithful. Hume contended that, in the first place, a miracle must defy all possible naturalistic interpretations of the occurrence regarded as miraculous. He pointed out that much which had been deemed miraculous in the past could in his day be explained by the new scientific discoveries. In the second place, to establish the existence of a miracle we need a witness with a reputation for integrity and credibility greater than that of the laws of nature which are violated by the miracle. After a miracle has been established by the fulfillment of such difficult conditions, it affords the faithful little satisfaction, for they admit the potency of the Devil to work miracles. One cannot tell whether it is God's miracle or the Devil's that is being venerated.

Alexander Pope in his *Universal Prayer* (1737), and other writers of like spirit, endeavored to express a theory of the physical universe and of God compatible with the new astronomy and natural science. The petty tribal God of the early Hebrews was manifestly not adequate to serve as the ruler of the new universe that had been revealed by the astronomers from Copernicus to Newton. It was necessary, therefore, greatly to magnify God in order to create a supernatural Being logically suitable to the requirements of the Newtonian cosmic perspective. Further, the Christian notion of God had been one of divine arbitrariness. God, to orthodox Christians, functioned vividly only when He was apparently leading nature to deviate from her natural and normal course in such manifestations as earthquakes, volcanic eruptions, tidal waves, comets, and the like. Pope and his associates, on the contrary, were impressed with the new laws and processes revealed by natural science and came to regard God as a lawmaking and law-abiding God. He was especially manifest in the unending repetitions and orderly behavior of nature. Natural law was identified with divine law, God being regarded as the source of all natural manifestations. God was not only enlarged and His acts made harmonious with orderly nature, but the conception of His character was reinterpreted and ennobled. This was especially the work of Anthony Ashley Cooper, the third Earl of Shaftesbury (1671-1713). He replaced the orthodox notion of a harsh, cruel, and arbitrary Deity by one whose kindliness, urbanity, and tolerance matched that of a typical cultivated English gentleman of the eighteenth century.

The various threads of Deistic argument were brought together and synthesized by Thomas Paine (1737-1809), one of the most interesting figures of the late eighteenth century and the early nineteenth. Paine was not only a propagandist for enlightenment but an important practical figure in two great revolutions, the American and the French. It was in France that he wrote his famous work, *The Age of Reason*.

Paine has suffered under the accusation, hurled at him by Theodore Roosevelt, of being a "dirty little atheist,"[1] but it is perfectly obvious to any reader of *The Age of Reason* (1796) that his only crime was to sum up the whole Deistic framework of ideas in a manner designed for successful distribution among the middle class and literate artisans. The civil authorities in England had reached the point where they tolerated religious heterodoxy in the "better classes," but they feared the unsettling effect of Deistic propaganda among the "lower orders" of mankind. Paine's brochure therefore came under the ban and his publisher was sent to prison. The work, however, has for many long years been the Bible of the village "atheist," usually, in reality, the village agnostic. The following passages from *The Age of Reason* well illustrate Paine's line of argumentation:

Everything we behold carries in itself the internal evidence that it did not make itself. Every man is an evidence to himself that he did not make himself; neither could his father make himself, nor his grandfather, nor any of his race; neither could any tree, plant, or animal make itself; and it is the conviction arising from this evidence, that carries us on, as it were, by necessity, to the belief of a first cause eternally existing, of a nature totally different to any material existence we know of, and by the power of which all things exist, and this first cause man calls God.

The true Deist has but one Deity; and his religion consists in contemplating the power, wisdom, and benignity of the Deity in his works, and in endeavoring to imitate him in everything moral, scientifical, and mechanical.

The God in whom we believe is a God of moral truth. . . .

Mankind have conceived to themselves certain laws, by which what they call nature is supposed to act, and that a miracle is something contrary to the operation and effect of those laws; but unless we know the whole extent of those laws, and of what are commonly called the powers of nature, we are not able to judge whether anything that may appear to us wonderful or miraculous, be within, or be beyond, or be contrary to, her natural power of acting.

It is a duty incumbent on every true Deist, that he vindicate the moral justice of God against the calumnies of the Bible. . . .

The character of Moses, as stated in the Bible, is the most horrid that can be imagined. If those accounts be true, he was the wretch that first began and car-

---

[1] See J. P. Bland, *President Roosevelt and Paine's Defamers*, Boston Investigator Co., 1903.

ried on wars on the score or the pretence of religion, and under that mask, or that infatuation, committed the most unexampled atrocities that are to be found in the history of any nation.

Anyone who has read the account of Deistic opinions given above will recognize these passages from Paine's book as either being common to all Deists, or borrowed from some particular writer. They can scarcely lay claim to originality. Nevertheless, *The Age of Reason* is one of the few great books in the history of religious controversy and intellectual emancipation. It sums up the whole Deistic case brilliantly, clearly, and with impressive force.

One thing, in particular, that should impress itself upon readers of these Deistic writers is the relatively moderate character of their doctrines when judged by contemporary attitudes. Scandalous and blasphemous as they may have seemed even to the learnedly devout in the seventeenth and eighteenth centuries, they have today become the commonplace dogmas of literate Protestant Christians and are shared personally by not a few professing Catholics. The all too common notion of these men as bellicose and crusading atheists is preposterous and completely nonhistorical.

4. RATIONALISM IN FRANCE

For the most colorful developments of this Rationalistic movement in religious thought it is necessary to cross the Channel into France. Pierre Bayle (1647-1706) was one of the most remarkable and ingenious of those engaged in the difficult task of advancing freedom of thought. He was a French Huguenot who was driven out of France by the Revocation of the Edict of Nantes. He settled in Holland and from that country prosecuted his battle. We have already noted his trenchant arguments for freedom of thought. Bayle was exceedingly wily in his methods, and by a pose of impartiality did a vast deal to break down prejudice. One of his earliest works was a critical consideration of the text "Compel them to come in" (Luke 14:23). In persecuting the Protestants, the Catholic authorities in France had used this text as a justification. Bayle worked the matter around into the argument that one can never be sufficiently certain about the truth of one's position to use force in compelling agreement with it. In his great work, *A Historical and Critical Dictionary,* he used, as John M. Robertson phrases it, a "Pyrrhonian impartiality." Never dropping the pose of being orthodox, he yet succeeded in advancing free thought on a scale never before equaled. He set forth the crimes of David in great detail and said that no gentleman would shake hands with such a fellow.[1] Bayle was not only very competent in his handling of Old Testament characters, but also equally devastating in his attack on the Christian epic. He was one of the first to understand its dualism in detached fashion and to hold it up to ridicule after the following manner:

However detestable the opinion of two principles has constantly appeared to all Christians, they have, nevertheless, acknowledged a principle of moral evil. Divines teach us that a great number of angels having sinned, made a party in the universe

[1] *Cf.* Howard Robinson, *op. cit.,* pp. 164-68.

against God. The devil—a brief name for this party—having declared war against God from the moment of his fall, has always continued in his rebellion. . . . He succeeded in his first hostilities with regard to man. In the Garden of Eden he became the master of mankind. But God did not abandon this prey to him, but delivered them out of their bondage by virtue of the satisfaction which the second person of the Trinity (Jesus, the Son) undertook to pay to his justice. This second person engaged to become a man, and to act as a mediator and redeemer. He took upon himself to combat the devil's party, so that he was the head of God's party against the devil.

The design of Jesus Christ, the Mediator and Son of God, was to recover the country which had been conquered. That of the devil was to hold it. The victory of the Mediator consisted in leading men into the paths of truth and virtue, that of the devil in seducing them into the road of error and vice. So that, in order to know whether moral good equals moral evil among men, we need only compare the victories of the devil with those of Jesus Christ. But in history we find very few triumphs of Jesus Christ, and we everywhere meet with the triumphs of the devil.[1]

Bayle took particular care to emphasize the moral excellence of all the freethinkers he had occasion to treat. When it was objected that he was not exactly serving the cause of orthodoxy thereby, he replied that he "would have been delighted to dwell on their vices," but he "knew of none." [2]

When criticism grew menacing, Bayle put forth an ingenious argument in favor of faith. He said that faith becomes more meritorious in proportion as revealed truth surpasses our capacity to reduce it to rational expression; and that in accepting what our minds simply cannot understand, we show how deep is our submission to God. This was followed by a long catalogue of the objections raised by reason to the doctrines usually supported by faith, with the subtle idea of showing that there was no hope of being religious on a rational basis. The upshot was that by glorifying faith and appealing to its power to save religion, he was really making faith repugnant to the minds of all intelligent men. By such adroit methods, Bayle advanced his cause in a way hitherto unparalleled, although many other writers of the time also took refuge in irony and satire as a foil against persecution.

In his famous *History of the Rise and Influence of the Spirit of Rationalism in Europe,* Lecky gives the following splendid summary of Bayle's qualities as a Rationalistic critic:

The intellect of Bayle was very different from those of his predecessors, and was indeed in some respects almost unique. There have been many greater men, but there never perhaps was one who was so admirably fitted by his acquirements and his abilities, and even by the very defects of his character, to be a perfect critic. With the most profound and varied knowledge he combined to an almost unrivalled extent that rare faculty of assuming the standing-point of the system he was discussing, and of developing its arguments as they would have been developed by its most skilful advocate. But while he possessed to the highest degree that knowledge and that philosophical perception which lay bare the hidden springs of past beliefs, he appeared to be almost absolutely destitute of the creative power, and almost absolutely indifferent to the results of controversy. He denied nothing. He inculcated nothing. He scarcely exhibited any serious preference. It was his delight to bring

[1] Cited in Robinson, *op. cit.,* p. 209. For further development of this idea, see *Ibid.,* pp. 209 ff.
[2] Bury, *op. cit.,* p. 136.

together the arguments of many discordant teachers, to dissect and analyse them with the most exquisite skill, and then to develop them till they mutually destroyed one another. His genius was never so conspicuous as when lighting up the wrecks of opposing systems, exhuming the shattered monuments of human genius to reveal their nothingness and their vanity. In that vast repertory of obscure learning [the *Historical and Critical Dictionary*] from which Voltaire and every succeeding scholar have drawn their choicest weapons, the most important and the most insignificant facts, the most sublime speculations to which man can soar, and the most trivial anecdotes of literary biography, lie massed together in all the irony of juxtaposition, developed with the same cold but curious interest, and discussed with the same withering sardonic smile. Never perhaps was there a book that evinced more clearly the vanity of human systems or the disintegrating power of an exhaustive enquiry. To such a writer nothing could be more revolting than an exclusive worship of one class of opinions, or a forcible suppression of any of the elements of knowledge. Intellectual liberty was the single subject which kindled his cold nature into something resembling enthusiasm. In all he wrote he was its earnest and unwavering advocate, and he diffused his own passion among the scholars and antiquarians of whom he was the chief.[1]

Much more famous than Bayle was Voltaire (1694-1778), the most influential and intriguing intellectual figure of the eighteenth century. When he took up Rationalism it comprised no more than the solemn observations of retiring and often fugitive savants in England or the detached and subtle satire of Montaigne and Bayle in his own country. He left it a powerful and popular intellectual force throughout the Western world. By native talents and personal experiences Voltaire was perfection itself for such a rôle. He lacked all paralyzing reverence for any human thought or institution. Nor was he hampered by any debilitating conception of conventional good taste. He had infinite courage. His versatility in the field of thought and letters has rarely been equaled in human history. He ranged from Newtonian physics to drama, and from anthropology to the novel. He could thus reach a remarkable variety and number of readers with his critical writings. He was immensely witty and entertaining, thereby escaping the oblivion of the erudite but solemn pedant. When thoroughly aroused in propagandist activity, he possessed an energy and capacity for work that was almost miraculous and was regarded by his enemies as veritably diabolic. Finally, he received lucky "breaks," attracted the attention of famous and influential persons, and was vested with a prestige that made him an international figure and gave his writings vast repute.

Voltaire absorbed the Deistic arguments in England.[2] He was also deeply impressed by the work of John Locke. It should be noted here that Voltaire was simply typical of the time in being a bit of an Anglomaniac, for England had temporarily assumed the leadership of the intellectual world. It was from its shores that most of the dissident doctrines were exported. Will Durant has admirably summarized the admiration for the English that Voltaire expressed in his suppressed *Letters on the English:*

What surprised him was the freedom with which Bolingbroke, Pope, Addison, and Swift wrote whatever they pleased; here was a people that had opinions of

[1] Lecky, *op. cit.,* Vol. II, pp. 64-65.
[2] *Cf.* N. L. Torrey, *Voltaire and the English Deists,* Yale University Press, 1930.

its own; a people that had remade its religion, hanged its king, imported another, and built a parliament stronger than any ruler in Europe. There was no Bastille here, and no *lettres de cachet* by which titled pensioners or royal idlers could send their untitled foes to jail without cause and without trial. Here were thirty religions and not one priest. Here was the boldest sect of all, the Quakers, who astonished all Christendom by behaving like Christians. Voltaire never to the end of his life ceased to wonder at them.[1]

Voltaire thus admired the English, and his career was based in considerable part on intellectual capital he borrowed from them.[2] One should not, of course, suppose that the France of Voltaire's youth was entirely barren of ideas. More recent scholarship has uncovered plenty of basis for many of his disconcerting ideas in the writings of Frenchmen in the generations previous to his work. Indeed, Voltaire's seeming intellectual indebtedness to English Rationalism was in part an outgrowth of his strategy of propaganda. Owing to the current Anglomania in France, arguments drawn from English writers had more prestige than similar ideas borrowed from earlier French Rationalists. Voltaire actually drew heavily upon his French predecessors, especially Bayle, but he often failed to acknowledge this intellectual debt.

Voltaire was a man of letters interested in science and social justice. This gave him unusual powers as a propagandist for science and Rationalism. E. M. Forster has well summarized the advantages he possessed in this respect as a popularizer of eighteenth-century science and the spirit of reform:

He did science one good turn: he impressed the general public with her importance. This is all that a literary man can do for science, and perhaps only a literary man can do it. The expert scientist is too conscious of the difficulties of his subject; he knows that he can only communicate his discoveries to us by simplifying and therefore falsifying them, and that even when he can state a fact correctly we receive it incorrectly, because we cannot relate it to the thousands of other facts relevant. The literary man has no such misgivings. His imagination is touched by the infinite variety of the natural world; he reads books about it, skipping the statistics and perhaps he does a few experiments, in order to grasp the meaning of research. Then, in the course of other activities, he writes about science, with a spurious lucidity that makes the expert smile. Spurious but stimulating; the public does realize, from the remarks of such men as Voltaire, Charles Kingsley, Samuel Butler, Mr. H. G. Wells, Mr. Aldous Huxley, Mr. Gerald Heard, that something is happening. It does get a misty idea of the expanding empire of mankind.[3]

Voltaire was a man of astounding intellectual fertility and versatility. Almost no form of writing adapted to propaganda escaped his exploitation. He poured forth a stream of histories, essays, dramas, poems, novels, and short stories, most of them designed to the one end of destroying the intolerant power of the Catholic Church and its political backers. In politics, while he was liberal, he was not revolutionary. He approved nothing more advanced than a liberal monarchy. But to be liberal in those days was nevertheless dangerous. Further-

[1] W. J. Durant, *The Story of Philosophy*, Simon & Schuster, 1926, pp. 226-27.
[2] He even chose as one of his mistresses a woman who had prepared an erudite translation of Newton's *Principia*.
[3] Forster, "Incongruities: Voltaire's Slugs," "Books," New York *Herald Tribune*, Aug. 30, 1931, p. 4.

more, he was not a lover of the common people, and aimed to convert only the cultivated classes. If his industry was astonishing and his versatility amazing, he was far from being always an original or independent thinker. It would have suited him to perfection if he could have eradicated Catholicism and substituted the liberal Deism that he had found in England.

What marks Voltaire for special admiration is certainly his courage and energy. The French liberal thinkers were confronted with a hostile Church and a hostile State. Their situation was infinitely more desperate than that of the English, and it required a proportionately greater amount of courage to defy the powers that ruled. By his wit, nimbleness, and persistence Voltaire carried on a "one-man revolution." His zealousness against every form of religious bigotry made him more than a single man; it made him a veritable intellectual movement. His famous biographer Lord Morley said of him:

> When the right sense of historical proportion is more fully developed in men's minds, the name of Voltaire will stand out like the names of the great decisive movements in the European advance, like the Revival of Learning, or the Reformation. The existence, character, and career of this extraordinary person constitute in themselves a new and prodigious Era.[1]

Will Durant has put it even more forcefully:

> Italy had a Renaissance and Germany had a Reformation, but France had Voltaire; he was for his country both Renaissance and Reformation, and half the Revolution. He carried on the antiseptic scepticism of Montaigne, and the healthy earthly humor of Rabelais; he fought superstition and corruption more savagely and effectively than Luther or Erasmus, Calvin or Knox or Melanchthon; he helped to make the powder with which Mirabeau and Marat, Danton and Robespierre blew up the Old Régime.[2]

The consummate controversial skill of his literary works gave him a reputation far beyond the boundaries of France. Not since Erasmus had there been a personality in the intellectual development of Europe with so wide a reputation, and Voltaire was a far more vigorous, dramatic, colorful, and spectacular figure than the essentially devout and mildly ironic Erasmus.

In spite of his vast importance in the history of the liberation of the human mind—he is one of the saints of this movement—the bulk of what he wrote is unread today, in which respect he resembles most of the figures with whom we are dealing. It is not his Rationalistic argumentation that has survived, but his clever fiction. His poetry and drama will put anyone to sleep and his essays have lost much of their savor, but few can read his short romances or his novel *Candide* without a chuckle of delight. Of such are the ironies of history. One's serious work molders unread, but one's jeux d'esprit continue to delight millions. The student who desires to gain a direct insight into Voltaire's mind, methods, and learning should read the famous *Philosophical Dictionary*, the best anthology of Voltaire's erudition, satire, courage, and critical observations.[3]

---

[1] John Morley, *Voltaire*, Macmillan, 1871, p. 1.   [2] Durant, *op. cit.*, p. 220.
[3] For a good selected abridgement, see the edition by H. I. Woolf of Voltaire's *Philosophical Dictionary*, Knopf, 1924. Students of the intellectual history of the eighteenth century have long since recognized that this work is very "Baylian" in content.

If Voltaire was a littérateur turned propagandist, Denis Diderot (1713-84) was essentially a journalist before the days of journalism, who got mixed up in the same general task. Diderot is one of the most appealing personalities of the period, for in spite of his brilliance Voltaire could be intensely disagreeable, while the other great Frenchman of the time, Rousseau, with whom we shall deal later, was positively hateful and inordinately suspicious and quarrelsome.

Diderot was the son of a cutlery-maker and with many of his contemporaries was educated by Jesuits. Like Voltaire and many other French writers of the day, he could read English and thus absorb the main English ideas then current. His philosophical and religious viewpoint was compounded of English and progressive French doctrines. But he was a man who easily dissipated his energies without accomplishing much, and a good deal of his time was taken up with hack work. He wrote many plays that are now considered very dull; some novels that are still readable but not exciting; and some very witty and admirable dialogues and essays. He was one of the first journalistic art critics and wrote reams of ephemeral comments on the current exhibitions. He also undertook to execute commissions of a strange sort, like the writing of a series of sermons for a Portuguese missionary who was going to Africa. Harold J. Laski thus summarizes Diderot's remarkable versatility:

Diderot's versatility is such that any picture of its achievement would end only at the boundaries of knowledge. If his political ideas have no claim to originality, at least they are well expressed and representative of all that is most creative in the liberalism of his time. The writings on education are more important. They show not only his sense that the problem was urgent; there is a modernity of temper about them—especially in his preference for modern languages and science over the scholastic discipline of his day—which is noteworthy. On physiology, on the principles of legislation, on music and mathematics there are vast collections of memoranda, never, indeed, of the first importance, but rarely without point and distinction. All of it is conceived in what may be termed the Baconian spirit; in all of it there is that restless and exciting sense that, to use his own words, "we touch the moment of a great revolution in the sciences." All of it also is inspired by a large humanism before which it is difficult not to feel humble. They are fragments from a great man's workshop, the outpourings of a mind so full of ideas, so rich in invention, that he can hardly stay to hold the pen which should express the thoughts which crowd one another. And even in their incompleteness, they make one understand why the range of Diderot's inventiveness fertilized so much of what was best in the creation of his age.[1]

Fortunately for Diderot, he was invited by a bookseller to take charge of an encyclopedia, and the production of it became his historic career. As originally planned, this work was to be a translation and adaption of an English work, but under Diderot's hand it became the great repository of Rationalistic thought. Although in the beginning the work had official sanction and although Diderot was aided by the chief of police of Paris even after it was banned, the work was produced under most difficult conditions.[2] It was soon apparent that the work was Rationalistic in tone, and so it became the butt of

---

[1] Laski, "Diderot: Homage to a Genius," *Harper's Magazine*, April, 1931.
[2] *Cf.* J. H. Robinson and C. A. Beard, *Readings in Modern European History*, Ginn, 1908, 2 vols., Vol. I, pp. 185 ff.

clerical opposition, to which in time was added the opposition of the King. Nevertheless, the popularity of the work was immense, and the subscribers increased in number almost in proportion as the difficulties of publication increased.

For his work Diderot drew upon all sorts of writers, but the backbone of his staff was made up of his freethinking friends. His chief assistant was D'Alembert, an able mathematician. He aimed to publish not only articles on scientific, religious, and philosophical topics, but also detailed accounts of the trades. Many of the latter articles he wrote himself, for his natural good-fellowship enabled him to approach the working people in a friendly manner. Furthermore, he made it a point to have articles on the practical arts written by one who practiced the particular art. For example, the article on brewing was prepared by an intelligent brewer. In this procedure he anticipated the attitude of the editors of the current Encyclopaedia Britannica. The total result was that *L'Encyclopédie* (1752-72), as it is known, was a work of genuine utility, and marks an epoch in the history of such monumental surveys of knowledge. An illuminating historical exercise would be to compare with it the spirit and the contents admitted to their compilations by Pliny, Isidore of Seville, Rhabanus Maurus, and Vincent of Beauvais.[1]

Diderot thus figures in the history of the time as the great editorial genius of the group. His charming personality enabled him to get along with all the various freethinkers of the day. It is recorded that he quarreled with but two men in all of his life, his father and Rousseau. Such a record marks him out as remarkably accommodating. How far it accounts for his success in getting the coöperation of naturally dissident folk is another matter. But he carried his project through and lived to old age at peace with the world.

Important and illuminating as were these Rationalistic writings from Locke to Diderot, we should not make the mistake of imagining that their authors cut loose from all connections with the past or failed to mirror the interests that had attracted earlier generations. As Carl Becker has indicated in his *Heavenly City of the Eighteenth-Century Philosophers,* many of the problems with which they dealt were those which they shared with Aquinas and Duns Scotus. Their thought was never fully humanized and secularized, in spite of much progress in that direction. Issues related to the supernatural attracted much of their attention, and their general mental frame of reference had as much in common with the thirteenth century as with the twentieth.

5. THE BARON HOLBACH AND ATHEISM

Diderot was not so "orthodox" in his Deism as Voltaire, but moved over towards materialistic atheism. This latter position was anticipated by Julien Offray de Lamettrie, who in 1748 denied the proofs of the existence of God and was openly defended by his friend Paul Henri Thiry, Baron d'Holbach (1723-89), a wealthy German who settled in Paris. Holbach was a chemist by training but, in harmony with the spirit of the times, engaged in anti-religious pamphleteering. Of course, the orthodox Catholics and Protestants re-

---

[1] See above, Vol. I, pp. 726, 738. On the character of *L'Encyclopédie*, see Lynn Thorndike, "L'Encyclopédie and the History of Science," *Isis,* Vol. VI (1924), pp. 362-86.

garded the classic Deistic writers as atheists, though one of the five basic tenets of the natural religion was the dogmatic belief in the existence of a Supreme Being. Religious liberalism has usually been denounced as atheism by the pious, the desire being to give the dog a bad name. As an actual matter of fact, it was only men like Holbach and his followers who were literally atheists in that they did directly deny the existence of God.

The several works of Holbach were issued anonymously or pseudonymously, but none of the rest of them is so powerful or memorable as *Le système de la nature* (1770). Of this work Höffding writes: "It contains no really new thoughts. Its significance lies in the energy and indignation with which every spiritualistic and dualistic view was run to earth on account of its injuriousness both in practice and in theory." [1] This judgment by Höffding is criticized by many students of the history of European thought who contend that *The System of Nature* is one of the most stimulating and provocative of all statements of the uncompromising naturalistic position—much clearer and more satisfactory than most nineteenth century attempts.

Holbach argued that it would be necessary to posit God as First Cause only if matter were passive. But if there is movement in matter then God serves no purpose other than to push the question of first cause back another step. This not only fails to make the whole question more intelligible, but indeed confuses matters. The assumption of two kinds of being, spiritual and material, leads, as Holbach contended, to all sorts of obscurity and evasion. The spiritual principle lets in the priests and the train of oppressions that naturally follow. Above all, it is not necessary to an explanation of the universe. The latter can be adequately accounted for on the basis of a materialistic determinism, a system in which God has no essential place. Everything from the cosmos to human conduct is a product of causal necessity. There is no place for arbitrary freewill. Man is simply a complex manifestation of nature. He is neither better nor worse than the rest. Indeed, in Holbach's scheme the subjective Christian judgments of good and bad have no application to man. It may be observed that Holbach's fundamental views of nature and causation do not, however, necessarily involve a dogmatic atheistic view. They represent the contemporary scientific view of nature and man, held by agnostics and not a few theists.

The position of Holbach was the logical outcome of the successive positions taken up by the eighteenth-century critics of religion. The progression was natural from (1) Locke's attempt to relate supernaturalism to Rationalistic natural religion to (2) the Deists' natural religion without supernatural sanctions, and to (3) the materialistic atheism of Holbach. The next move would require positing religion on entirely new bases—a nineteenth-century achievement.[2]

French Deists like Voltaire had important German disciples, among whom the more notable were the eminent philosopher Immanuel Kant, in his earlier days, and the philosopher-poet Lessing. Very important was the work of Hermann Reimarus (1694-1768).[3] In the course of a Deistic work designed to show that the moral teachings of the Bible were compatible with natural religion, he endeavored to separate the historical Jesus from the husk of dubious prophe-

---

[1] Harald Höffding, *History of Modern Philosophy*, Macmillan, 1908, 2 vols., Vol. I, p. 481.
[2] See below, pp. 672 ff.
[3] See F. C. Conybeare, *History of New Testament Criticism*, Putnam, 1910, pp. 108 ff.

cies, uncertain miracles, and extraneous theological dogmas. This was especially relevant to Deism, which had insisted that the teachings of Jesus were harmonious with natural or reasonable religion. It was highly desirable to discover what the real Jesus and His teachings were actually like.

6. RELIGIOUS RADICALISM IN AMERICA

We may now glance at the transfer of the Deistic doctrines to America. It is well established that Jefferson, John Adams, Franklin, and perhaps George Washington were Deists, though some of them occasionally tempered their opinions because of political exigencies.

Franklin was an out-and-out Deist. He once formulated his religious ideas in response to a request from the president of Yale University. He said: "I believe in one God, the Creator of the universe. That he governs it by his providence. That he ought to be worshipped. That the most acceptable service we render him is doing good to his other children. That the soul of man is immortal, and will be treated with justice in another life respecting its conduct in this." It would be difficult to imagine a more concise summary of the fundamental postulates of Deism. Washington was also cordial to Deistic doctrines, though he frequently attended the formal Episcopal services. He never received communion. John Adams was an advanced Unitarian—a type of belief that the leading historian of American religion during this period has called "respectable Deism." Jefferson was an aggressive Deist. He extolled reason and declared that we should follow wherever it leads, even if we must as a result deny the existence of God. He vigorously attacked the priesthood and the Calvinistic clergy. In the campaign of 1800 he was bitterly assailed as an atheist, but the charge was not well founded. Strange as it may seem, none of the first seven Presidents of the United States were professing Christians. As De Witt has sagely observed, the private beliefs of the Fathers were more advanced than their public utterances:

> In different degrees, Jefferson, Franklin, Gouverneur Morris, John Adams, were free-thinkers, but without intolerance or display, without ostentatious irony, quietly, almost privily; for the masses remained believers. Not to offend them, it was necessary to speak with respect of sacred things; to produce a deep impression upon them, it was requisite to appeal to their religious feelings; and prayers and public fasts continued to be instruments resorted to whenever it was found desirable, whether by agitators or the State, to act powerfully on the minds of the people.[1]

Religious radicalism was, naturally, not limited to our early Presidents.[2] That doughty Green Mountaineer, Ethan Allen, was an active foe of orthodoxy and evangelical religion. He composed several large books on the subject, the most notable of which was *Reason: The Only Oracle of Man* (1784). The chief organizer of militant Deism was Elihu Palmer, who also wrote many pamphlets, representative of which was *Thoughts on the Christian Religion* (1794). He vigorously assailed orthodoxy and was especially outspoken in his denunciation of the dogma that the Bible is the revealed word of God. While Allen and Palmer definitely believed in the existence of a Supreme Being, John

---
[1] C. H. de Witt, *Jefferson and the American Democracy*, London, 1862, p. 17.
[2] See especially G. A. Koch, *Republican Religion*, Holt, 1933.

Stewart, author of *The System of Reason and Nature* (1813), was inclined towards atheism, as also was Gouverneur Morris. Thomas Paine spent his last years in the United States and lent the weight of his influence to American skepticism.

Deism and Rationalism were, however, soon smothered in the United States under the rising tide of evangelism and the powerful Christian apologetics of President Timothy Dwight of Yale College. By the middle of the nineteenth century it is doubtful if any candidate holding Jefferson's religious views could have been elected President of the United States, or even have been nominated for the office. Ingersoll's views on religion in the eighties did not differ widely from those of Jefferson, and the Republican party sadly needed a man of his luster, oratorical powers, and personal integrity. But he was not regarded by party leaders as "available" on account of his agnostic notions.

7. THE ORIGINS OF BIBLICAL CRITICISM

Concurrent with the development of a new outlook on religious philosophy, there came a change in the attitude towards the Bible. It was reëxamined by certain critics as though it were a secular document, the authenticity of which they wished to determine. Some of the early Church Fathers in the later Roman Empire had questioned some of the conventional stories about the authorship of the Bible, but no truly critical attack on the problem was made before the Jewish scholar Aben Ezra, who about 1150 A.D. questioned the legend of the Mosaic authorship of the Pentateuch.

In the early modern period, however, the first to take an interest in this subject was Thomas Hobbes (1588-1679), who used the weapons of logic and common sense. He pointed out how strange it was that a writer of an autobiography should discuss his own death and burial. Yet the Pentateuch relates the secret burial of Moses and describes the sorrow of the Jews following his death. A somewhat similar attack was made by Baruch Spinoza (1632-77), who added linguistic scholarship to logic. He showed that the Book of Genesis could hardly have been written by a single author and drew upon his knowledge of Jewish literature to discredit the theory of Mosaic authorship. He further showed that the books of Judges, Joshua, Samuel, and Kings could not have been written by any of the persons mentioned in these books. In 1722 William Whiston called attention to the falsification of the text of the Old Testament in several places and suggested how the original might be restored. Five years later, in his *Literal Scheme of Prophecy Considered,* Anthony Collins proved the late date of the Book of Daniel, thus upsetting the legend of the prophetic powers of the author. In the middle of the eighteenth century (1753) a learned French physician, Jean Astruc (1684-1766), roughly sketched what has come to be accepted as the scholarly version of the nature and composition of the Pentateuch. And at the end of the century (1799) a German savant, Karl David Ilgen, indicated that there were at least seventeen different documents in Genesis, compiled by some three major groups of writers.

In one sense, work of this sort was of more permanent worth than that of the Deists, for it stood the test of time whereas Deism, except as a general religious attitude, long ago collapsed as a result of the progress of science and critical scholarship. It was essentially a reflex from the ideas embodied in the Newtonian world-machine. With the coming of new facts the underlying bases of this doctrine disintegrated. This should not be taken as an indication that in essence the doctrine was wrong, but merely to illustrate the fact that when the revelations of science change, the rationalizations built upon them shift as well.

VIII. SECULARIZING ETHICS

The development of a more liberal attitude towards religion was accompanied by comparable progress in ethical doctrine. With the exception of certain schools of Greek naturalists, ethics, or the science of conduct, was closely linked with religion down to modern times. This connection has no logical necessity, for religion is certainly not always the key to the discovery of right conduct. But the situation is easy enough to understand historically.

From earliest times it has been believed that the codes of conduct which man has followed implicitly have been revealed by the gods. This fact is illustrated at great length in Professor William Graham Sumner's *Folkways*,[1] the classic study of the actual evolution of moral codes. Since religion has been that body of thought and action primarily concerned with the supernatural, it is only natural that it should have had dominion over the field of conduct. Christianity accepted the doctrine of supernatural ethics with great enthusiasm and completeness. The Bible and the doctrines of the Church Fathers were regarded as the infallible sources of moral guidance. Such considerations as the bearing of a particular form of conduct on earthly happiness and well-being were given even a passing thought in determining questions of right and wrong only as they affected salvation in the world beyond life. Nor was the question of right and wrong related to the matter of individual differences in need, capacity, taste, or desire. There was, in theory at least, one rigid and undeviating course of right and wrong for king and slave, rich and poor, genius and moron, strong and weak.

There had been some skeptics who had questioned this absolutistic theory of revealed ethics, most notably the Epicureans. They had already arrived at something roughly similar to our modern scientific views. They held that notions of right and wrong had evolved naturally in a sort of trial-and-error fashion as man had been compelled to face life experiences under diverse conditions. While later generations might attribute a supernatural origin to codes of conduct, they were really man-made. Their validity depended upon their utility, namely, their relative capacity to promote human happiness. Aristotle, likewise, rejected supernatural ethics and held that right was to be ascertained by rigorous logical thinking. Specifically, it was that happy mean between overindulgence and asceticism.

In early modern times the Christian doctrine of supernatural ethics was attacked from many angles. We have already seen how Montaigne questioned its goal.[2] Francis Bacon, as we have indicated, held that the Kingdom of Man

[1] Ginn, 1907.   [2] See above, pp. 154-55.

is more important in a practical way than the Kingdom of God and maintained that science is the key to improving human and social conditions. Thomas Hobbes, while he heartily respected the existing moral conventions, tried to place them on scientific and logical foundations—a process that we now call rationalization. Above all, he tried to show that ethical standards are the product of enlightened self-interest.[1]

One of the most urbane and pleasing writers on ethical matters in early modern times was Shaftesbury, whose religious doctrines we have examined.[2] He held to an instinctive and sentimental view of morality. He contended that all men not corrupted and perverted are naturally inclined instinctively to seek the true, the good, and the beautiful for their own sake. He was notable for making beauty rather than chastity a major test of morality. He was the father of a modern school of ethics that makes "good taste" a leading test of ethical rectitude. He vigorously challenged the notion that high moral living was dependent upon supernatural religion, and pointed to the immaculate lives of many well-known Deists and atheists. If man instinctively and intuitively seeks the good, the true, and the beautiful, he does not require divine revelation to lead him to this goal. David Hume and Adam Smith developed more thoroughly a psychological theory of morality.[3] They based their doctrine upon the notion of reflective or subjective sympathy. An observer tends to project himself into the situation of others and to reflect upon how he would feel under the same circumstances. Happiness in others projects joy to the observer, while misery on the part of those observed generates sorrow in the mind of the observer. We are instinctively driven to consider how we would feel under the identical conditions. Hence we are naturally impelled to do those things which will promote happiness and avert evil. In remarkable contrast to the orthodox Christian attitude and in flat opposition to Kant's later and famous "categorical imperative," Hume contended that the soundness of morality is to be determined by its results in increasing human happiness here and now. This was the beginning of modern Hedonism. A similar doctrine was espoused in France by Helvétius and Holbach.

A thoroughly secular conception of ethics was suggested by Montesquieu, who is regarded by many as the founder of the comparative theory of ethics. He maintained that notions of right and wrong and codes of conduct naturally arise to meet conditions of life, especially those conditions which are geographical and climatic.[4] For example, polygyny is approved in warm climates, where women mature and fade early, but is frowned upon in temperate and cold climates. Drunkenness is denounced in warm zones because alcohol is not needed to create additional bodily warmth, whereas it is very common in cold areas. Despotism is the right kind of government for the torrid areas, constitutional monarchy for temperate zones, and republicanism for the colder regions. In short, whatever exists as a result of natural causes in any given area

---

[1] See Smith, *op. cit.*, Vol. I, pp. 542 ff.
[2] See Havelock Ellis, *The Dance of Life*, Houghton Mifflin, 1923, pp. 260 ff.; and Sir Leslie Stephen, *History of English Thought in the Eighteenth Century*, Putnam, 1902, 2 vols., Vol. II, pp. 15 ff.; E. P. Smith, in *Essays in Intellectual History; Dedicated to James Harvey Robinson*, Harper, 1929, pp. 21-42.   [3] See Höffding, *op. cit.*, Vol. I, pp. 433-37, 441-46.
[4] See Thomas, *The Environmental Basis of Society*, pp. 63-69, 158-59.

is looked upon by its people as right. The details of Montesquieu's theory have proved more vulnerable than his general hypothesis as to the origin of moral codes.

A highly practical view of morality appeared in the writings of the versatile and fertile British reformer Jeremy Bentham (1748-1832). He was the father of the Utilitarian theory of ethics.[1] According to Bentham's theory of human nature, man is a cold, calculating animal. He is governed chiefly by the desire to receive pleasurable sensations and to avoid pain. In his choice of conduct he is always controlled by this wish to secure pleasurable and avert painful experiences. Projected into society, this desire leads man to wish for the greatest happiness for the largest number of his fellow beings. The test of the moral validity of any practice is the degree to which it contributes to the greatest happiness of the largest possible number of mankind. This is the core of Utilitarian ethics.

In this way ethical doctrine was secularized and socialized. It was contended that morals have a natural origin, that they should be based upon considerations relative to human life here and now, and that the leading criterion of the soundness of a form of conduct is its ability to bring the greatest amount of happiness to the human race.

Morality was not, however, liberated from the medieval sex obsession[2] as quickly or as completely as one might have expected. Modern capitalism found the existing impurity-complex highly useful for its purposes. It therefore did everything possible to encourage a view of morality that identifies the good life with ostensible and public sexual purity, whatever degree of secret indulgence material wealth may procure and hide from the public gaze. This attitude was very useful to capitalism because, whatever a man's lack of honesty, integrity, or humanity in business or financial dealings, his morals are rarely attacked so long as he is not openly detected in a breach of chastity or fidelity.[3] Kant's classic effort to free ethics from supernaturalism played right into the hands of these nineteenth-century bourgeois "purists," a development which Kant himself would have probably deplored.

IX. THE ORIGINS OF THE THEORY OF PROGRESS

One of the more conspicuous results of the rise of science and the growth of Rationalism was the gradual rise of the idea of progress. It is a significant fact that more than 99 per cent of the period of man's existence upon the planet was passed through without any consciousness of the actual progress of human culture. Human progress down to the seventeenth century was natural and spontaneous, and in no sense the result of the collective effort to realize any conscious ideal of racial and cultural advancement.

The ancient Jews, holding the doctrine of the Fall of man, therefore believed perfection to be found in the past rather than to be sought in the future. The ancient pagans shared to some degree a comparable notion, namely, the dogma of a decline from a golden age. Even more popular with the Greeks and Ro-

---
[1] See W. L. Davidson, *Political Thought in England . . . from Bentham to J. S. Mill*, Holt, 1916, Chaps. III-IV; and W. C. Mitchell, "Bentham's Felicific Calculus," in *Political Science Quarterly*, June, 1918.   [2] See above, Vol. I, pp. 382 ff., 699 ff.
[3] *Cf.* Robert Briffault, *Sin and Sex*, Macaulay, 1931.

mans was the conception of the cyclical nature of human development. Culture would rise to a certain point and then decline to a level comparable to that which had existed at the beginning. Then the process would start all over again and the cycle would be repeated. The Christians took over the Jewish notion of the Fall of man and combined it with the pagan view of the decline from a golden age. Man could never expect any Utopia here on earth. The state of blessedness was to be attained only in the world to come. The final judgment and the end of things earthly was, according to the Christian view as stated in the Book of Revelation, to be preceded by unusually horrible and devastating earthly occurrences.

Gradually, however, there arose the conviction that better things might be in store for humanity here on this earth. Back in the thirteenth century Roger Bacon had a vision of what applied science might do for man. Montaigne had a glimmering of a new idea when he suggested that philosophy should be concerned with human happiness here on earth rather than with salvation in the life to come. Francis Bacon and Descartes united in decrying the authority of the past. Bacon had contended that the moderns were superior to the ancients and suggested that Utopia might be secured through applying science to human problems.

The doctrine of progress as it is conventionally understood began, however, with men like Jonathan Swift (1667-1745) and Bernard de Fontenelle (1657-1757). Swift's *Battle of the Books* (1697) was a telling satire on the defenders of the authority of the ancients and the worship of the classics and classical scholars. In his *Dialogues of the Dead* (1683) Fontenelle hardly went beyond the contention that the ancients were no better than the moderns, but five years later in his *Digression on the Ancients and the Moderns* he took a more advanced position. He held that the ancients and the moderns are essentially alike in a biological sense, there being no progress in this respect. In the fine arts, which are chiefly a spontaneous expression of the human spirit, there seems to be no law of progress. The ancient peoples achieved great things here, but the best modern works in art, poetry, and oratory equal the most perfect ancient examples. On the other hand, in science and industry we find an altogether different story. In these fields development is cumulative. There has been vast progress since antiquity and even greater things may be looked for in the future. Moreover, Fontenelle proceeded to state that unreasoning admiration for the ancients is a major obstacle to progress. It is doubtful if anybody, even in our own day, has more successfully stated the general principles involved in the problem of what we call progress than did Fontenelle.

Charles Perrault (1628-1703) was a contemporary of Fontenelle and expressed very much the same view in his *Parallel of the Ancients and Moderns* (1688-96). But he was so much impressed by what he regarded as the perfection of the culture of his own generation that he was not much concerned with future progress—if, indeed, he would have conceded that anything could be better than his own age. A more positive attitude towards future progress was also taken by the Abbé de Saint-Pierre in his *Plan for Perpetual Peace* (1712). He contended that progress was real and that the achievements of his own age were more notable than those of the era of Plato and Aristotle. He was particularly interested in social progress, and believed in the desirability of an Academy of Political Science to guide social advance. He placed great faith in the power of a wise government and was a forerunner of Helvétius and the Utilitarians. Helvétius, who flourished in the middle of the eighteenth century, was the foremost of the French social optimists of this period. He believed thoroughly in the possibility of human perfection and thought it could be achieved effectively through universal enlightenment and rational education. He believed in the equality of man, and held that existing inequalities can be eliminated through education.

In the first half of the eighteenth century the Italian Giovanni Battista Vico (1668-1744), a philosopher of history, worked out his conception of progress.[1] He held that human progress does not take place directly or in a straight line. Rather, it takes the form of a spiral. There may seem to be cycles of development, but they never go back to the original starting-point. Each turn is higher than the preceding. A little later in France a more realistic historical theory of progress was worked out by Anne Robert Jacques Turgot, Baron de l'Aulne (1729-81), himself an eminent contributor to the philosophy of history.[2] He laid great stress upon the continuity of history and the cumulative nature of progress. He contended that the more complex the civilization, the more rapid human progress. Hence advance was very slow in primitive times, but has been greatly accelerated in the modern epoch. Even more optimistic was the distinguished writer of the French revolutionary period, Condorcet.[3] He not only stated his belief in the reality of progress but presumed to divide the history of civilization into ten periods, each representing a definite stage in the development of mankind and human civilization. Nine of these periods had already been passed through, and the French Revolution and modern science were leading us to the brink of the tenth, which would produce an era of happiness and well-being the like of which had never been known.

There were other men who contributed variously to the notion of progress. The German philosopher Herder attempted to work out laws of progress based on the joint operation of nature and God. Immanuel Kant sought to prove the reality of moral progress. The English publicist William Godwin (1756-1836) believed that perfection might be obtained through the abolition of the state and property and the inculcation of reason through private instruction. Henri de Saint-Simon (1760-1825) followed the line of the Abbé de Saint-Pierre in holding that a definite social science must be provided to guide human progress. These notions culminated in the historical philosophy and sociology of Auguste Comte (1798-1857). He worked out a comprehensive system of "laws" concerning intellectual progress and formulated an expansive philosophy of history, embodying the division of the past into a large number of periods and subperiods, each characterized by some phase of cultural advance.

[1] See Benedetto Croce, *The Philosophy of Giambattista Vico,* Macmillan, 1913.
[2] See John Morley, *Critical Miscellanies,* Macmillan, 1886-1908, 4 vols., Vol. II, pp. 78 ff.
[3] See J. S. Schapiro, in *Essays in Intellectual History Dedicated to James Harvey Robinson,* pp. 165 ff.; *Condorcet and the Rise of Liberalism in France,* Harcourt, Brace, 1934, Chap. xiii; and A. E. Burlingame, *Condorcet, the Torch Bearer of the French Revolution,* Stratford Press, 1930, Chap. xi.

While the theory of progress has retained enthusiastic support from many since the time of Comte, pessimistic or chastened attitudes have also appeared.[1] Some, like the German philosophers Friedrich Nietzsche and Oswald Spengler, have reverted to something similar to the doctrine of cycles characteristic of classical times. More common, however, has been the tendency to substitute the notion of change for that of progress. The latter implies that things are certainly getting better. Of this we are not now so certain, but we are aware of change in many phases of life and thought. Most important has been the recognition that change takes place rapidly in the realm of science and material culture and very slowly in institutions and morals. This discrepancy in the rate of progress as between material culture and social institutions—now called "cultural lag"—seems to have placed modern civilization in particular jeopardy.[2]

The intellectual developments that have been briefly touched upon in this chapter marked a turning-point in the evolution of human civilization. The old static provincial and agrarian order that had dominated man since primitive days now definitely began to break up. Skepticism gradually made inroads upon faith. A world-perspective slowly replaced the neighborhood outlook. Natural and social science began to challenge logic and theology as the sovereign guides to human knowledge. Philosophy came to be concerned with the problem of living well here on earth and began to have some interest in the facts of experience. Ethics, or the science of conduct, was partially divorced from the supernatural, began to take an interest in earthly well-being, and studied existing ethical codes with profit. The trend towards skepticism was promoted by the slowly increasing freedom and safety with which the accepted system of belief and conduct might be challenged in the spoken and written word. Finally, man not only became conscious of change, but thought that he could detect progress therein.

While Rationalism was the most characteristic intellectual product of the early Modern era, it did not hold sway unchallenged. Its greatest rival gained much headway at the turn of the eighteenth century. Rationalism marked a definite break with both the medieval spirit and the Protestant past. It placed full reliance upon reason. To many this imposed too great a mental strain. They longed for the emotional richness and the dogmatic certainty of a less sophisticated age. Hence, they brought about the great emotional reaction against Rationalism that is customarily known as Romanticism—a tendency already quite apparent in the intellectual attitudes of Jean Jacques Rousseau.

X. THE ROMANTICISTS AND THE REVOLT AGAINST REASON

The Rationalists of the seventeenth and eighteenth centuries placed their faith in reason. The real world to them was the world revealed through sense perception, greatly extended and sharpened by the new instruments of scientific investigation and precision. They believed that the Newtonian system embodied a definitive synthesis. God lay behind the sum total of the natural phenomena and laws which were revealed through the scientific progress that

---

[1] See below, p. 683.   [2] See below, pp. 1101 ff.

culminated in Newton's scheme. God's laws were the laws of nature as discovered by science. Human progress could be forwarded through further scientific research and the application of its discoveries to human betterment. From Francis Bacon to Condorcet, this had been the theme of social optimism. The Rationalists did not despise the feelings and emotions, but they placed their reliance upon the intellect in all matters pertaining to truth and enlightenment. Towards the end of the eighteenth century, under the influence of the French Revolution some of these writers went to rather dubious extremes in their optimism concerning the possibility of uprooting human traditions and institutions and bringing about the rapid transformation of society through the application of a few "self-evident dictates of pure reason."

The conservatives inevitably reacted vigorously against any such doctrine. They not only opposed the specific attacks of the Rationalists upon religious beliefs and social institutions, but they also insisted upon developing a fundamental philosophical defense of their contrary position. This reaction in philosophy is often summarized under the term "Romanticism," though it soon developed into the transcendental "Idealism" of the Germanic philosophers. Whether termed Romanticism or Idealism, it was in any case a repudiation of the trust in the intellect and a buttressing of faith and the subjective attitude. It is not inaccurate to say that the metaphysics of the new philosophy may be termed Idealism, while its social and cultural applications are most appropriately designated as Romanticism. The writers of this school turned to the feelings and emotions with the same trust and confidence that the Rationalists had bestowed upon the intellectual faculties of man. The Idealistic and Romanticist philosophers frequently used the term "pure reason," but after Kant's day what they meant by the term was more literally "pure faith."

The inevitable reaction from a too great emphasis upon the intellectual side of man's personality was already hard at work in the writings of Rousseau. But he was merely one of a large group of writers who, in one way or another, aimed to undermine Rationalism and to replace it by something more appealing to the average sensuous man who cannot live by mind alone.

The metaphysical basis for Idealism and Romanticism was laid by the great German philosopher Immanuel Kant (1724-1804). Kant had originally been interested in scientific matters [1] and had inclined towards a Rationalistic view of things. But, as he tells us, he was aroused from his "dogmatic slumbers" by David Hume's destruction of the conventional conception of causation.[2] He devoted himself to composing one of the two or three leading contributions to critical metaphysics and epistemology in the whole history of philosophy, the *Critique of Pure Reason,* published in 1781. Here he showed clearly enough that science is but the description of phenomena as they appear to the human senses. From this standpoint it is accurate and reliable, provided the scientific research is complete and exacting. Yet this does not mean that science necessarily gives us an accurate portrayal of the universe in any absolute sense. In fact, the universe is basically unintelligible to man.[3] Science is at best only a presentation of phenomena as they appear to finite man, limited in knowledge

---

[1] He pretended a scientific interest to the last.   [2] See above, p. 162.
[3] Most of Kant's arguments relative to the unintelligibility of the world grew out of his ignorance of social science.

and experience. The so-called laws of nature are but the laws of the human mind. Kant thus distinguished sharply between the world as man perceives it to be—the sensual or phenomenal world—and the world as it actually is, namely, the so-called realm of "things-in-themselves."

There is no denying the truth or logic of this Kantian position. Man can only know and interpret the universe in terms of his own abilities and powers. How close his observations and conceptions come to the absolute actuality we do not and never can know because we shall always be limited to the human perspective. If this attitude is made the basis for enduring human humility, all is well. It furnishes the foundation for recognizing the slight and fragmentary character of human knowledge. It should discourage all dogmatism about absolutes and the ultimate character of the physical universe.

Unfortunately, the Kantian point of view has had exactly the opposite results. It opened the floodgates for a tidal wave of the most diversified imagination, speculation, and wishful thinking. That which should have sounded the death knell of all dogmatism became the bugle call that summoned forth the most dogmatic group of philosophers since the heyday of Scholasticism.

Once the supremacy of the intellect was challenged, an appeal was made on all sides to emotion-provoked wishful thinking. If the feelings were to be our guide, the sky was veritably the limit of philosophical gestures. The products of the intellect can be subjected to some degree of measurement, control, and criticism, but not so with the products of the emotions. One intuition or deep sentiment is as real and as good as another. Even the great Kant did not prove immune. In his *Critique of Practical Reason* he contended that the assumption of the existence of God, which he freely admitted could not be proved, is the only thing which can make much of human experience intelligible or can make truly moral conduct appear rational. While Kant assumed to build his ethics on Newtonian science, his moral doctrines were taken mainly from Rousseau, whom Kant regarded as the greatest moral teacher who ever lived.

While Kant's views encouraged the later Romanticist and Idealistic philosophers, the latter were scarcely true to his essential doctrines. Kant had clearly stated that the intellect is potent and valid only when applied to the realm of the knowable—to a description of the sensual world. The Idealists not only assumed that we must take the "real" or supersensual world on faith. They tried heroically to secure assurance concerning the mysterious realm of the unknowable—the supersensual world of God. Hence they evolved with great fertility all sorts of far-fetched hypotheses regarding the mystical and subjective union of man, intelligence, God, and nature.

The abandonment to feelings and experience was forcefully advocated by Johann Gottfried von Herder (1744-1803). He was bitterly opposed to Kant's critical philosophy, but congenial to opening the path of wisdom to the dictates of the emotions. He had little knowledge of, or talent for, technical metaphysics, really possessing no competent grasp of Kant's epistemological doctrines, which he attacked. He was strong for the unity of man and the Absolute, and resented the dualism that Kant implied here. He held that man and nature were united in God. He laid great emphasis on the reality of individual experience, and was especially attracted by art, poetry, and language. In the latter field he did much to launch the cultivation of comparative philology. His most distinguished work was done in the philosophy of history. He believed that historical evolution was a product of the interworking of external environment and of *Geist,* the dynamic totality of subjective impulses, for which there is no exact English term. Through his emphasis on the unity and individuality of national culture he became a powerful factor in founding the philosophy of nationalism in Germany.[1]

The Kantian distinction between the realm of reality and of human experience was even more vigorously attacked by Johann Gottlieb Fichte (1762-1814). He produced what he regarded as a destruction of this dualism. Man is a form of manifestation of God, and nature an expression of the spirit. "Knowledge is not mere knowledge of itself, but of being, and of the one being that truly is, namely, God." Along with the mystical Idealism in Fichte, one may discern a certain pragmatism in his emphasis on action and his notion that knowledge is important only for the sake of action. For Fichte, the motive of progress is the quest for human perfection, which will permit the maximum of human striving for further perfection. When there is nothing else left to strive for we can still strive to create God, which task we need never fear we shall finish. The best general summary of Fichte's outlook is contained in his lectures on *The Characteristics of the Present Age* (1804).

Fichte was especially interested in language as a mode of expression of personality and a precious element in national culture. One of the proofs of the superiority of the Prussians was their primordial *Ursprache* (original language). This mystical view of language provided the proper aura for the work of the philologists like the brothers Grimm and their successors. Fichte was the high priest of the revival of German nationalism after the defeat at Jena.[2] His *Lectures to the German Nation,* delivered during the winter of 1807-08, were the rallying-point of those who brought about the regeneration of Prussia.

Fichte's effort to unite nature and intelligence was carried forward by Friedrich Wilhelm Joseph von Schelling (1775-1854), who is especially noted for his work on the philosophy of esthetics. In his *System of Transcendental Idealism* he tried to effect this synthesis:

> Nature is visible soul, soul is invisible nature, and both advance incessantly by an uninterrupted succession of stages and gradation of forms. . . . Just as nature exhibits to us the series of dynamic stages by which spirit struggles towards consciousness of itself, so the world of intelligence and practice, the world of mind, exhibits the series of stages through which self-consciousness with its inevitable oppositions and reconciliations develops in its ideal form.

Neither nature nor man is static. As Professor Edward Caldwell Moore summarizes Schelling's basic thought:

> On the contrary, nature is always in the process of advance from lower, less highly organised and less intelligible forms, to those which are more highly organised, more nearly the counterpart of the active intelligence in man himself. The personality of man has been viewed as standing over against this nature, this last being thought of as static and permanent. On the contrary, the personality of man, with all of its intelligence and free will, is but the climax and fulfilment of a long succession of

[1] See R. R. Ergang, *Herder and the Foundations of German Nationalism,* Columbia University Press, 1931.
[2] See H. C. Engelbrecht, *Johann Gottlieb Fichte,* Columbia University Press, 1933.

intelligible forms in nature, passing upward from the inorganic to the organic, from the unconscious to the conscious, from the non-moral to the moral, as these are at last seen in man. . . . Philosophy has to treat of the inner life which moves the whole of nature as intelligible productivity, as subject, no longer as object. . . . Schelling has here rounded out the theory of absolute idealism which Fichte had carried through in a one-sided way.[1]

The unity and harmony of the inner life of man claimed the special attention of Karl Wilhelm Friedrich von Schlegel (1772-1829). Robert Flint thus summarizes Schlegel's conception of the central problem of philosophy and of the philosophy of history:

Philosophy . . . is the science of the inward life of man. It makes, he insists, but one presupposition, viz., the existence of the internal life; and its chief or central problem is to determine how unity and harmony may be conferred upon that life, how the image of God, which it has lost, may be restored in it. To point out how this may be effected in the individual consciousness, is the task of pure philosophy— the philosophy of life, distinctively so called. To point out how the process has been so far actually carried on among the different peoples and in the various ages of the world, is the task of the philosophy of history.[2]

Schlegel devoted himself primarily to the philosophy of history, though he did notable work in philology and in the history of literature. His survey of history is chiefly a record of the apostasy of man from God. He sought evidence from history that man would return to an "unquestioning and unqualified submission to authority," but even Schlegel had to admit that his investigation ended in the hope rather than the assurance that this blessed result would ever be realized. Like John Henry Newman, Schlegel himself sought refuge and certainty through going over to Catholicism.

The most heroic effort to unite God and the universe is found in the work of Friedrich Daniel Ernst Schleiermacher (1768-1834). The antithesis between the real and the ideal is only a practical and convenient working illusion of the world of fact. "We must assume a universal identity of the ideal and the real behind the antithesis which constitutes the world." It is the problem of man to reduce this conflict between the real and the ideal: "The whole effort and end of human thought and action is the gradual reduction of the realm and power of this antithesis in the individual, the race, and the world." Universal reason (faith) is the unifying principle of nature. The absolute unity behind all is God, in whom "the real is manifold and the spirit is one." In other words, "the universe is God, and God is the universe." Without such an attitude, no really great constructive work is possible. "No great man ever lived, no great work was ever done, save in an attitude towards the universe which is identical with that of the religious man towards God." Very important was Schleiermacher's identification of religious reality with personal religious experience. His views here were the source of the many and popular "religious experience" theories of religion today, and have also had no little influence upon the psychological treatment of religion by William James and others.

These philosophical trends culminated in the work of the ponderous and

[1] Moore, *Outline of the History of Christian Thought since Kant*, Scribner, 1915, pp. 61-62.
[2] Flint, *The Philosophy of History in France and Germany*, Scribner, 1874, p. 457.

prolific dialectician Georg Wilhelm Friedrich Hegel (1770-1831). Others of the group had sought the key to reality in religion, in art, or in language. In the works of Hegel we find the apotheosis of philosophy—serving as the master guide to reality: "At the basis of all reality, whether material or mental, there is thought. . . . It only appears in consciousness as the crowning development of the mind. Only with philosophy does thought become fully conscious of itself in its origin and development." Fichte had spoken of the universal process as a synthesis of opposites. With Hegel this notion of "thesis, antithesis, and synthesis" became the "perpetual law of thought."

The Kantian dualism was rejected outright by Hegel, who built his whole philosophy around the insistence that nothing is unknowable. He held that there is nothing real in the universe save the world and man's social experience of it—that there is no reality behind that which can be observed.

Hegel was concerned with the processes whereby the knowable, those things which "are observable within experience," manifest themselves and develop. Hegel looked at the universal problem in a dynamic manner. "The universe is a process of development to the eye of philosophy. It is the process of the Absolute—in religious language, the manifestation of God. The rhythmic movement of thought is the self-unfolding of the Absolute." It is not surprising, then, that one of the most notable works of Hegel was his subjective philosophy of history, devoted to portraying the unfolding of *Geist* in the development of mankind. In oriental times only the semidivine monarch was free. The Greeks, Romans, and medievals extended the scope of mental freedom to the aristocracy, and the "few" were then able to enjoy liberty. To the Germans of the post-Reformation period came the "mission" to bring liberty to all mankind. Hegel believed that progress comes through conflict and synthesis. A movement or idea—thesis—starts. Then its opposite—antithesis—appears. Out of the clash comes an ultimate synthesis that embodies truth and progress. No formula or dogma of the German Romanticist or Idealistic philosophers had more influence on human thought and action than this. Its relationship to Marxian dialectic, for example, is well known. Hegel exerted a wide influence in socializing philosophical thought and in promoting interest in the social sciences.

The outstanding things about all these philosophers is that whatever their intellectual pretensions, their systems were essentially based on faith. This fact has been admirably brought out by Professor Randall in the following paragraph:

Kant's book stimulated Romanticists to a flood of special systems founded on faith. Man, they claimed, is not fundamentally intellectual. Rather human nature is at bottom made up of instincts and feelings; and his instinctive and emotional life should dominate his career and paint for him both his conception of the world and his conception of human life. In other words, the poet or the saint is a truer and better guide on the pathway of life and thought than the scientist. Religion, morals, art, literature, social and political philosophy, and education should recognize this fundamental fact and build upon it. Religion is not a science to be demonstrated, but a matter of the heart, a life to be lived. Morality is not a science, but essentially the good will and the performance of one's duties. Art is not a matter of form and structure, but of rich sentiment and feeling. Society is not a cold-blooded enterprise founded on self-interest, but a vast organism pressing onward to realize dimly seen ideals, in which all are members one of another. The whole universe is not a machine, but a living body, to be interpreted on the analogy of man's life.[1]

The value and validity of the metaphysics of this Romanticist and Idealistic philosophy must be left to the judgment of other and more competent minds, but the whole discussion of the relative potency and significance of the intellectual versus the emotional faculties is of no more than curious interest to one acquainted with modern psychology. The notion that the intellect and the emotions function separately or independently is now an archaic absurdity. The most critical and Rationalistic of men may be operating under the influence of emotional complexes of the most deep-seated character. Our "self-evident dictates of pure reason" may be no more than the rationalization of impressions of childhood. As has often been pointed out, we can usually give a good reason for the attitude that we take, but rarely know the real reason. Modern psychology has emphasized the great importance of the emotions, but not as a comprehensive alibi for muddy thinking or as a dignified reservoir of ignorance and credulity.

Another important contrast between the Rationalists and the Romanticists lies in their quite different emphasis on the importance of the individual. The Rationalists were chiefly interested in social maladjustments, with the oppression of mankind as a whole, and with social progress for the race. The conflicts within society arrested their attention. Their great ethical slogan was "The greatest good for the greatest number," a phrase taken over from them by Bentham and the Utilitarians. The Romanticists were more concerned with the struggle within the individual—with his conflicts and problems. In modern terms, Romanticism was introverted and introspective. This led to a greater emphasis on the value and importance of the individual. Self-expression became a major impulse.

Finally, it should be made clear that while Romanticism and Idealism were, as an intellectual movement, conservative and reactionary, at least some of their representatives were what we would today call "Modernists." Moreover, Romanticism did help on a number of progressive intellectual achievements of the nineteenth century, such as the genetic view of the social process, the historical outlook, the theory of evolution, Marxian dialectic, and even certain attitudes of experimental science.

XI. THE RELIGIOUS REACTION

We have already seen that the great majority of the Rationalists were deeply religious men. They believed in the natural religion that was conformable to reason. But they generally repudiated faith, religious tradition, and the other rubrics of supernaturalism. Further, they judged moral conduct in large part in relation to its effect upon the promotion of virtue, that is, the improvement of human well-being here on earth. Their test of morals was essentially secular—those things were moral which helped to increase human happiness here and now.

These attitudes naturally stirred up a reaction on the part of the more con-

[1] Randall, op. cit., p. 410.

servative leaders of pious thought. Immanuel Kant not only let down the bars for the anti-Rationalist movement in philosophy; he also paved the way for a definite reaction in religious and moral philosophy. In his *Critique of Pure Reason* Kant has demolished all of the traditional arguments for the existence of God—the ontological argument, the argument from design, and the like. This work still remains a monument to philosophical agnosticism. Yet when Kant proceeded to build the philosophical basis for his own system of religion and morals, he suspended his agnosticism and became a pragmatic theist.

In his *Critique of Practical Reason* (1788) he assumed the existence of God as a necessary postulate of the moral will. We must take God for granted in order rationally to work for the highest good. Kant's ethics were not sociological or secular. He repudiated any such conception as that morality should be judged by its social effects on man. Instead, he adopted the conception of the "categorical imperative" or the notion of unconditioned and obligatory morality. We should not be guided by any thought of immediate benefits or punishments as a result of our earthly conduct. Rather, we must live in such a manner that our lives may seem a model for, or an imitation of, the moral law of the universe. This is in reality the deification of the solemn sense of pious duty. As Professor Moore puts Kant's conception:

> The claims of duty are the higher ones. They are mandatory, absolute. We do our duty whether or not we superficially desire to do it. We do our duty whether or not we foresee advantage in having done it. We should do it if we foresaw with clearness disadvantage. We should find our satisfaction in having done it, even at the cost of all our other satisfactions. There is a must which is over and above all our desires. This is what Kant meant by the categorical imperative.[1]

This is, obviously, a repudiation of the Hedonistic trends in Rationalism and dangerously near to a justification of the Puritan inner compulsion. Kantian ethics were in no small part a rationalization of the provincial and emotionally starved personal experience of the chaste bachelor philosopher of Königsberg.

In the field of religion Kant's mantle was passed on to Schleiermacher. We have just seen how the latter held that the religious attitude was essential to any truly great achievement. Schleiermacher contended that "religion is a condition of devout feeling, specifically the feeling of dependence upon God." He laid great stress upon the importance of the life and teachings of Jesus. It is chiefly through the character of Jesus that we may know God. "The real task of religion is the reproduction within the believer, as far as possible, of the consciousness, experience, and character of Jesus." The true religious experience will deliver us from the great sin—the dominion of the senses: "It is the dominance of the lower nature in us, of the sense-consciousness. It is the determination of our course of life by the senses. This preponderance of the senses over the consciousness of God is the secret of unhappiness, of the feeling of defeat and misery in men, of the need of salvation." The Christian experience will save us from all this and provide full redemption.

The Romanticist reaction in religion was chiefly centered in Germany. From England came another effort to combat Rationalism, namely, the "Christian evidences" propaganda. Deism had its birth in England. Here Rationalism had run its full course, even suggesting to Hume the notion that belief in God was

---

[1] Moore, *op. cit.*, p. 49.

by no means an inherent faculty of the human mind. The echoes of Holbach's materialistic atheism also reached British shores. Atheism had suggested that the universe and man might have come into existence without divine creation. The forces of the faith were rallied to repulse such alarming doctrines.

The most famous of the attacks upon Deism was *The Analogy of Natural and Revealed Religion* by Bishop Joseph Butler (1692-1752),[1] published in 1737, long before Holbach's time. Butler tried to meet the Deists on their own ground. The latter contended that their natural religion was a religion of reason and that revealed religion, when valid, was no more than a special pronouncement of the eternal truths of natural religion. Particularly did they repudiate historical Christianity. Butler tried to show that revealed religion would meet the tests of reason just as well as natural religion. But he almost overdid the job. To many it has seemed that what he proved was that both natural and revealed religion are equally unreasonable. At any rate, his *Analogy* was the most powerful answer to Deism that ever came from the camp of revealed religion.

A lesser intellect but a more indefatigable worker in behalf of revealed religion was William Paley (1743-1805).[2] He was the founder of what is known as the "Christian evidences" movement, and his two chief works were *A View of the Evidences of Christianity* (1794) and *Natural Theology, or Evidences of the Existence and Attributes of the Deity Collected from the Appearances of Nature* (1802). Paley's effort to demonstrate the existence of God was based upon the familiar "argument from design," namely, the contention that the wonders, perfections, and delicate adjustments of nature necessitate the assumption of a designing and creative intelligence, or God.

The works of nature want only to be contemplated. . . . Of the vast scale of operation through which our discoveries carry us, at one end we see an intelligent Power arranging planetary systems, fixing, for instance, the trajectory of Saturn, or constructing a ring of two hundred thousand miles to surround his body, and be suspended like a magnificent arch over the heads of his inhabitants; and, at the other, bending a hooked tooth, concerting and providing an appropriate mechanism for the clasping and reclasping of the filaments of the feather of the humming bird.

Paley was neither a great scholar nor an original mind, but he was a masterly expositor and advocate. Professor Bury has well said of his efforts, "Paley's defense is the performance of an able legal adviser to the Almighty." [3]

The culmination of this line of thought was the publication of the so-called Bridgewater Treatises. When Lord Bridgewater, president of the Royal Society, died he set aside £8,000 to be divided into eight equal parts and awarded to the writers of treatises showing "the power, wisdom, and goodness of God, as manifested in Creation." The best-known figures who won one of these awards are Peter M. Roget (of the celebrated *Thesaurus*), Sir Charles Bell, and William Whewell, philosopher and historian of the scientific method. Their books were entitled, respectively, *Animal and Vegetable Physiology with Reference to Natural Theology; The Hand, Its Mechanism as Evincing Design;* and *Astronomy and General Physics Considered with Reference to*

---

[1] See McGiffert, *op. cit.*, pp. 230 ff., and Stephen, *op. cit.*, Vol. I, Chap. v.
[2] See Stephen, *op. cit.*, Vol. I, pp. 405 ff.   [3] Bury, *History of the Freedom of Thought*, p. 168.

THE RELIGIOUS REACTION

Natural Theology. Other sciences suborned to the service of God were chemistry, meteorology, physiology, geology, and mineralogy. It was not until many years later that Helmholtz, the profound student of optics, remarked that he would be ashamed to lay claim to the invention of so clumsy and imperfect a mechanism as the human eye. For several generations the Bridgewater frame of mind dominated the natural sciences. It played a part in the Darwinian controversy, and occasionally pops up in the writings of the more apologetic scientists like Millikan and Pupin even today.

Courses in Christian evidences soon became an integral unit in higher education in England and America. Butler's *Analogy* and Paley's *Natural Theology* were the favorite texts, though later and lesser writers often prepared textbooks based on these and other works. These courses were usually taught by the president of the college, who was himself almost invariably a clergyman. This gave added prestige to the course and greater assurance to the students regarding their faith. Such courses long served to hold American higher education in line with orthodoxy. So effective was Mark Hopkins in presenting Christian evidences at Williams College about the time of the American Civil War that Stanley Hall, the famous American educator, then a student at Williams, was compelled to hide in a cow stable to read Darwin's *Origin of Species* by the light of a barn lantern.[1] Special college honors and emoluments were bestowed in the effort to turn attention to Christian evidences. The degrees of Doctor of Divinity and Doctor of Philosophy were freely given to those who would submit a thesis defending orthodox Christianity. These were for the most part rather wooden compilations culled from Paley and his successors.

Butler, Paley, and others also stirred up interest and activity among English Protestants, which took form in the creation of various societies devoted to the dissemination of Christian literature in the way of cheap books, appropriate pamphlets, and earnest tracts. The London Missionary Society, the Religious Tract Society, the British and Foreign Bible Society, the Church Missionary Society, and the Baptist Missionary Society expanded rapidly after their founding about the opening of the nineteenth century.[2] Clergymen paid more attention to their duties, and the institution of family prayers became exceedingly common. Even the popular magazines began to devote attention to religion.[3]

Still more momentous was the foundation of Methodism by John Wesley (1703-91). He firmly believed that religion should be based on human emotions rather than the intellect. It must rest upon Faith rather than Reason, and he fully agreed with Luther that Faith was entirely competent to "wring the neck of Reason." Methodism was a complete repudiation of the position of Locke and the Deists, who held that religion should be a calm following out of the dictates of reason. That which with Locke and the Deists was a dignified intellectual enterprise became with Wesley an emotional panic and orgy. Wesley also denounced the Deistic notion of the natural dignity and worth

---

[1] Personally recounted to the writer.
[2] The important Society for Promoting Christian Knowledge had been formed in 1698, and the Society for the Propagation of the Gospel in Foreign Parts in 1701.
[3] The interesting Oxford Movement will be considered later. See below, pp. 679-80.

of man. For this he substituted the old dogma of the Fall of man, his innately sinful nature, his total unworthiness, and his full dependence upon divine grace for restoration and redemption. This led him particularly to emphasize the doctrine of the Atonement and the saving power of Jesus Christ. Man must be brought to righteousness through the forceful and thorough conviction of sin. This led to ardent approval of evangelistic methods and the sheer appeal to brute emotion. Wesley was particularly harsh on men who were able to live a decent life on the basis of their own sense of honor and justice, without any feeling of dependence upon God—in short, the so-called men of honor. Such men were, in Wesley's view, far worse than the most dissolute and carnal sinners. For the latter there might be some hope, but none at all for the former.

Methodism, with its reliance upon the welling up of the emotions, made a strong appeal to the poor and miserable British workers and peasants during the distressing period of the great inclosures and the Industrial Revolution, which followed on the heels of Wesley's movement.

George Whitefield and Francis Asbury carried the gospel to America, where it likewise found fertile soil among those who had to bear the harsh and dangerous life of the frontier. It was the quasi-official religion of the frontier, and in the later history of this country some of its devotees have shown a desire to make it, in influence at least, our state religion. As it grew older Methodism turned from the question of personal righteousness, emotionally experienced and affirmed, to the regulation of social conduct. It became a strong force behind Prohibition, "moral" crusades, censorship, and similar movements.

The evangelical movement in America was not limited to the Methodists. It was soon joined by the Baptists. This sect, which started as the Anabaptists in Germany and had been brought to America by Roger Williams and others, was originally a very liberal and tolerant religious group. But it soon became ardently evangelical. It is probably true that the Southern Baptists of contemporary America represent the most devout religious group of any size in the New World. Another evangelical ally appeared in the Disciples of Christ, sometimes shortened to the single word "Christians." This sect was started by Alexander Campbell as a secession of devout and dissatisfied Baptists and Presbyterians who believed their parent sects had strayed from the essentials of the Apostolic faith. They laid great stress upon the literal word of the Bible, demanded total immersion of all converts, ordered weekly open communion, and believed in complete congregational government. The Presbyterians have often been lumped together with Methodists, Baptists, and Disciples as evangelicals. In general, however, the Presbyterians have maintained more dignity in their religious views and practices, though they are often more smug in their sectarianism and more coldly hostile to modern intellectual life and social reform.

Evangelical religion meant quite literally a strong reliance on evangelistic methods of conversion. Great pulpit orators like Lorenzo Dow went before congregations, camp meetings, and other gatherings to terrorize the sinners and unbelievers and to bring to them a sharp realization of their sinful unworthiness and the necessity of throwing themselves upon the saving grace of Christ to secure redemption. These evangelists, who had derived their model of procedure from Wesley and Whitefield themselves, revived the early medieval and Reformation emphasis upon the stark realities and unspeakable horrors of Hell, and a strong aroma of verbally created sulphur and brimstone hung over most early evangelistic enterprise. Professor McMaster presents plenty of material descriptive of these evangelistic methods in his account of American history in the middle of the last century. Much of this, with additional information, is collected in Dr. Frederick Morgan Davenport's *Primitive Traits in Religious Revivals*.[1] However emotional and antirationalistic may have been the evangelistic prowess of a Lorenzo Dow or a Dwight Moody, there is no doubt that such men were full of sincerity. There was little of the commercialized technique that has been exploited by some prominent contemporary evangelists and was forcefully exposed in Sinclair Lewis's *Elmer Gantry*.[2]

The religious reaction broke out in France as well as in Germany and England. In France it was strongly tinged not only with the Romanticist philosophy, but also with political and ecclesiastical elements. French freethinking of the eighteenth century had been identified with political revolution and with heavy inroads into the French Catholic Church. It was inevitable that the religious reaction should carry with it strong emphasis upon political authority and ecclesiastical restoration. It is not astonishing, then, that most of the outstanding leaders in the religious revival should be the same men whom we shall treat below as the assailants of revolutionary political theory.[3] In their zeal to restore Catholicism and authority, these writers laid great stress upon the importance and infallibility of the Church of Rome and the Pope. It was thus what is called an "ultramontane" movement.[4]

The man who put spirit into the religious attack upon French free thought was François Châteaubriand (1768-1848). His *Genius of Christianity* (1802), the outstanding expression of French Romanticism, was the gospel of the French revolt against Rationalism. It was an out-and-out apology for Catholicism, taking for granted the underlying thesis that Catholicism and Christianity are identical and coextensive. It was a masterpiece of style and appealed to the senses and emotions more than to the intellect. His *Martyrs* (1809) created an even greater sentimental attachment for the Church and its dramatic and moving origins.

Louis de Bonald (1754-1840) devoted more attention to arguments for the restoration of political authority than to religious matters, though he was intensely interested in the latter. His large work, *The Theory of Political and Religious Authority in Civil Society* (1796), embodied most of his religious doctrines. He laid more stress on language than had Fichte, pointing out its alleged divine origin and deducing therefrom much of his religious conviction. He supported with eloquence the infallibility of supernatural religion, spiritual truth, and the authority of the Church. He also defended with zest the orthodox conception of the supernatural sanctions and objectives of morality. The

---

[1] Macmillan, 1905. [2] Harcourt, Brace, 1927. [3] See below, pp. 232 ff.
[4] Meaning support of the ecclesiastical forces on the other side of the mountains (the Alps), in contrast to the Gallican or French nationalist movement in Catholicism. Some earlier "ultramontanes" had, of course, been antipapal at times.

writings of Joseph de Maistre (1754-1821) are still more decisively political, but he stoutly upheld Catholicism and religious authority. His *St. Petersburg Evenings* (1821) was a stanch defense of religious authority and an attack upon Voltaire and the freethinkers. More influential was his work *The Pope* (1819), which expounded forcefully the notion of the infallibility of the Pope as well as of secular monarchs.

Next to the works of Chateaubriand, the greatest popular influence was exerted by the early writings of the Abbé Hugues Félicité Robert de Lamennais (1782-1854). His *Reflections on the State of the Church* (1808) was a slashing criticism of the humiliation of the Catholic Church by the French Revolution and a protest against its limited powers under the Concordat of 1801. Much more widely read was his *Essay on Religious Indifference* (1818), which both assailed the doctrines of skepticism and indicated at length the indispensable services rendered by religion to man and society.

The majority of the writings associated with the religious reaction in France were by Catholics of ultramontane persuasion, but one author brought in the impulse of German Idealism as expressed by Kant and Schleiermacher, namely, Henri Benjamin Constant de Rebecque (1767-1830), who devoted to the subject a voluminous work, *The Sources, Forms and Developments of Religion* (1824-30). Incidentally, Constant assailed the Deists, particularly singling out Thomas Paine, about whom he knew little at first hand.

The French religious revival was short-lived and not by any means so influential with the populace as the pietistic revival in England. The Bourbon dynasty was thrown out in 1830 and a tolerant bourgeois government installed under the Orleanists. Even French Catholicism became much more liberal with writers like Lamartine, Buchez, and Leroux. Indeed, Lamennais himself showed great capacity for intellectual growth and became an antagonist of the Church that he had earlier so zealously defended. The social philosopher Count Henri de Saint-Simon wrote an influential book on *The New Christianity* (1825), in which he denounced religious formalism and ecclesiasticism and emphasized the social message of religion as an aid to reform and justice for the masses. His disciple Auguste Comte boldly cast aside all supernaturalism, theism, and otherworldliness, and created a frank religion of Humanity, which would glorify man and work for his betterment here and now. It was to rely upon sociology rather than theology for guidance. Before the end of the nineteenth century France had become the most openly skeptical of important modern states—perhaps the only one in which agnosticism and atheism were highly respectable in the best political, social and intellectual circles.

The total upshot of the Romanticist and obscurantist revolt was to reënforce the trend to reaction in religion, Catholic and Protestant, in politics and in social life. Protestantism retreated from every one of the advanced positions taken up under Deism and reverted to emotionalism. Politics was characterized by the revival of absolutism and reactionary statecraft under Metternich and the Quadruple Alliance. This trend was also stimulated by Napoleon's spectacular career, which likewise contributed to the retreat of many revolutionary Romanticists into conservatism—for instance, the English poet Wordsworth—and to the anti-French outburst in American politics in the early nineteenth century. In the field of morals, there was a withdrawal from the fruitful efforts of the Deists to find sound guidance for empirical investigations of man's constitution, sophisticated by esthetic considerations, into purely authoritarian formulations, based either upon an appeal to some "categorical imperative" or merely to the traditional Christian practice.

The fact remains, however, that Romanticism was in the full flush of its power for only about sixty years. The reaction was never sufficiently general to put an end to scientific progress, and when, following 1850, new scientific ideas began to appear, the success of the Modernists became more of a certainty. The acerbity of the controversies in the late nineteenth century may be attributed to the fact that Romanticism had intervened between the triumph of intelligence in the eighteenth century and the coming of the new science. It lent its strength to the traditionalists and the reactionaries. But in the face of the cumulative effect of the new knowledge, the reactionaries proved rather impotent in the long run among the educated classes.

In the world at large the rising tide of science gave birth to a social optimism that swept the intellectual world and continued in force well into the twentieth century. It required a social catastrophe like the World War to bring another period of intellectual reaction, that through which we are living at present. In this respect, the intellectual reaction to the World War is comparable to the reaction to the French Revolution.

SUGGESTED READING

Hammerton, *Universal History of the World,* Chaps. 147, 153-54, 158, 161
Abbott, *The Expansion of Europe,* Vol. I, pp. 477-90; Vol. II, pp. 133-40, 223-31, 261-67
Randall, *The Making of the Modern Mind,* Chaps. XI-XII
Woodbridge Riley, *From Myth to Reason,* Appleton, 1926, Bks. III-IV
J. R. Mayer, *The Seven Seals of Science,* Century, 1927, Chaps. V-VIII
Sir W. C. D. Dampier-Whetham, *History of Science,* Macmillan, 1930, Chaps. III-IV
Philipp Lenard, *Great Men of Science,* Macmillan, 1933, pp. 12-170
H. E. Cushman, *Beginner's History of Philosophy,* Houghton Mifflin, 1918-20, 2 vols., Vol. II, pp. 51-55, 74-92, 155-74, 192-210
Harald Höffding, *History of Modern Philosophy,* Macmillan, 1908, 2 vols., Vol. I
Ernest W. Nelson and others, *Persecution and Liberty: Essays in Honor of George Lincoln Burr,* Century, 1931, pp. 3-20, 171-226
Joseph McCabe, *The History and Meaning of the Catholic Index of Forbidden Books,* Haldeman-Julius, 1931
J. B. Bury, *History of the Freedom of Thought,* Holt, 1913, Chaps. IV-VI
——— *The Idea of Progress,* Macmillan, 1932
Lecky, *History of the Rise and Influence of the Spirit of Rationalism in Europe,* Chap. IV
McGiffert, *Protestant Thought before Kant,* Scribner, 1911, Chap. X
A. W. Benn, *History of English Rationalism in the Nineteenth Century,* Longmans, 1926, 2 vols., Vol. I, Chaps. III-V, VIII-IX; Vol. II, Chap. XI
H. M. Morais, *Deism in Eighteenth Century America,* Columbia University Press, 1934
Preserved Smith, *History of Modern Culture,* Holt, 1930-34, 2 vols., Vol. I (1543-1687), Chaps. II-VII, XIII, XV; Vol. II (1687-1776), Chaps. II-V, VII, XI, XIV-XV

Howard Robinson, *Bayle the Sceptic,* Columbia University Press, 1931
John Morley, *Voltaire,* Macmillan, 1871
J. S. Schapiro, *Condorcet and the Rise of Liberalism in France,* Harcourt, Brace, 1934
C. L. Becker, *The Heavenly City of the Eighteenth-Century Philosophers,* Yale University Press, 1932
J. M. Robertson, *Short History of Freethought, Ancient and Modern,* 2d ed. rev., Putnam, 1906, 2 vols.
—— *History of Freethought in the Nineteenth Century,* Putnam, 1930, 2 vols., Vol. I, Pt. I, Chap. 1
E. C. Moore, *Outline of the History of Christian Thought since Kant,* Scribner, 1915, Chaps. ii-iii
Webster, *Historical Selections,* Sec. XXVII
Robinson and Beard, *Readings in Modern European History,* Vol. I, Chap. ix
W. S. Knickerbocker, ed., *Classics of Modern Science,* Crofts, 1927, pp. 1-156
F. J. Teggart, ed., *The Idea of Progress, a Collection of Readings,* University of California Press, 1925

FURTHER REFERENCES

THE LIBERATION OF THE INTELLECT IN EARLY MODERN TIMES. On the temper of early modern times, see Smith, *op. cit.,* Vol. II, pp. 16 ff.; Robinson, *Mind in the Making,* Chap. vi; H. J. Laski, "The Rise of Liberalism," Encyclopaedia of the Social Sciences, Vol. I; Randall, *op. cit.,* Chaps. ix-x; Pt. IV of J. K. Hart, *The Discovery of Intelligence* (Century, 1924); Bury, *History of Freedom of Thought,* Chaps. iv-vi.

On the development of the secular attitude, see article "Secularism," Encyclopaedia of the Social Sciences; G. J. Holyoake, *The Origin and Nature of Secularism* (London, 1896) and *English Secularism* (Open Court Pub. Co., 1897).

SCIENCE. On the intellectual background of the rise of modern science, see Smith, *The Age of the Reformation,* Chaps. xii-xiii, and *History of Modern Culture,* Vol. I, pp. 7 ff., 144 ff.; H. E. Barnes, "The Historical Background and Setting of the Philosophy of Francis Bacon," *Scientific Monthly,* May, 1924. On the rise of modern science, by far the most satisfactory treatment for the non-technical student is Smith, *History of Modern Culture,* Vol. I, Pt. I; Vol. II, Chaps. ii-iv. See also Hammerton, *op. cit.,* Chap. 147; Chap. viii of F. S. Marvin, *The Living Past* (Oxford Press, 1913); Riley, *op. cit.,* Bk. III; Mayer, *op. cit.,* Chaps. iv-vi; A. E. Shipley, *The Revival of Science in the Seventeenth Century* (Princeton University Press, 1914); W. T. Sedgwick and H. W. Tyler, *Short History of Science* (Macmillan, 1917), Chaps. x-xiii; Pt. III of R. J. Harvey-Gibson, *Two Thousand Years of Science* (2d ed. rev., Macmillan, 1931).

On Newton, see Lenard, *op. cit.,* pp. 83 ff.; Selig Brodetsy, *Sir Isaac Newton* (Luce, 1928); L. T. More, *Isaac Newton,* Scribner, 1934. Interesting biographical studies of leading scientists of this period can be found in Lenard, *op. cit.,* pp. 12-123; and pp. 74-175 of Benjamin Ginzburg, *The Adventure of Science* (Simon & Schuster, 1930).

For a good history of time-telling devices from antiquity until today, see A. P. Usher, *History of Mechanical Inventions* (McGraw-Hill, 1929), Chaps. vi, x; Chap. v of T. C. Bridges, *The Book of Invention* (London, 1925).

On early equipment for scientific research, see George Forbes, *History of Astronomy* (Putnam, 1909), Bk. III; pp. 145 ff. of C. J. Singer, *The Story of Living Things* (Harper, 1931); Chaps. xi-xii of W. A. Locy, *The Growth of Biology* (Holt, 1925); Gillespie, *The Influence of Oversea Expansion on England,* Chaps. viii-ix;

David Murray, *Museums: Their History and Their Use* (Glasgow, 1904, 3 vols.).
On the rise of scientific societies, see Smith, *op. cit.*, Vol. I, pp. 164 ff.; Martha Ornstein, *The Rôle of Scientific Societies in the Seventeenth Century* (privately printed, 1913).
On natural science in the eighteenth century, see Randall, *op. cit.*, Chap. xi; Chap. vi of J. N. Leonard, *Crusaders of Chemistry* (Doubleday, Doran, 1930); Sedgwick and Tyler, *op. cit.*, Chap. xiv; Mayer, *op. cit.*, Chaps. vii-viii; Harvey-Gibson, *op. cit.*, Pt. V; Vol. I, Chaps. iv-viii of Sir Edward Thorpe, *History of Chemistry* (Putnam, 1909-10, 2 vols.).

PHILOSOPHY. On the emancipation of philosophy, see Smith, *op. cit.*, Vol. I, Chap. vii; Vol. II, Chap. v; Cushman, *op. cit.*, Vol. II, Chaps. iv-ix; Höffding, *op. cit.*, Vol. I, *passim;* Riley, *op. cit.*, Bk. IV.
On Montaigne, see Edward Dowden, *Michel de Montaigne* (Lippincott, 1905); E. H. Sichel, *Michel de Montaigne* (Dutton, 1911); I. C. Willis, *Montaigne* (Knopf, 1927); Montaigne, M. E. de, *Autobiography,* ed. by Marvin Lowenthal (Houghton Mifflin, 1935) and *Essays,* ed. by W. C. Hazlitt (Burt, 1933).
On Francis Bacon, a good introductory biography is Byron Steel (Francis Steegmüller), *Sir Francis Bacon* (Doubleday, Doran, 1930). More recent and thorough is Charles Williams, *Bacon* (Harper, 1934). On his thought, see Chap. iii of W. J. Durant, *The Story of Philosophy* (Simon & Schuster, 1926); Höffding, *op. cit.*, Vol. I, pp. 184 ff.; Chap. v of Walter Libby, *Introduction to the History of Science* (Houghton Mifflin, 1917); John Nichol, *Francis Bacon* (Lippincott, 1888-89, 2 vols.).
On Descartes, see Cushman, *op. cit.*, Vol. II, pp. 77 ff.; Höffding, *op. cit.*, Vol. I, pp. 212 ff.; Riley, *op. cit.*, Chap. xxxii; A. B. Gibson, *The Philosophy of Descartes* (Dutton, 1932); S. V. Keeling, *Descartes* (Smith, 1934).
On Locke's philosophy, see Cushman, *op. cit.*, Vol. II, Chap. vii; Höffding, *op. cit.*, Vol. I, pp. 377 ff.; James Gibson, *Locke's Theory of Knowledge* (Cambridge University Press, 1917); A. C. Fraser, *Locke* (Lippincott, 1890).
On Hume, see Cushman, *op. cit.*, Vol. II, pp. 192 ff.; pp. 330 ff. of A. K. Rogers, *Student's History of Philosophy* (3d ed., Macmillan, 1932); Höffding, *op. cit.*, Vol. I, pp. 424 ff.; T. H. Huxley, *Hume* (Harper, 1879); David Hume, *Letters,* ed. by J. Y. T. Grieg (Oxford Press, 1932, 2 vols.); B. M. Laing, *David Hume* (Smith, 1932); John Laird, *Hume's Philosophy of Human Nature* (Dutton, 1932); C. W. Hendel, *Studies in the Philosophy of David Hume* (Princeton University Press, 1925).

INTOLERANCE. On the history of intolerance and persecution, see Bury, *History of Freedom of Thought,* Chaps. iii-iv; Lecky, *op. cit.*, Chap. iv, Pt. 2; *Persecution and Liberty,* pp. 3 ff., 93 ff., 171 ff., 211 ff.; Chaps. vi-xii of A. J. Klein, *Intolerance in the Reign of Elizabeth* (Houghton Mifflin, 1925); E. S. P. Haynes, *Religious Persecution* (London, 1904); A. H. Verrill, *The Inquisition* (Appleton, 1931); W. E. Garrison, *Intolerance* (Round Table Press, 1934).
On the Inquisition, see further H. C. Lea's classic works on the subject, used widely in Verrill, *op. cit.* The latter is the most convenient and readable summary. For a Catholic apology, minimizing the savagery of the Inquisition, see A. L. Maycock, *The Inquisition* (Harper, 1927).
On the attempt to censor books, see Hendrik Van Loon, *Tolerance* (Boni & Liveright, 1925); Smith, *op. cit.*, Vol. I, pp. 511 ff.; Vol. II, pp. 567 ff.; G. H. Putnam, *The Censorship of the Church of Rome* (Putnam, 1906, 2 vols.); C. R. Gillett, *Burned Books* (Columbia University Press, 1927, 2 vols.)—especially the Introduction; McCabe, *op. cit.*
On the character of the economic intolerance that has been associated with the rise of capitalism, the following is representative literature: Chap. vi of Leon Whip-

ple, *The Story of Civil Liberty in the United States* (Vanguard Press, 1927); Chap. VI of E. S. Bates, *This Land of Liberty* (Harper, 1930); E. J. Hopkins, *What Happened in the Mooney Case* (Harcourt, Brace, 1932); O. K. Fraenkel, *The Sacco-Vanzetti Case* (Knopf, 1931); J. P. Clark, *The Deportation of Aliens from the United States to Europe* (Columbia University Press, 1931); L. F. Post, *The Deportation Delirium of Nineteen-Twenty* (Kerr, 1923); Gaetano Salvemini, *The Fascist Dictatorship in Italy* (Holt, Vol. I, 1927); Ernst Henri, *Hitler over Europe* (Simon & Schuster, 1934); H. H. Tiltman, *The Terror in Europe* (Stokes, 1932).

On the progress of tolerance, see D. S. Muzzey, pp. 3-20 of *Essays in Intellectual History; Dedicated to James Harvey Robinson* (Harper, 1929); Vol. II, Chaps. XXIV-XXV of J. H. Robinson, *Introduction to the History of Western Europe* (Ginn, 1924, 2 vols.); Van Loon, *op. cit.*, Chaps. XVI-XXVI; Bury, *History of Freedom of Thought*, Chaps. VI-VIII; Lecky, *op. cit.*, Chap. IV, Pt. 2; Smith, *op. cit.*, Vol. I, pp. 481 ff.; Vol. II, pp. 545 ff.; W. R. Jordan, *The Development of Religious Toleration in England . . . to the Death of Elizabeth* (Harvard University Press, 1932); A. A. Seaton, *The Theory of Toleration under the Later Stuarts* (Putnam, 1911); Francesco Ruffini, *Religious Liberty* (London, 1912); T. V. Smith, *Creative Sceptics* (Willett, Clark, 1934); H. M. Kallen, ed., *Freedom in the Modern World* (Coward-McCann, 1928).

THE RELIGIOUS REVOLUTION. On the Anabaptists, see McGiffert, *op. cit.*, pp. 100 ff.; Chap. I of Frederic Palmer, *Heretics, Saints and Martyrs* (Harvard University Press, 1925); E. B. Bax, *The Rise and Fall of the Anabaptists* (Macmillan, 1903). On the Socinians, see McGiffert, *op. cit.*, pp. 107 ff.; Vol. VII of Adolf von Harnack, *History of Dogma* (Little, Brown, 1895-1900, 7 vols.). On Rationalism and Deism, see Randall, *op. cit.*, Chap. XII; McGiffert, *op. cit.*, Chap. X; Smith, *op. cit.*, Vol. I, Chap. XIII; Vol. II, Chaps. XI, XIV; Lecky, *op. cit.*, Chap. II; Vol. I, Chaps. I-II of Sir Leslie Stephen, *History of English Thought in the Eighteenth Century* (Putnam, 1902, 2 vols.); Benn, *op. cit.*, Vol. I, Chaps. II-III; S. G. Hefelbower, *The Relation of John Locke to English Deism* (University of Chicago Press, 1918).

On Thomas Paine's ideas and contributions, see W. E. Dodd, "Tom Paine," *American Mercury*, December, 1930; pp. 100-40 of F. J. Hearnshaw, ed., *The Social and Political Ideas of Some Representative Thinkers of the Revolutionary Era* (Holt, 1932); H. H. Clark, "Historical Interpretation of Thomas Paine's Religion," University of California *Chronicle*, 1933; M. D. Conway, *Life of Thomas Paine* (Putnam, 1909, 2 vols.).

On French Rationalistic writings, for good surveys see Pt. II, Chap. XI and Pt. IV, Chaps. II, VII-IX of C. H. C. Wright, *History of French Literature* (Oxford Press, 1925); Pt. II, Bk. II, Chap. III and Pt. III, Bks. II, IV, of W. A. Nitze and E. P. Dargan, *History of French Literature;* Benn, *op. cit.*, Vol. I, Chaps. IV-V. See also Becker, *op. cit.* On Bayle's writings and methods, see Howard Robinson, *op. cit.*

On Voltaire, see Smith, *op. cit.*, Vol. II, pp. 369 ff.; Durant, *op. cit,* Chap. V; Morley, *op. cit.;* Victor Thaddaeus, *Voltaire, Genius of Mockery* (Coward-McCann, 1928)—impressionistic; C. B. Chase, *The Young Voltaire* (Longmans, 1926); André Maurois, *Voltaire* (Appleton, 1932); C. E. Vulliamy, *Voltaire* (Dodd, Mead, 1930); G. M. C. Brandes, *Voltaire* (Albert & Charles Boni, 1930, 2 vols.); M. M. H. Barr, *A Century of Voltaire Study* (Institute of French Studies, 1929); F. M. A. de Voltaire, *Philosophical Dictionary, selected, ed. and tr. by H. I. Woolf* (Knopf, 1924). On Voltaire as a historian, see J. B. Black, *The Art of History* (Crofts, 1926).

On Diderot, see John Morley, *Diderot and the Encyclopaedists* (Macmillan, 1878, 2 vols.); R. L. Cru, *Diderot as a Disciple of English Thought* (Columbia University Press, 1913).

On Holbach and atheism, see Smith, *op. cit.*, Vol. II, pp. 515 ff.; M. P. Cushing, *Baron d'Holbach* (Lemcke & Buechner, 1914).

FURTHER REFERENCES

On Deism in the United States, see Barnes, *History and Social Intelligence,* Chap. x; Chaps. III-IV of Woodbridge Riley, *American Thought from Puritanism to Pragmatism* (new ed., Holt, 1915); McGiffert, *op. cit.,* pp. 251 ff.; Morais, *op. cit.;* G. A. Koch, *Republican Religion* (Holt, 1933); S. A. Cobb, *The Rise of Religious Liberty in America* (Macmillan, 1902).

On the origins of biblical criticism, see Smith, *op. cit.,* Vol. I, pp. 279 ff.; Vol. II, pp. 265 ff.; Chaps. V-VII of Archibald Duff, *History of Old Testament Criticism* (Putnam, 1910); Chaps. III-VI of F. C. Conybeare, *History of New Testament Criticism* (Putnam, 1910).

On the Newtonian world-machine conception, see Riley, *From Myth to Reason,* Chaps. XXX-XXXI; Chap. IV of John Langdon-Davies, *Man and His Universe* (Putnam, 1910).

LIBERATING ETHICS FROM SUPERNATURALISM. On the ethical liberation, see Smith, *op. cit.,* Vol. I, pp. 542 ff.; Vol. II, pp. 608 ff.; R. C. Givler (pp. 495 ff.) in H. E. Barnes and others, *History and Prospects of the Social Sciences* (Knopf, 1925); Randall, *op. cit.,* Chap. XV; Chap. VI of Havelock Ellis, *The Dance of Life* (Houghton Mifflin, 1923); Chaps. VII-VIII of Prince P. A. Kropotkin, *Ethics; Origin and Development* (Dial Press, 1924); Chaps. VI-XIII of A. K. Rogers, *Morals in Review* (Macmillan, 1927); E. A. Shearer, *Hume's Place in Ethics* (Bryn Mawr College, 1915).

THE THEORY OF PROGRESS. On the rise of this theory, see Nitze and Dargan, *op. cit.,* Pt. III, Bk. I, Chap. 1; Smith, *op. cit.,* Vol. II, pp. 226 ff.; Bury, *The Idea of Progress,* Chaps. IV-XIII; Pt. II of W. D. Wallis, *Culture and Progress* (McGraw, 1930); Teggart, *op. cit.,* pp. 59-190; Becker, *op. cit.*

THE ROMANTICISTS AND THE REVOLT AGAINST REASON. On the Romanticist and Idealistic reaction against Rationalism, see Hammerton, *op. cit.,* Chap. 161; Randall, *op. cit.,* Chap. XVI; Cushman, *op. cit.,* Vol. II, Chaps. X-XI; Höffding, *op. cit.,* Vol. II, Bks. VII-VIII; Moore, *op. cit.,* Chaps. II-III; R. M. Wenley, *Kant and His Philosophical Revolution* (Scribner, 1911); Robert Adamson, *Fichte* (Lippincott, 1881); John Watson, *Schelling's Transcendental Idealism* (Griggs, 1882); W. B. Selbie, *Schleiermacher* (Dutton, 1913); William Wallace, *Prolegomena to the Study of Hegel's Philosophy* (2d ed. rev., Macmillan, 1894); G. S. Morris, *Hegel's Philosophy of the State and of History* (Scott, Foresman, 1892).

THE RELIGIOUS REACTION. On the religious conservatism of the Romanticist and Idealistic philosophers, see *Ibid.,* Chaps. II-III; A. C. McGiffert, *The Rise of Modern Religious Ideas* (Macmillan, 1915); C. C. J. Webb, *Kant's Philosophy of Religion* (Oxford, 1926); A. R. Osborn, *Schleiermacher and Religious Education* (Oxford Press, 1934). On the ethical theories of the Romanticists and Idealists, see Kropotkin, *op. cit.,* Chap. IX; Rogers, *op. cit.,* Chaps. XVI-XVIII; J. W. Scott, *Kant on the Moral Life* (Macmillan, 1924); H. A. Reyburn, *The Ethical Theory of Hegel* (Oxford Press, 1922).

On the religious reaction against Rationalism in England, see Stephen, *op. cit.,* Vol. II, pp. 383 ff.; Benn, *op. cit.,* Vol. I, Chaps. VIII-IX; Robertson, *History of Freethought in the Nineteenth Century,* Vol. I, Pt. I, Chap. I.

On the rise of Methodism and its intellectual and social significance, see C. T. Winchester, *Life of John Wesley* (Macmillan, 1906); G. C. Cell, *The Rediscovery of John Wesley* (Holt, 1935); Herbert Asbury, *A Methodist Saint* (Knopf, 1927); E. M. North, *Early Methodist Philanthropy* (Methodist Book Concern, 1915); Faulkner, *Chartism and the Churches.* See further bibliographies in Asbury, *op. cit.,* pp. 337-42; North, *op. cit.,* pp. 174-81.

On the religious reaction in France, good introductory surveys may be found in Robertson, *op. cit.,* Vol. I, pp. 24-38; pp. 351-53, 367-81 of Robert Flint, *Historical Philosophy in France, French Belgium and Switzerland* (Scribner, 1894).

CHAPTER VI

THE SOCIAL AND CULTURAL IMPACT OF THE NEW INSTITUTIONS AND INTELLECTUAL FORCES

I. THE GROWTH OF POPULATION AND THE INCREASING PROMINENCE OF THE MIDDLE CLASS

Among the more important social changes promoted by oversea expansion and the Commercial Revolution were the growth of population, the increasing mobility of peoples, the gradual change from status to class as the basis of society, and the greatly increased power of the middle class. A surplus economy was emerging, of which the marked increase in public building was an index.

Population, owing to inadequate food supply and the high death rate, had increased little in Europe until the later Middle Ages. Temporary gains were wiped out by epidemics like the Black Death of the middle of the fourteenth century. Aside from the few travelers, merchants, missionaries, and Crusaders there was little movement from place to place. Life was provincial and people usually were born, lived, and died in the same locality. The lord, the knight, the serf, the guildsman, and the apprentice had taken their respective positions in a society determined by status and function rather than by sharp class differentiation. For more than a thousand years the agricultural aristocracy had occupied the predominant position in society almost unchallenged. This whole social set-up was shaken to its foundations after 1500.

After 1600 the new commodities increased the food supply of Europe and made it possible to maintain a much larger population within the same area. Improved medical science played some part, especially in the eighteenth century, by helping to cut the death rate. The actual growth of population following 1600 was striking. Competent students of the problem have estimated that the population of Europe in 1650 was about 100,000,000. It is calculated to have increased to 140,000,000 in 1750, and to 187,000,000 in 1800. In 1500 the population of England and Wales is estimated to have been about 3,000,000. By 1600 it had reached 4,000,000; in 1700, 6,000,000; and in 1800, 9,000,000. At the close of the Middle Ages it is believed by the chief authorities that France had a population of about 12,000,000. By 1700 its population had increased to 21,000,000, in 1770 to 24,000,000, and in 1800 to 27,000,000. The population of Italy in 1700 is estimated as 14,000,000 and in 1800 as 18,000,000; of Prussia in

POPULATION GROWTH AND RISE OF MIDDLE CLASS 213

1740 as 3,300,000 and in 1800 as 5,800,000;[1] of Austria in 1754 as 6,100,000 and in 1800 as 8,500,000. There are no reliable statistics for the population of Russia. It is estimated that in 1720 it amounted to about 14,000,000 and in 1800 to about 29,000,000. The astonishing growth in population from the sixteenth century through the nineteenth is often attributed solely to the Industrial Revolution but, as the figures above show, the expansion of population was apparent much earlier. The Industrial Revolution was in part an effect of the increase of population, though it became, in turn, a very powerful cause of further growth.

While the urban age, as we now know it, was a product of the Industrial Revolution, which set in during the eighteenth century, the commercial and social changes in the period following 1500 had a considerable influence upon the character, size, and number of towns.[2] The older medieval cities, which owed their position and prominence to their location on the medieval trade routes along the seacoast, rivers, and mountain passes, were very generally displaced by the newer western seaboard towns, which were fortunately situated with respect to the rising oceanic trade to the westward. Cities in a position to profit by the new developments became larger. London had a population of 725,000 by 1740, and Paris one of 675,000 in 1750. There were 79 French cities with a population of over 10,000. Amsterdam, Vienna, Naples, Palermo, and Rome ran between 100,000 and 200,000. New suburban areas were developed outside the old and filthy city centers. Some slight start was made towards better sanitation and paving. The increasing volume of property and the growth of business ideals helped on a drive to lessen criminality and to protect life and property. Metropolitan standards gradually came into being. Speculation in city real estate also began on a considerable scale at this time.

The European population not only increased notably from 1500 to 1800; it also became much more mobile. There began an extensive movement of peoples from European lands to remote areas beyond the seas. The attraction of lands overseas for Europeans served to stimulate emigration and began that steady drain of European peoples to distant areas which has continued to our own day. In many cases the emigrants were disappointed in the economic opportunities of the country to which they went, but this did not prevent great numbers from voluntarily leaving Europe and going to the new regions overseas in the hope of making or increasing their fortunes. In addition to those who went overseas from choice, many moved under some form of coercion, all the way from actual kidnapping to the sending of convicted criminals, redemptioners, and indentured servants to work out their freedom in the new lands. A surprisingly large number from among these types were sent to foreign lands. It has been estimated that down to 1776 England shipped some 50,000 criminals to the American colonies. Professor Karl F. Geiser has shown that half or more of the settlers of the colony of Pennsylvania down to 1800 were indentured servants and redemptioners.[3]

---
[1] The increase in Prussia was partially accounted for by extensive annexation of former Polish and Austrian populations.
[2] See Botsford, *English Society in the Eighteenth Century*, Chap. VII; and M. D. George, *London Life in the XVIIIth Century*, Knopf, 1925.
[3] Geiser, *Redemptioners and Indentured Servants in the Colony and Commonwealth of Pennsylvania*, sup. to *Yale Review*, Vol. X, No. 2, 1901, especially pp. 40-41.

The curiosity aroused by vivid tales and colorful reports of strange lands and peoples led to a great stimulation of travel. This resulted in a notable increase of European knowledge concerning foreign regions. Such travel often led to the writing of new narratives and descriptions dealing with the areas visited. These, in turn, led to new voyages, and so on. Once the medieval provincialism of village and manor was broken up and "adventure," in its broadest sense, was really popularized, there was nothing particularly mysterious about the ensuing revolutions in social life, population conditions, cultural perspective, and social theories.

Even more significant for European history than emigration was the remarkable increase in the numbers, wealth, and power of the middle class or bourgeoisie. While this group had been slowly recruited from the medieval trading and manufacturing classes in the towns, its numbers had never been very impressive before the expansion of Europe and the Commercial Revolution. The upper ranks of the bourgeoisie were recruited from "merchant proprietors, financiers, slave traders, colonial entrepreneurs, tax farmers, munition makers and manufacturers of luxuries." During this period the largest single group in the middle class was made up of small-scale entrepreneurs, who took part in commercial operations, conducted small shops in the towns, or acted as merchant capitalists in the putting-out system. Besides those engaged in trade, manufacture, and finance, the professional branch of the middle class grew in numbers and influence. In the new national states it was the lawyer class that was mainly relied upon by the monarchs for administration and advice, and it became one of the chief bulwarks of absolute monarchy. Other groups, such as the bookkeepers, auditors, and agents, became indispensable to the efficient conduct of business enterprises.

The new economic attitudes, based on the notion that financial gain is the uppermost motive in economic activity and that "money talks," passed over into political life.[1] Corruption in colonial administration and in the operation of the chartered companies was rife. The trial of Warren Hastings was merely a dramatization of abuses that were common at the time. The British officials were outraged at American colonial smuggling after 1763, but the practice was "universal" in the mother country itself in the eighteenth century, and as Botsford points out: "Bribery was frankly the normal process of Parliamentary government, and the public knew it; there was no pretense at deception."[2] A strong reason for this was the failure of England from 1660 to 1832 to alter the political structure and methods to keep pace with the new alignment of economic interests. The middle class was not able to govern directly, since the landed aristocracy still controlled Parliament by means of a medieval system of representation: "The low tone of public life was due chiefly to the fact that the moneyed classes now so powerful an element in the state, did not as yet have representation in Parliament sufficient, according to their lights, for the protection and promotion of their vast interests."[3] Since the new mercantile class could not get into Parliament in sufficient numbers by legitimate methods, its members endeavored to offset this handicap by openly buying seats. The prices increased as competition became more intense and the merchants more wealthy: "In the time of George I, a fair price for a seat was £1,400 or £1,500.

---

[1] See Botsford, *op. cit.*, pp. 180 ff.   [2] *Ibid.*, p. 181.   [3] *Ibid.*

At the first general election in the reign of George III, a nomination could be purchased for £2,000. Within a short time the price had advanced to £4,000, while Chesterfield complained that the election at Northampton cost the contending parties £30,000 a side."[1]

The public policies of the middle class passed through two major stages from 1500 to 1800. During most of the period the bourgeoisie favored a strong state and extensive regulation of commerce and industry. Finding this policy irksome and restrictive the middle class began in the eighteenth century to adopt a more international point of view, to recommend that the state be limited to protecting life and property, and to demand rather complete freedom in economic affairs. This evolution can be well illustrated by the history of the English middle class to 1800.[2]

In the political life of the era the English bourgeoisie started out to establish a dominant middle-class administrative machine—it wished to preserve the monarchy but to subordinate it to the parliamentary administration, which this class hoped to dominate. When the Civil War came in the middle of the seventeenth century and a middle-class state was established in what is known as the Commonwealth, the bourgeoisie saw that they had gone too far. The naval wars disturbed trade, and commercial restrictions hampered the very class that had put them on the statute books. In short, the middle class saw its business injured by its own machinery. Hence it ceased to try to monopolize the administration, but endeavored instead to control the government that existed. As Mr. Gretton has well observed, this marked a turning-point: "The middle class abandoned the attempt to make a middle-class state, and successfully proceeded to make the State middle class."[3] The progress was natural from the middle-class revolution of 1645-49 to the Walpole régime of the early eighteenth century, in which the state was operated to advance the interests of the middle class.[4] In political theory the trend was decisively towards minimizing the legitimate functions of the state.

The English middle class pursued a policy of enlightened selfishness in its alignments and affiliations between 1500 and 1800. At first it stood with the workingmen against the landlords. Then it dropped the artisans and proceeded to attack the guilds. During the Civil War, it united with the town workers, but after 1660 the middle class generally returned to its selfish policy of "capital versus the community." It opposed James II and precipitated the "Glorious Revolution" of 1688-89, in part because it feared lest James's Catholic foreign policy might injure its trading operations.

The middle class was enlarged and enriched in various ways. It took the lead in foreign trade and obtained most of the lucrative monopolies. It went into banking, established the Bank of England, and made the state a debtor to itself. It carried on the industrial operations of the country, mainly under the putting-out system. As oversea demand for commodities grew, the manufacturing in-

---

[1] *Ibid.*, pp. 183-84.
[2] *Cf.* Gretton, *The English Middle Class;* and Gillespie, *The Influence of Oversea Expansion in England to 1700*, pp. 340 ff. [3] Gretton, *op. cit.*, p. 127.
[4] See *Cambridge Modern History*, Vol. VI, Chap. VI; Mottram, *History of Financial Speculation*, pp. 100 ff.; Botsford, *op. cit.*, Chap. VI; and Brisco, *op. cit.*

dustry became more prosperous. Finally, the middle class dominated the new speculative trend and made extensive profits out of stockjobbing. Becoming wealthy, it sought to achieve social and political prestige by buying up great landed estates and purchasing coats of arms and seats in Parliament. By 1830 a large part of the English landed aristocracy was made up of former merchants and industrialists who had become wealthy and retired to the country.[1]

More than any other class in modern society, the bourgeoisie have shaped and determined the destinies and trends of human development. It was not until near the close of the nineteenth century that a new and menacing rival appeared in the industrial proletariat. To a very large extent, modern economic and social history, as well as modern political history, is the record of the growth of bourgeois power and policies.

Though not so immediately raised to power, the lower classes were also considerably affected by the social changes from the sixteenth to the nineteenth centuries.[2] From the fourteenth century onward, there had been a more or less steady tendency towards the emancipation of the serfs.[3] While this movement was not completed in Russia, Italy, and Austria until the middle of the nineteenth century, or in Balkan Europe until somewhat later, the rise of capitalism was a constant threat to such a servile labor system. Those who profited by it understood this fact perfectly well. In the end, the landed aristocracy had to bow before the increased wealth and influence of the bourgeoisie. The peasantry, gradually freed from the old agrarian servility by the rising capitalism, was to find a new and more permanent type of bondage in the factories of the coming industrial era.[4]

The moral emancipation connected with Rationalism and Hedonism led to much greater sex freedom for women in Latin Europe.[5] Extra-marital relations were often maintained by both men and women with social impunity. But such freedom was curtailed in Teutonic, Dutch, and Anglo-Saxon countries, where a frank attitude towards sex was rather the exception than the rule. Even where women enjoyed remarkable sex freedom they had no political or economic equality with men. Not until the end of this period did a few daring women like Mary Wollstonecraft launch a feminist revolt and demand equal rights for women.

Such sweeping and dynamic changes as population growth and mobility, the rise of new social classes, and the growing ascendancy of the middle class all helped to create discontent with the antique institutional heritage from the Middle Ages and to promote interest and activity in the cause of social reform.[6]

II. THE SECULARIZATION OF POLITICAL PHILOSOPHY

The national state, of whatever form, was absolute in its power. Whatever the theoretical pretensions of the Church, the secular State was now supreme.

---

[1] On the French middle class in this period, see Sée, *Economic and Social Conditions in France during the Eighteenth Century*, Chaps. IX-XI.
[2] *Cf.* Sée, *op. cit.*, Chaps. II, IX; and Ogg and Sharp, *Economic Development of Modern Europe*, pp. 24 ff., 50 ff.   [3] See above, Vol. I, pp. 630 ff.
[4] See below, pp. 427 ff., 483 ff.
[5] See Hammerton, *op. cit.*, Chap. 151; and Smith, *History of Modern Culture*, Vol. II, pp. 600 ff.
[6] *Cf.* Sée, *op. cit.*, Chap. XIII.

Philosophical justifications of its supremacy had to be forthcoming. These were found in the doctrines of Roman law, in the theory of the divine right of kings, and in the conception of a social contract.

The rise of business and capitalism made private property far more significant than in earlier ages. Those who possessed property desired public protection and assurance against confiscation and robbery. The new bourgeois political theory therefore laid special stress upon the duty of the state to safeguard private property. In fact, private property came to be enumerated as one of the three or four inherent natural rights of man, and its protection was looked upon as a manifestation of natural law and a responsibility of civil law.

Finally, the development of Rationalism and religious liberalism, together with the rise of Protestantism, tended to destroy the vitality of the old struggle between the political State and the Roman Catholic Church. The foundations of political philosophy soon came to be sought in history and psychology rather than in divine revelation and approval. The Protestants took the side of the State in most cases and favored political control of the Church. The great Protestant slogan was that he who rules the territory also controls the religion thereof. Most of the bourgeois political philosophers were Rationalists, and they would accept none of the old arguments that relied primarily upon supernatural sanctions. By the end of the eighteenth century the modern psychological and historical interpretations of political origins had been firmly established and political philosophy was thoroughly secularized.

The last hangover of supernaturalism in political theory was directly related to the divine right of kings. The powerful monarchs of the new national states ruled for the most part in Protestant states or in Catholic states like France where a strong nationalist trend prevailed in Catholicism. There was a powerful impulse to find some basis for the authority of monarchs that could be set over against the pretensions of the Pope as the vicegerent of God on earth. This led to the argument for the divine right of kings.

Roman law had provided a secular basis for claims to political absolutism, and the Roman Emperors had claimed partial divinity. But this was not enough for Christian kings who abhorred pagan gods. Hence the kings and the apologists developed ingenious arguments to support the theory of divine approval of kingship by the Christian God. They took up and amplified the biblical arguments for the divine origin and approval of the state and kingly rule that had been used by the princes and their supporters during the Middle Ages.[1] They pointed to the divine selection and sanction of Old Testament kings by God, and showed how Peter and Paul had both gone out of their way to emphasize the divine origin of the state and the Christian duty of obedience to constituted political authority. An English writer, Sir Robert Filmer (died 1653), worked out an original defense of divine right in his *Patriarcha*. He held that God had in the beginning bestowed upon Adam complete secular power, extending even to life and death. Noah inherited this supreme power from Adam and handed it on to his sons. The latter passed it on to the biblical patriarchs, and from these all the later kings and princes of the earth inherited

---

[1] See above, Vol. I, pp. 769 ff., 807 ff.

absolute temporal power. The arguments for the divine right of kings from both the scriptural point of view and the patriarchal approach were combined by Bishop Bossuet, the great French Catholic writer. This indicates the strength of the nationalist and royalist tradition even in certain Catholic states.

The defense of divine right soon faded out, however, and in its place there arose the most important secular defense of the state in early modern times: the notion of a social contract.[1] This idea had been set forth in rudimentary form in antiquity, especially by the Epicurean philosophers. In Roman law it was implied that the people had originally consented to the assumption of absolute power by the Emperor, and this notion of popular sovereignty had been revived by Marsiglio of Padua and other students of Roman law in the late medieval period.[2] Certain medieval writers had believed in the doctrine of a contract between the rulers and their subjects. At the close of the medieval period writers were beginning to differentiate between this governmental contract and an earlier and more fundamental contract which lay at the basis of all orderly social relations among mankind.[3]

The historical tendencies of the times hastened this development. The heritage from feudalism emphasized charters, contracts and other limitations on the kings. Commerce and business emphasized the importance of contracts. The primitive natives discovered in oversea areas led the philosophers to believe that they had at last found concrete vindication of the theory of a pre-social state of nature.[4] The middle class often found the kings obstructive to their financial interests, and desired a doctrine of political origins that would justify resistance to royal authority. The social-contract theory was exactly to their liking, though some, like Hobbes, found that it could be used to buttress the opposed theory of royal absolutism.

Roughly, the social-contract theory of political origins and revolution ran as follows: Men originally lived in a pre-social state of nature without law or order. This condition was full of inconveniences and dangers because of avarice and struggles over property. Hence the more sensible people decided to leave this state of anarchy and to institute a well-ordered community life. The agreement to do so constituted the social contract. Next, they decided upon a form of government and entered into a second or governmental contract between the rulers and subjects. This—essentially what we now call a constitution—defined the rights and powers of each and the relations between the two. If the rulers violated this contract (really the constitution of the state), then the subjects possessed the right to rise up in active rebellion, pitch out their oppressive rulers, and install a new set. Such was the complete doctrine of the social contract as it appeared in well-developed form with Locke, Pufendorf, and Rousseau. Some writers did not present so elaborate a conception, and Hobbes refused to sanction the right of revolution at all.

The first thoroughgoing exposition of the social-contract idea appeared in

---

[1] Very important also in secularizing the conception of political authority was the doctrine of the sovereignty of the state—"supreme power, unrestrained by law"—developed by Bodin, Hobbes, Blackstone, Bentham, and others. The social-contract theory, in a way, was one explanation of how this sovereign power arose.   [2] See above, Vol. I, pp. 807 ff.

[3] See above, Vol. I, pp. 808-9.

[4] Cf. H. N. Fairchild, *The Noble Savage*, Columbia University Press, 1928.

THE SECULARIZATION OF POLITICAL PHILOSOPHY

The Laws of Ecclesiastical Polity (1594) by Richard Hooker, a famous English ecclesiastic. The Dutch publicist and founder of international law, Hugo Grotius, also accepted the social-contract notion, though he tried to combine it with Aristotle's view of the natural sociability of man.

In spite of the previous developments of the social-contract doctrine, it remained for the English philosopher Thomas Hobbes (1588-1679) to give that conception its first classic statement. Going far beyond any of the previous writers in the detail and "remorseless logic" with which he analyzed the situation, he assumed a pre-social state of nature that was "a state of war of all men against all men." He flatly denied the dictum of Aristotle that man is by nature social, and maintained that all social relations exist for gain or for glory. He held that any permanent social group must originate in the fear that all men feel towards each other in a state of nature. He was as cynical as Machiavelli in his analysis of human nature and agreed with the latter that all human activity springs from man's insatiable desires.

To escape the miseries of the turbulent and unregulated state of nature, Hobbes held that men agreed to unite in a civil society for their mutual protection. In doing so, they made an inalienable transfer of their individual powers to the general governing agent or sovereign. Hobbes did not, however, hold that either the state of nature or the contract was necessarily true in a historical sense. His analysis was psychological, and he has been correctly called the father of social psychology. It is the irrevocable nature of the social contract and the conception of unlimited sovereign power that distinguish the doctrines of Hobbes from those of the majority of the other members of the contract school. Besides this voluntary social contract, Hobbes contended that there might be another type based upon force where a conqueror compelled submission on the pain of death. Hobbes's conception of the nature and attributes of sovereignty was an importantly new contribution, but he confused the state with the government, and erroneously attributed sovereign power to the latter.

The German statesman and philosopher Samuel Pufendorf (1632-94) attempted a reconciliation of the doctrines of Grotius and Hobbes in his *Law of Nature and of Nations*. His ethics were primarily those of Grotius, while his political doctrines were mainly Hobbesian. He held that the social instinct in man would account for the existence of the family and lesser social groups, but that a contract was necessary to bring into being the state and government. While Pufendorf began his analysis of the state of nature with the assumption that it was a state of peace, he ended with practically the same conclusion as that arrived at by Hobbes. His conception of the contract was twofold. First, there was a social contract that embodied the agreement to unite; then a vote was taken to determine the form of government desired. Finally, the arrangement was ended by a governmental contract between the governors and the governed regarding the principles and limits of political administration.

The Jewish philosopher Baruch Spinoza (1632-77) was in his political theory a member of the contract school. He agreed with Hobbes on the existence of a pre-social state of nature that was one of war and universal enmity. Society, he maintained, had a purely utilitarian basis in the advantages of mutual aid and the division of labor. To render this advantageous association secure, it was necessary that its utilitarian basis be supplemented by a contract to give it a legal foundation and thus to guarantee to each the rights that he had possessed as an individual prior to the contract. Spinoza claimed that the contract was rendered valid only by the superior advantages which it offered, and that the sovereign was such only as long as he could maintain his authority. This justification of rebellion he considered to be the only real assurance of just rule and individual liberty. Spinoza was mainly interested in using the contract as a buttress for liberty, while Hobbes had been chiefly concerned in utilizing it to justify absolutism.

The *Patriarcha* of Filmer, defending the divine right of kings, called forth two better-known works in refutation of its thesis. The first was by Algernon Sidney (1622-83), *Discourses concerning Government.* He criticized Filmer's work in detail, discovered the origin of government in the consent of the governed, and declared himself for the indefeasible sovereignty of the people. Of all English writers in the seventeenth century Sidney was, perhaps, the most capable and spirited assailant of absolute monarchy. He favored a mixed government combining elements of monarchy, aristocracy, and democracy.

The second refutation of the *Patriarcha* constituted the first of John Locke's *Two Treatises of Government,* but the second treatise was far more epoch-making in its doctrines.[1] Locke here set forth his important conception of the social contract and his justification of revolution. In his views on the state of nature, Locke differed radically from Hobbes, Spinoza, and even Pufendorf, in that he denied that it was by any means a condition of war or disorder. It was not even a pre-social state, but was rather a pre-political situation in which every man had the personal right to execute the laws of nature. The very social nature of man, Locke contended, would prevent the state of nature from being one of isolation and unsociability. The most serious deficiency in the state of nature was the absence of an impartial judge who could settle all disputes in an equitable manner and take the power of executing the laws from the hands of each individual. The chief and immediate cause of man's leaving the state of nature was the increase of private property and the desire to use and preserve it in safety. This emphasis on the preservation of property might have been expected from the apologist of the bourgeois revolution of 1688. As we have seen, Locke frankly maintained that the chief end of government was the protection of property.

Locke made the most direct claim of any writer of the contract school for the historicity of the social contract as the actual mode of initiating civil society, and he maintained that it must be assumed to lie at the basis of all the civil societies in existence.

He differentiated clearly between the political community formed by the social contract and the government to which it delegated the functions of political control. By so doing he was able to show how the government might be dissolved without destroying civil society itself. Locke held this dissolution of the government, or revolution, is justifiable when the terms or purposes of the contract are violated by those in power. The majority of the citizens are the only ones qualified to judge when these infractions have become sufficient to

[1] S. P. Lamprecht, *The Moral and Political Philosophy of John Locke,* Columbia University Press, 1918.

warrant revolution. Locke thus laid the philosophical foundations for the American and French revolutions, as well as apologizing for the English Revolution of 1688.

The erratic and romantic Rousseau, whose general position we shall presently examine, was the last of the classical contract school. In his earlier writings he took the position, in opposition to Hobbes, that the condition of man in the state of nature was almost ideal in its rude simplicity, and that the state of war was unknown in those idyllic days. The whole progress of civilization, while bringing increasing enlightenment, had but contributed to the physical and moral degeneration of the race and the growth of inequality and corruption. In his later writings he abandoned his ecstatic praise of the natural state of man and took practically the same position as Locke, namely, that while this natural condition of man was not one of war, its inconveniences rendered the institution of civil society imperative. The only way in which civil society could be instituted, and united power and general protection secured, was through the medium of a social contract. This contract gave rise to the state or the civil community and not to the government. Rousseau, following Locke, thus distinguished between the state and government, making sovereign power the prerogative of the state and governmental power purely delegated. His definition of sovereignty as the absolute power in the state, growing out of an expression of the general will, was probably his outstanding contribution to political philosophy, and one that had much influence in the nineteenth century when representative government and democracy became more prevalent.

Though the seventeenth and eighteenth centuries marked the period of the greatest popularity of the social contract in political philosophy, this age ended with crushing attacks upon this point of view. The most effective theoretical assault was made by the philosopher, David Hume.[1] He offered a twofold psychological criticism. In the first place, the natural sociability of man would account for the origin of social groups without any conscious contract to live together. Further, the social contract implies a psychological impossibility, namely, knowledge prior to experience. Men could not well know the advantages of society and government before they had ever experienced them. Hume also turned to history and asked for examples of the origin of society and the state through a contract. He claimed that history fully supported the notion of the naturalistic evolution of society and the state, while it never revealed any examples of the artificial creations called for by the social and governmental contracts.

This historical attack on the social contract was continued with even more force and elaboration by Adam Ferguson in his *Essay on the History of Civil Society* (1764).[2] This was the first notable contribution to historical sociology since Herodotus, Lucretius, and Ibn Khaldun. Ferguson traced the development of society and the state in detail. He held that society was the product of innate human sociability, gradually expressing itself in ever larger human

[1] See Hume, *Essays, Moral, Political and Literary,* edited by T. H. Green and T. H. Grose, London, 1875, 2 vols., Vol. I, Pt. I, Essay V; Pt. II, Essay XII.
[2] *Cf.* W. C. Lehmann, *Adam Ferguson and the Beginnings of Modern Sociology,* Columbia University Press, 1930.

groupings. The state and government, on the other hand, have usually been the product of war and conquest. These are the notions held today by the majority of contemporary sociologists and cultural historians.

By implication, Montesquieu also undermined the social and governmental contracts.[1] It was his notion that societies and states grew up naturally in response to external conditions. The special forms of government were due to different climatic and other geographical factors, not to the arbitrary will of contracting parties who preferred a despotism, a monarchy, or a republic. We have already pointed out how Montesquieu introduced the comparative point of view into sociology, politics, and jurisprudence. With men like Hume, Montesquieu, Ferguson, and Bentham, political philosophy was gradually transformed and split up into the several social sciences of sociology, economics, politics, and ethics, a process that we shall describe in a later chapter.[2]

The first flush of the French Revolution produced the apotheosis of Pure Reason in political theory. Good examples are afforded by the doctrines of the Abbé Sieyès, Condorcet, and Godwin. The first two of these writers have already been considered. William Godwin's *Enquiry concerning Political Justice* (1793) was the first great keynote of Philosophical Anarchism.[3] He called for the reconstruction of society by means of the application of the dictates of reason. He believed that reason vindicated his proposal to wipe away repressive political institutions and to equalize the distribution of wealth. He would have abolished all political units larger than the parish and would not even concede the function of education to the state.

In discussing the progress in political thought in early modern times one should not overlook the criticisms of war and the plans for assuring perpetual peace. The history of peace plans will be dealt with more thoroughly later,[4] but we should mention in passing the sincere pacifism of George Fox and the Society of Friends and the plans for arbitration, international organization, or both, that were set forth by Emeric Crucé (1623), Sully (1638), the Abbé de Saint-Pierre (1712), Bentham (1789), and Immanuel Kant (1795). The horrors of the religious, dynastic, and French revolutionary wars prompted these men of noble sentiments to search for some manner of ending this barbarous heritage from an earlier era of civilization.

III. THE NEW DEVELOPMENTS IN LAW AND LEGAL PHILOSOPHY

The evolution of jurisprudence and legal philosophy during the early modern period was as notable as that in political thought, and it was conditioned by much the same developments that affected the course of political theory. The dominant note which runs through all phases of legal growth in this age is that of secularism—divorcement from revelation and a grounding of law in the experiences of mankind.

One conspicuous aspect of legal evolution was the triumph of Roman law and that sway of secular absolutism in law and politics to which brief reference

---

[1] See below, pp. 227 ff. [2] See below, pp. 665 ff.
[3] See H. N. Brailsford, *Shelley, Godwin and Their Circle,* Holt, 1913; and William Godwin, *An Enquiry concerning Political Justice,* ed. by R. A. Preston, Crofts, 1926, 2 vols., especially Vol. I, Introduction. [4] See below, pp. 914 ff.

has already been made. We have also noted how the revival of Roman law in the Middle Ages promoted royal power and the prestige of the State at the expense of the Church and other rivals of the secular arm. This movement reached its culmination in early modern times, when secular absolutism gained undisputed dominion in political affairs. It was helped along notably by the Protestant revolt, which favored the power of the prince at the expense of the Church. As we have noted, the dominant note in the political theory of Protestantism was that he who controls the politics of an area should also determine its religion.[1] Roman law influenced all western European states—and by imitation Russia as well. But it gained its main foothold in the Latin countries, where it still forms the foundation of the governing legal principles.

An effective secularizing influence was derived from the common law of England. We described the character and origins of the common law in treating of the institutional development of medieval England. The common law flourished and received wider application during the era under discussion, and its principles were transmitted to the English colonies in America.[2] It opposed by implication the doctrine of revealed law, since it was admittedly the collective legal wisdom of the nation as derived from the experiences of its various communities in dealing with all manner of cases over centuries. In France, Guy Coquille (1523-1603) tried to work out a similar doctrine of a French common law.

Perhaps the most influential type of legal development during this period was the doctrine of natural law. The notion of a law of nature is an old one: it goes back to Socrates and the Stoics. But in this period the conception was clarified and related more closely to specific political and legal applications. The law of nature was regarded as the body of rules and principles that governed men in pre-political days. Natural law was the norm by which to test the soundness of civil laws that were drawn up by the government after the state had been established.[3] The state should not terminate the law of nature, but rather should provide for the enforcement of its benign principles. The state should not restrict our natural freedom. It only frees us from the terrors and anarchy of unorganized prepolitical society. Hobbes, Pufendorf, Spinoza, and others contributed to the development of the doctrine of natural law, but it was John Locke who gave it the particular "slant" that has made it of such great significance in legal history and business operations. He found that the major tenets of the law of nature were the sanctity of personal liberty and of private property. The state was doing its supreme duty when it assured their protection and perpetuity.[4] This notion was seized upon by the rising capitalistic class, embodied in the constitutions that it wrote, and introduced into the jurisprudence that it fostered. Here we find the legalistic basis of the contemporary reverence for property and the impregnable defenses that have been erected about it.[5] Linked up with the power of the Supreme Court of the

---

[1] Especially in the case of a Protestant ruler.
[2] R. B. Morris, *Studies in the History of American Law*, Columbia University Press, 1930.
[3] O. F. Gierke, *Natural Law and the Theory of Society, 1500 to 1800*, tr. and ed. by Ernest Barker, Macmillan, 1934. Some writers regarded natural law as merely the body of rules inherent in the very nature of man and social relations.
[4] *Cf.* Larkin, *Property in the Eighteenth Century*.
[5] See C. G. Haines, *The Revival of Natural Law Concepts*, Harvard University Press, 1930, Pts. II-III.

United States to declare laws unconstitutional under the broad concept of "due process of law," it has all but removed private property from social control. As we shall point out later, it has also done much to block the road to orderly progress through legislation and to invite revolution.[1]

Much more accurate and illuminating than the application of natural law with which we are familiar, but of much less practical import for applied jurisprudence and legal processes at the time, was the rise of comparative jurisprudence in the work of Montesquieu and others. It represented in a rough way the application of the conception of the common law to the race as a whole. As the common law represented a pooling of the experiences of the various communities in a nation, so law as a whole was a product of the experiences of the many races and nations on the planet. Great interest was found in comparing the legal codes of diverse peoples, in pointing out their differences and similarities, and in trying to deduce general legal principles of broad application. No other school of law at the time was so civilizing. No man thoroughly appreciating the variety of legal concepts and practices could well be arrogant concerning the laws of his particular country.

A somewhat narrower application of this approach to law led to the origins of the historical school of jurisprudence. Montesquieu had been concerned with the laws of all peoples. The historical jurists were mainly interested in the evolution of law within the boundaries of their particular state. Most of them—notably Edmund Burke—regarded law as an outgrowth of the organic culture of the nation. Of these early historical jurists perhaps the best known was Burke. Adam Ferguson combined the historical and comparative approaches to law, a procedure that has become increasingly popular from his day to our own. It has served to lessen provincialism and patriotic conceit in jurisprudence.

Rationalism had a decisive but by no means uniform influence upon legal evolution. John Locke tended towards Rationalism, but he laid special stress upon the law of nature. Many later Rationalists departed widely from this precedent. They were prone to stress the artificial character of sound law and to regard it as the product of the dictates of reason applied to specific social problems. With this school, human legislation was the only valid source of law. There was also a tendency to lay special stress upon the responsibility of law to insure to every man equality in his right to enjoy life, liberty, and property. It was natural that this group should be in favor of the codification of law, while the historical school was opposed to such a notion. The latter held that an artificial product of reason might be codified, but a living, growing achievement, such as a historical system of law, could not be.

It was but a short step from the Rationalistic school of law to the Utilitarian. Both relied primarily upon human reason. Both were interested in reform. Utilitarian jurisprudence was merely a further development and refinement of the Rationalistic doctrine. What its chief exponent, Bentham, did was to hold that rational jurisprudence must be a science of social reform, designed in every part to increase the happiness of the largest possible number of men. There was still in it, however, a strong strain of individualism. Bentham be-

---

[1] See below, pp. 842 ff.; and Mott, *Due Process of Law*.

lieved that every man was the best judge of his own happiness. Hence there should be no restrictions on the acts of anyone except those necessary to secure equal freedom for others. Bentham especially eulogized the importance of freedom of contract. He came closer than others of his day, however, to the contemporary doctrine of law as an adjunct to, or even an instrument of, social engineering.

The most important practical product of the legal cogitation during this age was the afore-mentioned codification of French law that began in 1793 as a result of revolutionary enthusiasm and ended in the magnificent Code Napoléon. Legal codifications in other European countries followed in the nineteenth century.

Another very important legal development in this period was embodied in the rise of international law. In the Roman Empire there was little chance for the development of international law because Rome ruled most of the civilized world. Yet in the Roman conception of the *jus gentium* (law of nations) there lay an interesting germ, namely, the notion of a body of law embodying the combined and pooled wisdom of the peoples with whom the Romans had come into contact. This gave rise to the idea of a secular law distinct from the laws of any particular state.

In early modern times the growth of commercial relations, the rise of the national state, the increasing popularity of the dogma of the absolute sovereignty of the state, and the numerous and bloody wars of the period, all combined to create the necessity for a conception of equity rising above the laws of particular states and restricting the irresponsible conduct of the latter. While slightly earlier legalists, such as Ayala, Suárez, and Gentili, had contributed to the theory of international law, the man who really systematized the subject for the first time and put it forward in such form as to command public respect was Hugo Grotius (1583-1645), a Dutchman, whose great book, *The Law of War and Peace,* was published in 1625.

Sovereign states were in those days viewed as individuals, and efforts were made to introduce a sort of civilizing "law of nature" to govern the relations between these individual states. The conception of public war was brought in to replace the notion of private war, and attempts were made to civilize and regulate the conduct of nations in wartime. It was held that international law embodies ideals of right conduct which have a moral authority over the sovereign state, even though international law cannot be imposed by the force of any common superior. This served to mitigate somewhat the then popular conception that the state was wholly an end unto itself and owed no obligations whatever to humanity at large.

The Treaty of Westphalia in 1648 was the first international agreement to embody any considerable acceptance of the principles of international law. It recognized the doctrine of the sovereignty of the national state and proceeded upon the assumption that war is a public affair. It also served to clarify the rules of diplomatic practice at the time. The Treaty of Utrecht (1713) accepted such doctrines as those of the balance of power and the dictum that "innocent enemy goods under a neutral flag were free from capture; i.e., free ships make free goods." In the eighteenth century the highly systematic work of Emeric de Vattel (1714-67), *The Law of Nations*, helped still further to extend and clarify the field of international law.

IV. RATIONALISM AND SOCIAL PHILOSOPHY

We have dealt in an earlier chapter with the rise of Rationalism and the origins of a new set of doctrines that challenged the Age of Faith on many fundamental points. The opinions and activities of the Rationalists not only produced an intellectual revolution; they also helped along the effort to curb many cruelties and abuses in the old régime and to promote the cause of social reform.[1]

One of the major accomplishments of the Rationalists was to rehabilitate the dignity and prestige of man in his earthly setting. They upheld man as the supreme achievement of God's creative ingenuity and contended that to depreciate man was a direct insult to God. In thus raising man to a higher position of importance than he had been assigned by any previous thinkers save some of the Greeks and Romans and a few of the more radical Humanists of the Renaissance, the Deists made possible the rise of the social sciences, which are devoted to the study of the nature of man and his social relationships.[2]

With the growth of the interest in *man as man* there inevitably came about a great increase in the desire to improve social conditions by eliminating abuses and oppression and by increasing human happiness. In other words, secularism immediately suggested reforms in social institutions, something in which a logical orthodox Christian could scarcely find an absorbing interest.

Another conception that was espoused by Rationalists and their followers contributed notably to those aspects of social reform which were related to the sweeping aside of archaic and oppressive laws. Starting with the alleged mechanical laws governing the physical universe—laws formulated by Newton and other scientists—the Deists insisted that there is a natural order in the cosmos and society which has been established and approved by God. The laws of universal motion are the divine laws of the cosmic system. The latter includes the realm of social institutions, and our social system should conform completely to the natural order. Such a desirable result can best be assured through the creation of a situation of complete laissez faire and pure competition. To achieve this natural order in social relationships the old obstructive laws, which are really an affront to God and His wisdom, must be brushed away.[3] In surveying the rise of Rationalism in the preceding chapter we incidentally touched on a number of suggestions that were directly related to the

---

[1] See Robinson and Beard, *The Development of Modern Europe*, Vol. I, Chap. VIII; and C. C. Brinton, article "The Revolutions," Encyclopaedia of the Social Sciences, Vol. I.

[2] See Randall, *The Making of the Modern Mind*, Chaps. XIII-XV; and A. O. Hansen, *Liberalism and American Education in the Eighteenth Century*, Macmillan, 1926, Chap. 1. The more radical Humanists had, as we have seen, made "man the measure of all things," but their outlook was poetic and esthetic, and they had no knowledge of social science and little interest in social reform. The Rationalists glorified man in a sociological rather than an esthetic perspective.

[3] *Cf.* Riley, *From Myth to Reason*, pp. 167 ff.; Randall, *op. cit.*, pp. 253 ff., 323 ff.; and John Langdon-Davies, *Man and His Universe*, Harper, 1930, pp. 168 ff.

spirit of social reform. Montaigne insisted that the purpose of philosophy is to teach one how to live happily rather than how to die safely. Francis Bacon made the revolutionary recommendation that the Kingdom of Man be substituted for the Kingdom of God as the chief center of human interest. He also set forth a utopian plan whereby the best intellects would cultivate science in the effort to advance human prosperity and happiness. Shaftesbury tried to divorce ethics from supernatural religion and to base it upon philosophy and esthetics. He also suggested an interpretation of God that harmonized with the program of human betterment. Hume went even further and identified morality with the increase of human happiness here on earth. Alexander Pope especially praised the dignity of man and attempted to raise him from the low estate in which he had been left by orthodox theologians. The Abbé de Saint-Pierre argued for a definite science of political progress that would no longer leave reform a creature of fortune or accident. The French philosopher Helvétius was especially hopeful in regard to the ability of education to sharpen the human intellect and correct social abuses. Voltaire labored mightily and comprehensively to discredit abuses and promote social change. A number of practical reform movements, among them Beccaria's campaign for criminal law reforms, may be traced directly to Voltaire's stimulus.

We may now consider briefly some of the writers who attempted to free social and political theory from supernaturalism and tradition and bring it into accord with the dictates of human reason.

1. THE BARON DE MONTESQUIEU

Of all the writers in this field one of the most impressive to present-day readers is Charles de Secondat, Baron de la Brède et de Montesquieu (1689-1755). He was one of the main founders of "rational politics." A member of the French nobility, he was educated for the magistracy, in which he served for many years. Early attracted to the comparative study of human institutions, his first publication was a series of satirical compositions known as *The Persian Letters* (1721).[1] In these he ironically criticized contemporary European society from the standpoint of imaginary travelers. Through the fiction of two Persians traveling in Europe and writing of French society to their friends and relatives back home he was able to make a witty and spicy attack upon the whole French social system. This clever satire was widely read even in the court circles.

Like Montaigne, to whom we may reasonably compare him in spirit, Montesquieu was fascinated by Plutarch and by the Romans generally. He thought that their history offered a complete historical laboratory for the study of institutions. In 1734 he published the results of his years of reflection on Roman life under the title *The Greatness and Decadence of the Romans*. Fourteen years later there appeared what is incomparably his greatest work, *The Spirit of Laws*.

Montesquieu differed from most of the contemporary social thinkers in that he did not produce a mechanical solution for social difficulties, nor did he usu-

---

[1] For an excellent edition, see *The Persian Letters of Montesquieu*, ed. by Manuel Komroff, Dial Press, 1929.

ally bring his findings to the support of any special reform.[1] He developed the "comparative" study of institutions to a very high point. Instead of applying himself to a particular situation he ranged up and down the known fields of information about social groups, customs, and laws, seeking out the underlying spirit. In addition to feeding his interest through books, he traveled extensively, visiting nearly every country in Europe. Montesquieu distilled his carefully accumulated facts into *The Spirit of Laws*. Very few dogmatic generalizations found their way into this work. Perhaps the distinguishing feature of the book is the number of practical suggestions offered to lawmakers. On the other hand, he made no proposal of drastic reform, and even his admiration for the British constitution, which he misunderstood, did not lead him to advocate directly its adoption in France.

It was his underlying idea that laws, customs, and institutions are the product of geographical conditions, particularly climatic conditions, and that what might admirably serve one people would be quite unsuitable for another. This basic notion Montesquieu had derived from the writings of an English publicist, John Arbuthnot.[2] On this ground he rejected the British system for France, arguing that his country was better served by a more "Gothic" form of government. Yet in spite of his own distrust of formulas, his belief that the British government was designedly divided into three parts, the executive, the legislative, and the judicial, operating under a scheme of checks and balances, had a strong influence on the makers of the American Constitution.[3]

The general conception contained in Montesquieu's comparative view of institutions and morals was a direct and severe challenge to the Christian attitude. The Christians held that there was one revealed way of living and thinking, which was equally binding on Scandinavians and Hottentots.[4] Montesquieu dared to suggest that nothing of the sort is true, holding that institutions and ideas are "good" just in proportion as they are adapted to producing the most happy and prosperous existence in any particular place and time.

2. THE ABBÉ DE SIEYÈS

An enthusiastic manifesto of rational politics appeared in the works of the Count Joseph Emmanuel Sieyès (1748-1836), usually known as the Abbé Sieyès, a French writer of the Revolutionary period,[5] and author of *What Is the Third Estate?* He believed that man could alter the whole course of political evolution through the application of reason to politics. When one has worked out in his mind the type of government that is desirable, it is possible to set up such a system if adequate popular support can be enlisted for it. In short, institutions do not have to be allowed to change slowly while old abuses persist. They can be made over to suit the needs of the time, applied at once, and made to produce speedily the results desired by wise men. Such a view justified revo-

---

[1] The most notable exception here would be Montesquieu's advocacy of the reform of criminal law, which had a considerable influence on Beccaria. See below, pp. 399-400.
[2] See Thomas, *The Environmental Basis of Society*, pp. 58 ff.
[3] See the suggestive essay on this point by L. H. Jenks, "The Constitutional Trinity," *American Mercury*, March, 1926. Cf. also William Bondy, *The Separation of Governmental Powers*, Macmillan, 1896. [4] A view shared also by many Deistic Rationalists.
[5] See G. G. Van Deusen, *Sieyès: His Life and His Nationalism*, Columbia University Press, 1932, Chaps. II-IV.

RATIONALISM AND SOCIAL PHILOSOPHY

lution if desirable reforms could not be obtained in any other way. This doctrine was a threat to vested monarchical and aristocratic interests, which rested chiefly on tradition, inertia, and the superstition that what is must continue to be.

3. CONDORCET AND SAINT-SIMON

Further development of this idea appeared in the writing of two other distinguished Frenchmen, Marie Jean Antoine Nicolas Caritat, Marquis de Condorcet (1743-94) and Count Claude Henri de Saint-Simon (1760-1825). The former is chiefly noted for his stirring but perhaps extravagantly optimistic view of the possibilities of human progress, *The History of the Progress of the Human Spirit,* written in the midst of the French Revolution while he was in hiding as a result of incurring the enmity of the radical Jacobins.[1] Our interest here, however, lies in his strong belief in the virtues of applied science as an instrument of progress; his denunciation of Christianity as an obstacle to progress; and his anticipation of the idea of deliberate and directed progress. He was also one of the first to advocate universal education, coeducation, equality of the sexes, and woman suffrage.

The "practical" aspects of the new social optimism found expression in the works of Saint-Simon, who wrote after the French Revolution, when the deplorable social results of the new industrial order were beginning to be rather obvious in England. He proposed to organize society under the control of industrial experts who were to direct production with a view to bringing plenty to all mankind. The industrial experts, in turn, were to be instructed by a selected group of scientists. The latter would apply themselves to discovering new truths and to inculcating both the new information and all that was worthy in the old. Professor Dunning clearly summarizes the Saint-Simonian plan of social reconstruction:

> The new social order must rest on the political leadership of the useful class. Capacity rather than possessions must become the qualification for control of the public service. The producers must supplant the mere consumers—the bees the drones—in political authority. For the realization of which end in France Saint-Simon sketched out the reorganized political system. Without requiring the abolition of the monarchy, he called for a government with supreme power in a new species of parliament. This body should include, first, a house of invention, consisting of civil engineers, poets (*ou autres inventeurs en littérature*), painters, sculptors, architects and musicians; second, a house of examination, consisting of physicists and mathematicians; and third, a house of execution, consisting of captains of industry (*chefs des maisons d'industrie*), unsalaried, and duly apportioned among the various kinds of business. The first house would present projects of law, the second would examine and pass upon them, and the third would adopt them.[2]

In addition to this program, the Saint-Simonians proposed to abolish all existing religions and to substitute a new one based specifically on the actual social teachings of Jesus Christ. The religious aspect of their scheme would

---

[1] See Schapiro, *Condorcet,* Chaps. v, xii; and Burlingame, *Condorcet,* especially Chaps. vii-ix, xi.
[2] Dunning, *History of Political Theories from Rousseau to Spencer,* p. 357.

serve to provide the galvanizing idealism needed for the realization of their desire to improve the lot of the poor. Their scheme, while never given practical application, served as a social leaven, for interest in it stimulated social legislation of a very desirable kind. Saint-Simon's suggestive but fragmentary ideas were expanded in two enormous works on systematic sociology by his disciple Auguste Comte.[1]

4. JEREMY BENTHAM

While most of the social reformers of this age were Frenchmen, many of whom idealized British society, the most ingenious and active of them all was an English lawyer and publicist who had little esteem for British institutions as they existed from 1770 to 1830. This man was Jeremy Bentham (1748-1832), the greatest "social inventor" who has ever lived.[2] By this we mean that no other has ever lived who has been as fertile in suggesting reforms in so great a diversity of fields. He is comparable to Leonardo da Vinci in the realm of science and art. Bentham worked from the basic formula that had been suggested by Hutcheson, Helvétius, and others, namely, "the greatest happiness for the greatest number." By this test British society in 1776 left much to be desired, and Bentham flayed unmercifully men like the eminent jurist William Blackstone, who were full of smug self-satisfaction concerning their country. Bentham made epoch-making contributions to criminal law reform, prison reform, the reconstruction of the system of poor relief, the establishment of a public health system, the encouragement of public education, the recommendation of general thrift and savings banks, the reform of local government, colonial self-government, and the like. He is said to have carried in his pockets model constitutions for the leading countries of his time. Constructive legislation in England in the nineteenth century owed far more to Bentham than to any other person.

5. JEAN JACQUES ROUSSEAU

Jean Jacques Rousseau (1712-78) is usually included among eighteenth-century Rationalistic writers, but he was quite as much a forerunner of the Romanticists in his social philosophy. At any rate, he is at the same time one of the most fascinating and one of the most exasperating of the personalities in the period of the Enlightenment. It has been noted that the religious and social ideas of the century were usually reflections of the new mathematical and physical discoveries, and that while most Rationalists wished to rearrange their opinions, few had any desire to abolish the structure of civilization. Furthermore, and most important, they were all devoted to reason as opposed to emotion and feeling. In Rousseau we have a reversal of this emphasis, and he is unusual among the intellectual figures of his day in being a man of feeling. David Hume once rescued him from a most disagreeable period of exile in Switzerland and carried him off to England against all the warnings of solicitous friends. Rousseau almost invariably quarreled with those who attempted

[1] See below, p. 666.
[2] See Graham Wallas, "Jeremy Bentham," *Political Science Quarterly*, March, 1923; and Elie Halévy, *The Growth of Philosophical Radicalism*, Macmillan, 1928, Pt. I.

to have dealings with him, and in the end Hume proved no exception. The experience, however, allowed the Englishman to observe Rousseau closely, and he wrote as follows:

> He has read very little during his life, and he has now renounced reading altogether. He has seen very little, and he has not the slightest curiosity to see and observe. He has studied and reflected, strictly speaking, very little, and has, in truth, only a very slight stock of knowledge. He has simply *felt* throughout his life; and in that regard his sensitiveness has reached a point that surpasses anything I ever saw before; but it affords him a keener sensation of pain than of pleasure. He is like a naked man, not only stripped of his clothes, but stripped of his skin, who, thus flayed to the quick, should be forced to contend with the inclemency of the elements which incessantly keep this world in turmoil.

This was the man whose works became so popular that the announcement that a new volume was ready would lead to the mobbing of the printing establishment. His influence both at the time he lived and worked and since his death has been very great.

Rousseau's ideas, or his emotional reactions, were simple and direct. Typical of his method was one of his very first works—*Has the Progress of Science and the Arts Tended to Corrupt or Purify Morals?*—a discussion of the worth of civilization. It was written for submission in a literary competition, and the central thesis came to him with the swift and devastating suddenness of a conversion in a backwoods camp-meeting. He was walking along a country road when it flashed into his mind that the cause of all the troubles of mankind was the oppressive institutions under which men lived.[1] This "hunch" raised him to a state of ecstatic imagination, under the influence of which he elaborated his idea and won the prize. This unreasoned notion struck at the roots of the subject, and in its unsettlement of all the customary landmarks let loose the floodgates of destructive criticism.

While Rousseau believed barbarism preferable to civilization, he did not, as is so often said, regard barbarism as the most perfect state of man. The latter he found in that intermediate period, the patriarchal society of pastoral nomads.[2]

In attempting to discover why mankind was ever induced to abandon its original idyllic situation in barbarism and patriarchal civilization, Rousseau somewhat modified his original position in a later book, *The Social Contract* (1762). He held that while the early state of man was not, as Hobbes contended, one of war and misery, its inconveniences hastened the origins of the state through a social contract. Rousseau did not, however, contend that the state actually arose historically in any literal social contract. His discussion was purely abstract, and he was interested in the social-contract doctrine only as a logical explanation of political origins. While the importance of Rousseau's conception of popular sovereignty as the expression of the general will is generally conceded,[3] historians now tend to ascribe less importance to Rousseau's dogmas as direct causal influences in the French Revolution than was formerly

---

[1] Rousseau's biographer, Matthew Josephson, doubts the explanation that Rousseau gives of the origins of this notion. Mr. Josephson believes that Rousseau derived the idea from Diderot.
[2] *Cf.* A. O. Lovejoy, "The Supposed Primitivism of Rousseau's *Discourse on Inequality*," *Modern Philology*, November, 1923. [3] See above, p. 221.

the case. Few men have been further removed from the temperament of the practical revolutionist than was Rousseau.

His whole drive, however, was in the direction of razing artificial restrictions and enabling man to realize the expansive native powers within his personality. In his educational theory, for instance, as he developed it in *Emile,* he laid special emphasis upon the value of a spontaneous development of the whole inner personality, which he placed far above the mere acquisition of knowledge. He also tended to infuse a democratic tendency in education by declaring that every child had the natural right to an education. The same general trends are to be found in his more strictly literary ventures. He introduced into his novels excursions into emotion-shaking love affairs, and initiated the worship of idyllic nature that was to characterize a whole school of poets in the next century.

In fact, while he had certain alliances with the major writers of the eighteenth century (he was religiously something of a Deist), he was in general influence more a precursor of Romanticism than an ally of the proponents of reason. In the doctrines of Rousseau we come upon the frontiers of a period of reaction in the course of which many of the landmarks erected during the previous century were submerged, so to speak, in a sea of tears troubled by the gusty excesses of "storm and stress."

V. THE ROMANTICIST REACTION IN SOCIAL AND POLITICAL THEORY

The whole complex of Rationalistic reactions to political and social problems was vigorously attacked by the exponents of Romanticism [1] and conservatism in political theory, among whom the more conspicuous figures were Burke, De Bonald, De Maistre, and Von Haller. These men rejected the Rationalism of Sieyès and Godwin, as well as the intuition of Rousseau, and reverted to the worship of tradition and authority.

Edmund Burke (1729-97) was an early but eloquent representative of Romanticism in the political theory of the time.[2] As such he attacked with special fierceness the notion that institutions could be arbitrarily changed by means of revolution and legislative programs. Political institutions, like other manifestations of "national genius," are the result of a natural and gradual development. They are an organic unity that matures slowly as a result of the peculiar genius and the historical experiences of a given people. Institutions may alter, but all safe institutional changes must be left to the processes of natural and organic development.

Holding this view, Burke was inevitably exceedingly hostile to the French Revolution. In a famous essay he used irony and exaggeration to achieve a reductio ad absurdum of the social contract as a literal historical explanation of the origins of the state.[3] His own notion of the social contract was that of

---

[1] See above, pp. 194 ff.
[2] *Cf.* Stephen, *History of English Thought in the Eighteenth Century,* Vol. II, pp. 219 ff.
[3] "A Vindication of Natural Society," Edmund Burke, *Works and Correspondence,* 8 vols., London, 1852, Vol. II, pp. 520-51. See also A. K. Rogers, "Burke's Social Philosophy," *American Journal of Sociology,* June, 1912.

the implied corporate unity of history and society—a view appropriate to a Romanticist philosopher. He thus expressed this conception: "It is a partnership in all science, a partnership in all art, a partnership in every virtue and in all perfection. As the ends of such a partnership cannot be obtained in many generations, it becomes a partnership not only between those who are living, but between those who are living, those who are dead, and those who are to be born." His *Reflections on the Revolution in France* constituted the most powerful and bitter theoretical attack to which that movement was subjected. He used his every resource of oratory, invective, and irony to discredit the Revolution, its aims, and its achievements.[1]

In his own constructive political theory, Burke appears as a eulogist of the aristocratic British monarchy of the eighteenth century. To Burke this seemed a complete vindication of the political theory of Romanticism. The British constitution was the perfect product of centuries of the evolution of English culture. It was an evidence of national genius. Its workings were so perfect and harmonious as to constitute a very replica of nature itself. Its development illustrated the way to secure a desirable political system. This was not to be realized by such a violent upheaval as the French Revolution.

The most competent defense of the old régime that had been overthrown by the French Revolution appeared in the works of a French nobleman, the Vicomte Louis Gabriel Ambroise de Bonald (1754-1840), *An Essay on the Natural Laws of the Social Order,* and *Primitive Legislation*. In these he made a forceful plea for an absolute hereditary monarchy and a privileged nobility. De Bonald held that in any form of government a single will always dominates. In a popular government we never know just whose will is ruling. This produces instability and uncertainty. In a monarchy we know exactly whose will is ascendant, and this creates a sense of stability and security. The supreme sovereignty resides in God, the monarch rules through the will of God. De Bonald thus set forth the first powerful functional, and non-feudal defense of monarchy.

To De Bonald the privileged nobility is no mere social ornament. It constitutes the real agent of absolute monarchical authority. In a popular government there is no test of personal success except in the acquisition of wealth. Hence officials are bound to use their office for the sake of personal pecuniary gain, that is, graft. There is no such temptation in the case of nobles, whose superior status is already assured. They are in a position to give unselfish service to the state. Only through them can we secure competent and disinterested administration.

De Bonald held that the source of all valid law and legislation is to be discovered in the teachings of the Bible and in the customs and institutions of a particular people. He went beyond Burke in his contemptuous denunciation of the whole theory of written constitutions.

Medievalism was mingled with Romanticism in the political theory of Joseph de Maistre (1754-1821), a Savoyard publicist. His chief works were *Observations on France, An Essay on the Source of Political Constitutions,* and *The Pope*. The starting-point of his political theory is the typical authoritarian couplet—an infallible Pope and an absolute monarch. There is no need of seek-

---

[1] He was rather crushingly answered by Thomas Paine in *The Rights of Man*.

ing human justification for this. It is the will of God that it should be so. In harmony with Romanticist dogmas, he contended that constitutions exist in the spirit of a people as the result of their historical experience. They cannot ever be actually reduced to writing. A constitution is frail and inadequate in proportion as it is written down. The people can only give a name to what already exists in their nature. They can never suddenly create any new form of political organization. He agreed with Burke that the most perfect of modern constitutions was the British because it had remained unwritten. In De Maistre we find the classic subordination of alert rationality to the principle of comfortable resignation to authority and custom.

A highly realistic argument for absolutism appeared in the voluminous work of the Swiss political scientist Ludwig von Haller (1768-1854), *The Restoration of Political Science*. He held that the fundamental rule of nature is that of inequality. The situation of mastery and subjection, then, is a perfectly natural and inevitable condition. Political authority comes from above by nature and the grace of God, not from below by the consent of the people. Civil society is a matter of fact, not of right. There are no legal limitations on the absolute power of the monarch, though he may find practical moral limitations in the superior utility of a just and able administration. The people may rebel, but that will accomplish nothing, because if the monarch were not the stronger he would not be ruling. Von Haller admits the possibility of a republican form of government, but his discussion of a republic indicates that he confused it with what we ordinarily regard as an aristocracy.

The Romanticist philosophy in jurisprudence received its most impressive statement in the writings of the German jurist Friedrich Karl von Savigny (1779-1861).[1] It permeates all his extensive works, but was most clearly brought out in his debate with Thibaut, another German legalist. The latter proposed the codification of German law. The suggestion horrified Savigny. Law, he said, is an ever growing and expanding product of national culture. To codify it would be to kill it. It would be as preposterous as to embalm a growing plant.

The reactionary political philosophy found its practical champion in Prince Metternich, who was able to hold Continental Europe in subjection to absolutism from the defeat of Napoleon through the failure of the revolutions of 1848.[2]

VI. UTOPIAS, SOCIAL AND REVOLUTIONARY DOCTRINES AFFECTING THE LOWER CLASSES

The doctrines justifying revolution that we have discussed above [3] were concerned primarily with the transformation of political institutions and affected mainly the upper-class landowners and the middle-class merchants. But there were many writers between 1500 and 1800 who recognized that political progress means little unless accompanied by comparable social and economic

---
[1] See A. W. Small, *The Origins of Sociology*, University of Chicago Press, 1924, Chap. II.
[2] *Cf.* A. J. May, *The Age of Metternich*, Holt, 1933; and above, pp. 120 ff.
[3] See above, pp. 218 ff.

changes. Others recognized that no type of social reform is adequate unless it touches the life of the masses of agricultural and industrial workers. They admitted that the doctrine of the equality of man must go deeper than mere beautiful political phrases and must apply to the economic and social status of the various members of society. Some of these proposals for social change took the form of "Utopias," or pictures of ideal society envisaging novel principles not yet adopted in the civilizations of the writers.

Programs and movements for social reform date back in their origins almost to the dawn of written history. Oppression of certain classes existed in the first historical societies, and it is not surprising that some of the earliest literature reflects the growth of discontent among the subject groups. As Professor E. R. A. Seligman has pointed out,[1] the desire to improve the social environment has ever been the dynamic impulse back of the evolution of economic and social doctrines, though it is quite true that theories which have once been the harbingers of progress may later be utilized as a bulwark of the existing order.[2]

While proposals for the betterment of social conditions have appeared in all ages, they have been most numerous after great social and economic revolutions that have altered the status of existing classes and have brought an abnormal amount of misery to those whose condition was most seriously affected by the transition. As Professor Robert Flint has expressed it: "It is in their times of sorest depression that nations usually indulge most in dreams of a better future and that their imaginations produce most freely social ideals and utopias."

The growth of wealth and class differentiation in antiquity; the development of Athens into a commercial empire; the growth of the plutocracy in the Roman Republic; the disintegration of Roman society in the fourth and fifth centuries A.D.; the breakdown of feudalism and the origin of the national states; the rise of the bourgeoisie following the Commercial Revolution; and that greatest of all social and economic revolutions, the Industrial Revolution of the late eighteenth and nineteenth centuries—these are well-known examples of social and economic transformations that brought social upsets and human misery in their train and have provoked appropriate programs of social reform written by those who were distressed by the social suffering that ensued. We are here concerned with the transformations, confusion, and misery caused by the breakdown of the medieval system and the origins of modern industry, commerce, and agricultural methods following the close of the Middle Ages.

The first and the most famous of these Utopias was the work of an English scholar and official, Sir Thomas More (1478-1535). More wrote during the Tudor period, when English society, particularly the lower classes, was feeling the impact of the breakdown of the manorial system and the rise of large-scale sheep-farming. The break-up of the English monasteries by Henry VIII also increased the misery of the time. In the opening section of his famous *Utopia* More presents us with a vivid picture of the disorder and suffering of the time. In order to suggest a remedy for these sorry conditions, More por-

---

[1] "Owen and the Christian Socialists," *Political Science Quarterly,* June, 1886.
[2] Notably Economic Liberalism.

trayed an ideal society on the fanciful island of Amaurote. Here wealth was to be divided equally, so as to put an end to that avarice and covetousness which More, like Plato, regarded as the root of all human evils. The whole society on the island was to be a well-organized community based upon coöperative principles. Altruism would prevail and each would have in his mind the interests of the others. Everybody was to engage in agriculture and in addition to learn some trade. The government was to be a combination of aristocracy and the force of public opinion. More did not believe that many laws would be required, since equality and the coöperative principle would automatically bring to an end most of those evil desires and acts which require legislative restraint.

Francis Bacon, as has been noted, advocated the betterment of human society through the application of natural science. His ideal society, described in *The New Atlantis,* was located on an island off the coast of South America. Its central feature was the House of Solomon, already described. It also sent out travelers to visit the rest of the world and gather in advanced scientific knowledge. All this was to be applied to increasing the happiness and welfare of the population. All superstition was to be rooted out and social improvements were to be assured through the knowledge acquired by the scientists.

Much more radical were the proposals embodied in *The City of the Sun,* written by an Italian friar, Tommaso Campanella (1568-1639). He maintained that society is based upon the principles of power, love, and intelligence, and he contended that there could be no desirable social system unless these receive due recognition in the organs of social control and political administration. Campanella argued for the complete abolition of all slavery, the dignity and importance of labor, and the elimination of the leisure class. Everybody was to work, but he believed that a short day would suffice to produce all the required necessities of life. He favored communism in property. He believed that the home and the family were the chief cause of the property instinct. Hence property could not be done away with so long as the individual home was maintained. Community of wives and children he thought to be essential to the elimination of the acquisitive tendency.

The utopia of James Harrington (1611-77), an English publicist, had a much more aristocratic cast. In his *Oceana* he held that society must be organized on psychological principles, so as to make certain the leadership of the intellectual élite. Further, political organization must be so arranged as to secure the predominant influence of the landholding classes, which he believed would be largely identical with the intellectual aristocracy. He sponsored the equal division of landed property and a wide use of the elective principle in government.

The *Télémaque* of François Fénelon (1651-1715) was a long and fanciful pedagogical novel, which utilized the simple Homeric society in order to inculcate ideals suitable for the education of a prince.[1] It endeavored to teach sound principles of government which were at wide variance with the tyranny and exploitation that prevailed under the French Bourbons. Among the novel principles that Fénelon suggested was the education of women.

The beginning of true social radicalism is to be discerned in *The Code of*

---

[1] *Cf.* Geoffroy Atkinson, *The Extraordinary Voyage in French Literature before 1700,* Columbia University Press, 1920, Chap. VII.

Nature, written in 1755 by a Frenchman named Morelly about whose life little is known. He advocated a new social system based upon the rights of the masses and the laws of nature rather than something handed down from above by benevolent autocrats. He took man in a state of nature and primitive society as his standard of comparison. Here, without either property or force, Morelly pictured man as inherently good. The purpose of government and human institutions should be to preserve this inherent human goodness and social equality. Therefore he advocated the abolition of private property and the establishment of equality. His notion of communism was not merely equality of property, but actual communal ownership of goods by all members of society. He laid special stress upon the social distribution of the product of industry. He attacked the doctrine of innate ideas and contended that there is no natural idea or instinct of property. Hence there will be no great difficulty in putting an end to the institution of private property. As a form of government, Morelly proposed what he designated as democracy but what was really a benevolent rule by patriarchs.

Contemporary with Morelly and holding much the same ideas was the Abbé Gabriel Bonnot de Mably (1709-85). He attempted to reconcile the selfish and social tendencies in man by holding that while self-interest furnishes the basic drive in human efforts, true happiness can be found only in social life. Man originally lived in a state of relative perfection but fell from this happy estate into misery because of the rise of private property and the quarrels which this promoted. The underlying cause of human suffering and social evils has been the accumulation and the unequal distribution of wealth. The rise of money helped along this degradation of man and society. Mably held that we cannot suddenly return to perfection by establishing pure communism. We must start by restricting property rights and holdings. We can then work gradually towards communism. The proper governmental system through which to achieve this result is about what we would call a conservative republic.[1]

During the French Revolution a notable movement towards social radicalism was led by François Babeuf (1760-97). He took seriously the equality slogan of the French Revolution, and insisted that any equality of real significance must be social and economic, as well as political. These principles he embodied in his *Manifesto of the Equals*. He held that in primitive society economic and social equality were the rule. Society and government should exist to preserve this equality. To Babeuf, they seemed in his day rather to defend and perpetuate inequality. He therefore advocated communism in property and equality of individual status. He was especially bitter against private property in land. He warmly supported the doctrine of democracy as a form of government. Though Babeuf himself was guillotined, his doctrines cropped up again in the Revolution of 1848 and in the Paris Commune of 1871.

VII. THE ORIGINS OF PUBLIC RELIEF OF THE POOR

Interesting as the suggestions above respecting the betterment of the masses in some new social order may be, there remained the practical problem of

---

[1] Mably's political views are almost too complicated to classify.

relieving the actual suffering that existed in the society in which men lived in western Europe after the breakdown of the medieval order. The first resolute effort to deal with this perplexing and persistent issue was embodied in the English poor-law legislation from 1536 to 1796.

During the Middle Ages the very institutional set-up of society had after a fashion cared for much of the misery of the time. The medieval manor held within its confines the poor people of the country—and this meant the great majority of the poor, including serfs and a few slaves. They shared a common poverty and met their crises together. The guilds of the towns provided charitable relief for many of the indigent artisans of the urban regions. But there were still many poor and miserable people who could rely upon neither the communal manor nor the charity of the guildsmen. These were supported, so far as they received any relief at all, by the Church. The latter regarded the succor of the poor as one of its cardinal duties and responsibilities. But it aimed to ameliorate suffering rather than to eliminate poverty. It accepted the poor as a part of the divine order of things.

The origin of modern times brought in its train a whole complex of new circumstances that made a change in medieval poor-relief methods obligatory, particularly in Protestant states where the power and the wealth of the Catholic Church were severely curtailed. The manor broke up and disappeared in many countries, especially in England. The inclosure of land for sheep-raising led to the ejection of many of the poor peasants from their paltry holdings and wiped out their sole means of support. Monasteries, which had long aided many beggars, were suppressed, and the relief system of the Catholic Church was upset or terminated entirely. In a new era in which the secularization and nationalization of politics was a conspicuous trend, it was logical that the State should try to supplant the Church in relieving the poor, and this is exactly what happened in England, which took the lead in establishing public relief of the poor.

The first important English poor law was that of 1536, in the reign of Henry VIII. It well reflected the transition between religious and public relief. It forbade open begging, directed the local authorities to collect funds to relieve the poor, and ordered that collections be taken up in churches on Sundays, and at festivals and gatherings. Direct gifts to vagrants were forbidden, and it was directed that professional beggars were to be whipped and driven back to their own parishes. If the state was now to be in charge of relief, the churches were still relied upon as agencies for collecting the funds to be disbursed by the public authorities. Laws of 1547, 1555, and 1563 provided that places should be found to lodge the worthy and homeless poor, and that citizens who failed to contribute to poor relief were to be admonished and then publicly taxed to obtain funds. In 1572 a law created special officers, overseers of the poor and collectors, to take charge of poor relief, and in 1576 the first workhouse test was introduced. The justices of the peace were empowered to construct or procure workhouses and to provide raw materials for work by those who asked for relief. Only those willing to accept such work were to be aided, unless they were obviously incapacitated.

This earlier legislation was overhauled and systematically brought together in the famous Elizabethan Poor Law of 1601. The poor were divided into three classes: (1) The able-bodied; (2) the incapacitated; and (3) children. The first were to be relieved solely in the workhouses, as provided in the act of 1576. The second class was to be cared for in almshouses, while the children were ordered to be apprenticed—that is, bound out to those willing to support them in return for services rendered. A definite tax was to be levied for poor relief, and certain fines and gifts were also to be applied to this purpose. The officials in charge of poor relief were called overseers, were taken from each parish, and were appointed by the justices of the peace. This law of 1601 remained the backbone of the English poor-relief system until the great act of 1834 was passed as an outgrowth of the long agitation and many suggestions of Jeremy Bentham.

There were a few supplementary laws passed between 1601 and 1832. An act of 1662 was designed to prevent the exploitation of rich or generous parishes. It made each parish responsible for the relief of only those poor who could claim legal residence in the parish. A law of 1691 required more accurate records of poor relief, while another of 1696 extended the workhouse principle that had been embodied in the law of 1576. Then an act of 1723 enabled parishes too small to maintain a separate workhouse to combine in constructing joint institutions to serve as many parishes as united for this purpose. The workhouse test was made obligatory for the relief of all able-bodied poor.

The coming of the Industrial Revolution and the vast increase in the inclosure of lands in England during the second half of the eighteenth century put special strains on the poor-relief system and led to its near-disintegration. The Gilbert Act of 1782 abolished the farming-out of the poor, permitted in many cases relief in private homes instead of in workhouses and almshouses, and introduced the notorious and fatal "allowance system." Only the old, the infirm, mothers of illegitimate children, and young children were to be sent to almshouses, while for the able-bodied, relief was to be given in their homes and work to be found near by. Paid officials, known as guardians, were empowered to collect the wages of the able-bodied poor and then to contribute enough more from poor-relief funds to enable the individual and his family to live. This was an open invitation to unscrupulous employers to cut down wages, since the state would make them up in any event. This wrong-headed system was still further extended in 1795, and in 1796 the workhouse test was openly abolished. Allowances were to be in proportion to the size of the family, thus encouraging illegitimacy. The result was what might have been expected: (1) An increase in poor-relief expenditures from $10,000,000 in 1783 to $39,000,000 in 1818; (2) sweeping wage cuts; and (3) the demoralization of the poor and of many of the laboring classes.

So the poor-relief system of England started out with rudimentary inadequacy at the beginning of the period and ended in chaos at the end. It was from this condition that the Poor Law of 1834 was designed to rescue England. This pioneer poor-relief system of England was widely imitated on the Continent and in the English colonies in America.

VIII. MAJOR EDUCATIONAL DEVELOPMENTS IN EARLY MODERN TIMES

Education and pedagogy in one way or another felt the impact of the leading intellectual and institutional developments of the age—Humanism, the Protestant revolt, nationalism, Rationalism, and Romanticism. The Renaissance, as we have seen, promoted the introduction of the Greek language and literature in the curriculum of universities, colleges, and schools, substituted classical Latin for medieval Latin, and raised classical Latin to a position that demanded its cultivation as a literary medium. The Protestant Revolution led the Protestants to recommend that the State control education as well as religion, while the Counter-Reformation Catholics renewed their conviction that the Church should dominate education. New teaching orders, notably the Jesuits, sprang up. Nationalism gave added force to the Protestant support of public education. Though free public education of a compulsory sort did not appear on any considerable scale until the nineteenth century, the eighteenth century was the era in which western European society very widely accommodated itself to the idea that the state should assume extensive responsibility for education. Rationalism endeavored to free education from clerical influence and to end the fears arising from religious superstitions. It aimed to produce a sophisticated and urbane outlook upon life. The study of manners and customs among native peoples overseas tended to raise doubts about the harsh disciplinary methods then in vogue in European schools and to arouse interest in naturalness and spontaneity. This trend towards cultivating the innate qualities of the individual and allowing full and free expression to the human personality was further stimulated by Rousseau and Romanticism, though in the latter case it was often somewhat modified and restrained by pietistic strains and religious qualms.

Literary education during this period still remained a privilege of the noble and wealthy minority, though it was no longer so exclusively restricted to the preparation of the priest, the scholar, or the clerk. Its privileges were now extended to the sons of rural gentlemen and of the upper classes among the business groups. The religious wars of the sixteenth and seventeenth centuries were a blight on higher education for the time being and helped to perpetuate intellectual stagnation in the universities. A number of important new universities were established, such as Louvain in Belgium, Leyden in Holland, and Leipzig, Halle, and Göttingen in Germany. The classics supplanted the trivium as the most important item in the curriculum. While the university curricula before 1800 remained in most places incredibly archaic and sterile, there were rumblings of discontent and certain harbingers of progress. Notable here was the revolt against pedantry, Humanism, and irrelevance led by Christian Thomasius (1655-1728), a professor at Leipzig. He had the audacity to lecture in German [1] and to treat of manners, customs, and other problems of daily life. He was expelled from Leipzig for this breach of good taste and

---

[1] Classical Latin was everywhere the respectable language of university instruction.

"sound" pedagogical principles, but found a position at Halle. There was little progress in university instruction outside Germany during this period, though some slight impact on ossification was observable in the English universities as a result of the influence of the German Hanoverian dynasty, which came to England with George I. Technical schools appeared in the eighteenth century. The first was the School of Mines at Brunswick, Germany, opened in 1745, and the second the Freiberg School of Mines, opened in 1765.

The content of the information inculcated in the reputable schools and universities usually bore little relation to the facts of nature or the problems of society. Theology and the old arts curriculum predominated at the outset of the era we are discussing and the classics at the end. Such natural science as existed was welcomed in but few universities and would have found little equipment or encouragement in most of them even if it had been admitted. It was only towards the close of the eighteenth century that the influence exerted by Rationalism helped to make some institutions of higher learning more congenial to natural science, and the schools still remained impregnable against any advances here. The social sciences were even more rigorously and arrogantly excluded from universities, colleges, and schools, though here and there an occasional professor of history or political philosophy was appointed. Rousseau's recommendation that we ignore most of the content of formal education was less foolish and disastrous in 1762 than it would be today—a fact often overlooked by his critics.

One of the first important impulses to popular education, which we may well note here, came from a late medieval semi-monastic order, the Brethren of the Common Life, founded by Gerhard Groot (1340-84) of Deventer. It was a simple communistic order devoted to care of the sick and poor and to copying and teaching. In its later days it had distinguished members, such as Rudolph Agricola and Johann Reuchlin. In its educational tenets it opposed Scholasticism and laid emphasis upon the vernacular languages and the Bible. The order was highly congenial to the extension of education among the masses. By 1450 it had some hundred and fifty schools in Flanders, France, and Germany and exerted a strong influence upon the Jesuits, who later absorbed most of the schools maintained by the Brethren. The Jesuit Order, to which we have already made reference, was incorporated in 1540. It had become one of the chief educational influences in western Europe by the seventeenth century.[1] In the second quarter of the seventeenth century it is estimated that it had some 40,000 students in its schools in France alone. The curriculum was essentially that prescribed by the Scholastic tradition of the Middle Ages, to which was added instruction in Greek and in Aristotelian natural science. While vigorously opposing intellectual independence and originality on the part of the students, the Jesuits encouraged studiousness by stimulating the competitive spirit rather than by relying on the customary brutal whippings of the time. The educational activities of the Jesuits were limited by the expulsion of the order from France in 1761 and temporarily ended through its

[1] See Smith, *op. cit.*, Vol. I, pp. 323 ff.; Vol. II, pp. 429 ff.; and *St. Ignatius and the Ratio Studiorum*, ed. by E. A. Fitzpatrick, McGraw-Hill, 1933.

suppression by the Church in 1773. This termination of Jesuit education made all the more necessary secular education provided by the state.

The Renaissance and the interest in the classics helped along the foundation of schools of a more elementary character than the colleges and universities. In England, Winchester was founded in 1379, Eton in 1440, and St. Paul's in 1512. The gymnasium, the characteristic German secondary school to our own day, took its origins from the Strasbourg gymnasium established by Johannes Sturm in 1537. The Boston Latin School was opened in 1635. A step towards practicality and common sense in educational practice in the schools was embodied in the foundation of a so-called *Realschule* by Johann Hecker at Berlin in 1747. He proposed to prepare children for actual life and to teach them relevant subject matter from real models and directly from nature. There were, of course, few or no regular schools provided for the children of the poor—the lower working classes and the peasants. So far as they obtained any education at all, it was through charity schools maintained chiefly by Church and religious bodies. Some schools for girls were founded in the seventeenth and eighteenth centuries, but they made little headway.

The pedagogical ideals underlying education during this period underwent interesting modifications and shifts of emphasis. The revival of the classics did not actually bring with it any of the naturalness and sophistication that had characterized Hellenic education. Rather, Greek and Latin became mainly a severe mental discipline linked up with stern Christian tenets. Nothing in human experience has been less in accord with the spirit of Hellenism than the study of the classics in western European and American education. The classics themselves were looked upon more as a means of mental discipline than as an avenue to the true appreciation of a pagan civilization. Accompanying this went the general acceptance of the doctrine that rigorous physical discipline is essential to strengthen the will and toughen the pupil against fear. Professor Preserved Smith recounts the instance of a Württemberg schoolmaster who estimated that in fifty years of teaching he had given 911,527 strokes with a stick, 124,000 lashes with a whip, 136,715 slaps with the hand, and 1,115,800 boxes on the ear.[1] There was also a feeling that a care-free and joyous attitude on the part of the pupil was akin to sin. Nothing that a student really enjoyed could be a legitimate or useful unit of instruction.[2] In spite of their pagan background, the classics in European education were thus inculcated in a strongly religious atmosphere.

With the coming of Rationalism and the period of the Enlightenment there was a marked revolt against this religious severity and disciplinary rigor. Rationalism manifested a desire to wipe out the fears and worries that earlier religious superstitions had instilled into the minds of pupils. Tolerance, urbanity, and serenity were the great intellectual virtues that Rationalism wished to inculcate. The sophisticated gentleman was its most cherished product. An admirable example of this Rationalistic ideal appeared in the code of conduct drawn up by Lord Chesterfield for his son. Since Rationalism was prone to believe in the inherent equality of all men and to regard differences in achieve-

---

[1] Smith, *op. cit.*, Vol. II, p. 423.   [2] A view still, unfortunately, all too prevalent.

ment as due to inequalities in opportunity, it logically placed emphasis on education and its democratization. There could be no social utopia until education was open to all. Such a doctrine was especially urged by Helvétius and his followers.

The chief educational theorist of Rationalism was John Locke, who applied his empirical psychology and philosophy to educational doctrine. Holding that our minds are a blank at birth and that our knowledge and behavior are a result of experience, he logically argued that every opportunity should be given for the provision of such experiences as would produce the ideal personality and body of information. This led to emphasis upon the proper social environment as well as inculcated information. But Locke was frank enough to admit that his theory was applicable only to the children of the well-to-do. He suggested manual training for the children of the poor. Of generally similar views was the German philosopher Leibnitz, who laid special stress upon viewing education as a preparation for actual life. Accordingly, he advocated practical subjects, especially natural science. This emphasis on natural science was later warmly seconded by Diderot.

Romanticism brought with it an even more decided revolt against the older order of artificial disciplinary repression than Rationalism had incited. Viewing, as it did, the feelings and emotions as the most important item in the human make-up, it naturally rebelled against compressing them within the strait-jacket of conventional school discipline. It recommended an adaptation of the curriculum and discipline to our instincts and to the spontaneous expression of the individual human personality. It labored heartily to set up the freedom of the human spirit as a pedagogical ideal and practice.

These protests of the Romanticists against the stereotyped and repressive educational system bore fruit in a great pedagogical revolution. This was anticipated in Rousseau's *Emile* (1762). In this he argued for giving greater play to naturalness in education and for democratizing the educational process by opening its opportunities to all—at least to all boys. By the "natural" Rousseau did not mean the qualities of savage man so much as the inherent traits of the human personality. He bespoke an adjustment of educational practice to the actual character of human beings. Rousseau did, however, overwork his valid criticism of the old educational order. He minimized the value of utilizing the accumulated wisdom of the ages and useful techniques of inculcating information. Much time would be wasted if we depended as fully upon spontaneous forms of self-expression as he recommended.[1] The pedagogical revolution initiated by Rousseau was refined and developed by Johann Bernhard Basedow (1723-90), Heinrich Pestalozzi (1746-1827), and Johann Friedrich Herbart (1776-1841).

Basedow was converted from the views of a conventional pedagogue by his reading of the *Emile*. He devoted the rest of his life to promoting a qualified version of Rousseau's educational and psychological ideals. More influential was Pestalozzi, who "made positive and concrete the negative and general educational principles enunciated by Rousseau." Pestalozzi was, however, a

[1] See especially Smith, *op. cit.*, Vol. II, pp. 439 ff.

somewhat eccentric character and not an "accepted scholar." This created considerable resistance to his principles among those who demanded stability and erudition in educational leadership. This difficulty was remedied by Herbart, who was both a learned man and a distinguished university professor. He brought Pestalozzi's doctrines into accord with reputable learning and with such psychological principles as then existed. This supplied them with additional prestige. Herbart infused Rousseau's doctrines into formal pedagogy, but he still viewed educational problems primarily from the standpoint of the teacher. The new pedagogy was linked up directly with the learning process by Friedrich Wilhelm Froebel (1782-1852). He followed Rousseau by holding that in educational practice the nature of the child must be given precedence over educational machinery and artificial educational ideals. He maintained that the development of the personality is of more importance than the mere inculcation of information and the training of the intellect.[1] An interesting anticipation of modern genetic psychology, associated especially with the work of G. Stanley Hall in our own day,[2] is to be observed in the voluminous *Course of Studies* by Etienne Bonnot de Condillac (1715-80). Condillac held that in his educational experience the child should recapitulate the cultural evolution of the race and in the same order of development, that is, should proceed from myth to natural science. The education of women was defended by Fénelon in a treatise on this subject (1687), but he was no seventeenth-century feminist. Women were to be educated solely for family responsibilities and housekeeping. Condorcet was more advanced in his views on the education of women.

IX. HOW THE NEW CULTURAL CURRENTS AFFECTED LITERATURE

In describing the literature of the period conventionally known as the Renaissance we indicated that the dominating feature was the revival of interest in classical models and styles and the imitation of these in the writings of the time.[3] We pointed out, however, that classicism did not hold sway unchallenged. National literature, composed mainly in the vernacular, became increasingly popular. In the seventeenth and eighteenth centuries this nationalization of literature gained still further headway. It was inhibited to some extent by the wide influence of oversea factors and by the cosmopolitanism of the age. Another notable change in the literature and art of this period was its predominantly middle-class character. The culture of the Middle Ages had reflected primarily the nobility and the Church. It was upper-class and ecclesiastical. The Renaissance had helped to make a breach with this tradition, but it had not gone the whole way towards a bourgeois culture. By the eighteenth century, while there were still vestiges of the churchly and the noble in the literature and the fine arts, both of these were predominantly in the hands and at the service of the middle class.

The influence of oversea expansion on literary developments was very evident and extensive. The manners, customs, and ideas of oversea peoples figured widely in the literature of the sixteenth, seventeenth, and eighteenth centuries.

---

[1] See below, p. 689.   [2] See below, pp. 648, 689.   [3] See above, Vol. I, pp. 833 ff.

The settings of many of the Utopias, the romances, and the allegories of the time were found in real or imaginary spots in Africa, Asia, or the Americas.[1] This influence of the study of exploration, adventure, and the manners and customs of strange peoples in distant lands is evident in the poetry of Camoëns, Spenser, Milton, and Dryden; in the drama of Marlowe, Shakespeare, Dryden, and Molière; in the novels of Rabelais, Cervantes, Defoe, Swift, Rousseau, Bernardin de Saint-Pierre, and Samuel Johnson; in the essays of Montaigne, Bacon, and Pope; in the historical writings of Peter Martyr, Oviedo, Las Casas, Gómara, Herrera, De Barros, Raleigh, De Charlevoix, and Raynal; in the political philosophy of men like Hobbes, Locke, Rousseau, and Montesquieu; in Hakluyt's *Voyages;* and in the travel tales of Chardin, Dampier, Lafitau, Tavernier, and Bernier. Acquaintance with these descriptions of life overseas among a great diversity of peoples, and reflection thereupon, often served to develop a high degree of tolerance and urbanity on the part of writers thus instructed. An increased interest in humanity and its problems was another important effect. Rabelais's *Gargantua* and *Pantagruel,* Camoëns's *Lusiad,* Bernardin de Saint-Pierre's *Paul and Virginia,* Defoe's *Robinson Crusoe,* Swift's *Gulliver's Travels,* Johnson's *Rasselas: Prince of Abyssinia,* Joseph Addison's *Vision of Mirza,* and William Beckford's *History of the Caliph Vathek* were prominent examples of works in which the oversea or oriental influence was decisively predominant. Translations of oriental literature also assumed an important rôle in European literary interests. Galland's translation of the Arabian Nights appeared in 1704 and set the pace for a veritable oriental craze in France which was soon taken up in England. *The Persian Tales* and *The Turkish Tales* (the old *Book of Sindbad*) followed the Arabian Nights. Next came faked translations of imaginary oriental books, a practice led by Geullette in France. As Professor Gibb writes: "It was a very strange Orient that was reflected in the 'oriental' literature of the eighteenth century, an Orient which the romantic imagination of the time refashioned after its own ideas and peopled with grotesque figures clothed in the garb of caliphs, kadis, and jinns." These fakes and excesses were assaulted by Hamilton, Pope, Goldsmith and others.

Oversea expansion had a particularly important influence upon historical writing.[2] The old absorption in a narrow and stereotyped political and ecclesiastical history gave way before a new interest in humanity, manners and customs, and institutions. All this tended to humanize history and to stimulate the rise of the history of civilization. A new recognition also arose of the intimate relationship between geography and history. Further, the stilted classicism in style was supplanted by a fresh and direct descriptive mode of expression, and the annalistic method of presentation was generally abandoned. Representative of this historical literature were the *General and Natural History of the Indies* by Gonzalo Fernández de Oviedo (1478-1557); the *General History of the Indies* by Antonio de Herrera (1549-1625); and the *Philosophical and Political History of the Settlements and Trade of Europeans in the East and West Indies* by Guillaume Thomas Raynal (1713-96).

The gradual transition from the classicism of Humanism to national litera-

[1] *Cf.* Atkinson, *op. cit.*
[2] See H. E. Barnes, "History: Its Rise and Development," Encyclopedia Americana, Vol. XIV, pp. 226-8.

ture was well illustrated by the prevalence in the seventeenth century of what has been termed the baroque school of literary expression. It relied heavily upon classical forms and allusions and was studiously embellished with decorative devices. It reached its highest level in France and England. Its chief French representatives were the group of able writers who flourished in the days of Louis XIV. Pierre Corneille (1606-84), author of the immortal *Cid,* is often regarded as the father of the modern French drama. Jean Baptiste Poquelin Molière (1622-73) was probably the greatest master of comedy in modern times. Representative are his *Don Juan* and *Learned Ladies.* Jean Baptiste Racine (1639-99) was a keener psychologist than Molière, but he tended more towards tragedy and deep moralizing. His *Andromache* and *Athalie* are typical tragedies. Madame de Sévigné (1626-96) was the writer of witty and spicy letters. But a more daring scandal-monger was Jean de La Fontaine (1621-95), who was also the ablest short-story writer of his age and the composer of inimitable fables. In England the best representatives of the baroque tendency were John Milton (1608-74), a profound and learned poet and an able essayist and controversialist; John Dryden (1631-1700), the chief ornament of Restoration drama and a capable poet and song-writer; and Alexander Pope (1688-1744), regarded by most critics as the greatest English poet of the eighteenth century and one of the leading Deistic thinkers. In Germany this literary trend was represented by Martin Opitz (1597-1639), a learned and industrious but slavish copyist of classic verse.

The literature of Rationalism, strictly speaking, fell more in the fields of Deistic theology, critical and scientific philosophy, historical writing, and critical and satirical essays than it did in fiction or poetry. Much of this literature we have already touched upon. But there were, nevertheless, important novels produced by the Rationalists. Voltaire's *Candide* is probably the most devastatingly effective satirical novel ever written in any era. Anticipating Romanticism as much as they expressed Rationalistic ideas, Rousseau's *Emile* exerted a vast influence upon the liberalizing of education, while his *La nouvelle Héloïse* was one of the most popular love novels of the day. Daniel Defoe's *Robinson Crusoe,* with its picture of the state of nature, still retains its popularity, even more as a perennial children's story than as "a glorification of the resourceful individual bourgeois adventurer." In *Tom Jones,* Henry Fielding (1707-54) described and urbanely ridiculed the manners and customs of England in the first half of the eighteenth century. *Gulliver's Travels* by Jonathan Swift (1667-1745) was the most thorough and devastating satire on conditions of the time in England. Ironically enough, its current popularity is, like that of *Robinson Crusoe,* due to its descriptive charm for children. Rationalism was not devoid of great poets, since Pope might quite well be described as belonging to this school. But there were others, such as the brilliant Frenchman André de Chénier (1762-94), and the two eminent Germans Gotthold Ephraim Lessing and Johann Friedrich von Schiller (1759-1805). Lessing and Schiller also made notable contributions to the drama, the former in his *Nathan the Wise,* a Rationalistic discussion of the Jewish problem, and Schiller by the famous *Wallenstein* and *William Tell.* Schiller wavered between Rationalism and the Romanticism of his friend Goethe.[1]

[1] See below, p. 702.

HOW CULTURAL CURRENTS AFFECTED LITERATURE 247

In the realm of historical writing Rationalism left distinguished monuments.[1] In his work on the age of Louis XIV, Voltaire made a decisive break with the dull annalistic method of writing history and described the totality of French culture at the time. His *Essay on Manners and Customs* was the first modern history of civilization. Montesquieu's book on Roman history was obviously far less capable than his great work on law and politics. The philosopher David Hume wrote an urbane but not particularly enduring work on English history. William Robertson (1721-93) composed very competent histories of Scotland, America, and the reign of Charles V. By far the best known of the Rationalistic historical works was Edward Gibbon's (1737-94) classic *The Decline and Fall of the Roman Empire*. When provided with up-to-date critical notes this work is still dependable as a survey of the periods covered.

We have not the space to reconsider the writings of those Rationalistic essayists, controversialists, and scholars with whom we have already dealt. Merely to recall the names of Montaigne, Bacon, Bayle, Anthony Collins, Swift, Shaftesbury, Helvétius, Diderot, Condorcet, and Holbach will suffice to indicate the extent, power, and flavor of their writings.

The popularity of the philosophy of Romanticism at the end of the eighteenth century and the beginning of the nineteenth was of deep significance for literature. Its primary emphasis on the feelings and the emotions was more conducive to the stimulation of literary—particularly poetic—impulses than the more purely intellectual and analytic spirit of Rationalism. Further, the Romanticists laid great stress upon the unique character of national culture. This made for the nationalization of literature as contrasted with the primary cosmopolitanism of Rationalism. In France the writings of Rousseau marked a sort of turning-point at which Rationalism shaded into Romanticism.[2] We shall consider the literary products of the Romanticist school in dealing with the history of nineteenth-century literature.

X. ACHIEVEMENTS IN ART AND MUSIC

While there were no such epoch-making developments in art as took place during the Renaissance, the artistic achievements of the seventeenth and eighteenth centuries were notable. The most conspicuous tendencies were, perhaps, the ever increasing secularization, the increase of human interests, and the zest for synthetic unity.

Most Renaissance painting had been devoted to religious themes—the Virgin (Madonna), scenes from the life of Christ, martyrs, saints, miracles, and the like. But secularization had set in even within strictly Renaissance painting. In Italy some of the great painters like Titian and Correggio had depicted feminine beauty in truly sensuous fashion. Moreover, many of the painters were commissioned by princes and nobles to paint portraits and other secular subjects. There developed considerable commercial painting of a decidedly secular cast. The greatest of Spanish painters, Velásquez, had painted almost

---
[1] See Barnes, *loc. cit.*, pp. 228 ff.; Smith, *op. cit.*, Vol. II, pp. 247 ff.; and T. P. Peardon, *The Transition in English Historical Writing, 1760-1830*, Columbia University Press, 1933, Chaps. I-II.
[2] See below, pp. 690 ff.

exclusively royalty, men of state, military scenes, and figures from pagan mythology.

The Flemish and Dutch painters of the later Renaissance furnish the best example, however, of the growing secularization of artistic interests. Their art was less intellectual than that of the Italian masters. They gave way to artistic sensuousness and pursued art more for art's sake than as an instrument for conveying ideas. This encouraged the development of great technical skill, in which the Flemish and Dutch painting excelled—notably in color, line, and the use of light and shade. The Dutch painters were especially realistic and gave much attention to genre painting or the reproduction of homely scenes from everyday life. "More than any other nation they have left us a picture of their homes, their courtyards and streets and their everyday life." Nor were the Flemish and Dutch painters afraid to depict drinking scenes and other examples of joyous living. Another example of secularization is to be seen in the growing popularity of landscape-painting. Landscapes were now painted for their own intrinsic artistic beauty and not primarily to provide backgrounds for Madonnas and martyrs. Portrait-painting also attained unsurpassed excellence during this period and added its weight to the secularizing tendency.

Next to the secularization of art, the most noticeable aspect of artisic evolution in this period was the emergence of the new style called the baroque, comparable to the baroque manner in literature to which reference has already been made. Indeed, this development of baroque art was in itself a manifestation of the humanizing and secularizing process. As Professor Rogers pertinently observes: "The art of any age is the visual reflection of its central urges. For the seventeenth century these are the affirmation of the dignity of humanity and its institutions through the conquest of the tangible world of space, and a thoroughgoing application of the principle of organization and unification to every aspect of life." Baroque art represented an abandonment of the penchant for symbolic expression in favor of a realistic portrayal of human tangibilities. In particular, there was a striving for the conquest, organization, and unification of spatial relations. This type of art was calculated to make the same deep appeal to the feelings that was present in the artistic aspirations of the Middle Ages. It added to this the superior technique of the late Renaissance art, thus making it possible to express the emotional feeling more competently and to present a greater appeal to the senses. Professor Smith thus describes the general character of baroque art:

> The result was a union of the transcendental and the natural. The artist used the resources of a studied treatment to arouse the strongest possible emotions in the beholder. Thus was naturally evolved that exaggeration which is a marked characteristic of baroque, and which revealed itself in exuberance of ornament, in the emphasis of gesture, in the continued *fortissimo* of color and *prestissimo* of movement. In striking composition, in piquant detail, they sought that "strangeness of proportion" without which, said Francis Bacon, "there is no excellent beauty." Moreover, they sought to enhance the effect of each art of painting, sculpture, and architecture by a harmonious and grandiose combination of them all. Large dimensions, profuse ornament in the same style, skillful arrangements of lighting, or spacing, and even of landscape gardening and of town-planning, raised and exaggerated the effect of the whole. In color was sought a unifying as well as a pleasing element.[1]

[1] *Cf.* Smith, *op. cit.*, Vol. I, pp. 570 ff.

ACHIEVEMENTS IN ART AND MUSIC

In due time a much lighter and more decorative artistic style, helped on by oriental influences, appeared in the so-called rococo.[1] This particularly affected architecture and interior decoration. In part as a revolt against this, we find a return to pure, cool, and formal classicism near the end of this early modern age.

The supreme artistic talents of Italians and Spaniards did not fade suddenly with the close of the high Renaissance. As a matter of fact, many regard Tintoretto of the late Venetian school as the father of baroque painting. Certainly, the three great eclectics of the Bolognese school, the Caracci brothers of the last half of the sixteenth century, and their contemporary, Michelangelo Caravaggio (1569-1609), definitely represent the new baroque trend in painting. The leadership in painting definitely shifted, however, to northwestern Europe in the sixteenth and seventeenth centuries. Flanders and the Netherlands claimed most of the great artists of the early modern period. The preëminent artist of the baroque period in Flemish painting was Peter Paul Rubens (1577-1640). He was a very prolific painter, with great gift for both form and color. While he painted many pictures built about scriptural subjects, he also portrayed many secular themes, depicting the female form in a particularly sensuous and voluptuous fashion. His paintings, often very large compositions showing great capacity for the arrangement of detail, make a direct and powerful appeal to the eye and the senses. Rubens had many pupils and assistants and created a veritable school of painters. This accounts for the large number of pictures that obviously bear the mark of his influence.

Comparable to Rubens was Rembrandt van Rijn (1606-69) among the Dutch painters. Without, in all probability, any deliberate intent, he forwarded the secularizing process by following a practice already to be observed in Holland. While he painted many scenes from the Bible, he took his characters and settings for such pictures from daily scenes and living persons in the seventeenth-century Netherlands. The biblical story was thus transplanted into the Dutch culture of everyday life. If Rembrandt was less prolific and sensuous than Rubens, his art gives evidence of much more subtlety and insight. He was, incidentally, one of the first truly great landscape-painters. Rembrandt has left us some splendid examples of genre painting, but the most notable artists in the depiction of the day-by-day life and characters in Dutch culture were Pieter de Hoogh (1629-78) and Jan Vermeer (1632-75).

The foremost painter of court life, with all its gayety and display in this age, was a Frenchman, Jean Antoine Watteau (1684-1721), who portrayed the life of the nobility with great grace and delicacy. Even more in harmony with the gay spirit of these times and very popular with the court group were the prolific François Boucher (1703-70) and his pupil Jean Honoré Fragonard (1732-1806). They depicted with far more colorful realism than Watteau the erotic voluptuousness of the court life of their era. By this time Venus had in part supplanted the Virgin as a theme for artists. In the jovial moods—drinking scenes and the like—embodied in many of the pictures of Frans Hals (1580-1666) and David Teniers the Younger (1610-90) one finds a wide departure from the solemnity of religious themes. The social life of

---

[1] *Cf.* Reichwein, *China and Europe,* pp. 23 ff.

the English aristocracy and middle class in all of its characteristic phases was portrayed with a strong touch of satire by William Hogarth (1697-1764), perhaps the most capable and influential English painter of the eighteenth century. He also reveled in scenes of underworld character and unabashed realism in portraying the life of the lower classes. An interesting parallel in music to this side of Hogarth is found in *The Beggar's Opera* by John Gay.

In landscape painting the leading Dutch master was Jacob van Ruysdael (1628?-82). He was an extreme realist, reproducing natural scenes as they were, with little tendency towards idealization or classicism. In this faithful portrayal of nature Van Ruysdael proved himself a master of composition, light, and color. His chief rival in landscape-painting at the time was a Frenchman, Claude Lorraine (Gelée, 1600-82). But the latter in no way approached Van Ruysdael in realism. He painted exquisite imaginary landscapes in conventional style to serve as backgrounds for classical or mythological episodes and scenes. As a master in reproducing sunlight he had no peer in his day. Another very capable French painter of imaginative landscapes was Nicolas Poussin (1594-1665), whose "Shepherds in Arcady" is perhaps his best-known picture. At the very end of this period there appeared two very talented landscape-painters in England, John Constable (1776-1837) and Joseph M. W. Turner (1775-1851). The former rivaled Van Ruysdael in the fidelity with which he reproduced nature. Turner had a penchant for a quasi-poetic interpretation of the sun, sky, and sea. He was probably the ablest and most prolific landscape-painter who has ever lived.

Portrait-painting reached a far higher degree of popularity and perfection in this period than in any earlier age. Rembrandt did notable work in portraits, but the most famous painter of portraits was the Flemish master, Anthony van Dyck (1599-1641). He combined to a remarkable degree naturalness, dignity, and refinement. There is, however, little vigor or character in his pictures, owing in some measure probably to the fact that his subjects were chiefly from the monarchy and the nobility in appropriate poses. In the seventeenth century the English monarchs and nobles had depended upon foreign portrait-painters like Van Dyck, but in the eighteenth century England itself produced two of the ablest portrait-painters of the era, Sir Joshua Reynolds (1723-92) and Thomas Gainsborough (1727-88). Neither showed much psychological penetration, but they have rarely been surpassed for technical skill in portraiture. Reynolds idealized with classic dignity the English generals, statesmen, and ladies of his era. Gainsborough excelled him in delicacy of touch and skillful use of color. In France, Boucher and Fragonard were extremely popular portrait-painters, being widely employed by the nobility and court favorites. The most eminent French painter of the period, Jacques Louis David (1748-1825), also turned his attention to some degree to portrait-painting, but he was more famous for his revival of classicism. His interest in classical scenes, which was shared by his contemporary Pierre Paul Prud'hon (1758-1823), was definitely a move towards the secularization of art. In Spain realistic portrait painting attained the level of satire in the work of Francisco Goya (1746-1828), who had the splendid audacity to paint even monarchs as they actually looked in daily life.

ACHIEVEMENTS IN ART AND MUSIC

The influence of oversea expansion upon art was marked and diversified.[1] Novel secular themes appeared in the effort of painters to portray maritime life and the new peoples and cultures that had been discovered in oversea areas. The sailor, the adventurer, and the idealized Indian maiden displaced to some degree the saint, the martyr, and the Virgin. A number of the painters we have mentioned above, such as Boucher and Watteau, reflected oriental influences in their art. In portraying the American Indians and their life John White in England and Cornelis Ketel in the Netherlands took the lead.

Much more important than the direct influence of oversea expansion on painting was its effects upon various phases of personal adornment, decorative art, furniture, and landscape gardening.[2] The characteristic art of the age of the decadent French Bourbons, the well-known rococo, was profoundly influenced by contact with China and Japan. Newly discovered plants and animals, as well as purely imaginary creatures suggested thereby, were widely used in illustrating books and maps. The whole art of engraving was modified by oriental precedents. Oriental patterns were extensively adopted in making new designs for the decoration of jewelry and family plate. Imitation of the oriental love of jewelry in personal display and ostentation, coupled with the vast increase in the supply of precious metals and stones, served to give jewelry a position of new importance in European art. Porcelain ware was introduced from China and Japan and rather successfully imitated by the Dutch. Screens and lacquered work from the same source became increasingly popular. The fashion of interior decoration, in which at this time the oriental element was predominant, may almost be said to date from this period. From the Orient came such things as wall paper, porcelain, lacquer, and the like. Exotic woods were imported and widely utilized. There was a large demand for Chinese designs in furniture and these vied in popularity with Jacobean, Louis XIV, Queen Anne, and other European styles. Especially favored were the Chinese mirrors. From an imitation of Chinese dishes there evolved the more famous brands of European chinaware. Such were the Delft ware of Holland, the Dresden china of Germany, and the Wedgwood china of England. Landscape gardening in western Europe was both stimulated and revolutionized by oriental influences. Gardens were laid out after Chinese and Japanese models. In English parks even imitation pagodas, Chinese temples, and oriental bridges were erected. Frederick the Great constructed a Chinese pavilion on his palace grounds at Sans Souci in Potsdam. With these buildings there arose the European imitation of the fine oriental latticework.

All in all, the major items in the history of painting and decoration during the period from the decline of the Italian Renaissance to the nineteenth century were the secularization of artistic themes; the introduction of pagan motifs, including both the classical and the oriental; the emphasis on a realistic portrayal of everyday life and physical nature; a surrender to the sensuous, especially in France; the perfection of the art of portrait-painting; a remarkable development of the decorative arts, particularly interior decoration; and the reaction of adventure, maritime life, and exotic native culture upon many phases

---

[1] See Gillespie, *op. cit.*, pp. 310 ff.; Botsford, *op. cit.*, Chap. IV; and Reichwein, *op. cit.*
[2] See especially Reichwein, *op. cit.*

of art. The provincialism and supernaturalism of the art of the Middle Ages and the early Renaissance were to a large degree abandoned or outdistanced.

In the history of architecture during this period the two chief factors were the spread of the Renaissance styles to northern and western Europe and the influence of classical scholarship and the Orient. In France, the Italian Renaissance models had a strong influence, but they did not entirely obliterate the native French trends. The châteaux no longer needed to be built with a primary eye to fortification and protection. Beauty could be given freer sway, and such was the case with the Renaissance châteaux.[1] The Louvre, the façade of which was designed by Claude Perrault (1613-88), is one of the finest examples of French Renaissance architecture. The most pretentious expression of French architecture of this type is, of course, the collection of magnificent buildings erected at Versailles by Louis XIV. Of these Jules Hardouin-Mansart (1645-1708) was the chief architect. He also designed the famous dome of the chapel of the Hôtel des Invalides in Paris, as well as laying out the Place Vendôme and the Place des Victoires. The rococo trend, though somewhat restrained, was best represented by the work of Robert de Cotte (1651-1725), who designed the building now used as the Bank of France.

In England the two major architects of the period, likewise influenced by Italian Renaissance tastes, were Inigo Jones (1573-1652) and Sir Christopher Wren (1632-1723). Of the former's work the best-known example is the banquet hall of Whitehall Palace. The latter was the architect of the greatest of England's modern churches, St. Paul's Cathedral in London, a baroque structure topped by an impressive dome. Wren's work first brought real beauty to Protestant church structures. We have already described the oriental influence on architectural decoration in treating of the imitation of oriental pavilions, pagodas, temples, bridges, and the like, and the prominent oriental element in the interior decoration of the time.

One of the most notable innovations in architecture during this period was the building of homes with a view to beauty and comfort rather than to protection against military attack. The rise of the national state and the growth of political centralization produced law and order, and it was no longer necessary for every man's house to be architecturally as well as legally his castle. The invention of improved and cheaper methods of making window glass allowed more light to penetrate houses, and the improved technique in building chimneys helped to eliminate smoke within. These advances combined to bring about a revolution in interior decoration. Here the ornate rococo style predominated, and its masters were J. A. Meissonier (1695-1750) in France and Robert Adam (1728-92) in England.

There were only four sculptors of any real note aside from late Renaissance artists. They were the Frenchmen, François Girardon (1628-1715) and Jean Antoine Houdon (1741-1828), and the Italians, Lorenzo Bernini (1598-1680) and Antonio Canova (1757-1822). Girardon was the official sculptor of Louis XIV and is responsible for most of the sculptured work at Versailles. His best single piece is the statue of Richelieu. Houdon's masterpiece is his seated figure of Voltaire, deemed by many to rival the best work of Donatello. Bernini, who

---

[1] *Cf.* Abbott, *The Expansion of Europe*, Vol. I, p. 368.

was also a distinguished architect and did much work on St. Peter's at Rome, was a good representative of baroque sculpture, with its trend towards dramatic realism. Some of his best works were "Apollo and Daphne" and the "Rape of Persephone." Canova founded a new school of Italian sculpture noted for its grace, delicacy, and loveliness. Perhaps the most representative of his works were the Cupid and Psyche group and the "Weeping Italy."

The rise of modern music manifested much the same gradual secularizing tendency that had appeared in painting, sculpture, and architecture. Formal music in western Europe had hitherto been primarily religious and church music. While the great composers of early modern times like Bach still devoted most of their efforts to sacred music, they also wrote much secular music that supplemented the folk songs which had come down from an earlier period.

A fundamental transition in the history of music from the older to the early modern style thus took place at the beginning of the seventeenth century. The new music of this period was preponderantly secular in intention, and the older liturgical. But long before 1600 there had existed flourishing schools of secular composition—-notably, that of the troubadours; that of the Florentine School of the thirteenth century; that surrounding the court of the Medici; and, most particularly, the groups of men who worked for the court of Henry VIII and of Elizabeth. In the latter years of the Renaissance and of the late sixteenth century a widely cultivated secular form, the *madrigal,* flourished in many parts of Europe, especially in England and Italy. Foremost among the reasons why secular music became so rapidly and so widely cultivated in seventeenth-century Europe are these: (1) The pseudo-classical attitude of cultivated men and women of the baroque age, who found in the kind of music associated with revamped and revised classical drama precisely what was believed to be the classic formula of dramatic declamation; (2) the emergence of successful and wealthy merchant classes who supported lavish entertainments; (3) a veritable system of musical patronage by royalty and nobility which was well developed by the eighteenth century; and (4) the fact that secular music fitted in well with the highly mundane, ornate, and carefree tastes of the rococo culture of the eighteenth century. While it is thus true that most of the important music of western Europe before 1600 had been primarily religious and Church music, it would be misleading to convey the idea that secular music occupied the attention of serious composers for the first time during the seventeenth century. There had been important secular compositions before this date.

A popular musical product of this period was the oratorio, mainly sacred choral music, though secular themes were sometimes exploited. The oratorio occupied a sort of transitional position between the overwhelmingly sacred and vocal music of the medieval period and the preponderantly secular and instrumental music of the nineteenth century. The oratorio grew up as an attempt to revive the earlier Church plays in a new and more acceptable form. The outstanding early modern composer of oratorios and instrumental music was Georg Friedrich Handel (1685-1759), a German long resident in England. Best known is his *Messiah.* Handel, though remembered by posterity, and rightly so, chiefly for his oratorios, was also, it must be recalled, one of the half-dozen most famous and successful composers of opera in his age.

The earliest notable form of secular music was the opera, which first appeared in early modern Italy. The most capable composers of early operas were Claudio Monteverde (1568-1643) and Alessandro Scarlatti (1659-1725). From their day to our own the Italians have been especially productive in this field of artistic endeavor. The ascendancy in operatic composition in the eighteenth century passed from Italians to the Germans. Here the two great figures were Christoph Gluck (1714-87) and Wolfgang Amadeus Mozart (1756-91). So sweeping were Gluck's reforms that he is regarded by many as "the father of the modern opera." Looking upon the prevailing Italian operatic style and tradition as artificial and whimsical, he set out resolutely to give operatic music virility, sincerity, and consistency. He was also a master of melody and of dramatic exploitation of the chorus. Mozart was, perhaps, more of a musical genius but was less of a reformer. He conformed to the Italian models but carried operatic music to unparalleled heights by the sheer musical beauty and dramatic color of his great compositions, such as *Don Giovanni* and *Figaro*. While most operas were then, and have always remained, tragic in theme, one famous ballad opera was produced at this time. This was *The Beggar's Opera,* written by John Gay in 1728 as a satire on London society of his day. It was surprisingly modern in conception and technique and anticipated by two centuries many of the features of the modern musical comedy. The so-called *opera buffa* also became a flourishing institution in the early part of the eighteenth century—a manifestation of the extravagant rococo culture of the period. Perhaps the most important example was Pergolesi's *La serva padrona,* which precipitated the famous row known as the "Guerre des Bouffons" (Clowns' War) in Paris.

The preëminent musical genius of the age was Johann Sebastian Bach (1685-1750), not only the first real master of organ music—continuing and perfecting the methods of Frescobaldi and Pachelbel—but also one of the ablest composers of all time. Some rate him as the supreme figure in the whole history of music. He was an extremely prolific composer, but none of his many compositions was trivial or unworthy of a master. He possessed remarkable power in the way of welding diversified details into a harmonious and unified whole. Though inspired by religious impulses, notably the German Protestant chorals, he wrote many secular pieces, excelling in sonatas and concertos. Some of his secular compositions, like the *Coffee Cantata, The Thankful Thoughts of a Tobacco Smoker,* the *Capriccio on the Departure of a Well-beloved Brother,* and some of the dances in his suites, are gay and care-free and neither learned nor sober in their style and content. Bach was a devout Protestant, and in him the streams of tendency from both the secular and religious inheritance of the past converged. He was preëminent in all forms of composition except the opera, and he even borrowed certain forms, notably the aria, from the opera. He could make use of nearly all the varied stylistic craftsmanship of his age and create out of it something quite fresh and original. In particular—and this is the heart of his greatness—he could weld polyphonic contrapuntal methods (their origins running well back into the Middle Ages and their first complete realization achieved by the masters of the sixteenth century) with the harmonic style, which had been suggested long before 1600 and by the time of Bach had come to be the primary consideration in musical thought. Full appreciation of Bach's genius was not forthcoming until the nineteenth century. Along with Bach, Handel, Gluck, and Mozart in this period, one would need to mention Franz Josef Haydn (1732-1809), often designated "the father of the symphony and the string quartet," a title which he deserved as a result of his constructive synthesis and amplification of the earlier work in instrumental composition. In addition to further elaboration of the sonata form he devised the graceful rhythm of the minuet. While lacking profundity or grave dignity, Haydn has never been surpassed, if indeed equalled, as a composer of graceful, lively, and cheerful music. Mozart's contributions to the symphony and the string quartet were only less important than his operatic compositions to which we have already called attention. In England Henry Purcell (1658-95) was the outstanding composer of the period, possessing technical ability far in advance of most of his contemporaries and excelled only by Bach in this respect. John Dryden wrote the words for many notable musical compositions, best known perhaps being his *Ode for St. Cecelia's Day*.

The improvement of musical instruments was of great assistance to the advances made in instrumental music and helped on its popularity.[1] Flutes, bassoons, clarions, trumpets, trombones, lutes, guitars, viols, harps, and harpsichords had been in use before. The viols were adapted to produce our violins and violoncellos, and the height of violin craftsmanship was attained by Antonio Stradivari (1644-1737). The pianoforte was transformed into the modern piano by Bartolommeo Cristofori in 1710, and the organ was perfected by the time of Bach. Among the new instruments added to the orchestra were the horns, oboes, and clarinets. While vocal music predominated at the beginning of the age and held its own throughout, the transition to the ascendancy of instrumental music and orchestration was evident by the close of the eighteenth century. The advances in mathematics, physics, and acoustics promoted a growing interest in the exact science of music, and many efforts were made to formulate the precise mathematical laws of musical expression.

XI. THE CONTRIBUTIONS OF EUROPEAN EXPANSION AND THE PERIOD OF ENLIGHTENMENT

Before the close of the eighteenth century European culture began to feel the full impact of the new type of economic activities, commercial expansion, Rationalistic philosophy, and the world outlook. There was, to be sure, no sharp transition from medievalism and no full attainment of modernism. As we shall make clear later,[2] European society and thought in the year 1800 were decidedly archaic. But there is no escaping the remarkable changes since the days of Erasmus and Charles V.

The economy was still primarily agrarian, but the agricultural dominion was being challenged by the remarkable commercial developments and the rise of new industries. The ascendancy of the feudal aristocracy was undermined and a new power was manifested by the rising middle class of merchants and busi-

---
[1] *Cf.* Arthur Elson, *The Book of Musical Knowledge,* Houghton Mifflin, 1915, Pt. IV.
[2] See below, pp. 263 ff.

ness men. Orthodox Christianity was subjected to searching examination. Faith was no longer regarded by all as the sovereign guide to human conduct and individual happiness. There was an inclination to place more reliance upon reason, experience, and experimentation. The older absorption in eschatology and the world to come was tempered by a growing concern with happiness here and now and by a belief in the reality of human progress. Human nature was no longer viewed as inevitably evil, but was regarded as capable of being fully controlled by the experiences of life. It might be shaped through sound education so as to be almost wholly good. All of this made for earnest activity in bringing about social reform.

The state, which had long been looked upon as a product of divine revelation and approval, was now thoroughly secularized. It was regarded as a manmade product designed to protect humanity against the evils and chaos of the state of nature. Man might give it any form he chose and could alter it when conditions warranted. The right of revolution was fully conceded by progressive thinkers. The remarkable developments in world commerce helped to create a world outlook in the place of the provincialism that had dominated the Middle Ages in actual life. People came to be interested in the cultures of oversea areas and were no longer wholly absorbed with the doings of their neighbors and fellow townsmen. The new commerce profoundly influenced economic theory. As the mercantile classes grew more numerous and powerful they balked at the narrow mercantilism that had restricted their freedom, and they drew from the philosophers a doctrine which supported freedom of trade.

Education, literature, and art were influenced by Humanism, Rationalism, and expansion overseas. The secular trends in Humanism, which had been derived at second hand from the Greeks and Romans, were emphasized and encouraged by the tenets of Rationalism. Education was to some slight degree rescued from the supernaturalism of religion and the pedantry of classicism. In literature, while the spirit and tastes of Humanism were still powerful, romances of adventure were stimulated by the tales of discovery and exploration. The optimism and critical trends in Rationalism also exerted their influence. Art was no longer devoted primarily to the glorification of God and the clarification of the Scriptures. Secular themes, many of them drawn from maritime life and exploration in extra-European lands, gradually but surely supplanted biblical figures, scriptural scenes, saints, and martyrs. Pagan styles and tastes entered with the wide imitation of the art of China and Japan.

All in all, the period from 1650 to 1800 was the most disrupting and portentous era in human history since the rise of Athenian civilization in the sixth and fifth centuries before Christ.

SUGGESTED READING

Hammerton, *Universal History of the World*, Chaps. 154, 158-59
Hayes, *Political and Cultural History of Modern Europe*, Vol. I, Chap. xi
Nussbaum, *History of the Economic Institutions of Modern Europe*, Pt. II, Chap. iii
Gillespie, *History of Europe, 1500-1815*, Chaps. vi-vii
—— *The Influence of Oversea Expansion on England to 1700*, Chaps. i-iii, x-xi
Botsford, *English Society in the Eighteenth Century*, Chaps. v-vii

SUGGESTED READING

Smith, *History of Modern Culture*, Vol. I, Chaps. VIII, XI, XVII-XIX; Vol. II, Chaps. VI, IX-X, XII, XVI-XVII
Randall, *The Making of the Modern Mind*, Chaps. XIII-XIV, XVI
David Ogg, *Europe in the Seventeenth Century*, Macmillan, 1925
R. B. Mowat, *The Age of Reason*, Houghton Mifflin, 1934
W. H. Bruford, *Germany in the Eighteenth Century*, Macmillan, 1935
Ogg and Sharp, *Economic Development of Modern Europe*, Chap. I
W. F. Willcox, "The Expansion of Europe and Its Influence upon Population," pp. 4-70 of *Studies in Philosophy and Psychology by Former Students of Charles Edward Garman*, Houghton Mifflin, 1906
Sir Frederick Pollock, *Introduction to the History of the Science of Politics*, Macmillan, 1911, Chap. III
H. W. Laidler, *History of Socialist Thought*, Crowell, 1927, Chaps. IV-VIII
S. A. Queen, *Social Work in the Light of History*, Lippincott, 1922, Chaps. X-XI
Paul Munroe, *Textbook in the History of Education*, Macmillan, 1911, Chaps. VIII-X
Helen Gardner, *Art Through the Ages*, Harcourt, Brace, 1926, Chaps. XIX-XXV
Reichwein, *China and Europe*, pp. 13-72
Arthur Elson, *The Book of Musical Knowledge*, Houghton Mifflin, 1915, Chaps. VII-XI
T. M. Finney, *A History of Music*, Harcourt, Brace (forthcoming), Pts. V-VI
Robinson and Beard, *Readings in Modern European History*, Vol. I, pp. 191-99
Jerome Davis and H. E. Barnes, *Readings in Sociology*, Heath, 1927, pp. 172-80
F. W. Coker, ed., *Readings in Political Philosophy*, Macmillan, 1914, pp. 189-557
Henry Morley, *Ideal Commonwealths*, Colonial Press, 1901
T. P. Cross and C. H. Slover, *Heath Readings in the Literature of Europe*, Heath, 1933, pp. 801-909
Kenneth Bell and G. M. Morgan, eds., *The Great Historians*, Macmillan, 1925, Pts. III-IV

FURTHER REFERENCES

POPULATION. On the growth of population in early modern times, see article "Population," Encyclopaedia of the Social Sciences; Ogg and Sharp, *op. cit.*, pp. 10 ff.; Nussbaum, *op. cit.*, p. 244; Willcox, *loc. cit.* For a history of the efforts to estimate European population during this period, see *Ibid.*, pp. 42 ff.

On migrations of Europeans, see Gillespie, *The Influence of Oversea Expansion on England*, Chap. I; Schlesinger, *New Viewpoints in American History*, Chap. I; Edith Abbott, *Historical Aspects of the Immigration Problem* (University of Chicago Press, 1926); H. P. Fairchild, *Immigration* (rev. ed., Macmillan, 1925); L. G. Brown, *Immigration* (Longmans, 1933).

On the rise and growth of the middle class, see Nussbaum, *op. cit.*, Pt. II, Chap. III; Werner Sombart, *The Quintessence of Capitalism* (Dutton, 1915); Gretton, *The English Middle Class*; Traill and Mann, *Social England*, Vol. V, Chaps. XVII-XVIII; Sée, *Economic and Social Conditions in France during the Eighteenth Century*, Chaps. IX-XI.

THE SECULARIZATION OF POLITICAL PHILOSOPHY. On the secularization of politics and political philosophy, see Smith, *op. cit.*, Vol. II, pp. 189 ff.; Lecky, *History of . . . Rationalism*, Chap. V.

On the divine right of kings, for good treatments see Figgis, *The Divine Right of Kings*; Allen, *History of Political Thought in the Sixteenth Century*.

On the social-contract theory, see Chaps. VI-VIII, X, of W. A. Dunning, *History of Political Theories from Luther to Montesquieu* (Macmillan, 1905); G. P. Gooch, *Political Thought in England from Bacon to Halifax* (Holt, 1914); H. J. Laski,

Political Thought in England from Locke to Bentham (Holt, 1920); *Cambridge Modern History,* Vol. VI, Chap. XXIII; Vol. I of C. E. Vaughan, *Studies in the History of Political Philosophy* (Longmans, 1925, 2 vols.); R. G. Adams, *The Political Ideas of the American Revolution* (Duke University Press, 1922).

THE ROMANTICIST REACTION IN SOCIAL AND POLITICAL THEORY. On the political theory of Romanticism, see Dunning, *History of Political Theories from Rousseau to Spencer,* Chap. V; F. J. C. Hearnshaw, *Social and Political Ideas of Some Representative Thinkers of the Age of Reaction and Reconstruction* (Holt, 1932); Vaughan, *op. cit.,* Vol. II.

NEW DEVELOPMENTS IN LAW AND LEGAL PHILOSOPHY. On legal evolution in early modern times, for an excellent and learned survey see Chap. v of Fritz Berolzheimer, *The World's Legal Philosophers* (Macmillan, 1912). On Roman law, see Vinogradoff, *Roman Law in Mediaeval Europe.* On the common law, see article "Common Law," Encyclopaedia of the Social Sciences; Sir Frederick Pollock, *The Genius of the Common Law* (Lemcke & Buechner, 1912); Roscoe Pound, *The Spirit of the Common Law* (Marshall Jones Co., 1921). On the rise of natural law, see Pt. I of C. G. Haines, *The Revival of Natural Law Concepts* (Harvard University Press, 1930); O. F. Gierke, *Natural Law and the Theory of Society, 1500 to 1800* (Macmillan, 1934). B. F. Wright, Jr., *American Interpretations of Natural Law* (Harvard University Press, 1931). On the early history of American law, see R. B. Morris, *Studies in the History of American Law* (Columbia University Press, 1930).

On international law, for its history see Gettell, *History of Political Thought,* pp. 186-93, 234-35, 241; Henry Wheaton, *History of the Law of Nations in Europe and America* (Gould, Banks, 1845); Sir G. G. Butler and Simon Maccoby, *The Development of International Law* (Longmans, 1928); John Westlake, *International Law* (Putnam, 1910-11, 2 pts.).

On Grotius, see Dunning, *History of Political Theories from Luther to Montesquieu,* Chap. v; Hamilton Vreeland, *Hugo Grotius* (Oxford Press, 1917); W. S. M. Knight, *The Life and Works of Hugo Grotius* (London, 1925).

RATIONALISM AND SOCIAL PHILOSOPHY. On the rationalization of social and political theory, see Smith, *op. cit.,* Vol. II, pp. 204 ff.; F. J. C. Hearnshaw, ed., *Social and Political Ideas of Some Great French Thinkers of the Age of Reason* (Crofts, 1930) and *Social and Political Ideas of Some Representative Thinkers of the Revolutionary Era.*

On Montesquieu's social and political theories, see Dunning, *History of Political Theories from Luther to Montesquieu,* Chap. XII; and for his theory of climatic influences, see Thomas, *The Environmental Basis of Society,* pp. 63-69.

On the social doctrines of Rousseau, see Dunning, *History of Political Theories from Rousseau to Spencer,* Chap. I; Matthew Josephson, *Jean-Jacques Rousseau* (Harcourt, Brace, 1931, 2 vols.). On the cultural setting and implications of his "naturalism," see article "Primitivism," Encyclopaedia of the Social Sciences; Friedell, *Cultural History of the Modern Age,* Vol. II, Bk. III, Chap. IX.

On Condorcet, see Schapiro, *Condorcet;* Burlingame, *Condorcet.*

On Saint-Simon, see Dunning, *History of Political Theories from Rousseau to Spencer,* pp. 355 ff.; L. H. Jenks, pp. 221 ff. of *Essays in Intellectual History; Dedicated to James Harvey Robinson.*

On Bentham, see Chaps. II-V of W. L. Davidson, *Political Thought in England . . . from Bentham to Mill* (Holt, 1916); Elie Halévy, *The Growth of Philosophical Radicalism* (Macmillan, 1928).

On the social theory of Comte, see H. E. Barnes, "The Political and Social Philosophy of Auguste Comte," *Open Court,* July-August, 1922; Hearnshaw, *Social and*

Political Ideas of Some Representative Thinkers of the Age of Reaction and Reconstruction, Chap. VII.

UTOPIAS. On the utopians and social radicals, see W. B. Guthrie, *Socialism before the French Revolution* (Macmillan, 1907); Kingsley Martin, *French Liberal Thought in the Eighteenth Century* (Little, Brown, 1929); Lewis Mumford, *The Story of Utopias* (Boni & Liveright, 1922); J. O. Hertzler, *History of Utopian Thought* (Macmillan, 1923); Hearnshaw, *Social and Political Ideas of Some Representative Thinkers of the Revolutionary Era* and *Social and Political Ideas of Some Great French Thinkers of the Age of Reason;* J. B. Peixotto, *The French Revolution and Modern Socialism* (Crowell, 1901); H. J. Laski, *The Socialist Tradition in the French Revolution* (London, 1930). Texts of most of the Utopias may be found in Morley, *op. cit.*

THE ORIGINS OF POOR RELIEF. On the development of the poor-relief system in England, see Chap. XIII of J. L. Gillin, *Poverty and Dependency* (Century, 1926); Queen, *op. cit.,* Chaps. X-XI; E. M. Leonard, *The Early History of English Poor Relief* (Columbia University Press, 1900).

EDUCATION IN EARLY MODERN TIMES. On educational developments, see Smith, *op. cit.,* Vol. I, Chap. XI; Vol. II, Chap. XII; Hart, *The Discovery of Intelligence,* Chaps. XXII-XXX; Monroe, *op. cit.,* Chaps. VIII-IX.

HOW THE NEW CULTURAL CURRENTS AFFECTED LITERATURE. On European expansion and literature, see pp. 199 ff. of Sir T. W. Arnold and Alfred Guillaume, *The Legacy of Islam* (Oxford Press, 1931); Gillespie, *The Influence of Oversea Expansion on England to 1700,* Chap. X; Botsford, *op. cit.,* pp. 17-23; A. F. J. Remy, *The Influence of India and Persia on the Poetry of Germany* (Columbia University Press, 1901); M. P. Conant, *The Oriental Tale in England in the Eighteenth Century* (Lemcke & Buechner, 1908). On the history of literature from the sixteenth century to the nineteenth, see Smith, *op. cit.,* Vol. I, Chap. XVIII; Vol. II, Chaps. VII-X; Chaps. X-XIV of Emile Faguet, *Initiation into Literature* (Putnam, 1914); Bks. III-IV of Laurie Magnus, *History of European Literature* (Norton, 1934); Pt. III of J. A. Macy, *The Story of the World's Literature* (Boni & Liveright, 1925); Vol. II, Bks. I-III, of E. H. Legouis and L. F. Cazamian, *History of English Literature* (Macmillan, 1926-29, 2 vols.); Nitze and Dargan, *History of French Literature,* Pts. II-III; Wright, *History of French Literature,* Pts. II-IV; Pt. II of Ernest Mérimée, *History of Spanish Literature* (Holt, 1930); Chaps. XV-XXII of Richard Garnett, *History of Italian Literature* (Appleton, 1928); Chaps. VI-VIII of Kuno Francke, *History of German Literature* (Holt, 1901); Chaps. X-XVI of Calvin Thomas, *History of German Literature* (Appleton, 1909).

On early Romanticist French and English literature and the transition to the nineteenth century, see M. B. Finch and E. A. Peers, *The Origins of French Romanticism* (Dutton, 1920); H. N. Fairchild, *The Romantic Quest* (Columbia University Press, 1931).

On historical writing in the period, see Bks. III-IV of Eduard Fueter, *Histoire de l'historiographie moderne* (Paris, 1914); and J. B. Black, *The Art of History* (Crofts, 1926).

ACHIEVEMENTS IN ART. On artistic developments, see Smith, *op. cit.,* Vol. I, Chap. XIX; Vol. II, Chap. XVIII; Gardner, *op. cit.,* Chaps. XIX-XXIV; F. J. Mather, *Modern Painting* (Holt, 1927); Chaps. XXII-XXIV of Salomon Reinach, *Apollo* (Scribner, 1924); Chaps. XIV-XV of Thomas Craven, *Men of Art* (Simon & Schuster, 1931); Friedell, *op. cit.,* Vol. II, Bk. II, Chaps. I, III.

On Rembrandt, see the extremely entertaining and illuminating biography by Hendrik Van Loon, *R.v.R.: The Life and Times of Rembrandt van Rijn* (Garden

City Publishing Co., 1932). On overseas influences and rococo art, see Reichwein, *op. cit.;* and Mary Evans, *Costume Through the Ages* (Lippincott, 1930), Chap. VII. On the intellectual, cultural and social ramifications of rococo, see Karl Toth, *Woman and Rococo in France* (Lippincott, 1931).

ACHIEVEMENTS IN MUSIC. On the origins of modern music, see Smith, *op. cit.,* Vol. II, pp. 633 ff.; Chaps. VII-XIII of Paul Bekker, *The Story of Music* (Norton, 1927); Chaps. VIII-XI of Cecil Gray, *History of Music* (Knopf, 1928); Elson, *op. cit.,* Chaps. VI-IX; Pts. III-VI of W. S. Pratt, *History of Music* (6th ed., Schirmer, 1922); Sir C. V. Stanford and Cecil Forsyth, *History of Music* (Macmillan, 1925).

PART TWO

THE ERA OF INDUSTRIAL CAPITALISM, NATIONALISM, DEMOCRACY, AND IMPERIALISM

VII. THE NEW EMPIRE OF MACHINES AND THE RISE OF THE FACTORY SYSTEM

VIII. THE REVOLUTION IN POWER, TRANSPORTATION, AND COMMUNICATION

IX. THE TRANSIT OF THE INDUSTRIAL REVOLUTION TO CONTINENTAL EUROPE AND THE ORIENT

X. THE INDUSTRIAL REVOLUTION COMES TO THE UNITED STATES

XI. THE DEFENSE AND CRITICISM OF EARLY INDUSTRIAL CAPITALISM

XII. SOCIAL PHASES OF THE NEW RÉGIME

XIII. THE FOUNDATIONS OF CONTEMPORARY NATIONALISM

XIV. THE ORIGINS OF DEMOCRACY AND THE RISE OF PARTY GOVERNMENT

XV. THE COURSE OF MODERN IMPERIALISM

XVI. THE INFLUENCE OF CONTEMPORARY IMPERIALISM ON WESTERN CIVILIZATION

XVII. THE WORLD WAR, 1914-1918

XVIII. AFTER THE WORLD WAR

XIX. INTELLECTUAL AND CULTURAL ACHIEVEMENTS OF THE NINETEENTH CENTURY

PART TWO

THE ERA OF INDUSTRIAL CAPITALISM, NATIONALISM, DEMOCRACY, AND IMPERIALISM

VII. THE NEW EMPIRE OF MACHINES AND THE RISE OF THE FACTORY SYSTEM
VIII. THE REVOLUTION IN POWER, TRANSPORTATION, AND COMMUNICATION
IX. THE TRANSIT OF THE INDUSTRIAL REVOLUTION TO CONTINENTAL EUROPE AND THE ORIENT
X. THE INDUSTRIAL REVOLUTION COMES TO THE UNITED STATES
XI. THE DEFENSE AND CRITICISM OF EARLY INDUSTRIAL CAPITALISM
XII. SOCIAL PHASES OF THE NEW MACHINE
XIII. THE FOUNDATIONS OF CONTEMPORARY NATIONALISM
XIV. THE ORIGINS OF DEMOCRACY AND THE RISE OF PARTY GOVERNMENT
XV. THE COURSE OF MODERN IMPERIALISM
XVI. THE INFLUENCE OF CONTEMPORARY IMPERIALISM ON WESTERN CIVILIZATION
XVII. THE WORLD WAR, 1914-1918
XVIII. AFTER THE WORLD WAR
XIX. INTELLECTUAL AND CULTURAL ACHIEVEMENTS OF THE NINETEENTH CENTURY

CHAPTER VII

THE NEW EMPIRE OF MACHINES AND THE RISE OF THE FACTORY SYSTEM

I. THE EVE OF A NEW ERA IN HUMAN CIVILIZATION

In the chapters that have gone before we have reviewed many of the more important developments in human society which brought mankind out of the medieval age into modern times. Here were presented the outstanding developments from the sixteenth century through the eighteenth: explorations, settlements and colonization, the growth of commerce, the rise of capitalism, the growth of a strong middle class, the integration of the national state, the appearance of representative government, the revival of natural and experimental science, the revival of skepticism, the increasing toleration and freedom of thought, the emergence of an optimistic hope in human progress, and the rudimentary beginnings of the several social sciences that helped along the rising interest in social reform.

In spite of all these new achievements, however, the life of the majority of mankind in western Europe had changed but little since the Middle Ages. Society was still overwhelmingly agricultural. Most progressive developments had taken place in the towns or had mainly affected the town classes. If feudalism and serfdom had been undermined or wiped away in many rural areas, even here the technique of agriculture and the customs of everyday life had changed but slightly. The masses traveled little or not at all. The majority of men were ignorant of the most rudimentary scientific facts about nature and mankind. In spite of all-important beginnings, even the ablest scientists had little sound understanding of the universe, the physical traits of man, the underlying laws and processes of biology, or the character of human behavior. The supernatural was still generally accepted even by Rationalists, and this outlook dominated a good deal of science as well as the social perspective of most men. Education was superficial, was irrelevant in content, and was limited to the wealthier minority, the professional classes, and prospective clerics. The civilization of the middle of the eighteenth century showed many remarkable advances when compared to the state of affairs in the year 1000, but so far as material culture is concerned it was very rudimentary when viewed in relation to what prevails in the second quarter of the twentieth century.

II. THE ECONOMIC BACKWARDNESS OF SOCIETY IN 1750

The material culture of the West had not been revolutionized in its major outlines since the dawn of written history. Even the lake dwellers of Switzerland and northern Italy, who lived perhaps ten thousand years ago, possessed much the same industrial technique as that which existed in many parts of western Europe in the middle of the eighteenth century. Most types of domesticated animals, the chief fruits and cereals, and many aspects of manufacturing technique, particularly in the textile industry, had been widely known and utilized in the Neolithic Age. The two outstanding improvements in material culture since the Stone Age had been the art of utilizing metals and the development of the science and art of navigation.

Industry was still organized and conducted according to either the guild or the putting-out system. Industrial establishments were small and simple, and personal relationships between employer and employee existed in nearly every case. Life remained primarily agrarian. There were still very few manufacturing and commercial towns. The manufacturing industry was often carried on throughout the countryside in combination with agriculture, the finished product being taken to the distant towns for marketing.

Commercial institutions were of the most rudimentary sort. The largest bank in existence in the eighteenth century had less capital than is today possessed by the leading banks of second-class American cities. Only a start had been made in the development of modern instruments of credit, such as bank checks, drafts, and bills of exchange. The problems of modern capitalism and industrialism, as we now know them, had scarcely appeared on the economic horizon. All awaited the sweeping Industrial Revolution that was to install the "empire of machines" and create contemporary civilization.

As a result of these primitive economic conditions Western society was characterized by relative cultural stability and isolation. The rapid changes in the mode of living with which we are today familiar were unknown in eighteenth-century European society. Life went on much as it had in earlier generations. There were few changes in, or challenges to, the dominant social institutions. Custom, habit, and tradition reigned supreme, with only faint protests. Human existence was far more simple and provincial in its nature than the highly mechanized life of today. The outlook and interests of the average man were still circumscribed by the confines of the local neighborhood. The modern newspaper had not been fully enough developed or its circulation sufficiently extended to make it possible for the average citizen to familiarize himself from day to day with world-events as he can at the present time.

The nineteenth century may be described in one aspect as the period in which the group outlook of man was gradually being transformed from the provincialism and barbarism of the local community or neighborhood into the larger-scale but much more dangerous provincialism and savagery of the unrestrained national-state system.[1]

We shall now turn to a consideration of the remarkable series of achieve-

---

[1] See F. S. Chapin, *Historical Introduction to Social Economy*, Century, 1917, Chap. XVI; and A. W. Page and others, *Modern Communication*, Houghton Mifflin, 1932, Chap. I.

ments that have produced contemporary civilization: science, engineering, the rise of machinery, the growth of the factory system, the emergence of great industrial and commercial cities, the triumph of industrial capitalism, the evolution of imperialism, the striving for democratic government, the culmination of the national spirit, and the narrow escape of the whole resultant civilization from destruction in the World War.

It is the story of the transition from the quiet, placid, provincial life of rural neighborhoods, with the rudest of material equipment, to the day of telegraphs, telephones, newspapers, radios, airplanes, automobiles, concrete highways, subways, movies, and other characteristic manifestations of our present-day material life. It need not be alleged that we are always better or happier than mankind was in 1750, but we certainly live far differently from our ancestors of only two centuries ago—or even a century ago.[1]

In short, in the year 1750 the Western world was living in what may be accurately described as an archaic "folk culture." By 1900 most Western peoples had moved on into an urban and industrial world-civilization of a most progressive character in all of its mechanical aspects.

III. THE SCIENTIFIC BACKGROUND OF MODERN INDUSTRIALISM

1. CHANGES IN SCIENTIFIC PROBLEMS AND METHODS

Among the influences that have contributed to the development of our new world of material culture no others have been so potent and far-reaching as modern science and technology. This can perhaps best be demonstrated by a brief description of the bearing of some of the advances in scientific methods and research upon social and economic life in the past fifty or seventy-five years.

One of the most striking aspects of contemporary scientific progress is the growing breadth and complexity of modern science and the rapidity of the advances in the various fields.[2] In 1700 a versatile scientist like Leibnitz or Newton could be a master of the outstanding facts of all natural science. In 1875 an able scholar might still have under control the complete development of a single major branch of science such as physics or chemistry. Today it is difficult for one human mind to keep abreast of the discoveries made in a single subdivision of physics or chemistry.[3] This means that natural science must become ever more definitely a coöperative enterprise as between nations, departments of science, and those engaged in work in each special field of scientific endeavor.

Another important point to be noted is the great improvement in the organization and support of scientific research. Early modern natural science arose for the most part outside the universities in coöperative societies of enthusiastic amateurs of differing degrees of competence and training.[4] By the second half of the nineteenth century natural science had been accorded an established

[1] See Stuart Chase, "My Great-great Grandfather and I," in *The Nation*, September 1, 1926.
[2] See below, pp. 640 ff., 1035 ff.
[3] One of the most brilliant of contemporary mathematical physicists actually committed suicide a few years ago, in part because his subject was developing more rapidly than he could master it.
[4] See above, pp. 150 f.

place in the institutions of higher learning. Most of the eminent scientists of that period were university professors who had added to their research the burdens of teaching. In the last half-century extensive provision has been made for endowed foundations. These provide scientific research with ample facilities, leaving the research students free from all responsibility save that of penetrating more accurately and more extensively into the mysteries of nature.[1]

A third novel aspect of contemporary scientific progress has been the increasing rapidity with which discoveries in natural science have been taken up and exploited in the service of technology and industry. A century ago scientific discoveries, which have since proved of untold significance for technology and industry, were left relatively untouched for generations by those interested in the advance of material culture or economic enterprise. Today, the findings of the scientists are eagerly awaited and are immediately applied in the appropriate field of medicine, technology, or industry. Indeed, some of the best scientific research of our day is subsidized by great industrial concerns in laboratories that they support in connection with their factories, mines, or transportation lines. The linkage between science, technology, industry, and art has become ever more direct, more sensitive, and more effective.[2]

2. NATURAL SCIENCE AND THE INDUSTRIAL REVOLUTION

There is an intimate connection between the impact of science upon modern civilization and the remarkable technological changes that have produced the contemporary era of material culture. More and more, technological progress has become wrapped up with and dependent upon the antecedent developments of the physical sciences. James Hargreaves, a hundred and sixty years ago, without any esoteric knowledge of modern physics or chemistry, could invent the spinning jenny on the basis of suggestions derived from tipping over a spinning-wheel. Such things as the automobile, the airplane, the radio, and other contemporary mechanisms depend, however, very decisively upon antecedent discoveries in highly technical phases of physical science.

We often fail to realize that great practical industrial significance may ultimately reside in the most abstruse achievements of pure science. Willard Gibbs's [3] erudite paper on "The Equilibrium of Heterogeneous Substances" has been described by a great scientist as "one of the mightiest works of genius the human mind has ever produced." It was so abstract and difficult that even his fellow American physicists and chemists could hardly comprehend its significance at the time of its appearance (1867). In our day, however, it has been said of Gibbs's memoir that "never has an abstract investigation so influenced the fundamental basis of industry as the treatise of Gibbs on heterogeneous equilibrium."

A few illustrations of how science has directly aided in bringing about the

---

[1] See below, pp. 767 ff., on the socialization of invention.

[2] It is true, however, that in cases where scientific discoveries threaten to undermine extensive financial investments linked up with older and less efficient methods, strenuous efforts are sometimes made to suppress or delay the technical application of such discoveries. See below, pp. 427, 725, 820.

[3] See below, pp. 643, 645; and F. H. Garrison, "Josiah Willard Gibbs and His Relation to Modern Science," *Popular Science Monthly*, May-August, 1909.

technological wonders of today will serve to dissipate quickly an often expressed belief that there is little direct connection between research in pure science and the progress of mechanical methods and technology.

The fully developed steam engine depended for its perfection upon the study of gases by Boyle and Mariotte, research into the physics of heat by Black and Carnot, and the investigation of the conservation of energy by Joule, Mayer, and Helmholtz. Without the elaborate experimentation of Faraday on the physical basis of electricity and magnetism we should not have had the dynamo or the electric motor. Research into gases and electricity combined to make possible the internal-combustion engine and the use of modern projectiles. Modern chemistry lies behind the remarkable developments in the iron and steel industry, the petroleum industry, the modern chemical dye industry, the manufacture of explosives and the utilization of many by-products. Our modern methods of communication likewise have a very complicated scientific background. It was the researches of Oersted and Ampère that made possible the telegraph. Only extremely advanced work by Clerk Maxwell and Heinrich Hertz in mathematical and electrical physics enabled Marconi to launch the wireless telegraph. The radio depends not only upon research in electrical physics but also upon the invention of the thermionic valve, derived from a study of the release of electrons from heated bodies. We can well ponder the following cogent statement:

> The pure scientists are the advance guard of civilization. By their discoveries, they furnish to the engineer and industrial chemist and other applied scientists the raw material to be elaborated into manifold agencies for the amelioration of the conditions of mankind. Unless the work of the pure scientist is continued and pushed forward with ever increasing energy, the achievements of the industrial scientists will diminish and degenerate. Many practical problems now confronting mankind cannot be solved by the industrial scientist alone, but must await further fundamental discoveries and new scientific generalizations.[1]

We may now turn to a survey of the transition from the handicraft economy to what John Maurice Clark has aptly called the "empire of machines"[2]—either the greatest boon to humanity thus far achieved or a Frankenstein monster destined ultimately to confuse and destroy its baffled creator.

IV. THE GENERAL NATURE AND SIGNIFICANCE OF THE INDUSTRIAL REVOLUTION

1. THE NATURE OF THE INDUSTRIAL REVOLUTION

The term "Industrial Revolution" should not be confined to any single type of economic development in modern times. Rather, a sufficiently broad conception must be adopted so that the term will embrace all of the diverse economic changes that have produced contemporary material culture, including

---

[1] G. E. Hale, "Science and the Wealth of Nations," *Harper's Magazine*, January, 1928, p. 243. Those who desire to follow further this entrancing story of the impulse given to technology and industry by pure science will do well to read this striking article.

[2] *Yale Review*, October, 1922. See below, p. 766.

the alterations in social institutions that have followed those economic transformations.

For the sake of clarity, the Industrial Revolution may be divided into three main phases: (1) The revolutionary changes in the technical methods of manufacturing, transportation, and the communication of information; (2) the rise of the factory system, viewed as a new method for the organization of industry and the discipline of labor; and (3) the general economic, social, political, and cultural effects of the new technology and the factory system upon Western civilization.

2. FROM TOOL TO MACHINE

The technological changes that formed the basis for the mechanical aspects of the Industrial Revolution rested, as we have just seen, to no small degree upon the progress that had been made earlier in natural and applied science. In the broadest sense, the revolution in technique consisted, in the first place, in the transition from a handicraft to a machine basis. There probably has never been a more revolutionary transition in human society than was embodied in the abandonment of the tool economy and the entry into the machine age. Man now became able to harness nature and to adapt it to his service through the medium of iron slaves. Not only was a new machine technique provided for the manufacturing of textiles; cheaper and more effective methods for the manufacturing of metal products were also developed. An improved type of motive power was found to drive the new machinery and the novel mechanisms of transportation. The steam engine, the internal-combustion engine, and the electric motor supplanted the ox, the ass, and the horse. Electricity has been exploited in the interest of transportation facilities. It has also been made the basis for a marvelous revolution in the communication of information, so that facts can be disseminated over any distance known to this planet, with the practical elimination of the time handicap. Finally, this easily gathered and rapidly transmitted information is now broadcast widely through the medium of the daily newspaper as well as the radio.

3. THE RISE OF THE FACTORY SYSTEM

Equally novel was the appearance of the factory system as a new method of industrial organization and labor discipline. The old guild and putting-out systems had been based primarily upon personal relationships between the employer and employee in industry. Both of these older systems were compelled to give way to the factory system, once the machine technique had been introduced.

The term "factory system" is a little confusing, having been used in different senses by various writers.[1] It is here employed to mean the labor (personnel) organization of the modern machine-equipped plant. It has been used by excellent authorities to designate any considerable aggregation of workmen, even with simple handicraft tools, under a single management. Such units might

---

[1] See A. P. Usher, *Introduction to the Industrial History of England*, Houghton Mifflin, 1920, pp. 346 ff.; and Knight, Barnes, and Flügel, *Economic History of Europe*, Pt. II, Chap. IV.

GENERAL NATURE OF THE INDUSTRIAL REVOLUTION

better be called "central shops," to avoid confusing voluntary centralization for convenience with the intricate and compulsory centralization of the labor force so characteristic of the machine age.

In the precise sense in which it is used here, the factory system was a necessary consequence of the modern machine technique. The bulky and complicated machinery that came in with the Industrial Revolution could not be installed in households. The factory system immediately produced a radically different type of industrial discipline. Far larger numbers of individuals were brought within one establishment, the personal relations between the employer and the employee tended to disappear, and the worker became regimented in all of his activities. With the growth of the factory system and of impersonal business enterprise, labor tended to become a commodity, bought and sold in the open labor market according to competitive business ideals rather than in accord with considerations of humanity. The factory worker was essentially at the mercy of the employer class, except in so far as labor organizations have gradually provided a means for collective bargaining and the effective defense of the workers.

4. GENERAL MATERIAL AND CULTURAL RESULTS

The Industrial Revolution meant not merely a changed technique in manufacturing and transportation, and a new type of industrial organization. It also produced deep-seated and extensive economic, social, and cultural reactions.[1] The mechanical technique, carried on under the factory system, led to an enormous increase in the volume of commodities produced; stimulated commerce; called for a much larger application of capital; reduced labor to a condition of general dependence upon the capitalist class; produced larger and improved banking and credit institutions; created corporations, trusts, holding companies, and other forms of large-scale industrial organization; and stimulated vast business combinations tending towards monopoly.[2] Likewise, the new theory of business enterprise became triumphant. Immediate pecuniary profit became the chief motive of economic effort. The ledger circumscribed the economic perspective.

Social conditions were also profoundly altered.[3] Civilization changed from a rural to an urban basis. The modern industrial city, with all its varied social problems, came into being. Population increased rapidly, so that the number of people living in Europe in 1900 was, roughly, double that in 1800. Great international shifts of population took place as a result of emigration from backward regions to more highly developed industrial areas.

The intellectual results of the Industrial Revolution were notable.[4] The individual was enabled to receive information from all over the world, owing to the new methods of communication. He read books and journals to a far greater degree than ever before. Further, partly as a result of the gradual development of a class consciousness in the worker, came the achievement of free public education for the masses.

Along with these general intellectual and cultural gains of the Industrial

[1] *Cf.* Flick, *Modern World History,* Pt. IX.
[2] See below, Chaps. xv, xx-xxi.
[3] See below, Chap. xii.
[4] See below, pp. 438 ff.

Revolution a number of serious disadvantages have appeared. The nervous strains of the urban age have proved far greater than those of the earlier and simpler life of the country. Culture has tended to become standardized in terms of the machine technique. In enslaving the machine, man has himself been brought into bondage to the economic and social system that the machine technology created. The laborer has under capitalism become to a considerable degree merely a cog in a great industrial mechanism.

The political life of Europe and of the world was greatly modified by the Industrial Revolution. The middle class became all-powerful in the era of the industrialized state. This class provided political protection of its interests through constitutions and legislation based on the sanctity of property rights.[1] But its ascendancy was soon challenged by the rising proletariat, whose growing participation in politics has created what we have today of modern democracy.[2]

The development of the modern technique for transmitting information made it possible for citizens of each of the great national states to feel and think alike through stimulation by uniform information. In this way the emotions of nationalism and patriotism, which had been stimulated by the revolutions of the seventeenth and eighteenth centuries, were made relatively facile and enduring. Telegraphs, telephones, radios, newspapers, and rapid transit have now made even great states psychologically smaller and more compact than a New England township was in the days of John Adams. Finally, the greatly increased productivity brought about by the new machine technology and factory system led to the search for new colonies, raw materials, and markets in oversea areas. This movement we speak of in history as modern national imperialism.[3]

V. WHY THE INDUSTRIAL REVOLUTION CAME FIRST TO ENGLAND

Looking at the matter in broad historical perspective, it is safe to say that the Industrial Revolution emerged earliest in England, primarily because England had been more thoroughly affected than the Continent by the various results of the Commercial Revolution.

First, the medieval system of industry, as carried on in the small shops of the guild system, broke down earliest in England. In the textile industry at least it had practically disappeared there by the middle of the sixteenth century, having been supplanted by the domestic or putting-out system. The rigid "closed-shop" organization of the guild system was not well adapted to the introduction of a new type of industrial technique or to the large-scale application and discipline of labor. The coming of the putting-out system ended the ability of the guilds to maintain the earlier industrial technique and guild control of labor. This made it much easier to introduce mechanical processes and the factory system.

The disappearance of the guild system in England was but one phase of the earlier development of economic freedom and initiative in this region as compared to conditions existing in Continental countries. There was also a far

---

[1] See above, pp. 131 ff. [2] See below, pp. 427 ff., 482 ff. [3] See below, Chap. xv.

larger supply of surplus capital in England awaiting investment in the new industrial enterprise than was to be found elsewhere. This was primarily true because by the middle of the eighteenth century England had become the most important commercial state in Europe, having by this time thoroughly outdistanced the Dutch. It had created a great merchant marine and begun to control the markets of the world to an even greater degree. This mercantile expansion and the resulting accumulation of capital not only made possible extensive investment in industrial enterprises, but also stimulated the desire for this form of financial outlay. With the constantly expanding markets, there arose a need for less expensive commodities and for more extensive supplies of them.

Labor conditions also favored the development of machines in England. After 1700 the demand for staple textiles was so great as to create a shortage of skilled spinners and weavers. This created a real need for mechanical substitutes. No sooner, however, had machines appeared than changes in English agriculture provided plenty of unemployed men eager to operate them. The extensive inclosure and engrossing of land, which was carried on in England after about 1740, together with the Agricultural Revolution of the eighteenth century, ousted great numbers of the peasants from their petty and insecure holdings. This created an army of unemployed, who furnished reservoirs of labor for the new factories.[1] Again, England was amply supplied with water power, with large reserves of coal, and with some iron ore. These were all indispensable prerequisites to the later development of the textile and the iron and steel industries. Even atmospheric conditions in England were well adapted to the processes of the new era, the damp climate being very favorable to the processes of the textile industry.

Further, the leading English manufactures of 1750 were, in the main, staple products that were easily adapted to the new mechanical processes of manufacturing. Particularly was this true of English textiles, which had become specialized on a fairly rough type of cloth made partly of cotton, and readily produced by mechanical methods. This was in marked contrast to the finer goods made in France. The concentration of the French on the latter has helped to delay even in our day the complete transition of French manufacturing to a mechanical basis.[2]

English scientific activity was peculiarly well adapted, by its interests and achievements, to the needs of applied science, technology, and industrial invention. While not ignoring the remarkable earlier English contributions to pure science, historians of science have long pointed out that English scientific activity in the eighteenth century showed a decidedly practical bent, when compared with the concentration upon pure or abstract science on the Continent. An excellent illustration of this is to be seen in the experiments on latent heat, which were carried on by Joseph Black and were the basis of the important achievements of James Watt in devising the earliest true steam engine.

The political, legal, and military situation in England was likewise relatively favorable to the coming of the mechanical age. It achieved representative gov-

---

[1] See above, pp. 48 ff; and Witt Bowden, *Industrial Society in England Towards the End of the Eighteenth Century,* Macmillan, 1925, pp. 218 ff.
[2] See below, pp. 325 ff.

ernment and parliamentary supremacy at least a hundred years earlier than France.[1] The merchant classes were thus enabled to influence political policy and to turn both domestic institutions and international relations to the service of commerce. Arbitrary royal interference with economic activities and personal property rights were in large part terminated by the Revolution of 1688-89. Excessive and unjust taxation, contrary to the wishes of the middle class, was very greatly reduced. Laws were passed guaranteeing the security of property and the freedom and sanctity of contract. Some degree of freedom in industrial and commercial action had already been secured when the first mechanical inventions appeared. The average English investor was usually free to make the best possible use of his economic sagacity without fear of political interference.

Even international diplomatic policy in England had long been colored by economic and commercial considerations. One of the reasons for the Revolution of 1688-89 was that James II shaped English foreign policy in the interest of the advancement of Catholicism, instead of adapting it to the desires of the British commercial groups. In the first half of the eighteenth century, however, Walpole guided English foreign relations so far as he could in behalf of the English investors and merchants, and his precedent was widely followed thereafter.[2]

Finally, the general situation in political, diplomatic, and military affairs that prevailed in Europe from 1793 to 1815 was as favorable to industrial development in England as it was fatal to economic expansion on the Continent. The revolutionary and Napoleonic wars, which ravaged the continent of Europe and laid waste wide areas, did not reach English soil, in spite of the most vigorous efforts of Napoleon. At the same time, the military situation in Europe greatly stimulated British industry by producing new and extensive markets for British manufactured products in both the textile and iron industries. Great Britain sold vast quantities of clothing and munitions of war to the nations on the Continent that were engaged in war for most of a generation.

This latter advantage was one of the most important in hastening the development of the Industrial Revolution in England. It was in part because of his recognition of this favorable reaction of the European wars upon English industry that Napoleon vainly attempted to ruin England economically through his Continental System, designed to keep English products from the Continental European markets. It was this profitable English industrial activity which, more than anything else, made it possible for England to back the anti-Napoleonic coalitions and to push the wars against Napoleon to a successful conclusion. There is much truth in the remark of Professor Shotwell that "the wars against Napoleon were not won at Leipzig or Waterloo, but rather in the cotton factories of Manchester and the iron mills of Birmingham."

It is, of course, true that the work of Henri Sée and certain other Continental economic historians has shown that the priority of England in launching the Industrial Revolution was not so unique and absolute as some of the earlier English economic historians would have had us imagine. France and

---

[1] See above, pp. 98 ff.
[2] See *Cambridge Modern History,* Vol. VI, Chap. VI; Mottram, *History of Financial Speculation,* pp. 100 ff.; and Brisco, *The Economic Policy of Robert Walpole.*

Belgium were not so backward in industrial evolution in 1760 as we once believed them to be.[1] There was considerable concentration of capital in industrial enterprise and the preliminary steps were being taken in creating mechanical production and factory operations. Nevertheless, it can safely be held that the prevailing conception that the English did the pioneer work in this great industrial transformation remains substantially correct, requiring only occasional qualification in details.[2]

VI. THE NEW TEXTILE MACHINERY AND PROCESSES

First to be put on a thoroughgoing mechanical foundation in England was the textile industry, particularly the cotton branch. The manufacture of cotton goods in England goes back as far as the sixteenth century, having been introduced probably by Flemish immigrants. Gradually it expanded and was put upon a semi-capitalistic basis. Many spinners and weavers became more thoroughly specialized in the cotton industry and devoted their entire attention to this type of manufacturing. In many instances, there seems to have been some introduction of the central shop system in cotton manufacturing before 1760. Therefore the introduction of mechanical methods of spinning and weaving cotton cloth was simply the culmination of important developments in that industry running over a century or more. These new mechanical methods were part of a general continuous development and improvement in the technique and organization of cotton manufacturing. As Mr. G. W. Daniels puts it:

A continuous development can be traced in all directions. Even the inventions of the jenny and the water-frame, when viewed in their right relations, are seen as the outcome of efforts extending over more than thirty years preceding their appearance, and come as something expected, rather than as something sudden and unique.[3]

At the opening of the eighteenth century the cotton fiber was still being prepared for spinning by a tedious hand process of removing the seeds and tearing, sorting, and picking over the fiber. The spinning was done by the crude spinning-wheel, a medieval invention that was only a slight improvement over the old hand spindle, which comes down from the Stone Age.[4] The hand spindle was, in fact, still widely used in Europe in 1700 and is to be found in certain backward parts of southern and eastern Europe even today.

The weaving was done on the hand loom, which had also been invented thousands of years earlier in the Neolithic Age. The yarn that had been spun on the spinning-wheel was arranged in parallel lines on the loom. Those which ran lengthwise on the loom were known as the warp. The cross threads, the weft or woof, were then worked in as follows: Every other thread in the warp

---

[1] *Cf.* Sée, *Economic and Social Conditions in France during the Eighteenth Century,* Chap. VIII; and Henri Hauser, "The Characteristic Features of French Economic History from the Middle of the Sixteenth to the Middle of the Eighteenth Centuries," *Economic History Review,* October, 1933.
[2] An excellent account of the Industrial Revolution in England, including its effects upon English civilization, is contained in G. H. Perris, *Industrial History of Modern England,* Holt, 1914. For the course of industrial developments in Scotland, see Henry Hamilton, *The Industrial Revolution in Scotland,* Oxford Press, 1931.   [3] Daniels, *The Early English Cotton Industry,* p. 145.
[4] See above, Vol. I, pp. 22-23.

was fastened to a crossbar. Hence half the warp could be raised and drawn back at once and the shuttle containing the woof "fed" through. Then the other half of the warp threads was raised and drawn in the opposite direction and the shuttle returned. The woof had also to be crowded close together in order to give a solid compact cloth. This was a very slow and unsatisfactory process and required a large amount of hand labor to produce any considerable quantity of cloth.

After the cloth had been woven, it was finished and dyed by another set of workers. Only in the dyeing process had any important advances been made for centuries, and the improvements in this field were due primarily to the new sources of vegetable dyes that had been discovered in the oversea areas during the period of European expansion. Broadly speaking, it is safe to say that the textile industry at the opening of the eighteenth century was not profoundly different from that which had been in operation for thousands of years.

The first important break with traditional methods of cloth manufacture appeared in the invention of the so-called flying shuttle by John Kay, a Lancashire weaver, in 1738. This was an automatic spring-propelled shuttle, which carried the woof back and forth through the warp with no other attention than was needed to release it for each jump across the loom. Kay's invention decreased to a marked degree the amount of man power necessary in the weaving industry. Moreover, by 1730 the weavers were already able to work somewhat more rapidly than the spinners, and often had to wait for an adequate supply of yarn. Kay's invention therefore put the weavers still further ahead of the spinners and created an even greater need for improved spinning methods.

Ambitious inventors were not wanting in the efforts of a generation to provide this all-essential new spinning machinery. Indeed, Wyatt and Paul were attempting to devise a satisfactory spinning machine about the very time that Kay perfected his flying shuttle. Though they were unable to work out a machine efficient enough to revolutionize the spinning industry, their labors unquestionably prepared the ground for the notable advances that began with the invention of the spinning jenny.

The first fairly successful automatic spinning machine was this spinning jenny, invented by James Hargreaves about 1764. The story goes that Hargreaves noticed that a spinning-wheel continued to revolve after it had been tipped over, the wheel then turning in a horizontal plane. This led him to perceive that it would be possible to turn a number of spindles with a belt propelled by a single wheel. Accordingly he devised a machine that in its first important model turned eight spindles, thus increasing approximately eightfold the efficiency of the old spinning-wheel. Before his death, Hargreaves had increased the number of spindles that might thus be turned from eight to eighty. Hargreaves' machine was light and easy-running, but it had one serious defect, namely, that the yarn which was thus spun was coarse and loose and required a mixture of flax with the cotton.

The next important addition to the technique of mechanical spinning was embodied in the water frame of Richard Arkwright. It appears that little credit should be assigned to Arkwright for this invention, the original model having been made by a clock-maker named Kay, at the suggestion and under the supervision of a mechanic by the name of Highs.[1] Arkwright appropriated this invention, financed it, and made it a practical success about 1769. It had two sets of revolving rolls, the second set moving more rapidly than the first, thus pulling out the fiber and stretching it before it was wound in the yarn. This made a much tighter or harder yarn than could be produced by the spinning jenny, but still rather coarse. The term "water frame" was derived from the fact that it was so heavy and cumbersome a machine that it could not be turned by hand, as had been the case with the first spinning jenny, but required water power to run it. Another phase of the improvement embodied in the water frame was its ability to make yarn out of pure cotton fiber, instead of requiring the mixture of flax that was essential to the yarn made by the spinning jenny.

Yet the water frame was not the machine that was to create the future of the cotton industry. What was needed was a light and efficient machine that would spin fine, hard, and smooth yarn. This all-important innovation was the work of Samuel Crompton, who produced his famous spinning mule in 1779. It was essentially a combination of many of the better features of the spinning jenny and the water frame. The term "mule" was descriptive of its hybrid origin. Not only was Crompton's mule easier to operate than the water frame, but it also provided, for the first time, the possibility of making by mechanical processes a type of yarn that was both hard and fine. It devised a duplex process of pulling and twisting the fiber before it was wound on the spindles as yarn. With certain subsequent modifications, Crompton's mule has remained one of the most significant and widely used of the mechanical spinning machines from his day to our own.

By 1780 these innovations of Hargreaves, Arkwright, and Crompton had met the all-essential need for more effective methods of spinning yarn and now put the spinners further ahead of the weavers than the latter had been in advance of the spinners in 1740.

No one of the real inventors was adequately rewarded for his inventions. Hargreaves died leaving only a small estate (£7,000); Crompton did not patent his mule, and greedy and unscrupulous manufacturers took it over without giving him decent remuneration or royalties. It was not until 1812 that Parliament, on proof of obvious privation, finally made him a grant of some £5,000. Arkwright became a very wealthy man because of his work as a leading promoter in the new cotton industry. As we shall see later,[2] he was the most important of the early capitalists who established the factory system on the foundation of these technological improvements in the textile industry. Those who really supplied the inventive genius lying behind his water frame received practically nothing.

In order to bring weaving up to the level of efficiency that had been attained by the spinners, it was necessary to provide a practical mechanical loom. Edmund Cartwright, a mathematically inclined English clergyman of Kent, devised a power loom as early as the spring of 1785, but did not complete his

---

[1] *Cf.* P. J. Mantoux, *The Industrial Revolution in the Eighteenth Century*, Harcourt, Brace, 1928, pp. 234 ff.   [2] See below, p. 287.

machine until 1787. As a matter of fact, his great contribution was to furnish the practical suggestions upon which improved and thoroughly practical power looms could be constructed. The chief defect of the Cartwright loom was its clumsiness and the fact that it did not provide for an adequate dressing of the warp. These defects were largely eliminated through the ingenuity of Radcliffe and Horrocks in the first decade of the nineteenth century. They were unable, however, to finance their invention. The first extensive marketing of the improved loom was carried out by Sharp and Roberts, who successfully distributed the Horrocks loom as early as 1822.

This date is of very great significance in the textile industry, because it marked the period in which hand weaving was decisively supplanted by mechanical processes—with great suffering on the part of the displaced hand weavers.[1] Improvements in the mechanical loom have, of course, continued down to our own day, the most notable early advance being the Kenworthy and Bullough loom, which was brought out in 1841. The successful provision of power-weaving machinery put the weavers on a parity with spinners and put the textile industry on a thoroughgoing and successful mechanical basis.

An important type of cloth made during this early stage of the Industrial Revolution was calico, which was disposed of particularly in the warm climates.[2] At first, its manufacture was retarded because of the slow process of stamping the colors by hand blocks. In the latter part of the eighteenth century a method of printing calico by means of designs cut upon the surface of a revolving cylinder was introduced. This not only stimulated the calico industry, but also furnished the suggestions that later grew into the rotary printing press.

It should be borne in mind, however, that the new spinning and weaving machinery could not have been so widely and rapidly exploited had it not been for a very important invention on this side of the Atlantic, namely, the cotton gin, which was first made a success by Eli Whitney in 1792.[3] Down to this time, the only method known for separating the cotton seed from the fiber was picking it over by hand. This was a very slow and laborious process, which rendered the cleaned fiber too expensive ever to have made the cotton industry a paying outlet for extensive investment. Whitney invented a machine in which a cylinder studded with spikes rotated through a bed piece with spikes set in rows meshing with those on the cylinder. By feeding the fiber into this revolving cylinder, it was possible by mechanical methods to separate the seeds and to produce relatively cheap cotton fiber. The fiber was pulled through and the seeds left behind. It was not until nearly a century after Whitney's time that the cotton-growers in the South learned that those cotton seeds possessed great commercial value in the making of various types of cattle food and oil products. Commercial chemistry has since still further increased their value and uses.[4]

The cotton gin worked a revolution, not merely in the cotton manufacturing

---

[1] Well described in George Eliot's *Silas Marner,* and in Hauptmann's drama *The Weavers.*

[2] See P. J. Thomas, "The Beginnings of Calico-Printing in England," *English Historical Review,* April, 1924, pp. 206-16.

[3] See H. U. Faulkner, *American Economic History,* Harper, rev. ed., 1931, pp. 221 ff.; and George Iles, *Leading American Inventors,* Holt, 1912, pp. 75 ff. [4] See below, pp. 730-31.

THE NEW TEXTILE MACHINERY AND PROCESSES 277

industry, but also in the cotton-growing industry. In 1791 the United States exported but 200,000 pounds of cotton; by 1800 it was exporting 2,000,000 pounds, and the volume grew amazingly. By 1860 the average annual exportation of cotton had risen to 1,383,000,000 pounds. It was this which led the South to specialize in the cotton branch of the agricultural industry and did more than anything else to extend Negro slavery.

The effect of the new textile inventions upon the growth of Britain's cotton industry is well illustrated by the following figures of the volume of manufactured cotton goods exported from England at representative periods from 1710 to 1831:

Year	Export Value of Cotton Manufactures in Thousands of Pounds Sterling
1710	5
1751	45
1780	355
1790	1,662
1800	5,406
1831	17,200

In 1835 England produced 63 per cent of all the cotton cloth manufactured in the world.

The progress of the textile industry was, of course, bound up with the possibility of mechanizing the clothing industry. Unless clothing could be made up readily by machine methods the quantity of machine-made cloth that could be used was inevitably limited. The crucial invention here was made by an American, and his contribution is eminently worthy to rank with that of Eli Whitney. This was the sewing machine, invented by Elias Howe (1819-67), a Massachusetts machinist.[1] Howe worked on his device for several years and finally patented it in 1846. Its subsequent improvements lay at the basis not only of the important and flourishing clothing trades but also of the modern methods of making boots and shoes.[2]

VII. THE TECHNOLOGICAL REVOLUTION IN THE IRON AND COAL INDUSTRIES

The new textile machinery and the steam engine,[3] which was improved so that it might furnish the motive power for this machinery, required a far greater supply of iron and steel products, and also made it necessary that these should be produced at a cheaper cost than ever before.

At the opening of the eighteenth century the methods of making iron and steel remained very much the same that they had been for thousands of years. Especially was this true of the methods of manufacturing iron. The ore was smelted chiefly with charcoal. The furnaces were too small and the air-blast

---

[1] See Iles, *op. cit.*, pp. 338 ff.   [3] See below, pp. 299 ff.
[2] See below, pp. 359, 367.

machinery too crude to make large castings or even to produce small ones cheaply and in large quantities. In spite of the small output of iron, the use of charcoal had led to the gradual deforestation of those countries which had developed the iron industry to any large extent.

The first notable attempt to introduce coal as a fuel for smelting iron ore seems to have been associated with the work of an English blacksmith named Dud Dudley, following 1619.[1] While Dudley was certainly headed in the right direction, his methods were so crude as to render his efforts largely futile. Such success as he seemed likely to achieve was obstructed through the jealousy of neighboring blacksmiths, who feared lest his innovations might revolutionize their trade. It was not until after 1710 that the employment of coal as the main fuel in the smelting of iron ore was successfully established.[2]

At this time, the achievement was carried through by an English ironmaster named Abraham Darby, who utilized coke as fuel in his furnaces at Coalbrookdale. Coke, or coal from which the coal gas and other impurities have been burned out in closed furnaces, has since been found more satisfactory as a fuel in the smelting of iron ore than coal in its native form. Coke will burn much more rapidly and produce a greater amount of heat than coal, while the flame possesses fewer impurities likely to mix with the molten iron and thus lower its quality.

Another important contribution to the iron-making process came about 1760, when John Smeaton developed the air-blast furnace.[3] This was an improvement upon the old blacksmith's forge and bellows in that it provided a rotary fan to force air on the burning coal and coke and produced a very hot fire. This device was soon notably improved through Watt's achievements with the steam engine, the latter then being used to drive the rotary fan of the blower.

It was upon the basis of these innovations by Darby and Smeaton that Peter Onions and Henry Cort were able to work out independently in the years 1783-84 their new process for the manufacturing of malleable iron. The new textile machinery and engines had to be built of better stuff than the cast iron so far produced, which was relatively weak, brittle, and full of impurities. Onions and Cort hit upon a process of making malleable or pure wrought iron relatively cheaply and in large quantities. They started with the pig iron that is obtained by smelting crude iron ore. Their furnaces were arranged in such a way as to keep the pig iron out of contact with the fuel, thus preventing it from absorbing the impurities and gases arising from the burning coke. A hot flame was played over the molten pig iron, which was stirred vigorously, thus burning out those impurities which were not absorbed by the chemical lining of the furnace. This left a high-grade product—a tough metal known as wrought iron. It was from this stirring or "puddling" of the molten iron that the process came to be known as the puddling process.[4]

The methods of Onions and Cort were notably improved by Joseph Hall

[1] *Cf.* Mantoux, *op. cit.,* pp. 292 ff.; and J. U. Nef, *The Rise of the British Coal Industry,* Routledge, 1932, 2 vols.
[2] *Cf.* E. R. Turner, "The English Coal Industry in the Seventeenth and Eighteenth Centuries," *American Historical Review,* October, 1921.
[3] For a clear introductory treatment of the blowing apparatus and the development of blast furnaces, with ample illustrations, see Usher, *Industrial History of England,* pp. 317 ff.
[4] *Cf. Ibid.,* pp. 330-31.

about 1830 and by Henry Bessemer two decades later. Bessemer generated an exceedingly hot flame by the simple method of introducing a blast of air into the molten iron, the oxygen in the air igniting, and burning out most of the impurities in the iron. With this simple development of greater heat, the puddling or stirring became unnecessary. One of the most important contributions to cheaper methods of making iron was the hot-blast device introduced by James Beaumont Neilson, a Scotch inventor, in 1828. Though his suggestion was contemptuously rejected by the ironmasters for some time, it reduced the cost of making iron to about one-third of what it had been before.

An important allied improvement in the iron industry was also carried on by Cort in conjunction with Purnell, when they developed the rolling mill for eliminating impurities from molten iron and for cutting and shaping iron products.[1] Even sheet iron was rare and expensive when produced by the old methods of hand-hammering. This could never have produced the type of steam boiler plate, iron bars, railroad rails, and the like familiar to us today. The principle involved in rolling mills is to run the hot iron (and steel also after the improvement of steel production) through a series of notched and grooved rollers that produce any shape desired. The hot iron takes on the shape of the space between the rollers. This often overlooked contribution of Cort and Purnell was really one of the major steps in the evolution of our modern metal industry.

The organization of the early iron industry, based on the new inventions, was mainly the work of John Wilkinson, greatest of early ironmasters. He created the factory system in this line of work and was the first to devise sufficiently precise methods to make practicable the extensive manufacture of iron machinery. Next to Wilkinson, probably the most important of the early ironmasters was John Roebuck, who built the great Carron works in Scotland following 1760. But Roebuck's very ambition and versatility proved his undoing and he ultimately failed in business.

Iron and steel production were greatly aided by improvements in allied industries, such as coal-mining and the extraction of ore. Watt's steam engine[2] was much more efficient than the older atmosphere engine for pumping water from the coal mines. Sir Humphry Davy's invention of the safety lamp in 1815 lessened the frequency of those deadly gas explosions, which were set off in mines by open torches or candles. It provided for an inclosed lamp in which the open flame was no longer brought directly into contact with the gases in the mines. There is some justice in the remark of one writer that Davy's invention of the safety lamp was a much more important event in history than the battle of Waterloo, which took place the same year.

Since Davy's time coal-mining has been put on a mechanical foundation to such a degree that the modern mine is little less than a great factory with many of its technical devices operating underground. With its electric elevators, its elaborate network of underground car tracks and coal trains operated by electricity, its series of great steel beams and girders supporting the roof of the mine, its elaborate system of electrical illumination, its power drills and high explosives, the modern coal mine is one of the most remarkable examples

[1] See Usher, *op. cit.*, pp. 331-32.   [2] See below, pp. 300 ff.

of the triumph of the mechanical technique in the contemporary age. This revolution in technique is, of course, not limited to work that goes on beneath the ground, but applies to all processes of preparing coal for consumption. In particular should be mentioned the automatic system of coal pickers, sizers, and graders and the elaborate mechanical devices, such as steam and electric cranes for the loading and unloading of coal trains and boats.

No less remarkable have been the improvements in extracting iron ore.[1] In the eighteenth century the tools used were the hand pick and the shovel. At the present time, very much the same mechanical improvements and devices have been introduced in the extraction of ore that exist in the mining of coal. The ore is separated from its matrix by the use of steam drills and high explosives. It is then scooped up and loaded, not by hand shovels, but by steam shovels of the type that are utilized in railroad and canal construction. One shovel can scoop up as high as 6,000 tons of ore in a day. These steam shovels load the ore on ore cars, which are usually taken to the docks where ore steamers are ready. Even in the matter of unloading the cars of ore, the new mechanical technique has been of the utmost service in providing an elaborate series of hoists, traveling cranes, and many other ingenious mechanical devices competent to handle heavy products of this sort. A whole car of iron ore is picked up as though it were a feather, dumped into an ore steamer, and set back upon the tracks. As many as 12,000 tons of ore are loaded in an hour, where once it took hand shovelers days to load a smaller ship. The process is reversed with equal dispatch at the other end in such places as Conneaut Harbor, Ohio, where ore steamers are mechanically unloaded by great traveling cranes and the ore placed on trains bound for steel-manufacturing centers.

VIII. THE NEW STEEL INDUSTRY

At the close of the eighteenth century, steel was still produced by the slow, crude, and expensive process of baking the impurities out of the molten iron in sand boxes. The new machinery required not only the purer and cheaper iron provided by Cort's process, but also a considerable amount of steel for the parts subjected to the greatest wear or strain. In the first half of the nineteenth century many attempts were made to devise better methods of manufacturing steel. The first successful achievement was that of a Kentucky blacksmith by the name of William Kelly, who began his experiments about 1846.[2] Kelly's process was almost identical with that of the Englishman Bessemer a decade later, and consisted of introducing into molten iron a jet of cold air. This air, instead of cooling the molten iron, generated an even greater heat, because of the introduction of oxygen and the resulting combustion and burning out of impurities.

While it is well established that Kelly was the pioneer inventor in modern scientific steel-making, his methods were not given wide publicity and had relatively little significance in the history of the industry. Sir Henry Bessemer worked out the same process independently in England. Having already made a fortune by his numerous inventions, in the 1840's he attempted to improve

[1] See below, p. 756.   [2] See below, p. 359.

Cort's method of manufacturing malleable iron. A projectile that he invented in the early fifties required a high muzzle velocity and hence a heavy charge of powder in the cannon that fired it. In this way his attention was drawn to the scarcity and the high cost of good steel. He discovered by accident, because of a hole in one of his furnaces that had been stopped with a piece of iron, that the entry of air into the molten metal sets up a process of "internal combustion" which burns out the impurities. This is the principle of what we know as the Bessemer converter. Steel is pure (malleable) iron with the right proportion of carbon, manganese, and a few other substances added.

It was soon discovered that the Bessemer converter would not work well with ores containing considerable phosphorus, which refuses to be burned out by oxygen.[1] It was also inadequate for the finer grades of steel because of the impossibility of taking samples of molten metal during the process of manufacture. This is desirable in order to insure the complete elimination of impurities and to adjust exactly the amount of carbon, manganese, or other elements to be added. The great advantage of the Bessemer system lies in the cheapness of its product. It immediately reduced the price of good ordinary steel by more than 75 per cent.

On account of the above-mentioned defects of the Bessemer process in manufacturing an excellent grade of steel, a new method was devised by Karl W. Siemens in England about 1858 and first effectively put into practice by the firm of Martin in France in 1864. Before the close of the sixties it had proved a practical success for producing high-grade steel in relatively large quantities.

This Siemens-Martin or open-hearth process may be described briefly as follows: The iron ore is first melted in the blast furnace, and the molten iron is drawn off into small transverse receptacles known as pigs. Here it is allowed to harden, and the pigs are removed in blocks. They constitute the pig iron that is remelted in the process of making steel by the open-hearth method, as well as in making malleable iron. The pig iron is next mixed with scrap iron, put in the open-hearth furnace, and remelted. An air blast is introduced, which burns out the impurities, but the process is much less rapid than with the Bessemer process. It usually takes about four hours to prepare steel from the molten iron in the open-hearth furnace as compared with forty minutes in the Bessemer process.

The task involved is to burn out all of the impurities and then, after the impurities have been eliminated, to add exactly the right amount of carbon, manganese, and other ingredients to make the steel sufficiently tough and hard. The phosphorus and the silicon are burned out in the first and second hours, whereas the manganese and carbon are burned out primarily in the third and fourth hours.[2] Finally, when the impurities are gone the desired amounts of carbon and manganese are introduced, and then the product, as high-grade steel, is drawn off from the bottom of the furnace instead of being poured out at the top of the converter, as in the Bessemer process.

---

[1] Steel can be produced from phosphoric ore by the Bessemer process, but the quality is poor.
[2] The original carbon content of the molten pig iron has to be burned out so that the exact proportions can then be added artificially. To rely on the natural carbon content would be dangerous guesswork, though it has been overcome in part in the Krupp process.

The amount of carbon contained in steel varies from a mere trace to about 2 per cent, but most steel has a carbon content of under 1 per cent. If the carbon content is low, then the steel is very tough, but also soft, while a high carbon content makes the steel extremely hard, but also brittle.

While the open-hearth method provided for the possibility of making a higher grade of steel than the Bessemer process, yet it had one notable defect—the greater expense and the longer time element involved. On this account many of the more progressive steel-manufacturing concerns have introduced what is known as the duplex process, which is a combination of the Bessemer and the open-hearth processes. In this duplex process, the molten iron is conveyed directly from the blast furnace to a Bessemer converter. After the Bessemer process has been applied the product is poured into the open-hearth furnace and the further purification of the molten iron is here carried out. The advantage of the duplex process is that it greatly reduces the time required in the ordinary open-hearth process and at the same time gives a far better grade of steel than is possible with the Bessemer process if used alone.

One difficulty that was met in the earlier utilization of both the Bessemer and the Siemens-Martin processes grew out of the problem of using iron ore with a high content of phosphorus. For a time it was found impossible to eliminate the phosphorus so that the resulting steel product would be satisfactory. The solution of the problem was worked out by two English scientists and engineers, P. C. Gilchrist and Sidney Thomas. They developed in 1877-78 what is known as the basic limestone lining, which during the process of purification in the furnace absorbs the phosphorus from the molten iron. This basic limestone lining was first applied to the Bessemer retort, but soon came to be utilized in the open-hearth furnace. If the molten iron has a low percentage of phosphorus, the open-hearth furnace utilizes what is known as acid lining, instead of the limestone. The Thomas-Gilchrist invention, more than anything else, made possible the all-important development of the German steel industry, because of the high phosphoric content of the Lorraine iron beds.

The famous Krupp process of making steel is a very ingenious and highly scientific combination of the best modern methods. In this process, molten iron oxide is stirred rapidly into molten pig iron, at a temperature only a little above the melting-point of the metal. The phosphorus and silicon are thereby removed without taking out much of the carbon, which oxidizes only slowly. The result is the production of good steel in large quantities at moderate cost, coupled with an unusually high degree of uniformity. The better types of commercial steel are today made almost entirely by the Siemens-Martin or open-hearth and the Krupp processes, though the Bessemer process is still widely utilized for making railroad rails and cheap grades of steel. At present a far larger quantity of steel is made by the open-hearth method than by the Bessemer process. The better types of tool steel, case-hardened steel, crucible steel, and so on, are made by complicated processes that need not be described at this place because they involve no fundamentally different scientific principles and because the quality of these types of steel by far surpasses that of the products of the Bessemer and open-hearth processes. One of the recent methods of making unusually high-grade steel in relatively large quantities is provided by the electric furnace,[1] which has been widely utilized in Sweden. It need not be supposed that we have reached anything like perfection in the methods of making steel or that further revolutionary improvements are out of the question.[2]

Steel is today widely used in other ways than in the making of machinery, most notably in building operations, from great bridges and skyscrapers to ordinary dwellings and even articles of furniture. Concrete, reënforced by steel, has become one of the most common of building materials.[3] This has greatly increased the demand for steel as the framework of such concrete construction, whether in bridges or in office and factory buildings. Paralleling this increased use of steel as building material, the progress of engineering has made possible the rigorous testing of materials and the assurance of adequate strength in structural steel work without introducing any more than the necessary amount of steel. In this way, safety and economy are harmonized. No phase of modern engineering has been more significant in the building industry than that rather modest department of engineering endeavor known as the testing of materials.

An important development in the iron and steel industry, as well as in the history of all types of machinery, was the greater facility and precision attained in the manufacture of machines and machine parts. Considerable exactness was necessary to make even an early Watt engine. The man who first attained sufficient precision in ironwork to make this possible was the early ironmaster John Wilkinson. The standardization of parts was also necessary before machines could be made in large numbers at low cost, or repairs made with economy and expedition. Eli Whitney is usually given credit for this development, having introduced standardization in the manufacture of muskets. The machine-tool industry has also been another outstanding phase of the progress of mechanical invention. As machines have become more complicated there is ever greater need for mechanical precision of a refined character.

IX. ARTIFICIAL ILLUMINATION IN MODERN MATERIAL CULTURE

To an almost unbelievable degree modern industrial society is dependent upon cheap and efficient methods of producing artificial light. The modern factory is usually so constructed as to require a wide use of artificial light, particularly on dark days, in the early morning, and in the late afternoon hours. The same situation obtains in the great business blocks, subways, tunnels, and above all in the mines. Likewise, life in the modern city would be far more unsafe at night without elaborate provision for artificial lighting. The inconvenience and dangers that are experienced in the modern city by a temporary breakdown in the gas or electric-lighting systems are but a slight measure of the situation that would exist if we were to be deprived of all artificial illumination.

[1] *Cf.* Edward Cressy, *Discoveries and Inventions of the Twentieth Century,* 3d ed. rev., Dutton, 1930, Chap. IX.
[2] For a concise summary of contemporary mass-production methods of steel manufacture through the use of automatic machinery, see below, pp. 756-62.
[3] See H. E. Howe, *The New Stone Age,* Century, 1921.

Primitive man apparently relied chiefly upon the torch. Very early, however, we find the use of some form of tallow candle or of a dish of oil as a lamp. The candle and the oil lamp remained almost the sole methods of artificial lighting, even with the better classes, until well along in the nineteenth century. The chief type of oil used in the modern lamp down to about the middle of the nineteenth century was sperm or whale oil. This was produced in large quantities after the discovery of new fields for whaling during the expansion of Europe. About the time of the American Civil War, kerosene began to be introduced on a wide scale as the chief illuminant used in lamps, and the kerosene lamp is still very generally used by agricultural populations throughout the Western world. Improved oil lamps, generating gas, have today made kerosene lighting almost as efficient for domestic uses as electricity or gas.

The first revolutionary changes in lighting appeared with the development of gaslight. This was dependent primarily on notable advances in chemistry in the seventeenth and eighteenth centuries. Successful experiments with gaslight were conducted after 1800. In this progress the most notable names are those of R. W. von Bunsen and C. A. von Welsbach. Gaslighting did not become popular until about the middle of the nineteenth century, and its use was at that time chiefly limited to cities.

Nothing ever devised produces a better light, as such, than gas, but it has many incidental drawbacks, such as the slightly irritating odor and various dangers associated with its use, including possible asphyxiation. Most of the good qualities of gaslight have been combined with unique cleanliness, safety, and ease of operation in the electric light, which has been introduced since the middle of the last century. The electric arc light was worked out in theory by Sir Humphry Davy between 1801 and 1821. The inclosed arc light was devised by L. B. Marks, an American, in 1894. The incandescent electric light grew out of the researches of Grove (1840) in England and Starr (1845), Sawyer, Maxim, and Farmer (1878) in the United States. It was made a commercial success by Thomas A. Edison following his famous electric demonstration in 1879. It must be understood, of course, that the first types of both lamps were crude and imperfect. Even at the present time we are witnessing significant technical improvements in every form of electric lighting. The best electric lights of today are still very wasteful of electric current.

It would be hard to overestimate the economic, social, and intellectual significance of these improved modern lights. Their development has made possible many phases of modern industrial life and social concentration. Production, both manufacturing and agricultural, has been enormously increased by making it possible for people to work under conditions and during hours that would otherwise be impracticable for productive labor. Contemporary transportation would be virtually impossible without artificial light. Again, the significance of gas and electric lights for modern recreation, concentrated as it is chiefly in the hours after 6 p.m., is at once obvious. Their educational significance, in the broadest sense of the term, is apparent to anyone who will attempt to estimate the importance of the theater, movies, night schools, university extension work, evening lectures, illustrated lectures, and the like.

X. THE COMING OF THE FACTORY

The new empire of machines brought about a radical transformation in the mode of applying human labor in industrial processes. It produced the factory, the most characteristic modern form of concentrating and controlling labor. The factory could exist in a crude form without machines of a complicated sort. We have seen that, in the form of rudimentary "central shops," the factory was to be found in ancient Mesopotamia, in Greece and Rome, and in England in the merchant-capitalist system of the early eighteenth century.[1] But factories were unusual before the empire of machines came into being. From this time onward they became inevitable and today are well-nigh universal in modern industry. If factories of a sort could exist without complicated machines, at least modern machinery cannot be set to work outside factories, being too bulky and too expensive to be installed in private homes. It also requires more workers than can be assembled under one domestic roof.

In an earlier chapter we indicated some of the weaknesses of the putting-out system as it had developed in England by the eighteenth century.[2] Under this industrial system, a considerable amount of manufacturing was carried on in rural districts, some of it in combination with agriculture. This was due partly to guild opposition, which prevented any great consolidation of industrial plants in the towns. Once national governmental regulation had curbed the guilds, manufacturing, notably in new industries such as woolen and worsted cloth, grew up outside their jurisdiction. The new capitalist class of master clothiers came to control the textile industry.

The Commercial Revolution, with the resulting widening of the market, enlarged the potential sale of manufactured products, and the advantages of large-scale production began to be manifest. Industry was again in part drawn into towns by the force of greater economy, particularly in securing a labor supply and in reaching a market. In the eighteenth and nineteenth centuries the urbanization of industry was given irresistible force through the introduction of power-driven machines.

Industry now became concentrated in new localities where the essential water power, iron, and coal were available. With the introduction of machinery, manufacturing processes could be broken up into many routine operations, performed chiefly by machines and merely supervised by the workers. Not only were these machines too expensive for the individual workman to own, but each was linked up with all the others that contributed their special operations to a general process like the turning of cotton fiber into finished cloth. Such machines had to be installed in places where power to drive them was available, which were rarely the workmen's homes. For in those days, before the development of electrical appliances, power was transmitted by shafting and belts, which meant that it must be used fairly close to its source.

The gradual transition from hand weaving to factory looms well illustrates the general trend. There were many weavers in central shops in England before the power loom was invented. When the power loom appeared the more eco-

[1] See above, Vol. I, pp. 129, 208, 299; and above, pp. 46 ff.   [2] See above, pp. 47-8.

nomical machinery was installed and the shop became a factory. Hand weavers who still worked in their homes were gradually driven out of business as the power machines were improved and did the work too cheaply for the single operator of a hand loom to compete with them. The hand worker was obliged to seek employment in the factory or take up some other occupation that would yield a living. The factory soon proved itself a more efficient type of agency for manufacturing. Its general acceptance was therefore inevitable, and even desirable, in spite of the revolutionary social changes it involved, and the disorder and suffering that some of this entailed.

The rise of factories utilizing mechanical power dates mainly from the successful construction of Watt engines following 1780.[1] The first steam spinning-factory was opened by a man named Robinson in 1785. Other important figures in establishing the early textile factories were Richard Arkwright, Samuel Oldknow, Robert Peel, and Robert Owen. The energetic ironmaster John Wilkinson introduced the factory system into the metal industry.

XI. THE MAIN ELEMENTS IN THE FACTORY SYSTEM

Of the leading characteristics of the factory system, the most striking is the assembling of more workmen in one establishment than could be brought together in any earlier type of industrial discipline. While an establishment may be regarded as a factory when it employs only a dozen or a score of workmen, the characteristic modern factory has hundreds or even thousands of employees. Even the small factories normally employ a greater number of people than were ever brought together in any ordinary guild establishment.

The factory system also offers a far greater opportunity for the control, supervision, and discipline of labor. As compared with the earlier apprentices and journeymen, modern factory workers are normally more at the mercy of the employing class than was possible when the journeymen might become masters and when tools were relatively inexpensive. The superior discipline possible in the factory system is even more apparent when compared with the putting-out system, under which the capitalist or his representative visited the employees only sporadically while distributing raw material or collecting the finished products. Prior to the development of labor organizations, the factory workers were almost entirely dependent upon the will of the employer, while their daily presence in the plant made possible thorough supervision and discipline.

Not only did the factory make for easier control of labor; it rendered such discipline and regimentation absolutely inevitable if chaos and confusion were not to prevail. Informal supervision, based upon personal contacts, might have been adequate for the small guild establishment, but it was quite insufficient to meet the situation created by bringing hundreds of individuals under one roof. It became necessary to have rigorous rules defining the hours of labor, the assignment of individual tasks, the attitude of the employee in his relations with the employer, details of conduct within the factory, and even the

[1] See below, pp. 300 ff.

matter of orderly entering and leaving.[1] The following summary of the rules and penalties imposed in an early cotton factory near Manchester is cited by Mr. and Mrs. Hammond. It well illustrates the character of the new industrial discipline and the implied contrast between the new conditions and the relatively flexible and care-free nature of industrial life under the earlier putting-out system:[2]

	s.	d.
Any spinner found with window open	1	0
Any spinner found dirty at his work	1	0
Any spinner found washing himself	1	0
Any spinner leaving his oil can out of its place	1	0
Any spinner repairing his drum banding with his gas lighted	2	0
Any spinner slipping with his gas lighted	2	0
Any spinner putting his gas out too soon	1	0
Any spinner spinning with gaslight too long in the morning	2	0
Any spinner having his lights too large for each light	1	0
Any spinner heard whistling	1	0
Any spinner having hard ends hanging on his weights	0	6
Any spinner having hard ends on carriage band	1	0
Any spinner being five minutes after last bell rings	1	0
Any spinner having roller laps, no more than two draws for each roller lap	0	6
Any spinner going further than the roving-room door when fetching rovings	1	0
Any spinner being sick and cannot find another spinner to give satisfaction must pay for steam per day	6	0
Any spinner found in another's wheel gate	1	0
Any spinner neglecting to send his sweepings three mornings in a week	1	0
Any spinner having a little waste on his spindles	1	0

The first adequate code of factory discipline was worked out by Sir Richard Arkwright. In fact, his significance in the Industrial Revolution is far greater as a factory organizer than as the promoter of the roller water frame. Arkwright's own factories proved so successful and his code seemed so adequate that the latter was widely adopted in Europe, and became the parent of the later and fuller ones of the nineteenth century.

Of late years, observation and experiment have led to a belief that these conventional codes of factory discipline have serious defects in their reaction upon the human personality. They have been criticized for sacrificing to order and regimentation our normal human impulses towards creative effort—or for that matter towards any effort whatever beyond the amount compulsory for holding a job.

[1] So elaborate has this code of factory discipline become in some places that its complete and literal application would paralyze the operation of the plant. This situation has been seized upon by certain radical labor organizations, which have practiced peaceful sabotage solely by carrying out the factory rules with great thoroughness and literalness. See below, pp. 952 ff.
[2] J. L. LeB. and Barbara Hammond, *The Town Labourer*, Longmans, 1925, pp. 19-20.

It has been long evident that workers are subjected to a good deal of nervous strain by the monotony of mechanical routine and factory discipline. It even appears that this boredom often induces nervous illness that keeps workers at home:

> Boredom causes industrial workers in England to lose more time from their jobs than all the recognized industrial diseases put together, the report of the Chief Inspector of Factories and Workshops for 1931 shows. This is the result of the mechanization of industry, according to a comment in *The Lancet,* English medical journal. The vague nervous disabilities that have increased greatly in recent years are really the result of ennui on the part of the machine hand, it is thought. This state of boredom so great as to cause nervous ailments severe enough to lose time from work was almost unknown to the craftsman, *The Lancet* points out.[1]

The recognition that there is something wrong in this situation has led to the development of the modern sciences of personnel management and industrial psychology and psychiatry in an attempt to humanize the factory.

The machine technique itself has tended to mechanize the workman, who often carries on a narrowly specialized routine operation throughout most or all of his active career.[2] In this way, all those skills growing out of special training and of the repetition of familiar simple motions may be easily realized. Adam Smith pointed out long ago the great advantages inherent in this subdivision of industrial processes, but he never could have foreseen the elaborate and intricate application of the idea in the modern factory. This has culminated in the mass production and speed-up processes usually connected in the public mind with the achievements of Henry Ford in the automobile industry.[3]

It is well to remember that the factory system not only brought to industrial workers a new and rigorous type of industrial discipline; it also uprooted the older intellectual perspective and social attachments of mankind, which had been built up over tens of thousands of years of human experience. Nobody has more concisely and graphically presented this all-important consideration than Professor Sombart:

> First, there appears the important fact that the proletarian is a typical representative of that kind of man who no longer is in relation (either internal or external) to Nature. The proletarian does not realise the meaning of the movement of the clouds in the sky; he no longer understands the voice of the storm.
>
> He has no fatherland, rather he has no home in which he takes root. Can he feel at home in the dreary main streets, four stories high? He changes his dwelling often either because he dislikes his landlord or because he changes his place of work. As he moves from room to room, so he goes from city to city, from land to land, wherever opportunity (i.e. capitalism) calls. Homeless, restless, he moves over the earth; he loses the sense of local colour; his home is the world. He has lost the call of Nature, and he has assimilated materialism.
>
> It is a phenomenon of to-day that the great mass of the population has nothing to call its own. In earlier times the poorest had a piece of land, a cottage, a few animals to call his own; a trifle on which however he could set his whole heart. To-day a handcart carries all his possessions when a proletarian moves. A few old scraps are all by which his individual existence is to be known.

---

[1] New York *Times,* Aug. 28, 1932, Sec. 1, p. 4.   [3] See below, pp. 752 ff.
[2] See Arthur Pound, *The Iron Man in Industry,* Little, Brown, 1922.

THE MAIN ELEMENTS IN THE FACTORY SYSTEM

All community feeling is destroyed by the iron foot of capitalism. The village life is gone; the proletarian has no social home; the separate family disappears.[1]

XII. WORKING-CONDITIONS IN EARLY FACTORIES AND MINES

The misery and uncertainty of working-class life in the Flemish towns at the close of the Middle Ages has attracted the attention of many social and economic historians. Industrial concentration in cities had already produced the problems of woman and child labor, of unemployment and exploitation of the workers, long before the age of power-driven machines. The later scattering of industry over the countryside, incident to the struggle between the guilds and the rising capitalist class, made the worker under the putting-out system relatively independent of his employer. Unemployment, also, was less serious in the country, where land for cultivation might still be had. This independence was beginning to be lost in England, however, even before the coming of machines and factories. As we approach the eighteenth century, there is an evident tendency for the workers in the putting-out system to specialize in the spinning or weaving of cloth and to give up farming or gardening altogether.

As long as work continued to be done in the homes, the women and children labored chiefly with the men of their own families. They were certainly overworked, undernourished, and at times badly treated. The putting-out system was like the modern sweatshop in many particulars.[2] If misery was not always increased by the introduction of factories, it was at least concentrated and its horrors were made more conspicuous. The English agrarian inclosures following 1740 provided a peculiarly helpless and willing group of laborers for the new textile plants and the iron mills.[3] The dispossessed peasants faced the alternative of factory labor or sheer starvation.

When the workers entered the new industrial towns, they did not find well-equipped dwellings, but rather hastily erected shacks and tenements.[4] The factories themselves had arrived so swiftly that most of them were crudely built from the standpoint of safety and health as well as that of comfort. For the first time, both women and children were now employed on a large scale in work that separated them from their homes during the long working-day. It is estimated that at least three-fourths of the employees in the early cotton factories were either women or children, who could manage most of the machines with relative ease.[5] The women were in no position to demand men's wages, or to hold out successfully against even the most repulsive working-conditions. Consequently they were exploited and oppressed in shameful fashion.

Extensive as were the abuses of woman labor, the most distressing aspect of the new factory system lay in the general employment of young children.

---

[1] Translated and adapted from Sombart's *Das Proletariat*, in Milton Briggs, *Economic History of England*, London, 1914, pp. 213-14.   [2] See above, pp. 46 ff.
[3] *Cf.* J. L. LeB. and Barbara Hammond, *The Rise of Modern Industry*, Harcourt, Brace, 1926, Chap. VII; and Gilbert Slater, *The Growth of Modern England*, Houghton Mifflin, 1933, pp. 102 ff.
[4] See Hammond and Hammond, *The Town Labourer*, Chap. III; and *The Age of the Chartists*, Chap. VII.   [5] See Hammond and Hammond, *The Rise of Modern Industry*, p. 188.

Much the worst evil was that connected with the utilization of pauper apprentices. Large numbers of pauper children who were supported through poor relief were to be found in the cities of southern England. As soon as a demand for child labor developed, the poor-relief authorities tended to farm them out as apprentices to manufacturers in the northern industrial towns in order to escape the financial burden of supporting them. Once the poor-relief authorities of London, for example, had sent these children out of that part of the country and given up control over them, there was no one to look after their interests. The only curb upon employers was the fear of starvation, epidemics, or a mortality so terrific as actually to create a scarcity of labor. Some of the worst working-conditions revealed by the various factory investigations existed among these "apprenticed" pauper children. As Mr. Briggs has concisely and accurately observed: "The children lived the life of a machine when working, and at other times that of a beast."[1]

Hours of work in the factories were excessive, and the wages paid were ridiculously low. Sixteen and eighteen hour days were not uncommon for children under fourteen years of age. From fourteen to sixteen hours constituted a normal working-day. The following testimony of a father of two working boys given to the factory commissioners in 1833 is typical:

> My two sons (one ten, the other thirteen) work at the Milnes's factory at Lenton. They go at half past five in the morning; don't stop at breakfast or tea time. They stop at dinner half an hour. Come home at a quarter before ten. They used to work till ten, sometimes eleven, sometimes twelve. They earn between them 6s. 2d. per week. One of them, the eldest, worked at Wilson's for two years, at 2s. 3d. per week. He left because his overlooker beat him and loosened a tooth for him. I complained, and they turned him away for it. They have been gone to work sixteen hours now; they will be very tired when they come home at half past nine. I have been obliged to beat 'em with a strap in their shirts, and to pinch 'em, in order to get them well awake. It made me cry to be obliged to do it.[2]

Along with these atrocious hours went extremely inadequate wages. The following table taken from Bowley's *Wages in the United Kingdom in the Nineteenth Century*[3] indicates the average weekly wage paid at various representative periods to the leading types of male English laborers since 1795:

	1795		1807		1824		1833		1867		1897	
	s.	d.	s.	d.	s.	d.	s.	d.	s.	d.	s.	d.
London type of artisan ..	25	0	30	0	30	0	28	0	36	0	40	0
Provincial type of artisan	17	0	22	0	24	0	22	0	27	0	34	0
Town labourers	12	0	14	0	16	0	14	0	20	0	25	0
Agricultural labourers ...	9	0	13	0	9	6	10	6	14	0	16	0

These figures are for men. The highest (40s. for London in 1897) is equal to $10.00 a week, the lowest to only $2.25. The payment to women and children was of course much lower, averaging in the early days of the Industrial Revolution from 4s. to 9s. ($1 to $2.25) a week. With a considerable setback from 1820 to 1870, and occasional stationary periods, factory wages increased slowly

---

[1] Briggs, *op. cit.*, p. 357.
[2] Robinson and Beard, *Readings in Modern European History*, Vol. II, p. 283.
[3] Macmillan, 1900, p. 70.

in England between the middle of the eighteenth century and the close of the nineteenth. Yet the rise in wages was relatively slight for seventy years after 1800, as the following table from Bowley will make clear:

AVERAGE WEEKLY WAGES OF COTTON SPINNERS IN THE MANCHESTER DISTRICT

Year	Wage
1806	24s. 2d.
1810	30s. 0d.
1815	28s. 11d.
1819	28s. 11d.
1833	27s. 1d.
1841	22s. 0d.
1849	21s. 7d.
1859	24s. 1d.
1870	27s. 8d.
1880	33s. 6d.
1886	35s. 7d.
1893	37s. 0d.

Wage payments have thus failed utterly to keep pace with the increases in the income and fortunes of the capitalistic classes. As we shall see later, this fact has done more than anything else to undermine capitalism.

While wages may have risen slightly since the opening of the nineteenth century, the unskilled laborers in England have tended to hover around the line of primary poverty, a goodly number living below this line, as Charles Booth and Seebohm Rowntree showed in their famous studies of living-conditions in London and York at the close of the nineteenth century.[1] Booth showed that approximately 31 per cent of the population of London lived below the poverty line, while Rowntree revealed the fact that approximately 28 per cent in York were in poverty.

The moral situation in the new factories was not less deplorable than the economic. In many cases women were compelled to submit to involuntary sex relations in order to hold their positions, and there was a common saying in England in the first half of the nineteenth century, "Every man's factory is his harem." Immoral relations with women employees were not limited to the owners or managers of factories, but were indulged in by subordinate foremen as well. In fact, there was often general moral degradation within the factory, the results of which were rendered even more distressing on account of the presence of numbers of children. A large amount of illegitimacy naturally grew out of these illicit relations. The moral and social conditions in the life of the working classes in the new towns outside of working-hours were little if any better than in the factories. Healthy forms of recreation being denied the workers because of both poverty and the long working-day, drunkenness and sex immorality were strikingly prevalent. They were about the only available methods of breaking the unspeakable monotony and drabness of industrial life.

[1] Charles Booth, *Life and Labour of the People of London*, 17 vols., Macmillan, 1891-1903; and B. S. Rowntree, *Poverty: A Study of Town Life*, Longmans, 1902 (new ed., 1922).

Even the most elementary hygienic laws were ignored. Little or no consideration was given to adequate ventilation or heating. The factories were often filled with tepid and steamy air in the summer season and were excessively cold in the winter. No provision whatever was made for rest rooms or any of the other comforts now common in the well-equipped modern factory. Safety devices were unknown. Machinery was rarely provided with guards to protect workers from rapidly revolving wheels, or from being drawn into gears or whirled about shafts. Fatal accidents were frightfully frequent and maiming even more common. The relatives of the deceased or the injured were rarely able to collect damages, because at that time the law which prevailed was the so-called common-law rule. This provided that no damages could be collected unless it could be shown that the employer was directly responsible for the accident. This was rarely possible, because of the employer's superior capacity to engage clever counsel and prove that the employee or some "fellow servant" had been guilty of contributory negligence.

Such were the conditions in most English factories of the first half of the nineteenth century as revealed by a series of public and private investigations. There still remained a considerable number of handicraft workers in England as late as 1825, chiefly in the weaving and the boot and shoe industries. The introduction of improved looms after 1825 gradually but surely made the competition of these handicraft workers with the factory machine system more hopeless. The hand weavers were slowly driven out of the field before 1850, and the handicraftsmen in the boot and shoe industry disappeared during the next generation. There are still some handicraft workers in certain special trades, but the great bulk of modern industry is now located within the factory. It seems rather obvious that any practical plan for improving the lot of the factory worker must consist in creating a new set of conditions within the factory rather than introducing proposals like those of John Ruskin or Ralph Borsodi for closing the factories and returning to a handicraft economy. As a refuge for excess laborers this self-sufficing rural family industry may, however, prove increasingly important.

Labor conditions in the mines of England at this time were even worse than those which prevailed in the factories.[1] Women and children were extensively employed in underground pits from twelve to sixteen hours a day. Women were utilized to push or draw coal carts, particularly in places where the roof was too low to allow a donkey to pass through. Children four and five years of age were used in the mines as "trappers," opening and closing doors for the passage of carts of coal. The wages paid to these women and children were scandalously inadequate, averaging from 2s. 6d. for the young children to 12s. per week for the very best women. The following brief citation from the valuable work of Isabel Simeral gives a graphic summary of typical conditions which prevailed in the mines:

The work of these babies was usually that of "trappers." They sat beside the traps or doors in the coal seams through which the coal carts were passed to the roads leading to the main road where the coal was placed to be removed to the surface. It was dangerous to leave a door open as it caused great heat, closeness, and a pos-

[1] See Hammond and Hammond, *The Town Labourer*, Chap. IX; and Isabel Simeral, cited below.

sible explosion. These babies, then, sat in a spot hollowed out in the wall and when they heard the approach of a coal cart pulled open the trap by means of a cord and closed it after the cart had passed. They worked for twelve and fourteen hours daily with no light except what some kindly disposed miner was willing to give them in the shape of candle ends. The places were usually damp and no matter how monotonous the labor, the strap was applied if they delayed or endangered the work by falling asleep. They never saw sunlight except upon Sunday, and had no relaxation whatsoever except upon that day. Hodder, the biographer of Lord Ashley who uncovered the situation, says that instances were known where highly sensitive children became imbeciles from the fright of darkness, loneliness, and the vermin with which the mines were frequently infested. The seams were sometimes only twenty-two to twenty-eight inches high and only tiny children could pass through at all.[1]

Another notorious and terrible situation was that presented by the chimney sweeps.[2] Many of the early chimneys were less than a foot square inside. Children were taken at three or four years of age—and frequently stolen—for this work. They were pushed up through chimneys, often while still hot. Many were burned to death, lost inside flues, or smothered. Of course permanent disfigurement or loss of eyesight was commoner than death outright. Tuberculosis was a very usual result of chimney-sweeping. Running sores due to abrasions, infection, and lack of care were all but universal. The hardiest child could not get used to the work for many months. These unfortunates were treated practically like animals, having their food thrown to them and often going unwashed for years. Some firms cynically advertised "small children for small chimneys." Serious attempts to abolish this atrocious evil by law were initiated as early as 1804, but they were repeatedly blocked in Parliament, especially in the House of Lords, by the wealthy manufacturing interests. The disappearance of child chimney sweeps some three decades later was due in part to the introduction of larger chimneys and mechanical sweepers, which made the old method uneconomical. The movement was aided to a considerable extent by a more humanitarian state of public opinion in the reforming thirties.

Factory conditions were never quite so bad on a wide scale elsewhere as they were in England. France did not become so thoroughly industrialized. The same is true of the other European states with the exception of Germany. In Germany the Industrial Revolution had not advanced far before Bismarck introduced his system of factory legislation, which protected the workers from the worst abuses that had existed in England. In the United States the scarcity of workers and the existence of cheap land prevented for many years such extreme oppression of the workers as prevailed in England. Still, the following schedule of working-hours in a leading factory in Fall River in 1817 indicates that the laborers were far from the forty-four-hour or thirty-hour week in those days:

> Work started at five A.M. if light permitted.
> One-half hour off for breakfast at eight A.M.
> Half-hour for lunch at twelve M.
> Quit work at seven-thirty.

---

[1] Simeral, *Reform Movements in Behalf of Women and Children in England of the Early Nineteenth Century, and the Agents of Those Reforms*, privately printed, 1916, p. 109.
[2] See Hammond and Hammond, *The Town Labourer*, pp. 177 ff.

Adult males laboring in this factory received at this time from 83 cents to $1 a day, while women and children received from $2.00 to $3.00 a week.

Factory legislation and the growth of public sentiment since the middle of the nineteenth century have brought about a great improvement in working-conditions.[1] Woman and child labor have been restricted, factory conditions have improved tremendously, and labor organizations have helped to raise wage levels. That exploitation of the workers and gross evils in laboring-conditions have not yet entirely disappeared is, however, almost too well known to require mention. As will be pointed out later,[2] some of the worst of these evils exist close at home. Indeed, down at least to the application of the N.R.A. codes in 1933, the working-conditions in the soft-coal industry in western Pennsylvania, West Virginia, and Kentucky and in the Southern textile industry were almost as deplorable as those in English factories in 1830.[3]

In our day, however, it is usual for the worst abuses of the older type of factory to have disappeared. Wages are higher; hours are shorter; factories are cleaner; safety devices are fairly general; and welfare work is often present. At the same time, new abuses and evils have crept in, most of them incident to mass production and the speed-up processes that have come along with it.[4] A period of three or four years of steady labor in some of our mass-production plants of today breaks the health of the average workman and often unfits him for any steady work thereafter. It is obvious that a higher wage or a clean factory is of little permanent benefit to such a victim of our mania for profits at whatever disasters to the human material exploited to secure them.

XIII. THE REACTION OF THE INVENTIONS AND FACTORIES UPON BUSINESS: THE RISE OF INDUSTRIAL CAPITALISM

We shall reserve until a later chapter the thorough treatment of modern financial institutions and business practices.[5] But it is desirable in this place to say at least a word about the character of the important developments associated with what is called early industrial capitalism.[6]

The increased scale of business units, the greater need for credit and capital, and the expanding volume of business and trade combined to hasten and intensify those capitalistic developments which had first taken form in the pre-industrial capitalism that had grown up with the expansion of Europe and the Commercial Revolution.[7] Commercial banking took on substantial proportions.[8] Far greater financial resources were assembled and the use of commercial paper was extended and facilitated. The banking of the time was often rash and venal and inadequately supervised by state authorities. Especially was this so in the United States, where there were many banks founded on the proverbial shoestring and a scandalous number of failures. But, with all their

---

[1] See below, pp. 387 ff., 938 ff.   [2] See below, pp. 368-9.
[3] *Cf.* National Committee for the Defense of Political Prisoners, *Harlan Miners Speak*, Harcourt, Brace, 1932; and Thomas Tippett, *When Southern Labor Stirs*, Peter Smith, 1931.
[4] See below, pp. 752 ff.   [5] See below, Chap. XXI.
[6] *Cf.* Mantoux, *op. cit.*, Pt. III, Chap. II.   [7] See above, pp. 57 ff.
[8] See Arthur Birnie, *Economic History of Europe, 1760-1930*, Dial Press, 1930, Chap. VI.

weaknesses, the superior banks after 1800 were larger, better organized, and more perfectly adapted to assembling resources and extending credit than any that had been known in an earlier period. In order to promote new enterprises and float their securities, a special kind of bank or financial institution came into being, namely, the underwriting syndicate and the investment bank. These arose especially after the railroads had adopted the corporate method of organization and had placed their securities on the market in large volume.

With the appearance of corporations ownership began to be divorced to a certain degree from management. Ownership was scattered among many stockholders, while management was concentrated in a few officers and directors and in the experts whom they hired to operate the business. Here thus appeared the germs of that absentee ownership which has played so prominent and disastrous a rôle in contemporary financial operations and business enterprise.[1]

Business ideals were brought more thoroughly into conformity with the price system and the goal of profits. If quality was maintained, it was not primarily because of high ideals of craftsmanship but because loss of sales was feared if goods were of too inferior a grade. Profits, not workmanship, were at stake. The dominant business and financial aspiration of the day was to accumulate as much pecuniary gain as possible in the shortest time. Economic society took on rather purely acquisitive traits and the social viewpoint and controls of the medieval period disappeared. Bookkeeping concepts replaced the moral law. As enterprises became larger and corporations became popular, economic life became impersonal. A "cash nexus" and legal fictions took the place of personal relationships. Business was everywhere viewed as an enterprise to make money. Even labor was looked upon as a commodity to be bought and sold through a wage system. Engrossing, regrating, and forestalling, which had been outlawed in medieval economic life,[2] became the very cornerstones of the new industrial and financial order. Such a notion as the "just price" would have been looked upon as idiotic by the captains of industry of the nineteenth century.

In spite, however, of novel financial developments and the increased need for credit, capitalism still remained primarily industrial in character. Financial institutions and practices were designed to aid and further industry and were not yet ends in themselves. Industry was first and foremost in economic considerations. While corporations became numerous, though by no means universal, in the first half of the nineteenth century, they were still regarded as subsidiary to industrial purposes. They were not yet looked upon as instruments wherewith to manufacture paper pyramids or to turn out securities that might be exploited in financial gambles. The production of goods for profit rather than wholesale legal robbery through financial manipulation was the dominant ideal of capitalistic society. Finance was still the servant of industry.

As the scale of business units became larger and combinations were achieved in one way or another, concentration of control became more marked. After

[1] See below, pp. 798 ff. [2] See above, Vol. I, pp. 653 ff., 679 ff.

about 1870 American economic society moved away from early industrial capitalism into what is known as monopoly capitalism.[1]

[1] See below, pp. 751, 780 ff.

SUGGESTED READING

Hammerton, *Universal History of the World,* Chaps. 159, 163, 176
Ogg and Sharp, *Economic Development of Modern Europe,* Chap. VII
F. C. Dietz, *The Industrial Revolution,* Holt, 1927, pp. 3-73
Milton Briggs, *Economic History of England,* London, 1914, Chaps. V, VI, IX
Clive Day, *Economic Development in Modern Europe,* Macmillan, 1933, Chaps. I-II
H. G. Wells, *The Work, Wealth and Happiness of Mankind,* Doubleday, Doran, 1931, 2 vols., Vol. I, pp. 109-17, 233-37, 259-328
Marjorie and C. H. B. Quennell, *The Rise of Industrialism, 1733-1851,* Putnam, 1932
Usher, *Introduction to the Industrial History of England,* Chaps. XII-XIII
—— *History of Mechanical Inventions,* Chap. IX
J. L. LeB. and Barbara Hammond, *The Town Labourer, 1760-1832,* Longmans, 1925, Chaps. II, VI, VIII-XI, XIV
—— *The Rise of Modern Industry,* Chaps. VI, VII, IX, XI, XIII
Mantoux, *The Industrial Revolution in the Eighteenth Century,* Introduction, Pt. II, Chaps. I-III; Pt. III, Chap. II
Daniels, *The Early History of the Cotton Industry*
C. R. Gibson, *The Romance of Coal,* Lippincott, 1923
T. S. Ashton, *Iron and Steel in the Industrial Revolution,* Longmans, 1924
Matthew Luckiesch, *Artificial Light, Its Influence upon Civilization,* Century, 1920
W. B. Kaempffert, ed., *Popular History of American Invention,* Scribner, 1924, 2 vols., Vol. I, Pt. III, Chaps. I, III; Vol. II, Pt. IV, Chap. I
Allen Clarke, *The Effects of the Factory System,* Scribner, 1899
Robinson and Beard, *Readings in Modern European History,* Vol. II, Chap. XVIII
Marshall, *The Emergence of the Modern Order,* Vol. I, Pt. I, pp. 200-17, 245-66
Davis and Barnes, *Readings in Sociology,* pp. 190-220
J. F. Scott and Alexander Baltzly, eds., *Readings in European History since 1814,* Crofts, 1930, pp. 64-70, 78-94
Bland, Brown, and Tawney, *English Economic History; Select Documents,* pp. 495-521
Benjamin Rand, *Selections Illustrating Economic History since 1763,* Harvard University Press, 1911, Chaps. II, XII, XVIII

FURTHER REFERENCES

THE ECONOMIC BACKWARDNESS OF SOCIETY IN 1750. On the old régime in Europe before the Industrial Revolution, see Hammerton, *op. cit.,* Chap. 159; Flick, *Modern World History,* Chap. IV; Nussbaum, *History of the Economic Institutions of Modern Europe,* Pt. III, Chap. V; Vol. I, Chap. VIII, of J. H. Robinson and C. A. Beard, eds., *The Development of Modern Europe* (rev. ed., Ginn, 1929-30, 2 vols.); Chap. I of E. R. Turner, *Europe since 1789* (Doubleday, Page, 1920); Slater, *The Growth of Modern England,* Chap. II; Renard and Weulersse, *Life and Labor in Modern Europe,* pp. 343-83; Mantoux, *op. cit.,* Pt. I, Chap. I; Day, *op. cit.,* Chap. I; M. D. George, *England in Transition* (London, 1931).

NATURAL SCIENCE AND THE INDUSTRIAL REVOLUTION. On natural science and mechanical inventions, see Chap. VII of F. S. Marvin, ed., *Science and Civilization*

(Oxford Press, 1923); Hammerton, *op. cit.*, Chap. 176; Chap. xix of E. V. Cowdry, ed., *Human Biology and Racial Welfare* (Hoeber, 1930).

THE INDUSTRIAL REVOLUTION. On the general character of the Industrial Revolution, for introductory surveys see *Cambridge Modern History*, Vol. X, Chap. xxiii; Hammerton, *op. cit.*, Chap. 163; Birnie, *Economic History of Europe*, Chap. i; Robinson and Beard, *The Development of Modern Europe*, 1908 ed., Vol. II, Chap. xviii; Usher, *op. cit.*, Chap. x; Chap. xv of Chapin, *Historical Introduction to Social Economy* (Century, 1917); Turner, *op. cit.*, Chap. vi; Ogg and Sharp, *op. cit.*, Chap. vii; Day, *op. cit.*, Chap. ii; Hammond and Hammond, *The Rise of Modern Industry*, Pt. II; Dietz, *op. cit.*; Quennell and Quennell, *op. cit.*; Pt. IV of G. E. Hedger and others, *An Introduction to Western Civilization* (Doubleday, Doran, 1933).

On the tool economy, see Bk. II, Chap. i of F. C. Müller-Lyer, *History of Social Development* (Knopf, 1921). On the history of mechanical inventions, see Hendrik Van Loon, *Man the Miracle Maker* (Liveright, 1928); pp. 5-174 of L. C. Marshall, *The Story of Human Progress* (Macmillan, 1925); Ellison Hawks, *The Triumph of Man in Science and Invention* (Nelson, 1929); E. W. Byrn, *The Progress of Invention in the Nineteenth Century* (Van Nostrand, 1901); T. W. Corbin, *Mechanical Inventions of To-day* (Lippincott, 1912); Usher, *History of Mechanical Inventions*; George Iles, *Leading American Inventors* (Holt, 1912); F. W. Wile, ed., *A Century of Industrial Progress* (Doubleday, Doran, 1928); R. S. Holland, *Historic Inventions* (Jacobs, 1911); Holland Thompson, *The Age of Invention* (Yale University Press, 1921); Kaempffert, *op. cit.* Professor Usher's book is probably the most satisfactory single volume.

On reasons for English priority in the Industrial Revolution, see Ogg and Sharp, *op. cit.*, pp. 128 ff.; Lectures I-II of J. E. T. Rogers, *Industrial and Commercial History of England* (Putnam, 1892); Mantoux, *op. cit.*, Pt. I; Slater, *op. cit.*, Chap. iii; Chap. i of Witt Bowden, *Industrial Society in England towards the End of the Eighteenth Century* (Macmillan, 1925).

THE NEW TEXTILE MACHINERY AND PROCESSES. On the early history of the cotton industry, see Crawford, *The Heritage of Cotton*, Chap. viii; Daniels, *The Early English Cotton Industry*.

On the rise of mechanical methods of manufacture in the textile industry, see Crawford, *op. cit.*, Chap. ix; Daniels, *op. cit.*; Usher, *op. cit.*, Chap. xii; and *History of Mechanical Inventions*, Chap. ix; Mantoux, *op. cit.*, Pt. II, Chaps. i-ii; Hawks, *op. cit.*, Chap. v; Sir S. J. Chapman, *The Lancashire Cotton Industry* (Manchester, Eng., 1904); L. S. Wood and Albert Wilmore, *The Romance of the Cotton Industry in England* (Oxford Press, 1927).

IRON AND COAL. On the progress of science and invention in the iron and steel industry, see Hawks, *op. cit.*, Chap. x; Bridges, *The Book of Inventions*, Chap. iv; Usher, *Introduction to the Industrial History of England*, Chap. xiii; Hammond and Hammond, *op. cit.*, Chap. ix; Mantoux, *op. cit.*, Pt. II, Chap. iii; Ashton, *op. cit.* On the early history of the steel industry, see J. S. Jeans, *Steel: Its History, Manufacture and Uses* (Spon, 1880).

On modern methods of coal-mining, see Hawks, *op. cit.*, Chap. ix; Chaps. i, v-x of T. C. Cantrill, *Coal Mining* (Macmillan, 1914); F. H. Wilson, *Coal: Its Origin, Method of Working, and Preparation for the Market* (Pitman, 1913); W. A. Bone, *Coal, and Its Scientific Uses* (Longmans, 1918); Gibson, *op. cit.*; James Tonge, *Coal* (Van Nostrand, 1907); Homer Greene, *Coal and the Coal Mines* (Houghton Mifflin, 1928); E. C. Jeffrey, *Coal and Civilization* (Macmillan, 1925); R. E. Machin, *Science in a Coalfield* (Pitman, 1932); H. W. Hughes, *Text-book of Coal-Mining* (Lippincott, 1917); F. H. Kneeland, *Getting out the Coal* (McGraw-Hill, 1926).

MACHINES AND MACHINE PARTS. On precision methods of manufacture, see Usher, *History of Mechanical Inventions*, Chap. XII; Iles, *op. cit.*, pp. 75 ff.

ARTIFICIAL ILLUMINATION. On the history and significance of artificial illumination, see Bridges, *op. cit.*, Chaps. VII, XVIII; Luckiesh, *op. cit.*; H. C. Horstmann and V. H. Tousley, *Modern Illumination* (F. J. Drake, 1916); S. I. Levy, *Incandescent Lighting* (Pitman, 1922).

On the history of electric lighting, see pp. 138 ff. of R. M. Keir, *The Epic of Industry* (Yale University Press, 1926); Cyril Sylvester and T. E. Ritchie, *Modern Electrical Illumination* (Longmans, 1927); A. G. Worthing, *Series of Nine Radio Talks on the Origin and Development of Artificial Light Sources* (University of Pittsburgh, 1927).

THE COMING OF THE FACTORY. On the development of the modern factory system and methods, see Mantoux, *op. cit.*, Introduction and Pt. III, Chaps. II-III; Nussbaum, *op. cit.*, Pt. III, Chap. IV; Hammond and Hammond, *The Town Labourer*, Chaps. I-III. On the triumph of machines over the handicraft system, see Bowden, *op. cit.*, Chap. II. On the factory and the new industrial discipline, see Hammond and Hammond, *op. cit.*, Chap. II; Chapman, *op. cit.*; Halévy, *History of the English People in 1815*, Bk. II, Chap. II.

On Sir Richard Arkwright, see W. B. Kaempffert, "The First Captain of the Machine Age," New York *Times* Magazine, Dec. 18, 1932, pp. 4, 18; Mantoux, *op. cit.*, pp. 238-39; Bowden, *op. cit.*, p. 151; George Unwin, *Samuel Oldknow and the Arkwrights* (Longmans, 1924).

On working-conditions in the new factories and mines, see Hammond and Hammond, *op. cit.*, Chaps. II, VI, VIII-IX; pp. 1-42 of B. L. Hutchins and A. Harrison, *History of Factory Legislation* (London, 1911); Briggs, *op. cit.*, Chaps. IX, XIII; Clarke, *op. cit.*; Bowden, *op. cit.*, Chap. IV; G. H. Perris, *Industrial History of Modern England* (Holt, 1914); Mantoux, *op. cit.*, Pt. III; Friedrich Engels, *The Condition of the Working Class in England in 1844* (Scribner, 1892); Isabel Simeral, *Reform Movements in Behalf of Women and Children in England of the Early Nineteenth Century* (privately printed, 1916).

On working-conditions in early America, see pp. 287 ff. of H. U. Faulkner, *American Economic History* (rev. ed., Harper, 1931); Chap. IX of E. C. Kirkland, *History of American Economic Life* (Crofts, 1932); Vol. II, Chap. I of H. J. Carman, *Social and Economic History of the United States* (Heath, 1930-36, 3 vols.); Vols. III-V of J. R. Commons, ed., *Documentary History of American Industrial Society* (Clark, 1910, 10 vols.).

On the rise of industrial biology, psychology, and psychiatry, see Chap. V of E. M. East, ed., *Biology in Human Affairs* (McGraw-Hill, 1931); P. S. Florence, *The Economics of Fatigue and Unrest* (Holt, 1924); J. C. Goldmark, *Fatigue and Efficiency* (Russell Sage Foundation, 1912); V. V. Anderson, *Psychiatry in Industry* (Harper, 1929); Elton Mayo, *The Human Problems of an Industrial Civilization* (Macmillan, 1933).

On industrial capitalism, see G. D. H. Cole, article "Industrialism," Encyclopaedia of the Social Sciences; Nussbaum, *op. cit.*, Pt. III, Chap. IV; Pt. IV, Chap. VI; Hobson, *The Evolution of Modern Capitalism*; Sée, *Modern Capitalism*; H. G. Moulton, *The Formation of Capital* (Brookings Institution, 1935).

CHAPTER VIII

THE REVOLUTION IN POWER, TRANSPORTATION, AND COMMUNICATION

I. THE NEW POWER RESOURCES

1. THE STEAM ENGINE

With the introduction of the new spinning and weaving machinery and the cotton gin, the mechanical foundations of the textile industry were completed. Indispensable for the operation of the new mechanical technique was a satisfactory motive power for the new machinery in those areas where natural water power was not available or economical. Water power has been, and still remains, the best type of motive power where it is available in a form practicable for manufacturing purposes. Unfortunately, sufficient water power is not everywhere at hand to run as many factories as a country can readily support. Again, excellent water power is often located in regions so remote from raw materials or markets as to make it too costly to employ it. Only in our own day has it become possible to develop water power at inaccessible points and then transport it in the form of electricity to districts where factories can be economically established.

The steam engine was the first important form of motive power supplied to those factories where water power was not available. It owed its practical application in industry to the Scotch inventor James Watt. Apparently, the first development of the principle of the steam engine should be assigned to Hero of Alexandria (Egypt), who had provided a crude sort of engine as early as 100 B.C.[1] Hero did not make any practical commercial application of his invention, though he did utilize it for the amusement of royalty by fastening a rope to it and, through a series of drums, opening and closing temple doors. In the seventeenth century an Italian, Giovanni Branca, and an Englishman, Edward Somerset, revived the knowledge of Hero's device.[2]

The first important practical innovation, however, lying in direct line of ancestry to Watt's steam engine was the steam digester that was devised by Denis Papin (1647-1712). Papin, born at Blois, was a religious refugee in London after 1681. Here, as curator of the Royal Society, he conceived of his digester. In 1687 he became a professor of physics in the University of Marburg. About 1690 Papin invented a device whereby steam was generated in a cylinder,

[1] See above, Vol. I, p. 230.
[2] See R. H. Thurston, *History of the Growth of the Steam Engine*, Appleton, 1902, pp. 16 ff.

which had one end open to the air. When the expanding steam was generated, it would raise the piston to the top of the cylinder. The fire was then put out and the cylinder was cooled by pouring water on it. This condensed the steam and generated a vacuum under the piston. The pressure of the atmosphere on the piston pushed it back once more to the bottom of the cylinder. The fire could then be rebuilt, steam generated once more, and the process repeated. It will be seen that the power thus generated was produced chiefly by the pressure of the atmosphere rather than by the steam, which was utilized mainly to provide a vacuum against which atmospheric pressure might work effectively. Papin's digester engine was the first of a series of atmosphere engines that held the field until the time of Watt.

An Englishman, Thomas Savery, about 1702 devised a separate boiler in which the steam could be generated and rendered permanently available for use. Thereafter it was possible to keep the fire burning continuously under the boiler. A great saving was thus introduced, as compared with the old and expensive method that Papin had employed of putting the fire out each time that the steam was condensed to form the vacuum. The Savery engine had no piston and was, in reality, an atmospherically propelled pumping device.

The first important commercial combination of the Papin piston engine with the Savery boiler was the work of Thomas Newcomen, who worked this out about 1705. A lazy boy tending one of the Newcomen engines contrived an all-important improvement: an automatic device for opening and closing the steam valves in this dual process of raising the piston, condensing the steam, and allowing the atmosphere to return the stroke of the piston. This was the highest development that the atmosphere engine reached. It was the defects of a Newcomen engine, rather than the fabled teakettle, that furnished the incentive for Watt to transform the atmosphere engine into the true steam engine.

James Watt as a young man was a maker of mathematical instruments, employed in the University of Glasgow. He had remarkable mechanical ingenuity and no little scientific competence. He had been something of a student of physics and chemistry, and had worked with Dr. Joseph Black in the latter's notable investigations that led to the discovery of the theory of latent heat. This experience furnished Watt the scientific background for his invention of the steam engine.

The other set of impulses came from the actual problems arising in his work as maker of mathematical instruments in the university. In 1763, while repairing a model of Newcomen's engine, he clearly perceived the enormous waste of fuel and energy in the atmosphere engine due to the excessive and repeated heating and cooling of the cylinder. In attempting to solve this problem, Watt hit upon the expedient of closing both ends of the cylinder and applying steam to force the piston back and forth in the cylinder. He thus exploited steam pressure throughout the process, instead of relying upon the atmosphere to furnish the real power in the engine. This idea apparently dates back to 1765. He also worked out a separate condensing chamber for handling and applying the steam. Many regard this as Watt's most essential

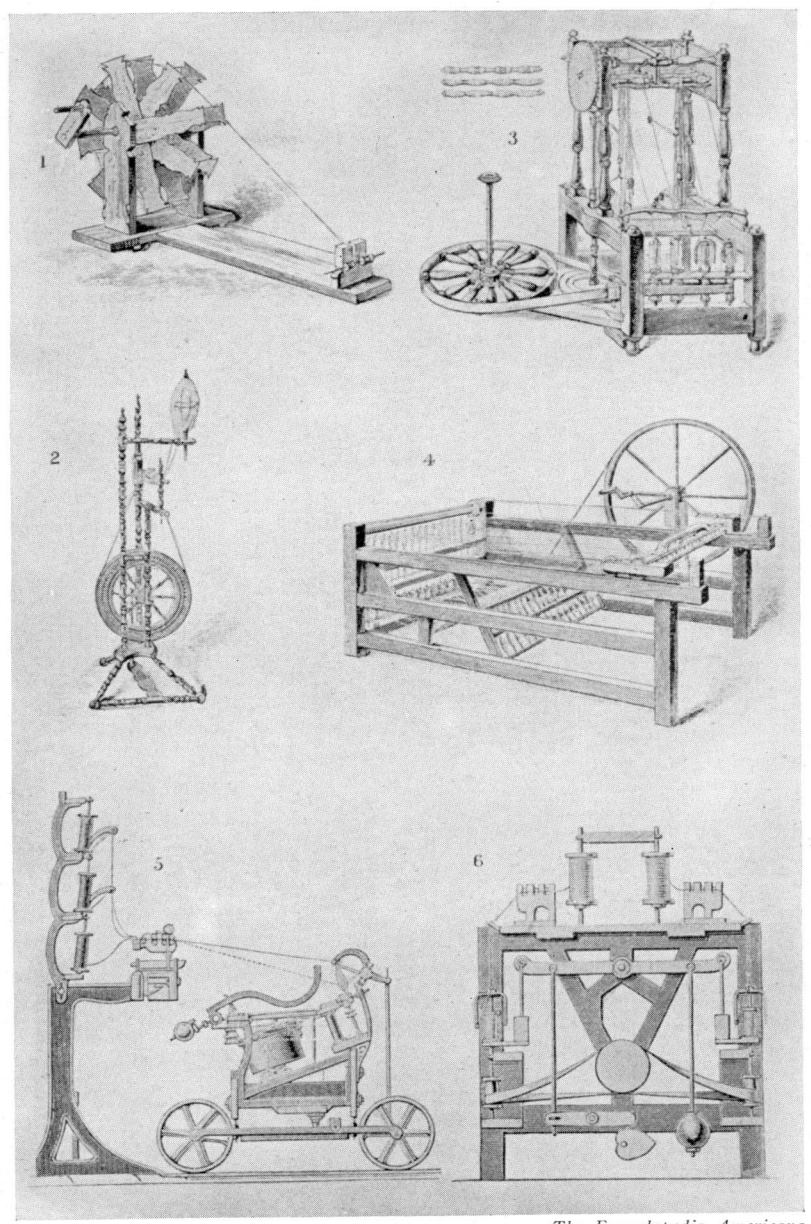

The Encyclopedia Americana

EARLY SPINNING MACHINERY

1. INDIAN SPINNING-WHEEL
2. SAXONY SPINNING-WHEEL
3. ARKWRIGHT'S WATER-FRAME
4. HARGREAVES' SPINNING-JENNY
5. CROMPTON'S MULE
6. THROSTLE

AN EARLY FACTORY *Old Print Shop*

A MODERN FACTORY *General Electric Company*

THE NEW POWER RESOURCES

contribution to the history of the steam engine. This condensing chamber is required on all true steam engines to our own day. By 1769 Watt had taken out his first patent for a successful steam engine. From now on the power in the engine was supplied by steam, and there was no longer any of the waste involved in cooling the cylinder with each stroke of the piston.

It was years, however, before Watt's steam engine was perfected and could be made a commercial success. There were no lathes for accurately turning the parts, casting was still a crude process, and the mechanics of the time made doubtful even the eventual construction of such large and complicated machines. Even with present-day mechanical engineering knowledge, it is often a long way from a small, soft-metal model embodying the idea of a machine to the full-sized, commercially practicable machine itself. Following the bankruptcy of the original firm, Watt was fortunate in securing as a partner in 1769 Matthew Boulton, whose experience in manufacturing mechanical toys proved invaluable in solving a myriad of practical problems.[1] Boulton also supplied the necessary financial backing to build and market the engines successfully. The superior methods of iron manufacture in the mills of John Wilkinson were also an indispensable aid to Watt and Boulton. Wilkinson supplied the first accurately bored cylinder and precise machine parts. By 1785 the Watt-Boulton engines were being introduced into factories, and by 1800 were very extensively used for pumping and for propelling the new textile machinery.[2]

While the great contribution of Watt to the development of the engine lay in the transformation of the atmosphere engine into the steam engine and the provision of a scientific steam condenser, he was also responsible for two other important improvements. One was the automatic governor, which maintained an even speed by regulating the flow of steam into the cylinder, adjusting it with mechanical exactness to the pull of the machinery. When much power is required the governor lets a large jet of steam into the cylinder; when the machinery is idling the governor cuts down the flow of steam. The other significant advance was the abandonment of the crude alternating-beam device, used in the earlier pumping engines. Watt devised the crank and shaft arrangement, which adapted the engine to the task of turning shafts equipped with a number of different-sized belt wheels. Numerous minor improvements greatly economized the amount of fuel and steam used in later engines.

The more important innovations in the building of the true steam engine since Watt's time have consisted in the provision of more complicated condensing chambers, devices for using steam over several times, each time at a lower pressure, and the creation of multiple-cylinder engines. The Watt engines were very low pressure engines and the trend has been towards ever higher internal pressure in the engines, thus permitting the re-use of the steam at lower pressures. The steam turbine, which came in about a century after Watt's invention of the steam engine, brought a sweeping revolution in the exploitation of steam power.

[1] *Cf.* Erich Roll, *An Early Experiment in Industrial Organization, Being a History of the Firm of Boulton & Watt, 1775-1805,* Longmans, 1930.
[2] See John Lord, *Capital and Steam Power, 1775-1800,* London, 1923.

The steam turbine was a revival, in improved form, of the first type of steam engine invented by Hero. The steam pressure is applied not to a piston, but to a series of revolving blades turning a large closed cylinder. These blades always turn in the same direction, hence there is no loss of energy through the necessity of a reversal of motion, as in the piston of the reciprocating engine. But the greatest advantage of the turbine construction lies in the fact that it furnishes a smooth pull without the use of a heavy flywheel. Its light weight and freedom from vibration have adapted it particularly to use in steamships. The first important patents were taken out by Sir Charles A. Parsons and Gustaf de Laval in the eighties of the last century. Parsons's turbine is the one that has been most generally adopted because of his scheme for reducing the speed of rotation of the blades so as to make it possible to drive machinery directly from the turbine shaft, without the necessity of "gearing it down."

The steam engine is still widely used in both the reciprocating and turbine types. But its exclusive dominion has long since been ended through the advent of an engine operated by the explosion of gas in a closed cylinder—the so-called internal-combustion engine.

2. THE INTERNAL-COMBUSTION ENGINE

The earliest anticipation of the principle of the internal-combustion engine was made in 1680 by the distinguished Dutch scientist Christiaan Huygens. He invented a crude engine, the piston of which was raised by the explosion of gunpowder in the cylinder. Huygens's device was of scientific interest but of no commercial significance. The first true gas engine was invented by an Englishman named Barber, in 1791. The earliest practical gas engine was produced by two German inventors, Nicholas Otto and Eugen Langen.

This gas engine of Otto and Langen, operated by the explosion of gas within the cylinder, was put on the market in the decade after the American Civil War. It was exhibited at the Paris World's Fair in 1867. A lighter and more efficient gas engine was invented by Gottlieb Daimler in 1883. The subsequent developments of the gas engine have been very closely associated with the progress in the application of electricity, improvements in gas mixture through carburization, and the origin and development of the petroleum industry. Down to the present time much the most important internal-combustion engine has been the gasoline engine. In this the power is produced by the explosion of gas within the cylinder by means of an electric spark carefully timed to the movement and position of the piston. The gas itself is prepared for quick explosion by a mixture of air and gasoline in a device known as a carburetor.

The chief defect in the utilization of the modern gasoline engine lies in the relative expensiveness of gasoline, and there have been many attempts to devise cheaper fuels. The most successful achievement in this direction thus far has been the Diesel engine, which was invented by a German scientist, Rudolf Diesel, about 1897. The Diesel engine uses much heavier and cheaper oil, which is introduced into the cylinders in the form of a spray and ignited by the heat of highly compressed air. This engine has proved unusually successful in marine service and in many instances has supplanted even the steam turbine. As over against the ordinary gasoline engine, it has the great advantage of cheaper fuel. As compared with the steam engine, it requires much less space on the ship because no fire box or boilers are necessary. A smaller crew can operate a Diesel-equipped boat of comparable tonnage, and the expense of keeping the ordinary steamship under steam at all times is avoided. While the Diesel engine has thus far been utilized chiefly in navigation, the trends at present indicate that it will eventually be more widely adapted to manufacturing processes. Its wide use in submarines during the World War has stimulated experiment, and various new models have been brought out, especially in Germany. Adapted to railroad locomotion, the Diesel engine has recently enabled the streamlined Burlington "Zephyr" to break all railroad speed records, and the Union Pacific streamlined train to break transcontinental train records. The Diesel engine is now being adapted for use in automobiles.[1]

The internal-combustion engines, even of the Diesel variety, are inferior to steam in one respect, namely, in ability to distribute the load gradually—its even, infinitely graduated application. This quality has also been achieved through the electric motor, but electricity has usually proved too expensive to drive out either steam or internal-combustion engines. The discovery in recent years of new methods of making steam with far greater economy of fuel may bring about a renaissance of steam power. Already, steam-driven turbines located near great cities are beginning to supplant turbine water wheels in the generation of electrical current in cases where the electricity would have to be transmitted some considerable distance from the water power.

II. THE REVOLUTION IN TRANSPORT

1. HIGHWAYS

Another advance bound up with the unfolding of the Industrial Revolution consisted in the revolution in transportation facilities. During their occupation of Gaul and England, the Romans had built a system of remarkable roads radiating throughout western Europe.[2] In some areas these had been the only really passable routes of communication during the medieval period. These Roman roads had, however, deteriorated owing to lack of repair, so that by the seventeenth century there were few or no highways in England that would be regarded as even tolerably good today. In the third chapter of his *History of England* Macaulay presents the classic, if somewhat exaggerated, description of the English roads at the time of the seventeenth-century Stuart Restoration.[3] These were little more than trails, the coaches requiring a large number of horses and crawling along at unbelievably slow speed. Not only were the physical conditions of travel extremely bad, but the matter of personal safety was by no means assured, the roads being as dangerous because of robbers as were the mountain highways of the western United States in pioneer days.

This intolerable condition of highway travel seriously hindered the development of internal commerce in England. The little that existed was carried on chiefly by means of pack horses. While, as Gibbins and others have since

---
[1] See article, "Diesels on Wheels!" *Fortune*, December, 1934.
[2] See above, Vol. I, pp. 317 ff. For the best brief account of the history of roads from primitive times to the present day, see the article "Roads," Encyclopaedia of the Social Sciences.
[3] *Cf.* Joan Parkes, *Travel in England in the Seventeenth Century*, Oxford Press, 1925.

pointed out,[1] it is possible that Macaulay somewhat exaggerated the condition of the English highways, yet we find a very similar picture of conditions a century later from the writings of Arthur Young, who probably traveled more widely in England than any other man of his generation.[2] On the Continent, roads were often in even worse condition than those in England, and improvements were usually even slower in coming.

The first determined effort to improve the English highways was embodied in the series of "turnpike acts" passed following 1663. These acts authorized individuals, corporations, and communities to build highways as a commercial enterprise. Those who built roads were to be indemnified by the privilege of levying tolls. While there were many of these turnpike acts passed during the seventeenth and eighteenth centuries, this policy resulted in few permanent improvements. After roads were constructed, those who had built them showed a far greater interest in collecting tolls than in keeping the highways in repair. The well-nigh complete failure of the English turnpike acts to achieve their ostensible purpose is well revealed in the vigor and flavor of the language employed by Arthur Young to describe the English road system at the close of the eighteenth century. Of a certain turnpike Young wrote: "A more dreadful road cannot be imagined. I was obliged to hire two men at one place to support my chaise from overturning. Let me persuade all travellers to avoid this terrible country, which must either dislocate their bones with broken pavements, or bury them in muddy sand."[3]

The beginning of scientific road-building in England is associated with the work of an intrepid English contractor, John Metcalf, and two Scottish engineers, Thomas Telford (1757-1834) and John McAdam (1756-1836).[4] Metcalf introduced into road-building after 1765 the scientific consideration of gradient. He wound his roads through valleys, and in other ways tried to eliminate long and steep grades. He also mastered the problem of constructing good road foundations in marshy or other soft lands. But he was never able to build a good top surface. One principle in road-building followed by Telford and McAdam was essentially the same, namely, careful preparation of the roadbed before the final surfacing, so as to insure adequate drainage by the use of gutters. The earlier roads had usually been laid out merely by scraping or digging a passageway through the countryside, without any scientific provision for the drainage of water from the center of the road. As a result, the roads were usually reservoirs for the accumulation of water, becoming more like ditches than roads during wet seasons.

The chief difference between the Telford and McAdam methods of road-building was to be found in the type of surfacing employed. Telford built his road in two main layers. After preparing the roadbed, Telford first put down a layer of stones about seven inches high, setting them by hand and putting the largest end downward. Then the space between was filled with smaller

---

[1] See H. de B. Gibbins, *Industry in England*, Scribner, 1916, p. 354; and Parkes, *op. cit.*
[2] See Prothero, *English Farming Past and Present*, Chaps. IX, XIII.
[3] Cited in Prothero, *op. cit.*, p. 203.
[4] The best histories of English roads are Sidney and Beatrice Webb, *English Local Government: the Story of the King's Highway*, Longmans, 1913; and Gilbert Sheldon, *From Trackway to Turnpike*, Oxford Press, 1928.

stones packed and tamped by hand to make a hard surface. On top of this he put down a second layer consisting of about seven inches of crushed stone. The road was surfaced with a binder of gravel about an inch thick. The Telford system produced an excellent road, but it was relatively expensive to build.

McAdam improved upon the Telford system by laying down a series of progressively larger stone coatings for the road surface. He began with very large cobblestones on the bottom and approached the surface with constantly smaller sizes, culminating in a dust surface on the top. The road was then rolled smooth and hard. In securing the hard surface McAdam relied primarily upon a mud binder between the stones and heavy pressure by the road-roller. On account of the greater simplicity and cheapness of the McAdam construction, the so-called macadamized road has furnished the model in highway-building down to our day. Most of our present improved automobile highways, other than concrete roads, are still based on the McAdam principle. The only important change has been the addition of an asphalt or tar surface to act as a binder and to aid in resisting wear. In 1930 there were some 664,321 miles of macadamized roads in the world, about 100,000 miles, or 15 per cent, being in the United States. Concrete roads are gradually supplanting macadamized highways now, because of their greater durability, especially under heavy truck traffic.

In France there was considerable improvement of the highways, particularly in the latter half of the eighteenth century.[1] Most of this construction was carried out by the central government, which trained highway engineers and financed construction. By 1788 there were about 30,000 miles of passable roads, of which the best radiated in a network from Paris to such towns as Strasbourg, Lyons, Marseilles, Brest, and Toulouse. Military considerations played as large a part in their construction as commercial needs. This could also be said in large measure of the great improvements in highways carried out under Napoleon, which put France far ahead of contemporary England in the excellence of its highway system. During the nineteenth century there was created in France one of the finest systems of highways in all Europe. The French roads were divided into three classes. The *routes nationales* are maintained by the state and connect Paris with the important provincial cities. The *routes départementales,* in the care of the departments under the supervision of the Minister of Public Works, are excellent macadamized roads. The *petites voies,* the country and district highways, are kept up by the communes. After the opening of the twentieth century, the excellent *routes nationales* had a total mileage of 24,000, the departmental roads amounted to almost 10,000, while the *petites voies* had a greater mileage than the *routes départementales.*

In Germany, owing to economic backwardness and political disunity, there could not be said to be any "system" of highways until well along in the nineteenth century, and travel over long distances except by water was very restricted. During the past seventy-five years an excellent system of highways has been constructed in Germany.[2]

[1] See J. H. Clapham, *The Economic Development of France and Germany, 1815-1914,* Macmillan, 1923, pp. 104 ff., 349-50. [2] See *Ibid.*, pp. 107 ff., 349-50.

While there was a notable improvement in highways in Europe and America during the nineteenth century, the greatest force accounting for the prevalence of good roads has been the general introduction of automobiles since 1900.[1] At first, the improved automobile roads were constructed chiefly on the McAdam plan with the addition of a tar or an asphalt surface. The trend now is generally towards the more durable concrete highways. There is considerable discussion now as to the feasibility of putting trucks and busses on railroad rails instead of on the roads—a sort of revised and improved tramway system. Models have been tried and demonstrated to be a technical success. The recent technical improvements in rubber tires have made this possible.

Automobiles have not only led to an immense increase in expenditures for better roads, but have also contributed heavily to their construction. In 1930 some $1,991,000,000 was spent for road construction in the United States, and some 43 per cent of this total was met by motor-vehicle fees and gasoline taxes. The latter represent a modified form of toll charge and a reversion in principle to the old turnpike method of making the users of roads pay in part for improvements.

2. EARLY CANAL BUILDING

Commercially much more significant than roads was canal construction in the earlier days of the Industrial Revolution in England and on the Continent. The art of canal-building is very old in human history: the Babylonians were building an elaborate system of canals in the third millennium before Christ. These were employed for transportation, irrigation, and defense.[2] In the second millennium the Egyptians constructed a canal connecting the Red Sea with one of the mouths of the Nile, thus anticipating the Suez Canal by more than three thousand years. Fairly extensive canal systems appeared in Italy late in the Middle Ages, and the ship canal connecting Lübeck with Hamburg also did heavy duty. In early modern times the French made some progress in canal-building under the direction of such statesmen as Colbert, and in the later eighteenth century renewed attention was paid by the state to internal navigation, particularly to canals.

It was not until the middle of the eighteenth century that any extensive development of canal-building began in England. The first important modern enterprises were promoted by the Duke of Bridgewater, who, disappointed in love, sought solace in the development of the canal industry. His first significant achievement followed the passage of the earliest English canal act in 1759. This canal was built (1761) from Worsley to Manchester, a distance of some seven miles. After this, canal-building progressed rapidly in England, guided largely by the promoting enthusiasm of Bridgewater and made practically possible by the engineering genius of James Brindley (1716-72). Brindley possessed no technical engineering training, having formerly been an illiterate millwright. He was, however, a man of very great native mechanical genius, and achieved more success in the solution of the elementary problems of canal-

---

[1] For a model study of the effect of automobiles on highway construction and operation, see F. G. Crawford and H. W. Peck, *Motor Vehicles and Highways in New York*, Syracuse University Press, 1927.   [2] See above, Vol. I, p. 129.

building than any other single individual. Largely by ingenuity, he solved some of the leading difficulties in canal engineering, such as the construction of locks, viaducts, and tunnels and the digging of extensive cuts through hilly country.

From 1760 to 1830 canal-building was carried on in England with much enthusiasm, so that by the latter date there were some three thousand miles of canals and canalized rivers. In fact, there was, if anything, an excess of canals when we consider the demand for transportation. The resulting oversupply of canals led to a considerable number of business failures and helped to check the building movement after this time. At the present time there are in England only some 3,700 miles of canals.

The canals were extremely useful in providing transportation facilities for heavier materials, such as coal and iron ore, which it was well-nigh impossible to transport on the miserable roads that existed at that time in England. Of all types of modern transportation the canals were most intimately related to the early developments of the Industrial Revolution in England.

In nineteenth-century France the canals, like the highways, were handled mainly by the central government, in contrast to England, where they were almost exclusively the product of private enterprise. The French canals were therefore more highly standardized as to depth, and so on, and they have been toll-free. Mainly because of these advantages the French canals have continued to play a significant part in transportation, particularly of bulky goods, whereas the English canals lost much of their importance after the construction of the railroads. By the twentieth century France had four chief canals and many lesser ones, with an aggregate mileage of over 3,000. Together with the navigable rivers, the commercial waterways of the country amount to over 7,500 miles.

In Germany the navigation system that came down from the medieval period was supplemented at various points, especially during the nineteenth century, by improvements in the river courses (as on the Rhine, for instance) and by the construction of canals. The latter came so late, however, that it was slowed down somewhat by the greater interest in railroad construction. By the outbreak of the World War there were, in addition to some 6,000 miles of navigable waterways, well over 2,000 miles of canals, and plans called for the construction of considerably more mileage. Germany resembles France in the large measure of government control and in the maintenance of inland waterways as a valuable supplement to overland routes. The improvement of waterways has continued even since the construction of the railroad net.

The early canal-building era in the United States from 1810 to 1837 was an interesting and characteristic aspect of this phase of the history of transportation.[1] Its treatment will be reserved for the section dealing with the economic development of the United States.[2]

The first important period of canal-building was brought to an end by the invention of the locomotive and the development of the railroads, although canals have remained an important element in domestic commerce during the

[1] See Faulkner, *American Economic History*, pp. 318 ff.   [2] See below, pp. 360 ff.

last century. As a transport system for heavy and non-perishable commodities they are still very efficient and economical.

3. THE FIRST RAILROADS

Neither roads nor canals provided a fully satisfactory method for rapid transportation of individuals or goods. Such an achievement was first brought about by the railroad. This involved the application of the Watt steam engine to the service of locomotion and transportation.[1]

While producing revolutionary results, the railroads developed naturally and gradually out of a number of previous achievements, both in the way of roadbed construction and in the provision of a satisfactory type of power. The earliest anticipation of the modern roadbed was to be found in the so-called tramways, which were introduced in Germany as early as the fifteenth century. In constructing tramways heavy square timbers were laid down in parallel rows, the distance between them being equal to the gauge of the ordinary cart or coach of the time. They were devised in order to provide some economical method of overcoming the obstacles presented by the miserable roads of the time. The timbers under the wheels kept the conveyance from sinking into the mud and becoming lodged there.

The tramway was introduced into England in the seventeenth century, usually for the transportation of heavy materials from quarries and mines. Until near the close of the next century the English tramways continued to utilize timbers for the tracks, at best placing strips of iron on top to prevent excessive wear. Gradually, with the improved methods of making iron, iron tracks tended to supersede both wooden ones and those made of a combination of wood and iron. In addition to the private tramways operated by miners, manufacturers, and merchants, public tramways, open to all upon the payment of a fee or toll, were built on a considerable scale. Carts and coaches on these public tramways were drawn by oxen, mules, or horses.

The modern railroad was at first little more than an attempt to substitute the steam engine for the horse as the means of propulsive locomotion. Almost synchronously with the appearance of the public tramway in England ingenious inventors sought to adapt the Watt engine to furnishing an adequate type of locomotive power. Among those who were earliest successful in this attempt were Richard Trevithick, William Hedley, and George Stephenson.

Stephenson completed his first reasonably efficient locomotive as early as 1814, and in 1825 the first English railroad, the Stockton and Darlington, was opened. Trains were run at a speed of from 10 to 15 miles per hour. Stephenson assiduously devoted himself to the improvement of his engine. By 1830 he had produced the famous "Rocket," which was able to make the unheard-of speed of some 29 miles per hour.[2] Before the close of the thirties the London

---

[1] *Cf.* T. W. Corbin, *The Romance of Modern Railways,* Lippincott, 1922.

[2] The fastest time ever made by a train drawn by a steam locomotive was recorded by the Empire State Express on the New York Central Railroad on May 10, 1893. Driving engine "999," Charles H. Hogan maintained an average speed of 112.5 miles per hour for a distance of one mile. Diesel-drawn trains have attained a speed of 120 miles an hour.

and Birmingham Railway had been opened over a distance of some 125 miles and was maintaining train schedules calling for a speed of about 25 miles per hour. There were also lines connecting London with Bath and Bristol.

The early English railroads were originally operated in a very simple manner. Following the model of the turnpikes and tramways, they were rented to any person who wished to pay the tolls. This confusing procedure soon proved utterly paralyzing and impossible of execution. It quickly gave way to some centralized and regulating agency. In due time the railroads were owned and operated by a commercial company which supplied its own trains and constructed and maintained its own right of way. Many of the freight cars on English railways are, however, still owned by private individuals, the figure in 1913 being only slightly below the number of railway-owned freight cars.[1] The shipper may provide his own cars, load and unload them himself, collect and deliver his goods, and even provide his own terminal stations, paying the railroad only for the use of the roadbed and the haulage.

In the course of the improvement of railroad transportation, many important contributions were made by American engineers. The latter had to face new and more serious problems, owing to the steeper grades and longer distances in North America.[2] The English railroads were at first built on approximately straight lines without sharp curves, and the trucks on the cars and locomotives were rigidly attached. It was impossible for such a locomotive or coach to take a sharp curve, for any such attempt would have snapped the trucks from the coach.

The Americans found it necessary to build railroads with sharp curves, and they solved this problem by putting a swivel axle on the trucks. This enabled the trains to take sharp curves and, further, made it possible to build much longer locomotives and coaches than would otherwise have been possible. Another innovation consisted in making the car wheel in the form of a truncated cone to enable it to take curves safely. Again, the first English railroads, following the tramway model, were built on a solid roadbed with the rails fastened to a series of piles driven into the ground. This was an expensive method and also produced a far greater degree of shock and wear and tear on the rolling stock. American engineers constructed a flexible roadbed through the use of transverse wooden ties laid on a ballast base. The latter was made of either gravel or crushed stone. This insured a relatively cheap type of roadbed and one that combined the necessary rigidity with sufficient flexibility to insure greater comfort to passengers and less wear upon the rolling stock.[3] The latest contribution of American engineers to greater safety and comfort on railway trains has been the adaptation of pneumatic tires to railway cars. A train using them has been installed in Germany.

Although one or two relatively long lines appeared fairly early, most of the English lines continued to be rather short. Between 1844 and 1847, some 637

---

[1] See L. C. A. Knowles, *The Industrial and Commercial Revolutions in Great Britain during the Nineteenth Century,* Dutton, 1926, p. 259.
[2] See Kaempffert, *Popular History of American Invention,* Vol. I, Pt. I, Chap. 1; and M. D. Stevers, *Steel Trails: The Epic of the Railroads,* Minton, Balch, 1933.
[3] For railroad construction in the United States, see below, Chap. x.

roads were chartered for operation or construction, with a total length of 9,400 miles—an average length of about 14 miles. By this time, however, it had become clear that the railroads were a success, that they would be used for passengers even more than for freight, contrary to the original expectation, and that they would produce serious competition with the canals. The year 1844 marks the real beginning of government regulation of the new mode of transportation. From that date onward, government regulation continued to increase, and the railroad companies began to consolidate and to form longer lines and railroad systems. By the end of 1850, over 6,500 miles of railroads out of the far larger mileage chartered for construction were actually in operation.[1]

The last quarter of the century was marked by growing government control, in spite of the laissez-faire principles so dominant in business during that period. By 1893, maximum rates had been fixed by statute for all the railways. From that time on, the more intense competition, together with the ever present demands for safety devices and new facilities, brought about fresh amalgamations. Before the outbreak of the World War, the question of the nationalization of the English railroads had become a pressing one—which still awaits solution.

England's experiments with railroads showed the way to the rest of Europe, not only with reference to many of the engineering problems involved, but also in relation to the social problems raised by the appearance of a public-service utility and what might almost be called a "natural monopoly."

4. RAILROAD DEVELOPMENT IN FRANCE AND GERMANY

During the nineteenth century, the transportation facilities of France underwent a veritable revolution. This was in part a result of the industrial changes that occurred during the same period, and in part a stimulus to those changes. France's belated entry into the field of railroad-building is to be ascribed to its retarded industrial development and to the excellence of its highways and its system of water transportation.[2]

The history of railroad-building in France was marked by careful planning, government interest and activity, and the comparative absence of the uncoordinated and haphazard growth characteristic of England and even more of the United States. After several years of investigation and consideration, a plan that provided for construction, management, and ownership was worked out under Thiers and adopted in 1842. According to this comprehensive scheme, nine great trunk lines were to be constructed radiating out from Paris. They were to bind the frontiers to the capital and to connect southern France with the Atlantic coast and the Rhine. The state itself contracted to contribute some 250,000 francs per mile to meet the cost of construction, and was to own the roadbed. Private companies chartered by the government were to contribute about 200,000 francs per mile to provide the rolling stock and all necessary equipment for the operation of the railroads.

It was stipulated that after forty years the railroads were to be taken over by the state. With this plan as a model the French railroad system and policy since

[1] See Knowles, *op. cit.*, p. 270.   [2] See below, pp. 325 ff.

1842 display a logic and uniformity that have often been lacking in railroad-building.

One year after the adoption of the scheme, in 1843, the first important railroad line was opened, operating between Rouen and Paris. From that year on, railroad-building has continued with regularity, interrupted only by the Revolution of 1848, the 1857 crisis, and the confusion after the Franco-Prussian War. The tendency towards combination, which was apparent at the very inception of railroad construction, resulted in the monopolistic control of the entire system by six companies in the fifties. With each company enjoying complete control in its particular region, there was little incentive for further construction. While the trunk lines were fully developed, the inadequate local branch lines were neglected. In order to rectify the situation, the government in 1859 extended the charters to ninety-nine years and undertook to guarantee profits. There was an additional provision that gave the state the right to buy out the roads after fifteen years. This effort was not very successful in developing adequate local service, and the government had to resort to other means of stimulating the private companies. Even the new efforts bore little fruit, although they did result in the construction of several railroad lines in southwestern France.

The contemporary dissatisfaction with the condition of the railroads was reflected in the active movement for state ownership, which reached its height in the years 1875-80. At the time of the Freycinet ministry (Freycinet was one of the active proponents of state ownership), however, the government refused to engage in a comprehensive scheme of railroad-building. It undertook instead to construct several scattered lines, which were later taken over by the private companies. With the dismissal of Freycinet in 1880 and the death of Gambetta the following year, the movement for state ownership lost its two outstanding leaders and declined in strength. In 1883-84, the government reverted to the system of guaranteed profits to railroad companies on newly built lines.

By law, the state has been given the right to take over through purchase any or all of the existing lines at any time it pleases. Later opinion on this point is illustrated by the acquisition of over 3,500 miles of railroad by the Clemenceau government in 1908 on the ground of corrupt mismanagement by the owners. It was expressly stated, however, that this action was not based on sympathy with the idea of state ownership. Those who were responsible for the purchase insisted that it was made because no other means could be found to remedy the abuses. On the eve of the World War, the government owned less than one-sixth of the railway lines in operation. Railway mileage had increased from 18,650 in 1885 to 31,553 in 1912, a figure that has not changed greatly since the World War.

Some decades before the revolution in German industry after 1870 far-reaching changes in transportation occurred, the most important of which was the development of railways. There had been no widespread construction of roads or canals before the introduction of the railroad, and the entry of the railroad into the field of transportation somewhat retarded, as we have seen, the subsequent road and canal building.

The first German railroad line was opened in 1835. It was four miles in length and ran from Nuremberg to Furth. The next line, between Dresden and Leipzig, began operating four years later. In the forties there was sufficient activity in railroad construction to bring the total extent of the railroads up to 3,633 miles by 1850. After that date, railroad-building continued apace. New lines connecting the more important industrial centers were opened. The figures for Prussia indicate the steady progress. The 290 miles of railroad in 1840 grew to 6,890 in 1860. By 1871, the main lines had been completed in large measure. Since 1871, the advance in railroad mileage has been fairly rapid and steady, as the following table shows:

Year	Total Trackage in Kilometers	Year	Total Trackage in Kilometers
1870	18,887	1900	49,878
1875	27,981	1905	53,822
1880	33,865	1910	59,031
1885	37,967	1914	61,749
1890	41,818	1920	55,556
1895	45,203		

The World War and the Versailles Treaty, it can be seen, cost Germany over 6,000 miles of railroad. The treaty also ordered the surrender of some of the best German trains and engines to France.

Railroad-building in Germany as a whole at first followed no such general plan as in France. The several German states constructed their lines as they saw fit, and the lack of coördination that resulted was lamentable.

From the very beginning of railway construction the German states faced the problem of government ownership. In the South German states, it was generally believed that the railroads were so important that to intrust them to private hands would be to risk the welfare of the state. In the forties a policy of government ownership and operation was adopted. In northeastern Germany, however, there was no similar clear-cut program of government ownership. Saxony had a mixed system of public and private lines, on the assumption that the advantages of both types might thus be enjoyed. As a matter of fact, however, the worst evils and abuses of each type were more apparent, and the state took over the private lines in the seventies.

In Prussia, the need of railroads was early recognized. Since the state did not feel inclined to finance their construction, railroad-building was at first a field for private enterprise. In 1842, Prussia adopted the policy of encouraging private construction by guaranteeing interest on railroad bonds. In 1848, the first state-built line was begun. The results of wars and annexations during the course of the century gave Prussia the state lines of Hesse-Cassel and Hanover and the private railroads of Nassau. As a result of the Franco-Prussian War, the new government took over the railway system of Alsace-Lorraine, the control of which was given to the Prussian Railway Administration.

When the German Empire was created in 1871, the railway system was a complicated mixture of private and government-owned lines. Many states owned and operated all the railroads within their frontiers; a third of the lines in Prussia were state-owned; and connecting lines had been built by private capitalists. The railroads thus constituted a complicated problem that had to be faced by the new imperial government.

There already existed considerable precedent in Germany for state-owned lines. Bismarck became the leading figure in an active movement for the creation of a coördinated railroad system, first to be administered by the imperial government and ultimately to be owned and operated by it. Through his efforts there were embodied in the imperial constitution a number of clauses that gave the Empire extensive rights over the railroads. One article (Number 4) declared that railways were to be "subject to the surveillance of the Empire and to imperial legislation"; another provided for uniform administration; a third declared that "railways which are considered necessary for the defense of Germany or for the purposes of general commerce may be constructed for the account of the Empire by an imperial law—even in opposition to the will of those members of the Confederation through whose territory the railways pass." These and other provisions offered Bismarck scope to press for his ultimate goal—the transfer of all the railroads in Germany to the hands of the Empire.

In addition to the usual arguments of greater disinterestedness and fairness in the construction of railway lines, the establishment of low and uniform rates, and the like, under state control or ownership, the advocates of state ownership claimed that state-owned railways would help to break down political particularism, establish a unified railroad system throughout Germany, and prevent speculation in railroad securities. Opponents of the Bismarck plan, led by Bavaria, claimed that it involved overcentralization, that it would give preponderant influence to Prussia and increase its political domination over the other states, that it would hinder private enterprise and destroy competition, and that it would subject the railroads to political influence. Owing to the strength of the opposition, Bismarck's plan for imperial ownership of the German railroads was never carried out until after the World War, though in 1873 a Central Railway Office (*Eisenbahnamt*) was created. Nevertheless, the movement for state ownership continued apace. In 1910, out of a total mileage of 36,894 of standard railroads in the German Empire, 34,596 miles were state-owned. Prussia showed the way in this nationalization of railroads. In 1878 there were only about 5,000 miles of railroads owned or operated by the state, while in 1910 there were 21,500 miles, only about 0.6 per cent remaining in private hands. The Prussia-Hesse railroad system in 1914 was perhaps the greatest business enterprise in the world—and conducted by the state. After the World War Bismarck's dream of imperial control of the German railroads was realized. Article 89 of the Weimar Constitution, which created the German Republic, directed that the Reich should take over all the railroads and administer them as a unit. State ownership of railroads has proved a great success in Germany, and the profits from these roads have constituted a major item in the revenues of the German states. This happy outcome of state ownership has been due in large part to the efficient German civil service and to the relative absence of political graft in German administration.

5. STEAM NAVIGATION

Even before steam power had been applied to railroads it was successfully exploited in the propulsion of vessels on inland waters. The steamship gradually supplanted the sailing vessel and man became a more undisputed master of the rivers, seas, and oceans. Roger Bacon, in his famous letter on the possibilities of applied science written in the latter part of the thirteenth century, vaguely anticipated the principle of the steam engine.[1] In 1690 Denis Papin set forth the possibility of using his digester engine to drive boats, and in 1707 he demonstrated the correctness of his idea by propelling a model boat with one of his engines at Cassel on the river Fulda. But the Elector of Hanover refused him freedom of the rivers, and a mob of river boatmen, who feared the possibilities of the steamboat, destroyed Papin's vessel and tried to kill Papin, who barely escaped to England with his life. In 1736-37 Jonathan Hulls in England clearly described a device to propel a boat through the use of stern paddle wheels under steam power. In 1752 further suggestions were offered by the eminent mathematician Bernoulli, and about the same time the Abbé Gauthier suggested the use of side paddle wheels with steam power.

The earliest authentic operation of a steamboat was the achievement of James Rumsey, a Virginia mechanic. He produced his craft in 1784, and it attracted the interest of both Benjamin Franklin and George Washington.[2] In the presence of the latter in 1785 he drove a boat at the rate of four miles an hour against the current of the Potomac. Between 1786 and 1796 John Fitch in America and William Symington in England successfully applied the steam engine to the problem of water locomotion. Fitch's work is particularly interesting in that one of his boats actually carried passengers for several months in 1790 and also in that he made use of a crude form of propeller instead of the paddle wheel that was employed on all the other early steamboats, including Fulton's, up to the 1840's. The inventions of Fitch and Symington were not, however, adopted on any significant scale.

The honor of having first achieved commercial success with the steamboat must be assigned to Robert Fulton, who was quite as much a promoter as an inventor.[3] He had traveled widely in Europe and was thoroughly familiar with the work of both Fitch and Symington. In 1807 he had the famous *Clermont* built and launched on the Hudson River and was rewarded by seeing his vessel make a satisfactory trip to Albany. He had the resources to hire first-rate builders to construct the hull, and to import a Watt-Boulton engine. The steamboat was thereafter rapidly developed to meet the need of water transportation in the inland waters of the United States and very soon for ocean transportation. In the process of successfully marketing the steamboat and securing its wide adoption, Fulton played a very important part. Steam was immediately applied to the navigation of inland waters.

By 1819 the *Savannah*, a rude early steamboat with an auxiliary sailing equipment, made a successful transatlantic trip, relying on steam most of the way across. The first really successful transatlantic trips made by true steamboats

[1] See above, Vol. I, pp. 789 ff.
[2] See Ritter, *Washington as a Business Man*, p. 155.
[3] See Iles, *Leading American Inventors*, pp. 40 ff.

THE REVOLUTION IN TRANSPORT

were those of the *Sirius* and the *Great Western,* which crossed the Atlantic in eighteen and fifteen days, respectively, in April, 1838. The next year the Cunard Line was established, this being the first marine organization for transatlantic steam navigation.

From the time of Fulton onward the progress of steam navigation has consisted mainly in certain technical improvements in the details of propulsion, in the type of motor used, in the material of which boats have been constructed, and in the method of commercially organizing and controlling the great fleet of steamboats that now carry the commerce of the world.

One very significant innovation was the invention of the screw propeller, which possessed very real advantages over the old side-wheel or stern-wheel paddle propellers, except for navigation in shallow water. Fitch had hit upon a rudimentary form of propeller, and early in the nineteenth century Colonel Stevens of New Jersey made improvements upon Fitch's device. There is good ground for according Stevens the honor of being the inventor of the screw propeller. The actual introduction of a successful screw propeller into navigation was, however, due to the labors of John Ericsson, later noted as the inventor of the *Monitor,* and F. P. Smith, an English inventor. Ericsson's model, perfected in 1839, was the one most widely adopted for application to steam vessels.[1] Even at the present time, however, the paddle wheel is retained on such large vessels as the Hudson River steamers because of the danger of damaging or entangling a screw propeller in shallow or grass-infested water.

Another very significant improvement in steamboats was found in the turbine engine, which gave much greater power and took up less space. The Parsons turbine engine had been invented in the eighties, but was first used in ocean navigation on the *Kaiser Wilhelm II* in 1901. Much more recently we have witnessed, in some cases, the superseding of steam engines by electric motors driven by steam turbines, or by a much more promising invention, the Diesel engine.[2]

Very important also has been the improvement in the material out of which vessels have been constructed. The early ships were, of course, made of wood, though iron scows were built as early as 1787 by the English ironmaster, Wilkinson. These iron scows were utilized for the transportation of coal and ore. At first it was commonly supposed that an iron boat would not float, though scientists familiar with Archimedes' law of floating bodies were convinced to the contrary. It was soon shown that iron construction actually lessened the weight of ships of comparable size, capacity, and strength. Wooden vessels were superseded by iron boats in the English navy and merchant marine following 1840, about the same time that the screw propeller was made available.[3]

The struggle for the ocean carrying trade between England and the United States, unfortunately for the latter, came to a head in the decades of the Civil War and Reconstruction. There was some question as to the all-round superiority of iron over wood, but the steel ship, made generally practicable by the Bessemer and open-hearth processes of steel manufacture,[4] served to make both

[1] See Iles, *op. cit.*, pp. 218 ff.   [2] See above, pp. 302-3.
[3] *Cf.* J. P. Baxter, *The Introduction of the Ironclad Warships,* Harvard University Press, 1933.
[4] See above, pp. 280 ff.

older types obsolete. Our preoccupation with the Civil War and its aftermath, together with absorption in westward expansion and the completion of our Industrial Revolution, gave Great Britain a lead in boat construction and the carrying trade that was never overcome. Some attempts have been made to introduce reënforced concrete into ship construction, but to date the success of this experiment has not been notable or encouraging.

The improvement in the materials out of which boats are constructed was paralleled by certain other technical advances, most notably the standardization of parts in shipbuilding. This made it possible to manufacture standardized parts of vessels in steel factories remote from shipyards, to be collected and assembled later. This process of standardization of parts in the building of steel steamships reached its height in the frenzied American efforts during the World War, and in German submarine construction in the same period.

It was but natural that the progress in the technique of steam navigation should be accompanied by a remarkable increase in the size and speed of ocean-going vessels. For example, the tonnage of the *Great Western* was only 1,340, whereas the *Bismarck*, the largest vessel constructed before 1934, and now known as the *Majestic*,[1] rates a little over 56,000. Her older and slightly smaller sister ship, the *Vaterland*, now the American *Leviathan*, has been refitted since the war to give her a tonnage of more than 59,000. The *Great Western* was 236 feet long, whereas the *Majestic* measures 915 feet, the *Leviathan*, 907. The engine of the *Great Western* had a horse power of 450, whereas the engines of the *Majestic* and the *Leviathan* develop about 100,000 horse power. The largest boat now afloat is the new French liner *Normandie*.[2] Its tonnage is 79,280 and its length 1,029 feet. It develops a horse power of 160,000. The engines in most of the great steamers today are either the improved turbine or a combination of turbine and reciprocating engines. Diesel engines, as has been noted, are being used more frequently, and Scandinavians have had much success with liners driven by electric motors. The increase in speed of transatlantic voyages may also be measured by the difference between the fifteen days occupied by the *Great Western* in making its trip and the four days, thirteen hours, and fifty-eight minutes in which the Italian liner *Rex* made the crossing from Gibraltar to New York during the summer of 1933. The distance covered is 3,181 sea miles and the average speed was 28.92 knots an hour. The record for the north-Atlantic passage is held by the German liner *Bremen*, at four days, fourteen hours, and twenty-seven minutes. This record voyage was made in November, 1934. The fastest time ever made by a boat was that recorded by Gar Wood, who drove his motor boat at the rate of 124.9 miles per hour.

The two great types of ocean traffic today are carried on by the liners on the one hand, and the "tramp steamers" on the other; in other words, the line traffic and the charter traffic. The average layman, in considering the subject of the steamboat, almost always concentrates his attention upon the great liners, because of the popular attention drawn to them by reports of their remarkable size, speed, or famous attendant disasters. As a matter of fact, the greater part

[1] Taken over from Germany by England at the close of the war.
[2] The Cunard Line has tried to match the *Normandie* with the *Queen Mary,* launched early in 1935. The *Queen Mary* is 1,018 feet long and has a tonnage of 73,000. But she surpasses the *Normandie* in horse power, with engines generating 200,000 horse power.

From Currier and Ives, *by Harry T. Peters, reprinted by permission from Doubleday, Doran and Company*

AN EARLY EXPRESS TRAIN

Union Pacific Railroad Company

A STREAMLINE TRAIN

U. S. Department of Agriculture

AN OLD-TYPE REAPER

Rittase Photo

LATER REAPING MACHINERY

of the commerce of the world is carried on by the relatively small and dingy tramp steamers, which bear what is known as the charter traffic. The liners are relatively large and speedy vessels that run along definite routes, according to pre-announced schedules, and land uniformly at certain selected ports. They specialize primarily in passenger, express, and mail transportation, all of which require a relatively high degree of speed and safety.

The tramp steamer is prepared to carry all types of cargoes to any part of the world. It is not usually a large vessel, because it must be small enough not to be required to wait too long in port to secure a normal cargo. No effort is made to develop excessive speed, because above a certain rate additional speed becomes disproportionately more expensive. The average tonnage of a tramp usually runs from 2,500 to 5,000, and its speed is usually around 8 to 12 knots an hour. It uses only from 25 to 40 tons of coal a day, whereas the *Mauretania* consumes something over 1,000 tons a day. Another reason for the relative cheapness of chartered tramp-steamer transportation lies in the fact that there is no expensive overhead shore organization of administrators, publicity men, and clerks.

The tramp steamers secure their connection with shippers desiring their services chiefly through brokerage houses that specialize in bringing the shippers and the boat-owners together. Usually the rate charged by the owner of the tramp steamer will depend upon the prospect of getting a return cargo from or near the port to which the original shipment is to be sent. Sometimes there is a tendency for even the charter traffic to develop rather regular lines of transit in order to build up a more permanent and reliable clientele, but it still remains relatively flexible and adapted to transporting all types of cargoes to and from all parts of the earth.

Since the World War the liner freight traffic has gained somewhat at the expense of the chartered traffic.[1] Many firms are willing to pay the higher prices demanded by liners in order to get quick service between ports. Moreover, liners have reduced their freight rates in many cases. There has been an excessive amount of liner construction since 1919, and the greater supply of boats and the more intense competition between them has worked in the direction of reduced rates. Finally, not a few of the liners themselves become tramps during the less busy periods of the year in ocean passenger transportation. They abandon their regular lanes and offer themselves for special trips.

The improvement of steam navigation has resulted in a great decrease in, and standardization of, rates. The shipping rates as a whole have been lowered about 50 per cent in the last half-century. The reduction and the standardization of shipping rates have reacted to increase the standardization and equalization of the prices of the commodities thus transported.

III. NEW DEVICES FOR THE TRANSMISSION OF INFORMATION

Another highly significant phase of the transformation in modern technology has been the development of new and revolutionary devices for communication and the transmission of information. These inventions are not only interesting

---

[1] *Cf.* Clair Price, "Heavy Weather for the Tramps of the Sea," New York *Times* "Magazine," Apr. 22, 1934.

and significant in themselves, but they have proved indispensable to the development of many other aspects of the newer technology. For example, modern transportation is almost completely dependent upon the telephone, the telegraph, and electric signals, while modern international trade has to depend upon the cable and the wireless telegraph.

Most of these new methods for rapid and extensive transmission of information have been made possible by the progress in our knowledge and control of electrical phenomena since the time of the American Revolution.[1] Benjamin Franklin showed the essential identity between lightning and electricity. Seebeck (1770-1831) for the first time worked out the theory and the practice of the magnetic field. Ampère (1775-1836) developed the basic law of electrodynamics, explaining the attraction and repulsion of electrical currents. Faraday constructed upon their foundations the electric dynamo. Electrical physics owed much to the work of Sir William Thomson (later Lord Kelvin). Hertz, in 1887, successfully established the electromagnetic theory of heat, light, and sound. Clerk Maxwell and Willard Gibbs developed mathematical physics to the point where a general synthesis of physico-chemical phenomena was possible of statement in certain fundamental and uniform mathematical equations. The Curies, building on the work of earlier students of physico-chemical and electrical theory, laid the basis for the modern knowledge of radioactivity. Along with these developments in the field of the pure science of electricity went various improvements in the methods of generating and transmitting electrical currents and many other phases of practical engineering associated with electricity. Thomas Alva Edison and such scientists in the General Electric laboratories as Steinmetz and Coolidge were important contributors here.

Crude devices for signaling between relatively distant points had existed from primitive times by such means as fires or smoke on hilltops or the beating of unusually resonant drums.[2] Down to the second quarter of the nineteenth century, however, the speediest method of communicating information known was the employment of carrier pigeons. They were swift but not always too dependable, and they could transport only fragmentary bits of information. In the last decade of the eighteenth century Claude Chappe and his brothers worked out an elaborate system of signaling by means of semaphores. This was adopted by Napoleon.

The first important achievement in the way of adapting electricity to the more rapid transmission of information over long distances was the invention of the electric telegraph by Carl A. Steinheil, Sir Charles Wheatstone, and Samuel F. B. Morse.[3] The first practical applications of the telegraph were made by Steinheil in the year 1837, when he sent a message from Munich to Bogenhausen, by the English in the same year in sending a message from Euston to Camden, and by Morse in 1844, when he transmitted a message from Baltimore to Washington. After Morse's time the successful extension of telegraph facilities on land developed speedily. The next problem lay in providing some sort of an adequate conductor for transmitting information across wide

---

[1] See above, p. 152, and below, p. 644.
[2] For a good summary of the background and development of the telegraph, see Beckles Willson, *The Story of Rapid Transit,* Appleton, 1903, Chap. v; and Kaempffert, *op. cit.,* Vol. I, Pt. II, Chaps. I-III.   [3] *Cf.* Iles, *op. cit.,* pp. 119 ff.

bodies of water. After a series of disheartening failures, which would have discouraged a man of less persistence, Cyrus W. Field succeeded in laying a cable across the Atlantic Ocean in 1866. At present a network of cables crosses all the major water bodies of the planet.

The electric telegraph and the cable represented the major achievements in the improvement of communication during the first phase of the Industrial Revolution. In a later chapter on "The Second Industrial Revolution" we shall deal with the much more striking and diversified inventions in this field during the last fifty years.[1] This will tell the story of the telephone, wireless telegraphy, the radio or wireless telephony, the transmission of pictures by electrical devices, television, and other well-nigh incredible accomplishments of pure and applied contemporary science.

IV. THE LIBERALIZATION OF COMMERCIAL POLICIES

The new machinery, the factory system, and the development of the railroad and the steamboat brought about a great increase of goods and made their transport and distribution far easier and cheaper.[2] It was natural that the new capitalist class should favor policies designed to increase the volume and the scope of commercial activities. It had once been thought that mercantilism would achieve this result, but experience had proved the contrary to be true. Therefore the mechanical revolution in production and transport was provided with a new liberal economic philosophy to undermine mercantilism and work for the liberalization of commercial policies.

The political and economic theories of the eighteenth and nineteenth centuries, together with the remarkable changes in manufacturing and commerce, thus combined to produce a notable alteration of trade policies. Beginning with the middle of the eighteenth century, a number of writers in France and England made a vigorous attack upon the old mercantilistic notions and practices.[3] The most notable of these writers were, as we have seen, the French Physiocrats and Adam Smith and his followers in England. There were some important later Continental writers who also adhered to this point of view, among whom may be noted J. B. Say and Frédéric Bastiat in France and J. H. von Thünen and K. H. Rau in Germany.[4]

Down to about 1820, this reaction against mercantilism chiefly took the form of polemical writings and oral argument, but from 1820 onward there developed a steady movement against restrictive legislation. This brought about far-reaching practical results in the repeal of laws restricting freedom of trade.

The first important steps in this direction were taken in Prussia and in England. In 1819 the King of Prussia, in counsel with his two ministers, Von Maassen and Von Bülow, removed the internal customs barriers from Prussia and made the state one fiscal unit. These reforms provided for admitting raw materials free and for a duty of about 10 per cent on imported manufactures. In the form of a Zollverein, by 1842 this Prussian system had been extended to all the

[1] See below, pp. 736 ff. [2] See Birnie, *Economic History of Europe*, Chap. IV.
[3] See above, pp. 77 ff., and below, pp. 378 ff.
[4] See Charles Gide and Charles Rist, *History of Economic Doctrines*, Heath, 1917, Bk. I.

leading German states except Austria.[1] In this manner, the archaic German customs system was very generally abandoned.

Shortly after the beginnings of Prussian trade liberalization in 1819, the movement against trade restriction took a practical form in England. Under the leadership of William Huskisson, president of the Board of Trade, an organized effort began about 1820 to induce other states to reduce their customs duties. In consequence, a series of reciprocity treaties was negotiated following 1820. Huskisson was killed in a railroad accident in 1830, but the spirit of his work continued, and in 1833 a very thoroughgoing reduction of duties on commodities imported into England was ordered.

The next important stage of the trade-liberalization movement in England took form in the campaign against the so-called Corn Laws. The Corn Laws embodied legislation providing for heavy duties on all wheat[2] imported into England. Such protective laws had been in existence from the time of medieval England, but towards the close of the Napoleonic wars and immediately following Waterloo the tariffs on wheat were raised very considerably. Exorbitant duties were imposed except when the price of grain was very high; in other words, wheat could not be profitably imported except at the time of a general crop failure or wheat famine in England itself.

The movement against the Corn Laws was led by Richard Cobden (1804-65) and John Bright (1811-89), two leading British manufacturers of the new Liberal party. The parliamentary campaign was in charge of Sir Robert Peel. The program of Cobden and Bright was based upon a type of economic theory worked out by the followers of Adam Smith, especially David Ricardo.[3] These economists argued that wages tend to equal the cost of subsistence on the part of the laborer. In other words, wages bear a constant and direct relation to the price of food. If food can be made cheaper, lower wages can be paid and the profits of the employer thus increased. Cobden and Bright and the manufacturing and commercial classes in England launched their campaign of propaganda against the Corn Laws on the basis of this doctrine. They felt that if the Corn Laws were abolished wheat might be imported cheaply and wages cut in proportion. While the policy of Cobden and Bright was thus clearly motivated by their economic interests and connections, there is little doubt that they rationalized it to the point of believing that they were carrying on an unselfish crusade for the betterment of all mankind.

From the standpoint of political propaganda and economic education, the anti-Corn-Law campaign was one of the best organized political and economic movements of modern times.[4] It was carried on from about 1836 to 1846. In the latter year the Anti-Corn-Law League succeeded in carrying through Parliament a law providing for the abolition of the Corn Laws on February 1, 1849. Accompanying the repeal came legislation removing or reducing duties on other commodities. The movement toward free trade went on, and by 1860 England had become practically a free-trade state. The Cobden reciprocity

---

[1] Most of them had come in by 1834.

[2] Wheat, outside the United States, usually being known as corn. Our corn (maize) has not been generally introduced elsewhere. For the best history of the Corn Laws and their political ramifications, see D. G. Barnes, *History of the English Corn Laws from 1660-1846*, Crofts, 1930.

[3] See below, pp. 378 ff.

[4] *Cf.* Archibald Prentice, *History of the Anti-Corn-Law League*, London, 1853, 2 vols.

THE LIBERALIZATION OF COMMERCIAL POLICIES

treaty with France was negotiated in this year (1860). W. E. Gladstone led the fight for free trade at this time.

Bearing in mind England's priority in the development of modern industry, it becomes easy to understand its adoption of a free-trade policy. It was not only that its economists and statesmen recognized more clearly than others the advantages of an international division of labor. Even more important, from a practical point of view, was the fact that its manufacturers were so firmly established that they could withstand unbridled competition with the producers of other less highly industrialized countries and remain prosperous. This consideration does not belittle England's endorsement of the free-trade policy. It merely explains how it was possible to carry such a policy into effect successfully.

It must be noted that England alone, of all modern industrial and commercial states, was able to reject the protectionist movement of the latter part of the nineteenth century, and remain a free-trade state down to the outbreak of the World War in 1914.[1]

In France, as in Germany and England, there came to be a distinct trend in the direction of free trade about the middle of the nineteenth century. A campaign for tariff reduction developed in the so-called Orleanist period from 1830 to 1848, led by Frédéric Bastiat (1801-50).[2] Though Bastiat died in 1850, the work that he had started was carried on by Sainte-Beuve, who succeeded in converting Napoleon III to the policy of free trade. From 1852 to 1860 notable progress was made in reducing and eliminating customs duties, and in 1860 the Cobden reciprocity treaty carried France far on the way towards free trade. Other reciprocity treaties were made during this same period with the sanction of Napoleon III.

Similar movements towards trade liberalization swept over the greater part of Europe about the middle of the last century. Even in the United States there was comparable progress, beginning with the Clay compromise tariff of 1833 and culminating in the very low tariff of 1857.[3] In all these Western industrial and commercial nations it was not only believed that cheaper food meant lower wages, but it was also contended that complete freedom of trade would encourage the growth of industries in every country along the lines that each particular state was best fitted to develop. Moreover, it was asserted that commerce would be greatly stimulated by an economic régime free from any restrictions. The period around the year 1860 represented the temporary triumph of the movement towards either free trade or great reduction in tariff schedules.

[1] See below, pp. 774-76.
[2] Bastiat's polemics against protectionism were probably the ablest writings of their kind in the nineteenth century.
[3] Cf. F. W. Taussig, *Tariff History of the United States,* 7th ed., Putnam, 1923, Pt. I, Chap. III.

SUGGESTED READING

Hammerton, *Universal History of the World,* Chap. 168.
Wells, *The Work, Wealth and Happiness of Mankind,* Vol. I, pp. 117-54
Usher, *History of Mechanical Inventions,* Chaps. XI, XIII
Kaempffert, *A Popular History of American Invention,* Vol. I, Pt. I, Chaps. I-II; Pt. II, Chaps. I-III; Pt. III, Chap. I

322   REVOLUTION IN POWER AND TRANSPORTATION

H. H. Webster, *Travel by Air, Land, and Sea,* Houghton Mifflin, 1934
Briggs, *Economic History of England,* Chap. VI
F. S. Chapin, *Historical Introduction to Social Economy,* Century, 1917, Chap. XVI
Beckles Willson, *The Story of Rapid Transit,* Appleton, 1903, Chaps. I-VII
Mantoux, *The Industrial Revolution,* Pt. II, Chap. IV
R. H. Thurston, *History of the Growth of the Steam Engine,* Appleton, 1902
Corbin, *Mechanical Inventions of To-day,* Chap. XXIV
Ogg and Sharp, *Economic Development of Modern Europe,* Chap. XI and pp. 246-76, 284-89
Gilbert Sheldon, *From Trackway to Turnpike,* Oxford Press, 1928
W. T. Jackman, *The Development of Transportation in Modern England,* Macmillan, 1916, 2 Vols.
E. A. Pratt, *History of Inland Transport and Communication in England,* Dutton, 1912
A. G. Nathan and Margaret Ernst, *The Iron Horse,* Knopf, 1931
M. D. Stevens, *Steel Trails: The Epic of the Railroads,* Minton, Balch, 1933
M. D. Stevens and Jones Pendlebury, *Sea Lanes: Man's Conquest of the Ocean,* Minton, Balch, 1935
F. C. Bowen, *A Century of Atlantic Travel,* Little, Brown, 1930
Day, *History of Commerce,* Chaps. XXVIII-XXXIV
P. W. L. Ashley, *Modern Tariff History,* 3d ed., Dutton, 1920, Pt. I, Chaps. I-IV; Pt. III, Chaps. I-IV
F. W. Taussig, *Tariff History of the United States,* 7th ed., Putnam, 1923, Pt. I, Chap. III
E. L. Bogart and C. M. Thompson, eds., *Readings in the Economic History of the United States,* Longmans, 1916, Chaps. XII, XIX
Scott and Baltzly, *Readings in European History since 1914,* pp. 94-98
Bland, Brown, and Tawney, *English Economic History; Select Documents,* pp. 689-711
Benjamin Rand, *Selections Illustrating Economic History since 1763,* 3d ed., J. Wilson, 1895, Chaps. I, V, VIII, IX, XVI

FURTHER REFERENCES

THE NEW POWER RESOURCES. On the history of the steam engine, the best account is Thurston, *op. cit.* See also Usher, *op. cit.,* Chaps. XI, XIII; Bridges, *The Book of Inventions,* Chap. VI; Corbin, *op. cit.,* Chaps. IV, XVI; and Chaps. I-V of T. W. Corbin, *Modern Engines* (London, 1918). On the development of the steam engine from Savery to Watt, see Mantoux, *op. cit.,* Pt. II, Chap. IV.

On the history of the turbine, see Thurston, *op. cit.,* pp. 4 ff.; Corbin, *Modern Engines,* Chap. VI; and *Mechanical Inventions of To-day,* Chaps. XVIII-XIX.

On the history of the internal-combustion engine, see Keir, *The Epic of Industry,* pp. 112 ff.; Corbin, *Mechanical Inventions of To-day,* Chap. XXIV; and *Modern Engines,* Chap. XII.

On the Diesel engine, see Keir, *op. cit.,* pp. 124 ff.; Corbin, *Modern Engines,* pp. 124 ff.; Chap. IV of Edward Cressy, *Discoveries and Inventions of the Twentieth Century* (3d ed. rev., Dutton, 1930); A. P. Chalkley, *Diesel Engines for Land and Marine Work* (Van Nostrand, 1927); Orville Adams, *Modern Diesel Engine Practice* (Henley, 1931); D. L. Jones, *Diesel Engines* (Henley, 1926); article, "Diesels on Wheels," *loc. cit.*

TRANSPORTATION. On the history of transportation, see Willson, *op. cit.;* A. W. Kirkaldy and A. D. Evans, *History and Economics of Transport* (Pitman, 1915); Pratt, *op. cit.;* Jackman, *op. cit.* For good introductory surveys, see Briggs, *op. cit.,*

FURTHER REFERENCES

Chap. VI; Ogg and Sharp, *op. cit.,* Chap. XI; Bridges, *op. cit.,* Chaps. XI, XVII, XIX; Hawks, *The Triumph of Man in Science and Invention,* Chaps. XI-XIII; Corbin, *Mechanical Inventions of To-day;* Birnie, *Economic History of Europe,* Chap. III; Webster, *Travel by Air, Land and Sea.*

On the development of roads, see article "Roads," Encyclopaedia of the Social Sciences; Joan Parkes, *Travel in England in the Seventeenth Century* (Oxford Press, 1925); Sheldon, *op. cit.;* F. G. Crawford and H. W. Peck, *Motor Vehicles and Highways in New York* (Syracuse University Press, 1927).

On the history of English canals, see Jackman, *op. cit.;* Kirkaldy and Evans, *op. cit.;* Pratt, *op. cit.;* H. G. Thompson, *The Canal System of England* (Unwin, 1903). On French and German canals, see pp. 104 ff., 350 ff., of J. H. Clapham, *The Economic Development of France and Germany, 1815-1914* (Macmillan, 1923); pp. 170-323 of H. G. Moulton, *Waterways versus Railways* (Houghton Mifflin, 1926).

On the rise of English railways, see Jackman, Pratt, and Kirkaldy and Evans, as cited; H. G. Lewin, *Early British Railways* (Spon, 1928); Sir W. M. Acworth, *The Railways of England* (Scribner & Welford, 1890); E. C. Cleveland-Stevens, *English Railways* (Dutton, 1915).

On American contributions to railroad engineering, see Kirkland, *History of American Economic Life,* pp. 296 ff.; J. E. Watkins, "The Development of the American Rail and Track," United States National Museum, *Report,* 1889, pp. 651-708; Chap. V of R. M. Keir, *The March of Commerce* (Yale University Press, 1927); Stevens, *op. cit.*

On French railroads, see Ogg and Sharp, *op. cit.,* pp. 234 ff.; Knight, Barnes and Flügel, *op. cit.,* pp. 597 ff.; Clapham, *op. cit.,* pp. 143 ff., 340 ff.

On German railroads, see *Ibid.,* pp. 150 ff., 345 ff.; Chap. III of W. H. Dawson, *Industrial Germany* (Colin, 1912). On the development of state ownership of railroads in Germany, see Sir W. M. Acworth, *Historical Sketch of Government Ownership of Railroads in Foreign Countries* (Joint Committee on Commerce, Washington, D. C., 1917).

On the evolution of the steamboat, see Keir, *The March of Commerce,* Chap. IV; Thurston, *op. cit.,* Chap. V; Henry Fry, *History of North Atlantic Steam Navigation* (Scribner, 1896); Bowen, *op. cit.*

On the history and methods of ocean shipping, see C. E. Fayle, *Short History of the World's Shipping Industry* (Dial Press, 1933); Kirkaldy, *British Shipping;* Abraham Berglund, *Ocean Transportation* (Longmans, 1931); E. R. Johnson and G. G. Huebner, *The Principles of Ocean Transportation* (Appleton, 1918) and *The Ocean Freight Service* (Appleton, 1925); G. G. Huebner, *Ocean Steamship Traffic Management* (Appleton, 1920). For a good summary of recent charter and liner ocean transportation, see Clair Price, "Heavy Weather for the Tramps of the Sea," New York *Times,* "Magazine," Apr. 22, 1934.

NEW DEVICES FOR THE TRANSMISSION OF INFORMATION. On the history of methods of communication, see Chapin, *op. cit.,* Chap. XVI; Willson, *op. cit.,* Chaps. V, VII; Chap. I of A. W. Page and others, *Modern Communication* (Houghton Mifflin, 1932); Bridges, *op. cit.,* Chaps. VIII-X, XV, XXIII-XXV; Kaempffert, *op. cit.,* Vol. I, Pt. II.

THE LIBERALIZATION OF COMMERCIAL POLICIES. On tariff liberalization, see Birnie, *op. cit.,* Chap. V; Hammerton, *op. cit.,* Chap. 168; Ogg and Sharp, *op. cit.,* pp. 247 ff., 269 ff., 284 ff.; William Cunningham, *The Rise and Decline of the Free Trade Movement* (Macmillan, 1905); Ashley, *op. cit.;* Taussig, *op. cit.;* A. L. Dunham, *The Anglo-French Treaty of Commerce of 1860* (University of Michigan Press, 1930).

CHAPTER IX

THE TRANSIT OF THE INDUSTRIAL REVOLUTION TO CONTINENTAL EUROPE AND THE ORIENT

I. THE GENERAL CHARACTER OF THE TRANSIT OF THE INDUSTRIAL REVOLUTION

During the course of the nineteenth century, the industrial changes that had already affected England made their way not only to continental Europe but to the United States and the Orient as well. In broad outlines, the industrial development of the Continent and of the other regions followed the pattern laid down in England.

Owing, however, to differences in time, natural resources, geography, and other conditioning factors, the process of industrialization exhibits variation in detail from one country to another. Similarly, in each of these regions definite variations from the English precedent in industrial development can be observed. But these differences should not be permitted to obscure the fact that, in terms of major essentials and consequences, the Industrial Revolution in continental Europe was primarily an extension and a later phase of the English Industrial Revolution.

Looking at the matter broadly, the Continent began to experience the characteristic industrial changes about seventy-five to a hundred years later than England did.[1] In small measure this was due to England's attempt to maintain up to 1825 an embargo on the exportation of the new industrial devices. The important reasons for the belated introduction of machinery, however, are much more satisfactorily sought and found in the local development, national peculiarities, and special conditions of the various countries themselves. As might be expected, the new industrial development brought with it: (1) The overthrow of the guild system wherever it was still functioning; (2) the widespread introduction of machinery and steam power; (3) the rise of the factory system; (4) marked improvements in the methods of transportation; and (5) a relative reduction in the importance of agriculture as compared with industry and trade.

In most countries, the general pattern of the Industrial Revolution was transplanted from England—en bloc, as it were. It came, therefore, with much more rapidity than it did in England. In Germany, for example, transformations in

---

[1] There were evidences of industrialization in France and Belgium before this.

industry were experienced in the fifteen- or twenty-year period after 1870 comparable to those which required a full century, from 1750 to 1850, in England. There was, of course, a preceding period of preparation in Germany, but even so the industrial changes in that country constituted a true "revolution" as measured in terms of rapidity and thoroughness of transformation.

Because the new industrial system in Germany, France, and other countries was taken rather completely from England, the cultural implications of the change have been very interesting. It has meant that the nonindustrial aspects of the cultures of these countries have been transformed by the Industrial Revolution to a far less degree than was England's. Veblen makes this clear in the case of Germany:

Germany combines the results of English experience in the development of modern technology with a state of the other arts of life more nearly equivalent to what prevailed in England before the modern industrial régime came on; so that the German people have been enabled to take up the technological heritage of the English without having paid for it in the habits of thought, the use and wont, induced in the English community by the experience involved in achieving it.[1]

In the later stages of the Industrial Revolution, towards the very close of the nineteenth century, England no longer remained the sole model for the countries then undergoing industrialization. Other industrial centers were by then well prepared to make contributions of their own. This is excellently shown in Russia's industrial awakening in the nineties, for which Germany served as a major model for imitation. Since 1900, the industrial influence of the United States upon other parts of the world has been very marked.

While England was the general model for technological and industrial imitation down to the close of the eighteenth century, the completeness and exactness of the duplication of English attitudes and methods should not be exaggerated. Countries like Germany, for example, were in an age of nascent electrical development when they came to introduce wholesale English methods that had been born in the age of steam and water power. While Germany has, of course, relied upon steam and water power, it has also tended to exploit electricity and chemistry far more than Britain. Such considerations as these led to modifications and adjustments in imitating England.

II. THE INDUSTRIAL REVOLUTION IN FRANCE

1. ORIGINS

France was the first Continental country to experience the transformations that led to the establishment of the new industrial order. At the opening of the nineteenth century agriculture predominated in France. During the preceding century French commerce had grown steadily. That there was no comparable advance in industry is attributable to the political situation at the close of the century, the relative scantiness of certain natural resources, the presence of the conservative industrial guilds, the absence of a sufficiently large body of skilled workmen, and a lack of adequate capital. The system of household manufac-

---

[1] T. B. Veblen, *Imperial Germany and the Industrial Revolution,* Huebsch, 1915, p. 82.

ture was firmly intrenched and the prejudice against the factory system was strong. Only after the third decade of the nineteenth century did the changes in industry occur on a wide and accelerated scale. These conditions explain why the active beginnings of the Industrial Revolution in France are dated from 1825.

The Revolutionary and Napoleonic periods were important in preparing the way for French industrial changes. During those years there was a general tendency towards the undermining of the guild system and the liberalization of industry. During the Consulate and the Empire, sincere efforts were made to encourage the use of machinery in the textile industry. They were not, however, very successful.

As early as 1774-76, under the inspiration of Turgot,[1] a serious attempt was made to destroy the privileges of the French guilds, and to liberalize industry by permitting every man to determine the manner, time, and place of any occupation it pleased him to pursue. These measures could not be pressed to their fullest advantage, and after Turgot's dismissal from the comptroller-generalship, the guilds made a rapid recovery from this assault. Much more effective in undermining the strength of the guilds was the economic development of France during the two centuries preceding the Revolution. The guild privileges were no longer so extensive. In fact, their monopolies were infringed upon, and their regulations often evaded. The putting-out system was well developed in certain areas.

Nevertheless, guild control and restriction were still characteristic of French industry on the eve of the Revolution. The guild problem was hotly debated, and the domestic workers of both rural and urban districts were insistent upon reform. The question received attention in the *cahiers* of 1789,[2] in which the guild system was attacked and defended in accordance with the interests of particular groups. Finally, the problem was decisively settled in 1791 by a law of the National Assembly which declared that after April 1, 1791, any person was "free to do such business, exercise such profession, art, or trade, as he may choose."

The guilds themselves were not expressly abolished, but they were shorn of their special privileges. They were left without any real reason for existence. Mainly as a result of the desire to suppress the agitation of workingmen for better wages and working-conditions, which followed the passage of the law destroying the guild monopoly, the National Assembly enacted a measure that remained to plague the French working class for almost a century. This was the law Le Chapelier (June 14, 1791). It definitely declared trade associations of workers to be illegal and proclaimed gatherings of workingmen to be "riotous" and punishable by law.[3]

The Napoleonic period was characterized by a partial attempt to restore the guilds, and the bakers, butchers, printers, and brokers were forced to assume guild organization. The bakers' and butchers' guilds were established after 1801 by Napoleon to avoid food riots; the printers were organized (1810) to

---

[1] See above, p. 111.   [2] See above, pp. 112 ff., 115 ff.
[3] It is significant that associations of merchants (Chambers of Commerce) were specifically excluded from the application of this measure.

make supervision of the press easier; and the brokers were restricted in number and placed under police control in order to regulate speculation in government securities. The motives behind the restoration of the guilds were more political than economic in nature. After the overthrow of Napoleon, the guild monopolies were once more removed and free competition again became the norm, though some of the associations persisted well into the nineteenth century.[1]

2. MECHANICAL INDUSTRY

The disappearance of the guilds signaled an age of free industrial competition in France and cleared the path for the introduction of machinery and the development of the factory system.[2] The 15 steam engines in use before the Congress of Vienna had jumped to 600 by 1830, but all notable mechanization of industry came after that date. Even after the third decade of the century, the process by no means reached the degree of completeness it did across the Channel. In 1834, there were only 5,000 mechanical looms in France compared to the 100,000 in England, and the 2,450 engines in use in France in 1839 had a total horse power of only 33,000. The following figures show the growing importance of power (steam engines) in French industry up to 1871:

Year	Number of Engines	Total Horsepower
1851	5,672	71,000
1861	15,805	191,000
1871	26,146	316,000

This development of power is reflected in the textile and iron and steel industries. By 1846, the number of mechanical looms in operation had increased to 31,000. Steam power was first employed in mining and in the metal industries, its application to textile manufacture coming later. After 1830, the methods that had been used in England for some time, such as puddling and smelting by coke, were introduced in France. The charcoal furnace, however, diminished in importance very slowly. Not until the sixties did the new coke furnaces exceed the number of charcoal furnaces. Between 1821 and 1847 the gross output of pig iron almost tripled.[3] France was not exceedingly rich in either coal or iron deposits between 1871 and 1918, and the two were not usually found close together. As early as 1840, France was compelled to import coal because its own resources were not adequate to meet the demands created by the growing iron industry. Some years before the World War the discovery of new iron deposits raised France in importance as a manufacturer of iron and steel products. The recapture of Alsace and Lorraine and the temporary seizure of the Saar Valley as a result of the World War brought a marked stimulus to the French iron and steel industry.

The first major advances in French industry came after the formation of the Third Republic, 1870-71, despite the loss of the valuable industrial regions of

---

[1] The demise of the butchers' guild came in 1858, that of the bakers in 1863, and that of the printers in 1870.   [2] The very first cotton mill was set up in 1785.
[3] When Alsace-Lorraine was under French rule.

Alsace and Lorraine to Germany. Rich in iron ore deposits, embracing one-quarter of the spindles of the French cotton industry, and a center for other manufactures, Alsace and Lorraine were among the most important of French industrial regions. Their loss was, as it has been said, a distinct "body blow" to French industry.[1]

Nevertheless, industrial expansion continued. The value of manufactured products in 1897 amounted to 15,000,000,000 francs against 5,000,000,000 in 1870. In the textile industry, hand looms were generally replaced by power looms, and on the eve of the World War France ranked fifth in the number of cotton spindles with 7,000,000.[2]

There was likewise a steady growth in the number of steam engines in use and a still more rapid increase in their total horse power. From 26,146 steam engines with a horse power of 316,000 in 1871, the figures increased to 82,238 and 2,913,013 respectively for 1910. Production in coal, iron, and steel steadily increased. Thirteen million metric tons of coal were produced in 1870; 26,000,000 metric tons in 1890; almost 33,000,000 tons in 1900; and 41,000,000 tons in 1912-13. A similar growth is to be observed in the production of iron ore and in the iron and steel output. Statistics of pig-iron production illustrate this gradual increase. In 1885, France produced 1,600,000 metric tons; and in 1910, 4,000,000 metric tons. The greatest expansion came during the first quarter of the twentieth century, for the French iron and steel industry became modernized relatively late. In many other fields of manufacture there was a comparable expansion.

Just as in England, the introduction of machinery meant the absorption of an increased number of people in industry, and the growth of factories. The Industrial Revolution in France, however, has been distinguished by several noteworthy differences from that in either Germany or England. The economic development of France was characterized by its gradualness and stability, and by the moderate expansion in many industrial fields. Because of the continued importance of agriculture and the nature of French manufactures, which specialized on fine work and luxury goods to a considerable degree, the application of mechanical methods was relatively slow. France has never been industrialized to the degree that England and Germany have been. At the turn of the century there were only nine departments in France in which half or more than half of the population was employed in mechanical industry as distinguished from agriculture. Even today, there are more people engaged in agriculture than in any other single occupation. The recovery of Alsace and Lorraine since the World War has, of course, reduced the excess of agricultural laborers over the number engaged in industry.

Because French industry has tended to produce either luxuries or articles of fine quality, hand labor has persisted. Though the French have been successful in producing "class" goods of outstanding quality, as well as cheap articles in quantity, there never has been the pressure for complete mechanization that

[1] The great iron and steel industry of this area was, however, almost purely a German development. The phosphoric iron ore in the region could only be worked satisfactorily by the Thomas-Gilchrist process, which was not discovered until after the Franco-Prussian War. The coal of the Saar Valley was also needed for coking purposes.

[2] Far behind the leader, Great Britain, which had 56,000,000.

existed in England and Germany. In England and Germany the general movement of industry has been towards large-scale production and ever growing combinations, while France has been conspicuous for a tendency in the other direction—towards industrial individualism. Small-scale production and small establishments characterize French industry outside of Alsace and Lorraine. In 1914, out of almost 20,000,000 persons connected with all types of French industry, there were only 10,665,000 wage-earners as against 8,996,000 employers and independent workers. This situation has been an obvious handicap to French industry in competition in the world-market with the large-scale production methods of the United States, Germany, and England. On the other hand, it has its compensation in the somewhat wider distribution of profits that obtains and in the large number of workingmen occupied in their homes and shops rather than in tremendous plants.

III. THE INDUSTRIAL REVOLUTION IN GERMANY

1. THE BACKGROUND

If the industrialization of France is characterized by its incompleteness and gradualness, by the prominence of hand labor, and by the persistence of small establishments, the mechanization of German industry after about 1870 is marked by breath-taking rapidity, great thoroughness, and remarkable efficiency.

As late as the middle of the nineteenth century the region we now know as Germany was industrially backward. The industry of Germany then did not even compare with that of France. Agriculture was the leading occupation; the factory system had been introduced but slightly. A contemporary observed that about 1850 the putting-out system still prevailed; that machines were relatively few; that the country was poor; and that adequate financial institutions were lacking.

The causes of this condition are easily apparent: (1) The guild system had disappeared very slowly in several regions in spite of adverse legislation; (2) political decentralization and the conflicting interests and jealousies of the some thirty-nine different German states hampered industry; (3) there were no beckoning markets for German manufactured goods, since home consumption was small and there were no German colonies; (4) transportation facilities were inadequate; (5) the high esteem placed upon agriculture acted as a brake upon industrial enterprise; (6) the highly developed forest industry absorbed many workers; (7) the Napoleonic wars had ravaged the land and stricken the country with poverty; and (8) free capital and a well-developed credit system were missing.

The decline and disappearance of the guild system in Germany duplicates rather closely what occurred in France. French conquests, especially in southern Germany, and the infiltration of French ideas during the Napoleonic period hastened the passing of guild monopoly and the establishment of a system of industrial freedom. During the Stein-Hardenberg régime rapid strides were taken to insure the liberalization of Prussian economic life. Between 1808 and

1811 the privileges of the guilds were in large measure removed and the licensing of craftsmen was introduced. Shorn of their monopolies and powers of compulsion, some of the guilds went out of existence completely, while others continued as "free associations." Similar changes took place in other parts of Germany, but many guilds still survived.

The importance of the handicraft system and the almost static nature of German industry are illustrated by the absence for over thirty years of any important new legislation touching the guilds. An act of 1845 was designed to give uniformity to Prussian industry and to create a high degree of industrial freedom. Certain guilds and some guild practices—the apprenticeship system, for example—were, however, retained. At first the measure promised to be successful, but the panic years of 1846-47 and the revolutionary year of 1848 upset the normal trend. The handicraft workers, who feared the factory system, played an active rôle in the Revolution of 1848, and through their efforts the act of 1845 was so modified as to curtail the industrial liberties it had granted. Had this modification been energetically enforced, it might have had unfortunate consequences for the advance of German industry. It is a commentary on the age to find that the public officials had been inoculated with laissez-faire doctrines to the point where they enforced the law with extreme laxity.

Changing economic conditions set up a strong current towards the further emancipation of industry throughout all the German states during the fifties and sixties. By 1860, the guild system was practically dead, although it was not yet formally buried. The final step came in 1868-69 with the passage of acts that fully legalized the industrial liberty existing in fact. Workers were given complete freedom of movement, and all checks and restraints were removed from industrial initiative.

Commercial freedom made much progress in Germany during the period from the Congress of Vienna to the Revolutions of 1848. Both mercantilism and the later trend towards Economic Liberalism and free trade helped in this matter. The former usually worked towards economic nationalism and the creation of national free-trade areas. Free-traders also urged the clearing away of tariff boundaries between the petty German states, as well as the development of free trading relations between the major German states and the rest of Europe. Therefore both the disciples of Adam Smith in Germany and Friedrich List and his followers aided in wiping out the customs lines between the German states. The resulting Zollverein helped to liberate commerce among the Germanic peoples. Industry was freed from restrictive bonds and many of the obstacles to the full development of economic enterprise and individual effort were cleared away. The legal destruction of the guild system, just mentioned, was another preparatory step towards the industrialization of Germany.

While the greatest progress came after 1870, the fundamental changes in industry, on the basis of which the new order arose, were being prepared for in the two decades preceding that date. The period 1850-70 was one of comparative peace and prosperity. The wars of 1864 and 1866 were short and had little effect on German industry or commerce. The Zollverein (Customs Union), which affected Prussia, Saxony, Bavaria, and many lesser German states,[1] not only facilitated commerce, thus broadening the German market, but still protected the German manufacturers against their French and English competitors. The growth of transportation facilities with the rise of the railroad likewise extended the bounds of the German market. Machinery was imported from England, and a considerable number of skilled English workingmen were induced to migrate to the industrial regions of Germany, such as the Rhine provinces, Silesia, and Saxony, where they served as instructors for the German workers. In the forties firms that were to be important in German industrial history sprang into being. Borsig set up a machine shop in Berlin in 1837 which was to grow into the great Borsig locomotive works. At Essen, Krupp and Company established a cast-steel factory which quickly created a reputation for the high quality of its product.

2. THE COMING OF MACHINERY

The most marked developments in German industry during this period took place in the manufacture of textiles and iron and steel. In 1846, the 136 cotton mills in Prussia were poorly equipped mechanically and they usually depended upon some form of power other than steam. All the German states together consumed on the average only some 18,500,000 pounds of raw cotton annually for the years 1846-50. After 1850, the number of mills grew, their equipment improved, and steam power came into increasing use. Between 1851 and 1855 the consumption of raw cotton averaged over 56,000,000 pounds annually. Ten years later over 97,000,000 pounds were used annually. As late as 1836 Germany had depended chiefly upon imported cotton yarn for its looms; by 1860 that dependence had disappeared. Similar advances were made in the manufacture of silk, linen, and woolen cloth.

The failure to adopt the newest methods in metallurgy and the continued use of crude equipment retarded the development of the iron and steel industry until almost the midway mark of the nineteenth century. Between 1848 and 1857, however, the production of iron ore trebled, and between 1862 and 1875 the output of the iron and steel furnaces of Germany jumped from 685,000 metric tons to over 2,000,000 metric tons.[2] Statistics on the home consumption of raw iron indicate the industrial growth during the two decades 1850-70. The per capita consumption of pig iron in 1850 was 10.6 kilograms; in 1870, it was 38.3 kilograms. Coal-mining experienced a commensurate acceleration. In 1846 Prussia produced about 3,000,000 metric tons of coal; in 1852, 5,000,000 tons were mined; in 1867 some 18,500,000 tons were produced; and in 1871 the output totaled 25,950,000 tons.

These advances, however, were but pygmy steps compared to the gigantic strides taken after 1871. "The growth of German industry and industrial organisation since the war of 1870-1871," writes Professor Ogg, "is one of the capital economic phenomena of modern times."[3] Another student speaks of the eco-

---

[1] See above, pp. 319 ff. Other states entered the Zollverein later.
[2] A significant portion of this gain came before 1871. The perfection of the Bessemer process in 1856 accounts, in part, for this rapid increase in the German iron and steel output.
[3] Ogg and Sharp, *Economic Development of Modern Europe*, p. 215.

nomic growth of Germany in the forty-three years between 1871 and 1914 as "truly miraculous." The following comparative figures on the coal production and the iron and steel output of Great Britain, France, and Germany pointedly show what took place:

I. COAL PRODUCTION
(in tons)

	United Kingdom	France	Germany
1875	99,760,000	11,840,000	28,330,000
1913	287,410,000	40,190,000	273,650,000

II. PIG-IRON AND STEEL PRODUCTION

	United Kingdom	France	Germany
1875	6,365,462	1,448,272	2,029,389
1913	8,923,773	2,690,546	14,389,852

III. STEEL INGOTS AND CASTINGS PRODUCTION

	United Kingdom	France	Germany
1875	707,754	223,467	242,206
1913	7,835,113	2,655,854	14,946,212 [1]

In the twenty years between 1875 and 1895, the number of persons employed in the iron and steel industry increased from 732,000 to 1,115,000; for the chemical industry the figures read 41,000 and 97,000; and the number engaged in mining jumped from 283,000 in 1875 to 430,000 in 1895.

An additional index of industrial growth lies in the changing proportion of the population engaged in agriculture and its allied activities. Between 1871 and 1910 the number of persons engaged in mechanical industry steadily mounted at the expense of the figures for agricultural workers. In 1871, about 64 per cent of the population was engaged in agriculture; twenty years later it was around 57.5 per cent; and in 1910 the percentage had dropped to approximately 40 per cent.

To what causes can we ascribe this tremendous spurt in German industry? First, the Franco-Prussian War was an important cause. It resulted in the unification of the German states and the creation of the German Empire, which, for the first time in German history, made possible the adoption of a thoroughgoing national program for industry. The acquisition of Alsace and Lorraine gave Germany two highly industrialized centers and invaluable natural resources, such as iron ore.[2] Moreover, the billion-dollar indemnity that France was compelled to pay increased at a timely moment the capital available for investment in industry. Second, the German mechanical equipment was new and hence of greater efficiency than the English, some of which was even obsolete. There is one kind of advantage in being first on the scene, as in the case of England, but there are some compensating advantages in starting in

[1] Sir Philip Dawson, *Germany's Industrial Revival*, Macmillan, 1926, p. 2. It should be noted that these figures give Germany a position in the coal production of the world that it scarcely deserves. This is due to the fact that German coal contains a considerable proportion of lignite, and a ton of lignite is usually rated as being equivalent only to a third of a ton of coal. The better quality of English coal helps to explain the fact that in 1913 England exported about a third of its coal product, while Germany had very little net coal export in that year.

[2] The iron-ore deposits became industrially important after 1878, when the Thomas-Gilchrist process for utilizing successfully phosphoric iron ore was made available.

later. Third, the rapid growth of an active market at home and abroad was of capital significance. The rise of colonization, clever diplomacy, astute business methods, and excellent products helped to create a large foreign market, while at home the population jumped from 41,058,792 to 64,925,993 between 1871 and 1910. Fourth, the development of transportation facilities of all kinds stimulated industrial production and brought a sharp decrease in freight rates.[1] Fifth, the active aid that the German government gave to industry operated effectively. Well-designed tariffs protected German industries; German embassies all over the world did whatever they could to help industry, and German diplomatic pressure was frequently exerted for commercial purposes; the state extended the opportunities for technical education; and there was no restrictive legislation to limit the size of industrial combinations. Sixth, the successful application of scientific research to industry was of great importance. The chemical and electrical industries of the Germans stand out as an example of their ability to take up and develop further the inventions of other countries—in these fields chiefly British. Seventh, the banking interests cooperated most intimately with industry and actively supported industrial undertakings.

Apart from the fact, already noted, that the new industrial order was not a native product but was taken over mainly from England, the chief characteristics of the Industrial Revolution in Germany are about what we might expect. All industrial activity increased. Old, established industries, such as textiles and iron and steel, expanded, and new industries, notably the chemical, the dye, and the electrical, appeared. Older methods of applying labor were replaced by the factory system. Agriculture became relatively less important in comparison with industry. German agriculture itself underwent both a structural and a functional change. It tended to give up staple crops, such as wheat, and went into specialty cropping, in which the sugar-beet industry later assumed great importance.

Iron and steel production has always been the backbone of the industry of modern Germany. The chief promoters of the industry have been Krupp, Thyssen, and Stinnes. The chief iron-ore deposits were found in Silesia, Lorraine, and the Siegerland region along the Rhine. Lorraine was lost to Germany as a source of supply after the World War. As a result of tariff rates favoring the iron and steel industries, improvements in transportation, and the adoption of new processes that made possible the use of phosphorous ores, the output of iron and steel expanded remarkably after 1880.[2] This industrial growth meant that England was being surpassed as an iron and steel manufacturer. At the opening of the World War, Germany possessed a comfortable lead as the chief European steel and iron producer. Only the United States had a greater output. The German iron and steel industry is located mainly in the Ruhr area, especially at Essen, the German Pittsburgh.

[1] See above, pp. 311 ff.
[2] For the decade 1880-89, Germany produced on an average 8,952,640 metric tons of iron ore annually and 3,619,590 tons of pig iron. The figures for the decade 1900-09 were 22,443,170 metric tons of iron ore and 10,550,000 tons of pig iron. Between 1880 and 1910 the steel output grew from about 1,500,000 metric tons to more than 13,000,000.

The development in coal-mining kept pace with that in other fields. Down to 1914, the bulk of the German coal was mined in the Rhineland-Westphalia and Saar districts and in Upper Silesia. In 1914, Germany stood third among the world's coal-producers, following on the heels of the United States and Great Britain. The World War, of course, affected the German coal industry disastrously.[1] Down to 1919 the increase in coal production was not only steady but very rapid.[2] Among the interesting developments in the coal industry was the entry of the state into that field of business enterprise. Of the 318 collieries operating in 1910, the state owned 27.

In the textile trades and in the manufacture of industrial machinery and other metal products, the years from 1871 to the World War witnessed progress of the same phenomenal nature. In 1911 Germany, with 10,500,000 spindles, was surpassed only by Great Britain and the United States in cotton manufacture. In almost every branch of industry Germany assumed a position of high importance or European leadership. Well worth noting is the growth of relatively new industries, such as the electric and the chemical. In these fields the thoroughness of German technical training and the employment of methods of scientific research, especially in organic chemistry, have been well rewarded. The discovery of the structure of the "benzene ring" by Kekulé in 1865 laid the basis for the remarkable development of industrial chemistry in Germany. A German chemist, Dr. Adolf von Baeyer, discovered how to make synthetic indigo in 1897. At the opening of the century Germany's leadership in the dye industry was unquestioned, and in 1913 at least three-fourths of the world's output came from that country.[3] No less successful were the Germans in the manufacture of medicines and serums, a field in which they excelled.

With the increasing use of electricity, those branches of German industry concerned with the manufacture of electrical equipment grew by leaps and bounds. The creators of the German electrical industry were Werner von Siemens and Emil Rathenau, who may be compared to Edison in our country. In 1914, this industry was among the leading German industries in the value of annual product, though not in the number of men employed. In 1890, the electrical industry employed well under 15,000 workers, and the value of its annual product was 78,000,000 marks; ten years later, over 50,000 persons were employed and the value of the annual product had jumped to 368,000,000 marks. This phenomenal gain was increased in succeeding years right down to 1914.

[1] See below, pp. 613 ff. The Saar voted in January, 1935, to return to Germany.
[2] The average annual output of bituminous coal for the decade 1880-89 was 57,039,660 metric tons; for the following decade it was 81,978,310 tons; and for 1900-09 it was 126,081,810. In the last year before the war, 190,109,400 metric tons of bituminous coal were produced. The amount of lignite, or "brown coal," mined increased in proportion.
[3] In spite of the German ascendancy in the chemical-dye industry, it is important to note that the first practical discovery in both the chemical-dye industry and in industrial chemistry was the work of an English scientist, William Henry Perkin. In 1868 he achieved the chemical synthesis of alizarin, formerly produced from the madder root cultivated in the East and used for the production of the color turkey-red. This discovery withdrew 400,000 acres from the cultivation of the madder root and depressed Eastern agriculture.

3. THE ORGANIZATION OF INDUSTRY: CARTELS AND SYNDICATES

The forms of business organization that German industry assumed were a logical outgrowth of those modern tendencies towards concentration which have manifested themselves in most countries, though not so much in France. Not only was German industry well organized in all its aspects, but it moved steadily towards a greater measure of centralized control. Although many small industrial establishments still exist in Germany, increasing concentration in industry was a leading trait of the country's economic development after 1880. Especially in the coal, iron, steel, and electrical industries did large establishments swallow up the smaller ones. More than that, various types of industrial agreements were developed in these large industries in order to limit competition and to centralize control still further.

One form of large-scale business organization was the *Interessengemeinschaft*—similar to what in America has been called a "community-of-interest" agreement. Under this, rival concerns subscribe to certain arrangements with reference to prices and markets and sometimes to the pooling of profits. More common are the cartel (*Kartell*) and the syndicate. These terms are frequently used as if they stood for the same thing, but even though they describe very similar practices, they can be distinguished from one another. The cartel in its simplest form is a combination of potentially competing firms in a single industry, bound by agreements involving prices. The purpose is obviously to lessen competition and to secure for all certain advantages that the producers could not gain individually. When the agreement progresses beyond this stage—when it becomes written rather than oral and when it covers aspects of industry other than prices—the form of organization becomes a syndicate. "The syndicate," writes Professor Ogg, "regulates, through its committees, quantity and quality of production, prices, and sales, leaving to the associated firms simply the functions of producing the commodities required and transmitting them to the designated markets."[1]

These are the forms that extended organization has taken in Germany. There were only a very few examples in German industry of huge mergers or actual consolidations comparable to those in the steel or the oil industry in the United States.[2] Had German industry been faced by hostile legislation similar to that directed against the trusts in the United States, it is possible that the merger or holding company might have been forced into existence.

The reaction to the cartel and syndicate upon German industrial evolution has naturally been very marked and there have been discussions without end as to their merits and defects. They have been sharply criticized on the ground that they place labor at a disadvantage, menace the consumer with higher prices, sacrifice the home market to the foreign market, and tend to reduce the spirit of innovation and enterprise in industry. These points are, of course, debatable. W. H. Dawson, that able and judicious student of modern Germany,

---

[1] Ogg and Sharp, *op. cit.*, pp. 222-23. For excellent studies of the nature and operation of cartels and syndicates, especially of the great Rhenish-Westphalian coal syndicate, see A. H. Stockder, *German Trade Associations: the Coal Kartell*, Holt, 1924; and *Regulating an Industry: The Rhenish-Westphalian Coal Syndicate*, Columbia University Press, 1932; and Hermann Levy, *Industrial Germany*, Macmillan, 1935. [2] See below, pp. 748 ff., 796 ff.

believes, on the other hand, that in expanding foreign markets, in bringing about more efficient industrial organization, and in regulating production and prices, the cartels and syndicates have been successful and beneficial.[1] They have also kept out of Germany the holding company. It seems quite evident that they have operated as a stabilizing force on industry and in some cases have encouraged industrial development. In the opinion of unbiased students, perhaps the chief disadvantage has been the way in which the cartels and syndicates have retarded the scrapping of obsolete plants and the introduction of more efficient technology. This has been an obstacle to the full realization of the traditional German zest for maximum efficiency.

The most active period of cartel and syndicate organization came after the turn of the century. It was unmistakably stimulated by the depression of 1900. The electrical, chemical, coal, and iron and steel industries have especially experienced extensive concentration. By 1914, almost the entire electrical industry had fallen into the control of two concerns, the Siemens-Schuckert and the Allgemeine Elektrizitätsgesellschaft. At the same time, there were some 62 cartels and syndicates in the iron and steel industry and 19 in the coal industry. A large portion of the German coal supply was in the hands of the Rhenish-Westphalian Coal Syndicate, while the output of German pig iron and steel was similarly centralized.

Altogether, there were about 400 interest conventions, cartels, and syndicates in Germany in 1914. The mere number of these cartel and syndicate organizations is of course no complete indication of how strongly the cartel and syndicate movement is intrenched in any branch of industry.[2] The establishment of cartels or syndicates in one important industry has often brought about the same form of organization in related and allied industries. The degree of centralized control established by the syndicates varies from one industry to another, and from one time to another. Since the World War, German industry has been rigorously organized and controlled according to the novel principle of "rationalization," to which attention will be devoted later.[3]

4. TRADE AND COMMERCE

Along with the reconstruction of its industry along modern lines Germany experienced a tremendous expansion in commerce. As late as 1870 the volume of German foreign trade was small, and the Germans had the unenviable reputation of selling cheap goods of poor quality. After that date Germany raised the quality of its goods, cultivated new markets, specialized in certain articles, and competed successfully with other industrial nations in the world-market. A valuable market was opened up in southeastern Europe, and Germany continually broadened the sphere of its commercial activities outside of Europe. A frankly protectionist tariff policy was adopted in 1879.

Around 1850 raw materials and foodstuffs still made up the bulk of German exports. After 1880 the exports became essentially industrial. Cotton manufac-

---

[1] W. H. Dawson, *Industrial Germany,* London, 1912, pp. 137 ff.

[2] One large cartel or syndicate may control more business than a hundred small organizations. A comparable situation exists in the United States with our holding companies. For example, there are over 300,000 non-financial corporations in the country, but the 200 largest holding companies and corporations control nearly half of all American business.   [3] See below, pp. 629 ff.

tures, hardware, other types of metal goods, and the products of the chemical and electrical industries, were among the leading industrial exports in 1914. Coal was the only raw material, and beet sugar the only foodstuff, exported in quantity. The imports were largely foodstuffs and raw materials. Only about one-fifth of the imports were manufactured goods.

In 1872, the value of German imports and exports combined came to 5,962,-000,000 marks. In 1905, the value of the exports alone almost equaled that figure, amounting to 5,840,000,000 marks, while the value of imports reached almost 7,500,000,000 marks. Britain alone surpassed Germany in foreign trade before the World War. The discrepancy between German imports and exports was more than made up by the same type of "invisible exports"—capital investments and the like—that balanced Great Britain's foreign-trade accounts.

The chief purchasers of German goods between 1894 and 1907 were Great Britain, Austria-Hungary, the United States, Holland, Russia, Switzerland, France, and Belgium, named in order of decreasing importance. Great Britain, Germany's foremost rival, was its best customer, and France, one of its poorest customers in this list, provided a larger market than all of Germany's colonies put together. Germany's imports came largely from the United States, Russia, Great Britain, Austria-Hungary, France and its colonies, British India, and the Argentine. Germany constructed a great merchant marine under the leadership of Albert Ballin of the Hamburg-American Line and others. Germany had the largest liners in the world when the war broke out in 1914.

Germany's industrial and commercial development set it upon the dangerous road of imperialistic expansion.[1] Dependence upon foreign trade, a need for raw materials, sharp competition with other nations, increased industrial productivity, and other factors, both economic and political, resulted in Germany's pursuing an active foreign and colonial policy in order to secure certain markets in the industrially undeveloped regions of the world. Germany centered its imperialistic activities in Asia Minor, Mesopotamia, Africa, the Far East, and Oceania. The Empire came into conflict with Great Britain in South Africa and in the region of the Persian Gulf, and with France in Morocco. The full implications of German imperialism and its connection with the economic development of the country are treated at greater length in another chapter.[2] Germany also developed a large trade with Latin America in the period before the World War.

IV. THE INDUSTRIAL REVOLUTION IN RUSSIA

Russia was the last of the great European nations to reconstruct industry along modern lines. Despite the efforts of Peter the Great to introduce manufacturing on an extensive scale, the building of some factories as early as the middle of the eighteenth century,[3] the attempts of the government to aid in the development of industry since Peter's time, and the not inconsiderable growth of industry in some sections of that vast country after the first quarter

---

[1] See M. E. Townsend, *The Rise and Fall of Germany's Colonial Empire, 1884-1918*, Macmillan, 1930; and Heinrich Schnee, *German Colonization Past and Future*, Knopf, 1926.
[2] See below, pp. 528, 532 ff., 540. On German industry since the World War, see below, pp. 613 ff., 629 ff.   [3] In 1765, there were 262 factories employing 37,862 workers.

of the nineteenth century, the true period of Russia's actual industrialization did not arrive until the decade of the 1890's. Apart from exceptional regions, Russian industry until 1890 can be described with much truth as still primitive. Despite its wealth of natural resources admirably suited to industrial exploitation, Russia was preponderantly an agricultural country. And a very large portion of the manufactured goods consumed were peasant handicraft products.

After 1890, following a preparatory period of industrial development in Polish Russia, Russian industry experienced a transformation similar in general nature, though not in extent, to that of England, France, and Germany. Machinery and the factory system were extensively introduced, the transportation system was revolutionized, industrial centers appeared, and the customary concomitant effects of industrialization were experienced. One of the distinguishing features of the Industrial Revolution in Russia was the rôle played by the state in the whole process. The driving force behind the industrial transformation was not the initiative of private individuals but, broadly speaking, the activities of the state. The industrial changes were in large measure virtually imposed upon the country.

Industrial development of a modern nature is almost an impossibility if a large portion of the population is in bondage. A free and mobile class of wage-earning workers is a prerequisite, and such a class was not present in Russia in large numbers before 1861. The peasant class was neither free nor mobile. It was a semiservile class. About the middle of the last century there were no fewer than 47,000,000 serfs in Russia. Of that number, 20,000,000 were tenants on Crown lands, another 4,700,000 on the appanages of the imperial family, while 21,000,000 were serfs on private estates and 1,400,000 were in domestic service. From early in the nineteenth century, plans were in the air for the general emancipation of the serfs, but the only results were the freeing of serfs in a few restricted regions of Russia. The movement finally came to fruition under Tsar Alexander II (1855-81), the "Tsar Liberator."[1] In 1858 the serfs on the imperial appanages were given their freedom, and in 1859 a series of measures were launched that resulted in the emancipation of the Crown serfs by 1866. Finally, by the famous Edict of Emancipation of March 3, 1861, the serfs on the private estates of the nobility were given their personal freedom.

Liberation, however, raised another problem. Personal freedom without the possession of land would be pointless. The transfer of parcels of land to the emancipated peasantry on the estates of the Crown could be accomplished without great difficulty. But it was too much to expect that the nobles would give up any large portion of their lands without full indemnification. In the end, the landlords were compensated for the lands that were transferred to the peasantry. These amounted to over 350,000,000 acres. In western Russia, individual peasants took over parcels of land and, with the aid of the state, were enabled to pay the landlords for them. Throughout the remainder of Russia, ownership fell to the village community, the mir, which took over the responsibility of compensation.

In addition to the lack of a suitable labor supply before the period of emancipation, there were other factors that militated against any extensive industrial development. The countryside had changed little since medieval days. The

---

[1] *Cf.* Stephen Graham, *Tsar of Freedom,* Yale University Press (forthcoming).

THE INDUSTRIAL REVOLUTION IN RUSSIA

rural estates and villages were generally self-sufficient and relatively isolated communities. There were no railways, and an adequate banking system and credit structure still belonged to the future.

What, then, were the causes of the vigorous industrial development of the decade of the nineties? First and foremost stood the encouraging attitude of the Russian government. Of considerable importance was the emancipation of the peasants in 1861. This increased the cheap, though not very efficient, labor supply that moved upon the cities seeking employment.[1] Internal changes in the life of the peasantry after the period of emancipation

have contributed to increase the supply of labor. . . . Among these may be observed the abolition of the method of taxation by "mutual guarantee" which had contributed to hold the village population in the villages, and to prevent them from going into the industrial centres. The abolition of the "mutual guarantee" rendered "separations" more easy by increasing the mobility of the peasant, and enabled him readily to become a workman.[2]

Still another factor led to the increase of the labor supply. The promotion of education by the local administrative units (the zemstvos) encouraged an appreciable portion of the young agricultural population to go to the cities and enter industry. The development of the Russian railroad system is regarded by some students as an outstanding cause of the growth of Russian industry. It is questionable whether it was the main cause, but the growth of railways was beyond doubt of much importance. Considerable impetus was given to industrial growth by the protective-tariff policy adopted by the government. Russia had long lacked capital, and during this period the investment of foreign capital began on a considerable scale. Frenchmen, Belgians, and Germans were the chief investors, and they were attracted to Russia not only by its magnificent resources, but also because their investments had suffered heavily in the United States as a result of the depressions of 1873 and 1893 in our country. Russia gave every promise of being a very profitable field, and the very able Count Sergius Witte, who long served as Minister of Finance under Alexander III and his successor, Nicholas II, offered alluring inducements to foreign capitalists.[3] Witte, who typified the new economic Russia in his progressive industrial program and policies—though he remained a conservative in social matters—engineered a ten-year commercial peace with Germany and established the gold standard, giving the Russian financial system a more dependable basis.

Even though the introduction of the new industrial technology proceeded quickly during and after the decade of the nineties, the domestic system of manufacturing retained a position of great importance in Russian industry, and the changes were not far-reaching enough to transform Russia from an agricultural nation into an industrial one before 1914. Nevertheless, remarkable

---

[1] It is to be understood, of course, that most of the former serfs remained as free peasants upon the land. Only a small minority at first sought employment in the cities. But the emancipation movement made the peasants free to move when industrialization had progressed far enough to call for their services in the manufacturing towns.

[2] James Mavor, *Economic History of Russia*, Dutton, 1925, 2 vols., Vol. II, pp. 376-77.

[3] French investments were, of course, promoted by the Franco-Russian military alliance of 1892. See below, pp. 578 ff.

advances were made between 1890 and 1914. The following table shows the increase in the numbers of industrial workers and railway employees in the thirteen-year period, 1887-1900.[1]

Year	Number of Establishments	Total Number of Miners and Factory Workers	Total Number of Persons Employed on the Railways	Total
1887	.....	1,318,048	218,077	1,536,125
1897	39,029	2,098,262	414,152	2,512,414
1900	38,141	2,373,419	450,000	2,823,419

It should be noted that these categories do not include all the industrial workers engaged in the respective years. It is quite possible that the figures for the workingmen in 1887 should be increased by almost 1,000,000, and those of 1897 and 1900 by at least 1,000,000. The rapidity of the increase between 1887 and 1897 is, however, easily seen. The number of industrial workers in factories was still far surpassed by that of the workingmen in domestic industries, of whom there were some 7,000,000 or 8,000,000 in 1904. The statistics above also indicate the growth of medium- and large-sized establishments, for although the number of factories decreased, the number of workers increased.

With the state taking the lead in inducing and encouraging private enterprises, Russia tripled its coal production between 1870 and 1900, surpassed Austria, France, and Belgium as an iron and steel producer, began to exploit its rich coal deposits, expanded all branches of the textile industry, and by 1914 had some 4,000,000 workers engaged in factory production. Polish Russia became the most extensively industrialized region of the Empire, followed by the districts around Moscow and Vladimir.

The road of industrial progress in Russia was by no means smooth. After the depression period, commencing in 1899, the industrial expansion, especially between 1905 and the opening of the World War, was characterized by marked irregularity.

The development of a railway system was, as we have seen, one of the primary causes for Russia's industrial expansion. In a country of Russia's size, an adequate transportation system is a necessity. In binding together the far-flung boundaries of the old Empire the railroads accomplished a task of extreme significance. The first railroad in Russia goes back to 1836, when a short line was constructed connecting St. Petersburg (now Leningrad) with the summer residence of the Tsar at Tsarskoe Selo. Seven years later the state undertook to build two lines with the aid of American engineers, one connecting St. Petersburg and Moscow and the other running from Warsaw to the Polish-Austrian frontier. The Crimean War flashed a strong light on the absolute need for an improved transportation system, and inspired Alexander III to undertake an investigation of the whole problem of railroad-building. From then (1856) on until 1878, railway construction progressed steadily, and some 13,000 miles of railroad were laid down. The general procedure was that private companies did

[1] Mavor, *op. cit.*, p. 386.

the actual building of the lines under supervision and control by the government.

After a short period of quiescence, railroad construction was again undertaken by the state in 1881. The most fruitful period of railway expansion occurred contemporaneously with the rapid growth in industry under Count Witte after 1893. The result was an increase in railway mileage in twenty years (1885 to 1905) from 16,155 to 40,500. Rather excessive attention was given after 1908 to lines running to the Polish-German frontier. The French made large loans to Russia for railroad-building. They insisted that Russia give special attention to strategic military railroads that would facilitate the shipment of Russian soldiers to the German frontier. The famous Trans-Siberian Railway, commenced in 1891, was virtually completed in 1901, and by 1905 it was possible to travel directly by rail from St. Petersburg to the Pacific. This not only opened up an immense home market, but it also made possible a migration movement into Siberia on a greater scale than ever before.

The policy of the government in regard to railroads from the time Witte assumed office proceeded beyond supervision to actual ownership of the lines. In 1914, 70 per cent of the total mileage was owned by the state. There were, altogether, in that year over 46,000 miles of railway. From the decade of the nineties onward, the state set the rates, both freight and passenger, for all railways. Throughout this whole period, and even today, water transportation, by way of rivers and canals, has retained a position of high importance in Russia. In 1914, one-third of the total freight was shipped by water, in spite of natural difficulties afforded by the course of the rivers.

The developments in Russia since the World War, and especially since the Communist Revolution of 1917, are of such vital importance that they deserve a separate chapter for thorough consideration.[1]

V. ECONOMIC PROGRESS IN OTHER EUROPEAN COUNTRIES

1. CONTRASTS AND SIMILARITIES

Since 1850 or even before, machinery, the new technology, and the factory system have been introduced into the other countries of Europe. To speak of an Industrial Revolution might, however, be misleading, if it is understood to mean that industry has in all of these countries assumed a position of importance comparable to that which it holds in England or Germany. With them, as with Russia, the term when applied often indicates only the kind of transformation in industrial methods that has begun, rather than the extent of the change. Some of these countries lack the proper natural resources to permit them to become heavily industrialized. Others are too small in area, population, or both. Some lack the outlet for goods that colonies might offer. One or two approach England and Germany very closely in industrial organization, but not in the gross importance of the manufacturing interests. In several there still persists a system of peasant farming that was abandoned by the industrialized

---

[1] See below, Chapter xxv.

nations many years ago. Belgium, alone, among these other states, was relatively thoroughly industrialized by 1914.

2. ITALY

Two difficulties stood in the way of the economic progress of Italy in the nineteenth century. One was the economic disunion resulting from the lack of political unity, which was not gained until 1860-71.[1] Eight tariff barriers divided the country in 1840, and the effect of their abolition in 1860 was immediately felt in the doubling of trade. The second difficulty was the paucity of coal and iron deposits in the peninsula. Italy has been forced to import the bulk of the coal and iron it consumes. The remarkable resources in water power, however, which have been systematically exploited only in recent years, have lessened the dependence upon English coal.[2] Unless sometime in the future Italy secures colonies that can supply adequate quantities of coal and iron—and this seems highly improbable—it is difficult to see how it can assume a position comparable to that of England, Germany, or France in the economic world. But Italy is making some headway even in iron and steel production. In 1931 the production of pig iron was 500,000 metric tons, of steel ingots 1,450,000 metric tons, and of rolling-mill stock 1,365,000 metric tons.[3]

The chief Italian manufacturing is still found in the textile industry. Silk-manufacturing is among the most important industries, though Italy trails far behind China and Japan as a grower and exporter of raw silk. In the important new rayon industry, however, Italy has taken first place in European output. Imported woolen and cotton yarn is woven into finished cloth, and linen is manufactured from home-grown flax. Within recent years, Italy has made headway as a producer of machinery and high-grade automobiles.

The first important period of railway-building followed the creation of the Italian kingdom in 1860. In the twenty years between that date and 1880, the main lines were laid out and the mileage increased more than sixfold. From 1881 to 1907 the railway mileage doubled. In the latter year it reached 9,800. There was little building from 1907 until Mussolini came into power in 1922. Since 1922 railroad service has been greatly improved and many beautiful railroad stations constructed. The expense and engineering problems in Italian railroad-building have been greatly increased by the mountains, especially the Apennines. The general European tendency towards state ownership of railroads quickly struck Italy. By 1914 some 8,300 miles out of about 10,000 were owned by the state.

Italian foreign commerce has grown markedly in the last half-century. In 1890 it amounted to about $420,000,000. By 1905 it had increased to $725,000,000. In 1913 it stood at $1,200,000. The merchant marine had in 1932 a gross tonnage of over 3,300,000. The chief customers of Italy are Switzerland, Turkey, Egypt,

---

[1] See below, pp. 459 ff.

[2] Of course, the new and cheaper methods of generating electricity through the use of steam turbines may ultimately increase the Italian use of British coal, once the Italian water-power sites are all fully developed.

[3] The fact that Italy produces three times as much steel as it does of pig iron might puzzle many readers who, quite naturally, think of steel as produced from pig iron. The explanation lies in the fact that Italy imports a large amount of scrap iron which is mixed with the pig iron to produce the steel.

and the Argentine. Textiles, silk, olive oil, dairy products, macaroni, spaghetti, and other wheat products, and wines are the main exports. In spite of all industrial advances since the period of unification, Italy still remains predominantly an agricultural country.

Since 1922 Italy has been engaged upon a remarkable experiment in state capitalism under what is known as Fascism. It arose under the leadership of Benito Mussolini, himself formerly an extreme radical, as an effort to check postwar radicalism in Italy. For a time it stabilized Italian economic life, balanced the budget, and promised to increase material prosperity. Considerable employment was provided by elaborate public-works projects. A special effort was made to foster Italian agriculture, especially wheat production. Too little attention, however, was given to the just distribution of the social income and to increasing the purchasing power and the well-being of the masses. As a consequence of this and of the world-wide depression, material conditions have become steadily worse since 1929, and a severe economic crisis cannot long be staved off.[1]

3. AUSTRIA-HUNGARY

Broadly speaking, the economic structure of Italy's old enemy fell into two sections coinciding closely with the two portions of the Dual Monarchy created in 1867.[2] Hungary was overwhelmingly an agricultural state, while Austria, in comparison, was a manufacturing region. That section of Austria touching on Germany had felt some impulse from the new industrial technology before the creation of the Dual Monarchy, but the real period of Austrian industrialization came after that date. Hungary still remains (1935) primarily agrarian, but in the intervening period up to the World War, Austria had made marked progress in industrialization, especially in Bohemia, Moravia, and Silesia.

At the opening of the World War, Austria-Hungary had developed a well-diversified group of manufactures. Textiles, leather goods, chemicals, hardware, scientific and musical instruments, and glassware, chinaware, and stoneware were among the leading products, and manufactured goods had an annual value of $500,000,000 in 1914. Austria stood next to France in leather goods. There were 2,500,000 cotton spindles, and 650,000 in the woolen industry.

Since the middle of the nineteenth century the whole of the Dual Monarchy has been knit together by an extensive transportation system in which the railroads and waterways interlock admirably. In 1860, there were less than a thousand miles of railroad; in 1914, the aggregate mileage was approximately 28,000, of which about 23,000 were state-owned.

The decimation of Austria after the World War, as provided for in the Treaty of St. Germain,[3] thoroughly disrupted the Austrian economy. The country was separated from Hungary, the territory reduced from 135,000 square miles to 32,000 square miles, and the population from 30,000,000 to 6,500,000. This destroyed the home market to a considerable degree and rendered Vienna,

---

[1] Cf. Hugh Quigley, "Fascism Fails Italy," (New York *Times*) *Current History*, June, 1934, pp. 257-65. The most thorough report in English on Fascist Italy today is to be found in *Fortune*, July, 1934, the whole issue being devoted to this subject.
[2] Cf. Geoffrey Drage, *Austria-Hungary*, Dutton, 1909.
[3] See below, p. 616.

with a population of 2,000,000, a city out of all proportion to its hinterland. These defects were for a time partially overcome through extensive foreign loans and through the relatively successful quasi-Socialist government of Austria, which lasted until 1933.[1]

A succession state, Czechoslovakia, inherited much of the mechanical industry of the old Austria—about 80 per cent of the industrial life of Austria before 1914.[2] Most notable in contemporary Czechoslovak industry are glass and pottery, brewing, textiles, leather works, coal-mining, and iron and steel production. The great Bata firm is the foremost shoe manufacturing concern in the world. A socialized land-reform program has also helped to increase the well-being of the people.

4. SWITZERLAND

Tiny Switzerland, mountainous and landlocked, having no colonies, and feeling the same lack of primary natural resources as does Italy, has nevertheless developed a type of economic life that is decidedly industrial. To compensate for the lack of coal, the ample water-power resources have been extensively used for some time, though by no means thoroughly exploited. The textile industry has been well developed, and before the World War Switzerland ranked as almost the equal of France as an exporter of cotton and silk goods. The clock-making and watchmaking industries of Switzerland have long been important, although within recent years Switzerland has not been able to withstand the competition of the United States in the finer grades of clocks and watches. Considerable machinery is manufactured in and around Zurich, Winterthur, St. Gall, and Basel. Other important Swiss products include chocolate, shoes, carved wood, aniline dyes, concentrated meats and soups, and aluminum. Not the least important industry was and is the "tourist industry," which even before the war brought about a million people annually to view the natural beauties of Switzerland.

5. SPAIN

From a position of primacy during the era of oversea expansion Spain experienced a sharp decline.[3] Deprived of nearly all its colonies and backward economically, Spain can be ranked at best as only a third-rate economic power. The pursuance of a deplorable colonial policy since the World War further added to Spain's misfortunes, although the new Republic, so recently created, promises to remedy some of the economic and political evils that have beset the country. Added to the disheartening factor of political instability, Spain was cursed with an atrocious landholding system and a technical incapacity to exploit the natural resources of the country.[4] Much of this has, of course, undergone radical change either within recent years or within the very last years (1931-35). Spain is rich in mineral deposits and produces a great deal of raw wool. It may some day become an important industrial state.

[1] Cf. C. A. Macartney, *The Social Revolution in Austria*, Macmillan, 1927. Radical Socialists controlled Vienna, while the conservative Catholic Socialists dominated the government of the country.
[2] See Josef Gruber, ed., *Czechoslovakia*, Macmillan, 1924.   [3] See above, pp. 25 ff.
[4] The plight of Spain is a magnificent illustration of the inability of agricultural economies to produce their own surplus capital and of their consequent dependence upon foreign capital for industrial exploitation.

ECONOMIC PROGRESS IN OTHER EUROPEAN COUNTRIES

The chief phase of industrial reconstruction in Spain came in the decade after the Spanish-American War (1898-1908). The belated industrial transformation was made possible by an expanding and protected home market, cheap labor, and an abundance of water power. The chief industrial activity was centered in Catalonia, and the conservatism that characterized Spanish capitalists throughout the nineteenth century and the early part of the twentieth began to break down only within recent years. Among the chief Spanish manufactures are cotton (a leading industry), wool, silk, iron and steel, leather goods, rope, soap, and cork. Since the World War, there has been a rapid development in the electrical industry, and the iron and steel industry has grown greatly in importance. An outstanding feature of the period of industrial reconstruction about the turn of the century was the growth of trusts, which took advantage of the high protective tariffs, and were able to limit competition, and, of course, to enhance prices.

Beginning in 1931, Spain underwent a frustrated revolution that was far more than a political change. It has profoundly modified the economy of the country. It was especially interesting as a moderately radical or advanced liberal movement in contrast to the extreme radicalism of the new Soviet régime in Russia.[1]

The outstanding achievement of the Spanish revolution in the realm of economics has been the nationalization of the land. The land was taken over from the great nobles and the Church, the former owners to be reasonably compensated. The cultivation of the land was administered by an Institute of Agrarian Reform, coöperating with self-governing peasant committees. The state provided ample financial aid in the reconstruction of Spanish agricultural methods. Economic decency and justice in manufacturing and allied industries were assured by the creation of committees made up of representatives of both labor and capital who fixed wages and standards of working-conditions and arbitrated disputes. The new labor code lined up the government behind organized labor. Of the 1,000 strikes since the overthrow of Alfonso, labor won 93 per cent. The evils and inadequacies of private charity and doles were eliminated through the adoption of a comprehensive system of social insurance. The strength shown by the counter-revolutionary forces in Spain in the autumn of 1934 makes it difficult to forecast with any certainty the ultimate outcome of the promising trend towards social reconstruction in that country.

6. HOLLAND AND BELGIUM

Of the small territory that constitutes present-day Holland (the Netherlands), almost 27 per cent is unproductive.[2] The natural resources are exceedingly limited: there are scant mineral deposits, little forest land, and a small

---

[1] In late October, 1934, the counter-revolutionary forces gained the upper hand in Spain and checked the progress of revolutionary reforms. On the new régime in Spain, see B. W. Diffie, in R. L. Buell, ed., *New Governments in Europe,* Nelson, 1934, pp. 396-440.

[2] Of course, this 27 per cent of unproductive land is a low percentage when compared to the situation in the world as a whole. Many regions, exclusive of the Arctic and Antarctic areas, run as high as 60 or 70 per cent. But it is a serious handicap in a country with such a limited area as Holland.

supply of coal. Nevertheless, Holland ranks among the important commercial nations of western Europe. This, of course, has been largely due to the highly advantageous commercial situation of Holland around the mouth of the Rhine and at a very strategic position on the coast of Europe, and to the highly profitable Dutch colonies.

Since separation from Belgium in 1830 the industry of Holland proper has developed steadily, and machinery and the new methods have generally been introduced wherever possible. The chief manufacturing industries include the linen, cotton, and woolen industries, shipbuilding, earthenware and faïence (fine porcelain) making, cigar-making, diamond-cutting, the manufacture of quinine, brewing, distilling. Among the materials that Holland gets from the colonies that make possible other trades not yet mentioned are spices, coffee, sugar, cinnamon, indigo, and petroleum. The Royal Dutch Shell Company is one of the great oil organizations of the world.

Holland is by no means a leading industrial country, as the large quantity of manufactured goods imported, especially from England, proves. Its great importance, outside of agriculture and dairying, lies in its commercial and financial activities. Before the World War, the foreign trade of Holland almost equaled that of France, a country many times its size and with a population five times as great. Imports on the eve of the war amounted to $1,632,500,000 and exports to $1,285,000,000. The gross tonnage of the merchant marine in 1932 was in excess of 3,000,000. The first railway line was opened in 1839, and after 1845 there began a period of steady railroad-building, with the state taking the lead in the enterprise. Before the close of the century, the main Dutch lines had been constructed. The present railroad mileage is 2,298, just about half the mileage of the Dutch canals.

Belgium was one of the first Continental countries to introduce the new industrial processes. Down to the sixteenth century, the Belgian Netherlands (Flanders) had been one of the main centers of European manufacturing. Even at the time of the French Revolution it stood high with reference to industry among other Continental nations. At the very end of the eighteenth century and early in the nineteenth, the new machinery and methods already in use in England were introduced. During the first half of the nineteenth century, Belgium was the only country that matched strides with England industrially. Textile and other types of machinery were installed during the first quarter of the century. With some of the richest of European coal deposits, Belgium was producing about 6,000,000 tons a year about 1830. It is significant that France did not achieve this figure until 1850. By 1913, the coal output had grown to 23,000,000 metric tons. Industrial development in other fields occurred at so rapid a pace that, despite the large coal output, the need of fuel was so great that Belgium had to import coal from England from 1840 onward.

The iron and steel industry has assumed important proportions though it has had to depend chiefly on imported ore. Textiles have long been among the chief Belgian products, and the cotton, woolen, and linen goods manufactured are noted for their high quality. The Belgian railway system developed in a fashion similar to that of the other European countries during the course of the nineteenth century. The colonies acquired in Africa, though rich in practically all types of natural resources, have not served as a market for the mother country to any such degree as have the Dutch colonies. Private individuals, including the royal family, have, however, profited handsomely.

7. THE SCANDINAVIAN COUNTRIES

Among the three Scandinavian countries, manufacturing is less important in Norway and Denmark than in Sweden. In all three, shipping and fishing interests are considerable, but these are less important than agriculture and dairying in Denmark. Scientific agriculture is highly developed in Denmark, where there is also to be found an extensive adoption of the coöperative movement. All lack adequate coal deposits, and water is called upon to supply power. The electric industry is extensively fostered. The economic life of all is necessarily bound up most intimately with that of their larger neighbors.

These states have a prominent place in the carrying trade. The merchant marine of Norway has a gross tonnage of 4,100,000, that of Sweden, 1,700,000, and that of Denmark, 1,175,000. There are many motor-driven vessels.

Sweden, with its rich beds of iron ore, has been able to develop the iron and steel industry, and to specialize in the manufacture of fine hardware for export. Next to the iron and steel industry, wood-pulp works, sawmilling, the cement industry, textiles, sugar-refining, and match-making are among the more important manufactures. Swedish iron and steel are distinguished for their fine quality. The lack of coal in Sweden is compensated for by the abundance of water power and the generation of cheap electricity. The electric furnace has been introduced with special success into the Swedish steel industry. Beginning in 1856, when the first railway line was constructed, more than 8,000 miles of railroad were opened by the time of the World War. As in other European countries, the government has become involved in the problems attendant upon railroad construction, operation, and regulation. Sweden has a total railroad mileage of 10,500, much of which has been recently electrified.

Contemporary Sweden is particularly interesting as one of the few successful examples of the realization of "controlled capitalism" under democratic institutions.[1] There are three main reasons for its remarkable achievements here: (1) The state has participated in industry in an active and intelligent fashion; (2) the coöperative movement is highly developed, and consumers have acted to protect their own interests; and (3) enlightened social education has been consistently carried on over a long period.

In 1929, the government investments in Swedish industry amounted to $613,-452,000 and a net profit of over 6 per cent was realized on this investment, a most remarkable achievement for a country with only 6,000,000 inhabitants scattered over a mountainous and forest-covered area. Among the industrial and commercial activities of the Swedish state are the operation of one-third of the mines of the country; the management of telegraph and telephone lines; the generation of 34 per cent of the electric power used in the country; and extensive profits through the control of the liquor, tobacco, and match trades. The monetary policy of Sweden is also very interesting and relevant. For more

[1] *Cf.* M. W. Childs, *Sweden: Where Capitalism Is Controlled*, Day, 1934.

than three years Sweden has successfully operated its monetary system on the basis of a true managed or commodity dollar.[1]

Supplementing this highly enlightened and efficient intervention of the government in business and trade is a strong development of the coöperative movement. Coöperatives own and operate at least 10 per cent of Swedish industry. Consumers' coöperatives are also very well developed. There are 340 consumers' stores in Stockholm alone. The coöperatives broke the power of three of the greatest trusts in Sweden when they were believed to be gouging the public—the margarine, flour-milling, and electric-bulb trusts. Not only has Sweden raised the living-standard of its people far above that of most capitalist countries, but it has also withstood the shock of the depression far better than any other important European state.

8. THE BALKAN COUNTRIES

Southeastern Europe has as yet been little affected internally by the new industrial order.[2] Generally speaking, agriculture and the allied industries employ most of the people. Until comparatively recent times, a landholding system roughly resembling that of feudal Europe was in force in many regions, and it is only since the World War that the great estates have been undergoing extensive partition. The complicated and confused history of the region throughout the course of the nineteenth century, and the fact that it was a field which the great European Powers were eager to exploit politically, explain in part its economic retardation. Most of southeastern Europe was controlled by Turkey until late in the nineteenth century. The Turks, down to 1908, were as backward economically as they were politically. Turkish domination thus helped notably to hold up the economic evolution of the Balkans.

Southeastern Europe is a region, however, that is rich in natural resources and whose future economic possibilities are great. They may be intelligently exploited in the next few decades. It still remains, nevertheless, primarily a rural area, though foreign capital since the war has promoted some industrialization, especially in Rumania and Yugoslavia. But the main progress since 1918 has consisted in the democratization of the landholding system, particularly in Rumania. The coöperative movement is strongly developed in the Balkans.

VI. THE INDUSTRIAL REVOLUTION IN THE ORIENT: JAPAN AND CHINA

1. JAPAN

Japan was the first of the oriental countries to undergo a process of Europeanization. Since the last quarter of the nineteenth century, the government, the army and navy, the educational system, and the landholding system have all been Westernized. There are few phases of history more interesting than the conscious adoption of the material, and many of the cultural, aspects of occidental civilization by Japan. The Europeanization of the nation was

---

[1] See E. T. H. Kjellstrom, *Managed Money: The Experience of Sweden*, Columbia University Press, 1934.
[2] *Cf.* Knight, Barnes and Flügel, *Economic History of Europe*, Pt. II, Chap. XIV.

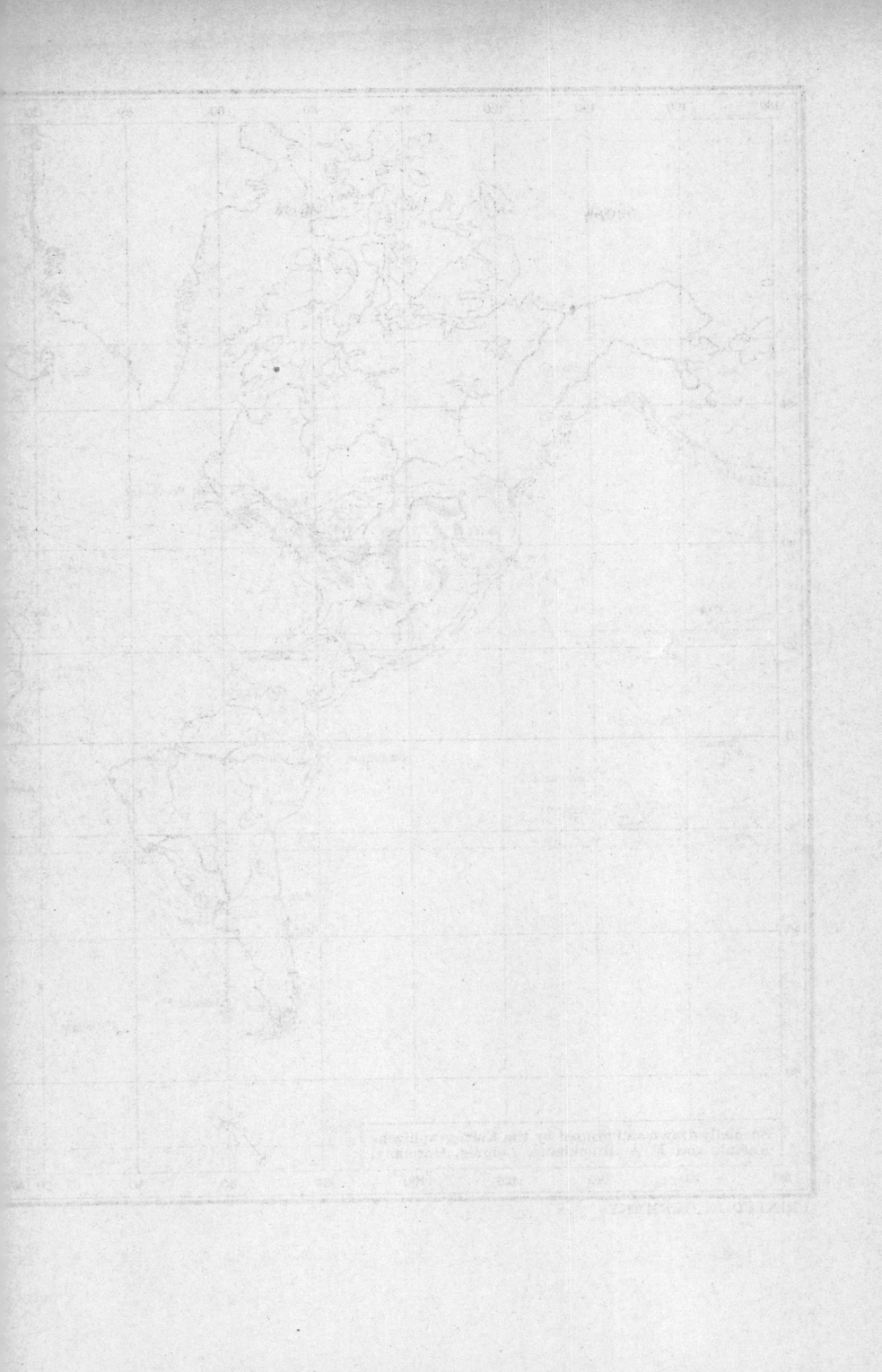

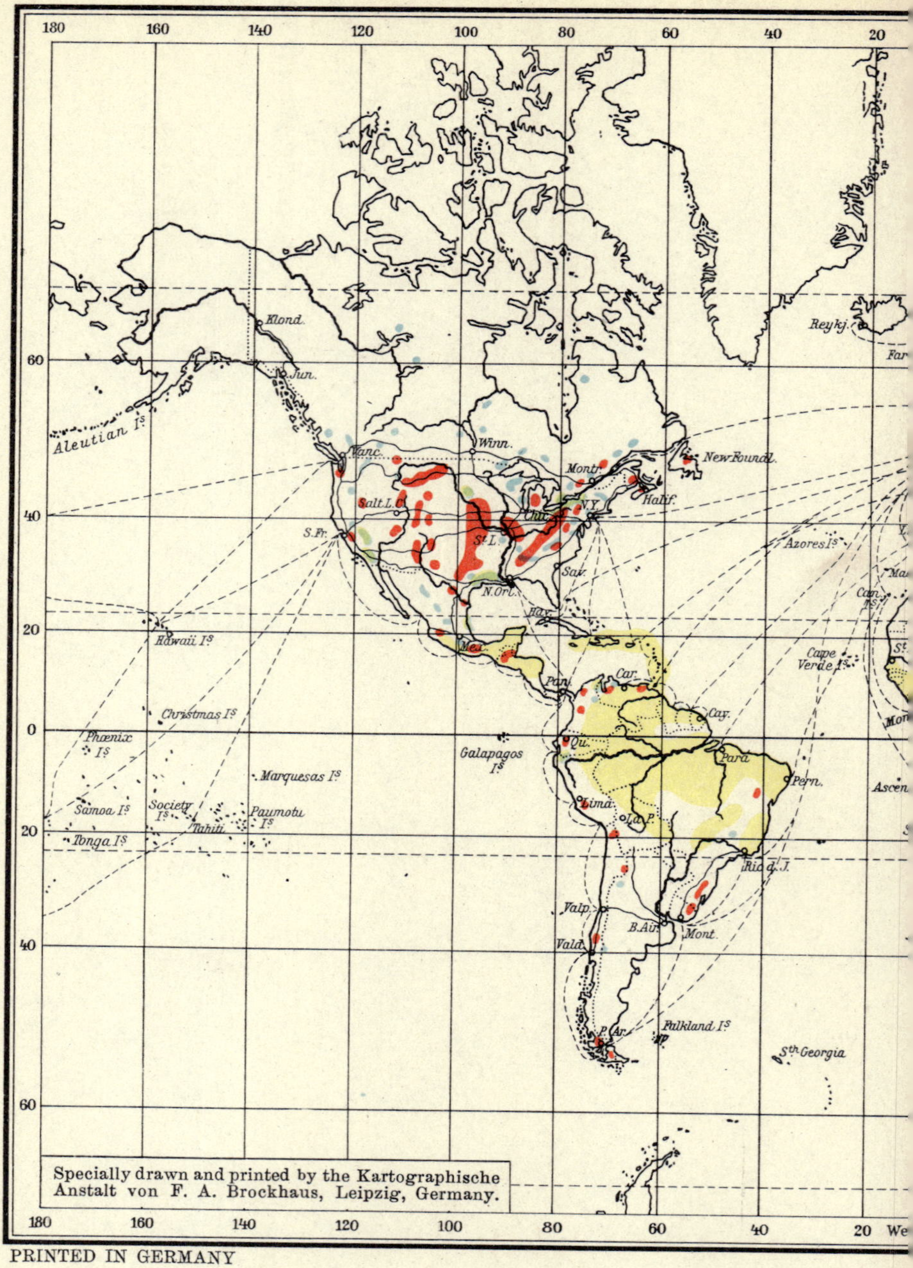

PRINTED IN GERMANY

WORLD MAP SHOWING ECONOMIC RESOURCES 1914

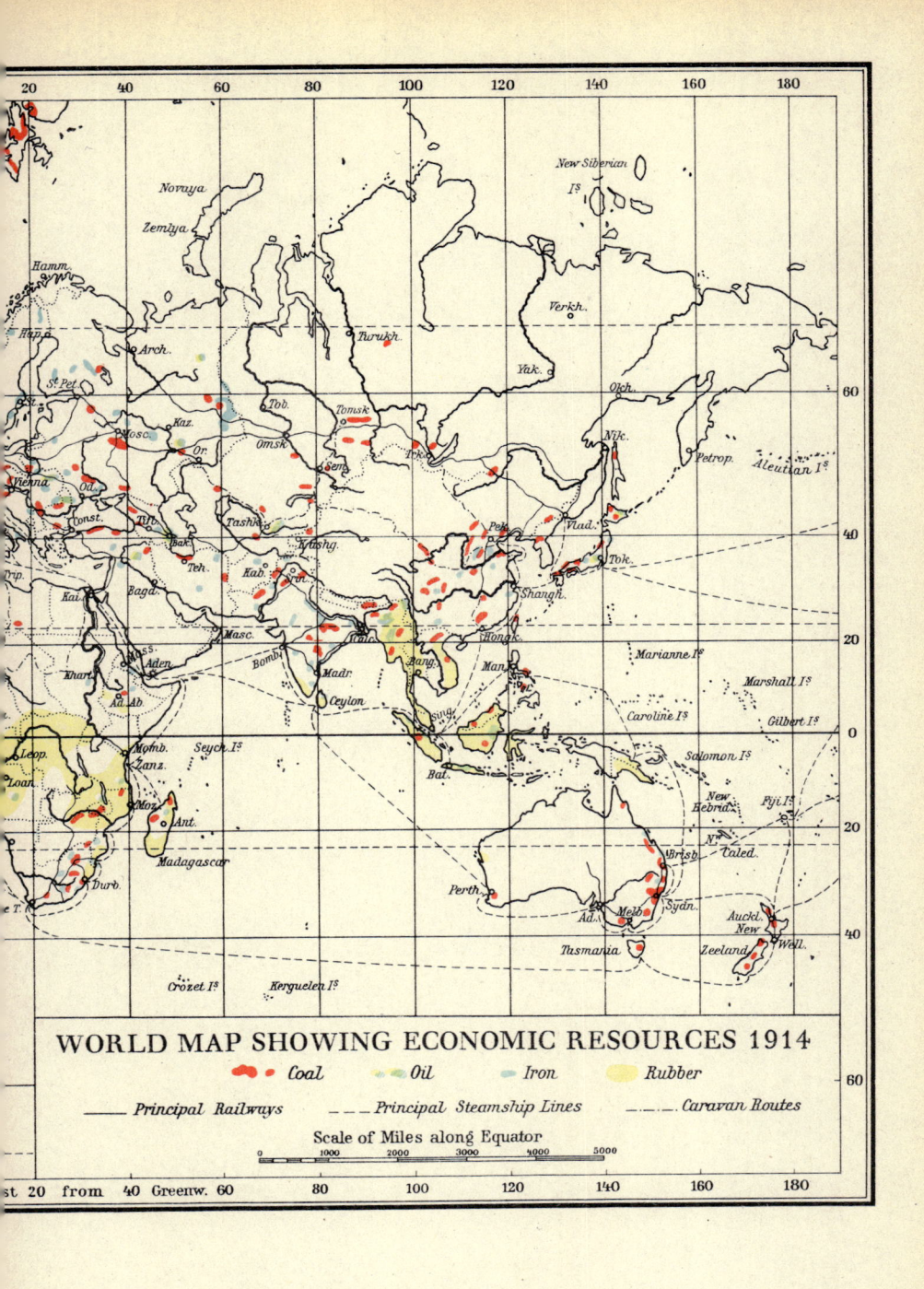

produced by a conscious effort of the Japanese. They were guided by the desire to protect themselves from the exploitation of occidentals by becoming—at least materially—a "European" nation. The history of Japan for the last half-century offers glowing testimony of the ability of the Japanese to imitate and adopt modern material culture so successfully as to surpass in many respects the Western nations at their own game, whether it be political imperialism, manufacturing, or commerce.

The industrialization of Japan has resulted in an entirely new situation in the Orient. The necessity of following in the footsteps of Japan has been made evident to its populous and long-immobile neighbor, China. America and Europe have been faced with a powerful competitor in the Far East. The imperialistic activities of Japan have unsettled conditions in the Orient. The Westernization of Japan has also had far-reaching effects upon its own culture, which is now a strange mixture of intensive industrialization, modern imperialistic thought, and the political mysticism that dominates many phases of life.[1]

Before 1870, Japan had few manufacturing industries as we understand the term. Within thirty years, largely through the activities of the national government, modern industry and technology had become an essential factor in the life of the country. By 1896, there were in Japan over 4,500 industrial and commercial companies. These were organized as joint-stock companies and partnerships. Twenty-five years earlier, the country had possessed not even one joint-stock company. By 1906, these enterprises had increased to over 9,000 in number, with paid-up capital amounting to $500,000,000. In 1870, no manufactured goods were exported. In 1901, the value of the manufactured goods exported came to almost $40,000,000. The figure rose to about $100,000,000 in 1906. By 1913 the annual foreign trade of Japan amounted to $680,000,000, increasing to $2,400,000,000 in 1925, the peak year of Japanese foreign commerce. In 1925 exports were valued at $1,150,000,000.

Prior to 1880 there existed no cotton manufacturing industry in Japan. By 1897 there were over 750,000 spindles in operation, and the industry provided employment for almost 45,000 persons. At the outbreak of the World War the industry employed some 127,000 men and women, and there were almost 2,500,000 spindles running. The war greatly stimulated the cotton industry, raising the number of spindles to 3,689,000 in 1920. By 1934 there were 8,525,000 spindles operating. A notable boom took place in the Japanese cotton industry in 1932-34, partly owing to the increased control of the Chinese market after the breakdown of the Chinese boycott. Considerable developments have taken place in other manufacturing industries. The silk, match, and toy industries are very important. The most spectacular recent development has come in the rayon industry, where Japan ranks next to the United States in production, with 345,600,000 square yards in 1934, valued at $55,000,000. This has, however, at the same time, weakened the silk industry. There is also a flourishing cement industry. Coal-mining is increasing in importance, producing 30,000,000 metric tons in 1933. In the peak year of 1929, Japan produced 34,000,000 tons of coal. It has been customary for writers on the Far East to predict that once Japan gained control of the Chinese iron-ore deposits there would be a vast increase in the iron and steel industry of Japan. More recent students, especially Bain

[1] *Cf.* F. R. Eldridge, *Dangerous Thoughts on the Orient,* Appleton-Century, 1933.

and Orchard, doubt this and believe that the Japanese possibilities are limited in this field of operation.[1]

Railway construction paralleled the growth of industry. The first railroad line was opened in 1872 despite heavy opposition from various quarters. When the government, without whose aid the railroads would never have been constructed so extensively, undertook a program of nationalization of private railway lines in 1906, railway mileage amounted to almost 5,000 in an area about as large as the State of Montana. The 6,000 miles of railroad operating in 1914 were nearly all owned by the state. By 1932 Japan had nearly 13,000 miles of railroad, of which 8,774 were state-owned. Japan had set out to model itself upon the West, and had succeeded beyond expectation.

Beginning in 1931, Japan moved in decisive fashion to occupy Manchuria and exploit its natural resources. It also took steps to secure economic dominion over China. If it succeeds in this ambitious program its economic position will be considerably strengthened.[2]

2. CHINA

Vast China could not save itself from the danger of European exploitation, which Japan so successfully avoided. The conservatism of the people and the obdurate unwillingness of the Manchu rulers to break with the past made it impossible for China to meet the threat of the West as Japan had done—namely, by conscious Westernization. Whatever industrialization occurred before 1914 was not initiated by the Chinese, generally speaking, but by foreign capitalists acting under concessions and privileges of one type or another. The almost limitless natural resources of the country, the cheap labor, and the potential market there for manufactured goods proved powerful attractions for foreign investors. With the coöperation of the governments of the respective European Powers, "spheres of influence" and concessions were won from the impotent government of China by European capitalists. This economic and political penetration reached its height in the decade 1890-1900.

As a result of the activities of foreign—and also Chinese—capitalists, the mineral deposits of China began to be exploited. Machinery and the factory system were introduced, and the textile industry was developed.[3] In 1914, there were 1,250,000 spindles in operation. In 1927, China had 133 cotton mills with 3,581,000 spindles and 25,980 looms. There were 4,211,000 spindles in 1932, of which 1,630,000 were owned by Japanese. The number of factories had dropped to 56, however, indicating the advance of large-scale production. In 1933, the foreign trade of China amounted to $424,647,000. The telephone and telegraph system has grown. The first railroad, constructed in 1875-76, was destroyed by the Chinese themselves. Overcoming this initial opposition, railway-building forged ahead, and in 1914 China possessed as large a railway

[1] *Cf.* H. F. Bain, *Ores and Industry in the Far East,* Council on Foreign Relations, 1927; and J. E. Orchard, *Japan's Economic Position,* McGraw-Hill, 1930.
[2] *Cf.* G. E. Sokolsky, *The Tinder Box of Asia,* Doubleday, Doran, 1932; and G. B. Rea, *The Case for Manchoukuo,* Appleton-Century (forthcoming).
[3] See especially K. S. Latourette, *The Chinese: Their History and Culture,* Macmillan, 1934, 2 vols., Vol. II, Chap. xv. For a selected bibliography on Chinese industrialization, see *Ibid.,* Vol. II, p. 119.

mileage as Japan—but spread over a vastly larger area. Today there are about 12,500 miles of railroad, exclusive of Manchuria. Recent civil wars have, however, seriously injured and confused the transportation system.

Just as important in the economic condition of China as its present backwardness are the future possibilities of the country. Once political stabilization has been achieved, the exploitation of its extensive natural resources systematically begun, and the new industrial technology fully introduced, China will possibly be transformed into a great industrial region. There has of late been a decided reversal of opinion concerning the potential mineral and iron and steel industries of China. Under the influence of the stories spread by the German geologist and geographer Ferdinand von Richthofen, after 1870, Europeans were wont to predict an untold development here. Since then, it has been found that while China has large coal reserves, much of the Chinese coal is not suitable for coking purposes. Moreover, the Chinese iron-ore deposits are far less rich than the coal reserves and are of a low grade. There are few ore deposits in China that will measure up to the requirements of modern large-scale manufacturing.[1] The remarkable, if little recognized, growth of Communism in China in the last decade makes it appear likely that the economic future of China may be associated with the collectivism that has dominated Russia since 1917.[2] It may present another notable example of a country exploited and developed according to Communistic methods and principles rather than by the typical methods of Western capitalistic imperialism.

VII. AUSTRALASIA AND OTHER AREAS

The main Australasian colonies of Great Britain, Australia and New Zealand, still remain primarily agricultural countries. This is due to a number of reasons. The resources for agricultural and pastoral industry have been so extensive as to absorb most of the energies of the population. The latter is not large enough as yet to furnish a home market for any remarkable manufacturing industry, while the distances are so great as to constitute a handicap to manufacturing for shipment to Europe, Asia, or the United States.

Nevertheless, there have been important manufacturing developments, especially since about 1890. Between 1894 and 1912 the number of persons employed in Australian factories increased from 133,000 to over 340,000. The horse power employed in Australian manufacturing in the year 1928-29 was 753,991. The total power generated in that year amounted to 1,679,314. Of this total, electricity supplied 537,000 horse power. The major industries are, in order of importance, textiles, metal work, food products, woodwork, and printing. There is also a considerable mining industry producing gold, coal, iron, and zinc. The following tables fully illustrate the status and nature of industrialization in Australia.[3]

[1] See Bain, *op. cit.*
[2] See Sokolsky, *op. cit.*, Chap. xii; and V. A. Yakhontov, *The Chinese Soviets*, Coward-McCann, 1934.
[3] D. B. Copland, ed., *An Economic Survey of Australia*, American Academy of Political and Social Science, *Annals*, Vol. CLVIII, 1931, pp. 20, 26, 77, 82.

TABLE I—Estimated Value of Australian Production
(In £ millions)

	1924-25	1928-29
Agriculture	107.2	89.4
Pastoral	126.8	116.7
Dairy produce, etc.	45.2	50.7
Forest and fish	12.4	11.6
Mining	24.6	19.6
Manufacture	138.0	15.8
Total	454.1	447.9

TABLE II—The Chief Manufacturing Groups

Group	No. of Employees 1908	1928-29	Value Added (£1000) 1908	1928-29
I. Clothing and textiles, etc.	70,075	109,108	5,089	24,499
II. Metal works, machinery, etc.	48,505	98,145	8,000	35,709
III. Food and drink, etc.	40,652	67,029	8,184	36,125
IV. Books, paper, printing, etc.	21,448	33,837	3,224	12,398
V. Vehicles and accessories, etc.	10,784	27,094	1,241	8,328
VI. Working in wood	21,310	25,762	2,739	8,715
VII. Stone, clay, glass, etc.	9,420	19,692	1,604	8,443
VIII. Furniture, bedding, etc.	7,117	16,006	832	4,614
IX. Heat, light and power	5,754	12,216	2,470	10,604
X. Rubber goods and leatherware	....	9,589	....	4,011

New Zealand remains more thoroughly agricultural. Only about 60,000 persons are engaged in any kind of manufacturing, and most of this is devoted to processing and conditioning food products of one kind or another, especially beef, mutton, and butter. The bituminous-coal deposits in New Zealand are especially rich and of good quality. As population increases, there is every probability that industrialization will proceed apace in both Australia and New Zealand. Its industrial leaders are in thorough rapport with the latest industrial and technological developments elsewhere.

The Industrial Revolution has spread to other parts of the world in some degree. There is a considerable textile industry in India. Quite contrary to general impressions in the West, India possesses remarkable possibilities in the way of the future development of the iron and steel industry. Indeed, India may take the place in actuality here that has been held for so long by China in the fanciful predictions of Westerners. In the provinces of Bihar and Orissa, India has one of the largest iron-ore deposits in the world, comparing favorably with the Lake Superior and Lorraine beds. The ore is of good quality, is easily mined, and is located close to ample mines of good coking coal. The lowest-cost pig iron in the world today is produced at the Jamshedspur plant of the Tata Iron and Steel Company. Japan is importing this Indian pig iron and some has been sent to Europe and the United States. No area in the world possesses greater industrial possibilities than India. This is one reason why England hangs on to India with bulldog perseverance.

AUSTRALASIA AND OTHER AREAS

Since the World War some progress has been made in reviving the industrial life of the Near Orient, once the center of the industry and commerce of antiquity. These developments have taken place in Turkey, Cyprus, Palestine, Syria, Iraq (the old Mesopotamia), and Persia. The textile industries, leather work, the cigarette industry, mining, and metal work are the more important manufacturing activities. In Palestine much has been done to promote the hydroelectric industry, while the petroleum industry is important in Iraq and Persia. The Zionist movement in Palestine has helped notably in the new industrial growth in that area. In Turkey, the able rule of Mustapha Kemal has aided and directed the industrial revival. In Africa there are mines and factories, such as the gold and coal mines of South Africa and the sugar, textile, and cigarette factories in Egypt. The little colony of the Gold Coast produces half of the cocoa used in the world. In Latin America, industrialization has made some headway, for example, in the nitrate works of Chile, the leather and textile factories of the Argentine, the coffee-processing industry of Brazil, the oil production of Colombia, Venezuela, and Mexico, and the mining industry of Mexico. The Dominion of Canada, while still primarily an agrarian economy, has made great advances in the last half-century, and promises to become a major industrial area. In 1881 the total investment in manufacturing was $165,000,000 and the total output was valued at $310,000,000. In 1932, a capital of $4,750,000,000 was invested, and the total output was valued at $2,125,000,000. The mineral products of Canada, especially asbestos, nickel, gold, silver and coal, are very important, as are also the lumber and paper industries. Canada has carried on extremely interesting and successful experiments in the government generation and distribution of hydroelectric power. The government has also entered widely and successfully into the ownership of railroads. In 1933-34, the foreign trade of Canada amounted to $1,019,000,000, ranking ninth among the nations of the world. The banking system of Canada is noted for its efficiency and integrity.

SUGGESTED READING

Hammerton, *Universal History of the World*, Chaps. 162, 165, 173, 175
Ogg and Sharp, *Economic Development of Modern Europe*, Chaps. x, xv
Knight, Barnes, Flügel, *Economic History of Europe*, Pt. II, Chaps. ix-x, xiii-xv
H. O. Rugg, *Changing Civilizations in the Modern World*, Ginn, 1930
F. Le R. McVey, *Modern Industrialism*, 2d ed. rev., Appleton, 1923
Day, *History of Commerce*, Chaps. xxxix-xliv, lvi-lvii
E. W. Zimmermann, *World Resources and Industries*, Harper, 1933
J. H. Clapham, *The Economic Development of France and Germany, 1815-1914*, Macmillan, 1923
James Mavor, *Economic History of Russia*, Dutton, 1925, 2 vols.
Gerhard Dobbert, ed., *Red Economics*, Houghton Mifflin, 1932
H. M. Vinacke, *History of the Far East in Modern Times*, rev. ed., Crofts, 1933, Chaps. xiv, xvi
H. G. Moulton and Junichi Ko, *Japan: An Economic and Financial Appraisal*, Brookings Institution, 1931
J. E. Orchard, *Japan's Economic Position*, McGraw-Hill, 1930

K. S. Latourette, *The Chinese: Their History and Culture,* Macmillan, 1934, 2 vols., Vol. II, Chap. xv
J. B. Condliffe, *China Today: Economic,* World Peace Foundation, 1932
R. H. Tawney, *Land and Labour in China,* Harcourt, Brace, 1932
F. V. Field, ed., *Economic Handbook of the Pacific Area,* Doubleday, Doran, 1934
E. O. A. Shann, *Economic History of Australia,* Macmillan, 1931
Vera Anstey, *The Economic Development of India,* Longmans, 1929
Kurt Grunwald, *The Industrialization of the Near East,* Palestine Economic Society, 1934
L. C. A. and C. M. Knowles, *Economic Development of the British Overseas Empire,* London, 1924-30, 2 vols.
Walter Fitzgerald, *Africa,* Dutton, 1934
Jacob Warshaw, *The New Latin America,* Crowell, 1922, Chaps. iii-v, xiii
H. F. Bain and T. T. Read, *Ores and Industry in South America,* Harper, 1934
C. F. Jones, *The Commerce of South America,* Ginn, 1928
Scott and Baltzly, *Readings in European History since 1814,* Chap. iv

FURTHER REFERENCES

THE TRANSIT OF THE INDUSTRIAL REVOLUTION TO CONTINENTAL EUROPE AND THE ORIENT. An elementary but extremely illuminating presentation of the transit of the Industrial Revolution is contained in Rugg, *op. cit.* The best single work is Zimmermann, *op. cit.*

FRANCE. On French economic life on the eve of the Industrial Revolution, see Henri Hauser, "The Characteristic Features of French Economic History from the Middle of the Sixteenth to the Middle of the Eighteenth Centuries," *Economic History Review,* October, 1933; Sée, *Economic and Social Conditions in France during the Eighteenth Century.* On the industrialization of France, see Ogg and Sharp, *op. cit.,* pp. 204 ff.; Knight, Barnes, and Flügel, *op. cit.,* Chap. x; Day, *Economic Development in Modern Europe,* Chaps. vii-x; Clapham, *op. cit.,* Chaps. iii, x; W. F. Ogburn and William Jaffé, *The Economic Development of Post-war France* (Columbia University Press, 1929).

GERMANY. On the slow development of German industry before 1871, see Day, *op. cit.,* Chap. xi; Clapham, *op. cit.,* Chap. iv. On the industrialization of Germany, see Chap. iv of G. P. Gooch, *Germany* (Scribner, 1925); Ogg and Sharp, *op. cit.,* pp. 210 ff.; Knight, Barnes, and Flügel, *op. cit.,* Chaps. xi-xii; Clapham, *op. cit.,* Chaps. iv, xi; Karl Helfferich, *Germany's Economic Progress, 1888-1913* (Germanistic Society of America, 1914); E. D. Howard, *The Cause and Extent of the Recent Industrial Progress of Germany* (Houghton Mifflin, 1907); Dawson, *Industrial Germany.* On the organization of German industry, see Knight, Barnes, and Flügel, *op. cit.,* Chap. xii; Chap. x of W. H. Dawson, *The Evolution of Modern Germany* (Scribner, 1914); and *Industrial Germany,* Chaps. v-vi; Chaps. viii-xii of Bruno Burn, *Codes, Cartels, National Planning* (McGraw-Hill, 1934).

On German commercial expansion, see Ogg and Sharp, *op. cit.,* Chap. xiv; Knight, Barnes, and Flügel, *op. cit.,* pp. 624 ff.; Clapham, *op. cit.,* pp. 314 ff., 355 ff.; Day, *History of Commerce,* Chaps. xxxix-xl; Dawson, *The Evolution of Modern Germany,* Chaps. iv, xviii.

RUSSIA. On Russian economic evolution, see Ogg and Sharp, *op. cit.,* Chap. xv; Knight, Barnes, and Flügel, *op. cit.,* Chap. xv; Day, *Economic Development in Modern Europe,* Chaps. xiv-xviii; Pokrovsky, *Brief History of Russia,* Vol. I, *passim;* Mavor, *op. cit.*

OTHER EUROPEAN COUNTRIES. On European industrialization outside England, Germany, France, and Russia, see Knight, Barnes, and Flügel, *op. cit.,* Chaps. XIII-XIV; E. F. Heckscher, "The Place of Sweden in Modern Economic History," *Economic History Review,* October, 1932; Josef Gruber, *Czechoslovakia* (Macmillan, 1924); C. A. Macartney, *The Social Revolution in Austria* (Macmillan, 1927); Laurent Duchesne, *Histoire économique et sociale de la Belgique* (Paris, 1932). For further literature on the subject, see Knight, Barnes and Flügel, *op. cit.,* bibliography, pp. 712-13, 747-48; pp. 132-41 of Felix Flügel and Allyn Lousely, *Syllabus of the Economic History of Europe* (University of California Press, 1929).

THE INDUSTRIAL REVOLUTION IN THE ORIENT. On the progress of industrialism in the Far East, see Latourette, *op. cit.,* Vol. II, Chap. XV; Joseph Barnes, ed., *Empire in the East* (Doubleday, Doran, 1934); Chaps. XI-XII of Stephen King-Hall, *Western Civilization and the Far East* (Scribner, 1924); H. M. Vinacke, *Problems of Industrial Development in China* (Princeton University Press, 1926) and *History of the Far East in Modern Times,* Chaps. IX, XIII-XIV, XVII; Chaps. VIII-IX, XXIV of E. T. Williams, *China, Yesterday and To-day* (5th ed. rev., Crowell, 1923); F. R. Eldridge, *Trading with Asia* (Appleton, 1921); Chaps. X, XV of H. C. Thomson, *The Case for China* (Scribner, 1933); Chaps. XI-XII of M. T. Z. Tyau, *China Awakened* (Macmillan, 1922); Pts. II-III of H. C. James, ed., *China* (American Academy of Political and Social Science, *Annals,* Vol. CLII, 1930); C. F. Remer, *Foreign Investments in China* (Macmillan, 1933); Condliffe, *op. cit.;* Tawney, *op. cit.;* Wilfred Smith, *Geographical Study of the Coal and Iron in China* (Liverpool, 1926); J. B. Taylor, *Farm and Factory in China* (London, 1928); D. K. Lieu, *China's Industries and Finance* (Peking, 1927); H. F. Bain, *Ores and Industry in the Far East* (Council on Foreign Relations, 1927); J. B. Gubbins, *The Making of Modern Japan* (Lippincott, 1922); A. S. and S. W. Hershey, *Modern Japan* (Bobbs-Merrill, 1919); Moulton and Ko, *op. cit.;* Orchard, *op. cit.; Facts and Factors in Economic History,* pp. 304-27.

INDIA. Chaps. XIII-XIV, XVII-XVIII of Sir J. G. Cummings, ed., *Modern India* (Oxford Press, 1932); Anstey, *op. cit.;* D. H. Buchanan, *The Development of Capitalistic Enterprise in India,* Macmillan, 1934.

THE NEAR ORIENT. Grunwald, *op. cit.;* Harry Viteles and Khalil Totah, eds., *Palestine: A Decade of Development* (American Academy of Political and Social Science, *Annals,* Vol. CLXIV, 1932); Chaps. XIII-XV of A. J. Toynbee and K. P. Kirkwood, *Turkey* (Scribner, 1927); Chaps. X-XI of A. C. Millspaugh, *The American Task in Persia* (Century, 1925).

AUSTRALASIA. For the economic history of Australasia, see W. K. Hancock, *Australia* (Scribner, 1931); C. H. Northcott, *Australian Social Development* (Columbia University Press, 1918); V. S. Clark, *The Labour Movement in Australasia* (London, 1906); Shann, *op. cit.;* D. B. Copland, ed., *Economic Survey of Australia* (American Academy of Political and Social Science, *Annals,* Vol. CLVIII, 1931); J. B. Condliffe, *Short History of New Zealand* (Christchurch, N. Z., 1927); and *New Zealand in the Making* (Columbia University Press, 1930); W. P. Reeves, *New Zealand* (3d ed. rev., Houghton Mifflin, 1925).

SOUTH AFRICA. The only good work in English is D. M. Goodfellow, *Modern Economic History of South Africa* (London, 1930). On Africa as a whole, see Fitzgerald, *op. cit.*

LATIN AMERICA. Warshow, *op. cit.;* Bain and Read, *op. cit.;* Jones, *op. cit.;* J. F. Normano, *Brazil* (University of North Carolina Press, 1935).

CANADA. H. A. Innis and A. F. W. Plumptre, *The Canadian Economy and Its Problems* (Canadian Institute of International Affairs, 1934); *Facts and Factors in Economic History,* pp. 328-56; Knowles, *op. cit.,* Vol. II; Gustavus Myers, *History of Canadian Wealth* (Kerr, 1914).

CHAPTER X

THE INDUSTRIAL REVOLUTION COMES TO THE UNITED STATES

I. AMERICAN ECONOMIC LIFE TO THE CIVIL WAR

1. INDUSTRIAL ORIGINS

The new forms of mechanized manufacture spread to the United States at about the same time as they did to continental Europe. At the close of the Revolutionary War, the United States was predominantly agricultural, over 90 per cent of the population being engaged in farming. Most goods needed by the colonists were manufactured in the homes or in small shops. Factory-made goods were imported from England, along with some luxury products not made in this country. England endeavored, in keeping with the mercantilist philosophy, to discourage home manufacture and to stimulate buying from England. But it was never able to compete successfully with the small-scale manufacture for home use in the colonies.

For several reasons the period immediately following the establishment of independence saw the development of considerable industry in the United States. Some of it was stimulated by the removal of the restrictions imposed by the British colonial system; some was the result of the ambition of the new republic to establish economic, as well as political, independence of England; and much of it was the product of the interference with American importations from Europe that arose out of the Napoleonic wars and particularly the War of 1812. This stimulated the home market for American products.

From a formative point of view, the years between 1790 and 1860 were the decisive ones in the establishment of American manufactures. These years witnessed the definite creation of the textile, the iron and steel, and the boot and shoe industries in the United States. During that period industry became increasingly mechanized. The factory system was established, and gradually replaced the method of household manufactures that had prevailed during the colonial period. Quantitatively considered, the second half of the nineteenth century was perhaps the more striking, in that it brought a remarkable increase in the scale of operations, the volume of manufactured products, and the capital invested in American manufactures.[1]

The most important factors that have contributed to the remarkable develop-

[1] For an admirably illustrated introduction to American industrial history, see R. M. Keir, *The Epic of Industry*, Yale University Press, 1926.

ment of the American industrial system were: (1) The wealth of the natural resources of the country, which included water power, lumber, rich coal and iron deposits, and the presence of many metallic ores; (2) the presence of small but increasing quantities of capital that could be invested in industry and the almost gullible zeal of Europeans for investment here; (3) the indirect stimulus offered by the government to home industry after 1816 by protective tariffs; (4) the introduction of machinery from Europe and the improvements made upon it here, as well as notable basic inventions by Americans; (5) the facilitation of the home market as a result of continued improvements in highway and water transportation and the development of the railroads after 1840; and (6) the influx of an ever growing body of Europeans ready to engage in industry as skilled or unskilled workers. Few facts so pertinently illustrate the changes that occurred as the growth in the amount of capital invested in manufacturing. In 1820 some $50,000,000 were so invested; in 1860 the figure was $1,000,000,000.

2. MECHANICAL INDUSTRY AND THE FACTORY SYSTEM

The beginnings of the factory system in America go back to 1789, when one Samuel Slater, an English mechanic, came to this country bearing in his memory the details of the construction of the spinning machinery he had used in England.[1] At this time England was still striving to prevent, so far as possible, the exportation of its new machinery or of plans for its construction elsewhere. Slater enlisted the interest of Moses Brown, a wealthy American merchant, and about 1790 they set up an Arkwright type of mill run by water power at Pawtucket, Rhode Island. This mill spun the first machine-made cotton warp in the United States. In 1803 Slater's brother brought from England the plan of one of the improved Crompton mules, and introduced this into the Slater factory. By this time a number of cotton mills using water power had been established in New England. The cotton industry in this country as well as in England was of course greatly stimulated by Eli Whitney's invention of the cotton gin.[2]

The next important figure in American textiles was Francis Cabot Lowell, who established the first textile factory in the United States that carried on both spinning and weaving by mechanical methods. This factory he opened at Waltham, Massachusetts, about 1813. His master mechanic, Paul Moody, made many additions to the machinery originally copied from British models. Lowell extended his operations to Chelmsford in 1822. The name of the town was soon changed to Lowell. Here he specialized in calico, having brought in the process of cylindrical printing of calico from England. Lawrence was started by Daniel Saunders, the town being originally named Merrimac, but renamed in 1848 after Abbott Lawrence, a prominent manufacturer who had moved there from Lowell. Fall River was started in 1811 by Colonel James

[1] See C. F. Ware, *The Early New England Cotton Manufacture,* Houghton Mifflin, 1931.
[2] See above, p. 276. This same Eli Whitney, as was noted before, is credited with the introduction of the idea of standardized and interchangeable machine parts, a principle that has been of fundamental importance in the development of American industry. Whitney applied the idea as early as 1807 in the manufacture of firearms.

Durfee, and in 1846 the first factory at New Bedford was established as an offshoot from Fall River.

In this textile aristocracy of the first half of the nineteenth century in New England, one detects the origins of many of the intellectual and political aristocrats in eastern New England—the Abbotts, Lawrences, Cabots, and Lowells—who succeeded the Adamses, Websters, and Sumners in economic and social eminence in New England.

Another leading center of the American textile industry was the upper Mohawk Valley in the region about Utica, New York. The industry in Utica was founded in 1807-08 by Benjamin Wolcott, Jr., the son of one of Slater's employees.

The cotton industry grew rapidly in the United States. In 1807 there were 8,000 spindles, in 1810 some 87,000, and in 1820 there were 250,000. Twenty years later, the value of cotton products reached almost $50,000,000 and 2,284,631 spindles were in operation. In 1860 there were over 5,000,000 spindles running, and the value of the product had mounted to $115,681,774.

No small part was played in the rapid development of this, as of other industries in the United States, by the protective attitude of the government. An important stimulus had been given to home manufactures by the Embargo and Non-Intercourse acts, followed by the War of 1812. These had served to cut off supplies from England and to give a temporary protection to the infant industries of America. They also diverted American capital from other fields, particularly foreign commerce, to the new manufactures. At the conclusion of the War of 1812, the large supplies of manufactured goods that had been accumulating in England during the interference with Continental and American trade were "dumped" in the American market at low prices. With these cheap foreign products the new industries in the United States could not compete. A protest arose, which resulted in the passage of a protective tariff in 1816 placing a fairly high duty on manufactured goods. It was felt that this would aid not only the manufacturing interests but, by stimulating the growth of cities, would also increase the market for our agricultural products. This argument constituted the basis of what Henry Clay called "the American System."

In the meantime, other branches of industry were experiencing a development somewhat similar to that in the manufacture of cotton. In the woolen industry the introduction of power machinery was slower, and it was not until about 1840 that household manufacture was displaced to any marked extent. Certain processes, particularly carding and fulling, were early carried on by machinery, and a carding machine invented by an American in 1826 was even adopted in Europe.[1] But the spinning and weaving processes continued to be carried on at home, especially in the frontier communities. The finer woolen and worsted products were imported from England. The American woolen industry experienced a steady and, after 1840, a fairly rapid growth until 1860.[2] By this time factory manufacture was almost everywhere predominant; there were almost 2,000 woolen mills operating, in which over

---

[1] See E. C. Kirkland, *History of American Economic Life*, Crofts, 1932, p. 326.
[2] See A. H. Cole, *American Wool Manufacture*, Harvard University Press, 1926, 2 vols.

$35,000,000 was invested. The value of the product came to $68,865,963 in that year.

The iron industry likewise underwent fundamental changes during this period.[1] It had made something of a start in colonial times, but was handicapped by the fact that soft coal had not yet been found in the United States. Indeed, until almost the middle of the nineteenth century, the bulk of American pig iron was smelted with charcoal, which was relatively plentiful and cheap because of the extensive forests. It was only after the introduction of the hot blast, about 1830, that it became possible to use anthracite coal, of which large supplies existed in eastern Pennsylvania. By 1855 anthracite smelting exceeded charcoal smelting in the making of pig iron. After iron ore was discovered in western Pennsylvania, near beds of soft coal, Pittsburgh became the center of the developing industry, especially after the use of coke gradually increased.[2] One of the great handicaps of the early iron industry was the cost and difficulty of transportation. Therein lay another advantage for Pittsburgh as the concentration point for the industry. That city was an accessible shipping-center for the West, since it could be reached and its products shipped over the Ohio and Mississippi river systems.

After 1820 the iron industry "grew up in western Pennsylvania and the Ohio Valley, extending by 1860 as far as the region of Lake Superior, where smelting was carried on in northern Michigan and near Detroit."[3] In 1851, a Kentucky blacksmith, William Kelly, as previously noted, invented independently the same process for making steel that the Englishman Bessemer patented five years later, and several years of litigation accompanied the first use of the Bessemer process in this country.[4]

Not the least important innovation in the iron and steel industry was the increasing specialization in the products that appeared after the second decade of the last century. The iron mills of Pennsylvania made kettles, nails, hinges, locks, firearms, plows, and tools of all kinds—the multifarious hardware products, mostly small, that were essential to pioneer life in the developing West. By 1860 not only these things, but a variety of agricultural machinery, textile machinery, iron rails for railways, steam engines, and locomotives were all being made in the United States on an extensive scale. The period of vast expansion and large-scale production in the American iron and steel industry came, however, after the Civil War.

One more industry may be mentioned as typical of industrial development before 1860.[5] The boot and shoe industry in colonial America was originally, like most others, a household affair. Of greater importance, however, were later stages, when the shoes were made either by traveling craftsmen who visited at the homes and made up the leather of the settlers, or in the small shops—"ten-footers," they were called—by the master craftsman, usually at the order of the customer. It was as late as about 1810 before a last was

[1] *Cf.* Keir, *op. cit.*, Chap. IX. Some iron products, however, long continued to be household manufactures.
[2] *Facts and Factors in Economic History; Articles by Former Students of Edwin Francis Gay*, Harvard University Press, 1932, pp. 424-45.
[3] Faulkner, *American Economic History*, p. 307.
[4] See above, p. 280. The litigation was, of course, carried on by the Kelly interests and was designed to prevent the introduction of the Bessemer equipment.
[5] See B. E. Hazard, *The Organization of the Boot and Shoe Industry in Massachusetts before 1875*, Harvard University Press, 1921.

introduced that enabled the cobbler to distinguish between rights and lefts. The shoes were sewed by hand and the uppers were fastened to the wooden soles by wooden pegs. Early in the nineteenth century merchant capitalists began to furnish leather to the cobblers, who made up the shoes, which were then sold to the country storekeepers. By 1825 most of the shoes, at least on the Atlantic Coast, were made in workshops where a number of workers were collected, but the greatest part of the work was still done by hand. Some of the processes were still "put out," as in the textile industry much earlier in England.[1]

By 1851 the sewing machine, which had been invented in the preceding decade, was applied to the manufacture of the uppers of shoes. The shoe industry had thus been centralized and partly mechanized by 1860, but power had not as yet been generally applied to it.

3. IMPROVEMENTS IN TRANSPORTATION

During the first half of the nineteenth century, the steady movement of settlement to the west, north and south, rapidly broadened the home market and placed new demands upon industry in the East. By 1860 a considerable degree of industrial concentration had already developed, particularly in the urban centers along the Atlantic Coast, and at western points such as Pittsburgh, Cincinnati, Chicago, and St. Louis.

The westward expansion and the increased shipment of goods from the East made imperative better and more rapid means of transportation and communication. Heavy inland traffic in the early nineteenth century necessarily moved up and down the rivers, but the rivers ran for the most part north and south, whereas the natural routes of trade ran inland to the west from the Atlantic Coast. Western settlement thus made essential the building of highways, and it was at the same time greatly facilitated by their construction.

A real drive for the building of improved roads swept the United States at the opening of the nineteenth century. Following the English example, a number of turnpike roads were constructed by private capital, which sought its return by the charging of tolls.[2] In the more sparsely settled districts, however, where the prospect of profits was not sufficient to entice the entrepreneur, state governments expended considerable capital in the construction of highways. A long and eloquent debate was waged as to the right of the national government to finance internal improvements, and one important highway, the Cumberland turnpike, running from Cumberland on the Potomac to Wheeling on the Ohio, was a federal project. Traffic on these roads was heavy, but freight charges remained prohibitively high for low-cost bulky products. These continued to move, when they moved at all, down the rivers or along the coast.

The canal-building era in American transportation opened approximately in 1820.[3] By that time the steamboat had demonstrated its practicability, and was increasing in size and speed. It was rarely used on canals, however, being limited mainly to coastwise and inland river transportation. But the use of the

---

[1] See above, pp. 46 ff. [2] *Cf.* J. A. Durrenberger, *Turnpikes*, privately printed, 1931.
[3] *Cf.* A. F. Harlow, *Old Towpaths,* Appleton, 1926.

steamboat increased the need of canals to connect the larger waterways. The year 1817 witnessed the beginnings of the Erie Canal, which after its completion in 1825 was an immediate and striking success. Plans for other canals multiplied, and before the middle of the century there was an imposing network of canals and canalized rivers, concentrated chiefly along the Atlantic Coast and in the Ohio Valley. In this chapter of transportation history, as in the preceding one, the West played a dominant rôle, the growing settlement of the region west of the Alleghenies being both a cause and a result of the improvement in the means of transportation.

As has often—and quite properly—been pointed out, the character of the canal network was in no small degree an outgrowth of the competition of the seaboard cities, notably Baltimore, Philadelphia, and New York, for a dominating position in this trade with the West. New York, with the Erie Canal, secured the major victory; Philadelphia and Baltimore were only poor rivals, with the Pennsylvania Main Line and the Chesapeake and Ohio canals, respectively. The difficulties of the terrain for canal-building in Pennsylvania, Maryland, and West Virginia explain this failure to duplicate New York's success in canal-building.

While many canal projects were just taking form, or were being carried to slow completion, there appeared the "iron horse," which was later to render canals relatively unimportant carriers except for slow and heavy freight.[1] As Professor Faulkner remarks:

The effects of railroads in opening up the West, in providing transportation for western products, in stimulating eastern manufacturing, in binding the sections together, in disseminating information and education to remote sections, provide a story intertwined with every phase of our economic, social, and political life since 1840.[2]

Reference was made earlier to the serious problems raised by the construction of the American railroads, because of the many curves and grades involved.[3] Another equally serious problem was that of finance, since mileage was necessarily great and capital was scarce in the new country. While neither of these problems was solved at all satisfactorily in the early period, the railroads soon came to be the very arteries of the nation's life. Owing to inexperience with the new means of transportation and haste to complete the projects and to secure a monetary return, many of the early railroads were constructed with grades that should have been eliminated; the roadbeds either wore out themselves or soon shook the rolling stock to pieces; and gauges differed so much on short lines that through traffic was impossible. The outcome of such defects as these was that many of the early lines soon had to be rebuilt at heavy additional expense.

Private capital being scanty and difficult to secure, state and city governments in their eagerness often advanced funds to speed the construction of railroads, and, as was true with the canals, much of the capital thus supplied was never returned. When the Western lines began to be built, much assistance was rendered by the federal government in the shape of large grants of land

---

[1] *Cf.* Stevers, *Steel Trails*.   [2] Faulkner, *op. cit.*, p. 342.   [3] See above, p. 309.

along the proposed lines.[1] This land could be sold by the railroads to settlers after construction of the road. Foreign capital, especially English and German, was eagerly invested in early American railways. In spite of all this assistance, bankruptcies and reorganizations were a characteristic feature of our early railroad history, and much capital, part of it American, but a great proportion foreign, was lost. A major reason for incompetence in the surveying, planning, and building of early American railroads (down to after 1880, at least) was that they were viewed as instruments for financial gambling with railroad securities even more than as agencies for transportation. So careless were the greedy promoters that Professor Ripley has remarked of one of the leading systems that it seems as though every possible grade had been sought and every important city avoided.[2]

The first railroads were opened in the thirties, and were built, as might be expected, from the coast towns into the interior. New York, well served by the Erie Canal, was not so eager for the new methods of transportation as were Baltimore and Philadelphia, and the New England rival, Boston. The latter city, prevented by topography from developing any important canals, was among the first to adopt the railroad, partly as a means of tapping the rich trade of the Erie Canal terminal at Albany. By 1850 Boston was the center of 3,000 miles of railroad.[3] Baltimore became the eastern terminus of the first long line, the Baltimore and Ohio; and Philadelphia, abandoning the costly and ineffective canal-and-railroad combination of the Pennsylvania Main Line, likewise turned its attention to a through railroad route.

Meanwhile, New York had not been caught napping, and by 1851 had supplemented its waterway by the New York and Erie Railroad. The construction of this line completed the ascendancy, so brilliantly inaugurated by the Erie Canal, of New York City over its commercial rivals. By the middle of the century it had far surpassed the other coast cities in population and in volume of trade, and this leadership has never since been seriously threatened.

Railroad mileage in the United States rose from nothing in 1830 to over 30,000 by 1860. At that time nine lines connected the Atlantic Coast with the interior of the continent, and a fairly extensive system of railroads had been constructed parallel to the Atlantic seaboard. The main channels of trade, which in the first half of the century had run north and south, were now definitely east and west, leaving New Orleans, once one of the proudest commercial centers in America, to fall into a decline from which it began to recover only in the twentieth century. By the time of the Civil War, the ultimate outcome of the competition between the waterway and the railroad was fairly clear, and a number of states that had invested large sums of money in the furtherance of canal projects had already been driven into bankruptcy.

The first half of the nineteenth century was marked by an expansion of agriculture in the United States no less striking than the growth of industry and transportation. The westward movement took place in three "waves,"

---

[1] See L. H. Haney, *A Congressional History of Railways in the United States 1850-1888*, University of Wisconsin, 1908-10, 2 vols., Vol. I.

[2] *Cf.* Forrest Davis, *What Price Wall Street?* Godwin, 1932, Chaps. v-ix; R. I. Warshow, *Jay Gould*, Greenberg, 1928; A. D. H. Smith, *Commodore Vanderbilt*, McBride, 1927; Bouck White, *The Book of Daniel Drew*, Doran, 1910; and Matthew Josephson, *The Robber Barons*, Harcourt, Brace, 1934.

[3] See Kirkland, *op. cit.*, p. 289.

each with its typical culture. First came the hunter and trapper, who explored the country and made known its possibilities. He was followed by the pioneer farmer, who cleared the land and started a subsistence agriculture. These two types of frontiersmen were usually driven on further by the appearance of the settled farmer, who brought in more of the comforts of civilization and began to produce a surplus of agricultural products, which sought the markets of the East and South. In the South, the westward movement proceeded differently. The first stages of exploration and pioneering were essentially the same. But the pioneer was followed by the cotton planter or some other type of plantation owner who bought up the land, consolidated the small farms, and introduced Negro slaves. Here agriculture was to a considerable degree commercial, as the planter did not usually produce his own food supply but specialized in cotton, tobacco, and other characteristic Southern products.

The exploitation of the vast expanse of virgin land in the West was the chief factor in shaping the culture of that area during much of the nineteenth century. The rolling wooded lands of the Ohio and Mississippi river basins made the clearing of the land the first necessity of the would-be farmer; his home was usually a log cabin, and his first salable product often the potash made from the logs that he had to destroy. The lumber industry accompanied the westward movement from Maine through New York and Pennsylvania to Indiana, northern Michigan, Wisconsin, and Minnesota. When the prairie lands west of the Mississippi were reached, the settler faced an entirely different set of problems. The land had only to be plowed and planted, but there were no trees to offer shelter from the weather, there was no wood to build with or to burn for fuel, and the prairie sod was a tough proposition for crude plows. For some time the prairies were avoided, but when the steel plow was introduced, and the lumber industry and railroads supplied the necessary timber, the prairie lands with their rich soil were found to be veritable "gold mines" for the farmer.

4. POPULATION GROWTH AND THE WESTERN FRONTIER

During much of the nineteenth century, land approached closely the status of a free commodity in America, while labor was relatively scarce. As a result, the farming methods were such that they have often been denounced by later writers as wasteful and exploitative, exhausting the natural resources of the soil. From our point of view there is some truth in this charge, but the methods fitted the needs of the time, and were not more detrimental to succeeding generations than some of the contemporary practices in the misuse of natural resources.[1] As another outgrowth of the scarcity of labor, the invention and introduction of agricultural machinery was rapid in this country, even in the first half of the nineteenth century. The steel plow was introduced in the thirties. Hussey and McCormick devised the reaper between 1833 and 1845. The mowing machine came in at the same time. A crude threshing machine was invented by 1850, to be vastly improved upon during the next half-century.

[1] The most serious complaint to be lodged against the early settlers is their deplorable waste of forests. For example, Indiana was once covered with superbly valuable hard woods. Wisconsin was also outrageously deforested by the pioneers.

The grain-binder appeared in 1878, followed by the much more impressive header and thresher combined. The gang plow and tractor have greatly expedited cultivation in the present century.

As can readily be imagined, the population of the United States grew rapidly after 1800. The total population of the colonies in 1700 has been estimated at 275,000; this figure had increased by 1750 to over 1,200,000; and in 1790 to almost 4,000,000. The increase was much more rapid after 1800; the figures of 1790 had more than doubled by 1820, and by 1860 the population stood at more than 30,000,000. A large part of this increase was due to immigration, particularly after about 1825. In the years 1850-54 inclusive, for example, over 350,000 immigrants came to the United States each year. Many of these immigrants were attracted by the opportunities in the West, which also drew many settlers from the more thickly populated Eastern sections. Some states in the West, such as Ohio and Kansas, developed a culture that was substantially transplanted from New England. By 1860 the land east of the Mississippi was fairly well taken up. In the decade of the fifties the first tier of states west of the Mississippi began to fill up, and settlement of the Pacific Coast proceeded rapidly after the discovery of gold in 1849.

It must not be thought that the economic expansion of the early nineteenth century occurred without a hitch. In general, this period was characterized by increasing prosperity in the United States, but it was marked, too, by several fairly serious economic setbacks, particularly those of 1819, 1837, and 1857. Various factors operated to bring about these crises, followed in each case by several years of depression. Among the more important were: (1) Overspeculation in land, many people buying large quantities on credit, for which they later found themselves unable to pay; (2) overinvestment in transportation projects, either canal or railroad; (3) rash speculation in the securities of these shaky enterprises; and (4) so-called wildcat banking, conservative principles of credit extension and of the issuance of paper money being insufficiently observed.[1] All of these are weaknesses in a business system such as might be expected in a new and rapidly expanding capitalistic community bent on quick profits. Each of the crises brought on numerous individual failures and slowed down economic development temporarily, but they did not alter the main lines of growth or teach the salutary economic lessons that were there to be learned if anybody cared to learn them.

II. THE GROWTH OF LARGE-SCALE INDUSTRY SINCE 1860

1. ECONOMIC EFFECTS OF THE CIVIL WAR

The Civil War is as significant for economic as for political development in the history of the United States. In the period preceding the war, machinery and the factory system were introduced, but it was not until after the Civil War that machine production, the factory system, and a definite wage-earning class colored the whole of American industrial life. With the demand for manufactured products that it created, the Civil War started a movement which

---

[1] *Cf.* Davis, *op. cit.*; W. W. Price, *We Have Recovered Before!* Harper, 1933, Chaps. II, VI-VII; and Horace White, *Money and Banking*, 5th ed., Ginn, 1914, Bk. III.

by 1890 had made manufacturing a principal source of American wealth. Since that time our factories and mines have transformed the United States into the greatest of industrial nations.

2. AGRICULTURE AFTER THE CIVIL WAR

The Civil War also proved a remarkable stimulus to agriculture in the North and to new agricultural developments in the Northwest, not only because of the great demand for food to supply the troops, but also because there was an increased market for our agricultural products abroad, due to crop failures there. As a result of these influences, the decade of the sixties saw a great increase in the use of the new agricultural machinery.

A number of factors served to continue this stimulation of the settlement of land and the expansion of American agriculture. Among these were the rapid growth of the domestic and foreign markets, at first for grain products and later, with the introduction of refrigeration on railroads and steamships, for meat and dairy products. The Homestead Act of 1862 facilitated the taking up of unoccupied land in order to exploit this increased demand for farm products. All this conspired to bring about the rapid exhaustion of the supply of desirable agricultural lands in this country. By 1890 what remained was chiefly land of poor quality, or land that necessitated precarious dry farming or extensive irrigation. Recent agrarian history has been marked by an increasing prevalence of tenancy, which now exceeds 50 per cent of the total number of farms in a number of leading agricultural states.

By the opening of the twentieth century diversified agriculture was beginning to supplant the one-crop system in the West, though there is still much room for improvement in that respect. Dairy farming is on the increase throughout the Middle West, and technical knowledge is being applied to agriculture to an increasing degree, in methods of crop rotation, the use of fertilizers, stock-breeding, the reduction or elimination of stock and crop diseases, and the problems of farm management in general. In spite of the increasing application of science and capital, however, the problems of American agriculture have in the past decade or two become serious, and are discussed in some detail later in the chapter.[1]

While the Civil War proved an almost unmixed blessing for the economic development of the North, its immediate effects on the South were disastrous in the extreme. Aside from the actual destruction inevitable in the area of military operations, the man power and the capital of the South were far more depleted than those of the North. Further, the political chaos of the Reconstruction period hampered economic development, which had already received a severe temporary setback from the abolition of the slave system. However unsound slave labor may have been from a broad socio-economic point of view, it was the system to which the South was adjusted, and its termination brought agricultural confusion. It has long been recognized by economic historians that the Civil War by no means entirely destroyed the plantation system, which was carried on in modified form in the later nineteenth century through the development of tenancy among the Negro and the

[1] See below, pp. 373 ff.

poor white populations. Small-scale farming became, however, the rule in the South for many years after 1865. The rudimentary agrarian organization of the South after 1865 was not conducive to rapid improvement in agricultural technique, through the increased application of either scientific methods or capital. During the last twenty-five years, however, large-scale corporation farming has made considerable headway. Cotton has continued to be the chief money crop, and is marketed in Southern factory towns, the North, or in Europe. Manufacturing made no considerable start in the South until the last decades of the nineteenth century. Since then the cotton textile and iron and steel industries have developed rapidly in the Carolinas, Georgia, Alabama, and Tennessee at the expense of older established Northern centers.[1]

3. POPULATION CHANGES AND IMMIGRATION

The concentration upon agriculture in the South and West helped to create a ready market for the ever growing industries of the East. The nation's population continued to increase after 1865 even more rapidly than in the first half of the century. By 1880 it had passed 50,000,000, in 1900 it was over 75,000,000, and by 1930 it had grown to 122,000,000. Until 1920 more than half of this population was classified as rural, but according to the United States Census of that year, the urban population exceeded 50 per cent of the total. This urban predominance continues to increase, though less rapidly since the great depression of 1929. In the decade after 1920, owing in part to immigration restriction and in part to a falling birth rate, the population growth of the United States fell off markedly. Students of population predict a static population for the country somewhere around 1975.[2] The social problems of urban life, among which housing, education, recreation, and the changing customs take a prominent place, are therefore of increasing importance.[3] Most of the large urban centers are in the East, but a number, such as Chicago, Detroit, Cleveland, Minneapolis, St. Louis, San Francisco, Los Angeles, Portland, and Seattle, have grown up at strategic points in the West.

No small part of the population increase was still due to continued immigration, over 10,000,000 persons coming in between 1860 and 1890.[4] In several years between 1905 and 1915, the annual number of immigrants ran over 1,000,000. In the earlier period, most of the immigrants came from northern and western Europe, and the majority of them engaged in agriculture in their new homes. But after about 1890 an increasing percentage belonged to the "new" immigration, coming from eastern and southern Europe. They entered in large numbers into industry and general urban occupations. Partly because this later immigration offered a sharper contrast to the existing racial stocks in this country and partly because of the larger numbers and the increasing concentration in our cities, immigration since about 1900 has raised many pressing social

[1] See Broadus and G. S. Mitchell, *Industrial Revolution in the South,* Johns Hopkins University, 1930; W. J. Carson, ed., *The Coming of Industry to the South,* American Academy of Political and Social Science, *Annals,* Vol. CLIII, 1931; and Tippett, *When Southern Labor Stirs.*
[2] See W. S. Thompson, *Population Problems,* McGraw-Hill, 1930, Chap. XIII.
[3] See below, pp. 405 ff.
[4] See Edith Abbott, *Historical Aspects of the Immigration Problem,* University of Chicago Press, 1926; and H. P. Fairchild, *Immigration,* rev. ed., Macmillan, 1925.

problems. A more critical sentiment has led in recent years to a policy of fairly rigid restriction.[1]

4. INDUSTRIAL EXPANSION

The attitude of the government in the later nineteenth century continued, on the whole, to be favorable to industrial development. The tariff of 1816 has already been referred to as protective, but the later tariffs, beginning in 1862, imposed much higher duties, at first in order to increase the federal revenue, but later chiefly to foster such home industries as iron and steel, textiles, sugar, and tin.[2] In the late nineteenth century and the early twentieth, some fairly strict measures, such as the Sherman Anti-Trust Act of 1890 and the Clayton Bill of 1914, were passed regulating industry and particularly industrial concentration. It was not expected, however, that these would check the growth of industry, but that they would guide it along socially beneficial lines. This legal restriction has been very effectively evaded by devious devices such as holding companies, which have brought in far worse evils than monopoly.

Finally, the development of American manufactures on any such scale as took place would not have been possible but for the improvements in the means of transportation.[3] While the skeleton of the railroad network in the East was fairly complete by 1860, the first railroad to span the continent—the Union Pacific—was not completed until 1869. Since then several other transcontinental roads have been built. A good deal of railroad construction was also carried on in the South to replace that destroyed in the war. After 1865 railroad mileage grew at a prodigious rate. It mounted to 95,261 in 1880 and twenty years later came to 198,964. In 1930 there were approximately 250,000 miles of railway in the United States—more than on the whole continent of Europe.

The need during the Civil War of providing uniforms for over a million soldiers greatly stimulated the introduction of mechanical methods in Northern industry, and thus helped to complete the mechanization of the woolen and the clothing industries, especially the former. Cotton manufacture was well advanced on a mechanical basis by 1850. The ready-made clothing industry received its initial impetus at this time—aided greatly by Howe's sewing machine. Substantially the same thing happened in the shoe industry. The application of the sewing machine to the industry in the fifties was soon followed by the introduction of power; and the McKay machine for sewing uppers on soles speeded up the development of the factory industry. Another important innovation was the Goodyear welting machine, which helped to make possible the manufacture of the finest grade of shoes by machinery. With the further application of power and the invention of lasting-machines, the way was prepared for the complete mechanization of the boot and shoe industry.

Aside from the growth in the scale of operations, the most important features in the later history of the textile and the shoe industries in America have been

---

[1] See below, pp. 423-24.   [2] See Taussig, *Tariff History of the United States.*
[3] *Cf.* John Moody, *Railroad Builders,* Yale University Press, 1919; A. C. Laut, *Romance of the Rails,* McBride, 1928, 2 vols.; J. B. Hedges, *Henry Villard and the Railways of the Northwest,* Yale University Press, 1930; and R. E. Riegel, *The Story of the Western Railroads,* Macmillan, 1926.

the changes in localization. Towards the end of the nineteenth century, cotton manufacturing began to be carried on in the South. It was for the most part the coarser qualities that were produced there at first. By the 1920's the shift of the industry from its old New England centers was so pronounced that some of the mills in the North had shut down, and in some instances capital and entrepreneurship had moved bodily to the newer area.[1] The hasty introduction of the textile industry into the South, together with the industrial inexperience and cheap labor supply there, combined to produce bad working-conditions reminiscent of the English factories a century ago. Discontent provoked thereby led to extensive and bitterly fought strikes in 1929-30.[2] This labor resentment flared up again in the short but widespread textile strike of 1934.

With the rise of Western industrial cities, the shoe industry gradually shifted, concentrating in the West, especially in St. Louis, which also became a center for the manufacture of shoe machinery. Massachusetts still retains its primacy in this industry, however, particularly in the manufacture of the finer grades of men's shoes and of women's shoes.

The great need for iron that the Civil War created increased its price and brought about a rapid opening of new iron mines and mills. The later nineteenth century was marked particularly by the discovery and exploitation of large and rich iron-ore deposits in northern Michigan and Minnesota, with the resulting development of a heavy coal and iron traffic on the Great Lakes. In 1925 these mines and ore beds produced nearly 84 per cent of the iron ore of the country. The production of pig iron first passed 1,000,000 long tons in 1870. By 1880 it was nearly 4,000,000, by 1890 over 9,000,000, and in 1900 almost 13,-800,000. This growth continued, though not steadily, to a high point of over 42,600,000 tons in 1929. In this year, the United Kingdom, Germany, France, and Belgium together produced less than 26,000,000 tons. These figures bear striking testimony to the increasing importance of iron in the mechanical age.[3]

The growth of the iron and steel industry was dependent to a considerable extent upon coal.[4] The late nineteenth century saw the increasing mechanization of coal-mining, marked by the introduction of cutting machines and mechanical loaders and a growing use of electricity to haul the loaded cars. These and other factors have helped to account for the overproduction that has constantly threatened the coal industry in recent years, and has done so much to preserve the bad working-conditions, more characteristic of soft-coal mining than of any other American industry. Competition of petroleum as a fuel has also helped to depress the coal industry. The following extracts from a description of living-conditions among the West Virginia miners in 1931 by Tom Tippett, an experienced investigator, cannot but remind the reader of mining-conditions in England at the beginning of the Industrial Revolution:

> The miners live in isolated company villages far up in the mountains. A small, unpainted shack on stilts, unceiled, with broken steps and leaky roof is a common type of home.... The miners must trade at the company store where prices

---

[1] See Mitchell and Mitchell, *op. cit.*   [2] See Tippett, *op. cit.*
[3] See J. R. Smith, *The Story of Iron and Steel*, Appleton, 1908; and E. D. McCallum, *The Iron and Steel Industry in the United States*, King, 1931.
[4] See W. H. Hamilton and H. R. Wright, *The Case of Bituminous Coal*, Macmillan, 1925.

usually range from 20 to 66 per cent higher than in the outside towns. The wages of many run about $2 and $3 a day—and work is far from steady. On pay day many workers receive, literally, no money whatever, their payments for rent, food, doctor, explosives for mining, etc., having used up all their earnings. . . . Since the men are in debt to the company, it is very difficult for them to leave. . . . There is the home of a 30-year-old striker, whom I will call Walter Robinson. We went inside. Some coals were burning in a grate, and around it huddled Mrs. Robinson and three small children. All of them were without shoes, all only half clothed. On the bed in the same room was a tiny baby, three months old. Still another child died this year. From where I stood I could easily see through the house whose walls were single planks separated by wide cracks. It was just as easy to see the sky through the roof. Nothing that is called furniture was in the place nor anything commonly associated in our minds with the word home. All the Robinsons were hungry and have been underfed for months.[1]

These conditions are further reflected in the prevalence of bitter strife between miners and employers.[2] While strong labor organizations, which at present the coal operators do not tolerate, could undoubtedly do much to alleviate the situation, a thoroughgoing reform of the coal industry would involve shutting down many of the less productive mines, and thus permanently throw out of work thousands of miners.[3] Such problems as this have no simple solution, and claim the earnest attention of all who are seriously interested in social welfare.

The development of coal-mining was accompanied by a growing importance of bituminous coal and coke as fuel for the smelting of iron. By 1875 they passed anthracite, and since 1925 coke has smelted practically all of the pig iron produced in this country. While no revolutionary technical changes have been introduced in smelting methods, the past fifty years have been marked by a notable enlargement in the scale of operations and by increased efficiency. They have been characterized, too, by the rise of the iron and steel industry in the South. In fact, the spread there of the iron and steel and textile industries has given rise to the term "the new South." There are excellent deposits of coal, iron, and limestone in close proximity, especially in Alabama. The chief center of the iron and steel industry in the South is Birmingham, Alabama. Iron and steel manufacture has also proceeded apace in Tennessee.

The production of steel has advanced along with that of iron.[4] Following the Bessemer process, which was fairly widely introduced in America in the seventies, the Thomas-Gilchrist process of working ores high in phosphorus content, the Siemens-Martin or open-hearth process, and finally the electric furnace were adopted. Since Kelly's day, the American steel industry has been marked not so much by its inventiveness as by its adaptation of foreign technology to large-scale production. The new processes have made possible the manufacture of the high-grade products demanded by the modern building trades and by the automobile, tool, and machinery industries. The United States now not only supplies most of the home market for iron and steel, but exports

---

[1] Brookwood College, *Report*, 1931.
[2] *Cf.* National Committee for the Defense of Political Prisoners, *Harlan Miners Speak*.
[3] *Cf.* Hamilton and Wright, *op. cit.*
[4] See H. N. Casson, *The Romance of Steel*, Barnes, 1907; and H. B. Vanderblue and W. L. Crum, *The Iron Industry in Prosperity and Depression*, A. W. Shaw, 1927.

large quantities to foreign countries. The remarkable growth of the steel industry in the United States may be discerned from the following figures of steel-ingot and castings production. In 1875 the yearly product was slightly under 400,000 long tons. By 1910 it had jumped to 26,095,000, and in 1929 to 56,433,470 long tons. The production of rolled and miscellaneous steel products advanced from 16,840,000 long tons in 1905 to 41,069,000 in 1929.

In addition to the marked expansion of the older industries, the late nineteenth century and the early twentieth have been distinguished by the development of a number of new ones, which belong to the story of the "Second Industrial Revolution."[1] Among the first was petroleum, the uses of which for industrial and lighting purposes began to be exploited in the 1860's. It has now come to be one of the leading American industries. Others are the electrical, automobile, chemical, rubber, and machinery industries, as well as the still newer motion-picture and radio industries. The electrical industry ranks with petroleum as the major business in this group. It has conquered the illumination market of the country and has made serious inroads upon steam and gasoline as a source of power. The electrical utilities have generally remained mainly privately owned in this country and have shown a special tendency towards concentration and financial manipulation.[2]

Perhaps the industrial growth can most strikingly be summarized by pointing out that, according to the Census of 1860, the total value of product of American manufactures in that year, including both factories and hand and neighborhood industries, was $1,886,000,000. By 1900 this figure had risen to $13,000,000,000; by 1915, excluding those establishments with a value of product of less than $500, it was well over $24,000,000,000. By 1929, excluding establishments with products valued at less than $5,000, it was $70,420,000,000.[3] Meanwhile the capital invested had increased in proportion. The leading industries in 1930, from the standpoint of value of product, were textiles, iron and steel, machinery, and transportation equipment, each running above $7,000,000,000 for the year.

The rapid growth in the volume of American manufactures has been accompanied, especially since about 1880, by an increasing tendency towards consolidation and combination. By 1890 the corporation had become the usual form of business organization for the large undertaking.[4] At the present time, some 80 per cent of the business enterprises of the country, including almost all of the larger ones, are organized as corporations. The outstanding exceptions are some express companies and a few private banks, which, largely in order to avoid publicity regarding their operations, have never incorporated.

Sharp distinctions have developed also as between corporations. Beginning in the last decades of the nineteenth century, a movement towards combination, either partial or complete,[5] in order to avoid competition and to reap the advantages of large-scale production, has finally created a small group of super-

---

[1] See below, Chapter xx.
[2] See W. E. Mosher, *Electrical Utilities*, Harper, 1929; and C. D. Thompson, *Confessions of the Power Trust*, Dutton, 1932.
[3] These figures, of course, take no account of changes in the purchasing power of the dollar.
[4] On the development of the corporate form of business organization, see below, pp. 796 ff.
[5] See below, pp. 748 ff.

corporations. The movement has been particularly marked in the past fifteen or twenty years and has been aided by the legal device of the holding company. We now have in this country ten or a dozen billion-dollar corporations.[1] A very important study[2] of America's 200 largest nonfinancial corporations indicates that their share of the country's total business assets is rapidly on the increase. In 1910 the 200 largest American nonfinancial corporations controlled one-third of the total assets of nonfinancial corporations reported as paying federal income taxes, while about 200,000 other corporations controlled the other two-thirds. In 1920 the 200 largest controlled 39 per cent of our business wealth, while over 250,000 others controlled the remainder. By 1931 the 200 controlled 55 per cent of the total business wealth, while the control of the other 45 per cent was divided among over 300,000 other companies. Though the number of corporations is on the increase, the larger ones are thus growing in power much more rapidly than the business community as a whole. In 1930 over 80 per cent of the total gross assets of the 573 largest companies on the New York Stock Exchange were controlled by 130 companies with assets of over $100,000,000 each. The social significance of this situation can scarcely be overrated for a country whose fundamental political and economic principles were at one time democracy and equality.

Not only are American industry, transportation, and utilities gravitating into the control of a few great supercorporations, but the control of each of these vast organizations has become centered in a few individuals who never today own anything like a majority of the stock. Indeed, it is unusual for the governing clique to own as much as 10 per cent of the stock. Legal devices have superseded the old necessity for a majority ownership of stock to achieve control. This control over great corporations through only slight ownership of securities has invited mismanagement and pillage from the inside rather than encouraging efficient management. The exploiting insiders get all the spoils from exploitation and yet bear only a small fraction of the loss as stockholders. This situation has contributed as much as anything else to the corruption and disintegration of American business in the last decade and has placed private property in greater jeopardy than any other single development in American history.[3]

A study of the growth in the size of manufacturing establishments in the United States leads to a similar conclusion as to the increasing control exercised by a relatively few large undertakings. As late as 1909, less than one-sixth of the workers in American factories were found in establishments employing 1,000 or more wage-earners; by 1923 the figure had risen to nearly one-fourth.[4] In 1904 establishments with an annual product value of $500,000 or over turned out 57 per cent of the total manufacturing product; in 1925 about 71 per cent was produced by such establishments.[5] In 1904 establishments with an annual

[1] See table on p. 750. There are today about 508,000 financial and nonfinancial corporations, combined, in the country.
[2] A. A. Berle and G. C. Means, *The Modern Corporation and Private Property*, Commerce Clearing House, 1932. See also I. M. Wormser, *Frankenstein, Incorporated*, McGraw-Hill, 1931.
[3] *Cf.* P. M. O'Leary, *Corporate Enterprise in Modern Economic Life*, Harper, 1933; Berle and Means, *op. cit.;* and W. Z. Ripley, "Our Corporate Revolution and Its Perils," New York *Times*, July 24, 1932, Sec. VIII, p. 1. See below, pp. 798 ff., 822 ff.
[4] See H. W. Laidler, *Concentration of Control in American Industry*, Crowell, 1931, p. 4.
[5] See *Ibid.*, p. 5.

product value of $1,000,000 or more included less than 1 per cent of the total number of establishments, and turned out only 38 per cent of the total value of product. In 1925 they numbered 5.6 per cent of the total number of establishments, and turned out over 67 per cent of the total product.

Such proofs of the growth of "big business" can be multiplied indefinitely. This growth can be illustrated by examples from such typical American industries as the iron and steel, the automobile, the telephone, the electric, and the oil industries. But enough has already been said to prove conclusively that the day of the small manufacturer has definitely passed in many American industries. While the number of establishments and even of stockholders in corporations may continue to increase, the actual control of industry is passing rapidly into the hands of a relatively small group. Whether this implies that America will be controlled by an industrial autocracy, or whether it will really simplify an eventual transfer of control to society by way of a Socialistic state remains to be decided by the events of the future.

It was only natural that the striking industrial expansion of the United States, manufacturing and agricultural alike, should be reflected in an increase of our foreign trade. In 1860 our imports amounted to $534,000,000 and our exports to $333,000,000; in 1900 our imports were valued at $850,000,000 and our exports at $1,395,000; in 1914 imports stood at $1,789,000,000 and exports at $2,114,000,000; in 1920 our imports had mounted to $5,279,000,000 and our exports to $8,228,000,000. Not only had our foreign trade increased greatly, but we had passed from a nation in which imports greatly exceeded exports into one with a large export balance. But our foreign trade remained insignificant when compared to our internal trade, amounting to not over 10 per cent of the latter at any time. Indeed, our domestic trade is greater than the foreign trade of all the nations of the world combined.

5. RECENT PROBLEMS

As in the first half of the nineteenth century, American economic development has been interrupted since 1860 by several crises, the most serious being those starting in 1873, 1893, and 1929.[1] An important factor in these, as in the earlier crises, was wild speculation, which helped to carry prices, particularly security prices, to an economically unjustified level, from which they dropped abruptly, causing numerous business failures. Recovery came in each case only gradually after a depression lasting several years, and recovery from the 1929 depression is not yet assured (1935). Another important item in the inability to maintain permanent prosperity under American capitalism has been the inequitable and unwise distribution of the social income, neither farmers nor wage-earners obtaining a just share. In the very prosperous year 1929, 6,000,000 families, or over 21 per cent of the total, had an income of less than $1,000 per family; 20,000,000 families, or 71 per cent of the total, had incomes of less than $2,500 each; and only 2,000,000 families, or 8 per cent of the total, had incomes in excess of $5,000. The richest 0.1 per cent of the families at the top—those receiving annually in excess of $75,000—enjoyed a total income as great

---

[1] On the business cycle, see below, pp. 836 ff.

as the poorest 42 per cent of all American families. The poorest 80 per cent of the population contributed only 2 per cent of the national savings. This appalling situation has prevented the masses from being sufficiently extensive consumers to maintain the market for goods.[1]

The transformation of America into an industrial state created a social class little known here before the Industrial Revolution—the proletariat. So long as small-scale industry prevailed, and virgin land awaited the arrival of the cultivator, there could be no considerable propertyless class dependent upon wages. But twentieth-century America has millions for whom daily bread depends upon a job in mine, factory, or mill. The significance of this is brought home to society most clearly when economic depression closes many establishments and thousands of laborers are thrown out of work. Class consciousness has not as yet taken sharp form among the American laborers; even when it is organized, American labor is not normally radical, as it often is in Europe. In England and most other European countries the working classes frankly recognize that they will remain in this status during their lives. In the United States the workers have been affected by past conditions and, under the spell of "the American dream," still like to think that they may rise to be capitalists. This has stifled their interest in purely working-class movements.[2]

American economic leadership of the Western world was almost won before 1914, and was assured by the developments arising out of the World War.[3] Accompanying the remarkable industrialization and leaving unmistakable imprints upon American culture have been the triumph of material considerations, the victory of the machine, and the increase of cultural standardization.[4]

American farming was hard hit as a result of the decline of demand for farm products after the close of the Civil War and was deeply affected by the crises of 1873 and 1893. These rebuffs, together with oppression by railroads, elevator companies, and loan sharks, led to several vigorous agrarian revolts from 1870 to 1896, such as the Greenback movement, the Granger movement, and the Populist movement. But farming still held its own, and reached its highest prosperity during the World War. Then came a sudden shift in the fortunes of agriculture, which we shall now describe.

III. THE CRISIS IN AMERICAN AGRICULTURE

American farming prosperity, which was maintained, with some serious lapses, on a passably decent level from 1850 to 1920, rested upon certain definite historical conditions. In the first place, English capitalism was unable to feed itself. After the repeal of the Corn Laws in 1846 it very frankly depended upon cheap foodstuffs from abroad, and the American farmers were the great source of this supply. At the same time, our capitalistic system was then in the state of evolution. We were a debtor economy and sent our farm products abroad to help pay the interest on our foreign borrowings and the bills for the raw

---

[1] *Cf.* R. R. Doane, *The Measurement of American Wealth*, Harper, 1933; and Maurice Leven, H. G. Moulton, and C. A. Warburton, *America's Capacity to Consume*, Brookings Institution, 1934.
[2] *Cf.* J. L. Spivak, "Bitter Unrest Sweeps the Nation," *American Mercury*, August, 1934.
[3] *Cf.* Ludwell Denny, *America Conquers Britain*, Knopf, 1930.
[4] J. H. Dietrich, *The Chief Danger in Our Civilization*, Minneapolis, 1930.

materials and semifinished goods that we needed for the building up of American industrial prosperity. The remarkable growth of American capitalistic industry after the Civil War created such a tremendous demand for foreign raw materials and services that every effort was made to stimulate the expansion and productivity of American agriculture as a leading means of meeting our foreign obligations. The marked increase of American urban population, with the development of our manufacturing industries and the rise of mass production, thus served to postpone for two or three decades the final reckoning with Canada, Australia, the Argentine, India, and Russia. American farmers were on the verge of evil days when the World War broke out and sent the prices of farm products to the dizziest heights known in the history of American farming.

With almost cruel suddenness, after 1918, American farming was plunged from the clouds into the abyss. British capitalism went into eclipse, could no longer spend so heavily for food products, and bought much of its agricultural imports elsewhere. American capitalism, in the meantime, had reached a state of monopolistic maturity. We became a creditor nation. No longer did we need to pay heavy interest charges on foreign investments or to import such large quantities of foreign services and goods. Therefore we did not have to export agricultural products to pay such debts. The further development of mechanization and efficiency in American farming greatly raised the agricultural productivity per unit of labor and capital expended, thus increasing the tendency to produce more farm products at a time when the demand was decreasing. The striking growth of the American population, which had created a constantly larger market for our farm products, slowed down decisively in the second and third decades of the present century. Our home market was thus reduced at the very time when the foreign demand was slackening. Further, new dietary conceptions, based upon our modern knowledge of vitamins and the like, brought about shifts in food uses, greatly to the detriment of the older and heavier standard farm products. There was a constantly greater use of fruits and vegetables. The hay market was undermined by the rise of the automobile and the decreased use of the horse. The foreign areas, which we mentioned above, entered into the race with full force after 1920. We find it as difficult to compete with them today as western-European farmers earlier found it to compete with us between 1850 and 1900. Further, many of our former customers in foodstuffs abroad have been so crushed by the economic effects of the World War that they have no surplus left to buy foreign foodstuffs from anywhere on the scale that prevailed before 1914. Moreover, they are making the most desperate efforts to create self-sufficiency as to foodstuffs through intensive cultivation, land reclamation, and the like.

In short, in the last ten years it has veritably seemed as though the heavens had fallen in on the American farmer. As late as 1920 he was still enjoying an almost fabulous and unprecedented prosperity. A decade later he was in a condition that made his state back in the days of Populism seem almost opulent by comparison. Such a tremendous and sudden shift in destiny not only quickly absorbed the farmer's reserves from the past but shook his morale to its very foundations.

The mortality list on the "morning after" is a long and sad one. In 1919 the total value of farm income in the United States was $15,000,000,000. By 1932 it had shrunk to $5,200,000,000. The share of farm income in the total national income dropped from 18.5 to 10 per cent in the boom decade from 1919 to 1929. In June, 1932, the prices of farm products were only 52 per cent of their prewar level, while the prices of the commodities the farmer had to buy were 10 per cent higher than they were in 1914. The farmer, therefore, could purchase with his farm products only 47 per cent of what he could have bought in 1914. On top of all this came a tremendous break in the value of farm property. Down to 1920 farm real estate had held up at a high price in spite of temporary setbacks to farming prosperity. Therefore a farmer who could no longer make what he believed to be an adequate living could at least sell out to some more optimistic soul and live for a time on the proceeds. Even this escape was now closed. The value of farm property in the United States dropped from $78,000,000,000 in 1919 to $44,000,000,000 in 1932, a fall of nearly 50 per cent. At the same time, the farm-mortgage indebtedness increased from $3,300,000,000 in 1910 to $7,900,000,000 in 1920 and to $9,500,000,000 in 1931. In 1931 the interest on mortgage debts absorbed no less than 8 per cent of the gross farm income of the United States, compared to 3 per cent in the days before the war. Paralleling this rise of mortgage indebtedness and interest charges went a comparable rise in taxes. In this same year, 1931, farm taxes equaled 11 per cent of the gross farm receipts, compared to 4 per cent in the period before the war. So staggering were these fixed charges on the farmer that in the five years prior to March 1, 1932, 9.5 per cent of the farms of the country passed out of the hands of their original owners through mortgage foreclosures and the like, and 3.5 per cent of American farms were sold because of failure to pay taxes. The per capita income of the American farming population, even in the boom year of 1929, was only $273 as compared with $908 for the non-farming groups.

President Roosevelt was quick to recognize that the farmers' plight was desperate and that speedy action must be taken to restore agricultural purchasing power. A series of acts were passed by Congress in the spring of 1933 designed to ease the mortgage burden, to control crop production, to give a bounty to farmers who would coöperate with the government in reducing crop acreage, and otherwise to rehabilitate this once prosperous but now sorely oppressed industry. The most serious error in these policies was the adoption of the conceptions of the "scarcity economy" and the resulting effort to reduce agricultural production at a time when millions of Americans were underfed through lack of income to provide even a minimum health diet. Even in 1929, out of twelve major food production categories, we had a shortage in no less than eight.[1]

[1] See below, pp. 417, footnote 2.

SUGGESTED READING

Hammerton, *Universal History of the World,* Chap. 169
Kaempffert, *Popular History of American Invention,* Vol. I, Pt. I, Chaps. i-ii; Vol. II, Pt. IV, Chaps. ii, v, vii
Faulkner, *American Economic History,* Chaps. xiii, xx-xxi
Kirkland, *History of American Economic Life,* Chaps. viii, x-xi

Isaac Lippincott, *The Economic Development of the United States*, 2d ed., Appleton, 1927, Chaps. ix, xi, xix-xxiii
L. M. Hacker, *Short History of the New Deal*, Crofts, 1934
―— and B. B. Kendrick, *The United States since 1865*, new ed., Crofts, 1934
H. J. Carman, *Social and Economic History of the United States*, Heath, 1931-36, 3 vols.
E. Q. Hawk, *Economic History of the South*, Prentice-Hall, 1934
D. R. Dewey, *Financial History of the United States*, Longmans, 1922
Taussig, *Tariff History of the United States*
A. M. Simons, *Social Forces in American History*, Macmillan, 1911
Oneal, *The Workers in American History*
M. W. Jernegan, *The Working and Dependent Classes in Colonial America, 1607-1783*, University of Chicago Press, 1931
H. A. Wallace, *New Frontiers*, Reynal and Hitchcock, 1934
E. G. Nourse and others, *America's Capacity to Produce*, Brookings Institution, 1934
Maurice Leven, H. G. Moulton and C. A. Warburton, *America's Capacity to Consume*, Brookings Institution, 1934
Bogart and Thompson, *Readings in the Economic History of the United States*, Chaps. viii-ix, xxi
L. B. Schmidt and E. D. Ross, eds., *Readings in the Economic History of American Agriculture*, Macmillan, 1925
W. Z. Ripley, *Railway Problems*, Ginn, 1921
―— ed., *Trusts, Pools and Corporations*, Ginn, 1916
J. R. Commons, ed., *Trade Unionism and Labor Problems*, Ginn, 1921
J. D. Magee, ed., *Collapse and Recovery*, Harper, 1934

FURTHER REFERENCES

THE INDUSTRIAL REVOLUTION COMES TO THE UNITED STATES. The standard works on American economic history are E. L. Bogart, *Economic History of the American People* (Longmans, 1930); T. W. Van Metre, *Economic History of the United States* (Holt, 1921); Lippincott, *op. cit.;* Faulkner, *op. cit.;* W. W. Jennings, *History of Economic Progress in the United States* (Crowell, 1926); Kirkland, *op. cit.;* E. F. Humphrey, *Economic History of the United States* (Century, 1929); F. A. Shannon, *Economic History of the People of the United States* (Macmillan, 1934). The fullest treatment in a single work is to be found in Carman, *op. cit.*

On early American manufactures, see Vol. I of V. S. Clark, *History of Manufactures in the United States* (McGraw-Hill, 1929, 3 vols.); R. M. Tryon, *Household Manufactures in the United States, 1640-1860* (University of Chicago Press, 1917).

On the tariff before 1860, see Taussig, *op. cit.;* C. W. Harris, *The Sectional Struggle* (Lippincott, 1902); Ashley, *Modern Tariff History*, Pt. II, Chaps. i-iii.

On American commerce, see E. R. Johnson and others, *History of Domestic and Foreign Commerce of the United States* (2d ed., Carnegie Institution, 1915, 2 vols. in 1); Keir, *The March of Commerce*.

On early transportation, see *Ibid.*, Chaps. iii-iv; A. B. Hulbert, *Paths of Inland Commerce* (Yale University Press, 1921); B. H. Meyer, *History of Transportation in the United States before 1860* (Carnegie Institution, 1917).

On early American agriculture, see P. W. Bidwell and J. J. Falconer, *History of Agriculture in the Northern United States, 1620-1860* (Carnegie Institution, 1925); U. B. Phillips, *Life and Labor in the Old South* (Little, Brown, 1929); Schmidt and Ross, *op. cit.*

On westward expansion, see R. H. Gabriel, *The Lure of the Frontier* (Yale Uni-

FURTHER REFERENCES

versity Press, 1929); F. L. Paxson, *History of the American Frontier, 1763-1893* (Houghton Mifflin, 1924); C. L. Goodwin, *The Trans-Mississippi West (1803-1853)* (Appleton, 1922); F. J. Turner, *The Frontier in American History* (Holt, 1921).

On the distribution of public land, see B. H. Hibbard, *History of the Public Land Policies* (Macmillan, 1924).

On the history of American agriculture, see R. H. Gabriel, *Toilers of Land and Sea* (Yale University Press, 1926); Schmidt and Ross, *op. cit.;* Bidwell and Falconer, *op. cit.;* Iles, *Leading American Inventors,* pp. 276 ff.

On the history of immigration into the United States, see Fairchild, *Immigration,* Chap. IV; Abbott, *Historical Aspects of the Immigration Problem;* G. M. Stephenson, *History of American Immigration, 1820-1924* (Ginn, 1926).

On American industry since 1860, see Clark, *op. cit.;* Keir, *The Epic of Industry,* Chaps. IV-XIV.

On the financial methods accompanying railroad development, see Matthew Josephson, *The Robber Barons* (Harcourt, Brace, 1934); C. F., Jr., and Henry Adams, *Chapters of Erie* (Osgood, 1871); R. I. Warshow, *Jay Gould* (Greenberg, 1928); A. D. H. Smith, *Commodore Vanderbilt* (McBride, 1927); John Moody, *Railroad-Builders* (Yale University Press, 1919); Bouck White, *The Book of Daniel Drew* (Doran, 1910). For at least an implied defense of their methods and of their bankers, see the various writings of Stuart Daggett, especially pp. 345 ff. of *Railroad Reorganization* (Harvard University Press, 1908), *Chapters on the History of the Southern Pacific* (Ronald Press, 1922), and *Principles of Inland Transportation* (Harper, 1928); and N. S. B. Gras, "Do We Need Private Bankers?" (New York Times) *Current History,* August, 1933.

On the commerce of the United States, see Chaps. III-IV of Clive Day, *History of Commerce of the United States* (Longmans, 1925); Johnson and others, *op. cit.*

On industrial crises in the United States, see Forrest Davis, *What Price Wall Street?* (Godwin, 1932); W. W. Price, *We Have Recovered Before!* (Harper, 1933); L. M. Graves, *The Great Depression and Beyond* (Brookmire Economic Service, 1932).

On the American labor movement, see J. R. Commons and others, *History of Labour in the United States* (Macmillan, 1921, 2 vols.); L. L. Lorwin and J. A. Flexner, *The American Federation of Labor* (Brookings Institution, 1933); C. E. Zaretz, *The Amalgamated Clothing Workers of America* (Ancon Publishing Co., 1934); P. F. Brissenden, *The I.W.W.: A Study of American Syndicalism* (Columbia University Press, 1920); W. Z. Foster, *Toward Soviet America* (Coward-McCann, 1932).

On the crisis in American agriculture since the World War, see Bernhard Ostrolenk, *The Surplus Farmer* (Harper, 1932); E. S. Mead and Bernhard Ostrolenk, *Voluntary Allotment* (University of Pennsylvania Press, 1933); L. M. Hacker, *The Farmer Is Doomed* (Day, 1933); W. G. Gee, *American Farm Policy* (Norton, 1934); E. S. Sparks, *History and Theory of Agricultural Credit in the United States* (Crowell, 1932); Vol. I, Chap. X of *Recent Social Trends in the United States* (McGraw-Hill, 1933, 2 vols.); Chap. VI of A. B. Adams, *Our Economic Revolution* (University of Oklahoma Press, 1933); Chap. V of C. A. Beard and G. H. E. Smith, *The Future Comes* (Macmillan, 1933); Wallace, *op. cit.*

On the inequitable distribution of wealth in the United States, see Leven and others, *op. cit.;* Whitney Coombs, *The Wages of Unskilled Labor in Manufacturing Industries in the United States, 1890-1924* (Columbia University Press, 1926).

CHAPTER XI

THE DEFENSE AND CRITICISM OF EARLY INDUSTRIAL CAPITALISM

I. ECONOMIC LIBERALISM AND THE IDEALIZATION OF CAPITALISTIC INDIVIDUALISM

Every important socio-economic system, if it has any duration, produces a compatible body of ideals designed to defend and justify it. Institutions and practices that are the accidental or fortuitous product of historical circumstances come to be invested with a sort of divine wisdom and perfection. This was true, among other forms of society, of the patriarchal empires and of the feudal system. It was not less true of the later capitalistic order that gradually gained dominance between the fifteenth century and the twentieth.[1]

But the social results of the new industrialism were not all happy. We have already described the inhumane factory and mine conditions that it created.[2] It was not long before there arose sharp criticisms of capitalistic methods and philosophy. In this chapter we shall be concerned chiefly with (1) the rise of the apology for capitalism in the form of Economic Liberalism; and (2) the attack upon this attitude from many angles of dissent.

In order that we may appreciate fully the nature and implications of the apologies for capitalism, it is desirable to have a clear conception of the character of capitalistic ideals as they had evolved by the close of the first Industrial Revolution. The ideals of competitive capitalism have been forcefully summarized by Stuart Chase in what he calls "the bible of free competition":

Buy in the cheapest and sell in the dearest market, that profit may be at a maximum. Charge all that the traffic will bear.

Tolerate no monopolies. Let supply and demand work unfettered. Prices for goods can thus never remain long too high. When Company A starts making an unreasonable profit, Company B will promptly come charging into the field, increase the supply of goods, and so force the price down to fairer levels.

Let every capitalist strive to outdo every other capitalist, in order that the weak may fall and the strong survive, and so keep the most vigorous and the most efficient at the top. Every man for himself, and the devil take the hindmost. Encourage individualism.

Let profit be the motive for every industrial action. Prayerfully followed, profit is the perfect guide.

Specialize and standardize the tasks of labor.

[1] See C. A. Beard, "Individualism and Capitalism," Encyclopaedia of the Social Sciences.
[2] See above, pp. 289 ff.

Tolerate no interference from labor, work it as hard as possible, and pay it not more than a survival wage.

Use all the resources of the Government and of its armed forces to find and hold foreign markets, but tolerate no government interference in internal matters.[1]

The first great body of doctrine that extolled the new capitalistic order is known as Economic Liberalism. It is also identified with the economic doctrine of laissez faire and the political theory of individualism.

This type of theory cannot be properly appraised unless the historical circumstances surrounding its origin and diffusion are taken into consideration. It began before the Industrial Revolution as an attack upon the archaic legislative restrictions that had grown up as a part of the mercantile commercial and colonial system. In so far as it helped to clear away these obstructions to economic freedom, it contributed to the coming of modern industrial society. After the Industrial Revolution had arrived, however, its later adherents utilized the laissez-faire concepts to defend the new capitalistic order and to prevent, so far as possible, the abolition, through remedial legislation, of the grave social evils it created.

The founders of Economic Liberalism were the group of French writers in the middle of the eighteenth century to whom we have earlier referred as the Physiocrats, so named from the work of one of their adherents, Dupont de Nemours, entitled *Physiocracy, or the Natural Constitution of That Form of Government Most Advantageous to the Human Race* (1767).[2] They derived their basic doctrine from the English Deists and the French *philosophes,* to the effect that social, political, and economic phenomena are governed by the same natural laws that Newton and his associates believed they had proved to rule the physical universe. They were convinced that the perfection of all human social institutions could best be realized by letting them freely conform to this natural order, a condition which they believed would most certainly be brought about under a régime of unlimited competition. If man refrained from legislation and any attempt to control economic processes by artificial means, then God and His natural order would have full sway. One reason for human unhappiness and prevailing misery, so they said, was the operation of a large number of archaic and restrictive laws which, being statutory and unnatural, were holding back the free dominion of natural law in the affairs of men.

Accordingly, the Physiocrats vigorously advocated the immediate and total abolition of all restrictive legislation and the introduction of an era of laissez-faire individualism. The only desirable functions of the state were the protection of life and property, the erection of public buildings and other public works, and the promotion of education, so that man might grasp more surely the principles of natural law. Extensive social legislation was regarded as dangerous, since it would surely impede the operation of those beneficent natural principles upon which these advocates placed their chief reliance. The Physiocrats contributed views of less significance through their interpretation of social progress in terms of the net product of agriculture and their scheme of a reform in public finance, which centered about the notion of a single tax on land.

[1] Stuart Chase, *Poor Old Competition,* League for Industrial Democracy, 1931, p. 13.
[2] See Henry Higgs, *The Physiocrats,* Macmillan, 1897.

The moving genius among the Physiocrats was François Quesnay (1694-1774), who was ably seconded by Gournay, Mirabeau, Dupont de Nemours, Mercier de la Rivière, Baudeau, and Le Trosne.

The general notions of the Physiocrats concerning individualism and the inactivity of the state received the support of the distinguished French economist and statesman Turgot (1727-81), and intrigued the first great systematic writer on political economy, the Scotch philosopher Adam Smith (1723-90).[1] The chief significance of Adam Smith for the history of social reform is that he embodied the laissez-faire thesis in a notable work, *An Inquiry into the Nature and Causes of the Wealth of Nations* (1776). This received so wide a circulation and attracted so extensive a following for Smith's doctrines that the eminent historian Buckle, nearly a century later, regarded this book as the most influential and beneficial one ever written. In spite of his general acceptance of the Physiocratic position as to the proper functions of the state, Smith abandoned to a considerable degree their excessive laudation of agriculture, and emphasized the prime value, to a state, of commerce and manufacturing industry. Especially did he revive the Platonic doctrine of the importance of the division of labor and specialization in increasing and improving productivity. His emphasis upon the part played by labor in production paved the way for the later views of Ricardo and the Socialists with respect to the "labor theory of value." His advocacy of free trade on the ground of the advantages of an international division of labor was one of the most forceful arguments ever advanced for commercial freedom.

Smith died before the Industrial Revolution had fully developed even in England, and there is good evidence for holding that he did not even foresee the complete course of this transformation, much less stand out as a conscious apologist of the new capitalist class. But his doctrines were of a sort that fitted in admirably with the policy of noninterference. This the capitalist manufacturers desired to have prevail, in order that they, if not their employees, might enjoy the alleged "blessings of the perfect freedom of contract." Smith's notions were therefore expanded and exploited by the middle class and sympathetic economists to provide an authoritative theoretical opposition to social legislation designed to advance the interests of the industrial proletariat.[2]

The most extensive development of the concepts of Adam Smith naturally took place in England, where he had written and where that commercialism which was most congenial to his views was the furthest advanced, but he was honored by reverent disciples in every important European state and in the United States. His most distinguished English disciples were Thomas Robert Malthus (1766-1834); David Ricardo (1772-1823); James Mill (1773-1836); John Ramsay McCulloch (1789-1864), and Nassau William Senior (1790-1864). The one thing that, in particular, distinguished the doctrines of Smith from those of his disciples was the greater social pessimism of the latter,[3] a difference

---

[1] See F. W. Hirst, *Adam Smith*, Macmillan, 1904; and Eli Ginzberg, *The House of Adam Smith*, Columbia University Press, 1934.

[2] For a good discussion of this bourgeois perversion of Smith's doctrines, see Ginzberg, *op. cit.*

[3] On the differences between Smith and Ricardo, see O. F. Boucke, *The Development of Economics, 1750-1900*, Macmillan, 1921, pp. 113 ff.

that may be explained in part by the sweeping changes in the economic and social environment in the interval that had elapsed since Smith's death.

While the chief importance of these writers consists in their elaboration of the supposed virtues of the competitive order, each contributed some special interpretation of some originality and significance. Malthus held that remedial legislation is not only harmful, as interfering with the natural order of things, but is also useless so far as any hope of improving the poorer classes is concerned.[1] He maintained that even though the distribution of wealth should be equalized, no permanent good could result. Since population tends to increase more rapidly than the means of subsistence, the normal disparity between population and the available means of support would ultimately be restored and with this would come a return of poverty and misery. The proletariat creates its own misery through an excessive birth rate, and the only hope of enduring relief lies in the restriction of the birth rate through the postponement of marriage.

Ricardo paid particular attention to the subject of the distribution of wealth. Mainly from the Physiocratic notion that the wages of agricultural laborers tend towards the minimum of subsistence and from Malthus's doctrine of population, he derived his famous "subsistence theory of wages." According to this dogma, wages tend towards a level that allows the laboring class to exist and perpetuate itself without either increase or decrease. If wages are increased the population grows accordingly. Hence the folly of legislation designed to enlarge the income of the proletariat, for the resulting increase of population would absorb the monetary gain and prevent any diminution of poverty and misery. Moreover, higher wages would lower profits, curtail industrial initiative, increase unemployment, and very soon increase poverty and misery. Further, Ricardo attacked the landlords by maintaining that rent tends to absorb an ever greater share of the social income, and that the interests of the landlords are opposed to those of all other economic classes. Finally, he laid the basis for the Marxian theory of value by holding that, within certain definite limitations, value is determined by the amount of labor involved in the production of goods—a doctrine vigorously attacked by many later economists.

James Mill brought into Economic Liberalism the Utilitarian philosophy of Bentham regarding the maximum good for the largest number.[2] This ideal Mill and his associates believed to be attainable only through the operation of the principles of Economic Liberalism. Mill's clearly written treatise did much to popularize the theories of Ricardo, who was a prolix and involved writer. Of all this group of writers, Mill had the most naïve and limitless confidence in the benevolence of the middle-class manufacturers and merchants. McCulloch was the chief systematizer of the principles of Economic Liberalism, and, somewhat illogically, was the most sympathetic member of the group towards the laboring classes, being a supporter of Place and Hume in their attempt to legalize trade-unionism. He is particularly known for his elaboration of the "wages-fund" doctrine, which held that only a specific sum could be diverted into wages without wrecking the whole industrial process. This is the

[1] For more detail on Malthus's theory of population, see below, pp. 416 ff.
[2] See above, pp. 78, 319, and below, p. 382.

reverse of a notion popular today to the effect that unless enough money is put into wages to produce mass purchasing power the whole capitalistic system will inevitably fold up.

Senior represented the final and most extreme stage of Economic Liberalism through his attempt to perfect economics as a purely abstract and objective science—a science of wealth and not of welfare—and by his ardent opposition to even the mildest form of legislation beneficial to the laboring classes. He warned against legislation to shorten the hours of labor, contending that profits are made only in the last hours of the day. Hence, to shorten the working-hours would end profits, discourage the industrialists, and lead to the closing of the factories and mines. Senior was dubbed by his critics "Last Hour" Senior.

In the writings of John Stuart Mill (1806-73) we detect a break with the most cherished traditions of Economic Liberalism. Mill held that only the processes of production were subject to the control of natural law and hence not to be disturbed by human legislation. This view, justifying social control of the distributive process, opened the way for extensive legislation regulating wages, interest, rent, and profits.

While most of these writers took little active part in politics, their ideal of "perfect competition for the employers and subjection for the workers" was eagerly adopted by Richard Cobden, John Bright, and other members of the Manchester School,[1] and by the new Liberal party. Such notions were very useful in the campaign to reduce the power and privileges of the landed aristocracy and to enforce and perpetuate the servile and helpless status of the laborers. Further, their notions were widely popularized, and their general views were as much the order of polite conversation in British parlors as Rousseau's notions of the state of nature had been in the French salons of half a century before.[2] The bourgeois entrepreneur had replaced the noble savage of the previous century as the recipient of idealized admiration.

In France, the doctrines of this later version of Economic Liberalism were espoused by a number of economists, the most notable of whom were Jean Baptiste Say (1767-1832) and Frédéric Bastiat (1801-50). Say's position was very similar to that of Senior. He maintained that political economy is purely a descriptive science and not in any way a practical art. The economist should simply study and formulate economic laws and should never usurp the functions of the statesman. Reversing the position of the Physiocrats, he laid special stress upon the social contributions of manufacturing. Say was the most enthusiastic of all the eulogists of the new era of mechanical industry. He was the French bourgeois economist of the period in much the same way as Guizot was the statesman of this group.[3] Bastiat revived the optimism of Adam Smith and, as an ardent admirer of Cobden, devoted his attention chiefly to an advocacy of free trade. The function of the state, he held, was solely to maintain "order, security and justice." So enthusiastic were Say and Bastiat over the supposed beneficial activities of the new manufacturing and commercial classes that some less scientific followers denied that poverty or misery even existed.

In Germany, Economic Liberalism was defended by Johann Heinrich von Thünen (1783-1850) and Karl Heinrich Rau (1792-1870), while in America

[1] See above, pp. 319 ff., below, pp. 490 ff. [2] See above, pp. 221, 231. [3] See above, pp. 122-23.

Henry C. Carey (1793-1879) first introduced the classical political economy, though he differed from Smith's English disciples by reviving the optimism of Smith and attacking the pessimism of Malthus. Moreover, he advocated national protectionism in contrast to the free-trade doctrines of most others of the liberal school.

Though it will be evident that Economic Liberalism was as distinctly a capitalistic movement as Socialism has been a proletarian agitation—that, as Cliffe Leslie expressed it, "they created a science for wealth rather than a science of wealth"—nevertheless, their efforts accomplished much that was good. Before state activity to solve the problems created by the Industrial Revolution could begin in an effective manner, it was necessary that the antique rubbish of mercantilism should be cleared away. This was the great contribution of the Economic Liberals and their political adherents, even though they offset much of the value of their destructive efforts by their opposition to progressive legislation. It should also be pointed out in passing that the Economic Liberals were aided (1) by the contemporary philosophy of Romanticism, with its denial of the possibility of artificially accelerating the rate of political progress; and (2) by the political individualism that had been set forth by Wilhelm von Humboldt, was later taken up by John Stuart Mill in his earlier days, and was eulogized by Herbert Spencer.

In England, the more notable practical effects of Economic Liberalism were: (1) The growth of free trade, associated with the work of Huskisson, Cobden, Bright, Peel, and Gladstone; (2) the abolition of such archaic political restrictions as the Test and Corporation acts, which had restricted the political rights of Dissenters; (3) the increase of the political powers of the middle class in the central and local government by the Reform Bills of 1832 and 1835; (4) the abolition of slavery in the colonies through the efforts of Wilberforce and Buxton; (5) the repeal of the savage criminal code as a result of the work of Romilly, Mackintosh, Buxton, and Peel; (6) the development of a policy of preventive treatment in the handling of the problem of poor relief, which was evident in the notable Poor Law of 1834; and (7) the first concessions to a more liberal policy of imperial government through the leadership of Lord Durham, Edward Gibbon Wakefield, and others.[1]

In France, serfdom and the guild monopolies were abolished before the close of the eighteenth century; Guizot directed the Orleanist régime solely in the interests of the capitalists; and Bastiat's doctrines were able to win Napoleon III for free trade.

In Prussia, Stein and Hardenberg secured legislation looking towards the complete abolition of serfdom and of guild monopolies, and the development of municipal self-government. Following 1819 a more liberal economic and commercial policy was embodied in the famous Zollverein, the work of Maassen, Bülow, Eichhorn, and Von Motz. Most of the other German states followed Prussia in this liberalizing policy, and some, like Baden, quite outdistanced it in this respect.

It will be apparent, however, that none of this legislation materially bene-

---

[1] In these reforms the Economic Liberals were, of course, aided by the Philosophical Radicals and the Utilitarians.

fited the new proletariat. Indeed, some of the legislation of this period was specifically designed to paralyze the efforts of the laborers for self-improvement, and the agitators for the abolition of Negro slavery in the colonies passed by unnoticed the industrial slavery that existed at home among their own white countrymen.

During the closing period of the popularity of Economic Liberalism this individualistic doctrine gained support from another source, namely, the evolutionary hypothesis as interpreted by Herbert Spencer (1820-1903).[1] The Deists and the Physiocrats had derived their notions from the hypothesis that the physical universe is presided over by a lawgiving and law-abiding Providence. Spencer invoked the new agnostic naturalism in support of individualism. He held that social evolution, like biological evolution, is a natural and spontaneous process with which man should not interfere. Human well-being can best be insured by letting evolution take its course. If man tries to intervene and hasten the process, disaster is likely to result. Cosmic evolution was thus assigned the place that had been given to God in the Deistic scheme adopted by the early Economic Liberals. To the latter, human legislation was an affront to God. To Spencerians, it was a defiance of the all-pervading evolutionary process. As late as 1905 the Supreme Court of the United States based an important decision on Herbert Spencer's *Social Statics,* and in 1912 the conservatives brought out a new edition of the book in the effort to defeat Theodore Roosevelt and his Progressive party.

II. ENGLISH PHILOSOPHICAL RADICALISM AND UTILITARIANISM

Utilitarianism, a term used by Jeremy Bentham and given wide currency by John Stuart Mill, is the designation usually applied to the school of writers headed by Bentham (1748-1832) and including, among others, James Mill, George Grote, John Austin, Alexander Bain, and John Stuart Mill. They represented primarily the spirit and tenets of Economic Liberalism as applied in political theory. Their work constituted about the only significant contribution of England to this field between the time of Burke and that of Spencer. Essentially, they were a further development of that Philosophical Radicalism in England which grew out of English sympathy with the French Revolution, and was represented by William Godwin, Thomas Paine, William Cobbett, Francis Place, and a group of literary figures, including Shelley, Byron, and Wordsworth.[2] This group of early Philosophical Radicals stood in direct opposition to the satisfaction that Blackstone and Burke expressed over the alleged perfection of British institutions. They maintained the necessity of sweeping changes to eliminate ancient superstitions, archaic laws, outgrown institutions, and brutal practices.

In his earlier years Bentham might have been logically classed with this earlier group, for his first notable work—*A Fragment on Government* (1776)—

---

[1] See Ernest Barker, *Political Thought in England from Spencer to the Present Day,* Holt, 1915. Chap. IV.

[2] See W. P. Hall, *British Radicalism, 1791-1797,* Columbia University Press, 1912; and Brailsford, *Shelley, Godwin and Their Circle.*

was a violent attack upon the complacency of Blackstone. But he gradually developed a broad and constructive philosophy of reform and thus remolded radicalism into Utilitarianism. His doctrines were based upon the hedonistic psychology, which aimed to increase human happiness,[1] and upon the ethical slogan of "the greatest happiness for the greatest number"—a principle earlier enunciated but not greatly developed by Hutcheson, Beccaria, and Priestley. Institutions were to be judged according to their contributions to the attainment of this "greatest happiness." Bentham's practical program of reform, however, indicated that, like the Economic Liberals, he regarded unrestricted competition and enlightened self-interest as the chief avenues through which his Utilitarian program could be realized. He was especially emphatic about the sanctity of contracts. Bentham's chief concern, in short, was with the abolition of archaic and restrictive legislation, but he did urge some positive reforms, such as education of the masses, the extension of savings institutions, public-health legislation, a new poor law, and prison reform. Bentham and his immediate followers might seem to have regarded the "greatest good for the greatest number" as best attainable through conferring "the greatest amount of goods upon the business classes." Yet his principles, if honestly and logically interpreted, were excellently suited to justify a large amount of positive remedial legislation in behalf of the proletariat.

In this way, indeed, the Utilitarian premises later became an important force supporting constructive social legislation. In fact, this evolution of Utilitarianism into social reform is evident even within the circle of its own adherents. John Stuart Mill eventually emerged from an exponent of marked individualism into a vigorous supporter of social legislation in the interest of the laboring classes and a not unappreciative student of distinctly Socialistic proposals.

Probably the most important achievements of this group in the way of directly aiding the lower classes were the work of Francis Place and Joseph Hume in securing the temporary legalization of trade-unionism, the Poor Law of 1834, and some indirect benefits from liberal political reforms and health legislation. They also made important contributions towards securing the abolition of outworn practices and obstructive legislation, an achievement that we described above in dealing with the practical results of Economic Liberalism.

III. THE RISE OF OPPOSITION TO ECONOMIC LIBERALISM

1. CRITICISM BY ECONOMISTS

There were a number of theoretical weaknesses in Economic Liberalism, which quickly attracted the opposition of political economists. While Smith had actually assumed to be more concerned with the wealth of a "nation" than that of a social class, it is nevertheless true that his followers seemed more agitated over the wealth of the new business class than over the problem of increasing the prosperity of the entire nation. This brought down upon Eco-

[1] Anticipated by Machiavelli, Hobbes, Hume, and Helvétius.

nomic Liberalism the criticism of economists who presented a national or social theory of wealth.

These latter writers maintained that the increase of the wealth of particular individuals or classes is no safe criterion in estimating the value to the state or society of an economic, social, or political policy. This was the point of view especially of the Englishman Lord Lauderdale (1759-1839) and the Scotch-Canadian John Rae (1786-1873). Lauderdale, in his *Inquiry into the Nature and Origin of Public Wealth* (1804), differentiated clearly between public wealth and private riches, and held that the latter were usually gained at the expense of the former. He showed how public wealth depends upon abundance and private riches upon scarcity—a vital fact not comprehended as yet by many statesmen of our own era. This led him to distinguish public from private interest and to justify legislation designed to protect the former. By appealing to authorities from Aristotle to his own day, as well as by logical analysis, Rae, in his *New Principles of Political Economy* (1834), proved to his own satisfaction that remedial state activity was more in harmony with the principles of nature and society than laissez faire and pure competition. He thus undermined the very foundations of Economic Liberalism.

The position of the Economic Liberals generally, and of Senior and Say in particular, that the economist must restrict his science to purely abstract and descriptive discipline and must rigidly refrain from advocating any positive policy of statesmanship or social reform, was vigorously attacked by Jean Charles Léonard (Simonde) de Sismondi (1773-1842), an itinerant but versatile Swiss scholar.[1] He was the most distinguished and effective exponent in his age of the notion that economics must assume responsibility for promoting general prosperity and social reform, a point of view since urged with vigor by such economists as Schmoller, Gide, Webb, Hobson, Hamilton, Douglas, and others. He saw clearly that economics should be intimately concerned with the problems of practical statesmanship and applied sociology, and more than any other writer of his time he foreshadowed modern social or "welfare" economics. Moreover, his actual program of reform embraced most of what is now included in trade-unionism, factory legislation, and social insurance. In taking this attitude he stood almost alone in his age, but his doctrines were later accorded respect, as economics swung back more to the social point of view.

The Economic Liberals were, as we have seen, internationalists and exponents of free trade. This position was attacked by the early nationalistic economists, Adam Heinrich Müller (1779-1829), Friedrich List (1789-1846), and Henry C. Carey. They defended the policy of a protective tariff to give national self-sufficiency and prosperity. The nation, rather than individuals, classes, or human society as a whole, received their special solicitude. They were not, however, inflexibly dogmatic in this position. List, in particular, held that after the Industrial Revolution had become thoroughly established in a country, free trade might be beneficial. To aid "infant industries" in the first stages of industrial development a protective tariff was, however, in his opinion indispensable. List was far more liberal and flexible in his ideas than contemporary protectionists.

[1] Mao-Lan Tuan, *Simonde de Sismondi as an Economist,* Columbia University Press, 1927.

The Economic Liberals erred in the direction of too great an abstraction and absolutism in economic doctrines. They generalized too much from contemporary conditions and were confident of the universal and eternal applicability of their economic laws and theories. They were also careless of facts that ran counter to their theories. Indeed, when Ricardo was once reproached because his doctrines did not tally with certain facts, he retorted that it was so much the worse for the facts. These defects were corrected in theory at least by the early representatives of the so-called Historical school of economics,[1] chiefly Richard Jones (1790-1885) in England and Bruno Hildebrand (1812-78), Wilhelm Roscher (1817-94) and Karl Knies (1821-98) in Germany. The predominance of the Germans in this group has led to the practical identification of the Historical school with German economists. These writers ridiculed the element of absolutism in the classical economic doctrines. They maintained that no type of economic theory could be true except for the age from which the facts or premises were drawn. Therefore, economic theories must change with historical alterations in the economic constitution of societies. There can be neither invariable economic laws nor valid economic theories that ignore the dynamic element of economic change. Their emphasis on the necessary relation between fact and theory also suggested careful statistical studies of actual social and economic conditions. The latter frequently and logically led to advocacy of remedial legislation.

2. POLITICAL OPPOSITION AND FACTORY LEGISLATION

It has been shown that Economic Liberalism was primarily an economic philosophy and a political program designed in the interest of the capitalists, who, in English politics, belonged for the most part to the Whig or Liberal party. It was but natural, therefore, that it would be assailed by the one powerful party whose economic and political interests were diametrically opposed to those of the business elements, that is, by the landed proprietors who made up the bulk of the Tory or Conservative party.

The Tories had a number of reasons for disliking the capitalists. In the first place, there was the social aversion of the aristocrats for what they regarded as the rich parvenu eager to break into their ranks. Then they feared that the new industrialism might destroy forever the "Merrie England" in which the landlords were supreme. Again, they entertained a jealousy of the growing political strength of the middle class, especially after the latter had forced through the Reform Bill of 1832 giving more power to the industrial cities. Finally, the economic interests of the two classes were fundamentally opposed; the Tories desired a continuation of the Corn Laws to keep the price of grain high, while the business class wished for their abolition to secure cheap wheat and therefore, according to the current economic reasoning, cheap labor.

The Tories were extremely fortunate in finding a point of attack upon the capitalists that enabled them to cloak their political and economic rivalry under the mantle of humanitarian sentiments and to entertain a reasonable hope of increasing their political following among the proletariat. The strategic line of

---

[1] *Cf.* J. K. Ingram, *History of Political Economy,* Macmillan, 1894, Chap. vi; L. H. Haney, *History of Economic Thought,* Macmillan, 1911, Chaps. xxiv-xxv; and Boucke, *op. cit.,* Chap. vi.

attack decided upon by the Tories was factory legislation. This would reduce the prosperity of the manufacturers by compelling them to grant higher wages, shorter hours, and the introduction of better physical conditions and appliances in their factories. Possibly, too much has been made of this point of Tory self-interest by recent writers who have followed Arnold Toynbee in emphasizing the political and economic selfishness that motivated the landlord factory-reformers. Some of the leaders in this movement, especially Lord Shaftesbury, were governed by real humanitarian impulses,[1] but it can at least be said that they were especially fortunate in finding a type of humanitarianism that harmonized particularly well with their economic and political interests. They showed little solicitude for the abuses that they themselves perpetuated among the rural workers.

The leaders in the earlier stages of this "Tory social reform" were Anthony Ashley Cooper, seventh Earl of Shaftesbury (1801-85), Michael Thomas Sadler (1780-1835), Richard Oastler (1789-1861), and John Fielden (1784-1849), a public-spirited manufacturer. They secured the appointment of the parliamentary investigating commissions whose reports have furnished the present generation with most of their sources of information concerning the conditions among the laboring classes in England during the first half of the nineteenth century, and they obtained much remedial legislation designed to alleviate or eliminate these evils of early industrialism.

It is impossible in the space available to describe in detail the contents of this legislation, but its general character can be indicated. The factory acts of 1802, 1819, 1831, 1833, 1844, 1847, 1850, and several minor laws of the sixties secured the ten-hour day for the laboring classes in practically all factories. They also provided real factory inspection, safety appliances, better sanitary conditions, and a general discouragement of child labor. Women and children were excluded from mines, and better hours and safety devices were provided for in mines by acts of 1842, 1855, and 1872. The distressing evils in the employment of juvenile chimney sweeps were eliminated by laws of 1834 and 1840. Particularly the result of the efforts of Shaftesbury were the important Factory Act of 1833 and the famous Ten-Hour Bill of 1847.

Political jealousy and economic rivalry between the upper classes and the middle classes were thus able to achieve for the betterment of the proletariat much more than the latter and their sympathizers were able to obtain for themselves. While Shaftesbury may have been motivated mainly by genuine humanitarian impulses in his campaign for social reform, it is doubtful if the same can be said for the continuator of his policy, Benjamin Disraeli (1804-81). That he thoroughly understood the oppression of the peasantry and the industrial proletariat no reader of his *Sybil* can doubt. Yet little evidence exists that he was touched by any real personal sympathy for the oppressed, and much leads one to the conclusion that his concessions to the lower classes were founded upon purely partisan motives and personal ambitions. In part, he continued Shaftesbury's social legislation, but his appeal for the support of the proletariat was primarily political. By the Reform Act of 1867 he extended the suffrage to the more prosperous portion of the urban laboring class.

[1] See J. L. LeB. and Barbara Hammond, *Lord Shaftesbury,* Harcourt, Brace, 1924.

This type of social reform again appeared in England during the Conservative-Unionist régime of the nineties, when it was particularly associated with the name of Joseph Chamberlain.[1] This benevolent paternalism, born of political rivalry, was confined in its earlier stages chiefly to England, for there alone had the new business class attained sufficient proportions to attract the organized opposition of the landed interests. It appeared at a later time in other European states, most notably in the Bismarckian social-insurance and labor legislation.[2]

3. EARLY CHRISTIAN SOCIALISM

The new capitalism and industrialism and the doctrines of its theoretical apologists among the Economic Liberals were frequently identified with the philosophy of materialism. This naturally led to opposition from the churchmen and the faithful of all types. While programs of social reform hostile to Economic Liberalism were put forward by Catholics, High Churchmen, Broad Churchmen, and Dissenters, one unifying purpose runs through all of their work, namely, the desire to socialize Christianity and thereby to capture social reform for the Church. They thus hoped to secure for religious institutions the gratitude and support of the numerous members of the proletariat.

The origins of modern Christian Socialism may be traced to the work entitled *The New Christianity* (1825) by the French sociologist Henri de Saint-Simon.[3] In this work the contrast between the social doctrines of Christ and the traditionalism and ritualism of the historical Church was clearly drawn, and a striking appeal was made for the socialization of religion.

In the field of Social Catholicism there were a number of interesting developments, particularly in France under the Bourbon restoration and the Orleanist monarchy. The movement began, as we have seen, as a revival of emotionalism, obscurantism, and political reaction in the doctrines of Châteaubriand, De Bonald, and De Maistre (1753-1821).[4] But the growth of democracy affected Church as well as State in France, and several exponents of the religious revival clearly understood that if they were to make any headway they would need to liberalize the Catholic standpoint. This was partially achieved by Antoine Frédéric Ozanam (1813-53), who founded the Society of St. Vincent de Paul and linked up Neo-Catholicism with practical philanthropy; by Alphonse de Lamartine (1790-1869), who attempted to connect the Catholic movement with the growth of republican sentiment in France; by Robert de Lamennais (1782-1854), who tried unsuccessfully to harmonize Catholicism with the principles of the French Revolution and political democracy; and by Philippe Joseph Buchez (1796-1865), who shared the historical viewpoint of the German school of economists, tried to prove the spirit of Christianity to be revolutionary, anticipated the "Guild Socialism"[5] of Bishop von Ketteler and Franz Hitze, and advocated a scheme of coöperative production and distribution.

The Protestant members of this first important group of Christian social re-

---

[1] See E. E. Gulley, *Joseph Chamberlain and English Social Politics*, Columbia University Press, 1926.
[2] See below, pp. 940 ff.
[3] See above, pp. 229 ff.
[4] See above, pp. 205 ff.
[5] See below, pp. 955 ff.

formers are those who have usually been specifically designated as Christian Socialists, but this title could with equal accuracy be extended to the Catholic reformers just named.

The leaders in the Protestant aspects of this movement were chiefly Anglican clergymen of the Broad Church party, though there was considerable support accorded by the Unitarians and the Methodists. The most prominent members of the Christian Socialist group in England were John Frederick Denison Maurice (1805-72), Charles Kingsley (1819-75), and Thomas Hughes (1822-96). Others of influence who adhered to their general point of view were John M. F. Ludlow (1821-1911) and John Lalor (1814-56).

Maurice, usually regarded as the founder of the movement in England, was especially interested in the education of the laboring class. Kingsley analyzed the social problems of his day in powerful sermons and such telling books as *Alton Locke, Yeast,* and *The Water-Babies*. Like Buchez, he urged the formation of workingmen's organizations and the institution of coöperative associations.

Probably the most enduring contribution of English Christian Socialism to social reform was the impulse that it gave to the organization of coöperative and profit-sharing societies, of which one, based on the work of Owen—the famous Rochdale Pioneers—has endured to the present day. The coöperative movement spread rapidly on the Continent and has developed particularly in Denmark and Belgium.[1] The English Christian Socialists actually imported their ideas on workers' associations and coöperation mainly from Buchez's work in France, since Owen's work in England was at the time associated with anti-Christian notions. The other important result of Christian Socialism in this first stage was the aid it gave to the cause of the education of the proletariat and to arousing the interest of the Anglican Church in social reform.

The impulse to social reform within the Anglican Church originated by the Christian Socialists attracted even members of the High Church party, and the leaders of that emotional reaction, the Oxford Movement, such as Hurrell Froude, Newman, Keble, and Pusey, lent their support to the development of trade-unionism and the betterment of housing-conditions among the poor.[2] Finally, even the dissenting sects, particularly the Quakers and the newer evangelical organizations, took a very significant part in agitating for remedial legislation for the poorer classes.[3] This social impulse in Christianity spread even to the United States, where much interest was shown by W. E. Channing and the New England Unitarians and Transcendentalists.[4]

4. THE ESTHETIC REVOLT AGAINST MATERIALISM AND MISERY

The Industrial Revolution has produced nearly all the material comforts of modern life and has created many new forms of art and beauty as well. Never-

---
[1] See below, pp. 947-48.
[2] See W. G. Peck, *The Social Implications of the Oxford Movement*, Scribner, 1933.
[3] *Cf.* E. M. North, *Early Methodist Philanthropy;* W. J. Warner, *The Wesleyan Movement in the Industrial Revolution,* Longmans, 1930; Methodist Book Concern, 1915; and Faulkner, *Chartism and the Churches.*
[4] See O. B. Frothingham, *Transcendentalism in New England,* Beacon Press, 1876; and Lindsay Swift, *Brook Farm,* Macmillan, 1900.

theless, at least in its first stages, the new industrialism, with its dismal factories, clouds of smoke, and filthy tenements, was extremely ugly and repulsive to the esthetic temperament and humanitarian impulses alike. Therefore, the new order of things and its supporters among the Economic Liberals were vigorously attacked by those who were the representatives of the literary and artistic standards of the age.[1]

This so-called esthetic revolt against the new industrial order was of a rather varied sort, ranging all the way from the purely cultural protest of such men as Matthew Arnold to the conversion of leading literary figures such as George Sand and William Morris to overt Socialistic programs. While most of the leading figures in art and literature during the second third of the nineteenth century were repulsed by the new industrial developments, a few can be singled out as the leaders in the esthetic protest. Among these were Robert Southey (1774-1843), Thomas Carlyle (1795-1881), Samuel Coleridge (1772-1834), Charles Dickens (1812-70), Charles Reade (1814-84), John Ruskin (1819-1900), Matthew Arnold (1822-88), William Morris (1834-96), Ralph Waldo Emerson (1803-82), George Sand (1804-76) and Leo Tolstoy (1828-1910). Of this group the most important were Dickens, Carlyle, Ruskin, George Sand, Tolstoy, and Arnold.

Dickens was probably the ablest and most effective critic among the literary figures who protested against the evils of the Industrial Revolution, as well as those which had come down from an earlier era—the criminal law and prisons, for example. He saw about him the miserable factory towns, the unspeakable conditions in the mines, the long hours of labor, insufficient wages, and the ruthless oppression of women and children. His whole personality was revolted by these products of laissez faire and the new capitalism. His reaction is mirrored in a classic passage from *Martin Chuzzlewit:*

> Bethink yourselves . . . that there are scores of thousands breathing now, and breathing thick with painful toil, who . . . have never lived at all, nor had a chance of life. Go ye . . . Teachers of content and honest pride, into the mine, the mill, the forge, the squalid depths of deepest ignorance, and uttermost abyss of man's neglect, and say can any hopeful plant spring up in air so foul that it extinguishes the soul's bright torch as fast as it is kindled! [2]

Dickens not only attacked the industrialists, but also the usurers who fattened upon the unfortunates in the England of his day. He also wrote effectively in behalf of the campaign for better housing and sanitation in the new industrial cities.[3]

Carlyle is significant chiefly as a devastating critic of the materialism and the economic abstractions of the classical school. He had little or no constructive program of reform beyond a willingness to wait for some unique genius to appear with a ready-made solution. Ruskin was as bitter as Carlyle in his criticism of the new industrial society and its ideals, but he offered a program for the solution of existing problems through his advocacy of the restoration

---

[1] On this movement in literature, see H. D. Lockwood, *Tools and the Man*, Columbia University Press, 1927.

[2] Chap. XIII.

[3] On Dickens as a social critic, see W. W. Crotch, *Charles Dickens, Social Reformer*, London, 1913.

of the dignity of labor, the institution of a régime of industrial coöperation, state education, government workshops, and state insurance for the working classes. A part of his program bordered on the Guild Socialism of a slightly later period, but he put education above all other types of relief for the situation. A trace of the temptation to a utopian flight from reality appeared in his "Gild of St. George."

George Sand, of a slightly earlier period, imbibed freely the utopian and revolutionary Socialism of the forties in France, and by her writings did much to popularize these notions, in particular the doctrines of Pierre Leroux. Tolstoy's reform program was somewhat retrogressive and irrational, though less so for a writer with the agrarian background of Russia than for one writing in the midst of Western industrialism. He advocated a complete abandonment of the new industrialism, a return to an agrarian age, and the organization of the agrarian economy according to the principles of the Russian mir, with its communistic and coöperative practices considerably expanded. Arnold, an admirer of the authoritarian and positive Prussian state, laid the literary basis for the introduction of the Hegelian theory of the state into England.[1]

While one can appreciate the real and valid motives for this revolt of the esthetic temperament against the repulsive features of modern industrial society, this group offered little in the way of workable constructive reforms. Few, except those who went over to Socialism, had any real reform program. Only an impractical person could accept the proposal of some of them that society should revert to a pre-Industrial Revolution economy in which kings lived with fewer personal comforts than the average workingman of today. Further, even those who, like Ruskin, had some program to offer, were scarcely in line with modern industrial democracy, but desired the establishment of some sort of authoritative and benevolent paternalism.

In spite of all this, the esthetic protest was a real contribution to the reform cause. It effectively insisted that an increase in material gain was no complete justification of a new order of civilization, and maintained that modern industrialism must make a place for the assertion of the ideal and the esthetic.

The more recent circle of literary critics of the social order, including Emile Zola, Anatole France, Bernard Shaw, H. G. Wells, John Galsworthy, Maurice Maeterlinck, Sinclair Lewis, Winston Churchill,[2] Theodore Dreiser, Sherwood Anderson, and Upton Sinclair, differ from most of their predecessors in that, instead of favoring a return to a more primitive economy and social order, they are among the most ardent exponents of advanced social reform.[3] Only a few, enamored of the best in older civilizations and seeing only the darkest phases of the present order, have looked back with longing eyes to a bygone age. In this class may be put J. P. Mahaffy, Ralph Adams Cram, J. J. Walsh, Jacques Maritain, Irving Babbitt, and the Neo-Humanists.[4]

[1] See below, pp. 936 ff.
[2] An American novelist, not to be confused with the English reactionary of this name.
[3] See below, pp. 1079, 1089. [4] See below, pp. 1055 ff.

5. UTOPIAN SOCIALISM AND THE RECONSTRUCTION OF THE SOCIAL AND ECONOMIC ENVIRONMENT

Those extremely daring schemes of social reform which are conventionally known as "utopian" appear most frequently after some great transition that brings with it an abnormal degree of misery. The Industrial Revolution, the greatest of all such transitions, and probably the most productive of accompanying misery, naturally brought forth an unprecedented number of utopian plans for the solution of existing social problems, but all of these programs were more realistic and practical than the somewhat fanciful utopias of the sixteenth and seventeenth centuries which we analyzed in an earlier chapter.

In the most fundamental sense Utopian Socialism of the first half of the nineteenth century was a revolt against the semifatalism of Economic Liberalism. The latter had represented society as the product of natural laws and forces, had accused the proletariat of being the authors of their own miseries, and had sharply denied the possibility of improving conditions artificially through constructive human legislation. Utopian Socialism denounced these assumptions of Romanticism, individualism, and Economic Liberalism, and revived the notions of the French Revolution to the effect that human intelligence and ingenuity are fully equal to the task of forging a new social and economic order. It held that human nature is primarily the product of the social environment and that, accordingly, the solution of contemporary evils is to be found in the creation of a better set of social institutions and practices. They maintained that man can, by rational thought, determine his own social system and social relations. Some, like Fourier, even claimed that man may by well-conceived legislation anticipate the normal course of social evolution and devise short cuts to the ideal goal.

The pioneer in the utopian literature of this period is conventionally assumed to be Count Henri de Saint-Simon.[1] But, as we have seen, he can be quite as truly regarded as the formulator of the chief theses of Comtian sociology or as a forerunner of Christian Socialism. The other utopias would have developed out of the surrounding conditions and ideas had Saint-Simon never written. Saint-Simon's most important contribution to social science and ultimately to social reform was his contention that the social problems created by the Industrial Revolution were so serious that a distinct science of social reconstruction must be evolved to deal with them. Comte attempted to systematize this new social science—Sociology—of which Saint-Simon had seen the need.[2]

The disciples of Saint-Simon further developed his diverse notions. Enfantin and Bazard emphasized the communistic principles to be found in that primitive Christianity which Saint-Simon so much admired. Leroux defended the notion of the social and moral equality of mankind and stressed the essential solidarity of society and the community of interests of all social classes.

The foremost of the French utopians was François Charles Marie Fourier (1772-1835). He was one of the most thorough believers in the possibility of

---

[1] See above, pp. 229 ff.
[2] On Saint-Simon's specific program of social reconstruction through expert direction of society, see above, p. 229.

reforming mankind through the creation of an ideal social environment. This he believed would be found in an "apartment-house utopia"—a coöperative community or *phalange* of some 1,800 individuals in which each would work at a congenial occupation. He hoped ultimately to see human society reconstituted as a world-federation of these phalansteries, the capital of which was to be located at Constantinople. Fourier did not envisage a society that would wholly abolish all private property or attempt to equalize all classes and individuals. He worked out what he believed to be a proper fractional distribution of the social income between labor, capital, and management. While he did not profoundly affect France, no other member of the utopian group attracted so large and sympathetic a following in America. Many Fourierian groups were established in the United States, the most famous of which was Brook Farm, founded and conducted by some of the most noted members of the "Brahman caste" of New England literary lights.[1] The other notable French utopian reformer was Etienne Cabet (1788-1856), whose followers established an experimental community first in Texas and later in Nauvoo, Illinois.

The leading English Utopian Socialist was Robert Owen (1771-1858), who came into the field of utopian theorizing fresh from a practical demonstration of the possibility of establishing an ideal industrial community. At his cotton mills in New Lanark he had organized an advanced industrial community, which, at the opening of the nineteenth century, possessed many of the features that characterize the most progressive industrial organizations of the present day. It was unique at that time. While Owen gave his support to almost every type of constructive philanthropy that was current in his day, he is known especially for his agitation in behalf of factory legislation and trade-unionism, his vigorous advocacy of industrial coöperation, and his concrete plan for ideal industrial communities. The latter did not differ markedly from that of Fourier, though the individual groups were to be slightly smaller. Although his plan was adopted in several places in the United States, most notably at New Harmony, Indiana, these trials resulted in little practical success. The enduring mark that Owen left on social reform consists chiefly in his support of many plans for aiding the solution of existing evils and in his emphasis upon the peculiar virtues inhering in coöperation. More recent echoes of the utopian movement have been William Morris's *News from Nowhere,* Edward Bellamy's *Looking Backward,* and several utopian novels by H. G. Wells.

Significant as were the notions of Utopian Socialism in emphasizing the ability of society consciously and artificially to solve its own problems, this type of Socialism could scarcely lead directly into Marxian Socialism. It was too impractical and, from the standpoint of the Marxians, it was not sufficiently democratic. The utopians did not set forth plans designed to aid the proletariat alone, but aimed at a reconstruction of all society. In a very real sense they were as much the forerunners of modern French "Solidarism" as of Marxian Socialism.[2] Between Utopian and Marxian Socialism there intervened the stage of "Transitional Socialism" through which Socialism was made a revolutionary and a proletarian movement.

---

[1] See Swift, *op. cit.*   [2] See below, pp. 933 ff., 957 ff.

While the great majority of the Utopian Socialists were concerned chiefly with the reformation of the new industrial society, there was one writer, the learned British physician Charles Hall (about 1740-1820), who anticipated Henry George and contended that the main cause of the evils of the age was private property in land and the concentration of land in great estates. In his *Effects of Civilization,* published in 1805, Hall argued for the nationalization of land as the remedy for the abuses and oppression of his age. Dr. Beer has thus summarized his doctrines:

The division of land into large dominions, and the inequality consequent upon that division, gave to the rich an absolute power over the non-possessors, whom they use for the purpose of increasing the stock of wealth. Private property in land led to manufactures, trade, and commerce, by which the poor are made poorer still, and the small possessors are deprived of the little they possess and thrown into poverty.

The division of the land being thus the original cause of the evil, the reform of society must evidently start by removing the cause. The land, therefore, should be nationalized and settled with small farmers. The land should be restored to the nation, and the nation to the land. Agriculture should be the main occupation of all. Of the sciences and arts only those should be preserved and promoted that are necessary for the prosperity of agricultural pursuits.[1]

Hall was not, however, unaware of the evils of industrialism and early capitalism. He clearly formulated the labor theory of value, the notion of surplus value, and the doctrine of the class struggle. He held that labor creates values but receives only wages. The difference between values and wages constitutes the basis of the private wealth of the industrialists and landlords. This private wealth is taken away from labor because of the weakness of the latter. Hall also laid stress upon the fact that the rich profit from the wars that the poor have to fight.

6. TRANSITIONAL OR REVOLUTIONARY SOCIALISM

The most important figures in the so-called Transitional Socialism were the "Ricardian Socialists," William Thompson (1785-1833), John Gray (died about 1850), Thomas Hodgskin (1787-1869), and John Francis Bray (about 1840); the Frenchmen Louis Blanc (1813-82) and Pierre Joseph Proudhon (1809-65); and the Germans Wilhelm Weitling (1808-70) and Ferdinand Lassalle (1825-64). Proudhon, however, played a more prominent part in founding modern Anarchism, and Lassalle is equally important as an advocate of State Socialism.

So far as his practical reform program is concerned, Thompson was a disciple of Robert Owen, but his *Inquiry into the Principles of the Distribution of Wealth Most Conducive to Human Happiness* (1824) contained a very clear statement of the famous Marxian conception of the doctrine of "surplus value." He maintained that labor produces all value and should get the whole product, but under capitalistic society it is cheated out of a great part of its just income. Gray criticized the bourgeois society of his day, accepted the labor theory of

---

[1] Max Beer, *History of British Socialism,* G. Bell & Sons, London, 1919-20, 2 vols., Vol. I, pp. 130-31, Vol. II, p. 373. See his *Social Struggles and Thought,* Small, Maynard, 1925, pp. 31 ff.

value, and advocated state intervention. Hodgskin turned the theory of the natural order against the Economic Liberals by attempting to show that capitalism was an artificial and not a natural product. Bray elaborated the economic interpretation of history as well as the labor theory of value.

Louis Blanc was one of the first to insist that the only effective help that the proletariat can expect must come from their own efforts. They themselves must make effective their most basic right—the right to labor. He believed that the laboring classes would have to triumph through an economic revolution, either peaceful or violent. His post-Revolutionary program consisted in "social workshops," which practically meant state support and control of industry according to a democratic plan of organization. In the French Revolution of 1848 his plan was ostensibly tried out, but since it was operated by his enemies, who only desired to discredit it, the scheme proved a hopeless failure. Certain phases of Blanc's doctrine roughly resemble the later programs of Syndicalism and Guild Socialism.[1]

Proudhon made an especially bitter attack upon the institution of private property, or rather upon the abuses of private property that then existed. But he was equally critical of the doctrine of Communism. He proposed to base the income of everyone solely upon the amount of labor performed, the unit value of which was to be equal and uniform among all members of society. Following the Revolution of 1848, he attempted to secure the establishment of a national banking system founded upon this labor scrip, but he failed utterly in this. Standing at the opposite pole from Say and Bastiat in his attitude towards modern capitalism, he is chiefly significant for his effective onslaught upon the abuses of the bourgeois régime.

Weitling, a Magdeburg tailor who later came to the United States, anticipated Marx by a comprehensive and trenchant review of the evils that modern capitalism had brought to the workingmen and by an eloquent appeal to the proletariat, urging them to rise in their own behalf and overthrow their capitalistic oppressors. His program was a curious combination of proposals similar to certain notions of Fourier, Saint-Simon, and Proudhon—Fourier's conception of "attractive industry," Saint-Simon's notion of expert direction of society, and Proudhon's proposal for an exchange bank based on labor scrip.

Lassalle made important historical, legal, and philosophical attacks on capitalism and private property, stressed the fact that the laborers can only escape from bondage through political activity, and assumed a leading part in urging and guiding the formation of the first significant labor party in Germany. His concrete plan for reform called for state workshops much like those proposed by Louis Blanc, but this phase of his doctrines and activity had little subsequent influence. Transitional Socialism thus in many obvious ways prepared Europe for Marxian Socialism.[2]

IV. EARLY PHILOSOPHICAL ANARCHISM

It might be thought that the Economic Liberals had achieved the most perfect apotheosis of the individual, but another contemporary school exceeded them in this respect, namely, the early Philosophical Anarchists. The Economic

---

[1] See below, pp. 952 ff., 955.   [2] See below, pp. 933 ff.

Liberals at least proposed to retain the state to preserve life and protect property, but the Anarchists advocated the total abolition of the state and all coercive juristic institutions.

The first of this group was William Godwin (1756-1836), whose *Enquiry concerning Political Justice* (1793) was the most enthusiastic elaboration of the extreme Rationalistic notions of the French Revolution by an English social philosopher. He held that all evils in society result from the detrimental effect of repressive human institutions. He proposed that all collective and coercive organizations larger than the parish should be abolished; that the unequal distribution of wealth should be done away with; that the institution of marriage should be wiped out; and that mankind should be free from everything save the moral censure of their associates, thereby being made ready for their ultimate perfection through the influence of reason.

Proudhon inveighed mightily against the bourgeois state, which he regarded solely as an institution for exploitation and oppression. His ideal society was to be founded upon that combination which may readily be created in abstraction, but has never yet been realized as a practical condition, namely, "the union of order and anarchy." He believed that if the obligations of contract could be enforced, society would function perfectly. But he scarcely comprehended that until human institutions have reached a higher state of perfection there can be no assured enforcement of contractual obligations without the authority of the law behind them. In the United States, Josiah Warren (1799-1874), earlier an enthusiastic follower of Robert Owen, developed doctrines somewhat similar to those of Proudhon but quite independent of Proudhon's influence. His more important works were *True Civilization* (1846) and *Equitable Commerce* (1852).

While Godwin, Proudhon, and Warren rejected the utility of the state, they stressed the importance of society—of the concept of humanity. It was left for Max Stirner (1805-56) in his *The Ego and His Own* (1844) to exalt the individual above even humanity and society, to assert that the individual constitutes the only true reality, to maintain that the only limitation upon the rights of the individual is his failure to obtain what he desires, and to contend that "the only right is might."

Though these early Anarchists were guilty of many excesses of statement and offered no well-reasoned substitute for the state that they proposed to destroy, they did perform a real service by insisting that the state, at least as long as it is undemocratized, may be unjustly oppressive and a legitimate object of suspicion on the part of those excluded from participation in it.

V. THE POLITICAL REVOLUTIONS OF 1848

We have already noticed how in the winter and spring of 1848, the masses throughout central, southern, and western Europe, led on by the bourgeoisie themselves in many areas, rose in the attempt to secure for themselves freedom from oppression through participation in political activity.[1] In the German states freedom from political autocracy was desired; in the Hapsburg realms and in Italy not only political liberty but also freedom from the social and

---

[1] See above, pp. 122 ff.

economic burdens of feudalism was aimed at; in France the political participation of the masses and the overthrow of the oppression of the bourgeoisie were the goal; and in England the Chartists hoped to achieve economic betterment and that participation in the world of politics which had been denied to the mass of Englishmen in the Reform Bill of 1832. For various reasons, primarily the fatal divisions of the revolutionists through national, party, or economic rivalry, the movements failed in every country, although the abolition of serfdom in the Hapsburg possessions was a permanent achievement. The failure of these political revolts of the masses turned many into economic channels of attack upon the forces of privilege and helped on the growth of revolutionary and Marxian Socialism.

VI. THE RISE OF HUMANITARIANISM

Associated with the rise of science, mechanical industry, and the new capitalism were not only various social and economic doctrines defending or criticizing capitalism, but many types of humanitarian reforms designed to increase the well-being of mankind.

In the middle of the eighteenth century, political oppression and arbitrary government were still common. A citizen might be imprisoned or executed in arbitrary fashion in most places outside England and the lesser asylums of freedom. Criminals were treated with atrocious brutality. In many states religious intolerance persisted, torture and imprisonment still being common in the handling of religious dissent. Dissenters were generally excluded from important political offices. The relief of the poor was imperfect and inadequate. In many places they were left to starve or shift for themselves. In others the responsibility was still that of the Church. Where public authorities had taken it up the organization was usually unscientific and inequitable. Human slavery among whites had been pretty much abandoned, but Negroes were still enslaved by the whites in colonies and in the Southern states of the United States. The Catholics had for centuries been interested in the salvation of peoples overseas, but the Protestants had done little missionary work before the end of the eighteenth century.

In an earlier chapter [1] we traced the evolution of political liberalism as partially achieved in the English revolutions of 1649 and 1689, the American Revolution, the French Revolution of 1789, the European revolutions of 1830 and 1848, and the Russian Revolution of 1905. These important political uprisings seriously curbed political autocracy, usually put the middle class into the saddle, established the right of revolution, and gained at least the semblance of equality for all before the law.

We shall now consider a series of important reforms which sought to reduce human misery and increase the happiness of man. The background for this movement lay in the rise of Deism, which we have treated above.[2] The humanitarian movement spread to the Quakers and the Evangelical groups. The antislavery crusade was led by the Evangelicals, who also took a prominent part in urging factory and mine reforms in the nineteenth century. They and

---

[1] See above, pp. 94 ff.   [2] See above, pp. 174 ff.

the Quakers also worked for educational reform, as well as for improvement of prison conditions.

One of the worst survivals of barbarism in Europe in the eighteenth century lay in criminal law. Men were still subjected to torture during the process of trial in many countries. Sentences were severe and punishments extremely brutal. The death sentence was often imposed for such a trivial offense as petty theft. Corporal punishment, including branding and mutilation, was still common. Debtors were commonly imprisoned. Prisons were reserved chiefly for debtors and those accused of crime prior to trial. These prisons were mostly filthy, uncomfortable, and brutally administered.

The barbarous criminal law was attacked by Voltaire and Montesquieu in the middle of the eighteenth century. The latter's *Persian Letters* especially satirized the European criminal law of this period. But the most influential reformer in the field of criminal law was the Italian nobleman Cesare di Beccaria (1738-94). His *Essay on Crimes and Punishments* (1764) was probably the most effective book written in the whole history of criminal-law reform. He argued that the prevention of crime is more important than punishment; that torture should be abolished; that punishment should be used to deter men from committing crimes rather than to inflict social revenge on an individual; that imprisonment should be substituted for corporal punishment; and that capital punishment should be abandoned. Indeed, with the exception of the recent application of psychology and psychiatry to crime, Beccaria suggested most of the essentials of criminological progress that have been achieved in the century and a half since his work was published.

Beccaria's ideas deeply influenced the reform of the criminal codes of the American states after 1776, the new criminal code of Revolutionary France, and the reform of the British criminal code by Bentham, Romilly, Buxton, Mackintosh, and Peel in the first half of the nineteenth century. In 1800 there were about two hundred capital offenses in the British criminal code. By 1861 they had been reduced to three: treason, murder, and piracy. Torture was gradually abolished in European criminal procedure and fair and humane trials were provided for accused persons. Imprisonment for debt was slowly outlawed. It did not disappear even in the United States until the Jacksonian period, when it was submerged by the rising tide of democratic enthusiasm.

The reform of the criminal law was paralleled by the increased use of imprisonment as the usual method of punishment and by an improvement in the character of the prisons.[1] We have already pointed out that down to the middle of the eighteenth century corporal punishment and fines were the chief devices employed in the punishment of criminals. Jails and prisons were used mainly for accused persons and debtors. But the American Quakers were repelled by the copious shedding of blood and the other barbarities connected with corporal punishment. Therefore, just as soon as Pennsylvania obtained its independence in 1776 it was ordered that imprisonment at hard labor should be instituted in the place of corporal punishment.[2] Soon the Pennsyl-

[1] See H. E. Barnes, *The Story of Punishment*, Stratford Press, 1930, Chaps. v-vi.
[2] See H. E. Barnes, *The Evolution of Penology in Pennsylvania*, Bobbs-Merrill, 1927.

vania system of prison discipline, based on continuous solitary confinement, became world-famous. But a competing type—the Auburn system—soon appeared. This provided for solitary confinement at night and for association in prison shops during the day. These two systems struggled for supremacy during the nineteenth century. The Auburn system won most favor in the United States, the Pennsylvania system in Europe. In either case, it meant the abandonment of brutal whippings, the lopping-off of ears, branding, and other usual brutalities of the preprison era. In England the work of the American Quakers and other reformers like Louis Dwight was paralleled by the prison-reform efforts of John Howard (1726-91) and Elizabeth Fry (1780-1845). The main progress in prison administration in the last century has consisted in the triumph of the notion that prisons are places for the reformation of convicts rather than for the mere punishment of criminals. Special institutions have been established for women, children, insane criminals, feeble-minded criminals, and the like, thus insuring more specialized and competent treatment of each type.

Religious intolerance was widely prevalent in the eighteenth century. Catholics, dissenting Protestants, and Jews were usually excluded from public office and often subjected to prolonged imprisonment. In England, for example, the Corporation Act of 1661 disqualified all but Anglicans from municipal government, and the Test Act of 1673 excluded orthodox Roman Catholics from both civil and military service. An act of 1678 also denied them membership in either house of Parliament. In some other countries religious persecution was far worse. After the Revocation of the Edict of Nantes in France the French Protestants were frequently butchered in droves. Jews were uniformly badly treated and almost always excluded from office.

Religious toleration first gained headway in Holland and Switzerland. In 1689 England passed the Toleration Act, which forbade the imprisonment of dissenting Protestants solely because of their religious views. The Test and Corporation Acts were repealed in 1828. The next year the Catholic Emancipation Act was passed, admitting Catholics to most of the important public offices in England.[1] The Jews had to wait until 1858 for the passage of laws admitting them to Parliament. In France religious toleration was very generally secured during the Revolution, following 1789, and the progress of the French Revolutionary principles in other states furthered religious toleration. The American Constitution of 1789 guaranteed religious freedom, and the several states soon abandoned their religious tests for suffrage. Rather barbarous treatment of Jews has continued down into the present century, but tolerance and decency in regard to religion, with some persistent and notorious lapses, have gradually won headway. The growth of science and Rationalism has been a powerful factor in bringing about this civilized result.

In the gradual establishment of scientific public relief of the poor England took the lead.[2] The marked increase of pauperism following the rise of sheep-farming in the fifteenth and sixteenth centuries made ecclesiastical relief of the poor inadequate. Between 1563 and 1601 a series of laws were passed pro-

---

[1] See Slater, *The Growth of Modern England*, pp. 292 ff.   [2] See above, pp. 237 ff.

THE RISE OF HUMANITARIANISM

viding for public support of paupers, but the administration of the law was left in the hands of local authorities. The system persisted with few changes down to 1795, when the so-called Berkshire method was established. According to this, relief was to be administered on the basis of the size of the family and inadequate wages were to be supplemented out of the poor-relief funds. This invited pauperism, illegitimacy, and the demoralization of the relief system. Reform finally came in the great Poor Law of 1834, which was an embodiment of the principles of Jeremy Bentham. It was based on the idea of the prevention of pauperism as well as the relief of the worthy poor. It forbade giving relief in homes except to the aged and the sick. It required others to enter a workhouse to get aid. It provided for a logical and economical unification of local areas in administering relief. Since that time the administration of poor relief has been better organized on a national basis in England.

The British precedents in poor relief were rather generally adopted in the United States, modified by the so-called Indiana system. Even more scientific have been some of the Continental schemes, especially in the cities. The most famous is the Hamburg-Elberfeld system, which insures careful inspection of needs along with maximum economy in the administration of relief. These earlier and more crude methods of administering relief have been supplemented in our own day by elaborate social-insurance codes designed to make direct relief less necessary.[1]

In the next chapter [2] we shall deal with the progress of public-health legislation, which was rendered necessary by the rise of the new factory towns. Here, once more, the influence of Jeremy Bentham was of primary importance.

More humane treatment of the insane was brought about during this era. In 1750 it was still generally the rule to keep the insane chained up in brutal fashion in jails and poorhouses. A French physician, Philippe Pinel (1745-1826), was the first to take a civilized attitude towards these unfortunates. As superintendent of a French institution for the insane, he ordered the chains stricken off the inmates. He showed that it was safe and effective to deal with most of the insane without fastening them with chains. The most influential figure in establishing hospitals for the insane was an American woman, Dorothea Lynde Dix (1802-87), perhaps the foremost American humanitarian of the first half of the nineteenth century.[3] She carried on an extensive and successful campaign in behalf of the building of hospitals for the insane and the transfer of these unfortunates from poorhouses, jails, and prisons.

Another phase of the humanitarian movement was the attack on Negro slavery.[4] An English clergyman, William Wilberforce, secured the passage of an act by the British Parliament abolishing the slave trade in 1807. But the reformers were further determined to end slavery in the British Empire. The Quakers, led by Thomas F. Buxton, took the lead in this, but they were aided by other clerical groups. Finally, in 1833 Parliament passed a bill abolishing slavery in the British Empire after August 1, 1834. It required a great Civil

---
[1] See below, pp. 938 ff.
[2] See below, pp. 409 ff.; and Hammerton, *Universal History of the World,* Chap. 189.
[3] See Francis Tiffany, *Life of Dorothea Lynde Dix,* Houghton Mifflin, 1892.
[4] See Hammond and Hammond, *The Rise of Modern Industry,* Chap. xii; and F. J. Klingberg, *The Anti-Slavery Movement in England,* Yale University Press, 1926.

War to abolish slavery in the United States, and it persisted in fact if not in law in many tropical colonies until well into the present century.

Missionary enterprise cannot be omitted from this brief summary of early humanitarianism.[1] The Catholics had been interested in saving the souls of the heathen ever since the Apostolic age, but the Protestants did not enter deeply into such activity until the eighteenth century. The Society for the Propagation of the Gospel in Foreign Parts (Anglican) was established in 1701. A large number of Protestant societies devoted to foreign missions were formed in the last decade of the eighteenth century. While these societies were theoretically devoted to saving souls, they also did much to introduce European ways of life among the backward peoples. In a later chapter [2] we shall deal more thoroughly with the results of missionary enterprise.

Finally, we may refer briefly to the rise of popular education.[3] Free public instruction first arose on a large scale in Prussia in the latter part of the eighteenth century. Here the benevolent despots saw the value of an educated public. The French revolutionists, influenced by Rousseau, also favored public instruction. In England the first public aid to education was authorized by an act of 1833. During the nineteenth century, British support of education mainly took the form of state aid to private schools. But in 1918 a national public education system was set up. Public education in the United States received its first great impetus from the wave of democratic optimism that came to a crest in the age of Andrew Jackson. Democracy was a powerful factor in promoting interest in public education. The democrats believed that all men were equal in native capacity and that equal opportunities in education would insure actual equality in life and achievement. In a later chapter we examine further the validity of this notion.[4]

[1] See C. H. Robinson, *History of Christian Missions*, Scribner, 1915; and K. S. Latourette, *History of Christian Missions in China*, Macmillan, 1929.   [2] See below, pp. 563 ff.
[3] See below, pp. 683 ff., 1070 ff.   [4] See below, Chapter XXII.

SUGGESTED READING

Hammerton, *Universal History of the World*, Chap. 164
Nussbaum, *History of the Economic Institutions of Modern Europe*, Pt. IV, Chap. VIII
Ginzberg, *The House of Adam Smith*
Max Beer, *Social Struggles and Thought (1750-1860)* Small, Maynard, 1929
Dunning, *History of Political Theories from Rousseau to Spencer*, pp. 57-64, 148-53, and Chaps. VI, IX
Davidson, *Political Thought in England from Bentham to J. S. Mill*
L. H. Haney, *History of Economic Thought*, Macmillan, 1911, pp. 133-437
Gide and Rist, *History of Economic Doctrines*, Bks. I-IV
Laidler, *History of Socialist Thought*, Chaps. VIII-XIII
R. T. Ely, *French and German Socialism in Modern Times*, Harper, 1886
C. J. H. Hayes, *Political and Social History of Modern Europe*, new ed., Macmillan, 1924, 2 vols., Vol. II, pp. 102-16
Slater, *The Growth of Modern England*, pp. 141-85, 301-85
Birnie, *Economic History of Europe*, Chaps. XII-XIV
Queen, *Social Work in the Light of History*, Parts III-IV
H. E. Barnes, *The Repression of Crime*, Doubleday, Doran, 1926

H. S. Spalding, *Chapters in Social History,* Heath, 1925, Chaps. XXI-XXIV
Webster, *Historical Selections,* pp. 776-88, 799-825
Robinson and Beard, *Readings in Modern European History,* Vol. II, pp. 270-86
Scott and Baltzly, *Readings in European History Since 1814,* pp. 64-93, 109-12
Bland, Brown, and Tawney, *English Economic History; Select Documents,* Pt. III, pp. 571-612, and Secs. IV-V
D. O. Wagner, ed., *Social Reformers: Adam Smith to John Dewey,* Macmillan, 1934, Pts. I-IV

FURTHER REFERENCES

THE DEFENSE AND CRITICISM OF EARLY INDUSTRIAL CAPITALISM. On Economic Liberalism, see *Cambridge Modern History,* Vol. X, Chap. XXIII; Gide and Rist, *op. cit.,* Bk. I; Chaps. II-IV of O. F. Boucke, *The Development of Economics, 1750-1900* (Macmillan, 1921); Haney, *op. cit.,* Chaps. IX-XVII; Chap. V of J. K. Ingram, *History of Political Economy* (Macmillan, 1894); Ginzberg, *op. cit.* On John Stuart Mill, see Gide and Rist, *op. cit.,* pp. 352 ff.; Haney, *op. cit.,* Chap. XXII. On Bastiat and Say, see *Ibid.,* Chaps. XIV, XVI. On Henry Carey, see *Ibid.,* Chaps. XVI-XVII. On political individualism, see Dunning, *op. cit.,* pp. 148 ff., 235 ff., 395 ff. On the effects of Economic Liberalism in England, see Slater, *op. cit.,* Chaps. IV, VI-VII, XI, XII.

On Bastiat, Napoleon III, and free trade, see Ogg and Sharp, *op. cit.,* pp. 205 ff., 269 ff. On developments in Prussia, see *Ibid.,* pp. 210 ff., 284 ff.

On Philosophical Radicalism and Utilitarianism, see W. P. Hall, *British Radicalism, 1791-1797* (Columbia University Press, 1912); Davidson, *op. cit.;* Halévy, *The Growth of Philosophical Radicalism;* Boucke, *op. cit.,* Chaps. IV-V; Graham Wallas, "Jeremy Bentham," *Political Science Quarterly,* March, 1923.

On legislation resulting from Economic Liberalism, see Slater, *op. cit.,* Chaps. VII, XII-XIII, XV. On attacks on Economic Liberalism, see Gide and Rist, *op. cit.,* pp. 170 ff., 264 ff., 379 ff.; Haney, *op. cit.,* Chaps. XVIII-XX.

On the Historical School of economics, see Ingram, *op. cit.,* Chap. VI; Boucke, *op. cit.,* Chap. VI; Haney, *op. cit.,* Chaps. XXIV-XXV.

On Tory social reform, see *Cambridge Modern History,* Vol. XII, Chap. XXIII; H. de B. Gibbins, *The English Social Reformers* (Scribner, 1902); Hutchins and Harrison, *History of Factory Legislation;* W. J. Wilkinson, *Tory Democracy* (Longmans, 1925).

EARLY SOCIALISM. On early Christian Socialism, see Gibbins, *op. cit.;* E. R. A. Seligman, "Owen and the Christian Socialists," *Political Science Quarterly,* June, 1886; Hugh Martin, ed., *Christian Reformers of the Nineteenth Century* (Doran, 1927); C. E. Raven, *Christian Socialism, 1848-1854* (Macmillan, 1920); Flint, *Historical Philosophy in France, French Belgium and Switzerland,* Chaps. VI-VII.

On the dissenting sects (especially the Quakers) and poor-relief legislation, see H. U. Faulkner, *Chartism and the Churches* (Columbia University Press, 1912); North, *Early Methodist Philanthropy;* W. J. Warner, *The Wesleyan Movement in the Industrial Revolution* (Longmans, 1930); Simeral, *Reform Movements in Behalf of Women and Children;* Hammond and Hammond, *The Age of the Chartists,* Chap. XIII.

THE ESTHETIC REVOLT AGAINST MATERIALISM AND MISERY. Martin, *op. cit.;* V. D. Scudder, *Social Ideals in English Letters* (new ed., Houghton Mifflin, 1933); H. D. Lockwood, *Tools and the Man* (Columbia University Press, 1927); J. W. Cunliffe, *Leaders of the Victorian Revolution* (Appleton-Century, 1934); Lindsay Swift, *Brook Farm* (Macmillan, 1900); G. C. Knight, *American Literature and*

Culture (Long and Smith, 1932). On George Sand, see K. T. B. Butler, *History of French Literature* (Dutton, 1923, 2 vols.); Lockwood, *op. cit.* On Tolstoy, see pp. 6 ff. of Prince Dmitry Svyatopolk-Mirsky, *Contemporary Russian Literature* (Knopf, 1926).

On Utopian Socialism, see Ely, *op. cit.,* Chaps. III-V; Chaps. II, IV of Thomas Kirkup, *History of Socialism* (5th ed. rev. and largely rewritten by E. R. Pease, Longmans, 1913); Laidler, *op. cit.,* Chaps. VIII-XII; Pt. I, Chaps. II-IV of Morris Hillquit, *History of Socialism in the United States* (5th ed., rev., Funk & Wagnalls, 1910).

On Transitional Socialism, see Ely, *op. cit.,* Chaps. V-VII, XII; Kirkup, *op. cit.,* Chaps. III, V; Laidler, *op. cit.,* Chaps. VIII, XIX; Esther Lowenthal, *The Ricardian Socialists* (Longmans, 1911); Vol. I, Introduction, of Sir J. A. R. Marriott, *The French Revolution of 1848 in Its Economic Aspects* (Oxford Press, 1913, 2 vols.).

On early Philosophical Anarchism, see Ely, *op. cit.,* Chap. VII; Kirkup, *op. cit.,* Chap. XI; Vol. I, Introduction, of William Godwin, *An Enquiry concerning Political Justice,* ed. by R. A. Preston (Crofts, 1926, 2 vols.); E. V. Zenker, *Anarchism* (Putnam, 1897); Paul Eltzbacher, *Anarchism* (B. R. Tucker, 1908).

On the rise of humanitarianism, see Birnie, *Economic History of Europe,* Chaps. XII-XIV; Hammerton, *op. cit.,* Chap. 164; Martin, *op. cit.;* Gibbins, *op. cit.;* Gilbert Slater, *Poverty and the State* (Long & Smith, 1931) and *The Growth of Modern England,* pp. 141 ff.

On the reform of criminal law, see Coleman Phillipson, *Three Criminal Law Reformers* (Dutton, 1923).

On the history of poor relief, see Gillin, *Poverty and Dependency,* Pt. III; Slater, *The Growth of Modern England,* pp. 182 ff., 315 ff.; Queen, *op. cit.,* Pt. III.

CHAPTER XII

SOCIAL PHASES OF THE NEW RÉGIME

I. THE FACTORY TOWN AND THE URBAN AGE

One of the major social results of the Industrial Revolution was the gradual transition of Western civilization from an agricultural to an urban basis—perhaps the chief social transformation in human history. The expansion of Europe and the Commercial Revolution stimulated the growth of towns and lessened the overwhelming predominance of agricultural life that had characterized the medieval age. But European culture was still of an agrarian pattern in 1800. The great majority of people lived in the country raising flocks, cultivating the soil, or working for merchant capitalists under the putting-out system.

The Industrial Revolution carried the urbanizing process forward very rapidly. The new machinery drove out the domestic or "putting-out" system of production and made the large workshop or factory inevitable. The factory rendered essential the assembling of a large number of workers close to factory sites. There were no trolleys, busses, or suburban trains in those days. The working-day was long and afforded little time for travel to and from work. Therefore the factory laborers were compelled by force of circumstances to gather together in drab industrial cities that spawned about the new and grim factories. Modern urban civilization thus got under way.

Our modern city-dominated culture is, then, a product of the factory system, and is very different from anything that preceded it. City life for the majority of a population is a decided novelty—so new that its results cannot as yet be foretold. Athens seems never to have had a population of much over 100,000 and the average in imperial Rome was only about five times that figure.[1] Only Alexandria and Baghdad, and perhaps Constantinople and Cordova, ever exceeded 1,000,000. In 1800 London had only 864,000 inhabitants, Paris 547,000, and Berlin 172,000. There were only 15 cities in England in 1801 with a population of over 20,000. Added together, their population totaled only about 1,500,000. By 1891 there were 185 English cities of over 20,000, with a combined population of over 15,500,000. In 1933 the population of London was 7,742,000; of Paris 3,783,000; of Berlin 4,288,000; and of New York 7,986,000. These figures are characteristic of the changed situation throughout the Western industrial states.

The rapid growth of city population after the industrializing process was

---

[1] Some authorities, however, estimate the maximum population of ancient Rome as 1,000,000.

under way is well illustrated by the following table showing the relative increase of the urban population of the United States since 1790:

GROWTH OF CITY POPULATION

Year	Total Population	Cities of 8,000 Inhabitants or over		
		Population	Number of Places	Percentage of Population
1790	3,929,214	131,472	6	3.3
1800	5,308,483	210,873	6	4.0
1820	9,638,453	475,135	13	4.9
1840	17,069,453	1,453,994	44	8.5
1860	31,443,321	5,072,256	141	16.1
1880	50,155,783	11,365,698	285	22.7
1900	75,994,575	25,018,335	547	32.0
1920	105,710,620	46,307,640	924	43.8
1930	122,775,046	60,333,452	1,208	49.1

Not only did the factories bring into being a larger number of cities and a more extensive urban population than ever existed before; the new cities were also of a novel type. Hitherto, cities had grown up chiefly because of their strategic or military significance, their position as the capital of a conquering or powerful state, their primacy in the arts, letters, and culture, their rich and brilliant society, or their commercial preëminence and activities. After the Industrial Revolution cities arose and flourished mainly because of their adaptability to industrial life, to which were often added the advantages that they had earlier possessed as commercial centers. Economic considerations overshadowed all other matters in the genesis of the more representative contemporary cities. Civilization was henceforth not only urban but also industrial in character. Many leading cities combined commercial, industrial, financial, and cultural advantages among the factors that promoted their rise and ascendancy. In our country this has been notably true of New York City.

The following statistics from the New York *Times,* illustrative of the population growth and occupational distribution in New York City, are illuminating as to urban situations as they have developed in the century of the Industrial Revolution:

THE CITY'S POPULATION

Year	New York City
1790	49,000
1800	79,000
1820	152,000
1840	391,000
1860	1,174,000
1880	1,911,000
1900	3,437,000
1920	5,620,000
1933	7,986,000

In the year 2000—which the generation just coming into consciousness will, in many cases, live to see—the metropolitan area of New York may contain three times its present population. According to the calculations of Professors Raymond Pearl and Lowell J. Reed of Johns Hopkins . . . the territory where 9,000,000 people now live and move and have their being will contain 29,000,000 seventy-five years hence. The whole of the area of present Greater New York, Newark, Jersey City, and Hoboken will by then be built up as solidly as Manhattan and the Bronx are today. The population, spreading out from the present city in all directions, will have settled in all of Westchester and Nassau counties and the wide stretches of Union, Essex, and Bergen counties that lie back of Staten Island and Newark and up along the west bank of the Hudson. This area will be built up to about half the present density of Greater New York.

The next table shows the number of persons in New York City engaged in gainful occupations, classified by the general nature of their work. The figures are based upon the Federal Census of 1920, but are increased in proportion to the gain in the city's population that is estimated to have taken place since then:

OCCUPATION OF NEW YORKERS

Kind of Work	Number of People (in thousands)	Percentage of Total
Manufacturing	863	30
Clerical	455	16
Trade: Retail stores, etc.	442	16
Domestic and personal	347	12
Transportation	272	10
Building trades	212	7
Professional	190	7
Public service	68	2

Another table gives a summary of the number of men and women employed in New York City in the main categories of employment according to an estimate based on the 1920 census. This illustrates the entry of women into industry:

MEN AND WOMEN WORKERS
(in thousands)

Occupations	Men	Women	Percentage of Women
Manufacturing	632	231	27
Trade	381	61	14
Clerical	246	209	46
Transportation	246	26	10
Building and construction	212	...	..
Domestic and personal service	170	177	52
Professional	113	77	41
Public service	67	1	2
Total	2,067	782	27 [1]

[1] New York *Times*. Many social biologists and students of population trends would seriously question the prognostication of Professor Pearl and Professor Reed as to the possible size of New York City in the year 2000. Their prediction is apparently based upon the assumption of a steady increase in the general population and a continuance of the trend towards urban concentration. In the last decade, population growth in the United States has slowed down and, as we shall point out later, there is a probability that it will be stabilized about 1975. Further, a trend towards the redistribution of urban population has already set in and the drift today is toward suburbs. The

The proportion of women to men in the city's offices, shops, and factories has, of course, changed with a swiftness that our grandfathers could not possibly have foretold. Modern industry has little respect for the slogan "Woman's place is in the home." What the future holds for women in the work of the community is, like other chapters of city prophecy, an interesting—even if not a strictly scientific—field for speculation.

Just in proportion as any state has been affected by the Industrial Revolution and has introduced the new machine methods, urban predominance has become characteristic of the population. In the more advanced industrial states, such as England, Belgium, Germany, and the United States, the city population is already in the majority.

Though the modern city sprang up because of the new industrial conditions, there was little in the way of order, planning, or sanitation in the growth of these early manufacturing towns. Crude dwellings appeared near the factories, often built back to back in long rows and separated only by board partitions. They were human rabbit warrens rather than decent dwelling-places. Little provision was made for personal hygiene and sanitation. Sewers and water systems were hardly thought of. Refuse was thrown out of the doors and windows or through trapdoors in the floor. Parks and recreation places were practically unknown. Except in the residential sections occupied by employers, the streets were rarely paved. Opportunities for recreation scarcely existed—hardly a primary defect with sixteen-hour working-days. Naturally, epidemics and pestilences were common in such surroundings. Not only did they threaten the existence of the working population; the lives of the employers and their families were but little safer. Whatever the relative proportion of humanitarian spirit and of self-preservation in their motives, influential citizens were ultimately compelled to line up behind public-health programs.

Jeremy Bentham's name is associated with early agitation for public hygiene, as with nearly every other important reform movement of the first third of the nineteenth century. Of his many disciples, Edwin Chadwick and Southwood Smith were the most active in this particular cause. The disastrous effects of neglecting sanitation were forcibly brought to public attention after 1837, in which year a law was passed providing for the registration of births and deaths, together with statistical evidence as to causes. Under the leadership of Smith and Chadwick, thorough investigations were undertaken. The reports of these committees served to arouse a public concern with health, which was further stimulated by the cholera epidemic of 1847. A Public Health Act was passed in 1848, creating a general Board of Health to advise Parliament and to coördinate the work of local health boards. Chadwick, Smith, and Lord Shaftesbury were on the first board. This was so hampered in its efforts by vested interests, which profited by conditions as they were, that very little was immediately accomplished. In due time, a series of acts was passed, from 1871 to 1875, codifying and extending sanitary legislation and providing for

population of Manhattan Island has been decreasing for over a decade. Yet the views of Pearl and Reed may not be so far short of the actuality, since they take into account not only Manhattan but also the region of Greater New York. The latter may become inhabited by a vastly greater population than exists there today, while the extreme concentration of population in Manhattan Island, the Bronx, and Brooklyn may be abated at the same time by a suburban trend.

THE FACTORY TOWN AND THE URBAN AGE 409

local enforcement. The separate Ministry of Health, created in 1919, was set up as an adequate central authority, thus curing the most serious administrative defect in the older system.

Other European countries had to meet the same problems of urban health when the Industrial Revolution reached them. Germany and one or two other Continental countries have gone even further than England in sanitary legislation. Besides the provisions for pure drinking-water and adequate drainage, good paving accompanied by sprinkling and flushing of streets has helped to ward off disease. Garbage is kept off the streets or covered.

Scientific knowledge of the causes of diseases and the main channels of their dissemination is a major achievement of recent times. To give an example, smallpox was formerly a terrible scourge, but now comparatively few people in the Occident contract it, and a small percentage of these die or are disfigured. Diphtheria has also been all but wiped out in up-to-date cities. Typhoid fever has been suppressed mainly by safeguarding the water supply. Preventive medicine is an illustration of an achievement that has extended far beyond remedying the original difficulties. Made necessary by the rise of the factory town, it has gone on reducing the death rate, and the latter has long since become lower than it was before the factory system started.

The coming of elementary forms of public-health provisions, through the efforts of reformers and physicians, was only the beginning of attempts to solve the difficult problem of adapting mankind to the novel facts of urban life. It has seemed desirable not only to make life possible within the city, but also to make it relatively pleasant and endurable. This has involved a multitude of significant experiments with respect to both city politics and the direction of city life in general.

As the population has become more and more concentrated in municipalities, the problems of municipal government vie in importance with those of state, provincial, and central governments. The conditions of city life have provided opportunities for a far greater degree of corruption and manipulation in city politics than exists elsewhere. The political boss, especially, has taken hold and fattened in city politics.[1] The problems of contemporary city government have centered very largely around the activities of the local bosses and the efforts of the more intelligent and honest citizens to free themselves from the octopus of the political machine. Various schemes have been suggested for achieving this desirable end, such as the commission form of government, the city-manager plan, and sundry other administrative novelties. Merely to throw one group of "rascals" out by a political upheaval accomplishes little of permanent value. City government must be placed upon a scientific and efficient basis if we wish to achieve any lasting improvement. The European municipalities

[1] J. T. Salter, *Boss Rule: Portraits in City Politics*, McGraw-Hill, 1935.

INCOME — CITY OF PITTSBURGH — EXPENDITURES					
Receipts Estimated For 1934			**Expenditures Authorized For 1934**		
Source	Amount	Percent of Total	Category	Amount	Percent of Total
TAXES ON LAND	9,809,040	49.83%	GENERAL GOVERNMENT (OVERHEAD)	1,502,675	7.07%
TAXES ON BUILDINGS	5,150,960	26.17%	POLICE	2,377,514	11.18%
WATER RENTS	2,698,000	13.71%	FIRE	1,863,690	8.77%
INTEREST ON BANK BALANCES	80,000	.40%	HEALTH	692,196	3.26%
FINES AND FORFEITS	80,500	.41%	GARBAGE & RUBBISH REMOVAL	1,240,000	5.83%
LICENSES	772,560	3.92%	LIBRARIES	551,525	2.60%
MARKET AND WHARF RENTALS	97,500	.50%	CHARITIES	915,047	4.30%
PUBLIC SERVICE PRIVILEGES	38,000	.19%	HIGHWAYS (MAINTENANCE)	518,730	2.44%
DEPARTMENTAL RENTALS AND CHARGES	525,000	2.67%	STREET LIGHTING	800,540	3.77%
MISCELLANEOUS	433,440	2.20%	STREET CLEANING	314,000	1.48%
			WATER	1,734,949	8.16%
			PARKS	395,487	1.86%
			RECREATION	221,710	1.04%
			INTEREST AND SINKING FUNDS	6,264,130	29.46%
			MISCELLANEOUS	1,867,856	8.78%
TOTAL	**$19,685,000**	**100%**	**TOTAL**	**$21,260,049**	**100%**

NOTE: The 1934 budget appears unbalanced, due to a conservative estimate of the amount that would be received from delinquent taxes. Collections from this source during the first five months indicate the possibility of the budget being balanced by the end of the year.

Copyright, 1934, by J. C. Slippy.

HOW A MODERN CITY ASSEMBLES AND DISBURSES ITS INCOME [1]

[1] From *Survey Graphic*, August, 1934, p. 373.

THE FACTORY TOWN AND THE URBAN AGE

have succeeded far better than those of the United States in solving the perplexing problems of urban politics. Especially has this been true of the German cities.

More important, perhaps, for modern city life than the attack upon the abuses of urban politics has been the related effort, in many cities, to secure control over the public utilities of municipalities, and to provide public facilities for divers forms of recreation. Considerable advance has been made in many great European states towards the municipal ownership of lighting plants, street railways, theaters, lecture halls, music halls, parks, gardens, and so on. Again this has notably been characteristic of the German cities. In this manner, the urban peoples, generally, have gained more and more control over the conditions that determine whether or not their own lives shall be healthy, safe, and inspiring.

In America, relatively little progress has been made in municipal ownership, but many writers believe that public ownership on a municipal scale is far more likely to be immediately successful than the more ambitious Socialist plan of the general state ownership of all the means of production. Certainly, municipal Socialism is in line with the opinion of many political and sociological writers that the local government units must be given a far greater degree of recognition in the politico-social system of the future.

Some especially difficult problems have appeared in connection with the vast public enterprises of the city under modern industrialism. A lighting plant, a street railway, a water system, or a telephone exchange is likely to be a perfect monopoly, or inefficient to the extent that it is not. In Germany and some other European states, the tendency has been to avoid both the abuses of private monopoly and the difficulties of government regulation by resorting, as we have noted, to municipal ownership of such public utilities.

One of the most interesting aspects of the effort to make cities more rational and attractive has been the development of the regional survey and of regional planning projects. City-planning dates back to ancient oriental times. Even in medieval towns there was some conception of planning.[1] Sir Christopher Wren worked out a plan for the rebuilding of London in 1666 after the great fire. This would have made London one of the most beautiful of the world's cities, but the plan was disregarded. Paris was partially rebuilt according to definite plans by Louis XIV, Napoleon I, and Napoleon III. Especially important was the work carried out by the latter under the direction of Baron Haussmann. Germany has given more attention to city-planning than any other state. The planning movement was given an impetus in the United States when Major L'Enfant laid out the design of the new capital, Washington.

But scientific city-planning on a social as well as an architectural basis really began with the work of Frédéric Le Play in France in the last half of the nineteenth century.[2] By his day the Industrial Revolution was sufficiently advanced to indicate the necessity of reckoning with the underlying geographical, biological, and economic factors involved, as well as planning for architectural

[1] Cf. F. J. Haverfield, *Ancient Town-Planning,* Oxford Press, 1913; and T. F. Tout, "Medieval Town Planning," *Town Planning Review,* April, 1919.
[2] See below, p. 945.

and scenic beauty. Le Play recognized that in any social planning of cities one must have a full knowledge of the city and its outlying environs, including population, resources, and topography. Hence he proposed the scientific social survey of urban areas and their environs. Le Play's ideas were taken up and related more directly to city-planning by the eminent Scottish biologist and sociologist Patrick Geddes.[1] He organized and conducted the Edinburgh Survey and gave it publicity through the Town Planning Exhibition of 1910. His ideas have gained support among pioneers in the city-planning movement elsewhere. Perhaps the most ambitious of all regional urban surveys was that carried on by a committee appointed to conduct a regional survey of New York City and its environs under the directions of Charles D. Norton and Frederick C. Delano. As a result, the committee published a voluminous and comprehensive report.[2]

There are three major programs of city-planning today (see diagram, p. 413)—the New York City tendency towards the massing of skyscrapers in the mid-urban areas;[3] the opposite extreme, known as the "garden-city" conception of Ebenezer Howard of England,[4] which spreads the population over suburban areas and avoids any marked urban congestion; and the proposals of a Frenchman, M. Le Corbusier, who aims at a compromise between these two extremes.[5] The garden-city program denies the necessity of urban congestion and distributes the population so that there shall never be more than fifty persons per housing acre. The New York trend is, as we have seen, towards massing the great skyscrapers and high apartments in the center of the city and encouraging the suburban spread of the shopping and working population. The plan of M. Le Corbusier is, perhaps, more sensible than either extreme. His plan is thus described by Mr. Abercrombie:

His City of Tomorrow (planned for 3,000,000 people) is as opposed to the New York tendency of jostling skyscrapers at the center, as it is to the Garden City low-over-all density. He proposes to maintain or slightly to increase the over-all Continental density but to reduce the ground covered by building to 15 per cent of the total area and to confine all business to a few isolated skyscrapers ¼ mile apart and 700 feet high; the intervening ground is open gardens and woodland of extremely naturalistic type, through which run great unimpeded traffic arteries. All housing is in two types of tenement, which being at least 110 feet high also leave a great deal of open space. . . . This is the extreme use of height in order to free ground space, rather than greatly to increase density. The four basic principles are given as follows:

1. We must de-congest the centers of our cities.
2. We must augment their density.
3. We must increase the means for getting about.
4. We must increase parks and open spaces.

[1] Patrick Geddes, *City Development*, London, 1904; and *Cities in Evolution*, London, 1915.
[2] *Regional Plan of New York and Its Environs*, 10 vols., New York, 1928-32, summarized and interpreted in R. L. Duffus, *Mastering a Metropolis*, Harper, 1932. See also R. M. Haig, "Toward an Understanding of the Metropolis," *Quarterly Journal of Economics*, February-May, 1926.
[3] See Patrick Abercrombie, *Town and Country Planning*, Holt, 1933, pp. 99 ff.
[4] Howard, *The Garden Cities of To-morrow*, London, 1902.
[5] See Abercrombie, *op. cit.*, pp. 116 ff. and diagram, p. 413.

THE FACTORY TOWN AND THE URBAN AGE

M. Le Corbusier is however sufficiently human to allow ... garden villages, both for those who wish to work in the factory zones (kept outside the city) and those who work in the skyscrapers but prefer to bring up their families in "garden" houses. There is an essential protective zone of woods and fields—a fresh-air reserve—between the city proper and these suburbs.[1]

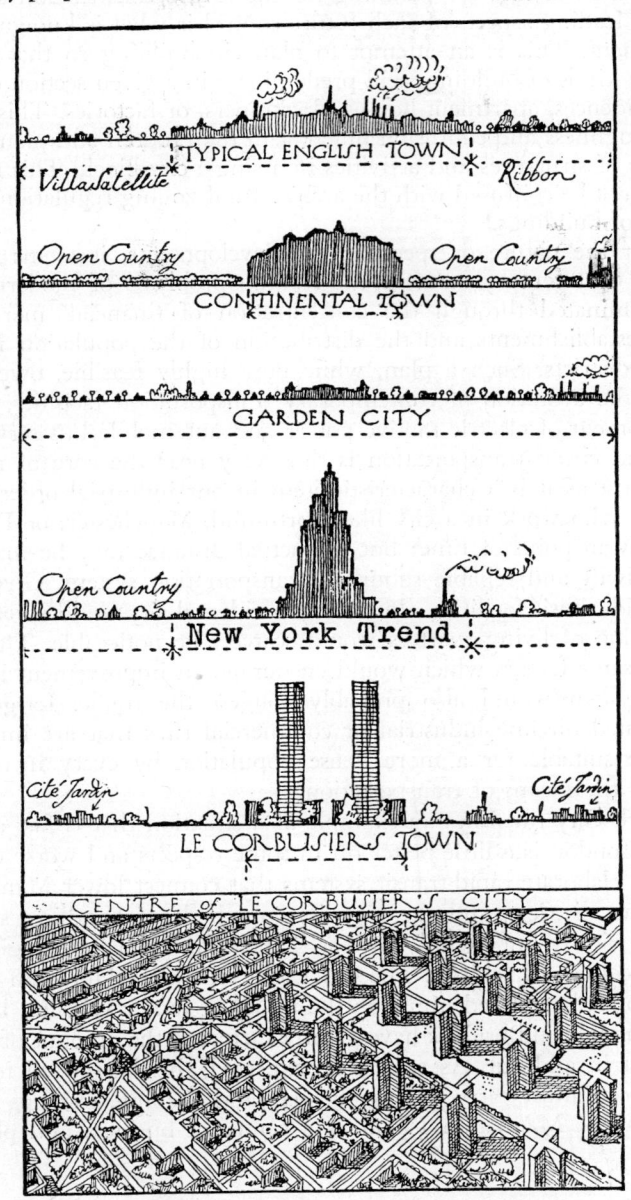

CITIES OF THE PRESENT AND THE FUTURE[2]

[1] See Abercrombie, *op. cit.*, pp. 116-18.
[2] Adapted from *Ibid.*, pp. 115, 117.

The chief obstacle to the adoption of so rational a plan is that it will require the abandonment or destruction of billions of dollars' worth of buildings already constructed in our planless era of city-building. This would arouse the bitter opposition of the vested real-estate interests. We are likely to make progress piecemeal through planning for the future construction of our cities. One of the leading aspects of such future control is what is known as the zoning movement. This is an attempt to plan city-building so that similar and appropriate kinds of buildings will predominate in a given section of the city—be they residences, apartment houses, skyscrapers, or factories. This is designed to end the ugliness and confusion inherent in the random and planless mixture of all kinds of structures and activities in a single city block. This type of zoning should not be confused with the architectural zoning regulations relating to the height of buildings.[1]

Whatever the nature or speed of the developments, it seems certain that within the next century some of the leading problems of modern urban life will be eliminated through the concentration of financial, mercantile, and industrial establishments and the distribution of the population in suburban residential districts. Such a plan, while now highly feasible, owes its practicability to the evolution of contemporary transportation facilities, particularly the development of electric motive power and automobile bus service.

Rapid and cheap transportation is thus very near the core of modern city problems, just as it is a characteristic item in our industrial order in general. The people who work in a city like Dortmund, Manchester, or Detroit must live close by in point of time; but the actual distance may be many miles if there is a swift and reliable suburban transportation system. Given twice its present rapid-transit facilities, almost any occidental city could spread out until the congestion of living-quarters would scarcely be noticeable. The drawback is that the same factors which would encourage an improvement in the transportation system would also probably congest the traffic. Large cities are usually located on fine industrial or commercial sites that are improved and made more suitable for a more dense population by every increase in the efficiency of the means of transportation.

New York City furnishes an example of a situation that is fast approaching absurdity; London is a little better off in some respects and worse off in many others. The elaborate rapid-transit systems that connect lower Manhattan with the suburban districts, and the ingenious methods of handling street traffic, have paradoxically but literally increased the congestion by bringing to town still more people and vehicles. The water that separates Manhattan from points west and south has placed limits on the utility of motor vehicles; but the new vehicular tunnels and bridges have greatly increased the amount of road traffic that can get in and out. As was to be expected, this has added to the traffic that the streets must carry during the day and evening. Perhaps the further specialization of Manhattan Island as a center of business and pleasure will

[1] See below, p. 1097.

crowd more people out of residence there, which would reduce the traffic late at night. There is more opportunity to spread out in London, but even there the swarms of pedestrians, busses, and cabs that surge to and fro on some streets are at times as vast as they are unnecessary.

Congestion in the urban areas being what it is, the question of decent housing is inevitably among the most vital of urban problems. This is particularly true because, owing to the cost and difficulty of transportation, it is chiefly the poorer economic groups that have to remain near the center. Some of the worst housing evils of the early industrial period have been reduced by legislation growing out of an increasingly sensitive public conscience; but the housing-conditions in the larger cities in both America and Europe are still far from satisfactory. Crowding, poor ventilation and lighting, and lack of sanitary facilities remain the chief evils.

Since the World War some of the European cities have found this another very promising field of municipal Socialism. Vienna, for instance, was left seriously handicapped by the peace treaty, which deprived it of most of its natural hinterland at the same time that it imposed heavy financial burdens. Yet Vienna has none the less managed to set a notable example for other cities in its construction of municipal apartments, with modern facilities and plenty of light and air.[1] These apartments rent at a moderate figure, and their social value has already been demonstrated, among other ways, by a reduction of infant mortality and tuberculosis rates. It is likely that the future will see similar policies adopted by many of the larger urban centers. The Amalgamated Clothing Workers have constructed model apartments for laboring classes in New York City that duplicate on a smaller scale the municipal achievements in Vienna. The public-works projects relied upon by President Franklin Roosevelt to restore prosperity embody large expenditures for improving municipal housing.

Unsolved though many of them are, there is no call for sentimental concern over city problems. The urban population is now about as healthy and lives nearly as long as that of the country. It has been observed that city people now make more, spend more, and save at least as much as their rural cousins. There is a certain danger, however, in concentrating half or more of the population of an enormous area in cities. An upheaval like the World War is likely so to change economic and political arrangements that great cities like Vienna are left without the food, clothing, or fuel necessary to sustain life. Against this point it might be urged that rural peoples have likewise suffered famine and decimation in all periods of history, including the present, and that the economic mechanism provided by the Industrial Revolution furnishes both the spirit and the sinews of relief on a scale never approached before. We shall recur later to a discussion of some of the leading effects of urban life upon the mental attitudes that dominate contemporary society.[2]

In addition to the general movement of population from country to town, there has been a wider movement of peoples from one region to another.[3]

---

[1] See R. E. Chaddock, "Housing in Vienna," *American Journal of Sociology*, January, 1932.
[2] See below, p. 438.
[3] See Thompson, *op. cit.*, Chap. XXIII.

The economic centers of great states have shifted from the older settlements, where life was based chiefly upon agricultural opportunities, into the sections that afford industrial and commercial advantages. In general, population has tended to flow to water-power sites, to those convenient to such natural resources as coal, iron ore, petroleum, and essential raw materials for manufacturing, or to regions having special harbor advantages.

II. MODERN INDUSTRIALISM AND POPULATION TRENDS SINCE 1800

1. POPULATION INCREASES

As striking as urban growth have been the net gains in population as a result of medical science and the Industrial Revolution. Population increase in Europe was comparatively slow until the middle of the eighteenth century. But from that time until the outbreak of the World War the population of Europe rose in round numbers from 140,000,000 to 463,000,000. In 1800, the population of Europe was 187,693,000; in 1830, 233,962,000; in 1860, 282,893,000; in 1890, 362,902,000. In 1801 the population of England and Wales was 8,892,000. In 1911 it had risen to 36,000,000. Germany was little affected by the Industrial Revolution up to 1871, and then had a population of about 41,000,000. By 1914 this had increased to 67,900,000. The United States was relatively an empty country in 1789, with a white population of about 4,000,000. This had grown to 122,775,000 in 1930 and to over 125,000,000 in 1935.

A number of interesting explanations have been offered as to the cause of this phenomenal growth in numbers. First and foremost were the new scientific agricultural methods, which vastly increased the food supply. The Industrial Revolution was also a direct cause of increased productive capacity, of food as well as of other things. It likewise created the possibility of concentrating in a few occidental countries a vast amount of food products brought from outside. Improvements in the artificial preservation and refrigeration of foodstuffs have also helped to insure a more efficient utilization of the food produced and to prevent the appalling food wastes of earlier ages. Another most significant factor in population growth has been the rise of modern medicine and public hygiene, which has markedly reduced the death rate.[1] For example, the population of Germany has increased remarkably during the past fifty years, and yet the birth rate has steadily fallen. In 1861-70 the German birth rate per 100,000 of the population was 37.2. In 1900-05 it was 35.5. By 1935 it had dropped to about half of the 1900-05 rate. The death rate dropped from 26.9 in 1861-70 to 20.8 in 1895-1904, and to 12.6 in 1931. Other factors than lowered death rate, of course, helped to account for the gains in the German population.

2. MALTHUSIANISM AND BIRTH CONTROL

When the rapid increase in population first began, most people who noted it at all considered it an unalloyed advantage, since a large supply of workers was an essential basis for the factory industry which was then being established. Even before the end of the eighteenth century, however, some more cautious

---

[1] See Edgar Sydenstricker, *Health and Environment,* McGraw-Hill, 1933.

thinkers began to have doubts. In 1798 appeared the first edition of Thomas Robert Malthus's *Essay on Population,* which was destined to have a remarkable influence upon economic and social discussions for more than a century. The substance of Malthus's argument was that population tends to increase at a geometric ratio (1,2,4,8,16, etc.), while the food supply can not possibly be made to increase at more than an arithmetic ratio (1,2,3,4, etc.); and that, as a result, population tends always to press upon the underlying means of subsistence.[1] Malthus saw two kinds of checks to the tendency of population to outrun its food supply—(1) positive (war, pestilence, and starvation), and (2) negative (postponement of marriages to a later age, and what he described as "moral restraint"). In the England of his day, Malthus could not see how a considerable part of the population could escape from a life of poverty and misery. He feared that, for the immediate future at least, any increase in the means of subsistence would tend to bring about a more than corresponding increase in the population.

The Malthusian theory of population growth has been widely criticized in view of the historical developments of the past century. It is obvious that, while in western Europe the population has increased notably, the rate of increase has not been greater but actually less than that of the food supply available. This does not necessarily invalidate the so-called Malthusian law, but it does point to other factors at work in the actual situation, most notably scientific agriculture and the artificial preservation of food. In fact, a careful statement of the law would immediately throw many of the criticisms out of court. For example, sudden and extensive increases in food supply cannot instantaneously lead to equal increases in the population.

Obviously, Malthus's law was intended to apply to a given population within a definite area. If the boundaries of the area are changed, as has been the case with Russia, the United States, or the British Empire, it must naturally take some time for numbers to reach what might be called the "saturation point."[2] The same qualification is obviously true when one considers the new sources of food supply from outside, such as modern transportation has made possible. Moreover, increasing wants and a higher standard of living tend to bring into play the voluntary abstention or "moral restraint" that reduces the birth rate. Finally, increasing knowledge of birth control and sterilization has led to restriction of the size of an increasing number of families without "moral restraint" or abstention in the Malthusian sense.

[1] Malthus has been subjected to a good deal of unfair and irrelevant criticism by those who have not taken the pains to read his doctrines with care. He has been alleged to hold that the food supply actually increases at an arithmetic ratio. Then it is pointed out that the food supply often fails to grow at any such ratio. Malthus's real statements on this point seem well within the bounds of accuracy. See H. P. Fairchild, *General Sociology,* Wiley, 1934, pp. 340-41.

[2] The alleged food surplus in the United States today is cited by some as a disproof of Malthus's ideas. But Mr. Robert Doane has shown that, even when judged on the basis of 1929 production, we had no general food surplus but actually imported billions of pounds of food. Out of twelve basic classes of foods consumed, we had a shortage in eight in 1929, on the basis of home production. See his "But Is It a Surplus Economy?" *New Outlook,* August, 1934. The root of the trouble is that the inequitable distribution of wealth does not give the masses enough money with which to buy the food they really need. Messrs. Leven, Moulton, and Warburton have shown that in 1929 three-fourths of American families did not have enough income to "provide an adequate diet at moderate cost," while nine-tenths of the families lacked an income sufficient to provide themselves with a liberal diet.

What the Neo-Malthusians too often overlook, however, is that the biological and food-producing issues are today complicated by the inequalities of social income and the inability of the masses to get money enough to buy the food which actually exists in abundance. Men starve or go hungry in the midst of plenty—indeed, even in the face of the deliberate destruction of food which cannot be sold at a profit. It is quite possible that population increases may go on to a point where, even in an equitable and efficient economy, men could not produce enough food to eat. But in advanced economic civilizations today, the food problem is mainly one of getting the income with which to buy available supplies, rather than any actual shortage of food. It is more a problem of securing purchasing power for adequate consumption than one of production.[1]

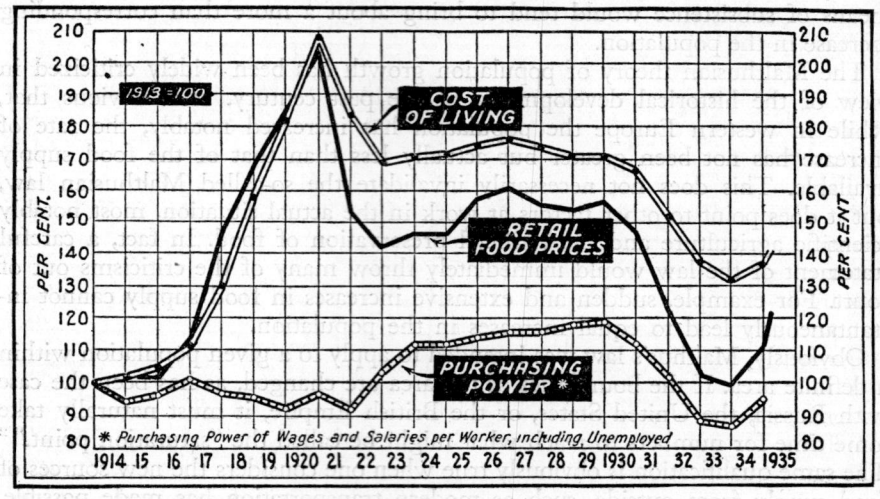

PURCHASING POWER AND FOOD AND LIVING COSTS [2]

While the nineteenth century was notable for population growth, the twentieth century has brought a marked decrease in the birth rate in many of the northwestern European countries as well as in America—so marked that some of these populations are scarcely more than reproducing themselves even with a constantly lowering death rate.[3] In France the population is almost static; in England, Germany, and the United States it promises to reach a static point within thirty years or so. As has been pointed out by a number of observers, particularly Dublin and Kuczynski,[4] it is in the highly industrialized countries that the birth rate has fallen off most rapidly. It may turn out that in-

---

[1] Cf. Leven, Moulton, and Warburton, *America's Capacity to Consume*.

[2] "Why People Cannot Get Food Today," New York *Times*, Mar. 10, 1935.

[3] Thompson, *op. cit.*, Chaps. VIII, XII, XXII; and *Recent Social Trends in the United States*, McGraw-Hill, 1933, 2 vols., Vol. I, Chap. I.

[4] Cf. R. R. Kuczynski, *The Balance of Births and Deaths*, Brookings Institution, 1928-31, Vol. I-II; and Conrado Gini and others, *Population*, University of Chicago Press, 1930, pp. 283 ff.

MODERN INDUSTRIALISM AND POPULATION TRENDS

dustrialization is associated first with marked population increases and then with a trend towards decrease and stabilization.[1]

A few figures on this situation will prove illuminating. The differential rate of population increase among the various continents of the world is revealed by the figures giving the percentage of net annual increase per 1,000, 1900-30: Europe, 7.8; Asia, 4.8; Africa, 0.3; North America, 15.6; South America, 26.3; Oceania, 16.8. For Europe, representative statistics of the percentages of net annual population increase per 1,000 are as follows: England and Wales (1929), 2.9; France (1929), —0.3; Germany (1929), 5.3; Italy (1929), 9.1; Poland (1929), 15.2; Russia (1927), 21.5. The rate for the Balkan countries averages about 16 per 1,000. In France, in 1931 the net natural increase of population—the excess of births over deaths—was only 46,639. In England, in 1932 it was 129,889. In Germany, in 1931 the net increase was some 305,525, with a birth rate about one-half what it was in 1901-05. Poland, with a population of approximately one-half that of Germany, had a net population increase of 470,000 in 1931. Italy, with a population intermediate between that of Germany and Poland, boasted a net increase of 417,000 in 1931. Russia gained 3,000,000 in 1931 as a result of net population increase, indicating that the new and more liberal sex ethics in that land [2] does not militate against reproduction. The map opposite p. 420 makes clear these notable inequalities in population growth in Europe today.

This differential in birth rate in Europe and Asia may have broad political consequences. If the population becomes static or actually decreases in certain countries, while it grows rapidly in others, the states with a growing population are likely to become relatively stronger in a military sense—unless the methods of warfare are so changed that mere numbers count for little.[3]

The political and military effects of the marked changes that are taking place in the rate of population growth receive frequent expression in speeches and print—most of us are familiar, for instance, with Mussolini's exhortations to Italians to prove their patriotism by producing children, preferably male children. From a social and cultural point of view, however, a falling birth rate is not only to be expected; it is, in reality, highly desirable at the present time. The hope of raising the general standard of living and of improving the quality of population is tied up with a reduction in the rate of population increase in areas where stabilization is not already imminent.[4]

Until conscious and artificial methods of controlling and limiting the population are widely and successfully adopted, the population of many areas may continue to press upon the means of subsistence, whatever the degree of development of technical efficiency in modern productive enterprise. Particularly does Malthus's contention seem valid if one broadens his doctrine somewhat and takes into consideration the higher standards of living that have been sought by the working classes in the last hundred years.[5] It has proved ex-

---

[1] Cf. F. H. Hankins, "Does Advancing Civilization Involve a Decline in Natural Fertility?" American Sociological Society, *Publications*, Vol. XXIV, No. 2, pp. 115-22.
[2] Including the utmost freedom in birth-control information and methods.
[3] See Thompson, *op. cit.*, Chap. XXII; and *Danger Spots in World Population*, Knopf, 1929.
[4] Cf. Thompson, *Population Problems*, Chaps. XX, XXIV-XXV.
[5] Cf. W. S. Thompson, *Population: A Study in Malthusianism*, Columbia University Press, 1915.

tremely difficult to prevent the population from increasing more rapidly than it has been possible to raise the standard of living for the working classes. Where the population has not pressed so harshly upon the sheer means of subsistence, it has invariably tended to exert pressure upon the standard of living. Some form of birth control must well become, as one writer has described it, "the pivot of civilization."[1] This is the point which many sociologists most persistently suggest to modify or supplement the Socialist contention that the only serious defect in modern industrial and social life lies in the private ownership of property and the means of producing wealth. Yet technicians make a very strong case in their contention that it is the low income permitted to the masses under contemporary capitalism, and the wastes of capitalism in production for profit, which create the low existing living-standards. If our production in industry and agriculture were expanded to the highest degree compatible with scientific knowledge and the resulting product equitably divided, an unprecedently high standard of living could be immediately realized. Economic practices restrain human betterment even more than does population growth.

Professor E. M. East points out that many eugenicists, failing to take a broad view of population problems, have generally concentrated their attention on insuring a reduction of the birth rate among the defectives and an increase among the better classes. As a matter of fact, says East, "the really useful eugenics is properly directed birth control, and the only practical directive agent is education." In many countries the birth rate needs to be reduced with increasing rapidity among all biologically inferior and economically dependent classes of the population. But this can hardly be expected to occur voluntarily save as the result of fairly pressing economic necessity, especially among that large fraction of the population which lacks either the intelligence to make the proper adjustment to modern life, or the knowledge without which no adequate adjustment can be made. Such knowledge "is not wanting," concludes Professor East, "but it is a serious question whether there is the required amount of that type of ability which will make a sustained effort to apply it."[2]

Because the rate of population growth is at present falling off in some of the older countries of western Europe and in the United States, certain biologists and statisticians, especially those in the employ of life-insurance companies, which naturally favor a high birth rate, have argued that we are in danger of underpopulation and race suicide.[3] These writers fail to make clear that the rate of population growth is still increasing even in a large part of Europe. Europe and the United States are, moreover, but a small part of the earth, so far as population is concerned. The backward peoples with low standards of living still have an enormous birth rate. If China were to keep its present birth rate, and at the same time could adopt medical methods that would reduce the staggering death rate, that country alone could overpopulate the planet in a century. If all the ships that sail the seven seas were devoted

---

[1] M. H. Sanger, *The Pivot of Civilization*, Brentano's, 1922.
[2] *Cf.* E. M. East, *Mankind at the Cross-Roads*, Scribner, 1923.
[3] *Cf.* Jerome Davis and H. E. Barnes, eds., *Readings in Sociology,* Heath, 1927, pp. 430-41.

DENSITY AND GROWTH OF POPULATION IN EUROPE

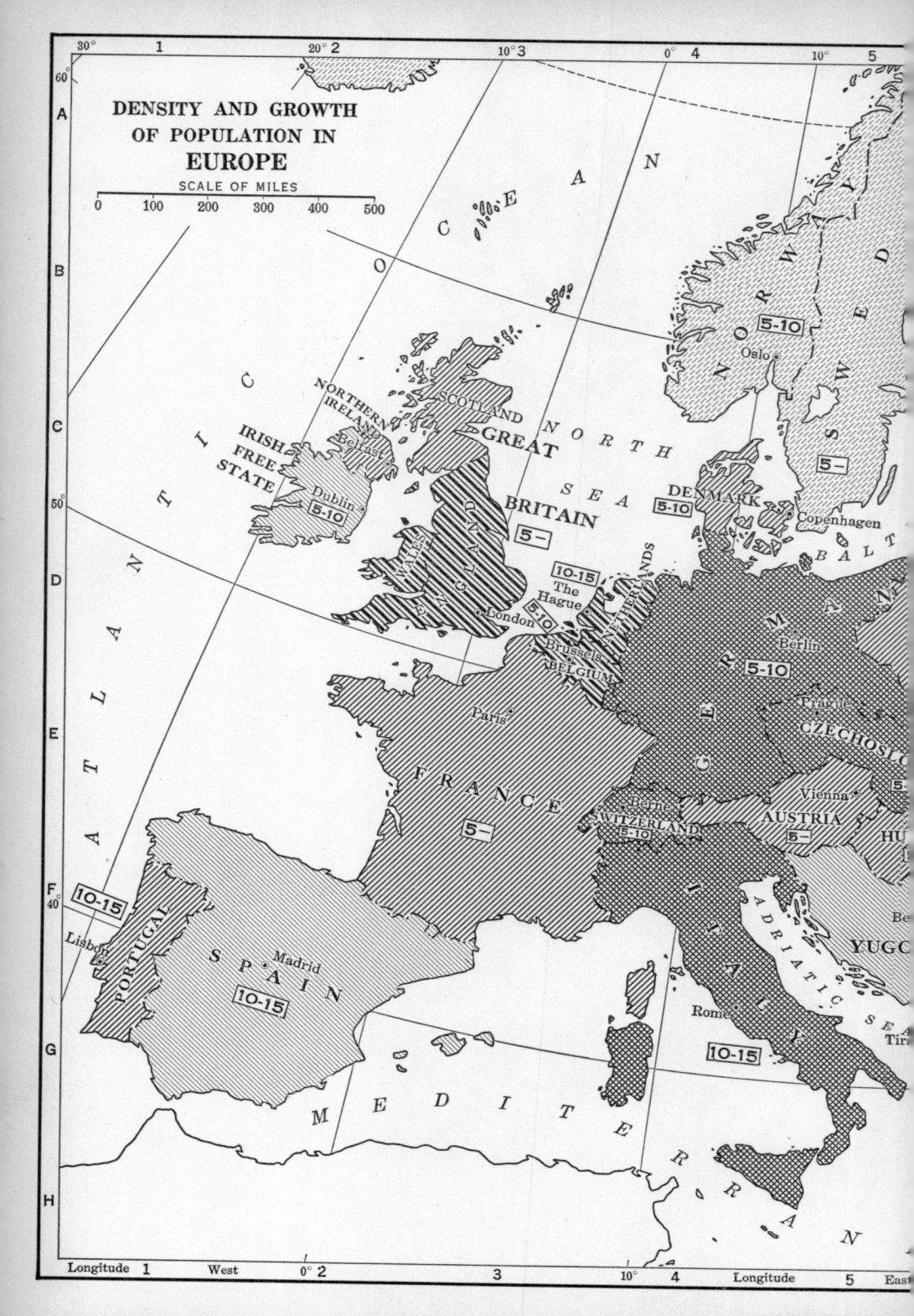

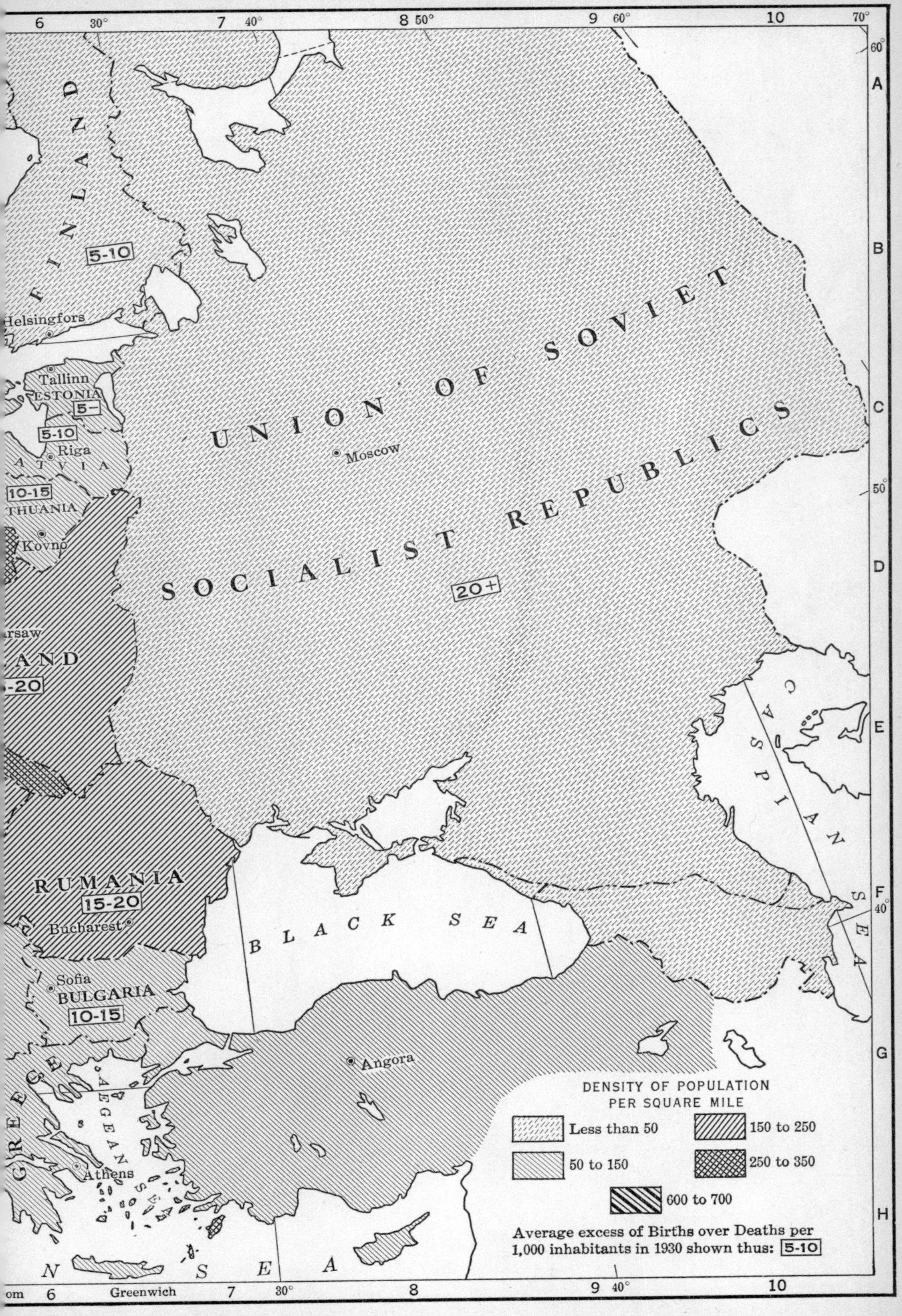

FINLAND
5-10
Helsingfors
Tallinn
ESTONIA
5−
5-10
Riga
ATVIA
10-15
THUANIA
Kovno
arsaw
AND
-20
UNION OF SOVIET SOCIALIST REPUBLICS
Moscow
20+
CASPIAN SEA
RUMANIA
15-20
Bucharest
BLACK SEA
Sofia
BULGARIA
10-15
Angora
GREECE
AEGEAN SEA
Athens
DENSITY OF POPULATION PER SQUARE MILE
Less than 50
50 to 150
150 to 250
250 to 350
600 to 700
Average excess of Births over Deaths per 1,000 inhabitants in 1930 shown thus: 5-10
Greenwich

H OF POPULATION

solely to this purpose, they could not carry away to foreign shores the Chinese infants that are born each year. So far, at least, the facts favor Professor East's thesis rather than that of the scare-mongers who would have us believe that the world is in real danger of depopulation.[1] At the present rate of population increase, Professor East predicts a population for the world of 5,000,000,000 in the year 2000 A.D.

3. THE MODERN IMMIGRATION PROBLEM

The age-long process of folk migration manifests itself today in the form of immigration. We have witnessed a steady trickle of peoples to the regions where the economic conditions of the working classes are reputed to be the best. The major movement since 1865 has been from Europe and Asia to the United States and South America.

The chief cause of this migration to the United States has been the attraction of the more highly developed economy and the more fluid social structure. Mechanical industry and the factory system have there offered far greater opportunities for steady and profitable employment than the more backward agricultural countries of Europe, particularly of central and eastern Europe, where the immigrant peoples were born. Free or cheap land has also been an incentive to bring immigrants both to the United States and to South America.

To a considerable extent, the hoped-for economic advantages to immigrants coming from one of these more backward countries have been vindicated by actual experience. Many, to be sure, have been induced to leave their native land on the basis of quite erroneous stories as to the rapidity with which wealth may be accumulated in countries like the United States. A book like Mary Antin's *The Promised Land*[2] admirably illustrates this point. In other cases, most unscrupulous methods have been used by steamship companies and others to attract immigrants to the United States, in order that profit might be made from passenger fares or from commissions paid by American contractors who have desired cheap European labor for their enterprises. Some legislation was passed in 1885 and thereafter to check this evil, though it has never been entirely eliminated. The main regions from which the immigrants came into the United States and other American areas during the first half of the nineteenth century were Great Britain, Ireland, and Germany. Since the Civil War, however, the largest volume of immigration has come from the southern, central, and eastern European areas, mainly as a result of adverse economic conditions in these European districts. In these latter regions, the immigration was at first heaviest from Italy, though more recently the majority of those who came to America hailed from Russia and mid-Europe.

Obscured though it is by other more local movements, the migration from Europe overseas has been an outstanding example of population shift after the rise of the factory system. The numbers leaving Europe between the sixteenth century and the early nineteenth were insignificant when compared to the later phase of the exodus from that continent. For example, 1,285,349 peo-

---

[1] *Cf.* Thompson, *Population Problems*, Chap. xxv.   [2] Houghton Mifflin, 1912.

ple left Europe for the United States in the single year 1907—a number approximately equal to the total population of the English colonies in America in 1725. From 1904 to 1914, no less than 10,000,000 immigrants came into the United States from Europe, or more than twice the population of the United States at the time of the adoption of the Constitution. A German social economist, Alexander Supan, estimated that during the nineteenth century 31,500,000 Europeans emigrated overseas.[1] This estimate is assuredly too low, because no less than 35,000,000 Europeans have come to the United States alone since 1820. The more usual figure for European migration from 1800 to 1914 is something over 50,000,000.

It has been frequently argued that we do not get the best European types from their respective countries as a result of contemporary immigration, but secure, rather, the less desirable types from the standpoint of both biological and sociological conditions.[2] This is probably in part a popular prejudice. The general history of immigration inclines the social historian to believe that almost invariably the more alert types tend to migrate, leaving behind them the more indolent and docile, though a considerable number of roving, restless, criminal spirits must incidentally find their way into the body of immigrants. Yet it is certainly true that the relative number of criminals and representatives of the lowest strata among the Europeans who migrate today is not so great as it was in the period of American settlement from 1600 to 1776.[3] Then the deported criminals and the indentured servants formed one of the largest elements in the stream of immigrants coming to the colonies. The question of European immigration into the United States is one that must be settled upon its merits, in the light of the relative need for more non-native labor and new racial types at any particular time. In other words, the matter should be dealt with on strictly sociological and scientific grounds, rather than upon the basis of race prejudice or doubtful dogmas.

There has been much discussion by sociologists and economists as to the net results of immigration. It would seem that, in general, the countries from which the immigrants have come have profited very little by the temporary release of the pressure of the population on the means of subsistence. The population losses through emigration have been made up by an immediate increase in the birth rate or the average of survival. It may safely be stated that it is doubtful if any European country, with the possible exception of Ireland, has been decreased notably in population through emigration. Therefore the rather common humanitarian argument that immigration ought to be tolerated by the country to which immigrants come, on the ground that it improves the living-conditions in the countries from which they came, is fallacious and superficial.

As to the results of immigration upon the country to which immigrants come, it seems certain that the process has been on the whole beneficial. Most of the advanced culture areas outside of Europe owe their superior condition in part to the fact that they have been populated by Europeans. It is almost a platitude to remark that all that separates the United States from a culture of

---

[1] See Ogg and Sharp, *The Economic Development of Modern Europe*, p. 337.
[2] *Cf.* W. C. Abbott, *The New Barbarians*, Little, Brown, 1925.   [3] See above, p. 213.

roving Indians is the process of immigration. At the same time, there is no doubt that immigrants may come too rapidly to allow them to be safely and adequately assimilated in the native population and that immigration may bring in altogether too divergent types to make full ultimate assimilation at all feasible. Particularly is this true when either Negro or Mongolian types are brought into a white population that has active race prejudices against intermixture.

When we come to the matter of the mixture of various branches of the white race, the problem is chiefly one of cultural assimilation and adjustment. There can be little doubt of the advantages coming from the immigration of any white type into an oversea area, provided the immigrants represent a level above the average of the native group, and provided there is a real need for a more rapid increase of the population than would be possible as a result of an excess of births over deaths. It must be said, however, that the population of the United States had reached a point by 1910 where immigration, if continued for many years at its old rate, would inevitably have forced down the American standard of living.

It is also very probable that countries like the United States have suffered severely from the coming of too great numbers of divergent cultural types, especially since about 1885. It has been contended by many writers that this overrapid immigration has tended to debase both the cultural and the economic level of the American population. This is essentially the thesis of Professor E. A. Ross's book on *The Old World in the New*.[1] On the other hand, however, Dr. Isaac A. Hourwich, in his work on *Immigration and Labor*,[2] has taken the point of view that the immigrant laborer has not debased the American standard of living or been willing to accept lower wages than the general run of American labor. Probably the most judicious appraisal of the impact of immigration on American culture and social life, backed by ample factual material, is contained in Professor H. P. Fairchild's definitive work *Immigration*. Here the social benefits of immigration are fully admitted and its dangers and abuses clearly pointed out.

This marked increase of emigration from the Old World has brought up sharply the problem of regulating or restricting the resulting immigration to the New. Any state has both the right and the duty to restrict immigration to that point which allows complete assimilation, social, economic, and cultural, as well as to exclude immigrants when the population has become adequate for the needs of the country. Restrictive regulations should aim at a selective immigration, which will admit the best types as measured by physical, mental, and cultural tests. Discrimination based upon racial dogmas and in no sense truly selective, such as governs contemporary American regulations, is highly dubious from both the scientific and the diplomatic standpoint. In 1921 the United States adopted a quota law restricting the entry of immigrants on the basis of the number of each nationality in the country in 1910 (later changed to 1890). In 1929 we adopted the "National Origins Plan" and limited the total immigration to 150,000 annually. No effort was made to provide for

---

[1] Century, 1914. More savage is the attack on immigration and recent immigrants by Abbott. *op. cit.*   [2] Viking Press, 1922.

a rigorous selection of superior types.[1] Since 1929 there has been an extensive deportation of aliens, especially radicals, from American shores.[2]

III. THE TRIUMPH OF THE BOURGEOISIE

Another major social result of the growth of modern industry has been the widespread triumph of the bourgeoisie in its struggle for power against the old agrarian vested interests. This means that the new capitalist, manufacturer, and merchant have very often secured a position of economic and political ascendancy, to which, in some countries, has been added social supremacy as well.

This happened quickly in the United States, which never had any considerable landed gentry except in the slaveholding South. This Southern gentry was ruined as a result of the Civil War. At the other extreme, free land long provided an avenue of escape for the industrial worker who found himself overdisciplined or oppressed. Hence a class-conscious American labor movement started relatively late and resistance to the bourgeoisie was delayed.

In England, the presence of both a deeply rooted landed upper class and a working class that was early pressed into a defensive solidarity against the new bourgeois-capitalist group retarded the latter's advance to acknowledged social leadership during the nineteenth century.[3] The situation was further confused by occasional opportunist alliances between the landed and working classes against their common rival, the bourgeoisie. Interestingly enough, most of Britain's advanced labor legislation in its earlier stages was the work of the conservative landlords. The bourgeois liberals, in turn, in order to bid for working-class support, without which they could not obtain control of legislation, were forced from 1905 to 1914 into a program of social reform quite at variance with their original laissez-faire economic ideas.[4]

English economic classes have taken on a new orientation during the twentieth century. The bourgeoisie and the landed aristocracy have gradually become fused through the purchase of estates by successful business men, intermarriage, the entrance of younger sons of country families into business, and the ennobling of middle-class families for economic services. Moreover, both the landed aristocracy and the middle class recognized a common threat in an aggressive working-class group, which escaped the tutelage of both older parties and actually formed a short-lived Labor government in 1924.

In Germany, the old landed aristocracy held its own with the bourgeoisie and forced the latter into a compromise.[5] Here also, aggressive popular groups took shape. For a time after the World War the bourgeoisie made notable concessions to the proletariat, but in 1933 they resorted to Fascism to suppress working-class movements altogether. In Russia and Hungary, little affected by

[1] Cf. W. A. Hamm and Oscar Dombrow, *Current Problems in American History*, College Entrance Book Co., 1933, pp. 70-74.
[2] See J. P. Clark, *The Deportation of Aliens from the United States to Europe*, Columbia University Press, 1931.
[3] Cf. O. F. Christie, *The Transition from Aristocracy, 1832-1867*, Putnam, 1928.
[4] Cf. L. T. Hobhouse, *Liberalism*, Holt, 1911; and C. J. H. Hayes, *British Social Politics*, Ginn, 1913.
[5] Cf. G. P. Gooch, *Germany*, Scribner, 1925, Chaps. III-IV, XIII, XVI; and C. B. Hoover, *Germany Enters the Third Reich*, Macmillan, 1933.

the Industrial Revolution before 1900, the old landlord class remained in the saddle until lower-class revolutions after 1917 very markedly altered the class situations in both countries. The landlords in postwar Hungary have now definitely reëstablished their power while in Russia they have been permanently ousted along with the bourgeoisie.

The winning of the war and the power wielded by great financial and industrial interests in politics have given the bourgeoisie an apparent supremacy in France, though they are jealously watched by the peasants, who form over half the population, and are counterbalanced by very determined proletarian and landlord groups. Italy has gone over frankly to Fascism.

In earlier days (1500-1800) the bourgeoisie were generally known as the "middle class"—intermediate between landlords and the peasantry. Today, where they have actually triumphed they usually constitute the "upper class." Where their ascendancy is not absolute the great industrialists and financiers join with the landed aristocracy in constituting the upper class.

In the United States the upper bourgeoisie constitute the only upper class that we have.[1] A new middle class is now being constituted out of professional men, the governmental bureaucracy, the salaried commercial groups, and the relatively solvent farmers.[2] This class is coming to be known even here as the "petite bourgeoisie." The proletariat or "lower" class is made up of the factory workers, miners, and other laborers, urban and rural. With the depression of farming, many of the agricultural classes are now being forced down to the level of quasi-servility. They will probably take their place in the proletariat along with the agricultural laborers, who are already thus classified.[3]

This split in the bourgeois ranks, largely determined by relative wealth, is today coloring our economic and political policy. The great masters of finance and monopoly capitalism support the old doctrine of governmental nonintervention, however much they may themselves unite to control finance, markets, and production and thus destroy true competition. They are opposed to extensive state supervision of economic affairs, though desperate economic straits may force them to make temporary concessions, as in 1933 in the United States. On the other hand, the new middle class or petite bourgeoisie, while not willing to go the whole way to Socialism, demands that the State shall step in and insure greater economic well-being and a more equitable division of the social income.[4] This group furnished a powerful backing for Mussolini and Hitler, and it was directly responsible for the great popular majority given to Franklin D. Roosevelt in 1932.

[1] *Cf.* Hoffman Nickerson, *The American Rich*, Doubleday, Doran, 1930, Pt. I.
[2] *Cf.* A. N. Holcombe, *The New Party Politics*, Norton, 1933, Chaps. IV-V; John Corbin, *The Return of the Middle Class*, Scribner, 1922; and W. B. Pitkin, *Capitalism Carries On*, McGraw-Hill, 1935.
[3] While these class divisions in the United States actually exist, they have not yet fully emerged in the form of class consciousness. The upper bourgeoisie, of course, recognizes and admits its status, but the lower middle class and the proletariat in the United States have not as yet been able to recognize or willing to admit their inferior status in our society. There has been a persistent tradition in this country, partly born of the frontier spirit, that there are no well-defined social and economic classes here and that every son of a laborer or small farmer is theoretically on his way to a bank presidency or to a position as an important industrial executive. While it is still possible to rise from the lowest to the highest economic class, the examples of so doing are far less frequent than they were even a half-century ago, and the class divisions described above are very real today.
[4] See Holcombe, *op. cit*, Chaps. IV-V.

Another break within capitalism is already becoming apparent, namely, the conflict between speculative finance and productive business.[1] The stock-market crash, the bank holiday, the Senate investigation of the great investment bankers in 1933-34, the collapse of some of the best-known investment houses and real-estate promoters, and other comparable episodes have served to emphasize the conflict between the interests of speculative financiers on the one hand and productive industrialists and business men on the other. Speculative finance profits most from instability and uncertainty, while business benefits from stability and predictability in the economic world. Speculative finance resents any reduction of purely financial gains, however necessary to economic health. Industry and business must insure ample wage payments and other measures designed to increase mass purchasing power. Otherwise, factories shut down and stores cease to do business. The most potent source of opposition between the interests of finance capitalism and those of industrial capitalism has come about as a result of the rise of the supercorporation and the holding company. By means of the latter and associated devices, a few insiders, with but slight ownership of stock, can dominate the management of the vast concern. Whatever they can appropriate as the result of mismanagement and manipulation is essentially all theirs, while their returns from dividends secured through efficient management are a relatively slight proportion of the whole body of dividends. Hence there is every incentive to inside manipulation and ultimate danger of wrecking the concern. This virtual robbery has been safely legalized through the intricacies of corporation-law practice. Not even in feudal days did lawful pillage exist on so vast a scale. In this way, finance devours business and undermines the whole capitalistic system.

Therefore, while most of the attention to the alleged class struggle in contemporary society has been devoted to the conflict between industrialists and their employees—who are theoretically allies under any sound theory of capitalism, since goods must be sold to those who earn wages—the really active and crucial conflict today is that between finance and industry, between finance capitalism and industrial capitalism. And finance capitalism has struck far heavier blows at the integrity and prosperity of industry and productive business than all the proletarians combined. Moreover, if capitalism disintegrates in our time, it will probably be a result of this subtle but effective looting from within by speculative finance rather than the product of outside attacks from the proletariat.[2]

The contributions and services of the bourgeoisie to society since 1750 form a subject that is warmly debated,[3] the radicals representing the bourgeoisie as ruthless exploiters, but admitting that they performed a service in overthrowing feudalism. In fairness, one would have to concede that the great industrial improvements which characterize contemporary society we owe in part to the bourgeois class.[4] It must not be forgotten, however, that we are even more

---

[1] See D. C. Coyle, *The Irrepressible Conflict: Business vs. Finance*, privately printed, 1932; J. T. Flynn, *Graft in Business*, Vanguard Press, 1931, and *Security Speculation*, Harcourt, Brace, 1934. See also below, Chap. xxi.   [2] See below, pp. 822 ff.
[3] *Cf.* Josephson, *The Robber Barons*, and Gustavus Myers, *History of the Great American Fortunes*, Kerr, 1910, 3 vols.
[4] *Cf.* M. H. Dobb, *Capitalist Enterprise and Social Progress*, London, 1925.

indebted to the scientists, engineers, and inventors than we are to the promoters and financiers who have exploited their technical discoveries and improvements.[1]

Whether the present alliance between financial resources on the one hand and the managerial and engineering brains on the other is temporary or permanent is still guesswork. Socialists claim that the latter can, should, and will be detached from the financial group and aligned with the workers, when society is reorganized. This has actually been achieved, albeit partially by force, in Russia. Technocracy especially urges the divorce of engineering genius from the profit system.[2] The Industrial Revolution is still too near us, and the class lines that it produced are still too chaotic, to permit any final judgment as to the social order that will result after the great forces which have been released have had time to shake society down to some sort of equilibrium.

IV. THE PROLETARIAN CHALLENGE TO CAPITALISM

While the bourgeoisie were still struggling with the landlords for control of the European governments, their own ascendancy was challenged from the other side by the rising proletarian element brought forth by the Industrial Revolution. The working classes—then living mostly in the country—had been scattered, illiterate, and generally docile down to the Industrial Revolution. Only when deeply stirred by the grossest abuses did they attempt any concerted action on a large scale, as for example in the sporadic peasants' revolts of medieval and early modern times. The Industrial Revolution concentrated many workers in relatively small areas. Here they were thrown together in large numbers daily and subjected to common abuses. A considerable solidarity and no little unanimity of opinion and class aspirations thus developed among the workers.

With the growth of capitalism and the concentration of control in business, it was inevitable that a sharper differentiation than ever before should arise between capital and labor. Under the guild system, the apprentices and journeymen in many crafts expected as a matter of course to rise to the status of master. The separation of employers and workers into distinct classes was much more marked under the putting-out system, but the talented and ambitious worker still had a very good chance of rising to the position of a merchant capitalist.

With the development of the machine technique and the factory system, so great an investment was required to establish and conduct an industry that only in the most unusual circumstances could a laborer hope to rise to the position of a prominent manufacturer or merchant. More and more, the classes that controlled manufacturing and commercial activities became specialized, exclusive, and sharply differentiated from labor. There was little solicitude for the poor among the new urban bourgeoisie, who were bent upon ever larger profits.

---

[1] *Cf.* F. W. Taussig, *Inventors and Money-Makers*, Macmillan, 1915; and H. S. Hatfield, *The Inventor and His World*, Dutton, 1933. For a very comprehensive exposition of how big business, dominated by the profit motive, often retards the progress of applied science and more efficient machines, see Felix Frazer, "Big Business Smashes the Machine: How Inventions Are Sabotaged" and "Business Smashes the Machine: Inventor's Dilemma, Capitalism's Iniquity, Society's Loss," *Common Sense*, October-November, 1934.

[2] See Frank Arkright, *The A B C of Technocracy*, Harper, 1933.

As Professor H. J. Laski has laconically remarked: "The poor were consigned to a God whose dictates were by definition beneficent; and if they failed to understand the curious incidence of his rewards that was because his ways were inscrutable." [1]

The industrial proletariat was greatly increased in numbers by the Industrial Revolution and became more distinct, more specific, and more dependent upon capital.[2] Concentrated in cities and held to a rigid schedule of hours, the workers found it impossible to eke out their living by agriculture, hunting, or fishing. In such countries as the United States, free land furnished a possible escape from factory conditions so long as the frontier lasted. But this safety valve is no longer operative. Widespread and prolonged unemployment would mean for the average factory worker nothing short of sheer starvation unless the state stepped in to administer relief.

This extreme dependence of labor upon capital has been denounced by the more radical working-class elements as an unjust and unnecessary type of servility that must be speedily done away with. Their contention, however, that the ultimate form of industrial organization shall be one in which labor will control all the processes and policies of production and distribution is, so far at least, little more than vague aspiration and an optimistic prophecy. Outside of Russia, the urban worker is still almost entirely dependent upon enterprises maintained by private capital.

Through various forms of protective activity, such as the growth of labor organizations, modern industrial workers have sought to improve their condition, mitigate the effects of unemployment, and share as much as possible in the product of their work.[3] So far, their success has been chiefly in the way of amelioration of working-conditions, little of a positive nature having been done outside of Russia to alter the worker's dependence upon the means of production owned and controlled by others.

The earlier capitalists were greatly influenced by the eighteenth-century notion of a "natural order," which, in economic matters, was believed to imply a régime of unlimited competition. Even the French revolutionaries had this conviction. They abolished the relatively light quitrents that had held over from the manorial order and preserved the much more oppressive *métayer* system because the latter represented contracts entered into by the tenants.

In this economic atmosphere, the employer tended to look upon labor in an impersonal manner—as little more than a commodity entering into the processes of manufacturing and commercial activity. Obliging economists informed employers that only a fixed and limited sum—the "wage fund"—could be diverted to labor without ending profits and ruining industry. This gave the employer an apparent scientific vindication of his avarice and selfishness. Preoccupied with his efforts to accumulate capital and secure pecuniary profit, he did not seem to comprehend that the free competition which he demanded for himself clashed essentially with the restrictive measures inherited from the older order that he wished to impose upon the lower classes. So many of the

---

[1] Laski, *Political Thought in England from Locke to Bentham*, p. 307.
[2] *Cf. Recent Social Trends*, Vol. II, Chap. xvi.
[3] See below, pp. 949 ff.; and Frank Tannenbaum, *The Labor Movement*, Putnam, 1921, Pt. I.

new urban workers were recruited from the poorer type of peasants, accustomed to servility and recently shorn of their lands, that there was at first astonishingly little resistance from below to the oppressive policies of the capitalist employers. The workers could accept abuse and low wages or starve.

However, the laboring classes began to conceive of the possible value of the vote, in order that they might influence public policy and pass legislation which would better their lot. Especially irritating were the laws in all European countries at the opening of the nineteenth century forbidding workers to unite in any way to match their collective bargaining strength against that of their employers, which was increasing with the size of business units. Obviously, the right of an individual to quit work is useless to him unless he can get a job elsewhere. When one man out of a force of five hundred or five thousand quits work by himself he has no coercive influence upon the employer, whose plant continues to operate just as before. On the employer's side, however, lay the effective power to close the plant and throw the whole five hundred or five thousand out of work. Without either the vote or the right to combine, the worker could not force either industry or the state to lessen the risks of injury and unemployment or to grant a living wage.

Therefore, one of the leading political aspirations of the proletariat during the nineteenth century was the realization of universal suffrage. At the opening of the century, the masses were everywhere deprived of suffrage; at its close they had gained this right in almost every Western country.[1]

The general legalization of unions and associations of workingmen, which had begun in the twenties, was roughly associated with the extension of the suffrage. The first law legalizing unionism in England was the work of Francis Place and Joseph Hume, two members of the group of Philosophical Radicals who were interested in widening the suffrage. Only a year after the vote was first given to a large group of English workers in 1867 a concession was made to unionism in the establishment of a trade-union council. Seven years later (1875) the conspiracy laws were practically withdrawn. Associations were first legalized in Germany in 1868, but unionism was pretty sharply repressed until a more liberal policy was introduced by William II after 1890. A French law of 1791 had prohibited all labor combinations, but a good deal of surreptitious association took place even before 1848, when universal manhood suffrage was established by law. Reaction set in under Louis Napoleon, and strikes were not made legal until 1864. The right of labor to organize was finally legalized by the Syndicat law of 1884. To give two more examples: the Austrian unions were legalized in 1869, following the new liberal constitution of December, 1867; and unions were made lawful in Italy in 1912, though they had long been in existence. Unionism was not widely encouraged in Russia before the Revolution of 1917. Then unionism was gladly embodied in the structure of the proletarian state. There were no longer any private employers to oppose unions.

Working-class influence has permeated practically every department of the economic policies of modern states, from industrial legislation and social-insurance schemes to taxation. It is impossible to estimate the exact impact of the

[1] See below, pp. 489 ff.

labor vote, primarily because it has rarely been exerted alone or along purely class lines. Measures protecting the workers in various ways have certainly gone ahead much faster than would have been possible without this proletarian unrest. For example, even the German program of social insurance was undertaken by Bismarck largely to placate the masses, and thus stave off an alignment by economic classes that might have produced far more radical changes. This whole question of social reform will be dealt with in some detail later.[1]

In spite of the tremendous numerical preponderance of workers, universal suffrage has not yet led to working-class rule outside of Russia. At the furthest, it has produced a balance of power between the various conflicting groups. This suggests either that there is not a laboring-class majority or that the majority does not rule. Obviously, society is not simply and sharply divided into two classes, "labor" and "capital," as some students appear to believe.[2] The truckman who owns his own vehicle and hires a helper is in a sense a capitalist, though he works with his hands. Even workers for wages or salaries often own shares of the capital stock of corporations, or get part of their income from interest on bonds. Employees in responsible positions, such as cashiers in banks, are often expected to own stock. Those who work with their hands by no means form a homogeneous group. They have their own hierarchies, from the highly paid, unionized specialists, such as the locomotive engineers, down to the common or unskilled laborers. Practically the same is true of capitalists, who range from the moguls of speculative finance, the great captains of industry, and inheritors of huge fortunes down to the widow who lives entirely but very modestly on the income from her corporate securities. The manner in which the petite bourgeoisie shade into the proletariat, as well as the many divisions of the latter, is well brought out in the following classification of the so-called gainful workers in the United States:

GAINFUL WORKERS IN THE UNITED STATES CLASSIFIED INTO SOCIAL-ECONOMIC GROUPS: 1920 TO 1930 [3]

Census Year	1930 Number	1930 Percentage	1920 Number	1920 Percentage
1. Professional Persons	2,945,797	6.0	2,050,163	4.9
2. Proprietors, Managers, etc.	9,665,540	19.8	9,180,583	22.1
2a Farmers (owners, tenants)	6,012,012	12.3	6,387,360	15.3
2b Wholesale and Retail Merchants	1,787,047	3.7	1,401,849	3.4
2c Other Owners, and Managers	1,866,481	3.8	1,391,374	3.3
3. Clerks and Kindred Workers	7,949,455	16.3	5,704,970	13.7
4. Skilled Workers	6,282,687	12.9	5,570,602	13.4
5. Semiskilled Workers	7,977,572	16.3	6,638,615	16.0
6. Unskilled Workers	14,008,869	28.7	12,469,316	30.0
Total	48,829,920	100.0	41,614,248	100.0

[1] See below, Chap. xxiv.
[2] Cf. T. N. Carver, *The Present Economic Revolution in the United States*, Little, Brown, 1925; and Anewrin Williams, *Co-partnership and Profit-sharing*, Holt, 1913.
[3] Condensed from A. M. Edwards, "Social-Economic Grouping of Gainful Workers," *Journal of the American Statistical Association*, Vol. 28 (1933), p. 383.

Critics of the present social order often charge it with being undemocratic because the bourgeoisie wield an influence in economic and political matters out of all proportion to their numbers.[1] This condition seems to be inseparable from a régime of private property. In practice it is usually impossible to draw a line between politics and economics. A very large proportion of the activities of governments, local and otherwise, consists in regulating and protecting the economic order. It is also obvious that it takes money as well as leaders to keep political party organizations afloat.

The domination of the bourgeoisie in politics today is nothing more than a manifestation of the fundamental truism that economic factors are primary and political elements secondary and derivative.[2] In oriental, classical, and medieval times the agrarian aristocracy prevailed in political life. The ascendancy of the business classes in politics today is but a reflection of their triumph in modern society. The proletarian domination in Russia is proof that if the workers and peasants attain sufficient power, politics will then express the aspirations and ideals of the classes that today are still in a semiservile position in bourgeois states.

The greatest obstacle, however, to the development of any effective proletarian movement to upset the capitalistic order is to be found in the operation of the psychological mechanism of "identification." This explains why workers and white-collar groups are unable to assert their interests and power even when in a definite numerical majority in any country. Karl Marx assumed that workers were acutely conscious of their own special interests and would conduct themselves accordingly in thoroughly rational fashion. Our experience in the last century has proved the opposite, namely, that the proletariat has shown itself at times incapable of realizing its real class interests and unbelievably susceptible to seduction by capitalistic propaganda. Especially has this been true of the more recently developed capitalistic countries.

Social psychology of the old type threw some light on this seemingly perplexing problem by showing how deeply men are affected by custom, convention, and tradition. But the newer dynamic psychology has gone much further in clearing up the situation, through its analysis of the mechanism of "identification" and its operation upon the lower classes. Not only the stockholders but even the employees in great businesses tend to identify themselves with the business or family that employs them. In this manner they get psychic "compensation" for their own lowly status. They thereby create in their minds much more real loyalty to the employing class than they have for their own group.

Professors Malcolm M. Willey and Melville J. Herskovits have described the operation of this psychic mechanism with astuteness in their article "Notes on the Psychology of Servitude." It uncovers a factor little discussed before, but it is beyond comparison the greatest obstacle radical leaders have to contend with and the most potent factor in the psychology of conservatism. We here quote a few cogent sections from this article:

[1] *Cf.* John McConaughy, *Who Rules America?* Longmans, 1934.
[2] *Cf.* C. A. Beard, *The Economic Basis of Politics*, new ed., Knopf, 1934; and H. L. Childs, *Labor and Capital in National Politics.* Ohio State University Press, 1930.

The problem with which we are presented may then be concisely stated as follows: . . . Why is it the despair of social reformers, labor leaders, and radicals, that a large proportion of the working men are so unresponsive to measures which should, to all intents and purposes, be highly attractive to them?

The notorious contempt of the head-waiter for those, who when coming under his aegis, do not seem "to the manner born," i.e., to be in possession of wealth and breeding, as he conceives the latter, needs only to be mentioned to be conceded. The fear and trepidation with which a person of the upper middle class will approach the ordeal of purchasing a major article of wearing apparel in one of the so-called exclusive shops, has been sufficiently commented upon by the comic weeklies. The haughty disdain with which the chauffeur of the wealthy family regards his master's poor relations has often been noticed. . . .

The bank clerk who swells with pride at the statement of the huge transactions of the institution which employs him, even though he does not share beyond an occasional small bonus in the profits, is motivated by something much deeper than a rational pride in his participation in the affairs of the bank. . . .

If in the light of the suggestions outlined in this discussion we return to the main problem, it would seem that in this psychological mechanism of unconscious identification lies the key to an understanding of the reluctance of large groups of workers to respond to the doctrines set forth for their economic betterment. Herein, it is believed, lies the answer to the puzzling occurrence of frequent vehement expositions of the conservative philosophy on the part of those least benefited by the system which they uphold.[1]

Not only are millions of the working classes rendered loyal to the capitalistic system through the operation of the mechanism of identification; the menace of the proletariat to capitalism is still further lessened by the understandable but senseless divisions within the working classes. We pointed out above that the bourgeoisie are by no means united. We have the fundamental conflict between the monopoly and finance capitalists on the one hand and the petite bourgeoisie on the other. Then there is the rising antagonism between finance capitalists and industrialists. In labor circles, as well, there is the most bitter antagonism. Orthodox trade-unionists detest Socialists, and Socialists denounce Communists. Moreover, within each group of unionists, Socialists, and Communists there are intense factional quarrels. Frequently, proletarians hate each other more deeply than they do the capitalists. The conservative unions are, indeed, much more closely linked to capitalism than to the radical labor movement. The American Federation of Labor held out against the recognition of Russia longer than many conservative capitalists.

Struggles between employers and employees over wages have often injured so many people besides the direct participants that attention has been drawn to a vaguely defined "middle class," generally mentioned as the "public," supposed to occupy a place between the urban worker and the capitalist.[2] It is sometimes more definitely indicated as consisting of the professional groups, the lesser manufacturers and merchants, the more highly skilled and successful artisans, and the farming classes. It is the general group we described above as the petite bourgeoisie. Many of these groups favor the capitalist side in labor controversies. Those who are not direct parties but are nevertheless affected by

[1] *Journal of Social Forces*, March, 1923, pp. 228, 230, 232, 234.   [2] *Cf.* Corbin, *op. cit.*

such contests include both capitalists and the workers in other industries. In fact, *all the consumers* are "the public" in case of a stoppage of a vital economic process. This is true to a certain degree with even the employers and workers who are the parties of the first and second part in a particular dispute, which usually turns about dividing the rewards between two sets of *producers*. The classification of society into different groups of producers thus often runs athwart another that is quite as real, namely, the classification as consumers.[1] The Guild Socialists would frankly recognize both, organizing people as producers into self-governing economic-interest groups and as consumers somewhat along the present political lines.[2]

In concluding this section on the proletarian challenge to capitalism it is well to emphasize the fact that the most powerful and significant challenge that has ever been launched is the present experiment with proletarian control in Soviet Russia.[3] Contemporary Russia is a great socio-economic laboratory in which are now being tested, under great handicaps, some of the basic tenets of proletarian social and economic theory. The facts of Russian industrial life today constitute more of a challenge to capitalism than all the vehement rhetoric and finely spun theory thus far mustered in behalf of the proletariat. We shall later examine this development in more detail.

V. WEALTH, SOCIAL CLASSES, AND ECONOMIC EQUALITY

In spite of its weaknesses and injustices, the new system of social classes, based on wealth, is in some ways more tolerable than the old, based on blood. Mere want of proper deference on the part of the lowly is no longer punishable with the lash or imprisonment. The employer's hold upon even his own laborers is limited by their freedom of movement to another position and by the existence of labor organizations that take some of the arbitrariness out of the relation of master and man. Still, the aristocracy of wealth has little to complain of so long as the lower classes enthusiastically yield it the sincerest flattery—by copying its ways, clothes, and speech.

The rôle played by the idea of equality in our factory-made civilization is very hard to appraise.[4] Once the first phase of the French Revolution had demolished most of the arbitrary legal and political privileges of the upper classes, it became evident that "equality" is a vague word that must not be taken too literally in practice. Napoleon defined it as the freedom of a person to follow any career for which his talents fitted him. Economically, it was identified in practice with the laissez-faire ideas of the economists. Even the Declaration of the Rights of Man had expressly stated that it did not mean equality in property, and the execution of Babeuf in Paris in 1797 effectively discouraged any such conception.

The nineteenth century used the word in the restricted Napoleonic sense of

---

[1] *Cf.* W. B. Pitkin, *The Consumer, His Nature and His Changing Habits*, McGraw-Hill, 1932; *Recent Social Trends*, Vol. II, Chap. XVII; and Leven, Moulton, and Warburton, *America's Capacity to Consume*.
[2] See below, pp. 955 ff.   [3] See below, pp. 979 ff.
[4] *Cf.* C. L. Becker, *The United States: An Experiment in Democracy*, Harper, 1920, and *The Declaration of Independence*; and T. V. Smith, *The American Philosophy of Equality*, University of Chicago Press, 1927.

legal or formal equality of economic opportunity. But there was no serious thought of removing the actual inequalities of opportunity due to the inheritance of property and family prestige. For practical purposes, "talent" is an inseparable mixture of heredity and early environment. The incentives furnished by youthful associations and family position tend to bring out native capacity, or even to take its place to some extent. The world is unquestionably full of mute, inglorious Morgans, Rothschilds, Rockefellers, and Fords whose early lives have not guided their feet into the path of wealth and fame. There is no more preposterous dogma than the biased thesis of the spokesmen of the upper bourgeoisie—often voiced also by pseudo-biological determinists—to the effect that wealth and income in contemporary society are roughly related to innate ability on the part of the holders thereof.

In spite of the rôle played by accident and the unequal start given people of comparable natural endowments, the popular belief in the existence of equality of opportunity was one of the moral pillars of the nineteenth-century economic order. It was freely stated that there were only two or three generations "from shirt sleeves to shirt sleeves" in cases where ability was not inherited with wealth. Today, on the contrary, the divorcing of ownership from management has almost ended the difficulty in founding and perpetuating a "family."[1] Economic privilege, in the form of safe bonds and incorporated ventures, can go on piling up indefinitely without any effort, personal concern, or real ability on the part of the owners. Lawyers, trust companies, or secretaries can take care of all responsibilities. The marked rises and falls in the financial status of individuals are today far more the product of varying fortune in gambling in speculative finance than of demonstrated ability or incompetence in productive industry. Nevertheless, the considerable number of shifts upward and downward from one economic class to another proves that inequalities of opportunity are still surmountable in some instances. Our society still gains in stability from a common belief—even though it be an illusion—that one's station in life corresponds in a general way to one's merits.

VI. FEMINISM AND THE CHANGING STATUS OF THE SEXES

One of the more interesting social results of the Industrial Revolution has been the growing independence of women and the changing status of the sexes. In primitive society woman often occupied a very prominent position in both social relationships and industrial operations,[2] even though there were few, if any, examples of the matriarchate that early anthropologists once believed to exist.[3] But from the so-called dawn of history down to the Industrial Revolution civilization was male-dominated, if not literally a "man-made civilization."[4] The Industrial Revolution slowly but surely upset this state of affairs.

The underlying cause was not any rational or altruistic conception of the

---

[1] *Cf.* T. B. Veblen, *Absentee Ownership,* Huebsch, 1923. See also below, pp. 798 ff.

[2] *Cf.* O. T. Mason, *Woman's Share in Primitive Culture,* Appleton, 1924; and A. G. Spencer, *Woman's Share in Social Culture;* Lippincott, 1913.

[3] See above, Vol. I, pp. 51 ff.; and V. F. Calverton, *The Making of Man,* Modern Library, 1931, pp. 157 ff.

[4] See C. P. Gilman, *The Man-Made World,* Charlton Co., 1910. For an opposite view, see Mathilde and Mathias Vaërting, *The Dominant Sex,* Doran, 1923.

FEMINISM AND THE CHANGING STATUS OF THE SEXES 435

equality of women on the part of the men. The whole issue turned on the fact that the mechanical methods of production opened the way for widespread employment of women, who were quite able to watch and tend the new machinery. We have already noted the deplorable conditions under which women first worked in the new factories of England.[1] The entry of women into industry progressed steadily in each country after the Industrial Revolution reached it.[2] In Germany the number of women workers increased from 5,500,-000 in 1882 to 11,400,000 in 1925. In France it increased from 6,400,000 in 1896 to 8,600,000 in 1921. In England the gain was from 3,800,000 in 1881 to 5,700,000 in 1921. A century before 1881 there had been almost no women employed in the few English factories. The situation in the United States offers an illuminating example.[3] In 1870 some 14.7 per cent of women were gainfully employed; in 1880 the percentage had increased to 16; in 1890 to 19; in 1900 to 20.6; and in 1920 to 25.5. In the latter year there were some 7,593,709 women wage-earners in this country. The Census of 1930 listed 10,752,000 women and girls gainfully employed. The industrial status of women improved markedly. In 1870, 60.7 per cent of all women gainfully employed outside of agriculture were servants of one kind or another. In 1920 only 18.2 per cent were listed as servants. The occupational distribution of the 10,752,000 American women gainfully employed in 1930 was as follows: Domestic and personal service, 29.6 per cent; clerical, 18.5 per cent; manufacturing and mechanical, 17.5; professional, 14.2 per cent; trade, 9 per cent; agriculture, 8.5 per cent; and transportation, 2.6 per cent. Especially striking has been the increase in the number of women in business and the professions. Higher education of women has helped here. One-half of the graduates of the better colleges for women are gainfully employed.

The wages and salaries paid to women still remain, however, relatively low.[4] The average weekly wage of all employed women in American manufacturing industries was approximately $12 in the half-year from July to December, 1933, the first half year of "New Deal" wage scales. Even before the depression the California minimum wage of $16 a week for experienced women workers was regarded as very high. In representative American industries the earnings of women run to from 20 to 70 per cent below men's earnings, and they average about 41 per cent lower. By and large, the mass of American women workers cannot maintain decent living-standards on the wages they receive. Of the nearly 700,000 women working in New York as wage-earners and in the professions, only 7 per cent earn over $60 a week even in boom times. A careful study of the income of women in business and the professions indicated that the median yearly salary is $1,548; that 88 per cent earn less than $2,500 yearly; that only 6 per cent earn over $3,000; and that only 1.3 per cent earn over $5,000. Among the reasons for the lower salaries and wages of women are: (1) Their physical strength does not permit them to carry on some of the heavy mechanical trades for which men receive relatively high wages; (2) there is a lack of labor organization among most women workers, so that they lose the

---

[1] See above, pp. 289 ff.   [2] *Cf.* Edith Abbott, *Women in Industry*, Appleton, 1910.
[3] See J. A. Hill, *Women in Gainful Occupations, 1870-1920*, United States Government Printing Office, 1929.
[4] *Cf.* Grace Hutchins, *Women Who Work*, International Publishers, 1934, Chap. VII.

advantages of collective bargaining; and (3) many women hope to marry and will accept low pay rather than fight for better conditions because they believe that their industrial situation is a temporary one. In spite of all this, however, the condition of the working woman today is distinctly better than it was even a half century ago.

The relatively unfortunate position of women industrially has been one of the main factors lying back of their demand for political equality.[1] By getting the vote they hoped to pass laws that would elevate their status and do away with their disabilities. In spite of the growth of democracy since 1825, women were denied political participation for three-quarters of a century. Only New Zealand enacted woman suffrage before 1900, taking this step in 1893. Australia followed suit in 1902, as did Norway and Finland before 1914. The devotion and sacrifices of women in the World War hastened the granting of the suffrage. England conceded limited suffrage rights in 1918 and completed the process in 1928 by giving the vote to all women over twenty-one years of age. The United States extended the right of suffrage to women through the Nineteenth Amendment in 1920. Most of the new constitutions of Europe embodied woman suffrage. The political equality of women has received a setback recently with the growth of dictatorship in Europe. The patriarchal male attitude has reasserted itself, and the tendency is to declare once again that woman's place is in the home raising children to make good soldiers.

Women have not only been given the right to vote; they have entered important public offices. We have had women Congressmen and governors—even one woman Senator in Washington. A woman, Frances Perkins, entered the cabinet of the President of the United States in March, 1933. Women have made much progress in the legal field. They have quite generally been admitted to jury service. Many of them are now practicing law. A woman, Florence Allen, was appointed to the United States Circuit Court of Appeals—the second highest court in the land—by President Roosevelt in 1934.

The victory in securing political equality has spurred on women to attempt to secure legal and economic equality.[2] In the United States, for example, in spite of woman suffrage, men are in a favored position so far as legal and property rights are concerned. In most states the husband has special rights in his claims on his wife's property and services. He can absolutely control her services in the home and to a considerable extent elsewhere. He is the "natural guardian" of their children and has special powers over them. These privileges are offset to some extent by the fact that it is the husband who still pays alimony in case of divorce. In France and some European countries the disabilities of women are even greater. For instance, in France, according to Mr. Maurois:

A married woman . . . cannot have a bank account without getting authorization from her husband. Though she may manage a large business while her husband does

---

[1] *Cf.* Slater, *The Growth of Modern England*, Chap. xxi; E. S. Pankhurst, *The Suffragette Movement*, Longmans, 1931; E. R. Hecker, *Short History of Women's Rights*, 2d ed. rev., Putnam, 1914; and I. H. Irwin, *The Story of the Woman's Party*, Harcourt, Brace, 1921.

[2] See S. P. Breckenridge, *Marriage and the Civic Rights of Woman*, University of Chicago Press, 1931.

nothing, she can make no important agreement without obtaining his signature. If she is a wage-earner, her husband has a claim on her pay. If she desires a passport for foreign travel, she must have her husband's consent.[1]

The State of Wisconsin set a precedent by passing an Equal Rights law in 1921, which declared that women should "have the same rights and privileges under the law as men in the exercise of suffrage, freedom of contract, choice of residence for voting purposes, jury service, holding office, holding and conveying property, care and custody of children, and in all other respects." This act has not been widely imitated as yet, though the Russian and Spanish revolutions conferred full equality on women. There can be no true equality between the sexes, however, until the law takes cognizance of the special burden imposed upon women in being the childbearing sex and offers appropriate protection to motherhood. In Russia alone does the law do so fully, and this is one of the reasons why the position of woman is higher in Russia today than in any other important country on the globe.[2]

In this struggle to secure equality for women a number of important figures stand out.[3] The first great feminist was Mary Wollstonecraft (1759-97), who defended women's rights at the very close of the eighteenth century. A century later Emmeline Pankhurst and her daughter Sylvia led the struggle in England for equal suffrage. In the United States, Elizabeth Cady Stanton (1815-1902), Susan B. Anthony (1820-1906), Belva Lockwood (1830-1917), Victoria Woodhull (1838-1927), Carrie Chapman Catt (1859-   ), and others have taken the lead in working for woman suffrage and other phases of the recognition of women. The most thoroughgoing advocate of the rights of women has been the Russian crusader Alexandra Kollontay, who argues not only for economic and legal equality but also for the full sexual equality of women. She has lived to see many of her ideals put into practice in Russia since 1917. In Sweden, Ellen Key (1849-1926) valiantly upheld women's rights and was especially noted for her courage in discussing sex problems. The birth-control movement, a great boon to women, has been valiantly supported by Marie Stopes in England and Margaret Sanger in the United States.

An important social effect of the emancipation of woman has been the inroads that feminine independence and economic initiative have made upon the patriarchal home.[4] The latter had dominated human society for centuries when life was primarily agricultural or pastoral in its economic foundations and when women were absolutely dependent for their support upon men. Today, many women prefer the economic independence offered by industry and professions to marriage purchased at the price of economic dependence upon a man. Moreover, if a woman does not find her husband congenial, starvation does not face her if she leaves him and tries to earn her own living. In many instances young women have to support relatives and continue working to an age when marriage becomes relatively difficult to contract. Moreover,

[1] New York *Times*, Apr. 8, 1934, Sec. VI, p. 5.   [2] See below, pp. 1022 ff.
[3] *Cf.* Pankhurst, *op. cit.*; I. H. Irwin, *Angels and Amazons*, Doubleday, Doran, 1933; and M. B. Smith, *Evangels of Reform*, Round Table Press, 1934.
[4] *Cf.* A. G. Spencer, *The Family and Its Members*, Lippincott, 1923; E. R. Groves and W. F. Ogburn, *American Marriage and Family Relationships*, Holt, 1928; and V. F. Calverton, *The Bankruptcy of Marriage*, Macaulay, 1928.

when a woman can exist by her own labors, she is more likely to be discriminating in the choice of a husband and may in the end not be able to find one to her liking. In these and other ways, the Industrial Revolution and the entry of women into industry, trade, and the professions have led to a great increase in the divorce rate, to a decrease in the number of marriages per capita, and to a diminished importance of the family as the unit of society. It is logical that in Russia, where the industrialization and emancipation of women have progressed further than anywhere else in the world, we find the old type of family life rather less important than in agrarian or bourgeois countries. It is possible that Plato's idea that the state should exert primary control and supervision over children will ultimately prevail.

VII. PSYCHOLOGICAL RESULTS OF THE INDUSTRIAL REVOLUTION

The Industrial Revolution has profoundly changed the volume and variety of the subject matter with which the human mind has to deal. Medieval man, in his slow-moving social environment, often without a single significant change in activities for generations, might seek for a final and decisive explanation of things or accept a fixed social order as a matter of course. In the early modern age, printing and the oversea explorations brought more changes than took place in many phases of civilization during the entire thousand years of the Middle Ages. Town life in western Europe in 1750 revealed sweeping effects of the Commercial Revolution.[1] But the bulk of the population still lived in the country and tilled the soil much as it had been doing for many thousand years—was, indeed, quite illiterate. The town laborers were little better off culturally. Most of their information related solely to the ordinary processes of life, the superstitious traditions of the locality, common gossip, and certain formal religious teachings imparted by the priesthood or ministry.

The laborer or farmer of today often stands in the midst of more striking changes in material culture in a decade than took place during a large part of the whole medieval period or during any century before the Industrial Revolution.[2] As a rule he has an elementary-school education. Hence he has at his disposal the modern newspaper, from which he may obtain a vast array of diversified and reasonably reliable information. So far as mere information is concerned, the town laborer of today in Western countries is often far better provided for than most scholars, statesmen, and diplomats of the thirteenth or fourteenth centuries. That it is mostly useless or trivial information, often unassimilated, uninterpreted, and unutilized in his daily work, does not alter the fact that the newspaper, the radio, news reels, and the like have transformed the mental life and activities of the members of his class.

The common man is thus made aware of great changes taking place—or at least of a certain instability of things.[3] Still further, a vastly increased variety of stimuli affect him personally. We need only compare the life of the peasant,

---

[1] *Cf.* George, *London Life in the XVIIIth Century.*
[2] *Cf.* C. H. Cochrane, *Modern Industrial Progress,* Lippincott, 1904; W. N. Polakov, *The Power Age,* Covici, Friede, 1933; and W. F. Ogburn, *You and Machines,* United States Government Printing Office, 1934. [3] Chapin, *Historical Introduction to Social Economy,* Chap. XVI.

who was still the typical laborer in western Europe in 1750, with that of one of his descendants of today. The stimuli to the laborers of old came largely from nature itself. Handicraft methods of manufacturing and the simple social order that went with them did not add greatly to the complication of life. The chances are about even that their descendants are industrial workers in a city. Even if they are not, popular education, periodicals, and the new communication facilities essentially urbanize their mental perspective and interests.

The noise, swiftness, and intricacy of present-day existence furnish a sharp contrast. Steam and electricity in a certain sense bring the activities of the whole world to each person's consciousness every day. He reads of a revolution in China, of the international struggle for oil in the Near East, and of the new devices for killing him, his fellow citizens, and their enemies in the event of war. The moving-picture film tries to explain the Einstein theory to him, and he often spends his evening tuning in on his radio to hear propaganda, music, educational lectures, or what not from places hundreds or thousands of miles away.

The change has been so swift and radical that man as an organism is subjected to new strains, for which his past has very imperfectly prepared him in many cases.[1] A human organism that has adjusted itself through thousands of years to a relatively simple agrarian environment, monotonously and slowly repeating certain functions and processes from one generation to another, finds itself facing a vastly different set-up in modern urban life. The increased nervous strain involved in meeting the new situations—noises, dangers, industrial disciplines, types of recreation, rapid adjustments and readjustments—constitutes the severest test ever placed upon man as a biological entity and a psychological mechanism.

New mental and nervous diseases have appeared, and the frequency of such disorders has greatly increased.[2] Dr. Mayo has recently told us that one out of every five hospital beds in the United States now holds a mental or nervous case. Perhaps the situation is not so bad as it looks in the statistics, some cases being hereditary, and others merely brought to light by the improved present-day social machinery for ferreting out and segregating the unfit. On the other hand, many people who now have to be cared for in institutions certainly got on fairly well in a simpler rural society. A large amount of mental and nervous wreckage has been caused by the wide gulf between our old customs, ethical standards, and institutions on the one hand, and on the other, the very different set-up that has arrived with the new industrial and urban era. This is one price we are paying for putting the "cave man in the modern city," namely, placing an animal, who attained his present physical and mental powers in the cave age, in a modern urban and industrial civilization. We must ever keep in mind the fact that man has not changed in any important respect as to bodily or mental equipment during the last thirty to fifty thousand years.

Not the least of the evils that have been charged to the Industrial Revolution, with its regimentation and repetition of processes, has been a certain

---

[1] *Cf.* Graham Wallas, *The Great Society*, Macmillan, 1914; W. F. Ogburn, *Social Change*, Viking Press, 1922, Pt. IV; and H. E. Barnes, *Can Man Be Civilized?* Coward-McCann, 1932, Chaps. III-IV.
[2] See below, pp. 968 ff.

materialism of outlook, and a standardization of ideas and attitudes.[1] Machines play so large a part in our lives that we want everything to be "efficient" in the mechanical sense. We tend to classify and evaluate even ideas in terms of the concrete and practical—which cannot be done, of course, unless they are roughly uniform, and therefore unoriginal. Such a spirit tends to stultify popular art, literature, and music, especially when the product must please so large an audience that there is little encouragement of the distinguished and original qualities which appeal only to a cultured few. What is more depressing than to look down upon a sea of straw hats in a summer crowd? Underneath the hats are standardized factory-made suits, neckties, and shoes. The only way to be distinctive is to spend more money than the others, which gives rise to what Veblen has aptly called "the pecuniary standard of taste." This pecuniary measuring stick is again a part of our deference to wealth and the social classification of people according to income. It is easy, especially with a decimal system of currency, to set down how much a person is "worth" in figures. Even excessive expenditures no longer can purchase absolute distinction. A Plymouth or Pontiac car looks much like one costing ten times as much.

Accompanying this cultural and psychic standardization there has thus developed a parallel and closely related tendency to base our social and cultural evaluations upon deference to great wealth. This is a manifestation of what Veblen has called the psychology of "the leisure class."[2] With the growth of great fortunes and the ascendancy of the very wealthy classes in industry and society there has come about a marked proclivity to attach high prestige to the possession of vast riches and to venerate the various social manifestations that opulence induces in conduct.

Of all of these attitudes, none is more important than the element of "conspicuous waste" as a criterion of the possession of wealth.[3] Nothing is a more dramatic proof of economic independence than the ability to waste huge sums of money on nonsocial and nonproductive enterprises, such as ostentatious dress and equipage, elaborate and wasteful forms of social entertainment, grotesquely pretentious and elaborate dwellings. Above all stands complete abstinence from any sign of manual labor. Since these forms of conduct and such psychic attitudes are supposed to characterize the most-to-be-envied of all classes in modern society, they have become the approved norms for the creation of reverence and deferential obeisance on the part of the masses.

Along with this reverence for the characteristic attitudes and practices associated with great wealth we have the parallel effort of the wealthy to insist upon the servility of the laboring classes. The latter are stigmatized by the necessity of manual labor, in the same way that the wealthy are distinguished by their general abstinence from any such menial effort. It has been possible thus far to make the industrial proletariat defer to the standards and tastes of the wealthy and, at the same time, to accept as somewhat inevitable their own lowly status. It is true that there are some signs of a decline of the theories and

---

[1] See Ralph Borsodi, *This Ugly Civilization*, 2d ed., Harper, 1933; and Dietrich, *The Chief Danger in Our Civilization*. For an opposite interpretation, see H. K. Norton, "The Age of Alarums," *Century Magazine*, April, 1930.

[2] T. B. Veblen, *The Theory of the Leisure Class*, Macmillan, 1899 (now Viking Press).

[3] Veblen, *op. cit.* See also Josephson, *op. cit.*, Chap. xiv; R. H. Fuller, *Jubilee Jim*, Macmillan, 1928; and Parker Morell, *Diamond Jim*, Simon & Schuster, 1934.

PSYCHOLOGICAL RESULTS OF INDUSTRIAL REVOLUTION

practices of the leisure class among the more wealthy. There is also a growing reluctance on the part of the industrial proletariat to accept as inevitable their lowly and servile station. Nevertheless, the situation described above has prevailed very generally during the last century or more.

In order to illustrate more fully what is meant by the theory of the leisure class and their methods of "honorific consumption" and "conspicuous waste," we shall quote from Veblen's remarkable book *The Theory of the Leisure Class:*

> So soon as the possession of property becomes the basis of popular esteem, therefore, it becomes also a requisite to that complacency which we call self-respect. In any community where goods are held in severalty it is necessary, in order to his own peace of mind, that an individual should possess as large a portion of goods as others with whom he is accustomed to class himself; and it is extremely gratifying to possess something more than others. But as fast as a person makes new acquisitions, and becomes accustomed to the resulting new standard of wealth, the new standard forthwith ceases to afford appreciably greater satisfaction than the earlier standard did. The tendency in any case is constantly to make the present pecuniary standard the point of departure for a fresh increase of wealth; and this in turn gives rise to a new standard of sufficiency and a new pecuniary classification of one's self as compared with one's neighbours. . . .
>
> In order to gain and hold the esteem of men it is not sufficient merely to possess wealth or power. The wealth or power must be put in evidence, for esteem is awarded only on evidence. And not only does the evidence of wealth serve to impress one's importance on others and to keep their sense of his importance alive and alert, but it is of scarcely less use in building up and preserving one's self-complacency. . . .
>
> Abstention from labour is not only a honorific or meritorious act, but it presently comes to be a requisite of decency. The insistence on property as the basis of reputability is very naïve and very imperious during the early stages of the accumulation of wealth. Abstention from labour is the conventional evidence of wealth and is therefore the conventional mark of social standing; and this insistence on the meritoriousness of wealth leads to a more strenuous insistence on leisure. . . .
>
> The quasi-peaceable gentleman of leisure . . . not only consumes of the staff of life beyond the minimum required for subsistence and physical efficiency, but his consumption also undergoes a specialization as regards the quality of the goods consumed. He consumes freely and of the best, in food, drink, narcotics, shelter, services, ornaments . . . amulets, and idols or divinities. . . .
>
> Conspicuous consumption of valuable goods is a means of reputability to the gentleman of leisure. As wealth accumulates on his hands, his own unaided effort will not avail to sufficiently put his opulence in evidence by this method. The aid of friends and competitors is therefore brought in by resorting to the giving of valuable presents and expensive feasts and entertainments. . . .
>
> From the foregoing survey of the growth of conspicuous leisure and consumption, it appears that the utility of both alike for the purposes of reputability lies in the element of waste that is common to both. In the one case it is a waste of time and effort; in the other it is a waste of goods. Both are methods of demonstrating the possession of wealth, and the two are conventionally accepted as equivalents.[1]

[1] Veblen, *op. cit.*, pp. 31, 36-37, 41, 73, 75, 85.

VIII. THE DAWN OF A NEW ERA OF LEISURE

If we may look for a decline in the influence of the ideals of the older and exclusive leisure class, we may also expect a greater amount of leisure time for the mass of mankind. If civilization endures, leisure is bound to cease to be a class privilege and to become a mass necessity. With the improvement of mechanical efficiency, the coming of the "power age," and the introduction of automatic machinery, the amount of time required to produce either necessities or luxuries has been vastly reduced. This means that man must face intelligently the problems of leisure.

The sane utilization of leisure time has thus become one of the serious social problems raised by the mechanical age. It is also one that has by no means received the extended attention it deserves. Until recently man's struggle for existence has always absorbed the major portion of his time; during much of history, the great majority of men have had to toil long hours at back-breaking work, almost justifying the statement of the college freshman that "often their only relief was in death."

But with the widespread use of machinery and the development of mass production, it has become possible in the past century for man to produce in a relatively short working-day as much as he needs to consume, and as much as his purchasing power will allow him to buy. If we put all able-bodied persons to work, the working day and week must become even shorter. As a consequence, large numbers of men find themselves with more leisure time on their hands than their ancestors ever had. And the amount of this leisure time is likely to increase in the future rather than to decrease.

If our economic system, therefore, continues to function efficiently and continuously, leisure is bound to become an even greater social problem.[1] Our old economic gospel of work for work's sake needs to be profoundly altered.[2] It has driven us to an overemphasis on wealth and materialism, to a consideration of production as the main object of human endeavor instead of emphasizing consumption, which is the only rational goal.

As we gradually come to realize that wealth-getting is by itself futile, and by no means synonymous with satisfaction or happiness, we are beginning to see that our chief attention in the future needs to be devoted not to the production of more goods, but to a more rational use of that increased leisure time which is, after all, the chief boon of the machine age.

Worth-while leisure is of course something far more than mere freedom from arduous toil and long hours of work. Mere idleness is not an end to be desired, as can be attested not only by the unemployed and the convalescent, but by many business men who have retired from work only to find that life has little significance left for them. Leisure must also be recognized as something beyond having more time for the consumption of material goods, the sale of which will pile up bigger profits for the few. The wise use of leisure time cannot be promoted solely through an increase in purchasing power, which

---

[1] *Cf. Recent Social Trends,* Vol. II, Chap. XVIII; and M. L. B. Greenbie, *The Arts of Leisure,* McGraw-Hill, 1935.

[2] *Cf.* H. P. Fairchild, "Exit the Gospel of Work," *Harper's Magazine,* April, 1931.

will only furnish more opportunity for seeking the excitement and distraction that seem to be the chief uses of leisure at present.

There is, in fact, no satisfactory leisure that does not refresh man, make life richer, increase happiness, promote mental health, and serve to make our terrestrial experience more worth while for the normal individual. We need a philosophy of leisure time that lays more emphasis on what man is and less on what he does. We need to learn to express ourselves more adequately along avenues that actually re-create us, instead of in ways that merely furnish us change and excitement.

But this involves a reëducation of man, a more or less fundamental change in our philosophy. The problem of a wise use of leisure is so complicated and important that it merits and requires prolonged scientific study, so that we may reconstruct our present wrong-headed ideals and readjust ourselves to an outlook that promises something more worth while in life. It is a problem which is weighty enough to deserve that serious attention from our social scientists which it is now just beginning to receive. Economics, the science of wealth-getting, will perhaps occupy a relatively less important position among the social sciences of the future, and sociology, which is concerned with man and his relationships, a relatively more important one. The new attitude has been admirably summarized by Professor Fairchild:

We must, most emphatically of all, have a new philosophy of idleness—or rather, we must substitute for the present philosophy of idleness a sound and comprehensive philosophy of leisure time. We must come to realize that leisure time, that is, time spent in pleasurable employment, is the only kind of time that makes life worth living. All other time is tolerable only as it contributes to the richness and developmental content of our leisure. But, of course, leisure, to be itself tolerable, must be immeasurably more than mere idleness. Leisure time should mean the opportunity for all those pursuits that really contribute to the realization and enlargement of personality. . . .

In this connection, the phrase "idle rich" must lose its current uncomplimentary significance. Idle is exactly what the rich ought to be. Idle, of course, in the sense that they are not doing remunerative work of a kind that keeps somebody else from getting the income that he can get only from work. . . . Let him [the rich man] devote his time to some noncompetitive pursuit—art, or philosophy, or research, or the breeding of Chow dogs or dahlias or what you will—and leave work to those who have to have it.[1]

All this is a far cry from the philosophy of John Calvin,[2] but it furnishes the perspective that we must adopt from this time forward if the fruits of science and industry are to mean very much to humanity.

IX. THE ECONOMIC BASIS OF CONTEMPORARY CULTURE

The general cultural, social, and psychological results of the Industrial Revolution present an admirable opportunity to test the validity of the economic determination of history, namely, the Marxian thesis that other aspects of civilization are determined by the economic conditions which prevail at the time. It

---

[1] Fairchild, *loc. cit.*, pp. 571-72. [2] See above, Vol. I, p. 862.

is, of course, possible to accept the Marxian doctrine of social causation as applied to Western society since 1800 without implying in any way blanket approval of the Socialist program of social reform. The facts afford a large degree of confirmation of Marx's thesis, though it was, in part, the development of Rationalism and science since 1500 that made possible the technological revolution which established capitalistic enterprise so firmly.

In Western society as a whole, our institutions have become adjusted in large part to the new economic order and its processes. Population growth has parallelled modern industrial evolution. The social stratification and the social hierarchy conform rather completely to the economic differentiation in society. Our social interests are primarily bound up with the economic interests, real or supposed, of each class. Social values have taken on the pecuniary coloring of the capitalistic order, the bourgeoisie desiring to acquire more, and the proletariat attempting to check this and to capture industrial processes for their own use. Social prestige tallies pretty closely with the bank account.

Government remains, as it has always been, fundamentally an expression of the struggle between economic classes, but this conflict has now become primarily one between the capitalists and the proletariat, with the intermediate groups tending as yet to side with capital in most industrial states.[1] In some of the economically more archaic states, like Hungary, the landlords still control politics. In most of the Western states the capitalists have come to dominate. In Russia we have the proletariat in the saddle. In certain countries, such as England, there is still a deadlock between the older agrarian interests, capital, and the proletariat. Not only domestic politics but also international relations have come into conformity with modern industrialism. The basic motive in international relations in recent years has been the effort to secure raw materials and markets for both goods and capital. It is not without reason that contemporary diplomacy has been variously denominated as "dollar diplomacy," "oil-burning diplomacy," and "rubber-neck diplomacy." [2]

Law has shaped itself in harmony with the outstanding aspects of modern industrialism. Where the bourgeoisie have come to control, the theory of a natural order based upon unlimited competition has furnished the cornerstone of juristic theory and practice; so much so, in fact, that Justice Holmes once accused his colleagues on the United States Supreme Court of attempting to read Herbert Spencer's *Social Statics* into the Constitution of the United States. The protection of private property, the perpetuity of contracts, the obstruction of state interference in business affairs, and the imposition of special disabilities on the proletariat have been the outstanding features of bourgeois jurisprudence. Where the proletariat have come into control, the situation has been reversed and legislation has been passed expropriating the capitalistic and agrarian owners and proclaiming a régime of coöperation or of Communism. Without passing judgment upon the question of which procedure is preferable, it may be remarked that in either case legal concepts and procedure have adapted themselves very closely to the dominating economic ideals and interests.

[1] See Franz Oppenheimer, *The State,* Vanguard Press, 1926; Beard, *op. cit.;* Childs, *op. cit.;* and Beer, *Social Struggles and Thought.*   [2] See below, pp. 546 ff., 769 ff.

THE ECONOMIC BASIS OF CONTEMPORARY CULTURE

Religion has not escaped from the contamination of the new industrial age. As Veblen pointed out nearly a generation ago in his *Theory of the Leisure Class*, the "pious observances" of the capitalists are mainly a manifestation of the "pecuniary taste" and "conspicuous waste" of the wealthy.[1] Certain psychologists have since suggested that they may also be a form of psychic compensation for the dubious economic ventures of week days. Capitalistic leaders have in many areas been able to use religion among the middle classes in such ways as to emphasize the sanctity of private property and the perpetuity of the capitalistic system. Churches are thus often taken advantage of to spread capitalistic propaganda.[2] In his *The Man Nobody Knows*,[3] the eminent publicist, Bruce Barton, has actually portrayed Jesus in the guise of a high-pressure contemporary salesman. The Rev. C. Everett Wagner has declared that a very popular trend in modern religion "rings the cash register," contending further that it is a "movement of sanctified commercialism, peculiarly a product of the twentieth century." He allies himself with "the many clergymen and laymen who are thoroughly disgusted with Big Business declaring dividends on religion." One must recognize with due respect the brave resistance to the misuse of religion by capitalism put up by such organizations as the Federal Council of the Churches of Christ and the late Interchurch World Movement, but the Federal Council is not, unhappily, representative of the dominant trends in contemporary bourgeois religion.

On the other hand, in a proletarian régime supernaturalism is discarded and a secularized religion based upon the Communist dogmas supplants it.[4] When proletarian leaders retain Christianity they represent it as primarily a program of secular economic revolution, a point of view vigorously maintained by Upton Sinclair in *They Call Me Carpenter,* and by Bouck White in *The Church of the Social Revolution.*

Ethical questions and solutions have not been free from economic influences. The capitalistic groups have been fiercely determined to retain the supernatural and conventional theory of ethical standards.[5] This represents morality as almost wholly dictated by religion and limited to sex—a moral man being one who is formally affiliated with an ecclesiastical organization and whose sex conduct in public is externally correct. This attitude is highly convenient to the plutocrat, since the reprehensible practices associated with finance capitalism and the theory of business enterprise thereby escape condemnation. He usually has the pecuniary resources to obscure any actual sex dereliction unless he is uncommonly stupid and unlucky.

The radicals, on the contrary, incline to minimize the significance of supernatural revelation and of the sex criteria of conduct. They contend that capitalism and economic waste and oppression are the really serious forms of immorality.[6] Moral standards, they maintain, must be secularized and socialized.

---

[1] Perhaps the most forceful and astute presentation of this situation is contained in Winston Churchill's novel, *The Inside of the Cup*, Macmillan, 1913.
[2] This is emphasized with much heat in Upton Sinclair's *The Profits of Religion*, privately printed, 1918.   [3] Bobbs-Merrill, 1925.   [4] See below, pp. 1021-22.
[5] For an excellent example of such capitalistic apologetic, see J. T. Adams, in Albert Einstein and others, *Living Philosophies*, Simon & Schuster, 1931, pp. 153 ff. On the capitalistic sponsorship of antivice societies, see H. C. Broun and Margaret Leech, *Anthony Comstock, Roundsman of the Lord*, Boni, 1927, p. 154.   [6] *Cf.* Ella Winter, *Red Virtue*, Harcourt, Brace, 1933.

They aver that books like Stuart Chase's *Tragedy of Waste,* Kallet and Schlink's *100,000,000 Guinea Pigs,* Berle and Means' *The Modern Corporation and Private Property,* Matthews and Shallcross's *Partners in Plunder,* and John T. Flynn's *Graft in Business* reveal a much more serious type of immorality than the works of Ovid, Boccaccio, and Casanova.

The economic classes in society have not failed to recognize the importance of capturing the school system in behalf of their cause. Capitalistic states base their education, so far as possible, on subjects perpetuating the old "humanities," which in no sense bring up the dangerous problems of property and economic justice. As educational progress has encouraged giving attention to the social sciences, the vested capitalistic interests have endeavored to see to it that the instruction given therein emphasizes the sanctity of private property and the perfection of the present scheme of things.[1] In the especially precarious field of economics there has been an effort to divert attention from the description and analysis of the contemporary economic order and to concentrate pedagogical instruction upon the classical "laws" of economics or upon methods of administering more profitably the present system of business enterprise. The risky nature of a straightforward presentation of the facts regarding the existing state of economic and social affairs has been indicated with an ample display of clinical material in the reports of the American Association of University Professors on academic freedom, in Upton Sinclair's slightly overdrawn *The Goose Step* and *The Goslings,* and with withering irony in Thorstein Veblen's *The Higher Learning in America.*

Not only do the capitalists insist upon correctness in all instruction pertaining to the existing economic and social system; they are also extremely sensitive in regard to respectable moral tradition, since they recognize the invaluable service of conventional moral codes in maintaining capitalist reputability.[2] Hence, there is little toleration of any effort to offer instruction in scientific ethics or to suggest that the whole problem of ethics must be given a broad social and economic setting. There has been a concerted attack on scientific sociology as especially dangerous in this regard.

When the industrial proletariat capture the educational system they see to it promptly that the schools become a powerful adjunct of radical proletarian propaganda and devote themselves to the task of training up young labor-unionists, Communists, or Syndicalists. Capitalism, private property, and profits are fiercely denounced.[3]

Art thoroughly reflects the age of contemporary materialism.[4] The new technology has made possible a new type of massive architecture, most notably exemplified by the metropolitan skyscrapers. These same technological advances have led to a remarkable standardization of architecture and of many other phases of art where products can be duplicated and produced on a vast scale and far more cheaply than by the old individualized methods of handi-

---

[1] *Cf.* G. A. Coe, *Educating for Citizenship,* Scribner, 1932; Pierce, *Citizens' Organizations for the Civic Training of Youth;* and Thompson, *Confessions of the Power Trust,* Pt. VI.
[2] *Cf.* H. E. Barnes, "Sex in Education," in V. F. Calverton and S. D. Schmalhausen, *Sex in Civilization,* Macaulay, 1929.   [3] *Cf.* Thomas Woody, *New Minds: New Men?* Macmillan, 1932.
[4] For an extreme view, see Upton Sinclair, *Mammonart,* privately printed, 1925.

THE ECONOMIC BASIS OF CONTEMPORARY CULTURE

craft manufacture.[1] It is not surprising that the New York *Evening Post* once carried as a prominent news item the following announcement: "Artist Aims to Be the Ford of Statuary."[2] The article continued:

> A combination of Henry Ford and Benvenuto Cellini was found in New York today. He is Simon Moselsic, a Russian sculptor, who follows the Detroiter in the use of quantity production and the Florentine in personally attending to every detail of manufacturing. He works in four materials—porcelain, wood, marble and bronze. Just now he is producing in quantity tiny bronzes, with the result that statuary may soon adorn any smoking stand, mantelpiece or whatnot where Americans keep their objects of art.

Nor can one overlook in this regard the growing importance of the movies and the radio as methods of producing highly standardized types of visual art and music.

Contemporary art has tended to specialize on motifs usually associated with some aspect or other of contemporary industrial society, and not infrequently eulogizes by implication the achievements of the bourgeoisie. The great financiers and industrialists use their pecuniary resources to acquire the great masterpieces and to endow metropolitan art museums, standing before the public as the real patrons and connoisseurs of art. How far they are actually removed in many cases from any real appreciation of the artistic spirit and values may be seen from the naïve surprise and indignation once expressed by a great American industrialist when the trustees of the Dresden gallery in Germany refused to sell him Raphael's "Sistine Madonna" at any price that they might choose to set upon this work. When the laboring classes dominate society, art is immediately drafted into the service of the proletariat. The example of Russia affords illuminating proof of this. In such cases the themes of art become even more frankly class-conscious and socialized.[3]

An interesting example of the economic interpretation of art was afforded in the clash between the Rockefeller interests and an able but radical artist, Diego Rivera. The latter was noted for his striking murals and was engaged by Mr. Rockefeller, in full knowledge of Rivera's radicalism, to paint a large mural in the great Rockefeller Center (Radio City) in New York City. Rivera painted a mural depicting current economic and social developments and, with true radical logic, included a large picture of Lenin. Whereupon Mr. Rockefeller dismissed Rivera and had the almost finished mural destroyed in February, 1934. Mr. Rivera was, however, paid for his services.

Journalism has long since become a class affair,[4] but the superior pecuniary power of the capitalistic press and its capacity to attract remunerative advertising have enabled it to present a better range of entertainment for its readers than can labor journals, and to print papers of a far more impressive physical appearance. The proletariat have, as a result, usually failed to support the papers of their class with adequate loyalty—a serious handicap to proletarian propaganda. Proletarian journalism outside of Russia is as yet relatively slight and inadequate, in spite of no lack of able editors and writers.

---

[1] *Cf.* Philip Johnson, *Machine Art,* Norton, 1934.   [2] Mar. 19, 1928, Home ed., p. 4.
[3] See Winter, *op. cit.,* Chap. XVII.
[4] For an exaggerated interpretation, see Upton Sinclair, *The Brass Check,* privately printed, 1919. For much valuable material, see N. D. Cochran, *E. W. Scripps,* Harcourt, Brace, 1933.

Finally, literature shadows forth the economic stratification of society.[1] The nonfiction works are given over in increasing degree to the description and analysis of questions connected with modern industrialism and to the plans for conserving, mitigating, or destroying it. Fiction, likewise, is in part devoted either to the eulogy or to the criticism of capitalistic institutions and practices. When not so employed it chiefly provides diverting entertainment for the leisure class or pictures thinly veiled utopias where the author portrays a better world in which to live. The controversy surrounding the critical attack on Thornton Wilder by Mike Gold well illustrates the contrast between the leisure-class conception of literature and the extreme proletarian version of its nature and purpose.[2]

The most extensive and ambitious effort to present an economic interpretation of contemporary industrial civilization has been executed by Upton Sinclair in his various books: *The Jungle, King Coal, Jimmie Higgins, The Profits of Religion, The Goose Step, The Goslings, Mammonart, The Brass Check,* and *Money Writes*. While we cannot avoid admiring the courage, industry, and information possessed by Sinclair, the work should be done over again with less indignation and with rather more humor and irony, a task partly executed by Thorstein Veblen, unfortunately in an involved literary style likely to render his works permanently obscure to all save the élite.[3]

It may be well, however, in this connection to call attention to the view of Mr. G. D. H. Cole, to the effect that in an economy based upon production for service rather than for private profit the doctrine of economic determination would not longer hold good. In other words, Socialism would terminate the validity of one of the chief Socialist dogmas:

In short, if economic classes and class-conflicts are done away with, the Marxian thesis will no longer hold good, and economic power will no longer be the dominant factor in Society. Economic considerations will lose their unreal and distorted magnitude in men's eyes, and will retain their place as one group among others round which the necessary social functions are centered. For the artificial material valuation of social things, which is forced upon us by the actual structure of present-day society, it will become possible to substitute a spiritual valuation. When once we have got the economic sphere of social action reasonably organized on functional lines, we shall be free to forget about it most of the time, and to interest ourselves in other matters. The economic sphere will not, of course, be any less essential than before; but it will need less attention. Always associations and institutions, as well as people, need most attention when they are least "themselves." Our preoccupation with economics occurs only because the economic system is diseased.[4]

[1] See V. F. Calverton, *The Liberation of American Literature*, Scribner, 1932; and Granville Hicks, *The Great Tradition: An Interpretation of American Literature since the Civil War*, Macmillan, 1933. See also below, pp. 1079, 1089.   [2] Carried on in the *New Republic*, principally.
[3] *Cf.* Joseph Dorfman, *Thorstein Veblen and His America*, Viking Press, 1934.
[4] G. D. H. Cole, *Social Theory*, Stokes, 1920, pp. 153-54.

SUGGESTED READING

Hammerton, *Universal History of the World*, Chaps. 166, 189
Nussbaum, *History of the Economic Institutions of Modern Europe*, Pt. IV, Chap. v
Randall, *The Making of the Modern Mind*, Chap. xxii
A. M. Schlesinger, *The Rise of the City, 1878-1898*, Macmillan, 1933
A. J. Todd, *Industry and Society*, Holt, 1933

SUGGESTED READING 449

Articles, "Birth Control," "City," "City and Town Planning," "Civilization," "Equality," "Food Industries," "Food Supply," "Industrialism," "Leisure," "Materialism," "Middle Class," "Municipal Government," "Population," "Proletariat," Encyclopaedia of the Social Sciences

M. N. Baker, *Municipal Engineering and Sanitation*, Macmillan, 1902
Nels Anderson and E. C. Lindeman, *Urban Sociology*, Crofts, 1928
Niles Carpenter, *The Sociology of City Life*, Longmans, 1931
N. P. Gist and L. A. Halbert, *Urban Society*, Crowell, 1933
R. D. McKenzie, *The Metropolitan Community*, McGraw-Hill, 1933
W. S. Thompson, *Population Problems*, McGraw-Hill, 1930, Chaps. II, VIII-IX, XII-XIII, XVI-XIX, XXII-XXIII
H. P. Fairchild, *General Sociology*, Wiley, 1934, Chaps. XV-XVII, XX
—— *Immigration*
John Corbin, *The Return of the Middle Class*, Scribner, 1922
N. A. Berdyaev, *The Bourgeois Mind*, Sheed & Ward, 1935
W. B. Pitkin, *Capitalism Carries On*, McGraw-Hill, 1935
M. H. Dobb, *Capitalist Enterprise and Social Progress*, London, 1925
Jerome Davis, *Capitalism and Its Culture*, Farrar & Rinehart (forthcoming)
Lewis Corey, *The Crisis of the Middle Class*, Covici, Friede, 1935
A. N. Holcombe, *The New Party Politics*, Norton, 1933, Chaps. II, IV, V
Beer, *Social Struggles and Thought*
René Fülöp-Miller, *Leaders, Dreamers and Rebels*, Viking Press (forthcoming)
Lillian Symes and Travers Clement, *Rebel America*, Harper, 1934
Louis Adamic, *Dynamite*, Viking Press, 1934
Wells, *The Work, Wealth and Happiness of Mankind*, Vol. II, Chaps. X, XIII-XIV
Slater, *The Growth of Modern England*, Chaps. III, IX, XXI
A. N. Pack, *The Challenge of Leisure*, Macmillan, 1933
Davis and Barnes, *Readings in Sociology*, pp. 333-46, 398-441, 875-91
J. C. Jones, Amry Vandenbosch, and M. B. Vandenbosch, eds., *Readings in Citizenship*, Macmillan, 1932, pp. 607-68, 779-820
F. G. Crawford, *Readings in American Government*, Knopf, 1927, Chaps. XXVII-XXVIII

FURTHER REFERENCES
SOCIAL PHASES OF THE NEW RÉGIME

On the population developments as a whole associated with the Industrial Revolution, see Nussbaum, *op. cit.*, Pt. IV, Chap. V.

On modern urban growth, see Ogg and Sharp, *The Economic Development of Modern Europe*, pp. 333 ff.; Gist and Halbert, *op. cit.*, Chap. II; A. F. Weber, *The Growth of Cities* (Columbia University Press, 1899); Chap. IV of F. C. Howe, *The Modern City and Its Problems* (Scribner, 1915).

On the growth of cities in the United States, see W. F. Ogburn and others in *Recent Social Trends in the United States*, Vol. I, Chap. IX.

On economic factors in modern urban development, see Chaps. V-VI of N. S. B. Gras, *Introduction to Economic History* (Harper, 1922); Anderson and Lindeman, *op. cit.*, Chap. XIV; Gist and Halbert, *op. cit.*, Chaps. III-IV. For a model study of the evolution of a great modern metropolis, see H. P. Ormsby, *London on the Thames: A Study of the Natural Conditions That Influenced the Birth and Growth of a Great City* (London, 1924).

On women in urban industry, see Edith Abbott, *Women in Industry* (Appleton, 1910); Grace Hutchins, *Women Who Work* (International Publishers, 1934).

On living-conditions in early industrial cities, see Hammond and Hammond, *The Age of the Chartists*, Chap. VII; Slater, *op. cit.*, pp. 375 ff.; M. C. Buer, *Health, Wealth and Population in the Early Days of the Industrial Revolution* (London, 1926).

On the beginnings of public-health legislation in England, see Slater, *op cit.*, pp. 375 ff.; Hammond and Hammond, *op. cit.*, Chap. XVI; Hammerton, *op. cit.*, Chap. 189; *Facts and Factors in Economic History*, pp. 240-60; J. H. H. Williams, *A Century of Public Health in Britain, 1832-1929* (Macmillan, 1932).

On preventive medicine and city life, see Cowdry, *Human Biology and Race Welfare*, Chap. XVIII; East, *Biology in Human Affairs*, Chaps. VII-VIII; Chaps. I-IV, XVI of H. H. Waite, *Disease Prevention* (Crowell, 1926); C. E. A. Winslow, *The Evolution and Significance of the Modern Public Health Campaign* (Yale University Press, 1923); Sir Arthur Newsholme, *The Evolution of Preventive Medicine* (Williams & Wilkins, 1927) and *The Ministry of Health* (Putnam, 1925).

On the need for scientific city government, see Chap. XIII of William Anderson, *American City Government* (Holt, 1925); *The Story of the City Manager Plan* (National Municipal League, 1931). On city problems, see Howe, *op. cit.*, Chap. XXIV; Thompson, *op. cit.*, Chaps. XVIII-XIX; Gist and Halbert, *op. cit.*, Chaps. XIV-XVI, XVIII-XIX; McKenzie, *op. cit.;* Carpenter, *op. cit.*

On problems of urban government, see Howe, *op. cit.*, Chaps. V-XIV, XVII, XXII; Anderson and Lindeman, *op. cit.*, Chap. XVII; E. S. Griffith, *Current Municipal Problems* (Houghton Mifflin, 1933); Gist and Halbert, *op. cit.*, Chap. XVII; W. B. Munro, *Municipal Administration* (Macmillan, 1934). On corruption in urban political rings, see Lincoln Steffens, *The Shame of the Cities* (McClure, Phillips, 1904); N. B. Thomas and Paul Blanshard, *What's the Matter with New York?* (Macmillan, 1932); W. B. and J. B. Northrop, *The Insolence of Office* (Putnam, 1932). On urban political corruption and the underworld of crime and rackets, see D. T. Lynch, *Criminals and Politicians: A History of the Rackets' Red Glare* (Macmillan, 1933); Fletcher Dobyns, *The Underworld of American Politics* (privately printed, 1932); Stephen Endicott, *Mayor Harding of New York, a Novel* (Mohawk Press, 1931).

On municipal-ownership projects, see Howe, *op. cit.*, Chaps. XIII-XIV, XXI; Chaps. VIII-XII of C. D. Thompson, *Public Ownership* (Crowell, 1925).

On urban surveys and city-planning, see Gist and Halbert, *op. cit.*, Chaps. XXI-XXIII; Howe, *op. cit.*, Chaps. XV-XVI, XIX-XX; Anderson and Lindeman, *op. cit.*, Chap. XVIII; Pts. I-II of Patrick Abercrombie, *Town and Country Planning* (Holt, 1933); Sir Raymond Unwin, *Town Planning in Practice* (Century, 1932); R. R. Kern, *The Supercity* (privately printed, 1924); R. L. Duffus, *Mastering a Metropolis* (Harper, 1932)—a popular digest of *Regional Plan of New York and Its Environs* (Regional Plan of N. Y., 1928-31, 10 vols.).

For the history of the subject, see Haverfield, *op. cit.;* T. F. Tout, "Medieval Town Planning," *Town Planning Review*, April, 1919; T. H. Hughes and E. A. G. Lamborn, *Towns and Town-Planning* (Oxford Press, 1923).

On rapid and cheap transportation as affecting the urban problem, see Anderson and Lindeman, *op. cit.*, Chap. VII; Kern, *op. cit.*, Chap. IX.

On municipal housing problems, see Howe, *op. cit.*, Chaps. XIX-XX; Gist and Halbert, *op. cit.*, Chaps. V-VIII; Anderson and Lindeman, *op. cit.*, Chap. XVI; *Housing America* by the editors of *Fortune* (Harcourt, Brace, 1932); Kern, *op. cit.*, Chaps. II-III.

POPULATION TRENDS. On the causes of modern population growth, see W. S. Thompson, *op. cit.*, Chaps. VI, IX, XIV-XV; Chap. IV of E. M. East, *Mankind at the Crossroads* (Scribner, 1923) and *Biology in Human Affairs*, Chaps. VII-VIII; Raymond Pearl, *The Biology of Population Growth* (Knopf, 1925); Frank Lorimer and Frederick Osborn, *Dynamics of Population* (Macmillan, 1934). For a model study of pre-Industrial Revolution population conditions, see E. B. Greene and V. D. Harrington, *American Population before the Federal Census of 1790* (Columbia University Press, 1932). On net population gains as the result of medical science and the Industrial Revolution, see Ogg and Sharp, *op. cit.,* Chap. xvi; Thompson, *op. cit.,* Chaps. iv, xii; E. M. East, *Mankind at the Crossroads.*

On the Malthusian controversy, see W. S. Thompson, *Population: A Study in Malthusianism* (Columbia University Press, 1915); and *Population Problems,* Chaps. i-iii; Chaps. i, x of J. A. Field, *Essays on Population* (University of Chicago Press, 1931); Ezra Bowen, *An Hypothesis of Population Growth* (Columbia University Press, 1931); H. G. Duncan, *Race and Population Problems* (Longmans, 1929).

On the eugenics problem, the best recent discussion is S. J. Holmes, *The Eugenic Predicament* (Harcourt, Brace, 1933).

IMMIGRATION. On migration to regions with improved economic conditions for the working classes, see Thompson, *Population Problems,* Chap. xxiii; Nussbaum, *op. cit.,* Pt. IV, Chap. iv.

On the immigration problem, see Ogg and Sharp, *op. cit.,* Chap. xvi; Fairchild, *Immigration* (the standard work); W. F. Willcox, ed., *International Migrations* (Pitman, 1929-31, 2 vols.); J. W. Jenks and W. J. Lauck, *The Immigration Problem* (Funk & Wagnalls, 1926); Edith Abbott, *Immigration: Select Documents and Case Records* (University of Chicago Press, 1924); *Recent Social Trends in the United States,* Vol. I, Chap. xi; R. D. McKenzie, *Oriental Exclusion* (University of Chicago Press, 1928); pp. 70-74 of W. A. Hamm and Oscar Dombrow, *Current Problems in American History* (College Entrance Book Co., 1933). The best comprehensive study of immigration is contained in the series edited by A. T. Burns, *Americanization Studies* (Harper, 1920-24, 10 vols.).

On the effects of immigration, for a reasonable critical estimate see E. A. Ross, *The Old World in the New* (Century, 1914). For a violent criticism, see W. C. Abbott, *The New Barbarians* (Little, Brown, 1925). For a favorable view, see I. A. Hourwich, *Immigration and Labor* (Viking Press, 1922). For an objective analysis, see W. M. Leiserson, *Adjusting Immigrant and Industry* (Harper, 1924).

THE TRIUMPH OF THE BOURGEOISIE. On the triumph of capitalism and the middle class, see article "Middle Class," Encyclopaedia of the Social Sciences; Hammerton, *op. cit.,* Chap. 166; Sombart, *The Quintessence of Capitalism;* Gretton, *The English Middle Class;* Gustavus Myers, *History of the Great American Fortunes* (Kerr, 1910, 3 vols.); John McConaughy, *Who Rules America?* (Longmans, 1934); Corbin, *op. cit.*

THE PROLETARIAN CHALLENGE TO CAPITALISM. On this subject, see article "Proletariat," Encyclopaedia of the Social Sciences; Holcombe, *op. cit.,* Chap. ii; Symes and Clement, *op. cit.;* Beer, *op. cit.;* Wells, *op. cit.,* Vol. II, Chap. x; W. Z. Foster, *Toward Soviet America* (Coward-McCann, 1932); S. D. Schmalhausen, ed., *Recovery through Revolution* (Covici, Friede, 1933); Austin Lewis, *The Rise of the American Proletarian* (Kerr, 1907) and *The Militant Proletariat* (Kerr, 1911); Nathan Fine, *Labor and Farmer Parties in the United States, 1828-1928* (Rand School of Social Science, 1928); S. A. Rice, *Farmers and Workers in American Politics* (Columbia University Press, 1924); John Strachey, *The Coming Struggle for Power* (Covici, Friede, 1933); Robert Briffault, *Breakdown* (Coward-McCann, 1932); Fülöp-Miller, *op. cit.*

FEMINISM. On the recent emancipation of women, see Slater, *op. cit.,* Chapter xxi; E. R. Hecker, *Short History of Women's Rights* (2d ed. rev., Putnam, 1914); Meyrick Booth, *Woman and Society* (Longmans, 1929); R. P. Mason, *Woman*

Walks Alone (Dial Press, 1931); I. H. Irwin, *Angels and Amazons* (Doubleday, Doran, 1933); H. W. Puckett, *Germany's Women Go Forward* (Columbia University Press, 1930).

On the condition of working women, see Abbott, *op. cit.;* pp. 253 ff. of C. A. Beard, ed., *A Century of Progress* (Harper, 1933); O. L. Thatcher, *Occupations for Women* (privately printed, 1927); Hutchins, *Women Who Work;* E. J. Hutchinson, *Women's Wages* (Longmans, 1919); American Woman's Association, *Women Workers through the Depression,* ed. by Lorine Pruette (Macmillan, 1934).

PSYCHOLOGICAL RESULTS OF THE INDUSTRIAL REVOLUTION. On the psychological changes and problems brought by the Industrial Revolution, see Graham Wallas, *The Great Society* (Macmillan, 1914); Chaps. x-xi of J. H. Randall, Jr., *Our Changing Civilization* (Stokes, 1929). Pt. IV of W. F. Ogburn, *Social Change* (Viking Press, 1922); Mayo, *The Human Problems of an Industrial Civilization*.

THE RISE OF A NEW ERA OF LEISURE. On the problem of leisure in our age, see C. D. Burns, *Leisure in the Modern World* (Century, 1932); G. A. Lundberg, *Leisure: A Suburban Study* (Columbia University Press, 1934); Gove Hambidge, *Time to Live* (McGraw-Hill, 1933); L. P. Jacks, *The Education of the Whole Man* (Harper, 1931); Harold Loeb, *Life in a Technocracy* (Viking Press, 1933).

GOVERNMENT AND ECONOMICS. C. A. Beard, *The Economic Basis of Politics* (new ed., Knopf, 1934); Oppenheimer, *The State;* E. P. Herring, *Group Representation before Congress* (Johns Hopkins Press, 1929); H. L. Childs, *Labor and Capital in National Politics* (Ohio State University Press, 1930).

LAW AND INDUSTRIALISM. Haines, *The Revival of Natural Law Concepts;* Jerome Frank, *Law and the Modern Mind* (Coward-McCann, 1930); Gustavus Myers, *History of the Supreme Court of the United States* (Kerr, 1918); Max Lerner, "The Supreme Court and Capitalism," *Yale Law Journal,* March, 1933; L. B. Boudin, *Government by Judiciary* (Godwin, 1931, 2 vols.).

ETHICS AND INDUSTRIALISM. Robert Briffault, *Sin and Sex* (Macaulay, 1931); H. C. Broun and Margaret Leech, *Anthony Comstock, Roundsman of the Lord* (Boni, 1927); M. L. Ernst and William Seagle, *To the Pure: A Study of Obscenity and the Censor* (Viking Press, 1928); Freda Kirchwey, ed., *Our Changing Morality* (Boni, 1924); H. S. Brock (Jonathan Leonard), *Meddlers* (Viking Press, 1929).

RELIGION AND INDUSTRIALISM. Chap. IV of J. H. and J. H., Jr., Randall, *Religion and the Modern World* (Stokes, 1929); H. F. Ward, *Which Way Religion?* (Macmillan, 1931); Paul Hutchinson, *The Ordeal of Western Religion* (Houghton Mifflin, 1933); Bouck White, *The Church of the Social Revolution* (Church of the Social Revolution, 1914).

EDUCATION AND INDUSTRIALISM. Pt. II of H. O. Rugg, *Culture and Education in America* (Harcourt, Brace, 1931); G. S. Counts, *The American Road to Culture* (Day, 1930); B. L. Pierce, *Citizens' Organizations and the Civic Training of Youth* (Scribner, 1933) and *Public Opinion and the Teaching of History in the United States* (Knopf, 1926).

LITERATURE AND INDUSTRIALISM. Scudder, *Social Ideals in English Letters;* V. F. Calverton, *The Liberation of American Literature* (Scribner, 1932); Granville Hicks, *The Great Tradition: An Interpretation of American Literature since the Civil War* (Macmillan, 1933).

ART AND INDUSTRIALISM. Pp. 136-54 of H. L. Mencken, *Prejudices, Second Series* (Knopf, 1925); Philip Johnson, *Machine Art* (Norton, 1934); Lewis Mumford, *Technics and Civilization* (Harcourt, Brace, 1934); H. E. Read, *Art and Industry* (Harcourt, Brace, 1935).

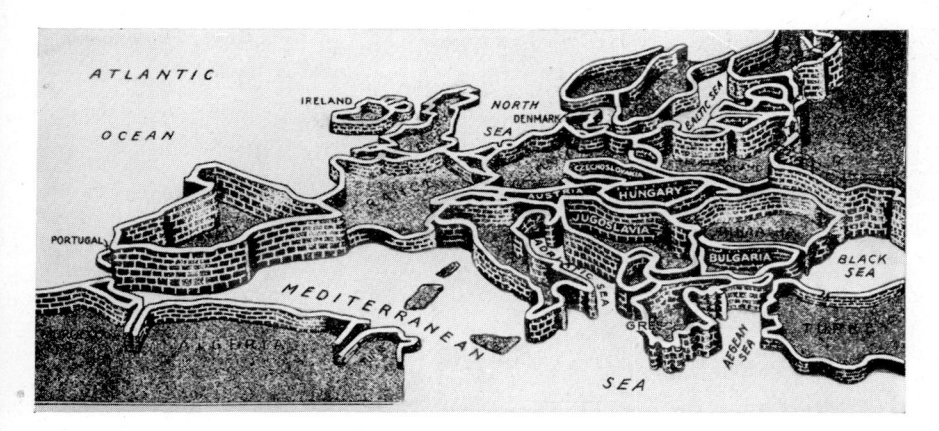

THE TARIFF WALLS OF EUROPE WITH THEIR RELATIVE HEIGHTS

First published in the London Illustrated News, *reproduced, for publication in the United States, with the permission of the New York* Times.

AN INDUSTRIAL CENTER

From Smoke Investigation Bulletin, *Mellon Institute of Industrial Research*

New York Public Library

FIFTH AVENUE AND FORTY-SECOND STREET,
NEW YORK CITY, 1850

Ewing Galloway

FIFTH AVENUE, NEW YORK CITY, 1889

CHAPTER XIII

THE FOUNDATIONS OF CONTEMPORARY NATIONALISM

I. THE POPULARIZATION OF NATIONAL SENTIMENT

The primary political innovations of the contemporary age were nationalism, liberalism, republicanism, democracy, and imperialism.[1] We have already considered the rise of liberalism and republicanism. We may now turn to a historical and analytical survey of those outstanding political developments of our times—nationalism, democracy, party government, and imperialism.

The growth of nationalism in modern times can probably be understood most intelligently if we regard it as having developed through something like the following stages of expression:[2]

1. *Nationality as a Popular Sentiment*

In this period, which lasted roughly from the French Revolution to the first quarter of the nineteenth century, nationalism carried with it no particular political connotation. It was chiefly a matter of irrational popular contagion.

2. *Nationality as the Idea of Political Self-Determination*

In this stage, which ran for about half a century after 1815 and continued longer in central and southeastern Europe, nationality was represented as the proper basis for the state. The oppressed and subject nations were to be freed, so that the boundaries of nationality would be generally identical with the boundaries of political groups.

3. *The Age of "Integral Nationalism"*

In this period, which dominated the generation before the World War, loyalty to nation-state was elevated above all other human loyalties—at least all loyalties to earthly things. It was held that religion, education, and culture must all subordinate themselves to national ends and shape their policies in harmony with the principles of nationalism.

4. *Economic Nationalism*

This stage set in before the World War but has become more marked in its developments since 1918. It is now held that economic life must be subordinated

[1] See Charles Seignobos, *History of Contemporary Civilization*, Scribner, 1909, Chaps. IV-V, X, XIV-XV, XIX; and Lynn Thorndike, *Short History of Civilization*, Crofts, 1926, Chaps. XXXIX-XL.
[2] This prospectus follows roughly the suggestions in the excellent books on nationalism by Professor C. J. H. Hayes.

to political considerations and power. The nation is to become an economic as well as a political unit. The final apparent goal is either state Socialism or state capitalism, the latter of which has become progressively Fascist in character.

These stages, of course, overlap somewhat in a strict chronological sense, but they hold good in broad outline and describe accurately the evolution of modern nationalism.

The expansion of Europe and the Commercial Revolution not only gave a great impetus to the autocratic national state, but in time created conditions that contributed more than anything else before the Industrial Revolution to its ultimate downfall.[1] The middle class increased in power and prestige and soon turned against the kings in the more progressive countries of western Europe. It destroyed the autocratic state and prepared the way for the growth of nineteenth-century democracy. Along with the destruction of the autocratic aspect of the early national state, there came an intensification and popularization of national sentiment quite unknown in the earlier aristocratic forms of political organization. The nature and significance of this all-important revolt of the middle class against the absolutist state is effectively set forth by Professor Carlton Hayes in the following illuminating citation:

Driven on by insatiable ambition, not content to be lords of the world of business, with ships and warehouses for castles and with clerks for retainers, the bourgeoisie have placed their lawyers in the royal service, their learned men in the academies, their economists at the king's elbow, and with restless energy they push on to shape state and society to their own ends. In England [by the close of the seventeenth century] they have already helped to dethrone kings and have secured some hold on Parliament, but on the Continent their power and place is less advanced.

For the eighteenth century is still the grand age of monarchs, who take Louis XIV as the pattern of princely power and pomp. "Benevolent despots" they are, these monarchs meaning well to govern their people with fatherly kindness. But their plans go wrong and their reforms fall flat, while the bourgeoisie become self-conscious and self-reliant, and rise up against the throne of the sixteenth Louis in France. It is the bourgeoisie that start the revolutionary cry of "Liberty, Equality, Fraternity," and it is this cry in the throats of the masses which sends terror to the hearts of nobles and kings. Desperately the old order—the old régime—defends itself. First France, then all Europe, is affected. Revolutionary wars convulse the Continent. Never had the world witnessed wars so disastrous, so bloody.[2]

In France the bourgeois triumph came a century later than it did in England. In the seventeenth century the middle class was too weak to defy the monarchy and the feudal nobility. But in 1789 and the years following it gave convincing evidence of increased power by crushing both royalty and nobility and establishing itself as the supreme element in the state. Threatened by the exiled French aristocracy and their foreign sympathizers, the Revolutionists, held together by the new shibboleth of *Fraternité,* arose as a "nation in arms" to defend their freshly won liberties against the champions of the old régime.

---

[1] See above, Chapter IV.
[2] C. J. H. Hayes, *Political and Social History of Modern Europe,* Macmillan, 1916, 2 vols., Vol. I, pp. 393-94.

THE POPULARIZATION OF NATIONAL SENTIMENT 455

A vast change took place in the nature of national sentiment as a result of this popularizing force of fraternity. At the close of the seventeenth century Louis XIV implied, if he did not say, that the state and the monarch were one and the same; at the close of the eighteenth, bourgeois officials were declaring that the French nation had a glorious existence quite independent of the king. Professor Hayes has well expressed the importance of this new Revolutionary watchword of Fraternity in the process of popularizing the sentiment of nationalism:

Of all the political and spiritual elements in the "old régime" of the nineteenth century, one of the most stubborn and most impressive was the growth of nationalism. Taking definite form in the days of the French Revolution, under the fair name of Fraternity, it appeared as a revolt of a self-conscious people in behalf of their individual liberty and equality against the tyranny or inefficiency of contemporaneous divine-right institutions. By the French idea of Fraternity every European country was soon affected, so that formerly latent sympathies were galvanized into a most lively sentiment, and theorists from the domains of history or philosophy or even of economics could find popular approval for their solemn pronouncements that "people speaking the same language and sharing the same general customs should be politically united as nations."[1]

As a result of the twenty-three years of general European war following 1792, the national sentiment of well-nigh every European country was transformed from the autocratic type to a popular form, generally diffused through the whole body politic.[2] This came about either directly, where Napoleon conquered and carried the French reforms, or indirectly, as a defense reaction against this great military genius by the other states, the leaders of which found it necessary to arouse a similar patriotism in their citizens in order to cope with Napoleon. The French Revolutionary patriotism was carried directly from France into the Rhine provinces, Italy, and Poland. It appeared as a defense reaction in Prussia and Austria, particularly Prussia,[3] in Spain and her colonies, and, to a lesser degree, even in England and Russia. No state in Europe wholly escaped the wave of patriotic enthusiasm that swept over Europe from 1792 to 1815.

The remarkable contribution of Napoleon to the growth of nationalism in modern European history, through giving widespread dissemination to the forces and tendencies of his time, is thus stated by Professor Robinson:

So long as states were composed of *subjects* rather than of *citizens,* the modern emotions of nationality could scarcely develop. Nationality, in our meaning of the term, is a concomitant of another mystical entity, democracy. The French Revolution began, it is true, in a period of philosophic cosmopolitanism, since that was the tradition of the *philosophes,*—and the French armies undertook to liberate other peoples from their tyrants in the name of the rights of *man,* not of *nations.* But Napoleon, in a somewhat incidental and left-handed fashion, did so much to promote the progress of both democratic institutions and of nationality in western Europe that he may, in a sense, be regarded as the putative father of them both. His

---

[1] C. J. H. Hayes, "The War of the Nations," *Political Science Quarterly,* December, 1914, pp. 687-88. [2] *Cf.* Rose, *Nationality in Modern History,* Lectures II-VI.

[3] *Cf.* Engelbrecht, *Johann Gottlieb Fichte;* and W. C. Langsam, *The Napoleonic Wars and German Nationalism in Austria,* Columbia University Press, 1930.

plebiscites were empty things in practice, but they loudly acknowledged the rights of peoples to decide on vital matters. He was a friend of constitutions—so long as he himself made them. Then his attempt to seat brother Joseph on the Spanish throne produced a really national revolt, and led to the Spanish constitution of 1812 and all its later revivals and imitations. In Italy he stirred a desire for national unity and the expulsion of the foreigner which had been dormant since the days of Machiavelli's hopeless appeal. He is the founder of modern Germany. He succeeded in a task which had baffled German emperors from the days of Otto the Great; for in 1803 he so far consolidated her disrupted territories that the remaining states, enlarged and strengthened, could in time form a strong union and become a great international power. His restrictions on the size of the Prussian army after his victory at Jena suggested to Scharnhorst, Gneisenau, and Boyen a subterfuge which made Prussia the military schoolmaster of Europe, and cost the millions of lives since offered up in the cause of nationality.[1]

To these European effects of the influence of the Napoleonic period upon the growth of nationalism should be added the contagion of this development which extended to America. The rise of national independence in Latin America was immediately related to the influence of Napoleon upon Spain.[2] As H. A. L. Fisher has written: "If the South American democracies value their independence, statues of Napoleon might with propriety be raised in the squares of Valparaiso and Buenos Aires." The naval and commercial aspects of the struggle between England and France after 1793 greatly stimulated the development of national unity in the United States. Clay and the "War Hawks" called upon our country to avenge the "insults" to its flag and the ravages on its trade. They impatiently demanded the opportunity to invade Canada. This culminated in the War of 1812, in which our naval victories did much to stimulate national pride.[3] Finally, the purchase of Louisiana, made possible by Napoleon, was perhaps the greatest "nationalistic" event in the first half-century of our history as an independent state.

So great a momentum did the newly popularized sentiment of nationality gain that not even Metternich, the most powerful conservative statesman of the first half of the nineteenth century, could check it. In spite of his temporarily successful efforts to leave Italy and Germany mere "geographical expressions" in 1815, his arrangement was cast to the winds in the unification of Italy and of Germany by those great nationalistic statesmen, Cavour and Bismarck. The nationalistic sentiment surged violently, if with less success in gaining full political expression, in the Balkans, Bohemia, Poland, and Hungary.

But the French Revolution only gave the initial impulse to this new or democratic phase of the development of nationality. A much more profound revolution was already in process of development in the factories and mines of England, where there was being prepared the greatest cultural transformation in the history of the race. This could not fail to have a far-reaching reaction upon the growth of national sentiment and the activities and attitudes of the national states.

[1] J. H. Robinson, "What Is National Spirit?" *Century Magazine,* November, 1916, p. 61.
[2] See Shepherd, *Latin America,* Chaps. VII-IX.
[3] See Barnes, *History and Social Intelligence,* Chaps. IX-XII.

II. NATIONALISM IN THE MACHINE AGE

The development of new means for the communication of information, as a result of the Industrial Revolution, through the railroad, telegraph, telephone, and cheap newspapers,[1] made possible a true psychic unity within each nation, broke up local isolation, and completed the process of popularizing national sentiment and perfecting national self-consciousness. It made the various national manifestations of the "herd instinct" more communicable, more responsive, and more liable to sudden and hysterical explosions.[2] This "instantaneous" character of contemporary national thought and its antagonism to reflective analysis has been well expressed by Newton D. Baker:

In our modern life there is more of instantaneousness than there has ever been in the world before. Never since the world began was it possible to conceive such a situation as this: that one hundred and twenty million people stretching over a continent, an imperial expanse, should think and feel simultaneously. By radio we all hear the same fact at the same time. It may happen to be six o'clock in New York when I hear it, and two o'clock in California when somebody else hears it; but however the clocks may vary, the instant in time is identical. The isolation that once existed when news traveled slowly, advancing in waves, reaching first one area, then another, then a third, with the first having time to meditate about it before it became a universal idea—all this is a thing of the past. Now we not only get the same idea at the same moment, but we all react to it at the same time. Therefore, what was once an inescapable moment of meditation vouchsafed to most of us before the universality of an idea was accomplished, is now abolished.[3]

So backward was the general level of thought and social interests on the eve of the Industrial Revolution that the sudden development of means for quickly communicating the prevalent attitudes throughout the modern national state tended to give to national thought and emotion the same self-satisfied provincialism that had earlier prevailed on a local scale. The inhabitants of whole national states came to entertain towards their neighbors much the same sentiments of suspicion and hostility that dwellers in local communities had once possessed towards strangers from outside.[4] Therefore it is not surprising when Professor Robinson finds that: "Our ancient tribal instinct evidently retains its blind and unreasoning characteristics despite the fact that we are able nowadays, by means of newspapers, periodicals, railroads, and telegraphs, to spread it over vast areas, such as are comprised in modern states like Germany, France, Russia, and the United States." [5] Professor Hayes has very effectively stated the relation of the Industrial Revolution to the spread of national sentiment and of nationalistic propaganda:

Without the Industrial Revolution, it would be impossible to raise funds, to supply textbooks and material equipment, or to exercise centralized supervision and control

---

[1] See above, pp. 317 ff.; and below, pp. 736 ff.
[2] *Cf.* W. B. Pillsbury, *The Psychology of Nationality and Internationalism*, Appleton, 1919, Chap. VI; and G. E. Partridge, *The Psychology of Nations*, Macmillan, 1919, Pt. I.
[3] Baker, "The Answer Is Education," *Journal of Adult Education*, June, 1931, p. 265.
[4] For a splendid socio-psychological analysis of the attitude towards strangers from primitive times to our own, see M. M. Wood, *The Stranger: A Study in Social Relationships*, Columbia University Press, 1934.
[5] Robinson, *loc. cit.*, p. 63. *Cf.* W. B. Kaempffert, ed., *Popular History of American Invention*, Scribner, 1924, 2 vols., Vol. I, Pt. II, and O. W. Riegel, *Mobilizing for Chaos*, Yale University Press, 1934.

requisite to the establishment and maintenance of great systems of free universal schooling. Without the Industrial Revolution, it would be impossible to take all able bodied young men away from productive employment and put them in an army for two or three years, feeding and clothing and housing them and providing them with transport, arms and hospitals. Without the Industrial Revolution, it would be impossible to produce huge quantities of journals, to collect news for them quickly, to print them in bulk, to distribute them widely, to have a numerous public to read them and much advertising to pay for them. Without the Industrial Revolution, it would be impossible for a propagandist society to flood a large country with written and oral appeals. . . .

The technological advance itself is not more favorable to one purpose [nationalism] than to the other [internationalism]. It can be used for either or for both. In fact it has been used for a century, and is still used, preëminently for nationalist ends. Societies, journals, and schools, as well as armies, are today predominantly nationalist, and the nationalism which they inculcate tends to be more exclusive and more vigorous. Indeed, economic development seems to be a handmaid to nationalist development, rather than the reverse.[1]

The world-wide extension of the new mechanism of communication also rendered "jingoistic" expressions in other countries better known and more likely to arouse antagonisms. Finally, as will be evident from succeeding chapters, the Industrial Revolution was the most influential force impelling the modern national states to build up new colonial empires in the era of modern imperialism after 1870.[2]

The European revolutions of 1848 promised to bring to a focus the two great principles of the first half of the nineteenth century—nationality and democracy—which had been produced by the combined action of the French and Industrial Revolutions. For the moment they seemed likely to realize the dream of the European liberals and create a political order that would give full recognition to both nationality and democracy. The enthusiasm thus stirred among the nationalists and democrats in Europe during these momentous years has been eloquently set forth by Lord Bryce:

So the sympathy, both of America and of Britain, or at least of British Liberals (among whom was then to found a great majority of the men of light and leading), went out when, in 1848, the crash of the Orleans Monarchy in France had shaken most European thrones, to the Italian revolutionaries, to the Polish revolutionaries, to the Czechs in Bohemia, to the Magyars in Hungary, who, under the illustrious Kossuth, were fighting in 1849 for their national rights against Hapsburg tyranny, to the German patriots who were trying to liberalize Prussia and the smaller kingdoms, and bring all Germans under one free constitutional Government. Men hoped that so soon as each people, delivered from a foreign yoke, became masters of their own destinies, all would go well for the world. The two sacred principles of Liberty and Nationality would, like twin guardian-angels, lead it into the paths of tranquil happiness, a Mazzinian paradise of moral dignity and liberty, a Cobdenian paradise of commercial prosperity and international peace.[3]

But the tragic sequence of events in 1848-1849 proved that nationality and democracy could even then scarcely coöperate in complete harmony. National

---

[1] C. J. H. Hayes, *Historical Evolution of Modern Nationalism*, Long & Smith, 1931, pp. 239-41.
[2] See below, pp. 521 ff.
[3] James Bryce, *Essays and Addresses in Wartime*, Macmillan, 1918, p. 141.

jealousy and particularism weakened the cause of democracy and ultimately led to the temporary downfall of both before the onslaughts of political reactionaries and antinational imperialists.[1]

The liberals of 1848 quite futilely believed that, when tempered with democracy, nationality would be divested of its chauvinistic and aggressive qualities and would insure the coming of perpetual peace. The discussion to follow will show that a more complete realization of nationality has thus far achieved even less than democracy in producing the political millennium. Rather, it has seemingly merited Lord Acton's indictment that "there is no principle of change, no phase of political speculation conceivable which is more comprehensive, more subversive, more arbitrary than nationality. Its course will be marked with material as well as moral ruin, in order that a new invention may prevail over the works of God and the interests of mankind."

The nineteenth century witnessed the belated completion of national unification in two major European states—Italy and Germany—through the efforts of Cavour and Bismarck in the decade and a half following 1855.[2] These statesmen, in deep sympathy with the national aspirations of their countrymen, gathered together under their leadership the various forces working in this direction and succeeded in giving concrete and effective expression to the generally diffused impulse to political unification. In a very real sense, they may be regarded as having carried to completion the forces and tendencies aroused in their respective states by the French Revolution and the Napoleonic conquests and statesmanship. The main obstacle to national unification which had to be overcome in both cases was the antagonism of that inveterate and implacable enemy of Napoleon and the "French Ideas"—the anachronistic empire of the Hapsburgs and Metternich.

Starting with the discouraging conditions after the collapse of the Revolution of 1848, Count Camillo di Cavour converted Victor Emmanuel II of Sardinia to liberalism and a program of unification, skillfully enlisted the aid of Napoleon III in 1858, and drove the Austrians out of Venetia in 1859 with the assistance of the French armies. A colorful patriotic adventurer, Giuseppe Garibaldi, overcame the opposition in Sicily and Naples in 1860, and vainly attacked Rome in 1862 and 1867. In 1870 the King of Sardinia was able to occupy Rome and to proclaim the complete unification of Italy. In Prussia, the able and domineering Count Otto von Bismarck crushed out liberalism and pacifism, defeated Austria in 1866, and eagerly exploited Napoleon III's foolish bid for war in 1870. Decisively defeating France in 1870-71, he was at last able to unite Germany and to create the second German Empire in 1871. King William I of Prussia was proclaimed Emperor William I of Germany in the Hall of Mirrors at Versailles in 1871.

The work of Cavour and Bismarck marked a significant stage in that incessant warfare against the medieval imperial concepts and practices which had begun at Westphalia in 1648, and was carried further at Utrecht (1713)

---

[1] See above, pp. 122 ff.
[2] See *Cambridge Modern History*, Vol. XI, Chaps. xiv, xvi, xix; Helmolt, *History of the World*, Vol. VIII, Chap. iii; Bolton King, *A History of Italian Unity, 1814-1871*, Scribner, 1899, 2 vols.; Sir A. W. Ward, *Germany, 1815-1890*, Macmillan, 1917-20, 3 vols., Vol. II; and W. H. Dawson, *The German Empire, 1867-1914*, Macmillan, 1919, 2 vols., Vol. I.

and in the creation of the Confederation of the Rhine (1806). It finally ended in the utter collapse of the Austrian Empire in the autumn of 1918, as a result of the growth of national sentiment among the subject peoples and the blow to its military prestige in the crushing defeat which marked the close of the "War of the Nations." Force, chicanery, duplicity, and intrigue were employed about equally by both Cavour and Bismarck in achieving their nationalistic ambitions, but the political systems they created were somewhat different. "Blood and iron" and *Realpolitik* were used by Cavour merely as a means to the end of creating a relatively liberal state and a parliamentary government, while with Bismarck they were used to repress the type of liberalism that Cavour had successfully established.

These wars of nationalism during the middle and the third quarter of the nineteenth century also revolutionized the arts of war. The firearms of the Napoleonic period were crude and inaccurate; as we have seen, some bows and arrows were actually used at the Battle of Leipzig. The rifling of muskets and cannon was introduced in the first half of the nineteenth century, giving greater accuracy and range. Revolvers became popular after 1850, being particularly promoted among the cowboys of the American West. Most of the rifles used in the Civil War were muzzle-loaders using a percussion cap—a real advance over the flintlock. Breechloaders were used slightly in the Civil War. The first conflict in which their use was of crucial importance was the Austro-Prussian War of 1866, in which the Prussians were armed with the so-called needle gun. Mortars and canister and shrapnel came into use in this period. Repeating rifles were not used until the Spanish-American War, when smokeless powder was also introduced. Machine guns came in at the close of the century.

In addition to these larger national states that have appeared upon the European map since 1815, a number of smaller nationalities have attained, in part at least, to statehood.[1] Greece achieved independence in 1829; Belgium gained its independence in 1830 and its neutralization in 1839; Luxembourg became an independent neutralized state in 1867; Serbia, Rumania, and Montenegro were recognized as states in 1878; Norway separated from Sweden in 1905; Bulgaria took advantage of the European confusion and tension of 1908 to declare her complete freedom from Turkey; and in 1913 Austria and Italy created the independent Albanian state to block Serbia from an outlet to the sea.

In spite of this considerable addition to the "family of nations" in Europe, nationalistic aspirations were by no means satisfied by 1914. Not only did the political map fail to coincide with the boundaries of nationality in the case of every one of the European national states created during the nineteenth century, but there were great historical nations like the Poles, the Irish, the Czechs of Bohemia, and the Finns that were denied any independent political existence whatever.

Had the psychology of peoples been the same in 1914 that it was a century and a half earlier, this condition of incomplete national independence would have produced no grave problems. Potential nations, as distinct in race, language, and historical traditions as these were at the beginning of the twentieth

---

[1] See Ferdinand Schevill, *History of the Balkan Peninsula*, rev. ed., Harcourt, Brace, 1933, Chaps. XIX-XXVI; and W. M. Gewehr, *The Rise of Nationalism in the Balkans, 1800-1930*, Holt, 1931.

Europeans Peoples

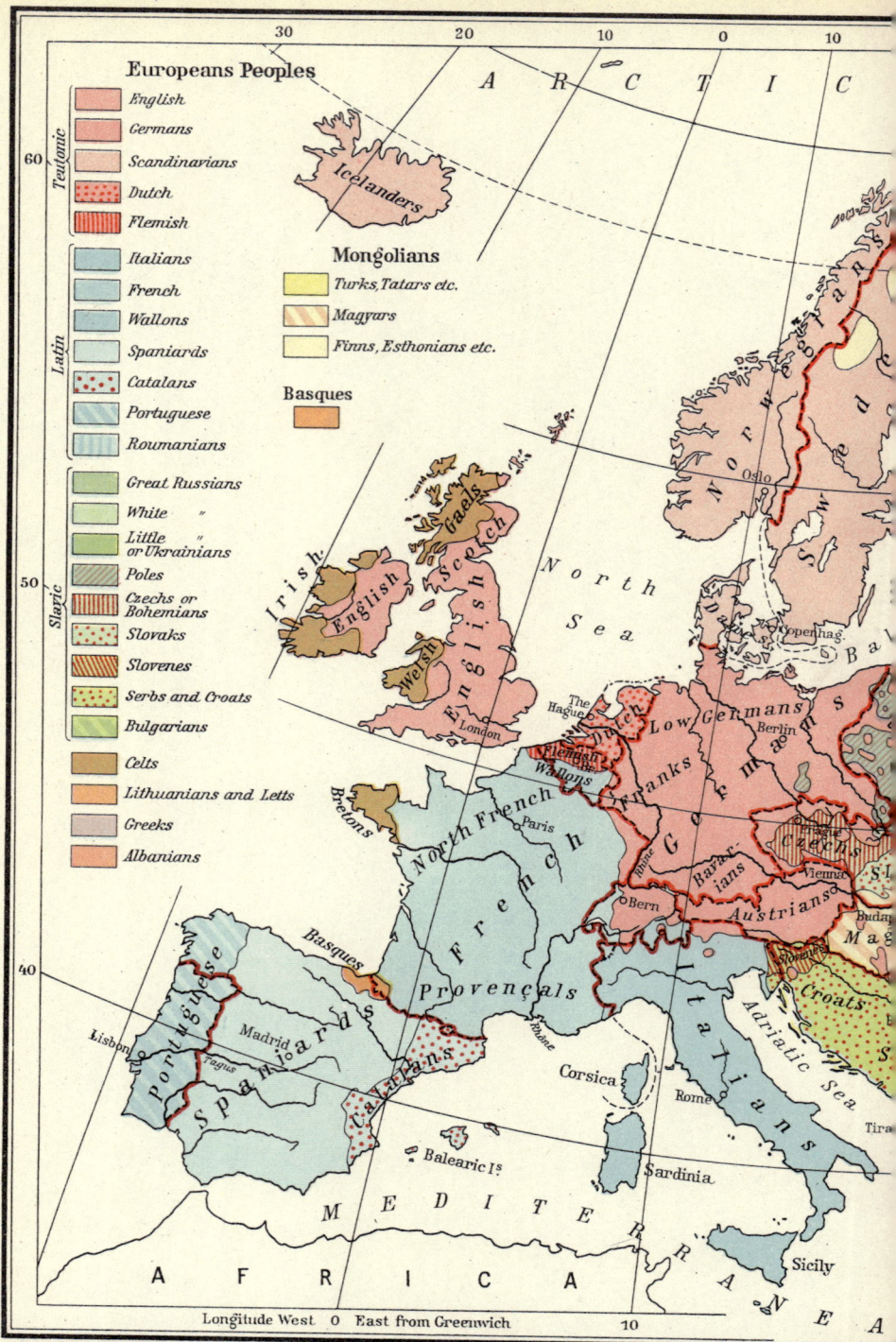

Teutonic
- English
- Germans
- Scandinavians
- Dutch
- Flemish

Latin
- Italians
- French
- Wallons
- Spaniards
- Catalans
- Portuguese
- Roumanians

Slavic
- Great Russians
- White "
- Little or Ukrainians
- Poles
- Czechs or Bohemians
- Slovaks
- Slovenes
- Serbs and Croats
- Bulgarians

- Celts
- Lithuanians and Letts
- Greeks
- Albanians

Mongolians
- Turks, Tatars etc.
- Magyars
- Finns, Esthonians etc.

Basques

PRINTED IN GERMANY

Longitude West 0 East from Greenwich

Peoples and Languages of MODERN EUROPE

Specially drawn and printed by the Kartographische Anstalt von F. A. Brockhaus, Leipzig, Germany.

century, had at an earlier date lived long without complaint when subjected to the domination of alien peoples. But the triumph of the autocratic national state, the psychological contagion generated by the French Revolution, the defense reactions produced by the Napoleonic conquests, and the impact of the popular democracy brought into being by the Industrial Revolution—all these served to arouse national sentiments. The net result of these forces in stirring the quiescent "herd instinct" and in giving it a nation-wide field of expression made any attempt to deny national aspirations a forlorn hope after 1900.[1]

There had developed in the greater states of Europe a boisterous and intolerant chauvinism which inevitably reacted upon the "repressed nationalities" and aroused like sentiments and ambitions among them. This tendency was powerfully forwarded by the unwise attempt of large national states to crush out by persecution the aspirations of the subject nationalities within their boundaries. Germany oppressed the Danes and Poles; Russia, the Finns, Letts, Lithuanians, Poles, and Ruthenians; Austria, the Czechs, Poles, and Serbs; Hungary, the Slovaks, the Rumanians, the Ruthenians, and the Croats; and Turkey, portions of most Balkan peoples and the embryonic nations of Asia Minor. Further, these lesser or "oppressed" nationalities followed the example of the greater states in arousing an interest in national history and literature. They stimulated the hope for independence by centering attention upon the past glory of their peoples, were it as remote as classical times or the early Middle Ages. Nothing could thwart this new force of nationality—not even the oldest monarchy in Europe nor the mightiest military state that the world had yet seen.

The general nature of the friction and dissatisfaction felt in the Europe of 1914 over the failure of the political units to coincide with the national groupings has been admirably summarized by Professor Charles Downer Hazen in the following synoptic outline:

1. Dissatisfaction in Germany on the part of
    a. The people of Alsace-Lorraine;
    b. The Poles of Eastern Prussia;
    c. The Danes of Northern Schleswig.
2. Dissatisfaction in Denmark over
    a. The position of the Danes in Northern Schleswig.
3. Dissatisfaction in Austria-Hungary on the part of
    a. The Czecho-Slovaks;
    b. The Rumanians of Eastern Hungary;
    c. The South- or Jugo Slavs;
    d. The Italians of the Trentino, Istria, and Trieste.
4. Dissatisfaction in France over
    a. Alsace-Lorraine.
5. Dissatisfaction in Italy over
    a. Italia Irredenta—Trentino, Istria, Trieste.
6. Dissatisfaction in Serbia over
    a. The oppression of millions of Serbs by Austria-Hungary;
    b. Lack of outlet to the sea.

[1] *Cf.* Hayes, *Historical Evolution of Modern Nationalism*, Chaps. III, V, VII.

7. Dissatisfaction in Rumania over
    a. The oppression by Hungary of millions of Rumanians.
8. Dissatisfaction in Bulgaria over
    a. The boundaries laid down by the Treaty of Bucharest, 10 Aug., 1913.
9. Dissatisfaction in Greece over
    a. Turkish rule of millions of Greeks.
10. Dissatisfaction of the Poles over the fact
    a. That Poland does not appear upon the map of Europe, but has been divided among and incorporated with the three partitioning powers of the 18th century, Russia, Prussia, and Austria.
11. Dissatisfaction in Russia on the part
    a. Of the Poles;
    b. Of the people of Finland [Letts, Lithuanians, Poles, Ruthenians, Ukrainians].[1]

To these, obviously, should be added the dissatisfaction felt by the Irish nationalists, who, in spite of the eloquent appeals of O'Connell and Redmond and the sympathy the Irish cause aroused in Gladstone and the English Liberals, were denied the realization of their aspirations for home rule.

Joined to these sources of friction and unrest produced by the imperfect realization of patriotic aspirations among oppressed national groups, were the deep-seated and ominous rivalries among the great national states of Europe over purely European national problems.[2] From 1870 to 1914 France was mourning over its "Lost Provinces." At the same time Bismarck alleged that Germany was maintaining and increasing its great armament chiefly as a protection against the contemplated French war of revenge, so fiercely urged by Déroulède and his fellow patriots. In spite of a formal alliance, Austria and Italy were fundamentally at odds over the solution of the problem of *Italia irredenta*. The *Mittel-Europa* plan of Germany and Austria was diametrically opposed to the Panslavic schemes of Russia, as well as to the national aspirations of the Balkan states. Finally, England's jealousy over Russian longing for Constantinople, which had led her into an aggressive and costly war in 1854-56 and threatened wars in 1878 and 1884, was not removed until the mutual looting and "strangling" of Persia had been consummated in 1907. After that date, British hatreds and suspicions in the Near Orient were directed chiefly against Germany and its Berlin-to-Baghdad project. Even in 1908, however, Lord Grey blocked Izvolsky's plan to control the Straits leading out of the Black Sea, a move that had been approved even by Austria in return for permission to annex Bosnia. This act of the English Foreign Minister was probably the most important indirect cause of the World War.

Ominous and troublesome as were the rivalries of national states in Europe over Continental problems, these were no more unsettling than those which arose from the struggle over the opening up of backward countries for investment and the planting of colonies in lands beyond the sea.[3]

In the period from the close of the Napoleonic Wars to 1870 there had

[1] C. D. Hazen, *Outline of Course on the Issues of the War, 1918*, Columbia University Press, Pt. I, Third Installment, pp. 11-12.
[2] See H. A. Gibbons, *Nationalism and Internationalism*, Stokes, 1930, Chaps. III-IV.
[3] See below, pp. 549 ff.

been a decided decline in imperialistic enterprises. Under the reign of Economic Liberalism European countries even went so far as to question the desirability of colonies. Richard Cobden and his followers believed that the British Empire was quite as much a liability as an asset to England.[1] But the results of the Industrial Revolution soon put an end to this amiable "cosmopolitan dream" of the Cobdenites. There arose a new scramble for the unappropriated parts of the earth, which could be utilized as sources of raw materials and as markets for the greatly increased volume of manufactured products.

This process of national expansion overseas, in its second or recent phase, set in about 1870, when the effects of the Industrial Revolution had been felt in England and France and were beginning to be experienced to an ever greater degree by Germany. France turned to Africa and Asia, and in Tunis, north-central Africa, Morocco, and Indo-China sought both compensation for the territorial loss of Alsace-Lorraine and investment opportunities for its growing body of capitalists. To obtain a more complete control over the routes leading to India, Disraeli bought the large block of Suez Canal stock in 1875 and started Great Britain on its second experiment in empire-building.[2] As a result, the British imperial possessions came to include Egypt, the Sudan, South Africa, Nigeria, southern Persia, and Tibet. Russia extended its sphere of political and economic control not only to the region of Manchuria in the Far East, but also to the district about the Caspian Sea, including the northern half of Persia. Germany sought its "place in the (imperialistic) sun" by colonization in Africa and in the islands of Oceania and the Pacific, and by an attempt at economic control of Asia Minor and Mesopotamia through its Berlin-Baghdad railroad project. Italy, after an unsuccessful attempt to get control of Abyssinia in 1896, was compelled to remain content with Somaliland and Eritrea until it was able, fifteen years later, to wrest Tripoli and Cyrenaica from Turkey. Finally, nearly all the above-mentioned states participated in the economic, if not the political, partition of China.

The conflict of ambitions in this process of European expansion created many instances of international friction. Germany and England clashed over the distribution of territory in South Africa and over the control of the Persian Gulf. France and Germany precipitated three European crises in the course of their disputes concerning Morocco. France and England nearly went to war through disputes over the territory surrounding the sources of the Nile. Russia went to war with Japan over Manchuria and Port Arthur, and came to an agreement with England concerning Persia only after a mutual division of the spoils in the arrangement of 1907.

Moreover, this new imperialism served to stimulate national pride and aggressiveness on the part of the great national states of Europe through the development of the "mapitis" psychosis, namely, the enthusiasm or chagrin felt by the citizens over the success or failure of their respective states in covering the map of the world with the brilliant colors designating their colonial possessions. Finally, economic nationalism, which had derived an early stimulus

---

[1] J. A. Hobson, *Richard Cobden, the International Man,* Holt, 1919; and W. H. Dawson, *Richard Cobden and Foreign Policy,* Frank-Maurice, 1926.
[2] *Cf.* C. W. Hallberg, *The Suez Canal,* Columbia University Press, 1931, Chap. xv.

from Fichte's book, *The Closed Commercial State* (1800), and from the writings of Friedrich List, was powerfully impelled by the struggle for markets and the desire to protect national trade and economic interests. This led to the inauguration of a neo-mercantilistic era of higher protective tariffs.[1] Beginning with the Bismarckian tariff bill of 1879, there ensued a general European movement towards nationalistic protective tariffs, so high that they would have caused even List[2] to gasp with astonishment, if not with dismay. Only England escaped from this tendency to introduce what practically meant perpetual economic warfare among the various continental European states even in times of political peace. These early manifestations of the very important trend towards economic nationalism are treated more thoroughly elsewhere in our discussions of tariff revivals, imperialism, the export of capital and the like.[3]

In this manner were events in and out of Europe contributing to the stimulation of jingoism and international distrust in the generation preceding the coming of the calamity of 1914. The writings or speeches of jingoists[4] presented to the world evidence of the various grandiose programs of national expansion and served to stir up mutual suspicions and antagonism.

The diplomacy of the latter part of the nineteenth century and the beginning of the twentieth was very poorly adapted to meet this difficult task of reaching a peaceful adjustment of conflicting international claims. While diplomatic theory and practice made some advance in candor during the century after Talleyrand, it is equally certain that it was still essentially Machiavellian. As Mr. Walter Weyl has well said, it was still controlled by "the approved diplomatic type, the aged, bemedaled, chilly, narrow, and conservative Excellency, very gentlemanly, very astute, fundamentally stupid."

The prospect of a peaceful settlement of the disputes between the European states over European and colonial problems was greatly diminished by the vast armaments that were created and increased, ostensibly in the interest of preserving peace, but actually, as subsequent events have proved, to encourage an aggressive nationalistic policy of expansion and annexation.[5]

In its origin this militaristic movement dates back to the French Revolution. In 1793 France first introduced the policy of conscription, and it confirmed this practice by law five years later. To prepare for the War of Liberation and to evade Napoleon's arbitrary limitation of the Prussian army to 42,000 men, the Prussian military leaders introduced into Prussia the system of universal liability to military service in the years following 1808. Austria, in the attempt to cope with Napoleon, moved in the same militaristic direction under Archduke Charles and Count Stadion.

After 1815, there was a decided slump in military sentiment and activity, associated to some degree with the prevalence of Economic Liberalism and its cosmopolitan tenets. The first important military revival was the work of Napoleon III, who assured France and Europe that "the Empire meant peace," but gave practical proof that it meant a restoration of the military traditions

---

[1] See below, pp. 769 ff.
[2] See above, p. 386. On economic elements in nationalism, see Hayes, *Historical Evolution of Modern Nationalism*, Chap. VII; and Partridge, *op. cit.*, Pt. I, Chap. IX.
[3] See below, pp. 546 ff., 769 ff.
[4] For example, Peters, Reventlow, Rohrbach, Tannenberg, Déroulède, Delcassé, Barrès, Rhodes, Kipling, Maxse, Lea, Balfour, D'Annunzio, Crispi, Pobiedonostsev, Plehve, Izvolsky and Aehrenthal.
[5] *Cf.* C. J. H. Hayes, *Essays on Nationalism*, Macmillan, 1926, Chap. VI.

of his illustrious uncle. But the Napoleonic restoration of the militarism of a half-century earlier was not nearly so fateful for the world as the contemporaneous developments across the Rhine. King William I of Prussia planned to reorganize the Prussian army as it had been in the great struggle against the first Napoleon. Calling to his aid, in 1862, the most forceful figure in the history of modern politics, Otto von Bismarck, he was not only able to carry out his army plans, but also to defeat Austria. Extending the new system to the North German Confederation, Bismarck, aided by foolish French aggression, was able to crush France and bring about the long-desired unification of Germany. Having "vindicated" the policy of "blood and iron" by three victorious wars, Bismarck fastened militarism upon Germany with a deadly grip through a series of laws passed between 1873 and 1887. The military octopus grew until it culminated in the army act of 1913. France adopted a similar system in 1872, and before 1914 its military establishment per capita far exceeded that of Germany. Most of the other great Powers, as well as the Balkan states, followed suit in the decade of the seventies. Even Turkey, in 1883, invited General von der Goltz to reorganize the army of the Sultan on the German plan.

Nor was the increase in armament limited to land forces; the great extension of new colonial enterprises and the development of a larger merchant marine seemed to demand new and bigger navies.[1] In view of Great Britain's greater colonial possessions and trade, it was but natural that it should favor the movement for larger sea forces. In 1889, Great Britain passed an act providing for a vast increase in its fleet and launched the policy of keeping its naval strength far in advance of any rival state. Not until 1898 did Germany's interest in *Weltpolitik* lead it to consider rivaling Britain on the seas. In that year the first great German naval act was passed. This was supplemented by other more extensive increases in acts of 1900, 1906, and 1912, thus providing ammunition for British jingoes like Lord Balfour and making an Anglo-German concord extremely improbable. Nor were England and Germany alone in this process. All the leading powers, but especially France and Russia, redoubled their speed in new naval preparations. With these great war machines at hand, the European states were all the more disinclined to submit their conflicts and disputes to what were regarded by the jingoistic patriots and imperialists as the pusillanimous and ignoble methods of arbitration.

Accompanying these political and economic forces making for a greater prevalence of jingoism in the last generation of European history were psychological causes not less effective in promoting mutual hatred and contempt.[2]

Linguistic and anthropological fallacies, growing out of Fichte's *Lectures to the German Nation* (1807-8), Count Arthur de Gobineau's grotesque *Essay on the Inequality of the Human Races* (1853-55) and Max Müller's hasty generalizations in his *Lectures on the Science of Language* (1861-64), led to an inflation of racial egotism, the intensification of racial misconceptions, and the fatal, if fruitless, search for the original "Aryan" bearers of civilization among the nations of Europe.[3] That writers, more patriotic than scientific, could find certain and irrefutable evidence that the original habitat of the primordial "Aryans"

---

[1] On armaments in 1914, see H. E. Barnes, *The Genesis of the World War*, 3rd ed. rev., Knopf, 1929, pp. 54 ff. [2] See Partridge, *op. cit.;* and Pillsbury, *op. cit.*
[3] See above, Vol. I, pp. 163 ff., 398 ff., 445 ff., and above, p. 197; F. H. Hankins, *The Racial Basis of Civilization*, Knopf, 1926, Pt. I; and Théophile Simar, *The Race Myth*, Boni, 1925.

was in France, Germany, Italy, Russia, Persia, and India is sufficient evidence not only of the hopeless scientific confusion, but also of the disastrous patriotic ardor that stimulated the absurd illusion.

Pseudo-Darwinian sociology represented war as the supreme principle making for social progress, in the same way that the struggle for existence forwards biological evolution.[1] This distortion of half-truth by the Austrian sociologist Gumplowicz and his school was eagerly seized upon by the militaristic and ultra-patriotic writers,[2] to provide a semiscientific cloak for their class and clique interests.

Superpatriotic history, literature, and philosophy magnified the former glory and the future heritage of each nation and proportionately disparaged the past and future of their rivals.[3] The emotional impulse derived from Romanticism, with its eulogy of medieval origins, led to a greatly increased interest in the study of national history. This was augmented by the patriotic enthusiasm accompanying the French Revolution and the Napoleonic era. Every country began the compilation of gigantic collections of the sources of national history, of which the *Monumenta Germaniae historica,* the *Documents inédits,* and the *Rolls Series* were only the most notable among many similar enterprises. National narrative histories, often breathing forth a fiery and defiant patriotic ardor, were prolifically produced and widely read.[4]

Literature also became even more chauvinistic.[5] Houston Stewart Chamberlain, building on the risky foundations of the anthropological fallacies of Gobineau, Pösche, and Penka, was able to discover that, almost without exception, every important figure in history since the beginning of the Christian era had been a German. Even St. Paul, Dante, Giotto, Michelangelo, and Raphael were included by this undaunted exponent of *Kultur* under the caption of "We Teutons"! Nisard detected the very essence of Reason herself in the spirit of French literature. Maurice Barrès found that French culture was a precious and indigenous product of Celtic blood, to which neither Roman nor Teuton had contributed in the slightest degree. He advocated its preservation by making it the center of a near-oriental cult of ancestor worship. Léon Daudet asserted that nations other than the French exhibited undoubted evidence of mental and moral decline. Leo Maxse, editor of the *National Review,* and Rudyard Kipling, the poet of "Saxondom" and British imperialism, indulged in frenzied exhortations to their countrymen, urging a greater assumption of the "white man's burden" throughout the non-European world. Carducci made the heroes of Italian unification the theme of the noblest of

---

[1] *Cf.* H. E. Barnes, "The Struggle of Races and Social Groups as a Factor in the Development of Political and Social Institutions," *Journal of Race Development,* April, 1919.

[2] Such as Moltke, Bernhardi, and Von der Goltz in Germany; Déroulède and Barrès in France; Lord Roberts, Wyatt, Cramb, and Maude in England; and Lea, Maxim, Mahan, and Gardner in America.

[3] See H. E. Barnes, "History: Its Rise and Development," Encyclopedia Americana, Vol. XIV, pp. 234 ff.

[4] Notably by Giesebrecht, Droysen, Treitschke, and Sybel in Germany; by Michaud, Raynouard, Mignet, Lamartine, Guizot, Thiers, Michelet, and Martin in France; by Freeman, Stubbs, Froude, Carlyle, Macaulay, and Napier in England; and by Bancroft and others in the United States.

[5] See Hayes, *Essays on Nationalism,* Chaps. III-IV, VII; and *Historical Evolution of Modern Nationalism,* Chap. VI.

modern Italian poems, while D'Annunzio wrought himself up into neo-Platonic ecstasy over the necessity of recovering *"Italia irredenta."*

Patriotic state education taught unquestioning loyalty to state or dynasty as the first principle of moral conduct, carefully obscured any questionable occurrences or policies in the national past, and frowned on national criticism and proposals of radical reform.[1]

Slowly but surely Europe was preparing for the cataclysm of August, 1914.[2] As Professor William Graham Sumner had long before predicted, the vast armaments that had been accumulated with the avowed purpose of defense alone invited the transformation of nationalistic and military philosophy from the advocacy of a purely "defensive war" into an exposition of the virtues and necessity of a "preventive war."

While the rise of modern nationalism has been most conspicuous in Europe, this should not obscure the fact that similar historical forces produced comparable developments elsewhere, most notably in America and Japan.

III. THE DEVELOPMENT OF CONTEMPORARY NATIONALISM OUTSIDE EUROPE

Of the examples of the rise and growth of nationalism in America the case of the United States has, of course, been the most impressive and significant.[3] As Professor Cheyney has so convincingly pointed out,[4] the settlement of America was even more deeply connected with the economic impulses arising from the Commercial Revolution in Europe than it was with the religious revolts from Catholicism on the Continent and the Established Church in England. These new commercial forces were even more influential in promoting unity among the colonists. A century of mutual ignoring of British commercial restrictions, making smuggling a powerful vested interest, gave the thirteen colonies a strong common motive for unified action in opposing the proposed enforcement of these long-dormant mercantilistic restrictions after 1763—a motive that Professor Schlesinger has fully proved to have been far more powerful than any theoretical or legal abstractions involved in colonial resistance to British imperial power.[5]

In addition to these economic foundations of the growth of American national sentiment, there was a fundamental sociological process, which has been aptly termed by Professor Becker "the beginnings of the American people."[6] A widely different geographical, social, political, and economic environment had long been operating upon a population originally psychologically variant from the great mass of less adventurous Englishmen. This tended inevitably to create in the colonies a people who became, generation after generation, more and more divergent from their kinsmen in the mother country

---

[1] *Cf.* J. F. Scott, *Patriots in the Making,* Appleton, 1916, and *The Menace of Nationalism in Education,* Macmillan, 1926.
[2] *Cf.* R. J. Sontag, *European Diplomatic History, 1871-1932,* Century, 1933, Chaps. I-V; and C. E. Playne, *The Neuroses of the Nations,* Seltzer, 1925.
[3] *Cf.* A. F. Pollard, *Factors in American History,* Macmillan, 1925, Chaps. III, V.
[4] *The European Background of American History.*   [5] See above, pp. 98 ff., 104 ff.
[6] C. L. Becker, *The Beginnings of the American People,* Houghton Mifflin, 1915.

across the Atlantic. Not only did these environmental influences tend to produce an essential dissimilarity between Englishmen and Americans; through the fundamental uniformity of the American social environment, there was being created a homogeneous and united American people and the beginnings of a national self-consciousness.[1]

The American Revolution, initiated, in part unintentionally, by the enterprising and recalcitrant merchants and favored by the debtor landlords and disgruntled frontiersmen, was carried to success by their courage and audacity, by the not disinterested aid of the French and, above all, by the aid of the British Whigs. This revolt from Britain furnished a unifying force of very great potency for a temporary period, but the reaction in the days of the Confederation threatened for the time being a lapse into anarchy and dismemberment. Thanks, however, to their desire for financial stability and commercial prosperity, the vigorous capitalistic class, led by that great constructive statesman of early nationalism, Alexander Hamilton, turned the tide of political opinion from separatism and provincialism to nationalism and unity. Their work was carried on by the strongly nationalistic decisions of John Marshall, whom not even Jefferson's enmity could remove from the Supreme Court. Indeed, the Jeffersonian Republicans, when they came into power in 1800, ceased their negativism and accepted most of the nationalistic program that they had criticized with such vigor and acrimony when executed by Hamilton and Adams. Jefferson could purchase Louisiana; Madison could be won for war with Great Britain; and Monroe could formulate a strongly nationalistic foreign policy.[2]

Nationalism in America thus took its origin from the reactions of the Commercial Revolution on the Western world; as in Europe, it was completed by the Industrial Revolution. The new factories in the North created an industrial interdependence between various sections of the country and attracted an immigrant population with no sectional sentiments. The new canals and railroads helped on that great nationalistic enterprise of the nineteenth century in America—the conquest of the West, studied with such fruitfulness by Professor Turner and his disciples.[3] While the territorial additions of the middle of the century were temporarily a cause of sectional dispute and friction, they ultimately became a matter of national pride and common interest. Though Negro slavery and the accompanying states-rights movement threatened to disrupt the embryonic nation, the success of the North in the Civil War demonstrated by the verdict of physical force that Webster, rather than Calhoun or Hayne, was right in his interpretation of the nature of the federal union. A permanent political sanction and buttress for nationalism was provided by the Reconstruction Amendments to the Federal Constitution.[4]

Events and tendencies since the Civil War have been even more conducive to the development of national unity than were those of the preceding half-

---

[1] *Cf.* Fisher, *The Struggle for American Independence.*
[2] K. C. Babcock, *The Rise of American Nationality,* Harper, 1906.
[3] F. J. Turner, *The Rise of the New West,* Harper, 1906, and *The Frontier in American History,* Holt, 1921; and F. L. Paxson, *History of the American Frontier, 1763-1893,* Houghton Mifflin, 1924.
[4] *Cf.* W. A. Dunning, *Reconstruction: Political and Economic,* Harper, 1906, Chaps. IV-VII.

century.[1] An Industrial Revolution, like that which affected New England in the first half of the nineteenth century, has come to the South, and the sharp sectional divisions of economic interests have now been greatly lessened. The further development of railroads, telegraph and telephone lines, the radio, and other means of rapid transportation and almost instantaneous communication of information have made our extensive country an economic and psychological unit to a degree unknown in a much smaller area in 1789. The intersectional investment of capital has also encouraged financial unity.

A national literature has been provided by such writers as Irving, Bryant, Cooper, Longfellow, Lowell, Whitman, Thoreau, Emerson, Hawthorne, Poe, Clemens, Howells, Riley, and Garland.[2] A collection of the sources of national history was planned and partially executed by Peter Force, and a national historical epic, eulogizing the American past, was created in the writings of Bancroft, Palfrey, Fiske, Holst, and Burgess. A "glorious" foreign war at the close of the century gave a great stimulus to the completion of national development.[3] Elaborate national expositions and public projects, such as the Chicago World's Fair (1893), the St. Louis Exposition (1904), and the Century of Progress Exposition (1933-34), have furnished a successive series of impulses to unity.

Many pessimistic publicists had believed that the great influx of foreigners into the United States in the last fifty years threatened national disruption as seriously as did the sectional divisions of the middle of the last century. But the experience of the United States in the World War definitely disproved their forebodings and demonstrated that, whatever the general results of immigration, they have not brought national disintegration. The participation of the United States in the deadly "War of the Nations" produced a welling-up of exuberant national sentiment and intolerant patriotism that caused both the Entente and the Central Powers to gasp with astonishment and incredulity.[4]

While national development in the United States has been the most notable exemplification of this process in the Western Hemisphere, it has not been the only one. Canada, in spite of a formal connection with Great Britain, has developed a very marked spirit of national self-consciousness,[5] while a century of independent political existence has created a strong feeling of national pride and unity in the various Latin-American states of Central and South America, especially the Argentine, Brazil, and Chile.[6] Nationalism, then, seems as well established in America as in Europe.

The most spectacular rise of nationalism in a nineteenth-century state was witnessed in Japan.[7] After having welcomed European adventurers and missionaries in the middle of the sixteenth century, Japan suddenly turned against the newcomers, murdered them or drove them from its shores, and returned

[1] Cf. P. L. Haworth, *The United States in Our Own Times*, rev. ed., Scribner, 1924.
[2] Cf. G. C. Knight, *American Literature and Culture*, Long and Smith, 1932.
[3] Cf. Walter Millis, *The Martial Spirit*, Houghton Mifflin, 1931.
[4] See Mark Sullivan, *Our Times*, Scribner, 1926-33, 5 vols., Vol. V, pp. 197 ff., 423 ff.
[5] See Carl Wittke, *History of Canada*, Crofts, 1928; and W. S. Wallace, *The Growth of Canadian National Feeling*, Macmillan, 1927.
[6] See J. F. Rippy, *The Historical Evolution of Hispanic America*, Crofts, 1932.
[7] See K. S. Latourette, *The Development of Japan*, 2d ed., Macmillan, 1926.

to immobility and isolation for three centuries. This artificial aloofness was broken down following 1853 by commercial concessions, obtained first by the United States and then by European states.

At first, the Japanese feudal princes opposed the entry of foreigners and their civilization, but the more farsighted among them recognized that Japan could hope to compete with the states of Europe and America only by adopting at least the superior mechanical features of their advanced civilization. Through the Revolution of 1867-68 and its immediate results, this reforming element abolished the Shogunate, brought the Mikado out of an inactive retirement, terminated feudalism, reorganized the army along European lines, and accepted the industrial methods and processes that had been produced in a century of economic development in Europe and America. Within a period of less than forty years Japan passed from a medieval feudal state to a modern industrial nation.

In no modern state is there such intense devotion to national ideals as is to be found in Japan. The veneration for the past practically reaches a condition of ancestor worship, while patriotism is in a real sense the official religion of Japan. By successful wars against China (1894-95) and Russia (1904-1905) Japan has become the great world-power of the Pacific, has acquired important territory on the mainland of Asia, and has endeavored to create and maintain a Japanese "Monroe Doctrine" in China and the Far East. The present-day exponents of internationalism seem likely to find Japan a most tenacious adherent to the old order of aggressive nationalism and imperialism. This fact was strikingly demonstrated by the Japanese occupation of Manchuria and the invasion of China following 1931. Not even the pressure exerted by the League of Nations was able to check Japanese advances. But it must be frankly admitted that Japan's contact with the diplomacy of the Western world could scarcely have taught it that the day of candor and generosity has yet arrived in the field of international relations. It has only learned all too well the lessons of Western imperialism.[1]

The rise of the new Japan stimulated the great inert mass of China. Stung by the defeat of their country by the microscopic Island Kingdom in 1895, the progressive Chinese patriots attempted to guard against another humiliation at the hands of the Japanese by imitating the Japanese adoption of Western civilization.[2] While this movement was temporarily obstructed by the reactionary element in the country, led by the Dowager Empress, the liberals overthrew the obstructionists in the Revolution of 1911-12, established a Chinese republic, and welcomed Western industrialism and culture. While this remarkable transformation was too rapidly consummated to remain secure and unchallenged, it has persisted to a remarkable degree in the face of sporadic setbacks, and China seems to be on its way towards development into a modernized national state, in spite of temporary separatist movements. Antipathy towards Japan makes even the growing Chinese Communism highly nationalistic in character.

In conclusion, it should be noted that no observations on the rise of nation-

[1] See H. C. Thomson, *The Case for China,* Scribner, 1933; and Eldridge, *Dangerous Thoughts on the Orient.*   [2] See M. T. Z. Tyau, *China Awakened,* Macmillan, 1922.

alism in the Far East can ignore the remarkable evidences of national self-consciousness in Australia and New Zealand that were brought out by the World War. One of its most prominent modes of manifestation has been the development of the "White Australia" policy with respect to oriental immigration.[1]

IV. NATIONALISM IN THE WORLD WAR

The disastrous "War of the Nations," which ceased in 1918, was not only a product of obsessed nationalism, but also brought with it an unprecedented inflation of national egotism and intolerant patriotism. Never before had a general war occurred when the machinery for disseminating both information and propaganda was so highly developed or so ruthlessly exploited. The slavish eulogy of national culture and history and the obscuring of national faults and mistakes had been prevalent in the half-century before the war. But they were as nothing compared to the tyrannical censorship and unabashed organized propaganda of every state immediately engaged in the conflict.[2]

Each of the opposing groups of Powers represented the gigantic conflict as a sort of Persian eschatology—a struggle between the forces of light and darkness, a clash of the powers of righteousness and iniquity.[3] Within each state an attempt was made to sustain morale by a curbing of all criticism of the "war aims" of the government or its allies and by a carefully planned presentation and reiteration of the past and present criminal record of the opposing states.[4]

So powerful and all-embracing was this tidal wave of patriotic defense reactions that it engulfed not only the "man on the street," but even the most eminent scholars and publicists, some of whom in the past had seen great virtue in the cultural complex of the enemy.[5] This disheartening spectacle perhaps reached its climax in the "manifesto" of the ninety-three German professors. But in no state were the intellectual classes immune from the contagion of fervid patriotism, and those few who maintained their poise were contemptuously derided as "flabby highbrows" by their overexcited colleagues and critics.

The astonishing effect of the wartime patriotism upon the public mind and its stimulating influence in creating a type of supernationalism has been trenchantly set forth by Professor Frank H. Hankins in the following citation:

Patriotism, like nationality, is not readily definable. It signifies loyalty to one's nation and implies the obligation to serve and defend it. It is thus a passion which all normal men feel, and which in time of our country's peril commands our instant

[1] See Myra Willard, *History of the White Australia Policy,* University of Melbourne Press, 1923.
[2] See H. D. Lasswell, *Propaganda Technique in the World War,* Knopf, 1927; C. E. Playne, *Society at War, 1914-1916,* Houghton Mifflin, 1931; and G. S. Viereck, *Spreading Germs of Hate,* Liveright, 1930. See below, pp. 599 ff.
[3] See Granville Hicks, "The Parsons and the War," *American Mercury,* February, 1927; and R. H. Abrams, *The Preachers Present Arms,* Round Table Press, 1933.
[4] See Sir A. A. W. H. Ponsonby, *Falsehood in War-Time,* Dutton, 1929; and I. C. Willis, *England's Holy War,* Knopf, 1928.
[5] See H. E. Barnes, *In Quest of Truth and Justice,* National Historical Society, 1928, pp. 141-64.

loyalty. Of all the emotions that move men to action it is the most capacious. When it is aroused there is no other social force comparable to it in the completeness with which it dominates all other springs of action in all sorts and conditions of men. It lifts the average man up out of the concerns of a work-a-day world into the noblest spirit of devotion; it quickens the pulse of the sluggard, reforms the wayward, forces generosity from the stingy, arouses the plodder to dreams of heroic deeds, gives courage to the cowardly, and makes the hearts of the shrewd and crafty wolves of society swell with an ostensible love of country. In its face local feuds are forgotten; the bitter struggles of parties and classes are submerged; differences of creed, of social status, and even of race are obliterated.

Under these circumstances only the group leaders may speak. The citizen must offer himself in silence as a willing sacrifice on the altar of his country in whatever manner those in authority may dictate. Even honest criticism is anathema; the conscientious objector, who in times of peace is praised as a courageous man who dares to stand against the world for what he believes right, is denounced as a sneaking coward and herded into prison. The individual rights of free speech, press, and assembly so essential to democratic government, so zealously guarded during peace, and so boastfully displayed to an admiring world on the national holidays, not only cease to exist but are even denounced and proscribed as inimical to the public safety. The noble sentiments of toleration are fiercely denounced, as is also individual variation from type which is vigorously defended during peace under the ideals of individual liberty and initiative. Every social institution is brought into line; all organs of public opinion send forth a constant stream of uniform suggestions; the appeal is made through church and lodge and every customary association, until the members of the social group coalesce into a solid sociality that surpasses the fondest imaginings of the utopian Socialist.

It is not unnatural that such a titanic social force should stir men's emotional nature to its depths; and especially during war, for war hallows every cause. At such times patriotism, like a resistless and mysterious genius, fills the entire fabric of society with its magical power. Few individuals escape its enchantment, and almost no one dares brook its hostility. While it ennobles the soul with the sublime spirit of self-sacrifice, it compels men to dilute the honesty of their thoughts; makes cowards of all but the most stalwart souls by forcing them to substitute the worse for the better reason and the lower ideal for one they feel to be higher. Under its guise every sort of sinister human purpose thrives, for anything which can be made to appear patriotic is instantly and deeply approved.

Any counsel of moderation is pounced upon as enemy propaganda, while the advocates of internationalism are accused of silly sentimentalism and treason. To encounter a suspicion of lack of patriotism creates a greater defilement than the violation of an ancient taboo. As in the days of witchcraft, suspects are whipped, tarred and feathered or hanged, or like the distinguished list in "Who's Who in Pacifism and Radicalism" are immolated on the altar of militarism amid the shouts of the mob and the secret glee of the patriots who find the established social system the best of all possible systems. In other words, patriotism gives full sway to fear, unbridles the lusts and brutalities of savage man, intensifies our innate suggestibility, and subordinates the mind to every sort of delusion and deceit.

Unfortunately, there is no printed guide for the proper conduct of human affairs, and so deep is the mystery of social processes that only the ignorant and the simple have complete confidence in their solution of social problems. In times of stress, therefore, the social mind finds refuge in those torrents of instinctive emotion which arise from the deepest recesses of human nature and which propel the social group

NATIONALISM IN THE WORLD WAR

like a rudderless vessel before the ocean winds. Patriotism makes of national thought not a cerebration but a contagion, not an activity but an epidemic.[1]

When one reflects that it was in the midst of such a psychological setting that the Peace Conference of 1918-19 had to carry on its work, it need cause little surprise that many of the liberal and generous sentiments expressed by the Allied leaders during the war vanished in thin air, and that the result of their "peacemaking" work bore very evident traces of revenge, a lust for spoil, and rampageous nationalism.[2] These defects, together with the crop of newly emancipated nations and recently established tariff areas, furnished enough problems to tax the ingenuity of the statesmen of the next generation.

V. NATIONALISM SINCE THE WORLD WAR

During the progress of the World War it was frequently asserted, especially by spokesmen of the Allies, that the great conflict would end the excesses of nationalism. An association of nations would be created. An international order would come into being. At the same time, these spokesmen announced a somewhat contrary determination, namely, the promise to liberate the small nations. The paradox was to be resolved through the provision of the League of Nations. This would insure that the emancipation of a number of small nations could not produce a resurgence of ardent nationalistic spirit. Further, the adoption of President Wilson's Fourteen Points was taken for granted. These would guarantee a just peace and the prevention of any desire for revenge upon the part of the vanquished peoples.

Unfortunately, these benign hopes were not realized. As a result of the emancipation of hitherto repressed nationalities and the creation of new states, there were thirty national states in Europe in 1920 instead of the eighteen that existed in 1914.[3] These provided just so many more centers of patriotic enthusiasm and the basis for so many more tariff walls. The vanquished peoples were humiliated and were made to feel very deeply the sting of defeat in a series of oppressive and unjust peace treaties. The peoples who had been repressed before 1914 were now permitted to become the oppressors, thus reversing the rôle. This may have evened up the old score, but the former masters bitterly protested their submerged status.

The period since the World War has also been very important in the history of nationalism as marking a further intensification of economic nationalism. This seems to be the latest and perhaps the most dangerous stage of nationalistic developments. Whereas in the late nineteenth and early twentieth centuries the national State subordinated the Church, education, and some other phases of culture to its dominion, in the postwar period nationalism has led the state to seek more than ever before to bend economic life to its own ends. The several states have sought as great a degree of economic self-sufficiency as possible, partly to attain a greater degree of economic security, if that be pos-

---

[1] Hankins, *Patriotism and Peace*, Clark University Press, 1919.
[2] See below, pp. 606 ff.; and Gibbons, *op. cit.*, Chap. v.
[3] See I. D. Levine, *The Resurrected Nations*, Stokes, 1919; P. S. Mowrer, *Balkanized Europe*, Dutton, 1921; and M. E. Ravage, *The Malady of Europe*, Macmillan, 1923.

sible, but even more to secure more adequate raw materials and other cogent economic weapons to be used in the next war. This attempt to subordinate economic life to the dictates of political nationalism has become an increasingly important manifestation of our contemporary civilization. It raises the question as to whether it may not ultimately culminate, for a time at least, in either State Socialism or state capitalism.[1]

The losses caused by the war made the economic struggle more intense than before 1914. Hence each state tried to promote industrial recovery by higher tariff rates, thus waging an economic war in a period of political peace. Capitalism was severely challenged by the rising economic radicalism, which won a complete triumph in Russia. Therefore it invoked patriotism in its behalf and created intensely nationalistic Fascist régimes and dictatorial governments.[2] In Hungary the ancient agrarian autocrats drew upon a similar psychology to prevent radical agrarian reforms. The desire to revise the Treaty of Versailles united with the fear of economic radicalism to bring into being a Fascist order in Germany under Hitler.[3] The Hitler régime has produced the most intense and solidified nationalism of our era outside of Japan. It has openly identified religion with patriotism and has subscribed to the most absurd racialism ever known. The postwar treaties created sore spots such as the Polish Corridor, the South Tyrol, and dismembered Hungary, all fertile breeding-places for fervent nationalism.[4] Mussolini, not satisfied with Italy's gains from the World War, talks of reviving the glories of the ancient Roman Empire. Nationalism was fanned in Britain by the threat of Indian secession and other challenges to the integrity of the Empire. The capitalistic states as a whole, however jealous and envious they might be of each other, have made common cause against Communist Russia. The latter, standing alone in the world, was in turn compelled to develop an ardent patriotic support of Bolshevik policies in order to preserve its integrity.[5] This stands in marked contrast to the international tenets of Communism, but self-preservation has precedence over abstract ideals.

Even in countries like the United States, which were not threatened with economic radicalism or with important Fascist tendencies, the severe economic depression after 1929 encouraged economic nationalism as a means of recovery. The vastly greater importance of the home market, as compared with foreign trade, suggested the desirability of a strongly nationalistic economic policy.[6] This has as yet outweighed the efforts of some statesmen, such as Secretary Cordell Hull, to lower tariff barriers. The London Economic Conference of 1933 made little headway in the direction of freer trade.

In the Far East, Japan, faced by the pressure of a growing population upon

---

[1] On recent economic nationalism, see Hayes, *Historical Evolution of Modern Nationalism*, pp. 262 ff.; Charles Schrecker, "The Growth of Economic Nationalism and Its International Consequences," *International Affairs*, March, 1934, pp. 208-25; G. D. H. Cole, "Planning International Trade," *International Conciliation*, April, 1934; and E. M. Patterson, ed., *The World Trend Towards Nationalism*, American Academy of Political and Social Science, *Annals*, Vol. CLXXIV, 1934.
[2] See John Strachey, *The Menace of Fascism*, Covici, Friede, 1933; H. W. Schneider, *Making the Fascist State*, Oxford Press, 1928; and Carmen Haider, *Do We Want Fascism?* Day, 1934.
[3] See Hoover, *Germany Enters the Third Reich;* and O. G. Villard, *The German Phoenix*, Smith & Haas, 1933.   [4] Sherwood Eddy, *The Challenge of Europe*, Farrar & Rinehart, 1933.
[5] See Hans Kohn, *Nationalism in the Soviet Union*, Columbia University Press, 1933.
[6] *Cf.* C. A. Beard, *The Open Door at Home*, Macmillan, 1934.

NATIONALISM SINCE THE WORLD WAR

a very limited habitat and scanty natural resources, decided to help itself to portions of eastern Asia that it felt it needed more intensely than either China or Russia.[1] It was encouraged to take such steps by the precedents in territorial larceny that had been set by Western Powers for more than a century. The latter had blandly carved out for themselves areas in the Orient without the excuse of any real need for more territory. The Japanese aggression still further stirred the patriotic emotions of China and Russia, and annoyed the United States. The League of Nations protested ineffectively. Indeed, some of the nations that joined in the protest were secretly egging the Japanese on in their aggressive action. Japan withdrew from the League, thus weakening this international association of states. It was further undermined by the withdrawal of Nazi Germany.

The League of Nations has found it difficult to create an international order, since its members are states that are, for the most part, pursuing a vigorous nationalistic policy at home. They can hardly act differently when assembled at Geneva for their noble rhetorical gestures.[2] Patriotic education has become more blatant and intellectually irresponsible than before the War.[3]

Nationalism, therefore, is as potent and omnipresent twenty years later as it was in 1914. In many areas it is more fierce and menacing than it was before the World War. It is no wonder, then, that many intelligent observers of the world-scene predict that we may be on the verge of another disastrous war of nations.[4]

VI. ANTI-SEMITISM COMBINES NATIONALISTIC FRENZY AND RACIAL VAGARIES

One of the most notable and the most absurd developments of nationalism in modern times has been the continuance of anti-Semitic propaganda and persecutions from medieval times. This movement has combined the usual nationalistic sentiments with the more preposterous versions of modern racial dogmas.[5]

The period following the discovery of America was a significant and important one in many fields of human endeavor, but probably most notably so in connection with the rise of modern capitalism. The long experience of the Jews in financial matters gave them an advantage here, and they played an active part in the rise of modern capitalistic institutions and practices. This story has been told with authority by Werner Sombart in his *The Jews and the Rise of Modern Capitalism* (1917) and in the biographies of leading Jewish capitalists like Rothschild. Jealousy of Jewish prowess prompted persecution, the char-

---

[1] See Sokolsky, *The Tinder Box of Asia;* and K. K. Kawakami, *Manchoukuo: Child of Conflict,* Macmillan, 1933.

[2] On internationalism and the League of Nations, see below, pp. 898 ff.

[3] See Scott, *The Menace of Nationalism in Education;* Mark Starr, *Lies and Hate in Education,* Hogarth Press, 1929; C. E. Merriam, *The Making of Citizens,* University of Chicago Press, 1931; and B. L. Pierce, *Civic Attitudes in American School Textbooks,* University of Chicago Press, 1930.

[4] See E. A. Powell, *Thunder over Europe,* Washburn, Ives, 1931; H. R. Knickerbocker, *The Boiling Point,* Farrar & Rinehart, 1934; and H. F. Armstrong, *Europe between Wars?* Macmillan, 1934.

[5] For a good review of anti-Semitism, see Benjamin Ginzburg, article "Antisemitism," Encyclopaedia of the Social Sciences.

acter of which has been made classic in Lion Feuchtwanger's widely-read novel *Power*.

Religious fanaticism also played its part in reviving Jewish persecution prior to the nineteenth century. Russian nationalists and orthodox Christians waged successive pogroms against the Jews. Persecution in many lands led hundreds of thousands of Jews to seek refuge in Poland, which, until the middle of the seventeenth century, showed a remarkably commendable tolerance towards religious dissenters. But in the latter part of the seventeenth century the Polish government came under the influence of the Jesuits and carried on a long series of bloody persecutions of the Jews. Economic motives entered also, for the Jews constituted the bulk of the Polish middle class.

At the opening of the nineteenth century the prospects for civilized treatment of the Jews seemed somewhat improved. The influence of Voltaire and the Rationalists had lessened the force of religious bigotry. The internationalism of the Classical Economists and the Cobdenite liberals temporarily checked the rising tide of nationalism and superpatriotism. But it was not long before the spirit of persecution was once more abroad in the land.

In Germany many elements contributed to produce two decades of violent anti-Semitism after 1879. This was the period of the so-called Aryan myth and of the theory that non-Aryan peoples were of inferior clay. This doctrine was extracted by vulgar pseudo-scientists from the linguistic studies of Max Müller and Ernest Renan. The imperial court preacher, Adolf Stoecker, rallied fanatical German Protestants to his side in the anti-Semitic crusade. A leader of the German patriots, the famous Professor Heinrich von Treitschke, proclaimed that the Jews must be erased. There had been disastrous speculation in Germany after the Franco-Prussian War, and two leading Jewish members of the Reichstag, Eduard Lasker and Ludwig Bamberger, had exposed the complicity of leading German financiers and politicians. Finally, the rising radicalism and Socialism was derived from the teachings of a Jewish philosopher, Karl Marx, and was organized in large part by Jewish leaders. All the Jew-haters united to produce a vigorous wave of anti-Semitism that ran wild in the early eighties and was revived in the early nineties. Only Bismarck's opposition prevented it from evolving into a general massacre. At the opening of the present century the hatred of the Jews in Germany had died down, and the Kaiser himself numbered many prominent Jews among his friends and advisers, most notable, perhaps, being Albert Ballin, of the Hamburg-American Line. In Austria the anti-Semitic movement was taken up following 1882, largely in imitation of Germany. The leaders here were Karl Lueger and Georg Schronerer.

France had its fling with anti-Semitism, culminating in the notorious Dreyfus case. The leader was an irresponsible writer, Edouard Drumont. In 1886 he published a scandalous book entitled *Jewish France*. In 1892 he founded an anti-Semitic newspaper, *La libre parole*. He not only revived the conventional arguments against the Jews as an inferior and grasping race but accused them of financial corruption at the top and revolutionary radicalism at the bottom. Dreyfus became the scapegoat of French anti-Semitism, but his ultimate vindication and the exposure of the baseness of his enemies served to discredit French anti-Semitism for many years to come.

The bloodiest anti-Semitism in the nineteenth century was carried on in Russia. It combined medieval religious intolerance with a fear of the growing radicalism of many Russian Jews. In 1882 Alexander III forbade the Jews to acquire land, limited them to city residence, and restricted them first to 10 per cent and then to 3 per cent of the student body in any Russian school or university. In 1890 he ordered all Jews not personally exempted to migrate from central Russia to the western provinces. Open massacre was common, and in the year 1891 alone more than three hundred thousand Jews left Russia. At the opening of the present century violence against the Jews became even more widespread under the leadership of the so-called Black Hundreds, the zealous reactionary bands encouraged by the government. There were many bloody massacres, of which that at Kishinev in 1903 was the most notable. Thousands of Jews were slain in the various butcheries.

Violence against the Jews in eastern Europe was not limited to the Russians. Rumania was a notorious offender. The Treaty of Berlin in 1878 had guaranteed religious equality in Rumania. But the Rumanian leaders hated the Jews, who were the dominant force in Rumanian finance and commerce. They refused to extend to the Jews citizenship or the right to own land. Local persecutions and massacres of the Jews were common.

It is probable that the wave of anti-Jewish feeling is as great today as at any time since the 1880's in France and Germany and two decades before the World War in Russia. What has been the cause of this revival of anti-Semitism in a supposedly civilized era?

In the first place, we have the extremely prevalent myth among reactionary Germans that the international Jewish bankers, in collusion with the European freemasons, plotted the World War in order to destroy the national state and the Christian religion. England is represented as having acted as the cat's paw for these two groups. This is a view generally shared by the Prussian reactionaries, and Ludendorff has shown himself somewhat unbalanced in elaborating this theme. It is easy to see how such a conception of world-politics leads to hatred of the Jews. The latter are held to be primarily responsible for a war that brought terrible calamities to Germany. The Nazis, in their present campaign against the Jews, make use of this myth, together with all the old "duds" utilized in Jew-baiting—the inferior Jewish race, Jewish radicalism and corruption, Jewish infidelity, and the like. Desirous of building up a strong patriotic backing, they know from the German past that anti-Semitism can always be counted on to gather together a certain nucleus of fanatics. Hitler himself seems to be fanatically sincere in his hatred of the Jews.

Another important item in the current anti-Semitic complex has been the elaborate international propaganda of Russian reactionaries against the Bolsheviks. Bolshevism has been represented as a Jewish product, making use of the fact that the Russian Communists derive their doctrines from Karl Marx and that several of the Russian Communist leaders have been Jews. Everything has been grist for the mill of these White Russians. The Jews have been accused, on the one hand, of trying to gain financial dominion over the rest of the world, and on the other, of trying to overthrow the whole capitalistic system. Moreover, the myth of Jewish responsibility for the World War is played up in quarters where it is likely to prove attractive. *The Secret World Government,* by Major General Count Cherep-Spiridovich, is the best example of such fantastically anti-Semitic literature.

Most dramatic and absurd of all the elements in recent anti-Semitism has been the world-wide dissemination of that palpable forgery *The Protocols of the Elders of Zion.* This first appeared in Russia in 1905, published by one Sergei Nilus. But the edition that was circulated most widely was that of 1917, a considerable expansion of the original text. It purported to reveal a great international conspiracy to bring the whole world under Jewish dominion. The theory of Nilus was that the *Protocols* were the notes that Theodor Herzl had submitted to the Council of Elders at the First Zionist Congress at Basel in 1897. The forged character of these *Protocols* was apparent to all competent students of Jewish life and policy. The fact of the forgery was actually proved by the correspondent of the London *Times* at Constantinople. The *Protocols* not only aroused excitement in the countries previously given to Jew-baiting but also led to an unprecedented rise of anti-Semitism in the United States and Great Britain. Singularly enough, much of this came after the London *Times* had exposed the forgery in 1921.

In the United States, Henry Ford, smarting under the enmity of Wall Street, was particularly impressed by the menace of Jewish capitalism. His Dearborn *Independent* was the chief organ of anti-Semitism in the United States. Ford later repudiated his charges against the Jews.

In Poland and Rumania a persistent anti-Jewish policy has been maintained since the World War. In these areas nationalism and economic jealousy have been the dominant factors. The Poles have desired to seize the control of business and finance from the Jewish middle class. They apparently have hoped to drive the Jews into desperation and then exploit the Red bogy against them. Rumania has continued the old prewar disabilities and persecutions. Even Great Britain, at first definitely committed to the support of the Jewish plan to rehabilitate Palestine, has more recently let the Jews down rather badly in this territory.

While deploring the savagery and imbecilities of contemporary anti-Semitism, the impartial historian cannot fail also to call attention to the incitement to the anti-Semites afforded by professional Judaism. This is still inculcated in an age when its intellectual foundations, in cultural, religious and anthropological doctrine, are as archaic and bankrupt as the racial bigotry that supports anti-Semitism. The notion of a "chosen people" is today on a par with Aryanism.[1]

[1] *Cf.* H. L. Mencken, "H. L. Mencken Believes that Hitler Has but His Own Throat to Cut," *American Hebrew,* Sept. 7, 1934.

SUGGESTED READING

Hammerton, *Universal History of the World,* Chaps. 156-57, 162, 165, 169, 172
Flick, *Modern World History,* Pt. V and Chaps. xxv-xxvi
W. B. Pillsbury, *The Psychology of Nationality and Internationalism,* Appleton, 1919, Chaps. I-II, IV, VI-VII
Muir, *Nationalism and Internationalism,* pp. 37-123
Rose, *Nationality in Modern History*

SUGGESTED READING 479

H. A. Gibbons, *Nationalism and Internationalism,* Stokes, 1930
H. E. Barnes, *The Genesis of the World War,* 3d ed. rev., Knopf, 1929, Chap. II
Hayes, *Essays on Nationalism*
—— *Historical Evolution of Modern Nationalism*
J. F. Scott, *Patriots in the Making,* Appleton, 1916
C. E. Merriam, *The Making of Citizens,* University of Chicago Press, 1931
C. A. Macartney, *National States and National Minorities,* Oxford Press, 1934
L. L. Snyder, *From Bismarck to Hitler,* Bayard Press, 1935
P. S. Mowrer, *Balkanized Europe,* Dutton, 1921
I. D. Levine, *The Resurrected Nations,* Stokes, 1919
Francis Delaisi, *Political Myths and Economic Realities,* Viking Press, 1927
C. A. Beard, *The Open Door at Home,* Macmillan, 1934
—— and G. H. E. Smith, *The Idea of National Interest,* Macmillan, 1934
F. H. Simonds and Brooks Emeny, *The Price of Peace,* Harper (forthcoming)
H. A. Miller, *The Beginnings of To-morrow,* Stokes, 1933
H. F. Armstrong, *Europe between Wars?* Macmillan, 1934
Webster, *Historical Selections,* pp. 655-91
Robinson and Beard, *Readings in Modern European History,* Vol. II, Chaps. XXI-XXII, XXIX
Scott and Baltzly, *Readings in European History since 1814,* pp. 238-67, 352-95, 593-601, 662-67
L. W. McMullen, ed., *Building the World Society,* McGraw-Hill, 1931, Chaps. I-II

FURTHER REFERENCES

NATIONALISM. Articles "Imperialism" (M. J. Bonn); "National Defense" (P. N. Baker); "National Economic Planning" (Emil Lederer); "Nationalism," "Nationality" (R. W. Flournoy, Jr.); and "Protection" (E. F. Heckscher), Encyclopaedia of the Social Sciences; Rose, *op. cit.;* Muir, *op. cit.;* Gibbons, *op. cit.;* G. E. Partridge, *The Psychology of Nations* (Macmillan, 1919); E. B. Krehbiel, *Nationalism, War and Society* (Macmillan, 1916).

THE FRENCH REVOLUTION AND NATIONAL SENTIMENT. Rose, *op. cit.,* Chap. II; Gibbons, *op. cit.,* Chap. II; Hayes, *Historical Evolution of Modern Nationalism,* Chap. III; Leo Gershoy, *The French Revolution, 1788-1799* (Holt, 1932); C. C. Brinton, *The Jacobins* (Macmillan, 1930) and *A Decade of Revolution, 1789-1799;* G. G. Van Deusen, *Sieyes: His Life and His Nationalism* (Columbia University Press, 1932). For the effect of the French Revolution on nationalism in Germany, Spain, and other European countries, see Rose, *op. cit.,* Chaps. III-VI; Hayes, *op. cit.,* Chap. IV; H. C. Engelbrecht, *Johann Gottlieb Fichte* (Columbia University Press, 1933); W. C. Langsam, *The Napoleonic Wars and German Nationalism in Austria* (Columbia University Press, 1930); Pt. II, Chaps. I-VII of L. M. E. Bertrand and Sir Charles Petrie, *History of Spain* (Appleton-Century, 1934); G. O. Griffith, *Mazzini, Prophet of Modern Europe* (Harcourt, Brace, 1932).

THE MACHINE ERA, MODERN COMMUNICATION, AND NATIONALISM. Chapin, *Historical Introduction to Social Economy,* Chap. XVI; Willson, *The Story of Rapid Transit;* Page and others, *Modern Communication;* Keir, *The March of Commerce,* Chaps. XI-XIII; *Recent Social Trends,* Vol. I, Chap. IV; G. O. Squier, *Telling the World* (Williams & Wilkins, 1933); K. A. Bickel, *New Empires* (Lippincott, 1930); N. B. Mavity, *The Modern Newspaper* (Holt, 1930); N. A. Crawford, *The Ethics of Journalism* (Crofts, 1924); J. K. Winkler, *W. R. Hearst: An American Phenomenon* (Simon & Schuster, 1928); O. W. Riegel, *Mobilizing for Chaos* (Yale

University Press, 1934); Walter Millis, *The Martial Spirit* (Houghton Mifflin, 1931); H. J. Forman, *Our Movie Made Children* (Macmillan, 1933).

THE REVOLUTIONS OF 1848 AND NATIONALISM. Chap. VII of James Bryce, *Essays and Addresses in Wartime* (Macmillan, 1918); Hayes, *op. cit.*, Chap. V; Gibbons, *op. cit.*, Chap. III; Andrews, *The Historical Development of Modern Europe,* Vol. I, Chaps. VII-X; Chaps. XVIII-XIX of C. A. Fyffe, *History of Modern Europe, 1792-1878* (new ed., Holt, 1896); Chaps. VI, XI, XIII-XIV, of Charles Seignobos, *Political History of Europe since 1814* (Holt, 1899).

NATIONALISTIC SENTIMENT AND UPRISINGS IN CENTRAL EUROPE AND THE BALKANS. Rose, *op. cit.*, Chap. VI; Gibbons, *op. cit.*, Chap. IV; R. W. Seton-Watson, *The Rise of Nationality in the Balkans* (Dutton, 1919); W. M. Gewehr, *The Rise of Nationalism in the Balkans 1800-1930* (Holt, 1931); Chaps. XIX-XXX of Ferdinand Schevill, *History of the Balkan Peninsula* (rev. ed., Harcourt, Brace, 1933); Chaps. VII-XII of W. A. Phillips, *Poland* (Holt, 1916); Chaps. V-VII of E. C. Corsi, *Poland, Land of the White Eagle* (Wyndham Press, 1933); J. W. Wuorinen, *Nationalism in Modern Finland* (Columbia University Press, 1931); John Buchan, ed., *The Baltic and Caucasian States* (Houghton Mifflin, 1923, *The Nations of To-day*).

NATIONALISM AND DIPLOMACY. D. P. Heatley, *Diplomacy and the Study of International Relations* (Oxford Press, 1919); De W. C. Poole, *The Conduct of Foreign Relations under Modern Democratic Conditions* (Yale University Press, 1924); M. J. Demiashkevich, *Shackled Diplomacy* (Barnes & Noble, 1934); Francis Neilson, *How Diplomats Make War* (Huebsch, 1916); G. P. Gooch, *Recent Revelations of European Diplomacy* (Longmans, 1928); F. R. Flournoy, *Parliament and War* (Columbia University Press, 1931).

NATIONALISM IN THE UNITED STATES. J. T. Adams, *The Epic of America* (Little, Brown, 1931); Becker, *The Beginnings of the American People;* C. H. Hamlin, *The War Myth in United States History* (Vanguard Press, 1927); K. C. Babcock, *The Rise of American Nationality* (Harper, 1906); F. R. Turner, *The Rise of the New West* (Holt, 1921); J. H. Smith, *The War with Mexico* (Macmillan, 1919, 2 vols.); J. F. Rhodes, *History of the Civil War, 1861-1865* (Macmillan, 1917); Millis, *op. cit.;* C. H. Grattan, *Why We Fought* (Vanguard Press, 1929); J. K. Turner, *Shall It Be Again?* (Huebsch, 1922); G. S. Viereck, *Spreading Germs of Hate* (Liveright, 1930); Knight, *American Literature and Culture.*

NATIONALISM IN THE FAR EAST. Hans Kohn, *History of Nationalism in the East* (Harcourt, Brace, 1929); Tyau, *China Awakened;* H. E. Wildes, *Japan in Crisis* (Macmillan, 1934); F. R. Eldridge, *Dangerous Thoughts on the Orient* (Appleton-Century, 1933); H. E. Wildes, *Social Currents in Japan* (University of Chicago Press, 1927); O. Tanin and E. Yohan, *Militarism and Fascism in Japan* (International Publishers, 1934); W. J. Durant, *The Case for India* (Simon & Schuster, 1930); H. T. Muzumdar, *Gandhi versus the Empire* (Universal Publishing Co., 1932); J. H. Nicholson, *The Re-making of Nations* (Dutton, 1925).

NATIONALISM IN THE WORLD WAR. C. E. Playne, *The Neuroses of the Nations* (Seltzer, 1925) and *Society at War, 1914-1916* (Houghton Mifflin, 1931); I. C. Willis, *England's Holy War* (Knopf, 1928); Viereck, *op. cit.*

NATIONALISM SINCE THE WORLD WAR. Levine, *op. cit.;* Mowrer, *op. cit.;* Valentine Thomson, *Young Europe* (Doubleday, Doran, 1932); R. M. Henry, *The Evolution of Sinn Fein* (Viking Press, 1920); Emil Lengyel, *The Cauldron Boils* (Dial Press, 1932); H. R. Knickerbocker, *The Boiling Point* (Farrar & Rinehart, 1934); Armstrong, *op. cit.;* Miller, *op. cit.;* G. M. Dutcher, *The Political Awakening of the East* (Abingdon Press, 1925); P. B. Potter, *This World of Nations* (Macmillan, 1929); H. C. Engelbrecht and F. C. Hanighen, *Merchants of Death* (Dodd, Mead, 1934).

FURTHER REFERENCES

ECONOMIC NATIONALISM. Hayes, *op. cit.,* Chap. VII; Chaps. V, IX-XI of H. E. Barnes, *World Politics in Modern Civilization* (Knopf, 1930); Delaisi, *op. cit.;* Beard, *The Idea of National Interest* and *The Open Door at Home;* E. M. Patterson, ed., *The World Trend Towards Nationalism* (American Academy of Political and Social Science, *Annals,* Vol. CLXXIV, 1934); Commission of Inquiry into National Policy in International Relations, *International Economic Relations* (University of Minnesota Press, 1934); Simonds and Emeny, *op. cit.;* Wallace, *New Frontiers.*

NATIONALISM AND EDUCATION. E. A. Reisner, *Nationalism and Education since 1789* (Macmillan, 1922); Mark Starr, *Lies and Hate in Education* (Hogarth Press, 1929); J. F. Scott, *The Menace of Nationalism in Education* (Macmillan, 1926) and *Patriots in the Making;* Merriam, *op. cit.;* J. M. Gaus, *Great Britain: A Study in Civic Loyalty* (University of Chicago Press, 1929); H. W. Schneider and S. B. Clough, *Making Fascists* (University of Chicago Press, 1929); B. L. Pierce, *Civic Attitudes in American School Textbooks* (University of Chicago Press, 1930).

NATIONALISM AND RACIAL DOCTRINES. F. H. Hankins, *The Racial Basis of Civilization* (Knopf, 1926); C. C. Josey, *Race and National Solidarity* (Scribner, 1923); T. L. Stoddard, *Racial Realities in Europe* (Scribner, 1924); John Oakesmith, *Race and Nationality* (Stokes, 1919); Théophile Simar, *The Race Myth* (Boni, 1925); J. L. Tenenbaum, *Races, Nations and Jews* (Bloch, 1934).

ANTI-SEMITISM. Benjamin Ginzburg, article "Antisemitism," Encyclopaedia of the Social Sciences; articles by various writers in the *Nation* (New York), Vol. CXVI, pp. 207-08, 240-42, 330-32, 409-11; Vol. CXVII, pp. 547-49; Vol. CXVIII, pp. 81-82; L. J. Levinger, *Anti-Semitism in the United States: Its History and Causes* (Bloch, 1925); J. W. Wise, *Swastika: The Nazi Terror* (Smith and Haas, 1933); H. M. Kallen, *Judaism at Bay* (Bloch, 1932); Maurice Samuel, *Jews on Approval* (Liveright, 1932); O. I. Janowsky, *Jews and Minority Rights (1898-1919)* (Columbia University Press, 1933); A. D. Margolin, *The Jews of Eastern Europe* (Seltzer, 1926); J. L. Spivak, "Plotting America's Pogroms," *New Masses,* October-December, 1934; Samuel Roth, *Jews Must Live* (Golden Hind Press, 1934), a bitterly anti-Semitic book by an American Jew; Herman Bernstein, *The Truth about the Protocols of Zion* (Covici, Friede, 1935).

CHAPTER XIV

THE ORIGINS OF DEMOCRACY AND THE RISE

OF PARTY GOVERNMENT

I. WHAT IS DEMOCRACY?

In an earlier chapter we traced the development of liberalism, constitutionalism, representative government, and republicanism.[1] While the earlier constitutions did not usually establish democratic government, the victories of the exponents of representative government and parliamentary supremacy helped along the democratic movement. Once the middle class established its right to participate in government, thus ousting the nobles and agrarian lords from their nearly complete dominion over political life, it was hard to prevent the lower classes from entertaining similar aspirations to participate in politics. The middle class had been induced to battle for its political rights because of the oppression to which it was subjected by kings and barons. The lower classes had to endure various burdens and restrictions at the hands of both the landlords and the bourgeoisie. They also, therefore, turned to the ballot as a means of terminating their servility and promoting their prosperity. The result was the gradual establishment of universal suffrage and majority rule—the fundamental machinery of political democracy.

One of the most interesting developments in the analysis of this political system has been the clarification of the definition of democracy.[2] The early definitions were formalistic and concerned chiefly with such problems as distinguishing between "direct" and "representative" democracy and analyzing the concept of democracy as a political system.[3]

Especially important has been the "democratizing" of the very conception of democracy. The old Aristotelian notion of the "people" as the upper-class and middle-class members of society, which persisted down to the close of the eighteenth century, has been supplanted by the contemporary view, which regards the people as embracing all members of society with no important exceptions. Consequently, the conception of "government by the people" meant quite a different thing when used by Lincoln from what it did in the days of Aristotle, the writers of the Magna Charta, Locke, or Rousseau.

Again, more recent students of the subject have come to see that democracy

---

[1] See above, Chapter IV.
[2] See H. E. Barnes, *Sociology and Political Theory*, Knopf, 1924, pp. 82 ff.; and C. A. Ellwood, article, "Democracy," Encyclopedia Americana.
[3] *Cf.* W. S. Carpenter, *Democracy and Representation*, Princeton University Press, 1925.

482

is something more than merely a form of government based on majority rule. Professor F. H. Giddings, whose views may be taken as typical of the recent comprehensive interpretation of democracy, finds that democracy is a particular kind of government, a specific form of the state, a special type of social organization, and a definite mode of social control.[1] As a method of government, a "pure democracy" implies the enfranchisement of the majority of the population and direct participation of all the citizens in public affairs. The much more common "representative democracy" is defined as one in which the citizens govern indirectly through periodically selected deputies or representatives. As a type of state, democracy implies the existence of popular sovereignty. As a type of social organization and control, democracy means both a popular organization of the community and the free control of non-political activities through the force of public opinion.

A number of students of democracy, among them James Harvey Robinson, have become dissatisfied with a formalistic and static analysis of democracy.[2] They have given it a pragmatic definition, and have identified it with a dynamic perspective. Professor Robinson, for example, holds that democracy not only requires the popular control of public policy, but also implies a type of social organization that will develop to the fullest extent the latent potentialities of every member of the society. It imposes upon society the moral obligation to do everything in its power to hasten the realization of such a state of affairs.

II. A BRIEF HISTORY OF DEMOCRACY

1. THE SLOW PROGRESS OF DEMOCRACY TO THE NINETEENTH CENTURY

Critical ethnologists agree that the earliest type of social organization among primitive men was the *local group* organized about the family and the village.[3] It is in these small social groupings that the nearest approach is found to the so-called primitive democracy. Here one finds small groups gathered together on the basis of intimate association, little affected by outside social or cultural influences. The individuals therein participate in the whole culture of the group to a degree little known in modern society outside isolated neighborhoods.

When one turns to examine what are usually the more advanced forms of primitive society organized on a kinship basis, with either maternal or paternal descent, less appears of the alleged democratic characteristics of primitive society. Every phase of life within the group was minutely ordered by a veritable maze of customary regulations, which were enforced with great rigidity. Within the group the freedom of the individual was further restricted by the prevalence of social ranks and grades. The much-vaunted tribal assemblies

---

[1] *Elements of Sociology*, pp. 311 ff.
[2] *The Mind in the Making*, Chaps. VII-VIII; *The Humanizing of Knowledge*, 2d ed. rev., Doran, 1926; and unpublished lectures.
[3] See above, Vol. I, pp. 44-45; and A. A. Goldenweiser, in Davis and Barnes, *Readings in Sociology*, pp. 51 ff.

have been reduced by modern critical research from the "original fountain springs of political liberty," as pictured by such writers as Kemble, Freeman and Fiske, to mere formal gatherings to confirm a preassured acquiesence in the policies of the leaders of the group—a function not dissimilar to that of the American party convention.[1] A distinguished authority has remarked that the defiance of the policies of the chiefs by a tribal assembly was such a rarity as to constitute no less than a political revolution.[2] As primitive society approached political or civil society the undemocratic features of its social organization markedly increased.

If any generalization of historical sociology can be regarded as definitely established, it is that political society and the state came into being through the amalgamation of tribal groups as a result of the incessant wars waged in what Walter Bagehot has called in his *Physics and Politics* the "nation-making age." A highly autocratic and hierarchical caste society thus developed, and it dominated early political society. There was, of course, nothing truly democratic in any field of social relations. In no other period of civilization has the individual counted for so little or been so circumscribed in his liberty as in this period of the formation of states and the development of early despotisms. The facts almost justify Hegel's famous dogma that in the ancient oriental age only the despot enjoyed freedom.

It is impossible to make any sweeping statement as to the degree of democracy realized in ancient Greece, for the situation varied greatly in different periods of Greek history.[3] The sweeping transformations of Greek governments from tyranny to aristocracy and from aristocracy to so-called democracy were so frequent as to give rise to the famous Platonic and Aristotelian theory of the cycle of governmental changes. True democracy was not, however, realized in Hellenic society. We have seen that even Athens, the most liberally inclined of the Greek city-states, could scarcely be regarded as a democracy in the modern implication of the term. While, as Professor Zimmern has pointed out, there has been a tendency to exaggerate the number of slaves in Athens, a majority of the population were excluded from citizenship at all times in Athenian history. Greek "democracy" meant relative social and political equality among only the citizen class—the class that, in the opinion of Aristotle, was "born to rule." Within this privileged citizen class, however, Athenian society made the closest approximation to democratic control of group activities that was achieved in antiquity.[4]

In republican Rome we find the same conception of exclusiveness in citizenship that had prevailed in Greece.[5] The numerous slaves and foreigners were excluded from the political life of the state. Within the citizen body itself there was less democratic control of political activities than had existed in Athens. Despite the gains made by the plebeians in the fourth century B.C. and the later attempts of the Gracchi to break down the dominion of the aristo-

---

[1] See above, Vol. I, pp. 50 ff.; and R. H. Lowie, *Primitive Society,* Boni & Liveright, 1920, Chap. XIII.

[2] Munroe Smith, *The Development of European Law,* Columbia University Press, 1928, pp. 14-24.

[3] See above, Vol. I, pp. 191 ff. On democracy in Greek and Roman antiquity, see T. R. Glover, *Democracy in the Ancient World,* Macmillan, 1927.

[4] See A. E. Zimmern, *The Greek Commonwealth,* Oxford Press, 1924; and R. J. Bonner, *Aspects of Athenian Democracy,* University of California Press, 1933.

[5] See above, Vol. I, pp. 268 ff., 305 ff., 311 ff.

Wide World Photos
THOMAS JEFFERSON

Wide World Photos
ANDREW JACKSON

ABRAHAM LINCOLN

Wide World Photos
WILLIAM JENNINGS BRYAN

LEADERS IN DEMOCRACY

Wide World Photos
JAMES RAMSAY MACDONALD

© *Wide World Photos*
FRANKLIN DELANO ROOSEVELT

MUSCLE SHOALS
Wide World Photos

cratic governing clique, the government of Rome drifted steadily into the control of the autocratic *ordo senatorius* and from that into the principate and the Empire.[1] The sodalities or industrial associations were the only approximation to social democracy, and they were discouraged by the government.

During the imperial period a slight movement towards democracy might be detected in the reduction of the number of slaves through manumission and the extinction of many sources of supply. But this minor symptom was more than offset by the growth of imperial despotism, the gains of the Senatorial plutocracy, the extinction of the *curiales* or urban middle class through the disproportionate burdens of taxation imposed upon it, and the rise of a caste system. As a result, the middle class, the lower-class freemen, and the slaves were very generally absorbed in the semiservile system known as the colonate.

Classical antiquity, then, never created real democracy in the political, social, or economic sense. It left behind it a more marked inequality than it had received from the rudimentary tribal society with which it had started.

The Roman Empire thus ended with the growth of plutocracy and the crushing out of the few democratic tendencies that had existed. With the barbarian "invasions" and the establishment of the Teutonic kingdoms the fruits of classical civilization were, for the most part, lost. Western Europe dropped back in a cultural sense into the conditions out of which ancient civilization had developed a thousand years earlier. Even the feeble advances of classical civilization in the direction of democracy had to be regained before any further progress could be made towards securing personal freedom, mass enfranchisement, and popular control of public policy.

Feudal society, developing from roots in the Gallo-Roman villa and in the German mark and comitatus,[2] offered little opportunity for the growth of democracy. With its slight perpetuation of the slavery of classical times and its retention on an extensive scale of the near-serfdom found in the colonate of the later Roman Empire, the feudal age was even less democratic in a political sense than were the classical city-states. On the manors there were some democratic tendencies in the intimate communal life of the serfs.[3] Professor Giddings has insisted that the real origin of modern social democracy is to be found in the enforced communal "equality" among the members of this servile peasantry in the Middle Ages. Some symptoms of democracy also appeared in the medieval free towns, but these were not extensive. The political, social, and economic organization became hierarchical and restrictive. Equality in the medieval town, as in the classical city-state, usually meant equality among the favored few. The most important contributions of the medieval towns to democracy consisted in the growth of representative government.

The Magna Charta as a harbinger of modern democracy has withered before modern historical research quite as much as the Teutonic folkmoot.[4] It did not mark a movement looking towards modern political liberalism, but was a reactionary manifesto of the feudal lords who were irritated by previous extensions of royal power. In 1215 they made an effort to pull England back

[1] See above, Vol. I, pp. 268 ff., 329 ff.
[2] See above, Vol. I, pp. 557 ff.
[3] See above, Vol. I, pp. 609 ff.
[4] See above, Vol. I, pp. 453-54, 799.

into the decentralized lawlessness and local tyranny of late Norman feudalism.

An interesting trend towards democracy in the Middle Ages occurred as an incident of the rise of Christianity.[1] A number of writers have claimed with some degree of justification that the first instances of real democratic society are to be found in the early Christian communities of the Apostolic age. Certainly, the only development of democracy in social organization in the medieval period occurred in the monastic movement—and this was limited. The organization of the secular clergy in the medieval Church, with its elaborate hierarchies for ecclesiastical administration and for the control of the sacraments, was scarcely less autocratic than the feudal society of the period. The only concession that the medieval Church made to democracy was that its offices were, in theory at least, open to all classes solely on the basis of merit. But the best positions were frequently filled by nobles. Perhaps the most significant contribution that the medieval Church made to the ultimate trend towards democracy lay in the political theory of the Conciliar Movement. This stressed the principle of representative government in the Church and led to the consideration of the applicability of the same principle to secular governments. Democracy, however, or any strong prophecy of democracy scarcely appeared during the thousand years that followed the collapse of the Western Roman Empire.

Those colorful developments intermediate between medievalism and modernity, the Renaissance and the Protestant Revolution, contributed little in themselves to the progress of democratic trends. The politics of the Renaissance period were mainly autocratic—whether of city-states or of the rising national states. But the Renaissance did, as we have seen, contribute notably to the rise of individuality and hence to the growth of that political individualism which was in line with the trends that emerged from early modern capitalism. The Protestant Revolution, contrary to the views of many apologists, added little to democratic trends. Indeed, it made the lot of the peasantry harder than before and helped along the development of the theory of the divine right of kings. But it did stimulate individualism from the religious angle, and it increased the power of the upper middle class, hence accelerating a tendency that was to be carried much further by the Commercial Revolution and the growth of capitalism. There were also some radical Protestant sects, such as the Anabaptists, who did espouse definitely democratic political notions.

Beginning with the sixteenth century and extending over about two centuries, there occurred that sweeping transformation which marks the dawn of modern society—the expansion of Europe and the Commercial Revolution.[2] The explorations and discoveries and the resulting contact with new cultures broke through the "cake" of medieval custom and opened the way for the development of modern institutions and ideas. The increased volume of wealth put at the disposal of the monarchs as a result of the "intervention of capital" enabled them to develop a paid officialdom and armies. With their assistance the kings crushed feudalism and perfected the national state.

But the most important of all the political results of the Commercial Revolu-

[1] See above, Vol. I, pp. 695 ff.; and S. J. Case, *The Social Origins of Christianity*, University of Chicago Press, 1923. [2] See above, Chapters I-III.

tion was the great increase of the bourgeoisie or middle class.[1] This element in society, as Werner Sombart has made amply clear, was destined for centuries to be the center from which most liberalizing influences spread. The bourgeoisie ultimately secured the well-nigh universal destruction of the autocratic social and political régime that had characterized the Middle Ages.

In England during this period the new middle class brought about the most notable transformation of the old social and political order that was accomplished before the nineteenth century.[2] By the beginning of the seventeenth century the power of the feudal nobility had generally vanished, serfdom had disappeared, and the restrictive guild system of industrial organization had been practically eliminated. Before the close of the century, through successive concessions from the king and through the revolutions of 1649 and 1689, the English bourgeoisie had dethroned two autocratic monarchs, had eliminated royal arbitrariness in politics and law, had brought about the predominance of Parliament in the government, and had enacted into a constitutional document those guarantees of civil liberty which have since come to be recognized as among the most fundamental human rights.

Oppressive religious disabilities, extensive property qualifications for participation in political life, and the perpetuation of many of the social phases of medieval feudal aristocracy continued to prevent England from being described as a democratic nation in 1700. But the fact that the middle class had created a constitutional system and had assured the ascendancy of Parliament—the popular branch of the government—constituted an epoch-making step towards the ultimate realization of democracy.

There was, moreover, one conspicuously democratic development in seventeenth-century England, namely, the rise of the so-called Levellers during the period of the Commonwealth. They were made up of real democrats both within the army and outside and were led by John Lilburne, who deserves a prominent rank among the few leading apostles of democracy. The Levellers boldly proclaimed the sovereignty of the people and held that Parliament should be the servant rather than the master of the mass of Englishmen. They demanded universal manhood suffrage, excluding only those who were servants or paupers, annual sessions of Parliament, and equal electoral districts. They also espoused a number of other democratic proposals, such as abolition of imprisonment for debt, elimination of monopolies and sinecures, abolition of tithes, and reform of the criminal law. In much of their program they anticipated the policies and demands of the Chartists just two centuries later.[3] The Levellers certainly constitute the most significant democratic development before the days of the Jacksonian Democrats in the United States and the Chartists in England.

In France, even more than in Tudor England, the Commercial Revolution at first encouraged the development of royal absolutism rather than the growth of constitutional and democratic government.[4] The Estates-General, summoned in 1614 for the last time in a hundred and seventy-five years, made a pathetic failure as compared with the achievements of the English Parliament a genera-

[1] See above, pp. 94 ff.
[2] See above, pp. 99 ff.
[3] See above, p. 127.
[4] See above, pp. 89 ff.

tion later. The hope of a gradual evolution of legislative supremacy in France, such as had taken place in England, perished. The political power of the feudal nobility was crushed by Richelieu's centralizing policies and by the suppression of the Fronde in 1652, but they retained many of their oppressive social and economic privileges until the "August Days" of 1789.

The French Revolution of 1789 to 1795 was the product of the abuses of the old régime, of the revolutionary political theory of the English Whigs, of the intellectual impulse from the French *philosophes,* and of the American example of a successful experiment with revolution and the beginnings of "democracy." The third estate had been too weak in 1614 to oppose successfully the combined strength of the monarch and the first two estates. Its strength had so increased by 1789, as a result of the effects of the Commercial Revolution, that it was able to coerce the monarch, the weakened nobility, and the clergy. It proceeded to clear away not only the vestiges of feudalism but also the oppression of the Church and the tyranny of the monarch.[1]

The calling of the Estates-General in 1789 is worthy of passing mention in any historical survey of the development of democracy because the first instance in history of the legal exercise of universal manhood suffrage occurred quite incidentally in the process of electing the deputies of the third estate. This partial exercise of universal suffrage was not, of course, a deliberate democratic gesture on the part of the government. It was a result of the carelessness, indifference, and ineptitude of the ministers in arranging for the election of the deputies.

The most significant achievements of the French Revolution were the abolition of those economic and social aspects of feudalism which still persisted, the establishment of a constitutional monarchy in 1791, and that of a republic in 1792. Though many of these reforms proved transitory, their effect was never entirely lost and they constituted the stimulus and precedent for the more gradual development of French democracy in the nineteenth century.[2]

In all other important European states, with the exception of the reforms attempted or executed by the Benevolent Despots, the old régime, with all its medieval institutions and practices, remained practically undisturbed until the nineteenth century.

The establishment of an aristocratic republic in America in the closing years of the eighteenth century marked an important step in the development of democracy. While American society and politics at the beginning of our national history abounded in undemocratic features, the new state had been founded on revolution from established authority. It was one of the first examples in history of an extensive federal republic and of a government organized on the basis of a written constitution formulated by a national constituent convention. It therefore stimulated the growth of constitutionalism and republicanism elsewhere, most notably in France, and it laid the foundations for what became in the nineteenth century the most ambitious experiment that has yet been conducted in the democratic control of political institutions.

---

[1] See above, pp. 109 ff.   [2] See above, pp. 120 ff.

2. DEMOCRATIC GAINS IN THE NINETEENTH AND TWENTIETH CENTURIES

At the opening of the nineteenth century democracy did not prevail in any country in the world. Only England, France, and the United States had made any notable progress in that direction. The slight progress elsewhere seemed destined to be crushed and the old order to be restored after 1815 through the sinister influence of Metternich, who had extended his reactionary system throughout continental Europe by 1823.[1] But in that year he received his initial reverse in Great Britain's challenge to the proposed intervention of the European reactionaries in the South American revolutions. Great Britain was not motivated by an abstract love of liberty and revolution, for those were scarcely more pleasing to its Tory ministry than to Metternich. It was impelled primarily by the fact that its trading interests, so greatly increased by the Industrial Revolution, were more likely to be improved by the freedom of the Spanish-American republics than through their return to Spanish control.[2]

The rapid growth of democracy in the nineteenth century was the product of two important socio-economic developments and their reactions upon political life. These were the Industrial Revolution and the expansion of American frontier society. The Industrial Revolution led to the triumph of the middle class, which continued its work of breaking down agrarian privilege, liberalizing politics and economics, and creating constitutional and representative government. The Industrial Revolution also brought into being a large industrial proletariat—the laboring classes—which wished to extend representative government into truly democratic government. In this aspiration it was aided, especially in the United States, by the individualistic and democratic spirit of the pioneers and frontiersmen.

The bourgeoisie, motivated in part by sentiments of enlightened humanity and in part by selfish class interests, carried the day against the autocracy of the old régime. This also made it possible for the industrial proletariat to consolidate the positions already won by the bourgeoisie and to begin the struggle for the final realization of democracy in the true sense of the word.

The battle for political and social democracy in the last century has centered in three successive achievements: (1) The elimination of the vestiges of the old régime—the heritage of the Middle Ages; (2) the establishment of the liberal régime of the "benevolent bourgeoisie"; and (3) the attack upon the supremacy of the bourgeoisie by the proletariat, beginning about the middle of the nineteenth century.

All these forces were created or set in motion by the Commercial and Industrial Revolutions, and our attention may now be turned to the manner in which they have been realized in the leading countries of the Western world. The most important achievements in these directions have consisted in (1) the extension of the suffrage; (2) the increase in the importance of the popular

[1] See above, pp. 120 ff.; and Arthur Herman, *Metternich*, Century, 1932.
[2] See L. A. Lawson, *The Relation of British Policy to the Declaration of the Monroe Doctrine*, Columbia University Press, 1922.

or legislative branch of the government as compared with the executive; (3) the growth of representative institutions; (4) a broadening of the conception of the scope and functions of government; and (5) the drafting of written constitutions that acknowledge and guarantee these progressive achievements.

As important as political democracy is economic democracy, or the equal right of all classes to carry on such activities as are necessary to advance or safeguard their material interests. At the beginning of the nineteenth century economic democracy was as far from realization as political democracy, and the progress made since that time has been notable. In 1800 most of the restrictive economic regulations that had been enacted during the two previous centuries favored the vested agricultural interests, even though they reflected the early commercial philosophy of mercantilism. As a result of the growth of the political power of the bourgeoisie most of the older restrictions on economic activities were abolished.

There was then instituted the reign of laissez faire that gave the middle-class manufacturers and merchants almost unrestricted opportunity for the development of their industrial and commercial enterprises and for the enjoyment of the "blessings" of the freedom of contract.[1] This individualistic movement was most thoroughgoing in England, where it was chiefly associated with the work of Cobden, Bright, Mill, and Gladstone, but no European country entirely escaped its influence.

Laissez faire, however, gave economic liberty only to the upper middle classes. It is to the development of labor-unionism and social legislation that one must look for the most effective means of advancing economic democracy among the laboring classes during the last century.[2]

In England, the new middle class secured its first important triumph of the nineteenth century in the parliamentary Reform Bill of 1832 and in the Municipal Reform Act of 1835. These reforms destroyed the almost medieval system of election and representation which had persisted in England until that time. They gave political recognition to the dislocation of economic interests and the population shifts that had been caused by the early Industrial Revolution. They were scarcely a direct victory for democracy, for they did not carry with them an enfranchisement of the masses. But they did constitute an indirect triumph in that they brought into power the bourgeoisie, who proceeded to clear away some of the most formidable obstacles to the ultimate realization of democracy. The democratic movement of this period—Chartism —proved a pathetic failure, but all except one of the Chartists' demands— (1) universal manhood suffrage; (2) vote by ballot; (3) equal electoral districts; (4) removal of property qualifications for members of Parliament; (5) annual sessions of Parliament; and (6) payment of members of Parliament— have since been realized, a significant testimony to the progress of political democracy in England.

The first important direct step in the actual realization of political democracy in England came in Disraeli's Borough Franchise Bill of 1867, which brought something approaching universal manhood suffrage to the residents of boroughs. A similar extension of the franchise to the working classes in the country districts by Gladstone's suffrage bill of 1884 further promoted political

[1] See above, pp. 319 ff., 378 ff.   [2] For more details, see below, pp. 938 ff., 949 ff.

democracy, even though universal manhood suffrage was not won. The process was carried further by the sweeping Franchise Act of February, 1918, which brought universal suffrage to men and introduced on a liberal scale the principle of woman suffrage. Woman suffrage won its final victory in 1928.

Two centuries earlier England had established the supremacy of Parliament. Therefore when the people secured the vote they were able to use it directly to influence the policies of the government and to secure for themselves some of the substance as well as the forms of political and social democracy. The grip of the people upon the legislative power in Great Britain was tightened by the Parliament Act of 1911, which finally assured the supremacy of the House of Commons.[1] A Labor government has twice been in office since the World War.

Beginning with the Elementary Education Act of 1870, the people endeavored to transform England into a social as well as a political democracy. Especially rapid was the progress in this direction under the Liberal party after 1905, as is abundantly proved by the remarkable series of reform measures passed. Among the most conspicuous of these were the Workmen's Compensation Act of 1906, the Education Act of 1906, the Old Age Pensions Act of 1908, the Labor Acts of 1909 and 1913, the Lloyd George Budget of 1909-10, the National Insurance Act of 1911, the Franchise and Education Acts of 1918, the National Health Insurance Act of 1924, and the Widows, Orphans, and Old Age Contributory Pension Acts of 1924 and 1929. These are a convincing demonstration that the English proletariat is on the way to gain for itself the position held in 1815 by the Tory squirarchy and after 1832 by the bourgeois liberals.

Economic democracy in England has profited by the abolition of the many restrictions upon the freedom of economic activity that existed in 1800. This was accomplished through the joint efforts of the middle class and the proletariat. Especially significant has been the development of labor-unionism. This was first legalized as a result of the activities of Francis Place and Joseph Hume in 1824-25. It received further legislative encouragement by the laws of 1871-76, 1906, and 1913. Despite adverse court decisions at the turn of the century, the right of trade-unions to organize and act seems firmly established in England. In spite of a titular monarchy and a social aristocracy, England is at the present time one of the most democratic of the great modern nations.

In France the ultra-conservative squirarchy, led by the arch-reactionary Charles X, made a most daring and determined effort, between 1815 and 1830, to restore the old régime.[2] The futility of the attempt to revive in France the order of things that had existed before 1789 was demonstrated by the Revolution of 1830, which sent into final oblivion the autocracy and corruption of Bourbon absolutism.

The bourgeois liberals, strengthened by the early effects of the Industrial Revolution, came into power with the Orleanist monarchy from 1830 to 1848. Louis Philippe, however, refused to square his policies with the growth of lib-

[1] On the triumph of the House of Commons, see Emily Allyn, *Lords versus Commons*, Century, 1931.
[2] See F. B. Artz, *Reaction and Revolution, 1814-1832*, Harper, 1934.

eralism. In 1848 he met the fate that Charles X had encountered in 1830. The new Republican government developed a fatal split over its policies, and the Bonapartist adventurer, aided by this division among Republicans and Socialists and by the romantic luster of his name, was able to establish a temporary autocracy. During its brief period of power the Provisional Government of 1848 secured the enactment of the first universal manhood suffrage law in European history, which has been retained with little change down to the present day. This gave France the double honor of being the nation that first permitted the practice of universal manhood suffrage (1789) and also the first powerful European state to adopt it as a permanent political policy.

Like his predecessors, Charles X and Louis Philippe, Louis Napoleon was unable to resist the growing forces of democracy and liberalism, which were being augmented by the effects of the Industrial Revolution, especially the growth of the bourgeoisie and the proletariat. Even before he was swept off the throne by the debacle of 1870 he had been compelled to relinquish most of the attributes of autocracy and to establish a liberal constitutional monarchy. The attempts to restore monarchy between 1871 and 1879 failed utterly. With the accession of President Grévy in 1879 it was definitely established that the constitution of 1875 would be interpreted to mean that France was henceforth to be a parliamentary republic. Gathering impetus in the decade of the eighties, through the vigor and wisdom of Jules Ferry, the Republic gained sufficient strength to withstand the onslaughts of monarchists and clericals in the Boulanger episode and the Dreyfus affair. It emerged from the latter stronger than ever.

Under the Third Republic the French proletariat has increased in political power until the progressive democratic element is today as firmly intrenched in its control of political policies as the conservative bourgeoisie was in 1840. Its power has been given objective expression in a series of social-reform acts that rival England's achievements in this field. In France, economic democracy was advanced by the law of 1864, giving workingmen the right to combine for strikes, and by that of 1884, granting general freedom of organization to the working class. The attempt of the government employees to establish their right to strike in 1909 and 1910 failed, however, almost completely. The systematization of sickness insurance in 1898, the Employers' Liability and Workmen's Compensation Act of 1898, the Old Age Pensions Act of 1910, and the comprehensive Social Insurance Act of 1930 constituted creditable achievements in the field of social legislation. The Act of 1930 was one of the most sweeping in the history of social insurance. Under its provisions about nine million workers are provided with benefit payments in the case of illness and invalidity and with old-age insurance. Provision is also made for maternity benefits in the families of the insured. In France, as in England, economic democracy is today well along towards realization.

Vastly different from the record of England and France was the course of events in central Europe in the nineteenth century. Stein and Hardenberg had abolished serfdom in Prussia in 1808-11, but Metternich was able to preserve the old régime intact in Austria after 1815. He was also able to nullify the decree of the Congress of Vienna that enabled each ruler in the German Confederation to give his state a constitution. Between 1815 and 1848 the power of the German middle class was increased by the early effects of the Industrial Revolution, and a disgruntled proletariat was created. A liberal and democratic régime would probably have come to exist in central Europe in 1848 had it not been that the issues of nationality and dynasty conflicted with the cause of liberalism and democracy. Taking advantage of this division of strength and interests among the liberals, the reactionaries, led by Schwarzenberg, were enabled to triumph in 1848-50 as they had under Metternich following 1815.

This failure of the liberal movement in mid-Europe in 1848 was a blow to democracy. In Germany it meant that unity was not to be accomplished under the benevolent auspices of the liberals of the Frankfort Parliament. It had to be worked out under the autocratic "blood and iron" policy of Bismarck, who, after creating the German Empire in this manner, was able, in part, to throttle subsequent attempts to liberalize and democratize it.

Taking over bodily the mechanical aspects of the Industrial Revolution from England, Germany presented, as Thorstein Veblen has convincingly pointed out,[1] the curious spectacle of a great modern industrial and commercial nation dominated by political autocracy and a medieval dynastic atmosphere. The semimedieval constitution given to Prussia by Frederick William IV in January, 1850, was retained practically unchanged to 1918, and no redistribution of seats in the Prussian Landtag took place between 1860 and 1918. This gave rise to a situation resembling that of the notorious "rotten boroughs" of England before 1832. Furthermore, the aristocratic three-class system of determining the suffrage and the archaic method of oral voting in Prussia destroyed even those slight traces of democracy which might have existed in spite of other limitations.

In the German Empire universal manhood suffrage was introduced in 1871 for elections to the Reichstag. Since, however, the Reichstag was dominated by the autocratic Bundesrat and the still more archaic government of Prussia, the representatives of the people could not make their will fully effective in the government. The universal suffrage and the alleged democratic Reichstag thus appear upon close examination to have been strongly qualified in practice. To make matters still worse, the distribution of electoral districts for seats in the Reichstag was not altered from 1870 to 1918. This excluded the great industrial cities of modern Germany from anything like an equitable representation after 1870, deprived the bourgeoisie and the proletariat of a true expression of their strength even in the representative branch of the German political organization, and perpetuated the dominating influence of the reactionary Prussian squirarchy.

Nor was there any greater degree of real social democracy in Germany. The elaborate social-legislation program of Bismarck came not from the influence of the masses, nor as a result of the modern democratic conception of the state as the servant of the people. It proceeded from Bismarck's highly undemocratic desire to crush the Social Democrats, to insure a healthy nation as the indispensable basis of a strong military system, and to attach the people to the autocratic German state through gratitude for its paternalism. The social legislation

[1] *Imperial Germany and the Industrial Revolution.*

of modern Germany was thus in no way a symptom of social democracy. It was a hangover of the same eighteenth-century enlightened despotism that had impelled Frederick the Great to undertake his internal reforms in Prussia.[1] Of the truth of this assertion overwhelming proof is afforded by the fact that the Social Democrats invariably opposed the social legislation of Bismarck, and by Bismarck's acknowledged purposes in undertaking his program of social reform. It should be remembered, however, that by 1914 the Socialist party had attained the strongest position in Germany that it had reached at that time anywhere in the world. This, together with the large measure of German municipal democracy, are facts which were often overlooked from 1914 to 1918 by Entente writers bent on emphasizing the German autocracy—a somewhat risky venture in the light of the fact that the governments of the Tsar and the Mikado were among the Entente forces, supposedly devoted to making the world safe for democracy.

Labor-unionism, as a movement towards economic democracy, made its first appearance as a significant movement in Germany in the decade of the sixties, but it was greatly weakened during the period of anti-Socialist legislation between 1878 and 1890. After 1890 it revived and enjoyed legal sanction for extensive economic activities until the advent of Hitler.

If Germany did not move far in the direction of democracy in the nineteenth century, the German Empire, and especially the Prussian kingdom, gave to the world an example of public-spirited devotion to the state and of efficiency in administration that no important democratic state has ever equaled.[2] Until democracy meets this challenge of the superior administrative efficiency of bureaucracy, it cannot be said to have fully vindicated its position in the modern world. This is especially true today, when we face constantly more complicated problems that must be wrestled with by statesmen.

The aftermath of the disasters of the World War brought to Germany at least temporarily a complete democratization. The Hohenzollern dynasty was repudiated, the Empire abolished, and a progressive Republic was created. Much additional social legislation was introduced. Many very advanced conceptions of social reconstruction were proposed and seriously considered.

The arrogant and oppressive treatment of Germany by the Allies, particularly France, at the Peace Conference and after has, however, greatly aided in discrediting democracy in Germany and in stimulating the revival of the autocratic and military clique. It is probable that M. Poincaré indirectly contributed more than any other single factor to the election of Von Hindenburg as the President of the Republic in 1925. What the ultimate outcome will be cannot be safely predicted, though for the time being democracy has been crushed in Germany. If German democracy disappears for good and all, the responsibility will lie chiefly at the door of the short-sighted French statesmen of 1918-33. Hitler and the National Socialists (Nazis) were a natural response to the oppression and degradation of Germany after 1918.

In the Austrian Empire political liberalism, after its defeat in 1850, met a somewhat kinder fate than it did in the Prussianized German Empire. No serious attempt was made to restore the feudal system that was abolished in

---

[1] See above, p. 92.
[2] Cf. H. G. James, *Principles of Prussian Administration*, Macmillan, 1913.

1848-49. In the period from 1860 to 1867 Francis Joseph, in order to placate his own subjects and the Hungarians for their disappointments in 1848-49, granted reforms that embodied many of the aspirations of the liberals of 1848. A real approach to parliamentary government was secured by the constitution of 1861 and the "fundamental laws" of 1867. These gave the Austrian parliament a legal position of much greater power than that possessed by the imperial German Reichstag. These reforms also embodied the institution of ministerial responsibility in the Parliament.

While the suffrage was at first extremely limited, the acts of 1896 and 1907 introduced universal manhood suffrage. The existence of a considerable degree of social democracy in Austria was also attested by the passage of a number of important social-reform acts after 1885. These laws were not wholly a revival of the benevolent despotism of Joseph II, but were partly a result of the agitation of Socialists and liberals. Social legislation in Austria was stimulated by the German precedent, and hence got an early start. A sweeping accident-insurance law was passed in 1887. This was followed by a systematic sickness-insurance act in 1888. Economic democracy has made headway in Austria as a result of the legalization of labor-unionism in 1869 and its subsequent growth. As in Germany, the World War brought to Austria a temporary stimulus to democracy and republicanism. The decade of democratic government in Austria after 1919 was especially notable for its work in the field of municipal housing.[1] A Fascist régime was set up in Austria in February, 1934, brought on, as in the case of Germany, mainly by the vindictive treatment of Austria in the peace treaty.

Hungary, however, the other member of the Dual Monarchy, was little affected by the progress of either political or social democracy. It made almost no advances in a liberal direction beyond the situation that existed in 1847, except to retain the act of the liberals of 1848 abolishing the political and economic aspects of feudalism. Universal manhood suffrage was not legalized until after 1918. The Hungarian reactionaries were able to defeat the efforts of Károlyi and other liberals to democratize the country in an economic sense after 1918. Hungary, while very efficiently governed, remains to the present day politically and socially one of the most illiberal of the important European nations. The great landlords still rule with little effective opposition. A cabinet brand of Fascism has been dominant in Hungary for nearly a decade.

In Italy the permanent establishment of parliamentary government was anticipated by Charles Albert of Piedmont in 1847-48 and was assured by the efforts of Cavour, a great admirer of the English system and one of the most vigorous advocates of parliamentary institutions among the liberal statesmen of the nineteenth century. The necessary complement of parliamentary government, universal manhood suffrage, was secured by the laws of 1882 and 1912. Finally, social and economic democracy made great strides in the laws of 1886, 1898, 1908, 1912, and 1919 that limited the labor of women and children, insured the working classes against accident, sickness, and old age, and established a national life-insurance system.

Labor-unionism had a very recent origin and development in Italy. Coming into existence along with the growth of radical parties recruited from the pro-

---

[1] On the postwar régime in Austria, see Macartney, *The Social Revolution in Austria*.

letariat, labor-unionism was at first little hampered in Italy by restrictive legislation. Since 1922 Italy has been governed by a Fascist dictatorship headed by a colorful personality, Benito Mussolini. Democratic institutions have been suspended. Social insurance, especially disability, old-age, and tuberculosis insurance, has been promoted and systematized under the Fascist government, but these advances can hardly be said to have been prompted by democratic motives or to have worked to the advantage of Italian democracy.

Despite some liberalization under Catherine II and Alexander I, Russia retained most aspects of the medieval system unimpaired down to the middle of the nineteenth century. An epoch-making step was taken in the formal abolition of serfdom by decree of Alexander II on March 3, 1861. The actual execution of emancipation, however, brought little progress in the direction of social democracy. It resulted essentially in the transformation of the peasantry from serfs of nobles to "serfs of the state." Not until Witte's decree of November 16, 1905, the edict of November, 1906, and the sweeping land reforms of July 27, 1910, and June 11, 1911, were the intended benefits of the Emancipation Act of 1861 and the real abolition of serfdom actually accomplished. Even then, these legislative reforms were only very slightly executed in actual practice before the World War.

The first important movement in the direction of political democracy in modern Russia came in 1864, when Alexander II issued his notable decree reviving the local assemblies or *zemstvos*, thereby introducing some degree of local self-government into Russia. This had not existed since the period of centralization under Peter the Great at the opening of the eighteenth century. After the Polish revolt of 1863 Alexander II, like his uncle, Alexander I, abandoned his early reforming tendencies and the night of reaction settled down once more upon Russia. It was not broken for forty years, in spite of revolutionary terrorism and the assassination of tsars, granddukes, and public officials.

The grip of absolutism, which assassinations could not break, was weakened by that deadly and persistent enemy of medievalism in politics and society, the Industrial Revolution. This first began to affect Russia on a considerable scale in the nineties during the ministership of Count Sergius Witte. It greatly strengthened the hitherto insignificant Russian middle class, in which lay the only hope of liberalism. The middle class was guided by such able leaders as Paul Milyukov and was aided by the discrediting of the old régime through the disasters of the Russo-Japanese War. Through the revolutionary movement of 1905-06, it was able to extort from the Tsar the liberalization of the suffrage and the creation of a constitutional parliamentary government in the Duma.

When freed from the strain of war, however, the Tsar, encouraged by his reactionary ministers, proceeded to abrogate his liberal measures by limiting the powers of the Duma and by altering the electoral law so as to defeat the principle of universal manhood suffrage. While this reactionary policy proved temporarily successful, military disasters after 1914 more serious than those of 1904-05 drove the distracted autocracy from Russia in complete humiliation. During the summer of 1917 the Russian Revolution passed through those stages so familiar to students of French history between 1789 and 1793. The control of affairs passed from conservative bourgeois statesmen to the leaders of the Bolshevik radicalism.[1] The ultimate outcome of the Russian Revolution cannot be predicted, but it is already apparent that it will be as impossible to reëstablish the conditions of 1914 in Russia as it was in France to bring about a return to the order of things that existed in 1788. In spite of the fact that the Allies proclaimed that they were fighting "to make the world safe for democracy," they intervened by force of arms in 1919-20 in the futile effort to crush radicalism in Russia.[2]

Spain has been the last important European addition to the fold of democracy and republicanism. In September, 1923, the constitution of 1876 was abolished and a dictatorship set up under General Primo de Rivera. The monarchy had been discredited by many things, but especially by the costly defeats in the Morocco War of 1921. Primo de Rivera ruled from 1923 to 1928, when he resigned under pressure. He was succeeded by General Berenguer who proved far less competent. His régime was also accompanied by severe economic crises. In 1931 came an uprising that drove out both dictatorship and monarchy. Alfonso XIII, last of the reigning Bourbons, fled the country and a Republic was declared on April 14, 1931.[3] The new Republic was Socialist and advanced liberal in backing, with considerable admixture of Syndicalism. It immediately took steps to promote social and economic, as well as political, democracy by passing legislation guaranteeing the rights of labor, providing for agrarian reform, reorganizing and emancipating education, and reducing the landholdings and power of the Catholic Church in Spain. In 1934 anti-republican and conservative forces gained revived power, and the Spanish Republic may go the way of the previous German and Austrian Republics.[4]

In the United States democracy was nearer to realization in 1800 than in most European countries, and consequently the advances made since that time have been more gradual and less spectacular than those in Europe. In the first half of the century the main achievements in democratizing the nation consisted in the abolition of the aristocratic property qualification for the exercise of the suffrage, the termination of imprisonment for debt, and the popularization of the concepts and practices of democracy as a result of the Jacksonian system.[5] The political theories of men like Jefferson had a strong Aristotelian flavor and they laid great emphasis upon special training, high intelligence, and expert direction of government. With the advent of the Jacksonians all this was changed. The "dangers" of special preparation for office were emphasized and supreme faith was placed in "pure" democracy. Rotation in office and the "spoils system" became characteristic of administrative procedure.[6]

[1] *Cf.* Leon Trotsky, *The History of the Russian Revolution*, Simon & Schuster, 1932, 3 vols.
[2] *Cf.* George Stewart, *The White Armies of Russia*, Macmillan, 1933.
[3] Spain had a brief period of republican rule in 1873-75.
[4] On the Spanish republican policies, see above, pp. 344-55; and Diffie, in Buell, *New Governments in Europe*, pp. 396 ff.
[5] A. E. McKinley, *The Suffrage Franchise in the Thirteen English Colonies in America*, University of Pennsylvania Press, 1905; K. H. Porter, *History of Suffrage in the United States*, University of Chicago Press, 1918; and C. F. Emerick, *The Struggle for Equality in the United States*, Science Press, 1914.
[6] See below, pp. 872 ff.; and C. E. Merriam, *History of American Political Theories*, Macmillan, 1903, Chap. v.

The scandals of the "spoils system" were in some degree curbed by the movement for civil-service reform that began in the administrations of Grant, Hayes, and Arthur.[1] This salutary tendency was courageously supported by Cleveland, particularly in his second term. Though it was weakened somewhat by McKinley, it was revived with renewed vigor by Theodore Roosevelt and Taft and has been extended since the World War. Even firmer and more extensive is the hold of the spoils system on American state and local government.

Democracy in America has thus failed to produce that efficiency in public service which has been realized in autocratic Germany or in democratic England. The most pressing problem in American politics is to work out a plan for the introduction of the principle of special fitness for public life.

One great obstacle to social democracy in America—Negro slavery—was removed in part as a result of the Civil War. But the Negro question has been one in which democracy has been complicated by race prejudice, and its final solution is not likely to be reached for another century. In many ways the show of strength of the Progressive party in 1912 and the victory of the Democratic party in 1912, 1916, and 1932 may be regarded as gains for social democracy. They were symptoms of popular protest against the domination of American politics and legislation by the conservative wing of the capitalistic class that became ascendent in American politics after the retirement of President Theodore Roosevelt and again after the liberalism of President Wilson had collapsed.

Unfortunately, the decline of morale and intellectual alertness in the United States, as a result of the reaction from the World War, led to a reign of the corrupt plutocratic interests quite unprecedented in our national history, if not in the whole history of representative government. The effort of the late Senator La Follette to lead the people in a crusade against this national disgrace in 1924 proved a most humiliating and portentous failure. The great economic depression beginning in 1929 may possibly stimulate a revival of idealism and progressivism. The "New Deal" of President Franklin D. Roosevelt was thought by many in 1933 to be a harbinger thereof.

Economic democracy in the United States has only begun to be attained. The use of "blanket injunctions" against trade-unions, so common in the labor disputes of the nineties, has declined somewhat, and the attempt of the conservative capitalists between 1908 and 1912 to bring the trade-unions within the reach of the anti-combination acts was restricted by the Clayton Bill. A federal anti-injunction bill was passed in 1932 and the rights of labor were given unprecedented legal recognition in the National Industrial Recovery Act of 1933. There has been little or no sweeping federal social legislation, but many states have passed workmen's compensation laws, legislation protecting women and children in industry, and the like. The backwardness of the country in this respect is well revealed by our inability as yet to ratify an amendment to the Constitution abolishing child labor, which was, however, actually condemned by the National Industrial Recovery Act. Even a belated and inadequate social-insurance program was proposed in Congress in 1935. The chief obstacle to economic and social democracy is the judicial interpretation of the "due process" clause of the Fourteenth Amendment, which has enabled a conservative

---

[1] See C. R. Fish, *Civil Service and the Patronage*, Longmans, 1905.

Supreme Court to set aside as unconstitutional much reform legislation.[1]

It must also be noted that "democracy in America" is no longer restricted, as in the time of De Tocqueville (about 1830), to the United States alone, but has become an assured fact in the Dominion of Canada and has made notable advances in some of the leading countries of Latin America.[2]

Nor is the United States, as it was in De Tocqueville's day, the most advanced and extensive laboratory in the democratic experiment. That position has passed to the Australian possessions of Great Britain and to Russia. Building on the precedent of England and the United States, Australia and New Zealand have passed beyond their models in the originality and extent of their experiments in social, economic, and political democracy. With their universal manhood and practically universal woman suffrage, their parliamentary government, their elaborate series of social-reform measures, and their original experiments in attempting to solve the perplexing problems of economic democracy, they are easily entitled to high rank in the vanguard of the world's progress towards ultimate democracy.[3] Soviet Russia will be treated in a later chapter.

The old patriarchal monarchy of China was finally ousted in 1912 and a Republic was proclaimed with Yuan Shi-kai as President. But the Republic had "tough sailing" as a result of further foreign penetration, the Japanese aggression during the World War, and splits between northern and southern China. As a result of the growing chaos and the success of Communism in Russia, Communism has made much headway in China, and the ultimate outcome may be a Communist state embracing much of the old Chinese territory.

The World War not only brought democracy to Germany, Austria, and Russia, but also created a number of new national states in central Europe, as well as adding much to the territory of certain existing states in the central-European and Balkan areas. Most of these new states were then organized on a democratic and republican plan. Some of them have gone beyond the major democratic states in their adoption of advanced types of political institutions and methods, such as proportional and vocational representation. Outstanding among the postwar democracies has been Czechoslovakia, guided by Thomas Masaryk and Edward Beneš. These immediate postwar gains for democracy and republicanism have been in part wiped out since by the growth of Fascism and dictatorship. The Russian Soviet organization is a novel and interesting experiment that may prove worthy of adoption later as a mode of decentralizing the overgrown modern state and adapting it to the economic realities of the modern age. It is an administrative scheme that could be exploited by capitalism as well as by Communism.

III. OBSTACLES TO DEMOCRACY

These notable achievements, which have been all too briefly enumerated above, have constituted great strides in the direction of political democracy since 1800. But they have left still unsolved many grave problems that will have

[1] *Cf.* L. B. Boudin, *Government by Judiciary*, Godwin, 1931, 2 vols. See below, pp. 842 ff.
[2] *Cf.* Wittke, *History of Canada;* and Rippy, *The Historical Evolution of Hispanic America*.
[3] C. H. Northcott, *Australian Social Development*, Columbia University Press, 1918; and V. S. Clark, *The Labour Movement in Australasia*. London. 1906.

to be met and conquered before democracy can be regarded as finally achieved. The securing of universal suffrage and representative government has made political democracy possible. It has not by any means assured its existence.

As Lord Bryce and Robert Michels have well pointed out, the political boss has proved quite as much of an obstacle to modern democracy as did the feudal lord to democratic tendencies in the medieval period.[1] Attempts have been made, which are as yet only partially successful, to eliminate his sinister influence through such devices as the direct primary and the civil-service laws.[2] Archaic forms of political institutions have often been found unsuited to advance the desires and needs of the people. Such machinery as the initiative, the referendum, and the recall has been introduced in the hope of making government more sensitive and more responsive to the public will.

Many of the problems concerning the perfection of representative institutions are yet to be solved. To meet this need such schemes are being proposed and adopted as the principle of minority and proportional representation, and the representation of professional and economic groups. Then, Sumner, Hobhouse, and others have reminded the world that most difficult and perplexing problems are involved in reconciling political democracy at home with the repression of subject peoples in imperial dominions.[3]

Finally, no one can seriously maintain that social and economic democracy exists when we have to face such economic and social inequalities as are revealed not in the vocal harangue of the soap-box orator, but in the sober and reliable statistics gathered by every great modern nation.[4] It is not desirable that society should permanently adopt any method of determining social and economic reward other than that based upon services rendered. It is a patent fact, however, that the prevailing methods of deciding the value of services is sadly antiquated and in need of revision, particularly in the direction of preventing rewards from being inherited instead of earned. It is, further, necessary to take such steps as shall be required to insure that all members of society, in proportion to their innate ability, receive approximate equality of opportunity and equipment for rendering services to society and receiving their reward for them.

A very real and practical obstacle to democracy that has appeared since the World War is to be seen in the rise of Fascism and the growing popularity of government by dictatorship.[5] Whether in Germany, in Italy, or in Hungary, dictatorship is believed by many to have proved more immediately efficient than democracy. The strains and stresses of the world in the economic depression have made many persons more impatient of the relatively inefficient and easy-going ways of democracy. The whole set-up today, at least superficially, seems to favor the propaganda in favor of Fascism and dictatorial government.

---

[1] James Bryce, *The American Commonwealth,* new ed., Macmillan, 1922-23, 2 vols.; and Robert Michels, *Political Parties,* Hearst's International Library, 1915.   [2] See below, pp. 879 ff.

[3] L. T. Hobhouse, *Democracy and Reaction,* Putnam, 1905.

[4] *Cf.* R. W. Kelso, *Poverty,* Longmans, 1929, Pt. I; Doane, *The Measurement of American Wealth;* and Leven, Moulton, and Warburton, *America's Capacity to Consume.*

[5] *Cf.* Strachey, *The Menace of Fascism;* Lindsay Rogers, *Crisis Government,* Norton, 1934; and Buell, *op. cit.*

IV. THE IMPORTANCE OF POLITICAL PARTIES IN MODERN GOVERNMENT

Democracy and representative government require for practical operation some method of assuring majority rule and of placing the representatives of the people in a position of political power. Thus far in human experience, no method of so doing has been discovered except party government. Representative government and the development of antagonistic social and economic interests in contemporary society—industrial, financial, commercial, agricultural, and proletarian—have begotten party politics as a natural and inevitable mode of procedure.

In contemporary Western society outside of Fascist states, party government has become the most prominent and publicly recognized phase of political activity. The average citizen participates in political life chiefly as a member of a party.[1] His interest in politics centers mainly in the victory of a certain group of candidates. The average voter has little conception of the general nature or purpose of government. He grasps feebly or not at all the fundamental issues that are involved in the contemporary political situation. His whole political outlook is concentrated upon the entity or organization known as the political party, and the candidates and symbols that give to the party vitality and personal interest.

Though parties are supposed to have distinct platforms or policies, these attract far less attention and arouse much less interest than the personal and symbolic aspects of party activity. In short, we may say that in modern representative and democratic government, the political party transcends in importance all other phases of political interest and activity. It may be further asserted that, whatever the defects of the party in actual practice, party government is the only feasible procedure in a representative democracy. Hence it is important to inquire into the nature, history, present defects, and future hopes in the conduct of political activities through the instrumentality of the party system.

V. THE NATURE AND FUNCTION OF POLITICAL PARTIES

Realistic students look upon the political party not as a spontaneous and voluntary benevolent association, but as the public organization through which the interest groups in modern society seek to promote their specific objects and ambitions. The party is an interest group or a combination of interest groups that can advance in a powerful way the aspirations of its adherents.[2] If the party represents a combination of interest groups and is at the same time a coherent and well-disciplined party, the specific interests of the constituent groups must have more common than divergent elements or the party will soon disintegrate.

Interest groups must compromise with each other in organizing a great party. For this reason, considerable latitude must exist in party platforms or

---

[1] *Cf.* C. E. Merriam and H. F. Gosnell, *The American Party System*, rev. ed., Macmillan, 1929, Chap. I; and H. R. Bruce, *American Parties and Politics*, Holt, 1927, Chap. XIV.
[2] See Barnes, *op. cit.*, pp. 114 ff.

whatever serves as the basis of party unity. The strongest parties are those which can unite the largest assemblage of persons in a single interest group or can combine in a harmonious manner, without sacrificing aggressiveness, the largest number of interest groups. This conception of the political party has been concisely summarized by Bentley:

> The party gets its strength from the interests it represents, the convention and executive committee from the party, and the chairman from the convention and committee. In each grade of this series the social fact actually before us is leadership of some underlying interest or set of interests.[1]

Sociologists are inclined to hold that, in spite of all obvious selfishness and corruption, party strife is the chief dynamic agency in promoting political progress and stimulating healthy political activity.[2] In the same way that the physical conflict of social groups created the state and modern political institutions, so the more peaceful struggle of parties within the state secures the continuance of political evolution. In no vital and progressive state can one expect a cessation of the conflict of interest groups, though, as Jacques Novicow long ago pointed out, the highest form of conflict is that which is carried on in the cultural realm.[3] This cultural conflict may ultimately be expected to supersede the prevailing economic struggles of the present day, in the same way that the latter have generally replaced the earlier biological contests of groups in the "state-making age."

Lester F. Ward, with his striving for scientific analogies, has defined party strife as "social synergy"—a powerful creative force or principle. Ward summarizes in the following paragraph his notion of the contributions of parties to political progress:

> ... the vigorous interaction of the two forces, which look so much like antagonism, strife, and struggle, transforms force into energy and energy into power, and builds social and political structures. And after they are constructed the same influences transform them, and it is this that constitutes social progress. Political institutions—the laws of every country—are the product of this political synergy, the crystallized action of legislative bodies created by political parties.[4]

Next to the nature and functions of political parties the most important sociological problem connected with them is the explanation of the seemingly inevitable inclination of such parties to become oligarchical in their organization.[5] There is a tendency to identify the party with the political machine and with its leaders. Professor Giddings has suggested that this is the result of the inevitable proclivity of the few to dominate in all social organization and activity. Linking this with his theory of social causation viewed as differential human response to stimulation, he finds that some react to new issues much more readily than others and, by their alertness and resourcefulness, dominate

---

[1] A. F. Bentley, *The Process of Government*, University of Chicago Press, 1908, p. 225.

[2] *Cf.* A. W. Small, *General Sociology*, University of Chicago Press, 1905, pp. 306 ff.; A. D. Morse, *Parties and Party Leaders*, Marshall Jones, 1923, Chaps. I-III; and Merriam and Gosnell, *op. cit.*, Chaps. XII-XIV.

[3] *Cf.* H. E. Barnes, "A Sociological Criticism of War and Militarism: An Analysis of the Doctrines of Jacques Novicow," *Journal of International Relations*, October, 1921.

[4] Ward, "The Sociology of Political Parties," *American Journal of Sociology*, January, 1908, pp. 440-41.

[5] *Cf.* Michels, *op. cit.*, Pts. II, VI.

social situations and activities. Oligarchy in parties, then, is a result of unlike or differential response to stimulation, and of the tendency to convert means into ends in all social organization:

Not all individuals react to a given stimulation with equal promptness, or completeness, or persistence. Therefore in every situation there are individuals that react more effectively than others do. They reinforce the original stimulation and play a major part in interstimulation. They initiate and take responsibility. They lead: they conduct experiments in a more or less systematic fashion.

Those individuals that react most effectively command the situation and create new situations to which other individuals must adjust themselves. Few or many, the alert and effective are a protocracy: a dominating plurum from which ruling classes are derived. Protocracy is always with us. We let George do it, and George to a greater or less extent "does" us.[1]

Every kleptocracy of brigands and conquerors, every plutocracy, every aristocracy, and every democracy begins as a protocracy. It comes into existence and begins its career as a little band of alert and capable persons who see the situation, grasp the opportunity, and, in the expressive slang of our modern competitive life, "go to it" with no unnecessary delay.

We have now arrived at the first induction, the fundamental principle of political science, which is, namely: *The few always dominate.*

Invariably the few rule, more or less arbitrarily, more or less drastically, more or less extensively. Democracy, even the most radical democracy, is only that state of politically organized mankind in which the rule of the few is least arbitrary and most responsible, least drastic and most considerate.[2]

A number of social psychologists have suggested explanations for this oligarchical tendency in parties. Sighele, LeBon, Tarde, Durkheim, and Ross have held that it is due to the domination of crowd psychology in modern political assemblies and even in states as a whole.[3] Psychic contagion is induced by the press and other modern agencies for expediting the communication of information and the creation of uniform emotional states. Under these circumstances the leaders can usually manipulate the masses almost at will, and hold the situation completely under their control.

The technique through which party leaders dominate the party and manipulate public opinion has been incisively analyzed from the psychological standpoint by Graham Wallas.[4] The political issues that concern mankind are not interpreted by the citizens as a complex of ideas and desires. They are recognized through the association of a political problem with some symbol. The most important political stimuli are furnished today by the political party. While a party may have a conscious intellectual origin and be designed to achieve a definite social end, it will have little strength or duration unless it secures symbols with sufficiently high emotional values, such as party animals, colors, tunes, names, rhetoric, catchwords, and the like.

A skillful party makes use of its symbols in the same way that a commercial

[1] F. H. Giddings, "Pluralistic Behavior," *American Journal of Sociology,* March, 1920, p. 539.
[2] F. H. Giddings, *The Responsible State,* Houghton Mifflin, 1918, pp. 19-20.
[3] *Cf.* Barnes, *Sociology and Political Theory,* pp. 73 ff.
[4] *Human Nature in Politics,* 3d ed., Crofts, 1921, Pt. I.

concern employs its trademarks and advertisements. If a candidate is not properly vested with symbols he has no chance of success. The most insignificant nonentity properly and fully identified with the party symbols is much more likely to be successful in an election than the strongest personality in the country if the latter has cut himself off from party connections and makes an appeal solely to the intelligence and good judgment of the citizens.

In this way the public is put at the mercy of the political organization. The latter soon comes to regard the party as an end in itself or as an agency for advancing the interests of the machine. The only means of escape from party tyranny lies in a removal of the psychological power of party symbols and in the discrediting of the political "spellbinder."

An illuminating synthesis of the causes of oligarchical tendencies in political parties is furnished in the monumental sociological analysis by Robert Michels.[1] He finds that oligarchical tendencies are inevitable in all forms of political organization and in all parties. This is true even though the political organization be that extreme form of decentralization known as Syndicalism or the parties be of a revolutionary character.

The average individual is stupid and lacking in initiative and resourcefulness. The more alert and intelligent naturally come to the top as leaders. But the psychological consequences of leadership are only too often vanity, arrogance, impatience of popular control, and a tendency on the part of the leaders to forget that they owe their position to popular consent.

Under modern conditions democracy, in a broad sense, is mass rule. But masses are incoherent and inarticulate; they must have leaders. Further, the masses cannot participate directly in government; they must choose representatives, and representative government means party organization. Wherever the masses do act directly in modern politics they are subject to mob psychology. In elections they are easily manipulated. The press, which is usually controlled by party leaders, can easily deceive them. Even modern parliaments, made up of chosen representatives, operate under psychological conditions very similar to those of the crowd. They are so large and unwieldy that they inevitably come under the domination of the able minority.

The main cause of oligarchy in political parties comes, however, from the necessity of organization. It is the inevitable organization which a political party must create if it is to function effectively that produces the necessity of leadership and the consequent development of oligarchy.

Probably no better summary statement of the real basis of party strife could be found than that contained in the last paragraph of Beard's brilliant brochure on *The Economic Basis of Politics:*

The grand conclusion, therefore, seems to be that advanced by our own James Madison in the Tenth Number of the Federalist. To express his thoughts in modern terms: a landed interest, a transport interest, a railway interest, a shipping interest, an engineering interest, a manufacturing interest, a public-official interest, with many lesser interests, grow up of necessity in all great societies and divide them into different classes actuated by different sentiments and views. The regulation of these various and interfering interests, whatever may be the formula for the ownership

[1] *Op. cit.*

of property, constitutes the principal task of modern statesmen and involves the spirit of party in the necessary and ordinary operations of government. In other words, there is no rest for mankind, no final solution of eternal contradictions. Such is the design of the universe. The recognition of this fact is the beginning of wisdom —and of statesmanship.[1]

VI. THE HISTORICAL EVOLUTION OF POLITICAL PARTIES

Factions representing distinct interest groups have existed from a very early day, though party government as a publicly recognized agency could scarcely appear until after the rise of representative government. We may here review some of the major features in the growth of parties and party government.[2]

In the Greek city-states, especially in Athens, there were political parties or factions. Aristotle, in fact, made an analysis of the genesis and nature of faction, party, and class activity, though he clearly disapproved of factions and party divisions. But there was no permanent party organization in Athenian democracy, much less any recognition of the party as a factor in political society. The Romans produced vigorous political factions, as Ferrero and others have explained in detail. Perhaps the factional situation at the time of the brothers Gracchi is as representative of Roman party development as any that might be chosen. But here again political factions and interests shifted rapidly.

After the collapse of Rome, the Western world broke up into the feudal system. With such world-order as existed being furnished by the Church and the unifying tradition of Rome, there was still no place for party government. The feudal political relations of the Middle Ages were based chiefly upon personal allegiance, a condition somewhat intermediate between the bond of blood relationship (real or fictitious) in primitive society and the political status of developed civil society. The chief struggle during the Middle Ages was that between the Church and the State, but such conflicts were partly international in their scope, and they rarely produced any permanent party alignment upon the questions at issue. The struggles within the Church, which culminated in the Conciliar Movement of the fifteenth century, were also international in scope and more directly productive of representative government than of the party system.

The factions or parties that at times existed in the medieval period are well exemplified by the historic conflict between the Guelphs and the Ghibellines.[3] These parties were produced by the struggle between the Holy Roman Emperor and the Italian city-states, but their conflicts were largely personal, family, or municipal feuds, carried on with great bitterness. There was little in them that closely resembled modern party conflict and organization. The other form of political conflict that prevailed in the Middle Ages, especially in the latter part of the period, namely, that between the newly developing cities and the feudal lords or the king, was a conflict of different types of society rather than party strife.

---

[1] Beard, *op. cit.*, p. 99.
[2] Some of the paragraphs that follow are adapted with permission from a memorandum on the history of political parties prepared for Mr. Dwight W. Morrow.
[3] *Cf.* J. W. Thompson, *Feudal Germany*, University of Chicago Press, 1928, Pt. I, Chap. VIII.

The origins of modern political parties are tied up with the Commercial Revolution and the rise of capitalism. The latter created a middle class powerful enough to challenge the old landed aristocracy and to constitute a significant opposition party. The first parties were fundamentally representatives of the aristocratic landed interests and of the growing urban middle class, respectively. This party development and struggle could, however, find significant expression only where the middle class had become strong enough to crush absolutism and to institute representative government. England was the only important European state where this was achieved before the middle of the eighteenth century. We have already described the political struggles in England in the seventeenth century and have indicated that the kings drew their support chiefly from the aristocratic landed groups, and that revolution was promoted mainly by the urban middle class.[1] The former grew into the Tories and the latter into the Whigs, this development taking place slowly between 1640 and 1700.

When William III came to the throne after the Revolution of 1689 English political parties were already a recognized element in parliamentary life. Many historians date their origin from the sharp divisions between Puritan and Royalist beginning in 1641. As a matter of fact, the effort to fix a date is misleading. The development of the political party as a means of holding a government in subjection came along haltingly.[2]

All through the seventeenth century men had acted in groups and with increasing self-consciousness. But the members of the groups shifted quickly and the groups themselves had little direct and recognized relation to the government. Parties were still unrecognized in public law. They were small associations of men in the Parliament, or directly related to the Parliament. There was little recognition that parties could be the servants of the state.

The important contribution of the reign of William III to party history was the creation between 1693 and 1696 of the first distinct party ministry in the history of England, the so-called Whig Junto.[3] For hundreds of years the king had appointed his ministry, but his choice was based largely upon personal considerations. William III's first ministry was made up of both Whigs and the Tories. But Parliament had been educating itself for a century. It now had a recognized position and authority. It was fortunate also that William's main interest lay in his Continental wars. This made it necessary for the new King to get on with Parliament since the latter controlled military finances. In 1693 the gradual process of replacing Tories by Whigs in the ministry began, and it continued to 1696. The Whigs generally supported the foreign policy of William and the Tories held back. Not only the King, but probably the parliamentary leaders, were unconscious of, or indifferent to, the important constitutional change that was being brought about.

The permanent development of something like strict partisanship in the con-

---

[1] See above, pp. 99 ff.
[2] On the early history of English political parties, see W. C. Abbott, "The Origin of English Political Parties," *American Historical Review*, July, 1919.
[3] On the rise of Whigs and Tories, see K. G. Feiling, *History of the Tory Party, 1640-1714*, Oxford Press, 1924.

stitution of ministries came with the rise of the cabinet system under Walpole during the reigns of George I and George II. George I, the founder of the Hanoverian dynasty, was a German by birth and culture, and never mastered either the English language or the English political system. He was content to rule through a minister who assumed actual charge of the political situation. He was fortunate in securing for his minister the leading representative of the middle-class Whigs, Robert Walpole. Walpole took all his ministers from the party that commanded the confidence of Parliament. In this way he built up the idea of the responsible partisan ministry. Walpole ruled with wisdom and discretion, avoiding foreign wars and entangling international relations.[1] Under his long leadership England became gradually accustomed to the party system. Though the party as such remained outside legal and constitutional theory, it ceased to be so regarded in practice.

When Walpole fell in 1742 there was an effort made to impeach him, as Bolingbroke and Oxford had been impeached upon their fall twenty-five years before. Walpole himself had spent a few days in the Tower when the Whig government, of which he was a subordinate member, had gone out in 1710. But a great change had come about in the conduct of public business during the administration of Walpole. The cabinet and the party system had been effectively established.

But party government in Parliament did not as yet involve a partisan organization of the electorate. English government was not sufficiently representative at this time to make this feasible. After Walpole's day a strong effort was made by George III to reverse the political tendencies of the preceding century and appoint ministers responsible to himself instead of to his Parliament. The effort succeeded for a while, with one disastrous result—the American Revolution. Then England settled down to a recognition of the principle that ministers "were responsible to Parliament for the conduct of the business of the government, even though this business continued to be called, for historical and sentimental reasons, the 'king's business.'"

Yet responsibility of the ministry to the House of Commons and the electorate meant something quite different, even at the close of the eighteenth century, from what it did at the close of the nineteenth. To account for this difference it is necessary to distinguish several important stages in the development of the English representative and party system.

The first stage came in the reign of William III, and especially later in the time of Walpole, when a ministry began to be drawn from a single party. This system was far different from the modern British party system, in which the ministry is fully responsible to Parliament. In case of a disagreement the ministry remained in power and used various types of fraud and intimidation on the House of Commons to obtain the desired support. Under the rotten-borough system it was usually possible for the governing ministry so to control the election as to secure the triumph of members favorable to the ministry.[2] While in theory the ministry was responsible to the majority party in Parliament, in actual fact the ministry rather than the Commons was supreme.

[1] Except for the brief and trivial "War of Jenkins' Ear" in 1739, which Walpole opposed.
[2] See above, pp. 214-15.

Though the ministry was supposed to bow to the will of the majority in the Commons, it usually made use of the existing political expedients to secure and maintain a parliamentary majority favorable to the ministry.

The next important stage in the development of the English party and representative system came after the Reform Bill of 1832, which did away with the rotten boroughs and widened the suffrage to some degree. It introduced the modern system of representative government in England. After that time, when there was a clash between ministry and Parliament and an appeal was taken to the constituencies, the ministry resigned if the election went against them. In 1834 we have the first instance of a ministry resigning because of a defeat in the general elections—the Peel ministry. In this way both the ministry and the House of Commons were rendered responsible to the electorate.

The electorate of 1834, however, differed from the electorate in England today. Only the property-owning classes and the more prosperous group of tenants could vote, even after the Reform Bill of 1832. The two important extensions of the suffrage granted by Disraeli and Gladstone in 1867 and 1884 tended to make control by the electorate more nearly identical with control by the people.

These suffrage acts, particularly that of 1867, had an important effect upon the development of English party machinery. In order to circumvent an undemocratic clause in the act of 1867 and to give the majority party maximum representation, the Radicals of Birmingham, under the leadership of Mr. William Harris, organized in October, 1867, the famous Birmingham Caucus.[1] This scheme had remarkable success as a type of local political machinery. It came to be known as the Local Liberal Association and was widely imitated throughout England. Because of its success the Conservatives were also compelled to develop a similar type of local party machinery, and the Birmingham Caucus thus became the prototype of the most important form of local party organization as it existed in England for a generation. This is particularly significant, because for elective purposes party organization in England for many years meant local party organization. In England the national organization of political parties did not for a long time even approximate the degree of development it had achieved in the United States. So far as England had a national party organization, it was chiefly a federation or union of these local associations. During the last quarter of a century, however, the Central Office in English political parties has come to play an ever larger part in the organization, the discipline, and the electioneering activities. It has tended to supersede the older unions or federations of local associations. While national organization has not even yet assumed the same high degree of centralization and control that exists in the United States, it is rapidly approaching this condition.[2] The extensions of the suffrage in 1918 and 1928 promoted the democratization of the British party system in the sense of giving the rank and file more sig-

---

[1] Fully to explain the Birmingham Caucus procedure would take more space than is at our disposal. Those interested will find a full explanation in A. L. Lowell, *The Government of England*, new ed., Macmillan, 1912, 2 vols., Vol. II, pp. 483 ff.

[2] *Cf.* J. K. Pollock, "British Party Organization," *Political Science Quarterly*, June, 1930.

THE HISTORICAL EVOLUTION OF POLITICAL PARTIES

nificance in the elections. It did not, of course, insure any direct control over English party organization by the mass of voters.

In England, the old division of Whigs and Tories began to break down after the Reform Bill of 1832, and the Liberals and Conservatives took their place before 1850. Their early battles turned about factory reform and free trade.[1] The Conservatives championed labor legislation and the Liberals the abolition of the Corn Laws and other protective measures. During the last half of the century, the Liberals became less rigidly laissez faire and came to favor social legislation, especially after 1905. The Conservatives were urged to do the same by Joseph Chamberlain, but he met with indifferent success. Irish Home Rule became a burning issue between the two parties from 1884 to the World War. The Liberals favored it. During the last decade of the nineteenth century the Labour party came into existence, and it assumed a definite part in English political life after 1906. It threw in its weight with the Liberal party for a time to forward social legislation. Growing in strength, it has been in office twice since the World War and recently seems to be regaining popularity. The World War hopelessly split the Liberal party, and British politics are now essentially divided between various groups of Conservatives and Laborites. The trend is now towards the group party system that prevails on the continent of Europe.

In France, the parties are numerous and have run all the way from the Action Française, royalist in sympathies, on the extreme right, to the Communists at the extreme left. The strongest party is the Radical Socialist party, which embraces the traditions of the Jacobins, the Republicans of 1848, and the Gambetta-Ferry group that founded the Third Republic. Its name is wholly a misnomer, since it is neither radical nor Socialist, but an anti-clerical bourgeois party of liberal inclinations, roughly comparable in backing and policies to the British Liberal party before the War. Its anti-clericalism is, however, far more advanced than that of the British Liberals at any time. Eminent leaders have been Clemenceau, Waldeck-Rousseau, and Caillaux. The French Socialists were strong before the World War, but they have never recovered from the loss of their great leader, Jean Jaurès, by assassination on the eve of the war.

In Germany, after the founding of the Empire the major political parties were the Conservative, drawing its strength chiefly from the great Prussian landlords (Junkers); the Center party, controlled by the Catholics, strongest in Bavaria and southern Germany, and social-reformist and clerical in policies; the National Liberal party, bourgeois, nationalist, protectionist, and imperialistic after 1879; the Progressive party, the radical and reformist party of the *petite bourgeoisie;* and the Social Democratic party, at first Marxian and after 1900 more and more Revisionist. As the World War approached the National Liberals tended to die out and the Socialists became stronger. After the World War the Socialists captured the new Republican government, only to be weakened by Allied vindictiveness and Communist opposition, and ultimately eclipsed and crushed by Nazi Fascism.

Austrian parties before the war were a reflection of the polyglot Empire as

[1] See above, Chapter XI.

well as of differing attitudes towards capitalism, social reform, and agrarian problems. The Centralists urged the consolidation of all national groups in one centralized empire. The Federalists favored a federal organization founded upon the chief racial and national groups. There was a Conservative party favoring landlords; a progressive bourgeois party; a Catholic Socialist party, somewhat like the German Center party but rather more radical in tone; and a Social Democratic group of Marxian proclivities. In addition to these, there were one or more parties drawn from each of the national groups in the empire, some based on nationalist platforms and some on the relative degree of their economic radicalism. The Austrian party system was thus a bewildering maze of cross-currents. It was the group system with a vengeance. After the election of 1907, there were no less than twenty-six different groups.

Italy after unification seemed for a time destined to follow the two-party system. It was governed by the conservative Right party, which hated democracy, until 1876. Then the liberal, democratic, and imperialistic Left came into power for a couple of decades. Crispi was its outstanding leader. After that time the trend was definitely towards the group system. Radical parties, not only the Socialist but also the Anarchist and the Syndicalist, gained in strength. Right after the World War a radical revolution seemed imminent, but Mussolini's "march on Rome" stemmed the radical tide, established Fascism, and crushed out party life in Italy. In 1934, Mussolini opened a new capital-labor parliament in which the party system was formally as well as literally abolished.

Before the adoption of our Constitution in 1789, the people of the United States had enjoyed more than one hundred and fifty years of practice in the organization of political institutions.[1] Although there was no widespread organization of parties until after the adoption of the Constitution, political parties had existed from the beginning of settlement in America. As John Adams said in 1812: "You say our divisions began with Federalism and anti-Federalism? Alas! they began with human nature; they have existed in America from its first plantation. In every colony, divisions always prevailed. In New York, Pennsylvania, Virginia, Massachusetts, and all the rest, a court and country party has always contended."

In surveying the development of political parties in the United States we shall consider first the development of party machinery and then examine the major party issues in our national history. The "Fathers" were familiar with the effects of parties, or better, factions. They regarded party government as detrimental and tried to guard against it in the new national government created by the Constitution of 1787. They provided for an Electoral College to select the President, and appear to have expected that this would operate in a nonpartisan manner.

Yet the very system of government created by the Constitution was one that strongly encouraged the origin and development of a party system. A twofold division of political activity and authority had been produced. There was a

[1] For a good treatment of early political parties in the United States, see G. W. Edwards, "New York City Politics before the Revolution," *Political Science Quarterly*, December, 1921; and C. L. Becker, *History of Political Parties in the Province of New York, 1760-1776*, University of Wisconsin Press, 1909.

division of political authority and responsibility between the federal and state governments, and, following the dictum of Montesquieu, there was a strict separation of the three phases of governmental power in the federal government. The executive, legislative, and judicial departments were, in formal theory at least, sharply separated and balanced against each other. It was necessary to have some organization that would produce unity of policy and action in state and federal governments and would also unify the three formally separated departments in the federal government, especially the executive and the legislature. The political party was the organization that achieved this goal of unification. Finally, the new American government was also one in which there were a vast number of elective offices of real importance. Organization was essential to provide candidates for these offices and to secure their election. The party fulfilled this need.

It was not long after 1789 that the party system arose and defied the nonpartisan scheme which the Fathers thought they had established. The Electoral College virtually ceased to operate as an independent body by 1796, and by 1800 it had already become a meaningless relic. Party development thus took place in spite of President Washington's earnest efforts to preserve the system contemplated by the framers of the Constitution. Washington chose the members of his cabinet from both parties, as English monarchs had done a hundred years before. The legitimate function of an opposition party was not comprehended by him. The party spirit of his administration and the bitterness of the party recriminations, with those in his own official family employing pamphleteers to attack their political opponents, reminds one of the party strife during the reigns of William and Anne.[1] Within a generation after Washington's Farewell Address, it was a well-recognized practice in our republic to form "associations" with the "real design to direct, control, counteract, or awe the regular deliberations of the constituted authorities."

County and town nominating conventions had developed in the latter part of the eighteenth century. When it became necessary to organize state and national governments, some form of party organization of comparable scope was rendered essential. The legislative *caucus,* that is, the nomination of candidates by party members of the legislatures, supplied this need. The legislators were usually prominent men from all sections of the political community and fairly represented the parties in the legislature. Owing to the difficulty of travel in those days, it was a great convenience to have a group of party men from all parts of the state or country already assembled in some central place. The legislative caucus became for a time the natural nominating convention and the one fairly permanent bit of party machinery. In its federal form this was known as the congressional caucus, and it controlled the party nominations for the Presidency from 1804 to 1824. Because parties were looked upon as extralegal and extraneous bodies of sinister potency at this time—being in fact literally without standing in public law—the central organization of the parties, the caucus, was naturally severely criticized. It was hailed as "King Caucus," and the deposition of this usurping monarch was eagerly sought.

[1] *Cf.* W. T. Morgan, *English Political Parties and Leaders in the Reign of Queen Anne,* Yale University Press, 1920.

The destruction of the caucus system as a factor in national politics was accomplished as a part of the democratic-frontier wave which brought Andrew Jackson to the Presidency. Jackson believed himself at a disadvantage with the smooth and devious politicians who controlled the caucus. He and his followers were still further enraged by the contested election for the Presidency in 1824, for Jackson believed that he had been cheated out of the election. He and his supporters began a thoroughgoing attack upon the congressional control of the party nominating system. By the time of the campaign of 1828 the caucus had disappeared, and in 1832 the national nominating convention had appeared in its place.

The first national nominating convention was that of the Anti-Masonic party, which met in Baltimore in 1831 and nominated William Wirt as its candidate for the Presidency. The Whigs met there later in the year and nominated Clay, and the next year the Democrats followed and nominated Jackson. An important revolution had been achieved and the party had grown out of the outlaw stage to some degree. The convention system soon supplanted the caucus in the local subdivisions of the government for nominating purposes. Along with this has come the development of permanent national, state, and county committees to look after party interests in the interval between the periodic nominating conventions. We may now turn to a brief review of the evolution of party issues in the United States.

The history of parties, as conventionally taught in the schools, is little more than a meaningless chronicling of the results of the quadrennial presidential campaigns. Yet the history of parties in America, if properly studied, furnishes an admirable introduction to the evolution of American society and the various phases of its progress. It is the basic purpose of government to mediate between the various conflicting ideals and interests in society and to adjust this conflict, as well as possible, in the interest of public order and progress. Parties have been the organization through which our major social interests have attempted to advance their causes. A study of parties and their activity reveals the more important public issues that have faced the country since the establishment of our national government.

At the outset, the Federalists under the lead of Hamilton planned to reorganize the government after the chaos of the Confederation, restore order, establish a sound system of public and private finance, and make it possible for business to resume with confidence. This program naturally called for much constructive legislation and for fairly high taxation. The program had the backing of the moneyed groups in the East, but it aroused the opposition of the agrarian interests in the South and West.

The latter had little to gain from a revival of business and sound finances. They did not feel that any important benefit would come from a redemption of the public securities and a funding of the public debt. In fact, they would be the losers, for many of the farmers were debtors and most of the certificates of indebtedness were held by the business classes. Further, they resented the greater burden of taxation put upon them by Hamilton's constructive program. Especially was this true of states, like Virginia, which had already paid off their state indebtedness. They found their slogan in the strict construction of

THE HISTORICAL EVOLUTION OF POLITICAL PARTIES   513

the Constitution, denying the validity of Hamilton's contention for "implied powers." They discovered an astute leader in Thomas Jefferson. As a result of the partial achievement of their program, fatal divisions within their ranks, and legislative indiscretions—as in the Alien and Sedition laws—the Federalists were weakened. In the party revolution of 1800 they were displaced by the Democratic-Republicans. This Jeffersonian party soon accepted the constructive policy of Hamilton, but put it on a more popular and democratic foundation.[1]

With the disappearance of the chief issues that had furnished the basis for party divisions from 1792 to 1815 and the development of new problems in our national evolution, there arose appropriate parties to expound these new programs and to defend these diversified interests. The remnants of the old Federalists and the more conservative Democratic-Republicans developed into the National Republican or Whig party, of which Clay and Webster were the spokesmen. They represented the business and financial interests of the East and the more nationalistic of the Middle-Westerners. They had for their program national improvement in the way of building roads, canals, and railroads, the fostering of manufactures, the increase of the tariff according to the so-called American system, the maintenance of a United States Bank, and the granting of loans to the West for sectional development.

To oppose this party there coalesced the more radical members of the old Democratic-Republican party and the new frontiersmen, together with some of the slaveholding element in the South. They also found many adherents among the oppressed laboring classes in the new textile towns of New England. The new party was called the Democratic party, and it chose for its leader Andrew Jackson.[2] The party members were in part a debtor group, came to a large degree from the frontier, where sentiments and practices of equality were the rule, and resented the domination of the business and financial element of the East. They desired state banks, that they might supply their own credit and be free from the economic control of the Easterners. The demand for the democratization of the suffrage appealed especially to the lower classes. In their effort to free themselves from the Eastern office-holder the Democrats drove this class from office and instituted the spoils system.

Soon after Jackson's death the issues that had confronted the parties in the thirties were superseded by the struggles over slavery.[3] The Whig party became divided on the slavery issue and gradually disintegrated. The Democratic party came more completely under the domination of the slavery group, for which Calhoun was the spokesman, and the Jacksonian element lost its control. The Democratic party became the party of the Slavocracy of the South. It was joined by the proslavery Whigs.

Out of the disintegrated Whig party and the newer radical and antislavery parties was formed the new Republican party. It was at first mainly a radical party, with its chief support, as in the case of the early Democrats, drawn from the laborers of the East and the frontiersmen of the West. Coming into power in 1860 through a destructive division of the Democratic party, it be-

---

[1] *Cf.* C. G. Bowers, *Jefferson and Hamilton*, Chautauqua Press, 1925.
[2] See Schlesinger, *New Viewpoints in American History*, Chap. IX; and C. G. Bowers, *Party Battles of the Jackson Period*, Houghton Mifflin, 1922.
[3] J. T. Adams, *America's Tragedy*, Scribner, 1934.

came the party that won the Civil War and thus gained the support of the banking and business classes, which had profited by the war. It soon lost its radical origins and became the party of the capitalistic conservatives.[1] It supported the new banking plans, railroad expansion, and the land grants, retention of the high war tariff, and the elimination of political interference with the freedom of business enterprise. The Democratic party, freed from the slavery octopus, became for the time being the minority party supporting political reform and a more liberal policy in Southern reconstruction.

Neither major party has been consistently either progressive or reactionary since 1865.[2] While the Republicans have been more uniformly conservative and dependable exponents of big business and the protective tariff, they have at times shown signs of liberalism, as under Theodore Roosevelt, and there has always been a powerful liberal wing in the Republican party, which has been known successively as Liberal Republican, Mugwump, and Progressive. The Democratic party has wabbled from marked liberalism, as under Bryan in 1896, to extreme conservatism, as under Parker in 1904, but it has tended rather to the moderate conservatism of the Cleveland type during most of the period since 1877. Under Wilson it ran the whole course from the liberalism of the "New Freedom" to the ultra-reactionary orgy during which the country was all but ruled by Attorney-General Palmer and the Department of Justice.

The more extreme liberals and radicals have tended to be skeptical of gaining their ends in either great party and have persistently organized radical minor parties, such as the Granger movement, the Greenback party, the Populist party, the Non-Partisan League (really a party), the Socialist and Socialist Labor parties, and, most recently, the Farmer-Labor party.[3] In one way these parties have been successful. They have forced the major parties to embody many of the progressive proposals in their platforms.

The logical party alignment in this country at present would probably be a clean sweep of the two old parties and the amalgamation of the conservative and liberal elements respectively into two new parties, one standing for conservative and the other for liberal tendencies.[4] This would probably have happened long before this had party organization been as fluid and undeveloped as in 1830. But so powerful has it become that party issues are now subordinated to party machinery, whereas the issues once made the parties and aided in perfecting their machinery. The means has been converted into the end. The two major parties have so much unreality and so few real differences because they exist chiefly to obtain the elective offices and the economic power that comes from being in control. It seems probable that the next great stage in party history is to be the struggle between the vested interests of the party machinery and the utility of the party as an exponent of ideals and interests. The difficulties inherent in thus reforming the party

---

[1] *Cf.* C. G. Bowers, *The Tragic Era*, Houghton Mifflin, 1929.
[2] *Cf.* Schlesinger, *op. cit.*, Chap. XII.
[3] *Cf.* F. E. Haynes, *Third Party Movements since the Civil War*, Iowa State Historical Society, 1916; Nathan Fine, *Labor and Farmer Parties in the United States, 1828-1928*, Rand School of Social Science, 1928; and S. A. Rice, *Farmers and Workers in American Politics*, Columbia University Press, 1924.
[4] *Cf.* S. G. Blythe, *Saturday Evening Post*, March 25 ("Why Not Scrap Them Both") and August 19, 1922 ("Flux"); and P. H. Douglas, *The Coming of a New Party*, McGraw-Hill, 1932.

THE HISTORICAL EVOLUTION OF POLITICAL PARTIES 515

system are well set forth in Graham Wallas's *Human Nature in Politics* and Robert Michels's *Political Parties*. The machinery, created gradually to give the party coherence and unity in advancing its ends, seems capable of becoming the great Frankenstein of modern political life.

In a recent stimulating book, Professor A. N. Holcombe predicts the end of the old rustic American party system based upon sections, and the rise of a new party alignment founded directly and openly upon class interests. The growing importance of the city in American life will, he believes, render such a transformation necessary:

> The passing of the frontier and the growth of urban industry have shaken the foundations of the old party system in national politics. The old sectional interests are changing and the old sectional alliances are breaking down. The old party politics is visibly passing away. The character of the new party politics will be determined chiefly by the interests and attitudes of the urban population. It will be less rustic than the old and more urbane. There will be less sectional politics and more class politics. That the old rustic sectional politics is passing is easy to demonstrate. What the new urbane class politics will be like and how it may be made most serviceable to the people of the United States are more difficult questions.[1]

VII. THE TWO-PARTY AND GROUP SYSTEMS

In the United States we have become so accustomed to the two-party system that we assume it to be the natural and inevitable alignment. Yet this is by no means true. Indeed, today, in both radical and conservative countries the tendencies are all working towards a multiplicity of parties and the group system. The two-party system of the United States is the exception rather than the rule.

It has been perpetuated in our country for a number of reasons. Down to 1861 there were numerous and frequent shifts in the major parties, thus inviting the coalescing of minor parties under the wing of some major party. Minor parties could participate in the formation of new major parties. There has been little real radicalism in the country since the Revolutionary War. Hence radical parties have not appeared with frequency and there has been a hostile popular psychology towards those which have arisen. When liberal third parties have developed it has been usual for one or both of the major parties to steal their thunder by appropriating the more attractive parts of their platforms. This has, of course, speedily ended the particular third party whose program has been absorbed by one of the older parties. Further, the two major parties have long had a special psychological hold on the masses. The Democrats appeal to tradition and proudly point to the fact that their party has endured for over a century unchanged even in name. The Republicans call attention to the fact that they saved the Union and allege with a straight face that they have been responsible for our remarkable economic evolution and material prosperity since 1861.

Moreover, labor and agriculture, nominally the source of distinct interests and party movements, have been unable here to form united and permanent political parties. Labor did not become well integrated until after the Civil

---

[1] Holcombe, *The New Party Politics*, pp. 1-2 and Chap. 1 *passim*.

War. The Knights of Labor might have formed a labor party, but their career was cut short too quickly. The policy of the American Federation of Labor under Samuel Gompers was to keep labor out of politics as a distinct party and to seek favors from one or another of the major parties. Moreover, there can be no real labor party until the American proletariat accepts the permanence of its status as laborers. This the American laborers have thus far refused to do. They have regarded themselves as potential capitalists and have been more interested in rising above the laboring groups than in improving themselves within the proletarian status. The frontier optimism and individualism of "the American dream" has persisted in them long after the frontier has ceased to exist. Radical labor in the United States has been too much divided into bitter cliques to form powerful and permanent party organizations. With the exception of sporadic developments such as the Greenback, Granger, Populist, Progressive, and Non-Partisan League movements, the farmers have been loyal to the old parties, rebelling only briefly in moments of near-starvation and losing their rebellious secession spirit with each rise in the price of agricultural products.

In Europe, before Fascism set in, there were in most countries a multiplicity of parties, a number of which were frequently united into "blocs" or groups.[1] This was because in Europe party organization has been more normally and naturally associated with the underlying interests of various groups and classes —the parties have, in other words, more closely assimilated themselves to the natural "interest groups" in the state. Moreover, there have been more classes and interests in Europe than in the United States—everything from monarchists to Communists and Anarchists. And within each major group there has been an inclination to split over minor divergencies in the interpretation of social, economic, or political doctrines. Further, party machinery is less powerful and cohesive in Europe than it is in the United States.

We may illustrate this tendency by the case of France. Take the Chamber of Deputies as constituted after the election of 1928. The 612 members were divided into no less than twelve parties, with two members who refused to join any of the twelve. The diagram on p. 517 well indicates the situation that results—the twelve parties being united into the three blocs of the Right, Center, and Left, with the Communists flanking the extreme left.

A similar situation has prevailed in Germany. In the election of 1930 there were some twenty-seven parties participating and no less than thirteen of these elected representatives to the Reichstag. Among the parties that existed in Germany from 1919 to the coming of Hitler and the Nazis were the following— roughly in order from the most conservative to the most radical: the German National People's party; the National Socialist party of Herr Hitler—the Nazis; the German People's party; the Christian People's party; the German Democratic party; the German Peasants' party; the Social Democratic party; the Independent Socialist party; and the Communist party. Under the dictatorship of Hitler there is no room for party differences. Party government is incompatible with dictatorship.[2]

[1] See E. M. Sait, *The Government and Politics of France*, World Book Co., 1920; and R. L. Buell, *Contemporary French Politics*, Appleton, 1920.
[2] See Rogers, *op. cit.*; and Buell, *New Governments in Europe*, pp. 126 ff.

THE TWO-PARTY AND GROUP SYSTEMS 517

The multi-party system naturally invites disorganization and chaos, as compared to the two-party system, but at least the parties do stand for something definite. The choice is, essentially, between the unreality of the two-party system of the United States and the chaotic character of the group and bloc system of Europe. The latter seems to be winning out. Even England, long the home of the two-party system, has now a half-dozen definite parties in the House of Commons. Even the old parties such as the Liberal are beginning to split up. The futility of the two-party system in the United States is becoming increasingly apparent.

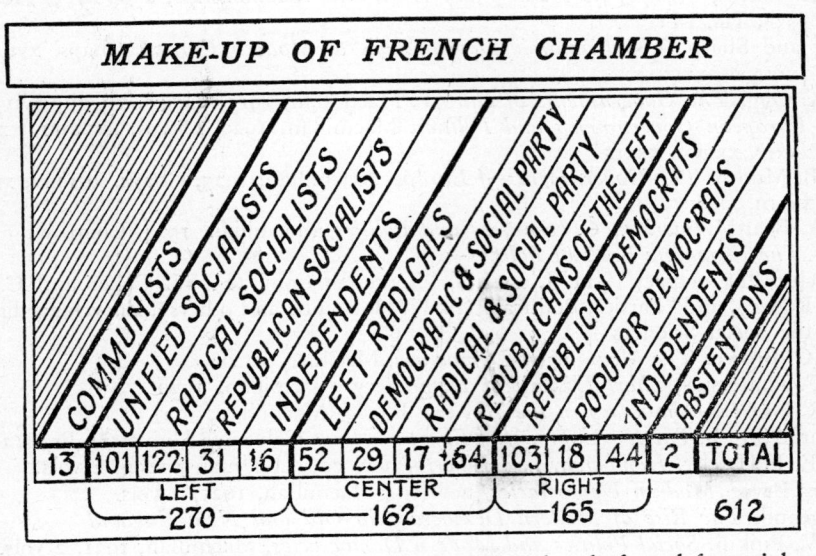

MAKE-UP OF FRENCH CHAMBER

COMMUNISTS	UNIFIED SOCIALISTS	RADICAL SOCIALISTS	REPUBLICAN SOCIALISTS	INDEPENDENTS	LEFT RADICALS	DEMOCRATIC & SOCIAL PARTY	RADICAL & SOCIAL PARTY	REPUBLICANS OF THE LEFT	REPUBLICAN DEMOCRATS	POPULAR DEMOCRATS	INDEPENDENTS	ABSTENTIONS	TOTAL
13	101	122	31	16	52	29	17	64	103	18	44	2	

LEFT — 270   CENTER — 162   RIGHT — 165   612

Party groups and their positions in the political scale from left to right are shown in the chart above for the Chamber elected in April, 1928. The Republican Socialists are split into two factions with twelve and nineteen votes and two "abstentions" were noted when the list was made up.

Whatever one's preferences in the matter, it certainly seems that the interests in modern society are too diversified and numerous to allow adequate expression through the medium of two political parties. This might have been possible in the old and simple agricultural days when there were only the court and country parties, but conservative and liberal labels are no longer inclusive enough to cover all the interests and attitudes of voters in our contemporary age.

A more serious challenge to the old party system than the group or bloc system is, of course, the increasing trend towards dictatorship. This dictatorial tendency may triumph in the form of various types of Fascism during the terminal stages of capitalism and may practically crush out all forms of real party life. If Fascism is ultimately followed by Communism, the latter will not be likely to foster aggressive party life. The parties representing private-property interests will disappear and, for a time at least, not too wide differences will be permitted among those who subscribe to Communism in a broad fashion.

SUGGESTED READING

Hammerton, *Universal History of the World,* Chaps. 160, 164, 166
Flick, *Modern World History,* Chaps. x-xi, xl
H. G. Plum and G. G. Benjamin, *Modern and Contemporary European Civilization,* Lippincott, 1923, Pt. VI
F. C. Palm and F. E. Graham, *Europe since Napoleon,* Ginn, 1934, Chaps. iv, vi, xi, xvi, xviii-xxi, xxv, xl
Hulme, *History of the British People,* Chaps. xxi-xxvii
A. H. Noyes, *Europe, Its History and Its World Relationships, 1789-1933,* Heath, 1934, Pts. I-IV
Ogg and Sharp, *The Economic Development of Modern Europe,* Chaps. xvii-xx, xxiv-xxv, xxix-xxx
F. A. Ogg, *The Governments of Europe,* Macmillan, 1913, Chaps. vii, xi, xvii
—— *European Governments and Politics,* Macmillan, 1929, Chaps. xvi-xvii, xxvii, xxxiv, xxxvii, xxxix
W. B. Munro, *The Governments of Europe,* Macmillan, 1925, Chaps. xiii-xiv, xxvi, xxxiii, xxxv
C. A. Beard, *American Government and Politics,* Macmillan, 1924, Chap. vii
—— *The Economic Basis of Politics*
Articles, "Democracy" (H. J. Laski), "Representation" (F. W. Coker and C. C. Rodee), and "Parties, Political" (A. N. Holcombe and others), Encyclopaedia of the Social Sciences
I. J. C. Brown, *The Meaning of Democracy,* McClurg, 1920
A. F. Hattersley, *Short History of Democracy,* Macmillan, 1930
T. R. Glover, *Democracy in the Ancient World,* Macmillan, 1927
Munroe Smith, *The Development of European Law,* Columbia University Press, 1928
W. E. H. Lecky, *Democracy and Liberty,* new ed., Longmans, 1899, 2 vols.
James Bryce, *Modern Democracies,* new ed., Macmillan, 1921, 2 vols.
Borgeaud, *The Rise of Modern Democracy in Old and New England*
C. W. Pipkin, *Social Politics and Modern Democracies,* Macmillan, 1931, 2 vols.
F. C. Howe, *Socialized Germany,* Scribner, 1915
W. J. Lauck, *Political and Industrial Democracy, 1776-1926,* Funk & Wagnalls, 1926
J. S. Penman, *The Irresistible Movement of Democracy,* Macmillan, 1923
Samuel Gompers, *Labor in Europe and America,* Harper, 1910
Schlesinger, *New Viewpoints in American History,* Chaps. iii-xii
A. N. Holcombe, *The Political Parties of To-day,* Harper, 1924
—— *The New Party Politics*
Robert Michels, *Political Parties,* Hearst's International Library, 1915
Jesse Macy, *Party Organization and Machinery,* Century, 1904
Webster, *Historical Selections,* Sec. XXI
Robinson and Beard, *Readings in Modern European History,* Vol. II, Chap. xxv, and pp. 467-77
Cheyney, *Readings in English History,* pp. 676-89, 702-15, 735-48
Scott and Baltzly, *Readings in European History since 1814,* pp. 106-09, 424-29
Crawford, *Readings in American Government,* Chaps. i-ii
C. A. Beard, *Readings in American Government and Politics,* Macmillan, 1925
P. S. Reinsch, ed., *Readings on American Federal Government,* Ginn, 1909

FURTHER REFERENCES

THE ORIGINS OF DEMOCRACY. On the history of democracy, see Hattersley, *op. cit.;* Glover, *op. cit;* Lecky, *op. cit.;* James Bryce, *The Holy Roman Empire* (new ed., Macmillan, 1919); and *Modern Democracies;* Penman, *op. cit.;* Lauck, *op. cit.;* Miller, *The Beginnings of To-morrow.* On the transformations brought about by the middle class in England in the seventeenth and eighteenth centuries, see Gretton, *The English Middle Class;* Borgeaud, *op. cit.;* Gooch, *Political Thought in England from Bacon to Halifax;* Laski, *Political Thought in England from Locke to Bentham.* On the Leveller movement, see Gooch, *op. cit.,* pp. 81 ff.; T. C. Pease, *The Leveller Movement* (American Historical Association, 1917).

On the historical evolution of democracy in the nineteenth century, see Ogg and Sharp, *op. cit.,* Pts. III-IV; Christie, *The Transition from Aristocracy, 1832-1867;* L. T. Hobhouse, *Liberalism* (Holt, 1911); James Bryce, *The American Commonwealth* (new ed., Macmillan, 1922-23, 2 vols.); and *Modern Democracies;* S. P. Orth, *Socialism and Democracy in Europe* (Holt, 1913); Hammond and Hammond, *The Age of the Chartists;* Paxson, *History of the American Frontier;* Penman, *op. cit.*

ENGLAND. On the growth of democracy in England and the British Empire in the nineteenth century, see Ogg and Sharp, *op. cit.,* Chaps. XVII, XIX, XXIII; Penman, *op. cit.,* Bk. III; Adams, *Constitutional History of England,* Chaps. XVII-XIX; Traill and Mann, *Social England,* Vol. VI, Chaps. XXI-XXIV; Slater, *The Growth of Modern England;* Hobhouse, *op. cit.;* Christie, *op. cit.;* E. M. Sait and D. P. Barrows, *British Politics in Transition* (World Book Co., 1925); A. B. Keith, *Responsible Government in the Dominions* (Oxford Press, 1912, 3 vols.)

FRANCE. On the democratic developments in France in the nineteenth century, see Penman, *op. cit.,* Bk. II; Chaps. XVII-XX of Charles Seignobos, *The Evolution of the French People* (Knopf, 1932); Vol. II, Chaps. XXXV-XXXIX of C. A. H. Guignebert, *Short History of the French People* (Macmillan, 1930, 2 vols.); Ogg and Sharp, *op. cit.,* pp. 380 ff., 438 ff., 512 ff.; Raymond Recouly, *The Third Republic* (Putnam, 1928); Joseph Barthélemy, *The Government of France* (Brentano, 1927); W. L. Middleton, *The French Political System* (Dutton, 1933).

GERMANY. On the slow course of democracy in Germany in the nineteenth century, see Ward, *Germany, 1815-1890;* W. H. Dawson, *The German Empire* (Macmillan, 1919, 2 vols.); Ogg and Sharp, *op. cit.,* pp. 389 ff., 431 ff., and Chaps. XXII, XXIV; K. F. Geiser, *Democracy versus Autocracy* (Heath, 1918); R. H. Fife, *The German Empire between Two Wars* (Macmillan, 1916).

On developments in Austria, see Vol. XV, Bk. II, Chaps. VI-VII, of H. S. Williams, *Historians' History of the World* (Encyclopaedia Britannica Co., 1904, 25 vols.); L. P. M. Léger, *Austria-Hungary* (John D. Morris, 1907); Drage, *Austria-Hungary;* Ogg and Sharp, *op. cit.,* pp. 396, 451, 536, 600-01.

On the rise of democracy in Czechoslovakia, see T. G. Masaryk, *The Making of a State* (Stokes, 1927).

ITALY. On democratic origins in Italy, see J. P. Trevelyan, *Short History of the Italian People* (Putnam, 1920); Ogg and Sharp, *op. cit.,* pp. 450-51, 537-39, 607-08; Tommaso Tittoni, *Modern Italy* (Macmillan, 1922).

SPAIN. On the democratic developments in Spain since 1868, see J. B. Trend, *The Origins of Modern Spain* (Macmillan, 1934); and pp. 396 ff. of R. L. Buell, *New Governments in Europe* (Nelson, 1934).

On Russian liberalization, see Pares, *History of Russia,* Chaps. XVII-XXIII; Chaps.

VII-XII of G. V. Vernadsky, *History of Russia* (rev. ed., Yale University Press, 1930); Ogg and Sharp, *op. cit.,* Chap. xv.

UNITED STATES. On democratic developments in the United States, see Penman, *op. cit.,* Bk. I; A. E. McKinley, *The Suffrage Franchise in the Thirteen English Colonies in America* (University of Pennsylvania Press, 1905); K. H. Porter, *History of Suffrage in the United States* (University of Chicago Press, 1918); Turner, *The Frontier in American History;* Guy Emerson, *The New Frontier* (Holt, 1920); C. L. Becker, *The United States: An Experiment in Democracy* (Harper, 1920); A. F. Pollard, *Factors in American History* (Macmillan, 1925); William McDonald, *Three Centuries of American Democracy* (Holt, 1923); Max Farrand, *The Development of the United States* (Houghton Mifflin, 1918); C. A. and Mary Beard, *The Rise of American Civilization* (Macmillan, 1927, 2 vols.); J. T. Adams, *The March of Democracy* (Scribner, 1932-33, 2 vols.); Kirkland, *History of American Economic Life;* A. C. McLaughlin, *A Constitutional History of the United States* (Appleton-Century, forthcoming); F. E. Haynes, *Social Politics in the United States* (Houghton Mifflin, 1924); T. V. Smith, *The Democratic Way of Life* (University of Chicago Press, 1926); Lauck, *op. cit.*

THE FAR EAST. On democracy in Australia and New Zealand, see Northcott, *Australian Social Development;* Clark, *The Labour Movement in Australasia;* Hancock, *Australia;* Condliffe, *New Zealand in the Making.*

On democracy and Communism in China, see Tyau, *China Awakened;* P. M. W. Linebarger, *Sun Yat Sen and the Chinese Republic* (Century, 1925); V. A. Yakhontov, *The Chinese Soviets* (Coward-McCann, 1931).

POLITICAL PARTIES. Much the best introduction to the theory, history, and present status of political parties is the article, "Parties: Political," Encyclopaedia of the Social Sciences; it contains an extensive bibliography. On the general theory of political parties, see A. F. Bentley, *The Process of Government* (University of Chicago Press, 1908); Michels, *op. cit.;* V. B. Boothe, *The Political Party as a Social Process* (University of Pennsylvania thesis, 1923).

On the history and organization of political parties, see Leonard Whibley, *Political Parties in Athens during the Peloponnesian War* (Putnam, 1889); Chaps. IV-VI of Max Beer, *Social Struggles in Antiquity* (International Publishers, 1929); F. F. Abbott, *Roman Politics* (Longmans, 1923); T. F. Tout, *The Empire and the Papacy, 918-1273* (Macmillan, 1898); Sir Richard Lodge, *The Close of the Middle Ages, 1273-1494* (Macmillan, 1901); H. A. L. Fisher, *The Medieval Empire* (Macmillan, 1908, 2 vols.); G. M. Trevelyan, *The Two-Party System in English Political History* (Oxford Press, 1926); Vol. I, Pt. II of A. L. Lowell, *The Government of England* (Macmillan, 1912, 2 vols.); and Vol. I, Chaps. II, IV, Vol. II, Chaps. VII-IX of *Governments and Parties in Continental Europe* (Houghton Mifflin, 1896, 2 vols.); Munro, *op. cit.,* Chap. XXVI; E. M. Sait, *The Government and Politics of France* (World Book Co., 1920); R. H. Soltau, *French Parties and Politics* (Oxford Press, 1930); Barthélemy, *op. cit.;* Middleton, *op. cit.;* Chaps. I-IV of R. L. Buell, *Contemporary French Politics* (Appleton, 1920); H. F. Gosnell, *Why Europe Votes* (University of Chicago Press, 1930); J. K. Pollock, "British Party Organization," *Political Science Quarterly,* June, 1930, "The German Party System," *American Political Science Review,* 1929; and *Money and Politics Abroad* (Knopf, 1932); E. E. Robinson, *The Evolution of American Political Parties* (Harcourt, Brace, 1924); Holcombe, *Political Parties of Today;* Fine, *Labor and Farmer Parties in the United States;* F. E. Haynes, *Third Party Movements since the Civil War* (Iowa Historical Society, 1916); F. R. Kent, *The Democratic Party* (Century, 1928); W. S. Myers, *The Republican Party* (Century, 1931); W. B. Munro, *The Invisible Government* (Macmillan, 1928); C. A. Beard, *The American Party Battle* (Macmillan, 1928).

CHAPTER XV

THE COURSE OF MODERN IMPERIALISM

I. THE HISTORICAL BACKGROUND OF MODERN IMPERIALISM

The greater portion of Part One of this volume was devoted to the expansion of Europe and its reactions upon Western civilization. The expansion movement did not cease in 1800, although there was a marked slump in European interest in oversea areas and their exploitation in the first seventy-five years of the nineteenth century.[1] The preoccupation of Britain and the United States with industrial development and the absorption of continental Europe in dynastic, nationalistic, and constitutional problems diverted attention from expansion. But the industrial and financial development produced by the Industrial Revolution laid the foundations for a new era of diffusion overseas that was, in many ways, more extensive than the achievements in the period from 1485 to 1800. The new industrialism required more and better markets. It produced an excess of capital for investment outside its borders. It had to seek new sources of raw materials. All of these factors joined with some of political derivation to create the new imperialism.

Perhaps the most conspicuous aspect of recent imperialism was the great swiftness of the occidental expansion. More territory was actually procured for white occupation of one sort or another within sixty years than was effectively appropriated in the three centuries of the old colonial movement. In 1800 about four-fifths of the land area of the world was untouched by civilized man through exploration. As late as 1870 more than half of the habitable surface of the earth had not been touched by Europeans. By the beginning of the twentieth century the whole planet outside of the extreme polar regions had been traversed by white men and its potentialities for exploitation had been catalogued.[2] Africa had been explored and partitioned. Oceania and Australasia had been occupied, and a commercial hegemony of Europe and the United States had been established in Asia and in Latin America.

The forces or causes lying back of this expansion movement are conventionally classified as economic, political, social, religious, and psychological. The economic causes of expansion grew directly out of the Industrial Revolution. The nature of the Industrial Revolution and its effect upon international economic relations have been admirably set forth by Professor Shotwell:

---

[1] *Cf.* Ramsay Muir, *The Expansion of Europe*, 3d ed. rev., Houghton Mifflin, 1928, Chap. v; C. A. Bodelsen, *Studies in Mid-Victorian Imperialism*, Knopf, 1925; and R. L. Schuyler, "The Climax of Anti-Imperialism in England," *Political Science Quarterly*, December, 1921.

[2] See *Cambridge Modern History*, Vol. XII, Chap. xxv; and Leonard Outhwaite, *Unrolling the Map: the Story of Exploration*, Day, 1935.

It has brought into existence a vast working population, embodied in iron and steel, drawn from mines and forests, from steam, gas, electricity by the mysterious genius of the human brain. It has transformed the face of nature and the life of the whole world. These are not mere economic facts. They form the largest and most wonderful chapter in the history of mankind. What is the Renaissance or Reformation, the empire of Charlemagne or of Caesar, compared with this empire of mind and industry, which has penetrated the whole world, planting its cities as it goes, binding the whole together by railroad and telegraph, until the thing we call civilization has drawn the isolated communities of the old régime into a great world organism, with its afferent and efferent nerves of news and capital reaching to its finger tips in the markets of the frontier? A nickel spent for thread in Uganda sets the spindles going in Manchester. Fellaheen by the Nile may be starving because the cigarette factories are building marble palaces for their owners on the banks of the Hudson.[1]

Following closely upon the heels of the first manifestations of the Industrial Revolution came the so-called Second Industrial Revolution, to which we shall devote our attention more thoroughly later. It gave a further powerful impulse to the expansionist movement that had been set in motion by the mechanical and capitalistic revolution taking place after 1738 in England. Professor Schapiro gives us an excellent and concise appraisal of this Second Industrial Revolution and of its influence upon imperialism:

Toward the end of the 19th century there took place a new Industrial Revolution, the results of which were almost as startling as those of its predecessor a century before. The application of science to industry through the extraordinary development of chemical and physical sciences, the better organization of business enterprise through combination, the larger use of capital and the opening up of new sources of raw material in Asia and Africa increased many fold the production of goods. Gigantic plants, equipped with scientific laboratories, worked by armies of laborers, and capitalized by millions of dollars, brought together in syndicates and "trusts," displaced the small factories, or "mills," as they were still called. It is estimated that the average increase in the commerce of all the countries of Europe during the 19th century was over 1,200 per cent. . . .

The Industrial Revolution at the beginning of the 19th century transformed the economic life of western Europe only; the new Industrial Revolution at the end of the century caused Europe to burst her industrial bonds and to encompass the entire world in its influences. The new industrialism multiplied production so enormously that markets had to be sought outside the limits of the home country. As competition for the home market within the leading industrial countries became very keen, the eyes of the captains of industry were naturally turned to the many regions that were at the same time densely populated and industrially undeveloped. The vast populations of Asia and Africa were so many potential customers for the business men of Europe. What fabulous profits awaited those who got the opportunity of clothing and shoeing the teeming millions of Chinese and Hindus![2]

This new industry, carried on by mechanical processes under the factory system, gave rise to an unprecedented increase in productivity and to an enormous accumulation of capital available for investment. The financial basis for the

---

[1] J. T. Shotwell, "The Industrial Revolution" (Lecture at Teachers College, Columbia University).
[2] J. S. Schapiro, *Modern and Contemporary European History*, Houghton Mifflin, 1919, pp. 650, 653.

development of modern imperialism is well revealed by the increased wealth and income of the United Kingdom and the United States since the Industrial Revolution in these countries:[1]

TOTAL WEALTH OF UNITED STATES		TOTAL WEALTH OF THE UNITED KINGDOM	
1850	$ 7,000,000,000	1700	$ 3,500,000,000
1870	30,000,000,000	1800	8,753,000,000
1900	88,000,000,000	1850	22,564,000,000
1922	322,000,000,000	1875	42,740,000,000
1925	355,000,000,000	1900	70,000,000,000
1929	361,800,000,000	1915	100,000,000,000
		1925	117,800,000,000

The total annual income of the United States increased from $31,400,000,000 in 1910 to $72,000,000,000 in 1920 and $89,400,000,000 in 1928. The national income of the United Kingdom in 1911 was $9,840,000,000 in 1911 and $18,730,000,000 in 1928. At the same time, the remarkable improvement in the technique of land and water transportation made possible the growth of world trade on a scale that exceeded anything before known. The total trade of the world (102 countries) amounted to $41,838,000,000 in 1913; to $57,189,000,000 in 1924; and to $68,526,000,000 in 1929. Since then there has been a steady decline, due to the depression and the growing economic nationalism.

As modern industrialism developed, the impulse to imperialism that resides in the search for markets for finished products was strongly supplemented by the desire to secure control of the supplies of indispensable raw materials. With the extensive development of the internal-combustion engine and the growing popularity of automobiles, essential minerals, rubber, and petroleum have become particularly important. Few other factors are more potent in contemporary diplomacy than the ambition to secure and safeguard an adequate supply of petroleum, minerals, and rubber.[2]

The desire to exploit Russian oil and trade was the main consideration inducing the British to recognize Soviet Russia. With the eclipse of the British interests and the growing ascendancy of the Standard Oil Company in the Russian fields, we find the spokesman of the Rockefeller interests discovering much to commend in the Bolshevist experiment.[3] The British restriction of the supplies of raw rubber a few years back proved sufficient to provoke decidedly anti-British protests from Mr. Herbert Hoover, certainly a man not previously known for anti-British proclivities.[4] The oil reserves of Colombia were sufficiently rich and essential to American needs to induce even adamant Rooseveltians like Henry Cabot Lodge to repudiate by implication Roosevelt's Panama policy and to enter into an arrangement to indemnify Colombia.[5]

Cheap transportation, the rapidity with which shipments could be made, and

---

[1] It is worth noting that the figures for the later years, especially those of 1929, owe their imposing size, in some part at least, to inflated prices and paper profits.
[2] See Pierre L'Espagnol de la Tramerye, *The World Struggle for Oil*, Knopf, 1924; Louis Fischer, *Oil Imperialism*, International Publishers, 1926; Ludwell Denny, *We Fight for Oil*, Knopf, 1928; F. C. Hanighen, *The Secret War*; Day, 1934; C. K. Leith, *World Minerals and World Politics*, Whittlesey House, 1931; and J. C. Lawrence, *The World's Struggle with Rubber, 1905-1931*, Harper, 1931.   [3] I. L. Lee, *Present-day Russia*, 2d ed., Macmillan, 1928.
[4] W. W. Liggett, *The Rise of Herbert Hoover*, Fly, 1932, pp. 329 ff.
[5] *Cf.* J. F. Rippy, *The Capitalists and Colombia*, Vanguard Press, 1931, Chaps. VI-VII, IX.

decreased losses in ocean shipments helped commerce to grow by leaps and bounds. All these developments inevitably led to a scramble for foreign markets and to unprecedented investment of capital in oversea areas. These markets and areas for capital investment were sought, when possible, in colonies carved out of backward and unoccupied tracts and, when these were not available, in older cultures that had not yet passed into the modern industrial age.

Political causes coöperated with the economic in producing the new movement of expansion.[1] The growth of modern nationalism stimulated and intensified the desire to secure colonial domains. Italy and Germany achieved national unification in 1870 and developed an intense patriotic fervor that encouraged the search for oversea possessions. France turned to colonial realms to secure compensation for the loss of Alsace-Lorraine. Russia, not satisfied with a vast area at home still awaiting exploitation and development, turned southward to seize more territory in Asia. England had long staked its future on maintaining its supremacy as a commercial and colonizing nation. Even the United States, before the close of the nineteenth century, had exhausted its great frontier and turned to Spanish-American lands for new areas of investment and exploitation. This process of expansion produced, as a sort of psychic and ethical compensation, the notion of the "civilizing mission" or the "white man's burden." This benevolent rationalization served to justify the seizure and spoliation of spacious regions belonging to both native peoples and old civilizations.

Sociological motives combined with political impulses to favor expansion.[2] Owing to a complex set of causes not yet perfectly understood, but closely connected with modern industrialism and the growth of medical science, the population of Europe increased from about 140,000,000 to over 463,000,000 between 1750 and 1914.[3] In many countries this led to a real pressure of the population on the means of subsistence, and emigration was stimulated or made absolutely necessary. It was natural that the mother country should desire to retain political control over its emigrants, but this could be achieved only when they migrated to colonies. In this way the socio-biological factor of population growth was linked up with the political drive of patriotism.

The age-old religious motives for developing oversea areas had not declined; they had actually increased. To the Catholic missionaries, who had never ceased activity since the beginning of oversea expansion, were now added an ever increasing number of Protestants. The appeal of the missionaries was further strengthened when it became possible to carry with them not only "the word which maketh wise unto salvation," but also modern industrial arts and the blessings of sanitary and medical science.

Broad psychological impulses served to extend the interests of Europeans to oversea lands. The love of adventure operated as always, while the compelling power of scientific curiosity had not abated. Again, the social prestige usually attached to colonial service acted as an incentive to the expansion movement.

---

[1] *Cf.* S. P. Orth, *The Imperial Impulse,* Century, 1916.
[2] See above, pp. 416 ff.; and Thompson, *Population Problems,* Chaps. IV, XXIII.
[3] See above, p. 416.

HISTORICAL BACKGROUND OF MODERN IMPERIALISM

Further, the psychological power of aggressive modern nationalism was utilized in the propaganda of skillful and unscrupulous imperialists to produce a popular espousal of their program. Finally, the "El Dorado complex" and the hope of acquiring great fortunes with little effort lay behind the recent imperialism, as it had behind the older colonialism of the sixteenth and seventeenth centuries.

The more recent expansion was a national movement rather than one of persons or privileged companies. Its chief area of operation was in the Eastern Hemisphere, whereas most of the activity in the earlier period of exploration and colonization was carried on in the Western Hemisphere. Africa, Oceania, and Australasia have been forcibly colonized since 1800, while economic exploitation has been vigorously promoted in Asia. This statement does not, however, ignore the extensive commercial exploitation of Latin America by European nations and the United States. Further, in the same way that the earlier movement of expansion overseas after 1500 brought into existence the Atlantic age, so the period of imperialism after 1870 may be said to have brought the Pacific age vividly into being. There are not a few writers who predict that the most active center of civilization and social development will sooner or later pass from western Europe and America to the Pacific and the Far East.[1] The significance of this more recent period of expansion overseas has been graphically described by Professor Shotwell:

In the twentieth century, conquistadors, clad in khaki or glittering in helmeted display, have proclaimed to most of the savages of the globe that they belong henceforth to European nations. On the wharves of London there are goods from German workshops for the merchant adventurers of to-day to carry off to Bantus or Negritos. Piles of coal from Cardiff lie inside the coral reefs of Australasian islands, for the ships which come to break the silence of farther Hebrides than Wordsworth dreamed of. But for the historian there is more significance than romance in such events. The men whom Joseph Conrad and Kipling describe are responsible for the transformation of Africa and Asia. And that transformation in its turn is mainly responsible for those policies of imperial expansion, of commercial and colonial rivalries which underlie the causes of the present world war.[2]

In studying contemporary imperialism it is necessary to place the emphasis somewhat differently from what it was in our treatment of the expansion of Europe from 1500 to 1800. In the earlier period the more notable results were to be observed in the reactions of the expansion movement upon Europe itself.[3] There was relatively little permanent penetration of oversea areas by Europeans. The most far-reaching influences were to be discerned in the impact of oversea products, practices, and ideas upon Europe.

After 1870 there was a much more extensive movement of Europeans overseas. As many as 50,000,000 Europeans migrated to oversea areas in the period between 1800 and the World War. A little over three-fifths of them came to

---

[1] For an interesting discussion on this point, see Hendrik Van Loon, "Kipling Was Right," *Cosmopolitan*, November, 1934.
[2] Introduction to N. D. Harris, *Europe and Africa*, new ed., Houghton Mifflin, 1927.
[3] See above, Chapters I-III, VI.

the United States and the rest went to other oversea areas. They carried the new technology and other aspects of Western civilization abroad and transformed the living-conditions of those dwelling in oversea areas. Therefore, if world-politics from 1500 to 1800 were of consequence chiefly because of the resulting European transformations, after 1870 world-politics found their most notable expression in the movement of European peoples and cultures to oversea areas. This should not be taken, of course, to mean any denial of the importance of European expansion abroad immediately after 1500 or as a minimizing of the reaction of the imperialistic process upon Europe after 1870. It is rather a matter of the relative significance of expansion and reaction, respectively, in these two periods. The following table provides an excellent summary statement of the extensive territorial expansion of the Western states up to the time of the World War.

COLONIAL EMPIRES OF THE WORLD IN 1914 [1]

Countries having colonial or non-contiguous territory	Number of colonies, etc.	Area (square miles) Mother country	Colonies and other non-contiguous territory	Population Mother country	Colonies and other non-contiguous territory
United Kingdom	55	120,953	12,043,806	46,052,741	391,582,528
France	29	207,076	4,110,409	39,602,258	62,350,000
Germany	10	208,830	1,230,989	64,925,993	13,074,950
Belgium	1	11,373	910,000	7,571,387	15,000,000
Portugal	8	35,500	804,440	5,960,056	9,680,000
Netherlands	8	12,761	762,863	6,102,399	37,410,000
Italy	4	110,623	591,250	35,238,997	1,396,176
United States	6	3,026,789	125,610	98,781,324	10,020,982

II. THE NATURE OF CONTEMPORARY IMPERIALISM

Economic imperialism has had far-reaching effects on modern society. It is not only a leading factor in modern commerce and investment, but has also profoundly affected many noneconomic aspects of our life. In the field of politics it has involved: (1) The development of a foreign policy conditioned by oversea ambitions and colonial dominion; and (2) the reaction of this type of foreign policy upon the domestic political institutions of those states which have participated to any extensive degree in imperialistic ventures. As L. T. Hobhouse long ago made clear, no country can expect to devote a part of its energy and resources to the acquisition and domination of lands and peoples overseas and still hope to keep its domestic politics free from the responsibilities and handicaps imposed by oversea dominion.[2]

In the field of social institutions far-reaching modifications have been produced both at home and abroad through the impact of widely different cultures. Likewise, cultural and intellectual activities have been deeply influenced by the interaction of divergent civilizations upon each other.[3]

---

[1] These figures are taken from the fuller table in the Encyclopedia Americana, Vol. VII, p. 297.
[2] *Cf.* his *Democracy and Reaction*.   [3] See above, pp. 6 ff., 31 ff., 244 ff.

Much heat and dogmatism have attended the effort to define and assess contemporary imperialism. Some regard it chiefly as a benevolent and unselfish civilizing process; to others it seems the most brutal and heartless manifestation of modern capitalism and the spirit of acquisitiveness. To the writer it appears that it is best to abandon, for the time being, the older and single-track dogmas concerning imperialism and to make a careful study of the actual facts, in order to find out just what contemporary imperialism really amounts to. In so doing, we may learn that some of our older dogmas are completely discredited, while other assumptions may be verified and extended. We have conventionally assumed that the imperialistic process develops through the following steps:

1. Merchants and bankers recognize the opportunities for pecuniary gain in certain relatively backward political and economic areas.

2. Their penetration is followed by appeals to the Foreign Offices of their respective states.

3. These requests ultimately lead to military or naval intervention and the political administration of such areas.

Such a sequence, however, while not uncommon, is by no means inevitable. Often there is no political or military intervention at all because the interested bankers and merchants feel that they can carry on their activities to better effect without the embarrassment of political friction.[1] This has been especially true of imperialism in the twentieth century. Hence on account of these variations in procedure it is necessary to make a careful and realistic study of imperialism in action. After all, the most useful definition of a thing is often a description of what it does.

It is certainly a mistake to conceive of modern imperialism solely in economic terms. Modern industrial states are impelled to build up an export trade and to seek sources of raw materials, but this does not necessarily force them to annex territory. The most important customers of the United States are Canada, Europe, and South American states, over which very few propose that we should exercise or attempt to exercise political control. Economic expansion has led to imperialism in considerable part because of nationalism and the patriotic pride in colonies. The French Congo and Indo-China have actually been economic liabilities on the hands of the French, and the same thing is true of the Italian possessions in Africa. The German colonial empire was certainly more a product of nationalism than of economic expansion. Germany's rivals, Great Britain and France, each bought more goods of Germany than did the whole German colonial empire. On the other hand, American and British imperialism has been produced more exclusively by economic motives. We may now turn our attention to a brief review of the outstanding facts connected with the occupation of oversea areas since about 1870.

[1] *Cf.* L. H. Jenks, *Our Cuban Colony,* Vanguard Press, 1928, Chaps. XI-XIII, XVI.

III. IMPERIALISM IN AFRICA

1. LEOPOLD OF BELGIUM AND THE FATE OF THE CONGO FREE STATE

On the very eve of the new imperialistic developments following the seventies, scientific curiosity, religious propaganda, and journalistic enterprise were leading men to undertake those epoch-making explorations which revealed to enthusiastic European and American capitalists the economic potentialities of the "Dark Continent." About a decade after most of the important African explorations had been concluded, the diplomatic and legal basis for the partition of Africa was arranged by the Berlin Conference, which sat from December, 1884, to February, 1885. The slave trade was branded as illegal; formal notice was ordered given of all protectorates assumed; it was declared that no territory should be annexed that was not "effectively occupied"; freedom was prescribed for all nations in the navigation of the Congo and Niger rivers; and provision was made for general freedom of trade in the Congo Basin.

The first notable apostle to Africa of modern capitalistic imperialism was King Leopold II of Belgium. Under his leadership an International Association for the Exploration and Colonization of Africa was formed in 1876, and two years later Stanley was employed to make a detailed geographic and economic survey of the Congo district. In 1882 Leopold organized the International Association of the Congo, with himself as president. Between April, 1884, and February, 1885, in part by intrigue at the Berlin Conference of 1884-85, he secured from the Great Powers the recognition of the International Association of the Congo as an independent sovereign state, and in April, 1885, he realized his full ambition by transforming it into the Congo Free State with himself as its king. It should be kept in mind that Leopold was not the sovereign of the Congo Free State by virtue of his position as King of the Belgians. The African district was his own private possession.

Indignant public opinion, aroused by the revelations of his cruel and extortionate exploitation of a backward people,[1] forced Leopold to surrender the Congo Free State to the Belgian government in 1908, for an ample indemnity.

2. GERMAN COLONIAL ENTERPRISE IN AFRICA

The real awakening of German interest in imperialism came about in 1878, when the German branch of the International African Association was established. In 1882 a society for the development of *Weltpolitik* was founded, the German Colonial Union, and two years later several mercantile marine companies and colonial societies openly sponsored a program of commercial and colonial expansion.

Within two years after 1884 Germany had acquired the substantial basis of its African domains. Dr. Gustav Nachtigal, the noted explorer, negotiated for the possession of Kamerun and Togoland in 1884 and both were taken over as German protectorates in that year. F. A. E. von Lüderitz, a Bremen merchant, in the summer of 1883 purchased what became German Southwest Africa when

---

[1] Chiefly by the English publicist E. D. Morel.

it was taken over by the German government in the next year. Carl Peters, one of the most enthusiastic of Pan-Germans and a representative of the German Colonial Union, acquired German East Africa in 1884, and his activity was approved and confirmed by the government in 1885. This German territory in Africa, totaling slightly over 1,000,000 square miles, was later defined and somewhat extended in its boundaries in the Anglo-German agreement of July, 1890, and the Franco-German arrangement of November, 1911, respectively.[1]

After the World War the German colonial empire, including not only the African but the Pacific colonies, was seized and divided among the Entente victors, going chiefly to the British Empire, Japan, and France.

3. GREAT BRITAIN AND THE BOERS IN SOUTH AFRICA

In 1854 two Boer (Dutch) republics, the Transvaal and the Orange Free State, announced their independent existence in South Africa. Disraeli, in the first enthusiasm of the new British imperialism, annexed the Transvaal in 1877. This led to the first Boer War of 1881, which ended in the complete defeat of somewhat insignificant British forces at Majuba Hill in 1881.

Foreigners, or "uitlanders," attracted by the discovery of rich gold and diamond mines in these Boer republics, came to own two-thirds of the land and about 90 per cent of the personal property in this region, and they paid about 95 per cent of the taxes. In spite of this, they were excluded from political rights and were subjected to extortionate taxes and irritating economic restrictions. In March, 1899, the uitlanders appealed to Great Britain for relief. The British imperialists gladly welcomed the opportunity to intervene. In this second Boer War (1899-1902) Great Britain was successful after serious early defeats, but its action was bitterly opposed at home by liberal statesmen like Lloyd George and by progressive publicists like J. A. Hobson and L. T. Hobhouse.

The triumph of the Liberal party in England in 1905 brought about a new policy of conciliation. The Union of South Africa—a new self-governing colony—was created out of Cape Colony, Natal, the Orange Free State, and the Transvaal. This action was approved by Great Britain on September 20, 1909.

4. GREAT BRITAIN IN EGYPT AND THE SUDAN

The completion of the Suez Canal in 1869 directed Great Britain's attention to Egypt. As has been noted, a fortunate combination of circumstances enabled Disraeli in 1875 to purchase some 177,000 shares of canal stock from the Khedive for £4,000,000 after France had refused the offer.

The reckless financial operations of the Khedive led to the establishment of a dual control over Egyptian finances by Great Britain and France in 1877. An Egyptian nationalist revolt broke out four years later. France was prevented from intervening by Clemenceau and other radical anti-imperialists, so Great Britain had to suppress the revolt unaided in the summer of 1882. This turn of events excluded France from a parity in the control of Egypt, and made Egypt an English protectorate in fact, although this relationship was not formally proclaimed until December 18, 1914—an action prompted by Turkey's al-

---

[1] On Germany and England in South Africa, see R. W. Bixler, *Anglo-German Imperialism in South Africa, 1880-1900*, Warwick & York, 1932.

liance with the Central Powers in the World War. Egypt was controlled during this intervening period by a series of British "financial advisers." In 1922 Egypt was proclaimed a formal, but not an actual, independent republic. At present, Egypt is seemingly on the verge of becoming a self-governing nation.

South of Egypt is the extensive district known as the Sudan. Nominally under Egyptian control, the inefficiency of the administration enabled a group of Muslim fanatics to secure control of that region and to massacre the distinguished English soldier General Charles George Gordon and his forces at Khartum in January, 1885. To protect Egypt from invasion and to safeguard the Egyptian water supply, General Kitchener was sent to conquer the Sudan. This was accomplished by September 2, 1898.

At the same time that Kitchener was subduing the Sudanese, a French force under Captain Marchand was moving eastward across Africa to the sources of the Nile, and it arrived at Fashoda in the lower Sudan on July 12, 1898. Pushing southward after his victories, Kitchener reached the same spot about two months later. War between Britain and France for a time seemed imminent, but France backed down and recalled Marchand. It was long held that this action was due to the conciliatory disposition of the French Foreign Minister, Delcassé, and that he gracefully surrendered at this time in order to promote an Anglo-French alliance. Professor Swain and others have exposed the falsity of this interpretation. In 1898-99 Delcassé was willing to fight England, but the Russians refused to support him, so he had to back down. For four years Delcassé sought a foreign alliance against Great Britain, and only desisted after the French radicals under Combes came into power in 1902 and threatened to dismiss him. The myth of an "Alphonse and Gaston" act between the French and the British in 1898-99 was a product of the Entente "ballyhoo" of 1914-18. The efforts of M. Paul Cambon, French Ambassador in London, did, however, bring about an Anglo-French understanding in 1903-04, which was confirmed in 1911, and given practical demonstration in 1914.[1] The seizure of German East Africa by Great Britain during the World War and the approval of this action by the Peace Conference gave Great Britain unobstructed control of a broad strip of territory from Cairo to Cape Town, assured the hegemony of Britain in African imperialism, and cleared the way for the Cape-to-Cairo Railroad.

5. FRENCH IMPERIALISM IN AFRICA

Excluded from Egypt by British action in 1882, France meanwhile had been laying elsewhere the basis for the huge French colonial empire in Africa. Algeria was occupied in the Orleanist period (1830-48). Settlements were made at Gabun following 1840, and these opened the way for the colonization of French Equatorial Africa. At the same time, posts were located on the Ivory and Guinea coasts, which prepared the way for the French expansion in the Senegal and Niger regions. Entry into Somaliland after 1846 put into French hands the key to the lower end of the Red Sea and the Gulf of Aden. Tunis was made a protectorate in 1881, and Italy was thereby estranged from France and impelled to enter the Triple Alliance with Germany and Austria. By the

[1] It is worth noting that the British were as bellicose over Fashoda as the Germans were in the next decade concerning Morocco.

Anglo-French agreement of 1890 French possession of the Sahara district was confirmed and a French protectorate allowed over Madagascar, which was transformed into a French colony in 1896. In the early nineties the French extended their possessions in the Senegal, Niger, and Congo districts. By the Anglo-French agreement of 1899 France acquired the central Sudan, and was enabled thereby to connect Algeria and the Sahara with the French Congo.

In 1900 and 1902 Italy agreed to a French protectorate over Morocco in return for French consent to Italian occupation of Tripoli. Italy, incidentally, secretly nullified its position in the Triple Alliance. In 1904 Great Britain gave its assent to the Moroccan protectorate in return for French willingness to see a British protectorate proclaimed in Egypt. But at this juncture Germany took a hand and the dispute over Morocco threatened the peace of Europe for some seven years. The Algeciras Conference of 1906 temporarily settled matters, but the French were unwilling to cease their political penetration, while the German economic interests and diplomatic aspirations led the German government on to more vigorous action. A less important crisis, arising over the action of the French and German authorities at Casablanca (1908), was settled without hostilities through referring the dispute to The Hague.

Three years later, as a counterpoise to the French occupation of Fez in violation of the Algeciras pact, a German gunboat anchored off the port of Agadir. War was averted only by the pacific policy of Caillaux and the German Emperor. Britain was more bellicose than France. The dispute was finally settled by the agreement of Germany to the convention of November, 1911, whereby it gave France a free hand in Morocco, in return for the cession of a part of the French Congo. Accordingly, France transformed Morocco into a French protectorate between March 30 and September 28, 1912. The French received some of the German African empire at the close of the World War. The French have experienced much trouble maintaining their power in Morocco. In the so-called Riff War of 1925-26, Abd-el-Krim, a native chieftain, successfully defied French power for more than a year and inflicted heavy losses and expense on the French.

6. ITALIAN IMPERIALISM IN AFRICA

In the very year of the occupation of Rome by Victor Emmanuel's army, Italy acquired the foothold on the Red Sea that soon developed into the colony of Eritrea. In 1889 the Italians occupied Italian Somaliland and attempted to reduce the neighboring region of Abyssinia to a protectorate. In this latter enterprise they were unsuccessful. A stinging defeat at the hands of King Menelek in 1896 caused the resignation of Crispi, the leader of Italian imperialism, and forced Italy to desist from further attempts to control Abyssinia, the independence of which was guaranteed by international agreement ten years later. Agreements of December, 1900, and November, 1902, obtained French consent to Italian aggressive action in Tripolitania. A successful war with Turkey secured for Italy, by the treaty of October 18, 1912, formal control over this area.

7. OTHER AFRICAN TERRITORY

In addition to the territories already enumerated, Great Britain by 1914 possessed Gambia, Sierra Leone, the Gold Coast, Nigeria, and Walfisch Bay in western Africa; Bechuanaland and Rhodesia in south-central Africa;[1] and British East Africa, Uganda, and British Somaliland and Nyasaland in eastern Africa. To these areas should now be added most of the German colonial possessions in Africa before the World War.

Portugal retains out of its former African possessions Guinea, Angola, and Portuguese East Africa. Spain has on the western coast three small areas of domination, northern Morocco, Rio de Oro, and Rio Muni. Finally, there are the independent states of Liberia, founded in 1822 under American auspices as a colony for emancipated slaves, and Ethiopia (formerly Abyssinia), a native Christian kingdom with its independence guaranteed in 1906.

From an almost untouched continent in 1870, Africa had by the outbreak of the World War passed into a well-traversed and completely partitioned area thoroughly subjected to imperialistic exploitation.

IV. MODERN IMPERIALISM IN WESTERN ASIA

1. THE BERLIN-BAGHDAD RAILROAD AND THE "DRANG NACH OSTEN"

Asia, as the cradle of Western civilization, had originally furnished Europe, and ultimately America, with those cultural elements which served to make contemporary civilization and imperialism possible. Capitalism and contemporary material culture were novel occidental achievements that gave the Occident a preponderance of strength over the Orient, and in the nineteenth and twentieth centuries enabled Europe to penetrate, subordinate, and humiliate its former Asiatic master and benefactor.

The German Empire attempted to gain control of the resources and means of communication in Asia Minor and Mesopotamia by means of the Berlin-Baghdad Railroad or the "Drang nach Osten" (Urge-to-the-East) plan.[2] The friendly gestures of the Kaiser to the Sultan, together with the subtle diplomacy of Von Bieberstein, won for Germany Turkish consent to the building of a railroad from Konia in western Asia Minor to Basra on the head of the Persian Gulf. A very considerable amount of international opposition was in the main removed by diplomatic activity. England, owing to the influence of Cecil Rhodes, was at first inclined to favor the German enterprise. Rhodes encouraged the German penetration of the Near East in return for the Kaiser's approval of Rhodes's last pet project, the Cape-to-Cairo Railroad. Russia was placated after a meeting of the Tsar and the Kaiser in November, 1910. These monarchs arranged an agreement made public on August 19, 1911. French objections did not prove serious, and a satisfactory adjustment was made with Great Britain by June 15, 1914, which safeguarded British interests in the East and gave Germany the desired transit rights.

---

[1] *Cf.* Harris, *op. cit.,* Chap. IX.
[2] *Cf.* E. M. Earle, *Turkey, the Great Powers and the Bagdad Railway,* Macmillan, 1923.

The actual building of the Baghdad railroad proceeded slowly and was often interrupted by financial and diplomatic obstacles. In the months just previous to the outbreak of the World War, however, construction was greatly hastened, and after 1914 the work progressed very rapidly. As the result of its defeat in the World War, Germany was ousted from this area. Under Bolshevik rule Russia also voluntarily withdrew, leaving England, France, Italy, and Greece to struggle over the spoils. Matters were still further complicated by the Chester Concessions of 1923, whereby American interests entered the field and an Ottoman-American Development Company was created to exploit Anatolia. The Chester Concessions were later annulled because of the failure of the company to secure adequate American support, but American oil interests continue to be active in this region and about Mosul.

During the World War, while the Entente was charming the world by its public declarations relative to its nonmaterial war aims and was especially stressing its intention to liberate the peoples oppressed by the "terrible Turk," it was actually arranging the partition of Turkey. This began in the Sykes-Picot agreement of 1916. Italy was kept in the dark at first, but demanded its share of the spoils when the secret treaty finally came to the attention of the Italian government. In a rough way, this partition was embodied in the peace treaties, but part of the plans were upset by the defiance and strength of Mustapha Kemal Pasha.

The World War produced an enormous dislocation of forces and alignments in the Near East.[1] The Germans were eliminated and the Turks defeated and humiliated. The latter, however, retained their foothold in Europe, ignored the Treaty of Sèvres, and established a strong national republic under the presidency of Mustapha Kemal Pasha, with its capital at Angora in Anatolia. Under Kemal's able rule Turkey has been consolidated and modernized.

Turkish dominion over the several million Arabs of Syria, Palestine, Mesopotamia, and the Arabian Peninsula was broken.[2] Syria was handed over as a mandate to France. Palestine and Kerak were organized into another mandate under British control. Mesopotamia was rechristened the Kingdom of Iraq and virtually made a British mandate. The Kingdom of Hejaz was conquered by Ibn Saud, and the scattered tribes of the Arabian Peninsula attained formal independence; but they are in reality under British supervision.

2. GREAT BRITAIN AND RUSSIA IN WESTERN ASIA

The natural contenders for Persia were Russia, working southward from European Russia and Turkestan, and Great Britain, slowly bearing down from India and Egypt. Russian occupation of Persian territory progressed after 1722, when the northern provinces were seized. By the close of the third quarter of the nineteenth century Russia had occupied all Persian territory as far south as the southern end of the Caspian Sea. British intrusion began early in the nineteenth century, and while no territory was permanently occupied, Great

[1] See A. J. Toynbee, *The Western Question in Greece and Turkey,* Houghton Mifflin, 1922; A. J. Toynbee and K. P. Kirkwood, *Turkey,* Scribner, 1927; and Dagobert von Mikusch, *Mustapha Kemal,* Doubleday, Doran, 1931.
[2] See J. de V. Loder, *The Truth About Mesopotamia, Palestine and Syria,* London, 1923; and Ernest Main, *Iraq,* London, 1934.

Britain established a firm hold upon Persian finances and commerce after its advances into this area in 1873, 1887, and 1889. This Anglo-Russian rivalry colored the Allied activity in the Greek War of Independence (1827); contributed to a general European conflict in the Crimean War of 1854-56; encouraged Disraeli's sinister interference with the Treaty of San Stefano in the short-sighted readjustment at the Congress of Berlin (1878); and served as one of the excuses for Great Britain's protection of the "intolerable Turk."

These disputes were finally terminated by the Anglo-Russian agreement of August 31, 1907, partitioning Persia. Northern Persia was put under Russian domination and the southern portion given over to the control of Great Britain. An intermediate neutral zone was created in which both Powers might operate. Germany was placated in part by obtaining the withdrawal of Russian opposition to the Berlin-Baghdad project, while France was partially consoled by the compromise and by the unity thereby effected between its two powerful allies. The Triple Entente came into being herewith.

After the World War Great Britain, erstwhile champion of small nations, taking advantage of Russia's weakness and the Soviet repudiation of its part in the agreement of 1907, extended British influence over that part of Persia formerly dominated by Russia. Through the aid of American interests, however, Persia has been able to maintain its formal political independence, only to be a victim of more extensive economic exploitation, stimulated by the rich oil deposits that have been discovered within Persian boundaries.

Afghanistan was another area of conflict between Russia and Great Britain.[1] In 1865 Turkestan was made a Russian province and was attached to Siberia. Afghanistan stood between Russia and India. So Great Britain, failing to capture it for itself, bent all its energies to maintain the independence of Afghanistan as a buffer state between India and Russian Turkestan. An agreement of 1880 gave Great Britain control over the foreign affairs of Afghanistan. The boundary of this state on the north was adjusted with Russia in 1885 and a possible war thereby averted. In 1907 a further agreement was made between Great Britain and Russia whereby the commercial equality of both states in Afghanistan was guaranteed, Great Britain was left in full control of the foreign affairs of the district, and the immunity of Afghanistan from annexation or occupation was guaranteed. Russian power in this region has waned since the Revolution of 1917, and the Amir has made some progress in obtaining freedom from British domination, receiving at least a recognition of formal independence by the treaty of November, 1922. Afghanistan was admitted to the League of Nations in 1934.

V. GREAT BRITAIN IN INDIA

During the first centuries of the old colonial movement Portugal, Holland, France, and England aspired to control parts of India, but the final rivalry lay between France and Great Britain. By 1803 France was curbed, and during the nineteenth century British occupation of India proceeded. The Mahratta Confederacy, encouraged by France, was overthrown in 1816-18; Nepal was over-

[1] See G. P. Tate, *The Kingdom of Afghanistan*, Bombay, 1911.

come in 1814-18; Burma was conquered in successive portions in 1826, 1852, and 1885; the Sind and Punjab areas were taken over in 1843-49; Sattari, Jhansi, Nagpur, and Oudh were annexed in 1852-56; Baluchistan was added in 1887; while Tibet was successfully "penetrated" in 1904-14. The long-standing difficulties with Russia, especially concerning Afghanistan, were settled by the above-mentioned Anglo-Russian Pact of 1907, and the safety of the Indian frontier was secured. There has been no uniformity in the government of India, some districts being under the direct control of British administrators, while others are ruled nominally by native princes subject to British oversight. The growth of the nationalist movement elsewhere since the early nineteenth century has made millions of Indians determined to achieve self-government. The famous Sepoy Mutiny of 1857 led to the transfer of the government of India from the East India Company to the Crown in 1858.[1] In 1877 Disraeli had Queen Victoria formally declared the Empress of India. The growth of Indian nationalism in the latter part of the nineteenth century led to the Indian Council Acts of 1892 and 1909. These promoted the growth of native representation in both central and local governing bodies. The World War did not bring independence for India, but it did promote to some degree concessions to Indian nationalism. India was allowed representation in Imperial Conferences on something like a parity with the self-governing Dominions and was promised administrative reforms. A notable step here was the India Act of 1919 which created a partly elective Indian Parliament and increased the native participation in government.[2] The most striking manifestation of Indian nationalism since the Sepoy Mutiny has been the Gandhi movement that has developed in the last decade. This is not only a nationalist challenge to British political control, but also an oriental repudiation of occidental industrial and financial methods, from which Britain derives most of its profits in India.[3] The essential character of this Gandhi revolt has been admirably summarized by Professor Shepherd:

According to the great Indian leader, well-nigh universally known as "Mahatma" or "Great Soul" Gandhi, the defects of British administration in his country may be summed up under a variety of heads. They comprise the "exploitation of India's resources for the benefit of Great Britain"; and "ever-increasing military expenditure and a civil service the most expensive in the world; extravagant working of every department in utter disregard of India's poverty; disarmament and consequent emasculation of a whole nation," lest the lives of the handful of British residents be imperilled; "traffic in intoxicating liquors and drugs," especially opium, "for the purpose of sustaining a top-heavy administration; progressively repressive legislation in order to suppress an ever-growing agitation seeking to give expression to a nation's agony," and "degrading treatment of Indians living in the British Dominions," and particularly the Union of South Africa.

Whether justifiable or not, these grievances certainly have strengthened the reaction of India to the impact of the West. Two important political evidences of it, which indicate the rise of a unifying self-consciousness among the articulate ele-

[1] See C. M. P. Cross, *The Development of Self-government in India, 1858-1914*, University of Chicago Press, 1922. [2] D. N. Banerjee, *The Indian Constitution*, Longmans, 1926.
[3] See Romain Rolland, *Mahatma Gandhi*, Century, 1924; and H. T. Muzumdar, *Gandhi versus the Empire*, Universal Publishing Co., 1932.

ments of the population, are the Indian National Congress, a body representative of the numerically preponderant Hindus, and the All-India Moslem League, voicing the sentiments of the powerful Mohammedan minority. This program may be summarized in two words—"swaraj" or self-government, and "swadeshi," or home manufacture. Fundamentally their objects are the same as those sought by Mahatma Gandhi, but the methods proposed for accomplishment differ. The radicals favor the gaining of independence by violent means to the extent of armed insurrection. The moderates look rather to cooperation with the British rulers in the gradual acquisition of self-government on the model of the Dominions and within the British Commonwealth of Nations. Gandhi and his followers, on the other hand, believe neither in violence nor cooperation, trusting to win the British over by appeals to conscience and to the spirit of fair play.[1]

The outcome of the Gandhi challenge cannot be foreseen at this time, though it has at least temporarily lost strength since 1932. Five years ago he and his followers would probably have accepted a grant of Dominion status as satisfactory, but now they demand complete independence. A Round Table Conference in 1932 resulted in a stalemate, with no substantial settlement, though a new constitution for India and greater self-government were promised. For the time being, the British Tory government seems to have suppressed the independence movement.

VI. WESTERN IMPERIALISM IN THE FAR EAST

1. THE WESTERN INTRUSION IN CHINA

The first notable incursion of Europeans into China followed the deplorable Opium War of 1840-42, through which Great Britain, in the Treaty of Nanking, forced China to open four additional important Chinese ports to European trade. The foreign intrusion was continued by the War of 1856-58, waged by the English and French against the Chinese, terminating in the Treaty of Tientsin of 1858, which opened six more Chinese ports to foreign trade and guaranteed the position and safety of foreign traders and missionaries in China. Between 1853 and 1864 the United States and Great Britain aided the Manchus in suppressing a patriotic native insurrection—the Taiping Rebellion. Further extension of foreign control followed the Chino-Japanese War of 1894-95, when the European Powers took from Japan part of its gains in the war. Germany followed the lead of Great Britain and France by seizing the port of Kiaochow in the province of Shantung in 1898, ostensibly as revenge for the murder of two German Catholic missionaries. Financial penetration and exploitation proceeded apace from 1895 to 1900. Finally, by the joint European and American armed intervention of 1900 to suppress the Boxer Revolt, nearly all barriers to Western commerce and economic penetration were removed and China was put under the commercial, and to a considerable extent the fiscal, tutelage of the Western Powers.

At the same time the Western Powers and Japan were also proceeding to encroach upon the Chinese dependencies and to wrest many of these from the Empire. Japan made various advances, beginning in the late nineteenth cen-

[1] W. R. Shepherd, "The Interaction of Europe and Asia: II, Western Ways in Eastern Lands," *World Unity*, January, 1928, p. 253.

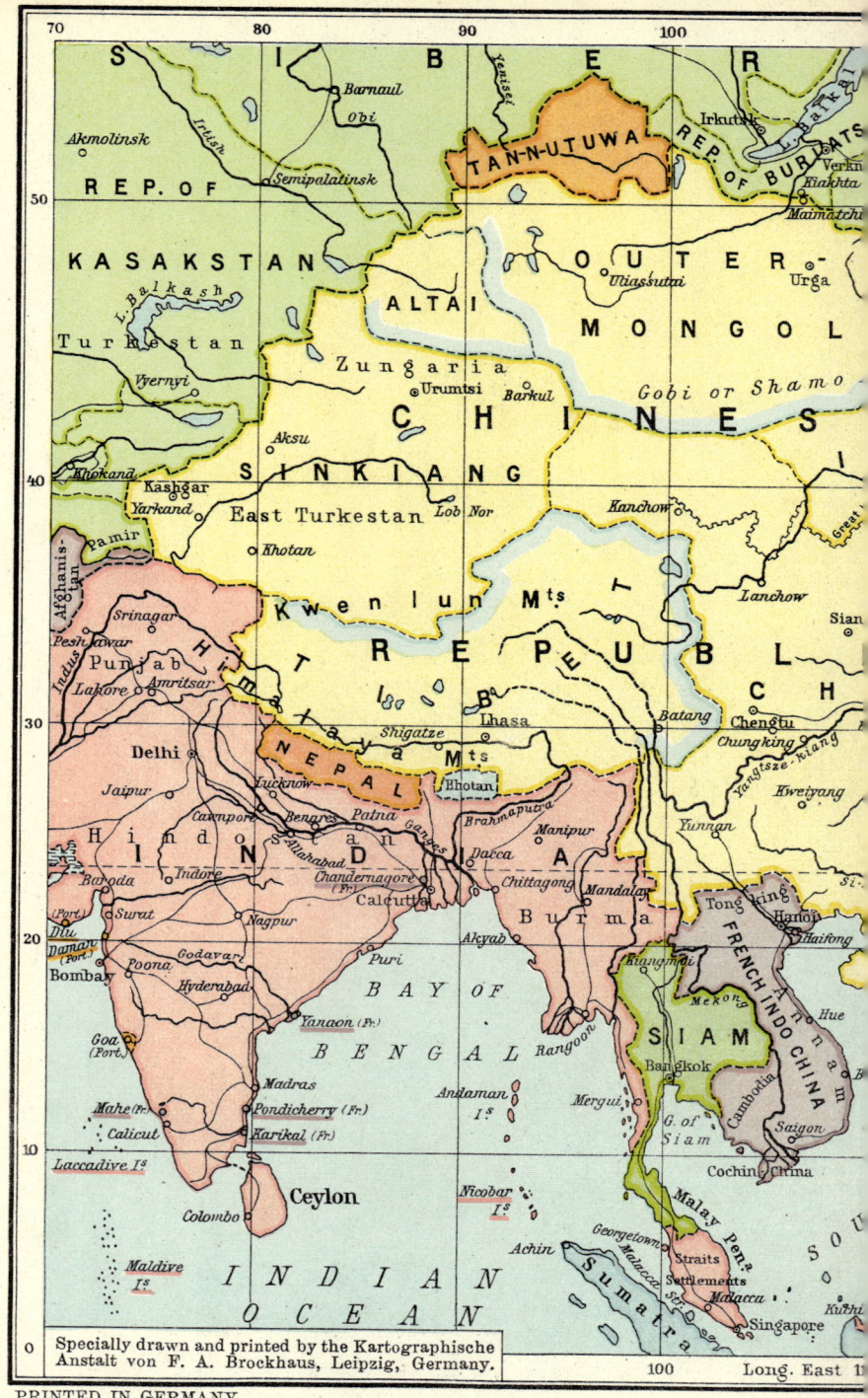

Specially drawn and printed by the Kartographische
Anstalt von F. A. Brockhaus, Leipzig, Germany.

PRINTED IN GERMANY

MAP OF THE FAR EAST

- Chinese Republic
- Russia
- Japan
- British possessions
- French possessions
- Portuguese "
- Dutch "
- United States possessions
- Principal Railways

Scale of Miles along Equator
0 100 200 400 600 800 1000

tury. Russia pushed southward from Siberia, took over Amur in 1860, occupied a portion of Chinese Turkestan in 1881, and threatened outer Mongolia in 1913, after losing its control of South Manchuria and the Liaotung Peninsula through the Russo-Japanese War of 1904-05. The British slowly permeated Tibet between 1904 and 1914, after having conquered Burma in 1885. France occupied eastern Indo-China between 1862 and 1885. Finally, some of the most valuable Chinese ports, such as Hongkong, Port Arthur, Kiaochow, Weihaiwei, and Kwangchanwan were handed over to foreign powers under military pressure.

The increasing strength of Chinese nationalism since the beginning of this century has now become a real challenge to the imperialism of foreign powers. The main reason why China has failed to unite and repel the invaders in recent years has been sectionalism within China itself—a disintegrating force that not even national sentiment can overcome. Under Sun Yat-sen in the South a radical republican government developed after the World War. The North remained more militaristic and monarchical. Of late the southern area has gravitated towards Communism, until today it is estimated that an area with around 100,000,000 inhabitants is now under firm Communist dominion. There are, of course, by no means as many actual Communists as this. The best estimates put the members of the Russian Communist party at about 500,000.[1] China is still involved in civil wars and brigandage, and those who wish to profit by China's weakness are not opposed to applying the method of "divide and rule."

Since the World War Japan has been far more of a menace to Chinese integrity than the Western Powers, though Japan learned its lessons in aggression from these same Western nations. The Chinese have been unable to develop the unity necessary for successful repulsion of Japan. Indeed, it is doubtful if a united China would have been entirely successful in so doing, because of the superior industrialization of Japan and the better Japanese mechanical equipment for war. The main weapon that the Chinese have been able to use against Japan is Chinese boycotting of Japanese goods, especially cotton textiles. One reason for the Japanese invasion of China in 1931 was to break down this boycott.

2. THE AWAKENING OF JAPAN

From 1600 to 1853 European relations with Japan were limited to one very severely restricted trading arrangement with the Dutch. In 1853-54 an American naval officer, Commodore Perry, obtained certain commercial concessions for American ships, and his success prompted other nations to attempt to secure similar privileges. Internal Japanese politics combined with antiforeign feeling to oppose this revival of amicable relations with foreigners. The inland sea was ordered closed to foreigners, and an Englishman, Richardson, was killed. In retaliation the American and European fleets bombarded the ports of Kagoshima and Shimonoseki in 1863 and 1864.

The aggressive action of foreigners proved successful and demonstrated the superiority of occidental material culture. After a political revolution terminating in 1871, drastic reforms were introduced into Japan. As a result, Japan has

[1] *Cf.* Sokolsky, *The Tinder Box of Asia,* Chap. XII; Yakhontoff, *The Chinese Soviets;* and Agnes Smedley, *China's Red Army Marches,* Vanguard Press, 1934.

advanced in less than a half-century from a feudal régime, with an archaic industrial and military technique, to a modern industrial nation, with imperialistic aspirations.

In the process of imperialistic expansion, Japan secured from China the Liukiu Islands in 1874; Formosa was retained from the spoil of the Chino-Japanese War of 1894-95; as a result of the Russo-Japanese War of 1904-05 the Liaotung Peninsula and Port Arthur, as well as southern Sakhalin, were obtained, and Korea and south Manchuria freed from Russian domination; in 1910 Korea was annexed and a political and economic penetration of Manchuria begun. As a result of altogether ineffective participation in the World War, Japan was awarded the German possessions in the Shantung Peninsula, with some political reservations, and the German island possessions in the Pacific north of the equator, including the Caroline, Pelew, Marianne, and Marshall islands. During the war period the notorious Twenty-one (later twenty-four) Demands upon China were in part imposed by Japan from January 18 to May 9, 1915. These meant for all practical purposes the reduction of China to a Japanese protectorate and the essential abrogation of Chinese sovereignty. They also gave Japan special economic advantages of a very important character in China. The Chinese protested bitterly, but their weakness and the involvement of the Western Powers in the World War made the Chinese protests futile.

Some two years later the Lansing-Ishii Agreement was signed, on November 2, 1917. By this the United States, while formally proclaiming that it recognized and continued the policy of an "open door" for China, actually gave up that position and conceded to Japan special interests in China and contiguous Asiatic territory. Thereby we confirmed in practice Japan's claim to a Japanese "Monroe Doctrine" for China, if not for the entire Far East. The Lansing-Ishii Agreement was terminated in 1921, according to the understanding of the United States, but its spirit was revived with much ardor from the Japanese standpoint in a rather defiant speech by the Japanese Foreign Minister in the summer of 1932. The United States has not seen fit to repudiate this revival.

Japan was awarded the Shantung Peninsula at the Paris Peace Conference, but at the Washington Conference of 1921-22 it agreed to evacuate this area. It later carried out its agreement, but in 1928 it took advantage of disorder in the peninsula, reoccupied it in part, and has remained there since.

More dramatic and portentous was the Japanese invasion of Manchuria in 1931 and its subsequent conquest of much of that area. The Western Powers protested through the League of Nations and invoked the Kellogg Pact. Japan defied the League and quite accurately showed that, so long as the British reservations to the Kellogg Pact were allowed to stand, it could not logically try to keep Japan out of an area of "special interest" like Manchuria. A new state called Manchukuo was created out of the territory in Manchuria seized by Japan, and a descendant of the old Manchu dynasty of China was placed on the throne. The state is wholly under the thumb of Japan. This new state has not yet (1935) obtained general recognition. In the winter of 1931-32 Japan invaded and destroyed a part of Shanghai.

The events of the period since 1931 indicate that Japan will be likely to defy any serious Western interference with its free hand in the Far East, especially in China. If it goes too far, however, it may meet with serious resistance from Russian and Chinese Communists. Much friction has developed with Russia over the Chinese Eastern Railroad. Certain powerful capitalistic states of Europe secretly uphold and encourage a strong Japanese policy in the Far East in order to checkmate the increased power and prestige of Communist Russia in this area.

3. THE PHILIPPINE ISLANDS AND AMERICAN INTERESTS IN THE FAR EAST

The Philippine Islands were conquered by Spain in 1571 and from this time to 1898, except for the period 1762-63, when Manila was occupied by the British, they were under Spanish control. As a result of the Spanish-American War, Spain agreed in 1898 to cede the Philippine Islands to the United States on the payment of $20,000,000 and the guarantee of the free entry of Spanish ships into Philippine ports for a period of ten years. In spite of their ability and desire to rule themselves, the United States did not provide for freeing the Philippines until 1932. A chief reason for our reluctance to free the Philippines is that we fear their subsequent occupation by Japan. This might jeopardize our other holdings in the Pacific, and would greatly increase the prestige and strategic power of Japan in this area. As a "Christmas present" the Congress of the United States passed the Hawes-Cutting bill over President Hoover's veto in December, 1932. This looked forward to the eventual freedom of the Philippines. It provided that a constitution must be drawn up which met the approval of the United States. After it had been in successful operation for a period of ten years, independence was to be granted. In the meantime, the islands were to be kept under the economic tutelage of the United States through the provision that the latter country would have control over the tariff regulations. The bill satisfied neither the nationalistic Filipinos nor the liberal citizens of the United States, and its provisions were not carried out. The Philippine legislature rejected the act, throwing the problem back into the Congress of the United States in the session of 1934. A new act, the Tydings-McDuffie Bill, was passed in March, 1934. Although it does not differ much from the Hawes-Cutting Act, the Filipinos appear likely to accept it as the best they can hope for.

In addition to the Philippines the United States possesses in the Pacific and Far Eastern area the Hawaiian Islands, annexed in 1898; the island of Tutuila in the Samoan group, obtained in 1899; an important coaling-station and naval base in Guam, obtained as a result of the Spanish-American War; and access to cable and radio stations on the island of Yap, guaranteed at the Washington Conference of 1921-22. None of these areas, however, figures prominently in contemporary imperialistic developments or controversies.

4. OCEANIA AND AUSTRALASIA

One of the areas of so-called backward races that has been most thoroughly appropriated by Western imperialistic nations is that which includes the islands, greatly varying in size and importance, which are situated south and east of Asia. These are usually divided into two major divisions, Oceania and Australasia. The former is further subdivided into Malaysia, Polynesia, Micronesia, and Melanesia, while the latter is composed of Australia, Tasmania, New Zealand, and the lesser adjacent islands.

Malaysia, sometimes known as the East Indies or the Malay Archipelago, is made up of the islands lying immediately to the southeast of Asia, the most important of which are Sumatra, Java, Borneo, Celebes, New Guinea, and Luzon and Mindanao of the Philippine group. The great majority of these belong to the Dutch, the only exceptions being the Philippines; eastern Timor, belonging to Portugal; the British possessions of Singapore and parts of Borneo and New Guinea; and the former German colony in northeastern New Guinea, formerly known as Kaiser Wilhelms Land.

Polynesia comprises the great majority of the islands of the western and mid-Pacific area, including the Fanning, Ellice, Tokelau, Tonga, Kermadec, and Cook islands, belonging to Great Britain; the Samoan Islands formerly belonging, with the exception of an American naval base, to Germany; the Austral, Society, Tuamotu, and Marquesas islands possessed by France; and the Hawaiian Islands, a territory of the United States.

Micronesia consists of the Marianne, Pelew, Caroline, and Marshall islands, formerly owned by Germany, and the Gilbert Islands possessed by Great Britain. Melanesia comprises the Santa Cruz, Banks, Fiji, D'Entre-Casteaux, and Louisiade islands, belonging to Great Britain; the former German colonies of the Admiralty, Bougainville, and Bismarck islands of the Bismarck Archipelago; the Solomon Islands, owned formerly by Great Britain and Germany; the French possessions of New Caledonia and the Loyalty Islands; and the New Hebrides, owned jointly by France and Great Britain.

The chief significance of the World War in this area was the disposition of the German possessions in Oceania. The Samoan Islands went to New Zealand. In general, the German islands north of the equator were handed over as mandatories to Japan, while those south of the equator were given to Australia.

Australia was scantily explored but claimed as an English possession in 1770 by Captain James Cook. By 1859 some six colonies had developed in Australia and Tasmania: New South Wales, Victoria, Queensland, South Australia, and Tasmania. The conventions of 1897-99 drafted a constitution for Australia, including Tasmania. This was embodied in the Australian Commonwealth Act of 1900, uniting the six colonies into a self-governing unit within the British Empire. The government of Australia combined essentially the federal republican structure of the United States with the British cabinet system of representative government.

From 1769 to 1839 New Zealand was nominally claimed by Great Britain. In 1839 Great Britain formally assumed possession of the region. In 1853 New Zealand was given self-government, and in 1865 it was separated in an administrative sense from Australia. In September, 1907, it was proclaimed the Dominion of New Zealand and renamed as another self-governing colony of the British Empire.

MODERN IMPERIALISM IN THE AMERICAS 541

VII. THE UNITED STATES AND LATIN AMERICA IN MODERN IMPERIALISM

It is obvious that the manifestation of contemporary imperialism most interesting and relevant to Americans is the expansion of American capital and colonial power beyond the old boundaries of the United States.[1] It has often been stated by patriotic orators that the United States is the one state that resolutely stood aloof from the imperialistic orgy of the last half-century. Yet the truth would seem to be that we were conceived in imperialism and dedicated to the principle of expansion. Founded as a phase of the first great period of imperialism and colonialism, ours has always been an imperialistic country from the standpoint of the development of control over new areas and the subjugation of lesser peoples.[2] The growth of our country has been, in one sense, mainly the record of imperialistic efforts and successes.

The history of the United States from 1607 to 1890 is in large part the portrayal of a continually expanding frontier, during which expansion we brought the original Indian population under our control and conquered much of a great continent.[3] This stage ended about 1890, at the very time when we had just passed through the important later stages of the Industrial Revolution. For the first time we had acquired a considerable volume of excess capital, and had developed a greater necessity for markets overseas. In other words, we needed to expand beyond our continental boundaries at the exact moment when we had the resources to do so and were under the control of a political party that was strongly dominated by American industry and finance. In the following summary paragraph Professor Moon gives a graphic statement of the actual extent of the "American Empire," which will doubtless astonish those readers who have not given special attention to imperialism and American expansion:

But if Canada is part of the British Empire, and if Egypt and Iraq are under British control, then by the same standards Cuba, Haiti, the Dominican Republic, Panama, and Nicaragua are to be reckoned as falling in some degree under the control of the United States, for they are subject to military intervention, which Canada is not; their foreign affairs are to some extent submitted to American guidance, or at least to an American veto; their economic life is in considerable measure under American supervision; and they are protected against non-American encroachment quite as genuinely as any French or British protectorate. Liberia may perhaps be added to the list, without serious dispute. Some readers would wish to add other Central American Republics, or Mexico, or Colombia and Venezuela; but these are excluded for the reason that American intervention in their affairs is less formal, less continuous, less analogous to the "protectorates" of European imperialism. Taking then, this fairly conservative list of quasi-dependencies—Cuba, Haiti, Santo Domingo, Panama, Nicaragua, and Liberia—and adding it to the list of territories and possessions, we obtain a grand total that will put the United States colonial empire in sixth place for area, and for population, and in second place for com-

---

[1] See R. G. Adams, *History of the Foreign Policy of the United States*, Macmillan, 1924.
[2] *Cf.* Cheyney, *The European Background of American History*.
[3] *Cf.* H. E. Bolton and T. M. Marshall, *The Colonization of North America, 1492-1783*, Macmillan, 1920; and Paxson, *History of the American Frontier, 1783-1893*.

mercial value. For a non-aggressive nation, the United States has done remarkably well, as compared with rivals candidly intent on imperial expansion. Only Great Britain has done better.[1]

It was natural that we should first turn to Latin America,[2] justifying our action in official rhetoric on the ground of advancing the cause of human justice, but not failing in the process to increase our facilities for investment and to acquire under favorable conditions the valuable natural resources of the extensive lands occupied.

Our intervention in Cuba was not in any sense a novel or accidental affair. We had aided the movement for Cuban independence from Spain, and considered intervention, at various times for more than half a century before 1898. At the end of the century things shaped up in such a way that we took the final step, with no special credit to our diplomatic ethics. From Cuba we extended our economic penetration and political pressure into other parts of Latin America: Mexico, Haiti, Santo Domingo, Nicaragua, Honduras, Salvador, Panama, and the Virgin Islands. During the same period we turned to the Pacific and entered the Hawaiian Islands and the Philippines. The United States also joined with alacrity in the commercial penetration of China.

With the outbreak of the World War came our remarkable investments in Allied bonds and the subsequent European loans, which have made us the most powerful influence in European finance. We now hold foreign securities, exclusive of war debts, to the face value of some $18,000,000,000. With the discovery of rich petroleum resources in Asia Minor and Mesopotamia we have recently interested ourselves in the Near Orient. There is no discernible limit to the nature or extent of our future investments in oversea areas—unless we profit by the lesson afforded by our stupendous losses through default.

The most striking aspects of our recent financial penetration beyond national boundaries are those connected with the expansion of our interests in Canada[3] and Latin America and our increasing importance in European international finance. We have now become the chief foreign investor in Canada; our trade and interests in South America have increased amazingly in about two decades; and Europe looks to our aid and direction in settling its outstanding financial problems, as the formulation of the Dawes and Young reports and the Hoover-Laval Moratorium bear eloquent witness.

Latin America, extending from the southern boundary of the United States to Cape Horn, was explored and settled mainly by the Spanish, with the exception of Portuguese Brazil, the Guianas, and a few French settlements in the West Indies. The trade of the Spanish colonies was regulated by the extremely rigid Spanish mercantilism administered through the so-called House of Trade, which was created in 1503 and extended and systematized during the next half-century.

Dwelling under a corrupt and inefficient officialdom and a stifled commercial activity, the inhabitants of Latin America made little administrative and

---

[1] P. T. Moon, *Imperialism and World Politics,* Macmillan, 1926, pp. 524-25.
[2] Excepting, of course, our purchase of Alaska in 1867.
[3] See H. L. Keenleyside, *Canada and the United States,* Crofts, 1929; and H. A. Innis and A. F. W. Plumptre, *The Canadian Economy and Its Problems,* Canadian Institute of International Affairs, 1934.

political progress until the era of the revolutions following 1810. From this year to 1830 and from 1838 to 1850, with two late additions at the very opening of the twentieth century, Latin America became a group of independent American states. Along with these there are the following foreign possessions: British Guiana, British Honduras, Jamaica, the Bahamas, Barbados, the Leeward and Windward islands, Trinidad, and Tobago controlled by Great Britain; French Guiana, Martinique, and Guadeloupe owned by France; Dutch Guiana, Curaçao, and some lesser islands belonging to Holland; and Puerto Rico and the Virgin Islands possessed by the United States.

The period from 1898 to the present has been conspicuous for the development of international relations in this district, namely: (1) The rise of a distinct Latin-American foreign policy under the direction of the so-called A. B. C. Powers (Argentina, Brazil, and Chile), which has questioned the Monroe Doctrine in Latin America generally and south of the equator in particular; (2) the counter-development of an opposing tendency in the aggressive imperialism of the United States in this region, with a bold extension of the Monroe Doctrine for Latin America; and (3) the attempt to compromise these two conflicting tendencies through the development of the Pan-American movement, which has been in progress since 1880.

The interpretation of the Monroe Doctrine [1] has kept pace with Latin-American progress and the development of the foreign relations of the United States. It originated in Monroe's administration as a warning to European reactionaries that they must not presume to interfere with the internal politics of states in the Western Hemisphere. In the days of Johnson and Grant the policy was extended to inform European nations that they could not annex any more American territory. In Benjamin Harrison's administration this attitude was still further expanded to warn Europeans against attempting to conquer American territory. For a number of years after 1870 we informed European countries of the paramount interest of the United States in an isthmian canal.

In 1903 President Theodore Roosevelt allowed the United States to support a secession party in a Latin-American government in order to secure our dominance in the canal scheme and the completion of the Panama Canal by the United States. Roosevelt stood firmly against territorial aggression by Europeans and declared that when any American state was unable to discharge the duties normally devolving on a civilized state or when it used force on representatives of foreign countries, it was the duty of the United States to intervene to maintain order and keep the peace. Following out this policy, he took over the financial administration of Santo Domingo in 1905, President Taft took similar action with regard to Nicaragua in 1912, and President Wilson did the same with Haiti in 1915.

The furthest extension of the Monroe Doctrine came in connection with Woodrow Wilson's announcement that we would not recognize states north of the equator which had established by force new governments that did not represent the will of the people; and in Coolidge's implication that we would censor the political morality of the Latin-American countries north of the Panama

[1] See D. Y. Thomas, *One Hundred Years of the Monroe Doctrine,* Macmillan, 1927.

Canal. Since 1928, however, the United States has receded markedly in maintaining a strong Monroe Doctrine. Through our interpretation of the doctrine when signing the Kellogg Pact, and in arbitration and conciliation treaties of Pan-American import signed in 1929, we all but nullified the earlier aggressive interpretations of the Monroe Doctrine. At the time of the Pan-American Conference in the winter of 1933-34, President Franklin D. Roosevelt declared our intention of allowing a policy of self-determination to prevail in Latin America. We are not likely, however, to go so far as is demanded by Costa Rica and allow the League of Nations to interpret the Monroe Doctrine.[1] The most remarkable step taken in years in liberalizing our Latin American policy came in May, 1934, when the Roosevelt Administration abrogated the Platt Amendment and gave Cuba the status of complete political independence.

The participation of the United States in the Algeciras Conference in 1906 proved that the older doctrine of the isolation and distinct separation of the two hemispheres was fast giving way before the growth of world commerce and international relations. What remained of this conception after 1906 was practically destroyed by the entry of the United States into the World War. Isolationists may still talk with vehemence, but they cannot obliterate our intervention in Europe, our part in making the peace treaties, or our vast and widely distributed investments abroad. Moreover, our isolationists are more opposed to our intervention abroad in behalf of peace than they are to our imperialistic ventures.

The commercial, and for practical purposes the political, domination of the United States over the Caribbean region and Central America appears to be assured. In line with the establishment of this ascendant position, the United States has retained control of Puerto Rico, has exercised a general supervision over Cuba, has administered the finances of Haiti, Santo Domingo, Nicaragua, and Salvador, has purchased the Virgin Islands from Denmark, has intervened in several Central American states and in Venezuela in the interest of promoting political stability and peace, and has connived at the disruption of Colombia in order to secure the Panama route for the isthmian canal. As Professor Rippy well insists, we "virtually control," in addition to our Puerto Rican colony, Cuba, Haiti, Santo Domingo, Mexico, Nicaragua, Honduras, Costa Rica, Salvador, Guatemala, and Panama, and dominate financially Venezuela and Colombia. There is slight wonder that we are viewed with suspicion and fear by Latin-American states, who look upon our protestations of anti-imperialism as gross hypocrisy.

While the United States dominates Latin America north of the equator in all matters pertaining to capital, industry, and commerce, down to 1914 a similar control was exerted south of the equator by Great Britain, Germany, and France, in the order given. The World War was a hard blow to German interests in South America, but they will probably revive, while those of Great Britain and France are expanding. Especially notable has been the development of the trade and investments of the United States in Colombia and Venezuela and south of the equator since the close of the World War. Our investments here have increased remarkably—nearly 1,000 per cent—since 1918.

[1] For a recent forceful and critical appraisal of the history and present status of the Monroe Doctrine, see Gaston Nerval, *Autopsy of the Monroe Doctrine,* Macmillan, 1934.

VIII. SUMMARY OF IMPERIALISTIC EXPANSION

Perhaps the best summary of the extent of modern imperialism can be offered by the following tables taken from Professor Moon's *Imperialism and World Politics*.[1]

PRESENT-DAY COLONIAL EMPIRES—AREAS

Areas of colonial possessions and protectorates
(in thousands of square miles)

	Africa	Asia	Pacific §§	Americas	Total
British *	4,203	2,126	3,279	4,008	13,616
Russian **		6,400			6,400
French †	3,773	317	10	36	4,136
Portuguese	927	7	1.6		936
Belgian	931				931
United States ††	37		122	752	911
Dutch			734	55	789
Italian	780				780
Spanish	129				132
Japanese §		86	28		114
Total					28,742

* Comprising the Dominions and all parts of the Empire as listed in the *Statesman's Year-Book*, excepting Great Britain and Ireland. Egypt is included, though nominally independent. Mandates are also added.

** Asiatic Russia, estimated, not including portions of Mongolia occupied by Soviet forces.

† Including mandates and Algeria, although the latter is in certain matters considered an integral part of France. Including also the French zone of the Moroccan protectorate.

†† Including Alaska, Hawaii, the Philippine Islands, Puerto Rico, the Virgin Islands, Samoa, Guam, the Wake and Midway Islands, the Panama Canal Zone, Guantanamo, Fonseca Bay, Corn Island, Cuba, Haiti, the Dominican Republic, Panama, Nicaragua, Liberia.

§ Including Chosen and Port Arthur on the mainland; and Formosa, southern Sakhalin, the Pescadores, and the mandated islands in the Pacific. One should add the protectorate, Manchukuo.

§§ Including the Malay Archipelago, Australasia, and all islands of the Pacific.

PRESENT-DAY COLONIAL EMPIRES—POPULATIONS

Populations (in millions) of Colonial Possessions and Protectorates

	Africa	Asia	Pacific	Americas	Total
British	65	333	8	11	417
French	35	23	x	x	59
Dutch			50	x	50
Russian		35			35
Japanese		19	4		23
United States	1.5		11.4	9	22
Belgian	11.5				11.5
Portuguese	8		x	x	9
Italian	1.9				2
Spanish	1				1
Total					630

x indicates population of less than one million.

[1] Moon, *op. cit.*, pp. 515-16.

IX. THE ECONOMICS OF CONTEMPORARY IMPERIALISM

It may safely be said that the guiding motive in contemporary imperialism today is an economic one; that however emphatically the "white man's burden" and the religious motives may be put forward, they are in part only disguises for the economic realities beneath.[1] Africa, the Near and Far East, and South America are vital factors in the industrial and commercial system of the Western world. From them come highly important commodities, including rubber, petroleum, cotton, coffee, cocoa, sugar, hemp, and minerals such as phosphate, manganese, copper, and gold. To them go the manufactured goods, chiefly textiles and iron and steel products, of which the industrialized nations produce a large surplus. As the Western nations become more highly industrialized their needs for a dependable supply of raw materials and a stable market are enhanced.

At the end of the nineteenth century, non-European countries took less than a quarter of the exports of the United States; in 1923, they took almost 50 per cent. During that period, too, the exports to and imports from colonial territories (our own and others) grew at a much more rapid rate than our foreign trade in general. Before the depression and the Gandhi movement England sent each year about $500,000,000 worth of goods to India alone, and imported somewhat less. The trade of the Congo grew from about $10,000,000 at the turn of the century to $44,500,000 in 1924. The trade of Java in 1920 amounted to about $1,500,000,000.

Statistical evidence of the commercial importance of colonies can be multiplied indefinitely. And while by no means all of the trade of the colonies is with the mother country, the latter usually enjoys a large advantage in that trade. Why else should Belgium secure valuable raw materials to the sum of 187,000,000 francs from the Belgian Congo in a year, while only 13,000,000 francs' worth go to England and 17,000,000 to all of America? And why else should America's share of Philippine imports increase from 6 per cent in 1893 to 55 per cent in 1925? And as the competition for markets becomes keener, the emphasis on control is almost certain to increase. Japan's aggressiveness towards China is, primarily, the result of its desire to control the valuable natural resources needed by its expanding industry, and to enjoy a preferential position in the market offered by the vast Chinese population.

Of course, as has already been pointed out, imperialism does not inevitably lead to political intervention or annexation. The United States, in particular, has often ostensibly justified the claims of its political spokesmen by avoiding the onus of political control, while at the same time achieving the actual imperialistic aims.[2] We have intervened in political affairs in Latin America on

---

[1] Of course, one must not overlook the power of political motives, especially patriotism and party gestures, even in recent imperialism. The desire to "keep up with the Joneses" in the international field and to see a lot of the map painted red or blue still persists. Even today, a good deal of the demand for colonies comes from newspapers, political rallies, and beer halls, as well as from banks and directors' offices.

[2] Probably the most skillful fusion of diplomatic decency and the furtherance of economic penetration in modern times is to be noted in the work of Mr. Dwight W. Morrow, in his handling of the Cuban situation after 1921 and his remarkable achievements as ambassador to Mexico from 1927 to 1930.

numerous occasions, and we have established financial receiverships, as for instance in our control of the customs duties in Haiti. But our defenders have illustrated our disinterestedness by pointing out that our intervention has always been temporary, and that we have rarely set up any permanent political control. It would be easy to answer that our ends have been served much better through establishing the measure of economic influence which was desired without taking on the burdens and expenses of political administration. And in large measure this is true.

The economic aspects of imperialism are by no means exhausted by a recitation of trade statistics. Undeveloped areas are also of great significance as avenues for the investment of surplus capital, which is attracted there by the relatively high rates of return.[1] Vast amounts of European capital went into the economic expansion of the United States from 1825 to 1895; and in more recent times, billions of dollars of capital have flowed from Europe and the United States into Africa, the Near East, the Far East, and South America. Coffee plantations, rubber plantations, oil wells, highways and railroads, commercial organizations—these are but a few of the channels into which European and American capital has been turned. The results have not always been profitable, but sometimes the return has been several hundred per cent. It has been estimated that England's investment in India alone before 1914 amounted to close to $2,000,000,000. French investments abroad had reached $10,000,000,000 by 1914; German investments amounted to about $7,000,000,000.[2]

Most startling of all, however, is the story of American foreign investments. In 1900 we had about $500,000,000 invested outside our own boundaries, chiefly in Mexico, Canada, and Cuba.[3] By 1913 this figure had increased to about $2,500,000,000, of which almost half was in Latin America and about one-quarter in Canada.[4] At the same time, however, we owed abroad nearly twice as much.

At the end of the World War, this position had altered completely. A large part of our securities owned abroad had been sold back to us, and at the same time we had advanced enormous sums, mainly to Europe. By 1926 we were the world's creditors to the extent of about $12,000,000,000, not counting war loans.[5] In 1925, the United States held almost $4,000,000,000 in government, state, and municipal bonds of foreign countries, of which the bulk was European; and over $5,000,000,000 of industrial loans, of which over 60 per cent had gone to Latin America, and more than a quarter to Canada. We also have extensive financial interests in Europe, chiefly in the electrical, telephone, automobile, motion-picture, and oil industries.[6] This was partly a natural result of our industrial expansion, but the speed with which it had occurred was due largely to the war and postwar conditions. The remarkable growth of American

---

[1] See Herbert Feis, *Europe, the World's Banker, 1870-1914,* Yale University Press, 1930.
[2] Moon, *op. cit.,* p. 31.
[3] Stuart Chase, New York *Times,* June 27, 1926.
[4] R. W. Dunn, *American Foreign Investments,* Viking Press, 1926; and Feis, *op. cit.*
[5] Chase, *loc. cit.*
[6] See F. A. Southard, Jr., *American Industry in Europe,* Houghton Mifflin, 1931.

investments abroad since 1914 is well presented in the following table (sums in millions of dollars):[1]

Region	1914	1932
Europe	350	5,765
Canada	750	4,601
South America	100	3,079
Central America	1,200	3,015
Australasia	175	1,012
Miscellaneous	50	495
Total	2,625	17,967

Before the war, our financial stake in Canada was about one-fourth that of England; now it is one-third greater than England's. It has even been said that if a war should break out between England and the United States, Canada's economic interests might align it on the side of America. Our investments in Latin America have grown by leaps and bounds, being especially heavy in Mexico, Cuba, Chile, and Argentina. While a large part of these investments has gone into mining, railways, public utilities, and oil, a considerable fraction has been put into state and municipal bonds.

From 1914 to 1929 the American public bought widely, optimistically, and indiscriminately almost any foreign securities offered, and American companies made heavy investment in plant and equipment, particularly in the South American countries. By the end of 1929 our investments abroad had reached the astonishing total of nearly $18,000,000,000.

Since 1929 the day of reckoning has come, and the United States is beginning to count the cost of becoming banker to the world. In excess of $6,000,000,000 of our investments, exclusive of war debts, are now in default, and the sum is mounting rapidly as compound interest piles up. No small part of this loss, the bulk of which falls on the individual investor, must be counted a cost of our imperialistic tendencies.[2]

The United States is not the only country, however, to discover that the imperialistic ledger has a heavy debit side. Libya, a relatively barren country, cost Italy nearly $600,000,000 up to 1924, and the trade amounts to less than the annual deficit in the cost of administration.[3] The Boer War, undertaken chiefly because of England's imperialistic ambition, cost that country 30,000 lives and £250,000,000.[4] And every country with imperialistic leanings has undergone similar heavy costs, among which must be counted a share of the upkeep of army and navy, maintained partly to protect the colonial empire. If imperialism be regarded, as it rightly should be, as a major cause of the World War, then a part of the colossal costs of that conflict must be assessed against it. Against these costs, which sometimes mount staggeringly, are to be placed the considerable gains in trade and the imponderable known as "national prestige," which finds not its least important expression in the colorings of a map of the world showing the extent of the colonial domain.

---

[1] The figures are taken from Max Winkler, *Foreign Bonds: An Autopsy*, Swain, 1933, p. xiv.
[2] See Winkler, *op. cit.*   [3] Moon, *op. cit.*, p. 223.   [4] *Ibid.*, p. 180, note 2.

THE ECONOMICS OF CONTEMPORARY IMPERIALISM 549

The depression beginning in 1929 has put a severe crimp in imperialism and the export of capital, as well as reduced the income from oversea investments. We have just noted the extensive defaulting on American investments abroad. This has not only lessened the income of American investors but has also discouraged further investment. The moratorium of 1932 was in part a recognition of this state of affairs. The citizens of other countries have suffered likewise from the defaulting on bonds by foreign countries. The falling-off of income from oversea investments is well illustrated by the case of England. The income from oversea investments was estimated as £285,000,000 in 1928, as £165,000,000 in 1930, and as £155,000,000 in 1933. It has fallen off even more since.

X. IMPERIALISM AND THE WORLD WAR

The relation of the expansionist movement to the state of mind that brought on the World War will be apparent from a bare summary of the international friction that it created. England and Germany clashed over territory in Africa and over the German attitude towards the British policy in dealing with the Boers; in Oceania, concerning the Samoan and other islands; and in Asia Minor, over the attempt of Germany to develop Mesopotamia and Asia Minor generally. England and Russia were led by jealousy over territory in the Near East into a bloody war in the middle of the century and nearly to another in 1878 and 1884; and mutual aggression in Afghanistan and Persia ended without war only through a parceling-out of the territory between them. England and France, after earlier friction over northern Egypt, came near to war over the Fashoda incident in 1898, and hostility was here averted solely by a redistribution of colonial ambitions and diplomatic alignments.

Germany and France threatened the peace of Europe thrice over Morocco before the matter was even temporarily adjusted. The rivalry of Germany and Russia in western Asia was not wholly settled by the "Willy-Nicky" correspondence or the convention of 1911; while the conflict between *Mittel-Europa* and Panslavic plans, and the mutual rivalry over Turkey, stimulated the diplomatic crisis that precipitated the war. Germany and the United States clashed over the Samoan Islands and in regard to the American conquest of the Philippines. Italy broke its long friendship with France over the latter's annexation of Tunis and made war on Turkey to secure Tripolitania after being sharply held up in Abyssinia. Russia and Japan fought over eastern Asiatic ports and Manchuria. Finally, the "glory" of the war with Spain served the better to prepare the United States to enter upon the World War.

Another important way in which imperialism helped on the World War was the contribution that it made to the creation of the great conflicting alliances in Europe that were thrown together in carnage in 1914. The writer does not subscribe to the theory that the existence of the Triple Alliance and the Triple Entente made a world-war inevitable, but it certainly made such a conflict far more likely, given the general setting of European politics in 1914.

Imperialism contributed its share to the coming of the great conflict: (1) Through the rivalry of the commercial empires of Great Britain and Germany;

(2) through British jealousy of German advances in the Near Orient; (3) through naval rivalry due to the naval increases believed to be essential to protect national commerce and colonies; (4) through French colonial ambitions as a compensation for European defeat; and (5) through the Russian desire to secure unimpeded access through, or complete control of, the Straits leading out of the Black Sea. Nationalism and imperialism welded the opposing alliances and turned Europe into an armed camp. When the crisis came in the summer of 1914 the forces and personalities favoring war triumphed over those which worked for peace.

The eminent English economist J. A. Hobson has admirably summarized the combined effects of capitalism, nationalism, and imperialism in creating the state of mind, attitudes, and policies that inevitably produced the World War, given the existing state of international relations and diplomatic methods.

> We have seen these two dominant forces emerging and moulding the course of actual events. Nationalism and capitalism in secret conjunction produced independent, armed and opposed powers within each country, claiming and wielding a paramountcy, political, social, and economic, within the nation and working for further expansion outside. This competition of what may fairly be called capitalist states, evolving modern forms of militarism and protectionism, laid the powder trains. The dramatic antithesis of aggressive autocracies and pacific democracies in recent history is false, and the failure to discern this falsehood explains the great surprise. Nowhere had the conditions of pacific democracy been established. Everywhere an inflamed and aggrandizing nationalism had placed the growing powers of an absolute state (absolute alike in its demands upon its citizens and in its attitude to other states) at the disposal of powerful oligarchies, directed in their operations mainly by clear-sighted business men, using the political machinery of their country for the furtherance of their private interests.[1]

In a later chapter we shall examine in more detail the cultural and diplomatic background of the World War.[2] This will enable us to arrive at a more precise estimate of the divers ways in which nationalism, capitalism, and imperialism coöperated to make the World War possible, even if they did not necessarily make it inevitable. Certainly, it is in the effects of nationalism and imperialism that we must seek the dynamic background of the diplomacy of 1870 to 1914.

XI. IMPERIALISM AND WORLD-POLITICS AFTER THE WORLD WAR

The chief effect of the World War on the course of modern imperialism was the capture of the German oversea possessions and their redistribution among the victorious Entente Powers. The imperialistic ambitions of the Entente, as embodied in the secret treaties, were substantially realized, though the details of the distribution of the German possessions were modified to a slight degree. In Africa the German colonies were divided between France and the British Empire as mandated territories. The major part of Togoland and Kamerun was given to France and the remainder to Great Britain. German Southwest Africa was placed under the Union of South Africa. German East Africa was awarded

---

[1] Hobson, "Why the War Came as a Surprise," *Political Science Quarterly,* September, 1920, p. 357.
[2] See below, Chapter XVII.

to Great Britain, with the exception of a small but rich portion—less than a tenth of the whole—Ruanda-Urundi, which was given to Belgium. Great Britain reduced Egypt to a literal protectorate. Turkey in Asia was partitioned, and most of the German interests in the Near East were absorbed by France and Great Britain. The latter took over Mesopotamia, which was organized under the quasi-mandate of Iraq. France took over Syria as a mandate. Palestine became a British mandate. Arabia, ostensibly independent, is under British control. The British virtually took over Persia upon the withdrawal of Russia from its sphere of interest in northern Persia. Persia has since, in part, regained its freedom.

The German interests in the Shantung Peninsula were awarded to Japan, although the latter agreed at the Washington Conference of 1921-22 to return them to China, which it later did for a time. The German island possessions in the Pacific Ocean were divided between Japan, Australia, New Zealand, and Great Britain. There were no German possessions in the New World, but the United States followed the European example of confiscating German property and patents. In short, the German Empire overseas disappeared as a result of the World War, and France and England gained elsewhere, notably at the expense of Turkey and Egypt.

The ideal of national self-determination could in some cases be invoked to justify the changes made in the map of Europe, but nothing beyond selfish interest could be alleged to defend the seizure of the German colonies. Of course, the Entente advanced the preposterous claim that the Germans deserved to forfeit their colonies because of their cruel and inefficient administration of these colonies, but this argument could impress only the ignorant and the self-righteous. The German colonial administration was far from perfect, but by 1914 it matched in wisdom, efficiency and moderation the British and French administration of peoples of comparable cultural and economic development.

Some writers have justified the procedure of the peacemakers at Paris in depriving Germany of its colonies on the ground that this made possible the establishment of the mandate system.[1] It may readily be conceded that the mandate system is preferable to the old national colonial system. This fact would, however, warrant the wholesale termination of the old system and the placing of the colonies of all the modern nations under the supervision of the Mandate Commission. If the mandate device was justifiable in relation to the German colonies, then it should have been extended to all other colonies.

The World War, the postwar treaties, and the League of Nations have exerted no appreciable influence in the way of restraining the progress of capitalistic imperialism, which was so potent a cause of the war. The same struggle for raw materials, markets, and capital investment goes merrily on. Indeed, the developments and investments since 1918 have far outdistanced anything known in any decade before 1914. The details of the struggle have, however, changed markedly. It is now more a contest between Great Britain and the United States than one between Great Britain and Germany. Japan and Italy have become more vigorous contenders for empire. Likewise, the struggle for raw materials is primarily over relatively novel products that

[1] See below, pp. 552 ff.

did not figure so prominently before 1914—petroleum and rubber. But the general nature of the process remains unchanged.

The struggle between Great Britain and the United States in Latin America is now far more keen than the conflict of interests between Germany and the United States in that area before 1914. The duel of Great Britain and the United States over the oil reserves of the Near East promises, with the next oil shortage, to be as bitter as was the contention of Germany and Great Britain over the Berlin-Baghdad Railway enterprise. Conciliatory and coöperative attitudes are as infrequent as in the old days. There is no prospect of any immediate internationalizing of raw materials, and the struggle for markets and investments is bound to become more intense. The tariff situation is far more nationalistic and protective than it was before the war.[1] Great Britain has temporarily gone over to the protectionist system and the United States proudly presents the highest tariff schedules in our history in spite of the fairly liberal views of Secretary Hull. If imperialism was a potential cause of war in 1914, it certainly remains such today on an even larger scale. The League of Nations is as powerless to curb imperialism as it is to check the dynamic factor behind imperialism, namely, modern capitalism. Japan openly defied both the League of Nations and the protest of the United States in 1931 and thereafter in its occupation of a large portion of Manchuria. The only way in which the League has affected or can affect imperialism lies in its minor and indirect capacity as a formal supervisory trustee of the territories taken from Germany, Turkey, and Arabia after the World War. This brings us to a discussion of the mandate question.

In his brochure *The League of Nations,* published in 1918,[2] General J. C. Smuts suggested that the national minorities taken from the Central Powers after the war should be subject to international scrutiny and supervision. His proposition was applied by President Wilson to colonial areas and later elaborated into the so-called mandate system, as embodied in Article 22 of the Covenant of the League of Nations:

> To those colonies and territories which as a consequence of the late war have ceased to be under the sovereignty of the States which formerly governed them and which are inhabited by peoples not yet able to stand by themselves under the strenuous conditions of the modern world, there should be applied the principle that the well-being and development of such peoples form a sacred trust of civilisation and that securities for the performance of this trust should be embodied in this Covenant.
>
> The best method of giving practical effect to this principle is that the tutelage of such peoples should be entrusted to advanced nations who by reason of their resources, their experience, or their geographical position can best undertake this responsibility, and who are willing to accept it, and that this tutelage should be exercised by them as Mandatories on behalf of the League.
>
> The character of the mandates must differ according to the state of the development of the people, the geographical situation of the territory, its economic conditions and other similar circumstances.
>
> In every case of mandate, the Mandatory shall render to the Council an annual report in reference to the territory committed to its charge.

---

[1] See below, pp. 769 ff., and B. B. Wallace and L. R. Edminster, *International Control of Raw Materials,* Brookings Institution, 1930.   [2] Nation Press.

The degree of authority, control, or administration to be exercised by the Mandatory shall, if not previously agreed upon by the Members and the League, be explicitly defined in each case by the Council.

A permanent Commission shall be constituted to receive and examine the annual reports of the Mandatories and to advise the Council on all matters relating to the observance of the mandates.

The mandated territory is by no means negligible either in area or in population. It is two-fifths as large as the United States in area and has a population more than half that of France. The distribution of the mandated regions among the victor states is revealed by the following figures:

MANDATED AREAS

	Area in square miles	Population
Britain	608,000	9,228,000
France	260,000	5,440,000
Belgium	20,000	5,000,000
Australia	93,000	404,000
South Africa	322,000	275,000
New Zealand	1,200	44,000
Japan	800	70,000
Total	1,305,000	20,261,000

The scrutiny and supervision of mandated territory is intrusted to the Mandates Commission, made up of eleven members, six of whom must be drawn from states that do not hold mandates. They serve for an indeterminate period. A member of the International Labor Organization serves with the Mandates Commission in an advisory capacity in matters relating to labor conditions in these areas.

The mandated territory is divided into three classes of mandates. The first class, or A Mandates, represent territory settled by advanced peoples and entitled to the right of local self-government. They are all found in the Near East: (1) Syria, a French mandate; and (2) Palestine and Iraq (Mesopotamia), British mandates. The B Mandates are made up of more backward areas administered under the supervision of the mandatory power. They are: (1) French and British Togoland; (2) French and British Kamerun; (3) British East Africa; and (4) Ruanda-Urundi, a Belgian mandate. The C Mandates are those which, for one reason or another, are ruled as integral parts of the mandatory states. They are made up of: (1) German Southwest Africa, a mandate of the Union of South Africa; (2) Samoa, a mandate of New Zealand; (3) Nauru Island, a British mandate; (4) the German islands south of the equator, mandates of Australia; and (5) the German islands north of the equator, mandates of Japan. Dr. Raymond Leslie Buell has estimated that the total mandated territory has a total annual trade of about $166,000,000.

The mandated territories have certain rights guaranteed by the League. The A Mandates are to be treated as states having general autonomy in matters of local self-government. The B and C Mandates are guaranteed: (1) Freedom of conscience and religion, in so far as these agree with the Christian conception of what constitutes morals and public order; (2) protection from such abuses as the slave trade, the sale of firearms, and the liquor traffic; and (3) freedom from military training and service aside from police duties.

The matter of supervision and the actual insurance of the execution of these guarantees is complicated by the fact that the ultimate authority resides in the Council of the League, in which the mandatory powers are ascendant. Another weakness of the mandate system is the inability of the Mandates Commission to subpoena witnesses and make investigations on the spot. Further, France has been allowed to set a dangerous precedent by introducing some military service in its African mandates. Nevertheless, the system has thus far worked in a fairly successful manner. France, Great Britain, and the Union of South Africa have been disciplined. An unwise choice of a French High Commissioner for Syria was made when the Herriot ministry chose General Sarrail for the post. He infuriated the Druses, and in the attempt to suppress the rebellion the French severely bombarded the ancient and precious city of Damascus.[1] The Mandates Commission presented a dignified but severe criticism of the French administration of Syria and General Sarrail was recalled, to be replaced by a more liberal and statesmanlike High Commissioner, Senator Henri de Jouvenel, who was reasonably successful in readjusting matters, though he, too, bombarded Damascus.

In drawing the Ruanda frontier between the Belgian and British mandates the British arranged the boundary in the interests of the best right of way for the Cape-to-Cairo Railroad. In doing so they fatally divided the native tribes of Ruanda. Missionaries in the area protested to the Mandates Commission and the latter induced Belgium and Great Britain to rectify the injustice in 1923. In 1921 the Union of South Africa levied an excessively high dog tax on Southwest Africa, and the Bondelzwarts tribe rebelled. The revolt was suppressed by the Union by modern methods of warfare, including bombing from airplanes, killing many natives. A Haitian representative at the League protested and the Mandates Commission investigated the affair, severely criticizing the administration of the Union of South Africa in this episode.

A more serious challenge to the mandate system may arise incident to the revival of German interest in the former German colonial possessions. A considerable agitation has recently developed in Germany for their restoration. This is led by Dr. Heinrich Schnee, the former Governor of German East Africa and an authority on modern imperialism and colonization.

As things now stand, there is little possibility that the League will seriously consider the German contentions, but with a marked realignment of European diplomacy the issue might well become a live and practical one. If Hitler gains enough European allies, the issue of returning the German colonies is bound to be revived with determination. Of course, a more statesmanlike move than the return of the German colonies would be to transform all colonies below the self-governing class into mandates. It is certainly smug hypocrisy for the Entente powers to declare their satisfaction with the mandate system and then limit its operation to the colonies seized from Germany and Turkey.

[1] Not restrained, it would appear, by earlier French indignation over the German bombardment of Reims.

SUGGESTED READING

Hammerton, *Universal History of the World,* Chaps. 162, 165, 167, 172-73
H. E. Barnes, *World Politics in Modern Civilization,* Knopf, 1930, Chaps. IX-XI
Flick, *Modern World History,* Pt. VII
P. T. Moon, *Imperialism and World Politics,* Macmillan, 1926
H. A. Gibbons, *Introduction to World Politics,* Century, 1922, Chaps. I-XX, XXVII-XXXIV, XLII-XLVI
R. L. Buell, *International Relations,* Holt, 1925, Pt. II
F. L. Schuman, *International Politics,* McGraw-Hill, 1933, Chaps. X-XV
C. H. Patton, *The Business of Missions,* Macmillan, 1924
C. B. Fawcett, *A Political Geography of the British Empire,* Ginn, 1933
N. D. Harris, *Europe and Africa,* Houghton Mifflin, 1927
―― *Europe and the East,* Houghton Mifflin, 1926
L. S. Woolf, *Empire & Commerce in Africa,* London, 1919
E. M. Earle, *Turkey, the Great Powers and the Bagdad Railway,* Macmillan, 1923
W. E. Hocking, *The Spirit of World Politics,* Macmillan, 1932
H. H. Dodwell, *Sketch of the History of India from 1858 to 1918,* Longmans, 1925
Cumming, *Modern India*
A. C. Osburn, *Must England Lose India?* Knopf, 1930
Savel Zimand, *Living India,* Longmans, 1928
Vinacke, *History of the Far East in Modern Times*
Barnes, *Empire in the East*
Remer, *Foreign Investments in China*
Eldridge, *Dangerous Thoughts on the Orient*
J. F. Rippy, *Latin America in World Politics,* Crofts, 1931
Jones, *The Commerce of South America*
F. A. Southard, Jr., *American Industry in Europe,* Houghton Mifflin, 1931
Max Winkler, *Foreign Bonds: An Autopsy,* Swain, 1933
Scott Nearing and Joseph Freeman, *Dollar Diplomacy,* Viking Press, 1925
Hiram Motherwell, *The Imperial Dollar,* Brentano's, 1929
Kemper Simpson, *Introduction to World Economics,* Harper, 1934
Quincey Wright, *Mandates Under the League of Nations,* University of Chicago Press, 1930
Webster, *Historical Selections,* Sec. XXII
Robinson and Beard, *Readings in Modern European History,* Vol. II, Chap. XXX
McMullen, *Building the World Society,* Chaps. III, VI, VIII

FURTHER REFERENCES

THE COURSE OF MODERN IMPERIALISM. HISTORICAL BACKGROUND. On the oversea expansion since 1870, see Muir, *The Expansion of Europe,* Chaps. VI-IX; H. E. Barnes, *op. cit.,* Chaps. IX-XI; Gibbons, *op. cit.;* Moon, *op. cit.*

On the motives of imperialism, see Moon, *op. cit.,* Chap. IV; Buell, *op. cit.,* Chap. XIII; Hammerton, *op. cit.,* Chap. 175; Simpson, *op. cit.*

On religious motives for developing oversea areas, see K. L. P. Martin, *Missionaries and Annexation in the Pacific* (Oxford Press, 1924); MacDonald, *Trade Politics and Christianity in Africa and the East;* Chaps. XIX-XX, XXV-XXVI, of K. S. Latourette, *History of Christian Missions in China* (Macmillan, 1929).

MODERN IMPERIALISM. On the benevolence and unselfishness versus the brutality and heartlessness of modern imperialism, compare, for example, Seeley, *The Expansion of England,* and Muir, *op. cit.,* Chaps. III, VI, VIII, with R. W. Fox, *The*

Colonial Policy of British Imperialism (International Publishers, 1934), J. A. Hobson, *Imperialism* (Pott, 1902), and Woolf, *op. cit.*

IMPERIALISM IN AFRICA. On imperialism and colonization in Africa, see H. L. Hoskins, *European Imperialism in Africa* (Holt, 1930); Helmolt, *History of the World,* Vol. III, Chap. III; Sir C. P. Lucas, *The Partition and Colonization of Africa* (Oxford Press, 1922); Harris, *Europe and Africa;* Woolf, *op. cit.;* R. L. Buell, *The Native Problem in Africa* (Macmillan, 1928, 2 vols.); E. D. Morel, *The Black Man's Burden* (Huebsch, 1920).

On the progress of imperialism in the Congo, see Harris, *op. cit.,* Chaps. II-III; A. B. Keith, *The Belgian Congo and the Berlin Act* (Oxford Press, 1919); E. D. Morel, *King Leopold's Rule in Africa* (London, 1904). On German imperialism in Africa, see Harris, *op. cit.,* Chaps. IV-V; M. E. Townsend, *The Rise and Fall of Germany's Colonial Empire, 1884-1918* (Macmillan, 1930); Heinrich Schnee, *German Colonization Past and Future* (Knopf, 1926).

On South Africa, see Harris, *op. cit.,* Chap. VIII; R. I. Lovell, *The Struggle for South Africa, 1875-1899* (Macmillan, 1934); J. A. Hobson, *The War in South Africa* (Macmillan, 1900); Goodfellow, *Modern Economic History of South Africa;* P. A. Silburn, *South Africa* (London, 1926); J. H. Hofmeyr, *South Africa* (Scribner, 1931).

On Egypt, see C. W. Hallberg, *The Suez Canal* (Columbia University Press, 1931); Harris, *op. cit.,* Chap. XIV; Edward Dicey, *The Story of the Khedivate* (Scribner, 1902); Sir V. G. Chirol, *The Egyptian Problem* (Macmillan, 1920); G. A. (Lord) Lloyd, *Egypt Since Cromer* (Macmillan, 1933-4, 2 vols.).

On the Sudan, see Harris, *op. cit.,* Chap. XV; P. F. Martin, *The Sudan in Evolution* (London, 1921).

On French imperialism in Africa, see Woolf, *op. cit.,* Pt. II; Harris, *op. cit.,* Chaps. VI, X-XII; S. H. Roberts, *History of French Colonial Policy (1870-1925)* (London, 1929, 2 vols.).

On Italy in Africa, see Harris, *op. cit.,* Chap. XIII; W. K. McClure, *Italy in North Africa* (Winston, 1914).

IMPERIALISM IN PERSIA AND THE NEAR ORIENT. On Persia, see W. M. Shuster, *The Strangling of Persia* (Century, 1912); E. G. Browne, *The Persian Revolution of 1905-1909* (Putnam, 1910); Vincent Sheean, *The New Persia* (Century, 1927); Millspaugh, *The American Task in Persia.*

On the Near Orient since the World War, see Hocking, *op. cit.;* J. A. Spender, *The Changing East* (Stokes, 1926).

INDIA. On modern India, see Hammerton, *op. cit.,* Chap. 167; E. A. Horne, *The Political System of British India* (Oxford Press, 1922); V. A. Smith, *Oxford History of India* (2d ed. rev., Oxford Press, 1928); E. J. Thompson, *Reconstructing India* (Dial Press, 1930); A. D. Innes, *Short History of the British in India* (London, 1902); Dodwell, *op. cit.;* Spender, *op. cit.;* Sir V. G. Chirol, *India, Old and New* (Macmillan, 1921).

For excellent descriptions of contemporary India, see Cumming, *op. cit.;* Monica Whatley and others, *The Condition of India* (Universal Publishing Co., 1934). Osburn, *op. cit.,* is a severe indictment of British rule by a British army officer long resident in India. On the Gandhi movement, see Muzumdar, *Gandhi versus the Empire;* Pyarelal, *The Epic Fast* (Universal Publishing Co., 1934).

WESTERN IMPERIALISM IN THE FAR EAST. D. E. Owen, *Imperialism and Nationalism in the Far East* (Holt, 1929); Helmolt, *op. cit.,* Vol. II, Chap. I; S. K. Hornbeck, *Contemporary Politics in the Far East* (Appleton, 1919); King-Hall, *Western Civilization and the Far East;* Barnes, *Empire in the East;* A. N. Holcombe, *The Chinese Revolution* (2d ed., Harvard University Press, 1931); Eldridge, *Trading with Asia;* Harris, *Europe and the East;* H. B. Morse and H. F. MacNair, *Far Eastern International Problems* (Houghton Mifflin, 1931); P. J. Treat, *The Far East* (Harper, 1928); Tyler Dennett, *Americans in Eastern Asia* (Macmillan, 1922); Etienne Dennery, *Asia's Teeming Millions* (Cape, 1931).

On China since the World War, see R. T. Pollard, *China's Foreign Relations, 1917-1931* (Macmillan, 1933); Bruno Lasker, ed., *Problems of the Pacific* (University of Chicago Press, 1932); Tyau, *China Awakened;* C. F. Remer, *A Study of Chinese Boycotts* (Johns Hopkins Press, 1933).

On Japan since the War, see Rikitaro Fujisawa, *The Recent Aims and Political Development of Japan* (Yale University Press, 1923); Eldridge, *op. cit.;* Wildes, *Japan in Crisis;* S. L. Gulick, *Toward Understanding Japan* (Macmillan, 1935).

On Manchuria and Manchukuo, see P. H. Clyde, *International Rivalries in Manchuria, 1689-1922* (Ohio State University Press, 1926); G. F. Sokolsky, *The Tinder Box of Asia* (Doubleday, Doran, 1932); Sherwood Eddy, *The World's Danger Zone* (Farrar & Rinehart, 1932); K. K. Kawakami, *Manchoukuo, Child of Conflict* (Macmillan, 1933); G. B. Rea, *The Case for Manchoukuo* (Appleton-Century, forthcoming).

On the Philippines, see D. P. Barrows, *History of the Philippines* (World Book Co., 1924); D. R. Williams, *The United States and the Philippines* (Doubleday, Page, 1924); W. C. Forbes, *The Philippine Islands* (Houghton Mifflin, 1929, 2 vols.); H. B. Hawes, *Philippine Uncertainty* (Century, 1932); H. H. Miller and C. H. Storms, *Economic Conditions in the Philippines* (new ed., Ginn, 1920); J. S. Reyes, *Legislative History of America's Economic Policy towards the Philippines* (Longmans, 1923).

For a good discussion of contemporary American imperial interests and policies in the Far East, see E. M. Patterson, ed., *American Policy in the Pacific* (American Academy of Political and Social Science, *Annals,* Vol. CLXIX, 1933); Nathaniel Peffer, *Must We Fight in Asia?* (Harper, 1935).

On Oceania, see Helmolt, *op. cit.,* Vol. II, Chap. III, pp. 299 ff.; K. L. P. Martin, *op. cit.;* G. H. Scholefield, *The Pacific; Its Past and Future* (Scribner, 1919); G. H. Blakeslee, *The Pacific Area* (World Peace Foundation, 1929); P. H. Clyde, *Japan's Pacific Mandate* (Macmillan, 1935).

On Australia and New Zealand, see Edward Jenks, *History of the Australian Colonies* (3d ed. rev., Putnam, 1912); Helmholt, *op. cit.,* Vol. II, Chap. III; Hancock, *Australia;* Shann, *Economic History of Australia;* Condliffe, *Short History of New Zealand* and *New Zealand in the Making.*

On Canada, see H. L. Keenleyside, *Canada and the United States* (Crofts, 1929); C. F. Wittke, *History of Canada* (Crofts, 1928); Innis and Plumptre, *The Canadian Economy and Its Problems.*

THE UNITED STATES AND LATIN AMERICA IN MODERN IMPERIALISM. Shepherd, *Latin America;* J. F. Rippy, *The Historical Evolution of Hispanic America* (Crofts, 1932); and *Latin America in World Politics;* J. F. Normano, *The Struggle for South America* (Houghton Mifflin, 1931). A series of volumes on American financial penetration in Latin America has been edited by H. E. Barnes, namely, L. H. Jenks, *Our Cuban Colony* (1928); M. M. Knight, *The Americans in Santo Domingo* (1928); M. C. A. Marsh, *The Bankers in Bolivia* (1928); B. W. and Justine Diffie, *Porto Rico: A Broken Pledge* (1931); J. F. Rippy, *The Capitalists and Colombia* (1931); and Charles Kepner, Jr., and Jay Soothill, *The Banana Empire* (1935). All are published by the Vanguard Press under the auspices of the American Fund for Public Service. Another study, originally intended as a volume in the same Series, has been published in part by R. R. Hill under the title, *Fiscal Intervention in Nicaragua* (privately printed, 1933). It contains much authoritative information but is regarded by some as overly favorable to the State Department and the bankers.

For a splendid analysis of the diplomacy of the Spanish-American War, see Chap. III of J. F. Rhodes, *The McKinley and Roosevelt Administrations* (Macmillan, 1922). For a good realistic account of the war, see Millis, *The Martial Spirit*.

THE ECONOMICS OF CONTEMPORARY IMPERIALISM. Buell, *op. cit.*, Chaps. XVII-XVIII; Achille Viallate, *Economic Imperialism and International Relations* (Macmillan, 1923); Nearing and Freeman, *op. cit.*; Motherwell, *op. cit.*; H. F. Fraser, *Foreign Trade and World Politics* (Knopf, 1926); Eldridge, *op. cit.*; J. C. Lawrence, *The World's Struggle with Rubber, 1905-1931* (Harper, 1931); Louis Fischer, *Oil Imperialism* (International Publishers, 1926); C. K. Leith, *World Minerals and World Politics* (Whittlesey House, 1931); Remer, *op. cit.*; Simpson, *op. cit.*; B. B. Wallace and L. F. Edminster, *International Control of Raw Materials* (Brookings Institution, 1930); Frank Tannenbaum, *Whither Latin America?* (Crowell, 1934).

IMPERIALISM AFTER THE WORLD WAR. Moon, *op. cit.*, Chaps. XVII-XVIII; Chaps. IV, IX, XI-XII, XXI, of W. C. Langsam, *The World since 1914* (Macmillan, 1933); Chaps. VII-IX, XXII-XXIII, of F. L. Benns, *Europe since 1914* (rev. ed., Crofts, 1934); Townsend, *op. cit.*, Chap. XII.

For a judicious discussion of the German colonial question, see Chaps. XI-XIII of W. H. Dawson, *Germany under the Treaty* (Longmans, 1933); Townsend, *op. cit.*, Chap. XII; and for the German case, Schnee, *op. cit.*

On the postwar Anglo-American rivalry, see Ludwell Denny, *America Conquers Britain* (Knopf, 1930).

On the imperial aggressiveness of Germany, Italy and Japan today, see Simonds and Emeny, *The Price of Peace*.

On the mandate system, see Moon, *op. cit.*, Chap. XVIII; Buell, *op. cit.*, Chap. XV; Wright, *op. cit.*; N. De M. Bentwich, *The Mandates System* (Longmans, 1930).

CHAPTER XVI

THE INFLUENCE OF CONTEMPORARY IMPERIALISM ON WESTERN CIVILIZATION

I. THE EFFECTS OF CONTEMPORARY EXPANSION ON OVERSEA AREAS

1. THE EXPORTATION OF MATERIAL CULTURE

The broader significance of modern imperialism, as Professor Shepherd has suggested, may best be comprehended by viewing it in two different aspects, namely: (1) The process of extending European civilization to lands overseas; and (2) the reciprocal influence of this expansion upon European culture itself. In keeping with this generalization by a master of the subject, we shall deal first with the leading effects of expansion upon oversea areas and then conclude with an estimate of the reaction of this expansion upon Western civilization.

Much the most important phase of the extension of European culture since 1870 has been the transit of the advanced material culture, especially the machine technology of Europe, throughout the world. In some countries Western material culture has not been widely adopted by the native populations, especially primitive tribes, but in the areas they inhabit it has been transplanted among the white settlers and has been the means whereby the white occidental has attained that supremacy over the colored native which has everywhere accompanied the coming of modern imperialism. The more conspicuous effects of the extension of the machine technology have been evident in such older civilizations as those of Japan, China, and India, where even a partial introduction of the more advanced industrial methods has wrought in many sections a striking transformation of the material aspects of their civilization. Further, if it be true that economic processes set in action tend ultimately to shape all accompanying phases of a civilization, then this economic transformation will some day bring about a more complete general cultural revolution.

The industrial changes in Asia that are now taking place should afford a most extensive social laboratory test of the validity of the Marxian theory of cultural development. Certainly, the political and educational changes that have already been observable in Japan and China indicate the prospect of a general cultural readjustment in those countries. Japan, however, is taking steps to avoid the loss of its racial and national characteristics while adopting the superior mechanical culture of the West. Along with the machine technology have come other phases of modern applied science, not only those directly related to industry, but also the sanitary and medical sciences that have done so much to save lives and reduce suffering.

Wherever the mechanical technology has been established in these undeveloped areas we may observe the characteristic aftermath of the introduction of the "empire of machines." The introduction of the factory system logically entailed the usual labor problems. Exploitation of labor, usually worse than that which took place a century ago in Europe and the United States, has followed. To the typical exploitative psychology characteristic of capitalism in general has been added the specially extortionate and heartless oppression of foreign capitalistic enterprise. With the development of capitalistic institutions the implied theory of business enterprise and the profit system have been substituted for the older and often more socially-minded ethical codes of the native orientals. Urban life has been promoted by the new industry. Population growth outside of Africa has been notable, though tempered by famine. This effect of European expansion on population growth is regarded by some writers as one of the major results of the movement. Professor W. F. Willcox writes: "The enormous increase in the population of the earth from 1750 to 1900 must be ascribed mainly to the expansion of Europe."[1] This has been due to the increase in the number of Europeans who have migrated and to the increase of natives resulting from the introduction of European agricultural, industrial, and medical knowledge overseas. Migration has developed apace, even if checked by legislation against orientals in Australasia and the United States. The new proletariat among the natives has gradually sensed its oppression and has begun a movement of protest. In short, there is being reproduced overseas, with differences resulting from a very different cultural, geographical, and racial setting, the Industrial Revolution that began nearly two centuries ago in England.

2. POLITICAL EXPERIMENTATION

In the political realm the extension of European institutions has been a mixed blessing. In the government of backward peoples there has been little real political education or liberalism, except perhaps in such cases as the government of the Philippine Islands. In most countries it has meant the superimposing of an autocratic white bureaucracy, which has usually been oppressive even if more efficient than the native governments. On the other hand, there can be no doubt that the imitation of Western political theories and institutions by such states as China and Japan may be conducive to a greater degree of liberty and political efficiency than would ever have been possible under the old imperial régimes. Thus far, however, it must be admitted that the study of the political institutions of the West has not notably liberalized Japan.

In addition to the policies of subjection and partial autonomy, which were typical of the administration in the old colonial movement, three other policies

[1] "The Expansion of Europe and Its Influence Upon Population," *Studies in Philosophy and Psychology by former students of Charles Edward Gorman,* Houghton Mifflin, 1906, p. 59; cf. W. F. Willcox, ed., *International Migrations,* Pitman, 1929-31, 2 vols.

have been developed in the more recent era: (1) Well-nigh complete autonomy, as in the British self-governing colonies;[1] (2) assimilation, or the adaptation of natives to Western culture, practiced, for example, by France in Algeria; and (3) association, in which native customs are respected and the native culture allowed to develop along natural lines, subject to a general oversight by Europeans. Examples of the last situation are Morocco, Egypt, and Zanzibar.

The most interesting recent innovation in the governmental field has been the mandate system, to which reference has already been made. This has introduced the conception of responsibility to world-opinion in the administration of colonial areas.

The political effects of the new imperialism have gone far beyond the development of methods of colonial government. There has been a notable adoption of European political methods and policies overseas.

First and foremost, of course, has been the transplanting of purely Western political systems into those colonial areas settled almost entirely by whites or governed by whites, such as Australasia and the Union of South Africa. Representative government has, however, made much progress even among oriental peoples and has served to challenge, and in some instances to uproot, the older absolutistic tradition. Even that advanced type of the representative system known as republican government has gained no little popularity in Eastern lands, though the monarchical influence is still strong, particularly in a psychological sense. In Japan there is an interesting combination of modern representative government with the retention of the typical oriental reverence for the imperial title and personality. The most conspicuous example of rapid modernization of Eastern political practices is that afforded by Mustapha Kemal in his new Turkish Republic in Asia Minor.[2]

No doubt the most striking and important political development that contemporary imperialism has produced in the East has been nationalism. This has been promoted in part by a direct imitation of European nationalism but has been more powerfully stimulated by the reaction of the oriental peoples against Western intervention, exploitation, and oppression. Nothing has done more to stimulate national self-consciousness among Eastern peoples than those persistent insults to their dignity and independence so characteristic of European imperialism in the last half-century.

Throughout the East there is growing resentment against Western exploitation, which has created a widespread expression of nationalistic sentiment and has challenged the ascendancy of the West. This is not only significant and ominous as to future relations between East and West, but also pregnant with dangerous possibilities as regards international relations among the Eastern peoples themselves. We know only too well what nationalism has produced in the way of international friction in the West since 1789. The one possible constructive contribution that nationalism might make in the East would be the promotion of internal reforms and the stimulation of national culture.

[1] *Cf.* R. G. Trotter, *The British Empire Commonwealth,* Holt, 1932.
[2] See Mikusch, *Mustapha Kemal.*

3. WESTERN SOCIAL INSTITUTIONS OVERSEAS

When we come to the extension of the social customs of Europeans overseas it is dangerous to dogmatize as to the results.[1] Most European governments have found it best to interfere as little as possible with native social customs, except in the case of what is obviously both cruel and useless. The abolition of infanticide, of the suttee, and of the more painful and repulsive religious rites of the natives are definite examples of progress due to contact with European customs. Much work has been done by missionaries in the attempt to change the sex customs of the African natives and the orientals. How much positive progress is involved in this introduction of the Puritan "impurity complex" among oversea populations is a question upon which students of anthropology, comparative ethics, and modern medical psychology have differed with the missionaries.[2]

The social contacts of the Westerners and the orientals have produced many interesting results and problems. For the most part the Westerners who have migrated to Asia and Africa have been relatively few in number compared to the numerous native populations. They have been compelled by cultural and economic considerations to dwell together in close contiguity as alien islands in the great ocean of native peoples. Partially because of their superior technological and economic power, and in part because of the necessity of compensating for their numerical inferiority, these foreign residents have all too often tended to assume an attitude of arrogant superiority towards the natives.[3] This has greatly irritated the cultivated natives, who regard themselves, often quite correctly, as much superior in culture and tradition to the parvenu European intruders. In this way friction has been generated and bad feeling intensified. At times the latter has progressed far enough to provoke anti-foreign riots, which have thus far done little more than to offer the foreigners a further excuse for exerting more force and tightening their grip on oversea regions.[4]

One should not overlook the effect of Western intrusion on the caste system of society in the Old World. The European influence has usually helped to overthrow the caste plan of social organization. This may be a desirable achievement in the long run, but the downfall of the caste system has been accompanied by much incidental and temporary social chaos and cultural distintegration. Moreover, the Westerner needs to be chastened in his satisfaction over the disruption of the caste system, since there is evidence that Western capitalism is creating a caste system of its own, which is just as indefensible as the oriental caste scheme that it is seeking to displace.

---

[1] *Cf.* H. A. Miller, *The Beginnings of To-morrow*, Stokes, 1933.
[2] For an able statement of the position that Westerners, including the missionaries, have usually done more harm than good in disturbing native customs, see G. H. L.-F. Pitt-Rivers, *The Clash of Culture and the Contact of Races*, London, 1927.
[3] This situation is very subtly but effectively presented in E. M. Forster's novel, *A Passage to India*, Harcourt, Brace, 1924; and with frank realism in A. C. Osburn's *Must England Lose India?* Knopf, 1930. [4] *Cf.* P. H. Clement, *The Boxer Rebellion*, Longmans, 1915.

4. MISSIONARY ENTERPRISE

In offering an estimate of the contributions of missionary enterprise, so closely associated with the expansion of Europe, to the progress of civilization, an observer's judgment is necessarily tempered by his attitude towards the validity of the orthodox Christian doctrines. If he accepts the orthodox contentions, then the salvation of the souls of the converted millions from the eternal tortures of hell would in itself alone justify the expansion movement. On the other hand, if a person takes the attitude of most contemporary critical scholarship and natural science and rejects the claims of orthodox Christianity to unique validity among religions, then missionary enterprise would have to be judged on the basis of whether the ideas and practices that Christians have introduced overseas were more suitable for the native population than those displaced. From this angle any verdict upon the results of Christian missions would need to be stated with much discrimination.

While one could scarcely question the material value of the introduction of Western medical science and some phases of Western technology, many native institutions were better adapted to serve the local needs than are the occidental practices that the missionaries have brought in.[1] Still further, if missionary activity is to be assessed primarily on the ground of its contributions to secular progress, then it is a valid question whether such work could not be carried on more competently by purely secular agents. For example, should not the extension of medical work to the Far East by the Rockefeller Institute under the control of trained medical specialists be preferred to the older medical missions? Cannot education be handled better by secular than by religious agencies?

In recent years the older optimism as to the possibility of rapid and thorough conversion of all the "heathen" and aborigines to Christianity has well-nigh disappeared among thoughtful people.[2] In spite of centuries of Catholic effort throughout the world and more than a century of Protestant activity in Africa and Asia, only an insignificant percentage of the inhabitants of these areas has been converted to Christianity, and the opposition to conversion was never more marked then it is today. To the older religious opposition we now find added the general cultural and political antipathy of the East to the West. In the nationalistic uprisings and other forms of opposition to Western intrusion the oriental religions have often been revived and promoted as a bulwark against imperialistic intrusion. In this way the native religions have become stronger and more determined in their opposition to Christianity.

In short, it would seem that the missionary movement was a logical by-product of orthodox Christianity, and when orthodoxy is being undermined at home, there is less hope of spreading it overseas. Certainly we cannot expect to take a sound body of morals abroad until science and esthetics provide such a code for us at home, something that is still far from realized in Western civilization.[3]

[1] *Cf.* Pitt-Rivers, *op. cit.;* and J. S. Huxley, *Africa View*, Harper, 1931.
[2] This is true in spite of the fact that it was about 1900 that Robert E. Speer and his co-workers were spreading the slogan "The World for Christ in Our Generation."
[3] *Cf.* H. M. Parshley, *Science and Good Behavior*, Bobbs-Merrill, 1928.

5. EDUCATING OVERSEA PEOPLES

One of the chief items in the justification of imperialism by its advocates has been the alleged "white man's burden" of civilizing the "heathen" and "natives." This civilizing function is supposed to be achieved chiefly through the instrumentality of education in the hands of missionaries and of teachers supported by the imperial and colonial administrative systems. A candid examination of the facts inclines one to doubt that the extent or the benefits of education in any way measure up to the conventional claims. In India, which is one of the areas most competently and expensively administered according to conventional standards of imperial control, 88 per cent of the men and 98 per cent of the women are illiterate, and not 1 per cent can read English. In French West Africa, also well and generously supported in the French budget, only one-twelfth of the administrative budget was devoted to educational purposes. The education given by missionaries is not only slight, but in many cases of dubious import. It consists in large part of religious instruction of an obscurantist type. There is little to be gained from inculcating a brand of education that is by no means generally accepted as valid in the West. About the only thoroughgoing and extensive system of education carried out in colonial areas has been associated with American administration of Puerto Rico, Hawaii, and especially the Philippine Islands. A few of the wealthier and more fortunate orientals have been able to come to America or Europe for higher education. Even this has not been an unmitigated benefit, for they often acquire ideas not applicable to the Orient today.

The results of educating orientals are dangerous for the imperialistic nations. As the oriental peoples become better acquainted with the history and culture of the Occident, they become to that degree better informed as to the questionable ideals, practices, and achievements of the West. This makes them more convinced of the essential hypocrisy involved in Western pretensions to disinterestedness in oversea areas and to the advancement of civilization and justice outside of Europe and America. Further, the more successful and widespread the educational progress, the less willing are the orientals to live under the heel of the foreigner.[1] The extension of education among the Filipinos has been paralleled by an increasingly comprehensive and determined movement for independence. We must conclude that if imperialism and colonialism are to be justified at all, other grounds must be sought than the pedagogical services of the West.

The "movies" are having a great popularity in the Orient just now, but when we reflect that some of our own movies probably degrade American culture and when we remember that the movies shown in the Orient are usually of the worst type—often those barred from exhibition in the United States—we may doubt their educational efficacy. They certainly increase in many instances the oriental disdain for the Occident.

6. THE DETRIMENTAL RESULTS OF EUROPEAN EXPANSION

Lest one might still be inclined to regard the European expansion as a beneficent process, it is necessary to call attention to certain other detrimental

---

[1] *Cf.* C. H. Peake, *Nationalism and Education in Modern China*, Columbia University Press, 1932.

THE EFFECTS OF CONTEMPORARY EXPANSION

effects of the contact of European peoples with those overseas. In economic matters Western industry and commerce, when introduced, have meant, as noted before, the development of modern capitalism with all the waste and misery that it has entailed in Western states. Further, there has been a general tendency to exploit native labor, not only in factories and mines, but also on rubber plantations and in agricultural activity, and to oust the natives from their lands when these possess valuable mineral deposits or other products of high commercial significance. The following description of a typical factory scene in China under foreign exploitation, cited by Professor Shepherd, well illustrates the unhappy state of affairs under the new labor conditions. It sounds remarkably like sections from the British Blue Books containing the Sadler and Ashley Reports on English laboring-conditions a century ago:

In the silk filatures women worked, standing, for twelve and thirteen hours a day, laying their babies on heaps of waste behind them. Children of six and seven worked similar hours, stirring the cocoons in boiling water, which scalded their hands. . . . They got their meal when the machinery was stopped, once a day for fifteen minutes, to stoke up. In the cotton mills there were two twelve-hour shifts for seven days a week, with a half day's break every ten days when the machinery was stopped; but then the other shift worked fourteen or sixteen hours. There were no meal-hours—they ate with one hand and worked with the other. The average wage was 16s. to 18s. ($4 to $4.50) a month. Even the reactionary Peking government had proposed the prohibition of boy labour under ten and girl labour under twelve and the limitation of hours for young persons to eight, with no night labour; the Shanghai Municipal Council (controlled wholly by Europeans) responded . . . with a report which proposed ten as the age limit for boys and girls alike, and that twelve-hour shifts, day and night, should be allowed for young persons.[1]

Even worse, however, than the bringing of factory conditions to oversea areas has been the practice of forced labor by natives under the direction of Western capitalists. This has often been cruel and barbarous beyond belief, and has led to frightful mortality in many cases, to say nothing of the sufferings of those who have not died.

The undoubtedly superior efficiency of European political control over colonies and the greater liberalism brought in as a result of the oriental imitation of Western constitutions have been paralleled by extreme autocracy and cruelty in colonial administration, especially in dealing with native revolts or crimes. Cases in point are the administration of Leopold in the Belgian Congo, the German suppression of the Herero Revolt in southwest Africa, the colonial administration of Carl Peters in German East Africa, the extermination of the natives by the English settlers in Tasmania, British massacres in India, and the conduct of the American military forces in coercing some of the more warlike tribes in the Philippines. Brutality in modern colonialism has been promoted to some degree by the hatreds and contempts engendered by racial and cultural contrasts. But it is probable that the chief inciting influence has been the association of colonial penetration with patriotism. This has permitted murder and rapine to be identified with a sense of public duty and devotion. As private individuals, few of the more brutal administrators could have

[1] Cited in W. R. Shepherd, "The Interaction of Europe and Asia," *loc. cit.*, p. 258. See also R. H. Tawney, *Land and Labour in China*, Harcourt, Brace, 1932; and Shuichi Harada, *Labor Conditions in Japan*, Columbia University Press, 1928.

been induced to perpetrate the deeds that they executed. Nobody has stated this "idealistic" patriotic impulse to colonial brutality better than Mr. Leonard Woolf in his *Empire & Commerce in Africa:*

... I have attempted to trace the general effects of European policy in Africa. In my judgment those effects have been almost wholly evil. The European went into Africa about forty years ago desiring to exploit it and its inhabitants for his own economic advantage, and he rapidly acquired the belief that the power of his State should be used in Africa to promote his own economic interests. Once this belief was accepted, it destroyed the idea of individual moral responsibility. The State, enthroned in its impersonality and a glamour of patriotism, can always make a wilderness and call it peace, or make a conquest and call it civilization. The right of Europe to civilize became synonymous with the right of Europe to rob or to exploit the uncivilized. The power of each European State was applied ruthlessly in Africa. In bitter competition with one another, they partitioned territory which belonged to none of them. By fraud or by force the native chiefs and rulers were swindled or robbed of their dominions. Any resistance by the inhabitants to the encroachments either of individual Europeans or of European States was treated as "rebellion," and followed by massacres known as wars or punitive expeditions. In this process tribe was used against tribe and race against race, and wherever any native administration existed it was destroyed.

This work was accomplished by men who were not more rapacious or evil than the ordinary man; it was accomplished by men often of ideals and great devotion, but who accepted a political dogma, namely, that their actions were justified by the right and duty of the European State to use its power in Africa for the economic interests of its European subjects. Just in the same way those who burnt and tortured heretics were probably no more cruel or evil than the majority of their fellows; they were men of ideals and great devotion who accepted the religious dogma that it was the right and duty of the Church to torture men's bodies for the sake of their souls.

The dogma of economic imperialism prevailed with the aid of modern rifle and gun. The slaughter of the most warlike Africans encouraged the survivors to submit, and peace descended upon the greater part of Africa. The first stage of economic imperialism was accomplished, and the European looked round and openly proclaimed that the work he had done was good. The reason which he gave and gives for this opinion is interesting and deserves a little examination. The policy of conquest and partition which we have described is usually defended on two grounds; first, that it was inevitable; and secondly, that it eventually substituted a system of law and order for one of lawless barbarism.[1]

One of the worst phases of European political intrusion overseas has been that juristic practice known as extraterritoriality, namely, the privilege of foreigners to be tried in their own courts and by their own laws, even when residing abroad. It is true that in some cases this has been necessary, namely, where native institutions are of a primitive sort or where anarchy exists temporarily in more civilized states. The insistence upon extraterritorial rights in well-developed countries such as China has been one of the most potent causes of friction and hatreds between native peoples and their foreign residents. The practice of appealing to State Departments and Foreign Offices to put armed forces behind the protection of private property or the collection of private

[1] Woolf, *op. cit.*, George Allen & Unwin, London, 1919, pp. 352-53. Used by permission.

debts, a practice comparable to calling out the militia to collect private debts at home,[1] has also been productive of a vast amount of brutality and hard feeling.

Nor has the social side of the contact between Europeans and natives been without unfortunate results. Antisocial European habits have been introduced for native imitation. At the same time that missionaries were trying to inculcate the practice of Western monogamy, white traders and others were systematically debauching the morals of the native women.

Then, over against the saving of native lives by the introduction of modern medical and sanitary science must be set the frequent introduction or encouragement of the unrestrained use of alcholic liquors and opium products, which has brought about not only a great loss of life among natives, but also unspeakable misery and serious physical deterioration.[2] Indeed, it may be doubted if it is desirable to provide hygienic methods for reducing the oriental death rate, unless at the same time the knowledge of birth control is widely provided in these lands to reduce the birth rate. More mouths to feed means a lower standard of living or increased frequency of famines. The dissemination of birth-control knowledge is obstructed by both native prejudice and the beliefs of influential groups of Western settlers in those regions. Population increase also stimulates the emigration movement in the Orient and leads to an increase of international friction in this as well as in other areas.[3]

In the Far East, Western medical science may halt epidemics and plagues and thereby lead to famine due to overpopulation. In many areas contact with the whites has, on the other hand, resulted in a type of subjection and oppression that has produced something approaching a decimation of population. The case of the French Congo is instructive. Between 1900 and 1921, under French exploitation the estimated population in this area fell from 10,000,000 to less than 3,000,000.

While one cannot well deny the fact that the expansion of European civilization overseas has brought a vast amount of material progress to the world at large, it seems equally true that the natives have probably lost more than they have gained by the "civilizing" process. If this be true, then the progress of modern imperialism can only be justified by the same argument through which Theodore Roosevelt upheld the conquest and expropriation of the American Indians, namely, that the "lower" civilizations must in the inexorable nature of things give way before the advance of the "higher."

II. THE REACTION OF CONTEMPORARY IMPERIALISM UPON EUROPE AND AMERICA

1. THE INFLUENCE OF ECONOMIC FACTORS UPON WESTERN EUROPE

Important and diversified as the various aspects of European penetration overseas may have been, the chief significance of these events and achievements

---

[1] This pertinent analogy was suggested to me by the late Dwight W. Morrow.
[2] *Cf.* E. N. La Motte, *The Ethics of Opium*, Century, 1924.
[3] *Cf.* Thompson, *Danger Spots in World Population*.

for Western civilization are to be sought in their reaction upon occidental civilization. It is what these things have done to Europeans and Americans as well as to the Hottentots and the Hereros.

Among the economic reactions of expansion upon the West one of the most significant has been the introduction of new commodities. These have included highly important articles of industry, such as silk and cotton products, rubber, petroleum, and nitrate of soda; food products and beverages, such as tropical fruits, rice, coffee, cocoa, and tea; and articles of ornament, as in the case of Chinese and Japanese ware and Indian ornamentation. Those beginnings in this field which we surveyed in an earlier chapter [1] have grown rapidly, and the earlier importations of commodities from the East have been extended and diversified. The discovery of these new articles of commerce and the stimulation of diversified industry overseas have promoted the development of a greatly extended international division of labor.

Commercial mechanisms and financial institutions have been greatly altered as a result of the discoveries and the increased trade that have accompanied the more recent phases of imperialism. While one should not neglect the significant beginnings of credit institutions and other devices to aid commerce in the old colonial movement, the mechanism of commerce in 1870 was certainly crude compared with that which has developed in the last fifty years to expedite world trade. International trade has produced an elaborate and complicated technology and commercial equipment.

The vast increase in world-trade has brought about the further development and perfection of international bills of exchange. There is little use of cash in making international transactions. Banks and brokerage houses devoted chiefly to handling commercial paper related to international trade have come into being on a wide scale. Machinery for handling trade balances has been expanded and simplified. Only enough bullion is transferred to square up periodic balances that cannot be taken care of by shipments of goods. Indeed, of late the shipment of bullion has been in part replaced by the practice of "earmarking" it and leaving it in vaults. In the old days, for example, if gold was due France by the banks of the United States the actual bullion would be shipped to France. Today this bullion may merely be set aside—"earmarked"— as belonging to France and left in New York vaults. International bankers, especially since 1900, have promoted extensive investment in foreign bonds, the soundness of which is not always guaranteed or certain.[2] Indeed the losses in foreign bonds recently have, temporarily at least, almost suspended the operation of this phase of finance.

Again, the volume of money in circulation has been markedly increased not only by the growth of business, but also by the discoveries of the precious metals in Australia, South Africa, and other oversea territories. This has affected price levels and other commercial conditions.[3] The growth of world-trade has stimulated the expansion of capitalism quite as much as trade has in turn been promoted by capitalism. The trading policies, involving questions of free trade versus protection, which have occupied so much attention in Europe and

---

[1] See above, pp. 32 ff.
[2] See Winkler, *Foreign Bonds: An Autopsy*.
[3] See G. F. Warren and F. A. Pearson, *Prices*, Wiley, 1933.

America, have been closely associated with the development of world-trade and modern imperialism.

The question is often asked whether modern imperialism actually pays when estimated on a purely economic and commercial basis. The verdict must be that while relatively rich and well-populated areas like India may yield a large income to the governing state, certainly imperialism as a whole has not paid. In estimating the economic value of imperialism to a state we cannot utilize as the basis of our appraisal the gross trade of a state with its dependencies. We can legitimately attribute to colonialism only that amount of the trade which can be attributed solely to political or economic control—obviously a rather indeterminate amount. Then, from this we would have to subtract the cost of administration and of armament for protection. When these qualifications are recognized, it at once becomes evident that imperialism is a dubious economic venture. Even in the case of India, it is doubtful if the difference between the revenue that England enjoys now and what it would possess if India were independent or the dependency of another state equals the expense of the imperial administration and the diplomatic, military, and naval responsibilities that go with it.

The possession of a colony can only in rare instances be made to bring about a complete monopoly over the trade of that colony. This is well illustrated by the case of England and Egypt. The total value of Egyptian trade in 1925 was $585,000,000, of which the British exports to Egypt amounted to $75,000,000, less than 40 per cent of the British exports to Argentina. The trade of France with its African possessions, outside Morocco and Algeria, in a year does not equal the French expenses incurred for one year in the Riff War alone. Further, in colonies populated by backward peoples there is little money and hence little opportunity for extensive native purchases.

Even less capable is the ruling state of making sure that it can secure a monopoly of the raw materials to be obtained from a colony. These raw materials are sold to those who offer the highest prices, and any effort to force exclusive sale to the citizens of the ruling state would be bitterly attacked by the colonial peoples, who naturally desire to make as much money as possible. When one balances these slight economic gains from the possession of colonies against the burdens of administration, it must be confessed that thus far imperialism seems to have been in the main an expensive economic illusion. After careful analysis Professor Moon comes to the following conclusions:

> Against the gain set the cost. Many colonies are operated at a deficit, so far as the government's finances are concerned, and the deficit is paid by the taxpayer of the mother-country. Most colonies are acquired at a considerable cost, whether in the form of a purchase price or in the form of military and naval expenditures. As one of the chief purposes of armaments, especially of naval armaments, has been to defend colonies against seizure, and to maintain the diplomatic prestige and influence which make colonial acquisitions possible, part of the armaments expenditures of the last half-century must be entered in the debit column of imperialism. Add to that the cost of occasional wars, such as the Russo-Japanese War, and of countless native insurrections, and the charges become so heavy as to cast some doubt on the net value of imperialism, measured in dollars and cents, to the tax-

paying public in general. In the case of Italy and of pre-war Germany, the net result of colonial ventures in Africa cannot be calculated as anything other than a loss. . . .

The general conclusions to be drawn from these facts seem to be: (1) Colonial trade is much more advantageous to a few industries, notably the cotton and iron industries, than to industry in general. (2) It is impossible to calculate the precise indirect gain, if there is any, which accrues to the public through increased general business prosperity, or to balance that gain against the direct costs, which are material. But the relative importance of colonial trade as compared with the total volume of internal and external trade is so slight, except in a few cases, as to afford little basis for imperialist oratory of the type made popular by Jules Ferry and Joseph Chamberlain, and to offer little compensation for the risks of war encountered by aggressively imperialist nations. Imperialist propaganda, however, exaggerates the supposed rewards and supports a policy of differential and monopolistic colonial tariffs. The result of such exaggeration is that for the sake of gaining relatively trifling increments of colonial trade great nations cheerfully incur heavy colonial and military expenses and too often deliberately jeopardize their largest markets and the peace of the world.[1]

In estimating the cost of modern imperialism one must take some notice of the expense of the World War. While extra-European factors were not exclusively responsible for the coming of the war, they played a prominent part in producing the diplomatic line-up and international hatreds that brought on the great conflict. But for imperialism the war would not have been likely to break out in 1914. The direct economic cost of the World War has been estimated at over $300,000,000,000, and the indirect economic costs were probably greater than this. Not in a century, if in a millennium, would the net profits of imperialism, if any, match these sums.

The fact that modern imperialism has not, as a whole, been a paying affair serves to strengthen the view that nationalism and patriotic pride must have been powerful factors in the promotion of the colonial movement. This does not mean that one needs to minimize the potency or even the primacy of the economic drive for oversea expansion, but it does indicate the necessity for caution in accepting the doctrine of economic determinism in any naïve and unquestioning manner.

2. IMPERIALISM AND THE POLITICAL LIFE OF THE WEST

The political reaction of imperialism upon Western society has been almost wholly unfortunate. The practice of autocratically governing natives abroad has tended to weaken democratic institutions at home. As Professor Hobhouse made clear years ago in his *Democracy and Reaction,* it is difficult for a state to pursue brutal and autocratic practices in its oversea dominions without having such procedure react unfortunately upon the administration of affairs at home. Professor Sumner repeatedly insisted that imperialism abroad cannot be harmonized with democracy at home.[2] The burden of imperial administration has proved to be a severe drain upon national resources and has lessened the funds available for advanced social legislation at home. Perhaps the only valu-

[1] Moon, *Imperialism and World Politics,* pp. 532, 534-35.
[2] W. G. Sumner, *War, and Other Essays,* Yale University Press, 1913, pp. 285-93, 337-52.

able contribution of imperialism in its political reaction upon Europe has been the training it has afforded in civil service and colonial administration, but this is only good training for a dubious profession. In England and France special emphasis is laid upon training for the colonial service. This field enlists some of the best-trained and most capable products of the educational system of the country. In England, especially, the cream of the college-educated classes has been drawn into this type of career. The German preparation for colonial administration was less extensive and exacting, but the Germans excelled both the French and the British in their careful study of commercial conditions and in their effort to exploit with adroitness and intelligence the foreign demand for German products.

3. CONTRIBUTIONS TO SCIENTIFIC ADVANCE IN THE WEST

In the field of natural science oversea expansion has been potent in leading to revolutionary progress.[1] It is conventionally supposed that scientific advances have come almost entirely from isolated work in European and American laboratories. It would be easy to demonstrate, however, that much of certain types of modern scientific progress has come from research in the greater laboratory of nature itself that has been opened to many by explorations overseas.

In the field of geography we must note not only the great mass of new data and the perfection of cartography, but also the development of physical geography in all its phases since the days of Alexander von Humboldt. Anthropogeography has promoted the analysis of the influence of the various physical environments of the earth upon man and social institutions in the writings of such students as Ritter, Peschel, Ratzel, and Reclus. Astronomy has been perfected through the wider and more accurate observation of the heavens made possible after modern explorations began. In biology and zoölogy, a vast amount of new data has been brought together, overthrowing much of the older systems of classification drawn up by Linnaeus, Buffon, and Cuvier. Moreover, the observation of the divers species of plants and animals throughout different parts of the world enabled Darwin, Huxley, and Wallace to formulate the most fruitful theory of the nineteenth century in biological science—the doctrine of organic evolution. Both chemistry and the materia medica have been infinitely enriched by discoveries made during the process of oversea expansion. Much of value to medicine has been secured as a result of contact with oversea areas, among such contributions being the introduction of quinine as a specific against malaria, and the discovery of the revolutionary malaria treatment for syphilis and paresis.[2] Various opiates have been of great assistance in fighting pain. The study and control of typically tropical diseases like yellow fever have added greatly to our medical knowledge. New or strange diseases, such as cholera, bubonic plague, beriberi, and sleeping sickness, have come to Europe from overseas and have presented an additional challenge to medical science.

[1] See below, pp. 145 ff. [2] See below, pp. 1048-49.

4. INFLUENCES ON WESTERN CULTURE

Not less significant has been the reaction of oversea discoveries on culture and the social sciences. Without the data supplied by the observation of a great number of different cultures and peoples there could have been no such social sciences as anthropology, ethnology, comparative philology, comparative religion, comparative jurisprudence, descriptive sociology, evolutionary politics, and historical economics.[1]

Nor has the oversea expansion been without its significance in providing the knowledge and motif for important contributions to philosophy, literature, the drama, and music. In philosophy we must note the influence of the *Sakuntala* of Kalidasa upon Herder, Goethe, and the Romanticist movement in European literature, of the Bhagavad-Gita on modern European philosophy, and of the teachings of Manu upon the doctrines of Nietzsche. More recently the views of Tagore and Gandhi have profoundly affected Western thinkers. The once popular philosophy of Count Keyserling owed much to the oriental stimulus that helped to create it.

The influence of the Orient and oversea expansion on literature since 1800 has been wide and varied.[2] We need mention only a few examples. Such are Oehlenschläger's drama *Aladdin's Lamp,* Goethe's "West-eastern Divan," with strong Persian influences, Thomas Moore's romantic interpretation of Hindu life in his *Lalla Rookh,* Coleridge's stirring poem, "Kubla Khan," Victor Hugo's *The Orientals,* combining the influence of the Greek struggle for independence with oriental influences, Prosper Mérimée's *Tamango,* portraying primitive passions on the African coast, Clara Reeve's novel *The History of Charoba,* Robert Southey's poem "Thalaba, the Destroyer," Charles Kingsley's *Westward Ho!* and *Hypatia,* Théophile Gautier's "One of Cleopatra's Nights" and his travel stories of the East, Gérard de Nerval's *Voyage in the Orient* and *Scenes of Oriental Life,* Charles Leconte de Lisle's graphic descriptive poems such as "The Elephants" and "The Jungles," Arnold's great poem "Sohrab and Rustum," the verses and romances of Kipling, Jules Verne's scientific romances, and the novels of Rider Haggard and Joseph Conrad.

In art the importation and adaptation of Japanese prints, screens, lacquered work, and silks, and of Chinese tapestry, rugs, and silks, exemplify the direct influence of extra-European areas. Then, painters like Turner and others have illustrated the effect of the interest in seafaring life and have portrayed the peoples and culture of oversea areas. Delacroix made much use of Algerian subjects in his paintings. The prolific Russian painter, Nicholas Roerich, has done much to introduce Mongolian, Tibetan, and Indian themes into modern painting. Likewise, a notable school of Modernistic art, known as Primitivism, has sought its inspiration and models in the figures and customs of oversea natives and native life. In music we may discern strong oriental influences in the compositions of Félicien David, especially *Le Désert,* in Verdi's *Aida,* in Massenet's *Thaïs,* in Puccini's *Madame Butterfly,* in Meyerbeer's opera *L'Africaine,* in Rimsky-Korsakov's orchestral suite *Scheherazade,* adapted from the Arabian

---

[1] See below, pp. 665 ff., 1057 ff.
[2] *Cf.* A. F. J. Remy, *The Influence of India and Persia on the Poetry of Germany,* Columbia University Press, 1931.

THE REACTION OF CONTEMPORARY IMPERIALISM

Nights, in Saint-Saëns's orientalized songs and his opera *Samson and Delila,* in Rubinstein's *Ocean Symphony* and *Golden at My Feet,* and in the exotic strains of many other compositions.

Professor Shepherd has summarized the outstanding contributions of the East to the cultural life of the West as: (1) The development of a civilized or secular outlook upon life and its problems; (2) the promotion of a spirit of philosophical and scientific inquiry; and (3) the development of imagination in philosophy and literature. While accepting and profiting by these to no small degree, we have also countered such influences by the exportation to oriental lands of our mechanical and matter-of-fact bookkeeping economy and our supernatural religion and ethics.

It is these little-recognized but very important cultural contributions which have accompanied recent oversea expansion that must be set off against its detrimental effects when one attempts to assess the total significance of modern imperialism for European civilization.

If, in conclusion, one were to raise the question of the probable future of imperialism, it seems that, as a creation of capitalism and *Machtpolitik*,[1] it is not likely to decline so long as these forces and principles remain operative, and their collapse does not appear so imminent as many radicals might wish. It would appear, however, that, except in the event of another world war, the imperialism of the future will have to be primarily economic and cultural rather than political, since most of the formerly unoccupied areas of the earth have now been appropriated by the stronger powers. If the age of imperialism is not yet finished, that of colonial expansion seems to be. To take even an optimistic view, the growing crisis of capitalism, the severe losses sustained in the export of capital by the defaulting on bonds, and the exhaustion of virgin areas for exploitation have all combined to take the edge off the buoyant imperialism of the period from 1870 to 1929.

[1] That is, rule through superior force, irrespective of ethics or the will of the ruled.

SUGGESTED READING

Hammerton, *Universal History of the World,* Chaps. 172-73
W. G. Sumner, *War, and Other Essays,* Yale University Press, 1913, pp. 285-93, 337-52
F. H. Giddings, *Democracy and Empire,* Macmillan, 1900, Chaps. I, XVII
Moon, *Imperialism and World Politics,* Chaps. IV, XIX
Schuman, *International Politics,* Chap. XI
P. S. Reinsch, *Intellectual and Political Currents in the Far East,* Houghton Mifflin, 1911
W. E. Soothill, *China and the West,* Oxford Press, 1925
M. F. Parmelee, *Oriental and Occidental Culture,* Century, 1928
Hans Kohn, *Orient and Occident,* Day, 1934
J. W. Slaughter, *East and West [in] China,* Rice Institute, 1927
Erwin Baelz, *Awakening Japan,* Viking Press, 1932
Miller, *The Beginnings of To-morrow*
H. C. Knapp-Fisher, *The Modern World,* Dutton, 1934
Sir A. F. Whyte, *The Future of East and West,* M. Saunders, 1932
K. J. Saunders, *The Ideals of East and West,* Macmillan, 1934
E. D. Harvey, *The Mind of China,* Yale University Press, 1933

Count Michimasa Soyejima and P. W. Kuo, *Oriental Interpretations of the Far Eastern Problem*, University of Chicago Press, 1925
G. H. L.-F. Pitt-Rivers, *The Clash of Culture and the Contact of Races*, London, 1927
G. L. Dickinson, *Letters from a Chinese Official*, Doubleday, Page, 1903
Daniel Crawford, *Thinking Black*, Doran, 1913
Morel, *The Black Man's Burden*
J. S. Huxley, *Africa View*, Harper, 1931
L. T. Hobhouse, *Democracy and Reaction*, Putnam, 1905
Webster, *Historical Selections*, Pt. V
Scott and Baltzly, *Readings in European History since 1814*, Chap. XII

FURTHER REFERENCES

THE INFLUENCE OF CONTEMPORARY IMPERIALISM ON WESTERN CIVILIZATION. As introductory reading on the subject matter of this chapter, see Moon, *op. cit.*, Chap. XIX; Parmelee, *op. cit.*; Kohn, *op. cit.*; Soothill, *op. cit.*

For the transit of material culture overseas, see Rugg, *Changing Civilizations in the Modern World*, pp. 415-612; Zimmermann, *World Resources and Industries*; McVey, *Modern Industrialism*.

On the exploitation of native workers, see Woolf, *Empire & Commerce in Africa*, pp. 315 ff.; Buell, *The Native Problem in Africa*; Tyau, *China Awakened*, Chaps. XII-XIII; Morel, *op. cit.*

On the government of oversea areas, see Buell, *International Relations*, Chaps. XV-XVI, XX; P. S. Reinsch, *Colonial Government* (Macmillan, 1902) and *Colonial Administration* (Macmillan, 1905); Sir V. G. Chirol, *The Occident and the Orient* (University of Chicago Press, 1924).

On nationalism overseas, see Dutcher, *The Political Awakening of the East*; Nicholson, *The Re-making of the Nations*; Miller, *op. cit.*; Hans Kohn, *Nationalism and Imperialism in the Hither East* (Harcourt, Brace, 1932); Frazier Hunt, *The Rising Temper of the East* (Bobbs-Merrill, 1922); Younghusband, *Dawn in India*.

On the education of natives, see Moon, *op. cit.*, pp. 558 ff.; T. J. Jones, *Education in Africa* (Phelps-Stokes Fund, 1922); Chaps. II-VI of C. W. Washburne, *Remakers of Mankind* (Day, 1932); C. M. Peake, *Nationalism and Education in Modern China* (Columbia University Press, 1932).

On extraterritoriality, see Buell, *op. cit.*, pp. 461 ff.; G. W. Keeton, *The Development of Extraterritoriality in China* (Longmans, 1928, 2 vols.); S. S. Liu, *Extraterritoriality: Its Rise and Its Decline* (Columbia University Press, 1925).

On foreign-exchange technique, see H. G. Brown, *International Trade and Exchange* (Macmillan, 1914); A. C. Whitaker, *Foreign Exchange* (Appleton, 1919).

On the economic balance sheet of imperialism, see Moon, *op. cit.*, pp. 526 ff.; Pt. I of Sir Norman Angell, *The Great Illusion* (4th ed. rev., Putnam, 1913) and Pt. I of *The Great Illusion, 1933* (Putnam, 1933); J. E. Baker, *Explaining China* (Van Nostrand, 1928); Simpson, *Introduction to World Economics*; Winkler, *Foreign Bonds: An Autopsy*.

For a stalwart defense of imperialism, see Giddings, *op. cit.*, Chaps. I, XVII.

On the interaction between East and West, see Parmelee, *op. cit.*; Huxley, *op. cit.*; Pitt-Rivers, *op. cit.*; Kohn, *Orient and Occident*; Slaughter, *op. cit.*; Peake, *op. cit.*; H. A. Van Dorn, *Twenty Years of the Chinese Republic* (Knopf, 1932); Paul Monroe, *China: A Nation in Evolution* (Macmillan, 1928); Crawford, *op. cit.*; Dickinson, *op. cit.*; Soothill, *op. cit.*; Reinsch, *Intellectual and Political Currents in the Far East*.

CHAPTER XVII

THE WORLD WAR, 1914-1918

I. LEVELS AND TYPES OF RESPONSIBILITY

In generalizing about responsibility for the World War it is necessary to be specific as to just what is meant by the term "responsibility."

There are some scholars who contend that all of the Great Powers involved were about equally responsible. There are others who state that France, Russia, and Serbia were the only important Powers in 1914 primarily responsible for a European war under conditions as they existed. Both of these opinions can be sustained if one clarifies what is meant by each interpretation.[1]

Those who argue for equal responsibility in this sense usually mean that, if we consider primarily the general causes of war in European society from 1870 to 1914, all the Great Powers were about equally responsible for the war system. They do not have in mind the crisis of 1914, but rather the cultural and institutional situation lying back of the July clash. Those who contend for the primary guilt of France, Russia, and Serbia have in mind the responsibility for unnecessarily forcing the Austro-Serbian dispute of 1914 into a general European conflict. It is necessary, therefore, to know just what one implies when he says that everybody was guilty or that this or that group of nations was guilty.[2]

The most thoughtful authorities on the question of responsibility for the World War contend that we must examine the problem on at least four levels: (1) Those general causes of war which made war possible if not inevitable in 1914; (2) the diplomatic history of Europe from 1870 to 1912; (3) the diplomatic revolution of 1912-14; and (4) the crisis of June 28 to August 5, 1914.

II. THE CAUSES OF WARS IN GENERAL

By the general causes of wars we mean those divers aspects of the European social order in the half-century before the World War which predisposed governments to war whenever a crisis of sufficient proportions arose. As representative factors making for war, one would naturally list such things as the cult of war, racial and national arrogance, the growth of great armaments, secret diplomacy, the struggle for raw materials and markets, the system of differential and discriminatory tariffs, population pressure, the doctrine of abso-

---

[1] The views of a third group who believe the Central Powers solely responsible no longer require serious consideration.

[2] The most judicious brief analysis and summary of the whole matter known to the writer is contained in C. L. Becker, *Modern History*, Silver, Burdett, 1931, Chap. xx. See also Sir C. R. Beazley, *The Road to Ruin in Europe, 1890-1914*, London, 1932.

lute national sovereignty, the conception of national honor, opposition to international organization and arbitration—in short, the whole complex of factors that led to what G. Lowes Dickinson has so well described as "the international anarchy" that prevailed throughout Europe in 1914.

When we consider such causes of war as the general factors listed above, it must be frankly admitted that all the nations involved in the war in 1914 were about equally guilty. They were all a part of the system; if one had a larger army than its neighbor, the neighbor was likely to have a greater navy. If one was more patriotic, another was more impelled by inexorable economic forces. If one pursued a more clever program of international duplicity through secret diplomacy, another disturbed the peace more by startling frankness in international behavior. Therefore it cannot be held that, so far as general causes of war are concerned, any one European state or group of powers was uniquely at fault.

During the war the Entente asserted and reiterated that Germany was, beyond comparison, the chief representative of the war system in Europe; that, for example, it had a larger army than any other state, was more given to enthusiastic reading of the prophets of war, such as Nietzsche and Bernhardi, whose names were on the tongues of every German schoolchild, and was dominated in its foreign policy by the bellicose and arrogant Pan-German League, which desired German dominion throughout the world. Let us look into the facts in regard to this Entente indictment of Germany.

A leading French authority on military organization, General Buat, has shown that on July 1, 1914, before a soldier had been called to the colors because of the crisis of that year, the active French army numbered 910,000 with 1,250,000 reservists, while the active Germany army at this time numbered 870,000 with 1,180,000 reservists.[1] The Russian army lacked little of being twice as large as the German. The British navy was actually twice as large as the German, while the combined British, Russian, and French navies made the Austro-German naval combination appear almost insignificant. Of course numbers do not mean efficiency, but they are surely the test of the existence and degree of armament, and the Entente contention was that Germany far surpassed any other nation in the world in 1914 in the extent of its armaments. The fact that the Germans proved the most efficient soldiers once war broke out does not alter the case in any degree. The French army was, in general, as well prepared for war as the German, and the Russian army was well prepared for the short war that the Russians expected if they were joined by France, Great Britain, and Serbia in a conflict against Austria and Germany.

Likewise, the assertion of the worship of Nietzsche and Bernhardi by the German people receives no support from the facts. In the first place, patriotic writing in Germany can easily be matched by cogent examples of jingoism in the other European states; for example, in the writings of Barrès and Déroulède in France; of Kipling, Lea, Cramb, and Maxse in England; of D'Annunzio in Italy; and of the Panslavists in Russia. In the second place, Nietzsche was in no sense an exponent of the Prussian military system. He hated the Prussian military oligarchy, and, as Professor Charles Andler, the foremost French au-

---

[1] E. A. L. Buat, *L'armée allemande pendant la guerre de 1914-18,* Paris, 1920, pp. 7-9.

thority on Nietzsche, has shown, he was by no means an indiscriminate eulogist of the war cult. As Andler says: "It is a mistake to continue to picture Nietzsche as the apologist of Saint Devastation." Yet even if we conceded the worst things said about Nietzsche by the Entente propagandists during the World War, it cannot be shown that he had any appreciable influence upon either the German masses or German officialdom before the war. He was vigorously anti-Christian in his philosophy, and hence anathema to the majority of the Germans, especially the Prussian bureaucracy and militarists, who were loyal and pious Protestants. No one could have been more repugnant to them than the prophet of the Antichrist. Nor was Bernhardi any more widely followed. He was not read by the masses, and the present writer once ascertained that not a single official in the German Foreign Office in 1914 had ever read his book on *Germany and the Next War*.

During the war Americans were frequently warned by André Chéradame and other propagandists as to the dangerous nature of the Pan-German plot to annex the world.[1] They were told that the German people and government were willingly in the grip of the Pan-German League and were eager abettors of its aggressive plans. The nature, activities, and influences of the Pan-German League were made the subject of a learned study by Dr. Mildred Wertheimer.[2] She showed that it was made up of a small group of noisy and reprehensible jingoes, who had no hold on the German government. The latter regarded the organization as a nuisance and an embarrassing handicap to German diplomacy. It could be matched by similar groups in any leading country in Europe, and had about as much influence on the Kaiser and Chancellor von Bethmann-Hollweg as the National Security League or the "preparedness" societies had on Wilson and Bryan in 1915. It may be true that the German people accepted the military yoke somewhat more willingly than some other European populations, but in 1914 the civil government in Germany retained control of affairs to the last and resolutely held out against war until all hope for peace was destroyed by the Russian general mobilization.[3]

We may therefore contend with complete assurance that, with respect to the general causes of war, the guilt from 1870 to 1914 was divided; in fact, about equally distributed. In holding Germany, along with England and Italy, as relatively less responsible for war in 1914,[4] we do not in any sense attempt to find these states innocent of an equal share in producing the system of international anarchy which made war probable whenever Europe faced a major diplomatic crisis. At the same time, it can no longer be asserted with any show of proof that Germany was uniquely black in its prewar record.

---

[1] *Cf.* André Chéradame, *The Pangerman Plot Unmasked*, Scribner, 1917.
[2] M. S. Wertheimer, *The Pan-German League, 1890-1914*, Columbia University Press, 1924.
[3] See below, p. 590. Von Moltke spoke only for himself, and the Austrians so understood it. The definitive treatment of the civil government versus the General Staff in Germany in 1914 is contained in M. H. Cochran, *Germany Not Guilty in 1914*, Stratford Press, 1931, Chap. VII.
[4] See below, pp. 592 ff.

III. EUROPEAN DIPLOMACY FROM 1870 TO 1912

Some may express surprise that the diplomatic history since 1870 is here divided into two sections: (1) 1870 to 1912; and (2) 1912 to 1914. Why should we not treat it as a single unit from 1870 to 1914? The answer is that down to 1912 the European system of alliances and European diplomacy were, at least ostensibly, devoted to the preservation of the balance of power and the maintenance of peace. Between 1912 and 1914, however, Russia and France, through their agents Izvolsky and Poincaré, abandoned this order of things and laid plans to exploit the appropriate European crisis in such a manner as either to humiliate the Central Powers or to enter upon a war that would bring to Russia the Straits and a warm-water port on the Black Sea, and to France the lost provinces of Alsace and Lorraine. They also endeavored, with much success, to get England so deeply involved with the Franco-Russian Alliance that it would be bound to come in on the side of France and Russia in the event of a European war. Therefore we have to draw a dividing line in European diplomacy at 1912, while fully realizing that the break was not sharp and that the policy which Izvolsky brought to fruition in 1914 was begun by him as early as 1908.

In the diplomatic history from 1870 to 1912 the developments and episodes of greatest moment were: (1) The genesis of the two great alliances—the Triple Alliance and the Triple Entente; (2) the French desire to recover Alsace-Lorraine; (3) the diplomatic clashes over the Near East and Morocco; (4) the superficial and somewhat hypocritical effort of the nations to secure disarmament and arbitration at the Hague Conferences of 1899 and 1907; and (5) the development of Anglo-German naval rivalry, especially after 1908.

The Triple Alliance was arranged by Bismarck between 1878 and 1882, and brought Germany, Austria, and Italy together in a defensive pact, designed primarily to frustrate a French war of revenge. Bismarck also secured benevolent relations with Russia through a Reinsurance Treaty made in 1884 and renewed in 1887. After Bismarck's retirement in 1890 the Kaiser abandoned the Russian link and turned to England as the most promising country outside of the Triple Alliance for Germany to cultivate. The French were on the alert and quickly picked up Russia. They had successfully negotiated a defensive military alliance by 1893.[1] When England and Germany failed to draw together between 1898 and 1903, because of the inadequacy and insincerity of the British offers and the opposition of the misanthropic Baron von Holstein, the French made a bid for British friendship. By 1904 they had succeeded in forming an Anglo-French agreement. Indeed, they even created a Triple Entente in 1907 through promoting an understanding between England and Russia; and they successfully tested British support in the second Morocco crisis of 1911, when England actually took a more bellicose stand than either France or Germany.[2]

The two great counter-alliances were certainly organized at the outset primarily to preserve the peace of Europe. Bismarck formed the Triple Alliance

---

[1] See Georges Michon, *The Franco-Russian Alliance, 1891-1917*, Macmillan, 1929, Chaps. I-IV; and W. L. Langer, *The Franco-Russian Alliance, 1890-1914*, Harvard University Press, 1929.

[2] Fully confirmed to the writer by M. Caillaux.

to prevent France from fomenting a war of revenge,[1] and Grey accepted the Triple Entente to preserve the balance of power, whatever may have been in the back of the heads of Paul Cambon and his associates, who led the English safely into the Entente. Yet in due time the counter-alliances became a menace to Europe, because both groups of Powers hesitated to back down in a serious crisis for fear of losing prestige. Further, as we shall show later, Izvolsky and Poincaré were successful in 1912 in transforming the purpose of the Triple Entente from a defensive and pacific organization into one that was preparing for a European war and was arming itself so as to be ready when the crisis arose.[2] This does not imply any deliberate plot on the part of Izvolsky and Poincaré to bring on a war for war's sake. It merely means that by the end of 1912 Izvolsky was convinced that Russia could gain its objectives only by war and that Poincaré was determined that France should gain its ends at the time of the same conflict. As between the two camps, it must be held that after 1911 the Triple Entente was much the greater menace to Europe [3] (1) because the Triple Alliance was gradually going to pieces on account of the secret Italian withdrawal in 1902 and because of Austro-German friction over Serbia in 1912-1913 and (2) because from 1912 to 1914 the Triple Entente was being transformed into a firm and potentially bellicose association.

At the close of the Franco-Prussian War of 1870 the Germans had annexed the two former German provinces of Alsace and Lorraine, which had been added to France by Louis XIV and other French monarchs. It proved an unwise move for Germany, as the French never ceased to hope for their recovery. France could not fairly hold Prussia responsible for the War of 1870, for even the Revanchard Clemenceau has admitted that "in 1870 Napoleon III, in a moment of folly, declared war on Germany without having even the excuse of being in a state of military preparedness. No true Frenchman has ever hesitated to admit that the wrongs of that day were committed by our side."[4] But the German annexations at the close of the war in 1871, whether justified or not, aroused a French aspiration for a war of revenge and laid a basis for the diplomatic maneuvers that ultimately led Europe to war in 1914. As Dr. Evart well states it:

> The Alsace-Lorraine annexation by Prussia, in 1871, was the principal factor in the counter-alliances, ententes, and antagonisms which perturbed continental Europe for forty-three years. . . . Not France only, but all Europe, kept in mind, between 1871 and 1914, with varying intensity, the prospect—one might say the assumed certainty—of the recurrence of the Franco-Prussian War.[5]

Since the time of the reign of Peter the Great, Russia had desired a good warm-water port to assure free and unimpeded passage for its commercial products and its war vessels. It had attempted to secure access through the Straits in the Crimean War and in the Russo-Turkish War of 1877-78, but was

---

[1] See W. L. Langer, *European Alliances and Alignments, 1871-1890,* Knopf, 1931.
[2] See below, pp. 582 ff.
[3] See S. B. Fay, *The Origins of the World War,* Macmillan, 1928, 2 vols., Vol. I, pp. 312-46.
[4] Georges Clemenceau, "The Cause of France," *Saturday Evening Post,* October 24, 1914.
[5] J. S. Evart, *The Roots and Causes of the Wars (1914-1918),* Doran, 1925, 2 vols., Vol. I, p. 671; Vol. II, p. 1169.

blocked by Great Britain and other European Powers. Russia next turned to the Far East and sought a warm-water port on the Pacific after the building of the Trans-Siberian Railroad. It secured this in Port Arthur, but was soon driven out of this commercial and naval base as a result of its defeat in the Russo-Japanese War. An attempt to get a port on the Persian Gulf also failed. Russia then returned to the Near East, to the Straits, which were now all the more desirable, as Russia had in 1907 come to terms with its old rival, Great Britain, which controlled the outlet from the Mediterranean to the Atlantic (Straits of Gibraltar).

The Russian Foreign Minister, Alexander Petrovich Izvolsky, first tried diplomacy. He proposed in 1908 that the Austrians should annex two south-Slav provinces, Bosnia and Hercegovina, in return for which Austria was to support the Russian demand for the Straits. Austria agreed and promptly annexed the two provinces, but England blocked the Russian plan in regard to the Straits. Izvolsky, usually bankrupt personally, did not dare openly to criticize England, as he was then being supported in part by gifts from Sir Arthur Nicolson, the British ambassador in St. Petersburg.[1] So he dishonestly alleged Austrian aggression and denied previous knowledge or approval of the annexation plan. This blocking by Grey of Izvolsky's plan to trade the annexation of Bosnia and Hercegovina by Austria for Russian control of the Straits must not only be regarded as a flagrant example of shortsighted British self-interest, but also as probably the most important single indirect cause of the World War. If Grey had shown generosity and foresight, the diplomatic revolution of 1912-14 would have been unnecessary and the World War unlikely.

Izvolsky next turned to Turkey, and in the fall of 1911 Russia made Turkey an offer of a defensive alliance if it would open the Straits to Russian war vessels. Turkey was still somewhat under the domination of the Germans in 1911 and did not care to accept this attractive offer of Russian protection against the Balkan states. A most significant aspect of the diplomacy of Izvolsky in 1908 and 1911 was that, on both occasions, he was prepared to sacrifice the interests of the Slavic states in the Balkans when Russia stood to gain by such action. In 1914, however, Russia justified the measures that brought on the war by the contention that it was bound by honor, tradition, and precedent to act as the protector of its little Slavic kinsmen in the Balkans.

After the failure of his Balkan diplomacy, Izvolsky became convinced that the Straits could only be obtained by a war. Therefore he logically decided to see if he could not get them by a local war rather than by a general European war, provided peace could be maintained on the larger scale. He helped to organize the Balkan League in 1912 and urged the Balkan states on to a war against Turkey, hoping that the former would be victorious and that Russia could use its influence with them to secure the Straits. The Balkan states, however, soon began fighting among themselves and this third plan of Izvolsky's was wrecked. He then became convinced that only a European war would bring the Straits to Russia, and the Russian government in time followed him in this decision. Such was the state of affairs in the Near East in 1914.

[1] A fact revealed to the writer by Count Pourtalès (German Ambassador to Russia in 1914) in 1927.

EUROPE IN 1871

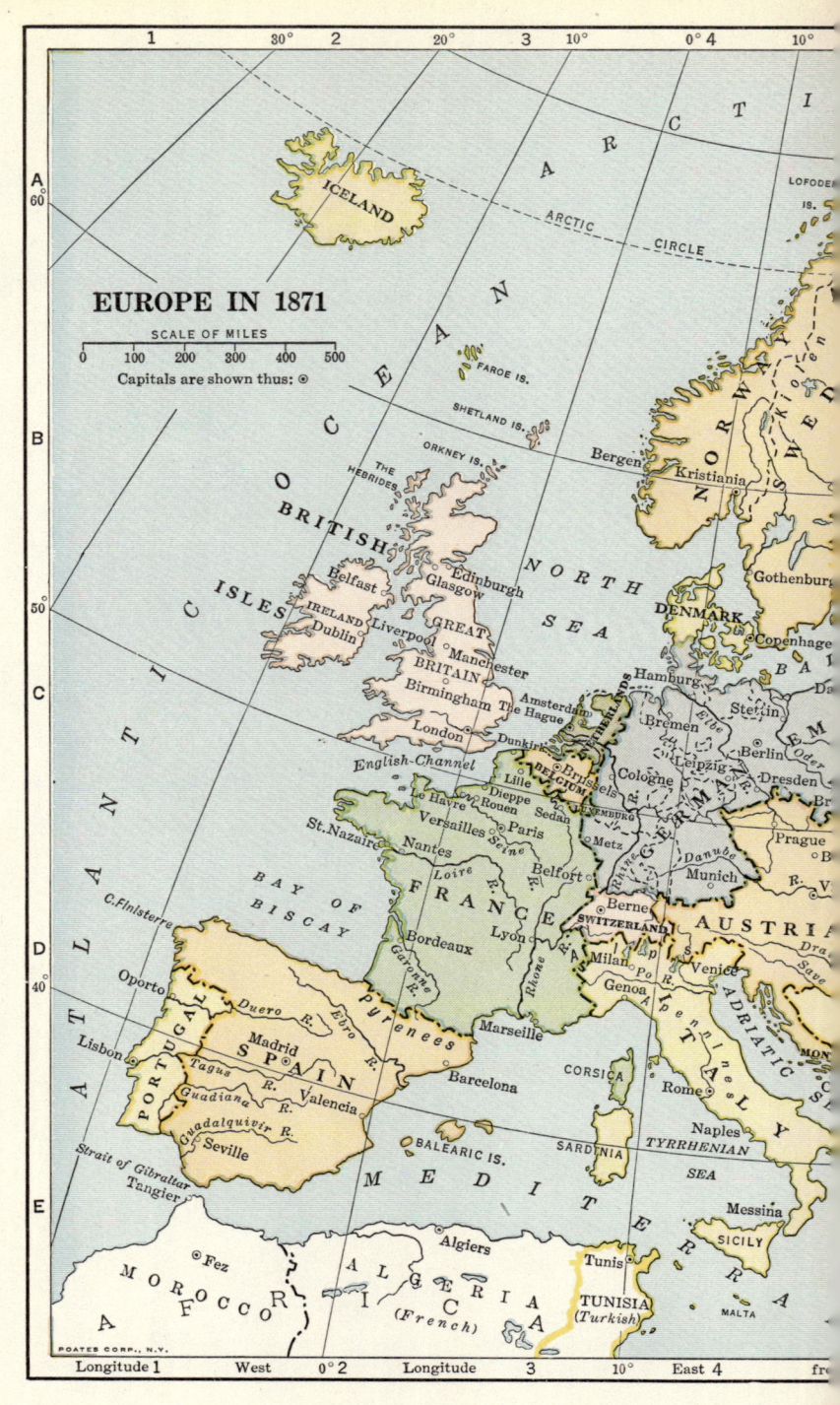

SCALE OF MILES
0 100 200 300 400 500
Capitals are shown thus: ⊙

O C E A N
White Sea
Dvina R.
L. Onega
L. Ladoga
Viborg
Kronstadt
Gulf of Finland
St. Petersburg
Riga
Duna R.
Volga R.
Moscow
Kazan
Samara
Tula
Orel
Saratov
Volga
Kharkov
Kiev
Dnepr R.
Don R.
Rostov
Astrakhan
Odessa
Pruth R.
Sea of Azov
R U S S I A
Ural Mountains
Ural R.
Ob R.
CASPIAN SEA
Caucasus Mts.
Tiflis
Baku
Batum
BLACK SEA
RUMANIA
Bucharest
Danube R.
Sofia
EUROPE
Constantinople
Bosporus
Sea of Marmara
Dardanelles
AEGEAN SEA
Athens
RHODES
CRETE
CYPRUS
TURKEY IN ASIA
Euphrates R.
Tigris R.
Baghdad
Greenwich
30°
40°
50°
60°
70°
6
7
8
9
A
B
C
D
E

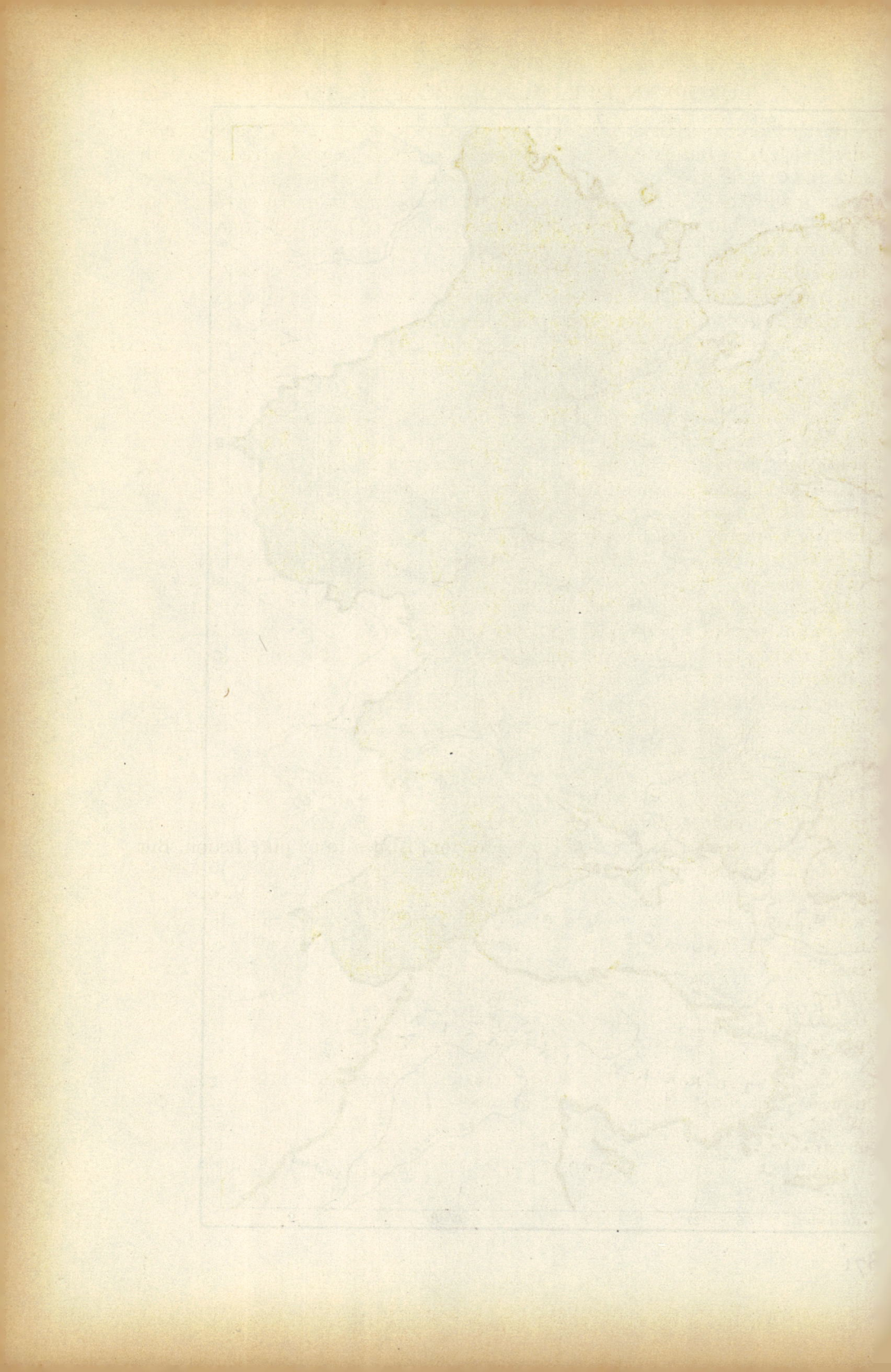

In the Morocco crises of 1905 and 1911, Germany was in the right both morally and legally, but its diplomatic methods left much to be desired as to both tact and finesse.[1] In 1905 Germany insisted that France should not be allowed to occupy northern Africa without taking the other European nations into consideration, and in 1911 it endeavored to prevent France from violating the Pact of Algeciras, which had been drawn up at the close of the first Morocco crisis. Incidentally, in the last Morocco crisis Germany had desired to break down the Anglo-French Alliance, but only made it firmer and more bellicose. Indeed, England seems to have been more eager for a test of arms in 1911 than either France or Germany. The writer possesses first-hand information that in 1911 the English urged Caillaux to adopt an attitude which would probably have led to war had he yielded to British advice.

The most important result of the second Morocco crisis was its effect upon internal French politics. The French jingoes attacked Caillaux for his pacific policies in 1911 and drove this great French statesman from power, supplanting him by the able and valiant but revengeful Raymond Poincaré. Had Caillaux remained in power, there is little probability that Izvolsky could have brought France around to a warlike policy by 1914.

In the two Hague Conferences of 1899 and 1907 Germany made rather a worse showing than the other major European states by being more honest, frank, and public about its attitude towards war and armament. Germany was no more opposed to land disarmament than France and no more averse to naval reduction that Great Britain, but it did not conceal its attitudes on these subjects from the public as carefully as did France and Great Britain, and made less hypocritical show of pacific intentions. To this degree Germany was diplomatically less competent than the other states. The Russian disarmament proposals were not made in good faith, as Count Witte later admitted. Finally, it must be made clear that there were no plans seriously submitted at The Hague for the arbitration of any of the real causes of wars. Therefore the common allegation that Germany at The Hague prevented Europe from putting an end to all wars a decade or more before 1914 is seen to be pure fiction. But Germany's candor, in other words, its diplomatic stupidity, enabled its enemies to portray Germany as the outstanding challenge to the peace of Europe.

We may therefore say that from 1870 to 1912 the responsibility for diplomatic arrangements likely to make for war was divided. On the whole, however, with the doubtful exception of England, Germany has the best record of any of the major states during this period. After a most careful examination of the *Grosse Politik*,[2] reviewing German policy from 1870 to 1914, Professor Sidney Bradshaw Fay has come to the following conclusions:

While it is true that Germany, no less than all the other Great Powers, did some things which contributed to produce a situation which ultimately resulted in the World War, it is altogether false to say that she deliberately plotted to bring it about or was solely responsible for it. On the contrary, she worked more effectively

---

[1] *Cf.* O. J. Hale, *Germany and the Diplomatic Revolution,* University of Pennsylvania Press, 1931. The Casablanca crisis of 1908 was not important; it was settled by the Hague Court.
[2] The official collection of documents on German foreign policy, 1870-1914.

than any other Great Power, except England, to avert it, not only in the last days of July, 1914, but also in the years immediately preceding.[1]

IV. THE DIPLOMATIC REVOLUTION: 1912-1914

In 1910 Izvolsky, who had been Russian Foreign Minister since 1906, resigned to accept the post of ambassador to France. This he did in part because of the Russian criticism of his failure to secure the Straits in 1908 and the resentment over the Russian humiliation that followed. He accepted the new appointment chiefly, however, because he believed that he could do more to forward the desirable Franco-Russian diplomatic maneuvers in Paris than in St. Petersburg. During 1910-11 he was unable to make much headway, as Caillaux and the friends of peace were in power in Paris and a pacifically inclined ambassador, Georges Louis, represented France at St. Petersburg. In January, 1912, the Caillaux group was superseded by Poincaré and his supporters. This marked a momentous turning-point in European international relations. These two able diplomats, Izvolsky and Poincaré, had at heart goals that could only be realized by one and the same method, namely, a war with Germany. Izvolsky admitted that "the road to Constantinople runs through Berlin," and Poincaré's life passion, as he himself confessed, was to recover Alsace-Lorraine, which could be achieved only by a victory over Germany. Poincaré once asserted in an address to university students:

In my years at school, my thoughts, made somber by the defeat, were always crossing the frontier that the Treaty of Frankfort had imposed upon us, and when I descended from my metaphysical clouds I could discover no other reason why my generation should go on living except for the hope of recovering our lost provinces.[2]

This is a matter of great importance, for Poincaré and his group represented the first Republican bloc willing to go to war for Alsace and Lorraine. Hitherto, the active French Revanchards had been, for the most part, royalists and enemies of the Third Republic. Plenty of Republicans had hoped for the return of the provinces, but no party of them had been willing to face the responsibility of waging a war to get them back for France. The linking of the Straits and Alsace-Lorraine as the common program of France and Russia, once a European war broke out, had of course been long taken for granted as a vital part of the Franco-Russian Alliance. As early as 1910, Georges Louis, the French ambassador in Russia, tells how, for many years, the Straits and Alsace-Lorraine had been inseparably connected in Franco-Russian diplomacy:

In the Alliance, Constantinople and the Straits form the counterpart of Alsace-Lorraine.

It is not specifically written down in any definite agreement, but it is the supreme goal of the Alliance that one takes for granted.

If the Russians open the question of the Straits with us, we must respond: "Yes, the day you aid us with respect to Alsace-Lorraine."

[1] *Die Kriegsschuldfrage,* December, 1926, p. 903.
[2] Cited by Mathias Morhardt, *Les preuves,* Paris, 1924, p. 135.

THE DIPLOMATIC REVOLUTION: 1912-1914

I have discovered the same idea in the correspondence of Hanotaux with Montebello.[1]

Izvolsky reported to his home government that he "felt like a new man" after his first conference with Poincaré, and while the two men disliked each other personally, distrusted each other to some degree, and differed frequently over details, they worked together cordially in all broad matters of diplomacy. Nothing that Poincaré has written in his apologetic memoirs can overthrow the impression of the essential unanimity of the two men in regard to the basic aspirations of Franco-Russian diplomacy from 1912 to the outbreak of the World War.

The first practical step in their diplomacy was the completion of a naval treaty between France and Russia in July, 1912, the military alliance of the two states having been completed nearly twenty years before. In August, 1912, Poincaré visited St. Petersburg. There he learned much more of the ambitious Russian plans in regard to the Straits and other territorial readjustments. He seems to have been convinced that France must coöperate enthusiastically to gain its objectives in the dual arrangement. It was perfectly clear to Poincaré that France had little prospect of obtaining Alsace-Lorraine unless it was done at the time Russia made war to obtain the Straits. His logic was faultless on this point. One of the most famous of contemporary French statesmen, in speaking to the present writer of Poincaré and Izvolsky, rather colorfully compared them to Jesus and the Devil, respectively, the difference being that in 1912 Poincaré actually capitulated to the diabolical suggestions of Izvolsky. It is the belief of some of the best historical students who have gone through the Russian source material that Poincaré's collapse before temptation was chiefly due to his Russian visit in 1912. Before that he had contemplated war as a possible eventuality. After the return from St. Petersburg he came to regard it as almost a certainty to be prepared for and accepted at the most advantageous moment; if inevitable, preferably not until after the Franco-Russian military plans had been completed.[2]

On November 17, 1912, Poincaré informed Izvolsky that if a crisis broke out in the Balkans and brought Russia in against Austria, and if Germany followed to protect Austria, then France would most certainly aid Russia and fulfill all the terms of the Franco-Russian Alliance. From then onward it was chiefly a matter of getting ready for the crisis when the latter arrived.[3]

November, 1912, was second in importance only to July, 1914, in witnessing events that helped on the World War. It was in this month (1) that Poincaré pledged France to execute its full obligations to Russia in support of Russian diplomacy in the Balkans; (2) that Grey pledged British naval, and by implication British military, support to France; and (3) that Russia drew up its secret military protocol in which it was stated that when the crisis came, diplomatic

---

[1] Cited by E. M. A. Judet, *Georges Louis*, Paris, 1925, p. 143.
[2] Some historians have pointed to the fact that Poincaré was scandalized in the summer of 1912 when he learned of Russia's patronage of the Balkan League and that France had been kept in the dark about it for four months. But it was the last fact—the Russian secrecy—that scandalized him, not the Russian policy of aggression in the Balkans.
[3] *Cf.* Friedrich Stieve, *Isvolsky and the World War*, Knopf, 1926, pp. 113-14.

negotiations were to be employed to screen military preparations leading to war.

The Russian army had made a poor showing against the Japanese in 1905. Though something had since been done to improve Russian military strength, the French believed that much further preparation was essential. Hence the French made large loans to the Russians, on condition that they should be spent under French supervision chiefly for munitions of war and for strategic railroads to the German frontier. The Russians also greatly increased the size of their army and the French reciprocated by enacting the Three-year Service Act, thus notably adding to the active French army.

In 1911-12 Izvolsky had found French opinion generally opposed to having France enter a European war over the Balkans. Something had to be done about this if the French public was to support the diplomatic plans of Poincaré and Izvolsky. Some of the French money lent to Russia was therefore sent back to be used by Izvolsky in bribing the leading French papers to publish incendiary articles against Austria and Germany and to make it appear that it was to the interest of France to block the alleged Austro-German intrigues in the Balkans.[1] Many of the greatest French papers were on the pay roll of Izvolsky. The list included the *Temps,* the leading Paris paper, as well as the organs of Millerand and Clemenceau. Hundreds of thousands of francs were dispensed in this way, Izvolsky ultimately putting the papers on a monthly-payment basis and withdrawing his subvention if they failed to be useful. He wrote home to his government frequently, telling them of the success of his campaign and asking for further funds. He told how, before the bribery campaign got under way, the French people were wont to complain about the danger of having France involved in Balkan controversies. After the press campaign had been operating for some time, so Izvolsky wrote, the French were impatient because the Russians were so complacent about Austria's threats against Serbia.

Izvolsky even imported Russian gold to assist in the election of Poincaré to the French Presidency early in 1913.[2] It was deemed wise to have Poincaré elected to the Presidency in order to give him official permanence. A French Prime Minister can be easily overthrown, but a President holds office for seven years, and a forceful man like Poincaré, by securing weak Foreign Ministers, could direct French foreign policy about as easily in the President's office as in the much more precarious position of Prime Minister. In fact, Poincaré told Izvolsky after his election to the Presidency that he proposed to be his own Foreign Minister, and this he was right down through the outbreak of the World War.[3]

In order to keep their plans moving smoothly it was desirable for Poincaré and Izvolsky to have a sympathetic French ambassador in St. Petersburg. M. Georges Louis, who held the office, was a member of the old Caillaux régime and was opposed to the bellicose schemes of Poincaré and Izvolsky. Therefore he was removed and replaced by M. Delcassé, a chief apostle of the war of revenge among the Republicans of France. Poincaré cleverly arranged it so that the Russians seemingly requested M. Louis's recall. With Delcassé

---

[1] See Barnes, *The Genesis of the World War* (1929 edition), pp. 119 ff. André Tardieu contributed many articles in this press campaign.   [2] Stieve, *op. cit.,* pp. 128-36.
[3] *Cf. Ibid., op. cit.,* p. 134.

and his successor, M. Paléologue, as the French ambassadors in St. Petersburg, there was no danger of opposition to the policies of Poincaré and Izvolsky from this quarter.

It was also necessary to convince Sazonov, the Russian Foreign Minister, of the necessity of a European war to obtain the Straits. This was done (1) by a ceaseless bombardment of letters written by Izvolsky from Paris; (2) by Sazonov's consciousness that the Balkan Wars had proved futile as a means of obtaining the Straits for Russia; and (3) by Sazonov's resentment when, in 1913, a German general, Liman von Sanders, was sent to Constantinople to train the Turkish army.[1] Hence on December 8, 1913, Sazonov sent a famous memorandum to the Tsar stating that Russia could not tolerate any other nation in control of the Straits, that Russia must have the Straits, and that Russia could obtain the Straits only by a European war. On December 31, 1913, and February 8, 1914, the Russians held long and secret ministerial councils at which they carefully laid out the strategy to be followed when this war came. The Tsar approved the minutes of these councils in March, 1914. Incidentally, Sazonov mentioned the fact that English aid must be assured if France and Russia were to hope to crush Germany, though he thought that they could probably defeat Germany and Austria even if England did not intervene on the side of France and Russia.[2]

It is quite true, as certain Russian writers have insisted, that the holding of these council meetings does not prove that Russia was planning war immediately, but it does show that Russia was very seriously considering the prospect of a war that would not be started by aggressive action against Russia.[3]

This brings us to the final scene in the dramatic revolution of European diplomacy from 1912 to 1914, namely, getting England so involved in the Franco-Russian net that it scarcely hesitated in the crisis of 1914. In 1911, through the Mansion House speech of Lloyd George, the British government had lined up decisively with France against Germany and had done all it could to inspire in the British press an anti-German tone. But Caillaux and the German leaders were inclined towards peace, and war was averted. In September, 1912, Sazonov visited London in behalf of an Anglo-Russian naval alliance. While he was not immediately successful in this, he received from the British hearty assurance of naval coöperation against Germany in the event of war and was told of a secret engagement to help France if war broke out.[4] In late November, 1912, Poincaré induced Sir Edward Grey to agree to an arrangement whereby the French fleet could be concentrated in the Mediterranean Sea while the British fleet could be relied upon to protect the French Channel ports. In 1912 also, France was able to frustrate a possible Anglo-German agreement growing out of Lord Haldane's visit to Germany. In April, 1914, the British King and Grey went to Paris and there Grey, with Izvolsky and Poincaré, laid the basis for an Anglo-Russian naval alliance that was moving towards completion in June, 1914.[5]

---

[1] This was no worse than what had already taken place, namely, that an English admiral had been put in charge of the Turkish navy, but England was friendly with Russia.
[2] A view shared by the French and Russian General Staffs in the spring of 1914.
[3] Compare Professor Schmitt's horror over the dubious Moltke-Conrad "understanding" of 1909. See below, p. 587.
[4] *Cf.* Stieve, *op. cit.,* pp. 89-90.   [5] *Cf. Ibid., op. cit.,* pp. 197 ff.

The fact that England and Germany seemed to be coming to an agreement over Portuguese colonies in Africa and over the Baghdad Railway project alarmed the French and Russians early in 1914 and probably explains why they decided in July, 1914, that the European war should be fought before England could slip away from the Triple Entente. France and Russia never felt absolutely certain of British support until August, 1914, though the recently published British documents show that the British Foreign Office never had any doubts about its obligations to the Entente in the crisis of 1914, and made its decision to come in on the side of France and Russia in July, 1914, without reference to the Belgian question.[1] As the eminent English publicist E. D. Morel once remarked, the French and Russians had thoroughly "hooked" the British by the close of 1912, even if Izvolsky and Poincaré did not entirely realize that they had done so. In his anti-German and pro-French policy Grey was egged on notably by Sir Eyre Crowe, Under-Secretary of State for Foreign Affairs. Crowe, who had a German mother, was even more Germanophobe than Francophile.

While Northcliffe was bringing the Tory public and the British masses round to his bellicose point of view,[2] the imperialistic and nationalistic propaganda was being successfully spread among the British Liberals by Mr. J. Alfred Spender, editor of the *Westminster Gazette,* and the chief upholder of imperialism and Continental entanglements among the Liberal newspaper men of England. Spender was probably a more dangerous influence than Northcliffe, for a Liberal government was in power in 1914 and the Liberals were not likely to be greatly influenced by the Tory press. A member of the British cabinet in 1914 informed the writer in 1927 that he regarded Spender as second only to the war clique in the cabinet among those who made it possible for Grey to throw England into the conflict. It might be mentioned in this connection that it was Spender who helped Grey write his apologia, *Twenty-five Years.*[3]

In this way Izvolsky and Poincaré transformed European diplomacy in the two years prior to 1914 and were ready for whatever crisis arose. They did not originally expect that 1914 would be the year of the decisive crisis which would bring on the European war. They had anticipated that this would come at the death of Francis Joseph, which they believed would bring about a serious Austro-Balkan clash. When the Archduke Francis Ferdinand was assassinated in the summer of 1914, they appear to have concluded that the potential Anglo-German rapprochement was too dangerous to allow the test to be postponed. England was known not to make wars lightly, and there was little hope that France and Russia unaided could speedily crush Germany and Austria. In any event, it seems certain that they decided that if a diplomatic crisis arose through Austrian demands upon Serbia, it would be better to fight than for Russia, and with it the Triple Entente, to accept humiliation and the resulting loss of prestige.

[1] Fully confirmed by Lord Morley's *Memorandum on Resignation,* Macmillan, 1928.
[2] See A. G. Gardner's slashing denunciation of the war-monger Northcliffe, reprinted in Barnes, *In Quest of Truth and Justice,* pp. 30 ff.
[3] See Spender's apology, *Fifty Years of Europe,* Stokes, 1933. In an amazing review of the book in the New York *Nation,* G. P. Gooch calls Spender a sincere friend of peace.

Poincaré has denied the truth of this indictment which we have been able to formulate on the basis of the Izvolsky correspondence and other documents, but he has been unable to bring forward any French documents that convincingly contradict Izvolsky's general interpretation of affairs. Moreover, there is little probability that Izvolsky would have dared to lie persistently to his chief, Sazonov, regarding matters of such vital concern for the foreign policy of his country and for his own diplomatic ambitions. He had suffered enough in 1909 from failure to make good his assurances.[1] Professor William L. Langer, the foremost American authority on prewar Russian diplomacy, in reviewing the latest edition of the Izvolsky correspondence writes:

When all is said and done this correspondence still formulates the most serious indictment of Franco-Russian pre-war policy and lends considerable color to the theory that there was a conspiracy against the peace of the world.[2]

While the Triple Entente was being thus more firmly cemented and made aggressive in character, so far as the Franco-Russian nucleus was concerned, the Triple Alliance was disintegrating. Italy, placated over northern Africa, had made a secret agreement with France in 1902 to the effect that it would enter no war against France. Though the Germans counted on Italian aid in 1914, we know there was little chance of their obtaining such assistance. Then from 1912 to 1914 there was considerable friction between Germany and Austria over Serbia. The Austrians felt that Serbia must be punished in order to stop Russo-Serbian intrigues in the Balkans. The Kaiser, however, under the influence of the pro-Serbian German minister in Belgrade, Baron von Griesinger, opposed the imminent Austrian aggression and twice prevented an Austrian offensive against Serbia. The Austrian journalist Heinrich Kanner, a disgruntled enemy of the old régime in Austria, together with Professor Bernadotte Schmitt, have claimed to find in the memoirs of Conrad von Hötzendorf, the former Austrian Chief of Staff, evidence of a dark Austro-German war plot secretly laid in 1909 and executed in 1914. Professor Fay, Count Montgelas, and others have shown that there is no factual foundation whatever for this "Schmitt-Kanner myth."[3]

V. THE EVE OF THE WORLD WAR

In the first half of 1914 many developments were taking place which were likely to make any crisis in that year pregnant with the probability of a European war. The growing Anglo-German amiability[4] greatly worried the French and Russians and made them feel that any considerable delay with the European war was dangerous. The Tory clique in England was favorable to a European war. Not only were the Tories bellicose and anti-German, but a war would help stop the menacing social reforms of the Liberal party in England, particularly the proposed land reforms, and also would make it more difficult

---
[1] This interpretation implies no faith in Izvolsky's integrity; merely his recognition of expediency.   [2] *Political Science Quarterly*, December, 1927, p. 656.
[3] *Cf.* S. B. Fay, *American Historical Review*, January, 1927, pp. 317-19; and Count M. M. K. S. Montgelas, "*Une nouvelle thèse relative à la question des responsabilités*," *Revue de Hongrie*, Nov. 15, 1926.
[4] Expressed by Lloyd George and Lichnowsky, for example, not by Grey and Crowe.

to enforce the Irish Home Rule Act. The Northcliffe press was demanding war against Germany, partly because of its Tory sympathies and partly because a war was good business for newspapers. As has been noted, Russia had decided that it must have the Straits and could only obtain them by a European war, and held two long ministerial councils in December, 1913, and February, 1914, to decide on the proper strategy for the war. In March, 1914, the Russian General Danilov congratulated his country on its readiness for the impending conflict and in June General Sukhomlinov, the Russian Minister of War, boasted that Russia was ready for war and that France must also be ready. This was done in part to silence the foes of the Three-year Service Act in France. In the spring of 1914 France had refused to allow the retirement into the reserves of the class normally entitled to leave active service that year, thus having four classes instead of two with the colors in July, 1914. The Tsar had received the Serbian Premier, Nikola Pašič, in February, 1914, had asked him how many men Serbia could put in the field if war came, promised him arms and ammunition from Russia, and told him to inform the Serbian King that Russia would do all in its power to aid Serbia.

In his memoirs, Sir Edward Grey represents Russia as drifting into war because of lack of any decisive policy or leadership: "Perhaps it may be true to say, of Russia, that she was like a huge, unwieldy ship, which in time of agitation kept an uncertain course; not because she was directed by malevolent intentions, but because the steering-gear was weak."[1] It is interesting to compare Grey's view with Sazonov's direct denial, embodied in his memorandum to the Tsar on December 8, 1913, telling him that Russia must have the Straits, and in all probability could secure them only by war:

In considering the future and in impressing upon ourselves that the maintenance of peace, so much desired, will not always lie in our power, we are forced not to limit ourselves to the problems of today and tomorrow. This we must do in order to escape the reproach so often made of the Russian ship of state, namely, that it is at the mercy of the winds and drifts with the current, without a rudder capable of firmly directing her course.

From the reports of the ministerial conferences of December 31, 1913, and February 8, 1914, we can readily perceive that Sazonov had seized the helm with determination and knew in what direction he was steering the Muscovite craft.

By January, 1914, the plot to murder the Archduke Francis Ferdinand, heir presumptive to the Austrian throne, was under consideration, and in March it had taken definite form. In May it was perfected by officers in the Serbian army, and it has been charged that high Russian military authorities had approved of it and had promised Russian aid in the event of an Austrian attack upon Serbia.[2] The Russian minister in Belgrade, Nicholas von Hartwig, was

[1] *Twenty-five Years, 1892-1916,* Stokes, 1925, 2 vols., Vol. II, p. 23.
[2] There is no evidence that Sazonov and the Russian Foreign Office knew anything about the Serbian assassination plot. Indeed, Count Pourtalès, the German ambassador in St. Petersburg in 1914, informed the writer in the summer of 1927 that he was thoroughly convinced that Sazonov was entirely innocent in this matter. Sazonov was at tea in the German Embassy when news was brought to him of the murder of the Archduke.

THE EVE OF THE WORLD WAR

organizing a widespread Balkan intrigue against Austria, and the Austrians captured many of his telegrams and decoded them. This enabled the Austrian statesmen to know of the Russo-Balkan menace to the Dual Monarchy. Before the murder of the Archduke they had drawn up a memorandum to be taken to Berlin, asking for German aid in thwarting the Russian intrigues in the Balkans. They particularly desired Germany to drop Rumania and to take on Bulgaria as the pivotal state for Austro-German diplomacy in the Balkans. The Serbian government was aware of the assassination plot for at least three weeks before the murder of Francis Ferdinand, but it took no active steps to frustrate the scheme or to warn Austria of the danger that was awaiting the Archduke when he visited Bosnia. Such was the state of affairs when the Archduke Francis Ferdinand was shot down on the streets of Sarajevo in Bosnia on St. Vitus's Day, June 28, 1914.

In regard to this third level of war responsibility, that residing in diplomatic developments from 1912 to 1914, we may hold that the guilt was mainly that of Russia, aided and abetted by Serbia, and to a lesser degree that of France; while Germany, England and Austria had the cleanest record.

VI. THE CRISIS OF JUNE-AUGUST, 1914

When the assassination came, the French and Russians recognized that the impending clash between Austria and Serbia might bring about a European conflict. The year 1914 was a particularly desirable time for the Entente, because there was imminent danger that England might develop more happy relations with Germany, and that the French Radicals might be able to secure the repeal of the French Army Bill. Russia, moreover, was threatened by another revolution. Poincaré went to St. Petersburg, and before even learning the terms of the Austrian ultimatum renewed his pledge of two years earlier to support Russia in a war over the Balkans, and indicated that the impending Austro-Serbian conflict would meet the conditions demanded by the French in supporting Russian intervention in that region.

The Franco-Russian program in 1914 was to indicate a formal show of conciliation and concessions on the part of Serbia, and apparent Franco-Russian willingness to settle the dispute through diplomacy. Underneath, secret Franco-Russian military preparations were carried on that ultimately made a diplomatic settlement impossible. Hence Russia urged Serbia not to declare war on Austria, and to insure a superficially conciliatory Serbian reply to Austria, the Serbian response to the Austrian ultimatum was drafted in outline by Berthelot and others in the French Foreign Office.[1] Russia did not desire to have Serbia precipitate matters prematurely by a declaration of war on Austria. This would have affected European opinion, particularly English opinion, unfavorably and would also have brought about military activities altogether too rapidly for Russia, whose mobilization over a vast area would necessarily be slow as compared to that of Austria and Germany.

On July 24, when the terms of the Austrian ultimatum to Serbia were made

---

[1] Berthelot once admitted to Jacques Mesnil, editor of *L'Humanité*, that he had drafted the Serbian reply in outline.

public, Russia and France began that dual program of a diplomatic barrage combined with secret military preparations which made a European war inevitable by the late afternoon of July 30. Russia sent a diplomatic message to Serbia counseling moderation, but at the same time prepared for the mobilization of the four great military districts of central and southern Russia, as well as of the Russian fleets. Russian money in Germany and Austria was also called in.

On the same day (July 24) Viviani, on his way back from St. Petersburg, telegraphed to the French Foreign Office that the Austro-Serbian situation was likely to develop serious European complications, and the French troops in Morocco were ordered home. Both countries began systematic military preparations for war on July 26. By July 29 the time had come when Russian military preparations had gone far enough to warrant a general mobilization, which would inevitably provoke war, and the Tsar was persuaded to consent to this order. A conciliatory telegram from the Kaiser urging peace, however, induced the Tsar to revoke the order, but the next day Sazonov and close associates once more extracted from the Tsar his reluctant consent to the order for general mobilization. The French and the Russians had understood for a generation that once Russian general mobilization was ordered there would be no way of preventing a general European war. General Dobrorolsky, chief of Russian mobilization in 1914, has told us with great candor that the Russian authorities in 1914 fully realized that a European war was *on* as soon as the mobilization order had been sent out from the general telegraph office in St. Petersburg late in the afternoon of July 30.

The French authorities had been informed as to the general nature and progress of the Russian military preparations, but they made no effort to restrain them, though the French well knew that these military activities were bound to render a European war inevitable. They actually urged the Russians to speed up their military preparations, but to be more secretive about them, so as not to alienate England or provoke Germany to rapid counter-mobilization. On the night of July 31 the French government went still further and finally decided for war, handing this information to Izvolsky about midnight on that day. As Izvolsky communicated the news to Sazonov shortly after midnight, "The French Minister of War disclosed to me with hearty high spirits that the French government has finally decided upon war."

The Austrian statesmen in 1914 decided that the time had come when it would be necessary to suppress the Serbian menace, and they consciously planned an ultimatum to Serbia of such severity that it would be highly unlikely that Serbia would concede all of these demands. The plan, then, was to make a show of diplomacy but to move towards probable war. This program was much like that of France and Russia, save for the crucial fact that Austria only desired to produce a local punitive war, while the plans of France and Russia envisaged a general European conflict. This is the most important point to be borne in mind when estimating the relative war guilt of Austria as against that of France and Russia.

Germany, lately friendly to Serbia, was alarmed by the assassination of the Archduke and the resulting menace to its chief ally. Germany therefore agreed to stand behind Austria in the plan of the latter to execute its program of punishing Serbia. The answer of the Serbians to the Austrian ultimatum, however, impressed the Kaiser as a satisfactory basis for further negotiations. On July 27, in coöperation with Sir Edward Grey, Germany began to urge upon Austria direct negotiations with Russia and the mediation of its dispute with Serbia. Austria refused to listen to this advice and declared war upon Serbia on July 28. Germany then became alarmed at the rumored Russian military preparations and vigorously pressed Austria for a diplomatic settlement of the dispute. Austria did not give way and consent to this until July 31, which was too late to avert a general European war because the Russian mobilization was then in full swing.[1] Germany endeavored without success to secure the suspension of military activities by Russia, and then, after unexpected hesitation and deliberation, declared war upon Russia.

The Russian general mobilization, undertaken with the full connivance of the French ambassador in St. Petersburg and approved by Paris before it was ordered, was decided upon at a time when diplomatic negotiations were moving rapidly towards a satisfactory settlement of the major problems in the crisis. Hence the Russian general mobilization not only precipitated military hostilities, but also was the main reason for the failure of diplomatic efforts in 1914.

England was for peace provided France was not drawn into the conflict, but was determined to come into the war in case France was involved. As France decided from the beginning to stand with Russia for war, and as England refused to attempt to restrain either France or Russia, England was inevitably drawn away from encouragement of its own and the German efforts towards a diplomatic settlement of the crisis and into support of the military action of France and Russia. England made the decision to enter the war after Germany had proposed to keep out of Belgium and to refrain from attacking France if England would remain neutral.[2] In fact, Germany even suggested that it might guarantee the integrity of France and the French colonies in the event of war if England would promise neutrality.[3] The Belgian issue in England was a pure subterfuge, cleverly exploited by Sir Edward Grey to inflame British opinion against Germany and to secure British support of his war policy. Even if Grey had wished personally to listen to his major ambassadors and to take steps to check the aggression of France and Russia, he would have found it difficult to do so because he was constantly inflamed by the passionate anti-Germanism of Crowe,[4] who put the worst interpretation on every

[1] Count von Berchtold, the Austrian Foreign Minister in 1914, explained fully and candidly to the writer why he did not heed Germany's pressure before July 31. He stated that the Austro-Hungarian statesmen were convinced that a continuance of the Serbian threat was a greater menace to the Dual Monarchy than a war between Germany and Austria on the one side and France and Russia on the other. He had plenty of assurance from the British Embassy in Vienna that England would most certainly not intervene to protect Serbia. Counting on English neutrality, he was determined to punish Serbia after the latter had refused to accede to the only really important items in the Austrian ultimatum. By July 31 Berchtold was finally convinced that England would come in if Germany and France went to war. He then moderated his policy, but the Russian mobilization made it too late. Lord Grey's evasive and two-faced conduct of British diplomacy in 1914 thus played a very important part in Austrian policy and in the coming of the war.
[2] Cf. *British Official Documents on the Origins of the War, 1898-1914*, ed. by G. P. Gooch and Harold Temperley, British Library of Information, 1926-32, 11 vols., Vol. XI, No. 448.
[3] *Ibid.*, Vol. XI, Nos. 419, 448, 453.
[4] English Undersecretary of State for Foreign Affairs in 1914.

German move in the crisis and held Britain's course steadfastly towards war.[1]

In estimating the order of guilt of the various countries we may safely say that the direct and immediate responsibility for the World War falls upon Serbia, France, and Russia, with the guilt about equally distributed. Next in order—far below France and Russia—would come Austria, though it never desired a general European war. Finally, we should place England and Germany, in the order named, both being opposed to war in the 1914 crisis. Probably the German public was somewhat more favorable to military activities than the English people, but, as we have amply explained above, the Kaiser made more strenuous efforts to preserve the peace of Europe in 1914 than did Sir Edward Grey. Germany worked hard to restrain Austria in the last days of the crisis, but Grey, defying the advice and information of all his important ambassadors, adamantly refused to restrain Russia or France or to discuss with Germany the inviolability of Belgium in return for British neutrality.

It has been declared futile, illogical, and impermissible to try to arrange the European Powers in any rank or order of guilt, on the ground that they were all involved in the morass of diplomatic squabbles and intrigues of 1914. This is to question the elementary logic applied every day in courts of law. Principals and accomplices are all involved, let us say, in a murder. But the court is able to distinguish between them, and pleas of first-degree murder, second-degree murder, and manslaughter are all permitted. It has further been maintained that it is unfair to say that Russia, for example, was guilty in 1914, because many Russians knew nothing about the issues of the war and many more were opposed to its onset. It should be obvious that we are not attempting the futile and unfair task of indicting a nation. We refer only to those statesmen who were responsible in 1914 for the public policy of their respective states and compelled each country to act as a unit.

Another good way of stating the ultimate conclusions about the crisis of 1914 would be to say that only Russia, Serbia, and France wished a general European war, under the conditions that existed in the summer of 1914; that Austria-Hungary wished a local punitive war against Serbia, but desired to avert, if possible, a general war; and that Germany, England, and Italy did not wish any kind of war, but were too stupid, dilatory, or involved in entanglements to prevent either the Austro-Serbian war or the wider conflict. The Kaiser had favored an immediate attack on Serbia by Austria right after the assassination, but following the Serbian reply to the Austrian ultimatum he favored negotiations.

Some writers whose accounts of prewar diplomacy do not differ materially from that presented in this chapter have nevertheless maintained that no important responsible statesman wanted war in 1914. Upon examining their position, it turns out that they mean that nobody wanted war for war's sake alone—or wanted war in the abstract. We might go even further than such historians and concede that nobody in 1914 wanted war if he could get what he wanted without war. Probably Alexander Izvolsky can be charged with

---

[1] *Cf.* Hermann Lutz, *Lord Grey and the World War*, Knopf, 1928, pp. 218-19, 235, 238, 244-45, 252-53, 266-67, 287, 289-90, 294, 300.

more responsibility for the World War than any other single person. Yet we have already made it clear that even Izvolsky accepted war only as a last resort in his campaign to get the Straits. He first tried diplomacy twice, in 1908 and in 1911, and then he quite humanely and discreetly had recourse to a "little war"—the Balkan Wars of 1912-13. Only when these efforts all failed did he reconcile himself to working for a European war to obtain the Straits. It is probable that only a handful of half-wits, neurotics, ultra-militarists, and the like wanted war in 1914 in preference to securing national ambitions by pacific means.

The question that we have to settle, however, is not who wanted or did not want war under conditions quite different from those which existed in Europe in 1914. This is both an insoluble and an irrelevant problem. What we have to deal with is the issue of what responsible statesmen wished war under the precise conditions that developed after June 30, 1914. To this a decisive answer can be given today, if such an answer can be given to any historical question since the dawn of written history. Certainly Izvolsky, Sazonov, and the Grand Duke Nicholas, among the Russians; Poincaré, Viviani, and Berthelot, among the French; and Pašić and the majority of the Serbian cabinet—these thought a European war preferable to permitting Austria to proceed with its justifiable punishment of Serbia.[1] The majority of the Austro-Hungarian cabinet believed a war involving France, Russia, Germany, and Austria to be better than refraining from the invasion of Serbia, but they did not think it worth a war in which England would fight on the side of France and Russia. The majority of the responsible statesmen of England and Germany would have preferred peace to war in 1914, but England accepted war rather than restrain its allies and Germany was unable to dissuade its ally from the Austro-Serbian conflict in time to save the peace of Europe. It is doubtful if any new facts or different logic will ever upset this general line of reasoning. The courageous and brilliant French publicist Georges Demartial has remarked that the theory of divided guilt in the crisis of 1914 is as discredited today as the older theory that Germany was solely responsible. If one means by "divided guilt" that war guilt in the 1914 crisis was *equally* divided between the two groups of Powers, then M. Demartial is right in his conclusion. Of course, he would agree to the theory of divided guilt in the sense that some responsibility in 1914 fell upon Germany. No sensible historian would contend that Germany's wish for European peace in 1914 was based upon any superior moral virtues of that nation. It is to be explained simply by the fact that Germany was gaining its ends, selfish ends if you wish, very well indeed by peaceful means, and its statesmen knew that war might place German progress in grave jeopardy.

VII. THE GREAT CONFLICT: THE OLD AND THE NEW WARFARE

The World War formally began July 28, 1914, when Austria-Hungary sent Serbia an official declaration of war, and continued for over four years, being

[1] Those in the Serbian, Russian and French cabinets, if any, who were personally opposed to war were, of course, in time carried along with the bellicose majority.

terminated with the signing of the Armistice by the Allies and Germany on November 11, 1918.

On July 30, 1914, mobilization of the Russian army was ordered, and on August 1, upon Russia's refusal to demobilize, Germany declared war against Russia. Before the end of that month France, Belgium, England, Montenegro, and Japan had joined Russia in the conflict, and in October of that year Turkey allied its forces with Germany. At the conclusion of 1914, the warring Central Powers included Germany, Austria-Hungary, and Turkey, and the Entente Allies were Russia, France, England, Japan, Belgium, Serbia, and Montenegro. Bulgaria's entrance in October, 1915, completed the ranks of the Central Powers. The years 1914-18 witnessed the increase of the Allied Powers by the entry of Italy (May, 1915), Portugal and Rumania (1916), the United States, Cuba, Panama, Greece, Siam, China, Liberia, and Brazil (1917), and Guatemala, Costa Rica, Nicaragua, Haiti, and Honduras (1918).

Some ten years before the war, the German General Staff had drawn up its campaign in the event of a general European war. The plan was to make a rapid drive through Belgium and envelop and capture the armies of France and of England, provided the latter should enter the conflict. Having disposed of the enemy in the west, all the German resources were then to be directed against Russia to oust it from the war. As the German Chief of Staff at the time was General von Schlieffen, this plan of campaign came to be known as the Schlieffen Plan.

When war broke out in August, 1914, this scheme was launched with clocklike precision. It worked perfectly, except for a bad blunder committed by General von Bülow in not attacking as ordered, and had it not been for the incompetence of the German Chief of Staff, General von Moltke, the Germans would, in all probability, have won the war with a smashing victory before the end of September, 1914.

But Von Moltke, nephew of the great leader of the Prussian army in 1870, was never an able military man. He had been chosen by the Kaiser chiefly for the legendary prestige of the family name. Moreover, in the summer of 1914 his health was so bad that he should have been in a hospital rather than in the headquarters of the General Staff.[1] Hence he was unable personally to direct hostilities.

At the height of the great German advance he sent to the front with absolute authority an incompetent subordinate, Lieutenant-Colonel Hentsch, who ordered a retreat at the very moment when the Germans might have entered Paris and at the same time have driven the British army back in disorder. The French followed up this retreat by what is usually known as the First Battle of the Marne.[2] This loss of the war through an utterly incompetent commander-in-chief is the major responsibility that the Kaiser must bear for the German defeat in 1914-18. Von Moltke's successor, Falkenhayn, was only a slight improvement. By the time Ludendorff and Hindenburg were placed in

---

[1] Von Moltke's physical incapacity in 1914 was fully described to the writer by Von Tirpitz.

[2] The common conviction, repeated by most non-expert historians of the war, that the German advance in 1914 was brought to an abrupt halt by the French counter-attack is quite mistaken. In spite of Von Bülow's blunder, the Germans could easily have taken Paris and paralyzed the English army if Colonel Hentsch had not advised retreat. Some of the German officers at the front threw their swords in the dust and others threatened to shoot Hentsch, but in the end they obeyed the order to retreat.

supreme command in 1916 it was too late for Germany to win a smashing military victory. Once the Germans retired, both sides settled down in the west to a dreary and terrible trench warfare that lasted for approximately four years.

The intrenched western front in 1914-15 stretched from Belfort northward to Verdun, westward to the Aisne River and then northward again to Ypres and Nieuport, covering a distance of six hundred miles. Although the Germans had vanquished most of Belgium and northern France and controlled many of the French mines and industries, they were unable to make substantial further advances and conquer all of France.

The army protecting Germany's eastern front, although inferior in size to the Russian, was able, under the leadership of Generals von Hindenburg and Ludendorff, to rout and partially annihilate the Russian army in the battle of Tannenberg in August, 1914.[1] This was the most decisive defeat administered to any army during the World War.

At this time, Austria-Hungary attempted to invade Russian Poland but was decisively defeated by the Russians and lost, as a consequence, eastern Galicia, including Lemberg. However, the counter-offensive launched by the Germans in the spring of 1915 under General von Mackensen drove the Russians from this region and returned practically all Galicia to Austria-Hungary.

Hindenburg, supported by huge armies, attacked Russian Poland, captured Warsaw and Vilna, and by October, 1915, most of Poland, Lithuania, and Courland was in the possession of the Central Powers. This offensive warfare, severely crippling the Russian forces, extended the German eastern front from Cernauti (Czernowitz) on the boundary of Rumania to Riga in the north. The reverses to Russia under the tsarist régime helped to bring on a revolution in the spring of 1917, in which the Tsar abdicated, to be succeeded first by Prince Lvov and then by Alexander Kerensky. Kerensky, as the head of the new Russian revolutionary government, attempted another invasion of Galicia in July, 1917, but this proved a dismal failure. When the Bolsheviks, under the leadership of Lenin and Trotsky, obtained control of Russia in November, 1917, they demobilized the armies, signed the crushing peace treaty of Brest-Litovsk in March, 1918, and withdrew from the war.

The Bulgarians, joining the Central Powers in October, 1915, assisted the Germans in attacking Serbia and Montenegro. Within two months they had succeeded in conquering these countries and Albania, and most of the Balkan Peninsula was occupied by the Central Powers. The Entente effort at a brilliant coup in southeastern Europe, namely, the attempt to force the Dardanelles and free the Russian man power and grain supply for the Entente, proved an expensive and dismal failure with the collapse of the gallant Gallipoli campaign early in 1916.

Rumania, joining the Allies in August, 1916, invaded Transylvania in Hungary, but Mackensen, seizing Bucharest, drove them from this region and,

---

[1] The amazing incompetence of the German High Command at the outset in 1914 not only lost the chance of a brilliant and speedy German triumph, but also came desperately near to bringing complete and rapid disaster upon Germany. General von Hindenburg was on the retired list when war broke out. He asked to be allowed to reënter the service but was arrogantly turned down. Not until the Russians seemed certain to overrun Prussia was he summoned frantically for the task of turning them back—so late that it put great risk and strain upon even Hindenburg's unique talent for warfare in East Prussia.

with the coöperation of Falkenhayn, soon occupied the greater portion of the country as the result of one of the most rapid and brilliant campaigns of the war.

The Italians, after the defeat at Caporetto in October, 1917, were pushed back from Austria as far as the Piave River in Italy, the Austrians taking about 200,000 men as prisoners and 2,000 pieces of artillery. However, thanks to efficient reorganization and British and French reënforcements, the Austro-Hungarians were halted. In June, 1918, they attempted to drive back the Italians stationed along the Piave, getting across the river at several points and even progressing five miles at one place. But the reënforced Italians, under the leadership of General Diaz, recovered their unity and- strength and, aided by floods, beat the enemy back and did not cease their offensive until November, 1918, when they invaded and occupied Trent and Trieste.

The strain of the war was becoming intense; people in many lands, but particularly in France, Russia, and Italy, expressed a desire for peace with Germany based on mutual concessions. The Germans, likewise, were disposed to welcome reasonable peace terms. The spread of an idea such as this implies the distintegration of morale and of the desire for victory. Russia's case has been discussed above. The defeat the Italians sustained at Caporetto at the hands of the Austro-Hungarian army in 1917 was a shock to Italian morale.

It seems highly probable that by the winter of 1915-16 Europe was headed towards a desirable negotiated peace. But the Entente was soon converted to a determination to continue the war through the intimation which Colonel House, as President Wilson's agent in Europe, had given that the United States would be likely to join the Entente if Wilson was reëlected. The new spirit was evident in the famous "knock-out victory" interview of Lloyd George, given out to Roy W. Howard of the United Press on September 29, 1916. This is an important item in the verdict of history against Woodrow Wilson. Lloyd George was also doubtless influenced by the entry of Rumania into the war in August, 1916, and by the British successes on the Somme. Another factor was the stupidity of German politics and diplomacy from 1916 to 1918. Ludendorff and Hindenburg were held back by the jealousy of the Kaiser and Falkenhayn when they might have won the war through bold and aggressive campaigns. Then they were given supreme control of both military and political power in 1916—the time when the war had to be won by Germany through clever diplomacy, if at all. Ludendorff, Hindenburg, and Tirpitz were poorly endowed with political acumen and diplomatic skill and finesse.

The United States entered the war in part because the British blockade of the ports of the Central Powers made us have our chief commercial stake in the Entente, and in part because of the pro-British sympathies of Ambassador Page and President Wilson, which made it difficult for them to attempt to hold England strictly to international law on the seas. The English violations of international law in regard to neutral rights provoked the German submarine warfare in retaliation. This submarine warfare furnished the ostensible excuse for the American entry into the conflict. Yet nearly a year before the resumption of submarine warfare early in 1917 Mr. Wilson had secretly conveyed to England his intention to enter the war on the side of the Entente if Germany would not accept terms of peace that only a conquered state could have been expected to concede.

During the winter of 1917-18, Ludendorff and Hindenburg made colossal preparations for a decisive attack against the Allies in France. Huge forces were placed on the western front; great guns of unprecedented range were installed for the purpose of firing upon Paris at a distance of seventy miles and thus shaking French morale; vast quantities of guns and ammunition were supplied to the soldiers; and everything possible was set in readiness for the great drive. The British were the first to feel the terrific impact of the German forces. The Germans attacked the British in March, 1918, near St. Quentin in the valley of the Somme River, and marched on to Amiens. In April the British west of Lille, and in May the French stationed along the Aisne River, were the recipients of the German onslaught. At a tremendous cost of both life and property, the Germans had advanced to the Marne at Château-Thierry, some forty miles distant from Paris. Here the tempo of the drives slowed down, owing to the rôle played by the fresh American forces.

After a month in which the opposing combatants faced each other, the Germans, in desperation, thrust forward in the Second Battle of the Marne. But by this time they were disheartened. Their reserves were exhausted, their ammunition was of an inferior grade, and the last great German offensive failed. The French, British, and Americans shifted from the defensive to the offensive and forced a widespread German retreat, taking St. Mihiel, St. Quentin, Cambrai, Lille, the Argonne Forest, and Sedan, until finally, on November 11, 1918, the Armistice was signed in the Forest of Compiègne.

In addition to the main battles fought on European soil, warfare was carried on in the Near Orient and in Africa. Soon after Japan's entry, the Japanese forces seized the German port of Kiaochow in China and, aided by the British, took the entire Shantung Peninsula, Tsingtao, and the German island possessions in the Pacific Ocean north of the equator, while those in the south were captured by the Australians and New Zealanders. Important sections of the Turkish Empire were seized by British and French armies; Turkish Armenia was occupied by Russian troops in 1916. Palestine surrendered to the English in 1917 after a brilliant campaign by General Allenby, who a year later, aided by Lawrence and the Arabs, captured Syria, cut the Baghdad Railroad, and forced Turkey out of the war. British and French armies took German Togoland in 1914 and Kamerun in 1916; the British troops stationed in South Africa crushed a Boer Rebellion in 1914 and took possession of German Southwest Africa in 1915 and of German East Africa in 1918.

The World War differed from other great wars in many respects. Never before had there been such an impressive agglomeration of men assembled to settle a human dispute. Whereas the figures of the armies ran into thousands in previous wars, they ran into millions in this catastrophic conflict. The strength of the Central Powers has been estimated at 29,787,000 and that of the Entente Allies at 80,108,000. These figures include troops ready for action, reserve forces, unorganized troops, militias, national guards, and colonial armies.

Fighting in the World War was a very complex matter and presented a radical change from warfare in the past.[1] Because of the great technical advance in making machine guns and artillery efficiently deadly, almost at the beginning of the war open fighting, except for brief attacks, was abandoned, and long and elaborate series of trenches were constructed. These were formed in

[1] *Cf.* Hammerton, *Universal History of the World*, Chaps. 178-80.

zigzag parallels, joined by laterals, and had subterranean rooms used for the storage of war supplies and for the resting-quarters of the soldiers. Some of these trench lines were most durably and securely built—notably the famous Hindenburg Line. Separating the opposing trenches was "no man's land," a mass of barbed wire and artificial banks of earth and stone that had to be traversed before reaching the enemy.

Artillery was developed with scientific acumen. The "barrage"—a terrific wall of coördinated artillery fire—was most ingeniously developed to lay down a protection for troops advancing behind it. Enormous numbers of machine guns, the most effective single instrument of the war, were employed by both sides. Huge cannon were placed behind the trenches to destroy with ruthless force the enemy's towns, fortifications, and larger targets. Explosives, both grenades and mines, were added to the shrapnel and shot. Poison gas, a deadly innovation, was first used by the Germans, but shortly by the Allies as well. Camouflage—the art of concealment of vulnerable objects both at sea and on land—was a new and widespread practice.

Gasoline engines played a significant rôle in this conflict as driving power for tanks, automobiles, and airplanes. The tank, first used by the British and probably the most remarkable of the many new instruments of warfare improvised during the struggle, was a huge caterpillar affair protected by an iron covering, crawling over the battlefield unstopped by ditches, barbed wire, or mounds, spewing forth bullets, and bringing death and havoc in its path.

The fighting in the air caught the interest of all peoples. One-man airplanes were used in the first year of the war as a means of discovering the position of the enemy and as a guide for the artillery. Later, two-seaters having an unprecedented swiftness were employed as bombing mediums, and for the use of photographers, spies, and scouts. Hydroplanes developed by the British assailed German submarines, and by 1916 squads and formations of airships were organized and the battles of the air were regarded as extraordinary feats of courage and valor. The emergence of air "aces," survivors of a succession of air duels, furnished much of the heroics of a war that was otherwise distinguished by a lack of romantic color.

The sea operations during the World War were less decisive in the form of battles than they were in their bearing upon the control of the commerce of the world, so important for the Entente countries, and only less significant for the Central Powers. Great Britain's naval superiority never proved of more critical importance. German commerce was swept from the sea, and very quickly also the German warships outside of the North Sea were captured or sunk and their raids upon British commerce terminated. An air-tight blockade was imposed on Germany, which did more than British arms ultimately to bring that country to its knees. Admiral von Spee destroyed a small British squadron off the coast of Chile on November 1, 1914, but his fleet was soon wiped out by the British in a battle off the Falkland Islands.

There was only one major naval conflict during the war, the Battle of Jutland, on May 31, 1916. While the Germans were ultimately compelled to retreat before overwhelming odds to their fortified cover, they inflicted heavy losses upon the British. Not since the rise of the British navy in the seventeenth century had the British come off so badly in a major naval battle. It is possible that Admiral Jellicoe might have repeated the feat of Nelson at Trafalgar had he been less timid or cautious, but he failed to rise to the opportunity. So the Germans had one brilliant exploit to their credit on the sea during the World War, but it proved only a futile show of superior bravery and strategy. The German fleet never again risked its fate.

Rather, the Germans concentrated upon building submarines to offset their inferiority in respect to capital ships. These submarines inflicted terrific losses upon British shipping, but in the end they undid those gains through bringing the United States into the war and turning the balance decidedly in favor of the Entente. It is true that Germany was able to justify its submarine warfare on the ground of the British blockade and that it offered to discuss discontinuing submarine activities if Britain would raise the blockade. It is also true that Great Britain interfered with the rights of neutral shippers far more extensively than did Germany. But Germany's depredations involved lives as well as property. This difference, together with the fact that the interest of American business and finance was linked with the cause of the Allies, served to bring us into the war.

The Germans exerted themselves most vigorously in the effort to drive British shipping from the seas before the United States could become effective in the war. But the industrial efficiency of the United States proved too much for them. Ships were rapidly and crudely built through the application, to the highest degree, of standardization in construction. The margin between new shipping and that sent to the bottom by submarines grew rapidly, and the destinies of Germany in the World War were doomed when sufficient American troops arrived in Europe to stem the tide of Ludendorff's last desperate drive in the spring and early summer of 1918. Approximately 4,000,000 tons of Allied shipping were destroyed by German submarines in the first half of 1917. But owing to the entry of the United States with its navy augmenting that of the British, the wreckage was diminished until in 1918 only 2,000,000 tons of shipping were sunk. The advice of Admiral von Tirpitz and others to disregard diplomacy in the interests of submarine warfare proved the second great German mistake during the World War. It lost the war in the last year of the conflict, as the Kaiser's unwisdom in maintaining Von Moltke in charge of the German army at the outset had destroyed the possibility of a brilliant and decisive German victory before snowfall in 1914.

VIII. PROPAGANDA IN THE WAR: THE PEN BEHIND THE SWORD

As novel and interesting as the vast scope of the conflict, the huge numbers involved, and the colossal costs exacted was the wide use of systematic propaganda by both sides. This, if it did not prove that the pen is mightier than the sword, at least showed that the pen can powerfully supplement the sword. Germany gave the Allies a great advantage in its invasion of Belgium, even though we now know that the Allies had intended to do the same thing if it proved necessary to their strategic advantage. A systematic campaign of exaggerations and falsifications regarding alleged German atrocities was planned and executed, and it helped mightily to turn neutral opinion against Germany as well as enraging still further the populace of each warring country. The eminent publicist Lord Bryce, very popular in America, was induced to endorse these stories and increase their credibility, especially in the United States. No sooner had the effect of the Belgian-atrocity campaign worn off than the Germans provided the Allies with another ace card by their submarine campaign, though this was less horrible in its results and no more illegal than the British blockade. But it lent itself better than the latter to dramatic and colorful exploitation. Moreover, the Entente control of the seas made it easier for them to get into contact with neutral sources of opinion. When the Germans did set up contacts with neutrals they were usually quite stupid in their propaganda methods. An exception was Count von Bernstorff, the German ambassador in Washington. As the propaganda plans reached a high development, systematic fabrications were deliberately planned and establishments were set up for the painting of faked scenes of devastation, falsification of postcards, manufacture of wax models of alleged mutilated figures, and the like.[1] A vast propaganda agency was created by the Entente in the United States, engineered by Lord Northcliffe and directed by Sir Gilbert Parker. Ministers of the Gospel entered enthusiastically into the fray and represented the war as a divinely guided crusade against the representatives of the Devil.[2] These extensive fabrications not only served to promote enlistments, convert neutrals, and intensify passions during the World War; they also made it difficult to secure a return to reason that would permit a statesmanlike peace settlement.

IX. THE TRAGIC BALANCE SHEET OF HOSTILITIES

The casualties of the World War were of such astounding magnitude as to be almost unbelievable. Kirby Page lists them in the table below:

CASUALTIES OF THE WORLD WAR [3]

	Known dead	Seriously wounded	Otherwise wounded	Prisoners or missing
Russia	2,762,064	1,000,000	3,950,000	2,500,000
Germany	1,611,104	1,600,000	2,183,143	772,522
France	1,427,800	700,000	2,344,000	453,500
Austria-Hungary	911,000	850,000	2,150,000	443,000
Great Britain	807,451	617,714	1,441,394	64,907
Serbia	707,343	322,000	28,000	100,000
Italy	507,160	500,000	462,196	1,359,000
Turkey	436,924	107,772	300,000	103,731
Roumania	339,117	200,000	......	116,000
Belgium	267,000	40,000	100,000	10,000
United States	107,284	43,000	148,000	4,912
Bulgaria	101,224	300,000	852,339	10,825
Greece	15,000	10,000	30,000	45,000
Portugal	4,000	5,000	12,000	200
Japan	300	......	907	3
Totals	9,998,771	6,295,512	14,002,039	5,983,600

[1] See Ferdinand Avenarius, *How the War Madness Was Engineered*, Berlin, 1926; *Behind the Scenes in French Journalism*, by a French Chief Editor, Berlin, 1925; and Sir Campbell Stuart, *The Secrets of Crewe House*, Doran, 1920.
[2] See Hicks, "The Parsons and the War," *loc. cit.*; and Abrams, *The Preachers Present Arms*.
[3] E. L. Bogart, *Direct and Indirect Costs of the Great World War*. Oxford Press, 1919, p. 172.

THE TRAGIC BALANCE SHEET OF HOSTILITIES

Page further summarizes the more prominent of the human costs of the war:[1]

    10,000,000 known dead soldiers
     3,000,000 presumed dead soldiers
    13,000,000 dead civilians
    20,000,000 wounded
     3,000,000 prisoners
     9,000,000 war orphans
     5,000,000 war widows
    10,000,000 refugees

The total immediate economic cost of the war has been estimated by a careful student, Professor Bogart, at $331,600,000,000. Some of the specific economic losses have been computed as follows: (1) Munitions and machines of war during the four years of fighting, $180,000,000,000; (2) property losses on land, $29,960,000,000; (3) losses to shipping, $6,800,000,000; (4) production losses through diverted and noneconomic production, $45,000,000,000.

These are simply immediate economic losses—those things which were actually consumed during the conflict. No account is taken of subsequent costs such as interest on loans, retirement of loans, pensions, and the like. President Coolidge, relying on Secretary Mellon's estimates, once frankly stated that the ultimate cost of the participation of the United States alone in the World War would, in his opinion, be $100,000,000,000. On January 16, 1935, the direct cost of the World War, exclusive of war loans abroad, to the United States was officially declared to be $50,000,000,000.

Writing shortly after the war was over, Professor E. L. Bogart said on the matter of immediate war costs:

The figures . . . are both incomprehensible and appalling, yet even these do not take into account the effect of the war on life, human vitality, economic well being, ethics, morality, or other phases of human relationships and activities which have been disorganized and injured. It is evident from the present disturbances in Europe that the real costs cannot be measured by the direct money outlays of the belligerents in the five years of its duration, but that the very breakdown of modern economic life might be the price exacted.[2]

The editor of the *Scholastic* made an effort to translate these figures of war costs into terms that we can visualize. He indicated that the cost of the World War would have been sufficient to furnish (1) every family in England, France, Belgium, Germany, Russia, the United States, Canada, and Australia with a $2,500 house on a $500 one-acre lot, with $1,000 worth of furniture; (2) a $5,000,000 library for every community of 200,000 inhabitants in these countries; (3) a $10,000,000 university for every such community; (4) a fund that at 5 per cent interest would yield enough to pay indefinitely $1,000 a year to an army of 125,000 teachers and 125,000 nurses, and (5) still leave enough to buy every piece of property and all wealth in France and Belgium at a fair market price. Such was what it cost to return Alsace-Lorraine to France, to try to get the Straits for Russia, and to punish Serbian plotters.[3]

[1] Compiled from figures in *Ibid.*, p. 161.
[2] E. L. Bogart, *Direct and Indirect Costs of the Great World War*, Oxford Press, 1919, p. 299.
[3] *Scholastic*, Nov. 10, 1934, p. 13.

X. DID THE WAR PAY?

Professor Bogart's words, cited above, we must sadly admit, are even more true and timely today than they were ten years ago. Where did all this carnage lead? Did it pay any nation involved?[1]

Austria-Hungary went down to ruin. Tsarist Russia passed away, failing to obtain the coveted Straits, in the effort to secure which Russia pushed Europe over the brink in 1914. France obtained Alsace-Lorraine, but there is now as much discontent with French rule in the lost provinces as there was over German dominion before 1914. Germany suffered appalling losses in every way, and Great Britain will probably never recover its prewar prestige and prosperity. Only Serbia, Rumania and Poland profited extensively, but 40,000,000 lives and over $300,000,000,000 were rather a high price to pay for inflating these backward Balkan states and liberating Poland.

Norman Angell showed clearly enough in his *Great Illusion* that war could never pay economically. This was derided, but he used the experience of the World War to vindicate the thesis in his *Fruits of Victory*, published more than a decade later.[2] No form of production or labor can be ultimately profitable —truly economic—unless it contributes in a permanent way to the increase of human well-being. Purely destructive forms of production make us "pay the piper" sooner or later. They are parasitical and non-economic.

One cannot blow to pieces dwellings and factories, flood and ruin mines, devastate the countryside, divert millions from the manufacture of the necessities of life into the making of engines of destruction, without ultimately being called to account. Europe is today paying the price—and it may be only the beginning of the total cost—for the abysmal carnage and destruction of 1914-18. It is doubtful whether European capitalism will be able to pull out of the morass created by the economic impact of the World War. Even at this date, democracy has had to be sacrificed on a wide front in the effort.

And we, also, are paying, and have been paying for more than a decade, the price exacted for our folly in entering the World War. Our enormously greater budget today is chiefly due to the stupendous debts placed on the shoulders of Uncle Sam by our entry into the "Great Crusade." In 1916 the total expenditures of the federal government amounted to only $735,056,202. Even before President Roosevelt's extensive relief appropriations began in 1933, our federal budget had increased to approximately $5,000,000,000, and a large part of this increase could be attributed to direct and indirect war costs.

The "war to end war" proved a huge travesty.[3] There have been wars and rumors of worse wars ever since November 11, 1918. Armaments have not been reduced. The nations are spending 70 per cent more today than in 1914 for the instruments of mass murder. The mythical "German military dictatorship" of 1914—when the German army was smaller than the French army—has been replaced by the appalling military dominance of France.

We have received no gratitude from our erstwhile Allies for our huge expenditures of money and men in their behalf. We have obtained little but

---

[1] It of course "paid" many private profiteers handsomely.   [2] Century, 1921.
[3] See next chapter, *passim*.

petulance and criticism. Though we have written off half the debts incurred, we have been branded as "Uncle Shylock." Our best friends abroad are our former enemies—and their disinterestedness is open to grave doubt. A considerable share of their ostensible amiability is certainly due to the hope that we may assist them in their present difficulties. Such are the results that we have obtained from the international foray that put our present deficit far above our total national budget of the prewar days. Moreover, the World War had

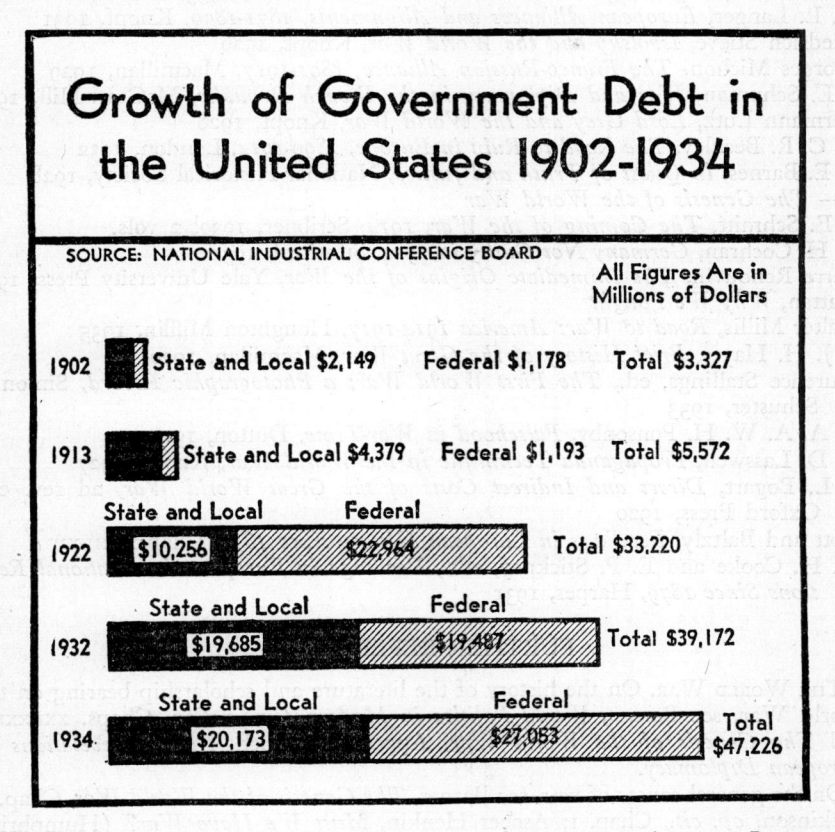

Growth of Government Debt in the United States 1902-1934

SOURCE: NATIONAL INDUSTRIAL CONFERENCE BOARD

All Figures Are in Millions of Dollars

Year	State and Local	Federal	Total
1902	$2,149	$1,178	$3,327
1913	$4,379	$1,193	$5,572
1922	$10,256	$22,964	$33,220
1932	$19,685	$19,487	$39,172
1934	$20,173	$27,053	$47,226

a disastrous influence on the private economy of the United States. It was the Liberty Loan drives that started us off on our craze for investment in securities, first government bonds and then all manner of both gilt-edge and dubious stocks and bonds. It gave finance capitalism a new and vast impulse and started us on our way to the orgy of the 1920's and the collapse of 1929.[1]

[1] Cf. Walter Rautenstrauch, *Who Gets the Money?* Harper, 1934, pp. 43 ff. See below, pp. 827-29.

SUGGESTED READING

Hammerton, *Universal History of the World,* Chaps. 175, 178-80
C. L. Becker, *Modern History,* Silver, Burdett, 1931, Chaps. xix-xx
Erik Achorn, *European Civilization and Politics since 1815,* Harcourt, Brace, 1934, Chaps. xiii-xvi

Noyes, *Europe—Its History and Its World Relationships,* Pt. VI
Langsam, *The World since 1914,* Chaps. I-III
Benns, *Europe since 1914,* Pt. I
Arthur Porritt, ed., *The Causes of War,* Macmillan, 1932
G. L. Dickinson, *The International Anarchy, 1904-1914,* Century, 1926
R. J. Sontag, *European Diplomatic History, 1871-1932,* Century, 1933, Chaps. I-VI
S. B. Fay, *The Origins of the World War,* Macmillan, 1928, 2 vols.
J. W. Swain, *Beginning the Twentieth Century,* Norton, 1933
W. L. Langer, *European Alliances and Alignments, 1871-1890,* Knopf, 1931
Friedrich Stieve, *Isvolsky and the World War,* Knopf, 1926
Georges Michon, *The Franco-Russian Alliance, 1891-1917,* Macmillan, 1929
F. L. Schuman, *War and Diplomacy in the French Republic,* McGraw-Hill, 1931
Hermann Lutz, *Lord Grey and the World War,* Knopf, 1928
Sir C. R. Beazley, *The Road to Ruin in Europe, 1890-1914,* London, 1932
H. E. Barnes, *In Quest of Truth and Justice,* National Historical Society, 1928
—— *The Genesis of the World War*
B. E. Schmitt, *The Coming of the War, 1914,* Scribner, 1930, 2 vols.
M. H. Cochran, *Germany Not Guilty in 1914,* Stratford, 1931
Pierre Renouvin, *The Immediate Origins of the War,* Yale University Press, 1928
Grattan, *Why We Fought*
Walter Millis, *Road to War: America 1914-1917,* Houghton Mifflin, 1935
C. J. H. Hayes, *Brief History of the Great War,* Macmillan, 1920
Laurence Stallings, ed., *The First World War; a Photographic Record,* Simon & Schuster, 1933
Sir A. A. W. H. Ponsonby, *Falsehood in War-Time,* Dutton, 1929
H. D. Lasswell, *Propaganda Technique in the World War,* Knopf, 1927
E. L. Bogart, *Direct and Indirect Costs of the Great World War,* 2d rev. ed., Oxford Press, 1920
Scott and Baltzly, *Readings in European History since 1814,* Chaps. XIII-XIV
W. H. Cooke and E. P. Stickney, eds., *Readings in European International Relations Since 1879,* Harper, 1931

FURTHER REFERENCES

THE WORLD WAR. On the history of the literature and scholarship bearing on the World War, see Barnes, *World Politics in Modern Civilization,* Chaps. XXI-XXIII; and *The Genesis of the World War,* Appendix; Gooch, *Recent Revelations of European Diplomacy.*

On the general causes of war, see Barnes, *The Genesis of the World War,* Chap. I; Dickinson, *op. cit.,* Chap. I; Ascher Henkin, *Must We Have War?* (Humphries, 1934); Porritt, *op. cit.* This last book is to be highly commended.

On the diplomatic history of Europe from 1870 to 1912, see Sontag, *op. cit.,* Chaps. I-IV; Swain, *op. cit.,* Pt. II; Fay, *op. cit.,* Vol. I; Erich Brandenburg, *From Bismarck to the World War* (Oxford Press, 1927); Langer, *op. cit.*

On the diplomatic revolution of 1912-14, see Fay, *op. cit.,* Vol. I, Chaps. IV-V; Sontag, *op. cit.,* Chap. V; Michon, *op. cit.,* Chaps. XI-XIV; Schuman, *op. cit.,* Chaps. IX-X; Stieve, *op. cit.*

On the crisis of 1914, see Swain, *op. cit.,* Chap. XVIII; Beazley, *op. cit.,* Chap. III; Sontag, *op. cit.,* pp. 191-205; Michon, *op. cit.,* Chaps. XIV-XV; Barnes, *The Genesis of the World War,* Chaps. IV-IX; Fay, *op. cit.,* Vol. II; Renouvin, *op. cit.*—an able apology for the Entente, to be compared with Count M. M. K. S. Montgelas, *The Case for the Central Powers* (Knopf, 1925).

FURTHER REFERENCES

The best balanced summary of the crisis of 1914 is Swain, *op. cit.,* Chap. xviii. The most authoritative work is Fay, *op. cit.,* Vol. II, excellent for its careful marshaling of facts, but often faulty in logic, especially as regards Austria, and very timid and illogical in conclusions. The concluding chapter is almost a non sequitur. For a full review, see Barnes, *World Politics,* Chap. xxiii. The second edition is fairer to Austria. The outstanding effort to preserve the wartime illusions concerning responsibility for the war is to be found in Schmitt, *op. cit.* It is crushingly answered by Cochran, *op. cit.* A much less scholarly effort than Schmitt's to reaffirm the major guilt of Germany is embodied in the work of the British journalist and naval enthusiast H. W. Wilson, *The War Guilt* (London, 1928). For the latest effort to discredit the present writer, see Jules Isaac, *Un débat historique* (Paris, 1933). His points were long since demolished in Barnes, *In Quest of Truth and Justice,* Pt. II; and Cochran, *op. cit.*

On England and the coming of the World War, see the lucid summary by Count M. M. K. S. Montgelas, *British Foreign Policy under Sir Edward Grey* (Knopf, 1928); and the excellent work of Lutz cited above—one of the ablest of all the books on the crisis of 1914. For an apology for Grey, see Margret Boveri, *Sir Edward Grey und das Foreign Office* (Berlin, 1933). On English psychology in prewar days, see C. E. Playne, *The Pre-war Mind in Great Britain* (London, 1928).

On the entry of the United States into the World War, the most illuminating works are Grattan, *op. cit.;* Millis, *op. cit.* For a generous estimate of Wilson's rôle in America, see J. W. Swain, "Woodrow Wilson's Fight for Peace," *Current History,* March, 1932; and *Beginning the Twentieth Century,* pp. 465-91. For a thorough but wholly conventional account of American diplomacy, see Charles Seymour, *American Diplomacy during the World War* (Johns Hopkins University Press, 1934). See review of this by Fay in the *New Republic,* Aug. 15, 1934, and the editorial comment in the same issue. The most amazing thing about Professor Seymour's book is his denial of pressure for war by the American bankers, a statement that is contradicted openly by the testimony of the bankers themselves. Indeed, the American documents show that Page and Wilson discussed our entry in terms of British credit and the status of American international bankers. For many facts overlooked by Seymour, see Turner, *Shall It Be Again?*

On the history of the World War, see Sontag, *op. cit.,* Chap. vi; Langsam, *op. cit.,* Chaps. i-iv; Benns, *op. cit.,* Pt. I; Chaps. xi-xv of P. W. Slosson, *Twentieth Century Europe* (Houghton Mifflin, 1927); Swain, *op. cit.,* Pt. III; Hayes, *op. cit.;* Louis Guichard, *The Naval Blockade, 1914-1918* (Appleton, 1930); M. F. Parmelee, *Blockade and Sea Power* (Crowell, 1924).

On science and the World War, see Hammerton, *op. cit.,* Chaps. 178-80.

On war propaganda, see Lasswell, *op. cit.;* Playne, *Society at War, 1914-1918;* Ponsonby, *op. cit.;* Viereck, *Spreading Germs of Hate;* Georges Demartial, *La guerre de 1914: comment on mobilisa les consciences* (Paris, 1922); Sir E. T. Cook, *The Press in War-time* (Macmillan, 1920); Sir Campbell Stuart, *The Secrets of Crewe House* (Doran, 1920); Willis, *England's Holy War;* pp. 578-611 of H. G. Wells, *An Experiment in Autobiography* (Macmillan, 1934); Ebba Dahlin, *French and German Public Opinion on Declared War Aims, 1914-1918* (Stanford University Press, 1933).

On the costs of the war, see Pt. II of Kirby Page, *National Defense* (Farrar & Rinehart, 1931); Bogart, *op. cit.*

CHAPTER XVIII

AFTER THE WORLD WAR

I. THE NOTE OF DISILLUSIONMENT

In the preceding chapter we have tried to make clear how important it is for an intelligent outlook upon contemporary problems of war and peace to assimilate in a discriminating fashion what we now know about the actual causes of the late World War. Nothing could constitute a more complete exposure of the shortsightedness and unreliability of the general run of diplomats and statesmen.[1] We now know that practically the entire body of Entente "war aims," including even the impressive and eloquent rhetoric of President Wilson, was for the most part false and misleading, setting up a verbal barrage behind which were hidden the most sordid and selfish plans of unscrupulous diplomats, foreign ministers, and international bankers.[2]

The acceptance of this view about the Entente position in no way carries with it any indiscriminate support of the diplomacy or viewpoint of the Central Powers, but we do not need to be "debunked" of anti-Entente propaganda in the United States. The German war lies gained little foothold among us. If we can but understand how totally and miserably we were "taken in" between 1914 and 1918 by the salesmen of "this most holy and idealistic world conflict," we shall be the better prepared to be on our guard against the lies and deceptions which, it may be expected, will be put forward by similar groups when urging the necessity of another world war in order to "protect the weak nations," "crush militarism," "make the world safe for democracy," "put an end to all further wars," and the like.

The period since the World War, from the standpoint of international relations, falls into three fairly well-defined periods.[3] First came the exuberance of victory and the Armistice terms based upon President Wilson's Fourteen Points. There was joy in the thought that the era of destruction, death, and sorrow was over. People still took seriously the Entente idealism of the war period. The mass acclaim with which Woodrow Wilson was greeted in Europe was probably without equal in history. He was hailed as the savior of the downtrodden peoples, as the prophet of a better day when peace and goodwill would reign over the earth. The masses awaited the peace conference that

---

[1] See Francis Neilson, *How Diplomats Make War*, Huebsch, 1916.
[2] See Ponsonby, *Falsehood in War-time;* F. C. Cocks, ed., *The Secret Treaties*, London, 1918; and Alcide Ebray, *A Frenchman Looks at Peace*, Knopf, 1927.
[3] See H. E. Barnes, *World Politics in Modern Civilization*, Knopf, 1930, Pt. IV; and G. B. Noble, *Policies and Opinions at Paris, 1919*, Macmillan, 1935.

should put the Wilsonian idealism into word and action. This period may well be called the Wilson epoch.

It was brought to an end by the realities of the postwar treaties—Versailles, St. Germain, Trianon, Neuilly, and Sèvres. When Wilson faced the hard-bitten diplomats who had fashioned or sanctioned the secret treaties during the World War, arranging the partition of the Central Powers and their possessions, he found that they had little sympathy with the noble sentiments which he had uttered during and after the conflict.[1] Mr. Wilson may have been sincere, but powerful statesmen of the Entente were all the time fully aware of the divergence between their secret plans and Mr. Wilson's campaign of idealism. Indeed, before he went to Paris President Wilson could have known what to expect, for he had already seen and discussed these secret treaties.[2] But he seems to have hoped that the Entente would tear them up and make peace on a just and statesmanlike basis. He was disappointed. A vindictive peace treaty was drawn up that wrecked his own program, saved much of the secret treaties, and treated Germany as a world-criminal. This launched the Versailles epoch, which lasted from 1919 to 1931.

The new facts discovered regarding the responsibility for the World War, the difficulty of keeping Germany under heel for an indefinite period, the financial dead weight of reparation payments and the war debts, the impossibility of collecting further reparation payments, the world-wide depression that was directly connected with postwar international finance—all these conspired to undermine the Versailles system. Beginning with the debt and reparations moratorium of 1931, and even more decisively shattered by the Lausanne Conference of 1932, the Versailles settlement began to totter. The Epoch of Revision lay at hand. Hitlerism threatened to make it a violent process.

II. NATIONAL SELF-DETERMINATION

The principle of national self-determination and the freedom of the oppressed nationalities was one of the leading slogans in the propaganda of the Entente during the World War. Almost alone of the Entente promises, this assurance was actually carried out with some thoroughness in the peace treaties. The treaties of Versailles, St. Germain, and Trianon gave free vent to the ambitions of nationalism. Never before in the history of Europe had so many new states been created as a result of the treaties following a European war. Indeed, the acquiescence in granting free rein to the nationalists was truly alarming, and resulted in a disastrous overdoing of the whole matter.[3]

Europe in 1928 could boast of thirty national states instead of the eighteen that existed in 1914, and the reallotment of nationals was so imperfectly done that about as many centers of dissatisfaction existed after 1919 as in 1914.[4] The thirty national states of today create almost twice as many potential causes of war as did the eighteen of 1914. In some cases, such as the Polish Corridor, the

---

[1] See J. M. Keynes, *The Economic Consequences of the Peace*, Harcourt, Brace, 1920.
[2] See Barnes, *op. cit.*, pp. 409-10.
[3] For the efforts to build an international order, see below, pp. 898 ff.
[4] *Cf.* Otto Junghann, *National Minorities in Europe*, Covici, Friede, 1932.

national dissatisfaction seems as pregnant with danger for European peace as the Serbian ambitions in 1914.

The postwar treaties restored Alsace-Lorraine to France, allowed Denmark to annex northern Schleswig, and handed over *Italia irredenta* to Italy. In the case of Italy the matter of restoration was overdone, and it received the almost wholly German population of the South Tyrol. While not directly involved in the peace treaties, Catholic Ireland received partial national emancipation during this period. A treaty of December, 1921, created the Irish Free State and made southern Ireland a self-governing Dominion in the British Empire.

The Baltic states were granted independence from Russia, and four new independent national states were created: Finland, Estonia, Latvia, and Lithuania. Granting the difficulties that existed, the territorial and ethnic assignments in this Baltic settlement were reasonably just, with the exception that Lithuanian claims were sacrificed to the demands of the stronger and more aggressive Poland, a situation rendered even more deplorable by the subsequent Polish seizure of the important Lithuanian city of Vilna.

Poland was restored as a great national state, with an area almost equal to that of the new German Republic. The Poles seemed to have learned little from the history of the past, and demanded a settlement well designed to alienate their neighbors and to constitute a standing impulse to destroy or reduce Poland as soon as diplomatic realignments permit. Not only did Poland encroach upon Russia and Lithuania, thus creating enmity on the north and east, but it also insisted upon German territory in Posen, East Prussia, and Upper Silesia, which will indefinitely postpone cordial relations with Germany. Most ill-advised of all was the Polish demand for a "corridor" separating East Prussia from the remainder of Germany. This is an arrangement to which Germany may never become reconciled, and it may make that country ever ready to anticipate and accept alliances designed to weaken or defeat Poland. Thirty per cent of the present population of Poland is non-Polish. Only the present French military alliance gives any extensive assurance of Polish safety or permanence.

The Ruthenians were granted their independence, and a separate Republic of the Ukraine was created. In 1922 the Ukraine rejoined Russia as one of the states federated in the Union of Socialist Soviet Republics. The Czechs and Slovaks were freed from Austro-Hungarian domination and a new national republic of Czechoslovakia was established. This has been the most democratically governed of the new states, but it contains many elements of serious internal weakness and potential discord. It is almost a miniature Austria-Hungary of the old days. The Slovaks are not unanimous in their enthusiasm for the union, and there is a great German minority in the west that may never cordially accept the Czech dominion. Finally, many Magyars have been included within the boundaries of the country. It is thought by many that upon the death of Masaryk, the great Czech statesman and national hero, whose person has been a powerful symbol of unity, Czechoslovakia may face great difficulties in maintaining its integrity.

Rumania was greatly enlarged at the close of the war, even though its military record on the side of the Entente was inglorious indeed and its administrative record one of the worst in Europe, constituting certainly no justification

LEGEND

- Formerly part of Russia
- Formerly part of Germany
- Formerly part of Austria-Hungary
- Formerly part of Bulgaria
- Plebiscite areas ceded or retained

SCALE OF MILES
0 50 100 150 200 250

POSTWAR T

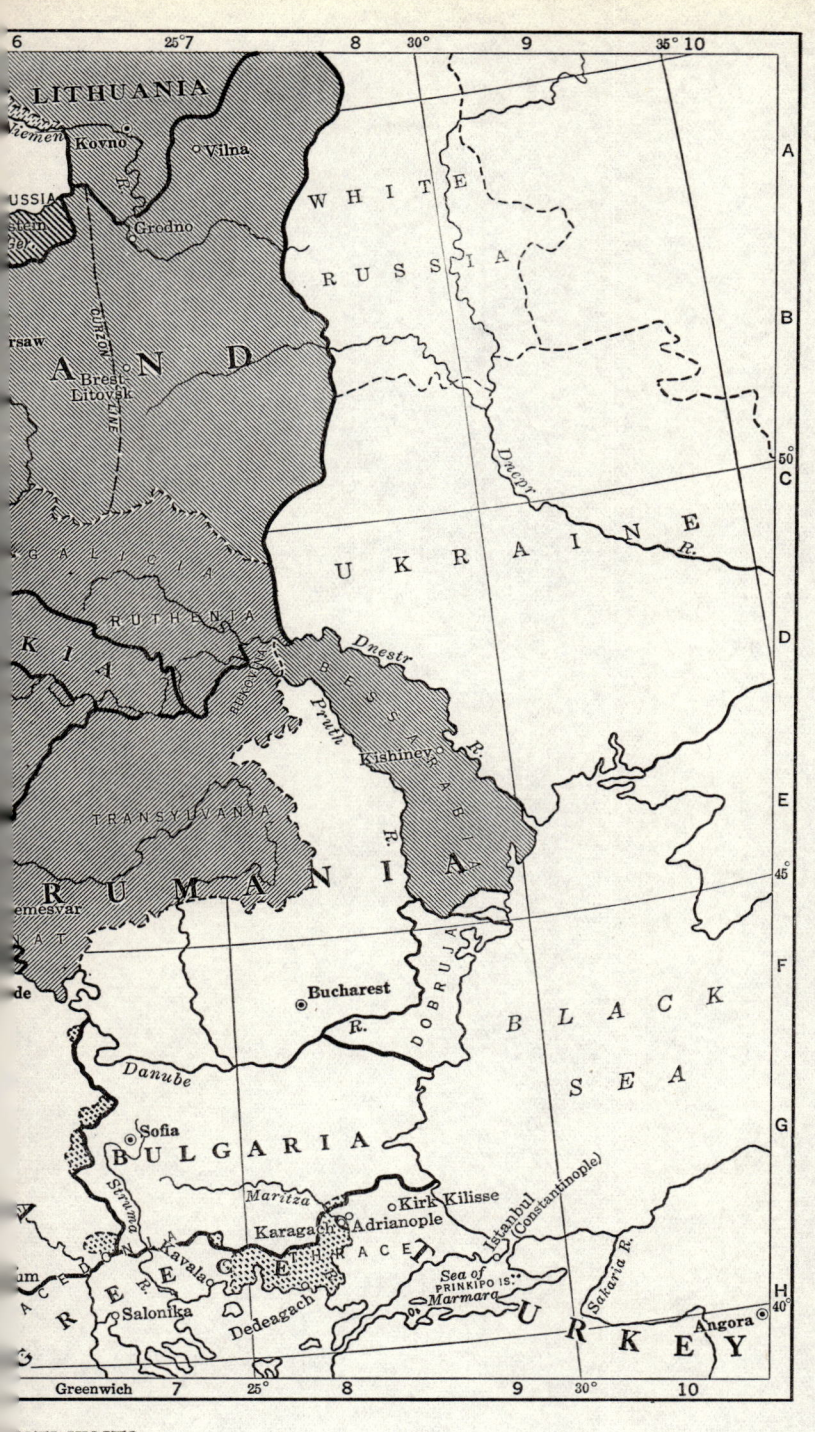

STMENTS

for intrusting it with even greater responsibilities. It was assigned Bessarabia, Transylvania, Bucovina, and part of the Banat, thus taking within its frontiers many Russians and Magyars. Neither the Russians nor the Magyars will be likely to acquiesce permanently in this settlement, and the gorged postwar Rumania constitutes one of the leading danger spots in Europe, though it is temporarily safe as one of the eastern outposts of the military hegemony of France.

The Serbs realized their highest ambitions at the peace table. To the prewar Serbia were added Bosnia, Hercegovina, Croatia, Montenegro, and smaller portions of other Balkan territory in the Banat and elsewhere. A great state, the kingdom of Yugoslavia, was created. It faces little danger at the hands of Austria or Hungary, but it is confronted with a serious challenge from Italy in regard to Albania and the Dalmatian coast. Albania was granted independence and an Albanian Republic (since become a monarchy) was created in 1925, but anarchy has prevailed, and Italy has a very definite ambition to control Albania as a part of its program of making the Adriatic an Italian lake. Greece was also rewarded for its delayed participation on the side of the Entente by territory taken chiefly from Bulgaria and Turkey. Greece developed large ambitions to become a strong imperialistic power in the Near East after the war. It overstepped itself, was treacherously abandoned by the French, and was driven from Asia Minor in disgrace by the Turks in the summer of 1922. The plan of creating a new Greek Empire collapsed.

The Entente had planned to extinguish Turkey in both Europe and Asia if victorious in the World War, and had assigned Turkey in Europe to Russia and its Balkan allies. By the time the war had been won, however, Russia had dropped out of the conflict and the tsarist régime had collapsed. The Entente Powers were too jealous of each other to assign Turkey to any one of themselves, and they did not trust their Balkan allies to retain all the loot in this area. Greece attempted to take things into its own hands, with the decisive defeat we have just mentioned. Taking advantage of the lack of unity among the victors, the Turks, under the leadership of one of the ablest figures in the postwar world, Mustapha Kemal Pasha, ignored the Treaty of Sèvres and established a modernized Turkish Republic in Asia Minor. They have retained a large part of their prewar European possessions, agreeing to internationalize the much-coveted Straits.

Partially to enlist the sympathy of the Jews of the world in the World War, the Balfour Declaration of 1917 promised to create a national home for the Jewish people in Palestine at the close of the war as a realization of the ardent Zionist aspirations. In July, 1922, Palestine was handed over to Great Britain as a Class A Mandate, and a High Commissioner, Sir Herbert Samuel, was appointed. A government for the area was created. Wealthy Jews throughout the world contributed to the development of Palestine as a refuge for the persecuted and impoverished Jewish peoples. More than $50,000,000 has been invested there since the war, modern industrial and power projects have been launched, and an important Hebrew University has been established. Between 1919 and 1931, some 115,690 Jews entered Palestine and 85,340 of them remained there.

About 30,000 Jews have been born in Palestine since 1919. Inasmuch as the Arabs outnumber the Jews in Palestine by more than five to one, much friction has been engendered as a result of Arab jealousy and apprehensiveness. An anti-Jewish outbreak in the summer of 1929 led to the slaying and wounding of several hundred Jews. In October, 1930, the British government announced a new policy more favorable to the Arabs, but it was bitterly criticized by the Jews. In 1932 a more lenient policy was renewed and the limitations on Jewish immigration to Palestine were lifted.

Near-Eastern nationalism has also been manifested in Syria, Arabia, and Egypt, and both England and France have been compelled to make some formal concessions to nationalist sentiment in these areas. Nationalism was also promoted in the Far East by the Japanese ambitions at the Peace Conference, by the Chinese resentment at the awards to Japan, by the aspirations for independence of the peoples of India, and by the enthusiasm of Australasia over its part in winning the war and its annexation of parts of the German colonial empire.

It now remains to catalogue briefly the outstanding mistakes and exaggerations of the national principle of which the peacemakers were guilty.[1] Alsace-Lorraine was restored to France, instead of being constituted a neutral state like Luxemburg, which was in every way the more desirable procedure. The inhabitants of Alsace-Lorraine do not desire to be closely joined to either Germany or France, but prefer autonomy. They have now been made an integral part of the highly centralized French Republic and have lost their former local autonomy and independence. Financial, judicial, administrative, and religious issues have developed and continued, and there is as much dissatisfaction in Alsace-Lorraine today over the restoration to France as there was over German rule in the decades before 1914.

Germany is justly outraged over the Polish Corridor, the partition of Upper Silesia, and the opposition of the Entente to union with German Austria. The latter was one of the most direct denials of the national principle by the peacemakers of 1919-20. The Magyars of Hungary bitterly resent the incredibly unjust treatment meted out in the Treaty of Trianon. This deprived them of about two-thirds of their territory and population, as well as of their natural boundaries and resources.[2] They especially protest the award of their former territories to peoples culturally much inferior to the Magyars and with a much less creditable economic and administrative record. They are determined never to abide by the oppressive Treaty of Trianon, and are putting themselves in readiness to take advantage of any situation that will give them justice by the sword, if it cannot be obtained by peaceful negotiations.

Bulgaria is smarting under the humiliation and deprivation forced upon it by the peace treaties, which denied it obviously Bulgarian territory and shut it off from any outlet through the Aegean. The independence spirit is strong in both Montenegro and Macedonia. The latter territory, split up among Greece, Yugoslavia, and Bulgaria, is probably the chief danger spot in the Balkan

---

[1] See especially Ebray, *op. cit.;* Mowrer, *Balkanized Europe;* and A. J. Toynbee, *The World After the Peace Conference,* Oxford Press, 1925.

[2] It is desirable to point out, however, that much of the territory lost by Hungary is occupied by peoples the majority of whom are non-Magyars.

Peninsula today.[1] Russia may be trusted to keep its weather eye open for any good opportunity to regain the rich province of Bessarabia.

One of the most tragic and indefensible denials of the national principle after 1918 was that in the South Tyrol. Here some 250,000 German Austrians were sacrificed to the Italian strategic aspirations to extend the Italian frontier to the top of the Brenner Pass. President Wilson consciously acquiesced in this award, in order to strengthen his stand against the impending Italian seizure of Fiume, but in the final outcome Italy obtained both the South Tyrol and Fiume. The Italian occupation of the South Tyrol would have been less serious a matter had the Italians kept their promise to respect the cultural autonomy of the Tyrolese, but they have not done so since 1921. Under the Fascist régime, Mussolini has initiated and pursued with ruthless thoroughness one of the most brutal programs of denationalization to be found in the records of modern European history. Protests have been uttered, not only by the German and Austrian governments, but also by numerous unbiased foreign students and observers, but thus far their voices have been raised in vain.[2]

In conclusion, then, it may be said that while the principle of nationality was more respected than any other at the Peace Conference, the territorial and ethnic readjustments were often ill-advised and unscientific. The new problems that have been created almost equal the older injustices in number, and sometimes exceed them in intensity and in potential danger to the peace of Europe. While the new readjustment of Europe actually reduced the repressed nationalities from about 50,000,000 to less than 20,000,000, the present set-up represents in many cases a more obviously flagrant violation of the principle of national self-determination than did the prewar situation. The chief present repressed national groups include about 8,000,000 Germans, 3,000,000 Magyars, and 1,500,000 Bulgars.[3]

Likewise, the creation of many new states is a step backward politically and economically, unless there is some accompanying guarantee of union and order, something that is by no means assured at the present time. The League of Nations gives little promise of being able to curb adequately the arrogance and insolence of the intensified national spirit that the World War and the peace treaties have created.[4] More tariff walls and higher tariffs increase economic friction.

The redistribution of the colonial empire of Germany and of the Turkish territory in Asia has already been described above in dealing with imperialism since the World War.[5]

III. MAKING THE WORLD SAFE FOR DEMOCRACY

We were solemnly informed from 1914 to 1918 that the World War was being fought "to make the world safe for democracy," and particularly to in-

---

[1] *Cf.* F. L. Benns, *Europe since 1914*, rev. ed., Crofts, 1934, pp. 695 ff.
[2] See C. H. Herford, *The Case of German South Tyrol against Italy*, London, 1927.
[3] Admittedly, it would be an almost impossible task so to reapportion Europe on a national basis that no nationals of one state would be in the territory of another. But recognition of this fact is quite different from conceding that the postwar treaties handled the problem as well as might have been done if reason and facts had prevailed.
[4] *Cf.* P. B. Potter, *This World of Nations*, Macmillan, 1929; Eddy, *The Challenge of Europe;* Knickerbocker, *The Boiling Point;* and J. F. Horrabin, *Atlas of Current Affairs*, Knopf, 1934.
[5] See above, pp. 550 ff.

sure the existence, safety, and stability of democracy in Germany. The end of the World War saw even the architect of that phrase acquiescing in the sending of American troops to assist in the Allied intervention to crush the Bolshevik government in Russia, which according to its Marxian theory would logically eventuate in a democracy more radical than any yet known.[1]

Even more serious is the fact that the Entente policy after the war seriously handicapped the once strong sentiment and movement for democracy in Germany, which would probably have triumphed in that country had it not been for the unconscious but real coöperation of Poincaré with the party of Ludendorff and the military monarchists in Germany. The continued rebuffs to the German democracy after 1919, the resolute efforts to collect crushing reparations, and the refusal to discuss a revision of the war-guilt thesis or to consider the revision of the Treaty of Versailles produced that state of German desperation which made it possible for a Hitler to rise to power and to crush out all remaining vestiges of democracy in Germany.

Since the war many Entente statesmen who during the conflict had been ostentatious champions of democracy as a panacea for world-ills have coöperated enthusiastically with Mussolini, the most autocratic personage who has risen to power in an important European state since the downfall of Napoleon III. In Greece, Turkey, Hungary, Rumania, Bulgaria, Yugoslavia, Spain, and Poland dictatorships of varying duration have been set up. There was much talk of dictatorship in France after 1926, to help in the solution of financial problems. Indeed, Poincaré enjoyed almost dictatorial power for some years. Not since the collapse of the Revolutions of 1848 has democracy been in greater peril in Europe than it is today.[2]

There are, of course, valid arguments for dictatorship, but we are here interested in indicating how the World War failed to advance the cause of democracy. Even in the United States, which was supposed to be interested far beyond any other country in making the war a great crusade for democracy, we have witnessed a strong reaction since 1917, so that individual liberty and freedom of expression were probably in greater jeopardy among us from 1917 to 1933 than at any other peace-time period since the period of the Alien and Sedition Laws of 1798.[3]

It is true that republicanism has made great formal progress since 1918 and that a crop of new republics has come into being. The events of the last twenty years, however, make it absolutely clear that republicanism is in itself no guarantee of either peace, justice, or freedom—or even of real democracy.

But we must go still further and recognize the fact that even had the World War most notably promoted the development of democracy and secured its complete domination on the planet, this would in itself alone be no guarantee of subsequent world-peace. When the Allied propaganda was in full bloom it was a constantly reiterated thesis that the war had been caused by autocracy. Democracy was held to be a sure bulwark against war. The facts we now

---

[1] See Stewart, *The White Armies of Russia*.
[2] *Cf.* M. J. Bonn, *The Crisis of European Democracy*, Yale University Press, 1925; Strachey, *The Menace of Fascism;* G. D. H. and M. I. Cole, *The Intelligent Man's Review of Europe To-day*, Knopf, 1933, Pt. IV; Buell, *New Governments in Europe;* and Rogers, *Crisis Government*.
[3] *Cf.* Bates, *This Land of Liberty;* and Leon Whipple, *The Story of Civil Liberty in the United States*, Vanguard Press, 1927.

possess about war guilt completely explode this view of democracy as a defense against war. A judicious American scholar, Professor Blakeslee, clearly tells us how the facts of modern history indicate the futility of relying upon democracy to assure peace unless we can combine with it an effective world organization:

> During the past century ... the great democracies have been making war, threatening war, and preparing for war, much of the time against each other. Their history shows clearly enough that if their neighbors had also been democratic this change alone would not have prevented wars. Nor is the outlook for the future encouraging. Democratic nations are still willing to fight to defend their national interests and policies; they demand their due share of over-sea trade, concessions and colonies—if they are a commercial or expansionist people—no less insistently because they are democratic. But the interest and policies of one nation conflict with those of another; what one democracy regards as a due share of over-sea trade, concessions, and colonies is an undue share to its rival. Each democracy becomes an excited partisan of its own view, ready to back it by force of arms; and the natural result is, as it always has been, wars and rumors of wars. There are enough conflicts in national policies today to lead to a dozen future conflicts, even if all the world should be democratic. There is Japan's insistence upon controlling China; our own Monroe Doctrine, when interpreted in a domineering or selfish spirit; England's Persian Gulf policy; the anti-oriental policy of the United States and the British self-governing colonies; the expansionist policy of all the Balkan states; and the Entente policy, formulated at the Paris Conference, of discriminating against the trade of the Central Powers after the present war shall be over. Unless present conditions are changed, the democratic nations of the world, with their conflicting interests, would find it difficult to maintain world peace, for the next century, even if they wished to maintain it. History, present conditions, and the logic of the situation show that democracy alone will never make the world safe. ...
>
> It is only by ... a definite concert of states ... that we may secure a reasonable promise of obtaining a permanent international peace and of becoming a nonmilitaristic world.[1]

IV. THE ECONOMIC ASPECTS OF THE TREATY OF VERSAILLES

The attitude of the Entente towards German economic prosperity and strength in 1914 is well set forth in a telegram of Izvolsky, then Russian ambassador to France, to his chief, Foreign Secretary Sazonov, on October 13, 1914:

> ... Very confidential. Delcassé ... earnestly asked me to draw your attention to the fact that the demands and aspirations of France remain unaltered, with the addition only of the necessary destruction of the political and economic power of Germany. The latter point is a sheer necessity in view of the existing situation, and especially in view of the participation of Great Britain in the war, and the French Government lays stress on the need for attaining this aim.[2]

This program of destroying Germany's economic power was embodied in the secret treaties.

[1] G. H. Blakeslee, "Will Democracy Make the World Safe?" *Journal of Race Development*, April, 1918, pp. 499-500, 505. [2] Stieve, *Isvolsky and the World War*, p. 248.

The Treaty of Versailles represented a robust effort to execute this ambition. The most serious blow to Germany in a long-time sense was the loss of its sources of coal and iron ore. The rich coal mines in the Saar Valley were given to France pending the results of a plebiscite in 1935. If the inhabitants at this time voted to return to Germany, then the latter was to purchase the coal mines from France.[1] Germany was further deprived of most of the coal supply in Upper Silesia, from which it derived a considerable proportion of its hard coal. These losses meant about 35 per cent of its entire coal reserves. This was not all; from this reduced reserve of coal Germany was required to make enormous free deliveries of coal to its victorious enemies. It was ordered to deliver 20,000,000 tons annually to France for five years and 8,000,000 tons annually for the next five years.[2] Further, as a part of the reparations system, it was directed to deliver 25,000,000 tons annually to other Entente states. Along with these great losses and depletions of its coal supply, Germany lost three-fourths of its iron ore through the restoration of Alsace-Lorraine to France.

Germany was also ordered, at a time when its own civilians were still dying of starvation as a result of the Entente blockade after the Armistice, to deliver to France great quantities of live stock and agricultural products. Germany was commanded to surrender its merchant marine to the Entente and to build 200,000 tons of shipping annually for the Entente. France took over the best rolling stock from the German railroads. German trade was further penalized by tariff and administrative arrangements. German products were boycotted in Entente countries, while Germany was compelled to put the Entente nations in the status of "most-favored nations" under the German tariff regulations. Germany was thus denied access to Entente markets for five years and exposed to Entente "dumping" during this same period. The main German commercial rivers were placed under administrative commissions manned chiefly by non-German members.

Most serious of all as an immediate burden were the reparations clauses of the treaty. Germany was compelled to indemnify the Entente for all the so-called "civilian damages" to Entente countries during the World War. In this category of damages to civilians were placed the potential pensions to Entente soldiers and their relatives, an enormous increase in the total reparations bill.[3]

No exact statement of the reparations account was formulated at the time, though one prominent British member of the commission put the figure at $125,000,000,000. On April 27, 1921, the Reparations Commission set the amount at $33,000,000,000 (about 132,000,000,000 gold marks). At the end of 1922 Germany was forced to default on reparation payments. The Dawes Plan, worked

---

[1] The Saar voted overwhelmingly in January, 1935, to return to Germany. It was formally returned in March, 1935.

[2] The French alleged in defense of these coal reparations that Germany had attempted to wreck the French mines during the war.

[3] This preposterous folly was due chiefly to the influence of Lloyd George, Clemenceau, and General Smuts. President Wilson consented against the almost unanimous advice of the American economic experts at Paris. When informed by his advisers that there was no logic in the inclusion of pensions as one of the items of damages to civilians during the war, Mr. Wilson is said to have remarked: "Logic! Logic! I don't give a damn for logic. I am going to include pensions." This decision practically doubled the amount of reparations demanded from Germany. See J. M. Keynes, *A Revision of the Treaty*, Harcourt, Brace, 1922, Chap. v.

out in the spring of 1924, did not set any final sum for the total payments, but specified the nature and amount of the annual payments to be made by Germany. An international commission to fix the total amount of reparation payments drew up its plan in the spring of 1929. Under this so-called Young Plan the figure was set at $27,600,000,000. In 1932 it was provisionally reduced to $714,000,000.

The treatment of Germany in a military and naval sense was fully as severe as the economic clauses of the treaty. It was compelled to surrender its navy intact to the British, but the German crew patriotically scuttled and sank the German ships at Scapa Flow. The German army was limited to 100,000 men to be raised by volunteer service.

Germany was forced by the fact of starvation and the threat of invasion to sign the Treaty of Versailles. The German representatives at Paris were treated like prisoners of war and their cogent arguments against the treaty in relation both to war responsibility and to Mr. Wilson's Fourteen Points were arrogantly ignored. The Germans were treated with even less civility and consideration than had been accorded to the French by Bismarck when concluding the treaty of 1871. As an integral part of the treaty, Germany was compelled to admit that it and Austria had willfully been the sole aggressors in bringing on the World War. This, the famous war-guilt clause (Article 231), was utilized as the special basis of the justification of German reparation payments.

The mode of enforcing the treaty was compatible with its nature. The Rhineland was placed under the direct control of some 75,000 Entente soldiers, to be supported by the Germans, and was divided into three zones. Provided the Germans executed the provisions of the treaty in a manner meeting the approval of the Entente, the Cologne zone was to be evacuated in 1925, the Coblenz zone in 1930, and the Mainz zone in 1935.[1] But the Locarno Agreement of 1925 promoted better relations, and at Thoiry in 1926 Briand promised Stresemann to do his best to secure an early evacuation of the Rhine territory. The American army had already been recalled in 1923. British public opinion demanded the return of the British troops, and they were brought back late in 1929. The French had to follow suit, and the last French soldier left the Rhine in June, 1930. Not only was the Rhineland made an occupied area; it was also converted into a neutralized zone. The Germans were forbidden to erect fortifications on the left bank or on the right bank within fifty kilometers of the river.

In this manner was formulated, signed, and enforced the "peace of justice, sympathy, fair play, and goodwill." It left many traces of "a rankling sense of injustice," which Mr. Wilson had warned against in his wartime speeches. William Allen White well summarized the situation when he wrote that Wilson traded "the substance of European demands for the shadow of American ideals." In spite of President Wilson's gradual surrender of his farsighted peace program, however, unbiased persons will probably have to concede that the Peace Treaty would have been worse but for his opposition to the European

[1] It has been pointed out that Germany occupied France in 1871, pending the fulfillment of the treaty obligations and the payment of the indemnity levied on France. The point that is forgotten here is that the indemnity levied on France was only $1,000,000,000, as against the more than $100,000,000,000 with which Germany was threatened in 1919 and the $33,000,000,000 actually settled upon by the Reparations Commission in 1921.

nationalists and imperialists at Paris. This fact affords still further cause for comment and reflection on the sincerity of the "holy war" talk of the Allies after 1914.

V. THE TREATIES WITH AUSTRIA, HUNGARY, BULGARIA, AND TURKEY

Separate treaties of a character similar to that of Versailles were made with Austria, Hungary, Bulgaria, and Turkey.[1] The Treaty of St. Germain was signed with Austria on September 10, 1919. It reduced the Austrian territory from 116,000 square miles to 32,000, and the population from 29,000,000 to 6,500,000. Reparation payments were demanded from Austria, but the total amount was not fixed and in 1922 Austria was freed from any reparation payments until 1942. Union with Germany—the much-wished Anschluss—was explicitly forbidden under threat of war.

Peace was made with Hungary by the Treaty of Trianon, signed on June 4, 1920. The Hungarian territory was reduced from 125,500 square miles to 36,000, and the population from 21,000,000 to 8,000,000. The Hungarian army was greatly restricted and reparation payments were levied—to begin with an annual payment of $2,000,000 for twenty years. As with Austria, though Hungary was required to pay reparations, the final extent of these was not fixed in the terms of the Treaty of Trianon. The Treaty of Neuilly was signed with Bulgaria in November, 1919. Bulgaria, already stripped of much Bulgarian territory as a result of its defeat in the Second Balkan War of 1913, was compelled to cede further territory to Serbia and Greece, to pay an indemnity of $450,000,000, and to limit its army.

Turkey was compelled to sign the Treaty of Sèvres on August 10, 1920; this restricted Turkey to a small state in Asia Minor. Owing, as previously noted, to Entente jealousies and distrust in their own camp, especially as to the disposition of Constantinople and the Near East, the Turks, under the able leadership of Mustapha Kemal, were able to defy the Entente and flout the Treaty of Sèvres. They secured a second treaty with the Entente, the Treaty of Lausanne, signed on July 24, 1923. This arrangement left Turkey in Europe in Turkish hands and recognized the powerful Turkish state in Asia Minor. As stated before, Turkey agreed to internationalize the Straits. In this manner was settled, at least temporarily, the issue of Constantinople and the Straits, which had been a strong factor in bringing on both the Crimean War and the World War.

The impossible nature of the treaties with Austria and Hungary soon had to be admitted tacitly by the Entente. Both states went bankrupt and had to be restored by Entente loans administered under the supervision of financial commissioners appointed by the Entente.

VI. THE EFFECT OF PEACE UPON LABOR

The World War introduced some notable temporary changes in the labor situation. In the warring European countries hostilities withdrew millions of men from industrial activity and brought many women into the factories. In

[1] See W. C. Langsam, *The World since 1914*, Macmillan, 1933, pp. 126-33.

some cases the laws against the labor of women were suspended. The shortage of labor produced by the emergency demands for clothing and munitions and by the huge numbers of men drafted into military service led to almost complete employment of all able-bodied laborers. There was a marked tendency to regiment labor, to fix wage limits, and to restrict severely the right to strike. These coercive measures were compensated for in part by the virtual elimination of unemployment and the payment of reasonably high wages. In the effort to eliminate strikes and loss of productive effort in the United States a War Labor Conference Board was created. It formulated a splendid code of working-conditions and recommended for the primary purpose of adjusting labor disputes the creation of a National War Labor Board, which came into being in April, 1918. Labor in the United States profited notably by the war, both through greater employment and higher wages and through enforced recognition of trade-unionism by the employers. In neutral states, as well, labor benefited by the increase of employment.[1]

These improved conditions and the idealism expressed by war leaders led many laborers to expect better things when the war had ended—virtually the retention of the gains made during the war. Some even hoped that a new era of social and industrial justice would emerge from the era of treaty-making. During the conflict President Wilson told the American Federation of Labor that one of the great results of the World War would be to free labor. The British Labour party proclaimed that the war must end in a great social and economic revolution.[2]

It should have been obvious to all realistically minded persons that no peace treaty could achieve very much of significance in the readjustment of the internal social and economic conditions of any state. The improvement of the condition of labor and any far-reaching social and economic reconstruction depend mainly upon the efforts of labor and its allies within national boundaries. The British Labour party probably understood all this. The Treaty of Versailles had to content itself with the enunciation of pious wishes and general aspirations.

In Part XIII of the Treaty there appears a general statement of noble abstract principles concerning the future condition of labor, and provision for an International Labor Organization and an active International Labor Office.[3] The latter has done important work in gathering information about laboring conditions throughout the world and has made enlightened recommendations as to progressive labor policies. But it has been able to accomplish little of practical import in the way of bringing about better conditions for labor in the major states of the world.

Once the war was over, the vested interests in the capitalistic nations made strenuous efforts to weaken or destroy labor organization and to nullify all the gains made by labor between 1914 and 1918. In countries that turned to Socialism or Communism during or after the war, the condition of labor was, naturally, thoroughly revolutionized.

[1] See Ogg and Sharp, *The Economic Development of Modern Europe*, Chaps. xxix-xxx.
[2] See below, pp. 958 ff.
[3] See below, pp. 905-06; G. N. Barnes, *History of the International Labour Office*, London, 1926; G. A. Johnston, *International Social Progress*, Macmillan, 1924; E. M. Oliver, *The World's Industrial Parliament*, London, 1925; and J. T. Shotwell, ed., *The Origins of the International Labor Organization*, Columbia University Press, 1934, 2 vols.

VII. THE FRENCH SECURITY PACT OF 1919

Before ending this section on the postwar treaties it is necessary to call attention to another attempted violation of President Wilson's pre-conference statement of Entente ideals and aims. In his famous speech of September 27, 1918, adding five new points to his peace program, he had said: "There can be no leagues or alliances or special covenants and understandings within the general and common family of the League of Nations." Yet he agreed to make the United States a party to a special security pact, signed on June 28, 1919, which bound the United States and Great Britain to come to the aid of France if the latter were attacked by Germany.[1] The United States Senate refused to ratify this treaty, but this does not affect the judgment we may pass on those who proposed and drafted the arrangement. The last echo of this effort of France to get special favor appeared in the Geneva Protocol of 1924. This time, however, the selfish policy of security for France was joined to the broader program of compulsory arbitration, insisted upon by Ramsay MacDonald.

The Geneva Protocol failed of ratification and in its place came the Locarno Agreements, which rested upon a more truly European basis. These covenants were characterized by mutual guarantees from which states other than France might derive benefits, and they also protected other states from French aggression. Though the French security treaty of 1919 was nullified, this did not prevent a wholesale violation of President Wilson's dictum that there should be no special alliances within the League of Nations. Between 1920, when the Franco-Belgian alliance was signed, and the Locarno Agreement of 1925 no less than twenty-six of these special treaties of alliance were signed, most of them involving France and its allies.

VIII. A WARNING TO FUTURE GENERATIONS

The conclusion of these preceding pages on the contrast between myth and fact in connection with the World War, and after, is the highly relevant opinion that war cannot be ended by more war any more than a drowning man can be resuscitated by pouring more water into his lungs.[2] The type of mind and the intellectual attitudes that are developed for and by war are those which bring to the surface all the baser traits of human nature. They intensify hatred and savagery, while reducing the potency of those mental attitudes which are conducive to pacific adjustments and mutual toleration.[3] It is only by attacking war head on, and making clear its multifarious contributions to human brutality and waste, as well as by proving the futile and unnecessary nature of every war, that we can make headway, if at all, against modern militarism and the war spirit.[4]

[1] The crushing and definitive answer to the plea of France that history proves it to be in special need of protection from Germany is contained in the article by Count Max Montgelas, *"Die drei Invasionen Frankreichs,"* Berliner Monatshefte, January, 1932. The article has been translated into English and published by the *Berliner Monatshefte* as a pamphlet, *Three Invasions of France.*

[2] Cf. Ebray, *op. cit.;* Sir Norman Angell, *The Great Illusion, 1933,* Putnam, 1933; and Jonathan Mitchell, *Goose Steps to Peace,* Little, Brown, 1931.

[3] Cf. Playne, *Society at War, 1914-1918.*

[4] As, for example, in Laurence Stallings, ed., *The First World War; a Photographic History,* Simon & Schuster, 1933.

It may have been worth while along this line to point out with more than usual frankness the imbecilities and disasters of the late World War, because this is a particularly recent and instructive instance for those now alive. It was not only a struggle through which we have lived, but also the war that was most universally exploited as the one uniquely necessary, idealistic, and justice-promoting conflict of all history. If we show how totally we were deluded, and how even the better natures of combatant peoples were enlisted in the struggle only to be betrayed, it may help us in the future to guard against being led astray by similar arguments in provoking or justifying another world-conflict.

It has doubtless been a consideration of these points that has led a few courageous spirits, such as Harry Emerson Fosdick, Sherwood Eddy, Kirby Page, and others, to declare that they would never again support or sanction any war. Even more impressive are the few rare spirits who in the heat of the war itself stood out, or proposed to stand out, against the prevailing madness. Among them were Jean Jaurès (the great French Socialist leader, perhaps the most enlightened statesman in Europe, who was assassinated at the very outset of the war), Romain Rolland, Karl Liebknecht, Ramsay MacDonald, Bertrand Russell, Norman Thomas, and many more. One can never be certain of a pledge to the future; the intelligence and the courage of these men have been proved by their past.

The manner in which we were deceived in the World War has been a chief cornerstone in the philosophy of the American isolationists. They may give consideration to the alleged warnings of the Revolutionary Fathers against European entanglements,[1] but such sentiments are given fresh meaning and cogency through the memory of the recent wartime idealism and its collapse. Though we may not fully approve of the isolationist attitude, one cannot fairly deny that men such as Senators Borah, Johnson, James Reed, and the like have much justification for their bias. The more sensible position is to avoid both extremes: sentimental enthusiasm for the Entente and internationalism, on the one hand, and backward-looking isolationism, on the other. Then we may cooperate effectively without being either an "international sucker" or a battler against the tide of world-history that makes actual isolation a page out of the human past.

IX. THE SETTLEMENT OF WAR DEBTS

During the World War and the post-Armistice period the Entente borrowed from the United States some $11,600,000,000, exclusive of loans from private bankers. By 1923, with accrued interest at the agreed rate of 5 per cent, this amounted to some $12,000,000,000. The United States refused to cancel these debts in response to the plea that the Entente had been fighting our war, but it did offer to make generous reductions of the debts owed to us by our former allies.

The settlement with England was made early in 1923, the agreement being signed on June 19, 1923. It placed the British debt at $4,604,128,085 and provided that it should be paid off in sixty-two annual installments. The interest rate for the first ten years was set at 3 per cent, after which time it was to be

---

[1] See below, pp. 922 ff.

3.5 per cent. The annual payments would, then, be about $160,000,000 a year for the first ten years and $180,000,000 a year for the remaining fifty-two years

The French debt settlement was signed on April 29, 1926. It fixed the principal of the French debt at $4,025,000,000 and provided that it should be paid off in sixty-two years at a gradually rising interest rate, interest payments to begin in 1931. The interest charges were very low. From 1931 to 1941 the rate was to be 1 per cent. Not until 1959 was it to rise to 3 per cent, and the highest rate, 3.5 per cent, was to be paid from 1966 to the end of the period in 1987.

The debt settlement with Italy was signed on November 14, 1925. The principal of the Italian debt was placed at $2,042,000,000, likewise to be paid in sixty-two annual installments. As regards interest payments the concessions were even more generous than those made to France. No interest was charged during the first five years. Not until 1970 was the interest rate to rise to 1 per cent, and the highest rate, 2 per cent, was to be paid only from 1980 to 1987.

There has been no settlement with Russia, because on January 21, 1918, the government of Soviet Russia issued a decree repudiating the foreign debts contracted by the former imperial government, as well as by the Lvov and Kerensky governments, on the ground that they were obligations contracted without reference to the will of the Russian people.[1] Since the United States recognized Russia in the late autumn of 1933, the Russian debt has been discussed, but no final settlement has yet been arranged (April, 1935).

The United States has also concluded generous debt settlements with the lesser European countries. The general nature of all the settlements is well set forth in the table from H. G. Moulton and Leo Pasvolsky's standard treatment, *World War Debt Settlements*.[2] (See first table on p. 621.)

It has been held that in making these agreements the United States has been very harsh and unyielding. As an actual matter of fact, these settlements represent a cancellation of a large part of the actual indebtedness. Just how great the cancellation is can be determined by comparing the principal of the original debt at 5 per cent interest with the so-called present value of the principal fixed in the debt settlement at the rate of interest specified. The present value is, in other words, the sum that would, at the original rate of 5 per cent interest, equal in sixty-two years the principal and interest payments arranged for in the debt settlements. On this basis of present-value computation we have actually canceled 60.3 per cent of the French indebtedness, 80.2 per cent of the Italian indebtedness, 30.1 per cent of the British indebtedness, and a grand average of 51.2 per cent.[3]

The second table from Moulton and Pasvolsky on page 621 indicates the percentage of cancellation involved in the whole series of debt settlements thus far arranged for. This table is a final and conclusive answer to the "Uncle Shylock" propaganda of the Entente and a full vindication of the American claims of unique and unprecedented generosity.

[1] *Cf.* Leo Pasvolsky and H. G. Moulton, *Russian Debts and Russian Reconstruction*, McGraw-Hill, 1924, pp. 197 ff.
[2] Brookings Institution, 1926.
[3] If present values of the debt are computed on a 4.25 per cent interest basis, the cancellation of the French debt would stand at 52.8 per cent; that of the Italian debt at 75.4 per cent; and that of the British debt at 19.7 per cent; with a grand average of 43 per cent. Even on this computation, the settlement would have to be regarded as extremely generous.

Wide World Photos
A WARSHIP THAT WAS SUNK BY A SUBMARINE

Wide World Photos
AN AIRPLANE

Wide World Photos
A BIG GUN

Wide World Photos
A TANK

SOME EQUIPMENT OF THE WORLD WAR

From F. A. Barber, The Horror of It, *reprinted by permission*
BLINDED AND MUTILATED

WORLD WAR LOSSES
(approximate)

HUMAN BEINGS
Fighting forces
Dead	10,000,000	
Severely wounded	6,300,000	
Other wounded	14,000,000	
Prisoners or missing	6,000,000	
	36,300,000	36,300,000

Civilians
Dead	13,000,000	
War orphans	9,000,000	
War widows	5,000,000	
Refugees	10,000,000	
	37,000,000	37,000,000
		73,300,000

IMMEDIATE MONEY COSTS
(Without pensions or debts) $332,000,000,000

Based on figures from Direct and Indirect Costs of the World War

RUINS—THE CATHEDRAL OF ARRAS   LOSSES AND GAINS

SOME RESULTS OF THE WORLD WAR

THE SETTLEMENT OF WAR DEBTS

TOTAL PRINCIPAL AND INTEREST TO BE PAID TO THE UNITED STATES BY 13 WAR DEBTORS

Country	Principal	Interest	Total	Average interest rate (approximate) over the whole period of payments, per cent
Great Britain	$4,600,000,000	$6,505,965,000.00	$11,105,965,000.00	3.3
Finland	9,000,000	12,695,055.00	21,695,055.00	3.3
Hungary	1,939,000	2,754,240.00	4,693,240.00	3.3
Poland	178,560,000	257,127,550.00	435,687,550.00	3.3
Esthonia	13,830,000	19,501,140.00	33,331,140.00	3.3
Latvia	5,775,000	8,183,635.00	13,958,635.00	3.3
Lithuania	6,030,000	8,501,940.00	14,531,940.00	3.3
Czechoslovakia	115,000,000	*197,811,433.88	312,811,433.88	3.3
Rumania	44,590,000	*77,916,260.05	122,506,260.05	3.3
Belgium	417,780,000	310,050,500.00	727,830,500.00	1.8
France	4,025,000,000	2,822,674,104.17	6,847,674,104.17	1.6
Yugoslavia	62,850,000	32,327,635.00	95,177,635.00	1.0
Italy	2,042,000,000	365,677,500.00	2,407,677,500.00	0.4
Total	$11,522,354,000	$10,621,185,993.10	$22,143,539,993.10	

* Includes deferred payments which will be funded into principal.

PRESENT VALUES OF FUNDED DEBTS AT 5 PER CENT
(In dollars, 000 omitted)

Country	Debt prior to funding	Present value of funded debt on the basis of a 5 per cent interest rate	Percentage of cancellation
Finland	$9,190	$6,452	29.8
Hungary	1,984	1,388	30.0
Poland	182,324	127,643	30.0
Esthonia	14,143	9,915	29.9
Latvia	5,893	4,137	29.8
Lithuania	6,216	4,322	30.5
Czechoslovakia	123,854	77,985	37.0
Rumania	46,945	29,507	37.1
Belgium	483,426	191,766	60.3
France	4,230,777	1,681,369	60.3
Yugoslavia	66,164	15,919	75.9
Italy	2,150,150	426,287	80.2
Total	$7,321,066	$2,576,690	64.8
Great Britain	$4,715,310	$3,296,948	30.1
Grand Total	$12,036,376	$5,873,638	51.2

Beginning in December, 1932, the European nations as a group ceased their full war-debt payments to the United States. Some defaulted entirely. Such was the case with France. Others made token payments—that is, they made a nominal payment on the interest due. Only Finland paid its annual quota in full. The European nations illogically alleged that when German reparation payments were practically wiped out at Lausanne this implied that war debts were to be canceled as well.[1]

The main case which the Allies have had against the United States did not consist in our refusal to cancel all debts or in the degree of our actual cancellation. Our policy here was most generous. The major valid grievance which the debtor nations actually possessed was our high tariff and the accompanying difficulty in obtaining dollars or gold with which to make payments on the debts. Our tariff wall kept out most foreign goods and made payment in kind almost impossible. But this proved, in fact, a specious argument, since when France did have ample gold after 1928 it made no effort to execute full payments. Moreover, when it was suggested at times that the Allies pay in silver or in commodities, this provoked no enthusiastic response.

X. THE REPARATIONS PROBLEM

Neither legally nor logically is there any direct connection between reparation payments and war debts due to the United States from the Entente. There is, nevertheless, a very practical economic link between German reparation payments and inter-Allied indebtedness. The Allied Powers have used their income from German reparation payments to pay the principal and interest on what they owe the United States, though in the case of France the reparation income far exceeded the required annual debt payments. The alleged connection between reparation payments and inter-Allied indebtedness has been clung to in desperation by the Entente in their campaign for cancellation of inter-Allied debts. The Entente states have done this because they wish to insist that any suggestion of lowering or canceling the German payments should carry with it by implication the necessity of canceling the inter-Allied debts.

While the United States tentatively conceded the Allied contention of a direct connection between the debt problem and the reparations problem as early as 1919, we later took a different view as the practical matter of the debt settlement came up. The official American attitude was that the debts owed to us by our former allies must be handled as a purely business matter, having no relation either to sentiment or to the financial relations between Germany and the Entente. The most resounding keynote of this view was embodied in Mr. Hoover's speech at Toledo in October, 1922. It was repeated by Secretary Hughes in New Haven in December, 1922. We have never officially surrendered this view, but our participation in making the Dawes Plan and in the Reparations Conference of 1929 certainly involved our tacit recognition of the alleged interrelationship between debts and reparation payments.

German reparation payments grew directly out of the Armistice terms demanding reparation for damages and out of the application of points seven and

---

[1] *Cf.* Dorsey Richardson, *Will They Pay?* Lippincott, 1933.

THE REPARATIONS PROBLEM

eight of Mr. Wilson's Fourteen Points in the construction of the Treaty of Versailles—the points concerning the evacuation and restoration of Belgium and France. The famous war-guilt clause of the Treaty of Versailles (Article 231) was specifically inserted and exploited to justify reparation payments. This article states that:

> The Allied and Associated Governments affirm and Germany accepts the responsibility of Germany and her Allies, for causing all the loss and damage to which the Allied and Associated Governments and their nationals have been subjected as a consequence of the war imposed upon them by the aggression of Germany and her Allies.

The basis of reparation payments had been the conception that they were not like the punitive indemnities of old but merely a just recompense for the war damages done by aggressive Germany and its associates. Further, the reparation payments were designed exclusively to pay for civilian damages and not for war costs, in spite of the fact that Lloyd George and many French leaders had early assured their fellow citizens that the Entente would make Germany pay for the war.

We have already pointed out that it was two years before the exact amount of German reparation payments was settled, though the Germans were ordered to pay 20,000,000,000 gold marks on account before May 1, 1921. During this interval there were the wildest estimates as to what would be exacted, and the French people were still hopeful and expectant that Germany would pay in full the expenses of the World War. A large number of conferences were held regarding the reparations situation between the signing of the Treaty of Versailles and the conclusion of the first general agreement about payments. Early in 1920 brief conferences were held at London, San Remo, and Hythe. In July, 1920, came the conferences at Boulogne and Spa. At these an arrangement was made regarding the proportional distribution of the German payments among the Entente states. This was later adopted and incorporated by the London Conference of 1921. Further conferences were held at Brussels and Paris in January and February, 1921. Then came the conference at London, which opened in March, 1921. Here the Entente Powers decided upon the exact amount of reparation payments to be demanded and the time and method of payment.

On April 27, 1921, the Reparations Commission announced that it had determined as the total amount $33,000,000,000, or 132,000,000,000 gold marks. It was stipulated that Germany should pay annually 2,000,000,000 gold marks in cash, 26 per cent of the proceeds of German export trade, and large amounts of coal and other products. It was provided that France should receive 52 per cent of the total reparation payments; Great Britain 22 per cent; Italy 10 per cent; Belgium 8 per cent; Japan and Portugal .75 per cent; with the remaining amount divided among Greece, Rumania, and Yugoslavia. Germany accepted the plan only under protest, correctly declaring that in its weakened and bankrupt condition it could make no such payments.[1]

In the summer of 1922 Germany defaulted and asked for a delay. The British

---

[1] German experts contended that by the end of 1922 Germany had made deliveries to the value of 41,600,000,000 gold marks. The American experts Moulton and McGuire and the English ex-

were inclined to sympathize with the German contention, but the French remained adamant, there being not a few French leaders who welcomed the prospect of German default as an ostensible justification for a French invasion of the Rhineland. Accordingly in January, 1923, the French and Belgians invaded the Ruhr area, on the ground that they would run the German industries and mines in this area and collect reparation payments directly. This was also an effort to realize one of the demands of the secret treaties that President Wilson had checked at Paris, namely, the detachment of the Rhineland from Germany and the creation of an independent Rhine Republic.

The Germans met the Franco-Belgian offensive by a campaign of passive resistance and by a frenzied but deliberate inflation of the German currency until the German legal tender possessed less value than the paper on which it was printed. After a struggle attended with great brutality and much violence the French were finally compelled by their economic failure in the Ruhr, and by the adverse opinion of Great Britain and the United States, to abandon the occupation policy and to accept the German proposal to submit the reparations problem to a board of experts, a procedure that had been anticipated by Charles Evans Hughes in a speech before the American Historical Association in December, 1922.[1]

There was accordingly created a commission of experts, known as the Dawes Commission because its chairman was Mr. Charles G. Dawes, later the Vice President of the United States. The commission did its work between January and April, 1924, and presented its report and plan to the Reparations Commission on April 9, 1924. It was adopted at the London Conference of Powers on July 16, 1924. Certain powerful American bankers appear to have had much to do in the way of giving preliminary advice to the American members of the commission, but the actual work of framing the plan was chiefly that of Owen D. Young and his advisers, Sir Josiah Stamp, and Sir Arthur Salter. It has come to be known as the Dawes Plan.

The Dawes Commission accepted by implication the German contention that the annual payments demanded by the Entente were too high and that Germany needed a moratorium period for recovery and resumption of full payments. The plan provided for gradually increasing payments, beginning with 1,000,000,000 gold marks in 1924-25 and increasing to the standard annual payment of 2,500,000,000 gold marks in 1928-29, the first year of the full payments. The payments were to be drawn from the interest on German railroad bonds, industrial debentures, transport taxes, and budget contributions. As the payment could be made in actuality only through the existence of an export balance, a Transfer Committee was created, made up of an Agent General of Reparations and five associates appointed by the Reparations Commission. The first Agent General was Mr. Seymour Parker Gilbert, an American.[2] Germany fully carried out the obligations imposed by the Dawes Plan, and at the end of 1928 Mr. Gilbert praised the German promptness in this regard.

pert Keynes estimated the value of the German deliveries at approximately 26,000,000,000 gold marks. The Reparations Commission set the value of the German deliveries at the absurdly low figure of 8,000,000,000 gold marks.

[1] The Germans, in the meantime, abandoned passive resistance.
[2] Later made a partner in the banking house of J. P. Morgan.

The German fulfillment of the Dawes Plan had been made possible primarily because of the large loans made by the United States, and it was obvious that a procedure based upon constantly greater loans could not persist indefinitely. Germany could not continue for years to make such payments without an industrial and financial collapse. Further, the Dawes Plan made no statement regarding the ultimate amount of reparation payments. The Germans very persistently demanded the reduction of the annual payments and the fixing of a definite final total to be paid. They had gone on the assumption that the 1921 determination was too large and must be abandoned.

In spite of the efforts of the Entente countries to preserve the Dawes Plan and to compel Germany to continue these payments, the latter country was able to secure the calling of a new international conference to revise the reparations schedules. It met in Paris on February 11, 1929, under the chairmanship of Owen D. Young. On the second day of the conference Dr. Hjalmar Schacht, the chief German delegate, informed the members that Germany could not continue payments under the Dawes Plan. On April 13 the Entente handed Germany their demands. These Germany refused, and an impasse resulted in the middle of April. Mr. Young held the conference together and submitted a compromise plan on May 4, which Germany accepted with reservations. After further negotiations, dickerings, and compromises an agreement was reached on May 29, and the Young Plan was signed by all parties on June 7.

The most striking single achievement of the Young Plan was to settle finally the total amount that Germany would be required to pay—some $27,600,000,000. It was stipulated that for thirty-seven years Germany would pay annuities averaging 2,050,000,000 gold marks. For the next twenty-one years it would be required to pay annuities averaging 1,700,000,000 gold marks, and for the last and final year the payment would be 900,000,000 marks. It will be seen that this arrangement not only determined the total amount to be paid but also markedly reduced the annuities that were required under the Dawes Plan—namely, 2,500,000,000 gold marks. An important administrative change in supervising reparation payments was also embodied in the Young Plan. The administration of the payments was removed from the Reparations Commission and lodged in an International Bank with a capital of $100,000,000, located in Basel, Switzerland.[1] The Young Plan also involved recognition of the fact that reparation payments and war debts are inseparably intertwined in European public finance, whatever the history or logic of the situation. Germany was placated in part by a promise of speedy evacuation of the Rhineland.

By the summer of 1931, it looked as though Germany would collapse financially. The United States had a great stake in German finances, owing chiefly to large loans by American bankers to the Germans for reparation payments and other expenditures. If Germany crumbled, we would be struck a heavy blow. Urged by leading American bankers and statesmen like Dwight W. Morrow, President Hoover secured a moratorium of a year on the payment of both debts and reparation. This saved the day temporarily. A year later (1932)

---

[1] By a strange and interesting freak of fortune, the director of the Bank of International Settlement was Leon Fraser, a brilliant young New York lawyer and banker who, as an instructor, had been dismissed from Columbia University as a result of his courage as a pacifist during the World War.

a conference of the European powers was held at Lausanne to consider Germany's claim that it could pay no more reparations. It was finally arranged that, if conditions allowed, Germany should pay $714,000,000 more on account.[1] In this way, the reparations problem was brought to an end and the Dawes and Young plans folded up. The Germans were forced to abandon their demand that the war-guilt clause of the Treaty of Versailles (Article 231) be wiped out, but their material victory was nearly complete.

The prospective loss of reparation payments at once intensified the Entente demand for cancellation of their debts to us. Many American statesmen have favored this proposal, provided the Allies will agree to disarm and not use their savings on war debts to build bigger and more menacing armies and navies. Thus far there has been no enthusiasm among the Allies for disarmament as the price of cancellation.

XI. INDUSTRIAL RESULTS OF THE WORLD WAR

It is obvious that the World War had a tremendous impact upon the economic life of Europe, and affected that of the rest of the world as well. We are not yet through, by any means, with the effects of the war upon the social, economic, and political structure of modern society. A greater period of time must elapse and more extensive studies will have to be undertaken and completed before the full significance of the cataclysm can be estimated. Indeed, it may turn out that the final collapse of Western capitalism will be the penalty exacted. It will satisfy our present purpose to note briefly some of the more important immediate economic results of the war upon western Europe.

Apart from the shocking losses in human life, it appears that the World War caused immediate material losses amounting to the staggering and "astronomical" figure that has been estimated at $332,000,000,000.[2] Regions in Austria, Italy, Rumania, Serbia, eastern Germany, Belgium, and France, varying in size and economic importance, were laid waste. France and Belgium suffered the heaviest damage. It is significant that all the chief industrial countries of Europe were participants in the war, and that many of the fronts along which the conflict raged lay in some of the most highly industrialized portions of Europe.

Among the most interesting of wartime developments was the new relationship between the government and all phases of economic activity that appeared in every belligerent nation. Long-cherished laissez-faire doctrines went by the board overnight. In the desire to win the war and as a result of the highly unusual conditions the war created, doctrines and practices long regarded as essentials of modern economic life were brusquely put aside. During the war labor, production, and distribution were all socialized or nationalized in varying degrees. Individual initiative was legislated out of existence to a surprisingly large extent, but the profit motive was only slightly curbed.

Broadly speaking, each nation functioned as a great economic unit under centralized national direction and control. The facilities of transportation fell

---
[1] See Walter Lippmann and others, *The United States in World Affairs . . . 1932*, Harper, 1933, Chap. VIII.
[2] Estimates, of course, vary considerably, but this figure seems to be acceptable to careful students.

completely under the control of the state, even in the United States. Labor was regimented to a degree never before known in Europe and America; new mechanisms were created to prevent labor disputes; and wages were regulated. Higher wages and nearly 100 per cent employment were held to compensate for the loss of freedom of action on the part of labor. Industrial production fell under the sway of national boards with dictatorial powers. Capital was commandeered to meet immediate needs. Agricultural production was administered by national agencies and the production of foodstuffs was stimulated. Prices were regulated in many instances, and the consumption of foodstuffs and essential war materials was surrounded by special limitations and regulations. In short, the economic life of each nation was integrated, unified, and placed under state control. As the war proceeded, this type of economic organization went beyond national boundaries—it became international in scope. "Each set of belligerents," writes Professor Sharp,[1] "in fact tended ... to evolve into a great coöperative, international unit, organised to achieve the all-important objective of winning the war." What happened during the war has convinced students of the possibilities of international coöperation in the future if certain national attitudes could be erased or at least given more constructive direction.[2]

The World War gave a tremendous impetus to the extension of machinery in industry and agriculture and to scientific and efficient management in production. The increased mechanization of industry was especially notable in those countries which had not yet accepted the new technology in entirety, such as France. Whatever knowledge America had to offer relative to scientific management, the purpose of which is to reduce labor costs and increase production, was applied to European industry in so far as possible. These laborsaving developments came about as a result of the increased burden placed upon industry by the war and because the armies withdrew so many male laborers from industry.

In addition to the changes in the technique of production, certain tendencies in the organization of industry were accentuated. The movement towards combinations and syndicates grew apace. Even in a country such as France, where small and medium-sized enterprises had been typical, the formation of huge industrial agglomerations was frequent. When the war forced the combination and concentration of industry it left an influence that has persisted to some degree. Characteristically enough, this tendency was reproduced in banking and finance. In those fields amalgamation proceeded at an even greater rate. As a result of the war, banking interests became more powerful in England, but they have not gained the same ascendancy over business that they have in the United States.

From the point of view of production, industry suffered in each of the belligerent nations except the United States. The latter, so long a neutral and entering the actual conflict late, capitalized the situation in Europe. It became the industrial giant of the world. In the case of both the Central Powers and the Allies, the shortage of labor, the scarcity of raw materials induced by either

[1] Ogg and Sharp, *op. cit.*, p. 657.
[2] *Cf.* S. P. H. Duggan, ed., *The League of Nations: The Principle and the Practice*, Little, Brown, 1919, Chap. III; and Sir J. A. Salter, *Allied Shipping Control*, Yale University Press, 1921.

the blockade or submarine warfare, the loss of foreign markets, the regimentation of industry to meet imperative war needs, actual invasion, and other factors particular to each country resulted in a decrease in the total industrial output. None of the European belligerents escaped this general let-down in production. Some, however, suffered more than others, France experiencing a sharp curtailment and Belgian industry being all but completely suspended. In Germany, all industries except munitions and chemicals suffered. War conditions made it possible for England to expand in textile and steel production, but the output of iron dropped sharply. The general situation is best made clear by the fact that the production of nonwar commodities in Europe has not yet regained prewar levels in all fields.

There is no space here to speak at length of the attempts at recovery or of the efforts to reconstruct industry during the postwar period. Suffice it is to say that the World War has cursed the world with problems of reconstruction of a magnitude such as has never before been known. Not the least of these have been the result of the territorial alterations brought about by the postwar treaties. Austria, for instance, was stripped by the Treaty of St. Germain of territory and natural resources, and has been reduced to little more than Vienna and a diminutive countryside. Whatever measure of economic unity and interdependence had been built up in the years preceding the war was broken. Austria became a baffling economic problem, for which there seems at present to be no satisfactory solution. The one attempt that held out hope of an adequate adjustment was that of an economic union, at least a tariff union, between Austria and Germany, but the League of Nations and the World Court withheld their consent to that proposal.

Serious problems were also raised by treaty provisions with regard to Silesia, which deprived Germany of an important fraction of its iron and steel industry, and broke up numerous well-established economic relationships. Likewise, the return to France of Alsace-Lorraine left Germany with a great deficiency in its iron-ore deposits, while it gave France many blast furnaces and rolling mills for which it had no fuel except in the temporarily occupied Saar Valley.[1] Changes like these in highly industrialized areas take many years to work themselves out fully and, for the time being at least, proved disrupting to a delicately balanced economic system.

The most striking and novel industrial development produced by the World War is, of course, the experiment in state-controlled industry carried on in Soviet Russia. To this a later chapter will be devoted.

By 1929 a widespread economic depression had settled down upon the Western world, bearing more heavily upon certain countries than upon others but affecting all states in serious fashion.[2] The causes of this were numerous. The oppressive economic terms forced on the Central Powers by the World War made their recovery impossible except through vast loans, which piled up a great burden of debt at home and placed in jeopardy the financial structure of the creditor countries when their debtors seemed unable to pay in full. The Hoover

---
[1] *Cf.* Guy Greer, *The Ruhr-Lorraine Industrial Problem*, Brookings Institution, 1925.
[2] *Cf.* Hammerton, *Universal History of the World*, Chaps. 182, 190; Cole and Cole, *op. cit.*, Pt. III; and G. D. H. Cole, *A Guide Through World Chaos*, Knopf, 1932, Chaps. I-II.

Specially drawn and printed by the Kartographische Anstalt von F. A. Brockhaus, Leipzig, Germany.

PRINTED IN GERMANY

EUROPE in 1920 showing Territorial Changes in World War

moratorium of 1931 was designed to prevent a collapse. Nowhere were wages and farm income sufficient to provide adequate purchasing power for a flourishing and dependable home market. Outside of Europe there was a notable postwar slump in agriculture that impoverished the farmers. Finance capitalism had fattened upon investments of capital abroad, but this field of activity grew more and more restricted, and debtor states often defaulted on their bonds. Few important new industries, such as the automobile industry of 1915 to 1929, appeared on the horizon to infuse renewed vitality into business. In the United States the breakdown was helped along by the vast growth of finance capitalism and the predatory psychology, and by the gutting and robbery of our great corporations from the inside that was made possible by the separation of management from ownership. The ominous situation was further intensified here by an orgy of stock-gambling that diverted financial resources and business attention from sound industrial enterprise. A vast burden of debt, public and private, was piled up by the World War, installment buying, and speculative losses. In short, finance capitalism was at last called upon to "pay the fiddler" as a penalty for shortsightedness and avarice of a generation's standing.

How and when the problems raised by the war and the Treaty of Versailles in all fields, political and social as well as economic, will be solved only the future will reveal. As things now stand only the most courageous dare utter prophecies, and only the most optimistic can envisage successful readjustment. Domestic and foreign debts, mounting tariff barriers, the intensification of national feeling, international relations pregnant with alarming possibilities, the world-wide economic crises, the blundering of statesmen—taken in their entirety, these problems make one pause and wonder if there is any way at all out of the present morass of world-affairs.[1]

XII. THE RATIONALIZATION OF INDUSTRY

The World War and the decade and a half since its close have been of the utmost importance in the technological and industrial evolution of the West. A great impetus was given to standardization in manufacture, especially of firearms, airplanes, and ships, during the war. Mass production was also encouraged to an unprecedented degree. It was carried furthest by Henry Ford and others, particularly in the automobile industry. The latter was the outstanding industrial development of the time. The period from 1918 to 1935 has been almost as decisively the gasoline age as the century from 1810 to 1910 was the age of steam. Our day has also been notable for the development of electric-power projects, the generation of current through water power, and the very recent technical improvements which indicate that coal and steam may be used more than water power for the generation of electricity in the future. Automatic machines became more numerous and efficient.[2]

These technological developments were not accompanied by comparable genius in the organization and administration of industry. The impact of the World War forced mankind to take note of this discrepancy, if waste and in-

---

[1] See below, pp. 769 ff., 859 ff., 910 ff., 917 ff., 961 ff.; and Cole and Cole, *op. cit.*
[2] These matters will be covered in detail in Chapter xx, "The Second Industrial Revolution."

efficiency were to be curbed. The result has been what is known as the *rationalization* of industry.

One of the most interesting developments in industry in postwar Europe, therefore, has been the frank admission in many quarters that economic conditions call for careful reconstructive planning rather than haphazard blundering if industry is to free itself from the quicksands into which it was thrust by the war and the events following. This new approach to industrial ills and the adjustments that have already been made are described by the term "rationalization." The Germans were the first to begin rationalization in a systematic fashion after the World War. They were impelled to do so in order to be able to meet the heavy burdens of the Treaty of Versailles and to reconstruct the German industries after the shock of war. The inflation following 1922 helped the industrialists greatly in their program of rationalization.

Despite the fact that rationalization is no longer a theoretical matter, the meaning of the term is widely misunderstood and is, in fact, extremely difficult to make clear in a short definition. The National Economic Advisory Board (Reichskuratorium für Wirtschaftlichkeit), which was established in Germany through state subsidy for the purpose of studying and encouraging rationalization, has defined the term as "the employment of all means of technique and ordered plans that serve to elevate the whole of industry, and to increase production, lower its costs, and improve its quality." In a more expanded definition, the World Economic Conference of 1927 described rationalization as "the methods of technique and organization designed to secure the minimum waste of either effort or material. It includes the scientific organization of labor, standardization of both material and products, simplification of processes, and improvements in the system of transport and marketing." Obviously, rationalization is a sweeping extension of some of the "scientific management" schemes that have developed in America,[1] and means much greater standardization and further cutting down of waste in industrial production.

It is in Germany that rationalization can best be observed.[2] The reorganization of industry and the changes that have obtained in the rest of western Europe outside of Russia, though they all aim at the rehabilitation of industry, have not been so thoroughgoing or so fundamental in their attack upon the problem. Those who understand the process of rationalization think in terms of an entire industry, however it may be organized, rather than of single establishments. The primary advantage to be gained is the elimination of the destructive cutting of prices that follows unrestricted competition. This is to be accomplished through some form of unification, either through the nationalization of industry, or trustification, or far-reaching coöperation among the various establishments engaged in the same industry. When unification is a fact, the groundwork for rationalization has been laid, since the adoption of a common policy by the whole industry is made possible. Then production must be controlled with a view to meeting the changes in demand in such a manner that prices are relatively stable. This, of course, is altogether in contrast to the old trust policy of restricting output so as to maintain high prices, without re-

---

[1] See below, pp. 762 ff.   [2] *Cf.* Levy, *Industrial Germany*.

gard to the greater demand if cheaper goods were made available. An English student says:

> Within this system of regulation, low production costs are aimed at by concentrating production in the most suitable works to reduce short-time working to the lowest limit; by the prevention of waste, either of material, labour, or mechanical energy; by closing down inefficient or unremunerative works or departments, with due regard to the maintenance of reserve plant to meet a sudden rise in demand; and by the extension of the most efficient works where necessary, and the installation of the best cost-saving plant available at all the works kept in production.[1]

Extensive specialization takes place in those plants which are best adapted to a particular type of production.

Centralized control and a common policy make possible great savings in the purchase and distribution of raw materials and partially completed goods, while expenses can be cut to a minimum in the disposition of the finished product. The whole process of rationalization as it has just been briefly sketched implies the fullest practice of coöperation in private industry, and the subordination of particular interests to general interests. It is a whole-hearted repudiation of the old competitive system. Rationalization, however, has value and safety only if imbued with social purpose. It must not have as its sole goal the profits of industrialists and stockholders, to be gained through monopoly practices. It must aim at a decrease in the cost of production, lower prices, and greater consumption. "The control of industry in this spirit," it has been observed, "may be described as a process of modified Socialism." Rationalization demands the coöperation of the worker. He must be willing to experience a temporary contraction of the labor market, so that industry in general may recover. In the meantime, however, sufficient support must be provided for the unemployed workers by the state. The process also implies a much more intimate relationship between government and industry.

Those who see in rationalization the only path to industrial recovery point out that its essential ideas can be extended to other economic fields apart from industry. They argue convincingly that the process of rationalization opens up a new era in society and constitutes a veritable revolution in its general significance. The remarkable recovery of the basic German industries after 1924 lends point to their arguments. The coal, steel, and chemical industries of Germany are three among many proofs of the possibilities that rationalization offers.

The National Industrial Recovery Act of 1933 in the United States was regarded by many as an ambitious, if modified, brand of rationalization.[2] It represented the acceptance by the government of the doctrine that the days of rugged individualism must come to an end if capitalism is to survive. Much the most sweeping example of the rationalization of all types of industry, manufacturing, power and agriculture is that which has been carried on in Soviet Russia and which will be described in some detail later.[3]

---

[1] Walter Meakin, *The New Industrial Revolution,* Coward-McCann, 1929, p. 21.
[2] *Cf.* C. A. Beard and G. H. E. Smith, *The Future Comes,* Macmillan, 1933; E. K. Lindley, *The Roosevelt Revolution,* Viking Press, 1933; S. C. Wallace, *The New Deal in Action,* Harper, 1934; and Benjamin Stolberg and W. J. Vinton, *The Economic Consequences of the New Deal,* Harcourt, Brace, 1935.   [3] See below, pp. 997 ff.

XIII. EUROPEAN AGRICULTURE SINCE 1914

During the nineteenth century, especially after the Stein-Hardenberg reforms and following the Revolutions of 1848, serfdom was pretty generally cleared away in the European agrarian system and the peasants were freed from servile dues. Little was accomplished, however, in ending the nonpersonal and nonpolitical aspects of feudal landholding, particularly in central and southeastern Europe. Great estates were perpetuated, and millions of the peasantry were left landless or with petty holdings incapable of supporting them on a decent standard of life. Indeed, in England during the first half of the nineteenth century the number of great estates was considerably increased as a result of the notable inclosure or engrossing movement to which we have made reference.[1] The major progress in agriculture during the nineteenth century lay in the development of improved agricultural implements, the gradual mechanization of agricultural processes, and the exploitation of chemistry to guide scientific fertilization. Most of these advances were limited, however, to non-European countries, such as the United States, Australia, and Argentina. Some of the more progressive European countries introduced the new agricultural machinery from the United States, but in the majority of the European agricultural areas crude methods of cultivating land and harvesting crops still prevailed. The scythe, sickle, flail, hoe, and the like were still common. So far as agricultural life was concerned, then, Europe in 1914 still bore many marks of the system of privilege, poverty and grinding labor that had dominated the medieval farming situation.

The World War provided a sudden and powerful stimulus to agriculture in Europe. Food had to be provided for soldiers, and since many of the latter were peasants, machinery had to be introduced when possible to make up for the withdrawal of human labor. Where submarine activities or blockade made it more difficult to import food supplies from abroad, feverish efforts had to be made to increase agricultural productivity at home. This also helped on the introduction of machinery and encouraged the cultivation of marginal lands earlier used for pasturage. It also necessitated the cultivation of lands that had been withdrawn for hunting and other nonproductive purposes. The high prices paid for grain during the war period gave a very effective impulse to increased acreage everywhere in the world. The wages of agricultural laborers were also notably improved. When the war was over and the demand resumed normality, prices of grain fell, producing a great slump in agricultural prosperity in many parts of the world, especially in the United States.[2] Since most of Europe never produces enough grain to meet its needs, the blow to European agriculture caused by the restoration of peace was less extreme.

The most striking revolution in European agriculture produced by the war was, of course, the complete obliteration of agrarian privilege in Russia, the nationalization of Russian farm lands, the introduction of extensive state farming, and the wholesale mechanization of agriculture on a scale and with a rapidity never before known in human history. This development will be described in the chapter on Soviet Russia.

[1] See above, pp. 48 ff.   [2] See above, pp. 373 ff.

The Russian example had profound effects upon neighboring states, but the impulse to agrarian reform in Europe was also stimulated by the growth of radicalism during the war and by the unsettling of the system of privilege in the warring states.[1] The latter trend was most marked in defeated states, for the dominant prewar nobility was saddled with much of the responsibility for entering and for losing the war. In succession states the zeal to expropriate the foreign landlords helped on the process. In the fifteen years after the World War there was a greater wave of agrarian reconstruction than had taken place in European agriculture since the downfall of the manorial system. This was especially true of central and southeastern Europe, where the old system of agrarian privilege and great estates was most strongly intrenched before 1914.

In England on the eve of the World War there was a strong movement in the Liberal-Labour coalition for land reform and the break-up of the scandalous system of great estates. The leader was Lloyd George.[2] But the strange ironies of war politics saw the conflict end with Lloyd George arm in arm with Bonar Law and Balfour, his two most malicious enemies of the prewar period. Liberalism in England was dissipated, and the radicals did not gain in power sufficiently to put through any notable land reforms. The conservatives have been able to keep English agriculture safe for privilege. The establishment of the Irish Free State did, however, lead to the ousting of some of the great English landlords in Ireland.

In Latin Europe the only notable progress was achieved in Spain as a result of the Revolution of 1931. The Revolutionary and Napoleonic agrarian reforms had made France a land of small peasant proprietors more than a century before. Right after the World War there was a strong movement in Italy for the further democratization of the landholding system, but the proprietors resisted it fiercely and supported the reactionary program of Mussolini. Under the latter there has been a very successful effort to mechanize Italian agriculture and to stimulate efficient production of wheat. Agricultural privilege was not, however, seriously tampered with, except in so far as it might impede productivity. In Spain, on the other hand, steps were taken that promised to produce real agrarian democracy. Not only were great private estates broken up, but the vast landholdings of the Catholic Church were appropriated by the state and made available for redistribution. Reaction set in during the summer and autumn of 1934, temporarily suspending the progress of the revolution.

In Germany the triumph of the Social Democrats and the establishment of a Socialist Republic might have been expected to lay the ground for a sweeping expropriation of the great Junker class of Prussia, but the Socialists feared to come to grips with the landlords and perhaps wreck the Republic. So they contented themselves with minor reforms in behalf of the peasantry. The civil and political restrictions imposed on the latter were abolished, collective bargaining was legalized in agriculture, the hours of work for agricultural laborers were shortened and fixed by law, and better working and living conditions for peas-

---

[1] *Cf.* Benns, *op. cit.*, pp. 571-78, 624 ff., 660-62; article "Agrarian Movements," Encyclopaedia of the Social Sciences; J. F. Scott, "The Crisis in European Agriculture," *American Mercury*, January, 1935; and the most thorough treatment in English, O. S. Morgan, ed., *Agricultural Systems of Middle Europe*, Macmillan, 1933.

[2] *Cf.* Hayes, *British Social Politics*, Chap. vii; and F. E. Green, *History of the English Agricultural Labourer, 1870-1920*, King, 1920.

ant workers were made mandatory on the employers. When Hitler was campaigning for power he promised the peasants that he would break up the great Junker holdings, but he failed signally to make any attempt to do so, and instead threw in his lot with the Ruhr-Junker industrial and agrarian hierarchy. The Socialist revolt in Austria after 1918 promised to promote agrarian reform there, but the split between the city radicals and the peasants prevented anything except trivial improvements in country districts. Agrarian reform was limited to a law of 1919 restoring to the peasants land taken over for sporting purposes since 1870. The growth of Fascism in Austria of late still further impedes any progress in agrarian reform. Moreover, great estates occupy only 6 per cent of arable Austrian land.

Hungary turned towards moderate Socialism under the leadership of Count Michael Károlyi immediately after the war. Károlyi proposed extensive agrarian reforms, including the partition and distribution of the vast Magyar estates, which presented an undemocratic agrarian situation matched only among the British gentry and the Prussian Junkers. But the landlords and the Reds proved too strong. Károlyi was driven out, and after the brief Communist interlude under Béla Kun, the landlords rode back into power in the Horthy régime. Scientific agriculture has made some headway since, but any attack on the great estates has been frustrated. As Professor Evans puts it, "Hungary is an island of Latifundia in a green sea of agrarian reform."

Poland is primarily an agricultural country, and the peasants clamored for agricultural reform the moment the new Polish state was created. But the landlord interests were strong enough to prevent any important reforms until 1925. Reform bills had been passed in 1919 and 1920 but were never executed, and another bill proposed in 1923 was defeated. In 1925, however, the citadel of privilege was penetrated and a law was passed providing for the redistribution of Polish land at the rate of 500,000 acres annually for a period of ten years. Ample provision for voluntary redistribution was made and generous terms were provided for the compensation of the noble owners.

The Baltic states took far more rapid and stringent steps than did Poland, urged on in part by the Russian example and in part by the demands of the peasants and radicals. In Finland, Latvia, Estonia, and Lithuania agrarian legislation of a drastic character was passed between 1919 and 1922, resulting in almost complete expropriation of the former large estates and the creation of a system of peasant proprietorship. In Estonia, for example, 97 per cent of the land held in great estates before the war was seized and distributed. The size of landholdings was strictly limited. The speed and the thoroughness of the reforms in the Baltic states were promoted by nationalistic as well as economic motives, for most of the great estates were owned by German and Polish landlords. It was an attack upon foreigners as well as upon landed privilege.

Czechoslovakia moved speedily against the great landlords as soon as the new republic was created. A law passed in April, 1919, made liable to expropriation all estates of over 625 acres in all or of over 375 acres of arable land. By the close of 1929 some 10,000,000 acres had been taken over and distributed among the peasants. The compensation provided for was limited, since it had to be accepted in terms of prices between 1913 and 1915, with no allowance for subsequent depreciation of currency.

Extensive agrarian readjustments have taken place in the Balkan states since the war. Reform began in Yugoslavia by an act of February, 1919, suppressing the vestiges of literal feudalism that still survived. The great estates belonging to Austrian and Magyar landlords were speedily seized, but the redistribution has proceeded more slowly with estates owned by Serbs. Nevertheless, considerable headway has been made, and no less than 3,000,000 acres have been taken from the former large landed domains and redistributed. In Bulgaria peasant proprietorship prevailed before the war, so there was less need for any expropriation. Sweeping legislation was passed, which limited the size of estates more sharply than elsewhere in Europe. A law of 1921 called for the seizure of Church and Crown lands and all private estates in excess of 75 acres. Owners who were not cultivators were limited to holdings of from 6 to 25 acres. More important were the agrarian reforms introduced in Rumania. Laws of December, 1918, and July, 1921, directed the seizure of estates of foreigners and absentee landlords, of Crown lands, and of private estates in excess of 1,250 acres. Because of currency depreciation, the compensation provided to the landlords amounted to little. The size of estates permitted varied in different parts of the new Rumania. It was most liberal in the Old Kingdom, where estates of 1,250 acres were permitted, and most stringent in Bessarabia, where holdings were limited to 250 acres. By 1932 about 90 per cent of Rumanian land was held by small proprietors.

These remarkable readjustments in European landholdings did not, of course, mean rapid increase of prosperity for peasants or the speedy modernization of agriculture. Depressed economic conditions in industry mean lower prices and decreased demand for agricultural products. The peasants could do little to overcome this handicap which has faced them, especially in immediate postwar days and since 1929. Moreover, the system of small estates that now prevails, together with the relative poverty and conservatism of the peasants, operate against any wholesale introduction of the best mechanical methods of the West. But certainly the legal and economic restrictions of the past have been well-nigh obliterated except in England, Germany, Italy, and Hungary. The peasants from now on will have little to contend against except the adverse conditions in manufacturing industry and lessened urban food demands, and their own lethargy and poverty. The blight of medievalism and agrarian privilege has been lifted. The efficiency and the prosperity of the European peasantry have been notably improved through the extensive development of the coöperative movement in agriculture. This enables the peasants to market their products to the best advantage and to get the maximum for the money they expend for consumers' needs.[1]

All in all, the peasantry in Europe were the only group, except a few wartime and postwar profiteers, that found their condition temporarily improved as a result of the conditions which followed in the wake of the great conflict. This situation presented a notable contrast to the condition of American farmers,

[1] See C. R. Fay, *Co-operation at Home and Abroad*, 3d ed. rev., King, 1925.

whose economic status has steadily declined since the World War.[1] In the New World the only agrarian improvement which in any way matched that in Europe took place in Mexico between 1915 and 1928.[2]

XIV. THE MONETARY CRISIS AND THE ABANDONMENT OF THE GOLD STANDARD

The general disruption of our financial and economic system by the World War, the coming of the world-depression in 1929, the striking fall in prices after 1929, and the vast burden of debt piled up as a result of the speculation and installment buying promoted by finance capitalism all contributed to a serious monetary crisis and the most extensive abandonment of the gold standard that has taken place during peace times in modern history.

While bimetallic or multimetallic standards of value, usually gold and silver, had prevailed for many centuries, the world very generally went over to the gold standard in the nineteenth century. England led off in 1816. Portugal came next in 1854. Then followed Germany in 1871; the Scandinavian countries in 1874; Holland in 1875; France in 1876; Austria-Hungary in 1892; India in 1893; Japan in 1898; Russia in 1899; and the United States in 1900. Only China, among the major countries of the world, did not adopt the gold standard.

The general use of gold for money implies nothing more than that for obvious reasons gold is acceptable the world over as a measure of the value of other commodities. It can be used for jewelry, the arts, and the like, therefore it has universal use and value. It is relatively scarce, light, durable, and easily coined. These factors have made it relatively suitable as a medium of exchange. The gold standard means a monetary system in which the unit of the nation's money is fixed in a definite weight of gold of a given degree of fineness. The government pledges itself to pay legal tender for all gold offered to it, and to redeem in gold all money presented to it. It also implies that bonds which state that payment will be made in gold upon demand—the so-called gold-clause bonds—will be paid off in gold upon the request of the holders at maturity. In actual fact, none of these implications of the gold standard could work out in fact. There is not enough gold in the United States, for example, to pay off more than a fraction of the paper money or credit currency of the country, should there be any substantial demand for such payment. All the monetary gold in the world—some $11,300,000,000—would not pay off more than about one-sixth of the gold-clause bonds now outstanding in the United States alone.

During the World War most of the warring countries temporarily abandoned the gold standard, and the diminished demand for gold made it cheaper. Hence it would not purchase as much in terms of other commodities, and prices rose when measured in terms of gold. During the years immediately following 1924, however, there was a vast increase in the demand for gold. Many countries returned to the gold standard, and the growth of business during the great speculative boom after 1924 required more gold to keep pace with the

---

[1] See above, pp. 373 ff. For evidence that the European farmers have also begun to face a crisis since 1929, see Scott, "The Crisis in European Agriculture," *loc. cit.*

[2] See Frank Tannenbaum, *The Mexican Agrarian Revolution*, Brookings Institution, 1929.

Wide World Photos

VITTORIO E. ORLANDO   DAVID LLOYD GEORGE   GEORGES CLEMENCEAU   WOODROW WILSON

THE BIG FOUR

Reproduced with permission of the Photographic Society, Berlin

Ewing Galloway

HERMANN HELMHOLTZ   GEORG WILHELM HEGEL

Keystone View Company

CHARLES DARWIN   FRANÇOIS MARIE AROUET DE VOLTAIRE

SCIENTISTS AND PHILOSOPHERS

business expansion. As a result, gold became more valuable, it would buy more in terms of other commodities, and prices fell. By February, 1934, prices had dropped to an index number of 66, even when prices from 1910 to 1914 were reckoned as 100. These low prices were a great blow to farmers and manufacturers, many of whom were unable to sell farm products and goods at a profit. They also worked a great hardship on debtors, a unit of whose money was worth far more in a low-price period than it was when they borrowed it during a high-price era. Another shock to the gold standard came as a result of speculation in foreign exchange and the raid on the gold supply of the world that was conducted, especially by France, after 1926.[1]

The result of all this has been a general abandonment of the gold standard, initiated by Great Britain in 1931 and followed by some thirty-three states, of which the United States was the last to take the step in 1933. In an effort to raise prices, stimulate business, and give justice to debtors, the United States depreciated the dollar to approximately 60 per cent of its former gold content and revalued it at this level.

There is now widespread insistence that there be some method provided for maintaining greater stability of prices than can be secured by reliance upon a gold dollar of fixed value and weight. The demand for and supply of gold changes like the demand for and supply of other commodities. This makes its value and the price level fluctuate. Hence there have been such proposals as a compensated gold dollar and a commodity dollar. In the case of the former, the amount of gold called for in the standard dollar would be varied in accordance with the price level, in the hope of stabilizing prices. The thoroughgoing commodity dollar would call for the termination of reliance upon any form of metallic standard. Prices would be controlled by a central bank, which would determine the issue of credit and currency on the basis of a composite price index, covering all the major commodities exchanged in the country. Sweden has operated on a commodity-dollar basis for several years with a considerable degree of success,[2] and England has maintained a "controlled currency" since 1931. Whatever the ultimate solution of the problem, it is evident that daring monetary policies will play a large part in the future of the capitalistic countries and that the old form of the gold standard is not likely to be restored.

[1] *Cf.* E. D. Schoonmaker, *Our Genial Enemy, France,* Long & Smith, 1932, Chaps. VI-VII.
[2] *Cf.* Kjellstrom, *Managed Money: The Experience of Sweden.*

SUGGESTED READING

Hammerton, *Universal History of the World,* Chap. 182
J. F. Horrabin, *Atlas of Current Affairs,* Knopf, 1934
Noyes, *Europe, Its History and Its World Relationships,* Pt. VII
J. H. Landman, *Since 1914,* Barnes & Noble, 1934
Langsam, *The World since 1914,* Chaps. IV-VII
Benns, *Europe since 1914,* Chaps. VII-VIII, X, XIII, XV, XX-XXI
G. B. Noble, *Policies and Opinions at Paris, 1919,* Macmillan, 1935
Count H. K. U. von Kessler, *Germany and Europe,* Yale University Press, 1923
Dawson, *Germany under the Treaty*
R. L. Buell, *Europe: A History of Ten Years,* new ed. rev., Macmillan, 1931
Article "Agrarian Movements," Encyclopaedia of the Social Sciences

J. H. Jackson, *Europe since the War,* Dutton, 1933
Quincy Howe, *World Diary, 1929-1934,* McBride, 1934
Ogg and Sharp, *The Economic Development of Modern Europe,* Pt. V
Day, *Economic Development in Modern Europe,* Chaps. v-vi, x, xiii
Alcide Ebray, *A Frenchman Looks at Peace,* Knopf, 1927
M. H. H. Macartney, *Five Years of European Chaos,* Dutton, 1923
Mowrer, *Balkanized Europe*
Jonathan Mitchell, *Goose Steps to Peace,* Little, Brown, 1931
Potter, *This World of Nations*
Patterson, *The World Trend towards Nationalism*
J. M. Keynes, *The Economic Consequences of the Peace,* Harcourt, Brace, 1920
—— *A Revision of the Treaty,* Harcourt, Brace, 1922
H. G. Moulton and Leo Pasvolsky, *World War Debt Settlements,* Brookings Institution, 1926
J. W. Angell, *The Recovery of Germany,* enl. and rev. ed., Yale University Press, 1932
Walter Meakin, *The New Industrial Revolution,* Coward-McCann, 1928
Bruno Burns, *Codes, Cartels, National Planning,* McGraw-Hill, 1934
O. S. Morgan, ed., *Agricultural Systems of Middle Europe,* Macmillan, 1933
G. D. H. Cole, *A Guide Through World Chaos,* Knopf, 1932
—— ed., *What Everybody Wants to Know about Money,* Knopf, 1933
—— and M. I. Cole, *The Intelligent Man's Review of Europe To-day,* Knopf, 1933
Sir Carles Morgan-Webb, *The Rise and Fall of the Gold Standard,* Macmillan, 1934
V. S. Clark, *What Is Money?* Houghton Mifflin, 1934
W. E. Atkins, *Gold and Your Money,* McBride, 1934
H. N. Brailsford, *Property or Peace?* Covici, Friede, 1934
Scott and Baltzly, *Readings in European History since 1814,* Chaps. xv-xvi
Jones, Vandenbosch, and Vandenbosch, *Readings in Citizenship,* pp. 459-93
Magee, *Collapse and Recovery: Readings in Current Economic Problems*
Cooke and Stickney, *Readings in European International Relations*

FURTHER REFERENCES

AFTER THE WORLD WAR. On the peace treaties, see Benns, *op. cit.,* Chaps. vii-viii; Langsam, *op. cit.,* Chaps. iv-v; Slosson, *Twentieth Century Europe,* Chap. xv; Swain, *Beginning the Twentieth Century,* Chaps. xxviii-xxix; A. J. Toynbee, *The World after the Peace Conference* (Oxford Press, 1925).

On the peace treaties and national self-determination, see Benns, *op. cit.,* Chaps. xix-xxi; Slosson, *op. cit.,* Chap. xviii; Langsam, *op. cit.,* Chaps. xvii, xix-xx; Lord C. B. Thomson, *Old Europe's Suicide* (Seltzer, 1920); Levine, *The Resurrected Nations;* Mowrer, *op. cit.;* Schevill, *History of the Balkan Peninsula,* new ed., Chaps. xxxi-xxxviii; Otto Junghann, *National Minorities in Europe,* Covici, Friede, 1932.

On nationalism in the Near East, see Hocking, *The Spirit of World Politics.*

On Palestine since the war, see Viteles and Totah, *Palestine;* F. F. P. Andrews, *The Holy Land under the Mandate* (Houghton Mifflin, 1931, 2 vols.).

On the economic aspects of the treaties, see Benns, *op. cit.,* Chap. x; Langsam, *op. cit.,* Chaps. vii, xv; Keynes, *The Economic Consequences of the Peace;* B. M. Baruch, *The Making of the Reparations and Economic Sections of the Treaty* (Harper, 1920); Kessler, *op. cit.;* P. P. Reinhold, *The Economic, Financial and Political State of Germany since the War* (Yale University Press, 1928); M. T. Florinsky, *The Saar Struggle* (Macmillan, 1934).

On Germany under the Treaty of Versailles, see Dawson, *op. cit.;* Kessler, *op. cit.*
On the abortive French security treaty of 1919 and the Geneva Protocol, see Langsam, *op. cit.,* Chap. VIII; P. J. N. Baker, *The Geneva Protocol* (King, 1925).
For a brilliant statement of the lessons of the World War for citizens of the United States, see Frederick Bausman, *Facing Europe* (Century, 1926).
On the war debts, see Moulton and Paslovsky, *op. cit.;* T. L. Stoddard, *Europe and Your Money* (Macmillan, 1932); Dorsey Richardson, *Will They Pay?* (Lippincott, 1933). For cancellationist propaganda, see Wildon Lloyd, *The European War Debts and Their Settlement* (Committee for the Consideration of Intergovernmental Debts, 1934).
On the reparations issue, see H. G. Moulton, *The Reparation Plan* (McGraw-Hill, 1924); D. P. Myers, *The Reparation Settlement* (World Peace Foundation, 1929); J. W. Wheeler-Bennett, *The Wreck of Reparations* (Morrow, 1933); Max Sering, *Germany under the Dawes Plan* (King, 1929); Chap. VIII of Walter Lippmann and others, *The United States in World Affairs . . . 1932* (Harper, 1933).
On the economic results of the war and on postwar industrial history, see Ogg and Sharp, *op. cit.,* Pt. V; Day, *op. cit.,* Chaps. V-VI, XIII; Benns, *op. cit.,* Chap. XV; Charles Gide, ed., *Effects of the War on French Economic Life* (Oxford Press, 1923); Ogburn and Jaffé, *The Economic Development of Post-war France;* Angell, *op. cit.;* Reinhold, *op. cit.;* André Siegfried, *Post-war Britain* (Dutton, 1925); R. C. Berkeley, *England's Opportunity* (London, 1931).
On the industrial experience of the United States during the war, see G. B. Clarkson, *Industrial America in the World War* (Houghton Mifflin, 1923).
On the rationalization of industry since 1918, see Angell, *op. cit.,* Chaps. IV-V, VII; Meakin, *op. cit.;* Doreen Warriner, *Combines and Rationalization in Germany* (King, 1931); R. A. Brady, *The Rationalization Movement in German Industry* (University of California Press, 1933); Burn, *op. cit.*
On postwar agricultural conditions, see articles "Agrarian Movements" and "Agricultural Coöperation" (B. H. Hibbard), Encyclopaedia of the Social Sciences; Benns, *op. cit.,* pp. 624 ff.; Zimmermann, *World Resources and Industries,* Pt. II; I. L. Evans, *The Agrarian Revolution in Roumania* (Macmillan, 1924); L. E. Textor, *Land Reform in Czechoslovakia* (London, 1923); Morgan, *op. cit.;* K. W. H. Scholz, ed., *Foreign Land Problems,* American Academy of Political and Social Science, *Annals,* July, 1930, Supplement; J. F. Scott, "The Crisis in European Agriculture," *American Mercury,* January, 1935.
On the monetary crisis and the gold standard, see Clark, *op. cit.;* Leo Pasvolsky, *Current Monetary Issues* (Brookings Institution, 1933); T. E. G. Gregory, *The Gold Standard and Its Future* (Dutton, 1932); Atkins, *op. cit.;* H. E. Barnes, *The Money-Changers vs. the New Deal* (Long & Smith, 1934); O. M. W. Sprague, *Recovery and Common Sense* (Houghton Mifflin, 1934); E. W. Kemmerer, *On Money* (Winston, 1934); L. D. Edie, *Dollars* (Yale University Press, 1934); Cole, *What Everybody Wants to Know about Money;* Morgan-Webb, *op. cit.;* Paul Einzig, *The Future of Gold* (Macmillan, 1935).
On the depression and current economic problems, see Cole, *A Guide Through World Chaos;* Brailsford, *op. cit.;* Soule, *The Coming American Revolution;* E. M. Patterson, *The World's Economic Dilemma* (McGraw-Hill, 1930).

CHAPTER XIX

INTELLECTUAL AND CULTURAL ACHIEVE-MENTS OF THE NINETEENTH CENTURY

I. THE DEVELOPMENT OF NATURAL SCIENCE

1. THE REMARKABLE GROWTH OF SCIENTIFIC ACTIVITY AFTER 1800

The progress of science in the nineteenth century was even more striking and extensive than it had been in the seventeenth. The main reason for this was that science in the nineteenth century was able to build upon the foundations that had been laid by many patient workers, extending over the centuries between Copernicus and Lavoisier. These earlier contributions acted as a sort of springboard from which the nineteenth-century scientific aspirations were able to leap to unprecedented heights of achievement. Especially important were the earlier developments in mathematics. These were indispensable to the further growth of many of the natural sciences, especially astronomy and physics. The possibilities in the application of mathematics to physical science had been set forth by Lagrange in his great work *Analytical Mechanics*.

The discoveries overseas had also placed a greater range and variety of natural phenomena at the disposal of scientists, something especially important for the development of geography and biology. During the eighteenth century scientific research also became better organized. Scientists were no longer banded together mainly in associations of enthusiastic amateurs. The universities slowly took up scientific work. Laboratories were established within university walls, one of the first of which was the chemistry laboratory opened at the University of Giessen by the great German chemist Justus von Liebig, in 1826. Science also became increasingly international with the rise of better means of communication. Savants in many countries kept in communication and pooled results.

In the seventeenth century astronomy had been the branch of scientific endeavor most successfully and dramatically cultivated. Chemistry had stood out particularly in the eighteenth. In the nineteenth century the most revolutionary developments occurred in the field of biology, with physics running a close second. In the twentieth century, the most startling results have been obtained in the fields of astronomy and physics, particularly electromechanics.

2. MATHEMATICS AND ASTRONOMY

In spite of the remarkable achievements in the three previous centuries, the advances in mathematics in the nineteenth century were revolutionary and opened up new vistas. Especially important were the demonstration of the limitations of the older algebra and geometry and the transcending of these restrictions by new concepts and processes. Augustin Cauchy (1789-1857) opened up the field of infinite functions and of residual and imaginary calculus, devoloped later by Professor Weierstrass of Berlin. Niels Abel (1802-29), the most precocious genius in the history of mathematics, showed the limitations of algebra in solving the higher equations and extended our knowledge of the theory of functions. Nicholas Lobatchewsky (1793-1856) and János Bolyai (1802-60) revealed the limitations of Euclidean geometry and founded non-Euclidean and hyper-geometry. Karl Jabobi (1804-51) carried further the theories of Abel, developed the field of elliptical functions, and advanced our knowledge of the theory of numbers. Georg Riemann (1826-66) contributed to non-Euclidean geometry, and did important work in the theory of functions and the geometry of curved surfaces, lines of investigation followed out by Felix Klein (1849-95). Karl Friedrich Gauss (1777-1855) not only was a very versatile mathematician but also did much to apply higher mathematics, particularly to astronomy and the theory of terrestrial magnetism.

In the realm of astronomy, there was very considerable progress in the nineteenth century. Larger and better telescopes were constructed. Better-equipped observatories were provided. New astronomical instruments—particularly the spectroscope—were invented. The spectroscope enabled astronomers to study light more scientifically and to determine the chemical composition of celestial bodies. Bessel succeeded for the first time in measuring the parallax of a star (1838). This was so small that previous astronomers had been unable to prove its existence. This confirmed the heliocentric theory and, in particular, enabled astronomers to compute the distance of the nearer stars. Neptune, the most remote of our planets,[1] was discovered in 1846 as the result of better astronomical instruments and the more accurate computations of the astronomers. Further striking progress in astronomy had to wait upon the development of electromechanics and thermodynamics in the latter part of the nineteenth century. These developments we shall discuss in a subsequent chapter.

3. NINETEENTH-CENTURY PHYSICS

The outstanding developments in the field of physics in the nineteenth century were the establishment of our modern scientific conceptions of the nature of heat, sound, light and electricity, and their unification in the broader domain of electromechanics through the use of advanced mathematical processes. This mathematical unification of physical nature was perhaps the most notable intellectual feat of the century. Two other important and related achievements must not be overlooked, namely, the discovery of the principle of the conservation of energy and the formulation of the laws of thermodynamics.

Down to the nineteenth century the prevailing theory had been that heat is a mysterious and imponderable fluid. The discovery of the actual character of

---

[1] Excepting the little planet Pluto, recently detected.

heat was the result of the work of Count Rumford and Sir Humphry Davy. In 1798-99 they showed that friction generates heat in proportion to the amount of work expended. Rumford discovered that in boring out a brass cannon both the cannon and the shavings became intensely hot. Davy found that two blocks of ice could be melted simply by rubbing them together, even though the surrounding atmosphere was kept below the freezing-point.

The study of heat was carried still further by an amateur English scientist, J. P. Joule (1818-89). He worked out (1843) what is known as the mechanical equivalent of heat, namely, the mechanical energy necessary to raise the heat of a given body by a certain amount. This suggested to others how energy might be converted into heat and furnished the key to the formulation of the very important principle of the conservation of energy.

This basic physical fact was confirmed between 1840 and 1850, the decade in which Joule's experiments were being carried on. In 1842, J. R. von Mayer suggested the possibility that the heat might be converted into work or work into heat, something that was proved to be true by Joule's experiments. In 1842, also, Sir W. R. Grove defended the idea of the interrelation of physical forces, a doctrine that he elaborated in a book some four years later. This conception had been anticipated in part by a French scientist, Sadi Nicolas Léonard Carnot, approximately twenty years earlier. It remained, however, for the most encyclopedic physicist of the nineteenth century, Professor Hermann von Helmholtz (1821-94) of Berlin,[1] to set forth a systematic presentation of the principle of the conservation of energy, a conclusion that he based upon his own independent experiments as well as upon those of his contemporaries. His monograph on the subject appeared in the year 1847. As a modern historian of science has put the matter concisely:

> The law of conservation of energy means that the sum total of the energy of the universe is a constant quantity. We cannot destroy energy and we cannot create it, we can only turn it from one form to another. It may be potential or it may be kinetic, but all the potential energy plus all the kinetic energy is a constant quantity.[2]

The concepts underlying the conservation of energy were linked up with electromechanics a generation later by Clerk Maxwell and Heinrich Hertz.

The scientific study of the character of heat and its mechanical equivalent not only led to the discovery of the principle of the conservation of energy; it also directly promoted the development of thermodynamics. The first law of thermodynamics was implicit in the conclusions of Joule. It was first enunciated by Helmholtz in 1847. It is: "When during any transformation of one form of energy into another heat is produced, the amount is always the same for the same amount of energy, whatever its form, and if heat disappears, exactly the same amount of some other kind of energy will appear in its place."

Even more important was the famous second law of thermodynamics, which relates to the dissipation and degradation of energy. According to this second

---

[1] Perhaps the most versatile mind of the century. Until he was fifty, Helmholtz was a professor of physiology.
[2] R. J. Harvey-Gibson, *Two Thousand Years of Science*, 2d ed. rev., Macmillan, 1931, p. 131.

law, while the total amount of energy in the universe theoretically remains constant, the amount of actually useful energy is always diminishing through its progressive transformation into nonuseful or dissipated heat. If this be true, it means that the supply of useful energy in the universe will ultimately be exhausted and the universe will gradually run down. The discovery of this second law of thermodynamics is attributed to Carnot (1824) and to Rudolf Clausius (1847), a German professor of physics. It was first systematically stated and explained by Sir William Thomson (Lord Kelvin) in 1852. It was carried over into the field of physical chemistry, in the form of what is known as the phase rule, by Josiah Willard Gibbs (1839-1903), probably the most profound American scientist of the nineteenth century.[1] In the second quarter of the twentieth century this second law of thermodynamics has provoked a bitter controversy among astronomers (for example, Jeans *vs.* Millikan) relative to its bearing upon the destiny of the physical universe as a whole.[2]

The first important work in the physical investigation of sound was done by Chladni and Bernoulli in the eighteenth century. They established the fact that sound is a manifestation of waves set up in the air by a vibrating body. The fundamental character of such vibrations and of the resulting waves was not, however, fully understood until sound-waves were linked up with the conception of electromagnetic waves as a result of the work of Hertz and others in the last quarter of the nineteenth century.

A scientific understanding of the character of light was first reached in the nineteenth century. The earliest wave theory of light had been anticipated by two seventeenth-century scientists, Hooke and Huygens, but it had been rejected by Sir Isaac Newton. It was revived, however, and Newton's objections were explained away by an English and a French scientist at the opening of the nineteenth century. Thomas Young (1773-1829) and A. J. Fresnel (1788-1827) were the first to state the wave theory of light in something like its modern form. A half-century later (1863), Clerk Maxwell showed that light seems to behave like electromagnetic waves, thus forwarding the ultimate unification of the analysis of heat, light, sound, and electricity.[3] Maxwell's work was carried further by a brilliant German physicist, Heinrich Hertz (1857-94).

Next in importance to the establishment of the electromagnetic theory of light stands the discovery of the spectroscope and the development of spectrum analysis. Spectrum analysis means the study of the radiations given off by various substances. Kirchhoff, in 1858, laid down its three fundamental principles: (1) Solid and liquid bodies and gases under high pressure give a continuous spectrum, crossed by neither dark nor bright lines; (2) gases under low pressure give off a discontinuous spectrum crossed by bright lines; and (3) when a white light passes through a gas we have a discontinuous spectrum crossed by dark lines. The earliest work in this field was that of an English doctor, W. H. Wollaston (1766-1828), and a German optician, Joseph von Fraunhofer (1787-

---

[1] *Cf.* Garrison, "Josiah Willard Gibbs and His Relation to Modern Science," *loc. cit.*
[2] See below, pp. 1041 ff.
[3] The wave theory has, of course, undergone considerable modification since 1905 as a result of the development of the quantum theory.

1826). In the first quarter of the nineteenth century they independently called attention to the dark lines (called since Fraunhofer lines) crossing the colored bands in the visible spectrum. Fraunhofer also demonstrated the fact that starlight is independent of sunlight. The modern science of spectrum analysis is the work of two German professors at Heidelberg, Robert Bunsen (1811-99) and G. R. Kirchhoff (1824-87). They invented the spectroscope and laid the basis for modern spectroscopy in 1859. Not only was this an important contribution to the physics of light, but it also enabled physicists and astronomers to detect the chemical constitution of distant heavenly bodies. An important practical result of the spectroscope was the discovery of helium gas by Lockyer and Ramsay. This noninflammable gas is a valuable, though expensive, substitute for hydrogen in the inflation of balloons.

The nineteenth century did much to advance our knowledge of electricity. In 1801 Wollaston proved the identity of "galvanism" and electricity. In 1819, H. C. Oersted (1777-1851), a Danish scientist, noted the agitating effects of an electric current on the needle of a compass. A. M. Ampère (1775-1836) further studied this phenomenon and not only reduced it to a law but also worked out the laws of the interaction of electric currents (1820). A further contribution was made by a German scientist, G. S. Ohm (1789-1854). He gave us our first important practical information about the nature of electric conductors and provided us with methods of measuring mathematically the resistance in the conduction of electric currents (1827). He put the laws of electromotive force in mathematical form. Perhaps the outstanding figure in the study of electricity in the nineteenth century was Michael Faraday (1791-1867). He showed that electric currents produce a magnetic field; elucidated the laws governing the flow of electric currents; investigated the mediums through which electromagnetic force is produced; and described the principles of electromagnetic induction.

Building on previous work, Maxwell brought forth a mathematical statement of the principles involved in electromagnetic waves. Not only was this in itself an important contribution to electromechanics, but also it laid the basis for the mathematical synthesis of physical nature in terms of electromagnetism. The next important development in electromechanics lay in the fields of the quantum theory and radioactivity, which will be described in dealing with the science of the twentieth century.

4. CHEMISTRY IN THE NINETEENTH CENTURY

The more important early developments in nineteenth-century chemistry represented a further extension of our knowledge of quantitative chemistry, which began with Lavoisier's discovery of the conservation of mass at the close of the eighteenth century. The first outstanding discovery was known as the law of multiple or definite proportions in the combination of chemical elements. The man who was responsible for formulating this law was an English scientist, John Dalton (1766-1844). Dalton was able to make use of the earlier suggestion of two French chemists, Proust and Berthollet. Dalton took hydrogen, the lightest element, as his unit. He showed (1805) that when one element unites with another, the weight ratios are some simple multiple of the lowest unit. The combining weight of an element is the weight of that element relative to that of the other elements. A French chemist, Joseph Louis Gay-Lussac (1778-1850), formulated in 1808 the law of the combination of gases, namely, that when gases combine they do so in volumes bearing a simple and direct ratio to each other. This law was supplemented in 1811 by that of the Italian chemist Count Amadeo Avogadro (1776-1856), who maintained that at the same temperature and pressure equal volumes of gases contain an equal number of molecules.

Dalton was not only famous for his law of multiple proportions but also for his atomic theory (1808). He contended that every element was composed of extremely minute particles or atoms completely incapable of division, a doctrine that has been greatly modified in recent years as a result of our study of electromechanics and radioactivity. But Dalton's doctrine encouraged a Swedish chemist, the Baron Berzelius (1779-1848), to undertake an elaborate study of atomic and molecular weights, which he estimated for some two thousand substances. Between 1869 and 1871 a Russian chemist, D. I. Mendelyeev (1834-1907), announced his famous periodic law, which explained that the elements, when arranged in the order of their atomic weights, fall into definite series or octaves. In this arrangement the eighth element above any one in the series possesses characteristics similar to the one from which the start has been made. The properties of the elements, therefore, stand in what is known as periodic dependence upon their atomic weights. Mendelyeev's thesis enabled chemists to predict, with later corroboration, the existence of chemical elements not yet observed to exist. The foremost American contribution to theoretical chemistry was the above-mentioned "phase rule" of Josiah Willard Gibbs, a complete mathematical statement of the fundamental principles underlying the problems of chemical equilibrium. In our day, this conception has also had very important practical applications in the realm of synthetic chemistry.

Next to the formulation of the laws of quantitative chemistry the most notable advance in chemical science in this century was that connected with the development of organic chemistry. It had been widely maintained that there is an impassable gulf between inorganic and organic matter. This illusion was broken down in 1828 when a German chemist, Friedrich Wöhler (1800-82), synthetically created urea out of inorganic materials. In 1832 Wöhler and Liebig began to unravel the mysteries of the benzene ring. At the same time, Berzelius showed that organic substances obey the same quantitative laws that had been established for the behavior of inorganic materials. The artificial manufacture of urea started organic chemistry on the road towards its marvelous achievements over a half-century later in the way of the artificial production of a large number of very interesting and often very valuable chemical compounds. In the meantime, the discoveries of the German chemist F. A. Kekulé (1829-96) gave a powerful impetus to these developments, especially his formulation of the theory of valency and his more comprehensive analysis of the benzene ring in 1865.

5. BIOLOGICAL DISCOVERIES IN THE NINETEENTH CENTURY

Much the most important advance in biology during this century was the apprehension and elucidation of the theory of organic evolution. This is so important a subject that it will be discussed separately in a subsequent section. We may call attention here, however, to the important doctrines of heredity set forth by Mendel, Weismann, and De Vries.

Gregor Mendel (1822-84) was an Austrian monk who in 1865 set forth the doctrine of heredity that is now most generally accepted by modern biologists. His views were not generally known at the time of his death and were not revived and accepted until the twentieth century. In 1885 August Weismann (1834-1914), a German biologist, challenged the popular view of the inheritance of acquired characters. According to Weismann, a blacksmith, for example, could not hand down to his children a tendency towards larger biceps. The germ plasm that carries our hereditary traits seems to be inappreciably affected by external changes in our anatomy during the life span or any succession of life spans that can be observed. Hugo de Vries (1848-   ), a Dutch botanist, proclaimed at the opening of the twentieth century his famous doctrine that new species arise through sudden mutations or sports rather than as the result of slowly accumulated changes.

Next to the doctrine of evolution, perhaps the most important biological innovation of the nineteenth century was the demonstration of the cellular nature of organic life by Theodor Schwann (1810-82) and Matthias Jakob Schleiden (1804-81) in 1838-39. They thereby founded what is known as cytology or the scientific study of the cell. They were greatly aided by the provision of the compound microscope in 1835. The significance of their achievement for the clarification of biological problems has been well summarized by Sir J. Arthur Thomson:

> As we have seen, not a few of the early microscopists made attempts to define the minute elementary parts that build up living creatures; but it was not till 1838 that the idea of the cell as a structural and functional unit was clearly focused in the Cell-Theory or, better, Cell-Doctrine (Zellenlehre) of Schwann and Schleiden. Its three propositions may be recalled. First, there is the *morphological* statement, that all living creatures have a cellular structure, and that all but the simplest, that is to say all that have what may be called a "body," are built up of cells and modifications of cells. Second, the Cell-Theory includes the *physiological* statement, that the activity of a many-celled organism is the sum of the activities of the component cells. This idea requires to be safeguarded by the fact of correlation, for the life of the whole cannot be described without recognising that it is more than the life of all its parts, just as the behaviour of a group of men with a common purpose cannot be adequately described merely in terms of the movements of the individuals. Third, the Cell-Theory includes the *embryological* statement, that the individual many-celled organism begins its life, in all ordinary cases, as a fertilised egg-cell, which divides and re-divides to form an embryo. In other words, developing and growing imply cell-division. Cellular structure is a condition of differentiation.[1]

[1] Sir J. A. Thomson and Patrick Geddes, *Life: Outlines of General Biology*, Harper, 1931, 2 vols., Vol. I, p. 701.

As soon as the cell theory was formulated, the cell was studied much more thoroughly. Karl von Nägeli and Hugo von Mohl examined carefully the contents of cells and in 1844 Von Mohl gave the name *protoplasm* to the plastic nitrogenous living matter within the walls of the cell. Soon after, Max Schultze declared (1863) that this protoplasm forms the physical basis of life. Not only healthy but also diseased tissues were made the subject of scientific study. The science of pathology was thus established on a sound basis by the two greatest pathologists of the nineteenth century, Rudolf Virchow (1821-1902) of Berlin and Louis Pasteur (1822-95) of Paris.[1] The latter was also preëminent in giving us our immensely important present understanding of bacteriology.

The science of embryology, or the study of the organism between fertilization and birth, did much to clarify a little-understood process and to assist in the study of heredity. Down to the nineteenth century it was commonly held that the fertilized egg (ovum) contains the complete mammal in miniature. This notion was overthrown by the Russian biologist Karl Ernst von Baer (1792-1876), who founded the modern science of embryology. The doctrine that the development of the individual organism between fertilization and birth roughly recapitulates or reproduces the whole biological history of the species was set forth by J. F. Meckel (1781-1833) and was greatly elaborated by the famous German biologist Ernst Heinrich Haeckel (1834-1919). While this dogma holds true only in part, it threw much light upon both biology and psychology and greatly stimulated the study of organic evolution and genetic psychology.

The growth of both biological and chemical knowledge helped to place the study of physiology, or the dynamics of human life, on a scientific basis. At the opening of the century François Bichat (1771-1802) had contended that the life of the whole organism is the result of the combined lives of the constituent tissues. The notion that life is primarily a matter of chemistry was given much greater thoroughness and precision. In addition to a more complete understanding of the processes of nutrition and metabolism, the physiologists discovered that animal heat is not an innate quality, but the result of chemical combustion within the body. Of the many men who contributed to the systematization of respectably scientific physiology in the nineteenth century, it is probable that the Frenchman Claude Bernard (1813-78) stands at the head, but we cannot overlook the work of the eminent German physiologist Johannes Müller (1801-58), who brought together all the existing physiological knowledge of his day in his *Outlines of Physiology*. Distinguished disciples of Müller like Emil Dubois-Reymond and Karl Ludwig carried on his work.

In the related field of botany the most important developments lay in the modification and improvement of Linnaeus' system of classification of plants and in the application of the theory of evolution to botany. In providing a new and more satisfactory system of classification the main contributor was Augustin de Candolle (1778-1841), who gave us what is still our generally accepted "system of nature." The man who showed that evolutionary principles apply to the plant kingdom, and did it largely independently of Darwin, was

---

[1] Pasteur was a chemist turned bacteriologist.

W. F. B. Hofmeister (1824-77), the outstanding botanist of the century. Hofmeister also made very important contributions to our knowledge of cytology and of the fertilization of plants. Further important work on cytology was carried on by Von Nägeli.

6. THE ORIGINS OF PSYCHOLOGY: THE SCIENCE OF MIND

The increasing knowledge of the human body that was gained by the progress in biology and chemistry enabled scientists to obtain their first rudimentary notions of the nature of the human mind. Even the most eminent of early scientists had possessed the most grotesque conceptions in regard to the basis of the mind. Aristotle, for example, had held that we think with our hearts and that the brain exists solely to pump phlegm on the heart to prevent it from overheating in moments of intense thought. Most studies of the mind between Aristotle and the nineteenth century were carried on in the field of metaphysics and philosophy, with a large tincture of theology. This approach was largely innocent of either biological or chemical knowledge.

The first truly scientific work on the brain and its functions was done by Franz Josef Gall (1758-1828), an Austrian physician. He carefully dissected the brain, described its real structure, and differentiated between the functions of the gray and the white matter in the brain. Some of his associates and successors debased his work by building upon it the pseudo-science of phrenology. Yet it was Gall who founded the scientific study of the brain that we now know as neurology and which constitutes the starting-point of all scientific psychology.

The science of physics was drawn upon to aid in the establishment of a science of the mind. Here two German scholars, Ernst Heinrich Weber (1795-1878) and Gustav Theodor Fechner (1801-87), did much to establish scientific and experimental psychology by an exact study of sensation. Fechner coined (1860) the term "psychophysics" to describe this line of work. It reached its highest development in the twentieth century in the work of E. B. Titchener of Cornell University, a student of Wundt.[1] After Darwin announced the doctrine of evolution this biological conception had a very considerable influence on the study of psychology, particularly in the work of Huxley and G. Stanley Hall (1846-1924). The latter used evolutionary biology to establish genetic psychology, which later became of great significance in the development of the science of education. Genetic psychology applied evolutionary conceptions to the mind as well as to the body.

The earliest important efforts in the nineteenth century to work out a systematic type of psychology came when scholars brought together the existing scientific knowledge and in its light tried to study our mental processes through the method of introspection. The most influential figures in this stage of psychological development were Alexander Bain (1818-1903) and Herbert Spencer (1820-1903).

This useful but rather elementary mode of investigating the human mind

[1] See E. G. Boring, *History of Experimental Psychology*, Century, 1929.

was outgrown in the experimental laboratory of the great German psychologist Wilhelm Wundt (1832-1920), of Leipzig, far and away the outstanding figure in nineteenth-century psychology. The scientific approach of Wundt was accepted by William James (1842-1910) in the United States. The latter wrote with great charm, and his *Principles of Psychology* (1891) was in every way the most effective summary of the state of psychological knowledge at the close of the nineteenth century. Not only was there much progress in the study of the normal mind; attention was also given to abnormal mental states by such students as Maudsley, Ribot, Charcot, and Bernheim. Medical, as well as academic, psychology gradually attained a scientific level.

It is hardly an exaggeration to say that we passed in this single century from relative ignorance of the nature of the human mind to a reasonably clear comprehension of mental processes. The psychologists did not rest content with merely investigating the human mind, but turned to a comparative study of the mind of man and of the other animals. This tendency was given a great stimulus by the growing popularity of the doctrine of evolution.

7. GEOLOGY AND GEOGRAPHY

We noted in an earlier chapter that in his *Theory of the Earth* James Hutton had supported the scientific and historical view of the origins of the Earth, in opposition to the orthodox biblical version of creation. In the half-century following the publication of Hutton's book in 1785 a great deal of important new knowledge was accumulated relative to the age and structure of the Earth. The extensive study of fossils by Cuvier and Lamarck was of great aid. All of this new information was brought together with great force and learning by Sir Charles Lyell (1797-1875) in his *Principles of Geology,* published in 1830-33.[1]

With the appearance of Lyell's able work, geology attained the rank of a true science and students became able to form some precise and reliable notion as to the origins, age and structure of the Earth, as well as of the extinct forms of life. The great French natural scientist Baron Georges Cuvier (1769-1832), through his extensive study of fossils, founded that branch of geology known as paleontology, or the study of the extinct forms of life on our planet; it was developed by Alcide d'Orbigny (1802-57), James Hall (1811-98), and others. Cuvier did not, however, accept the logical implication that these fossils upset the doctrine of a special creation.

Since the time of Lyell, geology has progressed mainly in the way of wider information and more exact description. It has also profited much by exploiting our growing knowledge of chemistry and zoölogy. In the latter part of the century special attention was given to the study of glaciation by James Geikie (1839-1915), Penck, Brückner, and others.

Towards the end of the nineteenth century the geologists no longer remained satisfied merely to describe the growth of the Earth, but set forth theories as to its origin that rejected Laplace's nebular hypothesis.[2]

The science of geology also came to have an important practical and eco-

---

[1] For an authoritative, encyclopedic and lucid summary of the history of geology, see H. E. Gregory, "History of Geology," *Scientific Monthly,* February, 1921.
[2] See below, p. 1047.

nomic value in the assistance it gave to the iron, coal, oil, and other extractive industries.[1]

The science of geography advanced to a comparable degree during this century. Physical geography was promoted in the first half of the century by such travelers and scholars as Baron Alexander von Humboldt (1769-1859) and Karl Ritter (1779-1859). Our knowledge of the physical features of the Earth became more extensive and precise and a special branch of the science, known as physiography, was founded to study and describe them. Geographical knowledge was vastly extended after 1850 as a result of the extensive explorations of oversea areas carried on by David Livingstone, Henry M. Stanley, Paul Belloni Du Chaillu, Gustav Nachtigal, Nikolai Prjevalsky, Baron Ferdinand von Richthofen, and others. This matched the growth of geographical knowledge in the earlier period of discoveries after 1500.[2]

Certain geographers became interested in the effect of geographical factors—such as climate, altitude, fertility, topography, and routes of travel—upon man himself. They thus founded what is called the science of anthropogeography, or human geography.[3] The foremost early figures in this field were Karl Ritter and his disciple, Friedrich Ratzel (1844-1904). The latter was the foremost anthropogeographer of the nineteenth century. His doctrines were brought into the United States by his student, Miss Ellen C. Semple. The eminent Philosophical Anarchist Elisée Reclus (1830-1903), a French refugee in Switzerland and Belgium, also did much to promote interest in this field.

8. THE PROGRESS OF MEDICAL SCIENCE IN THE NINETEENTH CENTURY

The progress of physical, chemical, and biological knowledge quite naturally had a revolutionary effect upon medical science. This century was auspiciously introduced in the field of medicine by the epoch-making discovery of the theory of immunity to disease made by the English physician Edward Jenner (1749-1823), who devised vaccination for smallpox. Jenner executed his first public vaccination for smallpox in the year 1796.

The most important contribution of physics to medicine in the nineteenth century is to be found in the use of "percussion" or tapping on the chest by Leopold Auenbrugger (1722-1809) and the invention of the stethoscope by Hyacinthe Laënnec (1781-1826). Through the concentration of the sense of hearing afforded by this instrument a physician can detect many diseases of the heart and chest. It taught physicians to pay attention to chest noises. Another outstanding contribution of physics to medicine lay in the application of electricity to medical diagnosis and cures, but this did not become very important until the twentieth century.

---

[1] See W. O. Hotchkiss, *The Story of a Billion Years,* Williams & Wilkins, 1933, and Gustav Egloff, *Earth Oil,* Williams & Wilkins, 1933.
[2] See H. B. Wetherill, *The World and Its Discovery,* Oxford Press, 1914; J. L. Mitchell (L. C. Gibbon), *Earth Conquerors,* Simon & Schuster, 1934; Edward Heawood, *History of Geographical Discovery in the 17th and 18th Centuries,* Putnam, 1912; Robert Brown, *The Story of Africa and Its Explorers,* Cassell, 1912, 4 vols.; Outhwaite, *Unrolling the Map;* and John Buchan, *Last Secrets: The Final Mysteries of Exploration,* Houghton Mifflin, 1924.
[3] *Cf.* Thomas, *The Environmental Basis of Society,* pp. 78 ff., 160 ff.

THE DEVELOPMENT OF NATURAL SCIENCE

Many helpful contributions were brought into medicine through the field of chemistry. Perhaps the most important was the development of surgical anaesthesia, or the use of chemicals (chloroform, ether and the like) to make surgery relatively painless. The honor of having first utilized a really effective anaesthetic must be assigned to a Boston dentist, William T. G. Morton, who demonstrated his success in October, 1846. It is doubtful if any other human discovery has done more to reduce pain and death.[1] Outstanding, also, was the compounding of effective germicides, especially after 1860.

The old theory that disease was caused by evil spirits was wiped out for all time by the announcement of the germ theory of disease in 1876. It was the work of Dr. Robert Koch (1843-1910), a brilliant German pathologist who had made use of the important earlier experiments of Pasteur on the germ basis of fermentation. Koch discovered the bacillus that causes tuberculosis in 1882. This germ theory of disease revolutionized the sciences of bacteriology and pathology. In this latter field, the work of Pasteur and Virchow was of great importance. The usual method of killing microörganisms in milk still bears Pasteur's name. His work on silkworm diseases saved the silk industry of France. His studies of anthrax helped to combat this dreaded disease of animals, while he was the first to give us a successful vaccine against hydrophobia.

If Morton and his successors made surgery more painless, Lord Lister (1827-1912) made it more safe against infection through his introduction of the principles of antiseptic surgery.[2] This meant the careful cleansing of the hands and instruments of the surgeon and the treatment of the wounds with the proper germicides. Down to this time, surgeons had been scandalously negligent with respect to such matters as even ordinary cleanliness, and a high death rate from infection had resulted. Another source of a frightfully high death rate from infection was puerperal, or childbed, fever. The man who discovered (1843) that this deadly malady was produced by unnecessary infections due to lack of cleanliness was a Boston physician, better known in the field of literature than in medicine, Oliver Wendell Holmes (1809-94). This disclosure led to antiseptic gynecology in the work of the Hungarian physician Ignaz Philipp Semmelweis (1818-65), and has saved the lives of countless thousands of mothers. Semmelweis's brave struggle against the inertia, jealousy, and malice of his fellow physicians constitutes one of the more stirring chapters in the history of medicine. It was his fight that put over this important new development in medical science and practice.[3]

While artificial germicides are extremely important in safeguarding us from infections, the body itself provides powerful shock troops in the battle against deadly germs. This fact was first proved by the eminent Russian scientist I. I. (Elie) Mechnikov (1845-1916), who showed that the function of the white corpuscles in the blood is primarily to fight off germs and to prevent infection and disease. The pus in an infected wound is mainly composed of the dead white corpuscles that have made the "supreme sacrifice" in our behalf.

[1] *Cf.* C. D. Leake, "The Historical Development of Surgical Anesthesia," *Scientific Monthly*, March, 1925.
[2] *Cf.* P. F. Clark, "Joseph Lister," *Scientific Monthly*, December, 1920.
[3] *Cf.* P. H. De Kruif, *Microbe Hunters*, Harcourt, Brace, 1926.

These various lines of medical progress made possible the emergence of a truly scientific surgery. It is usually conceded that the greatest surgeon of the nineteenth century was Theodor Kocher (1841-1917) of Switzerland, though he had many close rivals.

Medicine was applied not only to our bodies but also to our minds. Medical psychology appeared in the related fields of psychiatry and neurology.[1] In the latter part of the nineteenth century, psychologists and physicians, such as Henry Maudsley (1835-1918), T. A. Ribot (1839-1916), Jean Charcot (1825-93), Auguste Forel (1848-1931), Pierre Janet (1859-   ), S. Weir Mitchell (1829-1914), and others, raised the study of mental and nervous disease from the depths of witchcraft and diabolism. The stage was set for Sigmund Freud and the development of psychoanalysis.

The progress in medical science between Jenner and Kocher was most certainly far greater than the medical advances between Hippocrates and Jenner. This fact is usually obscured, at least by implication, even in our better medical histories, which devote far the greater amount of their space to the largely irrelevant, if curious and interesting, medical lore before 1800.

9. SCIENTIFIC THOUGHT AND POPULAR THOUGHT

The remarkable progress in natural science in the nineteenth century has led many to believe that mankind suddenly became scientific-minded and that an altogether new intellectual age had come into being by the time of the American Civil War. Nothing of the sort occurred.[2]

The mass of mankind in Western civilization were, it is true, vastly affected in an indirect way by the progress of nineteenth-century science. They were provided with all manner of wonderful new mechanical devices and conveniences, which vitally altered their lives. They were healed of diseases more surely and more frequently and operated upon by surgeons more successfully and more painlessly. In popular magazines and newspapers they read superficially about the wonders that modern science had uncovered. They looked through bigger and better telescopes, and through more powerful microscopes, in order to instruct or amuse themselves with respect to the heavens or the minute wonders of the animal and vegetable worlds.

In spite of all of this, however, as we have said in connection with technological advance, the mode of thinking of the great majority of men in the Western world was very slightly altered by the direct impact of science. To be sure, the perspective of a man who has traveled across a continent in a railroad train must be somewhat different from that of one whose travels have been limited to an oxcart within a rural township. But a transcontinental railroad trip may not prevent a person from thinking about the fundamental problems of life and society much as his grandfather did two generations before.

[1] See Bernard Hart, *Psychopathology: Its Development and Its Place in Medicine*, 2d ed., Macmillan, 1931; J. E. Nicole, *Psychopathology*, Dodd, Mead, 1930, Chaps. I-III; and W. L. Northridge, *Modern Theories of the Unconscious*, Dutton, 1924, Chaps. I-III.

[2] *Cf.* Robinson, *The Humanizing of Knowledge;* H. E. Barnes, *The New History and the Social Studies*, Century, 1925, Chap. x; *History and Social Intelligence*, Chap. XIX; *Can Man Be Civilized?;* and *The Twilight of Christianity*, Long & Smith, 1929, Chap. I; and R. B. Fosdick, *The Old Savage in the New Civilization*, Doubleday, Doran, 1928.

THE DEVELOPMENT OF NATURAL SCIENCE

Such was the case with Western civilization as a whole. In their thinking about God, the world, man, politics, law, wealth and economics, education, and the problems of right and wrong, the overwhelming majority of men were as much dominated by custom, tradition, folklore, and habit in 1885 as they had been in 1685. The power of the supernatural over human thought had been but little affected by scientific progress. Tradition and emotion rather than fact and logic still prevailed. Belief and conviction were supreme.

Even the scientists themselves, at least down to the very close of the century, rarely thought scientifically outside their laboratories. They usually rejected scientific discoveries in other fields if these challenged their personal prejudices or religious convictions. Even so great a scientist as Pasteur, at the very close of the nineteenth century, never accepted the implications of the theory of evolution or allowed his orthodoxy to be shaken in the slightest. A great English biologist, St. George Mivart, opposed evolution until his death in 1900. Among the scientists a Haeckel or a Huxley was the exception rather than the rule, and such men were very generally frowned upon by other members of the scientific fraternity.

Civilization in the year 1900 was, intellectually speaking, a great and unappreciative parasite thriving on the labors and discoveries of a few score outstanding scientists. In any popular sense, nothing approaching a scientific and skeptical age had yet dawned upon mankind.

II. THE RISE OF THE EVOLUTIONARY CONCEPT AND ITS EARLY INTELLECTUAL EFFECTS

1. THE DECLINING PRESTIGE OF BIBLICAL SCIENCE

As has been noted, the outstanding scientific and philosophical achievement of the nineteenth century was the establishment of the doctrine of evolution. It is so important an innovation that it deserves to be separated from the brief survey of natural science which has preceded and to be treated by itself as an epoch in science and human thought.

The victory of the evolutionary hypothesis was won, in the main, through the vindication of the biological propositions involved. But this phase of the triumph was powerfully aided by the parallel decline in the authority of the biblical sources that embodied and defended the special-creation conception. There is little logical or rational basis for believing in the doctrine of creation save for the biblical sanctions given it. Therefore any progress in undermining the dogma of the divinely revealed nature of the Scriptures helped to discredit creation and to buttress evolution.

Doubts were offered in regard to certain traditional notions of the authorship of the Bible by some of the more critical Church Fathers in the later Roman Empire. But the first critic to raise serious questions about the conventional view of the authorship of the Bible was a scholarly Spanish Jew, Aben Ezra, who about 1150 A.D. seriously challenged the notion of the Mosaic authorship of the Pentateuch. In the middle of the seventeenth century, as we have already noted, the distinguished critical philosopher Thomas Hobbes questioned the Mosaic authorship on the basis of considerations of logic and common sense as well as textual and historical scholarship. He pointed out how unusual it was for an author (Moses), while still writing his autobiography, to be able to call attention to his death and to boast that he was so well buried that no one for hundreds of years had been able to locate his grave. Yet the Pentateuch actually tells of this successful secrecy of the burial of Moses and describes in detail the grief of the Jews following his death.

The Jewish scholar Baruch Spinoza, a younger contemporary of Hobbes, began the truly critical study of the origin of the Book of Genesis, showed that it could not have been written by a single author at any one time, and offered further textual evidence to discredit the theory of the Mosaic authorship. In the middle of the eighteenth century a brilliant French physician, Jean Astruc, outlined crudely what has now come to be accepted as the accurate version of the nature and composition of the Pentateuch. The next decisive step was taken by Karl David Ilgen at the very close of the eighteenth century. He pointed out that there were some seventeen different documents in Genesis, with three major sources; this we have since accepted as correct.

In the century following Ilgen there was remarkable progress in the difficult problem of unraveling the authorship of the books of the Old Testament. Among the leading names associated with these marked advances in textual scholarship are W. M. L. De Wette, Hermann Hupfeld, Bishop John William Colenso, Abraham Kuenen, Bernhard Duhm, and Julius Wellhausen (1844-1918). Wellhausen brought Old Testament criticism near to perfection and is usually looked upon as the master scholar in this field. Splendid work has also been done in the last generation by such men as T. K. Cheyne, S. R. Driver, and B. W. Bacon.

The critical process has been carried beyond a mere study of the text of the Old Testament. The brilliant Cambridge professor William Robertson Smith, in his famous *Religion of the Semites* (1889), pointed out that there is little which is unique about the Jewish religion and indicated many points of similarity between the religion of the ancient Hebrews and the religious beliefs and practices of the other branches of the Semitic peoples.[1] Pursuing this line of investigation more thoroughly and precisely, scholars such as Delitzsch, Winckler, and Rogers have made clear the profound influence of Babylonian mythology and religious tradition upon the religion of the Hebrews, particularly in the way of the adoption of the Babylonian cosmology, creation tales, and early historical myths, such as the Garden of Eden, the Tower of Babel, and the Deluge. Such writers as R. H. Charles have done equally significant work in indicating the Indo-Persian derivation of the later Jewish conceptions that helped to produce the typically Christian version of the Devil, Heaven, and Hell.[2] It is today clearly evident that as literature

---

[1] See also G. A. Barton, *Sketch of Semitic Origins*, Macmillan, 1902.
[2] *Cf.* R. W. Rogers, *Cuneiform Parallels to the Old Testament*, Abingdon Press, 1912; R. H. Charles, *Religious Development between the Old and New Testaments*, Holt, 1914, Chap. IV; and *Critical History of the Doctrine of a Future Life in Israel*, 2d ed. rev., Macmillan, 1913.

the Bible is a purely secular product of human ingenuity, quite as much as the Gilgamesh epic, the Code of Hammurabi, the Homeric poems, Pliny's epistles, Virgil's Aeneid or Dante's *Divine Comedy*.[1] The following quotation from Professor Shotwell gives us a very illuminating statement of the character of the Bible as revealed by modern scholarship:

Let us imagine, for instance, that instead of the Jewish scriptures we are talking of those of the Greeks. Suppose that the heritage of Hellas had been preserved to us in the form of a Bible. What would be the character of the book? We should begin, perhaps, with a few passages from Hesiod on the birth of the gods and the dawn of civilization mingled with fragments of the *Iliad* and both set into long excerpts from Herodotus. The dialogues of Plato might be given by Homeric heroes and the text of the great dramatists (instead of the prophets) be preserved interspersed one with another and clogged with the uninspired and uninspiring comments of Alexandrian savants. Then imagine that the sense of their authority was so much obscured as centuries passed, that philosophers—for philosophers were to Greece what theologians were to Israel—came to believe that the large part of this composite work of history and philosophy had been first written down by Solon as the deliverance of the oracle of Apollo at Delphi. Then, finally, imagine that the text became stereotyped and sacred, even the words taboo, and became the heritage of alien peoples who knew nothing more of Greek history than what this compilation contained. Such, with some little exaggeration, would be a Hellenic Bible after the fashion of the Bible of the Jews. If the comparison be a little overdrawn there is no danger but that we shall make sufficient mental reservations to prevent us from carrying it too far. Upon the whole, so far as form and structure go, the analogy holds remarkably well.[2]

No informed and reasonable person, therefore, can expect the Bible to possess any greater reliability or wisdom relative to history or science than the civilization that produced the Bible could itself muster. The recognition of this fact was of vast significance for the subsequent acceptability of the doctrine of evolution. It undermined the chief obstacle to its espousal by the mass of mankind. There could not be any serious objection to the evolutionary philosophy in the Western world were it not for the rival doctrine of special creation set forth in the Bible. Once scholars understood that this dogma of creation was the product of an ancient generation of men, far less equipped to render an authoritative judgment on such matters than our present astronomers, geologists, and biologists, the creation stumbling-block no longer possessed for educated persons the prestige or potency that it had enjoyed in earlier times.

2. THE HISTORICAL DEVELOPMENT OF EVOLUTIONARY DOCTRINE

The history of the doctrine of evolution falls into two supplementary but quite different lines of development. One is the general philosophical conception of evolution as the master key to the understanding of the development of the cosmos, our universe, the Earth, organic life, man, social institutions,

---

[1] See Barnes, *The Twilight of Christianity*, Chap. IV; G. F. Moore, *The Literature of the Old Testament*, Holt, 1913; and J. A. Bewer, *The Literature of the Old Testament in Its Historical Development*, Columbia University Press, 1922.

[2] J. T. Shotwell, *Introduction to the History of History*, Columbia University Press, 1922, pp. 82-83.

and human culture. The other is the specific biological interpretation of the laws of heredity which explain how organic life has developed on this particular planet. These two are often confused, with the result that evolutionary biologists have often been given credit for achievements that really belong to cosmic philosophers.

The notion that change and development seem to be the basic processes of the physical universe was first enunciated, so far as we know, by Heraclitus, Empedocles, and Anaximander, all pre-Periclean Greek philosophers.[1] The best surviving statement of this point of view is contained in a late Epicurean product, Lucretius' great cosmological poem, *De rerum natura*. Here we find a sweeping conception of evolution, covering the development of the universe, life, man, society, and culture. Doubtless, the systematic Epicurean philosophers produced still more comprehensive and technical statements of the classical evolutionary theory, but if so the works have been lost.

There was no decisive advance beyond the Lucretian doctrine until the eighteenth century, when the evolutionary philosophy was revived and elaborated by Buffon, Diderot, the German *Naturphilosophen,* and some of the Romanticist philosophers. In the nineteenth century Herbert Spencer built up an equally broad philosophy of evolution on the basis of the remarkable progress of natural science between Copernicus and his own day. Spencer held that everything in nature from the whole physical cosmos to human institutions had evolved according to a specific formula or key, namely, the passage from an incoherent, disorganized homogeneous state to a well-differentiated and thoroughly coördinated heterogeneity. Differentiation, specialization, and coördination are the master processes in evolution in Spencer's system. Spencer applied this conception to every aspect of evolution, and introduced the evolutionary formula into every phase of human knowledge in his voluminous *System of Synthetic Philosophy* (1860-96).

It was, therefore, Herbert Spencer, not Charles Darwin, who made evolution an integral element in the intellectual equipment of every educated man of the twentieth century. Spencer's particular applications of his evolutionary formulae may have been premature, crude, inadequate, and often erroneous, but he must be given credit for the popularization of the most momentous notion in the whole history of human thought and social action. Others, from John Fiske to John Dewey, H. G. Wells, George Dorsey, and James Harvey Robinson, have carried on this task of clarifying and applying the evolutionary doctrine to human thought and social problems.

The other major phase of the history of evolution, that relating to the development of organic life on our particular planet, has had an equal heritage from the past. The question at issue here is the nature and origin of species. The biblical view was that all species of plants and animals were created by God once and for all some six thousand years ago—that from the moment of creation, these species have remained fixed and immutable. The evolutionary notion is that all existing species have descended from earlier and simpler forms of life—that no species is fixed and changeless. The history of evolutionary

---

[1] See above, Vol. I, pp. 221-22.

THE RISE OF THE EVOLUTIONARY CONCEPT

theory in this sense is the record of the gradual perception of the mutability of species.

Aristotle believed in an ascending series of organic life, proceeding from the more simple to the more complex types. He had at least a rudimentary notion of the facts of human reproduction, but he denied the sexuality of plants. In the Middle Ages, Albertus Magnus and other medieval biologists revived and tested the Aristotelian view. In early modern times Francis Bacon (1561-1626) and Leibnitz (1646-1716) both expressed their belief in variation and the mutability of species, thus breaking with the biblical view of specially created and immutable species. Joachim Camerarius (1500-74) proved the sexuality of plants. Kant (1724-1804) thought that widely differentiated species could be traced back to a common parent. Linnaeus (1707-78) worked out the first great scheme for the classification of organic life that suggested the common parentage of different existing species, although Linnaeus himself, until late in his life, believed in fixed and changeless species. Buffon (1707-88) clearly understood some of the broader implications of evolution, especially the relation between the environment and the slow differentiation of species.

The concept of adaptation to environment was developed more thoroughly by Erasmus Darwin (1731-1802), the grandfather of Charles Darwin. Malthus's law of population emphasized the importance of the struggle for existence. The poet-philosopher Goethe anticipated many of the basic conceptions of organic evolution, such as adaptation to environment, vital force, vestigial organs, and the like. Sir Charles Lyell brought together in his *Principles of Geology* (1830-33) all the rich evidence from geology that supports the evolutionary rather than the creationist hypothesis. Finally, Jean Lamarck (1744-1829) enunciated a definite doctrine of organic evolution in which the theory of mutability was based on the notion of the inheritance of acquired characters. Any changes in the body of a man or animal, so runs this doctrine, are handed along by hereditary processes to be the starting-point for the next generation. Lamarck's classic example was the giraffe, which, he thought, had developed its long neck through stretching it to reach high leaves and branches, handing on to progeny the slight gain in length in each generation. Most of these early contributions to the notion of the way in which the different species of plants and animals have developed were brought together in a very able popular book by a layman, Robert Chambers, *Vestiges of the Natural History of Creation* (1844).

These pre-Darwinian notions made a more plausible case for evolution than the traditionalists could make for creation, but it was Charles Darwin, more than any other man, who vindicated the notion of organic evolution and established it as the basic contribution of biology to human knowledge and enlightenment. He occupies much the same place as does Spencer in the history of the philosophical conception of evolution. Charles Darwin (1809-82) was for a time the naturalist on a chartered ship, the *Beagle,* which, voyaging widely, enabled him to study plant and animal life in various areas of the earth. This afforded many suggestions as to the differentiation and adaptation of species. Darwin was familiar with his grandfather's views, and was especially impressed with the Malthusian notion of the struggle for existence that is brought about through the pressure of organic life upon the means of subsistence. Further, Darwin carried on much experimental animal-breeding, especially with pigeons. At the same time, Alfred Russel Wallace was studying the evidence for evolution through field research in the Malay Archipelago. He sent a somewhat hesitant and discouraging résumé of his conclusions to Darwin, with the result that the latter felt compelled to publish his epoch-making work *On the Origin of Species* (1859).

The chief significance of Darwin's work was: (1) He systematized the doctrine of the origin and development of species on the basis of his own and preceding work; (2) he massed and marshaled the evidence for evolution; (3) he gave general currency to the notion that existing forms of plants and animals are descended from earlier and, in most cases, more rudimentary types; (4) he dealt in technical detail with certain main processes and factors of evolution, such as the struggle for existence, the survival of the fittest, natural selection, sexual selection, and the like; (5) he proved the basic interrelationships of organic life; and (6) he applied this reasoning not only to the lower animals but also to man himself.

Many of the specific details in Darwin's explanations of evolution have been abandoned or gravely modified as the result of the subsequent progress of biological research.[1] But his general thesis is even better established today than it was in 1859. Indeed, since Darwin's day evolution has passed from a working hypothesis to a well-established fact. This answers the frequent assertion of religious critics of evolution to the effect that "Darwinism is dead." Some of Darwin's minor theories like sexual selection are, indeed, dead, and even his doctrine of the survival of the fittest is questioned. But his evolutionary conception is of enduring validity and significance. Darwin occupies much the same position in biology that Newton does in the history of physics and astronomy. His work is no more dead than that of the author of the *Principia*.[2]

Darwin's work, undermining and assailing as it did the biblical theory of the origin of species, met with bitter resistance from nearly all clergymen, the present type of reconciling Modernist being a rare individual eighty years ago. But he was warmly supported by Wallace, Haeckel, Romanes, Huxley, and others, though some of them differed from him in regard to the details of his system. The years from 1860 to 1900 were a period that combined further research and bitter polemics. By the dawn of the present century the battle for evolution had been won, and the student of heredity is rarely called upon today in civilized areas to enter the battle lists against the straggling enemies of the evolutionary point of view.

The outstanding phases of the progress of evolutionary biology since Darwin's day have been:[3] (1) Weismann's hypothesis of the continuity of the germ plasm and the final disproof of the doctrine of the transmission of

---

[1] *Cf.* C. J. Singer, *The Story of Living Things*, Harper, 1931, Chap. xv.
[2] J. H. Robinson, "Is Darwinism Dead?" *Harper's Magazine*, June, 1922. *Cf.* C. C. Nutting, "Is Darwin Shorn?" *Scientific Monthly*, February, 1920; and J. S. Huxley, "Where Darwin's Theory Stands Today," New York *Times* "Magazine," Mar. 1, 1931.
[3] See Singer, *op. cit.*, Chap. xv; and S. J. Holmes, *The Eugenic Predicament*, Harcourt, Brace, 1933.

acquired characters as originally set forth by men like Lamarck; (2) De Vries's establishment of the fact of mutations or sports as the source of many new species; (3) the discovery and elaboration of Mendel's law of heredity; (4) the organization of extensive and well-controlled research facilities for the further study of the problems of heredity by T. H. Morgan and others; and (5) the development of the program of eugenics by Galton, Pearson, Ammon, and others, designed to apply the recently discovered laws of heredity to the improvement of the human race.

3. THE IMPLICATIONS OF EVOLUTION

The first striking implication of the evolutionary view of life is the complete revolution in our time perspective that the evolutionary conception has made necessary. In the place of a very brief period for the age of the Earth and all living matter, we must reckon with a time conception that defies both the human imagination and our conventional standards of measurement. From two to four billion years must be assigned to the age of the Earth in a minimum estimate, whereas the Sun had passed its maximum radiance before the Earth originated. When one turns to the probable amount of time involved in the evolution of the cosmos, the conceptions and standards that prevail in measuring time for earthly purposes seem quite trivial and inadequate. Jeans estimates the age of the cosmos as two hundred trillion years. Indeed, we may have to admit that in the new cosmic perspective the very notion of time, as we understand it, is nothing more than a convenient geocentric illusion. Einstein and others have already suggested that time and space are but secondary manifestations of energy. The era of human life in this new time perspective, instead of being coexistent with the duration of the Earth and all the heavenly bodies, must be regarded as but the briefest trifle in earth history, to say nothing of its utter insignificance in terms of cosmic history.

Along with this revolutionized time perspective has come the dynamic notion of change as the universal principle of cosmic development. This has provided the second main implication of evolution. In the place of the older static notions of a perfect creation a few thousand years back, with but slight subsequent alteration of the nature of the heavenly bodies, the Earth, and its organic life, we have to recognize that change appears to be the most vital principle in cosmic development and to realize that there is no such thing as a static condition to be observed in the universe. Everything is in a state of alteration, some of this being development and progress, while other changes definitely manifest disintegration and devolution. We have, then, the conception of a dynamic and ever changing universe in the place of the static outlook of a century ago.

A third vital implication of evolution is that man has been demonstrated to be a special biochemical entity,—a "colloidal aggregate." There seems to be nothing about human life or behavior that is not susceptible to explanation according to naturalistic laws and principles. This implication, combined with the other two aspects of evolution, proved as disruptive of the accepted views of man as it was of the older beliefs concerning creation. The scientific facts—in contrast to the older views—reveal man as neither a "worm" nor a being a

660 INTELLECTUAL AND CULTURAL ACHIEVEMENTS

little lower than the angels. He is, at least so far as science can say, only the leading member of the simian group, and therefore for the time being the dominant species in the animal kingdom on this planet.[1]

In addition to these three outstanding aspects of the cultural and intellectual impact of the doctrine of evolution, there were a number of other effects that are treated more in detail elsewhere in this book. The discovery of evolution meant that in the half-century following 1860 the biological sciences temporarily supplanted the mathematical sciences in general intellectual popularity. The notion that change seems to be one of the most universal processes of nature tended to undermine the absolutistic conceptions of some Romanticist and Idealist philosophers. Absolutes and the notion of final and ultimate Truth no longer possessed the standing that they did in the days of Schelling. Truth appeared to be merely a relative and changing product of evolution rather than an outgrowth of a divinely guided dialectic. It was something that could only be pragmatically tested through experience. The notion of progress could now, seemingly, be justified on cosmic and biological as well as historical and philosophical grounds. And the demonstration that biologists could control, in part, the course of biological development in organisms suggested to sociologists that society might find a way of artificially guiding and directing the course of social evolution. Progress might become a consciously controlled affair, bearing mankind on to higher levels of happiness and well-being.

The view of man as an animal, which was noted as the third important implication of evolution, has been extremely repellent to many traditionalists, but there is little logical ground for such an attitude, once it is understood what one really means by the inclusion of man in the animal kingdom. When one views the situation in a scientific and common-sense attitude he must recognize that the animal kingdom represents the highest order of life on the planet; that is, the highest known level of organic development. Therefore to be the temporary leader of the animal world is the highest form of achievement to which man could rationally aspire, and this title is the highest praise that can be bestowed upon Homo sapiens.

Further, not only is the conception that man is an animal a demonstrated fact in no way humiliating to the human race; it also has much greater practical significance. For once we come to recognize the fact that man is an animal, we immediately have the rich fields of comparative anatomy, physiology, and psychology to draw upon.[2] From these we can build a solid and illuminating approach to the study of human nature and behavior. These branches of science reveal man as a supersimian, and the study of simian psychology, as summarized in such books as those by Kohts, Köhler, and Yerkes,[3] are examples of the practical value of this approach to human behavior.

This new perspective for the human scene that science and evolution have created is admirably described by Professor Kirtley F. Mather—a conception far removed from the Christian epic of the Middle Ages:

---

[1] *Cf.* Sir Arthur Keith, *Man*, Holt, 1912.
[2] *Cf.* G. A. Dorsey, *Why We Behave Like Human Beings*, Harper, 1925.
[3] *Cf.* C. K. Ogden, *The Meaning of Psychology*, Harper, 1926, Chap. vii; and R. M. Yerkes, *Almost Human*, Century, 1925.

THE RISE OF THE EVOLUTIONARY CONCEPT

Joshua's World was made expressly for man. Everything in it was designed especially to contribute to his welfare or to punish him when he incurred the displeasure of his god. He occupied the summit of the tall pinnacle of superiority, not because he had won his way to that proud eminence, but because he had been placed there by the Creator. The locality where he lived was the center of the universe; sun, moon and stars revolved around him and it. Joshua's concept of man's place in nature has lingered long in the minds of his descendants; echoes of that concept are still with us. Did not Linnaeus give the name "Primates" to that order of mammals which he defined as including man?

But Our World is not so flattering. "What is man that thou art mindful of him?" has a new meaning since Betelgeuse was measured. In geologic time, man has lived for but a moment in the earthly day. In astronomic space, he is a speck of foam on the crest of a single wave in the midst of a Pacific Ocean. The earth is neither the smallest nor the biggest, the hottest nor the coldest, the most central nor the most remote among the planets of the solar system. Presumably there are many other similar bodies in the heavens. Except for the fact that you and I are on its surface, there is nothing especially distinguished about it. The sun is just an ordinary star. There are many larger, many smaller; many hotter, many colder; many brighter, many duller. Presumably many of its neighbors in the heavens have fully comparable planetary dependants in their train. The stellar galaxy is but one of the many far-flung aggregates of stars. So far as we are aware, it may be duplicated many times in space. Only our presence for a brief span of years upon this insignificant earth gives importance to one particular star in one of many galaxies of stars.

There is no reason for assuming that human life is the most superior expression of the vital impulse which the universe has yet achieved. It is scarcely likely that the Administration of the Universe has staked all on this one type of life in this one locality. Perhaps on some distant planet the achievements of the Universal Spirit far oustrip anything that man has yet attained. But for us, Our World in this particular geologic epoch gives The Opportunity. It is Man's hour; the prize is almost in his grasp. Dominion over his fellow-creatures is for all practical purposes his; mastery over the forces of inanimate nature is well-nigh assured; only Self, individual and aggregate, remains to be subdued. Our world is not a furnished stage on which the puppet man enacts a rôle; it is a challenge to the best in man to overcome all handicaps and emerge successful in the attempt to achieve a truly satisfactory life.[1]

The anthropologists and sociologists have made it clear that the evolutionary process applies not only to the physical development of the animal world and the human race, but to the growth and differentiation of human institutions as well. The same traditional argument for the idea of a special creation of the physical and organic world had held that all of our social institutions—the family, property, the state, law, religion, and the like—were likewise the product of a divine fiat. God had revealed to man His wishes as to the perfect type of family, religion, law, and so on.

The historians and social scientists have dealt as severely with this hypothesis as the astronomers, geologists, and biologists have with the dogma of a special creation of man. They have amply demonstrated that our every human institution, religious, economic, political, legal, educational, or moral, has been

[1] Mather, "The New World Revealed by Modern Science," *World Unity,* October, 1927, pp. 35-36.

the product of naturalistic influences operating from a very remote period in the human past.[1] Our culture is an outgrowth of trial, error, and accident, controlled by broad evolutionary processes. Man has faced nature under widely different circumstances. His efforts to preserve and perpetuate life have compelled him to attack the problems of existence in a variety of ways. The result has been an extensive differentiation of human institutions. In the struggles of communities, nations, and races these competing types of institutions and ideas have been subjected to the struggle for existence and those relatively best adapted to any given people, time, and place have tended to survive. The others have perished or have held over in remote or protected areas where peoples with a superior body of institutions could not penetrate successfully. All of our so-called sacred human institutions are thus only the naturalistic product of man's age-long struggle with nature to perpetuate his kind, to give them an ever greater surplus, and to protect them against suffering or extinction. It is, of course, recognized that even peoples with the most creditable institutions and beliefs have a vast baggage of archaic and mostly worthless institutions and convictions which clutter up the social scene, produce inertia, and lessen human well-being.

The writer to whom we are indebted more than to any other for the forceful statement and persistent reiteration of this thesis is Herbert Spencer, whom we have mentioned previously. Beginning with his *First Principles,* published in 1862, he devoted his life mainly to an application of the evolutionary hypothesis to all types of institutions and to every aspect of our mental life.[2] A group of sociologists who followed him went to an extreme in this direction and claimed that there is a complete identity between the processes of biological evolution and those of social evolution.[3] They asserted that society is an organism and that the same factors are at work therein as operate in the biological world. This contention is not widely accepted today, though there are some interesting analogies between organic and social evolution.

The most ambitious effort to work out universal laws of social evolution was that of an American anthropologist, Lewis Henry Morgan, in his *Ancient Society* (1877).[4] Morgan's general assumption of social evolution was more sound than most of his special interpretations of the evolution of primitive groups. Elaborate descriptive material on the evolution of human institutions and ideas was contained in the famous book *Folkways* (1907) by William Graham Sumner. His disciple, A. G. Keller, has presented a discriminating appraisal of the applicability of Darwinian evolutionary principles to social institutions in his *Societal Evolution* (1915, revised 1931), and has given us Sumner's ideas in full, *The Science of Society* (1927).

The recognition of the secular origin of our institutions has helped to promote a greater degree of urbanity and tolerance. It is less easy to be ferocious in the enforcement of a custom that we know to be of ancient and fallible human origin. We can no longer imagine that we are forcing the will of God

---

[1] *Cf.* A. G. Keller, *Societal Evolution,* rev. ed., Macmillan, 1931, and *Man's Rough Road,* Stokes, 1932; and G. A. Dorsey, *Man's Own Story: Civilization,* Harper, 1931.
[2] *Cf.* Barnes and Becker, *History of Sociological Thought.*
[3] See below, p. 667.   [4] See above, Vol. I, pp. 42 ff.

THE RISE OF THE EVOLUTIONARY CONCEPT

on our neighbors. The evolutionary point of view has also strengthened social optimism. If man has made our defective institutions in the past, he surely may, by the application of available knowledge, supplant them with far better ones without offering an affront to God in so doing. The whole foundation of the social philosophy of the Deists, the Physiocrats, the Classical Economists, and Spencerian individualists falls to pieces in this new perspective.[1]

Another important implication of the doctrine of evolution has been to emphasize and illuminate the fact that, for all practical purposes, "man is the measure of all things" in a far more thoroughgoing and satisfactory way than was the case with the early modern Humanists, or even the later Deists and eighteenth-century reformers. While the more resolute Humanists tended to glorify man and human experience, they had no scientific knowledge of man. Hence, their only tests and values had to be esthetic. They had no knowledge of biological or social science which would enable them to know just what this creature, man, who is the measure of all things, is actually like. Poetry and art are extremely valuable, but they fall far short of adequate guides for human values and conduct. The Deists and reformers also elevated man, but their views were tinged strongly with religious interests and values. Most of them believed in immortality and looked upon the future life as more important for man than earthly life. Moreover, while they made use of such biological and social science as existed, they had little that was reliable to exploit in this field. The evolutionary perspective and nineteenth-century natural and social science not only stressed the importance of man as man but also enabled us to know just what man is, what will make him happiest, and how to advance his well-being. These forward steps in our knowledge also emphasized the fact that life here on earth is the only life to which man may confidently look forward, and hence implied that our efforts should be concentrated on achieving the "good life" here and now.

III. THE INFLUENCE OF SCIENCE UPON INTELLECTUAL AND RELIGIOUS ATTITUDES

Nineteenth-century natural science had as revolutionary an influence on human thought and religious interpretations as did the remarkable scientific advances from Copernicus to Newton in an earlier age.[2] The notion of a world-machine best summarizes, perhaps, the general intellectual reaction to the new discoveries in science.[3] The new astronomy in the days of Newton had emphasized the element of law and order in the physical world and had identified natural law and divine law. God was pictured as standing behind the physical universe as the author of the invariable laws of nature. Nineteenth-century science led to an extensive elaboration of this conception of the physical universe as a vast and complicated machine obeying immutable

---

[1] See above, pp. 77 ff., 378 ff.
[2] On the part of the educated classes, of course.
[3] *Cf.* Woodbridge Riley, *American Thought from Puritanism to Pragmatism*, new ed., Holt, 1915, Bks. IV-V; Carl Snyder, *The World Machine*, Longmans, 1907; and John Langdon-Davies, *The New Age of Faith*, Viking Press, 1925.

laws. Moreover, the doctrine of evolution, as applied to astronomy, and the discoveries in the field of thermodynamics gave rise to the conception of the universe as a machine in motion. The notion of dynamic mechanism attained a well-nigh complete triumph in the minds of those whose thinking was at all attuned to scientific work and discoveries.

The logical and dogmatic foundation of this scientific approach to intellectual and physical problems was the invariable assumption of a definite cause-and-effect relationship in the realm of physical phenomena.[1] As Max Planck describes it, in the view of the nineteenth century causation was looked upon "as an expression of inviolable regulation which inheres in events, and is therefore a necessary framework in which experience comes to us, and without which experience is incomprehensible." In every field of nature, if one had a complete understanding of the causes, so it was believed, he could predict and describe the effects that flowed from them. This scientific conception of casual relationship was, of course, derived in considerable degree from the metaphysical notions of cause and effect that had been discussed by Hume, Kant, and other philosophers in an earlier period. The cause-and-effect relationship occupied much the same position in the assumptions and methods of the nineteenth-century scientists as God, the Perfect Being, had in the procedure of Descartes. The latter had also believed in the reality of certain definite categories of knowledge; so, likewise, the nineteenth-century scientists felt positive that they could fall back upon certain definitely established realities, such as energy, the transformation of energy, the conservation of energy, and the laws of radiant energies. A good statement of this view of cause and effect which dominated nineteenth-century thought is offered by Professor Mather:

In Joshua's World anything could happen. Magic played a most important part in everyday life. Happenings were determined by the caprice of ruling powers whose whims and intentions varied from day to day. Ours is a world of law. Effect follows cause with unvarying relations. Order and regularity reign where formerly magic and caprice held sway. The law of gravity operates relentlessly, the same yesterday, to-day and to-morrow, regardless of bribe or entreaty.[2]

This produced a prevailing air of certainty and assurance among those most devoted to scientific interests and points of view. Man was looked upon as capable of knowing the physical ultimates in the realm of science. He might not—as Spencer admitted—be capable of mastering the elusive ultimates in the fields of religion and philosophy, but he could be sure of handling with precision and accuracy the facts of the physical world. Such assumptions were conceded to the scientists even by many philosophers who held that science was quite incapable of dealing with the ultimate realities. Kant and his successors granted that science was capable of describing and understanding the facts of the phenomenal world that could be discerned by sense perception. In short, they admitted that science could master scientific data, however much it might fall short of understanding and interpreting the real or noumenal world.

[1] *Cf.* Karl Pearson, *Grammar of Science*, 3d ed. rev., Macmillan, 1911.
[2] Mather, *loc. cit.*, pp. 36-37.

Scientific discoveries in the nineteenth century also had, as we have hinted above in several places, a very marked influence upon that conception of progress which had been so popular in the previous century.[1] The doctrine of evolution seemed to offer complete scientific confirmation of the dogma of progress. Further, it gave this notion of progress greater precision and exactness. In the past man had turned primarily to history to enlist support for the doctrine of progress. Now he could have recourse to physical and biological science. Progress no longer seemed merely a matter of opinion. It was now regarded as a universal law. Moreover, it applied not only to man, culture, and things of this world, but involved the whole physical universe. Man possessed an affinity with the cosmos as a whole.

Not only did scientists and scientifically minded persons embrace such ideas as these. The more advanced minds in the field of religion, especially near the end of the nineteenth century, showed much hospitality towards these notions.[2] So far as the physical universe was concerned, they were inclined to accept what the scientists taught them. They might, following Schleiermacher, hold that faith is superior to reason or the laboratory and maintain that the scientist never touches the world of ultimate reality. In the realm of physical phenomena, however, the Modernists in religion were inclined to take science and its dogmas at their face value without any serious questioning.

IV. THE RISE OF THE SOCIAL SCIENCES

The nineteenth century not only witnessed incomparable developments in the natural sciences; it was also characterized by the rise and differentiation of definite social sciences, devoted to the accurate study of society and human relationships. From this time onward our analysis of human society and of the relations between men no longer had to depend either upon guesswork or upon revelation.

The importance attached to social science has varied with the emphasis laid upon man as a human being and as a member of secular human society. In the period before the Greeks, supernaturalism was too powerful to allow much place for a matter-of-fact study of man and society.[3] In the more highly developed Greek centers of civilization a remarkable degree of secularization and mundane interest made its appearance.[4] The Greek skeptics rejected supernaturalism and became interested in man as a member of earthly society. The Sophists, Plato, Aristotle, the Stoics, and Lucretius made many valuable contributions to the analysis of social relationships. But they possessed too little scientific knowledge to permit them to go far towards establishing true social science. Yet their attitude towards man and his problems was not unlike that of the Rationalists of the eighteenth century which permitted and encouraged the origins of social science.

With the triumph of Christianity human interest in social science declined rapidly.[5] Man was of importance as the custodian of an immortal soul and

---

[1] See J. B. Bury, *The Idea of Progress,* Macmillan, 1932, Chap. xix.
[2] *Cf.* W. N. Rice, *Christian Faith in an Age of Science,* Doran, 1903.
[3] See above, Vol. I, pp. 67 ff., 107 ff., 136 ff., 165 ff.   [5] See above, pp. 355 ff.
[4] See above, Chapter vii.

not as a unit of human society. For a millennium and a half this attitude towards man persisted. Theology then occupied the place held today by social science among emancipated intellects.

A number of factors contributed to bring about the rise of the social sciences between 1700 and 1850.[1] The Deists laid emphasis upon the dignity of man as man. The humanitarian impulse from the Abbé de Saint-Pierre and Helvétius to Bentham helped to divert man's attention from otherworldliness and tended to concentrate interest upon the good life here and now. The growth of science, especially of psychology, biology, and anthropology, made possible rudimentary beginnings in the study of human behavior and institutions. The rise of the conception of progress challenged the static notions of man and society that had been fostered by the special-creation hypothesis. It provided a dynamic interest in the future of man and civilization. The Industrial Revolution produced a tremendous dislocation of existing life and social institutions, and served to attract special attention to a study of these changes and their possible consequences.

One conspicuous aspect of the rise of the social sciences was their differentiation from the parent stock of political philosophy.[2] From Plato to Locke and later, the study of society, the state, economics, international relations, ethics, and the like had been merged in one inclusive body of subject matter known as political philosophy. Plato's *Republic*, Aristotle's *Politics*, Dante's *De monarchia*, Bodin's *Commonwealth*, and Pufendorf's *Law of Nature and of Nations* are good examples of this antique but inclusive political philosophy.

The need for broad and fundamental social science was first thoroughly recognized by Count Henri de Saint-Simon at the very opening of the nineteenth century. He saw that some scientific means must be provided to determine the need for and validity of the various programs of social reform that were invited by the miseries of the new economic conditions. His disciple Auguste Comte established such a science and called it sociology, or the science of associated life. Comte was particularly interested in what he believed to be the chief stages through which society has passed. These he held to be: (1) The theological and military stage of the ancient Orient; (2) the metaphysical and legalistic era from the Greeks to the eighteenth century; and (3) the scientific and industrial period since the eighteenth century. Comte was also deeply concerned with the problem of social reform. He forecast an ideal society, in which intellectual direction would be furnished by sociologists, practical control by business men, and moral stimulus by women.

The most influential sociologist of the nineteenth century was Herbert Spencer. He applied his version of the evolutionary hypothesis to an explanation of the nature and history of human society, and argued vigorously against any human scheme of social reform. He held that social progress must be an automatic outcome of evolutionary forces. Man will only muddle the process if he attempts to interfere. Spencer's notion that social progress must be

---
[1] See above, pp. 174 ff., 216 ff.
[2] See Dunning, *History of Political Theories from Rousseau to Spencer, passim.*

spontaneous was vigorously attacked by Lester F. Ward, the outstanding American sociologist of the century.

The new biology and the doctrine of evolution had a profound influence upon nineteenth-century sociology. One school, known as the Organicists, devoted itself mainly to describing at great length the alleged similarities or identities between human society and the individual biological organism. The foremost members of the school were a Russian, Paul von Lilienfeld, and a German, Albert Schäffle. Another group of writers, led by the Polish sociologist Ludwig Gumplowicz, misapplied Darwin's notion of the struggle for existence to the realm of social relationships. They identified war with the struggle for existence and contended that physical conflict is the chief factor in human progress. This doctrine was vigorously attacked by a Russian sociologist, Jacques Novicow. He held that the struggle for existence in human society should, as human society advances, pass from physical warfare to cultural competition.

The doctrine of evolution was directly instrumental in bringing into being in a systematic fashion another social science—anthropology, or the study of the bodily and cultural evolution of the human race. As Professor Marett has defined the subject: "Anthropology is the whole history of man as fired and pervaded by the doctrine of evolution. Man in evolution—that is the subject in its full reach." Once Darwin and others had proved that man has evolved from lower organic types, scientists attempted to trace human evolution in detail. Physical anthropologists discovered human skeletons of widely varying age and structure and sought to reconstruct from these the bodily evolution of man. Here scientists like Huxley, Broca, Topinard, and Virchow took the lead. Others were interested in reconstructing the cultural development of man in the so-called prehistoric period. They gathered, arranged, and classified his artifacts in stone, bone, copper, bronze, and iron, and gave names to the early culture ages. The most important early work in this field was carried on by Boucher de Perthes, Sir John Lubbock, and Gabriel de Mortillet. Lewis H. Morgan, Sir E. B. Tylor, Julius Lippert, William Graham Sumner, and others studied in detail the evolution of human ideas and institutions.

The beginnings of the science of economics, or the study of man's wealth-getting and wealth-using activities, has been described in the preceding chapter on the defense of early capitalism. The first important nineteenth-century economists were the so-called Classical Economists, Malthus, Ricardo, Senior, and James Mill, those disciples of Adam Smith who defended the new capitalism and the manufacturing class. They were fond of formulating abstract economic laws, which often had little relationship to the actual facts and usually turned out to favor the interests of the rising capitalistic class. They were criticized by the German Historical School, which emphasized the necessity of studying the evolution of economic institutions and of paying close attention to the facts of present-day economic life. An even more direct attack came from the welfare economists, led by Sismondi. Such writers held that economics should be a science of welfare rather than of wealth. Not until the latter part of the nineteenth century, when the economists made thorough use of the statistical and historical methods, were they able to make their subject truly scientific.

As is usually the case in the development of a distinct and well-demarcated science, the first steps in the growth of political science involved: (1) Concentration upon the definition of political terms; and (2) classifications of states, forms of government, and types of political institutions.

It was much the same service that was performed for the biological sciences by Linnaeus in the eighteenth century. Before institutional political history and the functional analysis of the state could proceed far in creating a science of politics it was necessary to have a uniform nomenclature and terminology and some clear understanding as to political forms and types. While it is often, and perhaps legitimately, criticized as formal and sterile, offering little insight into political processes and affording no guidance for political practice, it is possible to overlook the very real importance of this morphological stage in the development of the subject.[1] The most serious error that has arisen has been on the part of those who mistakenly regarded this preliminary stage of definition and classification as the mature perfection of political science.

While the professional political scientists were absorbed in definitions and classifications, practical statesmen made important contributions to a fuller understanding of the state and government, in particular suggesting that government is fundamentally a struggle of conflicting social and economic interests. It is the function of the state to act as umpire in this conflict and to see that justice is done. The men whose writings are most important in this respect were two Americans of the pre-Civil War period, James Madison and John C. Calhoun. Much later, sociologists emphatically supported the views of Madison and Calhoun.[2]

The first important step away from formal classification and definition that was taken by professional political scientists was a detailed description of contemporary political life. Here the first great work was Count Alexis de Tocqueville's famous study of *Democracy in America,* published exactly a century ago (1835). A half-century later appeared the equally well-known and much more exact and scientific description of American democracy by the eminent English publicist James Bryce, in his *American Commonwealth.*

Quite naturally, extensive attention was given by nineteenth-century political scientists to the question of the merits and possibilities of democracy.[3] By and large, European political scientists in the last century assailed democracy and American writers defended it. Among the most vigorous critics of democracy were J. F. Stephen, Sir Henry Sumner Maine, W. E. H. Lecky, and W. H. Mallock in England; Emile Faguet and Gustave Le Bon in France; and Heinrich von Treitschke and Friedrich Nietzsche in Germany. These critics were answered by James Russell Lowell, William Graham Sumner, Charles W. Eliot, Franklin H. Giddings, L. T. Hobhouse, and Graham Wallas.

---

[1] Among the writers most influential in forwarding work in the field should certainly be mentioned Jeremy Bentham, John Austin, J. K. Bluntschli, Robert von Mohl, J. G. Droysen, P. Laband, Georg Jellinek, Heinrich Marquardsen, Francis Lieber, Theodore Dwight Woolsey, John W. Burgess, and W. W. Willoughby.

[2] See Barnes, *Sociology and Political Theory,* Chap. vi.

[3] *Cf.* Merriam and Barnes, *History of Political Theories: Recent Times,* Chap. ii.

Democracy grew more popular and acquired more supporters as the nineteenth century drew to a close.

It was also quite inevitable that the triumph of party government in the last century should attract the attention of political science. The mode of choice of candidates for legislative offices, the methods of election, the nature and operation of the party machine, the genesis of platforms, party government in legislatures and committees, and the effect of party government on the several governmental departments are all problems that demand careful investigation and analysis. The first conspicuously successful effort to describe the formal workings of party government was achieved in Woodrow Wilson's *Congressional Government* (1885). The method was pursued further in certain sections of Bryce's *American Commonwealth,* and reached its culmination in the works of the Russian scholar Moisei Ostrogorsky.

Jurisprudence has passed through much the same stages as political science in the course of its development. The natural-law school, deriving much of its basic philosophy from Plato and the Stoics, looked upon law as the imperfect human appropriation of divine wisdom—the juristic expression of the Logos. It existed in essence prior to human society, and has been in potential form and content the same body of transcendental and normative rules, irrespective of time and place. Such differences as have existed in actual legal codes are simply expressive of the varying degrees of competence and success attained by various peoples in appropriating the legal manifestation of divine wisdom through the operation of the rational nature of man.

This metaphysical theory of law played a large part in the political and legal philosophy of the seventeenth and eighteenth centuries, and still persists in somewhat mitigated fashion in the minds and courtroom procedure of many jurists. The foremost adherents to this natural-law school of jurisprudence were such famous writers as Grotius, Pufendorf, Locke, and Vattel. As Professor Haines has done well to point out, it has enjoyed a revived popularity since late in the nineteenth century, when corporation lawyers and friendly judges apprehended its suitability to defend private property rights.

More popular among lawyers today, however, is the so-called analytical jurisprudence that took form in the writings of Hobbes, Bentham, and Austin.[1] This is concerned with the nature and content of law as the command of a determinate superior, the state. It does not normally deal with such problems as the genesis of the state and law, or with changes in the form of either. Nor does it assign any importance to those social forces which create and support law and legal administration. It rests satisfied with a consideration of what the law actually is at a given time and of the identity of the authoritative agents in its enforcement. Austin was the chief figure in this school and one of his main contributions was to divorce jurisprudence from ethics.

It is obvious that this is a practical and convenient theory of law for the judge and the attorney, and that it furnishes an admirable juristic orientation for the purely legalistic constitutional historian. It has distinguished modern theoretical exponents, among them the well-known jurist T. E. Holland. Yet

---

[1] Hearnshaw, *Social and Political Ideas of Some Representative Thinkers of the Age of Reaction and Reconstruction, 1815-1865,* Chap. VIII.

the analytical jurisprudence, whatever its advantages as a working philosophy of law, furnishes no clew to an intelligent understanding of the origins and nature of various legal codes, and no substantial suggestions as to the necessity or the methods of legal reform.

The weaknesses of the analytical school in failing thus to explore legal origins and development were overcome mainly through the efforts of the historical and comparative schools.[1] The historical school arose with such writers as Burke and Savigny, and has been developed, among others, by Sir Henry Sumner Maine, F. W. Maitland, Heinrich Brunner, J. C. Carter, and Sir Frederick Pollock. This school looks upon law as the product of the cultural forces inherent in the historical development of the nation. It is the gradually accumulated, selected, and codified wisdom of the nation. While in modern times law has come more and more to be legislative enactment and hence the literal command of the state, the nature of the legal system as a whole and the content of much contemporary legislation are determined primarily by the past history of the nation and by the peculiar institutions of any particular state that have grown out of the past.

The so-called comparative school of jurisprudence is simply an extension of the historical method in space. Its exponents contend that the "wisdom of a nation" has rarely been accumulated solely within its own borders. Cultural contacts and borrowing are as characteristic of legal as of other institutions. Hence one must study from a comparative and historical point of view the great legal systems of the world from the Code of Hammurabi to the German Imperial Code of 1900. The method was in large part suggested by the anthropologists of the comparative school in the last century, such as Lubbock, Tylor, Post, and Morgan. Perhaps its chief exponents have been Joseph Köhler and Sir Paul Vinogradoff.[2]

We have already noted how in the seventeenth and eighteenth centuries ethics, or the science of conduct, gradually tended to divorce itself somewhat from religion and to show more dependence upon science and art. This trend continued in the nineteenth century with much acceleration. Yet the orthodox body of ethical doctrine still received powerful support to the end of the last century.

The strongest impetus in this direction came, quite unintentionally, from the great German philosopher Immanuel Kant, whose doctrines we analyzed earlier in connection with the reaction against Rationalism. Kant held that one must assume a God in order to make good conduct seem rational, and he contended that we should be good for the sake of the Good alone and not because we might hope to increase our own happiness or the welfare of society thereby. Kant's doctrines were eagerly embraced by the religious groups, particularly by those inclined towards some degree of Modernism within the Protestant Church.

The other major stimulus to conventionality in ethical doctrine came from the capitalistic groups and their apologists. We have already noted how the

---

[1] F. J. C. Hearnshaw, ed., *Social and Political Ideas of Some Representative Thinkers of the Victorian Age,* Holt, 1933, Chap. IV.

[2] It is evident that no sharp line divides the historical and the comparative jurists; men like Pollock and Maitland have done real service in the field of comparative jurisprudence, while Vinogradoff has been one of the most productive contributors to historical jurisprudence.

Puritans laid great stress upon Sunday observance and the suppression of things carnal. The new capitalistic class reacted somewhat similarly in the nineteenth century. They ruthlessly exploited their laborers by working them for long hours in intolerable surroundings and for low wages. In other ways as well they had little regard for human happiness, the well-being of the masses or their own competitors, provided they could pile up large fortunes for themselves. If ethics was to include economic behavior, they recognized they would fare very badly in ethical judgments. Therefore they labored strenuously to restrict our notions of morality mainly to the realm of sex behavior, where their wealth would be able to protect them from detection with a high degree of success. It is not irrelevant to note that the chief society for the suppression of sexual immorality was founded in the late nineteenth century and was subsidized chiefly by one of the world's greatest bankers. Self-interest played its part along with self-defense. The capitalist employers thought their employees should be "good," because this was supposed to make for greater efficiency in the factory. All that goes by the name of vice demands leisure and emotional and physical resources. Whatever the laborers spend in sensation is lost for industry. The enthusiastic backing of Prohibition by great industrialists illustrates this attitude. This position and policy were powerful obstacles to the development of a broad type of social ethics during the nineteenth century.

The two most novel and progressive developments in the field of ethics were provided by the Utilitarian and Evolutionary schools. As we have seen, the Utilitarians, such as Bentham and Mill, contended that what is good is that which advances the greatest happiness of the greatest number of men. They had little regard for the hereafter, and meant by the greatest happiness our well-being here on earth. Spencer, from the Evolutionary school, held that in order to find out what is good we must examine the nature of man, physically and mentally. We must also observe the evolutionary process. Those things which contribute to bodily strength and mental growth and conform to the processes of evolution represent good forms of behavior. Whatever operates to the contrary is evil. Thomas Henry Huxley (1825-95), from the same general point of view, agreed mainly with Spencer, but held that possibly in our day mankind might control the evolutionary process in such a fashion as to make it more beneficial to humanity. The doctrines of the Utilitarian and Evolutionary schools were combined by Sir Leslie Stephen, who aspired to work out a naturalistic science of conduct as rigorous and exacting as any other branch of science.

There were, however, other interesting additions to ethical doctrine during the nineteenth century. The aspiration to make beauty and art the basis of moral judgments, which had been suggested by Lord Shaftesbury in the early eighteenth century, was revived with great force and eloquence in the nineteenth by John Ruskin and William Morris. A sociological theory of morality was suggested by Auguste Comte, who held that moral questions must be settled in the light of their relationship to social welfare and progress, with no consideration given to supernatural factors.

We pointed out how in the eighteenth century Montesquieu had contended that there is no such thing as absolute right and wrong. What is good must be decided on the basis of geographical influences and the social institutions resulting from them. Montesquieu thus founded what we know as the Comparative school of ethics. This point of view was elaborated in the nineteenth century by the students of historical and comparative jurisprudence, to whom we have just referred, and by the anthropologists and anthropogeographers.[1]

Though most historians in the nineteenth century insisted upon regarding their subject as a branch of literature rather than as a social science, this view is shared by few alert historians today. At least, we must here call attention to certain phases of the advance in historical writing in the nineteenth century. Romanticism stimulated nationalism, and the latter powerfully forwarded historical writing. This led to great nationalistic histories of Germany by such writers as Giesebrecht, Droysen, and Treitschke; of France by Michaud, Raynouard, Michelet, and Martin; of England by Kemble, Freeman, Froude, Macaulay, Napier, and Seeley; and of the United States by Bancroft and others. Patriotism also stimulated the great collections of national source material, such as the *Monumenta Germaniae historica,* the *Documents inédits,* the English *Rolls Series,* and the like. The enthusiasm for historical writing generated by nationalism reacted, in turn, to encourage more accurate historical narrative. There arose a desire to write history in exact accordance with the facts. The foremost figure in the rise of scholarly history in the nineteenth century was Leopold von Ranke (1795-1886), the eminent German historian. Historians like Mignet, Seignobos, Langlois, and others in France; Stubbs, Oman, Tout, Maitland, and their associates in England; and Osgood, G. B. Adams, Dunning, and many others in the United States—all followed the ideals of Von Ranke. Towards the end of the century, progressive historians like Karl Lamprecht became more favorably disposed to the idea of history as a social science and held that it should tell the story of human civilization as a whole.[2]

V. RELIGIOUS MOVEMENTS

The nineteenth was a century extremely important in the history of religion. There were very significant developments within the Christian Church, and this century also witnessed the rise of the first extensive attack upon supernaturalism as a whole. The earlier Rationalists, including even Voltaire and Thomas Paine, had been supernaturalists to a degree. With the exception of a few atheists, such as Baron d'Holbach, they all believed ardently in God. They merely asked that supernaturalism should also be reasonable. In the nineteenth century, many different groups of critical thinkers called for a complete rejection of all forms of supernaturalism.

The first striking development in religion in the nineteenth century was, however, a marked growth of religious fervor and pietism. There was a far wider popular enthusiasm for religion in 1850 than in 1775. There were a number of reasons for this increase of religious enthusiasm in the first half of the

[1] Notably Lewis H. Morgan, Sir John Lubbock, E. B. Tylor, Charles Letourneau, Julius Lippert, Friedrich Ratzel, and W. G. Sumner.
[2] *Cf.* Barnes, article "History: Its Rise and Development," Encyclopedia Americana, and G. P. Gooch, *History and Historians in the Nineteenth Century,* Longmans, 1913.

nineteenth century. The very attacks that had been leveled at orthodoxy by the Rationalists from Bayle to Voltaire and Thomas Paine [1] had produced a natural reaction and a swing of the pendulum to the other extreme. We have already noted how the "Christian evidences" movement got under way in the effort of Paley to combat Rationalism. The French Revolution had been in part an antireligious and especially an anti-Catholic movement in many of its policies. Therefore the political reaction after 1815 brought with it an increase in the fervor of Catholicism, especially French Catholicism.[2] The spirit of Chateaubriand was a product of this reaction. Kant and his disciples gave a new moral depth and philosophical dignity to Protestantism. Above all, the rise of evangelical sects that appealed to human emotions more than to reason helped to gain new converts and to increase the hold of religion on the masses. Methodism had taken the lead in the eighteenth century and other evangelical Protestant sects followed suit.[3] These new popular sects also gained strength among the common people because they took an active part in attacking the bad working and living conditions that followed the Industrial Revolution. Such religions also suited very well the harsh conditions of American frontier life and many new converts were gained in the United States. Pending real reforms, which did not come until the middle of the nineteenth century, Methodism offered a valuable release for the more sensitive and gentle element among the proletariat, who were hopelessly enmeshed in their earthly miseries. The Little Bethels with their congregations of weavers present a touching picture. It is easy to deride the "pie in the sky" motive, but this consolation was very real, given the conditions of the time and the type of mind involved. At least these poor unfortunates had that much sense of transcending their earthly lot.

Rationalism thus received a notable setback. It required the doctrine of evolution, biblical criticism, cultural history, anthropology, and psychology to put it back on its feet once more near the end of the nineteenth century.

Within Protestantism, the most notable development, perhaps, was its tendency to split up and develop extensive and somewhat bitter sectarianism. In the seventeenth century, for example, there had been only three or four leading branches of Protestantism, made up of those who followed Luther, Calvin, Zwingli, Knox, and some others, respectively. By the close of the nineteenth century there were literally nearly three hundred different Protestant sects, thus fulfilling the gloomy prophecy of Bishop Bossuet in the seventeenth century.

Though sectarianism may have weakened Protestantism, the latter was otherwise strengthened from a number of sources. It gained a new moral fervor as the result of the influence of Immanuel Kant and his followers, whom we have noted. Kant himself lived in the eighteenth century, but his religious influence was felt chiefly in the nineteenth. As an influence within Protestantism, he has

---

[1] *Cf.* A. W. Benn, *History of English Rationalism in the Nineteenth Century*, Longmans, 1926, 2 vols., Vol. I, Chaps. VIII-IX, Vol. II, Chap. XI; Koch, *Republican Religion*, Chap. VIII; and H. M. Morais, *Deism in Eighteenth Century America*, Columbia University Press, 1934, Chap. VI.
[2] *Cf.* James McCaffrey, *History of the Catholic Church in the Nineteenth Century*, Herder, 1909, 2 vols.
[3] See above, pp. 203 ff.; C. T. Winchester, *Life of John Wesley*, Macmillan, 1906; G. C. Cell, *The Rediscovery of John Wesley*, Holt, 1935; Herbert Asbury, *A Methodist Saint*, Knopf, 1927; and Mecklin, *The Story of American Dissent*.

probably been exceeded in power only by Martin Luther.[1] In his *Critique of Pure Reason,* Kant had demolished all arguments for the existence of God. He showed that in the phenomenal world the sense of duty is nonsense, since everything is inevitably determined by natural causes. Science gives man no justification whatever for a moral terminology. In his *Critique of Practical Reason,* however, he reversed the emphasis and held that only the assumption of God, freedom, and immortality can make moral conduct appear rational and make the categorical "ought" universally binding. Kant's religious influence was exerted mainly through the *Critique of Practical Reason,* and his chief disciples have been Schleiermacher, Harnack, Maurice, and McGiffert.

Another source of power in Protestantism in the nineteenth century was found in the rise and impressive growth of Protestant foreign missions.[2] The Catholics had carried on missionary enterprise among foreigners ever since the days of St. Paul. But the first important Protestant missionary activity was associated with the foundation of the Society for the Propagation of the Gospel in Foreign Parts in 1701, and of the Baptist Foreign Missionary Society in 1792. Other Protestant sects, in turn, founded foreign missionary societies and built up a very extensive work among the "heathen," particularly in Asia and Africa. This not only gained new converts overseas, but also stimulated the moral and religious fervor of those at home who contributed to missionary enterprise.

The remaining outstanding contribution to the strengthening of Protestantism was the rise and popularity of Methodism which we have discussed above. This was mainly the result of the work of John Wesley, George Whitefield, and Bishop Francis Asbury.[3]

It was inevitable that the Church, both Protestant and Catholic, should come into sharp conflict with the new scientific trends of the nineteenth century, especially evolutionary thought and the higher criticism of the Bible. The two latter tendencies merged in scholarly and well-unified fashion in the ninth edition of the Encyclopaedia Britannica, edited by T. S. Baynes following 1875. This great publication was the best summary of nineteenth-century Rationalism, fairly comparable to Diderot's Rationalistic *Encyclopédie,* which had appeared a century earlier.[4]

Certain of the Protestant sects, particularly the evangelical groups, rejected both evolution and the higher criticism root and branch. They clung to the literal word of the Bible and defended the special-creation doctrine and the view that the Bible had been directly and wholly inspired by God. These thoroughly devout and orthodox religionists came to be known, at the close of the century, as the Fundamentalists.[4] Some of the more liberal Protestants, particularly about this time, became inclined to accept the teachings of evolution and the findings of biblical scholarship. They made a real effort to reconcile the

---

[1] See Moore, *Outline of the History of Christian Thought since Kant,* Chaps. II-III, and A. C. McGiffert, *Rise of Modern Religious Ideas,* Macmillan, 1915.

[2] *Cf.* Robinson, *History of Christian Missions.*

[3] See Winchester, *op. cit.;* Asbury, *op. cit.;* and Hammerton, *Universal History of the World,* Chap. 158.

[4] See above, pp. 184 ff.

[5] *Cf.* S. G. Cole, *History of Fundamentalism,* Harper, 1931.

essentials of Christianity with modern science and criticism.[1] This school of Protestant religious thought came to be known as Devout Modernism. While accepting the idea that the universe, the Earth, and its inhabitants had been produced by evolutionary processes and conceding that the Bible was written by men without direct supernatural inspiration, the Devout Modernists vigorously maintained their belief in God and in the divinity of Jesus Christ.[2] This group laid special emphasis upon the importance of Jesus as a unique religious teacher and revived the old Deistic distinction between historical Christianity and the teachings of Jesus.

Nowhere within Protestantism during the nineteenth century was there any marked tendency to found a religious movement that rejected both the belief in God and the divinity of Jesus. There were two important humanistic religions, however, which did thus reject God and Jesus, but they were formed outside of conventional religious circles. The first of these was the so-called Positivism of Auguste Comte. Comte proposed a religious system that would be devoted to the worship of Humanity and in which the priests would be sociologists. It was espoused and warmly recommended by the thoughtful English historian and essayist Frederic Harrison.[3] The other outstanding humanistic cult was the Ethical Culture Society, founded in New York City in 1876 by Felix Adler, a high-minded Jewish professor of philosophy and ethics.[4] It aimed to bring together the best in the moral teachings of man from the earliest times to our own day. Recognizing the teachings of Jesus as an important contribution to our moral tradition, the movement did not ignore His ethical sayings. But it insisted upon regarding Jesus as a strictly human moral teacher. The Ethical Culture Society gained a considerable number of followers in both the United States and England, but it never became a major religious movement.

In contrast to the break-up of Protestantism into a large number of sects, the Catholic Church maintained its unity unimpaired from the time of the Counter-Reformation. This gave it a strength and coherence even out of proportion to its large number of communicants and accounts mainly for the remarkable vitality of Catholicism in our own day.

While the Roman Catholic Church maintained its formal unity, it was not wholly free from inner struggles. The first one of importance came around 1870, when a great Church Council was called at Rome.[5] It was packed with Italians and Jesuits and readily acceded to the demands of the conservative Pope and to the drive for absolutism in the Catholic Church. It was here that the famous dogma of papal infallibility was set forth, meaning that the Pope was infallible in his formal pronouncements on matters of faith and morals. In other words, there is no earthly superior to the Pope to whom an appeal may be carried in such matters. The Vatican Council of 1870 represented the essential collapse of that movement for Catholic representative government which had appeared in the great Church Councils of the fifteenth century.

[1] *Cf.* McGiffert, *op. cit.*
[2] *Cf.* A. C. Dieffenbach, *Religious Liberty,* Morrow, 1927.
[3] *The Positive Evolution of Religion,* Putnam, 1913.
[4] *Cf.* H. J. Bridges, ed., *Aspects of Ethical Religion,* American Ethical Union, 1926.
[5] *Cf.* Charles Seignobos, *Political History of Europe since 1914,* Holt, 1899, Chap. xxiii, and *Cambridge Modern History,* Vol. XI, Chap. xxv.

Liberal Catholics, particularly those outside of Italy, bitterly fought these ultramontane (referring literally to the Catholics over the mountains, namely, the Pope and his party on the other side of the Alps) and absolutistic tendencies in the Catholic Church. They called themselves the Old Catholics, and were led by Lord Acton in England, and by the great Church historian Von Döllinger in Germany. This group was, however, vastly outnumbered, and the movement it sponsored was speedily crushed.

The next struggle within the Roman Catholic Church took the form of a clash with scientific and scholarly tendencies. Theoretically, the Catholics have the better of the Protestants in reckoning with the advances in human knowledge. In theory, the Protestants are compelled to follow the literal word of the Bible, which is fixed once and for all and cannot be modified. In abstract Catholic theory, on the other hand, the Pope may reinterpret Catholic doctrine in such a fashion as to harmonize it with the findings of science and scholarship. In practice, however, the Catholic Church did not adapt its dogmas to scientific advances in the nineteenth century, whereas, as we have seen, many Protestants abandoned the literal word of the Bible and accepted much of the nineteenth-century science and scholarship.

From the beginning to the end of the century, the Catholic Church stood firmly against evolution, biblical scholarship, and other phases of the new learning that directly challenged Catholic dogmas. It did not, however, oppose science in those fields which in no way conflicted with religious interests. Therefore it freely permitted Mendel to carry on experiments with the facts of heredity as manifested by pea vines, allowed Pasteur to execute his studies on pathology and fermentation, and offered no objections to the work of Mivart in the fields of natural history and comparative anatomy. But the Catholic Church opposed with promptness and vigor those findings of scholarship which cut at the roots of Catholic doctrines. Many novel tendencies in nineteenth-century thought were denounced by Pope Pius IX in the famous papal *Syllabus of Errors* in 1864. Catholic works that were deemed in any way dangerous were placed upon the Catholic *Index of Forbidden Books*.

Towards the end of the century, a number of Catholic scholars, led by the great French biblical student Alfred Loisy, grew restive under the heavy hand of papal authority and sought to induce the Church to approve of the findings of modern scholarship.[1] They founded a Modernist movement within Catholicism, which was stamped out by a papal encyclical in 1907. Loisy was later subjected to major excommunication. Some recalcitrant Catholics have rebelled, left the Church, and conducted thereafter a violent attack upon its alleged obscurantist tendencies. Prominent among these was one of the most learned men of our age, Joseph McCabe, known to us already as the author of standard biographies of St. Augustine and Abélard.

While the religious developments of the nineteenth century took place for the most part within Catholicism and Protestantism, there were three rather important new religions that came into being in Western civilization during this period. The first was Mormonism, which was founded by Joseph Smith

---

[1] See A. F. Loisy, *My Duel with the Vatican*, Dutton, 1924.

and Brigham Young in the second quarter of the nineteenth century. The Mormons regard themselves as the religious descendants of the lost Ten Tribes of Israel, who according to Mormon tradition migrated to the United States by way of the Bering Strait. Their last survivors dictated the tenets of their religion on plates of gold, the location of which was said to have been revealed to Joseph Smith by an angel in 1823. Smith alleged that he dug up the plates near Palmyra, New York, in 1827. Smith was killed in Carthage, Illinois, after a riot (1844), but his followers were led to Utah in 1847 by his successor Brigham Young, a man of great physical force, resolution, and statecraft. Rapidly increasing their numbers both by missionary enterprise and by the practice of polygamy, the Mormons have built up a great religious and economic commonwealth in Utah and surrounding states, and they carry on a considerable missionary enterprise in Europe and other foreign lands. With certain important modifications, the Mormons accept the Jewish and Christian Bible, and the points of similarity to the Jewish and Christian faith are far more numerous than the differences.

The second major religious product of the nineteenth century was the foundation of Christian Science by Mary Baker Eddy (1821-1910). Mrs. Eddy was a nervous invalid, but withal a person of great zeal and determination. In the fall of 1862 she was treated by Dr. P. T. Quimby of Portland, Maine, one of the many mesmerists and faith-healers of that day. He was also somewhat of a metaphysician, being particularly interested in the ancient Stoics and a leading Irish thinker of early modern times, Bishop George Berkeley. He was, in addition, a Christian and a constant reader of the Bible. Mrs. Eddy's health was greatly improved as a result of her contact with Quimby, and she was profoundly interested in his ideas. Making use of them, she devoted herself for nearly twenty years to the composition of what became the Christian Science "Bible." She handed it over for final literary polishing to a Boston writer, Mr. James H. Wiggin, and it appeared in 1890 under the title *Science and Health*. It is a remarkable admixture of Christian doctrine, metaphysics, and "new thought." To the uninitiated it appears largely incomprehensible. At any rate, while there is considerable Christianity intertwined with the metaphysics, there is certainly no science there in any reasonable interpretation of the term "science."

A great "Mother Church" was constructed in Boston and the movement spread much more rapidly than did Mormonism. Not a few predicted that it would become the great American religion, but it now seems to have reached the apex of its growth. Its power to attract converts appears to have been based upon two fundamental sources of attractiveness. In the first place, by its "Father-Mother-God" symbolism, it made an emotional appeal to both sexes comparable to that of the Catholic Church. In the second place, it assumed to cure physical and mental diseases—in fact, regarded both as mainly imaginary and the product of "malicious animal magnetism." Through its power of suggestion, it probably did cure countless thousands of cases of imaginary disorders of a primarily neurotic origin. Hence the Christian Scientists have tended to appear unusually healthy, efficient, and optimistic—a trait that appeals particularly to an aggressive capitalistic civilization such as had become dominant in the United States by the close of the nineteenth century. The affinity between Christian Science and the "American dream"—frontier optimism and buoyancy—also helped on the popularity of the new religion in the United States.

The third religious innovation of wide importance in the nineteenth century was the formation of the Salvation Army by General William Booth (1829-1912). The Salvation Army has been compared by some writers to the Franciscans of the Middle Ages, with their passion for serving the poor. The quasi-military organization is more reminiscent of the Jesuits. There is some resemblance to the rise of the Methodists just a century earlier, in that both appealed at the outset especially to the poverty-stricken residents of London and England. Booth founded the Christian Mission in the London East End in 1865. He had originally been a Methodist evangelist of great persuasiveness, but he became convinced that even more sensational methods had to be adopted if the churchless masses were to be attracted. So he abandoned Methodism and established the above-mentioned mission. Aided by his wife, Catherine Booth, the ablest woman preacher of the century, he gradually developed the "army" organization and formally launched the Salvation Army in 1878. This has since grown into an international organization with headquarters in London. Its work has spread to more than sixty countries. It has nearly 10,000 posts, about 25,000 officers and nearly 30,000 brass bandsmen. The growth and organization of the Salvation Army after 1878 owed much to the energy of William's son, General Bramwell Booth. The Army makes its appeal not only through preaching but also by band music and quasi-military tactics and uniforms. Its meetings are held not only in halls, but also on the streets, in the attempt to attract the idle passers-by, stragglers, and others who have no religious affiliations.

The growth and strength of the Salvation Army have been due not only to its sensational preaching methods, but also to its relief and reform work. It early allied itself with the temperance movement and made total abstinence a condition of membership. It was thus able to do effective work in converting and reclaiming drunkards. It has also carried on much reform work in slums with prostitutes and discharged convicts. It took a leading part in bringing religious work into prisons and has helped to care for convicts upon release. Its extensive relief work with the urban poor has made it a powerful adjunct of public relief, especially in England and the United States. The Army gained added strength from the fact that it insisted from the beginning upon the absolute equality of women with men in preaching and leadership. Like Christian Science, it has made wide use of lay preachers and personal testimony. Its religious doctrine has remained of the most orthodox, emotional, and informal variety.

It was to be expected that the more aggressive scientists and others who were deeply affected by science and scholarship would attack Christianity directly. The able evolutionary philosopher Herbert Spencer contended in his *First Principles* that those ultimate issues connected with God and religion are unknowable to the human mind and hence might be ignored by man even if they could not be disproved. Spencer's friend Huxley, a much greater natural scientist, was rather more aggressive than Spencer in his assault upon religion. A brilliant debater and public speaker, he gloried in carrying his assault upon orthodoxy to the public platform, where he debated gayly with the greatest churchmen of England, as well as with the Prime Minister, W. E. Gladstone. Even more extreme in his attack upon Christianity was the eminent German biologist Ernst Haeckel.

The antireligious scientists did not lack allies in the world of practical affairs. Because the Catholic Church had opposed the Third French Republic, the leaders thereof tended to be decidedly anticlerical. Some, such as Georges Clemenceau, openly assaulted Christianity and the Church. In the opening years of the twentieth century, this French anticlericalism led to the complete separation of Church and State in France. In the United States, the antireligious forces were led by Colonel Robert G. Ingersoll, one of the foremost lawyers of his generation, a prominent Republican politician and one of the outstanding American orators of the last half of the nineteenth century. He did much to popularize evolution and biblical criticism before the vast and enthusiastic audiences who gathered to listen to him in all parts of the country. A prominent statesman and educator, President Andrew D. White of Cornell University, exercised a wide influence in behalf of free thought among the learned classes in the United States through his notable work *The History of the Warfare of Science with Theology* (1896). The Anarchist movement was based upon a frank repudiation of God as well as of the state. It maintained an attitude of bellicose atheism. Organizations such as the Rationalist Press Association started by Charles A. Watts in England were founded chiefly to publish and distribute important books and pamphlets attacking orthodox religion. Organized opposition to religion appeared in the International Freethinkers' League founded in 1880, with many national branches. Leaders of the movement were Ludwig Büchner, Ernst Haeckel, Georges Clemenceau, C. J. Holyoake, Charles Bradlaugh, Robert Ingersoll, and Lester F. Ward.

The religionists were not slow in organizing to defend themselves and in carrying the battle into the enemy's territory. To counteract the skeptical contention that there is little substantial ground for the belief in the special-creation conception, there grew up what was known as the Christian evidences movement, which we described earlier.[1] Another form of opposition to Rationalism appeared in the application of certain doctrines of Immanuel Kant, which we have mentioned in another connection in this chapter.[2]

Other movements were organized to repel disbelief. The Religious Tract Society was formed in 1799 to disseminate orthodox literature. But much more important was the so-called Tractarian Movement—generally known as the Oxford Movement—led by three young Oxford scholars,[3] Hurrell Froude, John Keble, and John Henry Newman. These scholars published between 1832 and 1838 a collection of very effective orthodox pamphlets called *Tracts for the Times*. They defended the faith with vigor and denounced the doctrines of skeptical science. In due time Newman found Protestantism, even of the most

---

[1] See above, pp. 201 ff.; Benn, *op. cit.*, Vol. I, Chap. VIII; and John Hunt, *Religious Thought in England in the Nineteenth Century*, London, 1896.
[2] See also above, pp. 670, 674.
[3] See R. W. Church, *The Oxford Movement, 1883-1845*, Macmillan, 1892, and Peck, *The Social Implications of the Oxford Movement*.

devout character, quite inadequate. He joined the Roman Catholic Church and in this organization he was ultimately elevated to the rank of Cardinal. Associated with the Tractarians was Henry Edward Manning, who also became a Catholic Cardinal.

The Christian churches also increased their popularity in the nineteenth century by entering directly into social reform and gaining the gratitude of the masses. We have already called attention to the Christian Socialism of Protestants such as Kingsley and Maurice in England and of Catholics like Buchez in France.[1] The evangelical Protestants, in particular, led in the attack upon the evils of the new factory system and of Negro slavery in the English colonies. The Society of Friends (Quakers) took a leading part in prison reform in the early nineteenth century. They were responsible for the famous Pennsylvania system of prison discipline.[2] The other outstanding figure in prison reform in the early nineteenth century was a devout American clergyman, Louis Dwight, who gained his first desire to labor for prison reform as a result of his work in distributing Bibles to prisoners. He was chiefly responsible for the spread of the Auburn prison system, the great rival of the Pennsylvania system. By and large, evangelical Protestantism was also strongly behind the democratic movement of the nineteenth century.[3] Catholicism, as well, came out for economic democracy under Pope Leo XIII.[4] In his famous encyclical, *Rerum novarum* (1891), he put the Catholic Church behind moderate labor-unionism and social justice. In Germany, Bishop von Ketteler powerfully espoused reform doctrines, while in the United States Cardinal Gibbons, with great courage for the time, defended the Knights of Labor and the right of labor to organize freely and unhampered.

VI. MAJOR TRENDS IN PHILOSOPHY

In an earlier chapter we dealt with that revolt against Rationalism which appeared in the form of Romanticism and Idealism in philosophy, particularly as expressed in the writings of leading German metaphysicians and theologians between 1750 and 1850. These men had dealt in sweeping and assured fashion with Absolutes. They had attempted to bring about a satisfactory reconciliation between Reason and Revelation and to place belief in God upon the solid foundations of epistemology and dialectic. They had many followers throughout the nineteenth century, especially in England and Scotland. Among their foremost British disciples were Thomas H. Green, F. H. Bradley,[5] and Bernard Bosanquet. In the United States modified Hegelianism was expounded by the famous Harvard philosopher Josiah Royce. With some variations, this absolutistic Idealism was later revived and defended in Germany by the influential philosopher Rudolf Eucken. It has been very popular with Devout Modernists.

Even the Idealists were, however, compelled to take account of scientific discoveries and to reason away any challenge that seemed to be embodied in sci-

---

[1] See above, pp. 389 ff.
[2] *Cf.* Barnes, *The Evolution of Penology in Pennsylvania*.
[3] *Cf.* Faulkner, *Chartism and the Churches;* North, *Early Methodist Philanthropy;* and Warner, *The Wesleyan Movement in the Industrial Revolution*.
[4] *Cf.* F. S. Nitti, *Catholic Socialism*, Macmillan, 1895. See also below, pp. 945 ff.
[5] Bradley's religious views were rather heretical.

entific procedure. Representative of this type of thought were the writings of Rudolf Hermann Lotze (1817-81), who attempted to reconcile the new mechanistic conceptions with the dogmas of Romanticism and Idealism. He conceded that cause-and-effect relationships prevail in the field of mechanical nature and suffice to explain the problems dealt with by scientists. But beyond and superior to the physical world lies the World of Value. This is characterized by a spiritual unity which is absent in the realm of purely material phenomena.

Lotze's basic conclusions had been philosophically optimistic. Those of Arthur Schopenhauer (1788-1860) were decidedly pessimistic. Schopenhauer held that natural science can only investigate and explain the realm of external phenomena—the World as Idea. Intuition alone enables us to get at the final realities. When we follow intuition we discover that the ultimate reality is Will. This absolute Will is, however, irrational, and from this conclusion we must deduce an inescapable and all-pervading pessimism. Human desires outrun human satisfactions both in number and in duration. The worst possible evil that can befall one is to be born. It is utterly futile to strive for happiness. We can only hope for some sustaining satisfaction through sympathizing with others over our mutual misery and hopelessness.

The outstanding advances in nineteenth-century philosophy, however, were those which embodied an effort to assimilate the discoveries and attitudes of science. The first important philosopher to build a system of philosophy upon the basis of scientific assumptions was Auguste Comte, whom we have discussed earlier.[1]

The able English philosopher John Stuart Mill was deeply affected by Comte in his earlier thinking, but his contribution to philosophy differed widely from Comte's voluminous and loosely reasoned writings. Mill aimed primarily to complete Francis Bacon's attack upon Aristotle and Scholasticism. He sought to provide the complete intellectual basis for a new type of scientific philosophy through working out a satisfactory inductive and experimental logic. This appeared in his famous *System of Logic* (1843), probably the most impressive and influential contribution made by any Englishman in the nineteenth century to the philosophical foundations of the scientific method.

The most extended exemplification of the conquest of philosophy by scientific concepts was embodied in the writings of Herbert Spencer, whom we have previously commented on in various connections. The essential points in his philosophy were expressed in a little book entitled *First Principles*.[2] Spencer's views were still further developed and popularized by the American writer John Fiske in his widely read *Outlines of Cosmic Philosophy* (1874).[3]

Some of the philosophical scientists were not willing to concede any such dualism as the unknowable and knowable worlds postulated by Spencer. They demanded the obliteration of the very notion of an unknowable world of ultimate reality closed to the ken of the scientist. They insisted upon a purely materialistic unity—a physical monism that denied completely the validity of the epistemology of Kant and the Idealistic philosophers. This type of reason-

[1] See above, p. 666.
[2] See above, p. 656.
[3] See Riley, *op. cit.*, Chap. VII.

ing represented the most extreme form of the influence of science on nineteenth-century philosophy and was perhaps most effectively set forth in Ernst Haeckel's *The Riddle of the Universe* (1899) and *Monism* (1906). This Monistic point of view was critically analyzed by Wilhelm Ostwald, a Neo-Kantian (1853-1932), and the empiricist Ernst Mach (1838-1916). Both Ostwald and Mach were skeptical of a crude materialism.

American philosophers made important contributions to this adjustment between scientific attitudes and philosophical formulations. The most important of these were Charles S. Peirce (1839-1914), William James (1842-1910), and John Dewey (1859-   ). Peirce doubted the absolute character of scientific laws and suggested that our main criterion of truth is experience as tested by experimentation. James was not only well read in science but was also the foremost American psychologist of the nineteenth century.[1] Hence he was the first important philosopher who approached the problems of knowledge well equipped with a store of passable information about the thinking machinery of man. He held that human thought is primarily a tool for action, thus suggesting what has come to be known in Dewey's hands as the doctrine of Instrumentalism in philosophy. Recognizing that the human mind could not fathom ultimates and arrive at absolute assurance of accuracy or error, he accepted a practical test known as Pragmatism, already suggested by Charles Peirce.[2] This, in a general way, means that the test of the accuracy of an idea or process is whether or not it seems to work out in human experience. James also rejected any effort to achieve either a spiritual or a materialistic unity. He abandoned Monism in favor of what he called Pluralism, roughly resembling in more developed form Montaigne's "hunch" that diversity is the rule of nature.

John Dewey was much affected by James's thought and approved his Pragmatism and Pluralism, but he differed from James in approaching philosophy from the logical and social point of view, whereas James's interests had been religious, ethical, and individualistic. Dewey went far beyond James in developing the notion of Instrumentalism, which he made the real foundation of his philosophical system. He possesses much more social consciousness than James and aims to put his philosophy to work for human betterment in the political and social field. He is a staunch supporter of democracy and became the most potent influence upon American education in the first quarter of the twentieth century. Dewey is also notable for his enthusiastic espousal of Darwinism in philosophy. Down to his day evolution had made its way into philosophy chiefly through the medium of Spencerianism. We shall have more to say about Dewey in other connections.[3]

The most ambitious effort to reconcile the old quasi-religious Idealism and the new scientific notions is contained in the philosophy of the Frenchman Henri Bergson (1859-   ).[4] While having respect for science, he falls back upon

---

[1] See C. H. Grattan, *The Three Jameses*, Longmans, 1932.

[2] See Riley, *op. cit.*, Chap. IX; and H. O. Rugg, *Culture and Education in America*, Harcourt, Brace, 1931, pp. 99-116. For an excellent introductory statement of the genesis and underlying notions of Pragmatism, see the article "Pragmatism," by H. M. Kallen, Encyclopaedia of the Social Sciences.

[3] See below, pp. 1067-68.

[4] See Riley, *op. cit.*, Chap. XI.

Kant's contention that science can never fathom ultimate reality. Yet a knowledge of the knowable world studied by science is necessary for our convenience and for the guidance of our conduct. The guide to an understanding of reality must be found in intuition, which Bergson believes to be far more powerful and profound than scientific reasoning. But intuition, to Bergson, is something more refined and precise than it was to Schopenhauer. It must reckon with the rules and findings of science as a starting-point and will, in time, come to be recognized as the highest form of science and empirical reasoning. Bergson, incidentally, wandered off into mystical flights in his conception of a so-called vitalistic Monism, and in his dogma of personal immortality, based upon the grotesque assumption that the consciousness of man is a continuous heritage from the past and must continue after the death of the individual.

The philosophical doctrines of Friedrich Nietzsche (1844-1900) do not fall within any of the major schools of nineteenth-century philosophy. We shall discuss later his pronounced anti-Christian views, his worship of the superman, and his contention that there is one morality for the strong and quite a different morality for the weak.[1] In his approval of the ruthless triumph of the strong over the weak, Nietzsche has been regarded by some as espousing a perverted form of Darwinism, but he did not accept evolution in either the Spencerian or the Darwinian form. Rather, he combined it with the ancient notion of recurring cycles of cultural development. In each cycle we go through an evolutionary process, but in due time we return to the same starting-point. In this respect there is a resemblance between his philosophy and that of Oswald Spengler, which became very popular after the World War.[2]

VII. EDUCATIONAL PROGRESS

The progress in education in the nineteenth century was very extensive and diversified. Among the outstanding features of educational development were the secularization of teaching and the popularization of education. Down to this time education had been in considerable part in the hands of the Church, and the religious content of education had been very prominent. The Protestant Revolution had weakened the power of the Catholic Church in education in Protestant lands and Protestantism tended to encourage state control of education. But even in Protestant lands ecclesiastical forces were prominent in education until the nineteenth century. In this century the state took an ever more active part in education and education became slightly more concerned with economic and political life, as well as with secular literature and art.

The declining influence of the Church in education was logically paralleled by the increasing prominence of the State and public authorities in educational enterprise. During the nineteenth century there was a marked movement for free, universal, and compulsory education. This was stimulated by the growth of democracy,[3] but even monarchical states participated in the promotion of

[1] See below, p. 704.
[2] In his latest work, Spengler also adopts Nietzsche's view of the superman. See his *Hour of Decision*, Knopf, 1934.
[3] See Hansen, *Liberalism and American Education in the Eighteenth Century*.

public education. In fact, the first move towards public education was that taken by the benevolent despot Frederick and Great, in 1763. By a decree of that year he took the initial step in establishing a public school system and in making attendance compulsory. It required thirty years to execute this plan because of opposition from the clergy and other conservative forces. A law of 1794 conclusively set up compulsory education in Prussia, and in 1811 the school system was put under direction of the learned scholar Alexander von Humboldt. The public school system of Prussia was expanded and strengthened by subsequent legislation, particularly laws of 1825, 1854, and 1872.

The French Revolutionists at the close of the eighteenth century possessed great enthusiasm for public education, and they started an excellent school system, later distorted by Napoleon. A national Normal School and a number of secondary schools were, however, established in 1794, and the University of France was brought into being in 1806 to control public education in France. Public elementary education began in France in 1833 as a result of the support that the movement received from the eminent historian Guizot, who was then Minister of Public Instruction. The Third Republic was especially favorable to public education, and free compulsory primary education was provided for in 1881-82. A thoroughgoing centralization of French public education was brought about in the law of 1886.[1] From this time on, public schools rapidly superseded Church schools in France, and early in the twentieth century the majority of the French Church schools were closed down by hostile legislation.

During the nineteenth century little was achieved in England in the way of establishing a real system of free public schools.[2] Not until 1833 did the government assume to interfere at all with education. Beginning in that year, the government began to make grants for educational purposes to Church and other private educational foundations. This policy was generally pursued with increasing liberality during the rest of the century. The first elementary schools were provided for in the Education Act of 1870, but they were long far outnumbered by the private schools that enjoyed state aid. Compulsory education was introduced by an act of 1876. Not until 1918, however, was a thoroughly adequate public school system set up in England.

In the United States Thomas Jefferson had advocated public education, but it made little headway until the era of Andrew Jackson, following 1828. The most important figures in the struggle for free public education in the United States were Horace Mann (1796-1859) and Henry Barnard (1811-1900). The first law providing for free public education was passed in Pennsylvania in 1834. In the half-century following this date free and compulsory public education was established in the great majority of the American states. Education thus ceased to be a privilege of the few and became the right of every child, however humble his economic circumstances. Most enlightened states also logically aided the movement for public education by laws restricting the working-hours of children in industry.

In Catholic countries the Church still exerts a dominant control over all but higher education, wisely deciding that this is the surest way to maintain the

[1] Jules Ferry was the most influential figure in reconstructing French education at this period.
[2] See Slater, *The Growth of Modern England*, Chap. XIII, and F. S. Marvin, *The Century of Hope*, Oxford Press, 1919, Chap. VIII.

faithfulness of the flock. Even in Protestant countries like the United States where full religious freedom exists, there are numerous parochial schools.

Another important educational innovation of the nineteenth century was the establishment of a well-differentiated and thoroughly graduated school system covering the entire educational evolution of the individual. The kindergarten was created for the preschool child. Then the child passed into elementary schools. From here he went to a grammar school, and then to a secondary or high school. If he was fortunate, he might proceed to a college, where he could obtain a Bachelor of Arts degree based on a so-called liberal education. Towards the end of the nineteenth century graduate schools were created in great universities, where young scholars might advance from college work to specialized studies under experts.[1] This development of graduate schools first became notable in Germany early in the nineteenth century and was introduced from Germany into other countries, especially the United States. Indeed, in Germany there is nothing strictly corresponding to our American colleges. Advanced high-school education and collegiate education are merged in Germany in the Gymnasium. Higher education was also gradually opened to women.[2]

With the increasing importance of public education, a greater need arose for professionally trained teachers. To meet this new demand, schools were created to educate teachers. At first they were somewhat superficial "normal" schools with relatively short terms of instruction. But in due time respectable teachers' colleges were created, which provided thoroughgoing instruction in the theories and methods of education.

Until well along towards the end of the nineteenth century the elementary and grammar schools were chiefly devoted to instruction in rudimentary subjects such as reading, writing, arithmetic, and grammar. But in the secondary schools, and especially in the colleges and universities, the curriculum was very considerably modified during the century. In the year 1800 the curriculum in the institutions of higher learning reflected primarily the influence of medievalism and Humanism. That is, instruction was chiefly limited to grammar, rhetoric, logic, Greek and Latin literature, and mathematics. The attacks on religion in the latter part of the eighteenth century had also stimulated the creation of courses in "Christian evidences," the character of which we have already described.

The first important novelty in curriculum changes in the nineteenth century consisted in instruction in vernacular languages and literature. Next came a very gradual introduction of courses in natural science, often established as accessory to departments of mathematics. Germany took the lead in making a place for natural science, while English colleges and universities were the most stubborn in resisting this new trend in education. Latest of all came tolerance of instruction in history and the social sciences, such as economics, politics, sociology, anthropology, and ethics. While respectable courses in these latter subjects had been established in Germany by the time of the American Civil War and had gained some headway in France during this same period, they were accorded little place in English or American higher education until the closing decades of the nineteenth century. Indeed, there was never a course

---
[1] Some were hangovers from medieval graduate schools.
[2] *Cf.* L. S. Boas, *Woman's Education Begins,* Wheaton College Press, 1935.

offered in sociology in an English college or university until the first decade of the twentieth century.

In spite of such concessions to new studies, the older and more respectable subjects that had come down from the Middle Ages and the Renaissance were given a very distinct advantage in the curriculum. Greater importance was attributed to them and students were required to devote to them most of their time. Little opportunity remained to take work in natural or social science, even if such courses were taught in the institution. Though Thomas Jefferson had favored such a system at the University of Virginia, it was not until 1869 that the so-called elective system, giving the student some freedom of choice in courses, was first introduced at Harvard University by President Charles W. Eliot, in the face of severe and even malicious criticism. But even under the elective system large doses of the traditional subjects were required in order to obtain the degree of Bachelor of Arts. Hence, in spite of these evidences of a growing discontent with the old system of education and with traditional subjects, at the close of the nineteenth century higher education still had little relation to preparation for everyday life. Nobody has made this more clear than Huxley, who once delivered the following stinging indictment of English higher education:

Now let us pause to consider this wonderful state of affairs; for the time will come when Englishmen will quote it as the stock example of the stolid stupidity of their ancestors in the nineteenth century. The most thoroughly commercial people, the greatest voluntary wanderers and colonists the world has ever seen, are precisely the middle classes of this country. If there be a people which has been busy making history on the great scale for the last three hundred years,—and the most profoundly interesting history,—history which, if it happened to be that of Greece or Rome, we should study with avidity—it is the English. If there be a people which, during the same period, has developed a remarkable literature, it is our own.

If there be a nation whose prosperity depends absolutely and wholly upon their mastery over the forces of nature, upon their intelligent apprehension of and obedience to, the laws of creation, and distribution of wealth, and of the stable equilibrium of the forces of society, it is precisely this nation. And yet this is what these wonderful people tell their sons: "At the cost of from one to two thousand pounds of our hard-earned money, we devote twelve of the most precious years of your lives to school. There you shall toil, or be supposed to toil; but there you shall not learn one single thing of all those you will most want to know directly you leave school and enter upon the practical business life. You will in all probability go into business, but you shall not know where, or how, any article of commerce is produced, or the difference between an export and an import, or the meaning of the word 'capital.' You will very likely settle in a colony, but you shall not know whether Tasmania is part of New South Wales, or *vice versa*. . . . Very probably you may become a manufacturer, but you shall not be provided with the means of understanding the working of one of your own steam engines, or the nature of the raw products you employ; and, when you are asked to buy a patent, you shall not have the slightest means of judging whether the inventor is an impostor who is contravening the elementary principles of science or a man who will make you as rich as Croesus. You will very likely get into the House of Commons. You will have to take your share in making laws which may prove a blessing or a curse to millions of men. But you shall not hear one word respecting the political organization of your country; the meaning of the controversy between free traders and protectionists shall never have been mentioned to you; you shall not so much as know that there are such things as economical laws. The mental power which will be of most importance in your daily life will be the power of seeing things as they are without regard to authority; and of drawing accurate general conclusions from particular facts. But at school and at college you shall know of no source of truth but authority; nor exercise your reasoning faculty upon anything but deduction from that which is laid down by authority. You will have to weary your soul with work, and many a time eat your bread in sorrow and in bitterness, and you shall not have learned to take refuge in the great source of pleasure without alloy, the serene resting place for worn human nature,—the world of art. Said I not rightly that we are a wonderful people? I am quite prepared to allow that education entirely devoted to these omitted subjects might not be a completely liberal education. But is an education which ignores them all a liberal education? Nay, is it too much to say that the education which should embrace these [neglected] subjects and no others would be a real education, though an incomplete one; while an education which omits them is really not an education at all, but a more or less useful course of intellectual gymnastics? [1]

Throughout the nineteenth century there was much talk about the so-called liberal education that was provided by the higher learning of the times. But the word "liberal" as thus used in no way meant progressive, free, or flexible education. It had reference to an education in the seven liberal arts of ancient derivation, to which were added classical languages and higher mathematics. A liberal education in this sense was then and still remains the very negation of liberalism as the term is logically to be understood.[2]

The nineteenth century was also notable for the establishment and promotion of various types of professional schools to provide training in law, medicine, engineering, the fine arts, and so on. Of course, there had been schools of theology, law, medicine, and clerical work in the Middle Ages, and in many areas they had been continued down to modern times. In the nineteenth century they became more numerous, better equipped, and more adequate. The growing importance of applied science and machinery led to a decisive need for efficient technical education. The earliest engineering instruction was given mainly in military schools and was a phase of army engineering. Military academies providing for some engineering training were established in Vienna in 1747, at Mézières in France in 1749, at Berlin in 1764, and at West Point in 1802. The first nonmilitary engineering school was established in Brunswick, Germany, in 1745, and another was opened in Freiburg in 1765. In the nineteenth century many civilian engineering schools were established, and by the end of the century they were fairly numerous and highly efficient. The first general engineering school devoted solely to civilian engineering was the Rensselaer Polytechnic Institute, opened in 1824 at Troy, New York. A number of specialized schools devoted to training in the fine arts appeared during the century. The first and most famous was the Ecole des Beaux Arts, opened in Paris in 1793. We have already called attention to the development of institutions for training teachers.

[1] Cited in Paul Monroe, *Text-book in the History of Education*, Macmillan, 1916, pp. 690-91.
[2] *Cf.* E. D. Martin, *The Meaning of a Liberal Education*, Norton, 1926.

The sweeping industrialization of modern society led to intensive economic rivalry between competing states. Therefore alert countries quickly saw the value of giving additional training that would produce more efficient workers.[1] Hence we find in the nineteenth century the first extensive emphasis placed upon industrial education. Practical instruction in manual training, needlework, cooking, agriculture, horticulture, and commercial transactions has been promoted by both public and private agencies. Night schools have been established to make these advantages available to those who work during the day. Continuation schools have been set up to allow students to supplement their academic education by work in the various practical trades.

Natural science, which exerted so tremendous an influence upon nineteenth-century religion, also widely affected education in this period. The doctrine of evolution was carried over from biology to psychology and pedagogy. It was shown that the human race had undergone mental as well as physical evolution. It was proved that we have mental as well as physical affinities with other animals. Especially important was the apprehension of the fact that an individual may pass through a sweeping experience of mental evolution from the immature and blank mentality of the newborn infant to the fully developed and well-stocked mind of the competent adult. This led to the placing of great emphasis upon the study of the mind of the child and upon the recognition of certain alleged parallelisms between the evolution of the mind of the race and the mental evolution of the individual (genetic psychology). The man who was chiefly responsible for linking evolutionary biology with psychology and educational practice was an American scholar, G. Stanley Hall, whom we have already commented on in this chapter in connection with the development of psychology in the nineteenth century.[2]

An important phase of the impact of science upon education was the increasing emphasis put upon scientific subjects in the curriculum. Though science made slow headway against the bitter and stubborn resistance of the old, established humanities, by the end of the nineteenth century scientific subjects had been pretty thoroughly installed in all reputable centers of the higher learning. Interestingly enough, scientific instruction in colleges and universities first appeared in the United States. This was probably due to the fact that in a new country the vested educational interests had less of a strangle hold upon the educational system. As early as 1642 Harvard University offered instruction in astronomy and botany, and in 1690 in physics. Very liberal concessions were made to natural science in Columbia University (King's College) in 1755, and in the University of Pennsylvania in 1756. The Normal School that had been established in Paris in 1794 provided some instruction in mathematics and physics. It was not until 1825 that a scientific (chemical) laboratory was opened in a German university—that of Professor Justus von Liebig at the University of Giessen. Courses in science were not established at Oxford or Cambridge until 1869, though scientific instruction was given in technical schools founded in England in the middle of the century. The United States enjoyed the same

[1] See F. W. Roman, *The Industrial and Commercial Schools of the United States and Germany*, Putnam, 1915.
[2] *Cf.* G. E. Partridge, *The Genetic Philosophy of Education*, Macmillan, 1912.

priority in the introduction of science into the secondary schools. Scientific subjects were taught in many academies of the American colonies by the time of the American Revolution. Science came into German secondary education in 1816. Science entered English secondary schools before it was able to get a footing in either Oxford or Cambridge. Elementary scientific subjects were gradually introduced into the English secondary schools after 1835. In no country, however, did natural science rank with the older disciplinary and literary items in the curriculum of either higher or secondary education in the year 1900.

Important advances were made in educational theory in this century. In a preceding chapter we referred to the important pedagogical development associated with the names of Rousseau, Herbart, and Pestalozzi. Their work was carried along with important modifications by Friedrich Froebel (1782-1852), mentioned in an earlier chapter as especially influenced by Pestalozzi.[1] The great pedagogical revolution that we associate with Froebel was his insistence that the child rather than the teacher must constitute the starting-point of all sound educational theory and practice, thus reversing the point of view of Herbart. Froebel believed that successful education consists in a shrewd, intelligent, and tolerant guidance of the spontaneous tendencies of the child. This was much in line with the basic doctrine of Rousseau. Quite logically, Froebel placed much emphasis upon emotional as well as intellectual elements in education. He looked upon the educational process as successfully directed self-activity. He established the first kindergarten and organized the first experimental school. No other man was so influential in assaulting the older type of disciplinary education of a cut-and-dried character. Froebel translated Rousseau's vague aspirations into formal educational theory and practice. His work was powerfully supplemented by the rise of biological science and reliable child psychology, which gave us a more exact and thorough knowledge of the actual character of the child personality. Especially important here was the genetic psychology and child study promoted by G. Stanley Hall and his disciples.

Another outstanding influence upon educational theory was that derived from the sociology which appeared in the work of Comte, Spencer, Lester F. Ward, F. H. Giddings, and others.[2] As we have seen, they laid great stress upon the social basis of human life and upon the way in which group life creates our ideas, customs, and institutions. Logically, they looked upon education as the only available means of attaining rational social control. They also viewed it as the medium through which our social traditions might be criticized, sorted, and transmitted. Finally, Ward and his followers believed that education would enable man artificially to control the course of social evolution and to build a better and happier world for man to dwell in. In this way sociology, while not ignoring the individual teacher or pupil, laid the necessary emphasis upon the social basis of the life of both teacher and student.

The democratic movement in the nineteenth century contributed its quota to educational theory.[3] Horace Mann was the most important early figure in

---

[1] See above, pp. 243 ff.
[2] *Cf.* E. P. Kimball, *Sociology and Education*, Columbia University Press, 1932.
[3] *Cf.* Hansen, *op. cit.;* C. R. Fish, *The Rise of the Common Man, 1830-1850*, Macmillan, 1927, Chap. x; and M. E. Curti, *The Social Ideas of American Educators*, Scribner, 1935.

linking democracy with educational doctrine. It was held that the apparent differences in ability and success were due primarily to differences in opportunity. If all were given a chance to secure a proper education, then all would show ability and would achieve relatively uniform success. Education seemed the logical avenue to the speedy attainment of Utopia. While much of this optimism has been subsequently abandoned, the democratic movement in education had a vast influence upon the provision of free public instruction from elementary schools to the college and university. In the twentieth century, democratic ideals were linked with scientific psychology and pedagogy by John Dewey and his associates.

These are only the more notable aspects of educational progress in the nineteenth century. Archaic tradition, pompous pedantry, specious "good taste," and solemn formalism were all too powerful even in the year 1900. But the developments in the preceding century had made a decisive breach with the past, and education was started on its way towards becoming a technique for the more rational and successful control of human life.

VIII. LITERATURE

1. CULTURAL FORCES IN NINETEENTH-CENTURY LITERATURE

Literature was profoundly affected by the intellectual, cultural, and institutional forces of the nineteenth century that we have already described. Romanticism, with its sentimentality, its deep emotional fervor, and its intense patriotism, challenged the classicism that had come down from the period of Humanism. It attached greater respect to national themes and vernacular literature and made possible a more richly emotional type of literary expression. Romanticism powerfully supported nationalism, and the latter promoted a patriotic literature glorifying various phases of the achievements of a particular country, especially as it magnified the heroes and deeds of the national past.[1] Nineteenth-century industrialism, the most striking aspect of the era, inevitably affected literature in many ways. The rise of industry became an epic, and this led to the widespread eulogy of business men and their success. Writers more thoughtful, however, were not so much impressed by the glories of modern capitalism as they were by the vulgarization and suffering that it often left in its wake. Therefore they wrote of the downtrodden working classes and the inadequate lives they were forced to lead as a result of bad working-conditions and insufficient incomes.[2] Modern capitalism also produced a large leisure class with ample time and money to read books, one that desired pure entertainment rather than a social message conveyed by literature. To meet this demand many works appeared in the tradition of belles-lettres—of stylistic purity and beauty rather than of any social import.

The individualistic sentiment, so successful in many quarters in the nineteenth century, rendered very popular the theme of the poor boy who made good in spite of handicaps and initial adversity. The appearance of three major social classes—agrarian aristocracy, bourgeois plutocracy, and proletariat

---

[1] See above, pp. 194 ff., 453 ff.   [2] See above, pp. 289 ff.

(urban and rural)—reacted upon the point of view and interests of writers. Democratic literature attacked the old aristocratic ideal that the upper level of human society is reserved for the rich and the gentle born. The extensive development of foreign travel and the dramatic adventures of explorers stimulated many contributions to the literature of adventure, maritime events, and the description of oversea life.[1] The numerous and bloody wars of the century afforded plenty of subject matter for writers eager to exploit the perennially popular themes of glory and death in the service of one's country. Natural science was not without its effect upon literature. The remarkable discoveries of science were frequently portrayed in literary masterpieces, and Utopias were written depicting the sweeping transformations that we might expect science to effect in human life. Science also enabled writers to get a more comprehensive and more exact knowledge of man and nature.

While the nineteenth century was a relatively self-satisfied and optimistic era of human development in Europe and the United States, there were many who predicted the doom of capitalism and envisaged the dawn of a better day to come. This gave us a considerable body of literature devoted to the theme of social change and revolution.

We may now turn to an examination of the way in which these various themes and trends expressed themselves in some of the more characteristic literary products of the major countries of the West. While it is impossible to divide the literary history of the West during the nineteenth century into precise chronological periods, it is roughly true that literary history in this era began with Romanticism and passed through Realism and Naturalism to social criticism. But any such chronological classification would need to provide for special tendencies—such as Symbolism—which fit into none of these categories.

Romanticism in literature differed from Romanticism in philosophy in one important particular. Literary Romanticism was inspired by the French Revolution and the zest for freedom, while philosophical Romanticism was usually reactionary. But the two united in stimulating spontaneity in expression and in opposing classicism. Realism was distinguished by factual precision and great thoroughness in the description of personal and social situations. When combined with a penchant for the physical, carnal, and sensuous, it evolved into Naturalism. Towards the end of the century, the increasing conflict of social classes promoted greater interest in social and economic problems.

2. ENGLAND

The Romanticist school in English literature dominated the period from the French Revolution to the reign of Queen Victoria. There were important contributions to both poetry and prose, but the poets were more numerous and more distinguished. While there were considerable differences in mood, manner, and style between the various English Romanticist poets, they were as a group characterized by rebellion against convention and tradition, enthusiasm for change, real appreciation of nature, and deep emotional fervor.

---

[1] See above, pp. 244 ff., 572 ff.

Among the outstanding English Romanticist poets were Percy Bysshe Shelley (1792-1822), George Noel Gordon, Lord Byron (1788-1824), John Keats (1795-1821), Samuel Taylor Coleridge (1772-1834), and William Wordsworth (1770-1850). Readers will differ in appraising the works of these brilliant poets, but Shelley's "Prometheus Unbound"; Byron's "Childe Harold" and "Don Juan"; Keats's "Hyperion" and "The Eve of St. Agnes"; Coleridge's "Rime of the Ancient Mariner"; and Wordsworth's "Tintern Abbey" and "Intimations of Immortality"—all these are certainly representative and brilliant ornaments of the English Romanticist movement in poetry. Other poets of this age worthy of mention were William Cowper, George Crabbe, William Blake, and Robert Southey. Shelley excelled in his revolutionary enthusiasm and burning high-mindedness, Byron in his satire and capacity to portray human passion, especially the extremes of love and hate, Keats in the sensuous and harmonious beauty of his expression, Coleridge in his ability to evoke the moods of magic and strangeness, and Wordsworth in the nobility of his perceptions of the transcendental union of man and nature.

Prose during the Romanticist period was represented, among others, by the novelists Sir Walter Scott (1771-1832) and Jane Austen (1775-1817), and by the essayists, William Hazlitt (1778-1830), Charles Lamb (1775-1834), and Thomas De Quincey (1785-1859). Jane Austen wrote with a quiet but most penetrating understanding of the ironies and foibles of the upper middle class and the aristocracy of her day that has made her work an enduring source of delight to no small body of readers. While himself a popular poet, Scott is better known for his historical fiction. He represented admirably the Romanticist sentimentality as to the Middle Ages. His extended and popular series of *Waverley Novels* deal with subjects and themes running all the way from medieval Scotland and the Crusades to the modern history of Scotland, England, France, and the South. Whatever the period covered, however, his emphasis and "values" are colored by the "stucco medievalism" that he drew from the Romanticist inspiration. Perhaps the most popular of his novels are *The Bride of Lammermoor, Ivanhoe, The Talisman,* and *Quentin Durward*.

William Hazlitt was the foremost English literary critic of the pre-Victorian period. He was deeply influenced by the German Romanticist writers, especially Schlegel, and sought to provoke emotional response on the part of his readers for any subject with which he chose to deal. In *The Spirit of the Age* he offered his opinions on his leading literary contemporaries, and his judgment still commands the respect of students of English literature. He is regarded by many as among the foremost prose stylists in the language. Charles Lamb was handicapped by poverty, the necessity of grinding clerical labor, and serious mental illness, but his work establishes him in the opinion of most as the greatest master of the personal essay in English literature. He was inimitably and unpredictably droll, capricious, incisive, and sentimental. No writer was ever more himself; and while par excellence an individualist, he exhibited a deep humanitarian interest in the abuses of his time, well exemplified in his essay "The Praise of Chimney-Sweepers." His humor is perhaps best shown in the famous "Dissertation upon Roast Pig," and the delicacy of his effects is particularly evident in "Old China." Thomas De Quincey was probably, next to Coleridge, the most learned of this group of English essayists. Born to wealth, he was a strange combination of waywardness and a zeal for erudition, especially in the field of language. He is best known for his *Confessions of an English Opium-Eater,* which describes his experiences as a drug addict. He was a supreme master of a rhapsodic prose style that is well illustrated by such essays as "The English Mail Coach."

The Victorian period in English literature, covering approximately three-quarters of a century, is so long that it cannot be characterized by identification with any single school, interest, or attitude.[1] It began in Romanticism and ended in the devastating criticism and the striking new tendencies of the early twentieth century—it ran the whole range from Scott to Shaw. But the true Victorian age, which fell approximately between 1850 and 1890, was characterized by serious moral purpose, with relatively little tolerance for frivolity, the deeper passions of mankind, or art for art's sake alone.

The most notable poets of the true Victorian age were Alfred, Lord Tennyson (1809-92), Robert Browning (1812-89), Matthew Arnold (1822-88), and Rudyard Kipling (1865-   ). Tennyson was most notable for his supreme mastery of the technique of poetic expression, though his great poem "In Memoriam" also well illustrated the philosophical trends of Victorianism. But Tennyson was not devoid of capacity for the portrayal of sentiment and passion, as is demonstrated by his "Idylls of the King," "The Lotus Eaters," "Ulysses," "Enoch Arden," and many other poems. Browning was less a master than Tennyson of the art of poetry as verbal sound, but he was more profound and thoughtful and illustrated better than any other Victorian poet the deep moral earnestness and underlying optimism that dominated the age. His *The Ring and the Book,* a philosophical analysis of murder and the response provoked from a group of human commentators, is quite generally regarded as his ablest poem. Matthew Arnold is best known as a critic and essayist, but in his early literary career he was viewed as a worthy competitor of Tennyson and Browning in the field of poetry. The most popular of his poems is one based upon an oriental motif, "Sohrab and Rustum." An enthusiastic student of the classics, Arnold based his poetry upon Greek models and traditions, and this prevented it from having wide popular appeal. Kipling, who belongs to the end of the Victorian era, was the enthusiastic poet of English imperialism. His poems deal chiefly with the experiences of English soldiers and adventurers in the Far East, especially India. There is nothing at all profound in Kipling, but his raciness and his appeal to the shallower and more blatant British imperialism have made him extremely popular with both English and American readers.

The best-known novelists of the first half of the Victorian age were Charles Dickens (1812-70), Charles Kingsley (1819-75), William Makepeace Thackeray (1811-63), and George Eliot (1819-80). These writers well illustrated the impact of the growing class differentiation in English society upon the fiction writers of that country. Dickens and Kingsley devoted themselves chiefly to an exposure of the miseries of the urban poor and the working classes in the

---

[1] Cf. S. T. Williams, *Studies in Victorian Literature,* Dutton, 1923, and J. W. Cunliffe, *Leaders of the Victorian Revolution,* Appleton-Century, 1934.

early days of the Industrial Revolution.[1] Dickens's masterpieces, *David Copperfield, Oliver Twist,* and *Hard Times,* portray the deplorable condition of the poor and oppressed in England, while Kingsley's *Yeast* and *Alton Locke* not only reveal the misery of the poor but argue for the desirability of improving their lot. But Dickens went beyond the literature of social exposure and made notable contributions to humor, satire, and historical romance. The last was best exemplified in his *Tale of Two Cities.* Thackeray described with mild cynicism and urbane satire the vanities, scandals, and snobberies of upper-class England of the first half of the nineteenth century. The most popular of his works was *Vanity Fair,* which turns about the battle of Waterloo and the character of the notorious Becky Sharp. George Eliot, whose real name was Mary Ann Evans (later Mrs. Cross), devoted herself chiefly to descriptions of the English middle class. Her works were distinguished by moral fervor, made effective by remarkable literary power. Her most enduring book is probably *Silas Marner,* partly reflecting the displacement of hand weaving by mechanical weaving.

In the later Victorian age the popular novelists were George Meredith (1828-1909), Thomas Hardy (1840-1928), Robert Louis Stevenson (1850-94), and Samuel Butler (1835-1902). Meredith was distinguished by great purity and luxuriance of style, high talent for character analysis, especially of underlying motives, and admiration for feminine intelligence and independence. Representative works were his *Beauchamp's Career, Diana of the Crossways,* and *The Egoist.* Hardy possessed a somber and sometimes almost animistic appreciation of physical nature matching in another mood that of Wordsworth and the early Romanticist poets, while in philosophy he was a pessimistic fatalist representing man as the helpless puppet of blind or unconscious Fate. Among his more famous books were *Tess of the D'Urbervilles* and *Jude the Obscure.* Stevenson had a rare lucidity and charm of style and has been particularly popular with youthful readers of *Treasure Island,* but his *Dr. Jekyll and Mr. Hyde* was written for adults and is perhaps the ablest literary analysis of what we now call the split personality. Samuel Butler was one of the most effective satirists in the whole history of English fiction. *The Way of All Flesh* was a devastating analysis of the inadequacies of conventional middle-class family life—its religion and morality—as a preparation for life. His *Erewhon* was a satirical assault upon the era of machines and industrialism and a description of a Utopia where modern problems were dealt with in scientific fashion. George Gissing (1857-1903) was the Zola of England in his realistic portrayal of the harsh and dismal life of the submerged classes. He especially emphasized the devastating effect of poverty on intellectually superior youth. Perhaps his best and most representative work was *The New Grub Street.*

The most influential and widely read critics and essayists of the Victorian age were Thomas Carlyle (1795-1881), Thomas Babington Macaulay (1800-59), Matthew Arnold, and John Ruskin (1819-1900). Better than any other figure in the whole Victorian age, probably, Carlyle exemplified the moral serious-

---

[1] On the social emphasis in English literature in the nineteenth century, see V. D. Scudder, *Social Ideals in English Letters,* new and rev. ed., Houghton Mifflin, 1923, Pt. II, and Hugh Martin, ed., *Christian Social Reformers of the Nineteenth Century,* Doran, 1927.

ness of the era. He attacked both democracy and industrialism, and worshiped the strong, self-guided man. In certain ways he was the precursor of Nietzsche and the contemporary apologists for dictatorship. Of his many and diversified works *Sartor Resartus* is probably the most representative of his thought. Of all the English essayists Lord Macaulay was the most flashily erudite. His enthusiasm for liberalism, suspect now for its rather uncritical acceptance of bourgeois progress, equaled that of Carlyle for authority and aristocracy. His most important essays were devoted to historical characters and historians, and his most enduring work was a monumental *History of England*. Arnold was the outstanding exponent of tolerance, urbanity, and culture and an everlasting foe of smugness and self-satisfied virtue. Yet he was no rebel and he had a considerable yearning for authority and organization, such as that exemplified by ancient Greece and modern Prussia. A highly representative work was his *Culture and Anarchy*. John Ruskin was in many ways a nineteenth-century Lord Shaftesbury who, like this great Deist of the eighteenth century, approached moral and social problems from the standpoint of the esthete and the lover of beauty. But this was supplemented by a profound humanitarianism that grew out of Ruskin's observation of the misery and ugliness brought into England by the Industrial Revolution. His ablest literary work was devoted to the defense of beauty and to exhortation to social reform. His interests are best represented by *The Seven Lamps of Architecture* and *Unto This Last*.

Outside of the field of formal literature important contributions to historical writing were made by men like James Anthony Froude, Macaulay, Carlyle, and their more scientific successors. This was also the golden age of the literature of science, which emerged from the pens of Darwin, Spencer, Huxley, Tyndall, Wallace, and others.

3. FRANCE

In France, Romanticism was represented in poetry by Alphonse de Lamartine (1790-1869), Victor Hugo (1802-85), Alfred de Vigny (1797-1863), and Alfred de Musset (1810-57).

Lamartine was a great lyricist and possessed all the power of portraying emotion and nature that had characterized the English Romanticists.[1] His *New Meditations*[2] have remained his most popular poems. Victor Hugo was one of the most versatile and productive poets in the whole history of literature. He wrote passionate lyrical ballads, satirical attacks upon political characters and abuses, and philosophical poems on the problems of life and the character of literature. His powers of visual imagery were remarkable and his feeling for the music of words unexcelled by any nineteenth-century poet, though his overintensity and bombasticism have lessened his appeal to readers of another age. His romantic sentimentalism is best exemplified in *The Orientals,* an early

---

[1] For French Romanticism, see M. B. Finch and E. A. Peers, *The Origins of French Romanticism,* Dutton, 1920, Bk. II.

[2] The titles of books in foreign languages are translated, the titles being those of translations in English when such are traceable. The date is that of first publication.

collection inspired by the Greek war for independence. His best political polemic in verse is *Punishments,* directed against Napoleon III; and his foremost philosophical contribution was contained in *Contemplations.* The main blots upon Hugo's genius were his colossal egotism and his utter lack of humor. De Vigny was the most restrained and austere of the French Romanticists. He excelled in elegance and beauty of style. Perhaps his most characteristic poem was his *The Bottle in the Sea,* a philosophical and descriptive poem of shipwreck. At the opposite extreme from De Vigny's restraint was the colorful emotionalism of De Musset, regarded by many as the French Byron. He was a self-centered and passionate poet of exotic love and strong emotions. The collection *Nights* contained his most representative work.

In the field of prose fiction the outstanding figures in French literature during the first half of the nineteenth century were Hugo, Prosper Merimée (1803-70), Théophile Gautier (1811-72), Alexandre Dumas the elder (1802-70), Amandine Lucile Aurore Dupin Dudevant (1804-76), usually known as George Sand, Marie Henri Beyle (1783-1842), who wrote under the pen name Stendhal, and Honoré de Balzac (1799-1850).

Hugo's most important prose work was his immortal *Les Misérables,* an unsurpassed exposure of the miseries, injustices, and sufferings of the masses in modern society. Merimée excelled as a delineator of primitive passions as exemplified by gypsies, brigands, and backward peoples. His remarkable power to portray love, jealousy, and revenge have led critics to regard him as a Romanticist forerunner of French Realism. Among Merimée's best-known works are *Carmen* and *Lokis.* Gautier was as talented in vivid description as Merimée, but he lightened his work with humor and a definite flair for the fantastic. Some of his best works are mildly satirical and realistic discussions of love and sex temptation. His best-known books are *The Beautiful Vampire (La morte amoureuse), One of Cleopatra's Nights,* and *Mademoiselle de Maupin.*

Dumas was an enormously prolific writer and many of his novels express a swashbuckling spirit of adventure. The most famous of these was *The Three Musketeers.* But certainly his greatest work was that masterpiece in the study of personal revenge, *The Count of Monte Cristo.* George Sand was a writer of singular grace and lucidity whose interest passed from Idealism to Humanitarianism and Utopian Socialism. She was one of the early feminists and some of her first novels were devoted to the theme of the emancipation of woman. Influenced by the Utopian Socialist Pierre Leroux, she became interested in the struggles of the working class and in a number of novels she warmly espoused the cause of social reform. Representative of her Idealism were such works as *The Devil's Pool* and *The Bagpipers,* while her humanitarianism and zeal for reform are best expressed in *The Journeyman Joiner.* Henri Beyle, under the pen name Stendhal, wrote from the emotional standpoint of Romanticism, but so keen was his insight that he later came to be regarded as the father of the psychological novel in France, anticipating by a half-century Paul Bourget, who warmly admired Stendhal. Stendhal's best-known novel was *Red and Black,* a study of experiences under Empire and Restoration, laying stress upon the manifestations of dominance, ambition, aggression, and self-advancement in the period.

LITERATURE

If Hugo was the great novelist of Romanticism and George Sand of Idealism, it was Balzac who thoroughly established French Realism. He was as prolific as Dumas and capable of even greater periods of relentless industry. He lacked distinction of style, but he was unrivaled for his power to describe human character and social settings with the most minute and devastating precision. His monumental *The Human Comedy* embraced more than a hundred novels and analyzed over five thousand personalities. He had, however, little of George Sand's grip upon the social and economic conditions of the age or upon the major intellectual currents of his time. His chief social sentiment was undying hatred for the avarice, sordidness, and smugness of the French middle class in the first half of the nineteenth century.

During the period of the Second Empire, 1852-71, French poetry was still dominated by Victor Hugo, but there were other eminent representatives of this literary art. Among these were Théodore de Banville (1823-91), a master of rhythm and rhyme and author of *A Rope Walker's Odes* (*Odes funambulesques*). Charles Leconte de Lisle (1818-94) was both a philosopher and a stylist, as well as a person of remarkable power in the description of nature, whether the snows of the mountains or the jungles of the tropics. He was also much interested in the description of animal life and alleged animal sentiments. Of his many poems we may cite as representative "Jungles," "Noon," and "Elephants." The most important innovation in poetry during the Second Empire was contained in the work of Charles Baudelaire (1812-67), author of *Flowers of Evil* (*Les fleurs du mal*), a verbal musician of the highest order. He was the outstanding precursor of French Symbolism.

The foremost figure in French fiction during the Empire was Gustave Flaubert (1821-80). His capacity for minute realistic description matched that of Balzac, while he infinitely surpassed the latter as a stylist. He heartily shared Balzac's contempt for the French bourgeoisie, whether their economics or their morality was in question. His outstanding works were *The Temptation of Saint Anthony* and *Madame Bovary*.

Probably the most distinguished prose writers of the period of the Empire were not novelists but essayists, critics, and scholars. Of these the most famous were Désiré Nisard (1806-88), Charles Augustin Sainte-Beuve (1804-69), Hippolyte Adolphe Taine (1828-93), and Ernest Renan (1823-92). Nisard was an intensely patriotic historian of French literature, with classic sympathies. He held that French literature was the embodiment of the very soul of human reason. Sainte-Beuve founded modern French literary criticism, endeavoring especially to show the relationship between the personality and experiences of an author and his works.[1] He also proved himself a most competent historian of culture in *The History of Port-Royal,* an account of the seventeenth-century Jansenists and their ideas. Taine looked upon man and culture as the inevitable outgrowth of the factors of race, heredity, and environment. The individual seemed less important to him than his background. As a historian, Taine wrote a very thoughtful but none too accurate history of the French Revolution and Napoleon. Renan was both the finest example of French Rationalism of this period and a great oriental scholar. His urbane and in-

---
[1] *Cf.* W. F. Giese, *Sainte-Beuve: A Literary Portrait,* University of Wisconsin Press, 1934.

triguing style gave him a wide popular following. His books did much to undermine the conventional notions regarding the Jews of Old Testament times and to promote a more intelligent understanding of the life and times of Jesus.[1] In the field of drama the foremost figure was Alexandre Dumas the younger (1824-95), the son of the great novelist whose work we have already described. He specialized in problems dealing with the themes of love, marriage, and the family. The best known of his works is *Camille*.

Under the Third Republic French poetry was most notably represented by René Sully-Prudhomme (1839-1907), Paul Verlaine (1844-96), and Arthur Rimbaud (1854-91). Sully-Prudhomme was defective in lyrical power but strong in philosophy, in which interest he was profoundly influenced by modern natural science. Many of his poems rely heavily upon scientific symbolism. His most famous poem is "The Broken Vase." Verlaine was the most musical of all French poets, though there is little depth of thought in his work. He was the supreme master of French lyric poetry. Among the best known of his poetic collections are *Parallels (Parallèlement)* and *Happiness*. Rimbaud was a friend of Verlaine and his poems reflect his wide travels and his urge for adventure. His experiences and his philosophy are best merged in his great poem *A Season in Hell*. The extreme lyrical tendency that was manifest in Baudelaire, Verlaine, and Rimbaud led to that exaggerated development of subtle communication known as Symbolism, in which the leading figures were Stéphane Mallarmé, Albert Samain, and Henri de Régnier.

In prose the Realistic tradition was carried on by Guy de Maupassant (1850-93) and Paul Bourget (1852-). De Maupassant employed Realism in achieving the greatest mastery of economy of means in short-story technique in all Western literature. Bourget introduced psychological analysis into realistic fiction. In his later writings, however, Bourget lapsed into piety and an espousal of traditional religion. His most important work was *The Disciple,* a consideration of the practical results of irresponsible philosophical teachings.[2] Realism passed over into what is known as Naturalism in the works of Emile Zola (1840-1902). He analyzed with the utmost frankness every aspect of the life of the middle class under the Second Empire. He even had no hesitation in candid portrayal of human degeneracy. Personally, he was inspired by courageous idealism and took a leading part in the exposure of the conspiracy against Dreyfus. Two of his best-known books are *Germinal* and *Nana*. Satire and humor in French fiction appeared at its best in the works of Alphonse Daudet (1840-97), whose most widely read book is the inimitable *Tartarin of Tarascon*.

The outstanding French essayists between 1880 and 1900 were in different ways relatively conventional and reactionary. Emile Faguet (1847-1916) was urbane and tolerant in his work in literary history and criticism, but in his political opinions he was fiercely critical of democracy. Ferdinand Brunetière (1849-1906) mingled literary criticism with an appreciation of natural science, in particular applying the theory of evolution to the explanation of the history of literature. But in other respects Brunetière was reactionary, being a de-

---

[1] *Cf*. L. F. Mott, *Ernest Renan*, Appleton, 1921.
[2] Bourget's *Outremer, Impressions of America*, was a caustic criticism of American civilization.

fender of literary tradition and discipline and of conventional moral judgments on literary figures. Jules Lemaître (1853-1914) had a catholic interest in French literature, which carried him from Racine to contemporary Impressionism. In religious, moral, and economic views he inclined towards severity and conservatism. Maurice Barrès (1862-1923) was perhaps the most fanatical patriot of the Third Republic and a leader of the movement for a war of revenge to recover Alsace-Lorraine. He had an intense admiration for the French past, which led some to accuse him of trying to revive ancestor worship.

4. ITALY AND SPAIN

Patriotism supplied the first important impetus to nineteenth-century Italian literature. Giuseppe Mazzini (1805-72) was the major literary figure engaged in the promotion of Italian unity. His studies of Dante inspired in him a vast zeal for the unification of Italy, and he wrote vigorously in support of this aspiration for a half-century. The theme of Italian unity also inspired the leading satirical and political poet of nineteenth-century Italy, Giuseppe Giusti (1809-50). He devoted his literary powers to a denunciation of foreign dominion in Italy. His masterpiece is his *St. Ambrose,* suggested by Austrian occupation of parts of Italy. The zeal for Italian emancipation also stirred the most scholarly of modern Italian poets, Count Giacomo Leopardi (1798-1837). Like Mazzini, he was deeply influenced by his studies of Dante. Another eminent poet impelled by patriotic sentiments was Gaetano Aleardo Aleardi (1812-78), whose best work was *Arnalda di Roca.* Sentimental and melancholy, rather than revolutionary and patriotic, Romanticism found its best expression in the *Edmenegarda* of Giovanni Prati (1815-84). The chief dramatic poet of nineteenth-century Italy was Pietro Cossa (1830-81), author of the popular *Nero.* The man who celebrated the unification of Italy in poetry was Giosuè Carducci (1833-1907), who praised with great eloquence and literary power the spirit of the new Italian kingdom.

In the realm of fiction, criticism, and drama the chief Italian writers of the nineteenth century were Alessandro Manzoni (1785-1873), Giovanni Verga (1840-1922), Luigi Capuana (1839-1918), Antonio Fogazzaro (1842-1911), Ruggiero Bonghi (1828-95), Guido Mazzoni (1859-   ), and Giuseppe Giacosa (1847-1906). Manzoni was the outstanding novelist among the Italian Romanticists. His foremost work was *The Betrothed* (*I promessi sposi*), a historical novel portraying the extremes of passive obedience under a régime of political oppression. Verga and Capuana introduced Realism into the Italian novel and short story. Verga was at his best in portraying and analyzing the life of the provincial peoples of Italy, especially the middle-class life of Sicilians. His classic work was *The House by the Medlar Tree* (*I Malavoglia*). Capuana also devoted himself to realistic descriptions of Italian regional life, likewise specializing in Sicilian manners and customs. His chief book was a naturalistic novel, *Giacinta.* He also wrote many short stories and several collections of fairy tales. The leading novelist of united Italy was Fogazzaro, who was particularly interested in portraying the future possibilities of the Catholic Church if it would renounce its worldly interests. Perhaps his best work was *The Man of the World* (*Il piccolo mondo antico*), a story of Austrian oppression. His book *The Saint* (*Il santo*) was placed on the *Index* because of its criticism of the alleged worldliness of churchmen. Bonghi was a superlative classical scholar and an able historian of culture as well as a foremost literary critic. Mazzoni was not only an able poet with a limpid and gracious style, but also a historian of literature, a classicist, and a literary critic of wide and varied historical learning. Giacosa was far and away the ablest Italian dramatist of the nineteenth century, notable for his psychological insight. His first plays were in the Romanticist strain, among the more important being *A Game of Chess* and *The Red Count*. But with *Hapless Love* he turned social dramatist. In this play he reflected the influence of Ibsen. Another notable play, *Like Falling Leaves,* portrayed the disintegration of an Italian family. Giacosa also wrote the librettos for Puccini's operas.

At the beginning of the nineteenth century the classical influence dominated in Spain and held first place until around 1830. Manuel José Quintana (1772-1857), known for his lyric poetry and his drama *Pelayo,* was one of the foremost figures, contributing to the field of literary criticism an important biography of Cervantes as well as other works. The invasion of Napoleon brought a change in Spanish literature. The strong reaction against the French led naturally to a comparable antipathy to the literary styles borrowed from France. Quintana, who had distinguished himself for his reverence for French models and French philosophy, now swung over and contributed his *Call to Arms against the French* and prose biographies of Pizarro, the Cid, and other heroic figures in Spanish history—*Lives of Celebrated Spaniards*. Another writer who was influenced by the patriotic motive was Juan Nicasio Gallego (1777-1853), whose *The Second of May* had a powerful patriotic appeal.

The classical and patriotic theme in Spanish literature was still predominant after the restoration of Ferdinand VII, but the reign of this monarch worked another change. His bitter hatred of all opposition forced the most prominent of the young literary men of the country to emigrate. While in exile many of them came into contact with the writings of Byron, Scott, Goethe, Châteaubriand, and other representatives of the Romanticist school. Francisco Martínez de la Rosa (1788-1862) was among the emigrants who spent some eight years out of Spain after 1824, changing his writings from the classical to the Romanticist school. Among his most important works are novels in imitation of Sir Walter Scott, and such dramas as *Aben-Humeya* and *The Conspiracy of Venice*. The same change from classicism to Romanticism may be seen in the writings of the Duke de Rivas (1791-1865) who followed the classical school until his exile led him to travel in France, England, and Italy. On his return to Spain he published his now famous *The Foundling Moor* (*El moro expósito*) and the drama *Don Alváro,* which, with his excellent lyric "To the Lighthouse of Malta," are among the best productions of the Romanticist period. The coming of Romanticism to Spain awakened an interest for literature in the people such as had not been known since the slavish imitation of the French classicists had succeeded the productions of the Spanish golden age, which had ended with the seventeenth century. This intense interest in literature and literary figures was related sharply to politics and the value of an author's books was frequently judged by the tendency he displayed in politics. José de Espronceda (1810-42) was among those authors who devoted themselves to both politics and literature. Many of his works are frankly imitations of Byron, but he is distinguished for his conspiracies and for the authorship of *The Devil World,* a work in which he sought to outdo Goethe's *Faust.* The best and most typical of the Romanticist novels was *Señor de Bembibre* by Enrique Gil y Carrasco (1815-46).

Living in the Romanticist age, though never thoroughly Romanticist, was Mariano José de Larra (1809-37), known also by his pen name of Figaro. Larra is justly famous for his biting criticism of the social customs of nineteenth-century Spain. He shot himself when he was twenty-eight and his death brought to light the poetic genius of José Zorrilla (1817-93). He, like Scott, popularized and revived national legends in such poems as *Granada* and *The Legend of the Cid,* but he distinguished himself most in *Don Juan Tenorio,* a play dealing with the favorite Spanish theme, which is still produced annually in Spain.

Realism entered nineteenth-century Spanish literature while Romanticism was still predominant. Larra was, of course, a Realist in his criticism of the social customs of the day. Manuel Bretón de los Herreros (1796-1873), a poet and dramatist, vividly portrayed the customs of his time. Ramón de Mesonero Romanos (1803-82) also commented, in prose, on the customs of Madrid, and left a good picture of that city in his *Handbook of Madrid.* It is difficult to discover, however, that any definite tendency dominated Spanish literature after the decline of Romanticism. Rather, there came about what one Spanish writer called "an enchanting anarchy." Among novelists an outstanding figure was Cecilia Böhl de Faber (1796-1877), who under the pen name of Fernán Caballero wrote in detail on the life and culture of southern Spain, especially Andalusia. Among her more important works were *The Alvareda Family* and *Andalusian Tales and Poetry.* Another novelist of wide popularity was Juan Valera (1824-1905), a diplomat, publicist, and poet as well as the "liberator of Spanish fiction." His novel *Pepita Jiménez* both revived Spanish fiction and freed it from dependence on French models.

The tendency towards regionalism in Spain produced a literature in which the form enabled an author to hang upon it sketches of provincial scenes and characters. This type of novel had appeared in José María de Pereda (1834-1905) and found two exponents in Emilia Pardo Bazán (1851-1921) and Armando Palacio Valdés (born 1853). Doña Pardo Bazán, daughter of a Galician nobleman, produced her best work, of which *Mother Nature (La madre naturaleza)* is her masterpiece, in the nineteenth century. Palacio Valdés also produced his best work in that century. His novel *Sister Saint Sulpice* is considered a model of character analysis, and has gained wide fame abroad. Benito Pérez Galdós (1845-1920) must be ranked among the great novelists of the nineteenth and twentieth centuries. *Trafalgar* is considered one of the best historical novels. He also dealt with social problems in a series of novels of which *Angel Guerra* and *Fortunata and Jacinta* are the best examples. He likewise distinguished himself as a dramatist, *The Foolish Wife (La loca de la casa)* being considered his best drama.

Spain was well represented in the nineteenth century by competent historians and literary critics. Among the most prominent were José Amador de los Ríos (1818-78) whose seven-volume *Critical History of Spanish Literature* brings the story to end of the reign of the Catholic kings; and Marcelino Menéndez y Pelayo (1856-1912), whose genius overshadowed that of all other Spaniards in his age. His works are numbered by the dozen, the most famous being *History of the Spanish Heretics,* and *History of Esthetic Ideas in Spain.* As an authority on esthetics and intellectual history he ranks with Croce in Italy.

5. GERMANY, AUSTRIA, AND SCANDINAVIA

German literature in the nineteenth century leads off with a dominant personality who far overshadows even Victor Hugo in France—Johann Wolfgang von Goethe (1749-1832), poet, novelist, dramatist, philosopher, and scientist. He is far and away the dominating figure in all Germanic literature. Some rate him as the leading philosophical poet of modern times, and others tend to put him almost in a class by himself in the history of all literature. Even a French critic, Emile Faguet, writes of him as "Goethe, whom posterity can only put in the same rank with Homer." To get away from such superlatives, one may say that while the two men were vastly different, Goethe brought a new intellectual era to Germany as truly as Voltaire did to France somewhat earlier. He was deeply affected by Romanticism in his earlier years and his writings of that period influenced other Romanticists, such as Sir Walter Scott. But in his later life he turned towards a pure classicism in style and thought. His finished work thus presented "a union of the German spirit with classical genius." Of his lyrical poems, perhaps the most popular was *Hermann and Dorothea,* a masterpiece of lyric classicism that portrayed a somewhat idealized version of German middle-class life. His *West-Eastern Divan* was a collection of lyrics that reflected oriental (Persian) influences. His best-known dramas were *Iphigenia* and *Tasso.* His chief novel was *Wilhelm Meister,* a study of the development of character through the interplay of fortune and experience. But the transcendent work of Goethe was his extended philosophical poem, *Faust,* on which he worked at intervals for over fifty years. It is a vast epic of human striving for knowledge through experience, developing Goethe's doctrine that serenity can only be achieved by a resignation in the face of eternal realities that enables one to face with calm the transient things of mortal life.

The outstanding poet in German Romanticism was the brilliant Jewish writer Heinrich Heine (1797-1856), quite generally regarded as the greatest German poet since Goethe. Patriotism and the War of Liberation inspired the poems of Ernst Moritz Arndt (1769-1860). Another important Romanticist poet in Germany was the Swabian Ludwig Uhland (1787-1862). An attempt to revive classicism and to merge it with lyricism and the traditions of the German folk song appeared in the important poems of Eduard Mörike (1804-75).

Among the leading novelists of the period were Gustav Freytag (1816-95) and Theodor Storm (1817-88). Freytag's best-known novel, *Debit and Credit* (*Soll und Haben*), eulogizes the German middle classes and denounces the nobility. Storm was influenced both by the growing realism in description and by his interest in the German past. Other important novelists of the time were Joseph Viktor von Scheffel (1826-86), who described German life of the tenth century in his historical novel *Ekkehard;* Felix Dahn (1834-1912), whose *A Struggle for Rome* was a moving account of the struggles between the Goths and the Eastern emperors for the control of Italy; and the Swiss writer, Gottfried Keller (1819-90), who passed from Romanticism to Realism and was a master of the short story as well as of the novel. His masterpiece, *Green Henry,* is an analysis of his own mental evolution.

Romanticism promoted a wide and sentimental interest in the German past, and during the middle of the century short stories placed in the setting of medieval Germany were especially popular. The foremost writer of this type of historical short story was Wilhelm Heinrich Riehl (1823-97). Historical novels abounded, some of the most important being Wilhelm Hauff's *Lichtenstein,* and Freytag's *Our Ancestors,* which traced the history of a German family from 400 to 1848. Freytag also composed a popular history of medieval German civilization.

Much the most important German dramatist in the middle of the nineteenth century was Friedrich Hebbel (1813-63). Among his more popular dramas are *Judith, Genoveva,* and *Maria Magdalena.* His plays especially stress the emancipation of individuality, feminism, and sex conflict. Another important dramatist of the period was Franz Grillparzer (1791-1872), a Viennese who wrote many historical plays glorifying the Hapsburgs and others treating Greek themes and figures according to classical models. Otto Ludwig (1813-65) not only was an able dramatist, excelling in poetic conceptions and mastery of detail, but also composed the most important of early realistic novels in Germany in his *Between Heaven and Earth.*

The unification of Germany in 1870 and the creation of the German Empire produced conditions encouraging literary activity, but there were few outstanding figures in German literature between 1870 and the close of the century. Thomas Mann (1875-   ), the leading contemporary German writer, completed his great novel of the generations of a burgher family during the nineteenth century, *Buddenbrooks,* at the very end of that century. The majority of German writers at this time were influenced by the Realism and Naturalism of French and Scandinavian writers, especially Zola and Ibsen. The more notable poets were Richard Dehmel (1863-1920), Baron Detlev von Liliencron (1844-1909), and Otto Julius Bierbaum (1865-1910). Influenced by the Realists and Naturalists, these poets were deeply concerned with eroticism, which they treated with great candor. Bierbaum was the least affected by the foreign trends of the time.

Among the German novelists of this period two stand out especially, Paul Heyse (1830-1914), and Theodor Fontane (1819-98). Heyse's most important works were *Children of the World* and *In Paradise.* He was distinctly anticlerical in his point of view and was accused of glorifying ancient paganism. A characteristic work by Fontane was *Effi Briest.* Through his persistent and frank discussion of sex and marriage problems Fontane was the forerunner of extreme Naturalism in German fiction. He had talent as a psychological analyst and his novels dealt mainly with upper-class German society.

704   INTELLECTUAL AND CULTURAL ACHIEVEMENTS

The most distinguished German contributions in the last third of the nineteenth century were made in the field of drama. A Viennese playwright, Ludwig Anzengruber (1839-89), possessed remarkable capacity for frank and realistic description of Austrian peasant life. Along with Arno Holz (1863-1929), he paved the way for Hauptmann, Sudermann, and thoroughgoing Naturalism in the German drama. Incomparably the two most famous German dramatists of this period were Gerhart Hauptmann (1862-   ) and Hermann Sudermann (1857-1928), thorough devotees of the Naturalistic cult of Zola. Hauptmann's first important play, *Before Dawn,* appeared in 1889 and set the precedent as to subject matter and procedure that was followed in his later plays. They deal with dypsomania, mental disorder, degeneracy, sex freedom, and the question of eugenics and marriage. The love motif was now complicated by conscious consideration of hereditary taints. Another famous play by Hauptmann, *The Weavers,* discusses the misery of Silesian weavers and their rights to social justice. Sudermann's first play, *Honor,* was also put on in 1889. This likewise forecast his later dramatic interests, playing up the conflict between social classes and between parents and children and bringing to the fore the whole problem of sex honor, all of these being treated in a cynical and satirical fashion. The same themes were repeated in *Magda* (*Die Heimat*) and other of Sudermann's leading plays. Both Hauptmann and Sudermann stress social rather than individual responsibility in human situations. Sudermann was also an important novelist, and his *Dame Care* (*Frau Sorge*) is one of the best of modern German Realistic and Naturalistic novels.

One of the most remarkable figures in modern German literature was the philosopher Nietzsche, already referred to, who ranks with Strindberg and Schopenhauer as a leading iconoclast of the nineteenth century. Nietzsche outdid Carlyle in his worship of the superman. He also vigorously attacked Christianity, especially denouncing its doctrine of altruism, which he held to be a glorification of weakness. He distinguished between two types of morality, the morality of the strong and powerful, based upon the application of intelligence and force, and the morality of the slave, founded upon weakness and resignation. He identified the slave morality very closely with that of Christianity. Characteristic works of Nietzsche are *Beyond Good and Evil, The Genealogy of Morals,* and *Thus Spake Zarathustra.* Nietzsche was discovered and popularized primarily by the Danish literary critic, Georg Brandes, and was later given large vogue in the United States through the influence of H. L. Mencken.

Among the remaining Germanic peoples, the Scandinavians have contributed important figures in the history of nineteenth-century literature. From Denmark came the work of Hans Christian Andersen (1805-75), famous for his children's stories and fairy tales;[1] and Georg Brandes (1842-1927), the most learned and capable literary critic of the last quarter of the nineteenth century. Brandes's linguistic facility made him at home in a wide range of literature. Among the outstanding Norwegian literary figures was the poet and dramatist Björnstjerne Björnson (1832-1910), author of many poems, plays concerning the legends of Norse heroes, and social dramas. Jonas Lie (1833-1908) was

---

[1] *Cf.* Signe Toksvig, *The Life of Hans Christian Andersen,* Harcourt, Brace, 1934.

the founder of the modern Norwegian novel. His work *The Visionary* (1870) was notable for its portrayal of the local color of the Scandinavian northland. His most famous book was *Go Ahead* (1882), a novel centering about the destinies of an old trading vessel. It well illustrated his humor and terse style. He was interested in the personal problems of men and women and in the elementary virtues of the home. Henrik Ibsen (1828-1906), one of the greatest of modern dramatists, was an implacable foe of bourgeois society and of democracy. He regarded the latter as the vehicle by which the middle class deceives and dominates the masses. In *An Enemy of the People* and *The Pillars of Society*, Ibsen satirized the middle class and democracy, while in *The Doll's House* he stated the case for the emancipation of woman. The major Swedish writer of the century was August Strindberg (1849-1912). He was a prolific writer in many fields—fiction, drama, history, and social polemics. He was a revolutionary Socialist in his earlier years, but later came under the influence of Nietzsche and passed over to extreme individualism. In his later life he became much interested in mystical and occult phases of religion. His Socialistic views appeared in his *Upper and Lower Classes* (1880). His bitterness towards women was evident in such dramas as *The Father, Countess Julia,* and the *Creditors*. Two of his best novels were *By the Open Sea* and *On the Seaboard*. His main historical work was an extended history of the Swedish people.

6. RUSSIA

In spite of the backwardness of Russian culture, Russian writers assumed an important place in European literature as a whole toward the close of the nineteenth century. While there were no poets of the first order, there were Russian novelists and dramatists worthy to rank with the best in western Europe. Foremost among these were Alexander Pushkin (1799-1837), Nikolai Gogol (1809-52), Mikhail Lermontov (1814-41), Ivan Turgenev (1818-83), Fedor Dostoevsky (1821-81), Count Leo Tolstoy (1828-1910), Vladimir Soloviev (1853-1900), and Anton Chekhov (1860-1904).

Pushkin, Lermontov, and Gogol founded modern Russian literature. The first two were primarily romantic poets, though Lermontov wrote an important novel, *A Hero of Our Time* (1840). It contrasts the rugged virtues of the Caucasus mountaineers with the social ideals, customs, and vices of the upper-class Russians of the time—including Lermontov himself. His epic poem *The Demon* is a vivid elaboration of themes drawn from Russian folklore. Pushkin first gave Russian literature form and style. He united the vigor and naturalism of Russian social themes with the finished style of the West. His best-known work is a tragic poem, *Boris Godunov,* describing the confusion in Russia following the death of Tsar Theodore II in 1682. Gogol was both a novelist and a dramatist, and the founder of modern Russian prose. He satirized and ridiculed serfdom and the corrupt Russian bureaucracy, especially the provincial governors, in his great drama *The Inspector* (1836) and his novel *Dead Souls* (1842).

Turgenev was especially adept in his powers of detached description. *The Diary of a Sportsman* gave interesting and accurate details on the life of the

Russian serfs, while his *Fathers and Sons* treated of the struggle between absolutism and revolution after the middle of the century. Dostoevsky, himself an epileptic and a victim of exile to a Siberian prison camp, excelled in the portrayal of the pathological and the maladjusted. His basic theme was that salvation comes to man only through suffering, and even crime. He has had no equal as an analyst of morbid motives and sentiments.[1] His most notable work was *Crime and Punishment*, a realistic study of the psychological effects of his deed upon a deliberate murderer.

Tolstoy occupied the leading position in Russian literature during the latter part of the nineteenth century. He had little capacity to work out a well-integrated plot, but he was a master in marshaling and utilizing in moving fashion loosely connected incidents and settings. His two long and most admired works are *War and Peace*, an epical account of Russia during the Napoleonic invasion, and *Anna Karénina*, which develops the notion that one can find happiness only in doing good to others.

Soloviev was a learned Russian scholar who was at first much interested in the problems of religion and particularly admired the Roman Catholic Church. He was called by some the Russian Newman, but he never became a Roman Catholic. In politics he was an idealist and a liberal, and he wrote brilliantly against the reactionary Russian régime. But in literature and philosophy he was a profound mystic and bitterly opposed agnosticism and materialism. His most important works were *Three Conversations on War, Progress and the End of Human History*, and *The Story of Antichrist*.

Chekhov was the outstanding Russian dramatist of the nineteenth century, but he was also the author of many important short stories. His most important plays were *The Seagull, Uncle Vanya, The Three Sisters,* and *The Cherry Orchard*. In technique these differ widely from the Western drama, but they are not incapable of arousing the interest of Western audiences. Chekhov's short stories emphasize the psychological isolation of the individual and the difficulties met in mutual human understanding. Among the most important of them were "A Dreary Story," "The Lady with the Dog," "The Ravine," and "My Life."

Poland and Lithuania were during this period a part of Russia and they produced literary figures of importance. The outstanding one was the Polish poet and novelist Adam Mickiewicz (1798-1855). He wrote charming romantic ballads; a great epic poem, *Pan Thaddeus* (1834), dealing with the struggles of Poland for freedom and equality; and a notable historical novel, *Konrad Wallenrod*.

7. THE UNITED STATES

The first important literary developments in the United States took place under the influence of the Romanticist movement. Our conspicuous Romanticist poet was William Cullen Bryant, who resembled his English contemporaries in his love of nature. His most important poem is, perhaps, "Green River." The outstanding prose-writer of American Romanticism was James

---

[1] *Cf.* N. A. Berdyaev, *Dostoievsky: An Interpretation*, Sheed and Ward, 1934.

Fenimore Cooper, the first really capable American novelist. He established his position by his novel *The Spy,* written in 1821, but his reputation depends primarily upon his series of *Leatherstocking Tales,* treating of love and adventure in the frontier area, where the Indians were gradually being pushed back before the white man's advance. Also writing under Romanticist influence, Washington Irving founded the short story in America. This type of writing is best represented by the collection in his classic *Sketch-Book.*

These early Romanticist writers were followed by a group who are usually known as Transcendentalists, or Idealists devoted to the cause of political and social reform. The intellectual leader of this group was Ralph Waldo Emerson, author of many essays, all distinguished by a ringing call to national righteousness. A representative collection will be found in his volume *The Conduct of Life* (1860). Henry David Thoreau was a prose poet of nature, as well as an arch-individualist and a bitter foe of Negro slavery. His *Walden* is his most characteristic work. The outstanding novelist of the period was Nathaniel Hawthorne, whose *Scarlet Letter* still ranks as one of the great American novels. The other leading novelist was Herman Melville, whose *Moby-Dick* has remained a classic to our own time. Beneath its interesting style and its absorbing plot lies an allegory of man's effort to pursue and conquer evil.

Poetry was most effectively cultivated by Henry Wadsworth Longfellow (1807-82), John Greenleaf Whittier (1807-92), Edgar Allan Poe (1809-49), and Emily Dickinson (1830-86). Longfellow brought to poetry the New England viewpoint and extensive linguistic learning, which enabled him to adapt much from the poetry of other languages and literatures. His most popular poems were *The Song of Hiawatha, Evangeline,* and "The Courtship of Miles Standish." Whittier, a Quaker, was stirred to poetic fire by his hatred of slavery. He also wrote beautifully of nature, as illustrated by his *Snow-Bound.* Poe wrote the best American lyrics. Walt Whitman (1819-92) was the outstanding poetic rebel of this age. He is especially notable for his revolt against Puritanism and for his contention that the things of the body are as pure and noble as the things of the mind. His most representative work was *Leaves of Grass,* first published in 1855 and much altered and expanded in later editions.

The last half of the nineteenth century in the United States was characterized by the triumph of capitalism, the completion of westward expansion, and the perfection of national consolidation. A national American literature emerged, in which the writers reflected and eulogized or criticized the prevailing economic and political developments.

The American novel reached its highest development during this time in the works of William Dean Howells (1837-1920), Henry James (1843-1916), Frank Norris (1870-1902), and Stephen Crane (1871-1900). In differing degrees, these writers were representative of American Realism. Howells was a restrained admirer of the American business man of the last quarter of the nineteenth century. This type is best portrayed in *The Rise of Silas Lapham.* Howells did not, however, hesitate to expose the abuses of American capitalism, and in such books as *Annie Kilburn* and *A Traveller from Altruria* he became rather bitter and caustic on this point. Henry James was the brother of the great Harvard psychologist, but spent most of his time in Europe as an expatriate. His importance in fiction lies chiefly in his marked capacity for psychological analysis and highly stylized "design." A characteristic work was *The American*. His novels portray with discriminating appreciation, but often quite devastatingly, that leisure class later cynically analyzed by the great economist Thorstein Veblen. His characters, however, usually reveal but little of that sordid industrialism that dominated the age in which James lived. His later works were mainly devoted to the life of Americans in Europe and to the contrasts between American and European traits. Frank Norris introduced into America in thoroughgoing fashion the Naturalism of Zola. In *The Octopus* and *The Pit* he began the critical portrayal of the avarice and irresponsibility of certain types of American capitalists. Crane greatly resembled Thomas Hardy in his emphasis upon the dominating influence of the environment over the individual. Perhaps his best work was *The Red Badge of Courage,* a psychological study of the volunteer soldier under fire in the Civil War.

American satire and humor attained its best expression in the works of Samuel L. Clemens (Mark Twain, 1835-1910) and Ambrose Bierce (1842-1914?). Mark Twain wrote charmingly of river life on the Mississippi and of frontier life in the middle of the century. Nobody represented better than he did the urbane side of the frontier spirit in American literature. His satirical work is contained primarily in his short stories and in *The Gilded Age,* in which he collaborated with Charles Dudley Warner—an unrivaled indictment of American politics and economics at the close of the Civil War. Through a number of his books and stories Mark Twain also established himself as the foremost American humorist of the century. His most important books in this field were *Huckleberry Finn, The Adventures of Tom Sawyer,* and *Innocents Abroad*. Bierce's writings were not relieved by any of the lightness or urbanity that characterize Mark Twain's work. He was the outstanding American iconoclast, and his spirit is well expressed in *The Cynic's Word Book,* later changed in title to *The Devil's Dictionary*.[1]

Literary criticism and the essay found worthy practitioners in the United States in Edgar Allan Poe, James Russell Lowell (1819-91), and Oliver Wendell Holmes (1809-94). Poe was also the outstanding American representative of short-story writing, being worthy to rank with De Maupassant himself. Lowell was the first distinguished literary defender of democracy, and was an outstanding foe of slavery and political corruption. His *Biglow Papers* best illustrate his intellectual attitudes. Holmes was one of the few New Englanders to possess intellectual detachment and urbanity, both of which qualities appear conspicuously in his well-known *Autocrat of the Breakfast Table* (1857-58). In any survey of American literature attention should also be called to the utopian forecast, *Looking Backward,* by Edward Bellamy (1850-98), which showed remarkable prophetic power in anticipating technological evolution and social reconstruction.

[1] *Cf.* C. H. Grattan, *Bitter Bierce,* Doubleday, Doran, 1929.

IX. TRENDS IN ART

While art was by no means dormant in the nineteenth century, it occupied no such position of supreme importance in culture as it had in some earlier periods of human civilization. During the nineteenth century men were primarily absorbed in the problems of industry that had been brought to the fore by the coming of machines and factories. Art was subordinated to economics. Writers like Ruskin and Rossetti recognized the threat to artistic appreciation embodied in the ruthless new industrialism and protested against this prospect. The new cities and buildings offered a remarkable field for the practical application of art, but the urge for rapid and immediate profits led the capitalists, for the most part, to ignore those possibilities which could not be turned into immediate economic gain. Therefore the new factories, office buildings, and cities as a whole tended to be extremely ugly. Even when wealth and leisure were attained, those who possessed them had so little understanding or appreciation of art that their efforts and expenditures in behalf of art usually resulted mainly in the increase and intensification of the vulgar and the ugly. Nevertheless, certain important artistic tendencies appeared in the nineteenth century that are eminently worthy of attention.

There was little of outstanding significance in English art during the nineteenth century. The last painter of international repute was Joseph M. W. Turner (1775-1851), for whom maritime and naval themes possessed special attraction. Turner was a master of color and was best in portraying a sunset or moonlight on the water. One of his great characteristic pictures is "The Fighting Téméraire." An important development in English art in this century was the establishment of the Pre-Raphaelite Brotherhood by Dante Gabriel Rossetti, William Holman Hunt, and William Morris. The movement was launched in 1848 and was designed as a humanistic protest against the ugliness and artificiality of the age. It was a notable effort to merge art, industry, and life and to make art an integral element in life instead of an artificial ostentation. The outstanding painter who followed the ideals of this group was G. F. Watts (1817-1904). The one important English sculptor of the nineteenth century was Alfred Stevens (1818-75), known especially for his remarkable statue of Wellington in St. Paul's Cathedral.

In nineteenth-century painting France easily took the lead. At the close of the eighteenth century the cold and austere classicism of painters like David had dominated. Romanticism, however, influenced painting as well as literature and the Romanticist revolt against French classicism was led by Eugène Delacroix (1798-1863). Romanticist painting was characterized by the dominance of emotionally dramatic themes, especially those drawn from the past, and by a pictorial treatment emphasizing movement and warmth and brightness of color. A characteristic picture was Delacroix's "The Entrance of Crusaders into Constantinople." Realism and Naturalism were stimulated by the works of Théodore Rousseau (1812-67), Jean Baptiste Corot (1796-1875), and Jean François Millet (1814-75). These painters were dominated by a vivid interest in the realities of physical nature, to which Millet added a deep concern with the traits of the French peasants and their lives. They aimed to reproduce these themes with realistic accuracy. This movement toward Realism and Naturalism was further stimulated by Gustave Courbet (1819-77) and Edouard Manet (1832-1883), both of whom were characterized by their determination to seek their subject matter in the everyday life that surrounded them.

Out of the revolt of Manet and his struggle for Realism arose the school of painters known as the French Impressionists, chiefly Claude Monet (1840-1926) and Pierre Auguste Renoir (1841-1919). Most of the Impressionists were landscape-painters who aspired to reproduce both light and color with great exactness as it appeared at any particular moment on any given landscape. Hence their work has been described as "pictorial stenography." This school frequently painted the same scene many times in order to catch and depict the fleeting alterations of light and color. Renoir also manifested great ability in a charmingly realistic portrayal of the human figure.

The weakness of French Impressionism with respect to structure and design provoked a reaction led by Paul Cézanne (1839-1906). Cézanne's paintings stress above all these very elements of structure and design and emphasize the principles of strength and power that were lacking in Impressionism. Cézanne had a wide influence upon Modernistic trends in painting in the twentieth century.[1] Pierre Puvis de Chavannes (1824-98) is held by some authorities to be the leading mural painter of the century and was the one French painter able to handle competently a large composition.

The outstanding French sculpture of the nineteenth century expressed the spirit of Naturalism. The major sculptors were François Rude (1784-1855), whose best work was his "Marseillaise" on the Arc de Triomphe; Jean Baptiste Carpeaux (1827-75), who produced the dancing group for the façade of the Paris Opera House; Paul Dubois (1829-1905), who revived the spirit of the Renaissance in his admiration of Donatello and Della Quercia, and is known for his statues of "The Young John the Baptist" and "The Florentine Singer"; and Auguste Rodin (1840-1917), best known for his impressive statue "The Thinker," which is reminiscent of the power of Michelangelo. Mention should also be made of the work of Constantin Meunier (1831-1905) in Belgium, who has been called the Millet of sculpture and who specialized in statues of miners and artisans.

In Germany the Romanticist school of painting found its best representative in Ludwig Richter (1803-84) and Moritz von Schwind (1804-71). The revolt to Realism found expression in the paintings of Adolf von Menzel (1815-1905) and Wilhelm Leibl (1844-1900). The latter was especially famous as a portrait-painter. German Impressionism found protagonists in Max Liebermann (1847-) and Fritz von Uhde (1848-1911), though neither of these painters abandoned completely their earlier Realism. Probably the most interesting of all German painters of the nineteenth century was the German-Swiss, Arnold Böcklin (1827-1901), who was distinguished especially for his artistic extravagance in the use of color and his effort to personify elemental natural forces. The three notable German sculptors of the nineteenth century

---

[1] See below, pp. 1095 ff.

were Christian Daniel Rauch (1777-1857), who produced the magnificent equestrian statue of Frederick the Great at Berlin; Ernst Rietschel (1804-61), known for his colossal statue of the King of Saxony at Dresden and for his busts of Goethe, Schiller, and Lessing; and Reinhold Begas (1831-1911), official sculptor of the German Empire and best known for his statues of William I and Bismarck, in Berlin.

Russians made contributions of significance to nineteenth-century art. The attempt to discredit tsardom entered into art in the illustrative realistic painting of Vassili Vereshchagin (1842-1904) and Ilya Repin (1844-1930). They portrayed with power the brutalities and superstitions of the Romanovs and their bureaucracy. A trend towards Modernism in the more lavish use of brilliant colors appeared in the later paintings of Boris Anisfeld (1879-) and Nicholas Roerich (1874-). The latter has been profoundly interested in the art of the Orient and has also founded a large institute in New York City to promote a varied artistic activity. The chief Russian sculptor of the century was Marc Antokolsky (1843-1902), an artist of great dramatic power whose statue of Ivan the Terrible is particularly well known. Another outstanding Russian sculptor is Prince Paul Troubetzkoy (1866-), famous for his Impressionistic statuettes, and for his equestrian statues of Alexander III and Tolstoy. A very important Russian contribution to art in the nineteenth century came in the Russian ballet and stage designing. Here the most prominent name is that of Leon Bakst (1867-1924).

The United States produced four first-rate painters in the nineteenth century. George Inness (1825-94), our foremost landscape-painter, was considerably influenced by such contemporary French painters as Corot. He was a master of composition and color. John La Farge (1835-1910) surpassed in his handling of light and color. He was also the one outstanding American artist in the field of stained-glass windows whose achievements could compare with the work done by the artists in the medieval cathedrals. He was the foremost decorator of the century in the United States. James Abbott McNeill Whistler (1834-1903) was our leading portrait-painter. John Singer Sargent (1856-1925) was also a very competent portrait-painter, but he is equally well known as a talented mural decorator.

American sculpture really began with Horatio Greenough (1805-52), whose "Greek Slave" is a landmark in the history of American sculpture. Perhaps the three outstanding American sculptors were Augustus Saint-Gaudens (1848-1907), Daniel Chester French (1850-1931), and Lorado Taft (1860-). Saint-Gaudens was easily preëminent and his work is notable for its serenity and its "monumental simplicity." Among his best work are the Lincoln statue in Lincoln Park, Chicago, and the Adams memorial in Rock Creek Cemetery in Washington. French became famous for his colossal "Republic" group at the Chicago Columbian Exposition. Among his other important works are the statues of John Harvard and of Lincoln at Lincoln, Nebraska, and the work on the Lincoln Memorial in Washington. Taft won distinction by his decoration of the Horticultural Building at the Chicago Exposition and has been especially noted for his memorial fountains.

It was in architecture that the American artistic genius found its most distinguished expression. First should be mentioned Charles Bulfinch (1763-1844), the Christopher Wren of the United States. The best example of Bulfinch's work was the original State House in Boston. The classical element in American architecture owes much to Benjamin H. Latrobe (1764-1820), who has been described as "the man who brought the Parthenon to America in his gripsack." Perhaps the best example of Latrobe's influence is the present Treasury Building in Washington, constructed by his disciple Robert Mills. An interesting effort to revive the Romanesque style in American architecture was associated with the work of Henry Hobson Richardson (1838-86), whose outstanding product was Trinity Church in Boston. The most important of the later American architects in the nineteenth century were Charles Follen McKim (1847-1909), first an assistant to Richardson, and Stanford White (1853-1906), the greatest genius in architectural decoration in the last half of the nineteenth century. A number of important buildings illustrate the beauty of their work. Of these the Boston Public Library is thoroughly representative. Louis Sullivan planned some of his earlier work, such as the Auditorium building in Chicago, according to Romanesque conceptions, but in his later career he was one of the first artists who adapted architectural ideals to the requirements of the coming age of skyscrapers. Perhaps the most striking episode in the history of American architecture in the nineteenth century was the designing of the buildings of the Chicago Exposition of 1892-93. This brought together such able architects as McKim, White, Sullivan, Daniel H. Burnham, Richard M. Hunt, and Charles B. Atwood. The classic style prevailed, and the best piece of designing was that of Atwood in creating the Palace of Fine Arts.

X. ACHIEVEMENTS IN MUSIC

As in the case of literature and art, the developments in musical art in the nineteenth century can only be intelligently understood or expounded when viewed against the background of the social and cultural trends of the period. First, there was the effect of revolutions, including the Industrial Revolution, on the society of the period, releasing a new public for musical entertainment. Second, there was the Romanticist movement with its deep emotional feeling. Third, there was lyricism—a direct stimulus to music. Fourth, there was the rising spirit of nationalism, which promoted patriotic music and national schools of music. Fifth, there was a marked growth of individualism, encouraging the release of the human ego. These, separately and together, give some clew to the new and quite general interest in the art of music on the part of classes of society that formerly had only occasional and tentative contact with it outside the Church. They also explain to some extent the emergence of strong personalities in music, and account for the new emphasis put on originality, as contrasted with the eighteenth-century habit of using the conventional and accumulated stock in trade. These reasons also clarify somewhat the new expansiveness of all the means used in music-making and, finally, explain in large part the experimentation, the heroic striving, and the melancholy that characterize the musical content of a large portion of the musical works of the nineteenth century.

ACHIEVEMENTS IN MUSIC

The musical art was one phase of nineteenth-century culture that exhibited forward strides about as striking and extensive as those manifested in the field of science and industry. In many ways the musical developments of the nineteenth century equaled those which had taken place in all previous history. This implies no tendency to depreciate men like Bach, Handel, and Haydn in the eighteenth century. There were several reasons for this large accomplishment. In the first place, nineteenth-century music was able to build on earlier developments in the field of musical art. In the second place, new musical instruments were invented and earlier instruments vastly improved upon.[1] Horns and other wind instruments were elaborated and improved in construction. The pipe organ made its appearance in modern form. The piano, which had been invented by Bartolommeo Cristofori in 1710, was made especially popular by Beethoven in the early nineteenth century. Music, like literature and art, was influenced by the succeeding esthetic and emotional influences of Romanticism, Realism, and Naturalism, but the Romanticist influence dominated the majority of musicians and musical products during the nineteenth century. It was a century characterized by expansion, harmony, and color in musical tone.

Perhaps the outstanding phase of musical progress in this century lay in the field of orchestral music.[2] The improvement and elaboration of musical instruments and the increasing complexity and perfection of the musical art naturally helped along this enthusiasm for orchestral composition. Outstanding figures were Ludwig van Beethoven (1770-1827), Felix Mendelssohn-Bartholdy (1809-47), Robert Schumann (1810-56), Franz Schubert (1797-1828), and Johannes Brahms (1833-97) in Germany; Hector Berlioz (1803-69), César Franck (1822-90), Charles Saint-Saëns (1835-1921), and Jules Massenet (1842-1912), in France; and the five great Russian composers, Alexander Borodin (1834-87), M. P. Moussorgsky (1839-81), Anton Rubinstein (1829-94), Peter Ilich Tchaikovsky (1840-93), and Nikolai Rimsky-Korsakov (1844-1908). The sensuous and melodic traits of Romanticist music dominated all of these men. Beethoven was not only one of the last of the great classicists, but a major forerunner of the Romanticists, some even including him among the latter. His versatility has been compared to that of Shakespeare in literature. He was the foremost individualist of the century. Of all these composers, easily the dominating figure was Beethoven, whose primacy among modern composers is only challenged by the name of Bach in the preceding century. If the orchestra was the preëminent mode of musical expression in the nineteenth century, one should also note the importance of the great musical literature of the piano, almost all of which was composed in this period, and the Wagner music-drama, regarded by some as the most characteristic musical product of the century.

In the realm of operatic music, the progress was striking and revolutionary.[3] Down to the nineteenth century the opera, while often highly refined, had been restricted to certain molds demanded by the public taste. The orchestra was incidental and subordinate to the vocal artists and there was little atten-

---

[1] See Elson, *The Book of Musical Knowledge*, Pt. IV.
[2] A. von A. Carse, *History of Orchestration*, Dutton, 1925; Elson, *op. cit.*, Pt. II, and Charles O'Connell, *The Victor Book of the Symphony*, Simon & Schuster, 1934.
[3] See H. E. Krehbiel, *Book of Operas*, Macmillan, 1919, 2 vols. in one.

tion given to providing real unity and harmony in the songs and instrumentation. The first notable success in harmonizing vocal music and instrumental music in the opera was attained by Karl Maria von Weber (1786-1826) in his immortal *Der Freischütz,* completed in 1820. This furnished the suggestions out of which were to grow the Wagnerian use of tone-painting and the development of the leit motif. Weber also deserves credit for his feat in writing a truly national Romanticist German opera in the face of the overwhelming tide of Italianism that had hitherto engulfed this field. The outstanding figure in nineteenth-century operatic music was Richard Wagner (1813-83). In this field he well-nigh measured up to Nietzsche's conception of the superman. He derived many of his themes from the legendary tales and figures of the old German folklore, particularly the Nibelungenlied. The Wagnerian demand for fullness and freedom of tone laid special stress upon orchestral music and at times even threatened to subordinate the vocal element to the instrumental. After Wagner's day there was no longer any danger that the orchestra would be subordinated to the vocal music. Among Wagner's major compositions were *Tristan and Isolde; Tannhäuser;* the famous trilogy, *Der Ring des Nibelungen; Die Meistersinger;* and *Parsifal.* His most famous follower, Richard Strauss (1864-), who was greatly aided by the masterly librettos of Hugo von Hofmannsthal, has composed such effective operas as *Salome, Elektra,* and *Der Rosenkavalier.* In Italian opera the great nineteenth-century figure was Giuseppe Verdi (1813-1901), who also gave much attention to the proper unification of voice and orchestra and wrote operatic music with a wealth of melody absent in Wagner's more majestic compositions. His chief operas were *Aïda, Rigoletto, La Traviata, Il Trovatore,* and *Otello.* Another eminent Italian operatic composer was Gaetano Donizetti (1797-1848), best known for his *Lucia di Lammermoor.* France produced a great operatic composer in Georges Bizet (1838-75), author of the lively and moving *Carmen.* At the end of the century Realism made its way into opera in such representative productions as Pietro Mascagni's *Cavalleria Rusticana* and Ruggiero Leoncavallo's *I Pagliacci.* The foremost composer of comic opera in this age was Gioachino Rossini (1792-1868), whose masterpiece was *Il Barbiere di Siviglia.* Ballad opera was united with social satire and lively musical scores in the numerous compositions of the British collaborators Gilbert and Sullivan.

Piano music owed its remarkable development in the nineteenth century to the fact that Beethoven showed such interest in this instrument in both his performances and his compositions.[1] Beside him the most prominent figures in the composition of music for the piano in the nineteenth century were the Hungarian musician Franz Liszt (1811-86) and the Polish artist Frédéric Chopin (1810-49). Liszt was a wizard in technique and Chopin a master of melody. Many of the more important composers of the nineteenth century wrote music for the violin, but the three outstanding technicians in violin music were Niccolò Paganini (1784-1840), Joseph Joachim (1831-1907), and Eugène Ysaÿe (1858-1931).[2] Paganini is generally regarded as the foremost violin technician who has ever lived and he also composed much music for this instrument. Vocal music as well was placed upon a truly artistic and scientific

---

[1] See Elson, *op. cit.,* Chap. LIV.   [2] *Ibid.,* Chap. LVI.

level during the nineteenth century.[1] Down to this time much of it had been spontaneous and traditional folk music or formal Church music, though one must not overlook the great oratorios of the eighteenth century. The man who was primarily responsible for linking vocal music with truly artistic musical conceptions and expression was Schubert, who first made the song a real lyric melody. He was notably followed in this field by Brahms, Schumann, and Robert Franz (1815-92). Among the outstanding vocal artists in the nineteenth century were Angelica Catalani, Jean de Reszke, Jenny Lind, Amalie Materna, Adelina Patti, Giuseppe Campanari, Christine Nilsson, Marcella Sembrich, Lilli Lehmann, and Italo Campanini.

[1] *Ibid.*, Chap. LV.

SUGGESTED READING

Hammerton, *Universal History of the World*, Chaps. 170-71, 176
Achorn, *European Civilization and Politics since 1815*, Chap. XII
Randall, *The Making of the Modern Mind*, Chaps. XVIII-XXI
F. S. Marvin, *The Century of Hope*, Oxford Press, 1919, Chaps. III, VI, VIII-X
Riley, *From Myth to Reason*, Bk. V
Robinson, *Introduction to the History of Western Europe*, Vol. II, Chaps. XXXVIII-XXXIX
────── and Beard, *The Development of Modern Europe*, Vol. II, Chaps. I, XVIII-XX
Flick, *Modern World History*, Pt. IX
A. R. Wallace and others, *The Progress of the Century*, Harper, 1901
Mayer, *The Seven Seals of Science*, Chaps. IX-XIV
Dampier-Whetham, *History of Science*, Chaps. V-VII
F. H. Garrison, *Introduction to the History of Medicine*, 4th ed., Saunders, 1929, Chaps. X-XI
Duff, *History of Old Testament Criticism*
Conybeare, *History of New Testament Criticism*
E. R. Trattner, *Unravelling the Book of Books*, Scribner, 1929
H. F. Osborn, *From the Greeks to Darwin*, Scribner, 1929
H. G. Wells, J. S. Huxley, and G. P. Wells, *The Science of Life*, Doubleday, Doran, 1931, 2 vols.
F. B. Mason, ed., *Creation by Evolution*, Macmillan, 1928
H. E. Barnes, *The New History and the Social Studies*, Century, 1925
────── *The Twilight of Christianity*
────── and others, *History and Prospects of the Social Sciences*
McGiffert, *The Rise of Modern Religious Ideas*
Robertson, *History of Freethought in the Nineteenth Century*
Cushman, *Beginner's History of Philosophy*, Vol. II, Chaps. XII-XIII
Höffding, *History of Modern Philosophy*, Vol. II
Monroe, *Text-book in the History of Education*, Chaps. XI-XIV
J. T. Merz, *History of European Thought in the Nineteenth Century*, new ed., University of Chicago Press, 1924, 4 vols.
Macy, *The Story of the World's Literature*, Pt. IV
Magnus, *History of European Literature*, Bk. V
Reinach, *Apollo*, Chap. XXV
Gardner, *Art through the Ages*, Chaps. XXII-XXVI
Craven, *Men of Art*, pp. 380-476
Mather, *Modern Painting*, pp. 48-345

T. E. Tallmadge, *The Story of Architecture in America,* rev. ed., Norton, 1929
Bekker, *The Story of Music,* Chaps. xiv-xix
Gray, *History of Music,* Chaps. xiii-xvi
Finney, *A History of Music,* Pt. VII
Elson, *The Book of Musical Knowledge,* Chaps. xii-xxx
David Ewen, ed., *From Bach to Stravinsky,* Norton, 1933
Webster, *Historical Selections,* pp. 830-36, 861-73, 898-910
Robinson and Beard, *Readings in Modern European History,* Vol. II, pp. 178-84, 224-32, 505-19
Scott and Baltzly, *Readings in European History since 1814,* pp. 414-24
Knickerbocker, *Classics of Modern Science,* pp. 157-384
W. P. Hall and E. A. Beller, eds., *Historical Readings in Nineteenth Century Thought,* Century, 1928, pp. 3-86, 201-40
C. S. Darrow and W. de G. C. Rice, eds., *Infidels and Heretics; an Agnostic's Anthology,* Stratford, 1929
R. W. Hinton, ed., *Arsenal for Skeptics,* Knopf, 1934
Cross and Slover, *Heath Readings in the Literature of Europe,* pp. 910-1190
P. H. Houston and R. M. Smith, eds., *Types of World Literature,* Doubleday, Doran, 1930
R. W. Chamberlain, ed., *Beacon Lights of Literature,* Iroquois Publishing Company, 1931-34, 4 vols.

FURTHER REFERENCES

INTELLECTUAL AND CULTURAL ACHIEVEMENTS OF THE NINETEENTH CENTURY. SCIENCE. On the history of science in the nineteenth century, see *Cambridge Modern History,* Vol. XII, Chap. xxiv; Hammerton, *op. cit.,* Chap. 170; Dampier-Whetham, *op. cit.,* Chaps. v-vii; Harvey-Gibson, *Two Thousand Years of Science,* Chaps. xv-xvii; Singer, *The Story of Living Things,* Chaps. viii-xv. The most readable account is Mayer, *op. cit.,* Chaps. ix-xiii.

On mathematics in the period, see Sedgwick and Tyler, *op. cit.,* Chap. xv; E. W. Brown, "History of Mathematics," *Scientific Monthly,* May, 1921; Florian Cajori, *History of Mathematics* (2d ed. rev., Macmillan, 1919); W. W. R. Ball, *Short Account of the History of Mathematics* (Macmillan, 5th ed., 1912); Vera Sanford, *Short History of Mathematics* (Houghton Mifflin, 1930); Roberto Bonola, *Non-Euclidean Geometry* (Open Court Publishing Co., 1912).

On astronomy and astrophysics, see Harvey-Gibson, *op. cit.,* pp. 73-89; Forbes, *History of Astronomy,* pp. 81-186; H. T. Stetson, *Man and the Stars* (McGraw-Hill, 1930).

On nineteenth-century physics, see Mayer, *op. cit.,* Chaps. ix-x; Dampier-Whetham, *op. cit.,* Chap. v; Sedgwick and Tyler, *op. cit.,* Chap. xvi; Harvey-Gibson, *op. cit.,* pp. 105-64, 223-304; Ginzburg, *The Adventure of Science,* Chaps. x-xi.

On nineteenth-century chemistry, see Harvey-Gibson, *op. cit.,* pp. 165 ff., 377 ff., Thorpe, *History of Chemistry,* Vol. I, Chaps. ix-xii; Vol. II, *passim;* John Johnston, "The History of Chemistry," *Scientific Monthly,* August, 1921.

On nineteenth-century biology, see Mayer, *op. cit.,* Chap. xii; Sedgwick and Tyler, *op. cit.,* Chap. xvii; Dampier-Whetham, *op. cit.,* Chap. vi; Ginzburg, *op. cit.,* Chaps. xii-xiv; Singer, *op. cit.,* Chaps. viii-xv; Locy, *The Growth of Biology,* Chaps. xv-xx, and Chaps. xviii-xx of *Biology and Its Masters* (3d ed. rev., Holt, 1928); Pt. III, Chaps. i-xvi, of Erik Nordenskiöld, *History of Biology* (Knopf, 1928).

On the history of psychology, see J. M. Baldwin, *History of Psychology* (Putnam, 1913, 2 vols.); G. K. Adams, *Psychology: Science or Superstition?* (Covici, Friede,

1931); Gardner Murphy, *Historical Introduction to Modern Psychology* (Harcourt, Brace, 1929); W. B. Pillsbury, *History of Psychology* (Norton, 1929); G. S. Hall, *The Founders of Modern Psychology* (Appleton, 1912); G. S. Brett, *History of Psychology* (Macmillan, 1912-21, 3 vols.).

On the history of geology and geography in this century, see Mayer, *op. cit.,* Chap. xi; Harvey-Gibson, *op. cit.,* pp. 89 ff., 342 ff.; Chaps. iii-viii of H. A. Woodward, *History of Geology* (Putnam, 1911); Keltie and Howarth, *History of Geography,* Chaps. ix-xiv; Franklin Thomas, *The Environmental Basis of Society* (Century, 1925).

On nineteenth-century medicine, see Chaps. x-xii of Victor Robinson, *The Story of Medicine* and Chaps. xx-xxix of *Pathfinders in Medicine* (Medical Life Press, 1929); H. E. Sigerist, *American Medicine* (Norton, 1934); Garrison, *op. cit.,* Chaps. x-xi; B. J. Stern, *Social Factors in Medical Practice* (Columbia University Press, 1927); H. W. Haggard, *The Doctor in History* (Yale University Press, 1934).

BIBLICAL CRITICISM. The best introduction to the scholarly view of the Bible is Trattner, *op. cit.* On the history of biblical criticism, see Duff, *op. cit.;* Conybeare, *op. cit.;* T. K. Cheyne, *Founders of Old Testament Criticism* (London, 1923). For an analysis of the Bible as a repository of knowledge, see C. F. Potter, *Is That in the Bible?* (Garden City Publishing Co., 1933).

THE RISE OF THE EVOLUTIONARY DOCTRINE. For the history of evolution, see Riley, *op. cit.,* Bk. V; Osborn, *op. cit.;* J. W. Judd, *The Coming of Evolution* (Putnam, 1910). On biological factors, the clearest presentation is Mason, *op. cit.;* the most technical detail is in Nordenskiöld, *op. cit.,* Pt. III, Chaps. x-xiii. On the evidence supporting evolution, see "Evidences for Evolution," *Scientific Monthly,* August-September, 1925. On the intellectual implications of evolution, see Langdon-Davies, *Man and His Universe,* Chap. vii; Riley, *op. cit.,* Bk. V; *Evolution in Modern Thought* (Modern Library, 1917); S. C. Schmucker, *The Meaning of Evolution* (Macmillan, 1913); G. A. Baitsell, ed., *The Evolution of Earth and Man* (Yale University Press, 1929).

THE SOCIAL SCIENCES. On the social sciences in the nineteenth century, see Randall, *op. cit.,* Chap. xix; Barnes, *The New History and the Social Studies;* Barnes and others, *op. cit.*

On the development of modern sociology, see H. E. Barnes and Howard Becker, *History of Sociological Thought* (Heath, forthcoming); P. A. Sorokin, *Contemporary Sociological Theories* (Harper, 1928); F. N. House, *The Range of Social Theory* (Holt, 1929). On the organicists, see F. W. Coker, *Organismic Theories of the State* (Columbia University Press, 1910).

On the development of anthropology, see A. C. Haddon and A. H. Quiggin, *History of Anthropology* (Putnam, 1910).

On the rise of modern economics, see Haney, *History of Economic Thought;* Gide and Rist, *History of Economic Doctrines.*

On the rise of political science, see Dunning, *History of Political Theories from Rousseau to Spencer;* Gettell, *History of Political Thought;* C. C. Brinton, *English Political Thought in the Nineteenth Century* (London, 1933).

On progress in jurisprudence, see Roscoe Pound, *Interpretations of Legal History* (Macmillan, 1923).

On ethical developments, see Barnes and others, *op. cit.,* Chap. ix; Kropotkin, *Ethics,* Chaps. ix-xiii; Rogers, *Morals in Review,* Chaps. xiv-xix.

NINETEENTH-CENTURY RELIGIOUS MOVEMENTS. On religious developments, see Randall, *op. cit.,* Chap. xix; McGiffert, *op. cit.;* Robertson, *op. cit.* On the religious reaction, see Benn, *History of English Rationalism,* Vol. I, Chap. viii.

718 INTELLECTUAL AND CULTURAL ACHIEVEMENTS

OXFORD MOVEMENT. J. H. Newman, *According to Cardinal Newman* (Dial Press, 1932); G. G. Atkins, *Life of Cardinal Newman* (Harper, 1931); pp. 1-130 of Lytton Strachey, *Eminent Victorians* (Harcourt, Brace, 1918); W. G. Peck, *The Social Implications of the Oxford Movement* (Scribner, 1933).

MORMONISM. J. Q. Adams, *The Birth of Mormonism* (Badger, 1916); H. M. Beardsley, *Joseph Smith and His Mormon Empire* (Houghton Mifflin, 1931); F. A. Golder, T. A. Bailey, and J. L. Smith, *The March of the Mormon Battalion* (Century, 1928); F. S. Harris and N. I. Butt, *The Fruits of Mormonism* (Macmillan, 1925).

CHRISTIAN SCIENCE. H. A. L. Fisher, *Our New Religion* (Peter Smith, 1930); E. F. Dakin, *Mrs. Eddy: The Biography of a Virginal Mind* (Scribner, 1929); E. S. Bates and J. V. Dittemore, *Mary Baker Eddy: The Truth and the Tradition* (Knopf, 1932); Sibyl Wilbur, *The Life of Mary Baker Eddy* (Concord Publishing Co., 1908).

SALVATION ARMY. Harold Begbie, *Life of General William Booth* (Macmillan, 1920, 2 vols.); F. de L. Booth Tucker, *Life of Catherine Booth* (Revell, 1893, 2 vols.); C. B. Booth, *Bramwell Booth* (Sears, 1934); John Manson, *The Salvation Army and the Public* (Dutton, 1906).

On the attack of scientists on Christianity, see Robert Eisler, article "Freethinkers," Encyclopaedia of the Social Sciences; Robertson, *op. cit.,* Chaps. IV, XI-XIII, XV; Benn, *op. cit.,* Vol. II, Chaps. XII-XIV, XVIII, XX; G. E. Macdonald, *Fifty Years of Freethought* (Truth Seeker Press, 1929-31, 2 vols.); Charles Bradlaugh, *Champions of Liberty* (Freethought Press, 1933); Joseph McCabe, *The Life and Letters of George Jacob Holyoake* (London, 1908, 2 vols.); Ingersoll, R. G., *The Complete Lectures* (Regan Publishing Corp., 1930).

On religion, social reform, and philanthropy, see Further References for Chapter XXIV, pp. 964-72, 977-78.

PHILOSOPHY. For philosophical development in the nineteenth century, see Cushman, *op. cit.,* Vol. II, Chap. XIII; Rogers, *Student's History of Philosophy,* pp. 425 ff.; Höffding, *op. cit.,* Vol. II, Bks. IX-X; Riley, *American Thought from Puritanism to Pragmatism;* Abraham Wolf, *The Philosophy of Nietzsche* (Macmillan, 1925).

EDUCATION. On educational advances, see Bradshaw, *Social History of England,* pp. 333-50; Hart, *The Discovery of Intelligence,* Chaps. XXVIII-XXXV; Monroe, *Textbook in the History of Education,* Chaps. XI-XIII; E. P. Cubberley, *History of Education* (Houghton Mifflin, 1920) and *Public Education in the United States* (Houghton Mifflin, 1919).

CHILD PSYCHOLOGY. E. A. Kirkpatrick, *Fundamentals of Child Study* (Macmillan, 1929); D. A. Thom, *The Mental Health of the Child* (Harvard University Press, 1928); M. W. Curti, *Child Psychology* (Longmans, 1930); J. J. B. Morgan, *Child Psychology* (Long & Smith, 1931); G. K. Adams, *Your Child Is Normal* (Covici, Friede, 1934).

LITERATURE. For introductory surveys of literary developments in this century, see Macy, *op. cit.,* Pt. IV; Magnus, *op. cit.,* Bk. V; Faguet, *Initiation into Literature,* Chaps. XV-XXI; Benedetto Croce, *European Literature in the Nineteenth Century* (Knopf, 1924); Friedell, *Cultural History of the Modern Age,* Vol. III, Bk. IV.

ENGLISH LITERATURE. Hammerton, *op. cit.,* Chap. 141; Chaps. XIV-XIX of B. G. Brawley, *New Survey of English Literature* (Crofts, 1925); Legouis and Cazamian, *History of English Literature,* Vol. II, Bks. V-VI; Vols. II-IV of Oliver Elton, *Survey of English Literature, 1780-1880* (Macmillan, 1920, 4 vols.); Chaps. I-V of J. W. Cunliffe, *English Literature during the Last Half-Century* (2d ed. rev., Macmillan, 1919) and *Leaders of the Victorian Revolution;* M. E. Speare, *The Political Novel* (Oxford Press, 1924).

FRENCH LITERATURE. Butler, *History of French Literature,* Vol. II; Nitze and Dargan, *History of French Literature,* Pt. III, Bks. VI-VIII; Wright, *History of French Literature,* Pt. V; Chaps. xxv-xxxiii of A. L. Konta, *History of French Literature* (Appleton, 1910); René Lalou, *Contemporary French Literature* (Knopf, 1924); Lockwood, *Tools and the Man* (for literature and social reform).

ITALIAN LITERATURE. Croce, *op. cit.,* Chaps. i-ii, viii, x, xii, xiv, xxv; Vol. II, Chap. xx of Francesco de Sanctis, *History of Italian Literature* (Harcourt, Brace, 1931, 2 vols.); R. S. Phelps, *Italian Silhouettes* (Knopf, 1924); Garnett, *History of Italian Literature,* Chaps. xxiii-xxv.

SPANISH LITERATURE. Croce, *op. cit.,* Chap. xvii; A. F. G. Bell, *Contemporary Spanish Literature* (Knopf, 1925); Mérimée, *History of Spanish Literature,* Pts. III-IV; James Fitzmaurice-Kelly, *New History of Spanish Literature* (Oxford Press, 1926).

GERMAN LITERATURE. Francke, *History of German Literature,* Chap. ix; Thomas, *History of German Literature,* Chaps. xvii-xx; R. M. Wernaer, *Romanticism and the Romantic School in Germany* (Appleton, 1910); Chaps. vi-viii of Jethro Bithell, ed., *Germany: A Companion to German Studies* (Dial Press, 1932).

SCANDINAVIAN LITERATURE. Macy, *op. cit.,* Chap. xlvi; Chaps. i-iii of H. G. Topsöe-Jensen, *Scandinavian Literature, from Brandes to Our Day* (Norton, 1929); Chaps. i-xii of Illit Gröndahl and Ola Raknes, *Chapters in Norwegian Literature* (Copenhagen, 1923); Chaps. xiv-xv of Theodore Jorgenson, *History of Norwegian Literature* (Macmillan, 1933).

RUSSIAN LITERATURE. M. J. Olgin, *Guide to Russian Literature* (Harcourt, Brace, 1920); Chaps. viii-xi of Kazimierz Waliszewsky, *History of Russian Literature* (Appleton, 1900); Svyatopolk-Mirsky, *Contemporary Russian Literature.*

AMERICAN LITERATURE. Knight, *American Literature and Culture;* S. T. Williams, *The American Spirit in Letters* (Yale University Press, 1926); Russell Blankenship, *American Literature as an Expression of the National Mind* (Holt, 1931); Calverton, *The Liberation of American Literature;* F. L. Pattee, *History of American Literature* (rev. ed., Silver, Burdett, 1909); V. L. Parrington, *Main Currents in American Thought* (Harcourt, Brace, 1927-30, 3 vols.); H. W. Boynton, *James Fenimore Cooper* (Century, 1931); Newton Arvin, *Hawthorne* (Little, Brown, 1929).

ART. Gardner, *op. cit.,* Chaps. xxii-xxvi; Reinach, *op. cit.,* Chap. xxv; Craven, *op. cit.,* Chaps. xvi-xix; Mather, *op. cit.,* pp. 48-345; Julius Meier-Graefe, *Modern Art* (Putnam, 1908, 2 vols.); D. S. MacColl, *Nineteenth Century Art* (Glasgow, 1918); Chaps. xxxv-xlii of E. R. Abbott, *The Great Painters* (Harcourt, Brace, 1927); pp. 1-161 of Clive Bell, *Landmarks in Nineteenth-Century Painting* (Harcourt, Brace, 1927); Bithell, *op. cit.,* Chaps. ix-x; F. J. Mather, C. R. Morey, and W. J. Henderson, *The American Spirit in Art* (Yale University Press, 1927).

On American architecture, see Tallmadge, *op. cit.;* T. F. Hamlin, *The American Spirit in Architecture* (Yale University Press, 1926).

MUSIC. W. R. Spalding, article "History of German Music," under "Germany," Encyclopedia Americana; Gray, *op. cit.,* Chaps. xiii-xvi; Pratt, *History of Music,* Pts. VIII-IX; Bekker, *op. cit.,* Chaps. xiv-xix; Bithell, *op. cit.,* Chap. xi; Stanford and Forsyth, *History of Music;* Elson, *op. cit.;* Ewen, *op. cit.*

PART THREE

THE CRISIS IN WESTERN CIVILIZATION

XX. THE SECOND INDUSTRIAL REVOLUTION

XXI. FINANCE CAPITALISM

XXII. THE CRISIS IN DEMOCRACY AND PARTY GOVERNMENT

XXIII. IN QUEST OF WORLD PEACE

XXIV. CONTEMPORARY PROGRAMS OF SOCIAL AND ECONOMIC REFORM

XXV. SOVIET RUSSIA

XXVI. INTELLECTUAL AND CULTURAL TRENDS IN THE TWENTIETH CENTURY

PART THREE

THE CRISIS IN WESTERN CIVILIZATION

XX. THE SECOND INDUSTRIAL REVOLUTION

XXI. FINANCE CAPITALISM

XXII. THE CRISIS IN DEMOCRACY AND PARTY GOVERNMENT

XXIII. IN QUEST OF WORLD PEACE

XXIV. CONTEMPORARY PROGRAMS OF SOCIAL AND ECONOMIC REFORM

XXV. SOVIET RUSSIA

XXVI. INTELLECTUAL AND CULTURAL TRENDS IN THE TWENTIETH CENTURY

CHAPTER XX

THE SECOND INDUSTRIAL REVOLUTION

I. THE MEANING OF THE SECOND INDUSTRIAL REVOLUTION

There is considerable justification for describing as a "new" or "Second" Industrial Revolution the changes in applied science and industry since the middle of the nineteenth century, and particularly since 1900. Obviously, such an expression is an arbitrary one, and is no more valid than others that are conveniently employed to designate outstanding historical periods or tendencies. But its use is justifiable on the ground that the development of industry within the past eighty years or so does give evidence of certain characteristics which, in several respects, differentiate the more recent period rather clearly from the earlier phase of mechanical production that began around 1750 in England. The term "Second Industrial Revolution" should mainly impress the student with both the complexity and the increased speed of the industrial transformations since about the halfway mark of the nineteenth century.

The choice of the year 1850 as the date that demarcates the terminal years of the first Industrial Revolution, while to a certain extent arbitrary, is convenient and not lacking in historical logic. The essentials of the new mode of industrial production—the machine and the factory system—were solidly established in at least one country, England, and had already taken root or were beginning to be introduced in other countries by that time. Large-scale mechanical industry was an impressive fact, factories had been established, and industrial capitalism had already assumed a position of dominance. The earliest factory legislation had been placed upon the statute books. The middle of the last century is as logical a break as can be found between the first and second periods of modern industrial development. In some countries, as in Germany and Japan, the first and second Industrial Revolutions followed in rapid sequence. Hardly had the machinery characteristic of the first been introduced when the early symptoms of the second began to appear. Our own generation is viewed as falling within the Second Industrial Revolution, but some students are now suggesting that certain postwar tendencies in Europe and the United States are so revolutionary in their significance that they give us grounds for speaking of still another or "Third" Industrial Revolution.[1] Some writers place the first Industrial Revolution between 1750 and 1918 and hold that the Second Revolution begins with the latter date. To the writer it seems better to regard a Third Industrial Revolution as getting under way after 1918.

[1] See above, pp. 629 ff.; and below, pp. 756 ff.

It is quite possible that the conventional historical categories that we now use to describe the development of the machine age and recent industrial changes will soon be abandoned. Very recently Lewis Mumford, following and elaborating Patrick Geddes's conceptions, has, in his very important book, *Technics and Civilization* (1934),[1] given up entirely the use of the term "Industrial Revolution." He divides the rise of the machine economy into three stages: (1) The *Eotechnic* or dawn age of machine technology, resting on a fire, wood, and water basis and involving such things as the water wheel, wooden ships, printing machinery, simple clocks, and the like; (2) the *Paleotechnic* or early machine age, based on coal and iron and embracing the inventions and devices we customarily associate with the first Industrial Revolution; and (3) the *Neotechnic* or recent machine age, depending on electricity and alloys and embodying the technological advances we shall describe in this chapter as the later stages of the Second Industrial Revolution. While Mr. Mumford's divisions and categories are more accurate and illuminating than the conventional historical terms we use, the latter are still so firmly intrenched in historical literature that it seems best to retain them for the time being.

What are some of the changes that justify the term "Second Industrial Revolution"? 1. The earlier processes and tendencies have been enormously accelerated and striking new inventions have been made. 2. The stimulus to and the methodology of invention have been greatly modified and systematized. 3. Novel forms of power—especially electricity—have been discovered and utilized. 4. New machines, greater in size, more complex in construction and operation, and more delicate in adjustment, have been developed. 4. Machinery is becoming automatic and intelligence is transferred to the machine. 5. Precision instruments and machines have appeared. 6. Industry is becoming more completely dominated by science. 7. Synthetic products are replacing natural materials to an impressive degree. 8. The volume of industrial production has grown vastly. 9. Older methods of communication and transportation have been improved upon and new ones have been introduced. 10. Industrial capital has increased tremendously. 11. New forms of industrial organization have developed; a new relationship has sprung up between finance, banking, and industry, creating the era of finance capitalism. 12. More persuasive methods for promoting the sale of products have been worked out and employed in contemporary high-pressure advertising. 13. The new industrial technique has become more generally diffused throughout Europe, America, and the Far East. 14. Industry has come to be more thoroughly concentrated in areas best suited to combine advantages of labor supply, cheap raw materials, and market facilities. 15. New politico-economic policies have been formulated and pursued with far-reaching international consequences. 16. The workingman has been faced with new and difficult problems of life interests and class relationships.

Upon some of these changes we have already touched. We have followed the spread of the first Industrial Revolution from England throughout the rest of the world, and we have spoken of the industrial cartels and syndicates

---

[1] Harcourt, Brace.

of Germany. To illuminate, with the necessary detail, all the changes we have just mentioned is impossible in the space at our disposal. For the most part, we can do no more than clarify their significance and indicate their broader implications.

The "Age of Steel" is among the most common phrases descriptive of our present era. The skyscraper, the modern factory, the ocean liner, the railroad and the miles of glistening tracks, the bridges—all attest the importance of steel in our civilization today. The widespread use of steel followed a series of inventions after the midway mark of the last century which made possible the large-scale production of steel and drastically reduced its price. Among the most important was the process invented (1856) by Sir Henry Bessemer, which, as we have already noted,[1] improved the quality of steel and reduced its price to less than a seventh of the former cost. The Siemens-Martin or open hearth process still further improved steel production. The Thomas-Gilchrist process made it possible, after 1877, to produce a good grade of steel from iron ores high in phosphorus content. These processes are in use today, both singly and in combination, and in recent years electric furnaces have been extensively employed in steel production. The effect of all this has extended the use of steel to a hitherto unheard-of degree and enabled the creation of new types of machinery. Steel is noted here simply as an example; inventions in other fields have been of comparable importance. In the more recent years oil and electricity have been even more intimately connected with the striking industrial changes than has steel.

The Second Industrial Revolution has stimulated invention tremendously, just as invention has also been responsible for so much of industrial development. Under the demands of industry, the ablest of technical minds have been led to concentrate on the solution of industrial problems. Science has become one of the most vital adjuncts of modern industry. Large firms engage scientists and support laboratories for industrial research. Present-day invention is a coöperative enterprise, the product of many minds rather than one. "In the new Industrial Revolution," aptly remarks Professor Schapiro, "the laboratory of industrial research supplanted the garret of the romantic 'inventor.'" Germany was a leader in this field, the government aiding and supporting private industry in its scientific investigations. Today, however, the United States shows the way to the rest of the world in the way of business subsidy to inventions. In capitalistic countries, however, business still dominates technology and science. There are potentially epoch-making inventions already made that are being kept secret or side-tracked by powerful interests, lest they have disastrous effects upon capital that has been invested in processes less efficient.[2] But this suppression of inventions has not been a widespread practice as yet.

[1] See above, pp. 280 ff.
[2] *Cf.* F. J. Frazer, "Big Business Smashes the Machine: How Inventions Are Sabotaged," *Common Sense*, October, 1934, and "Business Smashes the Machine: Inventor's Dilemma, Capitalism's Ingenuity, Society's Loss," *Idem*, November, 1934.

II. APPLIED CHEMISTRY AND THE NEW INDUSTRIAL ORDER

1. SYNTHETIC CHEMISTRY AND THE UTILIZATION OF BY-PRODUCTS

While science aided in many ways, as we have seen, in the promotion of the first Industrial Revolution, it has become much more closely and directly related to the achievements of the Second Industrial Revolution. This development has been clearly stated by Bertrand Russell:

> It is only in the nineteenth century that science came to be commonly regarded as affording a means of improving the general level of human life, not by moral regeneration, and not by political reform, but by increasing men's command over the forces of nature. This point of view was, of course, due to the Industrial Revolution, and to various inventions, such as steamships, railways and telegraphs. This view of science as the handmaid of industry has now become a commonplace.[1]

Chemistry, in particular, has to its credit remarkable accomplishments in the industrial field in recent years. Indeed, it is probable that no other department of science has had so large an influence in transforming our material culture.

The history of chemistry can be traced back to the alchemy of the ancients and the Muslims,[2] but the foundations that possess immediate practical significance were laid chiefly in the seventeenth and eighteenth centuries, the first stages culminating in the work of men like Lavoisier.[3] The first important workers in modern organic chemistry were Liebig and Wöhler, who, about 1832, laid the foundations for the general theory of the benzoic compounds, based upon the combinations in the so-called "benzene-ring." The final solution of the problem was achieved by Kekulé in 1865. A related contribution of great importance was Kekulé's conception of the valency of chemical radicles, which was made the foundation of our modern knowledge of the structure of organic compounds. Kekulé also greatly extended our knowledge of the carbon compounds. It remained, however, for Emil Fischer (1852-1919), probably the most energetic and constructive genius in the history of modern economic and synthetic chemistry, to make the contributions of synthetic chemistry thoroughly available for modern industrial life. This important work began about 1887. One of the most significant of these chemical discoveries was that of synthetic indigo, made by Dr. Adolf von Baeyer in 1897.

We are familiar enough with the fact of the remarkable achievements of contemporary synthetic chemistry in producing, from various by-products, perfumes, flavoring extracts, and a vast variety of other commercial products. We are also acquainted with the like achievements in creating cellulose, sugar, and other similar substances. We have also heard of the striking accomplishments of modern chemistry in revolutionizing the dye industry. We are not, however, always so conscious that the iron and steel industries,[4] the petroleum industry, the rubber industry, and many of the modes of contemporary illumination

---

[1] *Cf.* T. A. Boyd, *Research: The Pathfinder of Science and Industry,* Appleton-Century, 1935.
[2] See above, Vol. I, pp. 538 ff.
[3] On the history of chemistry, see above, pp. 644 ff.
[4] *Cf.* W. H. Voskuil, *Minerals in Modern Industry,* Wiley, 1930.

rest just as decisively upon the contributions of applied chemistry. The remarkable degree to which chemistry underlies contemporary industry has recently been summarized by Professor George Ellery Hale:

> The marvellous development of the chemical industries, which are now producing synthetically from coal-tar distillate most of the dyestuffs, antiseptics, high explosives, perfumes, flavors, and medicinals of commerce, became possible only after many years of painstaking scientific research had established the molecular theory of the structure of carbon compounds.
> Priestley's observation that electric sparks in the air produce compounds of nitrogen and oxygen and Cavendish's production of nitrate of potash from the resulting gases are the sources of the artificial nitrate industry, which has increased the yield of crops.
> Recent improvements in the fixation of nitrogen, the conversion of cheap oils into valuable fats, and the direct production of wood alcohol from coal and water have been made possible by scientific researches on the principles determining the equilibrium of chemical reactions and the possibilities of accelerating them by catalysis and by high pressures and temperatures.
> The discovery of calcium carbide and acetylene gas by Wöhler and the subsequent investigations of Moissan, Wilson, and Le Chatelier made possible the use of acetylene gas for illuminating purposes and its application in blow pipes to the cutting and welding of metals.
> The great industry of paper manufacture from wood pulp had its germ in Réaumur's studies of wasps, which construct their papery nests of materials produced by the mastication of bits of wood and other vegetable substances.[1]

Only the professional chemist or the layman who has read such works as Floyd Darrow's *Story of Chemistry* or E. E. Slosson's *Creative Chemistry*[2] can well understand the astonishing degree to which modern civilization depends upon various phases of applied chemistry. Modern chemical dyes, made from coal tar, have worked an even greater revolution in the dye and textile industries than was produced by the discovery of vegetable dyes during the period of European expansion. Some of the more important of the modern perfumes and flavoring extracts are likewise derived from coal tar. In fact, before the World War Germany exported something like $1,500,000 worth of synthetic perfumes each year. We are now able to manufacture synthetically those extremely important products, nitrogenous compounds, with various derivatives. Glucose, starch, sugar, syrups, and gums are made with ease by synthetic chemical processes. The beet-sugar industry has been built up primarily on the basis of modern chemistry. One of the most interesting and illustrative examples of the remarkable contributions of organic chemistry to modern economic life is to be discerned in the table on page 728, which lists the divers products that are extracted from ordinary maize or Indian corn.[3]

[1] Hale, "Science and the Wealth of Nations," *Harper's Magazine,* January, 1928, pp. 246-47.
[2] Century, new ed., 1930. See also L. V. Redman and A. V. H. Mory, *Romance of Research,* Williams & Wilkins, 1933; and W. J. Hale, *Chemistry Triumphant,* Williams & Wilkins, 1933.
[3] About twenty more products could be added today.

CORN PRODUCTS [1]

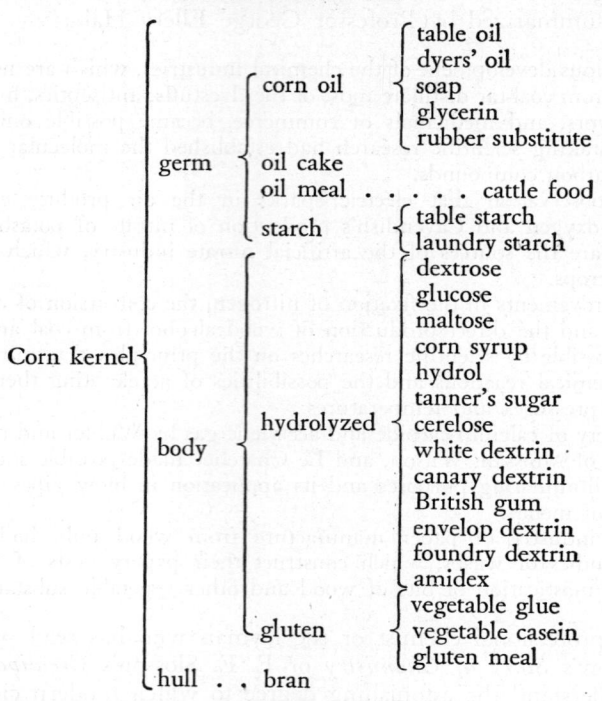

Corn kernel
- germ
  - corn oil
    - table oil
    - dyers' oil
    - soap
    - glycerin
    - rubber substitute
  - oil cake
  - oil meal . . . . . cattle food
- body
  - starch
    - table starch
    - laundry starch
  - hydrolyzed
    - dextrose
    - glucose
    - maltose
    - corn syrup
    - hydrol
    - tanner's sugar
    - cerelose
    - white dextrin
    - canary dextrin
    - British gum
    - envelop dextrin
    - foundry dextrin
    - amidex
  - gluten
    - vegetable glue
    - vegetable casein
    - gluten meal
- hull . . bran

Extremely important also are the various ways in which modern chemistry has been employed to utilize by-products and provide substitutes for more expensive natural products. The previously mentioned utilization of coal tar for the manufacturing of dyes, perfumes, flavoring extracts, and so on is an admirable example both of the utilization of by-products and of the development of substitutes for natural products. Equally interesting has been the utilization of cottonseed oil. Until relatively recent times cottonseed was regarded as entirely useless and was thrown away after it had been separated from the cotton fiber by the gin. At the present time the hulls are utilized as food for cattle, and the oil extracted has the most diverse uses, including the making of salad oil, soap, candles, glycerin, waterproofing material, and oleomargarine. The tables on pages 730 and 731 indicate some of the more important derivatives from cottonseed.

Not only is the manufacturing industry powerfully advanced by the new chemistry, but also the more important modern scientific methods of fertilizing the soil rest upon the discoveries and applications of contemporary chemical science.[2] Particularly important are the possibilities of manufacturing successfully artificial nitrogen on a large scale. Chemistry not only produces the par-

---

[1] Slosson, *Creative Chemistry*, p. 184. Used by the courtesy of the Appleton-Century Company.
[2] *Cf.* F. L. Darrow, *The Story of Chemistry*, rev. ed., Bobbs-Merrill, 1930, Chap. VI.

APPLIED CHEMISTRY AND NEW INDUSTRIAL ORDER

ticular types of fertilizers that are useful to modern agricultural chemistry, but it also provides a method for analyzing the soil in order to ascertain exactly what types of chemicals need to be added in each case in order to insure the maximum degree of fertility.

Another interesting application of chemistry (and physics) to modern industry has been the creation of new and more efficient methods of refrigeration and the resulting efficiency in the storage of meats, vegetables, and other foods.[1] Contemporary refrigeration, resting chiefly on chemical technique, is as far ahead of the old ice box and the refrigerator car as these were ahead of cooling-boxes in cellars. An unlimited supply of pure artificial ice can be made by the use of certain gases, especially ammonia gas. Man is no longer dependent upon a cold winter for his ice supply. Indeed, ice can be made in any quantity desired even in tropical areas. Electric, chemical, and oil-burning refrigerators manufacture their own ice. Even more remarkable and impressive is the production and use of the so-called dry ice, solid carbon dioxide, which freezes foods to a temperature far below what was possible before and preserves them at this low temperature for indefinite periods.

2. THE MODERN PETROLEUM INDUSTRY

Among the most important types of present-day businesses that are dependent to a major degree upon modern chemistry are the petroleum and rubber industries. With the development of modern machinery and its need for lubricants, and particularly with the appearance of the successful internal-combustion engine, the importance of petroleum and its derivatives in modern economic life has become increasingly apparent.[2] In many ways, it is not inaccurate to regard the present as the "Oil Age." Certainly there is, with the possible exceptions of steel and coal, no element in modern life more indispensable than petroleum and its derivatives in their various uses and services.

A general knowledge of the existence of petroleum has existed from ancient times. In the first half of the nineteenth century petroleum was extracted in small quantities and sold for its alleged medicinal properties. Because one of the chief promoters of this enterprise was Samuel Kier, petroleum was for a time known as Kier oil. Just before the American Civil War (1859), Edwin L. Drake and others successfully solved the problem of drilling shallow oil wells, and before the Civil War was over thousands of barrels of oil could be produced daily by the American oil industry.

There was, however, relatively little demand for this oil, and the slight supply exceeded the demand. But in the seventies the further utilization of petroleum, particularly in kerosene lamps, increased the demand. Soon the growing importance of the internal-combustion engine still further widened the market for petroleum products. At the same time, an increased market for the heavier petroleum derivatives was found in the use of lubricants for all types of modern machinery. Parallel with the growing demand for petroleum products

---

[1] *Cf.* Cressy, *Discoveries and Inventions of the Twentieth Century*, Chap. x.
[2] *Cf.* Egloff, *Earth Oil*, Chap. 1.

PRODUCTS AND USES OF COTTONSEED [1]

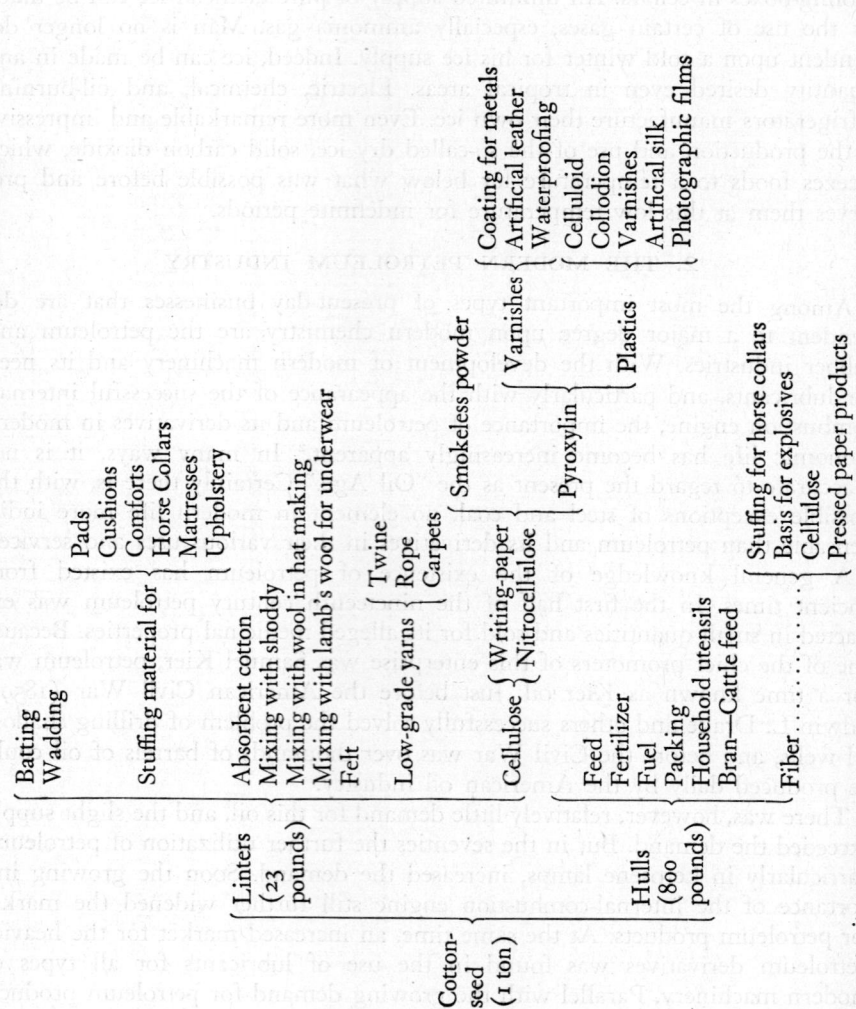

Cottonseed (1 ton)
- Linters (23 pounds)
  - Batting
  - Wadding
  - Stuffing material for
    - Pads
    - Cushions
    - Comforts
    - Horse Collars
    - Mattresses
    - Upholstery
  - Absorbent cotton
  - Mixing with shoddy
  - Mixing with wool in hat making
  - Mixing with lamb's wool for underwear
  - Felt
  - Low-grade yarns
    - Twine
    - Rope
    - Carpets
  - Cellulose
    - Writing-paper
    - Nitrocellulose
      - Smokeless powder
      - Varnishes
        - Coating for metals
        - Artificial leather
        - Waterproofing
      - Pyroxylin Plastics
        - Celluloid
        - Collodion
        - Varnishes
        - Artificial silk
        - Photographic films
- Hulls (800 pounds)
  - Feed
  - Fertilizer
  - Fuel
  - Packing
  - Household utensils
  - Bran—Cattle feed
- Fiber
  - Stuffing for horse collars
  - Basis for explosives
  - Cellulose
  - Pressed paper products

[1] Slosson, *op. cit.*, pp. 202–03.

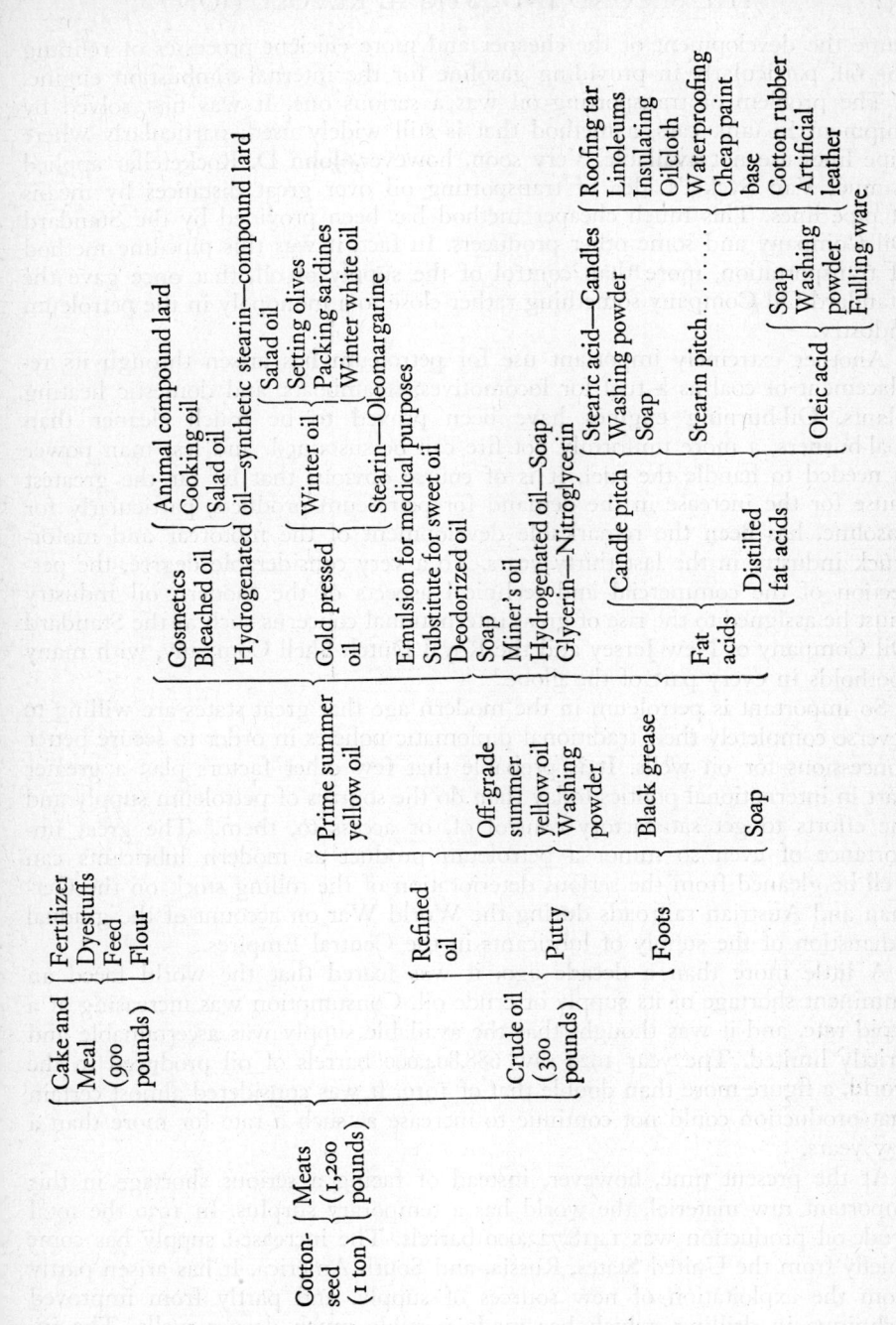

Cotton-seed (1 ton)
- Cake and Meal (900 pounds)
  - Fertilizer
  - Dyestuffs
  - Feed
  - Flour
- Meats (1,200 pounds)
- Crude oil (300 pounds)
  - Refined oil
    - Cosmetics
    - Bleached oil
      - Animal compound lard
      - Cooking oil
      - Salad oil
    - Hydrogenated oil—synthetic stearin—compound lard
      - Salad oil
      - Setting olives
      - Packing sardines
      - Winter white oil
    - Cold pressed oil
      - Winter oil
      - Stearin—Oleomargarine
    - Emulsion for medical purposes
    - Substitute for sweet oil
    - Deodorized oil
  - Prime summer yellow oil
    - Soap
    - Miner's oil
    - Hydrogenated oil—Soap
    - Glycerin—Nitroglycerin
      - Stearic acid—Candles
      - Washing powder
      - Soap
  - Putty
  - Off-grade summer yellow oil
  - Washing powder
  - Foots
    - Candle pitch
    - Stearin pitch
      - Roofing tar
      - Linoleums
      - Insulating
      - Oilcloth
      - Waterproofing
      - Cheap paint base
      - Cotton rubber
      - Artificial leather
    - Distilled fat acids
    - Fat acids
      - Oleic acid
        - Soap
        - Washing powder
        - Fulling ware
  - Black grease
  - Soap

came the development of the cheaper and more efficient processes of refining the oil, particularly in providing gasoline for the internal-combustion engine.

The problem of transporting oil was a serious one. It was first solved by shipment in tank cars, a method that is still widely used, particularly where pipe lines are not available. Very soon, however, John D. Rockefeller applied Samuel Van Syckel's idea of transporting oil over great distances by means of pipe lines. This much cheaper method has been provided by the Standard Oil Company and some other producers. In fact, it was this pipe-line method of transportation, more than control of the supply of oil, that once gave the Standard Oil Company something rather close to a monopoly in the petroleum industry.

Another extremely important use for petroleum has arisen through its replacement of coal as a fuel for locomotives, steamboats, and domestic heating plants. Oil-burning engines have been proved to be much cleaner than coal-burners, a more uniformly hot fire can be sustained, and less man power is needed to handle the fuel. It is of course obvious that by far the greatest cause for the increase in the demand for petroleum products, particularly for gasoline, has been the remarkable development of the motorcar and motor-truck industry in the last thirty years. To a very considerable degree, the perfection of the commercial and technical aspects of the modern oil industry must be assigned to the rise of great international concerns such as the Standard Oil Company of New Jersey and the Royal Dutch Shell Company, with many footholds in every part of the globe.[1]

So important is petroleum in the modern age that great states are willing to reverse completely their traditional diplomatic policies in order to secure better concessions for oil wells. It is probable that few other factors play a greater part in international politics today than do the sources of petroleum supply and the efforts to get satisfactory control of, or access to, them.[2] The great importance of even so minor a petroleum product as modern lubricants can well be gleaned from the serious deterioration of the rolling stock on the German and Austrian railroads during the World War on account of the gradual exhaustion of the supply of lubricants in the Central Empires.

A little more than a decade ago, it was feared that the world faced an imminent shortage of its supply of crude oil. Consumption was increasing at a rapid rate, and it was thought that the available supply was ascertainable and strictly limited. The year 1920 saw 688,804,000 barrels of oil produced in the world, a figure more than double that of 1910. It was considered almost certain that production could not continue to increase at such a rate for more than a few years.

At the present time, however, instead of facing a serious shortage in this important raw material, the world has a temporary surplus. In 1930 the total crude-oil production was 1,418,723,000 barrels. The increased supply has come chiefly from the United States, Russia, and South America. It has arisen partly from the exploitation of new sources of supply, and partly from improved technique in drilling, which has made possible much deeper wells. The in-

---

[1] *Cf.* Denny, *We Fight for Oil.*   [2] *Cf.* Fischer, *Oil Imperialism.*

crease in petroleum production has been so great that in the United States, at least, the annual output is being curtailed. Nevertheless, even the increased supply now available through the discovery of new oil fields and the improved methods of refining will not suffice for any great period in the future unless the abominable and unnecessary waste of today is checked.[1]

Of equal significance for the oil industry have been the technical improvements in the past decade in methods of refining. As a result, the amount of gasoline secured from a given quantity of crude oil has almost doubled—in 1921 it was 27 per cent; in 1930 it was 42 per cent; by 1932 it was over 50 per cent. This great increase is due chiefly to a new refining process known as cracking. It is not always a substitute for the older method of distillation, but is frequently applied to the residue after straight-run distilling has taken place. Instead of merely separating the crude oil into its various parts—benzine, gasoline, kerosene, fuel oil, lubricating oil, and asphaltum—as in the older distilling method, cracking brings about, through the use of great heat and high pressure,[2] a chemical decomposition of the gas and fuel-oil fractions in crude oil. The use of this process in the United States in 1930 yielded considerably more gasoline than all the refineries distilled in 1921. Forty per cent of the gasoline consumed in the United States today is "cracked" gasoline. This type is superior to distilled gasoline as a motor fuel, especially for the new high-compression motors. The refining and cracking plants of the United States today have a daily capacity of about 6,000,000 barrels. An even newer process, introduced from Germany and known as hydrogenation, still further increases the possible yield of gasoline from a given quantity of crude oil. It treats petroleum oils at a temperature of about 900° F. and a pressure of 3,000 pounds per square inch and adds hydrogen. Were it not for the cracking process there would not be gasoline enough to run the motorcars of the world today.

3. THE DEVELOPMENT OF THE RUBBER INDUSTRY

The rubber industry is also a child of modern chemistry.[3] Raw native rubber was known for centuries before it was utilized in a commercial way. Down to the middle of the nineteenth century the only uses of rubber were in spreading it on surfaces in its raw state in order to make them shed water or rolling it into balls for erasers and similar devices. Its successful utilization in the manufacture of clothing had to wait until some method was found to enable rubber to withstand extremes of temperature and to give it sufficient strength to prevent quick cracking or distintegration.

The only important utilization of rubber for clothing that was achieved before the time of Goodyear was an invention of Charles Mackintosh. About 1825 he conceived the idea of putting a layer of gum rubber between two pieces of cloth, thus rendering the product waterproof. The rubberized raincoat or "mackintosh," as it was called, has perpetuated the name of its inventor.

The honor of having discovered a method of adapting rubber to changes

---

[1] *Cf.* H. I. Ickes, "The Crisis in Oil: A Huge National Problem," New York *Times,* June 11, 1933, Sec. 8, p. 1.
[2] A temperature of 950° F. and a pressure of 400 pounds per square inch.
[3] *Cf.* B. D. Luff, *The Chemistry of Rubber,* Van Nostrand, 1924.

of temperature and to commercial uses on a large scale must be assigned to an American, Charles Goodyear, who in 1839 accidentally dropped on the stove a mixture of rubber gum and sulphur.[1] He noticed that these two substances tended to fuse under heat. In this way there was accidentally discovered the famous process known as the vulcanization of rubber. From subsequent improvements of this process all forms of modern commercial rubber are derived. Goodyear's discovery made possible a remarkable expansion of the rubber industry in the manufacture of rubber clothing and footwear. In this development, Goodyear himself and others, such as Goodrich and Candee, took a very prominent part. But, important as rubber clothing and footwear may be in modern life, the demand for rubber products of this sort never reached anything like the commercial significance of the market that has grown out of the manufacturing of bicycle and automobile tires.

The principle of the pneumatic tire was suggested by R. W. Thompson of London in the year 1845, but the first practical demonstration of the pneumatic tire was the work of an Irish veterinary surgeon, J. B. Dunlop, in 1888. Dunlop's invention was practically synchronous with the remarkable growth of the bicycle industry in the United States and Europe, which created an enormous demand for rubber. Scarcely had the bicycle industry become thoroughly established when the automobile or "horseless carriage" made its first appearance about 1895. Within ten years the automobile industry had become an important one, and it is now one of the major industries of the contemporary world.

The phenomenally rapid growth of the automobile industry has created the remarkable rubber industry of the present day, which devotes much of its efforts to the production of automobile tires. The total value of rubber products in the United States in 1930 was well over $1,000,000,000. The consumption of raw rubber in the United States rose from 100,000 tons in 1913 to 469,000 tons in 1929, and dropped to 349,000 in 1931. Over 143,000,000 automobile tires were produced in the United States in 1929. The maximum raw-rubber consumption of the world was reached in 1929, when no less than 808,000 long tons were absorbed.

The rubber industry, of course, has far wider ramifications than the transformation of raw rubber into rubber products and the distribution of these products to the consumer. It involves also the development of rubber plantations and other methods of insuring an adequate supply of raw rubber. As late as 1910, more than 90 per cent of the world's supply of crude rubber came from wild rubber trees. Ever since 1900, however, the cultivation of rubber has been on the increase, until at the present time over 95 per cent of the annual supply is from rubber plantations, located chiefly in Ceylon, the Malay Peninsula, and the Dutch East Indies.[2] More than 3,000,000 acres of rubber plantations are now under cultivation, producing annually over 800,000 long tons of crude rubber. Rubber production from wild rubber trees now amounts to only about 20,000 tons annually. In fact, the production of rubber increased so rapidly that it has now overtaken the demand, owing in part to the depression beginning in 1929. As a result, the period since the World War has been characterized by great fluctuations in the price of raw rubber, which at times

---

[1] See Iles, *Leading American Inventors,* pp. 176 ff. [2] See Zimmermann, *op. cit.,* pp. 382 ff.

fell below the cost of production. As the earliest plantations were mainly in English colonial territory, it seemed possible for Britain to restrict rubber production, or at least rubber export, by a graduated tax, which it attempted to do in 1922.[1] The ultimate result was to stimulate the planting of rubber trees, at first by the Dutch interests, and later by Americans, in Sumatra, Malaysia, and Liberia. As these plantations came to bearing age, it became impossible for England to control the price of raw rubber, and the restrictive plan was abandoned in 1928. British and Dutch interests have now joined hands. Raw rubber has now reached a condition similar to that of coffee, the productive capacity exceeding the demand by a considerable margin, with consequent falls in price disastrous to producers. Much experimental work is now being carried on in the manufacture of synthetic rubber. This may ultimately prove very successful and its threat already operates to keep down the price of raw native rubber.

The great increase in the production of raw rubber has been accompanied by equally striking changes in rubber manufacturing. Temporary high prices of raw rubber greatly stimulated the reclamation of used rubber, which increased by about 40 per cent between 1925 and 1929. Great economies have also been affected in the use of rubber, and many substitutes have come into use.

At the same time, new discoveries in synthetic chemistry have been applied to rubber,[2] the manufacturing technique has been improved, and high-speed machinery has been introduced within a few years so as to quadruple the output per worker. Greatly improved methods of vulcanization have been brought into use.

One of the most striking developments in the industry has been the reduction in the number of tire-manufacturing establishments, and the increase in their size. Census figures indicate that the number decreased by about 50 per cent between 1920 and 1929, while during the same period the number of wage-earners in the industry increased by about the same proportion. The rubber manufacturing industry is now in the same condition as the rubber plantations—able to produce more than the market can absorb at profitable prices.

In spite of the fact that rubber tires constitute overwhelmingly the largest single item in the rubber industry, other rubber products are of immense industrial and commercial significance. In 1929, rubber goods of all kinds to the value of $1,117,460,000 were produced in the United States. Of this total, rubber tires of all kinds accounted for only a little over half. An innovation of great promise is Lastex, an elastic cloth product made from silk and rubber thread, invented in 1930.[3] It is used especially in corsets, underwear, stockings, and bathing-suits. Lastex is, however, only one of many remarkable new rubber products.

In this brief space we have not, of course, in any sense pretended to do more than call attention very briefly to some of the outstanding ways in which contemporary chemistry has revolutionized modern material culture. To give anything like a complete account, one would certainly need to describe: (1) The development of the Portland cement industry and its effect upon the con-

---
[1] See C. R. Whittlesey, *Governmental Control of Crude Rubber,* Princeton University Press, 1931.
[2] See Slosson, *op. cit.,* Chap. VIII.
[3] See E. A. Hauser, *Latex,* Chemical Catalog Co., 1930.

struction of concrete buildings and roads; (2) the application of chemistry to the manufacture of high explosives for both peace-time and warfare purposes; (3) the rise and expansion of modern photography, as science, art, and industry; (4) the production and uses of industrial alcohol; (5) the application of chemical knowledge to the field of agriculture, in the way of soil analysis, and in the provision of nitrogen, potash, and other fertilizers; and (6) the varied uses of chemistry in modern medicine, from Pasteur's researches in pathology to radium therapy, the chemical reproduction of the hormones of the glands of internal secretion and of vitamins, and the application of chemicals in sanitation and preventive medicine.

III. NEW DEVELOPMENTS IN TRANSPORTATION AND COMMUNICATION

1. RECENT TRANSPORTATION CHANGES

Quite as revolutionary as the application of steam to industry after 1785 have been recent developments in new sources and quantities of power used in manufacturing and transportation.

The latest, and in some ways the most striking, phase of the development of motive power has been the result of our growing knowledge of methods of generating and utilizing electricity. Thanks to the work of physicists such as Galvani, Volta, Benjamin Franklin, Faraday, Kelvin, and others, and to the application of their researches by Westinghouse, Tesla, Ferranti, and Steinmetz, it is now possible to generate electricity in the regions where water power is available. It can then be conducted over high-tension wires for hundreds of miles to areas that are well located as manufacturing and commercial centers. In this manner modern science is overcoming the natural obstacles in the exploitation of water power remote from suitable industrial areas.

If some ingenious inventor is able to provide a method of conducting electrical current over great distances without the present serious waste in transit, there seems little question that in most modern states electricity will become by far the most important type of motive power. Already many countries, defective in their supply of coal for steam power or of petroleum for the internal-combusion engine, are taking vigorous steps to exploit their water power for generating electricity. This has been particularly true of Sweden, Italy, and Japan. Very recently, however, new and cheaper physico-chemical methods of producing steam—the "two-fluid systems"—have appeared. If commercially successful in their application to the production of electricity, these may eliminate the use of hydroelectric power, except in the immediate vicinity of its production.[1]

Since the middle of the last century the revolutionary changes in transportation and communication have, for practical purposes, operated so as to decrease the size of the world and create a unity new in history. The developments in this field fall into two categories: (1) Improvements in the older facilities of transportation and communication; and (2) the invention of new ones.

Transcontinental railroad lines have been constructed in America, Europe,

---

[1] See Cressy, *op. cit.,* Chap. III.

and Asia, and one in Africa is more than three-fourths completed. The steam locomotive has been so vastly improved that the engines of the fifties—or even of the nineties—are, by comparison, hardly more than puny curiosities. Steel has replaced wood in the construction of railway cars; the Pullman sleeping and dining cars have been introduced; and devices without number have helped to make railroad travel more safe and more comfortable. Comparable innovations, among which the refrigerator car is of the greatest significance, have favorably affected the shipment of freight. Perishables can now be shipped across a continent; flowers grown in Spain can be sold in the London market.[1] Service has been greatly speeded up, and express trains, in both Europe and America, travel long distances at a rate that would have been incredible to the Englishmen who first watched Stephenson's locomotive.

One of the latest developments in railroad technique has been the electric locomotive. It is much cleaner than the steam locomotive, is ever ready for service, and also offers far less danger of starting fires along the right of way. The use of this type of power is bound to increase with the gradual exhaustion of the world's coal and oil supplies. The electric car has proved of great convenience in urban and interurban transportation. It has reached its fullest development in the great metropolitan subways. Diesel-motored trains are increasing in use.

Increased speed of trains has been characteristic of our era. One hundred years ago a speed of 30 miles an hour was astonishing. In 1895 a train on the London and Northwestern Railway averaged 63.28 miles an hour for a distance of 540 miles. In the same year a train on the Pennsylvania Railroad averaged 76.5 miles an hour for the 58 miles between Atlantic City and Camden. In 1897 the Black Diamond Express of the Lehigh Valley Railroad averaged 80 miles an hour over the 44 miles between Alpine and Geneva, New York. In March, 1902, a Burlington train averaged 98.7 miles an hour over a test of 14 miles. In 1904 a Great Western train in England ran over the 118.5 miles from Paddington to Bristol at an average speed of 84.6 miles per hour. This record stood for thirty years. The fastest time ever made by a train drawn by a steam locomotive was hung up by the Chicago, Milwaukee and St. Paul Railroad on July 20, 1934. The train covered 68.9 miles between the suburbs of Chicago and the suburbs of Milwaukee at an average speed of 90.6 miles per hour, and at times attained a speed of 103 miles an hour. The engine pulled a train of five cars weighing 390 tons. But all speed records of steam trains were shattered by the Diesel-driven, streamline motor train, the Zephyr, of the Chicago, Burlington and Quincy Railroad in 1934. On a four-mile stretch in New Jersey (on a demonstration trip) it averaged 104 miles an hour. But its greatest feat was covering the 1,015 miles from Denver, Colorado, to Chicago, Illinois, in 785 minutes at an average speed of 77.6 miles an hour for the trip. It made a top speed of 112.5 miles per hour. This streamline train and Diesel engines may point the way to a revolution in railroad transportation. It is worth remembering, however, that way back in 1893 Engine 999 drew the Empire State Express on the New York Central Railroad at a speed of 112.5 miles an hour for one mile.[2] The most notable improvement in regard to speed is the possibility of maintaining high speed over long distances. In 1924 a combined Santa

---

[1] *Cf. Ibid.*, Chap. x.   [2] See above, p. 308.

Fe-New York Central train covered the 3,197 miles from Los Angeles to New York City in 69.7 hours of running time at an average speed of 46.25 miles per hour, while in 1925 a Canadian National train ran from Montreal to Vancouver, a distance of 2,938 miles, at an average speed of over 53 miles an hour. Late in October, 1934, a Diesel-driven, streamlined, Union Pacific train made the run from Los Angeles to New York City in 56 hours and 55 minutes. The time might have been much faster, since from Chicago to New York the train observed the scheduled speed of the Twentieth Century Limited. The trip could easily have been made in less than 50 hours. Gasoline cars propelled by an internal-combustion engine are coming to be commonly used where there is no need for a heavy locomotive and a train of cars. Great speed is secured by combining the automobile and locomotive, in other words, putting a motor-driven car on railroad tracks. The latest innovation is a streamlined car designed in the shape of a Zeppelin and deriving part of its power from a propeller. It is the work of a German named Krückenberg and is capable of maintaining a speed of over 100 miles an hour. It has not been adopted for commercial use thus far. The so-called Flying Hamburger, operating between Berlin and Hamburg, is a streamlined train much like the Burlington Zephyr.

Along with the technical phases of the improvement of locomotives, the building of larger and safer cars—particularly the employment of steel in car construction—and greater train speed, has come a remarkable development of safety appliances. These have rested mainly upon the utilization of electricity for purposes of communication. The telegraph, the telephone, and the electrically operated signaling system, together with the air brake and the automatic coupler, have made it possible to operate modern railroads with a reasonable degree of safety to passengers, operatives, and freight. The block signal system, introduced much earlier in Europe than in America, has perhaps done more than any other improvement to reduce accidents. It not only enables the engineer to ascertain whether the track is clear ahead of him; in its later form, it also automatically stops the train if a danger signal is passed by the engineer.

In our own day, the railroad has begun to meet very serious competition, particularly in America, from the motor truck and the motorbus. After all but eliminating the labor of the horse in some regions of the world, the automobile is now making serious inroads upon the railway. Present tendencies in the improvement of the motorcar and of the roads adapted for such traffic indicate that, for shipments of five hundred miles and under and confined to perishable or relatively light commodities, automobile trucking is proving a serious if not fatal competitor to railroad service. In passenger service, likewise, the railroads are now meeting heavy competition from motorbuses. Particularly interesting is the fact that the railroads have in a number of cases been compelled to install bus and truck service under their own auspices to meet the challenge of the independent buses and trucks, though the success of this protective measure is as yet in doubt.[1] Another mode of meeting the competition of buses in passenger traffic has been the installation not only of many conveniences but also much luxury in train service. Telephones and stock tickers have been placed in trains at terminals. Radios have been installed. The better trains frequently have shower baths, barber shops, beauty parlors, luxurious

---

[1] *Cf.* Charles Angoff, "The Railroads at Bay," *American Mercury,* January, 1928.

lounging quarters, and the like. Along with this have gone efforts to achieve greater speed, a matter already discussed. The streamlined Diesel-driven trains are a direct answer of the railroads to bus competition.

Trolley cars, both urban and interurban, have been decisively worsted by motorbuses. The latter are as yet only competitors of the railroads, but they have well-nigh wiped out the flourishing trolley service of a few years ago.

The first automobiles were really steam "road locomotives" which are hard to separate in their history from the early railroad locomotives. They were popular in England in the thirties of the last century, but were driven off the roads by the railroad monopolies. The modern automobile dates from the invention of the high-speed internal-combustion motor and the carburetor by Gottlieb Daimler in 1883. His motor was soon adapted to the "horseless carriage" by Panhard, Levassor, and Peugeot in France and by Carl Benz in Germany, and the automobile era was forthwith launched about 1886. Dunlop's pneumatic tire was, fortunately, made available at the same period.

The automobile industry, which got its real start in the last quarter of the nineteenth century, has now become one of the most typical of modern, large-scale, highly mechanized industries. The coming of the automobile has necessitated a new era of road-building, and has left an unmistakable imprint upon modern civilization, particularly upon that of America.

The automobile industry, especially in so far as mass production is concerned, is primarily centered in the United States. The total world-production of cars in 1928, the last year preceding the great depression, was 5,198,000. Of these no less than 4,601,000 were produced in the United States. At first, the motorcar industry was chiefly a luxury one. The cars were too expensive to encourage popular use. As late as 1912 only 43.8 per cent of the cars produced in the United States sold for less than $1,000. By 1915 over 72.3 per cent sold for less than this sum. In 1930, the average wholesale f.o.b. price of American cars, ranging from the Cadillac and Packard to the Ford, was $724. Henry Ford was the leading figure in marketing the low-priced car and making it a commodity for the majority of Americans. He utilized to a preëminent degree the mass-production methods that characterize the Second Industrial Revolution.[1] His example was followed by General Motors in their production of the Chevrolet car, and other manufacturers have since followed in their wake. By 1928 the automobile industry exceeded all other American industries in the wholesale value of products as well as in the value of exports. No less than 4,300,000 workers were employed and the wholesale value of cars produced is estimated at $3,162,798,000. A high degree of concentration has been achieved, over 90 per cent of the car production being carried on by the ten leading producers of the country. The automobile industry has vastly stimulated other industries, such as iron, steel, glass, electrical accessories, rubber tires, and rubberized textiles.

The enormous growth and extent of automotive traffic today is well summarized by Mr. George B. Galloway:

The growth of automotive traffic during the last decade may be seen in the statistics of motor vehicle registrations, motor passenger traffic, and motor truck traffic.

---

[1] See below, pp. 752 ff.

Stimulated by the development of hard-surfaced roads, improved with the aid of federal funds, motor vehicle registrations have greatly increased since 1920. In that year 8,225,859 passenger cars, taxis, and buses were registered in the United States compared with 23,121,589 in 1929, a growth of 180 per cent. Approximately 10,000 auto buses were included in the registrations for 1920, and in 1929 approximately 92,500, an increase of 825 per cent. The bus figures cover both revenue and non-revenue buses, the latter being those used for school purposes, by institutions, and the like. In 1920 there were 1,006,082 registered motor trucks compared with 3,379,854 in 1929, an increase of 235 per cent. During the decade the average carrying capacity of both passenger buses and motor trucks increased considerably.

Passenger traffic by private (that is, non-commercial) automobile is not easily calculable. It has been estimated, however, that passenger automobiles (other than buses) average about 5,000 miles annually, that an average of 2½ passengers are carried per car, and that about one-half of the total passenger-car mileage is made on the rural highways, that is, in interurban travel. On this basis, the total number of interurban passenger-miles in 1929 approximated 145 billion. Passenger-mileage on the steam railways in 1929 was less than 32 billion. Some general statistics are also available for autobus passenger traffic. Buses operating in interurban service represent about three-tenths of the total bus registration. Travel by interurban bus amounted to approximately 4,375,000,000 passenger-miles in 1926 and 6,797,000,000 passenger-miles in 1929, an increase during the four years of 55 per cent. In addition to the intercity service, 4,038,000,000 bus passenger-miles were traveled in city service in 1929, making a total of 10,835,000,000 bus passenger-miles in 1929.

Detailed information with respect to the extent of motor truck traffic is lacking, but some idea of its growth may be gained from the following figures. Motor truck registrations increased 235 per cent between 1920 and 1929. Making allowance for a gradual increase in unit capacity during that period, and for the more extensive use of trucks for the movement of freight in interurban service, it is estimated that in 1929 more than 15 billion ton-miles of commercial freight was moved by truck between cities and towns.[1]

Advances in speed have characterized automobiles as they have railroad trains and airplanes. A speed of twenty miles an hour was "fast" for the early models, whereas Sir Malcolm Campbell drove his Bluebird at a speed of 276.8 miles per hour on March 8, 1935, at Daytona Beach, Florida. "Cannon-ball" Baker drove an automobile across the continent in 69 hours, equaling the best steam-propelled train time, whereas the first automobile trip across the country—some thirty years ago—required 54 days.

The last and most novel addition to the means of transportation has been the airplane. The possibility of an airplane was first set forth by the medieval scientist Roger Bacon, in a famous letter written towards the close of the thirteenth century. The first important practical step towards aerial navigation was taken by the Montgolfiers when (1783) they demonstrated the practicability of an air trip by means of the balloon. The first airship was a combination of the air propeller and the balloon, the balloon having been designed in an elongated form to lessen air resistance. The first promising utilization of this so-called dirigible balloon was made by the Brazilian, Alberto Santos-Dumont, who circled the Eiffel Tower in 1901.

[1] G. B. Galloway, "Competition in Transportation," pp. 205-06, *Editorial Research Reports,* Vol. I, No. 12, 1931.

TRANSPORTATION AND COMMUNICATION

The first experiments with the practicability of the heavier-than-air machine were the work of Otto Lilienthal, Hiram Maxim, and S. P. Langley in the last decade of the nineteenth century. Langley's work was carried along by the Wright brothers, who, in 1903, made the first successful flight in a heavier-than-air motor-driven plane at Kitty Hawk, North Carolina. In 1906, they made a flight of over forty miles. A French aviator, Louis Blériot, flew the English Channel on July 25, 1909. Steady progress was made in the practical improvement of the airplane up to the outbreak of the World War.

The value of the airship in wartime for military observation was so apparent that the very best scientific ability in each of the warring countries was speedily utilized in the interest of devising better airplanes, and it is probable that no other phase of modern technology was so revolutionized during the war as the airplane service. The first nonstop transatlantic flight was made by Captain John Alcock and Lieutenant Arthur W. Brown on June 14, 1919. For sheer courage it has not been equaled by any later flight. The colorful flight of Charles A. Lindbergh from New York to Paris in 1927—the first solo flight across the Atlantic—served to make the public "air-conscious." In 1931 Post and Gatty flew around the world in 8 days and 15 hours. In 1933 Post made a round-the-world solo flight in 7 days, 18 hours, and 49 minutes.

Since the war regular passenger, mail, and express lines have been established in and between most of the European countries, within the United States, and between that country and several of the South American states. A hesitating beginning has also been made in transoceanic passenger and mail service, marked by the flights of the *Graf Zeppelin,* the *R-100,* and the *DO-X.* Airplane service had vastly increased the speed of travel and the consequent mobility of mankind. A man may leave Cleveland after a leisurely breakfast, lunch in New York City, conclude his business, and get back to Cleveland for dinner.

There is still much room for technical improvement in aviation, especially in the engines [1] and the terminal facilities, but air service is already assuredly a permanent and significant addition to modern rapid-transit facilities. The mortality in airship service in countries like Germany today is asserted to be only a little higher than that on the railroads, in proportion to the number of passengers carried. Not a passenger has ever lost his life in a Zeppelin in commercial service. The autogiro offers new possibilities in the way of safety in air travel.

That the airplane is more than a curiosity or a luxury and has become a vital element in transportation may be seen from the following facts about American air service in the year 1933. There were some 28 companies operating air transport lines, with 615 planes in service. The actual miles flown were 50,800,705 and the passengers carried, 546,235. The total of passenger miles [2] flown amounted to no less than 183,695,784. Some 1,884,545 pounds of air express were carried and 7,644,646 pounds of mail. While the element of safety in air travel is not what it will be in a few years, vast progress has been made in the safety factor. The following statement will make this clear: "At a travel rate of 130 miles per hour it would take a passenger, on the average, 3,000 days,

---
[1] The Diesel airplane motor seems likely to perfect airplane engines.
[2] A passenger mile represents one passenger carried one mile.

or over eight years, or 71,328 hours of continuous flying to run the risk of a fatal accident. This estimate is based upon the accidents and the approximate number of miles flown in scheduled operations in the United States from July 1, 1933, to July 1, 1934."

Great speed has been attained in airplane travel. On May 11, 1934, Colonel Roscoe Turner averaged 308.40 miles an hour between Detroit and New York City. On September 1, 1934, he flew from Burbank, California, to Brooklyn, New York, in 10 hours and 3 minutes. His average flying speed was 262 miles an hour. This is a far cry from "covered wagon" days, when, in 1842-43, it took Marcus Whitman five months of heroic effort to go from what is now the State of Washington to the City of Washington. The world's airplane speed record to the beginning of 1935 was hung up by an Italian aviator, Francesco Agello, who flew over Lake Garda at 440 miles an hour on October 23, 1934.

Since the eighties, when steel began to replace iron, which had earlier displaced wood, in the construction of ships, the changes in shipbuilding and in sea transportation have been startling. The modern liners, both coal-burning and oil-burning, bearing within their steel bodies a population equal to that of a small city, are striking examples of the remarkable progress that has been made. The supremacy of the steamship is now being threatened by vessels propelled by internal-combustion engines burning oil. Here the Diesel engine has been especially important. We have already made mention of the increased size and speed of ocean-going vessels and will not repeat it in this place.[1]

2. REVOLUTIONARY PROGRESS IN COMMUNICATION

Some of the most remarkable aspects of the Second Industrial Revolution are those connected with the improvement in the means of communication and in the transmission of information. These changes have transformed what would have been miracles to our grandfathers into commonplaces of our everyday life.

What was for a time the most picturesque and striking of these various methods of conquering space and the problems of the transmission of information was associated with the work of Guglielmo Marconi, a brilliant Italian physicist and inventor, who began his labors in wireless telegraphy about 1890. His achievements rested on the discoveries made by Heinrich Hertz relative to the transmission of electromagnetic waves through the ether.[2] Marconi was able to send a message across the English Channel in 1899, and in 1901 he sent the first wireless message across the Atlantic Ocean, a distance of over 3,000 miles. This demonstrated the practicability of the wireless telegraph. Subsequent developments of importance were the Fleming two-electrode valve and the De Forest three-electrode valve (the modern vacuum tube), one of the greatest inventions in the annals of electricity. Wireless telegraphy has revolutionized the methods of keeping in touch with moving vessels at sea.

The telephone, which was earliest installed as a practical instrument by Elisha Gray and Alexander Graham Bell in 1876, first solved the problem of transmitting the sound of the human voice over considerable distances by means of conductors and electromagnetically actuated diaphragms.

---

[1] See above, pp. 316 ff.   [2] See above, pp. 642-43.

TRANSPORTATION AND COMMUNICATION

Even more phenomenal than the wireless telegraph have been the developments since 1909 in the perfecting of wireless transmission or radio. The same general electrophysical theories lie behind this and Marconi's wireless telegraph. De Forest, Fessenden, Poulsen, and Colpitts made an application of these electrical theories to the transmission of the human voice over long distances without the necessity of a conductor. In the form that it assumed as a result of the work of De Forest, Fessenden, Poulsen, and others, the wireless telephone has already gone far towards revolutionizing the methods of long-distance transmission of information directly through the reproduction of the human voice. Aside from its commercial and recreational uses, radio has already demonstrated its social usefulness in such forms as transoceanic telephone messages, communication with remote and inaccessible points, and radios in police automobiles, now in fairly general use in American cities.

Even photographs can now be sent by wireless. Remarkable developments recently in television seem to make it certain that ere long one talking on the telephone may literally see the countenance of the person at the other end of the line. The full potentialities of the development of television can as yet scarcely be realized, but it may in the near future bring into our homes faithful pictures of predictable or arranged events at the moment they occur anywhere in the world—a political scene in France, an athletic meet in England, a musical event in Germany, a nationalist uprising in Asia.[1]

These new devices for transmitting information have tended to shrink our planet enormously through rapid communication between its most distant points. It is possible today to transmit news from central Siberia to New York City with greater ease and speed than it was to send information across the Hudson River in 1750. As a matter of fact, time has been almost eliminated as a factor in the transmission of information. Experiments during the Washington Conference on the Limitation of Armaments (1921-22) proved that it was well-nigh impossible to detect any difference in the time required to flash a result upon a screen in the room adjoining the Conference in Washington and that taken to transmit it to New York City. An even more dramatic illustration of the elimination of time in the communication of news was furnished by Admiral Byrd's flight across the South Pole in 1930. By means of the radio, the American newspaper offices concerned took note of the crossing of the Pole almost at the moment it took place,[2] instead of having to wait months or years, as was once the case, for the explorer to return to civilization with the story of his achievement. The moving-picture industry has been an important recent factor in the social dissemination of information, especially the news reels. This contribution will be discussed a little later on.

In this way the world has become a veritable psychological unity to a degree that Napoleon could not have dreamed in moments of the wildest imaginings.

3. SOCIAL APPROPRIATION AND DISSEMINATION OF INFORMATION

The instantaneous transmission of information has brought with it a wide expansion of devices and organizations for the social appropriation of news

---

[1] Page and others, *Modern Communication,* Chap. VII.
[2] The New York *Times,* through its own radio station in New York, picked up Byrd's crossing message when being sent to his own base station.

material. Most notable have been improvements in printing and news-gathering, making possible a cheap daily newspaper, and the growth of a better and more economical postal system.

The printing press had been invented by Coster and Gutenberg in the middle of the fifteenth century, but the mechanical processes still remained crude.[1] Pages were printed by pressing a flat frame of type on the sheet of paper, and all type had to be set by hand. The first important improvement was the cylindrical press, which made possible rotary printing. The cylindrical printing press was adapted from the similar device used for printing calicoes that was introduced during the early part of the Industrial Revolution.[2] It was successfully applied in the office of the London *Times* in 1812, and in America by the Philadelphia *Ledger* in 1846. The cylindrical press was not generally introduced in pressrooms, however, until about 1880. It was an enormous improvement over the old frame press with respect to both time and efficiency.

Since 1812 the evolution of printing presses has been one of the most notable features of the progress of modern mechanical ingenuity. The great modern presses not only print with great rapidity, but also make possible the automatic cutting and folding of pages and papers, in many cases performing difficult processes with a speed and dexterity incredibly superior to those of the human hand. One of the latest printing presses can print, fold, cut, and count no less than 1,000 thirty-two-page newspapers per minute.

The possibility of exploiting fully these improved printing presses would, however, have been remote were it not for an equally remarkable development of typesetting machinery. Originally, type was slowly set by hand, with the aid of a pair of tweezers. This crude method has since been supplanted by a typesetting machine which casts type from molten metal, the operator controlling the type-casting in a manner roughly identical with the technique of operating a typewriter. Credit for inventing typesetting machinery belongs to a German-American inventor, Ottmar Mergenthaler (1854-99), who began his work on the linotype machine in Baltimore about 1876. Through his achievements in this field he deserves to be ranked with Gutenberg in the history of printing.[3]

The linotype machine sets a solid line of metal type and represents the quickest method yet devised. Its one important defect is that an error made in one letter requires the resetting of an entire line. To get around this difficulty the montoype machine was invented by Tolbert Lanston in 1887, but it has not yet enabled the printer to set type as rapidly as with the linotype machine. This new linotype machinery has made it possible for typesetters to keep pace with the speed of the printing press, and it is through the combination of the telegraph, the telephone, the rotary press, and the linotype machine that we are now able to secure news about events in a remote area that may have taken place only about an hour before the moment in which the newspaper is delivered to customers on the street.

A remarkable new invention, the "teletypesetting" machine, has been worked out in recent years. A master copy is prepared cut in a perforated tape. This is corrected and put in a properly fitted typesetting machine. By electrical control

---

[1] See above, Vol. I, pp. 839 ff.
[2] See above, p. 276.
[3] *Cf.* Iles, *op. cit.,* pp. 393 ff.

this copy can then be set simultaneously and automatically on scores or hundreds of other typesetting machines with no human aid and without the slightest possibility of a typographical error. This seems bound to revolutionize the typesetting industry in newspaper plants.

Related to printing machinery and often acting as a substitute for it is the typewriter, an invention of vast practical significance but frequently overlooked in the story of invention. Proposals for a "writing machine" date from 1714 to the American Civil War. Most of them were designed to make raised or embossed letters for the blind. Among the inventors were W. A. Burt, Charles Thurber, Sir Charles Wheatstone, and Alfred E. Beach. Further work was done after 1860 by S. W. Francis and Thomas Hall of New York. The machine was finally made practicable by Charles L. Sholes, Samuel W. Soulé, and Carlos Glidden. It was placed on the market as the Sholes and Glidden typewriter and was first manufactured in 1874 by E. Remington & Sons of Ilion, New York. Since then there have been many improvements in typewriters, including a noiseless machine, first extensively marketed by Remington about 1916. By the outbreak of the World War the value of typewriters and supplies for them manufactured in this country amounted to over $30,000,000 annually. Only the invention of writing itself and of printing with movable type can compare with the invention of the typewriter in the history of the technique of human literary expression. More pages are typewritten each year than are printed. The mimeographing machine came into general use in the twentieth century and acted as a further substitute for printing. The typewriter and the teletype machine have revolutionized telegraphy by permitting the sending and reception of typed messages, so that it is no longer necessary to learn the Morse code.

The social significance of newer types of printing machinery would have been much less without the corresponding development of elaborate organization for gathering news. If every newspaper were compelled to support its own correspondents in all parts of the world and to maintain its own telegraphic and cable connections, the expense would be such as only a few great newspapers could meet. Instead of this, there has developed a specialized type of news-gathering agency, of which Reuter's, Wolff's, Havas, the Associated Press, and the United Press are examples. Such an agency is an elaborate organization of correspondents and the cables and telegraphic communications essential to the rapid transmission of the information gathered. Through this extensive machinery the significant information from all parts of the world is put at the disposal of newspapers that are willing to pay, directly or indirectly, for the service. They are thus able, by a relatively small expenditure, to obtain a variety and volume of news that would otherwise be denied to them.

While from the standpoint of technical efficiency these organizations have achieved remarkable progress, the accuracy of this service has occasionally been criticized. The type of news that will be gathered inevitably depends to no small extent upon the economic, social, and intellectual attitudes of the participating newspapers or their advertisers. News tends to be selected for its mass appeal and emotional content and not for its educational value. In short, the news-gathering agencies naturally gather the news that will "take" or sell. Further, the newspapers using the service often distort the facts by editing and rewriting the information secured. In this way much really significant news is lost to the public and much that is actually printed is highly unreliable. In spite of these defects, however, it is certain that we have profited enormously through securing more rapidly gathered and unprecedentedly varied information concerning what is taking place daily all over the face of the earth.

Another phase of progress in newspaper efficiency and economy has been the rise of newspaper chains, where a number of newspapers are under common ownership and management. This makes possible far greater economy of personnel in management, in editorial, news, and advertising service, and also permits greater economy in purchasing newsprint paper and other raw materials used. The chief danger lies in editorial tyranny exerted over a wide range of opinion-forming journals. Representative chains are those of Hearst, Scripps-Howard, Gannett, and Block.

Newspapers have not only been very important in spreading information, but have also contributed notably to further industrialization. The printing industry is an important one, as is also the manufacturing of printing presses and other allied machinery. But the most significant industrial accessory of modern newspapers is the paper and pulp industry. Wood pulp has supplied the only material capable of making practicable newsprint paper at a sufficiently low cost. The manufacture of wood-pulp paper began about the time of the Civil War. Paper production increased in volume in this country from 127,000 tons in 1867 to 11,000,000 tons in 1929. The total world-production in 1929 was 23,400,000 tons. The world production of newsprint (paper for newspapers) in 1929 was 7,319,000 tons, about one-third of the total paper production.

Another illustration of this progress towards better social appropriation of information is to be found in the improvement and cheapening of postal systems. Our modern business and financial system would be well-nigh paralyzed if it were compelled to return to the system of mail distribution that prevailed in the postal service of the world in 1850, when national postal systems were either unknown or privately owned, and letters had to be transmitted by coach or courier traveling slowly and on no regular schedule.[1]

In the first place, there has been a great technical improvement in the methods of distributing mail, particularly through closer coöperation with the railroad service. The mail service has thereby been able to improve with every advance in the technical efficiency of the railroad. The development of automobile trucking and pneumatic tubes for the distribution of mail in cities is a notable phase of the recent advances in the efficiency of the postal system. Air-mail service has been widely inaugurated and greatly reduces the time required for the delivery of letters. Aerial parcel-post service nows seems imminent.

Rowland Hill worked out a scheme for the cheapening of mail distribution in England about 1840, which has been widely imitated, with many variations, in the other countries of the modern world.[2] Particularly important has been the tendency toward standardization of the rates for the transmission of letters, irrespective of distance, within any national boundary, and such international agreements as those which formerly prevailed between England and the United

---

[1] *Cf.* W. E. Rich, *History of the United States Post Office to the Year 1829*, Harvard University Press, 1924.
[2] *Cf.* Sir Rowland and G. B. Hill, *The Life of Sir Rowland Hill*, London, 1880, 2 vols., and Clyde Kelly, *United States Postal Policy*, Appleton, 1931.

States, in which the same postage rates applied to a letter sent from Chicago to London or New Zealand as applied to a letter sent from Chicago to Springfield, Illinois. Of enormous importance in the improvement of the postal system has been the recent tendency in the United States towards the extension of the rural free delivery, beginning in 1899. This puts at the disposal of the agricultural population most postal advantages hitherto restricted to city populations. Here the automobile has recently proved of great utility. The parcel-post system established in the United States has been a great convenience to all, but especially to rural inhabitants who could not be served directly by express companies. It was established in January, 1913, and in 1930, out of a grand total of 7,000,000,000 pounds of mail matter carried, the parcel post accounted for 4,241,000,000 pounds.

The latest stage in the social appropriation of information is associated with the development of the moving-picture industry and the radio. We have already discussed the scientific and mechanical evolution of the radio. The moving picture in a crude form first appeared about 1900. Its development depended on remarkable progress in optics and the camera and film industries. The elements of photography were discovered by two Frenchmen, Louis Daguerre and Joseph Niepce, between 1826 and 1839, and extended by W. H. Fox Talbot in England and by J. W. Draper in the United States. But it could make little commercial headway until the celluloid film was produced at the end of the century. An important aid to the moving picture was the kinetoscope of Thomas A. Edison and the projector of Thomas Armat, invented in 1895. These made possible moving pictures, for the first anticipation of the "movie" consisted in the rapid shifting of a series of still pictures. By 1900 a crude movie of a train passing or a Negro boy eating a watermelon was produced. The first real story movie was turned out in 1905. It was made up of one reel of a thousand feet. The technique of large-scale movie production was revolutionized by D. W. Griffith, with his handling of massed actors and his use of the "close-up," "cut-back," and "fade-out." These were combined in the film "The Birth of a Nation" (1915), which revolutionized the movie art. The next advance was one that used popular personalities to achieve mass appeal. This brought in the "star" system, first promoted by Adolph Zukor. Such celebrities as Mary Pickford, Douglas Fairbanks, Charlie Chaplin, Theda Bara, and the like established the popularity of star performers. The sound picture was introduced after 1927 and helped to increase the mass following of the movies. By 1930 the average weekly attendance at movies in the United States was approximately 100,000,000. Aside from entertainment and information, the movies constitute an important unit in American industry. The news reels present a vivid visual reproduction of events that have happened in various parts of the world in the very recent past. Photographs can now be transmitted by cable and radio, and it is not unthinkable that we shall ultimately be able to transmit news reels by cable or wireless, so that an audience in Kansas City may see upon the screen in the evening events that took place in Capetown, South Africa, the same morning. An eminent journalist, Karl A. Bickel, has thus summarized the future prospects of the "movies" when linked up with radio and television:

The twist of a dial and the throw of a switch will enable you, in your sitting room, to see and hear the Kentucky Derby, to have a better vision of a great prize-fight or athletic contest than even the box-holders, to range the world, attending the theater or opera, visiting important banquets, sitting in with Congress in Washington, or viewing an airplane meet in Africa.[1]

The radio already permits a contemporaneous vocal account of events taking place over wide areas, and has proved of great value in transmitting information in case of floods and other natural disasters that have destroyed other means of communication. Even today it has considerably affected the "flash" extra editions of newspapers. The news summaries over the radio are beginning to constitute a serious competition with the newspapers.

In periods of peace and liberty these devices are of positive value to the community. But their possibilities in time of international tension and war, in the aid they lend to the development of the mob spirit, present a very great potential menace.[2] They also open up new channels for class and party oppression. There is the same tendency for the dominant economic groups to control the movies and the radio that has already been experienced in their dominion over the newspapers.[3] Communistic films and radio addresses are tabooed in capitalistic states, and capitalistic pronouncements likewise ruled out in Communist areas. The dominant economic convictions, political views, religious dogmas, and moral codes must be taken into careful consideration by those responsible for radio programs. So eminent a clergyman as Harry Emerson Fosdick was denied radio privileges for a very general talk on birth control. Programs are often excluded on the ground that they are "controversial," but it usually turns out that they are only presentations of a liberal or radical point of view. The conservative viewpoint on any subject is rarely found to be "controversial" outside of Russia. In the latter country the conservative point of view is "controversial."

IV. THE ERA OF LARGE-SCALE BUSINESS ENTERPRISE

The technological changes of the Second Industrial Revolution have been no more striking than the alterations that have taken place in the scale of business enterprise. The high degree of mechanization characteristic of modern industry is possible only when the average enterprise has an extensive command over capital and is turning out products in large volume. The first of these conditions has been greatly facilitated by the rise of the corporation as the typical business unit, and by the growing tendency towards combination, both of which will be discussed in the next chapter. Large-scale production has great natural advantages in the modern industrial order, with many of which we are already familiar. Among the more important are: (1) The opportunity of buying raw materials more cheaply in large quantities; (2) the greater possibility for the development of skill, specialization, and the division of labor; (3) smaller overhead costs; (4) the superior sales department that can be

[1] Bickel, *New Empires,* Lippincott, 1930, p. 43.
[2] *Cf.* Riegel, *op. cit.*
[3] See M. L. Ernst and Pare Lorentz, *Censored; the Private Life of the Movie,* Cape and Smith, 1930.

THE ERA OF LARGE-SCALE BUSINESS ENTERPRISE 749

maintained; and (5) the practicability of a profitable disposition of by-products, such as would not be feasible in a small concern.

As a result of these inherent advantages, there has been a widespread trend in the modern industrial world towards vast concentration of capital investment in gigantic industrial and commercial enterprises.[1] There is nothing unusual in our day of trusts, holding companies, and cartels in the capitalization of a concern at hundreds of millions. A manufacturing or a commercial concern with a capital of $100,000 in the year 1750 was an exceedingly large and thriving concern, while at the opening of the twentieth century the United States Steel Corporation was incorporated for around $1,000,000,000.[2] The table on page 750, showing some ten separate billion-dollar concerns in the United States by 1926, well indicates the remarkable concentration of capital in modern industrial activities. There are over twenty billion-dollar enterprises in the country today.

This industrial consolidation has also expressed itself in the increasing size of factories. One half of one per cent of the factories in the United States employ no less than 25 per cent of the workers engaged in manufacturing. Nine per cent of the factories employ 71 per cent of the wage-earners of our country. At the other end 85 per cent of the factories—the smaller units—employ only 20 per cent of the workers.

While industrial consolidation is doubtless more marked here than in Europe, it is also true that there, especially in Germany, the advantages of the large-scale enterprise in industries such as the iron and steel, the electrical, and the chemical have become quite clear.[3] It is a fact of great social significance that in many of the industries most fundamental to the modern economic order, the advantage lies with the very large industrial unit, with its high degree of mechanization, the tendency towards monopolistic control, and the large number of highly specialized workers.

Another outstanding characteristic of modern industry is the tendency towards a marked degree of localization of specific industries. This development has been due primarily to the operation of natural economic forces, which make it profitable to manufacture in those areas adjacent to or intermediate between the sources of the raw materials that enter into the process of manufacturing. In addition to nearness of raw materials, the matter of proximity to markets must be considered, so that a nice balance may be struck between the transportation costs of the raw materials and of the finished product.

Among the outstanding examples of this tendency are the location of the German iron and steel industry in the Ruhr Basin and in Silesia; the centering of the English iron and steel industry around Sheffield and Birmingham, and of the American around Pittsburgh, Gary, and Birmingham, Alabama; the concentration of the German cotton and silk industries around Elberfeld-Barmen and Krefeld; the establishment of the American collar and shirt industry at Troy, New York; the growth of the automobile industry around Detroit; the development of the flour-milling industry at Kansas City, Minneapolis, and Buffalo; the gradual shifting of the American cotton textile

---
[1] See below, pp. 784 ff., 796 ff.
[2] Abraham Berglund, *The United States Steel Corporation*, Macmillan, 1907.
[3] See Knight, Barnes, and Flügel, *Economic History of Europe*, pp. 538 ff., 548 ff., 643 ff.

BILLION DOLLAR CORPORATIONS

(Figures for 1926, where available, are given, otherwise for 1925)

Company	Total Assets	Market Value of Securities (Dow Jones)*	Value of Physical Properties	Gross Sales or Revenues	Net Profit	Dividends Paid	Number of Stockholders	Number of Employees	Date Founded
1. U. S. Steel Corporation	$2,446,000,000	$1,779,000,000	$1,692,000,000	$928,000,000	$117,000,000	$61,000,000	150,000	250,000	1901
2. Southern Pacific R. R.	2,147,000,000	†1,565,000,000	1,341,000,000	297,000,000	36,000,000	23,000,000	57,000	†71,000	1884
3. Pennsylvania R. R.	1,819,000,000	1,184,000,000	1,010,000,000	710,000,000	62,000,000	30,000,000	140,000	214,000	1845
4. American Telephone & Telegraph Co.	1,646,000,000	†2,066,000,000	197,000,000	180,000,000	107,000,000	81,000,000	362,000	293,000	1885
5. New York Central R. R.	1,449,000,000	1,251,000,000	1,020,000,000	399,000,000	49,000,000	27,000,000	64,000	†162,000	‡1914
6. Standard Oil of New Jersey	1,359,000,000	1,072,000,000	520,000,000	1,123,000,000	111,000,000	34,000,000	80,000	91,000	1882
7. Union Pacific R. R.	1,140,000,000	869,000,000	819,000,000	205,000,000	38,000,000	26,000,000	51,000	60,000	‡1897
8. Atchison, Topeka & Santa Fe R. R.	1,071,000,000	792,000,000	945,000,000	259,000,000	46,000,000	22,000,000	63,000	66,000	‡1895
9. General Motors Corporation	915,000,000	1,521,000,000	400,000,000	†1,000,000,000	†180,000,000	70,000,000	51,000	83,000	1908
10. Ford Motor Co.	*800,000,000	1,000,000,000	*300,000,000	751,000,000	†100,000,000	....	3	192,000	1903

* Includes market value of stocks and par value of bonds.
† Estimated.
‡ Date of present corporation, following reorganization.

industry to the South; the concentration of the French iron and steel industry in Alsace-Lorraine, and of the French silk industry in Lyons.

In general, this localization of industry has been produced by natural economies, but in some cases it would seem that it has a primarily historical basis, in that an industry may have been established more or less by chance at a certain point and maintained there chiefly as a result of the inertia of custom. Particularly in the iron and steel industry is the location of the great industrial centers determined by proximity of raw materials—in other words, "raw-material oriented."

These twin tendencies towards concentration and localization have been two of the most striking aspects of the general development of modern industrial and commercial enterprise in the late nineteenth and twentieth centuries.

While the extensive concentration of capital in business and commercial enterprise does not necessarily and invariably mean monopoly, the growth of modern large-scale business activity has almost inevitably tended towards monopolistic control of the product. Economists contend that a monopoly exists when a sufficient control over the supply of a particular product has been secured so that the price can be raised and, even with a decreased output, a greater profit can be secured. In other words, we have a commercial monopoly when a specific organization is able artificially to control the price of a particular commodity. Such a monopoly may exist as a result of a patent right or copyright, or through the prior discovery of certain sources of raw materials. But much more frequently modern monopolies have come into being primarily as a result of a concentration in the ownership of the various plants carrying on any particular industrial enterprise or of the railroads or steamship lines that control the transportation between given points. In few cases are monopolies complete, but any overwhelming concentration of the control over the manufacturing of a particular commodity or over the transportation lines in any specific area will give what is, for all practical purposes, a monopoly. In other words, it will enable the owners in such a combination practically to control the prices demanded for the commodity or the rates charged for the transportation service. The most important type of competition which has survived is that between alternate commodities, for example, copper versus aluminum, sulphate of ammonia versus nitrate, lumber versus steel, pianos versus radios, automobiles versus household furniture. Even here there has come about a tendency to centralize control.

The recent widespread appearance of the holding company as a legal device, which will be discussed in the following chapter, has played no small part in the growth of monopolistic control.[1] The holding company requires only a small amount of actual capital in proportion to the control secured over productive capacity; and it concentrates direction of policy in the hands of a small group. Monopolistic control of public utilities is particularly dangerous to public welfare, since these are so essential to modern life, and the possibilities of manipulation in the selfish interests of a few are so great.

Many statesmen and economists regard large-scale business combination as

[1] See J. C. Bonbright and G. C. Means, *The Holding Company, Its Public Significance and Its Regulation*, McGraw-Hill, 1932.

in itself a potential benefit to both producer and consumer, on account of the lower costs in production or service that may thereby come into existence. On the other hand, in actual practice the control over the production of a commodity or over transportation facilities has usually resulted not so much in cheaper and better service as in the provision of greater profits for the stockholders in the particular manufacturing and commercial concerns involved and in the holding companies that control the operation of these businesses.

At the same time, it should be frankly recognized that many great industrial organizations verging upon monopoly, such as the Standard Oil Company, the United States Steel Corporation, and the International Harvester Company, have introduced many labor-saving devices and have brought about many technical improvements that have increased to a marked degree the technical and commercial efficiency of the particular type of business involved. This has been especially true of the Standard Oil Company.[1]

It is this recognition of the potential benefits of big business, together with many actual abuses that have crept in as a result, that has led to the position taken by many statesmen, first notably by Theodore Roosevelt, who contend that the chief problem which the modern state faces is to secure that type of regulation which will bring about the social and economic advantages of greater economy in large-scale production and will at the same time prevent potential abuses in the way of exorbitant prices or limitation of output.

Hence there has been in many countries an effort to foster socially desirable types of combination and at the same time to prevent monopoly. In general, however, these efforts have not been highly successful. For example, Germany has always endeavored to encourage large-scale production, but without ever having brought into existence anything like the same universality of industrial consolidation that exists in the United States.[2] On the other hand, ever since 1890 the United States has, by various laws, endeavored to curb monopoly; but the net result has been a steady increase in the size and power of the great monopolistically inclined concerns.[3]

Paradoxically enough, both capitalists and Socialists regard this increased tendency towards concentration as favorable to their special views of economic organization and evolution. The capitalist looks upon it as desirable in the way of increasing his industrial power and profits, while the Socialist claims that it will be far easier for the state to take over the control of a few great business organizations than to attempt to operate a large number of small-scale concerns.

V. MASS PRODUCTION AND THE "SPEED-UP" SYSTEM

One of the outstanding traits of the Second Industrial Revolution is mass production. The assurance of production on a large scale depended primarily upon two factors: (1) The elimination of the waste due to inefficiency and

---

[1] *Cf.* J. W. Jenks, *The Trust Problem,* Doubleday, Page, 1917, Chap. III and pp. 334 ff.; J. T. Flynn, *God's Gold,* Harcourt, Brace, 1932; and Dobb, *Capitalist Enterprise and Social Progress.*

[2] See Knight, Barnes, and Flügel, *op. cit.,* Pt. II, Chap. XII, and Jenks, *op. cit.,* pp. 234 ff., 479 ff. There are, of course, great industrial consolidations in Germany. See above, pp. 335 ff.

[3] See Jenks, *op. cit.,* Chaps. I, XIII-XIV, and pp. 408 ff., and F. A. Fetter, *The Masquerade of Monopoly,* Harcourt, Brace, 1931.

MASS PRODUCTION AND THE "SPEED-UP" SYSTEM

duplication of effort in small plants; and (2) the manufacture of standardized and interchangeable parts by machinery. The first achievement was launched by the work of John D. Rockefeller, Sr., in the petroleum business. He brought it about through securing the domination of the Standard Oil Company in this industry.[1] Beginning about 1870, Rockefeller proceeded ruthlessly but effectively to root out small producers in the oil industry and to bring this field of economic effort under one centralized control. He was primarily concerned with eliminating waste and unnecessary expense in producing and distributing petroleum products. He understood that by controlling the industry as a whole in this country he could plan production, utilize the best equipment, secure superior talent in management and engineering, and otherwise insure that more oil could be produced and marketed in less time and with smaller expenditure of money. His conception of mass production involved especially the refining, shipment, and distribution of petroleum products—in particular, as has been noted, pipe lines for transporting oil. It embraced also the systematic utilization of by-products.

While Rockefeller was a pioneer in mass production, the process is associated in the public mind with Henry Ford more definitely than with any other single person.[2] In 1908 Mr. Ford decided to concentrate all of his attention on a single model of motorcar. Any extensive development of this program rested upon the fact that interchangeable parts can be turned out in great quantities by machinery and the whole quickly assembled into complete cars. The idea of interchangeable parts goes back at least to Eli Whitney, inventor of the cotton gin, who applied it in the manufacture of muskets.[3] The technique of turning out interchangeable parts had been solved in principle before Ford's day. His main contribution was to speed up the production of these parts and to invent a device for assembling them with all possible speed. The first was merely a matter of greater mechanical efficiency. The second meant the invention of the endless conveyor belt, which carried the parts to the place where they were needed by the workmen in assembling the car. At the end of the cumulative process a fully assembled car appeared. Charles Merz has graphically described the evolution of the Ford conveyor belt:

> The idea of the belt was borrowed from the Chicago packers, who used an overhead trolley to swing carcasses of beef down a line of butchers. Ford tried the idea first in assembling a small unit in his motor, the fly-wheel magneto, then in assembling the motor itself, and then in assembling the chassis.
>
> A chassis was hitched to a rope one day, and six workmen, picking up parts along the way and bolting them in place, travelled with it on an historic journey down a line two hundred and fifty feet in length as a windlass dragged it through the factory. The experiment worked, but developed one difficulty. God had not made men as accurately as Ford made piston rings. The line was too high for the short men and too low for the tall men, with a resultant waste in effort.
>
> More experiments were tried. The line was raised; then lowered; then two lines were tried, to suit squads of different heights; the speed of the line was increased; then lessened; various tests were made to determine how many men to put on one assembly line, how far to subdivide the operations, whether to let

---

[1] *Cf.* Flynn, *op. cit.*, Pts. V-VII.
[2] *Cf.* Charles Merz, *And Then Came Ford*, Doubleday, Doran, 1929, and Henry Ford and Samuel Crowther, *My Life and Work*, Doubleday, Page, 1922.   [3] *Cf.* Iles, *op. cit.*, pp. 75 ff.

one man who set a bolt in place put on the nut and the man who put on the nut to take time to tighten it. In the end, the time allotted for assembly on a chassis was cut from twelve hours and twenty-eight minutes to one hour and thirty-three minutes, the world was promised Model T's in new abundance, and mass production entered a new phase as men were made still more efficient cogs of their machines. . . .

"Every piece of work in the whole shop moves," Ford said in 1922. "It may move on hooks on overhead chains going to assembly in the exact order in which the parts are required; it may travel on a moving platform, or it may go by gravity, but the point is that there is no lifting or trucking of anything except raw materials." [1]

The results of these new methods of mass production were striking. In 1914 the Ford plant turned out 700 cars daily; in 1922 4,000 cars were manufactured per day. Between June 8 and December 7, 1923, 1,111,111 Ford cars were produced. On November 4, 1924, no less than 7,500 finished cars were turned out in the Ford plant. Ford not only attained new heights in mass production, but also made the country "mass-production conscious." His plants near Detroit became a mecca for visitors.

Closely associated with this mass-production process has come the "speed-up" of workers.[2] An intelligent former workman in a Ford plant, Robert L. Cruden, thus describes how this works out:

As a result of the conveyor system, upon which the whole plant is operated, the men have no time to talk to each other; have no rest except for fifteen or twenty minutes at lunch time; and can go to the toilet only when substitutes are ready to relieve them at the "belt." One operation upon which I worked required that I be on the job, ready to work, just as soon as the preceding shift went off; work up to the exact minute for lunch time; take a couple of minutes to clean up and get my lunch kit and be back thirteen minutes later ready to work. There was never a moment of leisure or opportunity to turn my head. . . .

A grinder told me recently, "The machines I'm running take up the distance of a short city block. By the time I am at the last one the first machine has already stopped. The boss is shouting at me and I have to run back there, then back down the line again to see that the last machine doesn't stand idle for a second. Now the boss tells me they're going to give me more machines." [3]

The results may be illustrated by tabulating the man power and productivity in the manufacturing of tire-carriers under the speed-up system as operated by Ford since 1925:

TIRE-CARRIER PRODUCTION [4]

Year	Produced	Men
1925	3,000 produced with	160 men
1926	3,400 " "	50 "
1927	4,095 " "	39 "
1928	4,950 " "	25 "
1930	6,650 " "	19 "
1931	6,970 " "	16 "

---

[1] Merz, *op. cit.*, pp. 198-200. [2] *Cf.* Cressy, *op. cit.*, Chap. VII.

[3] Cruden, "The Great Ford Myth," *New Republic*, Mar. 16, 1932, pp. 117-18. See also J. N. Leonard, *The Tragedy of Henry Ford*, Putnam, 1932, pp. 229 ff.

[4] Cruden, *op. cit.*, p. 118.

MASS PRODUCTION AND THE "SPEED-UP" SYSTEM

In short, the production increased by twofold while there were only one-tenth as many workers employed in 1931 as in 1925. Better machinery accounted only in part for the increased production.

The strain of working under such conditions is very great, and the average man risks a nervous or physical breakdown, or both, after two or three years of steady employment. But there are eager and hungry men standing in line to take the place of the discarded human wreckage. It is literally true that the perfectly sanitary modern factory using speed-up methods is more disastrous in its effect upon the mind and body of the workman than was the old, crude, unsanitary factory, devoid of safety devices, of a century ago.

Mass production has led its foremost practitioners to branch out into allied lines of production, to get control over the sources of raw materials, to secure important power sites, to control essential transportation systems, and to found appropriate publicity organs. The extent to which this can go is well illustrated by the scope of the Ford organization as summarized by George T. Odell:

The Ford organization represents a complete industrial chain independent of strikes or shortage of raw materials and of every means of transportation from the mines and forest to the finished product.

An announcement made public by the Ford organization in April, 1925, reveals the following lines of endeavor:

Automobiles—Two makes, with a production of 1,676,673 cars in 1924.

Tractors—A production of 64,450 in 1924.

Ford Airplanes—On February 7, 1927, it was announced that 6 three-motored Stout monoplanes had been completed at the Airplane factory of the Ford Motor Company at Dearborn, Mich. . . .

Railroad—Holds a 75-year lease on the Detroit, Toledo & Ironton line, which was purchased at a receivership sale for $5,000,000 and made into a paying line.

Ship Line—Operates vessels that complete the transportation system. The company controls its own ore boats and five ocean-going freighters.

Coal Mines—Buying coal in open market was unsatisfactory so the Ford organization purchased control of four fields, two in Kentucky and two in West Virginia. These mines have resources of 208,000,000 tons.

Timber—A million feet of lumber supplies Ford needs for one day. The company now owns nearly half a million acres of timber land in northern Michigan, and 120,000 acres in Kentucky.

Saw Mills—The largest mill is at Iron Mountain, and cuts as high as 300,000 feet of lumber a day. Complete towns are controlled by the company.

Blast Furnaces—About 400,000 tons of iron a year are required for production.

Hydro-electric Plants—Five plants in operation for harnessing of water power.

Foundry—The River Rouge Foundry is the largest in the world. It covers 30 acres and pours 2,000 tons of castings every 24 hours.

Glass—Ford Industries use about one-fourth of all plate glass produced in U. S. Glass is made at three places, Highland Park, River Rouge and at Glass-Mere, Pa.

Magazine—The *Dearborn Independent*, a weekly magazine, at Dearborn, Mich., was purchased by the Ford Company and now has a circulation of over 700,000.[1]

Mass production prevails in most other major industries. The manufacture of shoes is a typical example. Under the hand-manufacturing methods it

---

[1] Ford has a steel mill at River Rouge and is now building new steel mills to make himself virtually independent as an industrial unit.

was impossible for one man to turn out more than six pairs of shoes per week on the average. On this level of productivity it would require over 1,000,000 persons, working six days a week, to turn out as many shoes as were manufactured in the United States alone in 1932. With our modern mass-production and high-speed methods 185,000 employees produced no less than 313,000,000 pairs of shoes in this country in 1932. To illustrate the efficiency of modern shoe machinery it may be pointed out that it would require, for example, only 700 heeling machines running full capacity to put the heels on 1,000,000 pairs of shoes each day.

Another striking example of mass-production methods carried on by means of advanced mechanical devices is afforded by the iron and steel industry. Professor Kirkland thus vividly describes the contemporary process of making a steel rail for railroads:

> The ... continuous operation ... was worked out on a gigantic geographical scale by the iron and steel industry. Follow the raw iron from the Mesabi range. A steam shovel scoops it into railroad cars; the cars, hauled to Duluth or Superior, run onto the docks over pockets into which the contents of the car are discharged when its bottom folds outward; chutes lead the ore from the pockets into the hold of an ore vessel. At a Lake Erie port the vessel is unloaded by automatic machinery and the ore placed again in railroad cars; at Pittsburgh these cars are unloaded by dumpers which turn the car on its side and cascade the ore into bins; from these, skip cars carry the ore, as well as the coke and limestone, to the top of the blast furnace and dump them in. The blast then goes into operation. From the furnace the pig iron is transferred, still hot, by ladle cars to a mixer and then to the open-hearth furnaces. Savings in fuel are thus accomplished. When the open-hearth is tapped, the liquid steel is run into a gigantic ladle and thence poured into molds on flat cars, an engine pushes the cars to pits in which the steel ingots, left bare when the mold is stripped away, are kept warm until they are rolled. Conveyors carry the ingot to the rolls, and automatic platforms, rising and lowering, shoot the fashioning shape back and forth between the rolling apparatus. The resulting rail is so perfectly shaped that variations of a small fraction of an inch insure its rejection. Electric cranes, ladles, cars, conveyors, dumpers, unloaders, chargers make the production of iron from mine to rail a thing uncannily automatic, vibrantly alive.[1]

VI. POWER PRODUCTION, AUTOMATIC MACHINES, TECHNOLOGICAL UNEMPLOYMENT, AND THE EVE OF THE "THIRD" INDUSTRIAL REVOLUTION

The advance of science and technology as applied to the steam and electric power industries has revolutionized the whole character of modern economic and social life. We seem to be entering a new age. If there is anything that would justify the concept of a "Third" Industrial Revolution it is this new era of power and the associated development of automatic machinery, both dependent upon applied electrophysics.[2] Mr. Arkright has well summarized the character and significance of this revolutionary development in increased power:

[1] Kirkland, *History of American Economic Life*, pp. 453-54.
[2] See Kaempffert, *Popular History of American Invention*, Vol. II, Pt. V.

EVE OF THE "THIRD" INDUSTRIAL REVOLUTION

The largest single modern turbine has a capacity of 300,000 horsepower or three million times the output of a human being on an eight-hour-day basis. But the turbine runs twenty-four hours a day, which man does not do, and hence its total output is 9,000,000 times that of one man. To say it in another way—four of these turbines have a greater energy capacity than the entire adult working population of the United States. At the present moment the United States has an installed capacity of one billion horsepower in engines to do work.

What are these billion horses good for? Just one thing—to get work done. If these installed engines were operated continuously at capacity it would require fifty times the number of adult workers now living on the earth to equal this output by human labor alone. . . .

From these figures we may draw two conclusions:
1. The importance of man as a power unit in the United States is over.
2. The steady flow of this huge energy output has become so vital to our national existence that if we attempted to stop it and go back to hand labor we would die. Fire, disease, and starvation would do their work swiftly and ruthlessly.[1]

Another relatively novel and extremely portentous development in the realm of technology has been the recent growth of automatic machinery, namely, the removal of man two degrees from the actual burden of manual effort. Originally, man did the work himself or used tools. Then came the machines tended by men. Now we have machines watched and directed by other machines, thus vastly reducing the number of human beings needed to supervise mechanical processes and transferring intelligence from man to the machine. The basic nature of this change is well summarized by David Cushman Coyle:

In the power age there are two new mechanical factors. One is that electric power has made it possible to start and stop each machine in a factory independently by throwing a switch. The other is that the electric eye, the thermostat, and other instruments of the sort, have been developed to take the place of the human machine tender. From these inventions has grown a new conception, the automatic factory, where both the physical labor and the routine machine tending are done by non-human agencies. A few skilled mechanics and engineers are the only human beings about the shop.[2]

The divers ways in which the photo-electric cell or "electric eye" can be used to provide automatic control of economic processes has been well stated by Stuart Chase:

The photo-electric cell, which never makes a mistake and never knows fatigue, has been introduced to sort vegetables, fruits and eggs, to measure illumination, appraise colors, classify minerals, count bills and throw out counterfeits, time horse races, count people and vehicles, determine thickness of cloth, see through fog, record smoke in tunnels, inspect tin cans, substitute a new process for photo-engraving, direct traffic automatically, open doors at the approach of a waitress, count sheets of paper and measure their thickness, automatically control trains—to name only a few of its uses.[3]

What automatic machinery means in the way of increased productivity and saving of labor power can be illustrated by calling attention to the new ma-

[1] Arkright, *The A B C of Technocracy*, pp. 28-29.
[2] Coyle, *The Irrepressible Conflict: Business vs. Finance*, p. 6.
[3] Chase, *Technocracy; an Interpretation*, Day, 1933, p. 16.

chinery designed to make woolen cloth—still, in most factories, a process passing through the separate stages of washing, carding, spinning, weaving, fulling, dyeing, cutting, folding, and so on, each of these processes being done by machinery that requires direct human supervision.

Hitherto wool has required repeated handlings, frequently shipment from one plant to another before cleansing, fluffing, spinning, and weaving were completed. It is now possible through a straight-line automatic process to introduce into one end of a machine the raw wool and have the machine wash it, extract the wax and lanolin, fluff the wool, spin it into yarn, dye it, weave it into cloth and cut it into lengths, roll it into bolts and wrap it for shipment. This is the second leap in technology, and its application in one form or another can be seen in most industries in this country today.[1]

Equally striking has been the application of automatic machinery to such processes as making electric-light bulbs: "The electric-lamp plant at Corning, N. Y., can produce 650,000 lamps per machine per day. This represents an increase per man of 10,000 times that of the method previously employed in the making of electric bulbs." If one had space at his command he could illustrate these striking developments at greater length, but what has been said is sufficient to illustrate the principles and achievements involved.

The coming of the automatic machine has given a new significance and seriousness to technological unemployment, that is, the tendency of machines to throw men out of work through displacing human effort by mechanical appliances.[2]

Technological unemployment is no new thing. It is as old as the first stone culture of man—in other words, it goes back at least a quarter of a million years. The tool upset "prehistoric" industrial and social equilibrium as the machine has that of modern times. When men first began to use stone implements and weapons the labor involved in protecting life and gaining a crude livelihood was greatly reduced. One man with an early paleolithic fist hatchet, fashioned from a large flint nodule, was worth as much as several who had nothing but their big jaws, bare hands, and chance clubs and stones to depend on. Specialization in the flint industry threw many of our "prehistoric" forefathers out of work. One skilled workman could turn out more fist hatchets, scrapers, and drills than a half-dozen novices. Systematic flint-mining provided more good raw material than could be picked up sporadically by a multitude.

When animals were domesticated one shepherd could care for more potential food and clothing than a score of hunters could have provided in the earlier hunting economy. The labor of the donkey and the ox replaced that of thousands of oppressed human beings. When agriculture appeared, one farmer could produce more food than a pack of savages scouring around gathering nuts and berries.

[1] Arkright, *op. cit.,* pp. 35-36.
[2] *Cf.* C. E. Persons, "Technological Unemployment," pp. 709 ff. of *Facts and Factors in Economic History, by Former Students of Edwin Francis Gay,* P. H. Douglas and Aaron Director, *The Problem of Unemployment,* Macmillan, 1931, Pt. III; J. A. Hobson, *Rationalisation and Unemployment,* Macmillan, 1930; and G. E. Barnett, *Chapters on Machinery and Labor,* Harvard University Press, 1926.

The invention of the lever and the pulley released the labor of a whole procession employed in lifting and tugging by hand. The rise of commerce on a large scale displaced many a laborer and merchant by providing better goods brought in from other regions. Inasmuch as most human beings lived on farms until the nineteenth century, the major part of technological unemployment in historical times has been due to changes in agricultural methods and organization. The creation of the great estates cultivated by slave labor in the Roman Empire threw most of the old Roman freemen into the city rabble or into the servile colonate. When the rise of the corn market and sheep-farming at the end of the Middle Ages broke up the medieval manorial system there was wholesale dependency among the ejected serfs and peasants, whose sad condition is portrayed graphically in the opening pages of Sir Thomas More's *Utopia*. The inclosure of peasant holdings in England in the middle of the eighteenth century and thereafter threw tens of thousands out of their homes and made them eager to get work even in the wretched factories of early industrial England.

Then came the greatest revolution of them all down to that time—the invention of machines. The long age of the tool economy had come to an end. The hand spinners and weavers were soon left high and dry. The misery of the latter is immortalized in George Eliot's *Silas Marner*. It is worthy of note that the wage system first became important at this time, and technological unemployment assumed a new character. A man out of work was more helpless than before. He could not turn to a farm, except for a time in the United States. But the new factories at first soaked up the unemployed as industry expanded. A new line of industrial development seemed to appear whenever any group was thrown out of employment by some epoch-making invention of labor-saving machinery.[1] Moreover, as machines produced more units of goods, the price could be lowered, consumption greatly increased, and more men put to work to make the needed goods. Optimists believed that this would always be true and that technological unemployment was only the misleading bogey of the timorous.

About the time of the World War, as we have seen, there appeared, as a result of a combination of inventions and mechanical ingenuity, the most ominous of all developments in the history of human culture—the automatic, continuous-process machine and factory, capable of turning out incredible quantities of identical products and adapted to the production of everything from cigarettes to dwelling-houses. In the first Industrial Revolution man had to watch and run his machines. Now, in the Second, he can have machines watch and run other machines or run themselves.

This colossal new reservoir of productive capacity has scarcely been recognized as yet even by economic historians. Coupled with the improbability of any vast new industries remaining to be opened up, it puts the possible technological unemployment of the future entirely out of the range of comparison with the past. It is as futile to try to compare the oxcart and the automobile as to bring into comparison technological unemployment before and after the rise of automatic machinery.

[1] *Cf.* Isador Lubin, *The Absorption of the Unemployed by American Industry*, Brookings Institution, 1929.

While technological unemployment has thus existed from the fist hatchet of the early Stone Age down to one of our modern match machines, that which faces us in the future is not only different in degree from anything in the past —it actually differs in kind. Therefore those who would allay our fears regarding technological unemployment by referring to facts and figures bearing on the period prior to, say, 1925 are ignoring the data that are really relevant to their problem. Talk about technological unemployment that overlooks the future implications of automatic machinery is blind and misleading.

No one has brought together the import of the impressive developments in the new technology better than Stuart Chase:

1. In the United States we have developed energy resources from coal, oil, natural gas, and water power until the total consumed has grown from 75 trillion British Thermal Units in 1830 to 27,000 trillion B.T.U. in 1930; while population has increased only twelve-fold.

2. We have developed prime movers (engines) to convert this energy into horsepower, mechanical work, until the total now approaches one billion horse-power— capable of performing as much work as 10 billion men, some 250 times the working population.

3. We have developed a bewildering variety of clever machines to direct the brute power of the prime mover into thousands of useful operations, in manufacturing, agriculture, transportation, even in clerical work, merchandising, housework.

4. By virtue of these energy sources, prime movers and machines, the business of growing, manufacturing, and transporting economic goods is enormously accelerated. Due to the irresistible growth in the technical arts all three factors become constantly more efficient and more interlocked. The whole industrial system is approaching the status of one vast machine, the operation of every part of which depends upon the operation of every other part. If people in Texas do not consume automobiles, people in Detroit cannot consume as much food, whereupon farmers in Iowa cannot consume as many radios and harvesting machines, whereupon . . . The self-sufficient local community has gone forever. We are all tied together with chains of power and of steel.

5. The tendency in manufacturing and power production, and to a lesser degree in transportation, agriculture and clerical work, is in the direction of the full automatic process, where the machine does everything, the human muscle nothing. Such labor as is required increasingly takes the form of dial watching, control cabin work, switch throwing, inspection and set up. Even in this domain the photo-electric cell has been found to be a more dependable switch thrower than any human hand or eye.[1]

We have only scratched the surface of the remarkable developments that are taking place in the way of increasing energy for economic purposes and lessening the human factor in production. But even these sketchy summaries will demonstrate that if we are not already in the "Third" Industrial Revolution we are living on its eve. If the early power looms of a century ago symbolized the first Industrial Revolution, the great looms of 1900 stood for the Second. But the gulf between them is not so great as that which separates the new automatic machinery for making woolen cloth from the woolen-manufacturing technique at the opening of the twentieth century.

[1] Chase, *op. cit.*, pp. 23-24.

EVE OF THE "THIRD" INDUSTRIAL REVOLUTION

The Second Industrial Revolution has also extended to agriculture.[1] In the nineteenth century steel plows, grain drills, mowing machines, reapers, binders, and threshing machines became universal in all advanced agricultural areas. But in the twentieth century labor-saving devices of unheard-of efficiency began to be introduced. Agricultural chemistry enables the farmer to know and utilize the exact type of fertilizer needed to insure the maximum productivity. Chemistry also aids the farmer to clear his farms and orchards of insect pests. Specialization in one or two major crops makes possible the most efficient use of machinery and seasonal labor. Giant gasoline tractors, large gang plows, pulverizing harrows, and grain drills enable farmers to plow, harrow, and sow grain in one process. Likewise, at harvest time a combined header, thresher, cleaner, and bagger permits the execution of the harvesting process in a single act. Motor trucks facilitate the transportation of the grain from the farms to railroads and elevators. Hay-loaders speed up the gathering of hay. Milking machines, motor trucks, and refrigerator cars have revolutionized the dairy industry. Electric power is tapped by the farmer to provide light, power, and refrigeration. By electric or gas light agricultural work can be carried on, as at harvest time, twenty-four hours a day.

The net result of all this has been a great decrease in the unit cost of the production of wheat, barley, corn, oats, and the like. In 1900 it required three hours of man and horse time to produce a bushel of wheat. Today, with mass-production processes, a bushel of wheat can be produced in as little as three minutes of machine time. There has also been a marked increase of production, since these more efficient methods encourage the cultivation of marginal lands that could not be worked with profit by less economical technique. Coupled with decreased purchasing power on the part of the American urban public, these new labor-saving devices, and the resulting increase in output, have led to a notable overproduction in agriculture. There is little evidence that we have yet produced more than the American people can eat, but we have produced more than they can buy—one of the major maladjustments of capitalism. The extreme industrialization of agriculture has also worked havoc with the small farmer. The great corporation farmers can produce wheat profitably for 50 cents a bushel where the small farmer cannot make money at less than $1 a bushel. Agricultural labor has also been hard hit by mechanical competition.

There has been an intimate connection between mass production in manufacturing and in agriculture. Mass producers of intricate and expensive agricultural machinery, such as gang plows, headers, combination harvesters and threshers, and the like, have stimulated mass production in agriculture in order to market their products.[2] The latter can rarely be bought extensively by the small farmer, who has neither the money nor the land to utilize them fully.

How far we still are, however, from applying all of the new technology in farming may be seen from the authoritative statement of O. W. Willcox that by

---

[1] *Cf.* L. C. Gray, article "Agricultural Machinery," Encyclopaedia of the Social Sciences; R. H. Gabriel, *Toilers of Land and Sea,* Yale University Press, 1926, Chap. IX; and M. P. Taylor, *Common Sense about Machines and Unemployment,* Winston, 1933, Chap. VII.

[2] One of the most exuberant enthusiasts for mass production in farming has, for example, been Henry Ford, who manufactures extensively tractors and other machinery for the newer farming technology.

the most efficient use of known agricultural technique the eight principal crops in the United States could be produced on one-sixth of the land now used and by one-sixth of the farmers now engaged in producing them.

The most deliberate and extensive effort to introduce mass production into agriculture has been that carried on by Russia, especially under the Five Year Plan.[1] The agricultural phases of this plan were little more than a combination of mass-production methods and communal ownership.

II. THE GROWTH OF SCIENTIFIC BUSINESS MANAGEMENT

The industrial changes produced by the new technology of the Second Industrial Revolution rendered desirable revolutionary developments in the character of the organization and management of business enterprises.[2] As Arkwright was symbolic of the factory of the First Industrial Revolution, so F. W. Taylor has been of the better factories of the Second Industrial Revolution. The opportunities for gain and the responsibilities for loss became so great that they could not be left to chance and the rule-of-thumb methods of the early days of industrial capitalism.

The two main factors that led to the rise of new management methods were the greater size of industrial enterprises and their growing technicality. Both of these factors made more evident the necessity of expert management. In the old days there had been a few real "captains of industry," such as the elder Rockefeller, Andrew Carnegie, James J. Hill, and Marshall Field, who had a real genius for managerial efficiency and were not merely speculative gamblers and pirates. But there is no guarantee that great wealth always means executive competence, and the new scale and character of business made it desirable that each large organization should be expertly directed. In this way both the divorcement of ownership from practical management and the development of scientific management and administration in industrial enterprise were brought about.

The foremost figures in founding scientific management were three American engineers and industrialists, Frederick W. Taylor (1856-1915), Henry L. Gantt (1861-1919), and Frank B. Gilbreth (1868-1924).[3] Of these Taylor was the first and the moving spirit. He suffered from an eye trouble that interfered with his formal education. So he became an apprentice in a machine shop, mastered the practical aspects of the mechanical trades, and by the time he was twenty-one had become chief engineer of the Midvale Steel Company. He held important executive posts during the rest of his life, but he devoted himself mainly to management problems. He introduced the conception of scientific research into the efficiency of workers over a long period. The essentials of his system of management principles were the following: 1. Industrial

---
[1] See below, pp. 816 ff.
[2] Cf. H. R. Towne, "The Evolution of Industrial Management," *Industrial Management*, Apr. -, 1921; H. B. Drury, *Scientific Management*, 3d ed. rev., Longmans, 1922.
[3] Cf. F. W. Taylor, *The Principles of Scientific Management*, Harper, 1911; H. L. Gantt, *Work, Wages and Profits*, 2d ed. rev., Engineering Magazine, 1913, and *Organizing for Work*, Harcourt, Brace, 1919; and F. B. Gilbreth, *A Primer of Scientific Management*, Van Nostrand, 1912. Other important persons were Harrington Emerson, inventor of the "line-and-staff" system, and Carl G. Barth, who helped Taylor in the development of his system.

THE GROWTH OF SCIENTIFIC BUSINESS MANAGEMENT

operations must be studied in detail in objective fashion. 2. From such study standards of efficiency and operation can be derived. 3. The coördination of all departments in an industry must be carefully worked out to avoid duplication and waste. 4. A rigorous system of inspection must prevail in order to enforce the correct standards. 5. The whole management process must be regarded as a scientific experiment from which new discoveries and standards will constantly emerge. Taylor was widely in demand as a consultant, especially after 1900. The Taylor Society was founded in his honor and is devoted to the promotion of scientific management in this country.

Gantt was a well-trained mechanical engineer who was inspired by and associated with Taylor. He early recognized the necessity of bookkeeping honesty in cost accounting and insisted that the production cost of an article should be determined solely by the necessary expense involved in producing it—a fundamental divergence from the cost-accounting ethics often obtaining under finance capitalism. He also developed a well-known method for the graphic presentation of costs and the recording of results. His wage-payment plan is even more famous. He provided a regular daily wage scale, based on computation of the normal production of the average worker and then awarded a bonus to those who exceeded this minimum. This did away with the temptation to "soldier" and to limit output under the old piecework system. Gilbreth, who gained his main experience as a contractor and builder, devoted more attention to increasing the productivity per worker. He was influenced by Taylor, but went far beyond him in studying the problem of workers' motions in the factory and in analyzing the causes of fatigue. He exploited the moving picture in studying the standardized motions of workers and in trying to find the reasons for delayed motion.[1]

A subordinate but important department of scientific management is what is known as personnel administration. This has been defined by one of the leading authorities on the subject in the following words:

Personnel administration may be defined as the planning, supervision, direction and coordination of those activities of an organization which contribute to realizing its defined purposes with a minimum of human effort and friction, and with an animating spirit of cooperation and with proper regard for the genuine well being of all members of the organization.[2]

Special attention is given to the selection, placing, and training of workers, health and safety work in factories, control of negotiations leading to labor contracts, and the supervision of relationships between workers and employers. The movement began about 1912 in the United States. It has grown until today about 1,000 companies, making up a majority of all those with more than 1,500 employees, have some sort of personnel administration plan in operation. The movement has made some headway in Europe, an especially good example being the Rowntree Cocoa Works in York, England. One reason why the trend has been less marked in Europe is the existence of a strong

[1] F. B. Gilbreth, *Motion Study*, Van Nostrand, 1911, and F. B. and L. E. M. Gilbreth, *Fatigue Study*, Sturgis & Walton, 1916.
[2] Ordway Tead, article "Personnel Administration," Encyclopaedia of the Social Sciences, Vol. XII, p. 88.

labor movement that assumes much of this type of responsibility and makes the initiative of the employer less necessary.

A more advanced and humane development in improving the efficiency of workers has been an outgrowth of medical knowledge, psychology, and sociology.[1] An attempt has been made to give workers more insight into what they are doing and into the significance of the industrial processes that they carry on. Rest periods and recreation give them a better attitude towards work and increase productivity. The key to this sort of development has been the recognition that good health and morale must underlie all really permanent increase in the efficiency of the worker.

The need for more efficient business management was made apparent, even as late as 1921, by the report of the engineers who studied waste in industry. They assigned the responsibility for from 50 to 75 per cent of our appalling waste to management and less than 20 per cent to labor.[2] To a considerable degree this inefficiency in management is due to the restraints placed upon real scientific administration by the reckless gambling spirit of finance capitalism.

Scientific management has been held back markedly because this is an age of finance capitalism[3] and the latter is interested in immediate financial profits. These can be gained for a time by speculative methods more rapidly and voluminously than by sound industrial practices. Speculative finance can at times make more money out of mismanagement than from rigorous efficiency. For this reason, it may be expected that there will never be any truly scientific management on a general scale until finance capitalism is ended and a new type of control installed that is interested in efficient management at all times.[4]

VIII. THE CHAIN STORE AND MASS DISTRIBUTION

Mass-production methods have been paralleled by attempts to achieve mass distribution. Department stores selling a large variety of goods became common in the United States in the eighties of the last century. Mail-order houses began to appear about the same time. The most famous of these came to be Sears, Roebuck and Company and Montgomery Ward and Company, both of the parent concerns being located in Chicago.[5] After 1925 these two great organizations established many local stores for retail sales, thus combining the mail-order and chain-store methods. Mail-order houses were greatly aided by the establishment of the parcel-post system in January, 1913. The first of the important chain stores was the Great Atlantic and Pacific Tea Company, established in 1858. It expanded greatly from 1921 to 1932—from about 4,500 units to over 16,000. The Jones Brothers Tea Company[6] was launched in 1872 and the McCrory variety chain in 1882. The Woolworth five and ten cent stores opened in 1879 and the S. S. Kresge chain in 1885. Since 1900 there has been a mushroom growth of chain stores covering almost every field of commodities and services—extending even to gasoline stations, barber shops, and restaurants.

---

[1] *Cf.* Elton Mayo, *The Human Problems of an Industrial Civilization*, Macmillan, 1933; Ordway Tead, *Human Nature and Management*, McGraw-Hill, 1929; Harry Myers, *Human Engineering*, Harper, 1932; and W. D. Scott, *Increasing Human Efficiency in Business*, new ed., Macmillan, 1923.
[2] See below, pp. 818-19.   [3] See below, pp. 822 ff.
[4] *Cf.* Coyle, *op. cit.*, and R. S. Brookings, *Industrial Ownership*, 2d ed., Macmillan, 1925.
[5] *Cf.* V. E. Pratt, *Selling by Mail*, McGraw-Hill, 1924.   [6] Now the Grand Union Co.

THE CHAIN STORE AND MASS DISTRIBUTION 765

Today there are in the United States several thousand chain-store groups, operating some 141,603 local retail stores of one kind or another. In 1929 these chain-store companies had a total sales amounting to $10,772,000,000. This was about 21.5 per cent of all retail trade. In some types of commodities the proportion of the retail trade held by chain stores was much greater. For example, in variety goods chain stores handled 93.2 per cent of sales; in shoes, 46.2 per cent; and in groceries and meats, 33.3 per cent. The largest volume of sales is achieved by the Great Atlantic and Pacific Tea Company which, even in the depression year of 1931, had a total of sales amounting to $1,066,000,000.[1]

While the chain stores have certain definite advantages inhering in the very nature of their organization, such as mass purchasing at lower prices and cheaper advertising costs through mass publicity, the main reason for the success of such of them as have succeeded has been greater business enterprise and better business administration. The slipshod methods, unattractive stores, and frequent discourtesy that have characterized the less enterprising businesses conducted by individuals have been ruthlessly eliminated in the better chain stores. The latter take care to select locations that are convenient to potential patrons. They have the resources and the good sense to erect or remodel buildings for their stores, giving special attention to store fronts and interiors. They make use of the latest and most hygienic methods of storing, exhibiting, and handling commodities. They choose salesmen and saleswomen with care, and insist upon efficiency and courtesy. Some of the larger chains maintain schools for training in salesmanship. Chain stores often specialize in one general line of merchandise and abandon brands in even this one line if they do not sell rapidly. The resulting large volume of sales and quick turnover make possible large profits, even though the profit on each item sold is small. Detailed and scientific accounting systems enable chain-store administrators to know the course of business and to alter practices before overt failure stares them in the face. The chain-store administrators have a large assortment of facts to guide their judgment, whereas the independent owner usually has to rely mainly upon intuition and shrewd guessing. In short, the great advantage in chain stores lies in the superiority of management. As Professor Nystrom has expressed this fact:

In most of these points the essential difference between the chain store and independent store is nothing more or less than a difference in capability of management. The chain store can and does procure the best possible talent in its executive management. . . . It can afford to pay the necessary salaries to procure such talent. The independent store gets its management from its owner and no selecting agency other than ultimate failure determines who shall not become an independent store manager.[2]

The spread of chain stores has aroused strong opposition from independent stores, and various measures have been taken to check their growth. One mode of attack has been political, namely, disproportionate taxation of chain stores.[3] But their advantages will probably insure their continued development

---
[1] For latest statistics on chain stores, see *Census of American Business: Retail Distribution, 1933*, United States Department of Commerce, 1934.
[2] P. H. Nystrom, *Chain Stores*, rev. ed., United States Chamber of Commerce, 1930, p. 13.
[3] *Cf.* Gregory and C. A. Hankin, *Progress of the Law in the U. S. Supreme Court, 1930-1931*, Legal Research Service, 1931, pp. 264 ff.

and increased efficiency. The independent stores can survive if they adopt equally efficient and progressive methods. The main danger in chain-store development is the possibility of near-monopolistic control, which would encourage price-fixing at high levels. But the competition between chains, together with governmental control, will probably serve to prevent this.

The development of modern production, the greater volume of products to be marketed, and the like have not only produced mass distribution through chain stores. They have also tended to build up a science of managerial direction in the field of marketing. In other words, the scientific-management principle has been carried over into the marketing as well as into the production function of modern industrial life. Sales departments are recognized as an integral special department of industry. They are coming to be very efficiently organized and special training is provided for salesmen. The growth of advertising and the increasing expense involved in large-scale marketing efforts have promoted this trend towards more scientific control over the whole field of marketing. Scientific management in marketing has permeated not only the sales departments of industrial concerns, but the sales operations of mail-order houses, chain stores, department stores, and the like.[1]

IX. THE SOCIAL IMPACT OF THE MACHINE AGE

Every generation during the last century has imagined itself to have attained approximate finality in the development of mechanical technique. Our generation, owing to the remarkable introduction of mechanical devices into every phase of life, might perhaps be forgiven for special assurance on this point. Yet it is quite possible that we are today only in the beginning of the mechanical age, provided man is able to show sufficient inventiveness in the institutional field to allow him to operate successfully the revolutionized type of life that his machines inevitably create.[2]

In his striking article on "The Empire of Machines" Professor John Maurice Clark has stated in trenchant fashion some of the more important social and cultural implications of the coming of the machine era. We can quote but a few of the more relevant paragraphs from this remarkable analysis:

The fact is that humanity is suffering in the grip of forces beyond its control and of purposes not its own. There is a form of life on earth which is already giving man the "darn good lickin'" he has been inviting. It does not threaten our physical life, but it does threaten our supremacy, our freedom of will, and our control of our own destiny. It is driving man, lashing him onward at a racking pace towards some goal which he cannot even foresee, let alone choose for himself. Men speak of this form of life often. They call it "industrialism."

And where lies the vital principle of industrialism? With man, replies the Practical Man. It is the child of his brain, with all its qualities and defects; it is the extension of his dominion over nature through his new servants, science and machinery. True in part; yet servants have become masters before now, and modern industrialism is not anything man foresaw or desired. It is what it had to be to

---

[1] Cf. M. T. Copeland, "The Managerial Factor in Marketing," in *Facts and Factors in Economic History*, pp. 596 ff.

[2] Cf. T. B. Veblen, *The Theory of Business Enterprise*, Scribner, 1904, Chaps. II, IX.

conform to the racial needs and life processes of the machines. The more the historians learn the true significance of events, the more do machines crowd persons out of the places of prominence. . . .

We have brought into existence a race of monstrous beings, as indeed Samuel Butler has shown us; beings whose powers are vastly beyond our own in many respects, and whose natures, needs, and behavior are utterly foreign to ours. Such life as they have we gave them, but are we now free to take it away? They could not carry on their life processes for a day without our help, but is that help a thing we have the option to withhold?

The machines originally made bargains with man, in which they offered him things he much desired, and in exchange bound him to serve and maintain them, to eliminate the unfit among them and promote their racial progress, and to alter his own social and political arrangements in whatever ways might be necessary in keeping pace with the increasingly complex social organization of the machines themselves, and in keeping the children of man faithful to the service the machines require. The full nature of the terms of these bargains was not, however, revealed to man at the first. Some of the terms became evident only after generations had passed, and of some we cannot yet be sure.[1]

X. THE SPIRIT OF INVENTION

Perhaps the best conclusion that we could give to this discussion of material aspects of the Second Industrial Revolution would be to comment briefly upon the spirit of invention and the relation of inventions to modern civilization. As Gabriel Tarde pointed out, inventions are the chief source of innovation in modern culture. Only by inventions can culture be changed in any very fundamental way, except through the mere borrowing of the inventions that another group has earlier produced. Above all, the spirit of invention is a denial of the philosophy of repetition and stability, so characteristic of the old régime.

Inventions were few and relatively infrequent down to the middle of the eighteenth century. In fact, the state of technology was generally static for thousands of years prior to 1750. Relatively slight material progress was achieved between the close of the Stone Age and the Industrial Revolution. At the present time, inventions come in great numbers. Even such inventions as the airplane or the radio, which would have been regarded as nothing short of miraculous a century ago, are now complacently accepted. We have become so accustomed to the everyday occurrence of notable scientific and mechanical achievements that only the most striking inventions attract our full attention.

Furthermore, with the progress of modern technology, inventions are no longer the chance product of a unique genius, but are becoming more and more the inevitable result of well-planned scientific research.[2] Given a need for a definite invention, such an invention is well-nigh inevitable, as Professor Ogburn has clearly proved by citing numerous inventions arrived at independently and almost synchronously by a number of different inventors. At the present time, the limitations upon inventions are pecuniary rather than

---

[1] Clark, *op. cit.*, *Yale Review*, October, 1922, pp. 132-33. *Cf.* also R. A. Clemen, "The Effect of Scientific Inventions upon Economic Trends," in *Facts and Factors in Economic History*, pp. 666 ff., and W. B. Kaempffert, *Invention and Society*, American Library Association, 1930 (reading list).

[2] *Cf.* Zimmermann, *op. cit.*, Chap. III; Ogburn, *Social Change*, pp. 80 ff.; and Hatfield, *The Inventor and His World*.

scientific. It is not so much a question of whether an invention is possible as of whether it would pay to produce and market it. Walter Lippmann well summarizes the transformation in the nature of inventions in our day in saying that

a really new thing has come into the world. That thing is the invention of invention. Men have not merely invented the modern machines. There have been machines invented since the earliest days, incalculably important, like the wheel, like sailing ships, like the windmill and the watermill. But in modern times men have invented a method of inventing, they have discovered a method of discovery. Mechanical progress has ceased to be casual and accidental and has become systematic and cumulative. We know, as no other people ever knew before, that we shall make more and more perfect machines.[1]

Finally, it may be pointed out that with the number and rapidity of modern inventions contemporary civilization has assumed a dynamic character quite foreign to that of any earlier age. The chief danger in this situation lies in the possibility that mankind will not be able to carry out with sufficient rapidity the social and economic readjustments that are necessary to use successfully the new technical equipment. Modern technology has put at our disposal potential means for increasing human welfare unparalleled in the accomplishments of man. The future alone can determine whether or not humanity can safely be intrusted with this new machinery. There is a grave risk that modern inventors have created a Frankenstein monster quite capable of destroying modern civilization. There is special danger in the growing efficiency of the engines of destruction utilized in modern war. Indeed, it is highly probable, unless we are able to avert future wars, that modern technology will be little more than an instrument for collective human suicide.[2]

Our material surroundings have changed in the past century and a half with a rapidity out of all proportion to the very slight alteration of our social point of view. We have vastly increased human control over nature, without increasing correspondingly man's control over his own selfish passions. Our social ideals are still based on pecuniary standards; our conduct is founded on selfishness and exploitation rather than coöperation and service. In economics we still talk in terms of a "rugged individualism" that was outmoded in many areas before Lincoln split a rail. The state is still viewed with hostility as the collective policeman rather than as the instrument of social progress and justice. In politics we still trust to a crude form of majority rule and believe in a nose-counting democracy and corrupt party government, despite their betrayal of the interests of large groups of the population. Religion has made disappointingly little progress; the Modernists are too often in search of new phrases to encompass old ideas and practices. Morals are still largely based on theological formulas and unexamined custom, instead of secular and scientific guidance for well-being here and now. Broadly speaking, while we have been daring and imaginative in technology, we are evasive and over-conservative in our thought and conduct.[3]

[1] Lippmann, *Preface to Morals*, Macmillan, 1929, p. 235.
[2] *Cf.* Wells, *The Shape of Things to Come*, pp. 191 ff.; and Riegel, *op. cit.*
[3] See below, pp. 1101 ff.

THE SPIRIT OF INVENTION

Such is the present challenge of our social order. The chief need of the world today is for innovators such as Jeremy Bentham in the nineteenth century, who can apply in the social and institutional realms the imagination and the capacity that have been repeatedly demonstrated by our inventors in the field of technology, and a chief part of this new inventiveness must be an avenue of approach to the hearts and minds of men, persuasive of the urgent necessity of accepting a rational solution of social problems. Whatever secures and sustains these new social objectives will be the religion of the future.

XI. THE INTERNATIONAL RESULTS OF INCREASED PRODUCTION

The new technology and industrial consolidation introduced by the Second Industrial Revolution led to an enormous increase in the volume and variety of commodities produced for sale, greatly stimulated commerce and the development of the commercial classes, and led to a feverish search for wider markets both at home and in areas overseas. The following brief table indicates the growing value of manufactured cotton goods exported from England at representative periods from 1851 to 1881:

VALUE OF COTTON GOODS EXPORTED FROM GREAT BRITAIN [1]

Years	Annual average
1829–1831	$87,854,220
1859–1861	238,140,000
1889–1891	350,474,040
1911–1913	598,591,620
1920–1921	1,410,372,000

On the eve of the World War England was exporting no less than 7,000,000,000 yards of cotton cloth. The English cotton industry grew by 40 per cent from 1870 to 1900 and the woolen industry by over 100 per cent. Pig iron is another of the most typical products of the new industry. In 1861 the annual output of pig iron was 3,800,000 tons, but in 1900 and 1913 it averaged about 10,000,000.[2] After the war there was a slump, and since 1920 the annual production has not exceeded 7,500,000 tons. Annual coal production increased from 49,000,000 tons in 1850 to 287,000,000 in 1913.

Germany's industrial productivity increased even more strikingly.[3] While in 1800 that country was still largely agricultural, with relatively little trade and chiefly local industries, by the outbreak of the World War it had passed Great Britain in such a basic industry as iron and steel. The German iron output was only 685,000 metric tons in 1862; by 1880 it was 2,729,000. In 1910 it had increased to 14,794,000 tons. The ten-year averages for pig-iron production in later years were as follows:

---

[1] H. O. Rugg, *Changing Civilizations in the Modern World,* Ginn, 1930, p. 90.
[2] See J. H. Clapham, *Economic History of Modern Britain,* Macmillan, 1931-32, 2 vols., Vol. I, 1931, pp. 42-43. The decline of late in pig-iron production has been due in part to the increasing use of scrap iron.
[3] See above, pp. 329 ff.

PIG-IRON PRODUCTION [1]

1880–89	3,619,590 tons
1890–99	5,877,770 tons
1900–09	10,550,000 tons
1910–19	11,940,000 tons

Steel production increased from 1,548,000 tons in 1880 to over 13,149,000 in 1910; in 1900, Germany was already turning out more steel than England. The relative position of the chief producing countries in the iron and steel industry in 1913 was as follows:

PRODUCTION OF IRON AND STEEL, 1913
(millions of metric tons)

	United States	Germany	England	France
Iron	31	17	10	5
Steel	31	17	7	5

Germany's other industries increased comparably,[2] so that within fifty years that country had stepped into a leading position among the industrial nations of the world.

Statistics of American industrial development equally well reflect the amazing expansion of productivity in the past three-quarters of a century:

PRODUCTION IN THE UNITED STATES

1. Total Value of Manufactures
(in millions of dollars)

1850	$ 1,019
1860	1,886
1870	4,232
1880	5,369
1890	9,372
1900	11,406
1910	20,449
1920	62,041
1930	70,434

2. Mineral Production

1870	$ 200
1880	400
1890	606
1900	1,000
1910	1,988
1920	6,981
1930	4,810

---

[1] Knight, Barnes, and Flügel, *op. cit.*, p. 541.
[2] See above, pp. 331 ff.

3. Pig-Iron Production
(millions of tons)

1870	1,665
1880	3,897
1890	9,353
1900	14,000
1910	27,636
1920	36,956
1930	31,752

4. Crude-Petroleum Production
(thousands of barrels of 42 gallons)

1860	500
1870	5,260
1880	26,286
1890	45,823
1900	63,620
1910	209,557
1920	442,929
1930	896,265

What has actually happened, in fact, is that production has expanded since 1850 more rapidly than consumption, primarily because finance capitalism prevented an equitable distribution of wealth and thus restricted the purchasing power of the consuming masses.[1] Moreover, during the first Industrial Revolution population was growing so rapidly and markets were expanding at such a rate that production could scarcely keep pace. The twentieth century, however, offers few rich new areas for exploitation overseas, and the rate of population increase has slowed down considerably.[2] At the same time, increasing mechanization and the growth of large-scale enterprises have enabled the rate of production to continue to increase amazingly. Indeed, it would not be too gross a distortion of the truth to adapt the Malthusian formula and say that while markets have been increasing by arithmetical progression, productive capacity has tended to increase by geometrical progression.

Evidences of overproduction were not lacking even before the opening of the twentieth century. It was chiefly fear of this which led to the German cartel movement,[3] one of the declared purposes of the cartel being to ration production among the member firms. Production of many commodities received a great impetus in all countries from the pressure of war demands between 1914 and 1918, particularly since many countries were trying, so far as possible, to be self-sufficing with regard to vital products.

The period since the war has therefore witnessed a prolonged struggle for existence going on in many industries, aggravated by the general economic depression. The seriousness of the situation is typified by the English coal industry, where the conditions involve writing off a considerable fraction of the nation's wealth, and permanently depriving large numbers of people of the

---

[1] See below, pp. 798 ff., 805 ff., 822 ff.
[2] See above, pp. 416 ff., 546 ff., 550 ff.
[3] See above, pp. 335 ff.

only occupation for which they are trained. Realization of the dangers of overproduction has led to the formation of a number of international cartels, designed to restrain production and thus reduce price fluctuations. Among the most important have been the international steel cartel, formed in 1926, the zinc and aluminum cartels, and several agreements in the chemical industry.

In other lines, where limitation of production has not been feasible, overproduction has in some cases prevailed over a period of years, with results often disastrous to the producers. Notable examples are rubber, coffee, and wheat. In the United States, it is asserted that productive capacity exceeds market demand in many of our fundamental industries, including iron and steel, automobiles, boots and shoes, coal, petroleum, and textiles. That there is a direct relationship between this situation and the economic depression from which most of the world has suffered in the past few years, there can be little doubt. Its relationship to the postwar economic jealousies, to many newly created tariff barriers, and to the prevalent international financial difficulties is also close. What passes for overproduction is, however, all too often underconsumption due to inadequate mass purchasing power.

The swelling volume of manufactured products led, during the nineteenth century, to an increasingly effective effort to secure wider markets. While the most important of these markets were found in the more advanced and densely populated states of the world, the beliefs inherited from the earlier colonial era led many to feel that adequate markets could be discovered only in new and undeveloped territories, especially colonies. This conviction has played its part in the growth of modern colonialism since 1870. This subject has already been discussed in some detail in dealing with capitalistic imperialism.[1]

The decade following 1870 was a sort of turning-point, according to the belief of many economists, because about this time the new industrialism first reached the point in its growth where it seemed that production was outrunning the home markets. Selling competition between great industrial nations became keen. Business groups began to bring pressure upon their governments to acquire colonies or protectorates in regions that furnished indispensable raw materials or promised markets for finished goods.

Up to the World War, at least, the wisdom of attempting to get exclusive trade privileges by political means was not fully demonstrated. Most of the colonies acquired after 1870 provided relatively little demand for European products, and many were expensive to maintain and administer. England, as we have noted, was a far more important purchaser of German products than was the whole German colonial empire. The fact that the various nations looked forward to a period of even more serious competition for raw materials and markets in the future was, nevertheless, a first-rate factor in economic and commercial history. It gave a very great impulse to colonial aspirations and led to the exploration and settlement of those large areas of the earth which had not been seized and exploited during the earlier expansion of Europe and the first era of colonialism.

More illuminating than economic imperialism as a reflection of the growth of trade since the Industrial Revolution are, of course, the commercial statistics

[1] See above, pp. 521 ff., 546 ff.

Ewing Galloway

MODERN SPINNING MACHINERY

Thomas Hart Benton, New School for Social Research

POWER

From Ladies' Home Journal © *C. P. Co.*

AN OLD-TIME COUNTRY STORE

Worsinger Photo, Chain Store Agency

A MODERN CHAIN STORE

themselves, which testify eloquently to the expansion of world-trade since 1800. The growth of the foreign commerce of the world, gross and per capita, is well indicated by the following table:

FOREIGN COMMERCE AND PRODUCTION OF THE COUNTRIES OF THE WORLD [1]

Year	Gross commerce (in millions of dollars)	Commerce per capita
1800	1,400	$ 2.31
1820	1,600	2.13
1830	1,900	2.34
1840	2,700	2.93
1850	4,000	3.76
1860	7,200	6.01
1870	10,600	8.14
1880	14,700	10.26
1890	17,500	11.80
1900	20,100	13.02
1910	33,600	20.81
1913	40,400	24.47
1929	68,526	34.94
1931	39,300	19.65
1933	23,700	11.85

Europe carried about three-fourths of this trade at the opening of the nineteenth century, and about two-thirds at the close. All the continents shared in the increase. The gain of the other continents relative to Europe has been, however, surprisingly small. If we should group together Europe and the territories actually settled by Europeans, such as the United States, Canada, Argentina, and Australia, the apparent relative loss of trade by Europeans would practically disappear.

This marked increase in production brought about by the Second Industrial Revolution led to a revolution in trade policies. We have already noted how the earlier stages of the first Industrial Revolution and the capitalistic economic theories accompanying it worked decidedly in the direction of free trade.[2] The old mercantilistic legislation was swept away, and by the time of the American Civil War either free trade or low tariffs held the field throughout the Western world. The greater productivity of the new machinery and industrial organization after 1850 helped along the movement towards a revival of protection. The major prophet of this movement was Friedrich List, whose name we have already had occasion to mention as a critic of Economic Liberalism.[3]

List's epoch-making work, entitled *The National System of Political Economy,* was published in 1841. List was a German who had been driven out of his native land because of his progressivism. He came to America, and became acquainted with the political and economic writings of Alexander Hamilton. He was converted to Hamilton's views on national politics and

---

[1] Adapted from Day, *History of Commerce,* p. 271, and carried down to date.
[2] See above, pp. 319 ff.　　[3] See above, p. 386.

economics, and elaborated his views in the above-mentioned work and in numerous pamphlets.[1]

List contended that there was a wide diversity in the degree of economic evolution in the various states of the world, and that it was necessary for the less-developed states to safeguard their growing industries by means of a protective tariff. List's contention was what has become famous in economic theory as the "infant-industry argument." He admitted that as soon as a state had reached a condition of well-developed industrial life, it might then begin to reduce its tariff schedules until they approximated a condition of complete freedom of trade.

The first state to take a step towards the return to protection was the United States, during the Civil War. Following the Morrill Act of 1861 came several tariff bills, which were adopted ostensibly as fiscal measures designed to produce the greater national income that was much needed on account of the high expenditures caused by the Civil War. Beginning with the act of 1862, the tariff rates were raised, and when the war was over, there was no successful movement to restore something like the liberal schedules of the 1857 tariff. In spite of sporadic and temporary downward reductions in 1894 and 1913, under the Hawley-Smoot tariff of 1930 the United States had the highest tariff schedule in the history of American trade.

The first European state to make a break with the more liberal trend in trade policies was Germany. Bismarck, though originally a free-trader, believed that a protective tariff would be valuable for the stimulation of German home industries and agriculture and would produce a considerable increase of revenue. This would enable him to carry through successfully his military increases and his "State Socialism," and to promote nationalization. The bill was passed on June 7, 1879. Though this tariff of 1879 was fairly successful, it did not satisfy the vested interests, and higher schedules were provided in bills of 1885, 1887, and 1902. The tariff of December 25, 1902, was an extremely high one, an act in which the industrialists were aided by the great landlords.

France followed in the train of Germany with protectionist measures passed in 1881. As in Germany, this was merely a signal for still higher tariffs to come, and in the acts of 1892 and 1910 the schedules were raised. Other continental European states followed the example of Germany and France in a general revival of protectionism. Only Great Britain among leading states remained aloof. In spite of a vigorous campaign for a return to protectionism, led by Joseph Chamberlain, England decided, in 1905, to retain its free-trade system.

The stimulation of nationalism in the postwar period and the general economic depression beginning in 1929 have led to a great increase in tariffs and to the raising of numerous new barriers to the free circulation of goods. The new states created by the Treaty of Versailles have tried to further their nationalistic ambitions by neo-mercantilistic policies. And the older states, with their notable surplus productive capacity, have in a number of cases adopted a more highly protective policy than ruled before the war. Even in the United States, where the international competition and rivalry are felt less than in Europe, tariff rates have gone up noticeably since 1918. The situation is aggra-

[1] See Gide and Rist, *History of Economic Doctrines*, pp. 264 ff.

vated by the fact that continued payments of the tremendous reparations and war debts were possible only if the debtor nations could export goods and thus pile up credit balances. At the present time much of the Western world seems to be involved in a vicious economic circle that has done much to enhance the political instability of postwar Europe. A final blow was given to free trade when England, its staunchest advocate, put into force in 1932 several mildly protective tariff rates. It was hoped by many that the London Economic Conference of 1933 would lead to international agreements to revise tariffs downward, but it failed entirely in this respect.

The European tariff system possesses one trait that is not so prominent in the tariff regulations of the United States, namely, the tendency to use tariff schedules as a mode of economic warfare during times of political peace. In the United States the tariff is chiefly a business affair and is based mainly on a single flat rate to apply to imports from all countries whatever.[1] In Europe, on the contrary, tariff bills provide maximum and minimum rates, with a wide variation of schedules between the maximum and the minimum. In case a neighboring state will grant very favorable trade concessions, the minimum rates are applied in commercial relations with that particular state. If favorable concessions cannot be secured, then the maximum rates are applied. This European system of discriminatory and differential tariffs has been a prime economic cause of national friction and hatreds. With the possible exception of the struggle for raw materials and market overseas, it was probably the most significant economic factor in producing the belligerent spirit in contemporary Europe, thus helping to bring on the World War.

As to the relation of tariffs to national and world welfare, opinions differ. It seems that, in general, tariffs may prove helpful in the earlier stages of economic evolution, in order to protect promising industrial developments that are not as yet fully established. One may possibly go even further and agree with some experts on public finance that indirect taxes are better than direct taxes, and that a tariff for revenue only is one of the best forms of indirect taxation.

It is not difficult, however, to prove that the high protective tariffs which exist in modern states, alongside mature economic development, are a disastrous mode of protecting the vested interests, and that they prevent protected countries from enjoying a normal type of economic evolution. The world would probably be much better off if it were able to follow the policy advocated by Adam Smith and allow each state to develop to a high degree of excellence the types of industries that its natural resources, its geographical position, and the particular qualities of its population would seem to favor. Protective tariffs have enabled specific vested interests to force a country into many forms of industrial endeavor for which there exists little relative justification. This has withdrawn national economic efforts from lines of activity that would have been much more productive and desirable.

Further, it is certain that modern protective tariffs have been a leading cause

---

[1] In the Fordney-McCumber tariff of 1922 and the Hawley-Smoot tariff of 1930 there were "flexible clauses" giving the President some discretion in varying customs duties in accordance with the treatment of our goods by foreign countries.

of the rise and persistence of monopolies within a state. Many concerns, having practical control over the supply of a given commodity within a state, have been able to charge exorbitantly high prices because foreign firms have been unable, on account of the high tariff wall, to ship in such commodities and sell them at a cheaper price. Nothing could be more effective in reducing the oppressive policies of modern monopolistic concerns than general freedom of trade throughout the world. Nevertheless, in the light of the fact that the protective tariff system has now become pretty thoroughly ingrained in the political and economic system of every modern nation, with the possible exception of England, it is highly probable that any reduction of tariff rates will have to take place slowly and gradually, in order that modern business may adapt itself to these transformations in a safe and reasonable manner. One can scarcely hope for a rapid and successful transition from the exceedingly high protective tariffs that now exist to an era of real free trade.

SUGGESTED READING

Hammerton, *Universal History of the World*, Chaps. 176, 186.
Articles, "Automobile Industry," "Business Administration" (Herman Feldman), "Chemical Industries" (T. J. Kreps), "Holding Companies" (J. C. Bonbright and G. C. Means), "Invention" (Carl Brinkmann), "Large Scale Production" (M. W. Watkins), "Location of Industry" (Hermann Schumacher), "Management" (Oliver Sheldon), "Motion Pictures," "Oil Industry" (G. W. Stocking), "Personnel Administration" (Ordway Tead), "Protection" (E. F. Heckscher), "Radio," "Railroads," "Rubber" (C. R. Whittlesey), and "Tariff" (Jacob Viner), Encyclopaedia of the Social Sciences
Ogg and Sharp, *The Economic Development of Modern Europe*, Chaps. XIII-XIV, XXVIII
H. G. Wells, *The Shape of Things to Come*, Macmillan, 1933
—— *The Work, Wealth and Happiness of Mankind*. Vol. I, pp. 154-58
F. H. Hooper, ed., *These Eventful Years*, Encyclopaedia Britannica Co., 1924, 2 vols., Vol. II, Chaps. LXVII, LXIX, LXXVII, LXXXIII
Zimmermann, *World Resources and Industries*, Pt. III
Usher, *History of Mechanical Inventions*, Chaps. VIII-XIII
Thompson, *The Age of Invention*
Cressy, *Discoveries and Inventions of the Twentieth Century*
Kaempffert, *Popular History of American Invention*, Vol. I, Pt. I, Chaps. III-V, Pt. II, Chaps. IV-VII, Pt. III, Chaps. II-III; Vol. II, Pt. IV, Chap. VII, Pt. V
M. P. Taylor, *Common Sense about Machines and Unemployment*, Winston, 1933
Meakin, *The New Industrial Revolution*
Mumford, *Technics and Civilization*
Understanding the Big Corporations, by the editors of *Fortune*, McBride, 1934
F. L. Darrow, *The Story of Chemistry*, Bobbs-Merrill, 1927
E. E. Slosson, *Creative Chemistry*, new ed., Century, 1930
W. C. Geer, *The Reign of Rubber*, Century, 1922
W. H. Voskuil, *Minerals in Modern Industry*, Wiley, 1930
Gustav Egloff, *Earth Oil*, Williams & Wilkins, 1933
J. T. Flynn, *God's Gold*, Harcourt, Brace, 1932
Lawrence, *The World's Struggle with Rubber, 1905-1931*
W. N. Polakov, *The Power Age*, Covici, Friede, 1933
Bowen, *A Century of Atlantic Travel*

SUGGESTED READING

R. C. Epstein, *The Automobile Industry,* McGraw-Hill, 1928
J. E. Fechet, *Flying,* Williams & Wilkins, 1933
Squier, *Telling the World*
O. E. Dunlap, *The Story of Radio,* Dial Press, 1927
J. S. Thompson, *History of Composing Machines,* Inland Printer Co., 1904
Bickel, *New Empires*
B. B. Hampton, *History of the Movies,* Covici, Friede, 1931
H. W. Laidler, *Concentration in American Industry,* Crowell, 1931
F. A. Fetter, *The Masquerade of Monopoly,* Harcourt, Brace, 1931
Charles Merz, *And Then Came Ford,* Doubleday, Doran, 1929
R. L. Cruden, "The Great Ford Myth," *New Republic,* March 16, 1932
O. W. Willcox, *Reshaping Agriculture,* Norton, 1934
Stuart Chase, *Men and Machines,* Macmillan, 1929
H. O. Rugg, *The Great Technology,* Day, 1933
Frank Arkright, *The A B C of Technocracy,* Harper, 1933
Loeb, *Life in a Technocracy*
H. B. Drury, *Scientific Management,* 3d ed. rev., Longmans, 1922
H. S. Person, ed., *Scientific Management in American Industry,* Harper, 1929
F. A. Westbrook, *Industrial Management in This Machine Age,* Crowell, 1932
Ordway Tead and H. C. Metcalf, *Personnel Administration: Principles and Practice,* 3d ed. rev., McGraw-Hill, 1933
Mayo, *The Human Problems of an Industrial Civilization*
W. S. Hayward and Percival White, *Chain Stores,* McGraw-Hill, 1928
Arthur Pound, *The Iron Man in Industry,* Little, Brown, 1922
J. M. Keynes, Karl Pribram, and E. J. Phelan, *Unemployment as a World Problem,* University of Chicago Press, 1931
H. S. Hatfield, *The Inventor and His World,* Dutton, 1933
Ashley, *Modern Tariff History,* Pt. I, Chaps. v-ix, Pt. II, Chaps. iv-x, Pt. III, Chaps. v-vii
Taussig, *Tariff History of the United States,* Pt. II
G. M. Fisk and P. S. Peirce, *International Commercial Policies,* Macmillan, 1923
H. V. V. Fay, "Commercial Policy in Post-war Europe," *Quarterly Journal of Economics,* May, 1927
L. C. Marshall, *Industrial Society,* rev. ed., University of Chicago Press, 1929, 3 pts., Pt. II, *Production of the Modern Order,* Chap. iv, and pp. 925-45
Jones, Vandenbosch, and Vandenbosch, *Readings in Citizenship,* pp. 267-326
J. G. Frederick, ed., *For and Against Technocracy,* Business Course, 1933

FURTHER REFERENCES

THE SECOND INDUSTRIAL REVOLUTION. For introductory reading, see Taylor, *op. cit.,* Chaps. I-II; *Recent Social Trends,* Vol. I, Chap. III; Birnie, *Economic History of Europe,* Chap. xv; Rugg, *Changing Civilizations,* pp. 29-42, 60-83; Chase, *op. cit.;* Wile, *A Century of Industrial Progress;* Thompson, *op. cit.;* Cressy, *op. cit.;* Meakin, *op. cit.;* Nussbaum, *History of the Economic Institutions of Modern Europe,* Pt. IV.

On the chief technician of the Second Industrial Revolution, see W. A. Simonds, *Edison: His Life, His Work, His Genius* (Bobbs-Merrill, 1934).

On the contemporary coal, iron, and steel industries, see Zimmermann, *op. cit.,* Chaps. XXIV-XXV, XXX-XXXIII; Voskuil, *op. cit.*

CHEMISTRY. For major advances in organic chemistry, see Darrow, *op. cit.,* Chap. II. For the industrial applications of chemistry, see Slosson, *op. cit.*

PETROLEUM. For the history and essentials of the petroleum industry, see Keir, *The Epic of Industry,* Chap. VI; Cressy, *op. cit.,* Chap. II; Zimmermann, *op. cit.,*

Chaps. xxvi-xxvii; G. W. Stocking, *The Oil Industry and the Competitive System* (Houghton Mifflin, 1925); Egloff, *op. cit.*; S. S. Amdursky, *Handbook of the Petroleum Industry* (Taylor Instrument Companies, 1928); W. S. Tower, *The Story of Oil* (Appleton, 1909); J. H. Westcott, *Oil, Its Conservation and Waste* (4th ed., Beacon Publishing Co., 1930); L. G. Gurvich and Harold Moore, *The Scientific Principles of Petroleum Technology* (Van Nostrand, 1932).

RUBBER. On the chemistry of the rubber industry, see Slosson, *op. cit.*, Chap. viii; Darrow, *op. cit.*, Chap. viii; B. D. Luff, *The Chemistry of Rubber* (Van Nostrand, 1924).

On the rubber industry, see Lawrence, *op. cit.*; Geer, *op. cit.*; C. R. Whittlesey, *Governmental Control of Crude Rubber* (Princeton University Press, 1934).

POWER. On the power age, see Usher, *op. cit.*, Chap. xiii; Polakov, *op. cit.*, Chap. v; Fred Henderson, *The Economic Consequences of Power Production* (Day, 1933).

On electric-power developments, see Zimmermann, *op. cit.*, Chaps. xxviii-xxix; Keir, *op. cit.*, Chap. vii; Cressy, *op. cit.*, Chaps. v-vi.

TRANSPORTATION AND COMMUNICATION. For a clear account of the development in these fields, see Webster, *Travel by Air, Land, and Sea*—juvenile, but informing; Keir, *The March of Commerce*; Corbin, *Mechanical Inventions of To-day*; Hawks, *The Triumph of Man in Science and Invention*, Chaps. xi-xii; Bridges, *The Book of Inventions*, Chaps. xvii, xix.

On contemporary railroad technique, see Cressy, *op. cit.*, Chap. xiii.

On the automobile industry, see Keir, *op. cit.*, Chap. xvi; Cressy, *op. cit.*, Chap. xv; C. R. Gibson, *The Motor Car and Its Story* (Lippincott, 1927); Epstein, *op. cit.*; Arthur Pound, *The Turning Wheel* (Doubleday, Doran, 1934).

On the evolution of aviation, see Cressy, *op. cit.*, Chap. xvii; Keir, *op. cit.*, Chap. xvii; Hawks, *op. cit.*, Chap. xiii; Fechet, *op. cit.*; John Goldstrom, *Narrative History of Aviation* (Macmillan, 1930); Archibald Black, *Transport Aviation* (Simmons-Boardman, 1929).

On recent progress in ocean transport, see Cressy, *op. cit.*, Chap. xvi; Bowen, *op. cit.*; Berglund, *Ocean Transportation*.

COMMUNICATION. On the technique of modern communication, see Keir, *op. cit.*, Chaps. xi-xiii; Chapin, *Historical Introduction to Social Economy*, pp. 237 ff.; Bridges, *op. cit.*, Chaps. viii-x, xxiii-xxv; Chaps. i, iv-v, vii, of Page and others, *Modern Communication*; *Recent Social Trends*, Vol. I, Chap. iv; Squier, *op. cit.*

On the history and technique of the radio, see Cressy, *op. cit.*, Chap. xviii; Dunlap, *op. cit.*; F. E. Terman, *Radio Engineering* (McGraw-Hill, 1932); Clifford Kirkpatrick, "Intelligence and the Radio," *Sociology and Social Research*, January-February, 1935.

On typesetting machinery, see Usher, *op. cit.*, Chap. iii; Hawks, *op. cit.*, Chap. viii; Iles, *Leading American Inventors*, pp. 393 ff.; C. H. Cochrane, article "Composing Machines," Encyclopedia Americana; J. S. Thompson, *The Mechanism of the Linotype* (Inland Printer Co., 1928), and *op. cit.*

On news-gathering agencies, see Victor Rosewater, *History of Coöperative News-gathering in the United States* (Appleton, 1930); pp. 82 ff. of N. D. Cochran, *E. W. Scripps* (Harcourt, Brace, 1933).

On the development of the moving-picture industry, see Hampton, *op. cit.*; J. P. Kennedy, ed., *The Story of the Films* (McGraw-Hill, 1927); Will Irwin, *The House That Shadows Built* (Doubleday, Doran, 1928); Terry Ramsaye, *A Million and One Nights: The History of the Motion Picture* (Simon & Schuster, 1926, 2 vols.); Paul Rotha, *The Film till Now* (Peter Smith, 1931). The business and financial side of moving pictures is covered in H. T. Lewis, *The Motion Picture Industry* (Van Nostrand, 1933); H. B. Franklin, *Motion Picture Theatre Management*

(Doran, 1927); Upton Sinclair, *Upton Sinclair Presents William Fox* (American Book Supply Co., 1933). On educational and moral factors, see Forman, *Our Movie Made Children*.

LARGE-SCALE BUSINESS ENTERPRISE. On the concentration of industry, see Nussbaum, *op. cit.*, Pt. IV, Chap. VII; M. W. Watkins, article "Large Scale Industry," *loc. cit.;* Laidler, *op. cit.;* W. L. Thorp, *The Integration of Industrial Operations* (United States Census Bureau, 1924).

On the localization of industry, see Zimmermann, *op. cit.*, pp. 360 ff., 612 ff., 625 ff., 751 ff.; Hermann Schumacher, article "Location of Industry," *loc. cit.;* F. S. Hall, *The Localization of Industries* (United States Government Printing Office, 1902); Chap. VI of R. M. Keir, *Manufacturing* (Ronald Press, 1928); pp. 34 ff. of E. D. McCallum, *The Iron and Steel Industry in the United States* (King, 1931).

On the monopoly problem, see J. M. Clark, article "Monopoly," Encyclopaedia of the Social Sciences; Chaps. I, III-V, of J. W. Jenks, *The Trust Problem* (Doubleday, Doran, 5th ed., 1929); R. T. Ely, *Monopolies and Trusts* (Macmillan, 1900); Fetter, *op. cit.;* O. W. Knauth, *The Policy of the United States towards Industrial Monopoly* (Longmans, 1913).

UNEMPLOYMENT IN THE SECOND INDUSTRIAL REVOLUTION. P. H. Douglas and Aaron Director, *The Problem of Unemployment* (Macmillan, 1931); J. A. Hobson, *Rationalisation and Unemployment* (Macmillan, 1930); Keynes, Pribram, and Phelan, *op. cit.;* E. W. Bakke, *The Unemployed Man* (Dutton, 1934); R. C. Elbert, *Unemployment and Relief* (Farrar & Rinehart, 1934); N. M. Thomas, *Human Exploitation in the United States* (Stokes, 1934).

SCIENTIFIC MANAGEMENT. For a clear discussion of this subject, see Chap. IV of R. T. Bye and W. W. Hewett, *Applied Economics* (2d ed. rev., Crofts, 1934). The more important books on the subject are Person, *op. cit.;* Oliver Sheldon, *The Philosophy of Management* (Pitman, 1923); H. C. Metcalf, ed., *Business Leadership* (Pitman, 1931); E. D. Jones, *The Administration of Industrial Enterprises* (rev. ed., Longmans, 1925); Westbrook, *op. cit.;* G. T. Schwenning, ed., *Management Problems, with Special Reference to the Textile Industry* (University of North Carolina Press, 1930); Metcalf, *op. cit.;* Tead and Metcalf, *op. cit.;* H. B. Drury, *Scientific Management* (Columbia University Press, 1922).

CHAIN STORES. P. H. Nystrom, *Chain Stores* (rev. ed., United States Chamber of Commerce, 1930); Hayward and White, *op. cit.;* W. J. Baxter, *Chain Store Distribution and Management* (2d ed. rev., Harper, 1931); G. M. Lebhar, *The Chain Store—Boon or Bane?* (Harper, 1932).

THE SPIRIT OF INVENTION. On inventions, technology, and cultural history, see Usher, *op. cit.*, Chaps. I-III; Nussbaum, *op. cit.*, Pt. IV, Chap. III; Mumford, *op. cit.;* Ogburn, *Social Change,* pp. 80 ff.; and *You and Machines* (United States Government Printing Office, 1934); *Recent Social Trends,* Vol. I, Chap. III; Hatfield, *op. cit.;* W. B. Kaempffert, *Invention and Society* (American Library Association), 1930 —reading list.

For an optimistic analysis of machinery in modern life, see R. E. Flanders, *Taming Our Machines* (Harper, 1931). A more realistic view is given in Chase, *op. cit.;* and the most profound analysis in Mumford, *op. cit.*

PROTECTIONISM. On foreign-trade technique, see C. E. Griffin, *Principles of Foreign Trade* (Macmillan, 1924). On the return of protectionism, see Ashley, *op. cit.;* Taussig, *op. cit.;* Fay, *op. cit.;* Fisk and Peirce, *op. cit.;* Commission of Inquiry into National Policy, *International Economic Relations* (University of Minnesota Press, 1934); Patterson, *The World Trend towards Nationalism;* J. G. Smith, *Economic Planning and the Tariff* (Princeton University Press, 1934).

CHAPTER XXI

FINANCE CAPITALISM

I. STAGES IN THE EVOLUTION OF CAPITALISM

The Industrial Revolution and its associated economic transformations brought to completion the capitalistic system of industrial operations, economic ethics, and class relationships. It is confusing and misleading, however, to describe capitalism exclusively in terms of any single stage of its development. Nor would it be valid to attempt to envisage as a unified whole a system of economic life covering the period from the Fuggers to the Morgans. Capitalism can be intelligently understood only when we analyze it in the light of its major stages or periods of evolution, each of which had distinctive characteristics.

The most accurate and satisfactory conception of the evolution of capitalism is that which conceives of it as having passed through the following four successive stages of development: (1) Early or pre-industrial capitalism; (2) industrial capitalism; (3) monopoly capitalism; and (4) finance capitalism.[1]

The early or pre-industrial capitalism was that form which developed between the Commercial and Industrial revolutions. Society was still primarily agricultural, and capitalistic activities were chiefly associated with the rising world trade and small manufacturing units under either the guild or the putting-out system. Industrial capitalism prevailed during the earlier stages of the economic society produced by the first Industrial Revolution. It grew out of the rise of the machine technique, the factory system, the improvements in transportation growing out of the application of the steam engine, and the rise of urban industrial life.

Monopoly capitalism was primarily associated with the earlier developments in the Second Industrial Revolution, which demonstrated the superior efficiency of large industrial establishments and mass production. It was aided greatly by the growing popularity of the corporate form of business organization and the rise of trusts. Bold and unscrupulous figures in industry and transportation sought to get control of whole industries and to profit by the introduction of labor-saving devices and the advantages of large-scale operations. Price-fixing at a high level was another benefit sought in this period of rising monopolies. Ownership was not, however, divorced to any great extent from management.

---

[1] For discussions of the stages of capitalism, see Knight, Barnes, and Flügel, *Economic History of Europe*, pp. 337-41; N. S. B. Gras, "Types of Capitalism," in *Facts and Factors in Economic History*, pp. 580-95; Hobson, *The Evolution of Modern Capitalism*, Chap. 1; Werner Sombart, article "Capitalism," Encyclopaedia of the Social Sciences; and H. E. Sée, *Modern Capitalism*, Adelphi Co., 1928.

The industrial giants of those days still maintained an active personal control over their expanding enterprises.

Finance capitalism, as the name implies, was distinctively characterized by the rise of the great investment banker as the controlling figure in economic life. The financier replaced the industrialist in the supreme control of contemporary economic affairs. The process of consolidation launched by monopoly capitalism went on, this time directed by interested bankers rather than by ambitious industrialists. This unifying tendency was forwarded by the wellnigh universal adoption of the holding company in the place of the outlawed trusts. Management was divorced to an ever greater degree from ownership, and absentee ownership became all but universal. Productivity and service fell far into the background as the dominating motives of those in control of economic life. The economic ideal came to be that of making large and immediate financial profits through speculative manipulations. The latter were often definitely opposed to the long-time interests of the industries and transportation systems involved.

Applying this conception of the stages of capitalistic evolution to the economic history of the United States, the era of early or pre-industrial capitalism fell between the period of settlement and the first quarter of the nineteenth century.[1] Beginning about 1800, there came the introduction of machine methods into the cotton textile industry; the revolution in transportation brought about by canals, the building of river steamboats, and the rise of the railroads; the development of modern methods of making iron and steel; and the introduction of the factory system. This movement was powerfully forwarded by the industrial stimulus of the Civil War. No definite date can be assigned as marking the decisive end of this stage, known as industrial capitalism. Henry Ford may probably be most accurately regarded as an industrialist with the ideals of industrial capitalism, equipped with the technique afforded by the Second Industrial Revolution, and operating in a world dominated by finance capitalism. The anomalous character of Ford's ideals in the contemporary economic world has often been commented upon by historians and economists.

The last two decades of the nineteenth century, however, witnessed a definite transformation in the character of the dominant capitalistic processes and ideals. The chief objective was to achieve concentration of industrial power in order to obtain the advantages of large-scale production and monopoly prices. The outstanding and most representative figure of this period was John D. Rockefeller, Sr., and the Standard Oil Company was the most conspicuous and successful product of monopoly capitalism in this country. Other examples were the United States Steel Corporation, the International Harvester Company, and the American Tobacco Company. This monopolistic development was at first secured through the use of trusts, but these were outlawed by the Sherman Act of 1890. After this date the holding company was invented, and it has been fairly successful in keeping beyond the reaches of the law.

The age of finance capitalism overlaps the latter part of the period of monop-

---

[1] This chapter is devoted chiefly to American developments for two main reasons: (1) Finance capitalism has reached its highest and most characteristic developments in the United States; and (2) American data are more familiar to American readers.

oly capitalism.[1] The formation of the United States Steel Corporation at the opening of the twentieth century was as much the work of a banker, J. P. Morgan, as of the steel industrialists, Carnegie, Schwab, Frick, and others. This latest period has witnessed the creation of great banking combines and the increasing control of the great investment banks over manufacturing industries, mining, transportation, electric utilities, and insurance companies. If Rockefeller was the typical figure of the period of monopoly capitalism, J. P. Morgan was the outstanding personage in the triumph of finance capitalism.[2] Other leading banking concerns were Kuhn, Loeb & Co., Dillon, Read & Co., Lee Higginson & Co., and great metropolitan national banks such as the Chase National Bank and the National City Bank of New York City. Descendants of leaders in the period of monopoly capitalism often assumed a prominent position in the age of finance capitalism. For example, the younger Rockefeller has a controlling interest in the Chase National Bank, the greatest public banking organization in the United States.

It must not be supposed that the control of finance over legitimate business was limited to these giant investment banking houses and manipulators that we have just enumerated. There were lesser J. P. Morgans, Samuel Insulls, Albert Wiggins, Charles E. Mitchells and Clarence Dillons in every city and sizable town in the land who did in a small local way what these men did on a national scale. Moreover, they were helped by the big financial houses at the top, who unloaded on the smaller banks their less desirable securities, which the latter in turn sold to their trusting clients with disastrous results to the mass of Americans and to our banking system.

The growth of great banking institutions, together with the vast wealth that they have concentrated, has naturally made them the pivots in the development of finance capitalism. The first notable fact to be kept in mind is that the banks themselves, like industries and transportation lines, have combined into gigantic institutions and have created immense deposits.[3] The manner and extent of the combination of New York banks is made clear in the diagram on page 783.

In order that finance capitalism might reach full expression and reality, it was necessary that the banks gain essential control over industry, transportation, mining, and electric utilities. All of these require extensive credit, and the banks controlled the credit facilities of the country. Moreover, newly formed companies must have banking aid to float their securities. Old companies need similar help when they plan an extension or other activities necessitating the flotation of new issues of corporate paper. When a company fails and goes into receivership a great banking house may get control and supervise the reorganization, usually emerging with fairly complete control of the reorganized company. In this way nearly all forms of American business have fallen under the sway of the great American banks, private and public.

The actual character of finance capitalism in the United States today can

---

[1] For a good summary of the character and structure of finance capitalism in the United States, see *Recent Social Trends*, Vol. I, Chap. v.

[2] Rivaled later by Andrew W. Mellon. See Harvey O'Connor, *Mellon's Millions*, Day, 1933.

[3] *Cf.* J. M. Chapman, *Concentration of Banking*, Columbia University Press, 1934, and Bonbright and Means, *The Holding Company*, Chap. xii.

best be emphasized by a brief summary of the relevant facts.[1] The total national wealth of the country before the 1929 slump amounted to some $367,000,000,000. Of this total the business wealth may be assigned around $210,000,000,000. Some 78 per cent of all business wealth—$165,000,000,000—is corporate wealth. This is divided among some 300,000 nonfinancial corporations (that is, excluding banks and the like).

The degree of concentration of this corporate wealth under the management of a few individuals is almost incredible to all except technical students of re-

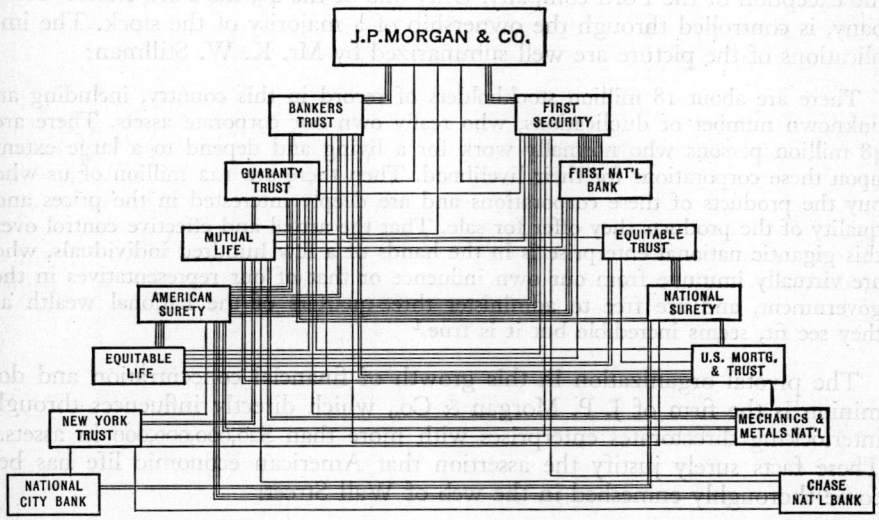

New York Bank Combine, 1920. Each Connecting Line Represents a Dictatorship.[2]

cent American economic and financial history. Two hundred of the largest corporations, representing only 0.7 per cent of the total number of corporations, control $81,000,000,000—namely, about half of all corporate assets, 35 per cent of all business wealth, and nearly 20 per cent of our total national wealth.

Within each of these great corporations there is a high degree of concentration of control. This is rarely based upon the actual ownership of a majority of the stock. In fact, only 10 of these 200 corporations are controlled by owners of a majority of the stock. And these are relatively small corporations within the group, since the 10 control only 2 per cent of the total assets of the 200 corporations. This divorce of control from investment and ownership is at times amazing. The Van Swerlingens built up control over 8 class A railroads with assets of more than $2,000,000,000 on the basis of an original investment of only $2,000,000, nearly all of which was borrowed from a Cleveland bank. This was expanded to $20,000,000 by various subsequent manipulative transactions. Henry L. Doherty and his associates control the Cities Service utility interests with some $1,000,000,000 of assets through the unbelievably small investment

---

[1] Cf. Berle and Means, *The Modern Corporation and Private Property*, Bk. I.
[2] Chart prepared by Senator Robert M. La Follette, Sr.

of $1,000,000. Likewise, an investment of $1,000,000 has given control over the $1,000,000,000 assets of the Standard Gas and Electric Company.

This is only part of the story. Among these 200 corporations there were 43 with assets of more than $500,000,000 each at the beginning of 1932. These are controlled by 166 individuals who serve as interlocking directors between these 43 corporations and 10 leading banks and 3 great insurance companies. In fact, these 10 banks and 3 insurance companies control in practice not only the 43 corporations, but all 10 of the $1,000,000,000 corporations of the country, with the exception of the Ford company. Only one of the 43, the Ford Motor Company, is controlled through the ownership of a majority of the stock. The implications of the picture are well summarized by Mr. K. W. Stillman:

> There are about 18 million stockholders of record in this country, including an unknown number of duplications, who really own our corporate assets. There are 48 million persons who normally work for a living and depend to a large extent upon these corporations for their livelihood. Then there are 122 million of us who buy the products of these corporations and are deeply interested in the prices and quality of the products they offer for sale. That the actual and effective control over this gigantic national enterprise is in the hands of a few hundred individuals, who are virtually immune from our own influence or that of our representatives in the government, and are free to administer three-quarters of the national wealth as they see fit, seems incredible but it is true.[1]

The pivotal organization in this growth of financial concentration and dominion is the firm of J. P. Morgan & Co., which directly influences through interlocking directorates enterprises with more than $20,000,000,000 in assets.[2] These facts surely justify the assertion that American economic life has become thoroughly enmeshed in the web of Wall Street.

II. NEW CREDIT INSTITUTIONS: COMMERCIAL AND INVESTMENT BANKS

"I believe it is safe to say that the revolution in the industrial field, to a certain degree at least, is responsible for a similar development in the field of banking, because the gigantic form assumed by corporations on both sides of the Atlantic renders their banking requirements so large and so all-encompassing that only banks with gigantic resources of their own are able to offer them commensurate facilities."

Paul Warburg thus explained the great growth and concentration in banking resources that has taken place. To serve institutions such as the United States Steel Corporation, General Motors, United States Rubber, and the like, each with over $1,000,000,000 sales annually (1928 figures), or such mer-

---

[1] Stillman, "Who Controls Business?" *New Republic,* July 26, 1933, p. 283. In his estimate that those in control of finance capitalism can administer three-fourths of our national wealth, Mr. Stillman takes into consideration the great banks as well as the nonfinancial corporations, and includes the control of the banks over manufacturing, mining, transportation, public utilities, insurance, and the like. His figure of 18,000,000 stockholders, implying that there are 18,000,000 separate individuals involved, is also somewhat misleading. Gardiner Means has made a study of the probable number of duplications—persons who hold stock in more than one corporation—and concludes that the actual number of shareholders is between 4,000,000 and 6,000,000.

[2] See below, pp. 790 ff.

COMMERCIAL AND INVESTMENT BANKS

chandising institutions as the A. & P. with over $1,000,000,000 sales, Sears, Roebuck & Co. with $347,000,000, Woolworth with $287,000,000, and Kresge Stores with $207,000,000, financial facilities of great magnitude are required. In response there have developed great banking institutions with resources well into the billions of dollars.

Modern corporate practices demand two types of financial services: (1) Short-term loans to finance the productive operations, and (2) long-term loans to provide funds for plant renovation, modernization, and extension. A complex group of financial institutions have developed to serve one or both of these financial needs. Roughly, the banks of the country may be divided into two groups: commercial banks, which are intended to deal in short-time loans for commercial, self-liquidating business transactions; and investment banks, which gather and supply capital for long-time investment, primarily floating corporate securities—that is, stocks and bonds.

The commercial bank performs a most important service in modern economic life. Its real function is to multiply credit on a large scale. The commercial bank provides the life-giving flow of credit to trade and industry. For example, the cotton merchant who is buying bales of cotton from the growers and collecting them in freight-train loads, to be shipped and sold to the cotton marketing center, finances his purchases by loans from his local bank, the collateral being the cotton, which will soon be sold to larger merchants. The larger merchants in turn borrow from larger banks to finance their purchases until they have shipped the cotton North to the converters. The converters in turn borrow from their banks to finance their operations till it reaches the handlers of cloth. And so, as the cotton moves on from the raw form to the finished product, there moves over it an ever increasing volume of bank loans, passed on from one bank to another, financing the collection, transportation, and manufacture of the product.

The commercial banker selects those to whom he will grant credit and thus virtually nominates the men who will temporarily control the commodity. In this selection the banker cannot be arbitrary. His selection must be limited to men who have adequate facilities to handle the commodity and who possess training and experience to carry on the economic processes so efficiently as to enable them to return the loan with the service charges.

This credit moves freely (is liquid) from bank to bank as the cotton moves on, leaving the first banker free to make new loans on fresh transactions. Only when the commodity ceases to move—when, along the line, there is a hitch, probably brought about by inability of the public to purchase the final products, thus backing the commodity up into retail, wholesale, manufacturing, or warehouse establishments—does the credit cease to flow (become frozen).

Where does the banker get the funds to lend to business? The truth is that he does not have them. He emits the credit. When he grants the original cotton merchant a loan, the banker gives him no money, merely a deposit credit. The merchant pays the growers by check; they in turn deposit these checks to their own credit. If we look at the banking system as a unit, we may say the banker provides credit for the merchant who applies for it and from then on it becomes a bookkeeping transaction, as he subtracts it from the account of one customer and adds it to another's.

Nearly all business transactions originate as bank loans. Let us assume a self-contained town in which there is $1,000,000 in cash. It is decided to form a bank with $1,000,000 capital. The whole money stock of the town is invested in the bank as capital, and no one has any money. Now Jones, the hardware man, decides to borrow $100,000 to pay his help and to purchase goods from the local machine factory. The loan is granted and he now pays his debts by check. From now on this loan circulates as money. Brown, his head clerk, deposits his pay check, pays his rent and his grocery and butcher bills by check, and draws $10 for pocket money. The pocket money is spent for cigarettes and carfare, and as rapidly as spent, returns to the bank as deposits for the tobacco shop or the transit company. Because the bank may think it prudent to have an actual reserve of say 10 per cent on its loans, it can extend loans to about ten times its cash. That is, a bank with $1,000,000 capital can make loans of about $10,000,000. The loans and deposits, it will be noted, are the same thing. A bank does not lend deposits out, it lends deposits in.

This assumed self-contained town and bank are not fantastic. In 1929, the bank capital in the United States totaled about $5,500,000,000. The total money in circulation also was about $5,500,000,000. In other words, all our money was invested as capital in banks. Then how did we do business? The banks had lent out, or had deposits of (which is the same thing), about $50,000,000,000. In brief, the entire business of the country was transacted in credit emitted from the banks.

One must not, however, overestimate the part played by the banker or his initiative. Banks do not literally "create" credit. Credit really comes into being when business and commercial transactions requiring credit arise. The business man's need for credit leads the banker to substitute his own credit for that of the business man by lending the latter money. Bank loans arise from business transactions that call for credit. As business expands, the need for credit and the outstanding volume of credit also expand. The degree to which credit depends upon the initiative of business is well illustrated by the situation in the United States from 1933 to 1935. The banks were prepared to provide credit in almost unlimited amounts, because of excess reserves in the Federal Reserve System. Nevertheless, owing to the fact that there was relatively little demand for credit because business and commercial transactions were not expanding rapidly, not much new credit was extended in the form of commercial bank loans. The "strike of credit" was more a business strike than a bank strike. The initiative in producing credit lies with business as well as with banks.

Modern bank checks, drafts, bills of exchange, and other types of commercial paper are today much more important as actual mediums of exchange than is ordinary cash. Only through the assistance of the modern bank is it possible to carry on anything like the volume of business transactions that take place in a given year in the modern economy.

Modern commercial banking has been greatly aided by the development of the clearing-house. This is an organization of the leading banks in any municipality or region, whereby the problems of balancing mutual credit or indebtedness are greatly facilitated. The total checks drawn upon any bank are set off against those which that particular bank holds against other banks, and no transfer of cash is required beyond what is required to balance the accounts between the member banks.

To provide industry with long-term credit, specialized banking institutions have been created, such as the underwriting syndicates, and investment banks. The underwriting syndicate is an organization that specializes in the sale of securities of some corporation about to be established or of one that desires more capital funds for extension or improvements. It performs the valuable function of putting its reputation and credit behind its client, thus creating confidence and encouraging the sale of securities. The work of the underwriting syndicate is carried on today chiefly by the great investment banks, which will be described below. The underwriting syndicate is thus not a separate and permanent institution in the ordinary sense of the term. It is a temporary organization of banks, investment banking houses, and dealers to market a certain group of securities. When these securities are disposed of the syndicate dissolves, or closes until it may be organized again to market another block of securities.

The trust company is a type of banking institution that accepts funds—inheritances and the like—in small or large quantities and takes over the task and responsibility of investing these funds. These trust companies are usually conservative investors of their clients' money and exercise great caution in buying securities. By and large, down to the great speculative orgy of 1927-29, the trust companies lived up to such expectations and to their responsibility. But in the wave of speculative contagion of these years the trust companies frequently lost their sense of caution, took long chances, and lost millions for their customers.[1] They appear to have learned something of a lesson from this experience, but it remains to be seen whether they will retain their chastened attitude if another "bull market" returns. As we shall point out more thoroughly below, even ordinary commercial banks became deeply involved in promoting speculation in securities from 1927 to 1929, with disastrous results to themselves and to their depositors and investment customers.

The ordinary savings bank, which by many, particularly in rural districts, is regarded as the bank par excellence, is not, from the standpoint of modern commercial analysis, a bank at all. Rather, it is a place of safe deposit for those who desire to gain a small but certain rate of interest on their deposits. These deposits are normally invested in long-time loans, such as real-estate mortgages. The savings bank does not ordinarily handle any commercial paper whatever, and is rather more of a conservative investment company than a commercial banking institution.

The reader need scarcely be reminded that modern banking operations extend far beyond national boundaries. International bills of exchange form the indispensable basis for the actual exchange of commodities between peoples of different countries. Their use makes it unnecessary to transport specie from

[1] *Cf.* Bernhard Ostrolenk and A. M. Massie, *How Banks Buy Bonds,* Harper, 1932, and J. T. Flynn, *Investment Trusts Gone Wrong!* New Republic, 1930.

one country to another, except at periodic intervals, and then merely enough to balance accounts.[1]

Further, it should be pointed out that modern financial institutions hold something like a pivotal position in the organization of modern business and transportation. It is the modern bank which has really made possible that development and specialization of the capitalistic class which was noted above. It is through the banks that the resources of modern capitalism are concentrated, deposited, and put at the disposal of the investor. Since business concerns have come to require very large amounts of both fixed and liquid capital, they are in considerable measure dependent upon the banks, which are the only agencies through which these needs can be satisfied promptly and economically.

In a broad way, it may be said that in modern economic life the leading banks of the country form the central point of concentration in the control of the financial and business interests of the nation. Usually the directors of great banks are represented on the boards of directors of the great manufacturing corporations and the great transportation and utility companies. In fact, as finance capitalism has attained its full development, the bankers have assumed a position of control over industry, transportation, and public utilities. This they have been able to do through their almost exclusive command over the credit and capital upon which all kinds of business under capitalism depend. Only Henry Ford among great American industrialists has been able to defy the bankers. Samuel Insull's great utility empire was wrecked because it was essentially unsound, but the antipathy of Eastern banking interests hastened the process and made the wreckage more complete.

In this development of financial dominion over modern economic life the investment bank has played an even greater part than the commercial bank. The corporation has become dominant as the approved form of business organization, and it is the investment bank which normally floats the original securities of corporations of all kinds and presides over the receiverships and reorganizations that are likely to follow after mismanagement has run its course.

Investment banks date from the very origin of banking. They did not float the securities of private corporations at first, since there were few or none of these, but they did accept and distribute the securities of states and thus created public credit. The original Bank of Venice was an investment bank. So was the Bank of England, which came into being primarily to raise a large loan for the government. In the United States the chief development of investment banks came after the Civil War. Before this time British capital had played a large part in handling our securities.[2] Railroad development exercised the dominant rôle in creating the American investment banks. Some of the earliest investment houses, appearing just before the Civil War, were E. W. Clark & Co. of Philadelphia, and Drew, Robinson & Co. of New York. They were interested in promoting the early railroads. Jay Cooke & Co. of Philadelphia was involved both in railroad promotion and in furnishing credit to

[1] *Cf.* A. C. Whitaker, *Foreign Exchange,* Appleton, 1919; and C. E. Griffin, *Principles of Foreign Trade,* Macmillan, 1924.
[2] *Cf.* L. H. Jenks, *The Migration of British Capital to 1875,* Knopf, 1927.

the government during the Civil War. After the war, the increased opportunities afforded for launching, manipulating, and merging railroads brought into existence other great investment houses, such as J. P. Morgan & Co., August Belmont & Co., Kuhn, Loeb & Co., and J. and W. Seligman of New York; the great House of Drexel in Philadelphia; and Lee Higginson & Co. in Boston. Next came the opportunities afforded by the age of monopoly capitalism and the holding company to form great industrial combines. The House of Morgan took charge of forming and launching the United States Steel Corporation, our first billion-dollar concern. It was the rise of the electric utility industry, however, which served to give investment bankers a new lease on prosperity and initiative. They made wide use of the superholding company and its possibilities of pyramiding paper so as to create great utility empires. In these the holding companies secured great financial profits without rendering any comparable service to society, while they drained the really essential operating companies and charged the public high rates for the electric service they furnished. The investment banks also played a large part in forming the greater mergers in the automobile industry. As business units have become larger, they have become more dependent upon the vast sums of capital that only the great investment houses can raise.

Owing to the lucrative business done by the investment banks, the commercial banks have sought to share in this remunerative activity and have organized security affiliates to engage in strictly investment activity. Such procedure was to some degree curtailed by the Glass-Steagall Bill of 1933.

There is nothing inherently evil in the raising of credit for business by the investment companies. Under capitalism, capital must be raised, and the investment banks raise it. The evil has come in their methods. The bonds floated were not always adequately protected by equities nor was the public always truthfully informed of all the conditions under which corporations secured loans. Not satisfied with raising capital, investment bankers have assumed control over business and have conducted it for the sake of immediate speculative profits, or with an eye on the speculative securities, seeming to care little if the methods followed might ruin American business as a whole at a later date. This menace has been the result of the gambling spirit of speculative finance and not of the credit-raising and capital-assembling activities of the investment banks. A major evil or defect in raising credit for a society by means of independent and irresponsible investment banks resides in the fact that although they have control of providing credit for business, they are subject only to their own individual profit motive in deciding where to supply capital. There is no broad social or economic attempt to view industry as a whole and to determine rationally the most desirable and useful place to which to direct capital. There is no central control and no attempt to ration credit and to place it where it would be most productive or to supply it to those industries where, socially speaking, it might be most desirable to expand business.

The House of Morgan is an illuminating example of how the great investment banking houses have been able to build up their control over American economic life as a whole. The remarkable interlacing of banks, transportation concerns, mines, and industries, together with the ultimate bank domination, are well shown in the following authoritative summary of the lordship of the House of Morgan and affiliated banks over the business of the United States by Lewis Corey. It is an admirable and impressive digest of the concentration of American money power:

Among the twenty dominant banks [and trust companies in the United States in 1929] were Bankers Trust, Guaranty Trust and First National (Morgan dependents) with resources of $3,403,000,000. The Morgan allies, National City and Chase National Banks, had resources of $4,855,000,000. These five banks in the Morgan combination, with their combined resources of $8,258,000,000, are interlocked with other banks by means of directorships, the aggregate resources being almost $20,000,000,000, equal to 33 per cent of total banking resources (in comparison with 13 per cent in 1912). In addition the Morgan combination is interlocked by means of directorships with insurance companies the combined resources of which in 1929 were $12,500,000,000, or 65 per cent of all insurance assets.

The increase in financial centralization parallels an increase in the financial control of industry. Ownership and management are becoming more and more separated, owing to the great increase of stockholders who own but do not manage. In 1929 J. P. Morgan and his seventeen partners held 99 directorships in seventy-two corporations with combined assets of approximately $20,000,000,000, as follows:

Financial: 23 directorships in 19 banks and other financial institutions, including Guaranty and Bankers Trusts (4), Mutual Life, First Security Co., Chase Securities Corporation, Corn Exchange Bank, New York Trust, Discount Corporation and Aetna Insurance. Combined resources, $5,250,000,000.

Industrial: 47 directorships in 35 corporations, including United States Steel (2), General Motors (2), Kennecott Copper (3), Standard Brands (2), Texas Gulf Sulphur, Continental Oil, Pullman Co. (3), International Harvester, General Electric, Philadelphia & Reading Coal & Iron, General Asphalt, Baldwin Locomotive, Associated Dry Goods, International Agricultural, General Steel Casting, and Montgomery-Ward. Combined assets, $6,000,000,000.

Railroad: 11 directorships in 10 railroads, including Northern Pacific (2), Atchison, Topeka & Santa Fe, Western Pacific and Chicago & Erie. Combined assets, $2,500,000,000.

Utility: 18 directorships in 13 utility combinations, including United Corporation (2), Philadelphia Electric (2), International Telephone & Telegraph, All-America Cables and Postal Telegraph & Cable. Combined assets, $6,250,000,000.

The Morgan dependents, Bankers Trust, Guaranty Trust, and First National Bank, have interlocking directorships of their own in corporations representing combined resources of $67,000,000,000, including American Telephone & Telegraph, International General Electric, Baltimore & Ohio, American Smelting & Refining, American International Corporation, Allied Chemical & Dye, American & Foreign Power, E. I. du Pont de Nemours, Equitable Trust, Erie, Goodrich Rubber, Houston Oil, Italian Superpower, New York Life, North American Aviation, New York, New Haven & Hartford, Radio Corporation, Aluminum Co. of America, Bethlehem Steel, Central Alloy Steel, Republic Iron & Steel, Cuba Co., Electric Bond & Share, Mellon National Bank, National City Bank, Western Union, Columbia Syndicate, Continental Illinois Bank & Trust Co. of Chicago, Curtiss-Wright Corporation, Equitable Life, Tidewater Oil and Goodyear Rubber & Tire. Eliminating duplications, J. P. Morgan & Co. and their dependents are represented in corporations with combined (net) assets of approximately $52,000,000,000.

In addition, the Morgan allies, Chase National and National City Banks, are represented by interlocking directorships in corporations with gross assets of $51,000,000,000 and net of $46,000,000,000, including Anaconda Copper, American Tobacco, Cuban-American Sugar, American Power and Light, Central Hanover Bank & Trust, Westinghouse Electric, American Sugar Refining, Illinois Central, International Match, New York Trust, International Power Securities, Consolidated Gas, Union Carbide & Carbon, United Aircraft, American Locomotive, Armour & Co., American Woolen, American Superpower, Bankers Trust, General Foods, Metropolitan Life, Hudson Coal, U. S. Industrial Alcohol, Republic Brass, Wickwire Spencer Steel, New England Power, St. Louis & San Francisco and Shell Union Oil.

The Morgan dependents and allies are interlocked in many corporations. Eliminating duplications, the Morgan combination is represented by directorships in corporations with net assets of approximately $74,000,000,000, equal to more than one-quarter of all corporate assets.

In addition, the Morgan combination dominated investment banking operations. During the first six months of 1930 J. P. Morgan & Co. floated issues amounting to $628,000,000, more than 18 per cent of the total. The percentage becomes much larger if the Morgan dependents and allies are included. The system of financial centralization and control comprises security issues as well as domination of corporate enterprises.

This immense power over American industry is concentrated in 167 persons in the Morgan combination who hold more than 2,450 interlocking directorships in corporations. Immense as the power is in itself, it is all the greater considering that it interlocks control and influence over those giant corporations which dominate their particular industries—and economic life as a whole. Financial centralization and control are now infinitely larger than in the elder Morgan's day.[1]

All of this vast financial and industrial control is exerted by the House of Morgan on the basis of an actual capital investment of only $53,000,000—a sum less than the capital stock of many a second-rate bank in the United States today. How the system secures and operates this vast command over the assets of the nation has been well described by Miss Ruth Finney in an article in the Scripps-Howard newspapers.[2] To quote from Miss Finney:

The Morgan firm is worth approximately 53 million dollars. Many others are worth more than that. But the Morgans have what no others have—influence in banks, insurance companies and corporations with assets 1,000 times as extensive as their own capital. They can, in other words, regiment something like 55 billion dollars to do their bidding. This figure is about 18 billion dollars larger than the whole national income in 1932. The concentration of its power in banks and other institutions with money to invest gives it greater power, proportionately, than even these figures would suggest.

This is the way the House of Morgan obtains influence over America's money:

By putting their partners on the boards of banks.

By making loans to high bank officials.

By letting high bank officials share easy profits in syndicate deals.

By inducing corporations over which it has power to deposit their money with

---

[1] Corey, *The House of Morgan*, Watt, 1930, pp. 446-48. A more complete statement of the Morgan holdings and interests is contained in *Reports of the Senate Banking and Currency Committee*, H. Res. 84 and Sen. Res. 56, Seventy-third Congress, First Session, Pt. 2, pp. 905 ff. But the Corey summary is ample for our purposes.

[2] May 30, 1933.

J. P. Morgan & Co., and by then passing on these deposits to favored banks. Thus the Morgans stand at the cross roads taking their toll of influence over the country's most important banks by acting as the dispenser of great patronage in the form of great deposits.

Insurance companies have available for investment more money than any other single institution. J. P. Morgan & Company has made sure that this money will be readily available for purchase of the securities it issues.

Hearings of the Senate banking and currency committee last week developed a wealth of detail showing how Morgan reaches into the pocketbooks of depositors in the biggest banks in the country, owners of life insurance policies, holders of stock in large industrial corporations.

It has been pointed out by several students [1] that the American banks in the period since the World War have showed marked tendencies towards leaving the field of true banking and becoming agents for speculative financial operations. It is true that between 1920 and 1929 the commercial banks, instead of merely extending commercial loans, were using their short-term deposits to purchase long-term bonds recommended by their correspondent banks or were selling securities to the investing public. As we have seen, most of the large commercial banks have had affiliated financing and investment companies, whose lists of stockholders are identical with those of the banks. Commercial banks have assisted in the flotation not only of bonds, but even of common stocks, often highly speculative in character. In the few years immediately preceding the crisis of 1929 the banks made large extensions of credit—some $7,000,000,000—which it was known would be used for speculating on the stock market. Often they borrowed from the Federal Reserve banks in order to relend to customers for use in the stock market. Even the Federal Reserve Board coöperated, at least to the extent of keeping the discount rate low, and thus encouraging the borrowing of money for speculation on the stock exchange.

All of this means that instead of exercising the conservative and stabilizing influence which had come to be expected of it, our banking system tolerated and even encouraged the speculative mania that led directly to the crisis. In the overissue of stocks, the pyramiding of holding companies, the overinvestment on the part of the public in speculative issues, and the flotation of billions of dollars' worth of dubious foreign bonds, the banks have played their part. Whether this is a permanent trend in banking policy remains to be seen.

In spite of the dominant position of banks in the modern economic order, American banking became amazingly unstable between 1921 and 1933. This has been primarily because our banking system has never emerged from the anarchy of rugged individualism, and it has been subordinated to the speculative ideals and processes of finance capitalism. The function of banks as the credit-supplying accessory of industry and transportation has gradually been invaded by the tendency to make banks the servants of speculative finance.

Notwithstanding the National Banking Act of 1863 and the Federal Reserve Act of 1913, two-thirds of our banks before 1933 remained state banks, and

[1] See particularly H. P. Willis, "Who Caused the Panic of 1929?" *North American Review*, February, 1930.

of these latter 94 per cent were outside of the Federal Reserve system.[1] This made impossible any adequate centralization, inspection, and regulation of banking. It also made it difficult for a small bank to draw upon adequate reserves in a period of crisis. Further, banks were allowed to use long-term commercial paper as security against demand deposits and short-term obligations. Finally, after 1920 the banks began to be more interested in supplying credit for speculative long-term bonds than in their legitimate function of furnishing short-term or self-liquidating credit.

As a result of all this, the bank failures, even in the extremely prosperous decade following 1920, were absolutely appalling in the United States. From 1920 through the year 1932 approximately 11,000 banks closed, with only 18,800 remaining open to do business on the eve of the "bank holiday" early in March, 1933. The deposits involved in these bank failures were approximately $5,000,000,000. The following table presents the bank mortality per year:

Year	Failures	Year	Failures	Year	Failures
1920	152	1925	612	1930	1345
1921	501	1926	956	1931	2298
1922	354	1927	662	1932	1453
1923	648	1928	491		
1924	776	1929	642		

This startling inefficiency and unreliability of the central institution of finance capitalism has done much to undermine its prestige and its power of financial domination in our country. To how great a degree the instability of American banking is due solely to anarchy and to speculative practices is well illustrated by comparing our record with that of the Dominion of Canada, where the inherent difficulties of banking are far greater and the opportunities for legitimate profit much slighter. Over against nearly 11,000 bank failures in the United States between 1920 and 1933 stands the fact that there has been only one bank failure in Canada since 1914. This occurred in 1923 when the Home Bank of Canada closed its doors with liabilities of $19,600,000.

This amazing contrast is to be explained by the fact that in Canada banking still remains primarily banking rather than an incidental servant of speculative finance. Along with this goes the superior organization of Canadian banks. Whereas we had approximately 30,000 banks in 1920, Canada has only 10 banks with some 3,970 branches. Each of these 10 great banks is able to maintain a highly efficient centralized research and service division with ample facilities to gather the necessary information for its hundreds of branches. Each bank can also concentrate its resources behind any weak members of the system as a whole. The same contrast exists between the banking system of the United States and that of England. There was not a single bank failure in England when England went off the gold standard, while nearly a thousand American banks closed their doors when Roosevelt called a halt on deflation by suspending gold redemption.

[1] Of course, a greater proportion of the total national banking assets were within the Federal Reserve system than this numerical statement of the banks outside the system might seem to imply.

Important provisions of the Glass-Steagall banking act of 1933 were designed to divorce commercial banks from speculation, to provide a better organization of our banks under national supervision through the Federal Reserve system, and to introduce a considerable degree of federal protection of depositors by a limited deposit guarantee. Unfortunately, the Glass-Steagall act barely scratched the surface in checking speculation and manipulation. It outlawed one special type of stock affiliates of banks and made an attempt to include in the banking examinations holding companies that own banks—something very difficult, if not impossible. But it left untouched the most serious menace to honest banking,—the growing system of holding-company control. Other provisions of this act broadened the credit base for the Federal Reserve system and allowed additional government securities to be eligible as the basis for the issuance of Federal Reserve notes. This, together with other related developments, has converted the Federal Reserve system from a commercial banking organization into an investment banking system loaded with government securities in which it is as possible to speculate, though within a somewhat more limited range, as it was formerly in corporate "cats and dogs."

One should not overlook the significance of the great insurance companies in the United States as money-gathering organizations. They collect more actual cash yearly than any other single type of financial concern in the country, and put vast sums at the disposal of banks and other investment institutions. The following table indicates the growth and status of life insurance in the United States since 1850:

LIFE INSURANCE

Number of policies and amount of insurance in force in ordinary and industrial companies of the United States, and income, payments, assets, liabilities, and surplus, on December 31, of years specified, 1850 to 1929.

A. INSURANCE IN FORCE FROM 1850 TO 1929

	Ordinary		Industrial		Total	
Year	Number of policies	Amount	Number of policies	Amount	Number of policies	Amount
1850	29,407	$ 68,614,189	....	$	29,407	$ 68,614,189
1860	60,000	180,000,000	....	....	60,000	180,000,000
1870	839,226	2,262,847,000	....	....	839,226	2,262,847,000
1880	685,531	1,581,841,706	236,674	20,533,469	922,205	1,602,375,175
1890	1,319,561	3,620,057,439	3,882,914	428,789,342	5,202,475	4,048,846,787
1900	3,176,051	7,093,152,380	11,219,296	1,468,928,342	14,395,347	8,562,080,722
1910	6,954,119	13,227,213,168	23,044,162	3,179,489,541	29,998,281	16,406,702,709
1920	16,695,000	35,092,000,000	49,805,000	7,190,000,000	66,500,000	42,281,000,000
1929	31,339,000	85,244,000,000	89,415,000	17,902,000,000	120,754,000	103,146,000,000

B. INCOME, PAYMENTS, ASSETS, ETC., FROM 1880 TO 1929

Year	Total income	Total payments to policyholders	Assets	Liabilities	Surplus
1880	$ 80,537,990	$ 55,881,794	$ 452,680,651	$	$ ....
1890	196,938,069	90,007,819	770,972,061	678,681,309	92,290,752
1900	400,603,257	168,687,601	1,742,414,173	1,493,378,709	249,035,464
1910	781,011,249	387,302,073	3,875,877,059	3,385,821,478	490,055,571
1920	1,764,000,000	745,000,000	7,320,000,000	6,989,000,000	330,688,000
1929	4,337,000,000	1,962,000,000	17,482,000,000	16,507,000,000	975,056,000

The great insurance companies have come under the control of the major banking interests of the country through interlocking directorates. They thus assume their natural and logical place in the picture of finance capitalism in the United States. The Morgan and Rockefeller banking interests, centered in the House of Morgan and the Chase National Bank, respectively, control most of the important life insurance companies of the United States today. This control was one of the most important unofficial and indirect results of the Hughes insurance investigation of 1905.[1]

The Second Industrial Revolution and the growing complexities of modern life have greatly extended the range of insurance and increased the volume of insurance business. Fire and life insurance have grown by leaps and bounds. Accident and theft insurance have developed substantial proportions. Almost every known personal risk is now insurable. Particularly important has been the rise and expansion of automobile insurance, some states making the insurance of automobiles and of driving risks compulsory.

III. THE INFLUENCE OF THE CORPORATION AND THE HOLDING COMPANY UPON INDUSTRIAL CONSOLIDATION

The new business enterprises required an improved form of industrial organization. In the seventeenth and eighteenth centuries the joint-stock company became a fairly common form of business organization, especially for commercial enterprises. It had marked advantages over the individual entrepreneur or the partnership, particularly in its command over capital. The development of the joint-stock principle led directly to the appearance of the corporation.

The origins of the corporation as a collective and legal unit are found back in Roman times. Not until the nineteenth century, however, did it become the characteristic type of business organization. It possessed all the advantages of the joint-stock company, together with the two important additional legal advantages of juristic personality and a liability limited to the proportional investment of each stockholder. There are other important advantages in the corporate form of business organization. The resources of the corporation are incomparably vaster than those of a single entrepreneur or those of a small group of partners, and the volume of capital it can raise permits the largest of enterprises to be undertaken. It enables large numbers of people from all classes to participate in business undertakings, and makes it possible to raise large sums of capital from individuals widely separated in space and differing greatly in financial assets. The corporation permits centralized control. It possesses permanence and continuity of existence, its life not being dependent upon that of the stockholders or officers. And, finally, corporate stock can be transferred from one person to another with ease.

The growing popularity of the corporation as the prevalent type of industrial organization has produced what Professors Berle and Means call "the Corporate Revolution," almost as important in many ways as the Industrial Revolution itself, though it is really a late legal and financial outgrowth of the Industrial Revolution:

[1] *Cf.* Gustavus Myers, *History of the Supreme Court of the United States*, Kerr, 1918, pp. 754 ff. See also the Senate report cited above, Vol. II, p. 934.

It is of the essence of revolutions of the more silent sort that they are unrecognized until they are far advanced. This was the case with the so-called "industrial revolution," and is the case with the corporate revolution through which we are at present passing.

The translation of perhaps two-thirds of the industrial wealth of the country from individual ownership to ownership by the large, publicly financed corporations vitally changes the lives of property owners, the lives of workers, and the methods of property tenure. The divorce of ownership from control consequent on that process almost necessarily involves a new form of economic organization of society.[1]

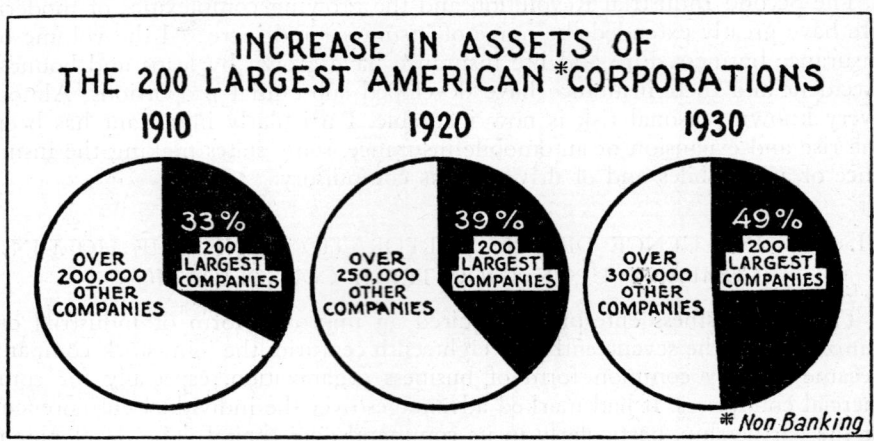

INCREASE IN ASSETS OF THE 200 LARGEST AMERICAN *CORPORATIONS

1910: OVER 200,000 OTHER COMPANIES — 200 LARGEST COMPANIES 33%
1920: OVER 250,000 OTHER COMPANIES — 200 LARGEST COMPANIES 39%
1930: OVER 300,000 OTHER COMPANIES — 200 LARGEST COMPANIES 49%

*Non Banking

N. Y. Times, July 24, 1932

The rapid growth of the assets of the larger corporations is indicated here. At this rate in 1950 they will constitute 65 per cent of the whole.

The corporation has greatly facilitated large-scale business organization by making possible the holding company, which is one of the most significant recent economic developments.[2] It is the most effective agent of the move towards combination, which has been a characteristic feature of the Second Industrial Revolution.[3] The holding company is itself a corporation, but its chief function is to acquire sufficient holdings of the stock of other corporations to shape or control their policy. The holding company may be an operating company as well—that is, it may carry on manufacturing or commercial operations. But its most vital, and often its sole, purpose is that of stockholding. The holding company has in America, partly on account of legislation restricting other methods of combination, tended to supplant the older pools and trusts. It is a particularly strategic instrument in business combination because of its possibilities of "pyramiding" stockholdings. Individual stockholders, geographically scattered, can exercise little effective control over the policy of a corporation. Any large block of stock, even though a minority, can thus often practically direct the policy. Corporate stock today is often of a nonvoting character, the insiders controlling through their ownership of a considerable share of the small quota of voting stock. This accounts, for example, for the control of H. L. Doherty over the giant Cities Service Company.

[1] Berle and Means, op. cit., Preface, pp. vii-viii.
[2] Cf. Bonbright and Means. op. cit., Chaps. I-II.
[3] See above, pp. 748 ff.

THE SUPERCORPORATION AND HOLDING COMPANY

In the past five or ten years, especially, it has not been uncommon, particularly in the electric utility business, for one holding company to be superimposed upon another, and upon mixed operating and holding companies, even to the fourth or fifth degree. At the top of the pyramid is a holding company that exercises the dominant control, though it carries on no commercial operations, its capitalization is only a small fraction of the total of that of the companies involved, and its very existence may not even be known to the stockholders in some of the subsidiary companies.[1] The potential evils of such a situation, in the way of stock manipulation, monopolistic control, and the sacrificing of one company to the interests of another, are vast, but there is as yet no effective means of controlling them in the public interest. A recent book on the subject makes this summary statement concerning the holding company:

The promoters of a business combination are likely to prefer the holding company to any other form of consolidation; first, because they can more readily secure the necessary stockholders' votes and the necessary financing by means of this device, and second, because they can effect combinations by means of the holding company that would otherwise be illegal or can avoid subsequent regulation to which an outright merger or amalgamation of companies would be subject.

It is this second characteristic of the holding company—its comparative freedom from social control—that justifies grave public concern and criticism. By means of the holding company, public utility operators have succeeded in drawing many of the teeth from the laws subjecting utility properties to control by public service commissions.[2]

No better summary of this section on the momentous "corporate revolution" which has swept over America could be found than the following comments of Professor Ripley on the leading traits and abuses of contemporary corporations and holding companies in the United States:

In many of the large corporations ownership is separated from control. While the number of stockholders is increasing, control is held by a minority, sometimes by a management which holds no appreciable amount of stock. This trend is fostered by the use of legal devices, including charter provisions giving boards of directors absolute powers.

Each State is free to grant any corporate powers it wishes, to be exercised anywhere in the Union. These powers are often based on company needs as determined only by the management, to the disadvantage of the stockholders.

If a shareholder with a grievance carries his case to court he is usually presumed to have acquiesced in all conditions set by law and charter; if the management can show itself within those conditions he has little chance to win. Moreover, lawsuits are too expensive for small and scattered stockholders to bear.

The small investor cannot get at the true facts regarding the corporations in which he contemplates investing.

Corporation managements possess information as to their companies' affairs which is not equally accessible to all stockholders. This gives them, on the stock exchanges, tremendous advantage over the isolated shareholder.[3]

---

[1] *Cf.* H. W. Laidler and H. S. Raushenbush, *Power Control,* New Republic, 1928, and Bonbright and Means, *op. cit.,* Chaps. v-vii.
[2] Bonbright and Means, *op. cit.,* pp. 338-39. On the abuse of subsidiaries by the holding companies, see pp. 343-84.
[3] W. Z. Ripley, "Our Corporate Revolution and Its Perils," New York *Times,* July 24, 1932, Sec. 2, p. 1.

The extensive development of the supercorporation and holding company on a national and international scale has brought the whole problem of corporate regulation into the realm of national issues. For many obvious reasons it is not possible for a single State to regulate the mammoth modern corporation. If a given State passes wise and fair laws regulating corporations it is easy for any corporations affected to move and incorporate in some State notorious for its lax laws on the subject. Hence, most careful students of the problem urge the necessity of a national incorporation law which will end the discrepancies between state laws on the subject and will subject corporations and holding companies to national supervision and control in the interest of society and sound business.[1] There is a growing conviction that holding companies should be abolished outright. As John T. Flynn observes, "They are the machine guns in the hands of the corporate promoters."

IV. FINANCE CAPITALISM AND ABSENTEE OWNERSHIP

As the amount of capital that could be applied to a single business enterprise increased, a further subdivision and differentiation *within* the capitalist class appeared. More elaborate organization enabled the possessor of great wealth to retire from active contact with industrial and commercial management, applying his resources to economic life through the agency of the industrial and commercial bank, the trust company, or the investment broker. This tendency has in turn contributed to the growing control of commerce and industry by these financial institutions. Absentee ownership has now become fully as feasible in many types of industry as it has long been in agriculture in aristocratic landholding countries like England.[2] Active management has gradually come to be handed over to salaried people specially trained in engineering or business administration.

In this way, the promoter and the technical and business expert have for the most part taken over the actual operation of concerns, the true capitalist supplying funds and often dealing with general policies only through his position as stockholder, director, or officer.[3] The executive offices of great manufacturing or trading corporations are not infrequently located at great distances from the factories, docks, or mines. For example, the offices of the United States Steel Corporation are in New York City; its factories in Pittsburgh, Gary, and so on. Often many of the investors and owners do not have even the most attenuated personal or official connection with the business concern.

Even more striking and ominous than the separation of ownership from active management is the divorce of ownership from actual and ultimate control. It is one thing for a great corporation to hire managers and technical experts who do their bidding. The latter can be discharged at the will of those

---

[1] *Cf.* J. T. Flynn, "Why Corporations Leave Home," *Atlantic Monthly,* September, 1932.

[2] In his *Absentee Ownership,* Thorstein Veblen lays much stress on the similarity of finance capitalism and the era of the supercorporation to the mode of control and exploitation of society which characterized the medieval feudal system.

[3] We refer here, of course, to the management of the operating phases of the concern, such as manufacturing, transportation, and the like, by experts in business administration or by technicians. The ultimate financial control lies in the hands of the officers and directors of the corporation, who may never come near the plants owned and operated by the concern.

who control the corporation. It is quite another matter for a small clique of insiders to be able to control and misuse a giant corporation, while those whose money has gone into the concern sit by and see their investments ruined or diverted without being able to do anything about it unless the controlling clique is foolish enough to commit some overt criminal act. It is a literal fact that in the majority of our great corporations in the United States today the average stockholder has practically no part in the control over the concern. As previously noted, Berle and Means have pointed out that some 65 per cent of our 200 largest nonbanking corporations, representing over 80 per cent of their combined wealth, are controlled by those who own only an insignificant minority of the stock.

We have already cited examples of this development of control on the basis of a very small investment.[1] The twenty largest stockholders in the Pennsylvania Railroad (the largest railroad) own only 2.7 per cent of the total; the twenty largest stockholders of the American Telephone and Telegraph Company (the largest utility) own only 4 per cent of the total; and the twenty largest stockholders of the United States Steel Corporation (the largest industrial) own only 5.1 per cent of the total. Yet these insignificant holdings, relative to the total, enable these twenty largest stockholders, in some cases less than the twenty, to control the policies of the whole corporation.

How this concentration of control, which represents no majority ownership, has been achieved is well described by Benjamin Mandel:

By means of "pyramiding" ownership through a chain of holding companies and subsidiary corporations, by issuance of non-voting stock, by the utilization of proxies, voting trusts and other legal legerdemain, the stockholder has been reduced to the rôle of a rubber stamp, while control remains firmly intrenched in the hands of a small group representing an insignificant proportion of stock ownership or invested capital. The right to exercise individual initiative remains in the hands of the board of directors exclusively.[2]

As in landholding, a major consequence of absentee ownership has been an emphasis upon immediate financial profits for the owners and management, at the possible sacrifice of public welfare and even of the stability of the concern itself. The sacrifice of the long-time interests of business concerns to the desire of stockholders for dividends is, however, far less serious than the sacrifice of every other consideration to the manipulations of the inside governing clique and to the greed of the latter for illegitimate profits to themselves which may mean in the end the failure of the whole business. But before the receivership comes, they will have received their rewards.[3] That this latter sacrifice often takes place was abundantly illustrated, during and after the crisis of 1929, by such later collapses as that of the Kreuger International Match concern and the Insull public-utility holdings. The holding company has played no small part in facilitating these practices. In the Insull and the Kreuger and Toll

[1] See above, pp. 783-84, for the facts about the Van Sweringen combination, the Cities Service Company, and the Standard Gas and Electric Company.
[2] Mandel, review of Berle and Means, *op. cit., Modern Monthly*, May, 1933, p. 253.
[3] For elaborate case material in point, see Flynn, *Graft in Business*, and *Security Speculation*, c. II, and Wormser, *Frankstein, Incorporated*, Chap. v.

concerns, there had been pyramiding of companies, overissue of securities, capitalization of future earnings, payment of dividends where none had been earned or there had been loss, in order to maintain credit—together with most of the other evils that have been enhanced by the use of the holding company and the increasing divorce between ownership and control. Kreuger and Insull provided only the most dramatic examples of these tendencies and evils.[1]

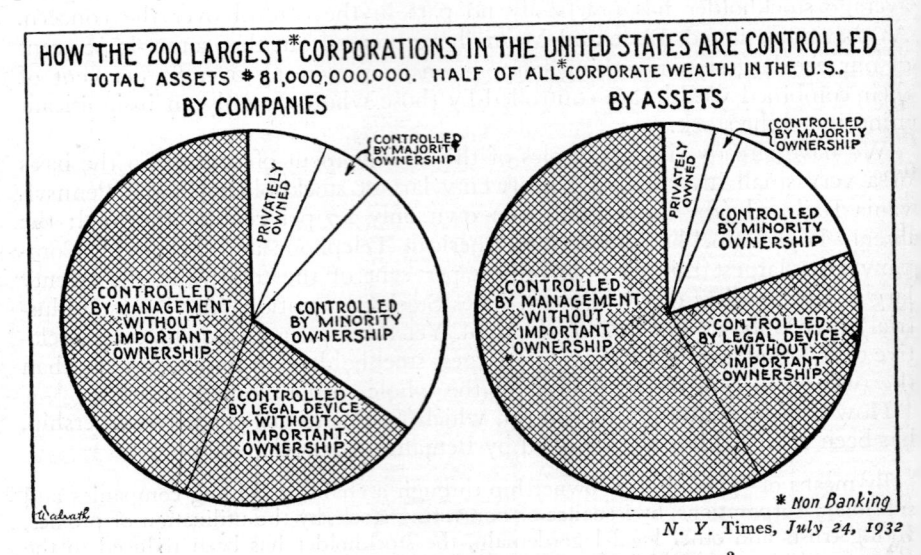

HOW THE 200 LARGEST*CORPORATIONS IN THE UNITED STATES ARE CONTROLLED
TOTAL ASSETS $81,000,000,000. HALF OF ALL*CORPORATE WEALTH IN THE U.S.

BY COMPANIES — BY ASSETS

*Non Banking

N. Y. Times, July 24, 1932

THE DIVORCE OF CONTROL FROM OWNERSHIP [2]

Showing how ownership and control are separated; the shaded area in each case indicates control without appreciable ownership.

The developments associated with business consolidation, absentee ownership, and corporate control have been emphasized especially by Professor William Z. Ripley.[3] He points out a combination of tendencies in the ownership and control of corporations that have developed in our generation: (1) The rise of the holding company and the growing concentration of control that have accompanied business consolidation; (2) the tendency, particularly since 1914, for the general public to invest widely in corporate securities as a source of private gain; (3) the issuance of nonvoting stock as well as the tendency of the owners of small blocks of voting stock to fail to exercise their voting privilege; (4) the actual control of the management of business by a small bloc of well-integrated stockholders who act as a unit; (5) the reduction of the per

---

[1] The Kreuger case was more flagrant than the Insull case. It involved, in addition to the typical offenses of finance capitalism, the downright forgery of Italian government bonds, which Kreuger put up for security.

[2] The charts were prepared from data contained in Berle and Means, *The Modern Corporation and Private Property.*

[3] See his article "From Main Street to Wall Street," *Atlantic Monthly,* January, 1926, and his later book, *Main Street and Wall Street,* Little, Brown, 1927.

FINANCE CAPITALISM AND ABSENTEE OWNERSHIP

centage of stockholding essential to control management that has paralleled the growth of business enterprise and the wider distribution of holdings; and (6) the resulting separation of ownership from management, culminating in "stripping the public shareholders of their voting rights" and "the nullification of the ordinary shareholder." A quotation from Professor Ripley shows some of the implications for the future of American economic life:

What an amazing tangle this all makes of the theory that ownership of property and responsibility for its efficient, farsighted, and public-spirited management shall be linked the one to the other. Even the whole theory of business profits, so painstakingly evolved through years of academic ratiocination, goes by the board. All the managers, that is to say the operating men, are working on salary, their returns, except on the side, being largely independent of the net result of company operation year by year. The motive of self-interest may even have been thrown into the reverse, occasionally, so far as long-time upbuilding in contradistinction to quick turnover in corporate affairs is concerned. And what has become of the relation between labor and capital? What guaranty may possibly be given by the *real owners* to the working class that there shall not be taken from it an opportunity for future welfare and development as a result of these changes? . . . Veritably the institution of private property, underlying our whole civilization, is threatened at the root unless we take heed.[1]

As he points out, the common practice of issuing stock with limited voting rights and conditional participation in profits not only deprives many stockholders of any vestige of control over the enterprise, but may cut them off from the major share of future earnings of the company. Yet the stockholders can usually be induced to consent to the arrangement because it is couched in terms that they do not understand, and the new stock for which they are asked to exchange their old often has an apparently greater market value.

Professor Ripley's warning is in substance that though the ownership of securities is becoming more widely distributed, the control of corporate enterprises is at the same time becoming ever more concentrated in the few great financial centers: "We have had experience, to our sorrow, with the old sectional divisions between the East and the West. Is there no smouldering spark in this matter of corporate control, which may some day flare up as a political issue of the first order?"[2]

Professor Ripley's book was a startling work for its day and it was one of the few professorial writings that for a moment actually "rocked Wall Street." But the later works of Berle and Means, *The Modern Corporation and Private Property,* and Wormser, *Frankenstein, Incorporated,* tell the story far more completely and with more revealing clarity. These authors make it especially plain that modern corporate procedure is the most devastating enemy of the sanctity and safety of private property that has ever appeared. In commenting on the volume by Berle and Means, Mr. Mandel emphasizes the important fact of the defiance of property rights by corporate manipulations:

The princes of corporate industry have not stopped with the mere deprivation of the voting rights of the individual stockholder. By various devices they have

[1] Ripley, *Main Street and Wall Street*, p. 83.   [2] *Ibid.*, p. 117.

even diverted profits in utter disregard of the amount of capital invested and have modified and negated ownership rights in defiance of the most sacred and hallowed rights of private property. Charters have been juggled by the small, initiative and controlling group, stock has been reclassified, "parasitic" shares have been issued and mergers, sales and leases have been entered into, over the heads of the stockholders, so that in the opinion of the authors, it has reached a point where the "share of stock . . . represents in a sense, a participation in corporate assets . . . subject to so many qualifications that the distinctness of the property right has been blurred to the point of invisibility." The powers of the controlling oligarchy have become in actual fact, confiscatory.

The "corporate revolution" has changed the very motives of those at the head of industrial enterprise. "In the operation of the corporation, the controlling group . . . can serve their own pockets better by profiting at the expense of the company than by making profits out of it. . . . As their proportion of the holdings decrease, and both profits and losses of the company accrue less and less to them, the opportunities of profiting at the expense of the corporation appear more directly to their benefit." The ruling princes of industry have become disloyal to the interests of the huge corporate empires they have themselves created, in their desire to pursue their own, private stock-jobbing designs. Thus the corporate monster devours its own children, the principles of private property, which have served as its legal justification and undermines the efficiency of the productive processes, its economic basis.[1]

There is another aspect of this movement "from Main Street to Wall Street" that neither Professor Ripley nor Berle and Means mention—but which is, nevertheless, of the utmost significance with reference to the ultimate destiny of economic radicalism. With the general diffusion of stockholding in corporations that are inseparably linked with the capitalistic system and the theory of business enterprise, it may be very difficult to persuade the more prosperous members of the proletariat and the lower middle class to be willing to stake their economic interests on any overthrow of capitalism. They are bound to grow less interested in the substitution of proletarian control, founded upon the principle of production for social need instead of private profit. Of course, if a time comes when there are no dividends for years, the psychology of the small stockholders may alter materially.

It may be noted, incidentally, that this demand of the stockholders for dividends is the chief check on utterly irresponsible looting of corporations by the inside management. But even this is entirely inadequate, as the large number of corporate failures and receiverships all too clearly reveals.

We must also reckon with the inevitable human tendency to ape one's superiors and to derive satisfaction from psychic identification with the economically and socially superior classes. If a person has even a tenuous connection with some important economic organization he is likely to "identify" himself with it rather than with the lower class with whom he associates daily and with whom his real interests lie. A laborer employed by the United States Steel Corporation who at the same time holds a single share of stock in the concern is much more likely to identify himself with this corporation than with the laboring class of which he is a member. It becomes "his" company

---

[1] Mandel, *loc. cit.*, pp. 253-54. One of the great ironies of history was the formation of the American Liberty League, in large part by Wall Street lawyers, in 1934, to protect private property

and the laborer develops a proprietary and protective sense that paralyzes his interest and efficiency as a member of a proletarian, and potentially revolutionary, group. Such a psychology of identification, of course, operates even more widely and immediately with the lower-middle-class investors.[1]

The paradoxical and self-defeating character of the contemporary trend towards wide stock ownership is worth noting. The lower-middle-class and wage-earning investors in stocks demand high dividends. But these are derived in part at the expense of the salaries and wages of these very white-collar and proletarian stockholders. The material as well as the psychological interests of the latter groups are split and divided in an utterly irreconcilable manner.

V. SPECULATION IN CORPORATE SECURITIES

A notable development in the modern financial world has been the growing speculation in the securities of various industrial, transportation, utility, and banking corporations. The securities of modern corporations—bonds, preferred stock, and common stock—are usually supposed to be of value chiefly as permanent investments to realize interest on bonds and dividends on stock. Those not so cautious as to leave their money in savings banks seek income on their capital by such investments.

Important and legitimate as such investment may be, it has of late been submerged under the enthusiasm bestowed upon what is virtually gambling in these securities. The aim of many purchasers is to profit not by the income from the earning power of these securities, but by the more or less arbitrary and temporary fluctuations in security values on the stock exchange. As bonds and preferred stocks, under normal conditions, change less rapidly and violently in market values, this form of gambling is limited chiefly to common stock. The most usual method is to buy these stocks on margin[2] at a given price, hold them until they rise in value, then sell and pocket the profits. Less frequent is "selling short," a more complicated process whereby the shrewd stock gambler can profit by declining prices in securities.

We may profitably review the history of the kind of trading represented in the present stock market.[3] It is actually a usage of modern origin. It first appeared early in modern times in the form of produce exchanges at Antwerp and elsewhere. The rise of world trade after the discovery of America assembled a much larger volume of commodities to be exchanged. Actual transfer of the goods in open market was often a difficult feat to perform. Consequently, strips of paper representing so much tobacco, rice, smoked herring, and the like were offered for sale. The purchaser presented these certificates to claim his goods. With the rise of the joint-stock company in the seventeenth century,

[1] See above, pp. 431-32.
[2] The term "buying on margin" is derived from the fact that in such operations the purchaser does not buy outright and pay full cash price for the securities. Instead, he deposits with the broker a sum of from 25 to 75 per cent of the price. This deposit is known as the margin. This device permits a much larger purchase of stocks than would be possible if the whole cost were paid, but the risk also is greater. The broker, of course, pays cash in full for the stock purchased at the exchange.
[3] See above, pp. 70 ff.

paper securities in the modern sense appeared on the market.[1] They represented a definite ownership of a share in a more or less legitimate business.

The growth of exchanges was accompanied by a number of wild booms and fatal crashes, among which the South Sea Bubble and the John Law venture are the best-known examples.[2] The public was hypnotized by the new commercial paper and easily drawn into supporting the most harebrained schemes of promotion. The loss of millions taught the investors a lesson and chastened their spirits. Bubbles became less frequent.

It is necessary to note that the losses sustained in these early crashes were mainly losses produced by foolish investments. The gambling was on the future earning power of the stocks rather than upon hoped-for rapid fluctuation in the market value of securities, though the two elements cannot be sharply separated.

The rise and triumph of the corporation in the nineteenth century provided the basic mechanism for the operations of the contemporary stock exchange.

The chief source of great profits in stock manipulation in the mid-nineteenth century remained for a time the practice of watering stock and issuing great blocks that did not rest upon actual investment or earning power. This was especially the case with the railroad finance of a half-century ago.[3] The present-day tendency to turn the stock market into a predominantly speculative institution, where the security values are shifted primarily upon the basis of current bidding, pools, and manipulation rather than upon changes in physical valuation, earning power, or capitalization, is primarily a development of the twentieth century.[4]

Blanket attacks on the stock exchange as a menace to the modern industrial world are foolish and misleading. The stock exchange has not only a legitimate but an indispensable function to perform in the contemporary economic order. This function is the exchange of securities desired for permanent investment or sold to obtain ready money. But when a man mentions "playing the market" today, he is likely to mean pure speculation—in reality, respectable gambling.[5]

This latest "get-rich-quick" craze has been intensified by the fact that the older forms of gambling—such as lotteries, race-track bets, and pools—have for the most part been outlawed, leaving the stock exchange as the great legitimate gambling institution of the nation. Even common laborers and clerks may invest their life's savings in the hope of getting rich quick. This speculative craze reached its height in America in the summer of 1929; it was followed by the great market crash of October, 1929, and the abysmal decline in the market value of stocks since that time.

Between October, 1929, and July 1, 1932, the value of securities listed on the

---

[1] See above, pp. 70 ff., and Mottram, *History of Financial Speculation.*
[2] See above, pp. 72 ff.
[3] *Cf.* Warshow, *Jay Gould;* C. F. Adams, Jr., and Henry Adams, *Chapters of Erie,* Osgood, 187 Josephson, *The Robber Barons;* Davis, *What Price Wall Street?;* Bouck White, *The Book of Dani Drew,* Doran, 1910; and Bonbright and Means, *op. cit.,* Chaps. VII-XI.
[4] Though not exclusively, by any means. See Davis, *op. cit.*
[5] *Cf.* Flynn, *Security Speculation.*

Wide World Photos
ANDREW MELLON

Wide World Photos
J. PIERPONT MORGAN, JR.

Ewing Galloway
WALL STREET

Wilfred Jones
THE MENACE OF THE GANGSTER

Cartoon by Talburt, Scripps-Howard Newspaper Alliance

THE WAY IT WORKS

New York Stock Exchange decreased by more than $75,000,000,000. The table and chart below give a few examples of declines in the prices of "gilt-edge" securities:

Name of Company	1929 highs	1932 (up to August 15) lows
American Telephone & Telegraph	310	70¼
Consolidated Gas	183	31½
Electric Bond & Share	101	8½
General Motors	92	7⅞
Kennecott Copper	105	4⅞
Radio Corporation of America	115	2½
United States Steel	261	21¼

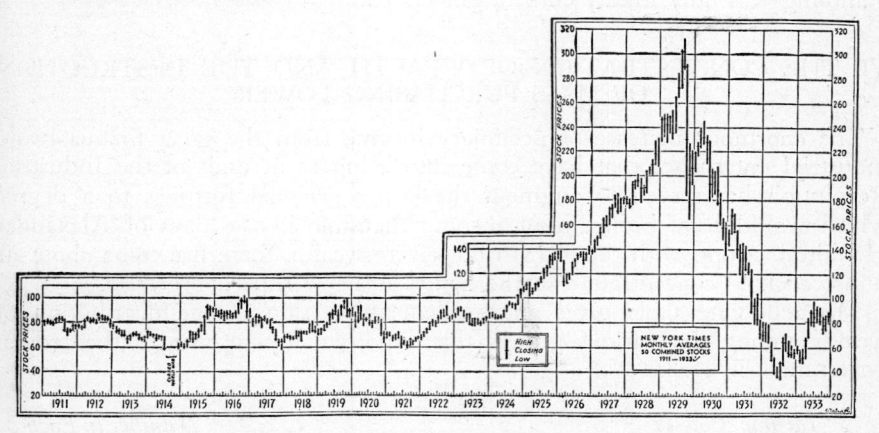

FLUCTUATION IN SECURITY PRICES ON NEW YORK STOCK EXCHANGE, 1911-1933[1]

This speculative gambling distracts attention from the sound services to be rendered by the exchange and obscures the real meaning of securities and the ultimate basis of their value. In addition, it produces deplorable psychological consequences. From the broker on the exchange to the sales girl at $15 a week, the nation becomes a population of ticker-tape watchers. An unreal sense of economic values prevails and the taste for patient and honest endeavor is lost.

There can be no real soundness in stock-exchange activities until steps are taken to repress speculation altogether. If one desires national industrial prosperity and financial security, while retaining the benefits of the capitalist system, the issues are clear enough. Let economic enterprises be run for the service of the public, with the legitimate profit that may be derived from rendering such service. Let security values be based on the earning power of the underlying companies. Let the activities of the stock exchange be limited to the transfer of securities between prospective investors.

Some legislation may be necessary to effect the necessary reforms, but experience has shown how difficult it is to regulate by law general economic tendencies. The necessary legislation must be supplemented by the education of the

[1] New York *Times*, Jan. 2, 1934.

public as to underlying realities in modern business and as to the precarious and antisocial nature of purely speculative enterprises.

An attempt was made to regulate the operations of the New York Stock Exchange in 1934, and a law was passed imposing regulations and creating a commission to exert supervision over the exchange. But the law went no further than to insure that the gambling would be reasonably honest by prohibiting pools, corners, and inside operations, and to make speculation less hazardous through requiring reasonable margins. Buying on margin was not otherwise curbed, and short selling was curtailed rather than abolished. No limitations whatever were placed upon the proper investment operations of the exchange. At most, the act was only a beginning in the right direction. Stock gambling was only mildly curbed, not ended.[1]

VI. THE CONCENTRATION OF WEALTH AND THE DESTRUCTION OF MASS PURCHASING POWER

The enormous increase of pecuniary income from the great financial and industrial enterprises that have come into being as a result of the Industrial Revolution has served to augment the larger personal fortunes to a degree which would have been almost incomprehensible in the days of Alexander Hamilton. Along with the growth of private wealth, there has come about its unprecedented concentration in the hands of a few superbourgeoisie.

The following table gives an excellent impression of the distribution of wealth among the various groups that reported any income to the federal government in 1928:

Income Classes	*Number in Each*
Under $1,000	111,123
Between $1,000 and $2,000	918,447
Between $2,000 and $3,000	837,781
Between $3,000 and $5,000	1,192,613
Between $5,000 and $10,000	628,766
Between $10,000 and $25,000	270,889
Between $25,000 and $50,000	68,048
Between $50,000 and $100,000	27,207
Between $100,000 and $150,000	7,049
Between $150,000 and $300,000	5,678
Between $300,000 and $500,000	1,756
Between $500,000 and $1,000,000	983
Over $1,000,000	511

This makes apparent the enormous concentration of wealth in the hands of a relatively few Americans. It becomes even more impressive when we reflect that the overwhelming majority of Americans did not have sufficient income to equal the low required minimum for reporting to the federal government under the income-tax provisions. Even in this extremely prosperous year, 1928, only 4,070,851 adults reported income to the federal government out of a total population of over 120,000,000, an adult population of at least 60,000,000 and a

---

[1] *Cf.* Flynn, *Security Speculation*, Pt. III.

working population of over 45,000,000. Those with enough income to be reportable to the federal government are thus only the small upper peak of the social pyramid. The broad center and the base of the social pyramid in the United States are made up of the great numbers whose income is below the small minimum set by the government as the point of exemption from reporting income.

Another estimate gives the following distribution of income for those receiving any income at all:

Range of 1929 Income	Number Income Recipients	Percentage of Total Income
1. $1,000,000 and over	504	1.511
2. $100,000 to $1,000,000	13,057	4.086
3. $25,000 to $100,000	88,493	5.057
4. $5,000 to $25,000	866,947	10.755
5. $3,000 to $5,000	1,874,538	10.040
6. $2,000 to $3,000	4,071,261	12.966
7. $1,000 to $2,000	22,799,967	38.825
8. $1,000 and under	18,465,951	18.760
	48,180,718	100.00

An interesting analysis of income by families has been offered by Leven, Moulton, and Warburton in their book on *America's Capacity to Consume*. They show that about 6,000,000 families in 1929—21 per cent of the total—had an income of less than $1,000; 12,000,000 families, or 42 per cent of the total, had incomes of less than $1,500; while 20,000,000 families, or about 71 per cent of the total, had incomes of less than $2,500. Only about 2,000,000 families, or 8 per cent of the total, had an income of over $5,000. Some 600,000 families, or 2.3 per cent of the total, had incomes of over $10,000. The 0.1 per cent of the families at the top, with incomes in excess of $75,000, received almost as much as the 42 per cent of the families at the bottom of the income ladder. In 1929, 36 persons had an income of over $5,000,000; 504 an income of over $1,000,000; and 14,701 an income of over $100,000.

These figures testify to the low income of the great majority of Americans. Yet the total income of the country in 1928 was sufficient to give an adequate income to every individual—at least if he lived as part of a family—had it been equally divided. The per capita income in 1928 was $749. If it had been equally divided, a family of five would have enjoyed an income of $3,745. Careful studies by the United States government have indicated that a family of five can maintain themselves in health and decency on a budget of approximately $2,000. Had wealth been equally divided in 1928, every family would have had sufficient income to live decently and to save at least a certain margin. As it was, the average income of all wage-earners gainfully employed in that year in the United States was $1,205. The unskilled wage-earners averaged less than $1,000, and the agricultural workers only slightly more than $500. More than 60 per cent of all American families received less than the $2,000 a year needed to maintain health and decency. This poorest 60 per cent of the families received only a quarter of the national income, while the richest 1.2 per cent of the families received approximately as much of it.

In 1928, 15,780 persons out of 120,000,000 received one-eighteenth of the total national income. In 1929 the richest 1 per cent of those receiving any income absorbed 12 per cent of the total, and the top 10 per cent took over 25 per cent of the total. Even more striking is the fact that the top 1 per cent of federal income-tax payers obtained three-fifths of the total increase in reported income from 1921 through 1928. A great deal is often made of the assertion that the number of persons with a reported income of over $5,000 a year increased by 92 per cent from 1921 through 1928. But this appears less significant when we learn that the number of those with incomes of over $100,000 increased by 597 per cent in the same period, and those with incomes in excess of $1,000,000 by 2,343 per cent. It is even more significant that approximately 99 per cent of the population received less than $5,000 a year, and that the proportion of the total national income going to this vast group was actually less in 1929 than in 1921. This shows that even in good years the relative group income of more than 98 per cent of our population has been steadily declining. This stands out in marked contrast to the astonishing increase in the incomes of the very wealthy during this same period.

The figures on incomes for 1933, published by the United States Bureau of Internal Revenue in December, 1934, showed that the New Deal, with its supposed solicitude for the "forgotten man," has not materially altered this tendency towards the concentration of wealth and income. Those with incomes of over $25,000 showed a marked gain in group and individual incomes, while those with incomes of less than $25,000 gave evidence of a marked falling-off. Moreover, corporate incomes showed a vast gain, while the total of individual incomes fell off.

Professor Walter B. Pitkin gives us a most illuminating picture of how the American people fare in an economic sense even under the New Deal:[1]

Income Classes in 1935

Number in Each Class		How Much They Receive per Capita
1. Upper class, very rich, about	500,000	$10,000 each, or $ 5,000,000,000
2. Middle class	12,000,000	1,000 each, or 12,000,000,000
3. Self-supporting workers, farmers, small business men	34,500,000	500 each, or 17,250,000,000
4. Marginals, earning most of living, but receiving some aid	15,000,000	300 each, or 4,500,000,000
5. Submerged idle, mostly on relief	65,000,000	75 each, or 4,875,000,000
Total	127,000,000	$43,625,000,000

It is not necessary here to go into the question of the ethical right or wrong of this vast concentration of wealth in the hands of a few, though it is quite obvious that those receiving vast incomes render no service to society at all proportionate to what they receive from it; nor does their ability correspond to their income. All that need concern us here is that this concentration of

---
[1] Adapted from Pitkin, *Capitalism Carries On*, pp. 180-81.

THE DESTRUCTION OF MASS PURCHASING POWER

income would by logical progression absolutely preclude the perpetuation of the present type of capitalistic society. It is axiomatic with realistic students of economics that capitalism, private property, and the profit system can be healthy only when there is a wide distribution of purchasing power among the masses.

The present concentration of wealth and income in this country makes impossible adequate mass purchasing power. The wealthy cannot purchase and consume in proportion to their income. They save the vast proportion of the latter and put it into so-called capital goods: new enterprises to manufacture more goods that cannot be bought by the masses who lack adequate income. Such are the elementary facts and logic revealing the prospect that capitalism may "fold up" in the future. The mechanism is well illustrated by the chart on page 810.

To be very practical, one may examine the figures for 1928. The 23,000,000 families made up of persons with incomes under $5,000 had a total money income of about $65,000,000,000. On a fair budget computation, the most they could spend for manufactured goods was $38,000,000,000. Yet in 1928 we manufactured goods (not including those exported) to the value of $55,000,000,000. The slightly more than 1,000,000 persons with incomes over $5,000 annually could hardly buy up the surplus $17,000,000,000 worth of manufactured goods out of the reach of those with incomes under $5,000 a year. How many more goods could be sold if income were more equitably divided has been indicated by Leven, Moulton, and Warburton. In 1929 over 70 per cent of American families had incomes of less than $2,500. If these 20,000,000 families had all had their incomes raised to $2,500 each they would, by the spending-standards of that year, have spent 40 per cent more for food, 65 per cent more for homes and living-quarters, 65 per cent more for clothing, and 115 per cent more for other consumers' goods and services. Another example of the inadequacy of mass purchasing power is afforded by the following statistics. Between 1923 and 1929 the value of manufactured products increased by some $10,000,000,000. But wages during this period advanced by only $600,000,000. The workers, salaried classes, and farmers were supposed to buy up this $10,000,000,000 worth of new goods. But the workers could not buy it with only $600,000,000 more at their disposal; the salaried classes had made gains in income only roughly comparable to those in wages; while the farmers were getting less in 1929 than in 1923.

If one wishes to put the social income to work in such fashion as to make it buy goods and services effectively, it must be contrived to place a larger share of that income in the hands of the masses. This is admirably demonstrated by the following table (top of page 811) giving the relative proportion of income spent and saved by the various income classes in the United States:

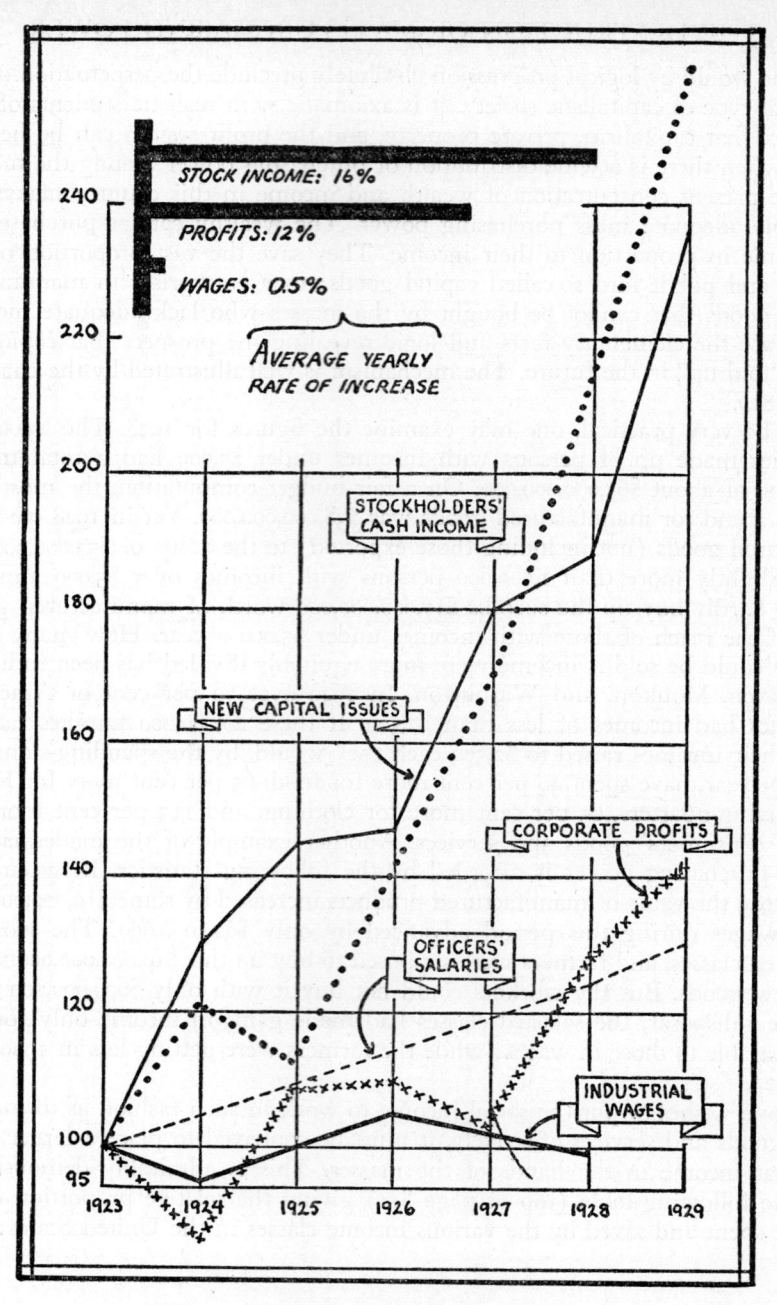

"PROSPERITY" IN ACTION, 1923-1929 [1]

[1] From Lewis Corey, *The Decline of American Capitalism,* Covici, Friede, 1934. This diagram reveals the excessive expansion of new enterprises and indicates how the income of the propertied classes completely outdistanced the wages of the workers. Mass purchasing power was thus fatally ignored and sacrificed.

THE DESTRUCTION OF MASS PURCHASING POWER

PERIOD FROM 1922 TO 1929 [1]

Income Classes	Per Cent Saved	Per Cent Taxes	Per Cent Spent for Goods and Services
$1,000 and under	3	3	94
$1,000, under $2,000	5	2	93
$2,000, under $3,000	11	2	87
$3,000, under $5,000	16	2	82
$5,000, under $10,000	14	3	83
$10,000, under $25,000	22	4	74
$25,000, under $50,000	30	8	62
$50,000, under $100,000	31	13	56
$100,000, under $150,000	35	15	50
$150,000, under $300,000	44	16	40
$300,000, under $500,000	67	17	16
$500,000, under $1,000,000	71	17	12
Over $1,000,000	77	17	6

Leven, Moulton, and Warburton add confirmation to this by calling attention to the fact that the top 2.3 per cent of American families—those with incomes in excess of $10,000 a year—contributed about two-thirds of the total savings in the United States. The poorest 80 per cent of the families contributed only 2 per cent of the savings.

The extreme concentration of wealth and income is frequently justified on the ground that the rich give liberally to support the poor through private charity, thus putting their money back into circulation and increasing mass purchasing power. In a striking article, Dr. Abraham Epstein brands this conception a myth. He says, "Among the masses of the well-to-do not many give anything to charity, even in the most generous city, New York. A negligible number of rich individuals support all charities. The vast bulk of the wealthy contribute to none." [2]

In those American cities where charitable contributions are raised through community chests or welfare federations the contributors have never exceeded 17 per cent of the population. There are 360 community chest drives in the United States each year. Combined, they do not raise more than $80,000,000, less than one-fourth of what England spends annually on unemployment insurance alone. New York is the richest and most free-spending American city. In Manhattan alone 357,000 persons filed income-tax reports in 1928. Yet only about 1 in 40 of these contributed to the Association for the Improvement of the Condition of the Poor or to the Charity Organization Society.

Neither do the rich remember the poor generously in their bequests and legacies. The New York Association for the Improvement of the Condition of the Poor has been in existence eighty-five years. It has been administered by very wealthy and reputable individuals. Yet it has received only 264 "legacies,

---

[1] Taylor, *Common Sense about Machines and Unemployment*, p. 97.
[2] "Do the Rich Give to Charity?" *American Mercury*, May, 1931, p. 23.

funds, and gifts." The Charity Organization Society received but 173 gifts or legacies between 1882 and 1930. The United Charities of Chicago received only 130. The Philadelphia Welfare Society has been remembered by only six persons in their wills. Likewise with foundations, Dr. Epstein says:

> The benevolences of a dozen individuals, such as Carnegie, the Rockefellers, Harkness, Rosenwald and a few others account for a considerable proportion of existing foundations. Of the estimated $1,000,000,000 now available in these funds, the gifts of the Rockefellers and Andrew Carnegie alone make up three-fourths of the total.[1]

Dr. Epstein concludes that private charity is utterly inadequate to the task of caring for the dependent classes either in normal times or in emergencies:

> Indeed, when we talk of caring for unemployment and drought by private philanthropy we talk nonsense. . . . Under this system the burden of social ills falls almost entirely upon the few generous rich and the bulk of poor wage-earners, who cannot refuse to give to charitable appeals when the boss asks them to contribute. It is altogether contrary to the modern principle of a fair proportional distribution of the burden. The bulk of the well-to-do escape entirely from paying their share.[2]

The National Bureau of Economic Research has published a report on the gifts of American corporations to community chests since 1920. The bureau selected for its study 129 representative cities. Of the $58,801,872 contributed in 1929 to the community chests of these 129 cities, $12,954,769, or 22 per cent, was contributed by corporations. Manufacturing corporations rated highest in percentage of gifts. They contributed 47.2 per cent of the total. Next came retail and trade companies with 22.4 per cent. Third were banks and trust companies with 10.7 per cent. Especially low were chain stores with 2.9 per cent, and insurance companies with 1.5 per cent.

The total benefactions look impressive until one goes deeper into the facts. The decade from 1920 to 1929 was unparalleled in corporate business and profits. Did corporate gifts to community chests increase accordingly? Hardly. Fourteen of the 129 community chests studied were in existence in 1920. Thirteen supplied information for the decade. In 1920 corporations contributed 23.8 per cent of the total of these 13 community chests. In 1929 they contributed only 22.9 per cent, and this was a boom year until mid-autumn. Moreover, the number of corporations contributing to these 13 community chests doubled between 1920 and 1929—2,652 in 1920 and 5,127 in 1929. Yet the total contributions from corporations increased but slightly—$2,535,000 in 1920 and $2,799,000 in 1929. Corporations fell far behind even in this bonanza decade in keeping up their share of the contributions to community welfare.

Without drawing any more decisive conclusions, these figures prove that corporate wealth cannot be permitted to expand unrestrainedly on the ground that its representatives will accept the responsibility of a square deal to society by means of a large refund through charity. Even if they could be so trusted,

---

[1] Epstein, *loc. cit.*, p. 27.
[2] *Ibid.*, p. 30. No less than 76 per cent of the money received for charity and philanthropy comes from those with incomes of less than $5,000 a year.

this would be an undesirable method of insuring general well-being. The only sensible way to proceed under capitalism is to see to it that workers obtain steady employment, high wages, tolerable working-conditions, and unemployment insurance. Then let corporate wealth take its legitimate earnings.[1]

In our discussions of the charity of the rich to the poor—inadequate though this charity may be—we usually lose sight of the extensive, if involuntary, charity of the poor towards the rich. This relevant point is well brought out by Mr. Gilbert Seldes in his booklet, *Against Revolution:*

I agree with revolutionaries that the charity system is outworn. But the charity of the rich to the poor is not the only one. There is the appalling charity of the poor to the rich. On the great lists of charitable contributions from the rich to the poor only a few items are anonymous; on the infinitely longer list of charity which the poor have given to the rich no names occur. The unmonied ones have had the exquisite tact to keep their benevolence a secret. The rich have given to the poor a little food, a little drink, a little shelter and a few clothes. The poor have given to the rich palaces and yachts, and an almost infinite freedom to indulge their doubtful taste for display, and bonuses and excess profits, under which cold and forbidding terms have been hidden the excess labor and extravagant misery of the poor. The poor have given . . . what is perhaps most precious to them, their security and their peace of mind, and have lived their lives precariously, always on the edge of danger, uncertain of the next day's food or the next month's rent, terrified of living lest they lose their jobs and terrified of dying lest their wives and children starve.[2]

The very wealthy have also reduced the available purchasing power of the less fortunate through the tax policies that prevail. They have prevented the adoption of the principle and practice of taxation in proportion to ability to pay. They have secured the adoption of sales taxes and other devices that throw the main burden upon the mass of purchasers. Even with respect to the income tax, they have invented ingenious methods of evasion through the "capital loss" and other provisions of the law, so that J. P. Morgan himself paid no income tax in 1931 or 1932.

Much has been written and spoken about the alleged overproduction of our time as a result of the increased efficiency of our machines and the lack of planning in our economy.[3] But most of the alleged overproduction to date has been, in reality, underconsumption due to the inability of the masses of workers and farmers to purchase even an adequate supply of necessities. It is doubtful if, outside of the automobile tire industry, there is any real menace of overproduction.[4] Even in the cotton textile industry and the shoe industry—frequently mentioned as distressing examples of overproduction—there is no proof that our factories, as at present equipped, could produce more shirts, dresses,

[1] For a broad-minded discussion of these considerations, see W. A. Robson, *The Relation of Wealth to Welfare,* Macmillan, 1925.
[2] Seldes, *op. cit.,* Day, 1932, p. 13.
[3] *Cf.* Stuart Chase, "The Enemy of Prosperity, Overproduction: What Shall We Do about It?" *Harper's Magazine,* November, 1930, and Scoville Hamlin, ed., *The Menace of Overproduction,* Wiley, 1930.
[4] *Cf.* Stuart Chase, *The Economy of Abundance,* Macmillan, 1934; Pitkin, *The Consumer;* Clark Foreman and Michael Ross, *The Consumer Seeks a Way,* Norton, 1935; W. H. Lough and M. R. Gainsbrugh, *High-Level Consumption,* McGraw-Hill, 1935; and Stuart Chase and others, *Rich Man, Poor Man,* Harper, 1935.

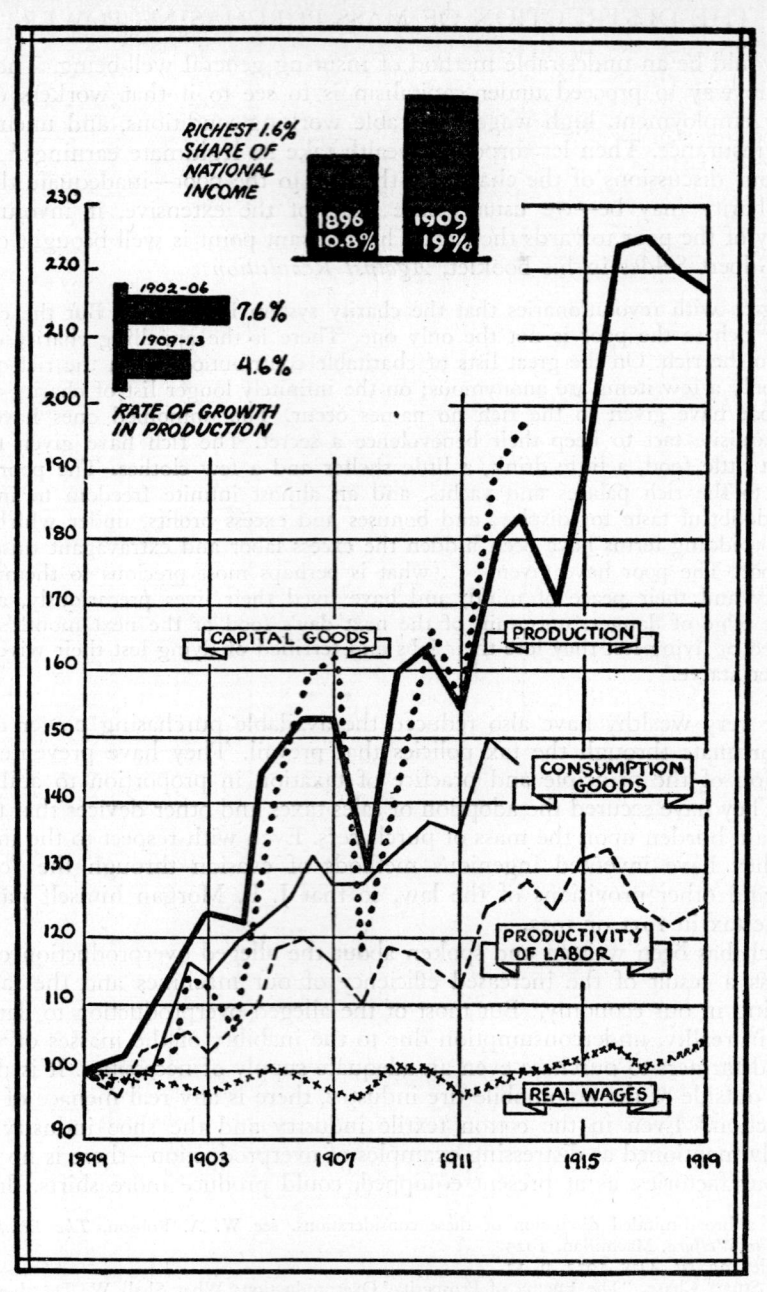

MAJOR ECONOMIC TRENDS—1896-1919[1]

[1] From Corey, *op. cit.* This chart further drives home the disparity between the profits of the business and financial groups and the wages of the working classes. This failure to consider and further mass purchasing power has seriously impaired capitalism.

and shoes than the population of the United States could legitimately consume. In 1928 and 1929 we did not turn out half as many clothes as could have been worn legitimately by the American population if it had possessed the requisite purchasing power. The Roosevelt Administration sought to limit farm production as a phase of the New Deal. Yet it is perfectly obvious that the American population has never even passably approached having all the bread, meat, milk, and vegetables that it could consume. Mr. Doane has shown that this is true even in boom periods. The following table deals with the food situation in the United States in the boom year, 1929. Out of twelve basic food items listed we had a production deficiency in eight:

STANDARD DIET [1]

Annual Liberal Diet * (pounds per capita per year) Items	Pounds	1929 Peak Production (thousands of pounds) Deficiency	Surplus
Flour and cereals	100	....	16,022,612
Milk	636	26,967,000	....
Potatoes	155	....	1,030,670
Beans, peas, nuts	7	....	1,396,240
Tomatoes, citrus fruits	110	1,382,926	....
Leafy and other green veg.	135	7,300,936	....
Other vegetables and fruits	325	12,326,000	....
Butter	35	2,234,688	....
Fats, bacon and lard	17	....	2,833,000
Sugar and molasses	60	2,461,450	....
Meats, including fish	165	1,986,265	....
Eggs (individual eggs)	360	13,723,370	....

* (Circular 296, U. S. Dept. of Agriculture.)

We had to import some 22,000,000,000 pounds of food. If the people of the country had enjoyed ample incomes in 1929, so that they could have bought all the food they wished, the deficit in our food production would have been much larger. In their important book *America's Capacity to Consume,* Leven, Moulton, and Warburton have pointed out that even in 1929 three-fourths of the nonrural families in the United States did not have enough income "to provide an adequate diet at a moderate cost," while nine-tenths of the nonrural families lacked the income to be able to provide themselves with a liberal diet. This underconsumption is the main menace to capitalism and it is one of the most obvious and self-destructive results of the avarice and shortsightedness of finance capitalism.

This failure of capitalism in the last half-century to insure mass purchasing power and to adjust consuming capacity to productive advances is what has brought the present-day decline of capitalism. Production has far outrun the power of the consumer to buy. The table on page 814 gives a good graphic presentation of how production completely outdistanced real wages from 1896 to the close of the World War. It also far outran the income of the farming and salaried classes.

[1] Cited in R. R. Doane, "But Is It a Surplus Economy?" *New Outlook,* August, 1934, p. 10.

Even more illuminating is the chart showing incomes in the boom decade of 1923 to 1929. The lines indicating industrial wages and salaries of corporation officers contrast vividly with the skyrocketing of corporate profits, stockholders' income, and new capital issues of corporations.

VII. THE THEORY OF BUSINESS ENTERPRISE AND THE PRICE SYSTEM

Along with the growth of a far more elaborate technique of organization in modern business there also appeared an equally significant attitude towards economic activities and financial gain. This has been well designated by Thorstein Veblen "the theory of business enterprise." The economy of the pre-industrial age had been moored to considerations of subsistence and to the fitness of materials to meet direct human needs. After the Industrial Revolution the economic order was governed by price mechanics and controlled by motives related to private pecuniary profits.

The dominant notions of the "theory of business enterprise" or the "pecuniary order" are essentially the following: In the first place, the modern economy may well be called the "bookkeeping economy," as was noted earlier in this volume, in that the results are to be measured quantitatively by means of an investigation of the amount of concrete pecuniary profits made by the concern. The ledger has taken the place of economic conscience. Profits are regarded as the mainspring of all industrial effort, and any force or influence that leads to the diminishing of immediate private pecuniary profits is viewed as a fatal obstruction to the development of modern industrial prosperity.

The point of view, then, which determines the desirability of modern industrial effort is that of the accountant. The volume of financial profit, rather than the excellence of the product or capacity to satisfy the actual needs of the population, is the basic factor to be considered. Of course, to manufacture goods without any adequate potential demand for the use of the product would entail serious loss. But the manufacturer does not have to concern himself with whether or not the public needs these goods, if by advertising he can induce the people to believe that they should buy the goods, and hence make them willing to purchase such materials. In case a manufacturer can by advertising induce customers to purchase a half-million dollars' worth of goods that they do not actually need, this is exactly as good business enterprise as though he were to sell them a half-million dollars' worth of the primary necessities of life. Much advertising is, of course, a legitimate attempt to bring to public notice new products or desirable qualities in old ones.[1] Not a little, however, is of a socially wasteful character, designed to persuade the public to buy something it does not need, or something that does not have the virtues claimed for it. Some advertising is personally and socially dangerous, and morally, if not legally, criminal. Dangerous or poisonous products are sold to unsuspecting customers, or the latter are led to place reliance in times of serious illness upon worthless nostrums that jeopardize their lives.[2] So powerful are predatory busi-

---

[1] *Cf.* F. S. Presbrey, *History and Development of Advertising,* Doubleday, Doran, 1929.
[2] On this point, see especially Arthur Kallett and F. J. Schlink, *100,000,000 Guinea Pigs,* Vanguard Press, 1933; J. B. Matthews and R. E. Schallcross, *Partners in Plunder,* Covici, Friede, 1935; T. S. Harding, *The Joy of Ignorance,* Godwin, 1932, and *The Popular Practice of Fraud,* Longmans, 1935. The classic exposition is H. G. Wells's famous novel, *Tono-Bungay,* Duffield, 1909.

ness interests that they can usually even prevent the people from obtaining important self-protective information gathered by the federal government, bearing upon food, drugs, and manufactured products, if this information might bring financial loss to the vendors of the inferior goods. This in spite of the fact that the people pay the taxes that support these government fact-finding bureaus.[1]

Further, excellence of product need not concern the manufacturer, except in so far as a rather variable minimum of quality must be maintained, lest the demand be reduced through disappointed customers. But it is not a social point of view or an interest in craftsmanship which leads him to maintain even this minimum of excellence in workmanship. Rather it is the purely pecuniary fear of a loss of monetary profits. If, through an interest in craftsmanship or a highly social conception of the function of the manufacturer, a modern employer actually reduces his profits by making a better type of commodity, he is, to the extent of the diminution of his profits, a bad business man, in the light of contemporary business standards.

The contemporary theory of business enterprise generally ignores long-time considerations as to profits. Immediate pecuniary profit to a particular employer is the basic element considered. Little thought is given as to whether this particular policy may not, in the end, result in economic loss to the business involved or in serious damage to the interests and prestige of the business class as a whole. It is this shortsighted immediacy of pecuniary judgment that has helped on the disastrous series of so-called business cycles of undue prosperity and calamitous depression which have characterized the history of industrial and commercial activity in every great modern state since the Industrial Revolution.

It is obvious that this attitude towards industrial effort is extremely wasteful and oppressive. It floods markets with great quantities of inferior and often socially undesirable products. It also stimulates incomplete consumption through the abandonment of commodities whose services have not yet been exhausted but which are discarded in the interest of whims of fashion or through the pressure of advertising.

One of the major indictments of the theory of business enterprise, the price system, and the competitive order is the vast amount of waste that they introduce into our productive and consumptive processes.[2] This has been made the subject of an interesting and comprehensive study by Mr. Stuart Chase entitled *The Tragedy of Waste*.[3] He holds that at least half of the available man power of America is wasted as a result of the unscientific methods originated and perpetuated by our competitive order:

An aeroplane view of America would disclose a very large fraction of the available man-power workless on any given working day; would disclose another large fraction making and distributing things which are of no real use to anybody; and a

---

[1] For conclusive evidence upon this point, see F. J. Schlink, "What Government Does and Might Do for the Consumer," American Academy of Political and Social Science, *Annals*, May, 1934.
[2] For a good summary treatment of the problem of waste, see R. T. Bye and W. W. Hewett, *Applied Economics*, Crofts, 1928, Chap. III.
[3] Macmillan, 1925.

third fraction taking two hours to do a job which engineers have found can be done in one—and which some men are actually doing in one. . . .

Half and more of our man-power counting for nothing; half and more of the yearly output of natural resources heedlessly scattered and destroyed . . . a billion slaves of energy turning useless wheels, dragging unneeded loads. Motion, speed, momentum unbounded—to an end never clearly defined, to a goal unknown and unseen. If there be a philosophy of waste, it lies in the attempt to clarify that goal, to turn men's eyes towards the whyfore of the sweat of their bodies and of their brains.[1]

In 1921 a Committee of the Federated American Engineering Societies published a comprehensive report on *Waste in Industry*. The introduction to this report was written by Mr. Herbert Hoover. Commenting on this report, Professors Bye and Hewett conclude that Mr. Chase's estimate of total waste is "very conservative." These authors present the following tabular summary of the conclusions of the Hoover report:

PERCENTAGE OF WASTE IN INDUSTRY

Industry	Points Assayed Against the Best Plant Studied Points	Points Assayed Against the Average of all Plants Studied Points	Ratio of the Best to the Average Plant
Men's Clothing Mfg.	26.73	63.78	1:2
Building Industry	30.15	53.00	1:1½
Printing	30.50	57.61	1:2
Boot and Shoe Mfg.	12.50	40.83	1:3
Metal Trades	6.00	28.66	1:4½
Textile Mfg.	28.00	49.20	1:1½

A plant in which all possible forms of waste were present would be charged with a hundred points in this table. As no plant is entirely wasteful in every respect, the number of points in any one case would be less than a hundred. In the men's clothing industry, for example, out of a hundred per cent possible waste, the best plant shows 26.73 as the actual waste found. The average clothing manufacturing concern runs almost three times that, or 63.78. It will be noticed that the average efficiency of industry is very far below that achieved by the best plant in each of the industries listed. The ratio of the best plant to the average is approximately one to two. . . .

The following table, taken from the Hoover Report, shows the relative responsibility for waste in industry as assayed against management, labor and other factors:

[1] Chase, *op. cit.*, pp. 269, 274-75.

Industry Studied	Responsibility Assayed Against Management	Responsibility Assayed Against Labor	Responsibility Assayed Against Outside Contacts (The Public, Trade Relationships, and Other Factors)
Men's Clothing Mfg.	75%	16%	9%
Building Industry	65%	21%	14%
Printing	63%	28%	9%
Boot and Shoe Mfg.	73%	11%	16%
Metal Trades	81%	9%	10%
Textile Mfg.	50%	10%	40%

The table indicates that more than half the waste in industry is due to faulty management, while less than one quarter of the total waste is due to labor. The remaining waste caused by various outside contacts of a plant is, with the exception of the textile business, apparently of little importance. If we are to eliminate waste and increase the efficiency of production, it is apparent that management must take the lead, for management has the greater part of the responsibility.[1]

Not only has business enterprise been wasteful in production but also it has squandered the natural resources of the world in a most disastrous manner.[2] Moreover, it has enormously weakened the financial integrity of manufacturing enterprise, transportation lines, and electric utilities through stock manipulation and other forms of undesirable, purely profit-getting activities. It may well be that a satisfactory type of economic and social system can coexist with private property and individual business initiative. But it is becoming very apparent that we can have no adequate and permanent type of economy that is founded upon this essentially antisocial theory of business enterprise and absentee ownership. From well-nigh every standpoint it must meet the condemnation of the objective industrial engineer, economist, and sociologist.

It is sometimes urged that the modern business entrepreneur or promoter is the man to whom we owe most of the advantages that have been brought to society by modern industrial and commercial life, but this attitude betokens an almost complete ignorance of the processes of industrial evolution. The classes to whom we owe most of those real improvements in economic life which we enjoy today are the applied scientists and technicians, who have provided us with the technological foundations of the contemporary economy. The pecuniary gains that have come about as a result of their efforts have usually been diverted to the business men who have exploited their achievements. Rarely has the scientist or the technician materially benefited to any comparable degree from his efforts.

To be sure, we owe something to the organizing capacity of great men of industry and finance like Carnegie, Krupp, Rockefeller, Edison, Ford, and

[1] Bye and Hewett, *op. cit.*, pp. 45-46.
[2] *Cf.* C. H. Van Hise, *The Conservation of Natural Resources in the United States*, rev. ed., Macmillan, 1914.

Stinnes,[1] but the great majority of business men have merely exploited the work of the inventors. The marked distinction between inventors and money-makers, which Professor Taussig has drawn,[2] is a valuable one for the modern economic historian to keep ever in mind. Such antisocial practices of the business man as stock gambling, railroad manipulation, misleading advertising, and wasteful exploitation of natural resources have really prevented society from making the most of the constructive achievements of the modern scientist and inventor. The domination of finance capitalism, with its consuming interest in immediate profits, has been especially fatal to a full realization of the possibilities of technical efficiency in modern industry.[3] Moreover, business sometimes puts a check on technological progress in cases where a new invention would be temporarily disastrous to the more powerful interests in the particular industry.[4]

The most that can be said for the old-line capitalism is that it helped to solve the early problems of industrial production. Through sensing the opportunity for gain in exploiting mechanical inventions and in improving business management, it helped to make production more efficient, though by no means so efficient as it would be if it were managed throughout by the technician. Of late, however, when inventions threaten at any point to reduce the private profits of intrenched industrial and commercial interests, the business men have consciously and deliberately held back productive efficiency. A good illustration of how competitive capitalism, either through waste, shiftlessness, or deliberate restriction of output, is today preventing maximum production is afforded by the recent Columbia University report on *Economic Reconstruction*. On the basis of a careful survey, it was estimated that production in the United States could be increased by 77.6 per cent if all industries were brought up to the best current practice in the most efficient plants. It was estimated that production could be increased by 90.1 per cent if equipment and management were brought up to the best current standards known to industrial engineers.[5] There was no attempt to reckon with what might be achieved if the best automatic machinery were introduced.

Moreover, by failing to take account of the necessity of providing for consumers' purchasing power, the old-line capitalists have undermined such contributions as they did actually make to productive enterprise. It is of little benefit to produce under capitalism if one cannot sell. By its shortsighted attitude towards the distribution of the social income, business enterprise has offset to a large degree its contributions to improved productive technique.

Not only does this disastrous theory of business enterprise apply to the employer class. It has also come to dominate in modified form the point of view of the great majority of modern industrial workers, particularly that of the

---

[1] *Cf.* Jenks, *The Trust Problem,* Chap. III and pp. 334 ff., and Dobb, *Capitalist Enterprise and Social Progress.*

[2] *Cf.* Taussig, *Inventors and Money Makers;* T. B. Veblen, *The Engineer and the Price System,* Huebsch, 1921; and F. W. Taussig and C. S. Joslyn, *American Business Leaders,* Macmillan, 1932.

[3] See below, pp. 822 ff.

[4] For particulars, see the two articles by F. J. Frazer cited in the last chapter.

[5] The Columbia University Commission, *Economic Reconstruction: Report,* Columbia University Press, 1934, pp. 6 ff., 87 ff. *Cf.* Chase and others, *Rich Man, Poor Man.*

better-organized skilled workers.[1] Business enterprise has operated on the principle of selling the largest possible volume of the poorest marketable quality of goods for the highest possible price. In time, well-organized labor in the older and more conservative types of unions adopted a similar philosophy and translated it into action in the form of the shortest possible working-day with the greatest permissible type of loafing for the highest possible wages. They were, of course, taught this by the dishonesty and oppression of their employers operating under the old piecework system. But the outcome is the same, whatever the cause. Limitation of output has become all too prevalent in conservative labor-union policy. Yet, as shown above, the waste due to labor policy is only a fraction of that due to inefficient management.

Some of the more up-to-date and constructive trade-unions are beginning to understand that strikes for higher wages, limitation of output, and lack of interest in craftsmanship and productivity must, in the end, lead to disaster and to the discrediting of the labor movement. Therefore, these unions are coming to embody in their program such things as the elimination of strikes, the substitution of compulsory arbitration, and the provision for increased output and greater technical efficiency on the part of labor.[2] Enlightened employers are gradually abandoning the grosser aspects of the theory of business enterprise, and the more intelligent labor leaders are emphasizing the necessity of adopting policies that will increase the volume and excellence of their product. In such tendencies lies the only hope of escape, within capitalism, from the expensive and wasteful methods of present-day business enterprise.

Veblen has cogently pointed out the possible profound import of the system of business enterprise, when superimposed upon our mechanical age, for the future of capitalism. Contemporary business enterprise is a system run by people who think only in terms of property rights, laws protecting property rights, and related items, and are interested only in immediate profits. Side by side with the institution of business enterprise has grown up the machine process, upon which business enterprise is completely dependent, but which is conceived and conducted by an entirely different set of persons. These latter are technicians and mechanical-minded folk who think mainly in terms of cause and effect. Veblen predicts that as these two basic elements in our contemporary capitalistic life develop further, the widely different types of persons who control each will become less and less able to understand each other or to talk the same language. The workers, likewise, will not understand the complex system of property rights supporting business enterprise or be able to comprehend or approve the justification for the property rights, privileges, and benefits of the system of business enterprise. As these groups grow further and further apart and understand each other less, the technicians will be highly susceptible to Communistic propaganda, especially if they are reduced to a low standard of living. Since they will not be able to see any justification for a system that they cannot understand but which is obviously oppressing them,

---

[1] *Cf.* L. L. Lorwin and J. A. Flexner, *The American Federation of Labor,* Brookings Institution, 1933.
[2] See J. M. Budish and G. H. Soule, *The New Unionism in the Clothing Industry,* Harcourt, Brace, 1920, and C. E. Zaretz, *The Amalgamated Clothing Workers of America,* Ancon Publishing Co., 1934.

they, along with the working classes, will become a fertile field for the propagation of ideas advocating the overthrow of the system.

VIII. THE EFFECT OF FINANCE CAPITALISM UPON BUSINESS

While it is necessary in any survey of recent economic history to make clear the defects of the philosophy of irresponsible business enterprise, one must, to be fair and accurate, indicate how the major part of such sound business as we once had has been undermined by the attitudes and methods of speculative finance in the era of finance capitalism.

Most attacks on the modern industrial order are lacking in discrimination and emphasis. We frequently assault modern "business," lumping in the term not only actual business pursuits but also speculative finance, which is really the major enemy of legitimate business. It is quite true, as we have just pointed out in preceding pages, that modern business enterprise leaves much to be desired. Nevertheless, it has been able to do great things for mankind. It has helped to supply us with those products which enable us to live in a manner different from early man. Modern business may be unscientific, may have exploited inventors, and may be harsh on labor. But, after all, its creations, even though they might have been much better achieved by the full use of technology, are the highest of man's economic achievements.[1] That they may prove self-destructive is another matter.

With finance it is a different story, but even here we are in danger of indiscriminate abuse. Legitimate banking, which supplies the credit machinery for modern business, renders an indispensable service to modern industrial life. Without it, large-scale business, with its increased efficiency and productivity, could not exist.

Banking and finance, which should be the servant of business, unfortunately have become its master in the United States. The furnishing of credit for business has become incidental and subordinate to speculative exploitation.[2]

A brief summary of some characteristic operations of finance capitalism will serve to illustrate its fundamental antagonism to sound business practice. The formula of the customary procedure of finance capitalism, with minor variations in individual cases, seems to be essentially the following:[3]

A new enterprise is proposed. There is little or no fundamental analysis of whether this enterprise is needed to serve the community. No serious study is made of whether society is already amply served, be the new enterprise a power plant, a shoe factory, or a transcontinental railroad. Rather, the only question raised is whether the securities of the proposed corporation can be floated successfully and profitably. If they can, the bankers get behind the proposal and market the securities at a handsome profit to themselves and with no serious concern as to how much water is thrown into the initial capitalization.

---

[1] *Cf.* Dobb, *op. cit.*
[2] *Cf.* Bonbright and Means, *op. cit.*, Chap. IV, and Flynn, *Security Speculation.*
[3] For an excellent clinical case history illustrating the following brief summary, see Max Lowenthal, *The Investor Pays,* Knopf, 1933, and the excellent review by G. C. Means in the New York *Times,* June 25, 1933. See also Bonbright and Means, *op. cit.*, pp. 343-84. For a defense of the policies of the big bankers, see N. S. B. Gras, "Do We Need Private Bankers?" (New York *Times*), *Current History,* August, 1933.

Then the actual plant or transportation system, as the case may be, is built at an unnecessarily high cost, the banking insiders often profiting through business or financial connections with construction and supply companies. After the original construction is over and business starts, we have a period of gross mismanagement and extravagance. Much of this is due to pressure placed upon the corporation by directors who in one way or another can profit more by such mismanagement than by legitimate and proper profits to themselves or to stockholders. They own but a small portion of stock, but get all of the proceeds of exploitation from the inside. Not even the insistence of the stockholders upon dividends can adequately check this tendency. Moreover, the stockholders are often kept in the dark until a receivership is inevitable.

Enough mismanagement makes a receivership plausible. The insiders and their bankers get together and decide upon the steps to be taken. Security-holders are usually lulled into a false sense of confidence lest they become panicky and take action that would delay or frustrate the plans of the controlling clique. A friendly judge is sought who will appoint receivers and committees favorable to those directing the reorganization. The host of small investors are then saddled with great losses while the insiders are enabled to own or control the new concern at relatively small cost. The little investor has only a substantial or total loss to show for his hard-earned and optimistically intrusted funds.[1]

In the meantime, from construction to reorganization, the service of the concern to the public has been a matter of incidental import compared to the financial profit that the interested insiders might make from underwriting, construction, mismanagement, and reorganization. Likewise, the value of the stock on the market—which should be determined by prudent investment and earning power—is actually mainly controlled by manipulations on the stock exchange, which is itself supported and made possible by the speculative bankers.

Launch, mismanage, wreck, and reorganize are, then, quite literally the slogans of finance capitalism. In between launching and wrecking, as high dividends as possible are secured. Hence wage cuts and other savings at the expense of mass purchasing power are favored. Professor Ripley has summarized the outcome very trenchantly: that "a multitude of people—a horde of bewildered investors—has little left in the world but ashes and aloes. These are all that remain of the precious fruits of years of self-denial and of hard labor. A raid upon the thrift and industry which lie at the very roots of our orderly civilization and culture has been, and still is, under way. This is becoming steadily more and more apparent as we set about clearing up the slash after the great timber cut of 1929." [2]

The inevitable result of the application of the methods of speculative finance to American business was the general paralysis of our economic order that set in during the autumn of 1929. The various ways in which finance capitalism has all but ruined American business can be briefly summarized.

---

[1] That this analysis of the nature of the operations of finance corporation capitalism is not overdrawn is evident from such careful works as those by Lowenthal, Berle and Means, Flynn, Wormser, and others. But even more cogent is the reported observation of Paul D. Cravath, one of the greatest of corporation lawyers, that in twenty years he has witnessed over half of the important American corporations pass through receivership.

[2] Ripley, "Our Corporate Revolution," *loc. cit.*

It induces the public to regard the securities of corporations as paper to be used in institutionalized gambling on the stock exchange. Attention is concentrated on the possibility of speculative profits in financial manipulation rather than upon the assurance of steady and permanent earnings on bona-fide capitalization.

Industry has been further placed in jeopardy through the tendency of finance capitalism to encourage excessive investment in plants. Money may be made for a time through floating securities of new companies, even though the field may be already overcrowded with producers. The final result, however, is overproduction, glutted markets, factories abandoned or running on part time, and other symptoms of industrial decline. Similarly, with real estate, finance capitalism encourages building out of all relationship to actual needs. Banks and investment companies can make large immediate profits selling mortgage bonds on new structures, even though these buildings when erected may have few or no tenants and will soon pass into bankruptcies and receiverships, placing the owners of these bonds in a position to endure heavy or total losses.

Finance capitalism has all but wrecked our transportation systems. In its early phases it promoted overinvestment in canals. Then came the fifty-year period in which railroads were viewed more as gambling machines than as transportation systems. But little or nothing was learned from the disastrous experience of the railroads with finance capitalism. The same methods were applied on a grander and more disastrous scale to our rising and essential electric utility industry, with results well illustrated by the collapse of the Insull interests in 1932. Insull was only one example. We have already noted how the converting of banks into adjuncts of speculative finance helped on the largest epidemic of bank failures in the history of the modern world.[1] The investment banks have also floated more than $10,000,000,000 worth of foreign bonds, many of which have defaulted on interest, principal, or both,[2] causing heavy losses to investors and reducing the purchasing power of the masses.[3]

Most fundamental of all, probably, is this antagonism of finance capitalism to the provision of that mass purchasing power upon which the very existence of the capitalistic system depends.[4] The speculative profits of finance capitalism are almost invariably derived by methods and from sources that deplete mass purchasing power. Finance capitalism takes the cream of the profits off every enterprise that it finances, "siphons" out the earnings and resources of these businesses, and drains the proceeds into the pockets of the bankers, underwriters, and security manipulators, to the disadvantage of wage-earners in these industries and enterprises. It also gouges the public in its rôle as security-holders and all too frequently leaves the industry or organization "financed" unable to function efficiently for any considerable period of time. It need hardly be pointed out that those who get these exploitative profits are the least needy class in society and contribute next to nothing to mass purchasing power. Conspicuous also has been the depression of the farmers, induced in many

---

[1] See above, pp. 792 ff.
[2] Cf. C. A. Beard and G. H. E. Smith, *The Idea of National Interest*, Macmillan, 1934, p. 556.
[3] Cf. Winkler, *Foreign Bonds: An Autopsy*, and Lawrence Dennis, *Is Capitalism Doomed?* Harper, 1933.
[4] Cf. G. W. Mallon, *Bankers vs. Consumers*, Day, 1933.

ways by finance capitalism,[1] as well as the antagonistic policies to labor such as wage cuts and antiunionism that make it difficult for the laborers to assure for themselves income sufficient for effective consumption.

Extremely ominous and difficult to reduce is the staggering burden of debt that finance capitalism has piled up as a result of its encouragement of overconstruction, its promotion of installment buying, and its backing of wildcat speculation.[2] It is quite possible that these lines of action will pull down the whole capitalistic system unless a very extensive "write-off" is effected—something that our finance capitalists will resist to the last.[3]

The long-term public and private debts of the United States amount to $134,000,000,000. The short-term debts at the end of 1932 amounted to approximately $104,000,000,000. This makes a total of $238,000,000,000. Obviously there is only a very slight margin between debts and total national wealth. The latter is variously estimated by experts today as somewhere between $200,000,000,000 and $300,000,000,000. It is therefore quite apparent that far the greater proportion of our national wealth is pledged to meet credit obligations incurred in the past. This leaves precious little surplus with which to meet the future.

Another important item to be considered is the relationship of debt to production. The capitalistic system is relatively safe only when there is a definite and fixed one-to-one relationship between the growth of debt and the growth of production. In his ultra-scientific volume on *Debt and Production*,[4] an able engineer, Mr. Bassett Jones, points out that this safe relationship has not existed in the United States since 1910. The curve of production growth has fallen off ever since that time, while the curve of debt growth has increased at an alarming rate during this same period. The result is that today our productive system cannot support more than one-sixth of the capital claims that have been piling up against it for the last twenty years. The implications of this situation are staggering. As Stuart Chase points out in commenting on Mr. Jones's book:

> Five-sixths of your accustomed profits, interest, rents, royalties, gentlemen, can no longer be counted upon; five-sixths of your principal, accordingly, in the form of stocks, bonds, leaseholds, mortgages, notes, has no real value, and, caught in the relentless laws of physical production, can have none in the calculable future. What all the radicals, revolutionists, defamers of capitalism, have been quite unable to do, the Second Law of Thermodynamics has done. Your property has been all but confiscated; you are left with dead paper in your vaults.[5]

These considerations, which are only the more conspicuous of those which could be adduced as illustrating the disastrous effects of finance capitalism, make it apparent that there is substantial validity in the charge that speculative finance is surely, and not so slowly, running the capitalistic system on the rocks. The subordination of speculative finance to the benefit of the industrialists and the business men by itself might not save capitalism, but it would cer-

---

[1] *Cf.* H. E. Gaston, *The Nonpartisan League*, Harcourt, Brace, 1920, Chap. III.
[2] *Cf.* E. R. A. Seligman, *The Economics of Instalment Selling*, Harper, 1927, 2 vols.
[3] *Cf.* Evans Clark and G. B. Galloway, eds., *The Internal Debts of the United States*, Macmillan, 1933.
[4] Day, 1933.
[5] Chase, "An Engineer's Report on the Recovery," *Common Sense*, September, 1933, pp. 14-15.

tainly be a step in the right direction. The system is unquestionably doomed if financial control by speculative bankers is perpetuated.

This basic theme is developed persuasively by D. C. Coyle in his interesting booklet, *The Irrepressible Conflict: Business versus Finance:*

> It is evident that in attempting to free itself of the poison of overbuilding, business is pulling the beard of that man-eating ogre Finance. It is only beginning to be dimly recognized that in a plenty economy there is and must be between the interests of business and those of finance an irrepressible conflict. The normal processes of finance are poisonous to business. Finance causes instability. One way to make financial profits is to wait until business starts to be profitable, and then lend money to someone to set up a competing plant. Then when everybody naturally goes bankrupt, the lender gets the property, and if recovery ever does take place, he is in on the ground floor. Business pays the cost. Another way is to buy securities when they threaten to go up, and hold them so that they will go up, and sell them when they threaten to go down, and sell short so as to help them go down. Business pays the cost. A third way to get financial profits is to set up an investment trust or a holding company that is so complicated that the small investor cannot see just how he is to be rooked. When his investment is gone, he becomes a poor customer for legitimate business. A fourth way is to take a commission from a foreign government for selling bonds to people who ask their banker for disinterested advice.[1] In any case, business pays the costs either in rising overhead or falling sales or both. Business needs stability to prosper, finance gets its profits from instability. . . . Over this conflict of interest there must be a battle, because so long as finance dominates business both are headed for the precipice, and finance will not loose its grip without a fight. The question whether they will go over the edge together will be settled by whether business has the vitality to rouse itself and muster the power to reduce finance to its proper place as the servant of production. . . .
>
> About one more shot of that kind of thing [the poison administered by finance to business before 1929], and it is hard to see how it will be possible to avoid the final collapse of our social order. The crossroads of history will be the place where we do or do not develop means for keeping money out of Wall Street and making it travel up and down Main Street where it belongs. No country has ever got out of a depression without some kind of expansion. The important thing to keep in mind now is that if the expansion is applied to the buying end it will not necessarily kill the patient.[2]

These are sound and relevant observations, provided one constantly remembers that when Mr. Coyle speaks of finance he means present-day speculative finance. No sane person can well question the enormous service rendered by sound financial processes and institutions to valid business.

The subordination of business to finance is admirably illustrated by the statistics concerning the profits of financial speculation, of financial corporations, and of ordinary business in the United States from 1923 to 1929—a period of supposedly vast prosperity. During these years the profits of nonfinancial corporations increased by only 14 per cent, while the profits of financial corporations increased by over 177 per cent. Speculative profits increased by no less than 300 per cent. Moreover, in 1928, the last full year of prosperity, the combined speculative and financial profits totaled much more than all the

---

[1] See Salter, *Recovery*, pp. 116-18 (Coyle's note). [2] Coyle, *op. cit.*, pp. 37 ff.

THE EFFECT OF FINANCE CAPITALISM UPON BUSINESS

profits of productive business. In that year, speculative profits amounted to $4,807,000,000, profits of financial corporations to $2,444,000,000, and profits of nonfinancial corporations to $5,192,000,000. Therefore, the much-heralded prosperity of the Coolidge era did not represent great gains for substantial business, but consisted primarily in the gambling and quasi-gambling accumulations of predatory finance. The chart on page 828 gives us a graphic presentation of this situation, which tells at a glance the story of American capitalism under financial dominion, even in what is conventionally regarded as a very prosperous period.[1]

A very disastrous influence of finance capitalism upon business in the way of lessening the relative income of productive business, cutting down income to producers—farmers and industrialists alike—decreasing the income going into wages and salaries, increasing living-costs and thus reducing mass purchasing power, is to be detected in the amazing increase of overhead costs since the World War. Overhead costs comprise all charges of any sort involved in moving goods from the producers—factories or farms—to the ultimate consumers and in distributing them to the latter. The total cost of operating all of our national industrial plant in 1917 was approximately equal to the cost of operating it in 1932. Yet the cost of overhead increased by no less than 230 per cent during those fifteen years. In 1917, when producers received $1 for raising or manufacturing consumers' goods, those who were engaged in the various overhead operations received $1 also. Today, for every dollar that goes to producers no less than $2.30 goes into overhead charges. For example, every consumer pays 62 cents out of every dollar of food costs for overhead charges on this food.

This increase of overhead has been due in large part to the creation of holding companies and the like that render little or no practical service in producing goods or in moving them to the consumers, but which do impose a vast charge upon society in order to pay dividends to these companies. In handling foods, there are great holding companies which demand dividends without making any substantial contribution to the distribution of the products. They are superimposed on the lesser corporations that perform the actual distributive services. They "milk" the latter of their proceeds and pass on the burden to society. As an instance, farmers producing milk in central New York have been paid as low as 2 cents a quart for milk delivered at the railroad, while the consumers of this milk in New York City, three hundred miles away, paid 14 cents a quart for it. The same condition prevails in other industries, notoriously in the field of the electric utilities, where holding companies "fleece" the operating companies and prevent the latter from producing and selling electric current at anything like as low a price as would otherwise be possible and profitable. As we have already seen, these holding companies dominate all phases of American economic life and add their parasitic charges to create the paralyzing overhead costs of today. The manner in which this came about through the propaganda and methods of finance capitalism has been very clearly summarized by Professor Walter Rautenstrauch:

> In 1918 the managers and workers of your national plant learned a new technique of operation. They discovered how to divert people's free money and savings into

[1] *Cf.* Corey, *The Decline of American Capitalism*, Chap. XXI.

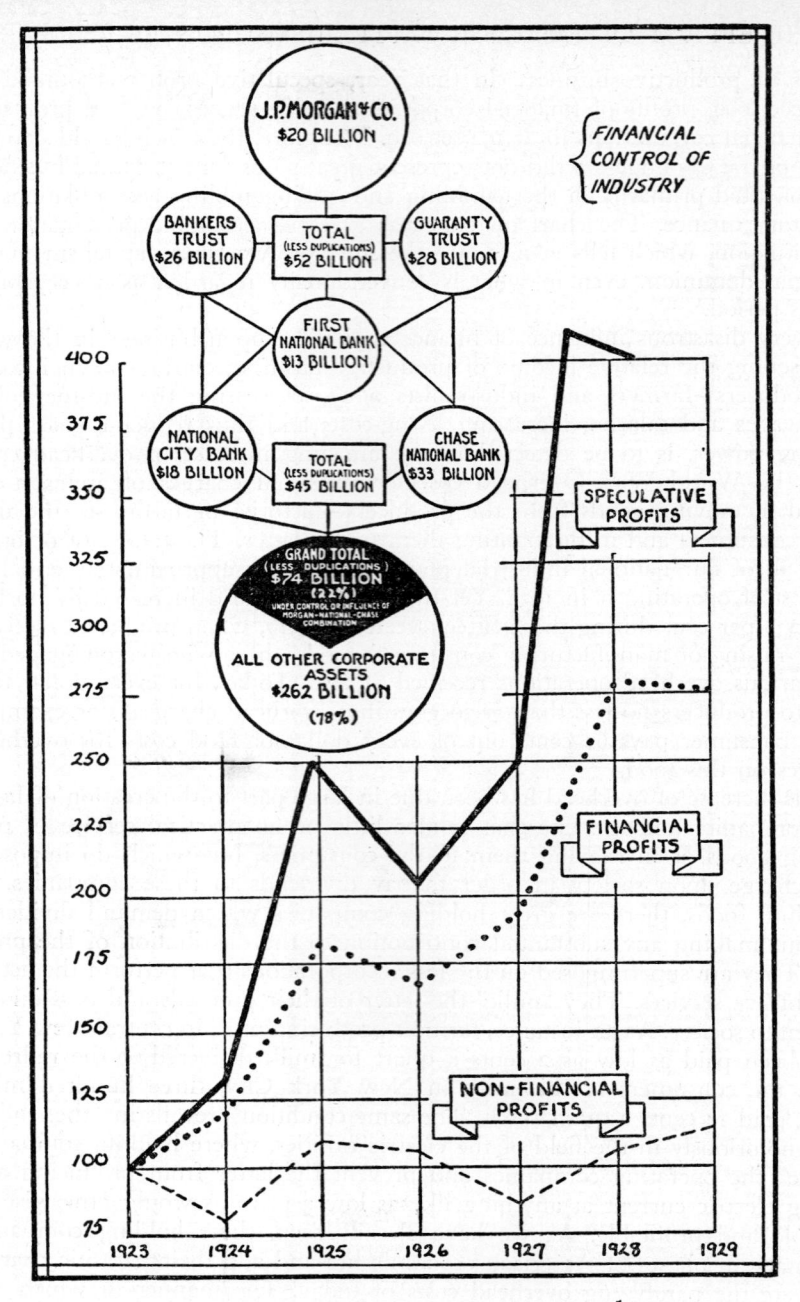

THE DYNAMICS OF FINANCE CAPITAL [1]

[1] From Corey, *op. cit.* This chart shows the concentration of financial and industrial power in the House of Morgan. It further indicates that the so-called prosperity of the Coolidge era was based upon speculative and exploitive financial profits and not on sound and substantial industrial growth and well-being—that is, how finance capitalism subordinated industrial capitalism.

stocks and bonds and first mortgages and similar securities. In that year, we began to create a nation, not of consumers, but of investors and speculators.

It began with the Liberty Loan drive. Tens of thousands of men and women turned bond salesmen. Patriotic citizens by the hundreds of thousands poured money into bonds so that your national plant could wage war to make the world safe for democracy and international bankers. The technique worked perfectly. Then along came other drives. Investment bankers began underwriting securities by the carload. Americans were urged to invest money in German railroads and Florida shore-front lots; in Texas oil-wells and Indiana retail stores; in anything and everything, from shoe stores to republics, from rubber tires to Rivieras-by-the-sea.

The rest is ancient history. For our purposes, however, let us see how the rise of the Great American Sucker affected the national economy and the habits of the workers within it. As more and more investors and speculators were created, the overhead in banking and finance rose apace. Indeed, production looked with envy upon prosperous bond and stock salesmen, investment bankers, busy brokers, and pompous financiers. Many a youth recently out of college earned upwards of $50,000 yearly through commissions on stock and bond sales alone. And so on. More and more the life of the overhead worker—the tradesman, the banker, the cashier, the salesman—seemed the life of Riley. There was little glamour, and there were certainly diminishing returns, in the life of the producer.

From 1918 on, then, more and more workers tended to attach themselves to the national payroll by rendering services of doubtful value, while fewer people produced the things by which we live. Between 1918 and 1928 loans and investments of commercial banks rose from $32,316,600,000 to $58,364,300,000. During the same period, the number of workers employed in overhead services rose from 15,360,000 in 1918 to 20,500,000 in 1929. But the number of producers remained almost constant, rising from 25,023,000 in 1918 to only 25,900,000 in 1928. Furthermore, the producers took in very little more money during the boom period, even though the total national income was steadily increasing, while the income of the overhead group increased still faster. Overhead got the money from 1918 to 1928 faster and in larger volume than the workers without whose labor we would starve, go naked, and die of exposure. Overhead is still getting the money. The situation has become a national habit.[1]

Professor Rautenstrauch has indicated the enviable condition that would exist if overhead costs had not been inflated in the period since 1917:

1. We would need 12,300,000 more producers;
2. And no more overheaders;
3. And an increase in the producers' income of 56 per cent over its 1932 level;
4. And an increase in the farmers' income of 216 per cent over its 1932 level.[2]

It is obvious that this inordinate increase of overhead charges has played a large part in causing the economic depression, decreasing the purchasing power of the mass of Americans, and bringing capitalistic society to its knees. There will be little chance of rehabilitating capitalism until this condition is corrected. It is true, of course, that there are many engaged in overhead services who receive modest incomes and contribute to the purchasing power of the country. But the majority of the overhead goes into earnings of relatively parasitic supercorporations and holding companies and swells the incomes of the rich at the top, who neither can nor will spend any large proportion of their in-

[1] Rautenstrauch, *Who Gets the Money?* pp. 43-45.   [2] *Ibid.*, p. 48.

comes. Moreover, every dollar added to overhead costs reduces by that amount the purchasing power of the whole community, which has to pay these charges in the rôle of the consuming public.

Those who believe that finance capitalism is likely to change its spots without rigorous governmental intervention and control will do well to go back and read some of the testimony given before the Pujo Committee in 1912. This congressional investigation of the money power took place almost a generation ago, but we find that the spirit was much the same as it is today. There was no admission of wrong—or even of power. The denial of elementary facts and logic by the elder Morgan and his partners approached the point of insolence.

Mr. Samuel Untermyer, counsel for the committee, clearly demonstrated that the Morgan interests and their affiliates then controlled some $22,500,000,000 in resources. They dominated great banks and trust companies. They controlled ten great railroad systems with 50,000 miles of track. They held dominion over five great industrial corporations—United States Steel, General Electric, American Telephone and Telegraph, International Harvester, and Western Union. They held interlocking directorates in 47 great corporations with aggregate resources of over $10,000,000,000.

For many years the House of Morgan had struggled hard to attain this position. The story is told in Lewis Corey's admirable history of the Morgan interests.[1] It would naturally be supposed that this struggle was carried on because the elder Morgan and his associates believed that it would bring them power and material advantage. Yet Morgan, who had for a generation bullied his associates and rivals,[2] denied that he possessed the slightest power in American economic life. The following is an excerpt from the 1912 testimony on this point:

UNTERMYER: When a man has got vast power, such as you have—you admit you have, do you not?
MORGAN: I do not know it, sir.
UNTERMYER: You do not feel it at all?
MORGAN: No, I do not feel it at all. . . .
UNTERMYER: Your power in any direction is entirely unconscious to you, is it not?
MORGAN: It is, sir; if that is the case.
UNTERMYER: You do not think you have any power in any department of industry in this country?
MORGAN: I do not.
UNTERMYER: Not the slightest?
MORGAN: Not the slightest.[3]

Mr. Morgan argued that while it was possible to gain a monopolistic control over business, transportation and the like, nobody could attain a monopoly over money and credit in the United States. He contended that the speculative spirit, even selling stocks short, is a "principle of life." He held that we cannot get along without it. On this point Mr. Untermyer asked him: "Why can you

[1] *The House of Morgan*, Pt. VIII.
[2] *Cf. Ibid.*, pp. 293 ff., and J. K. Winkler, *Morgan the Magnificent*, Vanguard Press, 1930, Chaps. VI-XIV.
[3] Corey, *op. cit.*, p. 403. *Cf.* top of chart on p. 828 for the facts.

THE EFFECT OF FINANCE CAPITALISM UPON BUSINESS

not get along without a man's selling something he has not got in the way of stocks?" Mr. Morgan answered, "That is a principle of life, I think."

In a prepared statement the Morgan firm denied that there was any danger in the concentration of money power:

> All power—physical, intellectual, financial or political—is dangerous in evil hands. If Congress were to fall into evil hands the results might be deplorable. But it seems to us as little likely that the citizens of this country will fill Congress with rascals as it is that they will entrust the leadership of their business and financial affairs to a set of clever rogues.[1]

As Lewis Corey observes: "The comparison limps. There is some popular control over Congress but none over the centralized financial mechanism presided over by J. Pierpont Morgan."[2] At least, we may emphasize the point that rascals in Congress have not outnumbered rogues in finance.

Henry P. Davison, in 1912 the leading Morgan partner, held that the vast financial dominion of J. P. Morgan gave the firm no advantage whatever. Mr. Untermyer asked him: "You recognize, do you not, that there is a great advantage in having the entrée and the interest in these banks and representation on the board; or do you think there is no advantage whatever?" Mr. Davison answered: "Absolutely no advantage at all."[3]

The culmination of the testimony was this:

"In other words," said Mr. Untermyer, "you know that J. P. Morgan & Co. can do no wrong?" Mr. Davison replied: "I know that J. P. Morgan & Co. could do no wrong if their endeavors and the circumstances permitted them to do as they wanted to do."[4]

Except from Mr. Otto H. Kahn and, to a lesser extent, from Winthrop D. Aldrich, there was no greater evidence of contrition or of a resolution to reform in 1933 than there had been twenty years before at the time of the Pujo investigation. Mr. Ferdinand Pecora, counsel of the committee in 1933, brought out at the senatorial investigation of banking methods facts even more disconcerting than those adduced by Mr. Untermyer. But the great financial overlords, with these few exceptions, defended their activities and policies. Their spirit is well illustrated by the attitude of Mr. Clarence Dillon, head of Dillon, Read & Co. The conduct of his company was regarded by many as rather more exceptionable and dubious than that of most other great investment houses. Yet Mr. Dillon, at the end of the investigation, blandly stated that he would repeat his behavior and methods if he had an opportunity. This is well revealed in the following account published by the Scripps-Howard newspapers:[5]

> The story of Dillon, Read and Company's financial operations was completed today in the records of the Senate banking committee with a final defense from Clarence Dillon, head of the investment house, and biting criticism and solemn warning from multimillionaire Senator James F. Couzens.

---

[1] Corey, *op. cit.*, p. 408.
[2] *Ibid.*
[3] *Ibid.*, pp. 399-400.
[4] *Ibid.*, p. 400. As an illustration of the seeming incapacity of the great bankers to recognize the social import of their doings, see T. W. Lamont, *Henry P. Davison: The Record of a Useful Life*, Harper, 1933.   [5] Oct. 14, 1933.

Professing pride in the record of his company, which since the war has issued nearly $4,000,000,000 of securities, the financier said he would pursue again with only minor changes the methods by which he gained control of huge sums of capital by a very small outlay in his investment trusts.

Going further, he defended the sale of large blocks of stock in the investment trusts by his partners in a syndicate operation that netted considerable profits—an operation in which he did not participate personally.

At this point what had been a sort of love feast between committee members and Mr. Dillon was interrupted by the wealthy Michigan Republican. Mr. Couzens addressed himself to the financier's formal statement that confidence is needed for new investments. Mr. Dillon had pointed out that $3,000,000,000 of industrial refinancing must be undertaken during the next three years, aside from new capital investment.

"Can you expect to gain public confidence in view of the committee's disclosures?" the Senator inquired.

Unperturbed, the financier nodded.

"I think if you are of this viewpoint after all this testimony you are in very grave error as to the return of public confidence and that you will have continued difficulty, if not utmost impossibility, of accomplishment of a refunding of these securities," Mr. Couzens continued.

"In other words, I cannot conceive of public confidence being returned to investment houses after the disclosure of Dillon, Read in the investigation of its foreign and domestic securities."

"I am sorry, Senator Couzens, that you feel that way," Mr. Dillon interjected.

"I don't want this hearing to end with a mere exchange of flowers when I feel the matter is much more serious than that," Senator Couzens continued. "You can often do something that externally looks good and you can exhibit it with pride but sometimes when you analyze the methods adopted to accomplish that result you may not be so proud of the methods as of the accomplishment."

"We are, in our case," Mr. Dillon said.

"I expected you would be, because we never expected to penetrate Wall Street," concluded the Senator.

The ramifications of finance capitalism have, of course, spread beyond the realm of corporation finance and have permeated every phase of our life. They have profoundly affected government finance, and for more than eight years one of the most successful and extreme practitioners of the principles of finance capitalism, Mr. Andrew W. Mellon, was Secretary of the Treasury and the most influential figure in the national administration. The federal government depends in considerable degree upon the great banks to float government bonds. Finance capitalism was able for years to dictate our federal tax policy, leaving those notorious loopholes for the rich which scandalized the nation during Mr. Pecora's investigation in 1933. The bankers have exerted pressure on the government in the case of our intervention abroad, especially in our investments in Latin America above the equator. Finance capitalism has been the chief force behind contemporary imperialism since 1900. It has been the main factor in urging reduction or cancellation of Allied war debts, so that Entente credit would be improved and new loans could be floated by the banks. The federal banking system has been deeply influenced by the speculative spirit of finance capitalism. The Federal Reserve system worked hand-in-glove with the bankers

THE EFFECT OF FINANCE CAPITALISM UPON BUSINESS

who placed great sums at the disposal of stockbrokers from 1926 to 1929 and encouraged the great orgy of stock gambling that rocked the nation when it collapsed in the latter year. Finance capitalism thoroughly dominated President Hoover's plan of recovery through the Reconstruction Finance Corporation. Bankers have also helped to finance state governments, which need banking support for their security issues even more than does the federal government. Through their control over the electric utilities of the country the bankers exert a powerful pressure on state politics, well illustrated by the utility scandal in the New York State Legislature in the spring of 1934. Especially were cities encouraged by the bankers in their reckless spending in the decade after the World War. In the end, many municipal bonds seriously depreciated and many cities were on the verge of bankruptcy. When hard times came the banks retrenched, curtailed their credit to city governments, demanded the most rigorous economy from city governments whose original extravagance the banks had light-heartedly encouraged, and got a strangle hold on impoverished city governments. This situation was not limited to smaller municipalities. The metropolis of the world, New York City, took its orders from the leading bankers of the city for several years during the depression following 1929.

The effect on education is also easily discernible. There has been an effort directly to influence teaching in the schools and colleges, most notoriously the propaganda carried on by the great electric utility concerns in our educational institutions.[1] But more often the influence is indirect and financial. In their demands for retrenchment in governmental expenditures, educational institutions are the first victims of the bankers' ax. Education appears to finance capitalism to be the least essential phase of modern life, and the teaching profession is too imperfectly organized to defend itself. The cutting of educational budgets by our finance-dominated states and cities since 1929 was one of the most deplorable scandals in all educational history.[2] Sometimes the results of finance capitalism go beyond curtailing educational income and result in complete cessation of pay to teachers, as was the case for many months in the second largest city in the United States. Public libraries, as a phase of adult education, likewise suffer grievously. These adverse effects of finance capitalism not only touch publicly supported institutions of learning, but even the privately endowed colleges and universities, which depend for their income mainly on corporate stocks and bonds, especially the latter, and are hit directly by those methods of finance capitalism which rob corporations from the inside, depress dividends, jeopardize interest payments, and bring receiverships.

IX. RACKETEERING AND ORGANIZED CRIME

The "something-for-nothing" ideals of the age of finance capitalism have borne fruit in an appalling development of organized crime and racketeering, obvious by-products of the system. Crime represents antisocial action clearly beyond the pale of the law and directly punishable by the force of the state.

[1] Cf. Thompson, *Confessions of the Power Trust*, Chaps. XXXVI-XL, and E. H. Gruening, *The Public Pays; a Study of Power Propaganda*, Vanguard Press, 1931, Chaps. II-V.
[2] Cf. Rex David, *Schools and the Crisis*, International Pamphlets, No. 39, 1934.

Racketeering embraces a wide variety of practices on the border line between crime and shady business practices. It rests primarily upon fear, and consists of diversified forms of extortion of money without any corresponding service rendered. Contemporary crime and racketeering have derived both inspiration and technique from certain business and financial practices of the last generation.[1]

The basis for our crime orgy was created quite inevitably by the developments of the last twenty years. It is a law of social psychology, formulated by Gabriel Tarde and others years ago, that the socially inferior tend to ape the socially superior. The upper classes capitulated pretty thoroughly to the prevailing something-for-nothing psychology of the past era. Freebooting in railroads, banks, utilities, receiverships, and the like became shockingly frequent.

It was inevitable that, sooner or later, a process of imitation would set in among the criminally inclined of the lower classes.

Many of the practices of finance capitalism have approached the border line of criminality.[2] This fact was recognized by President Franklin D. Roosevelt in his message to Congress on January 3, 1934:

. . . we have been shocked by many notorious examples of injuries done our citizens by persons or groups who have been living off their neighbors by the use of methods either unethical or criminal.

In the first category—a field which does not involve violation of the letter of our laws—practices have been brought to light which have shocked those who believed that we were in the past generation raising the ethical standards of business. . . .

In the other category, crimes of organized banditry, cold-blooded shooting, lynching, and kidnapping have threatened our security.

Crime has existed from primitive society, but the crime that is significant today—organized crime and racketeering—is a degenerate offshoot and by-product of finance capitalism. Not only has it derived much from the ethics and psychology of finance capitalism, but many an otherwise honest man has been driven into crime as a result of the inadequate income that finance capitalism has allotted to him.

The ancestors of our racketeers, if they lived in this country, had usually made an honest living conducting shoe-shining parlors, clothes-cleaning establishments, fruit stands, restaurants, and the like or at hard labor on farms, streets, and railroads. The younger generation looked with envy not at the bowed backs and wrinkled brows of their parents, but rather at the achievements of the American buccaneers who had made away with millions, with little service to society. If our usurers of high estate could "get theirs," why should anybody submit to hard labor? So the future racketeers reasoned. They had come to believe, as Courtenay Terrett expresses the idea, that "only saps work." So, for example, instead of cleaning clothes, they start a racket in the clothes-cleaning industry.

About the time this something-for-nothing psychology was making headway with these groups, the Eighteenth Amendment came into force. This provided

---

[1] *Cf.* Myers, *History of the Great American Fortunes*, and Josephson, *op. cit.*
[2] *Cf.* Flynn, *Graft in Business*; and E. D. MacDougall, ed., *Crime for Profit*, Stratford, 1933.

an ideal situation for the budding racketeers. Hardly anything could have been consciously designed better suited to their purposes. Public opinion was almost everywhere divided; in many sections of the country it was very definitely against Prohibition, and not a few regarded the bootleggers as allies in a common cause against this curtailing legislation. Bootlegging fostered other lawless pursuits—the hijacking racket among the "wet" outlaws, rackets in foods, milk, transportation, building construction, and the like. Legal remedy was extremely difficult: crowded dockets, timid witnesses, lenient juries, combined with all the delays and loopholes of the law which the culprits, money in hand, could take advantage of through competent legal advice. The legal profession has much to answer for on this latter score. Professional bondsmen were also an important part of the set-up to circumvent the law.

The depression further stimulated the growth of racketeering, since it threw out of work millions who might otherwise have preferred to earn an honest living. From these millions it was easy to recruit the few thousands needed as the underlings of the master minds of the underworld.

The belief that when Prohibition ended the criminals who made millions in illicit selling of liquor would meekly turn to lawful pursuits was downright naïve. They are already applying their perfected technique to the dope ring, kidnapping, bank robberies, hijacking of legitimate liquor supplies, and the like. And again there are not lacking crafty lawyers all too willing to defend them from the "strong arm of the law."

The combined crime and racket bill has been estimated by the latest competent inquiry to run between $12,000,000,000 and $18,000,000,000 a year.[1] Of this total, the racketeering bill amounts to around $4,000,000,000 to $5,000,000,000. This appalling crime bill is produced primarily by organized criminal gangs and racketeers, for the total depredations of isolated criminals—the lone wolves of the underworld—are slight by comparison. The criminal types of the last generation have all but disappeared. Once the great majority of all crimes, the old thefts and pocket-pickings are now insignificant in their costs, compared to the levies of the organized gangsters. The latter execute a great variety of anti-social acts—bank robberies, train robberies, looting of warehouses, and thefts of securities; the rackets in connection with liquor, dope, food, milk, the building trades, laundries, cleaning and dyeing establishments, garages, taxis, and the like; the use of gunmen in labor troubles; the swindles of the bucket-shop operators; and a host of lesser offenses against life, property, and personal liberty.

The fact that the racketeering underworld is directly linked up with urban political machines and political rings that have a powerful influence in selecting judges and district attorneys makes it relatively difficult to convict these offenders. Further, few dare to testify against them. The racketeers are very useful to politicians in intimidating reformers, stuffing ballot boxes, "repeating" on election day, and intimidating independent voters.[2]

---

[1] The nation's crime bill is best itemized and analyzed by A. B. Reeve, *The Golden Age of Crime*, Mohawk Press, 1931. Our national income in 1933 was $46,800,000,000.
[2] Cf. D. T. Lynch, *Criminals and Politicians: A History of the Racket's Red Glare*, Macmillan, 1933; Fletcher Dobyns, *The Underworld of American Politics*, privately printed, 1932; and Milton Mackaye, *The Tin Box Parade*, McBride, 1934.

X. THE BUSINESS CYCLE

No discussion of the modern business and financial system is complete without at least some reference to the problems of the business cycle, which at the present time seems to present a serious threat to the continuance of the capitalistic order. The phenomena of the business cycle have in recent years claimed the attention of some of the ablest economists and business men, both in the United States and in Europe. But no one seems to have found a completely satisfactory solution to the weighty problems involved.

By the business cycle is meant the more or less rhythmical variations in business activity, which seem ordinarily to pass through four fairly well-defined phases of expansion, boom, collapse, and depression. To describe the course of events very superficially: If we begin our examination at a hypothetical "normal" point [1] in business activity, we find that in the course of several months or perhaps as many years, business enterprises expand, new undertakings are established, production increases, and the volume of credit is multiplied.

As time goes on, the rate of expansion is speeded up and a boom period follows, usually distinguished by rising interest rates, leaping commodity and especially security prices, and a general state of business that can later, if not at the time, be described as "unhealthy." Usually, security prices rise out of all proportion to the earning capacity of the companies that have issued them; enterprises are founded that cannot in the long run be profitably operated; and very often an unsound relationship appears between the production of various types of commodities—goods for consumption as against goods used to produce more goods (machines, factories, and so forth), for instance.

Sooner or later a break occurs, perhaps brought on by some accidental factor. Often the first overt occurrence is the failure of a prominent business or banking firm. Once the process is started, a general liquidation inevitably takes place, involving other failures and large losses to investors in securities and to business men who have bought goods at the prevailing high prices and are forced to sell them in a falling market. Sometimes this collapse is so abrupt and serious as to be called a panic, with banks closed, specie payment suspended, and everyone trying desperately to realize on their assets before a further drop in values.

The crisis is of relatively short duration, but is commonly followed by months or years of depression—deflation—during which the pulse of business activity is slow, prices remain low, production is at a low ebb, unemployment becomes a serious problem, and the demand for credit, even at the prevailingly low interest rates, is sluggish.

Eventually, health is restored to the business organism, production begins to increase, prices begin to rise, and we are back where our description began.

The question of causes is of course paramount. Almost as many causes have been suggested as there have been investigators of the problem. In general, the emphasis is placed upon either external factors, such as the eight-year period in the planet Venus, which figures prominently in the explanation of the mathe-

[1] Hypothetical, for what is "normal," particularly if all phases of the business cycle are well-recognized components of the whole?

matical economist H. L. Moore,[1] or upon internal factors. Among the latter have been stressed: (1) Overproduction, either of consumers' or of capital goods; or the obverse of the same situation, underconsumption due to inadequate mass purchasing power; (2) maladjustments in prices, particularly as between raw materials and finished products; (3) variations in the interest rate, which encourage or discourage business expansion; (4) overcapitalization, involving a tendency to count too much on future growth; (5) a rise in the value of gold, bringing lower prices; and (6) the maladjustments resulting from the operations of the money economy itself, as well as from the contraction and expansion of money. Some economists, like Wesley Clair Mitchell, prefer to explain the cycle in terms of the interaction of several or all of these factors rather than of one or two. It seems to be generally believed that various measures, such as better business forecasting, plans for the stabilization of employment, or those for the control of credit or production, can moderate the full swing of the cycle through all its phases. But the assumption has prevailed widely that some cyclical movement of business is an inevitable accompaniment of an individualistic, competitive economic system, and must therefore be accepted along with the benefits of such a system.

The very serious and widespread depression of 1929 and succeeding years, which followed upon the heels of the postwar economic chaos, has directed more searching attention to this problem of the business cycle. In America, which came out of the war in possession of much of the liquid gold supply of the world, and with its business and financial system greatly stimulated by war opportunities, the ten or fifteen years following Versailles were marked by continued expansion, halted only temporarily by the set-back of 1920-21.

Then came the crash, and the country was plunged into a depression from which only limited signs of recovery have appeared up to the present. Unemployment passed 5,000,000, then 10,000,000, reached 12,000,000, and still continued to increase. Plants stood idle, or operated with reduced personnel which had suffered repeated wage cuts. And yet the real wealth of the country was not vastly different from what it had been at the peak of the boom. Economists, business men, and statesmen agreed that the capitalistic system could not stand repeated shocks of this kind.

Most important of all, voices have been raised to say that the periodic depressions are not inevitable accompaniments of the present economic order, that the economic fatalism which has accepted them is both wrong and dangerous. Forrest Davis makes the claim:

> The practical breakdown[s] of business enterprise ... are laid at the door of the semi-mythical business cycle, mysterious and foreboding, which is likely to descend upon an honest, well-meaning community of traders at any moment and out of clear skies. We maintain ... that the business cycle is not mysterious ... we are brought to the end of a productive period of prosperity invariably when the master traders for profit, enthroned in Wall Street, abuse the credit system of which they know so little; abstract too large a share of the nation's productive income, waste it in speculation, foolish foreign enterprises ... and, finally, overload the industry and thrift of the land with an intolerable burden of debt. ...

---

[1] *Economic Cycles,* Macmillan, 1914, and *Generating Economic Cycles,* Macmillan, 1923. Mention might also be made of Jenks's theory of the effect of sun spots upon terrestrial economic life.

The haphazard organism of capitalistic enterprise, centered in Wall Street, invariably does away with the goose that lays its golden eggs. Periodically, the profitable bird lies dismayingly stiff and spent in Wall Street's dooryard. Periodically—in 1837, 1857, 1873, 1893, 1907 and 1929—the "ruggedly individualistic," unsystematized economic order abruptly has ceased to function.[1]

Furthermore, Mr. Davis asserts that the recovery from these breakdowns is by no means automatic.

Acts of God, but not miracles, saved the floundering traders for profit—bankers, industrialists, promoters, etc.—from their sins in 1842, 1861, 1879, 1897 and 1915. . . .

War, famine, or foreign gold! Those, plus the underlying and God-given fact of an ever-present frontier, boundless deposits of mineral wealth, lush grain, cotton, and grazing land, pulled us out of the pits which greedy, inept and corrupt business enterprise dug for us.[2]

We cannot, therefore, count, according to Mr. Davis, on always coming out of these depressions. He is inclined to agree with Dr. Nicholas Murray Butler, who asserts:

The notion so often advanced here in the United States that we are simply passing through one more natural period of depression and panic from which we shall recover, as we recovered from others that preceded it, is wholly illusory. . . . Those ingenious persons who are drawing graphs and making tables to show when business will return to normal and when prices will rise, following the precedents of those earlier depressions, are wasting their time. Unless we remove the basic causes of this present depression, there is no assurance of any automatic check to it whatever until there comes about a complete paralysis of all business activity.[3]

The chart on page 839, together with its explanatory material, shows the fallacy of the assumed inevitability of the business cycle, of the assertions that economic history repeats itself, and that recovery is always automatic and certain.

Such points of view are encouraging, in that they give us hope of eliminating the worst evils of the business cycle. They are profoundly disturbing, on the other hand, in that they imply that if these defects are not eliminated, the system may break down under them. That this fact is beginning to be widely appreciated is indicated by the number of intellectual and business leaders who have come out in favor of a planned economy to replace the old system.[4] Some rational plan for our economic life seems to be the only way to mitigate effectively the business cycle and still preserve the capitalistic system—if planning and capitalism can be reconciled.

One of the most eloquent spokesmen for this solution to our business problems, Charles A. Beard, says that

[1] Davis, *op. cit.*, pp. 336, 330.
[2] *Ibid.*, pp. 319, 331.
[3] New York *Times*, Apr. 16, 1932; cited in Davis, *op. cit.*, p. 320.
[4] For good examples of this literature, see G. H. Soule, *A Planned Society*, Macmillan, 1932; Sir Norman Angell, *From Chaos to Control*, Century, 1933; and J. G. Frederick, ed., *Readings in Economic Planning*, Business Bourse, 1932.

the problem confronting us is not the simple issue of planning or no planning. The question presents aspects more complex: how much planning, by whom, under whose auspices, and to what ends? Planning there is already, on a large scale, by national, state, and municipal governments, by great corporations, and by individuals with reference to particular opportunities.[1]

Dr. Beard would utilize all those agencies, and would go further in the direction of integration of fundamental industries under federal supervision. He

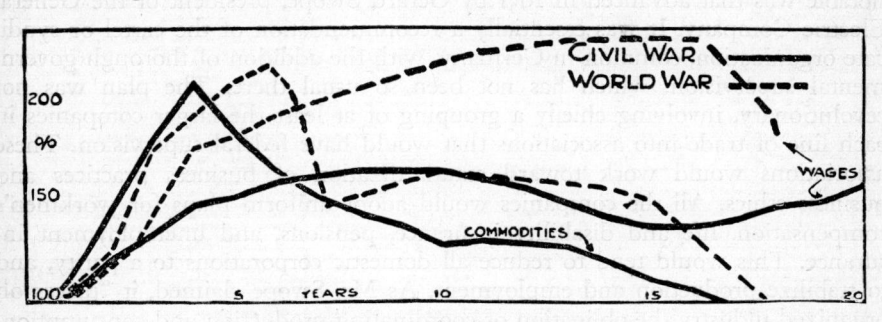

DOES HISTORY REPEAT ITSELF? [2]

According to this chart, compiled by Ford, Bacon & Davis, it does not. After the Civil War we had steadily rising wages and declining prices, which increased the purchasing capacity, improved the standard of living—and new opportunities offered new employment.

After the World War we have had falling prices too, but we have had faster falling wages which reduce the purchasing capacity, lower the standard of living, and diminish employment. Today we have no West to develop nor much of foreign trade and we are burdened with too many plants and railroads already built to think of immediate expansion.

visualizes the stabilization not merely of business, but of consumption through the maintenance of high wages and security for labor. He concludes that

the leadership of the nation has abandoned the philosophy of negation and is putting forward proposals for a better order of economy. To transform these blue-prints into workable plans and to realize them in actuality is the supreme task of this generation.[3]

Everyone agrees that planning is a hazardous and difficult problem. Not everyone will grant that it is feasible. Dr. Abraham Epstein points out[4] that industrial stabilization can exist under the capitalistic system only so long as it is financially profitable. If that is the case, it is fair to assume that, in a society motivated by the search for profit, it has already been carried into effect, so far as present knowledge permits. He further points out that the success of a plan for stabilization in one industry may mean ruin to another that supplies a competitive product. None of the plans thus far worked out for individual

[1] Beard, ed., *America Faces the Future,* Houghton Mifflin, 1932, p. 403.
[2] From W. N. Polakov, "Power as a Factor in Economic Readjustments," American Academy of Political and Social Science, *Annals,* January, 1933, p. 34.
[3] *Ibid.,* p. 410.
[4] "The Stabilization Nonsense," *American Mercury,* January, 1932. *Cf.* also Stolberg and Vinton, *The Economic Consequences of the New Deal.*

enterprises has saved its company from the evils of the depression, claims Dr. Epstein. He concludes that the essence of capitalistic economy is free competition, which is irreconcilable with economic planning.

Whether or not we agree with Dr. Epstein's argument, we are almost forced to accept the alternatives of some method of stabilization or an eventual breakdown of our present economic order. A number of plans were put forward after 1929, set forth with varying degrees of completeness. One of the most notable was that advanced in 1931 by Gerard Swope, president of the General Electric Company. It was essentially a recommendation of the cartel or syndicate organization, common in Germany, with the addition of thorough governmental supervision, which has not been so usual there. The plan was not revolutionary, involving chiefly a grouping of at least the larger companies in each line of trade into associations that would have federal supervision. These associations would work toward standardization of business practices and business ethics. All the companies would adopt uniform plans for workmen's compensation, life and disability insurance, pensions, and unemployment insurance. This would tend to reduce all domestic corporations to a parity, and to stabilize production and employment. As Mr. Swope claimed, it "places on organized industry the obligation of coordinating production and consumption, and of a higher degree of stabilization."[1]

The Swope plan attracted considerable public notice, and various business and political leaders declared themselves more or less completely in accord with its principles. No steps were then taken, however, to carry it into effect. The situation, grave as it was, apparently was not yet grave enough to stir the leaders of the country to effective action in 1931. Also it has been objected by some that this and like plans provide the machinery for complete monopoly and monopolistic prices. It has followed from this that the plans of Mr. Swope and his followers may not have been disinterested. The Swope plan may have had some little influence, however, upon the National Industrial Recovery Act of 1933. Mr. Swope was a leading adviser of President Roosevelt on the matter of industrial organization in 1933.

It is usually supposed that the National Industrial Recovery Act of 1933 was a determined program of economic planning by the federal government, but John T. Flynn has clearly shown that it was, in reality, a surrender by the government and the end of its long fight against the determination of big business to rule itself. Mr. Flynn admirably states the popular conception of the background and authorship of the NRA:

> There is a notion that NRA is the monster child of the Brain Trust. Whenever NRA bares its teeth and puts some little tailor in jail for pressing pants at a discount, the enemies of the Administration point their fingers in scorn and hatred at the flaming red rascal, Tugwell, who is supposed to have sovietized the good old U. S. A. through the NRA. . . .[2]

Mr. Flynn amply demonstrates that nothing could be further from the facts. Aside from Article 7A, the National Industrial Recovery Act was almost

---

[1] *The Swope Plan,* Business Bourse, 1931, pp. 43-44.
[2] Flynn, "Whose Child Is the NRA?" *Harper's Magazine,* September, 1934, p. 385.

exclusively the product of the thinking, policies, and pressure of American big business, particularly the United States Chamber of Commerce. For more than seventy years a powerful element among American business men have sought to regiment American business under their own dominion. Up to 1933 the United States government fought a winning, if waning, fight against this tendency. The NRA did not constitute a victory of the government over business men but was a surrender to them. A specific anticipation of the NRA appeared in the trade-practices codes worked out by the Trade Relations Committee of the United States Chamber of Commerce following 1925. Over forty such codes were adopted. Then in October, 1931, the United States Chamber of Commerce submitted a series of recommendations very similar in spirit to the NRA. About the same time a plan was set forth, as we have seen, by Mr. Gerard Swope which bore a marked resemblance to both the Chamber of Commerce proposals and the later NRA. Thus when Mr. Roosevelt came into office in March, 1933:

> The Chamber of Commerce and what is called Big Business had a program which included (1) modification of the Sherman anti-trust law; (2) self-rule by trade associations under codes of practice to regulate production, prices, and trade practices; (3) authority to shorten hours and establish minimum wages; (4) a long-term plan for setting up unemployment, disability, and old-age insurance.[1]

The National Industrial Recovery Act was in no important way a product of the so-called brain trust, but was rather an outcome of the pressure and guidance of American big business, functioning in part through the United States Chamber of Commerce and in part through Bernard Baruch and his protégé, General Hugh S. Johnson. The president of the Chamber of Commerce declared that it was "a complete victory for the Chamber." Mr. Flynn summarizes the facts:

> In short, with the exception of the collective bargaining provision—which as we have seen was subsequently robbed of much of its original strength—the NRA plan represented almost entirely the influence and ideal of big business men. The share of the Brain Trust in its paternity was microscopic; the share of the Chamber of Commerce and other business interests was predominant. There is little in the present outcry about government's regulating industry. The government has merely given up its long fight against the attempt of industry to regulate itself. It now says to industry: "Very well. You want to govern yourself. Go ahead. We will step aside. We will watch you while you are doing it and keep an eye on you later." That is all. As to the government eye that will be kept busy, General Johnson lost no time in announcing that he would expect the trades to police themselves.[2]

It was not the NRA that big business tried to sabotage, beginning in the summer of 1933. It was mainly the collective bargaining aspects of the Recovery Act and the other phases of the New Deal that interfered with the complete freedom of American business to run itself, and the United States in the bargain. Early in May, 1935, however, the United States Chamber of Commerce repudiated the NRA and declared war on the economic policies of the New Deal.

[1] *Ibid.*, p. 389. [2] *Ibid.*, p. 394.

XI. PROPERTY RIGHTS AND THE SUPREME COURT

The triumph of capitalism brought to its highest development that reverence for private property which first took form in the early days of Protestantism and the Commercial Revolution.

The New Testament set up a famous triad of virtues—faith, hope, and charity—but Paul explicitly stated that the greatest of these is charity. The theory of natural law, lying back of our Declaration of Independence and federal Constitution, created an equally historic triad in the form of the natural rights of man—life, liberty, and property. But the subsequent interpretation of these rights in our courts has elevated property to a preëminent place.

Perhaps as good a statement as was ever made of the philosophy of property rights that has been accepted by the Supreme Court is that made by the famous corporation lawyer Joseph B. Choate, when he argued in 1895 against the constitutionality of the income-tax law:

I believe that there are rights of property here to be protected; that we have a right to come to this Court and ask for this protection, and that this Court has a right, without asking leave of the Attorney General or of any counsel, to hear our plea. The Act of Congress (the income tax law) we are impugning before you is communistic in its purposes and tendencies, and is defended here upon principles as communistic, socialistic—what shall I call them?—populistic as ever have been addressed to any political assembly in the world. . . . I have thought that one of the fundamental objects of all civilized government was the preservation of the rights of private property. I have thought that it was the very keystone of the arch upon which all civilized government rests. . . . If it be true . . . that the passions of the people are aroused on this subject, if it be true that a mighty army of 60,000,000 citizens is likely to be incensed by this decision, it is the more vital to the future welfare of this country that this Court again resolutely and courageously declare, as Marshall did, that it *has* the power to set aside an Act of Congress violative of the Constitution, and that it will not hesitate in executing that power, no matter what the threatened consequences of popular or populistic wrath may be.[1]

One scarcely needs to be reminded that the Court accepted Mr. Choate's reasoning and set the law aside as unconstitutional. It required a constitutional amendment many years later to put the income-tax legislation beyond the reach of the Supreme Court. Whatever attitude the Court may take on property in the future, certainly it is fair and accurate to say that the majority of its members subscribed to Mr. Choate's philosophy from the close of the Civil War to the inauguration of Franklin D. Roosevelt in 1933.

Far more illuminating than any broad generalizations or blanket attacks on the Court is a calm factual statement of (1) just how it has stood, for the most part, like a stone wall in the path of progressive legislation; (2) the processes it makes use of; and (3) the decisions through which it has frustrated liberal and humane legislation.[2]

The foundation of the activities of the Court in obstructing progress is its

---

[1] Cited in Maurice Finkelstein, *The Dilemma of the Supreme Court: Is the N.R.A. Constitutional?* Day, 1933, p. 24.

[2] *Cf.* E. S. Corwin, *The Twilight of the Supreme Court,* Yale University Press, 1934.

PROPERTY RIGHTS AND THE SUPREME COURT

assertion of the right to set aside federal and state legislation as unconstitutional. This right it first claimed in 1803 in the case of *Marbury* vs. *Madison*. For a hundred and thirty years it has used this power with ever increasing frequency. This means that whenever the Court believes that a law does not square with the Constitution, as interpreted for the moment by five out of the nine judges on the bench, that law is declared invalid and of no account. Until 1886, however, the Court was relatively restricted in its field of operation in declaring laws unconstitutional. It had to be shown that the law in question clearly violated some explicit provision of the Constitution. Shortly after the Civil War a judicial perversion of one of the Reconstruction amendments gave the Court much greater leeway.

In order to protect the Negro against a return to servility, the Fourteenth Amendment had been added to the Constitution. It directed that no state should deprive any person of life, liberty, or property without due process of law. A drive was made at once to get corporations admitted as "persons" under the meaning of the Fourteenth Amendment.[1] Success came in 1886 in the Santa Clara County case, when the Court unanimously decided to include corporations in its interpretation of the Fourteenth Amendment and "due process of law." This let down the bars. As "due process of law" is quite literally anything the Supreme Court decides it to be at any moment, there is no limit whatever to its power to invalidate legislation. Whatever runs counter to the economic, social, or political philosophy of five judges can be set aside quite casually, no matter what the popular demand for the measures or what their logical legality may be. Professor E. S. Corwin has observed that

"due process of law" is not a regular concept at all, but merely a roving commission of judges to sink whatever legislative craft may appear to them, from the standpoint of the vested interests, to be of piratical tendency.[2]

With the exception of an occasional liberal, such as Harlan, Holmes, Brandeis, Stone, and Cardozo, who gets on the Supreme Court bench, the judges are almost invariably reactionary lawyers who have long been in the service of great corporate interests. Their experience, contacts, and outlook are those of business men and financiers who wish to preserve the old order intact.[3] The vague and broad character of the "due process of law" test of constitutionality gives them, as we have seen, almost unrestricted power to quash any law that conflicts with their conservative philosophy.

Let us look at some representative examples of the use of this power of the Supreme Court to set aside laws as unconstitutional and thus block the path to orderly progress through legislative action. The Supreme Court became a particularly aggressive champion of capitalism about the time we reached monopoly capitalism. The liberals, fearing the power of great mergers and monopolies to control prices at their will, endeavored to check this process by

---

[1] In his *Journal of the Joint Committee of Fifteen on Reconstruction, 39th Congress, 1865-67*, Longmans, 1914, Professor B. B. Kendrick has shown that this was the intention of some of those who drafted the Amendment.
[2] Cited by Max Farrand, *The Development of the United States*, Houghton Mifflin, 1918, p. 272.
[3] *Cf.* Zechariah Chafee, Jr., "The Economic Determination of Judges," in his *The Inquiring Mind*, Harcourt, Brace, 1928, pp. 254-65.

the Sherman Anti-Trust Act of 1890. In the E. C. Knight case (1895) the Supreme Court declared essentially that the Sherman Act applied only to monopolies in restraint of commerce between states and not to monopoly in manufacturing. In 1897-98 it admitted that the act covered both reasonable and unreasonable restraint of trade. But in 1911 the Court reinterpreted the Sherman Act according to the famous "rule of reason." It held that the Sherman Act was violated only by "unreasonable" restraint of trade. Some of the greatest mergers, such as the United States Steel Corporation, got through dissolution suits safely on the ground that their restraint was quite reasonable. The Clayton Act in Wilson's administration endeavored still further to control monopolies, but in the case of the *Federal Trade Commission* vs. *Gratz* (1920) the Court emasculated this as it had earlier undermined the Sherman Act. Some might allege that the "trust-busting" reformers were mistaken in their policies, but at least they had the support of the public, and the Court frustrated the popular will.

The railroads in this country were, in their early days, we know, the objects of much sharp practice. Some semblance of public control was essential, and the Interstate Commerce Commission was established in 1887 to supply this supervision. The Supreme Court was soon found decisively on the side of the railroads. Out of sixteen appeals made from the rulings of the Interstate Commerce Commission between 1887 and 1905 the Court decided in favor of the railroads fifteen times. In 1897 the Court further undermined the power of the commission by denying it authority to fix rates. About all that was left was the right to collect railroad statistics and give them publicity. Under Theodore Roosevelt's influence, the commission was strengthened, and in 1913 it was authorized to make a physical valuation of railroad properties as the basis for scientific determination of rates. Further power was bestowed in 1920, and liberals began to anticipate the day when the Interstate Commerce Commission would have both the authority to fix railroad rates and the knowledge requisite to do this in accurate and just fashion. This hope the Court upset in the O'Fallon case (1929) and in *United Railways* vs. *West* (1930). The Court held that not "prudent investment" but "reproduction cost new" must be taken into account in determining rates. It also held that anything less than 7.44 per cent return per year would be confiscatory. The Court further permitted the deduction of a depreciation charge from net income. Much the same obstructive principles favorable to corporate wealth were extended from the railroads to the electric utilities by the Court.

In the case of the *Burns Baking Company* vs. *Bryan* (1924) the Court declared unconstitutional a standard-weights law designed to protect buyers from short weight in sales. During the next year, in the case of *Weaver* vs. *Palmer Bros.*, the Court set aside a Pennsylvania law enacted to prevent the use of shoddy in comfortables. These are only representative examples of the way the Court has used its power to prevent the people from compelling elementary honesty, decency, and fairness on the part of American business when the latter is not willing to provide this of its own accord.

Even more fundamental and sweeping was the Court's clearly implied declaration in the case of *Allgeyer* vs. *Alabama* (1897) that business practices and callings are above the law and that the Fourteenth Amendment guarantees a man the right to live, work, and follow business activities as he wishes.

One of the most elemental principles of economic and social democracy is that when money has to be raised for public purposes taxation shall be based upon the principle of capacity to pay. The more a man is allowed to prosper in any society, the more may be exacted from him to support the existing political and social order. The wealthy have never been willing to concede this truism and have thus far prevented taxation measures from even approximating a real capacity-to-pay basis. The Supreme Court has not failed them in this struggle to evade equitable taxation. First came the notable decision in the case of *Pollock* vs. *Farmers' Loan and Trust Company* (1895), in which the Court declared an income-tax law unconstitutional. As has been noted, it took a constitutional amendment to enable our government to collect a tax on incomes. The Supreme Court then came to the rescue in the case of *Eisner* vs. *Macomber* (1920) and declared that stock dividends were not income and hence not liable to taxation. This provided a spacious loophole for the rich.

If there is any practice of capitalism that is open to criticism it is the transmission of vast wealth from one generation to the next. An able and energetic man may accumulate a fortune, in some cases to the benefit of the public as well as himself. But under our present system he may transmit a considerable proportion of it to a parasitical descendant who may never make even a gesture of public service during his lifetime. The only way to correct this is through drastic inheritance and estate taxes. Some states have tried to introduce such taxation. Wisconsin was a pioneer. The Supreme Court stepped into the breach and in the case of *Schlesinger* vs. *Wisconsin* (1925) declared unconstitutional the Wisconsin law designed to end evasions of the inheritance tax through spurious "gifts." In 1931 the Court continued its obstructive policies in regard to inheritances (*Farmers' Loan and Trust Company* vs. *Minnesota,* and *Coolidge* vs. *Long*).

If capitalism is to endure, it must make provision for safe and decent working-conditions, for an income sufficient to make each self-supporting adult an effective purchaser, and for sufficient leisure to produce a broad need for consumers' goods. Progressives have sought to bring such conditions into being. An Employers' Liability Act was passed in 1906, but the court set it aside. A decade later it reversed itself under the pressure of wartime conditions. The State of New York tried to eliminate atrocious working-conditions in bake-shops. The Court invalidated this legislation in the famous case of *Lochner* vs. *New York* (1905). Attempts have been made to establish minimum-wage laws. At first the Court, influenced by the masterly presentation of the case by Louis D. Brandeis, approved the Oregon minimum-wage law in 1908. But in 1923, in the case of *Atkins* vs. *Children's Hospital,* it set aside a minimum-wage law as unconstitutional because it infringed perfect "freedom of contract." Child labor was outlawed in Britain a century ago, but the Supreme Court tolerates the institution, lest interference destroy the sacred right of free contract. In the case of *Hammer* vs. *Dagenhart* (1917) it declared the federal anti-child-labor law unconstitutional.[1]

[1] Most of the NRA codes prohibit child labor, but they are of course only temporary as yet, and have not been efficiently enforced.

If labor is to be kept satisfied with the capitalistic system, it must be accorded justice and equality in treating with capital, yet in the famous Danbury hatters case (*Loewe* vs. *Lawlor,* 1908), labor was declared punishable for secondary boycott, under the Sherman Act. In 1911 the Court went still further (*Gompers* vs. *Bucks' Stove and Range Co.*) and declared that officials of the American Federation of Labor could be punished for encouraging boycotts against non-union employers. The labor clauses of the Clayton Act were specifically designed: (1) To prevent the prosecution of labor under the Sherman Act, which was aimed at business trusts and monopolies; and (2) to reduce the use of the injunction against unions. But in the case of the *Duplex Printing Company* vs. *Deering* (1920) the Court asserted that the Clayton Act did not prevent the issuing of injunctions against organized labor. In the same year, in the case of *Truax* vs. *Corrigan* the Court threw out an Arizona law forbidding the use of injunctions in labor cases. The case of *Hitchman Coal and Coke Company* vs. *Mitchell* (1917) was a particularly deadly blow to organized labor. It upheld the notorious "yellow-dog" contracts and reaffirmed the applicability of the Sherman Act to labor-union activities. In the Coronado case (1922) the court went still further and declared that a union might be sued for damages under the antitrust laws even though it was not incorporated. In the Bedford Cut Stone case (1927) the court went the limit and upheld the use of the injunction against union labor even if it could be proved that the strikers had in no way acted in an illegal manner. In short, Supreme Court decisions no less than paralyzed organized labor and collective bargaining, while sabotaging the efforts of the government to subject business and finance to social control.

We have now indicated a few of the ways in which the Supreme Court has frustrated or retarded the efforts of liberal leaders to establish a just and civilized social order in our country. It has opposed equitable taxation, permitted business to engage even in dishonest practices, interfered with efforts to provide decent wages and living-conditions, and all but ended the initiative of organized labor. In this way it has led many of the more hot-headed to feel that the only way out is through violence. While promoting revolution through its opposition to social change, the Supreme Court has, however, naturally tried to outlaw revolutionary movements in the United States. In the Gitlow case (1924) it outlawed revolutionary phrases and tactics and approved the prosecution of Communists and Syndicalists.[1] Three years later it took the same position in the Whitney case, upholding the California criminal Syndicalism law.

In our age, after witnessing the wastes, sorrows, and imbecilities of a war and a postwar period, most thoughtful people have come to agree upon the futility of war. More, they look upon war as a major menace to the race. But the Supreme Court still holds the obligation to bear arms an essential to citizenship. Capitalism and property cannot dispense with the right to wage war. Even a middle-aged and invalid woman of high culture will not be admitted to citizenship unless she will agree to the obligation to bear arms in case of war. In the Schwimmer case (1929) the Supreme Court, as Justice Holmes clearly implied, took a position of disapproval of the Golden Rule. The same

---

[1] Gitlow was convicted in 1919.

attitude was continued in the MacIntosh and Bland cases three years later.

The record of the Supreme Court in preventing us from moving forward in a sane and orderly fashion to a new and better day is revealed in the summary above. The character of the issues involved is clear enough. It is certain that the status quo ante in American society is hopeless. A new deal of some sort is inevitable. It may come in one of two ways: (1) By progressive and experimental legislation, such as that once promised by President Franklin D. Roosevelt; or (2) through a collapse of the older order and a radical new society built over the ruins. The Supreme Court seems to be heading us towards the second alternative. Only radicals can logically find delight in its practices. If the Court forces revolution it will destroy the system that sustains the conservatives. A progressive régime might preserve some part of the capitalistic order.[1]

The elimination of judicial review of legislation is probably the most promising proposed solution. In this way the Supreme Court would cease to function as the third and most conservative house of our national legislature. This would open the way to orderly social progress and reduce the probability of revolution. It would lessen the attacks on the Court and the demands for its abolition. Thus might be saved both its rightful judicial function and its prestige.

XII. "THE NEW CAPITALISM"

Much has been said in recent years about the rise of a "new capitalism." What such writers have in mind is the alleged appearance of a more rational and socialized form of capitalism which recognizes that the cut-throat methods of finance capitalism, with its concentration on immediate financial profits and its destructive influence on mass purchasing power, are fatal to the long continuance of the profit system and private property. Therefore the exponents of this improved form of capitalism stress the importance of steady employment for workers, high wages, and other policies likely to increase purchasing power. They understand that goods cannot be sold unless there is somebody to buy them and that no one can buy in a capitalistic economy unless he has some money.

Advocates of the "new capitalism" think that it offers the solution to our industrial ills.[2] The old capitalist, they say, motivated by profits, entered that field of industry and pursued that set of business principles—or the lack thereof —which appeared to insure him the greatest profits possible.[3] Those principles by which he guided his business invariably ran against the grain of decent

---

[1] In some indecisive opinions in 1933-34 the Supreme Court dealt kindly with New Deal legislation, leading some to think that a majority of the judges might line up behind the idea of progress through legislation. The sweeping and unanimous decision invalidating the National Industrial Recovery Act on May 27, 1935, settled the issue. It showed that the Court had not even caught up with President Roosevelt's mild liberalism.

[2] See E. A. Filene, "The New Capitalism," American Academy of Political and Social Sciences, *Annals*, May, 1930, Pt. I. This volume of the *Annals, The Second Industrial Revolution and Its Significance*, has much helpful material on this question. The best summary of the principles of the "new capitalism" by a business man—and apparently a sincere and honest statement—is S. S. Fels, *This Changing World*, Houghton Mifflin, 1933. See also J. D. Mooney, *The New Capitalism*, Macmillan, 1934, a much less whole-hearted work than that of Mr. Fels.

[3] See above, pp. 294 ff., 378 ff., 816 ff.

human sentiments. All competing industrialists were not only rivals, but often bitter enemies. The profits made were regarded as coming from two sources—labor and the consumer. It was the industrialist's task as an employer and a producer to take as much as he could from the consumer (the higher the price, the greater the profit), and to pay as little as possible to labor (for did not wages come out of profits?). "Each was out of his own pocket, and the way to get dollars into his own pocket, he supposed, was to take them out of someone else's pocket, or to see at least that they did not get into the pockets of the other fellow." This type of capitalism, of course, still persists, but, so claim the proponents of the new capitalism, another and quite opposed attitude is coming into being.

This new attitude, which in theory constitutes the new capitalism, is most extensively expounded in America. It, too, is motivated by profits. But it has abandoned some of the old rules and is somewhat less cruel in operation. Altruism and idealism do not lie at the bottom of the change. The new capitalism has its roots in purely practical and profitable ground. Therefore, its advocates make clear, it "pays" in every business sense. What, then, are the rules under which the game of increased profits is to be played? They are, in brief, higher wages, shorter hours, lower prices, and a planned economy. There are greater profits in selling large quantities at lower prices to the mass of the people than in selling a limited number of articles to a few people at high prices. High wages are profitable because they enable the mass of the people to become purchasers. Likewise, shorter hours are desirable. They give the necessary leisure time in which purchases are to be made and utilized by the masses. "If they are to buy automobiles," says one of the new capitalists, "they must have time in which to drive around."

Thus runs the argument: Fewer hours per day means greater efficiency on the part of labor, which in turn means greater production. Higher wages, too, demand that each laborer's productivity must be increased through greater efficiency, scientific management, and economy in production itself. All in all, the new capitalism is theoretically far less ruthless than the old. It implies, it is said, an ideal of social service and a planned economy.

While others have played a part in this movement known as the new capitalism, the first conspicuous propagandist was Henry Ford, and his name is more generally associated with it than that of any other American industrialist.[1]

In any critical consideration of the whole question of the new capitalism two things must be admitted. First, what has been described as the "old" capitalism still largely dominates the scene.[2] Second, there is not in practice quite so much that is new in the new capitalism as its proponents wish to assume. The significant changes that actually merit the term "the new capitalism" have not appeared so much in any new attitude towards labor and the consumer as in the more efficient organization and structure of productive industry. It is clear enough that the new capitalism we have just described has not yet stabilized

---

[1] Its foremost journalistic exponent was E. W. Scripps.

[2] To understand the contrast between the capitalistic conception of the "new capitalism" and what must be the essence of any real "new capitalism" cf. Mooney, op. cit., with Chase, The Economy of Abundance; H. P. Fairchild, Profits or Prosperity? Harper, 1932; and A. M. Newman, Enough for Everybody, Bobbs-Merrill, 1933.

industry or placed the essential industries upon a solid basis.[1] Critics also point out that while production has been increased, the problems of a more equitable and intelligent distribution still remain unsolved. To whatever degree the new capitalism has been practiced, it has not resulted in a greater equality of income, even in prosperous periods. Though it may have stimulated slightly the growth of welfare work affecting labor, it has not given labor any greater security. The reform of capitalism involves fundamentally a great increase in the income of the masses in order to promote mass purchasing power. The proponents of the new capitalism advocate this in principle, but most of them oppose it in practice and reject the specific policies, such as unrestricted collective bargaining, that might bring about such a result. Henry Ford, for example, has been one of the most bitter foes of organized labor, and his "speed-up" system is the most cruel and oppressive single item in our contemporary industrial world.

The fact is, to be candid, that the new capitalism of the writers is as yet mainly a verbal bubble on the very real ocean of finance capitalism.[2] Only a few important figures in our economic life have espoused the new capitalism even in rhetoric, and many of these have been talking for public consumption rather than for private practice. As just now observed, the most conspicuous representative of the new capitalism has been Henry Ford, and he has been compelled to fight bitterly with the finance capitalists, who have on more than one occasion tried to put him out of business. Further, Ford himself has shown far less zeal for the new ways since 1925. The enthusiasm for the new capitalism is most prevalent in periods of depression, when the bitter fruits of finance capitalism are most evident. This was particularly noticeable from 1929 to 1933. But no sooner did business begin to pick up in the summer of 1933 than there was a general pining for the old days of ruthless competition and exploitation. President Roosevelt's New Deal was a very mild brand of new capitalism, but the more powerful business and financial interests sharply criticized it and did their best to obstruct and destroy all parts of it that did not conform to selfish business interests. Their organizations, like the Liberty League of America, aimed to defend property and restore the old political individualism.

Thus far, the only new capitalism of any practical significance has been finance capitalism. Its leaders and achievements certainly do not measure up even to those of industrial capitalism or of monopoly capitalism.[3] The second generation of industrial leaders, including those who are supposed to typify the new capitalists, have not made any such contributions as did the earlier generation. They have not built great empires of industry and trade. They have, for the most part, built and administered great speculative financial combinations. In many cases these combinations have drained, through legalized looting by holding companies, the empires of industry, trade, transportation, mining, and public utilities, established by the earlier generation of capitalists, without rendering any direct or indispensable service.

[1] *Cf.* M. J. Bonn, *The Crisis of Capitalism in America,* Day, 1932.
[2] That the "new capitalism" might work if honestly espoused has been demonstrated by such men as Hapgood in Indianapolis and Rowntree in York, England.
[3] Compare the interesting effort to defend the opposite thesis in Ida Tarbell's history of the Standard Oil Company and her biographies of Judge Gary and Owen D. Young.

It is extremely doubtful if there will be any "new capitalism" on any important scale unless it is forced by state action.[1] If the political agencies are converted to the tenets of the constructive new capitalism that we outlined above, and introduce, by force if necessary, a system in which the interests of the masses—the forgotten men—are given primary consideration, then we may have a new capitalism, but it will be state capitalism and will be called Fascism by the radicals. A marked change is noticeable already in the attitude of the state towards industry even under capitalism. One expression of it is the "rationalization" of industry, which we have discussed in an earlier chapter. Increasing combination and centralization in industry have placed the whole problem of the regulation of business in the limelight. There are no countries today that even pretend to function under pure laissez-faire doctrines.

One of the results of the World War was the virtual repudiation of laissez-faire principles in the constitutions of the new European states.[2] The attitude towards the regulation and control of business varies, of course, from one country to another. In some, the constitutions grant extensive regulatory powers to the government; in some, the degree of control is specifically limited; certain states depend upon statute and judicial interpretation to dominate the field of industrial regulation. While "big business" and monopolies are traditionally frowned upon by some countries, others encourage their development. The whole problem of the relation of the state to industry has by no means been satisfactorily settled.

The "New Deal" introduced by President Roosevelt in 1933 was ostensibly designed to combine social control of the great industries with promotion of mass purchasing power.[3] It was held to represent an extensive adoption of the principles of the new capitalism, and the destinies of this movement may be rather definitely tied up with the outcome of the Roosevelt experiment. Others have contended that the New Deal was as deceptive in loyalty to any literal "new capitalism" as were the earlier pronouncements of men who called for a new system but went on in their own activities with a ruthless practice of finance capitalism. Such critics hold that the new capitalism in the New Deal exists only in its rhetoric, while its realities are in thorough accord with monopoly and finance capitalism. They assert that "it moves one speech ahead and two steps backward." Hence, they claim, it is destined to ultimate failure, if it is not already showing signs of collapse.[4]

[1] For an optimistic argument, see E. L. Heermance, *Can Business Govern Itself?* Harper, 1933.
[2] *Cf.* O. F. Boucke, *Laissez Faire and After,* Crowell, 1932.
[3] *Cf.* Beard and Smith, *The Future Comes;* and A. B. Adams, *Our Economic Revolution,* University of Oklahoma Press, 1933.
[4] *Cf.* Stolberg and Vinton, *op. cit.*

SUGGESTED READING

Thomas, *Human Exploitation in the United States*
Hammerton, *Universal History of the World,* Chap. 186
Nussbaum, *History of the Economic Institutions of Modern Europe,* Pt. IV, Chaps. II, IV, VI-VII
Wells, *The Work, Wealth and Happiness of Mankind,* Vol. I, pp. 348-54; Vol. II, pp. 457-520

SUGGESTED READING

Hobson, *The Evolution of Modern Capitalism*
C. F. Dunbar, *The Theory and History of Banking*, 5th ed. rev., Putnam, 1929
Horace White, *Money and Banking*, 5th ed., Ginn, 1914, Chaps. xiv-xxii
J. M. Chapman, *Concentration of Banking*, Columbia University Press, 1934
H. P. Willis and J. M. Chapman, *The Banking Situation*, Columbia University Press, 1934
L. E. Clark, *Central Banking under the Federal Reserve System*, Macmillan, 1935
L. D. Edie, *The Banks and Prosperity*, Harper, 1932
R. W. Goldschmidt, *The Changing Structure of American Banking*, London, 1934
Lewis Corey, *The House of Morgan*, Watt, 1930
—— *The Decline of American Capitalism*, Covici, Friede, 1934
A. H. Mowbray, *Insurance; Its Theory and Practice in the United States*, McGraw-Hill, 1930
Harvey O'Connor, *Mellon's Millions*, Day, 1933
Moulton, *The Formation of Capital*
P. M. O'Leary, *Corporate Enterprise in Modern Economic Life*, Harper, 1933
John Moody, *Masters of Capital*, Yale University Press, 1919
L. D. Brandeis, *Other People's Money and How the Bankers Use It*, Stokes, 1932
R. N. Owens, *Business Organization and Combination*, Prentice-Hall, 1934
A. J. Simons, *Holding Companies*, Pitman, 1927
J. C. Bonbright and G. C. Means, *The Holding Company, Its Public Significance and Its Regulation*, McGraw-Hill, 1932
A. A. Berle and G. C. Means, *The Modern Corporation and Private Property*, Commerce Clearing House, 1932
W. Z. Ripley, *Main Street and Wall Street*, Little, Brown, 1927
Myers, *History of the Great American Fortunes*
Josephson, *The Robber Barons*
Davis, *Capitalism and Its Culture*
Davis, *What Price Wall Street?*
L. F. and L. F. Lybarger, *The Big National Gamble*, Meredith Press, 1935
J. T. Flynn, *Investment Trusts Gone Wrong!* New Republic, 1930
—— *Graft in Business*, Vanguard Press, 1931
—— *Security Speculation*, Harcourt, Brace, 1934
Sinclair, *Upton Sinclair Presents William Fox*
Max Lowenthal, *The Investor Pays*, Knopf, 1933
Mottram, *History of Financial Speculation*
A. M. Wickwire, *The Weeds of Wall Street*, Newcastle Press, 1932
Evans Clark and G. B. Galloway, eds., *The Internal Debts of the United States*, Macmillan, 1933
T. B. Veblen, *The Theory of Business Enterprise*, Scribner, 1904
R. H. Tawney, *The Acquisitive Society*, Harcourt, Brace, 1920
John Strachey, *The Nature of Capitalist Crisis*, Covici, Friede, 1935
H. P. Fairchild, *Profits or Prosperity?* Harper, 1932
J. T. Adams, *Our Business Civilization*, Boni, 1929, Chaps. i-iii, v-vii
Dobb, *Capitalist Enterprise and Social Progress*
C. H. Van Hise, *The Conservation of Natural Resources in the United States*, rev. ed., Macmillan, 1914
Stuart Chase and F. J. Schlink, *Your Money's Worth*, Macmillan, 1927
James Rorty, *Our Master's Voice: Advertising*, Day, 1934
R. R. Doane, *The Measurement of American Wealth*, Harper, 1933
Taylor, *Common Sense about Machines and Unemployment*
E. D. McDougall, ed., *Crime for Profit*, Stratford Press, 1933

A. B. Reeve, *The Golden Age of Crime*, Mohawk Press, 1931
Lynch, *Criminals and Politicians*
Ernest Beaglehole, *Property; a Study in Social Psychology*, Macmillan, 1932
E. S. Corwin, *The Twilight of the Supreme Court*, Yale University Press, 1934
Boudin, *Government by Judiciary*
Price, *We Have Recovered Before!*
W. C. Mitchell, *Business Cycles*, University of California Press, 1913
S. S. Fels, *This Changing World*, Houghton Mifflin, 1933
J. D. Mooney, *The New Capitalism*, Macmillan, 1934
Stuart Chase, *A New Deal*, Macmillan, 1932
—— *The Economy of Abundance*, Macmillan, 1934
G. W. Mallon, *Bankers vs. Consumers*, Day, 1933
A. L. Deane and H. K. Norton, *Investing in Wages*, Macmillan, 1932
W. B. Pitkin, *The Consumer, His Nature and His Changing Habits*, McGraw-Hill, 1932
—— *Capitalism Carries On*
Bogart and Thompson, *Readings in the Economic History of the United States*, Chaps. xx, xxiii
Marshall, *Production in the Modern Order*, Vol. II, Chap. vii
Jones, Vandenbosch, and Vandenbosch, *Readings in Citizenship*, pp. 163-91, 389-429
J. B. Hubbard and others, eds., *Current Economic Policies*, Holt, 1934
Ripley, *Trusts, Pools and Corporations*
Frederick, *Readings in Economic Planning*
Magee, *Collapse and Recovery*
J. G. Smith, ed., *Facing the Facts*, Putnam, 1932
Samuel Crowther and others, *A Basis for Stability*, Little, Brown, 1932
H. W. Laidler, ed., *Socialist Planning and a Socialist Program*, Falcon Press, 1932

FURTHER REFERENCES

FINANCE CAPITALISM. For a good analysis of the stages of capitalism, see Max Lerner, "The Supreme Court and Capitalism," *Yale Law Journal*, March, 1933; Hammerton, *op. cit.*, Chap. 186. For more detail, see Hobson, *op. cit.*, especially Chap. 1; Sée, *Modern Capitalism*.

BANKS. On the evolution of modern banking, see article "Banking, Commercial," Encyclopaedia of the Social Sciences; J. I. Bogen, article "Investment Banking," *Ibid.*; Dewey, *Financial History of the United States*; Dunbar, *op. cit.*; White, *op. cit.*, Bk. III; C. A. Conant, *History of Modern Banks of Issue* (6th ed. rev., Putnam, 1927); Bernhard Ostrolenk, *The Economics of Branch Banking* (Harper, 1930); H. P. Willis and B. H. Beckhart, eds., *Foreign Banking Systems* (Holt, 1929).

On the investment bank, see Bogen, *loc. cit.*; H. G. Moulton, *The Financial Organization of Society* (3d ed. rev., University of Chicago Press, 1930); H. P. Willis and J. I. Bogen, *Investment Banking* (Harper, 1929); Willis and Beckhart, *op. cit.*

INSURANCE. Robert Riegel and H. J. Loman, *Insurance; Principles and Practice* (Prentice-Hall, 1921); Mowbray, *op. cit.*; S. S. Huebner, ed., *Modern Insurance Developments* (American Academy of Political and Social Science, *Annals*, Vol. CLXI, 1932); S. C. Cyzio, *Your Insurance* (London, 1934).

CORPORATIONS. On the history, character, and application of the corporation in modern life, see L. H. Haney, *Business Organization and Combination* (Macmillan, 1913); O'Leary, *op. cit.*; I. M. Wormser, *Frankenstein, Incorporated* (McGraw-Hill, 1931); D. H. Robertson, *The Control of Industry* (Harcourt, Brace, 1923); M. W.

FURTHER REFERENCES 853

Watkins, *Industrial Combinations and Public Policy* (Houghton Mifflin, 1927); Berle and Means, *op. cit.;* A. S. Dewing, *The Financial Policy of Corporations* (Ronald Press, 1926); Moulton, *op. cit.*

ABSENTEE OWNERSHIP. On absentee ownership and its problems, see Berle and Means, *op. cit.,* Bk. I, Chap. v; T. B. Veblen, *Absentee Ownership* (Huebsch, 1923); Ripley, *Main Street and Wall Street.*

SPECULATION. For an authoritative and sympathetic analysis of the mechanics of the modern stock exchange, see J. E. Meeker, *The Work of the Stock Exchange* (rev. ed., Ronald Press, 1930); Benjamin Graham and D. LeF. Dodd, *Security Analysis* (McGraw-Hill, 1934). For a competent criticism of stock-exchange methods, see J. T. Flynn, "Wall Street," New York *World Telegram,* Oct. 22-27, 1934, and *Security Speculation;* Wickwire, *op. cit.* For historical surveys, see Davis, *op. cit.;* J. L. Parker, *Unmasking Wall Street* (Stratford, 1932). For excellent discussions of stock-exchange regulation, see Evans Clark, ed., *Stock Market Control* (Appleton-Century, 1934); Flynn, *Security Speculation.* For a good primer, see G. L. Hoxie, *Stock Speculation and Business* (Stratford, 1930).

THE CONCENTRATION OF WEALTH. On wealth and income in the United States, see Doane, *op. cit.;* W. I. King, *The Wealth and Income of the People of the United States* (Macmillan, 1915); W. I. King and Lillian Epstein, *The National Income and Its Purchasing Power* (National Bureau of Economic Research, 1930); and W. I. King and others, *Income in the United States . . . 1909-1919* (National Bureau of Economic Research, 1921-22, Vols. I-II); A. L. Bowley, *The Division of the Product of Industry* (Oxford Press, 1919); Hugh Dalton, *Some Aspects of the Inequality of Incomes in Modern Communities* (Dutton, 1920). Excellent discussions of the necessity of purchasing power in a capitalistic system are contained in Fairchild, *op. cit.;* Kirby Page, *Individualism and Socialism* (Farrar & Rinehart, 1933); Deane and Norton, *op. cit.;* Mallon, *op. cit.;* Taylor, *op. cit.;* Fels, *op. cit.*

BUSINESS ENTERPRISE. On this and the profit system, see Veblen, *The Theory of Business Enterprise,* especially Chaps. III-IV. See also Adams, *op. cit.,* Chaps. I-III, VII; Nussbaum, *op. cit.,* Pt. IV, Chap. VI; Tawney, *op. cit.;* Fairchild, *op. cit.* For critical assessments of our acquisitive society and the pecuniary order, see Nussbaum, *op. cit.,* Pt. IV, Chap. VI; Veblen, *op. cit.;* Sidney and Beatrice Webb, *The Decay of Capitalist Civilization* (Harcourt, Brace, 1923); Corey, *The Decline of American Capitalism;* Taylor, *op. cit.;* Tawney, *op. cit.;* H. F. Ward, *Our Economic Morality and the Ethic of Jesus* (Macmillan, 1929); L. D. Brandeis, *Business—a Profession* (rev. ed., Hale, Cushman and Flint, 1925) and *The Curse of Bigness,* edited by O. K. Fraenkel (Viking Press, 1934); Fairchild, *op. cit.;* J. A. Hobson, *Work and Wealth* (Macmillan, 1914) and *Wealth and Life* (Macmillan, 1929); Thomas, *op. cit.*

ADVERTISING. The degree to which bogus advertising underlies modern business has been shown by Chase and Schlink in their striking book cited above. See also Arthur Kallet and F. J. Schlink, *100,000,000 Guinea Pigs* (Vanguard Press, 1933); Rorty, *op. cit.;* Silas Bent, *Ballyhoo: The Voice of the Press* (Boni & Liveright, 1927); J. B. Matthews and R. E. Shallcross, *Partners in Plunder* (Covici, Friede, 1935); T. S. Harding, *The Popular Practice of Fraud* (Longmans, 1935).

FINANCE CAPITALISM AND BUSINESS. On the disastrous effects of speculative finance upon American business, see D. C. Coyle, *The Irrepressible Conflict: Business vs. Finance* (4th ed., privately printed, 1933); Brandeis, *Other People's Money;* Flynn, *Investment Trusts Gone Wrong!* and *Graft in Business;* Berle and Means, *op. cit.;* Wormser, *op. cit.;* O'Connor, *op. cit.;* Sinclair, *op. cit.;* Davis, *op. cit.;* Lowenthal, *op. cit.;* Winkler, *Foreign Bonds: An Autopsy;* Lawrence Dennis, *Is Capitalism*

Doomed? (Harper, 1932); W. A. Robson, *The Relation of Wealth to Welfare* (Macmillan, 1925), Lybarger, *op. cit.*

RACKETEERING AND ORGANIZED CRIME. John McConaughy, *From Cain to Capone* (Coward-McCann, 1931); F. D. Pasley, *Al Capone, the Biography of a Self-made Man* (Washburn, 1930); Courtenay Terrett, *Only Saps Work* (Vanguard Press, 1930); Reeve, *op. cit.;* Lynch, *op. cit.;* C. R. Cooper, *Ten Thousand Public Enemies* (Little, Brown, 1935).

BUSINESS CYCLES. For general treatments, see Price, *op. cit.;* Mitchell, *op. cit.;* W. L. Thorp, *Business Annals* (National Bureau of Economic Research, 1926); A. B. Adams, *The Economics of Business Cycles* (McGraw-Hill, 1925). For able conventional analyses of the business cycle, see Mitchell, *op. cit.;* Adams, *op. cit.;* J. M. Clark, *Strategic Factors in Business Cycles* (Macmillan, 1934). For an admirable graphic presentation of the alleged business cycle in American history, see Price, *op. cit.*, p. 102. On economic planning see Burn, *Codes, Cartels, National Planning.*

PROPERTY RIGHTS AND THE SUPREME COURT. For a keen psychological analysis of the genesis and character of the property "instinct," see Beaglehole, *op. cit.* On the United States Supreme Court and property, see Hacker and Kendrick, *The United States since 1865,* pp. 196-99, 400-02, 622-23, 718-21; Lerner, *loc. cit.;* Myers, *History of the Supreme Court;* F. J. Goodnow, *Social Reform and the Constitution* (Macmillan, 1911); Haines, *The Revival of Natural Law Concepts,* Pts. II-III; Boudin, *op. cit.;* Felix Frankfurter and Nathan Greene, *The Labor Injunction* (Macmillan, 1930). For a clear and discerning, if unconventional, account of the present personnel and operations of the Supreme Court, see Chap. II of Drew Pearson and R. S. Allen, *More Merry-Go-Round* (Liveright, 1932). For legal and economic views of dissenting judges, see Felix Frankfurter, ed., *Mr. Justice Holmes* (Coward-McCann, 1931); O. W. Holmes, *The Dissenting Opinions of Mr. Justice Holmes,* ed. by Alfred Lief (Vanguard Press, 1929), and *Representative Opinions of Mr. Justice Holmes,* ed. by Alfred Lief (Vanguard Press, 1931); *The Social and Economic Views of Mr. Justice Brandeis,* ed. by Alfred Lief (Vanguard Press, 1930); A. T. Mason, *Brandeis, Lawyer and Judge in the Modern State* (Princeton University Press, 1933).

"THE NEW CAPITALISM." A large literature has grown up about this subject, especially since 1929. Representative books are: Henry Ford and Samuel Crowther, *My Life and Work* (Doubleday, Page, 1922); Mooney, *op. cit.;* A. O. Dahlberg, *Jobs, Machines, and Capitalism* (Macmillan, 1932); William KixMiller, *Can Business Build a Great Age?* (Macmillan, 1933); E. L. Heermance, *Can Business Govern Itself?* (Harper, 1933); Fels, *op. cit.;* W. B. Donham, *Business Looks at the Unforeseen* (McGraw-Hill, 1932); F. C. James, *The Road to Revival* (Harper, 1932); L. C. Walker, *Distributed Leisure* (Century, 1931); W. J. Lauck, *The New Industrial Revolution and Wages* (Funk & Wagnalls, 1929); B. A. Javits, *Business and the Public Interest* (Macmillan, 1932); L. S. Chadwick, *Balanced Employment* (Macmillan, 1933); Walter Lippmann, *The Method of Freedom* (Macmillan, 1934).

For a good presentation of the consumers' interests, see Pitkin, *op. cit.*

On the New Deal, see Hacker, *Short History of the New Deal;* Benjamin Stolberg and W. J. Vinton, *Economic Consequences of the New Deal* (Harcourt, Brace, 1935); E. K. Lindley, *The Roosevelt Revolution* (Viking Press, 1933); S. C. Wallace, *The New Deal in Action* (Harper, 1934); A. M. Bingham and Selden Rodman, eds., *Challenge to the New Deal* (Falcon Press, 1934).

For a splendid summary description and appraisal of industrial society today as shaped by the Second Industrial Revolution and finance capitalism, see Cole, *A Guide through World Chaos.*

CHAPTER XXII

THE CRISIS IN DEMOCRACY AND PARTY GOVERNMENT

I. THE CRITICAL TEST OF DEMOCRATIC INSTITUTIONS

In the latter part of the nineteenth century democratic institutions and party government were taken for granted as demonstrably successful achievements. They seemed as much assured as, say, the doctrine of evolution. At the opening of the second third of the twentieth century, democracy exists in any thorough degree in only two major Western states, Great Britain and the United States. Dictators have sprung up in many states and emergency governments rule with very nearly dictatorial power in others. Between 1900 and 1935 democracy was put to severe test and its tenets were submitted to scientific evaluation and rigorous political experience.

Democracy is inseparably linked up with party government. Thus far, democracy has been able to operate only by means of party institutions and activities. Similarly, when democracy vanishes there is no place for realistic party politics. Therefore the increasing jeopardy and the startling decline of democratic institutions have impaired the popularity and effectiveness of partisan politics. If present tendencies continue, both democracy and party government are likely to disappear before the onslaughts of Fascism and Communism.

In the following pages we shall examine more closely the ordeal through which democracy and party government have passed in the last generation, to emerge badly crippled and partially discredited. It is strangely ironical that the great World War, fought ostensibly to make the world safe for democracy, did more than anything else to set up trends that ultimately weakened or destroyed democracy in most of the Western world.[1]

II. THE FUNDAMENTAL ASSUMPTIONS OF DEMOCRACY

Having briefly surveyed the rise of democracy in an earlier chapter,[2] we may now consider the fundamental assumptions upon which the democratic move-

---

[1] While this chapter gives frank consideration to the weaknesses in democratic government that have been revealed in the last generation or so, it must not be regarded as in any sense a polemic against democracy. The author finds nothing charming in the substitutes for democracy that have of late emerged on the political horizon. The account of Fascism given here and in other sections of the work is as frank and critical as the observations on the democratic debacle. It is the duty of the historian to describe developments as he sees them in the historical record. A candid historian in England at the close of the fifteenth century, whatever his passion for feudalism, would have been compelled to call attention to many symptoms indicating the passing of that type of political order.   [2] See above, pp. 482 ff.

ment is based. To be fairly judged, the views of its supporters must be examined in terms of the state of political development and scientific knowledge between fifty and a hundred years ago, as well as in the light of the political experience and scientific data available today. Certain premises that we can now regard as discredited might once have been legitimately entertained by those not in possession of our present political experience or our contemporary scientific knowledge concerning man and society.

The early protagonists of democracy built their theory upon the assumption of the essential permanence of a simple agrarian type of society. Jefferson himself, scarcely a defender of any extreme type of democracy, frankly stated that he believed that even republican government could coexist only with a society founded on an agricultural basis. As he himself stated this:

> I think our governments will remain virtuous for many centuries . . . as long as there shall be vacant lands in any part of America. When they get piled upon one another in large cities, as in Europe, they will become as corrupt as in Europe.[1]

Hence we can scarcely condemn the original sponsors of democracy if the system which they promulgated failed to prove adequate to the problems forced upon it by the complex urban and industrial civilization of the present day. To be sure, this does not necessarily prove that democracy would have been successful even if society had remained agricultural in character.

Another assumption that was involved in the democratic complex was the laissez-faire theory of government. It was held by most of the exponents of democracy, whether Godwin, Jefferson, Cobden, or the German liberals of 1848, that the best government is the one that governs least, though it must not be forgotten that there were exceptions.[2] Such an exception was the Socialistic drive for democracy and universal suffrage under such leaders as Ferdinand Lassalle, who frankly repudiated the laissez-faire ideal. It will be conceded by most historians that a form of government which might have operated successfully under a Spencerian brand of individualism [3] would be far less capable of directing with efficiency a society dominated by ideals of extensive state interference.

[1] Thomas Jefferson, *Writings*, ed. by Paul Leicester Ford, Putnam, 1892-99, 10 vols., Vol. IV, pp. 479-80.

[2] Recent writers, among them some who are interested in seeking historical justification for the New Deal, have emphasized the fact that Jefferson was not a complete individualist and that the Jacksonians abandoned laissez-faire conceptions. See J. M. Jacobson, *The Development of American Political Thought*, Century, 1932, p. 256. Professor C. M. Wiltse goes even further and says, "The democratic and socialistic philosophies are closely related, both historically and logically." ("Jeffersonian Democracy: A Dual Tradition," *American Political Science Review*, October, 1934.)

Of course, there were exceptions to Jefferson's individualism, as there were to his strict constructionism, but he certainly believed that there should be no more governmental intervention than absolutely necessary. He once went so far as to say that a free press is worth more than all government. There were differences of opinion among Jacksonians, but the Jacksonian era as a whole witnessed a retrenchment of the public activities sponsored by the Whigs—especially the support of internal improvements. The tariff was progressively lowered. The United States Bank was brought to an end. Federal aid to public improvements was withdrawn and federal loans to the states became less lavish. It was the Jacksonians who blocked the possibility of public control or ownership of transportation facilities, such as developed widely in Europe. On the whole, it is certainly safe to conclude that in its germinal period democracy was closely intertwined with political individualism.

[3] See above, p. 384.

A central thesis of the supporters of historical democracy was the firm belief in the essential equality of all men, the observed existing differences being assigned to inequalities of opportunity.

The earlier American friends of a more liberal or republican political system did not believe in the equality of man, however much they may have subscribed to the formal equality of all before the law or their theological equality before God. Jefferson, for example, actually accepted with minor qualifications the Aristotelian dogma that some are born to rule and others to serve. He was only willing to accept the people's judgment as to who should rule them. He believed that the mass of the people could be trusted to choose the wisest men —men like Jefferson—to lead them, and his own experience seemed to vindicate his judgment.[1] For the people turned out his aristocratic opponents, the Federalists, and then proceeded to elect first Jefferson himself, and then his satellites, Madison and Monroe, consecutively for two terms each. The Sage of Monticello joined his fathers just after Monroe had been succeeded by the son of Jefferson's old Federalist rival. Jefferson's conception of the natural aristocracy that should rule society is well stated in the following passage from a letter to John Adams written in 1813:

> For I agree with you that there is a natural aristocracy among men. The grounds of this are virtue and talents. Formerly bodily powers gave place among the aristoi. But since the invention of gunpowder has armed the weak as well as the strong with missile death, bodily strength, like beauty, good humor, politeness and other accomplishments, has become but an auxiliary ground for distinction. There is also an artificial aristocracy, founded on wealth and birth, without either virtue or talents; for with these it would belong to the first class. The natural aristocracy I consider as the most precious gift of nature, for the instruction, the trusts, and government of society. And indeed it would have been inconsistent in creation to have formed man for the social state, and not to have provided virtue and wisdom enough to manage the concerns of society. May we not even say, that that form of government is the best, which provides the most effectually for a pure selection of these natural aristoi into the offices of government? The artificial aristocracy is a mischievous ingredient in government, and provision should be made to prevent its ascendency.[2]

The "honest-to-God" democrats of the Jacksonian and post-Jacksonian period, however, believed, or pretended to believe, that all men were essentially equal in ability, and hence were uniformly fitted to cast their votes. It was also held that no special training or experience was essential to the successful execution of the functions of any political office. Indeed, some of the Jacksonians even went so far as to declare that a long and successful career in office was a serious disqualification for political life, on account of the potential development of the bureaucratic spirit. It was held that a general system of education open to all

---

[1] It must, of course, be remembered that the electorate in Jefferson's day was quite different from what it was after the Jacksonian period. In the time of Jefferson the "people" who voted made up less than half of the adult males. The rest were excluded by property, religious, and other tests for voting.

[2] Jefferson, *op. cit.*, Vol. IX, p. 425.

would produce almost complete cultural and intellectual uniformity in society. Hence the democratic movement was associated with a strong impetus to popular education.[1]

Of course, this theory of equality and the associated doctrine of the fitness of all to hold office was not then so obviously absurd as it has now become as a result of our contemporary knowledge of differential psychology and the increasingly complicated nature of governmental problems. Particularly was this true of such views when held by those dwelling in the frontier society of Jackson's day. Here there was a much closer approximation to equality than in most modern societies. The severe selective processes active in frontier life served to make the surviving frontier settlers relatively uniform in ability.[2] Moreover, a man who could weather the dangers and hardships of westward migration in those days, and contend successfully against Indians and wild beasts after settling on the frontier, was likely to be able to carry out the crude functions of government that prevailed in such areas.

It was further contended by the exponents of democratic theory that the mass of the people were not only politically competent but would take a very ardent interest in all phases of political life, once the right to vote was extended to them.[3] There was full confidence that universal suffrage as a legal right would certainly and immediately produce universal suffrage as an actual political practice. It was believed and hoped that the people would veritably mob the polls at daybreak on each election morning in order to exercise the God-given privilege of casting their ballots. This assumption was not so absurd a century ago, when most of the functions of government related to local needs and problems and intimately touched the daily life of the people in ways that they could visualize and feel.

Closely associated with this assumption of universal interest in and use of the ballot was the crucial hypothesis that the people would very carefully examine both candidates and policies in a coolly rational manner, size up all political situations shrewdly, and then register a deliberate choice based upon careful reflection on all the salient facts available. Political campaigns, in short, were expected to be periods of intensive adult education in the field of politics.

The democratic dogmas were formulated when the popular type of individual and of social psychology was the so-called Benthamite "felicific calculus."[4] This assumed that man is a cool and eminently deliberative animal who calmly decides each and every act upon the basis of the relative amount of pleasure to be secured and pain to be avoided. Such a hypothesis of human nature implied that the voter would carefully scrutinize every political policy and party candidate from this angle. This rationalistic type of political psychology dominated political thinking from Bentham to Bryce, and was not thoroughly laid at rest until the appearance of Graham Wallas's *Human Nature in Politics,* published in 1908. Absurd as this view of human behavior

[1] *Cf.* Fish, *The Rise of the Common Man,* Chap. x, and Becker, *The United States: An Experiment in Democracy,* Chap. ix.
[2] *Cf.* Turner, *The Rise of the New West,* Chaps. v-vii.
[3] *Cf.* J. A. Smith, *The Growth and Decadence of Constitutional Government,* Holt, 1930, Chaps. iii-iv.
[4] See above, pp. 230, 384-85.

THE FUNDAMENTAL ASSUMPTIONS OF DEMOCRACY

may now seem, it was not so before experience had shown the contrary to be true. The doctrine was formulated prior to the rise of social psychology, which has proved the fundamentally nonrational nature of group behavior.[1]

Another of the arguments for democracy, usually formulated by those who had some apparent misgivings concerning the administrative efficiency of democracy or the rational qualities of the masses, was that even if the people are not capable of keen analytical reasoning powers, at least they are deeply sensitive to great moral issues.[2] They can be trusted to a far greater degree than the educated and capable minority in sensing injustice and promoting idealistic causes. As evidence in point, such things have been cited as the popular support of the movement against slavery and, more recently, the alleged democratic basis of the Prohibition movement.

The democratic theory was formulated for the most part, with the exception of the work of the Socialists, in an age that held to the theory of political determinism in history. It was asserted that political institutions are of primary importance in the field of social causation. It was believed that a particular political system might be able to alter fundamentally the whole character of civilization.[3]

The democratic theory was also worked out in general harmony with the philosophy of unmitigated nationalism.[4] It was believed that domestic political institutions could be developed *in situ* with little attention to the prevailing political tendencies of the world or the existing state of international relations. Democratic dogma was not, of course, unique in this respect, for the nationalistic obsession dominated the outlook of monarchs and aristocrats as well.

III. DEMOCRATIC ASPIRATIONS IN THE LIGHT OF SCIENCE AND EXPERIENCE

Such were the underlying premises upon which the democratic program was elaborated and synthesized. We have tried to make it apparent in passing that these premises were not necessarily preposterous in the light of social and cultural conditions a hundred years ago and in view of the existing state of psychological knowledge. But the basic socio-economic conditions out of which the democratic dogmas developed have since profoundly altered, and modern psychology has proved that many of the theoretical assumptions underlying the democratic hypothesis are untenable.[5]

---

[1] *Cf.* C. E. Gehlke, in Merriam and Barnes, *History of Political Theories: Recent Times*, Chap. x.

[2] *Cf.* H. W. Wright, *The Moral Standards of Democracy*, Appleton, 1925.

[3] A few, such as Madison, Calhoun, and others, understood the actual facts and expounded the doctrine that government is merely the umpire of fundamental and conflicting social and economic interests. See Beard, *The Economic Basis of Politics*. Even Jeffersonians and the agrarians implied that politics depends upon economics when they held that an agricultural society was essential to the success of democracy. But the general tendency of the age was to put trust in the political structure of society. The whole crusade for universal suffrage and democracy was based upon the notion that political democracy would bring a general reconstruction of society and culture. The ideas and program of the English Chartists afford a good illustration.

[4] *Cf.* Becker, *op. cit.*, Chap. v.

[5] *Cf.* Becker, *op. cit.*, Chap. x, and G. V. Price, *Optimistic America*, Western Baptist Publishing Co., 1933, Chap. ix.

Striking and extensive have been the changes in the social setting of political institutions since the days of the quasi-bucolic New England township of John Quincy Adams and the crude frontier society of Jackson. In the place of the simple agricultural civilization, with its relatively few and rudimentary political problems, we have our highly complicated urban industrial civilization, which presents an ever increasing variety of conditions that must be regulated in some degree by political action. In other words, the whole set-up of life conditions that lay back of the democratic movement has all but disappeared. Dr. Durant has admirably summarized this outstanding fact, so essential in evaluating the validity of the democratic pretensions today:

All those conditions are gone. National isolation has gone, because of trade, communication, and the invention of destructive mechanisms that facilitate invasion. Personal isolation is gone, because of the growing interdependence of producer, distributor, and consumer. Skilled labor is the exception now that machines are made to operate machines, and scientific management reduces skill to the inhuman stupidity of routine. Free land is gone, and tenancy increases. Free competition decays; it may survive for a time in new fields like the automobile industry, but everywhere it gravitates towards monopoly. The once independent shopkeeper is in the toils of the big distributor; he yields to chain drug stores, chain cigar stores, chain groceries, chain candy stores, chain restaurants, chain theaters—everything is in chains. Even the editor who owns his own paper and molds his own mendacity is a vestigial remnant now, when a thousand sheets across the country tell the same lie in the same way every day better and better. An ever decreasing proportion of business executives (and among them an ever decreasing number of bankers and directors) controls the lives and labors of an ever increasing proportion of men. A new aristocracy is forming out of the once rebellious bourgeoisie; equality and liberty and brotherhood are no longer the darlings of the financiers. Economic freedom, even in the middle classes, becomes rarer and narrower every year. In a world from which freedom of competition, equality of opportunity, and social fraternity have disappeared, political equality is worthless, and democracy becomes a sham.[1]

The laissez-faire theory of political inactivity has given way before differing degrees of state intervention, extending all the way to overt State Socialism. Even in the United States, under the sway of the Republican party with its theoretical individualistic philosophy, there came about a degree of state activity that would have caused Jefferson to be filled with the greatest alarm and the keenest disapproval. The industrialization and urbanization of modern life have created a host of new issues that not even a plutocratic and individualistic political organization can ignore.

The doctrine of the fundamental equality of all men has been dealt a rude shock by modern differential biology and psychology. These have revealed the existence of extensive individual differences of ability on the part of those inhabiting the same community. The most comprehensive effort to gain information along this line was embodied in the famous army mental tests given in 1917-18, which covered the unusually large and representative sample of 1,700,000 recruits. The following statistics indicate the distribution of mental capacity in this tested group, which certainly was fairly representative of the country at large:

[1] W. J. Durant, "Is Democracy a Failure?" *Harper's Magazine,* October, 1926, p. 557.

Grade	Mental Age	Percentage of the Total
A	18-19	4½
B	16-17	9
C+	15	16½
C	13-14	25
C—	12	20
D	11	15
D—	10	10

These series of tests, then, revealed the fact that only about 13 per cent of the population can be described as superior types and capable of distinguished leadership. The majority range from intellectual mediocrity to relative incompetence. While this does not mean that majority rule is always the rule of the stupid, since the leaders may on occasion guide the masses even in a democracy, still it does show that we cannot expect to secure sagacity or wisdom merely by counting noses.

Many writers, such as Professor Cooley, have contended that though the masses may not be intellectually distinguished, nevertheless they possess great innate shrewdness in selecting their leaders.[1] It would hardly seem that this thesis is borne out by such a concrete and convincing test as the selection of the Presidents of the United States since the Jacksonian period.[2] The outstanding Presidents through 1936—Lincoln, Cleveland, the two Roosevelts, and Wilson—have all been chosen as the result of an accident, a political fluke, or a special economic crisis. In other words, modern differential biology and psychology have unquestionably demonstrated that if we are to secure a type of political guidance adequate to cope with the difficult problems of today we must install in government the superior types with expert knowledge and not trust so implicitly the judgments of the common people. It would seem that such data as are now available would either justify the restriction of the voting privilege to those above the D grade or would support a selective system of voting in which additional voting power would be assigned to those possessed of a superior intelligence quotient. This reasoning does not imply that those of high intelligence are necessarily also supplied with superior social morality or civic idealism. But neither are the less intelligent any more rich in these qualities than they are in intellectual endowment. Stupidity and integrity are not invariably associated. Certainly the control of politics must be based on intelligence. The solution lies in socializing the élite, not in defying or denouncing intelligence.

The novel problems that have been created by contemporary civilization and must receive governmental attention are highly complex and technical in many cases.[3] Many political offices today require for an adequate grasp and solution of the problems facing the incumbent a degree of technical knowledge as great as that possessed by a distinguished economist, technician, physician, or law professor. A national legislator often needs to be more broadly and precisely educated than the average college teacher. Yet as Dr. Durant has well said, we require much more technical preparation for a physician or druggist than we

---

[1] Cf. C. H. Cooley, *Social Organization*, Scribner, 1909, Chap. XIII.
[2] Cf. Herbert Agar, *The People's Choice*, Houghton Mifflin, 1923.
[3] Cf. C. A. and William Beard, *The American Leviathan*, Macmillan, 1931, Chap. I.

insist upon for a Congressman, a governor, or even a President of the United States:

The evil of modern democracy is in the politician and at the point of nomination. Let us eliminate the politician, and the nomination.

Originally, no doubt, every man was his own physician, and every household prescribed its own drugs. But as medical knowledge accumulated and the *corpus prescriptionum* grew, it became impossible for the average individual, even for solicitous spinsters, to keep pace with the *pharmacopoeia*. A special class of persons arose who gave all their serious hours to the study of *materia medica,* and became professional physicians. To protect the people from untrained practitioners, and from those sedulous neighbors who have an interne's passion for experiment, a distinguished title and a reassuring degree were given to those who had completed this preparation. The process has now reached the point where it is illegal to prescribe medicines unless one has received such training, and such a degree, from a recognized institution. We no longer permit unprepared individuals to deal with our individual ailments or to risk our individual lives. We demand a lifetime's devotion as a preliminary to the prescription of pills.

But of those who deal with our incorporated ills, and risk our hundred million lives in peace and war, and have at their beck and call all our possessions and all our liberties, no specific preparation is required; it is sufficient if they are friends of the Chief, loyal to the Organization, handsome or suave, hand-shakers, shoulder-slappers, or baby-kissers, taking orders quietly, and as rich in promises as a weather bureau. For the rest they may have been butchers or barbers, rural lawyers or editors, pork-packers or saloon-keepers—it makes no difference. If they have had the good sense to be born in log cabins it is conceded that they have a divine right to be president.[1]

To be sure, the situation can be corrected to a slight degree by having expert guidance for ignorant legislators and administrators, but some modicum of education is essential in order to utilize expert advice with any competence after it has been offered. A governmental official in any line of work must have considerable intelligence and information even to be able to assimilate, weigh, and select the expert advice that is given to him. If he becomes merely a rubber stamp in the hands of his advisers, we do not have democracy but rather bureaucracy. The average Congressman or state legislator of today may well be capable of deciding whether or not a new plank should be added to a bridge or whether a common pound should be repaired, but it would be difficult for an untrained man to weigh or to utilize expert judgment with respect to international financial problems, the tariff, government control of railroads, state ownership of coal mines, public health, the NRA, or the regulation of radios and airplane traffic. In other words, the day is over when government can be conducted by rule of thumb, the rhetorical canons of Isocrates or Quintilian, or the spicy parliamentary repartee of the seasoned politician, such as the late charming Speaker Nicholas Longworth or Senator Pat Harrison.

Not only have the problems that must be settled by governmental control or supervision become much more numerous and complex in the last century, but the quality of our public officials has declined to an alarming degree. The writer is far from desiring to share in the conventional and unthinking eulogy

[1] Durant, *loc. cit.,* p. 563.

of the "Fathers," yet no informed person could well suggest that the caliber of our public servants today matches that of the officials in the period from 1790 to 1828.

In the last half-century we witnessed a transformation in political practice, as a result of which we seemingly no longer desired or expected real leadership in government. Rather the great economic interests, for all practical purposes, took over the running of the government and desired in political office those who would take orders with docility. Government practically became the servant of the interests. Men of great personal ability, real dignity, wide learning, and independence of character were not wanted in political offices by these groups. Such persons do not invariably take orders with complete servility and execute them with unwavering fidelity.

These considerations explain in large part the otherwise puzzling questions why the firm of J. P. Morgan & Co. engaged John W. Davis as the chief firm attorney but recommended Calvin Coolidge for the Presidency with enthusiasm in 1924; why the business interests were long highly suspicious of an able conservative like Herbert Hoover; and why an occasionally independent and outspoken scholar like Dr. Nicholas Murray Butler was not looked upon with favor by the business interests as presidential material. Yet, government by the interests is not so simple as some seem to believe. There is highly divided counsel in the orders given to the political servants of the interests, owing to the diversification and conflict of economic policies among the capitalists. For example, the international bankers wish freer trade so that their foreign debtors can pay in goods. The industrialists favor high tariffs to protect them against foreign competition. Industrialists desire inflation today to stimulate business. The main powers in speculative finance want "sound money" to insure full payment of debts due them.

Perhaps the chief service of the democratic illusion at present is that it enables countries such as the United States to operate the "bellhop" system successfully and yet keep the people reasonably well satisfied by means of the agreeable fiction that they themselves are running matters through their elected representatives. One can scarcely imagine, however, that this artifice constitutes any permanent or successful solution of the problems of contemporary political control. Cunningly contrived plutocracy is no suitable substitute for democracy.

The old assumption that the masses would evince an all-absorbing interest in public matters the moment that they received the vote has been discredited by experience as effectively as the dogma of mental equality has been dissipated by differential biology and psychology. Studies of nonvoting in the United States by Merriam, Gosnell, Schlesinger, Eriksson, and others have shown that even in presidential elections, which evoke the most widespread interest, only about half of the qualified voters turn out to cast their ballots.[1] The following statistics on the decline of the actual vote, as compared with the total number eligible to suffrage in the United States since 1856, present an illuminating picture of what Professors Schlesinger and Eriksson well designate "the vanishing voter":

[1] *Cf.* C. E. Merriam and H. F. Gosnell, *Non-voting,* University of Chicago Press, 1924.

United States Election Data [1]

Year	Actual Vote	Eligible Vote	Percentage Voting
1856	4,194,088	5,021,956	83.51
1860	4,676,853	5,555,004	84.19
1864	4,024,792	4,743,249	84.85
1868	5,724,686	7,208,164	79.42
1872	6,466,165	8,633,058	74.90
1876	8,412,733	9,799,450	85.84
1880	9,209,406	11,024,900	83.53
1884	10,044,985	12,412,538	80.92
1888	11,380,860	13,800,176	82.46
1892	12,059,351	15,488,748	77.85
1896	13,923,102	17,241,642	80.75
1900	13,959,653	18,272,264	76.39
1904	13,510,648	19,864,495	68.00
1908	14,888,442	21,598,493	68.93
1912	15,036,542	24,276,236	61.95
1916	18,544,579	28,484,046	65.10
1920	26,786,758	51,156,684	52.36
1924	29,091,492	54,421,832	53.45
1928	36,876,419	57,276,321	63.86
1932	39,734,351	60,389,827	65.13

Incidentally, it was shown in this table that even the excitement of the first opportunity to vote was not adequate to bring the expected number of women to the polls in 1920, their record being even worse than that of the men. The vote in state and local elections and in congressional elections in "off years" is far smaller than in presidential contests. The popular vote in direct primaries, which select the candidates for election, has proved so small as often to make the whole scheme of primaries, once a favorite reform fad, a travesty. Intensely important public issues no more call forth an eager populace than do the personal candidates for election. Those plebiscites in which important issues are submitted to the people in the form of the referendum do not seem to evoke any more enthusiastic response than the election of officials. In fact, a referendum by itself tends to elicit much less interest than a party election.

To a considerable extent this lack of interest in exercising the right of suffrage is due to the large-scale and complicated nature of contemporary politics. This has destroyed that sense of immediate local interest in elections and that personal curiosity about candidates which were characteristic of the earlier type of neighborhood politics. A sense of political vagueness and futility has today superseded the rather keen personal interest in policies that directly and visibly concerned the everyday life of the individual, and in candidates who were the personal acquaintances of all or most of the voters. Undoubtedly, another source

---

[1] Adapted and extended from A. M. Schlesinger and E. McK. Eriksson, "The Vanishing Voter," *New Republic*, Oct. 15, 1924, p. 167. An unprecedented number of votes were registered in 1928 and 1932, but this cannot be taken as an indication that the populace is taking a greater interest in politics. In 1928 the emotion-provoking Prohibition issue and the Catholic question were before the public. In 1932 the people were in a state of economic despair and longed to displace those officials they thought blameworthy or ineffectual.

of growing political indifference is the cynicism generated by modern partisan politics and the accompanying corruption and incompetence. This creates the impression that it makes little or no difference anyway as to which party or policy prevails. It might also be pointed out in passing that this cynically assumed absence of vital differences between major party methods and policies has become essentially the fact in American political life today. This state of affairs offers a decisive refutation of the thesis that representative government is bound always to create parties with marked differences as to policy and procedure in government.[1]

One of the most disconcerting aspects of the democratic debacle is that the people seem as indifferent and incompetent with respect to the so-called remedies for democratic failures as they are with regard to the processes of traditional democracy. It has often been held that the remedy for democracy is more democracy, namely, direct primaries, the initiative and the referendum, and the recall of judges and of judicial decisions. The unfortunate fact is that if the people could make use of such devices they would not need them. If they could develop the interest and intelligence essential to any effective exploitation of such mechanisms as the initiative and the referendum, they would be able to govern without them. These "remedies" for democratic failures make the same rigorous demands upon interest, attention, and deliberation that are required for the success of conventional democratic processes. The experience with these devices of radical democracy in the last generation has shown that they fail as often as democracy of a more moderate type, and for the same reasons.[2]

No less mythical in practice has been the democratic thesis of the capacity of the people for calm deliberation regarding the choice of candidates and for sober scrutiny of public policies. In the first place, as we have just shown, hardly half of the electorate, on the average, even shows enough interest in either candidates or policies to turn out at the polls. The nonvoters presumably neither deliberate nor scrutinize, and if they do so it is of no practical significance. It can hardly be held that even the actual voters do much deliberating. The methods of modern political parties during campaigns are not designed to promote calm reflection and penetrating insight into the real facts, issues, and personalities involved, but are rather calculated to stimulate emotion and to paralyze thought.[3] The psychopathology of the political party has been analyzed by Graham Wallas, Walter Lippmann, Robert Michels, Seba Eldridge, and others in detail and with precision. The successful party is usually the one that develops the best technique for stirring the emotions of the masses to a favorable reaction rather than the one which presents the most intelligent candidates or platform.

Further, as we noted previously, modern psychology has pulverized the old Benthamite felicific calculus and the rationalistic type of political psychology that grew out of it. It has been amply proved that man is not a cool, calculating entity, invariably choosing that line of conduct which he believes is sure to bring him a maximum of benefit and a minimum of discomfort. He is rather a

---

[1] See above, pp. 501 ff. [2] See below, pp. 879 ff.
[3] *Cf.* Bruce, *American Parties and Politics,* Chaps. XIII-XV, XVII.

creature dominated by such irrational factors as tradition, custom, convention, habit, and the passions of the mob.[1] These irrational influences are particularly present and potent in political campaigns. One's political preferences are determined chiefly by the circumstances of birth and upbringing, which lead the child to adopt the politics of his parents. Most of us are "biological" Democrats or Republicans. To this conventional or customary background are added the emotion-provoking antics of those who plan and execute campaigns so as to reduce them to the psychic level of a mob.

There is, therefore, little opportunity for any calm deliberation or careful scrutiny, or for the exercise of that shrewd insight into the qualities of candidates which was believed to be the particular attribute of the common people.

The argument that democracy is vindicated, if on no other grounds, by the special capacity of the masses for moral judgments and support of great idealistic causes, is easily seen to be mainly specious. In the first place, we now realize that there can be nothing really "moral" that is not scientifically sound.[2] The populace has neither the information nor the intelligence to ascertain what is actually valid in regard to social situations. The only way in which the public can be useful in moral questions is through the development of popular trust in the judgment of trained and informed leaders. Most of the great moral crusades have not had a popular origin, but have been the result of arousing popular support for movements begun by some educated and intellectually aristocratic reformer. The two great moral reforms carried on as a result of mass pressure in the United States have been Abolition and Prohibition, both of which have been widely regarded as ill-conceived and disastrous in their ultimate social results, fully conceding the desirability of freeing the slaves and arriving at a more rational control of the consumption of alcoholic liquor.

Progress in political science and social economics has made it clear enough that the old theory of political determinism is hopelessly superficial and inadequate. The laws of social causation which have now been established have proved that political institutions are derivative and not primary.[3] A political system does not create a social order, but a definite type of economic and social system produces in time a compatible political system, making due allowance for divergences in detail caused by differences of historical background and variations in culture. Hence democracy cannot be relied upon to mold a social system satisfactory to its requirements, but can only develop where conditions are adapted to encourage democratic institutions.

Another obstacle to the success of democracy in practical experience has been the rise of a permanent bureaucracy in the official civil service. In the United States, democracy has been weakened by the inefficiency and corruption growing out of our lack—at least until recently—of a well-trained and public-spirited civil service. England has been praised for having one. But while British administrative efficiency has gained as a result, democracy has suffered. So powerful has the permanent bureaucracy become that the initiative and authority of the ministry and the Parliament have become severely curtailed. It is literally a

---

[1] *Cf.* Wallas, *Human Nature in Politics;* Sumner, *Folkways;* and Gustave Le Bon, *The Crowd*, new ed., Macmillan, 1925.
[2] *Cf.* Parshley, *Science and Good Behavior.*   [3] *Cf.* Beard, *The Economic Basis of Politics.*

fact that the elected representatives in Great Britain today cannot seriously alter the policies and procedure of the permanent civil service. It would require a political revolution to do so. Ramsay MacDonald and the Labor government were criticized by radicals for not going further with the reconstruction of England. They were held back not only by their failure to have a clear majority in the House of Commons, but also by the fact that they did not dare to challenge the civil-service bureaucracy. In short, where we have no bureaucracy we have inefficiency; where we have bureaucracy we cease to have real democracy, whatever the external forms of government.

For reasons that we have outlined above, it would scarcely seem that democracy is suited to the exacting requirements of our complicated industrial civilization. Indeed, some of our best writers on contemporary society are coming to doubt the very adequacy of political institutions as a mode of social control and are demanding a new form of social control based upon and conforming to the economic and social realities of the present age. Technocracy is the most advanced proposal of this sort. W. K. Wallace's *The Passing of Politics*[1] is a representative example of a conservative advocacy of the abandonment of political institutions. Syndicalism is based upon the assumption of the archaic and antiquated character of political institutions. It recommends a simple and direct process of government through the economic groups that exist today. A Syndicalist congress would be an assembly of labor-unionists and professional men.[2] Again, the real dependence of government upon the social environment suggests the inadequacy of political democracy by itself alone. The vote is of little value to the socially submerged. Any real democracy would have to include social democracy as well as universal suffrage.[3]

Likewise, the nationalistic obsession has proved a dangerous doctrine for democracy in world-society.[4] Democracy cannot well ignore international conditions. A great war may come to any country in an age of "international anarchy" and destroy the political institutions that have been evolving and approaching perfection for many years. The democratic system in England at the outbreak of the World War was probably the highest pinnacle that democracy has attained—or may ever attain. Yet it was devastatingly shocked, if not permanently wrecked, by the impact of the World War.

Indeed, democracy as a defense against going to war was shown to be weak in the crisis of 1914, when even in a democracy like France or England, political leaders could plunge a fundamentally pacific population into the abyss.[5] Georges Demartial's *The War of 1914: How Consciences Were Mobilized* (1922), Caroline E. Playne's *Society at War,* Irene Cooper Willis's *England's Holy War,* C. H. Grattan's *Why We Fought,*[6] and Viereck's *Spreading Germs of Hate* present magnificent clinical pictures of the futility of democracy as a safeguard against war.

Though democracy cannot by itself cure war, the success of the World War in disposing of many of those symptoms of democracy which previously existed

---

[1] Macmillan, 1924.   [2] See below, pp. 952 ff.
[3] *Cf.* Hobhouse, *Liberalism;* and A. W. Small, *Between Eras from Capitalism to Democracy,* Intercollegiate Press, 1913.
[4] *Cf.* G. L. Dickinson, *The International Anarchy, 1904-14,* Century, 1926.
[5] See above, pp. 589 ff.   [6] Vanguard Press, 1929.

proved pretty convincingly that war can "cure" democracy. The World War was probably the greatest blow to democracy since the dismal failure of the Revolutions of 1848. There has been at one time or another since 1918 what amounted to a practical dictatorship by a person or a committee in Germany, Italy, Hungary, Austria, Russia, Spain, Portugal, Poland, Yugoslavia, Greece, Rumania, Bulgaria, and Turkey. In other European states emergency governments have ruled with quasi-dictatorial methods.

Lord Bryce, the outstanding student of the rise and character of modern democracy, was compelled to admit at the end of his studies that democracy had failed to achieve the main results that had been hoped from it:

It has brought no nearer friendly feeling and the sense of human brotherhood among peoples of the world towards one another. Neither has it created goodwill and a sense of unity and civic fellowship within each of these peoples. . . . It has not purified or dignified politics . . . and has not induced that satisfaction and contentment with itself as the best form of government which was expected.[1]

There is, perhaps, no other summary estimate of the contributions and defects of democratic government that is quite so authoritative or inclusive as that presented by Bryce:

I. It has maintained public order while securing the liberty of the individual citizen.

II. It has given a civil administration as efficient as other forms of government have provided.

III. Its legislation has been more generally directed to the welfare of the poorer classes than has been that of other Governments.

IV. It has not been inconstant or ungrateful.

V. It has not weakened patriotism or courage.

VI. It has often been wasteful and usually extravagant.

VII. It has not produced general contentment in each nation.

VIII. It has done little to improve international relations and ensure peace, has not diminished class selfishness (witness Australia and New Zealand), has not fostered a cosmopolitan humanitarianism nor mitigated the dislike of men of a different colour.

IX. It has not extinguished corruption and the malign influences wealth can exert upon government.

X. It has not removed the fear of revolutions.

XI. It has not enlisted in the service of the State a sufficient number of the most honest and capable citizens.

XII. Nevertheless it has, taken all in all, given better practical results than either the Rule of One Man or the Rule of a Class, for it has at least extinguished many of the evils by which they were effaced.[2]

---

[1] James Bryce, *Modern Democracies,* new ed., Macmillan, 1921, 2 vols., Vol. II, p. 533. *Cf.* Wallace, *op. cit.,* pp. 190 ff., and C. L. Becker, "Lord Bryce on Modern Democracies," in *Political Science Quarterly,* December, 1921.

[2] Bryce, *op. cit.,* Vol. II, p. 562. Democracy has hardly, however, as Bryce implies, obliterated class rule. The rule of the capitalist class has been more obvious and thorough in the United States than in prewar Germany, for example. The German Junkers were more successful than the American farmers in resisting the advances of plutocracy. While democracy originated in an agrarian age, the growing dominion of capitalism has coincided remarkably with the progress of political democracy.

The most important and direct challenge to democracy since the World War is Fascism.[1] This movement is not to be identified with dictatorship. Fascism can hardly exist without dictatorship, but not all dictatorships are Fascist in character. Fascism rests upon a sweeping antidemocratic philosophy. It repudiates natural rights, majority rule, representative government, parliamentarianism, and all other traditional categories and concepts of democracy. The individual and social groups must be subordinated to an absolutist guild state. The Aristotelian dogma that the few intellectually élite are born to rule is eagerly embraced. Dictatorship is accepted as necessary in order that the state may be swift and well integrated in its action. Gaining a footing first in Italy, the Fascist philosophy has more recently been accepted in Hitlerite Germany and is spreading to other countries.

The amazing spread of Fascism is well indicated by a United Press dispatch from London, dated January 11, 1934:

Fascism and parliamentary government were at death grips in all Europe today, with indications that 1934 might prove the decisive year in the struggle between the new and old political orders.

Governments of five nations—Austria, Roumania, Holland, Latvia, and the Irish Free State—have taken stern repressive measures since the new year, against Fascists or Nazis, their counterpart.

A premier, Ion G. Duca of Roumania, has fallen victim to a Nazi assassin. Roumanian and Austrian prisons are filling with Nazis.

With Nazi Germany as the center of the new Fascist movement, agitation and violence by those who believe the old form of government is doomed have spread over the continent.

Before the following summary was written, Austria had joined the impressive list of Fascist states (May 1, 1934). The extent of dictatorial rule in Europe under Fascism and Communism is well summarized in this communication from a competent European correspondent, Leland Stowe:

Twenty years after the outbreak of the war "to make the world safe for democracy," 354,000,000 out of Europe's 550,000,000 people are living under dictatorships in 12 different European countries, and democracy is banished from two-thirds of continental Europe. Twenty years after Aug. 1, 1914, Europe's political and social foundations are beset by the most serious disintegration yet recorded in the peace times of the 20th Century. Today more than ever Europe soberly realizes that the peace treaties have brought anything but peace.[2]

Students of modern European history are fairly familiar with the reaction after Metternich, with such oppressive measures as the Carlsbad Decrees of 1819, and with the flight of central-European liberals to America and other havens. But we hardly realize that repression is much more rife today than it was a century ago. Van Gheel Gildmeister, a Dutch Quaker who has been working for years among the victims of European political intolerance, revealed the fact that in the summer of 1934 there were no less than 3,500,000 political prisoners in central and southeastern Europe, excluding any in Russia. This is a far larger number than were imprisoned in the most palmy days of the Metternichian reaction.

[1] See below, pp. 961 ff.   [2] Syracuse *Herald*, Aug. 5, 1934.

Among the new states of Europe, Czechoslovakia has been the one consistent and successful outpost of democracy. But this has been due chiefly to the prestige of its distinguished democratic President, Professor Masaryk, and to the efficiency and industry of his able lieutenant, Professor Beneš. Many doubt whether democracy will long survive the removal of Masaryk from the scene.

The protagonists of autocracy now have at their disposal ample evidence that when democracy becomes threatening the movement can be easily checked by launching another war. There is little doubt that they will speedily make the effort, especially if the vested interests of plutocracy and autocracy stand to gain extensively in a material way by war. Therefore, one may safely say that democracy can safely coexist only with a pacific world order. It may well be that democracy is not even equal to the requirements of a peaceful society, but there is no doubt of its incapacity in the face of the strains of war. To point to the efficiency of the United States during the World War is no refutation of this statement. Such efficiency as we exhibited was purchased by disproportionately greater sacrifices of democratic institutions and intellectual freedom.[1]

IV. THE OUTLOOK FOR DEMOCRACY

One of the most frequently exploited of the apologies for democracy is the allegation that it is unfair to say that democracy is a failure, since it has really never been tried. It is pointed out that, even though we have long enjoyed universal suffrage in the United States, yet the real power in economic life and government is concentrated in the hands of a few very wealthy individuals —that we have plutocracy and not democracy. Mr. James W. Gerard once stated[2] that fifty-nine men rule America. The answer is that there could be no more effective proof of the futility of conventional democracy than the fact that we have enjoyed universal suffrage in the United States for a hundred years without realizing true democracy. If we have not been able to establish democracy in this country in the past century, when general social conditions were far better adapted to democracy than they are today or probably will be tomorrow, what hope is there that we shall be any closer to real democracy a hundred years hence? Especially when the world is much less liberal and democratic today than it was in 1900.

Several hundred years hence the historians of political theory and institutions may describe democracy as the most interesting political fiction of the nineteenth century. It may be shown to be something that, as originally understood, never did and never could exist on a large scale. The conditions that promoted it and in conjunction with which it might have existed—a simple agrarian society and a stable civilization—were already passing away when the democratic dogmas were first being fashioned. Before popular government was realized in practice those social conditions which were compatible with it had all but disappeared. Likewise, the theoretical assumptions upon which democracy was launched—the equality of man, high potential interest in public affairs on the part of the masses, and penetrating rationality of the populace in political

[1] *Cf.* Zechariah Chafee, Jr., *Freedom of Speech*, Harcourt, Brace, 1920.
[2] In American newspapers in August, 1931.

matters—have been disproved by the development of science and the test of experience. Hence, the political problem of the future is not to vindicate the old type of democracy, but to seek some form of social control more tenable in theory and more adapted in practice to the requirements of the contemporary age.

There is, then, no inherent reason why one should view with despair the debacle of the older democratic dogma, any more than one should lament the passing of absolute monarchy or feudal autocracy. There was once as much dismay among autocrats concerning the decay of absolutism as we now find in the writings of Bryce, Lippmann, and other even more disillusioned friends of democracy. The vital question before us is not that of retaining nineteenth-century democracy but that of finding some kind of government that will work.

It has been said by some that it is manifestly impossible to find another successful form of government. They contend that the friends of democracy may at least seek comfort in the thought that all other forms of government have proved to be worse. This implies, however, a retrospective attitude. The "worse" forms of government are those of the past. We have no means of knowing how greatly we may advance beyond those earlier methods and devices, all of which were worked out in a crude manner on the basis of limited experience and very little scientific knowledge. There is no reason why we should not employ in the political field some original and inventive ability, based upon the experience and social changes of the last century and the scientific knowledge concerning man and society that has been accumulated during this same period.

The problem is really one of getting efficient and social-minded leaders into positions of authority and responsibility.[1] We must have the efficiency, training, and professional political spirit of the old Prussian bureaucracy, divested of its class spirit, its arrogance, and its oppressiveness. Intelligence tests for weighing voting power; intelligence tests, information tests, special professional training, and successful experience for office-holding and promotion; the establishment of government schools for the training of officials in every branch of the government service, both domestic and foreign; and some combination of vocational and proportional representation to give justice and rationale to representative government—these would seem to be suggestions that are surely worthy of consideration and might be woven into the structure of the new state.[2] More power and vitality in local government units would doubtless help a good deal. The elimination of sumptuary legislation and much quite unnecessary state interference would relieve the strains upon administration and would decrease the burdens of political control. Many argue, however, that the fundamental changes in the economic and social structure in the last century render such reforms as these superficial, inadequate, and about as impossible as the old-fashioned democratic ideals and practices.

One must accustom himself, moreover, to considering the possible disappear-

[1] One of the most suggestive and sensible assessments of the future of democracy is the article "Is Democracy Doomed?" by Will Durant, *Saturday Evening Post*, Sept. 15, 1934. See especially his remedies for democracy, p. 82.

[2] On the interesting proposal of vocational representation, see H. A. Overstreet, "The Government of Tomorrow," *Forum*, July, 1915.

ance of what have in the past been called political institutions, as apart from the natural and functional social and economic groupings. He must envisage the possible development of a system of social control executed by the socio-economic organizations. It may well be that we shall pass on to highly novel and much more rational and effective types of social control than we now know how to make use of.[1] We may in the future look back upon the nineteenth-century democratic illusion much as a highly trained contemporary chemist views the aspirations of the old alchemists.

V. CONTEMPORARY ABUSES IN THE PARTY SYSTEM

In a previous chapter we traced the evolution of representative government, showed how this brought into being party government, and then followed the development of party government through its various stages down to the twentieth century. In spite of the indispensable nature of the political party in representative government, it inevitably developed serious abuses as by-products. Many of these abuses are not inherent in, and inseparable from, party government. Some of them were blunders inevitable in the first stages of experimentation with any procedure.

It may, perhaps, be helpful in understanding the critical state of party government to deal briefly with the abuses that have been most evident in the modern political party in the United States, and to indicate how we have attempted, in one way or another, to eradicate these defects.

First among the abuses of the modern party is the all-prevalent domination of the boss and the machine. It is a general and popular superstition in regard to the American government that the individual citizen is able directly to advance his interests and to make his opinion felt in governmental matters. In other words, the government is supposed to be the direct representative of the mass of citizens, whose wishes should dominate and direct all legislation.

All who have made even an elementary study of the processes of American government in the last fifty years know that this conception is but a pious aspiration and a misleading myth. It has been very difficult for any citizen or any group of public-spirited citizens to exert effective pressure directly upon any governmental organization. Legislation can usually be secured only through an advance negotiation with, and approval by, the boss and the machine. Instead of direct government, we have built what has been frequently called the "invisible government," controlling most phases of American political life. Elihu Root once said that for nearly a generation the center of the government of the Empire State was not at Albany, but in the private offices of Thomas C. Platt, of the United States Express Company. There has thus been built up an almost insuperable obstacle to true representative and democratic government.

Down to a generation ago, voting was not secret. It was possible for a boss or his representative to know how every citizen voted. This made it easy for the employer of a voter or for representatives of the political machine to intimidate the citizen and compel him to vote otherwise than he might have done had he been able to exercise complete independence.

---

[1] *Cf.* Wallace, *op. cit.*

CONTEMPORARY ABUSES IN THE PARTY SYSTEM

Again, the party machine has completely controlled the selection of delegates to the nominating conventions. Even the delegates themselves at the conventions have had relatively little part in the choice of candidates, the selection of whom has normally been prearranged and already decided upon by a narrow clique of the more powerful members of the machine. The people have then been given the opportunity to reject or ratify the candidates thus nominated, in whose selection the great mass of the citizens played no part whatever. In this way, political officers, who theoretically owed their position to popular election, were actually chosen by the machine.

The nomination of Warren G. Harding in 1920 was one of the most flagrant examples of the undemocratic nature of convention nominations. Mr. Harding was a relatively unknown machine politician in 1920. He was known only as a strictly regular Republican Senator of appearance and bearing above the average. He made a miserable showing in the preconvention primaries, and even his own manager was not elected to the Chicago convention. There was a long-drawn-out deadlock between Johnson, Lowden, and Wood, which apparently could not be broken. The weather was unbearably hot in Chicago at the time, and the delegates were disconsolate at the thought of another week-end in that city. The leaders of the plutocrats at the convention then saw their chance to exploit this desire of the delegates to get away from Chicago and to slip in a candidate who would be most plastic in their hands if elected to the Presidency. Harding seemed to be their man, as he was known to be wholly safe and complaisant, and his physiognomy seemed most promising to decorate the campaign pictures. Hence Myron T. Herrick, George Harvey, and a half-dozen others railroaded him through the convention. He was in no sense whatever the choice of the people. Had there been a popular plebiscite held throughout the United States on the eve of the Chicago convention of 1920, it is doubtful if Harding would have received 100,000 votes. He was nominated, and over 15,500,000 surged forward to place their stamp of approval upon him. The man the great majority of the people probably really desired to see nominated for the Presidency in 1920, Mr. Herbert Hoover, was not seriously considered by the convention.

Not only do the boss and the machine control the voting and nominations, they also control legislation. As we have already pointed out, the boss and the machine tend completely to dominate legislative processes. Even if the machine graciously allows a citizen or a group of citizens to introduce a bill embodying their desires, it stands no chance of being favorably reported out of committee and passed unless it meets the approval of the party leaders. In many cases, bills not approved by the party machine are not even introduced in the legislature. Legislation is mainly a matter secretly and effectively arranged between the favored groups and classes on the one hand, and the party machine on the other. The real government is centered in the collusion between the machine and the lobby.[1]

We are not, of course, arguing for any special diabolism on the part of American capitalism. Jefferson and the agrarians were politically as unscrupu-

[1] *Cf.* E. P. Herring, *Group Representation before Congress*, Johns Hopkins Press, 1929.

lous in their day, and if we were to have a society dominated by the proletariat we should certainly witness a most faithful continuance of much the same political methods that they now so warmly criticize when exploited by their plutocratic masters. It merely happens that we are now controlled by the business and financial classes.

In some few instances where the labor groups possessed an unusual degree of power, they also began to exert the same sorts of pressure upon legislation that had earlier been exerted by capitalistic representatives.[1] What we are concerned with now is the solemn fact that during the last fifty years popular wishes have had very little to do with the major part of the important legislation passed in our federal and state governments. The plutocracy have calmly used their power over the legislatures to embody their wishes and objectives in legislation. They have then utilized a generally willing and subservient press to convince the populace that such laws and policies were not only what the people really needed to advance the public welfare, but were also exactly what the mass of people actually desired. In most cases the press has been very successful in executing this technique of deception.

The only important limitation upon thoroughgoing government by the vested interests and the machine is the fact that, at least down to 1920, this collusion could not well be carried too far without leading to popular indignation and the development of a revolt against it. Such rebellion has appeared from time to time in the Liberal Republican movement, the Mugwump secession, Bryan Democracy, the Roosevelt Progressivism of 1912, the repudiation of Wilsonism and Palmerism in 1920, and the Farmer-Labor revolt of 1924. For the most part, however, the "interests" and the politicians have been able to deceive and reassure the public, and the revolts against plutocratic control have not been frequent or very successful. The failure to repudiate Coolidge and the Republican party in 1924 after the oil and Veterans' Bureau scandals well illustrates the contemporary docility or cynicism of the public in the face of the gravest abuses.[2]

As a reward for keeping the government in line with the interests of the dominant economic groups, the boss and the machine have been granted all sorts of gross and petty graft, and innumerable opportunities for public corruption. The "spoils system" has become something far more diversified, ingenious, and remunerative than in its primitive days under Andrew Jackson. Favorable contracts on government works, spoils of appointive office, "pork-barrel" legislation, and other types of positive rewards have been handed over to the boss for his efficient services in keeping the populace and the party subservient.[3]

With the growth of the population, the more perfect organization of the party, and the increased necessity for partisan alertness, the expenses that have been connected with successful party organization and campaigns have enormously increased. Vast sums of money have been spent to secure the nomination of favored candidates. In order to elect their candidates, political leaders have demanded large contributions from the powerful economic interests.

[1] *Cf.* Childs, *Labor and Capital in National Politics.*
[2] *Cf.* M. R. Werner, *Privileged Characters,* McBride, 1935.
[3] *Cf.* Merriam and Gosnell, *The American Party System,* Chaps. IV-VII, and R. C. Brooks, *Corruption in American Politics and Life,* Dodd, Mead, 1910.

This practice first became notorious in the Republican campaign of 1896, when Mark Hanna raised vast sums from Wall Street in order to secure the election of Major McKinley and to defeat what was believed to be the revolutionary program of William Jennings Byran. It had cost only $250,000 to elect Abraham Lincoln, but Hanna is said to have collected in all some $3,350,000 to put McKinley into the White House. This was far the largest sum ever expended in behalf of a single candidate up to that time. It was probably a good bargain for the economic interests that were faithfully shielded by McKinley's administration, though its value was in part lost by his assassination in 1901 and the succession of the more liberal Roosevelt. The Democrats spent only $700,000 on Bryan in 1896.

Though more money was spent for the election of McKinley than for any other candidate in our party history down to 1920, this was a very exceptional case at the time. The outlay for campaign expenses in the last thirty years has increased enormously in comparison with the situation before 1896. In 1916 the Republicans spent $3,500,000 in trying to elect Hughes. In no case has the Republican party spent less on its presidential candidate since that time. It spent $7,265,000 on Harding in 1920. The Democrats spent $2,300,000 for Cox. In the campaign of 1928 about $16,600,000 was expended by national and state committees—some $9,433,600 for Hoover and $7,152,500 for Smith. The following table gives the expenditures of the National Committees of the Republican and Democratic parties since 1896 in the presidential campaigns:

Year	Republican	Democratic
1896	$3,350,000	$ 675,000
1900	3,000,000	425,000
1904	1,900,000	700,000
1908	1,655,000	619,000
1912	1,076,000	1,134,000
1916	2,441,000	1,684,000
1920	4,022,000	1,318,000
1924	2,806,000	903,000
1928	3,529,000	5,342,000

That these sums are but a part of the total campaign expenditures is to be seen from the fact that the total Republican expenditures in the campaign of 1920 were $7,265,000 as compared with the $4,022,000 spent by the national committee. Most of this money is contributed by powerful individuals and interests that expect favors or protection. Five powerful interests—Standard Oil, Guggenheim, steel, automobiles, and public utilities—contributed approximately $1,000,000 to the Hoover chest in 1928. Some 239 individuals gave over $2,500,000 to the Hoover cause; one Republican contributed $175,000. Three Democrats each gave more than $100,000 to the Smith fund. In 1928 a new method of campaigning—radio addresses—was developed. The Republicans spent $600,000 in this way, and the Democrats $500,000.

Not only presidential but also congressional elections often involve colossal campaign expenditures. One senatorial candidate spent over $2,000,000 for his nomination and election. Since the World War three would-be Senators have been challenged by the Senate and refused seats because of excessive expenditures for nomination and election—Truman H. Newberry of Michigan in 1918; Frank L. Smith of Illinois in 1926; and William S. Vare of Pennsylvania in 1926.

More recently there has been a deplorable development of excessive expenditures for the securing of nominations for office, particularly the nomination for the office of President of the United States. So far did this go that Mr. Roosevelt's campaign for nomination in 1912 cost $750,000, while in the period preceding the Republican convention of 1920 so much money was expended by candidates in the struggle for delegates that two of the most prominent candidates were practically disqualified by the revelation of the preconvention expenditures in their campaign for nomination. The campaign of Leonard Wood for nomination at this time cost $1,775,000. Frank O. Lowden's expenses at the same time were $415,000. The Newberry, Smith, and Vare cases involved heavy nomination as well as election expenses. The direct primary has been in part responsible for this large increase in expenditures for nominations to office. It costs more to secure the support of the many who vote in primaries than it did to control the few who used to vote in caucuses and conventions. In states, like Pennsylvania, that are preponderantly one-party states the nomination is tantamount to election. Hence it is logical that more money should be spent in the primaries than in the formal election campaign.

Not only has there been a scandalous use of money in campaigns for nomination and election to public office. There has been much overt fraud and intimidation. Voters of minority parties are often kept away from the polls by violence, if necessary. Repeaters cast many ballots each for the candidates favored by the dominant machine. Ballots are fraudulently counted. It has been a persistent belief that Mr. Bryan was cheated out of hundreds of thousands, if not millions, of votes in the campaign of 1896 through fraudulent counts in centers controlled by the desperate and scared big-business forces. Fraudulent counts in city elections are regrettably common. Intimidation and fraud at the polls have become especially prevalent in the last fifteen years in connection with the rise of racketeering and gangdom and their affiliations with dominant political machines. Our election laws are archaic and provide inadequate protection to insure fair elections even when enforced. In a recent study, Dr. Joseph P. Harris concludes that:

Every investigation or election contest brings to light glaring irregularities, errors, misconduct on the part of precinct officers, disregard of election laws and instructions, slipshod practices, and downright frauds. The entire country has been shocked from time to time by the revelation of wholesale election frauds in some of our large cities. Competent political observers report that election frauds are by no means confined to these few cities, but are widely prevalent in less populous communities. Even these election scandals and the slipshod administration revealed by election recounts do not indicate the real state of affairs which prevails generally in election administration. The truth of the matter is that the whole administration—organizations, laws, methods and procedures, and records—are, for most states, quite obsolete. The whole system, including the election laws, requires a thorough revision and improvement.[1]

[1] Harris, *Election Administration in the United States,* Brookings Institution, 1934, p. 1.

In the course of party development, the machine and party organization, which are supposed to be a means for advancing the party program, have become ends in themselves. Since the campaign of 1900 there has been little vital contrast or conflict of principles between the Republican and Democratic parties.[1] They have rarely taken any fundamentally divergent stand upon any of the more significant public problems before us. The main goal of both parties in the last generation has been the spoils of office. An effort has been made to keep the machinery of the party intact, and to discourage any powerful insurgent movement that might wreck one of the grand old parties and substitute a new party with a definite and original party program.

For the last twenty-five years the citizen has merely been asked to decide which party machine he prefers. He has not been permitted to choose between two fundamentally different programs of public policy. The election of 1912 offered a slight exception to this situation, but even this episode demonstrated the power of the machine in the political party. Even the most dynamic and popular figure in American political life in the fifty years after the Civil War, with the most attractive and constructive party program that had been worked out since the original platform of the Republican party of 1856, was unable to carry through a successful revolt against the corrupt and reactionary Republican machine. The power of the machine was further demonstrated in 1912 through its ability to exclude from the Republican nomination for the Presidency the man who was most certainly the choice of the Republican voters of the country.

Another source of the corruption and of the defects of party government lies in the power of party symbols and party shibboleths, catchwords, and phrases, which are unreasoningly accepted by the mass of citizens.[2] The majority react to propositions and suggestions in a fundamentally emotional manner. Hence party symbols, party shibboleths, campaign catchwords—such as "the bloody shirt," "the full dinner pail," "the new freedom," references to "the grand old party" and to distinguished men who have led the party in the past—are relied upon to hold the voter in line and secure his allegiance, even though he knows nothing of the platform of the party, and would be likely to disapprove of it if it were made clear to him.

Those who wish to improve our political life and to wage a successful fight against the corruption and inefficiency that prevail find this power of party symbolism and phraseology an almost insuperable obstacle. To the average American audience, the sudden flashing upon the screen of the elephant, the donkey, the pictures of Jefferson, Jackson, Lincoln, Grant, McKinley, Bryan, or Roosevelt, weigh far more heavily and arouse more instant response and approval than the most carefully considered sound, scholarly, and informed political speech that one could imagine. Particularly significant is the fact that political campaigns are the periods in which the voter should employ the greatest amount of rationality, but they are actually the moment when he is most at the mercy of the emotions of party strife. The partisanship that between campaigns is but a mild aberration becomes inflated during the campaign periods

---

[1] *Cf.* Schlesinger, *New Viewpoints in American History*, Chap. XII, and Bruce, *op. cit.*, Chap. VII.

[2] *Cf.* Bruce, *op. cit.*, Chap. XIV.

into what is often downright hysteria and a paralysis of rational judgment.

A fundamental problem in party government relates to the very character of modern representative institutions. The old territorial units of representation are proving more and more inadequate to meet the problems of our complicated industrial civilization. Outside of purely rural districts a constituency is made up of the greatest diversity of social and economic classes and group interests. No man can truly "represent" them all, or any considerable proportion of them. If he really represents one or two of the stronger interests in his constituency, he dare not do so too openly lest he incur the displeasure of the others and risk defeat at the next election. As a result of this situation an extra-legal type of representation has arisen in the powerful and diversified lobby that has grown up in the national capital and in most state capitals. Here the representatives of the dominant interests—bankers, industrialists, exporters, farmers, war veterans, labor leaders, and the rest—assemble and deal directly with legislators. They try to secure the passage of laws favorable to their clients and to kill restrictive legislation. So powerful has this national lobby become that Professor Herring has well described it as a "third house of Congress." This development may be inevitable, but it is also a challenge to the existing type of representative government and to our party system. The importance of all this, not only for party government but even for the future of democracy itself, has been well expressed by Professor Becker when he says that

in place of nations of individuals, all more or less alike in respect to conditions and ideas, the Industrial Revolution has given us nations differentiated into classes and corporate and occupational groups, more or less different and often sharply antagonistic, in which lines of division have little or nothing to do with the territorial areas on which political representation is based. The government, nominally composed of persons chosen to represent the will of the people in certain territorial areas, finds that the crucial problems of the time, which are essentially economic, cannot be solved without taking into account the will of the people grouped in certain economic categories. Such is doubtless the real source of the diminished state of Deputies and Congressmen. What they too often legally represent is a group of people without any definite common will to be expressed; what they have to deal with are groups of people (and not labor groups only) who can get their will expressed only, or much better, by using their extra-legal power as a means of dictation.[1]

Another important issue is that raised by the exponents of proportional representation. They point out the injustice of leaving the defeated party members with no representatives, even though they may have lost the election by the narrow margin of only a few votes. They contend that valid representative government must give the parties representation in proportion to their strength. They hold that it is palpably unfair to give one party or group 100 per cent of the representation when they may have won the election by a majority of only 1 per cent of the votes cast. Yet it must be remembered that proportional representation would increase the number of parties in legislatures, thus creating the bloc system with its disadvantages.

[1] Becker, "Lord Bryce on Modern Democracies," *loc. cit.*, pp. 674-75.

VI. EFFORTS TO REFORM PARTY GOVERNMENT

The more enlightened citizens from the days of George William Curtis and Carl Schurz to our own have been thoroughly aware of the degradation of our political life that has been associated with the rise and domination of the party machine. There have been various attempts to reduce the prevalence of autocracy, corruption, and inefficiency in party government.[1]

One of the first modes of attack upon the party system came in the effort to substitute the civil-service system for the spoils system. This movement began to get thoroughly under way about 1872, and it has progressively developed until the majority of our federal offices are, at least in legal theory, filled upon the basis of merit as demonstrated by competitive examinations. But the federal civil service is by no means perfect at the present time, and the state and municipal civil-service systems are far inferior to that of the national government. Still, the situation has been greatly improved in comparison to that which prevailed in the time of President Grant. Of all the attempts to limit the complete rule of the boss, it is probable that the civil-service movement has been the most practically effective, even though the appointment of eligibles is still determined by partisan considerations and influence. Elective offices are still, of course, completely in the control of the party system.

The intimidation of the voter through a knowledge of how he is voting has been in part eliminated through the introduction of the Australian ballot, which came into this country in the decade following 1885.[2] At the present time, the secret ballot is in use in forty-seven of the forty-eight states. South Carolina remains the exception. Yet this secret or Australian ballot has not fully prevented the boss from knowing how a man votes, if it is in his power to intimidate the individual. Various special directions as to names to be written in the blank column of the ballot can serve to reveal the vote of an individual to the boss or his representatives about as adequately as in the earlier days when the vote was by show of hand or word of mouth. Voting machines make this more difficult, and the political machine has tended, though not always successfully, to resist their introduction.

In preventing the complete domination of legislation by the boss, there have been attempts by various groups of citizens and reform organizations to organize for the purpose of advancing certain types of legislation. By large-scale persistent efforts it has become occasionally possible for a sufficiently powerful group of citizens to secure the introduction, if not the passage, of bills looking towards political improvement and a better public policy.[3]

A notable effort to break down the control of the boss and the machine over legislation has been the so-called initiative and referendum. They were widely used in Switzerland and introduced into the United States in 1899 by South Dakota. Twenty states have adopted them in one form or another. When using the initiative, a stipulated number of citizens affix their names to a petition and

---

[1] *Cf.* R. C. Brooks, *Political Parties and Electoral Problems*, Harper, 1923, Pt. IV.
[2] *Cf.* E. C. Evans, *History of the Australian Ballot System in the United States*, University of Chicago Press, 1917.
[3] *Cf.* Herring, *op. cit.*

force the submission of the proposed legislation to the people of the state. The subsequent submission of a measure to the people is called a referendum. If the majority of the people approve, then this becomes law. In this way the law-making process may be taken entirely out of the hands of the boss-controlled legislature. The initiative and referendum may be worked together or separately. When they are applied together the law is initiated by the people and approved by them. When they are employed separately, a law may be initiated by petition and its fate be decided by the legislature with no popular referendum, or a proposition may be approved by the legislature in the first instance and then submitted to a referendum before it can become law.

These devices are intended to give the people a large share in the direct proposal and initiation of legislation and in the rejection of legislation passed by the machine-ridden legislature. But, excellent as these have been in theory, their practical operation has not been conspicuously successful. The people have shown a general apathy, popular organization has been difficult, and the general body of citizens have found it difficult to vote intelligently on the technical problems involved in many measures. If they vote at all on such matters they prefer to accept the suggestions of the party leaders. It is still true, therefore, that the vast body of legislation is introduced and passed at the behest, and under the control, of the machine leaders.

Attempts have been made to reduce the volume of corruption in politics through: (1) The impeachment or dismissal of legislators and public officials found guilty of receiving bribes; (2) through investigations of building scandals in connection with state and public works; and (3) through the introduction of a budget system, thus reducing the possibility of the wholesale graft and wild expenditures involved in the "pork-barrel" and "rider" devices.

The vast expenditures for nomination and election to public office have encouraged efforts to curb these abuses.[1] Laws—especially the federal Corrupt Practices acts from 1911 to 1925—designed to prevent elections from being a walkaway for the wealthy have outlawed contributions from employees of the federal government; forbidden contributions from national banks and public corporations; limited the amount that may be spent in election to federal offices; made it illegal to promise a job as a reward for political support; tabooed bribery in voting; and ordered publicity in campaign expenses.

But even such commendable measures as these have failed adequately to remedy the situation. The poor man is still handicapped. The laws exempt from inclusion under election expenses everything spent for personal expenses, stationery, postage, printing, telephone and telegraph charges, and the like—in short, most legitimate electioneering expenses. Friends or friendly interests may spend almost unlimited funds for the candidate. Expenditures may be made at other times than during the campaign without any severe restrictions. Great deficits may be piled up and paid off after the expense report has been filed. The much-heralded reporting of expenditures is often perfunctory and gets little publicity unless there are alert newspapers that scent a scandal. There is little machinery for enforcing existing legislation. Finally, primaries are usually exempted from these restrictive laws, and in many cases, as noted before, it is the primaries and not the elections that count.

[1] Cf. E. R. Sikes, *State and Federal Corrupt-Practices Legislation*, Duke University Press, 1928.

Rejection by legislative bodies of successful candidates who have spent too much in primaries or elections is no adequate expedient, for it cannot be relied upon to operate in every case. Also, this device affects only the successful contestant. His opponent may have spent more. For example, Mr. Vare's opponent for nomination in 1926, Mr. George Wharton Pepper, is said to have spent even more in the primaries than Mr. Vare did.

The complete dominance of the party machine in the matter of the selection of candidates has been lessened to some degree by the development of the direct-primary system.[1] Certain early anticipations of the principle came in the California law of 1866 and the Ohio law of 1871, but most of the progress has been made since the opening of the twentieth century. In large part, the contemporary movements towards direct primaries were the result of the agitation of Robert M. La Follette of Wisconsin in his struggle against the boss-dominated conventions of his state. The direct-primary system was thoroughly introduced in Minnesota in 1901, and is now utilized in widely varying degrees in all but three of the states of the Union—Connecticut, Rhode Island, and New Mexico.

The most spectacular use of the direct primary in the United States has been in connection with the nomination for the Presidency. The presidential preference primary was first established in Oregon in 1910. In the year 1912 some ten states used it. By 1916 some twenty-two states had mandatory presidential primary laws and three others permitted a preferential vote on presidential candidates. It was believed at this time that all states would soon have presidential primary laws, but the movement fell off sharply after 1916. No states have adopted it since then and three that once used it have abandoned it.

While in theory the direct primary provides admirable machinery to allow the voters to break down the control of the bosses over the nomination of party candidates, it has in practice proved to be rather unsatisfactory. This has not been due to the defects in the principle or mechanism of the direct primary, but rather to the lack of public interest and intelligence in its operation. The majority of the voters often remain away from the polls on primary day and allow the few faithful members of the old guard, who vote under the direction of the machine, to cast most of the votes for the candidates. In this way, the machine actually controls nominations much as it did under the old caucus and convention systems. The main difference is that it costs the state somewhat more under the primary system to select candidates. In fact, so indifferent have the people shown themselves to the direct primary in some states that they have allowed the bosses to reintroduce the convention system.

In dealing with the emotional power of party symbols and catchwords, the only effective antidote is education as to the real meaning of political parties, their true function in political life, and the manner in which politicians deceive the citizens by such means. As Graham Wallas pointed out in the first part of his famous work on *Human Nature in Politics,* these party symbols tend to lose much of their power once the people are shown how they have been duped by them in the past. Political education can thus furnish a real campaign psycho-

---

[1] *Cf.* Bruce, *op. cit.,* Chap. XII, and L. T. Beman, comp., *The Direct Primary,* H. W. Wilson, 1926.

therapy. Still, it cannot be hoped that education will entirely eliminate the emotional potency of the party symbols. The majority of the voters will be likely to react to political appeals on an emotional plane. Education is most effective with those who already consider public, as well as other, problems in a rational light.

Looking at the problem in its broadest light, one may say that the reform of contemporary party government is but a phase of the necessary reorganization of modern political life as a whole.[1] For it is doubtful if we can ever hope to provide for thoroughgoing direct majority rule, and it is even more doubtful that this would be desirable if we could obtain it. In all probability, we must accept the fact that society is destined always to be dominated by the superior intellects, unless certain unfair institutions and practices prevent real leadership from asserting itself. Hence the somewhat autocratic aspect of political parties is not in itself particularly to be deplored. It is probably both inevitable and desirable.

What is most disastrous in modern party autocracy is the type of leader who has dominated contemporary political parties. What must be achieved is the substitution for the corrupt boss and his plutocratic backers of properly educated and socialized leaders, who will realize their responsibility in public service and who will endeavor to use their position of ascendancy for the advancement and well-being of society. There is no doubt that this is in large part a pious aspiration, but the only way out lies in a series of successive approximations to this ultimate goal.

Intelligent political leadership is not likely to operate effectively unless linked with an active popular interest in political life. The latter is well-nigh impossible under the political conditions that exist in the modern state. The great territorial states of the present time, with their complexity of social and economic problems, have so far removed government from the interest and scrutiny of the average citizen that he is unable to grasp its nature and problems. The citizen has thus lost most of his interest in, and practical knowledge of, general political issues. His sole participation in politics usually lies in an unreasoning allegiance to some emotion-bearing party or personality.

We need to find various methods for reviving within the great national territorial states of the present day that active interest in government which characterized citizens in the earlier periods of small political units. This can be in part achieved by extending the degree of local government, thus bringing many important governmental problems closer to the people. Community interests and community organization, as Professor MacIver and Miss Follett have pointed out, might be greatly strengthened.[2] The powers of the central government could be restricted to certain large general interests that concern all the citizens of the entire country. By thus emphasizing the local political community, it is likely that the citizens will begin to take a greater interest in problems of government and be able to exert a more intelligent control over public affairs.

[1] *Cf.* Bruce, *op. cit.*, Chap. xix, and Brooks, *op. cit.*, Chap. xx.
[2] *Cf.* R. M. MacIver, *Community: A Sociological Study*, Macmillan, 1917, and M. P. Follett, *The New State: Group Organization the Solution to Popular Government*, Longmans, 1918.

Another promising proposal as to political reform lies in wiping out the irrational practice of basing representative government on territory and population, and the substitution of representation by professions and vocations.[1] Under such a system, every citizen would find his own occupation or profession directly and immediately represented in government. This would give a real rationale to political affairs. The voter might then take an active interest in the nomination and election of representatives. He would be likely to insist that the representatives of his profession be competent and worthy members of that particular calling. He would no longer be willing to be represented in a law-making body by a person whom he would be embarrassed to entertain in his home or recognize upon the street. A general adoption of proportional representation would also be likely to revive political interest, especially in areas where one party has been overwhelmingly powerful and the minority has possessed no part in actual representative government.

Finally, a great extension of realistic education upon public problems and political machinery must be provided.[2] At the present time, it may be pretty safely asserted that there is little realistic political education to be found in the public schools of the country, and surprisingly little even in the universities. Greater attention must be given to the study of government in the schools and universities, and the instruction in such courses must be something more than a superficial description of external forms of political institutions and pious generalizations as to the honest operation of political machinery. The real nature and purposes of existing party government must be candidly taught, and the defects of our present experiments along this line very clearly brought out. Above all, our teachers must cease inculcating in the minds of students, of whatever age, the fictitious dogma that our form of government is not only better than any other in existence, but is itself perfect and not subject to possible improvement. Humility is the beginning of wisdom no less in political affairs than in any other field of human activity.

The outlook for successful party government was for a time after 1918 brighter in some parts of Europe than in the United States. Vocational and proportional representation have made greater headway in the governments set up since 1918. Where these do not exist something which achieves roughly similar results, the group or bloc party system, does prevail. There tends to be more realistic political interest there than in our own country.[3] But this hopeful development is of late being rather more than offset by the virtual disappearance of any real party government in the states where dictatorship has been established—whether of Fascism or of Communism. In the larger part of Europe today party government is in eclipse or close to impotent. If dictatorship gains, it must be everywhere at the expense of the representative system and party government. Fascism and dictatorship present the same deadly challenge to party government that they do to democracy. Where there is no de-

---

[1] *Cf.* Barnes, *Sociology and Political Theory,* pp. 105-10; Overstreet, *loc. cit.;* and McBain and Rogers, *The New Constitutions of Europe,* Pt. I, Chap. VI.
[2] *Cf.* Coe, *Educating for Citizenship.*
[3] *Cf.* McBain and Rogers, *op. cit.,* Chaps. V-VI; A. J. Zurcher, *The Experiment with Democracy in Central Europe,* Oxford Press, 1933; and H. F. Gosnell, *Why Europe Votes,* University of Chicago Press, 1930.

mocracy there can be no party government in anything more than the name.

In the United States Professors Sait, Holcombe, and Douglas have argued for the necessity of breaking up the old and irrational Republican-Democrat dualism and creating a real conservative and liberal alignment.[1] In fact, Professor Douglas believes that we should have a definitely radical party to represent workers and farmers, even though this might produce a tripartite set-up of conservatives, liberals, and radicals. There are some rumblings which indicate that such a movement may be getting under way, but as yet the visible evidence of a new party alignment is less impressive than the logic of those who advocate such a development.

VII. GRAFT AND WASTE UNDER THE PARTY SYSTEM OF GOVERNMENT

The inevitable irritation associated with the annual task of making out federal and state income-tax returns and submitting to the even more distressing indignities of local assessors and tax-collectors has led many thrifty citizens to consider more seriously than previously the question of the nature of and need for the ever greater expenditures involved in the maintenance of public agencies and authorities. In the decade from 1791 to 1800 the total federal expenditures of our government were $68,256,000, which constituted an expenditure per individual, on the basis of the census of 1800, of approximately $13. In the decade from 1911 to 1920 the public expenditures of our federal government, on the basis even of the population of 1920, had increased to approximately $425 per head. For the year 1934 alone the federal expenditures were over $56 per individual, thus being over four times as great as the expenditures per individual during the whole first decade of our national history.

In this discussion we do not assume in any sense that democracy is necessarily accompanied by more graft and corruption than other forms of government. The most relevant fact in the contrast between democracy and autocracy or monarchy is that there is in the former a far more widely distributed invitation to individual enrichment at the hands of the government. In other words, as one contemporary writer has expressed it, democracy inevitably brings more "snouts to the trough" than any other of the leading forms of government.

Of course, we shall not in any sense contend that the enormous increase of government expenditures in the last century has been due exclusively to the growth of democratic ideas and practices or party rule. These ever increasing costs of government are to no small degree produced by the enormously greater complexity of the social problems that have arisen in the last hundred and fifty years. This increase of the practical problems that have to be dealt with by governmental agencies has made necessary an ever greater intervention of the government in social, economic, and cultural activities. Many writers have attributed this extension of governmental activity primarily to the growing popularity of bureaucracy and State Socialistic doctrines,[2] but to a very large

---

[1] E. M. Sait, "New Parties for Old," *Forum*, November, 1931; Holcombe, *The New Party Politics;* and Douglas, *The Coming of a New Party*.

[2] *Cf.* J. M. Beck, *Our Wonderland of Bureaucracy*, Macmillan, 1932.

degree such "State Socialism" has only been the practical acceptance of the actual realities forced upon society by scientific, technological, and economic revolutions. Wars, also, have become much more expensive, as have armaments preparatory to wars. There is much sumptuary legislation and inquisitorial intervention that is either useless or harmful and calls for lavish expenditures to maintain the officials who execute them.[1] But after making due allowance for these excesses, the fact remains that the historical changes of the last century have inevitably made necessary a remarkable increase in the scope and expense of state activities.

Some indication of the increase in the cost of our government since the early days will be apparent from the following figures. During the first ten years of our national history we spent through the federal government only $68,256,000. The appropriations for the fiscal year of 1932 ran to the staggering sum of $4,674,073,917. The "New Deal" has approximately doubled these expenditures. The total expenditures for the fiscal year 1933-34 were: ordinary expenditures of $3,100,914,000; extraordinary expenditures of $4,004,135,000, and a budget deficit of $3,989,496,000. Even the recently founded Department of Commerce uses up about as much in one year as the previously noted sum required to run our whole federal government for a decade in the days of Washington. The annual appropriation for the District of Columbia alone today is over seven times the annual budget for the federal government in Washington's administration. The percentage of the total income of the population of the United States which goes into governmental expenditures—federal, state, and local—has increased amazingly since 1913. In that year governmental expenditures amounted to 8 per cent of our total national (not governmental) income. By 1932 they had mounted to 31 per cent of the national income.[2] In 1932, according to the careful estimate of Ray Tucker, the total national income was $45,000,000,000, and the total cost of all governmental agencies was $14,000,000,000. Governmental costs have increased markedly since 1932, owing to the increasing expenditures for the relief of the unemployed.

The first point that should claim our attention in the analysis of government expenditures in the United States is the unscientific method of determining our federal expenditures and providing for the appropriations to meet them.[3] In England, for example, the Chancellor of the Exchequer is compelled to prepare an exact budget covering precisely the proposed expenditures for the coming year and also to determine the various sources or revenue that will meet the requirements of his budget. If the revenues greatly exceed or fall conspicuously beneath the expenditures, this official is regarded as manifestly unfit for the post. In the United States, however, there has been no such scientific coordination of effort.

Down to the time of the passage of the Budget and Accounting Act of 1921

[1] *Cf.* H. J. Brock (Jonathan Leonard), *Meddlers,* Viking Press, 1929; William Seagle, *There Ought to Be a Law,* Macaulay, 1933; and H. L. Mencken, *Notes on Democracy,* Knopf, 1926, pp. 35 ff.

[2] This was due in part, of course, to the shrinkage of the national income from 1929 to 1932.

[3] *Cf.* Beard and Beard, *op. cit.,* Chap. xi, and A. E. Buck, *The Budget in Governments of Today,* Macmillan, 1934.

the procedure in determining federal revenues and expenditures was essentially the following: In October the heads of the various cabinet departments would send to the Secretary of the Treasury their estimates for the expenditures for the ensuing year. It was invariably the practice for these departments to ask for more than they needed, because they feared that their requests would naturally be pruned by congressional committees. The Secretary of the Treasury had, however, no real power to reduce these estimates. While the executive department heads were in this way submitting their estimates to the Secretary of the Treasury, the committees in the House of Representatives in control of the various types of expenditures prepared their estimates largely on the basis of the expenditures of the previous year. Often there was no coöperation between the cabinet heads and the Secretary of the Treasury on the one hand and the House committees on expenditure on the other.

Even more striking is the fact that neither of these groups was directly in contact with or in any sense coördinated with the House committee on revenue, namely, the Committee on Ways and Means. There was opportunity for informal collaboration, but it was quite possible for the Committee on Ways and Means to work independently of the committees on appropriations and the executive departments, with the result that far too much or too little revenue might be raised in any particular year. If the revenues contemplated by the Committee on Ways and Means were not adequate to meet the federal expenditures, the President, the Secretary of the Treasury, and the Comptroller possessed the authority to decide what should be allotted to each department. This had to be done within the limitations imposed by the existence of specific appropriation bills designed for particular purposes and to be expended by a specified department. The unscientific and incoherent nature of such a financial system is obvious.

Much enthusiasm was generated by the passage in 1921 of the Budget and Accounting Act referred to above.[1] Many were led to suppose that this provided for something closely resembling the highly scientific English budget system. Nothing could be further from the truth. About all that the bill actually achieved was officially to invite and stimulate what had actually been possible before, namely, direct presidential scrutiny and leadership in the preparation of the estimated executive expenditures for the fiscal year. The President is required to lay before Congress at the time of the opening of each regular session a composite budget setting forth the revenues and expenditures of the previous year and the suggested revenues and expenditures of the next fiscal year. The specific information that is thus required is furnished to the President by the Director of the Budget Bureau, who is supposed to gather his information from the various executive departments and other disbursing agencies. It in no way gives the President or any cabinet official, such as the Secretary of the Treasury the authority to introduce bills to authorize these expenditures or to provide the specific basis for raising the revenue that they would require. The committees on appropriations can, in greater or less degree, ignore the President's recommendations, and the Committee on Ways and Means is not in any way legally

---

[1] *Cf.* W. F. Willoughby, *The National Budget System,* Brookings Institution, 1927.

required to respect the activities and proposals of either the President or the committees on appropriations.

Therefore our present budget system, as compared with the English plan and procedure, is no budget system at all. The direct and compulsory coordination of executive and legislative activity that characterizes the English system is still almost entirely absent from our plan. Most important of all is the fact that our budget scheme does not in any sense provide for effective control or reduction of the notorious pork-barrel system and logrolling. In his authoritative treatise Professor Beard concludes that "in actual practice, the first test of the new budget system . . . worked a number of economies, but it did not materially reduce the amount of logrolling or the size of the 'pork-barrel.'"[1] It does not need to be pointed out to any alert student of the situation that such a confused and uncoördinated system of controlling expenditures and receipts has been well-nigh perfectly adapted to fostering every sort of partisan, sectional, and class graft.

Two conspicuous and ingenious aspects of the technique of raiding the federal treasury have been the pork barrel and the omnibus bill. It may be well at this place to indicate the actual origins of these phrases. The term "pork barrel" originated from a usage on the Southern slave plantations.[2] Salt pork was given out to the slaves at definite times and a frequent method of distributing it was to smash a large barrel that contained pork and allow the slaves to crowd up to the broken barrel and seize as much as they could for themselves. The similarity in the procedure of Congressmen in their haste to include appropriations for their own localities in the general appropriation bill led certain cynical observers to designate the practice as the pork barrel, and the name has clung persistently.

The omnibus bill is self-explanatory. It simply means the elimination of the practice of passing specific appropriations for particular purposes for definite localities, and the substitution of the practice of lumping together in a single bill the appropriations of roughly similar type for the country at large. The advantages of the pork-barrel system and the omnibus bill in the forwarding of graft and corruption are at once evident.

In the old days, when appropriation bills were introduced for specific purposes in a particular area by individual Congressmen, any abuses or excesses in the proposal were eagerly and zealously criticized by fellow Congressmen who feared lest such inordinate appropriations might lead to the reduction of the revenue available for the needs of their own districts. Hence it was relatively difficult to get through any notorious example of graft or wasteful expenditure.

In due time, however, the typical legislative device of "logrolling" suggested a way out.[3] If appropriations of any particular type were provided for not in bills introduced by individual Congressmen for local needs but in the general or omnibus bill, then the majority of the Congressmen would all have fingers in the pie, and hence a very definite reason for supporting the general appro-

[1] C. A. Beard, *American Government and Politics,* Macmillan, 1924, p. 375.
[2] On the pork-barrel system, see C. C. Maxey, "A Little History of Pork," *National Municipal Review,* December, 1919.
[3] In logrolling those interested combine in supporting certain measures, with the understanding that each will help the others to secure legislation they desire.

priation bill. From this time on it became easy to embody proposals for gross and extravagant expenditures that would have been promptly excluded if they had been introduced as single bills by individual members of Congress.

We may now trace very briefly the history of the triumph of the combined pork-barrel system and the omnibus bill with respect to the three most notorious types of federal expenditures aside from the appropriations for armaments. The pork-barrel system triumphed in the appropriations for rivers and harbors by the time of the close of the American Civil War, and but two Presidents, namely, Arthur and Cleveland, have dared at any time to attempt to curtail the omnibus appropriation in river-and-harbor bills. The average annual river-and-harbor bills provided for an expenditure of around $50,000,000, and the best authorities estimate that probably 50 per cent of these expenditures are either wasted or devoted to projects that are well-nigh useless and add nothing to the well-being of the country.

The pork-barrel system, spreading from this beginning, entered into the methods of appropriation for federal buildings such as post offices and customhouses in 1901. Between 1902 and 1919 the appropriations for federal buildings were four times as great as those which had been provided for in the hundred and thirteen years preceding the advent of the pork-barrel method. Petty towns whose post-office needs would be amply provided for in the corner of a drug store or a portion of the first story of an ordinary store block were graced by elaborate granite or brick structures adequate for the needs of a sizable city. Professor Maxey cites the following interesting figures of the population of certain typical small American towns and the cost of the post offices erected in each village:

> Aledo, Ill., population 2,144, cost $65,000; Bad Axe, Mich., population 1,559, cost $55,000; Bardstown, Ky., population 2,136, cost $70,000; Basin, Wyo., population 763, cost $56,000; Big Stone Gap, Va., population 2,590, cost $100,000; Buffalo, Wyo., population 1,368, cost $69,000; Fallon, Nev., population 741, cost $55,000; Gilmore, Texas, population 1,484, cost $55,000; Jellico, Tenn., population 1,862, cost $80,000; Vernal, Utah, population 836, cost $50,000.[1]

In 1909 the Postmaster-General complained that Congress had appropriated no less than $20,000,000 for the construction of post offices in petty towns where his department believed that no changes at all were required.

Even more notorious has been the conquest of pension legislation by the pork barrel. Up to 1908 it had been necessary to consider pension bills independently and on their individual merit. There had, of course, been abuses in pension legislation before this time, particularly under President Harrison, when the effort was made to conceal the income from the protective tariff by reducing the treasury reserve through lavish expenditures for pensions. But earlier abuses were insignificant compared to those which have sprung up in the last two decades, and particularly since 1908. Fifty per cent more special pension grants were made between 1908 and 1916 than in the forty-seven preceding years between 1861 and 1908. As an actual matter of fact, at the present time the special pension grants each year exceed the number that were allowed in the

---

[1] Maxey, *loc. cit.*, pp. 696-97.

entire thirty years following 1865. Not only has the quantity of pension grants enormously increased but the graft and injustice connected with the system have also notoriously increased. Professor Maxey says on this point:

> To say that the majority of them have provided gratuities for persons who have absolutely no claim upon the benevolence of the country is to speak with great moderation. When we read of the deserters, the bounty jumpers, the unpensionable widows, the remote relatives, the post-bellum recruits, and the various other species of undeserving scoundrels who have had their names inscribed on the pension rolls by means of the special act, we wonder whether every omnibus bill is not a tissue of venality and corruption.

The expenditures for pensions in 1922 amounted to $252,576,000 as compared with the expenditure of $16,000,000 in 1865.

The World War has produced a vast increase in the money paid to soldiers for bonuses and pensions and other relief. The total expenditures for pensions in all our national history, exclusive of payments to World War veterans, has been $8,300,000,000. We have already paid to World War veterans in pensions and other aids some $6,000,000,000. Maintaining this outlay with no increase in the rate of payment, we shall have paid $21,500,000,000 to World War veterans by the close of 1945, when the final bonus payments become due. In the budget for 1933 the allotment for various payments to World War veterans was $1,020,000,000. This was some forty-seven times the payment made by European combatants for veterans' relief, when computed on the per capita basis of the men under arms in the great conflict.

The river-and-harbor bills, the appropriations for federal buildings, and the exploitation of the omnibus bill for private pension grants constitute the most notorious abuses in federal financial legislation aside from the expenditures for armament and war, with which we shall deal later. There are, however, certain other aspects of the pork-barrel system and allied practices to which we might call attention. Among them are the now abandoned provision for the distribution of tons of seeds to the constituents of Congressmen, the abuses in the congressional franking of mail, the waste in public printing, the maintenance of assay offices, the establishment and financing of unnecessary army posts and obsolete forts, and the support of Indian schools in districts remote from the Indian reservations. These forms of waste and graft, however, indefensible when considered particularly, are not significant when taken in their gross volume. They are perhaps more amusing than important, even though they embody expenditures far in excess of the congressional appropriations for educational, scientific, and cultural purposes.[1]

Another important source of increasing expenditures in the federal government is the increase in federal job-holders. This is usually associated in particular with democratic institutions and practices, though in all probability the increase of federal employees has been brought about to no small degree by the growth of state intervention in various aspects of social life and problems. In a trenchant article on "The Washington Job Holder," Mr. Harvey Fergus-

---

[1] *Cf.* L. L. Ludlow, *America Go Bust*, Stratford, 1933. Governmental franking of mail does, however, account in large measure for the annual deficit of the Post Office Department.

son thus calls attention to the remarkable development of the extensive bureaucracy that has grown up at Washington and elsewhere to provide employment for Americans who desire the security and dignity which goes with governmental servce:

The government job is very nearly the ideal job for the young fellow who wants above all to be sure of an easy living, made in a genteel way. All of the posts under Uncle Sam, except a few held mostly by Negroes, are white collar jobs with high-sounding titles. The salaries are fixed by law and guaranteed by the government. A Federal employé cannot be dismissed except for the rankest kind of incompetence or misconduct, and in case of trouble with his superiors he can always appeal to his Congressman, to the Civil Service Commission or to the Federal Employé's Union. When he is superannuated he draws a pension. His whole life is arranged for him. He has nothing to do but sit down in his swivel chair and wait for death, with light and agreeable work to pass the time while he is waiting. . . .

Few Americans are aware of the rate at which this horde of job-holders has grown, is growing, and will continue to grow, unless checked by some unprecedented and inconceivable act of God. The records of the Civil Service Commission show that in 1821 there were 8,211 civilian employés on the government rolls. The population of the United States was then about 9,000,000, which meant about 3,500,000 persons gainfully employed. There was thus one Federal civil employé, approximately, for every 425 Americans gainfully employed. In March, 1923, there were 504,778 civilian employés on the Federal roster. Calculating in the same way, this means that one out of every seventy-five American breadwinners had a hoof in the Federal trough. It means that the army of job-holders had grown five times as fast as the population.

The population is growing more and more slowly, as each successive census reveals, but the army of job-holders is increasing at a steadily accelerating rate. If both grow for the next hundred years at the same relative rates as in the past, there will be about 40,000,000 names on the Federal pay-roll a century hence, and one out of every twelve American wage-earners will have a government job. The roll has grown, not naturally, but by a series of rapid expansions, each of which involved stretching the Constitution to permit the founding of new bureaus. Every one of these bureaus began as a small office having from two to a dozen employés. But by a law which almost never fails to operate, each has grown until it now gives employment to dozens, hundreds, and in some instances thousands of job-holders.

The first additions to the simple governmental machine of the Fathers were the Interior Department and the Department of Agriculture, established under the constitutional power of the Federal government to promote industry and agriculture. They began as one-man or two-man offices. They grew quickly and each began to throw off branches. The second stage began with the era of government regulation of industry. The Interstate Commerce Commission was the first and remains a typical product of that movement. It began with less than a dozen employés and now has nearly two thousand. Its chief work has been the physical valuation of the railroads, upon which it has been engaged since 1917. This work is now generally conceded to be futile—but it has provided a thousand or more patriots with good livings for years.

The third stage in the expansion of the bureaucracy was begun by the brilliant political invention of the half-and-half plan, whereby the Federal government appropriates funds to be spent in States which raise an amount equal to the Federal allotment. By this ingenious device, which has just begun to work, the Federal government has gone into road-building, vocational education, the care of infants

GRAFT AND WASTE UNDER THE PARTY SYSTEM

and expectant mothers, and teaching housewives how to can beans, and has added many thousands of deserving incompetents to the Federal pay-roll. The fourth and last stage in the process now apparently impends. It will consist in the actual operation of industry by the government. Government ownership of railroads already looms ahead, and a project for the government manufacture and sale of fertilizer has strong support in both Houses. The Norris-Sinclair bill provides that the Federal government shall undertake the sale and exportation of food. The demand for the government operation of coal-mines is well known.[1]

The following facts will indicate to the reader the details of this enormous increase in federal service. In 1816 there were about 6,000 in the classified and unclassified federal positions. By 1861 the number had increased to about 50,000. By 1890 the number had more than trebled, reaching 166,000. By 1916, the year before we entered the World War, the federal civilian positions numbered 438,000. In 1918 the war increased these to some 917,760. By 1922 there was a shrinkage that brought the number down to 560,863. But in 1932 the number had risen to 732,460. The salaries amounted to $1,055,970,000. The total number of persons on the federal pay roll in 1932, both civil and military, amounted to 1,032,688. Their salaries ran up to $1,341,670,431. In October, 1934, the federal civilian employees in the executive branches alone totaled 680,181 and their salaries in this month amounted to $101,888,573.

When these figures are extended to include those holding state, municipal, and local positions they become even more impressive. Between 1870 and 1932 the number of persons in public service in the United States increased by 1000 per cent. Before the New Deal went into operation and produced an abnormal number of persons getting pay from the government, there were 2,500,000 on public pay rolls. They received $4,000,000,000 in salaries and wages—some 63 per cent of all tax money collected in the United States going for this purpose. This enormous bill makes it especially desirable that competent persons be employed in order that the public may get its money's worth.

It has been supposed by many that the gradual development of the civil-service system, which was introduced in a feeble fashion in 1883 and has been gradually extended and strengthened since that time, operates specifically and notably to reduce the graft and expense connected with federal offices. This is not true in any important sense. The civil-service system does not curtail the actual number of employees on the federal pay roll, but is designed, rather, to secure greater efficiency among those who are actually chosen for federal jobs. In one sense the civil-service system doubtless operates distinctly to increase the actual number of federal employees, in that it makes it more difficult to discontinue an obsolete or unnecessary branch of the service and to discharge supposedly faithful employees.

Most criticisms of our increasing federal expenditures attribute the increase primarily to the extravagance of Congressmen, petty waste, growth of State Socialistic enterprises, and the like. This attitude is notable in such a book as James M. Beck's *Our Wonderland of Bureaucracy*. But such critics overlook

[1] Fergusson, "American Portraits: The Washington Job-Holder," *American Mercury*, March, 1924, pp. 345-47.

what is far and away the chief source of public waste and mounting expenditures, namely, war and national defense. We may have an expensive civil-service bureaucracy and may waste large sums in petty graft and extravagance, but all this is pin money compared to the vast and unnecessary expenditures for warlike purposes. Moreover, it is well established that our civil servants are for the most part underpaid.[1]

Professor W. F. Willoughby of the Institute of Governmental Research in Washington prepared a detailed analysis of federal expenditures for 1930. This is reproduced below:

U. S. Expenditures, 1930, Analyzed by Functions

Functions	Amount	% of Total
1. GENERAL		
1. Legislative	$13,910,748.90	0.35
2. Judicial	11,299,752.92	.28
3. Executive	283,877.25	.01
	25,494,379.07	.64
4. General administration		
1. Fiscal administration	72,191,785.48	1.80
2. Government supply services	3,744,184.50	.09
3. Public-buildings service	21,945,393.17	.55
4. Civil pensions and allowances and federal payments to civil service and foreign service retirement funds	22,648,721.78	.58
5. Other general expenses	1,799,020.13	.05
Total: General administration	122,329,105.06	3.07
5. Construction of general government buildings, including sites	44,921,384.94	1.12
Total: General functions	$192,744,869.07	4.83
2. MILITARY		
1. National defense		
1. General	$599,234,935.88	15.02
2. Buildings, including sites	13,143,467.76	.3?
3. Aircraft	31,197,333.62	.7?
4. Naval construction, ships	58,050,214.67	1.4?
Total: National defense	701,625,951.93	17.5?
2. Pensions: compensation, war veterans, life insurance claims	835,275,349.10	20.9?
Total: Military functions	$1,536,901,301.03	38.5?

[1] A good answer to critics like Mr. Beck is contained in T. S. Harding, *T.N.T. Those Nationa? Taxeaters*, Long & Smith, 1934.

3. CIVIL
1. Foreign relations .... $14,460,125.94 .36
2. General law enforcement 45,245,312.29 1.13
3. Control of currency and banking .... 12,636,578.40 .32
4. Indian affairs .... 31,722,665.48 .80
5. Public domain .... 37,607,955.55 .94
6. Promotion and regulation of commerce and industry .... 23,414,521.40 .58
7. Promotion and regulation of aerial transportation 8,033,253.99 .20
8. Promotion, regulation, and operation of marine transportation
    1. General 76,731,561.32 1.92
    2. Capital stock, Inland Waterways Corporation 1,500,000.00 .04

    Total: Marine transportation 78,231,561.32 1.96
9. Promotion and regulation of land transportation. 7,397,042.80 .19
10. Postal Service (Deficiency in postal revenues) .. 91,772,649.80 2.30
11. Promotion and regulation of agriculture
    1. General 54,905,479.67 1.38
    2. Seed grain loans (net) .... 4,693,972.06 .12
    3. Agricultural marketing loans (net) 149,958,273.55 3.76

    Total: Agriculture 209,557,725.28 5.26
12. Promotion and regulation of fisheries .... 2,438,808.12 .06
13. Promotion of labor interests .... 10,256,778.36 .26
14. Immigration and naturalization .... 9,511,766.24 .24
15. Promotion of public health .... 14,295,360.10 .36
16. Promotion of public education .... 19,521,009.63 .49
17. Science and research, general .... 23,337,466.86 .59
18. Public improvements
    1. Roads 86,239,162.98 2.16
    2. Rivers and harbors 67,695,606.36 1.70
    3. Flood control .... 26,690,904.94 .67
    4. Other .... 15,488,666.72 .39

    Total: Public improvements 196,114,341.00 4.92
19. District of Columbia, territorial, and other local governments 48,375,821.79 1.21
20. Relief expenditures .... 1,897,291.05 .05

    Total: Civil functions $885,828,035.40 22.22

4. NONFUNCTIONAL
1. Refunds, losses, and miscellaneous $159,533,168.20 4.00
2. Fixed-debt charges
    1. Public-debt retirement chargeable to ordinary receipts 554,517,900.13 13.90
    2. Interest on public debt 659,347,613.07 16.53

    Total: Fixed-debt charges 1,213,865,513.20 30.43
    Total: Nonfunctional $1,373,398,681.40 34.43

    GRAND TOTAL .... $3,988,872,886.90 100.00[1]

[1] W. F. Willoughby, *Financial Condition and Operations of the National Government, 1921-1930*, Brookings Institution, 1931, pp. 173-76.

From this tabular exhibit of our federal expenditures it may be seen that war accounts for nearly 70 per cent of our federal outlay each year. Military and naval expenditures run to 38.5 per cent, and interest and retirement on the national debt, due chiefly to the cost of past wars, to 30.4 per cent. This brings the total up to 68.8 per cent. Payments to veterans are mounting each year. We are not likely to receive the promised payments from the foreign powers who owe us large war debts, which means that this financial burden will fall on the American people in the future. Therefore there is every probability that the already large fraction of the federal budget allotted to war expenses will become greater in the years to come.

The vast increase in our expenditures that the World War brought about is best revealed by the increase in the national budget since 1916. In that year the total federal expenditures amounted to some $735,056,000, as against $4,674,000,000 in 1932. The deficit that Congress faced in 1933-34 was about six times our total expenditures in 1916. The World War has not, to be sure, been the only reason for the increase in our federal expenses since 1916. But the war, in its direct and indirect effects upon our budget, was the outstanding single factor in producing the great increase of federal expenditures before the depression beginning in 1929. Other countries have been affected likewise. For example, the British national debt in 1914 stood at £700,000,000. By 1919 it had mounted to £6,750,000,000.

The governmental expenditures have also increased in state and local units in the last generation, though not in such dramatic fashion as in the federal government. In 1913 the total expenditures of the state governments amounted to $388,000,000. In 1932 they equaled $2,364,000,000. In 1913 the expenditures of local government units totaled $1,844,000,000. By 1932 they had increased to $8,292,000,000. In the case of the state and local governments much of this increase has been due to the heavy relief expenditures of the last few years since the depression set in. Expenditures for public works, such as improved highways and public buildings, have also figured prominently. In the cities there has been a considerable susceptibility to the boom psychology and urban rivalry, translating the "keeping up with the Joneses" attitude into the behavior of municipalities.[1] But public works and buildings have not absorbed all of the increase in expenditures.

[1] *Cf.* T. L. Stoddard, "Why Cities Go Broke," *Forum*, June, 1932.

SUGGESTED READING

Hammerton, *Universal History of the World*, Chaps. 182, 186, 190
F. W. Coker, *Recent Political Thought*, Appleton-Century, 1934, Pts. II-III
G. D. H. Cole, *A Guide to Modern Politics*, new ed., Knopf, 1934
Merriam, *Political Power*
C. E. Merriam and H. F. Gosnell, *The American Party System*, rev. ed., Macmillan, 1929, Chaps. XII-XIV
—— and Barnes, *History of Political Theories: Recent Times*, Chap. II
W. J. Durant, *Mansions of Philosophy*, Simon & Schuster, 1929, Chaps. XVIII-XX
Bryce, *Modern Democracies*
W. K. Wallace, *The Passing of Politics*. Macmillan, 1924, pp. 255-314

SUGGESTED READING

M. J. Bonn, *The Crisis of European Democracy,* Yale University Press, 1925
C. N. Callender, ed., *The Crisis of Democracy,* American Academy of Political and Social Science, *Annals,* Vol. CLXIX, 1933
M. A. Pink, *A Realist Looks at Democracy,* Stokes, 1931
Brown, *The Meaning of Democracy*
C. D. Burns, *Democracy: Its Defects and Advantages,* Macmillan, 1929
—— *Challenge to Democracy,* Norton, 1935
A. D. Lindsay, *The Essentials of Democracy,* University of Pennsylvania Press, 1929
E. M. Sait, *Democracy,* Century, 1929
—— *American Parties and Elections,* Century, 1927
H. S. McKee, *Degenerate Democracy,* Crowell, 1933
Samuel Everett, *Democracy Faces the Future,* Columbia University Press, 1935
Herbert Agar, *The People's Choice,* Houghton Mifflin, 1933
M. R. Werner, *Privileged Characters,* McBride, 1935
A. T. Hadley, *Economic Problems of Democracy,* Macmillan, 1923
H. W. Laidler, *Socializing Our Democracy,* Harper, 1935
H. J. Laski, *Liberty in the Modern State,* Harper, 1930
—— *Democracy in Crisis,* University of North Carolina Press, 1933
C. E. M. Joad, *Liberty To-day,* Dutton, 1935
Lippmann, *The Method of Freedom*
John Strachey, *The Menace of Fascism,* Covici, Friede, 1933
Lindsay Rogers, *Crisis Government,* Norton, 1934
R. G. Swing, *Forerunners of American Fascism,* Messner, 1935
H. L. McBain and Lindsay Rogers, *The New Constitutions of Europe,* Doubleday, Page, 1923, Pt. I
Buell, *New Governments in Europe*
R. C. Brooks, *Deliver Us from Dictators!* University of Pennsylvania Press, 1935
A. N. Holcombe, *The Foundations of the Modern Commonwealth,* Harper, 1923
—— *The Political Parties of To-day*
—— *The New Party Politics*
—— *Government in a Planned Democracy,* Norton, 1935
W. Y. Elliott, *The Need for Constitutional Reform,* McGraw-Hill (forthcoming)
Michels, *Political Parties,* Pts. V-VI
P. H. Douglas, *The Coming of a New Party,* McGraw-Hill, 1932
T. S. Harding, *T.N.T. Those National Taxeaters,* Long & Smith, 1934
A. E. Buck, *The Budget in Governments of Today,* Macmillan, 1934
Davis and Barnes, *Readings in Sociology,* pp. 492-518, 575-606, 778-810
Scott and Baltzly, *Readings in European History since 1814,* pp. 673-81
Jones, Vandenbosch, and Vandenbosch, *Readings in Citizenship,* pp. 83-110, 195-264, 779-818
Crawford, *Readings in American Government,* Chaps. III, XVII-XVIII, XXIII
R. L. Mott, *Materials Illustrative of American Government,* Century, 1925

FURTHER REFERENCES

THE CRISIS IN DEMOCRACY. Perhaps the most satisfactory and suggestive volume dealing with the present crisis in democratic theory and practice is Pink, *op. cit.* See also Coker, *op. cit.,* Pt. II; Durant, *Mansions of Philosophy,* Chaps. XVII-XIX; Smith, *The Democratic Way of Life;* Burns, *op. cit.;* Lindsay, *op. cit.;* Laski, *Democracy in Crisis;* Everett, *op. cit.*
On theories of equality and American democracy, see pp. 7 ff. of C. R. Fish, *The*

Rise of the Common Man, 1830-1850 (Macmillan, 1927); Becker, *The United States: An Experiment in Democracy,* Chap. x; T. V. Smith, *The American Philosophy of Equality* (University of Chicago Press, 1927).

On the debate concerning democracy today, see G. S. Hall, "Can the Masses Rule the World?" *Scientific Monthly,* May, 1924; M. M. Willey in Merriam and Barnes, *op. cit.,* Chap. III; Wallace, *op. cit.,* Chaps. xv-xvi; Durant, *op. cit.,* Chap. xviii; Sait, *Democracy;* Burns, *op. cit.;* Callender, *op. cit.;* Smith, *The Democratic Way of Life;* H. J. Laski, *The State in Theory and Practice* (Viking Press, 1935) and *Democracy in Crisis;* J. T. Shotwell, *Intelligence and Politics* (Century, 1921); Hans Delbrück, *Government and the Will of the People* (Oxford Press, 1923); Felix Frankfurter, *The Public and Its Government* (Yale University Press, 1930); H. L. Mencken, *Notes on Democracy* (Knopf, 1926); Emile Faguet, *The Cult of Incompetence* (2d ed., Dutton, 1916), Drew Pearson and R. S. Allen, *Washington Merry-Go-Round* (Liveright, 1931) and *More Merry-Go-Round.*

The most vigorous attacks on democracy are Mencken, *op. cit.;* Faguet, *op. cit.;* R. A. Cram, *The Nemesis of Mediocrity* (Marshall Jones, 1919); T. L. Stoddard, *The Revolt against Civilization* (2d ed., Scribner, 1932); Wyndham Lewis, *The Art of Being Ruled* (Harper, 1926); A. M. Ludovici, *A Defense of Aristocracy* (LeRoy Phillips, 1915) and *The False Assumptions of "Democracy"* (London, 1921).

On the extension of governmental action in the United States, see Haynes, *Social Politics in the United States; Recent Social Trends;* Lindley, *The Roosevelt Revolution;* Beard and Smith, *The Future Comes;* Hacker, *Short History of the New Deal;* R. G. Tugwell, *The Battle for Democracy* (Columbia University Press, 1935); Holcombe, *Government in a Planned Democracy;* Laidler, *op. cit.*

On the inequality of human ability, see Willey, *loc. cit.,* pp. 57 ff.; F. H. Hankins, in Davis and Barnes, *op. cit.,* pp. 492-516; R. S. Ellis, *The Psychology of Individual Differences* (Appleton, 1928). For the best estimate of the 1917-18 army intelligence tests, see E. G. Boring, "Intelligence as the Tests Test It," *New Republic,* June 6, 1923. See also C. C. Brigham, *A Study of American Intelligence* (Princeton University Press, 1923); William McDougall, *Is America Safe for Democracy?* (Scribner, 1921); Ordway Tead, *The Art of Leadership* (McGraw-Hill, 1935).

On American legislative methods, see P. S. Reinsch, *American Legislatures and Legislative Methods* (Century, 1907). For slashing criticisms of contemporary legislatures, see Chap. XI of Hoffman Nickerson, *The American Rich* (Doubleday, Doran, 1930); William Seagle, "The Clown as Lawmaker," *American Mercury,* March, 1933.

On the control of politics by economic interests, see H. D. Lloyd, *Wealth against Commonwealth* (Harper, 1894); McConaughy, *Who Rules America?;* Josephson, *The Robber Barons;* O'Connor, *Mellon's Millions;* Myers, *History of the Supreme Court;* R. C. Brooks, *Corruption in American Politics and Life* (Dodd, Mead, 1910); Werner, *op. cit.*

On bureaucracy and democracy, see Chap. v of Sir J. A. R. Marriott, *English Political Institutions* (3d ed., Oxford Press, 1925); C. K. Allen, *Bureaucracy Triumphant* (Oxford Press, 1931); J. M. Beck, *Our Wonderland of Bureaucracy* (Macmillan, 1932); L. D. White and others, *Civil Service Abroad* (McGraw-Hill, 1935).

On decentralization as an aid to democracy, see M. P. Follett, *The New State: Group Organization the Solution to Popular Government* (Longmans, 1918); R. K. Gooch, *Regionalism in France* (Century, 1932).

FASCISM. For the theoretical background of arbitrary political power, see Merriam, *op. cit.* On the rise of Fascism in Europe, see Coker, *op. cit.,* Chap. xvii; Otto Forst-Battaglia, ed., *Dictatorship on Trial* (Harcourt, Brace, 1931); Tiltman, *The Terror in Europe.* On Fascism versus democracy, see Strachey, *op. cit.;* H. W. Schneider,

Making the Fascist State (Oxford Press, 1928); Rogers, *op. cit.;* F. S. Nitti, *Bolshevism, Fascism and Democracy* (Macmillan, 1927); Carmen Haider, *Capital and Labor under Fascism* (Columbia University Press, 1930) and *Do We Want Fascism?* (Day, 1934). For the growth of dictatorship in both Fascism and Communism, see Emil Lengyel, *The New Deal in Europe* (Funk & Wagnalls, 1934). On Nazism, see Konrad Heiden, *History of National Socialism* (Knopf, 1935), F. L. Schuman, *The Nazi Dictatorship* (Knopf, 1935).

ABUSES OF THE PARTY SYSTEM. On the boss in politics, see Chap. II of W. B. Munro, *Personality in Politics* (Macmillan, 1924); Chap. IX of R. C. Brooks, *Political Parties and Electoral Problems* (Harper, 1923); Chap. VIII of H. R. Bruce, *American Parties and Politics* (Holt, 1927); D. T. Lynch, *Boss Tweed* (Boni & Liveright, 1927); D. B. Chidsey, *The Gentleman from New York* (Yale University Press, 1935); N. W. Stephenson, *Nelson W. Aldrich* (Scribner, 1930); Isaac Pennypacker, "Quay of Pennsylvania," *American Mercury,* November, 1926; Walter Davenport, *Power and Glory: The Life of Boies Penrose* (Putnam, 1931); S. B. Griffin, *W. Murray Crane, a Man and Brother* (Little, Brown, 1926)—eulogistic. On the "invisible government," see McConaughy, *op. cit.;* A. M. Kales, *Unpopular Government in the United States* (University of Chicago Press, 1914); Brooks, *Corruption in American Politics and Life.* On nominating conventions, see Brooks, *Political Parties,* Chaps. X-XI; Bruce *op. cit.,* Chaps. XI-XIII; F. W. Dallinger, *Nominations for Elective Office in the United States* (Longmans, 1897). For a severe attack on nominating conventions, see H. L. Mencken, *Making a President* (Knopf, 1932). On election expenditures, see Bruce, *op. cit.,* Chap. XV; Louise Overacker, *Money in Elections* (Macmillan, 1932); J. K. Pollack, *Party Campaign Funds* (Knopf, 1926) and *Money and Politics Abroad.* On lobbies, see Herring, *Group Representation before Congress.*

On proportional representation, see C. G. Hoag and G. H. Hallett, *Proportional Representation* (Macmillan, 1926). On the growth of the civil service in the United States, see C. R. Fish, *Civil Service and the Patronage* (Longmans, 1905).

EFFORTS TO REFORM PARTY GOVERNMENT. On the Australian ballot, see E. C. Evans, *History of the Australian Ballot System in the United States* (University of Chicago Press, 1917).

On the initiative and referendum, see Chaps. VI, VIII of A. B. Hall, *Popular Government* (Macmillan, 1921); Chaps. IV-VII of Felix Bonjour, *Real Democracy in Operation* (Stokes, 1920); E. P. Oberholtzer, *The Referendum in America* (new ed., Scribner, 1911).

On attempts to limit campaign expenditures, see E. R. Sikes, *State and Federal Corrupt-Practices Legislation* (Duke University Press, 1928).

GRAFT AND WASTE IN THE PARTY SYSTEM. For an account of increasing expenditures in the prewar period, see H. J. Ford, *The Cost of Our National Government* (Lemcke, 1910). For more recent material, see W. F. Willoughby, *The Financial Conditions and Operations of the National Government, 1921-1930* (Brookings Institution, 1931). On federal pensions prior to the World War, see W. H. Glasson, *Federal Military Pensions in the United States* (Oxford Press, 1918); J. W. Oliver, *History of the Civil War Military Pensions, 1861-1865* (University of Wisconsin Press, 1917). On recent expenditures for veterans, see Knowlton Durham, *Billions for Veterans* (Harcourt, Brace, 1932); Talcott Powell, *Tattered Banners* (Harcourt, Brace, 1933); Katherine Mayo, *Soldiers What Next?* (Houghton Mifflin, 1934).

For discussion of the merits of increased federal expenditures, see J. M. Beck, *Our Wonderland of Bureaucracy* (Macmillan, 1932); Harding, *op. cit.;* Ernest Greenwood, *Spenders All* (Appleton-Century, 1935). On the movement for public budgets, see Buck, *op. cit.*

CHAPTER XXIII

IN QUEST OF WORLD PEACE

I. HISTORIC PLANS FOR WORLD ORGANIZATION

Much has been written of wars and their effects upon human society. Much less has been said concerning the efforts to promote the cause of peace and goodwill among men. War has become the chief scourge of the human race and the main challenge to the stability of civilization. Unless war is eliminated, one may be reasonably sure that our advanced Western civilization cannot survive.[1] In this chapter we shall recount some of the more notable plans and achievements in working for the pacific adjustment of disputes among nations and for the reduction of the causes and frequency of the resort to arms.

The League of Nations has been regarded by many as a novel enterprise growing up in the minds of the more far-sighted statesmen at the Paris Peace Conference. Such a conception is quite misleading. Since the time of the Greeks many plans have been brought forth for international federation or international organization designed to decrease the frequency and probability of wars. A painstaking and enterprising editor, Mr. W. E. Darby, some two decades ago brought together the texts of the leading plans for international arbitration and international organization prior to 1910. The mere texts of these plans, as assembled in his useful *International Tribunals*,[2] served to make up a book of nearly a thousand pages of small print. Statesmen, philosophers, and humanitarians throughout the ages have been inspired with the hope of ridding the world of the menace of war. The plans were particularly numerous after the major wars of modern times. These bloody conflicts furnished their more thoughtful observers with very special and overwhelming evidence of the folly of war and its associated misery and suffering.

Dante, in his *De monarchia,* proposed a plan for the political harmony of Western Christendom that would put an end to the interminable struggles between the Holy Roman Empire and the Italian city-states. About the same time Pierre Dubois, in his *De recuperatione terrae sanctae,* expounded a plan for the unity of Europe in order to overcome the disasters of the Crusades and to promote the conquest of the Holy Land from the infidel. The devastating Thirty Years' War (1618-48) gave birth to the peace plans of Emeric Crucé (1623), Hugo Grotius (1625), and Sully (1638).

In his *The New Cyneas*[3] Crucé proposed a European assembly at Venice in

---

[1] Young, R. E., ed., *Why Wars Must Cease,* Macmillan, 1935.
[2] Fourth ed., American Peace Society, 1925.
[3] Allen, Lane & Scott, 1909.

which the sovereigns would be permanently represented by ambassadors who would attempt to settle the disputes arising between the member states. He laid special stress upon the necessity of controlling the commercial causes of wars. Hugo Grotius, the founder of systematic international law, suggested a comprehensive scheme of international arbitration to reduce the probability of war. Sully, in his *Great Design,* contemplated the federation of Europe into a Christian republic of some fifteen states. It was to be managed by a council of seventy representatives who would settle the quarrels among the various powers, their decisions being final and executed by force if necessary.

The dynastic wars of Louis XIV prompted the plans of William Penn (1693), the Abbé de Saint-Pierre (1713), and Leibnitz (1714). In his *Essay towards the Present and Future Peace of Europe,* William Penn suggested a general European parliament to handle disputes between states, with the power of coercing recalcitrant states. The Abbé de Saint-Pierre, who had been present in a secretarial capacity at the Peace Congress of Utrecht in 1713, set forth in the same year a plan that was really an elaboration of the scheme of Sully. He advocated a union of the sovereigns of Europe to preserve peace. They were to be represented by a general European diet of plenipotentiaries with full power to enforce decisions by resort to arms. Leibnitz endeavored to improve upon the plan of the Abbé by assigning a more prominent place to the Holy Roman Empire than had been contemplated by the French writer. He suggested a United States of Europe coextensive with the Catholic countries. The Pope was to be the leader in matters pertaining to religion and the Holy Roman Emperor the head of the organization in temporal affairs.

The Seven Years' War led Voltaire and Rousseau to endorse the plan of the Abbé de Saint-Pierre. Rousseau suggested elaborate additions to the original scheme. The Seven Years' War and the American Revolution helped to stimulate Jeremy Bentham's *Plan for a Universal and Perpetual Peace,* written between 1786 and 1789. The essence of his plan was a limitation of European armaments and the creation of a court for international arbitration.

The French Revolutionary and the Napoleonic wars were chiefly responsible for the appearance of three notable plans for promoting the peace of Europe. Immanuel Kant published his famous tract on *Perpetual Peace* in 1795. Believing that monarchs were the chief cause of wars, he anticipated Mr. Wilson and the British Liberals during the World War by proposing the universal establishment of popular governments. He proposed the ultimate abandonment of standing armies, the prohibition of the contraction of national debts in connection with the foreign affairs of a state, the federation of the free states of Europe, the prohibition of violent interference in the affairs of another state, and the reduction of the inhumanity of war. In an earlier work, *Universal Cosmo-Political History* (1784), Kant had gone into the problem far more profoundly, suggesting the social, cultural, and political changes necessary to produce political freedom and international federation.

The interesting and versatile Russian Tsar Alexander I was deeply concerned with the cause of European peace. He was especially attracted to the *Great Design* of Sully. As early as 1804, he sent to Pitt a somewhat premature plan for the reconstruction of Europe after the defeat of Napoleon. During the next decade he came under the influence of Christian mystics, especially the

Baroness von Krüdener. His peace scheme took on a decidedly theological cast, and he proposed to found his plan for European peace upon the principles of the Christian religion. On September 26, 1815, he induced his allied monarchs to sign the famous Holy Alliance.

Alexander's plan was primarily a pious rhetorical gesture, not taken seriously by his fellow signers. In the meantime, a much more realistic program was being worked out, chiefly under the guidance of the British statesman Lord Castlereagh, namely, the Concert of Europe. This grew out of the famous Quadruple Alliance of Russia, Prussia, Austria, and England, which had been initiated in 1814 and was formally renewed on November 20, 1815. This alliance, which has been frequently confused with Alexander's noble but impracticable and secretly ridiculed scheme, provided for the periodic assembling of the major European states (except France) to take common action against the threat to peace believed to reside in the revolutionary sentiments that had emanated from France. Castlereagh gave an excellent and candid description of his motives and ideals in the following paragraph from a letter that he wrote on December 28, 1815:

The necessity for such a system of connexion may recur, but this necessity should no longer be problematical when it is acted upon. The immediate object to be kept in view is to inspire the States of Europe, as long as we can, with a sense of the dangers which they have surmounted by their union, of the hazards they will incur by a relaxation of vigilance, to make them feel that the existing concert is their only perfect security against the revolutionary embers [that is, the sources of war, as then regarded] more or less existing in every State of Europe; and that their true wisdom is to keep down the petty contentions of ordinary times, and to stand together in support of the established principles of social order.[1]

The Concert of Europe remained in more or less active force from 1815 until the Conference of London in 1913, which temporarily settled the issues growing out of the Balkan Wars. It was invoked particularly in the Congress of Paris in 1856, following the Crimean War; in the Congress of Berlin in 1878, for the settlement of the Russo-Turkish issues and allied problems; and in the Algeciras Conference of 1906 to settle Moroccan disputes. Sir Edward Grey attempted to utilize it in 1914 to deal with the Austro-Serbian crisis, but his plan involved a set-up that would have been manifestly unfair to Austria; hence Austria and Germany refused to coöperate. The Concert of Europe, then, proved incapable of dealing with issues as complicated and formidable as the clash of the great systems of alliances before the World War.

In the interval between the Congress of Vienna in 1815 and the Conference of London in 1913, there were a number of plans submitted for international organization and the arbitration of international disputes. In his *Essay on a Congress of Nations for the Adjustment of International Disputes without Resort to Arms* (1840) an American, William Ladd, proposed a congress of ambassadors from all Christian nations and an international court of arbitration. Ladd's plan marked an advance on earlier schemes of this sort in that it was to be voluntary and accepted as its point of departure the existing state

---

[1] Viscount Castlereagh, *The Correspondence, Despatches, and Other Papers,* ed. by C. W. Vane Marquess of Londonderry, 3rd Ser., London, 1853, Vol. III, p. 105.

of affairs in Europe. James Mill and his more noted son, John Stuart Mill, both suggested plans for international arbitration, and John Stuart Mill proposed a European juristic federation. The prolific Swiss political philosopher Johann Kaspar Bluntschli, in *The Organization of European Federation* (1867), presented an elaborate plan for the federation of Europe for the purpose of international administration and unity. Finally, the indefatigable Russian sociologist and pacifist Jacques Novicow, in *International Politics* (1886) and *The Federation of Europe* (1901), produced extensive books arguing profoundly and eloquently for pacifism and European federation. That the establishment of the League of Nations has not precluded interest in this project of European union is to be seen in the publication of the suggestive work of R. N. Coudenhove-Kalergi on the United States of Europe (*Pan-Europe*).[1]

II. THE CREATION OF THE LEAGUE OF NATIONS

In his comprehensive book *The Drafting of the Covenant*[2] Mr. D. H. Miller has provided us with a detailed history of the genesis of the Covenant of the League of Nations, and we need concern ourselves only with the essential facts involved.[3]

A number of Americans, led by Hamilton Holt, organized the League to Enforce Peace during the World War. For the most part they were not pacifists, but members of the Republican party, strongly pro-Entente and favorable to an early entry of the United States on the side of the Entente. They accepted without critical examination the Entente fiction that the World War was a war to end war, but they were sufficiently statesmanlike to recognize that active steps must be taken to insure machinery for the actual termination of the war system. They favored the creation of some form of adequate international organization at the close of the World War.

President Wilson's initial interest in such a project appears to have come from the education he received at the hands of some of the more friendly members of the League to Enforce Peace, especially Mr. Holt.[4] The creation of a league of nations constituted the last of his Fourteen Points. In England opinion was moving along the same line in many circles. A group of prominent English lawyers, headed by Lord Phillimore, handed in a report in March, 1918, that was substantially similar in basic conceptions to the views formulated by the League to Enforce Peace.

Upon visiting Europe, Wilson fell in with the various foreign statesmen, among whom were Lord Robert Cecil, General Smuts, Léon Bourgeois, and others who were in favor of a league of nations to prevent further wars. Mr. C. J. B. Hurst, of the British delegation, and Mr. D. H. Miller, of the American delegation, finally reduced these various plans to definite form and drafted a Covenant for a League of Nations that furnished the basis for the first formal discussion by the Peace Conference on February 3, 1919. After further discus-

---
[1] Knopf, 1926.   [2] Putnam, 1928, 2 vols.
[3] *Cf.* Felix Morley, *The Society of Nations,* Brookings Institution, 1932, Pt. I.
[4] There is some evidence that Wilson was influenced by the British Union for Democratic Control even before a representative of the League to Enforce Peace spoke to him.

sions and redraftings, the Covenant was finally given the form in which it was embodied as an integral section of the Treaty of Versailles.

When he felt his peace of justice and progress slipping, President Wilson came to be more and more concerned with the League and less and less hopeful of the other provisions of the peace settlement. He believed that the League might ultimately serve to rectify the more inequitable aspects of the Treaty of Versailles. Though he was far from being the originator of the project, he was undoubtedly the most powerful personal force in the creation of the League and in securing the linkage of the League to the Treaty of Versailles.

President Wilson failed to secure American adherence to the League, primarily because of the narrow partisanship and provincialism of many of his opponents, but in part, also, because of his uncompromising attitude towards the not unreasonable reservations proposed by his critics. The Senate would probably have ratified the Treaty of Versailles and entered the League if Wilson had accepted even the reservations proposed by Senator Hitchcock, which certainly did not seriously impair our participation as a member of the League. But Wilson demanded all or nothing, and obtained the latter. It must also be recognized that certain Americans, such as Senators Borah and Johnson, opposed the League primarily because it was linked to the nefarious peace treaty that betrayed the promises which Mr. Wilson had made to the American people during his war administration.

In spite of American defection, the League has become a going concern, now claiming the membership of some sixty states. Its official headquarters are at Geneva, Switzerland. The Council of the League met for the first time in Paris on January 6, 1920, and the Assembly first convened in Geneva on November 15, 1920.

III. THE STRUCTURE AND OPERATION OF THE LEAGUE OF NATIONS

The fundamental objects of the League of Nations are well stated in the following paragraph:

The High Contracting Parties
In order to promote international co-operation and to achieve international peace and security

by the acceptance of obligations not to resort to war,
by the prescription of open, just and honourable relations between nations,
by the firm establishment of the understandings of international law as the actual rule of conduct among Governments, and
by the maintenance of justice and a scrupulous respect for all treaty obligations in the dealings of organised peoples with one another,

Agree to this Covenant of the League of Nations.

The League is made up of an Assembly, a Council, a Permanent Secretariat and numerous commissions and committees. The Assembly is constituted of representatives from the member states. No state may send more than three representatives, though they may also send alternates and expert advisers. Re-

STRUCTURE AND OPERATION OF LEAGUE OF NATIONS

gardless of the number of representatives sent, each state has but one vote in the Assembly. The Assembly elects its several officers. It deals primarily with matters of general and permanent international policy. It meets annually in September. The Council is made up of six permanent members, representing the six major participating states, and nine nonpermanent members selected by the Assembly. It meets at least four times yearly and often more frequently. It deals with the more serious immediate problems confronting the League. In a rough general way, one may say that the Assembly is the legislature of the League and the Council its responsible executive, leaving details of execution to the Permanent Secretariat. The vote of both the Assembly and the Council must be unanimous except in regard to procedure, where a majority vote is sufficient.

The Permanent Secretariat is composed of the Secretary-General and his assistants. The office of Secretary-General is the pivotal factor in the operation of the League as a going concern. The Secretary-General is a sort of acting president of the League. The personnel of his office is the only group in the major structure and organization of the League that sits permanently at Geneva. Therefore it devolves upon the Secretary-General's office to examine, assimilate, and interpret the business that is to come before the sessions of the Assembly and the Council, and to present this material to these meetings. After the Assembly and Council have adjourned, the Secretary-General must see to it that their decrees are announced and executed. These multifarious duties and responsibilities make the Secretary-General the most important single figure at Geneva. Much of the success of the League of Nations was due to the ability and devotion of the man who held this office for more than a decade, Sir James Eric Drummond. The Secretary-General has a force of nearly seven hundred persons in his office organization.

Most of the judicial functions of the League are intrusted to the Permanent Court of International Justice, commonly called the World Court. Its creation was provided for in the Covenant of the League and it was established in September, 1921. The eminent American jurist Elihu Root gave a large amount of expert advice in the actual creation of the Court, and Professor Manley O. Hudson has been one of the most competent and energetic protagonists of the Court.

As a foremost juridical step in behalf of peaceful settlement of disputes, the World Court is worthy of at least a brief analysis. In the first place, it is necessary to have a clear conception of the actual nature of the Court (the Permanent Court of International Justice). Many confuse it with the Hague Court of Arbitration, but there is no connection between the two, except that the World Court sits in the great Palace of Peace at The Hague. The Hague Court was created by the Hague Convention of 1899. It is not a permanent court at all. It is merely a list of one hundred and thirty-two able jurists of the world, from which disputing states may select arbitrators for a specific case. After the case has been settled these judges return to their homes. The World Court was created by Article 14 of the League of Nations Covenant, drafted just twenty years after the Hague Convention. It is made up of fifteen judges, chosen by the Council and Assembly of the League of Nations for a term of nine years. It is a permanent court and its members are paid a regular salary of a little over $6,000 a year. It is a court of law rather than of arbitration.

Down to 1929 the issues were voluntarily submitted to the Court. Article 36 of the statute of the World Court offered participating states the option of giving the Court compulsory jurisdiction in all legal disputes involving the interpretation of treaties, questions of international law, or a breach of international law. Germany was the only state to sign the compulsory clause before 1929, but since that time a considerable number of others have fallen into line. All states may still voluntarily sumbit cases to the Court. The United States has not joined the Court, though there have been three American judges in succession on the panel—John Bassett Moore, Charles Evans Hughes, and Frank B. Kellogg. In an interesting article on its tenth anniversary, in the New York *Times,* Clair Price has listed the more important cases to come before the Court:

> The closing of the Kiel Canal to ships bearing munitions in time of war; old Turkish concessions in Palestine; the reparations clauses of the Treaty of Neuilly; the boundary between Yugo-Slavia and Albania; the powers of the Danube Commission; a collision between French and Turkish ships in the Bosporus; the Turco-British dispute over the boundaries of the Mosul province of Iraq; the expulsion of the Ecumenical Patriarch from Constantinople; the Savoy free zones on the Franco-Swiss frontier; and the proposed Austro-German customs union—all have been grist to its mill.[1]

The World Court should in no sense be regarded as a safe bulwark against future war. Wars are due chiefly to political, economic, and psychological causes. The Court normally passes on only legal issues. As Judge Moore once stated in a lucid article, the task of the Court is to decide points of law, not to prevent wars. Most international-minded observers will regret that the United States is not in the Court. Some blame may be attached to our provincial-minded Senators. But, as usual, Europe can cast no stones. Thus far, the Court has acted as an instrument of Entente victory, perpetuating the spirit of the postwar treaties. Its most important cases, those of the Kiel Canal and the Austro-German customs union, would seem to have been decided on political rather than legal grounds. The eight-to-seven vote on the Austro-German customs union was a particularly severe blow to the prestige of the Court—a matter pointed out with great clarity by the eminent authority Professor E. M. Borchard in an editorial in the *American Journal of International Law*.[2] The question to be decided was the purely legal one of whether the proposed union violated Article 88 of the Treaty of St. Germain and Protocol No. 1 of the Geneva agreement of October 4, 1922. By a division of the Court largely according to the nationality of the judges (Austria having no judge on the Court) it was decided that the union did so violate these two clauses. But the majority was itself forced to agree that there was no precise legal justification for such a decision and that the opinion was founded upon political speculation about the future line-up of European Powers. Professor Borchard has well summarized the serious menace of this precedent:

[1] "When Nations Invoke the Law in Court," *Times,* Sept. 31, 1931, Sec. VI, p. 3.
[2] "The Customs Union Advisory Opinion," October, 1931.

STRUCTURE AND OPERATION OF LEAGUE OF NATIONS

The action of the court, with its new personnel, in confessedly permitting itself to be used as a political instrument, has created a danger which cannot be minimized. The court has behind it only public opinion and public confidence, not a sovereign state. The weakening of its judicial character threatens its very life.[1]

The League of Nations has dealt effectively with a number of minor clashes since 1920. Mrs. Mead has well summarized the achievements of the League to date with reference to the settlement of international disputes, especially those growing out of nationalistic sentiment:

League members are pledged to pacific settlement of disputes either by some form of arbitration, conciliation, judicial settlement or reference to the Council, and no loophole is left for possible use of force when an aggressor decides to abide by the verdict and nine months have elapsed after the submission of the case. Even then, in such remote contingency if the aggressor will not yield, use of military force would not occur until mild, and later drastic, economic pressure was used. No nation would dare stand out against the world. The League has settled the following disputes:

1. One between Finland and Sweden concerning the Aaland Islands which left them under Finnish sovereignty, neutralized and non-fortified, and with the Swedish language preserved to the inhabitants.

2. One between Poland and Lithuania, a very complex and difficult matter, still unsettled but the League prevented war.

3. A dispute over Upper Silesia, involving rights of Germans and Poles finally settled in the longest treaty ever made which provides for the administration of Upper Silesia as an economic whole for fifteen years.

4. Dispute between Jugo-Slavia and Albania, both members of the League; there was no bloodshed, though Jugo-Slav troops entered Albania, disputing the question of boundary line. For such hasty, improper action Jugo-Slavia found she could borrow no money from any European bankers, and she was obliged to withdraw.

5. Settlement of frontier questions involving Greece, Rumania, Serb-Croat-Slovene State, Austria, Hungary, and Czechoslovakia.

6. The outbreak between Italy and Greece, due to certain Greeks having murdered certain Italian officials, and the hasty action of Italy in a reprisal attack on the island of Corfu, in which about twenty refugee children were killed. The League instantly called a halt; all small nations were intensely concerned. Italy voluntarily paid 10,000,000 lire to the families affected; a settlement by the council of ambassadors in Paris was followed by the payment of damages by Greece to Italy and the painful episode which shocked the world ended without war, largely through energetic action by the League.

7. There has been settlement of the Memel difficulties; consideration of eastern Carelia which involved Russia; settlement of frontier between Poland and Czechoslovakia; of the minority question in Greece; settlement of the Iraq frontier and the controversy between Turkey and Great Britain over the Mosul region in Iraq. This was a serious and complicated matter, which resulted in a treaty between Great Britain and Iraq. Turkey received a percentage of Mosul oil and some rectification of her boundary.

8. The League called immediate halt to raids of Greek troops into Bulgaria in the autumn of 1925 on the appeal of Bulgaria, and at once sent an impartial commission to investigate which, on inquiry, showed Greece to be responsible. She was compelled to pay $224,000 damages, though her treasury could ill afford it.[2]

[1] Borchard, *loc. cit.*, p. 716.
[2] L. T. A. Mead, *Law or War?* Harper & Brothers, 1928, pp. 195-97.

The League of Nations has, quite naturally, done little or nothing to curb the capitalistic system or to secure social justice. To expect this would be to expect the impossible. The League has been made up of capitalistic states. Not until 1934 was Russia admitted to the League. Any effort at Geneva to restrict capitalism would have been met with more vigorous opposition than would interference with the basic foreign policies of major states. But at least some provision was made for fact-finding and publicity on labor problems. An International Labor Organization had been created at the Paris Peace Conference in 1919. Part XIII of the Treaty of Versailles incorporated the International Labor Organization as an integral part of the League of Nations. Its administrative branch is known as the International Labor Office, and the latter has carried on much research into labor conditions throughout the world, published its findings, and recommended progressive international labor legislation.

In addition to its major activities in dealing with the relations between states the League maintains a number of minor but interesting lines of endeavor, which are well summarized by Lucia Ames Mead:

> The League has established commissions and the holding of conferences on the manufacture and traffic of opium and other drugs; on Health Organization, including study of malaria, sleeping sickness, etc. It has established the Far Eastern Epidemiological Intelligence Bureau; a commission on Public Health training; on Quarantine of infected ships, etc.; committee and conference on White Slave Traffic; committee on Protection of Children; committee on Intellectual Co-operation with headquarters in Paris. This concerns itself, among other things, with the instruction of youth in the principles of the League. Almost every month in the year several committees or conferences dealing with these and other international matters are being held at Geneva, creating, as nowhere else, an international feeling and impartial treatment of international issues. Out of such conferences will probably come, eventually, a common coinage and a common system of weights and measures.[1]

The League has, as we have seen elsewhere, supervised the financial rehabilitation of Austria and Hungray. It has settled half a million Greek and Armenian refugees from Turkey in Macedonia. It has facilitated and guided the return of some 400,000 refugee soldiers from Russia. It does what it can to prevent the sale of arms to backward peoples. It fosters the exchange of scientific opinion, and aids in the exchange of teachers and students among the various states of the civilized world. In order to discourage secret diplomacy the League requires the registration of all treaties made between member states.

Many private organizations have also been set up at Geneva. As Dr. R. C Dexter points out:

> Equally important are the activities of the sixty-odd international private organizations, such as the International Migration Service, the International Society of Nurses, the Y.W.C.A., the International Social Institute, etc., which in the last ten years have established themselves at Geneva so that they might be in contact

[1] Mead, *op. cit.*, pp. 198-99.

STRUCTURE AND OPERATION OF LEAGUE OF NATIONS

with the work of the League itself. There is really growing up at Geneva a marvelous world center.

In spite of its extensive activities the League expenses amount annually to only some $5,000,000, about one-third the cost of a modern battle cruiser. These expenses are contributed by member states "in accordance with the apportionment of expenses of the International Bureau of the Universal Postal Union." England pays the largest sum, approximately $425,000, and Albania the least, $5,000.

If the League of Nations has notably failed to do what Mr. Wilson expected of it, namely, to rectify the injustices of the postwar treaties and to salvage the wreck of his "war aims," yet it is the most useful and promising political entity in existence in relation to international affairs, and the only apparent hope of securing a better set of conditions in the immediate future. At the same time, no sane person will expect it to be better than the major constituent states. Hence the real need is education and pressure by liberal opinion in the member states to induce their governments to adopt a more conciliatory and farsighted policy. The League cannot be fairly criticized because it has not proved an international institute of diplomatic alchemy.

Friends of world peace have been compelled of late to witness with no little sorrow a growing weakness of the League of Nations. The defiance of the League by Japan over Manchuria following 1931; the admission of Germany to the League, followed later by the rise of Hitler and belligerent nationalism in Germany; the tendency of Poland to break away from French tutelage; the disarmament farce under the aegis of the League; the antipathy of Fascism to international organization; the illogical attitude of the League towards Russia;[1] the withdrawal of Japan and Germany from the League; and the growth of war sentiment with the deepening crisis of world capitalism—these have been among the factors that have weakened the League almost to the point of impotence. It is too early to predict its actual dissolution, but the current trends in world-politics are certainly working in opposition to the principles upon which the League was founded.[2]

From the standpoint of the history of Western civilization, the League of Nations is even more interesting as a mild move in the direction of a world state than as an agency for adjusting world disputes. During the World War and immediately afterward many historians and publicists with real vision and imagination were filled with the hope that the World War would prove the last desperate and costly spasm of the national-state system. They predicted that the world would slowly but surely move on to the next logical stage in political evolution, namely, the world state. The most influential exponent of this noble but perhaps overoptimistic notion was the prolific and encyclopedic publicist H. G. Wells, who wrote, in addition to many articles and short books, a long

---

[1] Russia was admitted to the League in September, 1934, but this increased friction within the League.

[2] The League gained some renewed prestige in December, 1934, when it averted a war between Yugoslavia and Hungary, growing out of disputes over responsibility for the assassination of King Alexander of Yugoslavia in October, 1934. But most realistic observers took the ground that the League succeeded because the major Powers, as a result of inequalities in the line-up of the Powers, were not yet ready for the impending war.

and immensely popular *Outline of History* to justify the idea of the world-state as the culmination of the political development of mankind. The League of Nations was seized upon by such writers as Mr. Wells as cogent evidence that we were on our way to the world-state.[1]

The fact that the League has declined in strength and prestige rather than gathered force and become the center of a world political organization has been a bitter blow to those who wish humanity well. Mr. Wells is himself inclined to believe today that the world will probably have to undergo the ordeal of another general war, and even more grievous suffering than that which accompanied and followed the war of 1914-18, before mankind will accommodate itself to the idea that world political organization is indispensable to the orderly workings of a society such as has been produced by modern science and technology.[2] Of one thing we may be reasonably certain. That is that humanity must in the future move on to the world state—at least world-federation—unless we wish a reversion to near-barbarism among the inhabitants of our planet. We have today become a world civilization, and the latter cannot coexist for long with political separatism and international anarchy.

IV. THE LEAGUE OF NATIONS, DISARMAMENT, AND MILITARISM

It was hoped by many sincere internationalists and pacifists that the League of Nations would be particularly effective in reducing world armaments, thus carrying out one of the most frequently reiterated ideals of Entente leaders during the World War. Their aspirations have been rudely shattered since 1920. All of the member states are overwhelmingly committed to the maintenance of large armaments, and hence their representatives at Geneva can do little except to bluff and stall with respect to disarmament. The Covenant of the League is explicit about the desirability of definitive disarmament. Article 8 specifically says:

The Members of the League recognise that the maintenance of peace requires the reduction of national armaments to the lowest point consistent with national safety and the enforcement by common action of international obligations.

The Council, taking account of the geographical situation and circumstances of each State, shall formulate plans for such reduction for the consideration and action of the several Governments.

Such plans shall be subject to reconsideration and revision at least every ten years.

After these plans shall have been adopted by the several Governments, the limits of armaments therein fixed shall not be exceeded without the concurrence of the Council.

The Members of the League agree that the manufacture by private enterprise of munitions and implements of war is open to grave objections. The Council shall advise how the evil effects attendant upon such manufacture can be prevented, due regard being had to the necessities of those Members of the League which are not able to manufacture the munitions and implements of war necessary for their safety.

---

[1] See H. G. Wells, *An Experiment in Autobiography*, Macmillan, 1934, Chap. ix.
[2] See Wells, *The Shape of Things to Come*, Macmillan, 1933.

The Members of the League undertake to interchange full and frank information as to the scale of their armaments, their military, naval and air programmes and the condition of such of their industries as are adaptable to war-like purposes.

In the Third Assembly of the League of Nations (1922) the possibility of sincere action in regard to disarmament was delayed and evaded by the famous Resolution XIV, proclaiming that the member states of the League could not seriously contemplate disarmament unless some provision was made for security and protection. As a general principle this statement can hardly be criticized, but one can scarcely hold that Resolution XIV was made in good faith. It was the second great echo of the French aspiration for special protection, so that France might feel safe in retaining the spoils of victory. It fell between the abortive Security Pact of 1919 and the final effort in the Geneva Protocol.

There was certainly nothing to cause apprehension on the part of the Entente, which easily dominated the League. Germany, Austria, Hungary, and Bulgaria were disarmed and helpless. Russia was absorbed with internal problems and was ever fertile with plans and proposals for universal disarmament. If there was ever a favorable time for universal disarmament it was in 1922. The plain fact is that the Entente recognized the impossibility of a continuation of the treaties of Versailles, St. Germain, Trianon, and Neuilly without at the same time perpetuating their overwhelming military preponderance over the defeated powers.

The Covenant of the League of Nations authorized the Council to create a Permanent Advisory Commission on Armaments. This was done, but the body was packed with military and naval experts who were more interested in increasing armaments than in supporting disarmament. The first meeting of the Assembly did somewhat better in appointing a Temporary Mixed Commission of a nontechnical type on military and naval matters. This body was in part made up of laymen, some of whom were sincerely interested in disarmament, but they were unable to accomplish anything of moment. In December, 1925, the Council of the League decided to create a Preparatory Commission on Disarmament for an impending conference on the subject. It finally met in March, 1927, and carried on some interesting discussions. It did not, however, grapple seriously with the real issues involved or take any decisive steps towards practical disarmament. Nor has the regular conference which superseded it in 1932 done much better.[1]

If the League has done little to curb armaments, it has at least created machinery designed to curb hasty launching of an actual war, provided this machinery can be put into operation. Articles 10-16 of the Covenant: (1) Guarantee the protection of member states against aggression; (2) hold that war or a threat of war against a member state is a concern for the whole League; (3) commit all member states to the submission of disputes to arbitration or investigation; (4) bind these states not to go to war until at least three months after the arbitration award or the report of the investigating committee; and (5) prescribe economic action against any member state violating the terms of Articles 12, 13, or 15.

---

[1] *Cf.* J. W. Wheeler-Bennett, *The Pipe Dream of Peace*, Morrow, 1935 (pub. in England as *The Disarmament Deadlock*).

V. THE VAIN STRUGGLE FOR DISARMAMENT

In the period since the Hague Conferences the most important international gesture in the realm of disarmament has been the Washington Conference for the Limitation of Armaments, called by invitation of the United States on August 11, 1921, and opened in Washington on November 12, 1921.[1] Secretary of State Charles Evans Hughes set forth the view of the United States that the Conference should aim at the preservation of the status quo in naval armament and should disapprove all efforts of any one state to establish overwhelming naval preponderance. This involved a willingness to abandon existing building plans of capital ships for the future and to scrap capital ships of an older type. As a result, the United States, Great Britain, and Japan agreed to provide for the scrapping of some seventy-nine ships built or being built, with a tonnage of 2,200,000. These three states further consented to the proposal to attain in 1931 a naval ratio of capital ships of "five-five-three," namely, that Great Britain and the United States would be equal in strength as to capital ships and Japan should have a navy 60 per cent as strong as either. In this arrangement the United States made the greatest sacrifice, giving up fifteen ships to seven for Japan and four for Great Britain. This ratio is to be preserved from 1931 until 1937, when the time limit agreed upon expires.

Many hailed this plan as a great triumph for the principle of self-sacrifice and peace, but it was, for the most part, a hollow sham. The ships regarding which the agreement of limitation or scrapping was reached were essentially obsolete or approaching the obsolete in modern naval warfare. There was no decision reached as to the limitation of light cruisers, submarines, or aircraft. France refused to consider submarine limitation, in spite of the earnest endeavors of Great Britain to force an agreement to put an end to the existence of such craft. Hence Great Britain refused to consent to the limitation of light cruisers that were useful to combat submarines. There was no progress made in regard to land disarmament because France resolutely blocked any such proposal, on the absurd contention that it needed its vast army to protect itself against Germany, which had been effectively disarmed by the Treaty of Versailles.

The only notable progress growing out of the Washington Conference related to oriental affairs. A treaty, the so-called Nine Power Pact, was accepted, providing added protection for China, and guaranteeing more adequately its rights as a neutral state. Another treaty, the so-called Four Power Pact, insured Japan protection against an Anglo-American attack. Japan consented to abandon the Shantung Peninsula and return it to China, and an agreement was reached between Japan and the United States concerning the island of Yap, important to the United States as a cable-crossing. This advance in goodwill was impaired by the quite unnecessary affront to Japan in 1924 when the United States terminated the "Gentlemen's Agreement," which had satisfactorily controlled for some years the delicate subject of Japanese immigration into the United States. The United States later participated in European disarmament negotiations by sending delegations to confer with the League Preparatory Commission on Disarmament in 1927 and subsequent years.

[1] *Cf.* B. H. Williams, *The United States and Disarmament,* McGraw-Hill, 1931, Chaps. VIII-IX, and R. L. Buell, *The Washington Conference,* Appleton, 1922.

THE VAIN STRUGGLE FOR DISARMAMENT

The problem of further naval disarmament was again discussed at the Geneva Conference of June 20-August 4, 1927, once more called by the United States.[1] Here the chief impasse arose between the United States and Great Britain. The former desired to extend the five-five-three arrangement to all classes of craft, but Great Britain refused to consider such limitation of its light cruisers, which it deemed essential to the policing and defense of its great empire and extensive commerce. A naval agreement, secretly negotiated between France and Great Britain, was inadvertently announced in 1928 by Foreign Minister Chamberlain. As a result, publicity was forced, chiefly as a product of the work of the representatives of the Hearst papers in Paris. The agreement was ostensibly abandoned.

In the winter of 1929-30 a naval disarmament conference was held in London. Aside from the virtue residing in the very calling of an international conference, little of substantial significance was accomplished. The reductions provided for were trivial, as the following table will demonstrate:

TONNAGE AS OF JANUARY 15, 1930, CONTRASTED WITH TONNAGE UNDER LONDON CONFERENCE AGREEMENT

	United States		Great Britain		Japan	
	Tonnage Jan. 15, 1930	London Conference Agreement	Tonnage Jan. 15, 1930	London Conference Agreement	Tonnage Jan. 15, 1930	London Conference Agreement
Battleships	523,400	460,000	606,450	460,000	292,000	264,900
Aircraft carriers	90,086	135,000	115,350	135,000	68,870	81,000
Cruisers	250,500	......	406,911	......	206,815	......
Large	......	180,000	......	146,800	......	108,400
Small	......	143,500	......	192,200	......	100,450
Destroyers	290,304	150,000	196,761	150,000	129,375	105,450
Submarines	87,232	52,700	69,201	52,700	78,497	52,700
Total	1,241,522	1,121,200	1,394,673	1,136,700	775,557	712,900

The United States was theoretically for reduction of naval armament, but also insisted upon the right to parity of sea strength with Great Britain. The result was that we obtained the parity concession, but achieved little for disarmament. There was an effort made to conclude a Five Power agreement, which would include Great Britain, the United States, Japan, France, and Italy. But this came to nought because of the not unreasonable insistence of Italy on parity with France.

A general world disarmament conference was held at Geneva from February to August, 1932, but there was no substantial progress towards literal disarmament. Near the close of the conference President Hoover suggested far-reaching reductions in armament that would curtail current expenditures by about one-third, but his proposals were not officially accepted. A serious obstacle to progress in this conference was the logical German demand that the other Powers disarm to the German level or that the latter be allowed to arm on a parity with its neighbors. This proposal was blocked by France and its allies. So the conference broke up in stalemate. All moves for disarmament in 1933-35 have also proved futile.

[1] On the naval conferences since 1922, see Williams, *op. cit.*, Chaps. X-XIII.

The Russian government has repeatedly invited the League to consider real disarmament in an honest fashion, but its suggestions have been uniformly ignored or rebuffed.[1] So the world is actually spending over 75 per cent more for armaments today than in 1913—an increase from $2,500,000,000 to $4,500,000,000.

The following figures indicate the expenditures for armaments on the part of the dominant world Powers a decade after the World War:[2]

	1927-1928	1928-1929	1929-1930
United States	$624,600,000	$684,700,000	$741,000,000
United Kingdom	570,758,400	551,464,200	547,284,600
France	461,543,000	407,910,000	523,240,000
Italy	272,690,024	244,068,760	234,229,320
Japan	240,903,110	239,005,340	247,229,320

The following table gives the comparative armament expenditures for 1913 and 1934.

	National Currency (in Millions) 1913	1934	Percentage of Increase
France	1,807	2,273.8	25.8
Italy	927	1,171.6	26.3
Great Britain	77.2	114.9	48.8
Russia	869.5	1,795	106.4
Germany	1,947.7	894.3	117.9 (decrease)
United States	244.6	711.5	190.9
Japan	191.8	935.9	388

Further, there has never been such a disparity in armaments between conflicting groups of Powers as that which has existed between France, England, and their allies on the one hand, and Germany and its former allies on the other. In land armament France and its allies could muster a force more than forty times the paper strength of the armies and reserves of Germany and its allies. The naval discrepancy was even greater. This was the outcome, for over a decade at least, of President Wilson's crusade to end any military and naval hegemony in Europe.[3] While France's military increases are still aimed chiefly at Germany, the British naval plans are formulated chiefly with respect to the competitive threat of the naval strength of the United States.[4] We have superseded Germany as the great financial, commercial, imperialistic, and naval rival of Great Britain. It is too early to generalize as to the ultimate effect of the Hitler régime upon European armament. It seems certain that Hitler will either force disarmament to the German ratio, or will arm Germany in spite

[1] As a result of the Japanese threat, and dangers from European Fascism and Hitlerism, Russia has recently moderated its crusade for disarmament.

[2] European writers have frequently contended that the United States is pharisaical in urging disarmament on Europe. They point to the fact that our expenditures top the list. This fact is due to our relatively high payment of soldiers and sailors. Actually, our standing army is smaller than that of Belgium and our navy smaller than that of Great Britain. This consideration should not be taken, however, as any justification for our own all-too-high armament expenditures. See above, pp. 576, 894; and C. A. Beard, *The Navy: Defense or Portent?* Harper, 1932.

[3] *Cf.* K. B. Schmidt and Adolf Grabowsky, *The Problem of Disarmament*, Berlin, 1933, pp. 112-21.   [4] *Cf.* Denny, *America Conquers Britain.*

of the Treaty of Versailles. The latter move, openly initiated in March, 1935, will probably lead Germany's enemies to arm still more heavily. If the rest of Europe has political wisdom, it may well choose the former alternative and drop its armament to a parity with that of Germany.

In the last few years much attention has been devoted to the armament industries and to their propaganda against disarmament and world-peace. These industries include not only the manufacturers of powder, high explosives, bullets, shells, cannon, rifles, and other materials used directly in battle, but shipbuilding firms, steel companies, and the like that build war vessels and similar instruments of combat. Public interest was aroused by the senatorial investigation of the activities of one W. B. Shearer at the Geneva Arms Conference of 1927. It was revealed that Mr. Shearer had been engaged in propaganda for shipbuilding interests that were pushing the "big navy" campaign. He wrote articles and made speeches in behalf of naval expansion, conducted a lobby at Geneva against disarmament and for a large American navy, attempted to manipulate politics in favor of armament expansion, and organized a broad campaign of propaganda against the League of Nations, the World Court, and other pacific agencies.[1] Even more excitement was produced in the summer of 1934 when Senator Nye's investigating committee revealed the activities of the international "mystery man," Sir Basil Zaharoff, who was shown to have received large sums for his multifarious and devious doings in promoting the sale of various munitions of war, especially submarines. Much popular interest was also promoted during this same year by the publication of two forceful books on the armament industry, *Merchants of Death* by H. C. Engelbrecht and F. C. Hanighen,[2] and *Iron, Blood and Profits*[3] by George Seldes.

There is little doubt regarding the extensive character of the armament industry, its powerful propaganda, its insidious lobby, and its utter unscrupulousness, not stopping short of selling munitions that are obviously to be used to deal out death to fellow citizens. Yet, as Engelbrecht and Hanighen make clear, it is a mistake to blame the armament manufacturers for keeping alive the war system or to imagine that the closing of every armament factory in the world would end war. It is deeper forces, such as patriotism, imperialism, nationalistic education, and capitalistic competition, that cause wars. Nor is the greed of armament manufacturers at all unique. They simply follow the universal principles of finance capitalism, the theory of business enterprise, and the profit system. If British tank-makers hastened to sell Soviet Russia tanks when the British government was about to break off relations with Russia, so did leading moguls of finance capitalism sell short the stock of their own banks. If British airplane companies were ready to sell airplanes to Hitler, so did Mr. Sinclair and his associates make vast profits at the expense of their own stockholders. The armament propaganda and its serpentine manipulations should be relentlessly exposed, but friends of disarmament will have to go further afield if they wish to achieve success in ending war.[4]

[1] See C. A. Beard, *op. cit.*, pp. 111 ff.
[2] Dodd, Mead, 1934.
[3] Harper, 1934. See also Otto Lehmann-Russbüldt, *War for Profits*, King, 1930, and Seymour Waldman, *Death and Profits*, Harcourt, Brace, 1932.
[4] *Cf.* F. C. Hanighen and H. C. Engelbrecht, "Don't Blame the Munitions Makers," *American Mercury*, September, 1934.

VI. THE DEVELOPMENT OF THE PEACE MOVEMENT TO 1914

In the earlier pages of this chapter the various plans for international organization to reduce wars were sketched. Here we shall briefly review the development of peace sentiment and of the organizations designed to advance the attack upon war as an institution. Probably the origin of this pacifist attitude in Western civilization may be assigned to George Fox and the early Quakers.

In the nineteenth century a prominent position was taken by American writers in advancing the peace movement. David Low Dodge, a merchant who had lost much money as a result of the War of 1812, founded the New York Peace Society in 1815. In the same year Noah Worcester and William Ellery Channing founded the Massachusetts Peace Society. The contributions of William Ladd, a prosperous Maine farmer, have been noted. Among other things, he founded the American Peace Society in 1828. The Peace Society of England was founded by a Quaker, William Allen, in 1816. This led to the formation of the Peace Society of Geneva in 1830. By 1914 there were more than one hundred and fifty such societies in existence, each with many branches.

Charles Sumner and James Russell Lowell took a powerful stand against war in the middle of the last century, Sumner's essays and orations being particularly notable. Elihu Burritt, a self-educated blacksmith, became a world-figure by promoting the five great international peace congresses held in Europe between 1842 and 1851. These peace congresses met almost annually after 1889 and were very influential in bringing the Hague Conferences into existence. In 1889 William R. Cremer, a member of the British House of Commons, founded the Inter-parliamentary Union, and in its meeting in 1895 the plan that grew into the Court of Arbitration at The Hague was submitted. In 1896 Alfred Nobel, a Swedish inventor who had made a great fortune out of the invention and sale of dynamite and other high explosives, established an annual prize of about $40,000 for the most notable contribution during any year to the cause of world-peace.

In 1895 Albert K. Smiley established the annual peace conferences at Lake Mohonk in the Catskills, at which the presiding genius at the outset was Edward Everett Hale. In 1910 Edwin Ginn, a wealthy textbook manufacturer, founded the World Peace Foundation in Boston and gave it an endowment of $1,000,000. It was early headed by Edwin D. Mead. In 1911 Andrew Carnegie established the Carnegie Endowment for International Peace, the richest and most pretentious peace organization in the world. In addition, Carnegie donated the Peace Palace at The Hague, the structure occupied by the Pan-American Union at Washington, and the seat of the Central American Court in Costa Rica. The American Society for the Judicial Settlement of International Disputes was established in 1909, largely through the efforts of Theodore Marburg. It helped to strengthen the Hague Court conception. While capitalists were endowing peace palaces and peace foundations, the international Socialists and Anarchists were denouncing war and proclaiming the solidarity of labor throughout the world.

The Hague is famous in the history of the modern peace movement. Here were assembled the two Hague Peace Conferences at the suggestion of Russia in 1899 and 1907. At the first Conference provision was made for the establishment of a Permanent Court of Arbitration, which opened in April, 1901. Most of the proposals offered at the two Hague Conferences were hypocritical, ineffective, and submitted in bad faith, and little of practical import was accomplished because of the selfishness and conflicting interests of the participating states. But the Hague movement did help the world to accommodate itself to the rhetoric of peace and arbitration.[1]

The last important development in the peace movement prior to the World War was embodied in the series of arbitration treaties negotiated by Secretary of State Bryan with leading states of the world in 1913 and thereafter.[2] These treaties were intimately connected with the Hague Conferences, because the method embodied was that of the Commission of Inquiry that had been recommended at the first Hague Conference and was formulated at the second Hague Conference. The Bryan plan provided that in the case of an international dispute the states involved would not go to war until after a delay of a year, during which an international commission of inquiry would investigate the case and make its report. After the report was rendered the nations would be free to act as they saw fit. The main check upon aggression then would lie in the critical opinion of the world, which would condemn action by the state held by the Commission of Inquiry to be in the wrong. There are some writers [3] who regard these treaties as even more effective as a practical obstacle to war than the Kellogg Pact, though they are obviously far less sweeping as a rhetorical gesture against the war system. It must be remembered, however, that the Commission of Inquiry plan was useful chiefly as regards disputes arising out of questions of fact. It was of little use for persistent wrongs or wrongs committed under a claim of right.

Some twenty-one treaties of this sort were actually negotiated by the United States. Germany did not sign before 1917, a fact of much significance for the world. The attitude of the Kaiser and the German Foreign Office was realistic. Since Germany was surrounded by enemies far more powerful in ultimate resources than itself, the strength of that country lay in its ability to strike quickly and effectively in case war was forced upon it. Justifiable as this may have been from the military angle, such a decision played into the hands of the anti-German propagandists in other countries, who were able to play up Germany in an unfavorable light. Had Germany signed and had the United States delayed its declaration of war for a year, some believe that it is possible that the World War would have ended by a negotiated peace and the present intolerable European situation would have been in part averted.[4]

[1] Cf. H. M. Cory, *The Compulsory Arbitration of International Disputes,* Columbia University Press, 1932, Pt. I, Chaps. VI, XI.
[2] Cf. S. F. Bemis and others, eds., *American Secretaries of State and Their Diplomacy,* Knopf, 1927-29, 10 vols., Vol. X, pp. 3-44, and M. E. Curti, *Bryan and World Peace,* Smith College Press, 1931.
[3] For example, Professor E. M. Borchard.
[4] Cf. Curti, op. cit., pp. 155 ff. Unfortunate as the German attitude may have been in regard to the Bryan treaties, it was rather more lovely than that of Theodore Roosevelt, who suggested that "we would not pay the smallest attention to them in the event of their being invoked in any matter where our interests are seriously involved." (*Ibid.,* p. 155.) It is instructive to note

The sentiment of the world for peace was never stronger than in the years just before the World War, nor was the optimism of the pacifists ever greater than it was at that time. It was assumed by many that another great war was unthinkable in the light of the alignment of public opinion against war. Some arresting writers were proclaiming that war would be no more because it could no longer be made to pay economically. Socialists were declaring that the international bond of working-class consciousness was far stronger than patriotism, and they promised international sabotage of any war.

Of late years it has become the fashion even in certain antiwar circles to deride the pacifists of yesterday as impractical idealists, living in a fool's paradise, because their dream was not fulfilled. This is especially the slur cast by the recently popular formula-mongers. But we shall see the end of wars only when the aspirations of such persons are realized. War will disappear only when there are more persons of prominence and authority who hate war than there are who cherish it and desire to preserve it as an instrument of national policy. Especially important was the pacifist emphasis upon the necessity of considering and removing the causes of wars. In our present-day enthusiasm for legal devices and international formulas, such as League decrees, outlawry, renunciation, and the like, we are in danger of falling into the error of believing that war can be ended by a formal legal fiat enunciated in the face of social conditions making for war. Only the true pacifist can ever end war or will ever sincerely wish to terminate it, though this does not mean that the pacifist should not be progressive and ingenious and on the lookout for all new and potentially effective methods of attacking the war system. We must guard ourselves against either resting content with the stereotypes of the older pacifism or placing exuberant and exclusive faith in formal devices and legal machinery not based upon honest conversion to the pacifist program.[1] Perhaps a sensible way in which to view the situation is to regard the outlawry of war as one of the most promising types of contemporary pacifism. Certainly no one except a pacifist can render sincere and logical support to the outlawry program.

The World War rudely rent asunder all the structure of peace slowly erected in the generations before the war. Except in the United States and Italy, the Socialists raised little opposition to the World War. This was in part because of their failure to make arrangements through a prewar conference for a general strike in case war broke out. They had no war-resisting program and were caught in the general welter of patriotism. Then they lost their great leader, Jaurès, just as war came. There were, to be sure, certain brave war-resisters and conscientious objectors, but for the most part pacifism evaporated with the shock of war. Soon many leading pacifists of a few years before were participating in organizations for the zealous promotion of international hatred and collective murder. The prewar pacifists, of course, rationalized their war-

---

that this expression of the "scrap of paper" philosophy was uttered by Roosevelt at the very moment that he was denouncing Germany for the violation of Belgian neutrality. But Mr. Curti adds: "It is noteworthy, however, that Roosevelt did admit that a violation of the treaties would be morally damaging, but so did Bethmann-Hollweg in 1914."

[1] *Cf.* F. G. Tuttle, *Alternatives to War,* Harper, 1931, and Beard and Smith, *The Idea of National Interest.*

THE DEVELOPMENT OF THE PEACE MOVEMENT TO 1914

time savagery on the ground that this was a "war to end war," a "war of idealism," and the like. Even the Carnegie Endowment for International Peace espoused in 1917-18 the then popular slogan of "peace through victory," a sentiment to which Ludendorff or Foch would have heartily subscribed. The most dramatic pacifist gesture during the World War, the Ford Peace Ship, was contemptuously derided,[1] but today many thoughtful people regard Ford as being closer to right and sanity than Woodrow Wilson, and certainly far more praiseworthy in his sentiments than the war-mongers like Theodore Roosevelt. Not a few now view the Ford gesture as morally the most courageous and creditable act of Americans during the World War, whatever the excesses of optimism on the part of Mr. Ford and his associates in this colorful venture.[2]

VII. THE KELLOGG PACT: A CHALLENGE TO THE FUTURE

The first notable modification of the spirit of vindictiveness and rampant nationalism that had characterized the postwar treaties and the conduct of the Entente after 1920 appeared in the Locarno conventions of 1925.[3] Some five treaties grew out of this conference, which was attended by the major European Powers, including Germany. The most important was the treaty of mutual guarantee signed by Germany, Belgium, Great Britain, France, and Italy. It guaranteed the existing boundaries between France and Germany and between Belgium and Germany. Germany and France and Germany and Belgium mutually agreed not to attack, invade, or make war upon one another, except in self-defense. Several compulsory arbitration treaties were signed, and a Permanent Conciliation Commission was created. Locarno was an excellent gesture, but it did little to settle the basic differences that were agitating the peace of Europe.

The Locarno plan of 1925 to renounce war between a definite group of states was a first step towards a general treaty for the renunciation of war, which was signed by the majority of the more important states of the world in August, 1928. The Kellogg Pact of 1928 was a combined product of the Locarno gesture of renunciation and the campaign to secure the outlawry of war.

The conception of attacking war head-on through outlawry was launched as a practical movement during the World War by Salmon O. Levinson, a distinguished Chicago corporation lawyer, who had two sons at the front. He set forth his program for the first time in the *New Republic* for March 9, 1918. Mr. Levinson perceived an analogy between war and dueling. He held that though the causes of dueling had persisted, we have been able to outlaw this practice through the pressure of public opinion. He believed that we might do the same with regard to war. There is, however, one great difference between outlawing dueling and outlawing war, since in the latter case the interested parties have to do the outlawing. Levinson's first distinguished convert was Philander C. Knox. He later secured the support of eminent statesmen,

---

[1] *Cf.* Merz, *And Then Came Ford*, Chap. VIII; and Sullivan, *Our Times*, Vol. V (*Over Here*), pp. 162 ff.—an interesting but hostile patriotic account.
[2] On the half-hearted peace efforts since 1920, see Mitchell, *Goose Steps to Peace*.
[3] *Cf.* R. H. Buell, *Europe: A History of Ten Years*, Macmillan, 1928, Chap. VI, and J. S. Bassett, *The League of Nations*, Longmans, 1928, Chaps. XI-XII.

clergymen, scholars, jurists, and publicists, such as William E. Borah, Arthur Capper, John Dewey, C. C. Morrison, Raymond Robins, James T. Shotwell, John Haynes Holmes, Florence Allen, Joseph P. Chamberlain, and Harrison Brown. The last-named, an energetic young British publicist, was engaged by Mr. Levinson as his European representative to advance the cause abroad. There is an obvious distinction between the outlawry of war, which presupposes a common force to execute the sanctions of outlawry, and the mere renunciation of war, yet the Kellogg Pact to renounce war owed much to the outlawry project.

On April 6, 1927, the tenth anniversary of the entry of the United States into the World War, M. Briand, in a speech to American reporters in Paris, recommended the outlawry or renunciation of war (he identified these) as between the United States and France. It was a sudden stroke, but American newspaper men had suggested such action to Briand months before, and Professor Shotwell had intimated to Briand that the time was ripe for such a gesture.

It may well be, as Charles A. Beard has suggested, that Briand's real motive was to maneuver the United States into a position where we could not effectively block French aggression in maintaining the domination of France over the Continent, but in any event the most generous interpretation was put upon his suggestion. Mr. Levinson was in Paris at the time and immediately began to stir up support for the proposal. He was joined later in the summer by the Rev. Dr. C. C. Morrison, author of the standard treatise on the outlawry of war. In this country the most effective approval of the Briand proposal was embodied in a letter of Dr. Nicholas Murray Butler, president of Columbia University, to the New York *Times* on April 25, 1927. In May, 1927, Professor Shotwell and Professor J. P. Chamberlain of Columbia University prepared a draft treaty embodying the implications of the Briand proposal. Though the Kellogg Pact bears little resemblance to this draft treaty, the latter was important in an educational sense. On June 20, 1927, M. Briand sent to Washington the draft of a proposed treaty renouncing war.

The United States made no official answer, but on November 21, 1927, Senator Arthur Capper of Kansas proposed a set of resolutions, later introduced in Congress, expressing approval of the renunciation move. The more ambitious program of the outlawry of war was embodied in the resolution of Senator William E. Borah, introduced in Congress on December 12, 1927. Borah at this time had great influence over Secretary Kellogg as to the outlawry problem, and the ultimate American response was due chiefly to the support of the scheme by the Idaho Senator. On December 28, 1927, the United States made its formal reply to the Briand proposals by announcing a much broader plan. Instead of a Franco-American agreement, Secretary Frank B. Kellogg proposed a multilateral treaty with the other great Powers.

Mr. Levinson labored strenuously with Briand in order to induce him to accept the broader and more inclusive American proposal. France answered affirmatively on January 5, 1928, but confined the renunciation to aggressive war only, which was at first unacceptable to the United States. Ultimately Mr. Kellogg accepted essentially the original French proposal to limit the renunciation to wars of aggression. During the next few months there was a

THE KELLOGG PACT: A CHALLENGE TO THE FUTURE

campaign of education supported by liberal opinion in the United States and western Europe. The British Tory government and Tory sentiment did its best to sabotage the Kellogg proposal, but the strength of Labor and Liberal opinion in England compelled them to concede at least formal adherence, though with reservations fatal to the Kellogg Pact. On August 27, 1928, a pact renouncing war was signed at Paris by the United States, Great Britain, Germany, France, Italy, Belgium, Japan, Poland, and Czechoslovakia. On July 23, 1929, President Hoover proclaimed the treaty to be binding on the sixty-four signatory powers, most of whom had signed after August, 1928. The text is brief and we may quote it in full except for the list of names:

The President of the United States of America, the President of the French Republic, His Majesty the King of the Belgians, the President of the Czechoslovak Republic, His Majesty the King of Great Britain, Ireland and the British Dominions beyond the Seas, Emperor of India, the President of the German Reich, His Majesty the King of Italy, His Majesty the Emperor of Japan, the President of the Republic of Poland;

Deeply sensible of their solemn duty to promote the welfare of mankind;

Persuaded that the time has come when a frank renunciation of war as an instrument of national policy should be made to the end that the peaceful and friendly relations now existing between their peoples may be perpetuated;

Convinced that all changes in their relations with one another should be sought only by pacific means and be the result of a peaceful and orderly process, and that any signatory power which shall hereafter seek to promote its national interests by resort to war should be denied the benefits furnished by this treaty;

Hopeful that, encouraged by their example, all the other nations of the world will join in this humane endeavor and by adhering to the present treaty as soon as it comes into force bring their peoples within the scope of its beneficent provisions, thus uniting the civilized nations of the world in a common renunciation of war as an instrument of their national policy;

Have decided to conclude a treaty and for that purpose have appointed as their respective Plenipotentiaries . . .

ARTICLE 1

The high contracting parties solemnly declare in the names of their respective peoples that they condemn recourse to war for the solution of international controversies, and renounce it as an instrument of national policy in their relations with one another.

ARTICLE 2

The high contracting parties agree that the settlement or solution of all disputes or conflicts of whatever nature or of whatever origin they may be, which may arise among them, shall never be sought except by pacific means.

ARTICLE 3

The present treaty shall be ratified by the high contracting parties named in the preamble in accordance with their respective constitutional requirements, and shall take effect as between them as soon as all their several instruments of ratification shall have been deposited at ———.

This treaty shall, when it has come into effect as prescribed in the preceding paragraph, remain open as long as may be necessary for adherence by all the other powers of the world. Every instrument evidencing the adherence of a power shall be deposited at ———— and the treaty shall immediately upon such deposit become effective as between the power thus adhering and the other powers parties hereto.

It shall be the duty of the Government of ———— to furnish every Government named in the preamble and every Government subsequently adhering to this treaty with a certified copy of the treaty and of every instrument of ratification or adherence. It shall also be the duty of the Government of ———— telegraphically to notify such Governments immediately upon the deposit with it of each instrument of ratification or adherence.

In faith whereof the respective plenipotentiaries have signed this treaty in the French and English languages, both texts having equal force, and hereunto affix their seals.

Done at ———— the ———— day of August in the year one thousand nine hundred and twenty-eight.

One cannot assess the nature and significance of the Kellogg treaty merely by reading the text. The terms, taken literally, are unfortunately profoundly modified by the reservations and interpretations embodied in the exchanges of notes between the chief signatory powers prior to the signing of the treaty. The so-called Kellogg Pact does not *outlaw* war; it merely *renounces* war as an instrument of national policy. It does not, moreover, renounce all wars, but only those wars waged to advance national interests and policies. In other words, it actually renounces only aggressive wars, and the cynic would retort that there have been few admitted wars of aggression in history.[1]

Certain types of wars are specifically exempted in the interpretations and reservations exchanged by the signatory powers before the treaty was signed. Among these are collective wars to enforce the sanctions of the League of Nations and the Locarno covenants; wars of national defense; and wars in defense of special areas or interests in which Great Britain and other states are vitally concerned. The most flagrant type of reservation and exemption is that embodied in this matter of special British areas and interests, in defense of which England reserves the right to make war, justifying itself in part by the implied analogy of its attitude with the Monroe Doctrine. These British reservations are stated in the British note of May 19, 1928:

> There are certain regions of the world, the welfare and integrity of which constitute a special and vital interest for our peace and safety. His Majesty's Government has been at pains to make it clear in the past that interference with these regions cannot be suffered. Their protection against attack is to the British Empire a measure of self-defense. It must be clearly understood that His Majesty's Government accept the new treaty upon the distinct understanding that it does not prejudice their freedom of action in this respect. The Government of the United States has comparable interests, any disregard of which by a foreign power they have declared they would regard as an unfriendly act.

It is quite obvious that no diplomat would be worth his salt if he could not bring any conceivable type of war under one of these headings or classifications of exempted wars. In 1914 every participant in the World War could have justified its entry into it on the basis of one or another of these grounds—some

[1] That is, admitted to be aggressive by the actual aggressor.

could have held that their activities fell under two types of the Kellogg Pact exemptions, namely, a war of self-defense and a war in defense of an area of special interest.

There is no provision for enforcing the pact, which is its weakest point in a positive sense. If one of the signatory powers resorts to war, the other signatory powers are no longer bound by the treaty and simply recover their former freedom of action. It is evident, therefore, that the chief sanction of the Kellogg Pact is a moral sanction, and the main hope lies in popular support of the spirit of the treaty. Yet it must be remembered that the people are easily deceived, and clever leaders would probably be successful in inducing their fellow citizens to believe that any bellicose action of their state was in harmony with the treaty or was an answer to the violation of the treaty by another power.

The chief weaknesses of the treaty are then: (1) Obvious loopholes for crafty diplomats; (2) the lack of provision for rectification of the injustices contained in the postwar treaties; (3) the absence of any provision for disarmament; (4) the failure to attack resolutely any of the real causes of wars; and (5) the ignoring of the realities of the European situation.

A severely critical attitude towards the treaty as actually signed was set forth by Professor Edwin M. Borchard of Yale University.[1] He contends that the treaty, distorted and mutilated by the reservations, is worse than inadequate. It is, he says, a positive menace to peace and goodwill. He maintains that it does not provide for any effective obstruction of the majority of modern wars. Moreover, and particularly, it actually places the moral sanction of the world implicitly behind all the important types of wars reserved from the operation of the pact. The implication is, certainly, that the exempted types of wars are good and permissible wars. Therefore, by a very direct insinuation, the more than sixty signatory powers put their moral force on record in approval of most probable forms of war. For the first time in modern history, then, the stigma has been removed from war. As the reserved forms of wars amount in practice to almost every conceivable type, this means that the Kellogg Pact to renounce war may actually become a method of giving moral approval to war. It may make war more respectable than ever before in history. In short, the Kellogg Pact thus becomes transformed by the Franco-British reservations into the first great treaty in history that implicitly puts the moral approval of the world behind war. The British reservations to the Kellogg Pact afforded the Japanese a perfect pretext to deny its applicability to the Japanese invasion of Manchuria. The Japanese were not slow to seize the opportunity and to insist, quite logically, that Manchuria was certainly an area of "special interest" for Japan.

While we call attention to certain realistic matters that must be considered in connection with the Kellogg treaty, there is no valid reason for opposing the principle and there are many powerful arguments for supporting it. Merely as a gesture it is a most impressive departure, though we must remember the truth of Professor Shotwell's suggestion in his address at Yale University on March 13, 1928—that gestures in which a strain of apparent hypocrisy can be detected

[1] Address before the Williamstown Institute of Politics, Aug. 22, 1928.

may do more harm than good. At any rate, it is the point of departure from which other and better arrangements may be obtained. A most serious defect is that no cognizance is taken of the injustices perpetuated by the application of the postwar treaties. Professor Shotwell, one of the foremost supporters of the Kellogg Pact, admits this frankly and says that if the treaty assumes a perpetual continuance of these conditions "war will remain with us and the renunciation of war will be a hollow farce." In an article on "Bigger and Better Armaments"[1] Charles A. Beard draws a powerful and challenging contrast between the rhetoric of the Kellogg Pact and the realities of secret diplomacy, alliances, national interests, and great armaments in the world today. He makes it clear that we must be on guard against both the cynic who depreciates and mocks at any attempt to preserve peace and the naïve enthusiast who believes that merely by putting ink to parchment we can remake the world. The Kellogg Pact is, quite obviously, a challenge to the future and not an assured achievement. As it stands today it is, perhaps, the most somber and colossal monument to the folly of the formula enthusiasts.

VIII. THE ISOLATION MYTH IN THE UNITED STATES

One of the chief obstacles to the intelligent and active participation of the United States in world affairs has been the assertion of our isolationist leaders that the Fathers of our Republic were in favor of remaining aloof from world politics and urged our nonparticipation in European and world politics.

Isolationists can get no comfort from the doctrines of the Fathers of this country except through tearing statements from their context and ignoring the historical facts of those days.[2] Dr. Nicholas Murray Butler drove this point home in his address at the Cathedral of St. John the Divine in February, 1932, in commemoration of the two-hundredth anniversary of the birth of George Washington. Dr. Butler challenged the frequent assertion that Washington was the father of American isolation as well as of his country. He pointed out that Washington never used the phrase "entangling alliances with none," which has been frequently attributed to him. These words are found in Jefferson's first inaugural address.

It is clear to historical scholars that Dr. Butler is entirely right in this assertion. But he leaves the somewhat misleading impression that if Washington was not the father of the American isolation policy, Thomas Jefferson was. The only persistent principle in early American foreign policy was that of flexibility and expediency. We were a small and weak state in the early days. Therefore it behooved us not to line up in risky and unnecessary fashion with any European alliance that might put us at the mercy of its opponents. But we had no hesitation in accepting an alliance that would obviously benefit us. For example, in our preliminary negotiations for French aid in 1776, John Adams pointed out the necessity of avoiding an alliance "which should entangle us in any future wars in Europe." We quickly passed from such pre-

---

[1] *Harper's Magazine,* January, 1929.
[2] *Cf.* Duggan, *The League of Nations,* Chaps. xv-xvi; J. H. Latané, *From Isolation to Leadership,* rev. ed., Doubleday, Page, 1925, and *History of American Foreign Policy,* rev. and enlarged by D. W. Wainhouse, Doubleday, Doran, 1934; and R. M. Cooper, *American Consultation in World Affairs for the Preservation of Peace,* Macmillan, 1934.

cautions and allied ourselves with both France and Spain, even agreeing, if necessary, to declare war on Portugal. We also expressed our willingness to join in Catherine the Great's Armed Neutrality of 1780, but we were never officially invited to do so. At the close of the Revolution the Congress of the Confederation clearly stated our fundamental policy: "The true interest of the States requires that they should be as little as possible entangled in the politics and controversies of European nations." Here, then, we have the core of the American foreign policy that was adhered to by the Fathers. It can be interpreted as an isolationist policy only by those who are unacquainted with European conditions at the time. Such an attitude, if applied today, would advise against an alliance either with France and its satellites or with Germany and its associates. It could not be stretched to cover any advice to keep aloof from the League of Nations or the World Court.

George Washington continued the tradition of the Confederation with no essential change. John Jay was sent to negotiate a treaty with England that would settle difficulties involved in the unfulfilled Treaty of 1783. But when France called upon us to support its revolution against monarchical attacks in Europe Washington refused to allow us to be drawn into war in behalf of any European philosophy, system, or intrigue.

Consequently, he issued the Neutrality Proclamation of April 23, 1793. In his famous "Farewell Address" of September 17, 1796, he put the full force of his prestige behind the American foreign policy of flexibility and expediency:

> Why, by interweaving our destiny with that of any part of Europe, entangle our peace and prosperity in the toils of European ambition, rivalship, interest, humor or caprice?
> 'Tis our true policy to steer clear of permanent alliances with any portion of the foreign world. . . .
> Taking care always to keep ourselves, by suitable establishments, on a respectable defensive posture, we may safely trust to temporary alliances for extraordinary emergencies.

Washington recognized that revolution and change were sweeping over Europe. We might make an alliance with a friendly government and then see it pass suddenly into the control of another clique or party that would be opposed to the sound interests of the United States. Moreover, Washington made it clear in his annual message of 1793, as well as in other parts of his "Farewell Address," that even the degree of our discretion in avoiding foreign involvements was to depend upon our strength. Once the United States had become powerful and well established, "we may choose peace or war, as our interests, guided by justice, shall counsel."

Jefferson departed from the principles of Washington in no important way. Not even his sympathy with the French Revolutionists was able to draw him away from the established tradition. He lost no time in expressing his views. The famous phrase "Peace, commerce and honest friendship with all nations—entangling alliances with none" was set forth in his first inaugural address. Like Washington, he merely wished to be free from involvement in European parties, intrigues, and systems of alliance. In all his intellectual traits Jefferson was a broad-minded cosmopolitan, not an introverted isolationist.

Coming to the Monroe Doctrine of December 2, 1823, we find it to be no more than the logical and complete culmination of American foreign policy over the previous half-century. It was no isolationist policy, independent of Europe. Indeed it was actually suggested by George Canning, the British Foreign Secretary. The reactionary European powers, led by Prince Metternich, proposed to send armed forces to the New World to put down the revolutions in Latin America. President Monroe, in consultation with John Quincy Adams and Jefferson, set forth our attitude on this matter. In the first place, Monroe made clear our opposition to interfering in the domestic affairs of European states:

> In the wars of the European Powers, in matters relating to themselves we have never taken part, nor does it comport with our policy so to do. It is only when our rights are invaded or seriously menaced that we resent injuries or make preparation for our defense.

Accordingly, the United States demanded of Europe a similar policy of nonintervention in the domestic policies of American states:

> With the existing colonies or dependencies of any European Power we have not interfered and shall not interfere. But with the Governments who have declared their independence and maintained it, and whose independence we have, on great consideration and on just principles, acknowledged, we could not view any interposition for the purpose of oppressing them, or controlling in any other manner their destiny, by any European Power in any other light than as a manifestation of an unfriendly disposition towards the United States.

Brought down to date, the foreign policy of the Fathers would mean a warning against an alliance with Communism or Fascism, with France, Germany, or Russia, with Hitler or his opponents. We should hold aloof so that we may be free to decide our policy in regard to such truly world affairs as the League of Nations, the World Court, disarmament, and other issues of like import.

Further, one may remind the isolationists of their own inconsistency. Henry Cabot Lodge, for example, inveighed mightily in 1919 against our entering the League of Nations. Yet two years before he had struck a man who came to his office to ask him to help keep the United States out of the European war. To have urged our entry into the World War and then to raise the isolation bogey about the League is not unlike straining at the proverbial gnat and swallowing a camel. With strange irony, some of our isolationist senators who blocked our entry into the World Court early in 1935 urged at the same time our intervention in the internal affairs of Mexico.

IX. ELIMINATING THE BASIC CAUSES OF WARS

So long as the fundamental causes of wars are allowed to persist unimpaired there is little probability that any formal machinery will insure perpetual peace.[1] The problem, then, is the dual one of eliminating as many causes of wars as possible and of evolving machinery to hold the unremoved causes in check until they can be suppressed.

In the contemporary "race between education and catastrophe" man needs all

---

[1] *Cf.* Arthur Porritt, ed., *The Causes of War*, Macmillan, 1932.

DANGER SPOTS of TODAY

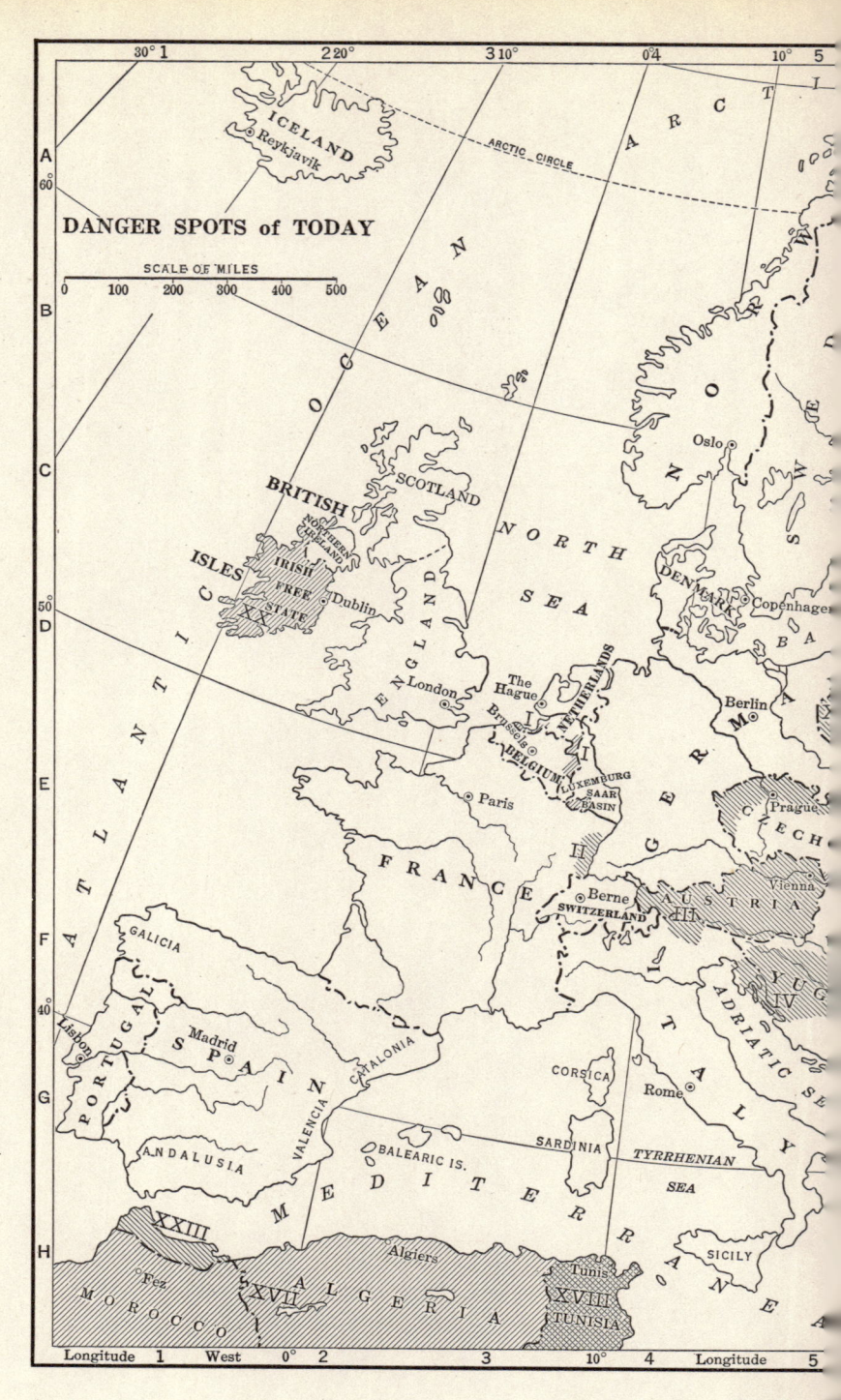

REFERENCE
I. Territory sought by Belgium
II. German speaking Alsatians
III. Germans in Upper Adige
IV. Slovenes and Croats in Jugoslavia and Italy
V. Albania
VI. Minorities in eastern Jugoslavia
VII. Bulgars in Greece, Jugoslavia, and the Dobrudja
VIII. Hungarians in surrounding countries
IX. Bessarabia
X. Minorities in eastern Poland
XI. Vilna
XII. Finns in Karelia
XIII. Transcaucasian peoples
XIV. Armenians
XV. Kurds
XVI. Danzig Corridor
XVII. African peoples under France
XVIII. Italians in Tunis
XIX. Greeks in the Dodecanese
XX. Catholic Ireland
XXI. Danzig
XXII. Arabs under France
XXIII. African peoples under Spain

of his intelligence and resources to solve social problems within national boundaries.[1] There is little hope that mankind will be able to cope successfully with the complexities of the modern age if its efforts are thwarted and destroyed by the periodic intervention of war and its attendant destruction and confusion. A very successful social policy and political system that may represent generations of untiring effort can be ruined in a few years by the ravages of war. As only one of many examples available, the contrast between the Liberal England of 1913, socially, economically, and politically, and the Tory England of 1935, with its poverty and misery and its visionless government, is most instructive of the ruination wrought by war.[2] There is little gain from working for a better social order within national boundaries if such efforts are to be wiped out in a few months of useless carnage. Hence the elimination of war is a basic prerequisite to any hope of a decent world order and to any assurance of enduring civilization.

The only way to end war is to face squarely the causes of wars and to attempt to reduce or mitigate these as rapidly and thoroughly as possible. It is of little avail merely to attack one or another of the symptoms of the war system. The fundamental causes must be sought out and resolutely assailed. This statement should not be taken as an attitude unfriendly to the movement for the outlawry of war. To the present writer it seems that the attack upon the causes of wars should be paralleled by the movement for the outlawry of war. If the latter should succeed it would provide a short cut to the objective to which all sane people aspire. At the same time, the more successful the achievements in the way of eliminating the causes of wars, the more likely is the outlawry program to succeed. The important thing to emphasize here is the desirability of avoiding a single-track outlook and allowing any one panacea or formula for ending war to usurp the field.

In considering the basic causes of wars it is highly essential to take a broad view of the question. One of the reasons why the former attacks upon war have proved inadequate is that enthusiastic pacifists have often tended to seize upon one cause of war, to the neglect of many others of equal or greater potency.

The causes of war may be summarized as biological, psychological, social, economic, political, and ethical. The biological causes of wars arise chiefly out of the nature of man. This permits a pugnacious as well as a pacific type of social conditioning, according to his social experience. Another biological cause of war is the tendency of populations to outrun the space and resources of their native habitats. The psychological causes of wars are comprehended chiefly within the war cult and "100 per cent" patriotism. The devotees of the latter condemn all pacific endeavor as a weak-kneed and flabby surrender of the manly virtues. The social causes of wars are found chiefly in the struggle of interests, in the doctrine of social Darwinism that war is the social analogue of the struggle for existence and hence the basis of all social and cultural progress, and in the racial dogmas which contend that some one race has been designed by God to inherit the earth. The economic causes of wars fall mainly under such headings as modern imperialism, the struggle for raw materials and

---

[1] *Cf.* L. W. McMullen, ed., *Building the World Society,* McGraw-Hill, 1931.
[2] Of course, it was the Liberal government of 1914 that headed straight for war and made possible the Tory government of 1935.

markets, trade rivalry, and the contemporary system of discriminatory and differential tariffs.

The political causes of wars emerge primarily as the doctrine of the finality of the national-state system and the dogma of the absolute nature of political sovereignty. These obstruct international organization and treaties that limit the complete independence of the state in every field. Along with these, as a combination of psychological and political factors, is to be found the conception of national honor, which leads to the view that arbitration of "vital issues" is a surrender of national dignity. Finally, the ethical and religious causes of wars are to be sought in the dogma that the state is an entity unto itself above all considerations of individual morality, in the assumption of the nobility of military sacrifice, in the view that war brings forth the loftiest ideals and sentiments that mankind is capable of entertaining, and in the assurance that God is invariably to be found rendering loyal support to the policies and arms of a particular state. Only in such a broad sweep of influences making for armed conflict can we hope to comprehend the multiplicity of the factors with which the ardent and disciplined pacifist must grapple if he is to have any prospect of success in his campaign against war.

It is obvious that the remedy is to be found in removing, so far as possible, those circumstances and influences which are likely to lead to open conflict.[1] A more pacific type of conditioning must be provided for man, so as to bring out his coöperative traits and obstruct his more pugnacious trends. Intellectual and cultural conflict must be substituted for physical combat. Birth control must be widely adopted to keep populations within those limits which may not peacefully be overstepped. The war cult must be undermined and the pacifist upheld as a higher type of citizen than the unreasoning and bellicose patriot. Indeed, pacifism must be shown to be the highest form of patriotism. Civic obligation and devotion must be represented as a higher ideal than "100-percentism."

The untenable dogma of social Darwinism must be uprooted. The fact that wars tend to leave a population biologically and institutionally worse than before should be thoroughly inculcated. It must be shown that the struggle of interests in the international field can be carried out pacifically, as it has already come to be for the most part within national boundaries. The racial obsession, which has arisen once more in crude form in recent years, can be laid at rest for all time by the corrosive action upon such error produced by even the most elementary scientific considerations relevant to the subject. Contemporary imperialism should be mitigated through the refusal of national states to put the armed forces of the state behind the private ambitions and claims of individual economic interests. There must be a progressive movement towards more thorough internationalization of the supply of raw materials and natural resources. We are also in immediate need of a revival of the healthy early-nineteenth-century movement for freer trade.

It should, moreover, be shown that the national state, like tribalism, feudalism, and other epochs in political development, is but a stage in political evolution, to be followed logically and historically by world organization in the

---

[1] *Cf.* T. B. Veblen, *An Inquiry into the Nature of Peace and the Terms of Its Perpetuation*, Huebsch, 1917, and Devere Allen, *The Fight for Peace*, Macmillan, 1930.

ELIMINATING THE BASIC CAUSES OF WARS

political field. It must be indicated that the dogma of absolute political sovereignty is a metaphysical fiction, whether applied within or beyond the boundaries of the state. It must be made clear that no state has been or can be completely free or independent in any field of activity. It must be emphasized that willingness to arbitrate is a far better proof of national honor than an eagerness to fight, in the same way that the private citizen commands confidence when he gives evidence of a willingness to take his case to court.

The musty fiction that a state occupies a special moral plane which renders the acts of its servants immune to moral judgments and condemnations should be relentlessly exposed.[1] It is also easy to prove that war, far from stimulating our more heroic virtues, actually debases man more than any other social and cultural situation. It brings forward the worst traits of Homo sapiens: his brutality, cupidity, and intolerance.[2] Finally, it is manifestly false that God can be assumed to give evidence of special favoritism towards any nation or group of nations or to set the stamp of divine approval upon carnage in any form.[3]

Those who have the interest of mankind at heart must be capable of visualizing the task that confronts them and must have the courage to risk unpopularity and opposition in the effort to solve these problems. Then there may be some prospect of ultimate success for the pacific program, especially if those interested in the reduction of the causes of war join hands cordially with those who are devoted to outlawing this leading scourge of humanity.

X. THE "AGGRESSIVE WAR" MYTH AND SUBSTITUTES FOR WAR

One of the major blind alleys in the recent propaganda of certain champions of peace has been the dissemination of the myth of the peculiarly dastardly and indefensible character of an "aggressive war." This has been an especially popular doctrine with those who wish for both peace and the perpetuation of the Treaty of Versailles, which assigned vast war booty to the Allies. Those who have been successful in a war usually become warm advocates of the maintenance of a peace that will sustain them in the possession of the spoils. They are all too prone to forget that they gained much of their far-flung territory or rich natural resources by aggressive wars in the past. Harold Nicolson has possessed the candor to bring out this point in commenting on England and Germany before 1914. In the introductory remarks to his biography of his father, *Portrait of a Diplomatist,* he says:

The Germans, during the period which I cover [the generation before the World War], were fired by exactly the same motives and energies which illuminate what we still regard as one of the most noble passages in our early history. We, for our part, were protected against all imprudence by the repletion, passivity, and, I should add, the selfishness, of old age.[4]

---

[1] *Cf.* W. W. Willoughby, *The Ethical Basis of Political Authority,* Macmillan, 1930; and E. F. Carritt, *Morals and Politics,* Oxford Press, 1935.
[2] *Cf.* Stallings, *The First World War; a Photographic History;* John Dos Passos, *Three Soldiers,* Doran, 1921; E. M. Remarque, *All Quiet on the Western Front,* Little, Brown, 1929; E. N. La Motte, *The Backwash of War,* Putnam, 1916; Walter Owen, *The Cross of Carl,* Little, Brown, 1931.
[3] Abrams, *The Preachers Present Arms.*   [4] Nicolson, *op. cit.,* Houghton Mifflin, 1930, p. xvi.

The essential truth of the whole matter has been admirably expressed by Professor Henry W. Lawrence:

> This harmonizing of national policies must deal with fundamentals; with the things that have commonly caused wars. The moral right to keep on possessing the best regions of the earth is directly balanced by the right to fight and capture them. It is amazing that so few people will admit this axiom of international morality. Popular opinion is widely befogged in the more comfortable countries by the childish notion that an aggressive war is wicked but a defensive war is righteous. They are, of course, precisely equal in moral quality, so long as war is the only adequate instrument by which vested wrongs can be righted and national needs supplied. The next rational step toward a tolerable world peace would be the broadcasting of this truth throughout Great Britain, France and the United States. It is already familiar to the peoples of Germany, Italy and Japan.[1]

In any event, before the causes of wars are eliminated and the wrongs of past wars are rectified we shall probably be faced with many a clash that threatens war. The prospect of riding safely through such crises will depend mainly upon how far we shall in the meantime have provided workable substitutes for war. When the war actually comes, the fair promises and declarations of peace-time fade out before mob hysteria like a late snowfall before a May sun at midday. Professor James T. Shotwell has well stated this important truism:

> While I fully appreciate the need of getting the discussion on to a practical purpose instead of re-asserting moral attitudes or calling for unrealizable reforms in international dealings, I do not think there is any single method which should be taken as a panacea. What is needed is the best pertinent substitute for war in any given dispute. This will vary from the refusal of the shipment of armaments to the pressure of financial and economic sanctions, and in some cases full measures of international police action, but recent history has shown that these processes cannot be safely employed in dealing with great nations. Compulsory arbitration is not acceptable to the United States, but has been taken on by most European powers.
>
> In view of all these complications the only sound policy, in my opinion, is to support the League of Nations, with a sufficiently elastic Covenant to accept the permissive sanctions which outlaw the rights of the aggressor as well as obligatory sanctions of joint co-operative police action. To help work out this constitution of co-ordinated policies is the only way that the world will slough off the primitive method of settling disputes on vital matters. If you wish to substitute for this some short cut, such as the refusal of military duty in time of war, you will be, I am sure, misleading the youth of the country, for when it comes to a test of the strength of emotional attitudes, patriotism will win.[2]

[1] H. W. Lawrence, "Peace Costs Too Much," *Christian Century*, Oct. 10, 1934, p. 1279. *Cf.* F. H. Simonds and Brooks Emeny, *The Price of Peace*, Harper, 1935, especially pp. 334 ff.

[2] Shotwell, "How Can We Prevent a New War?" *Scholastic*, Nov. 10, 1934, p. 17. Professor Shotwell's repetition of the "aggressor" fiction does not invalidate his powerful general argument.

SUGGESTED READING

Hammerton, *Universal History of the World*, Chap. 183
Langsam, *The World since 1914*, Chaps. vi, viii
Benns, *Europe since 1914*, Chaps. ix, xi
Buell, *Europe: A History of Ten Years*, Chaps. iv, vi, xix
────── *International Relations*, Pt. III

SUGGESTED READING

Jules Cambon and others, *The Foreign Policy of the Powers*, Harper, 1935
Jerome Davis, *Contemporary Social Movements*, Century, 1930, Book VIII
Wells, *The Work, Wealth and Happiness of Mankind*, Vol. II, Chap. XII
S. P. H. Duggan, ed., *The League of Nations: The Principle and the Practice*, Little, Brown, 1919, Chaps. II, XV
William Ladd, *An Essay on a Congress of Nations*, ed. by J. B. Scott, Oxford Press, 1916, Introduction
P. B. Potter, *Introduction to the Study of International Organization*, 3d ed. rev., Century, 1928
—— *This World of Nations*
H. M. Vinacke, *International Organization*, Crofts, 1934
Theodore Marburg, *The Development of the League of Nations Idea*, Macmillan, 1932, 2 vols.
J. S. Bassett, *The League of Nations*, Longmans, 1928
Felix Morley, *The Society of Nations*, Brookings Institution, 1932
J. W. Wheeler-Bennett, *The Pipe Dream of Peace*, Morrow, 1935 (pub. in England as *The Disarmament Deadlock*)
—— *Disarmament and Security since Locarno, 1925-1931*, Macmillan, 1932
—— and Maurice Fanshawe, *Information on the World Court, 1918-1928*, London, 1929
Engelbrecht and Hanighen, *Merchants of Death*
C. A. Beard, *The Navy: Defense or Portent?* Harper, 1932
B. F. Trueblood, *The Development of the Peace Idea*, privately printed, 1932
F. S. Marvin, ed., *The Evolution of World-Peace*, Oxford Press, 1921
A. C. F. Beales, *History of Peace*, Dial Press, 1931
Devere Allen, *The Fight for Peace*, Macmillan, 1930
Sir Norman Angell, *Peace and the Plain Man*, Harper, 1935
M. E. Curti, *The American Peace Crusade, 1815-1860*, Duke University Press, 1929
—— *Bryan and World Peace*, Smith College Press, 1931
H. M. Cory, *The Compulsory Arbitration of International Disputes*, Columbia University Press, 1932
Drew Pearson and Constantine Brown, *The American Diplomatic Game*, Doubleday, Doran, 1935
J. T. Shotwell, *War as an Instrument of National Policy and Its Renunciation in the Pact of Paris*, Harcourt, Brace, 1929
P. C. Jessup, *International Security*, Council on Foreign Relations, 1935
F. G. Tuttle, *Alternatives to War*, Harper, 1931
J. H. Latané, *From Isolation to Leadership*, Doubleday, Page, rev. ed., 1925
—— *History of American Foreign Policy*, rev. and enlarged by D. W. Wainhouse, Doubleday, Doran, 1934
H. D. Lasswell, *World Politics and Personal Insecurity*, McGraw-Hill, 1935
Scott Nearing, *War*, Vanguard Press, 1931
K. A. Bratt, *That Next War?* Harcourt, Brace, 1931
Inter-parliamentary Union, *What Would Be the Character of a New War?* Smith & Haas, 1933
Porritt, *The Causes of War*
Challenge to Death . . . prefaced by Viscount Cecil, Dutton, 1935
Leonidas Dodson, ed., *The Shadow of War*, American Academy of Political and Social Science, *Annals*, Vol. CLXXV, 1934
Economics of World Peace, American Academy of Political and Social Science, *Annals*, Vol. CL, 1930
Webster, *Historical Selections*, Sec. XXIII

Robinson and Beard, *Readings in Modern European History,* Vol. II, pp. 458-66
Scott and Baltzly, *Readings in European History since 1814,* pp. 682-89
Jones, Vandenbosch, and Vandenbosch, *Readings in Citizenship,* pp. 821-80
McMullen, *Building the World Society,* Chaps. IV-VIII
W. E. Darby, ed., *International Arbitration: International Tribunals,* 4th ed., American Peace Society, 1904
Cooke and Stickney, *Readings in European International Relations Since 1879*
F. B. Boeckel, *Between War and Peace,* Macmillan, 1928

FURTHER REFERENCES

IN QUEST OF PEACE. Davis, *op. cit.,* Bk. VIII. On the character of war under present conditions, see Will Irwin, *The Next War* (Dutton, 1921); Bratt, *op. cit.;* Interparliamentary Union, *op. cit.* For a brief history of plans for international organization, see Duggan, *op. cit.,* Chap. II; Chaps. II-IV of D. W. Morrow, *The Society of Free States* (Harper, 1919); Muir, *Nationalism and Internationalism,* pp. 124 ff.; Ladd, *op. cit.;* Marvin, *op. cit.*

On the League of Nations, see Hammerton, *op. cit.,* Chap. 183; Marburg, *op. cit.;* Bassett, *op. cit.;* Morley, *op. cit.,* Pt. II.

On the World Court, see M. O. Hudson, *The Permanent Court of International Justice* (Macmillan, 1934); Wheeler-Bennett and Fanshawe, *op. cit.*

On the International Labor Organization, see A. S. Cheyney, ed., *The International Labor Organization* (American Academy of Political and Social Science, Vol. CLXVI, 1933); J. T. Shotwell, ed., *The Origins of the International Labor Organization* (Columbia University Press, 1934, 2 vols.).

On the League of Nations and disarmament, see Pt. IV of B. H. Williams, *The United States and Disarmament* (McGraw-Hill, 1931); Schuman, *International Politics,* pp. 698 ff.; Wheeler-Bennett, *Disarmament and Security since Locarno, 1925-1931;* Salvador de Madariaga, *Disarmament* (Coward-McCann, 1929); K. B. Schmidt and Adolf Grabowsky, *The Problem of Disarmament,* Berlin, 1933.

On the history of the peace movement, see Allen, *op. cit.;* Beales, *op. cit.;* Trueblood, *op. cit.;* Curti, *The American Peace Crusade* and *Bryan and World Peace.*

On the history of the Kellogg Pact, see Pearson and Brown, *op. cit.;* Shotwell, *War as an Instrument of National Policy,* Pt. II; J. W. Wheeler-Bennett, *Information on the Renunciation of War* (London, 1929).

On world-organization, see Potter, *op. cit.;* Vinacke, *op. cit.;* J. H. Randall, *A World Community* (Stokes, 1930); Wells, *The Shape of Things to Come,* and Vol. II of *The World of William Clissold* (Doran, 1926, 2 vols.). On the American federal government as a model for international coöperation, see E. D. Fite, *Government by Cooperation* (Macmillan, 1932). On the psychological and historical foundations of world-organization, see F. S. Marvin, ed., *The Unity of Western Civilization* (3d ed., Oxford Press, 1929); C. D. Burns, *Short History of International Intercourse* (Oxford Press, 1924).

On the Isolation Myth in the United States, see Duggan, *op. cit.,* Chap. XV; Latane, *From Isolation to Leadership;* R. M. Cooper, *American Consultation in World Affairs* (Macmillan, 1934).

On the elimination of the causes of war, see Porritt, *op. cit.;* Tuttle, *op. cit.;* Cecil and others, *op. cit.*

On the aggressive war fiction, see Lawrence, "Peace Costs Too Much," *Christian Century,* Oct. 10, 1934; Simonds and Emeny, *The Price of Peace.*

CHAPTER XXIV

CONTEMPORARY PROGRAMS OF SOCIAL AND ECONOMIC REFORM

I. THE HISTORICAL BACKGROUND

The programs of social reform in the first half of the nineteenth century had cleared away the archaic obstructions inherent in mercantilism.[1] They had also made vigorous assaults upon the succeeding era of industrialism and Economic Liberalism from almost every angle, ranging from an esthetic protest to political and economic rivalry. In England and France some progress had been made towards the beginnings of constructive factory legislation, but elsewhere little had been achieved in this direction. Nowhere were workingmen freely allowed the right of self-protection through organization. In no major European country did political democracy exist in 1850. There were few constructive and practicable programs of social reform. Only in Prussia and the United States was there much free public education. But, in spite of these early failures to achieve permanent results, the ground had been prepared for the rise of those reform movements which have brought the beginnings of economic as well as political democracy into the modern world.[2]

Before 1850 the new industrial order had taken hold thoroughly only in England, though it had affected France to a considerable degree. Other major European countries, except for German beginnings, were little influenced by the Industrial Revolution until the last third of the century. When the new industrialism came to these states it created a wider enthusiasm for the programs of social reform. The first half of the nineteenth century was spent by the proletariat and its champions in groping about, feeling their way, in formulating impracticable programs and discovering successful methods of organization and achievement. After 1850 this preliminary training began to bear fruit in vigorous proletarian movements in both the political and the economic fields. Further, the mad rush for wealth tended to become less crude and harsh, and the more enlightened members of the capitalistic class became more resigned to a moderate restriction of their absolute industrial freedom. Finally, the Spencerian cosmology and the Darwinian biology made any static outlook upon social and economic problems scientifically untenable.

[1] See above, pp. 74 ff., 378 ff.
[2] Cf. F. W. Coker, *Recent Political Thought*, Appleton-Century, 1934, Chap. 1.

931

II. THE EFFECT OF THE IDEALISTIC PHILOSOPHY OF THE STATE

The political philosophy of both Economic Liberalism and Utilitarianism had been built on the thesis of the preëminence of the individual; the state was looked upon as merely the "communal policeman." Aside from the protection of life and property and the construction of public works, the main function of the state was held to be the abolition of restrictive legislation previously enacted. The notion of the state as the chief instrument of social reform was wholly repulsive to this school. Therefore, a new theory of the state was essential before extensive reform legislation could be given a respectable theoretical foundation. This new notion of the state was found in the doctrines of the German idealistic political philosophers, particularly Hegel. Here was discovered a conception of the state that was very reverent, took the community as the starting-point of political reasoning, and believed the individual capable of finding perfection only as a member of the state. This view was brought over into England by Matthew Arnold, T. H. Green, F. H. Bradley, and Bernard Bosanquet. Ernest Barker thus summarizes the nature and significance of this transformation in political philosophy:

> Not a modification of the old Benthamite premises, but a new philosophy was needed; and that philosophy was provided by the idealist school, of which Green is the greatest representative. That school drew its inspiration immediately from Kant and Hegel, and ultimately from the old Greek philosophy of the city-state. The vital relation between the life of the individual and the life of the community, which alone gives the individual worth and significance, because it alone gives him the power of full moral development; the dependence of the individual, for all his rights and for all his liberty, on his membership of the community; the correlative duty of the community to guarantee to the individual all his rights (in other words all the conditions necessary for his, and therefore for its own, full moral development) —these were the premises of the new philosophy. That philosophy could satisfy the new needs of social progress, because it refused to worship a supposed individual liberty which was proving destructive of the real liberty of the vast majority, and preferred to emphasise the moral well-being and betterment of the whole community, and to conceive of each of its members as attaining his own well-being and betterment in and through the community. Herein lay, or seemed to lie, a revolution of ideas. Instead of starting from a central individual, to whom the social system is supposed to be adjusted, the idealist starts from a central social system, in which the individual must find his appointed orbit of duty.[1]

This philosophy laid the foundation for extensive state activity, but it carried with it certain exaggerations and dangers, which Dewey and Hobhouse have revealed.[2]

III. THE RISE OF SCIENTIFIC SOCIOLOGY

The general science of society, or sociology, took its origin, as Professor Albion W. Small made clear, from the social conditions and reform programs of

---

[1] Barker, *Political Thought in England*, pp. 10-11.
[2] John Dewey, *German Philosophy and Politics*, Holt, 1915, and L. T. Hobhouse, *The Metaphysical Theory of the State*, Macmillan, 1918. Important books, but written under the influence of wartime psychology.

the first half of the nineteenth century, which called for some objective science capable of weighing the merits and detecting the defects in the many and varied plans for social reform.[1] Saint-Simon had recognized the need for such a science and it was founded by his disciple Auguste Comte and by Herbert Spencer, though the science of society would sooner or later have come into existence had these men never written.

The attitude of sociologists towards state activity has varied greatly.[2] Comte believed in a thoroughgoing program of social reform, but evolutionary biology affected most early sociological thought much as Newtonian mechanics had influenced political and economic thought for two centuries previously. Sociologists of individualistic leanings such as Ludwig Gumplowicz, Herbert Spencer, Jacques Novicow, and William Graham Sumner interpreted the evolutionary doctrine to mean that social institutions, like the animal organism, evolved in a spontaneous and automatic manner, and that human efforts could only be harmful—a view similar to that entertained by the Physiocrats towards interference with the "natural order" of physical and social phenomena. Others, particularly Lester F. Ward, Leonard T. Hobhouse, Ludwig Stein, and R. M. MacIver, have combated this view. They have maintained that while the earliest stages of social evolution were spontaneous, there comes a time when social progress can be artificially accelerated by the conscious direction of mankind.

Most sociologists, following Stanley Jevons, have avoided dogmatism on this point and have shown that laissez faire and State Socialism are policies which may each have their virtues in the degree to which they are adapted to the needs of a given society. But sociologists are tending to abandon the individualistic point of view and to stand with Ward and Hobhouse in favoring extensive state activity. While it can scarcely be said that every sociologist is on that account a potential statesman, it is certain that no scientific program of social reform can be formulated independent of sociological investigations or divorced from sociological principles.[3]

IV. THE DEVELOPMENT OF MARXIAN OR SCIENTIFIC SOCIALISM

The origins of the modern Scientific Socialism are generally and correctly associated with the work of Karl Marx (1818-1883) and Friedrich Engels (1820-1895). As Bertrand Russell has well said:

Socialism as a power in Europe may be said to begin with Marx. It is true that before his time there were Socialist theories, both in England and in France. It is also true that in France, during the revolution of 1848, Socialism for a brief period acquired considerable influence in the State. But the Socialists who preceded Marx tended to indulge in Utopian dreams and failed to found any strong or stable political party. To Marx, in collaboration with Engels, is due both the formulation of a coherent body of Socialist doctrine, sufficiently true or plausible to dominate the minds of vast numbers of men, and the formation of the International Socialist movement, which has continued to grow in all European countries throughout the last fifty years.[4]

[1] Small, *General Sociology,* Chap. III, and *The Origins of Sociology.*
[2] *Cf.* Barnes, *Sociology and Political Theory,* Chaps. IX-X.
[3] Implied in the Hoover report on *Recent Social Trends.*
[4] Russell, *Proposed Roads to Freedom,* Holt, 1919, pp. 24-25.

It would probably be futile to attempt to indicate all the sources of Marx's views, for he read deeply in the literature of his age and was in contact with most of its tendencies, but a few of his more conspicuous obligations may be set down: (1) To Hegel he was indebted for his dialectical system and his faith in state activity;[1] (2) his materialistic philosophy of history he took mainly from Feuerbach; (3) the labor theory of value was derived from Ricardo, Rodbertus, and the Ricardian Socialists; (4) the doctrine of surplus value was found by Marx in the writings of the Ricardian Socialist Thompson; (5) the notion of class conflict and of the necessity of a proletarian upheaval was emphasized in the works of Louis Blanc, Proudhon, and Weitling; (6) from Sismondi he received his conviction that capitalism would be weakened by the progressive concentration of wealth in the hands of a few men; and (7) from Rodbertus he may have derived the thesis that continually recurring crises were a phase of economic life under capitalism. In short, Marx synthesized three main currents of thought: (1) Hegelian philosophy; (2) Utopian and French Socialism; and (3) the Classical Economics.

The *Communist Manifesto,* a document drawn up by Marx and Engels for the German Communist League in Paris in January, 1848, contained the essence of Marxian Socialism. The document begins with the materialistic interpretation of history, that is, the contention that the successive systems of the production and distribution of wealth—pastoralism, agrarianism, and capitalism—have determined the accompanying social and cultural institutions.[2] Then comes the labor theory of value—the belief that labor produces all value. From this is derived the doctrine of surplus value by pointing to the difference between the total social product and the income received by labor.[3] This difference is the surplus value created by labor, out of which it is cheated by the capitalist, in the form of rent, interest, and profits. Hence arises the notion of an inevitable and irreconcilable class struggle between the proletariat and the capitalists. This will terminate in the final overthrow of the latter, for they are being continually weakened by the steady concentration of wealth, by repeated disastrous crises, and by the excesses and exhaustion of economic imperialism. The proletariat will become progressively stronger through economic solidarity, party organization, and the conquest of the right of suffrage. When the proletariat has secured sufficient power it will rise up and forcibly expropriate its oppressors and institute the régime of collectivism, which, in its first stages, will be a dictatorship of the proletariat. These doctrines were elaborated with greater thoroughness but in more ponderous and obscure language in the work on *Capital* written by Marx and edited and published by Engels.[4]

The question as to whether Marx and Engels believed that the proletarian state would be ushered in by violence or by democratic and constitutional

---

[1] Rebecca Cooper, *The Logical Influence of Hegel on Marx,* University of Washington Press, 1925.
[2] *Cf.* M. M. Bober, *Karl Marx's Interpretation of History,* Harvard University Press, 1927.
[3] The total surplus value is the sum of that created by individual laborers. Labor, according to Marx, is a commodity that produces more than its own value. If—following Marx's examples—the laborer works ten hours, he gets only the equivalent of roughly half what he has produced. The difference is surplus value (*Mehrwerth*).
[4] The ablest criticisms of Marxian doctrines are Gide and Rist, *History of Economic Doctrines,* Chap. III; O. D. Skelton, *Socialism; a Critical Analysis,* Houghton Mifflin, 1911; and T. B. Veblen, *The Place of Science in Modern Civilization,* Huebsch, 1919, pp. 405-56.

means has been bitterly debated. It is a crucial point, for upon it hinges the legitimacy of Revisionism versus Communism as the heir of Marx. The Revisionists claim that Marx favored constitutional methods, while the Communists contend that he stood for the violent overthrow of capitalism. The fact seems to be that he favored constitutional means wherever possible, but believed that violence might be necessary at some times and in some countries. In 1872, at the Hague Conference of the First International, Marx declared: "We do not assert that the way to reach this goal is the same everywhere. We know that the institutions, the manners, the customs of the various countries must be considered and we do not deny that there are countries like England and America, and if I understood the arrangements better, I might even add Holland, where the worker may obtain his object by peaceful means." Engels, also, in his Introduction to his famous book on *The Condition of the Working Class in England in 1844,* indicated a pretty definite feeling that more could be accomplished in the future through legal means than through violence. One must also bear in mind that when Marx used the term "revolution" he did not always mean a violent revolution, but rather a definite shift of economic and political power from the capitalist class to the proletariat. Even many of the followers of Karl Kautsky before the World War—the German Marxians—came to believe that Socialists should work for immediate reforms before the coming of the Socialist society.[1]

The enduring theoretical contributions of Marx are his materialistic interpretation of history and his extremely effective criticism of the individualistic industrialism of the first half of the nineteenth century, the second of which "cannot but stir into fury any passionate working-class reader, and into unbearable shame any possessor of capital in whom generosity and justice are not wholly extinct." Moreover, as a contributor to the science of economics he is generally regarded as the father of "institutional economics."[2]

Marx was also instrumental in establishing Socialism as a political force in Europe.[3] The International Workingmen's Association took its origins from a conference of workers at the London International Exhibition of 1862. It was organized at London two years later and its principles were drawn up by Marx and adopted at the Geneva conference of 1866. A German wing was started by Wilhelm Liebknecht in 1864 and, under his leadership and that of August Bebel, it was developed into the Democratic Workingmen's Association at Eisenach in 1869. In the meantime a German General Workingmen's Association had been organized and its program enunciated by Ferdinand Lassalle in 1863. These two groups coalesced at Gotha in 1875 and created the German Social Democratic party. Persecuted by Bismarck from 1878 to 1890, it grew in numbers and power until it commanded 110 out of 397 votes in the Reichstag of the old German Empire and after 1918 captured the preponderance of power of the government, holding it with fading fortunes until 1933.

---

[1] Perhaps the best discussion of this important issue is contained in S. H.-M. Chang, *The Marxian Theory of the State,* Vanguard Press, 1931, Chaps. IV-V.

[2] Since cultivated by Sombart, Weber, Hobson, Webb, Hammond, Veblen, Commons, Hamilton, Mitchell, Chase, Douglas, and others.

[3] *Cf.* Ogg and Sharp, *The Economic Development of Modern Europe,* Chaps. XXII-XXIII.

The beginning of the modern French political organization of labor dates back to 1878. Two years later French Marxism was originated under the leadership of Jules Guesde. But the French Socialists for a long time were unable to arrive at the same unity that characterized the party in Germany. Numerous sects developed and much bitter feeling grew up, particularly between the Marxians, led by Guesde, and the Revisionists or Opportunists, led by Jean Jaurès, perhaps the ablest figure in the history of contemporary Socialism. An effort to unite these factions failed in 1899, but met with more success in 1905. The United Socialist party was able to elect 102 out of 602 members of the Chamber of Deputies in 1914, besides 18 members of the allied Independent Socialist party.

The Socialist party organization made rapid progress in a number of the other chief European countries, notably Austria, Italy, and Russia, and reached remarkable strength in some of the lesser states, particularly Finland, Sweden, Denmark, and Belgium. In part this has been the result of the increased strength of the proletariat and in part an outgrowth of a moderation of Socialistic proposals that attracted many liberals who refuse to accept all the Marxian postulates.

The greatest success of Marxism has, however, come since the World War, in Russia.[1] Communism in Russia is quite literally the application of Marxian principles to the problems of economic, social, and political reconstruction. They have had to be modified to some extent because of the backward nature of the Russian economy. We shall devote a later chapter to this subject.[2]

Whatever the validity of the Socialist plans for economic revolution, there can be little doubt of the telling nature of the Socialistic critique of capitalism or of the soundness of the aspiration to base production on the motive of social service rather than private profit.

V. THE ENGLISH FABIANS AND THE GROWTH OF "REVISIONIST" SOCIALISM

In spite of the significance of Marxian Socialism in attracting a sufficient following to make it a political and economic movement of great importance, it seemed to many to possess certain obvious theoretical difficulties, which embarrassed its more thoughtful supporters and gave its enemies a vulnerable point of attack. These weaknesses were chiefly the debatable labor theory of value and the deductions from it, and the refusal of the Marxians to coöperate with existing capitalistic governments in securing immediate remedial legislation for the proletariat. A program of reform that was not to begin until a remote and complete economic and social revolution could be achieved was much less attractive to many reformers than one that would accept partial amelioration on the road to complete triumph.[3]

This attitude was first notably asserted by a group of English radicals known

---

[1] *Cf.* Chang, *op. cit.*, Chap. VIII, and Coker, *op. cit.*, Chap. VI.
[2] See below, Chap. XXV.
[3] *Cf.* H. W. Laidler, *History of Socialist Thought*, Crowell, 1927, Chap. XX, and Coker, *op. cit.*, Chap. IV.

as the Fabian Society.[1] They came together out of a general sympathy with Socialistic propositions that had been brought before them, in part by English followers of Marx, like William Morris and H. M. Hyndman, and in part by two American radicals, Henry George and Thomas Davidson. The most important members of this group have been Sidney Webb, Graham Wallas, Bernard Shaw, Chiozza Money, Edward Pease, H. G. Wells, and Stewart Headlam. They took their name from the cautious Roman general Fabius, since they had resolved to delay their final convictions until the Socialistic movement had further developed. They relied chiefly upon the hope of arousing an intellectual movement in favor of radical social reform. Their main significance lies in the fact that they repudiated the fatalism of Marx and came out for "opportunism," or remedial social legislation through the agency of the existing political organization. They thus made Socialism an evolutionary rather than a revolutionary movement. They were also less devoted to the internationalism of Marx and laid greater stress upon national progress in social reform.

While the Fabians originated the tenets of "Revisionism," the spread of this movement was due more to the agitation of a German Socialist savant, Eduard Bernstein (1850-1933). Bernstein lived in England during the period of the Socialist persecution in Germany and was converted to the ideas of the Fabians.[2] Returning to Germany in the early nineties, he began the dissemination of his new convictions. In his work on *Evolutionary Socialism* (1909) he systematized his principles, which were chiefly a denial of the Marxian economics, especially the labor theory of value, a declaration for opportunism or piecemeal remedial social legislation, a willingness to coöperate with existing governments and to concede more to the principles of nationalism and patriotism than the Marxians would allow. In other words, he aimed at the practical transformation of Socialism from a proletarian party of revolution into a party of radical social reform that could attract the support of non-Marxian liberals. While he was not able to dominate the German Socialist movement until after the death of Bebel and the elder Liebknecht, the Marxians came to constitute a definite minority among German Socialists, and many of the Revisionists even passed Bernstein in the degree to which they moderated the Marxian doctrine.[3]

The general history of Socialism in every important modern state before the war was much like that of German Socialism: Marxism served as the entering wedge of propaganda, while the growth of the movement witnessed the domination of Revisionism.[4] Only in Russia, where Socialism did not have a long enough period of development to allow the triumph of Revisionism, have the Marxians remained in the majority. The leading Revisionist Socialists have been Jean Jaurès in France, Emile Vandervelde in Belgium, Filippo Turati in Italy, and Peter Struve and M. Tugan-Baranovsky in Russia. At the outbreak of the World War most of the intellectual leaders of Socialism in the

---

[1] See E. R. Pease, *History of the Fabian Society,* Dutton, 1916.
[2] See Bernstein, *My Life in Exile,* Harcourt, Brace, 1921.
[3] Some German Marxians might challenge this statement and contend that even in 1914 Kautsky and the Marxians held their own with the Revisionists.
[4] In Austria before 1914 Socialism did remain pretty thoroughly Marxian and left-wing; and in the United States Debs was a fairly uncompromising Marxian. But even Debs was willing to flirt with Revision far more than was Daniel De Leon.

United States had also generally capitulated to Revisionism, though the majority of the party clung to Marxian principles.

As Socialism increased in strength it developed moderation for a time. This was due in part to the seemingly greater validity and practicability of Revisionism and in part to the very growth of Socialist power, for, as Professor Orth has put it, "ambition brings power, power brings responsibility, responsibility sobers the senses." Socialism before the World War appeared to be fairly well purged of the nightmare of violent revolution.

The collapse of international Socialism at the outbreak of the war under the pressure of the patriotic sentiment was a great disappointment to many. One factor that helped it on was the assassination of the greatest of prewar Socialist leaders, Jean Jaurès, on the eve of the war. He might have prevented the surrender of Socialist principles from being so abject. The war-mongers apparently perceived this, for it is believed upon good evidence that Izvolsky had a large part in the assassination plot.

The triumph and success of revolutionary Socialism in Russia and the crushing out of evolutionary Socialism in Italy and Germany by Fascism have reversed the prewar trend. It now appears to the radicals that they lost out in Germany and Italy because of moderation and constitutionalism. They believe they might have succeeded if they had resorted to revolution and force. Therefore the main current in Socialism today is more decidedly towards revolutionary Marxism.

VI. THE RISE AND EXPANSION OF STATE SOCIALISM

1. THE THEORY OF STATE SOCIALISM

Closely related to the principles and program of Revisionist Socialism and in part contributing to its growth and vitality is the so-called State Socialism. Their chief difference is that State Socialism has arisen primarily among radical bourgeoisie instead of moderate Socialists, though it must be remembered that in some cases, most notably in that of Bismarckian social legislation, State Socialism has been used to aid autocracy and check radicalism. A roughly similar program of remedial legislation is proposed by both, though their ultimate goal is slightly different. The Revisionist hopes for an ultimate proletarian state, but plans to ease as much as possible the passage of capitalism over into a real social democracy, while the State Socialist hopes to retain the capitalistic system, with large concessions to the laboring classes.[1]

State Socialism received some considerable impulse from Lassalle, but its chief early leaders were the German Karl Johann Rodbertus (1807-75), and the Frenchman, Charles Brook Dupont-White (1807-78).[2] More recently the program of State Socialism received the support not only of statesmen in the German Progressive party, the French Radical Socialist party,[3] and the English

---
[1] For this reason many writers, especially Socialists, would prefer to describe all the achievements listed in this section as state capitalism rather than State Socialism. They claim that the only true State Socialism yet achieved in the world is that in Russia today, which is on its way to Communism. This attitude appeals to the writer as logical and sound, but it runs so contrary to conventional usage that the term State Socialism is retained.

[2] Gide and Rist, *op. cit.*, Bk. IV, Chap. II.

[3] Not a true Socialist party, as its name would seem to imply.

Liberal party, but also, in different degrees, of the professorial champions of social reform within the capitalistic state, the so-called Socialists of the Chair,[1] such as Schäffle, Wagner, and Schmoller in Germany; Bouglé and Gide in France; Pigou, Hobson, and Hobhouse in England; and Commons, Patten, Hamilton, Seager, Douglas, and Tugwell in the United States.

2. STATE SOCIALISM IN ENGLAND

State Socialism began very informally, and with little conscious and deliberate philosophical basis, in the English efforts to better the horrible conditions existing in the early textile factories and the mines.

The alleviation of such conditions was a slow historical process of getting accustomed to a new type of industrial society. At first the peasants and artisans set afloat by the break-up of the old order were utterly alien to their new masters; but the two classes gradually got used to dealing with each other. The worst early factories were those situated away from the older cities, where use could be made of the water power of streams. With the growth of larger communities around these, and also with the increasing use of coal, which brought the factory into the town, outsiders became conscious of the dreadful working-conditions, and it was possible to mobilize public opinion against them. The general movement into towns increased the congestion, and this very fact brought many problems of the newer type of city to a head in such a way that remedial measures had to be taken. It also became obvious that the idealism and democratic enthusiasm of the end of the eighteenth century were not dead, but only temporarily bewildered by the currents of revolution, war, and industrial change that had swept down upon them.

The progress of this reform, through remedial legislation to the ten-hour bill of 1847, we have covered in an earlier chapter.[2] Other important acts were passed in 1850, 1878, and 1901, and a vast fabric of protective legislation and regulations has grown up. The growth of English labor unions will be dealt with later. A widening franchise for the working classes and the development of popular education have also been notable features of England's attempt to meet the new economic conditions with a more intricate and suitable type of social organization.

Though England was the early home of Economic Liberalism, even the party of Cobden was later converted to moderate State Socialism through a process of change that Professor Hobhouse has clearly explained in his little book *Liberalism*. Its vigorous leader, David Lloyd George, secured in the period between 1905 and 1914 the adoption of a legislative reform program sufficient to make Cobden turn in his grave. It was rivaled in content and decisiveness only by German achievements. Workman's compensation was secured by an act of 1906. Old-age pensions were introduced in 1908-09. Sickness, invalidity, and unemployment insurance were initiated in 1911. Thoroughgoing reform of the inequitable landholding system was forecast in the Small Holdings Act of 1907, but was cut short by the outbreak of the World War. The British social-insurance system has proved of untold value in the relief of the

---

[1] *Cf.* John Rae, *Contemporary Socialism*, Scribner, 1884, Chap. v., and D. O. Wagner, ed., *Social Reformers: Adam Smith to John Dewey*, Macmillan, 1934, pp. 486 ff.
[2] See above, pp. 387 ff.

unemployed and sick since the World War. The program of social insurance has been considerably expanded in England since 1918. The rules governing eligibility to old-age pensions were liberalized by an act of 1919 and the maximum pension rate slightly raised. This legislation was still further extended by the Widows, Orphans and Old Age Pensions Contributory Act of 1925 and the Contributory Pensions Act of 1929. A comprehensive National Health Insurance Act was passed in 1924 and those insured under it must also be insured for widows', orphans', and old-age pensions.[1] On March 1, 1935, the administration of the whole system of English unemployment insurance was placed in the hands of a new National Unemployment Insurance Board.

3. SOCIAL LEGISLATION IN GERMANY

Germany's experiments with State Socialism did not stop short with the developments in the field of railways. The program of social legislation that was undertaken under Bismarck resulted in the first outright repudiation of laissez-faire doctrines with reference to labor and the adoption of a paternalistic form of State Socialism.[2]

The late arrival of the factory system in Germany and the total lack of interest of government authorities retarded the first regulatory labor legislation until 1839. In that year a law was passed in Prussia limiting the working-day of children under sixteen to ten hours and prohibiting the employment of children under nine. It also forbade night work for those under sixteen. The law was miserably enforced and, though recognized as a failure, was not replaced until 1853. Legislation in that year prohibited children under twelve from working, set the working-day of children under fourteen at six hours, and stipulated that child workers were to receive three hours of school instruction every day. Here again, the administration of the statute was a farce. Neither employers nor government officials took it seriously. No other German state achieved any greater success with its industrial laws.

Increasing evils called imperatively for more extensive labor legislation, and the formation of the North German Confederation in 1867 set the scene for the adoption of a uniform labor code. After much debate, an industrial code surprisingly complete for that time was placed upon the statute books in 1869. This code amplified and reënforced the Prussian laws of 1839 and 1853, extending their provisions to mines and quarries. It also made obligatory the installation of safety devices by manufacturers. Again lax enforcement, largely as a result of the failure to provide for adequate inspection, took most of the teeth out of the measure. When the need for a complete and systematic code of industrial regulation became more clear as a result of the tremendous growth of industry after 1871, the movement for such legislation developed rapidly. Despite a bombardment of demands from all types of reformers, the imperial government could not be moved towards social radicalism. It remained intent on protecting labor in other ways.

Finally, in 1891, the movement was crowned with success. The Industrial Code of that year applied to factories, workshops, and home labor, other places

[1] E. M. Burns, "State Pensions and Old Age Dependency in Great Britain," *Political Science Quarterly*, June, 1930.

[2] *Cf.* Ogg and Sharp, *op. cit.*, pp. 389 ff. and Chap. xxiv; and W. H. Dawson, *Social Insurance in Germany*, Scribner, 1912.

of labor being provided for by other means. By its provisions, children under thirteen were prohibited from working, and females and males under sixteen were not permitted to work at night or to labor more than ten hours daily. Safety devices were made compulsory, and special regulations covered the more dangerous industries. The Industrial Code applied uniformly to the whole empire, but inspection and enforcement were left to the several states.

Far more important as social legislation were the more truly State Socialistic measures, the Sickness Insurance Law of 1883, the Accident Insurance Law of the following year, and the Old Age and Invalidity Law of 1889. Through such legislation, the empire assumed a policy of paternalistic State Socialism towards the working classes. Though not the originator of the social-insurance scheme, Bismarck was the one who supplied the necessary pressure to have the bills put through.[1] Social-insurance schemes were present in Germany before 1870, but the achievement of creating a national system and introducing the element of compulsion into their operation was that of the great Chancellor. In 1911, the social-insurance laws were unified into a single code which stands as a landmark in the history of social legislation.

The reasons that led Bismarck and his associates to the frank acceptance of social insurance by Germany can be considered under three headings: 1. It was hoped to entice the worker from the doctrines of Marxian Socialism, which were spreading rapidly, by assuring him of security and maintenance throughout his life and showing him that the state had his welfare at heart. 2. A paternalistic tradition was part and parcel of the Prussian heritage. The government was thought to be the proper authority to care for the workingman, and in so doing would create a healthier, more efficient nation. "In Prussia," Bismarck could say, "it is the kings, not the people, who make revolutions." 3. It was the function of the state to protect its citizens. The workingman served the state just as did the soldier or civil servant, and should be assured of as much security when his days of service were over as the soldier or state official. More than that, the workingman must be brought to regard the state as his benefactor and friend, not as his enemy. A contented, healthy working class is an asset to the state; a dissatisfied, unhealthy working class is a liability and a problem.

By the Sickness Insurance Law, all workers whose income fell below a stipulated amount were compelled to contribute to an insurance fund.[2] Workers' contributions made up two-thirds of the funds, those of the employers the remainder. Free medical attention and one-half of the wages for a period of twenty-six weeks were guaranteed to the insured person in case of sickness. The Accident Insurance Law provided compulsory workman's compensation for almost all industrial workers. Employers alone contributed to the funds, and they administered them in accordance with a scale set by law. In case of death, a yearly pension, which amounted to 20 per cent of the deceased's wages, was paid to the dependents of the insured person. Employees, employers, and the state all contributed to the fund from which the benefits were paid under the Old Age and Invalidity Law. The pensions varied in accordance with the

---

[1] Two German economists, Adolph Wagner and Gustav von Schmoller, abandoned laissez-faire doctrines and became active advocates of social-insurance ideas.
[2] In other words, all except highly paid skilled workers.

amount contributed by the worker. Insured persons of sixty-five (the age limit was first set at seventy) could draw their pensions.

As a result of the World War, the whole body of German social-insurance legislation underwent radical revision. Not only were the old laws liberalized and broadened in their application, and the money benefits readjusted to meet the new economic conditions, but in 1927 a measure was passed that provides for unemployment insurance. This type of insurance is also compulsory, and it applies to all workers whose incomes fall below a set standard. From funds made up of equal contributions of employers and employees and administered by the state at its own expense, insured persons receive a certain percentage of their wages for periods generally not exceeding twenty-six weeks in the year.[1]

The Hitler régime, which overthrew the German Republic in 1933, promised to extend the scope of conservative State Socialism in Germany.[2] The events of 1934 seem, however, to indicate a complete surrender of Hitler to Thyssen and the great German industrialists, who wish to restrict rather than extend labor and social legislation.[3]

4. SOCIAL LEGISLATION IN FRANCE

Accompanying the growth of the factory system in France there appeared the same evils and problems that had faced England. These brought a similar need for regulatory legislation. It is interesting to note that the first steps to regulate the hours and conditions of labor by the state go back to the Revolutionary period and Napoleon I. France was the first Continental country to offer legal protection to labor. Post-Industrial-Revolution legislation dates from the Child Labor Law of Louis Philippe's reign. This measure, which was passed in 1841, provided that no children under eight should be employed in industrial establishments, limited the working-day of children between eight and twelve to eight hours, and that of children between twelve and sixteen to twelve hours. Punishment was prescribed for violation of the law and special commissions were supposed to enforce it. The act was sharply criticized and it was very poorly enforced. The only partially successful and permanent labor legislation that resulted from the Revolution of 1848 was a twelve-hour law. There was no additional labor legislation until after the founding of the Third Republic.

Following the report of a commission, a law of 1874 applying to mines and industries provided for: (1) A general minimum age of twelve for children in industry; (2) a twelve-hour day for children between twelve and sixteen; (3) rest periods; (4) the prohibition of night work for females under twenty-one and for males under sixteen; (5) certain sanitary regulations; and (6) schooling for children under thirteen in industry. Between 1874 and 1914, labor was further protected by a series of regulatory measures that covered hours, working-conditions, the labor of minors, Sunday rest, and provisions for thorough inspection. On the eve of the World War the government had already published the first volumes of an excellent Labor Code that systematized the legal material on the question.

---

[1] There is a provision for the extension of the time, under certain circumstances.
[2] *Cf.* Hoover, *Germany Enters the Third Reich.*
[3] *Cf.* Ernst Henri, *Hitler over Europe,* Simon & Schuster, 1934, Pt. I; and F. L. Schuman, *The Nazi Dictatorship,* Knopf, 1935, Chaps. vi, xi.

THE RISE AND EXPANSION OF STATE SOCIALISM 943

With reference to social legislation such as old-age pensions, unemployment insurance, and the like, France lagged behind Germany. In 1898, the first workman's compensation law was passed, and not until 1905 was a system of old-age pensions instituted. The old-age law of that year was replaced by the more satisfactory Pensions Law of 1910, which was compulsory for all workers not otherwise provided for. By the Social Insurance Law of April, 1930, France finally established a thoroughgoing system of social insurance.[1] The workers, the employers, and the state all contribute, and the law provides for benefits for unemployment, death, old age, invalidity, maternity, and sickness. This act compels all workers, both male and female, whose incomes do not come up to a certain standard to insure themselves.

5. SOCIAL LEGISLATION IN OTHER EUROPEAN STATES

The example of Germany spread to other European countries.[2] Austria followed closely on its heels in social legislation. The Austrian accident-insurance law was passed in 1887 and has been strengthened since. Sickness insurance was provided in 1888. Since the World War, under a Socialist régime for a time, Austria has extended its State Socialism, including the most ambitious and commendable experiment thus far in the way of public subsidy of housing facilities. Austria would probably have gone further in social legislation after 1919 had it not been for the fact the reactionary Catholic Socialist party soon captured the country as a whole. True Socialism dominated only in Vienna and some other industrial cities. So the Viennese achievements in housing reform and the like were more precisely municipal Socialism than State Socialism.

In Italy, the state first aided the mutual insurance societies. A national accident insurance fund was created in 1885. The year 1898 marked the real introduction of Italian social insurance. In that year laws were passed providing for compulsory accident, sickness and invalidity, and old-age insurance. The law of 1898 was extended by the Socialist government in 1919 and modified somewhat by the Fascists in 1923. From 1921 to 1930 Italy paid out about 160,-000,000 lire for disability, old-age, and sickness relief.

The lesser European countries have also experimented extensively and successfully with social insurance. Especially has this been true of Belgium and the Scandinavian countries. The Australasian colonies of Great Britain have also gone far with social insurance projects.[3]

6. THE UNITED STATES LAGS BEHIND

Owing to administrative and juristic difficulties, to the confusion inherent in our federal system of government, to our laissez-faire philosophy, and to the hostile attitude of the Supreme Court, the United States has made much less

[1] See P. H. Douglas, "The French Social Insurance Act," in American Academy of Political and Social Science, *Annals,* November, 1932.

[2] *Cf.* Ogg and Sharp, *op. cit.,* pp. 395 ff., 597 ff.

[3] *Cf.* Clark, *The Labour Movement in Australia;* W. P. Reeves, *New Zealand,* 3d ed. rev., Houghton Mifflin, 1925; and Northcott, *Australian Social Development.*

progress than most European states in the matter of protective factory legislation. Some states have admirable codes, but others have made little progress in protecting labor. The most deplorable situation is now to be found in the Southern textile industries, where conditions often resemble those which existed in New England a century ago. An anti-child-labor amendment to the federal Constitution was before the country in 1935, but there seemed to be little probability of its immediate adoption.

State Socialism made scant progress in the United States until the death of McKinley put Mr. Roosevelt in the presidential chair. Down to that time the followers of the philosophy of Cobden and Bright, such as Roscoe Conkling and Mark Hanna, had maintained individualism in a position of dominance.[1] While Mr. Roosevelt achieved relatively little in the way of positive remedial legislation, he aroused the spirit of the people in this direction and made possible the very considerable progress in advanced economic and social legislation that took place in Mr. Wilson's administration. Down to the New Deal after 1933, local government units, such as states and cities, had gone much further than the federal government of the United States in the matter of positive social legislation. Some have rivaled European achievements. Notable here were the State of Wisconsin under the La Follette leadership and the city of Cleveland in the mayoralty of Tom Johnson.

Of all the enemies of the political postulates of Economic Liberalism, State Socialism has to date been the most deadly in practical results. It is really the "philosophical theory of the state" in action.

The New Deal under President Franklin D. Roosevelt in 1933 and thereafter made an ostensible effort to introduce some state control of industry, and offered a belated and inadequate program of social insurance.[2] The National Industrial Recovery Act, moreover, did promise to abolish child labor, though several hundred thousand children are still employed in American industries. The New Deal savored of State Socialism in some respects, especially in its entry into public works on an extensive scale and its mild sponsorship of state operation of selected electric utilities. Critics of the New Deal have, however, alleged that it is in reality a surrender of the government to industry, and is the Magna Charta of autonomy for big business—an impulse to capitalistic Syndicalism.

VII. RECENT DEVELOPMENTS IN CHRISTIAN SOCIALISM

The growth of social problems and the development of programs of relief have not been without their reaction upon ecclesiastical organizations and policies since 1850.[3] The chief contrast between the newer and the old Christian Socialism is the insistence today upon changes in the social and economic environment with less reliance upon the purely spiritual regeneration of the

---

[1] Even many reformers, such as E. L. Godkin, were stanch individualists.

[2] *Cf.* Cleveland Rodgers, *The Roosevelt Program,* Putnam, 1933; Lindley, *The Roosevelt Revolution;* Wallace, *The New Deal in Action;* and L. M. Hacker, *Short History of the New Deal,* Crofts, 1934.

[3] See above, pp. 389 ff., for the earlier developments in Christian Socialism.

individual. In other words, this means a transition from purely theological to partially sociological premises.

The Catholic group has been especially active in thus urging the Church to lead in social reform. In Germany, Adolf Kolping (1813-65) proposed associations of young workingmen for religious as well as economic betterment. Bishop von Ketteler (1811-77), Christoph Moufang (1817-90), and Franz Hitze (1851-1921) advocated not only social legislation, but also the organization of Guild Socialism [1] under Catholic auspices and aided by state financial support. This program was designed in part to weaken the State, the secular rival of the Church, and in part to attract the proletariat to the ecclesiastical authorities. The Catholic party in Germany has been strongest in Bavaria, from which the Center party, always an exponent of moderate social reform, has been chiefly recruited. In Austria, Karl Lueger (1844-1910) adopted the program of the German Catholic Guild Socialists and organized the powerful Austrian Christian Socialist party. This party gained greatly in strength after the World War. It elected a priest, Mgr. Ignaz Seipel, to the office of Chancellor in 1922, and he held office for some seven years.

In France, Frédéric Le Play (1806-82) proposed to solve modern social and economic problems by developing the "family group"—an organization midway between the old patriarchal family and the modern family organization. But much more important than this for social reform was his method of studying social problems, for he is rightly regarded as the real originator of the social-survey method of social investigation. More influential has been the work of Count Albert de Mun (1841-1914), who accepted the Guild Socialist program and organized the Action Libérale Française, virtually the Catholic Socialist party of France. Hilaire Belloc and Cecil and Gilbert Chesterton have tried without as notable success to organize a similar movement in England.[2]

The liberal Pope Leo XIII, in his encyclical *Rerum novarum* given out in 1891, advocated remedial social legislation for the laboring classes, espoused the program of Guild Socialism, and asserted the special solicitude of the Catholic Church for the lowly laborer, whether urban or agrarian. On May 15, 1931, the fortieth anniversary of Leo XIII's pronouncement, Pope Piux XI reaffirmed his principles and called for a fairer division between capital and labor. But he took pains to condemn materialistic Socialism. In the United States the work of social-minded Catholics such as the late Cardinal Gibbons, Father John A. Ryan, and Father Charles E. Coughlin has been notable alike for courage and zeal for social justice.[3]

The social impulse has also affected Protestantism in recent times. In Germany, the fanatical Hohenzollern court preacher Adolf Stoecker organized what was called a Christian Social Workingmen's party, but it was in reality more anti-Semitic than either Christian or Socialist. Friedrich Naumann in the nineties also made an unsuccessful attempt to capture German Protestantism for a liberal social-reform policy. In France, the Protestants have been noted for

---

[1] See below, p. 955.
[2] Of course, this Catholic Guild Socialism of Hitze, Count de Mun, Belloc, Chesterton, and so on is not the resolute program of the secular Guild Socialists like G. D. H. Cole. The last-named would doubtless resent the listing of Belloc and Chesterton as Guild Socialists.
[3] *Cf.* J. A. Ryan, *A Better Economic Order*, Harper, 1935. No other important public figure has so courageously or so openly attacked finance capitalism as has Father Coughlin.

their philanthropic organizations, but they have never been strong enough to create a powerful party of social reform. In England, the work of Maurice and Kingsley has been carried on by aggressive Anglicans like Bishop Westcott and Bishop Gore, who founded the Christian Socialist Union in 1889.[1] John Neville Figgis formulated an elaborate theoretical justification of what might be called ecclesiastical Syndicalism, namely, freedom and autonomy for the churches within the political state.

In America Christian Socialism was founded in the late eighties by Josiah Strong, Richard T. Ely, and George D. Herron, and received its most effective support from Walter Rauschenbusch in his famous works *Christianity and the Social Crisis*[2] and *Christianizing the Social Order*,[3] and from the writings of Harry F. Ward.[4]

The social point of view has attracted religious radicals as well as conservatives. Indeed, it is probable that the more critical adherents of Christian doctrine are most inclined to stress the social phases of Christianity. With them the social and ethical elements in religion are about all that seem worth saving and promoting.

VIII. THE NEWER ANARCHISM

Modern Anarchism is a revolt against the oppressiveness of both the agrarian and the capitalistic state. It is most significant that the two leading figures in the development of the modern Anarchist movement have been Russians. At a time when modern industrialism was creating new problems and bringing nearer the necessity for modern democracy, the Russian autocracy tried to maintain a government almost as medieval and intolerant as that of Peter the Great.

Of the two great leaders of modern Anarchism, Mikhail Bakunin (1814-76) was the revolutionary propagandist. He paid little attention to the details of the future Anarchist state. He regarded it as his chief task to spread the propaganda of hatred for the state and private property and to organize a movement committed to their destruction. To him the state was the great and central engine of human oppression, and its elimination seemed the one chief need of the time. Once the state was removed, the task of the reconstruction of society on Anarchistic principles could safely be left to the future generations. Hence the work of Bakunin centered upon the dissemination of the gospel of destruction, his views being most systematically expressed in his *God and the State,* published posthumously in 1882. Here he maintained that loyalty to the state and to religion is the chief obstacle to progress and liberty.

Prince Peter Kropotkin (1842-1921) was the chief systematic and constructive writer on modern Anarchism. According to him the ideal organization of so-

---

[1] See D. O. Wagner, *The Church of England and Social Reform since 1854,* Columbia University Press, 1930, and G. C. Binyon, *The Christian Social Movement in England,* Macmillan, 1931.
[2] Macmillan, 1907.   [3] Macmillan, 1912.
[4] Other adherents to this point of view have been Francis Peabody of Harvard, C. R. Henderson and Shailer Mathews of Chicago, C. A. Ellwood of Duke University, Reinhold Niebuhr of Union Theological Seminary, E. L. Earp of Drew Theological Seminary, A. P. Fitch, formerly of Amherst, P. A. Parsons of the University of Oregon, Jerome Davis of Yale, S. Ralph Harlow of Smith College, and David D. Vaughan of Boston University. The most active Christian Socialists in America today are Sherwood Eddy, Ward, Niebuhr, and Kirby Page. See Sherwood Eddy, *A Pilgrimage of Ideas,* Farrar & Rinehart, 1934, and Kirby Page, *Living Triumphantly,* Farrar & Rinehart, 1934.

ciety is the noncoercive community, without private property and functioning perfectly through mutual aid or coöperation. To support his position he not only put forth a theoretical defense of his system, but also made a thorough historical study of the importance of the principle of mutual aid from the first animal societies to the present day.[1] He brought forward a wealth of evidence to prove that coöperation is the chief factor in social evolution—thus combating Social Darwinism. The benign era of human coöperation was terminated by the rise of the modern dynastic and capitalistic state. This has created most subsequent evils without in any important way contributing to their effective removal. The state and private property, being the cause of human degradation and misery, must be brought to an end. The Communistic, coöperative, and non-political community, then, is the goal of the Philosophical Anarchist. Human nature having been perverted by private property and coercive political institutions, the removal of these two will restore the pristine virtues and coöperative spirit of the race. The Anarchistic views have also received the support of such writers as the Russian Ilya Mechnikov, the Frenchman Elisée Reclus and Jean Grave, and the Americans Benjamin R. Tucker, Emma Goldman, Alexander Berkman, and Roger N. Baldwin.

The economic program of the Anarchists is not greatly different from that of the Socialists, so far as the institution of private property is concerned, but their political ideals are diametrically opposed. The Socialist proposes a vast increase in state activity, while the Anarchist desires the complete extinction of political authority and the substitution of voluntary coöperation. The Anarchists have erred in generalizing too much from prewar Russian conditions, which were incomparably worse for the masses and for intellectuals than those in the more democratic states of western Europe. Further, the movement is unadapted to modern conditions. The proposals are mostly either antiquated or greatly ahead of their time. Voluntary coöperation may have been possible in a small primitive group or it may be practicable in the far distant future when human behavior and its social setting shall have been more nearly perfected. At the present time, when imperfect humanity faces problems of unprecedented complexity, the activity of the state is more than ever necessary.

IX. THE DEVELOPMENT OF THE COÖPERATIVE MOVEMENT

If the Anarchists went too far in their emphasis on the inherent goodness of man and on the nobility of human nature when uncontaminated by wealth or politics, they certainly made an important contribution in emphasizing the possibilities of coöperative activity. Indeed, the classic study of coöperation as a factor in human society is the above-mentioned work of Kropotkin. The coöperative movement may take on considerable proportions even within the structure of the political state. In fact, any immediate progress of the program must of necessity be worked out within the state.

It has been indicated previously that the modern coöperative movement had its origins in the work of Robert Owen and the Utopian Socialists and in the

[1] Kropotkin, *Mutual Aid; a Factor in Evolution*, Knopf, 1917. This book was written in 1902.

writings of William King, both in the second quarter of the nineteenth century. They were supported by Kingsley and the Christian Socialists. The impetus led to the formation of the Rochdale Equitable Pioneers' Society in 1844. This has been the most important coöperative organization in the English-speaking world.

In France, the first considerable encouragement of coöperative activity came from the work of Charles Fourier. Here again, the initial stimulus from the Utopian Socialists was aided and abetted by Christian Socialists. Buchez was particularly interested in coöperative societies. The coöperative movement in France was revived and reorganized after 1885, owing especially to the enthusiastic labors of Edouard de Boyve. In Germany, V. A. Huber and Hermann Schulze-Delitzsch put the coöperative movement on its feet. At the turn of the century, the Hamburg coöperative movement rehabilitated coöperation in Germany and made it an important factor in contemporary German society. Other European countries have developed coöperative activities and organizations to a considerable degree, especially notable being Denmark and Soviet Russia.[1] In the United States coöperation was launched by American followers of Owen and Fourier. After the Civil War it was taken up by the Granger movement in American agriculture, which stressed producers' coöperatives. In the last quarter of a century it has been promoted by Dr. J. P. Warbasse and his associates.

Coöperation has manifested itself in many forms. There has been producers' coöperation both in communal workshops and in agriculture. Even more widespread has been consumers' coöperation, or the practice of buying through coöperative stores and wholesale organizations. There has also been a considerable growth of coöperative credit, expressing itself in coöperative banks, building and loan associations, and the like. This form of coöperation has attained its highest development in Germany, owing especially to enthusiastic promotion by Wilhelm Haas (1839-1914).

There has been a tendency in each country for local coöperative associations to form national organizations. Representative of these is the British Coöperative Union, established in 1869. Even international coöperative organizations have come into being, such as the International Coöperative Alliance, constituted in 1895. The coöperatives have also lately made some use of the economic machinery of the League of Nations at Geneva.

In the majority of states, coöperation has shown the greatest vitality where it has been associated with some other progressive movement, such as labor-unionism, Socialism, Communism, or popular educational movements. With the exception of Russian Communism, few other radical movements have had as much practical effect to date in mitigating the evils of capitalistic business enterprise and speculation.

X. THE EXPANSION OF LABOR UNIONS

It was one of the cardinal points of Economic Liberalism that perfect freedom of contract should prevail in the economic relations of employer and

[1] *Cf.* E. T. Blanc, *The Co-operative Movement in Russia,* Macmillan, 1924, and F. C. Howe, *Denmark; a Cooperative Commonwealth,* Harcourt, Brace, 1921.

employee, but in actual practice the freedom was chiefly that of the employer to reject the services of the employee. Where one party to the contract could refrain from participation with equanimity while the other party would be threatened with starvation, there could be neither freedom nor equality of contract, and unorganized labor was wholly at the mercy of the capitalistic employer. On the other hand, if the laborers could combine and withhold the services not merely of one man but of a large number, the solicitude of the employer over failure to continue the labor contract could be greatly increased. The suffering of the employees could also be lessened through coöperation in bearing their mutual losses. The desire to meet the employer on relatively equal terms and thereby to realize security in employment and justice in wages has been the central impulse in the development of modern labor-unionism.

Labor unions have been often criticized for the lack of interest on the part of labor in efficient production, but this seems to be the result of easily understood circumstances. The modern methods of large-scale manufacture have eliminated most of the foundations of human interest in manual work, and the pay envelope is about all that can concretely appeal to the laborer. Then, the laborer has learned all too well the pecuniary philosophy of his employer. Inferior goods, dishonestly advertised and sold for high prices, represent a policy easily translated by the laborer into short hours and indifferent and slothful work for high wages. This emphasis of many unions on limitation of output was, of course, the result of dishonesty and unfairness on the part of employers in the old piecework system. Workers would be encouraged to greater production, and then the price per piece would be reduced. Limitation of output was the logical answer to such a policy. Whatever the excuse for it, however, such a procedure is antisocial in any large sense, though it probably cannot be abandoned when dealing with antisocial employers.

The question has often been raised as to the historical relation between the modern labor unions and the older guild organizations. It has been shown pretty conclusively that there was little genetic connection between them. In England there was a long hiatus between the end of the guilds and the origin of unions, and even on the Continent there is little evidence that labor unions grew up directly out of earlier guild organizations.[1]

In England, labor-unionism was early prohibited by the Combination Laws of 1799 and 1800. In 1824 Francis Place and Joseph Hume guided an act through Parliament legalizing labor organizations, but this was repealed in the following year. Owen's attempt to stimulate unionism in the thirties failed. In the sixties the cause of unionism was taken up by the so-called Junta, an interested group. By acts of 1871 and 1875 labor organization and strikes were legalized. Though the reactionaries, in the Taff Vale and the Osborne cases (1901 and 1909), tried to weaken the unions, the Liberal party, in legislation following 1905, has practically abrogated the effects of these decisions. Today labor organization is probably the most effective single social aid to the English urban proletariat. At the outbreak of the World War English unions had over 4,000,000 members. In 1921 the membership was given as 8,000,000. The number has dwindled since the general strike of 1921 to a little over half the 1921 figure. In

---

[1] The contrary opinion was maintained by the able German economic historian Lujo Brentano.

France, as we have seen, an act of 1864 gave the laborers the right to strike and a later law of 1884 authorized them to organize into unions. Since that time there has been a great increase in the number of unionists, accompanied by a bitter struggle between those who cling to orthodox methods of attempting to secure better conditions within the capitalistic system and those who incline towards the greater radicalism of the Syndicalist movement.

The French law of 1791 made labor organizations illegal and the strike a criminal act.[1] The industrialization of France, however, made the growth of trade-unions inevitable, but labor was forced to organize in secret or under the guise of benevolent societies. The workingmen struggled against such iniquitous legislation, but despite strikes and participation in the revolutionary activities of 1848, they were not strong enough to gain any recognition until the later years of the Second Empire. Only under special circumstances were workingmen's organizations permitted in the first years of Napoleon III's rule, and workers were still under the supervision of the police.[2] The growing strength of the labor associations and the pressure they exerted finally won the French worker the right to strike in 1864. Four years later the shaky government of the empire granted toleration to combinations of workingmen, though it did not repeal the Le Chapelier law of 1791. Until 1884 labor unions had no legal existence; they were simply "tolerated," as employers' associations had been tolerated during the course of the nineteenth century. In that year (1884)

a new law on syndicats [labor unions] was enacted, associated commonly with the name of Waldeck-Rousseau . . . which, although momentarily objectionable to labour in certain of its features, conferred upon syndicats for the first time the character of full legality and authorised them to combine in federations.[3]

This measure has been regarded as the "charter of liberties" of French labor. After its passage the organization of the working classes grew apace. The French labor unions now have about 2,500,000 members—about 2,000,000 in orthodox unions and 500,000 in Communist organizations.

The German trade-union movement did not really flourish until the decade of the seventies, and then its growth was hampered by the anti-Socialist legislation of 1878. After 1890, following the repeal of the anti-Socialist laws, labor organizations drove rapidly ahead. Between that date and the opening of the World War, the trade-unions won full recognition and definite privileges in the eyes of the law. By 1914, all workers except domestic servants, agricultural laborers, and seamen were granted the legal right to organize to obtain higher wages and better working-conditions. Strikes had been legalized by the Industrial Code of 1891. The state offered the strong anti-trade-union movements of the employers no assistance. Only when the trade-unions entered politics and "transcended the economic interests of their members as individuals and undertook to exercise an influence on public affairs" did they fall under the highly regulative measures pertaining to political clubs and societies. Under the new democratic constitution of the German Republic, labor was given special pro-

---

[1] On French social legislation, see Ogg and Sharp, *op. cit.*, pp. 380 ff., 594 ff., and C. W. Pipkin, *Social Politics and Modern Democracy*, Macmillan, 1931, 2 vols., Vol. II.

[2] This system of police surveillance was introduced by Napoleon I in 1803, and not completely removed until 1890.

[3] Ogg and Sharp, *op. cit.*, p. 443.

tection and the "right to labor was guaranteed." After that it was little restricted until the Hitler régime came into power in 1933. Most of the German unionists were organized in social democratic or "free" unions. The total union membership in 1921 was 13,000,000, but at present Hitler's restrictions have disrupted the old German unionism. In no other important country did the unionists so faithfully maintain the ideals of excellent craftsmanship that were so characteristic of the medieval guilds.

Labor-unionism has spread to most other European countries, though in many states, especially in the Latin nations, it has tended towards Syndicalism. There were 3,600,000 unionists in Italy in 1921, but their membership has since been dispersed by Mussolini. There were 2,000,000 labor-unionists in Czechoslovakia in 1921. In the United States extensive labor organization began after the Civil War with the Knights of Labor, an organization that declined after the violent strikes of 1886. It was superseded by the American Federation of Labor, which in March, 1933, claimed some 2,961,000 members. The National Industrial Recovery Act of 1933 somewhat increased the membership of labor unions. It ordered the free and unhampered right of organization and of collective bargaining, but the government has thus far failed to enforce the law. Some of the most powerful and alert American unions have remained outside the Federation, which has been restrained by the conservatism of its presidents, Samuel Gompers and William Green, and its vice president, Matthew Woll.[1]

Generally speaking, whereas in the earlier days of labor unions the organization was mainly based on trades, federated on a local basis, the trend is now towards the organization of both skilled and unskilled laborers by industries, the federated trade-union being replaced by the national industrial union.

The policies of labor unions have centered about two main avenues of attack upon the capitalists. Matters of immediate interest, such as wage agreements with employers, are arranged either by peaceful collective bargaining or, in last resort, by more violent action such as strikes and boycotts. For the more general advancement of the status of the proletariat the unions rely upon the possibility of obtaining legislation favorable to the interests of the laboring classes. Which of these two policies is most stressed varies with different unions and countries, but on the whole it is probable that the strike policy has predominated. This has been particularly true in the United States.

The degree to which the labor unions have attempted to gain political power has differed widely with time and nation. In Germany, most unionists were members of the Social Democratic party down to 1933. In France, orthodox unionists tend to affiliate with the Socialists, while the radicals who incline toward Syndicalism eschew all political activity. There are today many Communist labor-unionists in France. In England, the unionists have a distinct Labor party of considerable proportions, which has twice assumed control of the British government. In the United States, Samuel Gompers strove successfully to keep the American Federation of Labor out of formal partisan activity,

[1] Green and Woll, for example, opposed the recognition of Russia to the bitter end—long after recognition had been urged by conservative business men and even by the spokesman of the Rockefeller interests and Mr. S. Stanwood Menken of the National Security League. The conservative and obsolete policies and tactics of the A. F. of L. were largely responsible for missing the unique opportunity to organize American labor in 1933-35. See Stolberg and Vinton, *The Economic Consequences of the New Deal*, pp. 49 ff.

though he several times declared his own preferences for candidates at presidential elections.

No single fact needs to be more emphasized, in even a cursory survey of labor unions, than that there is the utmost diversity in modern labor organizations as to purpose, policy, organization, and tactics. An incidental but very important feature of labor-unionism has been the development of fraternal and coöperative activities among members.

While the growth of organized labor has been an outstanding feature of the social and economic history of the nineteenth century, the labor movement is still handicapped by many imperfections. The attempt to prevent violence through making arbitration of labor disputes compulsory has met with only temporary and local success, most notably in Australia, though the trend seemed for a time to be moving in this general direction. Again, many powerful employers and associations of employers have so little adjusted their economic orientation to the modern industrial world that they refuse to recognize the validity of either the principles or the practices of labor organizations. As a result, the relations between capital and labor are too frequently of the nature of only slightly mitigated industrial warfare. With the growing crisis of capitalism the employing class is becoming less tolerant of labor-unionism and inclining towards Fascism. The latter has no place for independent labor-unionism. As a result, there is a growing trend towards revolutionary philosophy and tactics in the labor movement. Events seem to point to a narrowing of the conflict to a death struggle between Fascism and Syndicalism or Communism.[1]

Our modern labor organizations have probably done more than anything else to advance the material interests of the laboring classes in the last half-century and have been the most potent factor in promoting industrial democracy. Yet labor-unionism is bound to be unsatisfactory to those who do not believe in merely alleviating the misery of the proletariat, but hope also to overthrow the whole modern capitalistic order. Orthodox labor-unionism aims chiefly to improve the lot of the laborer within a capitalistic industrial society, and accepts the implied persistence of this order. Therefore many workingmen who wish the institutions of society to be controlled by the proletariat and desire to achieve this revolution by economic means rather than by the political methods of Revisionist Socialism have tended to leave conventional labor-unionism and go over to the more radical labor movement that has found its greatest strength in Syndicalism. Others have espoused revolutionary Socialism or, as it is better known today, Communism.

XI. THE DEVELOPMENT OF SYNDICALISM AND THE RADICAL LABOR MOVEMENT

Syndicalism, which originated as a radical French labor movement and has since spread to other countries, particularly Italy and America, is the most recent radical proletarian movement to attain considerable proportions.

[1] It should in fairness and for the sake of accuracy be pointed out, however, that outside of Russia and Germany in the years just before Hitler, moderate Socialism had made more headway than either Syndicalism or Communism since 1919. But the prestige of Russia as a going concern more than offsets this, while the failure of moderate Socialism in Germany and Italy has helped to discredit Revisionism.

Syndicalism resembles Socialism in desiring to end the present capitalistic economic order; it has some similarity to labor-unionism in believing that the economic point of attack is likely to be most effective and in using labor organization as the chief instrument for gathering and disciplining the forces of the proletariat; and it is like Anarchism in desiring the aboliton of existing political forms of control over mankind. It differs from Socialism in rejecting the efficacy of political activity and in refusing to accept State Socialism, even in a proletarian state. It diverges from conservative labor-unionism in favoring as the unit of organization the industrial rather than the craft union and in aiming to get rid of the capitalistic employer altogether. While bearing a closer relation to Anarchism than to Socialism, it does not propose so thorough an abolition of all external social control as the Anarchist desires. It seems likely to retain a large amount of authoritative control over the members of the Syndicalist society, even though it may in theory try to evade this charge by refusing to designate such control as governmental or political.[1]

The historical origins of French Syndicalism are not difficult to understand. A vigorous theory of the necessity of a class war had come down from Proudhon in the middle of the nineteenth century. The many factions into which French Socialists had split and the bitter animosity that developed between them weakened the cause of the proletariat. The Socialist cause was further discredited in the minds of the radical laboring element because former Socialists, such as Millerand and Briand, had been willing when they entered the French government to use the forces of the capitalistic state against radical labor revolts. Therefore there arose a determination among a large number of French labor leaders to turn their backs upon all political activity and to distrust political methods of relief, whether from State Socialism or Marxian revolutionary quarters.

At the close of the eighties labor exchanges were organized, first in Paris, and later throughout the leading French cities, to act as general clearing-houses for local labor and employment problems. In 1892 there was established a national organization—the Federation of Labor Exchanges (Fédération des Bourses du Travail). This movement was guided by Fernand Pelloutier (1867-1901), a French disciple of Communistic Anarchism. About the same time another radical labor organization was developing in France. This was the General Confederation of Labor (Confédération Générale du Travail), founded in 1895 by uniting some seven hundred French local industrial unions or *syndicats,* from which the Syndicalist movement gets its name. In 1902 the Federation of Labor Exchanges and the General Confederation of Labor united and became the basis of the organized Syndicalist movement. The systematic theorist of French Syndicalism, curiously enough, was the aristocratic philosopher Georges Sorel (1847-1922).[2]

The Syndicalists reject any attempt to come to favorable terms with their capitalistic employers in any settlement that may be regarded as permanent. They aim frankly at conducting by industrial methods a class war that will sooner or later drive the capitalist from industry and overthrow his political defense—the modern national state. The type of organization at which the

[1] *Cf.* R. L. Mott, "The Political Theory of Syndicalism," *Political Science Quarterly,* March, 1922.
[2] *Cf.* Sorel, *Reflections on Violence,* Huebsch, 1914.

Syndicalists aim is the industrial union, the general organization of all laborers in a given industry. This, it is hoped, will give greater strength and less division of interests than craft-unionism, limited as the latter is chiefly to the minority of skilled laborers.

The Syndicalist method of carrying on the class war is "direct action," the two chief types of which are "sabotage" and the "general strike." The former is a temporary instrument designed to serve until the general strike finally drives the capitalist from the field. It consists of any mode of harassing the employer, from serious injury to machinery to slow and inferior workmanship in production. While some employers might be discouraged and abandon the fight merely as the result of sabotage, a more vigorous method will be needed to deal with the more obdurate capitalists and with the state. For this purpose the Syndicalists propose to resort to the general strike, which is not merely a suspension of labor to gain local victories, but a general "cessation of work, which would place the country in the rigor of death, whose terrible and incalculable consequences would force the government to capitulate at once."

If the Syndicalists were successful in destroying the capitalistic order they would institute a communistic economic society and a governmental organization based upon the industrial-union system. As Orth expresses it, "Syndicalists believe in a local or communal government. Their state is a glorified trade union whose activities are confined to economic functions, their nation is a collection of federated communal trade societies."[1] They would, then, take government out the front door of the state to bring it in by the back door of vocational regimentation.

Of all the radical modern reform movements Syndicalism has come the nearest, perhaps, to translating the class war into practical concrete action, and it is the form of organization into which the capitalists should most hesitate to drive the laboring classes.

Syndicalism has also attracted sympathetic consideration from many who are not willing to accept its whole economic program but feel that something must be done to decentralize the overgrown and unwieldy modern national state and to give representative government a more rational and practicable basis by allowing the representation of economic interests and classes. Further, many exponents of the more orthodox labor-unionism believe that they would gain greatly by giving up the craft-union organization and accepting the principles of the industrial-union organigation.

While Syndicalism began as a distinctly French movement, it has spread into other European countries, notably Italy. In the United States it has been adopted by a considerable group—the Industrial Workers of the World, who were greatly weakened by attacks upon them during the World War. From the combined influence of France and the United States, Syndicalism has built up a considerable following in Great Britain. Recent students have, however, held that militant Syndicalism is on the decline even in France.[2] Whether this will prove permanent or not remains to be seen. As a rallying-ground for revo-

---

[1] S. P. Orth, *Socialism and Democracy in Europe*, Holt, 1913, p. 108.
[2] *Cf.* D. J. Saposs, *The Labor Movement in Post-war France*, Columbia University Press, 1931.

lutionary labor Syndicalism is, from the standpoint of logic, more in harmony with advanced economic and political thought than is Communism.

XII. GUILD SOCIALISM AS A COMPROMISE BETWEEN SOCIALISM AND SYNDICALISM

The movement generally known as Guild Socialism means, in its essence, economic decentralization. It seeks the solution of the labor problem through the revival of industrial associations like the medieval guilds, adapted to the changed conditions of modern industrialism. Such a proposal dates back to the first half of the nineteenth century, when it was foreshadowed by some of the propositions of the English Christian Socialists and Ruskin. Guild Socialism of a clerical cast has been congenial to Catholic social reformers, such as Bishop Ketteler, Franz Hitze, Count de Mun, and Hilaire Belloc. The idea has been defended in a modified form by the French sociologist Emile Durkheim, while it has particularly attracted British intellectuals and labor leaders, such as G. D. H. Cole, S. G. Hobson, A. R. Orage, and A. J. Penty. In a much diluted and modified form it reached the United States in the so-called Plumb Plan for industrial democracy set forth at the close of the World War.[1]

In its modern and fully elaborated form Guild Socialism aims to effect a reconciliation between State Socialism and Syndicalism. The political control and administration, which represents society as consumers and receives the chief attention of the Socialists, will be retained by the political state. The management of industrial affairs, which pertains to society as producers and is emphasized by Syndicalism, will be turned over to guilds or associations of workingmen, properly federated into national organizations. This will give essential industrial autonomy and, it is hoped, will stimulate craftsmanship and productivity. Above both political and economic organization will be a joint committee composed of representatives of both the state and the guilds. This will have the final decision on disputed points and on those vital matters which concern the citizens as both producers and consumers.

To many, Guild Socialism seems the most promising of the modern reform policies and a clever synthesis of several other popular radical programs. Others, however, deny the possibility of any real separation of political and industrial functions. As Ernest Barker has expressed it:

> In truth, any doctrine of separation of powers, such as Guild-Socialism advocates, is bound to collapse before the simple fact of the vital interdependence of all the activities of the "great society" of to-day. . . . Either the State must go, as Syndicalists seem to advocate, and that means chaos, or the State must remain—and then, if you are to have Socialism, it must be State-Socialism.[2]

XIII. HENRY GEORGE, THE SINGLE TAX, AND LAND NATIONALIZATION

In spite of the attention given to land nationalization by Babeuf and Charles Hall, the great majority of radical reform programs in modern times have

[1] G. E. Plumb and W. G. Roylance, *Industrial Democracy*, Huebsch, 1923.
[2] Barker, *op. cit.*, p. 229.

centered about attacks upon the methods of production and distribution of the earnings in manufacturing industries and commercial enterprises. These ignored certain sources of modern social problems and some evident causes of poverty and misery involved in the unequal and undemocratic methods of landholding and absentee landlordship.[1] It was therefore natural that at least one important reform program should revolve about the proposal to reconstruct the methods of landholding in order to bring them more into harmony with modern democratic principles. The leader in this movement was an original and energetic American, Henry George (1839-97). Living in California in the early days of its civic and industrial development, he was struck with the great increase in land values that resulted in less than a decade from purely social causes. Coming to New York, the same phenomenon attracted his attention in the extreme land values created by social and economic concentration on Manhattan Island. So forcibly was he struck by these facts that he considered this increase of real-estate values, due to social influences, and its absorption by private persons to be the chief cause of poverty and misery. Consequently he proposed, in his notable work on *Progress and Poverty* (1879), a "single tax" on land, and the general abolition of other forms of taxes, a program that would turn into the public treasury the unearned or social increment in land values. This process would ultimately drive the absentee landlord out of existence and pave the way for the democratic nationalization of land.

George's theories attracted the greatest amount of interest in England, where the evils he exposed were especially prevalent and where the Liberal party found a modified version of his doctrines a suitable argument to be used in attacking their traditional enemies, the Tory or Conservative landlords. Among his followers was the famous scientist Alfred Russel Wallace, but it remained for David Lloyd George to give these doctrines some preliminary application in legislation. In the Small Holdings Act of 1907 and in his budget of 1909 he made definite attacks upon the vested land interests. At the outbreak of the World War he was preparing a radical program of agrarian reform for Great Britain, but the close of the conflict found him detached from the reform party and sitting at the Peace Conference with two of the most tenacious defenders of agrarian autocracy in England, Arthur James Balfour and Bonar Law.

The most extensive program of land nationalization is that which has been carried out by the Bolshevik government in Russia since 1917.[2] Most of the land of Russia has been taken from its former owners and turned over to the state for collective farming or public use. But this sweeping program is hardly an example of single-tax achievement. It is, rather, the application of Marxian Socialism in the field of agriculture and landholding, as well as the Socialistic repudiation of private property in real estate. Yet even in Bolshevik Russia the doctrines of George have been quoted with approval.

Most progressive thinkers differ from Henry George primarily in holding that the single tax should not be regarded as the sole remedy for modern social problems, though the majority of them would probably agree that society should in some manner and in large degree absorb these socially created values known as the unearned increment. All fair-minded readers will give George

---

[1] See above, pp. 237, 395.   [2] See below, pp. 1007 ff.

credit for having called attention to the fact that the capitalistic banker, manufacturer, or merchant is not solely responsible for the evils and misery of the present order.

XIV. BOURGEOIS ATTEMPTS TO ABSORB THE RADICAL PROLETARIAN MOVEMENTS

It could scarcely be supposed that the middle class would sit idly by and contemplate the growth of these threatening proletarian programs without attempting to counteract them—without trying, as G. Stanley Hall has expressed it, "to set a backfire." Probably the chief method employed has been State Socialism, or legislation designed to placate the laboring class, while retaining the essentials of the capitalistic system. It must not be forgotten, however, that much State Socialism has at times been a result of proletarian or landlord attacks upon the middle class.

The bourgeoisie have hoped to induce the proletariat to trust to the adequacy of the national capitalistic state as an agent for promoting the cause of social reform and the growth of industrial democracy. Further, certain specially adroit or generous members of the middle class have contributed great donations to social relief work and to modern scientific philanthropy. It has been hoped that such measures will lessen misery, reduce the pressure for more far-reaching reform, and attract the gratitude of those who receive aid. This has led certain radical writers to refer derisively to social work as "the wrecking-crew of capitalism."[1] These benefactions have not been made solely for the relief of physical privation and suffering. They have involved the intellectual and recreational improvement of the lower classes through libraries, Y.M.C.A. and Y.W.C.A. organizations, playgrounds, parks, and museums.

The more progressive and farsighted leaders of modern industrialism have developed policies of industrial conciliation designed either to placate the laborers or to get them practically interested in the preservation of the existing order. The best known of such methods are profit-sharing, coöperation, stock distribution, scientific management, labor legislation, and industrial welfare work.[2] Some have gone so far as to foster the growth of conservative trade-unionism, such as is represented by the American Federation of Labor.

Of course, most of the modern capitalists still hold tenaciously, with strange fatuity, to the attitude of John Bright and declare for a war to the end with State Socialism and industrial democracy. They may probably be regarded as among the most effective agents in promoting extreme forms of radicalism, however little they may intend to bring about such results.

A popular bourgeois plan for tinkering with the economic system is to be discerned in various proposals to restore prosperity by means of financial and credit manipulation that seek to put more purchasing power in the hands of the masses without fundamentally upsetting capitalism.[3] Perhaps the most significant and important of these is the social-credit program expounded by

---

[1] For example, Roger N. Baldwin, a veteran social worker.
[2] *Cf.* Birnie, *Economic History of Europe*, Chaps. x-xi.
[3] *Cf.* Emile Burns, *The Only Way Out*, International Publishers, 1932.

Major C. H. Douglas, which has gained much popularity in England, Australia, and the United States.[1]

A philosophy has been evolved that is designed to effect a liberal compromise between capital and labor. This has received its chief elaboration in France, where it is generally spoken of as the doctrine of Solidarism.[2] It takes its origin from the doctrines of Comte, the Positivists, and Leroux regarding the organic unity of human interests. It was further elaborated by the sociologists of the Organicist school and was much later expanded by Léon Bourgeois from the legal point of view; by Charles Gide from the standpoint of the progressive economist; by Emile Durkheim as a profound sociologist interested in practical social reform; by Georg Friedrich Nicolai from a sociobiological point of approach; and by Oscar Newfang from the angle of the "new capitalism."

This doctrine makes an honest and thoroughgoing attempt to reform the present order, so as to grant essential economic and social justice to the proletariat, while retaining the supposedly superior directive and inventive ability of capitalistic enterprise. In its practical program it proposes, on the one hand, an extension of remedial social legislation through State Socialism, and on the other, strong encouragement of the principle of voluntary coöperation. Its adherents also generally incline toward some considerable decentralization of the administrative powers and functions of the modern national state. Some members of the group lean rather distinctly towards Guild Socialism and the representation of economic groups and interests.

All in all, it is, perhaps, the one program of reform that embraces the interests of both capitalists and proletariat and which is, at the same time, sufficiently honest, disinterested, and progressive to entitle it to some respectful consideration.

There is little probability that President Roosevelt, or even his advisers of the so-called Brain Trust, know much about Solidarism as a social movement. Yet there seems to be a very considerable affinity between the New Deal and Solidarist principles. This is clear from President Roosevelt's own speeches and was even more apparent in the "big happy family" pronouncements of Professor Raymond Moley when he was the chief spokesman for the Administration.[3]

XV. THE GREAT WAR AND POLICIES OF RECONSTRUCTION

The World War will probably be regarded by the future historian as a dividing-point in the history of modern social-reform movements, but it is too early to predict just what the nature of the resulting social transformation will be. It may, perhaps, be seen by future historians that back of the conflict of nations was the beginning of the final struggle between the present social and economic classes—a struggle in which landlord and capitalist will unite against their common enemy, the proletariat. That the feudal landlord has generally succumbed already in the course of the struggle, except in England, Prussia and Hungary, is generally conceded.

---

[1] *Cf.* E. S. Holter, *The ABC of Social Credit*, Coward-McCann, 1934, and C. H. Douglas, *Social Credit*, rev. ed., Norton, 1933.
[2] *Cf.* Gide and Rist, *op. cit.*, Book V, Chap. III., and Coker, *op. cit.*, pp. 408 ff.
[3] *Cf.* Hacker, *op. cit.*, pp. 22-28.

THE GREAT WAR AND POLICIES OF RECONSTRUCTION 959

That labor hoped for the decisive termination of the modern order of individualistic industrialism as a result of the war is apparent from what is usually taken as the most profound utterance of labor during the war—the report of the Executive Committee of the British Labor party on reconstruction:

> The individualist system of capitalist production, based on the private ownership and competitive administration of land and capital, with its reckless "profiteering" and wage slavery; with its glorification of the unhampered struggle for the means of life and its hypocritical pretense of the "survival of the fittest"; with the monstrous inequality of circumstances which it produces and the degradation and brutalisation, both moral and spiritual, resulting therefrom, may, we hope, indeed have received a death-blow. With it must go the political system and ideas in which it naturally found expression.[1]

The committee expressed the further significant opinion that "what has to be reconstructed after the war is not this or that government department, or this or that piece of social machinery; but society itself."

During the great struggle, as a result of the necessity of maintaining the production of required munitions at the highest possible level, unusual concessions had to be made to labor. This did not make the proletariat any more readily inclined to acquiesce in the later restoration of the social and economic *status quo ante bellum*.

Many countries were compelled to take what in times of peace would have been regarded as alarming steps towards State Socialism. In Russia, the autocracy and bourgeoisie were overthrown and there followed the first attempt in history to apply Marxian Socialism to the reconstruction of a great state. In Germany, the rebuff of the Junker-bourgeois alliance paved the way for a temporary triumph of Revisionist Socialism in the political system, though the chaos after the war made possible the abortive Stinnes régime of industrial autocracy. The vindictive treatment of the German Republic by the Entente after 1919 gradually undermined radicalism in Germany and permitted the triumph of the Hitler party and other groups representing a combination of economic conservatism with extreme political nationalism.

The capitalists in wartime did not fail to recognize these various challenges to their very existence as a powerful organized class, nor did they hesitate to take steps to protect their system.[2] Their most effective strategy was to make patriotism just as far as possible synonymous with rigid adherence to a belief in the sanctity of the capitalistic system. All expressions of proletarian discontent and all plans for radical social reconstruction were branded as products of disloyalty or enemy propaganda. Radical leaders were assassinated or sentenced to long terms of imprisonment for far more mild and moderate criticisms of administrative policy than were passed by unnoticed when uttered by political opponents who were members of capitalistic parties. The treatment of Eugene V. Debs, as compared to that of Theodore Roosevelt and George Harvey, is a case in point. Severe espionage laws were passed. These were little utilized to

---

[1] Quoted in P. U. Kellogg and A. H. Gleason, *British Labor and the War*, Boni & Liveright, 1921, p. 373.
[2] *Cf.* Chafee, *Freedom of Speech*, and L. F. Post, *The Deportations Delirium of Nineteen-Twenty*, Kerr, 1923.

aid the military department, but were widely made use of to silence expressions of social and economic discontent.

The close of the conflict left a serious situation—a proletariat determined to end an oppressive social and economic order and militant capitalists bent upon preserving the system to which they owed their economic resources and political prestige.

Whether the adjustment will be made in a peaceful manner through a liberal compromise, in which both parties will concede much, or whether it will be made by violence in a bitter class war that can only end in the termination of capitalism in a most destructive manner, will depend wholly upon the sagacity and statesmanship of those who will lead in the negotiations. What plans of reconstruction will be most used cannot be foreseen. The conflict of today has called forth a reconsideration of every one of the proposals of the nineteenth century that have been discussed above, not even excepting a return to the complete individualism of the Economic Liberals. To the writer there seems little probability that the future will witness any complete and permanent adoption of any single program of reconstruction. It is more likely that an eclectic system will prevail, adapted to differing industries, and peoples.

The most interesting developments since the World War have been Communism in Russia [1] and Fascism in Italy [2] and elsewhere. These represent the most extreme forms of competing politico-economic systems. Fascism is the most militant and powerful expression of capitalism and private property, while Communism is the most menacing challenge to the capitalistic profit system. One maintains private property by force; the other uses force to dispossess its citizens of their property and create a collectivist system. Both systems have made most headway in the last decade. Many believe that as the struggle between capital and labor becomes more acute, all the states of the world will be drawn into one or the other of these forms of organization.

The depression of 1929 forced many capitalist leaders to reconsider the merits and defects of capitalism and to set forth what has been called the "new capitalism," namely, a planned economic order. In this system waste and overproduction will be severely curtailed and the consuming power of labor increased and maintained through higher wages, unemployment insurance, and the like. The most-discussed proposal has been the so-called Swope plan, mentioned earlier, as set forth by Mr. Gerard Swope of the General Electric Company. This envisages the nation-wide organization of our major industries in such a way as to forward planning and control of production. President Roosevelt's New Deal, especially the National Industrial Recovery Act, embraced much of the Swope plan, but seemed to administration enthusiasts to go further in the way of putting government in control of industrial planning. Mr. Swope had been in favor of industrial self-government. The radicals derided the New Deal and declared that it is only thinly veiled Fascism. Even liberal and authoritative commentators have contended that the National Industrial Recovery Act is actually the product of big business and that in this legislation the gov-

---

[1] *Cf.* Jerome Davis, *Contemporary Social Movements*, Century, 1930, Bk. IV. For a good survey of Communism and Fascism in action, see Emil Lengyel, *The New Deal in Europe*, Funk & Wagnalls, 1934; and E. T. Colton, *Four Patterns of Revolution*, Association Press, 1935.

[2] *Cf.* Davis, *op. cit.*, Bk. V.

ernment abandoned the long fight against self-government by big business.[1]

A final lesson regarding social-reform programs was taught by the World War. As Hobhouse pointed out a number of years ago in his *Democracy and Reaction,* the state is bound to be obstructed in effective programs of social reform while militarism menaces our civilization. So long as citizens are bowed beneath the burdens of taxation to supply munitions for active warfare, to support vast armament for "preparedness," and to prepare for future holocausts, there will never be adequate funds for thoroughgoing schemes of social reconstruction. A veritable social and economic paradise throughout the Western world could have been created out of the funds expended in the World War. In a very real sense the final solution of social problems is bound up with the discovery of some method for discouraging or eliminating war.[2]

XVI. FASCISM AND THE CORPORATIVE STATE

The World War sharpened the conflict between the middle class and the workers. Not only did it clarify the issue within individual capitalistic states; the rise of a great Communistic civilization in Russia also brought into sharp contrast the ideals and practices of capitalism and Communism. In some states there has been a frank effort to crush radicalism and to repress the workers and radical peasants. Such was the case in Hungary, for example.

The most novel and interesting development was, however, not a frank attempt to repress the proletariat but an ostensible effort to obliterate the class struggle. This took the form of a militant and dictatorial capitalism in what is known as Fascism.[3] It has been held by many commentators that the Marx of the Fascist movement is the Italian savant Vilfredo Pareto.[4] Fascism has been cogently described as an attempt to preserve capitalism by force, incidentally suppressing democracy and representative government. It may also be regarded in another sense as a movement that endeavors to promote, by forceful means if necessary, the alleged solidarity of interest between capital and labor. It is a complete reversal of the Marxian thesis of the class struggle, as well as of the doctrine of the popular will and majority rule.

Fascism is a merger of nationalism and bourgeois Syndicalism. The individual loses his identity and becomes a member of a guild state. The doctrine of natural rights, which dates from John Locke and other writers of the eighteenth century, is repudiated along with Rousseau's emphasis upon majority rule. The whole set of concepts that underlay nineteenth-century parliamentarianism are discarded. The existence of constituent groups within the state is fully admitted, but their subordination to the state is complete. All vocations find their logical place as a part of a great syndicate, the economic state. The Fascist doctrine, then, rests upon the conception of a corporative or guild state—the most complete adoption to date of the notions first crudely set

---

[1] See particularly J. T. Flynn, "Whose Child Is the NRA?" *Harper's Magazine,* September, 1934.
[2] See above, pp. 600 ff., 924 ff.
[3] Fascist apologists, in trying to make headway among liberals, represent Fascism as Solidarism in action.
[4] *Cf.* Malcolm Cowley, "A Handbook for Demagogues," *New Republic,* Sept. 12, 1934, a review of G. C. Homans and C. P. Curtis, *Introduction to Pareto,* Knopf, 1934.

forth by Johannes Althusius in the early seventeenth century.[1] This notion leaves little place for representative government. Majority rule is further rejected on the basis of the assumption that the élite are destined by nature to rule and are best fitted to express the national sentiments and traditions.

In its economic philosophy Fascism is capitalism with a vengeance. It challenges bluntly the Marxist thesis that there is an inherent and ceaseless clash of interests between capital and labor. It maintains the opposite dogma, namely, that their ultimate interests are identical—supplementary in the productive and distributive processes of economic life. Whether the Fascist thesis of solidarity is correct or not, the state forces capital and labor to operate in accordance with these tenets. The immediate control of productive processes is left to corporations constituted of employers and employees. But the state stands ready to step in whenever capital and labor come to an impasse or are inadequate to cope with an emergency. This makes the Fascist economic control, in theory at least, far more flexible than overt State Socialism.[2]

Fascism was first established on a large scale in Italy. The leader was Benito Mussolini, earlier an atheistically inclined radical who had at different times identified himself with Anarchism, Socialism, Syndicalism, radical labor-unionism, and birth control. He laid his plans and perfected his organization in 1919. Late in the year 1922 he marched on Rome, and virtually seized control of the government; he has since built up a relatively stable state along Fascist lines.

The term "Fascism" is very carelessly and inaccurately used, especially by its radical critics. Any form of State Socialism or of dictatorship is arbitrarily designated as Fascism. It has been rather loosely employed to describe the dictatorships in Hungary, Poland, Rumania, Bulgaria, Spain, and elsewhere. This is quite inaccurate in any precise use of the term. All Fascism means dictatorship, but not all dictatorship is Fascism. The latter is something more subtle and complicated than a crude effort to support capitalism by machine guns. Fully developed Fascism has appeared as yet only in Italy. It seems, however, that harsh Germany under Hitler is in the process of establishing a régime rather consciously based upon an imitation of the Italian system. Thus far, however, there have been notable differences between the Nazi and the Fascist programs, particularly in the anticlericalism of the former and their efforts to subordinate religion to nationalism.

In any event, Fascism represents the most powerful and articulate attempt in postwar society to challenge and oppose the doctrine of the class struggle and the rise of the workers' state. In promoting the so-called solidarity of interest between capital and labor, the Fascist government must interpret the interests of both. So far, Fascism has tended to suppress labor and to favor capital. With the increasing tension within capitalism, it is probable that labor will be even more obviously and completely sacrificed in the future.

[1] See Johannes Althusius, *Politica methodice digesta,* ed. by C. J. Friedrich, Harvard University Press, 1932, Introduction. It is held upon good authority that the doctrine of the corporative state was evolved some years after Fascism was established as a political fact in Italy. It is contended that it is purely a rationalization after the fact and an effort to devise a dignified "front" to obscure the harsh reality of dictatorial rule in behalf of capitalism.

[2] Even yet, however, the corporative state is mainly theory in Italy. The majority of the Italian industries are still organized in the old-fashioned way, under which the employing classes dominate.

XVII. THE PSEUDO-BIOLOGICAL APOLOGY FOR CAPITALISM, INDUSTRIAL AUTOCRACY, AND ECONOMIC INDIVIDUALISM

Not only have nationalism, political theory, and religion been invoked in the attempt to frustrate radical social and economic programs since the World War. Even biology has been enlisted in the cause of economic reaction—as it was in an earlier generation to support the war cult. It has been held that the struggle for existence operates freely and fully in the economic field, and that our present hierarchy of wealth and social status is a definite and defensible expression of the "survival of the fittest."

A widely popular doctrine of social reactionaries designed to discourage radical reform doctrines is that which is based upon an exaggerated and unwarranted interpretation of eugenic theories in biology. The more extreme eugenicists contend that biological factors are of primary importance in society and scoff at social reforms and cultural influences. They hold that no far-reaching improvements can be expected in human society until we create a race of supermen by selective breeding within the human race. Social legislation providing for more equitable distribution of wealth and opportunity, for just taxation, and for scientific social agencies is condemned as ineffective.

It is surely true that we would profit by eliminating the physically and mentally unfit and by producing an ever higher type of human being. There is also every probability that if the eugenicists were given their way they could produce a race of superior beings. Therefore it is desirable that we should encourage their program in every conceivable way. But it would be extremely dangerous to surrender to the extreme biological fatalism that is represented by the most thoroughgoing eugenicists. The obvious fact is that human society will perish or be saved before any eugenics program, taking into account existing opposition and inertia, can fashion a superrace. Our problems will not permit a century or more of evasion and postponement. If capitalism is not chastened and corrected long before that time it may surely be predicted that it cannot survive. Communism, likewise, will have to prove itself long before supermen can appear to run its machinery. If supermen ever come along they can then take up our institutions and run them more effectively, but radical reform will have to be brought about long before any eugenic platform can have begun to bear fruit.

The appeal to history is the best answer to the eugenicists' claim that nothing important can be done until the race is improved in a physical and intellectual way. It is conceded by most of these same anthropologists and biologists that the native physical and intellectual qualities of the race have not improved in the last fifty thousand years. Homo sapiens appeared about that time and has not increased in native intelligence since, whatever his subsequent accumulation of information. Indeed, some of the eugenically inclined biologists hold that the race is somewhat inferior today to what it was at the close of the cave age.[1] Yet all that we know as civilization has been achieved by this same race of men, inferior according to eugenic standards. Humankind with all its de-

---

[1] *Cf.* S. J. Holmes, *The Trend of the Race,* Harcourt, Brace, 1921.

fects has manifestly advanced from cave life to the modern city. Hence to claim that we could not, if sound knowledge were put to work, create a rational social system and intelligently exploit our vast natural resources is sheer nonsense. Even the less than superior people, if inculcated through proper education with correct information and standards, are competent to become worthy members of the society desired in the future—indeed more so than many superior people, for in all fairness it must be granted that the cause of stupid reaction has seldom lacked "brainy" and ingenious adherents.[1]

There is another biological fallacy that needs to be exposed, namely, the arrogant assumption of some that our present hierarchy of social classes and personal fortunes rest upon a valid biological basis—with the ablest at the top and the inferiors at the bottom of the pyramid. This illusion has been shattered by a very able biologist, Professor Hermann J. Muller of the University of Texas, who has said that

we are brought to realize that, in a society having such glaring inequalities of environment as ours, our tests [for I.Q.'s] are very unreliable for the determination of individual genetic differences in intelligence, except in some cases where these differences are extreme, or where essential likeness of both home and outer environment can be proved.[2]

The biologists themselves have been the best implicit critics of this notion of economic position under capitalism as an expression of the survival of the fittest. They have shown that able parents may have stupid children, thus upsetting any biological basis for a rigid hierarchy of wealth, based in large part today upon the inheritance of great fortunes. Further, it would require an expansive imagination and much wishful thinking to lead to the conclusion that an able engineer or scientist is usually biologically and intellectually inferior to his multimillionaire absentee employer.

XVIII. CONTEMPORARY HUMANITARIANISM: THE SCIENTIFIC CONTROL OF THE MALADJUSTED

Along with modern efforts to reconstruct the whole economic and social basis of civilization have come important humanitarian measures, which aim to make more tolerable the lot of the unfortunate, whatever the social system that prevails. In an earlier chapter we surveyed briefly the origins of modern humanitarianism in the eighteenth and nineteenth centuries.[3] We may now consider some of the more recent developments in this field of human activity.

There are several important traits of contemporary humanitarianism that are worth noting. In the first place, scientific knowledge is playing an ever larger part in this type of activity. Humane altruism and social sympathy have by no means been eliminated, but they have been chastened and controlled by expert knowledge. In other words, moral zeal and the "uplift" motive have been supplemented by scientific guidance. In the second place, relief of misery of

---

[1] For example, Metternich, Bismarck, Balfour, Churchill, Elihu Root, John W. Davis, and others
[2] Muller, "The Dominance of Economics over Eugenics," *Scientific Monthly*, July, 1933, p. 44
[3] See above, pp. 232 ff., 398 ff.

Wide World Photos
BENITO MUSSOLINI

© *Wide World Photos*
ADOLF HITLER

A CROWD GIVING THE NAZI SALUTE
Wide World Photos

Wide World Photos
THE LEAGUE OF NATIONS BUILDINGS, GENEVA

Wide World Photos
A THREE-YEAR-OLD FASCIST SOLDIER
SALUTES MUSSOLINI

whatever kind takes a position subordinate to the desire to eliminate the causes of such misery. The ameliorative goal has been supplanted by the preventive aim. Finally, it is coming to be widely recognized that most types of social maladjustment and their elimination are definitely linked up with the issue of modifying the whole social system. For example, there is little prospect of eliminating poverty in a régime of individualistic capitalism. Nor, to take another case, can nervous and mental disease be kept down to a reasonable level so long as economic insecurity and sex maladjustment are prevalent.

In dealing with poverty and pauperism, there has been much progress since the Poor Law of 1834. More adequate and comprehensive legislation relating to the relief of poverty has been put on the statute books. A better differentiation and balance has been attained between outdoor relief (that is, relief provided outside institutions) and institutional relief. Much the major part of our relief problems involve the aid of urban dependents. Much more efficient methods of administration have been introduced into urban charity. These began with the Hamburg-Elberfeld system mentioned above,[1] but the most important development was that associated with the growth of the Charity Organization societies.[2] This originated with the London society, founded in 1869 by Charles Loch and others. It spread to the United States after 1875; the first American Charity Organization Society was opened at Buffalo in 1877. Within fifteen years over fifty such organizations were established in this country.

The Charity Organization Society movement aims to eliminate the defects of earlier urban relief: inadequate grants to the really needy, graft by clever impostors, duplication of effort by a multiplicity of overlapping relief associations, and the absence of any proper coördination of relief agencies. In cities where a Charity Organization Society is established the claims of those seeking aid are carefully examined, so that the cases of actual need will be adequately handled and the fraudulent claims eliminated from any consideration. Duplication of effort and administrative waste are lessened by a proper coördination of all relief agencies. Systematic planning is made for the collection of funds, and wholesale drives, such as community-chest campaigns, are carried out. Educational activities are carried on in the effort to improve the living-standards of those who are inclined to ask for charity, and to acquaint potential givers with the ideals and methods of scientific social work. Finally, everything possible is done to take such steps as will lessen dependency—at least such steps as can be taken without any serious attack upon the existing order.

An important phase of the improved technique of social work—in part a product of the better methods introduced by the Charity Organization societies —is the growth of social case work, that is, the handling of individual cases according to scientific social-work standards, thus assuring just the attention that a particular applicant for relief really needs.

The massed misery of the new urban centers stimulated what is known as the social settlement movement. The settlement is a residence or meeting-place of social workers located in the midst of the slums. The aim is to bring workers

---

[1] See above, p. 401.
[2] *Cf.* A. G. Warner, *American Charities*, 3d ed., Crowell, 1919, Chap. XXII; H. D. Bosanquet, *Social Work in London, 1869-1912*, Dutton, 1914; and F. D. Watson, *The Charity Organization Movement in the United States*, Macmillan, 1922.

directly into contact with their problem and to extend the opportunities to aid the unfortunate right on the spot. Educational classes, health work, visiting-nurse activities, athletic opportunities, and the like are frequently maintained by the settlements. The settlements serve admirably as places for the practical training of social workers. They also offer an opportunity for those who wish to serve the poor but cannot make substantial financial contributions. They are oases of altruism and the application of scientific social-work principles in the deserts of misery created by the inequalities of our economic order.[1]

The first important settlement was Toynbee Hall, opened in East London in 1884 by Canon Barnett and named in honor of Arnold Toynbee, who had helped to promote the settlement idea. Over thirty settlement houses were established in Great Britain before 1900. In the United States the movement began with the establishment of the University Settlement in East Side New York by Stanton Coit in 1886. Other famous settlements have been Hull House in Chicago, established by Jane Addams in 1889; South End House, opened in Boston in 1891 by William J. Tucker and Robert A. Woods; Greenwich House and the Henry Street Settlement in New York City, the first headed since its foundation in 1902 by Mary Kingsbury Simkhovitch and the second (for health work) conducted since 1893 by Lillian D. Wald.[2]

While the settlement assumes the existence of slums, there has been a notable effort to eliminate them. This is known as the housing movement. Men like Robert W. De Forest and Lawrence Veiller have taken the lead in this movement in the United States. They propose to obliterate the scandalous tenement houses and slums that were a by-product of the wild scramble for profits in real estate and rentals during the last century. But the only really striking achievements that have been attained are those carried out by the Socialist government of Vienna and the Communist government of Russia since 1918,[3] though the Amalgamated Clothing Workers in New York City have shown in their coöperative apartments what might be done with a little social vision.

As social work has become more scientific its leaders have come to understand that it is especially important to get hold of children and to protect them from the unfortunate results of poverty, misery, and ignorance. Hence a movement to save children has gained much headway in the last half-century. Orphan asylums have been made more humane and natural by introducing the cottage and family systems in the place of the old jail-like discipline. Laws have been passed limiting the labor of children and insisting upon their education at public expense. Even among delinquent children we have introduced far more humane concepts and methods than prevail in our treatment of adult criminals.

Many social workers and sociologists have become convinced that whatever the improvements in the technique of social work, there can be no permanent betterment until the economic and other leading causes of dependency are eliminated. They hold that the only prevention which amounts to anything is that which prevents the causes of dependency. They contend that social work which operates short of that ideal is only "the wrecking-crew" that attempts

---

[1] *Cf.* A. J. Kennedy and others, *Social Settlements in New York City*, Columbia University Press, 1935.
[2] See P. U. Kellogg, article "Social Settlements," Encyclopaedia of the Social Sciences.
[3] See above, pp. 415 ff., and below, pp. 1017 ff.

to salvage the derelicts produced by our economic system. An important statement of this philosophy was embodied in the Minority Report on the British Poor Law in 1909, written largely by Mrs. Sidney Webb.[1] This made it clear that mere administrative changes in relief systems were of little consequence. This report helped greatly to encourage the passage of the British social legislation between 1909 and the outbreak of the World War.[2] Not even extended social insurance satisfies many commentators. They insist that nothing short of a modification of the whole capitalistic system will suffice. They point to the Russian experiment, which we shall discuss in the next chapter.

The treatment of criminals has come in for some notable changes in the last generation or two. The introduction of scientific and psychological methods for the understanding of all behavior, normal and criminal, has revolutionized our ideas of personal responsibility by undermining the old doctrine of free will and of the so-called free moral agent. It has been made clear that the criminal is a victim of heredity, bad environment, or both. Hence there is no logical ground for punishing him brutally. Logic will only support treatment in such a fashion as to protect society from the depredations of criminals and to reform, if possible, the individual offender. As a result, the ideal of reformation has gradually supplanted that of savage punishment and social revenge.[3] The first formal adoption of this ideal appeared in the Irish prison system, introduced by Sir Walter Crofton after 1853. It was brought to the United States by Franklin Sanborn, E. C. Wines, and others in the so-called Elmira system in 1877. This provided that the treatment and release of the prisoner should depend upon the evidence of his reformative efforts while incarcerated. Even in our conventional prisons there have been some improvements, particularly in eliminating shaved heads, striped suits, the lockstep, and other humiliating brutalities. But in the usual prison for adults the disciplinary system has not changed in fundamentals since prisons were first introduced a little over a century ago.[4] The most important effort to transform our prison discipline was embodied in the work of Thomas Mott Osborne at Sing Sing Prison in New York State and at the United States Naval Prison at Portsmouth, New Hampshire, between 1914 and 1921.[5] He believed that prisoners must be trained for freedom by giving them responsibility. He therefore proposed a scheme of inmate self-government. This worked wonders under Osborne's direction, and it may ultimately revolutionize prison administration.

More important, perhaps, than any progress within prisons has been the development of a movement to reduce the institutional treatment of delinquents to the lowest minimum compatible with social safety. Here the more important innovations have been probation and parole. A convict on probation is dealt

---
[1] *Cf.* S. A. Queen, *Social Work in the Light of History*, Lippincott, 1922, Chap. xii; and H. D. Bosanquet, *The Poor Law Report of 1909*, Macmillan, 1909.

[2] See above, pp. 938 ff.

[3] Among the more important persons who helped to transform our notions of criminals were Bentham, Archbishop Whateley, George Combe, Bonneville de Marsangy, E. C. Wines, Frank Sanborn, F. H. Wines, and Thomas Mott Osborne.

[4] *Cf.* Barnes, *The Story of Punishment*, Chap. vii., and J. L. Gillin, *Taming the Criminal*, Macmillan, 1931.

[5] See T. M. Osborne, *Prisons and Common Sense*, Lippincott, 1924; Frank Tannenbaum, *Osborne of Sing Sing*, University of North Carolina Press, 1933; and R. W. Chamberlain, *There Is No Truce*, Macmillan, 1935.

with outside an institution on a suspended sentence. If he reforms, he will never enter a prison. If he proves unruly, then the sentence may be invoked and the culprit remanded to an institution. Under the parole system a convict is freed conditionally from a penal institution upon evidence that he has shown fitness to be at large. He is then supervised and aided by parole officers until his sentence expires. The parole has been used mainly in connection with some form of indeterminate sentence that allows the prison authorities or parole authorities, rather than the judge, to determine when a convict is fit to be released.

Extremely important have been the introduction of psychiatry into the treatment of the convict and the resulting emphasis upon the necessity of individualized examination and treatment.[1] Psychiatry has been used with special success in dealing with juvenile delinquents. Here, scientific methods dominate. Physicians and social workers have supplanted lawyers, judges, and juries in the handling of young delinquents.[2] Russia is the only country that has as yet applied similar methods to the treatment of adult criminals.[3]

In no phase of humanitarian effort in our generation have there been more satisfactory results than in the improved methods of dealing with the so-called insane. Success here is especially important because of the notable increase in mental and nervous diseases in the last fifty years. The strains and stresses of city life and the worries connected with economic insecurity have contributed to a large increase in the number of persons who break down from nervous and mental disorders. The enormous extent of mental disease in contemporary times may be discerned from a recent statement by one of the leading American psychiatrists:

The 1928 hospital census of the American Medical Association showed that one out of every 325 persons in the United States was a patient in an institution for nervous and mental disorders, including patients in institutions for the feebleminded and the epileptic. There were about 438,000 patients in hospitals for mental diseases [alone] in the United States in 1928, maintained at a cost of over $80,-000,000 a year; the hospital population is increasing at the annual rate of approximately 10,000 and about 75,000 new cases are admitted to institutions every year. According to a recent study of mental disease expectancy, in New York state approximately one person out of every twenty-two of the population becomes a patient in a mental hospital at some time during his lifetime. There are more patients in mental hospitals than in all the general hospitals of the country at any one time.[4]

We noted above how Pinel, about the opening of the nineteenth century, started a movement to strike irons from the insane, and how Dorothea Dix led in the United States the crusade to establish hospitals for the insane.[5] In spite of the creation of the "lunatic asylums" after 1825, the treatment of these patients left much to be desired. They were herded like animals and locked up like criminals. Further, it was regarded as disgraceful to be a patient suffer-

[1] Cf. Barnes, op. cit., pp. 270 ff.
[2] Cf. C. L. Burt, The Young Delinquent, Appleton, 1925.
[3] See below, pp. 1024 ff.
[4] Bernard Glueck, article "Mental Hygiene," Encyclopaedia of the Social Sciences, Vol. X, p. 320.
[5] See above, p. 401.

ing from a mental or nervous disorder. Such ailments were not viewed calmly, as were other forms of sickness.

The revolution in our attitude toward such matters has been due mainly to the mental-hygiene movement, which received its initial impulse in the United States.[1] Mr. Clifford W. Beers, a student in Yale University, was compelled to take treatment in a Connecticut state hospital for the insane. He recovered and, remembering the unsatisfactory nature of his own treatment while in the hospital, resolved to devote the rest of his life to the improvement of our methods of treating the nervously and mentally afflicted. In 1908 he published his mental autobiography, *A Mind That Found Itself*.[2] This aroused much interest in psychologists like William James and in leading American psychiatrists and neurologists. Their aid enabled Beers to found the National Committee for Mental Hygiene in 1909. Many state societies were later founded in imitation of the national organization. In 1930 a great International Congress for Mental Hygiene was held in Washington and an International Committee for Mental Hygiene was founded. The mental-hygiene movement was powerfully forwarded by the growth in our knowledge of psychiatry between 1908 and 1930 as a result of the research of Freud and others of the psychoanalytic school.

The mental-hygiene movement has done much in an educational way to promote a sane attitude towards mental and nervous diseases. These disabilities are no longer regarded by civilized persons as mysterious or disgraceful. This has made it easier for afflicted persons to seek voluntary treatment and for relatives to send them to institutions for treatment before it is too late to effect a cure. This has diminished much of the old horror of becoming a patient in a hospital for the insane. Special stress has been laid on the necessity of preventive action in this field. Hence clinics have been set up to aid those in early stages of mental or nervous disorders. Particularly good work has been done with "problem children" in child-guidance clinics. Over fifty thousand American children are today benefiting each year from such aid. But it has been recognized that adequate preventive measures require the creation of healthy mental attitudes and ways of living. In this way mental hygiene has branched out into general mass education, and there are many who believe that mental hygiene will supply the new scientific morality that is required to adjust man to our novel ways of life and the changing mental perspective.

In any event, the mental-hygiene movement has already helped to check the spread of mental and nervous diseases and may ultimately reduce them to a minimum. Mental hygiene has also been found extremely useful in connection with social work and criminology, and some schools of social work, such as that at Smith College, are now conducted from the mental-hygiene point of view.

Closely related to the problem of mental and nervous disease is that of mental deficiency. The notion that some individuals are mentally superior and others defective in intelligence is an old one that dates back at least to Aristotle. But it was all a matter of guesswork until scientific mental testing was brought

---

[1] *Cf.* Barnes, *Can Man Be Civilized?* Chap. III; M. R. Davie, ed., *Social Aspects of Mental Hygiene*, Yale University Press, 1925; and W. L. Cross, ed., *Twenty-five Years After*, Doubleday, Doran, 1934.
[2] Macmillan.

into being with the rise of modern psychology. Most important in the development of mental testing were Galton in England, Binet and Simon in France, and Cattell, Farrand, Goddard, Terman, Yerkes, Otis, and others in the United States.

The profound social significance of the wide extent of mental deficiency had been suspected from our educational experience, but it was first demonstrated in a quantitative way by the tests administered to the men drafted for military service by the United States in 1917-18.[1] It was shown that about 40 per cent of the population fall within the classifications of dull normal, morons, imbeciles, and idiots. At the other extreme not more than about 10 per cent possess distinguished mental capacity.

These tests showed the necessity of revamping our educational, political, and economic procedure to harmonize with the discovered facts. Classes for retarded children were formed in our schools. The desirability of preponderantly vocational or manual-skills education for such children is being recognized. For the lower grades of the feeble-minded who require institutional segregation we have created many humane and intelligently administered schools and colonies. Trades are taught here—those who are not too low in the mental scale showing remarkable educability in handicraft work. The institutions for the feeble-minded are in the course of being made self-supporting. The inmates offer excellent material for the experimental study of feeble-mindedness and of intelligent ways of dealing with the problem. While we now recognize that not more than half of feeble-mindedness is due to hereditary causes, the social as well as the biological desirability of sterilizing these types has gradually been conceded. Even in cases of nonhereditary feeble-mindedness, mentally defective parents are not fitted to bring up children properly.

Another old and knotty social problem has been attacked with enlightenment and new resolution—that of the "social evil," prostitution and venereal disease. The old methods of direct repression of prostitution without removing its causes have been found very generally futile. Stress is therefore being laid on the necessity of dealing with causes. Here economic considerations are primary, namely, the inability of many women to earn a decent living in conventional modes of employment and the incapacity of many men to secure sufficient economic resources or security to enter permanent marriage relations. One mode of meeting the problem is the so-called companionate marriage advocated by the famous juvenile judge and social reformer Benjamin B. Lindsey of Denver. This is supposed to enable a young man and a young woman to pool their resources and permit both of them to continue in employment without the burden of children. Associated with this is the birth-control movement, sponsored by W. J. Robinson, Marie Stopes, Margaret Sanger, and others. This movement has a wider interest and implication, namely, to keep the population within limits that can be supported in any given economic order.

One of the worst by-products of prostitution has been venereal disease, which works more serious harm in the population than is popularly known. An effort has been made to offset this danger by the introduction of medical prophylaxis against such "social diseases." The various governments in the World War and

[1] See above, pp. 860 ff., and C. C. Brigham, *A Study of American Intelligence,* Princeton University Press, 1923.

since have made wide use of prophylaxis among soldiers and sailors with rather strikingly effective results. Russia has made more progress than any other country in dealing rationally and successfully with prostitution.[1] The equality of women, the guarantee of a livelihood by the state, and the realistic attitude toward sex have there combined to produce an almost complete elimination of the prostitution that was especially rife in Russian cities in the old tsarist days.

One of the most interesting and widely discussed of the humanitarian innovations of our day was the experiment of the United States, Finland, and other countries with the prohibition of the manufacture and sale of alcoholic liquors. The Prohibition movement started in the United States with the labors of John B. Gough, Neal Dow, and other leaders in the middle of the nineteenth century. But it did not gain any great practical headway until the Anti-Saloon League was founded in 1893 and began to apply the typical methods of practical political persuasion, namely, to threaten legislators with retaliation at the polls if they did not support prohibitive laws. By the end of 1914 some fourteen states had adopted Prohibition and about half of the country had outlawed the saloon. The Prohibition forces, under the leadership of Mr. Wayne B. Wheeler, head of the Anti-Saloon League, recognized the opportunity of capitalizing patriotic fervor and they redoubled their efforts after the United States entered the World War. They were aided by powerful industrialists who believed that sober workmen were more efficient and docile. In 1917 Congress sent a Prohibition amendment to the states for ratification. By January, 1919, the required number of states had approved and it became the Eighteenth Amendment, outlawing the manufacture and sale of alcoholic beverages.

From the beginning, powerful forces lined up against enforcement, some working for repeal of the amendment and others for nullification. Criminals and gangsters piled up great fortunes in the liquor racket as bootleggers, hijackers, and the like.[2] Wholesale corruption was threatened, and crime increased. A vast illicit sale and consumption of alcoholic liquors grew up in "blind tigers," speakeasies, and night clubs.[3] Drinking increased markedly among the youth of the land, a fact that alarmed many who were not greatly concerned with adult drinking. Finally, matters became so tense that President Hoover created a commission under the general direction of Mr. George W. Wickersham to study law enforcement, particularly as concerned Prohibition. The commission handed in its report in 1931 and inclined decisively towards a modification of the liquor policy of the Eighteenth Amendment. In the meantime, some of the prominent industrialists who had originally supported Prohibition fell away and advocated repeal. In the campaign of 1932 the Democratic party openly favored repeal and the Republican party gave it guarded approval. In February, 1933, a resolution for repeal was sent to the states by Congress and by December, 1933, the required number of states had approved. The question of liquor control was thrown back to the states for its solution. The legislation that has followed has generally aimed to correct the worst abuses in the use of alcoholic liquors while avoiding the excesses of outright Prohibi-

---

[1] See below, pp. 1022 ff.
[2] See above, pp. 833 ff.
[3] *Cf.* Stanley Walker, *The Night Club Era,* Stokes, 1933.

tion. Civilized and intelligent use of alcoholic liquor seems to be the aim. Rational temperance may be promoted by educational means.[1]

Finland tried a similar experiment, passing a prohibitory act in 1917.[2] Its experience with Prohibition was roughly similar to that of the United States and the law was repealed in December, 1931. Most unbiased observers in both the United States and Finland felt that while sanity in the use of alcoholic beverages is desirable, the Prohibition enthusiasts overshot their mark by the drastic, forceful, and overhasty character of their remedy. For the present, at least, control rather than prohibition seems to be the sensible approach to the handling of the liquor problem.[3] In spite of the impracticable nature of the stand for absolute Prohibition, the residual fact remains that the excessive use of alcoholic beverages has created a whole set of pathological social problems to bedevil human society. Alcohol misused is a poison that perhaps does not operate so harmfully upon the physiological organism as was once supposed, but psychologically and socially may have the most demoralizing effects.

XIX. CONCLUDING OBSERVATIONS

Most fair-minded and thoughtful readers will appreciate the fact that the writers considered in this chapter have discovered defects of the most serious nature in our industrial and social order and have made earnest efforts to suggest more efficient and equitable forms of social and economic organization. Yet there are obvious reasons why one may still remain unconvinced as to the complete adequacy of any one of them, confirmed as one may be in his belief of the well-nigh hopeless incompetence of the present order. In short, there is real uncertainty as to whether the intelligence of mankind is going to prove adequate to manage the complex problems that have followed in the train of the transformations of material civilization growing out of the Industrial Revolution.

Convincing statistical evidence of the almost indescribable waste and inefficiency of modern methods of producing and distributing commodities was published more than a decade ago by a group of anti-Socialistic engineers in the famous report sponsored by Herbert Hoover on *Waste in Industry*.[4] The situation was described at greater length by Stuart Chase in *The Tragedy of Waste*. Veblen in a number of works, most notably *The Theory of Business Enterprise,* has shown how social service and efficiency have almost disappeared from the concepts of the modern entrepreneur, whose thoughts are circumscribed by the narrow bookkeeping orientation of production for profit. More recently Ripley, Berle, Means, Bonbright, Corey, Flynn, and Lowenthal have revealed how the leaders of finance capitalism have seized control of the capitalistic order and have introduced a régime of selfishness, waste, and exploitation unheard of in the days of industrial capitalism. The Socialists, if they have done nothing else, have made clear for all time the gross inequalities of economic

---
[1] *Cf.* H. E. Barnes, *Prohibition versus Civilization,* Viking Press, 1932.
[2] *Cf.* J. H. Wuorinen, *The Prohibition Experiment in Finland,* Columbia University Press, 1931.
[3] *Cf.* R. B. Fosdick and A. L. Scott, *Toward Liquor Control,* Harper, 1933, and G. E. G. Catlin, *Liquor Control,* Holt, 1931.
[4] See above, pp. 818 ff.

possessions and opportunities in modern society. Only the most sycophantic adulator of wealth could imagine these social and material inequalities to be closely correlated with differences in ability.

Such are the facts; but most radical programs of social and economic reconstruction overlook the insuperable difficulties that reduce the practicability of their proposals. Bowley has shown, upon the basis of a careful study of the income of England in 1914, that an equal per capita distribution of the income of England before the World War would not have led to the enriching of the whole population to any revolutionary degree. He thus proved quite satisfactorily that the only hope for any general prosperity lay in increased production and greater mass purchasing power. But the capitalists since the World War have seemed determined to prove that these can only be secured under collectivism.

Even radically inclined but scientific-minded writers are beginning to question the complete validity of the schemes for industrial democracy that are involved in most of the programs analyzed above. The undeniably great differences in native ability that exist in every population raise the pertinent question of whether even political democracy can be permanently practicable in the face of the fact that only a small minority in society possesses superior creative and directive ability. If this fact is true, then the much more complicated economic and social problems will be even less susceptible to control and direction through the principles of majority rule.

The problem, then, would seem to be about that which was recognized by Saint-Simon and Auguste Comte, namely, the creation of a social order in which the able minority will dominate. Yet this domination must not be of the selfish and shortsighted type that has prevailed in modern capitalism. It must combine efficiency with a broad social point of view and in some manner stimulate the masses to their best efforts. In other words, the new order must be one in which the service motive has supplanted the profit incentive.[1] The problems of social reform are as pressing as they are complicated, and require the utmost freedom in discussion and proposals for improvement. Hence the folly of repressing liberal and radical movements.

As capitalism is sapped by depressions and the depredations of financial speculation it becomes more desperate. At the same time, the success of Russia gives the radicals new heart. As the conflict between capitalism and the workers' state becomes more acute, therefore, the lines tend to be more sharply drawn and the issue clarifies. It looks very much as though the industrial and social warfare of the next generation would narrow down to one between Fascism of some form and Communism. The intermediate grades of liberalism and moderate Socialism seem to be evaporating.[2] The one possible exception to this trend is the United States under President Franklin D. Roosevelt. This represents perhaps the last stand of democratic liberalism supported by the petit bourgeoisie. If the New Deal succeeds, it may prove that there is still some hope for democracy, liberalism, and middle-class social reform. If so, it will probably

---

[1] *Cf.* Coker, *op. cit.*, Chap. xx; J. A. Hobson, *Incentives in the New Industrial Order*, Seltzer, 1925; and H. F. Ward, *In Place of Profit*, Scribner, 1933.

[2] For a fierce attack on liberalism, see Robert Briffault, *Breakdown*, Coward-McCann, 1932, Chaps. x-xii. For interesting views on the future of capitalism, compare Pitkin, *Capitalism Carries On*, with John Strachey, *The Nature of Capitalist Crisis*, Covici, Friede, 1935.

mean that the capitalism which survives will be a "consumers' capitalism." In this the purchasing power of the consumer, rather than the monopolistic grip of the industrialist or the unrestrained greed of the financial speculator, will be the governing factor.[1]

[1] The trend at the present time seems to indicate that President Roosevelt is abandoning his petit-bourgeois supporters in a flirtation with big business, but his rebuff by the Chamber of Commerce of the United States early in May, 1935, may lead him to alter his program.

SUGGESTED READING

Hammerton, *Universal History of the World*, Chaps. 174, 185
Merriam and Barnes, *History of Political Theories: Recent Times*, Chaps. VI-VII
Bertrand Russell, *Proposed Roads to Freedom*, Holt, 1919
—— *Freedom versus Organization, 1814-1914*, Norton, 1934
Ogg and Sharp, *The Economic Development of Modern Europe*, Chaps. XVII-XVIII, XXIV-XXV
Thomas Kirkup, *History of Socialism*, 5th ed. rev. and largely rewritten by E. R. Pease, Macmillan, 1913
Davis, *Contemporary Social Movements*, Bks. III-VII
Laidler, *History of Socialist Thought*, Pts. II-V
Coker, *Recent Political Thought*, Pts. I, III
L. T. Hobhouse, *The Metaphysical Theory of the State*, Macmillan, 1918
H. E. Barnes, *Sociology and Political Theory*, Knopf, 1924
Sidney Hook, *Towards an Understanding of Karl Marx*, Day, 1933
G. D. H. Cole, *What Marx Really Meant*, Knopf, 1934
M. M. Bober, *Karl Marx's Interpretation of History*, Harvard University Press, 1927
S. H.-M. Chang, *The Marxian Theory of the State*, Vanguard Press, 1931
O. D. Skelton, *Socialism; a Critical Analysis*, Houghton Mifflin, 1911
E. R. Pease, *History of the Fabian Society*, Dutton, 1916
Eduard Bernstein, *Evolutionary Socialism*, Huebsch, 1909
Hillquit, *History of Socialism in the United States*
Thomas, *Human Exploitation*
M. S. Callcott and W. C. Waterman, *Principles of Social Legislation*, Macmillan, 1932
Pipkin, *Social Politics and Modern Democracy*
W. H. Dawson, *Social Insurance in Germany*, Scribner, 1912
I. M. Rubinow, *The Quest for Security*, Holt, 1934
C. A. Kulp, ed., *Social Insurance*, American Academy of Political and Social Science, Annals, Vol. CLXX, 1933
F. S. Nitti, *Catholic Socialism*, Macmillan, 1895
Ward, *Our Economic Morality*
—— *Which Way Religion?*
Zenker, *Anarchism*
Eltzbacher, *Anarchism*
C. R. Fay, *Co-operation at Home and Abroad*, 3d ed. rev., King, 1925
E. P. Harris, E. S. Wiers, and F. H. Hooke, *Co-operation, the Hope of the Consumer*, Macmillan, 1918
Gompers, *Labor in Europe and America*
Selig Perlman, *Theory of the Labor Movement*, Macmillan, 1928
Paul Blanshard, *Outline of the British Labor Movement*, Doran, 1923
M. R. Clark, *History of the French Labor Movement (1910-1928)*, University of California Press, 1930
Lorwin and Flexner, *The American Federation of Labor*

SUGGESTED READING

Zaretz, *The Amalgamated Clothing Workers of America*
Louis Levine, *Syndicalism in France*, 2d ed., Longmans, 1914
Brissenden, *The I.W.W.: A Study of American Syndicalism*
G. D. H. Cole, *Social Theory*, Stokes, 1920
——— *Guild Socialism; a Plan for Economic Democracy*, Stokes, 1921
Niles Carpenter, *Guild Socialism: An Historical and Critical Analysis*, Appleton, 1922
G. R. Geiger, *The Philosophy of Henry George*, Macmillan, 1933
Gide and Rist, *History of Economic Doctrines*, pp. 587-614 (on Solidarism)
Oscar Newfang, *Capitalism and Communism: A Reconciliation*, Putnam, 1932
G. H. Soule, *A Planned Society*, Macmillan, 1932
Lindley, *The Roosevelt Revolution*
Wallace, *The New Deal in Action*
Hacker, *Short History of the New Deal*
Stolberg and Vinton, *The Economic Consequences of the New Deal*
P. U. Kellogg and A. H. Gleason, *British Labor and the War*, Boni & Liveright, 1919
E. T. Colton, *Four Patterns of Revolution*, Association Press, 1935
Schneider, *Making the Fascist State*
Fausto Pitigliani, *The Italian Corporative State*, Macmillan, 1934
Haider, *Capital and Labor under Fascism*
C. B. Hoover, *Germany Enters the Third Reich*, Macmillan, 1933
Schuman, *The Nazi Dictatorship*
Holmes, *The Eugenic Predicament*
H. E. Barnes, *Can Man Be Civilized?* Coward-McCann, 1932
S. A. Queen and D. M. Mann, *Social Pathology*, Crowell, 1925
J. L. Gillin, *Social Pathology*, Century, 1933
R. C. Dexter, *Social Adjustment*, Knopf, 1927
Robinson and Beard, *Readings in Modern European History*, Vol. II, pp. 478-505
Scott and Baltzly, *Readings in European History since 1814*, pp. 396-414
Jones, Vandenbosch, and Vandenbosch, *Readings in Citizenship*, pp. 329-86, 541-604
Hall and Beller, *Historical Readings in Nineteenth Century Thought*, pp. 87-200, 241-306
Wagner, *Social Reformers*, Pts. V-IX
C. J. H. Hayes, *British Social Politics*, Ginn, 1913, Chap. x
Commons, *Trade Unionism and Labor Problems*
Mary Van Kleek and M. L. Fledderus, eds., *On Economic Planning*, Covici, Friede, 1935
Davis and Barnes, *Readings in Sociology*, Bk. IV
Wallis and Willey, *Readings in Sociology*, Chaps. v, xv-xvi
E. E. Southard and M. C. Jarrett, *The Kingdom of Evils*, Macmillan, 1922
James Ford, ed., *Social Problems and Social Policy*, Ginn, 1923

FURTHER REFERENCES

CONTEMPORARY PROGRAMS OF SOCIAL AND ECONOMIC REFORM. For good introductions to social-reform movements since 1850, see Helmolt and others, *History of the World*, Vol. VII, Chap. IV; Nussbaum, *History of the Economic Institutions of Modern Europe*, Pt. IV, Chaps. VIII-IX; Hammerton, *op. cit.*, Chap. 185; Birnie, *Economic History of Europe*, Chaps. VII-XIV; Russell, *Proposed Roads to Freedom;* C. E. M. Joad, *Introduction to Modern Political Theory* (Oxford Press, 1924);

John Rae, *Contemporary Socialism* (Scribner, 1884); Orth, *Socialism and Democracy in Europe;* Laidler, *op. cit.,* Pts. II-V; Coker, *op. cit.,* Pts. I, III; Wagner, *op. cit.,* Pts. III-IX; Davis, *op. cit.* The last-named is the most complete single survey.

IDEALISTIC THEORY OF THE STATE. Chaps. II-III of Ernest Barker, *Political Thought in England from Spencer to the Present Day* (Holt, 1915); Dunning, *History of Political Theories from Rousseau to Spencer,* Chap. IV; Coker, *op. cit.,* Chap XV; Hobhouse, *op. cit.*

MARX AND MARXISM. Birnie, *op. cit.,* Chap. VII; Coker, *op. cit.,* Chaps. II-III; Gide and Rist, *op. cit.,* Bk. IV, Chap. III; Hook, *op. cit.;* pp. 405-56 of T. B. Veblen, *The Place of Science in Modern Civilization* (Huebsch, 1919); Laidler, *op. cit.,* Pt. II; Karl Marx, *Capital,* ed. by Julian Borchardt (Kerr, 1925)—an abridgment, published in England as *The People's Marx;* Cole, *What Marx Really Meant;* Chang, *op. cit.;* Samuel Bernstein, *The Beginnings of Marxian Socialism in France* (Elliot Publishing Co., 1933).

REVISIONISM. Laidler, *op. cit.,* Chaps. XX-XXI; Coker, *op. cit.,* Chap. IV; Eduard Bernstein, *op. cit.*

STATE SOCIALISM. Coker, *op. cit.,* Chap. XVI; Birnie, *op. cit.,* Chap. XIV; Ogg and Sharp, *op. cit.,* Chap. XVII-XVIII and pp. 576 ff.; Callcott and Waterman, *op. cit.;* Dawson, *op. cit.;* Rubinow, *op. cit.;* Pipkin, *op. cit.;* Hayes, *op. cit.*

On social-insurance legislation in the United States, see Haynes, *Social Politics in the United States;* J. R. Commons and J. B. Andrews, *The Principles of Labor Legislation* (rev. ed., Harper, 1927); Callcott and Waterman, *op. cit.;* I. M. Rubinow, *Social Insurance* (Holt, 1913); Abraham Epstein, *Insecurity; a Challenge to America* (Smith & Haas, 1933).

CATHOLIC SOCIAL REFORM. C. E. McGuire, "Christian Thought and Economic Policy," *Catholic Historical Review,* January, 1934; Gide and Rist, *op. cit.,* pp. 483-502; Rae, *op. cit.,* pp. 228 ff.; Nitti, *op. cit.;* P. T. Moon, *The Labor Problem and the Social Catholic Movement in France* (Macmillan, 1921); G. P. McEntee, *The Social Catholic Movement in Great Britain* (Macmillan, 1927); George Metlake, *Christian Social Reform* (Dolphin Press, 1912); C. D. Plater, *The Priest and Social Action* (Longmans, 1914); Karl Waninger, *Social Catholicism in England* (Herder, 1914); J. A. Ryan, *A Better Economic Order* (Harper, 1935).

SOCIAL PROTESTANTISM. North, *Early Methodist Philanthropy;* Warner, *The Wesleyan Movement in the Industrial Revolution;* D. O. Wagner, *The Church of England and Social Reform since 1854* (Columbia University Press, 1930); William Cunningham, *Christianity and Social Questions* (Scribner, 1910); H. U. Faulkner in *Essays in Intellectual History; dedicated to James Harvey Robinson,* Chap. VIII; Laidler, *op. cit.,* Chap. XXXI; Ward, *Our Economic Morality.*

ANARCHISM. Coker, *op. cit.,* Chap. VII; Russell, *op. cit.,* pp. 32 ff.; Kirkrup, *op. cit.,* Chap. XI; Zenker, *op. cit.;* Eltzbacher, *op. cit.;* Peter Latouche, *Anarchy* (London, 1908); E. A. Vizetelly, *The Anarchists* (Lane, 1911); Emma Goldman, *Living My Life* (Knopf, 1931, 2 vols.).

THE COÖPERATIVE MOVEMENT. Davis, *op. cit.,* Bk. IV; Laidler, *op. cit.,* Chap. XXX; Charles Gide, *Consumers' Co-operative Societies* (Knopf, 1922); Fay, *op. cit.;* Harris, *op. cit.;* G. J. Holyoake, *History of Co-operation* (Dutton, 1906, 2 vols.)—chiefly England; F. C. Howe, *Denmark; a Cooperative Commonwealth* (Harcourt, Brace, 1921); Sidney and Beatrice Webb, *The Consumers' Co-operative Movement* (Longmans, 1921); Cedric Long, *The Consumers Cooperative Movement in the United States* (5th ed. rev., Cooperative League, 1930); J. P. Warbasse, *Co-operative Democracy* (Macmillan, 1927); article "Cooperation," Encyclopaedia of the Social Sciences.

FURTHER REFERENCES

THE LABOR MOVEMENT. Ogg and Sharp, *op. cit.*, Chaps. xix-xx; Sidney and Beatrice Webb, *History of Trade Unionism* (new ed., Longmans, 1911); Selig Perlman, *Theory of the Labor Movement* (Macmillan, 1928); B. M. and Sylvia Selekman, *British Industry Today* (Harper, 1929); R. H. Tawney, *The British Labor Movement* (Yale University Press, 1925); Blanshard, *op. cit.; The Labour Party's Aim: A Criticism and a Restatement,* by seven members of the Labour party (Macmillan, 1924); Clark, *op. cit.;* D. J. Saposs, *The Labor Movement in Post-war France* (Columbia University Press, 1931); W. S. Sanders, *Trade Unionism in Germany* (London, 1916); Commons and others, *History of Labour in the United States;* Lorwin and Flexner, *op. cit.*

SYNDICALISM. Laidler, *op. cit.*, Chap. xxii; Coker, *op. cit.*, Chap. viii; Levine, *op. cit.;* Saposs, *op. cit.*, Pt. I; J. R. MacDonald, *Syndicalism: A Critical Examination* (Open Court Publishing Co., 1913); John Spargo, *Syndicalism, Industrial Unionism and Socialism* (Huebsch, 1913); Brissenden, *op. cit.*

I.W.W. Brissenden, *op. cit.;* J. S. Gambs, *The Decline of the I.W.W.* (Columbia University Press, 1932).

GUILD SOCIALISM. Laidler, *op. cit.*, Chap. xxiii; Coker, *op. cit.*, Chap. ix; Carpenter, *op. cit.;* Cole, *Guild Socialism* and *Social Theory;* S. G. Hobson, *National Guilds and the State* (Macmillan, 1920).

HENRY GEORGE. L. P. Post, *The Prophet of San Francisco* (Vanguard Press, 1930); Geiger, *op. cit.;* A. N. Young, *The Single Tax Movement in the United States* (Princeton University Press, 1916).

BRITISH LABOR AND SOCIAL RECONSTRUCTION. Kellogg and Gleason, *op. cit.*

FASCISM, COMMUNISM, PLANNED CAPITALISM. On Fascism, see Schneider, *op. cit.;* H. R. Spencer, *The Government and Politics of Italy* (World Book Co., 1932); Pitigliani, *op. cit.;* Haider, *op. cit.* For the character and recent progress of Fascism, Communism, and planned capitalism in Europe, see Lengyel, *The New Deal in Europe;* Rogers, *Crisis Government;* Buell, *New Governments in Europe.* For the New Deal in the United States, see Hacker, *op. cit.;* R. M. Tugwell, *The Battle for Democracy* (Columbia University Press, 1934); Wallace, *op. cit.;* William MacDonald, *The Menace of Recovery* (Macmillan, 1934); H. S. Johnson, *The Blue Eagle from Egg to Earth* (Doubleday, Doran, 1935).

EUGENICS. For a very sensible analysis of the eugenics issue, see Holmes, *op. cit.*

POVERTY. On poverty and pauperism, see Gillin, *Poverty and Dependency,* Pt. III; R. W. Kelso, *Poverty* (Longmans, 1929); Slater, *Poverty and the State.* On social case work, see M. E. Richmond, *Social Diagnosis* (Russell Sage Foundation, 1917); and *What Is Social Case Work?* (Russell Sage Foundation, 1922). On the Charity Organization Society, see F. D. Watson, *The Charity Organization Movement in the United States* (Macmillan, 1922). On social settlements, see Jane Addams, *Twenty Years at Hull-House* (Macmillan, 1912); A. J. Kennedy and others, *Social Settlements in New York City* (Columbia University Press, 1935). On the housing problem, see R. W. De Forest and L. T. Veiller, eds., *The Tenement House Problem* (Macmillan, 1903, 2 vols.); E. E. Wood, *The Housing of the Unskilled Wage Earner* (Macmillan, 1919). On child problems, see Homer Folks, *The Care of Destitute, Neglected and Delinquent Children* (Macmillan, 1902); G. B. Mangold, *Problems of Child Welfare* (Macmillan, 1914); H. W. Thurston, *The Dependent Child* (Columbia University Press, 1930); J. P. Murphy and J. H. S. Bossard, eds., *Postwar Progress in Child Welfare* (American Academy of Political and Social Science, *Annals,* Vol. CLI, 1930).

THE TREATMENT OF CRIMINALS. Chaps. viii, x, of H. E. Barnes, *The Story of*

Punishment, Pt. I of *Battling the Crime Wave* (Stratford, 1931), and *The Repression of Crime,* Chap. v; J. L. Gillin, *Taming the Criminal* (Macmillan, 1931); L. N. Robinson, *Penology in the United States* (Winston, 1921); Lenka (Helene von der Leyen) von Koerber, *Soviet Russia Fights Crime* (Dutton, 1935).

MENTAL HYGIENE. Bernard Glueck, article "Mental Hygiene," Encyclopaedia of the Social Sciences; Barnes, *Can Man Be Civilized?* Chaps. III-IV; M. R. Davie, ed., *Social Aspects of Mental Hygiene* (Yale University Press, 1925); E. R. Groves and P. M. Blanchard, *Introduction to Mental Hygiene* (Holt, 1930); W. H. Burnham, *The Wholesome Personality* (Appleton, 1932).

MENTAL DEFICIENCY. The best work on feeble-mindedness is S. P. Davies, *Social Control of the Mentally Deficient* (Crowell, 1930). On mental testing, see Joseph Peterson, *Early Conceptions and Tests of Intelligence* (World Book Co., 1925); C. L. Burt, *Mental and Scholastic Tests* (King, 1922). On sterilization, see J. H. Landman, *Human Sterilization* (Macmillan, 1932).

ATTEMPTS TO ELIMINATE PROSTITUTION. On the attempt by repression, see W. C. Waterman, *Prostitution and Its Repression in New York City, 1900-1931* (Columbia University Press, 1932). For a sane survey of the problem, see W. J. Robinson, *The Oldest Profession in the World* (Eugenics Publishing Co., 1929).

On the companionate marriage, see B. B. Lindsey and Wainwright Evans, *The Companionate Marriage* (Boni & Liveright, 1927). On birth control, see M. H. Sanger, *The Pivot of Civilization* (Brentano's, 1922); D. D. Bromley, *Birth Control: Its Use and Misuse* (Harper, 1934).

PROHIBITION. J. A. Krout, *The Origins of Prohibition* (Knopf, 1925); Chap. IV of P. W. Slosson, *The Great Crusade and After, 1914-1928* (Macmillan, 1930); C. A. Warburton, *The Economic Results of Prohibition* (Columbia University Press, 1932); J. H. Wuorinen, *The Prohibition Experiment in Finland* (Columbia University Press, 1931). On the Anti-Saloon League, see P. H. Odegard, *Pressure Politics: The Story of the Anti-Saloon League* (Columbia University Press, 1928).

CIVILIZED DRINKING. H. E. Barnes, *Prohibition versus Civilization* (Viking Press, 1932); R. C. Binkley, *Responsible Drinking* (Vanguard Press, 1930); Yandell Henderson, *A New Deal in Liquor* (Doubleday, Doran, 1934).

CHAPTER XXV

SOVIET RUSSIA

I. THE SIGNIFICANCE OF SOVIET RUSSIA IN WORLD-HISTORY

We shall conclude our story of the history of civilization in its social and institutional aspects by a consideration of the system of institutions and intellectual attitudes that has developed within Soviet Russia since 1917. The propagandist is concerned about Russia either as an example of every conceivable evil of economics, morals, and politics or as a proof that a Utopia can be and is being brought down from dream to actuality. But the historian should, rather, be objectively interested in Russia as a strikingly novel experiment in the evolution of society. For the transformation in Russia ranks in its far-reaching implications with the transition from tribal to civil society, or with the emergence of capitalism and nationalism during early modern times. With respect to the Russian experiment we stand today much as an enlightened historian in the late seventeenth century stood in regard to nationalism and capitalism. The main interest in Russia is, then, to be found in the fact that it represents, for better or for worse, a vast experiment in the culture and institutions of a new and different era in human society.[1]

Whether one approves of it or not, the Russian Revolution has brought into existence a system of institutions and a social philosophy that repudiate or challenge much of human experience and achievement in the past. Many of its excited apostles exaggerate its virtues and achievements. They overlook the inherent continuity of human culture and the inescapable survival of vestiges of ancient folkways and prejudices. But all this should not obscure the fact that the events in Russia since 1917 have produced what is probably the most rapid, startling, and dramatic transformation in the whole history of the human race. Russia has set up a radically new way of living and thinking within less than two decades.

Supernaturalism is completely denied in the philosophy and beliefs of the party leaders and their followers. Instead the attempt is made to base their social structure upon a rationale derived exclusively from secular science and philosophy. The machine technology and natural science are about all that

[1] *Cf.* K. M. Gould, "Social Factors in Revolution," *American Scholar*, Winter, 1935; Davis, *Contemporary Social Movements*, pp. 221-41; E. A. Ross, *The Russian Bolshevik Revolution*, Century, 1921, and *The Russian Soviet Republic*, Century, 1923; E. W. Hullinger, *The Reforging of Russia*, Dutton, 1925; and L. A. White, "An Anthropological Appraisal of the Russian Revolution," *Open Forum*, May 9, 1931.

Russia has retained in whole-hearted fashion from the old régime of supernaturalism, capitalism, and nationalism.

Individualism has been supplanted by a true State Socialism. Private property and profit have given way before Communism and production for human service. Democracy has been suspended in behalf of temporary dictatorship. Class dominion, whether of landlords or business men, has been superseded by the alleged rule of the masses in behalf of the good of all. Representative government persists, but with grave modifications. The territorial type of representation has been abandoned, in part, in favor of the representation of professions and trades. Further, there are no parties that stand for capitalism or agrarian groups. Parties are, at most, cliques within the proletariat, and any considerable differences of opinion are suppressed or discouraged. The irrational planlessness of ultra-individualistic capitalism has been replaced by careful national planning of the whole economic life. The Russians do not approve nationalism, as it now exists in capitalist countries, but found their system upon the assumed brotherhood of the workers through the world—international Communism. They hope to attain thorough Communism, when the system is perfected, social and economic justice, real democracy, a high degree of freedom and world-peace.

II. THE RUSSIAN REVOLUTION

1. THE BACKGROUND

When Tsar Nicholas II was compelled to abdicate in March, 1917, not many observers were shocked. For many years the Western world had looked upon the tsarist régime as an autocratic despotism that had already outlived its day. The Allies, having made sure that the succeeding government would continue to prosecute the war against the Germans, were undisturbed.

When, however, the November Revolution overturned the Provisional Government and put the Bolsheviks (Communist party) in power, almost the whole world was struck with consternation. This was something different. The powerful agencies for dissemination of propaganda were set to work to attack—to cause internal dissension, to promote civil war, to force Russia to continue the war against Germany. Horror and "atrocity" stories were circulated about the Bolsheviks, as they had been against the Germans.

Civil war, turmoil, blockade followed the Revolution, and the circulation of propaganda against Russia continued. For a few years it was exceedingly difficult to get an objective picture of what had happened and what was happening in Russia.[1] It was even more difficult to get a proper perspective on the broader significance of this great event in the world's history.

Almost two decades have now passed since the Revolution. Facts in abundance are available for those who want facts.[2] And enough time has elapsed to enable us to take stock of the whole situation and begin to see what it all means in the record of Western civilization.

---

[1] *Cf.* Walter Lippmann and Charles Merz, "A Test of the News," *New Republic*, Aug. 4, 1920, Supplement. A similar campaign of propaganda was launched against Russia in the Hearst papers late in 1934.

[2] *Cf.* Walter Duranty, *Duranty Reports Russia*, Viking Press, 1934.

THE RUSSIAN REVOLUTION

That series of changes which we describe as the Russian Revolution were in progress in varying tempo during all the time from 1905 to 1917. They have succeeded in completely revolutionizing the Russia of the tsars.

Compared to the countries of western Europe, in whose footsteps Russia was following, nineteenth-century Russia presented a curious picture. There had been little of the characteristic liberalization of government through middle-class influence by the close of the century. Russia was still an autocracy in the fullest sense. The tsar and the bureaucracy governed. A national representative legislative body was lacking. The chief administrative posts were still in the hands of members of the landed aristocracy. There did exist county and provincial assemblies known as *zemstvos,* which had limited powers with reference to the local administration of public health and education. Similar bodies were to be found in the municipalities, but the decisions of these and of the zemstvos could be vetoed by the provincial governors, who were appointed by the tsar. Despite thoroughgoing reforms in the judicial system, there remained ground for frequent complaints because the peasantry did not come under the jurisdiction of the courts. They were subject to officials called land captains, who also possessed administrative powers. In the case of political offenses the judicial system simply did not have jurisdiction. A police order was sufficient to cause the arrest, imprisonment, and exile of any person regarded as endangering "public order." Such a person had no legal rights or means of defense. Nothing is more representative of the autocracy which then existed than the statement of policy by Nicholas II when he ascended the throne in 1894:

> I am glad to see here the representatives of all the different classes of the country assembled to express to me their submissive and loyal feelings. I believe in the sincerity of those feelings which are inherent in every Russian heart. But it has been brought to My knowledge that during the last months there have been heard in some zemstvos the voices of those who indulged in . . . senseless dreams with respect to the participation of the zemstvos in the general direction of the internal affairs of the State. Let it be known by all that I shall devote my whole power to the best service of the people, but that the principle of autocracy will be maintained by me as firmly and unswervingly as by my lamented father.[1]

Since nearly all measures proposing peaceful reform were met with repression, a radical terroristic movement grew up in Russia during the nineteenth century. The Narod (Towards Freedom) movement in the seventies, which attempted to lift the peasantry from squalor, ignorance, and misery and was marked by courageous self-sacrifice and profound idealism, failed to achieve the results hoped for.[2] At the close of the decade the terroristic acts grew in number and in 1881 Tsar Alexander II was assassinated. During the succeeding reigns of Alexander III and Nicholas II repressive measures were intensified, and the policy of autocratic reaction was elevated into a political philosophy.[3] The school system and all groups or individuals who dissented from orthodoxy, nationalism, and autocracy felt the heavy hand of reaction. Though they super-

---
[1] Cited in J. F. Scott and Alexander Baltzly, *Readings in European History since 1814,* Crofts, 1930, p. 343.
[2] *Cf.* M. N. Pokrovsky, *Brief History of Russia,* International Publishers, 1933, 2 vols., Vol. I, pp. 162-99.
[3] This was largely the work of Pobiedonostsev.

ficially appeared to be suppressed, the opposition movements could not be annihilated. They went on smoldering beneath the surface.

The reforms of Tsar Alexander II in the sixties had by no means eliminated discontent among the peasantry.[1] As a matter of fact, the peasant could be said to have simply changed his condition of dependence. He became a serf of the state rather than of a private landlord. Though they made up the bulk of the population, the peasants had a special status until 1906. They were subject to the regulations of the *mir* (village community), they could only move about with the permission of the mir, and the soil upon which they worked was regarded not as their private property but as part of a collective estate. Though the peasantry made up over 80 per cent of the population, they held but 353,-000,000 acres in the seventies as compared to the 200,000,000 acres in the hands of the nobility, who constituted less than 2 per cent of the population. In 1905 peasant holdings had increased to over 400,000,000 acres, and the nobility held 135,000,000.

Of privileges the peasantry knew little. The privileged groups included the landed nobility, members of the bureaucracy and army, and ecclesiastics of the Orthodox Catholic or Greek Church. The Greek Church, holding vast estates and enjoying a large annual revenue, was favored over all other religious denominations, and was one of the chief props of the autocratic régime. The burden of supporting the Church fell upon the masses. Other religious groups, especially nonconformist Catholics, suffered occasional persecutions. The Jews, who lived under special regulations, experienced severe and unwarranted persecution time and again.

Whereas in the western European countries the middle class rose to political dominance in the course of the eighteenth and nineteenth centuries, in Russia the government was still conducted in the interests of the large landowners. The slowness of Russia to industrialize checked the growth of a numerous middle class. Small as it was, however, it was vital and dynamic. The delayed expansion of the middle class also meant that there was a relatively small factory proletariat. As late as 1914 only 16 per cent of the population of Russia was urban. As had been the case in England and France, the interests of the middle class were opposed to those of the landlord. Its members, enjoying no political strength as yet, were eager to secure the same changes in the government that the bourgeoisie had earlier won in Western countries. The movement for "liberal" reform, in other words, was simply postponed in Russia. The great industrialists, financiers, and merchants of course exercised a definite influence, but it was not until after 1905 that the middle class as a whole secured any appreciable measure of political power.

Though the middle class was united with the workers as well as with the peasants against the landlords and autocracy, there was in most other respects a division of interest between the middle class and the proletariat. On a smaller quantitative scale the consequences of the Industrial Revolution experienced in other countries were likewise felt in Russia. This meant an alignment of bourgeoisie against proletariat. The liberal reforms demanded by the middle class in no sense involved such a modification of capitalism as would have

---

[1] See above, p. 338.

materially improved the economic condition of the workers or led to complete political and industrial democracy.

No more striking description of the condition and desires, not only of the working classes but of the Russian masses as a whole, can be found than in the moving words of a petition presented to the Tsar by a priest in 1905. It reads in part:

SIRE,—We, working men and inhabitants of St. Petersburg of various classes, our wives and our children and our helpless old parents, come to Thee, Sire, to seek for truth and defence. We have become beggars; we have been oppressed; we are burdened by toil beyond our powers; we are scoffed at; we are not recognized as human beings; we are treated as slaves who must suffer their bitter fate and who must keep silence. We suffered, but we are pushed farther into the den of beggary, lawlessness, and ignorance. We are choked by despotism and irresponsibility, and we are breathless. We have no more power, Sire, the limit of patience has been reached. There has arrived for us that tremendous moment when death is better than the continuation of intolerable tortures. . . . We beg but little; we desire only that without which life is not life, but hard labour and eternal torture. The first request which we made was that our masters should discuss our needs with us; but this they refused, on the ground that no right to make this request is recognized by law. They also declared to be illegal our requests to diminish the working hours to eight hours daily, to agree with us about the prices for our work, to consider our misunderstandings with the inferior administration of the mills, to increase the wages for the labour of women and of general labourers, so that the minimum daily wage should be one ruble per day, to abolish overtime work, to give us medical attention without insulting us, to arrange the workshops so that it might be possible to work there, and not find in them death from awful draughts and from rain and snow. All these requests appeared to be, in the opinion of our masters and of the factory and mill administrations, illegal. Every one of our requests was a crime, and the desire to improve our condition was regarded by them as impertinence, and as offensive to them.

Sire, here are many thousands of us, and all are human beings only in appearance. In reality in us, as in all Russian people, there is not recognized any human right, not even the right of speaking, thinking, meeting, discussing our needs, taking measures for the improvement of our condition. We have been enslaved, and enslaved under the auspices of Thy officials, with their assistance, and with their cooperation. Every one of us who dares to raise a voice in defence of working-class and popular interests is thrown into jail or is sent into banishment. For the possession of good hearts and sensitive souls we are punished as for crimes. . . . The people are deprived of the possibility of expressing their desires, and they now demand that they be allowed to take part in the introduction of taxes and in the expenditure of them.

The working men are deprived of the possibility of organizing themselves in unions for the defence of their interests. . . .

Russia is too great. Its necessities are too various and numerous for officials alone to rule it. National representation is indispensable. It is indispensable that the people should assist and should rule themselves. To them only are known their real necessities. Do not reject their assistance, accept it, order immediately the convocation of representatives of the Russian land from all ranks, including representatives from the working men. . . . Let everyone be equal and free in the right of election, and for this purpose order that the elections for the Constitutional Assembly be carried on under the condition of universal, equal, and secret voting. This is the most capital of our requests. . . . Yet one measure alone cannot heal our wounds. Other measures are also indispensable. Directly and openly as to a Father, we speak to Thee, Sire, about them in person, for all the toiling classes of Russia. The following are indispensable:

I. Measures against the ignorance and rightlessness of the Russian people:
1. The immediate release and return of all who have suffered for political and religious convictions, for strikes, and national peasant disorders.
2. The immediate declaration of freedom and of the inviolability of the person—freedom of speech and press, freedom of meetings, and freedom of conscience in religion.
3. Universal and compulsory elementary education of the people at the charge of the State.
4. Responsibility of the Ministers before the people and guarantee that the Government will be law-abiding.
5. Equality before the law of all without exception.
6. Separation of the Church from the State.

II. Measures against the poverty of the people:
1. Abolition of indirect taxes and the substitution of a progressive income tax.
2. Abolition of the Redemption Instalments, cheap credit, and gradual transference of the land to the people.
3. The orders for the military and naval ministries should be fulfilled in Russia, and not abroad.
4. The cessation of the war by the will of the people.

III. Measures against the oppression of labour:
1. Abolition of the factory inspectorships.
2. Institution at factories and mills of permanent committees of elected workers, which, together with the administration (of the factories) would consider the complaints of individual workers. Discharge of working men should not take place otherwise than by resolution of this committee.
3. Freedom of organization of co-operative societies of consumers and of labour trade unions immediately.
4. Eight-hours working day and regulation of overtime working.
5. Freedom of the struggle of labour against capital immediately.
6. Normal wages immediately.
7. Participation of working-class representatives in the working out of projects of law upon workmen's State insurance immediately.[1]

Only the blind could have failed to see the revolution in the offing.[2]

2. THE PRELIMINARY REVOLUTION OF 1905

The first phase of the active Russian Revolution is to be dated from 1905. The unpopularity of the imperialistic war with Japan and the overwhelming defeats suffered by Russian armies and navy set the stage for the open manifestation of the discontent that had been smoldering for many years in the

---

[1] Cited in Scott and Baltzly, *op. cit.,* pp. 344-46. This was the petition of Father Gapon, presented January 9, 1905, by a procession of workers which, without provocation, was fired upon by the police. The incident is known as Bloody Sunday. See below, p. 985.

[2] This Russian protest may fruitfully be compared with the protests (*cahiers*) before the French Revolution.

hearts and minds of Russian workers, peasants, professionals, and intellectuals. Throughout Russia in 1905 people found the courage to protest openly in strikes, peasant disturbances, mobilization riots, street meetings, and political demonstrations. Despite the repressive police measures and the fact that many of their leaders were outside of Russia, the different revolutionary organizations were very active.

The groups—which were quasi-secret and did not become true political parties until after 1905—were the Constitutional Democratic party (called the Cadets), composed of middle-class intellectual liberals, which demanded a parliamentary system; the Socialist Revolutionary party, essentially agrarian and concerned chiefly with land reform; and the Socialist Democratic party, Marxian in doctrine but split into two groups [1]—(1) the Revisionist *Mensheviki*, which means minority group, led by Plekhanov; and (2) the Marxian *Bolsheviki*, which means majority group, led by Lenin. The former favored working with the liberals, while the latter, complete revolutionaries, were for war to the end against capitalism.

Early in 1905, a peaceful parade of workers bearing a petition to the Tsar and led by a priest was fired upon by the soldiers seemingly without cause.[2] As a result, throughout Russia the working class swung to the revolutionary groups.

The situation was so critical that the government was faced with the necessity of either granting temporary and strategic reforms or being swept out of existence. A council of deputies (a soviet) was formed in St. Petersburg, strikes occurred throughout the country, the army was spotted with mutinies, acts of terrorism multiplied, and uprisings of peasants occurred throughout the land. It was impossible to continue the war with Japan.

On August 19, 1905, the Tsar issued a manifesto that granted a constitution and provided for a consultative legislative body. But further concessions were imperative, and on October 30 another manifesto was issued. This promised the classic civil liberties of person, speech, and organization which had been attained in many other countries, a more or less democratic electoral law, and the enactment of legislation by representative bodies.

The changes thus brought about constituted in a sense a liberal revolution. The parliamentary body organized was bicameral, consisting of a lower chamber, the Imperial Duma, and an upper chamber, the Imperial Council. Half the members of the latter were appointed by the Tsar and half elected by provincial assemblies, municipalities, lower nobility, and others. Members of the Duma were elected by nearly universal, though unequal, male suffrage. Educational, legal, land, and labor reforms, some of small moment, some of note, were carried through between 1905 and the opening of the World War, thus continuing the liberalization of Russia.

Dissatisfaction, however, remained very prevalent: 1. The revolutionaries and liberals alike distrusted the government. 2. The Tsar still controlled the cabinet, responsible only to him, the Imperial Council, and military and foreign affairs. 3. The Duma struggled with the cabinet, precipitating a crisis in 1906-07. 4. Changes were made in the electoral law in 1907 which gave the middle class

---

[1] After 1903.
[2] This is the Bloody Sunday episode described above, p. 983-84.

and landowners disproportionate strength. 5. Conditions among the workers were bad; the hours were long and wages were low. 6. The peasantry was still desirous of land reform. Despite the economic expansion that occurred during these years (1905-14) [1] and the statesmanlike labors of Stolypin, who was Prime Minister, the conditions making for social revolution were not eliminated. Had Stolypin not been removed from the scene by assassination in 1911, the subsequent history of Russia might have been different, for he was prepared to concede at least some of the reforms that were necessary.

Just as the Crimean War made possible the Emancipation edicts that followed, and the Russo-Japanese conflict the changes of 1905, so the World War opened the way for the "March" Revolution of 1917 (the February Revolution according to the O.S. Russian calendar), which completed the liberal stage of the Russian Revolution, and then the "November" Revolution (October according to the Russian calendar), which meant the introduction of Communism.

3. THE FUNDAMENTAL REVOLUTION OF 1917

The shock and strain of the World War was too great for the old order in Russia to bear, either economically or politically, though the people at first gave loyal support to the government. Every political group, with the exception of the Bolsheviks, had declared themselves in favor of the war in 1914.

When Russia entered the war in the summer of 1914 its leaders expected a short and gloriously successful conflict. The odds against Germany and Austria seemed overwhelming. Russia was unprepared, however, for a long war in any respect save that of man power. Its armies were badly led and they suffered defeat after defeat and great losses. Hindenburg all but annihilated its largest and best armies. However, there were also successful campaigns, and by the spring of 1917 Russia had improved its position in a purely military sense over that of 1915. But the situation was more ominous behind the lines than it was at the front. The nobility and even the court itself were honeycombed with treason. The financial demands of the war led to a critical condition of the Treasury and the issue of additional paper money. Such inflation, together with tremendous demand for goods caused by war needs, sent prices skyrocketing. The mobilization of 15,000,000 men withdrew much-needed man power from fields and factories, and the task of supplying them and supporting their families could not be carried through. The inadequacy of the railroad system under war conditions made it impossible to ship on time the men, supplies, and food to the destinations where they were most needed. Supplying the army with food led to a shortage of food in the countryside and cities. The result of the increased cost of living and food-rationing in the cities was strikes by factory workers.

Disregarding such dangerous conditions, the authorities failed to make those political readjustments which might have lessened the criticism which was directed against those in power. The Tsar was even opposed to the formation of voluntary organizations and committees to aid in the prosecution of the war, because he saw that these were aligned with the Duma, which he regarded as his enemy. There was no attempt at conciliation though the adoption of a

---

[1] See above, p. 338 ff.

more liberal policy, and the Duma came into open conflict with the Tsar on the question of a responsible cabinet. The Tsar refused to give way on this, but he found it necessary to change his ministers constantly because of the pressure of the Duma. The political leaders of the Duma mistrusted the Tsar, who was under the influence of the Tsarina, who, in turn, was but the tool of the enigmatic and hypnotic monk, Gregor Rasputin, a Siberian peasant. The Duma suspected, without adequate basis, that the imperial family contemplated peace with Germany. Aware that something had to be done to break the impasse, political leaders of all shades considered plan after plan. The result of one of these was the assassination of Rasputin by Prince Yussupov, the husband of the Tsar's niece, on December 30, 1916. A palace revolution was also being planned. But before it could be carried through, stronger forces intervened and made it an impossibility.

All classes, ominously discontented, were weary of the war. The army, suffering large-scale desertions, was shot through with a spirit of mutiny. The countryside witnessed peasant riots and the cities had their food disturbances in 1917. In Petrograd (as St. Petersburg was renamed in 1914, to become Leningrad in 1924) a general strike of factory workers was called in February, 1917. Nicholas did nothing; unrest and disturbances grew apace. Finally on March 11 he prorogued the Duma and ordered the strikers to return to work. But it was too late. The soldiers called in to create order mutinied and fraternized with the workers. On the twelfth, practically the entire Petrograd garrison mutinied. The Duma simply refused to pack up and go home. Coöperating with the Socialists, who had organized a Petrograd Soviet of Workers' and Soldiers' Deputies, it formed a Provisional Government headed by Prince Lvov. Its cabinet, composed chiefly of liberals, included monarchists as well as a stanch Social Revolutionary in the person of Alexander Kerensky. The Tsar, on his way to his palace at Tsarskoe Selo, was informed of the developments by two representatives of the Duma who requested his abdication. On March 15, he abdicated in favor of his brother, Grand Duke Michael, appointed Prince Lvov head of the new cabinet, and was then taken to Tsarskoe Selo, a virtual prisoner. The Grand Duke refused the crown, and tsardom in Russia became a thing of the past. The March Revolution was an accomplished fact.

The new government upon its organization issued a series of decrees that granted amnesty to political and religious prisoners and the usual Western civil liberties. It abolished all class distinctions, promised the convocation of a constituent assembly to decide upon a constitution and the form of government, and ordered the introduction of universal suffrage. Under pressure from the soviets it was forced to agree not to send the troops that had taken part in the revolution to the front. It also announced to the world that Russia would continue to prosecute the war and would "remain mindful of the international engagements entered into by the fallen régime." Together with the support offered to it by most of the civil and military officials throughout Russia, there came the rapid recognition of the Provisional Government, first by the United States and in turn by the Allied countries.

The new government, however, was destined to have a short life. Composed essentially of "liberals" of different shades, its temporary union with the Petrograd Soviet, which had been organized by Socialists, was bound to end in conflict. The liberals wanted energetic prosecution of the war and feared that the Socialists would desire immediate peace. The Socialists, on the other hand, accepting Marxian reasoning, were sure that the liberal revolution would promptly turn reactionary and introduce a dictatorship. They wished to prevent the creation of a strong central government. They desired, moreover, a thorough reconstruction of property-holding.

Almost from the very beginning, the Provisional Government lacked real strength. On March 14 the Petrograd Soviet had independently ordered the army and navy not to obey any of the government's commands unless they were sanctioned by itself. Soldiers' and sailors' soviets were established, and the army officers were stripped of all power. Rapidly the soviets multiplied throughout Russia, and Socialist propaganda was spread widely. Revolutionary leaders, including Lenin and Trotsky—Lenin came from Switzerland via Germany, and Trotsky from the United States via England—Lunacharsky, Kamenev, Krylenko, and Radek, arrived in Petrograd in April. The swing to Socialism continued apace. One by one, the bourgeois members of the Provisional Government were forced out and replaced by Socialists. By July, Kerensky was head of the government and Minister of War. He contemplated the democratization of the army and a general Russian military offensive the success of which would strengthen the government. The offensive, however, was turned into a rout of the Russian forces.

The strength of the soviets was meanwhile demonstrated by the convocation of the first All-Russian Congress of Soviets in Petrograd in June. The majority of the members, who numbered not far from 1,000, were Social Revolutionaries. The next largest group was composed of Mensheviks, while the Bolsheviks were in the minority. The Congress fully revealed through its speakers its opposition to the war. It elected an All-Russian Central Executive Committee of about 300 members. It was to function as a soviet parliament under the control of a presidium of about twenty men, who were, in the main, Mensheviks and Social Revolutionaries. Through the army soviets the Central Executive Committee could also exert considerable strength in the military department.

In the meantime, the Bolsheviks were extremely active both within Russia and along the front, where disgruntled troops could be easily converted. Taking advantage of a government crisis, the Bolsheviks carried on huge demonstrations of armed workers in Petrograd in which sailors from the Kronstadt fleet joined. But the premature uprising was suppressed and the leaders were either imprisoned or forced into hiding. The Bolsheviks were checked for the moment, and the cabinet headed by Kerensky seemed to be gaining force. Another danger faced Kerensky in General Kornilov, whom he had appointed commander in chief of the army. In the complicated game that was played before the Kornilov revolt collapsed in September, it appears that the able general may have contemplated the establishment of a military dictatorship. Kerensky, who tried to keep to the middle of the road between the Bolsheviks and the right-wing forces, and to solidify his own position, was apparently attempting to play off Kornilov and the soviets against each other. In the end the Kornilov rebellion strengthened the Bolsheviks. Kerensky had called upon their well-organized Red Guards for support against Kornilov, and they then capitalized the alleged attempt of Kerensky to destroy the soviets.

Added to the political difficulties was the fact that the army was daily disintegrating and the economic life of Russia was on the verge of complete collapse. Agriculture, industry, trade, transportation, and finance were all suffering serious dislocation. Industry was approaching complete paralysis. The transportation system had practically broken down. Prices were sky-high. Agricultural production was seriously curtailed, and the peasants in many regions were dividing land without waiting for legal measures. Kerensky's attempted solution of the economic problems produced nothing but heated discussion of measures that might be taken. The immediate action necessary was not forthcoming.

The Bolsheviks utilized the economic crisis to the utmost. In October the Petrograd Soviet was controlled by them, with Trotsky as its chairman. Bolshevik "cells" (local groups) were organized among workers and soldiers. Lenin, who was directing Bolshevik propaganda and tactics from Finland,[1] proposed a comprehensive plan of action that included immediate peace, land redistribution, workers' control of industry, nationalization of banks, and a system of food-rationing that had a strong appeal to soldiers and proletariat.

Late in October, the Bolsheviks decided upon an armed uprising. Orders were issued to the Petrograd garrison to obey only those commands sanctioned by the Military Revolutionary Committee of the Petrograd Soviet. Kerensky, incomprehensibly, did nothing. On November 6-7, the coup d'état came, the Bolsheviks controlled Petrograd, Kerensky fled, and the Provisional Government collapsed. On the seventh there convened the second All-Russian Congress of Soviets. This time the Bolsheviks were in control. The congress proclaimed itself supreme in the country, chose a new Central Executive Committee of Bolshevik membership, and appointed a Soviet of People's Commissars, which was to act as a cabinet.[2]

The program contemplated by the new government entailed: (1) Immediate peace; (2) suppression of counter-revolution and opposition groups within Russia; (3) the reconstruction of the economic, social, and political life of Russia; (4) the establishment of a "dictatorship of the proletariat which was to execute the above reconstruction and prepare the people for Communism"; and (5) the spreading of the proletarian revolution throughout the world.

At the close of November, elections for delegates to the Constituent Assembly were held, but the Social Revolutionaries were the dominant group. The Bolsheviks could only postpone the day of its meeting and meanwhile consolidate their strength. The assembly finally convened on January 18, 1918, and when it voted down a resolution to recognize the authority of the Bolshevik government it was dissolved by force. The November Revolution was thus established in fact. Within a little more than three months, the few non-Bolshevik mem-

---

[1] He fled there after the failure of the July uprising, to which he was opposed.
[2] Lenin was president of the Soviet of People's Commissars; Trotsky was Commissar for Foreign Affairs; Stalin was Commissar for Nationalities; Rykov, Commissar of the Interior.

bers of the Soviet of People's Commissars withdrew, and about the same time the Bolsheviks took the name of the Communist party.

4. CIVIL WAR, INTERVENTION, BLOCKADE

The new régime brought into being by the November Revolution was faced from the very beginning with civil war, and after the acceptance of the harsh terms of the Treaty of Brest-Litovsk with Germany (March 3, 1918), with foreign intervention and blockade. Opposition within the country came from those who supported the old régime, those who favored war and the program of the Kerensky government, those who stood to lose in property or position, and the nationalistic groups who demanded independence from Russia. The Allied countries and the United States, sharply antagonistic to the new régime, refused recognition. At first, they tried to induce individual generals to keep the armies in the field against Germany. After Brest-Litovsk, they brought the pressure of blockade to bear against Russia and gave full support to the various counter-revolutionary "White" armies in the field, sending them food, money, and supplies. They did even more to break the Bolsheviks. Two bodies of United States troops were stationed in Russia, a French fleet was sent to the Black Sea, English soldiers were dispatched to Murmansk, the Japanese penetrated into Siberia. By the middle of 1918, the position of the Russian Communists was critical.

Into the succession of wars and counter-revolutionary movements it is not necessary to enter.[1] It is sufficient to note that through several external factors—the lack of coöperation of the Whites, the organization and successful direction of the Red Army by Trotsky, and the adoption of a policy of political terror—the opposition groups were either crushed or they collapsed of themselves. By November, 1920, central Russia was fully under control of the Communists. The last of the White generals, Wrangel, fled the country, and Russia was at peace. One important reason why the Bolsheviks were able to succeed between 1917 and 1920 was the presence of a well-developed coöperative movement in Russia. The Soviet government was able to make good use of these coöperatives before it had perfected its own brand of collectivism.

In themselves, the events of November meant only transfer of power to the Communists. This in itself was not Socialism. A new social order had to be built, a new way of life had to be introduced. For this the leaders had as their equipment a burning idealism, a grim determination, and an unshakable faith in the doctrines of Marx. To make possible the introduction of Socialism new ideals would have to replace the old, a new political structure would have to be evolved, agriculture would have to be socialized, the country would have to be industrialized, the whole economic life of the nation would have to be carefully planned, and the "glorious doctrines of Socialism" would have to be made part and parcel of the mind of the masses.

Let us turn first to the changes made in the field of politics and government.

[1] See Stewart, *The White Armies of Russia*.

III. THE POLITICAL STRUCTURE OF THE U.S.S.R.

It was in central Russia about Moscow that the Communists were most strongly intrenched during the period of the civil war and the revolution. It was from this nucleus that there grew up the Russian Socialist Federative Soviet Republic—the R.S.F.S.R. This expanded until in 1923 it was made up of a vast federation of eleven autonomous republics and thirteen autonomous areas. Altogether, it constitutes 92 per cent of the area of the Union of Soviet Socialist Republics—the U.S.S.R.—and has about 70 per cent of the population. It is Soviet Russia proper, and is that part of the Union which is most important in both economics and politics. The U.S.S.R. as a whole is made up of the R.S.F.S.R. and six other constituent republics, the White-Russian, the Ukrainian, the Transcaucasian, the Turcoman, the Uzbek, and the Tadzhik. The following table indicates the distribution of territory and population among the

Constituent Republics	Area (in square kilometers)	Population, 1926
Russian S.F.S.R.	19,757,953	100,858,000
White Russian S.S.R.	126,792	4,983,900
Ukrainian S.S.R.	451,731	29,020,300
Transcaucasian S.F.S.R.	184,492	5,850,700
Turcoman S.S.R.	491,216	1,030,500
Uzbek S.S.R.	240,388	4,447,600
Tadzhik S.S.R.	100,000	822,600
U.S.S.R., Total	21,352,572	147,013,600 [1]

constituent republics of the U.S.S.R. The relationship of the various political units of the Soviet Union was established by the treaty of July 6, 1923, and this in turn made possible the promulgation of the constitution of the U.S.S.R. The diagram on page 992 illustrates its present federal structure.

The basic elements in the political structure [2] are the soviets (councils of deputies) of which there are three types, village, urban, and factory. Any village of over 300 population may have a soviet and every 100 people elect one deputy. The term of office in the village soviets is limited to one year, and these bodies meet twice a week. Voting is limited to the poorer peasants. The richer peasants (kulaks)—and, of course, members of the bourgeoisie and private traders—have no vote, and as a result lose all civil, economic, and educational privileges. The power of real local self-government in the village soviet is very slight. It possesses only police and administrative authority.[3]

Since 1925 all towns and factories have possessed soviets. Voting for these is

---

[1] The official estimate of the total population in 1934 was 168,000,000.
[2] The reader will keep in mind that the political system here described is that which exists at present and that the many changes which have occurred since the twenties—except where they are of the greatest importance—have not been described. It must be remembered that the present structure has not existed unchanged since 1918.
[3] In well-collectivized regions, the state administration of the collective farms (*kolkhozi*) for a time pushed the village soviets into the background, but this tendency has since been checked.

also restricted to workers.[1] The urban soviets also have special executive bodies (*presidiums*). Besides being political bodies, these urban soviets fulfill all the functions of municipal administration, which is their major preoccupation today. Important steps in liberalizing the elective system of Soviet Russia were taken by the Seventh Congress of Soviets on February 6, 1935. These provide

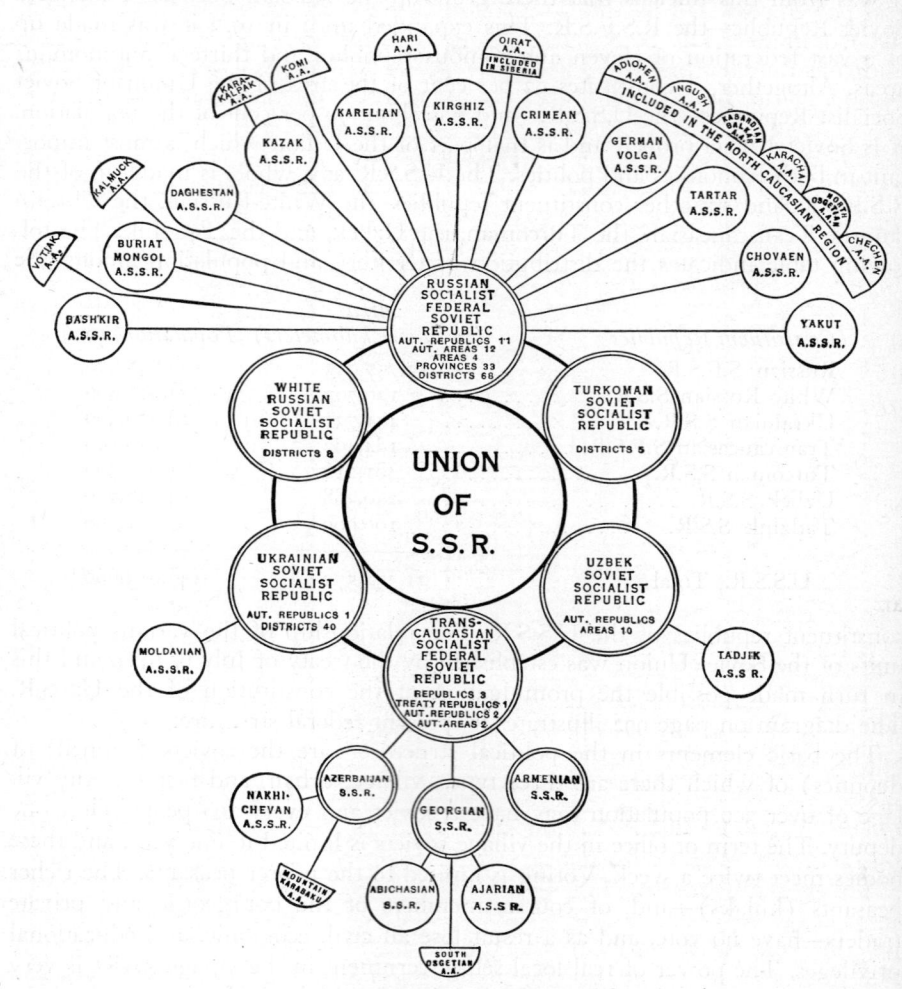

POLITICAL STRUCTURE OF THE U.S.S.R.

for the substitution of direct for indirect elections; equal representation of city and agricultural workers; and the adoption of the secret ballot.

As organs of local administration there are today the Regional Congresses of Soviets and the Territorial Congresses of Soviets, each of which possesses its own Executive Committee and Presidium. The local soviets elect the members

---

[1] The term "workers" in Russia includes both hand and brain workers.
[2] Reproduced by permission from *The Soviet Union*, Soviet Information Bureau, p. 23.

of these congresses. The political organization of the Federal Republic and of autonomous Republics are almost identical. The theoretical supreme authority in the Republic is the Congress of Soviets, the members of which are elected from the soviets and the lesser congresses. Actually the Congress of Soviets is run by and is dependent upon its own Central Executive Committee. The only real power possessed by the Congress of Soviets is the election of this Executive Committee. This body considers questions of legislation, local government, and constitutional problems. It meets three or four times a year. When not in session, its functions reside in its Presidium, whose members range from ten to

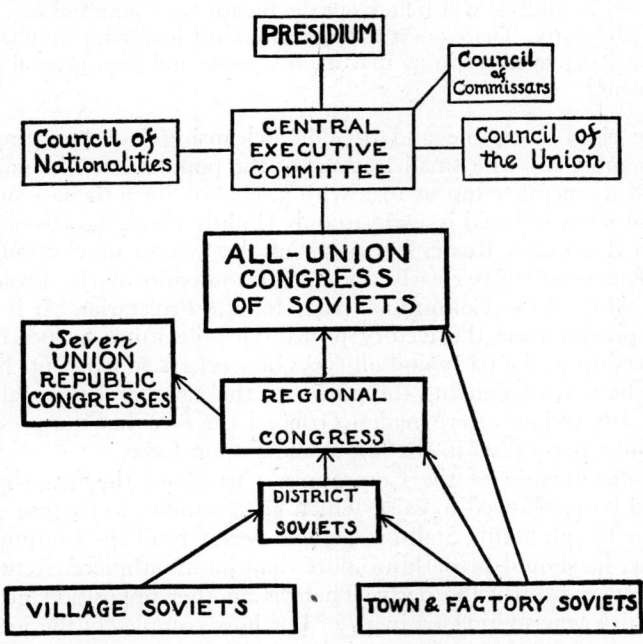

THE SOVIET ELECTORAL AND POLITICAL SYSTEM [1]

twenty. It is really the Presidium—together with the Council of People's Commissars—that runs the Republic.[2]

This system in the R.S.F.S.R. is duplicated for the Soviet Union as a whole. Here at the top of the structure there is the Union Congress of Soviets, ostensibly the supreme authority of the U.S.S.R., but actually not so. The Central Executive Committee of the Union consists of two chambers—the Council of the Union and the Council of Nationalities. The Central Executive Committee also has its Presidium, which with the Union Council of People's Commissars constitutes the real government of the U.S.S.R. The last-named Council of Commissars resembles a cabinet, and there are Commissars of Foreign Affairs, Armed Forces, Foreign Trade, Labor, Communication, and the like.

[1] Vera Micheles Dean, *Soviet Russia, 1917-1933,* Foreign Policy Association, 1933, p. 11.
[2] For another clear diagram of the structure of the government of the R.S.F.S.R. and the U.S.S.R., see also Langsam, *The World since 1914,* p. 501.

The elaborate constitutional structure here briefly sketched is in reality but the screen for the real governing agency of Russia, the Communist party. This, in turn, has an elaborate organization of its own.[1] This domination of the Communist party in Russia is denied by no responsible person today. While the Communist party at first operated behind the scenes, it has within recent years more and more frankly admitted its dictation of the Russian government. Stalin has bluntly asserted this in saying:

> To all responsible positions in the Government the Communist Party tries to nominate its candidates, and in 95 out of 100 cases those candidates are elected. Naturally, these candidates will follow out the theories of Communism . . . and the directions of the Party. Therefore a direct Communist leadership results. . . . Here in Russia the Party openly admits that it does guide and give general direction to the Government.[2]

Extremely rigid discipline and periodic "cleansings" or "purgings" restrict the party membership to a small fraction of the population. The party reached the height of its membership in 1932 with 3,500,000. Since then, a sweeping-out of undesirables has reduced it again to only slightly above 3,000,000. This small membership dominates Russia by virtue of the system of elections. What is present in Russia today is clearly not the Dictatorship of the Proletariat, but "the Dictatorship of the Communist party for the Proletariat." It is interesting that at the present time the factory proletariat constitutes 45 per cent of the total membership of the party and all types of workers 70 per cent. No pretense is made in the way of denying the power of the party and the reality of class rule. Nor is any serious effort made to conceal the fact that the present rule of the Communist party rests in the last analysis upon force.

It is this dictatorship of the Communist party, and the fact that it is the only political party allowed to exist, which gives validity to the use of the term "dictator" for Joseph Stalin. Stalin is General Secretary of the Communist party. Theoretically, he should be nothing more than its mouthpiece. Actually, Stalin and his followers control the party. There is another opposition group within its ranks, which was suppressed in 1930. But how completely the job was done cannot be determined. It is safe to say that Stalin at present enjoys tremendous influence and power, and that the use of the term "dictator" is warranted.

From the viewpoint of Communist ideology there is complete justification and necessity for the present dictatorship:

> In a bourgeois or Capitalist State any unconstitutional power acting behind the scenes and camouflaging its activities behind a constitutional screen, is conscious of a breach with established traditions and political ethics. This is not so with the Communist Party. In theory it reserves [to] itself a definite task—the transformation of human society from its present state to one of which the prophets of Communism speaks [sic] as the "earthly paradise." This task can only be accomplished through a dictatorship, and such a regime thus temporarily becomes, in Communist theory and practise, the only legal, ethical, moral and justifiable form of government. How long this will last, the Communists do not know; and much difference of opinion

---

[1] For a splendid diagram of Communist party structure, see Jerome Davis, ed., *The New Russia*, Day, 1933, pp. 122-23. For an elaborate chart of Russian political organization and of the structure of the Communist party, see Achorn, *European Civilization and Politics since 1815*, p. 520.
[2] Cited in Davis, *op. cit.*, p. 115.

exists among their leaders on the subject. Some believe in "Socialism in our time"; others [for example, Trotsky] maintain that such will not come about until the World Revolution takes place; others [for example, Stalin], again, believe that "Socialism in one State" can be achieved. Some speak of a single generation, and others of generations. But no orthodox Communist has ever assumed that the dictatorship will last permanently.[1]

Among the organs of government not yet mentioned, the O.G.P.U.—an abbreviation of the name that means United States Political Department—stood very high until recently.[2] In existence since 1917, this political police force was designed to operate against every type of counter-revolutionary activity, that is, anything and everything which might be considered inimical to the interests of the Communist state and party. To it fell the task of executing the political terror designed to make secure the gains of the revolution. The most efficient organization of its type the world has ever known, it was admitted by observers sympathetic with Russia to cover Russia with a network of its agents and to possess extraordinary powers of administration, justice, and punishment. It was frequently spoken of as the most powerful single governmental organ. It far surpassed in efficiency the old espionage and secret-police system of the tsars.[3]

At the head of the present judicial system, which is based upon a conception of law utterly opposed to the legal doctrines in existence elsewhere, there stands the Supreme Court of the U.S.S.R. It is broken up into a number of sections, whose broad powers involve "watching over legality within the confines of the Union." The other courts in the judicial system include the People's Courts, divided into Regional and Town, the Territorial Courts, and the High Courts of the Federal and Autonomous Republics, all having varying powers. Soviet justice is consciously and admittedly class justice. The judges are not limited by the written law when passing judgment and there are no "formal legal guarantees in law proceedings." It may be noted that while judicial proceedings are usually public, many trials are wholly secret. The framework of legal regulation is established by a set of codes. There is a civil code, a criminal code, a land code, a labor code, and codes of civil and criminal procedure. The conception and the categories of crime have undergone a transformation compatible with the new class character of Russian jurisprudence. Profiteering, for example, is regarded as a more serious offense than the ordinary murder.

There are many interesting differences between the Russian government of today and that of a capitalist republic. In the latter, parties tend to be representatives of different interests—capitalistic, agricultural, and proletarian. In Russia nobody has any official recognition except as a member of the working classes. In the United States capitalism dominates; in Russia it is outlawed. Representation in capitalist countries is generally founded almost solely upon territorial units. In Russia, while territorial facts have to be recognized in part, there is a general tendency towards the representation of various trades, vocations, or

[1] P. N. Malevsky-Malevich, ed., *Russia, U.S.S.R.; a Complete Handbook*, Payson, 1933, p. 222.
[2] *Cf.* Theodor Seibert, *Red Russia*, Century, 1932, Chap. XVI.
[3] The O.G.P.U. was formally abolished by a decree of July 10, 1934, and the secret service lodged in the Commissariat for Internal Affairs. This was done in order better to control arbitrary action by members of the secret service. Political crimes formerly handled by the judicial collegium of the O.G.P.U. have been transferred to the regular courts.

professions. In France, England, and the United States we have the forms, at least, of a democratic system. In Russia there is, for the time being, a frank dictatorship in the alleged interest of the mass of the Russian people. The dictatorship has, however, been somewhat mitigated in the last two years.

Much criticism has been launched in Russia against capitalist governments for the lack of freedom they accord to the lower classes, and for the gross favoritism shown to dominant sections of the bourgeoisie. But Russia is far more intolerant towards capitalists than is the United States, for example, towards the working class. There is far less personal freedom in Russia. Civil liberties, as they are understood in most capitalist democracies, are practically suspended.[1]

The Russians defend this situation on the ground that the repression of civil liberties is necessary during the transitional period of storm and stress and of danger from foreign attack. They contend that when technological progress has been completed and the danger of foreign onslaughts has diminished, more liberty will be possible. The Russians further allege that the formal civil liberties of capitalist countries are of little practical significance so long as the workers are in constant danger of starvation. They contend that if Russia curtails the abstract personal liberty of its citizens, it at least assumes the practical responsibility of making it possible for them to eat and live.

The Russian government also differs markedly from others in its attitude towards nationalism. This it repudiates, root and branch, and calls for world-union—not a union based on international capitalism but one of the "workers of the world." Russia has vigorously attacked—perhaps more in theory than in fact—imperialism and colonialism, and has proposed literal international disarmament, thus giving at least logical lip service to its international pretensions. The threat of foreign attack, pride in the achievements of Soviet Russia to date, the relative failure of the world-revolution hoped for in 1917 and immediately thereafter, and the resulting necessity of centering Communist activity upon Russia, have, however, all worked to prevent nationalism and patriotism from actually disappearing in the new Russia.[2]

The Soviet government has, as we just noted, condemned imperialism and colonialism. It surrendered its control over that part of Persia which had been awarded to Russia as a sphere of influence in the partition of 1907. But Soviet Russia has shown no inclination supinely to permit encroachments upon its territory. It has dealt firmly with the Japanese threat in the Far East. Yet it has not been bellicose. Had it been so, the Japanese policy in Manchuria since 1931 would have afforded many ample pretexts for a declaration of war by Russia. This Russian abandonment of imperialism is based partly upon idealism and partly upon sound sense. The leaders of Russia know full well that the task of rebuilding their own country will require all their energies and resources, and they realize that a foreign war might be as disastrous as the Russo-Japanese War was to tsarist Russia. The necessity of keeping strong forces in the Far East since 1931 has been mainly responsible for such slowing of the tempo in internal reconstruction as has actually taken place.

[1] *Cf.* W. H. Chamberlin, *Soviet Russia*, Little, Brown, 1930, Chap. XVIII; R. N. Baldwin, *Liberty under the Soviets*, new ed., Vanguard Press, 1929; and R. N. Baldwin, ed., *Letters from Russian Prisons*, Boni, 1925.

[2] *Cf.* Chamberlin, *op. cit.*, Chap. IX, and Kohn, *Nationalism in the Soviet Union*.

Keystone View Company
JOSEF STALIN

Ewing Galloway
KARL MARX

Ewing Galloway
NIKOLAI LENIN

Keystone View Company
LEON TROTSKY

A COLLECTIVE FARM, SOVIET RUSSIA

THE DNIEPROSTROY DAM, SOVIET RUSSIA

While Soviet Russia has abandoned for the time being its crusade in behalf of international Communism, it has remained steadfastly international in its outlook.[1] It has called for world-peace, disarmament, arbitration, and other basic international policies. The fact that it did not expect the capitalistic countries to accept such exhortations need not necessarily be regarded as any evidence of a lack of sincerity in the Russian policy. The Russian disarmament proposals have been the most straightforward of any offered since 1918, and the Russian criticism of the Kellogg Pact was the most cogent critique of that document set forth at the time. In Georgi Chicherin and Maxim Litvinov, Russia has possessed two of the most astute of contemporary diplomats.

IV. THE ECONOMY OF SOVIET RUSSIA

The transformations in the economic life of Russia have been even more startling and upsetting than those in the sphere of government.

There was no swift expropriation of the propertied classes immediately after the November Revolution. Lenin had hoped that in the field of industry the state would act as a controlling and integrating agent before actual ownership and management were transferred to it. He did suggest, however, that banks and trusts were to be immediately nationalized. Following their accession to power, the Bolsheviks issued a series of decrees that completely changed the nature of property-holding in Russia. In many cases these decrees simply legalized the expropriation on the part of local soviets and factory workers which had already taken place.

By decrees of November 7 and 8, 1917, private ownership in land was abolished,[2] and the property previously owned by the state—this included railroads —was given to the people. The banks were nationalized (or socialized) on December 14 of the same year. In the next month came the nationalization of shipping, and in the spring of 1918, companies engaged in foreign trade were also nationalized. Not until the close of June, 1918, was large-scale industry generally socialized, and only at the close of 1920 did the same happen to the smaller industrial concerns. The general replacement of former industrial owners by state managers in the larger enterprises did not come until 1919.

By these decrees and by "illegal" expropriation the first step towards ultimate Socialism—the socialization of the means of production—was taken. Land, mines, mills, forests, factories, and the like now belonged to society at large. The abolition of private property in this sense does not mean that the individual in Russia cannot own personal objects and effects. But there is no private ownership in the means of production as a whole.

The economic history of Soviet Russia to date can be divided into three periods. From the opening of 1918 until March of 1921, a system known as War Communism or Communism of Wartime characterized the Russian scene. War Communism meant in brief nothing more than extreme measures of rationing and requisitioning. Something similar to this took place in many of the countries engaged in the World War, but in Russia the system was applied to

[1] Cf. Louis Fischer, *The Soviets in World Affairs*, Ballou, 1930, 2 vols.
[2] The large estates were handed over to land committees and district soviets.

the limit after 1918. Agriculture was a state monopoly, and the government requisitioned everything from the peasant except what the latter needed for bare subsistence. Free trade was prohibited, and the laws that applied to trade in bread and grain were very rigid. This period saw a considerable use of force to increase production, a recourse to conscripted labor, a tremendous decline in production in all fields, and the gravest discontent, especially among the peasantry.

Faced with an industrial structure that failed to produce, a peasant class that refused to farm, and unrest the length and breadth of the land, Soviet leaders saw with increasing clearness that War Communism, either as an economic system or simply as a means to set Russia upon a pair of sturdy economic feet, was a failure. The continuation of War Communism might have meant a counter-revolution and the destruction of the Soviet state. While all the leaders were agreed that something had to be done, the actual determination of a policy almost split the Communist party wide open. It was Lenin who framed and forced through a solution with the New Economic Policy (the NEP), the first steps in which were adopted by the Communist party in March of 1921.

The NEP was designed primarily: (1) To appease and conciliate the peasants, so that the food supply might be increased and the agricultural classes won over to support the government; and (2) to bring about an industrial revival so that Russian commodities might be produced for exchange. Among the chief economic measures under the NEP were: (1) The substitution of a tax in place of the requisition of grain; (2) legalization of free trade in grain and other commodities; (3) self-government of coöperatives; (4) the placing of state trusts, under the supervision of the Supreme Economic Council, on a self-governing and commercial basis; (5) the abandonment of equal wages; (6) the leasing of factories to private enterprises; (7) the granting of concessions to foreign capitalists; and (8) the restoration of money as a medium of exchange.

In the end, the NEP meant that the state retained control of basic and large-scale industry, finance, credit, transportation, and foreign trade, while private capital was permitted to function in those fields which the state, lacking the means or resources, could not handle. It also implied some recognition of the principles of profit-making and free individual initiative. Though severely criticized at the time as an abandonment of Communist principles and a surrender to capitalism, Lenin insisted that it was only a "strategic retreat" that would enable the forces of Socialism to advance more rapidly later. Actually, it did solve the problems that had forced its adoption, and gave new strength to the economic position of Russia. In turn, it also created new problems in stimulating the rise of a new bourgeoisie, strengthening the position of the rich peasants (kulaks) and increasing the degree and harshness of the socialization that would be necessary later.

The last of the economic periods since the Revolution dates from 1928, and includes the First and Second Five Year Plans.[1] The first of these went into

[1] For the best introductory surveys of the Russian planned economy, see C. B. Hoover, *The Economic Life of Soviet Russia*, Macmillan, 1931, Chap. xii; M. Ilin (I. I. Marshak), *New Russia's Primer*, Houghton Mifflin, 1931; and W. H. Chamberlin, *The Soviet Planned Economic Order*, World Peace Foundation, 1931.

effect on October 1, 1928,[1] and was completed before the allotted five-year period. The Second Five Year Plan was inaugurated January 1, 1933, and is designed to run to December 31, 1937.

In the economic field, the First Five Year Plan sought primarily: (1) To increase agricultural production through collectivization and mechanization of farming, and (2) to industrialize the Soviet Union rapidly. Particular stress was placed upon basic industries rather than upon those engaged in the manufacture of consumers' goods. With this in mind, minimum and maximum control figures were set for all fields.

The main economic objectives of the Plan may be described as a large increase in the physical volume of industrial and agricultural production and an improvement in the daily standard of living of the population. As a result of the intensive development of its heavy industries, the Soviet Union might reasonably be expected to become more independent, economically, of the outside world and more formidable as a military power.[2]

An essential object of the plan was the increased socialization of commerce, industry, and agriculture. Other phases of the plan involved what has been called "moral socialization," as well. In other words, the plan also offered a blueprint for a planned development in such fields as education, criminology, sanitation, and housing. By and large, it may be said that the First Five Year Plan was completed on schedule. In the heavy industries it ran ahead of schedule.

The Second Five Year Plan follows the broad outlines of the first, and in the field of industry proposes an increase in output of 114 per cent.[3] In it, however, the manufacture of consumers' goods is given a more prominent place, and a twofold or threefold increase in foodstuffs and other necessities is expected by the time of its completion. It also is designed to make Russia economically independent of the outside world. Especially important in the second plan is the stress placed upon electrification of the country. Developments in noneconomic fields are also included in it. Should the plan run on schedule, the socialization of Russia's productive and distributive system ought to be completed in 1937. There is a special emphasis placed upon the final "liquidating" of the capitalist elements that still remain.

How these plans have affected the different fields of industry will be indicated below in the sections on industry, agriculture, transportation, education, and the like. We may point out here the degree of socialization that has already taken place as indicated by the following table for the years 1925-34:

[1] An earlier Five Year Plan, framed to cover the period 1926-31, had fallen through.
[2] Gerhard Dobbert, ed., *Red Economics,* Houghton Mifflin, 1932, p. 14.
[3] Roughly speaking, heavy industry is to increase 97 per cent, and light industry, including foods, 134 per cent. The increase in general industrial output during the First Five Year Plan (four and one-quarter years) was 133 per cent. See chart on p. 1000.

PERCENTAGES OF RUSSIAN INDUSTRIAL PRODUCTION [1]

Year	State Concerns	Coöperative Concerns	Private Concerns
1925-26	64.5	8.4	27.1
1926-27	66.3	8.5	25.2
1927-28	68.9	11.7	19.4
1928-29	70.7	14.1	15.2
1932	92.52	7.41	0.07
1933	92.76	7.17	0.07

Throughout these different periods there has been one constant factor—economic planning. The fact that it is and has been a planned system distinguishes Soviet Russia's productive and distributive system from the capitalist economy as much as any other single factor. In capitalist countries individual enterprises are often carefully planned and controlled. But since the interest of every individual enterprise conflicts in purpose—the making of profits—with every other, the whole of capitalist industrial life is characterized by a lack of coördination and regulation. At certain periods this irrational planlessness results in nothing short of economic anarchy. In Russia, however, the national economy forms a single, integral unit—completely so in theory and to a large degree in fact as well.

FIRST FIVE YEAR PLAN - SECOND FIVE YEAR PLAN

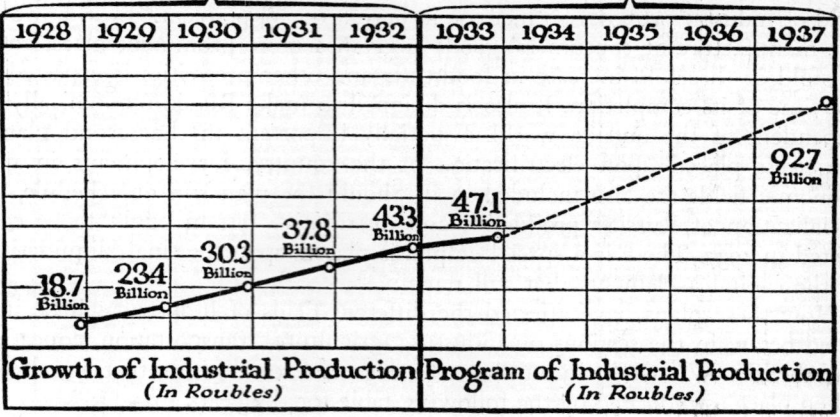

Growth of Industrial Production (In Roubles): 1928: 18.7 Billion; 1929: 23.4 Billion; 1930: 30.3 Billion; 1931: 37.8 Billion; 1932: 43.3 Billion.

Program of Industrial Production (In Roubles): 1933: 47.1 Billion; 1937: 92.7 Billion.

While the introduction of some sort of planned economy may not be impossible in capitalist countries—we can see an approach to economic planning in President Roosevelt's present industrial and agricultural measures in the United States—its operation in Russia is facilitated by: (1) Socialized ownership of the means of production; and (2) the presence of the principle of production for use and not for profit. A planned economy offers advantages in: (1) In-

[1] Adapted from Emile Burns, *Russia's Productive System,* Dutton, 1930, chart, p. 253, and brought down to date.

creased efficiency in production as a result of coördinated activities and the elimination of a duplication of effort; and (2) increased economy due to the elimination of overhead costs in the form of bonuses to officials, advertising, salesmen's and middlemen's profits, and the like.

The Communists have realized, nevertheless, that some form of competition between productive units is valuable if it results in increased production. A number of stimuli have been developed, therefore, to provide the individual drive that typifies capitalist activity and initiative. There are, thus, Socialist competitions between enterprises of the same size. Winners are rewarded generally with emblematic prizes. There are special industrial "shock brigades" who do more than the allotted tasks. Increased production is also stimulated by differential wage rewards. The point is constantly emphasized that the workers themselves enjoy the fruits of their increased labor.

The chief governmental agencies in Soviet Russia under which a planned economy is carried out include the Council for Labor and Defense, the Commission for Soviet Control, the State Planning Commission (Gosplan), the Central Statistical Bureau, the Commissariats for Heavy Industry, Light Industry and Lumber, the People's Commissariat for Supply, the Commissariat for Supplies and the Food Industry, and the Union Industrial Associations (one for each branch of industry). It should be observed that all industries in Russia are organized into government trusts, such as textile trusts, oil trusts, and so on. There may be a number of trusts in a given industry, as there are, for example, in the coal industry. These trusts are organized into syndicates which serve to coördinate production and distribution. Both trusts and syndicates are supervised and controlled by special governmental agencies from among those listed above. Nearly all industrial activity is thus organized into one thoroughly coördinated and regulated system.

In closing the first five-year period and starting on the second, Stalin and his associates made the following claims as to the broad general achievements under the First Five Year Plan:

A *two-fold* increase in the number of workers and office workers employed in large-scale industry compared with 1928, which represents an increase of 57 per cent in excess of the Five-Year Plan.

An increase in the national income—hence, an increase in the incomes of the workers and peasants—which in 1932 amounted to 45,100,000,000 rubles, an increase of 85 per cent compared with 1928.

An increase in the average annual wages of workers and office workers employed in large-scale industry by 67 per cent compared with 1928, which is an increase of 18 per cent in excess of the Five-Year Plan.

An increase in the social insurance fund by 292 per cent compared with 1928 (4,120,000,000 rubles in 1932 compared with 1,050,000,000 rubles in 1928), which is 111 per cent increase in excess of the Five-Year Plan.

An increase in public catering, which now caters for more than 70 per cent of the workers employed in the decisive branches of industry, which is an increase six times in excess of the Five-Year Plan. . . .

The adoption of the seven-hour day in industry affecting the overwhelming majority of the working class.[1]

[1] Joseph Stalin and others, *From the First to the Second Five-Year Plan*, International Publishers, 1934, pp. 42-43, 438.

Not only did the First Five Year Plan greatly increase the total industrial output of Russia—in 1932 it stood at 334 per cent of prewar output and 219 per cent of the 1928 output—but it also transformed Russia from a preponderantly agricultural to a dominantly industrial country. In 1927-28 industrial output amounted to only 48 per cent of the total national output, whereas in 1934 it constituted 72 per cent. No less than 1,500 new factories were built during the operation of the First Five Year Plan.

V. THE INDUSTRIAL PROGRESS OF SOVIET RUSSIA

Let us turn now to an analysis of specific aspects of Russian economic life since 1917, giving special stress to the period after 1927.[1] It will be evident from the material here presented that the Russian economy suffered greatly from almost seven years of warfare. In 1917, it may be noted, production in all fields averaged about 75 per cent of the prewar level. By 1920, production had fallen to one-fifth of the 1913 level. There had been a great physical loss in factories and machinery. The transportation system was crippled. Not until after 1921 was assistance from foreign nations in reconstruction forthcoming. The task of economic rehabilitation was, therefore, an extremely formidable one.

Pig-iron Production. In 1913 4,206,000 tons (metric) were produced. In 1920 only 104,000 tons were produced. Not until 1922-23 was this figure tripled. A great improvement was evident by 1924-25, when 1,290,000 were produced. In 1927-28 (the fiscal year) production had risen to 3,460,000; in 1928-29 it was 4,030,000; in 1929-30 it reached 5,000,000. Prewar production was already surpassed. In 1930-31, there was a slight decrease to 4,900,000 tons, but in 1933 it reached 7,250,000 tons. The production in 1934 was 10,440,000 tons. It is estimated that the gigantic Magnitogorsk plant alone will, when completed, turn out 2,500,000 tons of pig iron per year. According to figures set by the Second Five Year Plan, pig-iron production is supposed to reach the annual figure of 22,000,000 tons by the end of 1937—more than five times the prewar figure, and slightly in advance of American production for the exceedingly poor year of 1931.

Steel Production. Here the figures tell a similar story. In 1913, 4,140,000 metric tons were produced. In 1920-21 only 173,000 were turned out. From this point on production increased steadily. In 1924-25 it was 1,860,000 tons; in 1925-26, 2,910,000; in 1926-27, 3,590,000; in 1927-28, 4,150,000; in 1929-30, 5,800,000. The production in 1932 was 5,888,000 tons; in 1933, 6,920,000 tons; and in 1934, 9,600,000 tons.

The following table of steel production in metric tons shows how this branch of industrial progress in Russia compares with production in other countries. The variation in the figures from those given above is due to the fact that they come from different sources, those in the table being from a report of the German Association of Iron and Steel Manufacturers. They fully illustrate, nevertheless, the general trend:

---

[1] *Cf.* Hoover, *op. cit.*, Chaps. I-III.

THE INDUSTRIAL PROGRESS OF SOVIET RUSSIA

Steel Production

	1929	1930	1931	Change, 1931 compared with 1929 in percentage
United States	57.8	41.6	27.0	—53.3
Germany	16.2	11.5	8.3	—48.9
France	9.8	9.4	7.8	—20.4
U.S.S.R.	4.9	5.6	5.34	+ 9.0
Great Britain	10.1	7.6	5.26	—48.0
Belgium	4.1	3.3	3.2	—22.4
Other countries	19.1	16.5	13.3	—30.4
	122.0	95.5	70.2	—42.5

While steel production in the United States fell off 53.3 per cent in two years, and in Germany and Great Britain over 48 per cent, in Soviet Russia it gained by 9 per cent. Russia, therefore, was the only country in the world to show a gain in steel production during these years.

Though steel production in the U.S.S.R. was slightly lower in 1931 than in 1930, this is not to be attributed to the world-wide depression, for statistics in some other Russian industries show tremendous gains for this period. The decrease was due partly to the inability of the railroads to keep up with the increased demand of a rapidly growing industry and partly to the fact that many old mills were undergoing reconstruction. In view of the mechanization of both Russian industry and Russian agriculture, machine-building plants of giant size are important in Russian industrial production. There is a large one in the Urals, but the largest is that opened in September, 1934, at Kramatorsk in the Donetz coal basin—the Pittsburgh of Soviet Russia. It is the largest machinery-building plant in the world. It is scheduled, for example, to produce 60,000 tons of castings annually, about twice the production of the great Krupp works in Germany. It will employ about 24,000 workers, a third of them women.

Oil Production. In this field the production of recent years has left the prewar figures well behind. In 1913 there were 9,215,911 metric tons of oil produced in Russia. In 1920, production fell to 3,832,000 tons. In 1922-23 production advanced to 5,271,372 tons; in 1925-26, to 8,319,000 tons; in 1927-28, to 11,634,000 (in considerable excess of the prewar level); in 1928-29, to 12,300,000 tons; and in 1930-31, to 18,600,000. The production in 1932 went up to 21,380,000 tons; in 1933 to 21,500,000 tons; and in 1934 to 25,500,000 tons.

Coal Production. In 1913 there were 28,356,000 metric tons produced. In 1920 production had fallen to about one-fourth of that. By 1923-24 production had increased to 15,778,000 tons; in 1926-27 it went to 31,995,000 tons, well over the prewar figure; in 1927-28, to 36,095,000 tons. Production for 1930 went to 46,456,000 tons. The production in 1932 was 65,300,000 tons; in 1933, 76,700,000 tons; and in 1934, 93,500,000 tons.

Electrical Output. Nowhere in the plan of Soviet economy are the figures more amazing than in the electrical industry. Electrification of the land was one of Lenin's passionate aspirations, and rapid progress has been made in this field. Here, of course, comparison with the figures of 1913 is slightly misleading. In 1913 the output of electrical energy was 1,945,000,000 kilowatt hours. While figures for the years preceding 1922-23 are very poor, there is every evidence of a sharp decrease, at least one of 60 per cent. By 1925-26, however, it had risen to 3,135,000,000 kilowatt hours—more than 50 per cent increase over the prewar figure. Total production of electric power rose from 5,000,000,000 kilowatt hours in 1928 to 15,800,000,000 kilowatt hours in 1933. In 1934 it was 20,500,000,000 kilowatt hours. It is planned to have the output raised to 38,000,000,000 kilowatt hours by 1937.

Electric power plants are being constructed all over Russia. In 1928 there were only 18 district power stations, while in January, 1933, there were 44. Special effort is being made to harness the water power that is available in abundance. One of these projects is the much publicized Dnieprostroy plant, begun in 1927 and now practically completed, on the Dnieper River. Its estimated cost is over $113,000,000. Generating 900,000 horse power, it will be larger than any hydroelectric plant in Europe, and even larger than Muscle Shoals. Colonel Hugh L. Cooper, the American engineer who directed construction of Muscle Shoals, has been in charge of the construction of Dnieprostroy. The expected energy produced by this colossal plant will be equivalent to about 18,000,000 human workers. I. I. Marshak, a Russian engineer who wrote *New Russia's Primer* under the pseudonym M. Ilin, estimates that this power will be sold at the rate of 1 kopek for one kilowatt hour, or 1 kopek for the equivalent of the labor of a strong man for three days. A kopek is about half a cent in our money. If this is so, it would mean that electric power equal to the labor power of one man for one day would cost $0.0016—or that electric power equivalent to 30 days' labor of one man would cost about as much as a package of gum.

Electric power production has been increasing in Soviet Russia at the rate of about 35 or 40 per cent a year for the past few years. The percentage of electrification of industry rose from 47.7 per cent in 1925-26 to 73 per cent in 1933. In this respect the U.S.S.R. is exceeded only by the United States, where the corresponding percentage is about 75.

Cotton Cloth. In 1913 there were 2,238,000,000 meters of cloth produced in Russia. Production fell off so badly after the revolution that only 149,999,999 meters were turned out. By 1924-25 a sharp recovery had been made, and in the following year prewar production figures were almost equaled. In the following two years prewar production was surpassed, and in 1929, 3,068,000,000 meters were manufactured. There has been some falling off since. In 1932, 2,719,700,000 meters were turned out; and in 1934, some 2,711,000,000 meters.

Leather Shoes. In 1913 there were 5,500,000 pairs of boots and shoes made in Russia. Not until 1924-25 was prewar production surpassed. In 1925-26 9,000,000 pairs were made. With production increasing steadily, the number for 1927-28 was over 20,000,000; for 1929-30 it was over 39,000,000; and in 1934 it reached some 69,200,000 pairs.

The following tables will serve as a clear summary review of the remarkable

THE INDUSTRIAL PROGRESS OF SOVIET RUSSIA

progress of industrialization and of the increase of industrial production since the Five Year Plan was installed. The first table shows how industry has outdistanced agriculture in Russia since the World War. The second summarizes the growth of industrial production.

Relative Importance of Total Output of Industry and Agriculture

	1913	1929	1931	1932	1933	1934
1. Industry	42.1	54.5	66.7	70.7	70.4	72.4
2. Agriculture	57.9	45.5	33.3	29.3	29.6	27.6
Total	100	100	100	100	100	100

Percentage of Output of the Two Main Groups of Branches of Large-scale Industry

(In prices of 1926-27)

Total Volume of output (in billions of rubles)

	1929	1930	1931	1932	1933
Total large-scale industry	21.0	27.5	33.9	38.5	41.9 [1]
Of which:					
Group A, implements and means of production	10.2	14.5	18.8	22.0	24.3
Group B, consumers' goods	10.8	13.0	15.1	16.5	17.6

Percentages

	1929	1930	1931	1932	1933
Group A, implements and means of production	48.5	52.6	55.4	57.0	58.0
Group B, consumers' goods	51.5	47.4	44.6	43.0	42.0
Total	100	100	100	100	100

VI. TRANSPORTATION

The enormous size of Russia makes transportation problems at once very important and relatively difficult. Though most of Russia is a comparatively level country, the soil is of a type that requires stone surfacing if roads are to be passable during the wet season. There are not enough roads even of the unimproved variety—about 1,000,000 miles in European Russia—and only about 25,000 miles are stone-surfaced today. There are over 750,000 miles of surfaced highways in the United States. This shortage of good roads in Russia holds up what might otherwise be an enthusiastic development of automobile traffic. Russia's rivers are not well suited for commercial navigation. Most of them run north into the ice-bound Arctic Ocean, while the Volga, the most important river, empties into the Caspian, an inland sea. Moreover, most of the commodities that might be dispatched on the Volga must be sent upstream. But the level country does favor canal development, and the economic planning of

---

[1] The value of the total output of large-scale industry in 1934 was 49,500,000,000 rubles.

Russia calls for extensive canalization of rivers, especially the Volga, and the building of the Volga-Don Canal, the Beresina canal system, the Kama-Petchora Canal and a waterway from Moscow to the Volga.

In 1913 there were 46,000 miles of railway lines in operation in Russia. The World War, the Revolution, and the internal disturbances that followed almost completely dislocated the railroad system. Usable roads were cut almost in half, and the bulk of the available rolling stock was good for little more than junking. Until the adoption of the First Five Year Plan relatively little was done to rebuild the railways in comparison to the effort expended in other industrial fields. The plan contemplated the building of additional lines to bring the total length of lines to 50,000 miles in 1933. In the light of pressing needs, both the plan and the work done under it appear sorely inadequate, and technicians agree that the very important railway problem has in large measure remained unsolved. By 1931 official Soviet reports showed that only 41 per cent of the work contemplated in the construction of new and duplicate lines had been accomplished. Though the same thing is roughly true for replacement of rolling stock, locomotives, and the like, the figures there are slightly better. Whatever work has been done on the railways has resulted in a far greater financial burden than was contemplated, expenditures up to 1931 being 40 per cent above the estimates.

The entire railroad system—which is in part a key to the economic life of Russia—was in so serious a condition in 1931 that a thoroughgoing new program of construction, organization, and rehabilitation was announced. What results this has brought or will bring cannot yet be accurately determined, though the total mileage at the beginning of 1934 had been brought up to 1933 specifications. The following table of rolling stock gives comparative figures with 1913 and indicates the gravity of the problem in the light of the expansion of Russian industrial life and the need for better transportation facilities.

RUSSIAN ROLLING STOCK

	1913	1927-28	1931	1934
Locomotives	21,857	17,417	17,520	20,869
Freight cars	256,274	464,000	510,900	542,620
Passenger cars	20,868	22,360	31,080	31,940

Despite this, there has been growth in the total volume of traffic carried. Though it was not expected that the volume of traffic would reach prewar figures till 1932, it exceeded them in 1926-27. By 1930-31 the total volume of traffic was approximately three times that of 1913. Especially noteworthy has been the increase in passenger traffic, and it has been the comment of many observers that all Russia seems to be constantly on the move. Measures were recently adopted to reduce the movement of individuals wherever possible.

Very ambitious plans for the improvement of Russian railroads are involved in the Second Five Year Plan. The intention is to spend some $13,000,000,000 for transportation improvements. Approximately half of this will be put into railroads. Some 7,000 miles of new railroads are to be built and 6,000 miles of existing lines double-tracked. More than 3,000 miles are to be electrified. It is estimated that it would cost about $2,500,000,000 to bring Russia's approximately 52,000 miles of railroads up to American standards of equipment and operation. Compared to the United States, Russia has about one-seventh as much railroad mileage per capita and one-twelfth as much per square mile of territory.

In the field of aviation, the changes have been startling, and disproportionate attention has been given to aviation for obvious military as well as commercial reasons. The first air line, established in 1923, was only 430 kilometers long. By 1928 there were 11,927 kilometers of air lines in use. In 1933 the non-military air lines in operation reached 37,011 kilometers. There were 42,497 passengers carried, as well as 3,456 tons of mail and express. The flights covered some 6,000,000 kilometers. With one exception, the air lines are government-operated. Military aviation has developed rapidly, and Russia is today one of the most formidable powers in the air.

VII. THE AGRICULTURAL REVOLUTION

Among the gravest problems faced by the Communists in their reconstruction of Russia have been those connected with agriculture. The internal struggles, the three-year period of War Communism, and the changes in land-holding, which involved a general redistribution of land, played havoc with the productive end of agriculture.

Under War Communism (1918-21) agriculture was a state monopoly. All the farm produce above what was necessary for the sustenance of the producer and his family was taken over by the state to feed the armies and people. With most industries and the means of transportation functioning poorly or not at all, the peasants received little or nothing in the way of manufactured commodities in exchange for their foodstuffs. They logically refused to cultivate and then have their produce requisitioned by the state. They either decreased the acreage sown or hid the surplus. Compulsion of the severest kind was used to little avail. There was a grave scarcity of seed, fertilizer, live stock, and agricultural implements, and a serious impairment of man power. Many regions were hard hit by severe famine. Peasant uprisings occurred in southwest Russia and in the lower and middle Volga districts.

Agriculture had its worst year in 1921, and conditions had been only slightly better the year before. The peasant tended to produce solely for his own needs. All available statistics indicate that the yield of foodstuffs in 1921 came to only 30 per cent of the average annual yield for the ten-year period before the World War. In area cultivated there was approximately a 50 per cent decrease from 1915.

With the introduction of the NEP the system of requisitions was replaced by a food tax on sown areas amounting to approximately 10 per cent of the crop. The free marketing of the remainder of the produce was permitted. This and other measures alleviated to a large degree the peasant discontent, but it also later strengthened the position of the richer peasants (kulaks). A definite increase followed in foodstuffs produced and area cultivated. By 1925-26, the total sown area was a little over 89 per cent of that of 1913. In 1926-27 prewar production figures were almost approximated. It appeared, however, that if agriculture continued without technical modification neither the sown area nor the total amount produced would go far beyond that of prewar days.

As yet little had been accomplished in the socialization of agriculture. From 1928, accordingly, the government through the First Five Year Plan turned its energies in this direction. This meant a virtual reconstruction of agriculture and agricultural production. This has been carried on since that date in face of tremendous difficulties through the collective farm (kolhoz) and the state farm (sovhoz). These are the two forms of socialized agriculture, and of them the former is the more important.

The collective farm is produced by uniting individual peasant holdings. The richer peasants, through collectivization and accompanying tax measures, were simply to be exterminated as a class ("liquidated"). Along with the creation of the collectives, agriculture was to be mechanized. Statistics for 1930 indicate that in this year the number of collectives jumped from 59,400 in January to 110,200 in March, the average number of farms merged in one kolhoz from 73.9 to 129.2, and the average area under cultivation from 529.9 hectares to 797.4 for the two months. The process was too rapid and chaos resulted, together with hunger, discontent, and uprisings. A change in government policy that followed brought about a sharp drop in the number of farms collectivized. The process of collectivization has been going on steadily since then. The following tables will indicate the progress of agricultural collectivization since the First Five Year Plan got thoroughly under way. The state and collective farms embrace today some 85 per cent of all the land under actual cultivation in Soviet Russia, and 80 per cent of all peasants live on state or collective farms.

Progress of Collectivization

	1929	1930	1931	1932	1933
Number of collectives (*in thousands*)	57.0	85.9	211.1	211.05	224.5
Number of farms in collectives (*in millions*)	1.0	6.0	13.0	14.9	15.2
Percentage of collectivization of peasant farms	3.9	23.6	52.7	61.5	65.0

Seeded Area Under Grain According to Sectors
In millions of hectares

Sectors	1929	1930	1931	1932	1933	Percentage of the area of 1933
(1) State farms	1.5	2.9	8.1	9.3	10.8	10.6
(2) Collectives	3.4	29.7	61.0	69.1	75.0	73.9
(3) Individual peasants	91.1	69.2	35.3	21.3	15.7	15.5
Entire seeded area under grain in U.S.S.R.	96.0	101.8	104.4	99.7	101.5	100

In the collective farm the members pool their land and productive capital. The family keeps those things which have purely personal use, its house, and

THE AGRICULTURAL REVOLUTION

a small garden. The collective farm is managed by a board of directors elected yearly, and the work is done in gangs under the direction of foremen. At present the workers receive pay in kind and in money on a piecework basis.

The state farms have been developed mainly out of great estates of tsarist times or out of uncultivated regions. Highly specialized productive units, they frequently serve as experimental laboratories on a large scale. There were at the close of 1932 about 5,000 sovhozi, which cultivated some 43,000 square miles of land. By the spring of 1933 the collective farms and the state farms together embraced 85 per cent of all the land under cultivation in Soviet Russia. The farms of too great extent have been found unwieldy and the tendency is to break them up. A basic problem concerns the character of labor on the state farms. The workers admittedly lack initiative and responsibility and the sovhozi suffer as a result.

The Soviet government has done much to introduce the latest labor-saving devices into agriculture. The following table will make clear the remarkable progress in introducing tractors in agricultural work.

NUMBER OF TRACTORS EMPLOYED IN AGRICULTURE IN THE U.S.S.R.
(Allowance made for depreciation)

	1929	1930	1931	1932	1933
	\multicolumn{5}{c}{Number of tractors in thousands}
Total number of tractors	34.9	72.1	125.3	148.5	204.1
a. In machine and tractor stations	2.4	31.1	63.3	74.8	122.3
b. In Soviet farms (all systems)	9.7	27.7	51.5	64.0	81.8
	\multicolumn{5}{c}{Horse power in thousands}
Horse power of all tractors	391.4	1003.5	1850.0	2225.0	3100.0
a. In machine and tractor stations	23.9	372.5	848.0	1077.0	1782.0
b. In Soviet farms (all systems)	123.4	483.1	892.0	1043.0	1318.0 [1]

At present only about one-third of the farms and 15 per cent of the cultivated acreage in Russia remain under individual control. It is too early to judge the consequences of socialized agriculture in that country. The peasant is still very badly off and agricultural production remains a major problem. It is in the peasant and agriculture that Russia still has issues of the first importance. What happens there will determine much of the future of the Soviet Union. Of the amazing increase in the technical efficiency of agricultural methods since 1925 there can be no legitimate doubt. The great problem that lies ahead is to arouse proper enthusiasm on the part of the peasants in cooperating with the new order of agricultural affairs.

Collectivized farming under the First Five Year Plan certainly helped to bring more land under active cultivation. At the close of 1932 the area under cultivation had increased by 21,000,000 hectares—about 52,000,000 acres—over the 1927-28 figures. Under the new system of collectivized farming the production has also notably increased. The following tables will bring out clearly the increase in the amount of land under cultivation and in the production on this land since the First Five Year Plan went into operation.

[1] In 1934 the total number of tractors had increased to 311,000, and the horse power to 4,461,000.

Seeded Area for All Crops in the U.S.S.R.

In millions of hectares

	1913	1929	1930	1931	1932	1933
Entire Seeded Area	105.0	118.0	127.2	136.3	134.4	129.7
a. Grain Crops	94.4	96.0	101.8	104.4	99.7	101.5
b. Technical Crops	4.5	8.8	10.5	14.0	14.9	12.0
c. Vegetable Gardens	3.8	7.6	8.0	9.1	9.2	8.6
d. Fodder	2.1	5.0	6.5	8.8	10.6	7.3

Total Production of Grain and Technical Crops

In millions of centners

	1913	1929	1930	1931	1932	1933
Grain	801.0	717.4	835.4	694.8	698.7	898.0
Cotton (raw)	7.4	8.6	11.1	12.9	12.7	13.2
Flax (fiber)	3.3	3.6	4.4	5.5	5.0	5.6
Sugar beets	109.0	62.5	140.2	120.5	65.6	90.0
Vegetable-oil crops	21.5	35.8	36.2	51.0	45.5	46.0

The harvest of 1933 was a "bumper crop" and that of 1934 was only slightly less in spite of a severe drought. But for the latter it would have greatly exceeded the 1933 crop. These two good harvests have resulted in the abolition of the food-rationing system.

The World War and the succeeding famine did much to decimate the domestic animals of Russia. The tendency was increased by the stress of collectivization and the sabotage conducted by kulaks. But in the last two years some progress has been made in checking the losses in this essential element in agrarian life. The following table indicates the marked decline in the number of domestic animals, as well as the checking of this decline in 1933.

Live Stock in the U.S.S.R.

Millions of heads

	1916	1929	1930	1931	1932	1933
Horses	35.1	34.0	30.2	26.2	19.6	16.6
Large horned cattle	58.9	68.1	52.5	47.9	40.7	38.6
Sheep and goats	115.5	147.2	108.8	77.7	52.1	50.6
Hogs	20.3	20.9	13.6	14.4	11.6	12.2

The main obstacle to the more prolific rearing of live stock is the food shortage for man himself in Russia. The peasants have little incentive to raise more stock if it means taking food from their own mouths. When the grain production has become ample, there is little doubt that there will be sufficient live stock for the needs of the country. In February, 1935, V. A. Yakovlev asserted that all losses in live stock would be made up by the end of 1936.

VIII. SOVIET TRADE AND COMMERCE

However markedly the Soviet theories and practices have fluctuated in other fields, in that of foreign trade they have been remarkably constant. Since 1918, all foreign trade has been a state monopoly. This means that there does not exist in the Russian domestic market the same type of foreign competition that is to be found in other countries. It also means that foreign trade as such is controlled with a view to the general economic objectives of the state as a whole. Imports under such conditions are not subject to the same influences that they experience in markets which are characterized by a large degree of free competition.

Foreign trade emerged from the strain of the Revolutionary period and the blockade badly shattered. Compared to the export and import total for 1913, 2,894,167,000 rubles, the figure for 1920-21, 128,000,000 rubles, was ridiculously small. With the introduction of the NEP there came a steady increase in foreign trade. In 1926 exports and imports combined came to about 50 per cent of the prewar total. The best year for trade was 1930, when the total came to 2,070,-000,000 rubles, still below prewar levels. Since then there has been a decline in both exports and imports. The following table summarizes Russian foreign trade since 1930. A marked fall in foreign trade has characterized capitalistic states as well as Soviet Russia during the period of the world-wide depression.

	Soviet Exports (in rubles)	Soviet Imports (in rubles)
1930	1,002,300,000	1,068,700,000
1931	811,200,000	1,105,000,000
1932	574,928,000	704,040,000
1933	495,658,000	348,216,000
1934 (11 months)	378,600,000	206,700,000

In domestic trade the Soviet government has followed various policies. Under War Communism all private trade was banned. With the NEP, however, private capital was given the right to operate in internal trade. The state by no means abandoned the field, but the growth of private trade and traders was remarkable. The rejuvenation of private commercial activity at the time seemed to many to herald the beginning of the end of a purely Communistic economy. In 1923 private trade totaled 58.6 per cent of the retail trade and 22 per cent of the wholesale.

A real offensive was begun against private trading in 1924, with the result that socialized trade has grown tremendously. This is carried on either through state trading or through the coöperatives, which are under full state control. It might be observed that complaints are directed against the state-dominated organizations on the ground of inefficiency, inelasticity, and bureaucratic red tape. In 1928-29, however, only 1 per cent of the wholesale and 17.1 per cent of the retail trade was carried on privately.

In 1931 the government applied capitalistic methods to the field of socialized trade and established "commercial stores" where . . . goods were sold freely to all, in unlimited quantities, but at prices which were four, five and more times higher than those ruling in the cooperatives and approaching those obtaining on the free market. This was done for the purpose of extracting as many paper rubles from the population as possible. . . . The authorities knew that the "closed distributing centers" [the others] could provide no more than 75% of the rations.[1]

Stores known by the name Torgsin have also been opened, at which goods can be obtained at very low prices but only for foreign currency at par. In view of the fluctuation of the ruble throughout Russia this serves to nullify the low prices. All indications show that trade, both wholesale and retail, has been steadily increasing since 1922. In 1932, it should be noted, the crisis that resulted from lack of supplies brought remedial measures which promised to alter radically the existing state machinery of distribution. The free market has again assumed importance but it does not operate as under the NEP, and there seems no reason to expect a return to the NEP type of private trade.

IX. MONEY, BANKING, AND PUBLIC FINANCE

Those who have read much in theoretical Socialism have accustomed themselves to thinking of a Communistic economy as one in which there would be no money or banking in the conventional sense and none of the taxation devices that we know in capitalist states. Exchange in hypothetical Communist countries is usually portrayed as taking place through the exchange of certificates of labor effort, and where the state owns everything there would seem to be no rational need for taxation. That these theoretical situations do not exist in Russia today simply illustrates that the country is only on its way to Communism and is still predominantly in the stage of State Socialism.

Though there are banks in Russia, there is none of the finance capitalism that characterizes capitalist countries. There is no private bank of any sort in Russia. Banking and credit have been thoroughly socialized. There is no corporate stock issued as in capitalist countries, and in their security investments the banks are allowed to deal only in government bonds involved in internal loans. There is no investment allowed in foreign bonds.

At the head of the banking system stands the great State Bank established in November, 1921. It has 2,465 branches, a capital and surplus of over 600,000,000 rubles, assets of 20,000,000,000 rubles, and a gold and foreign-exchange reserve of about 725,000,000 rubles. This is the central credit institution for Russia and supplies the short-time or commercial credit of the country. Next comes the Industrial Bank, which is a long-term credit institution for financing industry and electrification—that is, the capital construction of the Soviet state. In short, it exercises roughly the function of the investment banks in capitalist countries. Supplementing it is the Municipal Bank, which finances municipal utilities and construction. A Coöperative Bank finances the capital construction which is carried on by the large number of Russian coöperatives. Then there is an Agricultural Bank, which furnishes capital and credit for the state farms.

[1] Malevsky-Malevich, *op. cit.*, p. 549.

MONEY, BANKING, AND PUBLIC FINANCE

The Soviet government has also encouraged the development of the State Savings Bank, which has about 50,000 branches and many depositors, about two-thirds of the deposits being the savings of individual citizens. The most distinctive character of the Russian banks is that credit and capital financing is wholly a state monopoly and is carried on for public advantage and not for private profit.

The State Bank was allowed to issue ten-ruble notes with 25 per cent gold backing. The need for currency grew as Russian industry developed. In the latest statement of the State Bank issue department, July 1, 1934, the coverage in gold, other precious metals, and foreign currency was 25.1 per cent. The figures, in thousands of chervontsi,[1] were:

Note issue	342,158.8
Gold	82,210.7
Other precious metals	865.3
Foreign currency	2,868.3

The Treasury also issues currency against its own gold reserve. The Treasury reserve is not made public. The Soviet government has tried to meet the problem of a growing shortage of currency by encouraging moneyless transactions. At the present time it is estimated that about two-thirds of all transactions are carried out by this method.

Public finance is designed to support the vast planned economy of Russia— to pay the bill for industrialization, electrification, the machinery and labor cost on the great state farms, new transportation facilities, and the like. The state revenues for these purposes are obtained through: (1) Levies on the profits of state enterprises; (2) taxation of commodities and incomes; (3) state borrowing; and (4) fixing high prices for consumers' goods, most of which are produced and sold by the state. About 10 per cent of the state revenue is derived from state profits on industry; about one-seventh at present comes from public borrowing. The rest is derived from taxation. The more important taxes are a turnover tax, which resembles our sales tax, an income tax, and the distasteful and relatively nonproductive agricultural tax, which is a source of much almost needless irritation of the peasants. The tax that most closely resembles our taxation procedure is the income tax, which takes from 1 to 25 per cent of the wages received, there being no important source of income save wages and salaries.

Since everything taxed is ultimately derived from the state, it would appear simpler for Russia to take the necessary income in the first place as state profits and avoid the necessity and expense of taxation. But the government thinks otherwise and resorts to this roundabout method of taxation as though it were a conventional capitalist state. Indeed, the Soviet government has reduced its share in the country's profits from 81 per cent to 10 per cent, preferring to derive the difference from taxation. It is thought to be a safer and more dependable device than arbitrarily appropriating a larger share of profits.

---

[1] The chervonets is worth $8.80 in American money.

X. SUMMARY OF ECOMONIC CONDITIONS IN SOVIET RUSSIA

Soviet Russia stands now in the middle of the Second Five Year Plan.[1] The first plan meant a constant drive under terrific strain. "We renounce butter and turn that butter into bricks," declared a Soviet official.[2] "We deny ourselves meats to convert them into machines." It involved great concentration upon producers' goods at the expense of consumers' goods. It has meant in many cases that the key and heavy industries could be built up only at the cost of a shortage in more immediate necessities.

Statistics indicating quantitative increases do not tell the whole story. It must be noted that key industries have at times lagged behind the growth in other fields. A shortage of basic raw materials hampers development in all fields. The weaknesses of the transportation system have the same effect. The inadequacy of the distribution system is felt keenly, sometimes in turn with very bad effect upon production. Industrial organization suffers unduly in many cases from too much bureaucracy. Lack of technical knowledge has led to the abuse of industrial machinery, cutting down its life and efficiency. Unskilled and inefficient labor provides grave problems. Despite the great willingness to learn that the Russian worker shows, his lack of training makes for high labor costs. Increased production at lower cost per worker comes with great slowness, if at all, in many fields. Increased production-costs in many industries have in turn created serious financial problems. To stimulate greater productiveness, the worker has been made to realize that he is working for himself as well as for society by the introduction of piecework and differential wage scales. This and the use of special "shock brigades" to speed up production have also increased industrial waste. A serious problem accompanies increased production when accompanied by decreased quality. Especially is this felt in the case of consumers' goods. Because of poor living-conditions, inadequate food, and the like, a disinclination or inability to work at top speed often exists even among workers who sympathize with the present régime.

In short, if anyone imagines that Soviet Russia has already been able to find the solvent for all of its economic problems he is seriously mistaken.[3] On the other hand, not even the most obstinate opponent of the Communist experiment can deny that, despite the major obstacles, there has been an amazing physical growth of Russian industry within recent years. The following table tells the story of Russian industrial progress, compared to that of the other major countries.

Industrial Production
Percentage of prewar level

	1913	1929	1933
U.S.S.R.	100	194.3	391.9
U.S.A.	100	170.2	110.2
England	100	99.1	85.2
Germany	100	113.1	75.4
France	100	139.0	107.6

[1] *Cf.* Stalin and others, *op. cit.*, and Davis, *op. cit.*, Chap. v.
[2] Mikhail Borodin, editor of the *Moscow Daily News*.
[3] The most severe criticism of the Russian economic experiment that is at all consistent with actual facts is contained in W. H. Chamberlin, *Russia's Iron Age*, Little, Brown, 1934.

The major defect in Russian industrial operations has been the great waste due to the difficulties of predicting and planning industrial development on so large a scale and for such rapid strides.[1] But one inclined to criticize this too sharply may profitably compare Russian waste with the waste under President Roosevelt's C.W.A. scheme and with the slow development of capitalist planning under the New Deal.

The Second Five Year Plan, differing from the first, is designed to organize new industries, perfect their organization, and raise the standard of living. The tempo is to be a bit more moderate than the first. Though its total aims are pretentious, the goals set, in view of the obstacles facing the first plan, are in a sense more modest:

With the completion of the second Five Year Plan, socialization is to be achieved, the distinction between the city and the village is to be eliminated, as agriculture is completely mechanized, and the discrimination between physical and intellectual labor is likewise to be done away with. A classless society of workers is to evolve at the conclusion of the Second Five Year Plan.[2]

XI. THE NEW SOCIAL ORDER IN RUSSIA

1. LIVING-CONDITIONS

Despite the large number of observers who have visited Russia and the impressive total of their comments, descriptions, and judgments—both unfavorably critical and otherwise—it is extremely difficult to determine to what extent the general standard of living of the average Russian has changed since prewar days. That the standard of living in Russia is definitely below that of capitalist countries, especially that of England, France, and the United States, there seems to be little question. But this difference is, of course, not to be ascribed to the Soviet régime as such, because even more striking differences in material well-being were present before the World War.

Whether the almost constant shortage of consumers' goods has meant a decline in the standard of living is hard to determine. Sympathetic observers report a definite increase of late. Others speak of constant hardships. That the process of industrialization has carried with it severe sacrifice of food and clothing there is no doubt. But this does not necessarily imply a lower standard than that which obtained before the Revolution. The worst that can be said is that the standard of living of the average Russian before the Revolution was comparatively low and that it has not sunk any lower. A marked improvement in material living-conditions has taken place since the first years of Soviet rule. It is hoped that the Second Five Year Plan will result in a major improvement.

From the viewpoint of sanitation, educational facilities, medical facilities, and social activities, the general standard of well-being has been undeniably raised to a remarkable degree. One observer comments that "The truth is far more is being done to promote their [the Russian workers'] social and cul-

---

[1] *Cf.* Clive Day, *Economic Development in Modern Europe*, Macmillan, 1933, pp. 411-12.
[2] Davis, *op. cit.*, pp. 91-92.

tural well-being than their material well-being."[1] If the extensive system of social insurance is also taken into consideration, there is reason to say that the social and cultural standard compares favorably with that of the average worker and farmer in capitalist countries. Production in all fields will have to be speeded up and the distributive system will have to function more smoothly before it can be said that the average Russian is well supplied with food, clothing, and other necessary commodities.

The mass of Russian people are workers—manual, clerical, administrative, or scientific. There is no class that lives by rent or dividends. Organization of the urban proletariat into unions is a governmental policy. Membership in the unions, of which there have been 47 of the industrial type, is not now compulsory, but in 1932 no less than 18,000,000 out of 23,000,000 workers were members. The unions are dominated by the Communist party, and are made responsible to a large extent for the disciplining of the masses. Members pay 2 per cent of their wages as dues. In addition to dealing with economic matters, the unions provide extensive cultural activities. It is hoped to transform the entire population into proletarians, and the growth of union membership shows the rapid strides being taken in this direction. During the present year the 47 unions were split up into 154. In 1933 the Commissariat for Labor was abolished and its functions were taken over by the trade-union organization. Union representatives in every plant have recognized functions in protecting the worker in respect to his working-conditions. The unions, of course, do not have the right to strike. They function not only to protect the worker, as such, but also to imbue him with Communist ideals. In the rural districts, the collective and state farms and the mechanization of agriculture serve to "proletarianize" the peasants. They are to become wage workers in the "grain factories."

An effort is made in the Soviet Union to induct as many people as possible into productive activities, that is, into some sort of industrial or cultural work. The number of wage-earners has increased rapidly. In 1930 there were 14,600,000 wage-earners; in 1932 the figure rose to 22,900,000. In spite of this and notwithstanding the fact that thousands of workers have been imported from the United States, Germany, and other countries, the speed of industrial expansion has been so great that a labor shortage, rather than unemployment due to a labor surplus, is still to be found.

Eighty-three per cent of the workers in large-scale state industry in 1931 were on an official seven-hour day. In the iron and steel, basic chemical, and rubber industries all workers, and in the oil, paper, textile, electrical, and nonferrous metals industries almost all workers (90 to 98 per cent) were on the seven-hour day. Persons between sixteen and eighteen are to work only six hours a day, those between fourteen and sixteen, four hours. On the whole, the Soviet worker has a shorter official working-day than any other worker and enjoys, in addition, 95 nonworking-days, including monthly vacations, during the course of the year.

The amount of wages paid to workers has increased even more than the in-

---

[1] Dobbert, *op. cit.*, p. 266.

crease in the number of workers. The total wage fund in 1931 was 21,100,000,-000 rubles, 68.8 per cent above the 1930 figure, and 34.5 per cent above the schedule for the last year of the First Five Year Plan, 1932-33. The average annual wage per worker for all branches of the national plant was 1,096 rubles for 1931, an increase of 23.5 per cent over 1930 and of 40 per cent over 1929. The average income per family increased even more, since more members of the family were gainfully occupied. Thus the monthly income per worker's family by the end of 1931 was 64 per cent higher than in 1929. Statistics here are, however, admittedly poor, and when allowance is made for the rate of exchange of the ruble wages in Russia, real wages in actual amount are probably below those in some leading industrial countries. If the very high prices are taken into consideration, real wages are perhaps somewhat below those in England and the United States. There are, however, no reliable statistics for movements in real wages. But it must be remembered that if real wages in Russia are low, at least every able-bodied adult is employed. Moreover, the state provides gratis many services for which workers in other countries must pay.

Huge housing programs are being carried out everywhere in the Soviet Union to solve the housing problem that has been almost constant. Houses, apartments, and even cities are being constructed to accommodate the tremendously increased number of workers. In 1925 the investment in housing projects for workers was 63,000,000 rubles. In 1930 it was 300,000,000 and in 1931, 575,000,000—over nine times as much as in 1925. In the coal regions alone investments for housing amounted to 201,000,000 rubles in 1931 as against 95,000,000 in 1930. Better than these figures are those in terms of square meters of floor space constructed. In 1925, 1,800,000 square meters (approximately 30,000 houses) were constructed. For 1930 it was 6,000,000 square meters (105,-000 houses) and for 1933, 7,200,000 square meters (approximately 150,000 houses). This remarkable building activity, however, has by no means cleared up the housing problem. Conditions for careful city-planning are propitious in Soviet Russia. Mr. Jacob Crane, an American engineer, writes that

for the first time in the modern world, cities may be built according to plans which utilize all of the land to the best advantage of city living because the land is publicly owned. In America big city building, and to a large degree city planning, has necessarily failed to produce good results because it has to be done within the very severe limitation of recognizing private property interests and the increase in and inflation of land values. This alone gives Russian city planning a tremendous advantage over that of America.[1]

In speaking of plans for industrial cities, he says:

In Giprogor I found the most completely organized designs for towns that I have seen. The whole town or city is one carefully worked out design, magnificent and beautiful.[2]

[1] Crane, "A New Conception of City Planning," *Economic Review of the Soviet Union*, Jan. 15, 1932, p. 36.
[2] *Ibid.*

To what extent complete use of these unusual opportunities will be made remains to be seen.

Improvements in municipal services are constantly being made. Paving of streets and installation of street railways, water systems, sewers, and so on are going on throughout the land. In 1917, only 162 cities had water-supply systems. In 1932 there were 369. In Russia under the tsars there were only 18 cities with sewer systems; in 1932 there were 55.

Those who most severely criticize Soviet Russia because it has not yet provided a sufficiently high standard of living for the masses often fail to consider the handicaps under which the Bolshevik régime began its work. It had to take over the most backward economy and social system that existed in any major country of the Western world. Moreover, it had to assume responsibility at a time when even this inefficient and archaic order had completely collapsed. The only fair way to judge the new Russian society is to hold it up against what would, in all probability, have happened if the tsarist régime had held over after 1917. There is hardly the possibility that living-conditions would have been as satisfactory as they are today for the mass of Russians. There is every probability that there would have been wholesale starvation, while, at the same time, there would have been no promise of a markedly better future. When one reflects upon the low standard of living that prevailed among the masses in normal times under the Romanovs, he is likely to shudder when he contemplates what would have happened if the incompetent old régime had been forced to cope with the economic and social wreck that was Russia in 1917.

2. THE NEW EDUCATION IN RUSSIA

In the field of education—or what the Russians prefer to call "public enlightenment"—noteworthy changes have taken place since the period of the Revolution. The statistics in this field are not altogether dependable nor do they tell the whole story, but they are indicative of a definite general tendency. Whereas previous to the Revolution only eight or nine million people in Russia received any kind of education, the total for 1934 was at least three times that number. This includes *all* types of education, and is in no sense limited to academic education. In 1914, it was estimated that only 51 per cent of the children were receiving education in the schools, while the percentage today is over 90. This has meant a remarkable increase, in view of the fact that in 1920 the number had dropped to 24.9 per cent. This was but one of the indications that the Russian educational system was largely a failure down to 1923.

Since 1923 there have been steadily increasing amounts expended for educational purposes, and an enthusiasm to learn seems to be evident throughout Russia. The educational cost per pupil has also been increasing. In 1934 the total number of pupils in schools of general education, including elementary, intermediate, and higher education, numbered 24,000,000. There were 602,000 students in intermediate technical schools. Some 271,000 were enrolled in workers' schools. The number of students in higher educational institutions was 472,000. The educational budget for the whole of the U.S.S.R. in 1934 was 8,900,000,000 rubles, and the estimated budget for 1935 is 10,100,000,000 rubles. The wiping out of illiteracy is strongly desired. The campaign against illiteracy has been remarkably successful, as the following figures will make clear. In 1907, 73 per cent of the Russians between ten and fifty years of age were illiterate; in 1913, 66 per cent; in 1927-28, 46 per cent; and in 1932, 7 per cent.[1]

In 1923 the aims of education were said to be the training of specialists and the preparation of a young group of Communists who could replace those now in power. Since 1925 energies have been concentrated upon compulsory primary education, a recognition of the fundamental problem of illiteracy. In 1929 another set of goals was formulated as part of the Five Year Plan, which emphasizes the training of "qualified workers," the eradication of illiteracy, religion, and other survivals of the old régime, and "the proletarianization of secondary and academic education." At the same time, education was extensively "militarized," and older pupils and university students are now subject to compulsory military training.

As late as August, 1932, the Central Executive Committee of the Communist party frankly admitted the inadequacies of the system then in operation and pointed out that "the main defect of the Soviet school—insufficiency of general knowledge, defective preparation for higher technical training and almost complete absence of knowledge in such matters as physics, chemistry, mathematics, the mother tongue and geography—has not been removed." [2] Plans drawn up since then are designed to remove these weaknesses. It is interesting to note that the latest system resembles in type of schooling, manner of instruction, development of material, and so on that which obtains in capitalist countries much more closely than did the other plans which the Soviet government has tried.

In the effort to provide trained and skilled workers, every available agency is made to function as a school—workers' clubs, the Red Army, prisons, the radio, the state farms, and so on. Not only is the entire force of the country designed to prepare people for labor but, naturally enough, education also functions to inculcate Communist ideals. This is done through both the schools and all young people's groups and societies. The educational system frankly rests upon class purposes and is conducted along class lines. The intolerance, the pointed propaganda, the absence of a critical attitude towards Communism, all find thorough justification in Communist thought on the ground that old notions, attitudes, and ideals must be destroyed and replaced by those of Communism, which alone prepares one for life in a socialized state. Whether the purpose or goal be admired or not, it is nevertheless true that never have all types of educational facilities been so thoroughly mobilized and so consciously directed towards a specific social goal as they are in Russia today.[3]

3. THE RELIGIOUS POLICY OF SOVIET RUSSIA

Among the most thoroughgoing changes introduced by the Communists have been those with reference to the Church and religion. An anticlerical and antireligious tendency was present in Russia before the Revolution as a protest against the unusually close connection between Church and State, the tre-

---

[1] Cf. Davis, op. cit., p. 218.
[2] Cited in Malevsky-Malevich, op. cit., p. 675.
[3] Cf. Klaus Mehnert, Youth in Soviet Russia, Harcourt, Brace, 1933, and Woody, New Minds: New Men? Chaps. I-III, XIII-XIV.

mendous wealth of the Greek Church, its extensive privileges and powers, the religious influence it exercised in fields that are today regarded as civil or secular, and the support it gave to the autocratic existing order. Among the props of the old régime, the Orthodox Church was one of the strongest.

Since the Communist program involves not only a material reconstruction of Russia and its economy but also a cultural and psychic transformation of its people, the religious policy of the Soviet Union—which has been so severely criticized throughout the world—can at least be understood. The Church and religion, in the eyes of Communists, not only served to perpetuate the existing order, but also acted as an "opiate" that kept the masses quiescent. A different people with new attitudes and ideals has to be created to operate the new Communist world. Not a religious conception of life, but a materialistic Communistic conception of life, must dominate. This meant alert opposition to supernatural religion—the adoption of a consciously directed antireligious program. Naturally, the chief attack was directed against the Orthodox Church, whose membership included at least 70 per cent of the population previous to the Revolution and whose leaders were a main bulwark of the old order. The antireligious program has expressed itself in strong atheistic propaganda, the placing of disabilities upon religious groups, and what may be called sporadic religious persecution.

The mediums utilized in spreading atheism are the school, the universities, and other educational agencies, the Red Army, printed matter, all the arts, unions—in short, almost any medium that will lend itself to the task. In this policy, however, it must be admitted that the Soviet government is doing no more than many states with an established religion and Church were accustomed to do but a short time ago. Indeed, the Soviet government has done little more than turn the tables on the Orthodox Church of Romanov days. Religious bodies or individuals are prohibited from propagating their particular beliefs, and have been prevented from exercising any influence in educational, political, economic, or social matters. Individuals holding official posts of an ecclesiastical nature cannot vote, and this in turn means increased taxation burdens and the deprivation of all types of advantages and privileges. Church property was, of course, early confiscated. Direct persecution, in the sense of the forcible suppression of religious bodies and the execution of ecclesiastics, has been sporadic and was most intense in 1918-23 and 1928-30. It has been charged by critics that many members of the Orthodox Church were put to death because of religious fidelity. The Russian government has alleged, however, with much supporting evidence, that they were executed for counter-revolutionary rather than religious offenses. Accurate statistics of the total number of persons suffering the death penalty for politico-religious reasons are lacking. In view of what is known, however, it seems likely that many of the newspaper reports of mass executions and atrocities can be regarded as wild exaggerations.

To all of this must be added, nevertheless, the fact that complete freedom of conscience is established by law. Any citizen may believe or disbelieve in religion as he pleases, so long as his belief does not lead to actions in conflict with existing law. While this theoretically grants every citizen the right to worship as he pleases, a law of 1929 materially modifies this. One of the articles reads: "In all state, public, coöperative, and private institutions and enterprises, the performance of any kind of religious service is forbidden, together with the display of articles of worship of any kind." Nevertheless, congregations do worship throughout Russia today, although they obviously labor under some difficulties. In general, those religious activities which are carried on are specially licensed by the government. Perhaps the best way to summarize the situation is to say that Russians are permitted to believe and worship, but there religion must end. It may no longer interfere in politics, economics, education, or morals.

On the whole, direct, forceful religious persecution is now in disfavor, and there is a concentration of energy upon antireligious propaganda. Wherever religious activity of any kind is deemed grave enough to constitute counter-revolutionary activity, punishment is severe and swift. Some priests are really active counter-revolutionaries and as such they are punished. But the government has realized that to deal with religious sentiment among the masses in terms of counter-revolution is ridiculous and dangerous.

What the results of the entire campaign have been cannot yet be estimated.[1] Of all the churches and religions in Russia, the Greek Church has suffered most in loss of members, wealth, position, and prestige. Its former extensive educational powers are today nonexistent. The other religious bodies have suffered too, but to a smaller extent. There has been a definite growth of atheism. But as late as 1929 a high Soviet official (Emelyan Yaroslavsky) stated that between sixty and seventy million people of the working population were still "actively religious." Especially notable has been the large number of Jews who are now classified as atheists.[2] The only religious groups that have been relatively unaffected are the non-Jewish and non-Christian—Mohammedans, Buddhists, Lamaists, and the rest—and of these only the first has any real importance. On the whole, it can be said that the objective of the Communists—the ultimate conversion of the Soviet citizen body to atheism—is still far from being attained.

In concluding this section on religion in the new Russia one should not fail to indicate that the Communist faith has indeed become the religion of millions of radical Russians. Some observers have marveled how a nation recently extremely pious could so quickly dispense with its accustomed religion. The answer is that those who hold fast to the old religions have gone on worshiping, while the enthusiastic supporters of the new régime have simply transferred their religious emotions to Communism and its leaders. In this way Communism may, in one sense, be regarded as the first great secular religion of mankind. Communistic ideology rests upon what is regarded as a very dogmatic body of historical philosophy and economic logic. But the fervor with which this ideology is supported and applied is of a thoroughly religious intensity. Moreover, there is already a Soviet Trinity—Marx, Lenin, and Stalin—special holy places like the tomb of Lenin, and periodic "purifications" of the party instigated by fervent Communists, comparable to Christian penitential

[1] Probably the most intelligent presentation of the issues involved in the new Russian religious policy is contained in Chaps. iv-vi of F. E. Williams, *Russia, Youth, and the Present-day World*, Farrar & Rinehart, 1934. See also Woody, *op. cit.*, Chap. viii; and J. F. Hecker, *Religion and Communism*, Wiley, 1935.

[2] Soviet Russia is one of the few states today where there is no anti-Semitism.

rites. And, interestingly enough, the Marxian materialistic philosophy of history is the Russian counterpart of the Christian epic. No less an expert than Professor Harry F. Ward has spoken of Communism as the most vital and dynamic religion in existence today. While Russian Communism has become, in effect, a powerful new religion, it is only fair to point out that Russian Communists bitterly resent this assertion. They claim for themselves complete rationality and conscious deliberation in their whole economic and social program.

4. MARITAL RELATIONS, THE FAMILY, AND MORALS

Marriage and morals have in the past been very closely related to, and dependent upon, supernatural religion. The rejection of supernatural religion in Soviet Russia has inevitably had a profound effect upon marriage mores, divorce codes, the relations between the sexes, the position of women, and the whole conception of the purpose of moral conduct. Whatever one's personal opinion of the present Russian doctrines and practices in such matters, it is certain that the transformation here has been quite as revolutionary and startling as it has been in the economic realm. To conventional-minded observers these changes have, indeed, been even more shocking than the economic reconstruction of Russia, though it should be noted that the much-publicized charge of the nationalization of women in Soviet Russia is a ridiculous fiction without an iota of evidence to support it.

Significant changes have taken place in the field of marital relationships in the new Russia. Civil marriage alone is recognized in the Soviet Union. Church marriages are not prohibited, but they have no legal status. In order to contract a marriage, both parties must be at least eighteen years old, and both must give their consent. Since 1926 what is known as de facto marriage has been recognized. This is similar to the common-law marriage of the United States, and the parties to it can register their union at any time. It is a legal union, and its dissolution simply involves the cessation of cohabitation. When registering a marriage, both parties must give evidence of their identity, information concerning family status, age, state of health, and so on. Persons found guilty of giving false information are punishable under the criminal code. A person may enter upon only one marriage at a time, and polygyny is punishable as a criminal offense. A person legally adjudged insane or mentally defective may not contract a marriage.

Since it accepts the theory that people marry because they would rather live together than apart, the Soviet union grants divorce when either or both of the parties no longer wish to live together. This simplification of divorce caused a tremendous increase in divorces up to 1926. After the many unhappy marriages of the old régime were terminated in the first rush for easy divorces, there was a remarkable falling off in the divorce rate. Russia has thus proved the often asserted contention of liberal writers on sex in Western lands that men and women who are congenial will continue to live together when legal pressure is removed. Both husband and wife are eligible to request alimony for a short period of time. Divorce in no sense frees the parents from responsibility for the children. Likewise, there is full responsibility for children born out of wedlock. The parents must contribute to their support and to their preparation for useful activity. Where this cannot be done, the state undertakes the task.

The conception of the family has naturally undergone a sharp modification. So thoroughly are the individual interests of the members of the family protected by law that the family as a unit no longer means what it does elsewhere. The positions of husband and wife are completely equalized. Husband and wife may keep or change their surnames, each may live where he or she pleases, or engage in any occupation. Husband and wife never hold property in common, and there is no "head of the family." If one is in need, either husband or wife has the right to demand support from the other. While recognized as guardians of their children, when such trusteeship is abused the right is lost. There are thus no parental rights of which the parents cannot be deprived by the courts. Both parents are assumed to be economically productive, and marriage as a means of feminine escape from economic responsibility is regarded as nonexistent. Nor can the family be viewed as a disciplinary agency for the children or as a mechanism for the transmission of accumulated property from parents to children. In theory, at least, what the Communists call the bourgeois family has disappeared in Russia.[1]

Implicit in much that has been said here is the absolute equality which exists between the sexes. The subjection of women ended with the Russian Revolution. They are now free and independent, the equals of men in every respect. In no other country do the same conditions exist. There can be found in Russia today no legal discrimination against women. They may enter any profession, hold any office, engage in any occupation. They receive the same wages as men for the same work. They no longer need depend upon men for a livelihood.

The moral and social consequences of this condition are potentially very great, but it is still too soon to get a clear picture of them. It is argued that already a result is apparent in the marked decrease of prostitution in Soviet Russia.[2] This has been the general impression of foreign visitors, and it is, of course, affirmed by official surveys. In few countries of the world do women play so prominent a part in all phases of social life as they do in the U.S.S.R. There women are often leaders in industry, education, science, or government.

Much of woman's newly won freedom has been the product of a changed attitude towards the bearing and rearing of children. Expectant mothers are relieved from work for a period of about sixteen weeks, which begins before the child is born and ends after recovery from confinement. During absence from work their pay goes on as before. When the mother returns to work her baby is deposited in a day nursery (crèche) in the custody of a trained nurse. The mother is allowed several periods during the day to rest and to nurse the baby. When the child grows older it is placed in a nursery or kindergarten during the day.

Since no legal stigma attaches either to children born out of wedlock or to "unmarried mothers," there is a virtual recognition of the right of every woman to bear children. This also implies the right not to bear children. Girls are given extensive clinical information in birth control, and all known contracep-

---

[1] *Cf.* Seibert, *op. cit.,* Chap. x, and Winter, *Red Virtue,* Chap. xiv.
[2] *Cf.* Winter, *op. cit.,* Chap. xii.

tive methods are made available. An unusual step has also been taken in the legalization of abortion, but only under certain conditions and under the closest supervision of the state. No deaths have occurred in the course of over 100,000 abortions.

The Communists, of course, completely reject "bourgeois" standards of ethics. The old conception of sin has officially gone by the board. Good and evil, they argue, are to be measured not in terms of the supernatural but in terms of human needs and activities. If a given act protects and furthers the interests of society and the individual, then it is, by virtue of that fact, good. If, on the contrary, it is injurious to social interests, it is bad. Such a code is obviously extremely flexible.

Next to the rejection of supernatural elements in morality, the most striking thing about ethics in Soviet Russia is the repudiation of the characteristic tendency in capitalistic countries to identify morals almost wholly with sex behavior. The Bolsheviks regard economic conduct as more germane to morals than sex activities.

5. THE NEW CRIMINOLOGY IN RUSSIA

Crimes, as such, are measured and classified in terms of their antisocial nature.[1] Three such rough categories may be established. The first includes conspiracy against the Soviet government, or counter-revolution; the second, inefficiency or mismanagement in industry; and the third, offenses such as theft, assault, murder, and so forth.

After Kerensky's experiment with the abolition of capital punishment, the death penalty was revived by Lenin, and is immediately visited upon all those deemed guilty of counter-revolutionary activities. Since so much depends upon the successful industrialization of the country and the solution of other economic problems, a person in a responsible position believed guilty of mismanagement, for any reason, may be tried. Inefficiency here is a crime against society. If the mismanagement was deliberate, then it would probably be classed with counter-revolution and treated accordingly. If due to stupidity or carelessness, the official is removed, demoted, publicly censured, and otherwise punished.

The third category of criminal offenses—the conventional crimes in most countries—can be regarded as antisocial acts due to improper training and education. In this sense, a person who steals is a person improperly educated. It follows, therefore, that such criminals are made by society. To cure crime the causes must be removed. Since in a large number of cases the object of crime is economic gain, the Communist argues that where personal acquisition does not lie at the core of human activities, such crimes decrease. Ultimately they should—with the proper education—theoretically disappear entirely.

For criminal acts that fall into the first two categories, punishment is swift and almost free from reformative principles. But for antisocial acts that fall into the third class, there is a conscious effort to reëducate instead of to punish. There is also a logical effort on the part of society to remove the causes that induce criminal action. There is in many regions of Russia now a growing use

[1] On Russian criminal jurisprudence, see M. S. Callcott, *Russian Justice*, Macmillan, 1935.

THE NEW SOCIAL ORDER IN RUSSIA

of the psychiatric method in the diagnosis of criminals, and, instead of punishment, a general adoption of the principle of treatment.[1]

In cases where antisocial offenders are put in prison, they are not punished and humiliated. They are not locked up in cells, but live in wards. In nearly all of the prisons there are factories where the prisoners are allowed to work, although they are not compelled to do so. They are paid wages for such work as they do in these factories. These wages they are allowed to send to their families or to save until their dismissal. Every prison has a library; almost all have a theater, a school, and club rooms. Ample provision is made for cultural and educational activities. Visitors have more than once found an inmate in one of these prisons who has "overstayed" his sentence by two or three months. Upon being asked why he was still there, when his sentence had expired long before, he replied that he had only begun his course in chemistry, or electricity, or biology a short time before his sentence was over. Hence he petitioned the prison authorities to allow him to remain until he had completed his course. This attitude may be fruitfully compared with the all-absorbing passion of those confined in our conventional prisons to escape or to secure legal release at the earliest possible moment. In Russia alone have the ideals of scientific criminology been realized.

6. MEDICINE, MENTAL HYGIENE, AND SOCIAL WELFARE

Soviet Russia demands complete devotion to the principles of the new régime on the part of its citizens. For its part, it accepts the reciprocal responsibility of caring for all the legitimate needs of each citizen. Consequently public-health service, mental hygiene, social welfare, and provisions for a sane use of leisure have undergone a most remarkable development in the new Russia.

Public-health activities and institutions have been completely revolutionized.[2] In the Russia of the tsars there were many eminent medical specialists, but adequate medical treatment was available only for the nobility and the upper middle class. The masses were neglected, and relied mainly on crude forms of self-medication, some of which were not far removed from primitive magic. There was little or no organized public-health service. Today, there is no country under the sun that places more stress upon proper medical facilities for its people and none which has laid out so ambitious a system of public-health work. A distinguished British physician who has visited Russia thus summarizes the remarkable layout that has been provided in this field of endeavor:

> Prophylactoria for the prevention of bodily diseases; official abortoria for those women who desire to avoid motherhood; lavishly equipped maternity institutes for mothers who decide to have children; crêches (day nurseries) for infants, polyclinics for the treatment of early and minor maladies; hospitals, infirmaries, and convalescent homes for persons who require more serious treatment; night homes for tuberculous town-workers still able to go to work in the day-time; rest-homes where workers can spend their official holidays: these and similar institutions are all provided by the State, free of cost.[3]

[1] *Cf.* Lenka (Helene von der Leyen) von Koerber, *Soviet Russia Fights Crime,* Dutton, 1935.
[2] *Cf.* A. J. Haines, *Health Work in Soviet Russia,* Vanguard Press, 1928.
[3] Sir James Purves Stewart, *A Physician's Tour in Soviet Russia,* Stokes, 1933, pp. 168-69.

It hardly needs to be pointed out that there is little or no private practice of medicine in the U.S.S.R. Medicine there is state medicine. Doctors are paid a definite salary by the state. The experience of Russia in this line of endeavor will afford a good basis for comparing the merits of state medicine with the thoroughly individualized medical practice that still persists in the United States. To date, the major criticism that may be made of state medicine in Russia is the low salaries paid to most doctors. Yet it should be borne in mind that all competent Russian doctors are employed and do make a living from their professional labors. No capable doctor in Russia is forced by sheer economic necessity to seek a livelihood in some other and less dignified activity.

In no field of Russian medicine or social welfare has the progress been more remarkable than in mental hygiene—that branch of medical science and psychology which is devoted to preventing mental and nervous diseases and to providing more efficient and humane treatment for such breakdowns as do occur.[1] Sex education, child-guidance clinics, hospitals for mental cases, and other agencies have been provided in profusion. Even more striking has been the effect of the Russian social order as a whole on mental health. In most Western countries there has been a vast increase of mental and nervous disease in the last generation. In Soviet Russia there has been a steady decrease in the prevalence of mental and nervous disorders—this in spite of the great privations and hardships to which the Russians have been subjected since 1917 in building up their new social order.

Competent observers of non-Communist persuasion have held that this striking decline in the frequency of mental disorders in Russia today has been due to the virtual elimination there of the chief causes of mental disease as they exist in other countries.[2] Among the major causes of mental and nervous disease are sex maladjustment, certain advanced stages of venereal disease, fear of the unknown or the supernatural, and the sense of economic insecurity. No one of these things exists to any marked degree in Soviet Russia. There is much frank sex education. Full knowledge is conveyed of the dangers of venereal disease and ample provision is made for venereal prophylaxis. Moreover, as has been noted, the changed attitude towards sex and property appears to have all but eliminated prostitution. The repudiation of supernatural religion has mitigated those psychoses and neuroses having a basis in religious fear. The state provides everybody willing to work with a job, so there is no longer the wearing fear of possible unemployment and want.

The changed attitude of the Russian state towards its citizens under Communism is also reflected in the elaborate provision for social-welfare projects. Russian workers today receive on the average, in addition to their regular wages, allotments for social insurance, pensions, education, and recreation that amount to approximately 40 per cent of their wage payments. There is a comprehensive system of social insurance providing protection against old age, incapacity, illness, unemployment, and time lost in labor disputes.[3] The remarkable attention given to promoting the health of the Russian people has been mentioned above in the brief description of the new medical service in Russia. Thorough care is provided in case of illness, elaborate instruction is

---

[1] *Cf.* Davis, *op. cit.,* Chap. II, and Williams, *op. cit., passim.*
[2] *Cf.* Williams, *op. cit.*   [3] *Cf.* Hoover, *op. cit.,* Chap. XI.

given as to how to prevent disease, and places for recuperation are supplied.

In spite of the charge of rank materialism that is very generally leveled against them, the Russians have devoted more attention to what used to be called "spiritual things" than any other existing civilization. While they hold that economic factors determine the other aspects of life, they do not necessarily regard material conditions as the most important matter in life. Rather, they look upon an assured livelihood as simply the basis for obtaining the so-called higher things of life. Hence they have made a systematic effort to create the essential facilities for a rational use of leisure.

The center of the cultural activities of the Russians today is the club, which resembles a well-equipped settlement house or a community center rather more than it does what is usually known as a club in this country. In these clubs are to be found libraries, music rooms, theaters, rooms for games, and the like. Special emphasis is placed upon the courses (circles) offered in a multiplicity of subjects, particularly those connected with the fine arts and the problems of leisure. There are nearly a million students enrolled in such classes today. These clubs are also a center of Communist propaganda. The existence of ample leisure is assured through the reasonably short working-day and the many holidays during the year.

XII. A TENTATIVE ESTIMATE

So much has happened in Russia since 1917, so much is planned for the future, so rapidly do events pass us by, so varied are the reports we receive, and so close are we to all that is going on, that it is with great trepidation that we dare attempt to draw a tentative estimate of the Russian experiment. Our brief sketch of Russia has been designed to show how a fundamental revolution not only overthrew the superstructure but also attempted to uproot the foundations of an old order. The Communists are attempting nothing less than the complete reorganization of the ideals as well as the mechanics of society. It is much more difficult to institute a new way of life, to replace personal acquisition and personal ambition with social service and social goals, than it is to manufacture a larger number of tractors or to electrify cities. To do this—to introduce Socialism as a way of life—the leaders of Soviet Russia have decided that a clean break with the old order and its characteristic modes of thought must be made wherever possible.[1] They have believed that to accomplish this result Russia must first be industrialized.

Starting with the paralyzing burden of the consequences of almost seven years of war (from 1914 to about the end of 1920), and with a country that was backward compared to other nations, they were confronted by a tremendous task. Already remarkable strides have been made in the physical rehabilitation of industry and in the reorganization of agriculture. From the most advanced countries of the Western world Russia has taken the best in the way of industrial technique and applied it to its own needs. It has done this even more rapidly than did Germany fifty years ago. Serious difficulties and problems are constantly faced and have to be solved. For some of these problems solutions have already been found. For others the solutions are still sought. All the in-

[1] *Cf.* Ward, *In Place of Profit.*

dications there are warrant the statement that at least the physical needs of the Russian people will be better satisfied within a year or two than they have been at any time in the past.

As in industry, so in education, religion, law, politics—in short, in all fields—new ideals and practices have been substituted for the old. Naturally, all of this has been done at terrific cost and at breath-taking speed—perhaps too rapidly. The whole body of the people is by no means sympathetic with what is being done. People find it difficult to sacrifice so completely the present for the sake of the future. The younger generation, it is hoped, since it is the product of a new environment, will be free from the antagonisms of the old, and will therefore be much more enthusiastic and loyal to the new régime. The dictatorship will of course have to continue until the whole people is ready for a Communistic life. How soon this will be no one can tell. Meanwhile, the leaders argue, if there is a deprivation of the usual democratic liberties, the population will find recompense in the improved material conditions. In their eyes, the paradox of starvation amid plenty that is to be found in capitalist countries can never exist in Russia, since production is for human welfare and distribution is socialized. In Russia overproduction cannot exist. The social and economic system is conducted not for the acquisition of private profits but for the well-being of the productive members of society.[1] Under the Soviet system, the workers are not regarded as commodities on the labor market.

Critics, of course, see many weaknesses and much to condemn in the Russian experiment. They point out that instead of preparing the way for the ideal classless society, the Communists have simply created new class lines and given dominance to different groups of people. They suggest that the bureaucracy which exists in Russia today is already top-heavy and will be bound to grow as the country advances economically. And bureaucracies, they argue, become self-perpetuating and tend, sooner or later, to function not for their original purpose but for the gain of the bureaucracy. Socialism, they say, is fundamentally incompatible with dictatorship. The regimented life that a dictatorship implies will ultimately make impossible the introduction of the contemplated complete democracy, they declare. The number of instances where a dictatorship has voluntarily stripped itself of power in the past, however, gives point to this objection. In present-day Russia, the critics point out, the autocracy of the Communist party has simply supplanted that of the tsar. They also claim that the rapid industrialization has placed too great a strain upon the Russian people, with insufficient recompense in an improved standard of living. They hold that the industrialization has been quantitatively so rapid that much which has been done will have to be done over because of qualitative inadequacies. How much validity these criticisms have, only the future will demonstrate.

In the field of international relations, the last few years have witnessed a marked improvement in the world position of the Soviet Union.[2] The Treaty of Brest-Litovsk and the threat of world Communism cut Russia out of the current of world-affairs as an active participant for several years. The abroga-

---

[1] *Cf.* Ward, *op. cit.*
[2] *Cf.* Fischer, *op. cit.*, and H. N. Brailsford, "Russia Enters the League," *New Republic,* Sept 12, 1934.

tion of past agreements entered into by the previous Russian governments added greatly to the difficulties. When actual intervention and the blockade proved unsuccessful in overthrowing Soviet Russia, the recognition of the new régime by the European and other Powers was unavoidable. The attractiveness of the vast Russian market also could not be disregarded. After 1921, therefore, country after country recognized Russia. The United States, the first state to recognize the Lvov government in March, 1917, was the last Great Power to grant recognition to Soviet Russia, despite the obvious advisability of such recognition.[1] President Roosevelt finally broke the deadlock and recognized Soviet Russia on November 16, 1933. The removal of emphasis by the Communists upon an immediate "world-revolution," and the increasing strength that the present régime has shown in internal affairs, as well as the fact that Russia simply cannot be discounted as a factor in world-affairs, serve to explain the de jure recognition of Russia by the leading states and its increasing international "respectability."

Since 1929 the leaders in Russia have done everything possible to convince the world of the peaceable intentions of the U.S.S.R., and have taken the lead in proposals for world-disarmament. The most recent international developments have served to strengthen Russia's position in world-affairs. In the West, Russia stands as a bulwark against the aggression of Nazi Germany. Because of this, it has drawn closer to France, not so long ago an archenemy. An insurance treaty against aggression was signed in 1934. This growing anxiety of France relative to Nazi Germany was a major reason why France withdrew its objections to the admission of Russia to the League of Nations and facilitated the admission of Russia to the League in the middle of September, 1934.[2] In the Far East, the U.S.S.R. is the only possible counterpoise to the imperial ambitions of a strongly armed Japan. Japanese penetration into China in Manchuria has at last brought Russia and Japan face to face. The Soviet Union is still apprehensive of Japanese encroachments, but the settlement of the Chinese Eastern Railway question in 1935 appears to have removed one serious source of friction. Informed observers see in Manchuria one of the major danger spots of the world. Whether the European powers, unable to check the Japanese advances in the Far East, will accept with keen relish an extended struggle between Japan and Russia, in the hope that both Powers will be seriously injured, remains to be seen. At any rate, Russia at present occupies a significant position in world affairs, and in the handling of international problems it cannot possibly be ignored. Fortunately for Russia, Japan did not attack it some years back. Then Japan would probably have won an easy victory or else put disastrous pressure on Russian economic resources. Today, Russia has soldiers, arms, and airplanes in the Far East sufficient to make a successful Japanese foray almost out of the question. But the energy and expense involved in rendering itself impregnable in the Far East have reduced the speed with which Russia might have gone ahead in economic development at home since 1931.

One of the major factors in securing for Russia a position of respect among the nations has been the creation of a great Red Army, second to none in the

[1] *Cf.* F. L. Schuman, *American Policy toward Russia since 1917,* International Publishers, 1928.
[2] *Cf.* Brailsford, *loc. cit.*

world for strength, discipline, and enthusiasm. Its development was due to Trotsky more than to any other person. Especially important since Trotsky's ejection from Russia has been the development of the Soviet air force. Russia has a fine military airplane division. More important, it can manufacture airplanes more rapidly than any other European state except Germany. And these plants are located so far from any powerful Western state that they cannot be bombed with much success—an advantage not enjoyed by the airplane plants of England, France, Germany, or Italy. This Russian air strength was a consideration in making the French willing to sign a defensive pact with Russia and to facilitate its entry into the League of Nations. As Mr. Brailsford has observed:

Here then was an acceptable ally. This Power had all the moral qualifications for membership in the League of Peace. Russia's pariah days are over: she can bomb with the best.[1]

As we have indicated, the real significance of these years of Communist control in Russia will only be revealed by the future. Whether the present efforts of the leaders to make the Soviet Union "an impregnable fortress of Socialism" in the midst of a capitalist world will succeed still remains an open question.[2] If they do, then two great systems will be opposed to one another. Ultimately Communism must seek to convert the world. Even if there is failure, at least Russia will remain the outstanding conscious experiment in social reconstruction in the history of the world. And the possibility of failure, under conditions as they now exist, will offer no final proof of the impracticability of Socialism or of the continued dominance of capitalism as we now know it. Already a new era has dawned in Russia, and whether one likes it or not, it is a fact that cannot be waved aside with a gesture of the hand. Perhaps as fair and intelligent an appraisal as any that has been made of the Russian experiment is that of Mr. Corliss Lamont, himself a son of the ranking partner of the firm of J. P. Morgan & Co.

In the kind of general estimate which we are trying to make, the promise of the future is just as important as the reality of the present. And it is this promise—we say with intent *promise* rather than merely *hope*—which is the most impressive thing of all, to our minds. The direction in the Soviet, from both the material and cultural standpoints, seems steadily and on the whole upward, and the problems those of growth. Elsewhere in the world the direction seems downward and the problems those of decay. In other words the many strains and stresses still existent in Russia are justified in the light of the great goal ahead. The masses of the people there are making what may be called *constructive* sacrifices, with a splendid purpose held consciously and continuously in mind. In capitalist countries, too, large masses of people are making sacrifices, but these sacrifices are chaotic, purposeless, and to a large extent useless. They are not leading anywhere. There is no plan behind them.

This makes all the difference in the world. For purposeful giving of all that is in you may lead to happiness not only in the future, but also in the present. And

---

[1] Brailsford, *loc. cit.*, p. 119.
[2] On the changed attitude of Russia towards world revolution since 1917, see M. T. Florinsky, *World Revolution and the U.S.S.R.*, Macmillan, 1933.

consequently we believe that there is a great deal of happiness in Russia today. People there are giving their complete allegiance to a great object of devotion which drives their personal worries and their Freudian complexes into the background. They are literally forgetting themselves. And in their adherence to the new, invigorating loyalties they are being released from age-long and century-long economic fears, sexual repressions, and religious feelings of guilt. All along the line what may legitimately be called a spiritual revolution has been accompanying the economic and political change—a revolution resulting in new motives and new ideals, in a new human nature, if you will.[1]

[1] Corliss and Margaret Lamont, *Russia Day by Day*, Covici, Friede, 1933, pp. 257-59. Probably the best work from which to get real insight into the social and economic spirit of the new Russia is Ward, *op. cit.*

SUGGESTED READING

Hammerton, *Universal History of the World*, Chap. 184
Day, *Economic Development in Modern Europe*, Chaps. xv-xix
Baron S. A. Korff, *Autocracy and Revolution in Russia*, Macmillan, 1923
G. V. Vernadsky, *The Russian Revolution*, Holt, 1932
M. J. Olgin, *The Soul of the Russian Revolution*, Holt, 1917
Pokrovsky, *Brief History of Russia*
G. T. Robinson, *Rural Russia under the Old Régime*, Longmans, 1932
Leon Trotsky, *History of the Russian Revolution*, Simon & Schuster, 1932, 3 vols.
W. H. Chamberlin, *History of the Russian Revolution, 1917-1921*, Macmillan, 1935, 2 vols.
R. W. Fox, *Lenin*, Harcourt, Brace, 1934
M. T. Florinsky, *World Revolution and the U.S.S.R.*, Macmillan, 1933
M. Ilin (I. I. Marshak), *New Russia's Primer*, Houghton Mifflin, 1931
Jerome Davis, ed., *The New Russia*, Day, 1933
—— *Contemporary Social Movements*, Bk. IV
Walter Duranty, *Duranty Reports Russia*, Viking Press, 1934
A. L. Strong, *I Change Worlds*, Holt, 1935
Bruce Hopper, *Pan-Sovietism*, Houghton Mifflin, 1931
W. H. Chamberlin, *Soviet Russia*, Little, Brown, 1930
—— *Russia's Iron Age*, Little, Brown, 1934
Theodor Seibert, *Red Russia*, Century, 1932
M. G. Hindus, *Humanity Uprooted*, rev. ed., Smith & Haas, 1930
Sherwood Eddy, *Russia Today*, Farrar & Rinehart, 1934
C. M. Hamilton, *Modern Russia as Seen by an Englishwoman*, Dutton, 1934
B. W. Maxwell, *The Soviet State*, Steves & Wayburn, 1934
Hans Kohn, *Nationalism in the Soviet Union*, Columbia University Press, 1933
V. A. Yakhontov, *Russia and the Soviet Union in the Far East*, Coward-McCann, 1931
H. F. Ward, *In Place of Profit*, Scribner, 1933
Joseph Stalin and others, *From the First to the Second Five-Year Plan*, International Publishers, 1934
Thomas Woody, *New Minds: New Men?* Macmillan, 1932
Ella Winter, *Red Virtue*, Harcourt, Brace, 1933
Klaus Mehnert, *Youth in Soviet Russia*, Harcourt, Brace, 1933
F. W. Halle, *Woman in Soviet Russia*, Viking Press, 1933
M. S. Callcott, *Russian Justice*, Macmillan, 1935

Koerber, *Soviet Russia Fights Crime*
F. E. Williams, *Russia, Youth, and the Present-day World,* Farrar & Rinehart, 1934
George Mecklenburg, *Russia Challenges Religion,* Abingdon Press, 1934
J. F. Hecker, *Religion and Communism,* Wiley, 1935
Sir Arthur Newsholme and J. A. Kingsbury, *Red Medicine,* Doubleday, Doran, 1933
Robinson and Beard, *Readings in Modern European History,* Vol. II, Chap. xxviii
Scott and Baltzly, *Readings in European History since 1814,* pp. 282-303, 330-51, 564-86, 633-62
Gerhard Dobbert, ed., *Red Economics,* Houghton Mifflin, 1932
J. R. Freeman, Joshua Kunitz, and Louis Lozowick, eds., *Voices of October,* Vanguard Press, 1930
George Reavey and M. L. Slonim, eds., *Soviet Literature,* Covici, Friede, 1934
Louis Fischer, *Soviet Journey,* Smith & Haas, 1935

FURTHER REFERENCES

SOVIET RUSSIA. For excellent surveys of the new Russia, see Davis, *Contemporary Social Movements,* Bk. IV; Ilin, *op. cit.*

On Russia before the Revolution of 1905, see Pares, *History of Russia,* Chap. xxi; Korff, *op. cit.,* Chaps. i-ii; M. M. Karpovich, *Imperial Russia, 1801-1917* (Holt, 1932); Pokrovsky, *op. cit.,* Vol. II, pp. 13-75. On the Russian Revolution of 1905, see Pokrovsky, *op. cit.,* Vol. II, *passim;* Olgin, *op. cit.*

RUSSIAN REVOLUTION OF 1917. Arthur Rosenberg, *History of Bolshevism* (Oxford Press, 1934); the colossal and authoritative work of Leon Trotsky cited above. For a brief anti-Bolshevik summary, see Vernadsky, *op. cit.* For the broader significance of the Revolution, see L. A. White, "An Anthropological Appraisal of the Russian Revolution," *Pravda,* Feb. 7, 1931, and *Open Forum* (Los Angeles), May 9, 1931. On Lenin, the leading figure in the new Russia, see I. D. Levine, *The Man Lenin* (Seltzer, 1924); Fox, *op. cit.* The authoritative biography by Trotsky is announced for publication by Doubleday, Doran.

COÖPERATIVES. On the rôle of the Russian coöperatives in the new Russia, see Chap. ix of C. B. Hoover, *The Economic Life of Soviet Russia* (Macmillan, 1931); E. T. Blanc, *The Co-operative Movement in Russia* (Macmillan, 1924).

For the best brief, up-to-date, official summary of all aspects of Soviet Russia, see Joseph Stalin, *The Political and Social Doctrine of Communism* (International Conciliation Bulletin, December, 1934).

SOVIET POLITICAL SYSTEM. On the political structure, see Chamberlin, *op. cit.,* Chaps. iii, ix; G. D. H. and M. I. Cole, "The Political System of Russia," *American Mercury,* June, 1934; Davis, *The New Russia,* Chaps. vii-ix; Seibert, *op. cit.,* Bks. II, V; Hopper, *op. cit.,* Chap. v; H. N. Brailsford, *How the Soviets Work* (Vanguard Press, 1927); Maxwell, *op. cit.*

On Stalin, see I. D. Levine, *Stalin* (Cosmopolitan Book Co., 1931). This is a rather hostile biography. A more sympathetic one is to be found in Henri Barbusse, *Stalin* (Macmillan, 1935).

SOVIET LEGAL SYSTEM. Davis, *The New Russia,* Chap. ix; Hopper, *op. cit.,* pp. 92-100; Seibert, *op. cit.,* Chap. xv; Judah Zelitch, *Soviet Administration of Criminal Law* (University of Pennsylvania Press, 1931).

SOVIET FOREIGN POLICY. Yakhontov, *op. cit.;* Chaps. xii-xiv of Andrei Lobanov-Rostovsky, *Russia and Asia* (Macmillan, 1933); Morse and McNair, *Far Eastern International Problems,* Chaps. xxviii, xxx; Sokolsky, *The Tinder Box of Asia;*

FURTHER REFERENCES

A. L. P. Dennis, *The Foreign Policies of Soviet Russia* (Dutton, 1924); Louis Fischer, *The Soviets in World Affairs* (Ballou, 1930, 2 vols.); T. A. Taracouzio, *Soviet Union and International Law* (Macmillan, 1935).

THE ECONOMIC REVOLUTION IN RUSSIA. Davis, *op. cit.*, Chap. v; Seibert, *op. cit.*, Bk. VI; Hopper, *op. cit.*, Chaps. vi-viii; Emile Burns, *Russia's Productive System* (Dutton, 1930); Dobbert, *op. cit.*, Chaps. i-v, xiii; Hoover, *op. cit.*; W. H. Chamberlin, *The Soviet Planned Economic Order* (World Peace Foundation, 1931) and *Russia's Iron Age;* Stalin and others, *op. cit.*

FIVE YEAR PLANS. For the official summaries of the First Five Year Plan and the prospectus of the Second Five Year Plan, see Stalin and others, *op. cit.*

TRANSPORTATION. On Russian transportation since 1918, see Dobbert, *op. cit.*, Chap. ix; Burns, *op. cit.*, Chap. ix; Chamberlin, *The Soviet Planned Economic Order*, pp. 85 ff.

AGRICULTURE. On Russian agriculture before 1917, see Robinson, *op. cit.* On Russian agriculture under the Bolsheviks, see Davis, *op. cit.*, Chap. iv; Dobbert, *op. cit.*, Chap. vi; Burns, *op. cit.*, Chap. xiii; Hoover, *op. cit.*, Chap. iv; Viacheslav Molotov, *The Success of the Five-Year Plan* (International Publishers, 1931); Hindus, *op. cit.* and *Red Bread* (Smith & Haas, 1931); Karl Borders, *Village Life under the Soviets* (Vanguard Press, 1927).

TRADE AND COMMERCE. On Soviet trade and commercial policy, see Dobbert, *op. cit.*, Chaps. iv, x, xiv; Hoover, *op. cit.*, Chaps. v-vi; Chamberlin, *Russia's Iron Age*.

MONEY, BANKING, AND FINANCE. Davis, *op. cit.*, Chap. viii; Dobbert, *op. cit.*, Chaps. vii-viii; Hoover, *op. cit.*, Chaps. vii-viii; Stalin and others, *op. cit.*, pp. 365-423.

SOVIET INDUSTRY. For widely contrasting estimates, see Stalin and others, *op. cit.*—exuberant; Louis Fischer, *Machines and Men in Russia* (Smith & Haas, 1932)—favorable; I. D. Levine, *Red Smoke* (McBride, 1932)—hostile; Ellery Walter, *Russia's Decisive Year* (Putnam, 1932)—hostile; Chamberlin, *Russia's Iron Age*—critical, and conflicting somewhat with his earlier books.

LIVING-CONDITIONS. On living-conditions in Russia today, see Davis, *op. cit.*, Chaps. vi, xi; Dobbert, *op. cit.*, Chap. xii; Hoover, *op. cit.*, Chaps. x-xi, xiii; Seibert, *op. cit.*, Chaps. xxi-xxii; Fischer, *op. cit.*, Pt. II. For severe attacks on Soviet living-conditions, see K. M. Stewart-Murray, Duchess of Atholl, *The Conscription of a People* (Columbia University Press, 1931); W. J. Durant, *The Tragedy of Russia* (Simon & Schuster, 1933); W. J. Robinson, *Soviet Russia as I Saw It* (Freethought Press, 1932). For more favorable reactions, see Thelma Nurenberg, *This New Red Freedom* (Wadsworth Press, 1932); Corliss and Margaret Lamont, *Russia Day by Day* (Covici, Friede, 1933); Hamilton, *op. cit.*; W. A. Rukeyser, *Working for the Soviets* (Covici, Friede, 1932); J. S. Huxley, *A Scientist among the Soviets* (Harper, 1932); Strong, *op. cit.*

SOVIET HOUSING ACHIEVEMENTS. Dobbert, *op. cit.*, Chap. xi; Davis, *op. cit.*, Chap. xii; Winter, *op. cit.*, Chap. xvi.

EDUCATION. On the new Russian education, see Chamberlin, *Soviet Russia*, Chap. xv; Davis, *op. cit.*, Chap. x; Seibert, *op. cit.*, Chap. x; Woody, *op. cit.*; G. S. Counts, *The Soviet Challenge to America* (Day, 1931); L. L. W. Wilson, *The New Schools of New Russia* (Vanguard Press, 1928); A. P. Pinkevich, *The New Education in the Soviet Republic* (Day, 1929).

RELIGION. On Soviet Russia and religion, see Chap. ix of Sherwood Eddy, *The Challenge of Russia* (Farrar & Rinehart) and *Russia Today*, Pt. I, Chap. iii; Pt. II, Chap. x; Williams, *op. cit.*, Chaps. iv-vi; Woody, *op. cit.*, Chap. viii; Seibert, *op. cit.*,

Chap. VIII; J. F. Hecker, *Religion under the Soviets* (Vanguard Press, 1927); Mecklenburg, *op. cit.*

On Communism as a new religion, see Ward, *Which Way Religion?* pp. 197 ff.; John Dewey, "Religion in the Soviet Union: An Interpretation of the Conflict," (New York *Times*), *Current History,* April, 1930; S. K. Ratcliffe, "Russian Communism as a Religion," *Yale Review,* December, 1931; Reinhold Niebuhr, "The Religion of Communism," *Atlantic Monthly,* April, 1931; H. R. Mussey, "Russia's New Religion," *Nation,* May 4, 1932; P. S. Bernstein, "Religion in Russia," *Harper's Magazine,* May, 1930; Hecker, *Religion and Communism.*

MORALITY. On the new morality and sex relations in Soviet Russia, the best work is Winter, *op. cit.* See also Eddy, *Russia Today,* Pt. II, Chap. VIII; Mehnert, *op. cit.,* Chap. VIII; Seibert, *op. cit.,* Chap. IX; Williams, *op. cit.*

WOMAN'S STATUS. On women in Soviet Russia, see Winter, *op. cit.,* Chap. VII; Jessica Smith, *Woman in Soviet Russia* (Vanguard Press, 1928); Halle, *op. cit.*

CRIME. On crime and punishments in Soviet Russia, see Seibert, *op. cit.,* Chaps. XV-XVI; Eddy, *The Challenge of Russia,* Chap. VII, and *Russia Today,* Pt. II, Chap. III; Davis, *op. cit.,* Chaps. IX, XIII; Winter, *op. cit.,* Chap. XIII; A. Shein, *Workers' Justice in the Soviet Union* (Moscow, 1932); Koerber, *op. cit.*

MEDICINE. On Russian medicine, see Newsholme and Kingsbury, *op. cit.;* A. J. Haines, *Health Work in Soviet Russia* (Vanguard Press, 1928).

SOCIAL WELFARE. On social-welfare activities, see Davis, *op. cit.,* Chap. XII; A. W. Field, *The Protection of Women and Children in Soviet Russia* (Dutton, 1932); Eddy, *Russia Today,* Pt. II, Chaps. II, IV, VI; G. M. Price, *Labor Protection in Soviet Russia* (International Publishers, 1928).

CULTURAL ACTIVITIES. Davis, *op. cit.,* Chap. XI; Winter, *op. cit.,* Chap. XVII; Chamberlin, *Soviet Russia,* Chaps. XII-XIII, XV; Hopper, *op. cit.,* Chap. IX; Freeman, Kunitz, and Lozowick, *op. cit.* The last is the best general account in English of all phases of Soviet culture. For a critical analysis of the frank attempt to make Soviet culture a department of Communist propaganda that has been carried on by Stalin, see Max Eastman, *Artists in Uniform* (Knopf, 1934).

PRESENT STATUS OF RUSSIA. For the latest official summary, see Stalin, *The Political and Social Doctrine of Communism.*

CHAPTER XXVI

INTELLECTUAL AND CULTURAL TRENDS IN THE TWENTIETH CENTURY

I. OUTSTANDING ACHIEVEMENTS IN SCIENCE

1. MATHEMATICS

In the notable scientific revival of the seventeenth century the achievements in mathematics and astronomy were the most remarkable of all. In the eighteenth century mathematics and chemistry took the lead. In the nineteenth century the outstanding discoveries were made in biology and physics. In the twentieth century by all odds the most notable developments took place in astrophysics and electromechanics. In these fields a veritable scientific upheaval was achieved, upsetting what appeared to be some of the most assured results of Newtonian astronomy and nineteenth-century physics. The twentieth century thus witnessed a revival of the priority of the mathematical and physical sciences, which had been temporarily forced into a subordinate position in popular interest through the remarkable progress in the biological sciences in the nineteenth century. The combination of mathematics and the new physics has produced a revolution in scientific notions unparalleled for novelty and disconcerting implications since the period from Copernicus to Newton. Applied to the investigation of the mysteries, vast expanse, and myriad stellar bodies of the heavens, this new mathematical and physical science has made necessary a transformation in the human perspective more striking and shocking than that involved in the evolutionary biology of the previous century.

In the field of mathematics the most important recent achievements of a practical sort have been the further development of the theory of functions and the application of advanced mathematics to the problems of astrophysics, physics and physical chemistry. This mathematical synthesis of physical nature executed by Clerk Maxwell, Willard Gibbs, Max Planck, Albert Einstein, and Poincaré is a most impressive intellectual achievement and promises ultimately to have a deep significance for the human race.[1] More abstruse and absorbing as phases of pure mathematical theory have been such research exercises as those dealing with imaginary numbers and the geometry of infinite dimensions.[2] The most

---

[1] *Cf.* Dampier-Whetham, *History of Science*, pp. 256, 260 ff., 425 ff. The work of Maxwell and Gibbs fell in the nineteenth century. See above, pp. 642 ff., 645, 727.

[2] *Cf.* W. T. Sedgwick and H. W. Tyler, *Short History of Science*, Macmillan, 1917, Chap. xv; Florian Cajori, *History of Mathematics*, 2d ed. rev., Macmillan, 1919; W. W. R. Ball, *Short Account of the History of Mathematics*, 5th ed., Macmillan, 1912; Vera Sanford, *Short History of Mathematics*, Houghton Mifflin, 1930; and Roberto Bonola, *Non-Euclidean Geometry*, Open Court Publishing Co., 1912.

significant aspect of contemporary mathematics, however, is not to be found so much in the subject itself as in the exploitation of mathematics in the service of the physical sciences, the implications of which Sinclair Lewis attempted to popularize in *Arrowsmith*.[1] Higher mathematics has become the indispensable instrument of progress in both pure and applied science, and the revolutionary developments in physics and astrophysics have done much to stimulate progress in pure mathematics.[2]

2. ASTRONOMY AND ASTROPHYSICS

In astrophysics perhaps the most sensational innovation has been Albert Einstein's modification of the Newtonian conception of gravitation and the motion of light and heavenly bodies in what is known as the doctrine of *relativity*. This he set forth in papers published in 1905 and 1915. Aside from its reconstruction of astrophysical concepts in relation to light and planetary motion, the main significance of the doctrine of relativity is its demonstration that the physical ultimate is energy, that matter is a manifestation of energy, and that gravitation is but a property of matter. It also breaks down the distinction between time and space. Time is regarded as a kind of fourth dimension of space.

One of the most important applications of the theory of relativity to astrophysics was Einstein's contention that light, as well as matter, is subject to the laws of gravitation. According to this theory, star images are distorted from their natural position because the rays of light coming from them are bent or curved as they pass close to the surface of the Sun—in other words, as they enter the Sun's gravitational field. The laws of gravitation and electromechanics are thus united. Einstein asserted that a study of solar eclipses would verify this doctrine, and several observations of eclipses since 1915 have tended to confirm his thesis. Another fruitful element of the theory of relativity is the emphasis it places upon the recognition, in the study of the motion of heavenly bodies, that all motion is relative to the observer and not absolute. Moreover, all points of observation in the universe are in motion:

It is impossible to detect any absolute motion in the universe. Another way of stating it is as follows: All motion is relative to the observer. This means that the uniform motion of an observer in a system cannot be detected by the observer from observations in that system. Einstein did not originate this "principle of relativity." It was known long before his day. But Einstein's importance is due to the deductions which he made from it.

For example, let us imagine that a man riding in a railway coach drops a stone out of the window. The man will see the stone fall to the ground in what seems to him to be a straight line. But a man standing on the railway embankment will observe that the train has been in motion and that the path of the stone to him is not a straight line but a parabola. A mythical observer on the sun would see yet another path for the stone, for he would observe that not only is the train in motion, but the earth itself is also in motion. An observer on a distant star would see yet another path for the stone, since he would realize that the sun itself is also in motion. But the star on which this last mythical observer has been placed, is also in motion.[3]

---

[1] Harcourt, Brace, 1925.
[2] *Cf.* E. T. Bell, *The Queen of the Sciences*, Williams & Wilkins, 1931.
[3] David Dietz, *The Story of Science*, rev. ed., Dodd, Mead, 1934, pp. 265-66.

Milton Pike

THE EMPIRE STATE BUILDING, NEW YORK CITY

Fairchild Aerial Surveys

AN AERIAL VIEW OF MODERN NEW YORK

The conceptions of Einstein thus necessitate a considerable modification of the old Newtonian doctrines:

Newton's views were:
Space is absolute.
Time is absolute.
Motion is absolute.
Intervals of time are identical everywhere and under all conditions.
The dimensions of rigid bodies are independent of the bodies' state of rest or motion.
The axioms of Euclidean geometry hold true for the entire universe.
Gravitation is due to an attraction between material bodies.
Rays of light travel in straight lines.
Einstein puts these views aside and in their place gives us the following:
Space and time are not independent of each other but united in a four-dimensional space-time continuum.
Rigid bodies contract in the direction in which they are moving.
Motion causes the clock to go slower.
These changes in measurements of space and time occur in such a way that the velocity of light remains a constant for all observers.
The gravitational field causes changes in measurements of space and time.
These changes are of such a nature and the nature of the four-dimensional space-time continuum is such that the interval between two events is the same for all observers although different observers will separate this interval into different components of distance and time.
A gravitational field alters the nature of space in such a way as to cause light rays to bend.
The geometry of the space-time continuum is non-Euclidean.[1]

The extension of our knowledge of the physical universe has been accompanied by literally amazing discoveries concerning the extent of the universe and the vast size of certain of the heavenly bodies. Better instruments, such as the improved spectroscope, spectrograph, spectro-comparator, and the interferometer, have also enabled scientists to discover the chemical constitution of the heavenly bodies, to measure the speed of light, to compute the size of the more distant heavenly bodies, and to detect the existence of stars hitherto invisible to the human eye through the most powerful telescopes. Here we owe the most to Wollaston, Fraunhofer, Bunsen, and Michelson. This as yet incomplete revelation of the vast extent and complex organization of the cosmos is perhaps the most striking intellectual achievement of the twentieth century. It deserves to rank with the confirmation of the doctrine of evolution in the last century and may well be regarded as more disconcerting to human presumption than the theory of evolution.

Modern astronomy, working with these newer instruments and conceptions, has completely destroyed the older limited, geocentric (earth-centered) picture of the universe. The Copernican revolution in astronomy, which substituted the Sun for the Earth as the dominating body in our own planetary system, brought about a notable revolution in the outlook of man upon the physical universe. Yet the Copernican transformation was but a beginning compared to the implications of modern astronomy. Contemporary astrophysics has com-

[1] *Ibid.*, pp. 274-75.

pletely annihilated the notion of a heliocentric cosmos and has shown that our Sun and its surrounding planets represent but a most insignificant item, even in our own galactic universe.

Our galactic universe, roughly identical with the Milky Way, is itself but one among an uncalculated number of island universes. Present-day astronomers estimate that there may be a million or more galaxies comparable to our Milky Way and its constituent stellar groups in the all-inclusive cosmos. Indeed, there seem to be cosmic organizations of a higher order than galaxies such as ours which is embodied in the Milky Way—actually, veritable clouds of galaxies, some of them containing apparently hundreds of galactic systems similar to ours. Our galactic system (contained in the Milky Way) is thought by many astronomers to be the largest single one. Yet the fact that distant galactic systems are far more complex and highly organized, being veritably galaxies of galaxies, makes our sidereal universe seem small and simple by comparison. The Coma-Virgo system is estimated to contain some three hundred galaxies. The distances of some of these remote galactic systems from the Earth are almost incredible. One already photographed is estimated to be some 170,000,000 light-years from our planet—that is, it would require 170,000,000 of our years for its light to reach the Earth.

In his interesting book *Exploring the Universe,* Mr. Henshaw Ward has well summarized some of these striking facts brought forward by the new astronomy, which demonstrate the extremely rudimentary nature of any such conception as a heliocentric cosmos, namely, a total physical universe dominated by our Sun and its attendant planets:

All sorts of uncanny knowledge about conditions in other suns are now the commonplaces of observatory talk. There are gaseous nebulae of vast area that whirl like pinwheels. There are stars in clusters, revolving about each other in courses so complicated and at such high speeds that even a mathematician must grow dizzy as he computes them. There are stars whose volume is a hundred million times that of our sun, composed of matter a million times less dense than the matter of our sun. Also there are stars composed of matter two thousand times as dense as gold, so that a pint of it would weigh nineteen tons. Some stars have an internal heat of many million degrees, and some move through space fifty times as fast as our sun travels athwart the Milky Way.[1]

We can, perhaps, best indicate the position of the Earth in the new cosmic perspective by (1) comparing the Earth with other planets in our system; (2) comparing the Earth and its fellow planets with the Sun; (3) comparing the Sun with some of the larger astral bodies that have been discovered and measured by modern astronomers; (4) indicating the nature and extent of our galactic system and the position of the Sun and its planets therein; and, finally, (5) making clear the relative insignificance of even our galactic system in the all-embracing cosmos as a whole.

The Earth is one of the smaller of the eight major planets revolving about our Sun. It has a mean diameter of 7,290 miles as compared with Jupiter's 87,000 and Saturn's 71,000. Professor David P. Todd has graphically described the relative masses of the planets and the Sun in our solar system:

[1] C. H. Ward, *op. cit.,* Bobbs-Merrill, 1927, p. 12.

Let an ordinary bronze cent piece represent the earth. So small are Mercury and Mars that we have no coin light enough to compare with them; but these two planets, if merged into a single one, might be well represented by an old-fashioned silver three-cent piece; Venus, by a silver dime; Uranus, a silver dollar, half dollar, and quarter together; Neptune, two silver dollars; Saturn, eleven silver dollars; and Jupiter, thirty-seven silver dollars (rather more than two pounds avoirdupois). An inconveniently large sum of silver would be required if this comparison were to be carried farther, so as to include the sun; for he is nearly 750 times more massive than all the planets and their satellites together, and on the same scale of comparison, he would somewhat exceed the weight of the long ton.[1]

As with relative size and mass, so with regard to distance from the Sun, the status of the Earth is not impressive. The Earth is some 93,000,000 miles distant from the Sun, whereas Neptune, the most remote planet,[2] is 2,795,-000,000 miles from the Sun and requires approximately 165 of our years to complete one revolution about the sun. While the distance of Neptune from the Sun represents a figure that it is almost impossible for the human mind to appreciate, it is most unimpressive indeed when compared with other cosmic distances that are commonplaces in astrophysical measurements.

If our Earth is fairly insignificant when compared with one of the larger planets such as Jupiter, it is much less considerable when compared with the Sun. The Sun's diameter is 110 times greater than that of the Earth, and its volume 1,300,000 times the volume of the Earth. Yet the Sun is but a mere cosmic speck compared with some of the great astral giants in our galactic system. Two of the larger stars that have been measured are Betelgeuse and Antares. The diameter of the Sun is approximately 865,000 miles. The diameter of Betelgeuse is about 240,000,000 miles, while that of Antares is approximately 400,000,000 miles. Astronomers estimate that we could pack into an astral space equal to the volume of Betelgeuse about 25,000,000 bodies equal in size to our Sun, while more than 50,000,000 bodies like our Sun could be conveniently stowed away within the surface of Antares. If Antares were placed with its center at the center of our solar system it would embrace the orbits of Mercury, Venus, the Earth, and Mars and extend out into space about 60,-000,000 miles beyond the orbit of Mars. Yet astronomers admit the possibility that stars larger than Antares exist in our own galactic system, and there is every probability that astral bodies decidedly larger than Antares are to be found in the million or more galactic systems that float in space beyond our own galaxy. Indeed, astronomers believe that most of the brighter stars in the Magellanic clouds are larger than Betelgeuse and some possibly larger than Antares.

The Sun and its encompassing planets constitute what is known as our solar system. Our solar system, however, is, along with countless other solar systems, a part of what is called our galactic system. This galactic system or sidereal universe, outlined by the Milky Way, of a shape suggesting a discus, is estimated to be more than 160,000 light-years in diameter and 10,000 light-years in thickness. If one desires to reduce these distances to miles he may do so by

[1] Todd, *A New Astronomy*, American Book Co., 1926, p. 335.
[2] Except for the insignificant Pluto.

multiplying each of them by 6,000,000,000,000, the number of miles light travels in a year, moving at the speed of 186,000 miles per second. Even this light-year of six trillion miles has been found too small for major astronomical computations. Hence, astronomers have adopted a new linear unit, the *parsec,* of nineteen million million miles. Indeed, for the greater cosmic distances, astronomers have had to have recourse to a *megaparsec,* which is equal to a million parsecs.

It is obvious that such a distance as the diameter of our galactic system completely transcends the capacity of human imagination. This galactic system of ours contains at the minimum estimate at least 100,000,000,000 stars (probably more than that number), many of which presumably involve great planetary systems.[1] The latest astronomical computations support the view that our galactic system revolves about a center close to the constellation Sagittarius, which is some 50,000 light-years from the Earth. Though this distance of the Earth from the center of our galactic system is staggering, the Earth is actually relatively close to the galactic center as compared with many other astral groups belonging to our galaxy. Astronomers believe that at the center of our galactic system there is a tremendous concentration of stars, thought to number at least 100,-000,000. It is estimated that our galactic system turns about this great cluster of stars near Sagittarius once in every 300,000,000 years. Therefore the galactic day of our galactic system is equal to 300,000,000 multiplied by 365 of our earthly days.

It is obvious from the preceding facts that our solar system almost disappears when viewed in terms of the galactic system of which it is a part. As Professor Shapley says: "Instead of being the center of this universe, our sun is but an insignificant speck around which flits a shadow called the earth." Yet, it must be recalled, our entire galactic system, with its diameter of more than 160,000 light-years and its family of more than 100,000,000,000 stars, is but a small and elementary unit in the physical cosmos as a whole. As we have indicated above, astronomers have not only discovered other galaxies similar to our galactic system or sidereal universe, but have even located or isolated what seem to them to be actual clouds of galaxies. Observers have already begun to conceive not only of a galaxy of galaxies but of a galaxy of galaxies of galaxies, and there seems to be no logical reason why we should stop at this point. It might be observed, however, that for practical purposes we might well stop with the conception of a single galactic system like our own sidereal universe. The human mind is quite incapable of grappling realistically even with what is involved in one galactic system. One brilliant astronomer has estimated that the cosmos as a whole may have a diameter of approximately one hundred and fifty sextillion miles. It is obvious that this can be only an intelligent gesture in assessing cosmic space. Even if approximately correct, it involves figures so immense as to mean little or nothing in a practical way to the human mind.

[1] Professor Eddington and some others have expressed a doubt that there are many suns with planets revolving about them. No astronomical instruments yet known will settle this question. It is not too easy to detect distant planets even in our own solar system. Pluto was only recently identified. So far, this matter has to be settled on the basis of cosmic logic, and that is certainly opposed to Eddington's view.

Professor Shapley presents a brilliant description of the nature, extent, and center of our single galactic system:

> From star clusters, from stellar motions, and from the study of variable stars, we appear to have found the center of our galactic universe. But obviously we have not even groped for the center of the universe of all material things. Our Galaxy is but one of hundreds of thousands. We know a little about ours, but practically nothing about the others except that they exist, that they are very remote, that the nearest ones are composed of stars, that their motions are high, and—most significant of all—that many of them are congregated into systems of still higher order. When we speak of the center of the universe, we should do better to consider the center of one of these systems of higher order, of the Coma-Virgo cloud of galaxies, for instance, with its three hundred members.
>
> But why not go further and see if the various clouds of galaxies that are now coming to light do not themselves form a still higher system? At two or three of the observatories, astronomers are busily engaged in investigating the outside galaxies. Several thousand new ones have been discovered and classified at the Harvard Observatory during the past year or two. With sufficient financial support for telescopes and observers, and a generous allowance of time, we shall be able to decide ultimately if there is evidence of a galaxy of these galaxies of galaxies within man's feeble though ambitious grasp.
>
> Finally, the astronomer is asked why he seeks out these vast facts about the center of the universe. "For the sake of pure knowledge," he might reply; "for the satisfaction of demonstrating the possible range of human thought and comprehension, regardless of the consequences." But alas! most of us do not rise to this high, unselfish, and unhuman ideal. We see in the new astronomical revelations the stuff that philosophic dreams are made of. We see the stars as providers of human interest of the deepest kind—as feeders of the inherent religious hunger.
>
> The study of the structure of the Milky Way is a part of the general advance of pure science designed to reveal man's place in the universe. If we are to forget the mean Earth and its brief day and year—and in our highest moments we all try to transcend such obsessions; if we are to contemplate the meaning of the universe: we must first try to know it, by measure, count, chemistry, and evolutionary tendencies. That is why the scientist labors on the description of a universe that has enmeshed man, time, thought, and galaxies, all in one complex aggregate.[1]

The progress of modern astrophysics has led to an interesting controversy as to whether the second law of thermodynamics applies to the physical universe as a whole. The majority of scientists hold that it does. If so, this means that the universe is almost infinitely slowly, but surely, running down through the ever continuing dispersal of energy that has, so to speak, filtered down to unusable levels. Applying this to our Sun, solar matter is being converted into energy with a resulting loss of 4,200,000 tons per second in the solar mass. At this rate, it is estimated that the Sun will radiate itself out of existence in fifteen trillion years. The same reasoning would apply to the universe as a whole, which may be compared to a fire slowly burning itself out:

> Eventually there will be nothing left but a great ocean of empty space in which float the cinders of burned-out stars and the frozen remnants of a few planets like

---

[1] Harlow Shapley, "The Center of the Universe," *Forum*, June, 1929, p. 375.

our earth, while the energy of the universe remains scattered in a uniform and unavailable state throughout space, the ghost of a once flourishing cosmos.[1]

The alleged degradation (unavailability) of heat energy has been reduced to scientific law—the law of entropy—by Eddington and others. The second law of thermodynamics showed that while all energy might be converted into heat, not all heat could be reconverted into energy, because heat will not pass from a colder to a warmer body. The law of entropy puts this principle in generalized form.

In effect this law states that,

as Time increases in any system, the amount of heat-energy available for the performance of useful work diminishes. Thus if a series of bodies is at different temperatures, so that a machine could be run by allowing heat to pass from the warmer bodies to the colder ones, the energy available in this way would continually decrease, the distribution of heat becoming more and more uniform. It is, in fact, by an extrapolation of this law over vast ranges of Space and Time that the death of the universe by heat uniformity has been predicted.[2]

This generally accepted view has been defended most ardently by Sir James Jeans. But Professor Robert A. Millikan disputes this theory and holds that energy is being reconverted into matter through bombardment by the short cosmic waves. It is his contention that while the stars are transforming their matter into energy, in other parts of the universe energy is being retransformed into matter. Thus far, this fundamental question must be regarded as unsettled, though the majority opinion is on the side of Jeans.[3]

So important has light become in modern discussions of astrophysics that some scientists have turned to it rather than to energy as a key to the understanding of physical nature. Sir William Bragg has recently interpreted the universe in terms of light, holding that this provides the key to the fundamental unity of radiation and matter. As he expresses it:

Meanwhile we have come into possession of a wonderful principle which unites all forms of radiation and all kinds of matter. We may rightly speak of light as constituting the universe when we give the word the full meaning which this prospect reveals to us.[4]

One of the most disconcerting of all recent hypotheses of science is the suggestion made by Dr. F. G. Pease that perhaps even the velocity of light is not constant. Dr. Pease is an eminent astrophysicist and is the successor of Professor Michelson in attempting to measure accurately the velocity of light. Carrying on Michelson's experiments, he came to the conclusion that the velocity of light is variable. Now the velocity of light is about the only thing that is assumed to be an invariable constant in the doctrine of relativity and the new astrophysics. If this is overthrown, it will require sweeping reformulations of both contemporary astronomy and contemporary physics. Dr. Pease set forth

[1] Dietz, *op. cit.*, p. 347.
[2] Hyman Levy, *The Universe of Science,* Century, 1933, p. 42. *Cf.* Benjamin Ginzburg, *The Adventure of Science,* Simon & Schuster, 1930, pp. 276 ff.
[3] Millikan's views are based upon the assumption that cosmic rays are energy rays. This is denied by Dr. A. H. Compton and others, who maintain that cosmic rays are charged particles.
[4] Sir W. H. Bragg, *The Universe of Light,* Macmillan, 1933, p. 279.

these views before the National Academy of Sciences at Cleveland in November, 1934. Mr. Dietz thus comments on their significance:

The world of science may have to rebuild the foundation stone upon which rest all its theories about the nature of the universe. . . . To the amazement of Mount Wilson astronomers, the experiments [designed to measure the velocity of light] have consistently failed to give a constant figure for light velocity. The whole world of science was amazed when rumors of this fact became known.

Dr. Pease revealed today that the experiment has continued to give such varying results and that all attempts to explain these variations have failed. What science is to do now is the big question.

The Einstein theory, which makes practically everything in the universe relative to the motion of the observer, recognizes only one constant thing in nature, namely, the velocity of light. The newest theory of the condition of the universe, the so-called theory of the expanding universe, likewise requires assumption that light velocity is constant.

If the assumption must be thrown away, then thousands of deductions about the distant stars, the interior of the atom and behavior of sub-atomic particles must be changed.[1]

3. THE NEW PHYSICS

At the opposite extreme from the magnitude revealed by the astrophysical measurements of sections of the cosmos are to be set the minuteness and complexity of the atom and its constituent electrons. Here we come to the core of the striking progress in electromechanics in the twentieth century. The contemporary physicists, such as Planck, Thomson, Rutherford, Bohr, De Broglie, Millikan, and Schrödinger, have shown that the supposed basic and integral atom is actually a highly composite and intricate physical system, almost as complex as the solar system itself. The study of the structure and activities of the atom has revealed a situation almost as impressive and startling as the astrophysical investigation of the universe. Dr. P. W. Slosson thus describes Bohr's view of atomic structure, which

pictures the atom as a sort of solar system in which the sun is represented by the nucleus and the planets by from one to ninety-two electrons revolving about it at high speeds in certain fixed orbits. When an electron jumps from a larger to a smaller orbit, energy is given off in the form of radiation of a certain wave length, according to Planck's law.[2]

In the past few years Bohr's theory of the atom has been challenged and substitute theories have been suggested. This development has been well summarized by Mr. David Dietz:

Within recent years, there have been disturbing factors to upset the Bohr theory. The emission of light is not as simple as it seemed. Sometimes the emission of a quantum of light seems to be the result of the simultaneous jump of two electrons. There were other difficulties. Why, for example, could the electrons which had hitherto been supposed to be little distinct particles, at times behave as waves? And so the theory of wave mechanics grew up, the result of the work of De Broglie, a

[1] David Dietz, New York *World-Telegram*, Nov. 19, 1934, p. 19.
[2] Slosson, *Twentieth Century Europe*, Houghton Mifflin, 1927, p. 703.

Frenchman, and Schroedinger, a German. According to this, the atom is not the miniature solar system of Bohr, but a vague pulsating sphere of electricity, something like an expanding and contracting balloon.[1]

In this new doctrine of Heisenberg, De Broglie, and Schrödinger the quantum theory is thus reconciled with the older wave theory of energy generation.

The smallest thing with which science deals is known as the electron, which has been thus described in telling fashion by Dr. E. E. Slosson:

... Professor Millikan put it this way: the quantity of electricity which courses through such an electric lamp *every second* is so large that if two and a half million persons were to begin to count out these electrons, and were to keep on counting them out, at the rate of two a second, and if no one of the counters were ever to stop to eat, sleep, or die, it would take them just 20,000 years to finish the task!

Thus the electron, of which all the atoms, molecules, and substances in the universe are composed (with a nucleus, in each atom, of positive electricity), is not only the smallest thing in the world, but also the entity possessing the greatest velocity—in some cases nearly 186,000 miles a second, the speed of light.[2]

Closely related to this intensive study of the structure of the atom has been the rise of what is known as the quantum theory, which has undermined the classic physics of the nineteenth century. The man who introduced the underlying conceptions in this doctrine was a German physicist, Professor Max Planck of Berlin. He found that the nineteenth-century notion concerning the radiation of energy in continuous waves did not seem to square with the facts. He suggested that energy is released in particles or bundles, which he called quanta. This explanation seemed to conform to observations in the laboratory. Einstein carried this doctrine further by urging that the old idea which held that energy exists in continuous waves should be discarded in favor of the view that energy exists as particles or corpuscles.

A dispute arose between those who desired to defend the old wave theory and the exponents of the quantum theory. Something of a compromise was worked out in the theory of the atom formulated by Schrödinger and Heisenberg. The problem must, however, still be regarded as unsettled and, perhaps, insoluble. The ultimate solution may be found in the suggestion of Professor Compton that "all the waves are particles and all the particles waves."

One of the major difficulties is that one cannot accurately measure both the velocity and the position of the electron. The more accurately we measure the velocity, the less precisely are we able to determine its position. This so-called law of indeterminacy, formulated by Heisenberg, has specifically challenged the basic rational postulate of cause-and-effect relationships operating without exception in the physical world.

Another outstanding achievement in physics consists in the work on X-rays and radium. In 1895 Röntgen produced the famous X-rays. Building upon the work of Crookes, Röntgen, and Becquerel, Madame Curie and her husband

---

[1] Dietz, Cleveland *Press,* Nov. 4, 1929. *Cf.* R. T. Cox, *Time, Space and Atoms,* Williams & Wilkins, 1933.

[2] Slosson, ed., *Keeping Up with Science,* Harcourt, Brace, 1924, p. 311. The more recent theory holds that while the nucleus has a positive charge of electricity, it is probably made up of protons and neutrons.

discovered radium and the principle of radioactivity at the very close of the nineteenth century. The diverse implications and varied modes of the practical exploitation of radium make it perhaps the most portentous of the many startling physiochemical discoveries of contemporary times. This work on X-rays and radium was of great importance for the above-mentioned investigation of the atom, for all modern study of the atom received its fundamental impetus from the discovery of X-rays and radium. Improved apparatus has been of great assistance in this further probing of the atomic mysteries. Among the more important devices recently provided have been the X-ray spectrometer of Sir William Bragg and the Coolidge X-ray tube. These have enabled physicists to pass beyond nuclei and electrons to the more intricate realm of neutrons, photons, protons, and positrons.[1]

4. CHEMISTRY

The most impressive phases of the progress in chemistry have been the researches in physical chemistry and the practical achievements in organic chemistry. In physical chemistry much work has been done in following up the pioneer achievements of Josiah Willard Gibbs in the study of the equilibrium of chemical reactions and other thermodynamic relations.[2] The physical chemists have also closely coöperated with the physicists in the recent study of the atom and the generation of energy. The X-ray has aided greatly in the progress of physical chemistry. As Sir William Bragg has expressed it: "The X-ray gives one a tremendous advantage in physical chemistry. The old way was to put things in a beaker and then break them up to see what they were made of. But with the X-ray solids can be studied without destroying them." The layman has, however, been more impressed with the remarkable practical consequences of the progress in organic chemistry.

A century ago Wöhler made synthetic urea and Hennell synthetic alcohol. The mysteries of the benzene ring, unraveled by Wöhler, Liebig, and Kekulé, then opened the way to the wonders of modern organic chemistry. Emil Fischer and others, building on these earlier discoveries, produced remarkable results in the way of creating organic substances synthetically. They veritably founded the important department of economic chemistry. We have already mentioned Von Baeyer's discovery of synthetic indigo. The marvels achieved in economic chemistry have been eloquently described by Floyd Darrow in his *Story of Chemistry* and by Professor Slosson in his *Creative Chemistry*. It requires two pages of fine print merely to catalogue the products derived from a ton of cottonseed, which was until very recently entirely wasted.[3] These synthetic products of cottonseed run from smokeless powder to photographic films, from felt to soap, and from salad oil to washing-powder. In other fields the chemists create artificially products running from vanilla flavoring to diamonds.

Chemical research into the field of colloids and conductivity has revealed

---

[1] *Cf.* Watson Davis, ed., *The Advance of Science,* Doubleday, Doran, 1934, Chaps. IV-V, and R. A. Millikan, *Electrons . . . Protons, Photons, Neutrons and Cosmic Rays,* University of Chicago Press, 1935.

[2] *Cf.* Darrow, *The Story of Chemistry,* Chap. III; and F. H. Garrison, "Josiah Willard Gibbs and His Relation to Modern Science," *Popular Science Monthly,* May-August, 1909.

[3] See above, pp. 730-31.

the colloidal character of protoplasm and has suggested that life and death are but different forms of chemical organization. Many persons have been almost literally "raised from the dead" by the introduction of certain chemicals such as adrenalin or pituitrin into their bodies. The problem of the creation of life can now be stated in chemical terms. Man himself is now technically described as a "colloidal aggregate of high complexity." Eminent biologists have lately contended that the determination of the sex of offspring is chiefly a matter of chemistry, depending mainly on the degree of acidity in the system of the mother. Physiological chemistry has revealed life itself to be a form of chemical behavior, "centering in an intricate mixture of carbon compounds."

In the domain of endocrinology, opened up by Cannon, Crile, and others, physiological chemists have revealed a novel and highly important set of chemical controls that are basic in human behavior. These endocrinologists have shown the determining influence of the hitherto mysterious glands of internal secretion in controlling metabolism, promoting the growth of the body, conditioning the emotions, conditioning sex characteristics, and, in their imperfections, giving rise to a great variety of physical and mental disorders.[1] Many of these basic secretions can now be produced artificially. Some of them, such as thyroxin and insulin, have revolutionized medical science.

5. BIOLOGY AND PHYSIOLOGY

In biology the foremost achievement has been, perhaps, the definite vindication of the evolutionary principle launched by Darwin and Wallace. While flaws have been revealed in some of the details of the processes regarded by Darwin as fundamental in the evolution of life, the vital principles that he suggested have been established as firmly as any law of science. The genetic processes of heredity have been studied thoroughly and have enabled contemporary biologists to correct the errors and to fill the gaps in Darwinian biology. The work of Weismann, overthrowing the Lamarckian hypothesis of the inheritance of acquired characters, and the enunciation of the principles of heredity associated with the names of De Vries and Mendel, have been the most significant here. The mechanism of heredity, involving the concepts of *chromosomes* and *genes,* has been studied in great detail by T. H. Morgan [2] and others. The modern notion of the gene is of particular importance. The stability and nonmodifiability of the gene (at least during a period of time short enough to be observed) by the organic or social environment destroys the old view of the possible inheritance of acquired characters. It vindicates the Weismann theory. Next to the work on the mechanism of heredity, probably the most important contributions to biology are those in the field of biochemistry which have been mentioned above—the discoveries as to the nature and influence of the endocrine system (glands of internal secretion) and the establishment of the colloidal character of protoplasm. The latter is worthy to rank with the discovery of the cell by Schwann and Schleiden a century ago.

[1] *Cf.* Walter Timme, *Lectures on Endocrinology,* Hoeber, 2d ed., 1932; W. J. Robinson, *Our Mysterious Life Glands and How They Affect Us,* Eugenics Publishing Co., 1934; and M. G. Schlapp and E. H. Smith, *The New Criminology,* Liveright, 1928, Bk. II.

[2] Morgan, *The Scientific Basis of Evolution,* Norton, 1932.

Biology and anthropology also enable man, for the first time, to arrive at a scientific conception of the notion of race and to trace the racial differentiation of mankind.[1]

Physiology has been given a more dynamic character and is now thoroughly linked up with contemporary physics and chemistry. Physiological chemistry has acquainted us with the nature of *calories* and *vitamins* and given many novel and important suggestions with respect to food values and metabolism. The conception of basal metabolism has afforded a clew to more penetrating and elemental conceptions of health and vitality. It has even been suggested that evolution can be artificially hastened by chemical means. It seems likely that there is not only a fundamental unity in all physical phenomena, but that physics, chemistry, and biology will prove the physicochemical unity of life and its processes. It appears possible that by hypothesis, if not by demonstration, the long-standing barrier between the organic and the inorganic will be broken down.

Optical and electrical progress is helping contemporary biology, as it has aided modern astrophysics. A new television supermicroscope has just been invented, providing both increased magnification and an artificial eye. This is expected to reveal impressive new data in both biology and physics.

6. GEOLOGY AND GEOGRAPHY

In geology more plausible hypotheses of the origins of the Earth have been suggested than the nebular hypothesis of Laplace, particularly the planetesimal theory of Chamberlin. Glaciation has been studied in a scientific fashion by Penck, Brückner, Geike, Chamberlin, and others from the standpoint of (1) its causes, periodicity, and physiographic results; and (2) its effects upon the oscillations of organic life. Economic geology has grown to be an indispensable adjunct of industry through its revelation of the nature and extent of deposits of oil, ore, and other natural resources highly important in the processes of modern industry.[2]

In geography much more exact knowledge has been acquired concerning the topography of the Earth's surface. Physical geography has been made a precise descriptive science. It has been given a sounder methodology through the development of regional geography by Paul Vidal de La Blache, Ferdinand von Richthofen, and their followers. Climatology, forwarded by Julius Hann and Robert De C. Ward, has come to be a true science, involving both physics and geography, and work in meteorology has gradually produced scientific methods of studying and predicting weather conditions. Above all, physical geography and climatology have been definitely linked up with the social sciences and the welfare of man through anthropogeography. This consists in the scientific analysis of the interrelation between man and his culture on the one hand and the geographic surroundings on the other. The earlier overgeneralized work of Ratzel has been superseded by more precise studies of the effect of geographical factors on man in definite regions of the Earth

---
[1] *Cf.* Hankins, *The Racial Basis of Civilization.*
[2] *Cf.* T. T. Read, *Our Mineral Civilization,* Williams & Wilkins, 1932.

pursued, among others, by Von Richthofen, Vidal de La Blache, Jean Brunhes, Lucien Febvre, and J. Russell Smith.

7. PSYCHOLOGY

Psychology, which fifty years ago was little more than a combination of theology, metaphysics, and phrenology, has now become in most respects a truly experimental science, and has proved itself of enormous importance to the understanding and guidance of human life.[1] Neurology, the study of the physical basis of the brain and nervous system, has made it possible to base psychology upon scientific biology and physiology. Endocrinology has indicated the highly important nature of the subtle chemical controls of human behavior and the processes of metabolism. Behaviorism, in its more extreme form as developed by John B. Watson, is an effort to make psychology a branch of biology and denies the significance of the subjective factors in human conduct. Its followers have done pioneer experimental work in the study of human habits and socially conditioned behavior. Psychophysics, as developed by Fechner, Weber, Titchener, and Boring, has made possible the establishment of almost as exact an experimental laboratory technique in certain restricted fields of psychology as that which prevails in the physical sciences. An attempt to create a synthetic and well-balanced study of mental life and behavior has been made by Köhler, Koffka, Wertheimer, and other exponents of the so-called Gestalt psychology.

Psychiatry, cultivated by Freud and more critical successors, has made use of medicine, psychology, and anthropology to produce a real revolution in our knowledge and control of abnormal behavior. It has, moreover, amply demonstrated the narrow gap between the normal and the abnormal mental life. The mechanisms of behavior that have been formulated by the psychiatrist have actually done more to explain even normal human behavior than the more abstract concepts of the formal psychologists. Social psychology has provided a means of studying scientifically the behavior of social groups and crowds, and has much of indispensable value to offer to students of the social sciences and modern social problems.

8. MEDICINE AND SURGERY

Modern medicine has kept pace with the progress in physics, chemistry, biology, and psychology, and has passed from a combination of magic and astrology into a relatively exact observational science, particularly in the field of surgery. Profiting by the development of anaesthetic and antiseptic surgery to a degree scarcely anticipated in 1900, by the provision of X-ray photography for surgical diagnosis, and by the discovery of chemical substances to stimulate the recovery of patients otherwise likely to succumb from the shock of a severe operation, contemporary surgery has achieved an astonishing precision. Bacteriology and the germ theory of disease have stimulated a high development of sanitation and preventive medicine, something quite as important as curative or therapeutic medicine.

Perhaps the most notable achievement in pathology in the twentieth century

---

[1] *Cf.* R. S. Woodworth, *Contemporary Schools of Psychology,* Ronald Press, 1931.

was the discovery of the germ of syphilis—the *spirochaeta pallida*—by Schaudinn in 1905, the provision of a blood test by Wassermann to determine its presence, and its experimental cultivation outside the body by the Japanese pathologist Noguchi, in 1911. Important curative measures were introduced by Ehrlich in 1910 when he discovered that salvarsan, an arsenic preparation, is very effective as a specific against syphilis. An Austrian pathologist, Julius Wagner von Jauregg, showed that malarial fever has remarkable curative effects upon hitherto incurable cases of paresis, the mental breakdown that may be one of the advanced stages of syphilis. Important advances have also been made in the utilization of antiseptics that prevent contraction of this disease. And it now appears that what has been one of the worst scourges of Western civilization since 1500 may be mitigated as effectively as smallpox, scarlet fever, or diphtheria has been. Cancer remains the chief plague that baffles medical science.

Finally, science is no longer limited to the physical and biological sciences, but has come to include the sciences of man and culture, namely, the so-called social sciences: anthropology, history, sociology, social psychology, economics, political science, and ethics. Slow but real progress is being made here in the way of developing an objective attitude towards human problems, in introducing the quantitative method of studying social phenomena, and in moving on from classification and definition into a real analysis of social processes.[1]

II. INTELLECTUAL IMPLICATIONS OF TWENTIETH-CENTURY SCIENCE

1. THE EVAPORATION OF CLASSIC THEORIES OF CAUSE AND EFFECT

The intellectual implications of the scientific advances made during the twentieth century have been the most revolutionary and unsettling that mankind has been forced to face since the days of Galileo and Newton. As we have noted above, nineteenth-century science, however much it might disturb and upset older notions, was always able to fall back upon one fundamental and reassuring conception—that a definite cause-and-effect relationship exists in all the operations of physical nature.[2] But the researches in mathematical physics and electromechanics in the twentieth century, embodied in the works of Planck, Heisenberg, Einstein, and others, have undermined this very cornerstone of the old scientific thought. A generation ago, the scientists believed that while the theologians and metaphysicians might be engaged in elaborate self-deception, the scientists were sure of their own ground. Today, the most candid scientists quite frankly confess that science cannot discover any ultimates, even in its own realm. This has been admirably stated by Professor P. W. Bridgman in the following paragraphs:

The thesis of this article is that the age of Newton is now coming to a close, and that recent scientific discoveries have in store an even greater revolution in our entire outlook than the revolution effected by the discovery of universal gravitation by Newton. The revolution that now confronts us arises from the recent discovery of new facts, the only interpretation of which is that our conviction that

[1] See below, pp. 1057 ff.   [2] See above, p. 664.

nature is understandable and subject to law arose from the narrowness of our horizons, and that if we sufficiently extend our range we shall find that nature is intrinsically and in its elements neither understandable nor subject to law. . . .

The same situation confronts the physicist everywhere; whenever he penetrates to the atomic or electronic level in his analysis, he finds things acting in a way for which he can assign no cause, for which he can never assign a cause, and for which the concept of cause has no meaning, if Heisenberg's principle is right. This means nothing more nor less than that the law of cause and effect must be given up. The precise reason that the law of cause and effect fails can be paradoxically stated; it is not that the future is not determined in terms of a complete description of the present, but that in the nature of things the present cannot be completely described. . . .

The physicist thus finds himself in a world from which the bottom has dropped clean out; as he penetrates deeper and deeper it eludes him and fades away by the highly unsportsmanlike device of just becoming meaningless. No refinement of measurement will avail to carry him beyond the portals of this shadowy domain which he cannot even mention without logical inconsistency. A bound is thus forever set to the curiosity of the physicist. What is more, the mere existence of this bound means that he must give up his most cherished convictions and faith. The world is not a world of reason, understandable by the intellect of man, but as we penetrate ever deeper, the very law of cause and effect, which we had thought to be a formula to which we could force God Himself to subscribe, ceases to have a meaning. The world is not intrinsically reasonable or understandable; it acquires these properties in ever-increasing degree as we ascend from the realm of the very little to the realm of everyday things; here we may eventually hope for an understanding sufficiently good for all practical purposes, but no more.[1]

Paradoxically enough, it thus seems that, when we get down to those ultimates involved in the world of the atom, the only certainty in science today is the certainty of uncertainty.[2] For all practical purposes, we may still follow many of the scientific laws and formulations worked out in the nineteenth century. Superficially and practically, they seem to describe the behavior of most physical phenomena as well as ever. Particularly is this true with respect to the exploitation of these older scientific conceptions in the various fields of technology. But when we get down to fundamentals we have to take over a new set of concepts: "Uncertainty reigns, and whether the universe is a world of fortuitous atoms or a world of freewill, it cannot be described in its fundamental physical aspects today as a world of causality."[3]

2. THE POSITION AND RÔLE OF MAN IN THE NEW
ASTROPHYSICAL PERSPECTIVE

A generation ago the background for the proper appraisal of evolution and of the story of man's rise in the physical world was sought in geology and historical biology. Now we recognize that we must go one step back of this and get some notion of cosmic perspective.

The older interpretations of the universe rested upon the assumption of the primary importance of the Earth in the cosmos. Hence man, as the domi-

---

[1] Bridgman, "The New Vision of Science," *Harper's Magazine*, March, 1929, pp. 444, 448, 450.
[2] *Cf.* G. W. Gray, "Science's New Certainty," *Scribner's Magazine*, December, 1933, and M. K. E. L. Planck, *Where Is Science Going?* Norton, 1932.
[3] Gray, *op. cit.*, p. 376.

IMPLICATIONS OF 20TH-CENTURY SCIENCE

nant element on our planet, was veritably "the lord of all creation." Taking these premises for granted, it did not appear unreasonable that man might be the product of God's direct creative endeavor. In the last half-century, however, these conventional assumptions have been completely shattered. This has given a new and devastating turn to our attitude towards man's place in the universe, his physical nature, and the manner in which he has reached his present position on the Earth.[1]

It is well-nigh impossible for us to envisage or describe in terms of mundane conceptions and standards of measurement the extent of even that small portion of the cosmos known to man. In even so incomplete a cosmic perspective as man may attain, our Earth immediately shrinks from the position of the largest and most important unit in the cosmos to a relatively insignificant and recent planet—a celestial juvenile and cosmic dwarf. It is, in time and space, certainly most inconsequential. Man likewise tends to shrink in the new cosmic outlook. Far from being "the lord of all creation," existing from the beginning of things, he now appears to be but a highly temporary biochemical episode on a very petty planet.[2] Astronomically speaking, man is almost totally negligible, while in biological antiquity and continuity he is far outdistanced by the lowly cockroach, which appears to have remained substantially unchanged for more than fifty million years. These facts regarding the insignificance of the Earth and man in the face of our modern views of the cosmos have been well stated by Professor Shapley:

> The thing that appalls me is not the bigness of the universe, but the smallness of us. We are in all ways small—little in foresight, shriveled in spirit, minute in material content, microscopic in the vastness of measured space, evanescent in the sweep of time—inconsequential in every respect, except, perhaps, in the chemical complexities of our mental reactions. In that alone our advance may surpass that of other terrestrial organisms.

But the sanctity of all protoplasm has practically disappeared in this, the heroic age of the physical sciences, when knowledge of the material universe, its content, structure, and dimensions, has so completely overthrown egocentrism. It should sufficiently deflate the organism, you would think, to find that his fountain of energy, the sun, is a dwarf star among thousands of millions of stars; to find that the star around which his little parasitic earth will-lessly plods is so far from the center of the known stellar universe that sunlight, with its incomprehensibly high velocity, cannot reach that center in a thousand generations of vain men.

The deflation, however, is not stopped at that point. We now reach much deeper into space than a few years ago, find millions of stars mightier than our sun, find greater velocities, larger masses, higher temperatures, longer durations than we have previously known. Even more illuminating, in this orientation of organisms in the physical universe, is the revelation that the earth, whose surface we infest, is not a parcel of grand antiquity. Rather recently, as astronomers now measure time, a singular incident happened in the life-history of the sun. Before that time the earth was not, nor were the animals of the earth. Nevertheless, for trillions of years, in the absence of the "Lords of all Creation," the stars had poured out their radiant energy, the celestial bodies had rolled on, law had governed the universe. Before

---

[1] *Cf.* Harlow Shapley, *Flights from Chaos*, McGraw-Hill, 1930, and H. P. Maxim, *Life's Place in the Cosmos*, Appleton, 1933.

[2] In Shapley's conception of the cosmos, man appears, low in the scale, as a colloidal aggregate subclass *beta*. See Shapley, *op. cit.*, p. 50.

that event, you and I, the material of our bodies, were electrons and atoms in the solar atmosphere. Since then we have been associated with the inorganic and organic evolution of a smaller concern.

The earth, as I have intimated, appeared only a few thousand million years ago. Our sun, it seems, had already passed its prime of radiance when in its wanderings through celestial space it met up with another star—a stellar romance—a marriage made in the heavens. From that affair—realistic astronomers call it an encounter—the planets of the sun were born. The passing star, ruffling up the exterior of the sun, detached some relatively small fragments of the solar atmosphere. Now we strut on one of the surviving fragments and wonder and speculate and discuss: "How can we *better* the world?" Crown of absurdities:—*we* repairing the world! That cast-off fragment, the ancestor from which and on which we descend, was composed wholly of gas! An emblem for us, that ancestral hot vapor.

The gaseous planet quickly liquefied as out in cold space it began its tireless revolutions around the parent sun. Soon after a crust formed, and, we may thank our lucky stars, the distance from the sun was right, the atmospheric and crustal chemistry was right, and other adjustments of the physical environment happened to be suitable for an elaboration of chemical reactions. The energy of the everflowing sunlight aided in complexifying this protoplasmic chemistry, a green mold formed in spots on the planet, and here we are—parasites on the energy of the sun that cast us forth.[1]

3. OUR COSMIC UNCERTAINTY

A general air of assurance and finality pervaded most members of the learned classes in previous generations. They felt convinced that they possessed precise and extended knowledge concerning God, the world, man, human destiny, the purpose and meaning of life, and all the other basic problems that confront man. Now all this is changed. We do have, to be sure, much more exact knowledge about the material universe and the biological nature of man, and we are coming to know more about the type of behavior most likely to insure human happiness on this planet. But the meaning of the whole human drama and its setting in the cosmic scheme of things has become ever more baffling. The dualistic cosmic philosophy, which probably originated with the Persians and found the ultimate meaning of the cosmos to lie in an all-inclusive struggle between good and evil, scarcely seems plausible in the light of modern knowledge. We are coming to have impressive confirmation of Descartes's intuition that if there is a divine purpose in the universe it is of a divine character, presumably beyond the comprehension of man. Indeed, the whole teleological conception, which insists that there is a purpose in everything, understandable in human terms, may, indeed, be nothing but a circumscribed human way of looking at things.

The older idea that there is a definite time limit set to the existence of the Earth and man, which will be terminated with a Day of Judgment, is now seen to possess no substantial foundation. It would seem that the creatures of the Earth may look forward to a future as extensive as their past has been, terminated only by natural processes so far distant as to be almost incalculable, albeit the occurrence of an annihilating cosmic accident is not outside the range of possibility.

[1] Harlow Shapley, "Man and His Young World," *Nation,* May 7, 1924, pp. 529-30.

Wide World Photos
SIGMUND FREUD

Wide World Photos
HERBERT GEORGE WELLS

Wide World Photos
JOHN DEWEY

Wide World Photos
ALBERT EINSTEIN

MODERN SCIENTISTS AND PHILOSOPHERS

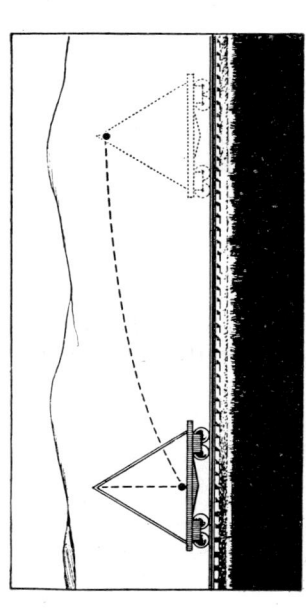

The truck has moved from right to left. The straight vertical line shows the falling ball as seen from the truck; the long curved line the same fall as seen from space.

Top right: When stationary, the train is apparently of the size indicated in the top illustration. If it were put into an extremely swift motion it would appear shortened as indicated in the lower illustration.

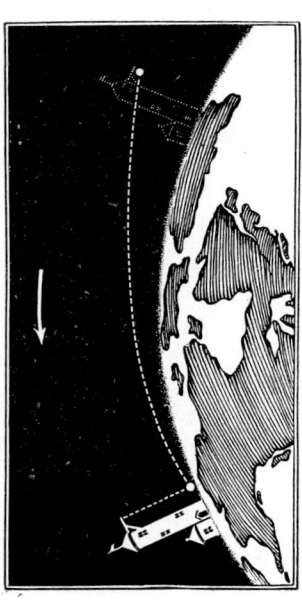

The tower has moved from right to left with the rotating earth. The straight dotted line shows the falling ball as seen by an observer on earth, the long curved line the same fall as seen by an observer out in space.

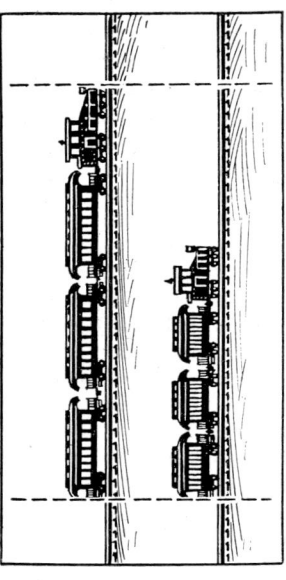

The positions of stars seen displaced during an eclipse of the sun. The crosses show where the stars would be if their light was not bent in passing the sun. The bending throws their images away from the sun.

RELATIVITY

From G. P. Serviss, The Einstein Theory of Relativity, *Edwin Miles Fadman*

Not only do we have to give up that sense of certainty and security based upon the older anthropomorphic and geocentric theology, but, as Charles Peirce suggested and recent physicists have indicated, the very conception of uniform, invariable, and universal scientific laws may also have to be abandoned.

The old symmetrical unity and completeness of knowledge, which seemed possible in an age of circumscribed information and outlook, was embodied in such works as those of Aristotle, the *Summa* of St. Thomas, and the *Encyclopédie* of the eighteenth-century *philosophes*. It was also reflected in the curriculum of the old "liberal college" of half a century ago. Today such inclusive unity is all but impossible. Montaigne's intuitive vision of the implications of Pluralism and Pragmatism has been confirmed in detail by Peirce, James, Dewey, and others, who have endeavored to state the implications of modern scientific discoveries for the reconstruction of philosophy.[1] The futile anguish of even cultured intellects with a retrospective yearning is well illustrated by the following lamentation of Nicholas Murray Butler in one of his annual reports as President of Columbia University:

> No small part of the social and political diseases and disorders that are now so generally discussed may be traced to the destruction through unsound educational methods of that common body of knowledge and intellectual and moral experience which held men together through a community of understanding and of appreciation. A steadily growing unity has been displaced for a chaotic multiplicity. Pluralism, the non-religious form of polytheism, is practically what William James, who was greatly enamored of it, described it to be, "a turbid, muddled, gothic sort of effort, without a sweeping outline and with little pictorial nobility." In all its forms, philosophical and other, it is a flat denial of all that is most worth while in human experience and an open surrender of any hope either to understand or to improve the universe. Moreover, it is self-contradictory, for if there is no One there cannot possibly be a Many. It might have been supposed that Socrates had made this postulate plain once for all, but perhaps it is no longer fashionable for philosophers to know either Greek or history.[2]

Indeed, the advances in human knowledge and their application to society and culture may have created too complicated a situation for man to wrestle with and may have spread before him a cosmic panorama too vast for him to comprehend or digest. His failure to grapple successfully with the issues of the present age may mark the last stages of the "divine experiment" when applied to man. Professor Lynn Thorndike, towards the close of his *Short History of Civilization,* has stated with much wisdom this uncertainty of the outcome of the perplexities of contemporary civilization:

> Furthermore, not only with the mass of contemporary writing is it difficult to keep track of the past masters in many lands, or *vice versa,* but science and learning have so ramified, so specialized, so progressed, that knowledge and theory have perhaps grown even faster than population or popular education. No one man, however learned and characterized by breadth of interest, can even fully appreciate, to

---

[1] *Cf.* Rugg, *Culture and Education in America,* Pt. III.
[2] Columbia University, *Annual Report of the President and Treasurer for the Year Ending June 30, 1921,* Columbia University Press, 1922, pp. 30-31.

say nothing of mastering, the achievements in all the different fields, while the ordinary man has no conception of the present state of knowledge. If the system of public education were more truly disciplinary, if the newspapers largely replaced crime, sensation, and sentimental matter by straightforward statement of political, social, and economic happenings, and the progress of knowledge, if the magazines minimized love stories, adventure, and personality in favor of matters of more moment to civilization, if advertisements gave sound advice as to good manners in public thoroughfares and conveyances, or sensible medical, legal, and financial counsel, if the moving pictures were employed more for purposes of instruction—perhaps the average man could keep up better with the onward march of civilization. Can science shepherd the herd? That is the question. Has scientific specialization proved fatal to the humanism which enabled many leaders of thought in previous generations to publish their views in an acceptable, graceful, and forceful form? Can we have only a caste of intellectuals, as in China and India? Will the popular demand, vulgar taste, and utilitarian attitude lower everything to its own level and swamp civilization? Or is civilization now unfolding in more varied flower than ever before with more individuals of high rank in each field and with an ever increasing public following which is able to appreciate their work? [1]

Whatever the difficulties of mankind that lie ahead, however, science has eliminated a number of bogeys and produced several epoch-making advantages. Professor J. Arthur Thomson has suggested some of these: First, science has destroyed "the old fear of forces leagued against man, and of evil spirits waiting eagerly for his destruction." We need only meet the foes that we can recognize and battle with. Second, we can abandon "the old sense of bewildering confusion, for almost everywhere there is order. A phantasmagoria has given place to a cosmos." Third, "gone is the old bogey of the capricious. . . . Given a reasonable acquaintance with the facts, it is far safer to predict the return of a comet than to tell how a cat will jump; yet there are laws of cat-jumping, and the Mendelian counts and describes his chickens before they are hatched." Fourth, "another of the dispiriting phobias which we are warranted in leaving behind is the picture of an eternal world-eddy—'nothing new but has already been, and nothing new under the sun.'" Evolution and change are real, whatever our new problems and difficulties. Finally, "gone too is the inhibiting belief that there are certain evils which cannot be got rid of." Many things that are so regarded might be eliminated immediately if we were to apply our present knowledge, and many problems that today seem insoluble may be easily wiped out with the further advance of human knowledge.

4. DECLINING CONFIDENCE IN THE DOCTRINE OF PROGRESS

The twentieth century has witnessed a decisive alteration in our attitude towards the doctrine of progress. In the nineteenth century the theory of progress was very generally accepted by the great majority of advanced minds. The emotional optimism that produced the theories of progress characteristic of the late seventeenth century and the eighteenth was taken over by nineteenth-century thinkers and given seeming vindication through the theory of evolution. The doctrine of progress appeared to be founded upon a basic law of nature.

[1] Thorndike, *op. cit.*, pp. 548-49.

IMPLICATIONS OF 20TH-CENTURY SCIENCE

Only the more optimistic thinkers of the twentieth century have been able to subscribe unqualifiedly to any such dogmatic conception of inevitable progress. Vast and unprecedented progress can be demonstrated in science and technology. Of the vast material progress since 1850 there can be no doubt whatsoever. But this material advance does not mean human progress unless man shows himself capable of controlling material gains in the interest of social well-being. The World War taught us a shocking lesson in this respect. Stupendous advances in science and technology were then used to expedite a type of group insanity and mass slaughter that came dangerously near being the suicide of Western civilization. A decade later the deep and prolonged economic depression demonstrated that unparalleled capacity to produce goods does not necessarily mean general prosperity or mass welfare. Democratic government and majority rule also seem recently not to be able to produce political rulers competent to cope with the ever increasing complexity of human problems. It is quite possible, therefore, that these very scientific and technological advances which seem to some the best proof of progress may prove the major cause of the downfall of civilization as a whole.

For this reason, in the place of progress, discriminating writers have tended to substitute the conception of social change. We can demonstrate the reality of change, but the notion of progress is very largely the product of wishful thinking. It will probably require another century or more before we can pass any judgment upon its validity. If we are able to socialize the advantages brought about by science and technology and to avert warfare, we may attain a degree of social well-being that will decisively substantiate the theory of progress. As yet, however, there is no such positive assurance before us.

Some contemporary writers have allowed their emotions to carry them to the other extreme from a belief in progress. Foremost here has been the presumptuous German philosopher and historian Oswald Spengler, whose voluminous work *The Decline of the West*[1] has become the Bible of contemporary social pessimists. Spengler repudiated the theory of progress and revived the older notion of cycles of change. He held that Western civilization has already passed its apex and is on its way towards general decline. This point of view was energetically attacked by another eminent German philosopher, Ludwig Stein, in his *Evolution and Optimism*,[2] which is specifically intended as a refutation of Spenglerism. The attitudes of both Spengler and Stein may be regarded as the outgrowth of wishful thinking.

5. THE NEW OBSCURANTISM

During the eighteenth and nineteenth centuries there was a definite hangover of that honest obscurantism which rested upon a sincere acceptance of orthodox religious concepts and traditions. This position frankly opposed the scientific method and rejected all scientific discoveries that in any way conflicted with the Scriptural record. The most systematic statement of this older obscurantism was set forth in Paley's *Natural Theology* and in the *Syllabus of*

---

[1] Knopf, 1926-28, 2 vols. Originally published in Germany in 1918. Spengler, regarded by many as an omniscient savant, punctured his own bubble by his naïve *Man and Technics*, Knopf, 1932.
[2] Boni, 1926.

Errors of Pope Pius IX (1864). In passing it may be recalled that Professor F. C. Conybeare once remarked that this papal collection of alleged "errors" of the day, condemned by His Holiness, constituted an admirable summary of the intellectual and scientific progress of the three previous centuries. In somewhat more sophisticated form this attitude of Pius IX is perpetuated today in the writings of Gilbert Chesterton and Hilaire Belloc.

Without in any way accepting either the premises or the contentions of this school of thought, one can have respect for the courage and logic underlying it, once one grants the assumed premises and understands the historical background out of which it has developed.

Scarcely as much can be said for another group of writers who protest that they are thoroughly conversant with contemporary scientific methods and achievements and in sympathy with intellectual progress and enlightenment. At the same time, they take a decidedly antagonistic attitude toward science, once it is brought out of the laboratory and given some application to our general evaluation of life and experience. It is undoubtedly a salutary thing, as Langdon-Davies has indicated,[1] to rebuke naïve and unrestrained advocates of the omniscience of contemporary science, but the "new obscurantism" has gone far beyond this.

Because the more original scientists, with a gift for cosmic perspective and a robust humanitarian motivation, have assumed to set forth a scientific interpretation of man and the world, these "highbrow obscurantists" have accused the scientists of developing a new cult, a new theology, or even a new mythology. When there are scientists brave and logical enough to contrast the scientific order of things with the old supernatural interpretation offered by orthodox religion, our contemporary obscurantists rush forward with the assertion that science is but offering a new religion for an older and scarcely less tenable variety. When scientists are modestly willing to admit differences of opinion, conflicting hypotheses, or incomplete knowledge, this new group hastily assumes such limitations to mean the general impotence of science.

The most conspicuous phase of this newer obscurantism has been known as the New Humanism, which must be differentiated from both the classical Humanism of the Renaissance and the new religious Humanism, which proposes to found a new cult divorced from belief in God. The New Humanism was most popular in the decade from 1920 to 1930. Its leaders were Professors Irving Babbitt of Harvard and Paul Elmer More of Princeton—Babbitt an expert on French literature and More an able conservative literary critic. It was warmly supported in England by an expatriate American poet and critic, T. S. Eliot. It has some affinity with the Neo-Thomism led by Jacques Maritain in France. A number of elements combined to produce the New Humanism. In part, the movement has been a reaction against the social interpretation of literature. It represents the leisure-class determination to keep literature free from the disturbing and unpleasant considerations involved in political, economic, and social reform. Then, there is a decided aristocratic strain in the movement. It constitutes a sort of literary feudalism, calculated to maintain

---

[1] *The New Age of Faith.*

literature and thought as an esoteric cult above the masses.[1] Another formative influence is the defensive reaction against the upsetting revelations of modern science. In the moral field, the New Humanism has represented an attack upon alleged Rousseauism, or the cult of the natural and spontaneous. The Humanists have adopted a Puritan solemnity in moral matters and demand an ascetic intellectual discipline over moral conduct. In its intellectual perspective this New Humanism constitutes a repudiation of the leadership of natural or social science and of the dictates of esthetics as a guide to life. It reverts to the supposedly stern guidance of Aristotle and Scholasticism, though Aristotle himself actually favored most of the ideas that the Humanists abhor. Their knowledge of philology and literary criticism is extensive, but their mastery of the history of thought is mostly confined to the few figures and limited periods congenial to their particular tastes.[2]

III. PROGRESS IN THE SOCIAL SCIENCES

The advances in the social sciences in the twentieth century have been extremely significant. These studies have become much less dominated by preconceived philosophical dogmas, and the historical and scientific methods have been extensively applied to them. More refined methods of statistical investigation and analysis have been introduced. There is somewhat less interest in working out a pseudo-scientific defense of the existing order and a more realistic determination to discover the actual facts, wherever they may lead. In the task of introducing the scientific method into the social sciences, perhaps the most widely discussed figure in the twentieth century has been the Italian economist and statistician Vilfredo Pareto (1848-1923), whose vast four-volume work, *The Mind and Society*,[3] is preëminently a book for specialists. Definitions, descriptions, classifications, and methodological disputes have given way to analysis of social functions and processes. To a very considerable degree, petty jealousies have been put aside in order to arrive at a more unified and coöperative conception of modern society. In the United States a determined movement has been launched to emphasize the teaching of the social sciences in the schools and colleges. A great Encyclopaedia of the Social Sciences has been edited by Professor E. R. A. Seligman and Dr. Alvin Johnson. It has come to be pretty generally recognized that the prospect of saving modern civilization through the application of intelligence to our problems will depend primarily upon the improvement and exploitation of social science.

In the field of history there has been a definite trend away from the older exclusive concern with annals of politics, diplomacy, and war.[4] Historians have shown much more concern about the evolution of civilization and about tracing the growth of human institutions. There has developed a real interest in describing the manner in which our twentieth-century civilization has evolved from earlier periods of culture. In Germany, Karl Lamprecht outlined

---

[1] *Cf.* Max Eastman, *The Literary Mind*, Scribner, 1931, pp. 15-53.
[2] Their weaknesses have been fully exposed by Mr. C. Hartley Grattan and his associates. *Cf.* C. H. Grattan, ed., *A Critique of Humanism*, Harcourt, Brace, 1930.
[3] Harcourt, Brace, 1935, 4 vols. On more rigorous methods in the social sciences, see G. A. Lundberg, *Social Research*, Longmans, 1929.
[4] *Cf.* H. E. Barnes, *Living in the Twentieth Century*, Long & Smith, 1928, Chap. XII, and *History and Social Intelligence*, Chaps. II-III.

the history of civilization in the light of the changing mental attitudes that have characterized the successive stages of human development. In France, Henri Berr edited a vast history of civilization designed to indicate in detail the evolution of human culture, and Georges Renard edited a comprehensive history of the evolution of economic institutions. In the United States, James Harvey Robinson led in developing an interest in the history of human thought and culture, a field in which he has been followed by such disciples as Carl L. Becker, Preserved Smith, and Lynn Thorndike.[1] James T. Shotwell did pioneer work in stimulating a concern with the history of civilization and social institutions, a field still cultivated more zealously by historical-minded economists such as Sombart, the Webbs, Tawney, and the Hammonds than by professional historians. Frederick J. Turner and Charles A. Beard penetratingly analyzed the data of economic and institutional history to give a better understanding of the development of the United States. An extensive history of civilization that will run to nearly two hundred volumes is now in the process of publication under the editorship of Professor Berr, C. K. Ogden, and the present writer. H. G. Wells and James Harvey Robinson have done much to popularize the conceptions of these newer types of history.

Sociology has advanced from controversies over definitions and classifications to a realistic analysis of social processes and institutions.[2] Gustav Ratzenhofer and Albion W. Small analyzed the relationship between social interests and the growth of social institutions. Emile Durkheim paid special attention to the domination of the group mind over the individual mind and made far the most extensive sociological analysis of the division of labor. Franklin H. Giddings sketched the evolution of civilization and worked out a systematic theory of social causation. Edward A. Ross described with force and ingenuity the operation of psychological factors in social control. Charles H. Cooley discussed with subtlety the character of group life and the nature of the social process. Leonard T. Hobhouse developed a system of sociology that drew heavily upon philosophy and anthropology, aiming fundamentally at rationally guided social reform. Leopold von Wiese produced an impressive systematization of sociological principles, based on the notion than sociology is a rigorously schematic exposition of the facts of interhuman behavior and social relationships. Trained specialists in social science have shown the bearing of historical, biological, psychological, and geographical factors upon group life.

Economics at the opening of the twentieth century was chiefly a collection of dubious laws and dogmas based upon pecuniary logic and the false Benthamite conception of human nature, neither of which had any great regard for the literal facts of economic life.[3] The systems of economics worked by Ricardo and others in his tradition and by John Bates Clark and his followers were truly impressive bodies of metaphysics and logic but scarcely social science. In the twentieth century, economics has become a real social science describing the evolution of economic institutions and the character of economic processes in contemporary life. Alfred Marshall (1842-1924) was the commanding figure

[1] *Cf.* H. E. Barnes, "James Harvey Robinson," in H. W. Odum, ed., *American Masters of Social Science*, Holt, 1927, pp. 321-408, and *History and Social Intelligence*, pp. 139 ff. (on Wells).
[2] *Cf.* L. L. Bernard, ed., *Fields and Methods of Sociology*, Long & Smith, 1934.
[3] *Cf.* P. T. Homan, ed., *Contemporary Economic Thought*, Harper, 1928.

in the transition of economics from pecuniary logic to empirical social science. Gustav von Schmoller and his associates and Karl Bücher introduced the historical method into economic science in a systematic way, thus enabling us to understand the evolution of the major stages of economic organization. Werner Sombart gave particular attention to the growth of modern capitalism, the outstanding economic development in the whole history of mankind. Max Weber was interested in the history of economic institutions and in the effect of religious and ethical teachings upon economic doctrines and practices. Emile Durkheim's studies of the social division of labor have been very important for realistic economics. Sidney and Beatrice Webb have studied in great detail the economic and social life of England since the Industrial Revolution, and John and Barbara Hammond have carried on similar investigations in the period of the Industrial Revolution itself. J. A. Hobson traced the development of modern capitalism, indicated the way in which economic science may promote social welfare, and suggested new incentives to supplant the profit motive. In the United States, Thorstein Veblen discussed economic institutions and modern capitalistic practices in many books in which realism is tempered with irony and satire. Along with John R. Commons, Veblen founded institutional economics in the United States. Statistical methods have been used by the economists with ever greater profusion and precision, one of the chief impulses here coming from Stanley Jevons. The economists have at last been able to provide us with information that will enable any honest student to understand the economic world in which we live and the stages through which we have passed in arriving at our present condition.

In political science, the older penchant for definitions of different forms of governments and for the description of party strife has been supplanted by a penetrating analysis of the influence of institutional forces upon political life and of the social functions executed by our political institutions.[1] Franz Oppenheimer showed the influence of economic factors upon political activity and institutions. Durkheim, Lippmann, and others analyzed the psychological basis of political behavior. Edward Jenks followed the teachings of Gumplowicz in tracing the effect of warfare and social struggles upon the creation and evolution of political institutions. J. N. Figgis and H. J. Laski carried further the studies of Gierke and Maitland with respect to the relation between social groups and political organization. Laski and other "Pluralists" have compelled a reconsideration of the whole conception of political sovereignty in the light of its social foundations. Charles A. Beard and C. E. Merriam have recognized the bearing of the newer sciences of man upon the reconstruction of political science. Beard has also laid special emphasis upon the economic basis of politics. Under the influence of such students as Eugen Ehrlich, Léon Duguit, Roscoe Pound, Justice Cardozo, and Felix Frankfurter the conceptions of law and jurisprudence have been socialized and law is conceived of as a technique for guiding social change.[2]

Anthropology, or the study of primitive man and his culture, was a slave to

---

[1] *Cf.* C. E. Merriam, *New Aspects of Politics,* 2d ed., University of Chicago Press, 1931, and Merriam and Barnes, *History of Political Theories: Recent Times.*

[2] *Cf.* Roscoe Pound, in H. E. Barnes and others, *History and Prospects of the Social Sciences,* Knopf, 1925, Chap. IX.

dogmatic conceptions of social evolution at the close of the nineteenth century.[1] Such studies as Lewis H. Morgan's *Ancient Society* (1877) were representative of this type of anthropology. It presented a very orderly conception of social evolution, but often failed notably to square with the facts. A new and critical school of anthropology has been developed by Franz Boas and his disciples and by some European anthropologists, such as Professor R. R. Marett. They have been interested in reinvestigating the character of primitive culture and society, in order to give us a literal picture in harmony with the facts, however poorly these facts may conform to any preconceived conception of cultural evolution. New discoveries of primitive human skeletons have enabled us to go much further in reconstructing the record of the evolution of man as a physical being. In this field such men as the famous English anatomist Sir Arthur Keith have taken the lead. Archaeology has given us new light upon the daily life of primitive man. This new information has been well digested and organized by George Grant MacCurdy.

Even ethics, so long the exclusive province of religion and metaphysics, has been placed upon a scientific basis by such men as Bertrand Russell, C. M. Joad, John Dewey, James H. Tufts, and R. C. Givler.[2] According to these more recent students of ethical problems, sound guidance for our conduct must be derived from a study of the nature of man and his social surroundings. The aim of ethics must be the provision of standards and knowledge leading to a complete and happy life here on earth. Scientific notions of conduct have been given esthetic interpretations by Havelock Ellis, George Santayana, and others.[3]

IV. OUTSTANDING PROBLEMS OF RELIGION

The intellectual and scientific advances of the twentieth century have possessed extremely significant implications for religion.

In Western Christendom we find essentially the following groupings with respect to religious convictions:[4] First, the completely orthodox, who believe in a personal God, accept the Bible as the literal word of God, proclaim the complete divinity of Jesus, and believe in the personal immortality of the human soul. This group still remains extremely numerous, particularly among the European peasantry and among the lower middle class in urban populations. It embraces all devout Catholics. The Protestant orthodox, particularly in the United States, have come to be rather generally known as Fundamentalists, because of their insistence upon rigorous adherence to certain indispensable "fundamentals" of the Christian faith.

In a second group we find what have been called the Devout Modernists. They have attempted to harmonize modern scholarship with deep religious conviction. They do not accept the idea that the Bible was directly dictated by God, but they regard it as the most important religious document of all history. While rejecting the notion of the literal divinity of Jesus, they regard Him as the unique religious and moral teacher of all time. They believe fervently in the reality and existence of God and most of them view God in a

---

[1] *Cf.* A. A. Goldenweiser, *ibid.*, Chap. v.   [2] *Cf.* R. C. Givler, *ibid.*, Chap. x.
[3] On the new morality, see J. H. Tufts, *America's Social Morality*, Holt, 1933, and Durant Drake, *The New Morality*, Macmillan, 1928.
[4] *Cf.* Barnes, *The Twilight of Christianity*, Chap. vii.

A T L A N T I C O C E A N
N O R T H S E A
GREAT BRITAIN
SCOTLAND
ENGLAND
WALES
NORTHERN IRELAND
IRISH FREE STATE
Belfast
Dublin
London
NORWAY
SWEDEN
Oslo
Stockho
DENMARK
Copenhagen
B A L
NETHERLANDS
The Hague
Brussels
BELGIUM
GERMANY
Berlin
Paris
FRANCE
Berne
SWITZERLAND
AUSTRIA
Vienna
CZECHO
Prague
HU
YUG
ITALY
Rome
ADRIATIC SEA
PORTUGAL
Lisbon
SPAIN
Madrid
M E D I T E R R A N
A F R I C A
20° 10° 0° 10°
50° 40°
1 2 3 4 5
A B C D E F G H
Longitude West
Longitude

EU

EUROPEAN RELIGIONS

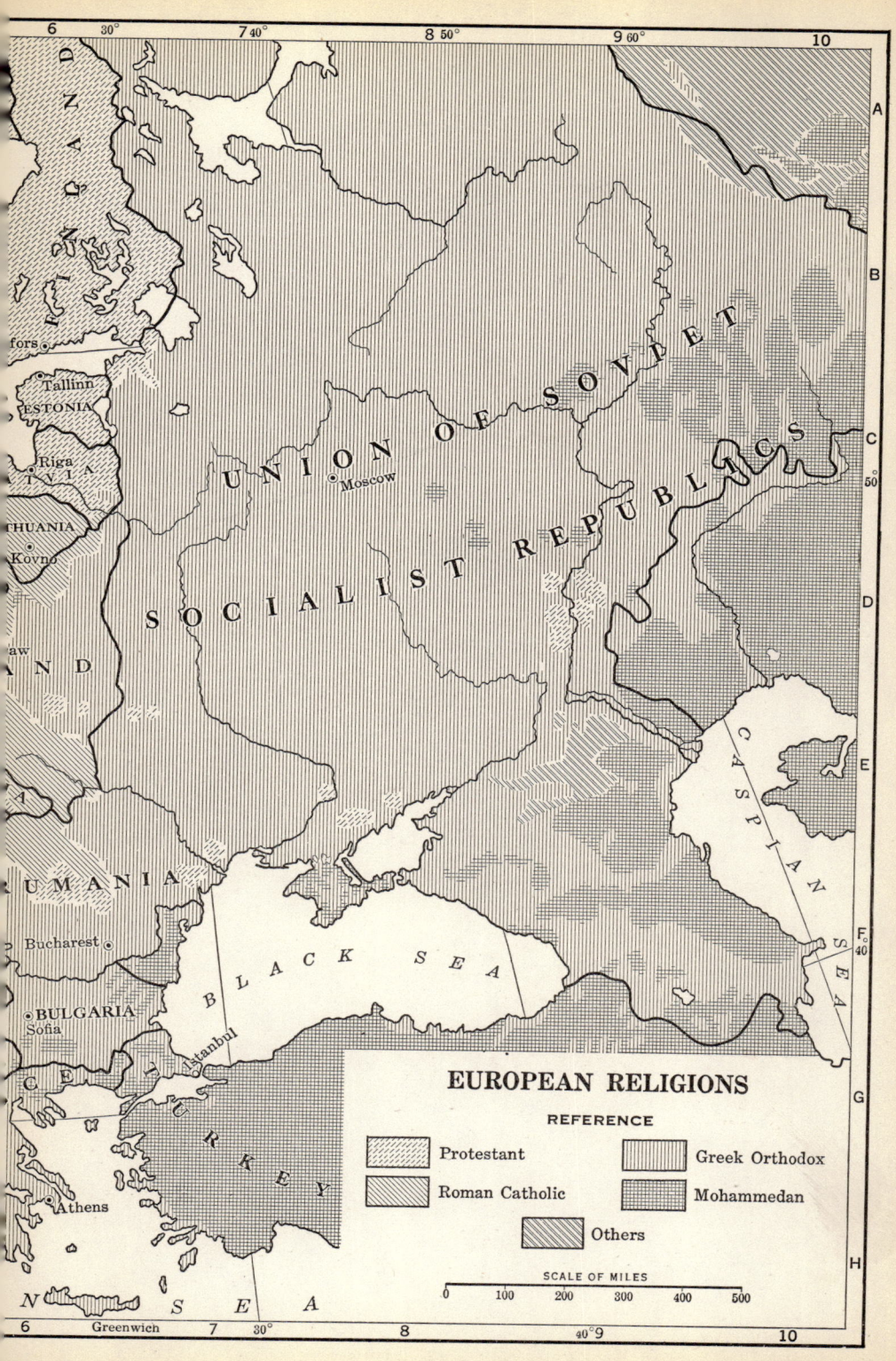

REFERENCE

- Protestant
- Roman Catholic
- Greek Orthodox
- Mohammedan
- Others

SCALE OF MILES
0   100   200   300   400   500

fatherly relationship to man. They are about equally divided in their acceptance or rejection of a literal immortality. These Devout Modernists have been drawn almost entirely from the ranks of the Protestants, all devout Catholic believers still adhering resolutely to the tenets of orthodoxy.

The most radical among those who still actively embrace religion are the so-called Advanced Modernists. The more conservative members of this group, while completely rejecting the divine inspiration of the Bible and the divinity of Jesus, still retain at least a shadowy loyalty to Christianity and at least a formal belief in the existence of God. Such are the extreme radical wing among the Congregationalists and the more conservative Unitarians and Universalists. The more resolute members of the Advanced Modernists take an agnostic position, holding that man cannot attain any certainty as to the existence of God, believe that the Bible has no unique claim to authority among other great religious and ethical works, reject not only the divinity of Jesus but also the notion that he was a unique religious and moral teacher, and surrender entirely any belief in personal immortality.[1] This more progressive wing of the Advanced Modernists is made up chiefly of the radical Unitarians and Universalists and others who have forsaken the more orthodox and devout of the Christian sects. A definite movement within Advanced Modernism has taken on the name of Humanism, because it bases its doctrines upon the service of man rather than the worship of God.[2] Most of its adherents have come from the Unitarian and Universalist circles. Its leaders have been such men as John H. Dietrich, A. Eustace Haydon, Charles Francis Potter, Curtis W. Reese, A. C. Dieffenbach, John Haynes Holmes, E. Burdette Backus, and A. Wakefield Slaten. The Humanist position has been supported by able philosophers, such as John Dewey, James H. Tufts, J. H. Leuba, Roy W. Sellars, Max C. Otto, Durant Drake and Corliss Lamont.

Such are the groups within Christendom today. Much the same divisions also exist among the Jews in Western civilization.[3] They range all the way from the dogmas of the fervently orthodox to those of Jewish Humanists, such as James Waterman Wise.

Taking Western civilization as a whole outside of Russia, approximately half of the populations are no longer formal communicants in any religious sect or denomination. The number who have fallen away from any religious connection is larger in Protestant than in Catholic countries. Most of this defection from formal religion has come as a result of growing indifference and the increasing absorption of time and human interest in new forms of secular activities. Relatively few among the general population have abandoned Christianity because of prolonged critical studies or well-documented agnosticism. It is probable that the automobile, Sunday newspapers, the movies, the radio, and golf have done more to separate man from active religious exercises than all the combined teachings of the skeptics in the last half-century.

From what has been said above, it is obvious that there is no uniformity in the reaction of these various religious groups to critical scholarship and science.[4]

[1] *Cf.* Corliss Lamont, *The Illusion of Immortality*, Putnam, 1935.
[2] Not to be confused with the reactionary literary Humanism described above.
[3] *Cf.* A. H. Silver, *Religion in a Changing World*, Harper, 1930, and Maurice Samuel, *Jews on Approval*, Liveright, 1932.
[4] *Cf.* Barnes, *op. cit.*, Chap. VII, and Clifford Kirkpatrick, *Religion in Human Affairs*, Wiley, 1929.

Whereas the Devout Modernists, as we pointed out earlier, were the advance guard of radical Christians in the year 1900, the Humanists occupy that position today. Perhaps the most interesting thing about the latter is that their very existence proves that religious enthusiasm can survive the abandonment of the belief in God, supernaturalism, and immortality.

The Catholics and Protestant Fundamentalists resolutely and logically resist both corrosive biblical criticism and those phases of science which conflict directly with the Christian epic.[1] Their views on the Bible and biblical science have not changed to any marked degree since the beginning of the nineteenth century. The Devout Modernists accept the facts, if not the implications, of biblical scholarship and have thoroughly adjusted themselves to the natural science of the nineteenth century, but rarely do they reveal any penetrating cognizance of twentieth-century science and its upsetting conclusions.[2] They have, however, shown an eagerness to assimilate the religious apologetics of certain twentieth-century scientists, such as Eddington, Pupin, Millikan, Mather and others. The Advanced Modernists have thoroughly adjusted themselves not only to nineteenth- but also to twentieth-century science. They endeavor to keep progressively informed in their scientific outlook. Hence there is little prospect of any conflict between science and Advanced Modernism.

The conflict between science and Fundamentalism, especially in the United States, took on a sharp and definite character when an effort was made following 1920 to make the teaching of evolution, biblical criticism, and economic materialism illegal in certain states.[3] The struggle came to a focus in the famous Scopes trial at Dayton, Tennessee, in the summer of 1925. Here the Fundamentalists convicted a local school-teacher of illegally teaching evolution in his biology classes. The Fundamentalists were led by William Jennings Bryan while Scopes was defended by the well-known lawyer and freethinker Clarence S. Darrow. Mr. Bryan died of overexertion in the closing days of the trial and American Fundamentalism lost aggressiveness from that moment.

One of the most interesting aspects of the reaction of science on religion in this century has been the application of psychology to the problems of religious experience, beliefs, and traditional mysteries.[4] The psychologists have assumed to be able to explain the origin and character of the belief in supernatural power, the conception of God as a father of mankind, the increased poise and energy often accompanying religious conversion, and the exalted mental state of the religious mystic. Psychologists also believe that they can make clear the relationship between various types of mental abnormalities and religious fanaticism. If the psychologists are right in these contentions, their work represents perhaps the most devastating challenge to supernaturalism and religious mystery thus far presented by scholarship.

The unsettling tendencies in twentieth-century science, particularly the destruction of the old theories of causation by the new electromechanics and the

---

[1] *Cf.* G. B. O'Toole, *The Case against Evolution*, Macmillan, 1925, and Maynard Shipley, *The War on Modern Science*, Knopf, 1927.

[2] An exception is E. W. Barnes, *Scientific Theory and Religion*, Macmillan, 1933, but there is not the slightest logical connection between the learned Bishop's scientific erudition and his religious dogmas.

[3] *Cf.* Shipley, *op. cit.*

[4] *Cf.* J. C. Flower, *An Approach to the Psychology of Religion*, Harcourt, Brace, 1927, and E. Martin, *The Mystery of Religion*, Harper, 1924.

revelation of the vast extent of the cosmos by contemporary astrophysics, have reacted upon religion as well. The candid modern scientist frankly admits that he is baffled in his search for, and understanding of, ultimates. The religionist has rushed into the breach and proclaimed that where science is baffled religion can supply the lacking certainty. The scientists have retorted that if the human mind could give any credible answers to the ultimate mysteries of the physical universe, science would supply these answers. They hold that where science is baffled religion must be far less capable of solving such unsettled problems.

The religionists have gained considerable encouragement from certain scientists with pietistic leanings. These men, such as Thomson, Pupin, Osborn, Eddington, Millikan, and Mather, recognizing that science cannot always give a final answer to physical ultimates, have reverted in their philosophy to their traditional religious views. This tendency has been sharply criticized as indefensible by other eminent scientists, such as Bertrand Russell, Dingle, and Levy.[1] These pietistic scientists have also been sternly rebuked by Professor Morris R. Cohen:

I have not been at all impressed by the religious and philosophic lessons drawn from science by men like Millikan, Eddington, Coulter, A. H. Compton, E. G. Conklin, and the like. I respect, as every one must, the great achievements of these distinguished workers in their special fields. But scientists do not always carry scientific method into their views of manners, morals, or politics, of justice between nations or social classes, of the reliability of mediums, etc. Neither are they scientific when they make their professional work a springboard from which to jump off into amateurish speculative flights in the fields of religion and philosophy.[2]

A reasonable attitude is that taken by Professor Compton. He is personally inclined towards the pietistic attitude, but frankly admits that it is purely an emotional yearning and is incapable of any scientific demonstration or defense.

The new natural science has also had a very decisive influence upon the discussion of the problem of the existence of God.[3] Few scientists have been foolish enough to declare that their findings have proved the nonexistence of God. But these very same findings have vastly increased the difficulty of settling this basic issue in religious controversy. Man can only determine the problem of the existence of God after he has thoroughly mastered all the relevant facts concerning the character of the whole physical universe. Only then can he decide whether the theory of divine creation or that of mechanistic evolution is most compatible with the facts. Philosophers, deeply affected by science, have indicated that it is well-nigh impossible for the human mind to fathom and interpret all the facts and mysteries of the physical universe. Hence it appears to such writers to be very difficult to settle definitively the more remote and perplexing question of the existence or nonexistence of God. This position has been very well stated by Professor James H. Leuba:

The claims of the religions and of philosophers that they have given an adequate answer to the problem of God are made in an adolescent conceit. An adequate solu-

---

[1] Bertrand Russell, *The Scientific Outlook,* Norton, 1931, Chaps. IV-V; Herbert Dingle, *Science and Human Experience,* Macmillan, 1932, Chap. XI; and Levy, *op. cit.*
[2] Cohen, *Reason and Nature,* Harcourt, Brace, 1931, p. xiv.
[3] *Cf.* J. H. Leuba, *God or Man?* Holt, 1933, and Baker Brownell, *Earth Is Enough,* Harper, 1933.

tion would demand a complete knowledge of all things in heaven and earth; it will therefore, be long delayed![1]

Religion and the Christian Church have not only been compelled to reckon with novel and disconcerting scientific discoveries. They have also had to face an even greater menace in the increasing secularization of life. With the growing number of practical inventions, the increasing prevalence of city life, and the extension of urban conveniences and attitudes to rural life, there has been a consequent and comparable lessening of human interest in supernatural affairs. Modern industrialism has been brought in for the most part by religious men, yet the results of modern industrialism have probably done more to weaken the hold of the old supernatural religion than all the skeptical and critical philosophy of the past. This has been admirably stated by Professor John Herman Randall, Jr.:

Industrialism and city life have been far more subversive than all the scientific theories put together. We are all too familiar with theological difficulties. We are apt to overlook the real religious revolution of the past forty years, the crowding of religion into a minor place by the host of secular faiths and interests. For every man alienated from the Church by scientific ideas, there are dozens dissatisfied with its social attitudes, and hundreds who, with no intellectual doubts, have found their lives fully occupied with the other interests and diversions of the machine age. What does it matter that earnest men have found a way to combine older beliefs with the spirit of science, if those beliefs have ceased to express anything vital in men's experience, if the older religious faith is irrelevant to all they really care for? A truly intelligent Fundamentalist, indeed, would leave biology alone as of little influence. He would instead try to abolish the automobiles and movies and Sunday papers and golf links that are emptying our churches. Even when the Church embraces the new interests, it seems to be playing a losing game. There is little of specifically religious significance in the manifold activities of the modern institutional church; a dance for the building fund is less of a religious experience than a festival in honor of the patron saint. And any minister knows that his "social activities" spring less from real need than from the fervent desire to attract and hold members. The church itself has been secularized. Its very members continue a half-hearted support, from motives of traditional attachment, of personal loyalty to the minister, of social prestige, because they do not want to live in a churchless community.[2]

The disintegrating influence of these new secular interests on conventional religion is especially effective because of its indirect nature. It is subtle and often unnoticed. Therefore it does not arouse the defensive reactions that are provoked by direct attacks of freethinkers upon traditional religion.

Not only have secular interests served to distract man's mind from the supernatural; secular institutions and practices have also tended to usurp duties and services formerly executed by the Church. Psychology, sociology, and medical science, together with the fine arts, have tended to take away from the Church its monopoly over the character of moral teachings and the control of moral conduct. Recreation was formerly rigorously supervised by the Church. Today

---

[1] Leuba, op. cit., p. 320.
[2] Randall, "The Forces That Are Destroying Traditional Beliefs" (New York Times), Current History, June, 1929, pp. 361-62.

there is a tendency to hand it over to control by medical experts, psychologists, and social workers. The Church once exerted a tremendous hold over the masses through the emotional appeal of its ritual, liturgy, and pageantry. Today the theater, the opera, the movies, and various types of secularized public pageantry compete extensively with churchly efforts along this line. Poetry and art tend in ever greater degree to act as a substitute for religion in meeting the mystical yearnings of mankind. The growth of secularism has lessened the influence of the Church upon education and has reduced the number and importance of Church schools. Moreover, the schools are assuming some of the responsibility for character-building and moral education that was once very thoroughly monopolized by the Church. The criticism and the guidance of public morality are now being exercised in ever greater degree by the lecture forum, university extension courses, institutions for adult education, and the press. The cause of social justice is here argued today as it used to be, more or less exclusively, from the pulpit. The radio threatens both church attendance and the preaching profession. One eminent clergyman can address millions of listeners over the air, whereas the largest churches will not seat more than a few thousand hearers. This may mean that we shall require far fewer preachers in the future.

The Church has not failed to recognize the challenge from these new social and cultural tendencies of the twentieth century. Organizations like the Lord's Day Alliance have attempted to perpetuate the old "blue laws" and restrict secular activities on Sunday. Progressive churches have instituted many and diverse types of social and cultural activities designed to appeal to the young and to uphold the strength of religion.[1] Such are church gymnasiums, dances and parties held under church auspices, educational classes maintained by ecclesiastical institutions, forums conducted on church premises, and plays produced by church members or held under the auspices of church authorities. These new social and educational activities of the more modernized churches may well have helped to keep up church attendance, but it must also be observed that they have failed rather completely to preserve an interest in supernatural religion. Their appeal is secular rather than spiritual.

The interest of the Church in social reform has continued into the twentieth century. The struggle between irresponsible capitalism and social justice goes on within religious circles as it does outside. The very rich have seen the value of religion enlisted upon their side in defending the accumulation of great fortunes. They have built great churches, supported religious activities, and endowed religious schools. They have been amply rewarded through the fervent defense of big business and large fortunes by preachers such as Chancellor Day, Pastor Bigelow, and other ardent admirers of plutocracy.[2]

In contrast, many religious reformers have appeared to denounce plutocracy and its alliance with the church. While Pastor Bigelow was unctuously eulogizing the steel barons, Bishop McConnell was courageously risking his position to support a thorough investigation of the social and economic policies of the

---

[1] *Cf.* Jerome Davis, ed., *Christianity and Social Adventuring*, Century, 1927.
[2] *Cf.* J. R. Day, *The Raid on Prosperity*, Appleton, 1907—an attack on Theodore Roosevelt's mild reform policies—and the Rev. Mr. Bigelow's attacks on the report of the Interchurch World Movement on the steel strike of 1919.

steel trust. Such religious crusaders have denounced economic injustice and have attempted to utilize the social momentum of religion as a means of undermining the old type of capitalism and setting up a more just and workable social and economic order. Harry F. Ward, Sherwood Eddy, Kirby Page, Reinhold Niebuhr, David Vaughan, and Ralph Harlow are representative of religious idealism enlisted in behalf of social justice. The Catholic Church has formally reiterated its friendliness toward social justice as stated in the nineteenth century by Pope Leo XIII. In 1931, Pope Pius XI reaffirmed and extended the doctrine of Leo XIII. Such spokesmen as Father John A. Ryan have matched the social radicalism of Protestants such as Harry F. Ward. The Christian Church, therefore, like secular society, is divided with respect to its attitude towards the old capitalistic order.[1] Some of the most whole-hearted support of capitalism has come from the Christian Church, but so also have some of the most forthright and devastating attacks upon the old economic order.

One of the most interesting religious innovations in the twentieth century has been the rise of secular religions such as Communism and Fascism. In the chapter on Russia we pointed out that Communism is supported by its Russian converts with fervor and enthusiasm of a truly religious character. We thus see established in a country that is extremely hostile to supernatural religion a secular cult which arouses as strong an emotional response from its followers as the old Greek Church ever did from an ignorant Russian village community. Italian Fascism also possesses a strong religious undercurrent. Hitler has attempted to give Nazism an open and avowed religious foundation.

It would be a rash person who would make any dogmatic prophecies as to the future of religion, but if it survives, its general tendencies will probably be along the lines suggested by Professor Kirsopp Lake:

One man may find much comfort in tobacco, while another may injure himself by smoking: one may err by playing too much, and another by never playing at all. I doubt whether the men of to-morrow will try to interfere with each other on these points, knowing that the thing which matters is ability to do good work, and that one man can do his best work in one way, another otherwise. Many of the things Puritans condemn are strictly indifferent. The religions of to-morrow will recognize this, it will give good advice to individuals, but not lay down general rules for universal observance.

On the other hand, it may have a sterner standard in business, industry and finance. It may insist more loudly that honesty applies to the spirit of business, not merely to its letter. It may even demand that men must be as trustworthy in advertisements, business announcements, and journalistic reporting as they are in private affairs. For these are the questions of morals which are the issues of life and death for the future. They are not covered by the teaching of Jesus or of historic Christianity, for neither ever discussed problems which did not exist in their time. Some of the principles which have been laid down by them will play a part in the solution of these problems but probably others will contain new elements and the religion of to-morrow will have to look for them.[3]

The generation following the World War witnessed a very marked revolt against the moral restraints of the prewar period. There was a determination to seek self-expression and to defy many of the more traditional conventions

---

[1] See the powerful portrayal of this theme in Winston Churchill's novel, *The Inside of the Cup*
[2] P. F. Douglass, *God among the Germans*, University of Pennsylvania Press, 1935.
[3] Lake, *The Religion of Yesterday and To-morrow*, Houghton Mifflin, 1925, p. 173.

especially as to sex and dress. This was due to the greater familiarity created by wartime association between the sexes, to the increase of mundane interests, to the impact of psychoanalytical psychology on the popular mind, to the growing secularism of life, to the popularity of erotic literature, to the wider use of the automobile, and to birth-control knowledge. It is too early to assess these developments as yet, though rational self-control seems to be setting in.

A very interesting manifestation of this "spirit of youth" was the growth of the nudist movement after the World War. This nakedness cult first gained considerable headway in connection with the youth movement in Germany and has since spread to other lands, including the United States. Its aim is said to be the restoration of the Greek naturalness with respect to the beauty and health of the human body. The findings of modern medicine and chemistry have been invoked in defense of the cult, much stress being laid upon the salutary effect of the exposure of the body to the air and direct solar rays.

V. DEVELOPMENTS IN PHILOSOPHY

In spite of its being a preëminently intellectual occupation that should promote independence of thought, philosophy has exhibited a remarkable capacity for continuity and inertia. The Germanic Idealism and Hegelianism, with later elaborations, carried over into the twentieth century, still attracting enthusiastic disciples. An effort was made by the Italian philosopher Benedetto Croce to harmonize Hegelianism with the modern scientific and critical spirit. Scholastic philosophy has been perpetuated not only in the Roman Catholic colleges and universities but also in a definite recent Thomistic revival led by Jacques Maritain and others. Even Aristotelianism has been recommended by the Humanist literary critics, such as Irving Babbitt and Paul Elmer More.

The most influential of the philosophical vestiges from the past has been the Neo-Transcendentalism which received its inspiration from the study of Kant. One branch, known as Neo-Kantianism, is led by Hermann Cohen and Wilhelm Windelband. Even more popular today is the branch known as Phenomenology, founded and cultivated by Franz Brentano, Alexius Meinong, Edmund Husserl, Max Scheler, and others. It aims to ascertain "essences" and universal characters by intuition. It holds that universals are something more than can be apprehended through empirical consciousness. Over and above the empirical ego is a transcendental ego. All transcendental egos merge to form a supreme transcendental Being, not unlike the Absolute of Hegel. This movement has affected ethics, especially through the work of Scheler. He tried to work out the objective values in our emotional and intuitive acts, and constructed a hierarchy of human values very reminiscent of the position of the Neo-Platonists.

The most characteristic development in twentieth-century philosophy has been, however, the sweeping triumph of the scientific method in progressive philosophical thought. This fact has been admirably stated by John Dewey:

It is a commonplace that since the seventeenth century science has revolutionized our beliefs about outer nature, and it is also beginning to revolutionize those about man.

When our minds dwell on this extraordinary change, they are likely to think of the transformation that has taken place in the subject matter of astronomy, physics, chemistry, biology, psychology, anthropology, and so on. But great as is this change, it shrinks in comparison with the change that has occurred in method. The latter is the author of the revolution in the content of beliefs. The new methods have, moreover, brought with them a radical change in our intellectual attitude and its attendant morale. The method we term "scientific" forms for the modern man (and a man is not modern merely because he lives in 1931) the sole dependable means of disclosing the realities of existence. It is the sole authentic mode of revelation. This possession of a new method, to the use of which no limits can be put, signifies a new idea of the nature and possibilities of experience. It imports a new morale of confidence, control, and security.[1]

The preëminent figure in twentieth-century philosophy is probably John Dewey. His Pragmatism, Pluralism, and Instrumentalism have been enriched, sharpened, and integrated as he has increased in knowledge and maturity of mind. His mature philosophy is best expressed in his *Experience and Nature* (1925) and *The Quest for Certainty* (1929). He has remained the most powerful exponent of the scientific method in philosophy in our era. In his earlier period his chief practical interest lay in education, but since 1920 he has shown an increasing concern with economic and political problems, having been greatly stimulated by the achievements of the Russian Revolution. Dewey has given ample proof of late that his outlook upon life is not a cold or narrow scientific dogmatism. His recent *Art as Experience* (1934) is regarded by many as the foremost American contribution to esthetics, while his *A Common Faith* (1934) is a calm and mature appraisal of religion from the point of view of philosophy and an able critique of supernaturalism.

The other outstanding American contributor to the scientific method in philosophy has been Professor Morris R. Cohen. His important books, *Reason and Nature* (1931) and (with Ernest Nagel) *Introduction to Logic and Scientific Method* (1934), constitute the most satisfactory formulation of the scientific point of view as applied to the problems of knowledge. In a sense they represent the completion of the task outlined by Francis Bacon and in part fulfilled by John Stuart Mill in his *System of Logic*.

In England the scientific method in philosophy has found a most learned and persuasive representative in Bertrand Russell. The author of numerous first-rate technical works on mathematics and logic, and the foremost mathematical logician of the day, he has most clearly expressed his intellectual attitude in *The Scientific Outlook* (1931). This is by far the most satisfactory work for the general reader who desires to acquaint himself with the scientific outlook in philosophy. Another younger and brilliant English exponent of this point of view has been Professor J. B. S. Haldane, who brought together representative examples of his thought in *Science and Human Life* (1933).[2] An effort to combine evolutionary science with a somewhat chastened mysticism appears in C. Lloyd Morgan's conception of "emergent evolution," set forth in his book of that title (1923) and in his *Life, Mind and Spirit* (1926). Dr. Morgan is an eminent physiologist and psychologist. An interesting contrast to Bertrand Russell is to be seen in his former collaborator, the learned mathematician

---

[1] Dewey in Einstein and others, *Living Philosophies*, p. 24.
[2] His father, J. S. Haldane, is also a distinguished philosophical biologist. See the latter's *The Philosophical Basis of Biology*, Doubleday, Doran, 1931.

Alfred North Whitehead. Whereas Russell turned sharply in the direction of science and social criticism, Whitehead, after playing a bit with "emergent evolution," reverted very definitely to Platonism and mysticism in his *Science and the Modern World* (1926) and *Religion in the Making* (1926). The best anthology of his thought is *Adventures of Ideas* (1933), a book more notable for its learning than for its intellectual adventuresomeness.

One of the most interesting and suggestive philosophers of the twentieth century was the German Hans Vaihinger (1852-1933), the leading exponent of what is known as Fictionism or the philosophy of "as if" (1911).[1] Many strands were woven into the pattern of Hans Vaihinger's philosophy. Born in 1852 in a Swabian parsonage and educated at Tübingen, he early felt the influence of Bauer with his legendary interpretations of the Bible. Kant's antinomies together with Schopenhauer's irrationally pessimistic Voluntarism impressed him. Most of all, his thought was shaped by the instrumental theory of mind taught by the biological sciences. For Vaihinger mental constructs are tools through which man adjusts himself to his environment. They fall into two general classes, those that look to verification in reality, such as hypothesis, theory, and law, and those that are aids to thought, or fictions. Thought never exhausts reality; truth is merely a minimum of error. Fictions serve as a means to fill out the gaps where informative thought fails and man is forced to act "as if" certain postulates were true. These "as ifs" are of two kinds, pure fictions or those that contradict reality and are self-contradictory (such as that parallel lines meet at infinity) and semifictions (such as Adam Smith's "enlightened selfishness") that are not self-contradictory. Fictions are of vast importance in the social sciences, religion, and philosophy. In the realm of his highest loyalties man lives largely in terms of fictions or "as ifs." The appeal of Vaihinger's philosophy lies in its many-sided contacts with life, its simplifications of ancient problems, and its tolerant Humanism. It is not skeptical, for it never raises doubt to the dignity of a principle. Its relativism and Pragmatism of course damn it in the eyes of the metaphysician who seeks finality and a closed system.

The growing importance of economic problems in modern life, the jeopardy of the capitalistic system, and the remarkable achievements of the Russian Revolution have led to increasing emphasis upon the significance of Marxism and Communism for philosophical analysis. It has been shown that we must not only reckon with the scientific method, but also with the chief economic realities of today. In many ways, the latter represent the most important practical outgrowth of the former. The importance of Marx for philosophy has been well stated by Dr. Sidney Hook in his book, *Towards an Understanding of Karl Marx* (1933). In *A Philosophic Approach to Communism* (1933), Dr. Theodore Brameld has presented a philosophical interpretation of the modifications of Marxian doctrines by Lenin and other leaders of Communist thought.

However satisfactorily economic problems may be solved, unless we devote proper attention to the fine arts we can never arise beyond the level of comfortable animals. An appreciation of this point of view has led to the systematic cultivation of the philosophy of esthetics by leading modern philosophers, most particularly Benedetto Croce, George Santayana, Havelock Ellis, and John

---

[1] *The Philosophy of "As If,"* Harcourt, Brace, 1924. In this chapter titles of foreign books are given in English, but the date is always that of publication in the original.

Dewey. Croce has exerted a wide influence upon the contemporary philosophy of esthetics through his works *Aesthetics* (1900) and *Problems of Aesthetics* (1911). Santayana has expounded the esthetic point of view in his notable work *The Sense of Beauty* (1896). Santayana has also established himself as the leading philosophical exponent of urbane skepticism in his famous series *The Life of Reason* (1905-06), of which one volume is *Reason in Art*. Ellis is an outstanding psychologist and sexologist, but he has given us one of the best statements of a skeptical and esthetic philosophy in his *Dance of Life* (1923). Dewey's important work on art has already been mentioned.

In the appreciation of the primary significance of scientific method and of the current revolution in scientific thinking; in the recognition of the necessity of dealing more satisfactorily with our economic problems; and in the apprehension of the fact that the true realization of civilization is to be discovered in due and proper attention to the fine arts, we find the outstanding issues and interests of contemporary philosophical thought. Other types of contemporary philosophical discussion are, for the most part, mere intellectual curiosities.

VI. SOME LEADING EDUCATIONAL ADVANCES

In the twentieth century free and universal education triumphed in all the more civilized countries of the Western world. Even in Russia, the Soviet government set up a thorough system of free public education in what had been the most illiterate of the major countries of Europe. Education has been further removed from the control of the Church and almost completely secularized, notwithstanding the considerable continuation of Church schools, especially Catholic schools. Consequently enormously increased numbers of children flocked to our schools and made necessary the extension of mass-production methods into educational practice.

Mass-production methods had first been introduced into education by Andrew Bell and Joseph Lancaster at the opening of the nineteenth century, in an effort to provide more economical instruction, first in orphan asylums and then in schools. But there was little general need for such procedure until education became free and universal a century later. For considerations of administrative convenience and financial economy, the control of our public schools then became rather decisively mechanized. Discipline and instruction were adapted to mass situations. This greatly facilitated education on a large scale but well-nigh eliminated the possibility of personal or individualized instruction. One of the major educational problems today is how to work out a successful compromise between mass production in education and proper attention to the special needs of the individual student.

In spite of the tendency towards overmechanization in our public education, great headway has been made in educational theory with respect to studying the mind of the individual child and adapting educational ideas and methods to the character of the child. This had, of course, been the basic conception of Froebel, but he possessed very little valid psychological knowledge upon the basis of which he might accurately understand the real nature of the child. Truly scientific child study was brought into being by G. Stanley Hall, whose

SOME LEADING EDUCATIONAL ADVANCES

work in linking psychology and education with evolution was referred to in an earlier chapter.[1] Hall's work in genetic psychology first placed child study upon a reasonably scientific plane. Froebel's emphasis upon cultivating and directing the spontaneous tendencies of the child was given a fresh impetus and further development by an Italian physician and educator, Dr. Maria Montessori. She was led into her educational doctrine in part by her work with feeble-minded children. She believed that the same methods which had proved so successful with them might well be applied to normal children. She carried on her first experiments with normal children in 1906. As Dr. Smith describes her work:

> The fundamental principles which distinguish Dr. Montessori's method are the complete liberty of the child in its spontaneous manifestations and the utilization of every atom of its natural energy.
>
> True discipline can be founded only on liberty, and must necessarily be active and not passive. A child who has been reduced to silence and immobility, who does only what he is told to do, is a paralyzed, not a disciplined child. . . . The liberty of the child must have as its limit only the collective interest. He must then be hindered from any acts offensive or harmful to others. All else that he does must not only be permitted but observed by the teacher, and the teacher must have not only the capacity, but the interest to observe this natural development. She must avoid rigorously the repression of spontaneous acts and the imposition of work at the will of another. To interfere with this spontaneity is, in Dr. Montessori's view, perhaps to repress the very essential of life itself. The aim of discipline is to train to activity, to work, for the welfare of self and of others. To this end the development of independence in the child is necessary.
>
> In Dr. Montessori's system rewards and punishments are banished. Reward comes in the child's own sense of mastery. Failure is a mere negation, to be taken as a sign that the child is not yet ready for that particular exercise. The teaching is almost entirely individual and the three fundamental rules for lessons are that they shall be brief, simple, and objective.[2]

Dr. Montessori's ideals have had a wide influence on twentieth-century education. Linked with those of Froebel and of psychologists and educators such as John Dewey, they have colored the development of the kindergarten and elementary education in our generation.

Another very important contribution to this emergence of a more rational and natural type of education was the creation of experimental and laboratory schools where the educational process might be studied and controlled and scientific deductions drawn therefrom.[3] The first of these experimental schools was founded by Francis W. Parker at Quincy, Massachusetts, between 1875 and 1880. In 1896 John Dewey and his wife linked the experimental school with formal education by establishing a laboratory school at the University of Chicago. Here the educators were perfectly free to direct education and observe its results without any hampering interference from formal administrators. Out of this laboratory school and other studies there grew Dewey's educational theories, which have had so much influence upon twentieth-century education

---
[1] See above, p. 648, 688.
[2] T. L. Smith, *The Montessori System in Theory and Practice*, Harper, 1912, pp. 6-8.
[3] *Cf.* Rugg, *op. cit.*, Chap. VII.

in the United States. They have also widely affected education in Europe and the Far East, particularly in Russia and China.

This development of a more natural and scientific educational procedure led to a revolt against the usual formal and rigid procedure of the public schools and produced the innovation known as Progressive Education. The need of this movement has been stated by Professor Melvin:

> Public school systems in many places today are bound in a net of tradition and established ways of doing things. The teacher finds herself caught in a web of timetables and systematic groupings, of statistical reports of administrators who don't use them, of supervision, of regulations, and of academic prejudice. The new teacher longs for freedom. She is anxious to teach well, she is able to teach well, but her wings are caught and damaged in the web of an antiquated system of school administration.[1]

The older conventional educational methods are just as disastrous to the mental life of the pupils. Education is an irksome compulsion rather than a spontaneous interest or pleasure. Probably few pupils would attend the public schools if not compelled to by parents and the law. Progressive education aims to enable the teacher to guide and instruct in an original and unhampered fashion and to make education so attractive to the pupils that they will cooperate spontaneously and enthusiastically. Education is designed to be an exciting adventure to teachers and pupils alike. Self-expression is encouraged, and the educational process is articulated, so far as possible, with real life situations. The expression and gratification of curiosity are encouraged. Education is not sharply divided into formal subjects. History and geography may be intermingled, or literature and drama. The old type of repressive discipline is absent. While disorderliness is discouraged, the discipline imposed is corrective and positive, rather than punitive.

Biological, psychological, and medical science have been applied to education in various ways.[2] A rational school hygiene, compatible with stimulating or conserving the health and energy of students, has been worked out in school construction and discipline. Physical training has been introduced on a wide scale aiming at the ideal of "a sound mind in a sound body." Mental testing has been used extensively to ascertain the innate mental endowment of students and to adapt instruction to the various levels of intelligence. This has enabled the teacher not only to handle more effectively the exceptionally able pupils but also to deal better with retarded types. Also, it has to be agreed, ordinary acaedmic education is rather futile for children with too low an intelligence level.[3] Manual training and other simple and direct types of instruction have been introduced as the best methods of training these more deficient types.

Democratic ideals have continued to influence education. The notion that education will iron out differences and eliminate inequalities has persisted in many circles, in spite of vigorous criticism by eugenicists and others. More

---

[1] A. G. Melvin, *The Technique of Progressive Teaching,* Day, 1932, p. 4.
[2] *Cf.* W. S. and Lena Sadler, *Piloting Modern Youth,* Funk & Wagnalls, 1931, and G. C. Myers, *Developing Personality in the Child at School,* Greenberg, 1931.
[3] *Cf.* S. P. Davies, *Social Control of the Mentally Deficient,* Crowell, 1930, Chap. xv.

important, however, has been John Dewey's insistence that to attain a successful democracy children must be educated to coördinate to democratic realities.[1] Schools and curricula must be organized in such a fashion as to visualize and reproduce the fundamental facts and processes of rational community life. Effective education cannot be a matter merely of instruction in isolated departments of knowledge, but must be a well-integrated preparation of the individual to function successfully as a member of society and a citizen of the state.

With the growth of Fascism in the twentieth century, democratic ideals have been repudiated in Fascist states, and an educational system created that is designed to produce unquestioning loyalty to the state and to military ideals. In Russian Communism, as well, while the ultimate aspiration is to create a classless and democratic society, the educational system today promotes fanatical devotion to the proletariat and to the state and leaves as small a place for democratic freedom as does Fascist education.[2]

The twentieth century has witnessed a continuance of the curriculum changes that had set in at the close of the nineteenth.[3] Less stress is being laid upon the old formal disciplines of mathematics and the ancient languages. More attention is paid to natural and social science, technology, modern literature, and art. Most of this progress in breaking away from the older type of studies has been achieved in the United States, postwar Germany, and Russia. In most English schools and in Continental schools outside Germany and Russia the curriculum still closely resembles that which existed at the opening of the nineteenth century. We have already dealt with educational innovations in Russia. The educational reforms in the German schools were a product of the German Revolution and the demand for a type of education adapted to preparing one for life as it is lived today. The Educational Reform Bill was finished in 1924, largely the work of Professor Hans Rickert. It was put into operation on Easter, 1925. All children who have passed through elementary schools are compelled to attend the grade school for the first four years. Then the more capable students enter the Gymnasium. The Gymnasium is divided into four types—one that studies ancient languages and literature; one that specializes in European history and civilization; one devoted mainly to mathematical and natural sciences; and one given over primarily to German history and culture. Students may elect which type they prefer to enter. Those who do not attend a Gymnasium are compelled to attend a public school for four more years and an evening vocational school for three years thereafter. Autocracy, paternalism, snobbery, and exclusive attention to an archaic classical curriculum were abolished from German schools. New German universities were established at Frankfort and Hamburg and an effort was made to encourage better teaching in the universities.[4] In French secondary education there has been retrogres-

---

[1] *Cf.* Dewey, *School and Society,* 1899 (rev. ed., University of Chicago Press, 1915), and *Democracy and Education,* Macmillan, 1916; and Rugg, *op. cit.,* Pt. VI.
[2] *Cf.* Merriam, *The Making of Citizens,* and H. W. Schneider and S. B. Clough, *Making Fascists,* University of Chicago Press, 1929.
[3] *Cf.* F. W. Roman, *The New Education in Europe,* Dutton, 1930; Fritz Kellermann, *The Effect of the World War on European Education,* Harvard University Press, 1928; R. G. Tugwell and L. H. Keyserling, eds., *Redirecting Education,* Columbia University Press, 1934-35, 2 vols.; and Rugg, *op. cit.*
[4] Much of this praiseworthy progress was upset by the Hitler régime.

sion rather than progress since the World War. The amount of instruction given in modern languages and natural science has been diminished as a result of a "reform" measure of 1923. No social science is taught. Attention is more than ever centered upon Greek, Latin, and French. Humanism still maintains its grip on French secondary education. Italian education clearly reflects the growing nationalism of the Fascist régime. As a result of the English Education Act of 1918 and other improvements, not only has a real public school system been established, but an effort has been made to break down the class character of English education, to provide better technical and scientific instruction, and to stimulate British patriotism. But the curriculum of the more respectable schools remains preponderantly classical, and there has been little modification of tradition in the universities outside of the University of London and one or two other newer universities.

In some continental European universities there has been a break with tradition. The most important curriculum change there has been the increased respectability of natural science in higher education and the greater amount of attention allotted to scientific studies. The social sciences have not as yet become thoroughly respectable in the more conventional European centers of learning, though they are more widely received today than they were in the last quarter of the nineteenth century.

In the last fifteen years in the United States a very considerable movement has been under foot to promote the cultivation of the social sciences, especially in the secondary schools, where they had made less headway than in higher education. Where the social sciences have been added extensively to the curriculum, they have as yet tended to be rather purely formal and descriptive and to defend the existing social system rather than to suggest a scientific critical attitude in the interest of an improved social order. It would seem, however, that within the next generation an extensive reception of a more realistic type of social science may prove to be the outstanding curriculum change in education.[1]

Another very interesting change in educational curricula is to be seen in the introduction of more practical studies, such as domestic science, manual training, graphic arts, and commercial studies. The devotees of traditional education have, however, vigorously resisted the proposition that such subjects can be truly educational in character, and most instruction along these lines has been carried on in specialized types of schools.

With the passage of laws limiting child labor, greater numbers of children have been able to carry their education on into secondary educational levels. These should give ample opportunity for the training of intelligent citizens of the modern world. But much attention is still given to archaic and irrelevant subjects having no relation to modern life and its problems. Moreover, it is very difficult for even progressive educators to make much headway in our high schools because of the tyranny exerted in many localities by the college entrance examinations. These are strongly conservative and make it necessary

[1] *Cf.* American Historical Association Commission on the Social Studies in the Schools, *Conclusions and Recommendations,* ed. by A. C. Krey, Scribner, 1934.

SOME LEADING EDUCATIONAL ADVANCES

for high-school students to devote most of their time to formal and traditional educational subjects if they hope to be admitted to institutions of higher learning. Since more and more high-school students wish to go to college, strength is lent to this domination of antiquated college ideals over high-school instruction, the latter of which for the most part should serve different and independent needs. The situation in Europe outside of Russia, and Germany from 1925 to 1933, is even more thoroughly characterized by the ascendancy of outworn ideals in secondary education.[1] By all means the most promising movement in secondary education has been the attempt to stimulate an increasing interest in the social sciences. W. H. Kilpatrick, Harold Rugg, George S. Counts, Leon C. Marshall, R. M. Tryon, C. H. Judd, C. A. Beard, and others have taken the lead in this important drive for a more realistic and modernized curriculum.

With the exception of growing interest in the natural sciences and slightly greater tolerance of the social sciences, European colleges and universities remain about as they were in 1890. There has been no such mass movement towards college education in Europe as in our country. Such higher education is still the privilege of the select few. The buildings devoted to higher education are mostly relatively few and simple, some of them having been occupied by the same institution for centuries.

At the close of the nineteenth century a large college or university in the United States rarely had more than a thousand students.[2] The typical college had less than 500 students. Today, there are several American universities that boast over 30,000 students (of all classifications) annually, and at least one university has over 15,000 full-time students. The twenty-five largest universities of the country all have in excess of 5,000 full-time students. Women's colleges have also become larger and more popular, one of them having an enrollment in excess of 6,000. Most of the important women's colleges of the country have an enrollment of more than 1,000. Accompanying this increased enrollment has been the construction of more commodious and pretentious buildings. A third-rate American college frequently has a more impressive architectural equipment than some of the oldest and most distinguished European universities. Some of the older and richer American universities have student residential buildings of an elegance matched only by the homes of the wealthy private citizens. These sumptuous surroundings create serious problems of psychic and economic readjustment when the students leave college life and attempt to make their way in the world, often having to live for years in straitened circumstances.

These large plants require much money for their operation. Outside of the state universities, this money has to be raised largely from contributions by the generous well-to-do. Hence the university president must be not only an educator, but also a business man. The dependence upon rich benefactors also makes it necessary to observe caution in university instruction, especially in matters pertaining to economics, politics, morals, and religion.

---

[1] *Cf.* Roman, *op. cit.*
[2] *Cf.* Barnes, in V. F. Calverton and S. D. Schmalhausen, eds., *The New Generation,* Macaulay, 1930, pp. 633 ff.

There has been a definite trend towards classification and differentiation in higher education. Junior colleges have been established to make possible two years of higher education for those who cannot pursue their work for the full four years. There has been a tendency to separate the undergraduate college from the postgraduate university. A generation ago most college professors gave both graduate and undergraduate instruction. Today, in our larger universities graduate instruction is given primarily by men who pay little or no attention to undergraduate work. Our more important professional schools have tended to become graduate schools requiring a Bachelor of Arts degree as a prerequisite. While normal schools for the technical training of teachers are still numerous and popular, we have now developed professional teachers' colleges that not only instruct in formal pedagogy but also give teachers some idea of the relationship between education and modern life. Indeed, it has been maintained that Teachers College at Columbia University provides a more thorough and realistic introduction to the problems of modern society than any general college or university in the United States.

Though most American higher education remains rather strictly conventional and traditional, there have been a number of notable experiments in the effort to make higher education more productive of intellectual curiosity and social realism. At Rollins College in Florida, formal classes are largely dispensed with in favor of directed reading and informal and voluntary conferences with instructors. At the University of Wisconsin, Dean Meiklejohn experimented with a radical alteration of the curriculum. This was divided between a study of Greek civilization and that of modern industrial civilization since 1750, the idea being to acquaint the student with the two outstanding types of civilization that have thus far appeared. At Antioch College in Ohio Arthur Morgan introduced an interesting combination of education and practical work. Each student devotes equal alternating periods of his time in college to (1) practical industry or professional work anywhere he chooses, and (2) to regular study at the college. This is designed to give greater realism to education. The University of Chicago has waived the strict time-requirement for the bachelor's degree and allows achievement, as ascertained by a comprehensive examination, to determine the length of residence required. An effort has also been made to extend the advantages of higher education to those unable to enter as regular students. Extension evening courses are numerous and elaborate summer-school curricula are offered by most leading universities and colleges.

One of the most astonishing developments in American higher education has been the increased popularity and commercialization of intercollegiate athletics, especially college football.[1] Athletic activities in institutions of higher learning are theoretically designed to promote the physical health of the whole student body, and most institutions do provide adequate gymnastic facilities for all their students. University football has, however, become highly commercialized. Great stadiums have been constructed, with a larger seating capacity than the Colosseum of ancient Rome, receipts from football games have totaled over $500,000 for a single institution in one season, football coaches have been paid higher salaries than university deans, and an otherwise entirely inconspicuous

---

[1] Cf. C. C. Little, *The Awakening College*, Norton, 1930, pp. 205 ff., and J. A. Krout, *The Annals of American Sport*, Yale University Press, 1929, pp. 240-58.

college or university has often been raised to a position of national prestige solely because of a successful football team. Other branches of intercollegiate athletics have been commercialized, but to nothing like so marked a degree. It has been alleged on good evidence by certain critics that intercollegiate athletics of this commercialized type has been a serious distraction from the fundamental purposes of education.[1]

The thoroughgoing industrialization of modern life and the importance of economic factors have reacted upon education in many notable ways. Industrial education of a technical type, which began in the nineteenth century, has been extended and has gained in popularity.[2] Our colleges and universities have established schools of business administration and schools of commerce. Some of these have been made graduate professional schools. Such schools have rarely taken an inquiring attitude towards modern economic life but have been designed to give the student technical training in operating business according to the theory of business enterprise and finance capitalism.

Some employers have established courses for their employees.[3] Progressive labor leaders have seen the necessity of training workers if labor is to be able to compete with the better-educated class of employers.[4] More than a century ago, Robert Owen in England and Thomas Skidmore in the United States urged the importance of educating the masses. In the middle of the nineteenth century both Karl Marx and Friedrich Engels did their best to promote the education of workers. The English Fabian Society, headed by leading English intellectuals, was especially sympathetic towards labor education. University-extension facilities have been made possible for workers by institutions of higher learning sympathetic with the cause of labor education. This has been particularly true with labor education in England. Labor colleges have been established, among the most notable being Ruskin College, Oxford, founded in 1899 by English and American radicals, and Brookwood Labor College at Katonah, New York, founded through the collaboration of academic radicals and American trade-unions. In Germany after the World War a number of important labor schools were set up, the most notable being the Berlin Trade Union School, opened in 1919, and the Academy of Labor at Frankfort, established in 1920. The Rand School of Social Science, opened in New York City in 1906, was intended to promote Socialistic education of both workers and any others who cared to matriculate. It has had an important influence in liberalizing the labor movement in the United States.

In spite of these promising beginnings in the field of labor education, only the surface has yet been scratched. Little has been accomplished beyond very inadequate provision for training labor leaders. The facilities have been so extremely limited that there has been little opportunity to educate the mass of workers with respect to either the realities of modern life or the technique of labor-union strategy. Education is still overwhelmingly in the control of the employing class and devoted to inculcating the point of view which characterizes this economically dominant group. In Russia, of course, the opposite is

---

[1] Cf. H. J. Savage and others, *American College Athletics*, Carnegie Foundation for the Advancement of Teaching, 1929.
[2] Cf. Roman, *The Industrial and Commercial Schools of the United States and Germany*.
[3] Cf. Nathaniel Peffer, *Educational Experiments in Industry*, Macmillan, 1932.
[4] Cf. Marius Hansome, *World Workers' Educational Movements*, Columbia University Press, 1931.

true, and education is controlled solely by the proletariat and sets forth a purely proletarian attitude.

The rapid changes in culture and the growing popularity of higher education have served to promote a very important educational movement known as adult education. Many who did not have the opportunity in youth to secure higher education have later developed the pecuniary resources required for educational experience, but cannot leave their business or professional work to matriculate in a formal institution of higher learning. They must remedy their past educational deficiencies by part-time education. Moreover, those who did have a college education a generation ago find themselves notoriously out of touch with present-day knowledge and intellectual interests. Some of these persons endeavor to bring themselves intellectually up to date. These two needs have led to a marked development of adult education. University-extension courses have endeavored to reach these groups. Such courses have been given not only in unviersity cities but also in outlying urban centers accessible to the teachers from the university center. Indeed, university instruction by mail has developed to considerable proportions, and the radio has been invoked in behalf of adult education.[1] There have been notable special institutions designed primarily to provide adult education. Cooper Union in New York City, long administered by Dr. Everett Dean Martin, has offered a diversified program for adults. But the foremost experiment in adult education to date has been the New School for Social Research, founded in 1919 by James Harvey Robinson, Charles A. Beard, Thorstein Veblen, Wesley C. Mitchell, and others. This has provided adult education in which instruction is given in a great diversity of fields by some of the most distinguished European and American scholars. The Labor Temple in New York City, presided over by Will Durant and Edmund B. Chaffee, has done good work in bringing adult education to the working classes.

Questions of academic freedom still persist. Indeed, with the increasingly critical state of the capitalistic system, we have witnessed extensive repression of independent thought upon the part of university professors. In Fascist countries, such as Italy and Germany, academic freedom has completely disappeared in all subjects that in any way relate to economics, politics, or other current issues. Russia, engaged in a life-and-death struggle to end capitalism, has likewise obliterated academic freedom. In those countries which still formally maintain both capitalism and democracy, to express radical views on economic, political, ethical, and religious topics is becoming increasingly more difficult. For a more subtle method than the older and crude procedure of summarily dismissing progressive teachers is employed by cautious university trustees and executives. Today the usual technique followed is to take every precaution that no radical or "dangerous" men shall be added to college or university faculties, whatever their scholarly achievements or capacity for efficient instruction. Then much ado is made about the complete freedom extended to this selected and cautious teaching staff.[2] The result is a great decline in the freshness, originality, vitality, and realism of instruction in institutions of higher learning. As was the

[1] *Cf.* W. S. Bittner and H. F. Mallory, *University Teaching by Mail,* Macmillan, 1933, and S. T. Granik, ed., *WOR Forum Book,* Falcon Press, 1933.

[2] The chief initiator of this procedure was President A. Lawrence Lowell of Harvard University.

case in the Middle Ages, there is less intolerance of ideas set forth in the classroom than of those expressed for popular consumption. Further, great educational endowments—"foundations"—have coöperated in this effort to promote academic docility. Under the guise of ultra-scientific rigor, they have extolled the spirit of research and condemned as unscholarly the venturing of any professorial opinion on current economic, political, or social matters. They assume that research, however devastating the facts uncovered, will never prove dangerous if the results are not clearly divulged to the public in intelligible and convincing fashion. Vast resources are squandered in many cases to investigate and formulate the obvious. Where startling facts are uncovered, it is not uncommon to obscure them by conclusions so cautious as to border on misinformation. The fact that the lavish grants of foundations go chiefly to professors and other scholars with a reputation for a delicate sense of discretion is another strong incentive to academic moderation.

In the United States an effort has been made to defend progressive college teachers through the organization of the American Association of University Professors, in which John Dewey and A. O. Lovejoy have been most active. But this group has been able to do little more than give publicity to the more outrageous examples of the abridgment of academic freedom. American teachers are not likely to assure for themselves complete academic liberty unless they are strongly organized in some guild or union of teachers such as that launched by Dr. Henry Linville, a movement that has thus far been firmly resisted by the majority of the teaching profession in the United States.

VII. LITERATURE IN OUR CENTURY

The major cultural developments of the twentieth century have been reflected in the literature of the period. Natural science has had its influence in impressing upon authors the remarkable scientific advances and their effects upon contemporary culture. This is, perhaps, best exemplified in the first volume of H. G. Wells's encyclopedic novel, *The World of William Clissold* (1926). Science has also improved certain types of literary technique, for example, in giving greater precision and exactitude to the psychological analysis of the human personality and mass movements. The maturity of capitalism has intensified the influence of economic factors upon literature.[1] On the one hand, the increased number of wealthy and leisured persons has created a demand for the literature of pure entertainment and spiritual cultivation. This has produced a definite type of leisure-class literature, well exemplified by such writers as Virginia Woolf, Hugh Walpole, Thornton Wilder, and Willa Cather. At the other extreme we find writers who insist that all worthy literature must stress the class struggle between worker and employer and espouse the cause of the former. Here we find such authors as Theodore Dreiser in his later books, John Dos Passos, Michael Gold, Jack Conroy, Ernst Toller, and many others.[2] In between these extremes we find those who are con-

[1] *Cf.* Calverton, *The Liberation of American Literature,* and Hicks, *The Great Tradition.*
[2] Especially (in different countries) Theodor Plivier, Rudolf Brunngraber, Grace Lumpkin, Robert Cantwell, Catharine Brody, André Malraux, and Ilya Ehrenburg. See Dorothy Brewster and J. A. Burrell, *Modern Fiction,* Columbia University Press, 1934, Chap. XI.

tent to describe realistically with either satire or indignation the economic realities of the present day. Such are John Galsworthy, Jakob Wassermann, and Sinclair Lewis. These last two groups of writers picture with great realistic detail modern life and its social institutions. The growing emancipation of the present generation from traditional ethical sanctions, the educational influence of psychoanalysis, and the unsettling influence of the World War upon morals have brought about a greater realism and freedom in dealing with sex problems, shown, for example, in the writings of Arthur Schnitzler, Victor Margueritte, Aldous Huxley, Frank Harris, F. Scott Fitzgerald, Ben Hecht, Floyd Dell, and many more. The World War produced a rich literature of description and psychological analysis, of which the works of Philip Gibbs, Henri Barbusse, Erich Remarque, John Dos Passos, and Walter Owen [1] are representative. Some genteel and conservative writers have been repelled by the frankness and realism of the modern scientific age and have reacted against the tendencies of our time. Such an attitude has characterized the literary Humanists led by Irving Babbitt, Paul Elmer More, and T. S. Eliot.

English poetry in the twentieth century has come into a period of decline. Two of its most popular exponents are Rudyard Kipling, whose work we have already discussed in dealing with nineteenth-century literature, and John Masefield. The latter is a realistic poet with a marked capacity to portray both natural phenomena and human passion. He was a sailor in his youth, and his sea ballads have attracted favorable attention. Among them are *Salt Water Ballads* (1902) and *A Mainsail Haul* (1913). He is also a master of the long narrative poem, exemplified by *The Everlasting Mercy* (1911) and *The Widow in the Bye-Street* (1912). D. H. Lawrence, while usually regarded as primarily a novelist, was far more natural and original a poet than Kipling or Masefield, and a poet of truly great promise, Wilfred Owen, was killed near the close of the World War. Many believe that William Butler Yeats, an Irishman, is immeasurably superior to any English poet of the recent period. Revealing the influence of his Gaelic studies, Yeats is probably the foremost lyric poet of the twentieth century.

The twentieth-century novel in England is represented by a number of very competent figures. Joseph Conrad specialized in novels of sea life, which he described in a strong and brilliant style. His acute psychological insight and his impressionistic power of natural description are wonderfully effective. Among his best-known books are *Victory* (1915) and *Lord Jim* (1900). Herbert George Wells has not only made important contributions to fiction but also has skillfully popularized the social import of history, biology, and economics. Few living persons equal him in encyclopaedic knowledge. He has been particularly fertile in producing Utopias that picture what life in society might be if man were able to apply his intelligence to the control of social affairs. While carrying a lighter freight of learning than his later works, Wells's earlier novels, such as *Kipps* (1905) and *The History of Mr. Polly* (1910), have more life and vitality. They are tender and true pictures of the lives of the

---

[1] Owen's little book *The Cross of Carl* has not received appropriate attention. It is far more devastating a portrayal of the horrors of the World War than the more popular books of Barbusse and Remarque.

shopkeeper class, which no other novelist since Dickens has known so well or handled with such delicate justice. Wells's best social novel is *Tono-Bungay* (1909). This portrays a typical business graft in the successful marketing of a bogus patent medicine and also indicates the social changes characterizing contemporary life. In his voluminous *World of William Clissold* Wells impressively unfolds the whole panorama of modern learning and describes its impact upon the human mind and social conduct. To a remarkable degree Mr. Wells combines realism and optimism. His political philosophy is that of a moderate Socialist and a vigorous internationalist.

John Galsworthy proved himself both an excellent literary artist and a competent social novelist. His *Forsyte Saga* (1906-22) is an incomparable picture of the property complex among the contemporary bourgeoisie and an illuminating account of the disintegration of Victorian society. Arnold Bennett is more a literary artist and a chronicler of his times than a social reformer, but his *Clayhanger* (1910) presents an excellent account of the entrance of a working-class family into the English bourgeoisie, and of the stuffy, overcarpeted moral life of the latter class, especially in its crippling effects on a young man of artistic aspirations. *The Old Wives' Tale* (1908) is generally considered his best work. Somerset Maugham's *Of Human Bondage* (1915), the story of a man's persistent devotion to a worthless woman, and his confused, but desperate, struggle to get along while enmeshed in the meaner levels of society, is one of the most powerful of modern novels. In *The Judge* (1922), Rebecca West presents an able social study of the problem of illegitimacy and a keen psychological analysis of the mother fixation. May Sinclair has achieved success in a number of novels that stress the evil influence of frustration, spiritual starvation, and self-sacrifice. The most important of her works are *The Divine Fire* (1904) and *Mary Olivier* (1919), a psychological study of the mental struggles of an intense and sensitive woman. Virginia Woolf is a superintellectualistic novelist, fond of bringing out the confused medley of tragedy, triviality and the fortuitous in life. Her best works are *Mrs. Dalloway* (1925) and *Jacob's Room* (1922). Hugh Walpole, author of *The Green Mirror* (1918) and *Above the Dark Circus* (1931), is perhaps the outstanding novelist for the entertainment of the English leisure class. In his *Crome Yellow* (1921), *Antic Hay* (1923), and *Point Counter Point* (1928), Aldous Huxley presents the best example of the complete emancipation of the younger generation from all Victorian standards and interests. His theme is the dominance of the body over the mind. In his much-discussed *Ulysses* (1922), James Joyce extended the frontiers of literature by his complete repudiation of any consideration of conventional plot and devoted a long book to an only partially successful, though verbally brilliant, chronicling of twenty-four hours of the lives of his characters and their minds, both on the conscious and the unconscious levels. Incidentally, the book gives a rich, if unnecessarily difficult, picture of early twentieth-century Dublin life—journalistic, medical, mercantile, artistic, and domestic. The stream of consciousness and its fantasies is keenly set forth.[1] D. H. Lawrence in such books as *Sons and Lovers* (1913), *The Lost Girl* (1920), *Women in Love* (1921), and *Lady Chatterley's Lover*

---

[1] *Cf.* P. J. Smith, *Key to the* Ulysses *of James Joyce*, Covici, Friede, 1934.

(1928), has dealt with the issues of sex, love and family situations in a manner characterized by realism and acute psychological analysis.

The most popular of contemporaneous English essayists and critics have been George Bernard Shaw and Gilbert K. Chesterton. Shaw has combined the attitudes of an esthete with those of a radical social realist, and he has employed wit and satire to great effect. Chesterton is a master of paradox and a firm supporter of the Catholic faith.

In the field of drama the major figures have been Shaw, Sir James M. Barrie, and Galsworthy. Most of Shaw's dramas are devoted to some social problem—*Widower's Houses* (1892) to profiteering in slum-area real estate, *Mrs. Warren's Profession* (1902) to prostitution and economic exploitation, *Androcles and the Lion* (1912) to religious conversion, and *Man and Superman* (1903) to eugenics and Socialism. In other plays, however, such as *Saint Joan* (1923), Shaw has dealt in historical fantasy. Barrie is a pleasant, semipoetical idealist and sentimentalist. Most famous of his plays has been the fantasy *Peter Pan* (1904). Galsworthy is regarded by many as a greater master of the social drama than Shaw. In *Strife* (1909) he portrays the struggle between capital and labor. In *Justice* (1910) he pleads for the reform of criminal law and prisons. *The Silver Box* (1906) and *Loyalties* (1922) deal with issues of race allegiance, professional loyalty, and class justice.

Far and away the most eminent figure in contemporary French literature—as dominant as Victor Hugo in his day—was Anatole France (Jacques Anatole Thibault). A spiritual disciple of the urbane Renan, and a rival of Voltaire in his mastery of mockery and satire, France combined great learning with notable grace and delicacy of expression.[1] His *Penguin Island* (1909), a satirical history of France and French society, is rivaled only by Voltaire's *Candide* as a satirical novel. In his *Thaïs* (1891) and other works on the period of early Christianity he treats of the early Christian Fathers and legends with sympathetic albeit devastating irony. In his *Contemporary History* (1897-1900) he satirically analyzes the political, economic, and religious life of modern France. Among his better-known fiction are *The Revolt of the Angels* (1914) and *The Crime of Sylvestre Bonnard* (1881), while in *The Red Lily* (1894) he strays realistically into the field of love and romance.

Recent French poetry is represented by Paul Valéry's classical perfection, Paul Fort's ballads of nature, Paul J. P. Toulet's verse fantasies, and Emile Verhaeren's symbolic poems. In the field of fiction Pierre Louÿs has written an eloquent defense of sensuality as the foundation of intellectual and artistic creation. He is an apostle of Hellenistic eroticism. His most representative work is *Aphrodite* (1896). The social novel has been developed in France by men like Paul and Victor Margueritte and Jules Romains. In their work *An Epoch* (1898-1904) the Margueritttes describe realistically the problems of the difficult days of 1870-71. The social background also appears in Romain Rolland's *Jean Christophe* (1907-12), regarded by many as the greatest monument of descriptive fiction in France since Victor Hugo's *Les Misérables*. Built around the fictional biography of a musical genius, Jean Christophe Krafft, the work is replete with pictures of social conditions, working-class struggles, love

---

[1] *Cf. The Opinions of Anatole France*, recorded by Paul Gsell, Knopf, 1922.

situations, and artistic problems. Henri Barbusse's *Under Fire* (1917) was a contribution to literary realism and to the literature of life on the front in wartime. It had a tremendous circulation. Marcel Proust resembles Joyce somewhat in his extensive excursions into the subjective and psychological. His extensive and intermittent work *Remembrance of Things Past* (1913-27) is a vast medley of psychological studies, character portraits, social realism, and essays on literary criticism. With all his shortcomings, he succeeded in producing an almost encyclopedic representation of contemporary French social life among the upper-middle and aristocratic classes, with occasional clairvoyant glances into the lives of the servant class. Snob and egotist that he was, he discerned with intuitive genius the evil destiny of "the rich and the well-born." André Gide has combined stylistic classicism and moral intensity applied to problems of conduct and personal relations of such a nature that he might be called a moral immoralist. Among his best-known books are *The Immoralist* (1902), *The Return of the Prodigal Son* (1907), and *The Counterfeiters* (1925).

The foremost French essayist of the twentieth century was Rémy de Gourmont, who combined to an amazing degree frankness and delicacy in treating of erotic themes. The chief figures in twentieth-century French drama were Edmond Rostand and Eugène Brieux. Rostand wrote somewhat imaginative and fantastic verse drama which appealed to those who were tired of Ibsen's realism. His foremost work was *Cyrano de Bergerac* (1897). Brieux is the author of many interesting problem plays. His *Red Robe* (1900) was a devastating exposure of the intrigues of lawyers determined to succeed in their profession even at the cost of the conviction of the innocent. *Damaged Goods* (1901) made a great sensation as the first important play to raise the question of marriage and venereal disease.

The most popular poet of contemporary Italy is Gabriele d'Annunzio, a passionate defender of beauty, sensuality, and patriotic sentiment. Other important contemporary Italian poets have been Giovanni Pascoli, noted for his capacity to idealize country life, and Salvatore di Giacomo, an able lyric poet who has described with great charm the colorful life of Naples. Giovanni Papini has shown ability as a poet, but he is best known for his eloquent controversial prose. Originally starting out as a critical pragmatist and a student of William James, he has reverted to emotionalism and religiosity. His *Life of Christ* (1921) gained world-wide popularity, but his point of view and style are also well represented in his quasi-autobiographical work *The Failure* (1912). At the opposite pole from Papini's florid emotionalism and anti-intellectualism stands Alfredo Panzini, a philosophic anti-academician, but with some of the qualities of personal intimacy that characterized such writings as those of Oliver Wendell Holmes. His novels are noted for their skillful handling of many incidents. Among his important works are *The Journey of a Poor Literary Man* (1919), *The Affairs of the Major* (1905), and *Wanted—a Wife* (1920). In Benedetto Croce, Italy possesses one of the most distinguished among the philosophers, esthetes, and literary critics of contemporary times. The foremost of recent Italian dramatists is Luigi Pirandello, who has been particularly successful in "dramatizing metaphysics." In other words, his plays are chiefly "dramas of ideas." In his problem plays he has laid special stress upon the necessity of holding together the biological father, mother, and child, whatever the social conventions. Pirandello's overcivilized skepticism is really decadent and he writes with a pessimistic conviction that all things, even personal identity, are illusory. While not a Fascist writer literally, his corrupt hopelessness and his distrust of all positive values, such as liberty, equality, and fraternity, render him inoffensive to the Fascists. He has recently been honored with the Nobel Prize in literature.

The effect of the War of 1898 on Spanish literature and life was almost instantaneous. During the last quarter of the nineteenth century Spain lived in a political atmosphere that had no reality. The political parties alternated in office every few months but the policies changed very little. Underlying social problems were left unsolved and the labor uprisings were crushed with no attempt at solution of the causes. Spain sank into insignificance abroad, but its remaining colonies gave the illusion of grandeur and to this the people and the politicians clung. Then came the blow of the Spanish-American War. Spain's real situation was laid bare and in the mortification of defeat old writers changed their course and a new school of novelists, dramatists, poets, and critics exposed the shams and weakness of Spanish life. Always a severe critic of itself, although too prone to resent criticism from foreigners, Spain now developed self-criticism to a marked degree. The full political effects of the criticism were not felt until the Revolution of 1931, but the effects on literature were immediate.

With Pérez Galdós,[1] Azorín, Joaquín Costa, Ganivet, Ortega, and Unamuno at the head, there began a Modernist movement that has lasted to the present day. No small part of this new movement was inspired by a closer study of the literature of Spanish America and the ideals of the Wars of Independence of the Spanish-American colonies. From such study came much inspiration for Spanish authors and the Spanish Americans were read and imitated. Rubén Darío, the Nicaraguan poet, became the master of a new school of poetry on both sides of the Atlantic. Inspiration was likewise received from England, France and Germany as well as other European nations to which young Spaniards went to find material for self-criticism, and the government fostered this migration of scholars and writers by granting many fellowships.

The foremost poet of contemporary Spain is Juan Ramón Jiménez, a master of simple and spontaneous lyric odes. His *Pastorals* (1905) are deservedly popular. Vicente Blasco Ibáñez was the author who achieved the most world renown, and early distinguished himself as a novelist of the social and economic life of Valencia. Down to 1904 his work was regional, but after that date it became more truly Spanish, and he contributed a series of novels dealing with social problems of Spain, his books serving as vehicles for his propaganda in an anticlerical and a prorepublican sense. The best novels are probably *The Shadow of the Cathedral* (1903), *Woman Triumphant* (1906), *Blood and Sand* (1908), and *The Dead Command* (1909); but a war novel, *The Four Horsemen of the Apocalypse* (1916), is his best-known work and reveals a cosmopolitan character. The Marqués Ramón del Valle-Inclán writes a poetic type of novel,

---

[1] See p. 702.

uses the device of the trilogy and is inclined to symbolism. His racy speech and his tilts with the authorities have made him a sort of George Bernard Shaw of Spain. Pío Baroja manifested a strong influence in the manner of Zola in his early writings, as have many other modern Spanish writers, but his best works are those dealing with his own Basque provinces, *Zalacaín, the Adventurer* (1909), and *The House of Aizgorri* (1900). The latter is one of a trilogy, which form Valle-Inclán used a number of times. Concha Espina is a woman novelist of great realistic powers whose best work is *The Sphinx of Clay* (1914). Ramón Pérez de Ayala is known as both a psychological novelist and short story writer, his best novel being probably *The Labors of Urbano and Simona* (1903). Serafín and Joaquín Alvarez Quintero are brothers who have gained Europe-wide fame with their witty and gay character sketches of Andalusian figures. Modern Spanish drama is best represented by Jacinto Benavente, who aims at an exact picture of life and has been very critical of Spanish politicians. His ablest works are probably *Created Interests* (1907) and *The School for Princesses* (1909). Gregorio Martínez Sierra and his wife Maria Martínez Sierra have written numerous plays and have contributed to the criticism of Spanish life.

The essay has had a strong influence in modern Spain. Angel Ganivet, although not living to the twentieth century, influenced it greatly by his masterpiece *Spanish Idearium* (1897), a long essay in which he outlined the Spanish character and recommended ways of reviving Spain's greatness. The War of '98, following the year after the publication of this work, gave it a wide and lasting influence. His successor was the fiery Miguel de Unamuno, who made his reputation as a liberal in politics and as an Anarchist in temperament. He writes the truth forcefully and impressively, however disagreeable it may be. This characteristic made him a critic of the monarchy and a prophet of republicanism, but his shafts have been aimed at republicanism since 1931. José Ortega y Gasset, frequently called Spain's leading intellect, has become known to the English-speaking world through his novel *The Revolt of the Masses* (1929). José Martínez Ruiz, better known as Azorín, is a journalist and novelist of great skill in writing unusual descriptions of commonplace things. In the field of scholarship and literary criticism the school founded by Menéndez y Pelayo has prospered. The greatest of the modern scholars is Ramón Menéndez Pidal, who is not so eloquent but more scientific than his master. In Rafael Altamira y Crevea, Spain has a historian who must be ranked with the greatest living. His masterful work, a fine example of the "new history," *History of Spain and Spanish Civilization* (1900-11), has been ably continued to 1923 in two additional volumes by Pío Zabala y Lera. A considerable literature has sprung up in Latin America, taking its inspiration from Spain and France rather than from the United States. Among the foremost of these writers are Darío, mentioned above; the publicist Francisco Garcia Calderón; José Enrique Rodó, an able Uruguayan poet; Rufino Blanco-Fombona, a Venezuelan critic and essayist; and Manuel Ugarte, an Argentine essayist and novelist. Much of this literature is characterized by bitter antipathy to the United States.

The foremost Germanic poets of contemporary times are Franz Werfel and Rainer Maria Rilke, representatives of expressionism and postwar disillusionment; Stefan George, an austere master of a faultless style and an esoteric manipulator of words; Hugo von Hofmannsthal, a colorful and dramatic poet; and Carl Spitteler (a German Swiss), both a philosophical poet and one capable of great power in descriptions of nature. The more important prose-writers in twentieth-century Germany have been Thomas Mann, Lion Feuchtwanger, Jakob Wassermann, Erich Maria Remarque, and Arthur Schnitzler. The major theme that permeates Mann's writing is the contrast between the physically normal but uncreative type and the creative artist, subnormal in health and abnormal in sensitivity. Mann has exhibited no little power in the subtle use of psychoanalysis. An impressive book is his *The Magic Mountain* (1924). A marvelously intricate though solid and balanced account is presented of the physical and psychic effects of disease and time upon the cosmopolitan population of a tuberculosis sanitarium in the Alps. It is a very revealing cross-section of the European society that was blindly hurrying to its own destruction just before the World War. He is now engaged on an even more ambitious epical three-volume work entitled *Joseph and His Brethren*, a psychological study of the patriarchs. Feuchtwanger's ablest novel, *Power (Jud Süss,* 1917), is a penetrating account of the Jewish problem in early modern times. Wassermann was influenced by Dostoevsky in his attitudes. He exhibited marked ability in local description, particularly of Franconia and the city of Nuremberg, in intimate analysis of the born-criminal types, and in his study of the Jewish problem in Germany. In *The Goose Man* (1915), however, he dealt in illuminating fashion with the problems of musical genius. His novels present the will to power as the chief cause of evil. Of his works, *The World's Illusion* (1919) is the best known. Remarque's *All Quiet on the Western Front* (1929) proved the most popular of all the books tragically and powerfully uncovering the horror of the war as it actually was fought. Arthur Schnitzler, a Viennese physician, is characterized by technical knowledge of psychology and finesse and delicacy in dealing with sensuous topics. His most popular novel is the brief *Casanova's Homecoming* (1918). Schnitzler has also been one of the most important of recent Germanic dramatists. His plays are notable for psychological acuteness and the prominence of brilliant dialogue. They are witty and realistic. Georg Kaiser's plays have been devoted to a symbolic handling of complex sex situations and to the effect of machines and capitalism upon the working classes. Ernst Toller frankly espouses a revolutionary philosophy in his bitter attack upon the enslavement of the workers by mechanical technique and the profit system. He is the foremost of German Communist playwrights.

Scandinavian writers have made contributions to twentieth-century literature out of all proportion to the population and political status of their homelands. In Denmark, Henrik Pontoppidan has resembled Russian writers like Gorki and Bunin in his capacity to deal in epic fashion with the life of simple people. His outstanding novel is *Lucky Peter* (1898-1905), a powerful study of the lives and emotions of simple pastoral and fishing people of Denmark. The outstanding recent Danish writer is Johannes Jensen, a master of themes drawn from both Danish history and the peasant life of his countrymen. His *The Fall of the King* (1899-1902) is an elaborate novel concerning the Renaissance king Christian II. His *Long Journey* (1909-21) is an epic story of the Gothic peoples. In *Jörgine* (1926) he wrote a very charming novel of the soil and the life of peasants. Denmark produced one of the ablest of proletarian novelists in Martin Andersen Nexö, whose *Pelle the Conqueror* (1906-10) is a powerful tale of the misery of the poor, of the labor movement and the general strike, and of the growth of the coöperative program.

Among recent Norwegian writers the most important are Sigrid Undset, Knut Hamsun, Johan Bojer, and Thomas Krag. Miss Undset first gained note by a daring erotic novel, *Jenny* (1912), but in *Spring* (1914) she appeared as a conventional moralist lauding the virtues of the home and domestic happiness. Her main work is a long pro-Catholic historical trilogy of fourteenth-century Norway, *Kristin Lavransdatter* (1920-22), published in English as *The Bridal Wreath, The Mistress of Husaby,* and *The Crown.* Knut Hamsun has told in strong and rugged style of the bitter struggle of the poor for life and self-expression. Two of his best-known books are *Hunger* (1890) and *The Growth of the Soil* (1917). Bojer is a realist after the manner of the seventies of the last century. He made his reputation with *A Public Procession* (1896), a novel of money in politics and of the moral degradation of the peasants after getting the vote and participating in politics. He produced an important psychological novel in *The Power of a Lie* (1903), a pessimistic study of moral degradation. Perhaps his most interesting novel is *The Last of the Vikings* (1913), a picture of the life of nineteenth-century Norwegian fishermen. Krag is a romantic and sentimental novelist, best known for his *Ada Wilde* (1896).

Recent Swedish literature is best represented by Selma Lagerlöf, Hjalmar Söderberg, Sigfrid Siwertz, Hjalmar Bergman, Verner von Heidenstam, and Ellen Key. Miss Lagerlöf is a gentle, sympathetic, and imaginative writer, famed for her charming *The Saga of Gösta Berling* (1891). She excels in fantasy and children's tales. Söderberg has written plays, short stories, and novels. He is especially able in his reproduction of the local color of Stockholm life and environment. Most important in this field is his *Martin Birck's Youth* (1901). His *Doctor Glas* (1905) is a psychological novel dealing with the doctor's right to take the life of dangerous and useless persons. His play *Gertrude* (1906) is an able portrayal of feminine emotion and is ranked by some with the best of Ibsen's plays. Siwertz has written important poems and short stories, but his best work is a novel, *Downstream* (1920), a bitter satire on the curse of wealth and avarice in our capitalist system. Bergman, both a playwright and a novelist, is distinguished for his wit and humor. He is best in depicting small-town life in Sweden, and his most significant book is *God's Orchid* (1919). Von Heidenstam is both a lyric poet of note and an outstanding novelist. His *Endymion* (1889) is a romantic novel, but more important is his *Saint Bridget's Pilgrimage* (1901), a psychological study of genius and its struggles against the stupidities of mankind. In his *King Charles's Men* (1897-98) he has produced an important collection of historical tales describing the tragedy of those who were sacrificed to the mad military ambitions of the boy king Charles XII. Ellen Key has been a courageous contributor to advanced sexology and liberal education in her *Love and Marriage* (1904), *The Century of the Child* (1903), and *Love and Ethics* (1911).

The outstanding contemporary poets in Russia, Fedor Sologub and Alexander Blok, were both representatives of the symbolic school. The foremost prose-writer of twentieth-century Russia is Maxim Gorki, an extreme representative of the realistic tradition and a champion of the submerged masses. To the time of the Russian Revolution in 1917 his sympathies were with the Russian Socialists, and since 1917 he has aligned himself with the Bolshevik group, though not identifying himself with the Communist party. He has been one of the few Russians able to maintain complete intellectual independence since the Revolution. His most famous novels, *Three of Them* (1900), *A Confession* (1908), and *The Mother* (1917), contain an unparalleled description of the bare, desolate, and semibarbarous Russian provincial life under the tsars. His latest writings have been autobiographical. They tell us little, however, about Gorki himself, but rather present remarkable portraits of his acquaintances and prominent figures of his era. Next to Gorki, the leading contemporary Russian writer is Ivan Bunin, also in his fiction a realistic social novelist. *The Village* (1910) describes with unfaltering realism the poverty and sordidness of Russian rural life under the old régime. Other important novels by Bunin present in detail phases of Russian peasant life and typical peasant characters. The four-volume novel of the Polish writer Ladislas Reymont, *The Peasants* (1904), is one of the most considerable literary works of the present century, ranking with the writings of Gorki and Bunin. The most popular of Russian short-story writers in our day is Leonid Andreev. His handling of sexual subjects with realism in *The Abyss* (1902) and "In Fog" (1902) aroused much controversy. His *The Governor* (1906) is a penetrating psychological study of the fear of assassination. The most important dramatic writing in Russia in the twentieth century was Gorki's play *The Lower Depths* (1902), but his other plays had little popularity. The Bolsheviks have shown much interest in the development of the drama, which they use as a mode of inculcating Communist ideals. Such dramas have been written by Lunacharsky, Wolkenstein, and Forsh.

The Bolshevik Revolution has colored literature as well as other aspects of Russian life since 1917. Literature has mirrored the great social transition; has become naturalistic in its frank descriptions; and has popularized the colloquial style of peasants and workers. Literature has become the interest of the many rather than the luxury of the few. It is a part of the new Russian life. In poetry, Alexander Blok has accepted the Revolution and eulogized the Red soldiers; Andrei Bely has extolled the messianic rôle of Bolshevism; and Boris Pasternak has even adapted the lyric to revolutionary ends. Naturalism in Russian revolutionary prose becomes evident in the novels of Vsevolod Ivanov. The new style has resembled the events—a harsh and rough description of terrible but significant occurrences. Naturalism and a wide use of the colloquial was forwarded by Leonid Leonov, author of *Soviet River* (1930), also a master in the psychological analysis of tense emotional situations. Even a romantic strain has been adapted to Soviet ends in Isaak Babel's colorful picture of the deeds of the Red cavalry. The foremost stylist of the new régime is Alexei Remizov. Two of the best of the new school of proletarian novelists are Ilya Ehrenburg and Valentin Kataaev.

Poetry in the United States in the twentieth century has found worthy representatives in such writers as Edwin Arlington Robinson, Edgar Lee Masters, Robert Frost, Vachel Lindsay, William Ellery Leonard, Carl Sandburg, Leonora Speyer, and Edna St. Vincent Millay. Robinson has united dignity of style with acute psychological insight. Masters has described with realism the life and conflicts of a typical Mid Western town. Leonard has made use of psychoanalysis in his poetry. Sandburg has been called a twentieth-century Whitman, defending democracy in the machine age. His style is racy and vigorous. Lindsay's poetry is notable for its moving rhythm. Frost has devoted himself primarily to describing the simple life and natural scenery of northern New England, tempering Puritanism with optimism. Mrs. Speyer is distinguished for the purity of her style, and Miss Millay is the outstanding lyrical poet of contemporary America.

The writers of fiction in twentieth-century America may be divided between those who have little or no social message and write primarily to entertain and edify, and those interested in one way or another in exposing the evils of contemporary society.

In the former group would fall such writers as Edith Wharton, Willa Cather, Mary Roberts Rinehart, Ellen Glasgow, Thornton Wilder, Elizabeth Madox Roberts, Mary Ellen Chase, Glenway Wescott, Joseph Hergesheimer, and James Branch Cabell. Almost without exception this group is distinguished by purity and dignity of style, Cabell being especially notable for his capacity for rarefied fantasy. These writers, however, draw the fire of the younger and revolutionary school, who regard them as "affected, strained, bookish, tiresomely traditional, and stuffy—the cosmetics of prose."

Outstanding problems of American society have been subjected to realistic portrayal and analysis in the books of such writers as David Graham Phillips, Robert Herrick, Theodore Dreiser, Winston Churchill, Upton Sinclair, Sherwood Anderson, Sinclair Lewis, F. Scott Fitzgerald, Erskine Scott Caldwell, John Dos Passos, and Michael Gold. Dreiser, Sinclair, and Anderson have devoted themselves mainly to analyzing the character and the evils of our industrial and capitalistic civilization. No other novelist, not even Hardy, has equaled Dreiser in his power to portray social determinism and the overwhelming dominion of the group and culture over the individual. This is best brought out in *An American Tragedy* (1925).[1] Though scandalously neglected by many historians of literature, Robert Herrick was perhaps the most substantial American writer of the period from 1898 to 1912.[2] He made a more serious and intelligent attempt than anyone else except Dreiser to write comprehensively and critically about American middle-class and upper-class life in the period beginning with the Cleveland era. He saw with astonishing clearness the general character of the period, with its money-making, greed, acquisitiveness, and ruthless individualism, and his best novels, *The Common Lot* (1904), *The Memoirs of an American Citizen* (1905), and *Clark's Field* (1914), are penetrating and unsparing recordings of the sordid epoch. Churchill best exhibited the attitude of the liberal reformer. In *Coniston* (1906) he exposed the political boss; in *Mr. Crewe's Career* (1908), corporate feudalism in American railroads, and in *The Inside of the Cup*, the hypocrisies of formal religion.[3] Lewis is the supreme satirist of small-town smugness and of conventional

---

[1] See Burton Rascoe, *Theodore Dreiser*, McBride, 1925.
[2] *Cf.* Newton Arvin, "Homage to Robert Herrick," *New Republic*, Mar. 6, 1935.
[3] *Cf.* M. E. Speare, *The Political Novel*, Oxford Press, 1924, Chap. XIII.

American business and professional types. *Babbitt* (1922) is perhaps his best novel. Fitzgerald has portrayed most realistically the "younger generation," especially in our colleges. In his *Tobacco Road* (1932) and *God's Little Acre* (1933), Erskine Caldwell has introduced extreme realism into his studies of the life of the Southern poor whites. Dos Passos and Gold are representative of the growing interest in portraying social problems from the frankly Communist point of view. Dos Passos's best novels are *Manhattan Transfer* (1925), *42nd Parallel* (1930), and *1919* (1931). Gold's important book is *Jews without Money* (1930). Postwar disillusionment, with its unwillingness to grapple with social and economic realities, found its ablest expression in Ernest Hemingway, whose best books are *The Sun Also Rises* (1926) and *A Farewell to Arms* (1929). Extreme Modernism and unconventionality have their most notable American representatives in Gertrude Stein and E. E. Cummings.

Criticism and the essay have been represented by writers such as James G. Huneker, H. L. Mencken, Ernest Boyd, Van Wyck Brooks, Joseph Wood Krutch, and Edmund Wilson. Huneker attacked the American tradition from the standpoint of Continental Bohemianism. Mencken introduced the basic ideas of Nietzsche and was once the chief American iconoclast of the twentieth century.[1] Boyd best represents the spirit of Continental esthetics in American criticism. Brooks, a master of limpid style, made wide use of the psychoanalytic technique. Krutch's criticism is characterized by precise academic learning, considerable use of the psychoanalytical method, and a general air of disillusionment. Edmund Wilson has of late introduced the methods of socio-economic criticism, in which field he has sympathetic associates in V. F. Calverton, Granville Hicks, Waldo Frank, Malcolm Cowley, Newton Arvin, and John Chamberlain.

The outstanding American dramatist of the contemporary era is the resolute realist Eugene O'Neill.[2] O'Neill's plays are rarely conventionally pleasant, and his power and popularity have been due chiefly to his sheer ability as a dramatic realist. He has dealt with a wide range of economic, racial, social, and sex issues. In most cases, he has been sharply critical of the intolerance, superficiality, oppression, and bigotry in contemporary American life. Next to O'Neill many would place Elmer Rice among contemporary American dramatists. He gained his first wide reputation with *Street Scene* (1929), a supremely realistic portrayal of the life and problems of the city proletariat. Recently, in such plays as *We, the People* (1933) he has taken bold steps in the direction of revolutionary drama. The unconventional originality of Mencken in literary criticism has been matched by that of his friend George Jean Nathan in dramatic criticism.

No brief survey of contemporary literature would be complete without at least a brief reference to periodical literature and present-day newspapers. The magazines not only publish the shorter work of some of the most important contemporary writers; they also furnish us with most of our information about books and our judgments on them. Reputable magazines, reflecting

---
[1] See Isaac Goldberg, *The Man Mencken*, Simon & Schuster, 1925.
[2] See B. H. Clark, *Eugene O'Neill*, rev. ed., McBride, 1933.

primarily the literary and social interests of capitalistic society and the leisure class, were well established in the nineteenth century. Representative of these are the *Fortnightly Review,* the *Contemporary Review,* the *Nineteenth Century,* the *Revue des deux mondes,* the *Deutsche Rundschau,* the *North American Review,* the *Atlantic Monthly, Scribner's, Century, Harper's,* and the *Outlook,* some of which have now ceased publication. There are some very interesting and valuable periodicals devoted almost exclusively to literary criticism and book-reviewing, such as the London *Athenaeum* and the *Saturday Review of Literature,* lately founded by Henry Seidel Canby. Iconoclastic criticism has been represented in such periodicals as the *Smart Set,* followed in a different pattern and on a more pretentious scale by the *American Mercury,* both magazines edited by Mencken and Nathan. Resolute political and social criticism dominates the pages of the *Forum,* the *New Republic,* the *Nation, Common Sense,* and a number of other excellent periodicals. Advanced Modernistic trends in literature have found expression in such publications as the *Dial* and *Hound and Horn.*

Periodical literature has mirrored the economic currents in the contemporary scene. In Europe, especially in England, there are some staid and respectable organs that reflect the vested interests of the agrarian aristocracy, the industrial oligarchy, or both. But in the United States, especially since the World War, there have been few if any important periodicals that are exclusively expressions of upper-class conservative opinion. The *Bookman*[1] has of late taken on such a cast, but its circulation and influence are limited. Even the *Atlantic Monthly* and *Scribner's* publish much important material severely criticizing rugged individualism and plutocracy. Likewise *Fortune,* a sumptuous monthly recently created for exclusive "class" circulation, has not hesitated to include much material that would have been branded as "muckraking" in the era of Theodore Roosevelt, when carried in *McClure's* and other reformist journals of that time.[2] The closest to upper-class periodical literature in the United States are such purely entertaining appeals to the leisure class as are represented by *Vanity Fair,* the *New Yorker* and *Esquire.* Here again, however, the critical note is not absent. Once mildly conservative periodicals like the *Forum* and *Harper's Magazine* have become leading agencies of social controversy and advanced liberal opinion. The *American Mercury* was founded by Mencken and Nathan in 1923 as an antireformist, antidemocratic magazine for the more cynical and detached members of the leisure class, but after 1933, under the editorship of Charles Angoff, it tended to rival the *Forum* and *Harper's* in the zeal and resolution with which it presented social, economic, and political criticism. Such weekly periodicals as the *Nation* and the *New Republic* have passed from organs of liberalism to at least mild radicalism, while the *New Masses* is frankly Communistic in tone. Critical humorous magazines have enjoyed wide popularity, among the leaders being *Simplicissimus, Puck, Life,* and *Judge.*

With the decline of the editorial domination of American newspapers and the growth of a mass appeal through sensational news, the intellectual leadership in American journalism has assuredly passed from the newspapers to

---
[1] Now *The American Review.*
[2] *Cf.* C. C. Regier, *The Era of the Muckrakers,* University of North Carolina Press, 1932.

periodical literature. Great commercial magazines with a wide popular appeal and large advertising revenue have flourished in the recent period, paralleling the rise of the commercial newspaper. Such are the *Saturday Evening Post,* the *American Magazine,* the *Cosmopolitan, Liberty,* the *Delineator,* the *Woman's Home Companion,* and the like. Their editorial courage and social enlightenment have usually declined in proportion to their commercial success.

Newspapers and newspaper problems are by no means uniquely contemporary. There were free-press battles in the Zenger case back in the first half of the eighteenth century in colonial America and in the Wilkes case in England shortly afterwards. Daniel Defoe had laid the basis of critical journalism long before. But the newspaper of the eighteenth century and the early nineteenth was quite a different affair from the great dailies of today. The contemporary newspaper has reached its highest development in the United States, though England follows closely. On the European continent there is nothing approaching the American newspaper for size or variety of content, though some Continental journals before the rise of Fascism and Hitlerism ranked ahead of most American and English papers for intelligent editorial interpretation of current events and world-trends.

Nothing in American life has more closely followed the trends in culture and economic development than the newspaper. At first the American newspapers were slight personal organs, usually founded to advance some individual or partisan project or to vent personal spite. They rarely appeared at precise intervals and were often vile and malicious. The "editorial" attitude dominated entirely and there was little news printed. In the second third of the century newspapers grew in quality, size, and influence, though the editorial interest and function still prevailed over the news element. News was published, but it was far more scanty than today, and the publisher all too often "editorialized" the news so as to make it seem to vindicate editorial opinion. The papers were read chiefly to enjoy the editorial judgment and flavor of the paper. Both editors and readers were usually bitterly partisan. Among the more representative papers of this era were the New York *Tribune,* edited by Horace Greeley; the Chicago *Tribune,* edited by Joseph Medill; the New York *Times,* edited by Henry Raymond; the New York *Evening Post,* edited by William Cullen Bryant; the New York *Sun,* edited by Charles A. Dana; the Springfield *Republican,* edited by Samuel Bowles; and the Albany *Evening Journal,* edited by Thurlow Weed.

With the improvement of the mechanics of newspaper fabrication,[1] the perfection of news-gathering technique, and the growth of American business, the commercial newspaper came into being between 1880 and the World War. The desire to express an editorial judgment was well subordinated to the aspiration to make a personal fortune through the newspaper, though of course the monetary aim did not wholly suppress editorial comment, especially editorials of a conservative cast. Papers now became *news*papers properly so called, but the news interest was secondary to the major economic motive of making money. The great motivating factor was the wish to exploit the vast potential revenues to be secured from commercial advertising. The

---

[1] See above, pp. 744 ff.

formula for success here was slowly but precisely worked out. Readers and mass circulation are to be attained through publishing attractive and often sensational news. Many interested readers insure wide circulation for the paper, and a newspaper with an extensive circulation presents a favorable medium for advertising. The latter constitutes the major source of newspaper income. Even a very large circulation would not pay the expenses of a great modern newspaper through subscriptions and news-stand sales. Wide circulation makes a profit indirectly through the gains from extensive advertising. The newspaper thus became an agency for selling lively news to attract a multitude of readers before whom commercial advertising could be placed with direct profits to the newspapers and indirect profits to the advertisers. The major figures in the transition from the editorial sheet to the true newspaper with commercial aims were James Gordon Bennett of the New York *Herald*, Charles A. Dana of the New York *Sun*, Joseph Pulitzer of the New York *World*, William Randolph Hearst of the New York *American* (and *Journal*), and E. W. Scripps of the Cleveland *Press*. Lord Northcliffe (Alfred Harmsworth) followed the procession with his London *Daily Mail*. Contrary to general impression, the most blatant attempt to gain circulation by sensational and scandalous news has not been made by an American paper, but by the London *News of the World*, owned by Lord Riddell, who died at the close of 1934.

The fact that newspapers go out to get news does not mean that they are interested in all news. They are primarily concerned with news that will sell and so build circulation. The test of the value of news is not the cultural significance of the items in question, but their power to excite and interest the populace. One of the greatest of living news-gatherers has lately said that the test of the importance of any news to the newspaper-man is its relative power to provoke strong and enduring human emotions.[1] Another demand is that news shall be up to the minute, and hence it quickly shifts to new events and interests. All this makes it difficult to get some of the intrinsically most important news before the public or to hold it there long enough for the readers to assimilate it intelligently. In spite of all this, however, the mass of citizens have gained greatly in their range of information as a result of the rise of the modern newspaper. One of the most prosperous of them all has not allowed the commercial motive to prevent it from constituting that true marvel of contemporaneous information, the New York *Times* of Adolph Ochs. A surprising amount of scientific, political, cultural, economic, and artistic news is sandwiched in among other features or printed in special magazine sections.

The desire to attract wide interest on the part of a reading public that is often neither too well educated nor too intelligent has given rise to a characteristic newspaper style—racy, pungent, staccato, and often not too solicitous of the facts. But certain great newspaper stylists have been produced, of whom the best-known contemporary examples are Heywood Broun, regarded by many as the outstanding journalistic writer in the history of American newspapers, and Walter Lippmann. The quest for circulation through mass appeal has more recently given rise to the "tabloid" newspapers with their small and convenient format, their visual appeal, and their sensational news. The

[1] K. A. Bickel.

experiment has, in general, proved successful, and the New York *Daily News* has the largest circulation of any newspaper in the world. The tabloid need not necessarily be sensational. The first tabloid, E. W. Scripps' Chicago *Day-Book,* was severely editorial and carried no advertising. One of the most dignified and reliable of modern newspapers, the Washington *Daily News*—a Scripps-Howard paper—is published in tabloid format.

The fact that the daily newspapers depend chiefly on advertising that is placed in newspapers by the great business interests inevitably makes the daily papers the spokesmen, in at least a broad general way, of the capitalistic groups. News and, above all, editorials are likely to be considered in the light of a desire to please, or at least not to alienate, conventional business. Labor and farmers are not likely to get a fair presentation of the facts bearing upon their interests when the latter conflict with the fundamental policies of business. Since labor, farming, and clerical groups can rarely gather the large capital needed to conduct a big daily paper today, they cannot publish papers that give as wide a variety of news and features as the press which serves capitalism. Moreover, these groups have thus far failed to support loyally the journals that have aimed to present their case fairly. They prefer to be excited and entertained by the capitalist press rather than to be instructed and exhorted by their own papers. Journalism is today, outside of Russia, capitalistic journalism. In Russia it is even more purely proletarian than it is capitalistic elsewhere. In Fascist countries a free press cannot exist. Editors are rubber stamps for the publicity bureau of the government, and even news is carefully censored, as it was in warring countries during the period from 1914 to 1918. With the trend toward Fascism, the outlook for a free press is not promising. In the United States, many of the great newspaper publishers have, with strange fatuity, sought to destroy the New Deal, their one defense against the coming of Fascism to this country.

In spite of the commercial and sensational trend and the subordination of the editorial function in contemporary journalism, there have been notable instances of papers that have gained an international reputation because of serious and honest editorial writing. Such have been the *Frankfurter Zeitung* under Adolph Sonnemann and his successors, *L'Eclair* under Ernest Judet, the Manchester *Guardian* under Charles P. Scott, the Springfield *Republican* under Samuel Bowles and Waldo Cook, the New York *Evening Post* under Oswald G. Villard, the St. Louis *Post-Dispatch* under the editorship of Clark McAdams, the New York *World-Telegram* under Roy Wilson Howard and Lee B. Wood, and the Philadelphia *Record* and New York *Evening Post* under J. David Stern.

VIII. MODERNISM IN ART AND MUSIC

The growing industrialism of our age has reacted in many and varied ways upon art. Popular interest in art for art's sake has declined. As a result, art has tended to become more divorced from real life—something apart, to be shown and inspected on special occasions in museums and exhibitions. It is not a natural part of everyday life. On the other hand, the need for decoration of buildings, vehicles, and other commercial products has produced a greatly increased demand for the use of certain elementary and conventional art designs that are capable of mass production. This form of art is all that very directly touches the daily life of the inhabitants of industrialized countries.

Art has been subjected to the same general unsettling influences that have affected other forms of contemporary life. In much of nineteenth-century art, especially in Impressionism, there had been a tendency toward precise but unimaginative reproduction. This almost seemed to imply that colored photography is the ideal to be sought in painting. Contemporary or Modernistic art represents an analytical and subjective revolt. It is comparable to the reaction against laissez faire in politics and economics. Modernistic art constitutes a trend towards emotional striving and esthetic reformation. The world must be taken apart and then put together again in human terms, that is, with human needs and emotions as a prime factor. An analysis of the way man can express himself in art is a necessary preliminary stage to the later synthetic achievement. This analytical and reflective mood explains much that otherwise seems unintelligible to the layman in Modernistic art. The first steps away from tradition and convention were taken by Cézanne and Vincent van Gogh. Cézanne had opposed the Impressionist tendency to "camera competition," namely, to reproduce the optical facts without creative interpretation:

> In his elemental simplicity, in his vision of nature in terms of geometric form and color, in his distortion, though slight, of natural form for the purpose of a forceful expression, and in his sense of design that was naturally a corollary of these principles—in all this he took issue with the Impressionists on the one hand and laid the foundations of contemporary art on the other.[1]

The process of revolt from "pictorial stenography" was even greater in the work of Van Gogh. He strove to represent essentials only and suppressed details. Bright color was put on in flat masses. By carrying such ideals into a study of primitive culture and going to the South Sea islands for his materials, Paul Gauguin helped to found "Primitivism," based upon special zeal for archaic and primitive art. Gauguin relied especially upon bold lines in his art, and was also famed for his flattening of forms and massing of colors.

The path to more extreme developments was opened by Henri Matisse. He simplified his drawings, sometimes to the point of unintelligibility, aiming to express subjective emotions rather than accurately to reproduce a visual image. The emotion depicted is more likely to be an aspiration of the artist than anything easily discernible to the casual observer. In the hands of a young Spaniard, Pablo Picasso, this trend produced about 1908 that exaggerated form of geometrical art known as Cubism. The geometrical design is simplified to an extreme degree on the theory that "everything in nature is modeled on the lines of a sphere, cone, and cylinder." The result is something distorted beyond all recognition. "Futurism" is another phase of the revolt against convention. It attempts to put into painting the thought of modern physics that the ultimate fact in nature is energy. It is not concerned with appearance but with giving an impression of motion and momentum. The Futurists try to depict "not the engine but the go." The leading Futurists are two Italians, Gino Severini and Luigi Russolo. The former has shown genius in the matter of decoration. "Synchromism" simplifies by placing entire reliance upon color, with more or

[1] Helen Gardner, *Art through the Ages*, Harcourt, Brace, 1926, p. 468.

less complete neglect of representation and design. Lavish and weird use of color alone is exploited to stimulate the imagination.

Amadeo Modigliani, an eccentric Italian, employed Modernistic technique in his handling of portraits and nudes. He was fond of portraying Negro types and neurotic females. He was skillful in his use of geometric design and of clear colors. George Grosz is the greatest of modern German painters. He opposed the World War, but managed to escape the death penalty. He flirted with Futurism at first, but later turned to grim illustrative realism employed in social studies and satire. He has attacked the existing order with vigor. His *Ecce Homo* (1908), a book of scenes from life, has been described as "the anatomy of degradation." Alfred Stieglitz established Modernism of a rather extreme form in the United States.[1] Modernistic mural decoration has been greatly developed in the United States by Thomas Benton and the Mexican painters, Diego Rivera and José Clemente Orozco. Bold figures, realism, and lavish use of strong color characterize their work. They have depicted American historical scenes and portrayed modern industry and occupational types. Orozco has satirized the leisure class and the bourgeois intelligentsia, while Rivera has openly used his art as propaganda for economic radicalism, a fact that led to the controversy attending the destruction of his murals at Rockefeller Center in New York City. Another Mexican, Miguel Covarrubias, has shown remarkable talent in caricature. Among other leading modernist painters whom we can mention here are André Derain, Henri Rousseau, André Lhote, Pierre Bonnard, and André Dunoyer de Segonzac.

In sculpture one may note a similar but not so well developed movement away from the conventional. George Grey Barnard has carried on in the tradition of Rodin in the United States without any conscious effort to imitate the great Frenchman. He is best known for his statue of Lincoln and for his war memorials. A similar tendency to unite the free technique of Rodin with strictly American subjects is to be observed in the sculpture of Gutzon Borglum. Simplification of design and a trend towards Primitivism are to be discerned in the work of Antoine Bourdelle and Aristide Maillol. In the more developed Modernism of Alexander Archipenko the human form is merely suggested and integral parts of it, like legs or arms, may be entirely omitted. The idea is to suggest form by adroit combination of line and mass. Jacob Epstein, a Russian Jew, has attracted attention through his architectural reliefs. His faces are bold and rough, and he has tried to adapt primitive and ancient art to a modern setting. His bronze work is especially good.

Architecture has exhibited more significant advances in the twentieth century than any other form of art and the most important achievements have been made in the United States.[2] The older classic and Gothic traditions have persisted, especially in church architecture. The Cathedral of St. John the Divine in New York City, designed by Ralph Adams Cram, is one of the most conspicuous examples of the continued popularity of Gothic design. The same is true of the great National Cathedral in Washington. But the most novel and important innovation has been in skyscraper architecture in the

---

[1] *Cf.* Rugg, *op. cit.*, pp. 198 ff.
[2] *Cf.* T. E. Tallmadge, *The Story of Architecture in America*, rev. ed., Norton, 1927, Chaps. IX-XI, and T. F. Hamlin, *The American Spirit in Architecture*, Yale University Press, 1926.

metropolitan centers. The guiding conception in skyscraper architecture was laid down by Louis H. Sullivan [1] in the notion that form should be determined by function. The increased land values and the necessity of housing many tenants made necessary the erection of skyscrapers. At first the tendency was to combine a tall tower with Gothic or classic trappings. The Woolworth Building, designed by Cass Gilbert, is a good example of the prewar "cathedral of commerce," with its great tower and Gothic embellishments. A later and more thoroughly Americanized structure of this sort is the Chicago Tribune Building.

A new style in skyscraper architecture was set by the New York City zoning law. The stipulation is that a tower of any height may be erected on one-fourth of the building space and that the height of the rest of the building fronting on the street must be in proportion to the width of the street. High towers are erected, flanked by massive terraces. The New York Telephone Building by Ralph Walker and the Hotel Shelton by Arthur Harmon are good early examples of this type of architecture, in which beauty is combined with an effort to secure the maximum efficiency in strength, floor space, light, and ventilation. These buildings are mostly free from any trace of classic or Gothic influences. Russia, since the revolution, has shown much interest in imitating American skyscraper architecture. Much progress has been made in building design and in materials in this type of structure, especially in the use of reënforced-concrete construction. Another novel type of urban architecture in which more lavishness than taste has been displayed is the giant moving-picture theater. Domestic architecture in small city, village, suburban, and country areas has been greatly influenced by the accepted precedent of the Colonial period and its English antecedents, as well as by the Spanish mission architecture of the Southwest.

In music, as well as in painting and other forms of art, the twentieth century witnessed a definite movement of revolt against the conventional forms. This started in France with Claude Debussy, who, in a general way, exerted an influence upon the musical revolution comparable to that of Cézanne in painting. We have already noted that in the music of the eighteenth century and the early nineteenth there was the cool, classic beauty of the masters of that period, Bach, Haydn, Handel, Mozart, and Beethoven, in his earlier compositions; music that was a model of form and self-control. Then came the Romanticist music of the nineteenth century, dominated by feeling, sentimentality, suggestion of mood, and rich self-expression. Wagner was the towering figure of Romanticist music. Down to the middle of the nineteenth century musical compositions had centered about a definite key—a fixed tonality and the use of a tonic chord. It was the period of the triumph of melodic and harmonic instrumental music, based upon an expansion and dispersion of tone.

Beginning about 1890, however, there was a revolt in music similar to the transition in painting associated with the French Modernists. This revolt was twofold: (1) Against everything that Romanticism in music had stood for—ideals and technique alike; and (2) against the conventional technical devices of composition. "Let us purify our music," wrote Debussy, one of the pioneers in the search for new musical possibilities. "Let us try to scarify it. Let us seek to obtain a music which will be barer (*plus nue*). We must guard against the

---

[1] *Cf.* Rugg, *op. cit.*, Chap. IX.

stifling of emotion under the heap of motives and superimposed designs." His *Prelude to the Afternoon of a Faun* (1892) admirably illustrated the transformation of music. Here "clear melody gave way to fragments lost in an ocean of harmony." In his *Pelléas and Mélisande* (1902), based on Maeterlinck's play, there is variety, color, and a freedom which is not hostile to tonality.

After Debussy, music gradually emancipated itself from the shackles of what was commonly considered to be the sole type of melody, harmony, and rhythm suitable for use in serious music. The contours of melodic lines changed. A tonal center of gravity was abandoned, producing *atonality*. Sometimes two keys were used at once, one superimposed on the other, bringing about *polytonality*. The more or less four-square rhythm gave way to an irregular, intangible, eccentric, and (to many ears) barbaric beat. Music became almost an experiment in acoustics, by which composers might work out an infinite range of sound-combinations. Owing to the disregard for the classical chord structure, as well as by the use of "tone clusters" and an involved polyphony, almost any resulting resonance became admissible. Musical ideas were stated with precision and as concisely as possible. Smaller combinations of solo instruments often replaced the former full, rich orchestras.

Musical Modernism has been manifested in different degrees, all the way from the subtle delicacy and refined elegance of Claude Debussy's harmonic versatility to Arnold Schönberg's uncompromising cacophony. Intermediate between Debussy and Schönberg is Igor Stravinsky, a Russian now long resident in Paris. His reputation spread after the rendition in Paris of his ballet *The Firebird* (1910) and his *Rite of Spring* (1913). He imitates in his music what is going on in the world about him. His music is noted for its complexity of rhythm and artistic use of dissonance. Mr. H. T. Finck says of his music:

> The importance of the melodic element in Stravinsky cannot be emphasised too much; it makes his music evolutionary as well as revolutionary. He, too, commits cacophonic outrages and deviltries and tomfooleries, but he usually has reasons for doing so and underlying them are real musical ideas, some of them strokes of genius. . . . In his *Firebird* what a riot of deliriously enchanting sound and fury! Here is proletarian jazz ennobled by genius and raised to the rank of a Bach fugue. Stravinsky's wit, his imagination, his ability to make cacophony agreeable, his inexhaustible fund of harmonic and orchestral tricks—why, this Russian can do more with twenty players than Richard Strauss or Gustav Mahler with a hundred and twenty! That way lies the future of music.[1]

Stravinsky has also been one of the most successful of the Modernists in achieving conciseness, an impersonal quality, and physical expression in music.

The most extreme among the influential Modernists is the German composer Arnold Schönberg. He has been called the king of cacophonists, to indicate supremacy in ability to compose a series or succession of harsh, discordant, and unpleasant sounds. Schönberg has gone further than any other prominent contemporary in abandoning the older musical concepts and ideals. Hence he is at once the most admired and the most hated of Modernists. His admirers assert that criticism of him is due to the musical limitations of his critics. On

---

[1] H. T. Finck, "Main Currents in Twentieth Century Music," in F. H. Hooper, ed., *These Eventful Years*, Encyclopaedia Britannica Co., 1924, 2 vols., Vol. II, pp. 413-14.

MODERNISM IN ART AND MUSIC

the other hand, his foes deny that he is really a musician at all. Typical of the conventional attitude toward Schönberg are the following observations of Professor R. O. Morris:

... I must confess to my total inability to foresee any possible future for this kind of thing. This complete upsetting of all traditional values, this disdain of all previously accepted melodic and harmonic relationships, suggests to me, not so much courage and sincerity, as an inflated arrogance of mind that can only be described as megalomania—a dreary wilderness of cacophony that somehow contrives to be pedantic and hysterical at the same time.[1]

The effect of Schönberg's music on the average listener—which will also go for that of the other extreme Modernists—has been well phrased by the late James Huneker when he says that "he mingles with his music sharp daggers at white heat, with which he pares away tiny slices of his victims' flesh. Anon he twists the knife in the fresh wound and you receive another horrible thrill."[2] It would be unfair, however, to deny Schönberg very great technical skill in musical composition. Since there is such a diversity of opinion regarding this composer, all we can do is to wait for the judgment of time. We are still too close for any definitive verdict. It should be recalled, however, that nearly all revolutionary composers have been compelled to overcome the prejudices and resistance of their contemporaries.

Not all Modernists have been so iconoclastic as Schönberg or so unpleasant to ears attuned to conventional melodic music. Next to Stravinsky, the leading Modernists of Russian birth are Sergei Prokoviev and Alexander Scriabin, both composers of symphonies of great depth and vigor. Many regard Scriabin as an influence equal to Debussy in the creation of modern music. In France, Maurice Ravel and Paul Dukas are the foremost composers of the Modernist school since Debussy. Ravel has moved on further in the tradition of Debussy, a characteristic work being his ballet *The Child and the Enchantments* (1925). In Italy, Alfredo Casella has repudiated the traditional Italian preoccupation with opera and has striven to compose purely instrumental music in the Modernist vein. More popular is Ottorino Respighi, who has proved very skillful in adapting the old music of the sixteenth and seventeenth centuries. He has produced emotional music of unusual beauty and colorfulness, well represented by his *Fountains of Rome* (1916). Frederick Delius, Gustav T. Holst, Vaughan-Williams, and some others have tried by using folk songs to create an English school of Modernism. Delius, a blind musician, is an able composer of choral music in which he combines exotic colorfulness with intellectualism. One of his best works is *In a Summer Garden* (1908). Cyril Scott has been Debussy's most notable follower in England. The Italian Swiss Ferruccio Busoni has achieved a "melodic classicism," and his *Turandot* (1918) is regarded by some as one of the most pleasing of Modernist compositions. In addition to Schönberg, the one eminent German Modernist is Paul Hindemith, a composer of progressive tendencies, held in high esteem. Ernest Bloch, a Swiss Jew who has come to America, is especially noted for his capacity to adapt Jewish music to Modernistic expression. His compositions are of an

[1] R. O. Morris, "An Introduction to Music," in William Rose, *An Outline of Modern Knowledge*, Putnam, 1931, p. 1046.
[2] Huneker, *Ivory Apes and Peacocks*, Scribner, 1915, p. 94.

intensely nationalistic character. Charles Loeffler, an Alsatian by birth and an American by adoption, has been strongly influenced by the French Impressionists, but his music nevertheless possesses a personal and distinctive quality. Aaron Copland, Roger Sessions, Leo Ornstein, and others, have developed the Modernist technique in the United States.

The trend towards extreme Modernism in music has not won over all contemporary musicians. Some have remained post-Romanticists and carried further certain developments of the nineteenth century. Richard Strauss, the disciple of Wagner, was at one time considered to be an arch-Modernist. It was thought that he had forced the art of musical expression far beyond its natural bounds. Today the "modernisms" are faded and his music is found to possess a rich melodiousness. He has become a conservative by contrast with Schönberg. He has composed tone poems that are extremely sensuous. His opera *Der Rosenkavalier* (1911) is one of the most intoxicating compositions ever put down. The music of Sir Edward Elgar—music of a high and noble character—is considered by many to be the work of the first English composer of real genius since Henry Purcell. Also devoted to the ideals of the previous century is the Finn Jean Sibelius, whose powerful music has stirred the national spirit of his countrymen. In Italy, Giacomo Puccini remained true to the traditions of the melodic opera in his well-known works *La Bohème* (1896), *Tosca* (1900), and *Madame Butterfly* (1904). If the great operas were chiefly a product of the eighteenth and nineteenth centuries, their appreciation and popularity have not waned in the twentieth. And the great vocalists, such as Caruso, Scotti, Nordica, Schumann-Heink, and Homer, will rank with the best of the preceding century. Mention should also be made of great instrumental performers, such as the Polish pianist Ignace Paderewski, the Austrian violinist Fritz Kreisler, and the Russian pianist and composer Sergei Rachmaninov.

Lighter music has been especially important among the musical developments of the twentieth century. The breezy and melodious operettas of Victor Herbert enjoyed great popularity in the decade before the World War. Even more outstanding in light music, and especially notable for its popular appeal, has been the development of the so-called jazz music. This type of music was promoted in large part by the growing emancipation from Puritanism and the increased popularity of informal dancing. Jazz is characterized by emphatic rhythm, exaggerated sentimental melody, and moving emotional appeal. Its sources are to be found chiefly in Negro rhythm, melodic idioms, and "blue" harmonies. It has also made adroit adaptations from the classic harmony and melody of earlier centuries.[1]

Jazz has been raised to a relatively dignified and serious form of modern musical expression through the efforts of such composers as George Gershwin, Irving Berlin, Arthur Schwartz, Jerome Kern and Cole Porter, and by conductors like Paul Whiteman. Gershwin's *Rhapsody in Blue* (1923) is representative of the more mature form of "symphonic" jazz. Jazz has thus not only drawn sustenance from sensuous music, but has itself contributed to, and influenced some types of, the more artistic products. An important by-product of

---

[1] For example, that popular jazz number of some years back, "Yes, We Have No Bananas," was produced by a combination of Handel's *Messiah* (Hallelujah Chorus) with "My Bonnie Lies Over the Ocean," and "I Dreamt That I Dwelt in Marble Halls."

jazz has been the American jazz band, a marvel of economy of means, ingenious instrumentation, and the like. It is a real contribution that exists nowhere else on earth save by direct imitation.

The invention of the phonograph, then of the radio, followed by musical sound-pictures, as well as the installation of symphony orchestras in the cheaper theaters, has done much to promote popular interest in music of every kind. A most portentous development in contemporary music has been the commercialization of music and its adaptation to mass production for financial profit. Jazz music helped along this trend, but even the classics have been adapted to mass production. Inasmuch as operas and symphonies represent a large financial investment today, they must be handled in businesslike fashion. The phonograph produced a very marked stimulus to the mass demand for music, but it has been the growing popularity of modern dancing, the radio, and musical pictures which "put over" commercial music. The result is that "toasted cigarettes" and *Tristan and Isolda* are lumped together for radio consumption. The names of the popular performers and orchestras are capitalized. And what do they perform? For the most part, music that will appeal to the largest numbers. Outside of the opera and such concerts as those of the New York Philharmonic Orchestra, most of the music is of an ultra-popular order, without variety and well-worn. There must be no risk that an untutored listener will tune out before the sales talk can be made. The popularization of poor music may lower, to a certain degree, the quality of compositions, but it may also mean that music will play a much larger part than previously in the cultural life of the people. In Soviet Russia, for instance, music has not only been cultivated as a phase of mass culture but has also been utilized to serve as an instrument of proletarian propaganda.

IX. CULTURAL LAG AND THE HUMAN OUTLOOK

In spite of the revolutionary changes that science has produced in our knowledge and technology has wrought in our material culture, our opinions and institutions have altered but slightly in a century. Any person who was a member of the Constitutional Convention in 1787 would be completely amazed and absolutely at sea when faced by our modern material culture, but he could discuss our economics, politics, education, and religion with a contemporary American citizen in terms that would be equally familiar to each of them. Indeed, the average member of the Constitutional Convention of 1787 would be viewed suspiciously as rather radical by the typical American conservative of today. Imagine, for example, such Revolutionary Fathers as Thomas Jefferson or Patrick Henry carrying on a Socratic dialogue on the principles of human liberty and good citizenship with Herbert Hoover or John W. Davis.

In contrasting our material culture with the mental life of Americans today, it is useful at the outset to emphasize the fact that the intellectual outlook of the masses remains much the same as it was in primitive times. Anthropologists have described the primitive mind as characterized chiefly by an all-pervading supernaturalism, lack of precise and logical thinking, credulity, and an ignorance of scientific methods and results. Judged by these standards, it is obvious that the great majority of moderns are still overwhelmingly primitive in their ways of thinking. Still further, much of the specific content of earlier superstitions has come down into the modern era. Professor A. M. Tozzer of Harvard University published some years ago an admirable book on primitive culture, *Social Origins and Social Continuities*. As an appendix he included examples of ancient superstitions persisting in the themes submitted by Harvard freshmen to the Department of English. He was able to make clear the striking similarity between the mental attitudes of primitive men and Harvard freshmen. There was a remarkable hangover of the primitive belief in luck, chance, and other prescientific attitudes and devices.

We may now consider more specifically the archaic nature of the prevailing opinions and institutions in contemporary society. Our political opinions and institutions represent a mosaic compounded of: (1) The veneration of the state derived from the oriental emperor worship; (2) Roman legalism and the conception of secular omnipotence; (3) the classical obsession with the merits of monarchy, aristocracy, and democracy; (4) archaic views of representative government that developed between the sixteenth century and the eighteenth; (5) seventeenth and eighteenth century doctrines of natural rights; and (6) the eighteenth-century view of the perfectibility of man, linked up with the nineteenth-century enthusiasm for democracy. While there is much vital political doctrine expounded by modern thinkers, this has found but slight adoption in practice, and there has been singularly little effort to adapt our political institutions to the needs of an urban, industrial age. We in America continue to revere a Constitution and a political system that were created in a simple agricultural society, in spite of the fact that material culture has been altered more in the last century in America than in the previous millennium.

Law, likewise, is founded upon ancient theories and practices. It is still based primarily upon oriental usages and conceptions, the formulations of the Roman jurists, the precedents of the English common law, and the eighteenth-century natural law. Very little progress indeed has been made in the way of introducing the historical and sociological point of view in the reconstruction of juristic theory and practice in America. We attempt to regulate a twentieth-century civilization by applying to it legal concepts and methods that have changed but little since the year 1700. The rules of legal evidence are hopelessly out of date and confused. In many ways they are almost exactly the opposite of the principles and processes applied in the field of scientific evidence, which is designed to ascertain the factual truth in regard to some specific problem. The attitude taken by the courts towards crime and criminal responsibility is a composite of archaic legalism, religious superstition, and metaphysical illusions. With the exception of certain advanced work in juvenile courts, there is not the slightest recognition of the modern socio-psychological conception of human conduct and its relation to the causation of crime. Even in the field of insanity, where the conventional legal conception of the free moral agent is in part suspended, the test for insanity is strictly legal and not medical. In a notorious case in Ohio—that of Mr. Remus—we witnessed the amusing spectacle of a group of learned and logical physicians branding the defendant as legally sane but medically and socially quite irresponsible.

Our attitudes and usages with respect to property are equally full of primitive vestiges. The notion of the unique sanctity of property is in part an outgrowth of primitive mysticism and superstition. Our contemporary view of property rights is a compound of ancient legalism and the prevailing sixteenth and seventeenth century Protestant views of God's approval of thrift and profit. To these have been added the seventeenth and eighteenth century notion that the chief purpose of the state and legal institutions is to protect private property. Nothing more modern than this is necessary to explain the majority decisions of the Supreme Court of the United States on matters pertaining to private property in the twentieth century. Critical writers have subjected the whole conventional theory of property to searching reëxamination, but their views have been for the most part ignored. When they have been taken into account they have been bitterly attacked as un-American, Bolshevistic, and the like. There is little or nothing in present-day American conceptions of property rights that cannot be discovered explicitly or implicitly in the writings of John Locke.

We have been especially reluctant to bring the control of sex and the family into harmony with contemporary scientific and esthetic considerations. Our sex mores and family institutions embody: (1) A primitive reaction to the mystery of sex and of women in particular; (2) Hebraic uxoriousness and conceptions of patriarchal male domination; (3) patristic and medieval views regarding the baseness of sex and sex temptation, especially as offered by women; (4) the medieval esteem for virginity in women; (5) the sacramental view of marriage, which leads us to regard marriage as a theological rather than a social issue; (6) the property views of the early bourgeoisie; and (7) the Kantian rationalization of personal inadequacy and inexperience. There is hardly a single item in the sex mores of a conventionally respectable American today that squares with either science or esthetics.

Our educational system has changed but little as compared with the vast alteration in our ways of living. Certain basic strains in our educational doctrine are derived from the oriental and medieval notion that the chief purpose of education is to make clear to man the will of the gods or of God. From the Greeks and Romans came the high esteem for training in rhetoric and argumentation as the prime essential of a successful career in politics. Humanism contributed the view that the classical languages embody the flower of secular learning and represent the most exquisite form of literary expression. The democratic obsession of the last century supports the idea that everybody is entitled to participate in a complete system of education, and that educational opportunities should be equal for all. The punitive psychology, which still dominates the greater part of our educational procedure, was derived from the Christian philosophy of solemnity and the exacting discipline of the will. Education in the natural and social sciences and in technology has not been regarded as relatively important or respectable, and occupies nothing like so great a part in our educational system as the older currents in our curriculum. As Professor Kallen has observed, education today is more of a distraction from life than a preparation for it. Few of the real problems involved in living intelligently and successfully in an urban and industrial society are touched upon vitally in our educational system, from the kindergarten to the graduate school. Nor has there been much effort to work over our educational methods in harmony with the modern psychological demonstration that vivid personal interest is the only sensible basis of a dynamic educational scheme.

Journalism has not yet achieved any considerable success as a method of informing the public of contemporary issues and providing general educational direction as to the problems of modern life. It still remains chiefly a method of providing for the wholesale dissemination of something like the old neighborhood gossip, now that the neighborhood has largely disappeared and face-to-face gossiping has become increasingly impossible. The same subjects that made juicy gossip in the prenewspaper days still constitute the best copy for the contemporary press. Personalities are much more highly esteemed than principles by the modern journal. No scientific discovery of modern times, no engineering achievement, nor any social-reform program, has received the same publicity as was bestowed upon the notorious murder trial of Ruth Snyder and Judd Gray or the kidnapping of the Lindbergh baby. No newspaper that has made a serious effort to devote itself primarily to public education on vital topics of economic, political, and sociological import has been able to survive.

It is scarcely necessary to point out the archaic elements of religion in our culture. The Fundamentalists today, among whom are numbered the majority of religious communicants, live under the domination of the same intellectual patterns that prevailed in primitive times. Mr. Bryan openly declared at the Dayton trial in 1925 that no statement whatever would appear to him preposterous or unsupportable provided it be found in Holy Writ. Even the great majority of liberal theologians today are in rebellion only against seventeenth and eighteenth century religious and philosophical views. It is probably no exaggeration to hold that not 10 per cent of Modernist theologians are really adjusted to contemporary knowledge and ways of thinking. The great majority of them are merely attempting to express archaic views in contemporaneous phraseology. Religion is slower in readjusting itself to new ways of living and thinking than any other phase of human culture. This fact was admirably demonstrated by the study of the relative change of opinions and attitudes in American culture since 1890 embodied in Dr. and Mrs. Lynd's important book, *Middletown*.[1] Even more, religion is a leading influence in promoting cultural lag in other fields of human opinion and activity. It is the primary intellectual factor that discourages a candid and secular approach to the reconstruction of human knowledge and social conduct in every field.

Not only is there a marked contrast between the degree and the rapidity of contemporary advances in the field of science and material culture on the one hand and of opinions and institutions on the other; there is also a marked difference of attitude with respect to antiques in our material surroundings and antiques among our ideas. So far as our means will allow, we desire to be strictly up to date in everything that is a manifestation of our material equip-

[1] R. S. and Helen Lynd, *op. cit.*, Harcourt, Brace, 1929.

ment. We demand the latest and most perfect bathroom equipment and the most up-to-date radio installation. Any American of even moderate means would be humiliated if compelled to own and operate an automobile ten years out of date. Yet this same person who demands a thoroughly contemporaneous vehicle in which to transport his body will probably even boast that his mind is furnished with information and opinions the great majority of which antedate the year 1800. Indeed, very few respectable opinions held by the majority of contemporary Americans have an origin as recent as the middle of the nineteenth century.

Another phase of this divergent attitude of humanity towards material culture, as compared to opinions and social institutions, relates to the reaction towards expert guidance. When a man desires to have a bathroom faucet repaired, a spark plug replaced in his car, or a tooth pulled, he at once deems it necessary to have recourse to an expert. Yet with respect to the much more difficult and complicated problems of social, economic, and political theory and practice, he is prepared to rest completely satisfied with the opinions of the man on the street or those of a slightly informed politician. He wants a "brain trust" to design his automobile, but not to plan his government.

The greatest danger that faces contemporary civilization is this alarming discrepancy between our natural science and technology on the one hand and our opinions and social institutions on the other. This situation cannot continue indefinitely. Unless we are able to bridge the gulf and bring our thinking and institutions up to date, the ultimate collapse of civilization seems inevitable. At present, far from closing this gap, the tendency is for the divergence to become constantly more extensive and notable. Our technology is progressing with dizzy speed, making more remarkable strides each year. At the same time, the forces of conservatism, which endeavor to obstruct the progress in opinions and institutions, appear to be getting stronger day by day with the rise of Fascism and other forms of reaction. The outlook, then, is one that is far from being conducive to easy-going optimism.

Even radicalism is hampered by cultural lag. Instead of linking their activities and interests with a program of contemporaneous perspective, such as Technocracy, most radicals conduct their discussions and plan their program within the restrictions imposed by the dialectic of Karl Marx, who is, in a way, as outmoded as Adam Smith or Herbert Spencer. Marx knew nothing of the Second Industrial Revolution or of contemporary finance capitalism. H. G. Wells may go too far when he writes, "Indeed from first to last the influence of Marx has been an unqualified drag upon the progressive reorganization of human society. We should be far nearer a sanely organized world system to-day if Karl Marx had never been born."[1] If, however, reverent Marxism were substituted for Marx himself, this severe indictment would be essentially true. We have already paid a high tribute to Marx as an economist and social prophet, but certainly the "parroting" of Marx by radicals today is as indefensible as the reverent citing of Smith and Spencer by "rugged individualists."

The discussion above enables us to comment intelligently upon the frequent assertion that we are living in a scientific age. The fact is, of course, that we

[1] Wells, *An Experiment in Autobiography*, p. 215.

are not doing anything of the sort. We are living in an era in which our opinions and institutions are overwhelmingly the product of contributions from the prescientific era. Our age is one in which our civilization has been profoundly affected in certain respects by scientific discoveries and their application to our material culture. In this way mankind, while still remaining primarily prescientific in its thinking and life interests, has been able to appropriate the results of the investigations and achievements of a few scientific-minded pioneers. It can probably be stated with accuracy that less than five thousand individuals have been responsible for those changes in our material civilization which separate us from the days of Franklin, Washington, and Jefferson. Modern civilization is essentially a venerable and ungrateful parasite, unintelligently exploiting the products of contemporary science and technology.

Very often those who most greedily accept and enjoy the products of modern science and technology are engaged in bitter attacks upon science as a whole and upon the scientific approach to life. Not infrequently persons who are most exacting in their demands for the most recent provisions in plumbing, the best medical attention, the most efficient and up-to-date automobiles, and the rest, are found at the same time defending classical or medieval civilization as the ideal period of human development. Many a plutocrat riding about in a Rolls-Royce car is at the same time disporting an intellect and a mental outlook that could be matched in every respect by the thought processes of a cave-dweller in the late Paleolithic period. In short, the real problem facing modern civilization is to make this actually a scientific age, that is, one in which we would not only insist upon contemporaneous bathtubs but also upon contemporaneous intellectual attitudes and assumptions.

The stupendous changes wrought by critical thought, science, and technology in our material civilization have given rise to problems that can be solved only by a corresponding development of the various social sciences which deal with the diverse aspects of social life that have been so thoroughly revolutionized since the days of George Washington.[1] We can no longer hope to receive adequate guidance in these matters solely from the theologian, the metaphysician, or the politician. Instead, we must bring the social sciences up to something like the same level of development and objectivity that has already been attained by the natural and applied sciences. Not only must we develop in this way accuracy and comprehensiveness in the particular social sciences, but we must also provide for proper and intelligent coöperation between them. As modern society is a unity of diverse processes and institutions, so these social sciences must be a coöperating group enriched by contributions from investigators in many realms of human endeavor. An excellent statement of this contrast between the progress of natural and social science in the last century, as well as an eloquent appeal for the development of the social sciences in the century to come, is embodied in the following quotation from the stimulating address delivered by President Walter Dill Scott of Northwestern University on "The Discovery of Truth in Universities":

[1] *Cf.* Barnes, *Can Man Be Civilized?* and Fosdick, *The Old Savage in the New Civilization.*

CULTURAL LAG AND THE HUMAN OUTLOOK

The universities justly claim first place as agencies for training men in effective methods of research and for formulating and teaching the principles that form the basis for later discoveries and applications. A survey of the progress of the agencies which promote human welfare reveals the fact that universities through the accomplishments of their teaching and research staffs have formulated principles and made discoveries and applications which have rendered the world a service much greater than is generally known.

Specific illustrations can be drawn most readily from such experimental sciences as physics, chemistry, and geology and their application to engineering; or from such observational sciences as zoology, botany, and bacteriology and their application to agriculture and to medicine. . . .

Advance in the physical and the biological sciences during future decades will certainly prove as helpful as at any previous time. But the most fruitful researches during the twentieth century will probably be conducted not in the natural sciences, but in the social sciences. We are at last coming to see that the proper study of mankind is man. We are beginning to direct our researches to the whole life of mankind—to the nature of man as a social and political being and to the achievements of man recorded in languages, literature, and institutions. There is recognized a need for a thorough rewriting of all our texts on history, economics, politics, sociology, psychology, esthetics, pedagogy, ethics, and religion. The social sciences are fostering a progress that may be measured not in mere billions of dollars or in millions of human lives, but rather in the finer, though less tangible, terms of appreciation, service, and sacrifice.

Research in the natural sciences has been effective in aiding the race to adjust itself to its physical environments. No such discovery of truth in the social sciences has been made in aiding the race to adjust itself to its human environments. Men are not now working together happily and effectively. There is said to be a lack of control in the home, restlessness in the school, apathy in the church, shirking in the shops, dishonesty in the counting houses, grafting in politics, crime in the city, and Bolshevism threatening all our institutions. . . .

All our human relations will be improved as rapidly as we make progress in the social sciences, and I am convinced that our universities will make as great a contribution in the social sciences during the twentieth century as they did by the discovery of truth in the natural sciences during the nineteenth century.

We may expect the most helpful contributions to the betterment of human relations from universities possessing certain favorable characteristics.

First, the university must be untrammeled by traditions or superstitions, by politics or cults; but must be animated by a love for truth, and the members of the teaching and research staff must be zealous in their pursuits of truth in their respective fields. . . .

Second, the university must sustain a graduate school and a group of professional schools, all in intimate contact with city life. [Only in such an atmosphere and in such an environment is the seeker after truth in touch with the most progressive thought and with the most persistent presentation of the problem of human relations.][1]

The "Gospel" of social science for the human future must be the tenets of a chastened, pragmatic, and scientifically guided open-mindedness so admirably summarized in the authoritative pronouncement of James Harvey Robinson:

---

[1] Scott, *op. cit., Century,* August, 1924, pp. 556, 559, 560. Bracketed sentence not published in the magazine article, but given in the original address, which was delivered at the inauguration of Chancellor C. W. Flint of Syracuse University, October, 1921.

Liberalism—and I have no great love for the word—may be conceived as the mood of the explorer, who notes the facts as he goes along. He does not know beforehand what he is going to find over the next mountain or across the next river or lake. He learns as he goes, and adjusts his beliefs to his increasing information. We have only just begun to explore man's nature and the world in which he is placed. We have new methods of research which were not available half a century ago. New experiments are being tried on a large scale, and conditions are vastly different from those with which our ancestors had to deal. Dogmas —ancient teachings which are protected in various ways from the fermentive influence of increasing knowledge—are still congenial to a creature such as man. But, while they are sometimes harmless, their chance of being suited to the present needs and best insight of men is so slight that we should have no least hesitation in calling them in question. The open-minded will do this so far as their powers permit. Open-mindedness, like dogma, demands faith and loyalty. It is a lofty ideal and one implying a new type of the mortification of the flesh—a new conception of righteousness and salvation. Whether one strives to fulfill the behests of ancient dogma or to follow those of open-mindedness, he will often stumble and have his moments of contrition and his renewals of faith. But the new gospel places far more onerous restraints on our natural impulses than did the old. It has its promises and its rewards—sometimes its beatific vision, but these glories are as yet for the scattered few. Yet the communion of saints grows daily.[1]

The fundamental fact that mankind must go ahead to better things or gradually be extinguished as another geological failure has been eloquently stated by Professor Harlow Shapley in a passage that merges the cosmic picture with social necessity in a most effective fashion:

Man, as a species, has had a short and brilliant career on the face of the earth. From ape-like ancestry to the editorial board of *The Nation* is at most a few million years. There are some cynics who think it is much less than that. Thousands of other species of animals besides *homo sapiens* have also risen rapidly to a high specialization, and then ceased to be. They paid for their brilliance with extinction. The dinosaurs lasted but a single era in geological history; they rose to a great climax of size, laid their eggs, and were gathered unto their fathers. They left no lineal descendants.

But the cockroach has a straight-line ancestry of two hundred million years or more. His is a stock sufficiently strong to carry him through numerous terrestrial upheavals, through desiccations and glaciations—and the cockroach today is just as good as he ever was. . . .

Biologically, it seems, we are as inexperienced as physically we are frail. Moreover, we are hampered with brains. We have mentality to burn, and many of us do burn it, at both ends. Our more or less primitive bodies cannot keep up in the evolutionary progress with our abnormal mentalities. . . .

Our concern mainly should be with the species—can *it* survive? It has no chance against the stars, of course; but can it long hold its own as a surviving form, or be ancestral to surviving forms, against other organisms, against primitive microbes and advanced insects? There is a fair chance, an optimistic scientist would say, if it were not that man's worst enemy is man.

The cockroach survives because it stands pat on form—it avoids experimental progress. Man, however, cannot stand still. He is delicately balanced in an unstable

---

[1] Robinson, "Open-mindedness: Faith and Loyalty," *American Hebrew*, Sept. 18, 1925, p. 595.

CULTURAL LAG AND THE HUMAN OUTLOOK

chemical complex; his abnormal mentality has led him to create an environment in which stagnation means extinction. Survival of the species appears to depend upon uninterrupted progress. Resignation is cowardice. Bended knees cannot help. The continued development of the reasoning intellect—our one conspicuous advantage—seems to be the only possibility. . . .

On these points the stellar perspective is clear. Protoplasm appears trivial and transient; but for man, the Drift prescribes progress and survival. If progression halts, we go to join the dinosaurs. If stagnation enters, in a million years or so, by the light of those undisturbed stars that heed life not at all, some conservative cockroach, crawling over the fossilized skull of an extinct primate, may be able to observe: "A relic here of another highly specialized organism which failed to recognize the laws of the universe, which preferred the current minor whims to the search for survival, and which missed its great opportunity to inherit the planet, perishing an early victim of the world's subtle chemistries." [1]

These passages from the pen of the man who is probably the most capable systematizer of contemporary astrophysical knowledge give the proper orientation and humility with which to close this survey of the origins of man and of his progress from the status of the supreme but untutored representative of simian life to the builder of an impressive world-civilization.

[1] Shapley, "Man and His Young World," *loc. cit.*, pp. 530-31.

SUGGESTED READING

Hammerton, *Universal History of the World,* Chaps. 181, 187-88, 190
Slosson, *Twentieth Century Europe,* Chaps. XXI-XXII
Hooper, *These Eventful Years,* Vol. II, Chaps. LXII-LXVIII, LXX-LXXVI
Friedell, *Cultural History of the Modern Age,* Vol. III, Bk. V
Randall, *Our Changing Civilization*
Gerald Heard, *These Hurrying Years,* Oxford Press, 1934
F. L. Allen, *Only Yesterday,* Harper, 1931
Wells, *The Work, Wealth and Happiness of Mankind,* Vol. II, Chaps. XV-XVI
——— *The World of William Clissold*
——— *The Shape of Things to Come*
John Langdon-Davies, *Man Comes of Age,* Harper, 1932
C. E. M. Joad, *Guide to Modern Thought,* Stokes, 1933
David Dietz, *The Story of Science,* rev. ed., Dodd, Mead, 1934
Watson Davis, ed., *The Advance of Science,* Doubleday, Doran, 1934
H. G. Garbedian, *The Major Mysteries of Science,* Covici, Friede, 1933
C. H. Ward, *Exploring the Universe,* new ed., Bobbs-Merrill, 1927
G. P. Serviss, *The Einstein Theory of Relativity,* Theosophical Press, 1923
R. T. Cox, *Time, Space and Atoms,* Williams & Wilkins, 1933
Harlow Shapley, *Flights from Chaos,* McGraw-Hill, 1930
Bertrand Russell, *The Scientific Outlook,* Norton, 1931
Hyman Levy, *The Universe of Science,* Century, 1933
R. S. Woodworth, *Contemporary Schools of Psychology,* Ronald Press, 1931
F. B. Karpf, *American Social Psychology,* McGraw-Hill, 1932
Barnes and others, *History and Prospects of the Social Sciences*
Recent Developments in the Social Sciences, ed. by E. C. Hayes, Lippincott, 1927
Odum, *American Masters of Social Science*
Joseph Dorfman, *Thorstein Veblen and His America,* Viking Press, 1934
Maynard Shipley, *The War on Modern Science,* Knopf, 1927

G. B. O'Toole, *The Case against Evolution,* Macmillan, 1925
H. E. Fosdick, *As I See Religion,* Harper, 1932
Barnes, *The Twilight of Christianity*
Kirchwey, *Our Changing Morality*
H. M. Parshley, *Science and Good Behavior,* Bobbs-Merrill, 1928
Walter Lippmann, *A Preface to Morals,* Macmillan, 1929
F. S. Marvin, ed., *Recent Developments in European Thought,* 2d ed., Oxford Press, 1929
W. T. Jones, ed., *Library of Contemporary Thought,* Knopf, 1927 *et seq.*
Albert Einstein and others, *Living Philosophies,* Simon & Schuster, 1931
Washburne, *Remakers of Mankind*
R. G. Tugwell and L. H. Keyserling, eds., *Redirecting Education,* Columbia University Press, 1934-35, 2 vols.
F. W. Roman, *The New Education in Europe,* Dutton, 1930
Counts, *The American Road to Culture*
Bertrand Russell, *Education and the Modern World,* Norton, 1932
Rugg, *Culture and Education in America*
A. L. Hall-Quest, *The University Afield,* Macmillan, 1926
Macy, *The Story of the World's Literature,* Pt. IV
J. M. Manly and Edith Rickert, *Contemporary American Literature,* new ed., Harcourt, Brace, 1929
Dorothy Brewster and J. A. Burrell, *Modern Fiction,* Columbia University Press, 1934
Hicks, *The Great Tradition*
D. M. Keezer, article "Press," Encyclopaedia of the Social Sciences
J. M. Lee, *History of American Journalism,* rev. ed., Houghton Mifflin, 1923
Bickel, *New Empires*
Gardner, *Art through the Ages,* Chap. xxx
Mather, *Modern Painting,* pp. 319-81
Thomas Craven, *Modern Art,* Simon & Schuster, 1934
Tallmadge, *The Story of Architecture in America,* Chaps. ix-xi
Elson, *The Book of Musical Knowledge,* Chap. lxi
George Dyson, *The New Music,* 2d ed., Oxford Press, 1926
Marion Bauer, *Twentieth Century Music: How It Developed and How to Listen to It,* Putnam, 1933
R. B. Fosdick, *The Old Savage in the New Civilization,* Doubleday, Doran, 1928
Ogburn, *Social Change*
J. W. Krutch, *Was Europe a Success?* Farrar & Rinehart, 1934
Burns, *Leisure in the Modern World*
Jones, Vandenbosch, and Vandenbosch, *Readings in Citizenship,* pp. 45-80
H. H. Newman, ed., *The Nature of the World and of Man,* University of Chicago Press, 1927
F. A. Cleveland, ed., *Modern Scientific Knowledge of Nature, Man, and Society,* Ronald Press, 1929
J. H. S. Bossard, ed., *Man and His World,* Harper, 1932, Chaps. iii-xi, xxiii-xxxiii
V. T. A. Ferm, ed., *Contemporary American Theology,* Round Table Press, 1932
C. W. Reese, ed., *Humanist Sermons,* Open Court Publishing Co., 1927
W. H. Kilpatrick, ed., *The Educational Frontier,* Century, 1933
Cross and Slover, *Heath Readings in the Literature of Europe,* pp. 910-1190.
C. C. Van Doren, ed., *Modern American Prose,* Harcourt, Brace, 1934
The Smart Set Anthology, ed. by Burton Rascoe, Reynal and Hitchcock, 1934

FURTHER REFERENCES

TWENTIETH-CENTURY SCIENCE. See the books referred to above, pp. 716-17, also Cleveland, *op. cit.;* Newman, *op. cit.;* Garbedian, *op. cit.;* Joseph McCabe, *The Riddle of the Universe Today* (Harper, 1934); Davis, *op. cit.;* H. B. Lemon, *From Galileo to Cosmic Rays* (University of Chicago Press, 1934).

On relativity, see Dampier-Whetham, *History of Science,* pp. 428 ff.; Ginzburg, *The Adventure of Science,* Chap. xv. For clear introductory summaries, see Ward, *op. cit.,* Chap. XII; Dietz, *op. cit.,* Chap. XXIII. For Einstein's own popular presentation, see Chap. I of his *The World as I See It* (Covici, Friede, 1934).

On the character of contemporary astronomical science, see Bks. VII-VIII of H. S. Williams, *The Great Astronomers* (Simon & Schuster, 1930); Herbert Dingle, *Modern Astrophysics* (Macmillan, 1924); Stetson, *Man and the Stars;* Shapley, *op. cit.;* R. H. Baker, *The Universe Unfolding* (Williams & Wilkins, 1932); Sir J. H. Jeans, *Through Time and Space* (Macmillan, 1934).

On contemporary electromechanics, see Ginzburg, *op. cit.,* Chap. XI; Dietz, *op. cit.,* Pt. III; Hammerton, *op. cit.,* Chap. 187; Cox, *op. cit.;* C. L. Mantell, *Sparks from the Electrode* (Williams & Wilkins, 1933); A. S. Eddington, *New Pathways in Science* (Macmillan, 1935).

On the quantum theory, see Dietz, *op. cit.,* Chap. XXII; Cox, *op. cit.,* Chap. XIII; M. K. E. L. Planck, *The Universe in the Light of Modern Physics* (Norton, 1931).

On radioactivity, see Dietz, *op. cit.,* Chap. XVIII; Cox, *op. cit.,* Chaps. IX-XI; Dampier-Whetham, *op. cit.,* pp. 382 ff., 391 ff.; Cressy, *Discoveries and Inventions of the Twentieth Century,* Chap. XX.

On contemporary chemistry, see Thorpe, *History of Chemistry,* Vol. II, Chaps. VIII-IX; Harvey-Gibson, *Two Thousand Years of Science,* pp. 377-415; Slosson, *Creative Chemistry;* B. L. Clarke, *The Marvels of Modern Chemistry* (Harper, 1932); L. V. Redman and A. V. H. Mory, *Romance of Research* (Williams & Wilkins, 1933); Darrow, *The Story of Chemistry.* On the chemistry of colloids, see Shapley, *op. cit.,* p. 50; Darrow, *op. cit.,* Chap. IX; Cleveland, *op. cit.,* Pt. III.

On endocrinology, see Walter Timme, *Lectures on Endocrinology* (2d ed., Hober, 1932); L. H. Mayers, *What We Are and Why* (Dodd, Mead, 1933); Louis Berman, *The Glands Regulating Personality* (Macmillan, 1921).

On contemporary biology, see Singer, *The Story of Living Things,* Pt. III; Dampier-Whetham, *op. cit.,* Chap. VIII; Harvey-Gibson, *op. cit.,* pp. 416 ff.; Nordenskiöld, *History of Biology,* Pt. III, Chaps. X-XVIII; H. H. Newman, *Evolution Yesterday and Today* (Williams & Wilkins, 1933).

On contemporary physiology, see Dampier-Whetham, *op. cit.,* pp. 359 ff.; Logan Clendening, *The Human Body* (rev. ed., Knopf, 1931); P. H. Mitchell, *Text Book of General Physiology* (McGraw-Hill, 1932).

On recent developments in geology, see Harvey-Gibson, *op. cit.,* pp. 342 ff.; Dietz, *op. cit.,* Pt. II; W. O. Hotchkiss, *The Story of a Billion Years* (Williams & Wilkins, 1933).

On geography and anthropogeography, see Barnes, *The New History and the Social Studies,* Chap. II; Barnes and others, *op. cit.,* Chap. II; *Recent Developments in the Social Sciences,* Chap. IV; Thomas, *The Environmental Basis of Society;* Isaiah Bowman, *Geography in Relation to the Social Sciences* (Scribner, 1934).

On the developments in contemporary psychology, see E. G. Boring, *History of Experimental Psychology* (Century, 1929); Murphy, *Historical Introduction to Modern Psychology;* Adams, *Psychology: Science or Superstition?* R. S. Woodworth, *Dynamic Psychology* (Columbia University Press, 1918), and *Contemporary Schools of Psychology;* Gardner Murphy, ed., *Outline of Abnormal Psychology* (Modern Library, 1929).

On recent psychiatry, see J. E. Nicole, *Psychopathology* (Dodd, Mead, 1930); Bernard Hart, *Psychopathology* (2d ed., Macmillan, 1931); A. P. Noyes, *Textbook of Psychiatry* (Macmillan, 1927); W. A. White, *Outlines of Psychiatry* (Nervous and Mental Disease Publishing Co., 13th ed., 1932); William Healy and others, *The Structure and Meaning of Psychoanalysis* (Knopf, 1930); Fritz Wittels, *Freud and His Time* (Liveright, 1931); E. S. Dummer, ed., *The Unconscious* (Knopf, 1927).

On social psychology, see Karpf, *op. cit.*

On contemporary medicine, see Robinson, *The Story of Medicine,* Chaps. xi-xii; Garrison, *Introduction to the History of Medicine,* Chap. xii; Morris Fishbein, *Frontiers of Medicine* (Appleton-Century, 1933); Sigerist, *American Medicine.*

For a critical review of some of the human faults of contemporary surgery, see R. H. McKay and Norman Beasley, *Let's Operate* (Long & Smith, 1932).

On preventive medicine, see Waite, *Disease Prevention;* Stanhope Bayne-Jones, *Man and Microbes* (Williams & Wilkins, 1932); P. H. De Kruif, *Microbe Hunters* (Harcourt, Brace, 1926); Hans Zinsser, *Rats, Lice and History* (Little, Brown, 1935).

INTELLECTUAL IMPLICATIONS OF SCIENCE. For good summaries of the new intellectual perspective, see Langdon-Davies, *Man and His Universe,* Chap. viii, and *Man Comes of Age;* Joad, *op. cit.;* Heard, *op. cit.;* Wells, *The World of William Clissold,* especially Vol. I; Levy, *op. cit.;* M. K. E. L. Planck, *Where Is Science Going?* (Norton, 1932); Herbert Dingle, *Science and Human Experience* (Macmillan, 1932); W. A. Neilson, ed., *Roads to Knowledge* (Norton, 1932); E. A. Kirkpatrick, *The Sciences of Man in the Making* (Harcourt, Brace, 1932).

On contemporary notions of the theory of progress, see Durant, *Mansions of Philosophy,* Chaps. xv-xvi; C. A. Beard, Introduction to Bury, *The Idea of Progress;* Hammerton, *op. cit.,* Chap. 191; Chaps. vi-vii, xxiii-xxxiv, of A. J. Todd, *Theories of Social Progress* (Macmillan, 1918); Wallis, *Culture and Progress,* Chaps. xviii-xxiv; Ogburn, *op. cit.*

For urbane examples of the "new obscurantism," see C. E. Ayres, *Science, the False Messiah* (Bobbs-Merrill, 1927); G. B. Munson, *The Dilemma of the Liberated* (Coward-McCann, 1930); Richard Rothschild, *Paradox* (Long & Smith, 1934), and *Reality and Illusion* (Harcourt, Brace, 1934). For an analysis of the trend, see Max Eastman, *The Literary Mind* (Scribner, 1931).

THE SOCIAL SCIENCES. On recent progress, see Barnes, *The New History and the Social Studies;* Barnes and others, *op. cit.; Recent Developments in the Social Sciences;* W. F. Ogburn and A. A. Goldenweiser, eds., *The Social Sciences and Their Interrelations* (Houghton Mifflin, 1927); Encyclopaedia of the Social Sciences (Macmillan, 1930-35, 15 vols.), especially Vol. I; L. F. Bernard, *The Fields and Methods of Sociology* (Long & Smith, 1934); Theo Surányi-Unger, *Economics in the Twentieth Century* (Norton, 1931); G. E. G. Catlin, *The Science and Method of Politics* (Knopf, 1927); Huntington Cairns, *Law and the Social Sciences* (Harcourt, Brace, 1935); Odum, *op. cit.;* Dorfman, *op. cit.;* J. R. Commons, *Myself* (Macmillan, 1934) and *Institutional Economics* (Macmillan, 1934).

RELIGION. On religion in the twentieth century, see Randall and Randall, *Religion and the Modern World;* E. A. Burtt, *Religion in an Age of Science* (Stokes, 1929); *Recent Social Trends,* Vol. II, Chap. xx; H. M. Kallen, *Why Religion?* (Boni & Liveright, 1927); Barnes, *The Twilight of Christianity.*

On Catholicism, see Michael Williams and Julia Kernan, *The Catholic Church*

FURTHER REFERENCES

in Action (Macmillan, 1934). On Protestantism, see H. P. Douglass and E. de S. Brunner, *The Protestant Church as a Social Institution* (Harper, 1935).

On Fundamentalism, see pp. 375 ff. of Clifford Kirkpatrick, *Religion in Human Affairs* (Wiley, 1929); S. G. Cole, *History of Fundamentalism* (Harper, 1931). On Devout Modernism, see G. H. Betts, *The Beliefs of 700 Ministers* (Abingdon Press, 1929). The most authoritative statement of Devout Modernist beliefs is Fosdick, *As I See Religion.* For an anthology, mainly of Devout Modernism, see Ferm, *op. cit.* For Advanced Modernism, see R. W. Sellars, *Religion Coming of Age* (Macmillan, 1928). On religious Humanism, see Reese, *op. cit.;* C. F. Potter, *Humanism* (Simon & Schuster, 1930) and *Humanizing Religion* (Harper, 1933); T. W. Darnell, *After Christianity—What?* (Brewer and Warren, 1930); J. H. Leuba, *God or Man?* (Holt, 1933); P. R. Heyl, *The Philosophy of a Scientific Man* (Vanguard Press, 1933); Gabriel Rombotis, "Haydon's Philosophy of Religion and His Method," *The New Humanist,* July-August, 1933; Corliss Lamont, *The Illusion of Immortality* (Putnam, 1935).

On the Church and economic reform, see Ward, *Which Way Religion?* Hutchinson, *The Ordeal of Western Religion;* E. B. Chaffee, *The Protestant Churches and the Industrial Crisis* (Macmillan, 1933).

On the new morality, see D. W. B. Russell, *The Right to Be Happy* (Harper, 1927); Kirchwey, *op. cit.;* Parshley, *op. cit.;* Lippmann, *op. cit.;* E. A. Westermarck, *Ethical Relativity* (Harcourt, Brace, 1932); Ezra Brudno, *Ghosts of Yesterday* (Appleton-Century, 1935).

On nudism, see M. F. Parmelee, *Nudism in Modern Life: The New Gymnosophy* (Knopf, 1931); Julian Strange, *Adventures in Nakedness* (Knopf, 1934).

PHILOSOPHY. On philosophy in the twentieth century, see Cushman, *Beginner's History of Philosophy,* Vol. II, Chap. XIII; Durant, *The Story of Philosophy,* Chaps. X-XI; Riley, *American Thought from Puritanism to Pragmatism;* Einstein and others, *Living Philosophies;* Jones, *op. cit.;* M. C. Otto, *Things and Ideals* (Holt, 1924).

EDUCATION. On recent educational tendencies, see *Recent Social Trends,* Vol. I, Chap. VII; Monroe, *Text-book in the History of Education,* Chap. XIV; Hart, *The Discovery of Intelligence,* Chaps. XXXIII-XXXIV; Washburne, *op. cit.;* Roman, *op. cit.;* Cubberley, *Public Education in the United States;* Kilpatrick, *op. cit.;* H. E. Buchholz, *Fads and Fallacies in Present-Day Education* (Macmillan, 1931); Tugwell and Keyserling, *op. cit.;* W. B. Curry, *Education in a Changing World* (Norton, 1935).

On genetic and child psychology, see G. E. Partridge, *The Genetic Philosophy of Education* (Macmillan, 1912); V. F. Calverton and S. D. Schmalhausen, eds., *The New Generation* (Macaulay, 1930); D. W. B. Russell, *Children: Why Do We Have Them?* (Harper, 1932); Curti, *Child Psychology;* Morgan, *Child Psychology;* Adams, *Your Child Is Normal;* Lorine Pruette, *The Parent and the Happy Child* (Holt, 1932); and *G. Stanley Hall: The Biography of a Mind* (Appleton, 1926).

On the social sciences and social reform in education, see Counts, *op. cit.;* W. H. Kilpatrick, *Education for a Changing Civilization* (Macmillan, 1927); Bertrand Russell, *op. cit.;* C. H. Judd, *Education and Social Progress* (Harcourt, Brace, 1934); H. E. Wilson, *The Fusion of Social Studies in Junior High Schools* (Harvard University Press, 1933); American Historical Association, Commission on Social Studies, *Conclusions and Recommendations* (Scribner, 1934); G. S. Counts, *The Social Foundations of Education* (Scribner, 1934). On the introduction of the social sciences into the schools, see *The Rugg Social Science Course* (Ginn, 1921 *et. seq.,* numerous vols.); Marshall, *The Story of Human Progress;* R. M. Tryon, *The Social Sciences as School Subjects* (Scribner, 1934); C. A. Beard, *A Charter for Social Sciences in the Schools* (Scribner, 1932); Tugwell and L. H. Keyserling, *op. cit.;* Henry Johnson, *Introduction to the History of the Social Sciences in Schools* (Scribner, 1932).

On innovations in American higher education, see Hamilton Holt, *The Rollins College Adventure in Education* (Rollins College, 1928); A. R. M. Stowe, *Modernizing the College* (Crofts, 1926); Alexander Meiklejohn, *The Experimental College* (Harper, 1932); A. E. Morgan, *What Is College For?* (Antioch College, 1930); C. C. Little, *The Awakening College* (Norton, 1930); *Five College Plans*, ed. by J. J. Coss (Columbia University Press, 1931); Marion Talbot, *The Education of Women* (University of Chicago Press, 1910); J. K. Hart, *Education for an Age of Power* (Harper, 1935).

For an incisive criticism of American higher education, see Chap. vii of Ludwig Lewisohn, *Up Stream* (Boni & Liveright, 1923); and for more detail and devastating satire, see T. B. Veblen, *The Higher Learning in America* (Huebsch, 1918).

On adult education and university-extension developments, see Nathaniel Peffer, *New Schools for Older Students* (Macmillan, 1926); Ruth Kotinsky, *Adult Education and the Social Scene* (Appleton-Century, 1933); Hall-Quest, *op. cit.*; J. F. Noffsinger, *Correspondence Schools, Lyceums, Chautauquas* (Macmillan, 1926); W. S. Bittner and H. F. Mallory, *University Teaching by Mail* (Macmillan, 1933). On workers' education, see Marius Hansome, *World Workers' Educational Movements* (Columbia University Press, 1931); O. D. Evans, *Educational Opportunities for Young Workers* (Macmillan, 1926); R. A. Beals, *Aspects of Post-collegiate Education* (American Association for Adult Education, 1935); M. A. Cartwright, *Ten Years of Adult Education* (Macmillan, 1935).

On academic freedom, see Veblen, *op. cit.*; the somewhat colorful books by Sinclair, *The Goose Step* and *The Goslings;* Buchholz, *op. cit.*, Chap. vi.

LITERATURE. On twentieth-century fiction in general, see Brewster and Burrell, *op. cit.*

On twentieth-century English literature, see Brawley, *New Survey of English Literature*, Chap. xix; Legouis and Cazamian, *History of English Literature*, Vol. II, Bk. VII; Cunliffe, *English Literature during the Last Half-Century*, Chaps. vii-xvi; Frank Swinnerton, *The Georgian Scene: A Literary Panorama* (Farrar & Rinehart, 1934); Chaps. xii-xiii of Lewis Ruckow, *Contemporary Political Thought in England* (Macmillan, 1925); Geoffrey West (G. H. Wells), *H. G. Wells* (Norton, 1930); Wells, *Experiment in Autobiography*.

On recent French literature, see Lalou, *Contemporary French Literature;* Wright, *History of French Literature*, Pt. VI; Nitze and Dargan, *History of French Literature*, pp. 723 ff.

On recent Italian literature, see Phelps, *Italian Silhouettes;* Garnett, *History of Italian Literature*, Chap. xxvi.

On recent Spanish literature, see Bell, *Contemporary Spanish Literature;* Mérimée, *History of Spanish Literature*, Pt. VI; L. A. Warren, *Modern Spanish Literature* (London, 1929, 2 vols.); Isaac Goldberg, *Studies in Spanish American Literature* (Brentano's, 1920); J. F. Rippy, "Literary Yankeephobia in Hispanic America," *Journal of International Relations*, January, 1922.

On recent German literature, see Bithell, *Germany*, Chap. viii; Arthur Eloesser, *Modern German Literature* (Knopf, 1933).

On contemporary Scandinavian literature, see Macy, *op. cit.*, Chap. xlvi; Topsöe-Jensen, *Scandinavian Literature*, Chap. iii; Gröndahl and Raknes, *Chapters in Norwegian Literature*, Chaps. xiii-xiv; Jorgenson, *History of Norwegian Literature*, pp. 390 ff.

On recent Russian literature, see Mirsky, *Contemporary Russian Literature;* Freeman, Kunitz, and Lozowick, *Voices of October;* Reavey and Slonim, *Soviet Literature.*

FURTHER REFERENCES

On recent American literature, see Manly and Rickert, *op. cit.;* Calverton, *The Liberation of American Literature;* Hicks, *op. cit.;* Knight, *American Literature and Culture,* Pt. III; Parrington, *Main Currents in American Thought,* Vol. III; Williams, *The American Spirit in Letters;* Blankenship, *American Literature as an Expression of the National Mind,* Chaps. xxii-xxviii; John Erskine in Beard, *A Century of Progress,* pp. 399 ff.; C. C. Van Doren, *The American Novel* (Macmillan, 1921), *Contemporary American Novelists, 1900-1920* (Macmillan, 1922), *Modern American Prose,* and *Sinclair Lewis* (Doubleday, Doran, 1933); *The Smart Set Anthology.*

On literature and the class struggle, see Louis Adamic, "What the Proletariat Reads," *Saturday Review of Literature,* December 1, 1934; Brewster and Burrell, *op. cit.,* Chap. xi; Calverton, *The Liberation of American Literature;* Hicks, *op. cit.;* John Strachey, *Literature and Dialectical Materialism* (Covici, Friede, 1934); Krutch, *op. cit.*

On American periodical literature, see Henri Klein, article "Periodical Literature," Encyclopedia Americana; Benjamin Stolberg, "The Liberal Journalism: A House Divided," *Vanity Fair,* September, 1933; A. de V. Tassin, *The Magazine in America* (Dodd, Mead, 1916); Allen, *op. cit.,* Chap. ix; C. C. Regier, *The Era of the Muckrakers* (University of North Carolina Press, 1932).

On newspapers, see Bickel, *op. cit.;* G. H. Payne, *History of Journalism in the United States* (Appleton, 1920); Lee, *op. cit.;* O. G. Villard, *Some Newspapers and Newspaper-Men* (Knopf, 1923); D. C. Seitz, *Joseph Pulitzer* (Simon & Schuster, 1924); Cochran, *E. W. Scripps;* Winkler, *W. R. Hearst;* F. F. Bond, *Mr. Miller of "The Times"* (Scribner, 1931); J. L. LeB. Hammond, *C. P. Scott of the Manchester Guardian* (Harcourt, Brace, 1934); Tom Clarke, *My Northcliffe Diary* (Cosmopolitan Book Co., 1931); Crawford, *The Ethics of Journalism.*

MODERN ART. Gardner, *op. cit.;* Hammerton, *op. cit.,* Chap. 188; Craven, *Men of Art,* Chap. xx, and *Modern Art;* E. A. Park, *New Backgrounds for a New Age* (Harcourt, Brace, 1927); S. W. Cheney, *Expressionism in Art* (Liveright, 1934); Abbott, *The Great Painters,* Chap. xliii; Clive Bell, *Since Cézanne* (Harcourt, Brace, 1922); Mather, Morey, and Henderson, *The American Spirit in Art;* R. L. Duffus, *The American Renaissance* (Knopf, 1928); W. D. Frank and others, eds., *America and Alfred Stieglitz* (Doubleday, Doran, 1934).

MUSIC. On contemporary music, see Elson, *op. cit.,* pp. 538-68; Bekker, *The Story of Music,* Chap. xx; pp. 191 ff. of Paul Rosenfeld, *Musical Portraits* (Harcourt, Brace, 1920); Dyson, *op. cit.;* Bauer, *op. cit.;* David Ewen, *Composers of Today* (Wilson, 1934).

CULTURAL LAG. J. H. Robinson, *The Humanizing of Knowledge* (2d rev. ed., Doran, 1926); Barnes, *The New History and the Social Sciences,* Chap. x; and *Can Man Be Civilized?;* G. S. Hall, "The Message of the Zeitgeist," *Scientific Monthly,* August, 1921; W. B. Pitkin, *Short Introduction to the History of Human Stupidity* (Simon & Schuster, 1932); F. S. Chapin, *Cultural Change* (Century, 1928); J. K. Folsom, *Culture and Social Progress* (Longmans, 1928); R. B. Fosdick, *The Old Savage in the New Civilization* (Doubleday, Doran, 1928); Lippmann, *op. cit.;* Ogburn, *op. cit.; Recent Social Trends,* Vol. I, Introduction; Randall, *op. cit.;* C. D. Burns, *Modern Civilization on Trial* (Macmillan, 1931); M. C. Otto, *Natural Laws and Human Hopes* (Holt, 1926); Frederick Soddy, ed., *The Frustration of Science* (Norton, 1935).

For splendid expositions of the failure of modern civilization, with all its technological improvements, to increase the sum total of human happiness, see Stuart Chase, "My Great-Great-Grandfather and I," *Nation,* Sept. 1, 1926; and Thomas, *Human Exploitation.*

INDEX

A. B. C. Powers, 543-44
Aaland Islands, 905
Abbott family, 358
Abd-el-Krim, 531
Abd-ul-Hamid, sultan of Turkey, 532
Abel, N. H., 641
Abélard, Pierre, 165, 676
Aben, Ezra, 188, 653
Abercrombie, Patrick, quoted, 412-13
Abolition. *See* Antislavery movement.
Absentee ownership, 295, 371, 434, 629, 781-803 *passim*, 819, 956
Absolute, the, 196, 199, 660, 680, 1067
Absolutism. *See* Church and State; Monarchy, absolute; State, the, absolute.
Abyssinia (Ethiopia), 17 n., 18, 463, 531, 532, 549
Acoustics, 152, 255
Acquapendente, G. F. d', 158
Acre (town), 19
Acta eruditorum, 150
Acton, J. E. E. D. Acton, 1st baron, 676; quoted, 459
Adam, 90, 217
Adam, Robert, 252
Adams, G. B., 672
Adams, J. Q., president of the United States, 860, 924
Adams, John, president of the United States, 134, 187, 270, 468, 857; quoted, 510, 922
Adams family, 358
Addams, Jane, 966
Addison, Joseph, 181, 245
Adler, Felix, 675
Admiralty Islands, 540
Adornment, personal, 32, 45, 251, 568
Adventure, spirit of, 8, 9, 21, 144, 214, 245, 251, 524, 691
Advertising, 63, 447, 724, 746-47, 765, 766, 816-17, 820, 1001, 1054, 1092-93, 1094
Aehrenthal, A. L., count von, 464 n.
Afghanistan, 534, 535, 549
Africa, 8, 19, 21, 25, 27 n., 57, 245, 337, 521, 522, 525, 546, 547, 549, 562, 566, 581, 597, 674; British East, 553; French West, 564; German East, 550-51, 565, 597; German Southwest, 528-29, 550, 553, 565; colonies in, 346-47, 463, 525-32 *passim*, 550-54, 570, 586; birth rate in, 419; trade with, 32, 33, 36, 37, 569. *See also* names of divisions.
Agadir, 531
Agello, Francesco, 742
Agnosticism, 178, 186, 188, 201, 206, 384, 678, 706, 1061, 1062
Agrarian economy, 6, 57, 60, 83, 85, 255, 263-64, 325-66 *passim,* 392, 395, 405, 438, 780, 856, 859 n., 868 n., 870, 873-74, 934, 1102
Agricola, Rudolph (Rodolphus), 241
Agriculture, 51, 78-79, 235, 324, 341-42, 318, 416, 420, 627, 229; progress in, 48-55, 632-36; dry farming in, 365; implements for, 49-50; mechanization of, 363-65, 374, 632, 759, 761-62, 1009, 1016
Agriculture in: Australia, 352; Baltic states, 634; Czechoslovakia, 634-35; Denmark, 347; the East, 334 n.; England, 49-55, 271, 633, 635; Europe, 632-36; France, 54; Germany, 54, 77, 229, 332, 333, 633-34, 635; Holland, 346; Hungary, 634, 635; Italy, 343, 633, 635; Mexico, 636; Prussia, 54; Roman Empire, 759; Rumania, 635; Russia, Soviet, 632-33, 762, 956, 991 n., 997, 999, 1005, 1007-10, 1016, 1027; Spain, 93, 345, 633; the United States, 365-66, 373-75, 515-16, 632, 635-36, 761-62, 824-25, 868 n., (income of) 375; Yugoslavia, 635
Agricultural Revolution, 48-55, 271
Airplanes, 265, 266, 740-41, 767; in the World War, 598, 741. *See also* Aviation.
Alabama, 366, 369
Alaska, 25, 28, 542 n., 545
Albania, 460, 595, 609, 904, 905, 907
Albany (N. Y.), 362; Congress (1754), 130; *Evening Journal*, 1092
Albertus Magnus (Albert of Cologne), 657
Albigenses, 165
Albuquerque, Affonso (Alphonso) da, the Great, 22
Alchemy, 146, 147, 148, 152, 726. *See also* Chemistry.
Alcock, Captain John, 741
Alcoholic liquors: total abstinence from, 678; traffic in, 535, 554, 835; use of, 33, 190, 567. *See also* Prohibition.
Aldrich, W. D., 831
Aleardi, Gaetano Aleardo, count, 699
Alembert, Jean Le Rond d', 151, 185
Alexander III, the Great, King of Macedon, 57
Alexander I, emperor of Russia, 121, 496, 899-900
Alexander II, emperor of Russia, 338, 496, 981-82
Alexander III, emperor of Russia, 128-29, 339, 340, 477, 711, 981
Alexander I, king of Yugoslavia, 907 n.
Alexandra Feodorovna, empress of Russia, 987
Alexandria, 57 n.; population of, 405
Alexius II (Comnenus), Eastern Roman emperor, 12
Alfonso XIII, king of Spain, 497

1117

Algarve, 21
Algebra, 146, 147, 641; Muslim, 147
Algeciras Conference (1906), 531, 544, 581, 900
Algeria, 530, 531, 545, 561
Al-Hazen, 146
Alien law, American, 513, 612
Allegory, 174, 175, 177, 245
Allen, Ethan, 187
Allen, F. E., 436, 918
Allen, William, 914
Allenby, Gen. E. H. H. Allenby, 1st viscount, 597
Allgemeine Elektrizitätsgesellschaft, 336
Almeida, Dom Francisco de, 22
Alsace-Lorraine, 312, 327-29, 332, 461-62, 463, 524, 578-614 *passim*, 628, 699, 751
Altamira y Crevea, Rafael, 1085
Althusius, Johannes, 962
Alvarez Quintero, Serafín and Joaquín, 1085
Amador de los Rios, José, 702
Amalfi, 38
Amalgamated Clothing Workers, 966
Amanullah, Amir of Afghanistan, 534
Ambassadors, Council of, 905
America, 6-8, 23-26, 33, 39, 42, 59, 63, 76; discovery of, 20, 21, 35, 63; trade with, 37. *See also* names of divisions of the Western Hemisphere.
American: Association of University Professors, 446; Civil Liberties Union, 172
American Civil War, 203, 315-16, 401-02, 460, 468, 514, 708, 789; effects of the, 364-68 *passim*, 424, 474, 498, 781, 839
American colonies (British), 24, 27, 34, 36, 130, 134, 166, 213, 214, 223, 239, 422, 467-68, 524, 1092. *See also* American Revolution.
American: culture, (criticized) 698 n., (influenced) 739; dream, 373, 516, 678
American: Federation of Labor, 432, 516, 617, 846, 951, 957; Liberty League, 802 n., 849; *Magazine*, 1092; *Mercury*, 1091; people, 467-68
American Revolution (1775-81), 37, 94, 97, 104-09, 111, 112, 118, 120, 127, 130, 178, 221, 468, 507; causes of the, 27, 34, 98, 468; influence of the, 398, 488, 899
American: system, the (tariff), 358, 513; Telephone and Telegraph Co., 750, 790, 799, 805, 830; Tobacco Co., 781, 791
Amiens, 597
Ammon, Otto, 659
Ampère, A. M., 267, 318, 644
Amsterdam, 38, 71; population of, 213; Bank of, 68
Amur, 537
Anabaptists. *See* Baptist Church.
Anaesthesia, 651, 1048
Anarchism, 395, 510, 516, 679, 914, 953, 962; Philosophical, 222, 396-97, 946-47
Anarchy. *See* Nature, state of.
Anatolia, 533
Anatomy, 145, 148, 153
Anaximander, 656
Ancestor worship, 466, 470

Andalusia, 701, 1085
Andaman Islands, 18
Andersen, H. C., 704
Anderson, Sherwood, 392, 1089
Andler, Charles, quoted, 577
Andreev, L. N., 1088
Angell, Sir Norman, 602
Angoff, Charles, 1091
Angola, 532
Angora, 533
Anisfeld, B. I., 711
Anne, queen of England, 104, 511
Annunzio, Gabriele d', 464 n., 467, 576, 1083
Anschluss (Germany-Austria), 610, 616, 904
Anselm, St., archbishop of, 160
Antares, 1039
Anthony, S. B., 437
Anthropogeography, 149, 571, 650, 1047-48
Anthropology, 153, 181, 572, 667, 1046, 1049, 1059-60; influence of, 666, 673, 1048
Antichrist, 577
Antilles, 24
Anti-Masonic party, American, 512
Antin, Mary, 421
Antioch College, 1076
Anti-Saloon League, 971
Anti-Semitism, 475-78, 945, 1021 n.
Antisepsis, 651, 727, 1048, 1049
Antislavery movement, 398, 401-02, 680, 707, 708, 866
Antokolsky, M. M., 711
Antwerp, 26, 38, 63, 71, 803
Anzengruber, Ludwig, 704
Apollo (god), 655
Apostles' Creed, 170
Apostolic Age, 486
Apprentices, 212, 239, 286, 290, 330, 427; Statute of, 77
Aquinas. *See* Thomas Aquinas, St.
Arabia, 533, 551, 552, 610; trade with, 34
Arabian Nights, 245, 572
Arabic numerals, 146
Arabs, 533, 610; in World War, 597. *See also* Muslims.
Arbitration: industrial, 345, 627, 821, 952; international, 576, 581, 898-928 *passim*, (treaties) 915
Arbuthnot, John, 149, 228
Archaeology, 1060
Archangel, 24
Archimedes, 315
Archipenko, Alexander, 1096
Architecture, 249, 252, 709; American, 711-12, 1096-97; baroque, 252; English, 252; French, 252; Italian, 252-53; rococo, 252; Soviet Russian, 1097; standardization of, 446
Argentina, 469, 543-44, 548, 632, 1085; trade with, 337, 343, 353, 374, 569, 773
Argonne Forest, 597
Ariosto, Lodovico, 86
Aristocracy, form of government, 220, 234, 484, 503, 1102
Aristocracy, social class, 135; landed, 3-4, 42, 49, 52-53, 94-108 *passim*, 125, 131, 132, 214-16, 234, 338, 382, 424-44 *passim*, 468-

INDEX

506 *passim,* 633-35, 690, 958, 981-82; natural, 857; the new, 860. *See also* Lords, feudal; Nobility.
Aristotle, 61, 134, 145 n., 148, 149, 151, 152, 156, 160, 163, 189, 192, 219, 241, 386, 482, 484, 497, 505, 648, 657, 665, 666, 681, 857, 869, 969, 1053, 1057, 1067
Arizona, 846
Arkright, Frank, quoted, 757, 758
Arkwright, Sir Richard, 54, 274-75, 286, 287, 762; machines of, 357
Armaments, modern, 464-65, 467, 569-70, 575, 602, 885, 961; cost of, 892, 894, 912; limitation of, 899 (*see also* Disarmament). *See also* Armies; Navies.
Armat, Thomas, 747
Armenia, Armenians, 597, 906
Armies, 13, 63, 75, 84, 85, 458, 486, 548; American, 599, 912 n.; Belgian, 912 n.; British, 103, 104; French, 576, 584, 588, 602; German, 576, 602, 615; Japanese, 348, 470; Prussian, 464-65; Russian, Soviet (Red), 989, 990, 1020, 1092-93; Russian, tsarist, 88, 576, 584, 986-87, 990; Turkish, 465, 585; World War, 597
Armistice (World War), 594, 597, 606
Arndt, E. M., 702
Arnold, Matthew, 391, 392, 572, 693, 694-95, 932
Art, 91, 92, 192, 196, 199, 233, 244, 247-53, 256, 391, 440, 446-47, 572, 663, 687, 709-12, 1094-97; and industry, 266, 709; baroque, 248, 249; criticism, 184; influence of, 670, 1064-65; mass production in, 1095; medieval, 248, 252; Renaissance, 247-53; rococo, 249, 251; standardization of, 446-47
Arthur, C. A., president of the United States, 498, 888
Articles of Confederation, American (1781), 108, 135
Artillery in the World War, 597-98
Arvin, Newton, 1090
Aryan myth, 465-66, 476-78
As if, philosophy of, 1069
Asbury, Francis, bishop, 204, 674
Ashley, Lord. *See* Shaftesbury, A. A. Cooper.
Ashley, Sir W. J., 66 n.
Asia, 5, 8, 13-23 *passim,* 28, 57, 245, 475, 521, 522, 524, 525, 532, 559, 674; colonies in, 463, 525; emigration from, 421; birth rate in, 419; trade with, 37, 351. *See also* East, the; and names of divisions.
Asia Minor, 11, 14, 16, 20, 337, 463, 542, 549, 609; peoples of, 461
Assemblies, parliamentary, 89, 94-109, 229, 482, 485, 490, 504, 869, 961; American, 132, 134, *see also* United States Congress; Australian, 499; Austrian, 125, 495; Bohemian, 124; British, *see* Parliament, British; East Indian, 535; French, 109-18 *passim,* 121, 135, 326, 487-88, 516-17, 936; German, 516, 935; Hungarian, 123-24; Italian, 510; New Zealand, 499; Philippine, 539; Prussian, 126, 493; Russian, Soviet, *see* Soviets; Russian,

tsarist, 128-29, 496, 981, 983, 985-87; Spanish, 135; tribal, 483-84
Assignats, French, 117
Associated Press, 745
Astrolabe, 31
Astrology, 158, 1048
Astronomy, 144, 147-48, 151-52, 154, 177, 571, 640-41, 644, 658, 663, 664, 1035, 1036-43
Astrophysics, 151-52, 1036-43, 1050-52, 1063
Astruc, Jean, 188, 654
Atheism, 66, 162, 170, 171, 178, 179, 185-206 *passim,* 672, 679, 962, 1020-21
Athenaeum, London, 1091
Athens, 134, 235, 256, 484, 505; population of, 405
Atlantic Monthly, 1091
Atomic: structure, 1043-45; theory, 645; weights, 152, 645
Atwood, C. B., 712
Atwood, H. F., 137
Auenbrugger, Leopold, 153, 650
Augsburg, 67-68
Augustine, St., bishop of Hippo, 158, 160, 169, 676
Austen, Jane, 692
Austin, John, 384, 668 n., 669
Austral Islands, 540
Australasia, 25, 521, 525, 539-42, 545, 560, 561, 610, 943. *See also* names of divisions.
Australia, 374, 436, 471, 499, 540, 551, 553, 568, 597, 632, 773, 868, 879, 952, 958
Austria (since 1918), 138, 499, 609, 610, 611, 616, 634, 868, 869, 905, 906, 943
Austrian Empire, 27-28, 48, 63, 113, 121-36 *passim,* 216, 397-98, 429, 455-65 *passim,* 476, 492-510 *passim,* 530, 580, 583, 584, 628, 636, 900, 943, 945; and the World War, 575-602 *passim,* 615, 626, 628, 900, 909, 986, (reparation payments) 616; population of, 213; trade with, 337; end of, 460
Austrians, 611
Austro-Prussian Wars (1864 and 1866), 88, 330, 460
Autogiro, 741
Autocracy. *See* Dictatorship.
Automobile: industry, 342, 629, 732, 734, (American) 288, 369, 370, 372, 739-40, 749, 753-54, 772, 789, 860, 875; insurance, 795
Automobiles, 265, 266, 440, 738, 739-40, 1005; effects of, 306, 374, 523, 848, 1067; in the World War, 598; power for, 303, 733; speed of, 740; tires for, 734, 735, 739
Autos da fe, 166
Avebury, John Lubbock, baron, 667, 670, 672 n.
Aviation, 740-42, 755, 862, 1007, 1030; for postal service, 746; military, 1007, 1030; speed in, 742. *See also* Airplanes.
Avogadro, Amedeo, count, 152, 645
Ayala, Ramón Pérez de, 1085
Ayala y Herrera, A. L. de, 225
Azorín. *See* Martínez Ruiz, José.
Aztec treasures, 40

Babbitt, Irving, 392, 1056, 1067, 1080
Babel, I. E., 1088

INDEX

Babeuf, F. N. (Gracchus), 168, 237, 433, 955
Babylonia, 57, 65, 306; religion of, 654
Bach, J. S., 253, 254-55, 713, 1097, 1098
Backus, E. B., 1061
Bacon, B. W., 654
Bacon, Francis, baron Verulam, viscount St. Albans, 86, 144 (quoted), 150, 154, 156-59, 172, 184, 189-90, 192, 195, 227, 236, 245, 247, 657, 681, 1068; quoted, 156-57, 248
Bacon, Roger, 146, 156, 157 n., 165, 192, 314, 740
Bacteriology, 647, 651, 1048
Baden, 127, 383
Baer, G. F., quoted, 65
Baer, K. E. von, 647
Baeyer, J. F. W. A. von, 334, 726, 1045
Bagehot, Walter, quoted, 484
Baghdad, 16, 57 n.; population of, 405
Bahama Islands, 23, 543
Bain, Alexander, 384, 648
Bain, H. F., 349-50
Baker, N. D., quoted, 457
Baker, "Cannon-ball," 740
Bakewell, Robert, 50-51, 54
Bakst, Leon, 711
Bakunin, M. A., 946
Balance. See Power, balance of; Trade, balance of.
Baldwin, R. N., 947, 957 n.
Balfour, A. J. Balfour, 1st earl of, 464 n., 465, 609, 633, 956, 964 n.
Balfour Declaration (1917), 609
Balkan: League, 580, 583 n.; peoples, 461
Balkan states, 89, 216, 348, 456, 462, 465, 499, 580, 583-84, 589, 613; in the World War, 595; birth rate in the, 419
Balkan Wars, 585, 593, 616, 900
Ballet, Russian, 711
Ballin, Albert, 337, 476
Balloons, 740
Ballot, secret, 127; Australian, 879, 992; by voting machine, 879
Baltic states and provinces, 14, 89, 608; trade with, 37
Baltimore, 361, 362, 512
Baluchistan, 535
Balzac, Honoré de, 696, 697
Bamberger, Ludwig, 476
Bancroft, George, 94, 466 n., 469, 672
Banat, the, 609
Banknotes. See Money, paper.
Bankruptcy, 824
Banks, banking, 58-72 passim, 215, 264, 269, 294-95, 333, 353, 396, 527, 568, 627, 782-98, 822, 829; branch, 793; coöperative, 948; failures of, 793; international, 787-88, 863; investment, 295, 426, 781-98 passim, 824-34 passim, (control by) 781-850 passim, 874; savings, 230, 787, 803, 1013. See also names of banks.
Banks: American, 294-95, 364, 513, 782-98 passim, 812, 824-34 passim; failures of, 793, 824; legislation on, 792-93; wildcat, 364. See also Federal Reserve system; and names of banks.

Banks, Soviet Russian, 997, 1012-13
Banks Islands, 540
Banville, T. F. de, 697
Baptist Church, 169-70, 204, 486
Bara, Theda, 747
Barbados, 24, 543
Barbarian invasions, 83, 485
Barber, John, 302
Barbusse, Henri, 1080, 1083
Barcelona, 67, 69
Barker, Ernest, 14; quoted, 12, 932, 955
Barnard, G. G., 1096
Barnard, Henry, 684
Barnes, E. W., bishop, 1062 n.
Barnes, H. E., 1058; Knight, M. M., and Flügel, Felix, quoted, 770
Barnett, Rev. S. A., 966
Baroja y Nessi, Pío, 1085
Barometer, 148
Barons, 482; robber, 88
Barrès, Maurice, 464 n., 466, 576, 699
Barrie, Sir J. M., 1082
Barros, Joao de, 245
Barth, C. G., 762 n.
Barton, Bruce, 65, 445
Baruch, B. M., 841
Basedow, J. B., 243
Basel, 344, 478, 625
Basques, 1085
Bastiat, Frédéric, 319, 321, 382, 383, 396
Bastille, 182; fall of the, 112
Bata firm (shoes), 344
Bates, E. S., 172
Baudeau, Nicolas, abbé, 380
Baudelaire, C. P., 697
Bauer, Bruno, 1069
Baumgartners, bankers, 67
Bavaria, 126, 313, 331, 509, 945
Baxter, Rev. Richard, 65
Bayle, Pierre, 150, 155, 162, 170-71, 179-81, 182, 183 n., 247, 673; quoted, 179-80
Baynes, T. S., 674
Bazán, Emilia Pardo, 701
Bazard, Saint-Amand, 393
Beach, A. E., 745
Beaconsfield, Benjamin Disraeli, earl of. See Disraeli, Benjamin.
Beard, C. A., 918, 922, 1058, 1059, 1075, 1078; quoted, 504-05, 839, 887; and Robinson, J. H., quoted, 8, 290
Beauty. See Esthetics.
Beazley, Sir C. R., and Yule, Sir Henry, quoted, 18
Bebel, F. A., 935, 937
Beccaria-Bonesana, Cesare, marquis de, 92, 93, 227, 228 n., 385, 399
Bechuanaland, 532
Beck, J. M., 137, 891
Becker, C. L., 27 n., 185, 1058; quoted, 467, 878
Beckford, William, 245
Becquerel, A. H., 1044
Bedford, Francis Russell, 5th duke of, 51
Beer, Max, quoted, 395
Beers, C. W., 969

INDEX

Beethoven, Ludwig van, 713, 714, 1097
Begas, Reinhold, 711
Behaviorism, 1048
Belfort, 595
Belgium, 93, 121, 122, 130, 135, 136, 368, 390, 408, 460, 528, 551, 553, 554, 618, 917, 919, 936, 943; imports of, 546; and the World War, 595, 596, 626, (debts of) 621, (reparations due) 623, 624, (invasion) 586-94 *passim,* 599, 916; trade with, 337
Bell, A. G., 742
Bell, Andrew, 1070
Bell, Sir Charles, 202
Bellamy, Edward, 394, 708
Bellarmine, R. F. R., cardinal, 169
Belloc, J. H. P., 945, 955, 1056
Belmont, August, & Co., 789
Bely, Andrei (B. N. Bugajev), 1088
Benavente, Jacinto, 1085
Beneš, Edward, 499, 870
Bengal, trade with, 37
Bennett, Arnold, 1081
Bennett, J. G., 1093
Bentham, Jeremy, 154, 191, 200, 218 n., 222, 224-25, 230, 239, 381, 384-85, 399, 401, 408, 666, 668 n., 669, 671, 769, 858, 865, 899, 932, 967 n., 1058
Bentley, A. F., quoted, 502
Benton, T. H., 1096
Benz, C. F., 739
Benzene ring, 334, 645, 726, 1045
Berchtold, Leopold, count von, 591 n.
Berenguer y Fusté, Gen. Damaso, count de Xauen, 497
Bergman, H. F. E., 1087
Bergson, Henri, 682-83
Bering, Vitus, 25
Berkeley, George, bishop, 677
Berkman, Alexander, 947
Berle, A. A., and Means, G. C., 446, 799, 800 n., 801, 802, 823 n., 972; quoted, 796
Berlin, Irving, 1100
Berlin, 126, 150, 242, 331, 687; population of, 405; Conference of (1884-85), 528; Congress of (1878), 534, 900; Treaty of (1878), 477
Berlin and Breslau, Bank of, 68 n.
Berlin-Baghdad Railway, 39, 462, 463, 532-33, 534, 552, 586, 597
Berlioz, Hector, 713
Bernard, St., abbot of Clairvaux, 165
Bernard, Claude, 647
Bernhardi, Friedrich von, 466 n., 576, 577
Bernheim, Hippolyte, 649
Bernier, François, 245
Bernini, G. L., 252-53
Bernoulli (Bernouilli), Daniel, 151, 314, 643
Bernoulli (Bernouilli), Jacques, 151
Bernoulli (Bernouilli), Jean, 151
Bernstein, Eduard, 937
Bernstorff, J. H. E., count von, 600
Berr, Henri, 1058
Berthelot, Philippe, 589, 593
Berthollet, C. L., 152, 644
Berzelius, J. J., baron, 645

Bessarabia, 609, 611, 635
Bessel, F. W., 641
Bessemer, Sir Henry, Bessemer process, 279, 280-82, 315, 331 n., 359, 369, 725
Betelgeuse, 661, 1039
Bethmann-Hollweg, Theobald von, 577, 916 n.
Beyle, M. H. *See* Stendhal, de.
Bhagavad-Gita, 572
Bible, 86, 166, 174, 175, 178, 186, 187, 189, 204, 233, 241, 249, 256, 378, 674-75, 676, 677, 680, 1055, 1060-61, 1069, 1104; higher criticism of the, 188-89, 653-55, 673, 674, 676, 679, 1062. *See also* New Testament; Old Testament.
Bichat, M. F. X., 153, 647
Bickel, K. A., 1093 n.; quoted, 748
Bicycle: industry, 734; tires, 734
Bieberstein. *See* Marschall von Bieberstein.
Bierbaum, O. J., 703
Bierce, Ambrose, 708
Bigelow, Rev. E. V., 65, 1065
Bimetallism, 636
Binet, Alfred, 970
Biology, 146-47, 148-49, 151, 152-53, 159, 571, 640, 646-48, 1035, 1046-47, 1050; and chemistry, 1046; influence of, 650, 666, 667, 689, 860-61, 931, 963-64, 1048
Birmingham: Ala., 369, 749; Eng., 272, 749, (Caucus) 508
Birth control, 416-21, 437, 567, 748, 926, 962, 970, 1023-24, 1067
Bismarck, O. E. L., prince von, 127, 293, 313, 389, 430, 456, 459-60, 462, 464, 465, 476, 493-94, 578-79, 615, 711, 774, 935, 938, 940, 941 (quoted), 964 n.
Bismarck Archipelago, Islands, 540
Bizet, Georges, 714
Björnson, Björnstjerne, 704
Black, Joseph, 152, 267, 271, 300
Black Death, 212
Blackstone, Sir William, 92, 218 n., 230, 384-85
Blake, William, 692
Blakeslee, G. H., quoted, 613
Blanc, (J. J. C.) Louis, 123, 395-96, 934
Blanco-Fombona, Rufino, 1085
Bland case, 847
Blasco Ibañez, Vicente, 1084
Blériot, Louis, 741
Bloch, Ernest, 1099-1100
Block press, 746
Blockade, 54, 596, 599, 628, 632, 990, 1029
Blok, A. A., 1087, 1088
Blood and iron, policy of, 460, 465, 493
Bloody Sunday, Russia, 983-84, 985 n.
Blount, Charles, 175
Blumenbach, J. F., 153
Bluntschli, J. K., 668 n., 901
Boas, Franz, 1060
Boccaccio, Giovanni, 446
Böcklin, Arnold, 710
Bodin, Jean, 149, 218 n., 666; quoted, 90
Boerhaave, Hermann, 148, 149, 153
Boers, Boer Wars, 138, 529, 548, 549, 597
Bogart, E. L., 602; quoted, 601

INDEX

Bohemia, 11, 68, 88, 123, 124, 130, 343, 456, 458, 460
Bohr, N. H. D., 1043-44
Bojer, Johan, 1087
Bolingbroke, Henry St. John, viscount, 176, 181, 507
Bolivia, 40
Bologna, 249
Bolshevik party, Russia, 129, 497, 595, 985-90 passim. *See also* Communist party, Russian.
Bolyai, János (John), 641
Bonald, L. G. A., viscount de, 205, 232-33, 389
Bonaparte, Joseph, king of Spain, 456
Bonaparte, Louis Napoleon. *See* Napoleon III.
Bonbright, J. C., 972; and Means, G. C., quoted, 797
Bondelzwarts rebellion (1921), 554
Bonghi, Ruggiero, 699-700
Bonds and stocks, 71-72
Bonnard, Pierre, 1096
Bonneville de Marsangy, Arnould, 967 n.
Bookkeeping, 63, 68; economy, 69, 295, 573, 816, 972
Bookman, 1091
Books, forbidden. *See* Censorship.
Boot and shoe industry. *See* Shoe industry.
Booth, Bramwell, 678
Booth, Catherine (Mrs. William), 678
Booth, Charles, 291
Booth, William (General), 678
Bootlegging, 835, 971
Borah, W. E., 619, 902, 918
Borchard, E. M., 904, 915 n., 921; quoted, 905
Bordeaux, 38
Borelli, G. A., 149, 159 n.
Borglum, Gutzon, 1096
Borneo, 540
Boring, E. G., 1048
Borodin, A. P., 713
Borodin, M. M., quoted, 1014
Borsig, August, 331
Borsodi, Ralph, 292
Bosanquet, Bernard, 680, 932
Bosnia, 462, 580, 589, 609
Bosporus, 904. *See also* Straits, the, 904
Boss, the political, 409, 500, 872, 874, 879, 881, 882
Bossuet, Jacques Bénigne, bishop, 90, 218, 673
Boston, 69, 362, 914, 966; Latin School, 242
Botany, 146-47, 148-49, 151, 153, 647-48
Botsford, J. B., quoted, 36, 36-37, 60, 72-73, 214-15
Boucher, François, 249, 250, 251
Boucher de Crèvecœur de Perthes, Jacques, 667
Bougainville Islands, 540
Bouglé, Célestin, 939
Boulanger, G. E. J. M., 492
Boulogne Conference (1920), 623
Boulton, Matthew, 301, 314
Bourbon dynasties, 27, 85, 87-88, 121, 206, 236, 251, 389, 491, 497
Bourdelle, E. A., 1096
Bourgeois, X. L., 901, 958
Bourgeoisie. *See* Middle class.
Bourget, P. C. J. 696, 698

Bourse. *See* Exchange.
Bowles, Samuel, 1092, 1094
Bowley, A. L., 973; quoted, 290, 291
Boxer Revolt (1900), 536
Boycotts, 846, 951
Boyd, Ernest, 1090
Boyen, L. H. L. von, 456
Boyle, Robert, 148, 152, 267
Boyve, Edouard de, 948
Bradlaugh, Charles, 679
Bradley, F. H., 680, 932
Bradley, James, 151
Bragg, Sir W. H., 1045; quoted, 1042, 1045
Brahms, Johannes, 713, 715
Brailsford, H. N., quoted, 1030
Brain Trust (Rooseveltian), 840-41, 958
Brameld, T. B. H., 1069
Branca, Giovanni, 299
Brandeis, L. D., 843, 845
Brandenburg, 88
Brandes, G. M. C., 704
Bray, J. F., 395-96
Brazil, 23, 24, 353, 469, 542-44; in the World War, 594; trade with, 34
Brentano, F. C., 1067
Brentano, Lujo, 949 n.
Brest-Litovsk, Treaty of (1918), 595, 990, 1028
Brethren of the Common Life, 241
Bretón de los Herreros, Manuel, 701
Briand, Aristide, 615, 918, 953
Bridgewater, Francis Egerton, 3d duke of, 306
Bridgewater, F. H. Egerton, 8th earl of (*Bridgewater Treatises*), 202-03
Bridgman, P. W., quoted, 1049-50
Brieux, Eugène, 1083
Briggs, Henry, 147
Briggs, Milton, quoted, 290
Bright, John, 320, 382, 383, 490, 944, 957
Brindley, James, 306-07
Brinton, C. C., quoted, 111
Bristol, 38, 60
British Empire, 94, 130, 165, 401, 417, 474, 541. *See also* England; names of Dominions.
Broca, Paul, 667
Brody, Catharine, 1079 n.
Broglie, Louis, prince de, 1043-44
Brook Farm, 394
Brooks, Van Wyck, 1090
Brookwood Labor College, 1077
Brotherhood. *See* Fraternity.
Broun, H. C., 1093
Brown, Lieut. A. W., 741
Brown, Harrison, 918
Brown, Moses, 357
Browning, Robert, 693
Brückner, Eduard, 649, 1047
Brunetière, Ferdinand, 698-99
Bruges, 71
Brunhes, Jean, 1048
Brunner, Heinrich, 670
Brunngraber, Rudolf, 1079 n.
Bruno, Giordano, 168
Brunswick, K. W. F., duke of (manifesto), 113
Brunswick, 121, 241, 687
Brussels Conference (1920), 623

Bryan, W. J., 514, 577, 874, 875, 876, 877, 915, 1062, 1104
Bryant, W. C., 469, 706, 1092
Bryce, James Bryce, viscount, 500, 599-600, 668, 669, 858, 871; quoted, 458, 868
Buat, Gen. E. L., 576
"Bubbles," 42, 65, 72-74, 804
Bucharest, 595; Treaty of (1812), 462
Bücher, Karl, 1059
Buchez, P. J. B., 206, 389, 390, 680, 948
Büchner, Ludwig, 679
Buckle, H. T., 380
Bucovina, 609
Buddhism, 16, 1021
Budget system, governmental, 880, 885-86
Buell, R. L., 553
Buenos Aires, 456
Buffalo, N. Y., 749, 965
Buffon, G. L. L., comte de, 151, 571, 656, 657
Building and loan associations, 948
Bulfinch, Charles, 712
Bulgaria, 460, 462, 589, 609, 610, 612, 635, 868, 905, 962; and the World War, 594, 595, 600, 616, 909
Bulgars, 611
Bullough, James, 276
Bülow, Heinrich, baron von, 319, 383
Bülow, Gen. Karl von, 594
Bunsen, R. W. von, 284, 644, 1037
Bunin, I. A., 1086, 1088
Bureaucracy, 425, 571, 862, 866-67, 884, 981-82; American, 857, 866-67, 889-92; German, 92, 313, 494, 577, 871; Soviet Russian, 1014, 1028. *See also* Civil-service reform and system.
Burgess, J. W., 469, 668 n.
Burke, Edmund, 224, 232-33 (quoted), 234, 384, 670
Burma, 18, 535, 537
Burnham, D. H., 712
Burns, Emile, quoted, 1000
Burritt, Elihu, 914
Burt, W. A., 745
Bury, J. B., quoted, 180, 202
Business: big, 445, 514, 748-52, 850, 944, 974 n.; class. *See* Merchant class; cycles, 64, 817, 836-42, 934
Business enterprise, 10, 60, 72, 79, 131, 139, 143-44, 214, 217, 269, 294-96, 426, 446, 552; and finance capitalism, 822-33; controlled by bankers, 782, 790-91, 860; large-scale, 335, 748-52; theory of, 60, 269, 445, 560, 802, 816-22, 913, 972
Business: ethics, 61-66, 72-73; forms and practices, 63, 68-69, 786, 787-88. *See also* Bookkeeping; unit, 61, 63
Busoni, Ferruccio, 1099
Butler, Joseph, bishop, 202, 203
Butler, N. M., 863, 918, 922; quoted, 838, 1053
Butler, Samuel, 182, 694, 767
Buxton, Sir T. F., 383, 399, 401
Bye, R. T., and Hewett, W. W., quoted, 818-19
By-products, 267, 728, 730-31, 749, 753
Byrd, Admiral R. E., 743

Byron, G. N. G. Byron, 6th baron, 384, 692, 696, 700, 701
Byzantine: culture, 15; Empire, 11-12, 14, 19, 58, (trade with) 45

Caballero, Fernán (C. B. de Faber), 701
Cabell, J. B., 168, 1089
Cabet, Etienne, 394
Cabinet government: American, 436, 511; Australian, 540; English, 104, 506-08
Cables, electric, 318-19. *See also* Telegraph.
Cabot, John, 23, 87
Cabot, Sebastian, 87
Cabot family, 358
Cabral, Pedro Alvarez, 23
Cadet party, Russia, 129, 130
Cádiz, 38
Caesar, Gaius Julius, 522
Cafés (coffeehouses), English, 34, 70
Cahiers, French, 326, 984 n.
Cahorsines (Caursines), bankers, 66
Caillaux, Joseph, 509, 531, 578 n., 581, 582, 584, 585
Calais, 67
Calculus, 145, 147, 159, 641
Calderón, F. G., 1085
Calderon de la Barca, Pedro, 86
Caldwell, E. S., 1089, 1090
Calendar, Egyptian and French revolutionary, 118
Calhoun, J. C., 468, 513, 668, 859 n.
Calicut, 22
California, 24, 435, 846, 881, 956
Caliphates, 16
Calonne, C. A. de, 112
Calverton, V. F., 1090
Calvin, John, 65, 166, 169, 183, 187, 443, 673
Cambon, P. P., 530, 579
Cambrai, 597
Cambridge University, 688
Cameralism. *See* Mercantilism, German.
Camerarius, Joachim, 657
Camerarius, R. J., 149
Camoëns, Luiz Vas de, 86, 245
Camouflage, World War, 598
Campanari, Giuseppe, 715
Campanella, Tommaso, 236
Campanini, Italo, 715
Campbell, Rev. Alexander, 204
Campbell, Sir Malcolm, 740
Canada, 24, 27, 353, 469, 499, 541; Home Bank of, 793; rebellion in (1837), 27; the United States and, 374, 456, 527, 542, 547-48
Canals, 77, 93, 119, 306-11 *passim,* 341, 346, 1005-06; American, 360-61, 362, 468, 781, 824
Canary Islands, 23, 33
Canby, H. S., 1091
Candee, Leverett, 734
Candolle, A. L. P. P. de, 647
Canning, George, 924
Cannon, W. B., 1046
Canova, Antonio, 252, 253
Canton, 22
Cantwell, Robert, 1079 n.

INDEX

Cape Colony, 529
Cape-Cairo Railway, 530, 532, 554
Cape Verde Islands, 22
Capital, 60, 294; commandeered, 627; concentration of, 73, 273, 748-52; increase in, 10, 49, 79, 269, 271, 357, 521-24, 541, 724; lack of, 329. *See also* Capitalism, finance.
Capitalism, 499, 528, 532, 552, 560, 565, 568, 752, 809, 934-36, 957-74 *passim,* 995, 999, 1059, 1065-66; attacked, 385-402, 707-08, (proletarian challenge to) 427-33; 953, 1087; controlled, 347; decline and threatened downfall of, 291, 602, 626, 631, 815, 825-26, 907, 934, 952, 960; defended, 168, 378-85, 667, 707-08, 963-64; development of, 780-84; rise of, 4, 39, 57-66, 143, 217, 263, 475, 506; influence of, 9, 10, 54, 132, 145-46, 168, 191, 216, 223, 270, 319, 424, 527, 550, 562, 573, 670-71, 690-91, 748, 761, 845, 868 n., 873, 913, 1078-79
Capitalism, early (pre-industrial), 46-48, 57-79, 214-15, 275, 285, 486, 780-81
Capitalism, finance, 421, 425, 426-27, 432, 445, 603, 629, 724, 780-850, 913, 1105; influence of, 109, 636, 764, 771, 816-17, 827-33, 972
Capitalism, industrial, 265, 288-89, 378-402, 426, 444-48, 498, 514, 723, 762, 780-81, 820, 828, 849, 972; effects of, 109, 773; rise of, 294-96
Capitalism, monopoly, 296, 374, 425, 432, 780-82, 843-44, 849, 850
Capitalism, "new." *See* Planning, economic.
Capitalism, state, 454, 474, 850, 938 n. *See also* Fascism.
Caporetto, battle of, 596
Capper, Arthur, 918
Capuana, Luigi, 699
Caracci, Agostino and Annibale, 249
Caravaggio, M. A. da, 249
Cardiff, 525
Cardozo, B. N., 843, 1059
Carducci, Giosuè, 466-67, 699
Carelia, 905
Carey, H. C., 383, 386
Carinthia, 68
Carlsbad Decrees, 869
Carron works, 279
Cartography, 146, 149, 571
Carlyle, Thomas, 94, 391, 466 n., 694-95, 704
Carnegie, Andrew, 762, 782, 812, 819, 914
Carnot, L. H., 120
Carnot, S. N. L., 267, 642, 643
Caroline Islands, 538, 540
Carpeaux, J. B., 710
Carpini, John (Giovanni) de Piano, 17, 19
Cartels, 335-36, 749, 771, 772, 840
Carter, J. C., 670
Cartier, Jacques, 24
Cartwright, Edmund, 275-76
Caruso, Enrico, 1100
Casablanca, 531, 581 n.
Casanova de Seingalt, G. J., 446
Casella, Alfredo, 1099
Caste system, 485, 562

Castlereagh, Robert Stewart, viscount (2d marquess of Londonderry), 900 (quoted)
Catalani, Angelica, 715
Catalonia, 345
Cathedrals: American, 1096; English, 252; medieval, 44
Cather, W. S., 1079, 1089
Catherine II, the Great, empress of Russia, 91-93, 131, 496, 923
Catt, C. C., 437
Cattell, J. McK., 970
Cauchy, A. L., 641
Causation, 162, 170 n., 186, 195, 664, 681, 1049-50, 1062-63; social, 859, 866, 1058
Cavendish, Henry, 152, 727
Cavour, Camillo Benso di, count, 125, 456, 459-60, 495
Cecil of Chelwood, E. A. R. Cecil, 1st viscount (Lord Robert), 901
Celebes, 540
Celestial mechanics. *See* Astrophysics.
Cellini, Benvenuto, 447
Celtic myth, 466
Cement, Portland, 347, 349, 735-36
Censorship, 110, 121, 163-68, 172, 184, 204, 471, 748, 1094
Centinel Letters, quoted, 108
Central America, 25, 469, 541, 548; trade with, 33, 34. *See also* names of countries.
Central American Court, 914
Century Magazine, 1091
Cernauti (Czernowitz), 595
Cervantes Saavedra, Miguel de, 86, 245, 700
Cesalpino, Andrea, 149
Ceuta, 21
Ceylon, 18, 734
Cézanne, Paul, 710, 1095, 1097
Chadwick, Sir Edwin, 408
Chaffee, E. B., 1078
Chain stores, 764-66, 860; gifts of, to charity, 812
Chamberlain, Austen, 911
Chamberlain, H. S., 466
Chamberlain, J. P., 918
Chamberlain, John, 1090
Chamberlain, Joseph, 389, 509, 570, 774
Chamberlin, T. C., 1047
Chambers, Robert, 657
Chambers of Commerce, French, 326 n. *See also* United States Chamber of Commerce.
Chancellor, Richard, 24
Channing, W. E., 390, 914
Chaplin, Charlie, 747
Chappe, Claude, I. U. J., and P. F., 318
Charcot, J. M., 649, 652
Chardin, Sir John, 149, 245
Charity: American, 811-13; organizations, 811-12, 965
Charlemagne (Charles the Great), Roman emperor, 522
Charles I, king of England, 100-03
Charles II, king of England, 103
Charles X, king of France, 120-21, 491-92
Charles V, medieval Roman emperor, 87, 255
Charles VI, medieval Roman emperor, 27 n.

INDEX

Charles III, king of Spain, 91, 93
Charles XII, king of Sweden, 88
Charles Albert, King of Sardinia (Piedmont), 125, 495
Charles Louis, archduke of Austria, 464
Charles Martel, king of the Franks, 59
Charles, R. H., 654
Charlevoix, P. F. X. de, 245
Chartist movement, 127, 398, 487, 490, 859 n.
Chase, M. E., 1089
Chase, Stuart, 446, 935 n., 972; quoted, 378-79, 757, 760, 817-18, 825
Chase National Bank, 782, 783, 790-91, 795, 828
Chateaubriand, F. R., viscount de, 205-06, 389, 673, 700
Château-Thierry, 597
Chekhov, A. P., 705-06
Chemical industry, 749; American, 370; German, 332, 333, 334, 336, 749
Chemistry, 146-53 *passim*, 265, 266-67, 325, 571, 640, 643, 644-45, 1035, 1045-46; and agriculture, 51-52, 736, 761; and industry, 522, 726-36; influence of, 284, 632, 647-51 *passim*, 736, 1047, 1067
Chénier, André de, 246
Chéradame, André, 577
Cherep-Spiridovich, Maj.-Gen., count, 478
Chester Concessions (oil), 533
Chesterfield, P. D. Stanhope, 4th earl of, 214, 242
Chesterton, Cecil (A. E.), 945, 1082
Chesterton, G. K., 174, 945, 1056
Cheyne, T. K., 654
Cheyney, E. P., 467
Chicago, 360, 366, 833, 966, 1097; expositions at, 469, 711, 712; party conventions at, 873; University of, 1076
Chicago newspapers: *Daily News,* 1094; *Day-Book,* 1094; *Tribune,* 1092
Chicherin, G. V., 997
Child study, 689, 1070-71
Child labor, 47, 289-90, 292-93, 388, 391, 495, 565, 940-41, 942; American, 498, 845, 944; English, 845; Soviet Russian, 1016
Children: guidance of, 969; protection of, 906, 966; treatment of, 239; state supervision of, 438, 1023
Chile, 353, 469, 543-44, 548, 598
Chillingworth, William, 170
China, 16-24 *passim,* 420-21, 463, 470, 475, 566, 610, 636, 910, 912, 1054; Civil War in, 351, 536; in the World War, 594, 597; open-door policy for, 538; trade with, 20, 22, 37, 44; Republic of, 499; Western intrusion in, 536-37, 542; Westernization of, 559-60; influence of, 31, 32, 34, 251, 256, 572. *See also* Japan and China.
Chinese Revolution (1911-12), 470
Chinghiz (Jenghiz) Khan, Mongol emperor, 16
Chino-Japanese War (1894-95), 536, 538
Chladni, E. F. F., 152, 643
Choate, J. B., quoted, 842
Chopin, F. F., 714
Chosen (Korea), 538, 545

Christian II, king of Denmark, Norway, and Sweden, 1086
Christian: epic, 144, 179-80, 660, 1022, 1062; evidences, 201-03, 673, 679, 685
Christian Science, 677-78
Christianity, 8, 14, 61, 155-207 *passim,* 226, 256, 389-90, 393, 445, 486, 554, 563, 654, 665-66, 672-80, 899-900, 1021-22, 1103; and Islam, 8, 14, 16-17, 88; attacked, 144, 175-76, 228, 229, 477, 678-79, 683, 704; defended, 173-75; persecutions by, 476; societies to promote, 203, 402, 674. *See also* Crusades; Missionaries, Christian; Socialism, Christian; and names of Christian churches.
Chronometer, 31, 45
Chubb, Thomas, 176
Church, Catholic. *See* Roman Catholic Church.
Church and State, 14-15, 89-90, 93, 102, 119, 169-70, 216-17, 223, 238, 473, 505, 679, 945, 984, 1019-20
Church Fathers, 177, 188, 189, 653, 1082
Churchill, W. L. S., 964 n.
Churchill, Winston (novelist), 392, 445 n., 1089
Cicero, Marcus Tullius, 145 n.
Cincinnati, 360
Cid, the (Rodrigo Diaz de Biyar), 700
Circumnavigation of the globe, 21, 23, 24
Cities: early, 213; modern, 283, 780; American, 515; population of, 405-07. *See also* Urbanization; and names of cities.
Cities Service Corporation, 783-84, 796
Citizenship: Athenian, 484; Roman, 484-85
City-planning, 248, 411-14; in Soviet Russia, 1017
City-states, 83; Dutch, 26; Greek, 932; Italian, 5, 8-21 *passim,* 61-62, 66-67, 83, 138, 505, 898
Civilization, modern, 38, 143-207, 263, 522, 725; origins of, 3-8; economic basis of, 443-48; the Orient and, 14, 15, 559-67; the outlook for, 1101-09; the threatened destruction of, 1055, 1057, 1105
Civil-service reform and system, 498, 500, 879, 891. *See also* Bureaucracy.
Clan, 82
Clark, E. W., & Co., 788
Clark, J. B., 1058
Clark, J. M., quoted, 267, 766-67
Clarke, Rev. Samuel, 174
Class conflict, 395, 448; 691, 934, 953-54, 960, 961, 962
Class consciousness, 269, 373, 425 n., 916
Classes, social, 212, 235, 433-34, 444, 448, 483-84, 562, 690-91; English, 52-53, 102; Roman, 484-85. *See also* names of classes.
Claude of Lorraine (Claude Gelée), 250
Clausius, R. J. E., 643
Clay, Henry, 456, 512, 513; tariff (1833), 321; quoted, 358
Clayton, H. De L., Clayton Act (1914), 367, 498, 844, 846
Clearing-houses, 69, 786-87
Clemenceau, Georges, 311, 509, 529, 584, 614 n., 679; quoted, 579
Clemens, S. L. (Mark Twain), 469, 708

INDEX

Clement IV, pope, 17
Clermont, Council of (1095), 12
Cleveland, Grover, president of the United States, 498, 861, 888
Cleveland, O., 366, 944; *Press,* 1093
Clock, pendulum, 148
Clothing, 32, 45; industry, 272, 277, 367; American, 813-14, 818, 819
Clowns' War (Guerre des Bouffons), 254
Coal-mines, 279-80, 292-93, 328-53 *passim,* 416, 769, 771-72, 1003; American, 357, 359, 368-69, 772
Coal: supply, 737; use of, 278, 729, 732, 736
Cobbett, William, 384
Cobden, Richard, Cobdenites, 320-21, 382, 383, 458, 463, 476, 490, 856, 939, 944
Cochin-China, 18
Coffeehouses, English, 34, 70
Cohen, Hermann, 1067
Cohen, M. R., 1068; quoted, 1063
Coinage, international, 906
Coit, Stanton, 966
Coke, Thomas, 49, 51, 52
Coke as fuel, 278
Colbert, J. B., Colbertism, 75, 77, 91, 119, 306
Cole, G. D. H., 945 n., 955; quoted, 448
Colenso, J. W., bishop, 654
Coleridge, S. T., 391, 572, 692, 693
Collective: bargaining, 269, 429, 436, 633, 841, 846, 849. *See also* Labor-unionism; farming. *See* Agriculture in Russia, Soviet.
Collectivism. *See* Communism.
Colleges. *See* Universities and colleges.
Collegia, Roman, 485
Collins, Anthony, 171-72, 174, 175, 188, 247
Colombia, 353, 523, 541, 544
Colonies, 7, 59, 76, 384, 398, 565, 613, 772, 996; population of, 545; trade with, 569-70
Colonies of: Belgium, 346-47, 526, 528, 545, 546, 551; Denmark, 544; England, 26-27, 87, 103, 130, 356, 383, 465, 526, 529-30, 532, 540, 542, 545, 613, 680, 735, 1084. *See also* American colonies (British); France, 24, 26-27, 112, 337, 524, 526, 527, 530-31, 540, 542-43, 545, 550; Germany, 333, 337, 524, 526, 528-29, 540, 544, 570, 772, (disposal of, 1919) 529, 532, 550-54, 610; Holland, 24, 346, 347, 526, 540, 543, 545; Italy, 342, 524, 526, 527, 531, 542, 545, 548, 570; Japan, 545; Portugal, 526, 532, 540, 542, 545, 586; Russia, 524, 545; Spain, 25-27, 100, 344, 455, 532, 541-42, 545; the United States, 524, 526, 539, 540, 542-45
Colonization, 3-13 *passim,* 24-28, 38, 85, 90, 263, 270, 379, 458, 462-65, 524-73 *passim.* *See also* Colonies.
Colpitts, E. H., 743
Columbia University, 625 n., 688; report on economic reconstruction, 820
Columbus, Christopher, 11, 19, 21, 22, 23, 33, 57 n.
Combe, George, 967 n.
Combes, J. L. E., 530
Combinations, 627, 849. *See also* Corporations; Holding companies; Trusts.

Comitatus, Germanic, 485
Commenda, Roman, 61
Commerce, foreign, 3-85 *passim,* 100, 122, 213, 235, 255, 256, 263, 269, 270, 318, 319, 380, 522-71 *passim,* 598, 759, 769, 780, 803; world total of, 523-24, 773; Aegean, 38; American, 349, 365, 372, 527, 537, 541, 773, (colonial) 105; Australian, 773; Austrian, 37; Canadian, 353, 773; Chinese, 349-50; Dutch, 24, 26, 34, 36, 37, 271, 346, 537; Egyptian, 38, 569; English, 24, 26-27, 35-37, 62, 98, 215-16, 271, 272, 337, 569, 598, 769; European, 349, 773; French, 24, 26-27, 35, 37, 54-55, 325, 569; German, 35, 38, 54-55, 77, 333, 336-37, 598, 614; Italian, 9, 37, 342-43; Japanese, 349; Muslim, 20; Portuguese, 25-26, 34; Prussian, 37-38; Russian (Soviet), 999, 1101-12, (tsarist) 524; Spanish, 25-26, 100
Commercial policies, liberalization of, 319-21
Commercial Revolution, 8, 9, 21, 31-48, 94, 780, 842; effects of, 43, 48, 84, 89, 99, 212, 235, 270, 285, 294, 405, 438, 454, 467, 468, 486-88, 489, 506
Commission business, 63
Common Sense, 1091
Commons, J. R., 60 n., 935 n., 939, 1059
Commons, House of, 104, 507-08, 517, 686, 867; supremacy of the, 491
Commonwealth. *See* England, Commonwealth in.
Commune. *See* Paris Commune.
Communication, 3, 10, 35, 38, 63, 83, 86, 152, 267-70, 317-19, 439, 457-58, 503, 736, 738, 742-48; American, 469
Communism, 392, 394, 396, 398, 432, 444, 446, 474, 476, 478, 517, 617, 634, 748, 821, 855, 869, 883, 924, 933-36, 937, 941, 947, 948, 950, 951, 952, 953, 959, 960, 963, 973, 1069; as a religion, 445, 1021-22, 1066; Chinese, 351, 470, 499, 537, 539; the United States and, 842, 846. *See also* Russia, Soviet.
Communist parties: European, 516; French, 509, 516-17; German, 509, 516; Russian, 537, 990, 994-95, 1028, (cleansings, purgings, of) 994, 1021-22. *See also* Bolshevik party.
Community chests, 811-12, 965
Companies, business: chartered, 62, 75, 85, 134, 214; regulated, 62; stock, 64. *See also* Joint-stock companies.
Company of the Indies, 74
Compass, mariner's, 31
Competition: free, 57, 61, 64, 78, 226, 327, 378-79, 385, 428, 444, 630, 751, 837, 840, 849, 860; international, 337, 772-76. *See also* Business enterprise.
Compiègne Forest, 597
Compton, A. H., 1042 n., 1063; quoted, 1044
Comte, Auguste, 193-94, 206, 230, 393, 666, 671, 675, 681, 689, 933, 958, 973
Conciliar Movement, 96, 486, 505, 675
Concordat of 1801, 119, 206
Concrete, uses of, 265, 283, 305, 306, 316, 736
Condillac, Etienne Bonnot de, 244

INDEX

Condorcet, M. J. A. N. Caritat, marquis de, 118, 193, 195, 222, 229-30, 244, 247
Confederation (social group), 82
Congo: Belgian, 528, 546, 565; Free State, 528; French, 527, 531, (population of) 567; trade of the, 546
Congregational Church, 107, 1061
Conklin, E. G., 1063
Conkling, Roscoe, 944
Conneaut Harbor, O., 280
Connecticut, 881
Conrad, Joseph, 525, 572, 1080
Conrad von Hötzendorf, Franz, count, 585 n., 587
Conroy, Jack, 1079
Conscientious objectors, 472, 846-47, 916
Conscription, military, 464
Conservative party, British, 387-89, 508-09, 536, 586, 587-88, 919, 925, 956
Conservatism, 232, 431-32, 514, 517, 633. See also Custom; Traditionalism.
Constable, John, 250
Constant de Rebecque, H. B., 206
Constantine I, the Great, Roman emperor, 169
Constantinople, 11, 147, 394, 462, 478, 582, 585, 616, 904; fall of, 4-5, 21; population of, 405
Constitutional Democratic party (Cadets), 129, 130
Constitutionalism, 136-38, 488
Constitutions, 94, 97, 111, 121, 129, 130, 223, 230, 233, 234, 436, 456, 489, 490, 521, 565, 850; definition of, 132, 218; origins of government by, 131-39; American federal, 98, 106, 108-09, 132-38 *passim*, 224, 228, 400, 444, 488, 510-11, 513, 842, 890, 1102, (Amendments to the) 104, 108, 133, 134-35, 436, 468, 498-99, 834-35, 944, 971, (the Supreme Court and) 842-47; American state, 103, 107, 134-35; Australian, 135, 540; Austrian, 125, 135, 425, 493, 495; Belgian, 121, 135, 136; Dutch, 136; English, 103, 132, 133-34, 135, 228, 233, 234, 487; French, 112-13, 117, 135, 136, 492; German, 136, 313; Greek, 136; Hungarian, 132, 136; Indian, 536; Italian, 135, 136; Latin American, 135, 136; Philippine, 539; Prussian, 126-27, 135, 493; Russian, (Soviet) 132, 136, (tsarist) 92, 128, 985; Sardinian, 135; Spanish, 135, 136, 456, 497; Swiss, 136; Turkish, 136
Consumption, economic, 433, 442
Contemporary Review, 1091
Contract, 64, 69, 132; freedom of, 225, 272, 380, 444, 490, 845, 948-49; importance of, 218; yellow-dog, 846
Conybeare, F. C., 1056
Cook, Captain James, 540
Cook, Waldo, 1094
Cook Islands, 540
Cooke, Jay, & Co., 788-89
Cooley, C. H., 861, 1058
Coolidge, Calvin, president of the United States, 543-44, 601, 827, 828, 863, 874
Coolidge, W. D., 318, 1045

Cooper, Col. H. L., 1004
Cooper, J. F., 469, 706-07
Cooper Union, 1078
Coöperation, 163, 236, 347-48, 389-94 *passim,* 444, 631, 635, 947-48, 957, 958, 966, 990, 998, 1011; intellectual, 906
Copernicus, Nicolaus, 78, 144, 145, 147, 151, 158, 167, 177, 640, 656, 663, 1035, 1037
Copland, Aaron, 1100
Copper money, 39, 41
Copyright, 751
Coquille, Guy, 223
Cordova, population of, 405
Corey, Lewis, 972; quoted, 790-91, 811, 814, 828, 830-31
Corfu, 905
Corn, Indian. See Maize.
Corn Island, 545
Corn Laws, British, 320, 387, 509
Corneille, Pierre, 86, 246
Corners, in speculation, 806
Cornwallis, Charles Cornwallis, 1st marquess, 107
Corot, J. B. C., 709, 711
Corporations, 62, 63, 71, 133, 269, 426, 430, 780; rise of, 295, 748; American, 336 n., 370-72, 629, 749, 781-827 *passim,* 840, 843, (charities, gifts to, by) 812-13, (controlled by bankers) 782-800 *passim,* (reorganization of) 782, 788, 823, (list of billion-dollar) 750. See also Receiverships; Roman, 96, 795
Correggio, 247
Corruption: in government, 110-12, 119, 214-15, 233, 409, 498, 768, 865, 868, 874-94 *passim;* in politics, 708, 835, 872-83, (elections) 835; of the papacy, 15
Cort, Henry, 278-79, 280-81
Corvée, France, 116
Corwin, E. S., quoted, 843
Cosmology, 144, 159, 931. See also Astronomy.
Cosmopolitan, 1092
Cosmopolitanism, 84, 244, 247, 463, 464
Cossa, Pietro, 699
Costa, Joaquín, 1084
Costa Rica, 544, 594, 914
Coster, Lourens Janszoon, 744
Cotte, Robert de, 252
Cotton textile industry. See Textile industries.
Cottonseed products, 728, 730-31, 1045
Coudenhove-Kalergi, R. N., 901
Coughlin, Rev. C. E., 945
Coulomb, C. A. de, 152
Coulter, J. M., 1063
Councils, Church. See also Conciliar Movement; names of Councils.
Counter-Reformation, 165, 166, 240
Counts, G. S., 1075
Courbet, Gustave, 710
Courland, 595
Couzens, James, 831-32 (quoted)
Covarrubias, Miguel, 1096
Cowley, Malcolm, 1090
Cowper, William, 692
Cox, J. M., 875

INDEX

Coyle, D. C., quoted, 757, 826
Crabbe, George, 692
Cracow, Republic of, 121
Cram, R. A., 392, 1096
Cramb, J. A., 466 n., 576
Crane, Jacob, quoted, 1017
Crane, Stephen, 707-08
Cravath, P. D., 823 n.
Credit, 42, 57, 64-69, 79, 264, 269, 294-95, 329, 568; coöperative, 948; in Soviet Russia, 1012; in the United States, 364, 782-825 *passim*
Cremer, W. R., 914
Crile, G. W., 1046
Crime: American, 833-36, 971; Soviet Russian, 1022, 1024; the newspapers and, 1104
Criminology, 967-69, 1102; Soviet Russian, 968, 995, 999, 1024-25. See also Punishment for crime.
Crimean War (1854-56), 340, 462, 534, 549, 579, 616, 900, 986
Crises, financial. See Business Cycle; Depression.
Crispi, Francesco, 464 n., 510, 531
Cristofori, Bartolommeo, 255, 713
Criticism: art, 184; literary, 694-708 *passim*, 1057, 1082, 1083, 1085, 1090, 1091
Croatia, 609
Croats, 124, 169, 461
Croce, Benedetto, 702, 1067, 1069-70, 1083
Croesus, king of Lydia, 60, 686
Crofton, Sir Walter, 967
Crompton, Samuel, 54, 275, 357
Cromwell, Oliver, lord protector of England, 26, 78, 102-03, 129, 134, 166
Crookes, Sir William, 1044
Crowe, Sir E. A., 586, 587 n., 591-92
Crucé, Emeric (Emeric de Lacroix), 222, 898-99
Cruden, R. L., quoted, 754
Crusades, 10-17, 165, 212, 898; influence of the, 5, 8-16, 20, 49, 54, 146; motives of the, 12-13
Cuba: in the World War, 594; the United States and, 541-48 *passim*
Cubism (art), 1095
Cultural lag, 194, 1101-09
Cummings, E. E., 1090
Cunaeus (physics), 152
Curaçao, 24, 543
Curie, M. S. and Pierre, 318, 1044-45
Curti, M. E., quoted, 915-16 n.
Curtis, G. W., 879
Custom, 155, 163, 233, 264, 431, 483, 653, 768, 866; study of, 228
Custozza, battle of, 125
Cutting, Bronson, 539
Cuvier, G. L. C. F. D., baron, 151, 571, 649
Cyprus, Kingdom of, 13 n.
Cyrenaica, 463
Cytology, 646-47, 648
Czechoslovakia, 138, 499, 608, 634-35, 870, 905, 919, 951; World War debts of, 621
Czechs, 124, 458, 460, 461, 608
Czernowitz (Cernauti), 595

Daguerre, L. J. M., 747
Dahn, (J. S.) Felix, 703
Daimler, Gottlieb, 302, 739
Dairying, 346, 347, 352; American, 365
Dalmatia, 609
Dalton, John, 152, 644-45
Damascus, 554
Dampier, William, 245
Dana, C. A., 1092, 1093
Danes, 461
Daniels, G. W., quoted, 273
Danilov, Gen. G. N., 588
Dante Alighieri, 466, 655, 666, 699, 898
Danton, G. J., 113, 183
Danube Commission, 904
Darby, Abraham, 278
Darby, W. E., 898
Dardanelles, 595. See also Straits, the.
Darío, Rubén, 1084, 1085
Dark Ages, 20
Darrow, C. S., 1062
Darrow, F. L., 727, 1045
Darwin, Charles, 203, 571, 647, 648, 656, 657-58, 667, 695, 931, 1046
Darwin, Erasmus, 657
Darwinism, 682; social, 466, 662, 683, 925, 926, 947
Daudet, Alphonse, 698
Daudet, Léon, 466
Davenport, F. M., 205
David, king of Israel, 179
David, F. C., 572
David, J. L., 250, 709
Davidson, Thomas, 937
Davis, Forrest, quoted, 837-38
Davis, J. W., 863, 964 n., 1101
Davis, Jerome, 946 n.; quoted, 1015
Davison, H. P., 831 (quoted)
Davy, Sir Humphry, 51, 279, 284, 642
Dawes, C. G., Dawes Plan, 542, 614-15, 622, 624-25, 626
Dawson, W. H., 335-36
Day, Clive, quoted, 36, 37, 773
Day, J. R., 65, 1065
Dayton, Tenn., 1062, 1104
Deák, Ferencz (Francis), 123
Dean, V. M., quoted, 993
Dearborn, 755; *Independent*, 755
Debs, E. V., 937 n., 959
Debts, foreign, 629. See also Loans, foreign; World War debts.
Decoration, interior, 249, 251, 252
Debussy, Claude, 1097, 1098, 1099; quoted, 1097-98
Declaration of: Independence, 106-07 (quoted), 134, 842; of Pilnitz, 113; of the Rights of Man, 104, 112-13, 115, 133, 433
Deflation. See Depression, financial.
Defoe, Daniel, 171, 245, 246, 1092; quoted, 65
De Forest, Lee, 742, 743
De Forest, R. W., 966
Dehmel, Richard, 703
Deism, 144, 151, 171-207 *passim*, 226, 228 n., 232, 246, 379, 384, 398, 663, 666, 675, 695
Delacroix, F. V. E., 572, 709

INDEX

Delano, F. C., 412
Delcassé, Théophile, 464 n., 530, 584-85, 613
De Leon, Daniel, 937 n.
Delft, 67
Delineator, 1092
Delitzsch, Friedrich, 654
Delius, Frederick, 1099
Dell, Floyd, 1080
Della Quercia, Jacopo, 710
Delphic oracle, 655
Demand (economics), 32, 61, 378
Demartial, Georges, 593, 867
Democracy, 4, 6, 84, 99, 127-38 *passim,* 220, 221, 237, 265, 270, 389, 402, 453-59 *passim,* 472, 503, 504, 550, 570, 668-90 *passim,* 768, 845, 855-94, 931, 973, 983, 1102; origins of, 482-502; and education, 402, 1072-73, 1078-79, 1103; attacked, 695, 698, 705, 961; defended, 482-84, 708, 1089; effect of World War on, 611-13; fundamental assumptions of, 855-59; history of, 483-99; obstacles to, 499-500; outlook for, 870-72, 973-74; weaknesses of, 1055
Democracy: American, 497-99, 668-69; Soviet Russian, 980
Democracy: economic, 490-500 *passim,* 845, 931, (American) 498-99; industrial, 392, 952, 955, 957, 973, 983
Democratic party, American, 487, 498, 512, 513-14, 515, 874-84, 971; early (Republican), 130
Denmark, 88, 390, 544, 608, 936, 948. *See also* Scandinavia.
D'Entrecasteaux Islands, 540
Department stores, 764-65, 766
Dependencies. *See* Colonies.
Deportation from U. S. A., 424
Depression, financial, beginning 1929, 343, 348, 372, 426, 474, 498, 500, 523, 549, 603, 607, 628-29, 636-37, 734, 771, 772, 774, 823, 829, 833, 835, 837-38, 849, 894, 960, 1055
Depressions, financial, 635, 849, 973; early American, 364, 372-73, 837. *See also* Business cycle.
De Quincey, Thomas, 692-93
Derain, André, 1096
Déroulède, Paul, 462, 464 n., 466 n., 576
Descartes, René, 145, 147, 148, 154, 159-60, 172, 192, 664, 1052; quoted, 160
Despotism, 190, 222, 484. *See also* Enlightened Despots.
Despots, Enlightened (Benevolent), 91-94, 454, 488, 494, 495. *See also* names.
Determinism: economic, 448, 570; philosophical, 162, 186; political, 859, 863
Detroit, 359, 366, 414, 749
Deutsche Rundschau, 1091
Devil, the Christian, 156, 171, 177, 180, 583, 600, 654
De Vries, Hugo, 646, 659, 1046
De Wette, W. M. L., 654
Dewey, John, 656, 682, 690, 918, 932, 1053, 1060, 1061, 1068, 1069-70, 1073, 1079, (and Mrs. Dewey) 1071-72; quoted, 1067-68

Dexter, R. C., quoted, 906-07
Diabolism, 652
Dial, 1091
Diaz, Gen. Armando, duke della Vittoria, 596
Diaz de Novaes, Bartholomeu, 21
Dickens, Charles, 391 (quoted), 693-94, 1081
Dickinson, Emily, 707
Dickinson, G. L., quoted, 576
Dictatorship, 884; modern, 136, 436, 474, 497, 499, 500, 517, 612, 695, 855, 868-70, 883-84; of the proletariat, 934. *See also* Fascism; Germany, Nazi; Italy, Fascist; Russia, Soviet.
Diderot, Denis, 92, 111, 151, 184-85, 231 n., 243, 247, 656, 674; quoted, 184
Dieffenbach, A. C., 1061
Dieppe, 38
Diesel, Rudolf, Diesel engines, 302-03, 308 n., 315, 316, 737-38, 741 n., 742
Dietrich, Rev. J. H., 1061; quoted, 163-64
Dietz, David, quoted, 1036, 1037, 1042, 1043, 1043-44
Dillon, Clarence, 782, 831-32 (quoted)
Dillon, Read & Co., 782, 831-32
Dingle, Herbert, 1063
Diplomacy, modern, 444, 464, 470, 550, 569, 578-82; 1912-14, 575, 582-87; secret, 575-76, 922; German, 333, 596
Direct action. *See* Sabotage; Strikes, general.
Directorates, interlocking, 783-84, 789-92, 795, 830
Disarmament, 581, 907, 908-13, 924, 996, 997, 1029, 1092. *See also* Washington (D. C.), Conference on Disarmament.
Disciples of Christ ("Christian" Church), 204
Discounting (banking), 68, 792
Discoveries. *See* Explorations.
Disease: causes of, 409; study of, 906; treatment of, 571, 677. *See also* Medicine.
Diseases: agricultural, 365; industrial, 288; venereal, 571, 970-71, 1026, 1049
Disraeli, Benjamin (earl of Beaconsfield), 388, 463, 490, 508, 529, 534, 535
Dissenters. *See* Nonconformists.
Distribution, mass, 764-66
District of Columbia, budget of the, 885, 893
Diu, battle of, 22
Divorce, 436, 438; in Soviet Russia, 1022
Dix, D. L., 401, 968
Dnieprostroy, 1004
Doane, R. R., 417 n.; quoted, 815
Dobbert, Gerhard, quoted, 999
Dobrorolsky, Gen. S., 590
Dodge, D. L., 914
Doherty, H. L., 783-84, 796
Dollar: commodity, 347-48, 637; compensated, 637
Döllinger, Ignaz von, 676
Domestic system. *See* Putting-out system.
Dominican order, 8, 19
Donatello, 252, 710
Donizetti, Gaetano, 714
Dope traffic, 835, 906
Dorsey, G. A., 656
Dortmund, 414
Dos Passos, John, 1079, 1080, 1089, 1090

Dostoevsky, F. M., 705-06, 1086
Douglas, C. H., 939, 958
Douglas, P. H., 386, 935
Dow, Rev. Lorenzo, 204-05
Dow, Neal, 971
Draconian laws, 167
Drake, Durant, 1061
Drake, E. L., 729
Drake, Sir Francis, 24, 59, 100
Drama, 572: American, 1090; English, 245, 246, 1082; French, 181, 182, 183, 184, 245, 246, 698, 1083; German, 246, 572, 702, 703, 704, 1086; Greek, 655; Italian, 700, 1083-84; Russian, 705, 706, 1088; Scandinavian, 704-05, 1087; Spanish, 700, 701, 1085
Drang nach Osten, 532-33
Draper, J. W. (photography), 747
Draper, J. W. (writer), quoted, 158-59
Dreiser, Theodore, 392, 1079, 1089
Drew, Robinson & Co., 788
Drexel & Co., 789
Dreyfus, Alfred, Dreyfus affair, 476, 492, 698
Driver, S. R., 654
Droysen, J. G., 466 n., 668 n., 672
Drug (dope) traffic, 835, 906
Drugs. *See* Materia medica.
Drummond, Hon. Sir J. E., 903
Drumont, Edouard, 476
Druses, 554
Dryden, John, 245, 246, 255
Dublin, L. I., 418
Dublin, 150, 1081
Dubois, Paul, 710
Dubois, Pierre, 89, 898
Dubois-Reymond, Emil, 647
Duca, I. G., 869
Du Chaillu, P. B., 650
Dudevant, A. L. A. D. *See* Sand, George.
Dudley, Dud, 278
"Due process" of law. *See* Law.
Du Fay, C. F. de C., 152
Duguit, Léon, 1059
Duhm, Bernard, 654
Dukas, Paul, 1099
Dumas, Alexandre, the elder, 696, 697
Dumas, Alexandre, the younger, 698
Dumouriez, Gen. C. F., 114
Dunkirk, 38
Dunlop, J. B., 734, 739
Dunning, W. A., 672; quoted, 229
Duns Scotus, John, 185
Dupont de Nemours, P. S., 379, 380
Dupont-White, C. B., 938
Durant, W. J., 1078; quoted, 94, 181-82, 860, 862
Durfree, James, 357-58
Durham, J. G. Lambton, 1st earl of, 27, 383
Durkheim, Emile, 503, 955, 958, 1058, 1059
Dutch: people, 34, 89; Republic, 138
Dwight, Rev. Louis, 400, 680
Dwight, Timothy, 188
Dyestuffs, 36, 44, 267, 274, 726-27, 728, 1045; German, 333, 334, 727
Dynamics, 148

Earth, age of the, 149, 150, 649, 659
East, E. M., 420-21 (quoted)
East, the, 3-25 *passim*, 57, 83, 164, 199, 337, 431, 470, 475, 525, 546, 547, 562-67, 580, 610, 666; route to the, 6, 19-21; trade with, 8, 9, 13, 32-45 *passim*, 62, 63, 77-78, 568; influence of, 16-25, 143, 251, 252, 572-73, 702, 711
East, the American, 363, 366, 367, 512-13, 801
East Africa: British, 532; German, 529, 530; Portuguese, 532
East India Company: Dutch, 24, 75; English, 24, 34, 59, 62, 75, 77-78, 535; French, 24
East Indian Archipelago. *See* Malaysia.
East Prussia, 14, 461, 595 n., 608
Eastern: Church. *See* Orthodox Eastern (Greek) Church; Roman Empire, *see* Byzantine Empire.
Eclair, L', 1094
Economic development, 4-10, 264-65, 931-74
Economic Liberalism, 9, 111, 134, 235 n., 330, 378-97, 463, 464, 773, 931, 932, 939, 944, 948-49, 960
Economics, 65, 154, 222, 378-97, 431, 443, 572, 667-68, 768, 859 n., 1049, 1058-59; in education, 446; Classical, 79, 387, 476, 663, 667, 934; Historical, 387, 667; institutional, 935, 1059
Eddington, A. S., 160, 1040 n., 1042, 1062, 1063
Eddy, Mary (Baker), 677
Eddy, Sherwood, 619, 946 n., 1066
Edison, T. A., 284, 318, 334, 747, 819
Education, 162, 184, 193, 199, 222, 227, 229, 232, 246, 256, 263, 284, 379, 385, 392, 399, 446, 453, 473, 563; adult, 1078; of girls, 242; of women, 229, 236, 244, 435; labor, 1077-78; professional, 684-88 *passim*, 1076; technical and industrial, 241, 687-88, 1077; vocational, 970; compulsory, 683-84; progressive, 1072; public, 230, 240, 269, 402, 438, 439, 457-58, 683-84, 857-58, 931; the Church and, 110, 241, 683-85, 1065, 1070. *See also* Universities.
Education in: China, 1072; England, 203, 242, 402, 491, 684, 939, 1073; Flanders, 241; France, 110, 118, 120, 241, 402, 684, 1073-74; Germany, 241, 242, 1073; (Nazi) 1073 n.; Greece (ancient), 242; Holland, 172; Italy (Fascist), 1074; Japan, 348; the Orient, 564; Prussia, 92, 402, 684, 931; Russia, (Soviet) 999, 1015-28 *passim*, 1070, 1072, 1073, (tsarist) 339, 981; Spain, 497; the United States, 203, 242, 402, 682, 684-85, 883, 931, 1057, 1068, 1071-73, 1103-04, (finance capitalism and) 833; United States dependencies, 564
Edwards, A. M., quoted, 430
Efficiency, industrial, 752-53, 848. *See also* Scientific management.
Egypt, 17, 14, 83, 306; and England, 463, 529-33 *passim*, 541, 545, 549, 551, 561, 569, 610; and France, 529, 549; trade with, 342; Republic of, 530
Ehrenburg (Erenburg), I. G., 1079 n., 1088

INDEX

Ehrlich, Eugen, 1059
Ehrlich, Paul, 1049
Eichhorn, K. F., 383
Einstein, Albert, 659, 1035, 1036-37, 1044, 1049
Eisenach, 935
Earp, E. L., 946 n.
Elba, 114
Elberfeld-Barmen, 749
El Dorado complex, 525
Eldridge, Seba, 865
Elections, American, 872-82
Electoral College, American, 510-11
Electric eye, 757, 760
Electrical industry, 345, 347, 353, 749; American, 370, 372; German, 333-36 *passim*, 749
Electricity, 152, 158, 267, 318, 342 n., 347, 641, 643, 644, 1044
Electricity, uses of, 724, 725; lighting, 284, 761; medical, 650; power, 268, 299, 302, 303, 315, 316, 325, 347, 351, 353, 414, 439, 629, 736, 737, 739, 761, 1004, 1006; refrigeration, 729, 761; signaling, 318, 738. *See also* Cable; Telegraph; Telephone; Radio.
Electromechanics, 640, 641, 644, 645, 1035, 1036, 1043, 1049, 1062-63
Electrons, 267, 1044
Electrophysics, 152, 318, 643-44, 756
Elgar, Sir Edward, 1100
Eliot, C. W., 668, 686
Eliot, George (Mary Ann Evans, Mrs. Cross), 276 n., 693-94, 759
Eliot, T. S., 1056, 1080
Elizabeth, queen of England, 26, 41, 59, 87, 100, 103, 239, 253
Ellice Islands, 540
Ellis, Havelock, 1060, 1069-70
Ellwood, C. A., 946 n.
Ely, R. T., 946
Emanuel I, the Fortunate, king of Portugal, 22
Embargo Act, American, 358
Embryology, 153, 647
Emerson, Harrington, 762 n.
Emerson, R. W., 391, 469, 707
Emigration, 12, 213-14, 269, 524; character of, 213-14; numbers of, 525-26
Emotionalism, 653, 1083. *See also* Romanticism.
Empedocles, 656
Emperor worship, 1102
Empires, 83, 378
Empiricism, 161
Employer-employee relationship, 133, 264, 268, 269, 286, 289, 427-33, 801. *See also* Labor-unionism.
Employer's liability. *See* Workmen's compensation legislation.
Employment, stabilization of, 813, 837-49 *passim*, 1026
Encyclopedia Americana quoted, 526
Encyclopaedia Britannica, 185, 674
Encyclopaedia of the Social Sciences, 1057
Encyclopedias, 167
Encyclopedists (*Encyclopédie*), 151, 184-85, 674, 1053

Endocrinology, 164, 736, 1046, 1048
Energy (physics), 267, 641-43, 664, 1042-44, 1045. *See also* Relativity.
Enfantin, B. P., 393
Engelbrecht, H. C., and Hanighen, F. C., 913
Engels, Friedrich, 933-35, 1077
Engineering, 147, 265, 283; education, 687
Engineers. *See* Technicians.
Engines: atmospheric, 279, 300-01; internal-combustion, 267, 268, 302-03, 370, 523, 598, 729, 732, 736, 738; oil-burning, 732, 742. *See also* Diesel; steam, 10, 32, 152, 267-86 *passim*, 299-302, 303, 308, 314, 324-28 *passim*, 370, 439, 629, 736-42 *passim*. *See also* Steamships; Turbine.
England, 3, 17, 23-112 *passim*, 120-22, 138, 139, 166-84, 201, 203, 214-16, 230, 235, 238-39, 250, 306-10, 319, 320, 373, 380-554 *passim*, 565, 569, 571, 609-37 *passim*, 672, 675, 678, 735, 746, 771, 774-75, 811, 855, 866-67, 885-87, 900-70 *passim*, 990, 996, 1015, 1059, 1091; Civil War in, 202, 215; Commonwealth in, 102-03, 129, 134, 215, 487; and the World War, 576-602 *passim*, 867, 925, (debts) 619-21, (reparation payments due to) 623. *See also* Versailles, Treaty of; and disarmament, 910-13; exports of, 35-36, 277, 546, 569, 769-70; imports of, 35-36, 546, 772; income and wealth of, 159, 973; national debt of, 894; population of, 212, 416, 418; birth rate in, 419; trade with, 337, 342, 346, 356, 358, 527; Bank of, 68, 215, 788; Church of, 87, 101-07 *passim*, 171, 389-90, 400, 467, 946. *See also* names of monarchs and wars.
English people, 331, 467-68; in France, 119
English revolutions, 4, 87, 94, 97-109 *passim*, 118-31 *passim*, 215, 220, 221, 272, 398, 487, 506
Engrossing, in trade, 295
Engrossing of land. *See* Inclosure.
Enlightenment, the, 92, 162, 230, 242, 255-56
Entail, 107
"Entangling alliances," 922-23
Entente, the Anglo-French, 530, 578, 581. *See also* Triple Entente.
Entrepreneurs, 58, 59, 63, 64, 74, 214, 382, 795-98, 819, 972
Entropy, law of, 1042
Epicurus, Epicureans, 155, 189, 218, 656
Epidemics, 212, 408, 567
Epstein, Abraham, 839-40; quoted, 811-12
Epstein, Jacob, 1096
Equality, 94, 97, 115, 119, 136, 193, 235, 236-37, 398, 402, 454-55, 485, 500, 513, 857-70 *passim*, 973; economic, 433-37 *passim*, 500
Erasmus, Desiderius, 156, 183, 255
Ericsson, John, 315
Eriksson, E. McK., 863; and Schlesinger, A. M., quoted, 864
Eritrea, 463, 531
Ernle, Lord. *See* Prothero, R. E.
Espina de Serna, Concha, 1085
Espronceda, José de, 701
Esquire, 1091

INDEX

Essays, 245, 246; American, 707, 708, 1090; English, 692-93, 694-95, 1082; French, 155-56, 182, 183, 184, 697, 698-99, 1083; Spanish, 1085
Essen, 331, 333
Estabrook, H. D., quoted, 137
Estate tax, 845
Estates, French, 112, 488; General. *See* Assemblies, parliamentary, French.
Esthetics, 156, 190, 197, 226 n., 227, 702, 1060, 1068, 1069-70, 1083, 1090; and materialism, 390-92; influence of, 663, 695, 1057
Estonia, 138, 608, 621, 634
Ethical Culture Society, 675
Ethics, 65, 154, 162, 189-91, 194, 196, 200, 222, 227, 446, 573, 669, 670-72, 675, 1049, 1060, 1067. *See also* Business ethics; Morality.
Ethiopia. *See* Abyssinia.
Ethnology, 572
Eton (school), 242
Eucken, R. C., 680
Euclid, 641, 1037
Eugenics, 420, 659, 963-64
Euler, Leonhard, 151
Europe, 3-6, 39, 415, 454, 691, 883-84; Concert of, 900; emigration from, 421-22, 525-26; influence of imperialism on, 567-73; population of, 269, 416, 524; birth rate in, 419; the United States and, 547-48, 922-24; trade with, 351, 527
Europe: expansion of, 3-28, 463, 486, 521, 562-67; effects of the, 31, 35, 49, 54, 58, 84, 99, 146, 212, 244-45, 251-52, 255-56, 274, 284, 294, 405, 454, 463, 525-26, 565-73
Evans, I. L., quoted, 634
Evolution, doctrine of organic, 200, 203, 466, 571, 646-65 *passim*, 676, 679, 1046-62 *passim*; influence of the, 667, 673, 674, 682, 688, 698
Evolution, social, 197, 221-22, 384, 466, 660-71 *passim*, 683, 689, 925, 926, 933, 947, 1060
Ewart, J. S., quoted, 579
Exchange: produce, 63, 70-71; stock, *see* Stock exchange.
Explorations and discoveries, 3-28, 38, 63, 97, 100, 144-63 *passim*, 263, 438, 486, 521, 525, 528, 640, 650, 690
Explosives, modern, 267, 727, 736; in the World War, 598
Extraterritoriality, 566-67

Faber, Cecilia Böhl de (Fernán Caballero), 701
Fabian Society, 936-37, 1077
Fabius Cunctator (Quintus Fabius Maximus), 937
Factories, 10, 47-48, 79, 128, 265, 268-69, 283, 337, 522, 725, 749, 759, 939. *See also* Factory system.
Factors (agents), 46
Factory legislation, 293, 294, 386, 387-89, 509, 723, 931; American, 944
Factory system, 3, 10, 47-48, 216, 268-69, 275, 285-86, 326-50 *passim*, 356, 357, 416, 421, 522, 723, 781, 940, 942; meaning of the term, 268-69; rise of the, 319, 405-16, 427, 560, 565, 680, 780; main elements in the, 286-94; effects of the, 268, 270, 294-96, 319, 405-16, 427, 560, 565, 680, 780. *See also* Industrial Revolution (first).
Facts and Factors in Economic History, quoted, 359
Faguet, Emile, 668, 698; quoted, 702
Fahrenheit, G. D., 148
Fairbanks, Douglas, Sr., 747
Fairchild, H. P., 423; quoted, 443
Fairs, 63, 66-67
Faith, 161-62, 180, 195, 199-200, 203, 226, 256, 665; Age of, 226
Falkenhayn, Erich von, 595, 596, 597
Falkland Islands, battle of the, 598
Fall River, Mass., 293, 357-58
Fame, desire for, 8
Family, 236, 289, 437-38, 483, 661, 945, 1103; in Soviet Russia, 1022-23; enterprise, 61; founding a, 434
Famine, 12, 560, 567
Fanning Islands, 540
Faraday, Michael, 267, 318, 644, 736
Farmer, M. G., 284
Farmer-Labor party, American, 514, 874
Farrand, Livingstone, 970
Fascism, 136, 168, 454, 474, 499, 500, 517, 850, 855, 869, 883-84, 907, 912 n., 924, 952, 960, 961-62, 973, 1073, 1078, 1094, 1105; meaning of the term, 962; as a religion, 1066; Austrian, 495, 634, 868; Hungarian, 495, 500, 868, 962. *See also* Germany, Nazi; Italy, Fascist.
Fashoda, 530, 549
Fatigue, industrial, 763
Faulkner, H. U., quoted, 361
Fay, S. B., 587; quoted, 581-82
Fear, effects of, 163-64, 472, 1026
Febvre, L. P. V., 1048
Fechner, G. T., 648, 1048
Federal Council of the Churches of Christ, 445
Federal Reserve banks, 68, 786, 792-94, 832-33
Federalist, 108, 504
Federalist party, American, 510, 512-13, 857
Federated American Engineering Societies report on waste in industry, 818-19
Feminism. *See* Women.
Fénelon, François de Salignac, 236, 244
Ferdinand II, the Catholic, king of Aragon, 87
Ferdinand I, emperor of Austria, 125
Ferdinand VII, king of Spain, 700
Ferdinand II, king of the Two Sicilies, 125
Ferguson, Adam, 154, 221-22, 224
Fergusson, Harvey, quoted, 890-91
Fermat, Pierre de, 147
Ferranti, S. Z., 736
Ferreira, Antonio, 86
Ferrero, Guglielmo, 505
Ferry, J. F. C., 120, 492, 509, 570, 684 n.
Fertilization (agriculture), 49, 51-52, 365, 632, 728-29, 736, 761
Fessenden, R. A., 743
Feuchtwanger, Lion, 476, 1086

INDEX

Feudalism, 4, 12-15 *passim*, 54, 59, 82-131 *passim*, 145, 218, 235, 263, 348, 378, 398, 426, 485-87, 488, 494-95, 505, 632, 635, 798, 871, 958; Japanese, 470
Feuerbach, Ludwig, 934
Fez, 531
Fichte, J. G., 197 (quoted), 199, 205, 464, 465
Fictionism (philosophy), 1069
Fiefs. *See* Feudalism.
Field, C. W., 319
Field, Marshall, 762
Fielden, John, 388
Fielding, Henry, 246
Figaro. *See* Larra, M. J. de.
Figgis, J. N., 946, 1059
Fiji Islands, 540
Filmer, Sir Robert, 90, 217, 220
Finance, 3-4, 8, 295. *See also* Capitalism, finance.
Finck, H. T., quoted, 1098
Finland, 129, 138, 436, 462, 608, 634, 905, 936, 971, 972; World War debts of, 621-22
Finney, Ruth, quoted, 791-92
Finns, 460, 461
Firearms, 45-46, 460
Fischer, Emil, 726, 1045
Fisher, S. G., 27 n.
Fisher, H. A. L., quoted, 456
Fishing industry, 48-49, 347
Fiske, John, 27 n., 469, 484, 656, 681
Fitch, A. P., 946 n.
Fitzgerald, F. S., 1080, 1089, 1090
Fitch, John, 314, 315
Fiume, 611
Five Year Plans, Soviet Russia, 762, 998-1002, 1006, 1009, 1014, 1015, 1017
Flanders, 43, 241, 289. *See also* Belgium.
Flaubert, Gustave, 697
Fleming, Sir J. A., 742
Fleming (Flemming), Paul, 86
Fleta, 41
Flick, A. C., quoted, 110, 136
Flint, Robert, quoted, 198, 235
Florence, 60, 67, 125, 253
Florida, 24
Flügel, Felix, Knight, M. M., and Barnes, H. E., quoted, 770
Fluvial (riparian) culture, 38
Flynn, J. T., 446, 823 n., 840-41 (quoted), 972; quoted, 798
Foch, Marshal Ferdinand, 917
Fogazzaro, Antonio, 699-700
Folkmoot, 485
Follett, M. P., 882
Fonseca Bay, 545
Fontane, Theodor, 703
Fontenelle, Bernard le Bovierde, 192
Food: cost of, 418; preservation of, 416. *See also* Refrigeration; supply, 33-34, 212, 374, 416-18; American, 815
Force, Peter, 469
Ford, Henry, Ford Motor Co., 288, 434, 447, 478, 629, 739, 750, 753-54, 761 n., 781, 784, 788, 819, 848-49; quoted, 754; peace ship of, 917

Ford, Bacon & Davis chart, 839
Fordney, J. W., Fordney-McCumber tariff, 775 n.
Foreign policy, 526-27; American, 538, 613, 922-24. *See also* Monroe Doctrine; English, 98, 215, 272, 613; German, 337; Latin American, 543; Russian (tsarist), 88-89
Forel, Auguste, 652
Forestalling, in trade, 295
Formosa, 538, 545
Forsh, O. D., 1088
Forster, E. M., quoted, 182
Fort, Paul, 1082
Fortnightly Review, 1091
Fortune, 1091
Fortunes, private, 57-58, 59-60, 430, 806-16. *See also* Plutocracy.
Forum, 1091
Fosdick, Rev. H. E., 619, 748
Foundations, endowed, 154, 266, 1079
Four Power Pact (1933), 910
Fourier, F. C. M., 393-94, 396, 948
Fourteen Points, Wilson's, 473, 606, 615, 623, 901
Fox, George, 222, 914
Fragonard, J. H., 249, 250
France, Anatole (J. A. Thibault), 392, 1082
France, 14, 17, 23-25, 48, 59, 73-91 *passim*, 99, 105, 112, 125, 131, 135, 136, 172, 179-87, 205-06, 217, 229, 247, 306, 307, 319, 321, 337, 382-40 *passim*, 425, 436-37, 454-94 *passim*, 509, 524, 529-44 *passim*, 561-68 *passim*, 609-22 *passim*, 636, 637, 651, 672, 774, 900-58 *passim*, 970, 996, 1015; Fronde in (1652), 87, 110, 488; Consulate in, 114, 118, 326; Directory in, 114; Provisional Government in (1848), 492; and the World War, 575-603 *passim*, 623, 626, 867, (debts) 620-22, (reparation payments due to) 622. *See also* Versailles, Treaty of; and America, 106, 107, 112, 468, 918-48; and Russia, 339, 341, 530, 578-79, 582-87, 990, 1029, 1030; and disarmament, 910-12; population of, 212, 418; birth rate in, 419; trade with, 337, 527; Bank of, 74, 119. *See also* French; and names of monarchs and wars.
Francis Ferdinand, archduke of Austria, assassination of, 586, 588-89, 590
Francis Joseph, emperor of Austria, 124, 125, 135, 495, 586
Francis, S. W., 745
Franciscan order, 8, 17, 19, 20, 678
Franck, César, 713
Franconia, 1086
Franco-Prussian War, 123, 127, 311, 312, 332, 459, 465, 579, 615 n.
Frank, Waldo, 1090
Frankenstein, 267, 515, 768
Frankfort: Parliament, 126, 493; Treaty of (1819), 582; University of, 1073
Frankfurter, Felix, 1059
Frankfurter Zeitung, 1094
Franklin, Benjamin, 105, 108, 152, 187 (quoted), 314, 318, 736, 1106
Franz, Robert, 715

Fraser, Leon, 625 n.
Fraternity, 94, 115, 130, 454-55, 860, 868, 980
Fraunhofer, Joseph von, 643-44, 1037
Frederick I, elector of Brandenburg, 88
Frederick I, king of Prussia, 89
Frederick II, the Great, king of Prussia, 77, 88, 91-92, 251, 494, 684, 711
Frederick William I, elector of Brandenburg (the Great Elector), 27 n., 37-38, 85-86, 88, 89, 92, 131
Frederick William I, king of Prussia, 88, 113
Frederick William III, king of Prussia, 319
Frederick William IV, king of Prussia, 126-27, 135, 493
Freedom: academic, 446, 1078-79; economic, 215, 272, 319, 860. *See also* Economic Liberalism; religious, 107, 128, 171, 172, 400, 477, 553-54, 1020-21. *See also* Tolerance; of assembly, 110, 123, 128, 472; of publication, 110, 115, 121, 123, 124, 128, 171, 172, 472, 1094. *See also* Censorship; of speech, 103, 110, 115, 128, 472, 612; of thought, 143-207 *passim*, 263, 679, 870. *See also* Liberty.
Free trade, 78-79, 320-21, 330, 380, 382, 383, 386, 509, 568-69, 773-74
Freeman, E. A., 466 n., 484, 672
Freemasonry, 477
Freewill, 186, 197
Freiberg, 241, 687
French, D. C., 711
French: Empire, (First) 114-20, 326, (Second) 123, 697, 698, 950; Republic, (First) 113, 138, 488, (Second) 122-23, 138, (Third) 138, 172, 327, 492, 509, 582, 679, 684, 698, 699
French and Indian War, 27, 105
French Revolution (1789-95), 6, 37, 52, 54, 94, 97, 98-99, 104, 109-20, 127, 135, 178, 183, 193, 195, 206, 221, 228, 229, 232-33, 237, 346, 389, 393, 400, 402, 428, 433, 455-56, 464, 488, 673, 684, 697, 923, 942; influence of, 79, 86, 121, 130, 131, 207, 222, 231-32, 326, 384, 397, 398, 455, 459, 461, 466, 633, 691; Reign of Terror of the, 109, 114, 128, 152. *See also* Fronde; Paris Commune; Revolutions of 1830 and 1848.
French Security Pact (1919), 618, 909
Frescobaldi, Girolamo, 254
Fresnel, A. J., 643
Freud, Sigmund, 652, 969, 1031, 1048
Freycinet, C. L. de S. de, 311
Freytag, Gustav, 702, 703
Frick, H. C., 782
Friends, Society of (Quakers), 170, 182, 222, 390, 398-400, 401, 680, 914
Frobisher, Sir Martin, 100
Froebel, F. W. A., 244, 689, 1070-71
Frontier, American, 99, 204, 363-64, 425 n., 468, 489, 512, 513, 515, 516, 524, 673, 678, 838, 858, 860. *See also* West, the American.
Frost, Robert, 1088-89
Froude, J. A., 466 n., 672, 695
Froude, R. H., 390, 679
Fry, Elizabeth, 400

Fuchs, Leonhard, 149
Fuggers, bankers, 58, 60, 67-68, 71, 780
Fulton, Robert, 314-15
Funck-Brentano, Frantz, 44 n.
Fundamentalism, religious, 674, 1060, 1062, 1064, 1104
Futurism (art), 1095-96

Gabun, 530
Gainsborough, Thomas, 250
Galdós, Benito Perez, 701, 1084
Galen, Claudius, 149
Galicia, 595
Galileo Galilei, 145, 148, 159, 1049
Gall, F. J., 154, 648
Galland, Antoine, 245
Gallego, J. N., 700
Gallipoli, 595
Galloway, G. B., quoted, 739-40
Galsworthy, John, 392, 1080, 1081, 1082
Galton, Sir Francis, 659, 970
Galvani, Luigi, galvanism, 152, 644, 736
Gama, Vasco da, 21-22, 25
Gambetta, Léon, 311, 509
Gambia, 532
Gandhi, Mohandas, 535-36, 572
Ganivet, Angel, 1084, 1085
Gannett press, 746
Gantt, H. L., 762-63
Gapon, Father Georgi, 983-84, 985
Garden cities, 412-13
Gardens, 33, 251. *See also* Landscape gardening.
Gardner, A. P., 466 n.
Gardner, Helen, quoted, 1095
Garibaldi, Giuseppe, 459
Garland, Hamlin, 469
Gary, E. H., 849 n.
Gary, Ind., 749, 798
Gaskell, quoted, 60
Gaslight, 284, 761
Gasoline, 370, 732, 733; engine, *see* Engines, internal-combustion.
Gatty, Harold, 741
Gauguin, Paul, 1095
Gaul, 44 n., 303
Gauss, K. F., 641
Gauthier, abbé, 314
Gautier, Théophile, 572, 696
Gay, John, 250, 254
Gay-Lussac, J. L., 152, 645
Geddes, Patrick, 412, 724
Geikie, James, 649, 1047
Geiser, K. F., 213
Geist, 197, 199
General Electric Co., 790, 830
General Motors Corporation, 750, 784, 790, 805
Geneva, 169, 902, 935; Agreement (1922), 904; Arms Conference (1927), 911, 913; Protocol (1924), 618, 909
Genoa, 18, 19-20, 23, 38, 67, 138
Gens, 82
Gentlemen's Agreement (United States-Japan), 910
Gentili, Alberico, 225

INDEX

Geography, 146, 149, 571, 640, 650, 1047-48; and history, 245
Geology, 146, 149, 153, 649-50, 657, 1047, 1050
Geometry, 145, 147, 159, 641, 1035, 1037; Muslim, 147
George I, king of England, 102, 104, 214, 241, 507
George II, king of England, 507
George III, king of England, 111, 215, 507
George V, king of England, 585
George William, elector of Hanover, 314
George, Henry, 395, 937, 956-57
George, Stefan, 1086
Georgia, 172, 366
Gerard, J. W., 870
German: Empire, (First) 332, 703; (Second) 459, 493; Republic, 313, 494, 499, 950-51; Revolution, 1073. See also Germany.
German Imperial Code, 670
Germanic (Teutonic, Nordic): kingdoms, 485; race, 11, 466; tribes, 82
Germans, 93, 124, 126, 608, 611, 905; as bankers, 58, 60, 67-68
Germany, 14, 26, 27-28, 42, 48, 58, 63, 75-89 passim, 122-27 passim, 136, 183, 197-205 passim, 306-21 passim, 339, 382, 397, 408, 409, 411, 424-25, 456-66 passim, 476, 492-93, 509, 524-47 passim, 565, 570, 571, 610, 616, 633, 636, 672, 676, 680, 774, 868 n., 904, 910, 915, 917, 923, 927, 928, 940-51 passim, 959, 1016; and the World War, 471, 549-54, 576-602 passim, 606-07, 626, 916 n., 980, 986, 987-90. See also Reparation payments and Versailles, Treaty of; and the League of Nations, 907; and the World Court, 904; emigration from, 421; population of, 416, 418; birth rate in, 418; exports of, 336-37, 727, 772; imports of, 337. See also German.
Germany, Nazi, 138, 424, 474, 475, 477, 494, 500, 509, 516, 554, 611, 612, 634, 868, 869, 907, 919, 924, 938, 942, 951, 959, 962, 1029, 1067, 1078; birth rate in, 419; and the League of Nations, 907; and disarmament, 911-13; and religion, 1066
Gershwin, George, 1100
Geullette, 245
Ghibellines, 505
Gibb, H. A. R., quoted, 245
Gibbins, H. de B., 303-04
Gibbon, Edward, 6, 177, 247
Gibbons, James, cardinal, 680, 945
Gibbs, J. W., 266, 318, 643, 645, 1035, 1045
Gibbs, Sir Philip, 1080
Gibraltar, 580
Giddings, F. H., 483, 485, 502-03 (quoted), 668, 689, 1058
Gide, A. P. G., 1083
Gide, Charles, 386, 939, 958
Gierke, O. F., 1059
Giesebrecht, Wilhelm von, 466 n., 672
Giessen, University of, 640, 688
Gil y Carrasco, Enrique, 701
Gilbert, Cass, 1097

Gilbert, Sir Humphrey, 152, 158
Gilbert, S. P., 624
Gilbert, W. S., 714
Gilbert Islands, 540
Gilbreth, F. B., 762-63
Gildmeister, Van Gheel, 869
Gilchrist, P. C., 282; Thomas-Gilchrist process. See Thomas, S. G.
Gilgamesh epic, 655
Gillespie, J. E., quoted, 18-19
Gillis, Rev. J. M., 169
Ginn, Edwin, 914
Giotto, 466
Giprogor, 1017
Girardon, François, 252
Gissing, G. R., 694
Gitlow, Benjamin, 172, 846
Giusti, Giuseppe, 699
Givler, R. C., 1060
Gladstone, W. E., 321, 383, 462, 490, 508, 679
Glands. See Endocrinology.
Glanvil (Glanvil), Joseph, 170
Glasgow, Ellen, 1089
Glass, Carter, Glass-Steagall Act, 794
Glass, 32, 44, 252, 344; stained, 44, 711
Glidden, Carlos, 745
Glory, desire for, 9, 10, 691
Gluck, C. W., 254, 255
Glueck, Bernard, quoted, 968
Gneisenau, August, count, 456
Giacomo, Salvatore di, 1083
Giacosa, Giuseppe, 699-700
Goa, 22
Gobineau, Count J. A. de, 465, 466
God, conceptions of, 65, 144, 150, 151, 155, 160, 173, 177-78, 186, 187, 194-95, 198, 199, 201-02, 226-28, 661, 663-64, 670, 926, 927, 1060-64 passim, 1103
Goddard, H. H., 970
Godfrey, Thomas, 31
Godkin, E. L., 944 n.
Godwin, William, 172, 193, 222, 232, 384, 397, 856
Goethe, J. W. von, 246, 572, 657, 700, 701, 702, 711
Gogh, Vincent van, 1095
Gogol, N. V., 705
Gold, Michael, 448, 1079, 1089, 1090
Gold, 36, 39-43, 58, 63, 546, 568, 837; earmarking, 568; mines, 63, 351, 353; money, 39, 41, 76, 636, 1013; rise in value of, 837; standard, (adopted) 339, 636, (abandoned) 636-37, 793
Gold Coast, 353, 532
Goldman, Emma, 947
Goldsmith, Oliver, 245
Goltz, Kolmar, baron von der, 465, 466 n.
Gómara. See Lopez de Gomara, Francisco.
Gomez, Diego (Diogo), 22
Gompers, Samuel, 516, 951-52
Goodrich, B. F., 734
Goodyear, Charles, and inventions, 367, 733-34
Gordon, Gen. C. G. ("Chinese"), 530
Gore, Charles, bishop, 946
Goremykin, I. L., 129

Gorki, Maxim (A. M. Pyeshkov), 1086, 1088
Gosnell, H. F., 863
Gotha, 935
Göttingen, University of, 240
Gough, J. B., 971
Gourmont, Rémy de, 1083
Gournay, J. C. M. V., 380
Government: origins of, 94-103, 135, 221; municipal, 102, 230, 409-11, (expenditures for) 894; representative, 3-4, 84, 90, 95, 107, 113, 114, 139, 263, 271-72, 482-508 *passim,* 561, 865, 869, 872, 878, 883, 954, 980, 1102, (tendency to abandon) 136, 961-62. *See also* Constitutions.
Government control (economic), 41, 42-43, 74-79, 96, 118, 132-33, 215, 310, 341, 347-48, 379, 396, 411, 425, 444, 626-27, 752, 850, 856, 860, 862, 871; in the United States, 367, 375, 627, 766, 846, 860. *See also* New Deal. *See also* Germany, Nazi; Italy, Fascist; Planning, economic; Russia, Soviet.
Government ownership, 307, 311, 312-13, 334, 341, 342, 343, 347, 350, 353, 411, 862. *See also* Communism; Socialism.
Goya y Lucientes, Francisco, 250
Gracchus, Gaius and Tiberius Sempronius, 484-85, 505
Grand Remonstrance, England, 102
Granger movement, 373, 514, 516, 948
Grant, U. S., president of the United States, 498, 543, 877, 879
Gras, N. S. B., quoted, 53
Grattan, C. H., 867, 1057 n.
Grave, Jean, 947
Gravitation, laws of, 145, 148, 152, 1036-37, 1049
Gray, Elisha, 152, 742
Gray, G. W., quoted, 1050
Gray, John, 395-96
Gray, Judd, 1104
Great Atlantic and Pacific Tea Company, 764-65, 785
Great Britain, 136; emigration from, 421; income of, 59, 523. For other references *see* England.
Great Elector. *See* Frederick William I.
Greece, ancient, 26, 57, 60, 83, 138, 143, 164, 191-92, 199, 226, 285, 431, 484, 505, 655, 898; influence of, 4, 146, 147, 256, 485, 665, 666, 693, 695, 1067. *See also* Greek.
Greece, modern, 136, 460, 462, 533, 609, 610, 612, 616, 868, 905; and the World War, 594, 600, (reparation payments due to) 623. *See also* Greek.
Greek: Church. *See* Orthodox Eastern (Greek) Church; language, 154, 240, 241, 242; literature. *See* Humanism (Renaissance).
Greek War of Independence (1827), 534; influence of, 572, 696
Greeks, modern, 462, 906
Greeley, Horace, 1092
Green, T. H., 680, 932
Green, William, 951
Greenback party; American, 373, 514, 516
Greenland, 73

Greenough, Horatio, 711
Grenville, George, 105
Gretton, R. H., quoted, 215
Grévy, F. P. J., president of France, 492
Grew, Nehemiah, 148
Grey of Fallodon, Edward Grey 1st viscount (Sir Edward), 462, 579-80, 583, 585-86, 587 n., 591-92, 900; quoted, 588
Griesinger, J. A., baron von, 587
Griffith, D. W., 747
Grillparzer, Franz, 703
Grimm, J. L. C. and W. C., 197
Groot, Gerhard, 241
Grosz, George, 1096
Grote, George, 384
Grotius, Hugo (Huig van Groot), 219, 225, 669, 898-99
Grove, Sir W. R., 284, 642
Guadeloupe, 24, 543
Guam, 539, 545
Guantanamo, 545
Guatemala, 544; in the World War, 594
Guelphs, 505
Guericke, Otto von, 148, 152
Guerre des Bouffons, 254
Guesde, J. B., 936
Guggenheim Brothers, 875
Guianas, the, 542-43
Guicciardini, Francesco, 86
Guild State, 869, 961-62
Guild system, 42, 44, 46, 47, 48, 58, 61, 77, 79, 118, 212, 215, 238, 264, 268, 270, 285, 286, 289, 324, 325-27, 329-30, 383, 427, 780, 949, 951
Guilford, Frederick North, 2d earl of. *See* North, Lord.
Guinea, 532
Guizot, F. P. G., 122, 382, 383, 466 n., 684
Gumplowicz, Ludwig, 466, 667, 933, 1059
Gunpowder, 45-46; smokeless, 460
Guns, 460, 597-98; machine, 460, 597
Gustavus II, Adolphus, king of Sweden, 88
Gustavus III, king of Sweden, 93
Gutenberg, Johann, 744

Haas, Wilhelm, 648
Habit, 164, 264, 653, 866
Hadley, John, 31
Haeckel, E. H., 647, 653, 658, 679, 682
Haggard, (H.) Rider, 572
Hague, The, 914-15, 935; Conferences, 578, 581, 914-15; Tribunal, 531, 581 n., 903, 914-15
Haines, C. G., 669
Haiti, 541-47 *passim,* 554; in the World War, 594
Hakluyt, Richard, 149, 245
Haldane, J. S., 1068 n.
Haldane, J. B. S., 1068
Haldane, R. B. H., viscount, 585
Hale, E. E., 914
Hale, G. E., quoted, 267, 727
Hall, C. M., 152
Hall, Charles, 395, 955

INDEX

Hall, G. S., 203, 244, 648, 688, 689, 1070-71; quoted, 957
Hall, James, 649
Hall, Joseph, 278-79
Hall, Thomas, 745
Halle, University of, 240-41
Haller, Albrecht von, 153
Haller, K. L. von, 232, 234
Hals, Frans, 249
Hamburg, 948; Bank of, 68 n.; University of, 1073
Hamilton, Alexander, 98, 108, 468, 512-13, 773-74, 806
Hamilton, Anthony (Antoine), 245
Hamilton, W. H., 386, 935 n., 939; quoted, 132, 136
Hammond, Barbara, 1058, 1059; and J. L. LeB., quoted, 287
Hammond, J. L. LeB., 60 n., 935 n., 1058, 1059; and Barbara, quoted, 287
Hammurabi, Code of, 655, 670
Hampden, John, 101
Hamsun, Knut, 1087
Handel, G. F., 253, 255, 713, 1097
Hankins, F. H., quoted, 471-73
Hann, Julius, 1047
Hanna, M. A., 875, 944
Hanotaux, A. A. G., 583
Hanover, 121, 126, 312
Hanoverian dynasty, 104, 241, 507
Hardenberg, K. A., prince von, 120, 329, 383, 492, 632
Hapgood, W. P., 849 n.
Hapsburg dynasty, 26, 27, 91, 123, 458. See also Austrian Empire; and names of Hapsburg monarchs.
Harding, W. G., president of the United States, 873, 875
Hardy, Thomas, 694, 708, 1089
Hargreaves, James, 54, 266, 274, 275
Harkness, E. L., 812
Harlan, J. M., 843
Harley, Robert, 1st earl of Oxford, 507
Harlow, S. R., 946 n., 1066
Harmon, A. L., 1097
Harnack, Adolf von, 674
Harper's Magazine, 1091
Harrington, James, 236
Harris, Frank, 1080
Harris, J. P., quoted, 876
Harris, William, 508
Harrison, Benjamin, president of the United States, 543, 888
Harrison, Frederic, 675
Harrison, John, 31
Harrison, Pat (Byron Patton), 862
Hartwig, Nicholas von, 588-89
Harvard, John, 711
Harvard University, 686, 688
Harvey, G. C., 873, 959
Harvey, William, 148, 158, 159
Harvey-Gibson, R. J., quoted, 642
Hastings, Warren, 214
Hauff, Wilhelm, 703
Hauptmann, Gerhart, 276 n., 704

Haussmann, G. E., baron, 411
Havas News Agency, 745
Hawaii, 539, 540, 542, 545, 564
Hawes, H. B., 539
Hawkins, Sir John, 100
Hawley, W. C., Hawley-Smoot tariff (1930), 774, 775 n.
Hawthorne, Nathaniel, 469, 707
Haydn, F. J., 255, 713, 1097
Haydon, A. E., 1061
Hayes, C. J. H., 453 n.; quoted, 454, 455, 457-58
Hayes, R. B., president of the United States, 498
Hayne, R. Y., 468
Hazen, C. D., quoted, 461-62
Hazlitt, William, 692
Headlam, S. D., 937
Health, public, 230, 385, 408-09, 416, 862, 906, 981, 1025-27; legislation, 401
Heard, Gerald, 182
Hearst, W. R., Hearst press, 746, 911, 980 n., 1093
Heat (physics), 267, 271, 300, 318, 641-43, 1042
Heating plants, 732
Heaven, Christian, 12, 192, 654
Hebbel, C. F., 703
Hebrew religion, 16, 177, 191-92, 654-55, 677, 698, 1021, 1061. See also Bible.
Hebrews, 63, 117, 609-10, 698, 1103; as financiers, 66, 475, 477; in Soviet Russia, 1021; persecution of, 26, 165-66, 400, 982. See also Anti-Semitism.
Hebrides, 525
Hecht, Ben, 1080
Hecker, J. J., 242
Hedley, William, 308
Hedonism, 190, 201, 216, 385
Hegel, G. W. F., 199 (quoted), 392, 484, 680, 932, 934, 1067
Heidenstam, Verner von, 1087
Heine, Heinrich, 702
Heisenberg, Werner, 1044, 1049-50
Hejaz, 533
Hell, Christian, 165, 205, 563, 654
Hellenistic culture, 143, 146
Helmholtz, H. L. F., von, 151, 203, 267, 642
Helvétius, C. A., 111, 155, 190, 193, 227, 230, 243, 247, 385 n., 666
Hemingway, Ernest, 1090
Henderson, C. R., 946 n.
Hennell, Henry, 1045
Henry VII, king of England, 23, 85, 86-87
Henry VIII, king of England, 59, 87, 235, 238, 253
Henry IV (of Navarre), king of France, 85, 87-88, 110
Henry of Portugal, the Navigator, duke of Viseu, 21-22
Henry IV, medieval Roman emperor, 12
Henry, Patrick, 105, 1101
Hentsch, Lieut.-Col. Richard, 594
Herbart, J. F., 243-44, 689
Heraclitus, 656

Herbert, Victor, 1100
Herbert of Cherbury, Edward Herbert, baron, 174-75
Hercegovina, 580, 609
Herd, instinct of the, 163-64, 457, 461
Herder, J. G. von, 149, 193, 196-97, 572
Heredity, 646, 656, 657-59, 1046. *See also* Evolution, doctrine of organic.
Herero Revolt, 565, 568
Heresy, 63, 163-68, 172, 566
Hergesheimer, Joseph, 1089
Herndon, Angelo, 172
Hero of Alexandria, 299, 302
Herodotus, 221, 655
Herrera y Tordesillas, Antonio de, 245
Herrick, M. T., 873
Herrick, Robert, 1089
Herring, E. P., quoted, 878
Herriot, Edouard, 554
Herron, G. D., 946
Herschel, Sir F. W., 152
Herskovits, M. J., and Willey, M. M., **quoted**, 432
Hertz, H. R., 267, 318, 642, 643, 742
Herzl, Theodor, 478
Hesiod, 655
Hesse-Cassel, 121, 312
Hessians, 111
Hewett, W. W., and Bye, R. T., quoted, 818-19
Heyse, P. J. L. von, 703
Hitze, Franz, 389, 945, 955
Hicks, Granville, 1090
Highland Society, 52
Highs, Thomas, 275
Highwaymen, 303
Hijacking, 835, 971
Hildebrand, Bruno, 387
Hill, J. J., 762
Hill, Sir Rowland, 746
Hindemith, Paul, 1099
Hindenburg, Marshal Paul von, president of the German Republic, 494, 595, 596, 986
Hindenburg Line (World War), 598
Hindus, 536, 572
Hipparchus, 149
Hippocrates, 149, 652
History, 1049; influence of, 217; philosophy of, 197, 198, 199; writing, 182, 245, 246, 247, 466, 469, 672, 695, 697, 702, 703, 705, 1057-58, 1085
Hitchcock, G. M., 902
Hitler, Adolf, 425, 474, 477, 494, 516, 554, 607, 612, 634, 907, 912-13, 924, 942, 951, 959, 962, 1066. *See also* Germany, Nazi.
Hobbes, Thomas, 90, 161, 188, 190, 218-21, 223, 245, 385 n., 654, 669
Hobhouse, L. T., 500, 526, 529, 570, 668, 932, 933, 939, 961, 1058
Hobson, J. A., 58 n., 60 n., 386, 529, 935 n., 939, 1059; quoted, 550
Hobson, S. G., 955
Hodder, Edwin, 293
Hodgskin, Thomas, 395-96
Höffding, Harald, quoted, 186
Hofmannsthal, Hugo von, 714, 1086

Hofmeister, W. F. B., 648
Hogan, C. H., 308 n.
Hogarth, William, 250
Hohenzollern dynasty, 88, 494
Holbach, P. H. D., baron d', 185-87, 190, 202, 247, 672
Holcombe, A. N., 884; quoted, 515
Holding companies, 269, 335-36, 426, 749, 751-52; American, 336 n., 367, 371, 781, 789-800 *passim,* 826, 827, 829
Holland, T. E., 669
Holland, 23-25, 35, 68, 83, 86, 87, 89, 121, 129, 136, 172, 179, 400, 534, 540, 636, 869, 935; trade with, 337
Holmes, Rev. J. H., 918, 1061
Holmes, O. W., Sr., 651, 708, 1083
Holmes, O. W., Jr., 444, 843, 846
Holst, G. T., 1099
Holst, H. E., von, 469
Holstein, Friedrich von, baron, 578
Holt, Hamilton, 901
Holy Alliance (1815), 900
Holy Roman Empire. *See* Roman Empire, medieval.
Holyoake, C. J., 679
Holz, Arno, 704
Homer, Louise, 1100
Homer, 236, 655, 702
Honduras, 542-44, 594
Hongkong, 537
Hoogh (Hooch), Pieter de, 249
Hook, Sidney, 1069
Hooke, Robert, 148, 149, 150, 643
Hooker, Richard, 219
Hoover, Herbert, president of the United States, 523, 539, 622, 625, 818, 833, 863, 873, 875, 911, 919, 971, 972, 1101. *See also* Moratorium.
Hopkins, Mark, 203
Horrocks, John, 276
Horthy, Nikolaus de Nagybánya, 634
Hospitalers, Knights, 14
Hottentots, 568
Houdon, J. A., 252
Hound and Horn, 1091
Hourwich, I. A., 423
House, Col. E. M., 596
House furnishing, 32-33, 44-45, 251
House of Solomon, 150, 158, 236
Housing, 32-33, 289, 390, 391, 408, 415, 495, 943, 968; in Soviet Russia, 999, 1017
Howard, Ebenezer, 412
Howard, John, 400
Howard, R. W., 596, 1094
Howe, Elias (sewing machine), 277, 360, 367
Howells, W. D., 469, 707-08
Huber, V. A., 948
Hudson, Henry, 24
Hudson, M. O., 903
Hudson's Bay Company, 75
Hughes, C. E., 622, 624, 875, 904, 910
Hughes, Thomas, 390
Hugo, V. M., 572, 695-96, 697, 702, **1082**
Huguenots, 37, 89
Hull, Cordell, 474, 552

INDEX

Hulls (Hull), Jonathan, 314
Humanism: New, 392, 1056-57, 1067, 1069, 1080; philosophical, 663; religious, 1056, 1061-62; Renaissance, 5, 144, 145, 154, 156, 159, 226, 240, 242, 244, 245-46, 256, 685, 690, 709, 1054, 1074, 1103
Humanitarianism, 391, 692, 693-94, 695, 696, 868, 964-72, 1056; rise of, 398-402
Humboldt, F. H. A., baron von, 571, 650, 684
Humboldt, K. W. von, 383
Hume, David, 154, 162-63, 170 n., 177, 190, 195, 201-02, 221-22, 227, 230-31 (quoted), 247, 385 n., 664
Hume, Joseph, 381, 385, 429, 491, 650, 949
Humor: in literature, 692, 698, 708, 1087, 1091; sense of, 169
Hundred Years' War, 85
Huneker, J. G., 1090; quoted, 1099
Hungary, 11, 16, 123-25, 130, 131, 136, 424-25, 444, 456, 458, 461-62, 474, 495, 609, 610, 612, 616, 634, 868, 905, 906, 907 n., 958, 961, 962; and the World War, 595-96, 909, (debts) 621
Hunt, R. M., 712
Hunt, W. H., 709
Hunter, John, 153
Hupfeld, Hermann, 654
Hurst, C. J. B., 901
Huskisson, William, 320, 383
Husserl, Edmund, 1067
Hussey, Obed, 363
Hutcheson, Francis, 230, 385
Hutten, Ulrich von, 86, 144
Hutton, James, 153, 649
Huxley, A. L., 182, 1080, 1081
Huxley, T. H., 172, 571, 648, 653, 658, 667, 671, 678-79, 695; quoted, 686-87
Huygens (Huyghens), Christian, 148, 302, 643, 648
Hyndman, H. M., 937
Hythe Conference (1920), 623

Ibañez, Vicente Blasco, 1084
Ibn Battuta, 19
Ibn Khaldun, 221
Ibn Saud, king of the Hejaz, 533
Ibsen, Henrik, 700, 703, 705, 1083, 1087
Idealism: philosophical, 195-200, 206, 660, 680-83, 696, 932, 1067; social, 64, 707
Identification, psychological, 431-32, 802-03
Ilgen, K. D., 188, 654
Ilin, M. (I. I. Marshak), 1004
Illegitimacy, 239, 291, 1022-24, 1081
Illinois, 876
Illiteracy, 438, 564, 1018-19
Illumination. *See* Lighting.
Immigration, 421-24; to Australasia, 471; to England, 273; to South America, 421; to the United States, 357, 364, 366-67, 421-24, 468, 525-26, 910, (character of) 422, 869, (in colonial period) 213-14; oriental, 613, 910
Immortality, belief in, 4, 164-65, 173, 175, 256, 663, 674, 683, 1060
Imperialism, 8, 9, 10, 265, 270, 337, 349, 453, 458, 463, 521-54, 616, 693, 772, 832, 926, 934, 996; the World War and, 549-50, 586; influence of, on modern civilization, 559-73, 913, 925
Impressionism: in art, 710, 711, 1095; in literature, 699; in music, 1100
Inca treasures, 40
Inclosure of land, 51-53, 54, 204, 238, 239, 271, 289, 632, 759
Income, social (national), 79, 825, 835; distribution of the, 237, 380-81, 394, 397, 418, 420, 425, 849, 945, (American) 372-74, 375, 417 n., 806-11, 820
Income tax: American, 813, 842, 845; French, 116; Soviet Russian, 1013. *See also* Income, social (national), distribution of.
Independence, political, 456-62 *passim*
Index of Forbidden Books, Church, 167, 676, 700
India, 17 n., 18-35 *passim*, 374, 466, 559, 564, 636, 734, 912, 1054; and England, 25, 27, 353, 474, 533, 534-36, 546, 547, 565, 569, 610; religion of, 654; routes to, 4, 9, 22-24, 63, 463; trade with, 27 n., 36, 43, 337, 546
Indiana, 363 n.; prison system, 401
Indianapolis, 849 n.
Indians, American, 82, 105, 251, 423, 541, 567, 707, 858, 889
Individualism, 78, 224-25, 378-84, 393, 397, 486, 631, 663, 690-91, 705, 712, 768, 849, 856, 860, 944, 959, 963-64, 980, 1105
Indo-China, 463, 527, 537
Indulgences, Church, 15
Industrial class. *See* Proletariat.
Industrial Revolution (first), 6, 32, 35, 37, 48, 79, 94, 122, 130, 235, 264, 266-67, 287, 306, 319, 324-53, 379, 386, 723, 726, 744, 759, 760, 767, 771, 773, 795-96, 931, 1059; meaning of the term, 10, 267-68; nature and significance of, 267-70; effects of the, 9, 10, 79, 86, 213, 239, 269-70, 303, 316, 383, 391-463 *passim*, 489-93, 496, 521-23, 560, 666, 673, 712, 780, 806, 878, 972, 982
Industrial Revolution (first) in: England, 37, 43, 48, 49, 53, 54, 204, 229, 270-77, 307, 321, 324, 333, 357, 368-69, 387-89, 695, 931; France, 293, 324 n., 325-29, 931; Germany, 293, 324-25, 329-37, 463, 931; Russia, 337-41, 425; the United States, 293-94, 356-75, 468-69, 541; other countries, (Australasian) 351-52, (Asiatic) 348-51, (European) 324 n., 342-48, 425
Industrial Revolution, Second, 319, 522, 723-76, 780, 781, 795, 796, 1105; meaning of the term, 723-25
Industrial Revolution, "Third," 723, 756
Industrial Workers of the World, 954
Industrialism, 47, 54, 119, 378, 444-48, 521, 666, 667, 748, 766-67, 772, 860, 931, 955, 959, 1064; and population trends, 416-24, 524; criticism of, 391-92, 935, 1086; literature and, 448, 690, 695, 709; effects of, 1077, 1094-95
Industry, American, (colonial) 105, 293-94, 325, 329, 344, 349, 364-73, 374, 426, 430,

INDEX

435, 630, 845 n., 1003, 1004, 1014; controlled by bankers, 781-823 *passim*
Industry, 3, 78-79, 192, 264, 285, 295, 324, 380, 398, 421, 427-29, 443, 565, 627, 780-81; beginning of modern, 31-48; rise and development of, 5, 7-8, 64, 68, 92, 122, 127, 235, 255; new impulses to, 43-46, 49; consolidation of, 795-98; large-scale. *See* Production; localization of, 285, 749-51; mechanization of, 627, 748-49, 771, 781, 860; organization of, 335-36, 724. *See also* Cartels; Factory system; Corporations; Holding companies; Syndicates; Trusts; power for, 299-319, 736, 756-62; rationalization of, 336, 629-31, 850; stabilization of, 839-40, 848-49. *See also* Industrial Revolution; Industrialization.
Industry, English, 35-36, 43-44, 46-48, 49, 100, 215-16, 270-77, 285-94 *passim*, 315-16, 329, 332, 368, 435, 456, 628, 723, 735, 759, 769-70, 845, 1003, 1014
Industry, French, 32, 43, 119, 271, 272-73, 327-29, 343, 344, 368, 435, 627-28, 770, 1003, 1014
Industry, German, 329-37, 368, 435, 628, 630, 631, 1014; Prussian, 92
Industry, Italian, 32, 43, 46, 342-43, 736, 962 n.
Industry, Russian: tsarist, 128, 325, 337-41; Soviet, 433, 628, 997, 999-1005, 1014-15, 1027-28
Industry in other countries: Asiatic, 342, 349-50, 352-53, 470, 723, 736; Australasian, 351-53; Canadian, 353; European, 46, 128 n., 289, 342-53, 724, 735
Inertia, effects of, 163-64, 229
Infanticide, 562
Inflation: German, 624, 630, 863; Russian, 896
Ingenhousz, Jan, 153
Ingersoll, R. G., 188, 679
Inheritance: of property, 119, 434, 1023; tax, 845
Initiative, the, 500, 865, 879-80
Injunctions, labor, 498, 846
Inness, George, 711
Innocent IV, pope, 17
Inquisition: Holy, 26, 93, 166; legal, 95
Insane, treatment of the, 401, 968-69
Installment buying, 629, 636, 825
Instrument of Government, English, 103
Instrumentalism, 682, 1068
Insull, Samuel, 782, 788, 799-800, 824
Insurance, 69-70, 840; automobile, 795; disability and sickness, 492, 495, 840, 939-43 *passim*. *See also* Social insurance.
Insurance companies, 70, 943; American, 783, 784, 794-95, (controlled by bankers) 790-92, 795, (charities, gifts of, to) 815
Intellectual life: of primitive man, 1101-02; medieval, 143-44; modern, 4-5, 78, 143-207, 652-53, 663-65, 963-64, 1101-02
Intelligence tests, 860-61, 871, 964, 970, 1072
Interchurch World Movement, 445
Intercursus Magnus, 87
Interessengemeinschaft, 335

Interest: attitude of the Church toward, 58, 61, 66, 67; rates, 58, 67, 69, 73, 836, 837
Interferometer, 1037
International Labor Organization, 553, 617, 906
International relations, 444, 561, 629, 859, 868, 1028-29. *See also* Arbitration, international; Foreign policy; Internationalism.
International: Harvester Company, 752, 781, 790, 830; Workingmen's Association (Communist), First, 935; Settlement, Bank of, 625
Internationalism, 8, 84, 90, 215, 222, 458, 470-76 *passim*, 576, 619, 996. *See also* Communism.
Interstate Commerce Commission, American, 844, 890
Intolerance: economic and political, 168-69, 172, 869, 959-60, (American) 107-08, 164, 168, 172; religious, 144, 146, 163-68, 398, 400, 477, 1019. *See also* Tolerance.
Inventions, 6, 31-32, 119, 271-72, 279, 294-96, 427, 724-26, 759, 767-69; exploitation of, 266, 725, 820, 822. *See also* Machines; and names of important inventions.
Investiture struggle, 12
Investment, 57-70 *passim*, 79, 271, 272, 469, 522, 803-06, 829; legislation concerning, 805-06; in Soviet Russia, 1012. *See also* Banks, investment.
Investment, foreign, 9, 61, 74 n., 76, 339, 344, 357, 362, 374, 463, 521, 524, 526, 542-51 *passim*, 629, 792, 824, 826, 829, 832, 837. *See also* Loans, foreign.
Iraq, Kingdom of. *See* Mesopotamia, modern.
Ireland, 27, 129, 166, 460, 462, 608, 967; emigration from, 421, 422; Home Rule for, 462, 509, 588. *See also* Irish Free State.
Irish: Free State, 608, 633, 869; Parliament Act, 27
Iron and steel industry, 32, 64, 267-86 *passim*, 327-53 *passim*, 725, 726-27, 749-51, 769-71, 1002-03; American, 333, 356, 359, 366-72 *passim*, 749, 756, 771, 772, 781
Iron mines, 280, 328-53 *passim*, 416; American, 357, 368
Iroquois Indians, 82
Irrigation, 306; American, 365
Irving, Washington, 469, 707
Isabella, the Catholic, queen of Castile, 23, 87
Ishii, Kikujiro, viscount, 538
Isidore, archbishop of Seville (Isidorus Hispalensis, Isidore Mercator), 185
Islam, 8-17 *passim*, 536, 1021
Ismail, Khedive of Egypt, 529
Isocrates, 862
Isolationism, 6, 83, 544, 619, 860, 922-24
Israel, Ten Tribes of, 677
Istria, 461
Italia irredenta, 461-62, 467, 608
Italians, 461, 675; as financiers, 58, 66
Italy, 4-21 *passim*, 37, 58, 69, 83, 89, 120, 121, 123, 124-25, 127, 130, 131, 135, 136, 144, 183, 216, 264, 306, 397-98, 429, 455-66 *passim*, 495-96, 505, 510, 524-51 *passim*,

INDEX

570, 578, 579, 587, 608, 609, 611, 620-21, 633, 699, 700, 703, 898, 905, 917, 943, 951, 952, 954; and the World War, 577, 592, 594, 596, 600, 626, 916, (debts) 620-21, (reparation payments due to) 623; emigration from. 421; population of, 212; birth rate in, 419; exports of, 342-43
Italy, Fascist, 343, 425, 474, 496, 500, 510, 611, 868, 919, 928, 938, 943, 951, 960, 962, 1066, 1078, 1084; and disarmament, 911-12
Ivan IV, the Terrible, tsar of Muscovy, 711
Ivanov, V. V., 1088
Izvolsky, A. P., 462, 464 n., 578-87, 590 (quoted), 592-93, 938; quoted, 613

Jackson, Andrew, president of the United States, Jacksonians, 399, 402, 487, 497, 512, 513, 684, 856 n., 857-58, 860, 874, 877
Jacobi, K. G. J., 641
Jacobins, 229, 509
Jamaica, 24, 60, 543
James I, king of England, 34, 90, 100
James II, king of England, 103, 215, 272
James, Henry, 707-08
James, William, 164, 198, 649, 682, 969, 1053, 1083
Janet, Pierre, 652
Jansenism, 697
Japan, 18-19, 467-75 *passim,* 529, 540, 549, 553, 561, 610, 636, 910, 919, 928, 990, 996, 1029; Westernization of, 348-50, 470, 537-39, 560; and China, 349-51, 470, 475, 499, 536-52 *passim,* 597, 610, 613, 1029; and Manchuria, 907, 921, 996, 1029; and the World War, 494, 594, 597, 600, (reparation payments due to) 623; and disarmament, 910-12; exports of, 349, 353; imports of, 353; trade with, 20, 537; influence of, 32, 45, 251, 256, 272. *See also* Russo-Japanese War.
Japanese Revolution (1867-68), 470
Jaurès, J. L., 509, 619, 916, 936, 937, 938
Java, 18, 24, 33, 34, 540; trade with, 546
Jay, John, 108, 923
Jeans, Sir J. H., 160, 643, 659, 1042
Jefferson, Thomas, president of the United States, 52, 97, 99, 104, 105, 108, 130, 137, 172, 187, 188, 468, 487, 513, 684, 685, 855-58 (quoted), 859 n., 860, 873-74, 877, 922-24 (quoted), 1101, 1106
Jehovah, 177
Jellicoe, Admiral J. R. Jellicoe, 1st earl, 598-99
Jellinek, Georg, 668 n.
Jena, battle of, 197, 456
Jenghiz Khan, Mongol emperor, 16
Jenkins' Ear, War of, 507 n.
Jenks, Edward, 837 n., 1059
Jenner, Edward, 147, 153, 650, 652
Jensen, J. V., 1086-87
Jerusalem, 11, 13; Kingdom of, 13. *See also* Crusades.
Jesuit order, 8, 93, 184, 240, 241-42, 476, 675, 678
Jesus Christ, 10, 57 n., 144, 174, 176, 180, 186-87, 201, 204, 205, 229, 247, 389, 445, 563 n., 583, 675, 698, 1060-61, 1066
Jevons, W. S., 933, 1059
Jews. *See* Hebrews.
Jhansi, 535
Jiménez, Juan Ramón, 1084
Joachim, Joseph, 714
Joad, C. M., 1060
John XXII, pope, 19
John II, the Perfect, king of Portugal, 31
John of Monte Corvino, 17, 19
Johnson, A. S., 1057
Johnson, Andrew, president of the United States, 543
Johnson, Gen. H. S., 841
Johnson, H. W., 619, 873, 902
Johnson, Dr. Samuel, 245
Johnson, T. L., 944
Joint-stock companies, 58, 61-63, 70, 71-72, 349, 795, 803-04
Jones, Bassett, 825
Jones, Inigo, 252
Jones, Richard, 387
Jones Brothers Tea Company, 764
Jordanus (Jordan Catalani), 19
Jonson, Ben, 86
Joseph I, king of Portugal, 93
Joseph II, medieval Roman emperor, 91, 93, 123, 495
Joseph (Bonaparte), king of Spain, 456
Josephson, Matthew, 231 n.
Joshua, 661, 664
Joule, J. P., 267, 642
Journal des savants, 150
Journalism, 447, 1104. *See also* Newspapers.
Journeymen, 42, 46, 286, 427
Jouvenel, Henri de, 554
Joyce, James, 1081, 1083
Judaism. *See* Hebrews.
Judd, C. H., 1075
Judet, E. M. G., 1094
Judge, 1091
July Ordinances, France, 121
Junkers, 509, 633-34, 868 n., 959
Junta, British, 19th century, 949
Junto, British Whig, 17th century, 506
Jupiter (planet), 1039
Jurisprudence, 154, 222-26, 234, 572, 669-70, 1059. *See also* Law.
Jury, trial by, 103, 110, 119, 123, 124, 436
Justice, social. *See* Social justice.
Jus gentium. *See* Law, of nations.
Justinian I, Eastern Roman emperor, 119
Jutland, battle of, 598-99

Kagoshima, 537
Kahn, O. H., 831
Kaiser, Georg, 1086
Kaiser Wilhelms Land, 540
Kalidasa, 572
Kallen, H. M., 1103-04
Kallet, Arthur, and Schlink, F. J., 446
Kamchatka, 25
Kamenev (L. B. Rosenfeld), 988
Kamerun, 528, 550, 553, 597

INDEX

Kanner, Heinrich, 587
Kansas, 364; City, Mo., 749
Kant, Immanuel, 162, 186, 190, 191, 193, 195-98, 199, 201, 206, 222, 657, 664, 670, 673-74, 679, 681, 682, 683, 899, 932, 1067, 1069, 1103
Karakorum, 16, 17
Károlyi, Michael, count, 125, 495, 634
Kataaev, V. P., 1088
Kautsky, Karl, 935, 937 n.
Kay, John (clock-maker), 275
Kay, John (inventor), 274
Keats, John, 692
Keble, John, 390, 679
Keith, Dr. (smallpox), 147
Keith, Sir Arthur, 1060
Kekulé von Stradonitz, F. A., 334, 645, 726, 1045
Keller, A. G., 662
Keller, Gottfried, 703
Kellogg, F. B., 904. *See also* Kellogg Pact.
Kellogg Pact, 538, 544, 915, 917-22, 997; text of the, 919-20
Kelly, William, 280, 359, 369
Kelvin, William Thomson, 1st baron, 318, 643, 736, 1043
Kemble, J. M., 484, 672
Kendrick, B. B., 843 n.
Kentucky, 294
Kenworthy, William, 276
Kepler, Johann, 147-48
Kerak, 533
Kerensky, A. F., 129, 595, 620, 987-90, 1024
Kermadec Islands, 540
Kern, J. D., 1100
Kerosene. *See* Petroleum.
Ketel, Cornelis, 251
Ketteler, W. E., baron von and bishop, 389, 680, 945, 955
Key, Ellen (K. S.), 437, 1087
Keynes, J. M., 623-24 n.
Keyserling, H. A., count, 572
Khartum, 530
Kiaochow, 536, 537, 597
Kidnaping, 834, 835, 1104
Kiel Canal, 904
Kier, S. M., 729
Kilpatrick, W. H., 1075
King, William, 948
Kings. *See* Monarchy.
Kings, divine right of, 89-90, 100, 136-37, 217-18, 220, 455, 486
Kingsley, Rev. Charles, 182, 390, 572, 680, 693-94, 946, 948
Kin-sai, 19
Kinship society, 82, 483
Kipling, Rudyard, 464 n., 466, 525, 572, 576, 693, 1080
Kirchhoff, G. R., 643, 644
Kirkland, E. C., quoted, 756
Kishinev pogrom, 477
Kitchener of Khartoum, H. H. Kitchener, 1st earl of, 530
Klein, Felix, 641
Kleptocracy, 503

Knies, Karl, 387
Knight, M. M., Barnes, H. E., and Flügel, Felix, quoted, 770
Knighthood, English, 101
Knights: medieval, 13, 212; of Labor, American, 516, 680, 951. *See also* names of orders.
Knox, John, 183, 673
Knox, P. C., 917
Koch, Robert, 651
Kocher, E. T., 652
Koffka, Kurt, 1048
Köhler, Joseph, 670
Köhler, Wolfgang, 660, 1048
Kohts, Nadie, 660
Kolhozi. *See* Agriculture, Soviet Russia.
Kollontay, Alexandra, 437
Kolping, Adolf, 945
Korea (Chosen), 538, 545
Kornilov, Gen. L. G., 988-89
Kossuth, Louis (Lajos), 123-24, 458
Krag, T. P., 1087
Kramatorsk, 1003
Krefeld, 749
Kreisler, Fritz, 1100
Kresge, S. S., chain stores, 764, 785
Kreuger, Ivar, International Match Co., 799-800
Kropotkin, P. A., prince, 946-47
Krückenberg, Franz, 738
Krüdener, B. J., baroness von, 900
Krupp: Friedrich, 333, 819; process and works, 281 n., 282, 331, 1003
Krutch, J. W., 1090
Krylenko, N. V., 988
Kublai Khan, Great Khan of Cathay, 17-19
Kuczynski, R. R., 418
Kuenen, Abraham, 654
Kuhn, Loeb & Co., 782, 789
Kulaks, 991, 998, 1007-08, 1010
Kun, Béla, 634
Kwangchanwan, 537

Laband, Paul, 668 n.
Labor, 79, 345, 627, 860, 934 n.; a commodity, 269, 428; attitudes toward, 236, 392, 441; discipline of, 53, 268, 270, 286-89; division of, 219, 380, 748, (international) 321, 568; exploitation of, 289, 294, 560, 565, 671; exchanges, 953; legislation, 118, 345, 429, 431, 491, 509, 940-41, 949, 957. *See also* Factory legislation; Social insurance; market, 54, 57, 269; state control of, 77; American, 515-16, (census of) 430. *See also* Proletariat.
Labo(u)r party, British, 424, 491, 509, 617, 633, 867, 919, 951; quoted, 959
Labor Temple, N. Y. City, 1078
Labor-unionism, 269, 286, 287 n., 294, 326, 345, 381-94 *passim,* 428-33 *passim,* 446, 490-97 *passim,* 617, 680, 821, 867, 948-62 *passim,* 984, 1077; for women, 435; opposition to, 118, 429, 825, 931; American, 369, 424, 432, 498, 516, 517, 846, 849, 874, 951-52, 1077; English, 939, 949-50; Soviet Russian, 1016

INDEX

Labrador, 23
Lacquer work, 32, 45, 251
Lacustrian (Lake-dwelling) Age, 264
Ladd, William, 900, 914
Laënnec, R. T. H., 650
La Farge, John, 711
Lafitau, J. F., 245
La Follette, R. M., Sr., 498, 783 n., 881, 944
La Fontaine, Jean de, 246
Lagerlöf, S. O. L., 1087
Lagrange, J. L., 151, 640
Laissez faire, 78 n., 96, 226, 330, 424, 433, 490, 850, 856, 860, 933, 940, 943. See also Economic Liberalism; Individualism.
Lake, Kirsopp, quoted, 1066
Lake-dwelling (Lacustrian) Age, 264
Lalor, John, 390
Lamaism, 1021
Lamarck, J. B. P. A. de Monet, 649, 657, 659, 1046
Lamartine, A. M. L. de Prat de, 206, 389, 466 n., 695
Lamb, Charles, 692
Lamettrie, Julien Offray de, 185
Lamennais, H. F. R. de, abbé, 206, 389
Lamont, Corliss, 1061; quoted, 1030-31
Lamprecht, Karl, 672, 1057-58
Lancaster, Sir James, 24
Lancaster, Joseph, 1070
Lancet, 288
Land: grants (U.S.A.), 363, 365-66, 424, 428, 514; nationalization of, 345, 395, 955-57; tenure, 52-53, 344, 348, 496, 632-36, 939, 982, 997-1007. See also Inclosure of land.
Landscape gardening, 248, 251
Langdon-Davies, John, 1056
Langen, Eugen, 302
Langer, W. L., quoted, 587
Langley, S. P., 740
Langlois, C. V., 672
Lannes, G. L., count de Montebello, 583
Lansing, Robert, 538
Lanston, Tolbert, 744
Laos, 18
Laplace, P. S., marquis de, 151-52, 649, 1047
Larra, M. J. de, 701
Las Casas, Bartolomé de, 245
Lasker, Eduard, 476
Laski, H. J., 1059; quoted, 184, 428
Lassalle, Ferdinand, 395-96, 856, 935, 938
Latin America, 120, 135, 136, 337, 456, 499, 521, 524, 525, 541-48, 552, 832, 924, 1084; revolutions of, 98, 120, 138, 489, 543
Latin: culture, 191-92, 199, 226, 256, 485; Empire of the East, *see* Byzantine Empire; language, 154, 240, 242; literature, *see* Humanism, Renaissance; people, 466
Latrobe, B. H., 712
Latvia, 138, 608, 621, 634, 869; World War debts, 621
Lauderdale, James Maitland, 8th earl of, 386
Lausanne: Conference of (1932), 607, 622, 626; Treaty of (1923), 616
Laval, Gustaf de, 302
Laval, Pierre, 542

Lavoisier, A. L., 145, 152, 640, 644, 726
Law, Andrew Bonar, 633, 956
Law, John, 73-74, 804
Law, 66, 115, 217, 227-28, 233, 234, 301, 379, 661, 1059, 1102; development of, 222-26, 444; codification of, 224-26, 234, 670; canon, 66; criminal, 92, 93, 116, 118, 119, 123, 383, 391, 399, 487; divine, 78, 177, 226, 663; international, 219, 225-26, 596; martial, 101, 104; natural, 78-79, 177-79, 195, 196, 217-25 *passim*, 237, 379, 382, 663, 669, 842, 1102; of nations, 225. See also Social reform.
Law: American, 560, 798, 880-81, (due process of) 133, 224, 498-99, 843-45; English, 101-02, 134, 223, 272, 383, 400-01, 436, 1102; French, 54, 116-19, 223, 225, 326, 436-37; Russian (tsarist) 223, (Soviet) 995, 1028; of other countries, (Australasian) 436, (European) 92, 116, 429, 436. See also Roman law.
Law courts, 61; American, 1102-03. See also United States Supreme Court; Church, 13; English, 101-02; French, 116-17; Russian (tsarist) 981, (Soviet) 995
Lawrence, Abbott, 357
Lawrence, D. H., 1080, 1081-82
Lawrence, H. W., quoted, 928
Lawrence, T. E. (T. E. Shaw), 597
Lawrence family, 358
Lawrence (Merrimac), Mass., 357
Lawyer class, 108, 214
Laziness. *See* Inertia.
Lea, Homer, 464 n., 466 n., 576
Leaders: importance of, 82, 871; political, 503-04, 882. See also Boss, political.
League of Nations, 470, 473, 475, 538, 544, 551, 552-54, 611, 618, 628, 898, 901-13, 916, 920, 948, 1029, 1030; Covenant of the, 902, (quoted) 552-53, 908-09; membership of the, 534, 902-03; the United States and the, 902, 923, 924, 928; and disarmament, 908-13
League to Enforce Peace, 901
Leather industry, 44, 343, 344, 345, 353. See also Shoe industry.
Le Bon, Gustave, 503, 668
Le Chapelier, I. R. G., Le Chapelier law, 326, 950
Le Chatelier, Henry, 727
Lecky, W. E. H., 27 n., 154, 165 n., 668; quoted, 180-81
Leconte de Lisle, C. M. R., 572, 697
Le Corbusier, M. (Jeanneret), 412-13
Lee Higginson & Co., 782, 789
Leeuwenhoek, Antony van, 149
Leeward Islands, 543
Lehmann, Lilli, 715
Leibl, Wilhelm, 710
Leibnitz, G. W., 147, 150, 159, 163 n., 243, 265, 657, 899
Leighton, Alexander, 167
Leipzig, 150; battle of, 272, 460; University of, 240
Leisure, problem of, 442-43, 845, 848, 1025-27
Leisure class, 91, 236, 690, 708; literature for

the, 448, 1079, 1081, 1089, 1091; psychology of the, 440-41
Lemaître, (F. E.) Jules, 699
Lemberg, 595
L'Enfant, P. C. (Major), 411
Lenin, V. I. (Nikolai, V. I. Ulyanov), 447, 595, 985-1004 *passim*, 1021, 1024, 1069
Leningrad, 987
Leo XIII, pope, 680, 945, 1066
Leonard, W. E., 1088-89
Leonardo da Vinci, 145 n., 148 n., 230
Leoncavallo, Ruggiero, 714
Leonov, L. M., 1088
Leopardi, Giacomo, count, 699
Leopold II, king of Belgium, 528, 565
Leopold II (of Austria), medieval Roman emperor, 93, 113
Le Play, Frédéric, 411-12, 945
Lermontov, M. Y., 705
Leroux, Pierre, 206, 392, 393, 696, 958
Leslie, Cliffe, quoted, 383
Lessing, G. E., 186, 246, 711
Letourneau, C. J. M., 672 n.
Le Trosne, G. F., 380
Letts, 461-62
Leuba, J. H., 1061; quoted, 1063-64
Levant, 22, 44; Company, 62; trade with the, 9, 13, 39. *See also* Asia Minor; Near East.
Levellers, British, 487
Leven, Maurice, Moulton, H. G., and Warburton, C. A., 417 n., 807, 809, 811, 815
Levinson, S. O., 917-18
Levy, Hyman, 1063; quoted, 1042
Lewis, Sinclair, 205, 392, 1036, 1080, 1089-90
Leyden, University of, 240
Lhote, André, 1096
Liaotung Peninsula, 537, 538
Liberal party, British, 320, 382, 458, 491, 509, 517, 529, 586, 587, 633, 899, 919, 925, 949, 956
Liberal Republican movement, American, 514, 874
Liberalism, 84, 128-38 *passim*, 162, 182-83, 398, 453, 458-60, 482-515 *passim*, 560, 565, 633, 695, 856, 973, 1108. *See also* Revolutions of 1830 and 1848.
Liberia, 532, 541, 545, 594, 735
Liberty, 78-79, 94, 96, 97, 106, 115, 126-38 *passim*, 220, 223, 224, 454-55, 458, 472, 483-84, 487, 560, 612, 842, 843, 860, 868, 899, 932, 980, 996
Liberty, weekly, 1092
Liberty Loan drives, 603, 829
Libraries, public, 833, 957
Libya, 548
Lichnowsky, K. M., prince, 587 n.
Lie, Jonas, 704-05
Lieber, Francis, 668 n.
Liebermann, Max, 710
Liebig Justus, baron von, 51, 640, 645, **688**, 726, 1045
Liebknecht, K. P. A. F., 619
Liebknecht, Wilhelm, 935, 937
Life, right to and protection of, 96, 106, 132, 133, 134, 213, 224, 379, 842, 843, 932

Life, weekly, 1091
Light (physics), 151, 318, 641, 643-44, 1035-37, 1042-43
Lighting, artificial, 283-86, 370, 726-27, 729
Lilburne, John, 487
Liliencron, Detlev von, baron, 703
Lilienfeld, Paul von, 667
Lilienthal, Otto, 740
Lille, 597
Liman von Sanders, Gen. Otto, 585
Lincoln, Abraham, president of the United States, 172, 482, 711, 768, 861, 875, 877, 1096
Lind, Jenny, 715
Lindbergh, Colonel C. A., 741; son of, 1104
Lindsay, Vachel, 1088-89
Lindsey, B. B., 970
Linnaeus, Carolus (Carl von Linné), 146, 151, 571, 647, 657, 661, 668
Linville, H. R., 1079
Lippert, Julius, 667, 672 n.
Lippmann, Walter, 865, 871, 1059, 1093; quoted, 768
Lisbon, 22, 38
List, Friedrich, 330, 386, 464, 773-74
Lister, Joseph, 1st baron, 651
Lister, Martin, 149
Liszt, Franz, 714
Literature, 198, 199, 256, 391, 440, 448, 1056-67; achievements in, 244-47, 572-73, 690-708, 1079-94; baroque, 246; promoted, 91, 92
Literature by countries: American, 469, 706-07, 1079-80, 1088-90; East Indian, 572; English 86, 245-47, 466, 572, 691-95, 1079-83, (influence of) 700-01, 702, 1084; French, 86, 183-84, 245-47, 466, 572, 695-708, 1084, 1085, (influence of) 700, 703, 704, 708, 1084, 1080, 1085-86, (influence of) 692, 700-01, 1084; Italian, 86, 466-67, 699-700, 1083-84; Latin American, 1084, 1085; oriental, influence of, 245, 572-73; Polish, 706, 1088; Portuguese, 86; Russian, 705-06, 1087-88; Scandinavian, 704-05, 1086-87, (influence of) 703; Spanish, 86, 245, 700-02, 1084-85, (influence of) 1085
Lithuania, 138, 608, 634, 706, 905; and the World War, 595, (debts) 621
Lithuanians, 461-62
Little brown brother, 7. *See also* Philippine Islands.
Litvinov, M. M., 997
Liukiu Islands, 538
Liverpool, 38
Living-conditions, 10, 48, 158, 291-92, 391, 633-34, 673; American, 368-69, 846; Soviet Russian, 1014, 1015-18
Living-cost, 42, 418, 827
Livingstone, David, 650
Lloyd George, David, 491, 529, 585, 587 n., 596, 614 n., 623, 633, 939, 956
Lloyd's (insurance), 70
Llwyd, Edward, 149
Loans, 71; security for, 58, 67; foreign, 341, 344, 628-29, (American) 542, 625
Lobatchewski, N. I., 641

INDEX

Lobbies, political, 673, 878, 913
Locarno Agreements (1925), 615, 618, 917, 920
Loch, C. S., 965
Locke, John, 97, 104, 106, 150, 154, 161-62, 170, 173-74, 176, 181, 185, 186, 203, 218-21, 223, 224, 243, 245, 482, 666, 669, 961, 1103; quoted, 161
Lockouts, 429
Lockwood, Belva, 437
Lockyer, Sir J. N., 644
Lodge, H. C., 523, 924
Loeffler, C. M. T., 1100
Log, mariner's, 31
Logarithms, 147
Logic, 154, 156, 194, 681, 1068
Logos, the, 669
Logrolling in legislation, 887
Loisy, A. F., 676
Lombardy, 67, 125; bankers, 66
London, 38, 46, 124, 127, 290, 291, 411, 414-15, 525, 678, 935, 965; population of, 213, 405
London: Conferences, (1813) 900, (1830-31) 121, (Disarmament, 1929-30) 623, (Economic, 1933) 474, 775, (Reparations, 1920) 623, (Reparations, 1924) 624; University of, 1074
London newspapers: *Daily Mail*, 1093; *News of the World*, 1093; *Times*, 478, 744
Londonderry, Robert Stewart, 2d marquess of. *See* Castlereagh.
Longfellow, H. W., 469, 707
Longworth, Nicholas, 862
Lopez de Gómara, Francisco, 245
Lords, feudal, 11-13, 54, 75, 83-85, 96, 109-10, 115, 212, 255, 454, 485-87, 500
Lords, House of, 293
Lord's Day Alliance, 1065
Lorraine, Claude (of), 250
Lorraine, 282, 333, 353. *See also* Alsace-Lorraine.
Los Angeles, 366
Lotteries, 64, 804
Lotze, R. H., 681
Louis, St. *See* Louis IX.
Louis IX, king of France (St. Louis), 17
Louis XIV, king of France, 26, 88, 89, 91, 137, 246, 247, 252, 411, 454, 455, 579, 899
Louis XV, king of France, 111 (quoted)
Louis XVI, king of France, 111-12, 117, 454
Louis XVIII, king of France, 120
Louis Philippe, king of the French, 121, 122, 491-92, 942
Louis, Georges, 582, 584; quoted, 582-83
Louisade Islands, 540
Louisiana, purchase of, 130, 456, 468
Louvain, University of, 240
Louÿs, Pierre, 1082
Lovejoy, A. O., 1079
Lowden, F. O., 873, 876
Lowell, A. L., 1078 n.
Lowell, F. C., 357
Lowell, J. R., 469, 668, 708, 914
Lowell family, 358
Lowell (Chelmsford), Mass., 357

Lowenthal, Max, 823 n., 972
Loyalist party, American, 106
Loyalty Islands, 540
Lubbock, Sir John. *See* Avebury.
Lucretius, 221, 656, 665
Ludendorff, Marshal Erich, 477, 595, 596, 599, 612, 917
Lüderitz, F. A. E. von, 528
Ludlow, J. M. F., 390
Ludwig, K. F. W., 647
Ludwig, Otto, 703
Lueger, Karl, 476, 945
Lumpkin, Grace, 1079 n.
Lunacharsky, A. V., 988, 1088
Luther, Martin, 42, 57 n., 86, 161, 171, 174, 183, 203, 673, 674
Luxembourg, 460, 610
Luzon, 540
Lvov, G. Y., prince, 595, 620, 987, 1029
Lybyer, A. H., 21 n.
Lyell, Sir Charles, 153, 649, 657
Lynching, 834
Lynd, R. S. and Helen, 1104
Lyons, 71, 751

Maassen, K. G. von, 319, 383
Mably, Gabriel Bonnot de, 99, 237
McAdam, J. L., 304-06
McAdams, Clark, 1094
Macaulay, T. B., Macaulay, baron, 130, 303-04, 466 n., 672, 694-95
McCabe, Joseph, 676
McClure's Magazine, 1091
McConnell, F. J., bishop, 1065-66
McCormick, C. H., 363
McCrory chain stores, 764
McCulloch, J. R., 380-81
McCumber, P. J., Fordney-McCumber tariff, 775 n.
MacCurdy, G. G., 1060
MacDonald, (James) Ramsay, 618, 619, 867
MacDonald, William, 137-38
McDuffie, 559
Macedonia, 169, 610-11, 906
McGiffert, A. C., 674
McGuire, C. E., 623 n.
Mach, Ernst, 682
Machiavelli, Niccolò, 86, 90, 219, 385 n., 456, 464
Machinery industry, 334, 342, 344, 746; American, 368, 369, 370
Machines, modern, 3, 10, 263-96, 324, 327, 341, 627, 723-25, 729, 748, 759, 768, 1014; effects of, 319, 440, 442, 766-67, 780; automatic, 280, 442, 557-60, 820; textile, 32, 43, 47, 268, 273-77, 278, 299, 346, 758. *See also* Technology.
Machtpolitik, 573
MacIntosh case, 847
MacIver, R. M., 882, 933
McKay, Gordon, 367
Mackensen, Marshal August von, 595-96
McKim, C. F., 712
Mackintosh, Charles, 733
Mackintosh, Sir James, 383, 399

McKinley, William, president of the United States, 498, 875, 877, 944
Maclaurin, Colin, 151
McMaster, J. B., 205
Madagascar, 18, 531
Madeira Islands, 33
Madison, James, president of the United States, 108, 468, 504, 668, 857, 859 n.
Madonna. See Mary, the Virgin.
Madrid, 93, 701
Maeterlinck, Maurice, 392, 1098
Magellan, Ferdinand, 21, 23, 24
Magic, 664, 1048
Magna Charta, 96, 101, 134, 482, 485, 944
Magnetism, 152, 158, 267, 641
Magnitogorsk, 1002
Magyars, 126, 458, 608-09, 610, 611, 634, 635
Mahaffy, J. P., 392
Mahan, A. T., 466 n.
Mahler, Gustav, 1098
Mahratta Confederacy, 534
Mail-order houses, 764, 766, 785
Maillol, Aristide, 1096
Maine, Sir H. J. S., 668, 670
Maine, State of, 363
Mainz, 167
Maistre, Joseph de, 206, 232-34, 389
Maitland, F. W., 670, 672, 1059
Maize (Indian corn), 33; by-products of, 728
Majority rule, 482, 768, 861, 869, 882, 961-62, 1055
Majuba Hill, battle of, 529
Malabar, 22
Malacca, 22
Malay Peninsula, 734
Malaysia (Malay Archipelago), 20, 540, 545, 658, 735
Malevsky-Malevich, P. N., quoted, 994-95, 1012, 1019
Mallarmé, Stéphane, 698
Mallock, W. H., 668
Malpighi, Marcello, 148, 149
Malraux, André, 1079 n.
Malthus, T. R., Malthusianism, 79, 380-81, 383, 416-21, 657-58, 667, 771
Man, status of, 226-27, 659-63, 665-66, 1050-54, 1107-09. See also Progress, human.
Manchester (Eng.), 272, 414, 522; Guardian, 1094; School, 382
Manchu dynasty, 350, 536
Manchukuo, 538, 545
Manchuria, 350, 463, 470, 537, 538, 549, 552, 907, 921, 996, 1029
Mandates, 533, 540, 545, 550-54, 561, 609
Mandel, Benjamin, quoted, 799, 801-02
Mandeville, Sir John, 19
Manet, Edouard, 710
Mangu Khan, Mongol emperor, 16
Manila, 539
Mann, Horace, 684, 689-90
Mann, Thomas, 703, 1086
Manning, H. E., cardinal, 680
Manorial system, 49, 51, 54, 58, 83, 235, 238, 428, 485, 759
Mansart, Jules Hardouin, 252

Manu, 572
Manufacturing. See Industry.
Manzoni, Alessandro, 699
Marat, J. P., 183
Marburg, Theodore, 914
Marchand, Capt. J. B., 530
Marconi, William (Guglielmo), 267, 742, 743
Marett, R. R., 1060; quoted, 667
March Laws, Hungary, 124
Margin, buying on, explained, 803, 806. See also Stock exchange.
Margueritte, Paul, 1082
Margueritte, Victor, 1080, 1082
Marianne Islands, 538, 540
Marie Antoinette, queen of France, 111
Mariotte, Edmé, 148, 267
Maritain, Jacques, 392, 1056, 1067
Mark, Germanic village, 485
Markets. See Commerce.
Marks, L. B., 284
Marlowe, Christopher, 86, 245
Marne, battles of the, 594, 597
Marquardsen, Heinrich, 668 n.
Marquesas Islands, 540
Marriage: attitudes toward, 397, 437-38, 1103; companionate, 970; in Soviet Russia, 1022
Mars (planet), 1039
Marschall von Bieberstein, Adolf von, baron, 532
Marshak, I. I. (M. Ilin), 1004
Marshall, Alfred, 1058-59
Marshall, John, 108, 468, 842
Marshall, L. C., 1075
Marshall Islands, 538, 540
Marsiglio (Marsilius) of Padua (Marsiglio Mainardino), 89, 218
Martin, E. D., 1078
Martin, Emile and Pierre, 281-82. See also Siemens, Sir William.
Martin, B. L. H., 466 n., 672
Martínez de la Rosa, Francisco, 700
Martínez Ruiz, José (Azorín), 1084, 1085
Martínez Sierra, Gregorio and Maria, 1085
Martinique, 24, 543
Marx, Karl, Marxism, 199, 200, 381, 395, 431, 443-44, 448, 476, 477, 509, 510, 559, 933-35, 961, 962, 1021, 1069, 1077, 1105; quoted, 935. See also Communism.
Mary, the Virgin, 247, 248, 249, 251
Mary II, queen of England, 103
Maryland, 361
Masaryk, T. G., president of Czechoslovakia, 499, 608, 870
Mascagni, Pietro, 714
Masefield, John, 1080
Mass: production. See Production; purchasing power. See Purchasing power.
Massachusetts, 368, 510
Massenet, J. E. F., 572, 713
Masters, E. L., 1088-89
Materia medica, 34, 147, 571, 862
Materialism, 66, 173, 186, 202, 390-92, 440, 442, 446, 682, 706, 934, 935, 1027, 1062
Materials. See Raw materials.
Materna, Amalie, 715

Maternity, protection of, 437, 492, 943, 1023, 1025
Mathematics, 15-16, 45, 146, 147, 151, 158-60, 184, 255, 640-41, 1035-36, 1068; Muslim, 146; oriental, 147
Mather, K. F., 1062, 1063; quoted, 661, 664
Mathews, Shailer, 946 n.
Matisse, Henri, 1095
Matriarchate, 434
Matthews, J. B., and Shallcross, R. E., 446
Maude, F. N., 466 n.
Maudsley, Henry, 649, 652
Maugham, W. S., 1081
Maupassant, Guy de, 698, 708
Maurice, J. F. D., 390, 674, 680, 946
Maurois, André, quoted, 436-37
Maxey, C. C., quoted, 888, 889
Maxim, Sir Hiram, 284, 740
Maxim, Hudson, 466 n.
Maxse, Leo, 464 n., 466, 576
Maxwell, J. C., 267, 318, 642, 643, 644, 1035
Mayer, J. R. von, 267, 642
Mayo, C. H., 439
Mazarin, Jules, cardinal, 87-88, 89, 110, 119, 131
Mazzini, Giuseppe, 124-25, 458, 699
Mazzoni, Guido, 699-700
Mead, E. D., 914
Mead, L. T. A., quoted, 905, 906
Mead, Richard, 149
Meakin, Walter, quoted, 631
Means, G. C., 446, 784 n., 799, 801, 802, 823 n., 972; and A. A. Berle, quoted, 796, 800; and Bonbright, J. C., 797
Mechanics, 149, 151, 640
Mechnikov, I. I. (Elie), 651, 947
Meckel, J. F., 647
Medici family, 253; as bankers, 58, 67
Medicine, 34, 147, 149, 153, 212, 262, 571, 650-52, 736, 862, 1015, 1025-26, 1048-49; influence of, 416, 524, 560, 563, 567, 764, 1048, 1064-65, 1067; preventive, 153, 409, 736, 1048. See also Diseases; Materia medica.
Medievalism, 35, 42, 61, 64, 145, 173, 194, 205, 216, 217, 233, 235, 255, 263, 338, 459-61, 466, 477, 487-96 passim, 632, 635, 685, 686, 692. See also Middle Ages.
Medill, Joseph, 1092
Meer, Jan van der (Vermeer), 249
Meiklejohn, Alexander, 1076
Meinong, Alexius, 1067
Meissonier, J. A., 252
Melancthon, Philipp, 166, 183
Melanesia, 540
Melinde, 22
Mellon, A. W., 601, 782 n., 832
Melville, Herman, 707
Melvin, A. G., quoted, 1072
Memel, 905
Mencken, H. L., 704, 1090, 1091
Mendel, Gregor, abbé, 646, 659, 676, 1046, 1054
Mendelssohn-Bartholdy, J. L. F., 713
Mendelyeev, D. L., 645
Menelek II, king of Ethiopia (Abyssinia), 531

Menéndez Pidal, Ramón, 1085
Menéndez y Pelayo, Marcelino, 702, 1085
Menken, S. S., 951 n.
Mental: deficients, 969-70; diseases. See Insanity; Nervous and mental disease; hygiene, 969, 1025-26; tests. See Intelligence tests.
Menshevik party, Russia, 985, 988
Menzel, A. F. E. von, 711
Mercantilism, 9, 26, 41, 43, 63, 75-78, 86, 256, 319, 330, 356, 379, 383, 464, 467, 490, 542, 773, 774, 931; German (cameralism), 54, 75-77, 92, 154
Mercator, Gerardus, 149
Merchant Adventurers, 62
Merchant class, 42-78 passim, 94, 98, 106, 234, 253, 468, 527, 666. See also Middle class.
Merchant marine: British, 45, 271, 465, 315; Dutch, 346; German, 614; Italian, 342; Scandinavian, 347; Spanish, 93
Merchant Staplers, 62
Mercier de La Rivière, Le, P. P., 380
Mercury (planet), 1039
Meredith, George, 694
Mergenthaler, Ottmar, 744
Mérimée, Prosper, 572, 696
Merriam, C. E., 863, 1059
Merz, Charles, quoted, 753-54
Mesnil, Jacques, 589 n.
Mesonero Romanos, Ramón de, 701
Mesopotamia (now Iraq), 65, 285, 337, 463, 532, 533, 541, 542, 549, 551, 553, 904, 905
Messiah, 175
Metal industry. See Iron and steel industry.
Metaphysics, 154, 163, 195, 200, 648, 669
Métayer system, 428
Metcalf, John, 304
Methodist church, 203-04, 390, 673, 674, 678
Metric system, 118
Metternich-Winneburg, C. W. L., prince, 120, 123, 124, 125, 127, 135, 206, 234, 456, 459, 489, 492-93, 869, 924, 964 n.
Meunier, Constantin, 710
Mexico, 24, 40, 353, 541-42, 544, 546 n., 547, 548, 636, 924; trade with, 33, 34
Meyerbeer, Giacomo (J. L. or J. M. Beer), 572
Mézières, 687
Michael, grand duke of Russia, 987
Michaud, J. F., 466 n., 672
Michelangelo Buonarroti, 466, 710
Michelet, Jules, 94, 466 n., 672
Michels, Robert, 500, 504, 515, 865
Michelson, A. A., 1037, 1042
Michigan, 359, 363, 368, 876
Mickiewicz, Adam, 706
Micronesia, 540
Microscope, 146, 148-49, 153, 646, 652, 1047
Middle Ages, 34, 38, 43, 44, 58-95 passim, 138, 143-46, 147, 165-68, 212, 218, 223, 238, 244, 254, 256, 289, 295, 306, 427, 431, 438, 461, 485-86, 487, 500, 657, 660, 687, 1079. See also Medievalism.
Middle class 3-5, 13, 32, 35, 42, 161, 244, 272, 380-98 passim, 432-97 passim, 506-10, 695, 697, 702, 705, 938, 957-61 passim, 981, 991, 996, 998, 1103; rise of the, 15, 82-139, 146,

235, 255-56, 263, 690; dominance of the, 89, 138, 212-16, 270, 387, 396-98, 431, 454, 982; triumph of the, 424-27; wealth of the, 216, 806-11
Middle class, lower (petite bourgeois), 89, 122, 425, 430, 432, 509, 973-74, 1060; American, 802-11 *passim*
Middle West, the American, 365, 513
Middleburg, Bank of, 68 n.
Middlemen, 63, 1001
Middleton, Conyers, 176-77
Midway Islands, 545
Mignet, F. A. A., 466 n., 672
Mikado, 470
Miles, William, 59-60
Militarism, 86, 458, 464-67, 472, 550, 576-77, 602, 961; German, 493, 576-77, 602. *See also* Armaments; Disarmament.
Mill, J. S., 79, 382, 383, 384-85, 490, 681, 901, 1068
Mill, James, 79, 380-81, 384, 667, 671, 901
Millay, E. St. V., 1089
Miller, D. H., 901
Millerand, Alexandre, president of France, 584, 953
Millet, J. F., 709-10
Millikan, R. A., 160, 203, 643, 1042, 1043, 1044, 1062, 1063
Mills, Robert, 712
Milton, John, 86, 150, 167-68, 245, 246
Milyukov, P. N., 129, 496
Mimeograph, 745
Mindanao, 540
Mines, mining, 39-40, 44, 59, 63, 79, 283, 292-93, 327, 328, 331-32, 347, 351, 353, 365, 388; controlled by bankers, 782. *See also* Coal-mining; Iron mines.
Ming dynasty, 20
Minneapolis, 366
Minnesota, 363, 368, 845, 881
Minority representation. *See* Proportional representation.
Mir. *See* Villages, Russian.
Mirabeau, H. G. de Riqueti, count de, 183
Mirabeau, Victor de Riqueti, marquis de, 380, 570
Miracle plays, 253
Miracles, 161-62, 173-74, 175-78, 187
Miranda, Francisco de Sá de, 86
Missionaries: Christian, 8-10, 20, 25, 203, 212, 398, 402, 469, 524, 536, 554, 562-64, 567, 674; Mormon, 677
Mississippi: Bubble, 73-74; Valley, 24, 27, 105
Mitchell, C. E., 782
Mitchell, S. W., 652
Mitchell, W. C., 837, 935 n., 1078
Mittel-Europa, 462, 549
Mivart, St. G. J., 653, 676
Mocha, 34
Modern era. *See* Civilization, modern.
Modernism: in art, 572, 710, 711, 1094-97; in literature, 1084, 1090, 1091; in music, 1097-1101; in religion, 144, 175 n., 207, 658, 665, 670, 676, 768, 1104, (Advanced) 1061, 1062, (Devout) 675, 680, 1060-62

Modigliani, Amadeo, 1096
Mohammedanism. *See* Islam.
Mohonk, Lake, 914
Mohl, Hugo von, 647
Mohl, Robert von, 668 n.
Moissan, Henri, 727
Moley, Raymond, 958
Molière, J. B. (Poquelin), 86, 245, 246
Moltke, Gen. H. J. L. von, 466 n., 577 n., 585 n., 594, 595, 599
Moluccas, 23
Monarchy, 75, 82-85, 108, 134, 138, 182, 206, 222, 223, 233, 454, 482, 486, 506, 884, 941, 1102; absolute, 4, 78, 83-100 *passim*, 130-31, 136, 139, 214, 217-20, 233-34, 455, 487, 496, 706, 871; constitutional (limited), 99, 111, 121, 126, 129, 135, 138, 139, 190, 215, 233, 488, 492. *See also* names of monarchs.
Monasticism, 51, 83, 93, 117, 119, 235, 238, 486
Monet, Claude, 710
Money, Sir L. G. Chiozza, 937
Money, 39-40, 568; depreciation of, 42, 60; exportation of, 77; labor scrip, 396; paper, 64, 69, 117, 364, 1013; "sound," 863; Soviet Russian, 998, 1012-13; Swedish, 347-48. *See also* Dollar; Gold money; Inflation; Silver money.
Money economy, 15, 41, 49, 54, 237, 837
Mongols, Mongolia, 16, 19-20, 423, 537, 545, 572
Monism, 681-82, 683
Monopolies, 42, 43, 62, 71, 73, 74-76, 85, 94, 100, 101, 215, 269, 326, 378, 383, 411, 487, 749, 751-52, 776, 780, 781, 797, 830, 840, 846, 850, 860, 974; state, 76, 92. *See also* Capitalism, monopoly.
Monroe, James, president of the United States, 468, 857, 924 (quoted)
Monroe Doctrine, 468, 543-44, 613, 920, 924
Montagu, Lady Mary Wortley, 147
Montaigne, Michel Eyquem de, 86, 150, 154-56, 158 n., 170, 181, 183, 189, 192, 227, 245, 247, 682, 1053
Montebello, G. L. Lannes, count de, 583
Monte Corvino, Giovanni di, 17, 19
Montenegro, 460, 594, 595, 609, 610
Montesquieu, C. L. de Secondat, baron de la Brède and de, 99, 111, 134, 149, 154, 190-91, 222, 224, 227-28, 245, 247, 399, 511, 671-72
Montessori, Maria, 1071
Monteverde, Claudio, 254
Montgelas, M. M. K. S., count, 587
Montgomery Ward and Company, 764, 790
Montgolfier, J. E. and J. M., 740
Moody, Rev. D. L., 205
Moody, Paul, 357
Moon, P. T., quoted, 541-42, 545, 569-70
Mooney, Tom, 168
Moore, E. C., quoted, 197-98, 201
Moore, H. L., 837
Moore, J. B., 904
Moore, Thomas, 572
Moors, 11, 26, 165-66

Morality, 175, 194, 199, 200, 201, 228, 291, 445-46, 563, 683, 704, 768, 969, 1064-67, 1080; Christian, 64-66, 173, 189-96; Puritan, 65, 1057, 1066; Soviet Russian, 1022-24. *See also* Ethics.
Moratorium, Hoover-Laval (1931), 542, 549, 607, 624, 625, 628-29
Moravia, Moravians, 124, 343
More, P. E., 1056, 1067, 1080
More, Sir Thomas, 86, 235-36, 759
Morel, E. D., 528 n., 586
Morelly, 237
Morgagni, G. B., 153
Morgan, A. E., 1076
Morgan, C. L., 1068
Morgan, J. P., Sr., 434, 782
Morgan, J. P., Jr., 813, 830-31 (quoted)
Morgan, J. P. & Co., 624 n., 780, 783-84, 789-92, 795, 828, 830-31, 863
Morgan, L. H., 662, 667, 670, 672 n., 1060
Morgan, T. H., 659, 1046
Mörike, E. F., 702
Morley of Blackburn, John Morley, viscount, 586 n.; quoted, 183
Mormon Church, 676-77
Moro, Lazzaro, 153
Morrill, J. S., Morrill Act, 774
Morris, Gouverneur, 187, 188
Morris, R. O., quoted, 1099
Morris, William, 391, 394, 671, 709, 937
Morocco, 337, 463, 530 n., 531, 532, 545, 561, 578, 581, 590, 900; War, 497
Morrison, Rev. C. C., 918
Morrow, D. W., 505 n., 546 n., 567 n., 625
Morse, S. F. B., 318; code of, 745
Mortillet, L. L. G. de, 667
Morton, John, cardinal, 86
Morton, W. T. G., 651
Moscow, 991
Moselsic, Simon, 447
Moses, 178-79, 188, 653-54
Mosul, 533, 904, 905
Motor: boats, 316; busses, 306, 414, 738-40; trucks, 306, 723, 738, 739-40, 761. *See also* Automobiles.
Motz, Friedrich von, 383
Moufang, Christoph, 945
Moulton, H. G., 623 n.; and Pasvolsky, Leo, 620, (quoted) 621; Warburton, C. A., and Leven, Maurice, 417 n., 807, 809, 811, 815
Moussorgsky, M. P., 713
Moving picture, 265, 439, 747, 748, 763; news reels of, 438, 743, 747; sound (talkies), 747, 1101; effects of, 447, 564; industry, 370, 743, 747
Mozart, W. A., 254, 255, 1097
Mugwump secession, 514, 874
Müller, A. H., 386
Muller, H. J., quoted, 964
Müller, J. P., 647
Müller, Max, 465, 476
Mumford, Lewis, 724
Mun, Albert, count de, 945, 955
Munro, D. C., 14
Münster, 170

Murmansk, 990
Muscovy Company, 24, 62
Muscle Shoals, 1004
Museums, 150, 957; art, 447
Music, 184, 250, 253-55, 440, 572-73, 712-15, 1097-1101; baroque, 253; jazz, 1098, 1100-01; rococo, 253, 254
Muslims, 11, 16-17, 20, 22, 57-58, 530; in commerce, 63; influence of, 8, 14, 15, 31, 146, 147, 726
Musschenbroek, Pieter van, 152
Musset, L. C. A. de, 695-96
Mussolini, Benito, 342, 343, 419, 425, 474, 496, 510, 611, 612, 633, 951, 962
Mustapha Kemal, president of the Turkish Republic, 353, 533, 561, 609, 616
Mysticism, 152, 899-900, 1062, 1068, 1069, 1103

Nachtigal, Gustav, 528, 650
Nagel, Ernest, 1068
Nägeli, K. W. von, 647, 648
Nagpur, 535
Nanking, Treaty of (1842), 536
Nantes, 38; Revocation of the Edict of (1685), 166, 179, 400
Napier, John, 147
Napier, Sir W. F. P., 466 n., 672
Napkin economy, 57, 60
Naples, 459, 1083; population of, 213; Kingdom of, *see* Two Sicilies.
Napoleon I, emperor of the French, 54, 99, 109, 114-20, 121, 130, 135, 206, 234, 272, 305, 318, 326-27, 411, 433, 455-56, 459, 461, 464, 465, 633, 684, 697, 700, 743, 899, 942, 950 n.; era of, 33, 37, 54, 91, 122, 123, 460, 466; Code of, 54, 117, 119, 225
Napoleon III (Louis Napoleon), emperor of the French, 122-23, 321, 383, 411, 429, 459, 464-65 (quoted), 492, 579, 612, 696, 950
Napoleonic wars, 52, 54, 130, 272, 320, 329, 356, 899
Narod movement (Russia), 981
Nassau, Germany, 312
Natal, 529
Nathan, G. J., 1090, 1091
Nation, N. Y. City, 1091
National Bureau of Economic Research, 812
National City Bank, N. Y. City, 782, 783, 790-91, 828
National Industrial Recovery Act and Administration, American, 294, 498, 631, 840-41, 845 n., 862, 944, 951, 960-61. *See also* New Deal.
National: Republican party, American, 513; Security League, 577, 951 n.; Socialist party, *see* Germany, Nazi.
Nationalism, 4, 6, 9, 75-76, 82-85, 110, 115, 121-36 *passim,* 197, 217, 240, 265, 270, 510, 521-37 *passim,* 550, 552, 561, 563, 570, 575, 607, 610, 616, 629, 634, 672, 690, 712, 774, 859, 867, 913, 917, 937, 959-63 *passim,* 980, 996; foundations of contemporary, 453-78; and the World War, 471-73, 586; Protestantism and, 65; American, 109, 467-69;

INDEX

economic, 330, 463-64, 473-74. *See also* Patriotism.
Naturalism: in art, 709-10; in literature, 691, 698, 703, 704, 708, 1088; *see also* Zola, Emile; in music, 713; in philosophy, 162, 186, 384
Nature: philosophers, 656; state of, 96-97, 218-19, 231, 237, 382
Naumann, Friedrich, 945
Nauru Island, 553
Nauvoo, Ill., 394
Navies, 548, 550, 569; in the World War, 598-99; American, 910-13; Austrian, 576; Dutch, 26; English, 26-27, 101, 103, 129, 315, 465, 576, 578, 585, 598-99, 910-12; French, 465, 576, 585, 910-11; German, 465, 576, 578, 615; Japanese, 348, 910-12; Russian, 465, 576, 585; Spanish, 24, 26-27, 87, 93; Turkish, 585 n.
Navigation, 31-32, 38, 45, 70, 149, 264; Acts, English, 27, 105
Near East, 9-16 *passim*, 39, 462, 532-34, 546-52 *passim*, 578, 580, 597, 610, 616; trade with, 9, 38
Necker, Jacques, 54
Negroes, 384, 398, 401, 423, 680; in the United States, 365, 498, 843, 890. *See also* Slavery, American.
Neilson, J. B., 279
Nelson, Horatio Nelson, viscount, 598; in the World War, 597
Neo-Catholicism, 389
Neo-Humanism. *See* Humanism, New.
Neo-Kantianism, 1067
Neo-Malthusianism, 417
Neolithic Age, 264, 273
Neo-Platonism, 467, 1067
Neo-Thomism, 1056, 1067
Neo-Transcendentalism, 1067
Nepal, 534-35
Neptune (planet), 641, 1039
Nerval, Gérard de, 572
Nervous and mental disease, 288, 439, 677, 965, 968-70. *See also* Mental hygiene.
Nestorians, 16
Netherlands, 26-27, 51, 63, 87. *See also* Belgium; Holland.
Neuilly, Treaty of (1919), 607, 616, 904, 909
Neurology, 648, 652
New Bedford, Mass., 358
Newberry, T. H., 876
New Caledonia, 540
Newcomen, Thomas, 300
New Deal, American, 435, 808, 815, 841, 847 n., 849, 850, 856 n., 885, 891, 944, 958, 960-61, 973-74, 1000, 1015, 1094. *See also* National Industrial Recovery Act.
New Economic Policy, Soviet Russia (NEP), 998, 1007, 1011-12
New England, 364, 513, 860; industry in, 357-58, 368, 469, 944
Newfang, Oscar, 958
Newfoundland, 24, 48
New Guinea, 540
New Harmony, Ind., 394
New Hebrides, 540

Newman, J. H., cardinal, 198, 390, 679-80, 706
New Masses, 1091
New Mexico, 881
New Netherlands, 24
New Orleans, 362
New Republic, 917, 1091
New School for Social Research, 1078
New South Wales, 686
New Testament, 57 n., 192, 217-18, 842; quoted, 8, 179
Newton, Sir Isaac, 78, 144, 147-48, 151, 152, 159, 177, 181, 182 n., 189, 194-95, 196, 226, 265, 379, 643, 658, 663, 933, 1035, 1036, 1037, 1049
New World. *See* America.
New York City, 361, 362, 412-13, 414-15, 711, 798, 811-12, 833, 956, 966, 1096-97; population of, 405-07
New York City newspapers: *American,* 1093; *Daily News,* 1094; *Evening Journal,* 1093; *Evening Post,* 1092, 1094, (quoted) 447; *Herald,* 1093; *Sun,* 1092, 1093; *Times,* 743 n., 1092, 1093, (quoted) 288, 406, 407, 418, 796, 800, 805; *Tribune,* 1092; *World,* 1093; *World-Telegram,* 1094
New York State, 361, 362, 363, 435, 510, 833, 845, 872, 968
New Yorker, 1091
New Zealand, 436, 471, 499, 540, 551, 553, 868; in the World War, 597
Newspapers, 63, 264, 265, 268, 270, 438, 457, 458, 503, 504, 652, 743-46, 748, 860, 874, 1054, 1065, 1090-92; news-gathering agencies for, 745-46. *See also* Journalism.
Nexö, Martin Andersen, 1087
Nibelungenlied, 714
Nicaragua, 541-45 *passim,* 594, 1084
Nicholas I, emperor of Russia, 124
Nicholas II, emperor of Russia, 339, 496, 532, 549, 585, 588, 590, 981 (quoted), 983-87 *passim;* abdication of, 595, 980
Nicholas, grand duke of Russia, 593
Nicobar Islands, 18
Nicolai, G. F., 958
Nicolson, Sir Arthur, 580
Nicolson, Harold, quoted, 927
Niebuhr, Reinhold, 946 n., 1066
Niepce, J. N., 747
Nietzsche, F. W., 194, 572, 576-77, 668, 683, 695, 704, 705, 714, 1090
Nieuport, 595
Nigeria, 463, 530-32
Nilsson, Christine, 715
Nilus, Sergei, 478
Nine Power Pact (1922), 910
Nineteenth Century, 1091
Nisard, J. M. N. D., 466, 697
Noah, 217
Nobel, A. B., 914
Nobel Prize in literature, 1084
Nobility, social class, 51, 52, 94, 108, 233, 244, 482, 486; French, 109-18 *passim,* 121, 123, 488; Russian, 92-93, 959. *See also* Aristocracy, landed; Lords, feudal.
Noguchi, Hideyo, 1049

Nomads, 231
Nominations, American party, 874-76, 880-81
Nonconformists, English, 100, 101, 102, 103, 104, 106, 166-67, 172, 383, 389, 390; persecution of, 400. *See also* Protestantism; and names of Evangelical churches.
Non-Intercourse Act, American (1809), 358
Non-Partisan League, American, 514, 516
Nordica, Lillian, 1100
Normans, Normandy, 11
Norris, Frank, 707-08
Norris, G. W., Norris-Sinclair bill, 891
North, Lord (Frederick, 2d earl of Guilford), 107, 111
North, the American, 365, 366, 367, 368, 468
North America, 25, 26, 44, 48; birth rate in, 419. *See also* America; and names of divisions.
North American Review, 1091
North Carolina, 73, 366
North German Confederation, 465, 940
Northcliffe, A. C. W. Harmsworth, 1st viscount, 586, 588, 600, 1093
Northmen, invasions of the, 83
Northwest, the American, 365
Norton, C. D., 412
Norway, 436, 460. *See also* Scandinavia.
Novara, battle of, 125
Novels, romances, 181, 182, 183, 184, 246, 256, 448, 692-706 *passim*, 1079-90 *passim*
Novicow, Jacques (Y. A. Novikou), 502, 667, 901, 933
Nudist movement, 1067
Nuremberg, 88, 1086
Nussbaum, F. L., quoted, 64
Nyassaland, 532
Nye, G. P., 913
Nystrom, P. H., quoted, 765

Oastler, Richard, 388
Obscurantism, 158, 206, 389, 1055-57
Oceania, 337, 463, 521, 525, 539-42, 549; birth rate in, 419
Oceanic (thalassic) culture, 3, 6
Ochs, Adolph, 1093
O'Connell, Daniel, 462
Odell, G. T., quoted, 755
Oderic (Odoric) of Pordenone, 19
Oehlenschläger, A. G., 572
Oersted, H. C., 267, 644
Ogburn, W. F., 769
Ogden, C. K., 1058
Ogg, F. A., quoted, 331, 335; and Sharp, W. R., quoted, 950
O.G.P.U., Russia, 995
Ohio, 364, 881
Ohm, G. S., 644
Oil: Age, 729; scandal, 874. *See also* Petroleum.
Old-age pensions or insurance, 491, 492, 495, 496, 841, 939-43 *passim*, 1026
Oldknow, Samuel, 286
Old Catholics, 676
Old régime, 109-23 *passim*, 183, 226, 233, 454-55, 488, 489, 491, 492, 496, 522, 767

Old Testament, 149, 179, 217-18, 649, 653-58 *passim*, 661, 698
Olmütz, Humiliation of, 126 n.
Oman, Sir C. W. C., 672
Omnibus bills, American, 887-89
O'Neill, E. G., 1090
Onions, Peter, 278
Open-hearth process, steel. *See* Siemens, Sir William.
Opera, 253-54, 572, 713-14, 1100, 1101
Opitz von Boberfeld, Martin, 86, 246
Opium, 535, 567, 906; War (1840-42), 536
Oppenheimer, Franz, 1059
Opportunism. *See* Socialism, Revisionist.
Optics, 146, 148, 203, 747
Orage, A. R., 955
Orange Free State, 138, 529
Oratorios, 253
Orbigny, A. D. d', 649
Orchard, J. E., 350
Oregon, 845, 881
Orford, 1st earl of. *See* Walpole, Sir Robert.
Organicism, 667, 958
Orleanist dynasty, 121, 122, 206, 321, 383, 389, 458, 491, 530
Ornstein, Leo, 1100
Orozco, J. C., 1096
Ortega y Gasset, José, 1084, 1085
Ortelius, (Oertel) Abraham, 149
Orth, S. P., quoted, 938, 954
Orthodox Eastern (Greek) Church, 12, 92, 982, 1019-21, 1066; persecution of the, 1020
Osborn, H. F., 1063
Osborne, T. M., 967
Osborne case (labor-unionism), 949
Osgood, H. L., 672
Osiander, Andreas, 167
Ostend Company, 27 n.
Ostentation, 32, 45, 91, 251, 440-41
Ostrogorsky, M. Y., 669
Ostwald, Wilhelm, 682
Otis, A. S., 970
Otto I, the Great, medieval Roman emperor, 456
Otto, M. C., 1061
Otto, Nicholas, 302
Oudh, 535
Outlook, 1091
Overcapitalization, 792, 800, 804, 837
Overhead costs, 748, 827, 1001
Overproduction, 761, 771-72, 813-15, 824, 837, 960, 1028
Ovid (Publius Ovidius Naso), 446; quoted, 160
Oviedo y Valdés, G. F. de, 245
Owen, Robert, 286, 390, 394, 395, 397, 947-48, 949, 1077
Owen, Walter, 1080
Owen, Wilfred, 1080
Oxford, Robert Harley, 1st earl of, 507
Oxford: Movement, 390, 679-80; University, 688
Ozanam, A. F., 389

Pachelbel, Johann, 254
Pacifism, 130, 172 n., 472, 625 n. *See also* Peace.

INDEX

Pacioli (Pacciuoli), Luigi, 63
Paderewski, Ignace, 1100
Paganini, Niccolò, 714
Page, Kirby, 619, 946 n., 1066; quoted, 600, 601
Page, W. H., 596
Paine, Thomas, 99, 171, 172, 178-79 (quoted), 188, 206, 233 n., 384, 672, 673
Painting: American, 711; Dutch, 248, 249, 250, 251; English, 250, 251, 572, 709; Flemish, 248, 249, 250, 709-10; French, 249, 250, 251, 572; German, 710-11; Italian, 247-48, 249, 251; Russian, 572, 711; Spanish, 247-48, 249, 250; medieval, 248; Renaissance, 247-53 *passim;* oriental influence on, 251
Palacio Valdés, Armando, 701
Paléologue, M. G., 585
Paleolithic Age, 1106
Paleontology, 649
Palermo, population of, 213
Palestine, 17, 19, 533, 551, 553, 597, 904; Hebrews in, 478, 609-10. *See also* Crusades.
Paley, Rev. William, 202, 203, 673, 1055
Palfrey, J. G., 469
Palmer, A. M., 514, 874
Palmer, Elihu, 187
Palos, 23
Panama: Canal, 543-44; Canal Zone, 545; Republic of, 523, 541-45 *passim,* 594
Pan-American Union, 914
Pan-Americanism, 543-44
Pandora's box, 108
Pan-German League, 576-77
Pan-Germanism, 529
Panhard & Levassor, 739
Panics, financial, 836. *See also* Business cycle.
Pankhurst, Emmeline and Sylvia, 437
Panslavism, 124, 130, 462, 549, 576
Panzini, Alfredo, 1083
Papacy, 12, 14-15, 17, 96, 205-06, 217, 233-34, 675-76, 899; corruption of the, 15. *See also* Church and State; and names of Popes.
Papal: curia, 67; infallibility, doctrine of, 675; States, 125
Paper, 746; wood pulp, 727, 746
Papin, Denis, 299-300, 314
Papini, Giovanni, 1083
Paracelsus, 148
Pardo Bazán, Emilia, 701
Pareto, Vilfredo, 961, 1057
Paris, 70, 87, 91, 112, 113, 120, 121, 252, 254, 411, 687, 902, 905, 953; in the World War, 594, 596-97; population of, 213, 405
Paris: Commune, (1789) 112, 113, (1871) 127-28, 237; Conferences on Reparations, (1920) 623, (1929) 625; Congress of (1878), 900; Peace Conference (1918-19), 473, 494, 530, 538, 544, 551, 610, 613, 898, 901, 906, 956. *See also* Versailles, Treaty of; Treaty of (1763), 27
Parker, A. B., 514
Parker, F. W., 1071
Parker, Sir Gilbert, 600
Parks, 408, 411, 957

Parliament, British, 52, 78, 79, 100, 127, 133, 134, 166, 167, 214-16, 275, 293, 400, 401, 408, 454, 490, 506-08, 866-67, 949; supremacy of, 98, 104, 121-22, 272, 487-88, 491. *See also* Commons, House of.
Parsons, Hon. Sir C. A., 302, 315
Parsons, P. A., 946 n.
Parthenon, 712
Parties, political, 431; evolution of, 484, 502, 511-12; nature and functions of, 501-05; importance of, 501. *See also* Communist parties; Socialist parties.
Parties, political, American, 510-17, 835; caucus system of, 511-12; conventions of, 484, 502, 511-12, 873, 881; machine of, 872-81 *passim. See also* names of American parties.
Parties, political: Austrian, 509-10; English, 517. *See also* names of English parties; European, 516-17; French, 509, 516-17, 936; German, 396, 493-94, 509, 516, 633, 935, 951; Italian, 510; Russian, 985. *See also* names of Russian parties.
Partnership, business, 61-62, 349, 795
Party system of government, 453, 669, 768, 855-94; group (bloc), 516-17, 878, 883; two-party, 515-17, 1059
Pascal, Blaise, 147, 148
Pascoli, Giovanni, 1083
Pašič, Nikola, 588, 593
Pasternak, Boris, 1088
Pasteur, Louis, 647, 651, 653, 676, 736
Pastoral economy, 351, 934
Pasvolsky, Leo, and Moulton, H. G., 620; quoted, 621
Patagonia, 23
Patents, 751
Pathology, 149, 153, 647, 651, 736, 1048-49
Patriarchy, 231, 237
Patriotism, 126, 270, 470-75 *passim,* 546 n., 565-66, 570, 672, 690, 699, 702, 868, 913, 916, 925, 926, 928, 937, 938, 959, 996, 1074. *See also* Nationalism.
Patten, S. N., 939
Patti, Adelina, 715
Paul, St., 217, 466, 674, 842
Paul IV, pope, 167
Paul, Lewis, 274
Pawtucket, R. I., 357
Peabody, F. G., 946 n.
Peace Conference, Paris (1918-19). *See* Paris Peace Conference.
Peace the natural state, 219, 221
Peace: the quest for international, 130, 222, 458-60, 464, 578, 612-13, 618-19, 868, 870, 898-928, 961, 980, 987; congresses and conferences of, 914-15; societies engaged in, 914, 917
Pearl, Raymond, 406
Pearson, Karl, 659
Peasantry, 5, 13, 53, 102, 109-20 *passim,* 216, 238, 271, 289, 338-39, 425-39 *passim,* 486, 496, 632-35, 710, 759, 981-1013 *passim,* 1060; revolts of the, 117, 427, 985, 1007. *See also* Proletariat.
Pease, Edward, 937

INDEX

Pease, F. G., 1042-43
Pecora, Ferdinand, 831, 832
Pedagogy, 243-44, 688-90
Peel, Sir Robert, 320, 383, 399, 508
Peel, Robert, 286
Peirce, C. S., 682, 1053
Peking, 16, 18-19, 20, 565
Pelew Islands, 538, 540
Pelloutier, Fernand, 953
Penck, Albrecht, 649, 1047
Penka, Karl, 466
Penn, William, 170, 899
Pennsylvania, 213, 294, 359, 361, 363, 399-400, 510, 844; Railroad, 362, 750, 799, 876; University of, 688
Pensions, 840, 890; veterans', 614 n., 888-89, 892, 894. See also Old-age pensions.
Penty, A. J., 955
Pepper, G. W., 881
Pereda, J. M. de, 701
Pérez de Ayala, Ramón, 1085
Pérez Galdós, Benito, 701, 1084
Pergolesi, G. B., 254
Periclean age, 143
Periodical literature, 439, 457, 652, 1090-92
Perkin, Sir W. H., 334 n.
Perkins, Frances, 436
Permanent Court of International Justice, 628, 903-05, 913; the United States and the, 904, 923, 924
Perrault, Charles, 192
Perrault, Claude, 252
Perry, Commodore M. C., 537
Persia, 16-17, 20, 39, 45, 462, 463, 466, 533-34, 549, 551, 613, 996; influence of, 572, 654, 702, 1052
Personnel administration, 288, 763-64
Peru, 24, 40; trade with, 34
Peruzzi, bankers, 58
Pescadores, 345
Peschel, Oskar, 571
Pestalozzi, J. H., 243-44, 689
Pestilence, 12, 212, 408, 417, 567
Peter, St., 174, 217
Peter I, the Great, emperor of Russia, 25, 85, 88, 89, 92, 131, 337, 496, 579, 946
Peter Martyr (Pietro Martire Vermigli), 245
Peter the Hermit, 11, 13
Peters, Carl, 464 n., 529, 565
Petite bourgeoisie. See Middle class, lower.
Petition, right of, 95; of Right, English (1628), 101, 134
Petrograd, 987
Petroleum, 267, 284, 302, 346, 353, 368, 370, 416, 523, 533, 534, 542, 546, 547, 548, 552, 568, 725, 726-27, 729-33, 736, 737; American, 370, 372, 729-33, 753, 771, 772; Russian, 732, 1003; South American, 732
Peugeot Frères, Les Fils de, 739
Phenomenology, 1067
Philadelphia, 70, 361, 362; *Ledger*, 744; *Record*, 1094
Philanthropy, scientific, 957. See also Charity.
Philip II (Philip Augustus), king of France, 3
Philip IV, the Fair, king of France, 14

Philip II, king of Spain, 85, 87, 93, 131
Philip V, king of Spain, 73
Philippine Islands, 23, 539, 540, 542, 545, 549, 560, 564, 565; imports of the, 546
Phillimore, W. G. F. Phillimore, 1st baron, 901
Phillips, D. G., 1089
Philology, 196, 197, 198, 205, 465, 476, 572, 1057
Philosophes, French, 111, 379, 455, 488, 1053
Philosophy, 143, 154-63, 173-207, 227, 572-73, 648, 664, 680-81, 932, 979, 1053, 1055-57, 1067-70; ancient, 155; Greek, 155, 655, 656, 932; medieval, 154-58. See also names of philosophies.
Phonograph, 1101
Photo-electric cell, 757, 760
Photography, 736, 747
Photographs, transmission of, 743, 747
Phrenology, 648
Physics, 147, 148, 151-52, 160, 181, 255, 265-67, 522, 640, 641-44, 658, 1035-36, 1043-45; influence of, 45, 648, 650, 729, 1047, 1049-50
Physiocrats, 54, 78-79, 111, 151, 154, 319, 379-80, 381, 382, 384, 663, 933
Physiology, 145, 148, 153, 184, 647, 1047, 1048
Picasso, Pablo, 1095
Pickford, Mary, 747
Picot, Georges, 533
Pidal, Ramón Menéndez, 1085
Piecework, 821, 949, 1014
Piedmont. See Sardinia.
Pigeons, carrier, 318
Pigou, A. C., 939
Pilgrimages, 11
Pilnitz, Declaration of, 113
Pinel, Philippe, 401, 968
Piracy, 9, 32, 70, 85. See also Privateering.
Pirandello, Luigi, 1083-84
Pisa, 38
Pitkin, W. B., quoted, 808
Pitt, William, 98, 899
Pittsburgh, 359, 360, 749, 798, 1003; income and expenditures of, 410
Pius VII, pope, 119
Pius IX, pope, 125, 676, 1056
Pius XI, pope, 945, 1066
Pizarro, Francisco, 33 n., 700
Place, Francis, 381, 384, 385, 429, 491, 949
Plague, the, 212. See also Pestilence.
Planck, M. K. E. L., 149, 1035, 1043-44, 1049; quoted, 664
Planning, economic, 838-41, 847-50, 960. See also Mercantilism, German; New Deal; Russia, Soviet.
Plato, Platonism, 145 n., 192, 236, 380, 438, 484, 655, 665, 666, 669, 1069
Platt, T. C., 544, 872
Playgrounds, 957
Playne, C. E., 867
Plebiscites, 456
Plehve, V. K., 128, 464 n.
Plekhanov, G. V., 985

INDEX

Pliny the Elder (Gaius Plinius Secundus), 19, 185, 655
Plivier, Theodor, 1079 n.
Plot, Robert, 149
Plumb, G. E., Plumb Plan, 955
Pluralism, 90, 682, 1053, 1059, 1068
Plutarch, 145 n., 227
Pluto (planet), 641 n., 1039 n., 1040 n.
Plutocracy, 146, 235, 442-43, 445, 447, 503, 690, 863, 868, 870, 963, 964; American, 498, 829-30, 870, 873-74, 880, 882, 1065-66. *See also* Fortunes, private.
Pobiedonostev, C. P., 128, 464 n., 981 n.
Poe, E. A., 469, 707, 708
Poetry, 192, 196, 663, 1065; American, 469, 706, 707, 1088-89; English, 245, 246, 572, 691-92, 693, 1080; French, 182, 183, 572, 695-96, 697-98, 1082; German, 246, 702, 703, 1085-86; Italian, 467, 699, 700, 1083; Latin American, 1084; Polish, 706; Russian, 705, 1087; Scandinavian, 704, 1087; Spanish, 700, 701, 1084
Poincaré, J. H., 1035
Poincaré, Raymond, president of France, 494, 578-87, 589, 593, 612; quoted, 582
Poison gas, 598
Polakov, W. N., quoted, 839
Poland, 11, 16, 88, 120, 121, 130, 138, 455-62 *passim*, 476, 478, 608, 612, 634, 706, 868, 905, 907, 912, 919, 962; and the World War, 595, 602; (debts) 621; population of, 418, 608; birth rate in, 419
Poles, 213 n., 461-62, 905
Polish Corridor, 474, 607-08, 610
Political economy, 383. *See also* Economics; Political science.
Political philosophy, 666; the secularization of, 216-22
Political science, 154, 222, 226-34, 378-97, 434, 572, 666, 668-69, 768, 859 n., 1049, 1059
Political society, beginning of, 484. *See also* State, the; and names of forms of government.
Pollock, Sir Frederick, 670
Polo, Maffeo and Nicolo, 17
Polo, Marco, 17-19
Polygyny, 190, 1022
Polynesia, 540
Pontoppidan, Henrik, 1086
Pools, financial term, 796, 804-06
Poor relief, 230, 237-40, 290, 383, 398, 400-01, 965, 967. *See also* Unemployment relief.
Pope, Alexander, 177, 181, 227, 245, 246
Population: growth and mobility of, 63, 212-16, 269, 381, 444, 524, 560, 575, (since 1800) 416-24; urbanization of, 405-16
Populist party, American, 373, 374, 514, 516
Porcelain, 251, 346
Pork-barrel legislation, 880, 887-89
Port Arthur, 463, 537, 538, 545, 580
Porter, Cole, 1100
Portland, Ore., 366
Portugal, 9, 21-23, 25-26, 35, 87, 130, 138, 534, 542, 586, 594, 600, 636, 868, 923; Republic of, 623

Pösche, Theodor, 466
Posen, 608
Positivism, 675, 958
Post, A. H., 670
Post, Wiley, 741
Postal system, 63, 746-47; aerial, 746; parcel post in the, 746, 747, 764; rural free delivery in the, 747; rates in the, 746-47
Potter, C. F., 1061
Pottery, 44, 344, 346
Poulsen, Valdemar, 743
Pound, Roscoe, 1059
Pourtalès, Friedrich, count von, 580 n., 588 n.
Poussin, Nicolas, 250
Poverty, 381, 965-67. *See also* Poor relief; Unemployment relief.
Power, E. E., quoted, 16-17, 18, 19-20
Power, balance of, 225, 578
Power, mechanical, 299-319, 736, 756-62. *See also* Engines.
Pragmatism, 197, 682, 1053, 1068, 1069, 1083
Prague, 124, 125
Prati, Giovanni, 699
Pre-Raphaelites, 709
Presbyterian Church, 204
Presidents, American; choice of, 861, 873, 881; methods of election of, 510-11; powers and duties of, 886-87. *See also* Elections; Nominations.
Prester John, 17
Price, Clair, quoted, 904
Price, the just, 295
Prices, price system, 57-58, 60, 295, 816-22, 837; control of, 118, 335, 627, 630-31, 637, 751; fixing, 71, 77, 335, 766, 780; fluctuations in, 41-43, 378, 630, 637, 836, 839, 848
Priestley, Joseph, 152, 385, 727
Primaries, 880; direct, 500, 864, 865, 876, 881
Primitivism (art), 572, 1095, 1096
Primo de Rivera y Orbaneja, Miguel, marquis de Estella, 497
Primogeniture, 12, 107, 121
Printing, 166-67, 438, 746; invention of, 5; licensed, 167; presses, 276, 744, 746
Prism, 146
Prisons, prison reform, 230, 385, 391, 399-400, 678, 680, 967; Auburn system, 401, 680; Elmira system, 967; Pennsylvania system, 400-01, 680; in Soviet Russia, 1025
Privateering, 32, 58, 59, 70, 75, 85, 100
Prjevalsky, N. M., 650
Production, economic, 374, 433, 442, 827; control of, 630-31; increase of, 769-76, 820-81, 825; and debt, 825; large-scale, 63, 285, 329, 370, 364-73, 748-52, 771, 780, 781, 822, 949; limitation of, 771-72, 821; mass, 10, 288, 294, 374, 442, 629, 739, 752-54, 780, (in agriculture) 761-62, (in education) 1070
Profit motive and system, 57, 62-69, 269, 294, 295, 378, 427-33 *passim*, 560, 781, 809, 816-48 *passim*, 913, 960, 972, 973, 1000, 1028, 1059; attitudes toward, 64, 65, 143, 168, 1103; in Soviet Russia, 980, 998. *See also* Speculation.
Profit-sharing, 390, 957

INDEX

Progress, human, 4, 144, 191-200 *passim,* 229, 256, 263, 660, 665, 666, 1054-55, 1102
Progressive party, American, 384, 498, 514, 516, 874
Prohibition (of alcohol), 671, 834-35, 859, 864 n., 866, 971-72; in America, 204, 834-35
Projectiles, 267, 281, 460
Projectors, financial term, 59, 65
Prokoviev, S. S., 1099
Proletariat, 4-5, 42-43, 64, 79, 91, 94, 99, 100, 102, 127, 136, 138, 178, 183, 235, 269-94 *passim,* 373, 380-454 *passim,* 482, 487-504 *passim,* 522, 560, 631, 673, 690-91, 705, 724, 749, 762-64, 859-68 *passim,* 931-74 *passim,* 1057; and religion, 178, 204; challenge of the, to capitalism, 427-33; dictatorship of the, 32, 874, 934. *See also* Russia, Soviet; effects of the World War on the, 616-18; in literature, 1079-88 *passim. See also* Class conflict; Class consciousness; Labor; Labor-unionism; Peasantry; Poor relief; Serfdom; Slavery.
Proletariat: American, 105-06, 132, 134, 364-75 *passim,* 515-16, 801-50 *passim,* 863-66, 874, 880, 935; English, 53-54, 134, 204, 215-16, 373, 387-88, 935; European, 373; French, 110-23 *passim;* Russian, 338-40. *See also* Russia, Soviet.
Propaganda, 457-58, 477, 525, 833; Soviet Russian, 446, 1019, 1020, 1027, 1088, 1101; World War, 471, 530, 533, 576-77, 586, 599-600, 606, 611-13, 980
Property: communism in, 236-37, 392
Property, private, 96, 131-39 *passim,* 168, 213, 217, 220, 223-24, 270, 272, 379, 420, 431, 434, 436, 441-46 *passim,* 487, 505, 517, 661, 669, 801-02, 809, 819, 821, 847, 849, 932, 946-60 *passim,* 1103; repudiated, 237, 396, 956, 959, 980, 997-1002; the United States Supreme Court and, 842-47
Prophecy, 175-76
Proportional representation, 136, 499, 500, 871, 878, 883
Prostitution, 970-71; Soviet Russia and, 971, 1023, 1026
Protectionism. *See* Tariffs, protective.
Protestant Episcopal Church, 187
Protestant Revolution, 4-5, 6, 21, 61, 65, 85, 86, 88, 145, 183, 205, 223, 240, 486, 522, 683
Protestantism, 63, 87, 117, 143-45, 166-206 *passim,* 217, 238, 389-90, 398-99, 402, 476, 524, 563, 577, 670-80 *passim,* 945-46, 1060-66, 1103; and capitalism, 65-66, 842; and education, 240-43, 683; persecutions by, 166; persecutions of, 166, 179, 400. *See also* Nonconformists; and names of Evangelical churches and divisions.
Prothero, R. E. (Lord Ernle), quoted, 50
Protocols of the Elders of Zion, 478
Protocracy, 503
Proudhon, P. J., 395-96, 934, 953
Proust, J. L., 152, 644
Proust, Marcel, 1083
Provence, 165

Provincialism, 4, 6, 252, 256, 264, 457, 468, 904
Prud'hon, P. P., 250
Prynne, William, 167
Psychiatry, 652, 969, 1048; criminal, 399, 968, 1025; industrial, 288
Psychoanalysis, 652, 969, 1067, 1080
Psychology, 159, 160, 163-64, 200, 647, 648-49, 688, 690, 1048, 1070-71; criminal, 399, 967; crowd (mob), 503, 504, 748, 866, 1048; dynamic, 431-32; genetic, 244, 647, 648, 688, 689, 1071; Gestalt, 1048; group, 859; industrial, 288, 764; of religion, 198, 1062; simian, 660; social, 219, 431, 858-59, 1048, 1049; influence of, 217, 243-44, 666, 673, 860-61, 1064-65, 1067
Psychophysics, 1048
Public opinion, 483
Public utilities, 370-71, 411, 751, 782-800 *passim,* 819-34 *passim,* 844, 875, 944
Public works, 77, 91-92, 120, 212, 252, 379, 415, 880, 932, 944
Puccini, Giacomo, 572, 700, 1100
Puck, 1091
Puerto Rico, 543-44, 545, 564
Prussia, 54, 77, 85-86, 88-89, 113, 120-35 *passim,* 197, 312, 313, 319-20, 329-30, 331, 383, 392, 455-65 *passim,* 477, 492-94, 509, 576-77, 579, 633, 695, 871, 900, 931, 940-41, 958; population of, 212-13; in the World War, 595 n. *See also* Germany; East Prussia.
Pufendorf, Samuel, 218-19, 220, 223, 666, 669
Punishments, 116, 163
Pujo, A. P., Pujo investigation, 830-31
Pulitzer, Joseph, 1093
Punishment: for crime, 398-400; Soviet, 1024-25. *See also* Prisons; for dissent, 398.
Punjab, the, 535
Pupin, M. I., 203, 1062, 1063
Purcell, Henry, 255, 1100
Purchasing power, mass, 382, 426, 765, 809-50 *passim,* 957, 960, 973-74
Puritanism, 63, 65, 100, 101, 104, 201, 506, 562, 671, 707, 1057, 1066, 1086, 1100
Purnell, 279
Pusey, E. B., 390
Pushkin, A. S., 705
Putting-out system, 46-48, 214, 215, 264, 268, 270, 285, 289, 325-26, 329, 339-40, 360, 405, 427, 780
Puvis de Chavannes, P. C., 710

Quadrant, 31, 45
Quadruple Alliance (1814), 206, 900
Quakers. *See* Friends, Society of.
Quantum theory, 643 n., 644, 1044
Quebec Acts, 27
Quesnay, François, 380
Quimby, P. T., 677
Quintana, M. J., 700
Quintero, Serafín and Joaquín Alvarez, 1085
Quintilian, 862

Rabelais, François, 86, 183, 245
Race: differentiation of, 1047; suicide, 420

Rachmaninov, S. V., 1100
Racialism, 197, 422-23, 474, 498, 575, 868, 925, 926. See also Anti-Semitism; Aryan myth.
Racine, J. B., 86, 246, 699
Racketeering, 833-36, 876
Radcliffe, William, 276
Radek, Karl (Karl Sobelson), 988
Radetsky, Josef, count of Radetz, 125
Radical party, British, 508
Radicalism, 66, 127, 136, 138, 236-37, 343, 431, 445-46, 472, 476, 477, 633, 961, 963; economic, 168, 474, 510, 802, 957-78; Philosophical, 383 n., 384-85, 429; in America, 107-08, 134, 164, 168, 172, 424, 840, 846
Radio, 265, 266, 267, 268, 270, 743, 747-48, 767, 862; influence of the, 438-39, 447, 457, 469, 748, 875, 1065, 1101; industry, 370
Radium, 1044-45; therapy, 736
Radioactivity, 318, 644, 645, 1045
Rae, John, 386
Railroads, 307, 457, 522, 725, 726, 732, 736-39, 740, 741, 751; early, 308-10; power for, 303; speed on, 308-09, 737-38; effects of, 319
Railroads: American, 295, 309, 357, 361-62, 365, 367, 468, 469, 736-38, 750, 781, 834, 844, 1007, (controlled by bankers) 783, 790-91, 820, 822-23, 824, 830, (rate-fixing by) 844; English, 308-10; French, 310-11; German, 309, 311-14, 331, 614, 732, 741; Russian; (tsarist) 339, 340-41, (Soviet) 997, 1006-07; of other countries, (African) 737, (Asiatic) 350-51, 737, (European) 342, 343, 346, 347, 732, 736-37
Raleigh, Sir Walter, 245
Ramsay, Sir William, 644
Ramus, Pierre (Petrus), 145 n.
Rand School of Social Science, 1077
Randall, J. H., Jr., quoted, 199-200, 1064
Ranke, Leopold von, 672
Raphael Sanzio, 447, 466
Rasputin, G. Y., 987
Rathenau, Emil, 334
Rationalism, 143-44, 150, 151, 155, 161-62, 172-87 passim, 205, 216, 217, 224-56 passim, 263, 397, 400, 444, 466, 476, 665, 670-80 passim, 697, 858, 865
Ratzel, Friedrich, 571, 650, 672 n., 1047
Ratzenhofer, Gustav, 1058
Rau, K. H., 319, 382
Rauch, C. D., 711
Rauschenbusch, Walter, 946
Rautenstrauch, Walter, quoted, 827-28
Ravel, Maurice, 1099
Raw materials, 9, 10, 43, 270, 319, 337, 374, 416, 444, 463, 474, 521, 522, 523, 527, 546, 551-52, 569, 575, 627, 631, 748, 749, 751, 837, 925, 926
Ray (Wray), John, 151, 153
Raymond, Henry, 1092
Raynal, G. T. F., 245
Raynouard, F. J. M., 466 n., 672
Ravaillac, François, 87
Rayon, 342, 349

Reade, Charles, 391
Realism: in art, 248, 250, 251, 709-10; in literature, 691, 696-707 passim, 1079-90 passim; in music, 713, 714
Reason, 4, 171, 203, 222, 665, 1068; and politics, 870-71, 877-78; French Goddess of, 118. See also Rationalism.
Réaumur, R. A. F. de, 727
Recall, the, 500, 865
Receiverships, 782, 788, 823, 824, 833, 834
Reclus, J. J. E., 571, 650, 947
Reconstruction Finance Corporation, American, 833
Reconstruction period (U. S. A.), 315-16, 365, 514
Recreation, 408, 411, 443, 764, 1026, 1064-65
Redi, Francesco, 149, 153
Redmond, J. E., 462
Reed, J. A., 619
Reed, L. J., 407
Reese, Rev. C. W., 1061
Reeve, Clara, 572
Referendum, the, 500, 864, 865, 879-80
Reflectors, 45
Reform. See Social reform.
Reform: Bills, British (franchise), 104, 122, 134, 383, 388, 490-91, 508; Bill of 1832, 104, 121-22, 134, 383, 387, 398, 490, 508, 509
Reformation. See Protestant Revolution.
Refrigeration, 365, 416, 729, 737, 761
Régnier, H. F. J. de, 698
Regrating, in trade, 295
Reimarus, H. S., 186-87
Reims, 554 n.
Reinsurance Treaty (1884), 578
Relativity, Einstein theory of, 439, 1036-43
Relief, economic, 603. See also Poor relief; Unemployment relief.
Religion, 4, 146, 156, 161, 199, 229-30, 445, 453, 471, 661, 670, 768, 963, 1060-67, 1068, 1104; revolution in, 172-91; comparative, 572; natural, see Deism; oriental, 563; persecutions of, 63, 146, 150, 166, 179, 400, 982, 1020-21; Persian, 471; in Nazi Germany, 962; in Soviet Russia, 1019-22, 1026, 1028. See also Science and religion; Supernaturalism; and names of religions.
Remarque, E. M., 1080, 1086
Rembrandt Harmens van Rijn, 249, 250
Remington, E., & Sons, 745
Remizov, A. M., 1088
Remus case, 1102-03
Renaissance, 4-5, 6, 20, 21, 183, 242, 247-53 passim, 486, 522, 686, 710. See also Humanism, Renaissance.
Renan, Ernest, 476, 697-98, 1082
Renard, G. F., 1058
Renoir, P. A., 710
Reparation payments, 616, 775, 904; German, 607, 612, 614-16, 622-26
Repin, I. J., 711
Representation. See Proportional representation; Government, representative; Vocational representation.

Republican party, American, 188, 513-14, 515, 541, 860, 873-84, 901, 971; first (now Democratic), 130, 468, 513
Republicanism, 84, 99, 131-39, 190, 222, 234, 237, 453, 488, 495, 497, 561, 612
Respighi, Ottorino, 1099
Reszke, Jean de, 715
Retail trade. *See* Chain stores; Department stores.
Reuchlin, Johann, 241
Reuter's Limited News Service, 745
Revanchard, French, 579, 699. *See also* Alsace-Lorraine.
Revelation, belief in divine, 173-76, 202, 217, 228, 680
Reventlow, Ernst, count zu, 464 n.
Revisionism. *See* Socialism, Revisionist.
Revolution: incitement to, 224, 846-47, 941; literature of, 691; right of, 96-97, 104, 162, 218-21, 228-29, 234-37, 256, 398; tendency toward, 84, 95, 161; world, 989, 995, 996, 1028-29
Revolutions, 4, 111, 270, 712, 868; of 1830, 104, 120-22, 130, 398, 491; of 1848, 104, 122-28, 130, 131, 135, 234, 237, 311, 330, 396, 397-98, 458-59, 509, 612, 632, 856, 868, 942, 950. *See also* names of revolutions.
Revue des deux mondes, 1091
Reymont, Ladislas, 1088
Reynolds, Sir Joshua, 250
Rhabanus Maurus Magnentius, 185
Rhenish-Westphalian coal syndicate, 335 n., 336
Rhetoric, 157
Rhine: Confederation of the, 460; Palatinate of the, 127; Republic, 624
Rhineland, the, 120, 331, 334, 455, 615, 624, 625
Rhode Island, 170, 881
Rhodes, C. J., 464 n., 532
Rhodesia, 532
Ribot, T. A., 649, 652
Ricardo, David, 79, 320, 380-81, 387, 667, 934, 1058
Rice, E. L., 1090
Richardson (killed in Japan), 537
Richardson, H. H., 712
Richelieu, A. J. du P. de, cardinal, 87-88, 89, 110, 119, 131, 252, 488
Richter, A. L., 711
Richtofen, Ferdinand, baron von, 351, 650, 1047-48
Rickert, Hans, 1073
Riddell, G. A. Riddell, baron, 1093
Riehl, W. H., 703
Riemann, G. F. B., 641
Rietschel, E. F. A., 711
Riff War, 531, 569
Riga, 595
Right, Petition of, English (1628), 101, 134
Rights: English Bill of, 103, 107, 108, 127, 134; natural, 96-97, 106-07, 113, 115, 217, 455, 487, 842, 869, 961, 1102. *See also* Declaration of Rights; Liberty; Life; Property.
Riley, J. W., 469

Rilke, R. M., 1086
Rimbaud, J. A., 698
Rimsky-Korsakov, N. A., 572, 713
Rinehart, Mary Roberts, 1089
Rio de Oro, 532
Rio Muni, 532
Riparian culture, 38
Ripley, W. Z., 362, 800, 802, 972; quoted, 797, 801, 823
Rippy, J. F., quoted, 544
Ritter, Karl, 571, 650
Rivas, Angel de Saavedra, duke de, 700
Rivera, Diego, 447, 1096
Roads: modern, 265, 303-06, 736-40 *passim;* American, 305, 306, 357, 360, 1005; English, 303-04; French, 119, 305, 310; Gallo-Roman, 305, 311; German, 305, 311; Roman, 303; Russian, Soviet, 1005; Spanish, 93
Roberts, E. M., 1089
Roberts, F. S. Roberts, earl, 466 n.
Roberts, Richard, 276
Robertson, J. M., quoted, 179
Robertson, William, 247
Robespierre, M. F. M. I. de, 114, 183
Robins, Raymond, 918
Robinson (spinning factory), 286
Robinson, E. A., 1088-89
Robinson, J. H., 483, 656, 1058, 1078; quoted, 167-68, 455-56, 457, 1108; and Beard, C. A., quoted, 8, 290
Robinson, W. J., 970
Rochdale Equitable Pioneers' Society, 390, 948
Rockefeller, J. D., Sr., 434, 732, 753, 762, 781, 782, 812, 819, 951
Rockefeller, J. D., Jr., 447, 782, 795, 812, 951, 1096
Rockefeller Institute, 563
Rodbertus, K. J., 934, 938
Rodin, Auguste, 710, 1096
Rodó, J. E., 1085
Roebuck, John, 279
Roerich, N. K., 572, 711
Rogers, J. E. T., 41-42
Rogers, M. R., quoted, 248
Rogers, R. W., 654
Roget, P. M., 202
Rohrbach, Paul, 464 n.
Rolland, Romain, 619, 1082-83
Romains, Jules (Louis Farigoule), 1082
Rollins College, 1076
Roman Catholic Church, **5, 12-15,** 58-67 *passim,* 85, 87, 93, 96, 100, 143-45, 162-206 *passim,* 217-18, 223, 238, 240, 242, 244, 389-90, 398, 402, 467, 486, 505, 524, 563, 566, 673-80 *passim,* 699, 706, 955, 1060-66 *passim;* persecution of the, 166, 982; wealth of the, 14-15; in Austria, 510, 943, 945; in Bulgaria, 635; in England, 101, 103, 104, 166-67, 172, 215, 272, 400, 945; in France, 109-21 *passim,* 205-06, 389, 488, 673, 679, 945, 1070; in Germany, 509, 945; in Spain, 497, 633; in the United States, 864 n., 945
Roman culture, and so forth. *See* Latin.
Roman Empire and Republic, 16, 53, 57, 83, 138, 164, 168, 188, 217, 225, 227, 235,

285, 484-86, 505, 653, 759; fall of the, 8, 83, 97
Roman Empire, medieval, 89, 505, 898, 899
Roman law, 172; influence of, 89, 116, 144, 217, 218, 222-23, 1102
Roman Republic, modern, 125
Romances. *See* Novels.
Romanes, G. J., 658
Romanov dynasty, 128, 129, 711, 1018
Romanticism, 173, 194-200, 201, 205-07, 230-34, 240, 243, 246-47, 383, 389, 393, 466, 572, 656, 660, 672, 680-81, 690-714 *passim,* 1097
Rome, 12, 125, 459, 531, 962; population of, 213, 405
Romilly, Sir Samuel, 383, 399
Romulus, 164
Röntgen, W. K., 1045
Roosevelt, F. D., president of the United States, 375, 415, 425, 436, 498, 544, 602, 793, 840-41, 842, 847, 849, 850, 861, 944, 958, 960, 973-74, 1000, 1015, 1029; quoted, 834. *See also* New Deal.
Roosevelt, Theodore, president of the United States, 178, 384, 498, 514, 523, 543, 567, 752, 844, 861, 874, 875, 876, 877, 915-16 n. (quoted), 917, 944, 959, 1065 n., 1091
Root, Elihu, 872, 903, 964 n.
Roscher, W. G. F., 387
Rosenwald, Julius, 812
Roses, Wars of the, 85, 86
Rosetti, D. G., 709
Ross, E. A., 423, 503, 1058
Rossini, G. A., 714
Rostand, Edmond, 1083
Rothschilds, bankers, 434, 475
Rotterdam, Bank of, 68 n.
Rousseau, H. J., 1096
Rousseau, J. J., 97, 99, 104, 111, 115, 184, 185, 194, 195, 196, 218, 221, 230-32, 240, 241, 243-44, 245, 246, 247, 382, 402, 482, 689, 899, 961, 1057
Rousseau, P. E. T., 709
Rowntree, B. S., Rowntree Cocoa Works, 291, 763, 849
Royal Dutch Shell Company, 346, 732
Royal Society of London for Improving Natural Knowledge, 150, 202; *Philosophical Transactions* of, 150
Royalist party, English, 106, 506
Royce, Josiah, 680
Ruanda-Urundi, 551, 553-54
Rubber, 523, 546, 547, 552, 568, 726-36 *passim;* American, 370, 733-36 *passim*
Rubens, P. P., 249
Rubianus, Crotus, 144
Rubinstein, A. G., 573, 713
Rubruquis (Rubruck), William of, 17, 19
Rude, François, 710
Rugg, H. O., 1075; quoted, 769
Ruhr, the, 333, 624, 634, 749
Ruiz, José Martínez (Azorín), 1084, 1085
Rumania, 33, 348, 460, 462, 477, 478, 589, 608-09, 612, 635, 868, 869, 905, 962; and the World War, 594, 595-96, 600, 602, 626, (debts) 621, (reparations) 623
Rumanians, 461-62
Rumford, Benjamin Thompson, count, 642
Rumsey, James, 314
Ruskin, John, 292, 391-92, 671, 694-95, 709, 955
Ruskin College, 1077
Russell, Bertrand, 619, 1060, 1063, 1068-69; quoted, 726, 933
Russia, Soviet, 90, 114, 129, 132, 136, 138, 168-69, 172, 345, 351, 427, 429, 431, 433, 437-38, 444, 447, 474, 475, 477, 499, 533-34, 539, 545, 608, 611, 612, 631, 632-33, 748, 868, 909, 924, 936, 937, 938, 948, 952 n., 959, 960, 961, 968, 971, 973, 979-1031, 1078, 1094, 1101; divisions of, 991; political structure of, 991-97; population of, 991; birth rate in, 419; national income of, 1001; exports and imports of, 1011; and the World War, 595, 980, 989, (debts) 620; and the League of Nations, 905, 906, 907, 1029, 1030; and disarmament, 912; the United States and, 432, 951 n., 990; trade with, 523
Russia, tsarist, 3, 16-17, 25, 28, 85-97 *passim,* 131, 216, 338, 374, 392, 417, 421, 424-25, 429, 455-66 *passim,* 476, 477, 478, 494, 496-97, 524, 532-51 *passim,* 636, 900, 914, 946-47, 956, 967, 971, 981-87, 1015, 1025; in the World War, 129, 494, 575-602 *passim,* 986-89; population of, 213; trade with, 24, 337, 523
Russian Revolution: of 1905, 4, 94, 97, 120, 128-29, 130, 398, 496, 984-86; of 1917, 114, 131, 437, 496-97, 595, 979, 980, 986-90, (influence of) 1068, 1069, 1088, (Provisional Government of the) 987-89
Russian Socialist Federative Soviet Republic, area and population of, 991
Russians, 609
Russo-Japanese War (1904-05), 128, 129, 130, 463, 470, 496, 537, 538, 549, 569, 580, 984-85, 986, 996
Russo-Turkish War (1877-78), 579
Russolo, Luigi, 1095
Rusticiano (Rustichello) of Pisa, 18
Ruthenians, 124, 461, 608
Rutherford of Nelson, Ernest Rutherford, baron, 1043
Ruysdael, Jacob van, 250
Ryan, Rev. J. A., 945, 1066
Rykov, A. I., 989 n.

Sá de Miranda, Francisco de, 86
Saar Valley, 327, 328 n., 334, 614, 628; plebiscite, 614
Sabotage, 287 n., 954
Sacco, Nicola, 168
Sachs, Hans, 86
Sadler, M. T., 388, 565
Sagittarius, 1040
Sahara, the, 531
St. Bartholomew's Day massacre, 166
St. Christopher (St. Kitts), 24

INDEX

Sainte-Beuve, C. A., 321, 697
St. Eustatius, 24
St. Gall, 344
Saint-Gaudens, Augustus, 711
St. Germain, Treaty of (1919), 343, 415, 495, 607, 616, 628, 904, 909
St. Helena's Bay, 22
St. John of Jerusalem, Knights of. *See* Hospitalers, Knights.
St. Lawrence Valley, 24, 105
St. Louis (Mo.), 360, 366, 368, 469; *Post-Dispatch*, 1094
St. Malo, 38
St. Mihiel, 597
St. Paul's School, Eng., 242
St. Petersburg (later Petrograd, Leningrad), 985, 987
Saint-Pierre, C. I. Castel, abbé de, 192-93, 222, 227, 666, 899
Saint-Pierre, J. H. B. de, 245
St. Quentin, 597
Saint-Saëns, C. C., 572-73, 713
Saint-Simon, C. H. de Rouvroy, count de, 193, 206, 229-30, 389, 393, 396, 666, 933, 973
St. Vincent de Paul, Society of, 389
Sait, E. M., 884
Sakhalin, 538, 545
Saladin, sultan of Egypt, 13
Salter, Sir J. A., 624
Salvador, 542, 544
Salvation Army, 678
Salvation of the soul, 170, 201, 204-05; preoccupation with the, 143, 145, 155, 162, 164-65, 189, 192
Samain, A. V., 698
Samoan Islands, 539, 540, 545, 549, 553
Sample, buying from, 63-64
Samuel, Sir H. L., 609
Sanborn, F. B., 967
Sand, George (A. L. A. D. Dudevant), 391, 392, 696, 697
Sandburg, Carl, 1088-89
San Francisco, 366
Sanger, M. H., 437, 970; quoted, 420
Sanitation, 213, 391, 408-09, 415, 524, 560, 567, 736, 999, 1015, 1048; factory, 292
San Lucar, 23
San Remo Conference (1920), 623
San Stefano, Treaty of (1878), 534
Santa Cruz, 540
Santayana, George, 1060, 1069-70
Santo Domingo, 24, 541-45 *passim*
Santos-Dumont, Alberto, 740
Sarai, 17
Sarajevo, 589
Sardinia (Piedmont), Kingdom of, 125, 135, 459
Sargent, J. S., 711
Sarrail, Gen. Maurice, 554
Satire, 144, 180-81, 192, 227, 246, 250, 254, 692, 694, 695, 698, 699, 708, 714, 1059, 1080, 1082, 1087, 1088, 1089
Sattari, 535
Saturday: Evening Post, 1092; *Review of Literature*, 1091

Saturn (planet), 202, 1039
Saunders, Daniel, 357
Saussure, H. B. de, 153
Savery, Thomas, 300
Savigny, F. K. von, 234, 670
Savoy, 904
Sawyer, W. E., 284
Saxons, 466
Saxony, 121, 126, 127, 312, 331
Say, J. B., 319, 382, 386, 396
Sazonov, S. D., 585, 587, 590, 593, 613; quoted, 588
Scandinavia, 636, 943. *See also* Denmark; Norway; Sweden
Scapa Flow, 615
Scarlatti, Alessandro, 254
Schacht, Hjalmar, 625
Schäffle, A. E. F., 667, 939
Schapiro, J. S., 42; quoted, 522, 725
Scharnhorst, G. J. D. von, 456
Schaudinn, Fritz, 1049
Scheele, K. W., 152
Scheffel, J. V. von, 703
Scheler, Max, 1067
Schelling, F. W. J. von, 197-98 (quoted), 660
Schiller, J. C. F. von, 246, 711
Schlegel, K. W. F. von, 198, 692
Schleiden, M. J., 646, 1046
Schleiermacher, F. D. E., 198 (quoted), 201 (quoted), 206, 665, 674
Schlesinger, A. M., 27 n., 98, 467, 863; and Eriksson, E. McK., quoted, 864
Schleswig, 461, 608
Schlieffen, Gen. Alfred, count von, Schlieffen Plan, 594
Schlink, F. J., and Kallet, Arthur, 446
Schmidt, J. K. (Max Stirner), 397
Schmitt, B. E., 585 n., 587
Schmoller, Gustav von, 386, 939, 941 n., 1059; quoted, 75
Schnee, Heinrich, 554
Schnitzler, Arthur, 1080, 1086
Scholastic, 601
Scholasticism, 144, 145, 154-56, 166, 184, 196, 241, 681, 1057, 1067
Schönberg, Arnold, 1098-99, 1100
Schopenhauer, Arthur, 681, 683, 704, 1069
Schrödinger, Erwin, 1043-44
Schronerer, Georg, 476
Schubert, F. P., 713, 715
Schultze, Max, 647
Schulze-Delitzsch, F. H., 948
Schumann, R. A., 713, 715
Schumann-Heink, Ernestine, 1100
Schurz, Carl, 879
Schwab, C. M., 782
Schwann, Theodor, 646, 1046
Schwartz, Arthur, 1100
Schwarzenberg, Felix, prince zu, 125, 126, 493
Schwimmer, Rosika, 846
Schwind, Moritz von, 710
Science, 4, 16, 146, 184, 192, 194, 207, 227, 229, 233, 236, 263, 314, 365, 398, 443, 573, 666, 979-80, 1105-07; progress in, 145-60, 571, 640-53, 656, 1043-49; promoted, 91,

92, 93, 143, 146, 182, 200; and industry, 265-68, 271, 333, 427, 522, 723-33, 756, 819; and invention, 767-69; and religion, 172-73, 177, 189-90, 195, 202-03, 207, 663-65, 674-83 *passim,* 1055-57, 1061-64; in education, 241, 685-86, 1103, 1107; societies and journals for, 150; influence of, 4-5, 10, 143-44, 400, 444, 560, 670, 681-83, 691, 698, 871, 964, 1049-57, 1079
Scientific management, 627, 629-31, 762-64, 766, 848, 860, 957. *See also* Efficiency.
Scopes, J. T., trial of, 1062, 1104
Scotland, 279
Scott, C. M., 1099
Scott, C. P., 1094
Scott, W. D., quoted, 1107
Scott, Sir Walter, 692, 693, 700, 701, 702
Scotti, Antonio, 1100
Scriabin, A. N., 1099
Scribner's Magazine, 1091
Scripps, E. W., 848 n., 1093, 1094
Scripps-Howard press, 746; quoted, 831-32
Sculpture, 252-53, 709, 710-11, 1096; baroque, 253
Seager, H. R., 939
Sears, Roebuck and Co., 764, 785
Seattle, 366
Secularism, 143-45, 163, 200, 222-23, 226, 256, 665, 1064-67; in art, 248-50. *See also* Rationalism; State, the absolute.
Securities (stocks and bonds), overissue of, 800, 804
Sedan, 597
Sedition: Act, English (1934), 172 n.; law, American (1798), 513, 612
Sée, Henri, 58 n., 60 n., 272
Seebeck, T. J., 318
Seeley, Sir J. R., 672
Segonzac, André Dunoyer de, 1096
Seignobos, Charles, 672; quoted, 15
Seipel, Mgr. Ignaz, 945
Seldes, George, 913
Seldes, Gilbert, quoted, 813
Self-denying Ordinance, France, 113
Self-determination, political, 453, 551, 607-13
Self-government: colonial or Dominion, 230, 535-36, 561; municipal, 102, 383
Seligman, E. R. A., 44, 235, 1057
Seligman, J. & W., 789
Seljuk Turks. *See* Turks.
Sellars, R. W., 1061
Semaphores, 318
Sembrich, Marcella, 715
Semmelweis, I. P., 651
Semple, E. C., 650
Seneca, Lucius Annaeus, 145 n.
Senegal, 530-31
Senior, N. W., 380, 382, 386, 667
Sepoy Mutiny (1857), 535
Serbia, 460, 461, 616, 905; and the World War, 575-76, 579, 584-85, 595, 600, 601, 602, 608, 609, 626, 900
Serbs, 124, 461, 635
Serfdom, 13, 54, 116-20, 212, 238, 263, 485, 759; emancipation from, 92, 93, 110, 117,
119, 120, 128, 131, 216, 338-39, 383, 487, 492, 496, 632
Servetus, Michael, 166, 168
Sessions, R. H., 1100
Seven Years' War (1756-63), 899
Severini, Gino, 1095
Sévigné, Marie de Rabutin-Chantal, marchioness de, 246
Seville, 38
Sèvres, Treaty of (1920), 533, 607, 609, 616
Sewing machine, 277, 360, 367
Sex: attitudes toward, 190, 191, 216, 445, 562, 671, 1026, 1067, 1103, (Soviet Russian) 971, 1022-24; conditioning, 1046; education, 1026; equality, 229, 971, 1023; problems in literature, 1080, 1081-82, 1086, 1087
Sextant, 31, 45
Shaftesbury, A. A. Cooper, 3d earl of, 178, 190, 227, 247, 408, 671, 695
Shaftesbury, A. A. Cooper, 7th earl of, 293, 388, 565
Shakespeare, William, 69, 86, 245, 713
Shallcross, R. E., and Matthews, J. B., 446
Shanghai, 538, 565
Shantung, 536, 538, 551, 597, 910
Shapley, Harlow, quoted, 1040, 1041, 1051-52, 1108-09
Sharp, John, 276
Sharp, W. R., quoted, 627; and Ogg, F. A., quoted, 950
Shaw, G. B., 392, 693, 937, 1082, 1085
Shays' Rebellion, 107
Shearer, W. B., 913
Sheen, Rev. F. J., 169
Sheffield, 749
Shelley, P. B., 384, 692
Shepherd, W. R., 10, 559, 573; quoted, 6-8, 535-36, 565
Sherman, John, Sherman Anti-Trust Act (1890), 367, 781, 841, 844
Shimonoseki, 537
Ship money, England, 101-02
Ships, shipbuilding, 31-32, 45, 742; American, 316; Dutch, 32, 346; English, 32, 45, 316; German, 316; Italian, 316; Scandinavian, 374. *See also* Mercantile marine; Steamships.
Shock brigades, Soviet Russia, 1001, 1014
Shoe industry, 44, 277, 292, 344, 755-56, 1004; American, 356, 359-60, 367-68, 756, 772, 813-15, 818-19
Shogunate, Japanese, 470
Sholes, C. L., 745
Short stories, 182, 183, 246, 698, 699, 703, 706, 707, 708, 1085, 1087, 1088
Shotwell, J. T., 918, 921-22 (quoted), 1058: quoted, 272, 522, 525, 655, 928
Shrapnel, 460
Siam, 18, 171, 594
Sibelius, Jean, 1100
Siberia, 16, 18, 25, 28, 341, 534, 537, 990
Sicily, 10-11, 69, 459, 699. *See also* Two Sicilies.
Sidney, Algernon, 220
Siegerland, 333
Siemens, E. W. von, 334

INDEX

Siemens, Sir William (K. W.), Siemens-Martin process, 281-82, 315, 369, 725
Siemens-Schuckert firm, 336
Sierra, Gregorio and Maria Martínez, 1085
Sierra Leone, 532
Sieyès, E. J., abbé, 222, 228-29, 232
Sighele, Scipio, 503
Sigismund, medieval Roman emperor, 88
Signaling, 318, 738
Silesia, 331, 333, 334, 343, 608, 610, 614, 628, 749, 905
Silk culture, introduction of, 32, 43
Silk industry. See Textile industries.
Silver, 39-43, 58, 63, 68, 76, 77, 568; mines, 63, 353; money, 39, 41, 76
Simeral, Isabel, quoted, 292-93
Simkhovitch, M. K. (Mrs. V. G.), 966
Simon, Thomas, 970
Simplicissimus, 1091
Sin, doctrine of, 175, 204
Sinclair, H. F., 913
Sinclair, J. H., Norris-Sinclair bill, 891
Sinclair, May, 1081
Sinclair, Upton, 392, 445, 446, 448, 1089
Sind, the, 535
Singapore, 540
Single tax, 379, 955-57
Sismondi, J. C. L. Simonde de, 386, 667, 934
Sitka, 25
Siwertz, P. S., 1087
Skepticism, 4, 16, 154-206 *passim,* 263, 665, 1084. See also Rationalism.
Skidmore, Thomas, 1077
Skyscrapers, 283, 412, 414, 446, 712, 725, 1096-97
Slaten, Rev. A. W., 1061
Slater, Samuel, 357
Slave trade, 36, 59, 401, 528, 554
Slavery, 59, 238, 398; abolition of (by England), 383; (by France) 118; Athenian, 484; Germanic, 485; Roman, 484-85, 759; in the United States, 277, 363, 365, 398, 468, 498, 513, 887; attitude toward, 236, 384, 859. See also Antislavery movement.
Slavs, 126. See also names of Slavic peoples.
Slosson, E. E., 727, 1045; quoted, 728, 730-31, 1044
Slosson, P. W., quoted, 1043
Slovaks, 461, 608
Small, A. W., 77, 932, 1058
Smallpox, 147, 153, 409, 650, 1049
Smart Set, 1091
Smeaton, John, 278
Smiley, A. K., 914
Smith, A. E., 875
Smith, Adam, 79, 154, 190, 288, 319, 320, 330, 380-81, 382, 383, 385, 667, 775, 1069, 1105
Smith, F. L., 876
Smith, F. P., 315
Smith, J. R., 1048
Smith, Joseph, 676-77
Smith, Preserved, 242, 1058; quoted, 248
Smith, T. L., quoted, 1071

Smith, T. S., 408
Smith, W. R., 654
Smith College, 969
Smithfield Club, 52
Smoot, Reed, Hawley-Smoot tariff (1930), 774, 775 n.
Smuggling, 24, 26, 214; American, 27, 105, 214
Smuts, Gen. J. C., 552, 614 n., 901
Snell, Willibrord (Snellius), 148
Snyder, Ruth, 1104
Social change, 1054-55
Social-contract theory, 97, 144, 218-22, 231, 232-33
Social control, 229, 236, 382, 689, 867, 871-72, 1058. See also Government control.
Social institutions, 661-62; new, 212-56
Social insurance, 345, 386, 389, 392, 401, 429-30, 492, 495, 498, 939-40, 984, 1001, 1016, 1026; American, 840. See also names of forms of insurance.
Social legislation. See Social reform.
Social philosophy. See Political science.
Social justice, 111, 144, 182, 446, 980, 1065-66
Social reform, 4, 216, 224-35 *passim,* 256, 263, 379-402 *passim,* 424, 444, 490-99 *passim,* 509, 666, 680, 695, 696, 707, 931-74, 985, 1058; Christian churches and, 1065-66; in the United States, 133, 498-99, 845-47. See also names of social reforms.
Social Revolutionary party, Russia, 129
Social sciences, 151, 154, 192-93, 195 n., 199, 226, 263, 443, 572, 665-72, 1048; enumerated, 1049; progress in the, 1057-60, 1106-07; in education, 241, 446, 685-87, 1057, 1074-75, 1103
Social settlements, 965-66
Social surveys, 945
Social work (welfare), 678, 957, 965-72; Soviet Russian, 1015-16, 1025-27; industrial, 294, 957. See also Charities; Poor relief.
Socialism, 344, 380, 383, 385, 391, 392, 411, 420, 425, 427, 432, 444, 617, 631, 752, 856, 859, 916, 933, 948, 950, 953, 962, 972-73; and the World War, 938; municipal, 411, 415
Socialism in: Austria, 495, 634, 937 n., 966; Belgium, 937; England, 933, 936-46 *passim,* 955; France, 392, 933, 934, 937-39, 953, 955; Germany, 633, 938-39, 952 n., 955, 959; Hungary, 634; Italy, 937, 938, 952 n.; Spain, 497; the United States, 372, 842, 891, 937, 939, 946, 1077. See also Socialist parties.
Socialism, Christian, 344 n., 389-90, 393, 680, 944-46, 948, 952, 955
Socialism, Fabian, 936-37
Socialism, Guild, 389, 392, 396, 433, 945, 955, 958
Socialism, International, 914, 933. See also Communism.
Socialism, Marxian (Scientific). See Communism.
Socialism of the Chair, 939

INDEX

Socialism, Revisionist (Opportunist), 509, 934-38 passim, 959, 985
Socialism, Ricardian, 380, 395, 934
Socialism, State, 395, 454, 474, 774, 860, 884-85, 933, 938-44, 953-62 passim. See also Fascism; Germany, Nazi; Italy, Fascist; Russia, Soviet.
Socialism, Transitional (Revolutionary), 394-97, 705
Socialism, Utopian, 393-95, 472, 696, 934, 947-48
Socialist parties: American, 514, 937-38, 945; Austrian, 510, 936, 937, 943, 945; French, 122, 492, 509, 517, 936, 938-39, 945-46, 951; German, 494, 509, 516, 935-36, 937, 938, 945; Italian, 510, 936; Russian, 936, 985; other European countries, 936
Society Islands, 540
Society, primitive, 82, 163, 164, 284, 434, 483-84, 1060. See also Nature, state of.
Socinians, 169-70. See also Unitarian Church.
Socinus (Sozzini), F. P. and L. F. M., 170
Sociology, 154, 156, 206, 221-22, 230, 386, 393; 443, 466, 572, 666-67, 1049, 1058; scientific, 932-33; influence of, 689, 764, 1064-65
Socrates, 223, 1053, 1101
Söderberg, H. E. F., 1087
Sokotra, 18
Solidarism, 394, 958, 961 n.
Sologub, Fedor (F. K. Teternikov), 1087
Solomon, House of, 150, 158, 236
Solomon Islands, 540
Solon, 655
Soloviev, Vladimir, 705, 706
Somaliland, 463, 530, 531, 532
Sombart, Werner, 58 n., 60 n., 475, 487, 935 n., 1058, 1059; quoted, 63-64, 69, 288-89
Somerset, Edward, 2d marquis of Worcester, 299
Somerville, J. S. Somerville, 15th baron, 51
Sonnemann, Adolph, 1094
Sophists, 665
Sorel, Georges, 953
Soulé, S. W., 745
Sound (physics), 152, 318, 641, 643
South, the American, 105, 277, 294, 363-69 passim, 398, 424, 512-14, 887; industry in the, 469, 944
South Africa, 138, 353, 463, 568, 597; Union of, 529, 535, 550, 553, 554, 561. See also names of divisions.
South America, 25, 26, 33 n., 34, 456, 469, 542, 544, 546-48, 741; trade with, 73, 527; birth rate in, 419. See also names of countries.
South Carolina, 73, 366, 879
South Dakota, 879
Southey, Robert, 391, 572, 692
Sovhozi. See Agriculture, Soviet Russia.
South Sea Bubble (Company), 73-74, 75, 804
Soviets, Russian, 985-93 passim
Soviet Union, The, quoted, 992
Spa Conference (1920), 623
Space concept. See Relativity.

Spain, 11, 21-40 passim, 58, 73, 76, 77, 85, 86, 87, 93, 100, 120, 130, 131, 135, 136, 165-66, 455, 456, 497, 539, 542, 549, 612, 633, 868, 912, 923, 962, 1085; Bank of, 68 n.; population of, 93; Republic of, 136, 138, 344, 497, 868
Spanish America. See Latin America.
Spanish Revolution (1931), 131, 136 n., 345, 437, 633, 1084
Spanish-American War (1898), 460, 469, 539, 549, 1084, 1085
Spanish Armada, 24, 26-27, 87
Spanish Succession, War of the, 130
Specialization: in agriculture, 333, 761; in industry, 347, 359, 378, 380, 631, 748, 749, 758
Spectro-comparator, 1037
Spectrograph, 1037
Spectrometer, 1045
Spectroscope, 641, 643-44, 1037
Speculation, financial, 42, 59, 64-65, 71, 72-74, 79, 213, 216, 295, 364, 426, 430, 434, 476, 629, 636, 637, 764, 781-838 passim, 849, 973-74; safeguarding, 805-06; American, 372, 787, 789, 792-94, 804-05, 820
Sipee, Admiral Maximilian, count von, 598
Speed: airplane, 742; automobile, 740; railroads, 308-09, 737-38; steamship, 316, 742
Speeding-up (industry), 288, 294, 754-55, 849
Speer, R. E., 563 n.
Spencer, Herbert, 383, 384, 444, 648, 656, 657, 662-67 passim, 671, 678, 681, 682, 683, 689, 695, 856, 931, 933, 1105
Spender, J. A., 586
Spengler, Oswald, 194, 683, 1055
Spenser, Edmund, 86, 245
Speyer, Leonora, 1089
Spice Islands, 20, 22, 23, 25
Spinoza, Baruch, 163 n., 188, 219-20, 223, 654
Spitteler, Carl, 1086
Spoils system, American, 497-98, 513, 874-79 passim
Springfield (Mass.) Republican, 1092, 1094
Stadion, Franz von, count, 464
Stage designing, 711
Stagecoaches, 63
Stahl, G. E., 148, 152
Stalin, Joseph (I. V. Dzhugashvili), 989 n., 994-95 (quoted), 1021; quoted, 1001
Stamp, Sir J. C., 624
Standard Gas and Electric Co., 784
Standard Oil Co., 523, 732, 750, 752, 753, 781, 849 n., 875
Standardization: of art and architecture, 446-47; of culture, 270, 373, 440; of labor, 378; of music, 447; of production, 283, 316, 357 n., 629-30, 753
Stanley, Sir H. M., 528, 650
Stanton, E. C., 437
Star Chamber, Court of the, 87, 101-02, 166, 167
Starr, J. W., 284
State, the national, 907, 926-27; rise of, 4, 63, 75, 82-139, 145, 225, 235, 263, 486; abso-

INDEX

lute, 75-78, 90, 144, 216-22, 225, 256, 264, 454, 506, 550, 561, 575-76, 926, 927, 1102; corporative (guild), 869, 961-62, 1102; proposed destruction of, 946-47, 953, 955
State, the, 484, 661; conceptions of, 223, 379-83, 392, 932; necessary, 96-97
Standards of living, 348, 417-23 *passim,* 435, 821, 839, 1015-16
States of the Church, 125
States rights, 468
Statistical Abstract of the United States, quoted, 40
Steagall, H. B., Glass-Steagall Act, 794
Steam power, 32. *See* Engines, steam.
Steamships and steamboats, 302, 303, 314-17, 361, 365, 725, 726, 732, 742, 751, 781; influence of, 319
Steel, 281; Age of, 725; uses of, 283, 316, 737, 738. *See also* Iron and steel industry.
Stein, Gertrude, 1090
Stein, H. F. K., baron vom and zum, 120, 329, 383, 492, 632
Stein, Ludwig, 933, 1055
Steinheil, C. A., 318
Steinmetz, C. P., 318, 736
Stendhal (M. H. Beyle), 696
Steno, Nicolaus, 149
Stephen, Sir J. F., 668
Stephen, Sir Leslie, 671
Stephenson, George, 308, 737
Sterilization of the unfit, 417, 970
Stern, J. D., 1094
Stethoscope, 650
Stevens, Alfred, 709
Stevens, Col. John, 315
Stevenson, R. L., 694
Stewart, Sir James Purves, quoted, 1025
Stewart, John, 187-88
Stieglitz, Alfred, 1096
Stillman, K. W., quoted, 784
Stinnes, Hugo, 333, 820, 959
Stirner, Max (J. K. Schmidt), 397
Stock-breeding and -raising, 49, 50-51, 54, 365, 1010
Stock exchange: origins of the, 63-64, 70-72; evolution of the, 803-05; London, 72; Paris, 72; New York, 72, 74 n., 371, 478, 784, 804-05, 826, 832, 837-38, 875. *See also* Speculation.
Stocks, 71-72; distribution of, to employees, 957. *See also* Speculation.
Stockholm, 1087
Stoecker, Rev. Adolf, 476, 945
Stoicism, Stoics, 223, 665, 669, 677
Stolypin, P. A., 129, 986
Stone, H. F., 843
Stone Age, 57 n., 145, 264, 273, 767
Stopes, M. C., 437, 970
Storm, T. W., 702-03
Stowe, Leland, quoted, 869
Stradivari (Stradivarius), Antonio, 255
Strain of modern life, 270, 439, 755, 969
Straits, the (the Dardanelles and the Bosporus), 462, 550, 578-88 *passim,* 593, 601, 602, 609, 616

Strasbourg Gymnasium, 242
Strauss, Richard, 714, 1098, 1100
Stravinsky, I. F., 1098, 1099
Streamlined trains, 303, 737-38
Street railways. *See* Tramways.
Stresemann, Gustav, 615
Strieder, Jakob, 58 n.
Strikes, 118, 345, 429, 492, 821, 950, 951, 954; general, 954; American, 368, 617, 846, 951
Strindberg, August, 704, 705
Strong, Rev. Josiah, 946
Struve, P. B., 937
Stuart dynasty, 90, 100-04, 166. *See also* England, Restoration period.
Stubbs, William, bishop, 466 n., 672
Sturm, Johannes, 242
Styria, 68
Suffrage, 99, 113, 122, 127, 129, 429-30, 482-509 *passim,* 856, 858, 859 n., 867, 870, 934, 984, 985, 992; woman, 122, 216, 219, 436-37, 491, 499, (American) 864; American, 107, 134, 135, 400, 497, 513, 857-58, 861, 863-66, 870, 872-73. *See also* Reform Bills, English.
Suárez, Francisco, 225
Submarines, 303, 316, 910, 911, 913; in the World War, 596, 598, 599, 600, 628, 632
Sudan, 463, 530, 531
Sudermann, Hermann, 704
Suez Canal, 39, 306, 463, 529
Sukhomlinov, Gen. V. A., 588
Sullivan, Sir A. S., 714
Sullivan, L. H., 1096
Sullivan, Louis, 712
Sully, Maximilien de Béthune, duke de, 87-88, 110, 222, 898-99
Sully-Prudhomme, R. F. A. P., 698
Sumatra, 18, 540, 735
Sumner, Charles, 914
Sumner, W. G., 189, 467, 500, 570, 662, 667, 668, 672 n., 933
Sumner family, 358
Sun Yat-sen, 537
Supan, Alexander, 422
Supernaturalism, 4, 143-207 *passim,* 217, 227, 252, 256, 263, 445, 573, 653, 665, 672, 979, 1062, 1068, 1101. *See also* Religion.
Superstition, 4, 145, 152, 157, 175, 229, 236, 240, 242, 438, 1102-03
Supply (economics), 61, 378
Surgery, 153, 651, 652, 1048-49
Surplus economy, 212
Survey Graphic, quoted, 410
Suttee, 562
Swadeshi (India), 536
Swain, J. W., 530
Swammerdam, Jan, 149
Swaraj (India), 536
Sweating workers, 47, 289
Sweden, 88, 89, 437, 460, 637, 905, 936; Bank of, 68 n. *See also* Scandinavia.
Swift, Jonathan, 181, 192, 245, 246, 247
Switzerland, 136, 138, 264, 400, 879, 904, 1086; trade with, 337, 342

INDEX

Swope, Gerard, 840-41 (quoted, Swope Plan), 960
Sybel, Heinrich von, 466 n.
Sydenham, Thomas, 149
Sykes, Sir Mark, 533
Symbolism in literature, 691, 697, 698, 1082, 1087
Symington, William, 314
Symphonies, 255, 573, 1101
Synchromism (art), 1095-96
Syndicalism, 90, 396, 446, 497, 504, 510, 867, 946, 950, 951, 952-55, 961, 962; the United States and, 846, 944, 954
Syndicates: industrial, 335-36, 522, 627, 749, 771, 772, 840, 1001, (German) 335-36; underwriting, 295, 787, 791
Synthetic products, 645, 724, 726-35 *passim*, 1045
Syracuse (N. Y.) *Herald* quoted, 869
Syria, 11-20 *passim*, 57, 533, 551, 553, 554, 597, 610; people of, as financiers, 66; trade with, 15, 45
Széchenyi, István, count, 123

Ta Manchu Tikuo (Henry Pu Yi), king of Manchukuo, 538
Taboos, 163, 164, 472
Tabriz, 17
Tadzhik Socialist Soviet Republic, area and population of, 991
Taft, Lorado, 711
Taff Vale case (labor unionism), 949
Taft, W. H., president of the United States, 498, 543
Tagore, Sir Rabindranath, 572
Taine, H. A., 697
Taille, France, 116
Taiping Rebellion (1853), 536
Talbot, W. H. F., 747
Tales. *See* Short stories.
Talking pictures. *See* Moving pictures, sound (talkies).
Talleyrand de Périgord, C. M. de, 118, 464
Tanks in the World War, 598
Tannenberg, O. R., 464 n.
Tannenberg, battle of, 595
Tapestry, 32, 45, 572
Tarbell, I. M., 849 n.
Tarde, Gabriel, 503, 767, 834
Tardieu, André, 584 n.
Tariffs, 59, 75, 85, 100, 105, 319-20, 473, 474, 575, 611, 614, 629, 773-76, 926; protective, 41, 339, 345, 383, 386, 464, 550, 552, 568-69, 773-76; American, 321, 357, 358, 367, 474, 513, 514, 622, 772, 856, 863, 888; French, 116, 123; German, 319-20, 330-31, 333, 336, 383, 628; Italian, 342; Philippine, 539; Russian, 339; Spanish, 345
Tasmania, 540, 565, 686
Tasso, Torquato, 86
Tatars, 16-17, 19
Taussig, F. W., 820
Tavernier, J. B., 245
Tawney, R. H., 60 n., 66 n., 1058; quoted, 65-66

Taxation, 85, 91, 94, 96, 485; American, 306, 375, 512, 813, 832, 845, 846; Austrian, 93; Bohemian, 124; English, 78, 86, 101, 103, 239, 272, (in American colonies) 27, 105; French, 110-19 *passim*; German, 92; Russian, (tsarist) 984, (Soviet) 1012, 1013. *See also* Income tax; Single tax.
Taylor, F. W., 762-63
Taylor, Jeremy, bishop, 170
Taylor, M. P., quoted, 811
Tchaikovsky, P. I., 713
Tea Act, British (1773), 105
Tead, Ordway, quoted, 763
Technicians, 229, 420, 427, 798, 819-22
Technocracy, 427, 867, 1105
Technology, modern, 63, 128, 265-71 *passim*, 317-18, 336, 341, 349, 444, 458, 524, 559-60, 563, 768, 822, 979-80; education in, 1103, 1105-06
Telegraph, 265, 267, 270, 318-19, 457, 469, 522, 726, 738, 744, 745, 747; wireless, 267, 318, 742, 743
Telephone, 265, 270, 318, 457, 469, 738, 742, 744; industry, American, 372; wireless, 743
Telescope, 31, 45, 146, 148, 150, 152, 159, 641, 652, 1037
Television, 743, 747-48; microscope, 1047
Telford, Thomas, 304-05
Temperance movement, 678. *See also* Prohibition.
Templars, Knights, 14
Temps, Le, Paris, 584
Tenancy, agricultural: American, 365-66, 860; English, 52-53
Teniers, David, the younger, 249
Tennessee, 366, 369
Tennis Court Oath, France (1789), 112, 129
Tennyson, Alfred Tennyson, 1st baron, 693
Terman, L. M., 970
Terrett, Courtenay, quoted, 834
Tesla, Nikola, 736
Teutonic. *See* Germanic.
Teutonic Knights, 14
Teutons. *See* Germanic (Teutonic, Nordic) race.
Texas (Réunion), 394
Textile industries, 43-48, 64, 299, 353, 727; American, 294, 356-59, 366-70 *passim*, 749-51, 772, 781, 813-15, 818-19, 944; English, 36, 43, 46-48, 270-77, 285-94, 769; French, 43, 326, 327-29; German, 331, 333, 334, 749; other countries, (Asiatic) 349, 350, (Australia) 351-52, (European) 43, 340-53 *passim*, 1004. *See also* Machines, textile.
Thackeray, W. M., 693-94
Theodosian Code, 172
Theology, 65, 151, 156, 158, 194, 241, 648, 666
Thermodynamics, 664, 1045; laws of, 641, 642-43, 825, 1041-42
Thermometer, 148
Thermostat, 757
Thibaut, A. F. J., 234
Thiers, L. A., 310, 466 n.
Thirty Years' War (1618-48), 54, 88, 91, 166, 898
Thoiry, 615

INDEX

Thomas Aquinas, St., 3, 156, 185, 1053. *See also* Scholasticism.
Thomas, Norman, 619
Thomas, S. G., Thomas-Gilchrist process, 282, 328 n., 332 n., 725
Thomasius, Christian, 240-41
Thompson, J. W., quoted, 11, 13
Thompson, R. W., 734
Thompson, William (economist), 395, 934
Thomson, Sir J. A., 1063; quoted, 646, 1054
Thomson, Sir William. *See* Kelvin, William Thomson, 1st baron.
Thoreau, H. D., 469, 707
Thorndike, Lynn, 145, 1058; quoted, 1053-54
Thought. *See* Freedom of thought; Intellectual life.
Thrift, 230, 823; Protestantism and, 65, 143, 1103
Thünen, J. H. von, 319, 382
Thurber, Charles, 745
Thyssen, August, 333, 942
Tibet, 18, 463, 535, 537, 572
Tientsin, Treaty of (1858), 536
Tillotson, John, archbishop, 174
Time concept, 659. *See also* Relativity.
Timor, 540
Tindal, Matthew, 171, 175, 176
Tintoretto, Jacopo Robusti, 249
Tippett, Tom, quoted, 368-69
Tirpitz, Admiral Alfred von, 594 n., 596, 599
Titchener, E. B., 648, 1048
Tithes, Church, 116, 117, 487
Titian (Tiziano Vecellio), 247
Tobacco, 34, 36, 44
Tobago, 543
Tocqueville, A. H. C. M. Clérel, count de, 499, 668
Todd, D. P., quoted, 1039
Togoland, 528, 550, 553
Tokelau Islands, 540
Toland, John (Janus Junius), 174
Tolerance, 16, 92, 93, 104, 110, 118, 119, 124, 146-78 *passim*, 204, 217, 242, 245, 400, 472, 476; growth of, 168-72, 217, 263, 662, 695. *See also* Freedom of conscience; Intolerance.
Toll Co., 799-800
Toller, Ernst, 1079, 1086
Tolstoy, L. N., count, 391, 392, 705-06, 711
Tonga Islands, 540
Tool economy, 268, 273-74, 758-59
Topinard, Paul, 667
Torricelli, Evangelista, 148
Tory party, British, 94, 100, 102, 103, 107, 122, 489, 491, 506, 509. *See also* Conservative party, British.
Toulet, P. J. P., 1082
Tout, T. F., 672
Townshend, Charles, 50-51, 54, 105
Towns, 438; factory, 102, 405-16; medieval, 15, 66, 75, 83, 134, 485. *See also* Cities; City-states; Urbanization.
Toynbee, Arnold, 388, 966
Tozzer, A. M., 1102
Tractarian Movement. *See* Oxford Movement.
Tracts for the Times, 679

Trade: balance of, 76, 77, 568, (American) 372, (English) 337; restraint of, 844
Trade-unions. *See* Labor unions.
Traditionalism, 227, 229, 232, 264, 431, 438, 662, 866
Trafalgar, battle of, 598
Tramways, 308-09
Transcaucasian Socialist Federative Soviet Republic, area and population of, 991
Transcendentalists, 390, 707, 1067
Transportation, 3, 10, 38, 86, 128, 268, 269, 270, 284, 303-17, 324, 329, 331, 333, 338, 340, 360-63, 414, 417, 523, 626-27, 736-42, 780; control of, 751, 752; American, 360-63, 367, 371, 469, 781, (interests) 780-81, (control of) 782, 788, 819; Soviet Russian, 1005-07, 1014. *See also* Canals; Railroads; Steamships; Tramways; Water transport.
Trans-Siberian Railway, 341, 580
Transvaal, 138, 529
Transylvania, 595, 609
Treaties, 583; American arbitration, 915; of 1783 (England-United States), 923; secret, 550, 607, 624; World War, 473-74, 606, 607. *See also* names of treaties.
Treitscke, Heinrich von, 466 n., 476, 668, 672
Trench warfare, 597-98
Trent, 596; Council of, 167
Trentino, 461
Trevelyan, Sir G. O., 27 n.
Trevithick, Richard, 308
Trianon, Treaty of (1920), 607, 610, 616, 909
Tribal society, 82, 483-84
Trieste, 461, 596
Trinidad, 543
Trinity, Holy, 64, 166, 168, 180
Triple Alliance (Italy, Germany, Austria), 530, 531, 549, 578-79
Triple Entente (England, France, Russia), 533, 534, 549, 550-51, 576-602 *passim*, 901. *See also* World War.
Tripoli, 463, 531
Tripolitania, 531, 549
Trolley cars, 739
Trotsky, Leo (L. D. Bronstein), 595, 988, 989, 990, 995, 1030
Troubadours, 253
Troubetzkoy, Paul, prince, 711
Troy, N. Y., 687, 749
Trust companies, 787, 798, 830; charity, gifts to, of, 812
Trusts (combinations), 269, 345, 348, 522, 630-31, 749, 780-81, 796; state, 997, 998, 1001. *See also* Clayton H. DeL., Clayton Act; Sherman (John) Anti-Trust Act.
Tryon, R. M., 1075
Tsz'e Hsi, dowager empress of China, 470
Tsingtao, 597
Tuamotu Islands, 540
Tucker, B. R., 947
Tucker, R. T., 885
Tucker, W. J., 966
Tudor dynasty, 52, 85, 86-87, 131, 166, 235, 487
Tufts, J. H., 1060, 1061

INDEX

Tugan-Baranovsky, M. I., 937
Tugwell, R. G., 840, 939
Tull, Jethro, 50-51, 54
Tunguses, 18
Tunis, 463, 530, 549
Turati, Filippo, 937
Turbines, 301-02, 303, 315, 342 n., 757
Turco-Italian War (1911-12), 531
Turcoman Socialist Soviet Republic, area and population of, 991
Turgenev, I. S., 705-06
Turgot, A. R. J., baron de l'Aulne, 79, 111, 193, 326, 380
Turkestan, 20, 533, 534, 537
Turkey, 33, 136, 348, 460-65 *passim*, 531, 532, 533-34, 549, 552, 580, 609, 612, 904, 905, 906; and the World War, 529-30, 594, 597, 616; Republic of, 561, 609, 868
Turks, 4, 11, 21, 39, 88, 164
Turner, F. J., 468, 1058
Turner, J. M. W., 250, 572, 709
Turner, Col. Roscoe, 742
Tuscany, 67, 125
Tutuila, 539
Twain, Mark (S. L. Clemens), 469, 708
Twenty-one Demands (Japan-China), 538
Two Sicilies, Kingdom of the, 125, 459
Tydings, M. E., 539
Tylor, Sir E. B., 667, 670, 672 n.
Tyndall, John, 695
Typesetting machinery, 744-45
Typewriters, 745
Tyrants, Greek, 484
Tyrol, the South, 474, 608, 611

Ugarte, Manuel, 1085
Uhde, F. K. H. von, 710
Uganda, 522, 532
Uhland, (J.) Ludwig, 702
Ukraine, the, 608, 991
Ukrainian Socialist Soviet Republic, area and population of, 991
Ukrainians, 462, 608
Ultramontane, meaning of, 205 n.
Unamuno, Miguel de, 1084, 1085
Underconsumption, 772, 813-15, 837
Underwriting, in insurance, 69-70; syndicates, 787
Undset, Sigrid, 1087
Unemployment, 271, 289, 381, 428-29, 617, 631, 758-60, 836; American, 812, 837, 839; insurance, 811, 813, 840, 841, 939-43 *passim*, 960; relief, (American) 885, 893, 894, (English) 602, 939-40
Union for Democratic Control, 901 n.
Union of Socialist Soviet Republics. *See* Russia, Soviet.
Unitarian Church, 169-70, 172, 187, 390, 1061
United Press Association, 745; quoted, 869
United States Chamber of Commerce, 841
United States Congress, 375, 511-12, 539, 830-31, 834, 842, 862, 886-94 *passim*, 918, 971; Senate, 426, 618, 792, 830-31, 902, 920; House of Representatives, 886-87; Congress of the Confederation, 923
United States Government, divisions and officials: Civil Service Commission, 890; Comptroller, 886; Departments, (Agriculture) 890, (Commerce) 885, (Interior) 890, (Justice) 514, (Labor) 436, (Post Office) 888, 889 n., (Treasury) 832, 886; Veterans' Bureau, 874
United States of America, 68, 74 n., 99, 136, 138, 167, 168, 170, 172, 187-88, 204, 206-07, 307, 314-15, 380-439 *passim*, 456-565 *passim*, 612-37 *passim*, 691, 704, 741-974 *passim*, 987, 990, 995-96, 1000, 1005, 1015, 1016, 1058, 1085, 1091; and the World War, 469, 498, 544, 577, 594, 596-97, 599-601, 606-07, 612, 615, 617, 829, 954, 971. *See also* World War debts; and the League of Nations, 901-02; and the World Court, 904; and disarmament, 910-13, 924; and imperialism, 567-73; and Latin America, 541-45; religion in the, 673-80 *passim*, 1060-66; national wealth, 783; income, 523; expenditures, 602, 884-94, 912; debts, 602-03, 825, 893-94; exports, 277, 372, 546; imports, 372, 546, 815; population, 364, 366-67, 374, 416; Bank of the, 513; trade with, 337, 351, 870, 889, 894, 901, 924. *See also* American.
United States of Europe proposed, 899, 901
United States Rubber Co., 784
United States Steel Corporation, 749, 750, 752, 781-82, 784, 789, 790, 798, 799, 802, 805, 830, 844, 875
United States Supreme Court, 108, 132, 223-24, 384, 444, 468, 498-99, 511, 842-47, 943, 1103
Universalist Church, 1061
Universities and colleges, 154, 240-42, 265-66, 640, 685-89, 1074-79, 1107; American, 154, 685-86, 688-89, 883, 1057, 1074-79, (for women) 1075; Belgian and Dutch, 240; English, 102, 241, 685-86, 688-89, 1074; French, 685; German, 240-41, 685, 688-89, 1073, 1077; Russian, Soviet, 1020
Untermyer, Samuel, 830-31 (quoted)
Uranus (planet), 152, 1039
Urban II, pope, 11-12
Urbanization, modern, 3, 53, 213, 265, 269, 285, 360, 408-16, 428, 515, 860; effects of, 270
Urbanity, 146, 154-56, 168, 169, 178, 190, 242, 245, 662, 695, 708
Ursprache, 197
Uruguay, 1085
Utah, 677
Utica, N. Y., 358
Utilitarianism, 191, 193, 200, 224-25, 381, 383 n., 384-85, 671, 932
Utopias, 158, 192, 227, 234-37, 245, 448, 691, 694, 708, 979, 1080
Utrecht, Congress of (1713), 899; Treaty of (1713), 225-26, 459
Uzbek Socialist Soviet Republic, area and population of, 991

Vaccination. *See* Smallpox.
Vaihinger, Hans, 1069

INDEX

Valdes, Armando Palacio, 701
Valencia, 1084
Valera y Alcalá Galiano, Juan, 701
Valéry, P. A., 1082
Valle-Inclán, Ramon, marquis del, 1084-85
Valparaiso, 456
Value, theories of: labor, 380, 381, 395-96, 934, 936, 937; surplus, 395-96, 934
Vandervelde, Emile, 937
Van Dyck, Sir Anthony, 250
Vanity Fair, 1091
Van Loon, Hendrik, 163
Van Sweringen, O. P. & M. J., 783
Van Syckel, Samuel, 732
Van Tyne, C. H., 27 n.
Vare, W. S., 876, 881
Varenius, Bernhardus, 149
Vatican Council, 675
Vattel, Emeric de, 226, 669
Vaughan, D. D., 946 n., 1066
Vaughan-Williams, Ralph, 1099
Veblen, T. B., 60 n., 168, 446, 448, 493, 708, 798 n., 821, 935 n., 972, 1059, 1078; quoted, 325, 440, 441, 445, 816
Vega (Carpio), Lope Felix de, 86
Veiller, L. T., 966
Velásquez, Diego Rodriguez de, 247-48
Venetia, 125, 459
Venezuela, 353, 541, 544, 1085
Venice, 17-19, 23, 37, 38, 67, 69, 249, 898; Bank of, 68 n., 788
Venus: goddess, 249; planet, 836, 1039
Verdi, G. F. F., 572, 714
Verdun, 595
Vereshchagin, V. V., 711
Verga, Giovanni, 699
Verhaeren, Emile, 1082
Verlaine, P. M., 698
Vermeer (van der Meer), Jan, 249
Verne, Jules, 572
Versailles, 91, 112, 459; Treaty of (1919), 312, 327-28, 333, 334, 474, 494, 533, 538, 540, 544, 550-54, 607-17, 623, 629, 630, 774, 902, 906, 909, 910, 913, 927, (war-guilt clause of the) 615, 623 (quoted), 626
Vesalius, Andreas, 145, 148
Viborg Manifesto (1906), 129
Vico, G. B., 193
Victor Emmanuel II, king of Italy, 125, 459, 531
Victoria, queen of England, proclaimed empress of India, 535; age of, 691, 693-95, 1081
Vidal de La Blache, P. M. J., 1047-48
Vienna, 39, 123-25, 343-44, 415, 628, 687, 943, 966; population of, 213; Bank of, 68 n.; Congress of (1815), 135, 327, 330, 492-93, 900
Viereck, G. S., 867
Vigny, Alfred de, 695-96
Viking invasions, 83
Villa, Gallo-Roman, 485
Villages, 483; Germanic, 485; Russian, 338-39, 392, 982
Villard, O. G., 1094
Vilna, 595, 608

Vincent of Beauvais, 19, 185
Vinogradoff, Sir P. G., 670
Virchow, Rudolf, 647, 651, 667
Virgil (Publius Vergilius Maro), 655
Virgin Islands, 542-44, 545
Virginia, 44, 73, 510, 512; University of, 685
Vitamins, 736, 1047
Vitello (Witelo), 146
Viviani, René, 590, 593
Vocational representation, 136, 499, 500, 871, 883, 995-96
Volta, Alessandro, 152, 736
Voltaire, F. M. Arouet de, 92, 111, 116, 155, 162, 174, 181-84, 185, 186, 206, 227, 246, 247, 252, 399, 476, 672, 673, 702, 899, 1082
Voluntarism, 681, 1069

Wages, 47, 239, 290-94 *passim,* 326, 369, 426, 429, 435, 565, 617, 632, 671, 759, 813, 825, 845, 847, 960, 984; fixing, 345, 627; fluctuations of, 41, 42-43; minimum, 435-36; theories of, 320-21, 379, 381-82, 428-29, 848-49; American, 809-10, 815-16, 839, 846; Soviet Russian, 998, 1001, 1014, 1016-17
Wagner, Adolph, 939, 941 n.
Wagner, Rev. C. E., quoted, 445
Wagner (Wilhelm), Richard, 713-14, 1097, 1100
Wagner von Jauregg, Julius, knight, 1049
Wake Islands, 545
Wakefield, E. G., 383
Wald, L. D., 966
Waldeck-Rousseau, Pierre, 509, 950
Walfisch Bay, 532
Walker, R. T., 1097
Wall Street. *See* Stock exchange, New York.
Wallace, A. R., 571, 658, 695, 956, 1046
Wallace, W. K., 867
Wallas, Graham, 503, 515, 668, 858, 865, 881, 937
Walpole, Hugh, 1079, 1081
Walpole, Sir Robert, 98, 215, 272, 507
Walsh, J. J., 392
Waltham, Mass., 357
War Communism, Soviet Russia, 997-98, 1007, 1011
War, 222, 225, 417, 484, 613, 618, 898, 916; causes of, 575-76, 613, 913, 924-27; "aggressive," 927-28; outlawry of, 917-27 *passim;* prevention of, *see* Peace, the quest for; substitutes for, 928; and democracy, 867-68, 870; attitudes toward, 219, 222, 225, 231, 466, 467, 472, 667, 846
Wars, 691, 885; European, 9, 54, 85, 91, 92, 93-94, 113-14, 146, 150, 222, 225, 240, 272, 330, 454, 455, 462, 464, 506, 702; Latin American, 1084; War of 1812, 356, 358, 456, 468, 914. *See also* names of wars.
Warbasse, J. P., 948
Warburg, J. P., quoted, 784
Warburton, C. A., Leven, Maurice, and Moulton, H. G., 417 n., 807, 809, 811, 815
Ward, C. H., quoted, 1038
Ward, H. F., 946, 1022, 1066
Ward, L. F., 667, 679, 689, 933; quoted, 502

INDEX

Ward, R. De C., 1047
Warfare, methods of, 10, 460, 768; World War, 597-99
Warner, C. D., 708
Warren, Josiah, 397
Warsaw, 595
Washington, George, president of the United States, 52, 105, 108, 187, 314, 511, 885, 922-23 (quoted), 1106
Washington (D. C.), 411, 914, 1096; Conference on Disarmament (1921-22), 538, 539, 551, 743, 910; *Daily News,* 1094
Wassermann, August, 1049
Wassermann, Jakob, 1080, 1086
Waste: conspicuous, 440-41, 445; in distribution, 972; in government, 868, 884-94; in production, 420, 817-19, 821, 960, 972, 1014; of natural resources, 819, 820
Waterloo, battle of, 120, 272, 279
Water power, 299, 303, 325, 342, 344, 345, 347, 357, 416, 629, 736
Water transport, 119, 307, 310, 341, 357, 360-61. *See also* Canals; Steamships.
Watson, J. B., 1048
Watt, James, 54, 152, 271, 278, 279, 283, 286, 299-301, 308, 314
Watteau, J. A., 249, 251
Watts, C. A., 679
Watts, G. F., 709
Wealth, 8-10, 12, 868; increase and concentration of, 63, 486, 806-16, 934; national, 79; theory of, 385-86; attitudes toward, 66, 143-44, 168, 214, 236, 433-34, 440, 442. *See also* Economics; Fortunes; Income; Plutocracy.
Webb, Beatrice (Mrs. Sidney), 967, 1058, 1059
Webb, Sidney, 60 n., 386, 935 n., 937, 1058, 1059
Weber, E. H., 648, 1048
Weber, K. M. F. E., baron von, 714
Weber, Max, 58 n., 60 n., 66 n., 935 n., 1059
Webster, Daniel, 468, 513
Webster family, 358
Weed, Thurlow, 1092
Weights and measures, 118, 906
Weierstrass, K. T. W., 641
Weihaiwei, 537
Weimar constitution (1919), 313
Weismann, August, 646, 658-59, 1046
Weitling, Wilhelm, 395-96, 934
Wellhausen, Julius, 654
Wellington, Arthur Wellesley, 1st duke of, 127, 709
Wells, H. G., 182, 392, 394, 656, 907-08, 937, 1058, 1079, 1080-81; quoted, 1105
Welsbach, C. A. von, 284
Welsers, bankers, 67
Werfel, F. V., 1085
Werner, A. G., 153
Wertheimer, M. S., 577
Wertheimer, Max, 1048
Wescott, Glenway, 1089
Wesley, John, 203-04, 205, 674
West, Rebecca, 1081
West, the American, 105, 107, 361, 364, 365, 366, 368, 460, 468, 512-13, 707, 801. *See also* Frontier.
Westcott, B. F., bishop, 946
Western Hemisphere. *See* America.
Western Union Telegraph Co., 790, 830
Westernization. *See* Civilization, Western.
West Indies, 24, 32, 33, 34, 49, 59, 112, 542; Company, Dutch, 24; trade with, 36, 60. *See also* names of islands.
Westinghouse, George, 736
Westminster Gazette, 586
Westphalia, 170, 334, 335 n., 336; Treaty of (1648), 87, 88, 129, 225, 459
West Point, 687
West Virginia, 294, 361, 368
Weyl, W. E., quoted, 464
Wharton, Edith, 1089
Whateley, Richard, archbishop, 967 n.
Wheatstone, Sir Charles, 318, 745
Wheeler, W. B., 971
Whewell, William, 202-03
Whig party; American, 512-13, 856 n.; British, 27, 100, 102, 103, 107, 122, 134, 468, 488, 506-07, 509
Whistler, J. A. McN., 711
Whiston, William, 188
White, A. D., 679
White, Bouck, 445
White, John, 251
White, Stanford, 712
White, W. A., quoted, 615
White-collar class. *See* Middle class, lower.
White man's burden, 7, 466, 524, 546, 564
White Russian Socialist Soviet Republic, area and population of, 991
White Russians, 477, 990
White-slave traffic, 906
Whitefield, George, 204, 205, 674
Whitehead, A. N., 1069
Whiteman, Paul, 1100
Whitman, Marcus, 742
Whitman, Walt, 469, 707, 1089
Whitney, Eli, 276, 277, 283, 357, 753
Whitney case (Syndicalism law), 846
Whittier, J. G., 707
Wickersham, G. W., 971
Wiese und Kaiserswaldau, L. M. W. von, 1058
Wiggin, A. H., 782
Wiggin, J. H., 677
Wilberforce, William, 383, 401
Wilder, T. N., 448, 1079, 1089
Wilkes, John, 172, 1092
Wilkinson, John, 279, 283, 286, 301, 315
Willcox, O. W., 761-62
Willcox, W. F., quoted, 560
Willey, M. M., and Herskovits, M. J., quoted, 432
William III, king of England, 89, 103, 506, 507, 511; income of, 59
William I, German emperor, 459, 465, 711
William II, German emperor, 429, 476, 531, 532, 549, 577, 578, 587, 590-96 *passim,* 599, 711, 915
William the Silent, prince of Orange, 87
Williams, Roger, 168, 170, 204

INDEX

Williams College, 203
Willis, I. C., 867
Willoughby, W. F., quoted, 892-93
Willoughby, W. W., 668 n.
Wilson, C. T. R., 727
Wilson, Edmund, 1090
Wilson, Woodrow, president of the United States, 498, 514, 543, 552, 577, 596, 606-07, 611, 614 n. (quoted), 615-16, 617, 618 (quoted), 624, 669, 844, 861, 874, 899, 901-02, 907, 912, 917, 944. See also Fourteen Points.
Wiltse, C. M., quoted, 856 n.
Winchester school, England, 242
Winckler, Hugo, 654
Windelband, Wilhelm, 1067
Windischgrätz, Gen. Alfred, prince, 124, 125
Windward Islands, 543
Wines, E. C., 967
Wines, F. H., 967 n.
Winkler, Max, quoted, 548
Winterthur, 344
Wirt, William, 512
Wisconsin, 363, 437, 845, 881, 944; University of, 1076
Wise, J. W., rabbi, 1061
Witchcraft, 146, 150, 158, 170, 472, 652
Witelo (Vitello), 146
Witt, C. H. de, quoted, 187
Witte, S. J., count, 128-29, 339, 341, 496, 581
Wöhler, Friedrich, 645, 726, 727, 1045
Wolcott, Benjamin, Jr., 358
Wolff, C. F., 153
Wolff Telegraph Bureau, 745
Wolkenstein, V. M., 1088
Woll, Matthew, 951
Wollaston, W. H., 643, 644, 1037
Wollstonecraft (Godwin), Mary, 216, 437
Woman's Home Companion, 1092
Women: position of, 118, 119, 434-38, 696, 705, 971, 1022-23; in industry, 47, 289, 291, 292, 388, 391, 407-08, 435-36, 495, 498, 565, 616-17; attitudes toward, 216, 666, 678, 705, 1103. See also Education of women; Suffrage, woman.
Wood, Gar, 316
Wood, L. B., 1094
Wood, Gen. Leonard, 873, 876
Woodhull, Victoria, 437
Woods, R. A., 966
Woolen industry. See Textile industries.
Woolf, L. S., quoted, 566
Woolf, Virginia (Stephen), 1079, 1081
Woolsey, T. D., 668 n.
Woolston, Thomas, 175-76 (quoted), 177
Woolworth chain (five and ten), 764, 785
Worcester, marquis of. See Somerset.
Worcester, Noah, 914
Wordsworth, William, 206, 384, 525, 692, 694
Work. See Labor.
Working class. See Proletariat.
Working-conditions, 289-94, 326, 345, 368, 391, 428, 565, 617, 633-34, 673, 690, 813, 845, 848, 939, 942
Working-hours, 236, 286, 290, 293, 294, 382, 388, 405, 408, 442, 633, 671, 821, 940-41, 942, 1001, 1006
Workmen's compensation, 292, 491, 492, 495, 840, 845, 939, 941, 943; in the United States, 498
World Court. See Permanent Court of International Justice.
World fairs: Chicago, 469, 711, 712; London (1862), 935; Paris, 302; St. Louis, 469
World War (1914-18), 84, 90, 114, 124, 125, 575-603, 899, 901, 907, 915, 920-21, 970; causes of the, 462, 477-78, 548, 575-93 *passim,* 606, 616, 775, (imperialism) 549-50; and policies of reconstruction, 958-61; naval operations, 598-99; equipment, 303, 597-99; cost, 570, 601-03, 626; losses, 474, 600-01; effects of the, 207, 265, 316, 349, 373, 374, 425, 436, 460, 471-73, 474, 495, 499, 509, 533, 535, 606-37 *passim,* 732, 839, 850, 855, 867-68, 916-17, 986, 1006, 1010, 1055, 1080. See also Propaganda; Reparations; names of treaties, especially Versailles.
World War debts, 607, 622, 625, 775; to the United States, 603, 619-22, 626, 832, 894
World organization, 898-901. See also League of Nations.
Wormser, I. M., 801, 823 n.
Wrangel, Gen. P. N., baron, 990
Wren, Sir Christopher, 252, 411, 712
Wright, Orville and Wilbur, 741
Wundt, W. M., 648, 649
Württemberg, 126, 242
Wyatt, H. F., 466 n.
Wyatt, John, 274

X-rays, 1044-45, 1048
Xenophanes, 155

Yahweh (God), 177
Yakovlev, V. A., 1010
Yakutat Bay, 25
Yale University, 187
Yap, 539, 910
Yaroslavsky, Y. Y., 1021
Yeats, W. B., 1080
Yemen, 34
Yerkes, R. M., 660, 970
York, Eng., 291, 763, 849 n.
Yorktown, 107
Young, Arthur, 51, 54, 304 (quoted)
Young, Brigham, 677
Young, O. D., Young Plan, 542, 615, 624, 625, 626, 849 n.
Young, Thomas, 643
Young Men's Christian Association, 957
Young Women's Christian Association, 906, 957
Youth movement, 1067
Ypres, 595
Ysaÿe, Eugène, 714
Yuan Shi-kai, president of the Chinese Republic, 499
Yugoslavia, 169, 348, 609, 610, 612, 635, 868, 904, 905, 907 n.; World War debts of, 621; reparation payments due to, 623

Yugoslavs, 461
Yule, Sir Henry, and Beazley, Sir C. R., quoted, 18
Yussupov, F. F., prince, 987

Zabala y Lera, Pío, 1085
Zaharoff, Sir Basil, 913
Zaiton, 20
Zanzibar, 18, 561
Zemstvos, 339, 496, 981
Zenger, J. P., trial of, 1092

Zeppelins, 741
Zimmern, A. E., 484
Zionist movement, 353, 478, 609
Zola, E. E. C. A., 392, 694, 698, 703, 704, 708, 1085
Zollverein, 319-20, 330-31, 383, 628
Zoölogy, 146-47, 148, 151, 571, 649
Zorrilla, José, 701
Zukor, Adolph, 747
Zwingli, Huldreich, 673
Zurich, 344